RCL

RESOURCES *for* COLLEGE LIBRARIES

2007

This Edition of ***Resources for College Libraries*** was prepared by:

ACRL & Choice:
Project Editor: Marcus Elmore
Editorial Director, Choice: Francine Graf
Editor & Publisher, Choice: Irving Rockwood

Special Thanks to Our Proofreaders:
Monika Maslowski, Jinna Anderson, Chris Sullivan, Jennifer Donahue, Judith Douville, Rebecca Bartlett, and Carolyn Wilcox

Record Entry Completed By:
Monika Maslowski, Laurie Trulock, and Sheila Laverty

R. R. Bowker LLC:
John Krafty: Product Manager, RCL
Ashley Ludwig: Managing Editor, RCL
Frank Morris: IT Director
Minh Huynh: Senior Programmer Analyst
Robert Zeisler: Senior Programmer Analyst

Editorial Staff:
Ian Singer: Vice President, Data Services
Roy Crego: Senior Managing Director, Editorial
Eleanor Schubauer: Managing Editor
Michael Olenick: Managing Editor
Beverly Palacio: Associate Editor

Production Department:
Doreen Gravesande: Senior Director, Production
Ralph Coviello, Manager, Manufacturing Services
Myriam Nunez: Project Manager, Product Development & Content Integrity
Kennard McGill: Production Consultant

Research Completed By:
Pat Diaz, Bobbie Ferraro, Kathy Griner, Becky Housel, and Diane Johnson.

Record Entry Completed By:
Jenny Marie DeJesus, Dorothy Perry-Gilchrist, Anthony Giuffra, and Steven Zaffuto

RCL

RESOURCES *for* COLLEGE LIBRARIES

2007

Volume 2:
Language and Literature

Mary Ellen Davis, Executive Director, ACRL

Published by
R. R. Bowker LLC
630 Central Avenue, New Providence
New Jersey 07974

Annie Callanan, President and CEO

URL: http://www.rclweb.net
E-mail address: rclfeedback@bowker.com

Readers may send any corrections and/or updates to the information in this work to:
rclfeedback@bowker.com

International Standard Book Number:

7 Volume Set:	ISBN: 0-8352-4855-0 ISBN13: 978-0-8352-4855-6
Vol. 1: Humanities:	ISBN: 0-8352-4856-9 ISBN13: 978-0-8352-4856-3
Vol. 2: Language & Literature:	ISBN: 0-8352-4857-7 ISBN13: 978-0-8352-4857-0
Vol. 3: History:	ISBN: 0-8352-4858-5 ISBN13: 978-0-8352-4858-7
Vol. 4: Social Sciences:	ISBN: 0-8352-4859-3 ISBN13: 978-0-8352-4859-4
Vol. 5: Science and Technology:	ISBN: 0-8352-4860-7 ISBN13: 978-0-8352-4860-0
Vol. 6: Interdisciplinary & Area Studies:	ISBN: 0-8352-4861-5 ISBN13: 978-0-8352-4861-7
Vol. 7: Indexes:	ISBN: 0-8352-4862-3 ISBN13: 978-0-8352-4862-4

Printed and bound in the United States of America

Table of Contents

Resources for College Libraries: General Introduction

Like its predecessors, the three editions of *Books for College Libraries* (BCL) that appeared in 1988, 1975, and 1964, *Resources for College Libraries* (RCL) is a bibliography of carefully selected works spanning the college curriculum and comprising a recommended core collection for all academic libraries. In the tradition of its predecessors, which drew on the such sources as the published catalog of Harvard's Lamont Library (1954), the shelflist of the undergraduate library of the University of Michigan, and, crucially, Charles Shaw's *List of Books for College Libraries* (1931), RCL attempts to balance multiple, often contradictory demands. It seeks to provide a balanced set of recommendations that take note of the weight of the various academic disciplines within the undergraduate curriculum, the degree to which those various disciplines depend on book materials for their essential teaching and research resources, and the extensive pattern of changes that have reshaped the academic curriculum since 1988, the year in which BCL3, the most recent edition of *Books for College Libraries,* appeared.

Of necessity, RCL also embodies a paradox identified by the late Virginia Clark, editor of BCL3: it "can fully succeed only by failing. It would be disastrous should the collection it suggests serve perfectly to ratify the finished work of book selection in any library."[1] Not only will individual institutions create collections significantly larger than the roughly 65,000 titles recommended by RCL, but they will tailor those collections to reflect the size and strength of their own individual departments, majors, and programs. RCL attempts to make general recommendations, within individual subject areas, of those titles most necessary for teaching the subject to undergraduates. In many cases, this means a foundation to which the smallest institutions should aspire but which larger collections will far surpass.

We describe RCL as a successor to, rather than a new edition of, BCL for two reasons. The first is formal, and lies behind the change in nomenclature: RCL includes in its recommendations a variety of electronic resources, including Web sites, subscription databases, e-books, and other electronic materials. The second, procedural reason follows from this: unlike its predecessors, RCL will appear as both a multivolume print edition and a searchable, continuously updated electronic database. In addition, there is a third, tacit distinction which may be made between RCL and the various editions of BCL: although bibliographers compiling subject lists for RCL often took the titles listed in BCL3 as a starting point, our bibliographic work emphasized building a comprehensive, retrospective list of titles by reference to the current undergraduate curriculum, and thus much of the work on RCL was from scratch. In contrast, the relationship between the various editions of BCL was demonstrably that of revision; from one edition to the next, there was an expectation that a title would be retained unless it was actively removed (if, for instance, it had been superseded by a more recent work). Because so much more time had passed between the appearance of BCL3 and the development of RCL than between any successive editions of BCL, bibliographers faced the simultaneously daunting and liberating prospect of creating a subject list *de novo.* That this same period (1988-2006) has seen momentous sea changes in many of the academic disciplines in the humanities and the sciences, as well as the growth of interdisciplinary study across all the academic disciplines, made this an opportunity to take measure of the way subjects are taught to undergraduates, as well as the sorts of subjects which are taught, when developing our core list.

One result of this reassessment was the decision to recognize and include as separate subject divisions in RCL a number of interdisciplinary fields, e.g., Environmental Studies and Gender Studies. The decision about which fields to include was based primarily on the degree to which those subjects function as areas of formal study at undergraduate institutions in the U.S., whether as major programs, academic minors, or areas of concentration housed within another department (film studies, for instance, is often offered as a program or concentration within the departments of English, Comparative Literature, or Theater). We recognized that the lists of titles recommended for teaching interdisciplinary subjects, e.g., Asian American Studies, might overlap significantly with the corresponding title lists for related traditional fields, e.g., American Literature. At the same time, we were confident that many of the recommended interdisciplinary titles would be unique, and so it has proved. The degree of overlap between the various sections of RCL is, throughout, fortuitous and reflects actual overlap between various undergraduate curricula. Effort was made to regularize the editions selected, but the work of compiling the various subject lists proceeded on an independent basis.

1. Virginia Clark, "Introduction," *Books for College Libraries: A Core Collection of 50,000 Titles,* (3rd ed., Chicago: American Library Association, 1988), vii.

The other dramatic difference between RCL and BCL is the decision to move away from Library of Congress classification as the primary framework for the selection and classification of titles. Though this is bound to be regarded by many librarians as a controversial decision, we are confident that it will prove in retrospect to be a sound one. The rationale for doing so is the desire to have titles classified in a fashion which closely follows the contours of the undergraduate curriculum. While LC accomplishes this for some subjects (for instance, British or American Literature, which are taught by chronological periods, and within periods by major authors and by forms such as poetry or drama), other curricula fail to mesh well with LC classification: Business Administration, for example, is responsible for the largest portion of baccalaureate degrees conferred by U.S. colleges and universities,[2] yet the classification of materials in the business curriculum in LC class HB-HJ, while sufficient for cataloging purposes, offers no insight on the relationship between materials so classified and the curriculum in which they are used. It is, furthermore, an arrangement which makes perfect sense to, but only to, librarians. Not all copies of BCL resided in technical services departments, but it seems unlikely that they were much consulted by students or faculty. Our hope is that the new classification scheme will work to the advantage of all the academic library's constituencies: librarians, especially those lacking strong background in a given subject, will be able to see not only the recommended titles but also, in the subject taxonomy, a map of the undergraduate curriculum; faculty will find recommendations of essential works in a form more accessible than LC, and bearing a closer correspondence to the way their courses and departments are organized; students, searching for a place to begin research on a particular topic, will also be able to recognize in the classification scheme something corresponding to their own encounter with the subject matter in the classroom and laboratory. Finally, since each entry in RCL retains its LC classification, those who prefer to search for materials in this fashion will still be able to.

RCL is the result of the collaborative efforts of 332 contributors, almost exclusively teaching faculty or librarians at U.S. colleges and universities. There were three kinds of contributors: subject editors, bibliographers, and referees. Subject editors were selected on the basis of their subject expertise and teaching or collection development experience: eighteen hold doctorates, four are members of the teaching faculty at research universities, two are independent scholars, and the remainder are academic librarians. Many have previously contributed to or authored major bibliographies in their subject areas. They were responsible for developing the subject classification taxonomy for their respective subject areas, for recruiting bibliographers and coordinating their efforts, and for reviewing the results. The subject editors represented a change from the various editions of BCL, where the bibliographers (mainly Choice reviewers) dealt directly with the project editor. By inserting a layer of subject experts we sought to ensure that the titles selected and the taxonomies in which they were classified reflected as much as possible the realities of the contemporary undergraduate curriculum. The second class of RCL contributors, bibliographers, was responsible for the bulk of the actual selection of titles. Like the subject editors, they were faculty and librarians selected for their subject knowledge, often with particular expertise in one specific aspect of a field. Finally, a pool of sixty-four referees, senior faculty or subject-specialist librarians, provided independent assessment of the initial lists developed by the bibliographers; the subject editors used this feedback to further refine their lists prior to publication.

The development of RCL had presumed from the beginning that bibliographers would be manipulating electronic bibliographic records in some sort of online environment, but the decision of the Association of College and Research Libraries (ACRL) Board of Directors to partner with publisher R. R. Bowker to produce RCL allowed us access to Bowker's massive database of bibliographic records, as well as the extensive technical support and expertise Bowker deployed on behalf of the project. Bibliographers selected titles in Bowker's *booksinprint.com* database, in a particular edition, and then imported them to the online RCL Authoring System, where they assigned subject headings and recommended audience levels. In those instances where no bibliographic record existed for a desired title, one was created from a reliable source (preferably with book in hand, though this was not always possible). At the same time, bibliographers submitted corrections to Bowker records when they identified errors or inconsistencies. While this system allowed us to avoid much of the brute effort which was expended on the creation of bibliographic records for the various editions of BCL, it also meant that bibliographers spent thousands of person-hours in the *booksinprint.com* database, identifying the most recent and reliable edition of particular works; in some cases, editors elected to include multiple editions, especially where the differences between them are significant for undergraduate teaching (see, for instance, the decision to include multiple, equally worthwhile translations of Dante's *Divine Comedy* in the Italian literature section).

The use of an online system for the manipulation of electronic bibliographic records was in part a matter of efficiency, but more importantly, it finally addresses one longstanding issue faced by BCL, that of obsolescence.

2. http://nces.ed.gov/fastfacts/display.asp?id=37: U.S. Department of Education, National Center for Education Statistics. (2006). *Digest of Education Statistics, 2005* (NCES 2006-030), chapter 3.

When *Choice* magazine was founded in 1964, it was envisioned as, among other things, an ongoing supplement to BCL1. This approach did not prove practical, and the second and third editions of BCL were required. In contrast, RCL will be updated on an ongoing basis beginning almost immediately after its initial publication; bibliographic records will reflect changes in print status, and new titles will be introduced at regular intervals, to supplement or replace extant titles.

In addition to the tireless efforts of the contributors, on whom I cannot lavish sufficient praise, special thanks to the ACRL Board of Directors and Mary Ellen Davis, ACRL Executive Director, without whose approval and generous support this project would not have been possible. Oversight and advice were provided throughout the project by the RCL Editorial Board: Carolyn Sheehy, North Central College, Chair; and other members Joan Ellen Broome, Georgia Southern University; Barbara Burd, College Misericordia; Brian E. Coutts, Western Kentucky University; Bradford Lee Eden, University of California, Santa Barbara; Stacey Marien, American University; and Richard Shaw, Technical College of the Lowcountry.

Thanks are also due the editorial staff of *Choice*, all of whom contributed effort and advice to the production of this work in varying degrees (and all of whom exhibited tremendous kindness in their efforts, especially in the final days): Becky Bartlett, Judith Douville, Fran Graf, Lisa Mitten, and Carolyn Wilcox. Fran Graf and Irv Rockwood, the Publisher of *Choice*, deserve another helping of praise for their advice, encouragement, and oversight of the project, as well as for handling negotiations of our partnership with R. R. Bowker. Judith Douville made superhuman contributions to a number of subject areas in addition to her own responsibilities in Chemistry. Although almost every member of the *Choice* office staff contributed to this work, Sheila Laverty deserves special praise for her work on the Dance section. Finally, the work would not have been completed if it had not been for the tireless effort of a small cadre of freelance staff, namely Jennifer Donahue, Monika Maslowski, Teri Staab, and Laurie Trulock, who proofread and edited subject headings and section notes, entered titles, cataloged records, and helped maintain communication with subject editors, with extraordinary care, intelligence, and persistence.

With our partners at R. R. Bowker, we enjoyed the highest degree of collegiality and cooperation. Special thanks are due to Angela D'Agostino, Vice-President of Marketing; John Krafty, Product Manager of *Books In Print*; Ashley Ludwig, Managing Editor; Todd Rudloff, Project Manager of *Books In Print*; Frank Morris, Senior Programmer; Minh Huynh, Senior Programmer Analyst, all of whom made significant contributions to bringing this work to the light of day.

Finally, my deep thanks to my family, Colleen and Graham, for their patience and support throughout this project.

Marcus Elmore,

Editor

A Note on the RCL Subject Taxonomy

One of the distinctive features of *Resources for College Libraries* is the subject taxonomy used to organize the titles included in RCL. Developed specifically for RCL by the RCL editorial team, and in particular by the subject editors, the RCL taxonomy reflects the contours of today's undergraduate curriculum. The RCL taxonomy's major headings, therefore, generally correspond to academic majors, departments, or courses of study, e.g., anthropology, business administration, or physics. (In some cases an academic discipline has been further subdivided in order to create sections of manageable size, e.g., the subdivision of History by geographical region.) The goal is a classification scheme, which organizes materials as they would be taught by faculty and encountered in the classroom and the laboratory by undergraduate students.

In some subject areas, e.g. British and American literature, the RCL subject taxonomy closely resembles the Library of Congress classification scheme used in *Books for College Libraries,* 3rd edition. In most cases, however, the differences between LC and today's undergraduate curriculum, have been so substantial as to require the development of a new taxonomy from scratch. This has been especially true for the interdisciplinary subjects such as African American Studies, Criminal Justice, and Native American Studies, which draw upon materials from a dizzying range of LC classes. Gender Studies, for example, draws from a large array of academic disciplines, including (but not limited to) psychology, sociology, literature, philosophy, political science, medicine, and history.

The coverage of interdisciplinary subjects in RCL is another of its distinguishing features, and one deemed essential from the very inception of the project. Although there is some overlap between the interdisciplinary title lists and those of related traditional subjects, e.g., American literature and Chicano/a literature (a subsection of Latino Studies), the interdisciplinary sections inevitably include many unique titles. In addition, the inclusion of the interdisciplinary subjects makes it possible to distinguish those titles which have been selected as essential resources for a traditional subject such as American literature (e.g., Carson McCullers' *Collected Novels*), from those selected for an interdisciplinary area (e.g., Pat Mora's *Communion,* selected for Latino Studies > Humanities > Literature > Chicano/a Literature), and also from those selected for both (e.g., Mora's *Borders*).

By making the ways in which titles are actually used in the classroom the focus for our classification of titles in RCL, we hope to both dramatically increase its usefulness to students and faculty members and also to underscore the extent to which titles were selected on the basis of their importance to undergraduate study and teaching.

RCL Contributors

John Abbott, Graduate Student, GSLIS, University of Illinois, Urbana-Champaign.
Subject Editor: European History.

Randy Abbott, Head Reference Librarian, University of Evansville.
Referee.

Anthony Adam, Assistant Director, John B. Coleman Library, Prairie View A&M University.
Bibliographer: GLBT Studies.

Jan Adamczyk, Slavic Reference Service, University of Illinois.
Bibliographer: Russian Languages and Literatures.

Michael Adams, Librarian, CUNY Graduate Center.
Bibliographer: American Literature.

Paulita Aguilar, Curator, Indigenous Nations Library Program, University of New Mexico.
Bibliographer: Native American Studies.

Flavia Alaya, Professor of English, Ramapo College of New Jersey.
Referee.

Jean Alexander, Head of Reference, Hunt Library, Carnegie Mellon University.
Referee.

Duncan Alford, Head of Reference, Law Library, Georgetown University.
Bibliographer: Law.

Karen Antell, Head, Reference Department, University of Oklahoma.
Bibliographer: Technology and Engineering.

Ralph Arcari, Director Emeritus, Health Center Library, University of Connecticut.
Subject Editor: Medicine.

Susan Ariew, University Librarian, University of South Florida.
Bibliographer: Education.

Jan Armstrong, Professor of Education, University of New Mexico.
Referee.

Teresa Arrington, Associate Professor of Modern Languages, Blue Mountain College.
Bibliographer: Spanish Language and Literature.

Susan Awe, Director of Parish Memorial Library, University of New Mexico.
Referee.

David Azzolina, Reference librarian, University of Pennsylvania.
Bibliographer: General Language and Literature.

Pete Banholzer, Technical Information Specialist, NASA.
Bibliographer: Geology.

Ron Banks, Human Subjects Coordinator, Institutional Review Board, University of Illinois.
Bibliographer: Education.

David Bantz, Chief Information Architect, University of Alaska.
Referee.

Adele Barsh, Business and Economics Librarian, Carnegie Mellon University.
Bibliographer: Business Administration.

Jennifer Bartlett, Head of Research & Instructional Services, Murray State University.
Bibliographer: American Literature.

Edwin Battistella, Dean of Arts and Letters and Professor of English, University of Southern Oregon.
Bibliographer: General Language and Literature.

Frederic Baumgartner, Professor of History, Virginia Tech University.
Bibliographer: European History.

Robert Beauregard, Professor, Urban Policy Analysis and Management, New School University.
Referee.

Linda Behrend, Cataloging Librarian, University of Tennessee, Knoxville.
Bibliographer: American Literature.

Penny Beile, Head, Curriculum Materials Center, University of Central Florida.
Bibliographer: Education.

Dean Bell, Dean and Chief Academic Officer, Spertus Institute of Jewish Studies.
Bibliographer: European History.

Dennis Benamati, Director, Ryan-Matura Library, Sacred Heart University.
Referee.

Riva Berleant-Schiller, Professor emerita of Anthropology, University of Connecticut, emerita.
Subject Editor: Anthropology.

Jay Bernstein, Reader Services Librarian, Kingsborough Community College.
Referee.

John Berry, Native American Studies Librarian, University of California, Berkeley.
Subject Editor: Native American Studies.

Sharon Black, Librarian, Annenberg School for Communication, University of Pennsylvania.
Bibliographer: Journalism and Communication.

Steve Blackburn, Library Director, Hartford Seminary.
Referee.

Robert Bland, Associate University Librarian Automation and Technical Services, University of North Carolina, Asheville.
Bibliographer: Philosophy.

Richard Bleiler, Humanities Bibliographer, University of Connecticut.
Bibliographer: General Language and Literature.

Laurel Blewett, Manager of Library Services, Edward Hospital.
Referee.

Christopher Bloss, Instructional Services Librarian, University of South Dakota.
Bibliographer: American Literature.

Ellen Bosman, Head of Technical Services, New Mexico State University.
Subject Editor: GLBT Studies.

Jesús Bottaro, Instructor, CUNY / Medgar Evers College.
Bibliographer: Spanish Language and Literature.

Steven Botterill, Professor of Italian, University of California, Berkeley.
Referee.

Sally Bowdoin, Head of Serials, Brooklyn College.
Subject Editor: British Literature.

Linda Bowles-Adarkwa, Subject Specialist, Black Studies and Women Studies, San Francisco State University.
Bibliographer: African American Studies.

James Boxall, Director, GIS Centre, Dalhousie University.
Subject Editor: Geography.

James Bracken, Assistant Director for Main Library Research and Reference Services, Ohio State University.
Subject Editor: Other Literatures in English.

Laura Braunstein, Research and Reference Services, Dartmouth University.
Bibliographer: General Language and Literature.

Tony Bremholm, Life Sciences Librarian, Texas A&M University.
Referee.

Karl Bridges, Coordinator of Electronic Instruction Resources, University of Vermont.
Bibliographer: U.S. and Canadian History.

JoEllen Broome, Reference Specialist, Georgia Southern University.
Subject Editor: Environmental Studies.

Mitchell Brown, Research Librarian for Chemistry and Earth System Sciences, University of California, Irvine.
Referee.

Mary Jane Brustman, Bibliographer for Social Welfare and Criminal Justice, SUNY Albany.
Subject Editor: Criminal Justice.

Mark Bullock, Graduate Student, History Department, University of Illinois at Chicago.
Bibliographer: European History.

Merry Burlingham, Chief Bibliographer and Collections Officer, University of Texas.
Bibliographer: Asian History, Languages, and Literatures.

Angela Cannon, Reference Librarian, Library of Congress.
Bibliographer: Russian Languages and Literatures.

Karen Cary, Head, Collection Management, Virginia Commonwealth University.
Bibliographer: Sociology.

Melissa Cast, Reference Librarian and Subject Specialist for Education, University of Nebraska Omaha.
Bibliographer: Education.

Rafaela Castro, Bibliographer, University of California, Davis.
Subject Editor: Latino Studies.

Tina Ching, Reference Librarian, Arizona State University.
Referee.

Diana Chlebek, English and Modern Languages and Literature Bibliographer, University of Akron.
Bibliographer: French Language and Literature.

Michael Chromey, Humanities Librarian, Atlanta University Center.
Bibliographer: African American Studies.

Hui Hua Chua, US Documents Librarian, Michigan State University.
Bibliographer: Journalism and Communication.

Alan Church, Professor of English, University of Texas at Brownsville.
Referee.

Janet Clarke, Asian American Studies Selector, Stony Brook University.
Bibliographer: Asian American Studies.

Kim Clarke, Assistant Librarian, Selector for Women's Studies, University of Minnesota, Twin Cities.
Subject Editor: Gender Studies.

Rudolph Clay, Subject Librarian, African and African-American Studies, Washington University.
Bibliographer: African American Studies.

Ana Maria Cobos, Library Department Chair, Saddleback College.
Subject Editor: Latino Studies.

Francesca Colecchia, Professor of Spanish, Duquesne University.
Referee.

Gerardo Colmenar, Associate Librarian, Asian American Studies, University of California, Santa Barbara.
Subject Editor: Asian American Studies.

Mark Connell, Director, Center for Advancement of Technology in Education, SUNY College at Cortland.
Referee.

Paul Connors, Research Analyst, Michigan Legislative Service Bureau.
Bibliographer: U.S. and Canadian History.

Miriam Conteh-Morgan, Collection Manager for African Studies, Ohio State University.
Bibliographer: African American Studies.

Kate Corby, Education and Psychology Bibliographer, Michigan State University.
Subject Editor: Education.

Ronald Cormier, Professor of French, Longwood College.
Referee.

Alice Crosetto, Acquisitions Librarian, University of Toledo.
Bibliographer: British Literature.

Cynthia Crosser, Social Sciences and Humanities Librarian, University of Maine.
Bibliographer: Education.

Gwyneth Crowley, Coordinator of Collection Development, Social Science Libraries, Yale University.
Subject Editor: Economics.

Alice Daugherty, Reference Librarian, Louisiana State University.
Bibliographer: American Literature.

Stephanie Davis, Librarian, Spring Arbor University.
Bibliographer: Education.

Judith de Luce, Professor of Classics, Miami University of Ohio.
Referee.

Kathy Dean, Humanities Bibliographer, Ohio State University.
Bibliographer: Other Literatures in English.

Louise Deis, Science & Technology Reference Librarian, Princeton University.
Subject Editor: Environmental Sciences; General Science.

JoAnn DeVries, Associate Librarian, Reference/Bibliographer, University of Minnesota.
Bibliographer: Agriculture.

Jan Dixon, Reference Librarian, University of Arkansas.
Bibliographer: Geology.

Deborah Dolan, Social Science Librarian, Hofstra University.
Bibliographer: Psychology.

Travis Dolence, Instruction Librarian, Minnesota State University Moorhead.
Referee.

Michael Doorley, Associate Lecturer in Humanities, American College, Dublin.
Bibliographer: European History.

Judith Douville, Visual Arts, Science and Technology Editor, CHOICE.
Subject Editor: Chemistry.

Bill Drew, Associate Librarian, Systems and Reference, SUNY – Morrisville.
Referee.

Heather Dubnick, Field Bibliographer, Modern Language Assoc.
Subject Editor: Spanish Language and Literature.

Dana Dunn, Professor of Psychology, Moravian College.
Referee.

Lisa Dunn, Head of Reference, Colorado School of Mines.
Bibliographer: Geology.

Karin Durán, Teacher Curriculum Center Librarian, California State University Northridge.
Bibliographer: Latino Studies.

David Eastman, Doctoral Candidate, Department of Religious Studies, Yale University.
Bibliographer: Religion.

Mary Edsall, Professor of Library and Information Science, Catholic University of America.
Subject Editor: Dance.

Marcus Elmore, CHOICE.
Subject Editor: General Language and Literature.

Robert Elsie, Independent scholar.
Bibliographer: European History.

Kimberly Embelton, Literature and Languages Librarian, California State University Northridge.
Bibliographer: British Literature.

Michael Emery, Professor of English, Cottey College.
Bibliographer: GLBT Studies.

Mark Emmons, Head, Instruction Services, University of New Mexico.
Subject Editor: Film.

Carlene Engstrom, Director, D'Arcy McNickle Library, Salish Kootenai College.
Bibliographer: Native American Studies.

Pam Enrici, Associate Librarian, University of Maryland.
Bibliographer: Technology and Engineering.

Robert Entenmann, Professor of History, St. Olaf College.
Referee.

Isabel Espinal, Librarian for Afro American Studies, Anthropology, Native American Indian Studies, University of Massachussetts.
Bibliographer: African American Studies.

James Allan Evans, Professor Emeritus of Classical Near Eastern and Religious Studies, University of British Columbia.
Bibliographer: European History.

Angel Falcon, Harvard University, formerly.
Bibliographer: African American Studies.

David Feldman, Professor of Mathematics, University of New Hampshire.
Referee.

Robert Fernekes, Information Services Librarian, Business Specialist, Georgia Southern University.
Bibliographer: Business Administration.

Anne Fields, OSU Libraries Coordinator for Research and Reference, Ohio State University.
Bibliographer: Education.

Jenifer Flaxbart, Head Librarian, Reference and Information Services, University of Texas, Austin.
Bibliographer: Journalism and Communication.

Adonna Fleming, GIS / Maps Librarian, University of Nebraska – Lincoln.
Bibliographer: Geology.

Nicole Fluhr, Professor of English, Southern Connecticut State University.
Referee.

Michael Fosmire, Science Librarian, Purdue University.
Subject Editor: Physics.

Stephen Foster, University Librarian, Wright State University.
Referee.

Gerri Foudy, Government and Politics, Public Affairs, and Law Librarian, University of Maryland.
Bibliographer: Political Science.

Kathleen Fountain, Political Science and Social Work Librarian, California State University, Chico.
Bibliographer: Political Science.

Kristine Fowler, Mathematics Librarian, University of Minnesota, Twin Cities.
Subject Editor: Mathematics.

Stephen Fowlkes, Bibliographer for Sociology, Social Work and Reference, Tulane University.
Bibliographer: Sociology.

Ann Fox, Professor of English, Davidson College.
Referee.

Joe Fugate, Professor of German, Kalamazoo College.
Referee.

Steve Fullwood, Manuscripts Librarian, Schomburg Center for Research in Black Culture, New York Public Library.
Bibliographer: African American Studies.

Ronald Ganze, Professor of English, Valparaiso University.
Bibliographer: Medieval Studies.

Bill Gargan, Reference Librarian and Bibliographer, Brooklyn College.
Bibliographer: British Literature.

Meryle Gaston, Islamic and Middle Eastern Studies Librarian, University of California, Santa Barbara.
Subject Editor: Middle Eastern History, Languages, and Literatures.

Cameron Gearen, Lecturer in English, Yale University.
Bibliographer: General Language and Literature.

Caroline Geck, Librarian, Kean University.
Referee.

Jennifer Geddes, Research Associate Professor of Religious Studies, University of Virginia.
Bibliographer: General Language and Literature.

Mary Gilles, Business Reference Librarian, Washington State University.
Subject Editor: Law.

David Giovacchini, Arabic Librarian, Middle East Collection, Stanford University.
Referee.

Ed Goedeken, Humanities Bibliographer, Iowa State University.
Subject Editor: U.S. and Canadian History.

Melissa Goldsmith, Lecturer, Louisiana State University.
Referee.

Millie Gonzalez, Reference Librarian, Framingham State College.
Bibliographer: Business Administration.

Olympia Gonzalez, Professor of Spanish, Loyola University of Chicago.
Referee.

David Goodman, Professor of Library and Information Science, Long Island University.
Subject Editor: Biology.

Candice Goucher, Professor of History, Washington State University, Vancouver.
Referee.

Malaika Grant, Reference/Instruction Librarian, University of Minnesota, Twin Cities.
Bibliographer: Gender Studies.

Laura Graves, Professor of History, South Plains College.
Bibliographer: Native American Studies.

Chip Green, Professor of Geology, University of South Carolina Upstate.
Referee.

Susan Green, Professor of History, California State University, Chico.
Referee.

Cheryl Grossman, Electronic Services Supervisor, LearningWork Connection, Ohio State University.
Bibliographer: Education.

Anna Marie Guengerich, Librarian, College of Education, University of Iowa.
Bibliographer: Psychology.

Richard Hacken, European Studies Bibliographer, Brigham Young University.
Referee.

Michael Handis, Associate Librarian for Collection Management, CUNY Graduate Center.
Bibliographer: European History.

Shaun Hardy, Librarian, Carnegie Institution of Washington.
Bibliographer: Geology.

Sara Harrington, Art Librarian, Rutgers University.
Referee.

Jon Harrison, Social Sciences Collections Coordinator, Missouri State University.
Bibliographer: Criminal Justice.

Elizabeth Hartung, Professor of Sociology, California Sate University Channel Islands.
Bibliographer: Sociology.

Laurence Hauptman, Professor of History, SUNY New Paltz.
Bibliographer: Native American Studies.

Peter Hayes, Professor of History, Northwestern University.
Bibliographer: European History.

Charles Hayford, Research Fellow, Department of History, Northwestern University.
Subject Editor: Asian History, Languages, and Literatures.

Jeremy Hein, Professor of Sociology, University of Wisconsin – Eau Claire.
Referee.

Eileen Herring, Agriculture Librarian, University of Hawaii.
Bibliographer: Agriculture.

Martin Hewitt, Head of History Department, Trinity and All Saints College, University of Leeds.
Referee.

Terry Hill, Customer Representative for North America, OTTO HARRASSOWITZ GmbH & Co. KG.
Bibliographer: Political Science.

Baraba Hillson, Public and International Affairs and Psychology Liaison Librarian, George Mason University.
Referee.

Lee Hilyer, Mathematics Subject Librarian, University of Houston.
Bibliographer: Education.

Keith Hitchins, Professor of History, University of Illinois.
Bibliographer: European History.

Adrian Ho, Assistant Librarian, University of Houston.
Bibliographer: Journalism and Communication.

David Hogg, Astronomer, National Radio Astronomy Observatory.
Referee.

Jane Holmquist, Astrophysics Librarian, Princeton University.
Subject Editor: Astronomy.

Emily Horning, Librarian for Philosophy, Religious Studies and Anthropology, Yale University.
Subject Editor: Religion.

John Hunter, Science/Engineering Librarian, Rice University.
Bibliographer: Geology.

Carol Hutchins, Head Librarian, Courant Institute of Mathematical Sciences, New York University.
Subject Editor: Computing.

Robin Imhof, Reference Librarian, University of the Pacific.
Bibliographer: GLBT Studies.

Richard Irving, Associate Librarian, SUNY Albany.
Bibliographer: Criminal Justice.

Kristin Jacobi, Head, Catologing Department, Eastern Connecticut State University.
Bibliographer: Native American Studies.

James Jaffe, Professor of History, University of Wisconsin – Whitewater.
Bibliographer: European History.

Arif Jamal, Social Sciences Bibliographer, University of Pittsburgh.
Bibliographer: African American Studies.

Sylvia James, Sylvia James Consultancy.
Bibliographer: Business Administration.

Fred Jenkins, Head of Collection Management, University of Dayton.
Subject Editor: Ancient History; Classics.

Donald Clay Johnson, Curator, Ames Library of South Asia, University of Minnesota.
Bibliographer: Asian History, Languages, and Literatures.

Melissa Johnson, Reference and Instruction Librarian, Lynn University.
Bibliographer: European History.

Sarah Johnson, Librarian, Eastern Illinois University.
Bibliographer: General Language and Literature.

Lisa Johnston, Head of Public Services, Sweet Briar College.
Bibliographer: British Literature.

Scott Johnston, Librarian, CUNY Graduate Center.
Subject Editor: Urban Studies.

David P. Jordan, Professor of History, University of Illinois at Chicago.
Bibliographer: European History.

Jonathan Judaken, Professor of History, University of Memphis.
Bibliographer: European History.

Jeannie Kamerman, Director, Curriculum Materials Library, University of West Florida.
Bibliographer: Education.

James Kelly, Humanities Bibliographer, University of Massachussetts.
Subject Editor: American Literature.

Marcia Keyser, Instruction and Reference Librarian, Drake University.
Bibliographer: Education.

Shayee Khanaka, Librarian, Middle Eastern Collection, University of California Berkeley.
Bibliographer: Middle Eastern History, Languages, and Literatures.

Sherise Kimura, Reference Librarian, University of San Francisco.
Bibliographer: Asian American Studies.

Douglas King, Librarian, University of South Carolina.
Bibliographer: American Literature.

Laura Kinner, Coordinator, Cataloging Services, University of Toledo.
Bibliographer: British Literature.

Harold Kirkwood, Librarian, Purdue University.
Bibliographer: Business Administration.

Patricia Kirkwood, Science Librarian, University of Arkansas.
Bibliographer: Technology and Engineering.

Sheila Kirven, Education Services Librarian, New Jersey City University.
Bibliographer: Education.

Linda Klein, Reference Librarian, Eastern Kentucky University.
Bibliographer: British Literature.

Michael Knee, Science Bibliographer and Reference Librarian, University of Albany.
Bibliographer: Computing.

Norma Kobzina, Head of Information Services, Marian Koshland Bioscience and Natural Resources Library, University of California, Berkeley.
Subject Editor: Agriculture.

David Koenigstein, Librarian, Brooklyn College.
Bibliographer: British Literature.

Gayla Koerting, Special Collections Librarian, University of South Dakota.
Bibliographer: U.S. and Canadian History.

Laura Koltutsky, Information Services Librarian, University of Houston.
Bibliographer: Education.

Kwasi Konadu, Professor of History, Winston Salem State University.
Bibliographer: African History, Languages, and Literatures.

Svetlana Korolev, Science Librarian, University of Wisconsin, Madison.
Referee.

Wade Kotter, Social Sciences Librarian, Weber State University.
Bibliographer: Criminal Justice.

Joe Kraus, Science Librarian, University of Denver.
Referee.

Eiko Kuwana, Professor of History, University of the Sacred Heart, Tokyo.
Bibliographer: European History.

Sharon Ladenson, Gender Studies and Communications Bibliographer, Michigan State University.
Bibliographer: Journalism and Communication.

Carolyn Laffoon, Earth and Atmospheric Sciences Librarian, Purdue University.
Bibliographer: Geology.

Blake Landor, Bibliographer for Philosophy, Classics, and Religion, University of Florida.
Subject Editor: Philosophy.

Jeffry Larson, Librarian for Romance Languages and Literatures, Linguistics, and Classics, Yale University.
Subject Editor: French Language and Literature; Italian Language and Literature.

Jason E. Lavery, Professor of History, Oklahoma State University.
Bibliographer: European History.

Bernadette Lear, Behavioral Sciences and Education Librarian, Pennsylvania State University.
Bibliographer: Psychology.

Patrick Leary, Research Fellow, Department of History, Northwestern University.
Subject Editor: Victorian Studies.

Richard S. Levy, Professor of History, University of Illinois at Chicago.
Bibliographer: European History.

Kevin Lindstrom, Behavioral Sciences and Education Librarian, University of British Columbia.
Bibliographer: Geology.

Ken Liss, Communication Librarian, Boston College.
Bibliographer: Journalism and Communication.

Carol Loranger, Professor of English, Wright State University.
Referee.

Jack Lynch, Professor of English, Rutgers University.
Bibliographer: British Literature.

Karen MacDonald, Business Subject Specialist Librarian, Texas A&M University.
Bibliographer: Business Administration.

Peter Magierski, Librarian for the Middle East Studies, New York University.
Bibliographer: Middle Eastern History, Languages, and Literatures.

Diane Maher, University Archivist, University of San Diego.
Bibliographer: American Literature; British Literature.

Janice Mathews, Librarian for Urban Studies and Social Work, University of Connecticut.
Referee.

Rhonda McGinnis, Business and Economics Librarian, Wayne State University.
Bibliographer: Business Administration.

Glenn McGuigan, Business Reference Librarian, Penn State University.
Subject Editor: Business Administration.

Peter McKay, Business Librarian, University of Florida.
Bibliographer: Business Administration.

Paula McMillen, Social Sciences Librarian, Oregon State University.
Bibliographer: Education.

Lori Mestre, Digital Learning Librarian, University of Illinois.
Bibliographer: Education.

Sue Metcalf, Social Sciences Librarian, New Mexico State University.
Referee.

Marion Miller, Professor of History, University of Illinois at Chicago, emerita.
Bibliographer: European History.

Lisa Mitten, CHOICE.
Subject Editor: Native American Studies.

Sandy Mooney, Design Librarian, Louisiana State University.
Referee.

Fred Muratori, Bibliographer for Anglo-American and Comparative Literature and Film, Cornell University.
Bibliographer: Drama and Theater.

Paula Murphy, Library Consultant.
Referee.

Linda Musser, Head, Fletcher L. Byrom Earth and Mineral Sciences Library, Pennsylvania State University.
Bibliographer: Geology.

Theodore Natsoulas, Professor of History, University of Toledo.
Bibliographer: European History.

Sharon Naylor, Education, Psychology and TMC Division Head, Illinois State University.
Bibliographer: Education.

Antoinette Nelson, Branch Manager, Science and Engineering Library, University of Texas Arlington.
Subject Editor: Technology and Engineering.

Jan Newberry, Professor of Anthropology, University of Lethbridge.
Referee.

Shawn Nicholson, Bibliographer for Sociology, Social Work, Urban Planning, Michigan State University.
Referee.

Jim Niessen, World History Librarian, Rutgers University.
Bibliographer: European History.

Byron Nordstrom, Professor of History, Gustavus Adolphus University.
Bibliographer: European History.

Akilah Nosakhere, Manager, Reference and Research Division, Auburn Avenue Research Library of African American Culture and History.
Subject Editor: African American Studies.

Nancy O'Brien, Head, Education and Social Science Library, University of Illinois.
Subject Editor: Education.

Darby Orcutt, Collection Manager for the Humanities and Data Analysis, North Carolina State University.
Bibliographer: Journalism and Communication.

Harriet Ottenheimer, Professor of Anthropology, Kansas State University.
Bibliographer: Anthropology.

Mark Padnos, Coordinator of Public Services, Bronx Community College.
Subject Editor: Germanic Languages and Literatures.

John Page, Associate Dean, Learning Resources Division, University of the District of Columbia.
Bibliographer: African American Studies.

Tim Parrish, Professor of English, Southern Connecticut State University.
Bibliographer: General Language and Literature.

Lucy Patrick, Head of Special Collections, Florida State University.
Referee.

Christopher Peebles, Associate Vice President for Information Technology and Professor of Anthropology, Indiana University.
Bibliographer: Anthropology.

Ed Peters, Professor of History, University of Pennsylvania.
Bibliographer: European History.

Carmelita Pickett, African American Studies Librarian, Emory University.
Bibliographer: African American Studies.

Lisa Pillow, Collection Development Librarian, University of Wisconsin – River Falls.
Bibliographer: African American Studies.

Chestalene Pintozzi, Science-Engineering Librarian, University of Arizona.
Bibliographer: Geology.

Don Polzella, Professor of Psychology and Associate Dean for Faculty Development and Graduate Programs, University of Dayton.
Subject Editor: Psychology.

Diethelm Prowe, Professor of History, Carleton College.
Bibliographer: European History.

Eleanor Randall, Reference Librarian, Edinboro University of Pennsylvania.
Bibliographer: Biology.

Brenda Reed, Public Services Librarian, Education Library, Queen's University.
Bibliographer: Education.

Ira Revels, Instruction Librarian, Cornell University.
Bibliographer: African American Studies.

Leslie Reynolds, Director of Policy Sciences and Economics Library, Texas A&M University.
Bibliographer: Business Administration.

Amy Robb, Field Librarian for Women's Studies and Communication, University of Michigan.
Bibliographer: Journalism and Communication.

Gloria Roberson, Reference Librarian, Adelphi University.
Bibliographer: African American Studies.

Beth Roberts, Earth and Mineral Sciences Librarian, Pennsylvania State University.
Bibliographer: Geology.

Elizabeth Robertson, Professor of English, University of Colorado.
Bibliographer: British Literature.

Martin Roden, Professor emeritus of Engineering, UCLA.
Bibliographer: Technology and Engineering.

Raquel Rodriguez, Librarian for the African American Collection, University of Pittsburgh.
Bibliographer: African American Studies.

Lisa Romero, Communications Librarian, University of Illinois.
Subject Editor: Journalism and Communication.

Lana Kay Rosenberg, Director, Dance Theatre, Miami University of Ohio.
Referee.

Tony Rosso, Professor of English, Southern Connecticut State University.
Bibliographer: British Literature.

Dana Roth, Chemistry Librarian, Caltech.
Bibliographer: Chemistry.

Linda Salem, Education Librarian, San Diego State University.
Bibliographer: British Literature.

Mark Sanders, Student Outreach Reference Librarian, East Carolina University.
Bibliographer: Environmental Studies.

Rachel Sandoval, Historical Records Project Archivist, University of California, Irvine.
Bibliographer: Latino Studies.

Victoria Santana, Electronic Services Librarian, Oklahoma City University.
Bibliographer: Native American Studies.

Román Santillán, Reference/Instruction Librarian, CUNY / College of Staten Island.
Bibliographer: Spanish Language and Literature.

Vernon Schlotzhauer, Social Science Librarian, Pennsylvania State University.
Bibliographer: Psychology.

Geoff Schmidt, Professor of English, Illinois State University – Edwardsville.
Bibliographer: General Language and Literature.

Alan Schroeder, Business Librarian, California State University Northridge.
Bibliographer: Business Administration.

Kate Schroeder, Doctoral Candidate, History Department, Indiana University.
Subject Editor: African History, Languages, and Literatures.

Friedrich Schuler, Professor of History, Portland State University.
Subject Editor: Latin American History.

Katrin Schultheiss, Professor of History, University of Illinois at Chicago.
Bibliographer: European History.

Jason Schultz, Communications Librarian, Georgia State University.
Bibliographer: African American Studies.

Catherine Shreve, Librarian for Public Policy and Political Science, Duke University.
Subject Editor: Political Science.

Jack Shreve, Professor of English, Allegany College.
Bibliographer: GLBT Studies.

Adam Siegel, Reference Librarian, University of California, Davis.
Bibliographer: Native American Studies.

Dorothy Siles, Librarian, Taylorville Public Library.
Bibliographer: Native American Studies.

Jane Sloan, Media Librarian, Rutgers University.
Subject Editor: Film.

Becky Smith, Head, Business and Economics Library, University of Illinois.
Bibliographer: Business Administration.

Helen Smith, Life Sciences Librarian, Penn State University.
Bibliographer: Agriculture.

Michael Smith, Business Librarian, Texas A&M University.
Bibliographer: Business Administration.

Jacqueline Snider, Librarian, ACT.
Bibliographer: Education.

Doug Southard, DRA International.
Bibliographer: Business Administration.

Roland Spickermann, Professor of History, University of Texas, Permian Basin.
Bibliographer: European History.

Jill Spreitzer, Assistant Librarian, Public Services, University of Detroit Mercy.
Bibliographer: Technology and Engineering.

Jennifer Stevens, Humanities Liaison Librarian, George Mason University.
Bibliographer: Other Literatures in English.

David Stoloff, Professor of Education, Eastern Connecticut State University.
Referee.

Fred Stoss, Biological Science Librarian, SUNY Buffalo.
Subject Editor: Biology.

Stephen Stratton, Head of Collection Development, California State University, Channel Islands.
Subject Editor: Sociology.

Cindy Stretch, Professor of English, Southern Connecticut State University.
Referee.

Leanne Strum, Library Liaison to the School of Business, Regent University.
Bibliographer: Business Administration.

Mila Su, Coordinator of Reference Services, Pennsylvania State University.
Subject Editor: Sport and Recreation.

Helen Sullivan, Head, Slavic Reference Service, University of Illinois.
Subject Editor: Russian Languages and Literatures.

Sarah Sussman, Curator, French and Italian Collections, Stanford University.
Bibliographer: European History.

Marek Suszko, Professor of History, Purdue University North Central.
Bibliographer: European History.

Laura Taddeo, Reference Librarian, SUNY Buffalo.
Bibliographer: British Literature.

Kornelia Tancheva, Director of Instructional Services, Cornell University.
Subject Editor: Drama and Theater.

Wendy Tann, Librarian, Federal Reserve Bank.
Bibliographer: Business Administration.

Cornelia Akins Taylor, Special Collections Librarian, Florida A & M University.
Bibliographer: African American Studies.

Betty Taylor-Thompson, Professor of English, Texas Southern University.
Referee.

Edward Teague, Head, Architecture & Allied Arts Library, University of Oregon.
Subject Editor: Visual Arts.

Samantha Teplitzky, Earth Sciences Librarian and Bibliographer, Stanford University.
Bibliographer: Geology.

Stephen Thompson, Co-Leader, Technical Services Department, Brown University.
Bibliographer: American Literature.

Erik Thomson, Collegiate Assistant Professor, Social Sciences, University of Chicago.
Bibliographer: European History.

Charles Thurston, Reference Librarian and Bibliographer, University of Texas at San Antonio.
Bibliographer: Education.

Judie Triplehorn, Librarian, Geophysical Institute, University of Alaska.
Bibliographer: Geology.

Markel Tumlin, English and American Literature Librarian, San Diego State University.
Bibliographer: American Literature.

Andrea Twiss-Brooks, Bibliographer for Chemical and Geophysical Sciences, University of Chicago.
Subject Editor: Geology.

Kent Underwood, Music Librarian, New York University.
Subject Editor: Music.

Alan Unsworth, Reference Librarian, University of Rochester.
Referee.

David Vaccari, Professor of Engineering, Stevens Institute of Technology.
Bibliographer: Technology and Engineering.

Susan Vega Garcia, Reference & Instruction Librarian, Bibliographer, Iowa State University.
Bibliographer: Latino Studies.

Tom Volkening, Engineering Librarian, Michigan State University.
Bibliographer: Technology and Engineering.

Heather Ward, University of Oregon, formerly.
Subject Editor: Medieval Studies.

Diane Warner, Monographs and Special Formats Cataloger, Texas Tech University.
Bibliographer: American Literature.

Gary Wasdin, Library Director, New School University.
Referee.

Matthew Wayman, Instruction Coordinator, Penn State University.
Bibliographer: U.S. and Canadian History.

Jeneen Willemssen, Librarian, Conserve School.
Bibliographer: Education.

Wendy Williamson, Economics Librarian, University of Minnesota.
Referee.

Suzanne Wise, Collection Development Librarian, Appalachia State University.
Referee.

Ada Woods, Reference Librarian, Towson University.
Bibliographer.

Peng Xu, Reference Librarian, Michigan State University.
Bibliographer: Business Administration.

Lisa Yuro, Reference Librarian/Humanities and Social Sciences Coordinator, University of Alabama.
Bibliographer: Journalism and Communication.

Ann Zawistoski, Reference and Instruction Librarian, Carleton College.
Bibliographer: Geology.

Linda Zellmer, Head, Geology Library, Indiana University.
Subject Editor: Geology.

HOW TO USE
RESOURCES FOR COLLEGE LIBRARIES

Resources for College Libraries (RCL) was designed to be easily searchable by author, title, and the RCL subject taxonomy. The set consists of seven volumes, Volumes 1-6 arranged by RCL Subject, and sorted alphabetically by author. Volume 7 is a comprehensive author, title and subject index. The volumes are arranged by *Resources for College Library* Subject Headings, a full listing of which is present in the Subject Headings Index in volume 7.

Each title in *Resources for College Libraries* has been classified with a specific RCL Subject and/or subjects. Titles can and often do appear within more than one RCL Subject area. Titles have been given a specific readership level through audience code: g=general, l=lower-division undergraduate, u=upper-division undergraduate graduate, and/or f=faculty level resources. Titles previously mentioned in *Books for College Libraries, 3rd Edition*, have been noted with a specific BCL3 icon. Non-book entries can be easily identified with the icons for Web, Ebook, or CD/DVD-ROM.

Title entries can include the following bibliographic information, when available: author, co-author, editor, co-editor, translator, co-translator, title, number of volumes, edition, series information, binding type, publisher, publisher location, date of publication, number of pages, ISBN, ISBN-13, Library of Congress Classification Number, Dewey Decimal Number, Library of Congress Control Number, Audience Code, and whether it has been reviewed in Choice Magazine.

Entries in the Author Index can include the following bibliographic information when available: author, co-author, editor, co-editor, translator, co-translator, along with page number(s) and volume number(s) of the selected works within the 6-volume set. Entries are not cross-referenced by other than primary author and/or first contributor. Entries in the Title Index include the title, page number(s) and volume number(s) of the selected works within the 6-volume set.

Titles in *Resources for College Libraries* have been alphabetized using the following rules:

- Initial articles of titles in English, French, German, Italian, and Spanish are not included for sorting purposes.
- Titles beginning with acronyms appear before those beginning with words. For example, B E A M A Directory would precede Baal, Babylon.
- As a general rule, U.S. and UN are filed in strict alphabetical order.

SAMPLE RCL ENTRY

1 DRAMA AND THEATER > Western Drama > United States

2 **Wilmeth, Don B. & Bigsby, Christopher (Editors)** **PN2221**
3 The Cambridge History of American Theater: 4 1870-1945. 5 Ed. 2
6 Don B. Wilmeth & Christopher Bigsby (Contribution by). 7 Trade Paper.
8 Cambridge University Press. 9 New York, NY. 10 2006. 11 608p.
12 Cambridge History of American Theater Ser. 13 ISBN: 0-521-67984-2, ISBN13: 978-0-521-67984-8. 14 Dewey:792/.0973.
15 LCCN: 00-000000
16 Audience: **l,u,f.** 17 *Choice, 2005*

1. RCL Subject Heading
2. Author/First Contributor
3. Title
4. Subtitle
5. Ed. Info
6. Additional Contributors
7. Binding Type
8. Publisher
9. Publisher Location
10. Publication Date
11. Number of Pages
12. Series Title
13. ISBN, ISBN-13
14. Dewey
15. LCCN
16. Audience Code
17. Choice Review and Date

- Numeric Titles may be found near the end of the Title Index

Authors in *Resources for College Libraries* have been alphabetized using the following rules:

- Proper names beginning with "Mc" and "Mac" are filed in strict alphabetical order. For example, entries for contributors' names such as MacAdam, MacAvory, and MacCarthy are located prior to the pages with entries for names such as McAdam, McCoy, and McDermott.
- When author names are represented with initials, they are alphabetized before author first names. For example, Smith, H. C. appears before Smith, Harold A.

Any errors in bibliographic data should be E-mailed directly to: rclwebfeedback@bowker.com

ABBREVIATIONS AND CODE LIST:

BCL3	*Books for College Libraries, 3rd Edition*
Bk.(s.)	Book(s)
Ed.	Edition
F	Faculty
G	General
Inc.	Incorporated
Jr.	Junior
ISBN	International Standard Book Number
L	Lower-Division Undergraduate
LCCN	Library of Congress Control Number
p.	Pages
RCL	Resources for College Libraries
Ser.	Series
Sr.	Senior
U	Upper-Division Undergraduate

Geographical Abbreviations

AL	Alabama
AK	Alaska
AB	Alberta
AE	American Europe
AS	American Samoa
AZ	Arizona
AR	Arkansas
ACT	Australian Capital Territory
BC	British Columbia
CA	California
CM	Central Marianas
CO	Colorado
CT	Connecticut
DE	Delaware
DC	District Of Columbia
FM	Federated States Of Micronesia
FL	Florida
GA	Georgia
GU	Guam
HI	Hawaii
ID	Idaho
IL	Illinois
IN	Indiana
IA	Iowa
KS	Kansas
KY	Kentucky
LA	Louisiana
ME	Maine
MB	Manitoba
MH	Marshall Islands
MD	Maryland
MA	Massachusetts
MI	Michigan
MP	Middle Pacific
MN	Minnesota
MS	Mississippi
MO	Missouri
MT	Montana
NE	Nebraska
NV	Nevada
NB	New Brunswick
NH	New Hampshire
NJ	New Jersey
NM	New Mexico
NSW	New South Wales
NY	New York
NF	Newfoundland
NC	North Carolina
ND	North Dakota
NP	Northern Marianas
N.T.	Northern Territory (Australia)
NT	Northwest Territory
NS	Nova Scotia
NU	Nunavut
OH	Ohio
OK	Oklahoma
ON	Ontario
OR	Oregon
TT	Pacific Territories
PW	Pacific West
PA	Pennsylvania
PE	Prince Edward Island
PR	Puerto Rico
PQ	Quebec
QLD	Queensland
RI	Rhode Island
SK	Saskatchewan
SA	South Australia
SC	South Carolina
SD	South Dakota
TAS	Tasmania
TN	Tennessee
TX	Texas
UT	Utah
VT	Vermont
VIC	Victoria
VI	Virgin Islands
VA	Virginia
WA	Washington
WV	West Virginia
W.A.	Western Australia
WI	Wisconsin
WY	Wyoming
YT	Yukon Territory

AMERICAN LITERATURE

This section contains works regularly taught in the course of the undergraduate major in English literature, and as such includes canonical works by major American authors, as well as other works regularly studied. These selections are supported by a variety of critical, biographical, and literary-historical works devoted to individual authors and to periods. Unlike BCL3, no effort was made to include the complete works of every author, and selection in general tended away from rather than toward the inclusion of complete letters, bibliographies of critical works, concordances, and other materials more appropriate to a research collection than one supporting the undergraduate curriculum. Although critical works tend to be more recent, an effort was made to include the most valuable of older works. For additional coverage of literary criticism and theory, see also the General Language and Literature section of RCL.

Particular attention was paid to the inclusion of works of writers of color and women writers; generally, these individual writers and works were selected on the basis of how commonly they are taught in the undergraduate curriculum. For additional coverage, see also the African American Studies; Asian American Studies; Gay, Lesbian, Bisexual, and Transgendered Studies; and Latino Studies sections of RCL.

Where possible, works are recommended in their newest, most reliable edition. Some works are available only as reprints, while a few are out of print, though still recommended.

—James Kelly

History, Criticism

Hart, James David, 1911- **PS21**
The Oxford Companion to American Literature. Ed. 6. Oxford University Press. 1995. ISBN:0-19-506548-4, ISBN13: 978-0-19-506548-0.
Audience: **g,l,u,f.**

History, Criticism > Criticism

PS78 .B56
Contemporary Literary Critics. Ed. 3. Trade Cloth. Thomson Gale. Farmington Hills, MI. 2005. ISBN:1-55862-187-3, ISBN13: 978-1-55862-187-9. Dewey:801/.95/0922 B.
Audience: **l,u,f.**

Allen, Paula Gunn **E98.W8**
The Sacred Hoop: Recovering the Feminine in American Indian Traditions. Ed. 2. Trade Paper. Beacon Press. Boston, MA. 1992. 336p. ISBN:0-8070-4617-5, ISBN13: 978-0-8070-4617-3. Dewey:970.004/97/0088042. LCCN:92-006332.
Audience: **u,f.** *Choice, 1986.*

Armstrong, Nancy & Tennenhouse, Leonard **PR431**
The Imaginary Puritan: Literature, Intellectual Labor, and the Origins of Personal Life. Trade Cloth. University of California Press. Berkeley, CA. 1992. 275p. The New Historicism Ser., No. 21:Studies in Cultural Poetics ISBN:0-520-07756-3, ISBN13: 978-0-520-07756-0. Dewey:820.9004. LCCN:91-040263.
Audience: **u,f.**

Ashton, Jennifer **PS323.5**
From Modernism to Postmodernism: American Poetry and Theory in the Twentieth Century. Albert Gelpi & Ross Posnock (Contribution by). Trade Cloth. Cambridge University Press. New York, NY. 2006. 212p. Cambridge Studies in American Literature and Culture Ser., Vol. 149 ISBN:0-521-85504-7, ISBN13: 978-0-521-85504-4. Dewey:811.509. LCCN:2006-296168.
Audience: **u,f.**

Baker, Barbara A. **PS261.B23 2003**
The Blues Aesthetic and the Making of American Identity in the Literature of the South. Trade Cloth. Peter Lang Publishing, Inc. New York, NY. 2003. 172p. Modern American Literature Ser., :New Approaches Ser. ISBN:0-8204-6220-9, ISBN13: 978-0-8204-6220-2. Dewey:810.9/357. LCCN:2002-029451.
Audience: **u,f.**

Benston, Kimberly W. **PS153.N5B45 2000**
Performing Blackness: Enactments of African-American Modernism. Paper over Boards. Routledge. New York, NY. 2000. 400p. ISBN:0-415-00948-0, ISBN13: 978-0-415-00948-5. Dewey:810.9/896073. LCCN:99-054173.
Audience: **u,f.**

Brooks, Cleanth **PS261.B75 1995**
Community, Religion and Literature: Essays. Trade Cloth. University of Missouri Press. Columbia, MO. 1995. 352p. ISBN:0-8262-0993-9, ISBN13: 978-0-8262-0993-1. Dewey:810.9/975. LCCN:94-043049.
Audience: **l,u,f.** *Choice, 1995.*

Crowley, John W. **PS374.A42C76 1994**
The White Logic: Alcoholism and Gender in American Modernist Fiction. Trade Paper. University of Massachusetts Press. Amherst, MA. 1994. 216p. ISBN:0-87023-944-9, ISBN13: 978-0-87023-944-1. Dewey:813/.509356. LCCN:94-014809.
Audience: **u,f.** *Choice, 1995.*

Davis, Charles T. & Gates, Henry Louis Jr. (Editors) **PS366.A35**
The Slave's Narrative. Paper Text. Oxford University Press, Inc. New York, NY. 1991. 384p. ISBN:0-19-506656-1, ISBN13: 978-0-19-506656-2. Dewey:818/.08.
Audience: **u,f.**

Dearborn, Mary V. **PS147.D43 1986**
Pocahontas's Daughters: Gender and Ethnicity in American Culture. Trade Cloth. Oxford University Press, Inc. New York, NY. 1985. 288p. ISBN:0-19-503632-8, ISBN13: 978-0-19-503632-9. Dewey:810/.9/9287. LCCN:85-005093.
Audience: **u,f.** *Choice, 1986.*

Eddy, Beth **PN75.B8E34 2003**
The Rites of Identity: The Religious Naturalism and Cultural Criticism of Kenneth Burke and Ralph Ellison. Trade Cloth. Princeton University Press. Princeton, NJ. 2003. 256p. ISBN:0-691-09249-4, ISBN13: 978-0-691-09249-2. Dewey:818/.5209. LCCN:2002-044719.
Audience: **u,f.** *Choice, 2004.*

Eliot, T. S. **PS78.C7**
Criticism in America: Its Functions and Status. Library Binding. Reprint Services Company. Temecula, CA. 1992. 30p. BCL1-PS American Literature Ser. ISBN:0-7812-6601-7, ISBN13: 978-0-7812-6601-7. Dewey:801/.95/0973.
Audience: **l,u,f.**

Faery, Rebecca B. **PS173.I6F34 1999**
Cartographies of Desire: Captivity, Race and Sex in the Shaping of an American Nation. Trade Paper. University of Oklahoma Press. Norman, OK. 1999. 288p. ISBN:0-8061-3150-0, ISBN13: 978-0-8061-3150-4. Dewey:810.9/35297. LCCN:98-054760.
Audience: **u,f.** *Choice, 2000.*

Foerster, Norman **PS78**
Toward Standards: A Study of the Present. Trade Paper. Kessinger Publishing, LLC. Whitefish, MT. 2005. ISBN:1-4179-3624-X, ISBN13: 978-1-4179-3624-3. Dewey:810.9005.
Audience: **l,u,f.**

Gates, Henry Louis Jr. **PS508.N3**
Afro-American Women Writers. Trade Cloth. Thomson Gale. Farmington Hills, MI. 1998. ISBN:0-8161-1848-5, ISBN13: 978-0-8161-1848-9. Dewey:810.8089607.
Audience: **g,l,u,f.**

Gates, Henry Louis Jr. **PS153.N5**
The Signifying Monkey: A Theory of African-American Literary Criticism. Trade Paper. Oxford University Press, Inc. New York, NY. 1989. 318p. ISBN:0-19-506075-X, ISBN13: 978-0-19-506075-1. Dewey:810/.9/896073.
Audience: **u,f.** *Choice, 1989.*

Glotfelty, Cheryll & Fromm, Harold (Editors) **PN81.E24 1996**
The Ecocriticism Reader: Landmarks in Literary Ecology. Paper Text. University of Georgia Press. Athens, GA. 1996. 448p. ISBN:0-8203-1781-0, ISBN13: 978-0-8203-1781-6. Dewey:801/.95. LCCN:95-032150.
Audience: **u,f.**

Habegger, Alfred **PS374.R37**
Gender Fantasy and Realism in American Literature. Trade Paper. Columbia University Press. New York, NY. 1984. 378p. ISBN:0-231-05397-5, ISBN13: 978-0-231-05397-6. Dewey:813/.4/0912. LCCN:82-001239.
Audience: **l,u,f.**

Hall, Donald **PS3515.A3152B74 2003**
Breakfast Served Any Time All Day: Essays on Poetry New and Selected. Trade Cloth. University of Michigan Press. Chicago, IL. 2003. 232p. ISBN:0-472-09852-7, ISBN13: 978-0-472-09852-1. Dewey:811/.009. LCCN:2003-008358.
Audience: **u,f.**

Hapke, Laura **PS374.P67H37 1989**
Girls Who Went Wrong: Prostitutes in American Fiction, 1885-1917. Trade Cloth. University of Wisconsin Press. Chicago, IL. 1989. 216p. ISBN:0-87972-473-0, ISBN13: 978-0-87972-473-3. Dewey:813.009/3520692. LCCN:89-085815.
Audience: **u,f.**

Hapke, Laura **PS374.W64H36 2001**
Labor's Text: The Worker in American Fiction. Trade Cloth. Rutgers University Press. Piscataway, NJ. 2001. xiv, 474p. ISBN:0-8135-2879-8, ISBN13: 978-0-8135-2879-3. Dewey:813.009/3523317. LCCN:00-039031.
Audience: **u,f.**

Hapke, Laura **PS374.W6H36 1992**
Tales of the Working Girl: Wage-Earning Women in American Literature, 1890-1925. Cloth Text. Macmillan Publishing Company, Inc. Old Tappan, NJ. 1992. 192p. Twayne's Literature and Society Ser., No. 2 ISBN:0-8057-8855-7, ISBN13: 978-0-8057-8855-6. Dewey:813/.5209352042. LCCN:92-010568.
Audience: **u,f.** *Choice, 1993.*

James, Henry **PS2112 1984**
The Art of the Novel: Critical Prefaces. R. W. B. Lewis (Foreword by), Richard P. Blackmur (Introduction by). Trade Paper. Northeastern University Press. Boston, MA. 1984. 399p. ISBN:0-930350-60-X, ISBN13: 978-0-930350-60-4. Dewey:813/.4. LCCN:84-005619.
Audience: **g,l,u,f.** B

James, Henry **PN761 .J27 1979**
Literary Reviews and Essays on American, English and French Literature. Albert Mordell (Editor). Trade Paper. Grove/Atlantic, Inc. New York, NY. 1979. ISBN:0-394-17098-9, ISBN13: 978-0-394-17098-5. Dewey:809/.034. LCCN:79-009213.
Audience: **g,l,u,f.** B

Jaskoski, Helen (Editor) **PS153.I52 E27 1996**
Early Native American Writing: New Critical Essays. LaVonne Brown Ruoff (Foreword by), Albert Gelpi & Ross Posnock (Contribution by). Trade Paper. Cambridge University Press. New York, NY. 1996. 257p. Studies in American Literature and Culture, No. 102 ISBN:0-521-55527-2, ISBN13: 978-0-521-55527-2. Dewey:810.9/897. LCCN:95-026723.
Audience: **l,u,f.**

Kazin, Alfred **PS369**
On Native Grounds: An Interrpetation of Modern American Prose Literature. Trade Paper. Harcourt Trade Publishers. New York, NY. 1995. 564p. Harvest Book Ser. ISBN:0-15-668750-X, ISBN13: 978-0-15-668750-8. Dewey:810.9. LCCN:42-024811.
Audience: **u,f.**

Leary, Lewis (Editor) **Z1225.L492**
Articles on American Literature: 1950-1967. Cloth Text. Duke University Press. Durham, NC. 1970. xxxi, 751p. ISBN:0-8223-0239-X, ISBN13: 978-0-8223-0239-1. Dewey:016.8109. LCCN:70-132027.
Audience: **l,u,f.**

Leary, Lewis **Z1225.L49**
Articles on American Literature: 1900-1950. Trade Cloth. Duke University Press. Durham, NC. 1954. xv, 437p. ISBN:0-8223-0241-1, ISBN13: 978-0-8223-0241-4. Dewey:16.81. LCCN:54-005024.
Audience: **l,u,f.**

Leary, Lewis & Auchard, John (Compiled by) **Z1225.L493**
Articles on American Literature, 1968-1975. Trade Cloth. Duke University Press. Durham, NC. 1979. xxv, 745p. ISBN:0-8223-0432-5, ISBN13: 978-0-8223-0432-6. Dewey:016.81/09. LCCN:79-052535.
Audience: **l,u,f.** B

McClure, Michael **PS3563.A262S35 1994**
Scratching the Beat Surface: Essays on New Vision from Blake to Kerouac. Trade Paper. Penguin Group (USA) Inc. New York, NY. 1994. 192p. ISBN:0-14-023252-4, ISBN13: 978-0-14-023252-3. Dewey:814/.54. LCCN:94-233382.
Audience: **l,u,f.**

McLendon, Jacquelyn Y. **PS3511.A864Z77 1995**
The Politics of Color in the Fiction of Jessie Fauset and Nella Larsen. Cloth Text. University Press of Virginia. Charlottesville, VA. 1995. 160p. ISBN:0-8139-1553-8, ISBN13: 978-0-8139-1553-1. Dewey:813/.52. LCCN:94-043835.
Audience: **u,f.** *Choice, 1995.*

Mencken, H. L. **PS3525.E43A6**
H. L. Mencken's Smart Set Criticism. Ed. 2. Trade Paper. Regnery Publishing, Incorporated, An Eagle Publishing Company. Washington, DC. 2001. 349p. ISBN:0-89526-231-2, ISBN13: 978-0-89526-231-8. Dewey:809. LCCN:87-023248.
Audience: **u,f.** B

Miller, Perry G. **PS74 .M5 1973**
The Raven and the Whale: The War of Words and Wits in the Era of Poe and Melville. Trade Cloth. Greenwood Publishing Group, Inc. Portsmouth, NH. 1973. 370p. ISBN:0-8371-6707-8, ISBN13: 978-0-8371-6707-7. Dewey:810/.9/003. LCCN:72-011741.
Audience: **l,u,f.**

Myers, Jeffrey **PS169.E25M94 2005**
Converging Stories: Race, Ecology, and Environmental Justice in American Literature. Trade Cloth. University of Georgia Press. Athens, GA. 2005. 188p. ISBN:0-8203-2744-1, ISBN13: 978-0-8203-2744-0. Dewey:810.93556. LCCN:2005-001133.
Audience: **u,f.**

Nicholls, David G. **PS153.N5N53 2000**
Conjuring the Folk: Forms of Modernity in African America. Trade Cloth. University of Michigan Press. Chicago, IL. 2000. 192p. ISBN:0-472-11034-9, ISBN13: 978-0-472-11034-6. Dewey:810.9/896073. LCCN:99-050557.
Audience: **u,f.** *Choice, 2001.*

Phillips, Dana **PS163.P48 2003**
The Truth of Ecology: Nature, Culture, and Literature in America. Trade Paper. Oxford University Press, Inc. New York, NY. 2003. 316p. ISBN:0-19-513769-8, ISBN13: 978-0-19-513769-9. Dewey:810.9/355. LCCN:2002-030735.
Audience: **u,f.**

Pritchard, John Paul **E210.A55**
Criticism in America: An Account of the Development of Critical Techniques from the Early Period of the Republic to the Middle Years of the Twentieth Century. Paper Text. Textbook Publishers. Temecula, CA. 2003. 325p. ISBN:0-7581-1781-7, ISBN13: 978-0-7581-1781-6. Dewey:973.311.
Audience: **l,u,f.**

Rohy, Valerie **PS153.L46R64 2000**
Impossible Women: Lesbian Figures and American Literature. Book, Other. Cornell University Press. Ithaca, NY. 2000. 208p. ISBN:0-8014-3728-8, ISBN13: 978-0-8014-3728-1. Dewey:810.9/9206643. LCCN:99-087706.
Audience: **l,u,f.**

Scharnhorst, Gary (Editor) **PS3 .A47**
American Literary Scholarship: An Annual, 1995. Library Binding. Duke University Press. Durham, NC. 1997. 500p. ISBN:0-8223-1952-7, ISBN13: 978-0-8223-1952-8. Dewey:810.
Audience: **u,f.**

Sundquist, Eric J. **PS153.N5S9 1993**
To Wake the Nations: Race in the Making of American Literature. Trade Cloth. Harvard University Press. Cambridge, MA. 1993. 720p. ISBN:0-674-89330-1, ISBN13: 978-0-674-89330-6. Dewey:810.9896073. LCCN:92-034164.
Audience: **u,f.** *Choice, 1993.*

Taylor, Carole Anne (Editor) **PS374.N4T38 2000**
The Tragedy and Comedy of Resistance: Reading Modernity Through Black Women's Fiction. Book, Other. University of Pennsylvania Press. Philadelphia, PA. 1999. 280p. Contemporary American Fiction Ser. ISBN:0-8122-3510-X, ISBN13: 978-0-8122-3510-4. Dewey:813/.5099287/08996. LCCN:99-029489.
Audience: **u,f.** *Choice, 2000.*

Thomas, Brook **PS374.R37T48 1997**
e American Literary Realism and the Failed Promise of Contract. E-Book. NetLibrary, Inc. Boulder, CO. 1997. ISBN:0-585-08239-1, ISBN13: 978-0-585-08239-4. Dewey:810.9/12.
Audience: **u,f.** *Choice, 1997.*

Thomas, Brook **PS374.R37T48 1997**
American Literary Realism and the Failed Promise of Contract. Trade Cloth. University of California Press. Berkeley, CA. 1997. 372p. ISBN:0-520-20647-9, ISBN13: 978-0-520-20647-2. Dewey:810.9/12. LCCN:96-003719.
Audience: **u,f.** *Choice, 1997.*

Trilling, Lionel **PS3539.R56 L5 1979**
The Liberal Imagination: Essays on Literature and Society. Trade Cloth. Harcourt Trade Publishers. New York, NY. 1979. 320p. ISBN:0-15-151197-7, ISBN13: 978-0-15-151197-6. Dewey:814/.5/2. LCCN:78-065749.
Audience: **g,l,u,f.**

True, Michael **PS169.N65T78 1995**
An Energy Field More Intense Than War: The Nonviolent Tradition and American Literature. Trade Cloth. Syracuse University Press. Syracuse, NY. 1995. 192p. Studies on Peace and Conflict Resolution ISBN:0-8156-2679-7, ISBN13: 978-0-8156-2679-4. Dewey:810.9/355. LCCN:95-013288.
Audience: **u,f.** *Choice, 1996.*

Vorlicky, Robert **PS338.M37V67 1995**
Act Like a Man: Challenging Masculinities in American Drama. Trade Cloth. University of Michigan Press. Chicago, IL. 1995. 400p. ISBN:0-472-09572-2, ISBN13: 978-0-472-09572-8. Dewey:812/.5409353. LCCN:94-038076.
Audience: **u,f.** *Choice, 1995.*

Winchell, Mark R. **PS29.B74W56 1996**
Cleanth Brooks and the Rise of Modern Criticism. Trade Cloth. University Press of Virginia. Charlottesville, VA. 1996. 608p. Minds of the New South Ser. ISBN:0-8139-1647-X, ISBN13: 978-0-8139-1647-7. Dewey:809. LCCN:95-046642.
Audience: **u,f.** *Choice, 1996.*

History, Criticism > History of American Literature

Aaron, Daniel **PS217.C58A27 2003**
The Unwritten War: American Writers and the Civil War. Trade Paper. University of Alabama Press. Tuscaloosa, AL. 2003. 432p. ISBN:0-8173-5002-0, ISBN13: 978-0-8173-5002-4. Dewey:810.9/358. LCCN:2002-073239.
Audience: **l,u,f.**

Ammons, Elizabeth & White-Parks, Annette (Editors) **PS217.T79T75 1994**
Tricksterism in Turn-of-the-Century American Literature: A Multicultural Perspective. Library Binding. University Press of New England. Lebanon, NH. 1994. 217p. ISBN:0-87451-680-3, ISBN13: 978-0-87451-680-7. Dewey:810.9/920693. LCCN:94-020520.
Audience: **u,f.** *Choice, 1995.*

Bercovitch, Sacvan **PS121**
The Cambridge History of American Literature, Set. Quantity Pack, Trade Cloth. Cambridge University Press. New York, NY. 2006. 6000p. The Cambridge History of American Literature Ser. ISBN:0-521-85760-0, ISBN13: 978-0-521-85760-4. Dewey:810.9.
Audience: **l,u,f.**

Bercovitch, Sacvan **PS121**
Reconstructing American Literary History. Trade Cloth. Replica Books. Bridgewater, NJ. 2000. 370p. ISBN:0-7351-0228-7, ISBN13: 978-0-7351-0228-6. Dewey:810/.9.
Audience: **l,u,f.** *Choice, 1986.*

Broaddus, Dorothy C. **PS255.B6B76 1998**
Genteel Rhetoric: Writing High Culture in 19th Century Boston. Trade Cloth. University of South Carolina Press. Columbia, SC. 1999. 128p. Studies in Rhetoric - Communication ISBN:1-57003-244-0, ISBN13: 978-1-57003-244-8. Dewey:810.9/974461. LCCN:98-019678.
Audience: **u,f.** *Choice, 1999.*

Brooks, Van Wyck **PS221 .B65**
On Literature Today. Library Binding. Reprint Services Company. Temecula, CA. 1993. 290p. BCL1-PS American Literature Ser. ISBN:0-7812-6578-9, ISBN13: 978-0-7812-6578-2. Dewey:810.904.
Audience: **l,u,f.**

Davidson, Cathy N. **Z1003.2.R424 1989**
Reading in America: Literature and Social History. Trade Paper. Johns Hopkins University Press. Baltimore, MD. 1968. 320p. ISBN:0-8018-3800-2, ISBN13: 978-0-8018-3800-2. Dewey:028/.9/0973. LCCN:88-035821.
Audience: **u,f.**

Davidson, Cathy N. **PS374.S67D38 2004**
Revolution and the Word: The Rise of the Novel in America. Ed. 2. Trade Paper. Oxford University Press, Inc. New York, NY. 2004. 480p. ISBN:0-19-514823-1, ISBN13: 978-0-19-514823-7. Dewey:810.9/358. LCCN:2004-275850.
Audience: **u,f.** *Choice, 2005, 1987.*

Elliott, Emory (Editor) **PS92.C64 1988**
The Columbia Literary History of the United States. Trade Cloth. Columbia University Press. New York, NY. 1988. 1263p. ISBN:0-231-05812-8, ISBN13: 978-0-231-05812-4. Dewey:810/.9. LCCN:87-014672.
Audience: **l,u,f.** *Choice, 1988.*

Kent, Kathryn R. **PS228.L47K46 2002**
Making Girls into Women: American Women's Writing and the Rise of Lesbian Identity. Trade Cloth. Duke University Press. Durham, NC. 2003. 344p. Series Q ISBN:0-8223-3030-X, ISBN13: 978-0-8223-3030-1. Dewey:813/.50935206643. LCCN:2002-008828.
Audience: **u,f.** *Choice, 2003.*

Kolodny, Annette **74-23950**
The Lay of the Land: Metaphor As Experience and History in American Life and Letters. Trade Paper. University of North Carolina Press. Chapel Hill, NC. 1984. 198p. ISBN:0-8078-4118-8, ISBN13: 978-0-8078-4118-1. Dewey:810.9/36. LCCN:74-023950.
Audience: **g,l,u,f.** B

Lewis, Leslie W. & Ardis, Ann L. **PS228.M63W66 2002**
Women's Experience of Modernity, 1875-1945. Trade Paper. Johns Hopkins University Press. Baltimore, MD. 2003. 304p. ISBN:0-8018-6935-8, ISBN13: 978-0-8018-6935-8. Dewey:820.9/9287/09034. LCCN:2001-008647.
Audience: **u,f.**

Ostrom, Hans & Macey, J. David (Editors) **PS153**
The Greenwood Encyclopedia of African American Literature. Cloth Text. Greenwood Publishing Group, Inc. Portsmouth, NH. 2005. 2196p. ISBN:0-313-32972-9, ISBN13: 978-0-313-32972-2. Dewey:810.9/896073. LCCN:2005-013679.
Audience: **g,l,u,f.** *Choice, 2006.*

Parrington, Vernon L. **PS88.P33**
Main Currents in American Thought: The Romantic Revolution in America, 1800-1860. Trade Paper. Harcourt Trade Publishers. New York, NY. 1955. 486p. ISBN:0-15-655135-7, ISBN13: 978-0-15-655135-9. Dewey:810/.9 s 810/.9/003.
Audience: **l,u,f.**

Parrington, Vernon L. **PS88 .P33**
Main Currents in American Thought: Beginnings of Critical Realism in America, 1860-1920. Trade Paper. Harcourt Trade Publishers. New York, NY. 1963. 429p. ISBN:0-15-611677-4, ISBN13: 978-0-15-611677-0. Dewey:810/.9 s 810/.9/004. LCCN:56-058467.
Audience: **l,u,f.**

Parrington, Vernon L. **PS88**
Main Currents in American Thought: The Colonial Mind, 1620-1800. Trade Paper. Harcourt Trade Publishers. New York, NY. 1955. 420p. ISBN:0-15-655134-9, ISBN13: 978-0-15-655134-2. Dewey:810.9.
Audience: **l,u,f.**

Perry, Bliss **E173 .C55 VOL. 34**
American Spirit in Literature: Chronicle. Trade Paper. Kessinger Publishing, LLC. Whitefish, MT. 2003. ISBN:0-7661-6428-4, ISBN13: 978-0-7661-6428-4. Dewey:810.9.
Audience: **l,u,f.**

Poirier, Richard **PS88.P6 1985**
A World Elsewhere: The Place of Style in American Literature. Trade Paper. University of Wisconsin Press. Chicago, IL. 1985. 272p. ISBN:0-299-09934-2, ISBN13: 978-0-299-09934-3. Dewey:810/.9. LCCN:85-040376.
Audience: **l,u,f.** B

Smyers, Virginia L. & Winship, Michael **Z1225.B55 2003**
Bibliography of American Literature. Jacob Blanck (Compiled by), Bibliographical Society of America Staff (Contribution by). Trade Cloth. Oak Knoll Press. New Castle, DE. 2003. ISBN:1-58456-109-2, ISBN13: 978-1-58456-109-5. Dewey:016.81. LCCN:2003-057968.
Audience: **l,u,f.**

Wendell, Barrett **PS88 .W4**
A Literary History of America. Trade Paper. Kessinger Publishing, LLC. Whitefish, MT. 2005. ISBN:1-4179-8346-9, ISBN13: 978-1-4179-8346-9. Dewey:810/.9.
Audience: **l,u,f.**

History, Criticism > Collected Essays. Collective Biography

CT103
American Writers, Set. Trade Cloth. Thomson Gale. Farmington Hills, MI. 1992. 2496p. ISBN:0-684-80586-3, ISBN13: 978-0-684-80586-3. Dewey:920.003.
Audience: **l,u,f.**

Applegate, E. C. **PS374**
American Naturalistic and Realistic Novelists: A Biographical Dictionary. Cloth Text. Greenwood Publishing Group, Inc. Portsmouth, NH. 2001. 456p. ISBN:0-313-31572-8, ISBN13: 978-0-313-31572-5. Dewey:813.009/12. LCCN:2001-023320.
Audience: **l,u,f.** *Choice, 2002.*

Bewley, Marius **PS124 .B45**
Complex Fate: Hawthorne, Henry James and Some American Writers. Trade Cloth. Gordian Press, Inc. Staten Island, NY. 1967. 248p. ISBN:0-87752-008-9, ISBN13: 978-0-87752-008-5. Dewey:810.9. LCCN:67-028474.
Audience: **l,u,f.** B

Blackmur, Richard P. **PS121 .B59 1977**
The Lion and the Honeycomb: Essays in Solicitude and Critique. Trade Cloth. Greenwood Publishing Group, Inc. Portsmouth, NH. 1977. ISBN:0-8371-9799-6, ISBN13: 978-0-8371-9799-9. Dewey:809. LCCN:77-010875.
Audience: **l,u,f.**

Brooks, Van Wyck **E169.1.B7985**
America's Coming-of-Age. Trade Cloth. Amereon, Ltd. Mattituck, NY. ISBN:0-8488-0433-3, ISBN13: 978-0-8488-0433-6. Dewey:973.
Audience: **l,u,f.**

Ehrlich, Eugene H. & Carruth, Gorton **PS141.E74 1982**
The Oxford Illustrated Literary Guide to the United States. Trade Cloth. Oxford University Press, Inc. New York, NY. 1982. 480p. ISBN:0-19-503186-5, ISBN13: 978-0-19-503186-7. Dewey:917.3/04. LCCN:82-008034.
Audience: **g,l,u,f.** B

Faulkner, Virginia & Luebke, Frederick C. (Editors) **PS0124.V5**
Vision and Refuge: Essays on the Literature of the Great Plains. Trade Paper. Books on Demand. Ann Arbor, MI. 1982. 160p. ISBN:0-608-01834-1, ISBN13: 978-0-608-01834-8. Dewey:810.9/978. LCCN:81-010418.
Audience: **g,l,u,f.** B

Flora, Joseph M. (Editor), et al. **PS261.S595 2006**
1979 Southern Writers: A New Biographical Dictionary. Amber Vogel & Bryan Albin Giemza (Editors). Cloth Text. Louisiana State University Press. Baton Rouge, LA. 2006. 616p. Southern Literary Studies ISBN:0-8071-3123-7, ISBN13: 978-0-8071-3123-7. Dewey:810.9/975/03 B. LCCN:2005-023668.
Audience: **g,l,u,f.**

James, Henry **PS121.J3 1956**
The American Essays of Henry James. Leon Edel (Editor). Trade Paper. Princeton University Press. Princeton, NJ. 1990. 320p. ISBN:0-691-01471-X, ISBN13: 978-0-691-01471-5. Dewey:810.9. LCCN:89-010684.
Audience: **l,u,f.**

Jones, Howard M. **PS121 .J6**
Ideas in America. Trade Cloth. A M S Press, Inc. New York, NY. ISBN:0-404-20144-X, ISBN13: 978-0-404-20144-9. Dewey:810.9. LCCN:83-045882.
Audience: **g,l,u,f.**

Kort, Carol **PS147**
American Women Writers: A Biographical Dictionary. Trade Paper. Facts On File, Inc. New York, NY. 2001. 288p. ISBN:0-8160-4434-1, ISBN13: 978-0-8160-4434-4. Dewey:810.9/9287 B.
Audience: **g,l,u,f.**

Lawrence, D. H. **PS121**
Symbolic Meaning, Uncollected Versions of 'Studies in Classic American Literature'. Trade Cloth. Penguin Group (USA) Inc. New York, NY. 1964. ISBN:0-670-68884-3, ISBN13: 978-0-670-68884-5. Dewey:810.9.
Audience: **l,u,f.**

Lawrence, D. H. **PR6023**
Studies in Classic American Literature. John Worthen, Lindeth Vasey & Ezra Greenspan (Editors). Trade Cloth. Cambridge University Press. New York, NY. 2002. 712p. The Cambridge Edition of the Works of D. H. Lawrence Ser. ISBN:0-521-55016-5, ISBN13: 978-0-521-55016-1. Dewey:810.9. LCCN:2003-272770.
Audience: **l,u,f.** B

Oates, Joyce Carol (Compiled by) **PS129.F5 1983**
First Person Singular: Writers on Their Craft. Trade Cloth. Ontario Review Press. Princeton, NJ. 1983. "viii, 280"p. ISBN:0-86538-037-6, ISBN13: 978-0-86538-037-0. Dewey:810/.9/0054. LCCN:83-021927.
Audience: **g,l,u,f.** B

Spiller, Robert E. **PS121**
Late Harvest: Essays and Addresses in American Literature and Culture. Trade Cloth. Greenwood Publishing Group, Inc. Portsmouth, NH. 1981. 280p. Contributions to American Studies, No. 49 ISBN:0-313-22023-9, ISBN13: 978-0-313-22023-4. Dewey:810/.9. LCCN:80-000543.
Audience: **l,u,f.** B

Spiller, Robert E. **PS88.L522 1974**
Literary History of the United States. Ed. 4. Trade Cloth. Macmillan Publishing Company, Inc. Old Tappan, NJ. 1974. xxvi, 1556p. ISBN:0-02-613160-9, ISBN13: 978-0-02-613160-5. Dewey:810/.9. LCCN:73-014014.
Audience: **l,u,f.** B

Warren, Robert Penn **PS3545.A748N4 1989**
New and Selected Essays. Trade Cloth. Random House, Inc. New York, NY. 1989. ISBN:0-394-57516-4, ISBN13: 978-0-394-57516-2. Dewey:810/.9. LCCN:88-026470.
Audience: **l,u,f.**

Winters, Yvor **PS121**
In Defense of Reason. Library Binding. Reprint Services Company. Temecula, CA. 1993. BCL1-PS American Literature Ser. ISBN:0-7812-6569-X, ISBN13: 978-0-7812-6569-0. Dewey:810/.9.
Audience: **l,u,f.**

History, Criticism > Women Authors

PS508.W7
☐ 19th Century American Women Writers. http://www.lehigh.edu/~dek7/SSAWW/eTextLib.htm
Audience: **g,l,u,f.**

Ammons, Elizabeth **PS374.W6**
Conflicting Stories: American Women Writers at the Turn into the Twentieth Century. Trade Paper. Oxford University Press, Inc. New York, NY. 1992. 248p. ISBN:0-19-508038-6, ISBN13: 978-0-19-508038-4. Dewey:813.4099287. LCCN:90-047290.
Audience: **u,f.**

Baym, Nina **PS149 .B38 1993**
Woman's Fiction: A Guide to Novels by and about Women in America, 1820-70. Ed. 2. Trade Paper. University of Illinois Press. Champaign, IL. 1993. 360p. ISBN:0-252-06285-X, ISBN13: 978-0-252-06285-8. Dewey:813/.3099287. LCCN:92-025929.
Audience: **l,u,f.**

Benbow-Pfalzgraf, Taryn **PS147.A42 2000**
American Women Writers: From Colonial Times to the Present: A Critical Reference Guide. Ed. 2. Trade Cloth. Thomson Gale. Farmington Hills, MI. 1999. ISBN:1-55862-433-3, ISBN13: 978-1-55862-433-7. Dewey:810.9/9287/03 B. LCCN:99-043293.
Audience: **l,u,f.**

Benstock, Shari (Editor) **88-1282**
The Private Self: Theory and Practice of Women's Autobiographical Writings. Trade Paper. University of North Carolina Press. Chapel Hill, NC. 1988. 326p. ISBN:0-8078-4218-4, ISBN13: 978-0-8078-4218-8. Dewey:809/.93592/088042. LCCN:88-001282.
Audience: **u,f.** *Choice, 1989.*

Burr, Zofia **PS151.B87 2002**
Of Women, Poetry, and Power: Strategies of Address in Dickinson, Miles, Brooks, Lorde, and Angelou. Trade Cloth. University of Illinois Press. Champaign, IL. 2002. 248p. ISBN:0-252-02769-8, ISBN13: 978-0-252-02769-7. Dewey:811.0099287. LCCN:2002-002332.
Audience: **l,u,f.** *Choice, 2003.*

Carby, Hazel V. **PS374.W6**
Reconstructing Womanhood: The Emergence of the Afro-American Woman Novelist. Trade Paper. Oxford University Press, Inc. New York, NY. 1989. 232p. ISBN:0-19-506071-7, ISBN13: 978-0-19-506071-3. Dewey:813/.4/099287. LCCN:87-011055.
Audience: **u,f.** *Choice, 1988.*

Douglas, Ann **PS152.D6 1998**
The Feminization of American Culture. Trade Paper. Farrar, Straus & Giroux. New York, NY. 1998. 416p. ISBN:0-374-52558-7, ISBN13: 978-0-374-52558-3. Dewey:810.9/9287/09034. LCCN:98-016732.
Audience: **l,u,f.** B

Engelhardt, Elizabeth S. D. **PS286.A6.E54 2003**
The Tangled Roots of Feminism, Environmentalism, and Appalachian Literature. Trade Cloth. Ohio University Press. Athens, OH. 2003. 248p. Ohio University Press Series in Ethnicity and Gender in Appalachia ISBN:0-8214-1509-3, ISBN13: 978-0-8214-1509-2. Dewey:810.9/974. LCCN:2003-048692.
Audience: **u,f.** *Choice, 2004.*

Hapke, Laura **PS374.W6 H357**
Daughters of the Great Depression: Women, Work, and Fiction in the American 1930s. Trade Paper. University of Georgia Press. Athens, GA. 1997. 312p. ISBN:0-8203-1908-2, ISBN13: 978-0-8203-1908-7. Dewey:813/.5209352042. LCCN:94-040316.
Audience: **u,f.**

Loeffelholz, Mary **PS147.L46 2004**
From School to Salon: Reading Nineteenth-Century American Women's Poetry. Trade Cloth. Princeton University Press. Princeton, NJ. 2004. 288p. ISBN:0-691-04939-4, ISBN13: 978-0-691-04939-7. Dewey:814.3099287. LCCN:2003-064126.
Audience: **l,u,f.**

Middlebrook, Diane W. & Yalom, Marilyn (Editors) **PS151.C65 1985**
Coming to Light: American Women Poets in the Twentieth Century. Trade Paper. University of Michigan Press. Chicago, IL. 1985. 288p. Women and Culture Ser. ISBN:0-472-08061-X, ISBN13: 978-0-472-08061-8. Dewey:811/.5/099287. LCCN:85-001145.
Audience: **g,l,u,f.** B *Choice, 1985.*

Newton, Judith L. & Rosenfelt, D. (Editors) **PS152.F46 1985**
Feminist Literary Criticism and Social Change. Trade Cloth. Routledge. New York, NY. 1986. 250p. ISBN:0-416-38700-4, ISBN13: 978-0-416-38700-1. Dewey:810/.9. LCCN:85-015209.
Audience: **l,u,f.** B *Choice, 1986.*

Ostriker, Alicia S. **PS147.O8 1986**
Stealing the Language: The Emergence of Women's Poetry in America. Trade Cloth. Beacon Press. Boston, MA. 1986. 291p. ISBN:0-8070-6302-9, ISBN13: 978-0-8070-6302-6. Dewey:811/.009/9287. LCCN:85-047949.
Audience: **l,u,f.** B *Choice, 1986.*

Papashvily, Helen Waite **PS149.P3 1972**
All the Happy Endings: A Study of the Domestic Novel in America, the Women Who Wrote It, the Women Who Read It, in the Nineteenth Century. Trade Cloth. Kennikat Press. Port Washington, NY. 1972. xvii, 231p. ISBN:0-8046-1497-0, ISBN13: 978-0-8046-1497-9. Dewey:813/.03. LCCN:76-153255.
Audience: **l,u,f.** B

Rabinowitz, Paula **91-50259**
Labor and Desire: Women's Revolutionary Fiction in Depression America. Trade Paper. University of North Carolina Press. Chapel Hill, NC. 1991. 236p. Gender and American Culture Ser. ISBN:0-8078-4332-6, ISBN13: 978-0-8078-4332-1. Dewey:813.5/2099287. LCCN:91-050259.
Audience: **u,f.** *Choice, 1992.*

Scheick, William **PS186.S34 1998**
Authority and Female Authorship in Colonial America. Trade Cloth. University Press of Kentucky. Lexington, KY. 1998. 168p. ISBN:0-8131-2054-3, ISBN13: 978-0-8131-2054-6. Dewey:810.9/9287/09032. LCCN:97-028918.
Audience: **u,f.** *Choice, 1998.*

Walker, Cheryl **PS147.W27 1982**
The Nightingale's Burden: Women Poets and American Culture Before 1900. Trade Cloth. Indiana University Press. Bloomington, IN. 1983. 208p. ISBN:0-253-34065-9, ISBN13: 978-0-253-34065-8. Dewey:811/.009/9287. LCCN:81-048514.
Audience: **l,u,f.** B

Wheeler, Lesley **PS147.W47 2002**
The Poetics of Enclosure: American Women Poets from Dickinson to Dove. Trade Cloth. University of Tennessee Press. Knoxville, TN. 2002. x, 201p. ISBN:1-57233-197-6, ISBN13: 978-1-57233-197-6. Dewey:811.009/9287. LCCN:2002-003608.
Audience: **l,u,f.** *Choice, 2003.*

History, Criticism > Literary history, by period > 17th-18th Centuries

Potkay, Adam & Burr, Sandra (Editors) **PR1297.B57 1995**
Black Atlantic Writers of the Eighteenth Century: Living the New Exodus in England and the Americas. Cloth over Boards. Palgrave Macmillan. New York, NY. 1995. 304p. ISBN:0-312-12133-4, ISBN13: 978-0-312-12133-4. Dewey:818/.108080896073. LCCN:94-036117.
Audience: **f.** *Choice, 1995.*

Shuffleton, Frank (Editor) **PS153.M56**
A Mixed Race: Ethnicity in Early America. Paper Text. Oxford University Press, Inc. New York, NY. 1993. 296p. ISBN:0-19-507523-4, ISBN13: 978-0-19-507523-6. Dewey:810.9920693. LCCN:92-043927.
Audience: **u,f.**

Slotkin, Richard **PS169.F7S57 2000**
Regeneration Through Violence: The Mythology of the American Frontier, 1600-1860. Trade Paper. University of Oklahoma Press. Norman, OK. 2000. 680p. ISBN:0-8061-3229-9, ISBN13: 978-0-8061-3229-7. Dewey:810.9/358. LCCN:99-053221.
Audience: **u,f.**

Zafar, Rafia **PS153.N5Z34 1997**
We Wear the Mask: African Americans Write American Literature, 1760-1870. Trade Cloth. Columbia University Press. New York, NY. 1997. 264p. ISBN:0-231-08094-8, ISBN13: 978-0-231-08094-1. Dewey:810.9/896073. LCCN:96-053974.
Audience: **u,f.** *Choice, 1998.*

History, Criticism > Literary history, by period > 19th Century

Bennett, Paula Bernat **PS310.F45B46 2003**
Poets in the Public Sphere: The Emancipatory Project of American Women's Poetry, 1800-1900. Trade Cloth. Princeton University Press. Princeton, NJ. 2003. 264p. ISBN:0-691-02645-9, ISBN13: 978-0-691-02645-9. Dewey:811/.3099287. LCCN:2002-069278.
Audience: **l,u,f.** *Choice, 2003.*

Broaddus, Dorothy C. **PS255.B6B76 1998**
Genteel Rhetoric: Writing High Culture in 19th Century Boston. Trade Cloth. University of South Carolina Press. Columbia, SC. 1999. 128p. Studies in Rhetoric - Communication ISBN:1-57003-244-0, ISBN13: 978-1-57003-244-8. Dewey:810.9/974461. LCCN:98-019678.
Audience: **u,f.** *Choice, 1999.*

Brodhead, Richard H. **PS201.B68 1993**
Cultures of Letters: Scenes of Reading and Writing in Nineteenth-Century America. Trade Paper. University of Chicago Press. Chicago, IL. 1995. 256p. ISBN:0-226-07526-5, ISBN13: 978-0-226-07526-6. Dewey:810.9003. LCCN:92-030967.
Audience: **u,f.** *Choice, 1993.*

Brown, Gillian **PS377**
Domestic Individualism: Imagining Self in Nineteenth-Century America. Nathaniel Hawthorne (Contribution by). Trade Paper. University of California Press. Berkeley, CA. 1992. 280p. The New Historicism Ser., No. 14:Studies in Cultural Poetics ISBN:0-520-08099-8, ISBN13: 978-0-520-08099-7. Dewey:813/.309. LCCN:90-011143.
Audience: **u,f.** *Choice, 1991.*

Brown, Herbert Ross **PS0377.B7**
The Sentimental Novel in America, 1789-1860. Trade Paper. Books on Demand. Ann Arbor, MI. 418p. ISBN:0-598-82814-1, ISBN13: 978-0-598-82814-9. Dewey:813.309. LCCN:59-006577.
Audience: **u,f.**

Cogan, Frances B. **HQ1419.C64 1989**
All-American Girl: The Ideal of Real Womanhood in Mid-Nineteenth Century America. Cloth Text. University of Georgia Press. Athens, GA. 1989. 312p. ISBN:0-8203-1062-X, ISBN13: 978-0-8203-1062-6. Dewey:305.4/2/0973. LCCN:88-008590.
Audience: **u,f.** *Choice, 1989.*

Kerkering, John D. **PS217.N38K47 2003**
The Poetics of National and Racial Identity in Nineteenth-Century American Literature. Albert Gelpi & Ross Posnock (Contribution by). Trade Cloth. Cambridge University Press. New York, NY. 2003. 366p. Cambridge Studies in American Literature and Culture, Vol. 139 ISBN:0-521-83114-8, ISBN13: 978-0-521-83114-7. Dewey:810.9/358. LCCN:2003-046081.
Audience: **u,f.** *Choice, 2004.*

Packard, Chris **PS217.H65P33 2005**
Queer Cowboys: And Other Erotic Male Friendships in Nineteenth-Century American Literature. Cloth over Boards. Palgrave Macmillan. New York, NY. 2005. 160p. ISBN:0-312-29340-2, ISBN13: 978-0-312-29340-6. Dewey:810.9/3526642. LCCN:2004-054124.
Audience: **u,f.** *Choice, 2005.*

Reid, Margaret **PS374.H5R45 2004**
Cultural Secrets As Narrative Form: Storytelling in Nineteenth-Century America. Trade Cloth. Ohio State University Press. Columbus, OH. 2004. xxxii, 259p. ISBN:0-8142-9038-8, ISBN13: 978-0-8142-9038-5. Dewey:813/.309358. LCCN:2003-023639.
Audience: **u,f.** *Choice, 2004.*

Reynolds, David S. **PS217.S6R49 1989**
Beneath the American Renaissance: The Subversive Imagination in the Age of Emerson and Melville. Trade Paper. Harvard University Press. Cambridge, MA. 1989. 640p. ISBN:0-674-06565-4, ISBN13: 978-0-674-06565-9. Dewey:810/.9/003. LCCN:89-031146.
Audience: **u,f.** *Choice, 1988.*

Samuels, Shirley (Editor) **PS217.S55C85 1992**
The Culture of Sentiment: Race, Gender, and Sentimentality in 19th-Century America. Trade Cloth. Oxford University Press, Inc. New York, NY. 1992. 358p. ISBN:0-19-506354-6, ISBN13: 978-0-19-506354-7. Dewey:810.9/003. LCCN:91-044238.
Audience: **u,f.** *Choice, 1993.*

Takaki, Ronald T. **E184.A1T337 2000**
Iron Cages: Race and Culture in 19th-Century America. Paper Text. Oxford University Press, Inc. New York, NY. 2000. 400p. ISBN:0-19-513737-X, ISBN13: 978-0-19-513737-8. Dewey:305.8/00973. LCCN:99-048268.
Audience: **u,f.**

Tarbox, Gwen **PS374.G55T37 2000**
The Clubwomen's Daughters: Collectivist Impulses in Progressive-Era Girls' Fiction. Cloth Text. Garland Publishing, Inc. New York, NY. 2000. 256p. Garland Studies in American Popular History and Culture ISBN:0-8153-3537-7, ISBN13: 978-0-8153-3537-5. Dewey:813/.40992827. LCCN:00-035331.
Audience: **u,f.** *Choice, 2000.*

Tompkins, Jane P. **PS374.S7T66 1986**
Sensational Designs: The Cultural Work of American Fiction, 1790-1860. Paper Text. Oxford University Press, Inc. New York, NY. 1986. 256p. ISBN:0-19-504119-4, ISBN13: 978-0-19-504119-4. Dewey:813/.2/09. LCCN:86-002492.
Audience: **u,f.** *Choice, 1985.*

Young, Elizabeth **PS217.C58Y68 1999**
Disarming the Nation: Women's Writing and the American Civil War. Trade Cloth. University of Chicago Press. Chicago, IL. 1999. 405p. Women in Culture and Society Ser. ISBN:0-226-96087-0, ISBN13: 978-0-226-96087-6. Dewey:810.9/358. LCCN:99-031518.
Audience: **u,f.** *Choice, 2000.*

Zafar, Rafia **PS153.N5Z34 1997**
We Wear the Mask: African Americans Write American Literature, 1760-1870. Trade Cloth. Columbia University Press. New York, NY. 1997. 264p. ISBN:0-231-08094-8, ISBN13: 978-0-231-08094-1. Dewey:810.9/896073. LCCN:96-053974.
Audience: **u,f.** *Choice, 1998.*

Zboray, Ronald J. **Z1003.2**
A Fictive People: Antebellum Economic Development and the American Reading Public. Trade Cloth. Oxford University Press, Inc. New York, NY. 1993. 348p. ISBN:0-19-507582-X, ISBN13: 978-0-19-507582-3. Dewey:028.90973. LCCN:91-046930.
Audience: **u,f.**

History, Criticism > Literary history, by period > 20th Century

PS221
Modern American Literature. Ed. 6. Trade Cloth. Thomson Gale. Farmington Hills, MI. 2004. ISBN:1-55862-440-6, ISBN13: 978-1-55862-440-5. Dewey:810.9/005.
Audience: **g,l,u,f.**

Campbell, James **PS226.B6C36 1999**
This Is the Beat Generation: New York, San Francisco, Paris. Trade Cloth. Martin Secker & Warburg, Ltd. London, 1999. xi, 320p. ISBN:0-436-20498-3, ISBN13: 978-0-436-20498-2. Dewey:810.9/0054. LCCN:00-302930.
Audience: **g,l,u,f.**

Carroll, Anne Elizabeth **E185.6.C33 2005**
Word, Image, and the New Negro: Representation and Identity in the Harlem Renaissance. Trade Cloth. Indiana University Press. Bloomington, IN. 2005. 288p. Blacks in the Diaspora Ser. ISBN:0-253-34583-9, ISBN13: 978-0-253-34583-7. Dewey:700/.89/9607307471. LCCN:2004-015335.
Audience: **u,f.** *Choice, 2005.*

English, Daylanne K. **PS228.E84E54 2004**
Unnatural Selections. Trade Cloth. University of North Carolina Press. Chapel Hill, NC. 2004. 288p. ISBN:0-8078-2868-8, ISBN13: 978-0-8078-2868-7. Dewey:810.9/3556. LCCN:2003-021778.
Audience: **u,f.** *Choice, 2004.*

Field, Edward **PS3556.I37Z47 2005**
The Man Who Would Marry Susan Sontag: And Other Intimate Portraits of the Bohemian Era. Trade Cloth. University of Wisconsin Press. Chicago, IL. 2005. 302p. Living Out Ser. ISBN:0-299-21320-X, ISBN13: 978-0-299-21320-6. Dewey:811/.54 B. LCCN:2005-005440.
Audience: **l,u,f.** *Choice, 2006.*

Filreis, Alan **PS3537.T4753 Z635 1**
Modernism from Right to Left: Wallace Stevens, the Thirties, and Literary Radicalism. Albert Gelpi & Ross Posnock (Contribution by). Trade Paper. Cambridge University Press. New York, NY. 2005. 394p. Cambridge Studies in American Literature and Culture Ser., Vol. 70 ISBN:0-521-61940-8, ISBN13: 978-0-521-61940-0. Dewey:811/.52. LCCN:2005-284230.
Audience: **u,f.**

Foley, Barbara H. **PS374.P6.F65 1993**
Radical Representations: Politics and Form in U. S. Proletarian Fiction, 1929-1941. Cloth Text. Duke University Press. Durham, NC. 1993. 484p. Post-Contemporary Interventions Ser. ISBN:0-8223-1361-8, ISBN13: 978-0-8223-1361-8. Dewey:813.5209358. LCCN:93-018687.
Audience: **u,f.** *Choice, 1994.*

Fone, Byrne R. S. **PR408.H65F66 1994**
Road to Stonewall. Trade Cloth. Thomson Gale. Farmington Hills, MI. 1994. 275p. Twayne's Literature and Society Ser., No. 14 ISBN:0-8057-8856-5, ISBN13: 978-0-8057-8856-3. Dewey:820.9/35206642. LCCN:94-017118.
Audience: **u,f.** *Choice, 1995.*

Foster, Edward H. **PS228.B6.F67 1992**
Understanding the Beats. Matthew J. Bruccoli (Editor). Cloth Text. University of South Carolina Press. Columbia, SC. 1992. 248p. Understanding Contemporary American Literature Ser. ISBN:0-87249-798-4, ISBN13: 978-0-87249-798-6. Dewey:810.9/0054. LCCN:91-036122.
Audience: **l,u,f.** *Choice, 1992.*

Francis, Elizabeth **HQ1426.F797 2002**
The Secret Treachery of Words: Feminism and Modernism in America. Trade Cloth. University of Minnesota Press. Minneapolis, MN. 2002. 248p. ISBN:0-8166-3327-4, ISBN13: 978-0-8166-3327-2. Dewey:305.42/0973. LCCN:2001-005641.
Audience: **u,f.**

Kalaidjian, Walter (Editor) **PS228.M63**
The Cambridge Companion to American Modernism. Cloth Text. Cambridge University Press. New York, NY. 2005. 358p. Cambridge Companions to Literature Ser. ISBN:0-521-82995-X, ISBN13: 978-0-521-82995-3. Dewey:810.9/112. LCCN:2005-283138.
Audience: **l,u,f.** *Choice, 2006.*

Kent, Kathryn R. **PS228.L47K46 2002**
Making Girls into Women: American Women's Writing and the Rise of Lesbian Identity. Trade Paper. Duke University Press. Durham, NC. 2003. 344p. Series Q ISBN:0-8223-3016-4, ISBN13: 978-0-8223-3016-5. Dewey:813/.50935206643. LCCN:2002-008828.
Audience: **l,u,f.** *Choice, 2003.*

Knight, Brenda **PS508.W7**
Women of the Beat Generation: The Writers, Artists, and Muses at the Heart of a Revolution. Anne Waldman (Foreword by), Ann Charters (Afterword by). Trade Cloth. DIANE Publishing Company. Collingdale, PA. 2004. 366p. ISBN:0-7567-7988-X, ISBN13: 978-0-7567-7988-7. Dewey:810.8/09287/09045.
Audience: **g,l,u,f.**

Meade, Marion **PS151.M43 2005**
Bobbed Hair and Bathtub Gin: Writers Running Wild in the Twenties. Trade Paper, Perfect. Harcourt Trade Publishers. New York, NY. 2005. 368p. A Harvest Book Ser. ISBN:0-15-603059-4, ISBN13: 978-0-15-603059-5. Dewey:810.9/9287/09042 B. LCCN:2004-056917.
Audience: **g,u,f.**

Miller, Tyrus **PR888.M63 M55 1999**
Late Modernism: Politics, Fiction, and the Arts Between the World Wars. Trade Cloth. University of California Press. Berkeley, CA. 1999. 280p. ISBN:0-520-21035-2, ISBN13: 978-0-520-21035-6. Dewey:823.91209112. LCCN:98-027436.
Audience: **u,f.** *Choice, 1999.*

Minter, David L. **PS379.M49 1994**
A Cultural History of the American Novel, 1890-1940: Henry James to William Faulkner. Trade Cloth. Cambridge University Press. New York, NY. 1994. 292p. ISBN:0-521-45285-6, ISBN13: 978-0-521-45285-4. Dewey:813.5/2/09. LCCN:93-030651.
Audience: **u,f.**

Nadell, Martha Jane **E185.6.N165 2004**
Enter the New Negroes: Images of Race in American Culture. Trade Cloth. Harvard University Press. Cambridge, MA. 2004. 224p. ISBN:0-674-01511-8, ISBN13: 978-0-674-01511-1. Dewey:305.896/073. LCCN:2004-052365.
Audience: **u,f.** *Choice, 2005.*

Rideout, Walter B. **PS379**
The Radical Novel in the U. S., 1900-1954: Some Interrelations of Literature and Society. Trade Paper. Edinburgh University Press. Edinburgh, 1992. 360p. ISBN:0-231-08077-8, ISBN13: 978-0-231-08077-4. Dewey:813/.5209355.
Audience: **u,f.**

Sherry, Vincent **PR478.W65S47 2004**
The Great War and the Language of Modernism. Trade Paper. Oxford University Press, Inc. New York, NY. 2004. 140p. ISBN:0-19-517818-1, ISBN13: 978-0-19-517818-0. Dewey:811/.5209358.
Audience: **u,f.**

Stone, Albert E. **PS228.W37S76 1994**
Literary Aftershocks: American Writers, Readers, and the Bomb. Trade Cloth. Thomson Gale. Farmington Hills, MI. 1994. 225p. Twayne's Literature and Society Ser. ISBN:0-8057-8853-0, ISBN13: 978-0-8057-8853-2. Dewey:810.9/358. LCCN:94-020030.
Audience: **l,u.** *Choice, 1995.*

Szalay, Michael **PS228.M63S93 2000**
New Deal Modernism: American Literature and the Invention of the Welfare State. Trade Paper. Duke University Press. Durham, NC. 2000. 320p. Post-Contemporary Interventions Ser. ISBN:0-8223-2562-4, ISBN13: 978-0-8223-2562-8. Dewey:810.9/112. LCCN:00-029390.
Audience: **u,f.** *Choice, 2001.*

Theado, Matt (Editor) **PS228.B6**
The Beats: A Literary Reference. Trade Paper. Avalon Publishing Group. New York, NY. 2002. 448p. ISBN:0-7867-1099-3, ISBN13: 978-0-7867-1099-7. Dewey:810.9/0054.
Audience: **l,u,f.**

Trask, Michael **PS228.M63T73 2003**
Cruising Modernism: Class and Sexuality in American Literature and Social Thought. Trade Cloth. Cornell University Press. Ithaca, NY. 2005. 256p. ISBN:0-8014-4170-6, ISBN13: 978-0-8014-4170-7. Dewey:810.9/112. LCCN:2003-010030.
Audience: **u,f.** *Choice, 2004.*

Van Wienen, Mark W. **PS310.W679 V36 1997**
Partisans and Poets: The Political Work of American Poetry in the Great War. Albert Gelpi & Ross Posnock (Contribution by). Trade Cloth. Cambridge University Press. New York, NY. 1997. 330p. Studies in American Literature and Culture, No. 107 ISBN:0-521-56396-8, ISBN13: 978-0-521-56396-3. Dewey:811.5/2/09. LCCN:96-015653.
Audience: **u,f.** *Choice, 1997.*

Wheeler, Elizabeth A. **PS374.C5W48 2001**
Uncontained: Urban Fiction in Postwar America. Cloth Text. Rutgers University Press. Piscataway, NJ. 2001. 312p. ISBN:0-8135-2972-7, ISBN13: 978-0-8135-2972-1. Dewey:813/.5409321732. LCCN:00-045894.
Audience: **u,f.** *Choice, 2001.*

Witalec, Janet (Editor) **PS153.N5H245 2003**
The Harlem Renaissance: A Gale Critical Companion. Trade Cloth. Thomson Gale. Farmington Hills, MI. 2002. Gale Critical Companion Collection ISBN:0-7876-6621-1, ISBN13: 978-0-7876-6621-7. Dewey:810.9/89607307471. LCCN:2002-010076.
Audience: **l,u,f.** *Choice, 2003.*

Zott, Lynn M. **PS228.B6Z68 2003**
The Beat Generation: A Gale Critical Companion. Trade Cloth. Thomson Gale. Farmington Hills, MI. 2003. 1500p. Gale Critical Companion Collection ISBN:0-7876-7569-5, ISBN13: 978-0-7876-7569-1. Dewey:810.9/0054. LCCN:2002-155786.
Audience: **l,u,f.** *Choice, 2004.*

History, Criticism > Literary history, by Region > New England

Broaddus, Dorothy C. **PS255.B6B76 1998**
Genteel Rhetoric: Writing High Culture in 19th Century Boston. Trade Cloth. University of South Carolina Press. Columbia, SC. 1999. 128p. Studies in Rhetoric - Communication ISBN:1-57003-244-0, ISBN13: 978-1-57003-244-8. Dewey:810.9/974461. LCCN:98-019678.
Audience: **u,f.** *Choice, 1999.*

Brooks, Van Wyck **PS243 .B72**
The Flowering of New England, 1815-1865. Trade Cloth. Amereon, Ltd. Mattituck, NY. ISBN:0-8488-0251-9, ISBN13: 978-0-8488-0251-6. Dewey:810.903.
Audience: **g,l,u,f.**

Brooks, Van Wyck **PS243.B72 1950**
New England Indian Summer. Trade Cloth. Amereon, Ltd. Mattituck, NY. 575p. ISBN:0-8488-2219-6, ISBN13: 978-0-8488-2219-4. Dewey:810.903.
Audience: **g,l,u,f.**

Buell, Lawrence **PS243.B84 1986**
New England Literary Culture: From the Revolution to the Renaissance. Cloth Text. Cambridge University Press. New York, NY. 1986. 529p. Studies in American Literature and Culture, No. 15 ISBN:0-521-30206-4, ISBN13: 978-0-521-30206-7. Dewey:810/.9/974. LCCN:85-014893.
Audience: **u,f.** B *Choice, 1987.*

Lowance, Mason I. Jr. **PS243**
The Language of Canaan: Metaphor and Symbol in New England from the Puritans to the Transcendentalists. Trade Cloth. Harvard University Press. Cambridge, MA. 1980. 345p. ISBN:0-674-50949-8, ISBN13: 978-0-674-50949-8. Dewey:810.9/974. LCCN:79-021179.
Audience: **u,f.** B

Nickels, Cameron C. **PS243.N53 1993**
New England Humor: From the Revolutionary War to the Civil War. Cloth Text. University of Tennessee Press. Knoxville, TN. 1993. 296p. ISBN:0-87049-804-5, ISBN13: 978-0-87049-804-6. Dewey:817.009/974. LCCN:93-000320.
Audience: **u,f.** *Choice, 1994.*

Sloane, David E. **PS538.L57 1983**
The Literary Humor of the Urban Northeast, 1830-1890. Cloth Text. Louisiana State University Press. Baton Rouge, LA. 1983. xii, 319p. ISBN:0-8071-1055-8, ISBN13: 978-0-8071-1055-3. Dewey:817/.3/080974. LCCN:82-012688.
Audience: **l,u,f.** B

Warren, Robert Penn **PS29.B74A4 1998**
Cleanth Brooks and Robert Penn Warren: A Literary Correspondence. James A. Grimshaw Jr. (Editor), Lewis P. Simpson (Foreword by), R. W. B. Lewis (Afterword by). Trade Cloth. University of Missouri Press. Columbia, MO. 1998. 472p. ISBN:0-8262-1165-8, ISBN13: 978-0-8262-1165-1. Dewey:809. LCCN:97-046078.
Audience: **u,f.** *Choice, 1998.*

Westbrook, Perry D. **PS243.W42 1988**
A Literary History of New England. Trade Cloth. Lehigh University Press. Cranbury, NJ. 1988. 368p. ISBN:0-934223-02-5, ISBN13: 978-0-934223-02-7. Dewey:810/.9/974. LCCN:87-045767.
Audience: **u,f.** *Choice, 1989.*

History, Criticism > Literary history, by Region > Middle States

Engelhardt, Elizabeth S. D. **PS286.A6.E54 2003**
The Tangled Roots of Feminism, Environmentalism, and Appalachian Literature. Trade Cloth. Ohio University Press. Athens, OH. 2003. 248p. Ohio University Press Series in Ethnicity and Gender in Appalachia ISBN:0-8214-1509-3, ISBN13: 978-0-8214-1509-2. Dewey:810.9/974. LCCN:2003-048692.
Audience: **u,f.** *Choice, 2004.*

Lanier, Parks Jr. (Editor) **PS286.A6P64 1991**
The Poetics of Appalachian Space. Cloth Text. University of Tennessee Press. Knoxville, TN. 1991. 232p. ISBN:0-87049-692-1, ISBN13: 978-0-87049-692-9. Dewey:810.9/3274. LCCN:90-045244.
Audience: **u,f.** *Choice, 1992.*

Miller, Danny L. (Editor), et al. **PS286.A6A83 2005**
An American Vein: Critical Readings in Appalachian Literature. Sharon Hatfield & Gurney Norman (Editors). Trade Cloth. Ohio University Press. Athens, OH. 2005. 352p. ISBN:0-8214-1589-1, ISBN13: 978-0-8214-1589-4. Dewey:810.9/974. LCCN:2004-023207.
Audience: **l,u,f.** *Choice, 2005.*

Quillen, Rita **PS325**
Looking for Native Ground: Contemporary Appalachian Poetry. Trade Paper. Appalachian Consortium Press. Boone, NC. 1989. ISBN:0-913239-58-5, ISBN13: 978-0-913239-58-2. Dewey:811.5409. LCCN:89-083315.
Audience: **u,f.**

History, Criticism > Literary history, by Region > The South

Abernathy, Jeff **PS261.A38 2003**
To Hell and Back: Race and Betrayal in the Southern Novel. Trade Paper. University of Georgia Press. Athens, GA. 2005. xii, 225p. ISBN:0-8203-2578-3, ISBN13: 978-0-8203-2578-1. Dewey:813/.509355. LCCN:2003-007992.
Audience: **u,f.** *Choice, 2004.*

Beck, Charlotte H. **PS261.B44 2001**
The Fugitive Legacy: A Critical History. Trade Cloth. Louisiana State University Press. Baton Rouge, LA. 2000. xii, 302p. Southern Literary Studies ISBN:0-8071-2590-3, ISBN13: 978-0-8071-2590-8. Dewey:810.9/975. LCCN:00-044389.
Audience: **u,f.** *Choice, 2001.*

Bradbury, John M. **PS261.B62**
The Fugitives. Trade Paper. Rowman & Littlefield Publishers, Inc. Lanham, MD. 1958. ISBN:0-8084-0139-4, ISBN13: 978-0-8084-0139-1. Dewey:810.975.
Audience: **u,f.**

Bryan, Violet H. **PS267.N49B78 1993**
The Myth of New Orleans in Literature: Dialogues of Race and Gender. Cloth Text. University of Tennessee Press. Knoxville, TN. 1993. 248p. ISBN:0-87049-789-8, ISBN13: 978-0-87049-789-6. Dewey:810.9/3276335. LCCN:92-042846.
Audience: **u,f.** *Choice, 1994.*

Clifford, Craig E. & Pilkington, Tom (Editors) **PS266.T4R36 1989**
Range Wars: Heated Debates, Sober Reflections, and Other Assessments of Texas Writing. Craig E. Clifford & Tom Pilkington (Preface by). Trade Cloth. Southern Methodist University Press. Dallas, TX. 1989. 208p. Southwest Life and Letters Ser. ISBN:0-87074-282-5, ISBN13: 978-0-87074-282-8. Dewey:810/.9/9764. LCCN:88-042632.
Audience: **u,f.**

Cook, Sylvia Jenkins **PS261.C57**
From Tobacco Road to Route 66: The Southern Poor White in Fiction. Trade Cloth. University of North Carolina Press. Chapel Hill, NC. 1976. xiv, 208 p. ;p. ISBN:0-8078-1264-1, ISBN13: 978-0-8078-1264-8. Dewey:813/.03. LCCN:75-035822.
Audience: **u,f.** B

Cowan, Louise **PN99.U52 C6**
The Southern Critics: An Introduction to the Criticism of John Crow Ransom, Allen Tate, Donald Davidson, Robert Penn Warren, Cleanth Brooks, and Andrew Lytle. Trade Cloth. Dallas Institute Publications, The. Dallas, TX. 1971. 84p. ISBN:0-911005-35-8, ISBN13: 978-0-911005-35-6. Dewey:801/.95/0975. LCCN:73-186934.
Audience: **u,f.**

Flora, Joseph M. (Editor), et al. **PS261.C55 2001**
The Companion to Southern Literature: Themes, Genres, Places, People, Movements and Motifs. Lucinda H. MacKethan & Todd Taylor (Editors). Trade Cloth. Louisiana State University Press. Baton Rouge, LA. 2004. xxvi, 1054p. Southern Literary Studies ISBN:0-8071-2692-6, ISBN13: 978-0-8071-2692-9. Dewey:810.9/975. LCCN:2001-029959.
Audience: **l,u.** *Choice, 2002.*

Flora, Joseph M. (Editor), et al. **PS261.S595 2006**
Southern Writers: A New Biographical Dictionary. Amber Vogel & Bryan Albin Giemza (Editors). Cloth Text. Louisiana State University Press. Baton Rouge, LA. 2006. 616p. Southern Literary Studies ISBN:0-8071-3123-7, ISBN13: 978-0-8071-3123-7. Dewey:810.9/975/03 B. LCCN:2005-023668.
Audience: **g,l,u,f.**

Folks, Jeffrey J. & Folks, Nancy Summers (Editors) **PS261.S618 2000**
The World Is Our Home: Society and Culture in Contemporary Southern Writing. Trade Cloth. University Press of Kentucky. Lexington, KY. 2000. 288p. ISBN:0-8131-2166-3, ISBN13: 978-0-8131-2166-6. Dewey:810.9/975. LCCN:99-089784.
Audience: **l,u,f.** *Choice, 2001.*

Foster, Edward H. **PS266.N8F67 1995**
Understanding the Black Mountain Poets. Trade Cloth. University of South Carolina Press. Columbia, SC. 1994. 224p. Understanding Contemporary American Literature Ser. ISBN:1-57003-014-6, ISBN13: 978-1-57003-014-7. Dewey:811/.54099756. LCCN:94-018677.
Audience: **l,u,f.**

Gray, Richard **PS261.G687 2000**
Southern Aberrations: Writers of the American South and the Problems of Regionalism. Trade Paper. Louisiana State University Press. Baton Rouge, LA. 2000. xiv, 535p. Southern Literary Studies ISBN:0-8071-2602-0, ISBN13: 978-0-8071-2602-8. Dewey:810.9/975. LCCN:99-059583.
Audience: **u,f.** *Choice, 2000.*

Gray, Richard J. & Robinson, Owen **PS261.C555 2004**
A Companion to the Literature and Culture of the American South. Trade Cloth. Blackwell Publishing, Inc. Malden, MA. 2004. 672p. Blackwell Companions to Literature and Culture Ser., Vol. 24 ISBN:0-631-22404-1, ISBN13: 978-0-631-22404-4. Dewey:810.9/975. LCCN:2003-020737.
Audience: **l,u,f.** *Choice, 2004.*

Hemingway, Ernest, et al. **PS266.F6K49 1989**
The Key West Reader: The Best of Key West's Writers, 1830-1990. John Dos Passos, Caputo, Lurie, Thomas McGuane & Tennessee Williams (Authors), George E. Murphy Jr. (Introduction by). Trade Cloth. Tortugas, Ltd. Key West, FL. 1990. 236p. ISBN:0-9624184-0-4, ISBN13: 978-0-9624184-0-2. Dewey:818.00803275941. LCCN:89-051565.
Audience: **l,u.**

Hobson, Fred **PS261**
Tell about the South: The Southern Rage to Explain. Paper Text. Louisiana State University Press. Baton Rouge, LA. 1998. xii, 396p. Southern Literary Studies ISBN:0-8071-1131-7, ISBN13: 978-0-8071-1131-4. Dewey:810.9/975. LCCN:83-005477.
Audience: **u,f.** B

Holman, C. Hugh **PS261.H65**
The Roots of Southern Writing; Essays on the Literature of the American South. Trade Cloth. University of Georgia Press. Athens, GA. 1972. xiii, 236p. ISBN:0-8203-0290-2, ISBN13: 978-0-8203-0290-4. Dewey:810/.9. LCCN:74-184774.
Audience: **u,f.** B

Inge, Tonette B. (Editor) **PS261.S58 1990**
Southern Women Writers: The New Generation. Doris Betts (Introduction by). Trade Paper. University of Alabama Press. Tuscaloosa, AL. 1990. 408p. ISBN:0-8173-0470-3, ISBN13: 978-0-8173-0470-6. Dewey:810.9/975. LCCN:89-033863.
Audience: **u,f.** *Choice, 1990.*

Jones, Paul C. **PS261.J657 2005**
Unwelcome Voices: Subversive Fiction in the Antebellum South. Trade Cloth. University of Tennessee Press. Knoxville, TN. 2005. 256p. ISBN:1-57233-327-8, ISBN13: 978-1-57233-327-7. Dewey:813/.309975. LCCN:2004-022784.
Audience: **u,f.**

King, Richard H. **PS261**
A Southern Renaissance: The Cultural Awakening of the American South, 1930-1955. Trade Paper. Oxford University Press, Inc. New York, NY. 1982. 364p. ISBN:0-19-503043-5, ISBN13: 978-0-19-503043-3. Dewey:810/.9/975.
Audience: **l,u,f.** *B*

Mackethan, Lucinda Hardwick **PS366.T73**
The Dream of Arcady: Place and Time in Southern Literature. Trade Paper. Louisiana State University Press. Baton Rouge, LA. 1980. x, 278p. ISBN:0-8071-2493-1, ISBN13: 978-0-8071-2493-2. Dewey:810.932. LCCN:79-016543.
Audience: **u,f.**

Madden, David **PS261.M26 2006**
Touching the Web of Southern Novelists. Trade Cloth. University of Tennessee Press. Knoxville, TN. 2006. 294p. ISBN:1-57233-463-0, ISBN13: 978-1-57233-463-2. Dewey:813/.009975. LCCN:2005-025947.
Audience: **u,f.**

Montgomery, Marion **PS261.M655 2005**
On Matters Southern: Essays about Literature and Culture, 1964-2000. Michael M. Jordan (Editor), Eugene D. Genovese (Foreword by). Trade Paper. McFarland & Company, Incorporated Publishers. Jefferson, NC. 2005. 214p. ISBN:0-7864-2224-6, ISBN13: 978-0-7864-2224-1. Dewey:810.9/975. LCCN:2005-013992.
Audience: **l,u,f.**

Perry, Carolyn & Weaks, Mary Louise (Editors) **PS261.H534 2002**
The History of Southern Women's Literature. Trade Cloth. Louisiana State University Press. Baton Rouge, LA. 2002. xvii, 689p. Southern Literary Studies ISBN:0-8071-2753-1, ISBN13: 978-0-8071-2753-7. Dewey:810.9/9287/0975. LCCN:2001-005342.
Audience: **l,u,f.** *Choice, 2002.*

Richards, Gary **PS374.H63R53 2005**
Lovers and Beloveds: Sexual Otherness in Southern Fiction, 1936-1961. Cloth Text. Louisiana State University Press. Baton Rouge, LA. 2005. 256p. Southern Literary Studies ISBN:0-8071-3051-6, ISBN13: 978-0-8071-3051-3. Dewey:813/.509353. LCCN:2004-023918.
Audience: **u,f.** *Choice, 2005.*

Rubin, Louis Decimus Jr. (Editor), et al. **PS261**
The History of Southern Literature. Blyden Jackson, Rayburn S. Moore, Lewis P. Simpson & Thomas D. Young (Editors). Trade Paper. Louisiana State University Press. Baton Rouge, LA. 1990. xiv, 626p. ISBN:0-8071-1643-2, ISBN13: 978-0-8071-1643-2. Dewey:810/.9/975/. LCCN:85-010183.
Audience: **l,u,f.** *B* *Choice, 1986.*

Rubin, Louis Decimus Jr. **PS261 .R65 1974**
South: Modern Southern Literature in Its Cultural Setting. Robert D. Jacobs (Editor). Trade Cloth. Greenwood Publishing Group, Inc. Portsmouth, NH. 1974. 434p. ISBN:0-8371-7224-1, ISBN13: 978-0-8371-7224-8. Dewey:810/.9/975. LCCN:73-016744.
Audience: **u,f.** *B*

Sullivan, Walter **PS261.S93**
A Requiem for the Renascence: The State of Fiction in the Modern South. Trade Cloth. University of Georgia Press. Athens, GA. 1976. xxiv, 81 p. ;p. ISBN:0-8203-0390-9, ISBN13: 978-0-8203-0390-1. Dewey:813/.009. LCCN:75-021176.
Audience: **l,u,f.** *B*

Ward, William S. **PS266.K4W37 1988**
A Literary History of Kentucky. Thomas D. Clark (Foreword by). Trade Cloth. University of Tennessee Press. Knoxville, TN. 1988. 416p. ISBN:0-87049-577-1, ISBN13: 978-0-87049-577-9. Dewey:810/.9/9769. LCCN:88-001277.
Audience: **u,f.**

Warren, James **PS407.W37 1999**
Culture of Eloquence: Oratory and Reform in Antebellum America. Cloth Text. Pennsylvania State University Press. University Park, PA. 1999. 272p. ISBN:0-271-01900-X, ISBN13: 978-0-271-01900-0. Dewey:815/.309. LCCN:98-041327.
Audience: **u,f.** *Choice, 2000.*

History, Criticism > Literary history, by Region > West and Central

PS277.M3 1972
Southwest Heritage; a Literary History with Bibliographies. Trade Cloth. University of New Mexico Press. Albuquerque, NM. 1972. x, 378p. ISBN:0-8263-0222-X, ISBN13: 978-0-8263-0222-9. Dewey:810/.997/9. LCCN:77-175507.
Audience: **u,f.**

Allmendinger, Blake **PS271.A434 2005**
Imagining the African American West. Saddle Stitched, Cloth over Boards, Dust Jacket. University of Nebraska Press. Lincoln, NE. 2005. 161p. Race and Ethnicity in the American West Ser. ISBN:0-8032-1067-1, ISBN13: 978-0-8032-1067-7. Dewey:810.9/3278. LCCN:2005-010261.
Audience: **u,f.** *Choice, 2006.*

Anzaldúa, Gloria **PS3551.N95B6 1999**
Borderlands - La Frontera: The New Mestiza. Ed. 2. Trade Cloth. Aunt Lute Books. San Francisco, CA. 1999. 260p. ISBN:1-879960-57-5, ISBN13: 978-1-879960-57-2. Dewey:811/.54. LCCN:99-022546.
Audience: **u,f.** *Choice, 1988.*

Barillas, William **PS273.B37 2006**
The Midwestern Pastoral: Place and Landscape in Literature of the American Heartland. Trade Cloth. Ohio University Press. Athens, OH. 2006. 272p. ISBN:0-8214-1660-X, ISBN13: 978-0-8214-1660-0. Dewey:810.9/3217340977. LCCN:2005-026992.
Audience: **u,f.** *Choice, 2006.*

Duffey, Bernard I. **PS285.C47 D8 1972**
The Chicago Renaissance in American Letters: A Critical History. Trade Cloth. Greenwood Publishing Group, Inc. Portsmouth, NH. 1973. 285p. ISBN:0-8371-6461-3, ISBN13: 978-0-8371-6461-8. Dewey:810.903. LCCN:72-006193.
Audience: **u,f.** *B*

Greasley, Philip A. **PS273.D53 2001**
e Dictionary of Midwestern Literature: The Authors, Vol. 1. E-Book. Indiana University Press. Bloomington, IN. 2001. 678p. ISBN:0-253-33609-0, ISBN13: 978-0-253-33609-5. Dewey:810.9/977/03. LCCN:00-040753.
Audience: **l,u,f.** *Choice, 2001.*

Lape, Noreen Groover **PS271.L37 2000**
West of the Border: The Multicultural Literature of the Western American Frontiers. Trade Cloth. Ohio University Press. Athens, OH. 2000. 234p. ISBN:0-8214-1345-7, ISBN13: 978-0-8214-1345-6. Dewey:810.9/3278. LCCN:00-028569.
Audience: **u,f.** *Choice, 2001.*

Major, Mabel **PS277.M3**
Southwest Heritage: Literary History with Bibliography. Library Binding. Reprint Services Company. Temecula, CA. 1993. 199p. BCL1-PS American Literature Ser. ISBN:0-7812-6581-9, ISBN13: 978-0-7812-6581-2. Dewey:810/.997/9.
Audience: **u,f.**

Rusk, Ralph Leslie **PS273.R8**
The Literature of the Middle Western Frontier. Paper Text. Classic Textbooks. Murrieta, CA. 1925. ISBN:1-4047-6627-8, ISBN13: 978-1-4047-6627-3. Dewey:810.977.
Audience: **l,u.**

Simonson, Harold P. **PS271.S5 1989**
Beyond the Frontier: Writers, Western Regionalism and a Sense of Place. Trade Cloth. Texas Christian University Press. Fort Worth, TX. 1989. 192p. ISBN:0-87565-040-6, ISBN13: 978-0-87565-040-1. Dewey:810/.9/3278. LCCN:89-004411.
Audience: **u,f.** *Choice, 1990.*

Weber, Ronald **PS273.W4 1992**
The Midwestern Ascendancy in American Writing. Trade Cloth. Indiana University Press. Bloomington, IN. 1992. 288p. Midwestern History and Culture Ser. ISBN:0-253-36366-7, ISBN13: 978-0-253-36366-4. Dewey:810.9/977. LCCN:91-046602.
Audience: **u,f.** *Choice, 1993.*

Western Literature Association Staff **PS271.U64 1997**
Updating the Literary West: Western Literature Association. Thomas J. Lyon (Editor). Trade Cloth. Texas Christian University Press. Fort Worth, TX. 1997. 1032p. ISBN:0-87565-175-5, ISBN13: 978-0-87565-175-0. Dewey:810.9/3278. LCCN:97-009120.
Audience: **u,f.** *Choice, 1998.*

History, Criticism > Literary history, by Form > Poetry

Beach, Christopher **PS323.5.B387 2003**
The Cambridge Introduction to Twentieth-Century American Poetry. Cloth Text. Cambridge University Press. New York, NY. 2003. 232p. Cambridge Introductions to Literature Ser. ISBN:0-521-81469-3, ISBN13: 978-0-521-81469-0. Dewey:811/.509. LCCN:2003-043580.
Audience: **l,u.**

Bennett, Paula Bernat **PS310.F45B46 2003**
Poets in the Public Sphere: The Emancipatory Project of American Women's Poetry, 1800-1900. Trade Cloth. Princeton University Press. Princeton, NJ. 2003. 264p. ISBN:0-691-02645-9, ISBN13: 978-0-691-02645-9. Dewey:811/.3099287. LCCN:2002-069278.
Audience: **l,u,f.** *Choice, 2003.*

Bloom, Clive & Docherty, Brian (Editors) **PS310.M57A59 1995**
American Poetry: The Modernist Ideal. Cloth over Boards. Palgrave Macmillan. New York, NY. 1995. 256p. Insights Ser. ISBN:0-312-12388-4, ISBN13: 978-0-312-12388-8. Dewey:811.5/09112. LCCN:94-003770.
Audience: **u,f.**

Clarke, Cheryl **PS310.N4C48 2004**
"After Mecca": Women Poets and the Black Arts Movement. Trade Cloth. Rutgers University Press. Piscataway, NJ. 2005. 208p. ISBN:0-8135-3405-4, ISBN13: 978-0-8135-3405-3. Dewey:811/.509896073. LCCN:2004-007530.
Audience: **g,l,u,f.** *Choice, 2005.*

Duplessis, Rachel Blau **PS310.S7D87 2001**
Genders, Races, and Religious Cultures in Modern American Poetry, 1908-1934. Albert Gelpi & Ross Posnock (Contribution by). Cloth Text. Cambridge University Press. New York, NY. 2001. 252p. Studies in American Literature and Culture, No. 125 ISBN:0-521-48300-X, ISBN13: 978-0-521-48300-1. Dewey:811.509355. LCCN:00-031284.
Audience: **u,f.**

Gray, Janet **PS310.R34G73 2003**
Race and Time: American Women's Poetics from Antislavery to Racial Modernity. Trade Cloth. University of Iowa Press. Iowa City, IA. 2004. 332p. ISBN:0-87745-877-4, ISBN13: 978-0-87745-877-7. Dewey:811/.3099287. LCCN:2003-060383.
Audience: **g,l,u,f.** *Choice, 2004.*

Nelson, Cary **PS324**
Repression and Recovery: Modern American Poetry and the Politics of Cultural Memory, 1910-1945. Trade Paper. University of Wisconsin Press. Chicago, IL. 1992. 352p. Wisconsin Project on American Writers Ser. ISBN:0-299-12344-8, ISBN13: 978-0-299-12344-4. Dewey:811/.5209. LCCN:89-040264.
Audience: **u,f.** *Choice, 1990.*

Parini, Jay & Miller, Brett C. (Editors) **PS303.C64 1993**
The Columbia History of American Poetry. Trade Cloth. Columbia University Press. New York, NY. 1993. 894p. ISBN:0-231-07836-6, ISBN13: 978-0-231-07836-8. Dewey:811.009. LCCN:92-029399.
Audience: **l,u,f.** *Choice, 1994.*

Spender, Stephen & Hall, Donald **PR19.S6**
The Concise Encyclopedia of English and American Poets and Poetry. Ed. 2. Trade Cloth. Hawthorn Books Ltd. 1963. 388p. ISBN:0-09-098810-8, ISBN13: 978-0-09-098810-5. Dewey:821/.003. LCCN:63-008015.
Audience: **g,l,u,f.** B

History, Criticism > Literary history, by Form > Drama

Krasner, David **PS338.N4K73 2002**
A Beautiful Pageant: African American Theatre, Drama, and Performance in the Harlem Renaissance, 1910-1927. Cloth over Boards. Palgrave Macmillan. New York, NY. 2002. 384p. ISBN:0-312-29590-1, ISBN13: 978-0-312-29590-5. Dewey:812/.5209896073. LCCN:2002-025109.
Audience: **u,f.** *Choice, 2003.*

Murphy, Brenda (Editor) **PS338.W6C36 1999**
The Cambridge Companion to American Women Playwrights. Trade Paper. Cambridge University Press. New York, NY. 1999. 324p. Companions to Literature Ser. ISBN:0-521-57680-6, ISBN13: 978-0-521-57680-2. Dewey:812.009/9287. LCCN:98-036593.
Audience: **g,l,u,f.**

Schanke, Robert A. & Marra, Kimberley B. (Editors) **PS338.H66S73 2001**
Staging Desire: Queer Readings of American Theater History. Trade Cloth. University of Michigan Press. Chicago, IL. 2002. 416p. Triangulations Ser., :Lesbian - Gay - Queer Theater - Drama - Performance ISBN:0-472-09749-0, ISBN13: 978-0-472-09749-4. Dewey:812.009/353. LCCN:2001-006446.
Audience: **u,f.** *Choice, 2003.*

Sinfield, Alan **PR739.H65S56 1999**
Out on Stage: Lesbian and Gay Theater in the Twentieth Century. Cloth over Boards. Yale University Press. Cumberland, RI. 1999. 416p. ISBN:0-300-08102-2, ISBN13: 978-0-300-08102-2. Dewey:820.9/3520664. LCCN:99-028103.
Audience: **l,u,f.** *Choice, 2000.*

History, Criticism > Literary history, by Form > Prose

Weisenburger, Steven C. **PS374.S2W4 1995**
Fables of Subversion: Satire and the American Novel. Trade Cloth. University of Georgia Press. Athens, GA. 1995. 336p. ISBN:0-8203-1668-7, ISBN13: 978-0-8203-1668-0. Dewey:813/.50917. LCCN:94-015268.
Audience: **u,f.** *Choice, 1995.*

History, Criticism > Literary history, by Form > Folk Literature

Abrahams, Roger D. **GR111.A47A38 1999**
African-American Folktales: Stories from Black Traditions in the New World. Book, Other. Knopf Publishing Group. New York, NY. 1999. 352p. Fairy Tale and Folklore Library ISBN:0-375-70539-2, ISBN13: 978-0-375-70539-7. Dewey:398.2/089/96073. LCCN:98-042200.
Audience: **l,u,f.**

Abrahams, Roger D. **GR103**
Deep down in the Jungle: Negro Narrative Folklore from the Streets of Philadelphia. Trade Paper. Aldine Transaction. Somerset, NJ. 1970. 278p. ISBN:0-202-01092-9, ISBN13: 978-0-202-01092-2. Dewey:398.3. LCCN:78-124404.
Audience: **g,l,u,f.** B

Briggs, Charles L. **GR111.M49B75 1988**
Competence in Performance: The Creativity of Tradition in Mexicano Verbal Art. Trade Paper. University of Pennsylvania Press. Philadelphia, PA. 1988. 448p. Conduct and Communication Ser. ISBN:0-8122-1260-6, ISBN13: 978-0-8122-1260-0. Dewey:398/.08968720789. LCCN:88-014427.
Audience: **u,f.**

Bronner, Simon J. **GR105**
American Folklore Studies: An Intellectual History. Trade Paper. University Press of Kansas. Lawrence, KS. 1986. xviii, 214p. ISBN:0-7006-0313-1, ISBN13: 978-0-7006-0313-8. Dewey:398/.072073. LCCN:86-009292.
Audience: **u,f.** *Choice, 1987.*

Bronner, Simon J. **GR105.B668 2002**
Folk Nation: Folklore in the Creation of American Tradition. Book, Other. Rowman & Littlefield Publishers, Inc. Lanham, MD. 2002. 256p. ISBN:0-8420-2891-9, ISBN13: 978-0-8420-2891-2. Dewey:398/.0973. LCCN:2002-021206.
Audience: **l,u,f.** *Choice, 2003.*

Bronner, Simon J. **GR105.B67 1998**
Following Tradition: Folklore in the Discourse of American Culture. Cloth Text. Utah State University Press. Logan, UT. 1998. 616p. ISBN:0-87421-239-1, ISBN13: 978-0-87421-239-6. Dewey:398/.0973. LCCN:97-045342.
Audience: **u,f.**

Bronner, Simon J. **GR55.S53B76 1996**
Popularizing Pennsylvania: Henry W. Shoemaker and the Progressive Uses of Folklore and History. Trade Paper. Pennsylvania State University Press. University Park, PA. 1996. 272p. ISBN:0-271-01487-3, ISBN13: 978-0-271-01487-6. Dewey:398/.092 B. LCCN:95-015354.
Audience: **u,f.** *Choice, 1996.*

Bronner, Simon J. **GR105.3.A44 1988**
American Children's Folklore. W. K. McNeil (Introduction by). Trade Cloth. August House Publishers, Inc. Atlanta, GA. 1988. 288p. American Folklore Ser. ISBN:0-87483-068-0, ISBN13: 978-0-87483-068-2. Dewey:398/.0973. LCCN:88-023469.
Audience: **l,u,f.**

Brunvand, Jan Harold (Editor) **GR101.A54 1998**
American Folklore: An Encyclopedia. Trade Paper. Garland Publishing, Inc. New York, NY. 1998. 816p. Reference Library of the Humanities ISBN:0-8153-3350-1, ISBN13: 978-0-8153-3350-0. Dewey:398.2/0973. LCCN:98-038863.
Audience: **g,l,u,f.** *Choice, 1996.*

Brunvand, Jan Harold **GR105.34.B78 2001**
Encyclopedia of Urban Legends. Library Binding. ABC-CLIO, Inc. Santa Barbara, CA. 2001. 525p. ISBN:1-57607-076-X, ISBN13: 978-1-57607-076-5. Dewey:398.2/0973/091732. LCCN:2001-000883.
Audience: **g,l,u,f.** *Choice, 2001.*

Brunvand, Jan Harold **GR105.B7 1998**
The Study of American Folklore: An Introduction. Ed. 4. Trade Cloth. W. W. Norton & Company, Inc. New York, NY. 1998. 646p. ISBN:0-393-97223-2, ISBN13: 978-0-393-97223-8. Dewey:398/.0973. LCCN:97-026188.
Audience: **l,u.**

Brunvand, Jan Harold **GR105**
Too Good to Be True: The Colossal Book of Urban Legends. Trade Paper. W. W. Norton & Company, Inc. New York, NY. 2001. 480p. ISBN:0-393-32088-X, ISBN13: 978-0-393-32088-6. Dewey:398.2/0973/091732.
Audience: **g,l,u,f.**

Cohen, David S. **GR110 N5 C64**
The Folklore and Folklife of New Jersey. Cloth Text. Rutgers University Press. Piscataway, NJ. 1983. 223p. ISBN:0-8135-0964-5, ISBN13: 978-0-8135-0964-8. Dewey:398/.09749.
Audience: **g,l,u,f.**

Dorson, Richard M. (Editor) **GR105**
Handbook of American Folklore. Trade Paper. Indiana University Press. Bloomington, IN. 1986. 608p. ISBN:0-253-20373-2, ISBN13: 978-0-253-20373-1. Dewey:398/.0973. LCCN:82-047574.
Audience: **g,l,u,f.**

Dundes, Alan (Editor) **GR111.A47M68 1990**
Mother Wit from the Laughing Barrel: Readings in the Interpretation of Afro-American Folklore. Trade Cloth. University Press of Mississippi. Jackson, MS. 1991. 640p. ISBN:0-87805-478-2, ISBN13: 978-0-87805-478-7. Dewey:398/.08996076. LCCN:90-040867.
Audience: **u,f.**

Fine, Gary Alan & Turner, Patricia A. **GR111.A47**
Whispers on the Color Line: Rumor and Race in America. Trade Paper. University of California Press. Berkeley, CA. 2004. 270p. ISBN:0-520-22855-3, ISBN13: 978-0-520-22855-9. Dewey:398/.089/96073. LCCN:2001-027089.
Audience: **g,l,u,f.** *Choice, 2002.*

Glassie, Henry H. **GR105**
Pattern in the Material Folk Culture of the Eastern United States. Book, Other. University of Pennsylvania Press. Philadelphia, PA. 1971. 344p. Publications of the American Folklore So ISBN:0-8122-1013-1, ISBN13: 978-0-8122-1013-2. Dewey:398.0973. LCCN:75-160630.
Audience: **u,f.**

Hurston, Zora Neale **GR111.A47H86 1990**
Mules and Men. Miguel Covarrubias (Illustrator), Arnold Rampersad (Foreword by), Franz Boas (Preface by). Trade Paper. HarperCollins Publishers. New York, NY. 1990. 336p. ISBN:0-06-091648-6, ISBN13: 978-0-06-091648-0. Dewey:398.2/09759. LCCN:89-045672.
Audience: **g,l,u,f.**

Mathias, Elizabeth & Raspa, Richard **GR111.I73M37 1988**
Italian Folktales in America: The Verbal Art of an Immigrant Woman. Trade Paper. Wayne State University Press. Detroit, MI. 1988. 346p. ISBN:0-8143-2122-4, ISBN13: 978-0-8143-2122-5. Dewey:398.2/08951073. LCCN:88-006598.
Audience: **u,f.**

Montell, William L. **GR110.K4**
Ghosts along Cumberland: Deathlore in the Kentucky Foothills. Trade Paper. University of Tennessee Press. Knoxville, TN. 1975. 272p. ISBN:0-87049-535-6, ISBN13: 978-0-87049-535-9. Dewey:398.2/7/097691. LCCN:74-032241.
Audience: **u,f.**

Roberts, John W. **GR111.A47**
From Trickster to Badman: The Black Folk Hero in Slavery and Freedom. Book, Other. University of Pennsylvania Press. Philadelphia, PA. 1990. 240p. ISBN:0-8122-1333-5, ISBN13: 978-0-8122-1333-1. Dewey:398/.352/0880396073. LCCN:88-020804.
Audience: **g,l,u,f.** *Choice, 1989.*

Stanley, David **GR110.U8F65 2004**
Folklore in Utah: A History and Guide to Resources. Trade Paper. Utah State University Press. Logan, UT. 2004. 360p. ISBN:0-87421-588-9, ISBN13: 978-0-87421-588-5. Dewey:398.2/09792/09. LCCN:2004-010411.
Audience: **u,f.**

Turner, Patricia A. **GR111.A47.T87 1993**
I Heard It Through the Grapevine: Rumor in African-American Culture. Trade Cloth. University of California Press. Berkeley, CA. 1993. 260p. ISBN:0-520-08185-4, ISBN13: 978-0-520-08185-7. Dewey:398.08996073. LCCN:93-017463.
Audience: **g,l,u,f.** *Choice, 1994.*

Weigle, Marta & White, Peter **GR110.N6W45 2003**
The Lore of New Mexico. Ed. 2. Trade Paper. University of New Mexico Press. Albuquerque, NM. 2004. 460p. ISBN:0-8263-3157-2, ISBN13: 978-0-8263-3157-1. Dewey:398.2/09789. LCCN:2003-006265.
Audience: **u,f.**

Zumwalt, Rosemary L. **GR48.Z86 1988**
American Folklore Scholarship: A Dialogue of Dissent. Trade Cloth. Indiana University Press. Bloomington, IN. 1988. 202p. Folkloristics Ser. ISBN:0-253-31738-X, ISBN13: 978-0-253-31738-4. Dewey:398/.0973. LCCN:87-045408.
Audience: **u,f.**

Collections of American Literature

PS507
American Hypertexts.
http://xroads.virginia.edu/~HYPER/hypertex.html
Audience: **g,l,u,f.**

PS507
American Literary Classics.
http://www.americanliterature.com/
Audience: **g,l,u,f.**

PS593.S67.T4 1980
Text--Sound Texts. Trade Cloth. HarperCollins Publishers. New York, NY. 1980. 441 p. :p. ISBN:0-688-08616-0, ISBN13: 978-0-688-08616-9. Dewey:811/.54/08. LCCN:79-093246.
Audience: **l,u,f.**

PS658

Wright American Fiction: 1851-1875.
http://www.letrs.indiana.edu/web/w/wright2/
Audience: **g,l,u,f.**

Allen, Paula Gunn (Editor) **PS508.I5 S62**
Song of the Turtle: American Indian Literature, 1974-1994. Trade Cloth. Ballantine Books. New York, NY. 1996. ISBN:0-614-96849-6, ISBN13: 978-0-614-96849-1. Dewey:813/.54080897.
Audience: **l,u,f.**

Andrews, William L. (Editor) **PS647.A35C56 2002**
Classic African American Women's Narratives. Trade Paper. Oxford University Press, Inc. New York, NY. 2003. 432p. ISBN:0-19-514135-0, ISBN13: 978-0-19-514135-1. Dewey:818/.308099287. LCCN:2002-003767.
Audience: **g,l,u,f.**

Augenbraum, Harold & Olmos, Margarite Fernández (Editors) **PS508.H57L4 1997**
The Latino Reader: An American Literary Tradition from 1542 to the Present. Trade Paper. Houghton Mifflin Company Trade & Reference Division. Boston, MA. 1997. 528p. ISBN:0-395-76528-5, ISBN13: 978-0-395-76528-9. Dewey:810.8/0868. LCCN:96-042277.
Audience: **l,u,f.**

Barksdale, Richard & Kinnamon, Keneth **PS508.N3**
Black Writers of America: A Comprehensive Anthology. Trade Paper. Prentice Hall PTR. Upper Saddle River, NJ. 1997. 944p. ISBN:0-13-779399-5, ISBN13: 978-0-13-779399-0. Dewey:810/.8/0896073.
Audience: **g,l,u,f.**

Baym, Nina (Editor) **PS507.N65 2002**
The Norton Anthology of American Literature: American Literature, 1820-1865. Ed. 6. Trade Paper. W. W. Norton & Company, Inc. New York, NY. 2002. 1700p. ISBN:0-393-97905-9, ISBN13: 978-0-393-97905-3. Dewey:810.8. LCCN:2002-141437.
Audience: **l,u,f.**

Baym, Nina (Editor) **PS507.N65 2002**
The Norton Anthology of American Literature: American Literature Between the Wars, 1914-1945. Ed. 6. Trade Paper. W. W. Norton & Company, Inc. New York, NY. 2002. 820p. ISBN:0-393-97900-8, ISBN13: 978-0-393-97900-8. Dewey:810.8. LCCN:2002-141437.
Audience: **l,u,f.**

Baym, Nina (Editor) **PS507.N65 2002**
The Norton Anthology of American Literature: Literature to 1820. Ed. 6. Trade Paper. W. W. Norton & Company, Inc. New York, NY. 2002. 900p. ISBN:0-393-97898-2, ISBN13: 978-0-393-97898-8. Dewey:810.8. LCCN:2002-141437.
Audience: **l,u,f.**

Baym, Nina (Editor) **PS507.N65 2002**
The Norton Anthology of American Literature: American Literature, 1865-1914. Ed. 6. Trade Paper. W. W. Norton & Company, Inc. New York, NY. 2002. 950p. ISBN:0-393-97899-0, ISBN13: 978-0-393-97899-5. Dewey:810.8. LCCN:2002-141437.
Audience: **l,u,f.**

Baym, Nina (Editor) **PS507.N65 2002**
The Norton Anthology of American Literature: American Literature since 1945. Ed. 6. Trade Paper. W. W. Norton & Company, Inc. New York, NY. 2002. 5,529p. ISBN:0-393-97901-6, ISBN13: 978-0-393-97901-5. Dewey:810.8. LCCN:2002-141437.
Audience: **l,u,f.**

Bradley, Sculley (Editor, Compiled by) **PS507.B74 1974**
The American Tradition in Literature, Vol. 2. Ed. 4. Trade Cloth. Penguin Group (USA) Inc. New York, NY. 1974. ISBN:0-448-13154-4, ISBN13: 978-0-448-13154-2. Dewey:810.8. LCCN:73-014128.
Audience: **l,u,f.** B

Brooks, Gwendolyn & Malcolm X **PS508.N3C5 2001**
Black Voices: An Anthology of African-American Literature. Abraham Chapman (Editor). Mass Market. Penguin Group (USA) Inc. New York, NY. 2001. 720p. Signet Classics Ser. ISBN:0-451-52782-8, ISBN13: 978-0-451-52782-0. Dewey:810.809.
Audience: **l,u,f.**

Butcher, Philip (Editor) **PS509.M5 E86**
The Ethnic Image in Modern American Literature: 1900-1950, Set. Trade Cloth. Howard University Press. Washington, DC. 1984. ISBN:0-88258-110-4, ISBN13: 978-0-88258-110-1. Dewey:810/.9/3520693.
Audience: **l,u,f.** B

Chametzky, Jules (Editor), et al. **PS508.J4J45 2000**
Jewish American Literature: A Norton Anthology. John Felstiner, Hilene Flanzbaum & Kathryn Hellerstein (Editors). Trade Cloth. W. W. Norton & Company, Inc. New York, NY. 2000. 1100p. ISBN:0-393-04809-8, ISBN13: 978-0-393-04809-4. Dewey:810.8/08924. LCCN:00-055393.
Audience: **l,u,f.**

Dandridge, Rita B. **PS508.N3 D25 1992**
Black Women's Blues: A Literary Anthology: 1934-Present. Trade Cloth. Macmillan Publishing Company, Inc. Old Tappan, NJ. 1992. 300p. G. K. Hall Reference Ser. ISBN:0-8161-9084-4, ISBN13: 978-0-8161-9084-3. Dewey:810.8/0352042. LCCN:92-019728.
Audience: **g,l,u,f.**

Dawidoff, Nicholas (Editor) **PS509.B37B37 2002**
Baseball: A Literary Anthology. Trade Cloth. Library of America, The. New York, NY. 2002. 721p. ISBN:1-931082-09-X, ISBN13: 978-1-931082-09-9. Dewey:810.8/0355. LCCN:2001-038654.
Audience: **l,u,f.**

Derleth, August (Editor) **PS648.S3N427 1998**
New Horizons: Yesterday's Portraits of Tomorrow. Joseph Wrzos (Introduction by, Notes by). Trade Cloth. Arkham House Publishers. Sauk City, WI. 1999. xv, 299p. ISBN:0-87054-174-9, ISBN13: 978-0-87054-174-2. Dewey:813/.0876208. LCCN:98-049573.
Audience: **g,l,u,f.**

Dunbar-Nelson, Alice M. (Editor) **PS663.N4M37 1997**
Masterpieces of Negro Eloquence: African-American Women

Writers, 1910-1940 by Dunbar-Nelson. Akasha Hull (Introduction by). Trade Cloth. Macmillan Publishing Company, Inc. Old Tappan, NJ. 1996. xxix, 512p. ISBN:0-7838-1424-0, ISBN13: 978-0-7838-1424-7. Dewey:815.008/0896073. LCCN:96-044327.

Audience: **g,l,u,f.**

Emanuel, James A. (Editor) **PS508.N3E4**
Dark Symphony. Trade Paper. Simon & Schuster. New York, NY. 1968. 628p. ISBN:0-02-909540-9, ISBN13: 978-0-02-909540-9. Dewey:810.8/09. LCCN:68-054984.

Audience: **l,u,f.**

Fernández, Roberto (Editor) **PS508.H57I5 1994**
In Other Words: Literatures of Latinas of the United States. Trade Paper. Arte Publico Press. Houston, TX. 1994. 592p. ISBN:1-55885-110-0, ISBN13: 978-1-55885-110-8. Dewey:810.8/0868. LCCN:94-009206.

Audience: **l,u,f.**

Flores, Lauro (Editor) **PS508.H57F58 1998**
The Floating Borderlands: Twenty-Five Years of U. S. Hispanic Literature. Trade Paper. University of Washington Press. Seattle, WA. 1999. 446p. ISBN:0-295-97746-9, ISBN13: 978-0-295-97746-1. Dewey:810.8/0868. LCCN:98-023924.

Audience: **l,u,f.**

Garcia, Cristina **PQ7237.E5B67 2006**
Bordering Fires: The Vintage Book of Contemporary Mexican and Chicana and Chicano Literature. Trade Paper. Knopf Publishing Group. New York, NY. 2006. 304p. ISBN:1-4000-7718-4, ISBN13: 978-1-4000-7718-2. Dewey:860.8/09720904. LCCN:2006-044721.

Audience: **g,l,u,f.**

Gilbert, Sandra M. (Editor) **PS508.W7N67**
Norton Anthology of Literature by Women: The Traditions in English. Ed. 3. Paper Text. W. W. Norton & Company, Inc. New York, NY. 2007. 2452p. ISBN:0-393-97923-7, ISBN13: 978-0-393-97923-7. Dewey:820.8/09287.

Audience: **g,l,u,f.**

Gopnik, Adam **PS509.P28A47 2004**
Americans in Paris: A Literary Anthology. Kate Chopin (Contribution by). Trade Cloth. Library of America, The. New York, NY. 2004. 650p. ISBN:1-931082-56-1, ISBN13: 978-1-931082-56-3. Dewey:810.8/03244361. LCCN:2003-066080.

Audience: **g,l,u,f.**

Halberstam, David & Stout, Glenn (Editors) **PS509.S65B47 1999**
The Best American Sports Writing of the Century. Trade Paper. Houghton Mifflin Company Trade & Reference Division. Boston, MA. 1999. xxxiii, 776p. The Best American Sports Writing Ser. ISBN:0-395-94514-3, ISBN13: 978-0-395-94514-8. Dewey:796/.0973. LCCN:2001-268588.

Audience: **g,l,u,f.**

Harjo, Joy **PS508.I5R38 1997**
Reinventing the Enemy's Language: Contemporary Native Women's Writing of North America. Trade Cloth. W. W. Norton & Company, Inc. New York, NY. 1997. 448p. ISBN:0-393-04029-1, ISBN13: 978-0-393-04029-6. Dewey:810.8/09287/08997. LCCN:96-036547.

Audience: **g,l,u,f.** *Choice, 1997.*

Harper's Magazine Staff **PS507 .H23 1972**
Gentlemen, Scholars and Scoundrels: A Treasury of the Best of Harper's Magazine; from 1850 to the Present. Horace Knowles (Editor). Trade Cloth. Ayer Company Publishers, Inc. Manchester, NH. 1977. Essay Index Reprint Ser. ISBN:0-8369-2554-8, ISBN13: 978-0-8369-2554-8. Dewey:810.8. LCCN:79-167352.

Audience: **g,l,u,f.**

Hobson, Geary (Editor) **PS508.I5 R4 1981**
The Remembered Earth: An Anthology of Contemporary Native American Literature. Trade Paper. University of New Mexico Press. Albuquerque, NM. 1981. 429p. ISBN:0-8263-0568-7, ISBN13: 978-0-8263-0568-8. Dewey:810/.8/0897. LCCN:80-054561.

Audience: **l,u,f.**

Huggins, Nathan I. (Editor) **PS509**
Voices from the Harlem Renaissance. Trade Paper. Oxford University Press, Inc. New York, NY. 1995. 448p. ISBN:0-19-509360-7, ISBN13: 978-0-19-509360-5. Dewey:810.8/0896073. LCCN:94-033190.

Audience: **l,u,f.**

Kanellos, Nicolás (Editor) **PS508.H57**
Herencia: The Anthology of Hispanic Literature of the United States. Paper Text. Oxford University Press, Inc. New York, NY. 2003. 656p. ISBN:0-19-513825-2, ISBN13: 978-0-19-513825-2. Dewey:810.8/0868.

Audience: **l,u,f.**

Kiernan, Kathy & Powers, Retha (Editors) **PS536.2**
This Is My Best: Great Writers Share Their Favorite Work. Trade Paper, Perfect. Chronicle Books LLC. San Francisco, CA. 2005. 448p. ISBN:0-8118-4829-9, ISBN13: 978-0-8118-4829-9. Dewey:820.8.

Audience: **g,l,u,f.**

Kilcup, Karen **PS508.I5N374 2000**
Native American Women's Writing: An Anthology c. 1800-1924. Trade Cloth. Blackwell Publishing, Inc. Malden, MA. 2000. 464p. Anthologies Ser. ISBN:0-631-20517-9, ISBN13: 978-0-631-20517-3. Dewey:810.8/09287/08997. LCCN:99-086315.

Audience: **l,u,f.**

Lapham, Lewis H. & Rosenbush, Ellen (Editors) **PS509.U52A39 2000**
An American Album: One Hundred of Fifty Years of Harper's Magazine. Trade Cloth. Harper's Magazine Foundation. New York, NY. 2000. 760p. ISBN:1-879957-53-1, ISBN13: 978-1-879957-53-4. Dewey:810.8/04. LCCN:99-087125.

Audience: **g,l,u,f.**

Lerner, Michael (Editor) **PS508.J4B47 2001**
The Best Contemporary Jewish Writing. Trade Cloth. John Wiley & Sons, Inc. Hoboken, NJ. 2001. 464p. ISBN:0-7879-5972-3, ISBN13: 978-0-7879-5972-2. Dewey:810.9/8924. LCCN:2001-003013.

Audience: **l,u,f.**

Lomax, John **PS595.C6**
Cowboy Songs and Other Frontier Ballads. Library Binding. Reprint Services Company. Temecula, CA. 1993. ISBN:0-7812-5890-1, ISBN13: 978-0-7812-5890-6. Dewey:782.4216.
Audience: **g,l,u,f.**

Long, Richard A. & Collier, Eugenia W. (Editors) **PS508.N3**
Afro-American Writing: An Anthology of Prose and Poetry. Ed. 2. Trade Paper. Pennsylvania State University Press. University Park, PA. 1990. 784p. ISBN:0-271-00376-6, ISBN13: 978-0-271-00376-4. Dewey:810/.8/0896073. LCCN:83-043224.
Audience: **g,l,u,f.** B

Ortiz, Simon J. **PS3565.R77**
After and Before the Lightning. Trade Cloth. University of Arizona Press. Tucson, AZ. 1994. 127p. Sun Tracks, :An American Indian Literary Ser. ISBN:0-8165-1448-8, ISBN13: 978-0-8165-1448-9. Dewey:813/.54. LCCN:94-005761.
Audience: **g,l,u,f.**

Roses, Lorraine E. & Randolph, Ruth E. (Editors) **PS508.N3H37 1996**
Harlem's Glory: Black Women Writing, 1900-1950. Trade Cloth. Harvard University Press. Cambridge, MA. 1996. 560p. ISBN:0-674-37269-7, ISBN13: 978-0-674-37269-6. Dewey:810.8/09287. LCCN:96-012342.
Audience: **g,l,u,f.** *Choice, 1997.*

Santiago, Roberto **PS508.P84B67 1995**
Boricuas: Influential Puerto Rican Writings - An Anthology. Trade Paper. Ballantine Books. New York, NY. 1995. 400p. ISBN:0-345-39502-6, ISBN13: 978-0-345-39502-3. Dewey:810.8/097295. LCCN:95-094411.
Audience: **g,l,u,f.**

Srikanth, Rajini & Iwanaga, Esther Y. (Editors) **PS508.A8B65 2001**
Bold Words: A Century of Asian American Writing. Cloth Text. Rutgers University Press. Piscataway, NJ. 2001. 480p. ISBN:0-8135-2965-4, ISBN13: 978-0-8135-2965-3. Dewey:810.8/0895/0904. LCCN:00-068346.
Audience: **l,u,f.** *Choice, 2002.*

Tamburri, Anthony J., et al. **PS508.I73F76 2000**
From the Margin: Writings in Italian Americana. Ed. 2. Paolo A. Giordano & Fred L. Gardaphe (Authors). Trade Paper. Purdue University Press. West Lafayette, IN. 2000. 501p. ISBN:1-55753-152-8, ISBN13: 978-1-55753-152-0. Dewey:810.8/0851073. LCCN:99-020903.
Audience: **l,u,f.**

Vizenor, Gerald R. **PS508.I5N37 1995**
Native-American Literature: A Brief Introduction and Anthology. Ishmael Reed (Editor). Trade Paper. Longman Publishing Group. White Plains, NY. 1997. 400p. Literary Mosiac Ser. ISBN:0-673-46978-6, ISBN13: 978-0-673-46978-6. Dewey:810.8/0897. LCCN:95-001693.
Audience: **g,l,u,f.**

Waldman, Anne **PS614.B33 1996**
The Beat Book: Poems and Fiction from the Beat Generation. Allen Ginsberg (Foreword by). Trade Cloth. Shambhala Publications, Inc. Boston, MA. 1996. 300p. ISBN:1-57062-000-8, ISBN13: 978-1-57062-000-3. Dewey:810.8/0054. LCCN:95-005326.
Audience: **g,l,u,f.**

Collections of American Literature > By Period

Charters, Ann **PS228.B6B39 2001**
Beat down to Your Soul. Trade Paper. Penguin Group (USA) Inc. New York, NY. 2001. 704p. ISBN:0-14-100151-8, ISBN13: 978-0-14-100151-7. Dewey:810.9/0054. LCCN:2001-024576.
Audience: **g,l,u,f.**

Charters, Ann (Editor) **PS536**
The Portable Beat Reader. Trade Paper. Penguin Group (USA) Inc. New York, NY. 2003. 688p. ISBN:0-14-243753-0, ISBN13: 978-0-14-243753-7. Dewey:810.8/0054.
Audience: **g,l,u,f.**

Fetterley, Judith (Editor) **PS647.W6P7 1985**
Provisions: A Reader from Nineteenth-Century American Women. Trade Cloth. Indiana University Press. Bloomington, IN. 1985. 480p. ISBN:0-253-17040-0, ISBN13: 978-0-253-17040-8. Dewey:818/.308/0809287. LCCN:84-042840.
Audience: **l,u,f.** B *Choice, 1986.*

Gutjahr, Paul C. (Editor) **PS535.P66 2001**
Popular American Literature of the 19th Century. Paper Text. Oxford University Press, Inc. New York, NY. 2001. 1,244p. ISBN:0-19-514140-7, ISBN13: 978-0-19-514140-5. Dewey:813/.308. LCCN:00-041647.
Audience: **g,l,u,f.**

Jehlen, Myra & Warner, Michael (Editors) **E187.E54 1997**
The English Literatures of America: 1500-1800. UK-B Format Paperback. Routledge. New York, NY. 1996. 1142p. ISBN:0-415-90873-6, ISBN13: 978-0-415-90873-3. Dewey:810.9/9/73. LCCN:96-047803.
Audience: **g,l,u,f.**

McCoy, Horace, et al. **PS648.D4C695 1997**
Crime Novels: American Noir of the 1930s and '40s. Cornell Woolrich, James M. Cain, Kenneth Fearing, Edward Anderson & William L. Gresham (Authors), Robert Polito (Editor). Trade Cloth. Library of America, The. New York, NY. 1997. 990p. Library of America ISBN:1-883011-46-9, ISBN13: 978-1-883011-46-8. Dewey:813/.087208052. LCCN:97-002485.
Audience: **g,l,u,f.**

Miller, Perry G. **PS541 .A67 1981**
The American Transcendentalists: Their Prose and Poetry. Trade Paper. Johns Hopkins University Press. Baltimore, MD. 1981. 388p. ISBN:0-8018-2701-9, ISBN13: 978-0-8018-2701-3. Dewey:810/.8/003. LCCN:81-047611.
Audience: **l,u,f.**

Mulford, Carla (Editor), et al. **E173.E28 2002**
Early American Writings. Angela Vietto & Amy E. Winans (Editors). Cloth Text. Oxford University Press, Inc. New York, NY. 2001. 1152p. ISBN:0-19-511840-5, ISBN13: 978-0-19-511840-7. Dewey:973. LCCN:2001-016384.
Audience: **g,l,u,f.**

Pizer, Donald **PS658.P5**
American Thought and Writing: The 1890's. Trade Cloth. Houghton Mifflin Company. New York, NY. 1972. xiii, 561p. ISBN:0-395-13493-5, ISBN13: 978-0-395-13493-1. Dewey:810/.8/004. LCCN:76-177497.
Audience: **l,u,f.**

Thompson, Jim, et al. **PS648.D4C697 1997**
Crime Novels: American Noir of the 1950s. David Goodis, Patricia Highsmith, Charles Willeford & Chester B. Himes (Authors), Robert Polito (Editor). Trade Cloth. Library of America, The. New York, NY. 1997. 892p. Library of America ISBN:1-883011-49-3, ISBN13: 978-1-883011-49-9. Dewey:813/.087208054. LCCN:97-002487.
Audience: **g,l,u,f.**

Waldman, Anne **PS614**
Beat Book: Poems and Fiction from the Beat Generation. Trade Cloth. Shambhala Publications, Inc. Boston, MA. 1999. 400p. ISBN:1-57062-427-5, ISBN13: 978-1-57062-427-8. Dewey:811.5408.
Audience: **g,l,u,f.**

Collections of American Literature > By Region

PS551
☐ Library of Southern Literature. http://docsouth.unc.edu/southlit/
Audience: **g,l,u,f.**

PS566.S59
Southwest: A Contemporary Anthology. Trade Cloth. Red Earth Press. Saint Louis, MO. 1977. xii, 418 p. :p. ISBN:0-918434-01-7, ISBN13: 978-0-918434-01-2. Dewey:810/.8/0978. LCCN:77-080002.
Audience: **l,u,f.**

Alurista & Rojas-Urista, Xeliina (Editors) **PS647.M49S68 1986**
Southwest Tales: A Contemporary Collection. Trade Paper. Maize Press. Pismo Beach, CA. 1986. 176p. ISBN:0-939558-09-2, ISBN13: 978-0-939558-09-4. Dewey:813/.01/0886872073. LCCN:85-061180.
Audience: **g,l,u,f.**

Ayers, Edward L. & Mittendorf, Bradley C. (Editors) **PS551**
The Oxford Book of the American South: Testimony, Memory, and Fiction. Trade Paper. Oxford University Press, Inc. New York, NY. 1998. 608p. ISBN:0-19-512493-6, ISBN13: 978-0-19-512493-4. Dewey:810.8/03275.
Audience: **g,l,u,f.**

Cohen, Hennig & Dillingham, William B. **PS645**
Humor of the Old Southwest. Ed. 3. Trade Cloth. University of Georgia Press. Athens, GA. 1994. 528p. ISBN:0-8203-1604-0, ISBN13: 978-0-8203-1604-8. Dewey:813/.008. LCCN:93-011281.
Audience: **l,u,f.**

Fetterley, Judith & Pryse, Marjorie (Editors) **PS508.W7 A48 1995**
American Women Regionalists: A Norton Anthology. Trade Paper. W. W. Norton & Company, Inc. New York, NY. 1995. 672p. ISBN:0-393-31363-8, ISBN13: 978-0-393-31363-5. Dewey:810.8092870903. LCCN:91-011583.
Audience: **g,l,u,f.**

Flanagan, John T. (Editor) **PS563**
America Is West: An Anthology of Middle Western Life and Literature. Trade Cloth. Greenwood Publishing Group, Inc. Portsmouth, NH. 1971. 677p. ISBN:0-8371-3358-0, ISBN13: 978-0-8371-3358-4. Dewey:810.8/032. LCCN:71-106687.
Audience: **l,u,f.**

Lopate, Phillip **PS549.N5**
Writing New York: A Literary Anthology. Trade Paper. Simon & Schuster. New York, NY. 2000. 1056p. ISBN:0-671-04235-1, ISBN13: 978-0-671-04235-6. Dewey:810.8/0327471.
Audience: **g,l,u,f.**

Lyons, Greg **PS561.L59 2002**
Literature of the American West. Trade Paper. Longman Publishing. Boston, MA. 2002. 496p. ISBN:0-205-32461-4, ISBN13: 978-0-205-32461-3. Dewey:810.8/03278. LCCN:2002-028672.
Audience: **l,u,f.**

Meine, Franklin J. **PS566.M4 1977**
Tall Tales of the Southwest: An Anthology of Southern and Southwestern Humor, 1830-1860. Trade Cloth. Scholarly Press, Inc. Saint Clair Shores, MI. 1977. xxxii, 456p. ISBN:0-403-07213-1, ISBN13: 978-0-403-07213-2. Dewey:817/.5/208. LCCN:76-051493.
Audience: **l,u,f.**

Randolph, Vance **GR110**
We Always Lie to Strangers: Tall Tales from the Ozarks. Glen Rounds (Illustrator). Trade Cloth. Greenwood Publishing Group, Inc. Portsmouth, NH. 1974. 309p. ISBN:0-8371-7765-0, ISBN13: 978-0-8371-7765-6. Dewey:398.2/09767/1. LCCN:74-012852.
Audience: **g,l,u,f.**

Ulin, David L. **PS572.L6W74 2002**
Writing Los Angeles: A Literary Anthology. Trade Cloth. Library of America, The. New York, NY. 2002. 880p. ISBN:1-931082-27-8, ISBN13: 978-1-931082-27-3. Dewey:810.8/0979494. LCCN:2002-069352.
Audience: **g,l,u,f.**

Collections of American Literature > By Form > Poetry

PS586

American Verse Project.
http://www.hti.umich.edu/a/amverse/

Audience: **g,l,u,f.**

PS591.N4

Database of African-American Poetry, 1760-1900. Chadwyck-Healey. 1995. ISBN:0-89887-108-5, ISBN13: 978-0-89887-108-1.

Audience: **g,l,u,f.**

PS3563.I334

Sixty-Seven Poems for Downtrodden Saints. Ed. 2. Library Binding. Downtrodden Saints, The Jack Micheline Foundation for the Arts. Tucson, AZ. 1999. 245p. ISBN:0-9666696-0-6, ISBN13: 978-0-9666696-0-2. Dewey:811/.54. LCCN:98-088040.

Audience: **g,l,u,f.**

Adoff, Arnold **PS615**

The Poetry of Black America: Anthology of the Twentieth Century. Gwendolyn Brooks (Introduction by). Trade Cloth. HarperCollins Publishers. New York, NY. 1973. 584p. ISBN:0-06-020089-8, ISBN13: 978-0-06-020089-3. Dewey:811/.5/408. LCCN:72-076518.

Audience: **l,u,f.** B

Allen, Donald **PS613 .N375 1999**

The New American Poetry, 1945-1960. Trade Paper. University of California Press. Berkeley, CA. 1999. 480p. ISBN:0-520-20953-2, ISBN13: 978-0-520-20953-4. Dewey:811/.5408. LCCN:98-032154.

Audience: **g,l,u,f.**

Bain, Robert (Editor) **PS607.W455 1996**

Whitman's and Dickinson's Contemporaries: An Anthology of Their Verse. Trade Cloth. Southern Illinois University Press. Carbondale, IL. 1996. 504p. ISBN:0-8093-2031-2, ISBN13: 978-0-8093-2031-8. Dewey:811/.308. LCCN:95-009867.

Audience: **g,l,u,f.** *Choice, 1996.*

Berg, Stephen & Mezey, Robert (Editors) **PS615.M58**

The New Naked Poetry: Recent American Poetry in Open Forms. Trade Paper. Macmillan Publishing Company, Inc. Old Tappan, NJ. 1976. xxvii, 478p. ISBN:0-672-61354-9, ISBN13: 978-0-672-61354-8. Dewey:811/.5/408. LCCN:75-012999.

Audience: **l,u,f.** B

Bontemps, Arna (Editor) **PS591.N4 B58**

American Negro Poetry. Library Binding. Sagebrush Education Resources. Caledonia, MN. 1996. ISBN:0-8085-7747-6, ISBN13: 978-0-8085-7747-8. Dewey:811/.5/08.

Audience: **l,u,f.**

Bruchac, Joseph (Introduction by) **PS591.I55.S66 1983**

Songs from This Earth on Turtle's Back: An Anthology of Poetry by American Indian Writers. Trade Paper. Greenfield Review Literary Center, Inc. Greenfield Center, NY. 1983. 300p. ISBN:0-912678-58-5, ISBN13: 978-0-912678-58-0. Dewey:811/.54/080897. LCCN:82-082420.

Audience: **l,u,f.** B

Carruth, Hayden & Podell, Susan Kagen **PS613 .C3 1989**

Voice That Is Great Within Us: American Poetry of the Twentieth Century. Trade Paper. Bantam Books. New York, NY. 1983. 768p. Bantam Classics Ser. ISBN:0-553-26263-7, ISBN13: 978-0-553-26263-6. Dewey:811.508. LCCN:77-022250.

Audience: **l,u,f.** B

Day, A. Grove **PM198**

The Sky Clears: Poetry of the American Indians. Trade Cloth. Greenwood Publishing Group, Inc. Portsmouth, NH. 1983. 218p. ISBN:0-313-23883-9, ISBN13: 978-0-313-23883-3. Dewey:897. LCCN:83-001576.

Audience: **l,u,f.** B

Ellmann, Richard (Editor) **PS584 .N4**

The New Oxford Book of American Verse. Trade Cloth. Oxford University Press, Inc. New York, NY. 1976. 1128p. Oxford Books of Verse ISBN:0-19-502058-8, ISBN13: 978-0-19-502058-8. Dewey:811.008. LCCN:75-046354.

Audience: **g,l,u,f.** B

Ellmann, Richard & O'Clair, Robert (Editors) **PS613.N67 1988**

The Norton Anthology of Modern Poetry. Ed. 2. Paper Text. W. W. Norton & Company, Inc. New York, NY. 1988. 1865p. ISBN:0-393-95636-9, ISBN13: 978-0-393-95636-8. Dewey:821/.008. LCCN:87-028310.

Audience: **g,l,u,f.**

Emrich, Duncan **PS593.L8.E5**

American Folk Poetry: An Anthology. Trade Cloth. Little Brown & Company. New York, NY. 1974. 864p. ISBN:0-316-23722-1, ISBN13: 978-0-316-23722-2. Dewey:811/.04. LCCN:74-003499.

Audience: **l,u,f.** B

Granger Book Company, Editorial Board Staff **PS507 .S827**

Survey of American Poetry: Revolutionary Era, 1766-1799, Vol. II. Trade Cloth. Roth Publishing, Inc. Farmingtn Hls, MI. 1983. 200p. ISBN:0-89609-214-3, ISBN13: 978-0-89609-214-3. Dewey:811/.008. LCCN:81-083526.

Audience: **l,u,f.**

Granger Book Company, Editorial Board Staff **PS507 .S827**

Survey of American Poetry: First Great Period, 1830-1860. Trade Cloth. Roth Publishing, Inc. Farmingtn Hls, MI. 1984. Series II, Vol. IV ISBN:0-89609-216-X, ISBN13: 978-0-89609-216-7. Dewey:811/.008. LCCN:81-083526.

Audience: **l,u,f.**

Granger Book Company, Editorial Board Staff **PS507 .S827**

Survey of American Poetry: Twilight Interval, 1890-1912, Vol. VI. Trade Cloth. Roth Publishing, Inc. Farmingtn Hls, MI. 1986. 400p. ISBN:0-89609-218-6, ISBN13: 978-0-89609-218-1. Dewey:811/.008. LCCN:81-083526.

Audience: **l,u,f.**

Granger Book Company, Editorial Board Staff **PS507 .S827 1982**

Survey of American Poetry: Colonial Period (1607-1765). Trade

Cloth. Roth Publishing, Inc. Farmingtn Hls, MI. 1982. 220p. ISBN:0-89609-213-5, ISBN13: 978-0-89609-213-6. Dewey:811/.008. LCCN:81-083526.
Audience: **l,u,f.**

Granger Book Company, Editorial Board Staff (Editor) **PS507 .S827**
Survey of American Poetry: Early Nineteenth Century, 1800-1829. Trade Cloth. Roth Publishing, Inc. Farmingtn Hls, MI. 1984. 286p. Series II, Vol. III ISBN:0-89609-215-1, ISBN13: 978-0-89609-215-0. Dewey:811/.008. LCCN:81-083526.
Audience: **l,u,f.**

Granger Book Company, Editorial Board Staff **PS507 .S827**
Survey of American Poetry: Civil War and Aftermath (1861-1889)., Vol. V+. Library Binding. Roth Publishing, Inc. Farmingtn Hls, MI. 1985. 400p. ISBN:0-89609-217-8, ISBN13: 978-0-89609-217-4. Dewey:811/.008. LCCN:81-083526.
Audience: **l,u,f.**

Hall, Donald (Editor) **PS615**
Contemporary American Poetry. Ed. 2. Trade Paper. Penguin Group (USA) Inc. New York, NY. 1989. 288p. Penguin Poets Ser. ISBN:0-14-058618-0, ISBN13: 978-0-14-058618-3. Dewey:811.5/4/08.
Audience: **g,l,u,f.** B

Hall, Donald (Editor) **PS586.3**
The Oxford Book of Children's Verse in America. Trade Paper. Oxford University Press, Inc. New York, NY. 1990. 368p. Oxford Books of Verse ISBN:0-19-506761-4, ISBN13: 978-0-19-506761-3. Dewey:811/.008/09282.
Audience: **g,l,u,f.** B

Heyen, William (Editor) **PS615.G38 1984**
The Generation of 2000: Contemporary American Poets. Trade Paper. Ontario Review Press. Princeton, NJ. 1984. 364p. Poetry Ser. ISBN:0-86538-043-0, ISBN13: 978-0-86538-043-1. Dewey:811/.5/08. LCCN:84-014745.
Audience: **l,u,f.** B

Hine, Daryl & Parisi, Joseph (Editors) **PS591.N4**
The Poetry Anthology, 1912-1977: 65 Years of America's Most Distinguished Verse Magazine. Trade Paper. Houghton Mifflin Company Trade & Reference Division. Boston, MA. 1978. ISBN:0-395-26547-9, ISBN13: 978-0-395-26547-5. Dewey:811/.5/208.
Audience: **l,u,f.** B

Hollander, John (Editor) **PS607.A56 1996**
American Poetry: The Nineteenth Century. Trade Paper. Library of America, The. New York, NY. 1996. 1040p. Library of America College Editions ISBN:1-883011-36-1, ISBN13: 978-1-883011-36-9. Dewey:811/.308. LCCN:96-008927.
Audience: **g,l,u,f.**

Hollander, John (Editor) **PS607.A56 1993**
American Poetry: Melville to Stickney, American Indian Poetry, Folk Songs and Spirituals. Trade Cloth. Library of America, The. New York, NY. 1993. 1050p. Library of America, Vol. 67 ISBN:0-940450-78-X, ISBN13: 978-0-940450-78-3. Dewey:811/.308. LCCN:93-010702.
Audience: **g,l,u,f.**

Hollander, John (Editor) **PS607.A56 1993**
American Poetry - The Nineteenth Century: Freneau to Whitman. Trade Cloth. Library of America, The. New York, NY. 1993. 1099p. Library of America, Vol. 66 ISBN:0-940450-60-7, ISBN13: 978-0-940450-60-8. Dewey:811/.308. LCCN:93-010702.
Audience: **g,l,u,f.**

Hollander, John (Editor) **PS595.H8A44 2003**
American Wits: An Anthology of Light Verse. Trade Cloth. Library of America, The. New York, NY. 2003. 200p. American Poets Project Ser. ISBN:1-931082-49-9, ISBN13: 978-1-931082-49-5. Dewey:811/.0708. LCCN:2003-046636.
Audience: **g,l,u,f.**

Howe, Florence (Editor) **PS589.N58 1993**
No More Masks: An Anthology of Twentieth-Century American Women Poets. Trade Paper. HarperCollins Publishers. New York, NY. 1993. 560p. ISBN:0-06-096517-7, ISBN13: 978-0-06-096517-4. Dewey:811.508. LCCN:92-054843.
Audience: **l,u,f.**

Kaufman, Alan & Griffin, S. A. (Editors) **PS613.O88 1999**
The Outlaw Bible of American Poetry. Trade Paper. Avalon Publishing Group. New York, NY. 1999. 720p. ISBN:1-56025-227-8, ISBN13: 978-1-56025-227-6. Dewey:811/.5408. LCCN:99-018930.
Audience: **g,l,u,f.**

Keillor, Garrison **PS586.G59 2005**
Good Poems for Hard Times. Trade Cloth. Penguin Group (USA) Inc. New York, NY. 2005. 368p. ISBN:0-670-03436-3, ISBN13: 978-0-670-03436-9. Dewey:811.008. LCCN:2005-042316.
Audience: **g,l,u,f.**

Keillor, Garrison (Selected by, Introduction by) **PS586.G58 2002**
Good Poems. Trade Cloth. Penguin Group (USA) Inc. New York, NY. 2002. 504p. ISBN:0-670-03126-7, ISBN13: 978-0-670-03126-9. Dewey:811.008. LCCN:2002-016881.
Audience: **g,l,u,f.**

Lehman, David **PS583.O82 2006**
The Oxford Book of American Poetry. John Brehm (Editor). Trade Cloth. Oxford University Press, Inc. New York, NY. 2006. 1100p. ISBN:0-19-516251-X, ISBN13: 978-0-19-516251-6. Dewey:811.008. LCCN:2005-036590.
Audience: **g,l,u,f.**

Library of America Staff (Editor) **PS613.A4 2000**
American Poetry: The Twentieth Century: Henry Adams to Dorothy Parker. Robert Hass, John Hollander, Carolyn Kizer, Nathaniel Mackey & Marjorie Perloff (Compiled by). Trade Cloth. Library of America, The. New York, NY. 2000. 1000p. Library of America, Vol. 115- ISBN:1-883011-77-9, ISBN13: 978-1-883011-77-2. Dewey:811/.508. LCCN:99-043721.
Audience: **g,l,u,f.** *Choice, 2000.*

Library of America Staff (Editor) **PS613.A4 2000**
American Poetry: The Twentieth Century: E. E. Cummings to May Swenson. Robert Hass, John Hollander, Carolyn Kizer, Nathaniel Mackey & Marjorie Perloff (Compiled by). Trade

Cloth. Library of America, The. New York, NY. 2000. 1000p. Library of America, Vol. 2 ISBN:1-883011-78-7, ISBN13: 978-1-883011-78-9. Dewey:811/.508. LCCN:99-043721.
Audience: **g,l,u,f.** *Choice, 2000.*

Mandelbaum, Allen & Richardson, Robert D. (Editors) **PS584.T48 2003**
A Treasury of American Poetry. Trade Cloth. Random House Value Publishing. New York, NY. 2003. 768p. ISBN:0-517-22153-5, ISBN13: 978-0-517-22153-2. Dewey:811.008. LCCN:2002-033876.
Audience: **g,l,u,f.**

Matthiessen, Francis O. **PS583 .O82**
Oxford Book of American Verse. Cloth Text. Oxford University Press, Inc. New York, NY. 1950. 1188p. Oxford Books of Verse Ser. ISBN:0-19-500049-8, ISBN13: 978-0-19-500049-8. Dewey:811.082.
Audience: **g,l,u,f.**

McClatchy, J. D. **PS595.C55P648 2005**
Poets of the Civil War. Trade Cloth. Library of America, The. New York, NY. 2005. 250p. American Poets Project Ser. ISBN:1-931082-76-6, ISBN13: 978-1-931082-76-1. Dewey:811/.4080358. LCCN:2004-061552.
Audience: **g,l,u,f.**

Meserole, Harrison T. (Editor) **PS601.A54 1985**
American Poetry of the Seventeenth Century. Trade Cloth. Pennsylvania State University Press. University Park, PA. 1986. 578p. ISBN:0-271-00418-5, ISBN13: 978-0-271-00418-1. Dewey:811/.1/08. LCCN:85-021701.
Audience: **g,l,u,f.**

Myers, Jack & Weingarten, Roger (Editors) **PS615**
New American Poets of the 80's. Trade Paper. Wampeter Press. Key West, FL. 1984. 480p. ISBN:0-931694-35-3, ISBN13: 978-0-931694-35-6. Dewey:811.08.
Audience: **l,u,f.** B

Roth Publishing, Inc. Staff **PS507 .S827**
Survey of American Poetry: Interval Between World Wars (1920-1939). Trade Cloth. Roth Publishing, Inc. Farmingtn Hls, MI. 1986. 380p. ISBN:0-89609-220-8, ISBN13: 978-0-89609-220-4. Dewey:811/.008. LCCN:81-083526.
Audience: **l,u,f.**

Roth Publishing, Inc. Staff **PS507 .S827**
Survey of American Poetry: Midcentury to 1984. Trade Cloth. Roth Publishing, Inc. Farmingtn Hls, MI. 1986. 370p. ISBN:0-89609-222-4, ISBN13: 978-0-89609-222-8. Dewey:811/.008. LCCN:81-083526.
Audience: **g,l,u,f.**

Roth Publishing, Inc. Staff **PS507 .S827**
Survey of American Poetry: World War II and Aftermath (1940-1950). Trade Cloth. Roth Publishing, Inc. Farmingtn Hls, MI. 1986. ISBN:0-89609-221-6, ISBN13: 978-0-89609-221-1. Dewey:811/.008. LCCN:81-083526.
Audience: **l,u,f.**

Roth Publishing, Inc. Staff **PS507 .S827**
Survey of American Poetry: Poetic Renaissance (1913-1919). Trade Cloth. Roth Publishing, Inc. Farmingtn Hls, MI. 1986. 380p. ISBN:0-89609-219-4, ISBN13: 978-0-89609-219-8. Dewey:811/.008. LCCN:81-083526.
Audience: **g,l,u,f.**

Smith, Dave & Bottoms, David (Editors) **PS615.M64 1985**
The Morrow Anthology of Younger American Poets. Anthony Hecht (Introduction by). Trade Paper. HarperCollins Publishers. New York, NY. 1985. 472p. ISBN:0-688-03450-0, ISBN13: 978-0-688-03450-4. Dewey:811/.54/08. LCCN:84-018044.
Audience: **l,u,f.**

Spengemann, William C. & Roberts, Jessica F. (Editors) **PS607.N56 1996**
Nineteenth-Century American Poetry. William C. Spengemann & Jessica F. Roberts (Introduction by, Notes by). Trade Paper. Penguin Group (USA) Inc. New York, NY. 1996. 496p. Classics Ser. ISBN:0-14-043587-5, ISBN13: 978-0-14-043587-0. Dewey:811.3/08. LCCN:96-003466.
Audience: **g,l,u,f.**

Stetson, Erlene **PS591.N4.B525**
Black Sister: Poetry by Black American Women, 1746-1980. Trade Cloth. Indiana University Press. Bloomington, IN. 1981. 336p. Midland Book Ser. ISBN:0-253-30512-8, ISBN13: 978-0-253-30512-1. Dewey:811/.008/09287. LCCN:80-008847.
Audience: **g,l,u,f.** B

Collections of American Literature > By Form > Drama

PS628.W6.P59 1985
Plays by American Women, 1900-1930. Trade Cloth. Applause Theatre Book Publishers. New York, NY. 1985. xxxiii, 261 pp. ISBN:0-87910-226-8, ISBN13: 978-0-87910-226-5. Dewey:812/.52/0809287. LCCN:84-024606.
Audience: **l,u,f.** B

Bonney, Jo **PS627.M63E98 2000**
Extreme Exposure: An Anthology of Solo Performance Texts from the 20th Century. Trade Paper. Theatre Communications Group, Inc. New York, NY. 1999. 450p. ISBN:1-55936-155-7, ISBN13: 978-1-55936-155-2. Dewey:812/.04508. LCCN:98-049391.
Audience: **g,l,u,f.**

Clum, John M. (Editor) **PS627.H67S73 1995**
Staging Gay Lives: An Anthology of Contemporary Gay Theater. Tony Kushner (Foreword by). Trade Paper. Westview Press. Boulder, CO. 1996. 496p. ISBN:0-8133-2505-6, ISBN13: 978-0-8133-2505-7. Dewey:812/.540809206642. LCCN:95-023652.
Audience: **g,l,u,f.** *Choice, 1996.*

Cohen, Sarah B. (Editor, Introduction by) **PS628.J47M35 1997**
Making a Scene: The Contemporary Drama of Jewish-American Women. Trade Cloth. Syracuse University Press. Syracuse, NY. 1996. 436p. ISBN:0-8156-2713-0, ISBN13: 978-0-8156-2713-5. Dewey:812/.540809287/08992. LCCN:96-021140.
Audience: **g,l,u,f.** *Choice, 1997.*

Garza, Roberto J. **PS628.M4**
Contemporary Chicano Theatre. Trade Cloth. University of Notre Dame Press. Notre Dame, IN. 1976. viii, 248p. ISBN:0-268-00709-8, ISBN13: 978-0-268-00709-6. Dewey:812/.5/408. LCCN:75-019876.
Audience: **l,u,f.** B

Gassner, John (Editor) **PS625.B47 2000**
Best Plays of the Early American Theatre, 1787-1911. Trade Paper. Dover Publications, Inc. Mineola, NY. 2000. 768p. ISBN:0-486-41098-6, ISBN13: 978-0-486-41098-2. Dewey:812.008. LCCN:00-027931.
Audience: **g,l,u,f.** B

Gassner, John (Editor, Introduction by) **PS625**
Best Plays of the Early American Theatre: From the Beginning to 1916. Trade Cloth. Crown Publishing Group. New York, NY. 1967. 716p. ISBN:0-517-50949-0, ISBN13: 978-0-517-50949-4. Dewey:812/.008.
Audience: **l,u,f.**

Gates, Robert A. (Editor) **PS631.A14 1984**
Eighteenth and Nineteenth Century American Drama. Trade Cloth. Irvington Publishers. New York, NY. 1985. 296p. ISBN:0-8290-1151-X, ISBN13: 978-0-8290-1151-7. Dewey:812/.008.
Audience: **g,l,u,f.**

Halline, Allan G. **PS634.S57**
Six Modern American Plays. Cloth Text. McGraw-Hill Higher Education. Burr Ridge, IL. 1966. 419p. Modern Library College Editions Ser. ISBN:0-07-553660-9, ISBN13: 978-0-07-553660-4. Dewey:812/.508. LCCN:51-008900.
Audience: **l,u,f.** B

Hatch, James V. & Shine, Ted (Editors) **PS628.N4.H3**
Black Theater, U. S. A.: Forty-Five Plays by Black Americans, 1847-1974. Children's Board Books. Simon & Schuster. New York, NY. 1974. 886p. ISBN:0-02-914160-5, ISBN13: 978-0-02-914160-1. Dewey:812/.008/0352. LCCN:75-169234.
Audience: **l,u,f.** B

Jacobus, Lee A. (Editor) **PN2080**
Longman Anthology of American Drama. Cloth Text. Longman Publishing Group. White Plains, NY. 1982. 512p. ISBN:0-582-28348-5, ISBN13: 978-0-582-28348-0. Dewey:822/.008. LCCN:80-021895.
Audience: **l,u,f.** B

King, Woodie & Milner, Ron (Editors) **PS628.N4**
Black Drama Anthology. Trade Cloth. Columbia University Press. New York, NY. 1972. 675p. ISBN:0-231-03644-2, ISBN13: 978-0-231-03644-3. Dewey:812/.54/080896073. LCCN:77-181833.
Audience: **l,u,f.** B

Kritzer, Amelia H. (Editor, Compiled by) **PS628.W6P595 1995**
Plays by Early American Women, 1775-1850. Trade Paper. University of Michigan Press. Chicago, IL. 1995. 448p. ISBN:0-472-06598-X, ISBN13: 978-0-472-06598-1. Dewey:812/.20809287. LCCN:94-045115.
Audience: **g,l,u,f.** *Choice, 1995.*

Moody, Richard (Author, Editor) **PS0623**
Dramas from the American Theatre, 1762-1909. Trade Paper. Books on Demand. Ann Arbor, MI. 913p. ISBN:0-598-53656-6, ISBN13: 978-0-598-53656-3. Dewey:812.008. LCCN:66-013958.
Audience: **l,u,f.** B

Moses, Montrose J. (Editor) **PS623.M7**
Representative Plays by American Dramatists, Vol. 1. Trade Cloth. Ayer Company Publishers, Inc. Manchester, NH. 2001. 678p. ISBN:0-405-08803-5, ISBN13: 978-0-405-08803-2. Dewey:812.082. LCCN:64-014707.
Audience: **l,u,f.**

Perkins, Kathy A. & Uno, Roberta (Editors) **PS627.M5C66 1996**
Contemporary Plays by Women of Color: An Anthology. Paper over Boards. Routledge. New York, NY. 1996. 336p. ISBN:0-415-11377-6, ISBN13: 978-0-415-11377-9. Dewey:812/.540809287. LCCN:95-007465.
Audience: **g,l,u,f.** *Choice, 1996.*

Richardson, Willis **PS627.N4P52 1993**
Plays and Pageants from the Life of the Negro. James L. Wells (Illustrator), Christine Gray (Introduction by). Trade Cloth. University Press of Mississippi. Jackson, MS. 1993. 400p. ISBN:0-87805-657-2, ISBN13: 978-0-87805-657-6. Dewey:812/.52080896073. LCCN:93-027075.
Audience: **g,l,u,f.**

Saldaana, Johnny (Editor) **PS627.S63E86 2004**
Ethnodrama: An Anthology of Reality Theatre. Trade Cloth. AltaMira Press. Walnut Creek, CA. 2005. 256p. Crossroads in Qualitative Inquiry Ser., Vol. 4 ISBN:0-7591-0812-9, ISBN13: 978-0-7591-0812-7. Dewey:812/.60803556. LCCN:2004-018673.
Audience: **g,l,u,f.**

Sandoval-Sanchez, Alberto & Sternbach, Nancy S. (Editors) **PS628.H57P87 2000**
Puro Teatro, a Latina Anthology: A Latina Anthology. Library Binding. University of Arizona Press. Tucson, AZ. 1999. 440p. ISBN:0-8165-1826-2, ISBN13: 978-0-8165-1826-5. Dewey:812/.540809287/08968. LCCN:99-006567.
Audience: **g,l,u,f.**

Turner, Darwin T. (Introduction by) **PS628.N4 B53 1994**
Black Drama in America: An Anthology. Ed. 2. Trade Paper. Howard University Press. Washington, DC. 1993. ISBN:0-88258-062-0, ISBN13: 978-0-88258-062-3. Dewey:812.008/0896073. LCCN:92-042322.
Audience: **g,l,u,f.**

Collections of American Literature > By Form > Prose

Andrews, William L. **PS647.A35C57 1994**
Classic Fiction of the Harlem Renaissance. Trade Paper. Oxford University Press, Inc. New York, NY. 1994. 410p. ISBN:0-19-508196-X, ISBN13: 978-0-19-508196-1. Dewey:813.52080896073. LCCN:93-011023.
Audience: **g,l,u,f.**

Baumbach, Jonathan & Spielberg, Peter (Editors) **PS659.S82**
Statements Two: New Fiction. Robert Coover (Introduction by). Trade Cloth. Fiction Collective Two, Inc. Tallahassee, FL. 1977. 217p. ISBN:0-914590-36-7, ISBN13: 978-0-914590-36-1. Dewey:813/.01. LCCN:76-056053.
Audience: **l,u,f.** B

Cassill, R. V. & Oates, Joyce Carol **PS648.S5N67 1998**
The Norton Anthology of Contemporary Fiction. Ed. 2. Trade Cloth. W. W. Norton & Company, Inc. New York, NY. 1998. 556p. ISBN:0-393-96833-2, ISBN13: 978-0-393-96833-0. Dewey:813/.010805. LCCN:96-051171.
Audience: **g,l,u,f.**

DeWitt, Henry (Editor) **PS648.S5**
The Ploughshares Reader: New Fiction for the 80's. Trade Cloth. Pushcart Press, The. Wainscott, NY. 1985. 514p. ISBN:0-916366-30-8, ISBN13: 978-0-916366-30-8. Dewey:813/.01/08.
Audience: **g,l,u,f.** B *Choice, 1985.*

Fox, Susan (Editor) **PS648.L47C56 1996**
Close Calls: New Lesbian Fiction. Trade Cloth. St. Martin's Press. Gordonville, VA. 1996. 288p. ISBN:0-312-14755-4, ISBN13: 978-0-312-14755-6. Dewey:813/.01089206643. LCCN:96-025585.
Audience: **g,l,u,f.**

Gillan, Maria **PS647.E85 G76**
Growing up Ethnic in America: Contemporary Fiction about Learning to Be American. Library Binding. Sagebrush Education Resources. Caledonia, MN. 1999. ISBN:0-613-21652-0, ISBN13: 978-0-613-21652-4. Dewey:813/.54080920693.
Audience: **g,l,u,f.**

Hills, L. Rust (Introduction by) **PS648.S5 G73 1983**
Great Esquire Fiction: The Finest Stories from the First Fifty Years. Phillip Moffitt (Preface by). Trade Cloth. Penguin Group (USA) Inc. New York, NY. 1983. 624p. ISBN:0-670-15922-0, ISBN13: 978-0-670-15922-2. Dewey:813/.01/08. LCCN:83-047877.
Audience: **g,l,u,f.**

Jones, Suzanne W. (Editor) **PS647.A35C76 2000**
Crossing the Color Line: Readings in Black and White. Trade Cloth. University of South Carolina Press. Columbia, SC. 2000. xv, 290p. ISBN:1-57003-376-5, ISBN13: 978-1-57003-376-6. Dewey:813/.0108355. LCCN:00-009501.
Audience: **g,l,u,f.**

King, Woodie (Editor) **PS647.N35**
Black Short Story Anthology. Cloth Text. Columbia University Press. New York, NY. 1972. 381p. ISBN:0-231-03711-2, ISBN13: 978-0-231-03711-2. Dewey:813/.01. LCCN:72-006773.
Audience: **l,u,f.** B

Martin, Wendy **PS647.W6W4 1990**
We Are the Stories We Tell: The Best Short Stories by North American Women since 1945. Trade Paper. Knopf Publishing Group. New York, NY. 1990. 352p. ISBN:0-679-72881-3, ISBN13: 978-0-679-72881-8. Dewey:813/.01089287. LCCN:89-039587.
Audience: **g,l,u,f.**

Naylor, Gloria (Editor) **PS647.A35C5 1995**
Children of the Night: The Best Short Stories by Black Writers, 1967 to the Present. Trade Cloth. Little Brown & Company. New York, NY. 1996. 592p. ISBN:0-316-59926-3, ISBN13: 978-0-316-59926-9. Dewey:813/.018896073. LCCN:95-016356.
Audience: **g,l,u,f.**

New Yorker Magazine Staff **PZ1.N48**
Fifty-Five Short Stories from the New Yorker. Library Binding. Reprint Services Company. Temecula, CA. 1993. 480p. BCL1-PS American Literature Ser. ISBN:0-7812-6935-0, ISBN13: 978-0-7812-6935-3. Dewey:813.08.
Audience: **g,l,u,f.**

Nguyen, B. Minh & Shreve, Porter **PS648.S5C73 2004**
The Contemporary American Short Story. Trade Paper. Longman Publishing. Boston, MA. 2003. 672p. ISBN:0-321-11727-1, ISBN13: 978-0-321-11727-4. Dewey:813/.0108054. LCCN:2003-058110.
Audience: **g,l,u,f.**

Oates, Joyce Carol (Editor) **PS648.S5O94 1992**
The Oxford Book of American Short Stories. Trade Cloth. Oxford University Press, Inc. New York, NY. 1992. 784p. ISBN:0-19-507065-8, ISBN13: 978-0-19-507065-1. Dewey:813.0108. LCCN:92-001353.
Audience: **g,l,u,f.**

O'Brien, Edward J. **PS643**
Fifty Best American Short Stories, 1915-1939. Library Binding. Reprint Services Company. Temecula, CA. 1993. 868p. BCL1-PS American Literature Ser. ISBN:0-7812-6936-9, ISBN13: 978-0-7812-6936-0. Dewey:813.0108.
Audience: **g,l,u,f.**

Ortiz, Simon J. **PS508.I5.E23 1983**
Earth Power Coming: Short Fiction in Native American Literature. Trade Paper. Dine College Press. Tsaile, AZ. 1983. 299p. ISBN:0-912586-50-8, ISBN13: 978-0-912586-50-2. Dewey:813/.01/08897. LCCN:83-060959.
Audience: **g,l,u,f.** B

Pack, Robert & Parini, Jay (Editors) **PS648.S5B7 1987**
The Bread Loaf Anthology of Contemporary American Short Stories. Library Binding. University Press of New England. Lebanon, NH. 1987. 341p. A Bread Loaf Anthology Ser. ISBN:0-87451-392-8, ISBN13: 978-0-87451-392-9. Dewey:813/.01/08. LCCN:86-040387.
Audience: **g,l,u,f.**

Parks, John G. **PS648.S5A475 2002**
American Short Stories since 1945. Paper Text. Oxford University Press, Inc. New York, NY. 2001. 912p. ISBN:0-19-513132-0, ISBN13: 978-0-19-513132-1. Dewey:813/.01054. LCCN:2001-021237.
Audience: **g,l,u,f.**

Pronzini, Bill & Adrian, Jack (Editors) **PS648.D4H375 1997**
Hardboiled: An Anthology of American Crime Stories. Trade Paper. Oxford University Press, Inc. New York, NY. 1997. 540p. ISBN:0-19-510353-X, ISBN13: 978-0-19-510353-3. Dewey:813/.0872/08.
Audience: **g,l,u,f.**

Pronzini, Bill & Greenberg, Martin H. (Editors) **PS648.W4**
The Arbor House Treasury of Great Western Stories. John Jakes (Introduction by). Trade Cloth. HarperCollins Publishers. New York, NY. 1982. ISBN:0-87795-439-9, ISBN13: 978-0-87795-439-2. Dewey:813/.0874/08. LCCN:82-072052.
Audience: **l,u,f.**

Quinn, Jay (Editor) **PS647.G39R43 2001**
Rebel Yell: Stories by Contemporary Southern Gay Authors. Trade Cloth. Haworth Press, Incorporated, The. Binghamton, NY. 2001. xiii, 168p. Gay Men's Fiction Ser. ISBN:1-56023-160-2, ISBN13: 978-1-56023-160-8. Dewey:813/.0108920642. LCCN:00-063370.
Audience: **g,l,u.**

Ruber, Peter A. **PS648.H6A75 2000**
Arkham's Masters of Horror: A 60th Anniversary Anthology Retrospective of the First 30 Years of Arkham House. Arkham House Staff (Editor). Trade Cloth. Arkham House Publishers. Sauk City, WI. 2000. xi, 443p. ISBN:0-87054-177-3, ISBN13: 978-0-87054-177-3. Dewey:813/.0873808. LCCN:00-026189.
Audience: **g,l,u,f.**

Shapiro, Gerald (Editor) **PS647.J4A49 1999**
American Jewish Fiction: A Century of Stories. Trade Cloth. University of Nebraska Press. Lincoln, NE. 1998. 445p. ISBN:0-8032-9252-X, ISBN13: 978-0-8032-9252-9. Dewey:813/.50808924. LCCN:98-014410.
Audience: **g,l,u,f.**

Showalter, Elaine (Editor, Introduction by, Selected by) **PS647.W6S37 1997**
Scribbling Women: Short Stories by 19th Century American Women. Cloth Text. Rutgers University Press. Piscataway, NJ. 1997. 515p. ISBN:0-8135-2392-3, ISBN13: 978-0-8135-2392-7. Dewey:813/.01089287. LCCN:96-038915.
Audience: **g,l,u,f.**

Simpson, Lewis P. (Editor), et al. **PS648.S5S45 1988**
Selected Stories from the Southern Review, 1965-1985. Donald E. Stanford, James Olney & Jo Gulledge (Editors). Trade Paper. Louisiana State University Press. Baton Rouge, LA. 1988. 384p. ISBN:0-8071-1490-1, ISBN13: 978-0-8071-1490-2. Dewey:813/.01/08. LCCN:87-021383.
Audience: **g,l,u,f.**

Stadler, Quandra P. (Editor) **PZ1**
Out of Our Lives: A Selection of Contemporary Black Fiction. Trade Paper. Howard University Press. Washington, DC. 1981. 324p. ISBN:0-88258-095-7, ISBN13: 978-0-88258-095-1. Dewey:813/.01. LCCN:74-007092.
Audience: **l,u,f.**

Stephenson, G. Ennis (Editor) **PS628.W6N56 1993**
Nineteenth Century Stories by Women: An Anthology. Trade Paper. Broadview Press. Peterborough, ON. 1993. 504p. ISBN:1-55111-000-8, ISBN13: 978-1-55111-000-4. Dewey:823/.80809287. LCCN:93-175166.
Audience: **g,l,u,f.**

Tuska, Jon (Editor, Introduction by) **PS648.W4W46 1995**
The Western Story: A Chronological Treasury. Cloth Text. University of Nebraska Press. Lincoln, NE. 1995. 404p. ISBN:0-8032-4428-2, ISBN13: 978-0-8032-4428-3. Dewey:813/.087408. LCCN:94-046857.
Audience: **g,l,u,f.**

Updike, John & Kenison, Katrina (Editors) **PS648.S5B45 2000**
The Best American Short Stories of the Century. John Updike (Introduction by). Trade Paper. Houghton Mifflin Company Trade & Reference Division. Boston, MA. 2000. 864p. ISBN:0-395-84367-7, ISBN13: 978-0-395-84367-3. Dewey:813/.010805. LCCN:00-269492.
Audience: **g,l,u,f.**

Walker, Scott **PS648.S5**
The Graywolf Annual: Short Stories. Trade Paper. Graywolf Press. St. Paul, MN. 1984. 176p. Short Fiction Ser. ISBN:0-915308-66-5, ISBN13: 978-0-915308-66-8. Dewey:813/.01/08.
Audience: **l,u,f.** *Choice, 1985.*

Zahava, Irene **PS648.H57L38 1994**
Lavender Mansions: 40 Contemporary Lesbian and Gay Short Stories. Trade Paper. Westview Press. Boulder, CO. 1994. 430p. ISBN:0-8133-2031-3, ISBN13: 978-0-8133-2031-1. Dewey:813/.01083520664. LCCN:94-007858.
Audience: **g,l.**

Collections of American Literature > By Form > Oratory. Diaries. Letters. Essays

American Mercury Staff **PS536.A56 1979**
The American Mercury Reader: A Selection of Distinguished Articles. Lawrence E. Spivak & Charles Angoff (Editors). Trade Cloth. A M S Press, Inc. New York, NY. 1979. 378 p. :p. BCL Ser., No. II ISBN:0-404-14765-8, ISBN13: 978-0-404-14765-5. Dewey:810/.8/0054. LCCN:75-041009.
Audience: **g,l,u,f.**

Brandt, Anthony **PS688 .P87**
The Pushcart Book of Essays. Trade Paper. Pushcart Press, The. Wainscott, NY. 2003. 550p. Pushcart Prize Ser., :Best of the Small Presses ISBN:1-888889-29-2, ISBN13: 978-1-888889-29-1. Dewey:80.
Audience: **g,l,u,f.**

Howard, Maureen (Editor) **PS688.P44 1984**
The Penguin Book of Contemporary American Essays. Trade Cloth. Penguin Group (USA) Inc. New York, NY. 1984. 320p. ISBN:0-670-23983-6, ISBN13: 978-0-670-23983-2. Dewey:814/.54/08. LCCN:84-040265.
Audience: **g,l,u,f.**

Hurd, Charles **PS0662.H8**
A Treasury of Great American Speeches, Our Country's Life and History in the Words of Its Great Men. Trade Paper. Books on Demand. Ann Arbor, MI. 392p. ISBN:0-598-50208-4, ISBN13: 978-0-598-50208-7. Dewey:815.082. LCCN:59-012175.
Audience: **l,u,f.**

Oates, Joyce Carol (Editor) **PS688**
The Best American Essays of the Century. Robert Atwan (Other Adaptation by). Trade Paper. Houghton Mifflin Company Trade & Reference Division. Boston, MA. 2001. 624p. ISBN:0-618-15587-2, ISBN13: 978-0-618-15587-3. Dewey:814.008.
Audience: **g,l,u,f.**

Orlean, Susan (Editor) **PS688**
The Best American Essays 2005. Robert Atwan (Contribution by). Trade Cloth. Houghton Mifflin Company Trade & Reference Division. Boston, MA. 2005. 320p. ISBN:0-618-35712-2, ISBN13: 978-0-618-35712-3. Dewey:814.008.
Audience: **g,l,u,f.**

Potter, David & Thomas, Gordon L. (Editors) **PS662 .P6**
Colonial Idiom. David Potter (Foreword by). Trade Paper. Southern Illinois University Press. Carbondale, IL. 1970. 653p. Landmarks in Rhetoric and Public Address Ser. ISBN:0-8093-9100-7, ISBN13: 978-0-8093-9100-4. Dewey:815/.1/08. LCCN:71-083669.
Audience: **l,u,f.** B

Reid, Ronald F. & Klumpp, James F. (Editors) **E173.A754 2005**
American Rhetorical Discourse. Ed. 3. Ronald F. Reid & James F. Klumpp (Commentaries by). Paper Text. Waveland Press, Inc. Prospect Heights, IL. 2004. 877p. ISBN:1-57766-367-5, ISBN13: 978-1-57766-367-6. Dewey:815.008. LCCN:2005-283754.
Audience: **u,f.**

Ryan, Halford R. **PS668 .C58 1992**
Contemporary American Public Discourse: A Collection of Speeches and Critical Essays. Ed. 3. Paper Text. Waveland Press, Inc. Prospect Heights, IL. 1992. 384p. ISBN:0-88133-629-7, ISBN13: 978-0-88133-629-0. Dewey:815/.010805. LCCN:92-190166.
Audience: **g,l,u,f.**

Straub, Deborah Gillan (Editor) **PS663.M55V64 1996**
Voices of Multicultural America: Notable Speeches Delivered by African, Asian, Hispanic and Native Americans. Trade Cloth. Thomson Gale. Farmington Hills, MI. 1995. 1372p. ISBN:0-8103-9378-6, ISBN13: 978-0-8103-9378-3. Dewey:815.008/0920693. LCCN:95-031473.
Audience: **g,l,u,f.**

Torricelli, Robert G. & Carroll, Andrew (Editors) **PS661.I53 1999**
In Our Own Words: Extraordinary Speeches of the American Century. Doris Kearns Goodwin (Foreword by). Trade Cloth. Kodansha America, Inc. New York, NY. 1999. 480p. ISBN:1-56836-291-9, ISBN13: 978-1-56836-291-5. Dewey:815/.508. LCCN:99-029995.
Audience: **g,l,u,f.**

Warner, Michael (Editor) **BV4241.A514 1999**
American Sermons: The Pilgrims to Martin Luther King Jr. Trade Cloth. Library of America, The. New York, NY. 1999. 939p. Library of America, Vol. 108 ISBN:1-883011-65-5, ISBN13: 978-1-883011-65-9. Dewey:252. LCCN:98-034295.
Audience: **g,l,u,f.**

Colonial Period (17th-18th Centuries)

PS712.C7 1983
Critical Essays on Anne Bradstreet. Trade Cloth. Thomson Gale. Farmington Hills, MI. 1983. xxv, 286 p. :p. ISBN:0-8161-8643-X, ISBN13: 978-0-8161-8643-3. Dewey:811/.1. LCCN:82-021339.
Audience: **u,f.** B

Austin, Mary H. **LB1607.C647**
Philip Freneau: The Poet of the Revolution. Library Binding. Classic Books. Murrieta, CA. 1998. 285p. The Collected Works of Mary Hunter Austin ISBN:1-58201-529-5, ISBN13: 978-1-58201-529-3. Dewey:373.73.
Audience: **l,u,f.**

Bosco, Ronald A. **PS871.A4 1989**
The Poems of Michael Wigglesworth. Trade Cloth. University Press of America, Inc. Lanham, MD. 1989. 374p. ISBN:0-8191-7345-2, ISBN13: 978-0-8191-7345-4. Dewey:821/.4. LCCN:88-034214.
Audience: **u,f.** *Choice, 1990.*

Bradstreet, Anne D. **PS0711.A1**
The Works of Anne Bradstreet in Prose and Verse. Trade Cloth. Scholarly Press, Inc. Saint Clair Shores, MI. 1976. ISBN:0-403-08995-6, ISBN13: 978-0-403-08995-6. Dewey:811.12.
Audience: **l,u,f.**

Cady, Edwin Harrison **PS507.C2 1969**
Literature of the Early Republic. Trade Cloth. Holt, Rinehart & Winston. Austin, TX. 1969. xiv, 686p. ISBN:0-03-080335-7, ISBN13: 978-0-03-080335-2. Dewey:810.8/002. LCCN:69-019909.
Audience: **l,u,f.** B

Dorson, Richard M. (Editor) **PS651.D6 1972**
America Begins: Early American Writings. Library Binding. Ayer Company Publishers, Inc. Manchester, NH. 1981. x, 438p. Folklore of the World Ser. ISBN:0-8369-2986-1, ISBN13: 978-0-8369-2986-7. Dewey:081. LCCN:72-005802.
Audience: **l,u,f.** B

Dunn, Richard S. & Yeandle, Laetitia (Editors) **F67.W7842 1996**
The Journal of John Winthrop, 1630-1649. Trade Cloth. Harvard University Press. Cambridge, MA. 1997. 374p. The John Harvard Library ISBN:0-674-48426-6, ISBN13: 978-0-674-48426-9. Dewey:974.4/02/092 B. LCCN:96-020644.
Audience: **g,l,u,f.** *Choice, 1997.*

Equiano, Olaudah **E185.97.T8**
The Interesting Narrative of the Life of Olaudah Equiano: Written by Himself. Ed. 2. Robert J. Allison (Introduction by). Cloth over Boards. Palgrave Macmillan. New York, NY. 2006. 208p. The Bedford Series in History and Culture Ser. ISBN:1-4039-7156-0, ISBN13: 978-1-4039-7156-2. Dewey:305.5/67/092 B.
Audience: **g,l,u,f.**

Ford, Arthur L. **PS705 .F6**
Joel Barlow. Library Binding. Irvington Publishers. New York, NY. 1971. Twayne's United States Authors Ser. ISBN:0-89197-809-7, ISBN13: 978-0-89197-809-1. Dewey:811/.2. LCCN:74-155944.
Audience: **l,u,f.**

Foster, Hannah Webster **PS744.F7 C6**
The Coquette; or, The History of Eliza Wharton: Founded on Fact by a Lady of Massachusetts. Trade Cloth. Scholarly Publishing Office, University of Michigan Library. Ann Arbor, MI. 2004. ISBN:1-4181-1392-1, ISBN13: 978-1-4181-1392-6. Dewey:813.2.
Audience: **g,l,u,f.**

Franklin, Benjamin **PS745.A2 2002**
Benjamin Franklin: Silence Dogood, the Busy-Body, and Early Writings. J. A. Leo Lemay (Editor). Saddle Stitched, Cloth over Boards, Dust Jacket. Library of America, The. New York, NY. 2005. 823p. ISBN:1-931082-22-7, ISBN13: 978-1-931082-22-8. Dewey:814/.1. LCCN:2001-050770.
Audience: **g,l,u,f.**

Franklin, Benjamin **E302.F82 1997**
Benjamin Franklin: Autobiography, Poor Richard, and Later Writings. J. A. Leo Lemay (Editor), Pre-Raphaelite Brotherhood (Notes by). Saddle Stitched, Cloth over Boards, Dust Jacket. Library of America, The. New York, NY. 1997. 816p. ISBN:1-883011-53-1, ISBN13: 978-1-883011-53-6. Dewey:973.2. LCCN:97-021611.
Audience: **g,l,u,f.**

Freibert, Lucy M. & White, Barbara A. (Editors) **PS647.W6H5 1985**
Hidden Hands: An Anthology of American Women Writers, 1790 to 1870. Cloth Text. Rutgers University Press. Piscataway, NJ. 1985. 400p. The Douglass Ser. ISBN:0-8135-1088-0, ISBN13: 978-0-8135-1088-0. Dewey:810/.8/09287. LCCN:84-022884.
Audience: **l,u,f.** B

Freneau, Philip M . **PS755 .A1**
Poems Written Between the Years 1768 and 1794. Trade Cloth. Gordon Press Publishers. New York, NY. 1972. ISBN:0-8490-0852-2, ISBN13: 978-0-8490-0852-8. Dewey:811/.2.
Audience: **l,u,f.**

Gates, Henry Louis **PS866.W5Z595 2003**
The Trials of Phillis Wheatley: America's First Black Poet and Her Encounters with the Founding Fathers. Trade Cloth. Basic Books. New York, NY. 2003. 144p. ISBN:0-465-02729-6, ISBN13: 978-0-465-02729-3. Dewey:811/.1 B. LCCN:2003-002717.
Audience: **g,l,u,f.** *Choice, 2003.*

Granger, Bruce I. **PS752**
Benjamin Franklin, an American Man of Letters. Trade Cloth. Greenwood Publishing Group, Inc. Portsmouth, NH. 1964. 280p. ISBN:0-313-26152-0, ISBN13: 978-0-313-26152-7. Dewey:818/.109 B. LCCN:87-023678.
Audience: **l,u,f.**

Guruswamy, Rosemary Fithian **Z8861**
The Poems of Edward Taylor: A Reference Guide. Cloth Text. Greenwood Publishing Group, Inc. Portsmouth, NH. 2003. 152p. Guides to Poetry ISBN:0-313-31781-X, ISBN13: 978-0-313-31781-1. Dewey:016.811/1. LCCN:2002-035330.
Audience: **l,u,f.**

Knight, Denise D. (Editor) **PS805.A17 1989**
Cotton Mather's Verse in English. Trade Cloth. University of Delaware Press. Newark, DE. 1989. 176p. ISBN:0-87413-349-1, ISBN13: 978-0-87413-349-3. Dewey:811/.1. LCCN:88-040313.
Audience: **l,u,f.**

Knight, Sarah Kemble & Winship, George Parker **F7 .K724**
The Journal of Madame Knight. Trade Paper. Kessinger Publishing, LLC. Whitefish, MT. 2004. ISBN:1-4179-6796-X, ISBN13: 978-1-4179-6796-4. Dewey:917.404/202.
Audience: **g,l,u,f.**

Lemay, J. Leo **PS752.O4**
The Oldest Revolutionary: Essays on Benjamin Franklin. Trade Cloth. University of Pennsylvania Press. Philadelphia, PA. 1976. x, 165p. ISBN:0-8122-7707-4, ISBN13: 978-0-8122-7707-4. Dewey:973.3/092/4. LCCN:75-041618.
Audience: **l,u,f.** B

Levy, Babette M. **PS805.Z5.L4**
Cotton Mather. Library Binding. Thomson Gale. Farmington Hills, MI. 1979. 188p. United States Authors Ser. ISBN:0-8057-7261-8, ISBN13: 978-0-8057-7261-6. Dewey:973.2/092/4. LCCN:78-023445.
Audience: **l,u,f.** B

Miller, Perry G. **PS530 .A48 1982**
The American Puritans: Their Prose and Poetry. Trade Paper. Columbia University Press. New York, NY. 1982. 346p. ISBN:0-231-05419-X, ISBN13: 978-0-231-05419-5. Dewey:810/.8/001. LCCN:81-010222.
Audience: **l,u,f.**

Philbrick, Thomas **PS737.C5 Z85**
St. John de Crevecoeur. Library Binding. Thomson Gale. Farmington Hills, MI. 1970. U. S. Authors Ser., No. 154 ISBN:0-8057-0191-5, ISBN13: 978-0-8057-0191-3. Dewey:818/.2/09.
Audience: **l,u,f.**

Rosenmeier, Rosamond **PS712.R6 1991**
Anne Bradstreet Revisited. Trade Cloth. Thomson Gale. Farmington Hills, MI. 1991. 200p. Twayne's United States Authors Ser., No. 580 ISBN:0-8057-7625-7, ISBN13: 978-0-8057-7625-6. Dewey:811/.1. LCCN:91-007835.
Audience: **l,u,f.**

Rowlandson, Mary White **E85.K38 2005**
The Account of Mary Rowlandson and Other Indian Captivity Narratives. Horace Kephart (Editor). Trade Paper, Perfect. Dover Publications, Inc. Mineola, NY. 2005. 112p. ISBN:0-486-44520-8, ISBN13: 978-0-486-44520-5. Dewey:973.2/092/2. LCCN:2005-045460.
Audience: **g,l,u,f.**

Rowson, Susanna **PS2736.R3C5 2004**
Charlotte Temple. Jane Smiley (Introduction by). Trade Paper. Random House, Inc. New York, NY. 2004. 144p. ISBN:0-8129-7121-3, ISBN13: 978-0-8129-7121-7. Dewey:813/.2. LCCN:2003-066519.
Audience: **g,l,u,f.**

Skemp, Sheila L. **PS808.M8Z88 1998**
Judith Sargent Murray: A Brief Biography with Documents. Trade Cloth. Palgrave Macmillan. New York, NY. 1998. 224p. Bedford Series in History and Culture ISBN:0-312-17770-4, ISBN13: 978-0-312-17770-6. Dewey:818/.209 B. LCCN:97-074971.
Audience: **u,f.**

St. John de Crevecoeur, J. Hector **E83.76**
Letters from an American Farmer. Susan Manning (Editor, Introduction by, Notes by). Trade Paper. Oxford University Press, Inc. New York, NY. 1999. 282p. Oxford World's Classics Ser. ISBN:0-19-283898-9, ISBN13: 978-0-19-283898-8. Dewey:973.2/7.
Audience: **g,l,u,f.**

Stanford, Ann **PS712.S8 1975**
Anne Bradstreet, the Worldly Puritan: An Introduction to Her Poetry. Trade Cloth. Bow Historical Books. New Providence, NJ. 1975. xiv, 170p. ISBN:0-89102-030-6, ISBN13: 978-0-89102-030-1. Dewey:811/.1. LCCN:74-022319.
Audience: **l,u,f.** B

Taylor, Edward **PS850.T2A6 1989**
The Poems of Edward Taylor. Donald E. Stanford (Editor). Trade Cloth. University of North Carolina Press. Chapel Hill, NC. 1989. 412p. ISBN:0-8078-4248-6, ISBN13: 978-0-8078-4248-5. Dewey:811/.1. LCCN:88-040555.
Audience: **l,u,f.**

Tyler, Royall **PS855.T7 C6 1970B**
Contrast: A Comedy. Trade Cloth. Burt Franklin Publisher. New York, NY. 1970. Dunlap Society Ser., No. 1 ISBN:0-8337-3583-7, ISBN13: 978-0-8337-3583-6. Dewey:812/.2. LCCN:72-130079.
Audience: **l,u,f.**

Ward, Nathaniel **PS0858.W2S5**
Simple Cobler of Aggawam in America. Library Binding. Reprint Services Company. Temecula, CA. 1993. 80p. BCL1-PS American Literature Ser. ISBN:0-7812-6942-3, ISBN13: 978-0-7812-6942-1. Dewey:274.2.
Audience: **l,u,f.**

Washington, George **E312.72 1997**
George Washington: From the Original Manuscript Sources, 1745-1799. John Rhodehamel (Editor). Trade Cloth. Library of America, The. New York, NY. 1997. 1184p. Library of America ISBN:1-883011-23-X, ISBN13: 978-1-883011-23-9. Dewey:973.4/1/092. LCCN:96-009665.
Audience: **g,l,u,f.**

Wheatley, Phillis **PS866**
Life and Works of Phillis Wheatley. Trade Cloth. Ayer Company Publishers, Inc. Manchester, NH. 1977. Black Heritage Library Collection ISBN:0-8369-8685-7, ISBN13: 978-0-8369-8685-3. Dewey:811. LCCN:70-083899.
Audience: **l,u,f.**

Wheatley, Phillis **PS866.W5 1989**
The Poems of Phillis Wheatley. Julian D. Mason Jr. (Editor). Trade Cloth. University of North Carolina Press. Chapel Hill, NC. 1989. 254p. ISBN:0-8078-4245-1, ISBN13: 978-0-8078-4245-4. Dewey:811/.1. LCCN:88-023280.
Audience: **l,u,f.** *Choice, 1990.*

19th Century > A

Adams, Henry **PS2124**
Democracy: An American Novel. Trade Cloth. Scholarly Press, Inc. Saint Clair Shores, MI. 1976. ISBN:0-403-05724-8, ISBN13: 978-0-403-05724-5. Dewey:813/.4.
Audience: **g,l,u,f.**

Adams, Henry **PS1004.A4E8 1997**
Esther: A Novel. Trade Cloth. Prometheus Books, Publishers. Amherst, NY. 1997. 310p. Literary Classics ISBN:1-57392-132-7, ISBN13: 978-1-57392-132-9. Dewey:818/.309. LCCN:96-040052.
Audience: **g,l,u,f.** B

Ade, George **PZ3.A228A**
Ade's Fables. John T. McCutcheon (Illustrator). Trade Paper. Kessinger Publishing, LLC. Whitefish, MT. 2005. ISBN:0-7661-9462-0, ISBN13: 978-0-7661-9462-5. Dewey:813.5.
Audience: **g,l,u,f.**

Ade, George **PS1006.A6S7 2003**
Stories of Chicago. Franklin J. Meine (Editor), John T. McCutcheon (Illustrator), Franklin J. Meine (Introduction by). Trade Cloth. University of Illinois Press. Champaign, IL. 2003. 312p. ISBN:0-252-02870-8, ISBN13: 978-0-252-02870-0. Dewey:813/.4. LCCN:2002-041619.
Audience: **g,l,u,f.**

Allen, James L. **PS1034**
A Kentucky Cardinal, Aftermath, and Other Selected Works. William K. Bottorff (Editor). Book, Other. Rowman & Littlefield Publishers, Inc. Lanham, MD. 1967. 192p. ISBN:0-8084-0200-5, ISBN13: 978-0-8084-0200-8. Dewey:813.
Audience: **g,l,u,f.**

Stevenson, Elizabeth **AC8 .A22**
A Henry Adams Reader. Trade Cloth. Peter Smith Publisher, Inc. Magnolia, MA. 1990. ISBN:0-8446-1423-8, ISBN13: 978-0-8446-1423-6. Dewey:81.
Audience: **g,l,u,f.**

19th Century > Alcott, Louisa May

PS1018.C7 1984
Critical Essays on Louisa May Alcott. Trade Cloth. Thomson Gale. Farmington Hills, MI. 1984. x, 295 p. ;p. ISBN:0-8161-8686-3, ISBN13: 978-0-8161-8686-0. Dewey:813/.4. LCCN:84-004499.
Audience: **g,l.** B

Alcott, Louisa May **PS1017**
Behind a Mask: The Unknown Thrillers of Louisa May Alcott. Trade Paper. Hesperus Press. London, 2004. 128p. ISBN:1-84391-086-1, ISBN13: 978-1-84391-086-2. Dewey:813/.4.
Audience: **g.** B

Alcott, Louisa May **PZ3.A355; PS1017**
Work: A Story of Experience. Trade Cloth. Scholarly Publishing Office, University of Michigan Library. Ann Arbor, MI. 2004. ISBN:1-4181-0183-4, ISBN13: 978-1-4181-0183-1. Dewey:813/.4.
Audience: **u,f.**

Alcott, Louisa May **PS10162005**
Louisa May Alcott: Little Women, Little Men, Jo's Boys. Elaine Showalter (Editor). Trade Cloth. Library of America, The. New York, NY. 2005. 1045p. The Library of America, Vol. 157 ISBN:1-931082-73-1, ISBN13: 978-1-931082-73-0. Dewey:813/.4. LCCN:2004-048828.
Audience: **g,l,u,f.**

Delamar, Gloria T. **PS1017.D45**
Louisa May Alcott and "Little Women": Biography, Critique, Publications, Poems, Songs, and Contemporary Relevance. Trade Paper. iUniverse, Inc. Lincoln, NE. 2001. 372p. ISBN:0-595-18722-6, ISBN13: 978-0-595-18722-5. Dewey:[B].
Audience: **g,l,u.**

Saxton, Martha **PS1018.S2 1978**
Louisa May: A Modern Biography of Louisa May Alcott. Trade Cloth. Andre Deutsch. London, 1978. xi, 428p. ISBN:0-233-96965-9, ISBN13: 978-0-233-96965-7. Dewey:813/.4. LCCN:78-324902.
Audience: **g,l.** B

Stern, Madeleine B. **PS1018.S75**
Louisa May Alcott: A Biography. Ed. 2. Paper Text. Northeastern University Press. Boston, MA. 1999. 422p. ISBN:1-55553-417-1, ISBN13: 978-1-55553-417-2. Dewey:813/.4 B. LCCN:99-015688.
Audience: **g,l.**

19th Century > B

Bellamy, Edward **PS1086.L6 2003**
Looking Backward: 2000-1887. Trade Cloth. Cork Hill Press. Carmel, IN. 2003. 224p. Cork Hill Classics Ser. ISBN:1-59408-488-2, ISBN13: 978-1-59408-488-1. Dewey:813/.4. LCCN:2003-111602.
Audience: **g,l,u,f.** B

Bellamy, Edward **PS1087.R48 2002**
Revisiting the Legacy of Edward Bellamy (1850-1898), American Author and Social Reformer: Uncollected and Unpublished Writings, Scholarly Perspectives for a New Millennium. Toby Widdicombe & Herman S. Preiser (Editors). Trade Cloth. Edwin Mellen Press, The. Lewiston, NY. 2002. 556p. Studies in American Literature Ser., Vol. 54 ISBN:0-7734-7105-7, ISBN13: 978-0-7734-7105-4. Dewey:813/.4 B. LCCN:2002-071435.
Audience: **u,f.** *Choice, 2003.*

Brown, Charles Brockden **PS1134.W5 1997**
Wieland: Or, the Transformation. Trade Cloth. Prometheus Books, Publishers. Amherst, NY. 1997. 234p. Literary Classics ISBN:1-57392-175-0, ISBN13: 978-1-57392-175-6. Dewey:813/.2. LCCN:97-026695.
Audience: **g,l,u,f.**

Brown, Charles Brockden **PZ3.B814**
The Novels and Related Works of Charles Brockden Brown: Edgar Huntly; or, Memoirs of a Sleep-Walker. Sydney J. Krause & S. W. Reid (Editors). Trade Cloth. Kent State University Press. Kent, OH. 1985. 510p. C.S.E. Edition Ser., No. 4 ISBN:0-87338-305-2, ISBN13: 978-0-87338-305-9. Dewey:813/.2 s. LCCN:84-004376.
Audience: **g,l,u,f.**

Brown, Charles Brockden **PZ3.B814**
The Novels and Related Works of Charles Brockden Brown: Clara Howard and Jane Talbot. Sydney J. Krause & S. W. Reid (Editors), Donald A. Ringe (Contribution by). Trade Cloth. Kent State University Press. Kent, OH. 1986. 539p. C.S.E. Edition Ser., Vol. 5 ISBN:0-87338-320-6, ISBN13: 978-0-87338-320-2. Dewey:813/.2 s. LCCN:85-008102.
Audience: **g,l,u,f.**

Niehardt, John G. & Elk, Nicholas Black **E99.03B48 2000**
Black Elk Speaks: Being the Life Story of a Holy Man of the Oglala Sioux. Ed. 21. Standing Bear (Illustrator), Vine Deloria Jr. (Introduction by). Trade Cloth. University of Nebraska Press. Lincoln, NE. 2000. 300p. ISBN:0-8032-1309-3, ISBN13: 978-0-8032-1309-8. Dewey:978.004/9752 B. LCCN:00-036382.
Audience: **g,l,u,f.**

19th Century > Bierce, Ambrose

Bierce, Ambrose **PS1097**
The Collected Writings of Ambrose Bierce. Trade Cloth. Amereon, Ltd. Mattituck, NY. ISBN:0-88411-859-2, ISBN13: 978-0-88411-859-6. Dewey:818.
Audience: **g,l,u,f.** B

Bierce, Ambrose **PS1097.D4 1999**
The Devil's Dictionary. Trade Cloth. Oxford University Press, Inc. New York, NY. 1999. 256p. ISBN:0-19-512626-2, ISBN13: 978-0-19-512626-6. Dewey:423.0207. LCCN:98-022576.
Audience: **g,l,u,f.** B

Bierce, Ambrose & Joshi, S. T. **PS1097.A6 2000**
The Collected Fables of Ambrose Bierce. Trade Cloth. Ohio State University Press. Columbus, OH. 2000. 413p. ISBN:0-8142-0842-8, ISBN13: 978-0-8142-0842-7. Dewey:818/.402. LCCN:99-052375.
Audience: **g,l,u,f.**

Bierce, Ambrose, et al. **PS1097.Z5A4 2003**
A Much Misunderstood Man: Selected Letters of Ambrose Bierce. T. S. Joshi & David E. Schultz (Authors). Trade Cloth. Ohio State University Press. Columbus, OH. 2003. 257p. ISBN:0-8142-0919-X, ISBN13: 978-0-8142-0919-6. Dewey:813/.4 B. LCCN:2002-154626.
Audience: **g,u.** *Choice, 2003.*

Bierce, Ambrose **PS1097.A6 2002**
Shadows of Blue and Gray: The Civil War Writings of Ambrose Bierce. Ed. 2. Brian M. Thomsen (Editor). Cloth over Boards. Tom Doherty Associates, LLC. New York, NY. 2002. 288p. ISBN:0-7653-0244-6, ISBN13: 978-0-7653-0244-1. Dewey:813.4. LCCN:2001-054547.
Audience: **g,l,u.**

19th Century > C

Cable, George W. **PS2124**
The Grandissimes. Trade Cloth. Amereon, Ltd. Mattituck, NY. ISBN:0-88411-796-0, ISBN13: 978-0-88411-796-4. Dewey:813/.4.
Audience: **g,l,u,f.**

Cable, George W. **PS1244**
Old Creole Days. Trade Cloth. Somerset Publishers, Inc. Santa Barbara, CA. 1974. ISBN:0-403-03056-0, ISBN13: 978-0-403-03056-9. Dewey:813/.4. LCCN:72-084524.
Audience: **g,l,u,f.** B

Cahan, Abraham **PZ3.C119**
Yekl: A Tale of the New York. Trade Paper. Kessinger Publishing, LLC. Whitefish, MT. 2004. ISBN:1-4191-9519-0, ISBN13: 978-1-4191-9519-8. Dewey:813.4.
Audience: **g,l,u,f.**

Chambers, Robert W. **PS1282.B55 2004**
The King in Yellow and Other Horror Stories. Everett Franklin Bleiler (Introduction by). Trade Paper. Dover Publications, Inc. Mineola, NY. 2004. 304p. ISBN:0-486-43750-7, ISBN13: 978-0-486-43750-7. Dewey:813/.52. LCCN:2004-047827.
Audience: **g,l,u,f.**

Child, Lydia Maria **PS1293 .A6**
Hobomok. Trade Paper. Kessinger Publishing, LLC. Whitefish, MT. 2004. ISBN:1-4191-2436-6, ISBN13: 978-1-4191-2436-5. Dewey:813/.2.
Audience: **g,l,u,f.**

Craddock, Charles Egbert **PS2454**
In the Tennessee Mountains. Trade Paper. Kessinger Publishing, LLC. Whitefish, MT. 2004. ISBN:1-4191-2613-X, ISBN13: 978-1-4191-2613-0. Dewey:813.
Audience: **g,l,u,f.**

Craddock, Charles Egbert **PS2454**
The Prophet of the Great Smoky Mountains. Trade Paper. Kessinger Publishing, LLC. Whitefish, MT. 2004. ISBN:1-4192-7921-1, ISBN13: 978-1-4192-7921-8. Dewey:813.4.
Audience: **g,l,u,f.**

Curtis, George William **PS1485 .A1**
From the Easy Chair, Vol. 1. Trade Paper. Kessinger Publishing, LLC. Whitefish, MT. 2004. ISBN:1-4191-2116-2, ISBN13: 978-1-4191-2116-6. Dewey:814.3.
Audience: **g,l,u,f.** B

19th Century > Chesnutt, Charles

Chesnutt, Charles Waddell **PS2124**
e The Conjure Woman. E-Book. Kessinger Publishing, LLC. Whitefish, MT. 2004. ISBN:1-4192-5745-5, ISBN13: 978-1-4192-5745-2. Dewey:813/.4.
Audience: **g,l,u,f.** B

Duncan, Charles **PS1292.C6Z69 1998**
The Absent Man: The Narrative Craft of Charles W. Chesnutt. Trade Cloth. Ohio University Press. Athens, OH. 1999. 234p. ISBN:0-8214-1239-6, ISBN13: 978-0-8214-1239-8. Dewey:810. LCCN:98-022063.
Audience: **g,l,u,f.** *Choice, 1999.*

McElrath, Joseph R. (Editor) **PS1292.C6Z684 1999**
Critical Essays on Charles Chesnutt. Trade Cloth. Thomson Gale. Farmington Hills, MI. 1999. xv, 306p. Critical Essays on American Literature Ser. ISBN:0-7838-0055-X, ISBN13: 978-0-7838-0055-4. Dewey:813/.4. LCCN:99-034852.
Audience: **g,l.** *Choice, 2000.*

McWilliams, Dean **PS1292.C6Z77 2002**
Charles W. Chesnutt and the Fictions of Race. Trade Cloth. University of Georgia Press. Athens, GA. 2005. 272p. ISBN:0-8203-2435-3, ISBN13: 978-0-8203-2435-7. Dewey:813/.4. LCCN:2002-002787.
Audience: **g,l.** *Choice, 2003.*

Render, Sylvia L. (Editor) **PS2124**
The Short Fiction of Charles W. Chesnutt. Trade Paper. Howard University Press. Washington, DC. 1981. 428p. ISBN:0-88258-092-2, ISBN13: 978-0-88258-092-0. Dewey:813/.4. LCCN:81-006314.
Audience: **g,l,u,f.** B

Wilson, Matthew **PS1292.C6Z94 2004**
Whiteness in the Novels of Charles W. Chesnutt. Trade Cloth. University Press of Mississippi. Jackson, MS. 2006. 248p. ISBN:1-57806-667-0, ISBN13: 978-1-57806-667-4. Dewey:813/.4. LCCN:2003-026568.
Audience: **u,f.**

19th Century > Chopin, Kate

Chopin, Kate **PS1294.C63**
The Awakening and Selected Short Fiction. Rachel Adams (Introduction by, Intro and Notes by). Cloth over Boards. Barnes & Noble, Inc. New York, NY. 2004. 288p. Barnes and Noble Classics Ser. ISBN:1-59308-158-8, ISBN13: 978-1-59308-158-4. Dewey:813/.4.
Audience: **g,l,u,f.**

Chopin, Kate **PS1294.C63 1970**
The Complete Works of Kate Chopin. Per Seyersted (Editor), Edmund Wilson (Foreword by). Cloth Text. Louisiana State University Press. Baton Rouge, LA. 1969. 1032p. Southern Literary Studies ISBN:0-8071-0849-9, ISBN13: 978-0-8071-0849-9. Dewey:813/.4. LCCN:73-080043.
Audience: **g,l,u,f.** B

Seyersted, Per **PS1294.C63**
Kate Chopin: A Critical Biography. Trade Cloth. Louisiana State University Press. Baton Rouge, LA. 1969. 256p. Southern Literary Studies ISBN:0-8071-0678-X, ISBN13: 978-0-8071-0678-5. Dewey:810.9. LCCN:77-088740.
Audience: **g,l,u.**

Skaggs, Peggy **PS1294.C63.S55 1985**
Kate Chopin. Trade Cloth. Macmillan Publishing Company, Inc. Old Tappan, NJ. 1985. 144p. Twayne's United States Authors Ser., No. 485 ISBN:0-8057-7439-4, ISBN13: 978-0-8057-7439-9. Dewey:813/.4. LCCN:84-027977.
Audience: **g,l,u.** B *Choice, 1985.*

19th Century > Clemens, Samuel (Mark Twain)

Anderson, Frederick **PS1338.A5 1971**
Mark Twain: The Critical Heritage. Trade Cloth. Barnes & Noble, Inc. New York, NY. 1971. xvi, 347p. ISBN:0-389-04213-7, ISBN13: 978-0-389-04213-6. Dewey:818/.4/09. LCCN:72-177519.
Audience: **g.** B

Brooks, Van Wyck **PS1331 .B7 1977**
The Ordeal of Mark Twain. Trade Cloth. A M S Press, Inc. New York, NY. BCL Ser. II ISBN:0-404-14512-4, ISBN13: 978-0-404-14512-5. Dewey:818/.4/03. LCCN:75-041039.
Audience: **g.**

Budd, Louis J. **PS1331.C76 1983**
Critical Essays on Mark Twain, 1910-1980. Trade Cloth. Thomson Gale. Farmington Hills, MI. 1983. 256p. Critical Essays on American Literature Ser. ISBN:0-8161-8652-9, ISBN13: 978-0-8161-8652-5. Dewey:818/.409. LCCN:83-004400.
Audience: **g,l.** B

Davis, Sara D. & Beidler, Philip D. (Editors) **PS1338.M9 1984**
The Mythologizing of Mark Twain. Trade Paper. University of Alabama Press. Tuscaloosa, AL. 1984. 208p. Alabama Symposium on English and American Literature ISBN:0-8173-0201-8, ISBN13: 978-0-8173-0201-6. Dewey:818/.409. LCCN:83-009166.
Audience: **u,f.** B

DeVoto, Bernard **PS1331.D4 1997**
Mark Twain's America. M. J. Gallagher (Illustrator), Louis J. Budd (Introduction by). Trade Cloth. University of Nebraska Press. Lincoln, NE. 1997. 351p. ISBN:0-8032-6607-3, ISBN13: 978-0-8032-6607-0. Dewey:818/.409. LCCN:96-037754.
Audience: **g,l.**

Hill, Richard & McWilliams, Jim (Editors) **PS1338 .M286 2002**
Mark Twain among the Scholars: Reconsidering Contemporary Twain Criticism. Trade Cloth. Whitston Publishing Company, Inc. Albany, NY. 2002. 168p. ISBN:0-87875-527-6, ISBN13: 978-0-87875-527-1. Dewey:818.409. LCCN:00-110016.
Audience: **g,l.**

Howells, William Dean **PS1331**
My Mark Twain: Reminiscences and Criticisms. Mark R. Godburn (Editor), Edwin H. Cady (Introduction by). Trade Cloth. Equator Books. Canaan, CT. 1991. 300p. ISBN:0-9628041-1-8, ISBN13: 978-0-9628041-1-3. Dewey:818/.409 B. LCCN:90-084577.
Audience: **l,u.** B

Kaplan, Fred **PS1331.K317 2003**
The Singular Mark Twain: A Biography. Trade Paper. Knopf Publishing Group. New York, NY. 2005. 768p. ISBN:1-4000-9527-1, ISBN13: 978-1-4000-9527-8. Dewey:818/.408 B. LCCN:2003-043558.
Audience: **g,l,u,f.**

Kaplan, Justin E. **PS1331.K33 1983**
Mr. Clemens and Mark Twain: A Biography. Trade Paper. Simon & Schuster. New York, NY. 1991. 432p. ISBN:0-671-74807-6, ISBN13: 978-0-671-74807-4. Dewey:818.4/09. LCCN:82-019597.
Audience: **g,l,u,f.**

Messent, Peter B. **PS1338.M48 2001**
The Short Works of Mark Twain: A Critical Study. Book, Other. University of Pennsylvania Press. Philadelphia, PA. 2001. 280p. ISBN:0-8122-3622-X, ISBN13: 978-0-8122-3622-4. Dewey:818/.409. LCCN:2001-027428.
Audience: **g,l.** *Choice, 2002.*

Neider, Charles **PS1331.A2 2000**
The Autobiography of Mark Twain. Trade Paper. HarperCollins Publishers. New York, NY. 2000. 560p. Perennial Classics Ser. ISBN:0-06-095542-2, ISBN13: 978-0-06-095542-7. Dewey:818/.409 B. LCCN:99-055390.
Audience: **g,l,u,f.**

Paine, Albert B. **PS1331.P3**
Mark Twain, a Biography: The Personal and Literary Life of Samuel Langhorne Clemens. Trade Paper. Books on Demand. Ann Arbor, MI. 868p. ISBN:0-598-77743-1, ISBN13: 978-0-598-77743-0. Dewey:928.1. LCCN:35-027375.
Audience: **g,l,u.** B

Pettit, Arthur G. **PS1342.P64.P47**
Mark Twain and the South. Trade Cloth. University Press of Kentucky. Lexington, KY. 1974. 240p. ISBN:0-8131-1310-5, ISBN13: 978-0-8131-1310-4. Dewey:818/.4/09. LCCN:73-086405.
Audience: **l,u,f.** B

Rasmussen, R. Kent **PS1330.R37 2004**
Mark Twain: The Essential Reference to His Life and Writings. Ed. 2. Trade Cloth. Facts On File, Inc. New York, NY. 2007. 1000+p. Critical Companion To Ser. ISBN:0-8160-5398-7, ISBN13: 978-0-8160-5398-8. Dewey:818/.409. LCCN:2004-046910.
Audience: **g,l.** *Choice, 1996.*

Salamo, Lin, et al. **PS1303 .S25 2004**
Mark Twain's Helpful Hints for Good Living: A Handbook for the Damned Human Race. Victor Fischer & Michael B. Frank (Authors), Mark Twain (Selected by), Bancroft Library, Mark Twain Project Staff (Contribution by). Trade Cloth. University of California Press. Berkeley, CA. 2004. 256p. Jumping Frogs Ser. ISBN:0-520-24245-9, ISBN13: 978-0-520-24245-6. Dewey:818/.409. LCCN:2003-024224.
Audience: **g,l,u,f.**

Twain, Mark **PS1302.T8**
The Devil's Race-Track: Mark Twain's Great Dark Writings. Ed. 2. Trade Paper. University of California Press. Berkeley, CA. 2005. 408p. ISBN:0-520-23893-1, ISBN13: 978-0-520-23893-0. Dewey:818.409.
Audience: **g.**

Twain, Mark **PS13022002**
The Gilded Age and Later Novels. Trade Cloth. Library of America, The. New York, NY. 2002. 1053p. The Library of America, Vol. 130 ISBN:1-931082-10-3, ISBN13: 978-1-931082-10-5. Dewey:813/.4. LCCN:2001-038053.
Audience: **g,l,u,f.**

Twain, Mark **PS1331**
Mark Twain's Notebooks and Journals, 1877-1883, Vol. 2. Frederick C. Anderson (Editor). Trade Cloth. University of California Press. Berkeley, CA. 1976. 718p. Mark Twain Papers, No. 8 ISBN:0-520-02542-3, ISBN13: 978-0-520-02542-4. Dewey:818/.409. LCCN:72-087199.
Audience: **g,l,u.** B

Twain, Mark **PS1302**
Huck Finn and Tom Sawyer among the Indians and Other Unfinished Stories. Dahlia Armon & Walter Blair (Foreword by). Trade Cloth. University of California Press. Berkeley, CA. 1989. 392p. The Mark Twain Library ISBN:0-520-05090-8, ISBN13: 978-0-520-05090-7. Dewey:813/.4. LCCN:88-027894.
Audience: **g,l,u,f.**

Twain, Mark **PS1331.A4 1987**
Mark Twain's Letters, 1853-1886, Vol. 1. Edgar M. Branch (Editor). Trade Cloth. University of California Press. Berkeley, CA. 1988. 664p. Mark Twain Papers, No. 9 ISBN:0-520-03668-9, ISBN13: 978-0-520-03668-0. Dewey:818/.409 B. LCCN:87-005963.
Audience: **g,l,u,f.** *Choice, 1988.*

Twain, Mark **PS2127.P67**
Early Tales and Sketches: 1864-1869. Edgar M. Branch, Robert H. Hirst & Harriet E. Smith (Editors). Trade Cloth. University of California Press. Berkeley, CA. 1981. 784p. Iowa-California Edition of the Works of Mark Twain, No. 15 ISBN:0-520-04382-0, ISBN13: 978-0-520-04382-4. Dewey:818/.408. LCCN:75-046045.
Audience: **g,l,u,f.**

Twain, Mark **PS2696**
Early Tales and Sketches: 1851-1864. Edgar M. Branch, Robert H. Hirst & Harriet Elinor Smith (Editors). Trade Cloth. University of California Press. Berkeley, CA. 1979. 811p. Early Tales and Sketches, 1851-1864 Ser., No. 15 ISBN:0-520-03186-5, ISBN13: 978-0-520-03186-9. Dewey:814/.4. LCCN:75-046045.
Audience: **g,l,u,f.**

Twain, Mark **PS1303**
Collected Tales, Sketches, Speeches and Essays. Louis J. Budd (Editor). Trade Cloth, Box or Slipcased. Library of America, The. New York, NY. 1992. ISBN:0-940450-80-1, ISBN13: 978-0-940450-80-6. Dewey:818/.409.
Audience: **g,l,u,f.**

Twain, Mark **PS1303 1992**
Collected Tales, Sketches, Speeches and Essays, 1852-1890, Vol. 1. Louis J. Budd (Editor). Trade Cloth. Library of America, The. New York, NY. 1992. 1120p. Library of America, Vol. 1 ISBN:0-940450-36-4, ISBN13: 978-0-940450-36-3. Dewey:818/.409. LCCN:92-052657.
Audience: **g,l,u,f.**

Twain, Mark **PS1303 1992**
Twain: Collected Tales, Sketches, Speeches and Essays, 1891-1910, Vol. 2. Louis J. Budd (Editor). Trade Cloth. Library of America, The. New York, NY. 1992. 1050p. Library of America, Vol. 2 ISBN:0-940450-73-9, ISBN13: 978-0-940450-73-8. Dewey:818/.409. LCCN:92-052657.
Audience: **g,l,u.**

Twain, Mark **PS1302 1984**
The Innocents Abroad and Roughing It. Guy Cardwell (Editor). Trade Cloth. Library of America, The. New York, NY. 1984. 1027p. ISBN:0-940450-25-9, ISBN13: 978-0-940450-25-7. Dewey:818/.403 B. LCCN:84-011296.
Audience: **g,l,u,f.**

Twain, Mark **PS2124**
Mark Twain : Mississippi Writings: Tom Sawyer; Life on the Mississippi; Huckleberry Finn; Pudd'Nhead Wilson. Guy Cardwell (Editor). Trade Cloth. Library of America, The. New York, NY. 1982. 1126p. ISBN:0-940450-07-0, ISBN13: 978-0-940450-07-3. Dewey:813/.4. LCCN:82-009917.
Audience: **g,l,u,f.**

Twain, Mark **PS1305.T93 1999**
Adventures of Huckleberry Finn: An Authoritative Text, Contexts and Sources, Criticism. Ed. 3. Thomas Cooley (Editor). Trade Paper. W. W. Norton & Company, Inc. New York, NY. 1998. xi, 402p. Critical Editions Ser. ISBN:0-393-96640-2, ISBN13: 978-0-393-96640-4. Dewey:813/.4. LCCN:98-006901.
Audience: **l,u.**

Twain, Mark **PS1331.A4 1987**
Mark Twain's Letters, 1870-1871, Vol. 4. Victor Fischer, Michael B. Frank & Lin Salamo (Editors). Trade Cloth. University of California Press. Berkeley, CA. 1995. 826p. The Mark Twain Papers, Vol. 4 ISBN:0-520-20360-7, ISBN13: 978-0-520-20360-0. Dewey:818/.409 B. LCCN:87-005963.
Audience: **g,l,u.**

Twain, Mark **PS1322 .I7 2003**
Is He Dead?: A Comedy in Three Acts. Shelley Fisher Fishkin & Barry Moser (Editors). Trade Cloth. University of California Press. Berkeley, CA. 2003. 270p. Jumping Frogs Ser., Vol. 1 ISBN:0-520-23979-2, ISBN13: 978-0-520-23979-1. Dewey:812/.4. LCCN:2003-050703.
Audience: **g,l,u,f.** *Choice, 2004.*

Twain, Mark **PS1331.A4 1987**
Mark Twain's Letters, 1874-1875, Vol. 6. Michael B. Frank & Harriet Elinor Smith (Editors). Trade Cloth. University of California Press. Berkeley, CA. 2002. 950p. Mark Twain Papers ISBN:0-520-23772-2, ISBN13: 978-0-520-23772-8. Dewey:813.4. LCCN:87-005963.
Audience: **g,l,u,f.**

Twain, Mark **PS2124**
Tom Sawyer Abroad and Tom Sawyer, Detective. John C. Gerber (Foreword by), Terry Firkins (Text by). Trade Cloth. University of California Press. Berkeley, CA. 1983. 207p. The Mark Twain Library, No. 2 ISBN:0-520-04560-2, ISBN13: 978-0-520-04560-6. Dewey:813/.4. LCCN:81-040325.
Audience: **g,l,u,f.**

Twain, Mark **PS1302 1992**
Historical Romances: The Prince and the Pauper; A Connecticut Yankee in King Arthur's Court; Personal Recollections of Joan of Arc. Susan K. Harris (Editor). Trade Cloth. Library of America, The. New York, NY. 1994. 1050p. Library of America, Vol. 71 ISBN:0-940450-82-8, ISBN13: 978-0-940450-82-0. Dewey:813/.4. LCCN:93-040246.
Audience: **g,l,u,f.**

Twain, Mark **PS1305.A2H43 2001**
The Annotated Huckleberry Finn: Adventures of Huckleberry Finn (Tom Sawyer's Comrade). Michael Patrick Hearn (Editor). Trade Cloth. W. W. Norton & Company, Inc. New York, NY. 2001. 512p. ISBN:0-393-02039-8, ISBN13: 978-0-393-02039-7. Dewey:813/.4. LCCN:2001-031507.
Audience: **g.** *Choice, 2002.*

Twain, Mark **PS1302.Q56 2004**
The Portable Mark Twain. Tom Quirk (Contribution by). Trade Paper. Penguin Group (USA) Inc. New York, NY. 2004. 816p. ISBN:0-14-243775-1, ISBN13: 978-0-14-243775-9. Dewey:818/.409. LCCN:2004-057341.
Audience: **g,l,u,f.** B

Twain, Mark **PS1302**
Mark Twain's Satires and Burlesques. Franklin R. Rogers (Editor). Trade Cloth. University of California Press. Berkeley, CA. 1966. 495p. Mark Twain Papers, No. 3 ISBN:0-520-01081-7, ISBN13: 978-0-520-01081-9. Dewey:817.4.
Audience: **g,l,u,f.**

Twain, Mark & Salamo, Lin **PS1331 .A4**
Mark Twain's Letters, 1872-1873. Harriet E. Smith (Editor). Trade Cloth. University of California Press. Berkeley, CA. 1997. 976p. Mark Twain's Letters, 1872-1873 Ser., Vol. 5 ISBN:0-520-20822-6, ISBN13: 978-0-520-20822-3. Dewey:818.409. LCCN:87-005963.
Audience: **g,l,u,f.**

Twain, Mark **PS1331.A3 H6**
Mark Twain-Howells Letters: The Correspondence of Samuel L. Clemens and William D. Howells, 1872-1910. Henry N. Smith & William M. Gibson (Editors). Trade Cloth. Harvard University Press. Cambridge, MA. 1960. 971p. ISBN:0-674-54900-7, ISBN13: 978-0-674-54900-5. Dewey:928.1. LCCN:60-005397.
Audience: **g,l,u,f.** B

19th Century > Cooper, James Fenimore

Clark, Robert (Editor) **PS1438.J33 1985**
James Fenimore Cooper: New Critical Essays. Trade Cloth. Rowman & Littlefield Publishers, Inc. Lanham, MD. 1986. 224p. Critical Studies ISBN:0-389-20592-3, ISBN13: 978-0-389-20592-0. Dewey:813/.2. LCCN:85-015701.
Audience: **l,u.** *Choice, 1986.*

Cooper, James Fenimore **PS1406**
The Deerslayer; or, The First War-Path: A Tale. Trade Cloth. Scholarly Publishing Office, University of Michigan Library. Ann Arbor, MI. 2004. ISBN:1-4181-1565-7, ISBN13: 978-1-4181-1565-4. Dewey:813.2.
Audience: **g,l,u,f.**

Cooper, James Fenimore **PS1408**
The Last of the Mohicans. A narrative of 1757. by J. Fenimore Cooper. Trade Cloth. Scholarly Publishing Office, University of Michigan Library. Ann Arbor, MI. 2004. ISBN:1-4181-0859-6, ISBN13: 978-1-4181-0859-5. Dewey:813/.2.
Audience: **g,l,u,f.**

Cooper, James Fenimore **PS1410**
The Pathfinder; or, the inland sea. by J. Fenimore Cooper. Trade Cloth. Scholarly Publishing Office, University of Michigan Library. Ann Arbor, MI. 2004. ISBN:1-4181-0382-9, ISBN13: 978-1-4181-0382-8. Dewey:813.2.
Audience: **g,l,u,f.**

Cooper, James Fenimore **PS1414**
The Pioneers; or, the sources of the Susquehanna. A descriptive tale. by J. Fenimore Cooper. Trade Cloth. Scholarly Publishing Office, University of Michigan Library. Ann Arbor, MI. 2004. ISBN:1-4181-0386-1, ISBN13: 978-1-4181-0386-6. Dewey:813.3.
Audience: **g,l,u,f.**

Cooper, James Fenimore **PS1416**
Prairie. Trade Cloth. Amereon, Ltd. Mattituck, NY. 411p. ISBN:0-8488-2546-2, ISBN13: 978-0-8488-2546-1. Dewey:813.2.
Audience: **g,l,u,f.**

Cooper, James Fenimore **PS1402**
Early Critical Essays, Eighteen Twenty to Eighteen Twenty-Two. James F. Beard (Introduction by). Trade Cloth. Scholars' Facsimiles & Reprints. Carefree, AZ. 1977. 160p. Scholars' Facsimiles and Reprints Ser. ISBN:0-8201-1228-3, ISBN13: 978-0-8201-1228-2. Dewey:814.2. LCCN:55011038.
Audience: **g,l.**

Cooper, James Fenimore **PS1431**
Letters and Journals, Vols. 3 & 4. James F. Beard (Editor). Trade Cloth. Harvard University Press. Cambridge, MA. 1964. 992p. ISBN:0-674-52551-5, ISBN13: 978-0-674-52551-1. Dewey:813.2.
Audience: **g,l,u.**

Ringe, Donald A. **PS1438.R5 1988**
James Fenimore Cooper. Trade Cloth. Macmillan Publishing Company, Inc. Old Tappan, NJ. 1988. 176p. Twayne's United States Authors Ser., No. 11 ISBN:0-8057-7527-7, ISBN13: 978-0-8057-7527-3. Dewey:813/.2. LCCN:88-012047.
Audience: **g,l.** B

19th Century > Crane, Stephen

Bassan, M. (Editor) **PS1449.C85**
Stephen Crane: A Collection of Critical Essays. Trade Cloth. John Wiley & Sons, Inc. Hoboken, NJ. 1967. ISBN:0-13-188888-9, ISBN13: 978-0-13-188888-3. Dewey:818/.4/09.
Audience: **g,l,u.**

Berryman, John **PS1449.C85Z56 2001**
Stephen Crane: A Critical Biography. Trade Paper. Cooper Square Publishers, Inc. New York, NY. 2001. 368p. ISBN:0-8154-1115-4, ISBN13: 978-0-8154-1115-4. Dewey:813/.4 B. LCCN:2001-028324.
Audience: **g.**

Cady, Edwin H. **PS1449.C85.Z575 1980**
Stephen Crane. Trade Cloth. Macmillan Publishing Company, Inc. Old Tappan, NJ. 1980. 184p. Twayne's United States Authors Ser. ISBN:0-8057-7299-5, ISBN13: 978-0-8057-7299-9. Dewey:813/.4. LCCN:79-026608.
Audience: **g,l.** B

Crane, Stephen **PS2124**
Maggie: A Girl of the Streets. Trade Paper. Wordsworth Editions, Ltd. Ware, 1998. 192p. Classics Library ISBN:1-85326-559-4, ISBN13: 978-1-85326-559-4. Dewey:813/.4.
Audience: **g.** B *Choice, 1999.*

Crane, Stephen **PS2124**
The Red Badge of Courage. Trade Paper. W. W. Norton & Company, Inc. New York, NY. 1999. 188p. ISBN:0-393-31954-7, ISBN13: 978-0-393-31954-5. Dewey:813/.4. LCCN:81-022419.
Audience: **g,l,u,f.**

Crane, Stephen **PS1449.C85**
Wounds in the Rain: A Collection of Stories Relating to the Spanish-American War of 1898. Trade Cloth. Ayer Company Publishers, Inc. Manchester, NH. 1977. Short Story Index Reprint Ser. ISBN:0-8369-4145-4, ISBN13: 978-0-8369-4145-6. Dewey:813/.4. LCCN:72-003294.
Audience: **g,l,u,f.**

Crane, Stephen **PS1449.C85 1969**
The Works of Stephen Crane: Bowery Tales; Maggie and George's Mother. Fredson Bowers (Editor). Trade Cloth. University Press of Virginia. Charlottesville, VA. 1969. 184p. ISBN:0-8139-0258-4, ISBN13: 978-0-8139-0258-6. Dewey:813/.4. LCCN:68-008536.
Audience: **g,l,u,f.** B

Nagel, James **PR6005.L37Z5**
Stephen Crane and Literary Impressionism. Trade Cloth. Pennsylvania State University Press. University Park, PA. 1980. 200p. ISBN:0-271-00267-0, ISBN13: 978-0-271-00267-5. Dewey:301.4314092. LCCN:80-016051.
Audience: **l,u.** B

Solomon, Eric **PS1449.C85Z8**
Stephen Crane: From Parody to Realism. Trade Paper. Books on Demand. Ann Arbor, MI. 311p. ISBN:0-598-20724-4, ISBN13: 978-0-598-20724-1. Dewey:813.4. LCCN:63-021347.
Audience: **g,l.** B

19th Century > D

Byerman, Keith E. **E185.97.D73B94 1994**
Seizing the Word: History, Art, and Self in the Work of W. E. B Du Bois. Trade Cloth. University of Georgia Press. Athens, GA. 1994. 256p. ISBN:0-8203-1624-5, ISBN13: 978-0-8203-1624-6. Dewey:305.896/73/092 B. LCCN:93-030368.
Audience: **g,l,u,f.** *Choice, 1995.*

Daly, Augustine **PS1499.D85**
Plays. Don B. Wilmeth & Rosemary Cullen (Editors). Trade Cloth. Cambridge University Press. New York, NY. 1984. 219p. British and American Playwrights Ser. ISBN:0-521-24090-5, ISBN13: 978-0-521-24090-1. Dewey:812/.4. LCCN:83-018929.
Audience: **g,l,u,f.** B

Davis, Rebecca Harding **PS1517.L5 1998**
Life in the Iron Mills. Cecilia Tichi (Editor). Trade Cloth. Palgrave Macmillan. New York, NY. 1997. 449p. Bedford Cultural Editions Ser. ISBN:0-312-16374-6, ISBN13: 978-0-312-16374-7. Dewey:813.3. LCCN:96-086795.
Audience: **g,l,u,f.**

De Forest, John W. **PS1525.D5M5 1998**
Miss Ravenel's Conversion from Secession to Loyalty. Sharon L. Gravett (Introduction by). Trade Cloth. University of Nebraska Press. Lincoln, NE. 1998. 466p. ISBN:0-8032-6615-4, ISBN13: 978-0-8032-6615-5. Dewey:813/.3. LCCN:98-020846.
Audience: **g,l,u,f.**

Deland, Margaret **PZ3.D371**
Dr. Lavendar's People. Trade Paper. Kessinger Publishing, LLC. Whitefish, MT. 2005. ISBN:1-4179-8851-7, ISBN13: 978-1-4179-8851-8. Dewey:813.
Audience: **g,l,u,f.**

Douglass, Frederick **E449.D749 1994**
Autobiographies: Narrative of the Life, My Bondage and My Freedom, Life and Times. Henry Louis Gates Jr. (Editor). Trade Cloth. Library of America, The. New York, NY. 1994. 1100p. Library of America, Vol. 68 ISBN:0-940450-79-8, ISBN13: 978-0-940450-79-0. Dewey:973.8/092 B. LCCN:93-024168.
Audience: **g,l,u,f.**

Du Bois, W. E. B. **E185.97.D73A2 1986**
Du Bois: Writings. Nathan I. Huggins (Editor). Trade Cloth. Library of America, The. New York, NY. 1987. 1334p. ISBN:0-940450-33-X, ISBN13: 978-0-940450-33-2. Dewey:973/.0496073. LCCN:86-010565.
Audience: **g,l,u,f.**

Dunbar, Paul Laurence **PS1556**
The Best Stories of Paul Laurence Dunbar. Paper Text. Classic Textbooks. Murrieta, CA. 1938. 258p. ISBN:1-4047-2715-9, ISBN13: 978-1-4047-2715-1. Dewey:813/.4.
Audience: **g,l,u,f.** B

Dunbar, Paul Laurence **PS1556 .A1**
The Complete Poems of Paul Laurence Dunbar. William Dean Howells (Introduction by). Trade Paper. Hakim's Publishers. Philadelphia, PA. 1993. 289p. ISBN:0-317-05269-1, ISBN13: 978-0-317-05269-5. Dewey:811/.4.
Audience: **g,l,u,f.**

19th Century > Dickinson, Emily

Anderson, Charles R. **PS1541**
Emily Dickinson's Poetry: Stairway of Surprise. Trade Cloth. Greenwood Publishing Group, Inc. Portsmouth, NH. 1982. 334p. ISBN:0-313-23733-6, ISBN13: 978-0-313-23733-1. Dewey:811/.4. LCCN:82-015844.
Audience: **u,f.** B

Benfey, Christopher E. G., et al. PS1541.Z5L43 2001
The Dickinsons of Amherst. Polly Longsworth & Barton Levi St. Armand (Authors), Jerome Liebling (Photographer). Trade Cloth. University Press of New England. Lebanon, NH. 2001. 220p. ISBN:1-58465-068-0, ISBN13: 978-1-58465-068-3. Dewey:811/.4. LCCN:2001-001810.
Audience: **g,l.**

Dickinson, Emily PS1541.A171999
The Poems of Emily Dickinson. R. W. Franklin (Editor). Trade Cloth. Harvard University Press. Cambridge, MA. 1999. 696p. ISBN:0-674-67624-6, ISBN13: 978-0-674-67624-4. Dewey:811/.4. LCCN:99-011821.
Audience: **g,l,u,f.**

Dickinson, Emily PS1541.Z5
Letters of Emily Dickinson. Thomas H. Johnson & Theodora Ward (Editors). Trade Cloth, Box or Slipcased. Harvard University Press. Cambridge, MA. 1958. 1042p. ISBN:0-674-52625-2, ISBN13: 978-0-674-52625-9. Dewey:811/.4. LCCN:58-005594.
Audience: **g,l,u.**

Eberwein, Jane Donahue PS1541.Z5E34 1985
Dickinson: Strategies of Limitation. Cloth Text. University of Massachusetts Press. Amherst, MA. 1986. 320p. ISBN:0-87023-473-0, ISBN13: 978-0-87023-473-6. Dewey:811/.4. LCCN:84-016335.
Audience: **g,l.** *Choice, 1985.*

Kirk, Connie Ann PS1541
Emily Dickinson: A Biography. Cloth Text. Greenwood Publishing Group, Inc. Portsmouth, NH. 2004. 216p. Greenwood Biographies Ser. ISBN:0-313-32206-6, ISBN13: 978-0-313-32206-8. Dewey:811/.4 B. LCCN:2003-058335.
Audience: **g,l.**

Pollak, Vivian R. (Editor) PS1541.Z5H57 2003
A Historical Guide to Emily Dickinson. Trade Cloth. Oxford University Press, Inc. New York, NY. 2004. 312p. Historical Guides to American Authors ISBN:0-19-515134-8, ISBN13: 978-0-19-515134-3. Dewey:811/.4. LCCN:2003-002308.
Audience: **u,f.**

Porter, David PS1541.Z5
Dickinson: The Modern Idiom. Trade Cloth. Harvard University Press. Cambridge, MA. 1981. 325p. ISBN:0-674-20444-1, ISBN13: 978-0-674-20444-7. Dewey:811/.4. LCCN:80-024322.
Audience: **g,l.**

Sewall, Richard Benson PS1541.Z5
The Life of Emily Dickinson. Cloth over Boards. Farrar, Straus & Giroux. New York, NY. 1994. 196p. ISBN:0-374-18694-4, ISBN13: 978-0-374-18694-4. Dewey:811/.4.
Audience: **g,l,u,f.**

Sielke, Sabine PS152.S54 1997
Fashioning the Female Subject: The Intertextual Networking of Dickinson, Moore, and Rich. Trade Cloth. University of Michigan Press. Chicago, IL. 1997. 280p. ISBN:0-472-10788-7, ISBN13: 978-0-472-10788-9. Dewey:811.009/9287. LCCN:96-045813.
Audience: **u,f.**

19th Century > E-F

Eggleston, Edward PS1582
The Circuit Rider: A Tale of the Heroic Age. Trade Cloth. Amereon, Ltd. Mattituck, NY. ISBN:0-88411-529-1, ISBN13: 978-0-88411-529-8. Dewey:813/.4.
Audience: **g,l,u,f.**

Eggleston, Edward PZ3.E29 HO27 PS1582
The Hoosier School-Master. Trade Cloth. Amereon, Ltd. Mattituck, NY. ISBN:0-89190-419-0, ISBN13: 978-0-89190-419-9. Dewey:813/.4.
Audience: **g,l,u,f.**

Fern, Fanny PS2384
Ruth Hall: A Domestic Tale of the Present Time. Susan Belasco Smith (Notes by). Trade Paper. Penguin Group (USA) Inc. New York, NY. 1997. 352p. Classics Ser. ISBN:0-14-043640-5, ISBN13: 978-0-14-043640-2. Dewey:813/.3.
Audience: **g,l,u,f.**

Frederic, Harold PS1707.D3 1997
The Damnation of Theron Ware. Trade Cloth. Prometheus Books, Publishers. Amherst, NY. 1997. 315p. Literary Classics ISBN:1-57392-169-6, ISBN13: 978-1-57392-169-5. Dewey:813/.4. LCCN:97-033406.
Audience: **g,l,u,f.**

Freeman, Mary E. Wilkins PS1711.P7 1983
Selected Stories of Mary E. Wilkins Freeman. Trade Cloth. W. W. Norton & Company, Inc. New York, NY. 1983. xix, 344p. ISBN:0-393-01726-5, ISBN13: 978-0-393-01726-7. Dewey:813/.4. LCCN:82-021179.
Audience: **g,l,u,f.**

19th Century > Emerson, Ralph Waldo

Burkholder, Robert E. & Myerson, Joel PS1638.C74 1983
Critical Essays on Ralph Waldo Emerson. Trade Cloth. Thomson Gale. Farmington Hills, MI. 1983. ix, 530p. Critical Essays on American Literature Ser. ISBN:0-8161-8305-8, ISBN13: 978-0-8161-8305-0. Dewey:814/.3. LCCN:82-015831.
Audience: **g,l.**

Emerson, Edward Waldo E467.1.L6
Life and Letters of Charles Russell Lowell. Trade Cloth. Associated Faculty Press, Inc. New York, NY. 1971. xiv, 499p. American History and Culture in the Nineteenth Century Ser. ISBN:0-8046-1477-6, ISBN13: 978-0-8046-1477-1. Dewey:973.78/1/0924. LCCN:71-137909.
Audience: **g,l,u,f.**

Emerson, Ralph Waldo PS1600
The Complete Works of Ralph Waldo Emerson.
http://www.hti.umich.edu/e/emerson/
Emerson, Edward Waldo (Editor).
Audience: **g,l,u,f.**

Emerson, Ralph Waldo **PS1624.A1 1994**
Emerson: Collected Poems and Translations. Harold Bloom & Paul Kane (Editors). Trade Cloth. Library of America, The. New York, NY. 1994. 640p. ISBN:0-940450-28-3, ISBN13: 978-0-940450-28-8. Dewey:811/.3. LCCN:93-040245.
Audience: **g,u,f.**

Emerson, Ralph Waldo **PS1602 1996**
Ralph Waldo Emerson: Essays and Poetry. Harold Bloom, Paul Kane & Joel Porte Jr. (Notes by). Trade Paper. Library of America, The. New York, NY. 1996. 1376p. Library of America College Editions ISBN:1-883011-32-9, ISBN13: 978-1-883011-32-1. Dewey:814/.3. LCCN:95-052464.
Audience: **g,l,u,f.**

Emerson, Ralph Waldo & Carlyle, Thomas **PS1631.A35C3**
The Correspondence of Emerson and Carlyle. Joseph Slater (Editor). Trade Paper. Books on Demand. Ann Arbor, MI. 632p. ISBN:0-8357-9063-0, ISBN13: 978-0-8357-9063-5. Dewey:816.3. LCCN:63-017539.
Audience: **g,l.** B

Emerson, Ralph Waldo, et al. **PS1606.A2W55 2003**
The Collected Works of Ralph Waldo Emerson: The Conduct of Life, Vol. VI. Barbara Packer, Joseph Slater & Douglas Wilson (Authors). Trade Cloth. Harvard University Press. Cambridge, MA. 2004. 560p. Collected Works of Ralph Waldo Emerson Ser. ISBN:0-674-01190-2, ISBN13: 978-0-674-01190-8. Dewey:814/.3. LCCN:2003-055760.
Audience: **g,l.**

Emerson, Ralph Waldo **PS3048**
Essays and Lectures. Joel Porte (Editor). Trade Cloth. Library of America, The. New York, NY. 1983. 1150p. ISBN:0-940450-15-1, ISBN13: 978-0-940450-15-8. Dewey:818/.308. LCCN:83-005447.
Audience: **g,l,u,f.**

Emerson, Ralph Waldo **PS1631 .A4**
Letters of Ralph Waldo Emerson, Set. R. L. Rusk (Editor). Trade Cloth. Columbia University Press. New York, NY. 1941. 3110p. ISBN:0-231-00724-8, ISBN13: 978-0-231-00724-5. Dewey:814/.3. LCCN:39-012289.
Audience: **g,l,u,f.**

Porte, Joel **PS1638.P665 2004**
Consciousness and Culture: Emerson and Thoreau Reviewed. Cloth over Boards. Yale University Press. Cumberland, RI. 2004. 256p. ISBN:0-300-10446-4, ISBN13: 978-0-300-10446-2. Dewey:810.9/003. LCCN:2004-043842.
Audience: **u,f.** *Choice, 2005.*

Porte, Joel **PS1631.P65 1988**
Representative Man: Ralph Waldo Emerson in His Time. Cloth Text. Columbia University Press. New York, NY. 1988. 361p. ISBN:0-231-06740-2, ISBN13: 978-0-231-06740-9. Dewey:814/.3 B. LCCN:88-000829.
Audience: **l,u.** B

Porte, Joel & Morris, Saundra (Editors) **PS1638**
The Cambridge Companion to Ralph Waldo Emerson. Trade Paper. Cambridge University Press. New York, NY. 1999. 300p. Companions to Literature Ser. ISBN:0-521-49946-1, ISBN13: 978-0-521-49946-0. Dewey:814.3. LCCN:98-036892.
Audience: **l,u,f.** *Choice, 2000.*

Sealts, Merton Miller, et al. **PS1613**
Emerson's 'Nature': Origin, Growth, Meaning. Ed. 2. Alfred R. Ferguson & Ralph Waldo Emerson (Authors). Trade Cloth. Southern Illinois University Press. Carbondale, IL. 1979. xi, 225p. ISBN:0-8093-0891-6, ISBN13: 978-0-8093-0891-0. Dewey:191. LCCN:78-013945.
Audience: **g,l.** B

Smith, Harmon **PS3053.S65 1999**
My Friend, My Friend: The Story of Thoreau's Relationship with Emerson. Cloth Text. University of Massachusetts Press. Amherst, MA. 2001. xii, 216p. ISBN:1-55849-186-4, ISBN13: 978-1-55849-186-1. Dewey:810.9/003 B. LCCN:98-053492.
Audience: **u,f.** *Choice, 2000.*

Teichgraeber, Richard F. 3rd **PS1638.T44 1995**
Sublime Thoughts - Penny Wisdom: Situating Emerson and Thoreau in the American Market. Trade Cloth. Johns Hopkins University Press. Baltimore, MD. 1995. 312p. New Studies in American Intellectual and Cultural History ISBN:0-8018-5000-2, ISBN13: 978-0-8018-5000-4. Dewey:810.9/003. LCCN:94-036088.
Audience: **u,f.** *Choice, 1995.*

Waggoner, Hyatt Howe **PS1638.W3**
Emerson As Poet. Trade Cloth. Princeton University Press. Princeton, NJ. 1974. xiii, 211p. ISBN:0-691-06269-2, ISBN13: 978-0-691-06269-3. Dewey:811/.3. LCCN:74-002983.
Audience: **g,l.** B

Williams, John B. **PS2388.P5W5 1991**
White Fire: The Influence of Emerson on Melville. Trade Cloth. National Film Network LLC. Lanham, MD. 1991. 208p. ISBN:1-878981-02-1, ISBN13: 978-1-878981-02-8. Dewey:813/.3. LCCN:90-028923.
Audience: **u,f.** *Choice, 1992.*

Yannella, Donald **PS1638.Y36 1982**
Ralph Waldo Emerson. Trade Cloth. Thomson Gale. Farmington Hills, MI. 1982. 160p. Twayne's United States Authors Ser., No. 414 ISBN:0-8057-7344-4, ISBN13: 978-0-8057-7344-6. Dewey:814/.3. LCCN:81-020321.
Audience: **l,u.** B

19th Century > Fuller, Margaret

Capper, Charles **PS2506**
Margaret Fuller: The Public Years. Trade Cloth. Oxford University Press, Inc. New York, NY. 320p. ISBN:0-19-506313-9, ISBN13: 978-0-19-506313-4. Dewey:818.309.
Audience: **u,f.**

Capper, Charles **PS2506.C36 1992**
Margaret Fuller, An American Romantic Life. Oxford University Press. 1992. ISBN:0-19-504579-3, ISBN13: 978-0-19-504579-6.
Audience: **l,u,f.**

Fuller, Margaret **PS2502**
Margaret Fuller, American Romantic: A Selection of Her Writings and Correspondence. Miller, Perry G., editor. Peter Smith Publisher, Inc. 1983. ISBN:0-8446-0802-5, ISBN13: 978-0-8446-0802-0.
Audience: **l,u,f.**

Hudspeth, Robert N. (Editor) **PS2506.A4 2001**
"My Heart Is a Large Kingdom": Selected Letters of Margaret Fuller. Margaret Fuller (Contribution by). Trade Cloth. Cornell University Press. Ithaca, NY. 2001. ISBN:0-8014-8653-X, ISBN13: 978-0-8014-8653-1. Dewey:818/.309 B. LCCN:00-010239.
Audience: **u,f.** *Choice, 2001.*

Urbawski, Marie (Editor) **PS2507 .M37**
Margaret Fuller: Visionary of the New Age. Trade Cloth. Northern Lights. Orono, ME. 1994. ISBN:1-880811-14-6, ISBN13: 978-1-880811-14-6. Dewey:818.309. LCCN:93-087696.
Audience: **u,f.** *Choice, 1995.*

Von Mehren, Joan **PS2506.V66 1994**
Minerva and the Muse: A Life of Margaret Fuller. Trade Cloth. University of Massachusetts Press. Amherst, MA. 1995. 416p. ISBN:0-87023-941-4, ISBN13: 978-0-87023-941-0. Dewey:818/.309 B. LCCN:94-018663.
Audience: **u,f.** *Choice, 1995.*

19th Century > Garland, Hamlin

Garland, Hamlin **PS1733.A42**
A Daughter of the Middle Border. Trade Paper. Kessinger Publishing, LLC. Whitefish, MT. 2005. ISBN:1-4179-0678-2, ISBN13: 978-1-4179-0678-9. Dewey:813.
Audience: **g,l.** B

Garland, Hamlin **PS1732**
Rose of Dutcher's Coolly. Trade Cloth. Somerset Publishers, Inc. Santa Barbara, CA. 1895. ISBN:0-403-00211-7, ISBN13: 978-0-403-00211-5. Dewey:813/.5/2. LCCN:76-108484.
Audience: **g,l,u,f.** B

Garland, Hamlin **PS1732.M3 1996**
Main-Travelled Roads. William Dean Howells & Joseph B. McCullough (Introduction by). Trade Cloth. University of Nebraska Press. Lincoln, NE. 1995. 247p. ISBN:0-8032-7058-5, ISBN13: 978-0-8032-7058-9. Dewey:813/.52. LCCN:95-034866.
Audience: **g,l,u,f.** B

Garland, Hamlin **PS1733.A44 1998**
Selected Letters of Hamlin Garland. Keith Newlin & Joseph B. McCullough (Editors). Cloth Text. University of Nebraska Press. Lincoln, NE. 1998. 469p. ISBN:0-8032-2160-6, ISBN13: 978-0-8032-2160-4. Dewey:[B]. LCCN:97-015356.
Audience: **g,l,u.**

Garland, Hamlin **PS1733.A47**
A Son of the Middle Border. Alice Barber Stephens (Illustrator). Trade Paper. Kessinger Publishing, LLC. Whitefish, MT. 2005. ISBN:0-7661-9393-4, ISBN13: 978-0-7661-9393-2. Dewey:813/.52 B.
Audience: **g,l,u.** B

19th Century > G-H

Clifford, Deborah **PS2018.C55**
Mine Eyes Have Seen the Glory: A Biography of Julia Ward Howe. Trade Cloth. Little Brown & Company. New York, NY. 1979. 313 p., [4] lp. ISBN:0-316-14747-8, ISBN13: 978-0-316-14747-7. Dewey:818/.4/09. LCCN:78-010379.
Audience: **g,l,u,f.** B

Gilman, Charlotte Perkins **PS1744.G57Z5 1975**
The Living of Charlotte Perkins Gilman: An Autobiography. Zona Gale (Foreword by). Trade Cloth. HarperCollins Publishers. New York, NY. 1975. xxxviii, 341p. Women's Studies ISBN:0-06-090422-4, ISBN13: 978-0-06-090422-7. Dewey:305.42/092 B. LCCN:75-324195.
Audience: **g,l,u,f.** B

Gilman, Charlotte Perkins & Golden, Catherine **PS1744.G57Y45 2004**
The Yellow Wallpaper: A Sourcebook. Paper over Boards. Routledge. New York, NY. 2004. 192p. Routledge Guides to Literature Ser. ISBN:0-415-26357-3, ISBN13: 978-0-415-26357-3. Dewey:813/.4. LCCN:2004-002077.
Audience: **l,u.**

Gilman, Charlotte Perkins **PS1744.G57Y45 2006**
The Yellow Wallpaper: A Dual-Text Critical Edition. Shawn St. Jean (Editor). Trade Cloth. Ohio University Press. Athens, OH. 2006. 144p. ISBN:0-8214-1653-7, ISBN13: 978-0-8214-1653-2. Dewey:813/.4. LCCN:2005-038051.
Audience: **l,u,f.**

Guiney, Louise I. **PS1767 .H3 1979**
Happy Ending: The Collected Lyrics of Louise I. Guiney. Trade Cloth. Greenwood Publishing Group, Inc. Portsmouth, NH. 1979. ISBN:0-313-20702-X, ISBN13: 978-0-313-20702-0. Dewey:811/.4. LCCN:78-011678.
Audience: **u,f.**

Harper, Frances Ellen Watkins **PS1799.H7I6 1988**
Iola Leroy, or Shadows Uplifted. Frances Smith Foster (Introduction by). Cloth Text. Oxford University Press, Inc. New York, NY. 1988. 336p. The Schomburg Library of Nineteenth-Century Black Women Writers ISBN:0-19-505240-4, ISBN13: 978-0-19-505240-4. Dewey:813/.4. LCCN:87-024794.
Audience: **g,l,u,f.**

Harris, George W. **PS1799.H87A6**
High Times and Hard Times: Sketches and Tales by George Washington Harris. M. Thomas Inge (Editor). Trade Cloth. Burt Franklin Publisher. New York, NY. 1976. ISBN:0-8337-5502-1, ISBN13: 978-0-8337-5502-5. Dewey:813/.3.
Audience: **g,l,u.**

Hearn, Lafcadio **PS1916**
Selected Writings. Henry Goodman (Editor). Trade Paper. Books on Demand. Ann Arbor, MI. 575p. ISBN:0-598-64629-9, ISBN13: 978-0-598-64629-3. Dewey:813.4. LCCN:49-011635.
Audience: **g,l,u,f.** B

19th Century > Harris, Joel Chandler

Bickley, R. Bruce Jr. **PS1813**
Joel Chandler Harris: A Biography and Critical Study. Trade Paper. iUniverse, Inc. Lincoln, NE. 2000. 180p. ISBN:0-595-13113-1, ISBN13: 978-0-595-13113-6. Dewey:818/.409.
Audience: **l,u.**

Brasch, Walter M. **PS1813 .B73 2000**
Brer Rabbit, Uncle Remus and the 'Cornfield Journalist': The Tale of Joel Chandler Harris. Trade Cloth. Mercer University Press. Macon, GA. 2004. xxxii, 399p. ISBN:0-86554-696-7, ISBN13: 978-0-86554-696-7. Dewey:817.4. LCCN:00-032878.
Audience: **g,l,u,f.** *Choice, 2001.*

Harris, Joel Chandler **PZ8.1.H233 UN 1983A**
The Complete Tales of Uncle Remus. Richard Chase (Compiled by). Reinforced. Houghton Mifflin Company Trade & Reference Division. Boston, MA. 2002. 864p. ISBN:0-618-15429-9, ISBN13: 978-0-618-15429-6. Dewey:813/.4. LCCN:2002-284107.
Audience: **g,l,u,f.** B

Harris, Joel Chandler **PS1801**
The Favorite Uncle Remus. A.B. Frost (Illustrator). Trade Cloth. Houghton Mifflin Company Trade & Reference Division. Boston, MA. 1973. 320p. ISBN:0-395-06800-2, ISBN13: 978-0-395-06800-7. Dewey:398.2.
Audience: **g,l,u,f.** B

Harris, Joel Chandler **PS1813.A4 1993**
Dearest Chums and Partners: Joel Chandler Harris's Letters to His Children: A Domestic Biography. Hugh T. Keenan (Editor). Trade Cloth. University of Georgia Press. Athens, GA. 1993. 576p. ISBN:0-8203-1480-3, ISBN13: 978-0-8203-1480-8. Dewey:818/.409. LCCN:92-008235.
Audience: **g,l.**

Harris, Julia F. **PS1813.H3 1973**
The Life and Letters of Joel Chandler Harris. Trade Cloth. A M S Press, Inc. New York, NY. 1973. ix, 620p. ISBN:0-404-00059-2, ISBN13: 978-0-404-00059-2. Dewey:818/.4/09. LCCN:72-168247.
Audience: **g,l,u.** B

19th Century > Harte, Bret

Harte, Bret **PS1831**
East and West. Trade Cloth. Scholarly Publishing Office, University of Michigan Library. Ann Arbor, MI. 2004. ISBN:1-4181-1752-8, ISBN13: 978-1-4181-1752-8. Dewey:811.4.
Audience: **g,l,u,f.**

Harte, Bret **PS1827**
The Luck of Roaring Camp and Other Sketches. Trade Cloth. Scholarly Publishing Office, University of Michigan Library. Ann Arbor, MI. 2004. ISBN:1-4181-1790-0, ISBN13: 978-1-4181-1790-0. Dewey:813.
Audience: **g,l,u,f.**

Harte, Bret **PS1830**
Poems. Trade Cloth. Scholarly Publishing Office, University of Michigan Library. Ann Arbor, MI. 2004. ISBN:1-4181-1722-6, ISBN13: 978-1-4181-1722-1. Dewey:811.
Audience: **g,l,u,f.**

Harte, Bret **PS1833.A4 1997**
Selected Letters of Bret Harte. Gary Scharnhorst (Editor). Trade Cloth. University of Oklahoma Press. Norman, OK. 1997. 480p. Literature of the American West Ser., Vol. 1
ISBN:0-8061-2897-6, ISBN13: 978-0-8061-2897-9. Dewey:[B]. LCCN:96-018191.
Audience: **g,l,u.** *Choice, 1997.*

Harte, Bret **PS1822**
Poems and Stories. Charles Swain Thomas (Introduction by). Trade Cloth. Scholarly Publishing Office, University of Michigan Library. Ann Arbor, MI. 2004. ISBN:1-4181-1723-4, ISBN13: 978-1-4181-1723-8. Dewey:813.45.
Audience: **g,l,u,f.**

Scharnhorst, Gary **PS1833.S38 2000**
Bret Harte: Opening the American Literary West. Trade Cloth. University of Oklahoma Press. Norman, OK. 2000. 272p. Oklahoma Western Biographies Ser., Vol. 17
ISBN:0-8061-3254-X, ISBN13: 978-0-8061-3254-9. Dewey:813/.4 B. LCCN:00-022412.
Audience: **g,l,u.** *Choice, 2001.*

Stewart, George R. **PS1833 .S7 1979**
Bret Harte, Argonaut and Exile. Trade Cloth. A M S Press, Inc. New York, NY. ISBN:0-404-15298-8, ISBN13: 978-0-404-15298-7. Dewey:813/.4 B. LCCN:76-006593.
Audience: **g,l,u,f.**

19th Century > Hawthorne, Nathaniel

Bell, Michael Davitt **PS1888.B4**
Hawthorne and the Historical Romance of New England. Trade Paper. Books on Demand. Ann Arbor, MI. 267p. ISBN:0-598-34873-5, ISBN13: 978-0-598-34873-9. Dewey:813/.3. LCCN:72-148169.
Audience: **l,u.** B

Brodhead, Richard H. **PS1888**
Hawthorne, Melville and the Novel. Trade Cloth. University of Chicago Press. Chicago, IL. 1976. viii, 216p. ISBN:0-226-07522-2, ISBN13: 978-0-226-07522-8. Dewey:813/.3/09. LCCN:75-005071.
Audience: **g,l,u.** B

Colacurcio, Michael J. **PS1892.R4**
The Province of Piety: Moral History in Hawthorne's Early Tales. Trade Cloth. Harvard University Press. Cambridge, MA. 1984. 680p. ISBN:0-674-71957-3, ISBN13: 978-0-674-71957-6. Dewey:813/.3. LCCN:83-026586.
Audience: **l,u.** B

Crews, Frederick C. **PS1892.P74C74 1989**
The Sins of the Fathers: Hawthorne's Psychological Themes. Trade Cloth. University of California Press. Berkeley, CA. 1989. 301p. ISBN:0-520-06817-3, ISBN13: 978-0-520-06817-9. Dewey:813/.3. LCCN:89-004955.
Audience: **g,l.** B

Crowley, Joseph Donald (Editor) **PS1881**
Hawthorne: The Critical Heritage. Trade Cloth. Routledge. New York, NY. 1978. xvi, 532p. ISBN:0-7100-6886-7, ISBN13: 978-0-7100-6886-6. Dewey:813/.3. LCCN:77-552816.
Audience: **g,l,u.** B

Gerber, John C. (Editor) **PS1868 .G38**
Twentieth Century Interpretations of The Scarlet Letter. Trade Cloth. John Wiley & Sons, Inc. Hoboken, NJ. 1968. Twentieth Century Interpretations Ser. ISBN:0-13-791582-9, ISBN13: 978-0-13-791582-8. Dewey:813.4. LCCN:68-023438.
Audience: **l,u.** B

Hawthorne, Julian **PS1881 .H35**
Nathaniel Hawthorne and His Wife a Biography, Vol. 1. Trade Paper. Kessinger Publishing, LLC. Whitefish, MT. 2004. ISBN:1-4179-4230-4, ISBN13: 978-1-4179-4230-5. Dewey:813/.3 B.
Audience: **u,f.**

Hawthorne, Julian **PS1881 .H35**
Nathaniel Hawthorne and His Wife a Biography, Vol. 2. Trade Paper. Kessinger Publishing, LLC. Whitefish, MT. 2004. ISBN:1-4179-4231-2, ISBN13: 978-1-4179-4231-2. Dewey:813/.3 B.
Audience: **u,f.**

Hawthorne, Nathaniel **PS2384**
The Blithedale Romance. Cloth Text. Amereon, Ltd. Mattituck, NY. 2000. ISBN:0-8488-2921-2, ISBN13: 978-0-8488-2921-6. Dewey:813/.3.
Audience: **g,u,f.** B

Hawthorne, Nathaniel **PS2384**
Collected Novels: Fanshawe, the Scarlet Letter, the House of the Seven Gables, the Blithedale Romance, the Marble Faun. Millicent Bell (Editor). Trade Cloth. Library of America, The. New York, NY. 1983. 1272p. Library of America Ser. ISBN:0-940450-08-9, ISBN13: 978-0-940450-08-0. Dewey:813/.3. LCCN:82-018031.
Audience: **g,l,u,f.**

Hawthorne, Nathaniel **PS1868.A2G76 1988**
The Scarlet Letter: An Authoritative Text. Ed. 3. Seymour L. Gross, E. Sculley Bradley, Richard C. Beatty & E. Hudson Long (Editors). Trade Cloth. W. W. Norton & Company, Inc. New York, NY. 1988. 480p. Critical Editions Ser. ISBN:0-393-95653-9, ISBN13: 978-0-393-95653-5. Dewey:813/.3. LCCN:87-018535.
Audience: **l.** B

Hawthorne, Nathaniel **PS1852 1996**
Hawthorne: Tales and Sketches. Roy H. Pearce (Editor). Trade Cloth. Library of America, The. New York, NY. 1996. 1200p. Library of America College Editions ISBN:1-883011-33-7, ISBN13: 978-1-883011-33-8. Dewey:813/.3. LCCN:95-052465.
Audience: **g,l,u,f.**

Hawthorne, Nathaniel **PS1852.S66 2005**
The Portable Hawthorne. William C. Spengemann (Contribution by). Trade Paper. Penguin Group (USA) Inc. New York, NY. 2005. 464p. Penguin Classics Ser. ISBN:0-14-303928-8, ISBN13: 978-0-14-303928-0. Dewey:813/.3. LCCN:2004-065791.
Audience: **g,l,u,f.**

Martin, Terence **PS1888.M34 1983**
Nathaniel Hawthorne. Trade Cloth. Thomson Gale. Farmington Hills, MI. 1983. 240p. United States Authors Ser., No. 75 ISBN:0-8057-7384-3, ISBN13: 978-0-8057-7384-2. Dewey:813/.3. LCCN:82-023419.
Audience: **g,l,u.** B

Martin, Terry J. **PS374.S5M38 1998**
Rhetorical Deception in the Short Fiction of Hawthorne, Poe and Melville. Trade Cloth. Edwin Mellen Press, The. Lewiston, NY. 1998. 120p. Studies in Comparative Literature Ser., Vol. 23 ISBN:0-7734-8240-7, ISBN13: 978-0-7734-8240-1. Dewey:813/.010903. LCCN:98-039987.
Audience: **u,f.**

Miller, Edwin H. **PS1881.M48 1991**
Salem Is My Dwelling Place: A Life of Nathaniel Hawthorne. Trade Cloth. University of Iowa Press. Iowa City, IA. 1991. 648p. ISBN:0-87745-332-2, ISBN13: 978-0-87745-332-1. Dewey:813/.3 B. LCCN:91-014543.
Audience: **g,l,u,f.** *Choice, 1992.*

Muirhead, Kimberly Free **PS1868.M85 2005**
Nathaniel Hawthorne's the Scarlet Letter: A Critical Resource Guide and Comprehensive Annotated Bibliography of Literary Criticism 1950-2000. Trade Cloth. Edwin Mellen Press, The. Lewiston, NY. 2004. 644p. Studies in American Literature Ser., 73 ISBN:0-7734-6196-5, ISBN13: 978-0-7734-6196-3. Dewey:813/.3. LCCN:2004-061070.
Audience: **l,u,f.** *Choice, 2005.*

Stoehr, Taylor **PS1889.S7**
Hawthorne's Mad Scientists: Pseudoscience and Social Science in Nineteenth-Century Life and Letters. Trade Cloth. Shoe String Press, Inc. North Haven, CT. 1978. 313p. ISBN:0-208-01710-0, ISBN13: 978-0-208-01710-9. Dewey:813/.3. LCCN:78-000050.
Audience: **l,u,f.** B

Swann, Charles **PS1892.H5 S9 1991**
Nathaniel Hawthorne: Tradition and Revolution. Albert Gelpi & Ross Posnock (Contribution by). Trade Cloth. Cambridge University Press. New York, NY. 1991. 294p. Studies in American Literature and Culture, No. 52 ISBN:0-521-36552-X, ISBN13: 978-0-521-36552-9. Dewey:813/.3. LCCN:90-002688.
Audience: **u,f.** *Choice, 1992.*

19th Century > Howells, William Dean

Borus, Daniel H. **PS374.R37B67 1989**
Writing Realism: Howells, James, and Norris in the Mass Market. Trade Cloth. University of North Carolina Press. Chapel Hill, NC. 1989. xii, 260p. ISBN:0-8078-1869-0, ISBN13: 978-0-8078-1869-5. Dewey:813/.5/0912. LCCN:89-031157.
Audience: **u,f.** *Choice, 1990.*

Cady, Edwin H. & Cady, Norma W. **PS2034.C7 1983**
Critical Essays on W. D. Howells, 1866-1920. Trade Cloth. Thomson Gale. Farmington Hills, MI. 1983. xxxii, 267p. Critical Essays on American Literature Ser. ISBN:0-8161-8651-0, ISBN13: 978-0-8161-8651-8. Dewey:818/.409. LCCN:83-006089.
Audience: **g,l.** B

Goodman, Susan & Dawson, Carl **PS2033 .G66 2005**
William Dean Howells: A Writer's Life. Trade Cloth. University of California Press. Berkeley, CA. 2005. 520p. ISBN:0-520-23896-6, ISBN13: 978-0-520-23896-1. Dewey:813/.4 B. LCCN:2004-026562.
Audience: **g,l,u,f.** *Choice, 2005.*

Howells, William Dean **PS2124**
Novels, 1875-1886: A Foregone Conclusion; A Modern Instance; Indian Summer; The Rise of Silas Lapham. Edwin H. Cady (Editor). Trade Cloth. Library of America, The. New York, NY. 1982. 1217p. ISBN:0-940450-04-6, ISBN13: 978-0-940450-04-2. Dewey:813/.4. LCCN:82-000112.
Audience: **g,l,u,f.**

Howells, William Dean **PS2022 1989**
Howells Novels, 1886-1888: The Minister's Charge; April Hopes; Annie Kilburn. Don L. Cook (Editor). Trade Cloth. Library of America, The. New York, NY. 1989. 900p. ISBN:0-940450-51-8, ISBN13: 978-0-940450-51-6. Dewey:813/.4. LCCN:88-082728.
Audience: **g,l,u,f.**

Howells, William Dean **PS1331**
My Mark Twain: Reminiscences and Criticisms. Mark R. Godburn (Editor), Edwin H. Cady (Introduction by). Trade Cloth. Equator Books. Canaan, CT. 1991. 300p. ISBN:0-9628041-1-8, ISBN13: 978-0-9628041-1-3. Dewey:818/.409 B. LCCN:90-084577.
Audience: **l,u.** B

Howells, William Dean **PS1331**
W. D. Howells: Selected Criticism. David Nordloh (Editor). Trade Cloth. Indiana University Press. Bloomington, IN. 1993. 352p. A Selected Edition of W. D. Howells Ser. ISBN:0-253-32857-8, ISBN13: 978-0-253-32857-1. Dewey:818/.409 s. LCCN:91-007615.
Audience: **g,l,u.**

Lynn, Kenneth S. **PS2033.L9**
William Dean Howells: An American Life. Trade Cloth. National Intermedia. New Castle, PA. 1971. 372p. ISBN:0-15-142177-3, ISBN13: 978-0-15-142177-0. Dewey:818/.4/09. LCCN:71-142091.
Audience: **g,l,u,f.** B

Simpson, James W. (Editor) **Z1035.A1.H69 1983**
Editor's Study: A Comprehensive Edition of William Dean Howell's Column. Trade Cloth. Whitston Publishing Company, Inc. Albany, NY. 1983. 465p. ISBN:0-87875-213-7, ISBN13: 978-0-87875-213-3. Dewey:028/.1. LCCN:81-050049.
Audience: **g,l,u.** B

19th Century > Irving, Washington

Brodwin, Stanley (Editor) **PS2092**
The Old and New World Romanticism of Washington Irving. William L. Hedges (Introduction by). Trade Cloth. Greenwood Publishing Group, Inc. Portsmouth, NH. 1986. 201p. ISBN:0-313-25441-9, ISBN13: 978-0-313-25441-3. Dewey:818/.209. LCCN:86-003168.
Audience: **u,f.** *Choice, 1987.*

Hedges, William L. & Irving, Washington **PS2088 .H4 1980**
Washington Irving: An American Study, 1802-1832. Trade Cloth. Greenwood Publishing Group, Inc. Portsmouth, NH. 1980. 274p. Goucher College Ser. ISBN:0-313-21159-0, ISBN13: 978-0-313-21159-1. Dewey:818/.209. LCCN:80-023564.
Audience: **l,u,f.** B

Irving, Pierre M. **PS2081 .A3**
Life and Letters of Washington Irving, Set. Trade Cloth. New Library Press.Net. Murrieta, CA. ISBN:0-7950-2344-8, ISBN13: 978-0-7950-2344-6. Dewey:818/.2/08.
Audience: **g,l,u,f.**

Irving, Washington **PS2052 1991**
Bracebridge Hall, Tales of a Traveller and the Alhambra. Andrew B. Myers (Editor). Trade Cloth. Library of America, The. New York, NY. 1991. 1104p. Library of America, Vol. 52 ISBN:0-940450-59-3, ISBN13: 978-0-940450-59-2. Dewey:813/.2. LCCN:90-062267.
Audience: **g,l,u,f.**

Irving, Washington **F592.I74 2004**
Washington Irving: Three Western Narratives. James P. Ronda (Editor). Trade Cloth. Library of America, The. New York, NY. 2004. 1024p. The Library of America, Vol. 146 ISBN:1-931082-53-7, ISBN13: 978-1-931082-53-2. Dewey:978/.02. LCCN:2003-044202.
Audience: **g,l,u,f.**

Irving, Washington **PS2081**
The Complete Works of Washington Irving: Journals and Notebooks, 1807-1822. Lillian Schlissel & Walter A. Reichart (Editors). Trade Cloth. Thomson Gale. Farmington Hills, MI. 1981. Critical Editions Program Ser. ISBN:0-8057-8501-9, ISBN13: 978-0-8057-8501-2. Dewey:818/.2/03.
Audience: **g,l,u,f.**

Irving, Washington **PS2052 1983**
History, Tales and Sketches: The Sketch Book, A History of New York, Salmagundi, Letters of Jonathan Goldstyle, Gent. James W. Tuttleton (Editor). Trade Cloth. Library of America, The. New York, NY. 1983. 1144p. ISBN:0-940450-14-3, ISBN13: 978-0-940450-14-1. Dewey:818/.209. LCCN:83-005474.
Audience: **g,l,u,f.**

Roth, Martin **PS2088.R6**
Comedy and America: The Lost World of Washington Irving. Trade Cloth. Associated Faculty Press, Inc. New York, NY. 1976. xiv, 205p. Literary Criticism Ser. ISBN:0-8046-9132-0, ISBN13: 978-0-8046-9132-1. Dewey:818/.2/09. LCCN:76-006870.
Audience: **g.** B

Steele, Linda **PS2084.S74 2004**
The Image and Influence of the Oklahoma Prairie in Washington Irving's Tour of the West. Trade Cloth. Edwin Mellen Press, The. Lewiston, NY. 2004. 120p. ISBN:0-7734-6459-X, ISBN13: 978-0-7734-6459-9. Dewey:818/.203. LCCN:2004-044850.
Audience: **u,f.**

19th Century > J-K

Bush, Robert **PS2178**
Grace King: a southern destiny. Louisiana State University Press. 1983. ISBN:0-8071-1111-2, ISBN13: 978-0-8071-1111-6.
Audience: **l,u,f.**

Jacobs, Harriet A. **E444.J17 2001**
Incidents in the Life of a Slave Girl. Trade Paper. W. W. Norton & Company, Inc. New York, NY. 2000. 416p. Critical Editions Ser. ISBN:0-393-97637-8, ISBN13: 978-0-393-97637-3. Dewey:305.5/67/092 B. LCCN:00-056877.
Audience: **g,l,u,f.**

Kennedy, John Pendleton **PS2162.S93 1986**
Swallow barn, or A sojourn in the Old Dominion. Mackethan, Lucinda H., editor. Louisiana State University Press. 1986. ISBN:0-8071-1322-0, ISBN13: 978-0-8071-1322-6.
Audience: **l,u,f.**

King, Grace Eilzabeth **PS2176**
Grace King of New Orleans; a selection of her writings. Bush, Robert, editor. Louisiana State University Press. 1973. ISBN:0-8071-0055-2, ISBN13: 978-0-8071-0055-4.
Audience: **l,u,f.**

Kirkland, Caroline M. **PS2191.N4 1990**
A New Home, Who'll Follow? Sandra A. Zagarell (Editor). Cloth Text. Rutgers University Press. Piscataway, NJ. 1990. 250p. American Women Writers Ser. ISBN:0-8135-1541-6, ISBN13: 978-0-8135-1541-0. Dewey:813/.3. LCCN:89-070088.
Audience: **g,l,u,f.**

19th Century > James, Henry

Beidler, Peter G. **PS2116.T83B39 1989**
Ghosts, Demons and Henry James: The Turn of the Screw at the Turn of the Century. Cloth Text. University of Missouri Press. Columbia, MO. 1989. 272p. ISBN:0-8262-0684-0, ISBN13: 978-0-8262-0684-8. Dewey:813/.4. LCCN:88-039776.
Audience: **u,f.** *Choice, 1989.*

Bellringer, Alan W. **PS2124.B44 1988**
Henry James. Cloth Text. Palgrave Macmillan. New York, NY. 1988. 180p. Modern Novelists Ser. ISBN:0-312-02056-2, ISBN13: 978-0-312-02056-9. Dewey:813/.4. LCCN:88-004486.
Audience: **g,u,f.** *Choice, 1989.*

Bradley, John R. (Editor) **PS2127.H63H46 1999**
Henry James and Homo-Erotic Desire. Cloth over Boards. Palgrave Macmillan. New York, NY. 1999. 169p. ISBN:0-312-21764-1, ISBN13: 978-0-312-21764-8. Dewey:813/.4. LCCN:98-026153.
Audience: **u,f.** *Choice, 1999.*

Bradley, John R. (Editor) **PS2127.F55H46 2000**
Henry James on Stage and Screen. Cloth over Boards. Palgrave Macmillan. New York, NY. 2000. 278p. ISBN:0-333-79214-9, ISBN13: 978-0-333-79214-8. Dewey:813/.4. LCCN:00-055696.
Audience: **g,u,f.** *Choice, 2001.*

Freedman, Jonathan (Editor) **PS2124 .C23 1998**
The Cambridge Companion to Henry James. Trade Paper. Cambridge University Press. New York, NY. 1998. 277p. Companions to Literature Ser. ISBN:0-521-49924-0, ISBN13: 978-0-521-49924-8. Dewey:813/.4. LCCN:97-018118.
Audience: **g,l,u,f.** *Choice, 1998.*

Funston, Judith **Z8447.F85 1991**
Henry James: A Reference Guide. Trade Cloth. Macmillan Publishing Company, Inc. Old Tappan, NJ. 1991. 592p. Reference Guides to Literature Ser. ISBN:0-8161-8953-6, ISBN13: 978-0-8161-8953-3. Dewey:016.813/4. LCCN:90-048856.
Audience: **g,l,u,f.** *Choice, 1991.*

Gale, Robert L. **PS2122**
A Henry James Encyclopedia. Cloth Text. Greenwood Publishing Group, Inc. Portsmouth, NH. 1989. 812p. ISBN:0-313-25846-5, ISBN13: 978-0-313-25846-6. Dewey:813/.4. LCCN:88-021388.
Audience: **g,l,u,f.** *Choice, 1989.*

Griffin, Susan M. (Editor) **PS2127.F55H45 2001**
Henry James Goes to the Movies. Trade Cloth. University Press of Kentucky. Lexington, KY. 2001. 320p. ISBN:0-8131-2191-4, ISBN13: 978-0-8131-2191-8. Dewey:813/.4. LCCN:00-012274.
Audience: **u,f.** *Choice, 2002.*

Habegger, Alfred **PS2127.F44H33 1989**
Henry James and the 'Woman Business'. Trade Cloth. Cambridge University Press. New York, NY. 1989. 298p. Studies in American Literature and Culture, No. 32 ISBN:0-521-36635-6, ISBN13: 978-0-521-36635-9. Dewey:813/.4. LCCN:2005-278321.
Audience: **u,f.** *Choice, 1990.*

Harden, Edgar F. **PS2122**
A Henry James Chronology. Cloth over Boards. Palgrave Macmillan. New York, NY. 2005. 344p. Author Chronologies Ser. ISBN:1-4039-4229-3, ISBN13: 978-1-4039-4229-6. Dewey:813/.4 B. LCCN:2004-050892.
Audience: **u,f.** *Choice, 2005.*

Hayes, Kevin J. (Editor) **PS2124 .H463 1996**
Henry James: The Contemporary Reviews. M. Thomas Inge (Contribution by). Trade Cloth. Cambridge University Press. New York, NY. 1996. 503p. American Critical Archives Ser., No. 7 ISBN:0-521-45386-0, ISBN13: 978-0-521-45386-8. Dewey:813.4. LCCN:95-008077.
Audience: **u,f.** *Choice, 1997.*

Heller, Terry **PS2116.T83H38 1989**
The Turn of the Screw: Bewildered Vision. Trade Paper. Macmillan Publishing Company, Inc. Old Tappan, NJ. 1989. Masterwork Studies, No. 26 ISBN:0-8057-8123-4, ISBN13: 978-0-8057-8123-6. Dewey:813/.4. LCCN:88-007583.
Audience: **g,l.** *Choice, 1989.*

Hocks, Richard A. **PS2124.H56 1990**
Henry James: A Study of the Short Fiction. Trade Cloth. Macmillan Publishing Company, Inc. Old Tappan, NJ. 1990. 200p. Twayne's Studies in Short Fiction, No. 17 ISBN:0-8057-8328-8, ISBN13: 978-0-8057-8328-5. Dewey:813/.4. LCCN:90-034509.
Audience: **l,u,f.** *Choice, 1991.*

James, Henry **PS2112.A3 2003**
The Portable Henry James. John Auchard (Editor). Trade Paper. Penguin Group (USA) Inc. New York, NY. 2003. 640p. ISBN:0-14-243767-0, ISBN13: 978-0-14-243767-4. Dewey:813/.4. LCCN:2003-048739.
Audience: **g,l,u,f.** B

James, Henry **PS2116.P6 1995**
The Portrait of a Lady: An Authoritative Text, Henry James and the Novel, Reviews and Criticism. Ed. 2. Robert D. Bamberg (Editor). Trade Paper. W. W. Norton & Company, Inc. New York, NY. 1995. 796p. Critical Editions Ser. ISBN:0-393-96646-1, ISBN13: 978-0-393-96646-6. Dewey:813/.4. LCCN:94-036709.
Audience: **g,l,u,f.**

James, Henry **PS21122006**
Henry James: Novels, 1901-1902. Leo Bersani (Editor). Trade Cloth. Library of America, The. New York, NY. 2006. 736p. The Library of America, Vol. 162 ISBN:1-931082-88-X, ISBN13: 978-1-931082-88-4. Dewey:813/.4. LCCN:2005-049443.
Audience: **g,l,u,f.**

James, Henry **PS2116.W5 2002**
The Wings of the Dove: Authoritative Text, the Author and the Novel, Criticism. Ed. 2. Joseph Donald Crowley & Richard A. Hocks (Editors). Trade Paper. W. W. Norton & Company, Inc. New York, NY. 2002. 608p. A Norton Critical Edition Ser. ISBN:0-393-97881-8, ISBN13: 978-0-393-97881-0. Dewey:813/.4. LCCN:2002-075395.
Audience: **g,l,u,f.**

James, Henry **PS2112 1996**
Henry James - Complete Stories, 1898-1910, Vol. 2. Denis Donoghue (Editor). Trade Cloth. Library of America, The. New York, NY. 1996. 960p. Library of America, Vol. 83 ISBN:1-883011-10-8, ISBN13: 978-1-883011-10-9. LCCN:95-023462.
Audience: **g,l,u,f.**

James, Henry **PS2123**
Henry James: Autobiography. Frederick W. Dupee (Editor). Trade Cloth. Princeton University Press. Princeton, NJ. 1983. 640p. ISBN:0-691-06584-5, ISBN13: 978-0-691-06584-7. Dewey:813/.4. LCCN:83-060460.
Audience: **g,l,u,f.** B

James, Henry **PS2111.E4 1990**
The Complete Plays of Henry James. Leon Edel (Editor). Cloth Text. Oxford University Press, Inc. New York, NY. 1991. 872p. ISBN:0-19-504379-0, ISBN13: 978-0-19-504379-2. Dewey:812/.4. LCCN:90-006754.
Audience: **g,l,u,f.** B

James, Henry **PS2123**
The Letters of Henry James, 1843-1875, Vol. 1. Leon Edel (Editor). Trade Cloth. Harvard University Press. Cambridge, MA. 1974. 489p. Letters of Henry Adams, 1843-1875 Ser., Vol. 1 ISBN:0-674-38780-5, ISBN13: 978-0-674-38780-5. Dewey:813.4. LCCN:74-077181.
Audience: **u,f.** B

James, Henry **PS2123**
The Letters of Henry James, 1875-1883, Vol. 2. Leon Edel (Editor). Trade Cloth. Harvard University Press. Cambridge, MA. 1975. 456p. Letters of Henry Adams, 1875-1883 Ser., Vol. 2 ISBN:0-674-38781-3, ISBN13: 978-0-674-38781-2. Dewey:813/.4 B. LCCN:74-077181.
Audience: **u,f.**

James, Henry **PS2123**
The Letters of Henry James, 1883-1895, Vol. 3. Leon Edel (Editor). Trade Cloth. Harvard University Press. Cambridge, MA. 1980. 612p. ISBN:0-674-38782-1, ISBN13: 978-0-674-38782-9. Dewey:816/.4. LCCN:74-077181.
Audience: **u,f.**

James, Henry **PS2123**
The Letters of Henry James, 1895-1916, Vol. 4. Leon Edel (Editor). Trade Cloth. Harvard University Press. Cambridge, MA. 1984. 872p. Letters of Henry Adams, 1895-1916 Ser., Vol. 4 ISBN:0-674-38783-X, ISBN13: 978-0-674-38783-6. Dewey:813.4. LCCN:74-077181.
Audience: **u,f.**

James, Henry **PS2123.A3 1987**
The Complete Notebooks of Henry James. Leon Edel & Lyall H. Powers (Editors). Trade Cloth. Oxford University Press, Inc. New York, NY. 1986. 528p. ISBN:0-19-503782-0, ISBN13: 978-0-19-503782-1. Dewey:818/.403. LCCN:86-021680.
Audience: **g,l,u,f.** B *Choice, 1987.*

James, Henry **PN761.J242 1984**
Henry James: Literary Criticism: Essays, American and English Writers. Leon Edel & Mark Wilson (Editors). Trade Cloth. Library of America, The. New York, NY. 1984. 1504p. Library of America, Vol. 1 ISBN:0-940450-22-4, ISBN13: 978-0-940450-22-6. Dewey:809/.034. LCCN:91-058224.
Audience: **g,l,u,f.**

James, Henry **PN761.J242 1984**
James: Literary Criticism: European Writers and Prefaces to the New York Edition. Leon Edel & Mark Wilson (Editors). Trade Cloth. Library of America, The. New York, NY. 1984. 1442p. Library of America, Vol. 2 ISBN:0-940450-23-2, ISBN13: 978-0-940450-23-3. Dewey:809/.034. LCCN:91-058224.
Audience: **g,l,u,f.**

James, Henry **PS2112 1989**
Novels, 1886-1890: The Princess Casamassima; The Reverberator; The Tragic Muse. Daniel M. Fogel (Editor). Trade Cloth. Library of America, The. New York, NY. 1989. 1312p. ISBN:0-940450-56-9, ISBN13: 978-0-940450-56-1. Dewey:813/.4. LCCN:88-082724.
Audience: **g,l,u,f.**

James, Henry **PS3511.A86**
The Bostonians. R. D. Gooder (Editor, Introduction by, Notes by). Trade Paper. Oxford University Press, Inc. New York, NY. 1998. 512p. Oxford World's Classics Ser. ISBN:0-19-283442-8, ISBN13: 978-0-19-283442-3. Dewey:813/.52. LCCN:84-007884.
Audience: **g,l,u,f.**

James, Henry & Hollander, John **PS2112 1996**
Henry James - Complete Stories 1892-1898, Vol. I. David

Bromwich (Editor). Trade Cloth. Library of America, The. New York, NY. 1996. 958p. Library of America, Vol. 82 ISBN:1-883011-09-4, ISBN13: 978-1-883011-09-3. LCCN:95-023463.
Audience: **g,u,f.**

James, Henry **DA625.J37 1993**
Collected Travel Writings: Great Britain and America. Richard Howard (Editor). Trade Cloth. Library of America, The. New York, NY. 1993. 868p. Library of America, Vol. 64 ISBN:0-940450-76-3, ISBN13: 978-0-940450-76-9. Dewey:917.304. LCCN:93-009192.
Audience: **g,l,u,f.**

James, Henry **D919 .J295 1993**
Henry James Collected Travel Writings: The Continent: A Little Tour in France; Italian Hours; Other Travels. Richard Howard (Editor). Trade Cloth. Library of America, The. New York, NY. 1993. 868p. Library of America, Vol. 65 ISBN:0-940450-77-1, ISBN13: 978-0-940450-77-6. Dewey:818/.403. LCCN:93-009193.
Audience: **g,l,u,f.**

James, Henry **PS21122003**
Henry James: Novels, 1896-1899. Myra Jehlen (Editor). Trade Cloth. Library of America, The. New York, NY. 2003. 1035p. Library of America, Vol. 139 ISBN:1-931082-30-8, ISBN13: 978-1-931082-30-3. Dewey:813/.4. LCCN:2002-030167.
Audience: **g,l,u,f.**

James, Henry (Editor), et al. **PS2116.T8 1998**
The Turn of the Screw. Ed. 2. Robert Kimbrough, Deborah Esch & Jonathan M. Warren (Editors). Trade Paper. W. W. Norton & Company, Inc. New York, NY. 1999. 286p. Critical Editions Ser. ISBN:0-393-95904-X, ISBN13: 978-0-393-95904-8. Dewey:813/.4. LCCN:98-031635.
Audience: **g,l,u,f.**

James, Henry **PS2112 1984**
The Art of the Novel: Critical Prefaces. R. W. B. Lewis (Foreword by), Richard P. Blackmur (Introduction by). Trade Paper. Northeastern University Press. Boston, MA. 1984. 399p. ISBN:0-930350-60-X, ISBN13: 978-0-930350-60-4. Dewey:813/.4. LCCN:84-005619.
Audience: **g,l,u,f.** B

James, Henry **PN761 .J27 1979**
Literary Reviews and Essays on American, English and French Literature. Albert Mordell (Editor). Trade Paper. Grove/Atlantic, Inc. New York, NY. 1979. ISBN:0-394-17098-9, ISBN13: 978-0-394-17098-5. Dewey:809/.034. LCCN:79-009213.
Audience: **g,l,u,f.** B

James, Henry **PS2116.A5 1994**
The Ambassadors: An Authoritative Text, the Author on the Novel, Criticism. Ed. 2. S. P. Rosenbaum (Editor). Trade Paper. W. W. Norton & Company, Inc. New York, NY. 1994. 558p. Critical Editions Ser. ISBN:0-393-96314-4, ISBN13: 978-0-393-96314-4. Dewey:813.4. LCCN:93-024724.
Audience: **g,l,u,f.** B

James, Henry **PS2116**
The Golden Bowl. Virginia Llewellyn Smith (Editor). Trade Paper. Oxford University Press, Inc. New York, NY. 1999. 640p. Oxford World's Classics Ser. ISBN:0-19-283542-4, ISBN13: 978-0-19-283542-0. Dewey:813/.4.
Audience: **g,l,u,f.**

James, Henry **PS2124**
Novels, 1871-1880: Watch and Ward; Roderick Hudson; The American; The Europeans; Confidence. William T. Stafford (Editor). Trade Cloth. Library of America, The. New York, NY. 1983. 1312p. ISBN:0-940450-13-5, ISBN13: 978-0-940450-13-4. Dewey:813/.4. LCCN:83-005475.
Audience: **g,l,u,f.**

James, Henry **PS2112 1985**
Novels, 1881-1886: Washington Square; The Portrait of a Lady; The Bostonians. William T. Stafford (Editor). Trade Cloth. Library of America, The. New York, NY. 1985. 1262p. ISBN:0-940450-30-5, ISBN13: 978-0-940450-30-1. Dewey:813/.4. LCCN:85-005207.
Audience: **g,l,u,f.**

James, Henry **PS2112.1999C**
Henry James: Complete Stories 1864-1874. Jean Strouse (Editor). Trade Cloth. Library of America, The. New York, NY. 1999. 975p. Library of America, Vol. 111 ISBN:1-883011-70-1, ISBN13: 978-1-883011-70-3. Dewey:813/.4. LCCN:98-053919.
Audience: **g,l,u,f.**

James, Henry **PS2124**
The American. James W. Tuttleton (Editor). Paper Text. W. W. Norton & Company, Inc. New York, NY. 1978. 496p. Critical Editions Ser. ISBN:0-393-09091-4, ISBN13: 978-0-393-09091-8. Dewey:813/.4.
Audience: **g,l,u,f.** B

James, Henry **PS2112 1999**
Henry James: Complete Stories, 1874-1884. William L. Vance (Editor). Trade Cloth. Library of America, The. New York, NY. 1999. 924p. Library of America, Vol. 106 ISBN:1-883011-63-9, ISBN13: 978-1-883011-63-5. Dewey:813/.4. LCCN:98-019252.
Audience: **g,l,u,f.**

Macnaughton, William R. **PS2124.M267 1987**
Henry James: The Later Novels. Trade Cloth. Macmillan Publishing Company, Inc. Old Tappan, NJ. 1987. 200p. United States Authors Ser., No. 521 ISBN:0-8057-7505-6, ISBN13: 978-0-8057-7505-1. Dewey:813/.4. LCCN:87-015030.
Audience: **u,f.** *Choice, 1988.*

Marshall, Adre **PS2127.P8M37 1998**
The Turn of the Mind: Constituting Consciousness in Henry James. Trade Cloth. Fairleigh Dickinson University Press. Cranbury, NJ. 1998. 280p. ISBN:0-8386-3695-0, ISBN13: 978-0-8386-3695-4. Dewey:813/.4. LCCN:97-018972.
Audience: **u,f.** *Choice, 1998.*

Martin, Walter R. & Ober, Warren **PS2124.M295 1994**
Henry James' Apprenticeship: The Tales, 1864-1882. Cloth Text. P. D. Meany Publishers. Lombard, IL. 1993. 240p. ISBN:0-88835-034-1, ISBN13: 978-0-88835-034-3. Dewey:813/.4. LCCN:95-224612.
Audience: **u,f.** *Choice, 1994.*

Rowe, John C. **PS2127.P6R69 1998**
The Other Henry James. Trade Cloth. Duke University Press. Durham, NC. 1998. 240p. New Americanists Ser. ISBN:0-8223-2128-9, ISBN13: 978-0-8223-2128-6. Dewey:813/.4. LCCN:98-018977.
Audience: **u,f.** *Choice, 1999.*

Seymour, Miranda **PS2123.S48 1989**
A Ring of Conspirators: Henry James and His Literary Circle, 1895-1915. Trade Cloth. Houghton Mifflin Company. New York, NY. 1989. 352p. ISBN:0-395-51173-9, ISBN13: 978-0-395-51173-2. Dewey:813/.4. LCCN:89-001686.
Audience: **u,f.** *Choice, 1990.*

Tintner, Adeline R. **PS2127.L5T55 1991**
The Cosmopolitan World of Henry James: An Intertextual Study. Cloth Text. Louisiana State University Press. Baton Rouge, LA. 1991. 352p. ISBN:0-8071-1663-7, ISBN13: 978-0-8071-1663-0. Dewey:813/.4. LCCN:91-002026.
Audience: **u,f.** *Choice, 1992.*

Tintner, Adeline R. **PS2127.L5T56**
The Pop World of Henry James: From Fairy Tales to Science Fiction. A. Walton Litz (Editor), Leon Edel (Foreword by). Trade Paper. Books on Demand. Ann Arbor, MI. 1989. 343p. Studies in Modern Literature, Vol. 89 ISBN:0-8357-1855-7, ISBN13: 978-0-8357-1855-4. Dewey:813/.4. LCCN:88-027725.
Audience: **u,f.** *Choice, 1989.*

19th Century > Jewett, Sarah Orne

Blanchard, Paula **PS2133**
Sarah Orne Jewett: Her World and Her Work. Trade Paper. Basic Books. New York, NY. 2002. 416p. ISBN:0-7382-0832-9, ISBN13: 978-0-7382-0832-9. Dewey:813/.4 B.
Audience: **g,l,u,f.**

Borus, Daniel H. **PS374.R37B67 1989**
Writing Realism: Howells, James, and Norris in the Mass Market. Trade Cloth. University of North Carolina Press. Chapel Hill, NC. 1989. xii, 260p. ISBN:0-8078-1869-0, ISBN13: 978-0-8078-1869-5. Dewey:813/.5/0912. LCCN:89-031157.
Audience: **u,f.** *Choice, 1990.*

Gale, Robert L. **PS2133**
A Sarah Orne Jewett Companion. Cloth Text. Greenwood Publishing Group, Inc. Portsmouth, NH. 1999. 368p. ISBN:0-313-30757-1, ISBN13: 978-0-313-30757-7. Dewey:813/.4 B. LCCN:98-046814.
Audience: **g,l,u,f.** *Choice, 2000.*

Howard, June (Editor) **PS2132.C643 N48 1994**
New Essays on the Country of the Pointed Firs. Emory Elliot (Contribution by). Cloth Text. Cambridge University Press. New York, NY. 1994. 132p. The American Novel Ser. ISBN:0-521-41574-8, ISBN13: 978-0-521-41574-3. Dewey:813.4. LCCN:93-033810.
Audience: **u,f.** *Choice, 1995.*

Jewett, Sarah Orne **PS2131 1999**
The Complete Poems of Sarah Orne Jewett. Ironweed Press Inc. 1999. ISBN:0-9655309-3-0, ISBN13: 978-0-9655309-3-4.
Audience: **l,u,f.**

Jewett, Sarah Orne **PS2132.C64 1997b**
The Country of Pointed Firs and Other Stories: Centennial Edition. Sherman, Sarah W., editor. University of New England Press. 1997. ISBN:0-87451-826-1, ISBN13: 978-0-87451-826-9.
Audience: **l,u,f.**

Jewett, Sarah Orne **PS2131 1994**
Novels and Stories: Deephaven; A Country Doctor; The Country of the Pointed Firs; Dunnet Landing Stories; Selected Stories and Sketches. Michael D. Bell (Editor). Trade Cloth. Library of America, The. New York, NY. 1994. 950p. Library of America, Vol. 69 ISBN:0-940450-74-7, ISBN13: 978-0-940450-74-5. Dewey:813/.4. LCCN:93-024167.
Audience: **g,l,u,f.**

Mobley, Marilyn Sanders **PS374.W6 M63 1994**
Folk Roots and Mythic Wings in Sarah Orne Jewett and Toni Morrison: The Cultural Function of Narrative. Trade Paper. Louisiana State University Press. Baton Rouge, LA. 1994. 193p. ISBN:0-8071-1964-4, ISBN13: 978-0-8071-1964-8. Dewey:813.0099287. LCCN:91-015031.
Audience: **u,f.**

Sherman, Sarah W. **PS2133.S54 1989**
Sarah Orne Jewett, an American Persephone. Trade Cloth. University Press of New England. Lebanon, NH. 1989. 347p. ISBN:0-87451-477-0, ISBN13: 978-0-87451-477-3. Dewey:813/.4. LCCN:88-040353.
Audience: **l,u,f.** *Choice, 1990.*

Silverthorne, Elizabeth **PS2133.S56 1993**
Sarah Orne Jewett: A Writer's Life. Trade Cloth. Overlook Press, The. New York, NY. 1993. 238p. ISBN:0-87951-484-1, ISBN13: 978-0-87951-484-6. Dewey:813/.4. LCCN:92-024589.
Audience: **g,l,u,f.** *Choice, 1993.*

19th Century > L-M

Miles, Emma B. **F217.A65**
Spirit of the Mountains. Roger D. Abrahams (Foreword by), David E. Whisnant (Introduction by). Trade Paper. University of Tennessee Press. Knoxville, TN. 1975. 250p. Tennesseana Editions Ser. ISBN:0-87049-465-1, ISBN13: 978-0-87049-465-9. Dewey:975. LCCN:75-019222.
Audience: **u,f.**

Mitchell, Silas Weir **PZ3.M695 Hu20 PS2414**
Hugh Wynne, Free Quaker; Sometime Brevet Lieutenant-Colonel on the Staff of His Excellency General Washington. Scholarly Press. 1968.
Audience: **l,u,f.**

Murfree, Mary N. **PZ3.M943 IT7 PS2454**
In the Tennessee Mountains. Library Binding. Reprint Services Company. Temecula, CA. 1999. Notable American Authors Ser. ISBN:0-7812-4591-5, ISBN13: 978-0-7812-4591-3. Dewey:813/.4.
Audience: **g,l,u,f.**

Murfree, Mary N. **PS2454**
The Prophet of the Great Smoky Mountains. Library Binding. Reprint Services Company. Temecula, CA. 1999. Notable American Authors Ser. ISBN:0-7812-4594-X, ISBN13: 978-0-7812-4594-4. Dewey:813.4.
Audience: **g,l,u,f.**

19th Century > Lanier, Sidney

De Bellis, Jack (Editor) **Z1227.D4**
Sidney Lanier, Henry Timrod and Paul Hamilton Hayne: A Reference Guide. Trade Cloth. Macmillan Publishing Company, Inc. Old Tappan, NJ. 1978. v, 213p. ISBN:0-8161-7967-0, ISBN13: 978-0-8161-7967-1. Dewey:016.811/4/09. LCCN:77-017203.
Audience: **u,f.**

Gabin, Jane S. **PS2213.G24 1985**
A Living Minstrelsy: The Poetry and Music of Sidney Lanier. Cloth Text. Mercer University Press. Macon, GA. 1985. viii, 182p. ISBN:0-86554-155-8, ISBN13: 978-0-86554-155-9. Dewey:811/.4 B. LCCN:85-005015.
Audience: **u,f.** *Choice, 1985.*

Lanier, Sidney **PS2202**
Poems and Letters. Library Binding. Reprint Services Company. Temecula, CA. 1995. 227p. American Autobiography Ser. ISBN:0-7812-8574-7, ISBN13: 978-0-7812-8574-2. Dewey:811/.4.
Audience: **g,l,u,f.**

Lanier, Sidney **PS2205.A2L35 1999**
Poems of Sidney Lanier. Mary D. Lanier (Afterword by). Trade Cloth. University of Georgia Press. Athens, GA. 1981. xli, 272p. ISBN:0-8203-0560-X, ISBN13: 978-0-8203-0560-8. Dewey:811/.4. LCCN:00-265133.
Audience: **g,l,u,f.**

Mims, Edwin **PS2213**
Sidney Lanier. Trade Cloth. Gordon Press Publishers. New York, NY. 1972. ISBN:0-8490-1052-7, ISBN13: 978-0-8490-1052-1. Dewey:818.4.
Audience: **l,u,f.**

19th Century > Longfellow, Henry Wadsworth

Calhoun, Charles C. **PS2281.C25 2004**
Longfellow: A Rediscovered Life. Trade Cloth. Beacon Press. Boston, MA. 2004. 304p. ISBN:0-8070-7026-2, ISBN13: 978-0-8070-7026-0. Dewey:811/.3 B. LCCN:2003-025980.
Audience: **g,l,u,f.** *Choice, 2005.*

Longfellow, Henry Wadsworth **PS22532000**
Henry Wadsworth Longfellow: Poems and Other Writings. J. D. McClatchy (Editor). Trade Cloth. Library of America, The. New York, NY. 2000. 825p. Library of America, Vol. 118 ISBN:1-883011-85-X, ISBN13: 978-1-883011-85-7. Dewey:811/.3. LCCN:00-026678.
Audience: **g,l,u,f.**

Wagenknecht, Edward **PS2288.W27 1986**
Henry Wadsworth Longfellow: His Poetry and Prose. Frederick Ungar. 1986. ISBN:0-8044-2960-X, ISBN13: 978-0-8044-2960-3.
Audience: **u,f.**

19th Century > Lowell, James Russell

Howard, Leon **PS2331.H6 1971**
Victorian Knight-Errant: A Study of the Early Literary Career of James Russell Lowell. Trade Cloth. Greenwood Publishing Group, Inc. Portsmouth, NH. 1971. 398p. ISBN:0-8371-5222-4, ISBN13: 978-0-8371-5222-6. Dewey:811/.3. LCCN:72-136072.
Audience: **u,f.**

Lowell, James Russell **PS2331.A3 N6**
Letters of James R. Lowell. Library Binding. Folcroft Library Editions. Folcroft, PA. 1984. ISBN:0-8414-5895-2, ISBN13: 978-0-8414-5895-6. Dewey:811/.3 B.
Audience: **g,l,u,f.**

Lowell, James Russell **PS2305 .A1 1978**
The Poetical Works of James Russell Lowell. Marjorie Kaufman (Revised by). Trade Cloth. Houghton Mifflin Company. New York, NY. 1978. 512p. Cambridge Editions Ser. ISBN:0-395-25726-3, ISBN13: 978-0-395-25726-5. Dewey:811/.3. LCCN:77-017274.
Audience: **g,l,u,f.**

Wagenknecht, Edward C. **PS2331 .W3**
James Russell Lowell: Portrait of a Many-Sided Man. Trade Cloth. Oxford University Press, Inc. New York, NY. 1971. 286p. Portraits of American Writers Ser. ISBN:0-19-501376-X, ISBN13: 978-0-19-501376-4. Dewey:811/.3 B.
Audience: **l,u,f.**

19th Century > Melville, Herman

Bickman, Martin **PS2384.M62A66 1985**
Approaches to Teaching Melville's Moby Dick. Trade Cloth. Modern Language Association of America. New York, NY. 1985. x, 157p. Approaches to Teaching World Literature Ser., No. 8 ISBN:0-87352-489-6, ISBN13: 978-0-87352-489-6. Dewey:813/.3. LCCN:85-004892.
Audience: **u,f.**

Branch, Watson G. (Editor) **PS2387**
Melville: The Critical Heritage. Trade Cloth. Routledge. New York, NY. 1985. xix, 444p. The Critical Heritage Ser. ISBN:0-7100-7774-2, ISBN13: 978-0-7100-7774-5. Dewey:813/.3. LCCN:73-086570.
Audience: **l,u,f.**

Brodhead, Richard H. **PS1888**
Hawthorne, Melville and the Novel. Trade Cloth. University of Chicago Press. Chicago, IL. 1976. viii, 216p. ISBN:0-226-07522-2, ISBN13: 978-0-226-07522-8. Dewey:813/.3/09. LCCN:75-005071.
Audience: **g,l,u.**

Gale, Robert L. **PS2386**
A Herman Melville Encyclopedia. Cloth Text. Greenwood Publishing Group, Inc. Portsmouth, NH. 1995. 560p. ISBN:0-313-29011-3, ISBN13: 978-0-313-29011-4. Dewey:813/.3. LCCN:94-029837.
Audience: **g,l,u,f.** *Choice, 1995.*

Gilmore, M. (Editor) **PS2384.M62**
Twentieth Century Interpretations of Moby Dick. Trade Cloth. Prentice-Hall. Upper Saddle, NJ. 1977. iv, 123p. ISBN:0-13-586057-1, ISBN13: 978-0-13-586057-1. Dewey:813/.3. LCCN:76-044426.
Audience: **g,l.**

Grenberg, Bruce L. **PS2388.Q5G7 1989**
Some Other World to Find: Quest and Negation in the Works of Herman Melville. Trade Cloth. University of Illinois Press. Champaign, IL. 1989. 248p. ISBN:0-252-01625-4, ISBN13: 978-0-252-01625-7. Dewey:813/.3. LCCN:88-038843.
Audience: **u,f.** *Choice, 1990.*

Gunn, Giles **PS2386.H54 2005**
A Historical Guide to Herman Melville. Trade Cloth. Oxford University Press, Inc. New York, NY. 2005. 272p. Historical Guides to American Authors Ser. ISBN:0-19-514281-0, ISBN13: 978-0-19-514281-5. Dewey:813/.3. LCCN:2004-063564.
Audience: **l,u.**

Kier, Kathleen E. (Compiled by) **PS2386 .A235 1994**
A Melville Encyclopedia: The Novels. Ed. 2. Trade Cloth. Whitston Publishing Company, Inc. Albany, NY. 1994. 1242p. ISBN:0-87875-453-9, ISBN13: 978-0-87875-453-3. Dewey:813/.3. LCCN:90-070385.
Audience: **l,u.** *Choice, 1991.*

Kirby, David **PS2386.K57 1993**
Herman Melville. Trade Cloth. Continuum International Publishing Group, Ltd. London, 1993. 192p. ISBN:0-8264-0608-4, ISBN13: 978-0-8264-0608-8. Dewey:813/.3. LCCN:93-012946.
Audience: **l,u.** *Choice, 1994.*

Martin, Terry J. **PS374.S5M38 1998**
Rhetorical Deception in the Short Fiction of Hawthorne, Poe and Melville. Trade Cloth. Edwin Mellen Press, The. Lewiston, NY. 1998. 120p. Studies in Comparative Literature Ser., Vol. 23 ISBN:0-7734-8240-7, ISBN13: 978-0-7734-8240-1. Dewey:813/.010903. LCCN:98-039987.
Audience: **u,f.**

McCall, Dan **PS2384.B28M3 1989**
The Silence of Bartleby. Book, Other. Cornell University Press. Ithaca, NY. 1989. 240p. ISBN:0-8014-2320-1, ISBN13: 978-0-8014-2320-8. Dewey:813/.3. LCCN:89-000627.
Audience: **u,f.** *Choice, 1990.*

Melville, Herman **PS2380.F68**
The Writings. Northwestern University Press. 1968.
Audience: **u,f.**

Melville, Herman **PS2382 1984**
Pierre, Israel Potter, the Confidence-Man, the Piazza Tale. Harrison Hayford (Editor). Trade Cloth. Library of America, The. New York, NY. 1985. 1478p. ISBN:0-940450-24-0, ISBN13: 978-0-940450-24-0. Dewey:813/.3. LCCN:84-011259.
Audience: **g,l,u,f.**

Melville, Herman **PS2384**
Redburn, White-Jacket, Moby-Dick. Thomas G. Tanselle (Editor). Trade Cloth. Library of America, The. New York, NY. 1983. 1436p. ISBN:0-940450-09-7, ISBN13: 978-0-940450-09-7. Dewey:813/.3. LCCN:82-018677.
Audience: **g,l,u,f.**

Melville, Herman **PS2384**
Typee, Omoo, Mardi. Thomas G. Tanselle (Editor). Trade Cloth. Library of America, The. New York, NY. 1982. 1333p. ISBN:0-940450-00-3, ISBN13: 978-0-940450-00-4. Dewey:813/.3. LCCN:81-018600.
Audience: **g,l,u,f.**

Melville, Herman **PS23822000**
Herman Melville: Moby-Dick, Billy Budd and Other Writings. Thomas G. Tanselle, Harrison Hayford & John Hollander (Editors). Trade Cloth. Library of America, The. New York, NY. 2000. 996p. Library of America College Editions ISBN:1-883011-89-2, ISBN13: 978-1-883011-89-5. Dewey:813/.3. LCCN:99-057965.
Audience: **g,l,u,f.**

Milder, Robert **PS2384.B7C75 1989**
Critical Essays on Melville's "Billy Budd". Trade Cloth. Thomson Gale. Farmington Hills, MI. 1989. 264p. Critical Essays on American Literature Ser. ISBN:0-8161-8889-0, ISBN13: 978-0-8161-8889-5. Dewey:813/.3. LCCN:88-035784.
Audience: **l,u.** *Choice, 1989.*

Parker, Hershel **PS2386.P37 1996**
Herman Melville: A Biography, 1819-1851. Trade Cloth. Johns Hopkins University Press. Baltimore, MD. 1996. 928p. ISBN:0-8018-5428-8, ISBN13: 978-0-8018-5428-6. Dewey:813.3. LCCN:96-018984.
Audience: **g,l,u,f.**

Parker, Hershel **PS2386.P37 1996**
Herman Melville: A Biography, 1851-1891. Trade Cloth. Johns Hopkins University Press. Baltimore, MD. 2002. 1056p. ISBN:0-8018-6892-0, ISBN13: 978-0-8018-6892-4. Dewey:813.3. LCCN:96-018984.
Audience: **g,l,u,f.** *Choice, 2003.*

Parker, Hershel **PS2384.B7P37 1990**
Reading Billy Budd. Trade Cloth. Northwestern University Press. Evanston, IL. 1990. 190p. ISBN:0-8101-0961-1, ISBN13: 978-0-8101-0961-2. Dewey:813/.3. LCCN:90-021487.
Audience: **u,f.** *Choice, 1991.*

Robertson-Lorant, Laurie **PS2386.R635 1996**
Melville. Trade Cloth. Crown Publishing Group. New York, NY. 1996. 928p. ISBN:0-517-59314-9, ISBN13: 978-0-517-59314-1. Dewey:813/.3 B. LCCN:95-004303.
Audience: **g,l,u.** *Choice, 1996.*

Rollyson, Carl & Paddock, Lisa **PS2386.A24 2001**
Herman Melville A to Z: The Essential Reference to His Life and Work. Trade Cloth. Facts On File, Inc. New York, NY. 2000. 288p. Facts on File Ser. ISBN:0-8160-3851-1, ISBN13: 978-0-8160-3851-0. Dewey:813/.3 B. LCCN:00-035338.
Audience: **g,l,u.** *Choice, 2001.*

Sten, Christopher **PS2388.T4S74 1996**
The Weaver-God, He Weaves: Melville and the Poetics of the Novel. Trade Cloth. Kent State University Press. Kent, OH. 1996. 376p. ISBN:0-87338-537-3, ISBN13: 978-0-87338-537-4. Dewey:813/.3. LCCN:95-037382.
Audience: **u,f.** *Choice, 1996.*

Wenke, John **PS2388.A35W46 1995**
Melville's Muse: Literary Creation and the Forms of Philosophical Fiction. Trade Cloth. Kent State University Press. Kent, OH. 1996. 272p. ISBN:0-87338-527-6, ISBN13: 978-0-87338-527-5. Dewey:813/.3. LCCN:95-003560.
Audience: **u,f.** *Choice, 1996.*

Williams, John B. **PS2388.P5W5 1991**
White Fire: The Influence of Emerson on Melville. Trade Cloth. National Film Network LLC. Lanham, MD. 1991. 208p. ISBN:1-878981-02-1, ISBN13: 978-1-878981-02-8. Dewey:813/.3. LCCN:90-028923.
Audience: **u,f.** *Choice, 1992.*

Yannella, Donald (Editor) **PS2384.B7 N49 2002**
New Essays on Billy Budd. Emory Elliot (Contribution by). Cloth Text. Cambridge University Press. New York, NY. 2002. 166p. The American Novel Ser. ISBN:0-521-41778-3, ISBN13: 978-0-521-41778-5. Dewey:813.3. LCCN:2001-052855.
Audience: **u,f.**

19th Century > N-R

Charvat, William & Kraus, Michael **PS2656 .A4**
William Hickling Prescott: Representative Selections with Introduction, Bibliography and Notes. Library Binding. Arden Library. Darby, PA. 1983. 466p. ISBN:0-8495-0962-9, ISBN13: 978-0-8495-0962-9. Dewey:810.81.
Audience: **g,l,u,f.**

Littlefield, Daniel F., Jr. **PS2649.P55Z76 1992**
Alex Posey: Creek Poet, Journalist, and Humorist. University of Nebraska Press. 1992. ISBN:0-8032-2899-6, ISBN13: 978-0-8032-2899-3.
Audience: **l,u,f.**

Page, Thomas Nelson **PS2514 .I6**
In Ole Virginia: Or, Marse Chan and Other Stories. Paper Text. Irvington Publishers. New York, NY. 1986. 230p. Americans in Fiction Ser. ISBN:0-8290-1864-6, ISBN13: 978-0-8290-1864-6. Dewey:813/.4.
Audience: **g,l,u,f.**

Parins, James W. **E99.C5R547 1991**
John Rollin Ridge: His Life and Works. Trade Cloth. University of Nebraska Press. Lincoln, NE. 2003. 260p. American Indian Lives Ser. ISBN:0-8032-3683-2, ISBN13: 978-0-8032-3683-7. Dewey:973/.0497502 B. LCCN:90-040464.
Audience: **u,f.** *Choice, 1991.*

Posey, Alexander Lawrence **PS2649.P55 1969**
Poems of Alexander Lawrence Posey, Creek Indian Bard. Hoffman Printing Company. 1969.
Audience: **l,u,f.**

Posey, Alexander **PS2649.P55.F87 1993**
The Fus Fixico Letters. Daniel F. Littlefield Jr. & Carol A. Petty Hunter (Editors), A. LaVonne Brown Ruoff (Foreword by). Trade Cloth. University of Nebraska Press. Lincoln, NE. 1993. 330p. ISBN:0-8032-3704-9, ISBN13: 978-0-8032-3704-9. Dewey:811.4. LCCN:92-046061.
Audience: **g,l,u,f.** *Choice, 1994.*

Ridge, John Rollins **PZ3.R4359 LI**
Joaquin Murieta: The Life and Adventures of Joaquin Murieta, the Celebrated California Bandit. Paul Reilly (Editor), Yellow Bird (As told by). Perfect. Poitin. Grass Valley, CA. 2003. 152p. ISBN:1-59108-000-2, ISBN13: 978-1-59108-000-8. Dewey:813.3.
Audience: **g,l,u,f.**

19th Century > Norris, Frank

Borus, Daniel H. **PS374.R37B67 1989**
Writing Realism: Howells, James, and Norris in the Mass Market. Trade Cloth. University of North Carolina Press. Chapel Hill, NC. 1989. xii, 260p. ISBN:0-8078-1869-0, ISBN13: 978-0-8078-1869-5. Dewey:813/.5/0912. LCCN:89-031157.
Audience: **u,f.** *Choice, 1990.*

French, Warren **PS2473 .F7**
Frank Norris. Trade Paper. N C U P, Inc. Albany, NY. 1962. Twayne's United States Authors Ser. ISBN:0-8084-0134-3, ISBN13: 978-0-8084-0134-6. Dewey:813.4.
Audience: **g,l,u,f.**

Graham, Don **PS2473.C7**
Critical Essays on Frank Norris. Library Binding. Thomson Gale. Farmington Hills, MI. 1980. li, 231 p. ;p. ISBN:0-8161-8307-4, ISBN13: 978-0-8161-8307-4. Dewey:813/.4. LCCN:80-021426.
Audience: **u,f.** B

Hochman, Barbara **PS2473.H6 1988**
The Art of Frank Norris, Storyteller. Cloth Text. University of Missouri Press. Columbia, MO. 1988. 160p. ISBN:0-8262-0663-8, ISBN13: 978-0-8262-0663-3. Dewey:813/.4. LCCN:87-019201.
Audience: **u,f.** *Choice, 1989.*

McElrath, J. **PS2473 .M34 1992**
Frank Norris Revisited. Trade Cloth. Macmillan Publishing Company, Inc. Old Tappan, NJ. 1992. 150p. Twayne's United States Authors Ser., Vol. 610 ISBN:0-8057-3965-3, ISBN13: 978-0-8057-3965-7. Dewey:813/.4. LCCN:92-004769.
Audience: **l,u,f.**

McElrath, Joseph R. Jr. & Crisler, Jesse S. **PS2473.M339 2005**
Frank Norris: A Life. Trade Cloth. University of Illinois Press. Champaign, IL. 2005. 520p. ISBN:0-252-03016-8, ISBN13: 978-0-252-03016-1. Dewey:813/.4 B. LCCN:2005-007105.
Audience: **g,l,u,f.** *Choice, 2006.*

Norris, Frank **PS2471 1986**
Novels and Essays: Vandover and the Brute; McTeague; The Octopus; Essays. Donald Pizer (Editor). Trade Cloth. Library of America, The. New York, NY. 1986. 1232p. Library of America, Vol. 33 ISBN:0-940450-40-2, ISBN13: 978-0-940450-40-0. Dewey:813/.4. LCCN:85-023133.
Audience: **g,l,u,f.**

Pizer, Donald **PS2473 .P5 1973**
The Novels of Frank Norris. Library Binding. M. S. G. Haskell House. Brooklyn, NY. 1972. Studies in Fiction, No. 34 ISBN:0-8383-1666-2, ISBN13: 978-0-8383-1666-5. Dewey:813/.4. LCCN:72-006785.
Audience: **u,f.** B

19th Century > Poe, Edgar Allen

Frank, Frederick S. & Magistrale, Anthony S. **PS2630**
The Poe Encyclopedia. Cloth Text. Greenwood Publishing Group, Inc. Portsmouth, NH. 1997. 480p. ISBN:0-313-27768-0, ISBN13: 978-0-313-27768-9. Dewey:818/.309. LCCN:96-022005.
Audience: **g,l,u,f.** *Choice, 1997.*

Hayes, Kevin J. (Editor) **PS2638 .C33 2002**
The Cambridge Companion to Edgar Allan Poe. Cloth Text. Cambridge University Press. New York, NY. 2002. 286p. Cambridge Companions to Literature Ser. ISBN:0-521-79326-2, ISBN13: 978-0-521-79326-1. Dewey:818.309 B. LCCN:2001-043972.
Audience: **g,l,u,f.** *Choice, 2003.*

Kennedy, J. Gerald & Weissberg, Liliane (Editors) **PS2642.R25R66 2001**
Romancing the Shadow: Poe and Race. Trade Cloth. Oxford University Press, Inc. New York, NY. 2001. 310p. ISBN:0-19-513710-8, ISBN13: 978-0-19-513710-1. Dewey:818/.309. LCCN:00-031365.
Audience: **u,f.** *Choice, 2001.*

Martin, Terry J. **PS374.S5M38 1998**
Rhetorical Deception in the Short Fiction of Hawthorne, Poe and Melville. Trade Cloth. Edwin Mellen Press, The. Lewiston, NY. 1998. 120p. Studies in Comparative Literature Ser., Vol. 23 ISBN:0-7734-8240-7, ISBN13: 978-0-7734-8240-1. Dewey:813/.010903. LCCN:98-039987.
Audience: **u,f.**

May, Charles E. **PS2642.F43M39 1991**
Edgar Allan Poe: A Study of the Short Fiction. Trade Cloth. Macmillan Publishing Company, Inc. Old Tappan, NJ. 1991. 192p. Twayne's Studies in Short Fiction, No. 28 ISBN:0-8057-8337-7, ISBN13: 978-0-8057-8337-7. Dewey:813/.3. LCCN:91-012225.
Audience: **l,u,f.** *Choice, 1992.*

Peeples, Scott **PS2638.P436 2003**
The Afterlife of Edgar Allan Poe. Trade Cloth. Camden House. Elizabethtown, NY. 2003. 216p. Studies in American Literature and Culture ISBN:1-57113-218-X, ISBN13: 978-1-57113-218-5. Dewey:818/.309. LCCN:2003-017325.
Audience: **u,f.** *Choice, 2004.*

Poe, Edgar Allan **PS2605.A1 2003**
Edgar Allan Poe: Poems and Poetics. Trade Cloth. Library of America, The. New York, NY. 2003. 200p. American Poets Project Ser. ISBN:1-931082-51-0, ISBN13: 978-1-931082-51-8. Dewey:811/.3. LCCN:2003-046637.
Audience: **g,l,u,f.**

Poe, Edgar Allan **PS2631 .A33 1966**
Letters of Edgar Allan Poe, Set. John Ostrom (Editor). Trade Cloth. Gordian Press, Inc. Staten Island, NY. 1966. 731p. ISBN:0-87752-085-2, ISBN13: 978-0-87752-085-6. Dewey:816.3. LCCN:66-020025.
Audience: **g,l,u,f.**

Poe, Edgar Allan **PS2631**
Poetry and Tales. Patrick F. Quinn (Editor). Trade Cloth. Library of America, The. New York, NY. 1984. 1408p. Library of America ISBN:0-940450-18-6, ISBN13: 978-0-940450-18-9. Dewey:818/.309. LCCN:83-019931.
Audience: **g,l,u,f.**

Poe, Edgar Allan **PS3048**
Essays and Reviews. G. R. Thompson (Editor). Trade Cloth. Library of America, The. New York, NY. 1984. 1544p. Library of America ISBN:0-940450-19-4, ISBN13: 978-0-940450-19-6. Dewey:818/.308. LCCN:83-019923.
Audience: **g,l,u,f.**

Sova, Dawn B. **PS2630.S68 2001**
Edgar Allan Poe A to Z: The Essential Reference to His Life and Work. Trade Cloth. Facts On File, Inc. New York, NY. 2001. 320p. [Facts on File Library of American Literature] ISBN:0-8160-3850-3, ISBN13: 978-0-8160-3850-3. Dewey:818/.309 B. LCCN:00-061039.
Audience: **g,l,u,f.** *Choice, 2001.*

Vines, Lois D. (Editor) **PS2638.P62 1999**
Poe Abroad: Influence, Reputation and Affinities. Trade Cloth. University of Iowa Press. Iowa City, IA. 1999. 284p. ISBN:0-87745-697-6, ISBN13: 978-0-87745-697-1. Dewey:818/.309. LCCN:99-036989.
Audience: **g,l,u,f.** *Choice, 2000.*

Walsh, John Evangelist **PS2631.W28 1998**
Midnight Dreary: The Mysterious Death of Edgar Allan Poe. Trade Cloth. Rutgers University Press. Piscataway, NJ. 1998. 180p. ISBN:0-8135-2605-1, ISBN13: 978-0-8135-2605-8. Dewey:818/.309 B. LCCN:98-024043.
Audience: **u,f.** *Choice, 1999.*

19th Century > Porter, Sydney (O. Henry)

Blansfield, Karen C. **PS2649.P5Z634 1988**
Cheap Rooms and Restless Hearts: A Study of Formula in the Urban Tales of William Sydney Porter. Trade Cloth. University of Wisconsin Press. Chicago, IL. 1988. 154p. ISBN:0-87972-420-X, ISBN13: 978-0-87972-420-7. Dewey:813/.52. LCCN:87-072837.
Audience: **u,f.**

Current-Garcia, Eugene (Editor) **PS2649.P5Z644**
O. Henry. Trade Cloth. Thomson Gale. Farmington Hills, MI. 1965. 192p. United States Authors Ser., No. 77 ISBN:0-8057-0368-3, ISBN13: 978-0-8057-0368-9. Dewey:813.52.
Audience: **g,l,u,f.**

Current-Garcia, Eugene (Editor) **PS2649.P5Z644 1993**
O. Henry. Trade Cloth. Thomson Gale. Farmington Hills, MI. 1993. 170p. Studies in Short Fiction, No. 49 ISBN:0-8057-0859-6, ISBN13: 978-0-8057-0859-2. Dewey:813.52. LCCN:93-000776.
Audience: **g,l,u,f.**

Harris, Richard C. **Z8706.2.H37**
William Sidney Porter (O. Henry): A Reference Guide. Library Binding. Macmillan Publishing Company, Inc. Old Tappan, NJ. 1977. xv, 229p. ISBN:0-8161-8006-7, ISBN13: 978-0-8161-8006-6. Dewey:016.813/52. LCCN:80-019508.
Audience: **g,l,u,f.**

Henry, O. & Porter, Sydney **PS2649**
Complete Works of O. Henry. Harry Hansen (Foreword by). Trade Cloth. Doubleday Publishing. New York, NY. 1960. ISBN:0-385-00961-5, ISBN13: 978-0-385-00961-4. Dewey:S C. LCCN:53-006098.
Audience: **g,l,u,f.**

19th Century > S-T

Moore, Jim & Vermilyea, Natalie **PS3014.T3Z77 1994**
Ernest Thayer's "Casey at the Bat": Background and Characters of Baseball's Most Famous Poem. Library Binding. McFarland & Company, Incorporated Publishers. Jefferson, NC. 1994. 376p. ISBN:0-89950-997-5, ISBN13: 978-0-89950-997-6. Dewey:811/.52 B. LCCN:94-18911.
Audience: **g,l,u,f.** *Choice, 1995.*

Sedgwick, Catharine Maria **PS2798.H63 1998**
Hope Leslie: Or, Early Times in the Massachusetts. Carolyn L. Karcher (Notes by). Trade Paper. Penguin Group (USA) Inc. New York, NY. 1998. 448p. Classics Ser. ISBN:0-14-043676-6, ISBN13: 978-0-14-043676-1. Dewey:813.2. LCCN:98-015385.
Audience: **g,l,u,f.** *Choice, 1987.*

Simms, William Gilmore **PS2840**
The writings of Willaim Gilmore Simms. Centennial edition. University of South Carolina Press. 1969. ISBN:0-87249-140-4, ISBN13: 978-0-87249-140-3.
Audience: **g,l,u,f.**

Stoddard, Elizabeth **PS2934.S3.A6 1984**
The Morgesons and Other Writings, Published and Unpublished. Lawrence Buell & Sandra A. Zagarell (Editors). Trade Cloth. University of Pennsylvania Press. Philadelphia, PA. 1984. 400p. ISBN:0-8122-7924-7, ISBN13: 978-0-8122-7924-5. Dewey:813/.4. LCCN:83-023439.
Audience: **g,l,u,f.** B

Thayer, Ernest Lawrence **PS3014.T3 C3**
Casey at the Bat: A Centennial Edition. Barry Moser (Illustrator), Donald Hall (Afterword by). Trade Paper. David R. Godine Publisher. Boston, MA. 1998. 32p. Godine Storyteller Ser. ISBN:1-56792-072-1, ISBN13: 978-1-56792-072-7. Dewey:811/.52. LCCN:88-045285.
Audience: **g,l,u,f.**

Tuckerman, Frederick Goddard **PS3104.T5 1965**
Complete poems. Momaday, N. Scott, editor. Oxford University Press. 1965.
Audience: **l,u,f.**

19th Century > Stowe, Harriet Beecher

Adams, John R. **PS2956.A6 1989**
Harriet Beecher Stowe. Trade Cloth. Macmillan Publishing Company, Inc. Old Tappan, NJ. 1989. 152p. United States Authors Ser. ISBN:0-8057-7532-3, ISBN13: 978-0-8057-7532-7. Dewey:813/.3. LCCN:88-026563.
Audience: **l,u.** B

Ammons, Elizabeth & Belasco, Susan (Editors) **PS2954.U6A66 2000**
Approaches to Teaching Stowe's Uncle Tom's Cabin. Trade Cloth. Modern Language Association of America. New York, NY. 2000. "ix, 240"p. Approaches to Teaching World Literature Ser., Vol. 66 ISBN:0-87352-755-0, ISBN13: 978-0-87352-755-2. Dewey:813/.3. LCCN:99-089158.
Audience: **u,f.**

Donovan, Josephine **PS2954.U6D66 1991**
Uncle Tom's Cabin: Evil, Affliction, and Redemptive Love. Robert Lecker (Editor). Trade Cloth. Macmillan Publishing Company, Inc. Old Tappan, NJ. 1991. 144p. Twayne's Masterworks Ser. ISBN:0-8057-8095-5, ISBN13: 978-0-8057-8095-6. Dewey:813/.3. LCCN:90-044091.
Audience: **g,l,u,f.** *Choice, 1991.*

Gossett, Thomas F. **PS2954.U6.G67 1985**
Uncle Tom's Cabin and American Culture. Trade Cloth. Southern Methodist University Press. Dallas, TX. 1985. 496p. ISBN:0-87074-189-6, ISBN13: 978-0-87074-189-0. Dewey:813/.3. LCCN:83-017245.
Audience: **u,f.** B *Choice, 1985.*

Hedrick, Joan D. **PS2956.H43 1994**
Harriet Beecher Stowe: A Life. Cloth Text. Oxford University Press, Inc. New York, NY. 1994. 544p. ISBN:0-19-506639-1, ISBN13: 978-0-19-506639-5. Dewey:813/.3. LCCN:93-016610.
Audience: **u,f.** *Choice, 1994.*

Lowance, Mason I. (Editor), et al. **PS2954.U53S76 1994**
The Stowe Debate: Rhetorical Strategies in Uncle Tom's Cabin. Ellen E. Westbrook & R. C. De Prospo (Editors). Library Binding. University of Massachusetts Press. Amherst, MA. 1994. 328p. ISBN:0-87023-951-1, ISBN13: 978-0-87023-951-9. LCCN:94-012254.
Audience: **u,f.** *Choice, 1995.*

Rosenthal, Debra J. (Editor) **PS2954.U6R68 2003**
A Routledge Literary Sourcebook on Harriet Beecher Stowe's Uncle Tom's Cabin. Trade Paper. Routledge. New York, NY. 2003. 168p. Literary Source Bks. ISBN:0-415-23474-3, ISBN13: 978-0-415-23474-0. Dewey:813/.3. LCCN:2003-004907.
Audience: **u,f.**

Stowe, Harriet Beecher **PS2954.U6S76 2005**
A Key to Uncle Tom's Cabin (large Facsimile): Presenting the Original Facts and Documents upon which the Story Is Founded. Trade Paper. Inkling Books. Seattle, WA. 2005. 268p. ISBN:1-58742-038-4, ISBN13: 978-1-58742-038-2. Dewey:813/.3. LCCN:2004-118108.
Audience: **g,l,u,f.**

Stowe, Harriet Beecher & Johnson, Charles **PS2954.U5 2002**
Uncle Tom's Cabin. Ed. 150. Trade Cloth. Oxford University

Press, Inc. New York, NY. 2002. 480p. Oxford World's Classics Hardcovers Ser. ISBN:0-19-515816-4, ISBN13: 978-0-19-515816-8. Dewey:813/.3. LCCN:2002-068424.
Audience: **g,l,u,f.** B

Stowe, Harriet Beecher **PS2384**
Dred: A Tale of the Great Dismal Swamp. Robert S. Levine (Editor). Trade Paper. University of North Carolina Press. Chapel Hill, NC. 2006. 664p. ISBN:0-8078-5685-1, ISBN13: 978-0-8078-5685-7. Dewey:813/.3.
Audience: **g,l,u,f.**

Stowe, Harriet Beecher **PS2951.5**
Stowe:Three Novels: Uncle Tom's Cabin; the Minister's Wooing; Oldtown Folks. Kathryn K. Sklar (Editor). Trade Cloth. Library of America, The. New York, NY. 1982. 1477p. ISBN:0-940450-01-1, ISBN13: 978-0-940450-01-1. Dewey:813/.3. LCCN:81-018629.
Audience: **g,l,u,f.**

19th Century > Thoreau, Henry David

Adams, Stephen & Ross, Donald Jr. **PS3054.A33 1988**
Revising Mythologies: The Composition of Thoreau's Major Works. Cloth Text. University Press of Virginia. Charlottesville, VA. 1989. 271p. ISBN:0-8139-1185-0, ISBN13: 978-0-8139-1185-4. Dewey:818/.309. LCCN:88-000801.
Audience: **u,f.** *Choice, 1989.*

Buell, Lawrence **PS3057.N3B84 1995**
The Environmental Imagination: Thoreau, Nature Writing, and the Formation of American Culture. Trade Cloth. Harvard University Press. Cambridge, MA. 1995. 600p. ISBN:0-674-25861-4, ISBN13: 978-0-674-25861-7. Dewey:818.3/09. LCCN:94-031321.
Audience: **u,f.** *Choice, 1995.*

Cain, William E. **PS3054.H57 2000**
A Historical Guide to Henry David Thoreau. Cloth Text. Oxford University Press, Inc. New York, NY. 2000. 286p. Historical Guides to American Authors ISBN:0-19-513862-7, ISBN13: 978-0-19-513862-7. Dewey:818/.309. LCCN:99-055276.
Audience: **u,f.** *Choice, 2001.*

Harding, Walter **PS3053**
The Days of Henry Thoreau: A Biography. Trade Cloth. Princeton University Press. Princeton, NJ. 1982. 544p. ISBN:0-691-06555-1, ISBN13: 978-0-691-06555-7. Dewey:818/.309. LCCN:82-061488.
Audience: **u,f.** B

Hodder, Alan D. **PS3057.R4H63 2001**
Thoreau's Ecstatic Witness. Cloth over Boards. Yale University Press. Cumberland, RI. 2001. 368p. ISBN:0-300-08959-7, ISBN13: 978-0-300-08959-2. Dewey:818/.309. LCCN:2001-033320.
Audience: **u,f.** *Choice, 2002.*

Mcgregor, Robert K. **PS3057.N3M28 1997**
A Wider View of the Universe: Henry Thoreau's Study of Nature. Trade Cloth. University of Illinois Press. Champaign, IL. 1997. 264p. ISBN:0-252-02318-8, ISBN13: 978-0-252-02318-7. Dewey:818/.309. LCCN:96-045799.
Audience: **u,f.** *Choice, 1998.*

Myerson, Joel (Editor) **PS3054 .C36 1995**
The Cambridge Companion to Henry David Thoreau. Cloth Text. Cambridge University Press. New York, NY. 1995. 248p. Companions to Literature Ser. ISBN:0-521-44037-8, ISBN13: 978-0-521-44037-0. Dewey:818.3/09. LCCN:94-029268.
Audience: **g,l,u,f.** *Choice, 1996.*

Myerson, Joel **PS3048.C75 1988**
Critical Essays on Henry David Thoreau's Walden. Trade Cloth. Thomson Gale. Farmington Hills, MI. 1988. 240p. Critical Essays Ser. ISBN:0-8161-8885-8, ISBN13: 978-0-8161-8885-7. Dewey:818/.303. LCCN:88-001818.
Audience: **u,f.** *Choice, 1989.*

Neufeldt, Leonard N. **PS3057.E25N48 1989**
The Economist: Henry Thoreau and Enterprise. Trade Cloth. Oxford University Press, Inc. New York, NY. 1989. 218p. ISBN:0-19-505789-9, ISBN13: 978-0-19-505789-8. Dewey:818/.309. LCCN:88-021000.
Audience: **u,f.** *Choice, 1989.*

Peck, H. Daniel **PS3054.P4 1990**
Thoreau's Morning Work: Memory and Perception in a Week on the Concord and Merrimack Rivers, the Journal and Walden. Cloth over Boards. Yale University Press. Cumberland, RI. 1990. 208p. ISBN:0-300-04823-8, ISBN13: 978-0-300-04823-0. Dewey:818/.309. LCCN:90-036011.
Audience: **u,f.** *Choice, 1991.*

Porte, Joel **PS1638.P665 2004**
Consciousness and Culture: Emerson and Thoreau Reviewed. Cloth over Boards. Yale University Press. Cumberland, RI. 2004. 256p. ISBN:0-300-10446-4, ISBN13: 978-0-300-10446-2. Dewey:810.9/003. LCCN:2004-043842.
Audience: **u,f.** *Choice, 2005.*

Schneider, Richard J. (Editor) **PS3057.N3T46 2000**
Thoreau's Sense of Place: Essays in American Environmental Writing. Lawrence Buell (Foreword by). Trade Cloth. University of Iowa Press. Iowa City, IA. 2000. 324p. American Land and Life Ser. ISBN:0-87745-708-5, ISBN13: 978-0-87745-708-4. Dewey:818/.309. LCCN:99-058112.
Audience: **u,f.** *Choice, 2000.*

Smith, Harmon **PS3053.S65 1999**
My Friend, My Friend: The Story of Thoreau's Relationship with Emerson. Cloth Text. University of Massachusetts Press. Amherst, MA. 2001. xii, 216p. ISBN:1-55849-186-4, ISBN13: 978-1-55849-186-1. Dewey:810.9/003 B. LCCN:98-053492.
Audience: **u,f.** *Choice, 2000.*

Tauber, Alfred I. **PS3057.P4 T38 2001**
Henry David Thoreau and the Moral Agency of Knowing. Trade Cloth. University of California Press. Berkeley, CA. 2001. 330p. ISBN:0-520-22527-9, ISBN13: 978-0-520-22527-5. Dewey:818/.309. LCCN:00-068283.
Audience: **g,l,u,f.** *Choice, 2002.*

Teichgraeber, Richard F. 3rd **PS1638.T44 1995**
Sublime Thoughts - Penny Wisdom: Situating Emerson and Thoreau in the American Market. Trade Cloth. Johns Hopkins University Press. Baltimore, MD. 1995. 312p. New Studies in American Intellectual and Cultural History ISBN:0-8018-5000-2, ISBN13: 978-0-8018-5000-4. Dewey:810.9/003. LCCN:94-036088.
Audience: **u,f.** *Choice, 1995.*

Thoreau, Henry David **PS3048.A2C73 2004**
Walden: A Fully Annotated Edition. Jeffrey S. Cramer (Editor). Cloth over Boards. Yale University Press. Cumberland, RI. 2004. 400p. ISBN:0-300-10466-9, ISBN13: 978-0-300-10466-0. Dewey:818/.303 B. LCCN:2004-009596.
Audience: **g,l,u,f.** *Choice, 2005.*

Thoreau, Henry David **PS2631**
A Week on the Concord and Merrimack Rivers; Walden, or, Life in the Woods; the Maine Woods; Cape Cod. Robert F. Sayre (Editor). Trade Cloth. Library of America, The. New York, NY. 1989. 1114p. ISBN:0-940450-27-5, ISBN13: 978-0-940450-27-1. Dewey:818/.309. LCCN:85-005175.
Audience: **g,l,u,f.**

Thoreau, Henry David **PS30422001**
Henry David Thoreau: Collected Essays and Poems. Elizabeth Hall Witherell (Editor). Trade Cloth. Library of America, The. New York, NY. 2001. 703p. Library of America, Vol. 124 ISBN:1-883011-95-7, ISBN13: 978-1-883011-95-6. Dewey:818/.309. LCCN:00-046234.
Audience: **g,l,u,f.**

19th Century > V-W

Ellis, R. J. **PR9191.5**
Harriet Wilson's 'Our Nig': A Cultural Biography of a 'Two-Story' African American Novel. Trade Paper. Rodopi. Kenilworth, NY. 2003. 228p. Costerus New Ser., 149 ISBN:90-420-1157-2, ISBN13: 978-90-420-1157-1. Dewey:812/.509384.
Audience: **u,f.**

Very, Jones **PS3126.L9**
Jones Very: Selected Poems. Nathan Lyons (Introduction by). Trade Paper. Books on Demand. Ann Arbor, MI. 156p. ISBN:0-598-06493-1, ISBN13: 978-0-598-06493-6. Dewey:811.3. LCCN:66-018878.
Audience: **g,l,u,f.**

Washington, Booker T. **E185.97.W4**
Up from Slavery: An Authoritative Text, Contexts and Composition History, Criticism. William L. Andrews (Editor, Introduction by). Trade Paper. Oxford University Press, Inc. New York, NY. 2000. 230p. Oxford World's Classics Ser. ISBN:0-19-283562-9, ISBN13: 978-0-19-283562-8. Dewey:370/.92 B.
Audience: **g,l,u,f.**

Westcott, Edward Noyes **PS3159.W12**
David Harum. Library Binding. Classic Books. Murrieta, CA. ISBN:0-7426-1105-1, ISBN13: 978-0-7426-1105-4. Dewey:813.
Audience: **g,l,u,f.**

Wilson, Harriet E. & Gates, Henry Louis Jr. **PS3334**
Our Nig: Or, Sketches from the Life of a Free Black. Ed. 3. Trade Paper. Random House, Inc. New York, NY. 2002. 304p. ISBN:1-4000-3120-6, ISBN13: 978-1-4000-3120-7. Dewey:813.3.
Audience: **g,l,u,f.**

19th Century > Whitman, Walt

Bowers, Fredson (Editor) **PS3201 1955**
Whitman's Manuscripts: Leaves of Grass, 1860. Trade Cloth. University of Chicago Press. Chicago, IL. 1955. ISBN:0-226-06886-2, ISBN13: 978-0-226-06886-2. Dewey:811.38. LCCN:55-007313.
Audience: **g,l,u,f.**

Callow, Philip **PS3231.C25 1992**
From Noon to Starry Night: A Life of Walt Whitman. Trade Cloth. Ivan R. Dee Publisher. Blue Ridge Summit, PA. 1992. 223p. ISBN:0-929587-95-2, ISBN13: 978-0-929587-95-0. Dewey:811/.3 B. LCCN:92-005311.
Audience: **u,f.** *Choice, 1993.*

Cherkovski, Neeli **PS129.C44 1988**
Whitman's Wild Children. Trade Cloth. Lapis Press. Venice, CA. 1988. 225p. ISBN:0-932499-57-0, ISBN13: 978-0-932499-57-8. Dewey:811/.54/09 B. LCCN:88-013366.
Audience: **u,f.**

Clarke, Graham **PS3238**
Walt Whitman: The Poem as Private History. Trade Cloth. Palgrave Macmillan. New York, NY. 1991. 176p. ISBN:0-312-03744-9, ISBN13: 978-0-312-03744-4. Dewey:811.3.
Audience: **u,f.** *Choice, 1992.*

Folsom, Ed **PS3242.A54.F65 1994**
Walt Whitman's Native Representations. Trade Cloth. Cambridge University Press. New York, NY. 1994. 215p. Studies in American Literature and Culture, No. 78 ISBN:0-521-45357-7, ISBN13: 978-0-521-45357-8. Dewey:811.3. LCCN:93-029689.
Audience: **u,f.** *Choice, 1995.*

Folsom, Ed & Price, Kenneth M. **PS3231.F65 2005**
Re-Scripting Walt Whitman: An Introduction to His Life and Work. Trade Cloth. Blackwell Publishing, Inc. Malden, MA. 2005. 176p. Blackwell Introductions to Literature Ser. ISBN:1-4051-1806-7, ISBN13: 978-1-4051-1806-4. Dewey:811/.3 B. LCCN:2004-029160.
Audience: **u,f.** *Choice, 2006.*

Folsom, Ed (Editor) **PS3238.W369 1994**
Walt Whitman: The Centennial Essays. Guido Villa (Illustrator). Cloth Text. University of Iowa Press. Iowa City, IA. 1994. 286p. ISBN:0-87745-459-0, ISBN13: 978-0-87745-459-5. Dewey:811/.3. LCCN:93-040838.
Audience: **u,f.** *Choice, 1994.*

Killingsworth, M. Jimmie **PS3238.K43 1993**
The Growth of Leaves of Grass: The Organic Tradition in Whitman Studies. Trade Cloth. Camden House. Elizabethtown, NY. 1993. xxii, 154p. LCENG Ser. ISBN:1-879751-44-5, ISBN13: 978-1-879751-44-6. Dewey:811/.3. LCCN:92-046142.
Audience: **u,f.** *Choice, 1993.*

Killingsworth, M. Jimmie **88-20579**
Whitman's Poetry of the Body: Sexuality, Politics, and the Text. Trade Paper. University of North Carolina Press. Chapel Hill, NC. 1991. 218p. ISBN:0-8078-4314-8, ISBN13: 978-0-8078-4314-7. Dewey:811/.3. LCCN:88-020579.
Audience: **u,f.** *Choice, 1989.*

Klammer, Martin **PS3242.S56K53 1995**
Whitman, Slavery and the Emergence of Leaves of Grass. Cloth Text. Pennsylvania State University Press. University Park, PA. 1995. 192p. ISBN:0-271-01315-X, ISBN13: 978-0-271-01315-2. Dewey:811/.3. LCCN:93-033495.
Audience: **u,f.** *Choice, 1995.*

Kramer, Lawrence **ML80.W5W35 2000**
Walt Whitman and Modern Music: War, Desire and the Trials of Nationhood. Cloth Text. Garland Publishing, Inc. New York, NY. 2000. 210p. Reference Library of the Humanities ISBN:0-8153-3154-1, ISBN13: 978-0-8153-3154-4. Dewey:782.43. LCCN:99-045480.
Audience: **u,f.** *Choice, 2000.*

Krieg, Joann P. **PS3231.A2 1998**
A Whitman Chronology. Trade Cloth. University of Iowa Press. Iowa City, IA. 1998. 176p. ISBN:0-87745-647-X, ISBN13: 978-0-87745-647-6. Dewey:811/.3 B. LCCN:98-025247.
Audience: **u,f.** *Choice, 1999.*

LeMaster, J. R. & Kummings, Donald D. (Editors) **PS3230.W35 1998**
Walt Whitman: An Encyclopedia. Cloth Text. Garland Publishing, Inc. New York, NY. 1998. 847p. Reference Library of the Humanities, Vol. 1877 ISBN:0-8153-1876-6, ISBN13: 978-0-8153-1876-7. Dewey:811/.3 B. LCCN:98-014072.
Audience: **g,l,u,f.** *Choice, 1999.*

Myerson, Joel (Editor) **PS3231.W47 1991**
Whitman in His Own Time: A Biographical Chronicle of His Life, Drawn from Recollections, Memoirs, Interviews by His Friends and Associates. Library Binding. Omnigraphics, Inc. Detroit, MI. 1991. xviii, 348p. Writers in Their Own Time Ser. ISBN:1-55888-424-6, ISBN13: 978-1-55888-424-3. Dewey:811/.3 B. LCCN:91-010301.
Audience: **u,f.** *Choice, 1992.*

Nathanson, Tenney **PS3238.N38 1992**
Whitman's Presence: Body, Voice, and Writing in Leaves of Grass. Trade Cloth. New York University Press. New York, NY. 1992. 528p. ISBN:0-8147-5770-7, ISBN13: 978-0-8147-5770-3. Dewey:811.3. LCCN:92-001309.
Audience: **u,f.** *Choice, 1993.*

Perlman, Jim **PS3238.W37 1998**
Walt Whitman: The Measure of His Song. Ed. 2. Trade Paper. Holy Cow! Press. Duluth, MN. 1997. 536p. ISBN:0-930100-78-6, ISBN13: 978-0-930100-78-0. Dewey:811/.3. LCCN:98-014190.
Audience: **u,f.** *Choice, 1999.*

Pollak, Vivian R. **PS3242.S47 P65 2000**
The Erotic Whitman. Trade Cloth. University of California Press. Berkeley, CA. 2000. 285p. ISBN:0-520-22189-3, ISBN13: 978-0-520-22189-5. Dewey:811/.3. LCCN:00-022229.
Audience: **u,f.** *Choice, 2001.*

Price, Kenneth M. **2003020181 [PS]**
To Walt Whitman, America. Trade Cloth. University of North Carolina Press. Chapel Hill, NC. 2004. 224p. ISBN:0-8078-2849-1, ISBN13: 978-0-8078-2849-6. Dewey:811/.3. LCCN:2003-020181.
Audience: **u,f.** *Choice, 2004.*

Reynolds, David S. **PS3231.R475 2005**
Walt Whitman. Trade Cloth. Oxford University Press, Inc. New York, NY. 2005. 172p. Lives and Legacies Ser. ISBN:0-19-517009-1, ISBN13: 978-0-19-517009-2. Dewey:811/.3. LCCN:2004-006715.
Audience: **g,u,f.** *Choice, 2005.*

Reynolds, David S. **PS3231.R48 1995**
Walt Whitman's America: A Cultural Biography. Trade Cloth. Alfred A. Knopf Inc. New York, NY. 1995. 671p. ISBN:0-394-58023-0, ISBN13: 978-0-394-58023-4. Dewey:811/.3 B. LCCN:94-012841.
Audience: **u,f.** *Choice, 1995.*

Sill, Geoffrey M. & Tarbell, Roberta K. (Editors) **PS3242.A66W3 1991**
Walt Whitman and the Visual Arts. Cloth Text. Rutgers University Press. Piscataway, NJ. 1991. 220p. ISBN:0-8135-1730-3, ISBN13: 978-0-8135-1730-8. Dewey:811/.3. LCCN:91-009551.
Audience: **u,f.** *Choice, 1992.*

Teller, Walter & Whitman, Walt **PS3222.W3 1973**
Walt Whitman's Camden Conversations. Trade Cloth. Rutgers University Press. Piscataway, NJ. 1973. 224p. ISBN:0-8135-0767-7, ISBN13: 978-0-8135-0767-5. Dewey:811/.3. LCCN:73-008509.
Audience: **u,f.** B

Thurin, Erik I. **PS3244.T48 1995**
Whitman Between Impressionism and Expressionism: Language of the Body, Language of the Soul. Trade Cloth. Bucknell University Press. Cranbury, NJ. 1995. 211p. ISBN:0-8387-5297-7, ISBN13: 978-0-8387-5297-5. Dewey:811/.3. LCCN:94-028805.
Audience: **u,f.** *Choice, 1995.*

Whitman, Walt **PS32042001**
Leaves of Grass. Ed. 2. Paper Text. W. W. Norton & Company, Inc. New York, NY. 2002. lii, 919p. Critical Editions Ser. ISBN:0-393-97496-0, ISBN13: 978-0-393-97496-6. Dewey:811/.3. LCCN:2001-045248.
Audience: **g,l,u,f.**

Whitman, Walt **PS3203.B624 2003**
Walt Whitman: Selected Poems. Harold Bloom (Editor). Trade Cloth. Library of America, The. New York, NY. 2003. 221p. American Poets Project Ser., Vol. 4 ISBN:1-931082-32-4, ISBN13: 978-1-931082-32-7. Dewey:811/.3. LCCN:2002-032124.
Audience: **g,l,u,f.**

Whitman, Walt **PS3231**
Whitman: Poetry and Prose. Justin Kaplan (Editor). Trade Cloth. Library of America, The. New York, NY. 1982. 1380p. ISBN:0-940450-02-X, ISBN13: 978-0-940450-02-8. Dewey:811/.3. LCCN:81-020768.
Audience: **g,l,u,f.**

Whitman, Walt **PS3203.R8 1972**
Walt Whitman of the New York Aurora, Editor at Twenty-Two: A Collection of Recently Discovered Writings. Joseph J. Rubin & Charles H. Brown (Editors). Library Binding. Greenwood

Publishing Group, Inc. Portsmouth, NH. 1972. 147p. ISBN:0-8371-5724-2, ISBN13: 978-0-8371-5724-5. Dewey:818/.3/07. LCCN:72-005277.
Audience: **g,l,u,f.** B

19th Century > Whittier, James Greenleaf

Kribbs, Jayne K. **PS3288.C7 1980**
Critical Essays on John Greenleaf Whittier. Trade Cloth. Thomson Gale. Farmington Hills, MI. 1980. xl, 228p. Critical Essays on American Literature Ser. ISBN:0-8161-8308-2, ISBN13: 978-0-8161-8308-1. Dewey:811/.3. LCCN:80-014207.
Audience: **u,f.** B

✓**Whittier, John Greenleaf** **PS3253.W3**
John Greenleaf Whittier's Poetry: An Appraisal and a Selection. Trade Paper. Books on Demand. Ann Arbor, MI. 220p. ISBN:0-608-15961-1, ISBN13: 978-0-608-15961-4. Dewey:811/.3. LCCN:79-152299.
Audience: **g,l,u,f.**

Whittier, John Greenleaf **PS3281**
The Letters of John Greenleaf Whittier, Set. John B. Pickard (Editor). Trade Cloth. Harvard University Press. Cambridge, MA. 1975. 2080p. Belknap Press Ser. ISBN:0-674-52830-1, ISBN13: 978-0-674-52830-7. Dewey:811/.3. LCCN:73-008805.
Audience: **g,l,u,f.** B

✓**Whittier, John Greenleaf** **PS3250.F75**
The Poetical Works of Whittier: Cambridge Edition. Hyatt H. Waggoner (Editor, Introduction by). Trade Cloth. Houghton Mifflin Company. New York, NY. 1975. xxxii, 538p. Cambridge Editions Ser. ISBN:0-395-21599-4, ISBN13: 978-0-395-21599-9. Dewey:811/.3. LCCN:75-025974.
Audience: **g,l,u,f.** B

Whittier, John Greenleaf & Wineapple, Brenda **PS3252.W47 2004**
John Greenleaf Whittier: Selected Poems. Trade Cloth. Library of America, The. New York, NY. 2004. 230p. American Poets Project Ser. ISBN:1-931082-59-6, ISBN13: 978-1-931082-59-4. Dewey:811/.3. LCCN:2003-060483.
Audience: **g,l,u,f.**

20th Century (1901-1960) > A

Ammons, A. R. **PS3501.M6.A17**
A. R. Ammons: Collected Poems, 1951-1971. Trade Paper. W. W. Norton & Company, Inc. New York, NY. 2001. 416p. ISBN:0-393-32192-4, ISBN13: 978-0-393-32192-0. Dewey:811.54. LCCN:72-005811.
Audience: **g,l,u,f.** B

Anderson, Maxwell & Stallings, Laurence **PS3501.N256**
Three American Plays. Cloth Text. Amereon, Ltd. Mattituck, NY. 2004. ISBN:0-8488-2750-3, ISBN13: 978-0-8488-2750-2. Dewey:812.
Audience: **g,l,u,f.** B

✓**Auchincloss, Louis** **PS3501.U25P67 1987**
Portrait in Brownstone. Paper Text. McGraw-Hill Companies, The. New York, NY. 1987. 320p. McGraw-Hill Paperbacks ISBN:0-07-002441-3, ISBN13: 978-0-07-002441-0. Dewey:813/.54. LCCN:87-005095.
Audience: **g,l,u,f.** B

✓**Auchincloss, Louis** **PS3501.U25R44 2002**
The Rector of Justin: A Novel. Trade Paper. Houghton Mifflin Company Trade & Reference Division. Boston, MA. 2002. 352p. ISBN:0-618-22489-0, ISBN13: 978-0-618-22489-0. Dewey:813/.54. LCCN:2002-725552.
Audience: **g,l,u,f.**

✓**Gilbert, Roger** **PS3501.M6Z73 2005**
Considering the Radiance. Trade Cloth. W. W. Norton & Company, Inc. New York, NY. 2005. 352p. ISBN:0-393-05999-5, ISBN13: 978-0-393-05999-1. Dewey:811/.54. LCCN:2004-027491.
Audience: **g,l,u,f.**

Kirschten, Robert **PS3501.M6Z63 1997**
Critical Essays on A. R. Ammons. Trade Cloth. Thomson Gale. Farmington Hills, MI. 1997. Critical Essays on American Literature Ser. ISBN:0-7838-0044-4, ISBN13: 978-0-7838-0044-8. Dewey:811/.54. LCCN:97-015750.
Audience: **l,u.**

20th Century (1901-1960) > A > Agee, James

✓**Agee, James** **PS3501.G35**
The Collected Poems of James Agee. Houghton-Mifflin. 1968. ISBN:0-395-07333-2, ISBN13: 978-0-395-07333-9.
Audience: **g,l,u,f.**

✓**Agee, James** **PS3501.G35.A6 2005**
James Agee: Film Writing and Selected Journalism. Michael Sragow (Editor). Saddle Stitched, Cloth over Boards, Dust Jacket. Library of America, The. New York, NY. 2005. 748p. The Library of America, Vol. 160 ISBN:1-931082-82-0, ISBN13: 978-1-931082-82-2. Dewey:791.43/75. LCCN:2005-045095.
Audience: **g,l,u,f.** *Choice, 2006.*

✓**Agee, James** **PS3501.G35A6 2005**
James Agee: Let Us Now Praise Famous Men, a Death in the Family, and Shorter Fiction. Michael Sragow (Editor). Saddle Stitched, Cloth over Boards, Dust Jacket. Library of America, The. New York, NY. 2005. 818p. The Library of America ISBN:1-931082-81-2, ISBN13: 978-1-931082-81-5. Dewey:818/.5209. LCCN:2005-045098.
Audience: **g,l,u,f.** *Choice, 2006.*

✓**Bergreen, Laurence** **PS3501.G35.Z59 1984**
James Agee: A Biography. Trade Cloth. Penguin Group (USA) Inc. New York, NY. 1984. 352p. ISBN:0-525-24253-8, ISBN13: 978-0-525-24253-6. Dewey:818/.5209. LCCN:83-025496.
Audience: **g,l,u,f.** B

Dardis, Tom **PS129.D3 1988**
Some Time in the Sun: The Hollywood Years of F. Scott Fitzgerald, William Faulkner, Nathanael West, Aldous Huxley, and James Agee. Trade Paper. Hal Leonard Corporation. Milwaukee, WI. 1989. 274p. ISBN:0-87910-116-4, ISBN13: 978-0-87910-116-9. Dewey:810/.9/0052 B. LCCN:88-021562.
Audience: **g,l,u,f.**

Kramer, Victor A. **PS3501.G35.Z74**
James Agee. Trade Cloth. Thomson Gale. Farmington Hills, MI. 1975. 182 p. :p. Twayne's United States Authors Ser., No. 252 ISBN:0-8057-0006-4, ISBN13: 978-0-8057-0006-0. Dewey:818/.5/209. LCCN:74-023882.
Audience: **l,u.** B

Lofaro, Michael A. & Davis, Hugh (Editors) **PS3501.G35A6 2004**
James Agee Rediscovered: The Notebooks for Let Us Now Praise Famous Men, and Other New Manuscripts. Trade Cloth. University of Tennessee Press. Knoxville, TN. 2005. 488p. ISBN:1-57233-355-3, ISBN13: 978-1-57233-355-0. Dewey:813/.52 B. LCCN:2004-002716.
Audience: **u,f.** *Choice, 2005.*

Spiegel, Alan **PS3501.G35Z894 1998**
James Agee and the Legend of Himself: A Critical Study. Trade Cloth. University of Missouri Press. Columbia, MO. 1998. 312p. ISBN:0-8262-1182-8, ISBN13: 978-0-8262-1182-8. Dewey:818.5209. LCCN:98-021590.
Audience: **g,l,u,f.** *Choice, 1998.*

20th Century (1901-1960) > A > Aiken, Conrad

Aiken, Conrad **PS3501.I5A15 1964**
Collected Novels of Conrad Aiken. Holt, Rinehart, and Winston. 1964.
Audience: **g,l,u,f.**

Aiken, Conrad **PR9230.9.B68**
Collected Poems, 1916-1970. Ed. 2. Cloth Text. Oxford University Press, Inc. New York, NY. 1970. 1064p. ISBN:0-19-501258-5, ISBN13: 978-0-19-501258-3. Dewey:811. LCCN:79-120179.
Audience: **g,l,u,f.**

Aiken, Conrad **PN710.A424**
A Reviewer's Abc: Collected Criticism of Conrad Aiken from 1916 to the Present. Paper Text. Textbook Publishers. Temecula, CA. 2003. 414p. ISBN:0-7581-8340-2, ISBN13: 978-0-7581-8340-8. Dewey:820/.9.
Audience: **l,u,f.** B

Aiken, Conrad **PS3501.I5**
Short Stories. Trade Cloth. Ayer Company Publishers, Inc. Manchester, NH. 1977. Short Story Index Reprint Ser. ISBN:0-8369-4034-2, ISBN13: 978-0-8369-4034-3. Dewey:813/.5/2. LCCN:72-178434.
Audience: **g,l,u,f.**

Seigel, Catharine F. **PS3501.I5 Z86 1993**
The Fictive World of Conrad Aiken: A Celebration of Consciousness. Library Binding. Northern Illinois University Press. DeKalb, IL. 1993. 232p. ISBN:0-87580-172-2, ISBN13: 978-0-87580-172-8. Dewey:818/.5209. LCCN:92-003804.
Audience: **u,f.** *Choice, 1993.*

20th Century (1901-1960) > A > Algren, Nelson

Algren, Nelson **PZ3**
A Walk on the Wild Side. Trade Cloth. Greenwood Publishing Group, Inc. Portsmouth, NH. 1978. 346p. ISBN:0-313-20294-X, ISBN13: 978-0-313-20294-0. Dewey:813/.52. LCCN:78-000509.
Audience: **g,l,u,f.**

Algren, Nelson **PS3501.L4625**
The Neon Wilderness: 24 Short Stories. Tom Carson (Introduction by), Studs Terkel (Afterword by). Trade Paper. Seven Stories Press. New York, NY. 2004. ISBN:1-58322-550-1, ISBN13: 978-1-58322-550-9. Dewey:813.5/2.
Audience: **g,l,u,f.**

Algren, Nelson **PS3501.L4625M3 1996**
The Man with the Golden Arm. James R. Giles (Introduction by). Trade Paper. Seven Stories Press. New York, NY. 2004. ISBN:1-888363-18-5, ISBN13: 978-1-888363-18-0. Dewey:813/.52. LCCN:89-071471.
Audience: **g,l,u,f.**

Heasley Cox, Martha & Chatterton, Wayne **PS3501.L4625.Z66**
Nelson Algren. Library Binding. Thomson Gale. Farmington Hills, MI. 1975. 192p. U. S. Authors Ser., No. 249 ISBN:0-8057-0014-5, ISBN13: 978-0-8057-0014-5. Dewey:813/.5/2. LCCN:74-019223.
Audience: **l,u.** B

Horvath, Brooke **PS3501.L4625Z69 2005**
Understanding Nelson Algren. Trade Cloth. University of South Carolina Press. Columbia, SC. 2005. 224p. Understanding Contemporary American Literature Ser. ISBN:1-57003-574-1, ISBN13: 978-1-57003-574-6. Dewey:813/.52. LCCN:2004-027126.
Audience: **g,l,u,f.**

20th Century (1901-1960) > A > Anderson, Sherwood

Anderson, David D. **PS3501.N4 Z57**
Critical Essays on Sherwood Anderson. Trade Cloth. Thomson Gale. Farmington Hills, MI. 1981. Critical Essays on American Literature Ser. ISBN:0-8161-8421-6, ISBN13: 978-0-8161-8421-7. Dewey:813/.52. LCCN:81-006815.
Audience: **l,u.**

Anderson, Sherwood **PS3501.N4 D3**
Dark Laughter. Library Binding. Classic Books. Murrieta, CA. 1998. 319p. The Collected Works of Sherwood Anderson ISBN:1-58201-500-7, ISBN13: 978-1-58201-500-2. Dewey:Fic.
Audience: **g,l,u,f.** B

Anderson, Sherwood **PS3501.N4 D4**
Death in the Woods and Other Stories. Library Binding. Amereon, Ltd. Mattituck, NY. ISBN:0-8488-1952-7, ISBN13: 978-0-8488-1952-1. Dewey:813/.52.
Audience: **g,l,u,f.** B

Anderson, Sherwood **PR6019.O9**
Marching Men. Trade Paper. 1st World Publishing, Inc. Fairfield, IA. 2005. 284p. ISBN:1-4218-0488-3, ISBN13: 978-1-4218-0488-0. Dewey:823/.9/1. LCCN:2004195673.
Audience: **g,l,u,f.** B

Anderson, Sherwood **PS3501.N4 P6**
Poor White. Library Binding. Classic Books. Murrieta, CA. 1998. 371p. The Collected Works of Sherwood Anderson ISBN:1-58201-505-8, ISBN13: 978-1-58201-505-7. Dewey:813/.52.
Audience: **g,l,u,f.**

Anderson, Sherwood **PS3501.N4Z5**
A Story Teller's Story. Library Binding. Classic Books. Murrieta, CA. 1998. 442p. The Collected Works of Sherwood Anderson ISBN:1-58201-506-6, ISBN13: 978-1-58201-506-4. Dewey:813/.52 B.
Audience: **g,l,u,f.** B

Anderson, Sherwood **PS3511.A86**
Winesburg, Ohio. Library Binding. Classic Books. Murrieta, CA. 1998. 303p. The Collected Works of Sherwood Anderson ISBN:1-58201-509-0, ISBN13: 978-1-58201-509-5. Dewey:813/.52.
Audience: **g,l,u,f.** B

Bassett, John Earl **PS3501.N4Z5484 2006**
Sherwood Anderson: An American Career. Trade Cloth. Susquehanna University Press. Cranbury, NJ. 2005. 152p. ISBN:1-57591-102-7, ISBN13: 978-1-57591-102-1. Dewey:813/.52. LCCN:2005-015407.
Audience: **g,l,u,f.** *Choice, 2006.*

20th Century (1901-1960) > A > Ashbery, John

Ashbery, John **PS3566.L27**
And the Stars Were Shining: Poems. Trade Cloth. Farrar, Straus & Giroux. New York, NY. 1995. 96p. ISBN:0-374-52434-3, ISBN13: 978-0-374-52434-0. Dewey:811/.54. LCCN:93-014255.
Audience: **g,l,u,f.**

Ashbery, John **PS3568.O243**
Can You Hear, Bird: Poems. Trade Cloth. Farrar, Straus & Giroux. New York, NY. 1997. 188p. ISBN:0-374-52501-3, ISBN13: 978-0-374-52501-9. Dewey:811.5/4. LCCN:95-000288.
Audience: **g,l,u,f.**

Ashbery, John **PS3501.S475H59 2000**
Hotel Lautreamont. Trade Cloth. Farrar, Straus & Giroux. New York, NY. 2000. 157p. ISBN:0-374-52755-5, ISBN13: 978-0-374-52755-6. Dewey:811/.54. LCCN:00-057659.
Audience: **g,l,u,f.**

Ashbery, John **PS3501.S475H6 1999**
Houseboat Days: Poems. Trade Paper. Farrar, Straus & Giroux. New York, NY. 1999. 88p. ISBN:0-374-52590-0, ISBN13: 978-0-374-52590-3. Dewey:811/.54. LCCN:99-018681.
Audience: **g,l,u,f.**

Ashbery, John **PS221.A84 2000**
Other Traditions. Trade Cloth. Harvard University Press. Cambridge, MA. 2000. 176p. The Charles Eliot Norton Lectures ISBN:0-674-00315-2, ISBN13: 978-0-674-00315-6. Dewey:811/.5209. LCCN:00-039648.
Audience: **g,u,f.** *Choice, 2001.*

Ashbery, John **PS3501.S475**
Self-Portrait in a Convex Mirror: Poems. Trade Paper. Penguin Group (USA) Inc. New York, NY. 1990. 96p. Penguin Poets Ser. ISBN:0-14-058668-7, ISBN13: 978-0-14-058668-8. Dewey:811/.54. LCCN:76-018814.
Audience: **g,l,u,f.**

Ashbery, John **PS3501.S475**
The Tennis Court Oath: A Book of Poems. Ed. 35. Trade Paper. Wesleyan University Press. Middletown, CT. 1977. 94p. Wesleyan Poetry Classics Ser. ISBN:0-8195-1013-0, ISBN13: 978-0-8195-1013-6. Dewey:811. LCCN:62-010569.
Audience: **g,l,u,f.** B

Ashbery, John **PS3566.L27**
Wakefulness: Poems. Trade Cloth. Farrar, Straus & Giroux. New York, NY. 1999. 96p. ISBN:0-374-52593-5, ISBN13: 978-0-374-52593-4. Dewey:811.5/4.
Audience: **g,l,u,f.**

Ashbery, John **PS3566.L27**
Where Shall I Wander: New Poems. Trade Paper. HarperCollins Publishers. New York, NY. 2006. 96p. ISBN:0-06-076530-5, ISBN13: 978-0-06-076530-9. Dewey:811/.54.
Audience: **g,l,u,f.**

Ashbery, John **PS3566.L27**
Your Name Here: Poems. Trade Paper. Farrar, Straus & Giroux. New York, NY. 2001. 144p. ISBN:0-374-52783-0, ISBN13: 978-0-374-52783-9. Dewey:811.5/4.
Audience: **g,l,u,f.**

Ashbery, John **PS3501.S475A6**
Selected Prose. Eugene Richie (Editor). Trade Paper. University of Michigan Press. Chicago, IL. 2005. 336p. Poets on Poetry Ser. ISBN:0-472-03139-2, ISBN13: 978-0-472-03139-9. Dewey:818/.5408.
Audience: **u,f.**

Herd, David **PS3501.S475Z69 2000**
John Ashbery and American Poetry. Cloth over Boards. Palgrave Macmillan. New York, NY. 2001. 240p. ISBN:0-312-23931-9, ISBN13: 978-0-312-23931-2. Dewey:811/.54. LCCN:00-051484.
Audience: **g,l,u,f.** *Choice, 2002.*

Hoeppner, Edward H. **PS323.5.H54 1994**
Echoes and Moving Fields: Structure and Subjectivity in the Poetry of W. S. Merwin and John Ashbery. Trade Cloth. Bucknell University Press. Cranbury, NJ. 1994. 259p. ISBN:0-8387-5279-9, ISBN13: 978-0-8387-5279-1. Dewey:811/.5409. LCCN:94-009960.
Audience: **u,f.** *Choice, 1995.*

Lehman, David (Editor) **PS3501.S475Z/**
Beyond Amazement: New Essays on John Ashbery. Book, Other. Cornell University Press. Ithaca, NY. 1980. 312p. ISBN:0-8014-1235-8, ISBN13: 978-0-8014-1235-6. Dewey:811/.5/4. LCCN:79-006850.
Audience: **u,f.** B

Schultz, Susan M. (Editor) **PS3501.S475Z87 1995**
The Tribe of John: Ashbery and Contemporary Poetry. Trade Paper. University of Alabama Press. Tuscaloosa, AL. 1995. 288p. ISBN:0-8173-0767-2, ISBN13: 978-0-8173-0767-7. Dewey:811/.54. LCCN:94-028820.
Audience: **g,l,u,f.**

Shoptaw, John **PS3501.S475Z86 1994**
On the Outside Looking Out: John Ashbery's Poetry. Trade Cloth. Harvard University Press. Cambridge, MA. 1995. 432p. ISBN:0-674-63612-0, ISBN13: 978-0-674-63612-5. Dewey:811/.54. LCCN:94-025956.
Audience: **g,l,u,f.** *Choice, 1995.*

20th Century (1901-1960) > B

Barnes, Djuna **PS3503.A614.A6 1962**
Selected Works of Djuna Barnes. Trade Cloth. Farrar, Straus & Giroux. New York, NY. 1980. 366p. ISBN:0-374-25936-4, ISBN13: 978-0-374-25936-5. Dewey:813.5/2. LCCN:62-007185.
Audience: **g,l,u,f.**

Barry, Philip **PS3503.A648 P5**
The Philadelphia Story: A Comedy in Three Acts. Trade Cloth. A M S Press, Inc. New York, NY. ISBN:0-404-20018-4, ISBN13: 978-0-404-20018-3. Dewey:812.5. LCCN:83-045700.
Audience: **g,l,u,f.** B

Benchley, Robert C. **PN6161**
The Benchley Roundup: A Selection by Nathaniel Benchley of his Favorites. William Gluyas (Illustrator). Trade Paper. University of Chicago Press. Chicago, IL. 1983. 359p. ISBN:0-226-04218-9, ISBN13: 978-0-226-04218-3. Dewey:814.5/2. LCCN:83-005111.
Audience: **g,l,u,f.**

Blackburn, Paul **PS3552.L342A17 1985**
The Collected Poems of Paul Blackburn. Edith Jarolim (Editor), M. L. Rosenthal (Foreword by). Trade Cloth. Persea Books, Inc. New York, NY. 1985. 728p. Lamplighter Ser. ISBN:0-89255-086-4, ISBN13: 978-0-89255-086-9. Dewey:811/.54. LCCN:85-009309.
Audience: **g,l,u,f.** *Choice, 1986.*

Bogan, Louise **PS3503.O195B5 1995**
The Blue Estuaries: Poems: 1923-1968. Trade Cloth. Farrar, Straus & Giroux. New York, NY. 1995. 136p. ISBN:0-374-52461-0, ISBN13: 978-0-374-52461-6. Dewey:813/.4 B. LCCN:95-020822.
Audience: **l,u,f.**

Bontemps, Arna (Editor) **PS3503.O474B5 1992**
Black Thunder: Gabriel's Revolt: Virginia 1800. Arnold Rampersad (Introduction by). Trade Paper. Beacon Press. Boston, MA. 1992. 256p. ISBN:0-8070-6337-1, ISBN13: 978-0-8070-6337-8. Dewey:813/.54. LCCN:91-034123.
Audience: **g,l,u,f.**

Bowles, Jane **F2551**
My Sister's Hand in Mine: The Collected Works of Jane Bowles. Truman Capote (Introduction by), Joy Williams (Preface by). Trade Paper. Farrar, Straus & Giroux. New York, NY. 2005. 496p. ISBN:0-374-52978-7, ISBN13: 978-0-374-52978-9. Dewey:818/.52. LCCN:2005-926649.
Audience: **g,l,u,f.**

Brautigan, Ianthe **PS3503.R2736**
You Can't Catch Death: A Daughter's Memoir. Trade Paper. St. Martin's Press. Gordonville, VA. 2001. 240p. ISBN:0-312-26418-6, ISBN13: 978-0-312-26418-5. Dewey:813/.54 B.
Audience: **g,l,u,f.**

Brautigan, Richard **PS3568.O243**
Trout Fishing in America. Trade Cloth. Amereon, Ltd. Mattituck, NY. 122p. ISBN:0-8488-2578-0, ISBN13: 978-0-8488-2578-2. Dewey:813.5/4.
Audience: **g,l,u,f.**

Broe, Mary L. (Editor) **PS3503.A614Z94 1991**
Silence and Power: A Reevaluation of Djuna Barnes. Trade Cloth. Southern Illinois University Press. Carbondale, IL. 1991. 438p. ISBN:0-8093-1250-6, ISBN13: 978-0-8093-1250-4. Dewey:818/.5209. LCCN:89-056358.
Audience: **u,f.** *Choice, 1991.*

Brossard, Chandler **PS3552.R67W48 2000**
Who Walk in Darkness. Ed. 3. Trade Paper. Herodias. New York, NY. 2000. 308p. ISBN:1-928746-12-8, ISBN13: 978-1-928746-12-6. Dewey:823/.9/1. LCCN:00-024248.
Audience: **g,l,u,f.**

Brown, Harry **PS3503.R81565.W35**
A Walk in the Sun. Trade Cloth. University of Nebraska Press. Lincoln, NE. 1998. 187p. ISBN:0-8032-6148-9, ISBN13: 978-0-8032-6148-8. Dewey:823.91. LCCN:98-029019.
Audience: **g,l,u,f.**

Brown, Sterling A. **PS3503.R833A17 1996**
The Collected Poems of Sterling A. Brown. Michael S. Harper (Editor). Trade Paper. Northwestern University Press. Evanston, IL. 1996. 267p. ISBN:0-8101-5045-X, ISBN13: 978-0-8101-5045-4. Dewey:811/.52. LCCN:95-053303.
Audience: **g,l,u,f.** B

Buck, Pearl S. **PS3503.U198 D7**
Dragon Seed. Library Binding. Buccaneer Books, Inc. Cutchogue, NY. 1993. ISBN:1-56849-133-6, ISBN13: 978-1-56849-133-2. Dewey:813.52.
Audience: **g,l,u,f.**

Buck, Pearl S. **PS3511.A86**
The Good Earth. Mass Market. Simon & Schuster. New York, NY. 2005. 448p. Enriched Classics Ser. ISBN:1-4165-0018-9, ISBN13: 978-1-4165-0018-6. Dewey:813/.52.
Audience: **g,l,u,f.**

Buck, Pearl S. **PS3503.U198 Z5**
My Several Worlds. Library Binding. Buccaneer Books, Inc. Cutchogue, NY. 1992. ISBN:0-89966-987-5, ISBN13: 978-0-89966-987-8. Dewey:928.1.
Audience: **g,l,u,f.**

Burdick, Eugene & Wheeler, Harvey **PS3552.U7116F35 1999**
Fail Safe. Eugene Burdick (Preface by). Trade Paper. HarperCollins Publishers. New York, NY. 1999. 288p. ISBN:0-88001-654-X, ISBN13: 978-0-88001-654-4. Dewey:813/.54. LCCN:98-035935.
Audience: **g,l,u,f.** B

Burke, Kenneth **PS3503.U6134A15 2004**
Here and Elsewhere: The Collected Fiction of Kenneth Burke. Denis Donoghue (Introduction by). Trade Paper, Perfect. David R. Godine Publisher. Boston, MA. 2005. 448p. ISBN:1-57423-201-0, ISBN13: 978-1-57423-201-1. Dewey:813/.52. LCCN:2004-017236.
Audience: **g,l,u,f.** *Choice, 2006.*

Burroughs, Edgar Rice **PS3503.U687P75 2005**
A Princess of Mars. Trade Paper, Perfect. Dover Publications, Inc. Mineola, NY. 2005. 160p. ISBN:0-486-44368-X, ISBN13: 978-0-486-44368-3. Dewey:813/.52. LCCN:2005-045419.
Audience: **g,l,u,f.**

Burroughs, Edgar Rice **PS3503.U687T3 2003**
Tarzan of the Apes. Trade Paper. Random House Adult Trade Publishing Group. New York, NY. 2003. 288p. The Modern Library Classics ISBN:0-8129-6706-2, ISBN13: 978-0-8129-6706-7. Dewey:813/.52. LCCN:2002-024543.
Audience: **g,l,u,f.**

Conn, Peter **PS3503.U198 Z624 19**
Pearl S. Buck: A Cultural Biography. Trade Paper. Cambridge University Press. New York, NY. 1998. 496p. ISBN:0-521-63989-1, ISBN13: 978-0-521-63989-7. Dewey:813.5/2.
Audience: **g,l,u,f.** *Choice, 1997.*

Skerl, Jennie (Editor) **PS3552.O837Z89 1997**
A Tawdry Place of Salvation: The Art of Jane Bowles. Trade Cloth. Southern Illinois University Press. Carbondale, IL. 1997. 240p. ISBN:0-8093-2100-9, ISBN13: 978-0-8093-2100-1. Dewey:818/.5409. LCCN:96-043454.
Audience: **u,f.**

Taliaferro, John **PS3503.U687**
Tarzan Forever: The Life of Edgar Rice Burroughs Creator of Tarzan. Trade Paper. Simon & Schuster. New York, NY. 2002. 400p. ISBN:0-7432-3650-5, ISBN13: 978-0-7432-3650-8. Dewey:813/.52.
Audience: **g,l,u,f.**

20th Century (1901-1960) > B > Baldwin, James

Baldwin, James **PS3552.A45B5 1995**
Blues for Mister Charlie: A Play. Trade Paper. Knopf Publishing Group. New York, NY. 1995. 144p. ISBN:0-679-76178-0, ISBN13: 978-0-679-76178-5. Dewey:812/.54. LCCN:94-023842.
Audience: **g,l,u,f.** B

Baldwin, James **E185.61.B195 2000**
The Fire Next Time. Trade Cloth. Holt, Rinehart & Winston. Austin, TX. 2000. 167p. HRW Library ISBN:0-03-055442-X, ISBN13: 978-0-03-055442-1. Dewey:305.896/073. LCCN:2001-265860.
Audience: **g,l,u,f.** B

Baldwin, James **PS3568.O243**
Go Tell It on the Mountain. Trade Paper. Dell Publishing. New York, NY. 2000. 240p. ISBN:0-385-33457-5, ISBN13: 978-0-385-33457-0. Dewey:[Fic].
Audience: **g,l,u,f.**

Baldwin, James **PS3552.A45G66 1995**
Going to Meet the Man. Trade Paper. Knopf Publishing Group. New York, NY. 1995. 256p. ISBN:0-679-76179-9, ISBN13: 978-0-679-76179-2. Dewey:823/.9/1. LCCN:94-041586.
Audience: **g,l,u,f.** B

Baldwin, James **PS3568.O243**
If Beale Street Could Talk. Trade Paper. Dell Publishing. New York, NY. 2000. 176p. ISBN:0-385-33459-1, ISBN13: 978-0-385-33459-4. Dewey:813/.54.
Audience: **g,l,u,f.**

Baldwin, James **PS3552.A45A6 1998**
Early Novels and Stories. Toni Morrison (Editor). Trade Cloth. Library of America, The. New York, NY. 1998. 992p. Library of America ISBN:1-883011-51-5, ISBN13: 978-1-883011-51-2. Dewey:813/.54. LCCN:97-023028.
Audience: **g,l,u,f.**

Baldwin, James **PS3552.A45A16 1998**
James Baldwin: Collected Essays. Toni Morrison (Contribution by). Trade Cloth. Library of America, The. New York, NY. 1998. 869p. Library of America, Vol. 98 ISBN:1-883011-52-3, ISBN13: 978-1-883011-52-9. Dewey:814/.54. LCCN:97-023496.
Audience: **g,l,u,f.**

McBride, Dwight A. (Editor) **PS3552.A45Z74 1999**
James Baldwin Now. Trade Paper. New York University Press. New York, NY. 1999. 356p. ISBN:0-8147-5618-2, ISBN13: 978-0-8147-5618-8. Dewey:818/.5409 B. LCCN:99-006546.
Audience: **u,f.**

Miller, D. Quentin (Editor) **PS3552.A45Z865 2000**
Re-Viewing James Baldwin: Things Not Seen. David A. Leeming (Foreword by). Trade Cloth. Temple University Press. Philadelphia, PA. 2000. 256p. ISBN:1-56639-736-7, ISBN13: 978-1-56639-736-0. Dewey:818/.5409. LCCN:99-033993.
Audience: **u,f.**

20th Century (1901-1960) > B > Bellow, Saul

Atlas, James **PS3503.E4488Z554**
Bellow: A Biography. UK-Trade Paper. Random House Adult Trade Publishing Group. New York, NY. 2002. 736p. ISBN:0-375-75958-1, ISBN13: 978-0-375-75958-1. Dewey:813/.52 B. LCCN:2001-056270.
Audience: **g,l,u,f.** *Choice, 2001.*

Bach, Gerhard (Editor) **PS3503**
The Critical Response to Saul Bellow. Cloth Text. Greenwood Publishing Group, Inc. Portsmouth, NH. 1995. 392p. Critical Responses in Arts and Letters Ser., Vol. 20
ISBN:0-313-28370-2, ISBN13: 978-0-313-28370-3.
Dewey:813/.52. LCCN:95-022756.
Audience: **g,l,u,f.**

Bellow, Saul **PS3511.A86**
Henderson the Rain King. Library Binding. Sagebrush Education Resources. Caledonia, MN. 1996.
ISBN:0-613-17274-4, ISBN13: 978-0-613-17274-5.
Dewey:813.5/2.
Audience: **g,l,u,f.**

Bellow, Saul **PS3503.E4488H56 1998**
Him with His Foot in His Mouth and Other Stories. Trade Paper. Penguin Group (USA) Inc. New York, NY. 1998. 304p. Great Books of the 20th Century Ser. ISBN:0-14-118023-4, ISBN13: 978-0-14-118023-6. Dewey:813/.52. LCCN:99-166191.
Audience: **g,l,u,f.** B

Bellow, Saul **PS3503.E4488M6 1996**
Mosby's Memoirs and Other Stories. Trade Paper. Penguin Group (USA) Inc. New York, NY. 1996. 192p. Great Books of the 20th Century Ser. ISBN:0-14-018945-9, ISBN13: 978-0-14-018945-2. Dewey:813.5/2. LCCN:96-160794.
Audience: **g,l,u,f.** B

Bellow, Saul **PS3503.E4488.M4**
Mr. Sammler's Planet. Trade Cloth. Penguin Group (USA) Inc. New York, NY. 1970. 313p. ISBN:0-670-33319-0, ISBN13: 978-0-670-33319-6. Dewey:813.5/2. LCCN:74-087248.
Audience: **g,l,u,f.** B

Bellow, Saul **PS3503.E4488H8 1996**
Humboldt's Gift. Martin Amis (Introduction by). Trade Paper. Penguin Group (USA) Inc. New York, NY. 1996. 496p. Great Books of the 20th Century Ser. ISBN:0-14-018944-0, ISBN13: 978-0-14-018944-5. Dewey:813.5/2. LCCN:96-159038.
Audience: **g,l,u,f.** B

Bellow, Saul **PR6019.O9**
Seize the Day. Cynthia Ozick (Introduction by). Trade Paper. Penguin Group (USA) Inc. New York, NY. 2003. 144p. Penguin Classics Ser. ISBN:0-14-243761-1, ISBN13: 978-0-14-243761-2. Dewey:823/.9/1.
Audience: **g,l,u,f.**

Bellow, Saul **PS3503.E4488H45 2003**
Herzog. Philip Roth (Introduction by). Trade Paper. Penguin Group (USA) Inc. New York, NY. 2003. 400p. Penguin Classics Ser. ISBN:0-14-243729-8, ISBN13: 978-0-14-243729-2. Dewey:813/.52. LCCN:2003-265266.
Audience: **g,l,u,f.** B

Bellow, Saul **PS3503.E4488A6 2003**
Saul Bellow: Novels, 1944-1953. James Wood (Editor). Trade Cloth. Library of America, The. New York, NY. 2003. 1029p. ISBN:1-931082-38-3, ISBN13: 978-1-931082-38-9. Dewey:813/.52. LCCN:2003-040144.
Audience: **g,l,u,f.**

Bradbury, Malcolm **PS3503.E4488Z/**
Saul Bellow. Trade Paper. Routledge. New York, NY. 1982. 96p. Contemporary Writers Ser. ISBN:0-416-31650-6, ISBN13: 978-0-416-31650-6. Dewey:813/.52. LCCN:81-022500.
Audience: **l,u.** B

Cronin, Gloria L. **PS3503.E4488Z619**
A Room of His Own: In Search of the Feminine in the Novels of Saul Bellow. Trade Cloth. Syracuse University Press. Syracuse, NY. 2000. xiii, 193p. Judaic Traditions in Literature, Music and Art Ser. ISBN:0-8156-2862-5, ISBN13: 978-0-8156-2862-0. Dewey:813/.52. LCCN:00-030087.
Audience: **u,f.** *Choice, 2001.*

Cronin, Gloria L. & Siegel, Ben (Editors) **PS3503.E4488Z55 1994**
Conversations with Saul Bellow. Trade Cloth. University Press of Mississippi. Jackson, MS. 1994. 236p. Literary Conversations Ser. ISBN:0-87805-717-X, ISBN13: 978-0-87805-717-7. Dewey:813/.52 B. LCCN:94-019474.
Audience: **g,l,u,f.**

Dutton, Robert R. **PS3503.E4488**
Saul Bellow. Trade Cloth. Macmillan Publishing Company, Inc. Old Tappan, NJ. 1982. 232p. United States Authors Ser., No. 181 ISBN:0-8057-7353-3, ISBN13: 978-0-8057-7353-8. Dewey:813/.52. LCCN:81-006977.
Audience: **l,u.** B

Moogk, Peter **PS3503.E4488Z859**
Small Planets: Saul Bellow and the Art of Short Fiction. Gerhard Bach & Gloria L. Cronin (Editors). Trade Paper. Michigan State University Press. East Lansing, MI. 2000. 425p. ISBN:0-87013-529-5, ISBN13: 978-0-87013-529-3. Dewey:813/.52. LCCN:99-023854.
Audience: **g,l,u,f.**

Pifer, Ellen **PS3511.A86**
Saul Bellow Against the Grain. Book, Other. University of Pennsylvania Press. Philadelphia, PA. 1991. 222p. Pennsylvania Studies in Contemporary American Fiction
ISBN:0-8122-1369-6, ISBN13: 978-0-8122-1369-0.
Dewey:813/.52. LCCN:89-022596.
Audience: **l,u,f.** *Choice, 1990.*

20th Century (1901-1960) > B > Benet, Stephen Vincent

Benet, Stephen Vincent **PS3503.E5325**
The Devil and Daniel Webster. Trade Cloth. Amereon, Ltd. Mattituck, NY. ISBN:0-8488-0789-8, ISBN13: 978-0-8488-0789-4. Dewey:818/.5209.
Audience: **g,l,u,f.** B

Benet, Stephen Vincent **PS3566.L27**
John Brown's Body. Library Binding. Buccaneer Books, Inc. Cutchogue, NY. 1982. ISBN:0-89966-405-9, ISBN13: 978-0-89966-405-7. Dewey:811/.54.
Audience: **g,l,u,f.**

Benet, Stephen Vincent **PS3503.E5325**
Selected Works of Stephen Vincent Benet. Trade Cloth. Henry Holt & Company. New York, NY. 1959. ISBN:0-03-028530-5, ISBN13: 978-0-03-028530-1. Dewey:818. LCCN:42-015523.
Audience: **g,l,u,f.**

Benet, Stephen Vincent **PS3503.E5325 Y7**
Young Adventure a Book of Poems by Stephen Vincent Benet. Trade Paper. Kessinger Publishing, LLC. Whitefish, MT. 2004. ISBN:1-4179-3636-3, ISBN13: 978-1-4179-3636-6. Dewey:811.
Audience: **g,l,u,f.**

Fenton, Charles A. **PS3503**
Stephen Vincent Benet: The Life and Times of an American Man of Letters, 1898-1943. Trade Cloth. Greenwood Publishing Group, Inc. Portsmouth, NH. 1978. 436p. ISBN:0-313-20200-1, ISBN13: 978-0-313-20200-1. Dewey:818/.5/209. LCCN:77-019015.
Audience: **g,l,u,f.**

Garrett, David & Konkle, Lincoln (Editors) **PS3503.E5325Z75 2002**
Stephen Vincent Benét: Essays on His Life and Work. Paper Text. McFarland & Company, Incorporated Publishers. Jefferson, NC. 2002. 256p. Contributions to Southern Appalachian Studies ISBN:0-7864-1364-6, ISBN13: 978-0-7864-1364-5. Dewey:818/.5209 B. LCCN:2002-035857.
Audience: **g,l,u,f.** *Choice, 2003.*

20th Century (1901-1960) > B > Berryman, John

Berryman, John **PS3566.L27**
The Dream Songs. Trade Paper. Farrar, Straus & Giroux. New York, NY. 1982. 427p. ISBN:0-374-51670-7, ISBN13: 978-0-374-51670-3. Dewey:811/.5/4. LCCN:74-093811.
Audience: **g,l,u,f.** B

Berryman, John **PS3503.E744A6 2004**
John Berryman: Selected Poems. Trade Cloth. Library of America, The. New York, NY. 2004. 200p. American Poets Project Ser. ISBN:1-931082-69-3, ISBN13: 978-1-931082-69-3. Dewey:811/.54. LCCN:2004-048570.
Audience: **g,l,u,f.**

Berryman, John **PS3566.L27**
John Berryman: Collected Poems, 1937-1971. Charles Thornbury (Editor). Trade Cloth. Farrar, Straus & Giroux. New York, NY. 1991. 512p. ISBN:0-374-52281-2, ISBN13: 978-0-374-52281-0. Dewey:811/.54. LCCN:89-030944.
Audience: **g,l,u,f.** *Choice, 1990.*

Haffenden, John **PS3503.E744.Z58**
John Berryman: A Critical Commentary. Cloth Text. New York University Press. New York, NY. 1980. vii, 216p. Gotham Library Ser. ISBN:0-8147-3404-9, ISBN13: 978-0-8147-3404-9. Dewey:811/.54. LCCN:79-003893.
Audience: **l,u.** B

Mariani, Paul L. **PS3503.E744Z79 1996**
Dream Song: The Life of John Berryman. Ed. 2. Trade Paper. University of Massachusetts Press. Amherst, MA. 1996. 584p. ISBN:1-55849-017-5, ISBN13: 978-1-55849-017-8. Dewey:811/.54 B. LCCN:95-039531.
Audience: **g,l,u,f.** *Choice, 1990.*

Travisano, Thomas **PS310.P63T73 1999**
Midcentury Quartet: Bishop, Lowell, Jarrell, Berryman and the Making of a Postmodern Aesthetic. Trade Cloth. University Press of Virginia. Charlottesville, VA. 1999. xvi, 325p. ISBN:0-8139-1887-1, ISBN13: 978-0-8139-1887-7. Dewey:811/.509113. LCCN:99-016426.
Audience: **u,f.** *Choice, 2000.*

20th Century (1901-1960) > B > Bishop, Elizabeth

Bishop, Elizabeth **PS3566.L27**
The Complete Poems, 1927-1979. Trade Paper. Farrar, Straus & Giroux. New York, NY. 1984. 287p. ISBN:0-374-51817-3, ISBN13: 978-0-374-51817-2. Dewey:811/.54. LCCN:69-015407.
Audience: **g,l,u,f.** B

Bishop, Elizabeth **PS3503.I785 A15**
The Collected Prose. Robert Giroux (Editor). Trade Paper. Farrar, Straus & Giroux. New York, NY. 1984. 278p. ISBN:0-374-51855-6, ISBN13: 978-0-374-51855-4. Dewey:818.5408. LCCN:83-016418.
Audience: **g,l,u,f.** B

Diehl, Joanne F. **PS3503.I785Z634 1993**
Elizabeth Bishop and Marianne Moore: The Psychodynamics of Creativity. Trade Cloth. Princeton University Press. Princeton, NJ. 1993. 136p. ISBN:0-691-06975-1, ISBN13: 978-0-691-06975-3. Dewey:811.54. LCCN:92-023533.
Audience: **u,f.**

Doreski, C. K. **PS3503.I785Z635 1993**
Elizabeth Bishop: The Restraints of Language. Trade Cloth. Oxford University Press, Inc. New York, NY. 1993. 190p. ISBN:0-19-507966-3, ISBN13: 978-0-19-507966-1. Dewey:811/.52. LCCN:92-030152.
Audience: **g,l,u,f.** *Choice, 1993.*

Fountain, Gary & Brazeau, Peter **PS3503.I785Z683 1994**
Remembering Elizabeth Bishop: An Oral Biography. Bonnie Costello (Afterword by). Cloth Text. University of Massachusetts Press. Amherst, MA. 1994. 456p. ISBN:0-87023-936-8, ISBN13: 978-0-87023-936-6. Dewey:811/.54 B. LCCN:94-014811.
Audience: **g,l,u,f.**

Goldensohn, Lorrie **PS3503.I785Z67 1992**
Elizabeth Bishop: The Biography of a Poetry. Trade Cloth. Columbia University Press. New York, NY. 1991. 306p. ISBN:0-231-07662-2, ISBN13: 978-0-231-07662-3. Dewey:811/.52. LCCN:91-021265.
Audience: **g,l,u,f.** *Choice, 1994.*

Kalstone, David **PS3503.I785Z75 2001**
Becoming a Poet: Elizabeth Bishop with Marianne Moore and Robert Lowell. Trade Paper. University of Michigan Press. Chicago, IL. 2001. 320p. ISBN:0-472-08720-7, ISBN13: 978-0-472-08720-4. Dewey:811/.54 B. LCCN:00-051174.
Audience: **l,u,f.**

Lombardi, Marilyn M. (Editor) **PS3503.I785.Z68 1993**
Elizabeth Bishop: The Geography of Gender. Cloth Text. University Press of Virginia. Charlottesville, VA. 1993. 288p. ISBN:0-8139-1444-2, ISBN13: 978-0-8139-1444-2. Dewey:811.54. LCCN:93-000908.
Audience: **g,l,u,f.** *Choice, 1994.*

McCabe, Susan **PS3503.I785Z77 1994**
Elizabeth Bishop: Her Poetics of Loss. Trade Cloth. Pennsylvania State University Press. University Park, PA. 1994. 272p. ISBN:0-271-01047-9, ISBN13: 978-0-271-01047-2. Dewey:811/.54. LCCN:93-030390.
Audience: **g,l,u,f.** *Choice, 1995.*

Millier, Brett C. **PS3503.I785.Z78**
Elizabeth Bishop: Life and the Memory of It. Trade Paper. University of California Press. Berkeley, CA. 1995. 620p. ISBN:0-520-20345-3, ISBN13: 978-0-520-20345-7. Dewey:811.54. LCCN:92-008548.
Audience: **g,l,u,f.** *Choice, 1993.*

Rotella, Guy **PS310.N3R68 1990**
Reading and Writing Nature: The Poetry of Robert Frost, Wallace Stevens, Marianne Moore, and Elizabeth Bishop. Trade Cloth. Northeastern University Press. Boston, MA. 1990. 253p. ISBN:1-55553-086-9, ISBN13: 978-1-55553-086-0. Dewey:811/.520936. LCCN:90-007576.
Audience: **u,f.** *Choice, 1991.*

Schwartz, Lloyd & Estess, Sybil P. (Editors) **PS3503.I785.Z65 1983**
Elizabeth Bishop and Her Art. Harold Bloom (Foreword by). Trade Paper. University of Michigan Press. Chicago, IL. 1983. 368p. Under Discussion Ser. ISBN:0-472-06343-X, ISBN13: 978-0-472-06343-7. Dewey:811.5/4. LCCN:82-020235.
Audience: **l,u.** B

Travisano, Thomas **PS310.P63T73 1999**
Midcentury Quartet: Bishop, Lowell, Jarrell, Berryman and the Making of a Postmodern Aesthetic. Trade Cloth. University Press of Virginia. Charlottesville, VA. 1999. xvi, 325p. ISBN:0-8139-1887-1, ISBN13: 978-0-8139-1887-7. Dewey:811/.509113. LCCN:99-016426.
Audience: **u,f.** *Choice, 2000.*

Zona, Kirstin H. **PS310.F45Z66 2003**
Marianne Moore, Elizabeth Bishop, and May Swenson: The Feminist Poetics of Self-Restraint. Trade Cloth. University of Michigan Press. Chicago, IL. 2002. 200p. ISBN:0-472-11304-6, ISBN13: 978-0-472-11304-0. Dewey:811/.50809287. LCCN:2002-008277.
Audience: **u,f.**

20th Century (1901-1960) > B > Bowles, Paul

Bowles, Paul **PS3552.O874A6 2002**
Paul Bowles: The Sheltering Sky/ Let It Come down/ the Spider's House. Trade Cloth. Library of America, The. New York, NY. 2002. 940p. ISBN:1-931082-19-7, ISBN13: 978-1-931082-19-8. Dewey:813/.54. LCCN:2002-019453.
Audience: **g,l,u,f.** *Choice, 2003.*

Bowles, Paul **PS3552.O874.A6 2002**
Paul Bowles: Collected Stories and Later Writings. Trade Cloth. Library of America, The. New York, NY. 2002. 1050p. ISBN:1-931082-20-0, ISBN13: 978-1-931082-20-4. Dewey:813/.54. LCCN:2002-019452.
Audience: **g,l,u,f.**

Caponi, Gena D. (Editor) **PS3552.O874.Z463**
Conversations with Paul Bowles. Trade Cloth. University Press of Mississippi. Jackson, MS. 1993. 175p. Literary Conversations Ser. ISBN:0-87805-649-1, ISBN13: 978-0-87805-649-1. Dewey:813/.54. LCCN:93-025038.
Audience: **g,l,u,f.** *Choice, 1994.*

Caponi, Gena Dagel **PS3552.O874Z6 1998**
Paul Bowles. Trade Cloth. Thomson Gale. Farmington Hills, MI. 1998. xiii, 152p. Twayne's United States Authors Ser., Vol. 706 ISBN:0-8057-4560-2, ISBN13: 978-0-8057-4560-3. Dewey:813/.54. LCCN:98-034789.
Audience: **g,l,u,f.**

Carr, Virginia **PS3552.O874Z625 2004**
Paul Bowles: A Life. Trade Cloth. Simon & Schuster. New York, NY. 2004. 432p. ISBN:0-684-19657-3, ISBN13: 978-0-684-19657-2. Dewey:813/.54 B. LCCN:2004-054748.
Audience: **g,l,u,f.**

Sawyer-Lauçanno, Christopher **PS3552.O874**
An Invisible Spectator: A Biography of Paul Bowles. Trade Paper. Grove/Atlantic, Inc. New York, NY. 1999. 544p. ISBN:0-8021-3600-1, ISBN13: 978-0-8021-3600-8. Dewey:813/.54 B.
Audience: **g,l,u,f.** *Choice, 1989.*

20th Century (1901-1960) > B > Boyle, Kay

Austenfeld, Thomas C. **PS159.G3A94 2001**
American Women Writers and the Nazis: Ethics and Politics in Boyle, Porter, Stafford and Hellman. Trade Cloth. University Press of Virginia. Charlottesville, VA. 2001. viii, 189p. ISBN:0-8139-2052-3, ISBN13: 978-0-8139-2052-8. Dewey:810.9/9287/0904. LCCN:00-068660.
Audience: **u,f.** *Choice, 2002.*

Boyle, Kay **PS3503.O9357A17 1991**
Collected Poems. Trade Paper. Copper Canyon Press. Port Townsend, WA. 1991. 192p. ISBN:1-55659-039-3, ISBN13: 978-1-55659-039-9. Dewey:811/.52. LCCN:90-085089.
Audience: **g,l,u,f.** B

Boyle, Kay **PS3511.A86**
Fifty Stories. Trade Paper. New Directions Publishing Corporation. New York, NY. 1992. 640p. Revived Modern Classic Ser., Vol. 741 ISBN:0-8112-1206-8, ISBN13: 978-0-8112-1206-9. Dewey:813/.52. LCCN:91-040229.
Audience: **g,l,u,f.** B

Boyle, Kay **PZ3.B69796 Un PS3503.O9357**
The Underground Woman. Doubleday. 1975. ISBN:0-385-07047-0, ISBN13: 978-0-385-07047-8.
Audience: **g,l,u,f.**

Elkins, Marilyn **PS3503.O9357Z58 1997**
Critical Essays on Kay Boyle. Trade Cloth. Thomson Gale. Farmington Hills, MI. 1997. Critical Essays on American Literature Ser. ISBN:0-7838-0012-6, ISBN13: 978-0-7838-0012-7. Dewey:813/.52. LCCN:97-008361.
Audience: **l,u.**

Lesinka, Zofia P. **PS228.W37L47 2002**
Perspectives of Four Women Writers on the Second World War: Gertrude Stein, Janet Flanner, Kay Boyle, and Rebecca West. Trade Cloth. Peter Lang Publishing, Inc. New York, NY. 2002. 200p. Studies in Literary Criticism and Theory Ser., Vol. 17 ISBN:0-8204-6103-2, ISBN13: 978-0-8204-6103-8. Dewey:810.9/358. LCCN:2002-023812.
Audience: **u,f.**

McAlmon, Robert & Boyle, Kay **PS3525.A1**
Being Geniuses Together, 1920-1930. Ed. 2. Trade Paper. Johns Hopkins University Press. Baltimore, MD. 1997. 374p. ISBN:0-8018-5584-5, ISBN13: 978-0-8018-5584-9. Dewey:818/.5/203. LCCN:96-035087.
Audience: **u,f.**

20th Century (1901-1960) > B > Bradbury, Ray

Bradbury, Ray **PS3503.R167D26 1999**
Dandelion Wine. Trade Cloth. HarperCollins Publishers. New York, NY. 1999. 288p. ISBN:0-380-97726-5, ISBN13: 978-0-380-97726-0. Dewey:813.5/4. LCCN:98-093914.
Audience: **g,l,u,f.**

Bradbury, Ray **PS3503.R167F3 2003**
Fahrenheit 451. Ed. 50. Trade Cloth. Simon & Schuster. New York, NY. 2003. 208p. ISBN:0-7432-4722-1, ISBN13: 978-0-7432-4722-1. Dewey:813/.54. LCCN:2003-066160.
Audience: **g,l,u,f.**

Bradbury, Ray **PS3568.O243**
The Martian Chronicles. Trade Cloth. HarperCollins Publishers. New York, NY. 1997. 288p. ISBN:0-380-97383-9, ISBN13: 978-0-380-97383-5. Dewey:813.5/4. LCCN:96-095071.
Audience: **g,l,u,f.**

Bradbury, Ray **PS3503.R167.A6 1980**
The Stories of Ray Bradbury. Trade Cloth. Alfred A. Knopf Inc. New York, NY. 1980. 912p. ISBN:0-394-51335-5, ISBN13: 978-0-394-51335-5. Dewey:813/.54. LCCN:80-007655.
Audience: **g,l,u,f.** B

Bradbury, Ray **PS3568.O243**
Something Wicked This Way Comes. Joe Muznaini (Illustrator). Trade Cloth. Gauntlet, Inc. Colorado Springs, CO. 1999. 230p. ISBN:1-887368-23-X, ISBN13: 978-1-887368-23-0. Dewey:813.5/4.
Audience: **g,l,u,f.**

Reid, Robin Anne **PS3503**
Ray Bradbury: A Critical Companion. Cloth Text. Greenwood Publishing Group, Inc. Portsmouth, NH. 2000. 152p. Critical Companions to Popular Contemporary Writers Ser. ISBN:0-313-30901-9, ISBN13: 978-0-313-30901-4. Dewey:813/.54. LCCN:00-022332.
Audience: **l,u.**

Weller, Sam **PS3503.R167Z94 2005**
The Bradbury Chronicles: The Life of Ray Bradbury. Trade Cloth. HarperCollins Publishers. New York, NY. 2005. 400p. ISBN:0-06-054581-X, ISBN13: 978-0-06-054581-9. Dewey:813/.54. LCCN:2004-059491.
Audience: **g,l,u,f.**

20th Century (1901-1960) > B > Brooks, Gwendolyn

Brooks, Gwendolyn **PS3503.R7244.Z524**
Report from Part One: An Autobiography. Trade Cloth. Broadside Press. Detroit, MI. 1972. 192p. ISBN:0-910296-82-0, ISBN13: 978-0-910296-82-3. Dewey:811/.5/4. LCCN:72-077308.
Audience: **g,l,u,f.**

Brooks, Gwendolyn **PS3503.R7244**
Report from Part Two, Vol. 2. Trade Cloth. Third World Press. Chicago, IL. 1996. 170p. ISBN:0-88378-162-X, ISBN13: 978-0-88378-162-3. Dewey:811/.54. LCCN:96-083057.
Audience: **g,l,u,f.**

Brooks, Gwendolyn **PS3503.R7244A6 1999**
Selected Poems. Trade Paper. HarperCollins Publishers. New York, NY. 1999. 160p. Perennial Classics Ser. ISBN:0-06-093174-4, ISBN13: 978-0-06-093174-2. Dewey:811.54. LCCN:98-054645.
Audience: **g,l,u,f.** B

Brooks, Gwendolyn **PS3503.R7244A6 2005**
The Essential Gwendolyn Brooks. Elizabeth Alexander (Editor). Saddle Stitched, Cloth over Boards, Dust Jacket. Library of America, The. New York, NY. 2005. 150p. American Poets Project Ser. ISBN:1-931082-87-1, ISBN13: 978-1-931082-87-7. Dewey:811/.54. LCCN:2005-044162.
Audience: **g,l,u,f.**

Brooks, Gwendolyn **PS3503.R7244Z5235**
Conversations with Gwendolyn Brooks. Gloria Jean Wade Gayles (Editor). Trade Cloth. University Press of Mississippi. Jackson, MS. 2003. xx, 167p. Literary Conversations Ser. ISBN:1-57806-574-7, ISBN13: 978-1-57806-574-5. Dewey:811/.54 B. LCCN:2003-047937.
Audience: **g,l,u,f.**

Kent, George E. **PS3503.R7244Z73**
A Life of Gwendolyn Brooks. Trade Paper. University Press of Kentucky. Lexington, KY. 1990. 296p. ISBN:0-8131-0827-6, ISBN13: 978-0-8131-0827-8. Dewey:811/.54 B. LCCN:89-031738.
Audience: **g,l,u,f.** *Choice, 1990.*

Wright, Stephen C. (Editor) **PS3503.R7244Z78 2001**
On Gwendolyn Brooks: Reliant Contemplation. Trade Paper. University of Michigan Press. Chicago, IL. 2001. 296p. Under Discussion Ser. ISBN:0-472-08839-4, ISBN13: 978-0-472-08839-3. Dewey:811/.54. LCCN:2002-284102.
Audience: **g,l,u,f.**

20th Century (1901-1960) > B > Burroughs, William

Burroughs, William S. **PN6162**
The Adding Machine: Selected Essays. Trade Paper. Arcade Publishing, Inc. New York, NY. 1993. 216p. ISBN:1-55970-210-9, ISBN13: 978-1-55970-210-2. Dewey:814/.54. LCCN:92-046690.
Audience: **g,l,u,f.**

Burroughs, William S. **PS3552.U75N3 2001**
Naked Lunch: The Restored Text. James Grauerholz & Barry Miles (Editors). Trade Cloth. Grove/Atlantic, Inc. New York, NY. 2003. 304p. ISBN:0-8021-1639-6, ISBN13: 978-0-8021-1639-0. Dewey:813/.54. LCCN:2001-023190.
Audience: **g,l,u,f.**

Burroughs, William S. **PS3552.U75**
Word Virus: The William S. Burroughs Reader. James Grauerholz & Ira Silverberg (Editors), Ann Douglas (Introduction by). Trade Paper. Grove/Atlantic, Inc. New York, NY. 2000. 576p. ISBN:0-8021-3694-X, ISBN13: 978-0-8021-3694-7. Dewey:813/.54.
Audience: **g,l,u,f.**

Burroughs, William S. **PS3552.U75J86 2003**
Junky. Ed. 50. Oliver Harris (Contribution by), Allen Ginsberg (Foreword by). Trade Paper. Penguin Group (USA) Inc. New York, NY. 2003. 208p. ISBN:0-14-200316-6, ISBN13: 978-0-14-200316-9. Dewey:813/.54. LCCN:2002-193008.
Audience: **g,l,u,f.** B

Harris, Oliver & Lieb, Frederick G. **PS3552.U75Z69 2003**
William Burroughs and the Secret of Fascination. Trade Cloth. Southern Illinois University Press. Carbondale, IL. 2003. 272p. ISBN:0-8093-2484-9, ISBN13: 978-0-8093-2484-2. Dewey:813/.54. LCCN:2002-004723.
Audience: **u,f.** *Choice, 2003.*

Hibbard, Allen (Editor) **PS3552.U75Z465 1999**
Conversations with William S. Burroughs. Trade Cloth. University Press of Mississippi. Jackson, MS. 2000. 226p. Literary Conversations Ser. ISBN:1-57806-182-2, ISBN13: 978-1-57806-182-2. Dewey:813/.54 B. LCCN:99-052249.
Audience: **u,f.**

Lardas, John **PS228.B6L37 2001**
The Bop Apocalypse: The Religious Visions of Kerouac, Ginsberg, and Burroughs. Trade Cloth. University of Illinois Press. Champaign, IL. 2000. 328p. ISBN:0-252-02599-7, ISBN13: 978-0-252-02599-0. Dewey:810.9/382. LCCN:00-008649.
Audience: **u,f.** *Choice, 2001.*

Morgan, Ted **PS3552.U75**
Literary Outlaw: The Life and Times of William S. Burroughs. Trade Paper. HarperCollins Publishers. New York, NY. 1990. ISBN:0-380-70882-5, ISBN13: 978-0-380-70882-6. Dewey:813/.54 B.
Audience: **g,l,u,f.** *Choice, 1989.*

Murphy, Timothy S. **PS3552.U75Z76 1997**
Wising up the Marks: The Amodern William Burroughs. Trade Paper. University of California Press. Berkeley, CA. 1998. 288p. ISBN:0-520-20951-6, ISBN13: 978-0-520-20951-0. LCCN:96-053094.
Audience: **l,u,f.** *Choice, 1998.*

Skerl, Jennie **PS3552.U75**
William S. Burroughs. Twayne. 1985. ISBN:0-8057-7438-6, ISBN13: 978-0-8057-7438-2.
Audience: **l,u,f.**

Skerl, Jennie & Lydenberg, Robin (Editors) **PS3552.U75Z93 1991**
William S. Burroughs at the Front: Critical Reception, 1959-1989. Trade Cloth. Southern Illinois University Press. Carbondale, IL. 1991. 281p. ISBN:0-8093-1586-6, ISBN13: 978-0-8093-1586-4. Dewey:813/.54. LCCN:90-009403.
Audience: **u,f.** *Choice, 1991.*

20th Century (1901-1960) > C

Cabell, James Branch **PS3511.A86**
Jurgen. Library Binding. Classic Books. Murrieta, CA. 1998. 325p. The Collected Works of James Branch Cabell ISBN:1-58201-561-9, ISBN13: 978-1-58201-561-3. Dewey:813/.52.
Audience: **g,l,u,f.**

Cain, James M. **PS3511.A86**
The Postman Always Rings Twice. Trade Cloth. Amereon, Ltd. Mattituck, NY. ISBN:0-89190-815-3, ISBN13: 978-0-89190-815-9. Dewey:813.5/2.
Audience: **g,l,u,f.**

Cassady, Neal **CT275.C3458 A3 1981**
The First Third and Other Writings. Trade Cloth. City Lights Books. San Francisco, CA. 1971. 225p. ISBN:0-87286-005-1, ISBN13: 978-0-87286-005-6. Dewey:973.92/092/4. LCCN:85-100975.
Audience: **g,l,u,f.**

Chandler, Raymond **PS3505.H3224 A6**
Chandler - Later Novels and Other Writings: The Lady in the Lake; The Little Sister; The Long Goodbye; Playback; Double Indemnity; Essays and Letters. Frank MacShane (Editor). Trade Cloth. Library of America, The. New York, NY. 1995. 1088p. ISBN:1-883011-08-6, ISBN13: 978-1-883011-08-6. Dewey:813.52.
Audience: **g,l,u,f.**

Chandler, Raymond **PS3505.H3224A6**
Chandler - Stories and Early Novels: Pulp Stories; The Big Sleep; Farewell, My Lovely; The High Window. Frank MacShane (Editor). Trade Cloth. Library of America, The. New York, NY. 1995. 1216p. ISBN:1-883011-07-8, ISBN13: 978-1-883011-07-9. Dewey:813/.52. LCCN:94-043705.
Audience: **g,l,u,f.**

Chayefsky, Paddy **PS3505.H632.A6 1994**
The Television Plays of Paddy Chayefsky. Arthur M. Schlesinger Jr. (Introduction by). Trade Paper. Applause Theatre Book Publishers. New York, NY. 1994. 277p. Collected Works of Paddy Chayefsky ISBN:1-55783-191-2, ISBN13: 978-1-55783-191-0. Dewey:812/.54. LCCN:94-185845.
Audience: **g,l,u,f.**

Cheever, Susan **PS3511.A86**
Home Before Dark. Trade Paper. Simon & Schuster. New York, NY. 1999. 256p. Contemporary Classics Ser. ISBN:0-671-02850-2, ISBN13: 978-0-671-02850-3. Dewey:813/.52.
Audience: **g,l,u,f.**

Ciardi, John **PS3505.I27A17 1997**
The Collected Poems of John Ciardi. Edward M. Cifelli (Editor). Trade Paper. University of Arkansas Press. Fayetteville, AR. 2003. 456p. ISBN:1-55728-449-0, ISBN13: 978-1-55728-449-5. Dewey:811/.52. LCCN:96-046331.
Audience: **g,l,u,f.**

Clark, Walter **PS3505.L376 O9**
Ox-Bow Incident. Library Binding. Sagebrush Education Resources. Caledonia, MN. 2001. ISBN:0-613-37164-X, ISBN13: 978-0-613-37164-3. Dewey:813/.52.
Audience: **g,l,u,f.**

Connelly, Marc **PS3505.O4814 G7**
Green Pastures. Cloth Text. Amereon, Ltd. Mattituck, NY. 2004. ISBN:0-8488-2703-1, ISBN13: 978-0-8488-2703-8. Dewey:812.5.
Audience: **g,l,u,f.**

Corso, Gregory **PS3566.L27**
Mindfield: New and Selected Poems. William S. Burroughs & Allen Ginsberg (Foreword by). Trade Cloth. Avalon Publishing Group. New York, NY. 1998. 288p. ISBN:0-938410-96-2, ISBN13: 978-0-938410-96-6. Dewey:811/.54.
Audience: **g,l,u,f.** *Choice, 1990.*

Cozzens, James Gould **PS3511.A86**
By Love Possessed. Library Binding. Buccaneer Books, Inc. Cutchogue, NY. 1994. ISBN:1-56849-549-8, ISBN13: 978-1-56849-549-1. Dewey:813/.52.
Audience: **g,l,u,f.** B

Cozzens, James Gould **PS3505.O99G8 1998**
Guard of Honor. Trade Cloth. Random House, Inc. New York, NY. 1998. 360p. Modern Library Ser. ISBN:0-679-60305-0, ISBN13: 978-0-679-60305-4. Dewey:813/.52. LCCN:97-039459.
Audience: **g,l,u,f.** B

Creeley, Robert **PS3505.R43.A17 1982**
The Collected Poems of Robert Creeley, 1945-1975. Trade Cloth. University of California Press. Berkeley, CA. 1983. 576p. ISBN:0-520-04243-3, ISBN13: 978-0-520-04243-8. Dewey:811/.54. LCCN:81-019668.
Audience: **g,l,u,f.** B

Creeley, Robert **PS3505.R43A15 2001**
Collected Prose. Trade Paper. Dalkey Archive Press. Normal, IL. 2001. 444p. ISBN:1-56478-303-0, ISBN13: 978-1-56478-303-5. Dewey:818/.5408. LCCN:2001-028786.
Audience: **g,l,u,f.**

Cullen, Countee **PS3505**
Color. Trade Cloth. Ayer Company Publishers, Inc. Manchester, NH. 1975. ISBN:0-88143-155-9, ISBN13: 978-0-88143-155-1. Dewey:811.
Audience: **g,l,u,f.** B

Cullen, Countee **PS3505.U287**
My Soul's High Song: The Collected Writings of Countee Cullen, Voice of the Harlem Renaissance. Early, Gerald. Doubleday. 1991. ISBN:0-385-41295-9, ISBN13: 978-0-385-41295-7.
Audience: **g,l,u,f.**

Hiney, Tom **PS3511.A86**
Raymond Chandler: A Biography. Book, Other. Knopf Publishing Group. New York, NY. 1998. x, 310p. ISBN:0-09-953351-0, ISBN13: 978-0-09-953351-1. Dewey:813.5/2.
Audience: **g,l,u,f.** *Choice, 1997.*

Hoopes, Roy **PS3505.A3113Z69 1987**
Cain: The Biography of James M. Cain. Trade Paper. Southern Illinois University Press. Carbondale, IL. 1987. 704p. ISBN:0-8093-1361-8, ISBN13: 978-0-8093-1361-7. Dewey:813/.52 B. LCCN:86-027926.
Audience: **g,l,u,f.**

Madden, David **PS3505.A3113 Z8**
James M. Cain. Trade Paper. Carnegie Mellon University Press. Pittsburgh, PA. 1987. 200p. ISBN:0-88748-045-4, ISBN13: 978-0-88748-045-4. Dewey:813/.5/2. LCCN:86-072297.
Audience: **g,l,u,f.**

Marling, William **PS374.D4M33 1995**
The American Roman Noir: Hammett, Cain and Chandler. Trade Cloth. University of Georgia Press. Athens, GA. 1995. 256p. ISBN:0-8203-1658-X, ISBN13: 978-0-8203-1658-1. Dewey:813/.0872/0905. LCCN:94-025550.
Audience: **u,f.**

Phillips, Gene D. **PS3505.H3224Z836**
Creatures of Darkness: Raymond Chandler, Detective Fiction and Film Noir. Trade Cloth. University Press of Kentucky. Lexington, KY. 2000. xxiv, 311p. ISBN:0-8131-2174-4, ISBN13: 978-0-8131-2174-1. Dewey:813/.52. LCCN:00-028306.
Audience: **g,l,u,f.** *Choice, 2001.*

20th Century (1901-1960) > C > Caldwell, Erskine

Arnold, Edwin T. (Editor) **PS3505.A322Z565 1990**
Erskine Caldwell Reconsidered. Trade Cloth. University Press of Mississippi. Jackson, MS. 1990. 120p. Southern Quarterly Ser. ISBN:0-87805-432-4, ISBN13: 978-0-87805-432-9. Dewey:813/.52 B. LCCN:89-049307.
Audience: **l,u.** *Choice, 1990.*

Caldwell, Erskine **PS3505.A322**
The Complete Stories of Erskine Caldwell. Trade Cloth. Amereon, Ltd. Mattituck, NY. ISBN:0-88411-455-4, ISBN13: 978-0-88411-455-0. Dewey:813.52.
Audience: **g,l,u,f.**

Caldwell, Erskine **PR6019.O9**
Tobacco Road. Library Binding. Bentley Publishers. Cambridge, MA. 1978. ISBN:0-8376-0422-2, ISBN13: 978-0-8376-0422-0. Dewey:823/.91. LCCN:78-055752.
Audience: **g,l,u,f.** B

Caldwell, Erskine **PS3505.A322G6 1995**
God's Little Acre. Lewis Nordan (Foreword by). Trade Paper. University of Georgia Press. Athens, GA. 1995. 232p. Brown Thrasher Bks. ISBN:0-8203-1663-6, ISBN13: 978-0-8203-1663-5. Dewey:813/.52. LCCN:94-025816.
Audience: **g,l,u,f.**

Devlin, James E. **PS3505.A322.Z56 1984**
Erskine Caldwell. Trade Cloth. Thomson Gale. Farmington Hills, MI. 1984. 189p. United States Authors Ser., No. 469 ISBN:0-8057-7410-6, ISBN13: 978-0-8057-7410-8. Dewey:813/.52. LCCN:83-026538.
Audience: **l,u.** B

Klevar, Harvey L. **PS3505.A322Z69 1993**
Erskine Caldwell: A Biography. Trade Paper. University of Tennessee Press. Knoxville, TN. 1993. 516p. ISBN:0-87049-775-8, ISBN13: 978-0-87049-775-9. Dewey:813/.52. LCCN:92-028494.
Audience: **g,l,u,f.** *Choice, 1994.*

McDonald, Robert L. (Editor) **PS3505**
The Critical Response to Erskine Caldwell. Cloth Text. Greenwood Publishing Group, Inc. Portsmouth, NH. 1997. 336p. Critical Responses in Arts and Letters Ser., Vol. 28 ISBN:0-313-30072-0, ISBN13: 978-0-313-30072-1. Dewey:813/.52. LCCN:97-016239.
Audience: **l,u.**

20th Century (1901-1960) > C > Capote, Truman

Capote, Truman **PS3505.A59A6 1994**
Breakfast at Tiffany's: A Short Novel and Three Stories. Trade Cloth. Random House, Inc. New York, NY. 1994. 176p. 360 Degrees Ser. ISBN:0-679-60085-X, ISBN13: 978-0-679-60085-5. Dewey:813/.54. LCCN:93-043633.
Audience: **g,l,u,f.** B

Capote, Truman **PS3505.A59.G7 1993**
The Grass Harp: Including a Tree of the Night and Other Stories. Trade Paper. Knopf Publishing Group. New York, NY. 1993. 224p. ISBN:0-679-74557-2, ISBN13: 978-0-679-74557-0. Dewey:813/.54. LCCN:93-019633.
Audience: **g,l,u,f.**

Capote, Truman **PS3568.O243**
Music for Chameleons. Trade Cloth. Amereon, Ltd. Mattituck, NY. 283p. ISBN:0-8488-2227-7, ISBN13: 978-0-8488-2227-9. Dewey:813/.54.
Audience: **g,l,u,f.** B

Capote, Truman **PS3505.A59O7 2004**
Other Voices, Other Rooms. John Berendt (Introduction by). Trade Cloth. Random House, Inc. New York, NY. 2004. 224p. ISBN:0-679-64322-2, ISBN13: 978-0-679-64322-7. Dewey:813/.54. LCCN:2004-046666.
Audience: **g,l,u,f.** B

Garson, Helen S. **PS3505.A59Z6553 1992**
Truman Capote: A Study of the Short Fiction. Trade Cloth. Macmillan Publishing Company, Inc. Old Tappan, NJ. 1992. 160p. Twayne's Studies in Short Fiction, No. 36 ISBN:0-8057-0851-0, ISBN13: 978-0-8057-0851-6. Dewey:813/.54. LCCN:92-010836.
Audience: **l,u.**

Inge, M. T. (Editor) **PS3505.A59Z475 1987**
Truman Capote: Conversations. Trade Cloth. University Press of Mississippi. Jackson, MS. 1987. 390p. Literary Conversations Ser. ISBN:0-87805-274-7, ISBN13: 978-0-87805-274-5. Dewey:813/.54 B. LCCN:86-019116.
Audience: **g,l,u.**

Nance, William L. **PS3505.A59.Z7 1970**
The Worlds of Truman Capote. Trade Cloth. Scarborough House. Chelsea, MI. 1970. 256p. ISBN:0-8128-1302-2, ISBN13: 978-0-8128-1302-9. Dewey:813/.5/4. LCCN:78-110940.
Audience: **g,l,u,f.** B

Plimpton, George **PS3568.O243**
Truman Capote: In Which Various Friends, Enemies, Acquaintances, and Detractors Recall His Turbulent Career. Trade Paper. Doubleday Publishing. New York, NY. 1998. 544p. ISBN:0-385-49173-5, ISBN13: 978-0-385-49173-0. Dewey:813.5/4.
Audience: **g,l,u,f.**

Waldmeir, Joseph J. & Waldmeir, John C. (Editors) **PS3505**
The Critical Response to Truman Capote. Cloth Text. Greenwood Publishing Group, Inc. Portsmouth, NH. 1999. 280p. Critical Responses in Arts and Letters Ser., Vol. 32 ISBN:0-313-30666-4, ISBN13: 978-0-313-30666-2. Dewey:813/.54. LCCN:98-048934.
Audience: **l,u.** *Choice, 1999.*

20th Century (1901-1960) > C > Cather, Willa

Bloom, Harold **PS3505.A87Z9382 1999**
Willa Cather. Trade Cloth. Facts On File, Inc. New York, NY. 1999. 120p. Bloom's Major Novelists Ser. ISBN:0-7910-5261-3, ISBN13: 978-0-7910-5261-7. Dewey:813/.52. LCCN:99-015164.
Audience: **l,u.**

Brown, E. K. **PS3505.A87Z584 1987**
Willa Cather: A Critical Biography. Leon Edel (Contribution by), James Woodress (Foreword by). Trade Paper. University of Nebraska Press. Lincoln, NE. 1987. xxxiv, 360p. ISBN:0-8032-6084-9, ISBN13: 978-0-8032-6084-9. Dewey:813/.52 B. LCCN:86-025097.
Audience: **g,l,u,f.** B

Cather, Willa **PS3511.A86**
Cather: Stories, Poems, and Other Writings. Sharon O'Brien (Editor). Trade Cloth. Library of America, The. New York, NY. 1992. 1039p. Library of America, Vol. 57 ISBN:0-940450-71-2, ISBN13: 978-0-940450-71-4. Dewey:813/.52. LCCN:91-062294.
Audience: **g,l,u,f.**

Cather, Willa **PS3505.A87A6 1990**
Cather: Later Novels: A Lost Lady; the Professor's House; Death Comes for the Archbishop; Shadows on the Rock; Lucy Gayheart; Sapphira and the Slave Girl. Sharon O'Brien (Editor). Trade Cloth. Library of America, The. New York, NY. 1990. 976p. Library of America, Vol. 49 ISBN:0-940450-52-6, ISBN13: 978-0-940450-52-3. Dewey:813/.52. LCCN:89-064130.
Audience: **g,l,u,f.**

Cather, Willa **PS3505.A87A6 1987**
Early Novels and Stories: The Troll Garden; O Pioneers!; The Song of the Lark; My Antonia; One of Ours. Sharon O'Brien (Editor). Trade Cloth. Library of America, The. New York, NY. 1987. 1336p. ISBN:0-940450-39-9, ISBN13: 978-0-940450-39-4. Dewey:813/.52. LCCN:87-010704.
Audience: **g,l,u,f.**

Goldberg, Jonathan **PS3505.A87Z647 2001**
Willa Cather and Others. Trade Cloth. Duke University Press. Durham, NC. 2001. 240p. Series Q ISBN:0-8223-2677-9, ISBN13: 978-0-8223-2677-9. Dewey:813/.52. LCCN:00-063658.
Audience: **g,l,u,f.** *Choice, 2001.*

Lee, Hermione **PS3511.A86**
Willa Cather: Double Lives. Trade Paper. Knopf Publishing Group. New York, NY. 1991. 432p. ISBN:0-679-73649-2, ISBN13: 978-0-679-73649-3. Dewey:813/.52 B. LCCN:91-050018.
Audience: **g,l,u,f.**

Meyering, Sheryl L. **PS3505.A87.Z7425**
A Reader's Guide to the Short Stories of Willa Cather. Trade Cloth. Macmillan Publishing Company, Inc. Old Tappan, NJ. 1993. 304p. Reference Publication in Literature Ser. ISBN:0-8161-1834-5, ISBN13: 978-0-8161-1834-2. Dewey:813/.52. LCCN:93-010381.
Audience: **l,u.** *Choice, 1994.*

Murphy, John J. (Editor) **PS3505.A87.Z593 1984**
Critical Essays on Willa Cather. Trade Cloth. Thomson Gale. Farmington Hills, MI. 1984. 344p. Critical Essays on American Literature Ser. ISBN:0-8161-8676-6, ISBN13: 978-0-8161-8676-1. Dewey:813/.52. LCCN:83-012612.
Audience: **l,u.** B

Randall, John H. 3rd **PS3505.A87 Z78 1973**
The Landscape and the Looking Glass: Willa Cather's Search for Value. Trade Cloth. Greenwood Publishing Group, Inc. Portsmouth, NH. 1973. 425p. ISBN:0-8371-6466-4, ISBN13: 978-0-8371-6466-3. Dewey:813/.5/2. LCCN:72-006207.
Audience: **l,u.**

Sergeant, Elizabeth S. **PS3505.A87Z83 1991**
Willa Cather: A Memoir. Marilyn Arnold (Foreword by). Trade Paper. Ohio University Press. Athens, OH. 1992. 312p. ISBN:0-8214-1009-1, ISBN13: 978-0-8214-1009-7. Dewey:813/.52 B. LCCN:91-013075.
Audience: **g,l,u.**

Stout, Janis P. **PS3505.A87Z863 2000**
Willa Cather: The Writer and Her World. Trade Paper. University Press of Virginia. Charlottesville, VA. 2000. xviii, 381p. ISBN:0-8139-1996-7, ISBN13: 978-0-8139-1996-6. Dewey:813/.52 B. LCCN:00-034975.
Audience: **g,l,u,f.** *Choice, 2001.*

Williams, Deborah Lindsay **PS374.F45W55 2001**
Not in Sisterhood: Edith Wharton, Willa Cather, Zona Gale and the Politics of Female Authorship. Cloth over Boards. Palgrave Macmillan. New York, NY. 2001. 240p. ISBN:0-312-22921-6, ISBN13: 978-0-312-22921-4. Dewey:813/.52099287. LCCN:2001-021549.
Audience: **u,f.** *Choice, 2001.*

20th Century (1901-1960) > C > Cheever, John

Bosha, Francis J. (Editor) **PS3505**
The Critical Response to John Cheever. Cloth Text. Greenwood Publishing Group, Inc. Portsmouth, NH. 1993. 352p. Critical Responses in Arts and Letters Ser., No. 6 ISBN:0-313-28355-9, ISBN13: 978-0-313-28355-0. Dewey:813.52. LCCN:93-008974.
Audience: **l,u.**

Cheever, John **PS3511.A86**
Bullet Park. Trade Paper. Knopf Publishing Group. New York, NY. 1992. 256p. Vintage International Ser. ISBN:0-679-73787-1, ISBN13: 978-0-679-73787-2. Dewey:813.5/2. LCCN:91-055304.
Audience: **g,l,u,f.**

Cheever, John **PS3505.H6428F3 1991**
Falconer. Trade Paper. Knopf Publishing Group. New York, NY. 1992. 224p. Vintage International Ser. ISBN:0-679-73786-3, ISBN13: 978-0-679-73786-5. Dewey:813.52. LCCN:91-055303.
Audience: **g,l,u,f.** B

Cheever, John **PS3505.H6428A6 2000**
The Stories of John Cheever. Trade Paper. Knopf Publishing Group. New York, NY. 2000. 704p. International Rediscovery Ser. ISBN:0-375-72442-7, ISBN13: 978-0-375-72442-8. Dewey:813.5/2. LCCN:00-267415.
Audience: **g,l,u,f.** B

Cheever, John **PS3505.H6428W3 2003**
The Wapshot Chronicle. Trade Paper. HarperCollins Publishers. New York, NY. 2003. 368p. Perennial Classics Ser. ISBN:0-06-052887-7, ISBN13: 978-0-06-052887-4. Dewey:813/.52. LCCN:2003-046572.
Audience: **g,l,u,f.**

Cheever, John **PS3505.H6428W32 2003**
The Wapshot Scandal. Trade Paper. HarperCollins Publishers. New York, NY. 2003. 320p. Perennial Classics Ser. ISBN:0-06-052888-5, ISBN13: 978-0-06-052888-1. Dewey:813/.52. LCCN:2003-048255.
Audience: **g,l,u,f.**

Donaldson, Scott (Editor) **PS3505.H6428Z463**
Conversations with John Cheever. Trade Cloth. University Press of Mississippi. Jackson, MS. 1987. 260p. Literary Conversations Ser. ISBN:0-87805-331-X, ISBN13: 978-0-87805-331-5. Dewey:813/.52. LCCN:87-017932.
Audience: **l,u.**

Donaldson, Scott **PS3511.A86**
John Cheever: A Biography. Trade Paper. iUniverse, Inc. Lincoln, NE. 2002. 450p. ISBN:0-595-21138-0, ISBN13: 978-0-595-21138-8. Dewey:813/.52 B.
Audience: **g,l,u,f.**

O'Hara, James **PS3505.H6428Z8 1989**
John Cheever: A Study of the Short Fiction. Trade Cloth. Macmillan Publishing Company, Inc. Old Tappan, NJ. 1989. 168p. Twayne's Studies in Short Fiction, No. 9 ISBN:0-8057-8310-5, ISBN13: 978-0-8057-8310-0. Dewey:813/.52. LCCN:89-032877.
Audience: **l,u.** *Choice, 1990.*

20th Century (1901-1960) > C > Crane, Hart

Crane, Hart **PS3505.R272 1968**
The Complete Poems and Selected Letters and Prose of Hart Crane. Trade Cloth. Oxford University Press, Inc. New York, NY. 1968. xvii, 302p. ISBN:0-19-212544-3, ISBN13: 978-0-19-212544-6. Dewey:818/.5/209. LCCN:77-376085.
Audience: **g,l,u,f.** B

Fisher, Clive **PS3505.R272Z66 2002**
Hart Crane: A Life. Cloth over Boards. Yale University Press. Cumberland, RI. 2002. 592p. ISBN:0-300-09061-7, ISBN13: 978-0-300-09061-1. Dewey:811/.52 B. LCCN:2002-000229.
Audience: **g,l,u,f.** *Choice, 2003, 2002.*

Harmon
Hart Crane Revisited. Library Binding. Thomson Gale. Farmington Hills, MI. 1996. ISBN:0-8057-3996-3, ISBN13: 978-0-8057-3996-1.
Audience: **l,u.**

Paul, Mariani **PS3505.R272Z753 1999**
The Broken Tower: A Life of Hart Crane. Trade Cloth. W. W. Norton & Company, Inc. New York, NY. 1999. 480p. ISBN:0-393-04726-1, ISBN13: 978-0-393-04726-4. Dewey:811/.52 B. LCCN:98-037726.
Audience: **g,l,u,f.** *Choice, 1999.*

Yingling, Thomas E. **PS3505.R272Z93 1990**
Hart Crane and the Homosexual Text: New Thresholds, New Anatomies. Trade Cloth. University of Chicago Press. Chicago, IL. 1990. 282p. ISBN:0-226-95634-2, ISBN13: 978-0-226-95634-3. Dewey:811/.52. LCCN:89-048053.
Audience: **u,f.** *Choice, 1991.*

20th Century (1901-1960) > C > cummings, e. e.

cummings, e e **PS3505.U334 A17**
100 Selected Poems. Trade Paper. Grove/Atlantic, Inc. New York, NY. 1988. 128p. ISBN:0-8021-3072-0, ISBN13: 978-0-8021-3072-3. Dewey:811.52. LCCN:59-015193.
Audience: **g,l,u,f.**

cummings, e e **PS3505.U334A6 2001**
22 and 50 Poems. Trade Paper. W. W. Norton & Company, Inc. New York, NY. 2001. 96p. ISBN:0-87140-177-0, ISBN13: 978-0-87140-177-9. Dewey:811/.52. LCCN:00-039118.
Audience: **g,l,u,f.**

cummings, e e **PS3505.U334A6 2000**
Etcetera: The Unpublished Poems of e e cummings. Trade Paper. W. W. Norton & Company, Inc. New York, NY. 2001. 192p. ISBN:0-87140-176-2, ISBN13: 978-0-87140-176-2. Dewey:811/.52. LCCN:00-039117.
Audience: **g,l,u,f.**

cummings, e e **PS3505.U334.Z5 1953**
I--Six Non-Lectures: The Charles Eliot Norton Lectures. Trade Paper. Harvard University Press. Cambridge, MA. 1991. 128p. The Charles Eliot Norton Lectures, 1952-1953 ISBN:0-674-44010-2, ISBN13: 978-0-674-44010-4. Dewey:818.5. LCCN:53-010472.
Audience: **u,f.** B

cummings, e e **PS3531.O82**
No Thanks. Trade Paper. W. W. Norton & Company, Inc. New York, NY. 1998. 96p. ISBN:0-87140-172-X, ISBN13: 978-0-87140-172-4. Dewey:811.52. LCCN:78-003827.
Audience: **g,l,u,f.**

cummings, e e **PS3505**
The Complete Poems, 1904-1962. George J. Firmage (Editor). Trade Cloth. Liveright Publishing Corporation. New York, NY. 1994. 1136p. ISBN:0-87140-152-5, ISBN13: 978-0-87140-152-6. Dewey:811/.52. LCCN:91-029158.
Audience: **g,l,u,f.** *Choice, 1992.*

cummings, e e **D570.9.C82 1999**
The Enormous Room. Samuel L. Hynes (Contribution by). Trade Paper. Penguin Group (USA) Inc. New York, NY. 1999. 304p. Twentieth Century Classics Ser. ISBN:0-14-118124-9, ISBN13: 978-0-14-118124-0. Dewey:365.6/0924. LCCN:98-011675.
Audience: **g,l,u,f.**

Friedman, Norman **PS3505.U334Z67 1996**
Re-Valuing Cummings: Further Essays on the Poet. Trade Cloth. University Press of Florida. Gainesville, FL. 1996. 200p. ISBN:0-8130-1443-3, ISBN13: 978-0-8130-1443-2. Dewey:811/.52. LCCN:95-046724.
Audience: **l,u.**

Kennedy, Richard **PS3505.U334 Z7**
Dreams in the Mirror: A Biography of E. E. Cummings. Ed. 2. Trade Paper. Liveright Publishing Corporation. New York, NY. 1994. 548p. ISBN:0-87140-155-X, ISBN13: 978-0-87140-155-7. Dewey:811.52. LCCN:79-018301.
Audience: **g,l,u,f.**

Sawyer-Lauçanno, Christopher **PS3505.U334Z84 2004**
E.E. Cummings: A Biography. Trade Cloth. Sourcebooks, Inc. Naperville, IL. 2004. 608p. ISBN:1-57071-775-3, ISBN13: 978-1-57071-775-8. Dewey:811/.52 B. LCCN:2004-012234.
Audience: **g,l,u,f.** *Choice, 2005.*

20th Century (1901-1960) > D

Dahlberg, Edward **PS3507.A33**
Bottom Dogs. Library Binding. Buccaneer Books, Inc. Cutchogue, NY. 1994. ISBN:1-56849-392-4, ISBN13: 978-1-56849-392-3. Dewey:813/.5/2.
Audience: **g,l,u,f.** B

Dahlberg, Edward **PS3507.A33**
Those Who Perish. Trade Cloth. A M S Press, Inc. New York, NY. ISBN:0-404-14528-0, ISBN13: 978-0-404-14528-6. Dewey:813/.5/2. LCCN:75-041071.
Audience: **g,l,u,f.** B

Day, Clarence **PS3507.A585**
The Best of Clarence Day. Trade Cloth. Amereon, Ltd. Mattituck, NY. ISBN:0-88411-528-3, ISBN13: 978-0-88411-528-1. Dewey:818.5.
Audience: **g,l,u,f.**

Di Donato, Pietro **PS3507.I37**
Christ in Concrete. Trade Cloth. Macmillan Publishing Company, Inc. Old Tappan, NJ. 1975. 320p. ISBN:0-672-52161-X, ISBN13: 978-0-672-52161-4. Dewey:813.52. LCCN:39-010762.
Audience: **g,l,u,f.** B

Donleavy, J. P. **PS3568.O243**
The Ginger Man. Trade Paper. Grove/Atlantic, Inc. New York, NY. 2001. 352p. ISBN:0-8021-3795-4, ISBN13: 978-0-8021-3795-1. Dewey:813/.54.
Audience: **g,l,u,f.** B

Dorn, Edward **PS3507.O73277.A17**
Selected Poems. Donald Allen (Editor), Robert Creeley (Preface by). Trade Paper. Grey Fox Press. San Francisco, CA. 1978. 108p. ISBN:0-912516-32-1, ISBN13: 978-0-912516-32-5. Dewey:811/.5/4. LCCN:78-002925.
Audience: **g,l,u,f.** B

Drury, Allen **PR6019.O9**
Advise and Consent. Library Binding. Buccaneer Books, Inc. Cutchogue, NY. 1991. ISBN:1-56849-060-7, ISBN13: 978-1-56849-060-1. Dewey:823/.9/1.
Audience: **g,l,u,f.** B

Duncan, Robert **PS3509.L43**
The Opening of the Field. Trade Paper. New Directions Publishing Corporation. New York, NY. 1973. 96p. ISBN:0-8112-0480-4, ISBN13: 978-0-8112-0480-4. Dewey:811/.5. LCCN:72-093976.
Audience: **g,l,u,f.** B

Duncan, Robert **PS3507.U629Y4**
The Years As Catches. Trade Cloth. Oyez. Berkeley, CA. 1977. ISBN:0-685-80007-5, ISBN13: 978-0-685-80007-2. Dewey:811/.5/4.
Audience: **g,l,u,f.**

Duncan, Robert **PS3507.U629A6 1997**
Selected Poems of Robert Duncan. Ed. 2. Robert J. Bertholf (Editor). Trade Paper. New Directions Publishing Corporation. New York, NY. 1997. 192p. Paperbook Ser. ISBN:0-8112-1345-5, ISBN13: 978-0-8112-1345-5. Dewey:811/.54. LCCN:96-043881.
Audience: **g,l,u,f.**

Duncan, Robert **PS3507.U629A6 1995**
Selected Prose of Robert Duncan. Robert J. Bertholf (Editor). Trade Cloth. New Directions Publishing Corporation. New York, NY. 1995. 200p. ISBN:0-8112-1278-5, ISBN13: 978-0-8112-1278-6. Dewey:811/.54. LCCN:94-012983.
Audience: **g,l,u,f.**

20th Century (1901-1960) > D > Dos Passos, John

Browder, Laura **PS228.R34B76 1998**
Rousing the Nation: Radical Culture in Depression America. Cloth Text. University of Massachusetts Press. Amherst, MA. 1998. 240p. ISBN:1-55849-125-2, ISBN13: 978-1-55849-125-0. Dewey:810.9/355. LCCN:97-033358.
Audience: **u,f.** *Choice, 1998.*

Dos Passos, John **PS3507.O743.C4**
Century's Ebb: The Thirteenth Chronicle. Trade Cloth. Harvard Common Press. Boston, MA. 1975. 448p. ISBN:0-87645-089-3, ISBN13: 978-0-87645-089-5. Dewey:813/.5/2. LCCN:75-000920.
Audience: **g,l,u,f.** B

Dos Passos, John **PS3507.O743.A6 2003**
John Dos Passos: Novels, 1920-1925. Trade Cloth. Library of America, The. New York, NY. 2003. 880p. The Library of America, Vol. 142 ISBN:1-931082-39-1, ISBN13: 978-1-931082-39-6. Dewey:813/.52. LCCN:2003-047529.
Audience: **g,l,u,f.**

Dos Passos, John **PS3507.O743A6 2003**
John Dos Passos: Travel Books and Other Writings 1916 to 1941. Townsend Ludington (Editor). Trade Cloth. Library of America, The. New York, NY. 2003. 860p. Library of America Ser., Vol. 143 ISBN:1-931082-40-5, ISBN13: 978-1-931082-40-2. Dewey:818/.5208. LCCN:2003-040143.
Audience: **g,l,u,f.**

Dos Passos, John **PS3507.O743A6 1996**
U. S. A.: The 42nd Parallel; 1919; The Big Money. Townsend Ludington & Daniel Aaron (Editors). Trade Cloth. Library of America, The. New York, NY. 1996. 1312p. ISBN:1-883011-14-0, ISBN13: 978-1-883011-14-7. Dewey:813/.52. LCCN:95-049282.
Audience: **g,l,u,f.**

Hook, Andrew **PS3507.O743Z/**
Dos Passos: A Collection of Critical Essays. Trade Cloth. Prentice-Hall. Upper Saddle, NJ. 1974. vi, 186p. ISBN:0-13-218867-8, ISBN13: 978-0-13-218867-8. Dewey:813/.52. LCCN:73-021561.
Audience: **l,u.** B

Maine, Barry **PS3507.O743Z72 2003**
e John Dos Passos: The Critical Heritage. E-Book. Taylor & Francis Group. Philadelphia, PA. ISBN:0-203-44475-2, ISBN13: 978-0-203-44475-7. Dewey:813/.52.
Audience: **l,u.**

Nanney, Donald C. **PS3507.O743J64 1998**
John Dos Passos Revisited. Trade Cloth. Thomson Gale. Farmington Hills, MI. 1998. xvii, 264p. Twayne's United States Authors Ser., Vol. 700 ISBN:0-8057-3971-8, ISBN13: 978-0-8057-3971-8. Dewey:813/.52. LCCN:98-034787.
Audience: **l,u.**

20th Century (1901-1960) > D > Dreiser, Theodore

Cassuto, Leonard & Eby, Clare Virginia (Editors) **PS3507.R55Z575 2003**
The Cambridge Companion to Theodore Dreiser. Trade Cloth. Cambridge University Press. New York, NY. 2004. 258p. Cambridge Companions to Literature Ser. ISBN:0-521-81555-X, ISBN13: 978-0-521-81555-0. Dewey:813/.52. LCCN:2003-055130.
Audience: **l,u,f.** *Choice, 2004.*

Dreiser, Theodore **PS3507.R55**
The Financier. Library Binding. North Books. Wickford, RI. 2003. Twelve-Point Ser. ISBN:1-58287-222-8, ISBN13: 978-1-58287-222-3. Dewey:Fic.
Audience: **g,l,u,f.** B

Dreiser, Theodore **B2248.M64**
Free and Other Stories. Trade Paper. Kessinger Publishing, LLC. Whitefish, MT. 2005. ISBN:1-4179-5936-3, ISBN13: 978-1-4179-5936-5. Dewey:146.4.
Audience: **g,l,u,f.**

Dreiser, Theodore **PZ3.D814**
The Genius. Library Binding. Classic Books. Murrieta, CA. 1998. 736p. The Collected Works of Theodore Dreiser ISBN:1-58201-619-4, ISBN13: 978-1-58201-619-1. Dewey:813/.52.
Audience: **g,l,u,f.** B

Dreiser, Theodore **PZ3.D814S41**
Sister Carrie: An Authoritative Text, Backgrounds and Sources Criticism. Trade Cloth. W. W. Norton & Company, Inc. New York, NY. 1970. x, 591p. Critical Editions Ser. ISBN:0-393-04325-8, ISBN13: 978-0-393-04325-9. Dewey:813/.5/2. LCCN:73-116120.
Audience: **g,l,u,f.** B

Dreiser, Theodore **PS3507.R55T5 2000**
The Titan. Library Binding. Classic Books. Murrieta, CA. 2000. 551p. The Collected Works of Theodore Dreiser ISBN:1-58201-626-7, ISBN13: 978-1-58201-626-9. Dewey:813/.52. LCCN:00-063911.
Audience: **g,l,u,f.** B

Dreiser, Theodore **PS3511.A86**
William James: Sister Carrie; Jennie Gerhardt; Twelve Men. Richard Lehan (Editor). Trade Cloth. Library of America, The. New York, NY. 1987. 1168p. Library of America ISBN:0-940450-41-0, ISBN13: 978-0-940450-41-7. Dewey:813/.52. LCCN:86-027583.
Audience: **g,l,u,f.**

Dreiser, Theodore & Riggio, Thomas P. **PS3507.R55A7 2003**
An American Tragedy. Trade Cloth. Library of America, The. New York, NY. 2003. 960p. The Library of America, Vol. 140 ISBN:1-931082-31-6, ISBN13: 978-1-931082-31-0. Dewey:823/.9/1. LCCN:2002-030168.
Audience: **g,l,u,f.**

Elias, Robert Henry **PS3507.R55.Z63 1970**
Theodore Dreiser, Apostle of Nature. Trade Cloth. Cornell University Press. Ithaca, NY. 1970. x, 435p. ISBN:0-8014-0603-X, ISBN13: 978-0-8014-0603-4. Dewey:813/.5/2. LCCN:70-129563.
Audience: **l,u.** B

Gerber, Philip L. **PS3507.R55 Z637 1992**
Theodore Dreiser Revisited. Trade Cloth. Macmillan Publishing Company, Inc. Old Tappan, NJ. 1992. 150p. Twayne's United States Authors Ser. ISBN:0-8057-3966-1, ISBN13: 978-0-8057-3966-4. Dewey:813/.52. LCCN:92-007283.
Audience: **l,u.**

Gogol, Miriam (Editor) **PS3507.R55Z848 1995**
Theodore Dreiser: Beyond Naturalism. Trade Cloth. New York University Press. New York, NY. 1995. 269p. ISBN:0-8147-3073-6, ISBN13: 978-0-8147-3073-7. Dewey:813/.52. LCCN:95-014447.
Audience: **l,u,f.** *Choice, 1996.*

Lingeman, Richard R. **PS3507.R55.Z66**
Theodore Dreiser: An American Journey. Trade Paper. John Wiley & Sons, Inc. Hoboken, NJ. 1993. 672p. ISBN:0-471-57426-0, ISBN13: 978-0-471-57426-2. Dewey:813/.52. LCCN:92-040559.
Audience: **l,u.**

Loving, Jerome **PS3507.R55 Z6655**
The Last Titan: A Life of Theodore Dreiser. Trade Cloth. University of California Press. Berkeley, CA. 2005. 526p. ISBN:0-520-23481-2, ISBN13: 978-0-520-23481-9. Dewey:813/.52 B. LCCN:2004-016270.
Audience: **g,l,u,f.** *Choice, 2005.*

Newlin, Keith (Editor) **PS3507**
A Theodore Dreiser Encyclopedia. Cloth Text. Greenwood Publishing Group, Inc. Portsmouth, NH. 2003. 456p. ISBN:0-313-31680-5, ISBN13: 978-0-313-31680-7. Dewey:813/.52. LCCN:2003-040841.
Audience: **l,u,f.** *Choice, 2004.*

20th Century (1901-1960) > E

Bartlett, Lee **PS3509.V65.Z56 1988**
William Everson: The Life of Brother Antoninus. Trade Cloth. New Directions Publishing Corporation. New York, NY. 1988. 288p. ISBN:0-8112-1060-X, ISBN13: 978-0-8112-1060-7. Dewey:811/.52. LCCN:87-011034.
Audience: **l,u,f.** *Choice, 1989.*

Eastlake, William **PS3555.A7C37 1999**
Castle Keep. Trade Cloth. Dalkey Archive Press. Normal, IL. 1999. 382p. ISBN:1-56478-208-5, ISBN13: 978-1-56478-208-3. Dewey:823/.9/1. LCCN:99-035096.
Audience: **g,l,u,f.** B

Eberhart, Richard **PS3509.B456.A6 1976**
Collected Poems, 1930-1976. Trade Cloth. Oxford University Press, Inc. New York, NY. 1976. xvi, 364p. ISBN:0-19-519849-2, ISBN13: 978-0-19-519849-2. Dewey:811/.5/2. LCCN:76-007288.
Audience: **g,l,u,f.**

Edmonds, Walter D. **PS3511.A86**
Drums along the Mohawk. Library Binding. Buccaneer Books, Inc. Cutchogue, NY. 1981. 320p. ISBN:0-89966-291-9, ISBN13: 978-0-89966-291-6. Dewey:813/.52.
Audience: **g,l,u,f.**

Engle, Paul **PS3509.N44 A7 1979**
American Song, a Book of Poems. Trade Cloth. A M S Press, Inc. New York, NY. BCL Ser., II ISBN:0-404-15285-6, ISBN13: 978-0-404-15285-7. Dewey:811/.5/2. LCCN:76-011505.
Audience: **g,l,u,f.**

Everson, William **PS3509.V65A17**
The Integral Years: Poems, 1966-1994. Trade Cloth, Box or Slipcased. David R. Godine Publisher. Boston, MA. 1999. 400p. ISBN:1-57423-110-3, ISBN13: 978-1-57423-110-6. Dewey:811.5/2. LCCN:00-504134.
Audience: **g,l,u,f.**

Everson, William **PS3531.O82**
The Residual Years: Poems, 1934-1948. Trade Paper. HarperCollins Publishers. New York, NY. 1997. 412p. ISBN:1-57423-055-7, ISBN13: 978-1-57423-055-0. Dewey:811/.52. LCCN:97-043682.
Audience: **g,l,u,f.** *Choice, 1998.*

Everson, William **PS3509.V65A17**
The Veritable Years: Poems, 1949-1966. Trade Cloth. David R. Godine Publisher. Boston, MA. 1998. 375p. ISBN:1-57423-084-0, ISBN13: 978-1-57423-084-0. Dewey:811/.52. LCCN:99-175517.
Audience: **g,l,u,f.**

Gelpi, Albert (Editor) **PS3509.V65A6 2003**
Dark God of Eros: A William Everson Reader. Trade Paper. Heyday Books. Berkeley, CA. 2003. 448p. California Legacy Ser. ISBN:1-890771-64-3, ISBN13: 978-1-890771-64-5. Dewey:811/.52. LCCN:2003-000532.
Audience: **g,l,u,f.**

20th Century (1901-1960) > E > Eliot, T. S.

Alldritt, Keith **PR605.W66A45 1989**
Modernism in the Second World War: The Later Poetry of Ezra Pound, T. S. Eliot, Basil Bunting and Hugh MacDiarmid. Cloth Text. Peter Lang Publishing, Inc. New York, NY. 1989. 135p. ISBN:0-8204-0865-4, ISBN13: 978-0-8204-0865-1. Dewey:821/.91/09358. LCCN:88-023059.
Audience: **u,f.**

Asher, Kenneth **PS3509.L43Z598 1995**
T. S. Eliot and Ideology. Cloth Text. Cambridge University Press. New York, NY. 1995. 211p. Studies in American Literature and Culture, No. 86 ISBN:0-521-45284-8, ISBN13: 978-0-521-45284-7. Dewey:821.9/12. LCCN:94-001312.
Audience: **u,f.** *Choice, 1995.*

Brooker, Jewel S. **PS3509.L43**
Mastery and Escape: T. S. Eliot and the Dialectic of Modernism. Trade Paper. University of Massachusetts Press. Amherst, MA. 1996. 288p. ISBN:1-55849-040-X, ISBN13: 978-1-55849-040-6. Dewey:821/.912. LCCN:93-045634.
Audience: **u,f.** *Choice, 1995.*

Childs, Donald J. **PS3509.L43**
From Philosophy To Poetry: T. S. Eliot's Study of Knowledge and Experience. Trade Cloth. Continuum International Publishing Group, Ltd. London, 2001. 232p. ISBN:0-485-11550-6, ISBN13: 978-0-485-11550-5. Dewey:821/.912.
Audience: **l,u.**

Chinitz, David E. **PS3509.L43Z64926**
T. S. Eliot and the Cultural Divide. Trade Cloth. University of Chicago Press. Chicago, IL. 2003. 274p. ISBN:0-226-10447-8, ISBN13: 978-0-226-10447-8. Dewey:821/.912. LCCN:2002-155085.
Audience: **u,f.**

Donoghue, Denis **PS3509.L43Z668 2002**
Words Alone: The Poet T. S. Eliot. Trade Paper. Yale University Press. Cumberland, RI. 2002. 352p. ISBN:0-300-09719-0, ISBN13: 978-0-300-09719-1. Dewey:821/.912.
Audience: **g,l,u,f.** *Choice, 2001.*

Eliot, T. S. **PS3509.L43**
Collected Poems: 1909-1962. Trade Cloth. Faber & Faber, Ltd. London, 1965. 3-238p. Fabor Paperbacks Ser. ISBN:0-571-05549-4, ISBN13: 978-0-571-05549-4. Dewey:821/.9/12. LCCN:76-358335.
Audience: **g,l,u,f.**

Eliot, T. S. **PS3509.L5**
The Complete Plays of T. S. Eliot. Trade Cloth. Harcourt Trade Publishers. New York, NY. 1969. ISBN:0-15-120755-0, ISBN13: 978-0-15-120755-8. Dewey:822.912. LCCN:50-014646.
Audience: **g,l,u,f.**

Eliot, T. S. **PS3509.L43055**
Old Possum's Book of Practical Cats. Trade Cloth. Harcourt Trade Publishers. New York, NY. 1995. ISBN:0-15-600277-9, ISBN13: 978-0-15-600277-6. Dewey:821.912.
Audience: **g,l,u,f.**

Eliot, T. S. **PS3509.L43 T6 1991**
To Criticize the Critic and Other Writings. Trade Paper. University of Nebraska Press. Lincoln, NE. 1992. 189p. ISBN:0-8032-6721-5, ISBN13: 978-0-8032-6721-3. Dewey:809. LCCN:91-041601.
Audience: **g,l,u,f.**

Frye, Northrop **PS3509.L43 Z674 1981**
T. S. Eliot: An Introduction. Paper Text. University of Chicago Press. Chicago, IL. 1996. 112p. ISBN:0-226-26649-4, ISBN13: 978-0-226-26649-7. Dewey:821/.912. LCCN:80-029344.
Audience: **l,u.**

Gordon, Lyndall **PS3509.L43Z6794 1999**
T. S. Eliot: An Imperfect Life. Trade Cloth. W. W. Norton & Company, Inc. New York, NY. 1999. 672p. ISBN:0-393-04728-8, ISBN13: 978-0-393-04728-8. Dewey:3509 L43 Z864. LCCN:98-046864.
Audience: **l,u,f.** *Choice, 2000.*

Gray, Piers **PS3509.L43Z**
T. S. Eliot's Intellectual and Poetic Development 1909-1922. Trade Cloth. Bow Historical Books. New Providence, NJ. 1982. xii, 273p. ISBN:0-391-02506-6, ISBN13: 978-0-391-02506-6. Dewey:821/.912. LCCN:81-208217.
Audience: **l,u.** B

Jain, Manju **PS3509.L43 Z6846 19**
T. S. Eliot and American Philosophy: The Harvard Years. Trade Paper. Cambridge University Press. New York, NY. 2004. 363p. ISBN:0-521-60439-7, ISBN13: 978-0-521-60439-0. Dewey:821.912.
Audience: **u,f.**

Kenner, Hugh (Editor) **PS3509.L43**
T. S. Eliot: A Collection of Critical Essays. Trade Paper. John Wiley & Sons, Inc. Hoboken, NJ. 1962. vii, 211p. ISBN:0-13-274324-8, ISBN13: 978-0-13-274324-2. Dewey:821.912.
Audience: **l,u.** B

Lentricchia, Frank **PS310.M57L46 1994**
Modernist Quartet. Cloth Text. Cambridge University Press. New York, NY. 1994. 319p. ISBN:0-521-47004-8, ISBN13: 978-0-521-47004-9. Dewey:811.5209. LCCN:93-050239.
Audience: **u,f.** *Choice, 1995.*

McDonald, Gail **PS3531.O82Z752 1993**
Learning to Be Modern: Pound, Eliot and the American University. Cloth Text. Oxford University Press, Inc. New York, NY. 1993. 256p. ISBN:0-19-811980-1, ISBN13: 978-0-19-811980-7. Dewey:807.1173. LCCN:92-020940.
Audience: **u,f.**

Menand, Louis **PS3509.L43**
Discovering Modernism: T. S. Eliot and His Context. Ed. 2. Trade Paper. Oxford University Press, Inc. New York, NY. 2005. 240p. ISBN:0-19-515992-6, ISBN13: 978-0-19-515992-9. Dewey:821/.912.
Audience: **l,u.** *Choice, 1987.*

Miller, James E. & Miller, James E. Jr. **PS3509.L43Z7856 2005**
T. S. Eliot: The Making of an American Poet, 1888-1922. Saddle Stitched, Cloth over Boards, Dust Jacket. Pennsylvania State University Press. University Park, PA. 2005. 468p. ISBN:0-271-02681-2, ISBN13: 978-0-271-02681-7. Dewey:B. LCCN:2005-005092.
Audience: **l,u,f.** *Choice, 2006.*

Moody, A. David (Editor) **PS3509.L43 Z64728 1**
The Cambridge Companion to T. S. Eliot. Trade Paper. Cambridge University Press. New York, NY. 1994. 279p. Companions to Literature Ser. ISBN:0-521-42127-6, ISBN13: 978-0-521-42127-0. Dewey:821/.912. LCCN:93-043558.
Audience: **l,u,f.** *Choice, 1996.*

Schuchard, Ronald **PS3509.L43Z86352**
Eliot's Dark Angel: Intersections of Life and Art. Trade Cloth. Oxford University Press, Inc. New York, NY. 1999. 284p. ISBN:0-19-510417-X, ISBN13: 978-0-19-510417-2. Dewey:821/.912. LCCN:98-054730.
Audience: **u,f.** *Choice, 2000.*

Southam, B. C. **PS3509.L43Z869 1996**
A Guide to the Selected Poems of T. S. Eliot. Ed. 6. Trade Paper. Harcourt Trade Publishers. New York, NY. 1996. 288p. ISBN:0-15-600261-2, ISBN13: 978-0-15-600261-5. Dewey:821/.912. LCCN:96-004007.
Audience: **l,u.**

Stead, C. K. **PR605.M63S7 1986**
Pound, Yeats, Eliot and the Modernist Movement. Cloth Text. Rutgers University Press. Piscataway, NJ. 1985. 300p. ISBN:0-8135-1075-9, ISBN13: 978-0-8135-1075-0. Dewey:821/.912/09. LCCN:84-029831.
Audience: **u,f.** *Choice, 1986.*

Williamson, George **PS3509.L43Z898 1998**
A Reader's Guide to T. S. Eliot: A Poem-by-Poem Analysis. Trade Paper. Syracuse University Press. Syracuse, NY. 1998. 248p. Reader's Guide Ser. ISBN:0-8156-0500-5, ISBN13: 978-0-8156-0500-3. Dewey:821/.912. LCCN:97-043467.
Audience: **l,u.** B

20th Century (1901-1960) > F

Chopin, Kate & Fearing, Kenneth **PS3511.E115 A6 2004**
Kenneth Fearing: Selected Poems. Trade Cloth. Library of America, The. New York, NY. 2004. 230p. American Poets Project Ser. ISBN:1-931082-57-X, ISBN13: 978-1-931082-57-0. Dewey:811. LCCN:2003-060482.
Audience: **g,l,u,f.**

Fante, John **PS3511.A594F85 1988**
Full of Life. Ed. 2. Trade Cloth. HarperCollins Publishers. New York, NY. 1996. 166p. ISBN:0-87685-719-5, ISBN13: 978-0-87685-719-9. Dewey:813/.52. LCCN:87-027630.
Audience: **g,l,u,f.**

Fante, John **PS3511.A86**
Ask the Dust. Charles Bukowski (Preface by). Trade Cloth. HarperCollins Publishers. New York, NY. 1996. 165p. ISBN:0-87685-444-7, ISBN13: 978-0-87685-444-0. Dewey:813.5/2. LCCN:79-022399.
Audience: **g,l,u,f.**

Fante, John **PS3511.A594B54 2000**
The Big Hunger: Stories, 1932-1959. Stephen Cooper (Editor). Trade Cloth. HarperCollins Publishers. New York, NY. 2000. 319p. ISBN:1-57423-121-9, ISBN13: 978-1-57423-121-2. Dewey:813/.52. LCCN:99-088227.
Audience: **g,l,u,f.**

Fante, John & Cooper, Stephen **PS3511.A594**
The John Fante Reader. Trade Paper. HarperCollins Publishers. New York, NY. 2003. 336p. ISBN:0-06-095948-7, ISBN13: 978-0-06-095948-7. Dewey:813/.52.
Audience: **g,l,u,f.**

Farrell, James T. **PS3511.A738A6 2004**
James T. Farrell: Studs Lonigan a Trilogy. Pete Hamill (Editor). Trade Cloth. Library of America, The. New York, NY. 2004. 1024p. The Library of America, Vol. 148 ISBN:1-931082-55-3, ISBN13: 978-1-931082-55-6. Dewey:813/.52. LCCN:2003-044207.
Audience: **g,l,u,f.**

Fast, Howard **PS3511.A784 T59**
Time and the Riddle: Thirty-One Zen Stories. Trade Paper. Crown Publishing Group. New York, NY. 1986. ISBN:0-517-53769-9, ISBN13: 978-0-517-53769-5. Dewey:813/.5/2.
Audience: **g,l,u,f.**

Fearing, Kenneth **PS3511.A86**
The Big Clock. Trade Cloth. Amereon, Ltd. Mattituck, NY. 1976. ISBN:0-8488-1000-7, ISBN13: 978-0-8488-1000-9. Dewey:813/.52.
Audience: **g,l,u,f.**

Fearing, Kenneth **PS3511.E115A17 1994**
Complete Poems. Robert M. Ryely (Editor). Trade Cloth. National Poetry Foundation. Orono, ME. 1994. 310p. Poet's Ser. ISBN:0-943373-24-7, ISBN13: 978-0-943373-24-9. Dewey:811.52. LCCN:93-086980.
Audience: **g,l,u,f.** *Choice, 1994.*

Ferber, Edna **PS3551.E46**
Cimarron. Library Binding. Buccaneer Books, Inc. Cutchogue, NY. 1992. ISBN:0-89968-279-0, ISBN13: 978-0-89968-279-2. Dewey:FIC.
Audience: **g,l,u,f.**

Ferber, Edna **PR6019.O9**
Show Boat. Library Binding. Buccaneer Books, Inc. Cutchogue, NY. 2002. ISBN:0-89968-281-2, ISBN13: 978-0-89968-281-5. Dewey:823/.91.
Audience: **g,l,u,f.**

Ferber, Edna **PS3511.E46S6**
So Big. Library Binding. Buccaneer Books, Inc. Cutchogue, NY. 1992. ISBN:0-89968-280-4, ISBN13: 978-0-89968-280-8. Dewey:823.91.
Audience: **g,l,u,f.**

Foote, Shelby **PS3568.O243**
Shiloh: A Novel. Trade Cloth. Amereon, Ltd. Mattituck, NY. 1985. ISBN:0-8488-0158-X, ISBN13: 978-0-8488-0158-8. Dewey:813.5/4.
Audience: **g,l,u,f.**

Landers, Robert K. **PS3511.A738Z76 2004**
An Honest Writer: The Life and Times of James T. Farrell. Trade Cloth. Encounter Books. New York, NY. 2004. 562p. Ser. ISBN:1-893554-95-3, ISBN13: 978-1-893554-95-5. Dewey:813/.52 B. LCCN:2003-064219.
Audience: **l,u.** *Choice, 2004.*

20th Century (1901-1960) > F > Faulkner, William

Blotner, Joseph **PS3511.A86.Z63 1984**
Faulkner: A Biography, Vol. 1. Trade Cloth. Random House, Inc. New York, NY. 1984. 778p. ISBN:0-394-50413-5, ISBN13: 978-0-394-50413-1. Dewey:813/.52 B. LCCN:83-017663.
Audience: **g,l,u,f.**

Brooks, Cleanth **PS3511.A86Z642 1990**
William Faulkner: Toward Yoknapatawpha and Beyond. Trade Paper. Louisiana State University Press. Baton Rouge, LA. 1990. xviii, 446p. ISBN:0-8071-1602-5, ISBN13: 978-0-8071-1602-9. Dewey:813/.52. LCCN:89-013317.
Audience: **l,u.**

Brooks, Cleanth & Faulkner, William **PS3511.A86Z64 1990**
William Faulkner: The Yoknapatawpha Country. Trade Paper. Louisiana State University Press. Baton Rouge, LA. 1990. xiv, 500p. ISBN:0-8071-1601-7, ISBN13: 978-0-8071-1601-2. Dewey:813/.52. LCCN:63-017023.
Audience: **l,u.**

Broughton, Panthea Reid **PS3511.A86**
William Faulkner: The Abstract and the Actual. Trade Paper. Louisiana State University Press. Baton Rouge, LA. 1974. 240p. ISBN:0-8071-2456-7, ISBN13: 978-0-8071-2456-7. Dewey:813/.5/2. LCCN:74-077324.
Audience: **l,u.**

Caron, Timothy P. **PS261.C35 2000**
Struggles over the Word: Race and Religion in O'Connor, Faulkner, Hurston and Wright. Trade Cloth. Mercer University Press. Macon, GA. 2000. 162p. ISBN:0-86554-669-X, ISBN13: 978-0-86554-669-1. Dewey:813/.50938220. LCCN:00-056252.
Audience: **u,f.**

Cox, Dianne L. (Editor) **PS3511.A86A869 1985**
William Faulkner's As I Lay Dying: A Critical Casebook. Trade Cloth. Garland Publishing, Inc. New York, NY. 1984. 246p. ISBN:0-8240-9228-7, ISBN13: 978-0-8240-9228-3. Dewey:813/.52. LCCN:84-013793.
Audience: **l,u.**

Dardis, Tom **PS129.D3 1988**
Some Time in the Sun: The Hollywood Years of F. Scott Fitzgerald, William Faulkner, Nathanael West, Aldous Huxley, and James Agee. Trade Paper. Hal Leonard Corporation. Milwaukee, WI. 1989. 274p. ISBN:0-87910-116-4, ISBN13: 978-0-87910-116-9. Dewey:810/.9/0052 B. LCCN:88-021562.
Audience: **g,l,u,f.**

Fargnoli, A. Nicholas **PS3511.A86 Z459**
William Faulkner A to Z: The Essential Reference to His Life and Work. Library Binding. Sagebrush Education Resources. Caledonia, MN. 2002. ISBN:0-613-64778-5, ISBN13: 978-0-613-64778-6. Dewey:813/.52 B.
Audience: **g,l,u.** *Choice, 2002.*

Faulkner, William **PS3511.A86A15 1995**
Collected Stories of William Faulkner. Trade Paper. Random House, Inc. New York, NY. 1995. 912p. ISBN:0-679-76403-8, ISBN13: 978-0-679-76403-8. Dewey:813/.5'2. LCCN:76-040938.
Audience: **g,l,u,f.**

Faulkner, William **PS3511 .A86**
Soldier's Pay. Mass Market. Penguin Group (USA) Inc. New York, NY. 1968. ISBN:0-451-50411-9, ISBN13: 978-0-451-50411-1. Dewey:813/.52 s 813/.52.
Audience: **u.**

Faulkner, William **PS3511.A86**
A Summer of Faulkner: Three Novels: As I Lay Dying, the Sound and the Fury, Light in August, Set. Box or Slipcased, Slip Sleeve. Knopf Publishing Group. New York, NY. 2005. Oprah's Book Club Ser. ISBN:0-307-27532-9, ISBN13: 978-0-307-27532-5. Dewey:813/.52.
Audience: **g,l,u,f.**

Faulkner, William **PS3511.A86**
Mosquitoes. J. Blotner (Editor). Cloth Text. Garland Publishing, Inc. New York, NY. 1987. 504p. William Faulkner Manuscripts ISBN:0-8240-6804-1, ISBN13: 978-0-8240-6804-2. Dewey:813/.52 s. LCCN:86-025823.
Audience: **g,l,u,f.**

Faulkner, William **PS3511.A86A6 1990**
Novels, 1936-1940: Absalom, Absalom!; If I Forget Thee, Jerusalem (The Wild Palms); The Unvanquished; The Hamlet. Joseph Blotner & Noel Polk (Editors). Trade Cloth. Library of America, The. New York, NY. 1990. 1148p. Library of America, Vol. 48 ISBN:0-940450-55-0, ISBN13: 978-0-940450-55-4. Dewey:813/.54. LCCN:89-062931.
Audience: **g,l,u,f.**

Faulkner, William **PS3511.A86A6 1994**
Novels, 1942-1954: Go Down Moses; Intruder in the Dust; Requiem for a Nun; A Fable. Joseph Blotner & Noel Polk (Editors). Trade Cloth. Library of America, The. New York, NY. 1994. 1110p. Library of America, Vol. 73 ISBN:0-940450-85-2, ISBN13: 978-0-940450-85-1. Dewey:813/.52. LCCN:94-002942.
Audience: **g,l,u,f.**

Faulkner, William **PS3511.A86**
William Faulkner Novels 1930-35: As I Lay Dying, Sanctuary, Light in August, Pylon. Joseph Blotner & Noel Polk (Editors). Trade Cloth. Library of America, The. New York, NY. 1985. 1056p. Library of America ISBN:0-940450-26-7, ISBN13: 978-0-940450-26-4. Dewey:813/.52. LCCN:84-023424.
Audience: **g,l,u,f.**

Faulkner, William **823.91**
Mayday. Carvel Collins (Introduction by). Cloth Text. University of Notre Dame Press. Notre Dame, IN. 1980. 96p. ISBN:0-268-01339-X, ISBN13: 978-0-268-01339-4. Dewey:823/.9/1. LCCN:76-022410.
Audience: **g,l,u,f.** B

Faulkner, William **PS3511.A86**
Requiem for a Nun. Thomas McHaney, Michael Millgate & Noel Polk (Editors). Cloth Text. Garland Publishing, Inc. New York, NY. 1987. 504p. William Faulkner Manuscripts ISBN:0-8240-6825-4, ISBN13: 978-0-8240-6825-7. Dewey:813.5/2. LCCN:87-008741.
Audience: **g,l,u,f.** B

Faulkner, William **PS3511.A86A6 2004**
Essays, Speeches and Public Letters. Ed. 2. James B. Meriwether (Editor). Trade Paper. Random House Adult Trade Publishing Group. New York, NY. 2004. 384p. ISBN:0-8129-7137-X, ISBN13: 978-0-8129-7137-8. Dewey:818/.5208. LCCN:2003-044278.
Audience: **g,l,u,f.**

Faulkner, William **PS3511.A86A6 1999**
Novels, 1957-1962: The Town; The Mansion; The Reivers. Noel Polk (Editor). Trade Cloth. Library of America, The. New York, NY. 1999. 1020p. Library of America, Vol. 112 ISBN:1-883011-69-8, ISBN13: 978-1-883011-69-7. Dewey:813/.52. LCCN:99-018348.
Audience: **g,l,u,f.**

Faulkner, William **PS3511.A86A6 2006**
Novels, 1926-1929. Noel Polk & Joseph Blotner (Editors). Trade Cloth. Library of America, The. New York, NY. 2006. 1170p. The Library of America, Vol. 164 ISBN:1-931082-89-8, ISBN13: 978-1-931082-89-1. Dewey:813/.52. LCCN:2005-049444.
Audience: **g,l,u,f.**

Hannon, Charles **PS3511.A86Z78453**
Faulkner and the Discourses of Culture. Trade Cloth. Louisiana State University Press. Baton Rouge, LA. 2004. 208p. Southern Literary Studies ISBN:0-8071-2986-0, ISBN13: 978-0-8071-2986-9. Dewey:813/.52. LCCN:2004-011545.
Audience: **u,f.** *Choice, 2005.*

Hoffman, Frederick J. **PS3511.A86**
William Faulkner. Ed. 2. Trade Cloth. Macmillan Publishing Company, Inc. Old Tappan, NJ. 1966. 160p. United States Authors Ser. ISBN:0-8057-0244-X, ISBN13: 978-0-8057-0244-6. Dewey:813.5.
Audience: **l,u.**

Howe, Irving **PS3511.A86Z84 1991**
William Faulkner: A Critical Study. Ed. 4. Book, Other. Ivan R. Dee Publisher. Blue Ridge Summit, PA. 1991. 308p. ISBN:0-929587-69-3, ISBN13: 978-0-929587-69-1. Dewey:813/.52. LCCN:91-015016.
Audience: **l,u,f.**

Kerr, Elizabeth M. **PS3511.A86**
William Faulkner's Yoknapatawpha: "A Kind of Keystone in the Universe". Trade Paper. Fordham University Press. Bronx, NY. 1983. 438p. ISBN:0-8232-1135-5, ISBN13: 978-0-8232-1135-7. Dewey:813/.52. LCCN:82-083490.
Audience: **l,u.** B

Levins, Lynn Gartrell **PS3511.A86.Z877**
Faulkner's Heroic Design: The Yoknapatawpha Novels. Trade Cloth. University of Georgia Press. Athens, GA. 1976. x, 202p. ISBN:0-8203-0374-7, ISBN13: 978-0-8203-0374-1. Dewey:813/.5/2. LCCN:74-018585.
Audience: **l,u.** B

Minter, David **PS3511.A86Z913 1997**
William Faulkner: His Life and Work. Ed. 2. Trade Paper. Johns Hopkins University Press. Baltimore, MD. 1997. 344p. ISBN:0-8018-5747-3, ISBN13: 978-0-8018-5747-8. Dewey:813/.52. LCCN:80-013089.
Audience: **l,u,f.** B

Moreland, Richard C. **PS3511.A86Z9135 1990**
Faulkner and Modernism: Revision and Rewriting. Paper Text. University of Wisconsin Press. Chicago, IL. 1990. 270p. ISBN:0-299-12504-1, ISBN13: 978-0-299-12504-2. Dewey:813/.52. LCCN:90-012049.
Audience: **u,f.**

Parini, Jay **PS3511.A86Z9445 2004**
One Matchless Time: A Life of William Faulkner. Trade Cloth. HarperCollins Publishers. New York, NY. 2004. 512p. ISBN:0-06-621072-0, ISBN13: 978-0-06-621072-8. Dewey:B. LCCN:2004-042891.
Audience: **g,l,u,f.**

Rollyson, Carl **PS3511.A86Z962 1998**
Uses of the Past in the Novels of William Faulkner. Trade Cloth. International Scholars Publications. Lanham, MD. 1998. 298p. ISBN:1-57309-279-7, ISBN13: 978-1-57309-279-1. Dewey:813/.52. LCCN:98-015060.
Audience: **l,u,f.**

Smith, Patrick A. **PS3558.A67Z88 2002**
William Faulkner: Six Decades of Criticism. Trade Paper. Michigan State University Press. East Lansing, MI. 2002. 256p. ISBN:0-87013-612-7, ISBN13: 978-0-87013-612-2. Dewey:813/.54. LCCN:2002-006806.
Audience: **l,u.** *Choice, 2003.*

Vickery, Olga W. **PS3511.A86Z98 1995**
Novels of William Faulkner: A Critical Interpretation. Paper Text. Louisiana State University Press. Baton Rouge, LA. 1995. 318p. ISBN:0-8071-2006-5, ISBN13: 978-0-8071-2006-4. Dewey:813/.52. LCCN:64-023150.
Audience: **l,u.** B

Volpe, Edmond Loris **PS3511.A86Z983 2003**
A Reader's Guide to William Faulkner: The Novels. Trade Paper. Syracuse University Press. Syracuse, NY. 2003. 427p. ISBN:0-8156-3001-8, ISBN13: 978-0-8156-3001-2. Dewey:813/.52. LCCN:2002-032756.
Audience: **l,u.**

Volpe, Edmond Loris **PS3511.A86Z9835 2004**
A Reader's Guide to William Faulkner: The Short Stories. Trade Paper. Syracuse University Press. Syracuse, NY. 2004. 256p. ISBN:0-8156-3047-6, ISBN13: 978-0-8156-3047-0. Dewey:812/.54. LCCN:2004-005262.
Audience: **l,u.** *Choice, 2004.*

Watson, James G. **PS3511.A86Z985354 20**
e William Faulkner: Self-Presentation and Performance. E-Book. University of Texas Press. Austin, TX. ISBN:0-292-79799-0, ISBN13: 978-0-292-79799-4. Dewey:813.5/2.
Audience: **u,f.** *Choice, 2001.*

Weinstein, Philip M. (Editor) **PS3511.A86Z745 1995**
The Cambridge Companion to William Faulkner. Trade Paper. Cambridge University Press. New York, NY. 1995. 262p. Cambridge Companions to Literature Ser. ISBN:0-521-42167-5, ISBN13: 978-0-521-42167-6. Dewey:813.5/2. LCCN:94-007335.
Audience: **l,u,f.**

Williamson, Joel **PS3511.A86**
William Faulkner and Southern History. Trade Paper. Oxford University Press, Inc. New York, NY. 1995. 544p. ISBN:0-19-510129-4, ISBN13: 978-0-19-510129-4. Dewey:813/.52.
Audience: **l,u,f.**

20th Century (1901-1960) > F > Ferlinghetti, Lawrence

Ferlinghetti, Lawrence **PS3511.E7**
A Coney Island of the Mind. Trade Paper. New Directions Publishing Corporation. New York, NY. 1958. 94p. ISBN:0-8112-0041-8, ISBN13: 978-0-8112-0041-7. Dewey:811.5. LCCN:58-007150.
Audience: **g,l,u,f.**

Ferlinghetti, Lawrence **PS3511.E557 H4**
Her. Trade Paper. New Directions Publishing Corporation. New York, NY. 1960. 156p. ISBN:0-8112-0042-6, ISBN13: 978-0-8112-0042-4. Dewey:813.5. LCCN:60-009221.
Audience: **g,l,u,f.** B

Ferlinghetti, Lawrence **PS3566.L27**
These Are My Rivers: New and Selected Poems, 1955-1993. Trade Paper. New Directions Publishing Corporation. New York, NY. 1994. 320p. ISBN:0-8112-1273-4, ISBN13: 978-0-8112-1273-1. Dewey:811/.54. LCCN:93-010383.
Audience: **g,l,u,f.**

Ferlinghetti, Lawrence **PS3511.E557 U5 1963**
Unfair Arguments with Existence. Trade Paper. New Directions Publishing Corporation. New York, NY. 1963. ISBN:0-8112-0048-5, ISBN13: 978-0-8112-0048-6. Dewey:812.54. LCCN:63-021384.
Audience: **g,l,u,f.**

Skau, Michael **PS3511.E557**
Constantly Risking Absurdity: The Writings of Lawrence Ferlinghetti. Trade Cloth. Whitston Publishing Company, Inc. Albany, NY. 1989. 103p. ISBN:0-87875-353-2, ISBN13: 978-0-87875-353-6. Dewey:811.54. LCCN:87-050835.
Audience: **u,f.** *Choice, 1989.*

Smith, Larry **PS3511.E557 Z88 1983**
Lawrence Ferlinghetti: Poet-at-Large. Trade Paper. Southern Illinois University Press. Carbondale, IL. 1983. 256p. ISBN:0-8093-1102-X, ISBN13: 978-0-8093-1102-6. Dewey:811/.54. LCCN:82-010835.
Audience: **l,u,f.**

20th Century (1901-1960) > F > Fitzgerald, F. Scott

Berman, Ronald **PS3511.I9Z55774 2001**
Fitzgerald, Hemingway and the Twenties. Trade Cloth. University of Alabama Press. Tuscaloosa, AL. 2001. 192p. ISBN:0-8173-1057-6, ISBN13: 978-0-8173-1057-8. Dewey:813/.5209. LCCN:00-010158.
Audience: **l,u.** *Choice, 2001.*

Bruccoli, Matthew J. (Editor) **PS3511.I9G838 2000**
The Great Gatsby: A Documentary. Cloth Text. Thomson Gale. Farmington Hills, MI. 1999. xviii, 387p. Dictionary of Literary Biography Ser., Vol. 219 ISBN:0-7876-3128-0, ISBN13: 978-0-7876-3128-4. Dewey:813/.52. LCCN:99-056682.
Audience: **l,u.**

Bruccoli, Matthew Joseph **PS3511.I9Z566 2002**
Some Sort of Epic Grandeur: The Life of F. Scott Fitzgerald. Ed. 2. Scottie Fitzgerald Smith (Afterword by). Trade Cloth. University of South Carolina Press. Columbia, SC. 2002. 656p. ISBN:1-57003-455-9, ISBN13: 978-1-57003-455-8. Dewey:813/.52 B. LCCN:2002-001553.
Audience: **g,l,u,f.**

Bruccoli, Matthew J. & Baughman, Judith S. **PS3511.I9T4515 1996**
Reader's Companion to F. Scott Fitzgerald's Tender Is the Night. Trade Cloth. University of South Carolina Press. Columbia, SC. 1995. 274p. ISBN:1-57003-078-2, ISBN13: 978-1-57003-078-9. Dewey:813/.52. LCCN:95-004408.
Audience: **l,u.**

Bryer, Jackson R. (Editor) **PS3511.I9A6 2000**
F. Scott Fitzgerald: Novels and Other Stories 1920-1922. Trade Cloth. Library of America, The. New York, NY. 2000. 1075p. Library of America, Vol. 117 ISBN:1-883011-84-1, ISBN13: 978-1-883011-84-0. Dewey:813/.52. LCCN:00-024287.
Audience: **g,l,u,f.**

Bryer, Jackson R. (Editor), et al. **PS3511.A86**
F. Scott Fitzgerald: New Perspectives. Alan Margolies & Ruth Prigozy (Editors). Perfect. University of Georgia Press. Athens, GA. 2000. 296p. ISBN:0-8203-2375-6, ISBN13: 978-0-8203-2375-6. Dewey:813/.52. LCCN:99-088355.
Audience: **l,u,f.**

Bryer, Jackson R. (Editor), et al. **PS3511.I9Z667 1996**
F. Scott Fitzgerald in the 21st Century. Ruth Prigozy & Milton R. Stern (Editors). Trade Cloth. University of Alabama Press. Tuscaloosa, AL. 2003. 392p. ISBN:0-8173-1216-1, ISBN13: 978-0-8173-1216-9. Dewey:813/.52. LCCN:2002-009352.
Audience: **l,u,f.** *Choice, 2003.*

Claridge, Henry (Editor) **PS3511.I9.Z555 1991**
F. Scott Fitzgerald: Critical Assessments, Set. Library Binding. Routledge. New York, NY. 1992. 2040p. Critical Assessments of Writers in English Ser. ISBN:1-873403-02-X, ISBN13: 978-1-873403-02-0. Dewey:813.52. LCCN:92-238106.
Audience: **l,u.**

Curnutt, Kirk (Author, Editor) **PS3511.I9Z6623 2004**
A Historical Guide to F. Scott Fitzgerald. Trade Cloth. Oxford University Press, Inc. New York, NY. 2004. 296p. Historical Guides to American Authors ISBN:0-19-515302-2, ISBN13: 978-0-19-515302-6. Dewey:813/.52. LCCN:2003-022931.
Audience: **l,u.** *Choice, 2005.*

Dardis, Tom **PS129.D3 1988**
Some Time in the Sun: The Hollywood Years of F. Scott Fitzgerald, William Faulkner, Nathanael West, Aldous Huxley, and James Agee. Trade Paper. Hal Leonard Corporation. Milwaukee, WI. 1989. 274p. ISBN:0-87910-116-4, ISBN13: 978-0-87910-116-9. Dewey:810/.9/0052 B. LCCN:88-021562.
Audience: **g,l,u,f.**

Donaldson, Scott (Editor) **PS3511.I9.G832 1984**
Critical Essays on F. Scott Fitzgerald's "The Great Gatsby". Trade Cloth. Thomson Gale. Farmington Hills, MI. 1984. 304p. Critical Essays on American Literature Ser. ISBN:0-8161-8679-0, ISBN13: 978-0-8161-8679-2. Dewey:813/.52. LCCN:83-018646.
Audience: **l,u.** B

Donaldson, Scott **PS3515.E37Z58574**
Hemingway vs. Fitzgerald: The Rise and Fall of a Literacy Friendship. Trade Cloth. Overlook Press, The. New York, NY. 1999. 320p. ISBN:0-87951-711-5, ISBN13: 978-0-87951-711-3. Dewey:813/.5209 B. LCCN:99-037835.
Audience: **g,l,u,f.** *Choice, 2000.*

Eble, Kenneth E. **PS3511.I9.Z6 1977**
F. Scott Fitzgerald. Ed. 2. Trade Cloth. Macmillan Publishing Company, Inc. Old Tappan, NJ. 1977. 192p. Twayne's United States Authors Ser., No. 36 ISBN:0-8057-7183-2, ISBN13: 978-0-8057-7183-1. Dewey:813/.5/2. LCCN:77-000429.
Audience: **l,u.** B

Fitzgerald, F. Scott **PS3511.I9T4 1996**
Tender Is the Night. Trade Cloth. Simon & Schuster. New York, NY. 1996. 320p. Scribner Classics ISBN:0-684-83050-7, ISBN13: 978-0-684-83050-6. Dewey:813.5/2. LCCN:96-015215.
Audience: **g,l,u,f.**

Fitzgerald, F. Scott **PS3511.I9G7 1996**
The Great Gatsby. Matthew J. Bruccoli (Preface by). Trade Cloth. Simon & Schuster. New York, NY. 1996. 176p. Scribner Classics ISBN:0-684-83042-6, ISBN13: 978-0-684-83042-1. Dewey:813.5/2. LCCN:96-016596.
Audience: **g,l,u,f.**

Fitzgerald, F. Scott **PS3511.I9L3 1994**
The Love of the Last Tycoon: The Authorized Text. Matthew J. Bruccoli (Editor). Trade Paper. Simon & Schuster. New York, NY. 1995. 192p. Scribner Classics ISBN:0-02-019985-6, ISBN13: 978-0-02-019985-4. Dewey:813.5/2. LCCN:94-006650.
Audience: **g,l,u,f.**

Fitzgerald, F. Scott **PS3511.I9Z463 2004**
Conversations with F. Scott Fitzgerald. Matthew Joseph Bruccoli & Judith Baughman (Editors). Trade Cloth. University Press of Mississippi. Jackson, MS. 2003. xx, 133p. Literary Conversations Ser. ISBN:1-57806-604-2, ISBN13: 978-1-57806-604-9. Dewey:813/.52 B. LCCN:2003-010741.
Audience: **l,u.**

Fitzgerald, F. Scott **PS3511.I9A6 2005**
My Lost City: Personal Essays, 1920-1940. Matthew J. Bruccoli & James L. W. West III (Editors). Trade Cloth. Cambridge University Press. New York, NY. 2005. 366p. The Cambridge Edition of the Works of F. Scott Fitzgerald Ser. ISBN:0-521-40239-5, ISBN13: 978-0-521-40239-2. Dewey:814/.52. LCCN:2005-002870.
Audience: **g,l,u,f.**

Fitzgerald, F. Scott **PS3511.I9C7 1993**
The Crack-Up. Edmund Wilson (Editor). Trade Paper. New Directions Publishing Corporation. New York, NY. 1993. 347p. ISBN:0-8112-1247-5, ISBN13: 978-0-8112-1247-2. Dewey:818.5. LCCN:93-001100.
Audience: **g,l,u,f.** B

Gale, Robert L. **PS3511**
An F. Scott Fitzgerald Encyclopedia. Book, Other. Greenwood Publishing Group, Inc. Portsmouth, NH. 1998. 544p. ISBN:0-313-30139-5, ISBN13: 978-0-313-30139-1. Dewey:813/.52 B. LCCN:98-013976.
Audience: **l,u,f.** *Choice, 1999.*

Kennedy, J. Gerald & Bryer, Jackson R. (Editors) **PS379**
French Connections: Hemingway and Fitzgerald Abroad. Trade Paper. Palgrave Macmillan. New York, NY. 1999. 368p. ISBN:0-312-22450-8, ISBN13: 978-0-312-22450-9. Dewey:813.5/2/09. LCCN:96-049632.
Audience: **u,f.** *Choice, 1998.*

Mellow, James R. (Author, Illustrator) **PS3511.I9Z686 1984**
Invented Lives: The Marriage of F. Scott and Zelda Fitzgerald. Trade Cloth. Houghton Mifflin Company. New York, NY. 1984. 569p. ISBN:0-395-34412-3, ISBN13: 978-0-395-34412-5. Dewey:813/.52 B. LCCN:84-009002.
Audience: **g,l,u,f.** B

Milford, Nancy **PS3511.I9234 Z8 1983**
Zelda: A Biography. Trade Paper. HarperCollins Publishers. New York, NY. 1983. 464p. ISBN:0-06-091069-0, ISBN13: 978-0-06-091069-3. Dewey:813/.52. LCCN:83-047568.
Audience: **g,l,u,f.** B

Mizener, Arthur **PS3511.I9Z/**
F. Scott Fitzgerald. Trade Paper. Thames & Hudson. New York, NY. 1999. 128p. Literary Lives Ser. ISBN:0-500-26024-9, ISBN13: 978-0-500-26024-1. Dewey:813.5/2. LCCN:86-051196.
Audience: **l,u.**

Prigozy, Ruth (Editor) **PS3511.I9 Z575 2002**
The Cambridge Companion to F. Scott Fitzgerald. Cloth Text. Cambridge University Press. New York, NY. 2001. 294p. Companions to Literature Ser. ISBN:0-521-62447-9, ISBN13: 978-0-521-62447-3. Dewey:813/.52 B. LCCN:2001-025957.
Audience: **l,u,f.**

Tate, Mary J. & Bruccoli, Matthew J. **PS3511.I9Z873 1997**
F. Scott Fitzgerald A to Z: The Essential Reference to His Life and Work. Trade Cloth. Facts On File, Inc. New York, NY. 1997. 352p. Literary A to Z Ser. ISBN:0-8160-3150-9, ISBN13: 978-0-8160-3150-4. Dewey:813/.52. LCCN:97-011321.
Audience: **g,l,u.** *Choice, 1998.*

Turnbull, Andrew **PS3511.I9**
Scott Fitzgerald. UK-B Format Paperback. Knopf Publishing Group. New York, NY. 2004. 368p. ISBN:0-09-946662-7, ISBN13: 978-0-09-946662-8. Dewey:813.5/2.
Audience: **l,u,f.** B

West, James L. W. III **PS3511.I9Z918 2005**
The Perfect Hour: The Romance of F. Scott Fitzgerald and Ginevra King, His First Love. Trade Cloth. Random House Adult Trade Publishing Group. New York, NY. 2005. 240p. ISBN:1-4000-6308-6, ISBN13: 978-1-4000-6308-6. Dewey:813/.52 B. LCCN:2004-051088.
Audience: **g,l,u,f.**

20th Century (1901-1960) > F > Frost, Robert

Brower, Reuben A. **PS3511.R94**
Poetry of Robert Frost: Constellations of Intention. Trade Paper. Oxford University Press, Inc. New York, NY. 1969. 256p. ISBN:0-19-631833-5, ISBN13: 978-0-19-631833-2. Dewey:811.52.
Audience: **l,u.**

Faggen, Robert (Editor) **PS3511.R94 Z559 2001**
The Cambridge Companion to Robert Frost. Cloth Text. Cambridge University Press. New York, NY. 2001. 304p. Companions to Literature Ser. ISBN:0-521-63248-X, ISBN13: 978-0-521-63248-5. Dewey:811/ .52. LCCN:00-052917.
Audience: **l,u,f.** *Choice, 2002.*

Frost, Robert **PS3511.R94A6 1995**
Frost: Collected Poems, Prose, and Plays. Richard Poirier & Mark Richardson (Editors). Trade Cloth. Library of America, The. New York, NY. 1995. 976p. ISBN:1-883011-06-X, ISBN13: 978-1-883011-06-2. Dewey:811/.52. LCCN:94-043693.
Audience: **g,l,u,f.**

Hoffpauir, Richard **PS310.C67H64 2002**
The Contemplative Poetry of Edwin Arlington Robinson, Robert Frost, and Yvor Winters. Trade Cloth. Edwin Mellen Press, The. Lewiston, NY. 2002. 280p. ISBN:0-7734-7198-7, ISBN13: 978-0-7734-7198-6. Dewey:811/.5209384. LCCN:2001-051331.
Audience: **l,u.** *Choice, 2002.*

Lentricchia, Frank **PS310.M57L46 1994**
Modernist Quartet. Cloth Text. Cambridge University Press. New York, NY. 1994. 319p. ISBN:0-521-47004-8, ISBN13: 978-0-521-47004-9. Dewey:811.5209. LCCN:93-050239.
Audience: **u,f.** *Choice, 1995.*

Newman, Lea & Frost, Robert **PS3511.R94Z845 2000**
Robert Frost: The People, Places and Stories Behind His New England Poetry. Trade Paper. New England Press, Incorporated, The. Shelburne, VT. 2000. 160p. ISBN:1-881535-39-8, ISBN13: 978-1-881535-39-3. Dewey:811/.52. LCCN:00-048074.
Audience: **l,u.**

Pack, Robert **PS3531.O82**
Belief and Uncertainty in the Poetry of Robert Frost. Trade Paper. University Press of New England. Lebanon, NH. 2005. 264p. ISBN:1-58465-456-2, ISBN13: 978-1-58465-456-8. Dewey:811/.52.
Audience: **u,f.** *Choice, 2004.*

Parini, Jay **PS3511.R94Z868 1999**
Robert Frost: A Biography. Cloth over Boards. Henry Holt & Company. New York, NY. 1999. 528p. ISBN:0-8050-3181-2, ISBN13: 978-0-8050-3181-2. Dewey:811/.52 B. LCCN:98-026690.
Audience: **g,l,u,f.** *Choice, 1999.*

Poirier, Richard **PS3531.O82**
Robert Frost: The Work of Knowing. John Hollander (Foreword by). Trade Cloth. Stanford University Press. Palo Alto, CA. 1990. 384p. ISBN:0-8047-1741-9, ISBN13: 978-0-8047-1741-0. Dewey:811/.5/2. LCCN:89-060362.
Audience: **u,f.** B

Pritchard, William H. **PS3531.O82**
Frost: A Literary Life Reconsidered. Ed. 2. Trade Paper. University of Massachusetts Press. Amherst, MA. 1993. 312p. ISBN:0-87023-838-8, ISBN13: 978-0-87023-838-3. Dewey:811/.52 B. LCCN:92-036872.
Audience: **l,u.** B

Rotella, Guy **PS310.N3R68 1990**
Reading and Writing Nature: The Poetry of Robert Frost, Wallace Stevens, Marianne Moore, and Elizabeth Bishop. Trade Cloth. Northeastern University Press. Boston, MA. 1990. 253p. ISBN:1-55553-086-9, ISBN13: 978-1-55553-086-0. Dewey:811/.520936. LCCN:90-007576.
Audience: **u,f.** *Choice, 1991.*

Timmerman, John H. **PS3511.R94Z595 2002**
Robert Frost: The Ethics of Ambiguity. Trade Cloth. Bucknell University Press. Cranbury, NJ. 2002. 200p. ISBN:0-8387-5532-1, ISBN13: 978-0-8387-5532-7. Dewey:811/.52. LCCN:2002-018610.
Audience: **u,f.** *Choice, 2003.*

Tuten, Nancy Lewis & Zubizarreta, John (Editors) **PS3511**
The Robert Frost Encyclopedia. Cloth Text. Greenwood Publishing Group, Inc. Portsmouth, NH. 2000. 488p. ISBN:0-313-29464-X, ISBN13: 978-0-313-29464-8. Dewey:811/.52 B. LCCN:00-025246.
Audience: **l,u,f.** *Choice, 2001.*

Wilcox, Earl J. & Barron, Jonathan N. (Editors) **PS3511.R94Z9156 2000**
Roads Not Taken: Rereading Robert Frost. Trade Paper. University of Missouri Press. Columbia, MO. 2000. 264p. ISBN:0-8262-1305-7, ISBN13: 978-0-8262-1305-1. Dewey:811/.52. LCCN:00-062891.
Audience: **l,u,f.**

20th Century (1901-1960) > G

Ben-Zvi, Linda **PS3513.L35Z595 2005**
Susan Glaspell: Her Life and Times. Trade Cloth. Oxford University Press, Inc. New York, NY. 2005. 492p. ISBN:0-19-511506-6, ISBN13: 978-0-19-511506-2. Dewey:813/.52 B. LCCN:2004-010804.
Audience: **g,l,u,f.** *Choice, 2005.*

Boyle, Anne M. **PS3513.O5765Z57 2002**
Strange and Lurid Bloom: A Study of the Fiction of Caroline Gordon. Trade Cloth. Fairleigh Dickinson University Press. Cranbury, NJ. 2002. 208p. ISBN:0-8386-3932-1, ISBN13: 978-0-8386-3932-0. Dewey:813/.52. LCCN:2001-054534.
Audience: **u,f.** *Choice, 2003.*

Gainor, J. Ellen **PS3513**
Susan Glaspell in Context: American Theater, Culture, and Politics, 1915-48. Trade Paper. University of Michigan Press. Chicago, IL. 2003. 344p. ISBN:0-472-03010-8, ISBN13: 978-0-472-03010-1. Dewey:818/.5209.
Audience: **u,f.** *Choice, 2002.*

Gale, Zona **PS3513.A34**
Miss Lulu Bett - Birth. Marv Balousek (Editor), Dianne Lynch (Introduction by). Trade Paper. Badger Books, Inc. Oregon, WI. 1994. 384p. ISBN:1-878569-19-8, ISBN13: 978-1-878569-19-6. Dewey:813.5.
Audience: **g,l,u,f.**

Gardner, Erle Stanley **PS3513.A6322**
The Case of the Sulky Girl. Library Binding. Amereon, Ltd. Mattituck, NY. 1976. Perry Mason Books Ser. ISBN:0-88411-402-3, ISBN13: 978-0-88411-402-4. Dewey:813/.5/2.
Audience: **g,l,u,f.** B

Glaspell, Susan **PS3513.L35 A6 1987**
Plays by Susan Glaspell. Christopher W. Bigsby (Editor), Martin Banham & Peter Thomson (Contribution by). Trade Paper. Cambridge University Press. New York, NY. 1987. 174p. British and American Playwrights Ser. ISBN:0-521-31204-3, ISBN13: 978-0-521-31204-2. Dewey:812/.52. LCCN:86-030986.
Audience: **g,l,u,f.**

Gordon, Caroline **PS3513.O5765**
The Strange Children. Trade Paper. Books on Demand. Ann Arbor, MI. 305p. ISBN:0-598-53421-0, ISBN13: 978-0-598-53421-7. Dewey:813/.5/2. LCCN:51-012447.
Audience: **g,l,u,f.**

Gordon, Caroline **PS3511.A86**
Penhally. M. E. Bradford (Introduction by). Trade Paper. Ivan R. Dee Publisher. Blue Ridge Summit, PA. 1991. 282p. Southern Classics Ser. ISBN:1-879941-03-1, ISBN13: 978-1-879941-03-8. Dewey:813/.5/2. LCCN:91-062456.
Audience: **g,l,u,f.** B

Gordon, Caroline **PS3513.O5765.A6 1981**
The Collected Stories. Robert Penn Warren (Introduction by). Trade Cloth. Farrar, Straus & Giroux. New York, NY. 1981. 352p. ISBN:0-374-12630-5, ISBN13: 978-0-374-12630-8. Dewey:813/.52. LCCN:80-028675.
Audience: **g,l,u,f.** B

Goyen, William **PS3513.O97H6 1999**
The House of Breath. Ed. 50. Trade Paper. Northwestern University Press. Evanston, IL. 1999. 191p. ISBN:0-8101-5067-0, ISBN13: 978-0-8101-5067-6. Dewey:813/.54. LCCN:99-025343.
Audience: **g,l,u,f.**

Grey, Zane **PS3513.R6545R5 2005**
Riders of the Purple Sage. Trade Cloth. Thomson Gale. Farmington Hills, MI. 2005. 362p. ISBN:1-59414-130-4, ISBN13: 978-1-59414-130-0. Dewey:813/.52. LCCN:2004-060017.
Audience: **g,l,u,f.**

Guthrie, A. B. Jr. **PS3513.U855B53**
The Big Sky. Library Binding. Buccaneer Books, Inc. Cutchogue, NY. 1993. ISBN:1-56849-121-2, ISBN13: 978-1-56849-121-9. Dewey:813/.52.
Audience: **g,l,u,f.** B

Guthrie, A. B. Jr. **PS3511.A86**
The Way West. Library Binding. Buccaneer Books, Inc. Cutchogue, NY. 1992. 350p. ISBN:0-89968-305-3, ISBN13: 978-0-89968-305-8. Dewey:813/.52.
Audience: **g,l,u,f.** B

Guthrie, Ramon **PS3513.U875.A6 1984**
Maximum Security Ward and Other Poems. Trade Cloth. Persea Books, Inc. New York, NY. 1984. xxi, 213 p. ;p. ISBN:0-89255-079-1, ISBN13: 978-0-89255-079-1. Dewey:811/.52. LCCN:83-022067.
Audience: **g,l,u,f.** B

Ozieblo Rajkowska, Barbara **00-021108 [PS]**
Susan Glaspell: A Critical Biography. Library Binding. University of North Carolina Press. Chapel Hill, NC. 2000. 368p. ISBN:0-8078-2560-3, ISBN13: 978-0-8078-2560-0. Dewey:813/.52 B. LCCN:00-021108.
Audience: **g,l,u,f.** *Choice, 2001.*

20th Century (1901-1960) > G > Ginsberg, Allen

Cassady, Carolyn **PS3521.E735**
Off the Road: My Years with Cassady, Kerouac, and Ginsberg. William Morrow & Co.. 1981.
Audience: **g,l,u,f.**

Ginsberg, Allen **PS3513.I74 2006**
Collected Poems 1947-1997. Trade Cloth. HarperCollins Publishers. New York, NY. 2006. 1216p. ISBN:0-06-113974-2, ISBN13: 978-0-06-113974-1. Dewey:811/.54. LCCN:2006-041191.
Audience: **g,l,u,f.**

Ginsberg, Allen **PS3513.I74Z476 2001**
Spontaneous Mind: Selected Interviews, 1958-1996. David A. Carter (Editor), Václav Havel (Preface by), Edmund White (Introduction by). Trade Cloth. HarperCollins Publishers. New York, NY. 2001. 624p. ISBN:0-06-019293-3, ISBN13: 978-0-06-019293-8. Dewey:811.5/4. LCCN:00-040849.
Audience: **l,u,f.**

Ginsberg, Allen & Ginsberg, Louis **PS3513.I74Z485 2001**
Family Business: Two Lives in Letters and Poetry. Michael Schumacher (Editor). Cloth over Boards. Bloomsbury Publishing. New York, NY. 2001. 452p. ISBN:1-58234-107-9, ISBN13: 978-1-58234-107-1. Dewey:811/.54. LCCN:2001-035431.
Audience: **g,l,u,f.** *Choice, 2002.*

Ginsberg, Allen **PS3513.I74D45 2000**
Deliberate Prose: Selected Essays, 1952-1995. Bill Morgan (Editor). Trade Cloth. HarperCollins Publishers. New York, NY. 2000. 560p. ISBN:0-06-019294-1, ISBN13: 978-0-06-019294-5. Dewey:814/.54. LCCN:99-041360.
Audience: **g,l,u,f.**

Hyde, Lewis (Editor) **PS3513.I74Z82 1984**
On the Poetry of Allen Ginsberg. Trade Paper. University of Michigan Press. Chicago, IL. 1985. 480p. Under Discussion Ser. ISBN:0-472-06353-7, ISBN13: 978-0-472-06353-6. Dewey:811/.54. LCCN:84-013000.
Audience: **l,u,f.**

Lardas, John **PS228.B6L37 2001**
The Bop Apocalypse: The Religious Visions of Kerouac, Ginsberg, and Burroughs. Trade Cloth. University of Illinois Press. Champaign, IL. 2000. 328p. ISBN:0-252-02599-7, ISBN13: 978-0-252-02599-0. Dewey:810.9/382. LCCN:00-008649.
Audience: **u,f.** *Choice, 2001.*

Miles, Barry **PS3566.L27**
Ginsberg: A Biography. Ed. 2. Trade Paper. Holtzbrinck Publishers. Gordonsville, VA. 2001. 627p. ISBN:0-7535-0486-3, ISBN13: 978-0-7535-0486-4. Dewey:811.5/4.
Audience: **g,l,u,f.**

Raskin, Jonah **PS3513.I74 H636 2004**
American Scream: Allen Ginsberg's Howl and the Making of the Beat Generation. Trade Cloth. University of California Press. Berkeley, CA. 2004. 324p. ISBN:0-520-24015-4, ISBN13: 978-0-520-24015-5. Dewey:811/.54. LCCN:2003-059527.
Audience: **u,f.**

Schumacher, Michael **PS3513.I74Z86 1994**
Dharma Lion: A Biography of Allen Ginsberg. Trade Cloth. St. Martin's Press. Gordonville, VA. 1994. 784p. ISBN:0-312-11263-7, ISBN13: 978-0-312-11263-9. Dewey:811/.54. LCCN:94-018378.
Audience: **u,f.**

20th Century (1901-1960) > G > Glasgow, Ellen

Glasgow, Ellen **PS3511.A86**
Barren Ground. Library Binding. Buccaneer Books, Inc. Cutchogue, NY. 1995. ISBN:1-56849-623-0, ISBN13: 978-1-56849-623-8. Dewey:813/.52.
Audience: **g,l,u,f.**

Glasgow, Ellen **PS3513.L34**
In This Our Life. Library Binding. Buccaneer Books, Inc. Cutchogue, NY. 1995. ISBN:1-56849-627-3, ISBN13: 978-1-56849-627-6. Dewey:813/.5/2.
Audience: **g,l,u,f.**

Glasgow, Ellen **PS3513.L34S5 1994**
The Sheltered Life. Carol S. Manning (Afterword by). Trade Paper. University Press of Virginia. Charlottesville, VA. 1994. 352p. ISBN:0-8139-1514-7, ISBN13: 978-0-8139-1514-2. Dewey:813/.52. LCCN:93-041095.
Audience: **g,l,u,f.**

Glasgow, Ellen **PS3513.L34Z47 1994**
The Woman Within. Pamela R. Matthews (Editor). Paper Text. University Press of Virginia. Charlottesville, VA. 1994. 319p. ISBN:0-8139-1563-5, ISBN13: 978-0-8139-1563-0. Dewey:813/.52 B. LCCN:94-003635.
Audience: **g,l,u,f.**

Glasgow, Ellen **PS3513.L34V4 1995**
Vein of Iron. Anne F. Scott (Afterword by). Trade Paper. University Press of Virginia. Charlottesville, VA. 1995. 408p. ISBN:0-8139-1636-4, ISBN13: 978-0-8139-1636-1. Dewey:[Fic). LCCN:95-014153.
Audience: **g,l,u,f.**

Goodman, Susan E. **PS3511.A86**
Ellen Glasgow: A Biography. Trade Paper. Johns Hopkins University Press. Baltimore, MD. 2003. 344p. ISBN:0-8018-7314-2, ISBN13: 978-0-8018-7314-0. Dewey:813/.52 B.
Audience: **g,l,u,f.** *Choice, 1998.*

Scura, Dorothy M. (Editor) **PS3513.L34Z6534 1995**
Ellen Glasgow: New Perspectives. Cloth Text. University of Tennessee Press. Knoxville, TN. 1995. 272p. Tennessee Studies in Literature, Vol. 36 ISBN:0-87049-879-7, ISBN13: 978-0-87049-879-4. Dewey:813/.52. LCCN:94-018726.
Audience: **u,f.** *Choice, 1996.*

Taylor, Welford Dunaway & Longest, George C. (Editors) **PS3513.L34Z76 2001**
Regarding Ellen Glasgow: Essays for Contemporary Readers. Trade Cloth. Library of Virginia, The. Richmond, VA. 2001. 202p. ISBN:0-88490-188-2, ISBN13: 978-0-88490-188-4. Dewey:813/.52. LCCN:00-112049.
Audience: **l,u.** *Choice, 2002.*

20th Century (1901-1960) > G > Goodis, David

Goodis, David **PS3511.A86**
The Blonde on the Street Corner. Trade Paper. Serpent's Tail Ltd. London, 1997. 250p. Midnight Classics Ser. ISBN:1-85242-447-8, ISBN13: 978-1-85242-447-3. Dewey:813.5/2. LCCN:97-066231.
Audience: **g,l,u,f.**

Goodis, David **PS3511.A86**
Dark Passage. Trade Paper. Prion. London, 1999. xi, 244p. The Film Ink Ser. ISBN:1-85375-309-2, ISBN13: 978-1-85375-309-1. Dewey:813.5/2.
Audience: **g,l,u,f.**

Goodis, David **PS3511.A86**
The Moon in the Gutter. Trade Paper. Serpent's Tail Ltd. London, 1998. 192p. Midnight Classics Ser. ISBN:1-85242-449-4, ISBN13: 978-1-85242-449-7. Dewey:813.5/2. LCCN:98-086406.
Audience: **g,l,u,f.**

Goodis, David **PS3513.O499S56 1990**
Shoot the Piano Player. Trade Paper. Knopf Publishing Group. New York, NY. 1990. 176p. Vintage Crime/Black Lizard Ser. ISBN:0-679-73254-3, ISBN13: 978-0-679-73254-9. Dewey:813.5/2. LCCN:90-050255.
Audience: **g,l,u,f.**

Sallis, James **PS374.D4**
Difficult Lives: Jim Thompson, David Goodis, Chester Himes. Ed. 2. Trade Paper. Gryphon Books. Brooklyn, NY. 2000. 102p. ISBN:1-58250-029-0, ISBN13: 978-1-58250-029-4. Dewey:813/.087209 B.
Audience: **g,l,u,f.**

20th Century (1901-1960) > H

Boyd, Valerie **PS3515.U789Z63 2002**
Wrapped in Rainbows: The Life of Zora Neale Hurston. Trade Cloth. Simon & Schuster. New York, NY. 2002. 528p. ISBN:0-684-84230-0, ISBN13: 978-0-684-84230-1. Dewey:813/.52 B. LCCN:2002-017011.
Audience: **g,l,u.**

Carter, Steven R. **PS3515.A515Z57 1991**
Hansberry's Drama: Commitment amid Complexity. Trade Cloth. University of Illinois Press. Champaign, IL. 1990. 216p. ISBN:0-252-01749-8, ISBN13: 978-0-252-01749-0. Dewey:812/.54. LCCN:90-033681.
Audience: **l,u,f.**

Croft, Robert W. **PS3515.U789Z6 2004**
A Zora Neale Hurston Companion. Trade Cloth. University Press of Florida. Gainesville, FL. 2004. 272p. ISBN:0-8130-2793-4, ISBN13: 978-0-8130-2793-7. Dewey:813/.52. LCCN:2004-049335.
Audience: **g,l,u.** *Choice, 2003.*

Cronin, Gloria L. (Editor) **PS3515.U789Z67 1998**
Critical Essays on Zora Neale Hurston. Trade Cloth. Thomson Gale. Farmington Hills, MI. 1998. 271p. Critical Essays on American Literature Ser. ISBN:0-7838-0021-5, ISBN13: 978-0-7838-0021-9. Dewey:813/.52. LCCN:98-019113.
Audience: **l,u.** *Choice, 1999.*

Hammett, Dashiell **PS3515.A4347.A6 1999**
Dashiell Hammett: Five Complete Novels. Steven Marcus (Editor). Trade Cloth. Library of America, The. New York, NY. 1999. 967p. Library of America, Vol. 110 ISBN:1-883011-67-1, ISBN13: 978-1-883011-67-3. Dewey:813/.52. LCCN:98-053911.
Audience: **g,l,u,f.**

Hammett, Dashiell **PS3515.A4347A6 2001**
Dashiell Hammett: Crime Stories and Other Writings. Steven Marcus (Editor). Trade Cloth. Library of America, The. New York, NY. 2001. 934p. The Library of America, Vol. 125 ISBN:1-931082-00-6, ISBN13: 978-1-931082-00-6. Dewey:813/.52. LCCN:00-054594.
Audience: **g,l,u,f.**

Hansberry, Lorraine **PS3515.A515**
A Raisin in the Sun and the Sign in Sidney Brustein's Window. Robert Nemiroff (Editor, Foreword by), Amiri Imamu Baraka (Commentaries by). Trade Paper. Knopf Publishing Group. New York, NY. 1995. 368p. ISBN:0-679-75531-4, ISBN13: 978-0-679-75531-9. Dewey:812.54. LCCN:94-040843.
Audience: **g,l,u,f.**

Hardwick, Elizabeth **PS3515.A5672G47 1989**
The Ghostly Lover. Trade Paper. HarperCollins Publishers. New York, NY. 1989. 278p. ISBN:0-88001-240-4, ISBN13: 978-0-88001-240-9. Dewey:813/.52. LCCN:89-016864.
Audience: **g,l,u,f.** B

Harris, Mark **PS3515**
Bang the Drum Slowly. Trade Cloth. University of Nebraska Press. Lincoln, NE. 2005. 265p. ISBN:0-8032-7338-X, ISBN13: 978-0-8032-7338-2. Dewey:813/.54. LCCN:2004-269963.
Audience: **g,l,u,f.**

Harris, Mark **PS3515.A757S6 2003**
The Southpaw. Trade Cloth. University of Nebraska Press. Lincoln, NE. 2005. 360p. ISBN:0-8032-7337-1, ISBN13: 978-0-8032-7337-5. Dewey:813/.54. LCCN:2003-012956.
Audience: **g,l,u,f.**

Hayden, Robert **PS3515.A9363 A6 1975**
Angle of Ascent: New and Selected Poems. Trade Cloth. Liveright Publishing Corporation. New York, NY. 1975. 131p. ISBN:0-87140-613-6, ISBN13: 978-0-87140-613-2. Dewey:811/.5/2. LCCN:75-020493.
Audience: **g,l,u,f.** B

Hecht, Ben **PS3515.E18 E7**
Erik Dorn. Trade Paper. Kessinger Publishing, LLC. Whitefish, MT. 2004. ISBN:1-4179-2389-X, ISBN13: 978-1-4179-2389-2. Dewey:818.5209.
Audience: **g,l,u,f.**

Heggen, Thomas **PS3568.O243**
Mister Roberts. Library Binding. Buccaneer Books, Inc. Cutchogue, NY. 1983. 230p. ISBN:0-89966-445-8, ISBN13: 978-0-89966-445-3. Dewey:813/.54.
Audience: **g,l,u,f.**

Heinlein, Robert A. **PS3515.E288; PZ3.H64**
The Past Through Tomorrow. Mass Market. Penguin Group (USA) Inc. New York, NY. 1987. ISBN:0-441-65304-9, ISBN13: 978-0-441-65304-1. Dewey:[Fic].
Audience: **g,l,u,f.** B

Heinlein, Robert A. **PS3568.O243**
Stranger in a Strange Land. Library Binding. Buccaneer Books, Inc. Cutchogue, NY. 1994. ISBN:1-56849-290-1, ISBN13: 978-1-56849-290-2. Dewey:813/.54.
Audience: **g,l,u,f.** B

Herbst, Josephine **PS3511.A86**
Rope of Gold. Mass Market. Warner Books, Inc. New York, NY. 1986. 416p. ISBN:0-446-32871-5, ISBN13: 978-0-446-32871-5. Dewey:813/.52.
Audience: **g,l,u,f.** B *Choice, 1985.*

Herbst, Josephine **PS3515.E596Z47 1999**
Starched Blue Sky of Spain and Other Memoirs, Reissued Ed. Paper Text. Northeastern University Press. Boston, MA. 1999. 192p. ISBN:1-55553-399-X, ISBN13: 978-1-55553-399-1. Dewey:813/.52 B. LCCN:99-010759.
Audience: **g,l,u,f.**

Hersey, John **PS3515.E7715B5 1988**
A Bell for Adano. Trade Paper. Knopf Publishing Group. New York, NY. 1988. 288p. Vintage Ser. ISBN:0-394-75695-9, ISBN13: 978-0-394-75695-0. Dewey:813/.54. LCCN:87-045943.
Audience: **g,l,u,f.** B

Hersey, John **PS3515.E7715W3 1988**
The Wall. Trade Paper. Knopf Publishing Group. New York, NY. 1988. 640p. ISBN:0-394-75696-7, ISBN13: 978-0-394-75696-7. Dewey:813/.52. LCCN:87-045944.
Audience: **g,l,u,f.** B

Heyward, DuBose **PS3511.A86**
Porgy. Library Binding. Buccaneer Books, Inc. Cutchogue, NY. 1991. 196p. ISBN:0-89966-768-6, ISBN13: 978-0-89966-768-3. Dewey:813/.52.
Audience: **g,l,u,f.**

Holmes, John Clellon **PS3558.O3594G6 1997**
Go. James Atlas (Foreword by), Seymour Krim & Ann Charters (Afterword by). Trade Paper. Avalon Publishing Group. New York, NY. 2002. 344p. ISBN:1-56025-424-6, ISBN13: 978-1-56025-424-9. Dewey:813.54. LCCN:2003-270481.
Audience: **g,l,u,f.**

Horgan, Paul **PS3515.O6583D57 1990**
A Distant Trumpet. C. P. Snow (Introduction by). Trade Paper. David R. Godine Publisher. Boston, MA. 1991. 656p. Nonpareil Bks., Vol. 65 ISBN:0-87923-863-1, ISBN13: 978-0-87923-863-6. Dewey:813/.54. LCCN:90-055278.
Audience: **g,l,u,f.** B

Hugo, Richard **PS3515.U3.A17 1984**
Making Certain It Goes On: The Collected Poems of Richard Hugo. Trade Cloth. W. W. Norton & Company, Inc. New York, NY. 1984. 456p. ISBN:0-393-01784-2, ISBN13: 978-0-393-01784-7. Dewey:811/.54. LCCN:83-008016.
Audience: **g,l,u,f.** B

Humphries, Rolfe **PS3515.U4835 A6**
Collected Poems of Rolfe Humphries. Trade Cloth. Indiana University Press. Bloomington, IN. 1965. 288p. Poetry Ser. ISBN:0-253-11250-8, ISBN13: 978-0-253-11250-7. Dewey:811.52. LCCN:65-019700.
Audience: **g,l,u,f.**

Hurston, Lucy **PS3515.U789Z74 2004**
Speak, So You Can Speak Again: The Life of Zora Neale Hurston. Trade Cloth. Doubleday Publishing. New York, NY. 2004. 32p. ISBN:0-385-49375-4, ISBN13: 978-0-385-49375-8. Dewey:813/.52 B. LCCN:2003-055598.
Audience: **g,l,u,f.**

Hurston, Zora Neale **PS3515.U789Z465 2006**
Dust Tracks on a Road: An Autobiography. Trade Paper. HarperCollins Publishers. New York, NY. 2006. 336p. P. S. Ser. ISBN:0-06-085408-1, ISBN13: 978-0-06-085408-9. Dewey:813/.52 B. LCCN:2005-052616.
Audience: **g,l,u.** B *Choice, 1985.*

Hurston, Zora Neale **GR55.H86A3 1995**
Folklore, Memoirs, and Other Writings. Cheryl A. Wall (Editor). Trade Cloth. Library of America, The. New York, NY. 1995. 1024p. Library of America, Vol. 75 ISBN:0-940450-84-4, ISBN13: 978-0-940450-84-4. Dewey:398/.092 B. LCCN:94-021384.
Audience: **g,l,u.**

Hurston, Zora Neale **PS3515.U789A6 1995**
Novels and Stories: Jonah's Gourd Vine; Their Eyes Were Watching God; Moses, Man of the Mountain; Seraph on the Suwanee. Cheryl A. Wall (Editor). Trade Cloth. Library of America, The. New York, NY. 1995. 1054p. Novels and Stories Ser., Vol. 74 ISBN:0-940450-83-6, ISBN13: 978-0-940450-83-7. Dewey:813/.52. LCCN:94-025757.
Audience: **g,l,u,f.**

Jones, Sharon L. **PS153**
Rereading the Harlem Renaissance: Race, Class, and Gender in the Fiction of Jessie Fauset, Zora Neale Hurston, and Dorothy West. Trade Cloth. Greenwood Publishing Group, Inc. Portsmouth, NH. 2002. 176p. Contributions in Afro-American

and African Studies, No. 207 ISBN:0-313-32326-7, ISBN13: 978-0-313-32326-3. Dewey:813/.5209896073. LCCN:2002-067840.
Audience: **u,f.** *Choice, 2003.*

Marling, William **PS374.D4M33 1995**
The American Roman Noir: Hammett, Cain and Chandler. Trade Cloth. University of Georgia Press. Athens, GA. 1995. 256p. ISBN:0-8203-1658-X, ISBN13: 978-0-8203-1658-1. Dewey:813/.0872/0905. LCCN:94-025550.
Audience: **u,f.**

Patterson, Tiffany Ruby **PS3515.U789Z797 2005**
Zora Neale Hurston and a History of Southern Life. Trade Cloth. Temple University Press. Philadelphia, PA. 2005. 248p. Critical Perspectives on the Past Ser. ISBN:1-59213-289-8, ISBN13: 978-1-59213-289-8. Dewey:813/.52. LCCN:2004-058855.
Audience: **l,u.** *Choice, 2006.*

West, Margaret Genevieve **PS3515.U789Z94 2005**
Zora Neale Hurston and American Literary Culture. Perfect, Paper over Boards, Dust Jacket. University Press of Florida. Gainesville, FL. 2005. 300p. ISBN:0-8130-2830-2, ISBN13: 978-0-8130-2830-9. Dewey:813/.52. LCCN:2005-042285.
Audience: **l,u.** *Choice, 2006.*

20th Century (1901-1960) > H > Hall, Donald

Hall, Donald **PS3515.A3152B74 2003**
Breakfast Served Any Time All Day: Essays on Poetry New and Selected. Trade Cloth. University of Michigan Press. Chicago, IL. 2003. 232p. ISBN:0-472-09852-7, ISBN13: 978-0-472-09852-1. Dewey:811/.009. LCCN:2003-008358.
Audience: **u,f.**

Hall, Donald **PS3515.A3152Z463**
Death to the Death of Poetry: Essays, Reviews, Notes, Interviews. Trade Cloth. University of Michigan Press. Chicago, IL. 1995. 168p. Poets on Poetry Ser. ISBN:0-472-09571-4, ISBN13: 978-0-472-09571-1. Dewey:811/.5409. LCCN:94-027082.
Audience: **g,l,u,f.**

Hall, Donald **PS3515.A312 E9**
Exiles and Marriage. Trade Cloth. Penguin Group (USA) Inc. New York, NY. 1955. ISBN:0-670-30102-7, ISBN13: 978-0-670-30102-7. Dewey:811.5.
Audience: **g,l,u,f.**

Hall, Donald **PS3566.L27**
Here at Eagle Pond. Trade Paper. Houghton Mifflin Company Trade & Reference Division. Boston, MA. 2000. 168p. ISBN:0-618-08473-8, ISBN13: 978-0-618-08473-9. Dewey:811/.54 B. LCCN:90-037582.
Audience: **g,l,u,f.**

Hall, Donald **PS3515.A3152Z475**
Life Work. Ed. 2. Trade Paper. Beacon Press. Boston, MA. 2003. 136p. ISBN:0-8070-7133-1, ISBN13: 978-0-8070-7133-5. Dewey:811/.54 B. LCCN:2002-043867.
Audience: **g,l,u,f.**

Hall, Donald **PS3566.L27**
The Old Life. Trade Paper. Houghton Mifflin Company Trade & Reference Division. Boston, MA. 1997. 130p. ISBN:0-395-85600-0, ISBN13: 978-0-395-85600-0. Dewey:811.5/4.
Audience: **g,l,u,f.**

Hall, Donald **PS3515.A3152P35 2002**
The Painted Bed: Poems. Trade Cloth. Houghton Mifflin Company Trade & Reference Division. Boston, MA. 2002. 112p. ISBN:0-618-18789-8, ISBN13: 978-0-618-18789-8. Dewey:811/.54. LCCN:2001-051620.
Audience: **g,l,u,f.**

Hall, Donald **PS3515.A3152.W4 1982**
The Weather for Poetry: Essays, Reviews, and Notes on Poetry, 1977-1981. Trade Paper. University of Michigan Press. Chicago, IL. 1983. 352p. Poets on Poetry Ser. ISBN:0-472-06340-5, ISBN13: 978-0-472-06340-6. Dewey:811/.009. LCCN:82-008544.
Audience: **g,l,u,f.** B

Hall, Donald **PS3515.A3152A6 2006**
White Apples and the Taste of Stone: Poems 1946-2006. Mixed Media. Houghton Mifflin Company. New York, NY. 2006. 448p. ISBN:0-618-53721-X, ISBN13: 978-0-618-53721-1. Dewey:811/.54. LCCN:2005-020047.
Audience: **g,l,u,f.**

Hall, Donald **PS3515.A3152W58 1998**
Without: Poems. Trade Cloth. Houghton Mifflin Company Trade & Reference Division. Boston, MA. 1998. 96p. ISBN:0-395-88408-X, ISBN13: 978-0-395-88408-9. LCCN:97-039925.
Audience: **g,l,u,f.**

Hall, Donald
The Man Who Lived Alone. Mary Azarian (Illustrator). Trade Paper. David R. Godine Publisher. Boston, MA. 1998. 36p. ISBN:1-56792-050-0, ISBN13: 978-1-56792-050-5. Dewey:[Fic].
Audience: **g,l,u,f.**

Rector, Liam (Editor) **PS3515.A3152Z65 1989**
The Day I Was Older: Writings on the Poetry of Donald Hall. Trade Cloth. Story Line Press. Ashland, OR. 1989. 289p. ISBN:0-934257-20-5, ISBN13: 978-0-934257-20-6. Dewey:811/.54. LCCN:89-004403.
Audience: **u,f.**

20th Century (1901-1960) > H > Hawkes, John

Hawkes, John **PS3568.O243**
The Blood Oranges. Trade Paper. New Directions Publishing Corporation. New York, NY. 1972. 284p. ISBN:0-8112-0061-2, ISBN13: 978-0-8112-0061-5. Dewey:813/.54. LCCN:74-152516.
Audience: **g,l,u,f.** B

Hawkes, John **PS3558.A82S4 2005**
Second Skin. Jeffrey Eugenides (Preface by). Trade Paper, Perfect. New Directions Publishing Corporation. New York, NY. 2005. 210p. New Directions Paperbook Ser., Vol. 1027 ISBN:0-8112-1644-6, ISBN13: 978-0-8112-1644-9. Dewey:813/.54. LCCN:2005-021516.
Audience: **g,l,u,f.**

Hawkes, John **PS3558.A82**
The Lime Twig. L. A. Fiedler (Introduction by). Trade Paper. New Directions Publishing Corporation. New York, NY. 1961. 175p. ISBN:0-8112-0065-5, ISBN13: 978-0-8112-0065-3. Dewey:813.54. LCCN:60-014719.
Audience: **g,l,u,f.**

Hawkes, John **PS3558.A82**
The Cannibal. A. Guerard (Introduction by). Trade Paper. New Directions Publishing Corporation. New York, NY. 1962. ISBN:0-8112-0063-9, ISBN13: 978-0-8112-0063-9. Dewey:813.5. LCCN:49-048130.
Audience: **g,l,u,f.** B

20th Century (1901-1960) > H > Hellman, Lillian

Austenfeld, Thomas C. **PS159.G3A94 2001**
American Women Writers and the Nazis: Ethics and Politics in Boyle, Porter, Stafford and Hellman. Trade Cloth. University Press of Virginia. Charlottesville, VA. 2001. viii, 189p. ISBN:0-8139-2052-3, ISBN13: 978-0-8139-2052-8. Dewey:810.9/9287/0904. LCCN:00-068660.
Audience: **u,f.** *Choice, 2002.*

Griffin, Alice & Thorsten, Geraldine **PS3515.E343**
Understanding Lillian Hellman. Trade Cloth. University of South Carolina Press. Columbia, SC. 1999. 184p. Understanding Contemporary American Literature Ser. ISBN:1-57003-302-1, ISBN13: 978-1-57003-302-5. Dewey:812/.52. LCCN:98-058042.
Audience: **l,u.** *Choice, 2000.*

Hellman, Lillian **PS3525.I5156**
Pentimento. Trade Paper. Little Brown & Company. New York, NY. 2000. 320p. ISBN:0-316-35288-8, ISBN13: 978-0-316-35288-8. Dewey:812/.52.
Audience: **g,l,u,f.** B

Hellman, Lillian **PS3515.E343 A6 1979**
Six Plays by Lillian Hellman: The Children's Hour, Days to Come, The Little Foxes, Watch on the Rhine, Another Part of the Forest, The Autumn Garden. Book, Other. Knopf Publishing Group. New York, NY. 1979. 512p. ISBN:0-394-74112-9, ISBN13: 978-0-394-74112-3. Dewey:812/.5/2. LCCN:79-002160.
Audience: **l,u,f.**

Hellman, Lillian & Bates, Kathy **PS3515.E343Z475 2000**
Scoundrel Time. Gary Wills (Contribution by). Trade Paper. Little Brown & Company. New York, NY. 2000. 176p. ISBN:0-316-35294-2, ISBN13: 978-0-316-35294-9. Dewey:812/.52 B. LCCN:00-702622.
Audience: **g,l,u,f.** B

Hellman, Lillian **PS3515.E343Z5 1999**
An Unfinished Woman: A Memoir. Wendy Wasserstein (Contribution by), Garry Wills (Introduction by). Trade Paper. Little Brown & Company. New York, NY. 1999. 304p. ISBN:0-316-35285-3, ISBN13: 978-0-316-35285-7. LCCN:99-462694.
Audience: **g,l,u,f.**

Martinson, Deborah **PS3515.E343Z773 2005**
Lillian Hellman: A Life with Foxes and Scoundrels. Trade Cloth. Basic Books. New York, NY. 2005. 480p. ISBN:1-58243-315-1, ISBN13: 978-1-58243-315-8. Dewey:812/.52 B. LCCN:2005-016616.
Audience: **g,l,u,f.**

20th Century (1901-1960) > H > Hemingway, Ernest

Baker, Carlos **PS3515.E37 Z575**
Ernest Hemingway Life Story. Trade Cloth. Thomson Gale. Farmington Hills, MI. 1976. ISBN:0-685-45827-X, ISBN13: 978-0-685-45827-3. Dewey:813/.52.
Audience: **l,u.**

Baker, Sheridan Warner **PS3515.E37 Z582**
Ernest Hemingway: An Introduction and Interpretation. Holt, Rinehart and Winston. 1967.
Audience: **l,u.**

Benson, Jackson J. (Editor) **PS3515.E37Z7466 1991**
New Critical Approaches to the Short Stories of Ernest Hemingway. Paul Smith (Contribution by). Cloth Text. Duke University Press. Durham, NC. 1991. 528p. ISBN:0-8223-1065-1, ISBN13: 978-0-8223-1065-5. Dewey:813/.52. LCCN:90-003463.
Audience: **l,u.**

Berman, Ronald **PS3511.I9Z55774 2001**
Fitzgerald, Hemingway and the Twenties. Trade Cloth. University of Alabama Press. Tuscaloosa, AL. 2001. 192p. ISBN:0-8173-1057-6, ISBN13: 978-0-8173-1057-8. Dewey:813/.5209. LCCN:00-010158.
Audience: **l,u.** *Choice, 2001.*

Broer, Lawrence R. & Holland, Gloria (Editors) **PS3515**
Hemingway and Women: Female Critics and the Female Voice. Trade Paper. University of Alabama Press. Tuscaloosa, AL. 2004. 376p. ISBN:0-8173-5150-7, ISBN13: 978-0-8173-5150-2. Dewey:813/.52.
Audience: **u,f.** *Choice, 2003.*

Burwell, Rose M. **PS3515.E37Z584162**
Hemingway: The Postwar Years and the Posthumous Novels. Trade Cloth. Cambridge University Press. New York, NY. 1996. 272p. Studies in American Literature and Culture, No. 96 ISBN:0-521-48199-6, ISBN13: 978-0-521-48199-1. Dewey:813.5/2. LCCN:95-014539.
Audience: **u,f.**

Comley, Nancy R. & Scholes, Robert **PS3511.A86**
Hemingway's Genders: Rereading the Hemingway Text. Trade

Paper. Yale University Press. Cumberland, RI. 1996. 168p. ISBN:0-300-06464-0, ISBN13: 978-0-300-06464-3. Dewey:813.5/2.
Audience: **u,f.** *Choice, 1995.*

Donaldson, Scott **PS3515.E37**
The Cambridge Companion to Hemingway. Cloth Text. Cambridge University Press. New York, NY. 1996. 335p. Companions to Literature Ser. ISBN:0-521-45479-4, ISBN13: 978-0-521-45479-7. Dewey:813.5/2. LCCN:95-008398.
Audience: **l,u,f.**

Donaldson, Scott **PS3515.E37Z58574**
Hemingway vs. Fitzgerald: The Rise and Fall of a Literacy Friendship. Trade Cloth. Overlook Press, The. New York, NY. 1999. 320p. ISBN:0-87951-711-5, ISBN13: 978-0-87951-711-3. Dewey:813/.5209 B. LCCN:99-037835.
Audience: **g,l,u,f.** *Choice, 2000.*

Fantina, Richard **PS3515.E37Z5885 2004**
Ernest Hemingway: Machismo and Masochism. Cloth over Boards. Palgrave Macmillan. New York, NY. 2005. 224p. ISBN:1-4039-6907-8, ISBN13: 978-1-4039-6907-1. Dewey:813/.52. LCCN:2005-043182.
Audience: **u,f.** *Choice, 2006.*

Fleming, Robert E. (Editor, Introduction by) **PS3515.E37Z617915**
Hemingway and The Natural World. Trade Cloth. University of Idaho Press. Moscow, ID. 2004. 276p. ISBN:0-89301-214-9, ISBN13: 978-0-89301-214-4. Dewey:813/.52. LCCN:98-042679.
Audience: **u,f.** *Choice, 2000.*

Hemingway, Ernest **PS3515.E57A7 1998**
Across the River and into the Trees. Trade Cloth. Simon & Schuster. New York, NY. 1998. 272p. Classic Ser. ISBN:0-684-84464-8, ISBN13: 978-0-684-84464-0. Dewey:823/.9/1. LCCN:98-159867.
Audience: **g,l,u,f.** B

Hemingway, Ernest **GV1107.H4 1999**
Death in the Afternoon. Trade Cloth. Simon & Schuster. New York, NY. 1999. 400p. Scribner Classics ISBN:0-684-85922-X, ISBN13: 978-0-684-85922-4. Dewey:791.8/2/0946. LCCN:99-231717.
Audience: **g,l,u,f.** B

Hemingway, Ernest **PS3515.E37F3 1997**
A Farewell to Arms. Trade Cloth. Simon & Schuster. New York, NY. 1997. 304p. Scribner Classics ISBN:0-684-83788-9, ISBN13: 978-0-684-83788-8. Dewey:813/.52. LCCN:96-053356.
Audience: **g,l,u,f.**

Hemingway, Ernest **PS3525.I5156**
The Fifth Column: And Four Stories of the Spanish Civil War. Trade Cloth. Thomson Gale. Farmington Hills, MI. 1978. 160p. ISBN:0-684-15815-9, ISBN13: 978-0-684-15815-0. Dewey:812/.52. LCCN:70-182369.
Audience: **g,l,u,f.** B

Hemingway, Ernest **PS3515.E37F6 1996**
For Whom the Bell Tolls. Trade Cloth. Simon & Schuster. New York, NY. 1996. 496p. Scribner Classics ISBN:0-684-83048-5, ISBN13: 978-0-684-83048-3. Dewey:813.52. LCCN:96-007706.
Audience: **g,l,u,f.**

Hemingway, Ernest **PS3515.E37I5 1986**
In Our Time. Trade Cloth. Simon & Schuster. New York, NY. 1980. 156p. ISBN:0-684-16480-9, ISBN13: 978-0-684-16480-9. Dewey:[Fic]. LCCN:86-012965.
Audience: **g,l,u,f.** B

Hemingway, Ernest **PS3515**
Islands in the Stream: A Novel. Trade Cloth. Simon & Schuster. New York, NY. 2003. 448p. ISBN:0-7432-5342-6, ISBN13: 978-0-7432-5342-0. Dewey:823/.91.
Audience: **g,l,u,f.**

Hemingway, Ernest **PS3515.E37Z475 1996**
A Moveable Feast. Trade Cloth. Simon & Schuster. New York, NY. 1996. 208p. Scribner Classics ISBN:0-684-83363-8, ISBN13: 978-0-684-83363-7. Dewey:813/.52. LCCN:96-030237.
Audience: **g,l,u,f.**

Hemingway, Ernest **PZ3.H3736**
The Nick Adams Stories. Trade Cloth. Thomson Gale. Farmington Hills, MI. 1987. 268p. Hudson River Editions Ser. ISBN:0-02-550780-X, ISBN13: 978-0-02-550780-7. Dewey:813/.5/2.
Audience: **g,l,u,f.** B

Hemingway, Ernest **PS3515.E37A6 1997**
The Short Stories. Trade Cloth. Simon & Schuster. New York, NY. 1997. 464p. Scribner Classics ISBN:0-684-83786-2, ISBN13: 978-0-684-83786-4. Dewey:[Fic]. LCCN:96-053349.
Audience: **g,l,u,f.** B

Hemingway, Ernest **PS3515.E37S8 1996**
The Sun Also Rises. Trade Cloth. Simon & Schuster. New York, NY. 1996. 224p. Scribner Classics ISBN:0-684-83051-5, ISBN13: 978-0-684-83051-3. Dewey:813/.52. LCCN:96-011420.
Audience: **g,l,u,f.**

Hemingway, Ernest **PS3515.E37T6 1999**
To Have and Have Not. Trade Cloth. Simon & Schuster. New York, NY. 1999. 176p. Scribner Classics ISBN:0-684-85923-8, ISBN13: 978-0-684-85923-1. Dewey:813.5/2. LCCN:00-266244.
Audience: **g,l,u,f.** B

Hemingway, Ernest, et al. **PS3515.E37U53 2005**
Under Kilimanjaro. Robert W. Lewis & Robert E. Fleming (Authors). Trade Cloth. Kent State University Press. Kent, OH. 2005. 472p. ISBN:0-87338-845-3, ISBN13: 978-0-87338-845-0. Dewey:813/.52. LCCN:2005-006235.
Audience: **g,l,u,f.**

Hemingway, Ernest **PS3515.E37Z464 1997**
The Dangerous Summer. James A. Michener (Introduction by). Trade Paper. Simon & Schuster. New York, NY. 1997. 240p. ISBN:0-684-83789-7, ISBN13: 978-0-684-83789-5. Dewey:914.6/04825. LCCN:97-018113.
Audience: **g,l,u,f.** B *Choice, 1985.*

Hemingway, Ernest **PS3515.E37G37 1995**
The Garden of Eden. Charles Scribner Jr. (Preface by). Trade Paper. Simon & Schuster. New York, NY. 1995. 256p. ISBN:0-684-80452-2, ISBN13: 978-0-684-80452-1. Dewey:813/.52. LCCN:95-015326.
Audience: **g,l,u,f.** B *Choice, 1986.*

Hemingway, Ernest **PS3515.E37O52 1996**
The Old Man and the Sea. C. F. Tunnicliffe & Raymond Sheppard (Illustrators). Trade Cloth. Simon & Schuster. New York, NY. 1996. 96p. Scribner Classics ISBN:0-684-83049-3, ISBN13: 978-0-684-83049-0. Dewey:813/.52. LCCN:96-011419.
Audience: **g,l,u,f.**

Hemingway, Ernest **PN6161**
By-Line Ernest Hemingway: Selected Articles and Dispatches of Four Decades. William White (Editor). Trade Cloth. Thomson Gale. Farmington Hills, MI. 1981. 512p. ISBN:0-684-16600-3, ISBN13: 978-0-684-16600-1. Dewey:814/.52. LCCN:67-015483.
Audience: **g,l,u,f.**

Kennedy, J. Gerald & Bryer, Jackson R. (Editors) **PS379**
French Connections: Hemingway and Fitzgerald Abroad. Trade Paper. Palgrave Macmillan. New York, NY. 1999. 368p. ISBN:0-312-22450-8, ISBN13: 978-0-312-22450-9. Dewey:813.5/2/09. LCCN:96-049632.
Audience: **u,f.** *Choice, 1998.*

Laurence, Frank M. **PS3515.E37.Z689 1981**
Hemingway and the Movies. Trade Cloth. University Press of Mississippi. Jackson, MS. 1980. 336p. ISBN:0-87805-115-5, ISBN13: 978-0-87805-115-1. Dewey:813/.52. LCCN:79-001437.
Audience: **u,f.** B

Leff, Leonard J. **PS3515.E37**
Hemingway and His Conspirators: Hollywood, Scribners, and the Making of the American Dream. Trade Paper. Rowman & Littlefield Publishers, Inc. Lanham, MD. 1999. 256p. ISBN:0-8476-8545-4, ISBN13: 978-0-8476-8545-5. Dewey:813/.52 B.
Audience: **u,f.**

Mellow, James R. **PS3515.E37Z74176**
Hemingway: A Life Without Consequences. Trade Cloth. Houghton Mifflin Company. New York, NY. 1992. 576p. ISBN:0-395-37777-3, ISBN13: 978-0-395-37777-2. Dewey:813/.52. LCCN:92-009549.
Audience: **g,l,u,f.** *Choice, 1993.*

Meyers, Jeffrey **PS3515.E37Z7418 1999**
Hemingway: A Biography. Trade Paper. Da Capo Press, Inc. Cambridge, MA. 1999. 734p. ISBN:0-306-80890-0, ISBN13: 978-0-306-80890-6. Dewey:813/.52. LCCN:98-054965.
Audience: **g,l,u,f.** B *Choice, 1986.*

Meyers, Jeffrey (Editor) **PS3515.E37Z/**
Hemingway: The Critical Heritage. Trade Cloth. Routledge. New York, NY. 1982. 632p. The Critical Heritage Ser. ISBN:0-7100-0929-1, ISBN13: 978-0-7100-0929-6. Dewey:813/.52. LCCN:81-020998.
Audience: **l,u.** B

Oliver, Charles M. **PS3515.E37Z7484 1999**
Ernest Hemingway A to Z: The Essential Reference to His Life and Work. Trade Cloth. Facts On File, Inc. New York, NY. 1999. 464p. Literary A to Z Ser. ISBN:0-8160-3467-2, ISBN13: 978-0-8160-3467-3. Dewey:813/.52. LCCN:98-030042.
Audience: **l,u.** *Choice, 1999.*

Reynolds, Michael S. **PS3511.A86**
Hemingway: The Paris Years. Trade Paper. W. W. Norton & Company, Inc. New York, NY. 1999. 402p. ISBN:0-393-31879-6, ISBN13: 978-0-393-31879-1. Dewey:813/.52 B. LCCN:89-030910.
Audience: **g,l,u,f.** *Choice, 1990.*

Reynolds, Michael S. **PS3515.E37Z75469**
Hemingway: The Final Years. Trade Cloth. W. W. Norton & Company, Inc. New York, NY. 1999. 352p. ISBN:0-393-04748-2, ISBN13: 978-0-393-04748-6. Dewey:813/.52 B. LCCN:99-017141.
Audience: **g,l,u,f.** *Choice, 2000.*

Reynolds, Michael S. **PS3515.E37**
Hemingway: The 1930s. Trade Paper. W. W. Norton & Company, Inc. New York, NY. 1998. 380p. ISBN:0-393-31778-1, ISBN13: 978-0-393-31778-7. Dewey:813/.52 B. LCCN:96-043113.
Audience: **g,l,u,f.** *Choice, 1997.*

Reynolds, Michael S. **PS3515.E37 Z7549**
The Young Hemingway. Trade Cloth. W. W. Norton & Company, Inc. New York, NY. 1998. 298p. ISBN:0-393-31776-5, ISBN13: 978-0-393-31776-3. Dewey:813/.52 B. LCCN:85-022936.
Audience: **g,l,u,f.** *Choice, 1986.*

Scafella, Frank (Editor) **PS3515.E37Z61793**
Hemingway: Essays of Reassessment. Trade Cloth. Oxford University Press, Inc. New York, NY. 1990. 288p. ISBN:0-19-506546-8, ISBN13: 978-0-19-506546-6. Dewey:813/.52. LCCN:90-032976.
Audience: **u,f.** *Choice, 1991.*

Smith, Paul (Editor, Contribution by) **PS3515.E37 Z7467 19**
New Essays on Hemingway's Short Fiction. Nancy Comley, Robert Scholes, James Phelan, Susan F. Beegel & Debra A. Moddelmog (Contribution by). Trade Cloth. Cambridge University Press. New York, NY. 1998. 153p. The American Novel Ser. ISBN:0-521-55382-2, ISBN13: 978-0-521-55382-7. Dewey:813/.52. LCCN:97-023485.
Audience: **l,u.** *Choice, 1998.*

Strychacz, Thomas F. (Translator) **PS3515.E37Z8826 2003**
Hemingway's Theaters of Masculinity. Trade Cloth. Louisiana State University Press. Baton Rouge, LA. 2004. 344p. ISBN:0-8071-2906-2, ISBN13: 978-0-8071-2906-7. Dewey:813/.52. LCCN:2003-012837.
Audience: **u,f.** *Choice, 2004.*

Wagner-Martin, Linda (Editor) **PS3515.E37Z58676**
Ernest Hemingway: Seven Decades of Criticism. Trade Paper. Michigan State University Press. East Lansing, MI. 1998. 427p. ISBN:0-87013-489-2, ISBN13: 978-0-87013-489-0. Dewey:813/.52. LCCN:98-042861.
Audience: **l,u,f.**

Wagner-Martin, Linda (Editor) **PS3515.E37Z6325 2000**
A Historical Guide to Ernest Hemingway. Cloth Text. Oxford

University Press, Inc. New York, NY. 2000. 256p. Historical Guides to American Authors ISBN:0-19-512151-1, ISBN13: 978-0-19-512151-3. Dewey:813/.52 B. LCCN:99-010910.
Audience: **l,u.**

Waldhorn, Arthur **PS3515.E37Z92 2002**
A Reader's Guide to Ernest Hemingway. Trade Paper. Syracuse University Press. Syracuse, NY. 2002. xiv, 284p. ISBN:0-8156-2950-8, ISBN13: 978-0-8156-2950-4. Dewey:813/.52. LCCN:2002-022789.
Audience: **l,u.** B

Young, Philip **PS3515.E37 Z982**
Ernest Hemingway: A Reconsideration. Trade Paper. Pennsylvania State University Press. University Park, PA. 2000. 308p. ISBN:0-271-02092-X, ISBN13: 978-0-271-02092-1. Dewey:813.52. LCCN:65-026101.
Audience: **u,f.**

20th Century (1901-1960) > H > Highsmith, Patricia

Harrison, Russell **PS3558.I366Z69 1997**
Patricia Highsmith. Trade Cloth. Thomson Gale. Farmington Hills, MI. 1997. xvi, 156p. Twayne's United States Authors Ser., Vol. 683 ISBN:0-8057-4566-1, ISBN13: 978-0-8057-4566-5. Dewey:813/.54. LCCN:97-018792.
Audience: **l,u.**

Highsmith, Patricia **PS3558.I366**
The Price of Salt. Trade Paper. W. W. Norton & Company, Inc. New York, NY. 2004. 288p. ISBN:0-393-32599-7, ISBN13: 978-0-393-32599-7. Dewey:813/.54.
Audience: **g,l,u,f.**

Highsmith, Patricia **PS3558.I366A6 2001**
The Selected Stories of Patricia Highsmith. Trade Cloth. W. W. Norton & Company, Inc. New York, NY. 2001. 672p. ISBN:0-393-02031-2, ISBN13: 978-0-393-02031-1. Dewey:813/.54. LCCN:2001-030878.
Audience: **g,l,u,f.**

Highsmith, Patricia **PS3558.I366S77 2001**
Strangers on a Train. Trade Paper. W. W. Norton & Company, Inc. New York, NY. 2001. 281p. ISBN:0-393-32198-3, ISBN13: 978-0-393-32198-2. Dewey:813.5/4. LCCN:2001-030821.
Audience: **g,l,u,f.**

Highsmith, Patricia **PS3558.I366A6 1999**
The Talented Mr. Ripley; Ripley under Ground; and Ripley's Game. Trade Cloth. Alfred A. Knopf Inc. New York, NY. 1999. 880p. Mr. Ripley Ser. ISBN:0-375-40792-8, ISBN13: 978-0-375-40792-5. Dewey:813/.54. LCCN:99-038147.
Audience: **g,l,u,f.**

Mawer, Noel **PS3558.I366Z76 2004**
A Critical Study of the Fiction of Patricia Highsmith--from the Psychological to the Political. Trade Cloth. Edwin Mellen Press, The. Lewiston, NY. 2004. 320p. Studies in American Literature Ser. ISBN:0-7734-6508-1, ISBN13: 978-0-7734-6508-4. Dewey:813/.54. LCCN:2003-068610.
Audience: **l,u.**

Wilson, Andrew **PS3568.O243**
Beautiful Shadow: A Life of Patricia Highsmith. Cloth over Boards. Bloomsbury Publishing. New York, NY. 2003. 534p. ISBN:1-58234-198-2, ISBN13: 978-1-58234-198-9. Dewey:813/.54 B.
Audience: **g,l,u,f.** *Choice, 2004.*

20th Century (1901-1960) > H > Himes, Chester

Fabre, Michel J. & Skinner, Robert E. (Editors) **PS3515.I713Z467 1995**
Conversations with Chester Himes. Trade Cloth. University Press of Mississippi. Jackson, MS. 1995. 320p. Literary Conversations Ser. ISBN:0-87805-819-2, ISBN13: 978-0-87805-819-8. Dewey:813/.54. LCCN:95-004762.
Audience: **l,u.**

Himes, Chester B. **PS3515.I713.Z5**
The Autobiography of Chester Himes. Trade Cloth. Doubleday Publishing. New York, NY. 1972. ISBN:0-385-08909-0, ISBN13: 978-0-385-08909-8. Dewey:813/.5/4. LCCN:71-157601.
Audience: **g,l,u,f.**

Himes, Chester B. **PS3568.O243**
The Collected Stories of Chester Himes. Trade Cloth. Avalon Publishing Group. New York, NY. 2002. ISBN:1-56025-311-8, ISBN13: 978-1-56025-311-2. Dewey:813/.54.
Audience: **g,l,u,f.** *Choice, 1991.*

Himes, Chester B. **PS3515.I713F67 1989**
A Rage in Harlem. Trade Paper. Knopf Publishing Group. New York, NY. 1989. 160p. Vintage Crime Ser. ISBN:0-679-72040-5, ISBN13: 978-0-679-72040-9. Dewey:813/.54. LCCN:89-040064.
Audience: **g,l,u,f.**

Himes, Chester B. **PS3515**
If He Hollers Let Him Go. Hilton Als (Introduction by). Trade Paper. Avalon Publishing Group. New York, NY. 2002. 216p. ISBN:1-56025-445-9, ISBN13: 978-1-56025-445-4. Dewey:813/.54. LCCN:2002-727758.
Audience: **g,l,u,f.**

Muller, Gilbert H. **PS3515.I713Z78 1989**
Chester Himes. Cloth Text. Thomson Gale. Farmington Hills, MI. 1989. 184p. Twayne's United States Authors Ser., No. 553 ISBN:0-8057-7545-5, ISBN13: 978-0-8057-7545-7. Dewey:813/.54. LCCN:89-032310.
Audience: **l,u.** *Choice, 1990.*

Sallis, James **PS3515.I713Z84 2001**
Chester Himes: A Life. Cloth over Boards. Walker & Company. New York, NY. 2000. 350p. ISBN:0-8027-1362-9, ISBN13: 978-0-8027-1362-9. Dewey:813/.54 B. LCCN:00-063328.
Audience: **u,f.** *Choice, 2001.*

Sallis, James **PS374.D4**
Difficult Lives: Jim Thompson, David Goodis, Chester Himes. Ed. 2. Trade Paper. Gryphon Books. Brooklyn, NY. 2000. 102p. ISBN:1-58250-029-0, ISBN13: 978-1-58250-029-4. Dewey:813/.087209 B.
Audience: **g,l,u,f.**

20th Century (1901-1960) > H > Hollander, John

Hollander, John **PS3515.O3485**
A Crackling of Thorns. Trade Cloth. A M S Press, Inc. New York, NY. Yale Series of Younger Poets, No. 54 ISBN:0-404-53854-1, ISBN13: 978-0-404-53854-5. Dewey:811.5. LCCN:73-011023.
Audience: **g,l,u,f.** B

✓**Hollander, John** **PS3515.O3485 P53**
Picture Window: Poems. Trade Paper. Alfred A. Knopf Inc. New York, NY. 2005. 96p. ISBN:0-375-71013-2, ISBN13: 978-0-375-71013-1. Dewey:811/.54.
Audience: **g,l,u,f.**

Hollander, John **PS3515.O3485P55 1998**
The Poetry of Everyday Life. Trade Cloth. University of Michigan Press. Chicago, IL. 1999. 184p. Poets on Poetry Ser. ISBN:0-472-09684-2, ISBN13: 978-0-472-09684-8. Dewey:811/.54. LCCN:98-039034.
Audience: **l,u,f.**

Hollander, John **PS3515.O3485R4 1999**
Reflections on Espionage: The Question of Cupcake. Trade Paper. Yale University Press. Cumberland, RI. 1999. 104p. ISBN:0-300-07966-4, ISBN13: 978-0-300-07966-1. Dewey:811/.54. LCCN:99-044253.
Audience: **g,l,u,f.**

Hollander, John **PS3515.O3485.S6**
Spectral Emanations: New and Selected Poems. Trade Cloth. Simon & Schuster Children's Publishing. New York, NY. 1978. xi, 238 p. ;p. ISBN:0-689-10888-5, ISBN13: 978-0-689-10888-4. Dewey:811/.5/4. LCCN:77-020645.
Audience: **g,l,u,f.** B

20th Century (1901-1960) > H > Hughes, Langston

De Santis, Christpher C. (Editor) **PS3515.U274 2001**
Essays on Art, Race, Politics and World Affairs, Vol. 9. Trade Cloth. University of Missouri Press. Columbia, MO. 2005. 632p. The Collected Works of Langston Hughes, Vol. 9 ISBN:0-8262-1394-4, ISBN13: 978-0-8262-1394-5. Dewey:818/.5209. LCCN:00-066601.
Audience: **g,l,u,f.**

✓**Gates, Henry Louis Jr. & Appiah, Anthony** **PS3515.U274Z672 1993**
Langston Hughes: Critical Perspectives Past and Present. Trade Cloth. HarperCollins Publishers. New York, NY. 1993. 255p. Literary Ser. ISBN:1-56743-016-3, ISBN13: 978-1-56743-016-5. Dewey:818/.5209. LCCN:92-045756.
Audience: **l,u.** *Choice, 1994.*

Hughes, Langston **PS3515.U274 A6**
The Langston Hughes Reader. Trade Cloth. Amereon, Ltd. Mattituck, NY. 1976. ISBN:0-8488-0698-0, ISBN13: 978-0-8488-0698-9. Dewey:810.81.
Audience: **g,l,u,f.** B

Hughes, Langston **PS3515.U274**
Laughing to Keep from Crying. Library Binding. Amereon, Ltd. Mattituck, NY. ISBN:0-88411-060-5, ISBN13: 978-0-88411-060-6. Dewey:813.52.
Audience: **g,l,u,f.** B

Hughes, Langston **PS3515.U274W3 1990**
The Ways of White Folks. Trade Paper. Knopf Publishing Group. New York, NY. 1990. 272p. Vintage Bks. ISBN:0-679-72817-1, ISBN13: 978-0-679-72817-7. Dewey:813/.52. LCCN:90-050180.
Audience: **g,l,u,f.** B

✓**Hughes, Langston** **PS3515.U274.G6 1973**
Good Morning, Revolution: Uncollected Writings of Social Protest. Faith Berry (Editor). Trade Cloth. Chicago Review Press, Inc. Chicago, IL. 1973. 160p. ISBN:0-88208-023-7, ISBN13: 978-0-88208-023-9. Dewey:818/.5/209. LCCN:73-081747.
Audience: **l,u,f.** B

Hughes, Langston **PS3515.U274 2001**
Fight for Freedom and Other Writings on Civil Rights. Christopher C. De Santis (Editor). Trade Cloth. University of Missouri Press. Columbia, MO. 2005. 232p. The Collected Works of Langston Hughes, Vol. 10 ISBN:0-8262-1371-5, ISBN13: 978-0-8262-1371-6. Dewey:818/.5209. LCCN:00-066601.
Audience: **g,l,u,f.** *Choice, 2002.*

✓**Hughes, Langston** **PS3515.U274 2001**
The Novels: Not Without Laughter and Tambourines to Glory. Dolan Hubbard (Editor, Introduction by). Trade Cloth. University of Missouri Press. Columbia, MO. 2005. 320p. The Collected Works of Langston Hughes, Vol. 4 ISBN:0-8262-1342-1, ISBN13: 978-0-8262-1342-6. Dewey:818/.5209. LCCN:00-066601.
Audience: **g,l,u,f.**

Hughes, Langston, et al. **PS3515.U274 2001**
The Collected Works of Langston Hughes, Vol. 11. Dolan Hubbard & Leslie Catherine Sanders (Authors), Arnold Rampersad (Introduction by). Trade Cloth. University of Missouri Press. Columbia, MO. 2005. 392p. ISBN:0-8262-1498-3, ISBN13: 978-0-8262-1498-0. Dewey:818/.5209. LCCN:00-066601.
Audience: **g,l,u,f.**

✓**Hughes, Langston** **PS3515.U274 2001**
Autobiography: The Big Sea. Joseph McLaren (Editor). Trade Cloth. University of Missouri Press. Columbia, MO. 2005. 272p. The Collected Works of Langston Hughes, Vol. 13 ISBN:0-8262-1410-X, ISBN13: 978-0-8262-1410-2. Dewey:818/.5209. LCCN:00-066601.
Audience: **g,l,u,f.** *Choice, 2003.*

✓**Hughes, Langston** **PS3515.U274 2001**
Autobiography: I Wonder as I Wander. Joseph McLaren (Editor, Introduction by). Trade Cloth. University of Missouri Press. Columbia, MO. 2005. 408p. The Collected Works of Langston Hughes, Vol. 14 ISBN:0-8262-1434-7, ISBN13: 978-0-8262-1434-8. Dewey:818/.5209. LCCN:00-066601.
Audience: **g,l,u,f.**

Hughes, Langston **PS3515.U274 2001**
The Short Stories. R. Baxter Miller (Editor). Trade Cloth. University of Missouri Press. Columbia, MO. 2005. 488p. The Collected Works of Langston Hughes, Vol. 15
ISBN:0-8262-1411-8, ISBN13: 978-0-8262-1411-9. Dewey:818/.5209. LCCN:00-066601.
Audience: **g,l,u,f.**

Hughes, Langston **PS3515.U274 2001**
The Poems, 1921-1940. Arnold Rampersad (Introduction by). Trade Cloth. University of Missouri Press. Columbia, MO. 2005. 280p. The Collected Works of Langston Hughes, Vol. 1
ISBN:0-8262-1339-1, ISBN13: 978-0-8262-1339-6. Dewey:818/.5209. LCCN:00-066601.
Audience: **g,l,u,f.** *Choice, 2001.*

Hughes, Langston **PS3515.U274 2001**
The Poems. Arnold Rampersad (Editor, Introduction by). Trade Cloth. University of Missouri Press. Columbia, MO. 2005. 352p. The Collected Works of Langston Hughes, Vol. 3
ISBN:0-8262-1341-3, ISBN13: 978-0-8262-1341-9. Dewey:818/.5209. LCCN:00-066601.
Audience: **g,l,u,f.**

Hughes, Langston **PS3515.U274 2001**
The Poems, 1941-1950. Arnold Rampersad (Editor, Introduction by). Trade Cloth. University of Missouri Press. Columbia, MO. 2005. 296p. The Collected Works of Langston Hughes, Vol. 2
ISBN:0-8262-1340-5, ISBN13: 978-0-8262-1340-2. Dewey:818/.5209. LCCN:00-066601.
Audience: **g,l,u,f.**

Hughes, Langston **PS3525.I5156**
Five Plays by Langston Hughes. Webster Smalley (Editor). Trade Cloth. Indiana University Press. Bloomington, IN. 1963. 280p. ISBN:0-253-32230-8, ISBN13: 978-0-253-32230-2. Dewey:812.5/2. LCCN:63-007169.
Audience: **g,l,u,f.**

Ostrom, Hans A. **PS3515**
A Langston Hughes Encyclopedia. Cloth Text. Greenwood Publishing Group, Inc. Portsmouth, NH. 2001. 520p. ISBN:0-313-30392-4, ISBN13: 978-0-313-30392-0. Dewey:818/.5209 B. LCCN:00-061047.
Audience: **l,u.** *Choice, 2002.*

Rampersand, Arnold **PS3537.T323**
The Life of Langston Hughes, Set. Ed. 2. Trade Cloth. Oxford University Press, Inc. New York, NY. 2002.
ISBN:0-19-521936-8, ISBN13: 978-0-19-521936-4. Dewey:818/.5209 B.
Audience: **u,f.**

Tracy, Steven C. (Editor) **PS3515.U274Z663 2003**
A Historical Guide to Langston Hughes. Trade Paper. Oxford University Press, Inc. New York, NY. 2003. 264p. Historical Guides to American Authors ISBN:0-19-514434-1, ISBN13: 978-0-19-514434-5. Dewey:811/.52. LCCN:2003-002111.
Audience: **g,l,u,f.**

Tracy, Steven C. **PS3515**
Langston Hughes and the Blues. Trade Paper. University of Illinois Press. Champaign, IL. 2001. 328p. ISBN:0-252-06985-4, ISBN13: 978-0-252-06985-7. Dewey:818/.5209.
Audience: **u,f.** *Choice, 1989.*

20th Century (1901-1960) > H > H. D.

Camboni, Marina (Editor) **PS3507.O726Z718 2002**
H. D.'s Poetry: "The Meanings That Words Hide": Essays. Trade Cloth. A M S Press. Pittsburgh, PA. 2002. xix, 208p. AMS Studies in Modern Literature, No. 24
ISBN:0-404-61594-5, ISBN13: 978-0-404-61594-9. Dewey:811/.52. LCCN:2002-026237.
Audience: **l,u.** *Choice, 2004.*

Chisholm, Dianne **PS3507.O726 Z6**
H. D.'s Freudian Poetics: Psychoanalysis in Translation. Book, Other. Cornell University Press. Ithaca, NY. 1992. 304p. Reading Women Writing Ser. ISBN:0-8014-2474-7, ISBN13: 978-0-8014-2474-8. Dewey:811/.52. LCCN:91-055558.
Audience: **u,f.**

Collecott, Diana **PS3507.O726 Z615 19**
H. D. and Sapphic Modernism 1910-1950. Trade Cloth. Cambridge University Press. New York, NY. 1999. 364p. ISBN:0-521-55078-5, ISBN13: 978-0-521-55078-9. Dewey:811.5/2. LCCN:98-038426.
Audience: **u,f.** *Choice, 2000.*

Connor, Rachel **PS3507.O726**
H. D. and the Image. Cloth over Boards. Manchester University Press. Manchester, 2005. 160p. ISBN:0-7190-6122-9, ISBN13: 978-0-7190-6122-6. Dewey:813/.52. LCCN:2005-272348.
Audience: **u,f.** *Choice, 2005.*

H. D. **PS3507.O726.T74 1973**
Trilogy: The Walls Do Not Fall; Tribute to the Angels; The Flowering of the Rod. Trade Cloth. New Directions Publishing Corporation. New York, NY. 1973. xii, 172p.
ISBN:0-8112-0490-1, ISBN13: 978-0-8112-0490-3. Dewey:811/.52. LCCN:73-078848.
Audience: **g,l,u,f.** B

H. D. **PS3507.O726T74 1998**
Trilogy: The Walls Do Not Fall; Tribute to the Angels; The Flowering of the Rod. Aliki Barnstone (Introduction by, Notes by). Trade Paper. New Directions Publishing Corporation. New York, NY. 1998. 224p. ISBN:0-8112-1399-4, ISBN13: 978-0-8112-1399-8. Dewey:811/.52. LCCN:98-022882.
Audience: **g,l,u,f.** B

H. D. **PS3507.O726**
Helen in Egypt. Horace Gregory (Introduction by). Trade Paper. New Directions Publishing Corporation. New York, NY. 1974. 320p. Book Ser. ISBN:0-8112-0544-4, ISBN13: 978-0-8112-0544-3. Dewey:811/.5/2. LCCN:74-008563.
Audience: **g,l,u,f.** B

H. D. **PS3507.O726A6 1986**
Collected Poems 1912-1944. Louis L. Martz (Editor). Trade Paper. New Directions Publishing Corporation. New York, NY. 1986. 668p. ISBN:0-8112-0971-7, ISBN13: 978-0-8112-0971-7. Dewey:811/.52. LCCN:83-006380.
Audience: **g,l,u,f.**

H. D. **PS3531.O82**
Hermetic Definition. Norman H. Pearson (Introduction by). Trade Paper. New Directions Publishing Corporation. New York, NY. 1972. ISBN:0-8112-0453-7, ISBN13: 978-0-8112-0453-8. Dewey:811/.5/2. LCCN:72-080980.
Audience: **g,l,u,f.** B

H. D. **PS3531.O82**
The Gift. Perdita Schaffner (Introduction by). Trade Paper. New Directions Publishing Corporation. New York, NY. 1982. 160p. ISBN:0-8112-0854-0, ISBN13: 978-0-8112-0854-3. Dewey:811/.52 B. LCCN:82-008027.
Audience: **g,l,u,f.** B *Choice, 1999.*

H. D. **PS3511.A86**
Bid Me to Live: A Madrigal. Perdita Schaffner (Introduction by), John Walsh (Afterword by). Paper Text. Black Swan Books, Ltd. Redding Ridge, CT. 1993. 220p. Imagist Ser. ISBN:0-933806-66-3, ISBN13: 978-0-933806-66-5. Dewey:813/.52.
Audience: **g,l,u,f.** B

Hollenberg, Donna Krolik **PS3507.O726Z74 1991**
H. D.: The Poetics of Childbirth and Creativity. Cloth Text. Northeastern University Press. Boston, MA. 1991. 224p. ISBN:1-55553-104-0, ISBN13: 978-1-55553-104-1. Dewey:811/.52. LCCN:91-010588.
Audience: **u,f.** *Choice, 1992.*

Korg, Jacob **PS3531.O82Z7142 2003**
Winter Love: Ezra Pound and H. D. Trade Cloth. University of Wisconsin Press. Chicago, IL. 2003. xii, 236p. ISBN:0-299-18390-4, ISBN13: 978-0-299-18390-5. Dewey:811/.52. LCCN:2002-010205.
Audience: **u,f.** *Choice, 2004.*

Laity, Cassandra **PS3507.O726 Z77 1996**
H. D. and the Victorian Fin de Siècle: Gender, Modernism, Decadence. Albert Gelpi & Ross Posnock (Contribution by). Trade Cloth. Cambridge University Press. New York, NY. 1996. 236p. Studies in American Literature and Culture, No. 104 ISBN:0-521-55414-4, ISBN13: 978-0-521-55414-5. Dewey:811.5/2. LCCN:96-003827.
Audience: **u,f.**

Morris, Adalaide Kirby **PS3507.O726Z78 2003**
How to Live/What to Do: H. D. 's Cultural Poetics. Trade Cloth. University of Illinois Press. Champaign, IL. 2003. 280p. ISBN:0-252-02796-5, ISBN13: 978-0-252-02796-3. Dewey:811/.52. LCCN:2002-007555.
Audience: **u,f.** *Choice, 2004.*

20th Century (1901-1960) > I

Ignatow, David **PS3517.G53 A6 1993**
Against the Evidence: Selected Poems, 1934-1994. Trade Paper. Wesleyan University Press. Middletown, CT. 1994. 196p. Wesleyan Poetry Ser. ISBN:0-8195-1214-1, ISBN13: 978-0-8195-1214-7. Dewey:811/.54. LCCN:93-004303.
Audience: **g,l,u,f.**

Ignatow, David **PS3517.G53L58 1999**
Living Is What I Wanted: Last Poems. Trade Cloth. BOA Editions, Ltd. Rochester, NY. 1999. 100p. American Poets Continuum Ser., Vol. 55 ISBN:1-880238-77-2, ISBN13: 978-1-880238-77-6. Dewey:811/.54. LCCN:99-072449.
Audience: **g,l,u,f.**

Ignatow, David **PS3517.G53**
New and Collected Poems, 1970-1985. Trade Paper. Wesleyan University Press. Middletown, CT. 1986. 349p. Wesleyan Poetry Ser. ISBN:0-8195-6174-6, ISBN13: 978-0-8195-6174-9. Dewey:811/.54. LCCN:85-015311.
Audience: **g,l,u,f.**

Inge, William **PS3517.N265 F6**
Four Plays: Come Back Little Sheba; Picnic; Bus Stop; The Dark at the Top of the Stairs. Trade Paper. Grove/Atlantic, Inc. New York, NY. 1994. 320p. ISBN:0-8021-3209-X, ISBN13: 978-0-8021-3209-3. Dewey:812. LCCN:78-073032.
Audience: **g,l,u,f.**

Inge, William **PS3517.N265 P5**
Summer Brave. Trade Paper. Dramatists Play Service, Inc. New York, NY. 1979. ISBN:0-8222-1098-3, ISBN13: 978-0-8222-1098-6. Dewey:812.54.
Audience: **g,l,u,f.**

Inge, William **PS3517.N265**
Splendor in the Grass. F. Andrew Leslie (Adapted by). Trade Paper. Dramatists Play Service, Inc. New York, NY. 1967. ISBN:0-8222-1066-5, ISBN13: 978-0-8222-1066-5. Dewey:812.54.
Audience: **g,l,u,f.**

20th Century (1901-1960) > J

Jackson, Laura Riding **PS3531.O82**
Laura Riding: Selected Poems in Five Sets. Trade Paper. Persea Books, Inc. New York, NY. 1993. 96p. ISBN:0-89255-189-5, ISBN13: 978-0-89255-189-7. Dewey:811/.5/2. LCCN:92-038484.
Audience: **g,l,u,f.** B

Jackson, Laura Riding & Jacobs, Mark **PS3519.A363A17 2001**
The Poems of Laura Riding: A Newly Revised Edition of the 1938-1980 Collection. Ed. 2. Trade Paper. Persea Books, Inc. New York, NY. 2001. ISBN:0-89255-258-1, ISBN13: 978-0-89255-258-0. Dewey:811/.52. LCCN:2001-016434.
Audience: **g,l,u,f.**

Johnson, James Weldon **PS3519.O2625A6 2004**
James Weldon Johnson: Writings. Library of America (Firm) Staff (Contribution by). Trade Cloth. Library of America, The. New York, NY. 2004. 828p. The Library of America, Vol. 145 ISBN:1-931082-52-9, ISBN13: 978-1-931082-52-5. Dewey:818/.52. LCCN:2003-044227.
Audience: **g,l,u,f.**

Johnson, James Weldon **PS3519.O2625Z463**
Along This Way: The Autobiography of James Weldon Johnson. Sondra K. Wilson (Introduction by). Trade Paper. Da Capo Press, Inc. Cambridge, MA. 1999. 440p. ISBN:0-306-80929-X, ISBN13: 978-0-306-80929-3. Dewey:818/.5209 B. LCCN:99-058436.
Audience: **g,l,u.**

Johnson, Joyce **PS3560.O3795Z47 1999**
Minor Characters: A Beat Memoir. Ann Douglas (Introduction by). Trade Paper. Penguin Group (USA) Inc. New York, NY. 1999. 304p. ISBN:0-14-028357-9, ISBN13: 978-0-14-028357-0. Dewey:818/.5403 B. LCCN:99-462665.
Audience: **g,l,u,f.**

Jones, James **PS3560.O49 F7**
From Here to Eternity. Trade Paper. Dell Publishing. New York, NY. 1998. 864p. ISBN:0-385-33364-1, ISBN13: 978-0-385-33364-1. Dewey:813.
Audience: **g,l,u,f.**

Jones, James **PS3560.O49**
The Thin Red Line. Trade Cloth. Macmillan Publishing Company, Inc. Old Tappan, NJ. 1985. ISBN:0-02-559780-9, ISBN13: 978-0-02-559780-8. Dewey:813.54.
Audience: **g,l,u,f.** B

Justice, Donald **PS3519.U825 A6 1991**
A Donald Justice Reader: Selected Poetry and Prose. Library Binding. University Press of New England. Lebanon, NH. 1991. 185p. Bread Loaf Series of Contemporary Writers Ser. ISBN:0-87451-567-X, ISBN13: 978-0-87451-567-1. Dewey:811/.54. LCCN:91-050369.
Audience: **g,l,u,f.**

Justice, Donald Rodney **PS3519.U825A6 2004**
Collected Poems. Trade Cloth. Alfred A. Knopf Inc. New York, NY. 2004. 304p. ISBN:1-4000-4239-9, ISBN13: 978-1-4000-4239-5. Dewey:811/.54. LCCN:2003-065735.
Audience: **g,l,u,f.**

Logan, William & Gioia, Dana (Editors) **PS3519.U825Z65 1997**
Certain Solitudes: On the Poetry of Donald Justice. Trade Cloth. University of Arkansas Press. Fayetteville, AR. 2003. 368p. ISBN:1-55728-475-X, ISBN13: 978-1-55728-475-4. Dewey:811/.54. LCCN:97-040809.
Audience: **u,f.**

Wilson, Sondra Kathryn (Editor) **PS3519.O2625A6 1995**
The Selected Writings of James Weldon Johnson: Social, Political, and Literary Essays, Vol. II. Trade Cloth. Oxford University Press, Inc. New York, NY. 1995. 474p. ISBN:0-19-507645-1, ISBN13: 978-0-19-507645-5. Dewey:814/.52. LCCN:94-031400.
Audience: **g,l,u,f.**

20th Century (1901-1960) > J > Jackson, Shirley

Hall, Joan W. **PS3519.A392.Z69 1993**
Shirley Jackson. Trade Cloth. Macmillan Publishing Company, Inc. Old Tappan, NJ. 1993. 180p. Twayne's Studies in Short Fiction, Vol. 42 ISBN:0-8057-0853-7, ISBN13: 978-0-8057-0853-0. Dewey:813/.54. LCCN:92-036432.
Audience: **l,u.** *Choice, 1993.*

Hattenhauer, Darryl **PS3519.A392Z7 2003**
Shirley Jackson's American Gothic. Cloth Text. State University of New York Press. Albany, NY. 2003. x, 236p. ISBN:0-7914-5607-2, ISBN13: 978-0-7914-5607-1. Dewey:813/.54. LCCN:2002-075874.
Audience: **u,f.** *Choice, 2003.*

Jackson, Shirley **PS3568.O243**
The Haunting of Hill House. Library Binding. Buccaneer Books, Inc. Cutchogue, NY. 1993. ISBN:0-89968-430-0, ISBN13: 978-0-89968-430-7. Dewey:813.5/4.
Audience: **g,l,u,f.**

Jackson, Shirley **PS3519.A392 L6 1991B**
The Lottery. Library Binding. Buccaneer Books, Inc. Cutchogue, NY. 1993. ISBN:0-89968-429-7, ISBN13: 978-0-89968-429-1. Dewey:Fic.
Audience: **g,l,u,f.**

Jackson, Shirley **PS3568.O243**
We Have Always Lived in the Castle. Library Binding. Buccaneer Books, Inc. Cutchogue, NY. 1994. 214p. ISBN:0-89968-532-3, ISBN13: 978-0-89968-532-8. Dewey:813/.54.
Audience: **g,l,u,f.** B

Jackson, Shirley **PS3568.O243**
Just an Ordinary Day: The Uncollected Stories of Shirley Jackson. Laurence J. Hyman & Sarah H. Stewart (Editors). Trade Paper. Bantam Books. New York, NY. 1997. 448p. ISBN:0-553-37833-3, ISBN13: 978-0-553-37833-7. Dewey:813/.54.
Audience: **g,l,u,f.**

20th Century (1901-1960) > J > Jarrell, Randall

Burt, Stephen **PS3519.A86Z596 2002**
Randall Jarrell and His Age. Trade Cloth. Columbia University Press. New York, NY. 2002. 320p. ISBN:0-231-12594-1, ISBN13: 978-0-231-12594-9. Dewey:811/.52. LCCN:2002-071257.
Audience: **l,u,f.** *Choice, 2003.*

Ferguson, Suzanne **PS3519.A86.Z62 1983**
Critical Essays on Randall Jarrell. Trade Cloth. Thomson Gale. Farmington Hills, MI. 1983. ix, 327 p. ;p. Critical Essays on American Literature Ser. ISBN:0-8161-8486-0, ISBN13: 978-0-8161-8486-6. Dewey:811/.52. LCCN:82-012100.
Audience: **l,u.** B

Jarrell, Randall **PS3519 .A86 A17**
The Complete Poems. Trade Paper. Farrar, Straus & Giroux. New York, NY. 1981. 520p. ISBN:0-374-51305-8, ISBN13: 978-0-374-51305-4. Dewey:811. LCCN:68-029469.
Audience: **g,l,u,f.** B

Jarrell, Randall **PS3531.O82**
Kipling, Auden and Company: Essays and Reviews, 1935-1964. Trade Cloth. Farrar, Straus & Giroux. New York, NY. 1982. 392p. ISBN:0-374-51668-5, ISBN13: 978-0-374-51668-0. Dewey:811/.52.
Audience: **u,f.** B

Jarrell, Randall **PS3519.A86P5 1986**
Pictures from an Institution. Trade Paper. University of Chicago Press. Chicago, IL. 1986. 286p. Phoenix Fiction Ser. ISBN:0-226-39374-7, ISBN13: 978-0-226-39374-2. Dewey:811/.52. LCCN:85-020965.
Audience: **g,l,u,f.**

Travisano, Thomas **PS310.P63T73 1999**
Midcentury Quartet: Bishop, Lowell, Jarrell, Berryman and the Making of a Postmodern Aesthetic. Trade Cloth. University Press of Virginia. Charlottesville, VA. 1999. xvi, 325p. ISBN:0-8139-1887-1, ISBN13: 978-0-8139-1887-7. Dewey:811/.509113. LCCN:99-016426.
Audience: **u,f.** *Choice, 2000.*

20th Century (1901-1960) > J > Jeffers, Robinson

Brophy, Robert J. (Editor, Introduction by) **PS3519.E27Z747 1995**
Robinson Jeffers: The Dimensions of a Poet. Trade Cloth. Fordham University Press. Bronx, NY. 1995. 248p. ISBN:0-8232-1565-2, ISBN13: 978-0-8232-1565-2. Dewey:811/.52. LCCN:94-045792.
Audience: **u,f.**

Carpenter, Frederick Ives **PS3519.E27**
Robinson Jeffers. Library Binding. Thomson Gale. Farmington Hills, MI. 1983. U. S. Authors Ser., No. 22 ISBN:0-8057-0412-4, ISBN13: 978-0-8057-0412-9. Dewey:818.52.
Audience: **l,u.**

Everson, William **PS3519.E27Z59 1988**
The Excesses of God: Robinson Jeffers As a Religious Figure. Albert Gelpi (Foreword by). Trade Cloth. Stanford University Press. Palo Alto, CA. 1988. 208p. ISBN:0-8047-1415-0, ISBN13: 978-0-8047-1415-0. Dewey:811/.52. LCCN:87-018077.
Audience: **u,f.** *Choice, 1988.*

Jeffers, Robinson & Gelpi, Albert **PS3519.E27A6 2003**
The Wild God of the World: An Anthology of Robinson Jeffers. Trade Cloth. Stanford University Press. Palo Alto, CA. 2003. 256p. ISBN:0-8047-4591-9, ISBN13: 978-0-8047-4591-8. Dewey:811/.52. LCCN:2002-153166.
Audience: **l,u,f.**

Jeffers, Robinson **PS3519.E27A6 2001**
The Selected Poetry of Robinson Jeffers. Tim Hunt (Editor). Trade Cloth. Stanford University Press. Palo Alto, CA. 2001. 747p. ISBN:0-8047-3890-4, ISBN13: 978-0-8047-3890-3. Dewey:811/.52. LCCN:00-048490.
Audience: **g,l,u,f.** B

Jeffers, Robinson **PS3519.E27Z5**
The Selected Letters of Robinson Jeffers, 1897-1962. Ann N. Ridgeway (Editor), Mark Van Doren (Foreword by). Trade Paper. Books on Demand. Ann Arbor, MI. 429p. ISBN:0-598-20976-X, ISBN13: 978-0-598-20976-4. Dewey:816/.5/2. LCCN:67-029318.
Audience: **g,l,u,f.** B

Karman, James **PS3519.E27Z578 1990**
Critical Essays on Robinson Jeffers. Trade Cloth. Thomson Gale. Farmington Hills, MI. 1990. 288p. Critical Essays on American Literature Ser. ISBN:0-8161-8897-1, ISBN13: 978-0-8161-8897-0. Dewey:811/.52. LCCN:90-036796.
Audience: **l,u.** *Choice, 1991.*

Zaller, Robert (Editor) **PS3519.E27Z576 1991**
Centennial Essays for Robinson Jeffers. Trade Cloth. University of Delaware Press. Newark, DE. 1991. 288p. ISBN:0-87413-414-5, ISBN13: 978-0-87413-414-8. Dewey:811/.52. LCCN:90-050542.
Audience: **u,f.** *Choice, 1992.*

20th Century (1901-1960) > K

Kanin, Garson **PS3521.A45**
Born Yesterday. Trade Paper. Dramatists Play Service, Inc. New York, NY. 1951. ISBN:0-8222-0136-4, ISBN13: 978-0-8222-0136-6. Dewey:812.5.
Audience: **g,l,u,f.**

Kantor, MacKinlay **PZ3.K14AN**
Andersonville. Library Binding. Buccaneer Books, Inc. Cutchogue, NY. 1994. ISBN:1-56849-297-9, ISBN13: 978-1-56849-297-1. Dewey:FIC.
Audience: **g,l,u,f.** B

Kaufman, Bob **PS3561.A84 A8**
Ancient Rain: Poems. 1956-1978. Raymond Foye (Editor). Trade Paper. New Directions Publishing Corporation. New York, NY. 1981. 96p. ISBN:0-8112-0801-X, ISBN13: 978-0-8112-0801-7. Dewey:811/.54. LCCN:81-001250.
Audience: **g,l,u,f.**

Kazin, Alfred & Solotaroff, Ted **PS29.K38A25**
Alfred Kazin's America: Critical and Personal Writings. Trade Paper. HarperCollins Publishers. New York, NY. 2004. 592p. ISBN:0-06-051276-8, ISBN13: 978-0-06-051276-7. Dewey:810.9.
Audience: **u,f.**

Kees, Weldon **PS3521.E285**
The Ceremony and Other Stories. Dana Gioia (Introduction by). Trade Cloth. Graywolf Press. St. Paul, MN. 1984. 147p. ISBN:0-915308-53-3, ISBN13: 978-0-915308-53-8. Dewey:813/.52. LCCN:83-083186.
Audience: **g,l,u,f.**

Kees, Weldon **PS3521.E285A17 2003**
The Collected Poems of Weldon Kees. Ed. 3. Donald Justice (Editor), David Wojahn (Introduction by). Trade Paper. University of Nebraska Press. Lincoln, NE. 2003. 208p. ISBN:0-8032-7809-8, ISBN13: 978-0-8032-7809-7. Dewey:811/.52. LCCN:2003-051362.
Audience: **g,l,u,f.** B

Kelley, Edith S. **PS3521.E4117W4 1996**
Weeds. Ed. 3. Charlotte M. Goodman (Afterword by). Trade Paper. Feminist Press at The City University of New York. New York, NY. 1996. 295p. ISBN:1-55861-154-1, ISBN13: 978-1-55861-154-2. Dewey:813/.52. LCCN:81-022061.
Audience: **g,l,u,f.** B

Kesselring, Joseph **PS3521.E775**
Arsenic and Old Lace. Trade Paper. Dramatists Play Service, Inc. New York, NY. 1944. ISBN:0-8222-0065-1, ISBN13: 978-0-8222-0065-9. Dewey:812.5.
Audience: **g,l,u,f.**

Kinnell, Galway **PS3521.I582A95 2002**
The Avenue Bearing the Initial of Christ into the New World: Poems: 1953-1964. Trade Paper. Houghton Mifflin Company Trade & Reference Division. Boston, MA. 2002. 160p. ISBN:0-618-21912-9, ISBN13: 978-0-618-21912-4. Dewey:811/.54. LCCN:2002-524045.
Audience: **g,l,u,f.**

Kinnell, Galway **PS3521.I582A6 2001**
A New Selected Poems. Trade Paper. Houghton Mifflin Company Trade & Reference Division. Boston, MA. 2001. 192p. ISBN:0-618-15445-0, ISBN13: 978-0-618-15445-6. Dewey:811/.54. LCCN:2001-039523.
Audience: **g,l,u,f.**

Knowles, John **PR6019.O9**
A Separate Peace. Library Binding. Sagebrush Education Resources. Caledonia, MN. 2003. ISBN:0-613-70530-0, ISBN13: 978-0-613-70530-1. Dewey:813/.54.
Audience: **g,l,u,f.**

Koch, Kenneth **PS3521.O27A17 2005**
The Collected Poems of Kenneth Koch. Trade Cloth. Random House, Inc. New York, NY. 2005. 784p. ISBN:1-4000-4499-5, ISBN13: 978-1-4000-4499-3. Dewey:811/.54. LCCN:2004-063827.
Audience: **g,l,u,f.**

Koch, Kenneth **PS3521.O27A6 2005**
The Collected Fiction of Kenneth Koch. Jordan Davis & Ron Padgett (Editors). Trade Cloth. Coffee House Press. Minneapolis, MN. 2005. 394p. ISBN:1-56689-180-9, ISBN13: 978-1-56689-180-6. Dewey:813/.54. LCCN:2005-012570.
Audience: **g,l,u,f.**

Kumin, Maxine **PS3521.U638A6 1997**
Maxine Kumin: Selected Poems, 1960-1990. Trade Cloth. W. W. Norton & Company, Inc. New York, NY. 1997. 320p. ISBN:0-393-04073-9, ISBN13: 978-0-393-04073-9. Dewey:811/.54. LCCN:96-042433.
Audience: **g,l,u,f.**

Kunitz, Stanley **PS3521.U7A17 2000**
The Collected Poems of Stanley Kunitz. Trade Cloth. W. W. Norton & Company, Inc. New York, NY. 2000. 288p. ISBN:0-393-05030-0, ISBN13: 978-0-393-05030-1. Dewey:811/.52. LCCN:00-041130.
Audience: **g,l,u,f.**

Orr, Gregory **PS3521.U7Z84 1985**
Stanley Kunitz: An Introduction to the Poetry. Trade Cloth. Columbia University Press. New York, NY. 1985. 297p. ISBN:0-231-05234-0, ISBN13: 978-0-231-05234-4. Dewey:811/.52. LCCN:84-023213.
Audience: **g,l,u.** *Choice, 1985.*

20th Century (1901-1960) > K > Kerouac, Jack

Cassady, Carolyn **PS3521.E735**
Off the Road: My Years with Cassady, Kerouac, and Ginsberg. William Morrow & Co.. 1981.
Audience: **g,l,u,f.**

Charters, Ann **PS3521.E735Z6 1987**
Kerouac: A Biography. Trade Paper. St. Martin's Press. Gordonville, VA. 1987. 432p. ISBN:0-312-00617-9, ISBN13: 978-0-312-00617-4. Dewey:813/.5/4. LCCN:86-033832.
Audience: **g,l,u,f.** B

Clark, Tom **PS3568.O243**
Jack Kerouac: A Biography. Carolyn Cassady (Introduction by). Trade Paper. Avalon Publishing Group. New York, NY. 2001. 272p. ISBN:1-56025-357-6, ISBN13: 978-1-56025-357-0. Dewey:813.5/4.
Audience: **g,l,u,f.**

French, Warren **PS3521.E735Z6328**
Jack Kerouac. Trade Cloth. Macmillan Publishing Company, Inc. Old Tappan, NJ. 1986. 168p. Twayne's United States Authors Ser., No. 507 ISBN:0-8057-7467-X, ISBN13: 978-0-8057-7467-2. Dewey:813/.54. LCCN:86-004817.
Audience: **l,u,f.** *Choice, 1987.*

Giamo, Ben **PS3521.E735Z634**
Kerouac, the Word and the Way: Prose Artist As Spiritual Quester. Trade Cloth. Southern Illinois University Press. Carbondale, IL. 2001. 272p. ISBN:0-8093-2431-8, ISBN13: 978-0-8093-2431-6. Dewey:813.54. LCCN:99-053205.
Audience: **u,f.** *Choice, 2001.*

Gifford, Barry & Lee, Lawrence **PS3521.E735Z635**
Jack's Book: An Oral Biography of Jack Kerouac. Trade Paper. Avalon Publishing Group. New York, NY. 2005. 304p. ISBN:1-56025-739-3, ISBN13: 978-1-56025-739-4. Dewey:813/.54 B.
Audience: **g,l,u,f.** B

Hayes, Kevin J. (Editor) **PS3521.E735Z625 2005**
Conversations with Jack Kerouac. Saddle Stitched, Cloth over Boards. University Press of Mississippi. Jackson, MS. 2005. 100p. Literary Conversations Ser. ISBN:1-57806-755-3, ISBN13: 978-1-57806-755-8. Dewey:813/.54 B. LCCN:2004-026277.
Audience: **l,u,f.**

Holton, Robert **PS3521.E735O533 1999**
On the Road: Kerouac's Ragged American Journey. Trade Cloth. Thomson Gale. Farmington Hills, MI. 1999. xv, 137p. Twayne's Masterwork Studies, Vol. 172 ISBN:0-8057-1692-0, ISBN13: 978-0-8057-1692-4. Dewey:813/.54. LCCN:99-033122.
Audience: **l,u,f.**

Jones, James T. **PS3521.E735Z734 1999**
Jack Kerouac's Duluoz Legend: The Mythic Form of an Autobiographical Fiction. Trade Cloth. Southern Illinois University Press. Carbondale, IL. 1999. 272p. ISBN:0-8093-2263-3, ISBN13: 978-0-8093-2263-3. Dewey:813/.54. LCCN:98-049222.
Audience: **u,f.** *Choice, 2000.*

Kerouac, Jack **PS3568.O243**
The Dharma Bums. Library Binding. Buccaneer Books, Inc. Cutchogue, NY. 1976. 192p. ISBN:0-89966-135-1, ISBN13: 978-0-89966-135-3. Dewey:813/.54. LCCN:84-672444.
Audience: **g,l,u,f.** B

Kerouac, Jack **PS3568.O243**
Doctor Sax. Library Binding. Buccaneer Books, Inc. Cutchogue, NY. 1976. 245p. ISBN:0-89966-133-5, ISBN13: 978-0-89966-133-9. Dewey:813/.54.
Audience: **g,l,u,f.**

Kerouac, Jack **PS3521.E735M4 1990**
Mexico City Blues: Two Hundred Forty-Two Choruses. Trade Paper. Grove/Atlantic, Inc. New York, NY. 1987. 256p. ISBN:0-8021-3060-7, ISBN13: 978-0-8021-3060-0. Dewey:811/.54. LCCN:90-002748.
Audience: **g,l,u,f.**

Kerouac, Jack **PS3568.O243**
On the Road. Trade Cloth. Penguin Group (USA) Inc. New York, NY. 2002. 320p. ISBN:0-14-200274-7, ISBN13: 978-0-14-200274-2. Dewey:813.5/4.
Audience: **g,l,u,f.** B

Kerouac, Jack **PS3521.E735**
The Subterraneans. Trade Paper. Grove/Atlantic, Inc. New York, NY. 1994. 128p. ISBN:0-8021-3186-7, ISBN13: 978-0-8021-3186-7. Dewey:813/.54. LCCN:58-006703.
Audience: **g,l,u,f.** B

Kerouac, Jack **PS3568.O243**
The Town and the City. Trade Cloth. Amereon, Ltd. Mattituck, NY. 1976. ISBN:0-8488-1068-6, ISBN13: 978-0-8488-1068-9. Dewey:813.5/4.
Audience: **g,l,u,f.**

Kerouac, Jack **PS3521.E735V36 1994**
Vanity of Duluoz: An Adventurous Education, 1935-1946. Trade Paper. Penguin Group (USA) Inc. New York, NY. 1994. 272p. ISBN:0-14-023639-2, ISBN13: 978-0-14-023639-2. Dewey:813/.54. LCCN:94-181669.
Audience: **g,l,u,f.**

Kerouac, Jack **PS3521.E735V47 1991**
Visions of Gerard: A Novel. Trade Paper. Penguin Group (USA) Inc. New York, NY. 1991. 144p. ISBN:0-14-014452-8, ISBN13: 978-0-14-014452-9. Dewey:813/.54. LCCN:90-022198.
Audience: **g,l,u,f.**

Kerouac, Jack **PS3568.O243**
Jack Kerouac: Selected Letters, 1957-1969. Ann Charters (Editor). Trade Paper. Penguin Group (USA) Inc. New York, NY. 2000. 656p. ISBN:0-14-029615-8, ISBN13: 978-0-14-029615-0. Dewey:813/.54 B.
Audience: **l,u,f.** *Choice, 2000.*

Kerouac, Jack **PS3568.O243**
The Portable Jack Kerouac. Ann Charters (Editor). Trade Paper. Penguin Group (USA) Inc. New York, NY. 1996. 656p. ISBN:0-14-017819-8, ISBN13: 978-0-14-017819-7. Dewey:813/.54.
Audience: **g,l,u,f.**

Kerouac, Jack **PS3521.E735V5 1993**
Visions of Cody. Allen Ginsberg (Featuring). Trade Paper. Penguin Group (USA) Inc. New York, NY. 1993. 448p. ISBN:0-14-017907-0, ISBN13: 978-0-14-017907-1. Dewey:813.5/4. LCCN:93-022466.
Audience: **g,l,u,f.** B

Kerouac, Jack **PS3521.E735D46 1995**
Desolation Angels. Joyce Johnson (Introduction by). Trade Paper. Penguin Group (USA) Inc. New York, NY. 1995. 432p. ISBN:1-57322-505-3, ISBN13: 978-1-57322-505-2. Dewey:813.5/4. LCCN:95-021092.
Audience: **g,l,u,f.**

Kerouac, Jack **PS3521.E735B5 1992**
Big Sur. Aram Saroyan (Foreword by). Trade Paper. Penguin Group (USA) Inc. New York, NY. 1992. 256p. ISBN:0-14-016812-5, ISBN13: 978-0-14-016812-9. Dewey:813.5/4. LCCN:92-251691.
Audience: **g,l,u,f.**

Lardas, John **PS228.B6L37 2001**
The Bop Apocalypse: The Religious Visions of Kerouac, Ginsberg, and Burroughs. Trade Cloth. University of Illinois Press. Champaign, IL. 2000. 328p. ISBN:0-252-02599-7, ISBN13: 978-0-252-02599-0. Dewey:810.9/382. LCCN:00-008649.
Audience: **u,f.** *Choice, 2001.*

Maher, Paul **PS3521.E735Z46 2005**
Empty Phantoms: Interviews and Encounters with Jack Kerouac. Trade Paper. Avalon Publishing Group. New York, NY. 2005. 352p. ISBN:1-56025-658-3, ISBN13: 978-1-56025-658-8. Dewey:813/.54 B. LCCN:2006-272980.
Audience: **l,u,f.**

Maher, Paul A. Jr. **PS3521.E735Z77 2003**
Kerouac: The Definitive Biography. David Amram (Foreword by). Trade Cloth. Taylor Trade Publishing. Blue Ridge Summit, PA. 2004. 484p. ISBN:0-87833-305-3, ISBN13: 978-0-87833-305-9. Dewey:813/.54 B. LCCN:2003-011738.
Audience: **g,l,u,f.**

McNally, Dennis **PS3521.E735Z775 2003**
Desolate Angel: Jack Kerouac, the Beat Generation, and America. Trade Paper. Da Capo Press, Inc. Cambridge, MA. 2003. 416p. ISBN:0-306-81222-3, ISBN13: 978-0-306-81222-4. Dewey:813/.54 B. LCCN:2003-276290.
Audience: **l,u,f.** B

Nicosia, Gerald **PS3521.E735**
Memory Babe: A Critical Biography of Jack Kerouac. Grove Press. 1983. ISBN:0-394-52270-2, ISBN13: 978-0-394-52270-8.
Audience: **g,l,u,f.**

Theado, Matt **PS3521.E735Z9 2000**
Understanding Jack Kerouac. Trade Cloth. University of South Carolina Press. Columbia, SC. 2000. 200p. Understanding Contemporary American Literature Ser. ISBN:1-57003-272-6, ISBN13: 978-1-57003-272-1. Dewey:813/.54. LCCN:98-040291.
Audience: **l,u,f.** *Choice, 2000.*

Weinreich, Regina **PS3521.E735Z945 2002**
Kerouac's Spontaneous Poetics. Trade Paper. Avalon Publishing Group. New York, NY. 2002. xx, 180p. ISBN:1-56025-387-8, ISBN13: 978-1-56025-387-7. Dewey:813/.54. LCCN:2002-018067.
Audience: **u,f.**

20th Century (1901-1960) > L

Bruccoli, Matthew Joseph (Editor, Translator) **PS3523.A7A6 2003**
Ring Around the Bases: The Complete Baseball Stories of Ring Lardner. Ring Lardner (Foreword by), Matthew Joseph Bruccoli (Introduction by). Trade Paper. University of South Carolina Press. Columbia, SC. 2003. 656p. ISBN:1-57003-531-8, ISBN13: 978-1-57003-531-9. Dewey:813/.52. LCCN:2003-016348.
Audience: **g,l,u,f.**

Carey, Gary **PS3523.O557.Z6 1988**
Anita Loos: A Biography. Trade Cloth. Bloomsbury Publishing Plc. London, 1988. xiii, 331p. ISBN:0-7475-0294-3, ISBN13: 978-0-7475-0294-4. Dewey:813/.52. LCCN:89-204802.
Audience: **g,l,u,f.**

Evans, Elizabeth **PS3523.A7.Z655**
Ring Lardner. Trade Cloth. Frederick Ungar A Book. Dulles, VA. 1980. 160p. Literature and Life Ser. ISBN:0-8044-2185-4, ISBN13: 978-0-8044-2185-0. Dewey:818/.5/209. LCCN:79-004829.
Audience: **g,l,u,f.** B

Lamantia, Philip **PS3562.A42B43 1997**
Bed of Sphinxes: Selected Poems. Trade Cloth. City Lights Books. San Francisco, CA. 1997. 200p. ISBN:0-87286-320-4, ISBN13: 978-0-87286-320-0. Dewey:811/.54. LCCN:96-009667.
Audience: **g,l,u,f.**

Lardner, Ring W. **PZ3.L323**
The Love Nest and Other Stories. Trade Paper. Kessinger Publishing, LLC. Whitefish, MT. 2005. ISBN:1-4179-0510-7, ISBN13: 978-1-4179-0510-2. Dewey:813.5.
Audience: **g,l,u,f.**

Lardner, Ring W. **PS3511.A86**
Round Up: The Stories of Ring W. Lardner. Trade Paper. Kessinger Publishing, LLC. Whitefish, MT. 2005. ISBN:1-4179-1447-5, ISBN13: 978-1-4179-1447-0. Dewey:813.5.
Audiencc: **g,l,u,f.**

Lardner, Ring W. **PN6161**
The Story of a Wonder Man Being the Autobiography of Ring Lardner. Margaret Freeman (Illustrator). Trade Paper. Kessinger Publishing, LLC. Whitefish, MT. 2004. ISBN:1-4179-1318-5, ISBN13: 978-1-4179-1318-3. Dewey:813.5.
Audience: **g,l,u,f.**

Larsen, Nella **PS3511.A86**
Passing. Library Binding. Sagebrush Education Resources. Caledonia, MN. 2002. ISBN:0-613-70752-4, ISBN13: 978-0-613-70752-7. Dewey:813/.52.
Audience: **g,l,u,f.**

Larsen, Nella **PZ3**
Quicksand. Trade Cloth. Greenwood Publishing Group, Inc. Portsmouth, NH. 1970. 310p. ISBN:0-8371-1127-7, ISBN13: 978-0-8371-1127-8. Dewey:813/.52. LCCN:74-075553.
Audience: **g,l,u,f.** B

Lea, Tom **PS3523.E1142B73 2002**
The Brave Bulls. John Graves (Foreword by). Trade Paper. University of Texas Press. Austin, TX. 2002. 296p. Southwestern Writers Collection ISBN:0-292-74733-0, ISBN13: 978-0-292-74733-3. Dewey:813/.54. LCCN:2002-069558.
Audience: **g,l,u,f.**

Lederer, William J. & Burdick, Eugene **PS3562.E3**
The Ugly American. Trade Paper. W. W. Norton & Company, Inc. New York, NY. 1999. 288p. ISBN:0-393-31867-2, ISBN13: 978-0-393-31867-8. Dewey:327. LCCN:58-007388.
Audience: **g,l,u,f.** B

Lee, Harper **PS3562 .E353 T6**
To Kill a Mockingbird. Trade Paper. HarperCollins Publishers. New York, NY. 2006. 336p. ISBN:0-06-112008-1, ISBN13: 978-0-06-112008-4. Dewey:813/.54.
Audience: **g,l,u,f.**

Lindsay, Vachel **PS3531.O82**
Collected Poems by Vachel Lindsay. Trade Paper. Kessinger Publishing, LLC. Whitefish, MT. 2005. ISBN:1-4179-0345-7, ISBN13: 978-1-4179-0345-0. Dewey:811.52.
Audience: **g,l,u,f.**

Loos, Anita **PS3523.O557G4 1998**
Gentlemen Prefer Blondes and but Gentlemen Marry Brunettes: The Illuminating Diary of a Professional Lady. Ralph Barton (Illustrator), Regina Barreca (Introduction by). Trade Paper. Penguin Group (USA) Inc. New York, NY. 1998. 288p. Twentieth Century Classics Ser. ISBN:0-14-118069-2, ISBN13: 978-0-14-118069-4. Dewey:813/.52. LCCN:98-015422.
Audience: **g,l,u,f.**

Loos, Anita (Editor), et al. **PS3523.O557 A6 2003**
Anita Loos Rediscovered: Film Treatments and Fiction. Cari Beauchamp & Mary Anita Loos (Editors). Trade Cloth. University of California Press. Berkeley, CA. 2003. 304p. ISBN:0-520-22894-4, ISBN13: 978-0-520-22894-8. LCCN:2003-003883.
Audience: **g,l,u,f.**

Lovecraft, H. P. **PS3523.O833**
The Case of Charles Dexter Ward. Trade Paper. Ballantine Books. New York, NY. 1987. 128p. ISBN:0-345-35490-7, ISBN13: 978-0-345-35490-7. Dewey:813.5.
Audience: **g,l,u,f.**

Lovecraft, H. P. **PS3523.O833A6 2005**
H. P. Lovecraft: Tales. Peter Straub (Editor). Trade Cloth. Library of America, The. New York, NY. 2005. 850p. The Library of America, Vol. 156 ISBN:1-931082-72-3, ISBN13: 978-1-931082-72-3. Dewey:813/.52. LCCN:2004-048979.
Audience: **g,l,u,f.**

Lowell, Amy **PS3523.O88A6 2004**
Amy Lowell: Selected Poems. Trade Cloth. Library of America, The. New York, NY. 2004. 200p. American Poets Project Ser. ISBN:1-931082-70-7, ISBN13: 978-1-931082-70-9. Dewey:821/.912. LCCN:2004-048505.
Audience: **g,l,u,f.**

Lowell, James Russell **PS2305.A1**
The Complete Poetical Works of James Russell Lowell. Horace E. Scudder (Editor). Trade Paper. Kessinger Publishing, LLC. Whitefish, MT. 2005. ISBN:0-7661-9485-X, ISBN13: 978-0-7661-9485-4. Dewey:811/.3.
Audience: **g,l,u,f.**

Lumpkin, Grace **PR6019.O9**
The Wedding: A Novel. Trade Cloth. Southern Illinois University Press. Carbondale, IL. 1976. 325p. Lost American Fiction Ser. ISBN:0-8093-0767-7, ISBN13: 978-0-8093-0767-8. Dewey:823/.9/1. LCCN:75-028481.
Audience: **g,l,u,f.** B

Lytle, Andrew **PS3523.Y88**
Velvet Horn. George Core (Afterword by). Trade Paper. University of the South Press. Sewanee, TN. 1987. 370p. ISBN:0-918769-03-5, ISBN13: 978-0-918769-03-9. Dewey:813.51.
Audience: **g,l,u,f.**

Lytle, Andrew **PS3523.Y88L66 1988**
The Long Night. Frank L. Owsley Jr. (Introduction by). Trade Paper. University of Alabama Press. Tuscaloosa, AL. 1988. 336p. Library of Alabama Classics ISBN:0-8173-0415-0, ISBN13: 978-0-8173-0415-7. Dewey:813/.52. LCCN:88-012101.
Audience: **g,l,u,f.**

Munich, Adrienne & Bradshaw, Melissa (Editors) **PS3523.O88Z54 2004**
Amy Lowell, American Modern. Trade Cloth. Rutgers University Press. Piscataway, NJ. 2004. 240p. ISBN:0-8135-3356-2, ISBN13: 978-0-8135-3356-8. Dewey:811/.52 B. LCCN:2003-005859.
Audience: **g,l,u,f.** *Choice, 2004.*

20th Century (1901-1960) > L > Lewis, Sinclair

Bucco, Martin **PS3523.E94Z555 2004**
Sinclair Lewis as Reader and Critic. Trade Cloth. Edwin Mellen Press, The. Lewiston, NY. 2004. 560p. Studies in American Literature Ser. ISBN:0-7734-6482-4, ISBN13: 978-0-7734-6482-7. Dewey:813/.52. LCCN:2004-040233.
Audience: **u,f.**

Hutchisson, James M. (Editor) **PS3523.E94Z835 1997**
Sinclair Lewis: New Essays in Criticism. Trade Cloth. Whitston Publishing Company, Inc. Albany, NY. 1997. 265p. ISBN:0-87875-492-X, ISBN13: 978-0-87875-492-2. Dewey:813/.52. LCCN:96-061675.
Audience: **l,u.**

Lewis, Sinclair **PS3523.E94**
Cass Timberlane. Trade Cloth. Amereon, Ltd. Mattituck, NY. 1976. ISBN:0-8488-1411-8, ISBN13: 978-0-8488-1411-3. Dewey:813.52.
Audience: **g,l,u,f.**

Lewis, Sinclair **PS3523.E94A6 2002**
Lewis: Arrowsmith, Elmer Gantry, Dodsworth. Trade Cloth. Library of America, The. New York, NY. 2002. 1346p. ISBN:1-931082-08-1, ISBN13: 978-1-931082-08-2. Dewey:813/.52. LCCN:2002-019451.
Audience: **g,l,u,f.**

Lewis, Sinclair **PS3523.E94M2 1992**
Main Street and Babbitt. John Hersey (Editor). Trade Cloth. Library of America, The. New York, NY. 1992. 898p. Library of America, Vol. 59 ISBN:0-940450-61-5, ISBN13: 978-0-940450-61-5. Dewey:813/.52. LCCN:91-058224.
Audience: **g,l,u,f.**

Lewis, Sinclair **PS3523.E94I8 2005**
It Can't Happen Here. Michael Meyer (Introduction by). Mass Market. Penguin Group (USA) Inc. New York, NY. 2005. 400p. ISBN:0-451-52929-4, ISBN13: 978-0-451-52929-9. Dewey:813/.52. LCCN:2004-061606.
Audience: **g,l,u,f.**

20th Century (1901-1960) > L > London, Jack

Auerbach, Jonathan **PS3523.O46Z53 1996**
Male Call: Becoming Jack London. Trade Cloth. Duke University Press. Durham, NC. 1996. 304p. New Americanists Ser. ISBN:0-8223-1827-X, ISBN13: 978-0-8223-1827-9. Dewey:813/.52. LCCN:96-014682.
Audience: **l,u,f.** *Choice, 1997.*

London, Jack **PR6023.E15**
Novels and Social Writings: The People of the Abyss, the Road, the Iron Heel, Martin Eden, John Barleycorn, Essays. Donald Pizer (Editor). Trade Cloth. Library of America, The. New York, NY. 1982. 1192p. ISBN:0-940450-06-2, ISBN13: 978-0-940450-06-6. Dewey:818/.5208. LCCN:82-006940.
Audience: **g,l,u,f.**

London, Jack **PS3511.A86**
Novels and Stories: The Call of the Wild, White Fang, The Sea-Wolf, Klondike and Other Stories. Donald Pizer (Editor). Trade Cloth. Library of America, The. New York, NY. 1982. 1021p. Library of America, Vol. 6 ISBN:0-940450-05-4, ISBN13: 978-0-940450-05-9. Dewey:813/.52. LCCN:82-000249.
Audience: **g,l,u,f.**

London, Jack **PS3523.O46.C8**
Curious Fragments: Jack London's Tales of Fantasy Fiction. Dale L. Walker (Editor), Philip Jose Farmer (Preface by). Trade Cloth. Associated Faculty Press, Inc. New York, NY. 1975. x, 223 p. ;p. ISBN:0-8046-9114-2, ISBN13: 978-0-8046-9114-7. Dewey:813/.5/2. LCCN:75-029450.
Audience: **g,l,u,f.** B

Nuernberg, Susan M. (Editor) **PS3523**
The Critical Response to Jack London. Cloth Text. Greenwood

Publishing Group, Inc. Portsmouth, NH. 1995. 336p. Critical Responses in Arts and Letters Ser., No. 19 ISBN:0-313-28927-1, ISBN13: 978-0-313-28927-9. Dewey:818/.5209. LCCN:95-015448.
Audience: **l,u.**

Reesman, Jeanne Campbell **PS3523.O46Z8665 1999**
Jack London. Trade Cloth. Simon & Schuster. New York, NY. 1999. 15p. Twayne's Studies in Short Fiction, Vol. 75 ISBN:0-8057-1678-5, ISBN13: 978-0-8057-1678-8. Dewey:813/.52. LCCN:98-055670.
Audience: **l,u.** *Choice, 1999.*

Walker, Dale L. (Editor) **PS3523.O46.A6 1999**
"No Mentor but Myself": Jack London on Writing and Writers. Ed. 2. Jeanne C. Reesman (Introduction by). Trade Cloth. Stanford University Press. Palo Alto, CA. 1999. xxii, 243p. ISBN:0-8047-3635-9, ISBN13: 978-0-8047-3635-0. Dewey:818/.5209. LCCN:99-067022.
Audience: **l,u,f.** *Choice, 2000.*

20th Century (1901-1960) > L > Lowell, Robert

Axelrod, Stephen Gould (Editor) **PS3523**
The Critical Response to Robert Lowell. Cloth Text. Greenwood Publishing Group, Inc. Portsmouth, NH. 1999. 344p. Critical Responses in Arts and Letters Ser., Vol. 33 ISBN:0-313-29037-7, ISBN13: 978-0-313-29037-4. Dewey:811/.52. LCCN:99-011307.
Audience: **l,u.** *Choice, 1999.*

Axelrod, Steven G. **PS3531.O82**
Robert Lowell: Life of Art. Trade Paper. Princeton University Press. Princeton, NJ. 1979. 304p. ISBN:0-691-01364-0, ISBN13: 978-0-691-01364-0. Dewey:811/.52. LCCN:78-051155.
Audience: **l,u.** B

Doreski, William **PS3523.O89Z649 1999**
Robert Lowell's Shifting Colors: The Poetics of the Public and the Personal. Trade Cloth. Ohio University Press. Athens, OH. 1999. 286p. ISBN:0-8214-1279-5, ISBN13: 978-0-8214-1279-4. Dewey:811/.52. LCCN:99-013112.
Audience: **u,f.**

Hamilton, Ian **PS3523.O89**
Robert Lowell: A Biography. Trade Paper. Knopf Publishing Group. New York, NY. 1983. 576p. ISBN:0-394-71646-9, ISBN13: 978-0-394-71646-6. Dewey:811/.52 B. LCCN:82-040121.
Audience: **g,l,u,f.** B

Haralson (Editor) **PS3523.O89**
Critical Essays on Robert Lowell. Trade Cloth. Thomson Gale. Farmington Hills, MI. 1998. ISBN:0-7838-0010-X, ISBN13: 978-0-7838-0010-3. Dewey:811/.5/2.
Audience: **l,u,f.**

Hart, Henry **PS3523.O89Z684 1995**
Robert Lowell and the Sublime. Jay Parini (Introduction by). Cloth Text. Syracuse University Press. Syracuse, NY. 1995. 260p. ISBN:0-8156-2610-X, ISBN13: 978-0-8156-2610-7. Dewey:811/.52. LCCN:94-038430.
Audience: **g,l,u,f.** *Choice, 1995.*

Lowell, Robert **PS3523.O89A17 1997**
Collected Poems. Trade Cloth. Farrar, Straus & Giroux. New York, NY. 1997. xvii, 1186p. ISBN:0-374-12553-8, ISBN13: 978-0-374-12553-0. Dewey:811/.52. LCCN:96-017254.
Audience: **g,l,u,f.**

Lowell, Robert **PS3523.O89 F56**
For Lizzie and Harriet. Trade Paper. Farrar, Straus & Giroux. New York, NY. 1975. 48p. ISBN:0-374-51291-4, ISBN13: 978-0-374-51291-0. Dewey:811/.5/2.
Audience: **g,l,u,f.** B

Lowell, Robert **PS3523.O89**
Life Studies and for the Union Dead. Trade Paper. Farrar, Straus & Giroux. New York, NY. 1967. 72p. ISBN:0-374-50628-0, ISBN13: 978-0-374-50628-5. Dewey:813.
Audience: **g,l,u,f.**

Lowell, Robert **PS3523.O89**
The Old Glory: Endecott and the Red Cross; My Kinsman, Major Molineux; and Benito Cereno. Robert Brustein (Introduction by), Jonathan Miller (Contribution by). Trade Cloth. Farrar, Straus & Giroux. New York, NY. 2000. 208p. ISBN:0-374-52704-0, ISBN13: 978-0-374-52704-4. Dewey:812.
Audience: **g,l,u,f.**

Mariani, Paul **PS3531.O82**
Lost Puritan: A Life of Robert Lowell. Trade Paper. W. W. Norton & Company, Inc. New York, NY. 1996. 560p. ISBN:0-393-31374-3, ISBN13: 978-0-393-31374-1. Dewey:811/.52 B.
Audience: **g,l,u,f.** *Choice, 1995.*

Meyers, Jeffrey (Editor) **PS3523.O89Z8555 1988**
Robert Lowell: Interviews and Memoirs. Trade Cloth. University of Michigan Press. Chicago, IL. 1988. 384p. ISBN:0-472-10089-0, ISBN13: 978-0-472-10089-7. Dewey:811/.52 B. LCCN:87-019172.
Audience: **l,u.** *Choice, 1988.*

Procopiow, Norma **PS3523.O89Z835 1984**
Robert Lowell: The Poet and His Critics. Library Binding. American Library Association. Chicago, IL. 1984. 337p. Poet and His Critics Ser. ISBN:0-8389-0411-4, ISBN13: 978-0-8389-0411-4. Dewey:811/.52. LCCN:84-000467.
Audience: **l,u.** B

Tillinghast, Richard (Editor) **PS3523.O89Z885 1995**
Robert Lowell's Life and Work: Damaged Grandeur. Trade Cloth. University of Michigan Press. Chicago, IL. 1996. 136p. Poets on Poetry Ser. ISBN:0-472-09570-6, ISBN13: 978-0-472-09570-4. Dewey:811/.52 B. LCCN:95-013706.
Audience: **l,u,f.**

Travisano, Thomas **PS310.P63T73 1999**
Midcentury Quartet: Bishop, Lowell, Jarrell, Berryman and the Making of a Postmodern Aesthetic. Trade Cloth. University

Press of Virginia. Charlottesville, VA. 1999. xvi, 325p. ISBN:0-8139-1887-1, ISBN13: 978-0-8139-1887-7. Dewey:811/.509113. LCCN:99-016426.
Audience: **u,f.** *Choice, 2000.*

20th Century (1901-1960) > M

Brittin, Norman A. **PS3525.I495 Z62 1982**
Edna St. Vincent Millay. Trade Cloth. Macmillan Publishing Company, Inc. Old Tappan, NJ. 1982. 184p. United States Authors Ser., No. 116 ISBN:0-8057-7362-2, ISBN13: 978-0-8057-7362-0. Dewey:811/.52. LCCN:82-012049.
Audience: **l,u.** B

Burkhardt, Barbara A. **PS3525.A9464Z58 2005**
William Maxwell: A Literary Life. Trade Cloth. University of Illinois Press. Champaign, IL. 2005. 336p. ISBN:0-252-03018-4, ISBN13: 978-0-252-03018-5. Dewey:813/.54 B. LCCN:2004-018508.
Audience: **g,l,u,f.** *Choice, 2005.*

Epstein, Daniel Mark **PS3525.I495Z636 2001**
What Lips My Lips Have Kissed: The Loves and Love Poems of Edna St. Vincent Millay. Cloth over Boards. Henry Holt & Company. New York, NY. 2001. 288p. ISBN:0-8050-6727-2, ISBN13: 978-0-8050-6727-9. Dewey:811/.52 B. LCCN:2001-024543.
Audience: **g,l,u,f.**

MacDonald, Ross **PS3525.I486G3 1996**
The Galton Case: A Lew Archer Novel. UK-Trade Paper. David McKay Company, Inc. New York, NY. 1996. 256p. Lew Archer Mystery Ser. ISBN:0-679-76864-5, ISBN13: 978-0-679-76864-7. Dewey:813/.52. LCCN:97-118474.
Audience: **g,l,u,f.**

March, William **PS3505.A53157T7 1987**
Trial Balance: The Collected Short Stories of William March. Rosemary Canfield-Reisman (Introduction by). Trade Paper. University of Alabama Press. Tuscaloosa, AL. 1987. 536p. Library of Alabama Classics ISBN:0-8173-0372-3, ISBN13: 978-0-8173-0372-3. Dewey:813/.52. LCCN:87-005900.
Audience: **g,l,u,f.**

Marquand, John P. **PS3525.A6695H2 1986**
H. M. Pulham, Esq. Trade Cloth. Academy Chicago Publishers, Ltd. Chicago, IL. 1986. 432p. ISBN:0-89733-231-8, ISBN13: 978-0-89733-231-6. Dewey:813/.52. LCCN:86-022150.
Audience: **g,l,u,f.**

Marquand, John P. **PS3511.A86**
The Late George Apley: A Novel. Library Binding. Buccaneer Books, Inc. Cutchogue, NY. 1994. ISBN:1-56849-446-7, ISBN13: 978-1-56849-446-3. Dewey:813/.52.
Audience: **g,l,u,f.**

Marquis, Don **PS3525.A67 L5**
The Lives and Times of Archy and Mehitabel. Trade Cloth. Doubleday Publishing. New York, NY. 1949. ISBN:0-385-04262-0, ISBN13: 978-0-385-04262-8. Dewey:817.5.
Audience: **g,l,u,f.** B

Masters, Edgar Lee **PS3525**
Spoon River Anthology. Library Binding. Classic Books. Murrieta, CA. 1999. 248p. The Collected Works of Edgar Lee Masters ISBN:1-58201-776-X, ISBN13: 978-1-58201-776-1. Dewey:811.52.
Audience: **g,l,u,f.** B

Maxwell, William **PS3568.O243**
All the Days and Nights: The Collected Stories of William Maxwell. UK-Trade Paper. Knopf Publishing Group. New York, NY. 1995. 432p. ISBN:0-679-76102-0, ISBN13: 978-0-679-76102-0. Dewey:813/.54.
Audience: **g,l,u,f.**

Maxwell, William **PS3525.A9464F6 1996**
The Folded Leaf. UK-Trade Paper. Alfred A. Knopf Inc. New York, NY. 1996. 304p. ISBN:0-679-77256-1, ISBN13: 978-0-679-77256-9. Dewey:813/.54. LCCN:96-005454.
Audience: **g,l,u,f.** B

Maxwell, William **PS3525.A9464T44 1997**
They Came Like Swallows. Trade Paper. David McKay Company, Inc. New York, NY. 1997. 192p. Vintage International Ser. ISBN:0-679-77257-X, ISBN13: 978-0-679-77257-6. Dewey:813/.54. LCCN:96-046880.
Audience: **g,l,u,f.** B

McBain, Ed **PZ4.H945 Ei PS3515.U585**
87th Precinct. Simon and Schuster. 1959.
Audience: **g,l,u,f.**

McCoy, Horace **PS3511.A86**
They Shoot Horses, Don't They? Library Binding. Buccaneer Books, Inc. Cutchogue, NY. 1993. ISBN:1-56849-241-3, ISBN13: 978-1-56849-241-4. Dewey:813.5/2.
Audience: **g,l,u,f.** B

McKay, Claude **PS3525.A24785A6**
The Passion of Claude McKay. Trade Cloth. Knopf Publishing Group. New York, NY. 1973. vii, 363p. Negro History Ser. ISBN:0-8052-3498-5, ISBN13: 978-0-8052-3498-5. Dewey:818/.5/209. LCCN:72-095662.
Audience: **g,l,u,f.** B

McNickle, D'Arcy **PS3525.A2844**
The Surrounded. Trade Cloth. University of New Mexico Press. Albuquerque, NM. 1978. 305p. Zia Book Ser. ISBN:0-8263-0469-9, ISBN13: 978-0-8263-0469-8. Dewey:813/.5/2. LCCN:77-091886.
Audience: **g,l,u,f.** B

Mencken, H. L. **PS3525.E43**
Days of H. L. Mencken: Three Volumes in One: Happy Days, Newspaper Days, and Heathen Days. Trade Cloth. Dorset Press. New York, NY. 1990. 925p. ISBN:0-88029-417-5, ISBN13: 978-0-88029-417-1. Dewey:928.1.
Audience: **g,l,u,f.**

Meredith, William **PS3525.E588E37 1997**
Effort at Speech: New and Selected Poems. Trade Cloth. Northwestern University Press. Evanston, IL. 1997. 231p. ISBN:0-8101-5070-0, ISBN13: 978-0-8101-5070-6. Dewey:811/.54. LCCN:97-009679.
Audience: **g,l,u,f.**

Merton, Thomas **PS3525.E7174 A6 1974**
A Thomas Merton Reader. Ed. 2. Thomas P. McDonnell (Editor), M. Scott Peck (Introduction by). Trade Paper. Doubleday Publishing. New York, NY. 1974. 528p. ISBN:0-385-03292-7, ISBN13: 978-0-385-03292-6. Dewey:818/.5/409. LCCN:74-000029.
Audience: **g,l,u,f.** B

Merton, Thomas **PS3525.E7174A6 2005**
In the Dark Before Dawn: New Selected Poems of Thomas Merton. Szabo (Introduction by), Kathleen Norris (Preface by). Trade Paper. New Directions Publishing Corporation. New York, NY. 2005. 256p. ISBN:0-8112-1613-6, ISBN13: 978-0-8112-1613-5. Dewey:811/.54o. LCCN:2004-030957.
Audience: **g,l,u,f.**

Micheline, Jack **PS3563.I334R5 1986**
River of Red Wine. Trade Paper. Water Row Press. Sudbury, MA. 1986. 60p. ISBN:0-934953-04-X, ISBN13: 978-0-934953-04-7. Dewey:811/.54. LCCN:85-052168.
Audience: **g,l,u,f.**

Michener, James **PS3525.I19 T3**
Tales of the South Pacific. Library Binding. Sagebrush Education Resources. Caledonia, MN. 1973. ISBN:0-8085-7707-7, ISBN13: 978-0-8085-7707-2. Dewey:813/.54.
Audience: **g,l,u,f.**

Michener, James A. **PS3568.O243**
The Bridges at Toko-Ri. Trade Paper. Ballantine Books. New York, NY. 1984. 128p. ISBN:0-449-20651-3, ISBN13: 978-0-449-20651-5. Dewey:813/.54.
Audience: **g,l,u,f.**

Miles, Josephine **PS3525.I4835.A6 1983**
Collected Poems, 1930-1983. Trade Cloth. University of Illinois Press. Champaign, IL. 1984. 280p. ISBN:0-252-01017-5, ISBN13: 978-0-252-01017-0. Dewey:811/.52. LCCN:82-011014.
Audience: **g,l,u,f.** B

Milford, Nancy **PS3525.I495Z72 2002**
Savage Beauty: The Life of Edna St. Vincent Millay. Ed. 1. Trade Cloth. Thomson Gale. Farmington Hills, MI. 2002. ISBN:0-7862-3965-4, ISBN13: 978-0-7862-3965-8. Dewey:811/.52 B. LCCN:2001-056366.
Audience: **g,l,u,f.** *Choice, 2002.*

Millay, Edna St. Vincent **PS3525.I495**
Collected Poems. Trade Cloth. HarperCollins Publishers. New York, NY. 2004. ISBN:0-06-018788-3, ISBN13: 978-0-06-018788-0. Dewey:811.52.
Audience: **g,l,u,f.** B

Millay, Edna St. Vincent **PS3525.I495A6 2003**
Edna St. Vincent Millay: Selected Poems. J. D. McClatchy (Editor). Trade Cloth. Library of America, The. New York, NY. 2003. 231p. American Poets Project Ser., Vol. 7 ISBN:1-931082-35-9, ISBN13: 978-1-931082-35-8. Dewey:811/.52. LCCN:2002-032126.
Audience: **g,l,u,f.**

Miller, Walter **PS3563.I4215 C3**
Canticle for Leibowitz. Library Binding. Sagebrush Education Resources. Caledonia, MN. 1997. ISBN:0-8085-2093-8, ISBN13: 978-0-8085-2093-1. Dewey:813/.54.
Audience: **g,l,u,f.**

Mitchell, Joseph **PS3525.I9714**
Up in the Old Hotel. UK-Trade Paper. Knopf Publishing Group. New York, NY. 1993. 736p. ISBN:0-679-74631-5, ISBN13: 978-0-679-74631-7. Dewey:813/.54. LCCN:92-050835.
Audience: **g,l,u,f.**

Mitchell, Margaret **PS3511.A86**
Gone with the Wind. Mass Market. Warner Books, Inc. New York, NY. 1993. 1024p. ISBN:0-446-36538-6, ISBN13: 978-0-446-36538-3. Dewey:813/.52.
Audience: **g,l,u,f.**

Moody, William Vaughn **PS2425 .A2 1969**
Poems and Plays. Trade Cloth. A M S Press, Inc. New York, NY. ISBN:0-404-04388-7, ISBN13: 978-0-404-04388-9. Dewey:818/.5/209. LCCN:70-080719.
Audience: **g,l,u,f.**

Morley, Christopher **PS3525 O71 F6X**
The Haunted Bookshop. Trade Paper. Kessinger Publishing, LLC. Whitefish, MT. 2004. ISBN:1-4179-2603-1, ISBN13: 978-1-4179-2603-9. Dewey:813.52.
Audience: **g,l,u,f.**

Pyron, Darden A. (Editor) **PS3525.I972.G687**
Recasting: "Gone with the Wind" in American Culture. Trade Paper. University Press of Florida. Gainesville, FL. 1983. 242p. ISBN:0-8130-0747-X, ISBN13: 978-0-8130-0747-2. Dewey:813/.52. LCCN:82-020310.
Audience: **u,f.** B

Thesing, William B. **PS3525.I495.Z634**
Critical Essays on Edna St. Vincent Millay. Trade Cloth. Thomson Gale. Farmington Hills, MI. 1993. 200p. Critical Essays on American Literature Ser. ISBN:0-8161-7310-9, ISBN13: 978-0-8161-7310-5. Dewey:811/.52. LCCN:92-038698.
Audience: **l,u.** *Choice, 1993.*

20th Century (1901-1960) > M > MacLeish, Archibald

MacLeish, Archibald **PS3525.A27**
J. B.: A Play in Verse. Trade Paper. Houghton Mifflin Company Trade & Reference Division. Boston, MA. 2000. 160p. ISBN:0-395-08353-2, ISBN13: 978-0-395-08353-6. Dewey:821.1.
Audience: **g,l,u,f.**

Macleish, Archibald **PS3525.A27.S3**
Scratch. Trade Cloth. Houghton Mifflin Company. New York, NY. 1971. ix, 116p. ISBN:0-395-12346-1, ISBN13: 978-0-395-12346-1. Dewey:812/.5/2. LCCN:73-145912.
Audience: **g,l,u,f.** B

MacLeish, Archibald **PS3525.A27A17 1985**
Collected Poems 1917 to 1982. Richard B. McAdoo (Preface by). Trade Paper. Houghton Mifflin Company Trade & Reference Division. Boston, MA. 1985. 544p. ISBN:0-395-39569-0, ISBN13: 978-0-395-39569-1. Dewey:811/.52. LCCN:85-014392.
Audience: **g,l,u,f.**

20th Century (1901-1960) > M > Mailer, Norman

Dearborn, Mary V. **PS3568.O243**
Mailer: A Biography. Trade Paper. Houghton Mifflin Company Trade & Reference Division. Boston, MA. 2001. 478p. ISBN:0-618-15460-4, ISBN13: 978-0-618-15460-9. Dewey:813/.54 B.
Audience: **g,l,u,f.** *Choice, 2000.*

Glenday, Michael K. **PS3525.A4152Z655**
Norman Mailer. Trade Cloth. Palgrave Macmillan. New York, NY. 1995. 163p. Modern Novelists Ser. ISBN:0-312-12644-1, ISBN13: 978-0-312-12644-5. Dewey:813/.54. LCCN:95-003705.
Audience: **l,u.** *Choice, 1996.*

Mailer, Norman **PS3525.A4152A78 1997**
An American Dream. Trade Paper. Knopf Publishing Group. New York, NY. 1999. 288p. Vintage International Ser. ISBN:0-375-70070-6, ISBN13: 978-0-375-70070-5. Dewey:813.5/4. LCCN:97-006684.
Audience: **g,l,u,f.** B

Mailer, Norman **PS3525.A4152**
The Armies of the Night: History As a Novel - The Novel As History. Trade Paper. Penguin Group (USA) Inc. New York, NY. 1995. 304p. ISBN:0-452-27279-3, ISBN13: 978-0-452-27279-8. Dewey:818.
Audience: **g,l,u,f.** B

Mailer, Norman **HV6248.P43**
Executioner's Song. Library Binding. Sagebrush Education Resources. Caledonia, MN. 1998. ISBN:0-613-10087-5, ISBN13: 978-0-613-10087-8. Dewey:364.1/523/0924.
Audience: **g,l,u,f.**

Mailer, Norman **PS3568.O243**
Harlot's Ghost. Trade Paper. Ballantine Books. New York, NY. 1992. 1200p. ISBN:0-345-37965-9, ISBN13: 978-0-345-37965-8. Dewey:813/.54. LCCN:92-090052.
Audience: **g,l,u,f.**

Mailer, Norman **PS3525.A4152N34 1998**
The Naked and the Dead: With a New Introduction by the Author. Ed. 50. Cloth over Boards. Henry Holt & Company. New York, NY. 1998. 736p. ISBN:0-8050-6018-9, ISBN13: 978-0-8050-6018-8. Dewey:813/.54. LCCN:98-006700.
Audience: **g,l,u,f.**

Merrill, Robert **PS3525.A4152Z774**
Norman Mailer. Trade Cloth. Thomson Gale. Farmington Hills, MI. 1992. 160p. Twayne's United States Authors Ser. ISBN:0-8057-3967-X, ISBN13: 978-0-8057-3967-1. Dewey:813/.54. LCCN:92-007282.
Audience: **l,u.**

20th Century (1901-1960) > M > McCarthy, Mary

Abrams, Sabrina Fuchs **PS3525.A1435Z58 2004**
Mary McCarthy: Gender, Politics, and the Postwar Intellectual. Trade Cloth. Peter Lang Publishing, Inc. New York, NY. 2004. 143p. ISBN:0-8204-6807-X, ISBN13: 978-0-8204-6807-5. Dewey:818/.5209. LCCN:2003-011709.
Audience: **u,f.**

Gelderman, Carol (Editor) **PS3525.A1435Z6 1991**
Conversations with Mary McCarthy. Trade Cloth. University Press of Mississippi. Jackson, MS. 1991. xviii, 273p. Literary Conversations Ser. ISBN:0-87805-485-5, ISBN13: 978-0-87805-485-5. Dewey:818/.5209. LCCN:90-049282.
Audience: **l,u.**

Kiernan, Frances **PS3525.A1435Z69 2000**
Seeing Mary Plain: A Life of Mary McCarthy. Trade Cloth. W. W. Norton & Company, Inc. New York, NY. 2000. 768p. ISBN:0-393-03801-7, ISBN13: 978-0-393-03801-9. Dewey:818/.5209 B. LCCN:99-041098.
Audience: **g,l,u,f.** *Choice, 2000.*

McCarthy, Mary **PS3525.A1435.C36**
Cast a Cold Eye. Trade Paper. Harcourt Trade Publishers. New York, NY. 1992. 228p. ISBN:0-15-615444-7, ISBN13: 978-0-15-615444-4. Dewey:813/.52. LCCN:92-021660.
Audience: **g,l,u,f.** B

McCarthy, Mary **PS3525.A1435 C4 1992**
A Charmed Life. Trade Paper. Harcourt Trade Publishers. New York, NY. 1992. 324p. ISBN:0-15-616774-3, ISBN13: 978-0-15-616774-1. Dewey:813/.52. LCCN:92-004322.
Audience: **g,l,u,f.** B

McCarthy, Mary **PS3525.A1435**
The Company She Keeps. Library Binding. Buccaneer Books, Inc. Cutchogue, NY. 1994. ISBN:1-56849-400-9, ISBN13: 978-1-56849-400-5. Dewey:813/.5/2.
Audience: **g,l,u,f.** B

McCarthy, Mary **PS3511.A86**
The Group. Library Binding. Buccaneer Books, Inc. Cutchogue, NY. 1991. 400p. ISBN:0-89966-856-9, ISBN13: 978-0-89966-856-7. Dewey:813/.52.
Audience: **g,l,u,f.**

McCarthy, Mary **PS3511.A86**
The Groves of Academe. Trade Paper. Harcourt Trade Publishers. New York, NY. 2002. 312p. ISBN:0-15-602787-9, ISBN13: 978-0-15-602787-8. Dewey:813/.52.
Audience: **g,l,u,f.** B

Stwertka, Eve & Viscusi, Margo (Editors) **PS3535**
Twenty-Four Ways of Looking at Mary McCarthy: The Writer and Her Work. Trade Cloth. Greenwood Publishing Group, Inc. Portsmouth, NH. 1996. 240p. Contributions to the Study of World Literature Ser., Vol. 70 ISBN:0-313-29776-2, ISBN13: 978-0-313-29776-2. Dewey:818/.5209. LCCN:96-005801.
Audience: **l,u.** *Choice, 1997.*

20th Century (1901-1960) > M > McCullers, Carson

Carr, Virginia Spencer **PS3525.A1772Z58 2003**
The Lonely Hunter: A Biography of Carson McCullers. Trade Paper. University of Georgia Press. Athens, GA. 2005. 680p. ISBN:0-8203-2522-8, ISBN13: 978-0-8203-2522-4. Dewey:813/.5/2. LCCN:2002-040930.
Audience: **g,l,u,f.**

Carr, Virginia Spencer **PS3525.A1772Z582**
Understanding Carson Mcculllers. Matthew J. Bruccoli (Editor). Trade Paper, Perfect. University of South Carolina Press. Columbia, SC. 2005. 181p. Understanding Contemporary American Literature Ser. ISBN:1-57003-615-2, ISBN13: 978-1-57003-615-6. Dewey:813.52.
Audience: **l,u.**

Friedman, Melvin J. **PS3525.A1772.Z594**
Critical Essays on Carson McCullers. Beverly Lyon Clark (Editor). Trade Cloth. Macmillan Publishing Company, Inc. Old Tappan, NJ. 1996. 240p. Critical Essays on American Literature Ser. ISBN:0-7838-0037-1, ISBN13: 978-0-7838-0037-0. Dewey:813/.52. LCCN:95-043272.
Audience: **l,u.**

Gleeson-White, Sarah **PS3525.A1772Z635**
Strange Bodies: Gender and Identity in the Novels of Carson McCullers. Trade Cloth. University of Alabama Press. Tuscaloosa, AL. 2003. 166p. ISBN:0-8173-1267-6, ISBN13: 978-0-8173-1267-1. Dewey:813/.52. LCCN:2002-012921.
Audience: **g,l,u,f.** *Choice, 2003.*

McCullers, Carson **PS3525.A1772 A6 1998**
Collected Stories of Carson McCullers. Trade Paper. Houghton Mifflin Company Trade & Reference Division. Boston, MA. 1998. 416p. ISBN:0-395-92505-3, ISBN13: 978-0-395-92505-8. Dewey:813/.52. LCCN:98-040781.
Audience: **g,l,u,f.**

McCullers, Carson **PS3525.A1772S63 1990**
The Square Root of Wonderful. Trade Cloth. Cherokee Publishing Company. Marietta, GA. 1990. 169p. ISBN:0-87797-188-9, ISBN13: 978-0-87797-188-7. Dewey:812/.52. LCCN:90-047728.
Audience: **g,l,u,f.**

McCullers, Carson **PS3525.A1772M5 2006**
The Member of the Wedding: A Play. Dorothy Allison (Introduction by). Trade Paper. New Directions Publishing Corporation. New York, NY. 2006. 144p. ISBN:0-8112-1655-1, ISBN13: 978-0-8112-1655-5. Dewey:813/.52. LCCN:2005-036493.
Audience: **g,l,u,f.** B

McCullers, Carson & Dews, C. L. Barney **PS3525.A1772Z74 1999**
Illumination and Night Glare: The Unfinished Autobiography of Carson McCullers. Cloth Text. University of Wisconsin Press. Chicago, IL. 1999. xxii, 233p. Wisconsin Studies in American Autobiography ISBN:0-299-16440-3, ISBN13: 978-0-299-16440-9. Dewey:813.52. LCCN:99-019805.
Audience: **g,l,u,f.** *Choice, 2000.*

McCullers, Carson **PS3525.A1772A6 2001**
Carson McCullers: Complete Novels. Carlos L. Dews (Editor). Trade Cloth. Library of America, The. New York, NY. 2001. 827p. The Library of America, Vol. 128 ISBN:1-931082-03-0, ISBN13: 978-1-931082-03-7. Dewey:813/.52. LCCN:2001-029049.
Audience: **g,l,u,f.**

McCullers, Carson **PS3525.A1772A6 2005**
The Mortgaged Heart: Selected Writings. Margarita G. Smith (Editor). Trade Paper. Houghton Mifflin Company Trade & Reference Division. Boston, MA. 2005. 320p. ISBN:0-618-05705-6, ISBN13: 978-0-618-05705-4. Dewey:813/.52. LCCN:2005-273976.
Audience: **g,l,u,f.**

McDowell, Margaret B. **PS3525.A1772.Z76**
Carson McCullers. Trade Cloth. Thomson Gale. Farmington Hills, MI. 1980. 160p. United States Authors Ser., No. 354 ISBN:0-8057-7297-9, ISBN13: 978-0-8057-7297-5. Dewey:813/.5/2. LCCN:79-013361.
Audience: **l,u.** B

Savigneau, Josyane **PS3525.A1772Z8513**
Carson McCullers: A Life. Joan E. Howard (Translator). Trade Cloth. Houghton Mifflin Company Trade & Reference Division. Boston, MA. 2001. 384p. ISBN:0-395-87820-9, ISBN13: 978-0-395-87820-0. Dewey:813.5/2. LCCN:00-046547.
Audience: **g,l,u,f.** *Choice, 2002.*

20th Century (1901-1960) > M > Merrill, James

Adams, Don **PS3525**
James Merrill's Poetic Quest, 81. Trade Cloth. Greenwood Publishing Group, Inc. Portsmouth, NH. 1997. 192p. Contributions to the Study of World Literature Ser. ISBN:0-313-30250-2, ISBN13: 978-0-313-30250-3. Dewey:811/.54. LCCN:96-035022.
Audience: **u,f.**

Merrill, James **PS3566.L27**
The Changing Light at Sandover: Including the Whole of the Book of Ephraim, Mirabell's Books of Number, Scripts for the Pageant, and a New Coda, The Higher Keys. Trade Cloth. Simon & Schuster. New York, NY. 1983. 512p. ISBN:0-689-11282-3, ISBN13: 978-0-689-11282-9. Dewey:811/.54. LCCN:81-070062.
Audience: **g,l,u,f.**

Merrill, James **PS3525.E6645A6 2004**
Collected Prose. Trade Cloth. Knopf Publishing Group. New York, NY. 2004. 752p. ISBN:0-375-41136-4, ISBN13: 978-0-375-41136-6. Dewey:818/.548. LCCN:2004-040914.
Audience: **l,u,f.**

Merrill, James **PS3568.O243**
The Diblos Notebook. Trade Paper. Simon & Schuster. New York, NY. 1975. ISBN:0-689-70519-0, ISBN13: 978-0-689-70519-9. Dewey:813/.54. LCCN:65-012401.
Audience: **g,l,u,f.** B

Merrill, James **PS3525.E6645A6 2002**
Collected Novels and Plays: James Merrill. J. D. McClatchy & Stephen Yenser (Editors). Trade Cloth. Random House, Inc. New York, NY. 2002. 688p. ISBN:0-375-41137-2, ISBN13: 978-0-375-41137-3. Dewey:818/.5408. LCCN:2002-020953.
Audience: **l,u,f.**

Merrill, James **PS3525.E6645A17 2001**
Collected Poems. Stephen Yenser & J. D. McClatchy (Editors). Trade Cloth. Alfred A. Knopf Inc. New York, NY. 2001. 912p. ISBN:0-375-41139-9, ISBN13: 978-0-375-41139-7. Dewey:811/.54. LCCN:00-040542.
Audience: **g,l,u,f.**

Rotella, Guy L. **PS3525.E6645Z63 1996**
Critical Essays on James Merrill. Trade Cloth. Thomson Gale. Farmington Hills, MI. 1996. 251p. Critical Essays on American Literature Ser. ISBN:0-7838-0031-2, ISBN13: 978-0-7838-0031-8. Dewey:811/.54. LCCN:95-043252.
Audience: **l,u.**

20th Century (1901-1960) > M > Merwin, W. S.

Frazier, Jane **PS3563.E75Z67 1999**
From Origin to Ecology: Nature and the Poetry of W. S. Merwin. Trade Cloth. Fairleigh Dickinson University Press. Cranbury, NJ. 1999. 144p. ISBN:0-8386-3799-X, ISBN13: 978-0-8386-3799-9. Dewey:811/.54. LCCN:98-054595.
Audience: **u,f.** *Choice, 2000.*

Hix, H. L. **PS3563.E75Z69 1997**
Understanding W. S. Merwin. Trade Cloth. University of South Carolina Press. Columbia, SC. 1997. 190p. Understanding Contemporary American Literature Ser. ISBN:1-57003-154-1, ISBN13: 978-1-57003-154-0. Dewey:811/.54. LCCN:96-051241.
Audience: **l,u.** *Choice, 1997.*

Merwin, W. S. **PS3563.E**
The First Four Books of Poems: Including a Mask for Janus, the Dancing Bear, Green with Beasts, the Drunk in the Furnace. Trade Cloth. Macmillan Publishing Company, Inc. Old Tappan, NJ. 1989. ISBN:0-02-584381-8, ISBN13: 978-0-02-584381-3. Dewey:811/.5/4. LCCN:89-012760.
Audience: **g,l,u,f.**

Merwin, W. S. **PS3563.E75A6 2000**
The First Four Books of Poems. Trade Paper. Copper Canyon Press. Port Townsend, WA. 2000. 256p. ISBN:1-55659-139-X, ISBN13: 978-1-55659-139-6. Dewey:811/.54. LCCN:00-008343.
Audience: **g,l,u,f.**

Merwin, W. S. **PS3563.E75M54 2005**
Migration: New and Selected Poems. Trade Cloth. Copper Canyon Press. Port Townsend, WA. 2005. 534p. ISBN:1-55659-218-3, ISBN13: 978-1-55659-218-8. Dewey:811/.54. LCCN:2004-017473.
Audience: **u,f.**

20th Century (1901-1960) > M > Miller, Arthur

Bigsby, Christopher **PS3525.I5156Z5445**
Arthur Miller: A Critical Study. Cloth Text. Cambridge University Press. New York, NY. 2004. 524p. ISBN:0-521-84416-9, ISBN13: 978-0-521-84416-1. Dewey:812/.52 B. LCCN:2004-045813.
Audience: **g,l,u.**

Bigsby, Christopher (Editor) **PS3525.I5156 Z548 1**
The Cambridge Companion to Arthur Miller. Trade Paper. Cambridge University Press. New York, NY. 1997. 297p. Companions to Literature Ser. ISBN:0-521-55992-8, ISBN13: 978-0-521-55992-8. Dewey:812.5/2. LCCN:96-037707.
Audience: **l,u,f.** *Choice, 1998.*

Brater, Enoch (Editor) **PS3525.I5156**
Arthur Miller's America: Theater and Culture in a Time of Change. Trade Cloth. University of Michigan Press. Chicago, IL. 2005. 280p. Theater Ser., :Theory/Text/Performance Ser. ISBN:0-472-11410-7, ISBN13: 978-0-472-11410-8. Dewey:812/.52. LCCN:2004-063695.
Audience: **u,f.** *Choice, 2005.*

Gottfried, Martin **PS3525.I5156**
Arthur Miller: His Life and Work. Trade Paper. Da Capo Press, Inc. Cambridge, MA. 2004. 504p. ISBN:0-306-81377-7, ISBN13: 978-0-306-81377-1. Dewey:812/.52 B.
Audience: **l,u,f.** *Choice, 2004.*

Griffin, Alice **PS3525.I5156Z675**
Understanding Arthur Miller. Matthew Broccoli (Editor). Trade Cloth. University of South Carolina Press. Columbia, SC. 1996. 220p. Understanding Contemporary American Literature Ser. ISBN:1-57003-101-0, ISBN13: 978-1-57003-101-4. Dewey:818/.5209. LCCN:95-041776.
Audience: **l,u.** *Choice, 1996.*

Miller, Arthur **PS3525.I5156**
After the Fall. Trade Paper. Penguin Group (USA) Inc. New York, NY. 1980. 128p. Plays Ser. ISBN:0-14-048162-1, ISBN13: 978-0-14-048162-4. Dewey:812/.52. LCCN:78-012045.
Audience: **g,l,u,f.**

Miller, Arthur **PS3525.I5156F59 1997**
Focus. Trade Paper. Syracuse University Press. Syracuse, NY. 1996. 217p. The Library of Modern Jewish Literature ISBN:0-8156-0437-8, ISBN13: 978-0-8156-0437-2. Dewey:813/.52. LCCN:96-029204.
Audience: **g,l,u,f.**

Miller, Arthur **PS3511.A86**
I Don't Need You Any More. Trade Cloth. Penguin Group (USA) Inc. New York, NY. 1967. ISBN:0-670-38989-7, ISBN13: 978-0-670-38989-6. Dewey:813.5/2.
Audience: **g,l,u,f.**

Miller, Arthur **PS3525.I5156I5 1985**
Incident at Vichy. Trade Paper. Penguin Group (USA) Inc. New York, NY. 1985. 80p. Penguin Plays Ser. ISBN:0-14-048193-1, ISBN13: 978-0-14-048193-8. Dewey:812.5/2. LCCN:84-026556.
Audience: **g,l,u,f.**

Miller, Arthur **PS3525.I5156.D4356**
Salesman in Beijing. Trade Cloth. Penguin Group (USA) Inc. New York, NY. 1984. 256p. ISBN:0-670-61601-X, ISBN13: 978-0-670-61601-5. Dewey:792.92. LCCN:83-047999.
Audience: **g,l,u,f.** B

Miller, Arthur **PN1997**
The Misfits: An Original Screenplay. George P. Garrett (Editor). Trade Paper. Irvington Publishers. New York, NY. 1989. Film Scripts Ser. ISBN:0-89197-850-X, ISBN13: 978-0-89197-850-3. Dewey:812/.52. LCCN:71-135273.
Audience: **g,l,u,f.**

Miller, Arthur **PS3525.I5156A6 2006**
Arthur Miller: Collected Plays, 1944-1961. Tony Kushner (Editor). Trade Cloth. Library of America, The. New York, NY. 2006. 864p. The Library of America, Vol. 163 ISBN:1-931082-91-X, ISBN13: 978-1-931082-91-4. Dewey:812/.52. LCCN:2005-049442.
Audience: **g,l,u,f.**

Miller, Arthur, et al. **PS3525.I5156T5 1996**
Theater Essays of Arthur Miller. Ed. 2. Robert A. Martin & Steven R. Centola (Authors). Trade Paper. Da Capo Press, Inc. Cambridge, MA. 1996. 628p. ISBN:0-306-80732-7, ISBN13: 978-0-306-80732-9. Dewey:809.2. LCCN:96-016452.
Audience: **l,u,f.**

Moss, Leonard **PS3525.I5156**
Arthur Miller. Trade Cloth. Thomson Gale. Farmington Hills, MI. 1980. 200p. United States Authors Ser., No. 115 ISBN:0-8057-7311-8, ISBN13: 978-0-8057-7311-8. Dewey:812/.5/2. LCCN:79-025071.
Audience: **l,u.** B

Savran, David **PS338.P6**
Communists, Cowboys, and Queers: The Politics of Masculinity in the Work of Arthur Miller and Tennessee Williams. Trade Paper. University of Minnesota Press. Minneapolis, MN. 1992. 256p. ISBN:0-8166-2123-3, ISBN13: 978-0-8166-2123-1. Dewey:812/.5209358. LCCN:92-004267.
Audience: **u,f.** *Choice, 1993.*

20th Century (1901-1960) > M > Miller, Henry

Miller, Henry **PS3525.I5454**
The Books in My Life. Trade Paper. New Directions Publishing Corporation. New York, NY. 1969. 322p. ISBN:0-8112-0108-2, ISBN13: 978-0-8112-0108-7. Dewey:28.9. LCCN:71-088728.
Audience: **g,l,u,f.** B

Miller, Henry **PS3525.I5454.C6**
The Cosmological Eye. Trade Paper. New Directions Publishing Corporation. New York, NY. 1961. ISBN:0-8112-0110-4, ISBN13: 978-0-8112-0110-0. Dewey:814.5. LCCN:75-088729.
Audience: **g,l,u,f.** B

Miller, Henry **PS3525.I5454N4**
The Rosy Crucifixion. Trade Cloth, Box or Slipcased. Grove/Atlantic, Inc. New York, NY. 1980. 1600p. ISBN:0-394-17774-6, ISBN13: 978-0-394-17774-8. Dewey:813/.52. LCCN:80-008064.
Audience: **g,l,u,f.** B

Miller, Henry **PS3525.I5454 T7**
Tropic of Cancer. Library Binding. Sagebrush Education Resources. Caledonia, MN. 1989. ISBN:0-613-70619-6, ISBN13: 978-0-613-70619-3. Dewey:818.52.
Audience: **u,f.**

Miller, Henry **PS3525.I5454T8 1987**
Tropic of Capricorn. Trade Paper. Random House, Inc. New York, NY. 1987. ISBN:0-394-62379-7, ISBN13: 978-0-394-62379-5. Dewey:813/.52. LCCN:86-033510.
Audience: **g,l,u,f.** B

Miller, Henry **PS3525.I5454 A6 1972**
The Henry Miller Reader. Lawrence Durrell (Editor). Trade Cloth. Ayer Company Publishers, Inc. Manchester, NH. 1977. Essay Index Reprint Ser. ISBN:0-8369-2664-1, ISBN13: 978-0-8369-2664-4. Dewey:818/.5/209. LCCN:73-038712.
Audience: **g,l,u,f.** B

20th Century (1901-1960) > M > Moore, Marianne

Diehl, Joanne F. **PS3503.I785Z634 1993**
Elizabeth Bishop and Marianne Moore: The Psychodynamics of Creativity. Trade Cloth. Princeton University Press. Princeton, NJ. 1993. 136p. ISBN:0-691-06975-1, ISBN13: 978-0-691-06975-3. Dewey:811.54. LCCN:92-023533.
Audience: **u,f.**

Engel, Bernard F. **PS3525.O5616Z65 1988**
Marianne Moore. Trade Cloth. Thomson Gale. Farmington Hills, MI. 1988. 176p. ISBN:0-8057-7525-0, ISBN13: 978-0-8057-7525-9. Dewey:811/.52. LCCN:88-019157.
Audience: **l,u.** B

Heuving, Jeanne **PS3525.O5616Z683**
Omissions Are Not Accidents: Gender in the Art of Marianne Moore. Trade Cloth. Wayne State University Press. Detroit, MI. 1992. 196p. ISBN:0-8143-2335-9, ISBN13: 978-0-8143-2335-9. Dewey:811/.52. LCCN:92-015343.
Audience: **u,f.** *Choice, 1993.*

Joyce, Elisabeth W. (Editor) **PS3525.O5616.Z685**
Cultural Critique and Abstraction: Marianne Moore and the Avant-Garde. Trade Cloth. Bucknell University Press. Cranbury, NJ. 1998. 160p. ISBN:0-8387-5371-X, ISBN13: 978-0-8387-5371-2. Dewey:811/.52. LCCN:97-041274.
Audience: **u,f.** *Choice, 1999.*

Kalstone, David **PS3503.I785Z75 2001**
Becoming a Poet: Elizabeth Bishop with Marianne Moore and Robert Lowell. Trade Paper. University of Michigan Press. Chicago, IL. 2001. 320p. ISBN:0-472-08720-7, ISBN13: 978-0-472-08720-4. Dewey:811/.54 B. LCCN:00-051174.
Audience: **l,u,f.**

Miller, Cristanne **PS3525.O5616Z696**
Marianne Moore: Questions of Authority. Trade Cloth. Harvard University Press. Cambridge, MA. 1995. 319p. ISBN:0-674-54862-0, ISBN13: 978-0-674-54862-6. Dewey:811/.52. LCCN:95-007167.
Audience: **u,f.** *Choice, 1996.*

Moore, Marianne **PS3525.O5616A17 2003**
The Poems of Marianne Moore. Grace Schulman (Editor). Trade Cloth. Penguin Group (USA) Inc. New York, NY. 2003. 480p. ISBN:0-670-03198-4, ISBN13: 978-0-670-03198-6. Dewey:811/.52. LCCN:2003-050159.
Audience: **g,l,u,f.** *Choice, 2004.*

Moore, Marianne **PS3525.O56 A14 1986**
The Complete Prose of Marianne Moore. Patricia C. Willis (Editor). Trade Cloth. Penguin Group (USA) Inc. New York, NY. 1986. 816p. ISBN:0-670-80451-7, ISBN13: 978-0-670-80451-1. Dewey:818/.5208. LCCN:85-041064.
Audience: **g,l,u,f.** *Choice, 1987.*

Paul, Catherine E. **PS310.M57P38 2002**
Poetry in the Museums of Modernism: Yeats, Pound, Moore, Stein. Trade Cloth. University of Michigan Press. Chicago, IL. 2002. 312p. ISBN:0-472-11264-3, ISBN13: 978-0-472-11264-7. Dewey:811/.5209112. LCCN:2002-002089.
Audience: **u,f.**

Rotella, Guy **PS310.N3R68 1990**
Reading and Writing Nature: The Poetry of Robert Frost, Wallace Stevens, Marianne Moore, and Elizabeth Bishop. Trade Cloth. Northeastern University Press. Boston, MA. 1990. 253p. ISBN:1-55553-086-9, ISBN13: 978-1-55553-086-0. Dewey:811/.520936. LCCN:90-007576.
Audience: **u,f.** *Choice, 1991.*

Zona, Kirstin H. **PS310.F45Z66 2003**
Marianne Moore, Elizabeth Bishop, and May Swenson: The Feminist Poetics of Self-Restraint. Trade Cloth. University of Michigan Press. Chicago, IL. 2002. 200p. ISBN:0-472-11304-6, ISBN13: 978-0-472-11304-0. Dewey:811/.50809287. LCCN:2002-008277.
Audience: **u,f.**

20th Century (1901-1960) > M > Morris, Wright

Madden & Wydeven, Joseph F. **PS3525.O7475Z95 1998**
Wright Morris Revisited. Trade Cloth. Thomson Gale. Farmington Hills, MI. 1998. 212p. Twayne's United States Authors Ser., Vol. 703 ISBN:0-8057-4531-9, ISBN13: 978-0-8057-4531-3. Dewey:813/.52. LCCN:98-010001.
Audience: **l,u.**

Morris, Wright **PS3525.O7475 F5**
The Field of Vision. Library Binding. Buccaneer Books, Inc. Cutchogue, NY. 1997. ISBN:1-56849-687-7, ISBN13: 978-1-56849-687-0. Dewey:813.5.
Audience: **g,l,u,f.** B

Morris, Wright **PS3525.O7475L66 1995**
The Loneliness of the Long Distance Writer: The Works of Love and the Huge Season. Trade Cloth. HarperCollins Publishers. New York, NY. 1996. 575p. ISBN:0-87685-991-0, ISBN13: 978-0-87685-991-9. Dewey:813/.52. LCCN:95-047580.
Audience: **g,l,u,f.**

Morris, Wright **PS3525.O7475P5 2000**
Plains Song: For Female Voices. Charles Baxter (Introduction by). Trade Cloth. University of Nebraska Press. Lincoln, NE. 2000. 229p. ISBN:0-8032-8267-2, ISBN13: 978-0-8032-8267-4. Dewey:813/.52. LCCN:00-033784.
Audience: **g,l,u,f.**

Morris, Wright **PS3525.O7475C4 2001**
Ceremony in Lone Tree. Keith Botsford (Introduction by). Trade Cloth. University of Nebraska Press. Lincoln, NE. 2005. 304p. ISBN:0-8032-8276-1, ISBN13: 978-0-8032-8276-6. Dewey:813/.52. LCCN:2001-027957.
Audience: **g,l,u,f.** B

20th Century (1901-1960) > N

Nash, Ogden **PS3527.A637.A6 1975**
I Wouldn't Have Missed It: Selected Poems of Ogden Nash. Isabel Eberstadt (Editor), Linell N. Smith (Compiled by), Archibald MacLeish (Introduction by). Trade Cloth. Little Brown & Company. New York, NY. 1975. 407p. ISBN:0-316-59830-5, ISBN13: 978-0-316-59830-9. Dewey:811/.52. LCCN:75-014008.
Audience: **g,l,u,f.** B

Neihardt, John G. **PS3531.O82**
Lyric and Dramatic Poems. Trade Paper. University of Nebraska Press. Lincoln, NE. 1991. 239p. ISBN:0-8032-5143-2, ISBN13: 978-0-8032-5143-4. Dewey:811/.52. LCCN:65-023374.
Audience: **g,l,u,f.**

Nims, John Frederick **PS3527.I863P6 2002**
The Powers of Heaven and Earth: New and Selected Poems. Trade Cloth. Louisiana State University Press. Baton Rouge, LA. 2002. xiv, 247p. ISBN:0-8071-2826-0, ISBN13: 978-0-8071-2826-8. Dewey:811/.54. LCCN:2002-030055.
Audience: **g,l,u,f.**

Nordhoff, Charles & Hall, James Norman **PS3568.O243**
Mutiny on the Bounty. Trade Cloth. University Publishing House, Inc. Mannford, OK. 2002. 375p. ISBN:1-57002-198-8, ISBN13: 978-1-57002-198-5. Dewey:813/.54.
Audience: **g,l,u,f.**

Parker, Douglas M. **PS3527.A637Z79 2005**
Ogden Nash: The Life and Work of America's Laureate of Light Verse. Dana Gioia (Foreword by). Book, Other. Ivan R. Dee Publisher. Blue Ridge Summit, PA. 2005. 336p. ISBN:1-56663-637-X, ISBN13: 978-1-56663-637-7. Dewey:811/.52 B. LCCN:2004-059912.
Audience: **g,l,u,f.** *Choice, 2006.*

20th Century (1901-1960) > N > Nabokov, Vladimir

Alexandrov, Vladimir E. (Editor) **PG3476.N3Z668 1995**
The Garland Companion to Vladimir Nabokov. Library Binding. Garland Publishing, Inc. New York, NY. 1995. 848p. ISBN:0-8153-0354-8, ISBN13: 978-0-8153-0354-1. Dewey:813/.54. LCCN:94-037409.
Audience: **l,u.** *Choice, 1996.*

Boyd, Brian **PS3568.O243**
Nabokov's Pale Fire: The Magic of Artistic Discovery. Trade Paper. Princeton University Press. Princeton, NJ. 2001. 316p. ISBN:0-691-08957-4, ISBN13: 978-0-691-08957-7. Dewey:813.5/4.
Audience: **u,f.**

Boyd, Brian **PS3568.O243**
Vladimir Nabokov: The American Years. Trade Paper. Princeton University Press. Princeton, NJ. 1993. 798p. ISBN:0-691-02471-5, ISBN13: 978-0-691-02471-4. Dewey:813/.54 B.
Audience: **u,f.** *Choice, 1992.*

Boyd, Brian **PS3568.O243**
Vladimir Nabokov: The Russian Years. Trade Paper. Princeton University Press. Princeton, NJ. 1993. 622p. ISBN:0-691-02470-7, ISBN13: 978-0-691-02470-7. Dewey:813/.54 B.
Audience: **u,f.** *Choice, 1991.*

Connolly, Julian W. (Editor) **PG3476.N3**
The Cambridge Companion to Nabokov. Cloth Text. Cambridge University Press. New York, NY. 2005. 286p. Cambridge Companions to Literature Ser. ISBN:0-521-82957-7, ISBN13: 978-0-521-82957-1. Dewey:813/.54. LCCN:2005-046987.
Audience: **g,l,u,f.** *Choice, 2006.*

Connolly, Julian W. (Editor) **PG3476.N3 Z776 1999**
Nabokov and His Fiction: New Perspectives. Anthony Cross, Caryl Emerson, Barbara Heldt, Malcolm Jones, Catriona Kelly, Donald Rayfield, G. S. Smith & Victor Terras (Contribution by). Trade Cloth. Cambridge University Press. New York, NY. 1999. 268p. Studies in Russian Literature ISBN:0-521-63283-8, ISBN13: 978-0-521-63283-6. Dewey:813/.54. LCCN:98-047176.
Audience: **u,f.**

Grayson, Jane (Editor), et al. **PG3476.N3Z794 2001**
Nabokov's World: Reading Nabokov. Arnold B. McMillan & Priscilla Meyer (Editors). Cloth over Boards. Palgrave Macmillan. New York, NY. 2002. 264p. Studies in Russian and Eastern European History Ser. ISBN:0-333-96417-9, ISBN13: 978-0-333-96417-0. Dewey:813.54. LCCN:2001-032720.
Audience: **u,f.**

Johnson, Kurt & Coates, Steven L. **QL31.N23J644 2001**
Nabokov's Blues: The Scientific Odyssey of a Literary Genius. Trade Paper. McGraw-Hill Companies, The. New York, NY. 2001. 372p. ISBN:0-07-137330-6, ISBN13: 978-0-07-137330-2. Dewey:595.78/092 B. LCCN:2001-030270.
Audience: **u,f.** *Choice, 2000.*

Larmour, David H. J. **PG3476.N3Z6996 2002**
Discourse and Ideology in Nabokov's Prose. Paper over Boards. Routledge. New York, NY. 2002. 192p. Studies in Russian and European Literature, Vol. 7 ISBN:0-415-28658-1, ISBN13: 978-0-415-28658-9. Dewey:813/.54. LCCN:2002-069658.
Audience: **u,f.**

Nabokov, Vladimir **PS3527.A15A6 1995**
The Stories of Vladimir Nabokov. Trade Paper. Random House, Inc. New York, NY. 1996. 704p. ISBN:0-679-72997-6, ISBN13: 978-0-679-72997-6. Dewey:813.5/4. LCCN:95-023466.
Audience: **g,l,u,f.**

Nabokov, Vladimir **PS3527.A15S7 1990**
Strong Opinions. Book, Other. Knopf Publishing Group. New York, NY. 1990. 368p. Vintage International Ser. ISBN:0-679-72609-8, ISBN13: 978-0-679-72609-8. Dewey:813/.54. LCCN:89-035741.
Audience: **g,l,u,f.** B

Nabokov, Vladimir Vladimirovich **PS3551.N464**
Nabokov's Butterflies. Brian Boyd & Robert Michael Pyle (Editors), Dmitri Nabokov (Translator). Trade Cloth. Beacon Press. Boston, MA. 2000. 800p. ISBN:0-8070-8542-1, ISBN13: 978-0-8070-8542-4. Dewey:818.5/4/09. LCCN:98-042846.
Audience: **g,l,u,f.**

Nabokov, Vladimir **PS3527.A15L6 1991**
The Annotated Lolita. Alfred Appel Jr. (Editor, Introduction by, Notes by). Trade Paper. Knopf Publishing Group. New York, NY. 1991. 544p. ISBN:0-679-72729-9, ISBN13: 978-0-679-72729-3. Dewey:813.5/4. LCCN:90-050264.
Audience: **g,l,u,f.**

Nabokov, Vladimir **PG3476.N3Z476 1999**
Speak, Memory: An Autobiography Revisited. Brian Boyd (Introduction by). Trade Cloth. Alfred A. Knopf Inc. New York, NY. 1999. 320p. Everyman's Library, Vol. 188 ISBN:0-375-40553-4, ISBN13: 978-0-375-40553-2. Dewey:813.5/4. LCCN:98-049237.
Audience: **g,l,u,f.**

Nabokov, Vladimir **PS3527.A15.A6 1996**
Vladimir Nabokov, 1941-1951: The Real Life of Sebastian Knight; Bend Sinister; Speak, Memory. Brian Boyd (Editor). Trade Cloth. Library of America, The. New York, NY. 1996. 734p. Library of America, Vol. 87 ISBN:1-883011-18-3, ISBN13: 978-1-883011-18-5. Dewey:813/.54. LCCN:96-015257.
Audience: **g,l,u,f.**

Nabokov, Vladimir **PS3527.A15.A6 1996**
Vladimir Nabokov, 1955-1962: Lolita; Pnin; Pale Fire; Lolita: A Screenplay. Brian Boyd (Editor). Trade Cloth. Library of America, The. New York, NY. 1996. 916p. Library of America ISBN:1-883011-19-1, ISBN13: 978-1-883011-19-2. Dewey:813/.54. LCCN:96-015256.
Audience: **g,l,u,f.**

Nabokov, Vladimir **PS3527.A15A6 1996**
Vladimir Nabokov, 1969-1974: ADA, or Ardor; Transparent Things; Look at the Harlequins!. Brian Boyd (Editor). Trade Cloth. Library of America, The. New York, NY. 1996. 862p. Library of America ISBN:1-883011-20-5, ISBN13: 978-1-883011-20-8. Dewey:813/.54. LCCN:96-015255.
Audience: **g,l,u,f.**

Nabokov, Vladimir **PS3527.A1**
Vladimir Nabokov Lolita: A Reader's Guide to Essential Criticism. Christine Clegg (Editor). Trade Paper. Palgrave Macmillan. New York, NY. 2003. 176p. Readers' Guides to Essential Criticism Ser. ISBN:1-84046-173-X, ISBN13: 978-1-84046-173-2. Dewey:813.4.
Audience: **l,u.**

Pifer, Ellen (Editor) **PS3527.A15L638 2002**
Vladimir Nabokov's Lolita: A Casebook. Trade Cloth. Oxford University Press, Inc. New York, NY. 2002. 218p. Casebooks in Criticism Ser. ISBN:0-19-515032-5, ISBN13: 978-0-19-515032-2. Dewey:813/.54. LCCN:2002-066796.
Audience: **l,u.**

Schiff, Stacy **PS3568.O243**
Vera: Mrs. Vladimir Nabokov. Trade Paper. Random House Adult Trade Publishing Group. New York, NY. 2000. 480p. Modern Library Ser. ISBN:0-375-75534-9, ISBN13: 978-0-375-75534-7. Dewey:813/.54 B. LCCN:99-042413.
Audience: **g,l,u,f.**

20th Century (1901-1960) > N > Nemerov, Howard

Nemerov, Howard **PS3566.L27**
The Collected Poems of Howard Nemerov. Trade Paper. University of Chicago Press. Chicago, IL. 1981. 534p. ISBN:0-226-57259-5, ISBN13: 978-0-226-57259-8. Dewey:811/.54. LCCN:77-000544.
Audience: **g,l,u,f.**

Nemerov, Howard **PS3527.E5H6 1992**
The Homecoming Game: A Novel. Trade Paper. University of Missouri Press. Columbia, MO. 1992. 264p. ISBN:0-8262-0870-3, ISBN13: 978-0-8262-0870-5. Dewey:813.54. LCCN:92-015687.
Audience: **g,l,u,f.**

Nemerov, Howard **PS3527.E5.A6 1991**
A Howard Nemerov Reader. Trade Cloth. University of Missouri Press. Columbia, MO. 1991. 552p. ISBN:0-8262-0776-6, ISBN13: 978-0-8262-0776-0. Dewey:817/.54. LCCN:90-020174.
Audience: **g,l,u,f.**

Nemerov, Howard **PS3527.ES S8 1971B**
Stories, Fables and Other Diversions. Trade Cloth. David R. Godine Publisher. Boston, MA. 1971. ISBN:0-87923-030-4, ISBN13: 978-0-87923-030-2. Dewey:813/.54. LCCN:75-143388.
Audience: **g,l,u,f.**

20th Century (1901-1960) > N > Nin, Anais

Bair, Deirdre **PS3511.A86**
Anais Nin: A Biography. Trade Paper. Penguin Group (USA) Inc. New York, NY. 1996. 672p. ISBN:0-14-025525-7, ISBN13: 978-0-14-025525-6. Dewey:813.5/2.
Audience: **g,l,u,f.** *Choice, 1995.*

Evans, Oliver **PS3527.I865**
Anais Nin. H. T. Moore (Preface by). Trade Cloth. Southern Illinois University Press. Carbondale, IL. 1968. 239p. Crosscurrents-Modern Critiques Ser. ISBN:0-8093-0285-3, ISBN13: 978-0-8093-0285-7. Dewey:813/.5/2. LCCN:67-011703.
Audience: **u,f.**

Jason, Philip K. (Editor) **PS3527**
The Critical Response to Anais Nin. Cloth Text. Greenwood Publishing Group, Inc. Portsmouth, NH. 1996. 296p. Critical Responses in Arts and Letters Ser., Vol. 23 ISBN:0-313-29626-X, ISBN13: 978-0-313-29626-0. Dewey:818/.5209. LCCN:96-006344.
Audience: **l,u.** *Choice, 1997.*

Nalbantian, Suzanne **PS3527.I865Z54 1997**
Anais Nin: Literary Perspectives. Trade Cloth. Palgrave Macmillan. New York, NY. 1997. 301p. ISBN:0-312-16523-4, ISBN13: 978-0-312-16523-9. Dewey:813.5/2. LCCN:96-003084.
Audience: **u,f.**

Nin, Anais **PS3527.I865D42 2004**
Delta of Venus. Trade Paper. Harcourt Trade Publishers. New York, NY. 2004. 320p. ISBN:0-15-602903-0, ISBN13: 978-0-15-602903-2. Dewey:813/.52. LCCN:2003-047835.
Audience: **g,l,u,f.**

Nin, Anais **PS3527.I865**
Winter of Artifice. Trade Paper. Swallow Press. Athens, OH. 1961. 130p. ISBN:0-8040-0322-X, ISBN13: 978-0-8040-0322-3. Dewey:813.52. LCCN:61-017530.
Audience: **g,l,u,f.**

Nin, Anais **PS3527.I865C57 1991**
Cities of the Interior. Sharon Spencer (Introduction by). Trade Paper. Swallow Press. Athens, OH. 1975. 609p. ISBN:0-8040-0666-0, ISBN13: 978-0-8040-0666-8. Dewey:813/.52. LCCN:91-014523.
Audience: **g,l,u,f.**

Nin, Anais **PS3527.I865U6 1995**
Under a Glass Bell. Gunther Stuhlmann (Foreword by). Trade Paper. Swallow Press. Athens, OH. 1995. 101p. ISBN:0-8040-0302-5, ISBN13: 978-0-8040-0302-5. Dewey:813.5/2. LCCN:94-032163.
Audience: **g,l,u,f.**

Nin, Anais **PS3527.I865H6 1989**
House of Incest. Val Telberg (Photographer). Trade Paper. Swallow Press. Athens, OH. 1958. 72p. ISBN:0-8040-0148-0, ISBN13: 978-0-8040-0148-9. Dewey:811/.54. LCCN:61-065487.
Audience: **g,l,u,f.**

Richard-Allerdyce, Diane **PS3527.I865Z86 1998**
Anais Nin and the Remaking of Self: Gender, Modernism, and Narrative Identity. Library Binding. Northern Illinois University Press. DeKalb, IL. 1997. 256p. ISBN:0-87580-232-X, ISBN13: 978-0-87580-232-9. Dewey:818/.5209. LCCN:97-014215.
Audience: **u,f.** *Choice, 1998.*

20th Century (1901-1960) > O

O'Hara, Frank **PS3529.H28.A6 1996**
Poems Retrieved. Ed. 2. Donald Allen (Editor). Trade Paper. Grey Fox Press. San Francisco, CA. 1996. 272p. ISBN:0-912516-19-4, ISBN13: 978-0-912516-19-6. Dewey:811/.54. LCCN:77-000554.
Audience: **g,l,u,f.**

O'Hara, Frank **PS3529.H28A17 1995**
The Collected Poems of Frank O'Hara. Allen Donald (Editor), John Ashbery (Introduction by). Trade Paper. University of California Press. Berkeley, CA. 1995. 620p. ISBN:0-520-20166-3, ISBN13: 978-0-520-20166-8. Dewey:811/.54. LCCN:94-024660.
Audience: **g,l,u,f.**

Oppen, George **PS3529.P54 1975**
The Collected Poems of George Oppen. Trade Cloth. New Directions Publishing Corporation. New York, NY. 1975. 263 p. ;p. ISBN:0-8112-0583-5, ISBN13: 978-0-8112-0583-2. Dewey:811/.5/2. LCCN:75-006965.
Audience: **g,l,u,f.** B

Perloff, Marjorie **PS3529.H28Z8 1998**
Frank O'Hara: Poet among Painters. Trade Paper. University of Chicago Press. Chicago, IL. 1998. 270p. ISBN:0-226-66059-1, ISBN13: 978-0-226-66059-2. Dewey:811/.54. LCCN:97-036184.
Audience: **g,l,u,f.**

Thackrcy, Susan **E162.A3**
George Oppen: A Radical Practice. Trade Paper. O Books. Oakland, CA. 2001. 82p. ISBN:1-882022-41-6, ISBN13: 978-1-882022-41-0. Dewey:973.2.
Audience: **l,u,f.**

Whitaker, Rick **PS153.G38W47 2003**
The First Time I Met Frank O'Hara: Reading Gay American Writers. Trade Cloth, Pictures or Photographs. Avalon Publishing Group. New York, NY. 2003. 208p. ISBN:1-56858-272-2, ISBN13: 978-1-56858-272-6. Dewey:810.9/920664. LCCN:2003-060172.
Audience: **g,l,u,f.** *Choice, 2004.*

20th Century (1901-1960) > O > O'Connor, Flannery

Di Renzo, Anthony **PS3565.C57Z646 1995**
American Gargoyles: Flannery O'Connor and the Medieval Grotesque. Trade Cloth. Southern Illinois University Press. Carbondale, IL. 1995. 269p. ISBN:0-8093-2030-4, ISBN13: 978-0-8093-2030-1. Dewey:813.5/4. LCCN:95-011478.
Audience: **u,f.** *Choice, 1994.*

Giannone, Richard **PS3565.C57Z6794 2000**
Flannery O'Connor, Hermit Novelist -- Richard Giannone. Trade Cloth. University of Illinois Press. Champaign, IL. 2000. 304p. ISBN:0-252-02528-8, ISBN13: 978-0-252-02528-0. Dewey:813/.54. LCCN:99-006653.
Audience: **l,u.** *Choice, 2000.*

Giannowe, Richard **PS3565.C57Z679 1999**
Flannery O'Connor and the Mystery of Love. Trade Cloth. Fordham University Press. Bronx, NY. 1999. 268p. ISBN:0-8232-1910-0, ISBN13: 978-0-8232-1910-0. Dewey:813/.54. LCCN:99-011718.
Audience: **u,f.** *Choice, 2000.*

O'Connor, Flannery **PS3565.C57 A6**
Mystery and Manners: Occasional Prose. Robert Fitzgerald & Sally Fitzgerald (Editors). Trade Paper. Farrar, Straus & Giroux. New York, NY. 1969. 256p. ISBN:0-374-50804-6, ISBN13: 978-0-374-50804-3. Dewey:818/.5/408. LCCN:69-015409.
Audience: **u,f.**

O'Connor, Flannery **PS3565.C57 1988**
O'Connor: Collected Works: Wise Blood; a Good Man Is Hard to Find; the Violent Bear It Away; Everything That Rises Must Converge; Essays and Letters. Sally Fitzgerald (Editor). Trade Cloth. Library of America, The. New York, NY. 1988. 1300p. Library of America, Vol. 39 ISBN:0-940450-37-2, ISBN13: 978-0-940450-37-0. Dewey:813/.54. LCCN:87-037829.
Audience: **g,l,u,f.** *Choice, 1989.*

20th Century (1901-1960) > O > O'Hara, John

Bruccoli, Matthew J. (Editor)
John O'Hara's Hollywood: Stories. Trade Paper. Avalon Publishing Group. New York, NY. 2003. 208p. ISBN:0-7867-1194-9, ISBN13: 978-0-7867-1194-9.
Audience: **g,l,u,f.**

Bruccoli, Matthew J. **PS3529.H29Z59 1995**
The O'Hara Concern: A Biography of John O'Hara. Trade Paper. University of Pittsburgh Press. Pittsburgh, PA. 1995. 488p. ISBN:0-8229-5559-8, ISBN13: 978-0-8229-5559-7. Dewey:813/.54. LCCN:95-010698.
Audience: **g,l,u,f.** B

Eppard, Philip B. (Editor) **PS3529.H29Z63 1994**
Critical Essays on John O'Hara. Trade Cloth. Thomson Gale. Farmington Hills, MI. 1994. 280p. Critical Essays on American Literature Ser. ISBN:0-7838-0026-6, ISBN13: 978-0-7838-0026-4. Dewey:813/.54. LCCN:94-006642.
Audience: **l,u.**

Goldleaf, Steven **PS3529.H29Z69 1999**
John O'Hara: A Study of the Short Fiction. Trade Cloth. Thomson Gale. Farmington Hills, MI. 1999. xviii, 191p. Twayne's Studies in Short Fiction, Vol. 76 ISBN:0-8057-1680-7, ISBN13: 978-0-8057-1680-1. Dewey:813/.54. LCCN:98-049014.
Audience: **l,u.** *Choice, 1999.*

O'Hara, John **PS3511.A86**
Appointment in Samarra. Library Binding. Sagebrush Education Resources. Caledonia, MN. 2003. ISBN:0-613-68488-5, ISBN13: 978-0-613-68488-0. Dewey:813.5/2.
Audience: **g,l,u,f.** B

O'Hara, John **PS3511.A86**
From the Terrace. Ed. 2. Trade Paper. Avalon Publishing Group. New York, NY. 1999. 897p. ISBN:0-7867-0682-1, ISBN13: 978-0-7867-0682-2. Dewey:813.5/2.
Audience: **g,l,u,f.**

O'Hara, John **PS3529.H29.G6**
Good Samaritan and Other Stories. Trade Cloth. Random House, Inc. New York, NY. 1974. ix, 296p. ISBN:0-394-49070-3, ISBN13: 978-0-394-49070-0. Dewey:813/.5/2. LCCN:74-001483.
Audience: **g,l,u,f.**

O'Hara, John **PS3529.H29P34 1983**
Pal Joey. Trade Paper. Knopf Publishing Group. New York, NY. 1983. 224p. ISBN:0-394-71188-2, ISBN13: 978-0-394-71188-1. Dewey:813.52. LCCN:82-040417.
Audience: **g,l,u,f.**

O'Hara, John **PS3529.H29**
Ten North Frederick. Mass Market. Avalon Publishing Group. New York, NY. 1985. 408p. ISBN:0-88184-173-0, ISBN13: 978-0-88184-173-2. Dewey:813.5.
Audience: **g,l,u,f.**

O'Hara, John **PS3529.H29A6 2003**
Selected Short Stories of John O'Hara. Louis Begley (Introduction by). Trade Paper. Random House Adult Trade Publishing Group. New York, NY. 2003. 256p. ISBN:0-8129-6697-X, ISBN13: 978-0-8129-6697-8. Dewey:813/.52. LCCN:2002-026423.
Audience: **g,l,u,f.**

O'Hara, John **PS3529**
Butterfield 8. Fran Lebowitz (Introduction by). Trade Paper. Random House Adult Trade Publishing Group. New York, NY. 2003. 320p. The Modern Library Classics ISBN:0-8129-6698-8, ISBN13: 978-0-8129-6698-5. Dewey:813/.54. LCCN:94-068391.
Audience: **g,l,u,f.**

Wolff, Geoffrey **PS3529.H29Z93 2003**
The Art of Burning Bridges: A Life of John O'Hara. Trade Cloth. Alfred A. Knopf Inc. New York, NY. 2003. 400p. ISBN:0-679-42771-6, ISBN13: 978-0-679-42771-1. Dewey:813/.52 B. LCCN:2002-043095.
Audience: **l,u,f.** *Choice, 2004.*

20th Century (1901-1960) > O > O'Neill, Eugene

Alexander, Doris **PS3529.N5Z5555 2005**
Eugene O'Neill's Last Plays: Separating Art from Autobiography. Trade Cloth. University of Georgia Press. Athens, GA. 2005. 264p. ISBN:0-8203-2709-3, ISBN13: 978-0-8203-2709-9. Dewey:812/.52. LCCN:2004-026982.
Audience: **u,f.** *Choice, 2005.*

Black, Stephen A. **PS3529.N5Z5676 1999**
Eugene O'Neill: Beyond Mourning and Tragedy. Cloth over Boards. Yale University Press. Cumberland, RI. 1999. 568p. ISBN:0-300-07676-2, ISBN13: 978-0-300-07676-9. Dewey:812/.52 B. LCCN:99-033897.
Audience: **u,f.** *Choice, 2000.*

Bogard, Travis **PS3529.N5.Z568 1988**
Contour in Time: The Plays of Eugene O'Neill. Trade Cloth. Oxford University Press, Inc. New York, NY. 1988. 528p. ISBN:0-19-505341-9, ISBN13: 978-0-19-505341-8. Dewey:812/.52. LCCN:87-034860.
Audience: **l,u,f.** *Choice, 1988.*

Estrin, Mark W. (Editor) **PS3529.N5Z626 1990**
Conversations with Eugene O'Neill. Trade Cloth. University Press of Mississippi. Jackson, MS. 1990. 272p. Literary Conversations Ser. ISBN:0-87805-447-2, ISBN13: 978-0-87805-447-3. Dewey:812/.52. LCCN:90-038144.
Audience: **l,u.**

Falk, Doris V. **PS3529.N5 Z64 1982**
Eugene O'Neill and the Tragic Tension. Ed. 2. Trade Cloth. Gordian Press, Inc. Staten Island, NY. 1982. 236p. ISBN:0-87752-222-7, ISBN13: 978-0-87752-222-5. Dewey:812/.52. LCCN:81-006739.
Audience: **l,u,f.**

Gallup, Donald C. **PS3529.N5Z6455 1998**
Eugene O'Neill and His Eleven-Play Cycle: A Tale of Possessors Self-Dispossessed. Cloth over Boards. Yale University Press. Cumberland, RI. 1998. 320p. Henry McBride Series in Modernism and Modernity ISBN:0-300-07187-6, ISBN13: 978-0-300-07187-0. Dewey:812/.52. LCCN:97-032718.
Audience: **l,u,f.** *Choice, 1999.*

Houchin, John H. (Editor) **PS3529**
The Critical Response to Eugene O'Neill. Cloth Text. Greenwood Publishing Group, Inc. Portsmouth, NH. 1993. 344p. Critical Responses in Arts and Letters Ser., No. 5 ISBN:0-313-27617-X, ISBN13: 978-0-313-27617-0. Dewey:812.52. LCCN:93-006562.
Audience: **l,u.**

Manheim, Michael (Editor) **PS3529.N5Z575 1998**
The Cambridge Companion to Eugene O'Neill. Cloth Text. Cambridge University Press. New York, NY. 1998. 274p. Companions to Literature Ser. ISBN:0-521-55389-X, ISBN13: 978-0-521-55389-6. Dewey:812/.52. LCCN:97-042228.
Audience: **g,l,u,f.** *Choice, 1999.*

Martine, James J. **PS3529.N5.Z62727**
Critical Essays on Eugene O'Neill. Trade Cloth. Thomson Gale. Farmington Hills, MI. 1984. 224p. Critical Essays on American Literature Ser. ISBN:0-8161-8683-9, ISBN13: 978-0-8161-8683-9. Dewey:812/.52. LCCN:83-026540.
Audience: **l,u.**

O'Neill, Eugene **PS3529.N5A6 1995**
Ten Lost Plays. Trade Paper. Dover Publications, Inc. Mineola, NY. 1995. 320p. ISBN:0-486-28367-4, ISBN13: 978-0-486-28367-8. Dewey:812/.52. LCCN:94-037321.
Audience: **g,l,u,f.**

O'Neill, Eugene **PS3529.N5 1988**
O'Neill Complete Plays, 1913-1920, Vol. 1. Travis Bogard (Editor). Trade Cloth. Library of America, The. New York, NY. 1988. 1100p. ISBN:0-940450-48-8, ISBN13: 978-0-940450-48-6. Dewey:812/.52. LCCN:88-050685.
Audience: **g,l,u,f.** *Choice, 1989.*

O'Neill, Eugene **PS3529.N5 1988**
O'Neill Complete Plays, 1920-1931, Vol. 2. Travis Bogard (Editor). Trade Cloth. Library of America, The. New York, NY. 1988. 1072p. ISBN:0-940450-49-6, ISBN13: 978-0-940450-49-3. Dewey:812/.52. LCCN:88-050685.
Audience: **g,l,u,f.** *Choice, 1989.*

O'Neill, Eugene **PS3529.N5 1988**
O'Neill Complete Plays, 1933-1943, Vol. 3. Travis Bogard (Editor). Trade Cloth. Library of America, The. New York, NY.

1988. 1000p. Library of Congress Classics
ISBN:0-940450-50-X, ISBN13: 978-0-940450-50-9.
Dewey:812/.52. LCCN:88-050685.
Audience: **g,l,u,f.** *Choice, 1989.*

Shaughnessy, Edward L. **PS3529.N5Z79696**
Down the Nights and down the Days: Eugene O'Neill's Catholic Sensibility. Trade Cloth. University of Notre Dame Press. Notre Dame, IN. 2000. 240p. Irish in America Ser. ISBN:0-268-00895-7, ISBN13: 978-0-268-00895-6. Dewey:[B]. LCCN:96-027117.
Audience: **u,f.** *Choice, 1997.*

Sheaffer, Louis **PS3529.N5Z797 2002**
O'Neill: Son and Playwright. Trade Paper. Cooper Square Publishers, Inc. New York, NY. 2002. 568p.
ISBN:0-8154-1243-6, ISBN13: 978-0-8154-1243-4.
Dewey:812.52. LCCN:2002-073617.
Audience: **l,u,f.**

Sheaffer, Louis **PS3529.N5**
O'Neill: Son and Artist. Trade Paper. Cooper Square Publishers, Inc. New York, NY. 2002. 768p. ISBN:0-8154-1244-4, ISBN13: 978-0-8154-1244-1. Dewey:812/.52.
Audience: **l,u,f.**

20th Century (1901-1960) > O > Odets, Clifford

Cantor, Harold **PS3529.D46Z6 2000**
Clifford Odets: Playwright-Poet. Ed. 2. Trade Cloth. Scarecrow Press, Inc. Lanham, MD. 2000. 256p. ISBN:0-8108-3731-5, ISBN13: 978-0-8108-3731-7. Dewey:812/.52. LCCN:99-046820.
Audience: **l,u.** B

Herr, Christopher J. **PS3529**
Clifford Odets and American Political Theatre. Trade Cloth. Greenwood Publishing Group, Inc. Portsmouth, NH. 2003. 200p. Contributions in Drama and Theatre Studies, No. 103
ISBN:0-313-31594-9, ISBN13: 978-0-313-31594-7.
Dewey:812/.52. LCCN:2003-046329.
Audience: **u,f.** *Choice, 2004.*

Miller, Gabriel **PS3529.D46Z65 1991**
Critical Essays on Clifford Odets. Trade Cloth. Macmillan Publishing Company, Inc. Old Tappan, NJ. 1991. 288p. Critical Essays on American Literature Ser. ISBN:0-8161-7300-1, ISBN13: 978-0-8161-7300-6. Dewey:812/.52. LCCN:91-006424.
Audience: **l,u.** *Choice, 1991.*

Odets, Clifford **PS3529.D46B5**
The Big Knife. Trade Paper. Dramatists Play Service, Inc. New York, NY. 1963. ISBN:0-8222-0115-1, ISBN13: 978-0-8222-0115-1. Dewey:811.5.
Audience: **g,l,u,f.** B

Odets, Clifford **PS3529.D46**
The Country Girl. Trade Paper. Dramatists Play Service, Inc. New York, NY. 1953. ISBN:0-8222-0243-3, ISBN13: 978-0-8222-0243-1. Dewey:812.5.
Audience: **g,l,u,f.**

Odets, Clifford **PS3529.D46 A6**
Waiting for Lefty and Other Plays. Library Binding. Sagebrush Education Resources. Caledonia, MN. 1993.
ISBN:0-613-29379-7, ISBN13: 978-0-613-29379-2.
Dewey:812.54.
Audience: **g,l,u,f.**

Weales, Gerald **PS3529.D46 Z9 1985**
Odets the Playwright. Ed. 2. Trade Paper. Heinemann. Portsmouth, NH. 1988. 205p. Modern Theatre Profiles
ISBN:0-413-58020-2, ISBN13: 978-0-413-58020-7.
Dewey:812/.52. LCCN:85-176840.
Audience: **l,u.**

20th Century (1901-1960) > O > Olson, Charles

Fredman, Stephen **PS3529.L655 Z65 1993**
The Grounding of American Poetry: Charles Olson and the Emersonian Tradition. Albert Gelpi & Ross Posnock (Contribution by). Cloth Text. Cambridge University Press. New York, NY. 1993. 184p. Studies in American Literature and Culture, No. 67 ISBN:0-521-44303-2, ISBN13: 978-0-521-44303-6. Dewey:811.009. LCCN:92-040123.
Audience: **u,f.** *Choice, 1994.*

Maud, Ralph **PS3529.L655Z482 1996**
Charles Olson's Reading: A Biography. Trade Cloth. Southern Illinois University Press. Carbondale, IL. 1996. 448p.
ISBN:0-8093-1995-0, ISBN13: 978-0-8093-1995-4.
Dewey:811/.54. LCCN:94-044403.
Audience: **u,f.** *Choice, 1996.*

Olson, Charles **PS3566.L27**
Collected Poems of Charles Olson: Excluding the Maximus Poems. Trade Paper. University of California Press. Berkeley, CA. 1997. 710p. ISBN:0-520-21231-2, ISBN13: 978-0-520-21231-2. Dewey:811/.54.
Audience: **g,l,u,f.**

Olson, Charles **PS3529.L655**
Selected Writings of Charles Olson. Trade Paper. New Directions Publishing Corporation. New York, NY. 1966. 262p.
ISBN:0-8112-0335-2, ISBN13: 978-0-8112-0335-7.
Dewey:818/.5/409.
Audience: **g,l,u,f.** B

Olson, Charles **PS3566.L27**
The Maximus Poems. George F. Butterick (Editor). Trade Paper. University of California Press. Berkeley, CA. 1995. 654p.
ISBN:0-520-05595-0, ISBN13: 978-0-520-05595-7.
Dewey:811/.5/4. LCCN:79-065759.
Audience: **g,l,u,f.** B

20th Century (1901-1960) > P

Busby, Mark & Heaberlin, Dick (Editors) **PS3531.O752Z62 2001**
From Texas to the World and Back: Essays on the Journeys of Katherine Anne Porter. Betsy Coloquitt (Introduction by). Trade

Paper. Texas Christian University Press. Fort Worth, TX. 2001. xiii, 249p. ISBN:0-87565-237-9, ISBN13: 978-0-87565-237-5. Dewey:813/.52 B. LCCN:00-064863.
Audience: **u,f.** *Choice, 2001.*

Ervin, Hazel Arnett & Holladay, Hilary (Editors) **PS3531**
Ann Petry's Short Fiction: Critical Essays. Trade Cloth. Greenwood Publishing Group, Inc. Portsmouth, NH. 2004. 208p. Contributions in Afro-American and African Studies, No. 209 ISBN:0-313-32291-0, ISBN13: 978-0-313-32291-4. Dewey:813/.54. LCCN:2004-000646.
Audience: **l,u,f.** *Choice, 2004.*

Gates, Henry Louis Jr. & Appiah, Anthony (Editors) **PS3568.O243**
Ann Petry: Critical Perspectives Past and Present. Trade Cloth. HarperCollins Publishers. New York, NY. 1994. Literary Ser. ISBN:1-56743-054-6, ISBN13: 978-1-56743-054-7. Dewey:813/.54.
Audience: **l,u,f.**

Givner, Joan **PS3531.O752Z64 1991**
Katherine Anne Porter: A Life. Trade Cloth. University of Georgia Press. Athens, GA. 1991. 616p. ISBN:0-8203-1348-3, ISBN13: 978-0-8203-1348-1. Dewey:813/.54 B. LCCN:90-023496.
Audience: **g,l,u,f.** B

Paredes, Americo **PS3531.A525B48 1990**
Between Two Worlds. Trade Paper. Arte Publico Press. Houston, TX. 1990. 142p. ISBN:1-55885-022-8, ISBN13: 978-1-55885-022-4. Dewey:811/.54. LCCN:90-038832.
Audience: **g,l,u,f.**

Paredes, Americo **PS3531.A525H36 1994**
The Hammon and the Beans and Other Stories. Trade Paper. Arte Publico Press. Houston, TX. 1994. 230p. ISBN:1-55885-071-6, ISBN13: 978-1-55885-071-2. Dewey:813/.54. LCCN:93-045644.
Audience: **g,l,u,f.**

Paredes, Americo **PS3531.A525S54 1998**
The Shadow. Trade Paper. Arte Publico Press. Houston, TX. 1998. 128p. Pioneers of Modern U.S. Hispanic Literature Ser. ISBN:1-55885-230-1, ISBN13: 978-1-55885-230-3. Dewey:813/.54. LCCN:98-010313.
Audience: **g,l,u,f.**

Paredes, Américo **PQ7297.A1**
With His Pistol in His Hand: A Border Ballad and Its Hero. Trade Paper. University of Texas Press. Austin, TX. 1970. 275p. ISBN:0-292-70128-4, ISBN13: 978-0-292-70128-1. Dewey:398.22.
Audience: **g,l,u,f.**

Peterkin, Julia **PS3511.A86**
Black April. Trade Cloth. Norman S. Berg Publisher, Ltd. Atlanta, GA. 1973. 316p. ISBN:0-910220-42-5, ISBN13: 978-0-910220-42-2. Dewey:813/.52. LCCN:27-005080.
Audience: **g,l,u,f.**

Peterkin, Julia Mood **PS3531.E77.C6**
Collected Short Stories of Julia Peterkin. Trade Cloth. University of South Carolina Press. Columbia, SC. 1970. xii, 384p. ISBN:0-87249-184-6, ISBN13: 978-0-87249-184-7. Dewey:813/.5/2. LCCN:70-120576.
Audience: **g,l,u,f.** B

Petry, Ann **PS3531.E933M57 1999**
Miss Muriel and Other Stories. Trade Paper. Houghton Mifflin Company Trade & Reference Division. Boston, MA. 1999. 304p. ISBN:0-618-00709-1, ISBN13: 978-0-618-00709-7. Dewey:813/.54. LCCN:99-035548.
Audience: **g,l,u,f.**

Petry, Ann **PS3531.E933N3 1999**
The Narrows. Trade Paper. Houghton Mifflin Company Trade & Reference Division. Boston, MA. 1999. 464p. ISBN:0-618-00710-5, ISBN13: 978-0-618-00710-3. Dewey:813/.54. LCCN:99-016611.
Audience: **g,l,u,f.**

Petry, Ann **PS3568.O243**
The Street. Trade Paper. Houghton Mifflin Company Trade & Reference Division. Boston, MA. 1998. 448p. ISBN:0-395-90149-9, ISBN13: 978-0-395-90149-6. Dewey:813/.54. LCCN:90-019880.
Audience: **g,l,u,f.** B

Porter, Katherine Anne **PS3531.O752**
The Collected Stories of Katherine Anne Porter. Trade Paper. Harcourt Trade Publishers. New York, NY. 1979. 504p. Harvest Book Ser. ISBN:0-15-618876-7, ISBN13: 978-0-15-618876-0. Dewey:813/.52 19. LCCN:79-010398.
Audience: **g,l,u,f.**

Porter, Katherine Anne **PS3531.O752**
The Old Order: Stories of the South from the Leaning Tower, Pale Horse, Pale Rider and Flowering Judas. Trade Paper. Harcourt Trade Publishers. New York, NY. 1955. 180p. ISBN:0-15-668519-1, ISBN13: 978-0-15-668519-1. Dewey:813.52. LCCN:66-000380.
Audience: **g,l,u,f.**

Porter, Katherine Anne **PS3531.O752P3 1990**
Pale Horse, Pale Rider: Three Short Novels. Cloth over Boards. Harcourt Trade Publishers. New York, NY. 1990. 216p. HBJ Book Ser. ISBN:0-15-170755-3, ISBN13: 978-0-15-170755-3. Dewey:813/.52. LCCN:89-026886.
Audience: **g,l,u,f.**

Porter, Katherine Anne **PZ3.P8315**
Ship of Fools. Trade Cloth. Amereon, Ltd. Mattituck, NY. ISBN:0-8488-1129-1, ISBN13: 978-0-8488-1129-7. Dewey:(Fic).
Audience: **g,l,u,f.**

Porter, Katherine Anne **PS3531.O752A17 1996**
Katherine Anne Porter's Poetry. Darlene H. Unrue (Editor, Introduction by). Trade Cloth. University of South Carolina Press. Columbia, SC. 1996. 224p. ISBN:1-57003-084-7, ISBN13: 978-1-57003-084-0. Dewey:811/.52. LCCN:95-032494.
Audience: **g,l,u,f.**

Purdy, James **PS3531.U426**
Color of Darkness. Trade Cloth. Greenwood Publishing Group, Inc. Portsmouth, NH. 1975. 175p. ISBN:0-8371-7874-6, ISBN13: 978-0-8371-7874-5. Dewey:813/.5/4. LCCN:74-026739.
Audience: **g,l,u,f.**

Purdy, James **PS3531.U426M34 1994**
Malcolm. Trade Paper. Serpent's Tail Ltd. London, 1994. 196p. ISBN:1-85242-368-4, ISBN13: 978-1-85242-368-1. Dewey:813.5/4. LCCN:94-028945.
Audience: **g,l,u,f.**

Stout, Janis P. **PS3531.O752Z815 1995**
Katherine Anne Porter: A Sense of the Times. Trade Cloth. University Press of Virginia. Charlottesville, VA. 1995. 400p. ISBN:0-8139-1568-6, ISBN13: 978-0-8139-1568-5. Dewey:813/.52 B. LCCN:94-042285.
Audience: **u,f.** *Choice, 1995.*

Titus, Mary **PS3531.O752Z826 2005**
The Ambivalent Art of Katherine Anne Porter. Saddle Stitched, Cloth over Boards, Dust Jacket. University of Georgia Press. Athens, GA. 2005. 252p. ISBN:0-8203-2756-5, ISBN13: 978-0-8203-2756-3. Dewey:813/.52. LCCN:2005-017312.
Audience: **l,u,f.** *Choice, 2006.*

Unrue, Darlene H. **PS3531.O752Z54 1997**
Critical Essays on Katherine Anne Porter. Trade Cloth. Thomson Gale. Farmington Hills, MI. 1997. xiii, 280p. Critical Essays on American Literature Ser. ISBN:0-7838-0022-3, ISBN13: 978-0-7838-0022-6. Dewey:813/.52. LCCN:97-004104.
Audience: **u.** *Choice, 1998.*

Unrue, Darlene Harbour **PS3531.O752Z828 2005**
Katherine Anne Porter: The Life of an Artist. Perfect, Paper over Boards, Dust Jacket. University Press of Mississippi. Jackson, MS. 2005. 381p. Willie Morris Books in Memoir and Biography ISBN:1-57806-777-4, ISBN13: 978-1-57806-777-0. Dewey:813/.52 B. LCCN:2005-001791.
Audience: **l,u,f.** *Choice, 2006.*

20th Century (1901-1960) > P > Parker, Dorothy

Meade, Marion **PS3531.A5855Z77 1989**
Dorothy Parker: What Fresh Hell Is This? Trade Paper. Penguin Group (USA) Inc. New York, NY. 1989. 496p. ISBN:0-14-011616-8, ISBN13: 978-0-14-011616-8. Dewey:817/.52. LCCN:88-023782.
Audience: **g,l,u,f.**

Parker, Dorothy **PS3531.A5855A17 1999**
Complete Poems. Trade Paper. Penguin Group (USA) Inc. New York, NY. 1999. 320p. Penguin Twentieth-Century Classics Ser. ISBN:0-14-118022-6, ISBN13: 978-0-14-118022-9. Dewey:811/.52. LCCN:98-047392.
Audience: **g,l,u,f.**

Parker, Dorothy R. **PS3531.A5855A6 2006**
The Portable Dorothy Parker. Ed. 2. Marion Meade (Contribution by). Trade Paper. Penguin Group (USA) Inc. New York, NY. 2006. 640p. Penguin Classics Deluxe Edition Ser. ISBN:0-14-303953-9, ISBN13: 978-0-14-303953-2. Dewey:818/.5209. LCCN:2005-054626.
Audience: **g,l,u,f.**

Parker, Dorothy **PS3531.A5855A6 1995**
Complete Stories. Colleen Breese (Editor), Regina Barreca (Introduction by). Trade Paper. Penguin Group (USA) Inc. New York, NY. 2002. 480p. ISBN:0-14-243721-2, ISBN13: 978-0-14-243721-6. Dewey:813/.52. LCCN:95-015524.
Audience: **g,l,u,f.**

Pettit, Rhonda S. **PS3531.A5855Z624**
The Critical Waltz: Essays on the Work of Dorothy Parker. Trade Cloth. Fairleigh Dickinson University Press. Cranbury, NJ. 2005. 384p. ISBN:0-8386-3968-2, ISBN13: 978-0-8386-3968-9. Dewey:818/.5209. LCCN:2004-019978.
Audience: **u,f.** *Choice, 2006.*

Pettit, Rhonda S. **PS3531.A5855Z83 2000**
A Gendered Collision: Sentimentalism and Modernism in Dorothy Parker's Poetry and Fiction. Trade Cloth. Fairleigh Dickinson University Press. Cranbury, NJ. 2000. 248p. ISBN:0-8386-3818-X, ISBN13: 978-0-8386-3818-7. Dewey:818/.5209. LCCN:99-051766.
Audience: **u,f.** *Choice, 2001.*

20th Century (1901-1960) > P > Patchen, Kenneth

Morgan, Richard G. (Editor) **PS3531.A764 Z73**
Kenneth Patchen: A Collection of Essays. Miriam Patchen (Foreword by). Library Binding. A M S Press, Inc. New York, NY. 1977. 262p. Studies in Modern Literature, No. 2 ISBN:0-404-16005-0, ISBN13: 978-0-404-16005-0. Dewey:811/.5/4. LCCN:77-078319.
Audience: **l,u,f.**

Patchen, Kenneth **PS3531.A764 A6**
Collected Poems of Kenneth Patchen. Trade Paper. New Directions Publishing Corporation. New York, NY. 1969. 512p. ISBN:0-8112-0140-6, ISBN13: 978-0-8112-0140-7. Dewey:811./5/4. LCCN:67-023487.
Audience: **g,l,u,f.** B

Patchen, Kenneth **PS3531.A764.J6 1961**
The Journal of Albion Moonlight. Trade Paper. New Directions Publishing Corporation. New York, NY. 1961. 313p. ISBN:0-8112-0144-9, ISBN13: 978-0-8112-0144-5. Dewey:818.54. LCCN:68-028283.
Audience: **g,l,u,f.** B

Patchen, Kenneth **PS3531.A764M46 1999**
The Memoirs of a Shy Pornographer. Jonathan Williams (Introduction by). Trade Paper. New Directions Publishing Corporation. New York, NY. 1999. 256p. Classics Ser. ISBN:0-8112-1411-7, ISBN13: 978-0-8112-1411-7. Dewey:813/.54. LCCN:98-037235.
Audience: **g,l,u,f.**

Smith, Larry **PS3531.A764Z88 2000**
Kenneth Patchen: Rebel Poet in America. Trade Cloth. Bottom Dog Press. Huron, OH. 2000. 312p. ISBN:0-933087-60-8, ISBN13: 978-0-933087-60-6. Dewey:811/.54 B. LCCN:00-711252.
Audience: **l,u,f.** *Choice, 2000.*

20th Century (1901-1960) > P > Perelman, S. J.

Gale, Steven H. (Editor) **PS3531.E6544Z693**
S. J. Perelman: Critical Essays. Cloth Text. Garland Publishing, Inc. New York, NY. 1991. 336p. Studies in Humor, Vol. 1 ISBN:0-8240-3422-8, ISBN13: 978-0-8240-3422-1. Dewey:818/.5209. LCCN:91-021460.
Audience: **l,u,f.**

Perelman, S. J. **PS3531.E6544A6 2000**
Most of the Most of S. J. Perelman. Trade Paper. Random House Children's Books. New York, NY. 2000. 572p. Modern Library Humor and Wit Ser. ISBN:0-679-64037-1, ISBN13: 978-0-679-64037-0. Dewey:818/.5209. LCCN:99-462419.
Audience: **g,l,u,f.**

Perelman, S. J. **PS3531.E6544W4 1998**
Westward Ha!. Trade Paper. Watson-Guptill Publications, Inc. New York, NY. 1998. 160p. ISBN:1-58080-067-X, ISBN13: 978-1-58080-067-9. Dewey:813/.52. LCCN:98-019493.
Audience: **g,l,u,f.**

Teicholz, Tom (Editor) **PS3531.E6544Z464**
Conversations with S. J. Perelman. Trade Cloth. University Press of Mississippi. Jackson, MS. 1995. 152p. Literary Conversations Ser. ISBN:0-87805-789-7, ISBN13: 978-0-87805-789-4. Dewey:818/.5209. LCCN:94-042526.
Audience: **l,u.**

20th Century (1901-1960) > P > Pound, Ezra

Alexander, Michael **PS3531.O82**
The Poetic Achievement of Ezra Pound. Trade Paper. Edinburgh University Press. Edinburgh, 1998. 256p. ISBN:0-7486-0981-4, ISBN13: 978-0-7486-0981-9. Dewey:811/.52.
Audience: **l,u,f.** B

Barnhisel, Gregory **PS3531.O82Z5454 2005**
James Laughlin, New Directions Press, and the Remaking of Ezra Pound. Trade Cloth. University of Massachusetts Press. Amherst, MA. 2005. 272p. Studies in Print Culture and the History of the Book Ser. ISBN:1-55849-478-2, ISBN13: 978-1-55849-478-7. Dewey:811/.52. LCCN:2004-026482.
Audience: **u,f.** *Choice, 2006.*

Beach, Christopher **PS323.5.B38 1992**
ABC of Influence: Ezra Pound and the Remaking of American Poetic Tradition. Trade Cloth. University of California Press. Berkeley, CA. 1992. 279p. ISBN:0-520-07527-7, ISBN13: 978-0-520-07527-6. Dewey:811/.509. LCCN:91-003972.
Audience: **u,f.** *Choice, 1992.*

Davie, Donald **PS3531.O82**
Ezra Pound. Trade Paper. University of Chicago Press. Chicago, IL. 1993. viii, 134p. ISBN:0-226-13753-8, ISBN13: 978-0-226-13753-7. Dewey:811/.5/2. LCCN:81-021857.
Audience: **u,f.** B

Furia, Philip **PS3531.O82.C2853**
Pound's Cantos Declassified. Trade Cloth. Pennsylvania State University Press. University Park, PA. 1984. 160p. ISBN:0-271-00373-1, ISBN13: 978-0-271-00373-3. Dewey:811/.52. LCCN:83-043227.
Audience: **l,u.** B

H. D. **PS3531.O82.Z595 1979**
End to Torment: A Memoir of Ezra Pound. Trade Cloth. New Directions Publishing Corporation. New York, NY. 1979. xii, 84p. ISBN:0-8112-0719-6, ISBN13: 978-0-8112-0719-5. Dewey:821/.912. LCCN:78-027149.
Audience: **u,f.** B

Heymann, C. David **PS3531.O82**
Ezra Pound: The Last Rower: A Political Profile. Trade Paper. Carol Publishing Group. Secaucus, NJ. 1992. 384p. ISBN:0-8065-1324-1, ISBN13: 978-0-8065-1324-9. Dewey:811/.52.
Audience: **u,f.**

Kearns, George **PS3531.O82.C294**
Guide to Ezra Pound's Selected Cantos. Trade Cloth. Rutgers University Press. Piscataway, NJ. 1980. x, 306p. ISBN:0-8135-0886-X, ISBN13: 978-0-8135-0886-3. Dewey:811/.52. LCCN:80-010306.
Audience: **l,u.** B

Kenner, Hugh **PS3531.O82**
The Pound Era. Trade Cloth. University of California Press. Berkeley, CA. 1973. xiv, 606p. ISBN:0-520-02427-3, ISBN13: 978-0-520-02427-4. Dewey:811.5/2. LCCN:72-138349.
Audience: **g,l,u.** B

Kenner, Hugh **PS3531.O82Z7 1985**
The Poetry of Ezra Pound. James Laughlin (Foreword by). Paper Text. University of Nebraska Press. Lincoln, NE. 1985. 342p. ISBN:0-8032-7756-3, ISBN13: 978-0-8032-7756-4. Dewey:811/.52. LCCN:85-008622.
Audience: **l,u,f.** B

Korg, Jacob **PS3531.O82Z7142 2003**
Winter Love: Ezra Pound and H. D. Trade Cloth. University of Wisconsin Press. Chicago, IL. 2003. xii, 236p. ISBN:0-299-18390-4, ISBN13: 978-0-299-18390-5. Dewey:811/.52. LCCN:2002-010205.
Audience: **u,f.** *Choice, 2004.*

Lan, Feng **PS3531.O82Z7195 2005**
Ezra Pound and Confucianism: Remaking Humanism in the Face of Modernity. Dust Jacket. University of Toronto Press. Toronto, ON. 2005. 270p. ISBN:0-8020-8941-0, ISBN13: 978-0-8020-8941-0. Dewey:811/.52. LCCN:2005-277635.
Audience: **u,f.** *Choice, 2005.*

Lentricchia, Frank **PS310.M57L46 1994**
Modernist Quartet. Cloth Text. Cambridge University Press. New York, NY. 1994. 319p. ISBN:0-521-47004-8, ISBN13: 978-0-521-47004-9. Dewey:811.5209. LCCN:93-050239.
Audience: **u,f.** *Choice, 1995.*

Levy, Alan **PS3531.O82 Z738**
Ezra Pound: Voice of Silence. Trade Cloth. Amereon, Ltd. Mattituck, NY. 160p. ISBN:0-8488-2638-8, ISBN13: 978-0-8488-2638-3. Dewey:811/.52.
Audience: **l,u.**

Makin, Peter **PS3531.O82C28517**
Ezra Pound's Cantos: A Casebook. Trade Cloth. Oxford University Press, Inc. New York, NY. 2006. 320p. Casebooks in Criticism ISBN:0-19-517528-X, ISBN13: 978-0-19-517528-8. Dewey:811/.52. LCCN:2005-022298.
Audience: **l,u.**

McDonald, Gail **PS3531.O82Z752 1993**
Learning to Be Modern: Pound, Eliot and the American University. Cloth Text. Oxford University Press, Inc. New York, NY. 1993. 256p. ISBN:0-19-811980-1, ISBN13: 978-0-19-811980-7. Dewey:807.1173. LCCN:92-020940.
Audience: **u,f.**

Nadel, Ira B. (Editor) **PS3531.O82 Z5517 19**
The Cambridge Companion to Ezra Pound. Cloth Text. Cambridge University Press. New York, NY. 1999. 352p. Companions to Literature Ser. ISBN:0-521-43117-4, ISBN13: 978-0-521-43117-0. Dewey:811/.52. LCCN:98-012923.
Audience: **l,u,f.** *Choice, 1999.*

Nadel, Ira B. **PS3531.O82Z758 2004**
Ezra Pound: A Literary Life. Trade Cloth. Palgrave Macmillan. New York, NY. 2004. 240p. Literary Lives Ser. ISBN:0-333-58256-X, ISBN13: 978-0-333-58256-5. Dewey:811/.52 B. LCCN:2004-041502.
Audience: **g,l,u.** *Choice, 2005.*

Norman, Charles **PS3531.O82**
The Case of Ezra Pound. William Carlos Williams, Ezra Pound, e e cummings, Louis Zukofsky & Conrad Aiken (Contribution by). Library Binding. Norwood Editions. Norwood, PA. 1986. 71p. ISBN:0-8482-1989-9, ISBN13: 978-0-8482-1989-5. Dewey:811/.5/2 B.
Audience: **l,u.**

Paul, Catherine E. **PS310.M57P38 2002**
Poetry in the Museums of Modernism: Yeats, Pound, Moore, Stein. Trade Cloth. University of Michigan Press. Chicago, IL. 2002. 312p. ISBN:0-472-11264-3, ISBN13: 978-0-472-11264-7. Dewey:811/.5209112. LCCN:2002-002089.
Audience: **u,f.**

Pound, Ezra **PS3531.O82.C24 1972**
The Cantos of Ezra Pound, Nos. 1-117. Trade Cloth. New Directions Publishing Corporation. New York, NY. 1970. 824p. ISBN:0-8112-0350-6, ISBN13: 978-0-8112-0350-0. Dewey:811.5/2. LCCN:70-117217.
Audience: **g,l,u,f.** B

Pound, Ezra **PS3531.O82**
Selected Prose of Ezra Pound, 1909-1965. William Cookson (Editor). Trade Paper. New Directions Publishing Corporation. New York, NY. 1975. 480p. Paperbook Ser. ISBN:0-8112-0574-6, ISBN13: 978-0-8112-0574-0. Dewey:814/.5/2. LCCN:72-093978.
Audience: **g,l,u,f.**

Pound, Ezra **PS3531.O82A6 2003**
Ezra Pound: Poems and Translations. Richard Sieburth (Editor). Trade Cloth. Library of America, The. New York, NY. 2003. 1300p. The Library of America, Vol. 144 ISBN:1-931082-41-3, ISBN13: 978-1-931082-41-9. Dewey:811/.52. LCCN:2003-040142.
Audience: **g,l,u,f.**

Pound, Ezra & Williams, William Carlos **PS3531.O82Z4976 1996**
Selected Letters of Ezra Pound and William Carlos Williams. Hugh Witemeyer (Editor). Trade Cloth. New Directions Publishing Corporation. New York, NY. 1996. 480p. Correspondence of Ezra Pound Ser. ISBN:0-8112-1301-3, ISBN13: 978-0-8112-1301-1. Dewey:811/.52 B. LCCN:95-038462.
Audience: **g,l,u,f.**

Qian, Zhaoming (Editor) **PS3531.O82Z62165**
Ezra Pound and China. Trade Cloth. University of Michigan Press. Chicago, IL. 2003. 296p. ISBN:0-472-09829-2, ISBN13: 978-0-472-09829-3. Dewey:811/.52. LCCN:2003-040230.
Audience: **u,f.** *Choice, 2004.*

Selby, Nick **PS3531.O82C28775**
Poetics of Loss in the Cantos of Ezra Pound: From Modernism to Fascism. Trade Cloth. Edwin Mellen Press, The. Lewiston, NY. 2005. 286p. Studies in British Literature Ser., Vol. 98 ISBN:0-7734-6055-1, ISBN13: 978-0-7734-6055-3. Dewey:811/52. LCCN:2005-049615.
Audience: **u,f.**

Singh, G. **PS3531.O82**
Ezra Pound As Critic. Trade Cloth. Palgrave Macmillan. New York, NY. 1994. 240p. ISBN:0-312-12056-7, ISBN13: 978-0-312-12056-6. Dewey:811/.52. LCCN:93-039872.
Audience: **u,f.** *Choice, 1995.*

Stead, C. K. **PR605.M63S7 1986**
Pound, Yeats, Eliot and the Modernist Movement. Cloth Text. Rutgers University Press. Piscataway, NJ. 1985. 300p. ISBN:0-8135-1075-9, ISBN13: 978-0-8135-1075-0. Dewey:821/.912/09. LCCN:84-029831.
Audience: **u,f.** *Choice, 1986.*

Tryphonopoulos, Demetres P. & Adams, Stephen J. (Editors) **PS3531**
The Ezra Pound Encyclopedia. Cloth Text. Greenwood Publishing Group, Inc. Portsmouth, NH. 2005. 368p. ISBN:0-313-30448-3, ISBN13: 978-0-313-30448-4. Dewey:811/.52 B. LCCN:2004-028176.
Audience: **l,u,f.** *Choice, 2005.*

20th Century (1901-1960) > P > Powell, Dawn

Page, Tim **PS3531.O936Z46 1998**
Dawn Powell: A Biography. Cloth over Boards. Henry Holt & Company. New York, NY. 1998. 362p. ISBN:0-8050-5068-X, ISBN13: 978-0-8050-5068-4. Dewey:813/.52 B. LCCN:98-019907.
Audience: **g,l,u,f.**

Powell, Dawn **PS3531.O936A6 2001**
Dawn Powell: Novels 1930-1942. Tim Page (Editor). Trade Cloth. Library of America, The. New York, NY. 2001. 1068p. The Library of America, Vol. 126 ISBN:1-931082-01-4, ISBN13: 978-1-931082-01-3. Dewey:813/.52. LCCN:00-054595.
Audience: **g,l,u,f.**

Powell, Dawn **PS3531.O936.A6 2001**
Dawn Powell: Novels 1944-1962. Tim Page (Editor). Trade Cloth. Library of America, The. New York, NY. 2001. 969p. The Library of America, Vol. 127 ISBN:1-931082-02-2, ISBN13: 978-1-931082-02-0. Dewey:813/.52. LCCN:00-054596.
Audience: **g,l,u,f.**

Powell, Dawn **PS3531.O936S86 1999**
Sunday, Monday and Always: Stories by Dawn Powell. Tim Page (Introduction by). Trade Paper. Steerforth Press. Hanover, NH. 1999. 220p. ISBN:1-883642-60-4, ISBN13: 978-1-883642-60-0. Dewey:813/.52. LCCN:99-043312.
Audience: **g,l,u,f.**

Rice, Marcelle Smith **PS3531.O936Z86 2000**
Dawn Powell. Trade Cloth. Thomson Gale. Farmington Hills, MI. 2000. xxiii, 181p. United States Authors Ser., Vol. 715 ISBN:0-8057-1602-5, ISBN13: 978-0-8057-1602-3. Dewey:813/.52. LCCN:99-059564.
Audience: **l,u.** *Choice, 2000.*

20th Century (1901-1960) > R

Balakian, Peter **PS3531.O82**
Theodore Roethke's Far Fields: The Evolution of His Poetry. Paper Text. Louisiana State University Press. Baton Rouge, LA. 1989. 192p. ISBN:0-8071-2454-0, ISBN13: 978-0-8071-2454-3. Dewey:811/.52. LCCN:88-029212.
Audience: **u,f.** *Choice, 1989.*

Gale, Robert L. **PS3535.O25Z459 2005**
An Edwin Arlington Robinson Encyclopedia. Trade Cloth. McFarland & Company, Incorporated Publishers. Jefferson, NC. 2006. 279p. ISBN:0-7864-2237-8, ISBN13: 978-0-7864-2237-1. Dewey:811/.52. LCCN:2005-024674.
Audience: **l,u.**

Gladstein, Mimi Reisel **PS3535**
The New Ayn Rand Companion. Ed. 2. Cloth Text. Greenwood Publishing Group, Inc. Portsmouth, NH. 1999. 176p. ISBN:0-313-30321-5, ISBN13: 978-0-313-30321-0. Dewey:813/.52. LCCN:98-050226.
Audience: **l,u.**

Kellman, Steven G. **PS3535.O787Z75 2005**
Redemption: The Life of Henry Roth. Trade Cloth. W. W. Norton & Company, Inc. New York, NY. 2005. 384p. ISBN:0-393-05779-8, ISBN13: 978-0-393-05779-9. Dewey:813/.52 B. LCCN:2005-011979.
Audience: **g,l,u,f.** *Choice, 2006.*

Kertesz, Louise **PS3535.U4Z/**
The Poetic Vision of Muriel Rukeyser. Kenneth Rexroth (Introduction by). Cloth Text. Louisiana State University Press. Baton Rouge, LA. 1980. xxii, 416p. ISBN:0-8071-0552-X, ISBN13: 978-0-8071-0552-8. Dewey:811/.5/2. LCCN:79-001131.
Audience: **l,u.** B

Levi, Jan H. **PS3535.U4 A6**
A Muriel Rukeyser Reader. Muriel Rukeyser (Editor). Trade Cloth. W. W. Norton & Company, Inc. New York, NY. 1995. 320p. ISBN:0-393-31323-9, ISBN13: 978-0-393-31323-9. Dewey:811/.52.
Audience: **g,l,u,f.**

Rand, Ayn **PS3511.A86**
Atlas Shrugged: Centennial Edition. Trade Cloth. Penguin Group (USA) Inc. New York, NY. 2005. 1192p. ISBN:0-525-94892-9, ISBN13: 978-0-525-94892-6. Dewey:813/.52.
Audience: **g,l,u,f.**

Rand, Ayn **PS3535.A547**
The Fountainhead: Centennial Edition. Leonard Peikoff (Afterword by). Trade Cloth. Penguin Group (USA) Inc. New York, NY. 2005. 752p. ISBN:0-452-28675-1, ISBN13: 978-0-452-28675-7. Dewey:RAN.
Audience: **g,l,u,f.**

Ransom, John Crowe & Mazer, Ben **PS3535.A635A17 2005**
The Complete Poems of John Crowe Ransom. Trade Cloth. Other Press, LLC. New York, NY. 2006. ISBN:1-59051-138-7, ISBN13: 978-1-59051-138-1. Dewey:811/.52. LCCN:2005-000315.
Audience: **g,l,u,f.**

Rawlings, Marjorie Kinnan **PS3511.A86**
The Yearling. Library Binding. Buccaneer Books, Inc. Cutchogue, NY. 1991. 250p. ISBN:0-89966-841-0, ISBN13: 978-0-89966-841-3. Dewey:813/.52.
Audience: **g,l,u,f.**

Richter, Conrad **PS3535.I429S66**
The Light in the Forest. Trade Cloth. Knopf Publishing Group. New York, NY. 2005. 176p. ISBN:1-4000-4426-X, ISBN13: 978-1-4000-4426-9. Dewey:813.52.
Audience: **g,l,u,f.**

Richter, Conrad **PS3535.I429S4**
The Sea of Grass. Trade Cloth. Amereon, Ltd. Mattituck, NY. 138p. ISBN:0-8488-2590-X, ISBN13: 978-0-8488-2590-4. Dewey:813/.52.
Audience: **g,l,u,f.**

Roberts, Elizabeth Madox **PZ3.R54145**
The Great Meadow. Trade Paper. Kessinger Publishing, LLC. Whitefish, MT. 2005. ISBN:1-4179-1424-6, ISBN13: 978-1-4179-1424-1. Dewey:813.52.
Audience: **g,l,u,f.** B

Roberts, Kenneth **PS3535.O176N6 2001**
Northwest Passage. Trade Paper. Down East Books. Camden, ME. 2001. 712p. ISBN:0-89272-542-7, ISBN13: 978-0-89272-542-7. Dewey:813/.52. LCCN:2001-094852.
Audience: **g,l,u,f.**

Robins, Elizabeth **PS2719.R4 1996**
The Convert. Jane Marcus (Introduction by). Trade Paper. Feminist Press at The City University of New York. New York, NY. 1996. 320p. ISBN:1-55861-162-2, ISBN13: 978-1-55861-162-7. Dewey:823/.9/1. LCCN:96-019635.
Audience: **g,l,u,f.** B

Robinson, Edward Arlington **PS3535.O25A6 1997**
Robinson: Selected Poems. Robert Faggen (Introduction by), Joseph Brodsky (Foreword by). Trade Paper. Penguin Group (USA) Inc. New York, NY. 1997. 288p. Twentieth Century Classics Ser. ISBN:0-14-018988-2, ISBN13: 978-0-14-018988-9. Dewey:811/.52. LCCN:97-013727.
Audience: **g,l,u,f.**

Roethke, Theodore **PS3535.O39A17 1991**
The Collected Poems of Theodore Roethke. Trade Paper. Doubleday Publishing. New York, NY. 1974. 288p. ISBN:0-385-08601-6, ISBN13: 978-0-385-08601-1. Dewey:811/.54. LCCN:65-023785.
Audience: **g,l,u,f.**

Roethke, Theodore **PS3535.O39A6 2005**
Theodore Roethke: Selected Poems. Edward Hirsch (Editor). Trade Cloth. Library of America, The. New York, NY. 2005. 200p. American Poets Project Ser. ISBN:1-931082-78-2, ISBN13: 978-1-931082-78-5. Dewey:811/.54. LCCN:2004-061553.
Audience: **g,l,u,f.**

Roth, Henry **PS3511.A86**
Call It Sleep: A Novel. Library Binding. Buccaneer Books, Inc. Cutchogue, NY. 1995. ISBN:1-56849-634-6, ISBN13: 978-1-56849-634-4. Dewey:813/.52.
Audience: **g,l,u,f.** B

Roth, Henry **PS3535.O787M47 1994**
Mercy of a Rude Stream. Trade Cloth. St. Martin's Press. Gordonville, VA. 1994. 304p. ISBN:0-312-10501-0, ISBN13: 978-0-312-10501-3. Dewey:813.54. LCCN:93-037270.
Audience: **g,l,u,f.**

Rukeyser, Muriel **PS3535.U4A17 2005**
The Collected Poems of Muriel Rukeyser. Janet E. Kaufman, Anne F. Herzog & Jan Heller Levi (Editors). Trade Cloth. University of Pittsburgh Press. Pittsburgh, PA. 2005. 600p. ISBN:0-8229-4247-X, ISBN13: 978-0-8229-4247-4. Dewey:811/.52. LCCN:2005-001790.
Audience: **g,l,u,f.**

Rukeyser, Muriel & Rich, Adrienne **PS3535.U4A6 2004**
Muriel Rukeyser: Selected Poems. Trade Cloth. Library of America, The. New York, NY. 2004. 230p. American Poets Project Ser. ISBN:1-931082-58-8, ISBN13: 978-1-931082-58-7. Dewey:811/.52. LCCN:2003-060484.
Audience: **g,l,u,f.**

Runyon, Damon **PS3511.A86**
Guys and Dolls. Haywood Broun (Introduction by). Library Binding. Amereon, Ltd. Mattituck, NY. ISBN:0-89190-438-7, ISBN13: 978-0-89190-438-0. Dewey:813.5/2.
Audience: **g,l,u,f.** B

Runyon, Damon **PS3535.U52**
Treasury of Damon Runyon. Clark Kinnaird (Editor). Trade Cloth. Random House, Inc. New York, NY. 1978. ISBN:0-394-60444-X, ISBN13: 978-0-394-60444-2. Dewey:817.5. LCCN:58-006363.
Audience: **g,l,u,f.**

Schwarz, Daniel R. **PS3535.U52Z75 2003**
Broadway Boogie Woogie: Damon Runyon and the Making of New York City Culture. Cloth over Boards. Palgrave Macmillan. New York, NY. 2003. 352p. ISBN:0-312-23948-3, ISBN13: 978-0-312-23948-0. Dewey:813/.52. LCCN:2002-074885.
Audience: **l,u,f.** *Choice, 2003.*

Seager, Allan **PS3535.O39Z83 1991**
The Glass House: The Life of Theodore Roethke. Trade Paper. University of Michigan Press. Chicago, IL. 1991. 320p. ISBN:0-472-06454-1, ISBN13: 978-0-472-06454-0. Dewey:811/.54 B. LCCN:91-011016.
Audience: **g,l,u,f.** B

20th Century (1901-1960) > R > Rexroth, Kenneth

Gutierrez, Donald **PS3535.E923Z74 1996**
The Holiness of the Real: The Short Verse of Kenneth Rexroth. Trade Cloth. Fairleigh Dickinson University Press. Cranbury, NJ. 1996. 280p. ISBN:0-8386-3651-9, ISBN13: 978-0-8386-3651-0. Dewey:811/.52. LCCN:96-010461.
Audience: **l,u,f.** *Choice, 1997.*

Hamalian, Linda **PS3535.E923**
A Life of Kenneth Rexroth. Trade Paper. W. W. Norton & Company, Inc. New York, NY. 1992. 464p. ISBN:0-393-30915-0, ISBN13: 978-0-393-30915-7. Dewey:811/.52 B. LCCN:90-038002.
Audience: **g,l,u,f.** *Choice, 1991.*

Rexroth, Kenneth **PS3535.E923.B4**
Beyond the Mountains. Trade Paper. New Directions Publishing Corporation. New York, NY. 1974. 192p. ISBN:0-8112-0552-5, ISBN13: 978-0-8112-0552-8. Dewey:811.52. LCCN:51-009631.
Audience: **g,l,u,f.**

Rexroth, Kenneth **PS3535.E923A95 1991**
An Autobiographical Novel. Linda Hamalian (Editor). Trade Paper. New Directions Publishing Corporation. New York, NY. 1991. 560p. Classics Ser. ISBN:0-8112-1179-7, ISBN13: 978-0-8112-1179-6. Dewey:813/.54. LCCN:91-004785.
Audience: **g,l,u,f.**

Rexroth, Kenneth **PS3535.E923A17 2002**
The Complete Poems of Kenneth Rexroth. Sam Hamill & Bradford Morrow (Editors). Trade Cloth. Copper Canyon Press. Port Townsend, WA. 2002. ISBN:1-55659-164-0, ISBN13: 978-1-55659-164-8. Dewey:811/.52. LCCN:2002-001706.
Audience: **g,l,u,f.**

Rexroth, Kenneth **PS3535.E923W6 1987**
World Outside the Window: The Selected Essays of Kenneth Rexroth. Bradford Morrow (Editor). Trade Cloth. New Directions Publishing Corporation. New York, NY. 1987. 352p. ISBN:0-8112-1024-3, ISBN13: 978-0-8112-1024-9. Dewey:814/.52. LCCN:86-028610.
Audience: **l,u,f.**

20th Century (1901-1960) > R > Rich, Adrienne

PS3535.I233 Z88
Adrienne Rich. Trade Cloth. Thomson Gale. Farmington Hills, MI. 1999. 192p. ISBN:0-8057-1673-4, ISBN13: 978-0-8057-1673-3. Dewey:811/.54.
Audience: **u,f.**

Langdell, Cheri Colby **PS3535**
Adrienne Rich: The Moment of Change. Trade Cloth. Greenwood Publishing Group, Inc. Portsmouth, NH. 2004. 296p. Contributions in Women's Studies ISBN:0-313-31605-8, ISBN13: 978-0-313-31605-0. Dewey:811.54.
Audience: **u,f.** *Choice, 2005.*

Rich, Adrienne **PS3535.I233A6**
Collected Early Poems, 1950-1970. Trade Paper. W. W. Norton & Company, Inc. New York, NY. 1995. 464p. ISBN:0-393-31385-9, ISBN13: 978-0-393-31385-7. Dewey:811.54.
Audience: **g,l,u,f.**

Rich, Adrienne **PS3535.I233.D7**
The Dream of a Common Language: Poems, 1974-1977. Trade Paper. W. W. Norton & Company, Inc. New York, NY. 1993. 88p. ISBN:0-393-31033-7, ISBN13: 978-0-393-31033-7. Dewey:811.54.
Audience: **g,l,u,f.**

Rich, Adrienne **PS3535.I233.A**
The Fact of a Doorframe: selected poems, 1950-2001. Norton. 2002. ISBN:0-393-32395-1, ISBN13: 978-0-393-32395-5.
Audience: **g,l,u,f.**

Rich, Adrienne **PN6162**
On Lies, Secrets and Silence: Selected Prose, 1966-1978. Trade Paper. W. W. Norton & Company, Inc. New York, NY. 1995. 320p. ISBN:0-393-31285-2, ISBN13: 978-0-393-31285-0. Dewey:814.5/4.
Audience: **g,l,u,f.**

Rich, Adrienne Cecile **PS3535.I233.W5**
The Will to Change; Poems 1968-1970. Trade Cloth. Norton. Farnborough, 1971. 67p. ISBN:0-393-04346-0, ISBN13: 978-0-393-04346-4. Dewey:811/.5/4. LCCN:78-146842.
Audience: **g,l,u,f.** B

Rich, Adrienne **PS3535.I233.A6 1975**
Adrienne Rich's Poetry. Barbara Gelpi & Albert J. Gelpi (Editors). Trade Cloth. W. W. Norton & Company, Inc. New York, NY. 1975. 150p. Critical Editions Ser. ISBN:0-393-04399-1, ISBN13: 978-0-393-04399-0. Dewey:811/.5/4. LCCN:75-315494.
Audience: **g,l,u,f.** B

Templeton, Alice **PS3535.I233Z89 1994**
The Dream and the Dialogue: Adrienne Rich's Feminist Poetics. Cloth Text. University of Tennessee Press. Knoxville, TN. 1994. 208p. ISBN:0-87049-859-2, ISBN13: 978-0-87049-859-6. Dewey:811/.54. LCCN:94-028324.
Audience: **u,f.**

20th Century (1901-1960) > S

Andrews, Tom (Editor) **PS3566.L27**
On William Stafford: The Worth of Local Things. Trade Paper. University of Michigan Press. Chicago, IL. 1995. 296p. Under Discussion Ser. ISBN:0-472-08321-X, ISBN13: 978-0-472-08321-3. Dewey:811/.54.
Audience: **l,u,f.**

Barnard-King, Caroline H. **PS3537.E915Z69 1989**
Anne Sexton. Trade Cloth. Thomson Gale. Farmington Hills, MI. 1989. 208p. Twayne's United States Authors Ser., Vol. 548 ISBN:0-8057-7538-2, ISBN13: 978-0-8057-7538-9. Dewey:811./54. LCCN:89-030986.
Audience: **l,u.** *Choice, 1990.*

Middlebrook, Diane W. **PS3537.E915**
Anne Sexton: A Biography. UK-Trade Paper. Knopf Publishing Group. New York, NY. 1992. 528p. ISBN:0-679-74182-8, ISBN13: 978-0-679-74182-4. Dewey:811/.54 B. LCCN:92-050093.
Audience: **g,l,u,f.** *Choice, 1992.*

Niven, Penelope **PS3531.O82**
Carl Sandburg: A Biography. Trade Paper. Eastern National. Fort Washington, PA. 2001. 888p. ISBN:1-888213-66-3, ISBN13: 978-1-888213-66-9. Dewey:811/.52 B.
Audience: **g,l,u,f.** *Choice, 1992.*

Sandburg, Carl **PS3531.O82**
The Complete Poems of Carl Sandburg. Cloth over Boards. Harcourt Trade Publishers. New York, NY. 2003. 832p. ISBN:0-15-100996-1, ISBN13: 978-0-15-100996-1. Dewey:811/.5/2.
Audience: **g,l,u,f.** B

Sandburg, Carl **PS3537.A618R4 1991**
Remembrance Rock. Trade Paper. Harcourt Trade Publishers. New York, NY. 1991. 1088p. ISBN:0-15-676390-7, ISBN13: 978-0-15-676390-5. Dewey:813/.54. LCCN:91-025215.
Audience: **g,l,u,f.** B

Schulberg, Budd **PR6019.O9**
What Makes Sammy Run? Library Binding. Buccaneer Books, Inc. Cutchogue, NY. 1994. ISBN:1-56849-333-9, ISBN13: 978-1-56849-333-6. Dewey:823/.9/1.
Audience: **g,l,u,f.** B

Schulberg, Budd **PR6019.O9**
The Disenchanted. Anthony Burgess (Introduction by). Trade Paper. Penguin Group (USA) Inc. New York, NY. 1987. 408p. ISBN:1-55611-027-8, ISBN13: 978-1-55611-027-6. Dewey:823/.91. LCCN:86-046387.
Audience: **g,l,u,f.**

Settle, Mary Lee **PS3569.E84O2 1996**
O Beulah Land. Trade Paper. University of South Carolina Press. Columbia, SC. 1996. 368p. The Beulah Quintet Ser., Bk. II ISBN:1-57003-115-0, ISBN13: 978-1-57003-115-1. Dewey:813/.54. LCCN:96-002226.
Audience: **g,l,u,f.**

Sexton, Anne **PS3537.E915A17 1981**
The Complete Poems: Anne Sexton. Maxine Kumin (Foreword by). Trade Paper. Houghton Mifflin Company Trade &

Reference Division. Boston, MA. 1999. 628p. ISBN:0-395-95776-1, ISBN13: 978-0-395-95776-9. Dewey:811/.54. LCCN:81-002482.
Audience: **g,l,u,f.** B

Shapiro, Karl Jay **PS3537.H27A6 2003**
Karl Shapiro: Selected Poems. John Updike (Editor). Trade Cloth. Library of America, The. New York, NY. 2003. 197p. American Poets Project Ser., Vol. 3 ISBN:1-931082-34-0, ISBN13: 978-1-931082-34-1. Dewey:811/.52. LCCN:2002-032123.
Audience: **g,l,u,f.**

Sherwood, Robert E. **PS3537.H825A63**
Abe Lincoln in Illinois. Trade Paper. Dramatists Play Service, Inc. New York, NY. 1939. ISBN:0-8222-0001-5, ISBN13: 978-0-8222-0001-7. Dewey:812.008.
Audience: **g,l,u,f.**

Sherwood, Robert E. **PS3537.H825 P4**
The Petrified Forest. Trade Paper. Dramatists Play Service, Inc. New York, NY. 1948. 74p. ISBN:0-8222-0889-X, ISBN13: 978-0-8222-0889-1. Dewey:812.5.
Audience: **g,l,u,f.** B

Shulman, Max **PS3537.H9919**
Barefoot Boy with Cheek. Will Crawford (Illustrator). Trade Cloth. A M S Press, Inc. New York, NY. ISBN:0-404-15296-1, ISBN13: 978-0-404-15296-3. Dewey:813/.5/2. LCCN:76-011506.
Audience: **g,l,u,f.** B

Simon, Neil **PS3545.I5365**
The Collected Plays of Neil Simon, Vol. 3. Trade Cloth. Random House, Inc. New York, NY. 1992. ISBN:0-679-40889-4, ISBN13: 978-0-679-40889-5. Dewey:812/.5/4.
Audience: **g,l,u,f.**

Simon, Neil **PS3545.I5365**
The Collected Plays of Neil Simon, Vol. 2. Trade Paper. HarperCollins Publishers. New York, NY. 1980. ISBN:0-380-51904-6, ISBN13: 978-0-380-51904-0. Dewey:812/.5/4.
Audience: **g,l,u,f.**

Simon, Neil **PS3545.I5365**
The Collected Plays of Neil Simon, Vol. 4. Trade Paper. Simon & Schuster. New York, NY. 1998. 368p. ISBN:0-684-84785-X, ISBN13: 978-0-684-84785-6. Dewey:812/.5/4. LCCN:86-012639.
Audience: **g,l,u,f.**

Simon, Neil **PS3545.I5365**
The Collected Plays of Neil Simon, Vol. 1. Trade Paper. Penguin Group (USA) Inc. New York, NY. 1986. 672p. Collected Plays of Neil Simon Ser., Vol. 1 ISBN:0-452-25870-7, ISBN13: 978-0-452-25870-9. Dewey:812/.5/4. LCCN:86-012639.
Audience: **g,l,u,f.**

Simpson, Louis **PS3537.I75A6 2003**
The Owner of the House: New Collected Poems 1940-2001. Trade Cloth. BOA Editions, Ltd. Rochester, NY. 2003. 416p. American Poets Continuum Ser., No. 78 ISBN:1-929918-38-0, ISBN13: 978-1-929918-38-6. Dewey:811/.54. LCCN:2003-045241.
Audience: **g,l,u,f.**

Simpson, Louis Aston Marantz **PS3537.I75.Z5 1972**
North of Jamaica. Trade Cloth. Harper & Row Ltd. London, 1972. 285p. ISBN:0-06-013887-4, ISBN13: 978-0-06-013887-5. Dewey:811/.5/4. LCCN:72-181647.
Audience: **g,l,u,f.** B

Smith, Betty **PS3537.M2895T7 2002**
A Tree Grows in Brooklyn. Trade Cloth. HarperCollins Publishers. New York, NY. 2001. 512p. ISBN:0-06-000194-1, ISBN13: 978-0-06-000194-0. Dewey:813/.52. LCCN:2001-039509.
Audience: **g,l,u,f.**

Smith, Lillian **PS3511.A86**
Strange Fruit. Library Binding. Buccaneer Books, Inc. Cutchogue, NY. 1994. ISBN:1-56849-420-3, ISBN13: 978-1-56849-420-3. Dewey:813/.52.
Audience: **g,l,u,f.**

Smith, Lillian **PN6161**
The Winner Names the Age: A Collection of Writings. Michelle Cliff (Editor). Trade Paper. W. W. Norton & Company, Inc. New York, NY. 1982. 224p. ISBN:0-393-30044-7, ISBN13: 978-0-393-30044-4. Dewey:814/.5/2.
Audience: **g,l,u,f.** B

Smith, Thorne **PS3511.A86**
Topper. Library Binding. Buccaneer Books, Inc. Cutchogue, NY. 1990. ISBN:0-89968-550-1, ISBN13: 978-0-89968-550-2. Dewey:813/.52.
Audience: **g,l,u,f.**

Snodgrass, W. D. **PS3537.N32 H4 1983**
Heart's Needle. Trade Paper. Alfred A. Knopf Inc. New York, NY. 1983. ISBN:0-394-72220-5, ISBN13: 978-0-394-72220-7. Dewey:811/.54. LCCN:83-048099.
Audience: **g,l,u,f.** B

Snodgrass, W. D. **PS3566.L27**
Selected Poems, 1957-1987. Trade Paper. Soho Press, Inc. New York, NY. 1991. 270p. ISBN:0-939149-61-3, ISBN13: 978-0-939149-61-2. Dewey:811/.54. LCCN:87-009463.
Audience: **g,l,u,f.**

Spencer, Elizabeth **PS3537.P4454S68 2001**
The Southern Woman: New and Selected Fiction. Trade Cloth. Random House Adult Trade Publishing Group. New York, NY. 2001. 480p. ISBN:0-679-64218-8, ISBN13: 978-0-679-64218-3. Dewey:813/.54. LCCN:00-054612.
Audience: **g,l,u,f.**

Spencer, Elizabeth **PS3537.P4454L54 1996**
The Light in the Piazza and Other Italian Tales. Robert Phillips (Introduction by). Trade Cloth. University Press of Mississippi. Jackson, MS. 1995. 304p. A Banner Bk. ISBN:0-87805-836-2, ISBN13: 978-0-87805-836-5. Dewey:813/.54. LCCN:95-039929.
Audience: **g,l,u,f.**

Spillane, Mickey **PS3568.O243**
I, the Jury. Trade Cloth. Simon & Schuster. New York, NY. 1994. 224p. Mike Hammer Ser. ISBN:1-883402-20-4, ISBN13: 978-1-883402-20-4. Dewey:813/.54.
Audience: **g,l,u,f.**

Stafford, William **PS3537.T143.S58 1983**
Smoke's Way: Poems from Limited Editions, 1968-1981. Trade Cloth. Graywolf Press. St. Paul, MN. 1988. 112p. ISBN:0-915308-40-1, ISBN13: 978-0-915308-40-8. Dewey:811/.54. LCCN:83-080525.
Audience: **g,l,u,f.**

Stafford, William **PS3537.T143.S7**
Stories That Could Be True: New and Collected Poems. Trade Cloth. HarperCollins Publishers. New York, NY. 1977. xvii, 267p. ISBN:0-06-013988-9, ISBN13: 978-0-06-013988-9. Dewey:811/.54. LCCN:77-003775.
Audience: **g,l,u,f.**

Stafford, William **PS3537.T143 A6 1993**
The Darkness Around Us Is Deep: Selected Poems of William Stafford. Robert Bly (Editor, Introduction by). Trade Paper. HarperCollins Publishers. New York, NY. 1993. 160p. ISBN:0-06-096916-4, ISBN13: 978-0-06-096916-5. Dewey:811/.54. LCCN:93-020696.
Audience: **g,l,u,f.**

Stewart, George R. **PS3537.T48545S7 2003**
Storm. Ernest Callenbach (Foreword by). Trade Paper. Heyday Books. Berkeley, CA. 2003. 352p. ISBN:1-890771-74-0, ISBN13: 978-1-890771-74-4. Dewey:813/.52. LCCN:2003-015860.
Audience: **g,l,u,f.**

Still, James **PS3537.T5377F76 2001**
From the Mountain, from the Valley: New and Collected Poems. Ted Olson (Editor). Trade Cloth. University Press of Kentucky. Lexington, KY. 2001. 144p. ISBN:0-8131-2199-X, ISBN13: 978-0-8131-2199-4. Dewey:811/.52. LCCN:00-012280.
Audience: **g,l,u,f.**

Still, James **PS3537.T5377W59 1991**
The Wolfpen Notebooks: A Record of Appalachian Life. Eliot Wigginton (Foreword by). Trade Cloth. University Press of Kentucky. Lexington, KY. 1991. 192p. ISBN:0-8131-1741-0, ISBN13: 978-0-8131-1741-6. Dewey:818/.5209. LCCN:90-022978.
Audience: **g,l,u,f.** *Choice, 1992.*

Stout, Rex **PS3537.T733**
And Be a Villain. Maan Meyers (Introduction by). Trade Paper. Bantam Books. New York, NY. 1994. 256p. ISBN:0-553-23931-7, ISBN13: 978-0-553-23931-7. Dewey:813/.52.
Audience: **g,l,u,f.**

Stuart, Jesse (Introduction by) **PS3537.T92516A6 2003**
A Jesse Stuart Reader: Stories and Poems. Trade Paper. Jesse Stuart Foundation, The. Ashland, KY. 2003. xiii, 342p. ISBN:1-931672-24-5, ISBN13: 978-1-931672-24-5. Dewey:818/.5209. LCCN:2004-301216.
Audience: **g,l,u,f.**

Stuart, Jesse H. **PS3537.T92516**
Taps for Private Tussie. Rocky Zornes (Illustrator), James M. Gifford (Introduction by), Chuck D. Charles (Contribution by). Trade Cloth. Jesse Stuart Foundation, The. Ashland, KY. 1992. 255p. ISBN:0-945084-24-2, ISBN13: 978-0-945084-24-2. Dewey:813/.52. LCCN:91-062582.
Audience: **g,l,u,f.**

Suckow, Ruth **PS3511.A86**
Country People. Library Binding. Classic Books. Murrieta, CA. 1999. 213p. The Collected Works of Ruth Suckow ISBN:1-58201-838-3, ISBN13: 978-1-58201-838-6. Dewey:813/.5/2.
Audience: **g,l,u,f.**

Suckow, Ruth **PS3537.U34.I6**
Iowa Interiors. Elizabeth Hardwick (Editor). Library Binding. Ayer Company Publishers, Inc. Manchester, NH. 1977. 283p. Rediscovered Fiction by American Women Ser. ISBN:0-405-10057-4, ISBN13: 978-0-405-10057-4. Dewey:813.52. LCCN:76-051679.
Audience: **g,l,u,f.**

Swenson, May **PS3537.W4786A6 2003**
The Complete Love Poems of May Swenson. Trade Paper. Houghton Mifflin Company Trade & Reference Division. Boston, MA. 2003. 160p. ISBN:0-618-34084-X, ISBN13: 978-0-618-34084-2. Dewey:811/.54. LCCN:2003-047836.
Audience: **g,l,u,f.**

Swenson, May **PS3537.W4786.N4**
New and Selected Things Taking Place: Poems. Trade Cloth. Little Brown & Company. New York, NY. 1978. ix, 301p. ISBN:0-316-82520-4, ISBN13: 978-0-316-82520-7. Dewey:811/.5/4. LCCN:78-016671.
Audience: **g,l,u,f.**

Wagner-Martin, Linda **PS3537.E915Z64 1989**
Critical Essays on Anne Sexton. Trade Cloth. Thomson Gale. Farmington Hills, MI. 1989. 272p. Critical Essays on American Literature Ser. ISBN:0-8161-8891-2, ISBN13: 978-0-8161-8891-8. Dewey:811/.54. LCCN:89-030569.
Audience: **l,u.** *Choice, 1990.*

20th Century (1901-1960) > S > Salinger, J. D.

Alsen, Eberhard **PS3537**
A Reader's Guide to J. D. Salinger. Cloth Text. Greenwood Publishing Group, Inc. Portsmouth, NH. 2002. 288p. ISBN:0-313-31078-5, ISBN13: 978-0-313-31078-2. Dewey:813/.54. LCCN:2002-067919.
Audience: **l,u.** *Choice, 2003.*

French, Warren **PS3537.A426Z614 1988**
J. D. Salinger, Revisited. Trade Cloth. Macmillan Publishing Company, Inc. Old Tappan, NJ. 1988. 152p. Twayne's United States Authors Ser. ISBN:0-8057-7522-6, ISBN13: 978-0-8057-7522-8. Dewey:813/.54. LCCN:88-004851.
Audience: **l,u.**

Hamilton, Ian **PS3568.O243**
In Search of J. D. Salinger. Trade Cloth. Knopf Publishing Group. New York, NY. 1989. ISBN:0-685-25524-7, ISBN13: 978-0-685-25524-7. Dewey:813/.54 B.
Audience: **g,l,u,f.**

Salinger, J. D. **PS3568.O243**
The Catcher in the Rye. Cloth Text. John Wiley & Sons, Inc. Hoboken, NJ. 2000. ISBN:0-8220-7038-3, ISBN13: 978-0-8220-7038-2. Dewey:813.5/4.
Audience: **g,l,u,f.**

Salinger, J. D. **PS3537.A426 F7**
Franny and Zooey. Library Binding. Sagebrush Education Resources. Caledonia, MN. 1991. ISBN:0-8085-1900-X, ISBN13: 978-0-8085-1900-3. Dewey:813.54.
Audience: **g,l,u,f.** B

Salinger, J. D. **PS3537.A426**
Nine Stories. Library Binding. Sagebrush Education Resources. Caledonia, MN. 1991. ISBN:0-613-70749-4, ISBN13: 978-0-613-70749-7. Dewey:813.5.
Audience: **g,l,u,f.** B

Salinger, J. D. **PS3537.A426 R3**
Raise High the Roof Beam, Carpenters, and Seymour: An Introduction. Library Binding. Sagebrush Education Resources. Caledonia, MN. 1991. ISBN:0-613-70753-2, ISBN13: 978-0-613-70753-4. Dewey:813/.54.
Audience: **g,l,u,f.**

Wenke, John **PS3537.A426Z97 1991**
J. D. Salinger: A Study of the Short Fiction. Trade Cloth. Macmillan Publishing Company, Inc. Old Tappan, NJ. 1991. 160p. Twayne's Studies in Short Fiction, No. 25 ISBN:0-8057-8334-2, ISBN13: 978-0-8057-8334-6. Dewey:813/.54. LCCN:91-011574.
Audience: **l,u.**

20th Century (1901-1960) > S > Saroyan, William

Foster, Edward H. **PS3537.A826Z67 1991**
William Saroyan: A Study of Short Fiction. Trade Cloth. Macmillan Publishing Company, Inc. Old Tappan, NJ. 1991. 168p. Twayne's Studies in Short Fiction, No. 26 ISBN:0-8057-8335-0, ISBN13: 978-0-8057-8335-3. Dewey:813/.52. LCCN:91-022003.
Audience: **l,u.**

Keyishian, Harry (Editor) **PS3537.A826Z626 1995**
Critical Essays on William Saroyan. Trade Cloth. Thomson Gale. Farmington Hills, MI. 1995. 192p. Critical Essays on American Literature Ser. ISBN:0-7838-0018-5, ISBN13: 978-0-7838-0018-9. Dewey:818/.5209. LCCN:94-048129.
Audience: **l,u.**

Leggett, John **PS3537.A826Z78 2002**
A Daring Young Man: A Biography of William Saroyan. Trade Cloth. Random House, Inc. New York, NY. 2002. 480p. ISBN:0-375-41301-4, ISBN13: 978-0-375-41301-8. Dewey:818/.5209 B. LCCN:2002-067149.
Audience: **g,l,u,f.** *Choice, 2003.*

Saroyan, William **PS3537.A826B6 1995**
Boys and Girls Together: A Novel. Trade Paper. Barricade Books, Inc. Fort Lee, NJ. 1995. 160p. ISBN:1-56980-047-2, ISBN13: 978-1-56980-047-8. Dewey:813/.52. LCCN:95-021745.
Audience: **g,l,u,f.**

Saroyan, William **PS3537.A826D3 1997**
The Daring Young Man on the Flying Trapeze. Trade Paper. New Directions Publishing Corporation. New York, NY. 1997. 270p. Classics Ser. ISBN:0-8112-1365-X, ISBN13: 978-0-8112-1365-3. Dewey:813/.52. LCCN:97-011718.
Audience: **g,l,u,f.**

Saroyan, William **PS3537.A826A6 2005**
Essential Saroyan. Trade Paper, Perfect. Heyday Books. Berkeley, CA. 2005. 192p. A California Legacy Book Ser. ISBN:1-59714-001-5, ISBN13: 978-1-59714-001-0. Dewey:813/.52. LCCN:2004-028318.
Audience: **g,l,u,f.**

Saroyan, William **PS3537.A826H7 1989**
Human Comedy. Cloth over Boards. Harcourt Trade Publishers. New York, NY. 1989. 256p. HBJ Book Ser. ISBN:0-15-142301-6, ISBN13: 978-0-15-142301-9. Dewey:813./52. LCCN:89-032785.
Audience: **g,l,u,f.**

Saroyan, William **PS3537.A826 T47**
Three Plays: My Heart's in the Highlands, The Time of Your Life, Love's Old Sweet Song. Harcourt, Brace and Company. 1940.
Audience: **g,l,u,f.**

Saroyan, William **PS3537.A826A6 1994**
The William Saroyan Reader. Trade Paper. Barricade Books, Inc. Fort Lee, NJ. 1994. 498p. ISBN:1-56980-019-7, ISBN13: 978-1-56980-019-5. Dewey:818/.5209. LCCN:94-025439.
Audience: **g,l,u,f.**

Saroyan, William **PS3511.A86**
The Man with the Heart in the Highlands and Other Early Stories. Herb Caen (Introduction by). Trade Paper. New Directions Publishing Corporation. New York, NY. 1992. 160p. Classics Ser., Vol. 740 ISBN:0-8112-1205-X, ISBN13: 978-0-8112-1205-2. Dewey:813/.52. LCCN:89-031604.
Audience: **g,l,u,f.**

20th Century (1901-1960) > S > Sarton, May

Evans, Elizabeth **PS3537.A832Z66 1989**
May Sarton, Revisited. Trade Cloth. Thomson Gale. Farmington Hills, MI. 1989. 160p. United States Authors Ser., No. 551 ISBN:0-8057-7542-0, ISBN13: 978-0-8057-7542-6. Dewey:811/.52. LCCN:89-030751.
Audience: **l,u.**

Fulk, Mark **PS3537.A832Z67 2001**
Understanding May Sarton. Trade Cloth. University of South Carolina Press. Columbia, SC. 2001. 160p. Understanding Contemporary American Literature Ser. ISBN:1-57003-422-2, ISBN13: 978-1-57003-422-0. Dewey:811/.52. LCCN:2001-001661.
Audience: **l,u.** *Choice, 2002.*

Ingersoll, Earl G. (Editor) **PS3537.A832Z464 1991**
Conversations with May Sarton. Trade Cloth. University Press of Mississippi. Jackson, MS. 1991. xxiii, 213p. Literary Conversations Ser. ISBN:0-87805-532-0, ISBN13: 978-0-87805-532-6. Dewey:811/.52. LCCN:91-027647.
Audience: **g,l,u.**

Sarton, May **PS3537.A832A17 1993**
The Collected Poems of Sarton, 1930-1993. Trade Cloth. W. W. Norton & Company, Inc. New York, NY. 1993. 576p. ISBN:0-393-03493-3, ISBN13: 978-0-393-03493-6. Dewey:811/.52. LCCN:92-032688.
Audience: **g,l,u,f.**

Sarton, May **PS3537.T323**
I Knew a Phoenix: Sketches for an Autobiography. Trade Cloth. W. W. Norton & Company, Inc. New York, NY. 1996. 300p. ISBN:0-393-31248-8, ISBN13: 978-0-393-31248-5. Dewey:818.5/2/09.
Audience: **g,l,u,f.** B

Sarton, May **PS3511.A86**
Mrs. Stevens Hears the Mermaids Singing. Trade Paper. W. W. Norton & Company, Inc. New York, NY. 1993. 240p. ISBN:0-393-30929-0, ISBN13: 978-0-393-30929-4. Dewey:813.5/2.
Audience: **g,l,u,f.**

Sarton, May **PS3537.A832**
The Small Room. Trade Cloth. W. W. Norton & Company, Inc. New York, NY. 1976. 256p. Norton Library, Vol. N832 ISBN:0-393-00832-0, ISBN13: 978-0-393-00832-6. Dewey:813.5/2. LCCN:76-025230.
Audience: **g,l,u,f.**

Sarton, May **PS3531.O82**
May Sarton: A Self Portrait. Marita Simpson & Martha Wheelock (Editors). Trade Paper. W. W. Norton & Company, Inc. New York, NY. 1988. 82p. ISBN:0-393-30535-X, ISBN13: 978-0-393-30535-7. Dewey:811/.52 B.
Audience: **g,l,u,f.**

20th Century (1901-1960) > S > Schwartz, Delmore

Atlas, James **PS3537.C79Z56 1985**
Delmore Schwartz: The Life of an American Poet. Trade Paper. Harcourt Trade Publishers. New York, NY. 1985. 432p. ISBN:0-15-625272-4, ISBN13: 978-0-15-625272-0. Dewey:811/.52 B. LCCN:85-005501.
Audience: **g,l,u,f.** B

Ford, Edward **PS3537.C79Z67 2005**
A Reevaluation of the Works of American Writer Delmore Schwartz, 1913-1966. Trade Cloth. Edwin Mellen Press, The. Lewiston, NY. 2005. iii, 168p. Studies in American Literature Ser. ISBN:0-7734-6150-7, ISBN13: 978-0-7734-6150-5. Dewey:811/.52. LCCN:2005-047903.
Audience: **u,f.**

McDougall, Richard **PS3537.C79.Z77**
Delmore Schwartz. Trade Cloth. Thomson Gale. Farmington Hills, MI. 1974. 156p. ISBN:0-8057-0657-7, ISBN13: 978-0-8057-0657-4. Dewey:818/.5/209. LCCN:73-017285.
Audience: **l,u.** B

Schwartz, Delmore **PZ3.S405 Wo PS3537.C79**
The World Is a Wedding. New Directions. 1948.
Audience: **g,l,u,f.**

Schwartz, Delmore **PS3537.C79A6 2004**
Screeno: Stories and Poems. Cynthia Ozick (Introduction by). Trade Paper. New Directions Publishing Corporation. New York, NY. 2004. 128p. ISBN:0-8112-1573-3, ISBN13: 978-0-8112-1573-2. Dewey:818/.52. LCCN:2004-004050.
Audience: **g,l,u,f.**

Schwartz, Delmore **PS3537.C79A6 1989**
Last and Lost Poems. Robert Phillips (Introduction by). Trade Paper. New Directions Publishing Corporation. New York, NY. 1989. 192p. Paperbook Ser., Vol. 673 ISBN:0-8112-1096-0, ISBN13: 978-0-8112-1096-6. Dewey:811/.52. LCCN:88-031396.
Audience: **g,l,u,f.**

20th Century (1901-1960) > S > Sinclair, Upton

Dell, Floyd **PS3537.I85 Z6**
Upton Sinclair A Study in Social Protest. Trade Paper. Kessinger Publishing, LLC. Whitefish, MT. 2005. ISBN:1-4179-0589-1, ISBN13: 978-1-4179-0589-8. Dewey:813/.5/2.
Audience: **l,u.** B

Scott, Ivan **PS3537.I85Z87 1997**
Upton Sinclair, the Forgotten Socialist. Trade Cloth. Edwin Mellen Press, The. Lewiston, NY. 1997. 412p. Studies in American Literature Ser., Vol. 23 ISBN:0-7734-8679-8, ISBN13: 978-0-7734-8679-9. Dewey:813/.52. LCCN:97-002194.
Audience: **l,u.**

Sinclair, Upton **PS3511.A86**
American Outpost: A Book of Reminiscences. Library Binding. Reprint Services Company. Temecula, CA. 1992. ISBN:0-7812-5088-9, ISBN13: 978-0-7812-5088-7. Dewey:813/.5/2.
Audience: **g,l,u,f.** B

Sinclair, Upton **PS3537.I85 Z517**
Autobiography. Harcourt, Brace & World. 1962.
Audience: **g,l,u,f.**

Sinclair, Upton **PS3537.I85**
Dragon's Teeth I. Trade Paper. Simon Publications, Inc. 2001. 324p. World's End Ser., Vol. 5 ISBN:1-931313-03-2, ISBN13: 978-1-931313-03-2. Dewey:813.52. LCCN:67-058718.
Audience: **g,l,u,f.**

Sinclair, Upton **PS3537.I85 Z54**
My Lifetime in Letters. Trade Cloth. University of Missouri Press. Columbia, MO. 1960. ISBN:0-8262-0002-8, ISBN13: 978-0-8262-0002-0. Dewey:928.1. LCCN:59-014141.
Audience: **g,l,u,f.** B

Sinclair, Upton **PS3537.I85**
Plays of Protest: The Naturewoman, the Machine, the Second-Story Man, Prince Hagen. Trade Paper. University Press of the Pacific. Miami, FL. 2004. 240p. ISBN:1-4102-1301-3, ISBN13: 978-1-4102-1301-3. Dewey:812/.5/2.
Audience: **g,l,u,f.**

Sinclair, Upton **PS3537.I85J85 2006**
The Jungle. Ronald Gottesman & Eric Schlosser (Introduction by). Trade Paper. Penguin Group (USA) Inc. New York, NY. 2006. 464p. Penguin Classics Deluxe Edition Ser. ISBN:0-14-303958-X, ISBN13: 978-0-14-303958-7. Dewey:813/.52. LCCN:2006-043248.
Audience: **g,l,u,f.**

20th Century (1901-1960) > S > Singer, Isaac Bashevis

Alexander, Edward **PJ5129.S49Z575 1990**
Isaac Bashevis Singer: A Study of the Short Fiction. Trade Cloth. Macmillan Publishing Company, Inc. Old Tappan, NJ. 1990. xv, 147 p. :p. Twayne's Studies in Short Fiction, No. 18 ISBN:0-8057-8329-6, ISBN13: 978-0-8057-8329-2. Dewey:839/.0933. LCCN:90-037724.
Audience: **l,u.** *Choice, 1991.*

Farrell Lee, Grace **PJ5129.S49 Z65 1987**
From Exile to Redemption: The Fiction of Isaac Bashevis Singer. Trade Cloth. Southern Illinois University Press. Carbondale, IL. 1987. 160p. ISBN:0-8093-1330-8, ISBN13: 978-0-8093-1330-3. Dewey:839/.0933. LCCN:86-020302.
Audience: **u,f.** *Choice, 1987.*

Farrell, Brace **PJ5129.S49Z63 1996**
Critical Essays on Isaac Bashevis Singer. Trade Cloth. Thomson Gale. Farmington Hills, MI. 1996. 227p. Critical Essays on American Literature Ser. ISBN:0-7838-0028-2, ISBN13: 978-0-7838-0028-8. Dewey:839/.0933. LCCN:95-023576.
Audience: **l,u.**

Hadda, Janet **PJ5129.S49Z695 2003**
Isaac Bashevis Singer: A Life. Trade Paper. University of Wisconsin Press. Chicago, IL. 2003. 272p. ISBN:0-299-18694-6, ISBN13: 978-0-299-18694-4. Dewey:839/.133 B. LCCN:2004-557589.
Audience: **g,l,u,f.** *Choice, 1997.*

Singer, Isaac Bashevis **PJ5129.S49A2 2004**
Isaac Bashevis Singer: Collected Stories. Ilan Stavans (Editor). Trade Cloth. Library of America, The. New York, NY. 2004. 915p. Library of America, Vol. 151 ISBN:1-931082-63-4, ISBN13: 978-1-931082-63-1. Dewey:839/.133. LCCN:2003-066081.
Audience: **g,l,u,f.**

Singer, Isaac Bashevis **PJ5129.S49A273 2004**
Isaac Bashevis Singer: Collected Stories. Ilan Stavans (Editor). Trade Cloth. Library of America, The. New York, NY. 2004. 832p. Library of America, Vol. 149 ISBN:1-931082-61-8, ISBN13: 978-1-931082-61-7. Dewey:839/.133. LCCN:2003-066055.
Audience: **g,l,u,f.**

Singer, Isaac Bashevis **PJ5129.S49A27 2004**
Isaac Bashevis Singer: Collected Stories. Ilan Stavans (Editor). Trade Cloth. Library of America, The. New York, NY. 2004. 800p. Library of America, Vol. 150 ISBN:1-931082-62-6, ISBN13: 978-1-931082-62-4. Dewey:839/.133. LCCN:2003-066057.
Audience: **g,l,u,f.**

20th Century (1901-1960) > S > Stafford, Jean

Austenfeld, Thomas C. **PS159.G3A94 2001**
American Women Writers and the Nazis: Ethics and Politics in Boyle, Porter, Stafford and Hellman. Trade Cloth. University Press of Virginia. Charlottesville, VA. 2001. viii, 189p. ISBN:0-8139-2052-3, ISBN13: 978-0-8139-2052-8. Dewey:810.9/9287/0904. LCCN:00-068660.
Audience: **u,f.** *Choice, 2002.*

Hulbert, Ann **PS3568.O243**
The Interior Castle: The Art and Life of Jean Stafford. Trade Paper. University of Massachusetts Press. Amherst, MA. 1993. 448p. ISBN:0-87023-870-1, ISBN13: 978-0-87023-870-3. Dewey:813/.54 B. LCCN:93-022870.
Audience: **u,f.**

Roberts, David **PS3569.T2Z83**
Jean Stafford: Life of a Writer. Trade Paper. St. Martin's Press. Gordonville, VA. 2003. 524p. ISBN:0-312-30217-7, ISBN13: 978-0-312-30217-7. Dewey:813/.54.
Audience: **g,l,u,f.**

Stafford, J. **PS3511.A86**
Mountain Lion. Trade Paper. Random House. London, 1988. 231p. ISBN:0-7012-0711-6, ISBN13: 978-0-7012-0711-3. Dewey:813/.52.
Audience: **g,l,u,f.**

Stafford, Jean **PS3511.A86**
Boston Adventure. Trade Paper. Harcourt Trade Publishers. New York, NY. 1984. 552p. ISBN:0-15-613611-2, ISBN13: 978-0-15-613611-2. Dewey:813/.52. LCCN:44-040176.
Audience: **g,l,u,f.** B

Stafford, Jean **PS3569.T2 C3 1981**
The Catherine Wheel. Trade Paper. HarperCollins Publishers. New York, NY. 1981. 283p. Neglected Books of the 20th Century Ser. ISBN:0-912946-87-3, ISBN13: 978-0-912946-87-0. Dewey:813/.54. LCCN:81-002065.
Audience: **g,l,u,f.**

Stafford, Jean **PS3569.T2A6 2005**
The Collected Stories of Jean Stafford. Trade Paper. Farrar, Straus & Giroux. New York, NY. 2005. 528p. ISBN:0-374-52993-0, ISBN13: 978-0-374-52993-2. Dewey:813/.54. LCCN:2005-047705.
Audience: **g,l,u,f.** B

Wilson, Mary A. **PS3569.T2Z93 1996**
Jean Stafford: A Study of the Short Fiction. Trade Cloth. Thomson Gale. Farmington Hills, MI. 1995. 176p. Twayne's Studies in Short Fiction, No. 62 ISBN:0-8057-7807-1, ISBN13: 978-0-8057-7807-6. Dewey:813/.54. LCCN:95-023493.
Audience: **l,u.** *Choice, 1996.*

20th Century (1901-1960) > S > Stegner, Wallace

Benson, Jackson J. **PS3537.T316Z58 2001**
Down by the Lemonade Springs: Essays on Wallace Stegner. Trade Paper. University of Nevada Press. Reno, NV. 2001. 256p. Western Literature Ser., : ISBN:0-87417-446-5, ISBN13: 978-0-87417-446-5. Dewey:813/.52. LCCN:2001-001408.
Audience: **u,f.**

Benson, Jackson J. **PS3511.A86**
Wallace Stegner: A Biography. Trade Paper. Penguin Group (USA) Inc. New York, NY. 1997. 496p. ISBN:0-14-024796-3, ISBN13: 978-0-14-024796-1. Dewey:813/.52 B.
Audience: **g,l,u,f.**

Benson, Jackson J. **PS3537.T316Z59 1998**
Wallace Stegner: A Study of the Short Fiction. Trade Cloth. Thomson Gale. Farmington Hills, MI. 1998. 180p. Twayne's Studies in Short Fiction, Vol. 73 ISBN:0-8057-1669-6, ISBN13: 978-0-8057-1669-6. Dewey:813/.52. LCCN:98-027650.
Audience: **l,u.** *Choice, 1999.*

Hepworth, James R. (Editor) **PS3537.T316Z469 1998**
Stealing Glances: Three Interviews with Wallace Stegner. Trade Cloth. University of New Mexico Press. Albuquerque, NM. 1998. 118p. ISBN:0-8263-1835-5, ISBN13: 978-0-8263-1835-0. Dewey:[B]. LCCN:98-022302.
Audience: **u,f.**

Stegner, Wallace **PS3511.A86**
The Big Rock Candy Mountain. Library Binding. Buccaneer Books, Inc. Cutchogue, NY. 1995. ISBN:1-56849-671-0, ISBN13: 978-1-56849-671-9. Dewey:813/.52.
Audience: **g,l,u,f.**

Stegner, Wallace **PS3537.T316**
City of the Living and Other Stories. Trade Cloth. Ayer Company Publishers, Inc. Manchester, NH. 1977. Short Story Index Reprint Ser. ISBN:0-8369-3028-2, ISBN13: 978-0-8369-3028-3. Dewey:813/.5/2. LCCN:73-081276.
Audience: **g,l,u,f.**

Stegner, Wallace **PS3537.T316A6 1991**
The Collected Stories of Wallace Stegner. Trade Paper. Penguin Group (USA) Inc. New York, NY. 1991. 544p. Contemporary American Fiction Ser. ISBN:0-14-014774-8, ISBN13: 978-0-14-014774-2. Dewey:813/.52. LCCN:90-044965.
Audience: **g,l,u,f.** *Choice, 1990.*

Stegner, Wallace **F591.S8235**
Marking the Sparrow's Fall: Wallace Stegner's American West. Trade Cloth. Henry Holt & Company. New York, NY. 1999. ISBN:0-8050-6253-X, ISBN13: 978-0-8050-6253-3. Dewey:978.
Audience: **g,l,u,f.**

Stegner, Wallace **PS3511.A86**
The Women on the Wall. Trade Paper. University of Nebraska Press. Lincoln, NE. 1981. 279p. ISBN:0-8032-9110-8, ISBN13: 978-0-8032-9110-2. Dewey:813/.52. LCCN:80-022461.
Audience: **g,l,u,f.**

20th Century (1901-1960) > S > Stein, Gertrude

Bay-Cheng, Sarah **PS3537.T323Z548 2003**
Mama Dada: Gertrude Stein's Avant-Garde Theater. Paper over Boards. Routledge. New York, NY. 2003. 208p. Studies in Modern Drama Ser. ISBN:0-415-96893-3, ISBN13: 978-0-415-96893-5. Dewey:812/.52. LCCN:2003-011575.
Audience: **u,f.**

Bridgman, Richard **PS3537.T323 Z56**
Gertrude Stein in Pieces. Trade Cloth. Oxford University Press, Inc. New York, NY. 1971. 428p. ISBN:0-19-501280-1, ISBN13: 978-0-19-501280-4. Dewey:818/.5/209.
Audience: **l,u,f.** B

Brinnin, John M. **PS3537.T323Z57 1987**
The Third Rose: Gertrude Stein and Her World. John Ashbery (Introduction by). Trade Paper. Addison-Wesley Longman, Inc. Boston, MA. 1987. 464p. ISBN:0-201-05880-4, ISBN13: 978-0-201-05880-2. Dewey:818/.5209 B. LCCN:87-014577.
Audience: **u,f.**

Dydo, Ulla E. **PS3537.T323Z5885**
The Language That Rises, 1923-1934. Gertrude Stein (Contribution by). Trade Cloth. Northwestern University Press. Evanston, IL. 2003. 704p. Avant-Garde and Modernism Studies ISBN:0-8101-1919-6, ISBN13: 978-0-8101-1919-2. Dewey:823/.912. LCCN:2002-153016.
Audience: **u,f.** *Choice, 2004.*

Ford, Sara J. **PS3537.T323Z5895**
Gertrude Stein and Wallace Stevens: Performance of Modern Consciousness. Paper over Boards. Routledge. New York, NY. 2002. 144p. Studies in Major Literary Authors, Vol. 14 ISBN:0-415-93944-5, ISBN13: 978-0-415-93944-7. Dewey:810.9/112. LCCN:2002-002529.
Audience: **l,u.**

Gygax, Franziska **PS3537**
Gender and Genre in Gertrude Stein. Trade Cloth. Greenwood Publishing Group, Inc. Portsmouth, NH. 1998. 168p. Contributions in Women's Studies, Vol. 169 ISBN:0-313-30755-5, ISBN13: 978-0-313-30755-3. Dewey:818.5209. LCCN:98-012150.
Audience: **u,f.** *Choice, 1999.*

Hobhouse, Janet **PS3537.T323**
Everybody Who Was Anybody: A Biography of Gertrude Stein. Trade Paper. Doubleday Publishing. New York, NY. 1999. ISBN:0-385-50009-2, ISBN13: 978-0-385-50009-8. Dewey:818/.5209.
Audience: **g,l,u.**

Lesinka, Zofia P. **PS228.W37L47 2002**
Perspectives of Four Women Writers on the Second World War: Gertrude Stein, Janet Flanner, Kay Boyle, and Rebecca West. Trade Cloth. Peter Lang Publishing, Inc. New York, NY. 2002. 200p. Studies in Literary Criticism and Theory Ser., Vol. 17 ISBN:0-8204-6103-2, ISBN13: 978-0-8204-6103-8. Dewey:810.9/358. LCCN:2002-023812.
Audience: **u,f.**

Neuman, Shirley & Nadel, Ira B. (Editors) **PS3537.T323.Z615**
Gertrude Stein and the Making of Literature. Trade Cloth. Northeastern University Press. Boston, MA. 1988. 236p. ISBN:1-55553-025-7, ISBN13: 978-1-55553-025-9. Dewey:818/.5209. LCCN:87-022122.
Audience: **u,f.** *Choice, 1988.*

Paul, Catherine E. **PS310.M57P38 2002**
Poetry in the Museums of Modernism: Yeats, Pound, Moore, Stein. Trade Cloth. University of Michigan Press. Chicago, IL. 2002. 312p. ISBN:0-472-11264-3, ISBN13: 978-0-472-11264-7. Dewey:811/.5209112. LCCN:2002-002089.
Audience: **u,f.**

Stein, Gertrude **PS3537.T323 A6 1970**
Selected Operas and Plays of Gertrude Stein. University of Pittsburgh Press. 1970. ISBN:0-8229-3195-8, ISBN13: 978-0-8229-3195-9.
Audience: **g,l,u,f.**

Stein, Gertrude **PS3537.T323A6 1990**
Selected Writings of Gertrude Stein. Book, Other. Knopf Publishing Group. New York, NY. 1990. 736p. ISBN:0-679-72464-8, ISBN13: 978-0-679-72464-3. Dewey:818/.5209. LCCN:74-019117.
Audience: **g,l,u,f.** B

Stein, Gertrude **PS3537**
Tender Buttons: Objects, Food, Rooms. Trade Cloth. Penguin Group (USA) Inc. New York, NY. 2003. 78p. ISBN:1-931243-42-5, ISBN13: 978-1-931243-42-1. Dewey:811.5.
Audience: **g,l,u,f.** B

Stein, Gertrude **PS3537.T323M3 1995**
The Making of Americans: An Opera and a Play from the Novel by Gertrude Stein. William H. Gass (Foreword by), Steven Meyer (Introduction by). Trade Cloth. Dalkey Archive Press. Normal, IL. 1995. 925p. American Literature Ser. ISBN:1-56478-088-0, ISBN13: 978-1-56478-088-1. Dewey:813/.52. LCCN:95-016357.
Audience: **g,l,u,f.**

Stein, Gertrude **PS3537.T323**
A Primer for the Gradual Understanding of Gertrude Stein. Robert B. Haas (Editor). Trade Cloth. David R. Godine Publisher. Boston, MA. 1975. ISBN:0-87685-137-5, ISBN13: 978-0-87685-137-1. Dewey:818/.5/209.
Audience: **g,l,u,f.** B

Stein, Gertrude **PS3537.T323**
The Yale Gertrude Stein. Richard Kostelanetz (Introduction by). Trade Cloth. Yale University Press. Cumberland, RI. 1980. 480p. ISBN:0-300-02574-2, ISBN13: 978-0-300-02574-3. Dewey:818/.5209. LCCN:80-005398.
Audience: **g,l,u,f.** B

Stein, Gertrude **PS3537.T323A6 1998**
Stein, 1903-1932: Q. E. D. ; Three Lives; Autobiography of Alice B. Toklas; Portraits. Catharine Stimpson & Harriet Chessman (Editors). Trade Cloth. Library of America, The. New York, NY. 1998. 960p. Library of America, Vol. 99 ISBN:1-883011-40-X, ISBN13: 978-1-883011-40-6. Dewey:818/.5209. LCCN:97-028915.
Audience: **g,l,u,f.**

Stein, Gertrude **PS3537.T323A6 1998**
Stein, 1932-1946: Stanzas in Meditation; Lectures in America; the Geographical History of America; Ida, Brewsie and Willie and Other Works. Catharine Stimpson & Harriet Chessman (Editors). Trade Cloth. Library of America, The. New York, NY. 1998. 864p. Library of America, Vol. 100 ISBN:1-883011-41-8, ISBN13: 978-1-883011-41-3. Dewey:818/.5209. LCCN:97-028916.
Audience: **g,l,u,f.**

Wagner-Martin, Linda **PS3537.T323Z87 1995**
Favored Strangers: Gertrude Stein and Her Family. Trade Cloth. Rutgers University Press. Piscataway, NJ. 1997. 400p. ISBN:0-8135-2169-6, ISBN13: 978-0-8135-2169-5. Dewey:818/.5209 B. LCCN:94-023700.
Audience: **u,f.** *Choice, 1996.*

Watson, Dana Cairns **PS3537.T323Z96 2004**
Gertrude Stein and the Essence of What Happens. Cloth Text. Vanderbilt University Press. Nashville, TN. 2005. 272p. ISBN:0-8265-1462-6, ISBN13: 978-0-8265-1462-2. Dewey:818/.5209. LCCN:2003-027602.
Audience: **u,f.** *Choice, 2005.*

Watts, Linda S. **PS3537.T323Z887 1999**
Gertrude Stein: Study of Short Fiction. Trade Cloth. Simon & Schuster. New York, NY. 1999. xiii, 153p. Twayne's Studies in Short Fiction, Vol. 77 ISBN:0-8057-1696-3, ISBN13: 978-0-8057-1696-2. Dewey:813/.52. LCCN:99-043647.
Audience: **l,u.** *Choice, 2000.*

Weiss, M. Lynn **PS3537.T323Z913 1998**
Gertrude Stein and Richard Wright: The Poetics and Politics of Modernism. Trade Cloth. University Press of Mississippi. Jackson, MS. 1998. 144p. ISBN:1-57806-100-8, ISBN13: 978-1-57806-100-6. Dewey:818/.5209. LCCN:98-007786.
Audience: **u,f.** *Choice, 1999.*

Will, Barbara **PS3537.T323Z925 2000**
Gertrude Stein: Modernism and the Problem of Genius. Trade Cloth. Edinburgh University Press. Edinburgh, 2000. 240p. ISBN:0-7486-1198-3, ISBN13: 978-0-7486-1198-0. Dewey:818/.5209. LCCN:00-421412.
Audience: **u,f.** *Choice, 2001.*

20th Century (1901-1960) > S > Steinbeck, John

Benson, Jackson J. (Editor) **PS3537.T3234Z8666**
The Short Novels of John Steinbeck: Critical Essays. Paper Text. Duke University Press. Durham, NC. 1990. 360p. ISBN:0-8223-0994-7, ISBN13: 978-0-8223-0994-9. Dewey:813/.52. LCCN:89-027255.
Audience: **l,u.** *Choice, 1991.*

Fensch, Thomas (Editor) **PS3537.T3234Z464**
Conversations with John Steinbeck. Cloth Text. University Press of Mississippi. Jackson, MS. 1988. 144p. Literary Conversations Ser. ISBN:0-87805-359-X, ISBN13: 978-0-87805-359-9. Dewey:813/.52 B. LCCN:88-017538.
Audience: **l,u,f.**

French, Warren (Editor) **PS3511.A86**
John Steinbeck. Ed. 2. Paper Text. Macmillan Publishing Company, Inc. Old Tappan, NJ. 1975. Twayne's United States Authors Ser. ISBN:0-672-61501-0, ISBN13: 978-0-672-61501-6. Dewey:813/.5/2.
Audience: **l,u.**

George, Stephen K. (Editor) **PS3537**
John Steinbeck: A Centennial Tribute. Terry Gorton (Foreword by). Trade Cloth. Greenwood Publishing Group, Inc. Portsmouth, NH. 2002. 232p. Contributions to the Study of American Literature Ser., Vol. 15 ISBN:0-313-32325-9, ISBN13: 978-0-313-32325-6. Dewey:813/.52 B. LCCN:2002-072542.
Audience: **l,u.**

Levant, Howard **PS3537.T3234.Z717**
The Novels of John Steinbeck: A Critical Study. Trade Cloth. University of Missouri Press. Columbia, MO. 1983. 328p. ISBN:0-8262-0164-4, ISBN13: 978-0-8262-0164-5. Dewey:813/.5/2. LCCN:74-076251.
Audience: **l,u.** B

Parini, Jay **PS3537.T3234**
John Steinbeck: A Biography. Trade Paper. Henry Holt & Company. New York, NY. 1996. 576p. ISBN:0-8050-4700-X, ISBN13: 978-0-8050-4700-4. Dewey:813/.52 B.
Audience: **g,l,u,f.** *Choice, 1995.*

Schultz, Jeffrey **PS3537.T3234**
Critical Companion to John Steinbeck: A Literary Reference to His Life and Work. Trade Cloth. Facts On File, Inc. New York, NY. 2005. 416p. Literary A to Z Ser. ISBN:0-8160-4300-0, ISBN13: 978-0-8160-4300-2. Dewey:813.52. LCCN:2004-026100.
Audience: **l,u.** *Choice, 2006.*

Shillinglaw, Susan & Hearle, Kevin (Editors) **PS3537.T3234Z619**
Beyond Boundaries: Rereading John Steinbeck. Trade Cloth. University of Alabama Press. Tuscaloosa, AL. 2002. 320p. ISBN:0-8173-1151-3, ISBN13: 978-0-8173-1151-3. Dewey:813/.52. LCCN:2002-000360.
Audience: **u,f.**

Steinbeck, John **PS3537.T3234S5 1994**
The Short Reign of Pippin IV: A Fabrication. Trade Paper. Penguin Group (USA) Inc. New York, NY. 1994. 192p. Great Books of the 20th Century Ser. ISBN:0-14-018749-9, ISBN13: 978-0-14-018749-6. Dewey:813/.52. LCCN:94-167774.
Audience: **g,l,u,f.** B

Steinbeck, John **PS3511.A86**
Sweet Thursday. Library Binding. Sagebrush Education Resources. Caledonia, MN. 1996. ISBN:0-613-70841-5, ISBN13: 978-0-613-70841-8. Dewey:813.5/2.
Audience: **g,l,u,f.** B

Steinbeck, John **PS3511.A86**
The Wayward Bus. Library Binding. Sagebrush Education Resources. Caledonia, MN. 1995. ISBN:0-613-70922-5, ISBN13: 978-0-613-70922-4. Dewey:813/.52.
Audience: **g,l,u,f.**

Steinbeck, John **PS3537**
The Winter of Our Discontent. Trade Paper. Penguin Group (USA) Inc. New York, NY. 1996. 288p. Great Books of the 20th Century Ser. ISBN:0-14-018753-7, ISBN13: 978-0-14-018753-3. Dewey:813/.52. LCCN:86-012251.
Audience: **g,l,u,f.**

Steinbeck, John **PS3537.T3234A6 2002**
John Steinbeck Novels 1942-1952, Vol. 3. Robert DeMott (Editor). Trade Cloth. Library of America, The. New York, NY. 2002. 983p. Library of America, Vol. 132 ISBN:1-931082-07-3, ISBN13: 978-1-931082-07-5. Dewey:813/.52. LCCN:2001-038119.
Audience: **g,l,u,f.**

Steinbeck, John **PS3537.T3234A6 1996**
John Steinbeck, 1936-1941: The Long Valley; the Grapes of Wrath; the Log from the Sea of Cortez; the Harvest Gypsies. Robert DeMott & Elaine A. Steinbeck (Editors). Trade Cloth. Library of America, The. New York, NY. 1996. 1088p. Library of America ISBN:1-883011-15-9, ISBN13: 978-1-883011-15-4. Dewey:813/.52. LCCN:96-003725.
Audience: **g,l,u,f.**

Steinbeck, John **PS3537.T3234A6 1994**
Steinbeck, 1932-1937: The Pastures of Heaven; To a God Unknown; Tortilla Flat; In Dubious Battle; Of Mice and Men. Robert DeMott & Elaine A. Steinbeck (Editors). Trade Cloth. Library of America, The. New York, NY. 1994. 912p. Library of America, Vol. 72 ISBN:1-883011-01-9, ISBN13: 978-1-883011-01-7. Dewey:813/.52. LCCN:94-002943.
Audience: **g,l,u,f.**

20th Century (1901-1960) > S > Stevens, Wallace

Axelrod, Steven G. & Deese, Helen (Editors) **PS3537.T4753Z624**
Critical Essays on Wallace Stevens. Trade Cloth. Thomson Gale. Farmington Hills, MI. 1988. 272p. Critical Essays on American Literature Ser. ISBN:0-8161-8886-6, ISBN13: 978-0-8161-8886-4. Dewey:811/.52. LCCN:88-005245.
Audience: **l,u.** *Choice, 1989.*

Baird, James **PS3537.T4753**
The Dome and the Rock: Structure in the Poetry of Wallace Stevens. Trade Cloth. Johns Hopkins University Press. Baltimore, MD. 1982. 368p. ISBN:0-8018-0048-X, ISBN13: 978-0-8018-0048-1. Dewey:811/.5/2. LCCN:68-019701.
Audience: **u,f.** B

Brogan, Jacqueline Vaught **PS3537.T4753Z619**
The Violence Within/The Violence Without: Wallace Stevens and the Emergence of a Revolutionary Poetics. Trade Cloth. University of Georgia Press. Athens, GA. 2005. 224p. ISBN:0-8203-2519-8, ISBN13: 978-0-8203-2519-4. Dewey:811/.52. LCCN:2003-000795.
Audience: **u,f.**

Filreis, Alan **PS3537.T4753 Z635 1**
Modernism from Right to Left: Wallace Stevens, the Thirties, and Literary Radicalism. Albert Gelpi & Ross Posnock (Contribution by). Trade Paper. Cambridge University Press.

New York, NY. 2005. 394p. Cambridge Studies in American Literature and Culture Ser., Vol. 70 ISBN:0-521-61940-8, ISBN13: 978-0-521-61940-0. Dewey:811/.52. LCCN:2005-284230.
Audience: **u,f.**

Ford, Sara J. **PS3537.T323Z5895**
Gertrude Stein and Wallace Stevens: Performance of Modern Consciousness. Paper over Boards. Routledge. New York, NY. 2002. 144p. Studies in Major Literary Authors, Vol. 14 ISBN:0-415-93944-5, ISBN13: 978-0-415-93944-7. Dewey:810.9/112. LCCN:2002-002529.
Audience: **l,u.**

Lentricchia, Frank **PS310.M57L46 1994**
Modernist Quartet. Cloth Text. Cambridge University Press. New York, NY. 1994. 319p. ISBN:0-521-47004-8, ISBN13: 978-0-521-47004-9. Dewey:811.5209. LCCN:93-050239.
Audience: **u,f.** *Choice, 1995.*

Rotella, Guy **PS310.N3R68 1990**
Reading and Writing Nature: The Poetry of Robert Frost, Wallace Stevens, Marianne Moore, and Elizabeth Bishop. Trade Cloth. Northeastern University Press. Boston, MA. 1990. 253p. ISBN:1-55553-086-9, ISBN13: 978-1-55553-086-0. Dewey:811/.520936. LCCN:90-007576.
Audience: **u,f.** *Choice, 1991.*

Sharpe, Tony **PS3537.T4753Z7658**
Wallace Stevens: A Literary Life. Trade Cloth. Palgrave Macmillan. New York, NY. 2000. 236p. Literary Lives Ser. ISBN:0-312-22069-3, ISBN13: 978-0-312-22069-3. Dewey:811.5/2. LCCN:99-013314.
Audience: **l,u.** *Choice, 2000.*

Stevens, Wallace **PS3537.T4753.A6 1990**
Opus Posthumous: Poems, Plays, Prose. Trade Cloth. Knopf Publishing Group. New York, NY. 1990. 352p. ISBN:0-679-72534-2, ISBN13: 978-0-679-72534-3. Dewey:811/.52. LCCN:89-070573.
Audience: **g,l,u,f.**

Stevens, Wallace & Kermode, Frank **PS3537.T4753A6 1997**
Stevens: Collected Poetry and Prose. Joan Richardson (Editor). Trade Cloth. Library of America, The. New York, NY. 1997. 1030p. Library of America ISBN:1-883011-45-0, ISBN13: 978-1-883011-45-1. Dewey:811/.52. LCCN:97-007023.
Audience: **g,l,u,f.**

20th Century (1901-1960) > T

Tarkington, Booth **PS2972.M25 1989**
The Magnificent Ambersons. Trade Cloth. Indiana University Press. Bloomington, IN. 1989. 536p. Library of Indiana Classics ISBN:0-253-35875-2, ISBN13: 978-0-253-35875-2. Dewey:813/.52. LCCN:89-045565.
Audience: **g,l,u,f.**

Teasdale, Sara **PS3539.E15**
The Collected Poems of Sara Teasdale. Library Binding. Buccaneer Books, Inc. Cutchogue, NY. 1996. ISBN:1-56849-345-2, ISBN13: 978-1-56849-345-9. Dewey:811.
Audience: **g,l,u,f.** B

Thurman, Wallace **PS3539.H957**
Blacker the Berry. Library Binding. Sagebrush Education Resources. Caledonia, MN. 1996. ISBN:0-613-37719-2, ISBN13: 978-0-613-37719-5. Dewey:813/.5/2.
Audience: **g,l,u,f.**

Thurman, Wallace **PS3511.A86**
Infants of the Spring. Trade Cloth. Ayer Company Publishers, Inc. Manchester, NH. 1977. Black Heritage Library Collection ISBN:0-8369-9129-X, ISBN13: 978-0-8369-9129-1. Dewey:813/.52. LCCN:72-004615.
Audience: **g,l,u,f.**

Thurman, Wallace **PS3539.H957A6 2003**
The Collected Writings of Wallace Thurman: A Harlem Renaissance Reader. Amritjit Singh & Daniel M. Scott (Editors). Library Binding. Rutgers University Press. Piscataway, NJ. 2003. 544p. ISBN:0-8135-3300-7, ISBN13: 978-0-8135-3300-1. Dewey:813/.52. LCCN:2002-152302.
Audience: **g,l,u,f.** *Choice, 2004.*

Toklas, Alice B. **PS3537.T323**
What Is Remembered? Trade Paper. Farrar, Straus & Giroux. New York, NY. 1985. 224p. ISBN:0-86547-180-0, ISBN13: 978-0-86547-180-1. Dewey:928.1. LCCN:84-062304.
Audience: **g,l,u,f.**

Tolson, Melvin B. **PS3539.O334A6 1999**
Harlem Gallery: And Other Poems. Raymond Nelson (Editor), Rita Dove (Introduction by). Trade Cloth. University Press of Virginia. Charlottesville, VA. 1999. 472p. ISBN:0-8139-1864-2, ISBN13: 978-0-8139-1864-8. Dewey:811/.52. LCCN:98-052063.
Audience: **g,l,u,f.**

20th Century (1901-1960) > T > Thompson, Jim

McCauley, Michael J. **PS3539.H6733Z78 1991**
Jim Thompson: Sleep with the Devil. Trade Cloth. Warner Books, Inc. New York, NY. 1991. ISBN:0-89296-392-1, ISBN13: 978-0-89296-392-8. Dewey:813/.54 B. LCCN:90-050548.
Audience: **g,l,u,f.**

Polito, Robert **PS3568.O243**
Savage Art: A Biography of Jim Thompson. Trade Cloth. Knopf Publishing Group. New York, NY. 1996. 560p. Vintage Ser. ISBN:0-679-73352-3, ISBN13: 978-0-679-73352-2. Dewey:813.5/4.
Audience: **g,l,u,f.**

Sallis, James **PS374.D4**
Difficult Lives: Jim Thompson, David Goodis, Chester Himes. Ed. 2. Trade Paper. Gryphon Books. Brooklyn, NY. 2000. 102p. ISBN:1-58250-029-0, ISBN13: 978-1-58250-029-4. Dewey:813/.087209 B.
Audience: **g,l,u,f.**

Thompson, Jim **PS3539.H6733A69 1990**
After Dark My Sweet. Trade Paper. Knopf Publishing Group. New York, NY. 1990. 144p. Vintage Crime/Black Lizard Ser. ISBN:0-679-73247-0, ISBN13: 978-0-679-73247-1. Dewey:813/.54. LCCN:90-050250.
Audience: **g,l,u,f.**

Thompson, Jim **PS3539.H6733G4 1990**
The Getaway. Trade Paper. Knopf Publishing Group. New York, NY. 1990. 192p. Vintage Crime/Black Lizard Ser. ISBN:0-679-73250-0, ISBN13: 978-0-679-73250-1. Dewey:813/.54. LCCN:90-050256.
Audience: **g,l,u,f.**

Thompson, Jim **PS3539.H6733G7 1990**
The Grifters. Trade Paper. Knopf Publishing Group. New York, NY. 1990. 208p. Vintage Crime/Black Lizard Ser. ISBN:0-679-73248-9, ISBN13: 978-0-679-73248-8. Dewey:813/.54. LCCN:90-050251.
Audience: **g,l,u,f.**

Thompson, Jim **PZ7.N4875 IAC 1990**
Pop. 1280. Trade Paper. Knopf Publishing Group. New York, NY. 1990. 224p. Vintage Crime/Black Lizard Ser. ISBN:0-679-73249-7, ISBN13: 978-0-679-73249-5. Dewey:[Fic]. LCCN:90-008292.
Audience: **g,l,u,f.**

Thompson, Jim **PS3539.H6733 S9 1991**
A Swell-Looking Babe. Trade Paper. Knopf Publishing Group. New York, NY. 1991. 156p. Vintage Crime/Black Lizard Ser. ISBN:0-679-73311-6, ISBN13: 978-0-679-73311-9. Dewey:813/.54. LCCN:91-050071.
Audience: **g,l,u,f.**

Thompson, Jim **PS3539.H6733 W5 1993**
Wild Town. Trade Paper. Knopf Publishing Group. New York, NY. 1993. 176p. Crime - Black Lizard Ser. ISBN:0-679-73312-4, ISBN13: 978-0-679-73312-6. Dewey:813/.54. LCCN:92-056367.
Audience: **g,l,u,f.**

20th Century (1901-1960) > T > Tate, Allen

Brooks, Cleanth & Tate, Allen **PS29.B74A4 1998**
Cleanth Brooks and Allen Tate: Collected Letters, 1933-1976. Alphonse Vinh (Editor), Louis Decimus Rubin Jr. (Introduction by). Trade Cloth. University of Missouri Press. Columbia, MO. 1998. 312p. ISBN:0-8262-1207-7, ISBN13: 978-0-8262-1207-8. Dewey:809 B. LCCN:98-034156.
Audience: **u,f.** *Choice, 1999.*

Meiners, R. K. **PS3539.A74.Z7 1973**
Last Alternatives: Allen Tate. Library Binding. M. S. G. Haskell House. Brooklyn, NY. 1972. 217p. American Literature Ser., No. 49 ISBN:0-8383-1594-1, ISBN13: 978-0-8383-1594-1. Dewey:818/.5/209. LCCN:72-004614.
Audience: **l,u.** B

Tate, Allen **PR6029.C33A6**
Collected Essays. Paper Text. Textbook Publishers. Temecula, CA. 2003. ISBN:0-7581-3352-9, ISBN13: 978-0-7581-3352-6. Dewey:828.
Audience: **g,l,u,f.** B

Tate, Allen **PS3539.A74A17 1989**
Collected Poems, 1919-1976. Trade Paper. Louisiana State University Press. Baton Rouge, LA. 1989. x, 218p. ISBN:0-8071-1533-9, ISBN13: 978-0-8071-1533-6. Dewey:811/.52. LCCN:88-027385.
Audience: **g,l,u,f.** B

Tate, Allen **PS3539.A74.Z52**
Memoirs and Opinions, 1926-1974. Trade Cloth. Swallow Press. Athens, OH. 1975. 225p. ISBN:0-8040-0662-8, ISBN13: 978-0-8040-0662-0. Dewey:818/.5/209. LCCN:75-010757.
Audience: **u,f.** B

Tate, Allen **PS3539.A74F3 1984**
The Fathers. Arthur Mixener (Introduction by). Trade Paper. Swallow Press. Athens, OH. 1984. 323p. ISBN:0-8040-0108-1, ISBN13: 978-0-8040-0108-3. Dewey:813/.52. LCCN:84-000212.
Audience: **g,l,u,f.** B

Underwood, Thomas A. **PS3539.A74Z93 2004**
Allen Tate: Orphan of the South. Trade Paper. Princeton University Press. Princeton, NJ. 2003. 456p. ISBN:0-691-11568-0, ISBN13: 978-0-691-11568-9. Dewey:818/.5209 B.
Audience: **u,f.**

20th Century (1901-1960) > T > Thurber, James

Fensch, Thomas (Editor) **PS3539.H94Z464 1989**
Conversations with James Thurber. Trade Cloth. University Press of Mississippi. Jackson, MS. 1989. 144p. Literary Conversations Ser. ISBN:0-87805-409-X, ISBN13: 978-0-87805-409-1. Dewey:818/.5209. LCCN:89-032215.
Audience: **g,l,u,f.**

Holmes, Charles S. **PS3539.H94**
The Clocks of Columbus: The Literary Career of James Thurber. Trade Paper. Simon & Schuster. New York, NY. 1978. ISBN:0-689-70574-3, ISBN13: 978-0-689-70574-8. Dewey:818/.5/209. LCCN:72-078287.
Audience: **g,l,u,f.**

Kinney, Harrison **PS3537.T323**
James Thurber: His Life and Times. Trade Paper. Henry Holt & Company. New York, NY. 1997. 1238p. ISBN:0-8050-5368-9, ISBN13: 978-0-8050-5368-5. Dewey:818.5/2/09. LCCN:95-009989.
Audience: **g,l,u,f.** *Choice, 1996.*

Kinney, Harrison (Editor) **PS3539.H94**
The Thurber Letters: The Wit, Wisdom, and Surprising Life of James Thurber. Rosemary A. Thurber (Contribution by). Trade Cloth. Simon & Schuster. New York, NY. 2003. 816p. ISBN:0-7432-2343-8, ISBN13: 978-0-7432-2343-0. Dewey:818/.5209 B. LCCN:2003-045718.
Audience: **g,l,u,f.**

Thurber, James **PS3539.H94.M9**
My World and Welcome to It. Trade Paper. Harcourt Trade Publishers. New York, NY. 1969. 324p. Harvest Book Ser. ISBN:0-15-662344-7, ISBN13: 978-0-15-662344-5. Dewey:818.52. LCCN:42-036350.
Audience: **g,l,u,f.**

Thurber, James **PS3539.H94 T5 1978B**
Thurber Carnival. Cloth Text. Amereon, Ltd. Mattituck, NY. 2004. ISBN:0-8488-2749-X, ISBN13: 978-0-8488-2749-6. Dewey:818/.5209.
Audience: **g,l,u,f.** B

Thurber, James **PN4874.R65T5 2001**
The Years with Ross. Adam Gopnick (Foreword by). Trade Paper. HarperCollins Publishers. New York, NY. 2001. 336p. Perennial Classics Ser. ISBN:0-06-095971-1, ISBN13: 978-0-06-095971-5. Dewey:070.4/1/092 B. LCCN:00-045290.
Audience: **g,l,u,f.** B

Thurber, James **PS3539.H94A6 1996**
James Thurber: Writings and Drawings. Garrison Keillor (Editor). Trade Cloth. Library of America, The. New York, NY. 1996. 1024p. Library of America ISBN:1-883011-22-1, ISBN13: 978-1-883011-22-2. Dewey:818/.5209. LCCN:96-005853.
Audience: **g,l,u,f.**

20th Century (1901-1960) > T > Toomer, Jean

Fabre, Genevieve & Feith, Michel (Editors) **PS3539.O478Z685 2001**
Jean Toomer and the Harlem Renaissance. Trade Cloth. Rutgers University Press. Piscataway, NJ. 2000. xii, 235p. ISBN:0-8135-2845-3, ISBN13: 978-0-8135-2845-8. Dewey:813/.52. LCCN:00-025193.
Audience: **u,f.** *Choice, 2001.*

Ford, Karen Jackson **PS3539.O478Z64 2005**
Split-Gut Song: Jean Toomer and the Poetics of Modernity. Saddle Stitched, Cloth over Boards, Dust Jacket. University of Alabama Press. Tuscaloosa, AL. 2005. 232p. ISBN:0-8173-1456-3, ISBN13: 978-0-8173-1456-9. Dewey:813/.52. LCCN:2004-022371.
Audience: **u,f.** *Choice, 2005.*

Grant, Nathan **PS374.N4G73 2004**
Masculinist Impulses: Toomer, Hurston, Black Writing, and Modernity. Trade Cloth. University of Missouri Press. Columbia, MO. 2004. 256p. ISBN:0-8262-1516-5, ISBN13: 978-0-8262-1516-1. Dewey:813/.5099286. LCCN:2003-026040.
Audience: **u,f.** *Choice, 2004.*

Kerman, Cynthia E. & Eldridge, Richard **PS3539.O478**
The Lives of Jean Toomer: A Hunger for Wholeness. Trade Paper. Louisiana State University Press. Baton Rouge, LA. 1989. 448p. ISBN:0-8071-1548-7, ISBN13: 978-0-8071-1548-0. Dewey:813/.52 B. LCCN:86-027622.
Audience: **g,l,u,f.** *Choice, 1988.*

McKay, Nellie Y. **PS3539.O478Z/**
Jean Toomer, Artist: A Study of His Literary Life and Work, 1894-1936. Trade Cloth. University of North Carolina Press. Chapel Hill, NC. 1984. xiv, 262p. ISBN:0-8078-1583-7, ISBN13: 978-0-8078-1583-0. Dewey:813/.52. LCCN:83-021570.
Audience: **l,u.** B

Rusch, Frederik L. (Editor) **PS3539.O478A6 1993**
A Jean Toomer Reader: Selected Unpublished Writings. Trade Paper. Oxford University Press, Inc. New York, NY. 1993. 312p. ISBN:0-19-508329-6, ISBN13: 978-0-19-508329-3. Dewey:813.52. LCCN:93-016374.
Audience: **g,l,u,f.** *Choice, 1994.*

Toomer, Jean **PS3511.A86**
Cane. Trade Cloth. Peter Smith Publisher, Inc. Magnolia, MA. 1990. ISBN:0-8446-6367-0, ISBN13: 978-0-8446-6367-8. Dewey:813/.52.
Audience: **g,l,u,f.** B

Toomer, Jean **PS3539.O478A6 1996**
Jean Toomer: Selected Essays and Literary Criticism. Robert B. Jones (Editor). Cloth Text. University of Tennessee Press. Knoxville, TN. 1996. 160p. ISBN:0-87049-938-6, ISBN13: 978-0-87049-938-8. Dewey:814/.52. LCCN:95-041825.
Audience: **u,f.** *Choice, 1997.*

Toomer, Jean **87-19203**
The Collected Poems of Jean Toomer. Robert B. Jones & Margery T. Latimer (Editors). Trade Paper. University of North Carolina Press. Chapel Hill, NC. 1988. 148p. ISBN:0-8078-4209-5, ISBN13: 978-0-8078-4209-6. Dewey:811/.52. LCCN:87-019203.
Audience: **g,l,u,f.**

Turner, Darwin T. (Editor) **PN6161**
The Wayward and the Seeking: A Collection of Writings by Jean Toomer. Trade Paper. Howard University Press. Washington, DC. 1980. ISBN:0-88258-028-0, ISBN13: 978-0-88258-028-9. Dewey:818/.5207. LCCN:74-011026.
Audience: **g,l,u,f.** B

20th Century (1901-1960) > V

Van Duyn, Mona **PS3566.L27**
Merciful Disguises: Published and Unpublished Poems. Trade Paper. Simon & Schuster. New York, NY. 1982. ISBN:0-689-11294-7, ISBN13: 978-0-689-11294-2. Dewey:811/.5/4. LCCN:73-078407.
Audience: **g,l,u,f.** B

Van Vechten, Carl **PS3543.A653**
Nigger Heaven. Trade Cloth. Farrar, Straus & Giroux. New York, NY. 1973. ISBN:0-374-98069-1, ISBN13: 978-0-374-98069-6. Dewey:813/.52. LCCN:73-003471.
Audience: **g,l,u,f.** B

Viereck, Peter R. **PS3543**
Terror and Decorum: Poems, 1940-1948. Trade Cloth. Greenwood Publishing Group, Inc. Portsmouth, NH. 1973. 110p. ISBN:0-8371-6296-3, ISBN13: 978-0-8371-6296-6. Dewey:811/.5/4. LCCN:78-178796.
Audience: **g,l,u,f.** B

20th Century (1901-1960) > V > Vidal, Gore

Baker, Susan & Gibson, Curtis S. **PS3543**
Gore Vidal: A Critical Companion. Cloth Text. Greenwood

Publishing Group, Inc. Portsmouth, NH. 1997. 232p. Critical Companions to Popular Contemporary Writers Ser. ISBN:0-313-29579-4, ISBN13: 978-0-313-29579-9. Dewey:813.54. LCCN:96-026809.
Audience: **l,u.**

Dick, Bernard F. **PS3543.I26.Z65**
The Apostate Angel; a Critical Study of Gore Vidal. Trade Cloth. Random House, Inc. New York, NY. 1974. 203p. ISBN:0-394-48108-9, ISBN13: 978-0-394-48108-1. Dewey:818/.5/409. LCCN:73-020553.
Audience: **l,u,f.** B

Harris, Stephen **PS3543.I26Z69 2005**
Gore Vidal's Historical Novels and the Shaping of American Political Consciousness. Trade Cloth. Edwin Mellen Press, The. Lewiston, NY. 2005. 292p. Studies in Historical Novel, Vol. 4 ISBN:0-7734-6031-4, ISBN13: 978-0-7734-6031-7. Dewey:813/.54. LCCN:2005-049783.
Audience: **u,f.**

Kaplan, Fred **PS3568.O243**
Gore Vidal: A Biography. Trade Paper. Knopf Publishing Group. New York, NY. 2000. 896p. ISBN:0-385-47704-X, ISBN13: 978-0-385-47704-8. Dewey:813.5/4.
Audience: **g,l,u,f.**

Kiernan, Robert F. **PS3543.I26.Z75 1982**
Gore Vidal. Trade Cloth. Frederick Ungar A Book. Dulles, VA. 1982. 182p. Literature and Life Ser. ISBN:0-8044-2461-6, ISBN13: 978-0-8044-2461-5. Dewey:818/.5409. LCCN:81-070962.
Audience: **l,u.** B

Parini, Jay **PS3543.I26Z67 1992**
Gore Vidal: Writer Against the Grain. Trade Cloth. Columbia University Press. New York, NY. 1992. 321p. ISBN:0-231-07208-2, ISBN13: 978-0-231-07208-3. Dewey:813.54. LCCN:91-045312.
Audience: **u,f.**

Peabody, Richard & Ebersole, Lucinda (Editors) **PS3543.I26Z464 2005**
Conversations with Gore Vidal. Trade Cloth. University Press of Mississippi. Jackson, MS. 2005. 208p. Literary Conversations Ser. ISBN:1-57806-672-7, ISBN13: 978-1-57806-672-8. Dewey:818/.5409. LCCN:2004-059554.
Audience: **l,u.**

Vidal, Gore **PS3568.O243**
1876: A Novel. Trade Paper. Knopf Publishing Group. New York, NY. 2000. 384p. Ace's Exambusters Ser. ISBN:0-375-70872-3, ISBN13: 978-0-375-70872-5. Dewey:813/.54.
Audience: **g,l,u,f.** B

Vidal, Gore **PS3543.I26B4 1996**
The Best Man. Trade Paper. Dramatists Play Service, Inc. New York, NY. 1996. ISBN:0-8222-1527-6, ISBN13: 978-0-8222-1527-1. Dewey:812/.54. LCCN:97-209147.
Audience: **g,l,u,f.**

Vidal, Gore **PZ3.V6668BU**
Burr. Trade Paper. Knopf Publishing Group. New York, NY. 2000. 448p. Ace's Exambusters Ser. ISBN:0-375-70873-1, ISBN13: 978-0-375-70873-2. Dewey:813.5/4. LCCN:73-003985.
Audience: **g,l,u,f.**

Vidal, Gore **PS3568.O243**
The City and the Pillar. Trade Paper. Knopf Publishing Group. New York, NY. 2003. 240p. ISBN:1-4000-3037-4, ISBN13: 978-1-4000-3037-8. Dewey:813.5/4.
Audience: **g,l,u,f.** B

Vidal, Gore **PS3543**
Julian. Trade Paper. Alfred A. Knopf Inc. New York, NY. 2003. 528p. ISBN:0-375-72706-X, ISBN13: 978-0-375-72706-1. Dewey:813/.54. LCCN:2003-276587.
Audience: **g,l,u,f.**

Vidal, Gore **PN6162**
The Last Empire: Essays, 1992-2000. Trade Paper. Alfred A. Knopf Inc. New York, NY. 2002. 480p. ISBN:0-375-72639-X, ISBN13: 978-0-375-72639-2. Dewey:814/.54.
Audience: **g,l,u,f.**

Vidal, Gore **PS3568.O243**
Lincoln: A Novel. Library Binding. Buccaneer Books, Inc. Cutchogue, NY. 1995. ISBN:1-56849-626-5, ISBN13: 978-1-56849-626-9. Dewey:813.5/4.
Audience: **g,l,u,f.** B

Vidal, Gore **PS3543.I26M9 1987**
Myra Breckinridge and Myron. Trade Paper. Penguin Group (USA) Inc. New York, NY. 1997. 432p. Twentieth Century Classics Ser. ISBN:0-14-118028-5, ISBN13: 978-0-14-118028-1. Dewey:813/.54. LCCN:87-040002.
Audience: **g,l,u,f.**

Vidal, Gore **PS3568.O243**
Palimpsest: A Memoir. Trade Paper. Penguin Group (USA) Inc. New York, NY. 1996. 480p. ISBN:0-14-026089-7, ISBN13: 978-0-14-026089-2. Dewey:813.5/4.
Audience: **g,l,u.** *Choice, 1996.*

Vidal, Gore **PS3543.I26U55 2001**
United States: Essays, 1952-1992. Trade Paper. Broadway Books. New York, NY. 2001. 1312p. ISBN:0-7679-0806-6, ISBN13: 978-0-7679-0806-1. Dewey:814/.54. LCCN:00-069799.
Audience: **g,l,u,f.**

Vidal, Gore **PS3543 ID2**
Visit to a Small Planet. Library Binding. Amereon, Ltd. Mattituck, NY. ISBN:0-8488-2040-1, ISBN13: 978-0-8488-2040-4. Dewey:812.5.
Audience: **g,l,u,f.**

Vidal, Gore **PS3543.I26W3 2000**
Washington, D. C. Trade Paper. Knopf Publishing Group. New York, NY. 2000. 432p. International Ser. ISBN:0-375-70877-4, ISBN13: 978-0-375-70877-0. Dewey:813/.54. LCCN:2002-278296.
Audience: **g,l,u,f.**

Vidal, Gore **PS3568.O243**
Williwaw. Trade Cloth. Arion Press. San Francisco, CA. 1996. 136p. ISBN:0-910457-34-4, ISBN13: 978-0-910457-34-7. Dewey:813/.54.
Audience: **g,l,u,f.** B

20th Century (1901-1960) > W

Bassett, Mark T. (Editor) **PS3515.O6455**
Blues of a Lifetime: The Autobiography of Cornell Woolrich. Trade Cloth. University of Wisconsin Press. Chicago, IL. 1991. 152p. ISBN:0-87972-535-4, ISBN13: 978-0-87972-535-8. Dewey:813/.52. LCCN:91-073287.
Audience: **g,l,u,f.**

Butts, William (Editor) **PS3545.I32165Z464**
Conversations with Richard Wilbur. Cloth Text. University Press of Mississippi. Jackson, MS. 1990. 288p. Literary Conversations Ser. ISBN:0-87805-424-3, ISBN13: 978-0-87805-424-4. Dewey:811/.52. LCCN:89-028839.
Audience: **l,u.**

Comito, Terry **PS3545.I765Z6 1986**
In Defense of Winters: The Poetry and Prose of Yvor Winters. Cloth Text. University of Wisconsin Press. Chicago, IL. 1986. 400p. Wisconsin Project on American Writers Ser. ISBN:0-299-10580-6, ISBN13: 978-0-299-10580-8. Dewey:811/.52. LCCN:85-040759.
Audience: **u,f.** *Choice, 1986.*

Edgecombe, Rodney S. **PS3545.I32165Z65**
A Reader's Guide to the Poetry of Richard Wilbur. Paper Text. University of Alabama Press. Tuscaloosa, AL. 1995. 224p. ISBN:0-8173-0715-X, ISBN13: 978-0-8173-0715-8. Dewey:811/.52. LCCN:94-037229.
Audience: **l,u.**

Graulich, Melody & Tatum, Stephen (Editors) **PS3345.V53R43 2003**
Reading the Virginian in the New West. Paper Text. University of Nebraska Press. Lincoln, NE. 2003. xix, 300p. ISBN:0-8032-7104-2, ISBN13: 978-0-8032-7104-3. Dewey:813/.52. LCCN:2002-028522.
Audience: **u,f.**

Wagoner, David **PS3545.A345T69 1999**
Traveling Light: Collected and New Poems. Trade Paper. University of Illinois Press. Champaign, IL. 1999. 320p. Illinois Poetry Ser. ISBN:0-252-06803-3, ISBN13: 978-0-252-06803-4. Dewey:811/.54. LCCN:98-058032.
Audience: **g,l,u,f.**

Walker, Margaret **PS3545.A517 F6**
For My People. Trade Cloth. Ayer Company Publishers, Inc. Manchester, NH. 1978. American Negro, :His History and Literature, Series 2 ISBN:0-405-01902-5, ISBN13: 978-0-405-01902-9. Dewey:810.8/09.
Audience: **l,u,f.** B

Wallace, Lew **PS3134.B4 1998**
Ben-Hur. David Mayer (Editor, Introduction by, Notes by). Trade Paper. Oxford University Press, Inc. New York, NY. 1998. 560p. Oxford World's Classics Ser. ISBN:0-19-283199-2, ISBN13: 978-0-19-283199-6. Dewey:813/.4. LCCN:97-043634.
Audience: **g,l,u,f.**

Ward, Mary J. **PS3545.A695**
The Snake Pit. Library Binding. Buccaneer Books, Inc. Cutchogue, NY. 1981. 6p. ISBN:0-89966-260-9, ISBN13: 978-0-89966-260-2. Dewey:813/.54.
Audience: **g,l,u,f.**

Wescott, Glenway **PS3545.E827G7 1996**
The Grandmothers: A Family Portrait. Sargent Bush (Introduction by). Trade Cloth. University of Wisconsin Press. Chicago, IL. 1996. 412p. ISBN:0-299-15020-8, ISBN13: 978-0-299-15020-4. Dewey:813/.52. LCCN:96-001902.
Audience: **g,l,u,f.** B

Wescott, Glenway **PS3545.E827P5 2001**
The Pilgrim Hawk: A Love Story. Michael Cunningham (Introduction by). Trade Paper. New York Review of Books, Incorporated, The. New York, NY. 2001. 136p. New York Review Books Classics Ser. ISBN:0-940322-56-0, ISBN13: 978-0-940322-56-1. Dewey:813/.52. LCCN:00-011548.
Audience: **g,l,u,f.** B

Wescott, Glenway **PS3545.E827A845 2004**
Apartment in Athens. David Leavitt (Introduction by). Trade Paper. New York Review of Books, Incorporated, The. New York, NY. 2004. 296p. New York Review Books Classics Ser. ISBN:1-59017-081-4, ISBN13: 978-1-59017-081-6. Dewey:813/.52. LCCN:2004-003860.
Audience: **g,l,u,f.** B

Whalen, Philip **PS3545.H117A6 1999**
Overtime: Selected Poems. Michael Rothenberg (Editor), Leslie Scalapino (Introduction by). Trade Paper. Penguin Group (USA) Inc. New York, NY. 1999. 304p. Penguin Poets Ser. ISBN:0-14-058918-X, ISBN13: 978-0-14-058918-4. Dewey:811/.54. LCCN:98-048926.
Audience: **g,l,u,f.**

Wilbur, Richard **PS3545.I32165A6 2004**
Collected Poems, 1943-2004. Cloth over Boards. Harcourt Trade Publishers. New York, NY. 2004. 608p. ISBN:0-15-101105-2, ISBN13: 978-0-15-101105-6. Dewey:811/.54. LCCN:2004-009228.
Audience: **g,l,u,f.**

Wilbur, Richard **PS3545.I32165R4 2000**
Responses: Prose Pieces, 1953-1976. Trade Paper. Story Line Press. Ashland, OR. 1999. 284p. ISBN:1-885266-82-0, ISBN13: 978-1-885266-82-8. Dewey:809.1. LCCN:99-048578.
Audience: **g,l,u,f.**

Wilson, Sloan **PS3573.I475.M3**
The Man in the Gray Flannel Suit. Library Binding. Buccaneer Books, Inc. Cutchogue, NY. 1991. 250p. ISBN:0-89966-862-3, ISBN13: 978-0-89966-862-8. Dewey:813.54.
Audience: **g,l,u,f.** B

Winters, Yvor **PS3545.I765A6 2003**
Yvor Winters: Selected Poems. Trade Cloth. Library of America, The. New York, NY. 2003. 200p. American Poets Project Ser. ISBN:1-931082-50-2, ISBN13: 978-1-931082-50-1. Dewey:811/.52. LCCN:2003-046638.
Audience: **g,l,u,f.**

Wister, Owen **PS3511.A86**
The Virginian: A Horseman of the Plains. Robert Shulman (Editor, Introduction by, Notes by). Trade Paper. Oxford University Press, Inc. New York, NY. 1998. 388p. Oxford World's Classics Ser. ISBN:0-19-283226-3, ISBN13: 978-0-19-283226-9. Dewey:813/.52. LCCN:97-030325.
Audience: **g,l,u,f.** B

Wouk, Herman **PQ2605.A3734**
The Caine Mutiny. Trade Cloth. Little Brown & Company. New York, NY. 2003. ISBN:0-316-95736-4, ISBN13: 978-0-316-95736-6. Dewey:843/.914.
Audience: **g,l,u,f.** B

Wright, James **PS3566.L27**
Collected Poems. Trade Paper. Wesleyan University Press. Middletown, CT. 1971. 229p. Wesleyan Poetry Ser. ISBN:0-8195-6022-7, ISBN13: 978-0-8195-6022-3. Dewey:811/.5/4. LCCN:70-142727.
Audience: **g,l,u,f.** B

Wylie, Elinor H. **PS3545.Y45V4 1984**
The Venetian Glass Nephew. Trade Paper. Academy Chicago Publishers, Ltd. Chicago, IL. 1988. 182p. ISBN:0-89733-112-5, ISBN13: 978-0-89733-112-8. Dewey:813/.52. LCCN:84-014557.
Audience: **g,l,u,f.**

20th Century (1901-1960) > W > Warren, Robert Penn

Bohner, Charles H. **PS3545.A748 Z6 1981**
Robert Penn Warren. Trade Cloth. Thomson Gale. Farmington Hills, MI. 1981. 176p. United States Authors Ser. ISBN:0-8057-7345-2, ISBN13: 978-0-8057-7345-3. Dewey:813/.52. LCCN:81-004269.
Audience: **l,u.** B

Bradley, Patricia L. **PS3545.A748Z625 2004**
Robert Penn Warren's Circus Aesthetic and the Southern Renaissance. Trade Cloth. University of Tennessee Press. Knoxville, TN. 2004. 196p. ISBN:1-57233-311-1, ISBN13: 978-1-57233-311-6. Dewey:813/.52. LCCN:2004-012280.
Audience: **u,f.** *Choice, 2005.*

Burt, John **PS3545.A748Z64 1988**
Robert Penn Warren and American Idealism. Cloth over Boards. Yale University Press. Cumberland, RI. 1988. 238p. ISBN:0-300-04067-9, ISBN13: 978-0-300-04067-8. Dewey:813/.52. LCCN:87-014742.
Audience: **u,f.** *Choice, 1989.*

Cronin, Gloria L. & Siegel, Ben (Editors) **PS3545.A748Z656 2005**
Conversations with Robert Penn Warren. Trade Cloth. University Press of Mississippi. Jackson, MS. 2005. 240p. Literary Conversations Ser. ISBN:1-57806-733-2, ISBN13: 978-1-57806-733-6. Dewey:813/.52. LCCN:2004-053642.
Audience: **l,u.**

Warren, Robert Penn **PS3545.A748**
All the King's Men. Trade Paper, Perfect. Harcourt Trade Publishers. New York, NY. 2005. 672p. ISBN:0-15-603096-9, ISBN13: 978-0-15-603096-0. Dewey:813/.52.
Audience: **g,l,u,f.** *Choice, 2002.*

Warren, Robert Penn **PS3545.A748B3 1994**
Band of Angels. Trade Paper. Louisiana State University Press. Baton Rouge, LA. 1994. 375p. Voices of the South Ser. ISBN:0-8071-1946-6, ISBN13: 978-0-8071-1946-4. Dewey:813/.52. LCCN:55-005814.
Audience: **l,u,f.** B

Warren, Robert Penn **PS3545.A748B7 1996**
Brother to Dragons: A Tale in Verse and Voices. Trade Paper. Louisiana State University Press. Baton Rouge, LA. 1996. 148p. Voices of the South Ser. ISBN:0-8071-2123-1, ISBN13: 978-0-8071-2123-8. Dewey:811/.52. LCCN:96-042223.
Audience: **g,l,u,f.** B

Warren, Robert Penn **PS3545.A748 C6 1983**
The Circus in the Attic and Other Stories. Trade Paper. Harcourt Trade Publishers. New York, NY. 1968. 288p. Harvest Book Ser. ISBN:0-15-618002-2, ISBN13: 978-0-15-618002-3. Dewey:813/.52. LCCN:83-008461.
Audience: **g,l,u,f.** B

Warren, Robert Penn **PS3545.A748A17 1998**
Collected Poems of Robert Penn Warren. John Burt (Editor), Harold Bloom (Foreword by). Trade Cloth. Louisiana State University Press. Baton Rouge, LA. 1998. 830p. ISBN:0-8071-2333-1, ISBN13: 978-0-8071-2333-1. Dewey:811/.52. LCCN:98-026104.
Audience: **l,u,f.**

Warren, Robert Penn **PS3545.A748 N5 1992**
Night Rider. George Core (Introduction by). Trade Paper. Ivan R. Dee Publisher. Blue Ridge Summit, PA. 1992. 460p. Southern Classics Ser. ISBN:1-879941-14-7, ISBN13: 978-1-879941-14-4. Dewey:813/.52. LCCN:92-082382.
Audience: **g,l,u,f.** B

Warren, Robert Penn **PS3545.A748**
The Cave. James H. Justus (Introduction by). Trade Paper. University Press of Kentucky. Lexington, KY. 2006. 424p. Kentucky Voices Ser. ISBN:0-8131-9155-6, ISBN13: 978-0-8131-9155-3. Dewey:813/.52. LCCN:2005-034196.
Audience: **g,l,u,f.**

20th Century (1901-1960) > W > Welty, Eudora

Abadie, Ann J. & Dollarhide, Louis D. (Editors) **PS3545 E6 Z66**
Eudora Welty: A Form of Thanks. Cloth Text. University Press of Mississippi. Jackson, MS. 1979. 138p. ISBN:0-87805-089-2, ISBN13: 978-0-87805-089-5. Dewey:813/.52 19. LCCN:78-013285.
Audience: **l,u.**

Devlin, Albert J. (Editor) **PS3545.E6.Z64 1983**
Eudora Welty's Chronicle: A Story of Mississippi Life. Cloth Text. University Press of Mississippi. Jackson, MS. 1983. 240p. ISBN:0-87805-176-7, ISBN13: 978-0-87805-176-2. Dewey:813/.52. LCCN:82-019996.
Audience: **l,u,f.** B

Johnston, Carol A. **PS3545.E6Z73 1997**
Eudora Welty: A Study of the Short Fiction. Trade Cloth. Thomson Gale. Farmington Hills, MI. 1997. 259p. Twayne's Studies in Short Fiction, No. 67 ISBN:0-8057-7936-1, ISBN13: 978-0-8057-7936-3. Dewey:813/.52. LCCN:96-041770.
Audience: **g,l.** *Choice, 1997.*

Kreyling, Michael **PS3545.E6Z752 1999**
Understanding Eudora Welty. Trade Cloth. University of South Carolina Press. Columbia, SC. 1999. 272p. Understanding Contemporary American Literature Ser. ISBN:1-57003-283-1, ISBN13: 978-1-57003-283-7. Dewey:813/.52. LCCN:98-040292.
Audience: **l,u.** *Choice, 2000.*

MacNeil, Robert **TR140.W43M33 1990**
Eudora Welty: Seeing Black and White. Trade Paper. University Press of Mississippi. Jackson, MS. 1990. 15p. ISBN:0-87805-471-5, ISBN13: 978-0-87805-471-8. Dewey:770/.92. LCCN:90-012640.
Audience: **u,f.**

Marrs, Suzanne **PS3545.E6Z7728 2005**
Eudora Welty: A Biography. Cloth over Boards. Harcourt Trade Publishers. New York, NY. 2005. 672p. ISBN:0-15-100914-7, ISBN13: 978-0-15-100914-5. Dewey:813/.52 B. LCCN:2004-030490.
Audience: **g,l,u,f.** *Choice, 2005.*

Marrs, Suzanne **PS3511.A86**
One Writer's Imagination: The Fiction of Eudora Welty. Trade Paper. Louisiana State University Press. Baton Rouge, LA. 2002. xix, 280p. Southern Literary Studies ISBN:0-8071-2841-4, ISBN13: 978-0-8071-2841-1. Dewey:813/.52.
Audience: **l,u,f.** *Choice, 2003.*

McHaney, Pearl A. **PS3545.E6Z6735 2005**
Eudora Welty: The Contemporary Reviews. M. Thomas Inge (Contribution by). Trade Cloth. Cambridge University Press. New York, NY. 2005. 420p. American Critical Archives Ser., Vol. 15 ISBN:0-521-65317-7, ISBN13: 978-0-521-65317-6. Dewey:813/.52. LCCN:2004-051102.
Audience: **l,u.**

Prenshaw, Peggy W. (Editor) **PS3545.E6Z775 1996**
More Conversations with Eudora Welty. Trade Cloth. University Press of Mississippi. Jackson, MS. 1996. 328p. Literary Conversations Ser. ISBN:0-87805-864-8, ISBN13: 978-0-87805-864-8. Dewey:813/.52. LCCN:95-025720.
Audience: **l,u.**

Turner, W. Craig & Harding, Lee E. **PS3545.E6Z63 1989**
Critical Essays on Eudora Welty. Trade Cloth. Thomson Gale. Farmington Hills, MI. 1989. 288p. Critical Essays on American Literature Ser. ISBN:0-8161-8888-2, ISBN13: 978-0-8161-8888-8. Dewey:813/.52. LCCN:88-024737.
Audience: **l,u.** *Choice, 1989.*

Waldron, Ann **PS3511.A86**
Eudora Welty: A Writer's Life. Trade Paper. Knopf Publishing Group. New York, NY. 1999. 432p. ISBN:0-385-47648-5, ISBN13: 978-0-385-47648-5. Dewey:813/.52 B. LCCN:98-005708.
Audience: **l,u.** *Choice, 1999.*

Welty, Eudora **PS3545.E6Z475 1984**
One Writer's Beginnings. Trade Paper. Harvard University Press. Cambridge, MA. 1998. 118p. The William E. Massey Sr. Lectures in the History of American Civilization Ser. ISBN:0-674-63927-8, ISBN13: 978-0-674-63927-0. Dewey:813/.52 B. LCCN:83-018638.
Audience: **g,l,u,f.** B

Welty, Eudora **PS3545.E6.A6 1998**
Eudora Welty: The Robber Bridegroom; Delta Wedding; The Ponder Heart; Losing Battles; The Optimist's Daughter. Richard Ford & Michael Kreyling (Editors). Trade Cloth. Library of America, The. New York, NY. 1998. 1012p. Library of America, Vol. 101 ISBN:1-883011-54-X, ISBN13: 978-1-883011-54-3. Dewey:813/.52. LCCN:97-046702.
Audience: **g,l,u,f.**

Welty, Eudora **PS3545.E6A6 1998**
Stories, Essays and Memoir: A Curtain of Green; The Wide Net; The Golden Apples; The Bride of the Innisfallen; Selected Essays One Writer's Beginnings. Richard Ford & Michael Kreyling (Editors). Trade Cloth. Library of America, The. New York, NY. 1998. 980p. Library of America, Vol. 102 ISBN:1-883011-55-8, ISBN13: 978-1-883011-55-0. Dewey:813/.52. LCCN:97-046691.
Audience: **g,l,u,f.**

Welty, Eudora **PS3545.E6W75 1994**
A Writer's Eye: Collected Book Reviews. Pearl A. McHaney (Editor). Trade Cloth. University Press of Mississippi. Jackson, MS. 1994. 308p. ISBN:0-87805-683-1, ISBN13: 978-0-87805-683-5. Dewey:028.1. LCCN:93-033643.
Audience: **g,l,u,f.**

Weston, Ruth D. **PS3545.E6Z97 1994**
Gothic Traditions and Narrative Technique in the Fiction of Eudora Welty. Cloth Text. Louisiana State University Press. Baton Rouge, LA. 1994. xiv, 264p. Southern Literary Studies ISBN:0-8071-1897-4, ISBN13: 978-0-8071-1897-9. Dewey:813/.52. LCCN:94-006067.
Audience: **l,u,f.** *Choice, 1995.*

20th Century (1901-1960) > W > West, Jessamyn

Shivers, Alfred S. **PS3545.E8315**
Jessamyn West. Trade Cloth. Macmillan Publishing Company, Inc. Old Tappan, NJ. 1992. 160p. Twayne's United States Authors Ser. ISBN:0-8057-3979-3, ISBN13: 978-0-8057-3979-4. Dewey:813/.54. LCCN:92-029077.
Audience: **l,u.** B

West, Jessamyn **PS3545.E8315A6 1986**
The Collected Stories of Jessamyn West. Trade Cloth. Harcourt Trade Publishers. New York, NY. 1986. 352p. ISBN:0-15-119010-0, ISBN13: 978-0-15-119010-2. Dewey:813/.54. LCCN:86-012031.
Audience: **g,l,u,f.**

West, Jessamyn **PR6019.O9**
The Friendly Persuasion. Trade Paper. Harcourt Trade Publishers. New York, NY. 2003. 228p. ISBN:0-15-602909-X, ISBN13: 978-0-15-602909-4. Dewey:823/.91.
Audience: **g,l,u,f.**

West, Jessamyn **PS3545.E8315**
Love, Death and the Ladies' Drill Team. Trade Paper. Harcourt Trade Publishers. New York, NY. 1968. ISBN:0-15-653905-5, ISBN13: 978-0-15-653905-0. Dewey:813.5. LCCN:55-010809.
Audience: **g,l,u,f.** B

20th Century (1901-1960) > W > West, Nathanael

Barnard, Rita **PS228.P67 B37 1995**
The Great Depression and the Culture of Abundance: Kenneth Fearing, Nathanael West and Mass Culture in the 1930s. Albert Gelpi & Ross Posnock (Contribution by). Trade Cloth. Cambridge University Press. New York, NY. 1995. 283p. Studies in American Literature and Culture, No. 87 ISBN:0-521-45034-9, ISBN13: 978-0-521-45034-8. Dewey:810.9/0052. LCCN:94-016668.
Audience: **u,f.** *Choice, 1996.*

Comerchero, Victor **PS3545.E8334 Z6**
Nathanael West: The Ironic Prophet. Trade Paper. University of Washington Press. Seattle, WA. 1967. 202p. ISBN:0-295-97876-7, ISBN13: 978-0-295-97876-5. Dewey:813.52. LCCN:64-023342.
Audience: **l,u.** B

Malin, Irving **PS3545.E8334.Z76**
Nathanael West's Novels. Trade Cloth. Southern Illinois University Press. Carbondale, IL. 1972. 152p. Crosscurrents-Modern Critiques Ser. ISBN:0-8093-0577-1, ISBN13: 978-0-8093-0577-3. Dewey:813/.5/2. LCCN:75-188697.
Audience: **l,u.** B

Martin, Jay **PS3511.A86**
Nathanael West: The Art of His Life. Trade Paper. Avalon Publishing Group. New York, NY. 1984. 435p. ISBN:0-88184-030-0, ISBN13: 978-0-88184-030-8. Dewey:813/.5/2.
Audience: **l,u.** B

Reid, Randall **PS3545 ES82 Z5 R2**
Fiction of Nathanael West: No Redeemer, No Promised Land. Paper Text. University of Chicago Press. Chicago, IL. 1992. ISBN:0-226-70925-6, ISBN13: 978-0-226-70925-3. Dewey:813/.5/2. LCCN:67-030949.
Audience: **u,f.** B

Siegel, Ben **PS3545.E8334Z63 1994**
Critical Essays on Nathanael West. Trade Cloth. Thomson Gale. Farmington Hills, MI. 1994. 248p. Critical Essays on American Literature Ser. ISBN:0-7838-0027-4, ISBN13: 978-0-7838-0027-1. Dewey:813/.52. LCCN:94-014474.
Audience: **l,u.**

Veitch, Jonathan **PS3545.E8334Z9 1997**
American Superrealism: Nathanael West and the Politics of Representation in the 1930's. Trade Paper. University of Wisconsin Press. Chicago, IL. 1997. 182p. Wisconsin Project on American Writers Ser. ISBN:0-299-15704-0, ISBN13: 978-0-299-15704-3. Dewey:813/.52. LCCN:97-014031.
Audience: **u,f.** *Choice, 1998.*

West, Nathanael **PS3545.E8334A6 1997**
Nathanael West - Novels and Other Writings: The Dream Life of Balso Snell; Miss Lonelyhearts; A Cool Million; The Day of the Locust; Other Writings; Letters. Sacvan Bercovitch (Editor). Trade Cloth. Library of America, The. New York, NY. 1997. 840p. Library of America, Vol. 93 ISBN:1-883011-28-0, ISBN13: 978-1-883011-28-4. Dewey:813/.52. LCCN:96-049007.
Audience: **g,l,u,f.**

20th Century (1901-1960) > W > Wharton, Edith

Bell, Millicent (Editor) **PS3545.H16 Z636 1995**
The Cambridge Companion to Edith Wharton. Cloth Text. Cambridge University Press. New York, NY. 1995. 229p. Cambridge Companions to Literature Ser. ISBN:0-521-45358-5, ISBN13: 978-0-521-45358-5. Dewey:813.5/2. LCCN:94-034704.
Audience: **l,u,f.**

Bendixen, Alfred & Zilverfsmit, Annette (Editors) **PS3545.H16Z6454 1991**
Edith Wharton: New Critical Essays. Cloth Text. Garland Publishing, Inc. New York, NY. 1991. 342p. ISBN:0-8240-7848-9, ISBN13: 978-0-8240-7848-5. Dewey:813/.52. LCCN:91-027844.
Audience: **l,u.**

Benstock, Shari **PS3545.H16Z595 2004**
No Gifts from Chance: A Biography of Edith Wharton. Trade Paper. University of Texas Press. Austin, TX. 2004. 575p. ISBN:0-292-70274-4, ISBN13: 978-0-292-70274-5. Dewey:813/.52 B. LCCN:2003-055569.
Audience: **g,l,u,f.**

Erlich, Gloria C. **PS3545.H16Z646 1992**
The Sexual Education of Edith Wharton. Trade Cloth. University of California Press. Berkeley, CA. 1992. 223p. ISBN:0-520-07583-8, ISBN13: 978-0-520-07583-2. Dewey:813/.52 B. LCCN:91-016671.
Audience: **l,u,f.**

Kassanoff, Jennie A. **PS3545.H16Z686 2004**
Edith Wharton and the Politics of Race. Albert Gelpi & Ross Posnock (Contribution by). Trade Cloth. Cambridge University Press. New York, NY. 2004. 238p. Cambridge Studies in American Literature and Culture Ser. ISBN:0-521-83089-3, ISBN13: 978-0-521-83089-8. Dewey:813.52. LCCN:2003-063281.
Audience: **u,f.** *Choice, 2005.*

Killoran, Helen **PS3545.H16Z6868 2001**
The Critical Reception of Edith Wharton. Trade Cloth. Camden House. Elizabethtown, NY. 2004. 192p. Studies in American Literature and Culture ISBN:1-57113-101-9, ISBN13: 978-1-57113-101-0. Dewey:813/.52. LCCN:2001-035774.
Audience: **l,u.** *Choice, 2002.*

Lewis, R. W. B. **PS3545.H16Z696 1985**
Edith Wharton: A Biography. Trade Paper. Fromm International Publishing Corporation. New York, NY. 1985. 592p. ISBN:0-88064-020-0, ISBN13: 978-0-88064-020-6. Dewey:813/.52 B. LCCN:85-013035.
Audience: **g,l,u,f.** B

Montgomery, Maureen E. **PS3545.H16Z747 1998**
Displaying Women: Spectacles of Leisure in Edith Wharton's New York. UK-B Format Paperback. Routledge. New York, NY. 1998. 272p. ISBN:0-415-90566-4, ISBN13: 978-0-415-90566-4. Dewey:813/.52. LCCN:97-031983.
Audience: **u,f.** *Choice, 1999.*

Peel, Robin **PS3545.H16Z758 2005**
Apart from Modernism: Edith Wharton, Politics, and Fiction Before World War I. Trade Cloth. Fairleigh Dickinson

University Press. Cranbury, NJ. 2005. 352p. ISBN:0-8386-4079-6, ISBN13: 978-0-8386-4079-1. Dewey:813/.52. LCCN:2005-004432.
Audience: **u,f.** *Choice, 2006.*

Price, Alan **PS3511.A86**
The End of the Age of Innocence: Edith Wharton and the First World War. Trade Paper. Palgrave Macmillan. New York, NY. 1997. 238p. ISBN:0-312-17677-5, ISBN13: 978-0-312-17677-8. Dewey:813.5/2.
Audience: **l,u,f.** *Choice, 1996.*

Rae, Catherine M. **PS3545.H16O437 1984**
Edith Wharton's New York Quartet. R. W. B. Lewis (Introduction by). Trade Cloth. University Press of America, Inc. Lanham, MD. 1984. 96p. ISBN:0-8191-4028-7, ISBN13: 978-0-8191-4028-9. Dewey:813/.52. LCCN:84-011813.
Audience: **l,u,f.** B

Singley, Carol J. (Editor) **PS3545.H16Z663 2002**
A Historical Guide to Edith Wharton. Cloth Text. Oxford University Press, Inc. New York, NY. 2003. 312p. Historical Guides to American Authors ISBN:0-19-513590-3, ISBN13: 978-0-19-513590-9. Dewey:813/.52. LCCN:2002-034613.
Audience: **l,u.** *Choice, 2003.*

Tinter, Adeline R. **PS3545.H16Z8786 1999**
Edith Wharton in Context: Essays on Intertextuality. Trade Cloth. University of Alabama Press. Tuscaloosa, AL. 1999. 304p. ISBN:0-8173-0975-6, ISBN13: 978-0-8173-0975-6. Dewey:813/.52. LCCN:99-006206.
Audience: **u,f.** *Choice, 2000.*

Tuttleton, James W. (Editor), et al. **PS3545.H16 Z6456 19**
Edith Wharton: Early Critical Responses. Kristin O. Lauer & Margaret P. Murray (Editors), M. Thomas Inge (Contribution by). Cloth Text. Cambridge University Press. New York, NY. 1992. 586p. American Critical Archives Ser., No. 2 ISBN:0-521-38319-6, ISBN13: 978-0-521-38319-6. Dewey:813.4. LCCN:91-043206.
Audience: **u,f.**

Wharton, Edith **PS3511.A86**
Old New York. Library Binding. Classic Books. Murrieta, CA. 1998. The Collected Works of Edith Wharton ISBN:1-58201-990-8, ISBN13: 978-1-58201-990-1. Dewey:813.5/2.
Audience: **g,l,u,f.** B

Wharton, Edith **PS3531.O82**
Edith Wharton: Selected Poems. Louis Auchincloss (Editor). Saddle Stitched, Cloth over Boards, Dust Jacket. Library of America, The. New York, NY. 2005. 183p. American Poets Project Ser. ISBN:1-931082-86-3, ISBN13: 978-1-931082-86-0. Dewey:811/.52.
Audience: **g,l,u,f.**

Wharton, Edith **PS3545.H16A6 2001**
Edith Wharton: Collected Stories 1891-1910. Maureen Howard (Editor). Trade Cloth. Library of America, The. New York, NY. 2001. 928p. Library of America, Vol. 121 ISBN:1-883011-93-0, ISBN13: 978-1-883011-93-2. Dewey:813/.52. LCCN:00-057596.
Audience: **g,l,u,f.**

Wharton, Edith **PS3545.H16A6 2001**
Edith Wharton: Collected Stories 1911-1937. Maureen Howard (Editor). Trade Cloth. Library of America, The. New York, NY. 2001. 848p. Library of America, Vol. 122 ISBN:1-883011-94-9, ISBN13: 978-1-883011-94-9. Dewey:813/.52. LCCN:00-057595.
Audience: **g,l,u,f.**

Wharton, Edith **PS3545.H16A6 1985**
Novels: The House of Mirth; The Reef; The Custom of the Country; The Age of Innocence. R. W. B. Lewis (Editor). Trade Cloth. Library of America, The. New York, NY. 1986. 1328p. ISBN:0-940450-31-3, ISBN13: 978-0-940450-31-8. Dewey:813/.52. LCCN:85-019816.
Audience: **g,l,u,f.**

Wharton, Edith **PS3545.H16A6 1996**
Edith Wharton: Four Novels. R. W. B. Lewis & Cynthia Griffin Wolff (Editors). Trade Paper. Library of America, The. New York, NY. 1996. 1168p. Library of America ISBN:1-883011-37-X, ISBN13: 978-1-883011-37-6. Dewey:813/.52. LCCN:96-008934.
Audience: **g,l,u,f.**

Wharton, Edith **PS121.W43**
Edith Wharton: The Uncollected Critical Writings. Frederick Wegener (Editor). Paper Text. Princeton University Press. Princeton, NJ. 1998. 350p. ISBN:0-691-00269-X, ISBN13: 978-0-691-00269-9. Dewey:810.9.
Audience: **g,l,u,f.**

Wharton, Edith **PS3545.H16.A6 1990**
Wharton:Novellas and Other Writings: Madame de Treymes; Ethan Frome; Summer; Old New York; the Mother's Recompense; a Backward Glance. Cynthia G. Wolff (Editor). Trade Cloth. Library of America, The. New York, NY. 1990. 1137p. Library of America, Vol. 47 ISBN:0-940450-53-4, ISBN13: 978-0-940450-53-0. Dewey:813/.52. LCCN:89-062930.
Audience: **g,l,u,f.**

White, Barbara A. **PS3545.H16Z93 1991**
Edith Wharton: A Study of the Short Fiction. Trade Cloth. Macmillan Publishing Company, Inc. Old Tappan, NJ. 1991. 190p. Twayne's Studies in Short Fiction, No. 30 ISBN:0-8057-8340-7, ISBN13: 978-0-8057-8340-7. Dewey:813/.52. LCCN:91-024547.
Audience: **l,u.** *Choice, 1992.*

Williams, Deborah Lindsay **PS374.F45W55 2001**
Not in Sisterhood: Edith Wharton, Willa Cather, Zona Gale and the Politics of Female Authorship. Cloth over Boards. Palgrave Macmillan. New York, NY. 2001. 240p. ISBN:0-312-22921-6, ISBN13: 978-0-312-22921-4. Dewey:813/.52099287. LCCN:2001-021549.
Audience: **u,f.** *Choice, 2001.*

Wright, Sarah B. **PS3545.H16Z459 1998**
Edith Wharton A to Z: The Essential Guide to the Life and Work. Trade Cloth. Facts On File, Inc. New York, NY. 1998. 352p. Literary A to Z Ser. ISBN:0-8160-3481-8, ISBN13: 978-0-8160-3481-9. Dewey:813/.52. LCCN:97-045574.
Audience: **l,u.** *Choice, 1999.*

Wright, Sarah B. **PS3545.H16Z99 1997**
Edith Wharton's Travel Writings: The Making of a Connoisseur. Cloth over Boards. Palgrave Macmillan. New York, NY. 1997. 208p. ISBN:0-312-15842-4, ISBN13: 978-0-312-15842-2. Dewey:813/.52. LCCN:96-048920.
Audience: **u,f.**

20th Century (1901-1960) > W > White, E. B.

Agosta, Lucien L. **PS3545.H5187Z524**
E. B. White: The Children's Books. Trade Cloth. Thomson Gale. Farmington Hills, MI. 1995. 179p. Twayne's United States Authors Ser., Vol. 621 ISBN:0-8057-4631-5, ISBN13: 978-0-8057-4631-0. Dewey:818/.5209. LCCN:95-008467.
Audience: **l,u.**

Elledge, Scott **PS3545.H5187Z64 1986**
E. B. White: A Biography. Trade Paper. W. W. Norton & Company, Inc. New York, NY. 1986. 348p. ISBN:0-393-30305-5, ISBN13: 978-0-393-30305-6. Dewey:818/.5209 B. LCCN:83-004032.
Audience: **g,l,u,f.**

Root, Robert **PS3545.H5187Z62 1994**
Critical Essays on E. B. White. Trade Cloth. Thomson Gale. Farmington Hills, MI. 1994. 224p. Critical Essays on American Literature Ser. ISBN:0-8161-7321-4, ISBN13: 978-0-8161-7321-1. Dewey:818/.5209. LCCN:93-038334.
Audience: **l,u.** *Choice, 1994.*

Root, Robert L. Jr. **PS3545.H5187Z86 1999**
E. B. White: The Emergence of an Essayist. Trade Cloth. University of Iowa Press. Iowa City, IA. 1999. 256p. ISBN:0-87745-667-4, ISBN13: 978-0-87745-667-4. Dewey:818/.5209. LCCN:98-048375.
Audience: **l,u,f.** *Choice, 1999.*

Sampson, Edward C. **PS3545.H5187.Z9**
E. B. White. Library Binding. Thomson Gale. Farmington Hills, MI. 1974. 190p. United States Authors Ser. ISBN:0-8057-0787-5, ISBN13: 978-0-8057-0787-8. Dewey:818/.5/209. LCCN:73-021582.
Audience: **l,u.**

White, E. B. **PZ7.W58277**
E. B. White: Charlotte's Web, Stuart Little, and the Trumpet of the Swan, Set. Trade Paper. HarperCollins Publishers. New York, NY. 2003. ISBN:0-06-055416-9, ISBN13: 978-0-06-055416-3. Dewey:813.4.
Audience: **g,l,u.**

White, E. B. **PN6161**
Essays of E. B. White. Trade Cloth. Peter Smith Publisher, Inc. Magnolia, MA. 2001. ISBN:0-8446-7195-9, ISBN13: 978-0-8446-7195-6. Dewey:814/.52.
Audience: **g,l,u,f.**

White, E. B. **PN6161**
One Man's Meat. Trade Cloth. Amereon, Ltd. Mattituck, NY. 360p. ISBN:0-8488-2412-1, ISBN13: 978-0-8488-2412-9. Dewey:814/.52.
Audience: **g,l,u,f.**

White, E. B. **PS3537.T323**
Poems and Sketches of E. B. White. Mass Market. HarperCollins Publishers. New York, NY. 1983. 232p. ISBN:0-06-090969-2, ISBN13: 978-0-06-090969-7. Dewey:818/.5209. LCCN:81-047240.
Audience: **g,l,u,f.**

White, E. B. **PS3545.H5187S4 1984**
The Second Tree from the Corner. Trade Cloth. HarperCollins Publishers. New York, NY. 1984. 272p. ISBN:0-06-015354-7, ISBN13: 978-0-06-015354-0. Dewey:818/.5209. LCCN:84-047609.
Audience: **g,l,u,f.**

20th Century (1901-1960) > W > Wilder, Thornton

Blank, Martin (Editor) **PS3545.I345Z645 1996**
Critical Essays on Thornton Wilder. Trade Cloth. Thomson Gale. Farmington Hills, MI. 1996. Critical Essays on American Literature Ser. ISBN:0-7838-0020-7, ISBN13: 978-0-7838-0020-2. Dewey:818/.5209. LCCN:95-002274.
Audience: **l,u.**

Burbank, Rex J. **PS3545.I345.Z57 1978**
Thornton Wilder. Ed. 2. Trade Cloth. Macmillan Publishing Company, Inc. Old Tappan, NJ. 1978. 152p. United States Authors Ser. ISBN:0-8057-7223-5, ISBN13: 978-0-8057-7223-4. Dewey:818.5209. LCCN:77-026237.
Audience: **l,u.**

De Koster, Katie (Editor) **PS3545.I345Z86 1998**
Thornton Wilder. Trade Paper. Thomson Gale. Farmington Hills, MI. 1998. 189p. Literary Companion to American Literature Ser. ISBN:1-56510-814-0, ISBN13: 978-1-56510-814-1. Dewey:818/.5209. LCCN:98-009891.
Audience: **l,u.**

Goldstein, Malcom L. **PS3545.I345Z**
The Art of Thornton Wilder. Trade Paper. University of Nebraska Press. Lincoln, NE. 1986. ISBN:0-8032-5074-6, ISBN13: 978-0-8032-5074-1. Dewey:812.52.
Audience: **l,u.**

Haberman, Donald **PS3545.I345 Z68**
The Plays of Thornton Wilder: A Critical Study. Wesleyan University Press. 1967.
Audience: **l,u.**

Lifton, Paul **PS3545**
Vast Encyclopedia: The Theatre of Thornton Wilder. Trade Cloth. Greenwood Publishing Group, Inc. Portsmouth, NH. 1995. 240p. Contributions in Drama and Theatre Studies Ser., Vol. 61 ISBN:0-313-29356-2, ISBN13: 978-0-313-29356-6. Dewey:812/.52. LCCN:95-005675.
Audience: **u,f.**

Wilder, Thornton **PZ3.W6468**
The Eighth Day: A Novel. Trade Paper. HarperCollins Publishers. New York, NY. 2007. 512p. ISBN:0-06-008891-5, ISBN13: 978-0-06-008891-0. Dewey:813/.52. LCCN:2006-046743.
Audience: **g,l,u,f.**

Wilder, Thornton **PS3545.I345H4 2003**
Heaven's My Destination: A Novel. Trade Paper. HarperCollins Publishers. New York, NY. 2003. 240p. ISBN:0-06-008889-3, ISBN13: 978-0-06-008889-7. Dewey:813/.52. LCCN:2003-047116.
Audience: **g,l,u,f.**

Wilder, Thornton **PS3511.A86**
The Ides of March: A Novel. Library Binding. Buccaneer Books, Inc. Cutchogue, NY. 1994. ISBN:1-56849-445-9, ISBN13: 978-1-56849-445-6. Dewey:813/.52.
Audience: **g,l,u,f.**

Wilder, Thornton **PS3545.I345 A19**
Three Plays: Our Town/The Skin of Our Teeth/The Matchmaker. Trade Paper. HarperCollins Publishers. New York, NY. 2007. 496p. Perennial Classics Ser. ISBN:0-06-051264-4, ISBN13: 978-0-06-051264-4. Dewey:812/.52. LCCN:2006-046741.
Audience: **g,l,u,f.**

Wilder, Thornton **PS3545.I345Z64 1992**
Conversations with Thornton Wilder. Jackson R. Bryer (Editor). Trade Cloth. University Press of Mississippi. Jackson, MS. 1992. xxiv, 130p. Literary Conversations Ser. ISBN:0-87805-513-4, ISBN13: 978-0-87805-513-5. Dewey:818/.5209. LCCN:91-029421.
Audience: **g,l,u,f.**

20th Century (1901-1960) > W > Williams, Tennessee

Crandell, George W. (Editor) **PS3545**
The Critical Response to Tennessee Williams. Cloth Text. Greenwood Publishing Group, Inc. Portsmouth, NH. 1996. 352p. Critical Responses in Arts and Letters Ser., No. 24 ISBN:0-313-29372-4, ISBN13: 978-0-313-29372-6. Dewey:812/.54. LCCN:96-018345.
Audience: **l,u.**

Falk, Signi L. **PS3545.I5365**
Tennessee Williams. Ed. 2. Trade Cloth. Macmillan Publishing Company, Inc. Old Tappan, NJ. 1978. 200p. Twayne's United States Authors Ser., No. 10 ISBN:0-8057-7202-2, ISBN13: 978-0-8057-7202-9. Dewey:812/.5/4. LCCN:77-016575.
Audience: **l,u.**

Griffin, Alice **PS3545.I5365.Z664**
Understanding Tennessee Williams. Cloth Text. University of South Carolina Press. Columbia, SC. 1994. 288p. Understanding Contemporary American Literature Ser. ISBN:1-57003-017-0, ISBN13: 978-1-57003-017-8. Dewey:812/.54. LCCN:94-018690.
Audience: **l,u.**

Heintzelman, Greta & Smith Howard, Alycia **PS3545.I5365Z459**
Tennessee Williams A to Z: The Essential Reference to His Life and Work. Trade Cloth. Facts On File, Inc. New York, NY. 2005. 448p. Critical Companion Ser. ISBN:0-8160-4888-6, ISBN13: 978-0-8160-4888-5. Dewey:812/.54. LCCN:2004-007362.
Audience: **l,u.** *Choice, 2006.*

Holditch, Kenneth & Leavitt, Richard Freeman **PS3545.I5365Z69 2002**
Tennessee Williams and the South. Trade Cloth. University Press of Mississippi. Jackson, MS. 2002. 184p. ISBN:1-57806-410-4, ISBN13: 978-1-57806-410-6. Dewey:812/.54 B. LCCN:2002-000631.
Audience: **l,u,f.**

Kolin, Philip C. (Editor) **PS3545**
The Tennessee Williams Encyclopedia. Cloth Text. Greenwood Publishing Group, Inc. Portsmouth, NH. 2004. 384p. ISBN:0-313-32101-9, ISBN13: 978-0-313-32101-6. Dewey:812/.54. LCCN:2003-059583.
Audience: **l,u.** *Choice, 2004.*

Leavitt, Richard F. **PS3545.I5365.Z735**
The World of Tennessee Williams. Tennessee Williams (Introduction by). Other. Penguin Group (USA) Inc. New York, NY. 1978. 168p. ISBN:0-399-11773-3, ISBN13: 978-0-399-11773-2. Dewey:812/.5/4. LCCN:76-028473.
Audience: **l,u.** B

Leverich, Lyle **PS3545.I5365**
Tom: The Unknown Tennessee Williams. Trade Paper. W. W. Norton & Company, Inc. New York, NY. 1997. 644p. ISBN:0-393-31663-7, ISBN13: 978-0-393-31663-6. Dewey:812.5/4.
Audience: **l,u,f.** *Choice, 1996.*

Martin, Robert A. **PS3545.I5365.Z615**
Critical Essays on Tennessee Williams. Trade Cloth. Thomson Gale. Farmington Hills, MI. 1997. 350p. Critical Essays on American Literature Ser. ISBN:0-7838-0042-8, ISBN13: 978-0-7838-0042-4. Dewey:812/.54. LCCN:97-021446.
Audience: **l,u,f.**

Murphy, Brenda **PS3545.I5365 Z78 19**
Tennessee Williams and Elia Kazan: A Collaboration in the Theatre. Trade Cloth. Cambridge University Press. New York, NY. 1992. 217p. ISBN:0-521-40095-3, ISBN13: 978-0-521-40095-4. Dewey:812/.54. LCCN:91-016237.
Audience: **l,u,f.** *Choice, 1992.*

Paller, Michael **PS3545.I5365Z799**
Gentlemen Callers: Tennessee Williams, Homosexuality, and Mid-Twentieth-Century Drama. Cloth over Boards. Palgrave Macmillan. New York, NY. 2005. 288p. ISBN:1-4039-6775-X, ISBN13: 978-1-4039-6775-6. Dewey:812/.54. LCCN:2004-054129.
Audience: **l,u,f.** *Choice, 2006.*

Roudané, Matthew C. (Editor) **PS3545.I5365 Z614 1**
The Cambridge Companion to Tennessee Williams. Cloth Text. Cambridge University Press. New York, NY. 1997. 301p. Companions to Literature Ser. ISBN:0-521-49533-4, ISBN13: 978-0-521-49533-2. Dewey:812/.54. LCCN:96-040036.
Audience: **l,u,f.** *Choice, 1998.*

Savran, David **PS338.P6**
Communists, Cowboys, and Queers: The Politics of Masculinity in the Work of Arthur Miller and Tennessee Williams. Trade Paper. University of Minnesota Press. Minneapolis, MN. 1992. 256p. ISBN:0-8166-2123-3, ISBN13: 978-0-8166-2123-1. Dewey:812/.5209358. LCCN:92-004267.
Audience: **u,f.** *Choice, 1993.*

Spoto, Donald **PS3545.I5365.Z836**
Kindness of Strangers: The Life of Tennessee Williams. Trade Paper. Da Capo Press, Inc. Cambridge, MA. 1997. 448p. ISBN:0-306-80805-6, ISBN13: 978-0-306-80805-0. Dewey:812/.54 B. LCCN:97-008428.
Audience: **g,l,u,f.**

Vannatta, Dennis **PS3545.I5365Z857**
Tennessee Williams: A Study of Short Fiction. Trade Cloth. Macmillan Publishing Company, Inc. Old Tappan, NJ. 1988. 168p. ISBN:0-8057-8304-0, ISBN13: 978-0-8057-8304-9. Dewey:813/.54. LCCN:88-010977.
Audience: **l,u.**

Voss, Ralph F. (Editor) **PS3545.I5365Z756**
Magical Muse: Millennial Essays on Tennessee Williams. Trade Cloth. University of Alabama Press. Tuscaloosa, AL. 2002. 314p. ISBN:0-8173-1127-0, ISBN13: 978-0-8173-1127-8. Dewey:812/.54. LCCN:2001-005097.
Audience: **u,f.** *Choice, 2002.*

Williams, Tennessee **PS3545.I5365**
Clothes for a Summer Hotel. Trade Paper. Dramatists Play Service, Inc. New York, NY. 1981. ISBN:0-8222-0221-2, ISBN13: 978-0-8222-0221-9. Dewey:812/.54.
Audience: **g,l,u,f.** B

Williams, Tennessee **PS3545.I5365**
Dragon Country, Eight Plays: In the Bar of a Tokyo Hotel, Mutilated, Gnadiges Fraulein, I Rise in Flames Cried the Phoenix, I Can't Imagine Tomorrow, Confessional, Frosted Glass Coffin and Perfect Analysis Given by a Parrot. Trade Paper. New Directions Publishing Corporation. New York, NY. 1970. 288p. ISBN:0-8112-0219-4, ISBN13: 978-0-8112-0219-0. Dewey:812/.5/4. LCCN:76-079724.
Audience: **g,l,u,f.**

Williams, Tennessee **PS3545.I5365.T95**
Out Cry. Trade Cloth. New Directions Publishing Corporation. New York, NY. 1973. 72p. ISBN:0-8112-0500-2, ISBN13: 978-0-8112-0500-9. Dewey:812/.5/4. LCCN:73-078789.
Audience: **g,l,u,f.** B

Williams, Tennessee **PS3545.I5365R58 1993**
The Roman Spring of Mrs. Stone. Ed. 2. Trade Paper. New Directions Publishing Corporation. New York, NY. 1993. 122p. Bibelots Ser. ISBN:0-8112-1249-1, ISBN13: 978-0-8112-1249-6. Dewey:813.5/4. LCCN:50-009067.
Audience: **g,l,u,f.** B

Williams, Tennessee **PS3545.I5365**
Tennessee Williams: Memoirs. Mass Market. Doubleday Publishing. New York, NY. 1983. 288p. ISBN:0-385-19186-3, ISBN13: 978-0-385-19186-9. Dewey:812/.5/4. LCCN:74-001523.
Audience: **g,l,u,f.** B

Williams, Tennessee **PS3545.I5365.A19**
The Theatre of Tennessee Williams: Twenty-Seven Wagons Full of Cotton and Other Short Plays, Vol. 6. Trade Cloth. New Directions Publishing Corporation. New York, NY. 1981. 368p. ISBN:0-8112-0794-3, ISBN13: 978-0-8112-0794-2. Dewey:812/.54. LCCN:90-005998.
Audience: **g,l,u,f.** B

Williams, Tennessee **PS3545.I5365A6 1984**
Stopped Rocking and Other Screenplays. Richard Gilman (Introduction by). Trade Cloth. New Directions Publishing Corporation. New York, NY. 1984. 352p. ISBN:0-8112-0901-6, ISBN13: 978-0-8112-0901-4. Dewey:791.43/75/0973. LCCN:84-006948.
Audience: **g,l,u,f.** B

Williams, Tennessee **PS3545.I5365A6 2000**
Tennessee Williams: Plays 1957-1980. Mel Gussow & Kenneth Holditch (Editors). Trade Cloth. Library of America, The. New York, NY. 2000. 975p. Library of America, Vol. 119 ISBN:1-883011-87-6, ISBN13: 978-1-883011-87-1. Dewey:812/.54. LCCN:00-030190.
Audience: **g,l,u,f.**

Williams, Tennessee **PS3545.I5365A6 2000**
Tennessee Williams: Plays 1937-1955. Mel Gussow & Kenneth Holditch (Editors). Trade Cloth. Library of America, The. New York, NY. 2000. 975p. Library of America, Vol. 119 ISBN:1-883011-86-8, ISBN13: 978-1-883011-86-4. Dewey:812/.54. LCCN:00-030190.
Audience: **g,l,u,f.**

Williams, Tennessee **PS3545.I5365A17 2002**
The Collected Poems of Tennessee Williams. David E. Roessel & Nicholas Rand Moschovakis (Editors). Trade Cloth. New Directions Publishing Corporation. New York, NY. 2002. 384p. ISBN:0-8112-1508-3, ISBN13: 978-0-8112-1508-4. Dewey:811/.54. LCCN:2001-055760.
Audience: **g,l,u,f.**

Williams, Tennessee **PS3568.O243**
Collected Stories. Gore Vidal (Introduction by). Trade Paper. New Directions Publishing Corporation. New York, NY. 1994. 602p. ISBN:0-8112-1269-6, ISBN13: 978-0-8112-1269-4. Dewey:813.5/4. LCCN:85-010642.
Audience: **g,l,u.** *Choice, 1986.*

20th Century (1901-1960) > W > Williams, William Carlos

Ahearn, Barry **PS3545.I544 Z55 1994**
William Carlos Williams and Alterity: The Early Poetry. Albert Gelpi & Ross Posnock (Contribution by). Trade Cloth. Cambridge University Press. New York, NY. 1994. 199p. Studies in American Literature and Culture, No. 75 ISBN:0-521-45200-7, ISBN13: 978-0-521-45200-7. Dewey:811/.52. LCCN:93-022980.
Audience: **u,f.** *Choice, 1994.*

Beck, John **PS3545.I544Z5745**
Writing the Radical Center: William Carlos Williams, John Dewey, and American Cultural Politics. Cloth Text. State University of New York Press. Albany, NY. 2001. 256p. ISBN:0-7914-5119-4, ISBN13: 978-0-7914-5119-9. Dewey:811/.52. LCCN:2001-049041.
Audience: **u,f.** *Choice, 2002.*

Bremen, Brian **PS3545.I544Z5766**
William Carlos Williams and the Diagnostics of Culture. Cloth Text. Oxford University Press, Inc. New York, NY. 1993. 248p. ISBN:0-19-507226-X, ISBN13: 978-0-19-507226-6. Dewey:811/.52. LCCN:92-008956.
Audience: **u,f.** *Choice, 1993.*

Crawford, T. Hugh **PS3545.I544Z5835**
Modernism, Medicine and William Carlos Williams. Trade Cloth. University of Oklahoma Press. Norman, OK. 1993. xi, 195p. Project for Discourse and Theory Ser. ISBN:0-8061-2550-0, ISBN13: 978-0-8061-2550-3. Dewey:811.52. LCCN:93-019161.
Audience: **u,f.** *Choice, 1994.*

Deese, Helen & Axelrod, Steven G. **PS3545.I544Z5837**
Critical Essays on William Carlos Williams. Trade Cloth. Thomson Gale. Farmington Hills, MI. 1994. vii, 232p. Critical Essays on American Literature Ser. ISBN:0-7838-0015-0, ISBN13: 978-0-7838-0015-8. Dewey:811/.52. LCCN:94-032339.
Audience: **l,u.**

Koehler, G. Stanley **PS3545.I544Z614 1998**
Countries of the Mind: The Poetry of William Carlos Williams. Trade Cloth. Bucknell University Press. Cranbury, NJ. 1998. 176p. ISBN:0-8387-5332-9, ISBN13: 978-0-8387-5332-3. Dewey:811/.52. LCCN:98-011453.
Audience: **u,f.** *Choice, 1999.*

Larson, Kelli A. **Z8976.44.L37 1995**
Guide to the Poetry of William Carlos Williams. Trade Cloth. Thomson Gale. Farmington Hills, MI. 1995. 182p. Guides to 20th Century Poets Ser. ISBN:0-8161-1986-4, ISBN13: 978-0-8161-1986-8. Dewey:811/.52. LCCN:94-040682.
Audience: **l,u.**

Lowney, John **PS3545.I544Z62 1997**
The American Avant-Garde Tradition: William Carlos Williams, Postmodern Poetry, and the Politics of Cultural Memory. Trade Cloth. Bucknell University Press. Cranbury, NJ. 1997. 176p. ISBN:0-8387-5333-7, ISBN13: 978-0-8387-5333-0. Dewey:811/.52. LCCN:96-007249.
Audience: **u,f.** *Choice, 1997.*

Morris, Daniel **PS3545.I544Z656 1995**
The Writings of William Carlos Williams: Publicity for the Self. Cloth Text. University of Missouri Press. Columbia, MO. 1995. 232p. ISBN:0-8262-1002-3, ISBN13: 978-0-8262-1002-9. Dewey:811/.52. LCCN:95-007718.
Audience: **l,u,f.** *Choice, 1996.*

Ostrom, Alan **PS3545.I544 Z8**
Poetic World of William Carlos Williams. Trade Cloth. Southern Illinois University Press. Carbondale, IL. 1966. 191p. Crosscurrents-Modern Critiques Ser. ISBN:0-8093-0217-9, ISBN13: 978-0-8093-0217-8. Dewey:811.52. LCCN:65-016536.
Audience: **l,u.** B

Pound, Ezra & Williams, William Carlos **PS3531.O82Z4976 1996**
Selected Letters of Ezra Pound and William Carlos Williams. Hugh Witemeyer (Editor). Trade Cloth. New Directions Publishing Corporation. New York, NY. 1996. 480p. Correspondence of Ezra Pound Ser. ISBN:0-8112-1301-3, ISBN13: 978-0-8112-1301-1. Dewey:811/.52 B. LCCN:95-038462.
Audience: **g,l,u,f.**

Williams, William Carlos **PS3545.I544**
Build-Up. Trade Paper. New Directions Publishing Corporation. New York, NY. 1968. 334p. Stecher Trilogy, Vol. 3 ISBN:0-8112-0227-5, ISBN13: 978-0-8112-0227-5. Dewey:813.5. LCCN:52-005166.
Audience: **g,l,u,f.**

Williams, William Carlos **PR6019.O9**
In the Money. Trade Paper. New Directions Publishing Corporation. New York, NY. 1967. Stecher Trilogy, Vol. 2 ISBN:0-8112-0231-3, ISBN13: 978-0-8112-0231-2. Dewey:823/.9/1. LCCN:40-035170.
Audience: **g,l,u,f.**

Williams, William Carlos **PS3545**
Selected Essays of William Carlos Williams. Trade Paper. New Directions Publishing Corporation. New York, NY. 1969. 352p. ISBN:0-8112-0235-6, ISBN13: 978-0-8112-0235-0. Dewey:814/.5. LCCN:54-007815.
Audience: **g,l,u,f.**

Williams, William Carlos **PS3545.I544**
A Voyage to Pagany. Library Binding. Reprint Services Company. Temecula, CA. 1988. ISBN:0-7812-0459-3, ISBN13: 978-0-7812-0459-0. Dewey:813.
Audience: **g,l,u,f.** B

Williams, William Carlos **PZ3.W67667**
White Mule. Trade Paper. New Directions Publishing Corporation. New York, NY. 1967. Stecher Trilogy, Vol. 1 ISBN:0-8112-0238-0, ISBN13: 978-0-8112-0238-1. Dewey:813.52. LCCN:37-011249.
Audience: **g,l,u,f.**

Williams, William Carlos **PS3531.O82**
William Carlos Williams: Autobiography. Library Binding. Reprint Services Company. Temecula, CA. 1995. 402p. American Autobiography Ser. ISBN:0-7812-8663-8, ISBN13: 978-0-7812-8663-3. Dewey:811.5/2.
Audience: **g,l,u,f.**

Williams, William Carlos **PS3545.I544A6 2004**
William Carlos Williams: Selected Poems. Trade Cloth. Library of America, The. New York, NY. 2004. 200p. American Poets Project Ser. ISBN:1-931082-71-5, ISBN13: 978-1-931082-71-6. Dewey:811/.52. LCCN:2004-048523.
Audience: **g,l,u,f.**

Williams, William Carlos **PS3531.O82**
The Collected Poems of William Carlos Williams, 1909-1939, Vol. 1. A. Walton Litz & Christopher J. MacGowan (Editors). Trade Paper. New Directions Publishing Corporation. New York, NY. 1991. 600p. ISBN:0-8112-1187-8, ISBN13: 978-0-8112-1187-1. Dewey:811/.52. LCCN:86-005448.
Audience: **g,l,u,f.** *Choice, 1987.*

Williams, William Carlos **PS3545.I544A17 1986**
The Collected Poems of William Carlos Williams, 1939-1962, Vol. 2. Christopher J. MacGowan (Editor). Trade Cloth. New

Directions Publishing Corporation. New York, NY. 1988. 576p. ISBN:0-8112-1063-4, ISBN13: 978-0-8112-1063-8. Dewey:811/.52. LCCN:86-005448.
Audience: **g,l,u,f.** *Choice, 1989.*

Williams, William Carlos **PS3545.I544A6 1996**
The Collected Stories of William Carlos Williams. Sherwin B. Nuland (Introduction by). Trade Paper. New Directions Publishing Corporation. New York, NY. 1996. 384p. ISBN:0-8112-1328-5, ISBN13: 978-0-8112-1328-8. Dewey:813/.52. LCCN:96-014710.
Audience: **g,l,u,f.**

20th Century (1901-1960) > W > Wilson, Edmund

Castronovo, David **PS3545.I6245.Z587**
Edmund Wilson. Trade Cloth. Thomson Gale. Farmington Hills, MI. 1998. 170p. Twayne's United States Authors Ser., Vol. 695 ISBN:0-8057-1642-4, ISBN13: 978-0-8057-1642-9. Dewey:818/.5209. LCCN:97-031613.
Audience: **l,u.** B *Choice, 1998, 1985.*

Dabney, Lewis **PS3545.I6245Z594**
Edmund Wilson: A Life in Literature. Cloth over Boards. Farrar, Straus & Giroux. New York, NY. 2005. 656p. ISBN:0-374-11312-2, ISBN13: 978-0-374-11312-4. Dewey:818/.5209 B. LCCN:2004-057148.
Audience: **l,u.** *Choice, 2006.*

Douglas, George H. **PS3545.I6245.Z595**
Edmund Wilson's America. Trade Cloth. University Press of Kentucky. Lexington, KY. 1983. 272p. ISBN:0-8131-1494-2, ISBN13: 978-0-8131-1494-1. Dewey:818/.5209. LCCN:83-019696.
Audience: **l,u.** B

Groth, Janet **PS3545.I6245Z67 1989**
Edmund Wilson: A Critic for Our Time. Trade Cloth. Ohio University Press. Athens, OH. 1989. 295p. ISBN:0-8214-0919-0, ISBN13: 978-0-8214-0919-0. Dewey:818/.5209. LCCN:88-032467.
Audience: **g,l,u,f.** *Choice, 1989.*

Meyers, Jeffrey **PS3545.I6245Z76 1995**
Edmund Wilson: A Biography. Trade Paper. Cooper Square Publishers, Inc. New York, NY. 2003. 592p. ISBN:0-8154-1111-1, ISBN13: 978-0-8154-1111-6. Dewey:818.5/2/09.
Audience: **g,l,u,f.** *Choice, 1995.*

Wilson, Edmund **PS3545**
Five Plays: Cyprian's Prayer, the Crime in the Whistler Room, This Room and This Gin and These Sandwiches, Beppo An. Ed. 1. Trade Paper. Farrar, Straus & Giroux. New York, NY. 1999. 541p. ISBN:0-374-52665-6, ISBN13: 978-0-374-52665-8. Dewey:812. LCCN:54-005432.
Audience: **g,l,u,f.**

Wilson, Edmund **PS3545.I6245**
A Prelude. Trade Cloth. Farrar, Straus & Giroux. New York, NY. 1967. ISBN:0-374-23696-8, ISBN13: 978-0-374-23696-0. Dewey:818/.5/203.
Audience: **g,l,u,f.**

Wilson, Edmund **PS3537.A832**
The Forties: From Notebooks and Diaries of the Period. Leon Edel (Editor). Trade Cloth. Farrar, Straus & Giroux. New York, NY. 1984. 397p. ISBN:0-374-51835-1, ISBN13: 978-0-374-51835-6. Dewey:818/.5203. LCCN:82-021028.
Audience: **g,l,u,f.** B

Wilson, Edmund **PS3545.I6245.Z535**
The Thirties: From Notebooks and Diaries of the Period. Leon Edel (Editor). Cloth over Boards. Farrar, Straus & Giroux. New York, NY. 1980. 800p. ISBN:0-374-27572-6, ISBN13: 978-0-374-27572-3. Dewey:818/.5209. LCCN:79-028700.
Audience: **g,l,u,f.** B

Wilson, Edmund **PS3545.I6245M4 2004**
Memoirs of Hecate County. Louis Menand (Introduction by). Trade Paper. New York Review of Books, Incorporated, The. New York, NY. 2004. 472p. New York Review Books Classics ISBN:1-59017-093-8, ISBN13: 978-1-59017-093-9. Dewey:813/.52. LCCN:2004-016635.
Audience: **g,l,u,f.**

Wilson, Edmund **PS3545.I6245I12 2001**
I Thought of Daisy. Neale Reinitz (Preface by, Afterword by). Trade Paper. University of Iowa Press. Iowa City, IA. 2001. 278p. ISBN:0-87745-769-7, ISBN13: 978-0-87745-769-5. Dewey:813/.52. LCCN:00-066998.
Audience: **g,l,u,f.** B

Wilson, Edmund **PS3545.I6245.Z54**
Letters on Literature and Politics, 1912-1972. Elena Wilson (Editor). Trade Cloth. Farrar, Straus & Giroux. New York, NY. 1977. 750p. ISBN:0-374-18508-5, ISBN13: 978-0-374-18508-4. Dewey:818/.5/209. LCCN:76-058460.
Audience: **g,l,u,f.** B

20th Century (1901-1960) > W > Wolfe, Thomas

Donald, David Herbert **PS3545.O337Z674 2002**
Look Homeward: A Life of Thomas Wolfe. Trade Paper. Harvard University Press. Cambridge, MA. 2003. 608p. ISBN:0-674-00869-3, ISBN13: 978-0-674-00869-4. Dewey:813/.52 b. LCCN:2003-267711.
Audience: **l,u,f.** *Choice, 1987.*

Wolfe, Thomas **PS3545.O337A15 1989**
The Complete Short Stories of Thomas Wolfe. Trade Paper. Simon & Schuster. New York, NY. 1989. 656p. ISBN:0-02-040891-9, ISBN13: 978-0-02-040891-8. Dewey:813/.52. LCCN:88-038324.
Audience: **g,l,u,f.** *Choice, 1987.*

Wolfe, Thomas **PS3545.O337H54 2000**
The Hills Beyond. Trade Paper. Louisiana State University Press. Baton Rouge, LA. 2000. 348p. Voices of the South Ser. ISBN:0-8071-2567-9, ISBN13: 978-0-8071-2567-0. Dewey:813/.52. LCCN:00-038441.
Audience: **g,l,u,f.** B

Wolfe, Thomas **PS3545.O337L6 1997**
Look Homeward, Angel. Trade Cloth. Simon & Schuster. New York, NY. 1997. 528p. Scribner Classics ISBN:0-684-84221-1, ISBN13: 978-0-684-84221-9. Dewey:813/.52. LCCN:97-013090.
Audience: **g,l,u,f.**

Wolfe, Thomas **PS3545.O337W4 1999**
The Web and the Rock. Trade Paper. Louisiana State University Press. Baton Rouge, LA. 1999. 712p. Voices of the South Ser. ISBN:0-8071-2389-7, ISBN13: 978-0-8071-2389-8. Dewey:813/.52. LCCN:98-054651.
Audience: **g,l,u,f.**

Wolfe, Thomas & Conroy, Pat **PS3545.O337O4 1999**
Of Time and the River: A Legend of Man's Hunger in His Youth. Trade Cloth. Simon & Schuster. New York, NY. 1999. 896p. Scribner Classics ISBN:0-684-86785-0, ISBN13: 978-0-684-86785-4. Dewey:813/.52. LCCN:99-032905.
Audience: **g,l,u,f.**

20th Century (1901-1960) > W > Wright, Richard

Caron, Timothy P. **PS261.C35 2000**
Struggles over the Word: Race and Religion in O'Connor, Faulkner, Hurston and Wright. Trade Cloth. Mercer University Press. Macon, GA. 2000. 162p. ISBN:0-86554-669-X, ISBN13: 978-0-86554-669-1. Dewey:813/.50938220. LCCN:00-056252.
Audience: **u,f.**

Fabre, Michel J. **PS3545.R815.Z6**
The Unfinished Quest of Richard Wright. Ed. 2. Isabel Barzun (Translator). Trade Paper. University of Illinois Press. Champaign, IL. 1993. 680p. ISBN:0-252-06264-7, ISBN13: 978-0-252-06264-3. Dewey:813/.52. LCCN:92-014493.
Audience: **u,f.**

Fishburn, Katherine **PS3545.R815.Z66**
Richard Wright's Hero: The Faces of a Rebel-Victim. Trade Cloth. Scarecrow Press, Inc. Lanham, MD. 1977. 228p. ISBN:0-8108-1013-1, ISBN13: 978-0-8108-1013-6. Dewey:813/.5/2. LCCN:76-051787.
Audience: **l,u.**

Gayle, Addison **PS3511.A86**
Richard Wright: Ordeal of a Native Son. Trade Cloth. Peter Smith Publisher, Inc. Magnolia, MA. 1983. ISBN:0-8446-6000-0, ISBN13: 978-0-8446-6000-4. Dewey:813/.52.
Audience: **l,u,f.**

Kinnamon, Keneth **PS3545.R815**
The Emergence of Richard Wright. Trade Cloth. University of Illinois Press. Champaign, IL. 1972. 224p. ISBN:0-252-00201-6, ISBN13: 978-0-252-00201-4. Dewey:813/.52. LCCN:72-078023.
Audience: **u,f.**

Macksey, Richard & Moorer, Frank E. (Editors) **PS3545.R815.Z815**
Richard Wright: A Collection of Critical Essays. Trade Cloth. Prentice Hall Press. Paramus, NJ. 1984. "x, 240"p. Twentieth Century Views Ser. ISBN:0-13-780924-7, ISBN13: 978-0-13-780924-0. Dewey:813/.52. LCCN:83-019285.
Audience: **l,u.**

Reilly, John M. (Editor) **PS3545.R815.Z82**
Richard Wright: The Critical Reception. Library Binding. Burt Franklin Publisher. New York, NY. 1978. xlvii, 400p. American Critical Tradition Ser. ISBN:0-89102-110-8, ISBN13: 978-0-89102-110-0. Dewey:813/.5/2. LCCN:78-005476.
Audience: **l,u.**

Weiss, M. Lynn **PS3537.T323Z913 1998**
Gertrude Stein and Richard Wright: The Poetics and Politics of Modernism. Trade Cloth. University Press of Mississippi. Jackson, MS. 1998. 144p. ISBN:1-57806-100-8, ISBN13: 978-1-57806-100-6. Dewey:818/.5209. LCCN:98-007786.
Audience: **u,f.** *Choice, 1999.*

Wright, Richard **PS3545.R815E4 1996**
Eight Men: Short Stories. Trade Paper. HarperCollins Publishers. New York, NY. 1996. 272p. ISBN:0-06-097681-0, ISBN13: 978-0-06-097681-1. Dewey:813/.52. LCCN:96-021614.
Audience: **g,l,u,f.**

Wright, Richard **PS3511.A86**
Wright: Early Works: Lawd Today!; Uncle Tom's Children; Native Son. Arnold Rampersad (Editor). Trade Cloth. Library of America, The. New York, NY. 1991. 936p. Library of America, Vol. 55 ISBN:0-940450-66-6, ISBN13: 978-0-940450-66-0. Dewey:813/.52.
Audience: **g,l,u,f.**

Wright, Richard **PS3545 .R815 1991**
Wright: Later Works: Black Boy and the Outsider. Arnold Rampersad (Editor). Trade Cloth. Library of America, The. New York, NY. 1991. 887p. Library of America, Vol. 56 ISBN:0-940450-67-4, ISBN13: 978-0-940450-67-7. Dewey:813/.52. LCCN:91-060540.
Audience: **g,l,u,f.**

Wright, Richard **PS3511.A86**
The Richard Wright Reader. Ellen Wright & Michel J. Fabre (Editors). Trade Paper. HarperCollins Publishers. New York, NY. 1978. ISBN:0-06-014736-9, ISBN13: 978-0-06-014736-5. Dewey:813/.52. LCCN:77-076690.
Audience: **g,l,u,f.**

20th Century (1901-1960) > Z > Zukofsky, Louis

Ahearn, Barry **PS3549.U47A683**
Zukofsky's A: An Introduction. Trade Cloth. University of California Press. Berkeley, CA. 1983. 254p. ISBN:0-520-04378-2, ISBN13: 978-0-520-04378-7. Dewey:811/.52. LCCN:81-013000.
Audience: **l,u.**

Zukofsky, Louis **PS3549.U47.A734**
A 22 and 23. Trade Paper. Penguin Group (USA) Inc. New York, NY. 1975. 60p. ISBN:0-670-00598-3, ISBN13: 978-0-670-00598-7. Dewey:811/.5/2. LCCN:75-017777.
Audience: **g,l,u,f.** B

Zukofsky, Louis **PS3549.U47A68 1993**
A. Trade Paper. Johns Hopkins University Press. Baltimore, MD. 1982. 832p. ISBN:0-8018-4668-4, ISBN13: 978-0-8018-4668-7. Dewey:811.52. LCCN:92-038357.
Audience: **g,l,u,f.**

Zukofsky, Louis **PS3549.U47**
Arise, Arise. Trade Paper. Penguin Group (USA) Inc. New York, NY. 1973. ISBN:0-670-13260-8, ISBN13: 978-0-670-13260-7. Dewey:812/.5/2.
Audience: **g,l,u,f.** B

Zukofsky, Louis & Scroggins, Mark **PS3549.U47A16 2000**
Prepositions + the Collected Critical Essays: The Wesleyan Cenntential Edition of the Complete Critical Writings of Louis Zukofsky. Charles Bernstein (Foreword by). Trade Paper. Wesleyan University Press. Middletown, CT. 2001. 264p. Wesleyan Centennial Edition of the Complete Critical Writing Ser., Vol. 2 ISBN:0-8195-6428-1, ISBN13: 978-0-8195-6428-3. Dewey:814/.52. LCCN:00-035169.
Audience: **g,l,u,f.**

20th Century (1961-2000) > A

Abbey, Edward **PS3551.B2M6 1985**
The Monkey Wrench Gang. R. Crumb (Illustrator). Trade Cloth. Dream Garden Press. Salt Lake City, UT. 1999. 368p. ISBN:0-942688-18-X, ISBN13: 978-0-942688-18-4. Dewey:813.5/4. LCCN:75-000831.
Audience: **g,l,u,f.**

✓**Albee, Edward** **PS3551.L25**
Seascape. Trade Paper. Dramatists Play Service, Inc. New York, NY. 1975. ISBN:0-8222-1004-5, ISBN13: 978-0-8222-1004-7. Dewey:812.54.
Audience: **g,l,u,f.**

✓**Albee, Edward (Author, Author)** **PS3551.L25T48**
Three Tall Women: A Play in Two Acts. Library Binding. Sagebrush Education Resources. Caledonia, MN. 1995. 110p. ISBN:0-613-36705-7, ISBN13: 978-0-613-36705-9. Dewey:812/.54.
Audience: **g,l,u,f.**

✓**Alexie, Sherman** **PS3551.L35774.I56**
Indian Killer. Trade Paper. Warner Books, Inc. New York, NY. 1998. 432p. ISBN:0-446-67370-6, ISBN13: 978-0-446-67370-9. Dewey:813.5/4. LCCN:97-027448.
Audience: **g,l,u,f.**

✓**Alexie, Sherman** **PS3551.L35774T46**
Ten Little Indians: Stories. Trade Cloth. Grove/Atlantic, Inc. New York, NY. 2003. 256p. ISBN:0-8021-1744-9, ISBN13: 978-0-8021-1744-1. Dewey:813/.54. LCCN:2003-044832.
Audience: **g,l,u,f.**

Alexie, Sherman **PS3568.O243**
The Toughest Indian in the World. Trade Paper. Grove/Atlantic, Inc. New York, NY. 2001. 256p. ISBN:0-8021-3800-4, ISBN13: 978-0-8021-3800-2. Dewey:813.5/4.
Audience: **g,l,u,f.**

Alurista **PS3554.L84**
Tremble Purple: Seven Poems. Trade Paper. Getting Together Publications. La Jolla, CA. 1986. 29p. ISBN:0-945308-00-0, ISBN13: 978-0-945308-00-3. Dewey:813.54.
Audience: **g,l,u,f.**

✓**Angelou, Maya** **PS3551.N464Z466 2002**
I Know Why the Caged Bird Sings. Trade Cloth. Random House, Inc. New York, NY. 2002. 288p. ISBN:0-375-50789-2, ISBN13: 978-0-375-50789-2. Dewey:818/.5409 B. LCCN:2001-041914.
Audience: **g,l,u,f.**

Aronofsky, Darren & Selby, Hubert Jr. **PN1997 .R475 2000**
Requiem for a Dream. Trade Paper. Faber & Faber, Inc. New York, NY. 2000. 144p. ISBN:0-571-20631-X, ISBN13: 978-0-571-20631-5. Dewey:791.43/72. LCCN:2003-427180.
Audience: **g,l,u,f.**

✓**Auburn, David** **PS3551.U28.P7 2001**
Proof. Trade Paper. Dramatists Play Service, Inc. New York, NY. 2001. 74p. ISBN:0-8222-1782-1, ISBN13: 978-0-8222-1782-4. Dewey:812/.6. LCCN:2002-278945.
Audience: **g,l,u,f.**

✓**Auster, Paul (Editor)** **PS3568.O243**
The Book of Illusions: A Novel. Trade Paper. Picador. New York, NY. 2003. 336p. ISBN:0-312-42181-8, ISBN13: 978-0-312-42181-6. Dewey:813/.54.
Audience: **g,l,u,f.**

Auster, Paul **PS3551.U77A6 2004**
Collected Poems. Trade Cloth. Overlook Press, The. New York, NY. 2004. 192p. ISBN:1-58567-404-4, ISBN13: 978-1-58567-404-6. Dewey:811/.54. LCCN:2003-064980.
Audience: **g,l,u,f.**

Auster, Paul **PS3551.U77**
Collected Prose: Autobiographical Writings, True Stories, Critical Essays, Prefaces, and Collaborations with Artists. Trade Paper. Picador. New York, NY. 2005. 528p. ISBN:0-312-42468-X, ISBN13: 978-0-312-42468-8. Dewey:81.
Audience: **g,l,u,f.**

Auster, Paul **PS3551.U77I45 1988**
In the Country of Last Things. Trade Paper. Penguin Group (USA) Inc. New York, NY. 1988. 208p. Contemporary American Fiction Ser. ISBN:0-14-009705-8, ISBN13: 978-0-14-009705-4. Dewey:813.5/4. LCCN:87-025640.
Audience: **g,l,u,f.** *Choice, 1987.*

✓**Auster, Paul** **PS3551.U77**
Oracle Night: A Novel. Trade Paper. Picador. New York, NY. 2004. 256p. ISBN:0-312-42366-7, ISBN13: 978-0-312-42366-7. Dewey:Fic. LCCN:2003-051063.
Audience: **g,l,u,f.**

Auster, Paul **PS3551.U77N49 2006**
New York Trilogy. Ed. 60. Luc Sante (Introduction by). Trade Paper. Penguin Group (USA) Inc. New York, NY. 2006. 400p. Penguin Classics Deluxe Edition Ser. ISBN:0-14-303983-0, ISBN13: 978-0-14-303983-9. Dewey:813/.54. LCCN:2006-041771.
Audience: **g,l,u,f.**

20th Century (1961-2000) > B

Banks, Russell **PS3568.O243**
Cloudsplitter: A Novel. Trade Paper. HarperCollins Publishers. New York, NY. 1999. 768p. ISBN:0-06-093086-1, ISBN13: 978-0-06-093086-8. Dewey:813.5/4. LCCN:97-022163.
Audience: **g,l,u,f.**

Banks, Russell **PS3568.O243**
Continental Drift. Trade Paper. HarperCollins Publishers. New York, NY. 2000. 432p. Perennial Classics Ser. ISBN:0-06-095673-9, ISBN13: 978-0-06-095673-8. Dewey:813.5/4.
Audience: **g,l,u,f.**

Banks, Russell **PS3568.O243**
The Sweet Hereafter. Trade Paper. HarperCollins Publishers. New York, NY. 1992. 272p. ISBN:0-06-092324-5, ISBN13: 978-0-06-092324-2. Dewey:813.54. LCCN:90-056404.
Audience: **g,l,u,f.**

Baraka, Amiri Imamu **PS3551.N464**
The Autobiography of Leroi Jones- Amiri Baraka. Trade Cloth. Freundlich Books. New York, NY. 1984. 329p. ISBN:0-88191-000-7, ISBN13: 978-0-88191-000-1. Dewey:818/.5409. LCCN:83-020576.
Audience: **g,l,u,f.**

Baraka, Amiri Imamu **PS3552.A583A6 2000**
The LeRoi Jones - Amiri Baraka Reader. Ed. 2. Trade Paper. Avalon Publishing Group. New York, NY. 1999. xxxiii, 586p. ISBN:1-56025-238-3, ISBN13: 978-1-56025-238-2. Dewey:818/.5409. LCCN:99-032364.
Audience: **g,l,u,f.**

Baraka, Amiri Imamu & Jones, LeRoi **PS3552.A583A6 2000**
The Fiction of Leroi Jones - Amiri Baraka. Greg Tate (Foreword by). Trade Cloth. Chicago Review Press, Inc. Chicago, IL. 2000. 480p. The Library of Black America ISBN:1-55652-346-7, ISBN13: 978-1-55652-346-5. Dewey:813/.54. LCCN:99-025770.
Audience: **g,l,u,f.** *Choice, 2000.*

Baraka, Amiri Imamu **PR9230.9.B68**
Transbluesency: The Selected Poems of Amiri Baraka/Leroi Jones. Paul Vangelisti (Editor). Trade Cloth. Marsilio Publishers. New York, NY. 1995. 292p. ISBN:1-56886-013-7, ISBN13: 978-1-56886-013-8. Dewey:811.
Audience: **g,l,u,f.**

Barrett, Andrea **PS3552.A7327S47 2002**
Servants of the Map: Stories. Trade Cloth. W. W. Norton & Company, Inc. New York, NY. 2002. 320p. ISBN:0-393-04348-7, ISBN13: 978-0-393-04348-8. Dewey:813.5/4. LCCN:2001-044209.
Audience: **g,l,u,f.**

Barthelme, Donald **PN6162**
Not-Knowing: The Essays of Donald Barthelme. Trade Cloth. Random House Value Publishing. New York, NY. 1999. ISBN:0-609-00076-4, ISBN13: 978-0-609-00076-2. Dewey:814/.54.
Audience: **g,l,u,f.**

Barthelme, Donald **PS3552.A76P3 2005**
Paradise. Trade Paper. Dalkey Archive Press. Normal, IL. 2005. 208p. American Literature Ser. ISBN:1-56478-403-7, ISBN13: 978-1-56478-403-2. Dewey:813/.54. LCCN:2005-049206.
Audience: **g,l,u,f.** *Choice, 1987.*

Barthelme, Donald **PR6019.O9**
Snow White. Trade Paper. Simon & Schuster. New York, NY. 1996. 192p. ISBN:0-684-82479-5, ISBN13: 978-0-684-82479-6. Dewey:823/.9/1. LCCN:67-014324.
Audience: **g,l,u,f.** B

Barthelme, Donald **PS3552.A76D4 2004**
The Dead Father. Donald Antrim (Introduction by). Trade Paper. Farrar, Straus & Giroux. New York, NY. 2004. 192p. ISBN:0-374-52925-6, ISBN13: 978-0-374-52925-3. Dewey:813/.54. LCCN:2004-047064.
Audience: **g,l,u,f.**

Barthelme, Donald **PS3552.A76K56 2006**
The King. Barry Moser (Illustrator). Trade Paper. Dalkey Archive Press. Normal, IL. 2005. 157p. American Literature Ser. ISBN:1-56478-413-4, ISBN13: 978-1-56478-413-1. Dewey:813/.54. LCCN:2005-056079.
Audience: **g,l,u,f.**

Bass, Rick **F735.B37**
Winter: Notes from Montana. Trade Cloth. Peter Smith Publisher, Inc. Magnolia, MA. 1999. ISBN:0-8446-7015-4, ISBN13: 978-0-8446-7015-7. Dewey:978.6.
Audience: **g,l,u,f.**

Bass, Rick **PS3552.A8213F53 1998**
Fiber. Elizabeth Hughes Bass (Illustrator). Trade Cloth. University of Georgia Press. Athens, GA. 1998. 64p. ISBN:0-8203-2063-3, ISBN13: 978-0-8203-2063-2. Dewey:813/.54. LCCN:98-015556.
Audience: **g,l,u,f.**

Beattie, Ann **PS3552.E177**
The Doctor's House. Trade Paper. Simon & Schuster. New York, NY. 2003. 288p. ISBN:0-7432-3501-0, ISBN13: 978-0-7432-3501-3.
Audience: **g,l,u,f.**

Beattie, Ann **PS3552.E177F65 2005**
Follies: New Stories. Trade Cloth. Simon & Schuster. New York, NY. 2005. 320p. ISBN:0-7432-6961-6, ISBN13: 978-0-7432-6961-2. Dewey:813/.54. LCCN:2004-065087.
Audience: **g,l,u,f.**

Beattie, Ann **PS3568.O243**
Perfect Recall: New Stories. Trade Cloth. Simon & Schuster. New York, NY. 2000. ISBN:0-7432-1525-7, ISBN13: 978-0-7432-1525-1. Dewey:813/.54.
Audience: **g,l,u,f.**

Berry, Wendell **PS3566.L27**
The Collected Poems of Wendell Berry, 1957-1982. Trade Paper. Farrar, Straus & Giroux. New York, NY. 1987. 288p. ISBN:0-86547-197-5, ISBN13: 978-0-86547-197-9. Dewey:811/.54. LCCN:84-062305.
Audience: **g,l,u,f.**

Berry, Wendell **PS3552.E75A6 1998**
Selected Poems of Wendell Berry. Trade Cloth. Basic Books. New York, NY. 1998. 160p. ISBN:1-887178-84-8, ISBN13: 978-1-887178-84-6. Dewey:811.5/4. LCCN:98-034793.
Audience: **g,l,u,f.**

Berry, Wendell **PS3552.E75**
Three Short Novels. Trade Paper. Basic Books. New York, NY. 2003. 336p. ISBN:1-58243-237-6, ISBN13: 978-1-58243-237-3. Dewey:813/.54.
Audience: **g,l,u,f.**

Bidart, Frank **PS3552.I33**
Desire: Poems. Trade Paper. Farrar, Straus & Giroux. New York, NY. 1999. 64p. ISBN:0-374-52599-4, ISBN13: 978-0-374-52599-6. Dewey:811/.54.
Audience: **g,l,u,f.**

Bidart, Frank **PS3552.I33M87 2002**
Music Like Dirt. Trade Paper. Sarabande Books, Inc. Louisville, KY. 2002. 31p. Quarternote Chapbook Ser. ISBN:1-889330-78-7, ISBN13: 978-1-889330-78-5. Dewey:811/.54. LCCN:2001-034866.
Audience: **g,l,u,f.**

Boyle, T. C. **PS3568.O243**
T. C. Boyle Stories: The Collected Stories of T. Coraghessan Boyle. Trade Paper. Penguin Group (USA) Inc. New York, NY. 1999. 704p. ISBN:0-14-028091-X, ISBN13: 978-0-14-028091-3. Dewey:813/.54.
Audience: **g,l,u,f.**

Boyle, T. C. **PS3568.O243**
World's End. Trade Paper. Penguin Group (USA) Inc. New York, NY. 1990. 480p. Contemporary American Fiction Ser. ISBN:0-14-029993-9, ISBN13: 978-0-14-029993-9. Dewey:813/.54. LCCN:87-032827.
Audience: **g,l,u,f.**

Boyle, T. C. **PS3568.O243**
Water Music. James R. Kincaid (Contribution by). Trade Paper. Penguin Group (USA) Inc. New York, NY. 1983. 464p. Penguin Contemporary American Fiction Ser. ISBN:0-14-006550-4, ISBN13: 978-0-14-006550-3. Dewey:813.5/4. LCCN:83-002137.
Audience: **g,l,u,f.**

Bradley, Marion Zimmer **PS3552.R228M5 2000**
The Mists of Avalon. Trade Cloth. Ballantine Books. New York, NY. 2000. 912p. ISBN:0-345-44118-4, ISBN13: 978-0-345-44118-8. Dewey:813/.54. LCCN:00-712415.
Audience: **g,l,u.** B

Brautigan, Richard **PS3503.R2736A6 1991**
A Confederate General from Big Sur; Dreaming of Babylon; The Hawkline Monster. Trade Paper. Houghton Mifflin Company Trade & Reference Division. Boston, MA. 1991. 608p. ISBN:0-395-54703-2, ISBN13: 978-0-395-54703-8. Dewey:813/.54. LCCN:90-020524.
Audience: **g,l,u,f.**

Brautigan, Richard **PS3503.R2736A6 1995**
Revenge of the Lawn; The Abortion; So the Wind Won't Blow It All Away. Trade Paper. Houghton Mifflin Company Trade & Reference Division. Boston, MA. 1995. 544p. ISBN:0-395-70674-2, ISBN13: 978-0-395-70674-9. Dewey:813/.54. LCCN:94-026177.
Audience: **g,l,u,f.**

Brautigan, Richard **PS3503.R2736A6 1989**
Trout Fishing in America; The Pill Versus the Springhill Mine Disaster; In Watermelon Sugar. Trade Paper. Houghton Mifflin Company Trade & Reference Division. Boston, MA. 1989. 400p. ISBN:0-395-50076-1, ISBN13: 978-0-395-50076-7. Dewey:813/.54. LCCN:88-038993.
Audience: **g,l,u,f.** B

Brewer, Gay **PS3552.U4Z56 1997**
Charles Bukowski. Trade Cloth. Thomson Gale. Farmington Hills, MI. 1997. xvi, 215p. Twayne's World Authors Ser., Vol. 684 ISBN:0-8057-4558-0, ISBN13: 978-0-8057-4558-0. Dewey:811/.54. LCCN:97-005880.
Audience: **l,u.** *Choice, 1998.*

Broumas, Olga **PS3566.L27**
Beginning with O. Stanley Kunitz (Foreword by). Trade Paper. Yale University Press. Cumberland, RI. 1977. 87p. Younger Poets Ser., Vol. 72 ISBN:0-300-02111-9, ISBN13: 978-0-300-02111-0. Dewey:811/.54. LCCN:76-049697.
Audience: **g,l,u,f.** B

Buechner, Frederick **PS3552.U35**
Godric: A Novel. Trade Paper. HarperCollins Publishers. New York, NY. 1983. 192p. ISBN:0-06-061162-6, ISBN13: 978-0-06-061162-0. Dewey:813/.54. LCCN:83-047717.
Audience: **g,l,u,f.**

Bukowski, Charles **PS3568.O243**
Ham on Rye. Trade Cloth. HarperCollins Publishers. New York, NY. 1998. 288p. ISBN:0-87685-558-3, ISBN13: 978-0-87685-558-4. Dewey:813/.54. LCCN:82-009631.
Audience: **g,l,u,f.**

Bukowski, Charles **PS3552.U4**
Run with the Hunted: A Charles Bukowski Reader. John Martin (Editor). Trade Paper. HarperCollins Publishers. New York, NY. 1994. 512p. ISBN:0-06-092458-6, ISBN13: 978-0-06-092458-4. Dewey:811.54. LCCN:92-053353.
Audience: **g,l,u,f.**

Busch, Frederick **PS3552.U814M8 1994**
The Mutual Friend. Trade Paper. New Directions Publishing Corporation. New York, NY. 1994. 240p. Paperbook Ser., Vol. 774 ISBN:0-8112-1258-0, ISBN13: 978-0-8112-1258-8. Dewey:823/.9/1. LCCN:93-031458.
Audience: **g,l,u,f.** B

Butler, Robert Olen **PS3552.U8278G66 2001**
A Good Scent from a Strange Mountain: Stories. Trade Paper. Grove/Atlantic, Inc. New York, NY. 2001. 269p. ISBN:0-8021-3798-9, ISBN13: 978-0-8021-3798-2. Dewey:813/.54. LCCN:00-066310.
Audience: **g,l,u,f.**

Harris, William J. **PS3552.A583Z68 1985**
The Poetry and Poetics of Amiri Baraka: The Jazz Aesthetic. Cloth Text. University of Missouri Press. Columbia, MO. 1985. 184p. ISBN:0-8262-0483-X, ISBN13: 978-0-8262-0483-7. Dewey:811/.54. LCCN:85-001000.
Audience: **l,u,f.** *Choice, 1986.*

Reilly, Charlie (Editor) **PS3552.A583Z465 1994**
Conversations with Amiri Baraka. Trade Cloth. University Press of Mississippi. Jackson, MS. 1994. 288p. Literary Conversations Ser. ISBN:0-87805-686-6, ISBN13: 978-0-87805-686-6. Dewey:818/.5409. LCCN:93-043532.
Audience: **l,u.**

Watts, Jerry G. **PS3552.A583Z93 2001**
Amiri Baraka: The Politics and Art of a Black Intellectual. Trade Cloth. New York University Press. New York, NY. 2001. 592p. ISBN:0-8147-9373-8, ISBN13: 978-0-8147-9373-2. Dewey:818/.5409. LCCN:2001-002006.
Audience: **l,u,f.**

20th Century (1961-2000) > Barth, John

Barth, John **PS3552.A75 B37 2005**
The Book of Ten Nights and a Night: Eleven Stories. Trade Paper, Perfect. Houghton Mifflin Company Trade & Reference Division. Boston, MA. 2005. 304p. ISBN:0-618-56208-7, ISBN13: 978-0-618-56208-4. Dewey:813/.54. LCCN:2003-067532.
Audience: **g,l,u,f.**

Barth, John **PS3552.A75C6 2001**
Coming Soon!!!: A Narrative. Trade Cloth. Houghton Mifflin Company Trade & Reference Division. Boston, MA. 2001. 416p. ISBN:0-618-13165-5, ISBN13: 978-0-618-13165-5. Dewey:813/.54. LCCN:2001-024988.
Audience: **g,l,u,f.**

Barth, John **PS3552.A75**
Further Fridays: Essays, Lectures and Other Nonfiction, 1984-1994. Trade Paper. Little Brown & Company. New York, NY. 1996. 392p. ISBN:0-316-08691-6, ISBN13: 978-0-316-08691-2. Dewey:814/.54.
Audience: **g,l,u,f.**

Barth, John **PS3552.A75G5 1987**
Giles Goat-Boy. Trade Paper. Doubleday Publishing. New York, NY. 1987. 748p. Anchor Literary Library ISBN:0-385-24086-4, ISBN13: 978-0-385-24086-4. Dewey:813/.54. LCCN:87-008886.
Audience: **g,l,u,f.**

Barth, John **PS3552.A75L6 1988**
Lost in the Funhouse. UK-Trade Paper. Doubleday Publishing. New York, NY. 1988. 224p. Anchor Literary Library ISBN:0-385-24087-2, ISBN13: 978-0-385-24087-1. Dewey:813/.54. LCCN:87-026214.
Audience: **g,l,u,f.**

Barth, John **PS3568.O243**
On with the Story: Stories. Trade Paper. Little Brown & Company. New York, NY. 1998. ISBN:0-316-19094-2, ISBN13: 978-0-316-19094-7. Dewey:813/.54.
Audience: **g,l,u,f.**

Barth, John **PS3552.A75S6 1987**
The Sot-Weed Factor. Trade Paper. Doubleday Publishing. New York, NY. 1987. 768p. Anchor Literary Library ISBN:0-385-24088-0, ISBN13: 978-0-385-24088-8. Dewey:813.54. LCCN:87-001399.
Audience: **g,l,u,f.**

Barth, John **PS3552.A75W47 2005**
Where Three Roads Meet: Novellas. Trade Cloth. Houghton Mifflin Company Trade & Reference Division. Boston, MA. 2005. 176p. ISBN:0-618-61016-2, ISBN13: 978-0-618-61016-7. Dewey:813/.54. LCCN:2005-040325.
Audience: **g,l,u,f.**

20th Century (1961-2000) > C

Carver, Raymond **PS3566.L27**
All of Us: The Collected Poems. Trade Paper. Alfred A. Knopf Inc. New York, NY. 2000. 416p. ISBN:0-375-70380-2, ISBN13: 978-0-375-70380-5. Dewey:811.5/4.
Audience: **g,l,u,f.**

Carver, Raymond **PS3568.O243**
Cathedral. Trade Paper. Random House, Inc. New York, NY. 1989. 240p. ISBN:0-679-72369-2, ISBN13: 978-0-679-72369-1. Dewey:813.5/4. LCCN:84-040009.
Audience: **g,l,u,f.**

Carver, Raymond **PS3553.A7894W43 1989**
Where I'm Calling From: Selected Stories. UK-Trade Paper. Knopf Publishing Group. New York, NY. 1989. 544p. Vintage Contemporaries Ser. ISBN:0-679-72231-9, ISBN13: 978-0-679-72231-1. LCCN:88-040366.
Audience: **g,l,u,f.**

Cervantes, Lorna Dee **PS3553.E79D75 2005**
Drive: The First Quartet; New Poems 1980-2005. Trade Cloth. Wings Press. San Antonio, TX. 2006. 312p. ISBN:0-930324-54-4, ISBN13: 978-0-930324-54-4. Dewey:811/.54. LCCN:2005-018878.
Audience: **g,l,u,f.**

Cervantes, Lorna Dee **PS3553.E79F7 1991**
From the Cables of Genocide: Poems on Love and Hunger. Trade Paper. Arte Publico Press. Houston, TX. 1991. 78p. ISBN:1-55885-033-3, ISBN13: 978-1-55885-033-0. Dewey:811/.54. LCCN:91-008721.
Audience: **g,l,u,f.**

Chabon, Michael **PS3553.H15A82 2000**
The Amazing Adventures of Kavalier and Clay. Trade Cloth. Random House, Inc. New York, NY. 2000. 656p. ISBN:0-679-45004-1, ISBN13: 978-0-679-45004-7. LCCN:00-029063.
Audience: **g,l,u,f.**

Chappell, Fred **PS3568.O243**
I Am One of You Forever. Library Binding. Sagebrush Education Resources. Caledonia, MN. 1987. ISBN:0-613-12758-7, ISBN13: 978-0-613-12758-5. Dewey:813/.54.
Audience: **g,l,u,f.**

Chappell, Fred **PS3566.L27**
Midquest: A Poem. Trade Paper. Louisiana State University Press. Baton Rouge, LA. 1981. 188p. ISBN:0-8071-1580-0, ISBN13: 978-0-8071-1580-0. Dewey:811/.54. LCCN:81-008474.
Audience: **g,l,u,f.**

Choi, Susan **PS3553.H584A64 2003**
American Woman: A Novel. Trade Cloth. HarperCollins Publishers. New York, NY. 2003. 384p. ISBN:0-06-054221-7, ISBN13: 978-0-06-054221-4. Dewey:813/.54. LCCN:2002-191935.
Audience: **g,l,u,f.**

Clifton, Lucille **PS3553.L45B58 2000**
Blessing the Boats: New and Selected Poems, 1988-2000. Trade Cloth. BOA Editions, Ltd. Rochester, NY. 2000. 145p. American Poets Continuum Ser., Vol. 59 ISBN:1-880238-87-X, ISBN13: 978-1-880238-87-5. Dewey:811/.54. LCCN:00-131741.
Audience: **g,l,u,f.**

Clifton, Lucille **PS3553.L45 G63 1987**
Good Woman: Poems and a Memoir, 1969-1980. Trade Paper. BOA Editions, Ltd. Rochester, NY. 1987. 276p. American Poets Continuum Ser., No. 14 ISBN:0-918526-59-0, ISBN13: 978-0-918526-59-5. Dewey:811/.54. LCCN:87-071302.
Audience: **g,l,u,f.**

Cole, Henri **PS3566.L27**
Middle Earth: Poems. Trade Paper. Farrar, Straus & Giroux. New York, NY. 2004. 80p. ISBN:0-374-52928-0, ISBN13: 978-0-374-52928-4. Dewey:811/.54.
Audience: **g,l,u,f.**

Cunningham, Michael **PS3553.U484H68 1998**
The Hours: A Novel. Cloth over Boards. Farrar, Straus & Giroux. New York, NY. 1998. 230p. ISBN:0-374-17289-7, ISBN13: 978-0-374-17289-3. Dewey:813/.54. LCCN:99-041903.
Audience: **g,l,u,f.**

20th Century (1961-2000) > D

De Haven, Tom **PS3554.E1116**
Derbys Dugan's Depression Funnies: A Novel. Trade Paper. Picador. New York, NY. 2002. 320p. ISBN:0-312-42133-8, ISBN13: 978-0-312-42133-5. Dewey:813/.54.
Audience: **g,l,u,f.**

Del Vecchio, John M **PS3554.E4327.A613**
The 13th Valley: A Novel. Trade Cloth. Bantam Books. New York, NY. 1982. 606 p. :p. ISBN:0-553-05022-2, ISBN13: 978-0-553-05022-6. Dewey:813/.54. LCCN:81-070920.
Audience: **g,l,u,f.** B

DeLillo, Don **PS3554.E4425**
Mao II: A Novel. Trade Paper. Penguin Group (USA) Inc. New York, NY. 1992. 256p. ISBN:0-14-015274-1, ISBN13: 978-0-14-015274-6. Dewey:813/.54. LCCN:90-050917.
Audience: **g,l,u,f.**

DeLillo, Don **PS3554.E4425U53 1997**
Underworld: A Novel. Trade Paper. Simon & Schuster. New York, NY. 1998. 832p. ISBN:0-684-84815-5, ISBN13: 978-0-684-84815-0. Dewey:813.5/4. LCCN:97-013825.
Audience: **g,l,u,f.**

Di Prima, Diana **PS3507.I68L6 1998**
Loba. Trade Paper. Penguin Group (USA) Inc. New York, NY. 1998. 256p. Penguin Poets Ser. ISBN:0-14-058752-7, ISBN13: 978-0-14-058752-4. Dewey:811/.54. LCCN:97-041144.
Audience: **g,l,u,f.**

Di Prima, Diane **PS3507.I68**
Dinners and Nightmares. Ed. 3. Trade Paper. Last Gasp Eco-Funnies, Inc. San Francisco, CA. 159p. ISBN:0-86719-395-6, ISBN13: 978-0-86719-395-4. Dewey:811.54.
Audience: **g,l,u,f.**

Di Prima, Diane **PS3507.I68M4 1998**
Memoirs of a Beatnik. Trade Paper. Penguin Group (USA) Inc. New York, NY. 1998. 208p. ISBN:0-14-023539-6, ISBN13: 978-0-14-023539-5. Dewey:813/.54. LCCN:99-158607.
Audience: **g,l,u,f.**

Di Prima, Diane **PS3566.L27**
Recollections of My Life as a Woman: The New York Years: A Memoir. Trade Paper. Penguin Group (USA) Inc. New York, NY. 2002. 432p. ISBN:0-14-023158-7, ISBN13: 978-0-14-023158-8. Dewey:811/.54 B.
Audience: **g,l,u,f.**

Dickey, James **PS3554**
Buckdancer's Choice: Poems. Trade Paper. Wesleyan University Press. Middletown, CT. 1965. 79p. Wesleyan Poetry Program Ser., Vol. 28 ISBN:0-8195-1028-9, ISBN13: 978-0-8195-1028-0. Dewey:811. LCCN:65-021079.
Audience: **g,l,u,f.**

Dickey, James **PS3568.O243**
Deliverance. Trade Cloth. Amereon, Ltd. Mattituck, NY. 1976. ISBN:0-8488-0476-7, ISBN13: 978-0-8488-0476-3. Dewey:813.5/4.
Audience: **g,l,u,f.**

Didion, Joan **F1488.3.D53 1994**
Salvador. Trade Paper. Knopf Publishing Group. New York, NY. 1994. 112p. ISBN:0-679-75183-1, ISBN13: 978-0-679-75183-0. Dewey:972.8405/2. LCCN:93-042217.
Audience: **g,l,u,f.**

Didion, Joan **PN6162**
Slouching Towards Bethlehem: Essays. Trade Paper. Farrar, Straus & Giroux. New York, NY. 1990. 238p. ISBN:0-374-52172-7, ISBN13: 978-0-374-52172-1. Dewey:814.5/4. LCCN:68-014916.
Audience: **g,l,u,f.**

Didion, Joan **PS3554.I33A6 2004**
Vintage Didion. Trade Paper. Knopf Publishing Group. New York, NY. 2004. 208p. Vintage Readers Ser. ISBN:1-4000-3393-4, ISBN13: 978-1-4000-3393-5. Dewey:814/.54. LCCN:2003-053754.
Audience: **g,l,u,f.**

Didion, Joan **PN6162**
The White Album. Trade Paper. Farrar, Straus & Giroux. New York, NY. 1990. 224p. ISBN:0-374-52221-9, ISBN13: 978-0-374-52221-6. Dewey:814.5/4.
Audience: **g,l,u,f.**

Didion, Joan **PS3554.I33Z63 2005**
The Year of Magical Thinking. Trade Cloth. Alfred A. Knopf Inc. New York, NY. 2005. 240p. ISBN:1-4000-4314-X, ISBN13: 978-1-4000-4314-9. Dewey:813/.54 B. LCCN:2005-045132.
Audience: **g,l,u,f.**

Dillard, Annie **PS369**
An American Childhood. Library Binding. Sagebrush Education Resources. Caledonia, MN. 1988. ISBN:0-613-13220-3, ISBN13: 978-0-613-13220-6. Dewey:818/.5409 B.
Audience: **g,l,u,f.** *Choice, 1988.*

Dillard, Annie **PS3551.N464**
The Annie Dillard Reader. Trade Paper. HarperCollins Publishers. New York, NY. 1995. 464p. ISBN:0-06-092660-0, ISBN13: 978-0-06-092660-1. Dewey:818/.5409. LCCN:94-019482.
Audience: **g,l,u,f.**

DiPrima, Diane **PS3507.I68P5 1990**
Pieces of a Song: Selected Poems of Diane DiPrima. Trade Cloth. City Lights Books. San Francisco, CA. 1989. 205p. ISBN:0-87286-237-2, ISBN13: 978-0-87286-237-1. Dewey:811/.54. LCCN:89-025243.
Audience: **g,l,u,f.**

Doctorow, E. L. **PS3554.O3B55 1998**
Billy Bathgate. Trade Paper. Penguin Group (USA) Inc. New York, NY. 1998. 336p. ISBN:0-452-28002-8, ISBN13: 978-0-452-28002-1. Dewey:813/.54. LCCN:98-019318.
Audience: **g,l,u,f.**

Doctorow, E. L. **PS3554.O3R34 1997**
Ragtime. Trade Cloth. Random House, Inc. New York, NY. 1997. 336p. Modern Library Ser. ISBN:0-679-60297-6, ISBN13: 978-0-679-60297-2. Dewey:[Fic]. LCCN:97-042251.
Audience: **g,l,u,f.** B

Dorn, Edward **PS3507.O73277G8 1989**
Gunslinger. Cloth Text. Duke University Press. Durham, NC. 1989. 202p. ISBN:0-8223-0964-5, ISBN13: 978-0-8223-0964-2. Dewey:811/.54. LCCN:89-007901.
Audience: **g,l,u,f.**

Dorn, Edward **PS3507.O73277**
Way West: Stories, Essays and Verse Accounts, 1963-1993. Trade Paper. HarperCollins Publishers. New York, NY. 1993. 281p. ISBN:0-87685-905-8, ISBN13: 978-0-87685-905-6. Dewey:811/.54. LCCN:93-024338.
Audience: **g,l,u,f.**

Dubus, Andre III **PS3554.U265H68 1999**
House of Sand and Fog. Trade Cloth. W. W. Norton & Company, Inc. New York, NY. 1999. 320p. ISBN:0-393-04697-4, ISBN13: 978-0-393-04697-7. Dewey:813.54. LCCN:98-035255.
Audience: **g,l,u,f.**

Dubus, Andre III **PS3568.O243**
The Last Worthless Evening: Four Novellas and Two Stories. Trade Paper. David R. Godine Publisher. Boston, MA. 1986. 184p. ISBN:1-56792-067-5, ISBN13: 978-1-56792-067-3. Dewey:813/.54. LCCN:86-045530.
Audience: **g,l,u,f.**

Dubus, Andre III **PS3554.U265**
The Times Are Never So Bad: A Novella and Eight Short Stories. Trade Paper. David R. Godine Publisher. Boston, MA. 1986. 184p. ISBN:0-87923-641-8, ISBN13: 978-0-87923-641-0. Dewey:813/.54. LCCN:82-048703.
Audience: **g,l,u,f.**

Duncan, Robert Edward **PS3507.U629G725 2006**
Ground Work: Before the War/In the Dark. Robert J. Bertholf & James Maynard (Editors), Michael Palmer (Introduction by). Trade Paper. New Directions Publishing Corporation. New York, NY. 2006. 288p. ISBN:0-8112-1653-5, ISBN13: 978-0-8112-1653-1. Dewey:811/.54. LCCN:2005-035052.
Audience: **g,l,u,f.**

Dunn, Stephen **PS3554.U49D54 2000**
Different Hours: Poems. Trade Cloth. W. W. Norton & Company, Inc. New York, NY. 2000. 112p. ISBN:0-393-04986-8, ISBN13: 978-0-393-04986-2. Dewey:811/.54. LCCN:00-030556.
Audience: **g,l,u,f.**

Dykeman, Wilma **PS3554.Y5**
Return the Innocent Earth. Ed. 2. Trade Paper. Wakestone Books. Newport, TN. 1994. 444p. ISBN:1-884450-01-6, ISBN13: 978-1-884450-01-3. Dewey:813.54.
Audience: **g,l,u,f.**

Dykeman, Wilma **PS3554.Y55**
The Tall Woman. Trade Paper. Wakestone Books. Newport, TN. 1999. 315p. ISBN:0-9613859-1-X, ISBN13: 978-0-9613859-1-0. Dewey:813/.54. LCCN:62-011580.
Audience: **g,l,u,f.**

20th Century (1961-2000) > E

Edson, Margaret **PS3545.I5365**
Wit: A Play. Library Binding. Sagebrush Education Resources. Caledonia, MN. 1999. ISBN:0-613-36752-9, ISBN13: 978-0-613-36752-3. Dewey:812/.54.
Audience: **g,l,u,f.**

Ellison, Ralph **PS3555.L625I5 2002**
Invisible Man. Trade Cloth. Random House, Inc. New York, NY. 2002. 448p. ISBN:0-375-50791-4, ISBN13: 978-0-375-50791-5. Dewey:813/.54. LCCN:2001-048541.
Audience: **g,l,u,f.**

Engels, John **PS3555.N42A6 2005**
Recounting the Seasons: Poems, 1958-2005. David Huddle (Foreword by). Trade Cloth. University of Notre Dame Press. Notre Dame, IN. 2005. 592p. ISBN:0-268-02770-6, ISBN13: 978-0-268-02770-4. Dewey:811/.54. LCCN:2005-025263.
Audience: **g,l,u,f.**

Erdrich, Louise **PS3568.O243**
The Bingo Palace. Trade Cloth. Turtleback Books. Madison, WI. 2004. 274p. ISBN:0-606-29840-1, ISBN13: 978-0-606-29840-7. Dewey:813/.54.
Audience: **g,l,u,f.**

Erdrich, Louise **PS3555.R42F68 2004**
Four Souls: A Novel. Trade Cloth. HarperCollins Publishers. New York, NY. 2004. 224p. ISBN:0-06-620975-7, ISBN13: 978-0-06-620975-3. Dewey:813/.54. LCCN:2003-065243.
Audience: **g,l,u,f.**

Erdrich, Louise **PS3568.O243**
Love Medicine. Trade Paper. HarperCollins Publishers. New York, NY. 2005. 400p. Perennial Classics Ser. ISBN:0-06-078646-9, ISBN13: 978-0-06-078646-5. Dewey:[Fic]. LCCN:92-056263.
Audience: **g,l,u,f.**

Erdrich, Louise **PS3568.O243**
Love Medicine. Library Binding. Sagebrush Education Resources. Caledonia, MN. 2001. ISBN:0-613-70664-1, ISBN13: 978-0-613-70664-3. Dewey:[Fic].
Audience: **g,l,u,f.**

Erdrich, Louise **PS3566.L27**
Original Fire: Selected and New Poems. Trade Paper. HarperCollins Publishers. New York, NY. 2004. 176p. ISBN:0-06-093534-0, ISBN13: 978-0-06-093534-4. Dewey:811/.54.
Audience: **g,l,u,f.**

Eugenides, Jeffrey **PS3555.U4M53 2002**
Middlesex: A Novel. Cloth over Boards. Farrar, Straus & Giroux. New York, NY. 2002. 544p. ISBN:0-374-19969-8, ISBN13: 978-0-374-19969-2. Dewey:813/.54. LCCN:2002-019921.
Audience: **g,l,u,f.**

20th Century (1961-2000) > F

Forche, Carolyn **PS3556.O68**
The Angel of History. Trade Paper. HarperCollins Publishers. New York, NY. 1995. 96p. ISBN:0-06-092584-1, ISBN13: 978-0-06-092584-0. Dewey:811.54. LCCN:93-037208.
Audience: **g,l,u,f.**

Forche, Carolyn **PS3566.L27**
Gathering the Tribes. Trade Paper. Yale University Press. Cumberland, RI. 1976. 74p. Yale Younger Poet Ser., No. 71 ISBN:0-300-01985-8, ISBN13: 978-0-300-01985-8. Dewey:811/.54. LCCN:75-023672.
Audience: **g,l,u,f.**

Ford, Richard **PS3568.O243**
Independence Day. Trade Paper. Knopf Publishing Group. New York, NY. 1996. 464p. ISBN:0-679-73518-6, ISBN13: 978-0-679-73518-2. Dewey:813.5/4.
Audience: **g,l,u,f.**

Fuller, Charles **PS3556.U367**
A Soldier's Play. Trade Paper. Farrar, Straus & Giroux. New York, NY. 1982. 100p. Dramabook Ser. ISBN:0-374-52148-4, ISBN13: 978-0-374-52148-6. Dewey:812. LCCN:82-015395.
Audience: **g,l,u,f.**

Silesky, Barry **PS3566.L27**
Ferlinghetti: The Artist in His Time. Mass Market. Warner Books, Inc. New York, NY. 1991. ISBN:0-446-39289-8, ISBN13: 978-0-446-39289-1. Dewey:811/.54 B.
Audience: **g,l,u,f.**

20th Century (1961-2000) > G

Gaines, Ernest J. **PS3568.O243**
The Autobiography of Miss Jane Pittman. Trade Cloth. Sagebrush Education Resources. Caledonia, MN. 1972. ISBN:0-88103-562-9, ISBN13: 978-0-88103-562-9. Dewey:813/.54.
Audience: **g,l,u,f.**

García, Cristina **PS3568.O243**
The Aguero Sisters. Trade Paper. Ballantine Books. New York, NY. 1998. 336p. Ballantine Reader's Circle Ser. ISBN:0-345-40651-6, ISBN13: 978-0-345-40651-4. Dewey:813.5/4. LCCN:98-084511.
Audience: **g,l,u,f.**

García, Cristina **PS3568.O243**
Dreaming in Cuban. Trade Paper. Ballantine Books. New York, NY. 1999. ISBN:0-345-91367-1, ISBN13: 978-0-345-91367-8. Dewey:813/.54.
Audience: **g,l,u,f.**

García, Cristina **PS3557.A66M66 2004**
Monkey Hunting. Trade Paper. Ballantine Books. New York, NY. 2004. 288p. Ballantine Reader's Circle Ser. ISBN:0-345-46610-1, ISBN13: 978-0-345-46610-5. Dewey:813/.54. LCCN:2004-275538.
Audience: **g,l,u,f.**

Gardner, John **PS3568.O243**
Grendel. Library Binding. Sagebrush Education Resources. Caledonia, MN. 1989. ISBN:0-8085-6648-2, ISBN13: 978-0-8085-6648-9. Dewey:813/.54.
Audience: **g,l,u,f.**

Gates, David **PS3557.A87J47 1992**
Jernigan. Trade Paper. Knopf Publishing Group. New York, NY. 1992. 256p. Vintage Contemporaries Ser. ISBN:0-679-73713-8, ISBN13: 978-0-679-73713-1. Dewey:813.54. LCCN:91-050720.
Audience: **g,l,u,f.**

Gilbert, Jack **PS3557.I34217R44**
Refusing Heaven: Poems. Trade Cloth. Alfred A. Knopf Inc. New York, NY. 2005. 112p. ISBN:1-4000-4365-4, ISBN13: 978-1-4000-4365-1. Dewey:811/.54. LCCN:2004-048844.
Audience: **g,l,u,f.**

Gilchrist, Ellen **PS3557.I34258A82**
The Annunciation. Trade Paper. Louisiana State University Press. Baton Rouge, LA. 2001. 368p. Voices of the South Ser. ISBN:0-8071-2736-1, ISBN13: 978-0-8071-2736-0. Dewey:813/.54. LCCN:2001-038208.
Audience: **g,l,u,f.**

Gilchrist, Ellen **PS3568.O243**
Ellen Gilchrist: Collected Stories. Trade Paper. Little Brown & Company. New York, NY. 2001. 576p. ISBN:0-316-19365-8, ISBN13: 978-0-316-19365-8. Dewey:813/.54.
Audience: **g,l,u,f.**

Gilchrist, Ellen **PS3568.O243**
I, Rhoda Manning, Go Hunting with My Daddy: And Other Stories. Trade Paper. Little Brown & Company. New York, NY. 2003. 304p. ISBN:0-316-73868-9, ISBN13: 978-0-316-73868-2. Dewey:813/.54.
Audience: **g,l,u,f.**

Gilchrist, Ellen **PS3568.O243**
In the Land of Dreamy Dreams: Short Fiction. Trade Paper. Louisiana State University Press. Baton Rouge, LA. 2002. 184p. Voices of the South Ser. ISBN:0-8071-2829-5, ISBN13: 978-0-8071-2829-9. Dewey:813/.54.
Audience: **g,l,u,f.**

Giovanni, Nikki **PS3557.I55.A6 2003**
The Collected Poetry of Nikki Giovanni: 1968-1998. Trade Cloth. HarperCollins Publishers. New York, NY. 2003. 496p. ISBN:0-06-054133-4, ISBN13: 978-0-06-054133-0. Dewey:811/.54. LCCN:2004-302269.
Audience: **g,l,u,f.**

Glück, Louise **PS3566.L27**
The First Four Books of Poems. Ed. 2. Trade Paper. HarperCollins Publishers. New York, NY. 1990. 240p. ISBN:0-88001-477-6, ISBN13: 978-0-88001-477-9. Dewey:811/.54.
Audience: **g,l,u,f.**

Glück, Louise **PS3557.L8S4 2001**
The Seven Ages. Trade Cloth. HarperCollins Publishers. New York, NY. 2001. 80p. ISBN:0-06-018526-0, ISBN13: 978-0-06-018526-8. Dewey:811.5/4. LCCN:00-046654.
Audience: **g,l,u,f.**

Glück, Louise **PS3557.L8W5 1992**
The Wild Iris. Trade Cloth. HarperCollins Publishers. New York, NY. 1992. 240p. ISBN:0-88001-281-1, ISBN13: 978-0-88001-281-2. Dewey:811.5/4. LCCN:91-036419.
Audience: **g,l,u,f.** *Choice, 1994.*

20th Century (1961-2000) > H

Hacker, Marilyn **PS3558.A28D47 2003**
Desesperanto: Poems, 1999-2002. Trade Cloth. W. W. Norton & Company, Inc. New York, NY. 2003. 128p. ISBN:0-393-05418-7, ISBN13: 978-0-393-05418-7. Dewey:811/.54. LCCN:2002-154390.
Audience: **g,l,u,f.**

Hacker, Marilyn (Compiled by) **PR1195.S65**
Poetry to Heal Your Blues. Saddle Stitched, Cloth over Boards. M Q Publications. London, 2005. 151p. ISBN:1-84072-668-7, ISBN13: 978-1-84072-668-8. Dewey:811.
Audience: **g,l,u,f.**

Hacker, Marilyn **PS3558.A28A6 1994**
Selected Poems of Marilyn Hacker, 1965-1990. Trade Cloth. W. W. Norton & Company, Inc. New York, NY. 1994. 288p. ISBN:0-393-03675-8, ISBN13: 978-0-393-03675-6. Dewey:811/.54. LCCN:94-027507.
Audience: **g,l,u,f.**

Harjo, Joy **PS3558.A62423H69**
How We Became Human: New and Selected Poems, 1975-2001. Trade Cloth. W. W. Norton & Company, Inc. New York, NY. 2002. 192p. ISBN:0-393-05101-3, ISBN13: 978-0-393-05101-8. Dewey:811/.54. LCCN:2002-000871.
Audience: **g,l,u,f.**

Harjo, Joy **PS3566.L27**
A Map to the Next World. Trade Paper. W. W. Norton & Company, Inc. New York, NY. 2001. 144p. ISBN:0-393-32096-0, ISBN13: 978-0-393-32096-1. Dewey:811/.54. LCCN:99-041099.
Audience: **g,l,u,f.**

Hass, Robert **PS3566.L27**
Field Guide. Trade Paper. Yale University Press. Cumberland, RI. 1973. 100p. Younger Poets Ser., Vol. 68 ISBN:0-300-07633-9, ISBN13: 978-0-300-07633-2. Dewey:811/.5/4. LCCN:98-176087.
Audience: **g,l,u,f.** B

Hass, Robert **PS3566.L27**
Sun under Wood. Trade Paper. HarperCollins Publishers. New York, NY. 1998. 96p. ISBN:0-88001-557-8, ISBN13: 978-0-88001-557-8. Dewey:811/.54.
Audience: **g,l,u,f.**

Heat-Moon, William Least **E158**
Blue Highways: A Journey into America. Trade Cloth. Little Brown & Company. New York, NY. 1999. 448p. ISBN:0-316-35391-4, ISBN13: 978-0-316-35391-5. Dewey:917.304/927.
Audience: **g,l,u,f.**

Hecht, Anthony **PS3558.E28A6 2003**
Collected Later Poems. Trade Cloth. Alfred A. Knopf Inc. New York, NY. 2003. 256p. ISBN:1-4000-4138-4, ISBN13: 978-1-4000-4138-1. Dewey:811.54. LCCN:2003-044601.
Audience: **g,l,u,f.**

Hecht, Anthony **PS3558.E28D37 2001**
The Darkness and the Light: Poems. Trade Cloth. Alfred A. Knopf Inc. New York, NY. 2001. 80p. ISBN:0-375-41194-1, ISBN13: 978-0-375-41194-6. Dewey:811/.54. LCCN:00-062007.
Audience: **g,l,u,f.**

Hecht, Anthony **PS3566.L27**
Flight among the Tombs: Poems. Trade Paper. Alfred A. Knopf Inc. New York, NY. 1998. 88p. ISBN:0-679-76592-1, ISBN13: 978-0-679-76592-9. Dewey:811.5/4.
Audience: **g,l,u,f.**

Heller, Joseph **PS3558.E476C3 1999**
Catch-22: A Novel. Trade Cloth. Simon & Schuster. New York, NY. 1999. 416p. Simon and Schuster Classic Editions ISBN:0-684-86513-0, ISBN13: 978-0-684-86513-3. Dewey:813/.54. LCCN:00-265132.
Audience: **g,l,u,f.** B

Henley, Beth **PS3558.E4962 C7**
Crimes of the Heart. Trade Paper. Dramatists Play Service, Inc. New York, NY. 1982. 106p. ISBN:0-8222-0250-6, ISBN13: 978-0-8222-0250-9. Dewey:812.54.
Audience: **g,l,u,f.**

Herbert, Frank **PS3558.E63D8 1984**
Dune. Trade Cloth. Penguin Group (USA) Inc. New York, NY. 1999. 528p. Ace Science Fiction Ser. ISBN:0-441-00590-X, ISBN13: 978-0-441-00590-1. Dewey:813.5/4. LCCN:83-016030.
Audience: **g,l,u,f.**

Hijuelos, Óscar **PS3558.I376M36 2000**
The Mambo Kings Play Songs of Love. Trade Paper. HarperCollins Publishers. New York, NY. 2000. 464p. Perennial Classics Ser. ISBN:0-06-095545-7, ISBN13: 978-0-06-095545-8. Dewey:813/.54. LCCN:99-053997.
Audience: **g,l,u,f.**

Hijuelos, Óscar **PS3568.O243**
Mr. Ives' Christmas. Trade Paper. HarperCollins Publishers. New York, NY. 1996. 256p. ISBN:0-06-092754-2, ISBN13: 978-0-06-092754-7. Dewey:813/.54. LCCN:95-038434.
Audience: **g,l,u,f.**

Hillman, Brenda **PS3558.I4526.B75**
Bright Existence. Library Binding. Wesleyan University Press. Middletown, CT. 1993. 112p. Wesleyan Poetry Ser. ISBN:0-8195-2204-X, ISBN13: 978-0-8195-2204-7. Dewey:811.54. LCCN:92-053862.
Audience: **g,l,u,f.** *Choice, 1993.*

Hogan, Linda **PS3568.O243**
Mean Spirit. Trade Paper. Ballantine Books. New York, NY. 1991. 384p. ISBN:0-8041-0863-3, ISBN13: 978-0-8041-0863-8. Dewey:813/.54.
Audience: **g,l,u,f.**

Hongo, Garrett **TD426.G721**
The River of Heaven. Trade Cloth. Carnegie Mellon University Press. Pittsburgh, PA. 2001. 67p. Classic Contemporaries Ser. ISBN:0-88748-358-5, ISBN13: 978-0-88748-358-5. Dewey:363.7394. LCCN:00-111579.
Audience: **g,l,u,f.**

Hwang, David Henry **PS3558.W83**
M. Butterfly: With an Afterword by the Playwright. Trade Paper. Penguin Group (USA) Inc. New York, NY. 1993. 112p. ISBN:0-452-27259-9, ISBN13: 978-0-452-27259-0. Dewey:812.54.
Audience: **g,l,u,f.**

20th Century (1961-2000) > I

Irving, John **PS3559.R8C5 1999**
The Cider House Rules. Trade Cloth. Random House, Inc. New York, NY. 1999. 592p. Modern Library Ser. ISBN:0-679-60335-2, ISBN13: 978-0-679-60335-1. Dewey:813.5/4. LCCN:99-030034.
Audience: **g,l,u,f.**

Irving, John **PS3559.R8W67 1998**
The World According to Garp. Trade Cloth. Random House, Inc. New York, NY. 1998. 720p. Modern Library Ser. ISBN:0-679-60306-9, ISBN13: 978-0-679-60306-1. Dewey:FIC. LCCN:97-039458.
Audience: **g,l,u,f.**

Kennedy, William **PS3568.O243**
Ironweed. Trade Paper. Penguin Group (USA) Inc. New York, NY. 1984. 240p. Contemporay American Fiction Ser. ISBN:0-14-007020-6, ISBN13: 978-0-14-007020-0. Dewey:813.5/4. LCCN:83-013470.
Audience: **g,l,u,f.**

20th Century (1961-2000) > J

Jin, Ha **PS3560.I6W34 1999**
Waiting: A Novel. Trade Cloth. Random House Children's Books. New York, NY. 1999. 320p. ISBN:0-375-40653-0, ISBN13: 978-0-375-40653-9. Dewey:813.5/4. LCCN:99-021334.
Audience: **g,l,u,f.**

Jin, Ha **PS3560.I6W37 2004**
War Trash: A Novel. Trade Cloth. Knopf Publishing Group. New York, NY. 2004. 368p. ISBN:0-375-42276-5, ISBN13: 978-0-375-42276-8. Dewey:813/.54. LCCN:2004-043428.
Audience: **g,l,u,f.**

Johnson, Diane **PS3560.O3746P4 1998**
Persian Nights. Trade Paper. Penguin Group (USA) Inc. New York, NY. 1998. 368p. William Abrahams Book Ser. ISBN:0-452-27958-5, ISBN13: 978-0-452-27958-2. Dewey:813/.54. LCCN:97-039783.
Audience: **g,l,u,f.**

Jones, Edward P. **PS3560.O4813K58 2003**
The Known World: A Novel. Trade Cloth. HarperCollins Publishers. New York, NY. 2003. 400p. ISBN:0-06-055754-0, ISBN13: 978-0-06-055754-6. Dewey:813/.54. LCCN:2003-040389.
Audience: **g,l,u,f.**

Jones, Rodney **PS3560.O5263E44 1999**
Elegy for the Southern Drawl. Trade Cloth. Houghton Mifflin Company Trade & Reference Division. Boston, MA. 1999. 128p. ISBN:0-395-95616-1, ISBN13: 978-0-395-95616-8. Dewey:811/.54. LCCN:98-043792.
Audience: **g,l,u,f.**

Just, Ward **PS3560.U75U54 2004**
An Unfinished Season: A Novel. Trade Cloth. Houghton Mifflin Company Trade & Reference Division. Boston, MA. 2004. 256p. ISBN:0-618-03669-5, ISBN13: 978-0-618-03669-1. Dewey:813/.54. LCCN:2004-042722.
Audience: **g,l,u,f.**

20th Century (1961-2000) > K

Kaufman, Bob **PS3521.A7265**
Solitudes Crowded with Loneliness. Trade Paper. New Directions Publishing Corporation. New York, NY. 1965. ISBN:0-8112-0076-0, ISBN13: 978-0-8112-0076-9. Dewey:811.54. LCCN:65-015673.
Audience: **g,l,u,f.**

Kaufman, Bob **PS3561.A84C73 1996**
Cranial Guitar. Gerald Nicosia (Editor), David Henderson (Introduction by). Trade Paper. Coffee House Press. Minneapolis, MN. 1995. 192p. ISBN:1-56689-038-1, ISBN13: 978-1-56689-038-0. Dewey:811/.54. LCCN:95-031960.
Audience: **g,l,u,f.**

Keillor, Garrison **PS3568.O243**
Lake Wobegon Days. Mike Lynch (Illustrator). Trade Paper. Penguin Group (USA) Inc. New York, NY. 2004. 352p. ISBN:0-14-013161-2, ISBN13: 978-0-14-013161-1. Dewey:813.5/4.
Audience: **g,l,u,f.**

Kelly, Brigit Pegeen **PS3561.E3927O73 2004**
The Orchard. Trade Paper. BOA Editions, Ltd. Rochester, NY. 2004. 88p. American Poets Continuum Ser., Vol. 82 ISBN:1-929918-48-8, ISBN13: 978-1-929918-48-5. Dewey:811/.54. LCCN:2004-001483.
Audience: **g,l,u,f.**

Kesey, Ken **PS3561.E667O5 2002**
One Flew over the Cuckoo's Nest. Ed. 40. Trade Cloth. Penguin Group (USA) Inc. New York, NY. 2002. 320p. Penguin Lives Ser. ISBN:0-670-03058-9, ISBN13: 978-0-670-03058-3. Dewey:813/.54. LCCN:2001-046923.
Audience: **g,l,u,f.** B

Kesey, Ken **PR6019.O9**
Sometimes a Great Notion. Charles Bowden (Introduction by). Trade Paper. Penguin Group (USA) Inc. New York, NY. 2006. 736p. ISBN:0-14-303986-5, ISBN13: 978-0-14-303986-0. Dewey:823/.9/1.
Audience: **g,l,u,f.**

Kesey, Ken **PS3573.A797O535 1996**
One Flew over the Cuckoo's Nest: Text and Criticism. John Clark Pratt (Editor). Trade Paper. Penguin Group (USA) Inc. New York, NY. 1996. 688p. The Viking Critical Library ISBN:0-14-023601-5, ISBN13: 978-0-14-023601-9. Dewey:813/.54. LCCN:95-031069.
Audience: **g,l,u,f.**

Keyes, Daniel **PS3561.E769F56 2004**
Flowers for Algernon. Trade Paper. Harcourt Trade Publishers. New York, NY. 2005. 324p. ISBN:0-15-603030-6, ISBN13: 978-0-15-603030-4. Dewey:813/.54. LCCN:2004-005049.
Audience: **g,l,u,f.** B

King, Stephen **PS3561.I483**
Salem's Lot. Trade Paper. Simon & Schuster. New York, NY. 2000. 480p. ISBN:0-671-03975-X, ISBN13: 978-0-671-03975-2. Dewey:[Fic].
Audience: **g,l,u,f.** B

King, Stephen **PS3561.I483**
The Shining. Trade Cloth. Doubleday Publishing. New York, NY. 1990. 464p. ISBN:0-385-12167-9, ISBN13: 978-0-385-12167-5. Dewey:[Fic]. LCCN:76-024212.
Audience: **g,l,u,f.**

King, Stephen **PS3561.I483S7 2001**
The Stand. Trade Cloth. Random House Value Publishing. New York, NY. 2001. 1200p. ISBN:0-517-21901-8, ISBN13: 978-0-517-21901-0. Dewey:813.54. LCCN:2001-023968.
Audience: **g,l,u.**

Kingsolver, Barbara **PS3568.O243**
The Poisonwood Bible: A Novel. Trade Cloth. HarperCollins Publishers. New York, NY. 2000. 560p. Oprah's Book Club Ser. ISBN:0-06-018579-1, ISBN13: 978-0-06-018579-4. Dewey:813.5/4.
Audience: **g,l,u,f.**

Kooser, Ted **PS3561.O6D45 2004**
Delights and Shadows: Poems. Trade Paper. Copper Canyon Press. Port Townsend, WA. 2004. 96p. ISBN:1-55659-201-9, ISBN13: 978-1-55659-201-0. Dewey:811/.54. LCCN:2003-018447.
Audience: **g,l,u,f.**

Kosinski, Jerzy N. **PZ4.K858**
Painted Bird. Library Binding. Sagebrush Education Resources. Caledonia, MN. 1995. ISBN:0-613-18075-5, ISBN13: 978-0-613-18075-7. Dewey:813.54.
Audience: **g,l,u,f.** B

Kushner, Tony **PS3561.U778A85 1993**
Angels in America: Perestroika. Trade Paper. Theatre Communications Group, Inc. New York, NY. 1993. 128p. ISBN:1-55936-073-9, ISBN13: 978-1-55936-073-9. Dewey:812/.54. LCCN:92-044011.
Audience: **g,l,u,f.**

Kushner, Tony **PS3561.U778A85 1993**
Millennium Approaches. Trade Paper. Theatre Communications Group, Inc. New York, NY. 1993. 136p. ISBN:1-55936-061-5, ISBN13: 978-1-55936-061-6. Dewey:812/.54. LCCN:92-044011.
Audience: **g,l,u,f.**

20th Century (1961-2000) > L

Lahiri, Jhumpa **PS3562.A316I58 1999**
Interpreter of Maladies. Trade Cloth. Houghton Mifflin Company Trade & Reference Division. Boston, MA. 2000. 160p. ISBN:0-618-10136-5, ISBN13: 978-0-618-10136-8. Dewey:813.54. LCCN:98-050895.
Audience: **g,l,u,f.**

Le Guin, Ursula K. **PS3562.E42L39 1994**
The Left Hand of Darkness. Ed. 25. Trade Cloth. Walker & Company. New York, NY. 1994. 325p. ISBN:0-8027-1302-5, ISBN13: 978-0-8027-1302-5. Dewey:813.5/4. LCCN:94-027147.
Audience: **g,l,u,f.** B

Le Guin, Ursula K. **PS3568.O243**
Unlocking the Air: Stories. Trade Paper. HarperCollins Publishers. New York, NY. 2005. 224p. ISBN:0-06-092803-4, ISBN13: 978-0-06-092803-2. Dewey:813/.54.
Audience: **g,l,u,f.**

Lea, Sydney **PS3562.E16P87 2000**
Pursuit of a Wound: Poems. Trade Paper. University of Illinois Press. Champaign, IL. 2000. 96p. Illinois Poetry Ser. ISBN:0-252-06817-3, ISBN13: 978-0-252-06817-1. LCCN:99-006987.
Audience: **g,l,u,f.**

L'Engle, Madeleine **PR9272.9.J35**
A Circle of Quiet, Set. Trade Cloth. HarperCollins Publishers. New York, NY. 1977. 246p. The Crosswicks Journal Trilogy Ser. ISBN:0-685-06341-0, ISBN13: 978-0-685-06341-5. Dewey:818.
Audience: **g,l,u,f.**

L'Engle, Madeleine **PS3523.E55O74 2005**
The Ordering of Love: The New and Collected Poems of Madeleine L'Engle. Trade Cloth. WaterBrook Press. Colorado Springs, CO. 2005. 384p. ISBN:0-87788-086-7, ISBN13: 978-0-87788-086-8. Dewey:811/.54. LCCN:2004-026880.
Audience: **g,l,u,f.**

L'Engle, Madeleine **PS3568.O243**
A Swiftly Tilting Planet. Cloth over Boards. Farrar, Straus & Giroux. New York, NY. 1978. 288p. ISBN:0-374-37362-0, ISBN13: 978-0-374-37362-7. Dewey:813.54. LCCN:78-009648.
Audience: **g,l,u,f.**

L'Engle, Madeleine **PR6019.O9**
A Wind in the Door. Library Binding. Sagebrush Education Resources. Caledonia, MN. 1976. ISBN:0-613-72383-X, ISBN13: 978-0-613-72383-1. Dewey:823/.9/1.
Audience: **g,l,u,f.**

L'Engle, Madeleine **PZ7.L5385**
A Wrinkle in Time. Trade Cloth. Book Wholesalers, Inc. Lexington, KY. 2002. ISBN:0-7587-6754-4, ISBN13: 978-0-7587-6754-7. Dewey:[Fic].
Audience: **g,l,u,f.**

L'Engle, Madeleine **PS3523.E55Z47 2001**
Madeleine L'Engle Herself: Reflections on a Writing Life. Carole F. Chase (Read by). Trade Cloth. WaterBrook Press. Colorado Springs, CO. 2001. 384p. Writers' Palette Ser. ISBN:0-87788-157-X, ISBN13: 978-0-87788-157-5. Dewey:813/.54 B. LCCN:2001-026827.
Audience: **g,l,u,f.**

Levertov, Denise **PS3562.E8876A6 2002**
The Selected Poems of Denise Levertov. Paul A. Lacey (Editor), Robert Creeley (Produced by). Trade Cloth. New Directions Publishing Corporation. New York, NY. 2002. 224p. ISBN:0-8112-1520-2, ISBN13: 978-0-8112-1520-6. Dewey:811/.54. LCCN:2002-011891.
Audience: **g,l,u,f.**

Levine, Philip **PS3562.E9B73 2004**
Breath: Poems. Trade Cloth. Alfred A. Knopf Inc. New York, NY. 2004. 96p. ISBN:1-4000-4291-7, ISBN13: 978-1-4000-4291-3. Dewey:811/.54. LCCN:2004-040839.
Audience: **g,l,u,f.**

Lopez, Barry **PS3562.O67A6 2003**
Vintage Lopez. Trade Paper. Knopf Publishing Group. New York, NY. 2004. 208p. Vintage Readers Ser. ISBN:1-4000-3398-5, ISBN13: 978-1-4000-3398-0. Dewey:813/.54. LCCN:2003-053807.
Audience: **g,l,u,f.**

Lopez, Barry **PS3562.O67W5 1999**
Winter Count. Trade Paper. Knopf Publishing Group. New York, NY. 1999. 128p. ISBN:0-679-78141-2, ISBN13: 978-0-679-78141-7. Dewey:813/.54. LCCN:99-021325.
Audience: **g,l,u,f.**

Lorde, Audre Geraldine **PS3562.O75A17 1997**
The Collected Poems of Audre Lorde. Trade Cloth. W. W. Norton & Company, Inc. New York, NY. 1997. 500p. ISBN:0-393-04090-9, ISBN13: 978-0-393-04090-6. Dewey:811/.54. LCCN:97-010878.
Audience: **g,l,u,f.** *Choice, 1998.*

Lurie, Alison **PS3562.U7**
Foreign Affairs. Trade Paper. Random House Adult Trade Publishing Group. New York, NY. 2006. 304p. ISBN:0-8129-7631-2, ISBN13: 978-0-8129-7631-1. Dewey:813.5/4.
Audience: **g,l,u,f.**

20th Century (1961-2000) > M

Malamud, Bernard **PS3568.O243**
The Natural. Trade Paper. Farrar, Straus & Giroux. New York, NY. 2003. ISBN:0-374-96037-2, ISBN13: 978-0-374-96037-7. Dewey:813/.54.
Audience: **g,l,u,f.**

Malamud, Bernard **PS3563.A4F5 2004**
The Fixer. Jonathan Safran Foer (Introduction by). Trade Paper. Farrar, Straus & Giroux. New York, NY. 2004. 352p. ISBN:0-374-52938-8, ISBN13: 978-0-374-52938-3. Dewey:813/.54. LCCN:2003-116991.
Audience: **g,l,u,f.**

Mamet, David **PS3545.I5365**
Glengarry Glen Ross. Trade Paper. Grove/Atlantic, Inc. New York, NY. 1984. 112p. ISBN:0-8021-3091-7, ISBN13: 978-0-8021-3091-4. Dewey:812.5/4. LCCN:83-049380.
Audience: **g,l,u,f.**

Marguiles, Donald **PS3563.A653D56 2000**
Dinner with Friends. Trade Paper. Theatre Communications Group, Inc. New York, NY. 2000. 112p. ISBN:1-55936-194-8, ISBN13: 978-1-55936-194-1. Dewey:812/.54. LCCN:00-041784.
Audience: **g,l,u,f.**

Matthews, William **PS3563.A855A17 2004**
Search Party: Collected Poems. Sebastian Matthews & Stanley Plumly (Editors). Trade Cloth. Houghton Mifflin Company Trade & Reference Division. Boston, MA. 2004. 336p. ISBN:0-618-35007-1, ISBN13: 978-0-618-35007-0. Dewey:811/.54. LCCN:2003-056795.
Audience: **g,l,u,f.**

Matthiessen, Peter **PS3568.O243**
At Play in the Fields of the Lord. Trade Cloth. Peter Smith Publisher, Inc. Magnolia, MA. 1992. ISBN:0-8446-6636-X, ISBN13: 978-0-8446-6636-5. Dewey:813/.54.
Audience: **g,l,u,f.**

Matthiessen, Peter **PS3563.A8584F3 1988**
Far Tortuga: A Novel. Trade Paper. Knopf Publishing Group. New York, NY. 1988. 416p. ISBN:0-394-75667-3, ISBN13: 978-0-394-75667-7. Dewey:813/.54. LCCN:87-040154.
Audience: **g,l,u,f.**

Matthiessen, Peter **PS3563.A8584A6 2000**
The Peter Matthiessen Reader. McKay Jenkins (Editor, Introduction by). Trade Paper. Knopf Publishing Group. New York, NY. 2000. 400p. ISBN:0-375-70272-5, ISBN13: 978-0-375-70272-3. Dewey:813/.54. LCCN:99-035246.
Audience: **g,l,u,f.**

McCarthy, Cormac **PS3563.C337 A79 1992**
All the Pretty Horses. Trade Cloth. Alfred A. Knopf Inc. New York, NY. 1992. 320p. The Border Trilogy, Vol. 1 ISBN:0-394-57474-5, ISBN13: 978-0-394-57474-5. Dewey:813.5/4. LCCN:91-058560.
Audience: **g,l,u,f.**

McClatchy, J. D. **PS3563.A26123H39**
Hazmat. Trade Paper. Alfred A. Knopf Inc. New York, NY. 2004. 96p. ISBN:0-375-70991-6, ISBN13: 978-0-375-70991-3. Dewey:813/.54. LCCN:2002-020529.
Audience: **g,l,u,f.**

McClure, Michael **PS3563.A262H84 1999**
Huge Dreams: San Francisco and Beat Poems. Trade Paper. Penguin Group (USA) Inc. New York, NY. 1999. 208p. Penguin Poets Ser. ISBN:0-14-058917-1, ISBN13: 978-0-14-058917-7. Dewey:811/.54. LCCN:98-047393.
Audience: **g,l,u,f.**

McClure, Michael **PS3563.A262**
Selected Poems. New Directions. 1986. ISBN:0-8112-0950-4, ISBN13: 978-0-8112-0950-2.
Audience: **g,l,u,f.**

McDermott, Alice **PS3568.O243**
At Weddings and Wakes. Trade Paper. Dell Publishing. New York, NY. 1998. 224p. ISBN:0-385-31985-1, ISBN13: 978-0-385-31985-0. Dewey:813.5/4.
Audience: **g,l,u,f.**

McDermott, Alice **PS3545.I5365**
That Night. Trade Paper. Dell Publishing. New York, NY. 1999. 192p. ISBN:0-385-33330-7, ISBN13: 978-0-385-33330-6. Dewey:813.5/4.
Audience: **g,l,u,f.**

McGuane, Thomas **PS3568.O243**
The Bushwhacked Piano. Trade Paper. Random House, Inc. New York, NY. 1994. ISBN:0-394-25886-X, ISBN13: 978-0-394-25886-7. Dewey:813/.54.
Audience: **g,l,u,f.**

McGuane, Thomas **PS3568.O243**
Keep the Change. Trade Paper. Random House, Inc. New York, NY. 1994. ISBN:0-394-25889-4, ISBN13: 978-0-394-25889-8. Dewey:813/.54.
Audience: **g,l,u,f.**

McGuane, Thomas **PS3568.O243**
To Skin a Cat: Stories. Trade Paper. Random House, Inc. New York, NY. 1994. ISBN:0-394-25888-6, ISBN13: 978-0-394-25888-1. Dewey:813/.54.
Audience: **g,l,u,f.**

McHugh, Heather **PS3563.A311614E94**
Eyeshot. Trade Cloth. Wesleyan University Press. Middletown, CT. 2003. 64p. Wesleyan Poetry Ser. ISBN:0-8195-6671-3, ISBN13: 978-0-8195-6671-3. Dewey:811/.54. LCCN:2003-053526.
Audience: **g,l,u,f.**

McMurtry, Larry **PS3568.O243**
The Last Picture Show: A Novel. Trade Cloth. Amereon, Ltd. Mattituck, NY. 1976. Last Picture Show Trilogy, No. 1 ISBN:0-89190-889-7, ISBN13: 978-0-89190-889-0. Dewey:813.5/4.
Audience: **g,l,u,f.**

McMurtry, Larry **PS3563.A319L6 2000**
Lonesome Dove: A Novel. Trade Cloth. Simon & Schuster. New York, NY. 2000. 864p. Simon and Schuster Classic Editions, No. 3 ISBN:0-684-87122-X, ISBN13: 978-0-684-87122-6. Dewey:813/.54. LCCN:00-712553.
Audience: **g,l,u,f.**

McPherson, James Alan **PS3568.O243**
Elbow Room: Stories. Trade Paper. Ballantine Books. New York, NY. 1986. 288p. Black History Titles Ser. ISBN:0-449-21357-9, ISBN13: 978-0-449-21357-5. Dewey:813/.54.
Audience: **g,l,u,f.** B

Miller, Jason **PS3545.I5365**
That Championship Season. Trade Paper. Dramatists Play Service, Inc. New York, NY. 1972. ISBN:0-8222-1126-2, ISBN13: 978-0-8222-1126-6. Dewey:812/.5/4.
Audience: **g,l,u,f.** B

Millhauser, Steven **PS3568.O243**
Martin Dressler: The Tale of an American Dreamer. Trade Paper. Knopf Publishing Group. New York, NY. 1997. 304p. ISBN:0-679-78127-7, ISBN13: 978-0-679-78127-1. Dewey:813.5/4. LCCN:96-000683.
Audience: **g,l,u,f.**

Mobley, Marilyn Sanders **PS374.W6 M63 1994**
Folk Roots and Mythic Wings in Sarah Orne Jewett and Toni Morrison: The Cultural Function of Narrative. Trade Paper. Louisiana State University Press. Baton Rouge, LA. 1994. 193p. ISBN:0-8071-1964-4, ISBN13: 978-0-8071-1964-8. Dewey:813.0099287. LCCN:91-015031.
Audience: **u,f.**

Momaday, N. Scott **PS3563.O47H6 1996**
House Made of Dawn. Trade Cloth. University of Arizona Press. Tucson, AZ. 1996. 212p. The Momaday Collection ISBN:0-8165-1705-3, ISBN13: 978-0-8165-1705-3. Dewey:813/.54. LCCN:96-031832.
Audience: **g,l,u,f.**

Momaday, N. Scott **E99.K5M64 1996**
The Way to Rainy Mountain. Al Momaday (Illustrator). Trade Cloth. University of Arizona Press. Tucson, AZ. 1996. 88p. ISBN:0-8165-1701-0, ISBN13: 978-0-8165-1701-5. Dewey:398.2/089/974. LCCN:96-028570.
Audience: **g,l,u,f.**

Mora, Pat **PS3563.O73B67 1986**
Borders. Ed. 2. Trade Paper. Arte Publico Press. Houston, TX. 1986. 88p. ISBN:0-934770-57-3, ISBN13: 978-0-934770-57-6. Dewey:811.54. LCCN:85-073352.
Audience: **g,l,u,f.**

Mora, Pat **PS3563.O73 C48 1984**
Chants. Ed. 2. Trade Paper. Arte Publico Press. Houston, TX. 1985. 52p. ISBN:0-934770-24-7, ISBN13: 978-0-934770-24-8. Dewey:811/.54. LCCN:83-070677.
Audience: **g,l,u,f.**

Morales, Alejandro **PS3563.O759B7 1988**
The Brick People. Ed. 2. Trade Paper. Arte Publico Press. Houston, TX. 1992. 320p. ISBN:0-934770-91-3, ISBN13: 978-0-934770-91-0. Dewey:863. LCCN:88-010409.
Audience: **g,l,u,f.** *Choice, 1989.*

Morales, Alejandro **PQ7082.N7**
The Rag Doll Plagues. Trade Paper. Arte Publico Press. Houston, TX. 1992. 200p. ISBN:1-55885-104-6, ISBN13: 978-1-55885-104-7. Dewey:863. LCCN:91-002381.
Audience: **g,l,u,f.**

Morgan, Robert **PS3568.O243**
Gap Creek: The Story of a Marriage. Trade Cloth. Algonquin Books of Chapel Hill. Chapel Hill, NC. 1999. 326p. Oprah's Book Club Ser. ISBN:1-56512-296-8, ISBN13: 978-1-56512-296-3. Dewey:813.5/4. LCCN:99-034995.
Audience: **g,l,u,f.**

Morgan, Robert **PS3563.O87147G67**
Green River: New and Selected Poems. Library Binding. Wesleyan University Press. Middletown, CT. 1991. 98p. Wesleyan Poetry Ser. ISBN:0-8195-2179-5, ISBN13: 978-0-8195-2179-8. Dewey:811/.54. LCCN:90-050912.
Audience: **g,l,u,f.**

Morgan, Robert **PS3563.O87147S87**
The Strange Attractor: New and Selected Poems. Trade Cloth. Louisiana State University Press. Baton Rouge, LA. 2004. 144p. ISBN:0-8071-2951-8, ISBN13: 978-0-8071-2951-7. Dewey:811/.54. LCCN:2003-020200.
Audience: **g,l,u,f.**

Morrison, Toni **PS3563**
Beloved. Trade Paper. Knopf Publishing Group. New York, NY. 2004. 352p. ISBN:1-4000-3341-1, ISBN13: 978-1-4000-3341-6. Dewey:813/.54. LCCN:2004-555136.
Audience: **g,l,u,f.** *Choice, 1988.*

Morrison, Toni **PS3568.O243**
The Bluest Eye. Trade Cloth. Knopf Publishing Group. New York, NY. 1993. 224p. Oprah's Book Club Ser. ISBN:0-375-41155-0, ISBN13: 978-0-375-41155-7. Dewey:813.5/4. LCCN:93-043124.
Audience: **g,l,u,f.**

Morrison, Toni **PS3563.O8749**
Sula. Trade Cloth. Alfred A. Knopf Inc. New York, NY. 2002. 192p. ISBN:0-375-41535-1, ISBN13: 978-0-375-41535-7. Dewey:813/.54.
Audience: **g,l,u,f.** B

Morrison, Toni **PS3563.O8749S6 1995**
Song of Solomon. Reynolds Price (Introduction by). Trade Cloth. Knopf Publishing Group. New York, NY. 1995. 416p. Everyman's Library ISBN:0-679-44504-8, ISBN13: 978-0-679-44504-3. Dewey:813/.54. LCCN:96-101651.
Audience: **g,l,u,f.** B

20th Century (1961-2000) > N

Naylor, Gloria **PS3564.A895W6 1983**
The Women of Brewster Place. Trade Paper. Penguin Group (USA) Inc. New York, NY. 1983. 208p. Penguin Contemporary American Fiction Ser. ISBN:0-14-006690-X, ISBN13: 978-0-14-006690-6. Dewey:813.54. LCCN:82-024533.
Audience: **g,l,u,f.** B

Nichols, John **PS3568.O243**
The Milagro Beanfield War: A Novel. Trade Paper. Henry Holt & Company. New York, NY. 2000. 464p. ISBN:0-8050-6374-9, ISBN13: 978-0-8050-6374-5. Dewey:813/.54. LCCN:93-011937.
Audience: **g,l,u,f.**

Norman, Marsha **PS3545.I5365**
'Night, Mother. Trade Paper. Dramatists Play Service, Inc. New York, NY. 1983. 67p. ISBN:0-8222-0821-0, ISBN13: 978-0-8222-0821-1. Dewey:812/.54.
Audience: **g,l,u,f.**

Notley, Alice **PS3564.O79M97 1998**
Mysteries of Small Houses. Trade Paper. Penguin Group (USA) Inc. New York, NY. 1998. 160p. Penguin Poets Ser. ISBN:0-14-058896-5, ISBN13: 978-0-14-058896-5. Dewey:811/.54. LCCN:97-042195.
Audience: **g,l,u,f.**

20th Century (1961-2000) > O

O'Brien, Tim **PS3565.B75J85 2002**
July, July: A Novel. Trade Cloth. Houghton Mifflin Company Trade & Reference Division. Boston, MA. 2002. 336p. ISBN:0-618-03969-4, ISBN13: 978-0-618-03969-2. Dewey:813/.54. LCCN:2002-032232.
Audience: **g,l,u,f.**

O'Brien, Tim **PS3568.O243**
The Things They Carried. Library Binding. Sagebrush Education Resources. Caledonia, MN. 1998. ISBN:0-8335-7486-8, ISBN13: 978-0-8335-7486-2. Dewey:813/.54.
Audience: **g.** *Choice, 1990.*

Ortiz, Simon J. **PS501.S85 VOL.42**
From Sand Creek: Rising in This Heart Which Is Our America. Trade Cloth. University of Arizona Press. Tucson, AZ. 1999. 96p. Sun Tracks, Vol. 42:An American Indian Literary Ser. ISBN:0-8165-1993-5, ISBN13: 978-0-8165-1993-4. Dewey:810.8/0054 s 811/.54. LCCN:99-028803.
Audience: **g,l,u,f.**

Ortiz, Simon J. **PS3565.R77**
Woven Stone. Trade Cloth. University of Arizona Press. Tucson, AZ. 1992. 367p. Sun Tracks, Vol. 21:An American Indian Literary Ser. ISBN:0-8165-1330-9, ISBN13: 978-0-8165-1330-7. Dewey:810.8. LCCN:92-012507.
Audience: **g,l,u,f.**

Ozick, Cynthia **PS3565**
The Bear Boy. Saddle Stitched. Weidenfeld & Nicolson, Ltd. London, 2005. 320p. ISBN:0-297-84808-9, ISBN13: 978-0-297-84808-0. Dewey:813.54. LCCN:2005-412717.
Audience: **g,l,u,f.**

Ozick, Cynthia **PS3565.Z5A6 1996**
A Cynthia Ozick Reader. Trade Cloth. Indiana University Press. Bloomington, IN. 1996. 400p. ISBN:0-253-33039-4, ISBN13: 978-0-253-33039-0. Dewey:813/.54. LCCN:95-039500.
Audience: **g,l,u,f.**

Ozick, Cynthia **PS3565.Z5H45 2004**
Heir to the Glimmering World. Trade Cloth. Houghton Mifflin Company Trade & Reference Division. Boston, MA. 2004. 320p. ISBN:0-618-47049-2, ISBN13: 978-0-618-47049-5. Dewey:FIC. LCCN:2004-042723.
Audience: **g,l,u,f.**

20th Century (1961-2000) > Oates, Joyce Carol

Daly, Brenda **PS3565.A8Z635 1996**
Lavish Self-Divisions: The Novels of Joyce Carol Oates. Trade Cloth. University Press of Mississippi. Jackson, MS. 1996. 232p. ISBN:0-87805-885-0, ISBN13: 978-0-87805-885-3. Dewey:813/.54. LCCN:96-011684.
Audience: **g,l,u,f.** *Choice, 1997.*

Oates, Joyce Carol **PS3565.A8B4318 1991**
Because It Is Bitter, and Because It Is My Heart. Trade Paper. Penguin Group (USA) Inc. New York, NY. 1991. 416p. ISBN:0-452-26581-9, ISBN13: 978-0-452-26581-3. LCCN:90-019681.
Audience: **g,l,u,f.**

Oates, Joyce Carol **PS3565.A8B47 1992B**
Black Water. Trade Paper. Penguin Group (USA) Inc. New York, NY. 1993. 160p. Plume Contemporary Fiction Ser. ISBN:0-452-26986-5, ISBN13: 978-0-452-26986-6. Dewey:813.54. LCCN:92-042773.
Audience: **g,l,u,f.**

Oates, Joyce Carol **PS3565.A8F355 2004**
The Falls: A Novel. Trade Cloth. HarperCollins Publishers. New York, NY. 2004. 496p. ISBN:0-06-072228-2, ISBN13: 978-0-06-072228-9. Dewey:813/.54. LCCN:2004-043310.
Audience: **g,l,u,f.**

Oates, Joyce Carol **PS3565.A8F69 1994**
Foxfire: Confessions of a Girl Gang. Trade Paper. Penguin Group (USA) Inc. New York, NY. 1994. 336p. ISBN:0-452-27231-9, ISBN13: 978-0-452-27231-6. Dewey:813/.54. LCCN:94-003897.
Audience: **g,l,u,f.**

Oates, Joyce Carol **PS3565.A8H54 2006**
High Lonesome: Stories 1966-2006. Trade Cloth. HarperCollins Publishers. New York, NY. 2006. 672p. ISBN:0-06-050119-7, ISBN13: 978-0-06-050119-8. Dewey:813/.54. LCCN:2005-051147.
Audience: **g,l,u,f.**

Oates, Joyce Carol **PS3568.O243**
I Am No One You Know: Stories. Trade Paper. HarperCollins Publishers. New York, NY. 2005. 304p. ISBN:0-06-059289-3, ISBN13: 978-0-06-059289-9. Dewey:813/.54.
Audience: **g,l,u,f.**

Oates, Joyce Carol **PS3568.O243**
Man Crazy: A Novel. Trade Paper. Penguin Group (USA) Inc. New York, NY. 1998. 288p. ISBN:0-452-27724-8, ISBN13: 978-0-452-27724-3. Dewey:813.5/4. LCCN:97-012725.
Audience: **g,l,u,f.**

Oates, Joyce Carol **PS3565.A8R29 2003**
Rape: A Love Story. Trade Cloth. Avalon Publishing Group. New York, NY. 2003. 128p. ISBN:0-7867-1294-5, ISBN13: 978-0-7867-1294-6. Dewey:813/.54. LCCN:2004-272106.
Audience: **g,l,u,f.**

Oates, Joyce Carol **PS3568.O243**
We Were the Mulvaneys. Prebound. Turtleback Books. Madison, WI. 2001. ISBN:0-606-20982-4, ISBN13: 978-0-606-20982-3. Dewey:813.5/4.
Audience: **g,l,u,f.**

Oates, Joyce Carol **PS3568.O243**
You Must Remember This. Trade Paper. Penguin Group (USA) Inc. New York, NY. 1998. 448p. ISBN:0-452-28019-2, ISBN13: 978-0-452-28019-9. Dewey:813/.54. LCCN:86-024337.
Audience: **g,l,u,f.**

Oates, Joyce Carol **PS3568.O243**
Blonde: A Novel. Jayne Atkinson (Read by). Trade Paper. HarperCollins Publishers. New York, NY. 2001. 752p. ISBN:0-06-093493-X, ISBN13: 978-0-06-093493-4. Dewey:813/.54.
Audience: **g,l,u,f.**

Oates, Joyce Carol **PS3565.A8W43 1994**
Where Are You Going, Where Have You Been?: Selected Early Stories. Elaine Showalter (Editor, Introduction by). Cloth Text. Rutgers University Press. Piscataway, NJ. 1995. 160p. Women Writers: Text and Contexts Ser. ISBN:0-8135-2134-3, ISBN13: 978-0-8135-2134-3. Dewey:813/.54. LCCN:94-011284.
Audience: **g,l,u,f.**

Wesley, Marilyn C. **PS3565**
Refusal and Transgression in Joyce Carol Oates' Fiction, 135. Trade Cloth. Greenwood Publishing Group, Inc. Portsmouth, NH. 1993. 192p. Contributions in Women's Studies, No. 135 ISBN:0-313-28462-8, ISBN13: 978-0-313-28462-5. Dewey:813.54. LCCN:92-039467.
Audience: **u,f.** *Choice, 1993.*

20th Century (1961-2000) > P

Paley, Grace **PS3568.O243**
The Collected Stories. Trade Paper. Farrar, Straus & Giroux. New York, NY. 2006. 386p. ISBN:0-374-53028-9, ISBN13: 978-0-374-53028-0. Dewey:813.5/4.
Audience: **g,l,u,f.**

Parks, Suzan-Lori **PS3566.A736T66 2001**
Topdog-Underdog. Trade Paper. Theatre Communications Group, Inc. New York, NY. 2001. 112p. ISBN:1-55936-201-4, ISBN13: 978-1-55936-201-6. Dewey:812/.54. LCCN:2001-027316.
Audience: **g,l,u,f.**

Percy, Walker **PS3566.E6912L64 1999**
Love in the Ruins. Trade Paper. Picador. New York, NY. 1999. 416p. ISBN:0-312-24311-1, ISBN13: 978-0-312-24311-1. Dewey:813/.54. LCCN:99-032173.
Audience: **g,l,u,f.**

Percy, Walker **PS3566.E6912**
The Moviegoer. Trade Paper. Knopf Publishing Group. New York, NY. 1998. 256p. ISBN:0-375-70196-6, ISBN13: 978-0-375-70196-2. Dewey:813.5/4. LCCN:61-007754.
Audience: **g,l,u,f.** B

Petesch, Natalie L. **PS3568.O243**
After the First Death There Is No Other. Trade Paper. University of Iowa Press. Iowa City, IA. 1974. 208p. Iowa Short Fiction Award Ser. ISBN:0-87745-064-1, ISBN13: 978-0-87745-064-1. Dewey:813/.5/4. LCCN:74-008851.
Audience: **g,l,u,f.** B

Piercy, Marge **PS3568.O243**
Braided Lives. Trade Cloth. Ultramarine Publishing Company, Inc. Hastings-on-Hudson, NY. 1982. 441p. ISBN:0-671-43834-4, ISBN13: 978-0-671-43834-0. Dewey:813/.54. LCCN:81-016695.
Audience: **g,l,u,f.**

Piercy, Marge **PS3566.I4C65 2003**
Colors Passing Through Us: Poems. Trade Cloth. Alfred A. Knopf Inc. New York, NY. 2003. 176p. ISBN:0-375-41537-8, ISBN13: 978-0-375-41537-1. Dewey:811/.54. LCCN:2002-066145.
Audience: **g,l,u,f.**

Piercy, Marge **PS3566.I4Z477 2002**
Sleeping with Cats: A Memoir. Trade Cloth. HarperCollins Publishers. New York, NY. 2002. 368p. ISBN:0-06-621115-8, ISBN13: 978-0-06-621115-2. Dewey:813.5/4. LCCN:2001-016845.
Audience: **g,l,u,f.**

Piercy, Marge **PS3566.I4O94 1999**
Three Women. Trade Cloth. HarperCollins Publishers. New York, NY. 1999. 309p. ISBN:0-688-17106-0, ISBN13: 978-0-688-17106-3. Dewey:813.5/4. LCCN:99-013324.
Audience: **g,l,u,f.**

Pinsky, Robert **PS3566.L27**
The Figured Wheel: New and Collected Poems, 1966-1996. Trade Paper. Farrar, Straus & Giroux. New York, NY. 1997. 320p. ISBN:0-374-52506-4, ISBN13: 978-0-374-52506-4. Dewey:811/.54.
Audience: **g,l,u,f.**

Pinsky, Robert **PS3566.I54F57 2006**
First Things to Hand: Poems. Trade Paper. Consortium Book Sales & Distribution. Saint Paul, MN. 2006. 24p. Quarternote Chapbook Ser., Vol. 5 ISBN:1-932511-34-2, ISBN13: 978-1-932511-34-5. Dewey:811/.54. LCCN:2005-022249.
Audience: **g,l,u,f.**

Pinsky, Robert **PS3566.I54H5 1997**
History of My Heart: Poems. Trade Paper. Farrar, Straus & Giroux. New York, NY. 1997. 64p. ISBN:0-374-52530-7, ISBN13: 978-0-374-52530-9. Dewey:811/.54. LCCN:99-178792.
Audience: **g,l,u,f.** B

Pirsig, Robert M. **PS3566.I66 L54 1992**
Lila: An Inquiry into Morals. Trade Paper. Bantam Books. New York, NY. 1992. 480p. ISBN:0-553-29961-1, ISBN13: 978-0-553-29961-8. Dewey:813.54. LCCN:91-016417.
Audience: **g,l,u,f.**

Plath, Sylvia **PS3566.L27**
Ariel. Trade Cloth. Buccaneer Books, Inc. Cutchogue, NY. 1999. ISBN:1-56849-723-7, ISBN13: 978-1-56849-723-5. Dewey:811/.54.
Audience: **g,l,u,f.** B

Plath, Sylvia **PS3566.L27**
Collected Poems. Trade Cloth. Buccaneer Books, Inc. Cutchogue, NY. 1998. ISBN:1-56849-703-2, ISBN13: 978-1-56849-703-7. Dewey:811.5/4.
Audience: **g,l,u,f.**

Plath, Sylvia **PS3566.L27.B4 1996**
The Bell Jar. Ed. 20. Frances McCullough (Foreword by), Lois Ames (Notes by). Trade Cloth. HarperCollins Publishers. New York, NY. 1996. 320p. ISBN:0-06-017490-0, ISBN13: 978-0-06-017490-3. Dewey:813/.54. LCCN:96-211742.
Audience: **g,l,u,f.**

Plumly, Stanley **PS3566.L78N69 2000**
Now That My Father Lies down Beside Me: New and Selected Poems, 1970-2000. Trade Cloth. HarperCollins Publishers. New York, NY. 2000. 176p. ISBN:0-06-019659-9, ISBN13: 978-0-06-019659-2. Dewey:811/.54. LCCN:99-057297.
Audience: **g,l,u,f.**

Price, Reynolds **PS3566.R54A6 1993**
The Collected Stories of Reynolds Price. Trade Cloth. Simon & Schuster. New York, NY. 1993. 640p. ISBN:0-689-12147-4, ISBN13: 978-0-689-12147-0. Dewey:813/.54. LCCN:92-036807.
Audience: **g,l,u,f.** *Choice, 1993.*

Price, Reynolds **PS3566.R54L6 1987**
A Long and Happy Life. Ed. 25. Trade Cloth. Simon & Schuster. New York, NY. 1987. 208p. ISBN:0-689-11947-X, ISBN13: 978-0-689-11947-7. Dewey:813/.54. LCCN:61-012790.
Audience: **g,l,u,f.** B

Proulx, Annie (Author, Adapted by) **PS3566.R697S4 1999**
The Shipping News: A Novel. Trade Cloth. Simon & Schuster. New York, NY. 1999. 352p. Scribner Classics ISBN:0-684-85791-X, ISBN13: 978-0-684-85791-6. Dewey:813/.54. LCCN:99-234809.
Audience: **g,l,u,f.**

Pynchon, Thomas **PS3568.O243**
The Crying of Lot 49. Prebound. Turtleback Books. Madison, WI. 1999. ISBN:0-606-19195-X, ISBN13: 978-0-606-19195-1. Dewey:813.5/4.
Audience: **g,l,u,f.** B

Pynchon, Thomas **PS3566.Y55G7 1995**
Gravity's Rainbow. Trade Paper. Penguin Group (USA) Inc. New York, NY. 1995. 768p. Twentieth Century Classics Ser. ISBN:0-14-018859-2, ISBN13: 978-0-14-018859-2. Dewey:813/.54. LCCN:95-220312.
Audience: **g,l,u,f.** B

20th Century (1961-2000) > R

Rabe, David **PS3568.A23**
The Vietnam Plays: The Basic Training at Paulo Hummel and Sticks and Bones. Trade Paper. Grove/Atlantic, Inc. New York, NY. 1994. 208p. Vietnam Plays Ser., Vol. 1 ISBN:0-8021-3313-4, ISBN13: 978-0-8021-3313-7. Dewey:812/.54. LCCN:92-037145.
Audience: **g,l,u,f.**

Rechy, John **PS3568.E28B6 2001**
Bodies and Souls: A Novel. Trade Paper. Grove/Atlantic, Inc. New York, NY. 2001. 448p. ISBN:0-8021-3846-2, ISBN13: 978-0-8021-3846-0. Dewey:813/.54. LCCN:2001-040158.
Audience: **g,l,u,f.**

Rechy, John **PS3568.O243**
The Coming of the Night. Trade Paper. Grove/Atlantic, Inc. New York, NY. 2000. 256p. ISBN:0-8021-3742-3, ISBN13: 978-0-8021-3742-5. Dewey:813/.54.
Audience: **g,l,u,f.**

Rechy, John **PS3568.E28L54 2003**
The Life and Adventures of Lyle Clemens. Trade Cloth. Grove/Atlantic, Inc. New York, NY. 2003. 352p. ISBN:0-8021-1746-5, ISBN13: 978-0-8021-1746-5. Dewey:813/.54. LCCN:2003-049070.
Audience: **g,l,u,f.**

Rechy, John **PS3568.E28M5 2001**
The Miraculous Day of Amalia Gómez: A Novel. Trade Paper. Grove/Atlantic, Inc. New York, NY. 2001. 224p. ISBN:0-8021-3847-0, ISBN13: 978-0-8021-3847-7. Dewey:813/.54. LCCN:2001-040159.
Audience: **g,l,u,f.**

Reed, Ishmael **PS3568.E365**
Mumbo Jumbo. Trade Paper. Simon & Schuster. New York, NY. 1996. 224p. ISBN:0-684-82477-9, ISBN13: 978-0-684-82477-2. Dewey:813.54.
Audience: **g,l,u,f.** B

Reed, Ishmael **PS3568.E365**
New and Collected Poems, 1966-2006. Cloth over Boards. Avalon Publishing Group. New York, NY. 2006. 384p. ISBN:0-7867-1788-2, ISBN13: 978-0-7867-1788-0. Dewey:811.54.
Audience: **g,l,u,f.**

Reed, Ishmael **PS3568.O243**
Reed Reader. Trade Paper. Basic Books. New York, NY. 2001. 524p. ISBN:0-465-06894-4, ISBN13: 978-0-465-06894-4. Dewey:813/.54.
Audience: **g,l,u,f.**

Reed, Ishmael **PS3568.E365Y4 2000**
Yellow Back Radio Broke Down. Trade Paper. Dalkey Archive Press. Normal, IL. 2000. 177p. ISBN:1-56478-238-7, ISBN13: 978-1-56478-238-0. Dewey:813/.54. LCCN:00-020976.
Audience: **g,l,u,f.**

Robinson, Marilynne **PS3568.O3125G55 2004**
Gilead: A Novel. Trade Cloth. Farrar, Straus & Giroux. New York, NY. 2004. 256p. ISBN:0-374-15389-2, ISBN13: 978-0-374-15389-2. Dewey:813/.54. LCCN:2004-047063.
Audience: **g,l,u,f.**

Robinson, Marilynne **PS3568.O243**
Housekeeping: A Novel. Cloth over Boards. Farrar, Straus & Giroux. New York, NY. 2005. 224p. ISBN:0-374-17313-3, ISBN13: 978-0-374-17313-5. Dewey:813/.54. LCCN:80-024061.
Audience: **g,l,u,f.**

Roth, Philip **PS3568.O855A77 1998**
American Pastoral: A Novel. Trade Paper. Knopf Publishing Group. New York, NY. 1998. 432p. Vintage International Ser. ISBN:0-375-70142-7, ISBN13: 978-0-375-70142-9. Dewey:813.5/4. LCCN:97-035623.
Audience: **g,l,u,f.**

Roth, Philip **PS3568.O855G48 1995**
The Ghost Writer. Trade Paper. Knopf Publishing Group. New York, NY. 1995. 192p. ISBN:0-679-74898-9, ISBN13: 978-0-679-74898-4. Dewey:813/.54. LCCN:95-006782.
Audience: **g,l,u,f.** B

Roth, Philip **PS3568.O855O6 1994**
Operation Shylock: A Confession. Trade Paper. Knopf Publishing Group. New York, NY. 1994. 400p. Vintage International Ser. ISBN:0-679-75029-0, ISBN13: 978-0-679-75029-1. Dewey:813.5/4. LCCN:93-044045.
Audience: **g,l,u,f.** *Choice, 1993.*

Roth, Philip **PS3568.O855A6 2005**
Philip Roth: Novels, 1967-1972. Ross Miller (Editor). Trade Cloth. Library of America, The. New York, NY. 2005. 672p. The Library of America, Vol. 158 ISBN:1-931082-80-4, ISBN13: 978-1-931082-80-8. Dewey:813/.54. LCCN:2005-040917.
Audience: **g,l,u,f.**

Roth, Philip **PS3568.O855A6 2005**
Philip Roth: Novels and Stories, 1959-1962. Ross Miller (Editor). Trade Cloth. Library of America, The. New York, NY. 2005. 913p. The Library of America, Vol. 157 ISBN:1-931082-79-0, ISBN13: 978-1-931082-79-2. Dewey:813/.54. LCCN:2005-040916.
Audience: **g,l,u,f.**

Rush, Norman **PS3568.U727 W47 1992**
Whites: Stories. Trade Paper. Knopf Publishing Group. New York, NY. 1992. 160p. ISBN:0-679-73816-9, ISBN13: 978-0-679-73816-9. Dewey:813/.54. LCCN:92-050099.
Audience: **g,l,u,f.**

Russo, Richard **PS3568.U812E4 2001**
Empire Falls. Trade Cloth. Alfred A. Knopf Inc. New York, NY. 2001. 496p. ISBN:0-679-43247-7, ISBN13: 978-0-679-43247-0. Dewey:813.5/4. LCCN:2001-088568.
Audience: **g,l,u,f.**

20th Century (1961-2000) > S

Hunt, Anthony **PS3569**
Genesis, Structure, and Meaning in Gary Snyder's Mountains and Rivers Without End. Cloth Text. University of Nevada Press. Reno, NV. 2004. 328p. Western Literature Ser. ISBN:0-87417-545-3, ISBN13: 978-0-87417-545-5. Dewey:811.5/4. LCCN:2003-017449.
Audience: **l,u,f.** *Choice, 2004.*

Murphy, Patrick D. (Editor) **PS3569.N88Z625 1990**
Gary Snyder. Trade Cloth. Thomson Gale. Farmington Hills, MI. 1990. Critical Essays on American Literature Ser. ISBN:0-8161-8900-5, ISBN13: 978-0-8161-8900-7. Dewey:811/.54. LCCN:90-041684.
Audience: **l,u.**

Murphy, Patrick D. **PS3569.N88Z788 2000**
A Place for Wayfaring: The Poetry and Prose of Gary Snyder. Trade Cloth. Oregon State University Press. Corvallis, OR. 2000. 256p. ISBN:0-87071-479-1, ISBN13: 978-0-87071-479-5. Dewey:811/.54. LCCN:99-088384.
Audience: **l,u,f.**

Murphy, Patrick D. **PS3569.N88**
Understanding Gary Snyder. University of South Carolina Press. 1992. ISBN:0-87249-821-2, ISBN13: 978-0-87249-821-1.
Audience: **l,u,f.**

Santiago, Esmeralda **F128.9.P85 S267**
Almost a Woman: Combined with When I Was Puerto Rican. Trade Cloth. Knopf Publishing Group. New York, NY. ISBN:0-676-59092-6, ISBN13: 978-0-676-59092-0. Dewey:974.7/1004687295/009.
Audience: **g,l,u,f.**

Santiago, Esmeralda **F128.9.P85S269 2005**
The Turkish Lover: A Memoir. Trade Paper, Perfect. Da Capo Press, Inc. Cambridge, MA. 2005. 368p. ISBN:0-306-81451-X, ISBN13: 978-0-306-81451-8. Dewey:974.7043092.
Audience: **g,l,u,f.**

Schenkkan, Robert **PS3569.C4833K46 1994**
The Kentucky Cycle. Trade Paper. Dramatists Play Service, Inc. New York, NY. 1994. ISBN:0-8222-1309-5, ISBN13: 978-0-8222-1309-3. Dewey:812. LCCN:94-164308.
Audience: **g,l,u,f.**

Scott, Joanna **PS3568.O243**
The Manikin: A Novel. Trade Paper. Picador. New York, NY. 2002. 288p. ISBN:0-312-42138-9, ISBN13: 978-0-312-42138-0. Dewey:813/.54.
Audience: **g,l,u,f.**

Selby, Hubert Jr. **PS3568.O243**
Last Exit to Brooklyn. Trade Paper. Grove/Atlantic, Inc. New York, NY. 1988. 304p. ISBN:0-8021-3137-9, ISBN13: 978-0-8021-3137-9. Dewey:813.54. LCCN:85-045940.
Audience: **g,l,u,f.**

Shaara, Michael **PS3569.H2K55 2004**
The Killer Angels: A Novel of the Civil War. Trade Cloth. Random House, Inc. New York, NY. 2004. 368p. ISBN:0-679-64324-9, ISBN13: 978-0-679-64324-1. Dewey:813/.54. LCCN:2004-046877.
Audience: **g,l,u,f.**

Shanley, John Patrick **PS3569.H3337D68 2005**
Doubt: A Parable. Trade Paper, Perfect. Theatre Communications Group, Inc. New York, NY. 2005. 58p. ISBN:1-55936-276-6, ISBN13: 978-1-55936-276-4. Dewey:812/.54. LCCN:2005-005284.
Audience: **g,l,u,f.**

Shepard, Sam **PS3569.H394B87 1997**
Buried Child. Trade Paper. Dramatists Play Service, Inc. New York, NY. 1996. ISBN:0-8222-1511-X, ISBN13: 978-0-8222-1511-0. Dewey:812/.54. LCCN:98-115330.
Audience: **g,l,u,f.**

Silko, Leslie Marmon **PS3569.I44C4 1986**
Ceremony. Trade Paper. Penguin Group (USA) Inc. New York, NY. 1986. 272p. Contemporay American Fiction Ser. ISBN:0-14-008683-8, ISBN13: 978-0-14-008683-6. Dewey:813'.54. LCCN:85-019216.
Audience: **g,l,u,f.** B

Silko, Leslie Marmon **PS3569.I44**
Gardens in the Dunes. Trade Paper. Simon & Schuster. New York, NY. 2000. 480p. ISBN:0-684-86332-4, ISBN13: 978-0-684-86332-0. Dewey:813/.54.
Audience: **g,l,u,f.**

Silko, Leslie Marmon **PS3568.O243**
Storyteller. Trade Paper. Arcade Publishing, Inc. New York, NY. 1989. 278p. ISBN:1-55970-005-X, ISBN13: 978-1-55970-005-4. Dewey:813/.54.
Audience: **g,l,u,f.**

Simic, Charles **PS3569.I4725A6 1999**
Charles Simic: Selected Early Poems. Ed. 3. Trade Cloth. George Braziller Inc. New York, NY. 1999. 264p. ISBN:0-8076-1456-4, ISBN13: 978-0-8076-1456-3. Dewey:811/.54. LCCN:99-034872.
Audience: **g,l,u,f.**

Simic, Charles **PS3569.I4725U55 1986**
Unending Blues: Poems. Trade Cloth. Harcourt Trade Publishers. New York, NY. 1986. 64p. ISBN:0-15-192830-4, ISBN13: 978-0-15-192830-9. Dewey:811/.54. LCCN:86-009800.
Audience: **g,l,u,f.**

Smiley, Jane **PS3568.O243**
Moo. Trade Paper. Ballantine Books. New York, NY. 1996. 432p. ISBN:0-449-91023-7, ISBN13: 978-0-449-91023-8. Dewey:813.5/4.
Audience: **g,l,u,f.**

Smiley, Jane **PS3569.M39T47 2003**
A Thousand Acres: A Novel. Trade Paper. Knopf Publishing Group. New York, NY. 2003. 384p. ISBN:1-4000-3383-7, ISBN13: 978-1-4000-3383-6. Dewey:813/.54. LCCN:2003-283902.
Audience: **g,l,u,f.**

Smith, Bruce **PS3569.M512O84 2000**
The Other Lover. Trade Cloth. University of Chicago Press. Chicago, IL. 2000. 98p. Phoenix Poets Ser. ISBN:0-226-76407-9, ISBN13: 978-0-226-76407-8. Dewey:811/.54. LCCN:99-022588.
Audience: **g,l,u,f.**

Smith, Lee **PS3568.O243**
Fair and Tender Ladies. Trade Paper. Ballantine Books. New York, NY. 1993. 336p. ISBN:0-345-38399-0, ISBN13: 978-0-345-38399-0. Dewey:813/.54. LCCN:92-097544.
Audience: **g,l,u,f.**

Smith, Lee **PS3568.O243**
Oral History: A Novel. Trade Paper. Ballantine Books. New York, NY. 1996. 320p. ISBN:0-345-41028-9, ISBN13: 978-0-345-41028-3. Dewey:813/.54. LCCN:96-096632.
Audience: **g,l,u,f.**

Smith, Patti **PS3569.M53787A6 1994**
Patti Smith: Early Works, 1970-1979. Trade Cloth. W. W. Norton & Company, Inc. New York, NY. 1994. 180p. ISBN:0-393-03605-7, ISBN13: 978-0-393-03605-3. Dewey:811.54. LCCN:93-023898.
Audience: **g,l,u,f.**

Snyder, Gary **PS3569.N88**
Earth House Hold. Trade Paper. New Directions Publishing Corporation. New York, NY. 1969. 143p. ISBN:0-8112-0195-3, ISBN13: 978-0-8112-0195-7. Dewey:818/.5/408. LCCN:68-028281.
Audience: **g,l,u,f.**

Snyder, Gary **PS3566.L27**
Gary Snyder Reader: Prose, Poetry, and Translations. Trade Paper. Basic Books. New York, NY. 2000. 640p. ISBN:1-58243-079-9, ISBN13: 978-1-58243-079-9. Dewey:811.5/4.
Audience: **g,l,u,f.**

Snyder, Gary **PS3566.L27**
Mountains and Rivers Without End. Trade Paper. Basic Books. New York, NY. 1997. 184p. ISBN:1-887178-57-0, ISBN13: 978-1-887178-57-0. Dewey:811/.54.
Audience: **g,l,u,f.**

Snyder, Gary **PS3569.N88.T8**
Turtle Island. Trade Cloth. New Directions Publishing Corporation. New York, NY. 1974. 114p. A New Directions Bk Ser. ISBN:0-8112-0545-2, ISBN13: 978-0-8112-0545-0. Dewey:811/.5/4. LCCN:74-008542.
Audience: **g,l,u,f.** B

Spicer, Jack **PS3566.L27**
The Collected Books of Jack Spicer. Robin Blaser (Editor). Trade Paper. HarperCollins Publishers. New York, NY. 1995. 382p. ISBN:0-87685-241-X, ISBN13: 978-0-87685-241-5. Dewey:811/.5/4. LCCN:75-009864.
Audience: **g,l,u,f.** B

Spiegelman, Art **DS135.P62**
Maus: A Survivor's Tale: My Father Bleeds History. Trade Cloth. Knopf Publishing Group. New York, NY. 1991. ISBN:0-394-54155-3, ISBN13: 978-0-394-54155-6. Dewey:940.53/15/03924024.
Audience: **g,l,u,f.**

Spiegelman, Art (Author, Illustrator) **D810.J4**
Maus: A Survivor's Tale: And Here My Troubles Began. Trade Cloth. Book Wholesalers, Inc. Lexington, KY. 2002. Maus Ser. ISBN:1-4046-2911-4, ISBN13: 978-1-4046-2911-0. Dewey:741.59/73.
Audience: **g,l,u,f.**

Stern, Gerald **PS3566.L27**
This Time: New and Selected Poems. Trade Paper. W. W. Norton & Company, Inc. New York, NY. 1999. 288p. ISBN:0-393-31909-1, ISBN13: 978-0-393-31909-5. Dewey:811/.54. LCCN:97-043670.
Audience: **g,l,u,f.**

Still, James **PS3537.T5377**
River of Earth. Dean Cadle (Foreword by). Trade Cloth. University Press of Kentucky. Lexington, KY. 1978. 256p. ISBN:0-8131-1372-5, ISBN13: 978-0-8131-1372-2. Dewey:813/.5/2. LCCN:77-092928.
Audience: **g,l,u,f.**

Stone, Robert **PS3568.O243**
Bear and His Daughter. Trade Paper. Houghton Mifflin Company Trade & Reference Division. Boston, MA. 1998. 222p. ISBN:0-395-90134-0, ISBN13: 978-0-395-90134-2. Dewey:813.5/4. LCCN:96-036737.
Audience: **g,l,u,f.**

Stone, Robert **PS3568.O243**
A Flag for Sunrise. Trade Paper. Knopf Publishing Group. New York, NY. 1992. 448p. ISBN:0-679-73762-6, ISBN13: 978-0-679-73762-9. Dewey:813/.54. LCCN:91-050278.
Audience: **g,l,u,f.**

Strand, Mark **PS3569.T69A6 1990**
Selected Poems. Trade Paper. Alfred A. Knopf Inc. New York, NY. 1990. 176p. ISBN:0-679-73301-9, ISBN13: 978-0-679-73301-0. Dewey:811/.54. LCCN:90-004902.
Audience: **g,l,u,f.**

Styron, William **PS3568.O243**
The Confessions of Nat Turner. Trade Cloth. Random House Adult Trade Publishing Group. New York, NY. 1994. ISBN:0-685-70622-2, ISBN13: 978-0-685-70622-0. Dewey:813/.54.
Audience: **g,l,u,f.**

Styron, William **PS3569.T9 L52 1992**
Lie Down in Darkness. Trade Paper. Knopf Publishing Group. New York, NY. 1992. 416p. ISBN:0-679-73597-6, ISBN13: 978-0-679-73597-7. Dewey:813/.54. LCCN:91-050036.
Audience: **g,l,u,f.**

Styron, William **PS3568.O243**
Set This House on Fire. Trade Paper. Random House, Inc. New York, NY. 1993. 528p. ISBN:0-679-73674-3, ISBN13: 978-0-679-73674-5. Dewey:813.5/4. LCCN:91-050737.
Audience: **g,l,u,f.** B

Styron, William **PS3569.T9S67 1998**
Sophie's Choice. Trade Cloth. Random House, Inc. New York, NY. 1998. 608p. Modern Library Ser. ISBN:0-679-60289-5, ISBN13: 978-0-679-60289-7. Dewey:813.5/4. LCCN:97-036895.
Audience: **g,l,u,f.** B

Styron, William **PS3568.O243**
A Tidewater Morning: Three Tales from Youth. Trade Paper. Knopf Publishing Group. New York, NY. 1994. 160p. ISBN:0-679-75449-0, ISBN13: 978-0-679-75449-7. Dewey:813.5/4.
Audience: **g,l,u,f.**

20th Century (1961-2000) > T

Tan, Amy **PS3570.A48J6 1989**
The Joy Luck Club. Trade Cloth. Penguin Group (USA) Inc. New York, NY. 1989. 288p. ISBN:0-399-13420-4, ISBN13: 978-0-399-13420-3. Dewey:813.5/4. LCCN:88-026492.
Audience: **g,l,u,f.**

Taylor, Peter **PS3539.A9633 A6 2001**
The Collected Stories of Peter Taylor. Trade Paper. Picador. New York, NY. 2001. 544p. ISBN:0-312-42020-X, ISBN13: 978-0-312-42020-8. Dewey:813/.54. LCCN:2001-036963.
Audience: **g,l,u,f.**

Taylor, Peter **PS3539.A9633I5 2002**
In the Miro District and Other Stories. Trade Paper. Louisiana State University Press. Baton Rouge, LA. 2002. 204p. Voices of the South Ser. ISBN:0-8071-2843-0, ISBN13: 978-0-8071-2843-5. Dewey:813/.5/4. LCCN:2002-727975.
Audience: **g,l,u,f.** B

Toole, John Kennedy **PS3568.O243**
A Confederacy of Dunces: A Novel. Ed. 20. Walker Percy (Foreword by), Andrei Codrescu (Introduction by). Trade Cloth. Louisiana State University Press. Baton Rouge, LA. 2004. 338p. ISBN:0-8071-2606-3, ISBN13: 978-0-8071-2606-6. Dewey:813.5/4. LCCN:79-020190.
Audience: **g,l,u,f.** B

Tyler, Anne **PS3568.O243**
The Accidental Tourist. Trade Paper. Ballantine Books. New York, NY. 2002. 352p. ISBN:0-345-45200-3, ISBN13: 978-0-345-45200-9. Dewey:813.5/4. LCCN:2002-090731.
Audience: **g,l,u,f.**

Tyler, Anne **PS3570.Y45**
Breathing Lessons: A Novel. Trade Paper. Ballantine Books. New York, NY. 2005. 352p. ISBN:0-345-48557-2, ISBN13: 978-0-345-48557-1. Dewey:813/.54.
Audience: **g,l,u,f.**

Tyler, Anne **PS3570.Y45D5 2005**
Dinner at the Homesick Restaurant. Trade Paper. Ballantine Books. New York, NY. 1996. 336p. Ballantine Reader's Circle Ser. ISBN:0-449-91159-4, ISBN13: 978-0-449-91159-4. Dewey:813/.54. LCCN:96-096729.
Audience: **g,l,u,f.**

20th Century (1961-2000) > U

Uhry, Alfred **PS3545.I5365**
Driving Miss Daisy. Trade Paper. Dramatists Play Service, Inc. New York, NY. 1987. 39p. ISBN:0-8222-0335-9, ISBN13: 978-0-8222-0335-3. Dewey:812/.54.
Audience: **g,l,u,f.**

Unger, Douglas **PS3571.N45L4 1995**
Leaving the Land. Trade Cloth. University of Nebraska Press. Lincoln, NE. 1995. 277p. ISBN:0-8032-9560-X, ISBN13: 978-0-8032-9560-5. Dewey:813/.54. LCCN:95-010945.
Audience: **g,l,u,f.**

Updike, John **PS3566.L27**
Collected Poems, 1953-93. Trade Paper. Alfred A. Knopf Inc. New York, NY. 1995. 416p. ISBN:0-679-76204-3, ISBN13: 978-0-679-76204-1. Dewey:811.54.
Audience: **g,l,u,f.**

Updike, John **PS3568.O243**
The Early Stories, 1953-1975. Book, Other. Ballantine Books. New York, NY. 2004. 864p. ISBN:0-345-46336-6, ISBN13: 978-0-345-46336-4. Dewey:813/.54.
Audience: **g,l,u,f.**

Updike, John **PN6162**
More Matter: Essays and Criticism. UK-Trade Paper. Ballantine Books. New York, NY. 2000. 928p. ISBN:0-449-00628-X, ISBN13: 978-0-449-00628-3. Dewey:814.5/4.
Audience: **g,l,u,f.**

Updike, John **PS3571.P4A6 2003**
Rabbit Novels, Vol. 1. Trade Paper. Ballantine Books. New York, NY. 2003. 640p. ISBN:0-345-46456-7, ISBN13: 978-0-345-46456-9. Dewey:813/.54. LCCN:2003-283420.
Audience: **g,l,u,f.**

Updike, John **PS3571.P4.A6 2003**
Rabbit Novels, Vol. 2. Trade Paper. Ballantine Books. New York, NY. 2003. 912p. ISBN:0-345-46457-5, ISBN13: 978-0-345-46457-6. Dewey:813/.54. LCCN:2003-283420.
Audience: **g,l,u,f.**

Updike, John **PS3568.O243**
Roger's Version. Trade Paper. Ballantine Books. New York, NY. 1996. 352p. ISBN:0-449-91218-3, ISBN13: 978-0-449-91218-8. Dewey:813/.54.
Audience: **g,l,u,f.**

Updike, John **PS3571.P4W5 1996**
The Witches of Eastwick. Ed. 1. Trade Paper. Ballantine Books. New York, NY. 1996. 320p. ISBN:0-449-91210-8, ISBN13: 978-0-449-91210-2. Dewey:813.5/4. LCCN:96-096642.
Audience: **g,l,u,f.** B

Updike, John **PS3571.P4A6 2001**
The Complete Henry Bech. Malcolm Bradbury (Introduction by). Trade Cloth. Alfred A. Knopf Inc. New York, NY. 2001. 544p. Everyman's Library ISBN:0-375-41176-3, ISBN13: 978-0-375-41176-2. Dewey:813/.54. LCCN:00-053488.
Audience: **g,l,u,f.**

20th Century (1961-2000) > V

Vogel, Paula **PS3572.O296H88 1997**
How I Learned to Drive. Trade Paper. Dramatists Play Service, Inc. New York, NY. 1997. 60p. ISBN:0-8222-1623-X, ISBN13: 978-0-8222-1623-0. Dewey:812/.54. LCCN:98-128331.
Audience: **g,l,u,f.**

20th Century (1961-2000) > Vonnegut, Kurt

Marvin, Thomas F. **PS3572**
Kurt Vonnegut: A Critical Companion. Cloth Text. Greenwood Publishing Group, Inc. Portsmouth, NH. 2002. 184p. Critical Companions to Popular Contemporary Writers Ser. ISBN:0-313-32634-7, ISBN13: 978-0-313-32634-9. Dewey:813/.54.
Audience: **l,u.**

Merrill, Robert **PS3572.O5Z62 1990**
Critical Essays on Kurt Vonnegut. Trade Cloth. Thomson Gale. Farmington Hills, MI. 1989. 248p. Critical Essays on American Literature Ser. ISBN:0-8161-8893-9, ISBN13: 978-0-8161-8893-2. Dewey:813/.54. LCCN:89-011130.
Audience: **l,u.** *Choice, 1990.*

Morse, Donald E. **PS3572**
The Novels of Kurt Vonnegut: Imagining Being an American. Trade Cloth. Greenwood Publishing Group, Inc. Portsmouth, NH. 2003. 232p. Contributions to the Study of Science Fiction and Fantasy Ser., Vol. 103 ISBN:0-313-31914-6, ISBN13: 978-0-313-31914-3. Dewey:813/.54. LCCN:2002-192775.
Audience: **l,u.** *Choice, 2004.*

Vonnegut, Kurt **PS3568.O243**
Bagombo Snuff Box: Uncollected Short Fiction. Trade Paper. Penguin Group (USA) Inc. New York, NY. 2000. 384p. ISBN:0-425-17446-8, ISBN13: 978-0-425-17446-3. Dewey:813/.54.
Audience: **g,l,u,f.**

Vonnegut, Kurt **PR6019.O9**
Breakfast of Champions. Trade Paper. Dell Publishing. New York, NY. 1999. 320p. ISBN:0-385-33420-6, ISBN13: 978-0-385-33420-4. Dewey:813/.54. LCCN:2005-285162.
Audience: **g,l,u,f.**

Vonnegut, Kurt **PS3568.O243**
Deadeye Dick. Trade Paper. Dell Publishing. New York, NY. 1999. 288p. ISBN:0-385-33417-6, ISBN13: 978-0-385-33417-4. Dewey:813.54.
Audience: **g,l,u,f.**

Vonnegut, Kurt **PS3568.O243**
Galapagos. Trade Paper. Dell Publishing. New York, NY. 1999. 336p. Delta Fiction Ser. ISBN:0-385-33387-0, ISBN13: 978-0-385-33387-0. Dewey:813/.54. LCCN:2005-285163.
Audience: **g,l,u,f.**

Vonnegut, Kurt **PS3568.O243**
God Bless You, Mr. Rosewater. Trade Paper. Dell Publishing. New York, NY. 1998. 288p. ISBN:0-385-33347-1, ISBN13: 978-0-385-33347-4. Dewey:813.54.
Audience: **g,l,u,f.**

Vonnegut, Kurt **PS3568.O243**
Mother Night. UK-Trade Paper. Dell Publishing. New York, NY. 1999. 288p. ISBN:0-385-33414-1, ISBN13: 978-0-385-33414-3. Dewey:813/.54. LCCN:2005-285167.
Audience: **g,l,u,f.**

Vonnegut, Kurt **PS3568.O243**
Player Piano. UK-Trade Paper. Dell Publishing. New York, NY. 1999. 352p. ISBN:0-385-33378-1, ISBN13: 978-0-385-33378-8. Dewey:813.54.
Audience: **g,l,u,f.** B

Vonnegut, Kurt **PS3568.O243**
The Sirens of Titan. Trade Paper. Bantam Books. New York, NY. 1998. 336p. ISBN:0-385-33349-8, ISBN13: 978-0-385-33349-8. Dewey:813.54.
Audience: **g,l,u,f.**

Vonnegut, Kurt **PR6019.O9**
Slapstick: Or Lonesome No More!. Trade Paper. Dell Publishing. New York, NY. 1999. 288p. ISBN:0-385-33423-0, ISBN13: 978-0-385-33423-5. Dewey:813/.54. LCCN:2005-285165.
Audience: **g,l,u,f.**

Vonnegut, Kurt **PS3572.O5S6 1994**
Slaughterhouse-Five: Or the Children's Crusade. Ed. 25. Trade Cloth. Dell Publishing. New York, NY. 1994. 224p. ISBN:0-385-31208-3, ISBN13: 978-0-385-31208-0. Dewey:813/.54. LCCN:94-171120.
Audience: **g,l,u,f.**

Vonnegut, Kurt **PS3572.O5**
Welcome to the Monkey House. Trade Paper. Dell Publishing. New York, NY. 1998. 352p. ISBN:0-385-33350-1, ISBN13: 978-0-385-33350-4. Dewey:813.5.
Audience: **g,l,u,f.**

20th Century (1961-2000) > W

Waldman, Anne **PS3573.A4215H4 1989**
Helping the Dreamer: New and Selected Poems, 1966-1988. Trade Paper. Coffee House Press. Minneapolis, MN. 1989. 240p. ISBN:0-918273-50-1, ISBN13: 978-0-918273-50-5. Dewey:811/.54. LCCN:89-015706.
Audience: **g,l,u,f.**

Waldman, Anne **PS3573.A4215I49 2003**
In the Room of Never Grieve: New and Selected Poems, 1985-2003. Mixed Media. Coffee House Press. Minneapolis, MN. 2003. 400p. ISBN:1-56689-145-0, ISBN13: 978-1-56689-145-5. Dewey:811/.54. LCCN:2003-055096.
Audience: **g,l,u,f.**

Walker, Alice **PS3568.O243**
The Color Purple. Ed. 10. Cloth over Boards. Harcourt Trade Publishers. New York, NY. 1992. 304p. ISBN:0-15-119154-9, ISBN13: 978-0-15-119154-3. Dewey:813/.54. LCCN:91-047202.
Audience: **g,l,u,f.** B

Wasserstein, Wendy **PS3573.A798H4 1990**
The Heidi Chronicles and Other Plays. Trade Cloth. Harcourt Trade Publishers. New York, NY. 1990. ISBN:0-15-139985-9, ISBN13: 978-0-15-139985-7. Dewey:812.54. LCCN:89-028114.
Audience: **g,l,u,f.**

Welch, Lew **PS3573.E45**
Ring of Bone: Collected Poems, 1950-1971. Donald Allen (Editor). Trade Paper. Grey Fox Press. San Francisco, CA. 1979. 244p. ISBN:0-912516-03-8, ISBN13: 978-0-912516-03-5. Dewey:811/.5/4. LCCN:72-085644.
Audience: **g,l,u,f.**

Whalen, Philip **PS3545.H117A6 1985**
Two Novels: You Didn't Even Try and Imaginary Speeches for a Brazen Head. Trade Cloth. Zephyr Press. Brookline, MA. 1985. 272p. ISBN:0-939010-07-0, ISBN13: 978-0-939010-07-3. Dewey:813/.54. LCCN:85-051335.
Audience: **g,l,u,f.** *Choice, 1986.*

Wharton, William **PS3573.H32 B57 1992**
Birdy. Trade Paper. Knopf Publishing Group. New York, NY. 1992. 320p. ISBN:0-679-73412-0, ISBN13: 978-0-679-73412-3. Dewey:813/.54. LCCN:91-050020.
Audience: **g,l,u,f.** B

Whitehead, Colson **PS3568.O243**
John Henry Days: A Novel. Trade Paper. Knopf Publishing Group. New York, NY. 2002. 400p. ISBN:0-385-49820-9, ISBN13: 978-0-385-49820-3. Dewey:813.5/4.
Audience: **g,l,u,f.**

Wideman, John Edgar **PS3573.I26F4 1990**
Fever: Twelve Stories. Trade Paper. Penguin Group (USA) Inc. New York, NY. 1990. 176p. ISBN:0-14-014347-5, ISBN13: 978-0-14-014347-8. Dewey:813/.54. LCCN:90-007015.
Audience: **g,l,u,f.**

Wideman, John Edgar **PS3573.I26H6 1992**
The Homewood Books. Cloth Text. University of Pittsburgh Press. Pittsburgh, PA. 1992. 536p. ISBN:0-8229-3831-6, ISBN13: 978-0-8229-3831-6. Dewey:813/.54. LCCN:91-018997.
Audience: **g,l,u,f.**

Wideman, John Edgar **PS3573.I26S4 1997**
Sent for You Yesterday. Trade Paper. Houghton Mifflin Company Trade & Reference Division. Boston, MA. 1998. 208p. ISBN:0-395-87729-6, ISBN13: 978-0-395-87729-6. Dewey:813/.54. LCCN:97-035019.
Audience: **g,l,u,f.**

Wieners, John **PS3573.I35A6 1986**
Selected Poems, 1958-1984. Raymond Foye (Editor), Allen Ginsberg (Foreword by). Trade Paper. HarperCollins Publishers. New York, NY. 1985. 322p. ISBN:0-87685-661-X, ISBN13: 978-0-87685-661-1. Dewey:811/.54. LCCN:86-001046.
Audience: **g,l,u,f.**

Wiggins, Marianne **PS3573.I385E94 2003**
Evidence of Things Unseen. Trade Cloth. Simon & Schuster. New York, NY. 2003. 400p. ISBN:0-684-86969-1, ISBN13: 978-0-684-86969-8. LCCN:2003-045611.
Audience: **g,l,u,f.**

Williams, C. K. **PS3566.L27**
The Vigil: Poems. Trade Cloth. Farrar, Straus & Giroux. New York, NY. 1998. 96p. ISBN:0-374-52554-4, ISBN13: 978-0-374-52554-5. Dewey:811/.54.
Audience: **g,l,u,f.**

Williams, Joy **PS3573.I4496Q53**
The Quick and the Dead. UK-Trade Paper. Knopf Publishing Group. New York, NY. 2002. 320p. Vintage Contemporaries Ser. ISBN:0-375-72764-7, ISBN13: 978-0-375-72764-1. Dewey:813.54.
Audience: **g,l,u,f.**

Wilson, August **PS3573.I45677F4**
Fences: A Play. Library Binding. Sagebrush Education Resources. Caledonia, MN. 1986. ISBN:0-7857-9611-8, ISBN13: 978-0-7857-9611-4. Dewey:812.54.
Audience: **g,l,u,f.**

Wilson, August **PS3545.I5365**
The Piano Lesson. Library Binding. Sagebrush Education Resources. Caledonia, MN. 1990. ISBN:0-613-03323-X, ISBN13: 978-0-613-03323-7. Dewey:812.5/4.
Audience: **g,l,u,f.**

Wilson, Lanford **PS3573.I458 T3**
Talley's Folly. Trade Paper. Dramatists Play Service, Inc. New York, NY. 1998. ISBN:0-8222-1626-4, ISBN13: 978-0-8222-1626-1. Dewey:812/.5/4.
Audience: **g,l,u,f.**

Wolfe, Tom **PS3573.O526**
The Bonfire of the Vanities. Trade Paper. Bantam Books. New York, NY. 2001. 656p. ISBN:0-553-38134-2, ISBN13: 978-0-553-38134-4. Dewey:813/.54. LCCN:2005-281883.
Audience: **g,l,u,f.**

Wolfe, Tom **DS422.C3**
The Electric Kool-Aid Acid Test. Trade Paper. Bantam Books. New York, NY. 1999. 432p. ISBN:0-553-38064-8, ISBN13: 978-0-553-38064-4. Dewey:305.5/68. LCCN:68-013008.
Audience: **g,l,u,f.**

Wolfe, Tom **PS3511.A86**
Mauve Gloves and Madmen, Clutter and Vine. UK-Trade Paper. Bantam Books. New York, NY. 1999. 240p. ISBN:0-553-38059-1, ISBN13: 978-0-553-38059-0. Dewey:813/.5/2. LCCN:76-043968.
Audience: **g,l,u,f.** B

Wright, Charles **PS3566.L27**
Black Zodiac: Poems. Trade Paper. Farrar, Straus & Giroux. New York, NY. 1998. 96p. ISBN:0-374-52536-6, ISBN13: 978-0-374-52536-1. Dewey:811/.54.
Audience: **g,l,u,f.**

Wright, Doug & Mahlsdorf, Charlotte von **PS3573.R53252I3 2004**
I Am My Own Wife: A Play. Trade Paper. Faber & Faber, Inc. New York, NY. 2004. 112p. ISBN:0-571-21174-7, ISBN13: 978-0-571-21174-6. Dewey:812/.54. LCCN:2003-021583.
Audience: **g,l,u,f.**

Wright, Franz **PS3573.R5327B44 2001**
The Beforelife. Trade Paper. Alfred A. Knopf Inc. New York, NY. 2002. 96p. ISBN:0-375-70943-6, ISBN13: 978-0-375-70943-2. Dewey:811/.54. LCCN:00-042854.
Audience: **g,l,u,f.**

20th Century (1961-2000) > Y

Yates, Richard **PS3568.O243**
The Collected Stories of Richard Yates. Richard Russo (Introduction by). Trade Paper. Picador. New York, NY. 2002. 496p. ISBN:0-312-42081-1, ISBN13: 978-0-312-42081-9. Dewey:813/.54.
Audience: **g,l,u,f.**

20th Century (1961-2000) > Z

Zindel, Paul **PS3576.I518**
The Effect of Gamma Rays on Man-in-the-Moon Marigolds. Trade Paper. Dramatists Play Service, Inc. New York, NY. 1970. ISBN:0-8222-0350-2, ISBN13: 978-0-8222-0350-6. Dewey:812.54.
Audience: **g,l,u,f.** B

Zweig, Paul **PS3576.W4A6 1989**
Selected and Last Poems. C. K. Williams (Editor, Introduction by). Trade Paper. Wesleyan University Press. Middletown, CT. 1989. 111p. Wesleyan Poetry Ser. ISBN:0-8195-1159-5, ISBN13: 978-0-8195-1159-1. Dewey:811/.54. LCCN:89-005417.
Audience: **g,l,u,f.** *Choice, 1990.*

21st Century

Albom, Mitch **PS3601.L335F59 2003**
The Five People You Meet in Heaven. Trade Cloth. Hyperion Press. New York, NY. 2003. 208p. ISBN:0-7868-6871-6, ISBN13: 978-0-7868-6871-1. Dewey:813/.6. LCCN:2003-047888.
Audience: **g.**

Allen, Ed **PS3601.L425A84 2003**
Ate It Anyway: Stories. Trade Cloth. University of Georgia Press. Athens, GA. 2005. viii, 182p. The Flannery O'Connor Award for Short Fiction Ser. ISBN:0-8203-2558-9, ISBN13: 978-0-8203-2558-3. Dewey:813/.6. LCCN:2003-008495.
Audience: **g.**

Campbell, Barbara **PS3603.A46E76 2003**
Erotic Distance. Trade Cloth. Truman State University Press. Kirksville, MO. 2003. 77p. New Odyssey Ser. ISBN:1-931112-31-2, ISBN13: 978-1-931112-31-4. Dewey:811/.6. LCCN:2003-007959.
Audience: **g.**

Cruz, Nilo **PS3603.R895A83 2003**
Anna in the Tropics. Trade Paper. Theatre Communications Group, Inc. New York, NY. 2003. 112p. ISBN:1-55936-232-4, ISBN13: 978-1-55936-232-0. Dewey:812/.6. LCCN:2003-015859.
Audience: **g.**

Davis, Jennifer S. **PS3604.A96H47 2002**
Her Kind of Want. Trade Paper. University of Iowa Press. Iowa City, IA. 2002. 152p. The Iowa Short Fiction Award Ser. ISBN:0-87745-818-9, ISBN13: 978-0-87745-818-0. Dewey:813/.6. LCCN:2002-018061.
Audience: **g.**

Ducey, Kevin **PS3604.U29R48 2004**
Rhinoceros. Yusef Komunyakaa (Introduction by). Trade Cloth. American Poetry Review, The. Philadelphia, PA. 2004. 0p. ISBN:0-9718981-5-4, ISBN13: 978-0-9718981-5-8. Dewey:811/.6. LCCN:2004-103258.
Audience: **g.**

Feitell, Merrill **PS3606.E38H47 2004**
Here Beneath Low-Flying Planes. Trade Paper. University of Iowa Press. Iowa City, IA. 2004. 138p. The Iowa Short Fiction Award Ser. ISBN:0-87745-911-8, ISBN13: 978-0-87745-911-8. Dewey:813/.6. LCCN:2004-045979.
Audience: **g.**

Fracis, Sohrab Homi **PS3606.R33T53 2001**
Ticket to Minto: Stories of India and America. Trade Paper. University of Iowa Press. Iowa City, IA. 2001. 226p. Iowa Short Fiction Award Ser. ISBN:0-87745-779-4, ISBN13: 978-0-87745-779-4. Dewey:813/.6. LCCN:2001-033590.
Audience: **g.** *Choice, 2002.*

Franzen, Jonathan **PS3556.R352C67 2001**
The Corrections: A Novel. Cloth over Boards. Farrar, Straus & Giroux. New York, NY. 2001. 576p. ISBN:0-374-12998-3, ISBN13: 978-0-374-12998-9. Dewey:813/.54. LCCN:2001-033478.
Audience: **g,l,u,f.**

Garcia, Ricardo L. **PS3607.A725C633 2005**
Coal Camp Justice: Two Wrongs Make a Right. Trade Cloth. University of New Mexico Press. Albuquerque, NM. 2005. 317p. ISBN:0-8263-3697-3, ISBN13: 978-0-8263-3697-2. Dewey:813/.6. LCCN:2005-005925.
Audience: **g.**

Halpern, Sue **PS3608.A549B66 2003**
The Book of Hard Things: A Novel. Cloth over Boards. Farrar, Straus & Giroux. New York, NY. 2003. 240p. ISBN:0-374-11559-1, ISBN13: 978-0-374-11559-3. Dewey:813/.6. LCCN:2003-044067.
Audience: **g.**

Haslett, Adam **PS3608.A85Y68 2002**
You Are Not a Stranger Here. Trade Cloth. Doubleday Publishing. New York, NY. 2002. 256p. ISBN:0-385-50167-6, ISBN13: 978-0-385-50167-5. Dewey:813/.6. LCCN:2001-054839.
Audience: **g.**

Hosseini, Khaled **PS3608.O832 K58**
The Kite Runner. Trade Cloth. Doubleday Canada, Ltd. Toronto, ON. 2003. 352p. ISBN:0-385-66006-5, ISBN13: 978-0-385-66006-8. Dewey:813.6.
Audience: **g.**

Kidd, Sue Monk **813/.54**
The Secret Life of Bees. Trade Cloth. Penguin Group (USA) Inc. New York, NY. 2002. 320p. ISBN:0-670-03237-9, ISBN13: 978-0-670-03237-2. Dewey:PS3611.I44.
Audience: **g.**

Kim, Suji Kwock **PS3611.I455N68 2003**
Notes from the Divided Country: Poems. Trade Cloth. Louisiana State University Press. Baton Rouge, LA. 2003. x, 74p. ISBN:0-8071-2873-2, ISBN13: 978-0-8071-2873-2. Dewey:811/.6. LCCN:2002-155402.
Audience: **g.**

Tost, Tony **PS3620.O88I58 2004**
Invisible Bride: Poems. Trade Cloth. Louisiana State University Press. Baton Rouge, LA. 2004. 58p. ISBN:0-8071-2964-X, ISBN13: 978-0-8071-2964-7. Dewey:811/.6. LCCN:2003-019397.
Audience: **g.**

BRITISH LITERATURE

This section contains works regularly taught in the course of the undergraduate major in English literature, and as such includes canonical works by major British authors, as well as other works regularly studied (e.g., Dracula). Following the usual practice in undergraduate curricula, major Irish, Scots, and Welsh authors are classified along with British authors, without distinction. These selections are supported by a variety of critical, biographical, and literary-historical works devoted to individual authors and to periods. Unlike BCL3, no effort was made to include the complete works of every author, and selection in general tended away from rather than toward the inclusion of complete letters, bibliographies of critical works, and other materials more appropriate to a research collection than one supporting the undergraduate curriculum. Although critical works tend to be more recent, an effort was made to include the most valuable of older works.

Where possible, works are recommended in their newest, most reliable edition. Some works are available only as reprints, while a few are out of print, though still recommended.

—Sally Bowdoin

Cox, Michael & Drabble, Margaret (Editors) **Z2011 .C65 PR87**
The English Literature Set: Consisting of the Oxford Chronology of English Literature and the Oxford Companion to English Literature. Trade Cloth. Oxford University Press, Inc. New York, NY. 2003. ISBN:0-19-522040-4, ISBN13: 978-0-19-522040-7. Dewey:820.9/002/02.
Audience: **g,l,u,f.**

Criticism

PR85
The Internet Public Library Online literary criticism collection.
http://www.ipl.org/div/litcrit
Audience: **l,u.**

Altick, Richard D. **PR56.A7 1987**
The Scholar Adventurers. Paper Text. Ohio State University Press. Columbus, OH. 1987. 338p. ISBN:0-8142-0435-X, ISBN13: 978-0-8142-0435-1. Dewey:820/.72/0922. LCCN:87-011064.
Audience: **l,u,f.**

Altick, Richard D. & Fenstermaker, John J. **PR56.A68 1993**
The Art of Literary Research. Ed. 4. Trade Cloth. W. W. Norton & Company, Inc. New York, NY. 1992. 368p. ISBN:0-393-96240-7, ISBN13: 978-0-393-96240-6. Dewey:807.2. LCCN:91-036247.
Audience: **l,u.** *Choice, 1993.*

Baldwin, Anna & Hutton, Sarah (Editors) **PR127 .P57 1993**
Platonism and the English Imagination. Trade Paper. Cambridge University Press. New York, NY. 2005. 373p. ISBN:0-521-02168-5, ISBN13: 978-0-521-02168-5. Dewey:820.9384. LCCN:93-009341.
Audience: **u,f.** *Choice, 1994.*

Browning, D. S. **PR19**
Everyman's Dictionary of Literary Biography. Ed. 3. Trade Cloth. Biblio Distribution. Lanham, MD. 1969. 812p. Everyman's Reference Library ISBN:0-460-03008-6, ISBN13: 978-0-460-03008-3. Dewey:928.2.
Audience: **g,l,u,f.**

Corbett, Edward P. J. **PR14**
Rhetorical Analyses of Literary Works. Trade Cloth. Oxford University Press, Inc. New York, NY. 1969. ISBN:0-19-500855-3, ISBN13: 978-0-19-500855-5. Dewey:820.9.
Audience: **l,u.** B

Donoghue, Denis **PR21.D66 1998**
The Practice of Reading. Cloth over Boards. Yale University Press. Cumberland, RI. 1998. 320p. ISBN:0-300-07466-2, ISBN13: 978-0-300-07466-6. Dewey:820.9. LCCN:97-042549.
Audience: **l,u.** *Choice, 1999.*

Drabble, Margaret (Editor) **PR19.O94 2000**
The Oxford Companion to English Literature. Ed. 6. Trade Cloth. Oxford University Press, Inc. New York, NY. 2000. 1184p. ISBN:0-19-866244-0, ISBN13: 978-0-19-866244-0. Dewey:820.9. LCCN:00-036741.
Audience: **g,l,u,f.** B *Choice, 2001, 1996.*

Felluga, Dino **PN86**
Introductory Guide to Critical Theory.
http://www.cla.purdue.edu/academic/engl/theory/
Audience: **l,u.**

Guillory, John **PR21.G85 1993**
Cultural Capital: The Problem of Literary Canon Formation. Trade Cloth. University of Chicago Press. Chicago, IL. 1993. 408p. ISBN:0-226-31043-4, ISBN13: 978-0-226-31043-5. Dewey:820.9. LCCN:92-034597.
Audience: **u,f.**

Hogan, Robert T. (Editor) **PR8706 .D5 1979**
Dictionary of Irish Literature. Trade Cloth. Greenwood Publishing Group, Inc. Portsmouth, NH. 1979. 815p. ISBN:0-313-20718-6, ISBN13: 978-0-313-20718-1. Dewey:820/.9/9415. LCCN:78-020021.
Audience: **g,l,u,f.**

Holmes, Charles S. (Editor), et al. **PR67 .H6**
The Major Critics: The Development of English Literary Criticism. Edwin Fussell & Ray Frazer (Editors). Trade Cloth. A M S Press, Inc. New York, NY. ISBN:0-404-20123-7, ISBN13: 978-0-404-20123-4. Dewey:820.9. LCCN:83-045783.
Audience: **l,u,f.** B

Jeffares, A. Norman **PR8711.J4 1982**
Anglo-Irish Literature. Trade Cloth. Knopf Publishing Group. New York, NY. 1982. 360p. History of Literature Ser. ISBN:0-8052-3828-X, ISBN13: 978-0-8052-3828-0. Dewey:820.9/9415. LCCN:82-005753.
Audience: **g,l,u,f.**

Kelleher, Margaret & O'Leary, Philip (Editors) **PB1306.C36 2006**
The Cambridge History of Irish Literature, Set. Trade Cloth. Cambridge University Press. New York, NY. 2006. 1286p. ISBN:0-521-82224-6, ISBN13: 978-0-521-82224-4. Dewey:820.9/9417. LCCN:2005-006448.
Audience: **g,l,u,f.**

Klarer, Mario **PR21.K5213 2004**
An Introduction to Literary Studies. Ed. 2. Paper over Boards. Routledge. New York, NY. 2004. 192p. ISBN:0-415-33381-4, ISBN13: 978-0-415-33381-8. Dewey:820.9. LCCN:2003-020775.
Audience: **l,u.**

Knapp, Jeffrey **PR129.A4K58 1994**
An Empire Nowhere: England, America, and Literature from Utopia to the Tempest. Ed. 1994. E-Book. NetLibrary, Inc. Boulder, CO. 1994. ISBN:0-585-24982-2, ISBN13: 978-0-585-24982-7. Dewey:820.9/003.
Audience: **l,u.**

Leavis, F. R. **PR83 .L399 1998**
The Living Principle: "English" As a Discipline of Thought. Paul Dean (Introduction by). Trade Paper. Ivan R. Dee Publisher. Blue Ridge Summit, PA. 1998. 280p. ISBN:1-56663-172-6, ISBN13: 978-1-56663-172-3. Dewey:801. LCCN:97-017238.
Audience: **l,u,f.**

Leavis, Frank R. **PR67 .D4 1970**
Determinations: Critical Essays. Library Binding. M. S. G. Haskell House. Brooklyn, NY. 1970. English Literature Ser., No. 33 ISBN:0-8383-1081-8, ISBN13: 978-0-8383-1081-6. Dewey:820.9. LCCN:70-119085.
Audience: **u,f.**

Leavis, Frank R. (Editor) **PN94 .L37**
Towards Standards of Criticism: Selections from the Calendar of Modern Letters, 1925-1927. Trade Cloth. Johnson Reprint Corporation. New York, NY. 1969. Belles Letters in English Ser. ISBN:0-384-31925-4, ISBN13: 978-0-384-31925-7. Dewey:801/.95.
Audience: **g,l,u,f.**

Lentricchia, Frank & Dubois, Andrew (Editors) **PR21.C58 2003**
Close Reading: The Reader. Library Binding. Duke University Press. Durham, NC. 2003. 424p. ISBN:0-8223-3026-1, ISBN13: 978-0-8223-3026-4. Dewey:820.9. LCCN:2002-009198.
Audience: **u,f.** *Choice, 2003.*

Lewis, C. S. **PN682.C6**
The Allegory of Love: A Study of Medieval Tradition. Paper Text. Oxford University Press, Inc. New York, NY. 1985. 390p. ISBN:0-19-281220-3, ISBN13: 978-0-19-281220-9. Dewey:809/.93354.
Audience: **l,u,f.**

Lewis, C. S. **PN671 .L4 1994**
The Discarded Image: An Introduction to Medieval and Renaissance Literature. Trade Paper. Cambridge University Press. New York, NY. 1994. 242p. A Canto Book Ser. ISBN:0-521-47735-2, ISBN13: 978-0-521-47735-2. Dewey:809/.02. LCCN:94-213150.
Audience: **l,u.** B

Lewis, C. S. **PR99.L4 1972**
Rehabilitations and Other Essays. Trade Cloth. Ayer Company Publishers, Inc. Manchester, NH. 1977. viii, 197p. Essay Index Reprint Ser. ISBN:0-8369-2559-9, ISBN13: 978-0-8369-2559-3. Dewey:820.9. LCCN:71-167377.
Audience: **l,u,f.** B

Lewis, C. S. **PR6023.E926.O5 1982**
On Stories: And Other Essays on Literature. Walter Hooper (Editor). Trade Cloth. Harcourt Trade Publishers. New York, NY. 1982. 144p. ISBN:0-15-169964-X, ISBN13: 978-0-15-169964-3. Dewey:809. LCCN:81-048014.
Audience: **l,u,f.** B

Lindsay, Maurice **PR8511**
History of Scottish Literature. Trade Cloth. Dufour Editions, Inc. Chester Springs, PA. 1977. 496p. ISBN:0-7091-5642-1, ISBN13: 978-0-7091-5642-0. Dewey:820.99411. LCCN:77-360000.
Audience: **g,l,u,f.**

MacKillop, Ian (Editor) **PR55.L43F2 2005**
F. R. Leavis: Essays and Documents. Trade Paper, Perfect. Continuum International Publishing Group, Ltd. London, 2005. 314p. ISBN:0-8264-8576-6, ISBN13: 978-0-8264-8576-2. Dewey:801/.95/092. LCCN:2005-050276.
Audience: **l,u,f.**

Marcus, Jane **PR119.M37 1988**
Art and Anger: Reading Like a Woman. Cloth Text. Ohio State University Press. Columbus, OH. 1988. 320p. ISBN:0-8142-0453-8, ISBN13: 978-0-8142-0453-5. Dewey:820/.9/352042. LCCN:88-001223.
Audience: **u,f.**

McGann, Jerome J. **PR7.T49 1985**
Textual Criticism and Literary Interpretation. Library Binding. University of Chicago Press. Chicago, IL. 2000. 250p. ISBN:0-226-55842-8, ISBN13: 978-0-226-55842-4. Dewey:801/.95. LCCN:84-016174.
Audience: **u,f.**

McGann, Jerome J. **P47**
A Critique of Modern Textual Criticism. David C. Greetham (Foreword by). Paper Text. University Press of Virginia. Charlottesville, VA. 1992. 160p. ISBN:0-8139-1418-3, ISBN13: 978-0-8139-1418-3. Dewey:801/.959. LCCN:92-014702.
Audience: **u,f.** B

Miller, J. Hillis Jr. **PN3355.M48 1992**
Ariadne's Thread: Story Lines. Cloth over Boards. Yale University Press. Cumberland, RI. 1992. 320p. ISBN:0-300-05216-2, ISBN13: 978-0-300-05216-9. Dewey:809.3. LCCN:91-032842.
Audience: **u,f.** *Choice, 1993.*

Miller, J. Hillis Jr. **PN45.M495 2002**
On Literature. Trade Cloth. Routledge. New York, NY. 2002. 176p. Thinking in Action Ser. ISBN:0-415-26124-4, ISBN13: 978-0-415-26124-1. Dewey:801/.3. LCCN:2002-021331.
Audience: **l,u,f.**

Miller, J. Hillis Jr. & Wolfreys, Julian **PN83**
J Hillis Miller Reader. Trade Paper. Stanford University Press. Palo Alto, CA. 2005. 464p. ISBN:0-8047-5056-4, ISBN13: 978-0-8047-5056-1. Dewey:809.
Audience: **l,u,f.**

Oueijan, Naji B. **PR129.A78O94 1996**
The Progress of an Image: The East in English Literature. Trade Cloth. Peter Lang Publishing, Inc. New York, NY. 1996. 152p. American University Studies, Ser. IV:English Language and Literature ISBN:0-8204-2712-8, ISBN13: 978-0-8204-2712-6. Dewey:820.9/325. LCCN:94-042894.
Audience: **u,f.**

Parrinder, Patrick & Parr, Adrian **PR63.P3 1991**
Authors and Authority. Trade Paper. Columbia University Press. New York, NY. 1991. 400p. ISBN:0-231-07647-9, ISBN13: 978-0-231-07647-0. Dewey:801/.95/0941. LCCN:90-028520.
Audience: **u,f.**

Polonsky, Rachel **PR129.R8 P65 1998**
English Literature and the Russian Aesthetic Renaissance. Catriona Kelly, Anthony Cross, Caryl Emerson, Barbara Heldt, Malcolm Jones, Donald Rayfield, G. S. Smith & Victor Terras

(Contribution by). Trade Paper. Cambridge University Press. New York, NY. 2006. 264p. Cambridge Studies in Russian Literature Ser. ISBN:0-521-02747-0, ISBN13: 978-0-521-02747-2. Dewey:820.9.
Audience: **u,f.** *Choice, 1999.*

Praz, Mario **PR129.I8 P7 1973**
The Flaming Heart. Trade Paper. W. W. Norton & Company, Inc. New York, NY. 1973. 400p. Norton Library ISBN:0-393-00669-7, ISBN13: 978-0-393-00669-8. Dewey:820/.9. LCCN:72-010369.
Audience: **l,u,f.**

Rajan, Balachandra **PR129.I5R35 1999**
Under Western Eyes: India from Milton to Macaulay. Trade Paper. Duke University Press. Durham, NC. 1999. 288p. Post-Contemporary Interventions Ser. ISBN:0-8223-2298-6, ISBN13: 978-0-8223-2298-6. Dewey:820.9/3254. LCCN:98-030647.
Audience: **u,f.** *Choice, 1999.*

Rollyson, Carl & Magill, Frank N. (Editors) **PN3451.C75 2000**
Critical Survey of Long Fiction. Ed. 2. Trade Cloth. Salem Press. Mississauga, ON. 2000. ;p. ISBN:0-89356-883-X, ISBN13: 978-0-89356-883-2. Dewey:809.3. LCCN:00-020195.
Audience: **g,l,u.** *Choice, 2001.*

Rushdie, Salman **PR6068.U757 I4 1991B**
Imaginary Homelands: Essays and Criticism 1981-1991. Trade Cloth. Penguin Group (USA) Inc. New York, NY. 1991. 432p. ISBN:0-14-014224-X, ISBN13: 978-0-14-014224-2. Dewey:828. LCCN:92-188054.
Audience: **l,u,f.** *Choice, 1991.*

Ruthven, K. K. **PR77 .R88 1990**
Feminist Literary Studies: An Introduction. Trade Paper. Cambridge University Press. New York, NY. 1990. 160p. A Canto Book Ser. ISBN:0-521-39852-5, ISBN13: 978-0-521-39852-7. Dewey:801/.95/082. LCCN:90-034404.
Audience: **l,u,f.**

Saintsbury, George E. **PR63 .S3**
A History of English Criticism. Library Binding. Reprint Services Company. Temecula, CA. 1992. 551p. BCL1-PR English Literature Ser. ISBN:0-7812-7001-4, ISBN13: 978-0-7812-7001-4. Dewey:820.1.
Audience: **l,u,f.**

Scholes, Robert E. **PR21.S36 2001**
The Crafty Reader. Cloth over Boards. Yale University Press. Cumberland, RI. 2001. 288p. ISBN:0-300-09015-3, ISBN13: 978-0-300-09015-4. Dewey:028. LCCN:00-013134.
Audience: **u,f.**

Singh, Jyotsna G. **PR129.I5S46 1996**
Colonial Narratives/Cultural Dialogues: Discoveries of India in the Language of Colonialism. Trade Paper. Routledge. New York, NY. 1996. 208p. ISBN:0-415-08519-5, ISBN13: 978-0-415-08519-9. Dewey:820.9/358. LCCN:96-007428.
Audience: **u,f.**

Spencer, T. J. **PR129.G8 S6**
Fair Greece, Sad Relic. Paper Text. Classic Textbooks. Murrieta, CA. 1954. 310p. ISBN:1-4047-0250-4, ISBN13: 978-1-4047-0250-9. Dewey:820.903.
Audience: **u,f.**

Starkie, Enid **PR129.F8.S8 1971**
From Gautier to Eliot: The Influence of France on English Literature, 1851-1939. Trade Cloth. Scholarly Press, Inc. Saint Clair Shores, MI. 1971. 236p. ISBN:0-403-01303-8, ISBN13: 978-0-403-01303-6. Dewey:820.9/008. LCCN:73-158509.
Audience: **l,u,f.** B

Thomson, James A. **PR127**
The Classical Background of English Literature. Paper Text. Classic Textbooks. Murrieta, CA. 1950. ISBN:1-4047-0576-7, ISBN13: 978-1-4047-0576-0. Dewey:820.9.
Audience: **l,u,f.**

Thorpe, James **PR65 .T5 PR65.T48**
Principles of Textual Criticism. Trade Paper. Huntington Library Press. San Marino, CA. 1972. 216p. ISBN:0-87328-055-5, ISBN13: 978-0-87328-055-6. Dewey:801/.959. LCCN:72-179135.
Audience: **l,u,f.** B

Tillyard, Eustace M. **PR125 .T5 1976**
The English Epic and Its Background. Trade Cloth. Greenwood Publishing Group, Inc. Portsmouth, NH. 1976. 548p. ISBN:0-8371-8781-8, ISBN13: 978-0-8371-8781-5. Dewey:809.1/3. LCCN:76-002543.
Audience: **l,u,f.**

Trilling, Lionel **PS3539.R56B4 1978**
Beyond Culture. Trade Cloth. Harcourt Trade Publishers. New York, NY. 1978. 256p. ISBN:0-15-111987-2, ISBN13: 978-0-15-111987-5. Dewey:809. LCCN:79-011660.
Audience: **u,f.**

Trilling, Lionel **PS3539.R56 G3 1977**
A Gathering of Fugitives. Trade Cloth. Harcourt Trade Publishers. New York, NY. 1978. 180p. ISBN:0-15-134582-1, ISBN13: 978-0-15-134582-3. Dewey:809. LCCN:77-017318.
Audience: **u,f.** B

Watson, George **PN99.G7 W3 1973C**
The Literary Critics. Ed. 2. Trade Cloth. Woburn Press. Andover, 1973. 240p. ISBN:0-7130-0085-6, ISBN13: 978-0-7130-0085-6. Dewey:801/.95/0942. LCCN:74-155895.
Audience: **l,u,f.**

Wittig, Kurt **PR8511.W5**
The Scottish Tradition in Literature. Paper Text. Textbook Publishers. Temecula, CA. 2003. viii, 352p. ISBN:0-7581-7350-4, ISBN13: 978-0-7581-7350-8. Dewey:820/.9/941.
Audience: **u,f.**

Wynne-Davies, Marion (Editor) **PR19.B5 1990**
Prentice Hall Guide to English Literature. Trade Cloth. John Wiley & Sons, Inc. Hoboken, NJ. 1990. 1088p. ISBN:0-13-083619-2, ISBN13: 978-0-13-083619-9. Dewey:820/.3. LCCN:90-032465.
Audience: **l,u.**

Literary History, by Period

Alexander, Michael **PR83.A44 2000**
A History of English Literature. Cloth over Boards. Palgrave Macmillan. New York, NY. 2000. 400p. Foundations Ser. ISBN:0-333-91397-3, ISBN13: 978-0-333-91397-0. Dewey:820.9. LCCN:00-042201.
Audience: **l,u.**

Bagehot, Walter **PR99**
Literary Studies (Miscellaneous Essays). Richard H. Hutton (Editor). Library Binding. Reprint Services Company. Temecula, CA. 357p. The Works of Walter Bagehot, 1826-1877 ISBN:0-7812-0893-9, ISBN13: 978-0-7812-0893-2. Dewey:820.4.
Audience: **u,f.**

Baldick, Christopher **PR85**
Oxford English Literary History. Trade Paper. Oxford University Press, Inc. New York, NY. 2006. 496p. Oxford English Literary History Ser., Vol. 10 ISBN:0-19-928834-8, ISBN13: 978-0-19-928834-2. Dewey:820.9.
Audience: **l,u,f.**

Barnard, Robert (Author, Author) **PR83.B27 1994**
A Short History of English Literature. Ed. 2. Trade Paper. Blackwell Publishing, Inc. Malden, MA. 1994. 248p. ISBN:0-631-19088-0, ISBN13: 978-0-631-19088-2. Dewey:820.9. LCCN:93-043242.
Audience: **g,l,u,f.**

Baugh, Albert C. (Editor) **PR83**
Literary History of England. Ed. 2. Trade Paper. Prentice Hall PTR. Upper Saddle River, NJ. 1997. 2280p. ISBN:0-13-537605-X, ISBN13: 978-0-13-537605-8. Dewey:820.9.
Audience: **g,l,u,f.**

Bradley, Andrew C. **PR99.B66 1969**
A Miscellany. Trade Cloth. Ayer Company Publishers, Inc. Manchester, NH. 1977. 267p. Essay Index Reprint Ser. ISBN:0-8369-0005-7, ISBN13: 978-0-8369-0005-7. Dewey:820.9. LCCN:72-076894.
Audience: **l,u,f.** B

Carter, Ronald & McRae, John **PR83.C28 1997**
The Routledge History of Literature in English: Britain and Ireland. Paper over Boards. Routledge. New York, NY. 1997. 608p. ISBN:0-415-12342-9, ISBN13: 978-0-415-12342-6. Dewey:820.9. LCCN:96-041221.
Audience: **g,l,u,f.**

Carter, Ronald & McRae, John **PR83.C28 2001**
The Routledge History of Literature in English: Britain and Ireland. Ed. 2. Paper over Boards. Routledge. New York, NY. 2001. 592p. ISBN:0-415-24317-3, ISBN13: 978-0-415-24317-9. Dewey:820.9. LCCN:00-046009.
Audience: **g,l,u,f.**

Conrad, Peter **PR83**
Cassell's History of English Literature. Cloth over Boards. Cassell P L C. London, 2003. 780p. ISBN:0-304-36610-2, ISBN13: 978-0-304-36610-1. Dewey:820.9. LCCN:2004-270725.
Audience: **g,l.** *Choice, 2004.*

Daiches **PR83 .D29**
Critical History of English Literature. Ed. 99. Trade Cloth. John Wiley & Sons, Inc. Hoboken, NJ. 1970. 1211p. ISBN:0-471-06961-2, ISBN13: 978-0-471-06961-4. Dewey:820.9.
Audience: **g,l,u,f.**

Dyson, H. V. & Dyson, B. **PR83 .I615 VOL. 3**
Augustans and Romantics, Sixteen Eighty-Nine to Eighteen Thirty. Library Binding. Reprint Services Company. Temecula, CA. 1988. ISBN:0-7812-0133-0, ISBN13: 978-0-7812-0133-9. Dewey:820.903.
Audience: **l,u,f.**

Eagleton, Terry **MLCS 91/06433 (P)**
Against the Grain: Essays Nineteen Seventy-Five to Nineteen Eighty-Five. Cloth Text. Analytical Psychology Club of San Francisco, Inc. San Francisco, CA. 1986. 200p. ISBN:0-86091-134-9, ISBN13: 978-0-86091-134-0. Dewey:820.9. LCCN:86-190678.
Audience: **l,u,f.** B

Fowler, Alastair **PR99**
A History of English Literature. Trade Paper. Harvard University Press. Cambridge, MA. 1991. 424p. ISBN:0-674-39664-2, ISBN13: 978-0-674-39664-7. Dewey:820/.9.
Audience: **g,l,u,f.** *Choice, 1988.*

Greene, Graham **PR99 .G6843**
Lost Childhood and Other Stories. Trade Paper. Penguin Group (USA) Inc. New York, NY. 1962. ISBN:0-670-00116-3, ISBN13: 978-0-670-00116-3. Dewey:820.4.
Audience: **g,l,u,f.**

Grierson, Herbert J. **PR99 .G686 1978**
The Background of English Literature: Classical and Romantic, and Other Collected Essays and Addresses. Trade Cloth. Greenwood Publishing Group, Inc. Portsmouth, NH. 1978. 290p. ISBN:0-313-20306-7, ISBN13: 978-0-313-20306-0. Dewey:820/.9. LCCN:78-002920.
Audience: **u,f.**

Hazlitt, William **PR99 .H35**
Lectures on the English Comic Writers. Paper Text. Classic Books. Murrieta, CA. 2001. The Complete Works of William Hazlitt ISBN:0-7426-8501-2, ISBN13: 978-0-7426-8501-7. Dewey:820.9.
Audience: **l,u,f.** B

Jusserand, Jean A. **PR93**
A Literary History of the English People, Set. Library Binding. Reprint Services Company. Temecula, CA. 1992. BCL1-PR English Literature Ser. ISBN:0-7812-7003-0, ISBN13: 978-0-7812-7003-8. Dewey:820.9.
Audience: **l,u,f.**

Renwick, W. L. **PR83.I615**
The Beginnings of English Literature to Skelton 1509. Paper Text. Textbook Publishers. Temecula, CA. 2003. 450p. ISBN:0-7581-3186-0, ISBN13: 978-0-7581-3186-7. Dewey:820.9/001.
Audience: **u,f.**

Sampson, George **PR85.S34 1970**
The Concise Cambridge History of English Literature. Ed. 3. Reginald C. Churchill (Revised by). Trade Cloth. Cambridge University Press. New York, NY. 1970. 990p. ISBN:0-521-07385-5, ISBN13: 978-0-521-07385-1. Dewey:820.9. LCCN:69-016287.
Audience: **u,f.**

Sanders, Andrew **PR83.S26 2004**
Short Oxford History of English Literature. Ed. 3. Paper Text. Oxford University Press, Inc. New York, NY. 2004. 768p. ISBN:0-19-926338-8, ISBN13: 978-0-19-926338-7. Dewey:820.9. LCCN:2004-049555.
Audience: **g,l,u,f.**

Stapleton, Michael **PR19**
The Cambridge Guide to English Literature. Norman Cousins (Foreword by). Trade Cloth. Cambridge University Press. New York, NY. 1983. 1000p. ISBN:0-521-25647-X, ISBN13: 978-0-521-25647-6. Dewey:820/.3/21. LCCN:83-001967.
Audience: **g,l,u,f.**

Taine, Hippolyte A. **PR93**
History of English Literature, Set. Library Binding. Reprint Services Company. Temecula, CA. 1992. BCL1-PR English Literature Ser. ISBN:0-7812-7005-7, ISBN13: 978-0-7812-7005-2. Dewey:820.9.
Audience: **l,u,f.**

Literary History, by Period > Anglo-Saxon

Anderson, George Kumler **N40.B47**
The Literature of the Anglo: Saxons. Paper Text. Textbook Publishers. Temecula, CA. 2003. 431p. ISBN:0-7581-4407-5, ISBN13: 978-0-7581-4407-2. Dewey:927.
Audience: **u,f.**

Cherniss, Michael D. **PR205 .C5**
Ingeld and Christ: Heroic Conceptions and Values in Old English Christian Poetry. Cloth Text. Walter de Gruyter GmbH & Co. KG. Berlin, 1972. 267p. Studies in English Literature Ser., No. 74 ISBN:90-279-2335-3, ISBN13: 978-90-279-2335-6. Dewey:829/.1.
Audience: **l,u.**

Donoghue, Daniel **PR173.D66 2004**
Old English Literature: A Short Introduction. Trade Cloth. Blackwell Publishing, Inc. Malden, MA. 2004. 160p. Blackwell Introductions to Literature Ser. ISBN:0-631-23485-3, ISBN13: 978-0-631-23485-2. Dewey:829/.09. LCCN:2003-018469.
Audience: **l,u.** *Choice, 2004.*

Frantzen, Allen J. **PR179.H66F73 1998**
Before the Closet: Same-Sex Love from Beowulf to Angels in America. Trade Cloth. University of Chicago Press. Chicago, IL. 1998. 380p. ISBN:0-226-26091-7, ISBN13: 978-0-226-26091-4. Dewey:829/.09353. LCCN:98-014935.
Audience: **l,u,f.** *Choice, 1999.*

Fulk, R. D., et al. **PR173.F85 2002**
A History of Old English Literature. Christopher M. Cain & Rachel S. Anderson (Authors). Trade Cloth. Blackwell Publishing, Inc. Malden, MA. 2002. 360p. Blackwell Histories of Literature Ser. ISBN:0-631-22397-5, ISBN13: 978-0-631-22397-9. Dewey:829.09. LCCN:2002-020896.
Audience: **l,u.** *Choice, 2003.*

Gardner, John **PR201.G37**
Construction of Christian Poetry in Old English. Trade Cloth. Southern Illinois University Press. Carbondale, IL. 1975. 159p. Literary Structures Ser. ISBN:0-8093-0705-7, ISBN13: 978-0-8093-0705-0. Dewey:829/.1. LCCN:74-028475.
Audience: **u,f.**

Godden, Malcolm R. & Lapidge, Michael (Editors) **PR173 .C36 1991**
The Cambridge Companion to Old English Literature. Trade Paper. Cambridge University Press. New York, NY. 1991. 314p. Companions to Literature Ser. ISBN:0-521-37794-3, ISBN13: 978-0-521-37794-2. Dewey:829/.09. LCCN:90-002673.
Audience: **u,f.** *Choice, 1992.*

Greenfield, Stanley B. **PR173**
A New Critical History of Old English Literature. Trade Paper. New York University Press. New York, NY. 1996. 372p. ISBN:0-8147-3088-4, ISBN13: 978-0-8147-3088-1. Dewey:829/.09.
Audience: **u,f.**

Horner, Shari **PR179.W65H67 2001**
The Discourse of Enclosure: Representing Women in Old English Literature. Paper Text. State University of New York Press. Albany, NY. 2001. viii, 207p. SUNY Series in Medieval Studies ISBN:0-7914-5010-4, ISBN13: 978-0-7914-5010-9. Dewey:829/.09352042. LCCN:00-049237.
Audience: **u,f.** *Choice, 2001.*

Howe, Nicholas **PR179.M53H68 2001**
Migration and Mythmaking in Anglo-Saxon England. Trade Cloth. University of Notre Dame Press. Notre Dame, IN. 2001. xxi, 198p. ISBN:0-268-03463-X, ISBN13: 978-0-268-03463-4. Dewey:829/.09355. LCCN:2001-018919.
Audience: **u,f.** *Choice, 1990.*

Lambdin, Laura Cooner & Lambdin, Robert Thomas (Editors) **PR166**
A Companion to Old and Middle English Literature. Cloth Text. Greenwood Publishing Group, Inc. Portsmouth, NH. 2002. 448p. ISBN:0-313-31054-8, ISBN13: 978-0-313-31054-6. Dewey:829/.09. LCCN:2001-057726.
Audience: **u.** *Choice, 2003.*

Liuzza, R. M. (Editor) **PR171.O44 2001**
Old English Literature: Selected Essays. Trade Cloth. Yale University Press. Cumberland, RI. 2001. xxxviii, 479p. ISBN.0-300-09138-9, ISBN13: 978-0-300-09138-0. Dewey:829.09. LCCN:2001-035968.
Audience: **u,f.**

Magennis, Hugh **PR203 .M24 1996**
Images of Community in Old English Poetry. Trade Cloth. Cambridge University Press. New York, NY. 1996. 221p. Studies in Anglo-Saxon England, No. 18 ISBN:0-521-49566-0, ISBN13: 978-0-521-49566-0. Dewey:829/.1. LCCN:95-026344.
Audience: **l,u.** *Choice, 1997.*

Opland, Jeff **PR0203.O6**
Anglo-Saxon Oral Poetry: A Study of the Traditions. Trade Paper. Books on Demand. Ann Arbor, MI. 1980. 301p. ISBN:0-8357-3754-3, ISBN13: 978-0-8357-3754-8. Dewey:398.2. LCCN:79-024202.
Audience: **l,u,f.** B

Quinn, Karen J. & Quinn, Kenneth P. **PR221.Q5 1990**
A Manual of Old English Prose. Trade Cloth. Garland Publishing, Inc. New York, NY. 1990. 454p. ISBN:0-8240-9032-2, ISBN13: 978-0-8240-9032-6. Dewey:016.8298. LCCN:83-048285.
Audience: **u,f.** *Choice, 1990.*

Treharne, Elaine **PR173.C66 2001**
A Companion to Anglo-Saxon Literature. Phillip Pulsiano (Editor). Trade Cloth. Blackwell Publishing, Inc. Malden, MA. 2001. 552p. Companions to Literature and Culture Ser., Vol. 11 ISBN:0-631-20904-2, ISBN13: 978-0-631-20904-1. Dewey:829.09. LCCN:2001-025924.
Audience: **u,f.** *Choice, 2002.*

Wu, Duncan & Treharne, Elaine (Editors) **PR1203.O43 2002**
Old and Middle English Poetry. Trade Cloth. Blackwell Publishing, Inc. Malden, MA. 2002. 176p. Blackwell Essential Literature Ser. ISBN:0-631-23073-4, ISBN13: 978-0-631-23073-1. Dewey:829/.108. LCCN:2002-020868.
Audience: **l,u,f.**

Literary History, by Period > Medieval. Middle English

Cooper, Helen **PR408.A7**
The English Romance in Time: Transforming Motifs from Geoffrey of Monmouth to the Death of Shakespeare. Trade Cloth. Oxford University Press, Inc. New York, NY. 2004. 560p. ISBN:0-19-924886-9, ISBN13: 978-0-19-924886-5. Dewey:821/.03309. LCCN:2004-301649.
Audience: **g,l,u,f.** *Choice, 2005.*

Dinshaw, Carolyn & Wallace, David (Editors) **PN671**
The Cambridge Companion to Medieval Women's Writing. Cloth Text. Cambridge University Press. New York, NY. 2003. 312p. Cambridge Companions to Literature Ser. ISBN:0-521-79188-X, ISBN13: 978-0-521-79188-5. Dewey:809/.89287/0902. LCCN:2003-273212.
Audience: **u,f.** *Choice, 2004.*

Duncan, Thomas G. (Editor) **PR313.C66 2005**
A Companion to the Middle English Lyric. Trade Cloth. Boydell & Brewer, Ltd. Woodbridge, 2005. 328p. ISBN:1-84384-065-0, ISBN13: 978-1-84384-065-7. Dewey:821/.1093823. LCCN:2006-295904.
Audience: **u,f.** *Choice, 2006.*

Goldie, Matthew Boyd (Editor) **PR291**
Middle English Literature: An Historical Sourcebook. Trade Cloth. Blackwell Publishing, Inc. Malden, MA. 2003. 344p. ISBN:0-631-23147-1, ISBN13: 978-0-631-23147-9. Dewey:820.9/001.
Audience: **l,u.** *Choice, 2004.*

Kane, George **PR311**
Middle English Literature: A Critical Study of the Romances, the Religious Lyrics, "Piers Plowman". Trade Cloth. Greenwood Publishing Group, Inc. Portsmouth, NH. 1980. 252p. ISBN:0-313-21992-3, ISBN13: 978-0-313-21992-4. Dewey:820/.9/001. LCCN:79-014146.
Audience: **u,f.**

Kirkpatrick, Robin **PQ4050.E5K57 1995**
English and Italian Literature from Dante to Shakespeare: A Study of Sources, Analogy and Divergence. Trade Paper. Longman Publishing Group. White Plains, NY. 1995. 384p. Medieval and Renaissance Library ISBN:0-582-06558-5, ISBN13: 978-0-582-06558-1. Dewey:820.9. LCCN:94-021998.
Audience: **u,f.** *Choice, 1995.*

Krueger, Roberta L. (Editor) **PN671 .C36 2000**
The Cambridge Companion to Medieval Romance. Cloth Text. Cambridge University Press. New York, NY. 2000. 310p. Companions to Literature Ser. ISBN:0-521-55342-3, ISBN13: 978-0-521-55342-1. Dewey:809/.02. LCCN:99-034240.
Audience: **u,f.** *Choice, 2001.*

Lambdin, Laura Cooner & Lambdin, Robert Thomas (Editors) **PR166**
A Companion to Old and Middle English Literature. Cloth Text. Greenwood Publishing Group, Inc. Portsmouth, NH. 2002. 448p. ISBN:0-313-31054-8, ISBN13: 978-0-313-31054-6. Dewey:829/.09. LCCN:2001-057726.
Audience: **u.** *Choice, 2003.*

Lewis, C. S. **PN681 .L4 1998**
Studies in Medieval and Renaissance Literature. Walter Hooper (Editor). Trade Paper. Cambridge University Press. New York, NY. 1998. 210p. A Canto Book Ser. ISBN:0-521-64584-0, ISBN13: 978-0-521-64584-3. Dewey:809/.02. LCCN:99-174745.
Audience: **u,f.** B

Simpson, James **PR85.O96 2002**
The Oxford English Literary History: 1350-1547: Reform and Cultural Revolution. Trade Cloth. Oxford University Press, Inc. New York, NY. 2002. 680p. Oxford English Literary History Ser., Vol. 2 ISBN:0-19-818261-9, ISBN13: 978-0-19-818261-0. Dewey:820.9. LCCN:2002-025038.
Audience: **u,f.** *Choice, 2003.*

Strohm, Paul **PR275.P63S77 2005**
Politique. Trade Cloth. University of Notre Dame Press. Notre Dame, IN. 2005. 312p. The Conway Lectures in Medieval Studies ISBN:0-268-04114-8, ISBN13: 978-0-268-04114-4. Dewey:820.9/358/0902. LCCN:2005-004934.
Audience: **g,u,f.** *Choice, 2005.*

Thomas, P. G. **PR166.T5**
English Literature Before Chaucer. Library Binding. M. S. G. Haskell House. Brooklyn, NY. 1969. Studies in Poetry, No. 38 ISBN:0-8383-0683-7, ISBN13: 978-0-8383-0683-3. Dewey:820/.9/001. LCCN:68-001069.
Audience: **l,u,f.**

Wallace, David (Editor) **PR255 .C35 1999**
The Cambridge History of Medieval English Literature. Trade Paper. Cambridge University Press. New York, NY. 2002. 1070p. The New Cambridge History of English Literature Ser. ISBN:0-521-89046-2, ISBN13: 978-0-521-89046-5. Dewey:820.9/001.
Audience: **u,f.**

Wu, Duncan & Treharne, Elaine (Editors) **PR1203.O43 2002**
Old and Middle English Poetry. Trade Cloth. Blackwell Publishing, Inc. Malden, MA. 2002. 176p. Blackwell Essential Literature Ser. ISBN:0-631-23073-4, ISBN13: 978-0-631-23073-1. Dewey:829/.108. LCCN:2002-020868.
Audience: **l,u,f.**

Literary History, by Period > Modern

Ezell, Margaret J. M. **PR438.S63E94 2003**
Social Authorship and the Advent of Print. Trade Paper. Johns Hopkins University Press. Baltimore, MD. 2003. 200p. ISBN:0-8018-7737-7, ISBN13: 978-0-8018-7737-7. Dewey:820.9/004.
Audience: **u,f.** *Choice, 2000.*

Gertz, SunHee Kim **PR251.G47 2001**
Chaucer to Shakespeare, 1337-1580. Cloth over Boards. Palgrave Macmillan. New York, NY. 2001. 262p. Transitions Ser. ISBN:0-333-72198-5, ISBN13: 978-0-333-72198-8. Dewey:820.9. LCCN:00-042067.
Audience: **u,f.**

Lodge, David **PR830.P75**
Consciousness and the Novel: Connected Essays. Trade Paper. Harvard University Press. Cambridge, MA. 2004. 336p. The Richard Ellmann Lectures in Modern Literature Ser. ISBN:0-674-01377-8, ISBN13: 978-0-674-01377-3. Dewey:823/.083091.
Audience: **u,f.**

Showalter, Elaine **PR115 .S5 1999**
A Literature of Their Own: British Women Novelists from Brontë to Lessing. Trade Paper. Princeton University Press. Princeton, NJ. 1998. 382p. ISBN:0-691-00476-5, ISBN13: 978-0-691-00476-1. Dewey:828/.8/099287. LCCN:98-089253.
Audience: **u,f.** *Choice, 1999.*

Williams, Raymond **DA566.4.W48 2001**
The Long Revolution. Trade Paper. Broadview Press. Peterborough, ON. 2001. 399p. ISBN:1-55111-402-X, ISBN13: 978-1-55111-402-6. Dewey:941.082. LCCN:2001-268334.
Audience: **u,f.** B

Literary History, by Period > Modern > 16th C., Elizabethan Era

Fernie, Ewan, et al. **PR421**
Reconceiving the Renaissance: A Critical Reader. Ramona Wray, Mark Thornton Burnett & Clare McManus (Authors). Trade Paper. Oxford University Press, Inc. New York, NY. 2005. 512p. ISBN:0-19-926557-7, ISBN13: 978-0-19-926557-2. Dewey:820.9/003. LCCN:2004-026580.
Audience: **u,f.**

Hadfield, Andrew **PR428.T73H33 1998**
Literature, Travel, and Colonial Writing in the English Renaissance, 1545-1625. Trade Cloth. Oxford University Press, Inc. New York, NY. 1999. 320p. ISBN:0-19-818480-8, ISBN13: 978-0-19-818480-5. Dewey:820.9/32171241/09031. LCCN:98-034187.
Audience: **u,f.** *Choice, 1999.*

Hamlin, William M. **PR129.A4H36 1995**
The Image of America in Montaigne, Spenser and Shakespeare: Renaissance Ethnography and Literary Reflection. Trade Cloth. Palgrave Macmillan. New York, NY. 1995. 256p. ISBN:0-312-12506-2, ISBN13: 978-0-312-12506-6. Dewey:820.9/3273. LCCN:94-045082.
Audience: **u,f.** *Choice, 1996.*

Jones, Edmund D. **PR67**
English Critical Essays: Sixteenth, Seventeenth and Eighteenth Centuries. Library Binding. Arden Library. Darby, PA. 1983. 394p. ISBN:0-8495-2806-2, ISBN13: 978-0-8495-2806-4. Dewey:824.7.
Audience: **l,u,f.**

Kinney, Arthur F. (Editor) **PR413 .C29 2000**
The Cambridge Companion to English Literature, 1500-1600. Cloth Text. Cambridge University Press. New York, NY. 1999. 363p. Companions to Literature Ser. ISBN:0-521-58294-6, ISBN13: 978-0-521-58294-0. Dewey:820.9/002. LCCN:99-021654.
Audience: **u,f.** *Choice, 2000.*

Kirkpatrick, Robin **PQ4050.E5K57 1995**
English and Italian Literature from Dante to Shakespeare: A Study of Sources, Analogy and Divergence. Trade Paper. Longman Publishing Group. White Plains, NY. 1995. 384p. Medieval and Renaissance Library ISBN:0-582-06558-5, ISBN13: 978-0-582-06558-1. Dewey:820.9. LCCN:94-021998.
Audience: **u,f.** *Choice, 1995.*

Lewis, C. S. **PR411**
Poetry and Prose in the Sixteenth Century. Trade Cloth. Oxford University Press, Inc. New York, NY. 1990. 704p. Oxford History of English Literature Ser., Vol. IV ISBN:0-19-812231-4, ISBN13: 978-0-19-812231-9. Dewey:820.9.
Audience: **u,f.**

Lewis, C. S. **PN681 .L4 1998**
Studies in Medieval and Renaissance Literature. Walter Hooper (Editor). Trade Paper. Cambridge University Press. New York, NY. 1998. 210p. A Canto Book Ser. ISBN:0-521-64584-0, ISBN13: 978-0-521-64584-3. Dewey:809/.02. LCCN:99-174745.
Audience: **u,f.** B

Loewenstein, David & Mueller, Janel (Editors) **PR421.C26 2002**
The Cambridge History of Early Modern English Literature. Trade Cloth. Cambridge University Press. New York, NY. 2003. 1050p. The New Cambridge History of English Literature Ser. ISBN:0-521-63156-4, ISBN13: 978-0-521-63156-3. Dewey:820.9/003. LCCN:2002-023792.
Audience: **u,f.** *Choice, 2003.*

Loewenstein, David & Mueller, Janel (Editors) **PR421**
The Cambridge History of Early Modern English Literature. Trade Paper. Cambridge University Press. New York, NY. 2006. 1050p. ISBN:0-521-68499-4, ISBN13: 978-0-521-68499-6. Dewey:820.9/003.
Audience: **u,f.** *Choice, 2003.*

Murphy, Andrew **PR129.I7M87 1999**
But the Irish Sea Betwixt Us: Ireland, Colonialism and Renaissance Literature. Trade Cloth. University Press of Kentucky. Lexington, KY. 1999. xii, 227p. Irish Literature, History, and Culture Ser. ISBN:0-8131-2086-1, ISBN13: 978-0-8131-2086-7. Dewey:820.9/32417/09031. LCCN:98-041607.
Audience: **u,f.**

Ruoff, James E. **PR19.R8 1975**
Crowell's Handbook of Elizabethan and Stuart Literature. Trade Cloth. Thomas Y. Crowell Company. New York, NY. 1975. 576p. ISBN:0-690-22661-6, ISBN13: 978-0-690-22661-4. Dewey:820/.9/003. LCCN:73-022097.
Audience: **l,u,f.** B

Shrank, Cathy **PR421**
Writing the Nation in Reformation England, 1530-1580. Trade Cloth. Oxford University Press, Inc. New York, NY. 2004. 304p. ISBN:0-19-926888-6, ISBN13: 978-0-19-926888-7. Dewey:820.9/358. LCCN:2004-303331.
Audience: **g,l,u,f.** *Choice, 2005.*

Woodbridge, Linda **PR429.W64.W66 1984**
Women and the English Renaissance: Literature and the Nature of Womankind, 1540-1620. Trade Cloth. University of Illinois Press. Champaign, IL. 1984. 376p. ISBN:0-252-01027-2, ISBN13: 978-0-252-01027-9. Dewey:820/.9/352042. LCCN:82-024792.
Audience: **u,f.** B

Worden, Blair **PR2342.A6W67 1996**
The Sound of Virtue: Philip Sidney's Arcadia and Elizabethan Politics. Cloth over Boards. Yale University Press. Cumberland, RI. 1997. 432p. ISBN:0-300-06693-7, ISBN13: 978-0-300-06693-7. Dewey:823/.3. LCCN:96-018713.
Audience: **u,f.** *Choice, 1997.*

Literary History, by Period > Modern > 17th C.

Achinstein, Sharon **PR438.D57A25 2002**
Literature and Dissent in Milton's England. Trade Cloth. Cambridge University Press. New York, NY. 2003. 314p. ISBN:0-521-81804-4, ISBN13: 978-0-521-81804-9. Dewey:820.9/3823. LCCN:2002-031062.
Audience: **u,f.** *Choice, 2004.*

Gallagher, Catherine **PR113.G35 1994**
Nobody's Story: The Vanishing Acts of Women Writers in the Marketplace, 1670-1820. Trade Cloth. University of California Press. Berkeley, CA. 1994. 339p. The New Historicism Ser., Vol. 31:Studies in Cultural Poetics ISBN:0-520-08510-8, ISBN13: 978-0-520-08510-7. Dewey:820.9/9287/09032. LCCN:94-009202.
Audience: **u,f.** *Choice, 1995.*

Jones, Edmund D. **PR67**
English Critical Essays: Sixteenth, Seventeenth and Eighteenth Centuries. Library Binding. Arden Library. Darby, PA. 1983. 394p. ISBN:0-8495-2806-2, ISBN13: 978-0-8495-2806-4. Dewey:824.7.
Audience: **l,u,f.**

Linton, Joan P. **PR129.A4 L56 1998**
The Romance of the New World: Gender and the Literary Formations of English Colonialism. Anne Barton, Jonathan Dollimore, Marjorie Garber, Jonathan Goldberg, Peter Holland, Kate McLuskie, Stephen Orgel & Nancy Vickers (Contribution by). Trade Cloth. Cambridge University Press. New York, NY. 1998. 288p. Studies in Renaissance Literature and Culture, No. 27 ISBN:0-521-59454-5, ISBN13: 978-0-521-59454-7. Dewey:820.9/358. LCCN:97-030145.
Audience: **u,f.**

Morse, David **PR448.V57M67 2000**
The Age of Virtue: British Culture from the Restoration to Romanticism. Cloth over Boards. Palgrave Macmillan. New York, NY. 2000. 340p. ISBN:0-312-22353-6, ISBN13: 978-0-312-22353-3. Dewey:820.9/353. LCCN:99-018157.
Audience: **u,f.** *Choice, 2000.*

Patrides, C. A. & Waddington, Raymond B. **PR421**
The Age of Milton: Backgrounds to Seventeenth-Century Literature. Trade Cloth. Bow Historical Books. New Providence, NJ. 1980. x, 438p. ISBN:0-389-20051-4, ISBN13: 978-0-389-20051-2. Dewey:820.9/003. LCCN:80-511211.
Audience: **l,u,f.** B

Patterson, Annabel **PR421.P38 1993**
Reading Between the Lines. Library Binding. University of Wisconsin Press. Chicago, IL. 1993. 350p. ISBN:0-299-13540-3, ISBN13: 978-0-299-13540-9. Dewey:820.9. LCCN:92-050257.
Audience: **u,f.**

Richetti, John (Editor) **PR442**
The Cambridge History of English Literature, 1660-1780. Trade Cloth. Cambridge University Press. New York, NY. 2005. 964p. The New Cambridge History of English Literature Ser. ISBN:0-521-78144-2, ISBN13: 978-0-521-78144-2. Dewey:820.9/005. LCCN:2005-298683.
Audience: **u,f.** *Choice, 2005.*

Womersley, David (Editor) **PR441.C66 2001**
A Companion to Literature from Milton to Blake. Trade Cloth. Blackwell Publishing, Inc. Malden, MA. 2001. 632p. Companions to Literature and Culture Ser. ISBN:0-631-21285-X, ISBN13: 978-0-631-21285-0. Dewey:820.9. LCCN:00-031018.
Audience: **l,u,f.** *Choice, 2002.*

Zwicker, Steven N. (Editor) **PR437 .C36 1998**
The Cambridge Companion to English Literature, 1650-1740. Margaret Anne Doody, Michael Seidel, Paul Hammond, James

A. Winn, John Spurr, Jessica Munns & Joshue Scodel (Contribution by). Trade Cloth. Cambridge University Press. New York, NY. 1998. 358p. Companions to Literature Ser. ISBN:0-521-56379-8, ISBN13: 978-0-521-56379-6. Dewey:820.9/004. LCCN:97-030165.
Audience: **u,f.** *Choice, 1998.*

Literary History, by Period > Modern > 18th C., Romanticism

Abrams, M. H. **PN751 .A2 1971**
The Mirror and the Lamp: Romantic Theory and the Critical Tradition. Paper Text. Oxford University Press, Inc. New York, NY. 1971. 406p. ISBN:0-19-501471-5, ISBN13: 978-0-19-501471-6. Dewey:801.950941.
Audience: **u,f.** B

Backscheider, Paula R. & Ingrassia, Catherine **PR851.C57 2005**
A Companion to the Eighteenth-Century English Novel and Culture. Trade Cloth. Blackwell Publishing, Inc. Malden, MA. 2005. 576p. Blackwell Companions to Literature and Culture Ser., Vol. 30 ISBN:1-4051-0157-1, ISBN13: 978-1-4051-0157-8. Dewey:823/.509. LCCN:2004-008398.
Audience: **u,f.** *Choice, 2006.*

Bhattacharya, Nandini **PR129.I5B49 1998**
Reading the Splendid Body: Gender and Consumerism in Eighteenth-Century British Writing on India. Trade Cloth. University of Delaware Press. Newark, DE. 1998. 232p. ISBN:0-87413-612-1, ISBN13: 978-0-87413-612-8. Dewey:820.9/3254/09033. LCCN:97-005222.
Audience: **u,f.**

Butler, Marilyn **PR457**
Romantics, Rebels and Reactionaries: English Literature and Its Background, 1760-1830. Paper Text. Oxford University Press, Inc. New York, NY. 1985. 220p. Opus Ser. ISBN:0-19-289132-4, ISBN13: 978-0-19-289132-7. Dewey:820.9/145. LCCN:80-042404.
Audience: **u,f.**

Chase, Cynthia **PR457**
Romanticism. Ed. 1. Cloth Text. Addison-Wesley Longman, Inc. Boston, MA. 1992. 304p. ISBN:0-582-05000-6, ISBN13: 978-0-582-05000-6. Dewey:820.9/145/09034.
Audience: **l,u,f.**

Clery, E. J. **PR448.F45C54 2004**
Feminization Debate in Eighteenth-Century Britain: Literature, Commerce and Luxury. Trade Paper. Palgrave Macmillan. New York, NY. 2004. 256p. Palgrave Studies in the Enlightenment, Romanticism and the Cultures of Print ISBN:0-333-77732-8, ISBN13: 978-0-333-77732-9. Dewey:820.9/3522/09033. LCCN:2003-070193.
Audience: **g,u,f.** *Choice, 2005.*

Craciun, Adriana & Lokke, Kari E. (Editors) **PR129.F8R39 2001**
Rebellious Hearts: British Women Writers and the French Revolution. Trade Paper. State University of New York Press. Albany, NY. 2001. xiii, 395p. Suny Series, Feminist Criticism and Theory Ser. ISBN:0-7914-4970-X, ISBN13: 978-0-7914-4970-7. Dewey:821/.7099287. LCCN:00-044069.
Audience: **u,f.**

Damrosch, Leopold Jr. (Editor) **PR442.M57 1988**
Modern Essays on Eighteenth-Century Literature. Trade Cloth. Oxford University Press, Inc. New York, NY. 1988. 502p. ISBN:0-19-504923-3, ISBN13: 978-0-19-504923-7. Dewey:820/.9/005. LCCN:87-005786.
Audience: **l,u,f.**

Day, Aiden **PR457.D38 1996**
Romanticism. Paper over Boards. Routledge. New York, NY. 1995. 240p. The New Critical Idiom Ser. ISBN:0-415-12266-X, ISBN13: 978-0-415-12266-5. Dewey:820.9/145. LCCN:95-008288.
Audience: **l,u,f.** *Choice, 1997.*

Fay, Elizabeth **PR468.F46F39 1998**
A Feminist Introduction to Romanticism. Trade Paper. Blackwell Publishing, Inc. Malden, MA. 1998. 264p. ISBN:0-631-19895-4, ISBN13: 978-0-631-19895-6. Dewey:820.9/145/082. LCCN:98-005902.
Audience: **u,f.** *Choice, 1999.*

Feldman, Paula R. & Kelley, Theresa M. (Editors) **PR457.R4568 1995**
Romantic Women Writers: Voices and Countervoices. Trade Paper. University Press of New England. Lebanon, NH. 1995. 336p. ISBN:0-87451-724-9, ISBN13: 978-0-87451-724-8. Dewey:820.9/9287/0903. LCCN:94-039710.
Audience: **u,f.** *Choice, 1995.*

Ferber, Michael (Editor) **PN603.C65 2005**
Companion to European Romanticism. Trade Cloth. Blackwell Publishing, Inc. Malden, MA. 2005. 600p. Blackwell Companions to Literature and Culture Ser., Vol. 38 ISBN:1-4051-1039-2, ISBN13: 978-1-4051-1039-6. Dewey:809/.9145. LCCN:2005-022100.
Audience: **u,f.**

Gerrard, Christine (Editor) **PR553.C66 2006**
A Companion to Eighteenth-Century Poetry. Trade Cloth. Blackwell Publishing, Inc. Malden, MA. 2006. 624p. Blackwell Companions to Literature and Culture Ser., Vol. 42 ISBN:1-4051-1316-2, ISBN13: 978-1-4051-1316-8. Dewey:821/.509. LCCN:2005-034701.
Audience: **u,f.**

Gilman, Ernest B. **PR933**
The Curious Perspective. Trade Cloth. Yale University Press. Cumberland, RI. 1978. xii, 267p. ISBN:0-300-02222-0, ISBN13: 978-0-300-02222-3. Dewey:820/.9/003. LCCN:78-006075.
Audience: **u,f.**

Heath, Duncan, et al. **B836.5**
Introducing Romanticism. Judy Boreham & Richard Appignanesi (Authors). Trade Paper. Totem Books. Cambridge, 2006. 176p. ISBN:1-84046-671-5, ISBN13: 978-1-84046-671-3. Dewey:141.6.
Audience: **g,l,u,f.**

Jarvis, Robin **PR447**
The Romantic Period: The Intellectual and Cultural Context of English Literature, 1789-1830. Trade Paper. Longman Publishing Group. White Plains, NY. 2004. 224p. Longman Literature in English Ser. ISBN:0-582-38239-4, ISBN13: 978-0-582-38239-8. Dewey:820.9/145. LCCN:2004-558702.
Audience: **u,f.**

Jones, Edmund D. **PR67**
English Critical Essays: Sixteenth, Seventeenth and Eighteenth Centuries. Library Binding. Arden Library. Darby, PA. 1983. 394p. ISBN:0-8495-2806-2, ISBN13: 978-0-8495-2806-4. Dewey:824.7.
Audience: **l,u,f.**

Keymer, Thomas & Mee, Jon (Editors) **PR441.C36 2004**
The Cambridge Companion to English Literature, 1740-1830. Cloth Text. Cambridge University Press. New York, NY. 2004. 328p. Cambridge Companions to Literature Ser. ISBN:0-521-80974-6, ISBN13: 978-0-521-80974-0. Dewey:820.9/005. LCCN:2003-069668.
Audience: **u,f.** *Choice, 2005.*

McGann, Jerome J. **PR590**
The Romantic Ideology: A Critical Investigation. Trade Paper. University of Chicago Press. Chicago, IL. 1985. 184p. ISBN:0-226-55850-9, ISBN13: 978-0-226-55850-9. Dewey:821/.7/09145. LCCN:82-017494.
Audience: **u,f.**

McGann, Jerome J. **PR4392.R63 .M37 2002**
Byron and Romanticism. James Soderholm (Editor), Marilyn Butler & James Chandler (Contribution by). Cloth Text. Cambridge University Press. New York, NY. 2002. 326p. Cambridge Studies in Romanticism, Vol. 50 ISBN:0-521-80958-4, ISBN13: 978-0-521-80958-0. Dewey:821/.7. LCCN:2001-052891.
Audience: **u,f.**

Mellor, Anne K. **PR468.F46M45 1992**
Romanticism and Gender. UK-B Format Paperback. Routledge. New York, NY. 1992. 288p. ISBN:0-415-90664-4, ISBN13: 978-0-415-90664-7. Dewey:820.9928709034. LCCN:92-022902.
Audience: **u,f.** *Choice, 1993.*

Morse, David **PR448.V57M67 2000**
The Age of Virtue: British Culture from the Restoration to Romanticism. Cloth over Boards. Palgrave Macmillan. New York, NY. 2000. 340p. ISBN:0-312-22353-6, ISBN13: 978-0-312-22353-3. Dewey:820.9/353. LCCN:99-018157.
Audience: **u,f.** *Choice, 2000.*

Nussbaum, Felicity (Editor) **D292.G56 2003**
The Global Eighteenth Century. Trade Cloth. Johns Hopkins University Press. Baltimore, MD. 2003. ISBN:0-8018-7224-3, ISBN13: 978-0-8018-7224-2. Dewey:909.7. LCCN:2002-012550.
Audience: **u,f.** *Choice, 2004.*

Potkay, Adam & Burr, Sandra (Editors) **PR1297.B57 1995**
Black Atlantic Writers of the Eighteenth Century: Living the New Exodus in England and the Americas. Cloth over Boards. Palgrave Macmillan. New York, NY. 1995. 304p. ISBN:0-312-12133-4, ISBN13: 978-0-312-12133-4. Dewey:818/.108080896073. LCCN:94-036117.
Audience: **f.** *Choice, 1995.*

Prickett, Stephen **PR457 .R645 1981**
The Romantics: The Context of English Literature. Cloth Text. Holmes & Meier Publishers, Inc. Teaneck, NJ. 1981. 270p. ISBN:0-8419-0723-4, ISBN13: 978-0-8419-0723-2. Dewey:820/.9/007.
Audience: **l,u,f.**

Raimond, Jean & Watson, Richard (Editors) **PR457.H26 1992**
A Handbook to English Romanticism. Cloth Text. Palgrave Macmillan. New York, NY. 1992. 328p. ISBN:0-312-07914-1, ISBN13: 978-0-312-07914-7. Dewey:820.9145. LCCN:91-041426.
Audience: **l,u,f.** *Choice, 1993.*

Richetti, John (Editor) **PR851 .C36 1996**
The Cambridge Companion to the Eighteenth-Century Novel. Cloth Text. Cambridge University Press. New York, NY. 1996. 297p. Companions to Literature Ser. ISBN:0-521-41908-5, ISBN13: 978-0-521-41908-6. Dewey:823.5/09. LCCN:95-043083.
Audience: **u,f.** *Choice, 1997.*

Richetti, John (Editor) **PR442**
The Cambridge History of English Literature, 1660-1780. Trade Cloth. Cambridge University Press. New York, NY. 2005. 964p. The New Cambridge History of English Literature Ser. ISBN:0-521-78144-2, ISBN13: 978-0-521-78144-2. Dewey:820.9/005. LCCN:2005-298683.
Audience: **u,f.** *Choice, 2005.*

Rivers, Isabel (Editor) **PR442.B57 2001**
Books and Their Readers in Eighteenth-Century England: New Essays. Trade Cloth. Continuum International Publishing Group, Ltd. London, 2001. 256p. ISBN:0-7185-0189-6, ISBN13: 978-0-7185-0189-1. Dewey:028.9/0942/09033. LCCN:00-054586.
Audience: **u,f.**

Roe, Nicholas **PR457.R4575 2005**
Romanticism: An Oxford Guide. Paper Text. Oxford University Press, Inc. New York, NY. 2005. 776p. ISBN:0-19-925840-6, ISBN13: 978-0-19-925840-6. Dewey:820.9/145. LCCN:2004-025235.
Audience: **g,l,u,f.**

Spacks, Patricia Meyer **PR858.P72S67 2003**
Privacy: Concealing the Eighteenth-Century Self. Trade Cloth. University of Chicago Press. Chicago, IL. 2003. 256p. ISBN:0-226-76860-0, ISBN13: 978-0-226-76860-1. Dewey:823/.509353. LCCN:2002-152993.
Audience: **u,f.** *Choice, 2003.*

Stevens, David **PR468.R65**
Romanticism. Adrian Barlow (Contribution by). Trade Paper. Cambridge University Press. New York, NY. 2004. 128p. Cambridge Contexts in Literature Ser. ISBN:0-521-75372-4, ISBN13: 978-0-521-75372-2. Dewey:820.9/007.
Audience: **g,l.**

Tobin, Beth Fowkes **PR129.T76T63 2004**
Colonizing Nature: The Tropics in British Arts and Letters, 1760-1820. Book, Other. University of Pennsylvania Press. Philadelphia, PA. 2004. 280p. ISBN:0-8122-3835-4, ISBN13: 978-0-8122-3835-8. Dewey:820.9/3213. LCCN:2004-052630.
Audience: **u,f.** *Choice, 2005.*

Wahl, Elizabeth S. **PR448.H65W35 1999**
Invisible Relations: Representations of Female Intimacy in the Age of Enlightenment. Trade Cloth. Stanford University Press. Palo Alto, CA. 1999. viii, 358p. ISBN:0-8047-2956-5, ISBN13: 978-0-8047-2956-7. Dewey:820.9/3538/086643. LCCN:99-025086.
Audience: **u,f.** *Choice, 2000.*

Wall, Cynthia (Editor) **PR442**
Concise Companion to the Restoration and the Eighteenth Century. Trade Cloth. Blackwell Publishing, Inc. Malden, MA. 2005. 296p. Blackwell Concise Companions to Literature and Culture Ser. ISBN:1-4051-0117-2, ISBN13: 978-1-4051-0117-2. Dewey:820.9/005. LCCN:2004-012930.
Audience: **u,f.** *Choice, 2006.*

Williams, Raymond **PR409.C5**
The Country and the City. Trade Paper. Oxford University Press, Inc. New York, NY. 1975. 344p. ISBN:0-19-519810-7, ISBN13: 978-0-19-519810-2. Dewey:820.9/32. LCCN:72-098128.
Audience: **u,f.** B

Williams, Raymond **DA533.W6 1983**
Culture and Society, 1780-1950. Ed. 2. Trade Cloth. Columbia University Press. New York, NY. 1983. 363p. A Morningside Bk. ISBN:0-231-02287-5, ISBN13: 978-0-231-02287-3. Dewey:306/.4/0941. LCCN:85-005195.
Audience: **g,u,f.** B

Womersley, David (Editor) **PR441.C66 2001**
A Companion to Literature from Milton to Blake. Trade Cloth. Blackwell Publishing, Inc. Malden, MA. 2001. 632p. Companions to Literature and Culture Ser. ISBN:0-631-21285-X, ISBN13: 978-0-631-21285-0. Dewey:820.9. LCCN:00-031018.
Audience: **l,u,f.** *Choice, 2002.*

Woodard, Helena **PR129**
African-British Writings in the Eighteenth Century: The Politics of Race and Reason. Trade Cloth. Greenwood Publishing Group, Inc. Portsmouth, NH. 1999. 208p. Contributions to the Study of World Literature Ser., Vol. 94 ISBN:0-313-30680-X, ISBN13: 978-0-313-30680-8. Dewey:820.9/358. LCCN:98-006758.
Audience: **u,f.** *Choice, 1999.*

Wordsworth, Jonathan **PR457.W73 1997**
The Bright Work Grows: Women Writers of the Romantic Age. Trade Cloth. Woodstock Books. Otley, 2003. xiii, 304p. Revolution and Romanticism, 1789-1834 Ser. ISBN:1-85477-212-0, ISBN13: 978-1-85477-212-1. Dewey:820.9/9287/09034. LCCN:96-042228.
Audience: **l,u,f.**

Wu, Duncan (Editor) **PR457.C58 1998**
A Companion to Romanticism. Trade Cloth. Blackwell Publishing, Inc. Malden, MA. 1997. 576p. Companions to Literature and Culture Ser., Vol. 1 ISBN:0-631-19852-0, ISBN13: 978-0-631-19852-9. Dewey:820.9/145. LCCN:97-000928.
Audience: **l,u,f.**

Zwicker, Steven N. (Editor) **PR437 .C36 1998**
The Cambridge Companion to English Literature, 1650-1740. Margaret Anne Doody, Michael Seidel, Paul Hammond, James A. Winn, John Spurr, Jessica Munns & Joshue Scodel (Contribution by). Trade Cloth. Cambridge University Press. New York, NY. 1998. 358p. Companions to Literature Ser. ISBN:0-521-56379-8, ISBN13: 978-0-521-56379-6. Dewey:820.9/004. LCCN:97-030165.
Audience: **u,f.** *Choice, 1998.*

Literary History, by Period > Modern > 19th C., Victorian Era

Abrams, M. H. **PN751 .A2 1971**
The Mirror and the Lamp: Romantic Theory and the Critical Tradition. Paper Text. Oxford University Press, Inc. New York, NY. 1971. 406p. ISBN:0-19-501471-5, ISBN13: 978-0-19-501471-6. Dewey:801.950941.
Audience: **u,f.** B

Adams, James E. **PR468.M38A33 1995**
Dandies and Desert Saints: Styles of Victorian Masculinity. Trade Paper. Cornell University Press. Ithaca, NY. 1995. 264p. ISBN:0-8014-8208-9, ISBN13: 978-0-8014-8208-3. Dewey:820.9/353. LCCN:95-011320.
Audience: **u,f.** *Choice, 1996.*

Altick, Richard D. **PR878.R4A48 1991**
The Presence of the Present: Topics of the Day in the Victorian Novel. Cloth Text. Ohio State University Press. Columbus, OH. 1991. 854p. Studies in Victorian Life and Literature ISBN:0-8142-0518-6, ISBN13: 978-0-8142-0518-1. Dewey:823/.80912. LCCN:90-034806.
Audience: **l,u,f.** *Choice, 1991.*

Andres, Sophia **PR878.A7A53 2004**
The Pre-Raphaelite Art of the Victorian Novel: Narrative Challenges to Visual Gendered Boundaries. Trade Cloth. Ohio State University Press. Columbus, OH. 2004. 288p. ISBN:0-8142-5129-3, ISBN13: 978-0-8142-5129-4. Dewey:823/.809357. LCCN:2004-012887.
Audience: **u,f.** *Choice, 2005.*

Ardis, Ann **PR878.F45A74 1990**
New Women, New Novels: Feminism and Early Modernism. Cloth Text. Rutgers University Press. Piscataway, NJ. 1990. 225p. ISBN:0-8135-1581-5, ISBN13: 978-0-8135-1581-6. Dewey:823/.809352042. LCCN:90-035039.
Audience: **u,f.** *Choice, 1991.*

Armstrong, Isobel **PR595.H5 A76 1993**
Victorian Poetry: Poetry, Poetics, Politics. Paper over Boards. Routledge. New York, NY. 1993. 560p. Critical History of Victorian Poetry Ser. ISBN:0-415-03016-1, ISBN13: 978-0-415-03016-8. Dewey:821.809. LCCN:92-002451.
Audience: **u,f.**

Armstrong, Isobel & Blain, Virginia (Editors) **PR585.W6W66 1999**
Women's Poetry, Late Romantic to Late Victorian: Gender and Genre, 1830-1900. Cloth over Boards. Palgrave Macmillan. New York, NY. 1999. 428p. ISBN:0-312-21536-3, ISBN13: 978-0-312-21536-1. Dewey:821.8/09/9287. LCCN:98-003709.
Audience: **u,f.** *Choice, 1999.*

Armstrong, Nancy **PR821**
Desire and Domestic Fiction: A Political History of the Novel. Trade Paper. Oxford University Press, Inc. New York, NY. 1990. 310p. ISBN:0-19-506160-8, ISBN13: 978-0-19-506160-4. Dewey:823/.009. LCCN:86-016482.
Audience: **u,f.** *Choice, 1987.*

Auerbach, Nina **GR830.V3**
Our Vampires, Ourselves. Trade Paper. University of Chicago Press. Chicago, IL. 1997. 240p. ISBN:0-226-03202-7, ISBN13: 978-0-226-03202-3. Dewey:820.9/375. LCCN:95-001044.
Audience: **u,f.** *Choice, 1996.*

Auerbach, Nina **PR830.W6**
Woman and the Demon: The Life of a Victorian Myth. Trade Cloth. Harvard University Press. Cambridge, MA. 1982. 270p. ISBN:0-674-95406-8, ISBN13: 978-0-674-95406-9. Dewey:823.8/09352/042. LCCN:82-009298.
Audience: **u,f.** B

Berry, Laura **PR878.C5B47 1999**
The Child, the State and the Victorian Novel. Trade Cloth. University Press of Virginia. Charlottesville, VA. 2000. 192p. Victorian Literature and Culture Ser. ISBN:0-8139-1909-6, ISBN13: 978-0-8139-1909-6. Dewey:823/.809352054. LCCN:99-035304.
Audience: **u,f.** *Choice, 2000.*

Boardman, Kay & Jones, Shirley (Editors) **PR115**
Popular Victorian Women Writers. Cloth over Boards. Manchester University Press. Manchester, 2004. 256p. ISBN:0-7190-6450-3, ISBN13: 978-0-7190-6450-0. Dewey:820.9/9287/09034.
Audience: **l,u,f.** *Choice, 2005.*

Bodenheimer, Rosemarie **PR878.D65**
The Politics of Story in Victorian Social Fiction. Trade Paper. Cornell University Press. Ithaca, NY. 1991. 264p. ISBN:0-8014-9920-8, ISBN13: 978-0-8014-9920-3. Dewey:823.8/09355. LCCN:87-017313.
Audience: **u,f.** *Choice, 1988.*

Brantlinger, Patrick **PR868.P68B73 1998**
The Reading Lesson: The Threat of Mass Literacy in Nineteenth-Century British Fiction. Trade Cloth. Indiana University Press. Bloomington, IN. 1998. 320p. ISBN:0-253-33454-3, ISBN13: 978-0-253-33454-1. Dewey:823/.809. LCCN:98-019906.
Audience: **u,f.** *Choice, 1999.*

Brantlinger, Patrick **PR463**
Rule of Darkness: British Literature and Imperialism, 1830-1914. Book, Other. Cornell University Press. Ithaca, NY. 1990. 336p. ISBN:0-8014-9767-1, ISBN13: 978-0-8014-9767-4. Dewey:820.9/008. LCCN:87-047823.
Audience: **u,f.** *Choice, 1988.*

Brantlinger, Patrick **PR0469.P6B65**
The Spirit of Reform: British Literature and Politics, 1832-1867. Trade Paper. Books on Demand. Ann Arbor, MI. 1977. 303p. ISBN:0-7837-4450-1, ISBN13: 978-0-7837-4450-6. Dewey:820/.9/3. LCCN:76-030537.
Audience: **u,f.** B

Bristow, Joseph (Editor) **PR591 .C36 2000**
The Cambridge Companion to Victorian Poetry. Cloth Text. Cambridge University Press. New York, NY. 2000. 353p. Companions to Literature Ser. ISBN:0-521-64115-2, ISBN13: 978-0-521-64115-9. Dewey:821/.809. LCCN:00-020013.
Audience: **l,u,f.** *Choice, 2001.*

Bristow, Joseph **PR468.H65B75 1995**
Effeminate England: Homoerotic Writing after 1885. Trade Cloth. Columbia University Press. New York, NY. 1995. 193p. Between Men, Between Women Ser. ISBN:0-231-10348-4, ISBN13: 978-0-231-10348-0. Dewey:820.9/353. LCCN:95-010836.
Audience: **u,f.** *Choice, 1996.*

Bristow, Joseph **PR592 .V527 1987**
The Victorian Poet: Poetics and Persona. Trade Cloth. Croom Helm, Ltd. London, 1987. 256p. World and Word Ser. ISBN:0-7099-3925-6, ISBN13: 978-0-7099-3925-2. Dewey:821/.8/09. LCCN:87-023720.
Audience: **u,f.**

Buckley, Jerome H. **PR461**
The Victorian Temper: A Study in Literary Culture. Trade Paper. Cambridge University Press. New York, NY. 1981. 304p. ISBN:0-521-28448-1, ISBN13: 978-0-521-28448-6. Dewey:820.9/008. LCCN:81-006142.
Audience: **u,f.**

Butler, Marilyn **PR457**
Romantics, Rebels and Reactionaries: English Literature and Its Background, 1760-1830. Paper Text. Oxford University Press, Inc. New York, NY. 1985. 220p. Opus Ser. ISBN:0-19-289132-4, ISBN13: 978-0-19-289132-7. Dewey:820.9/145. LCCN:80-042404.
Audience: **u,f.**

Campbell, Matthew **PR595.W45 C36 1999**
Rhythm and Will in Victorian Poetry. Gillian Beer (Contribution by). Trade Paper. Cambridge University Press. New York, NY. 2004. 288p. Cambridge Studies in Nineteenth-Century Literature and Culture Ser., Vol. 22 ISBN:0-521-60422-2, ISBN13: 978-0-521-60422-2. Dewey:821.809384.
Audience: **u,f.** *Choice, 2000.*

Chapman, Alison (Editor), et al. **PR591.C66 2002**
A Companion to Victorian Poetry. Richard Cronin & Anthony Harrison (Editors). Trade Cloth. Blackwell Publishing, Inc. Malden, MA. 2002. 632p. Blackwell Companions to Literature and Culture Ser., Vol. 15 ISBN:0-631-22207-3, ISBN13: 978-0-631-22207-1. Dewey:821/.809. LCCN:2001-004354.
Audience: **l,u,f.** *Choice, 2003.*

Davis, Philip **PR85.O96 2002**
The Oxford English Literary History: 1830-1880: the Victorians. Trade Cloth. Oxford University Press, Inc. New York, NY. 2002. 648p. Oxford English Literary History Ser. ISBN:0-19-818447-6, ISBN13: 978-0-19-818447-8. Dewey:820.9. LCCN:2002-025038.
Audience: **u,f.** *Choice, 2003.*

Dijkstra, Bram **N8219.L2**
Idols of Perversity: Fantasies of Feminine Evil in Fin-de-Sìecle Culture. Trade Paper. Oxford University Press, Inc. New York, NY. 1988. 478p. ISBN:0-19-505652-3, ISBN13: 978-0-19-505652-5. Dewey:704.9/424/09034.
Audience: **u,f.** *Choice, 1987.*

Fulford, Timothy, et al. **PR468.S34F85 2004**
Literature, Science and Exploration in the Romantic Era: Bodies of Knowledge. Peter J. Kitson & Debbie Lee (Authors), Marilyn Butler & James Chandler (Contribution by). Trade Cloth. Cambridge University Press. New York, NY. 2004. 346p. Cambridge Studies in Romanticism Ser., Vol. 60 ISBN:0-521-82919-4, ISBN13: 978-0-521-82919-9. Dewey:820.9/36. LCCN:2003-063280.
Audience: **g,l,u,f.** *Choice, 2005.*

Gilbert, Sandra M. & Gubar, Susan **PR115.G5 2000**
The Madwoman in the Attic: The Woman Writer and the Nineteenth-Century Literary Imagination. Ed. 2. Trade Paper. Yale University Press. Cumberland, RI. 2000. 768p. ISBN:0-300-08458-7, ISBN13: 978-0-300-08458-0. Dewey:820.9/9287/09034. LCCN:99-086038.
Audience: **g,l,u,f.**

Goodlad, Lauren M. E. **PR468.P57G66 2003**
Victorian Literature and the Victorian State: Character and Governance in a Liberal Society. Trade Cloth. Johns Hopkins University Press. Baltimore, MD. 2004. 320p. ISBN:0-8018-6963-3, ISBN13: 978-0-8018-6963-1. Dewey:820.9/358. LCCN:2002-154081.
Audience: **u,f.** *Choice, 2004.*

Green, Laura Morgan **PR788.W6G74 2001**
Educating Women: Cultural Conflict and Victorian Literature. Trade Cloth. Ohio University Press. Athens, OH. 2001. 166p. ISBN:0-8214-1402-X, ISBN13: 978-0-8214-1402-6. Dewey:823/.809352042. LCCN:2001-036060.
Audience: **u,f.** *Choice, 2002.*

Gross, John **PR63 .G7 1992**
The Rise and Fall of the Man of Letters: English Literary Life since 1800. Trade Paper. Ivan R. Dee Publisher. Blue Ridge Summit, PA. 1992. 372p. ISBN:1-56663-000-2, ISBN13: 978-1-56663-000-9. Dewey:820.9. LCCN:92-016011.
Audience: **u,f.**

Guy, Josephine (Editor) **HN385**
The Victorian Age. Trade Paper. Routledge. New York, NY. 2004. 632p. ISBN:0-415-27114-2, ISBN13: 978-0-415-27114-1. Dewey:306/.0941/09034.
Audience: **g,l,u,f.**

Harrison, Antony H. **PR595.H5H37 1998**
Victorian Poets and the Politics of Culture: Discourse and Ideology. Trade Cloth. University Press of Virginia. Charlottesville, VA. 1998. 192p. Victorian Literature and Culture Ser. ISBN:0-8139-1818-9, ISBN13: 978-0-8139-1818-1. Dewey:821/.809358. LCCN:98-014577.
Audience: **u,f.** *Choice, 1999.*

Homans, Margaret **PR469.W65H66 1986**
Bearing the Word: Language and Female Experience in Nineteenth-Century Women's Writing. Catherine R. Stimpson (Foreword by). Trade Cloth. University of Chicago Press. Chicago, IL. 1993. xiv, 326p. ISBN:0-226-35107-6, ISBN13: 978-0-226-35107-0. Dewey:820/.9/9287. LCCN:85-020960.
Audience: **u,f.** *Choice, 1987.*

Jack, Ian **PR457.J24**
English Literature, 1815-1832: Scott, Byron, and Keats. Trade Cloth. Oxford University Press, Inc. New York, NY. 1990. 656p. Oxford History of English Literature Ser., Vol XII ISBN:0-19-812238-1, ISBN13: 978-0-19-812238-8. Dewey:820.903. LCCN:63-025209.
Audience: **u,f.**

James, Louis **PR871.J36 2006**
Victorian Novel. Trade Cloth. Blackwell Publishing, Inc. Malden, MA. 2006. 272p. Blackwell Guides to Literature Ser. ISBN:0-631-22627-3, ISBN13: 978-0-631-22627-7. Dewey:823/.809145. LCCN:2005-012331.
Audience: **u,f.**

Jenkins, Alice & John, Juliet (Editors) **PR873.R47 1999**
Rereading Victorian Fiction. Cloth over Boards. Palgrave Macmillan. New York, NY. 2000. 236p. ISBN:0-312-22643-8, ISBN13: 978-0-312-22643-5. Dewey:823/.809. LCCN:99-015615.
Audience: **u,f.** *Choice, 2000.*

Jenkins, Alice & John, Juliet (Editors) **PR461.R48 2000**
Rethinking Victorian Culture. Cloth over Boards. Palgrave Macmillan. New York, NY. 2000. 262p. ISBN:0-312-22679-9, ISBN13: 978-0-312-22679-4. Dewey:820.9/008. LCCN:99-029985.
Audience: **u,f.**

Jones, Edmund D. (Editor) **PR503**
English Critical Essays: Nineteenth Century. Library Binding. Darby Books. Darby, PA. 1983. 522p. ISBN:0-89987-448-7, ISBN13: 978-0-89987-448-7. Dewey:821/.009.
Audience: **l,u,f.**

Kucich, John & Sadoff, Dianne F. (Editors) **PR461.V5 2000**
Victorian Afterlife: Postmodern Culture Rewrites the Nineteenth Century. Book, Other. University of Minnesota Press. Minneapolis, MN. 2000. xxx, 344p. ISBN:0-8166-3323-1, ISBN13: 978-0-8166-3323-4. Dewey:820.9/008. LCCN:00-008492.
Audience: **u,f.** *Choice, 2001.*

Levenson, Michael (Editor) **PN56.M54C36 1999**
The Cambridge Companion to Modernism. Cloth Text. Cambridge University Press. New York, NY. 1999. 263p. Companions to Literature Ser. ISBN:0-521-49516-4, ISBN13: 978-0-521-49516-5. Dewey:809.9/112. LCCN:98-013355.
Audience: **u,f.** *Choice, 1999.*

Levine, George L. **PR878.S34L4 1991**
Darwin and the Novelists: Patterns of Science in Victorian Fiction. Trade Paper. University of Chicago Press. Chicago, IL. 1992. 334p. ISBN:0-226-47574-3, ISBN13: 978-0-226-47574-5. Dewey:823/.8/09356. LCCN:87-036201.
Audience: **u,f.** *Choice, 1989.*

Levine, George & Madden, William **PR783.L4**
Art of Victorian Prose. Trade Cloth. Oxford University Press, Inc. New York, NY. 1968. ISBN:0-19-500953-3, ISBN13: 978-0-19-500953-8. Dewey:828/.8/08.
Audience: **u,f.**

Low, Gail C. **PR868.C6L69 1996**
White Skins/Black Masks: Representation, Colonialism and Cultural Cross-Dressing. Paper over Boards. Routledge. New York, NY. 1995. 312p. ISBN:0-415-08147-5, ISBN13: 978-0-415-08147-4. Dewey:303.4/82. LCCN:95-008889.
Audience: **u,f.**

Miller, J. Hillis Jr. **PR469.R4M5 2000**
The Disappearance of God: Five Nineteenth-Century Writers. Trade Paper. University of Illinois Press. Champaign, IL. 2000. 400p. ISBN:0-252-06910-2, ISBN13: 978-0-252-06910-9. Dewey:820.9/382117. LCCN:00-029938.
Audience: **u,f.** B

Miller, J. Hillis Jr. **PR463.M55 1990**
Victorian Subjects. Cloth Text. Duke University Press. Durham, NC. 1991. 336p. ISBN:0-8223-1110-0, ISBN13: 978-0-8223-1110-2. Dewey:820.9/008. LCCN:90-044885.
Audience: **u,f.**

Nelson, Claudia **PR830.C513N45 1991**
Boys Will Be Girls: The Feminine Ethic and British Children's Fiction, 1857-1917. Cloth Text. Rutgers University Press. Piscataway, NJ. 1991. 216p. ISBN:0-8135-1681-1, ISBN13: 978-0-8135-1681-3. Dewey:823/.8099287. LCCN:90-020004.
Audience: **u,f.**

Oergel, Maike **PR129.G3O37 1998**
The Return of King Arthur and the Nibelungen: National Myth in Nineteenth-Century English and German Literature. Trade Cloth. Walter De Gruyter Inc. Ossining, NY. 1997. 325p. Studies in Literature and the Arts, No. 10 ISBN:3-11-015084-0, ISBN13: 978-3-11-015084-1. Dewey:820.9/351. LCCN:97-050164.
Audience: **u,f.**

O'Gorman, Francis **PR871.C65 2005**
A Concise Companion to the Victorian Novel. Trade Cloth. Blackwell Publishing, Inc. Malden, MA. 2004. 304p. Blackwell Concise Companions to Literature and Culture Ser. ISBN:1-4051-0319-1, ISBN13: 978-1-4051-0319-0. Dewey:823/.809. LCCN:2003-026895.
Audience: **u,f.**

O'Gorman, Francis (Editor) **PR871.V53 2002**
The Victorian Novel: A Guide to Criticism. Trade Paper. Blackwell Publishing, Inc. Malden, MA. 2002. 368p. Blackwell Guides to Criticism Ser. ISBN:0-631-22704-0, ISBN13: 978-0-631-22704-5. Dewey:823/.809. LCCN:2002-022321.
Audience: **u,f.** *Choice, 2003.*

Polhemus, Robert M. **PR830.C63**
Comic Faith: The Great Tradition from Austen to Joyce. Library Binding. University of Chicago Press. Chicago, IL. 1996. x, 408p. ISBN:0-226-67320-0, ISBN13: 978-0-226-67320-2. Dewey:823/.009. LCCN:79-024856.
Audience: **u,f.** B

Poovey, Mary **HQ1075.5.G7P66 1988**
Uneven Developments: The Ideological Work of Gender in Mid-Victorian England. Trade Paper. University of Chicago Press. Chicago, IL. 1988. 289p. Women in Culture and Society Ser. ISBN:0-226-67530-0, ISBN13: 978-0-226-67530-5. Dewey:305.3/0942/09034. LCCN:88-004783.
Audience: **u,f.** *Choice, 1989.*

Powell, John (Editor), et al. **Z1039**
Biographical Dictionary of Literary Influences: The Nineteenth Century, 1800-1914. Derek W. Blakeley & Tessa Powell (Editors). Cloth Text. Greenwood Publishing Group, Inc. Portsmouth, NH. 2000. 536p. ISBN:0-313-30422-X, ISBN13: 978-0-313-30422-4. Dewey:028/.9/09034. LCCN:99-462057.
Audience: **g,l,u,f.** *Choice, 2001.*

Powell, Kerry (Editor) **PN2594**
The Cambridge Companion to Victorian and Edwardian Theatre. Trade Paper. Cambridge University Press. New York, NY. 2004. 308p. Cambridge Companions to Literature Ser. ISBN:0-521-79536-2, ISBN13: 978-0-521-79536-4. Dewey:792/.0942/09034. LCCN:2002-041552.
Audience: **u,f.** *Choice, 2004.*

Prickett, Stephen **PR468.F35P7 2005**
Victorian Fantasy. Ed. 2. Trade Paper. Baylor University Press. Waco, TX. 2005. 310p. Provost Ser. ISBN:1-932792-30-9, ISBN13: 978-1-932792-30-0. Dewey:820.9/15. LCCN:2005-015940.
Audience: **g,l,u,f.** B *Choice, 2006.*

Prins, Yopie **PR129.G8P75 1999**
Victorian Sappho. Trade Paper. Princeton University Press. Princeton, NJ. 1999. 294p. ISBN:0-691-05919-5, ISBN13: 978-0-691-05919-8. Dewey:821/.809. LCCN:98-028067.
Audience: **u,f.** *Choice, 1999.*

Reed, John R. **PR468.S6.R4**
Victorian Conventions. Trade Cloth. Ohio University Press. Athens, OH. 1975. 574p. ISBN:0-8214-0147-5, ISBN13: 978-0-8214-0147-7. Dewey:820/.9/008. LCCN:73-092908.
Audience: **u,f.** B

Regan, Stephan (Editor) **PN3499.N56 2001**
The Nineteenth Century Novel: A Critical Reader. Trade Paper. Routledge. New York, NY. 2001. 592p. The Nineteenth-Century Novel Ser. ISBN:0-415-23828-5, ISBN13: 978-0-415-23828-1. Dewey:809.3/034. LCCN:2002-319255.
Audience: **u,f.**

Roberts, Adam **DA552**
Victorian Culture and Society: The Essential Glossary. Trade Paper. Oxford University Press, Inc. New York, NY. 2003. 272p. An Arnold Publication ISBN:0-340-80762-8, ISBN13: 978-0-340-80762-0. Dewey:941.081/03. LCCN:2004-270205.
Audience: **g,l,u,f.** *Choice, 2004.*

Robinson, Solveig C. (Editor) **PR463.S47 2003**
A Serious Occupation: Literary Criticism by Victorian Women Writers. Trade Paper. Broadview Press. Peterborough, ON. 2003. xv, 307p. ISBN:1-55111-350-3, ISBN13: 978-1-55111-350-0. Dewey:820.9/08. LCCN:2003-277525.
Audience: **g,l,u,f.**

Shattock, Joanne (Editor) **Z2011 .N45 1999 PR83**
The Cambridge Bibliography of English Literature: 1800-1900. Ed. 3. Cloth Text. Cambridge University Press. New York, NY. 2000. 1536p. Cambridge Bibliography of English Literature Ser., Vol. 4 ISBN:0-521-39100-8, ISBN13: 978-0-521-39100-9. Dewey:016.82. LCCN:99-055526.
Audience: **l,u,f.** *Choice, 2000.*

Showalter, Elaine **PR468.S48S56 1990**
Sexual Anarchy: Gender and Culture at the Fin de Siecle. Trade Cloth. Penguin Group (USA) Inc. New York, NY. 1990. 304p. ISBN:0-670-82503-4, ISBN13: 978-0-670-82503-5. Dewey:820.9/9287/09034. LCCN:89-040697.
Audience: **l,u,f.**

Smith, Andrew **PR1111**
Victorian Demons: Medicine, Masculinity and the Gothic at the Fin-de-Siecle. Cloth over Boards. Manchester University Press. Manchester, 2004. 200p. ISBN:0-7190-6356-6, ISBN13: 978-0-7190-6356-5. Dewey:820.80353. LCCN:2004-426530.
Audience: **u,f.** *Choice, 2004.*

Stewart, Garrett **PR878.A79S74 1996**
Dear Reader: The Conscripted Audience in Nineteenth-Century British Fiction. Trade Paper. Johns Hopkins University Press. Baltimore, MD. 1996. 472p. ISBN:0-8018-5283-8, ISBN13: 978-0-8018-5283-1. Dewey:823/.809. LCCN:95-052372.
Audience: **u,f.** *Choice, 1997.*

Sutherland, John **PR871**
Victorian Fiction: Writers, Publishers, Readers. Ed. 2. Trade Paper. Palgrave Macmillan. New York, NY. 2005. 224p. ISBN:1-4039-3985-3, ISBN13: 978-1-4039-3985-2. Dewey:823/.809. LCCN:2005-049320.
Audience: **u,f.** *Choice, 1995.*

Thesing, William B. **PR871.C643 2005**
A Companion to the Victorian Novel. Patrick Brantlinger (Editor). Trade Paper. Blackwell Publishing, Inc. Malden, MA. 2005. 528p. ISBN:1-4051-3291-4, ISBN13: 978-1-4051-3291-6. Dewey:823/.809.
Audience: **g,l,u,f.** *Choice, 2003.*

Thompson, Nicola D. (Editor) **PR878.F45 W66 1999**
Victorian Women Writers and the Woman Question. Gillian Beer (Contribution by). Trade Cloth. Cambridge University Press. New York, NY. 1999. 274p. Studies in Nineteenth-Century Literature and Culture, No. 21 ISBN:0-521-64102-0, ISBN13: 978-0-521-64102-9. Dewey:823/.8099287. LCCN:98-035820.
Audience: **u,f.**

Tucker, Herbert F. (Editor) **PR461.C597 1999**
A Companion to Victorian Literature and Culture. Book, Other. Blackwell Publishing, Inc. Malden, MA. 1999. 512p. Companions to Literature and Culture Ser., Vol. 2 ISBN:0-631-20463-6, ISBN13: 978-0-631-20463-3. Dewey:820.9/008. LCCN:98-019517.
Audience: **g,l,u,f.** *Choice, 1999.*

Turner, Paul **PR461.T87 1989**
English Literature, 1832-1890, Excluding the Novel. Trade Cloth. Oxford University Press, Inc. New York, NY. 1989. 536p. Oxford History of English Literature Ser., Vol. 11, Pt. 1 ISBN:0-19-812217-9, ISBN13: 978-0-19-812217-3. Dewey:820/.9/008. LCCN:88-019501.
Audience: **l,u,f.**

Vicinus, Martha **PR468.L3.V5 1975**
The Industrial Muse: A Study of Nineteenth Century British Working-Class Literature. Trade Cloth. Thomson Heinle. Boston, MA. 1975. "x, 357"p. ISBN:0-06-497210-0, ISBN13: 978-0-06-497210-9. Dewey:820/.9/007. LCCN:75-314327.
Audience: **u,f.** B

Walder, Dennis (Editor) **PN3499.N564 2001**
The Nineteenth-Century Novel: Identities. Trade Paper. Routledge. New York, NY. 2001. 320p. The Nineteenth-Century Novel Ser. ISBN:0-415-23827-7, ISBN13: 978-0-415-23827-4. Dewey:809.3/034. LCCN:2002-319274.
Audience: **l,u.**

Wheeler, Michael **PR468.D42 W4 1994**
Heaven, Hell, and the Victorians. Cloth Text. Cambridge University Press. New York, NY. 1994. 295p. ISBN:0-521-45516-2, ISBN13: 978-0-521-45516-9. Dewey:820.9/354. LCCN:94-000787.
Audience: **u,f.**

Williams, Raymond **PR409.C5**
The Country and the City. Trade Paper. Oxford University Press, Inc. New York, NY. 1975. 344p. ISBN:0-19-519810-7, ISBN13: 978-0-19-519810-2. Dewey:820.9/32. LCCN:72-098128.
Audience: **u,f.** B

Williams, Raymond **DA533.W6 1983**
Culture and Society, 1780-1950. Ed. 2. Trade Cloth. Columbia University Press. New York, NY. 1983. 363p. A Morningside Bk. ISBN:0-231-02287-5, ISBN13: 978-0-231-02287-3. Dewey:306/.4/0941. LCCN:85-005195.
Audience: **g,u,f.** B

Wullschlager, Jackie **PR990.W84 1995**
Inventing Wonderland: Victorian Childhood as Seen Through the Lives and Fantasies of Lewis Carroll, Edward Lear, J. M. Barrie, Kenneth Grahame, and A. A. Milne. Trade Cloth. Simon & Schuster. New York, NY. 1996. 240p. ISBN:0-684-82286-5, ISBN13: 978-0-684-82286-0. Dewey:820.9/352054. LCCN:95-049924.
Audience: **u,f.**

Literary History, by Period > Modern > 20th C.

Allen, Brooke **PR471.A44 2003**
Twentieth-Century Attitudes: Literary Powers in Uncertain Times. Trade Cloth. Ivan R. Dee Publisher. Blue Ridge Summit, PA. 2003. 256p. ISBN:1-56663-520-9, ISBN13: 978-1-56663-520-2. Dewey:820.90091. LCCN:2003-040909.
Audience: **u,f.**

Ayers, David **PR478.M6A98 2004**
Modernism: A Short Introduction. Trade Cloth. Blackwell Publishing, Inc. Malden, MA. 2004. 168p. Blackwell Introductions to Literature Ser. ISBN:1-4051-0854-1, ISBN13: 978-1-4051-0854-6. Dewey:820.9/112. LCCN:2003-025564.
Audience: **l,u.**

Baldick, Chris **PR85**
The Oxford English Literary History: The Modern Movement (1910-1940), Vol. 10. Trade Cloth. Oxford University Press, Inc.

New York, NY. 2004. 496p. Oxford English Literary History Ser. ISBN:0-19-818310-0, ISBN13: 978-0-19-818310-5. Dewey:820.9.

Audience: **u,f.** *Choice, 2005.*

Bradshaw, David (Editor) **PR478.M6C66 2003**
A Concise Companion to Modernism. Trade Cloth. Blackwell Publishing, Inc. Malden, MA. 2002. 304p. Blackwell Concise Companions to Literature and Culture Ser. ISBN:0-631-22054-2, ISBN13: 978-0-631-22054-1. Dewey:820.9/112. LCCN:2002-066419.

Audience: **u,f.**

Brannigan, John **PR471.B68 2002**
Orwell to the Present: Literature in England, 1945-2000. Cloth over Boards. Palgrave Macmillan. New York, NY. 2003. 256p. Transitions Ser. ISBN:0-333-69616-6, ISBN13: 978-0-333-69616-3. Dewey:820.9/00914. LCCN:2002-026765.

Audience: **l,u.** *Choice, 2003.*

Bristow, Joseph **PR468.H65B75 1995**
Effeminate England: Homoerotic Writing after 1885. Trade Cloth. Columbia University Press. New York, NY. 1995. 193p. Between Men, Between Women Ser. ISBN:0-231-10348-4, ISBN13: 978-0-231-10348-0. Dewey:820.9/353. LCCN:95-010836.

Audience: **u,f.** *Choice, 1996.*

Caplan, David **PS325.C37 2004**
Questions of Possibility: Contemporary Poetry and Poetic Form. Trade Cloth. Oxford University Press, Inc. New York, NY. 2004. 176p. ISBN:0-19-516957-3, ISBN13: 978-0-19-516957-7. Dewey:811/.509. LCCN:2004-002168.

Audience: **u,f.** *Choice, 2005.*

Cunningham, Valentine **PR478.S57C86 1988**
British Writers of the Thirties. Trade Cloth. Oxford University Press, Inc. New York, NY. 1988. 544p. ISBN:0-19-212267-3, ISBN13: 978-0-19-212267-4. Dewey:820/.9/00912. LCCN:87-007630.

Audience: **l,u,f.** *Choice, 1988.*

Daiches, David **PR471 .D3**
Present Age in British Literature. Trade Cloth. Indiana University Press. Bloomington, IN. 1958. 388p. ISBN:0-253-16890-2, ISBN13: 978-0-253-16890-0. Dewey:820.900912. LCCN:58-006954.

Audience: **u,f.** B

Dettmar, Kevin J. H. **PR478.M6C65 2005**
Companion to Modernist Literature and Culture. David Bradshaw (Editor). Trade Cloth. Blackwell Publishing, Inc. Malden, MA. 2006. 616p. Blackwell Companions to Literature and Culture Ser., Vol. 39 ISBN:0-631-20435-0, ISBN13: 978-0-631-20435-0. Dewey:820.9/112. LCCN:2005-019721.

Audience: **u,f.** *Choice, 2006.*

English, James (Editor) **PR881.C658 2006**
A Concise Companion to Contemporary British Fiction. Trade Cloth. Blackwell Publishing, Inc. Malden, MA. 2006. 288p. Blackwell Concise Companions to Literature and Culture Ser. ISBN:1-4051-2000-2, ISBN13: 978-1-4051-2000-5. Dewey:823/.91409. LCCN:2005-012329.

Audience: **u,f.** *Choice, 2006.*

Fussell, Paul **PR478.E8F8 2000**
The Great War and Modern Memory. Ed. 25. Trade Paper. Oxford University Press, Inc. New York, NY. 2000. 384p. ISBN:0-19-513332-3, ISBN13: 978-0-19-513332-5. Dewey:820.9/358. LCCN:99-043295.

Audience: **g,l,u,f.**

Gilbert, Sandra M. & Gubar, Susan **PR111**
No Man's Land: The Place of the Woman Writer in the Twentieth Century: Sexchanges. Trade Paper. Yale University Press. Cumberland, RI. 1991. 483p. ISBN:0-300-05025-9, ISBN13: 978-0-300-05025-7. Dewey:820.9/9287. LCCN:87-010560.

Audience: **l,u,f.**

Gilbert, Sandra M. & Gubar, Susan **PR116 .G5 1994**
No Man's Land, The Place of the Woman Writer in the Twentieth Century: Letters from the Front. Cloth over Boards. Yale University Press. Cumberland, RI. 1994. 496p. ISBN:0-300-05631-1, ISBN13: 978-0-300-05631-0. Dewey:820.99287. LCCN:87-010560.

Audience: **l,u,f.**

Gilbert, Sandra M. & Gubar, Susan **PR111**
No Man's Land, The Place of the Woman Writer in the Twentieth Century: The War of the Words. Trade Paper. Yale University Press. Cumberland, RI. 1989. 336p. ISBN:0-300-04587-5, ISBN13: 978-0-300-04587-1. Dewey:820.9/9287.

Audience: **l,u,f.**

Hamilton, Ian (Editor) **PR601.O9 1994**
The Oxford Companion to Twentieth-Century Poetry in English. Trade Cloth. Oxford University Press, Inc. New York, NY. 1994. 618p. ISBN:0-19-866147-9, ISBN13: 978-0-19-866147-4. Dewey:821.9/1/09. LCCN:93-001436.

Audience: **u,f.** *Choice, 1994.*

Jones, Phyllis M. (Editor) **PR67 .J65**
English Critical Essays: Twentieth Century. Trade Cloth. Oxford University Press, Inc. New York, NY. 1968. Oxford World's Classics Ser. ISBN:0-19-250405-3, ISBN13: 978-0-19-250405-0. Dewey:820.4.

Audience: **l,u,f.**

Kenner, Hugh **PR8750.K46 1983**
A Colder Eye: The Modern Irish Writers. Trade Cloth. Alfred A. Knopf Inc. New York, NY. 1983. xiv, 301 p. ;p. ISBN:0-394-42225-2, ISBN13: 978-0-394-42225-1. Dewey:820/.9/89162. LCCN:82-048723.

Audience: **g,l,u,f.**

King, Bruce **PR85**
The Oxford English Literary History, 1948-2000: The Internationalization of English Literature. Trade Cloth. Oxford University Press, Inc. New York, NY. 2004. 400p. Oxford English Literary History Ser., Vol. 13 ISBN:0-19-818428-X, ISBN13: 978-0-19-818428-7. Dewey:820.9/920693. LCCN:2004-273375.

Audience: **g,l,u,f.**

Levenson, Michael (Editor) **PN56.M54C36 1999**
The Cambridge Companion to Modernism. Cloth Text. Cambridge University Press. New York, NY. 1999. 263p. Companions to Literature Ser. ISBN:0-521-49516-4, ISBN13: 978-0-521-49516-5. Dewey:809.9/112. LCCN:98-013355.
Audience: **u,f.** *Choice, 1999.*

Marcus, Laura & Nicholls, Peter (Editors) **PR471.C36 2004**
The Cambridge History of Twentieth-Century English Literature. Cloth Text. Cambridge University Press. New York, NY. 2005. 900p. The New Cambridge History of English Literature Ser. ISBN:0-521-82077-4, ISBN13: 978-0-521-82077-6. Dewey:820.9/0091. LCCN:2004-045922.
Audience: **u,f.** *Choice, 2006.*

Matthews, Steven **PR471**
Modernism. Trade Paper. Oxford University Press, Inc. New York, NY. 2004. 170p. A Hodder Arnold Publication ISBN:0-340-76325-6, ISBN13: 978-0-340-76325-4. Dewey:820.9/112/0904. LCCN:2004-303693.
Audience: **l,u,f.**

Miller, J. Hillis Jr. **PR601 .M5**
Poets of Reality: Six Twentieth-Century Writers. Trade Cloth. Harvard University Press. Cambridge, MA. 1965. 386p. ISBN:0-674-68050-2, ISBN13: 978-0-674-68050-0. Dewey:821.00912.
Audience: **l,u,f.** B

Miller, J. Hillis Jr. **PR473.M55 1990**
Tropes, Parables, Performatives: Essays on Twentieth-Century Literature. Cloth Text. Duke University Press. Durham, NC. 1991. 288p. ISBN:0-8223-1111-9, ISBN13: 978-0-8223-1111-9. Dewey:820.9/0091. LCCN:90-044886.
Audience: **u,f.**

Parker, Peter & Kermode, Frank (Editors) **PR471.R43 1996**
A Reader's Guide to Twentieth-Century Writers. Trade Cloth. Oxford University Press, Inc. New York, NY. 1996. 846p. ISBN:0-19-521215-0, ISBN13: 978-0-19-521215-0. Dewey:820.9/004 B. LCCN:95-025697.
Audience: **l,u.**

Shaffer, Brian W. (Editor) **PR881.C655 2005**
A Companion to the British and Irish Novel 1945-2000. Trade Cloth. Blackwell Publishing, Inc. Malden, MA. 2004. 608p. Blackwell Companions to Literature and Culture Ser. ISBN:1-4051-1375-8, ISBN13: 978-1-4051-1375-5. Dewey:823/.91409. LCCN:2004-007691.
Audience: **u,f.** *Choice, 2005.*

Sherry, Vincent B. & Sherry, Vincent **PS310.W679S47 2003**
The Great War and the Language of Modernism. Trade Cloth. Oxford University Press, Inc. New York, NY. 2003. 416p. ISBN:0-19-510176-6, ISBN13: 978-0-19-510176-8. Dewey:811/.5209358. LCCN:2002-070921.
Audience: **u,f.** *Choice, 2003.*

Stevenson, Randall **PR85**
The Oxford English Literary History: 1960-2000: The Last of England? Trade Cloth. Oxford University Press, Inc. New York, NY. 2004. 640p. Oxford English Literary History Ser., Vol. 12 ISBN:0-19-818423-9, ISBN13: 978-0-19-818423-2. Dewey:820.9. LCCN:2002-025038.
Audience: **u,f.**

Wachman, Gay **PR888.L46W34 2001**
Lesbian Empire: Radical Crosswriting in the Twenties. Paper Text. Rutgers University Press. Piscataway, NJ. 2001. 256p. ISBN:0-8135-2942-5, ISBN13: 978-0-8135-2942-4. Dewey:823/.912099206643. LCCN:00-045683.
Audience: **l,u,f.** *Choice, 2002.*

Williams, Raymond **DA533.W6 1983**
Culture and Society, 1780-1950. Ed. 2. Trade Cloth. Columbia University Press. New York, NY. 1983. 363p. A Morningside Bk. ISBN:0-231-02287-5, ISBN13: 978-0-231-02287-3. Dewey:306/.4/0941. LCCN:85-005195.
Audience: **g,u,f.** B

Williams, Raymond **NX465.5**
The Politics of Modernism: Against the New Conformists. Trade Cloth. Verso Books. London, 1996. 224p. Classics Ser. ISBN:1-85984-161-9, ISBN13: 978-1-85984-161-7. Dewey:700.1.
Audience: **u,f.**

Literary History, by Form > Poetry

Brooks, Cleanth **PR503**
The Well Wrought Urn: Studies in the Structure of Poetry. Trade Paper. Harcourt Trade Publishers. New York, NY. 1956. 324p. Harvest Book Ser. ISBN:0-15-695705-1, ISBN13: 978-0-15-695705-2. Dewey:821/.009. LCCN:47-003143.
Audience: **g,l,u,f.** B

Caplan, David **PS325.C37 2004**
Questions of Possibility: Contemporary Poetry and Poetic Form. Trade Cloth. Oxford University Press, Inc. New York, NY. 2004. 176p. ISBN:0-19-516957-3, ISBN13: 978-0-19-516957-7. Dewey:811/.509. LCCN:2004-002168.
Audience: **u,f.** *Choice, 2005.*

Courthope, William John **PR502.C8**
A History of English Poetry. Paper Text. Textbook Publishers. Temecula, CA. 2003. ISBN:0-7581-4375-3, ISBN13: 978-0-7581-4375-4. Dewey:821.09.
Audience: **l,u,f.**

Fairer, David (Editor) **PR503**
Warton's History of English Poetry, Set. Library Binding. Routledge. New York, NY. 1998. 616p. Cultural Formations Ser., :The Eighteenth Century ISBN:0-415-14871-5, ISBN13: 978-0-415-14871-9. Dewey:821/.009.
Audience: **u,f.**

Fenton, James **PR502.F46 2002**
An Introduction to English Poetry. Trade Paper. Farrar, Straus & Giroux. New York, NY. 2004. 152p. ISBN:0-374-52889-6, ISBN13: 978-0-374-52889-8. Dewey:821.009.
Audience: **l,u.**

Fenton, James **PR502**
An Introduction to English Poetry. Trade Cloth. DIANE Publishing Company. Collingdale, PA. 2004. 137p. ISBN:0-7567-7623-6, ISBN13: 978-0-7567-7623-7. Dewey:821.009.
Audience: **l,u,f.**

Fenton, James **PR601.F46 2001**
The Strength of Poetry: The Oxford Lecturers on Poetry, 1994-1999. Trade Cloth. Oxford University Press, Inc. New York, NY. 2001. 288p. ISBN:0-19-818707-6, ISBN13: 978-0-19-818707-3. Dewey:821/.91409. LCCN:2001-274640.
Audience: **u,f.**

Fry, Paul H. **PR502.F78 1995**
A Defense of Poetry: Reflections on the Occasion of Writing. Trade Cloth. Stanford University Press. Palo Alto, CA. 1995. xii, 256p. ISBN:0-8047-2452-0, ISBN13: 978-0-8047-2452-4. Dewey:821.009. LCCN:94-034286.
Audience: **g,l,u,f.** *Choice, 1995.*

Hamilton, Walter **PR505 .H3 1970**
Poets Laureate in England: Being a History of the Office. Trade Cloth. Burt Franklin Publisher. New York, NY. 1970. ISBN:0-8337-1560-7, ISBN13: 978-0-8337-1560-9. Dewey:821/.009.
Audience: **g,l,u,f.**

Lonsdale, Roger (Editor) **PR55B**
Samuel Johnson's Lives of the Poets: Boxed Set. Trade Cloth. Oxford University Press, Inc. New York, NY. 2006. 2,220p. Oxford English Texts ISBN:0-19-927897-0, ISBN13: 978-0-19-927897-8. Dewey:821.009. LCCN:2006-276111.
Audience: **g,l,u,f.**

Magill, Frank N. (Editor) **PR503**
Critical Survey of Poetry, Revised Edition, Vol. 8. Library Binding. Salem Press, Inc. Hackensack, NJ. 1992. 4254p. Critical Survey of Poetry, :English Language Ser. ISBN:0-89356-834-1, ISBN13: 978-0-89356-834-4. Dewey:821/.009. LCCN:92-003727.
Audience: **l,u.** *Choice, 1993.*

Mahood, Molly M. **PR549.R4 M3 1970**
Poetry and Humanism. Trade Paper. W. W. Norton & Company, Inc. New York, NY. 1970. 335p. Norton Library ISBN:0-393-00533-X, ISBN13: 978-0-393-00533-2. Dewey:821/.3/0931. LCCN:70-019684.
Audience: **l,u.**

Ricks, Christopher **PR508.A44R43 2004**
Allusion to the Poets. Trade Paper. Oxford University Press, Inc. New York, NY. 2004. 352p. ISBN:0-19-926915-7, ISBN13: 978-0-19-926915-0. Dewey:821.009.
Audience: **u,f.** *Choice, 2003.*

Ricks, Christopher **PR503**
The Force of Poetry. Trade Paper. Oxford University Press, Inc. New York, NY. 1995. 462p. ISBN:0-19-818326-7, ISBN13: 978-0-19-818326-6. Dewey:821/.009. LCCN:87-001579.
Audience: **l,u.**

Sacks, Peter M. **PR1181**
The English Elegy: Studies in the Genre from Spenser to Yeats. Trade Paper. Johns Hopkins University Press. Baltimore, MD. 1987. 392p. ISBN:0-8018-3471-6, ISBN13: 978-0-8018-3471-4. Dewey:821/.04. LCCN:84-023381.
Audience: **l,u,f.** B *Choice, 1985.*

Schmidt, Michael **PR502.S35 1999**
Lives of the Poets. Trade Cloth. Alfred A. Knopf Inc. New York, NY. 1999. 992p. ISBN:0-375-40624-7, ISBN13: 978-0-375-40624-9. Dewey:821.009. LCCN:98-051913.
Audience: **l,u.** *Choice, 2000.*

Shaw, W. David **PR508.E5S5 1994**
Elegy and Paradox: Testing the Conventions. Trade Cloth. Johns Hopkins University Press. Baltimore, MD. 1984. 296p. ISBN:0-8018-4836-9, ISBN13: 978-0-8018-4836-0. Dewey:821.009/354. LCCN:93-050617.
Audience: **u,f.** *Choice, 1995.*

Spender, Stephen & Hall, Donald **PR19.S6**
The Concise Encyclopedia of English and American Poets and Poetry. Ed. 2. Trade Cloth. Hawthorn Books Ltd. 1963. 388p. ISBN:0-09-098810-8, ISBN13: 978-0-09-098810-5. Dewey:821/.003. LCCN:63-008015.
Audience: **g,l,u,f.** B

Winters, Yvor **PR502 .W58**
Forms of Discovery: Critical and Historical Essays on the Forms of the Short Poem in English. Paper Text. Swallow Press. Athens, OH. 1967. 378p. ISBN:0-8040-0119-7, ISBN13: 978-0-8040-0119-9. Dewey:821/.009. LCCN:66-030433.
Audience: **l,u.**

Woodring, Carl R. & Shapiro, James (Editors) **PR502.C62 1994**
The Columbia History of British Poetry. Trade Cloth. Columbia University Press. New York, NY. 1993. 732p. ISBN:0-231-07838-2, ISBN13: 978-0-231-07838-2. Dewey:821.009. LCCN:93-018226.
Audience: **u,f.** *Choice, 1994.*

Literary History, by Form > Poetry > Collected Essays

Eliot, T. S. **PR503.E45 1986**
The Use of Poetry and the Use of Criticism: Studies in the Relation of Criticism to Poetry in England. Trade Paper. Harvard University Press. Cambridge, MA. 1986. 160p. The Charles Eliot Norton Lectures ISBN:0-674-93150-5, ISBN13: 978-0-674-93150-3. Dewey:821/.009. LCCN:86-011926.
Audience: **u,f.** B

Frye, Northrop (Author, Introduction by) **PR503**
Fables of Identity: Studies in Poetic Mythology. Trade Paper. Harcourt Trade Publishers. New York, NY. 1963. 276p. ISBN:0-15-629730-2, ISBN13: 978-0-15-629730-1. Dewey:821.09. LCCN:63-020974.
Audience: **l,u,f.** B

Graves, Robert **PR503.G65 1970**
The Common Asphodel. Library Binding. M. S. G. Haskell House. Brooklyn, NY. 1970. xi, 335p. English Literature Ser., No. 33 ISBN:0-8383-1023-0, ISBN13: 978-0-8383-1023-6. Dewey:809.1. LCCN:78-117590.
Audience: **u,f.** B

Graves, Robert **PR503.G66 1970**
The Crowning Privilege. Trade Cloth. Ayer Company Publishers, Inc. Manchester, NH. 1977. 311p. Essay Index Reprint Ser. ISBN:0-8369-1751-0, ISBN13: 978-0-8369-1751-2. Dewey:821/.009. LCCN:70-117797.
Audience: **u,f.** B

Hazlitt, William **PR403 .H35**
Lectures on the dramatic literature of the age of Elizabeth. by William Hazlitt. Trade Cloth. Scholarly Publishing Office, University of Michigan Library. Ann Arbor, MI. 2004. ISBN:1-4181-6205-1, ISBN13: 978-1-4181-6205-4. Dewey:820/.9/003.
Audience: **u,f.**

Hopkins, David **PR503.E53 1994**
The Routledge Anthology of Poets on Poets. Trade Paper. Routledge. New York, NY. 1994. 288p. ISBN:0-415-11847-6, ISBN13: 978-0-415-11847-7. Dewey:821.009. LCCN:94-019754.
Audience: **l,u,f.**

Leavis, Frank R. **PR503**
Revaluation: Tradition and Development in English Poetry. Book, Other. Greenwood Publishing Group, Inc. Portsmouth, NH. 1975. 275p. ISBN:0-8371-8297-2, ISBN13: 978-0-8371-8297-1. Dewey:821/.009. LCCN:75-017192.
Audience: **l,u.**

Literary History, by Form > Poetry > Special Topics

Brittan, Simon **PR508.M43B75 2003**
Poetry, Symbol, and Allegory: Interpreting Metaphorical Language from Plato to the Present. Trade Cloth. University Press of Virginia. Charlottesville, VA. 2003. xiii, 226p. ISBN:0-8139-2156-2, ISBN13: 978-0-8139-2156-3. Dewey:809.1. LCCN:2002-155372.
Audience: **u,f.** *Choice, 2003.*

Hobsbaum, Philip **PR508.V45H53 1996**
Metre, Rhythm and Verse Form. Paper over Boards. Routledge. New York, NY. 1995. 208p. The New Critical Idiom Ser. ISBN:0-415-12267-8, ISBN13: 978-0-415-12267-2. Dewey:801.9/51. LCCN:95-008576.
Audience: **l,u.** *Choice, 1997.*

Langbaum, Robert **PR509.M6L3 1985**
The Poetry of Experience: The Dramatic Monologue in Modern Literary Tradition. Paper Text. University of Chicago Press. Chicago, IL. 1996. 256p. ISBN:0-226-46872-0, ISBN13: 978-0-226-46872-3. Dewey:821/.02. LCCN:85-014861.
Audience: **g,l,u,f.**

Ricks, Christopher **PR508.A44R43 2002**
Allusion to the Poets. Trade Cloth. Oxford University Press, Inc. New York, NY. 2002. 320p. ISBN:0-19-925032-4, ISBN13: 978-0-19-925032-5. Dewey:821.009. LCCN:2002-067181.
Audience: **l,u,f.** *Choice, 2003.*

Literary History, by Form > Poetry > History of Poetry, by Period

Scarry, Elaine (Editor) **PR502.F56 1995**
Fins de Siècle: English Poetry in 1590, 1690, 1790, 1890, 1990. Trade Cloth. Johns Hopkins University Press. Baltimore, MD. 1994. 160p. Parallax Ser., :Re-Visions of Culture and Society ISBN:0-8018-4928-4, ISBN13: 978-0-8018-4928-2. Dewey:821.009. LCCN:94-015399.
Audience: **u,f.** *Choice, 1995.*

Vendler, Helen H. **PR502.V46 2003**
Coming of Age as a Poet: Milton, Keats, Eliot, Plath. Trade Cloth. Harvard University Press. Cambridge, MA. 2003. 192p. ISBN:0-674-01024-8, ISBN13: 978-0-674-01024-6. Dewey:820.9. LCCN:2002-027287.
Audience: **u,f.** *Choice, 2003.*

Literary History, by Form > Poetry > History of Poetry, by Period > Medieval

Pearsall, Derek Albert **PR502.R58 VOL. 1**
Old English and Middle English Poetry. Trade Cloth. Routledge & Kegan Paul, Ltd. 1977. xiv, 352 p. ;p. ISBN:0-7100-8396-3, ISBN13: 978-0-7100-8396-8. Dewey:821/.009. LCCN:77-357401.
Audience: **u,f.** B

Pearsall, Derek Albert & Wu, Duncan (Editors) **PR1203.P64 2002**
Poetry from Chaucer to Spenser. Trade Cloth. Blackwell Publishing, Inc. Malden, MA. 2002. 208p. Blackwell Essential Literature Ser. ISBN:0-631-22986-8, ISBN13: 978-0-631-22986-5. Dewey:821.008. LCCN:2002-023955.
Audience: **u,f.**

Literary History, by Form > Poetry > History of Poetry, by Period > 16th C., Elizabethan Era

Corns, Thomas N. (Editor) **PR541 .C36 1993**
The Cambridge Companion to English Poetry, Donne to Marvell. Cloth Text. Cambridge University Press. New York, NY. 1993. 326p. Companions to Literature Ser. ISBN:0-521-41147-5, ISBN13: 978-0-521-41147-9. Dewey:821.309. LCCN:92-044508.
Audience: **u,f.** *Choice, 1994.*

Erskine, John **PR539.L8E8**
Elizabethan Lyric. Trade Cloth. Gordian Press, Inc. Staten Island, NY. 1967. 344p. ISBN:0-87752-031-3, ISBN13: 978-0-87752-031-3. Dewey:821/.04. LCCN:67-021712.
Audience: **l,u.**

Heale, Elizabeth **PR535.S44H43 2003**
Autobiography and Authorship in Renaissance Verse: Chronicles of the Self. Cloth over Boards. Palgrave Macmillan. New York, NY. 2003. 288p. Early Modern Literature in History Ser. ISBN:0-333-77397-7, ISBN13: 978-0-333-77397-0. Dewey:821/.309353. LCCN:2002-032698.
Audience: **u,f.** *Choice, 2003.*

Low, Anthony **PR535.L7 L68 1993**
The Reinvention of Love: Poetry, Politics and Culture from Sidney to Milton. Trade Cloth. Cambridge University Press. New York, NY. 1993. 272p. ISBN:0-521-45030-6, ISBN13: 978-0-521-45030-0. Dewey:821.309354. LCCN:93-018184.
Audience: **u,f.** *Choice, 1994.*

Martz, Louis L. **PR533.M37 1991**
From Renaissance to Baroque: Essays on Literature and Art. Cloth Text. University of Missouri Press. Columbia, MO. 1991. 298p. ISBN:0-8262-0796-0, ISBN13: 978-0-8262-0796-8. Dewey:821/.309. LCCN:91-022889.
Audience: **l,u.** *Choice, 1992.*

May, Steven W. **PR535.C69M3 1999**
The Elizabethan Courtier Poets: The Poems and Their Contexts. Trade Paper. Pegasus Press. Chandler, AZ. 1999. 424p. ISBN:1-889818-05-4, ISBN13: 978-1-889818-05-4. Dewey:821/.309. LCCN:99-024514.
Audience: **l,u.** *Choice, 1991.*

McClung, William A. **PR545.C/**
The Country House in English Renaissance Poetry. Trade Cloth. University of California Press. Berkeley, CA. 1977. 172p. ISBN:0-520-03137-7, ISBN13: 978-0-520-03137-1. Dewey:821/.4/09355. LCCN:75-027928.
Audience: **l,u.**

Pearsall, Derek Albert & Wu, Duncan (Editors) **PR1203.P64 2002**
Poetry from Chaucer to Spenser. Trade Cloth. Blackwell Publishing, Inc. Malden, MA. 2002. 208p. Blackwell Essential Literature Ser. ISBN:0-631-22986-8, ISBN13: 978-0-631-22986-5. Dewey:821.008. LCCN:2002-023955.
Audience: **u,f.**

Phillippy, Patricia B. **PR535.L7P48 1995**
Love's Remedies: Recantation and Renaissance Lyric Poetry. Trade Cloth. Bucknell University Press. Cranbury, NJ. 1995. 261p. ISBN:0-8387-5263-2, ISBN13: 978-0-8387-5263-0. Dewey:821/.0409354. LCCN:94-021457.
Audience: **u,f.** *Choice, 1995.*

Post, Jonathan F. S. (Editor) **PR533 .G74 2002**
Green Thoughts, Green Shades: Essays by Contemporary Poets on the Early Modern Lyric. Trade Cloth. University of California Press. Berkeley, CA. 2002. 316p. ISBN:0-520-21455-2, ISBN13: 978-0-520-21455-2. Dewey:821/.040903. LCCN:2001-048051.
Audience: **l,u,f.** *Choice, 2002.*

Rivers, Isabel **PR535.R4R58 1994**
Classical and Christian Ideas in English Renaissance Poetry: A Student's Guide. Ed. 2. Trade Paper. Routledge. New York, NY. 1994. 248p. ISBN:0-415-10647-8, ISBN13: 978-0-415-10647-4. Dewey:821/.3093. LCCN:94-012710.
Audience: **l.** *Choice, 1995.*

Smith, A. J. **PR539.L7S65 1985**
The Metaphysics of Love: Studies in Renaissance Love Poetry from Dante to Milton. Trade Cloth. Cambridge University Press. New York, NY. 1985. 368p. ISBN:0-521-25908-8, ISBN13: 978-0-521-25908-8. Dewey:809.1/9354. LCCN:84-014945.
Audience: **l,u.** B *Choice, 1986.*

Literary History, by Form > Poetry > History of Poetry, by Period > 17th C.

Bloom, Harold (Introduction by) **PR545.M4J55 1986**
John Donne and the Seventeenth-Century Metaphysical Poets. Trade Cloth. Facts On File, Inc. New York, NY. 1986. 200p. Bloom's Modern Critical Views Ser. ISBN:0-87754-677-0, ISBN13: 978-0-87754-677-1. Dewey:821/.3/09. LCCN:86-004208.
Audience: **l,u.**

Corns, Thomas N. (Editor) **PR541 .C36 1993**
The Cambridge Companion to English Poetry, Donne to Marvell. Cloth Text. Cambridge University Press. New York, NY. 1993. 326p. Companions to Literature Ser. ISBN:0-521-41147-5, ISBN13: 978-0-521-41147-9. Dewey:821.309. LCCN:92-044508.
Audience: **u,f.** *Choice, 1994.*

Ellrodt, Robert **PR545.M4E43 2000**
Seven Metaphysical Poets: A Structural Study of the Unchanging Self. Trade Cloth. Oxford University Press, Inc. New York, NY. 2000. 382p. ISBN:0-19-811738-8, ISBN13: 978-0-19-811738-4. Dewey:821/.309384. LCCN:99-086586.
Audience: **l,u.** *Choice, 2001.*

Post, Jonathan F. S. **PR541.P67 1999**
English Lyric Poetry: The Early Seventeenth Century. Paper over Boards. Routledge. New York, NY. 1999. 352p. ISBN:0-415-02949-X, ISBN13: 978-0-415-02949-0. Dewey:821.040904. LCCN:98-048933.
Audience: **u,f.** *Choice, 2000.*

Post, Jonathan F. S. (Editor) **PR533 .G74 2002**
Green Thoughts, Green Shades: Essays by Contemporary Poets on the Early Modern Lyric. Trade Cloth. University of California Press. Berkeley, CA. 2002. 316p. ISBN:0-520-21455-2, ISBN13: 978-0-520-21455-2. Dewey:821/.040903. LCCN:2001-048051.
Audience: **l,u,f.** *Choice, 2002.*

Reid, David **PR545.M4R45 2000**
The Metaphysical Poets. Trade Cloth. Longman Publishing Group. White Plains, NY. 2001. 296p. Longman Medieval and Renaissance Library ISBN:0-582-29834-2, ISBN13: 978-0-582-29834-7. Dewey:821/.309. LCCN:99-086025.
Audience: **l,u,f.**

Williamson, George **PR541.W54 2001**
Six Metaphysical Poets: A Reader's Guide. Trade Paper. Syracuse University Press. Syracuse, NY. 2001. 274p. Reader's Guide Ser. ISBN:0-8156-0698-2, ISBN13: 978-0-8156-0698-7. Dewey:821/.309384. LCCN:00-053172.
Audience: **l,u.**

Literary History, by Form > Poetry > History of Poetry, by Period > 18th C., Romanticism

Abrams, M. H. **PN751 .A2 1971**
The Mirror and the Lamp: Romantic Theory and the Critical Tradition. Paper Text. Oxford University Press, Inc. New York, NY. 1971. 406p. ISBN:0-19-501471-5, ISBN13: 978-0-19-501471-6. Dewey:801.950941.
Audience: **u,f.**

Abrams, M. H. **PN603 .A3 1973**
Natural Supernaturalism: Tradition and Revolution in Romantic Literature. Trade Paper. W. W. Norton & Company, Inc. New York, NY. 1973. 550p. ISBN:0-393-00609-3, ISBN13: 978-0-393-00609-4. Dewey:809/.9/14. LCCN:73-007855.
Audience: **u,f.**

Baum, Joan **PR575.S53B38 1994**
Mind-Forg'd Manacles: Slavery and the English Romantic Poets. Trade Cloth. Shoe String Press, Inc. North Haven, CT. 1994. xiv, 253p. ISBN:0-208-02187-6, ISBN13: 978-0-208-02187-8. Dewey:821/.709353. LCCN:93-045722.
Audience: **u,f.** *Choice, 1994.*

Bloom, Harold (Editor) **PR590.E48 2004**
English Romantic Poetry. Trade Paper. Facts On File, Inc. New York, NY. 2004. 350p. Bloom's Period Studies Ser. ISBN:0-7910-7983-X, ISBN13: 978-0-7910-7983-6. Dewey:821/.7/09.
Audience: **l,u.**

Bloom, Harold **PR590.B39 1971**
The Visionary Company; a Reading of English Romantic Poetry. Trade Cloth. Cornell University Press. Ithaca, NY. 1971. xxv, 477p. ISBN:0-8014-0622-6, ISBN13: 978-0-8014-0622-5. Dewey:821/.7/09. LCCN:73-144032.
Audience: **l,u.**

Butler, Marilyn **PR457**
Romantics, Rebels and Reactionaries: English Literature and Its Background, 1760-1830. Paper Text. Oxford University Press, Inc. New York, NY. 1985. 220p. Opus Ser. ISBN:0-19-289132-4, ISBN13: 978-0-19-289132-7. Dewey:820.9/145. LCCN:80-042404.
Audience: **u,f.**

Fairer, David **PR561**
English Poetry of the Eighteenth Century, 1700-1789. Trade Paper. Longman Publishing. Boston, MA. 2003. 320p. ISBN:0-582-22777-1, ISBN13: 978-0-582-22777-4. Dewey:821.5/09.
Audience: **l,u.**

Gerrard, Christine (Editor) **PR553.C66 2006**
A Companion to Eighteenth-Century Poetry. Trade Cloth. Blackwell Publishing, Inc. Malden, MA. 2006. 624p. Blackwell Companions to Literature and Culture Ser., Vol. 42 ISBN:1-4051-1316-2, ISBN13: 978-1-4051-1316-8. Dewey:821/.509. LCCN:2005-034701.
Audience: **u,f.**

Heath, Duncan, et al. **B836.5**
Introducing Romanticism. Judy Boreham & Richard Appignanesi (Authors). Trade Paper. Totem Books. Cambridge, 2006. 176p. ISBN:1-84046-671-5, ISBN13: 978-1-84046-671-3. Dewey:141.6.
Audience: **g,l,u,f.**

Jordan, Frank (Editor) **PR590 .J6**
The English Romantic Poets. Ed. 4. Trade Cloth. Modern Language Association of America. New York, NY. 1985. 750p. ISBN:0-317-34914-7, ISBN13: 978-0-317-34914-6. Dewey:016.821/7/09.
Audience: **l,u,f.**

McGann, Jerome J. **PR590**
The Romantic Ideology: A Critical Investigation. Trade Paper. University of Chicago Press. Chicago, IL. 1985. 184p. ISBN:0-226-55850-9, ISBN13: 978-0-226-55850-9. Dewey:821/.7/09145. LCCN:82-017494.
Audience: **u,f.**

McGann, Jerome J. **PR4392.R63 .M37 2002**
Byron and Romanticism. James Soderholm (Editor), Marilyn Butler & James Chandler (Contribution by). Cloth Text. Cambridge University Press. New York, NY. 2002. 326p. Cambridge Studies in Romanticism, Vol. 50 ISBN:0-521-80958-4, ISBN13: 978-0-521-80958-0. Dewey:821/.7. LCCN:2001-052891.
Audience: **u,f.**

Roe, Nicholas **PR457.R4575 2005**
Romanticism: An Oxford Guide. Paper Text. Oxford University Press, Inc. New York, NY. 2005. 776p. ISBN:0-19-925840-6, ISBN13: 978-0-19-925840-6. Dewey:820.9/145. LCCN:2004-025235.
Audience: **g,l,u,f.**

Stevens, David **PR468.R65**
Romanticism. Adrian Barlow (Contribution by). Trade Paper. Cambridge University Press. New York, NY. 2004. 128p. Cambridge Contexts in Literature Ser. ISBN:0-521-75372-4, ISBN13: 978-0-521-75372-2. Dewey:820.9/007.
Audience: **g,l.**

Literary History, by Form > Poetry > History of Poetry, by Period > 19th-20th C.

Armstrong, Isobel **PR595.H5 A76 1993**
Victorian Poetry: Poetry, Poetics, Politics. Paper over Boards. Routledge. New York, NY. 1993. 560p. Critical History of Victorian Poetry Ser. ISBN:0-415-03016-1, ISBN13: 978-0-415-03016-8. Dewey:821.809. LCCN:92-002451.
Audience: **u,f.**

Armstrong, Isobel & Blain, Virginia (Editors) **PR585.W6W66 1999**
Women's Poetry, Late Romantic to Late Victorian: Gender and Genre, 1830-1900. Cloth over Boards. Palgrave Macmillan. New York, NY. 1999. 428p. ISBN:0-312-21536-3, ISBN13: 978-0-312-21536-1. Dewey:821.8/09/9287. LCCN:98-003709.
Audience: **u,f.** *Choice, 1999.*

Bradshaw, David (Editor) **PR478.M6C66 2003**
A Concise Companion to Modernism. Trade Cloth. Blackwell Publishing, Inc. Malden, MA. 2002. 304p. Blackwell Concise Companions to Literature and Culture Ser. ISBN:0-631-22054-2, ISBN13: 978-0-631-22054-1. Dewey:820.9/112. LCCN:2002-066419.
Audience: **u,f.**

Bristow, Joseph (Editor) **PR591 .C36 2000**
The Cambridge Companion to Victorian Poetry. Cloth Text. Cambridge University Press. New York, NY. 2000. 353p. Companions to Literature Ser. ISBN:0-521-64115-2, ISBN13: 978-0-521-64115-9. Dewey:821/.809. LCCN:00-020013.
Audience: **l,u,f.** *Choice, 2001.*

Bristow, Joseph **PR592 .V527 1987**
The Victorian Poet: Poetics and Persona. Trade Cloth. Croom Helm, Ltd. London, 1987. 256p. World and Word Ser. ISBN:0-7099-3925-6, ISBN13: 978-0-7099-3925-2. Dewey:821/.8/09. LCCN:87-023720.
Audience: **u,f.**

Butler, Marilyn **PR457**
Romantics, Rebels and Reactionaries: English Literature and Its Background, 1760-1830. Paper Text. Oxford University Press, Inc. New York, NY. 1985. 220p. Opus Ser. ISBN:0-19-289132-4, ISBN13: 978-0-19-289132-7. Dewey:820.9/145. LCCN:80-042404.
Audience: **u,f.**

Campbell, Matthew **PR595.W45 C36 1999**
Rhythm and Will in Victorian Poetry. Gillian Beer (Contribution by). Trade Paper. Cambridge University Press. New York, NY. 2004. 288p. Cambridge Studies in Nineteenth-Century Literature and Culture Ser., Vol. 22 ISBN:0-521-60422-2, ISBN13: 978-0-521-60422-2. Dewey:821.809384.
Audience: **u,f.** *Choice, 2000.*

Chapman, Alison (Editor), et al. **PR591.C66 2002**
A Companion to Victorian Poetry. Richard Cronin & Anthony Harrison (Editors). Trade Cloth. Blackwell Publishing, Inc. Malden, MA. 2002. 632p. Blackwell Companions to Literature and Culture Ser., Vol. 15 ISBN:0-631-22207-3, ISBN13: 978-0-631-22207-1. Dewey:821/.809. LCCN:2001-004354.
Audience: **l,u,f.** *Choice, 2003.*

Draper, R. P. **PR601.D67 1999**
An Introduction to Twentieth-Century Poetry in English. Trade Paper. Palgrave Macmillan. New York, NY. 1999. 320p. ISBN:0-312-21981-4, ISBN13: 978-0-312-21981-9. Dewey:821. LCCN:98-038114.
Audience: **l,u.** *Choice, 1999.*

Hamilton, Ian (Editor) **PR601.O9 1994**
The Oxford Companion to Twentieth-Century Poetry in English. Trade Cloth. Oxford University Press, Inc. New York, NY. 1994. 618p. ISBN:0-19-866147-9, ISBN13: 978-0-19-866147-4. Dewey:821.9/1/09. LCCN:93-001436.
Audience: **u,f.** *Choice, 1994.*

Harrison, Antony H. **PR595.H5H37 1998**
Victorian Poets and the Politics of Culture: Discourse and Ideology. Trade Cloth. University Press of Virginia. Charlottesville, VA. 1998. 192p. Victorian Literature and Culture Ser. ISBN:0-8139-1818-9, ISBN13: 978-0-8139-1818-1. Dewey:821/.809358. LCCN:98-014577.
Audience: **u,f.** *Choice, 1999.*

Johnson, Edward D. **PR593 .J6**
Alien Vision of Victorian Poetry: Sources of the Poetic Imagination in Tennyson, Browning and Arnold. Trade Cloth. Shoe String Press, Inc. North Haven, CT. 1963. ISBN:0-208-00090-9, ISBN13: 978-0-208-00090-3. Dewey:821.809.
Audience: **u,f.**

Persoon, James **PR610.P43 1999**
Modern British Poetry, 1900-1939. Trade Cloth. Thomson Gale. Farmington Hills, MI. 1999. xvi, 207p. Twayne's Critical History of Poetry Ser. ISBN:0-8057-1681-5, ISBN13: 978-0-8057-1681-8. Dewey:821/.91209. LCCN:99-029212.
Audience: **l,u.** *Choice, 2000.*

Powell, John (Editor), et al. **Z1039**
Biographical Dictionary of Literary Influences: The Nineteenth Century, 1800-1914. Derek W. Blakeley & Tessa Powell (Editors). Cloth Text. Greenwood Publishing Group, Inc. Portsmouth, NH. 2000. 536p. ISBN:0-313-30422-X, ISBN13: 978-0-313-30422-4. Dewey:028/.9/09034. LCCN:99-462057.
Audience: **g,l,u,f.** *Choice, 2001.*

Roberts, Neil (Editor) **PR601**
A Companion to 20th-Century Poetry. Trade Paper. Blackwell Publishing, Inc. Malden, MA. 2003. 648p. ISBN:1-4051-1361-8, ISBN13: 978-1-4051-1361-8. Dewey:821.9/1/09.
Audience: **l,u.**

Rosenberg, John D. **PR599.E45 R67 2005**
Elegy for an Age: The Presence of the Past in Victorian Literature. Trade Cloth. Wimbledon Publishing Company. London, 2005. 292p. Anthem Nineteenth Century Studies ISBN:1-84331-156-9, ISBN13: 978-1-84331-156-0. Dewey:821/.04. LCCN:2005-482247.
Audience: **l,u.** *Choice, 2006.*

Williams, Raymond **NX465.5**
The Politics of Modernism: Against the New Conformists. Trade Cloth. Verso Books. London, 1996. 224p. Classics Ser. ISBN:1-85984-161-9, ISBN13: 978-1-85984-161-7. Dewey:700.1.
Audience: **u,f.**

Literary History, by Form > Drama

Evans, Benjamin I. **PR625 .E8 1978**
A Short History of English Drama. Trade Cloth. Greenwood Publishing Group, Inc. Portsmouth, NH. 1978. 146p. ISBN:0-8371-9072-X, ISBN13: 978-0-8371-9072-3. Dewey:822/.009. LCCN:77-027446.
Audience: **l,u.**

Leech, Clifford (Editor), et al. **PR625.R44 1996**
The Revels History of Drama. T. W. Craik & Lois Potter (Editors). Children's Board Books. Routledge. New York, NY. 1997. 3342p. ISBN:0-415-14379-9, ISBN13: 978-0-415-14379-0. Dewey:822.009. LCCN:97-224912.
Audience: **l,u,f.**

Nicoll, Allardyce **PN2581**
English Theatre: A Short History. Trade Cloth. Greenwood Publishing Group, Inc. Portsmouth, NH. 1971. 252p. ISBN:0-8371-3133-2, ISBN13: 978-0-8371-3133-7. Dewey:792/.09421. LCCN:75-098861.
Audience: **u.**

Shepherd, Simon & Womack, Peter **PR625.S54 1996**
English Drama: A Cultural History. Trade Paper. Blackwell Publishing, Inc. Malden, MA. 1996. 424p. ISBN:0-631-19938-1, ISBN13: 978-0-631-19938-0. Dewey:822/.009. LCCN:95-032852.
Audience: **u,f.** *Choice, 1996.*

Trussler, Simon **PN2581.T78 1994**
The Cambridge Illustrated History of British Theatre. Trade Paper. Cambridge University Press. New York, NY. 2000. 416p. Illustrated Histories Ser. ISBN:0-521-79430-7, ISBN13: 978-0-521-79430-5. Dewey:792/.0941.
Audience: **g,l,u,f.** *Choice, 1995.*

Literary History, by Form > Drama > By Period > Medieval

Cox, John D. & Kastan, David S. **PR641.N49 1997**
A New History of Early English Drama. Cloth Text. Columbia University Press. New York, NY. 1997. 580p. ISBN:0-231-10242-9, ISBN13: 978-0-231-10242-1. Dewey:822/.009. LCCN:96-029670.
Audience: **l,u,f.** *Choice, 1997.*

Gibson, Gail M. **PR644.E28G53 1989**
The Theater of Devotion: East Anglican Drama and Society in the Late Middle Ages. Trade Cloth. University of Chicago Press. Chicago, IL. 1996. 268p. ISBN:0-226-29101-4, ISBN13: 978-0-226-29101-7. Dewey:822/.0516/0901. LCCN:89-004741.
Audience: **u,f.** *Choice, 1990.*

Harty, Kevin J. (Editor) **PR644.C4 C47 1993**
The Chester Mystery Cycle: A Casebook. Cloth Text. Garland Publishing, Inc. New York, NY. 1992. 344p. Medieval Casebooks Ser., Vol. 6 ISBN:0-8153-0497-8, ISBN13: 978-0-8153-0497-5. Dewey:822.051609. LCCN:92-036513.
Audience: **l,u.**

Kershaw, Baz & Milling, Jane (Editors) **PN2581.C36 2004**
The Cambridge History of British Theatre: Origins to 1660. Peter Thomson (Editor, Contribution by). Trade Cloth. Cambridge University Press. New York, NY. 2004. 570p. Cambridge History of British Theatre Ser. ISBN:0-521-65040-2, ISBN13: 978-0-521-65040-3. Dewey:792/.0941. LCCN:2003-055890.
Audience: **u,f.**

Robinson, J. W. **PR644.W3.R63 1991**
Studies in Fifteenth-Century Stagecraft. Trade Cloth, Box or Slipcased. Medieval Institute Publications. Kalamazoo, MI. 1990. xiv + 262p. Early Drama, Art and Music Monograph Ser., No. 14 ISBN:0-918720-38-9, ISBN13: 978-0-918720-38-2. Dewey:822.1. LCCN:92-223158.
Audience: **u,f.** *Choice, 1991.*

Travis, Peter W. **PR644.C4**
Dramatic Design in the Chester Cycle. Paper Text. University of Chicago Press. Chicago, IL. 1996. 328p. Chicago Original Paperback Ser. ISBN:0-226-81164-6, ISBN13: 978-0-226-81164-2. Dewey:822/.0516. LCCN:81-013047.
Audience: **u,f.**

Wilson, F. P. **PR641.W58 1969**
The English Drama, 1485-1585. Trade Cloth. Oxford University Press, Inc. New York, NY. 1969. [7], 244p. ISBN:0-19-812209-8, ISBN13: 978-0-19-812209-8. Dewey:822/.2/09. LCCN:70-386045.
Audience: **l,u,f.**

Literary History, by Form > Drama > By Period > 16th C., Elizabethan Era

Bradbrook, Muriel C. **PR651**
Themes and Conventions of Elizabethan Tragedy. Ed. 2. Trade Paper. Cambridge University Press. New York, NY. 1980. 280p. ISBN:0-521-29695-1, ISBN13: 978-0-521-29695-3. Dewey:822/.3/09.
Audience: **u,f.**

Braunmuller, A. R. & Hattaway, Michael (Editors) **PR651.C36 2003**
The Cambridge Companion to English Renaissance Drama. Ed. 2. Cloth Text. Cambridge University Press. New York, NY. 2003. 484p. Cambridge Companions to Literature Ser. ISBN:0-521-82115-0, ISBN13: 978-0-521-82115-5. Dewey:822/.309. LCCN:2002-035073.
Audience: **g,l,u,f.** *Choice, 2004, 1991.*

Dillon, Janette **PR658.S47 D55 2000**
Theatre, Court and City, 1595-1610: Drama and Social Space in London. Trade Paper. Cambridge University Press. New York, NY. 2006. 197p. ISBN:0-521-02990-2, ISBN13: 978-0-521-02990-2. Dewey:822/.30932421.
Audience: **u,f.** *Choice, 2000.*

Goodman, Jennifer R. **PR651.G66 1990**
British Drama Beginnings to Sixteen Hundred Sixty. Trade Cloth. Thomson Gale. Farmington Hills, MI. 1990. 264p.

Twayne's Critical History of British Drama Ser. ISBN:0-8057-8953-7, ISBN13: 978-0-8057-8953-9. Dewey:822.009. LCCN:90-041056.
Audience: **l,u.** *Choice, 1991.*

Hamlin, William M. **PR658.T7H35 2005**
Tragedy and Scepticism in Shakespeare's England. Trade Cloth. Palgrave Macmillan. New York, NY. 2005. 304p. Early Modern Literature in History Ser. ISBN:1-4039-4598-5, ISBN13: 978-1-4039-4598-3. Dewey:822/.05120903. LCCN:2004-062851.
Audience: **u,f.** *Choice, 2006.*

Hopkins, Lisa **PR658.W6H66 2002**
The Female Hero in English Renaissance Tragedy. Cloth over Boards. Palgrave Macmillan. New York, NY. 2002. 248p. ISBN:0-333-98791-8, ISBN13: 978-0-333-98791-9. Dewey:822/.051209352042. LCCN:2002-072344.
Audience: **u,f.** *Choice, 2003.*

Kershaw, Baz & Milling, Jane (Editors) **PN2581.C36 2004**
The Cambridge History of British Theatre: Origins to 1660. Peter Thomson (Editor, Contribution by). Trade Cloth. Cambridge University Press. New York, NY. 2004. 570p. Cambridge History of British Theatre Ser. ISBN:0-521-65040-2, ISBN13: 978-0-521-65040-3. Dewey:792/.0941. LCCN:2003-055890.
Audience: **u,f.**

Knapp, Jeffrey **PR658.R43K58 2004**
Shakespeare's Tribe: Church, Nation, and Theater in Renaissance England. Trade Paper. University of Chicago Press. Chicago, IL. 2004. 277p. ISBN:0-226-44570-4, ISBN13: 978-0-226-44570-0. Dewey:820.9/358.
Audience: **u,f.** *Choice, 2003.*

Mousley, Andy **PR651.M83 2000**
Renaissance Drama and Contemporary Literary Theory. Trade Paper. Palgrave Macmillan. New York, NY. 2000. 252p. ISBN:0-312-23174-1, ISBN13: 978-0-312-23174-3. Dewey:822/.309. LCCN:99-056334.
Audience: **u,f.** *Choice, 2000.*

Neill, Michael **PR658.P65N45 2000**
Putting History to the Question: Power, Politics and Society in English Renaissance Drama. Trade Cloth. Columbia University Press. New York, NY. 2000. 464p. ISBN:0-231-11332-3, ISBN13: 978-0-231-11332-8. Dewey:822/.309358. LCCN:99-029886.
Audience: **l,u,f.** *Choice, 2001.*

Nicoll, Allardyce (Editor) **PR2900**
Elizabethan Theatre. Jonathan Bate, Margreta De Grazia, Michael Dobson, Inga-Stina Ewbank, R. A. Foakes, Andrew Gurr, Lena Cowen Orlin, Terence Hawkes, John Jowett & A. D. Nuttall (Contribution by). Trade Paper. Cambridge University Press. New York, NY. 2002. 182p. Shakespeare Survey Ser., Vol. 12 ISBN:0-521-52348-6, ISBN13: 978-0-521-52348-6. Dewey:822.3/3.
Audience: **u,f.**

Pinciss, G. M. **PR658.R43P56 2000**
Forbidden Matter: Religion in the Drama of Shakespeare and His Contemporaries. Trade Cloth. University of Delaware Press. Newark, DE. 2000. 144p. ISBN:0-87413-706-3, ISBN13: 978-0-87413-706-4. Dewey:822/.3093823. LCCN:99-038700.
Audience: **u,f.** *Choice, 2000.*

Sullivan, Garrett A., et al. **PR653.E17 2006**
Early Modern English Drama: A Critical Companion. Patrick Gerard Cheney & Andrew Hadfield (Authors). Trade Paper. Oxford University Press, Inc. New York, NY. 2005. 351p. ISBN:0-19-515386-3, ISBN13: 978-0-19-515386-6. Dewey:822/.309. LCCN:2004-066273.
Audience: **g,l,u,f.**

Wells, Henry W. **PR651 .W4 1975**
Elizabethan and Jacobean Playwrights. Trade Cloth. Greenwood Publishing Group, Inc. Portsmouth, NH. 1975. 327p. ISBN:0-8371-7777-4, ISBN13: 978-0-8371-7777-9. Dewey:822/.009. LCCN:74-012953.
Audience: **l,u.**

Wilson, Wilson & Dutton, Richard **PR654.N49 1992**
New Historicism and Renaissance Drama: Longman Critical Readers. Ed. 1. Paper Text. Longman Publishing Group. White Plains, NY. 1992. 249p. ISBN:0-582-04554-1, ISBN13: 978-0-582-04554-5. Dewey:822/.309. LCCN:91-023851.
Audience: **l,u,f.**

Literary History, by Form > Drama > By Period > 17th C.

Dobree, Bonamy **PR698.C6 D6 1981**
Restoration Comedy, 1660-1720. Trade Cloth. Greenwood Publishing Group, Inc. Portsmouth, NH. 1981. 182p. ISBN:0-313-22722-5, ISBN13: 978-0-313-22722-6. Dewey:822/.0523/09. LCCN:81-001230.
Audience: **l,u.**

Donohue, Joseph (Editor) **PN2581.C36 2004**
The Cambridge History of British Theatre, 1660-1895. Peter Thomson (Contribution by). Trade Cloth. Cambridge University Press. New York, NY. 2004. 572p. Cambridge History of British Theatre Ser., Vol. 2 ISBN:0-521-65068-2, ISBN13: 978-0-521-65068-7. Dewey:792/.0941. LCCN:2003-055890.
Audience: **u,f.**

Fisk, Deborah Payne (Editor) **PR691 .C35 2000**
The Cambridge Companion to English Restoration Theatre. Trade Paper. Cambridge University Press. New York, NY. 2000. 322p. Companions to Literature Ser. ISBN:0-521-58812-X, ISBN13: 978-0-521-58812-6. Dewey:822/.409. LCCN:99-015230.
Audience: **l,u,f.** *Choice, 2001.*

Harwood, John T. **PR698.C6.H3 1982**
Critics, Values, and Restoration Comedy. Trade Cloth. Southern Illinois University Press. Carbondale, IL. 1982. 196p. ISBN:0-8093-1049-X, ISBN13: 978-0-8093-1049-4. Dewey:822/.0523. LCCN:81-018397.
Audience: **l,u.**

Hughes, Derek **PR691.H75 1996**
English Drama, 1660-1700. Trade Cloth. Oxford University Press, Inc. New York, NY. 1996. 512p. ISBN:0-19-811974-7, ISBN13: 978-0-19-811974-6. Dewey:822/.409. LCCN:95-040292.
Audience: **l,u,f.** *Choice, 1997.*

Hume, Robert D. **PR691.H8**
The Development of English Drama in the Late Seventeenth Century. Trade Cloth. Oxford University Press, Inc. New York, NY. 1976. 546p. ISBN:0-19-812063-X, ISBN13: 978-0-19-812063-6. Dewey:822/.4/09. LCCN:76-365768.
Audience: **u,f.** B

Kershaw, Baz & Milling, Jane (Editors) **PN2581.C36 2004**
The Cambridge History of British Theatre: Origins to 1660. Peter Thomson (Editor, Contribution by). Trade Cloth. Cambridge University Press. New York, NY. 2004. 570p. Cambridge History of British Theatre Ser. ISBN:0-521-65040-2, ISBN13: 978-0-521-65040-3. Dewey:792/.0941. LCCN:2003-055890.
Audience: **u,f.**

Lowenthal, Cynthia **PR698.I33L69 2002**
Performing Identities on the Restoration Stage. Trade Cloth. Southern Illinois University Press. Carbondale, IL. 2002. 272p. ISBN:0-8093-2462-8, ISBN13: 978-0-8093-2462-0. Dewey:822/.409353. LCCN:2002-021677.
Audience: **u,f.** *Choice, 2003.*

Milhous, Judith & Hume, Robert D. (Editors) **PR691.M55 1985**
Producible Interpretation: Eight English Plays, 1675-1707. Cloth Text. Southern Illinois University Press. Carbondale, IL. 1985. 352p. ISBN:0-8093-1167-4, ISBN13: 978-0-8093-1167-5. Dewey:822.4/09. LCCN:84-005634.
Audience: **u,f.** B

Orr, Bridget **PR698.I45 O75 2001**
Empire on the English Stage 1660-1714. Trade Cloth. Cambridge University Press. New York, NY. 2001. 360p. ISBN:0-521-77350-4, ISBN13: 978-0-521-77350-8. Dewey:822/.409358. LCCN:00-065091.
Audience: **u,f.** *Choice, 2002.*

Owen, Sue **PR691.C66 2001**
A Companion to Restoration Drama. Susan J. Owen (Editor). Trade Cloth. Blackwell Publishing, Inc. Malden, MA. 2001. 472p. Companions to Literature and Culture Ser., Vol. 12 ISBN:0-631-21923-4, ISBN13: 978-0-631-21923-1. Dewey:822/.409. LCCN:2001-025987.
Audience: **l,u,f.** *Choice, 2002.*

Waith, Eugene M. **PR691.W3 1971**
Ideas of Greatness; Heroic Drama in England. Trade Cloth. Barnes & Noble, Inc. New York, NY. 1971. xii, 292p. ISBN:0-389-04181-5, ISBN13: 978-0-389-04181-8. Dewey:822/.0080353. LCCN:79-030481.
Audience: **l,u.** B

Literary History, by Form > Drama > By Period > 18th C.,

Anderson, Misty G. **PR708.W6A53 2002**
Female Playwrights and Eighteenth-Century Comedy: Negotiating Marriage on the London Stage. Cloth over Boards. Palgrave Macmillan. New York, NY. 2002. 272p. ISBN:0-312-23938-6, ISBN13: 978-0-312-23938-1. Dewey:822/.0523099287. LCCN:2001-036573.
Audience: **u,f.** *Choice, 2002.*

Bernbaum, Ernest **PR711**
The Drama of Sensibility: A Sketch of the History of English Comedy and Domestic Tragedy. Trade Cloth. Peter Smith Publisher, Inc. Magnolia, MA. 1990. ISBN:0-8446-1074-7, ISBN13: 978-0-8446-1074-0. Dewey:822.509.
Audience: **l,u.**

Bevis, Richard W. **PR708.C6.B4 1980**
The Laughing Tradition: Stage Comedy in Garrick's Day. Trade Cloth. University of Georgia Press. Athens, GA. 1980. 292p. ISBN:0-8203-0514-6, ISBN13: 978-0-8203-0514-1. Dewey:822/.6/09. LCCN:79-048001.
Audience: **l,u.** B

Boas, Frederick S. **PR701 .B6 1978**
An Introduction to Eighteenth Century Drama, 1700-1780. Library Binding. Greenwood Publishing Group, Inc. Portsmouth, NH. 1978. ISBN:0-313-20193-5, ISBN13: 978-0-313-20193-6. Dewey:822/.5/09. LCCN:77-027612.
Audience: **l,u.** B

Donohue, Joseph (Editor) **PN2581.C36 2004**
The Cambridge History of British Theatre, 1660-1895. Peter Thomson (Contribution by). Trade Cloth. Cambridge University Press. New York, NY. 2004. 572p. Cambridge History of British Theatre Ser., Vol. 2 ISBN:0-521-65068-2, ISBN13: 978 0 521-65068-7. Dewey:792/.0941. LCCN:2003-055890.
Audience: **u,f.**

Hume, Robert D. **PR708.C6.H8 1983**
The Rakish Stage: Studies in English Drama, 1660-1800. Trade Cloth. Southern Illinois University Press. Carbondale, IL. 1983. 382p. ISBN:0-8093-1100-3, ISBN13: 978-0-8093-1100-2. Dewey:822/.009. LCCN:82-016984.
Audience: **l,u.** B

Kavenik, Frances M. **PR708**
British Drama, 1660-1779: A Critical History. Trade Cloth. Thomson Gale. Farmington Hills, MI. 1995. 282p. Twayne's Critical History of British Drama Ser. ISBN:0-8057-4533-5, ISBN13: 978-0-8057-4533-7. Dewey:842/.91409. LCCN:94-026538.
Audience: **l,u,f.** *Choice, 1995.*

Loftis, John **PR714.C6.L6 1979**
Comedy and Society from Congreve to Fielding. Trade Cloth. A M S Press, Inc. New York, NY. 1979. ix, 154 p. :p. Stanford University, Stanford Studies in Language and Literature, 19 ISBN:0-404-51829-X, ISBN13: 978-0-404-51829-5. Dewey:822/.052. LCCN:76-051940.
Audience: **l,u.**

Literary History, by Form > Drama > By Period > 19th-20th C.

Abbott, Anthony S. **PN1861**
The Vital Lie: Reality and Illusion in Modern Drama. Trade Paper. University of Alabama Press. Tuscaloosa, AL. 2003. 256p. ISBN:0-8173-1202-1, ISBN13: 978-0-8173-1202-2. Dewey:809.2/04.
Audience: **u,f.** *Choice, 1989.*

Berney, Kate & Templeton, N. G. (Editors) **PR736.C577 1994**
Contemporary British Dramatists. Michael Billington (Introduction by). Trade Cloth. Thomson Gale. Farmington Hills, MI. 1994. 768p. Contemporary Literature Ser. ISBN:1-55862-213-6, ISBN13: 978-1-55862-213-5. Dewey:822/.9109 B. LCCN:94-013899.
Audience: **l,u.**

Booth, Michael Richard **PN2594 .B58 1991**
Theatre in the Victorian Age. Trade Paper. Cambridge University Press. New York, NY. 1991. 238p. ISBN:0-521-34837-4, ISBN13: 978-0-521-34837-9. Dewey:792/.0941/09034. LCCN:90-021003.
Audience: **g,l,u,f.** *Choice, 1992.*

Booth, Michael R. & Kaplan, Joel H. (Editors) **PN2595 .E35 1996**
The Edwardian Theatre: Essays on Performance and the Stage. Trade Cloth. Cambridge University Press. New York, NY. 1996. 256p. ISBN:0-521-45375-5, ISBN13: 978-0-521-45375-2. Dewey:792/.09041. LCCN:97-006260.
Audience: **u,f.**

Buse, Peter **PR736.B88 2001**
Drama + Theory: Critical Approaches to Modern British Drama. Cloth over Boards. Manchester University Press. Manchester, 2002. 224p. ISBN:0-7190-5721-3, ISBN13: 978-0-7190-5721-2. Dewey:822/.91409. LCCN:2001-044923.
Audience: **g,l,u,f.** *Choice, 2002.*

Dietrich, Richard **PR721.D54 1989**
British Drama, Eighteen Ninety to Nineteen Fifty. Trade Cloth. Thomson Gale. Farmington Hills, MI. 1989. 330p. Critical History of British Drama Ser. ISBN:0-8057-8951-0, ISBN13: 978-0-8057-8951-5. Dewey:822/.912/09. LCCN:88-037964.
Audience: **l,u,f.** *Choice, 1989.*

Donohue, Joseph (Editor) **PN2581.C36 2004**
The Cambridge History of British Theatre, 1660-1895. Peter Thomson (Contribution by). Trade Cloth. Cambridge University Press. New York, NY. 2004. 572p. Cambridge History of British Theatre Ser., Vol. 2 ISBN:0-521-65068-2, ISBN13: 978-0-521-65068-7. Dewey:792/.0941. LCCN:2003-055890.
Audience: **u,f.**

Hays, Michael & Nikolopoulou, Anastasia (Editors) **PN1922**
Melodrama: The Cultural Emergence of a Genre. Trade Paper. Palgrave Macmillan. New York, NY. 1999. 304p. ISBN:0-312-22127-4, ISBN13: 978-0-312-22127-0. Dewey:809.2/52.
Audience: **u,f.** *Choice, 1997.*

Innes, Christopher **PR736.I53 2002**
Modern British Drama: The Twentieth Century. Ed. 2. Cloth Text. Cambridge University Press. New York, NY. 2002. 600p. ISBN:0-521-81651-3, ISBN13: 978-0-521-81651-9. Dewey:822/.9109. LCCN:2002-071567.
Audience: **l,u,f.** *Choice, 2003.*

Innes, Christopher **PN1851.S56 2000**
A Sourcebook on Naturalist Theatre. Trade Paper. Routledge. New York, NY. 2000. 272p. ISBN:0-415-15229-1, ISBN13: 978-0-415-15229-7. Dewey:809.2/912. LCCN:99-039133.
Audience: **u,f.** *Choice, 2001.*

Jenkins, Anthony **PR734.S5 J46 1991**
The Making of Victorian Drama. Trade Cloth. Cambridge University Press. New York, NY. 1991. 311p. ISBN:0-521-40205-0, ISBN13: 978-0-521-40205-7. Dewey:822/.809355. LCCN:90-002687.
Audience: **u,f.** *Choice, 1992.*

Kerensky, Oleg **PR736.K4 1979**
The New British Drama: 14 Playwrights since Osborne and Pinter. Trade Cloth. Taplinger Publishing Company, Inc. Marlboro, NJ. 1979. xx, 276 p. ;p. ISBN:0-8008-5499-3, ISBN13: 978-0-8008-5499-7. Dewey:822/.9/1409. LCCN:78-056986.
Audience: **l,u.** B

Kershaw, Baz (Editor) **PN2581.C36 2004**
The Cambridge History of British Theatre: Since 1895. Peter Thomson (Contribution by). Trade Cloth. Cambridge University Press. New York, NY. 2004. 596p. Cambridge History of British Theatre Ser., Vol. 3 ISBN:0-521-65132-8, ISBN13: 978-0-521-65132-5. Dewey:792/.0941. LCCN:2003-055890.
Audience: **u,f.**

King, Kimball **PR736.M56 2001**
Modern Dramatists: A Casebook of the Major British and American Playwrights. Cloth Text. Garland Publishing, Inc. New York, NY. 2001. 325p. Studies in Modern Drama, Vol. 14 ISBN:0-8153-2349-2, ISBN13: 978-0-8153-2349-5. Dewey:822/.9109. LCCN:00-065297.
Audience: **l,u,f.**

Nicoll, Allardyce **PR736**
English Drama: The Beginnings of the Modern Period, 1900-1930. Trade Cloth. Cambridge University Press. New York, NY. 1973. 1093p. ISBN:0-521-08416-4, ISBN13: 978-0-521-08416-1. Dewey:822/.9/1209. LCCN:70-171679.
Audience: **l,u.**

Powell, John (Editor), et al. **Z1039**
Biographical Dictionary of Literary Influences: The Nineteenth Century, 1800-1914. Derek W. Blakeley & Tessa Powell (Editors). Cloth Text. Greenwood Publishing Group, Inc. Portsmouth, NH. 2000. 536p. ISBN:0-313-30422-X, ISBN13: 978-0-313-30422-4. Dewey:028/.9/09034. LCCN:99-462057.
Audience: **g,l,u,f.** *Choice, 2001.*

Powell, Kerry (Editor) **PN2594**
The Cambridge Companion to Victorian and Edwardian Theatre. Trade Paper. Cambridge University Press. New York, NY. 2004. 308p. Cambridge Companions to Literature Ser. ISBN:0-521-79536-2, ISBN13: 978-0-521-79536-4. Dewey:792/.0942/09034. LCCN:2002-041552.
Audience: **u,f.** *Choice, 2004.*

Powell, Kerry (Editor) **PN2594**
The Cambridge Companion to Victorian and Edwardian Theatre. Trade Cloth. Cambridge University Press. New York, NY. 2004. 308p. Cambridge Companions to Literature Ser. ISBN:0-521-79157-X, ISBN13: 978-0-521-79157-1. Dewey:792/.0942/09034. LCCN:2002-041552.
Audience: **g,l,u,f.** *Choice, 2004.*

Puchner, Martin **PN1851.P83 2002**
Stage Fright: Modernism, Anti-Theatricality, and Drama. Trade Cloth. Johns Hopkins University Press. Baltimore, MD. 2002. 248p. ISBN:0-8018-6855-6, ISBN13: 978-0-8018-6855-9. Dewey:809.2/9112/0904. LCCN:2001-006622.
Audience: **u,f.** *Choice, 2003.*

Rebellato, Dan **PR736.R35 1999**
1956 and All That: The Making of Modern British Drama. Paper over Boards. Routledge. New York, NY. 1999. 280p. ISBN:0-415-18938-1, ISBN13: 978-0-415-18938-5. Dewey:822/.91409353. LCCN:98-029159.
Audience: **l,u,f.** *Choice, 1999.*

Rusinko, Susan **PR736.R87 1989**
British Drama, 1950 to Present. Trade Cloth. Thomson Gale. Farmington Hills, MI. 1989. 285p. Twayne's Critical History of British Drama Ser. ISBN:0-8057-8952-9, ISBN13: 978-0-8057-8952-2. Dewey:822/.914/09. LCCN:88-037951.
Audience: **l,u.** *Choice, 1989.*

Schoch, Richard W. **PR2880.A1 S32 2002**
Not Shakespeare: Bardolatry and Burlesque in the Nineteenth Century. Trade Cloth. Cambridge University Press. New York, NY. 2002. 224p. ISBN:0-521-80015-3, ISBN13: 978-0-521-80015-0. Dewey:822/.809. LCCN:2001-037924.
Audience: **u,f.** *Choice, 2002.*

Sternlicht, Sanford **PR736**
Masterpieces of Modern British and Irish Drama. Trade Cloth. Greenwood Publishing Group, Inc. Portsmouth, NH. 2005. 128p. Greenwood Introduces Literary Masterpieces Ser. ISBN:0-313-33323-8, ISBN13: 978-0-313-33323-1. Dewey:822/.91099417. LCCN:2005-014518.
Audience: **g,l,u,f.**

Sternlicht, Sanford V. **PR736.S74 2004**
A Reader's Guide to Modern British Drama. Trade Paper. Syracuse University Press. Syracuse, NY. 2004. 244p. ISBN:0-8156-3076-X, ISBN13: 978-0-8156-3076-0. Dewey:822/.9109. LCCN:2004-018690.
Audience: **l,u,f.**

Taylor, John Russell **PR736.T3 1969**
The Angry Theatre; New British Drama. Trade Cloth. Farrar, Straus & Giroux. New York, NY. 1969. 391p. ISBN:0-8090-2663-5, ISBN13: 978-0-8090-2663-0. Dewey:822/.9/1409. LCCN:78-088010.
Audience: **u,f.** B

Wu, Duncan **PR736. M34 2000**
Making Plays: Interviews with Contemporary British Dramatists and Directors. Trade Paper. Palgrave Macmillan. New York, NY. 2000. 272p. ISBN:0-312-23372-8, ISBN13: 978-0-312-23372-3. Dewey:822.9/14/09. LCCN:00-035266.
Audience: **l,u,f.**

Literary History, by Form > Prose Fiction. The Novel

Backscheider, Paula R. & Ingrassia, Catherine **PR851.C57 2005**
A Companion to the Eighteenth-Century English Novel and Culture. Trade Cloth. Blackwell Publishing, Inc. Malden, MA. 2005. 576p. Blackwell Companions to Literature and Culture Ser., Vol. 30 ISBN:1-4051-0157-1, ISBN13: 978-1-4051-0157-8. Dewey:823/.509. LCCN:2004-008398.
Audience: **u,f.** *Choice, 2006.*

Bradbury, Malcolm **PR821.B7**
Possibilities: Essays on the State of the Novel. Trade Cloth. Oxford University Press, Inc. New York, NY. 1973. xiii, 297p. ISBN:0-19-212189-8, ISBN13: 978-0-19-212189-9. Dewey:823/.009. LCCN:73-168713.
Audience: **l,u.** B

Brown, Homer O. **PR851.B75 1997**
Institutions of the English Novel: From Defoe to Scott. Trade Cloth. University of Pennsylvania Press. Philadelphia, PA. 1996. 244p. ISBN:0-8122-3383-2, ISBN13: 978-0-8122-3383-4. Dewey:823.009. LCCN:96-047118.
Audience: **u,f.** *Choice, 1997.*

Eagleton, Terry **PR821.E15 2005**
The English Novel: An Introduction. Trade Cloth. Blackwell Publishing, Inc. Malden, MA. 2004. 376p. ISBN:1-4051-1706-0, ISBN13: 978-1-4051-1706-7. Dewey:823.009. LCCN:2003-026893.
Audience: **l,u.**

Hart, Francis R. **PR8597.H37**
The Scottish Novel: From Smollett to Spark. Trade Cloth. Harvard University Press. Cambridge, MA. 1978. xii, 442 p. ;p. ISBN:0-674-79584-9, ISBN13: 978-0-674-79584-6. Dewey:823/.03. LCCN:77-020680.
Audience: **u,f.**

Larson, Jill **PR878.E67 L37 2001**
Ethics and Narrative in the English Novel, 1880-1914. Trade Cloth. Cambridge University Press. New York, NY. 2001. 186p. ISBN:0-521-79282-7, ISBN13: 978-0-521-79282-0. Dewey:823/.809353. LCCN:00-033706.
Audience: **u,f.** *Choice, 2001.*

Lodge, David **PR821.L6 2002**
Language of Fiction: Essays in Criticism and Verbal Analysis of the English Novel. Cloth Text. Routledge. New York, NY. 2002. 336p. Classics Ser. ISBN:0-415-29002-3, ISBN13: 978-0-415-29002-9. Dewey:823.009. LCCN:2002-031675.
Audience: **u,f.**

Parrinder, Patrick **PR830.N356.P37 2006**
Nation and Novel: The English Novel from Its Origins to the Present Day. Trade Cloth. Oxford University Press, Inc. New York, NY. 2006. 512p. ISBN:0-19-926484-8, ISBN13: 978-0-19-926484-1. Dewey:823.009/358. LCCN:2005-029735.
Audience: **u,f.**

Richetti, John J., et al. **PR821.C65 1994**
The Columbia History of the British Novel. John Bender, Deirdre David & Michael Seidel (Authors). Trade Cloth. Columbia University Press. New York, NY. 1994. 1064p. ISBN:0-231-07858-7, ISBN13: 978-0-231-07858-0. Dewey:823.009. LCCN:92-035749.
Audience: **l,u,f.** *Choice, 1994.*

Saintsbury, George E. **PR821.S3 1971**
English Novel. Trade Cloth. Scholarly Press, Inc. Saint Clair Shores, MI. 1971. vii, 319p. ISBN:0-403-01192-2, ISBN13: 978-0-403-01192-6. Dewey:823/.03. LCCN:78-145277.
Audience: **l,u.** B

Watt, Ian P. **PR851**
The Rise of the Novel. W. B. Carnochan (Foreword by). Trade Paper. University of California Press. Berkeley, CA. 2001. 339p. ISBN:0-520-23069-8, ISBN13: 978-0-520-23069-9. Dewey:823.509.
Audience: **g,l,u,f.**

Literary History, by Form > Prose Fiction. The Novel > Special Topics, A-Z

Adams, David **PR888.I54A33 2003**
Colonial Odysseys: Empire and Epic in the Modernist Novel. Book, Other. Cornell University Press. Ithaca, NY. 2003. 288p. ISBN:0-8014-4161-7, ISBN13: 978-0-8014-4161-5. Dewey:823/9109358. LCCN:2003-012660.
Audience: **u,f.** *Choice, 2004.*

Adams, James E. **PR468.M38A33 1995**
Dandies and Desert Saints: Styles of Victorian Masculinity. Trade Paper. Cornell University Press. Ithaca, NY. 1995. 264p. ISBN:0-8014-8208-9, ISBN13: 978-0-8014-8208-3. Dewey:820.9/353. LCCN:95-011320.
Audience: **u,f.** *Choice, 1996.*

Armstrong, Nancy **PR821**
Desire and Domestic Fiction: A Political History of the Novel. Trade Paper. Oxford University Press, Inc. New York, NY. 1990. 310p. ISBN:0-19-506160-8, ISBN13: 978-0-19-506160-4. Dewey:823/.009. LCCN:86-016482.
Audience: **u,f.** *Choice, 1987.*

Auerbach, Nina **GR830.V3**
Our Vampires, Ourselves. Trade Paper. University of Chicago Press. Chicago, IL. 1997. 240p. ISBN:0-226-03202-7, ISBN13: 978-0-226-03202-3. Dewey:820.9/375. LCCN:95-001044.
Audience: **u,f.** *Choice, 1996.*

Berry, Laura **PR878.C5B47 1999**
The Child, the State and the Victorian Novel. Trade Cloth. University Press of Virginia. Charlottesville, VA. 2000. 192p. Victorian Literature and Culture Ser. ISBN:0-8139-1909-6, ISBN13: 978-0-8139-1909-6. Dewey:823/.809352054. LCCN:99-035304.
Audience: **u,f.** *Choice, 2000.*

Bloom, Clive **PR888.P68B58 2002**
Bestsellers: Popular Fiction since 1900. Cloth over Boards. Palgrave Macmillan. New York, NY. 2002. 312p. ISBN:0-333-68742-6, ISBN13: 978-0-333-68742-0. Dewey:823/.9109. LCCN:2002-020886.
Audience: **l,u,f.** *Choice, 2003.*

Bloom, Clive (Editor) **PR888.D4T83 1990**
Twentieth-Century Suspense: The Thriller Comes of Age. Cloth Text. Palgrave Macmillan. New York, NY. 1990. 300p. Insights Ser. ISBN:0-312-03708-2, ISBN13: 978-0-312-03708-6. Dewey:823.087209. LCCN:89-037805.
Audience: **l,u.**

Brantlinger, Patrick **PR463**
Rule of Darkness: British Literature and Imperialism, 1830-1914. Book, Other. Cornell University Press. Ithaca, NY. 1990. 336p. ISBN:0-8014-9767-1, ISBN13: 978-0-8014-9767-4. Dewey:820.9/008. LCCN:87-047823.
Audience: **u,f.** *Choice, 1988.*

Cawelti, John G. & Rosenberg, Bruce A. **PR888.S65C38 1987**
The Spy Story. Trade Cloth. University of Chicago Press. Chicago, IL. 1987. 270p. ISBN:0-226-09868-0, ISBN13: 978-0-226-09868-5. Dewey:823/.0872/09. LCCN:86-030716.
Audience: **u,f.** *Choice, 1987.*

Ch'ien, Evelyn Nien-Ming **PR888.L35C47 2004**
Weird English. Trade Cloth. Harvard University Press. Cambridge, MA. 2004. 352p. ISBN:0-674-01337-9, ISBN13: 978-0-674-01337-7. Dewey:823/.9109. LCCN:2004-040509.
Audience: **l,u,f.** *Choice, 2004.*

Cvetkovich, Ann **PR878.F45 C85 1992**
Mixed Feelings: Feminism, Mass Culture and Victorian Sensationalism. Paper Text. Rutgers University Press. Piscataway, NJ. 1992. x, 227p. ISBN:0-8135-1857-1, ISBN13: 978-0-8135-1857-2. Dewey:823/.809352042. LCCN:92-004457.
Audience: **u,f.**

DeKoven, Marianne **PR888.M63D45 1991**
Rich and Strange: Gender, History, Modernism. Trade Cloth. Princeton University Press. Princeton, NJ. 1991. 257p. ISBN:0-691-06869-0, ISBN13: 978-0-691-06869-5. Dewey:823/.91091. LCCN:91-003571.
Audience: **l,u,f.** *Choice, 1992.*

Dijkstra, Bram **N8219.L2**
Idols of Perversity: Fantasies of Feminine Evil in Fin-de-Sìecle Culture. Trade Paper. Oxford University Press, Inc. New York, NY. 1988. 478p. ISBN:0-19-505652-3, ISBN13: 978-0-19-505652-5. Dewey:704.9/424/09034.
Audience: **u,f.** *Choice, 1987.*

Gilmour, Robin **PR788.U/**
The Idea of the Gentleman in the Victorian Novel. Trade Paper. Routledge. New York, NY. 1981. 208p. ISBN:0-04-800005-1, ISBN13: 978-0-04-800005-7. Dewey:823/.8/093520621. LCCN:81-010869.
Audience: **l,u,f.** B

Green, Laura Morgan **PR788.W6G74 2001**
Educating Women: Cultural Conflict and Victorian Literature. Trade Cloth. Ohio University Press. Athens, OH. 2001. 166p. ISBN:0-8214-1402-X, ISBN13: 978-0-8214-1402-6. Dewey:823/.809352042. LCCN:2001-036060.
Audience: **u,f.** *Choice, 2002.*

Hackett, Robin **PR888.L46H33 2004**
Sapphic Primitivism: Productions of Race, Class, and Sexuality in Key Works of Modern Fiction. Trade Cloth. Rutgers University Press. Piscataway, NJ. 2004. 200p. ISBN:0-8135-3347-3, ISBN13: 978-0-8135-3347-6. Dewey:823/.91099287. LCCN:2003-005944.
Audience: **u,f.** *Choice, 2004.*

Hanley, Lynne **PR888.W37H36 1991**
Writing War: Fiction, Gender, and Memory. Cloth Text. University of Massachusetts Press. Amherst, MA. 1991. 168p. ISBN:0-87023-738-1, ISBN13: 978-0-87023-738-6. Dewey:823/.9109358. LCCN:90-049252.
Audience: **l,u,f.** *Choice, 1992.*

Hanson, Clare **PR888.F45H36 2000**
Hysterical Fictions: The "Woman's Novel" in the Twentieth Century. Cloth over Boards. Palgrave Macmillan. New York, NY. 2000. 201p. ISBN:0-312-23529-1, ISBN13: 978-0-312-23529-1. Dewey:823.9/1/099287. LCCN:00-033344.
Audience: **u,f.** *Choice, 2001.*

Heilman, Anna **PR115**
New Woman Strategies: Sarah Grand, Olive Schreiner, and Mona Caird. Cloth over Boards. Manchester University Press. Manchester, 2004. 304p. ISBN:0-7190-5758-2, ISBN13: 978-0-7190-5758-8. Dewey:823.8099287.
Audience: **u,f.** *Choice, 2005.*

Hepburn, Allan **PR888.S65H47 2004**
Intrigue: Espionage and Culture. Cloth over Boards. Yale University Press. Cumberland, RI. 2005. 352p. ISBN:0-300-10498-7, ISBN13: 978-0-300-10498-1. Dewey:823/.087209091. LCCN:2004-015680.
Audience: **l,u,f.** *Choice, 2005.*

Heyns, Michiel **PR868.S32H49 1994**
Expulsion and the Nineteenth-Century Novel: The Scapegoat in English Realist Fiction. Trade Cloth. Oxford University Press, Inc. New York, NY. 1995. 304p. ISBN:0-19-818270-8, ISBN13: 978-0-19-818270-2. Dewey:823/.809353. LCCN:94-012798.
Audience: **u,f.** *Choice, 1995.*

Humble, Nicola **PR888.W6H86 2001**
The Feminine Middlebrow Novel, 1920s to 1950s: Class, Domesticity and Bohemianism. Trade Cloth. Oxford University Press, Inc. New York, NY. 2002. 282p. ISBN:0-19-818676-2, ISBN13: 978-0-19-818676-2. Dewey:823/.912099287. LCCN:2002-265884.
Audience: **u,f.** *Choice, 2002.*

Joshi, Priya **PR9492.2.J68 2002**
In Another Country: Colonialism, Culture, and the English Novel in India. Trade Cloth. Columbia University Press. New York, NY. 2002. 368p. ISBN:0-231-12584-4, ISBN13: 978-0-231-12584-0. Dewey:823/.809954. LCCN:2001-047921.
Audience: **u,f.** *Choice, 2003, 2002.*

Katz, Tamar **PR888.M63K38 2000**
Impressionist Subjects: Gender, Interiority and Modernist Fiction in England. Trade Cloth. University of Illinois Press. Champaign, IL. 2000. 256p. ISBN:0-252-02584-9, ISBN13: 978-0-252-02584-6. Dewey:823/.9109112. LCCN:99-050859.
Audience: **u,f.** *Choice, 2001.*

Kort, Wesley A. **PR888.P525K67 2004**
Place and Space in Modern Fiction. Trade Cloth. University Press of Florida. Gainesville, FL. 2004. 320p. ISBN:0-8130-2731-4, ISBN13: 978-0-8130-2731-9. Dewey:823/.9109384. LCCN:2004-042559.
Audience: **u,f.** *Choice, 2004.*

Latham, Sean **PR888.S58L38 2003**
Am I a Snob?: Modernism and the Novel. Trade Cloth. Cornell University Press. Ithaca, NY. 2003. 272p. ISBN:0-8014-4022-X, ISBN13: 978-0-8014-4022-9. Dewey:820.9/353. LCCN:2002-014604.
Audience: **u,f.** *Choice, 2003.*

Levine, George L. **PR878.S34L4 1991**
Darwin and the Novelists: Patterns of Science in Victorian Fiction. Trade Paper. University of Chicago Press. Chicago, IL. 1992. 334p. ISBN:0-226-47574-3, ISBN13: 978-0-226-47574-5. Dewey:823/.8/09356. LCCN:87-036201.
Audience: **u,f.** *Choice, 1989.*

Marcus, Jane **PR888.R34M37 2003**
Hearts of Darkness: White Women Write Race. Trade Cloth. Rutgers University Press. Piscataway, NJ. 2003. 224p. ISBN:0-8135-2962-X, ISBN13: 978-0-8135-2962-2. Dewey:823/.91209355. LCCN:2002-068044.
Audience: **u,f.** *Choice, 2004.*

McGann, Jerome J. **PN98.E4M39 2001**
Radiant Textuality: Literature after the World Wide Web. Cloth over Boards. Palgrave Macmillan. New York, NY. 2001. 288p. ISBN:0-312-29352-6, ISBN13: 978-0-312-29352-9. Dewey:801/.959/0285. LCCN:2001-021795.
Audience: **u,f.** *Choice, 2002.*

Polhemus, Robert M. **PR830.C63**
Comic Faith: The Great Tradition from Austen to Joyce. Library Binding. University of Chicago Press. Chicago, IL. 1996. x, 408p. ISBN:0-226-67320-0, ISBN13: 978-0-226-67320-2. Dewey:823/.009. LCCN:79-024856.
Audience: **u,f.**

Prickett, Stephen **PR468.F35P7 2005**
Victorian Fantasy. Ed. 2. Trade Paper. Baylor University Press. Waco, TX. 2005. 310p. Provost Ser. ISBN:1-932792-30-9, ISBN13: 978-1-932792-30-0. Dewey:820.9/15. LCCN:2005-015940.
Audience: **g,l,u,f.** *Choice, 2006.*

Priestman, Martin (Editor) **PR830.D4C36 2003**
The Cambridge Companion to Crime Fiction. Trade Paper. Cambridge University Press. New York, NY. 2003. 308p. Cambridge Companions to Literature Ser. ISBN:0-521-00871-9, ISBN13: 978-0-521-00871-6. Dewey:823/.087209. LCCN:2003-046056.
Audience: **g,l,u,f.** *Choice, 2004.*

Reitz, Caroline **PR830.D4R45 2004**
Detecting the Nation: Fictions of Detection and the Imperial Venture, 1788-1927. Trade Cloth. Ohio State University Press. Columbus, OH. 2004. 184p. Victorian Critical Interventions Ser. ISBN:0-8142-5135-8, ISBN13: 978-0-8142-5135-5. Dewey:823/.087209358. LCCN:2004-009551.
Audience: **u,f.** *Choice, 2005.*

Scanlan, Margaret **PR888.H5S3 1990**
Traces of Another Time: History and Politics in Postwar British Fiction. Cloth Text. Princeton University Press. Princeton, NJ. 1990. 215p. ISBN:0-691-06824-0, ISBN13: 978-0-691-06824-4. Dewey:823/.91409358. LCCN:89-035996.
Audience: **u,f.** *Choice, 1990.*

Sedgwick, Eve K. **PR409.M/**
Between Men: English Literature and Male Homosocial Desire. Carolyn G. Heilbrun & Nancy K. Miller (Editors). Paper Text. Columbia University Press. New York, NY. 1993. 244p. Gender and Culture Ser. ISBN:0-231-05861-6, ISBN13: 978-0-231-05861-2. Dewey:820.9/353. LCCN:84-017583.
Audience: **u,f.** *Choice, 1985.*

Smith, Andrew **PR1111**
Victorian Demons: Medicine, Masculinity and the Gothic at the Fin-de-Siecle. Cloth over Boards. Manchester University Press. Manchester, 2004. 200p. ISBN:0-7190-6356-6, ISBN13: 978-0-7190-6356-5. Dewey:820.80353. LCCN:2004-426530.
Audience: **u,f.** *Choice, 2004.*

Stableford, Brian M. **PR888.S35S73 1985**
Scientific Romance in Britain, 1890-1950. Cloth Text. Palgrave Macmillan. New York, NY. 1985. 288p. ISBN:0-312-70305-8, ISBN13: 978-0-312-70305-9. Dewey:823/.0876/09. LCCN:85-014610.
Audience: **l,u,f.** B *Choice, 1986.*

Sutherland, John **PN3331**
Can Jane Eyre Be Happy?: More Puzzles in Classic Fiction. Trade Paper. Oxford University Press, Inc. New York, NY. 2000. 248p. Oxford World's Classics Ser. ISBN:0-19-283603-X, ISBN13: 978-0-19-283603-8. Dewey:809.3.
Audience: **g,l,u,f.**

Sutherland, John **PR4168**
Is Heathcliff a Murderer?: Great Puzzles in Nineteenth-Century Fiction. Trade Paper. Oxford University Press, Inc. New York, NY. 2002. 268p. Oxford World's Classics Ser. ISBN:0-19-283468-1, ISBN13: 978-0-19-283468-3. Dewey:823.8/09.
Audience: **g,l,u,f.**

Suvin, Darko **PR878.S35.S8 1983**
Victorian Science Fiction in the U. K.: The Discourses of Knowledge and of Power. Trade Cloth. Macmillan Publishing Company, Inc. Old Tappan, NJ. 1983. 460p. ISBN:0-8161-8435-6, ISBN13: 978-0-8161-8435-4. Dewey:823/.0876/09. LCCN:83-010768.
Audience: **g,l,u,f.** B

Wachman, Gay **PR888.L46W34 2001**
Lesbian Empire: Radical Crosswriting in the Twenties. Paper Text. Rutgers University Press. Piscataway, NJ. 2001. 256p. ISBN:0-8135-2942-5, ISBN13: 978-0-8135-2942-4. Dewey:823/.912099206643. LCCN:00-045683.
Audience: **l,u,f.** *Choice, 2002.*

Literary History, by Form > Prose Fiction. The Novel > History of the Novel, by Period

Hunter, J. Paul **PR442**
Before Novels: The Cultural Contexts of Eighteenth Century English Fiction. Trade Paper. W. W. Norton & Company, Inc. New York, NY. 1992. 448p. ISBN:0-393-30861-8, ISBN13: 978-0-393-30861-7. Dewey:820.9/005.
Audience: **l,u.**

McKeon, Michael (Author, Introduction by) **PR841.M3 2002**
The Origins of the English Novel, 1600-1740. Ed. 15. Trade Cloth. Johns Hopkins University Press. Baltimore, MD. 2002. 560p. ISBN:0-8018-6995-1, ISBN13: 978-0-8018-6995-2. Dewey:823/.009. LCCN:2002-016072.
Audience: **u,f.** *Choice, 1987.*

Perry, Ruth **PR858.F29P47 2004**
Novel Relations: The Transformation of Kinship in English Literature and Culture, 1748-1818. Trade Cloth. Cambridge University Press. New York, NY. 2004. 476p. ISBN:0-521-83694-8, ISBN13: 978-0-521-83694-4. Dewey:823/.6093552. LCCN:2003-064022.
Audience: **u,f.** *Choice, 2005.*

Richetti, John (Editor) **PR851 .C36 1996**
The Cambridge Companion to the Eighteenth-Century Novel. Cloth Text. Cambridge University Press. New York, NY. 1996. 297p. Companions to Literature Ser. ISBN:0-521-41908-5, ISBN13: 978-0-521-41908-6. Dewey:823.5/09. LCCN:95-043083.
Audience: **u,f.** *Choice, 1997.*

Turner, Cheryl **PR858.W6**
Living by the Pen. Trade Paper. Routledge. New York, NY. 1994. 272p. ISBN:0-415-11196-X, ISBN13: 978-0-415-11196-6. Dewey:823.5099287. LCCN:91-045967.
Audience: **u,f.**

Literary History, by Form > Prose Fiction. The Novel > History of the Novel, by Period > 19th C.

Andres, Sophia **PR878.A7A53 2004**
The Pre-Raphaelite Art of the Victorian Novel: Narrative Challenges to Visual Gendered Boundaries. Trade Cloth. Ohio State University Press. Columbus, OH. 2004. 288p. ISBN:0-8142-5129-3, ISBN13: 978-0-8142-5129-4. Dewey:823/.809357. LCCN:2004-012887.
Audience: **u,f.** *Choice, 2005.*

Armstrong, Nancy **PR821**
Desire and Domestic Fiction: A Political History of the Novel. Trade Paper. Oxford University Press, Inc. New York, NY. 1990. 310p. ISBN:0-19-506160-8, ISBN13: 978-0-19-506160-4. Dewey:823/.009. LCCN:86-016482.
Audience: **u,f.** *Choice, 1987.*

Baker, William & Womack, Kenneth (Editors) **PR871**
A Companion to the Victorian Novel. Cloth Text. Greenwood Publishing Group, Inc. Portsmouth, NH. 2002. 464p. Literary Companions Ser. ISBN:0-313-31407-1, ISBN13: 978-0-313-31407-0. Dewey:823/.809. LCCN:2001-042326.
Audience: **l,u.** *Choice, 2002.*

da Sousa Correa, Delia (Editor) **PN3499**
Realisms: A Nineteenth-Century Novel. Trade Paper. Routledge. New York, NY. 2001. 320p. The Novel in History Ser. ISBN:0-415-23826-9, ISBN13: 978-0-415-23826-7. Dewey:823/.083/0908.
Audience: **l,u.**

Feltes, N. N. **PR878.C25.F44 1993**
Literary Capital and the Late Victorian Novel. Trade Cloth. University of Wisconsin Press. Chicago, IL. 1993. 185p. ISBN:0-299-13660-4, ISBN13: 978-0-299-13660-4. Dewey:823.809. LCCN:92-035455.
Audience: **u,f.** *Choice, 1993.*

Gallagher, Catherine **PR878.D65**
The Industrial Reformation of English Fiction: Social Discourse and Narrative Form, 1832-1867. Paper Text. University of Chicago Press. Chicago, IL. 1996. xvi, 320p. ISBN:0-226-27933-2, ISBN13: 978-0-226-27933-6. Dewey:823/.8/09355. LCCN:84-016272.
Audience: **u,f.** *Choice, 1986.*

James, Louis **PR871.J36 2006**
Victorian Novel. Trade Cloth. Blackwell Publishing, Inc. Malden, MA. 2006. 272p. Blackwell Guides to Literature Ser. ISBN:0-631-22627-3, ISBN13: 978-0-631-22627-7. Dewey:823/.809145. LCCN:2005-012331.
Audience: **u,f.**

Jenkins, Alice & John, Juliet (Editors) **PR873.R47 1999**
Rereading Victorian Fiction. Cloth over Boards. Palgrave Macmillan. New York, NY. 2000. 236p. ISBN:0-312-22643-8, ISBN13: 978-0-312-22643-5. Dewey:823/.809. LCCN:99-015615.
Audience: **u,f.** *Choice, 2000.*

Lovell, Terry **PR861**
Consuming Fiction. Cloth Text. Analytical Psychology Club of San Francisco, Inc. San Francisco, CA. 1987. 188p. Questions for Feminism Ser. ISBN:0-86091-173-X, ISBN13: 978-0-86091-173-9. Dewey:823/.009. LCCN:87-203939.
Audience: **u,f.** *Choice, 1988.*

Menon, Patricia **PR868.M47M46 2003**
Austen, Eliot, Charlotte Bronte and the Mentor-Lover. Cloth over Boards. Palgrave Macmillan. New York, NY. 2003. 240p. ISBN:1-4039-0259-3, ISBN13: 978-1-4039-0259-7. Dewey:823/.8099287. LCCN:2003-040474.
Audience: **g,l,u,f.** *Choice, 2004.*

Miller, D. A. **PR861**
The Novel and the Police. Trade Paper. University of California Press. Berkeley, CA. 1989. xv, 222p. ISBN:0-520-06746-0, ISBN13: 978-0-520-06746-2. Dewey:823/.8/09355. LCCN:87-025470.
Audience: **l,u,f.** *Choice, 1988.*

Nunokawa, Jeff **PR878.D65N86 2003**
The Afterlife of Property: Domestic Security and the Victorian Novel. Trade Paper. Princeton University Press. Princeton, NJ. 2003. 160p. ISBN:0-691-11467-6, ISBN13: 978-0-691-11467-5. Dewey:828.8.
Audience: **u,f.** *Choice, 1994.*

O'Gorman, Francis **PR871.C65 2005**
A Concise Companion to the Victorian Novel. Trade Cloth. Blackwell Publishing, Inc. Malden, MA. 2004. 304p. Blackwell Concise Companions to Literature and Culture Ser. ISBN:1-4051-0319-1, ISBN13: 978-1-4051-0319-0. Dewey:823/.809. LCCN:2003-026895.
Audience: **u,f.**

O'Gorman, Francis (Editor) **PR871.V53 2002**
The Victorian Novel: A Guide to Criticism. Trade Paper. Blackwell Publishing, Inc. Malden, MA. 2002. 368p. Blackwell Guides to Criticism Ser. ISBN:0-631-22704-0, ISBN13: 978-0-631-22704-5. Dewey:823/.809. LCCN:2002-022321.
Audience: **u,f.** *Choice, 2003.*

Powell, John (Editor), et al. **Z1039**
Biographical Dictionary of Literary Influences: The Nineteenth Century, 1800-1914. Derek W. Blakeley & Tessa Powell (Editors). Cloth Text. Greenwood Publishing Group, Inc. Portsmouth, NH. 2000. 536p. ISBN:0-313-30422-X, ISBN13: 978-0-313-30422-4. Dewey:028/.9/09034. LCCN:99-462057.
Audience: **g,l,u,f.** *Choice, 2001.*

Reed, John R. **PR468.S6.R4**
Victorian Conventions. Trade Cloth. Ohio University Press. Athens, OH. 1975. 574p. ISBN:0-8214-0147-5, ISBN13: 978-0-8214-0147-7. Dewey:820/.9/008. LCCN:73-092908.
Audience: **u,f.**

Regan, Stephan (Editor) **PN3499.N56 2001**
The Nineteenth Century Novel: A Critical Reader. Trade Paper. Routledge. New York, NY. 2001. 592p. The Nineteenth-Century Novel Ser. ISBN:0-415-23828-5, ISBN13: 978-0-415-23828-1. Dewey:809.3/034. LCCN:2002-319255.
Audience: **u,f.**

Stewart, Garrett **PR878.A79S74 1996**
Dear Reader: The Conscripted Audience in Nineteenth-Century British Fiction. Trade Paper. Johns Hopkins University Press. Baltimore, MD. 1996. 472p. ISBN:0-8018-5283-8, ISBN13: 978-0-8018-5283-1. Dewey:823/.809. LCCN:95-052372.
Audience: **u,f.** *Choice, 1997.*

Sutherland, John **PR871**
The Stanford Companion to Victorian Fiction. Trade Paper. Stanford University Press. Palo Alto, CA. 1989. 700p. ISBN:0-8047-1842-3, ISBN13: 978-0-8047-1842-4. Dewey:823/.809/03. LCCN:88-061462.
Audience: **g,l,u,f.** *Choice, 1989.*

Thesing, William B. **PR871.C643 2005**
A Companion to the Victorian Novel. Patrick Brantlinger (Editor). Trade Paper. Blackwell Publishing, Inc. Malden, MA. 2005. 528p. ISBN:1-4051-3291-4, ISBN13: 978-1-4051-3291-6. Dewey:823/.809.
Audience: **g,l,u,f.** *Choice, 2003.*

Thompson, Nicola D. (Editor) **PR878.F45 W66 1999**
Victorian Women Writers and the Woman Question. Gillian Beer (Contribution by). Trade Cloth. Cambridge University Press. New York, NY. 1999. 274p. Studies in Nineteenth-Century Literature and Culture, No. 21 ISBN:0-521-64102-0, ISBN13: 978-0-521-64102-9. Dewey:823/.8099287. LCCN:98-035820.
Audience: **u,f.**

Tillotson, Kathleen **PR871**
Novels of the 1840s. Trade Paper. Oxford University Press, Inc. New York, NY. 1983. 344p. ISBN:0-19-871109-3, ISBN13: 978-0-19-871109-4. Dewey:823/.8/09.
Audience: **g,l,u,f.**

Vicinus, Martha **PR468.L3.V5 1975**
The Industrial Muse: A Study of Nineteenth Century British Working-Class Literature. Trade Cloth. Thomson Heinle. Boston, MA. 1975. "x, 357"p. ISBN:0-06-497210-0, ISBN13: 978-0-06-497210-9. Dewey:820/.9/007. LCCN:75-314327.
Audience: **u,f.**

Walder, Dennis (Editor) **PN3499.N564 2001**
The Nineteenth-Century Novel: Identities. Trade Paper. Routledge. New York, NY. 2001. 320p. The Nineteenth-Century Novel Ser. ISBN:0-415-23827-7, ISBN13: 978-0-415-23827-4. Dewey:809.3/034. LCCN:2002-319274.
Audience: **l,u.**

Watt, Ian (Editor) **PR873**
Victorian Novel: Modern Essays in Criticism. Trade Cloth. Oxford University Press, Inc. New York, NY. 1971. viii, 485p. ISBN:0-19-501322-0, ISBN13: 978-0-19-501322-1. Dewey:823/.8/09. LCCN:77-135978.
Audience: **l,u,f.**

Williams, Raymond **PR871**
English Novel from Dickens to Lawrence. Random House of Canada, Ltd. 1987. ISBN:0-7012-0558-X, ISBN13: 978-0-7012-0558-4.
Audience: **l,u,f.**

Literary History, by Form > Prose Fiction. The Novel > History of the Novel, by Period > 20th C.

Booker, M. Keith **PR888**
The Modern British Novel of the Left: A Research Guide. Cloth Text. Greenwood Publishing Group, Inc. Portsmouth, NH. 1998. 424p. ISBN:0-313-30343-6, ISBN13: 978-0-313-30343-2. Dewey:823/.9109358. LCCN:97-043861.
Audience: **u,f.** *Choice, 1999.*

Bradbury, Malcolm **PR881**
The Modern British Novel. Ed. 2. Trade Paper. Penguin Group (USA) Inc. New York, NY. 2001. 656p. ISBN:0-14-029695-6, ISBN13: 978-0-14-029695-2. Dewey:823/.9109. LCCN:2003-427747.
Audience: **l,u.**

David, Deirdre (Editor) **PR871 .C17 2001**
The Cambridge Companion to the Victorian Novel. Cloth Text. Cambridge University Press. New York, NY. 2000. 288p. Companions to Literature Ser. ISBN:0-521-64150-0, ISBN13: 978-0-521-64150-0. Dewey:823/.809. LCCN:00-028928.
Audience: **g,l,u,f.** *Choice, 2001.*

English, James (Editor) **PR881.C658 2006**
A Concise Companion to Contemporary British Fiction. Trade Cloth. Blackwell Publishing, Inc. Malden, MA. 2006. 288p. Blackwell Concise Companions to Literature and Culture Ser. ISBN:1-4051-2000-2, ISBN13: 978-1-4051-2000-5. Dewey:823/.91409. LCCN:2005-012329.
Audience: **u,f.** *Choice, 2006.*

Head, Dominic **PR881 .H43 2002**
The Cambridge Introduction to Modern British Fiction, 1950-2000. Cloth Text. Cambridge University Press. New York, NY. 2002. 316p. Cambridge Introductions to Literature Ser. ISBN:0-521-66014-9, ISBN13: 978-0-521-66014-3. Dewey:823.91409. LCCN:2001-043261.
Audience: **l,u.** *Choice, 2002.*

Hunter, Jefferson **PR881**
Edwardian Fiction. Trade Cloth. Harvard University Press. Cambridge, MA. 1982. 291p. ISBN:0-674-24030-8, ISBN13: 978-0-674-24030-8. Dewey:823/.912/09. LCCN:81-006729.
Audience: **u,f.**

Karl, Frederick Robert **PR881.K25 2001**
A Reader's Guide to the Contemporary English Novel. Trade Paper. Syracuse University Press. Syracuse, NY. 2001. 304p. Reader's Guide Ser. ISBN:0-8156-0697-4, ISBN13: 978-0-8156-0697-0. Dewey:823/.9109. LCCN:00-053173.
Audience: **l,u.**

Kemp, Sandra (Editor), et al. **PR881.K39 1997**
Edwardian Fiction: An Oxford Companion. Charlotte Mitchell & David Trotter (Editors). Trade Cloth. Oxford University Press, Inc. New York, NY. 1997. 464p. ISBN:0-19-811760-4, ISBN13: 978-0-19-811760-5. Dewey:823/.91209 B. LCCN:96-037878.
Audience: **l,u,f.**

Matz, Jesse **PR888.M63M37 2004**
The Modern Novel: A Short Introduction. Trade Cloth. Blackwell Publishing, Inc. Malden, MA. 2004. 200p. Blackwell Introductions to Literature Ser. ISBN:1-4051-0048-6, ISBN13: 978-1-4051-0048-9. Dewey:809.3/04. LCCN:2003-018399.
Audience: **l,u.**

Monteith, Sharon, et al. **PR881**
Contemporary British and Irish Fiction: An Introduction Through Interviews. Jenny Newman & Pat Wheeler (Authors). Trade Paper. Oxford University Press, Inc. New York, NY. 2004. 192p. A Hodder Arnold Publication ISBN:0-340-76087-7, ISBN13: 978-0-340-76087-1. Dewey:823/.91409. LCCN:2004-445836.
Audience: **l,u,f.**

Morrison, Jago **PR881.M67 2003**
Reading Contemporary Fiction. Paper over Boards. Routledge. New York, NY. 2003. 272p. ISBN:0-415-19455-5, ISBN13: 978-0-415-19455-6. Dewey:823/.91409. LCCN:2002-151162.
Audience: **g,l,u,f.**

Shaffer, Brian **PR881.S53 2006**
Reading the Novel in English 1950-2000. Trade Cloth. Blackwell Publishing, Inc. Malden, MA. 2005. 256p. Reading the Novel Ser. ISBN:1-4051-0113-X, ISBN13: 978-1-4051-0113-4. Dewey:823/.91409. LCCN:2005-006122.
Audience: **l,u.**

Shaffer, Brian W. (Editor) **PR881.C655 2005**
A Companion to the British and Irish Novel 1945-2000. Trade Cloth. Blackwell Publishing, Inc. Malden, MA. 2004. 608p.

Blackwell Companions to Literature and Culture Ser. ISBN:1-4051-1375-8, ISBN13: 978-1-4051-1375-5. Dewey:823/.91409. LCCN:2004-007691.
Audience: **u,f.** *Choice, 2005.*

Williams, Raymond **NX465.5**
The Politics of Modernism: Against the New Conformists. Trade Cloth. Verso Books. London, 1996. 224p. Classics Ser. ISBN:1-85984-161-9, ISBN13: 978-1-85984-161-7. Dewey:700.1.
Audience: **u,f.**

Literary History, by Form > Humor. Satire

Barreca, Regina **PR830.H85B37 1994**
Untamed and Unabashed: Essays on Women and Humor in British Literature. Cloth Text. Wayne State University Press. Detroit, MI. 1994. 192p. Humor in Life and Letters Ser. ISBN:0-8143-2136-4, ISBN13: 978-0-8143-2136-2. Dewey:823.009/9287. LCCN:93-030645.
Audience: **l,u,f.** *Choice, 1994.*

Colletta, Lisa **PR888.H85C65 2003**
Dark Humor and Social Satire in the Modern British Novel. Cloth over Boards. Palgrave Macmillan. New York, NY. 2003. 184p. ISBN:1-4039-6365-7, ISBN13: 978-1-4039-6365-9. Dewey:823/.9109355. LCCN:2003-053657.
Audience: **u,f.** *Choice, 2004.*

Connery, Brian A. & Combe, Kirk (Editors) **PN6149.S2T44 1995**
Theorizing Satire: Essays in Literary Criticism. Cloth over Boards. Palgrave Macmillan. New York, NY. 1994. 256p. ISBN:0-312-12302-7, ISBN13: 978-0-312-12302-4. Dewey:809.7. LCCN:94-029335.
Audience: **u,f.** *Choice, 1996.*

English, James F. **PR937.E54 1994**
Comic Transactions: Literature, Humor, and the Politics of Community in Twentieth-Century Britain. Book, Other. Cornell University Press. Ithaca, NY. 1994. 280p. ISBN:0-8014-8166-X, ISBN13: 978-0-8014-8166-6. Dewey:827.009. LCCN:93-042073.
Audience: **u,f.** *Choice, 1995.*

Fritzer, Penelope J. & Bland, Bartholomew **PS438.F74 2002**
Merry Wives and Others: A History of Domestic Humor Writing. Paper Text. McFarland & Company, Incorporated Publishers. Jefferson, NC. 2002. 272p. ISBN:0-7864-1305-0, ISBN13: 978-0-7864-1305-8. Dewey:817/.509355. LCCN:2002-006090.
Audience: **l,u.** *Choice, 2003.*

Gale, Steven H. (Editor) **PR931.E54 1996**
Encyclopedia of British Humorists: Geoffrey Chaucer to John Cleese, Set. Trade Cloth. Garland Publishing, Inc. New York, NY. 1996. 1368p. ISBN:0-8240-5990-5, ISBN13: 978-0-8240-5990-3. Dewey:827.009. LCCN:95-002282.
Audience: **g,l,u,f.** *Choice, 1996.*

Griffin, Dustin H. **PN6149.S2G75 1994**
Satire: A Critical Reintroduction. Trade Cloth. University Press of Kentucky. Lexington, KY. 1994. 256p. ISBN:0-8131-1844-1, ISBN13: 978-0-8131-1844-4. Dewey:809.7. LCCN:93-032688.
Audience: **u,f.** *Choice, 1994.*

Knight, Charles A. **PN6149.S2K48 2004**
The Literature of Satire. Trade Cloth. Cambridge University Press. New York, NY. 2004. 338p. ISBN:0-521-83460-0, ISBN13: 978-0-521-83460-5. Dewey:809.7. LCCN:2003-055287.
Audience: **l,u,f.** *Choice, 2004.*

McRae, Andrew **PR934.M38 2003**
Literature, Satire and the Early Stuart State. Trade Cloth. Cambridge University Press. New York, NY. 2004. 260p. ISBN:0-521-81495-2, ISBN13: 978-0-521-81495-9. Dewey:827/.409358. LCCN:2003-053189.
Audience: **u,f.** *Choice, 2004.*

Nilsen, Don L. **Z2014**
Humor in Eighteenth and Nineteenth-Century British Literature: A Reference Guide. Book, Other. Greenwood Publishing Group, Inc. Portsmouth, NH. 1998. 312p. ISBN:0-313-29705-3, ISBN13: 978-0-313-29705-2. Dewey:016.827009. LCCN:98-014819.
Audience: **u,f.** *Choice, 1999.*

Ogborn, Jane & Buckroyd, Peter **PR931 .O43 2001**
Satire. Adrian Barlow (Contribution by). Trade Paper. Cambridge University Press. New York, NY. 2001. 128p. Cambridge Contexts in Literature Ser. ISBN:0-521-78791-2, ISBN13: 978-0-521-78791-8. Dewey:827.009. LCCN:2001-267906.
Audience: **l,u,f.**

Ross, Alison **PR931.R67 1998**
The Language of Humour. Trade Paper. Routledge. New York, NY. 1998. 128p. Intertext Ser. ISBN:0-415-16912-7, ISBN13: 978-0-415-16912-7. Dewey:827.009. LCCN:97-024610.
Audience: **l,u.**

Sitter, John **PR935.S58 1991**
Arguments of Augustan Wit. Cloth Text. Cambridge University Press. New York, NY. 1991. 202p. Studies in Eighteenth-Century English Literature and Thought, No. 11 ISBN:0-521-41120-3, ISBN13: 978-0-521-41120-2. Dewey:827/.409. LCCN:90-028116.
Audience: **u,f.** *Choice, 1992.*

Weinbrot, Howard D. **PR935.W39 1988**
Eighteenth Century Satire: Essays on Text and Context from Dryden to Peter Pindar. Cloth Text. Cambridge University Press. New York, NY. 1988. 272p. ISBN:0-521-32513-7, ISBN13: 978-0-521-32513-4. Dewey:827/.5/09. LCCN:87-026836.
Audience: **u,f.** *Choice, 1989.*

Collections of British Literature

Gilbert, Sandra M. & Gubar, Susan (Editors) **PS508.W7N67 1985**
Norton Anthology of Literature by Women: The Tradition in English. Trade Cloth. W. W. Norton & Company, Inc. New

York, NY. 1985. 295p. ISBN:0-393-01940-3, ISBN13: 978-0-393-01940-7. Dewey:784.9/63. LCCN:84-027276.
Audience: **g,l,u,f.** BCL3

Greenblatt, Stephen (Editor) **PR1109.N6 2005**
The Norton Anthology of English Literature, Eighth Edition, Volume 2: the Romantic Period through the Twentieth Century. Ed. 8. Trade Paper. W. W. Norton & Company, Inc. New York, NY. 2005. 3052p. ISBN:0-393-92532-3, ISBN13: 978-0-393-92532-6. Dewey:820.8. LCCN:2005-052313.
Audience: **g,l,u,f.**

Collections of British Literature > By Period

PR1502 .A7
Anglo-Saxon Poetic Records: A Collectve Edition. Trade Cloth. Somerset Publishers, Inc. Santa Barbara, CA. 1983. ISBN:0-403-03306-3, ISBN13: 978-0-403-03306-5. Dewey:829.
Audience: **u.**

Abrams, M. H. & Greenblatt **PR1109**
The Norton Anthology of English Literature: Middle Ages. Ed. 7. Trade Paper. W. W. Norton & Company, Inc. New York, NY. 2000. ISBN:0-393-97565-7, ISBN13: 978-0-393-97565-9. Dewey:820.8.
Audience: **u,f.**

Armstrong, Isobel (Editor), et al. **PR1177.N56 1996**
Nineteenth-Century Women Poets: An Oxford Anthology. Joseph Bristow & Cath Sharrock (Editors). Trade Cloth. Oxford University Press, Inc. New York, NY. 1997. 872p. ISBN:0-19-811290-4, ISBN13: 978-0-19-811290-7. Dewey:821.8/08/09287. LCCN:96-034552.
Audience: **g,l,u,f.** *Choice, 1997.*

Ballaster, Ros (Editor) **PR1127**
Fables of the East: Selected Tales 1662-1785. Trade Cloth. Oxford University Press, Inc. New York, NY. 2005. 288p. ISBN:0-19-926734-0, ISBN13: 978-0-19-926734-7. Dewey:398.2/095. LCCN:2005-020146.
Audience: **g,l,u,f.**

Blamires, Alcuin (Editor) **PR1912.A2 W65 1992**
Woman Defamed and Woman Defended: An Anthology of Medieval Texts. Karen Pratt & C. W. Marx (Contribution by). Trade Paper. Oxford University Press, Inc. New York, NY. 1992. 342p. ISBN:0-19-871039-9, ISBN13: 978-0-19-871039-4. Dewey:808. LCCN:92-003338.
Audience: **u,f.**

Broomfield, Andrea & Mitchell, Sally **PR1286.W6P76 1996**
Prose by Victorian Women: An Anthology. Cloth Text. Garland Publishing, Inc. New York, NY. 1995. 752p. Garland Reference Library of the Humanities, Vol. 1893: ISBN:0-8153-1970-3, ISBN13: 978-0-8153-1970-2. Dewey:828/.8080809287. LCCN:95-024400.
Audience: **g,l,u,f.** *Choice, 1996.*

Cook, Albert Stanburrough & Tinker, Chauncey B. **PR1508**
Select Translations from Old English Poetry: The Literature Which Inspired Tolkien's Lord of the Rings. John H. Costello & Dimitar D. Guetov (Produced by). Perfect. Capricorn Publishing. Appleton, WI. 2005. 208p. ISBN:0-9753970-6-0, ISBN13: 978-0-9753970-6-0. Dewey:829.1.
Audience: **l,u.**

Crossley-Holland, Kevin **PR1508**
The Anglo-Saxon World. Trade Cloth. Boydell & Brewer, Ltd. Woodbridge, 2004. 296p. ISBN:0-85115-885-4, ISBN13: 978-0-85115-885-3. Dewey:829/.08.
Audience: **l,u.**

DeMaria, Robert Jr. (Editor) **PR1134.B74 2001**
British Literature, 1640-1789: An Anthology. Ed. 2. Trade Paper. Blackwell Publishing, Inc. Malden, MA. 2001. 976p. Anthologies Ser. ISBN:0-631-21769-X, ISBN13: 978-0-631-21769-5. Dewey:820.9. LCCN:00-067510.
Audience: **g,l,u,f.**

Dobson, R. B. & Taylor, J. **PR2125.D6 1976**
The Rhymes of Robyn Hood: An Introduction to the English Outlaw. Trade Cloth. University of Pittsburgh Press. Pittsburgh, PA. 1976. x, 330 p. :p. ISBN:0-8229-1126-4, ISBN13: 978-0-8229-1126-5. Dewey:820/.8/0351. LCCN:75-031564.
Audience: **u,f.** BCL3

Fowler, Alistair (Editor) **PR1209 .N49 2002**
The New Oxford Book of Seventeenth-Century Verse. Trade Paper. Oxford University Press, Inc. New York, NY. 2002. 880p. Oxford Books of Verse ISBN:0-19-284087-8, ISBN13: 978-0-19-284087-5. Dewey:821/.408. LCCN:2002-282572.
Audience: **g,l,u,f.**

Gerould, Gordon H. **PR5684**
Old English and Medieval Literature. Library Binding. Reprint Services Company. Temecula, CA. 1988. ISBN:0-7812-0479-8, ISBN13: 978-0-7812-0479-8. Dewey:823/.8.
Audience: **l,u.** BCL3

Graham, Elspeth (Editor), et al. **PR1127.H38 1989**
Her Own Life: Autobiographical Writings by 17th Century Englishwomen. Hilary Hinds & Elaine Hobby (Editors). Trade Cloth. Routledge. New York, NY. 1989. 224p. ISBN:0-415-01699-1, ISBN13: 978-0-415-01699-5. Dewey:820.8/.09287. LCCN:89-006220.
Audience: **g,l,u,f.**

Greenblatt, Stephen (Editor) **PR1109.N6 2005**
The Norton Anthology of English Literature: The Middle Ages through the Restoration and the Eighteenth Century. Ed. 8. Trade Cloth. W. W. Norton & Company, Inc. New York, NY. 2005. 3058p. ISBN:0-393-92713-X, ISBN13: 978-0-393-92713-9. Dewey:820.8. LCCN:2005-052313.
Audience: **g,l,u,f.**

Harrison, G. B. **PR1125**
England in Shakespeare's Day. Perfect, Paper over Boards. Routledge. New York, NY. 2005. 256p. ISBN:0-415-35311-4, ISBN13: 978-0-415-35311-3. Dewey:820.8'0355.
Audience: **g,l,u,f.**

Jones, Emrys (Editor) **PR1205**
The New Oxford Book of Sixteenth-Century Verse. Trade Paper. Oxford University Press, Inc. New York, NY. 2002. 816p. Oxford Books of Verse ISBN:0-19-280195-3, ISBN13: 978-0-19-280195-1. Dewey:821.3/08.
Audience: **g,u,f.**

Kennedy, Charles W. **PR1508.K36**
An Anthology of Old English Poetry. Paper Text. Textbook Publishers. Temecula, CA. 2003. 174p. ISBN:0-7581-7069-6, ISBN13: 978-0-7581-7069-9. Dewey:829.1082.
Audience: **u.**

Knight, Stephen, et al. **PR2125.R63 2000**
Robin Hood and Other Outlaw Tales. Ed. 2. Thomas H. Ohlgren, Thomas E. Kelly & Consortium for the Teaching of the Middle Ages Staff (Authors). Trade Paper. Medieval Institute Publications. Kalamazoo, MI. 2000. xvi + 725p. Middle English Texts Ser. ISBN:1-58044-067-3, ISBN13: 978-1-58044-067-7. Dewey:820.8/035106927. LCCN:00-040115.
Audience: **u,f.**

Leighton, Angela & Reynolds, Margaret (Editors) **PR1177.V53 1995**
Victorian Women Poets: An Anthology. Trade Cloth. Polity Press. Cambridge, 1995. 800p. Anthologies Ser. ISBN:0-631-17608-X, ISBN13: 978-0-631-17608-4. Dewey:821/.80809287. LCCN:95-002697.
Audience: **g,l,u,f.**

McGann, Jerome J. (Editor) **PR1222.N48 2002**
The New Oxford Book of Romantic Period Verse. Trade Paper. Oxford University Press, Inc. New York, NY. 2002. 864p. Oxford Books of Verse ISBN:0-19-860432-7, ISBN13: 978-0-19-860432-7. Dewey:821/.7080145. LCCN:2002-511437.
Audience: **l,u.**

Olsen, Alexandra Hennessey (Editor) **PR1508.P59 1998**
Poems and Prose from the Old English. Ed. 2. Burton Raffel (Translator). Trade Paper. Yale University Press. Cumberland, RI. 1998. 254p. ISBN:0-300-06995-2, ISBN13: 978-0-300-06995-2. Dewey:829/.08. LCCN:97-022556.
Audience: **l,u.** *Choice, 1998.*

Ricks, Christopher (Editor) **PR1223**
The New Oxford Book of Victorian Verse. Trade Paper. Oxford University Press, Inc. New York, NY. 2002. 688p. Oxford Books of Verse ISBN:0-19-284084-3, ISBN13: 978-0-19-284084-4. Dewey:821/.808.
Audience: **g,l,u,f.**

Rudrum, Alan (Editor), et al. **PR1127.B76 2000**
The Broadview Anthology of Seventeenth-Century Verse and Prose. Joseph Black & Holly Nelson (Editors). Trade Paper. Broadview Press. Peterborough, ON. 2000. 1303p. Anthologies of English Literature Ser. ISBN:1-55111-053-9, ISBN13: 978-1-55111-053-0. Dewey:820.8/004. LCCN:2001-272401.
Audience: **g,l,u,f.**

Sands, Donald B. (Editor) **PR2064.M46 1986**
Middle English Verse Romances. Trade Cloth. University of Exeter Press. Exeter, 1986. 408p. Medieval English Texts and Studies ISBN:0-85989-228-X, ISBN13: 978-0-85989-228-5. Dewey:821/.1/08. LCCN:88-168272.
Audience: **u,f.**

Trapp, J. B. (Editor), et al. **PR1120.M37 2001**
The Oxford Anthology of English Literature: Medieval English Literature. Ed. 2. Douglas Gray, Julia Boffee & Julia Boffey (Editors). Paper Text. Oxford University Press, Inc. New York, NY. 2002. 650p. The Oxford Anthology of English Literature Ser. ISBN:0-19-513492-3, ISBN13: 978-0-19-513492-6. Dewey:820.8/001. LCCN:00-067754.
Audience: **u,f.**

Treharne, Elaine M. **PR1120.O39 2004**
Old and Middle English C.890-C.1400: An Anthology. Ed. 2. Trade Cloth. Blackwell Publishing, Inc. Malden, MA. 2004. 712p. Blackwell Anthologies Ser. ISBN:1-4051-1312-X, ISBN13: 978-1-4051-1312-0. Dewey:829.08. LCCN:2003-056057.
Audience: **u,f.**

Tucker, Herbert F. & Mermin, Dorothy (Editors) **PR1145.V52 2002**
Victorian Literature: 1830-1900. Herbert F. Tucker & Dorothy Mermin (Compiled by). Cloth Text. Thomson Heinle. Boston, MA. 2001. 1168p. ISBN:0-15-507177-7, ISBN13: 978-0-15-507177-3. Dewey:820.8/008. LCCN:2001-086294.
Audience: **l,u.**

Witherspoon, Alexander M. & Warnke, Frank J. **PR1127.S39 1982**
Seventeenth Century Prose and Poetry. Ed. 2. Cloth Text. Harcourt College Publishers. Fort Worth, TX. 1983. 1124p. ISBN:0-15-580237-2, ISBN13: 978-0-15-580237-7. Dewey:820/.8/004. LCCN:82-083867.
Audience: **g,l,u,f.**

Collections of British Literature > By Form

AC1.E8
British Historical and Political Orations, from the 12th to the 20th Century. Trade Paper. Books on Demand. Ann Arbor, MI. 384p. ISBN:0-598-55395-9, ISBN13: 978-0-598-55395-9. Dewey:825.08. LCCN:37-005615.
Audience: **u,f.**

Bryant, D. C., et al. **PN6122.H54**
An Historical Anthology of Select British Speeches. C. C. Arnold & F. W. Haberman (Authors). Trade Cloth. Books on Demand. Ann Arbor, MI. 558p. ISBN:0-8357-9904-2, ISBN13: 978-0-8357-9904-1. Dewey:808.85. LCCN:67-021676.
Audience: **g,l,u,f.**

Goodrich, Chauncey Allen **PR1325.G7**
Select British Eloquence: Embracing the Best Speeches. . . for the Last Two Centuries. Trade Paper. Books on Demand. Ann Arbor, MI. 960p. ISBN:0-598-86331-1, ISBN13: 978-0-598-86331-7. Dewey:825.082. LCCN:34-001469.
Audience: **g,l,u,f.**

Rosen, Greg **PR1322**
Old Labour to New: The Dreams That Inspired, the Battles That Divided. Trade Cloth. Politico's Publishing Ltd. Tunbridge Wells, 2005. 400p. ISBN:1-84275-045-3, ISBN13: 978-1-84275-045-2. Dewey:324.2/4107.
Audience: **g,l,u,f.**

Collections of British Literature > By Form > Poetry

Amis, Kingsley (Editor) **PR1175.N37**
The New Oxford Book of English Light Verse. Trade Cloth. Oxford University Press, Inc. New York, NY. 1978. 416p. Books of Verse ISBN:0-19-211862-5, ISBN13: 978-0-19-211862-2. Dewey:821/.08/08. LCCN:77-025756.
Audience: **g,l,u,f.** B

Appelbaum, Stanley (Editor) **PR1219.E54 1996**
English Romantic Poetry: An Anthology. Trade Paper. Dover Publications, Inc. Mineola, NY. 1996. 256p. Thrift Editions Ser. ISBN:0-486-29282-7, ISBN13: 978-0-486-29282-3. Dewey:821/.7080145. LCCN:97-177016.
Audience: **g,l,u,f.**

Armstrong, Isobel (Editor), et al. **PR1177.N56 1996**
Nineteenth-Century Women Poets: An Oxford Anthology. Joseph Bristow & Cath Sharrock (Editors). Trade Cloth. Oxford University Press, Inc. New York, NY. 1997. 872p. ISBN:0-19-811290-4, ISBN13: 978-0-19-811290-7. Dewey:821.8/08/09287. LCCN:96-034552.
Audience: **g,l,u,f.** *Choice, 1997.*

Auden, W. H. & Holmes, Norman (Editors) **PR1175**
The Portable Victorian and Edwardian Poets. Trade Paper. Penguin Group (USA) Inc. New York, NY. 1977. 672p. Portable Library, No. 53 ISBN:0-14-015053-6, ISBN13: 978-0-14-015053-7. Dewey:821/.008.
Audience: **g,l,u,f.**

Bender, Robert M. & Squier, Charles L. (Editors) **PR1195.S5**
The Sonnet: An Anthology. Mass Market. Simon & Schuster. New York, NY. 1987. ISBN:0-671-63732-0, ISBN13: 978-0-671-63732-3. Dewey:808.8142.
Audience: **g,l,u,f.**

Bernbaum, Ernest **PR1215 .B4**
English Poets of the Eighteenth Century. Trade Paper. Kessinger Publishing, LLC. Whitefish, MT. 2004. ISBN:1-4191-1790-4, ISBN13: 978-1-4191-1790-9. Dewey:821.508.
Audience: **g,l,u,f.**

Blain, Virginia (Editor) **PR1177.V5 2001**
Victorian Women Poets: A New Anthology. Trade Cloth. Longman Publishing Group. White Plains, NY. 2000. 400p. Longman Annotated Texts Ser. ISBN:0-582-27568-7, ISBN13: 978-0-582-27568-3. Dewey:821/.80809287. LCCN:00-055722.
Audience: **g,l,u,f.**

Brooks-Davies, Douglas (Editor, Introduction by) **PR1205**
Silver Poets of the Sixteenth Century. Ed. 2. Trade Paper. Tuttle Publishing. Boston, MA. 1994. 485p. ISBN:0-460-87440-3, ISBN13: 978-0-460-87440-3. Dewey:821/.308. LCCN:93-158442.
Audience: **g,l,u,f.**

Child, Francis James **PR1181.E47 2003**
The English and Scottish Popular Ballads, Vol. 5. Trade Paper. Dover Publications, Inc. Mineola, NY. 2003. 640p. 0 ISBN:0-486-43149-5, ISBN13: 978-0-486-43149-9. Dewey:821/.04408. LCCN:2003-053052.
Audience: **g,l,u,f.** B

Child, Francis James **PR1181.E47 2003**
The English and Scottish Popular Ballads, Vol. 1. Trade Paper. Dover Publications, Inc. Mineola, NY. 2003. 544p. 0 ISBN:0-486-43145-2, ISBN13: 978-0-486-43145-1. Dewey:821/.04408. LCCN:2003-053052.
Audience: **g,l,u,f.** B

Child, Francis James **PR1181.E47 2003**
The English and Scottish Popular Ballads, Vol. 3. Trade Paper. Dover Publications, Inc. Mineola, NY. 2003. 544p. 0 ISBN:0-486-43147-9, ISBN13: 978-0-486-43147-5. Dewey:821/.04408. LCCN:2003-053052.
Audience: **g,l,u,f.** B

Child, Francis James **PR1181**
The English and Scottish Popular Ballads, Vol. 4. Trade Paper. Dover Publications, Inc. Mineola, NY. 2003. 544p. 0 ISBN:0-486-43148-7, ISBN13: 978-0-486-43148-2. Dewey:821/.04408. LCCN:2003-053052.
Audience: **g,l,u,f.** B

Child, Francis James **PR1181.E47 2003**
The English and Scottish Popular Ballads, Vol. 2. Trade Paper. Dover Publications, Inc. Mineola, NY. 2003. 544p. 0 ISBN:0-486-43146-0, ISBN13: 978-0-486-43146-8. Dewey:821/.04408. LCCN:2003-053052.
Audience: **g,l,u,f.** B

Cummings, Robert (Editor) **PR1209.S53 2000**
Seventeenth-Century Poetry: An Annotated Anthology. Trade Cloth. Blackwell Publishing, Inc. Malden, MA. 2000. 624p. Annotated Anthologies Ser. ISBN:0-631-21065-2, ISBN13: 978-0-631-21065-8. Dewey:821/.408. LCCN:99-033568.
Audience: **g,l,u,f.**

Cunningham, Valentine & Wu, Duncan (Editors) **PR1223.V53 2002**
Victorian Poetry. Trade Cloth. Blackwell Publishing, Inc. Malden, MA. 2002. 200p. Blackwell Essential Literature Ser. ISBN:0-631-23075-0, ISBN13: 978-0-631-23075-5. Dewey:821/.808. LCCN:2002-020878.
Audience: **g,l,u,f.**

Cutts, John P. (Editor) **PR1209 .C8 1969**
Seventeenth Century Songs and Lyrics. Trade Cloth. Ayer Company Publishers, Inc. Manchester, NH. 1977. Granger Index Reprint Ser. ISBN:0-8369-6055-6, ISBN13: 978-0-8369-6055-6. Dewey:821/.4/08Z. LCCN:70-080373.
Audience: **g,l,u,f.**

Davie, Donald **PR1195.C48**
The New Oxford Book of Christian Verse. Trade Paper. Oxford University Press, Inc. New York, NY. 2003. 350p. ISBN:0-19-280486-3, ISBN13: 978-0-19-280486-0. Dewey:821.008/03823. LCCN:2003-279055.
Audience: **g,l,u,f.**

Feldman, Paula R. **PR1177.B76 1997**
British Women Poets of the Romantic Era: An Anthology. Trade Cloth. Johns Hopkins University Press. Baltimore, MD. 1997. 920p. ISBN:0-8018-5430-X, ISBN13: 978-0-8018-5430-9. Dewey:821/.70809287. LCCN:96-047417.
Audience: **g,l,u,f.** *Choice, 1998.*

Feldman, Paula R. & Robinson, Daniel (Editors) **PR1195.S5C46 1999**
A Century of Sonnets: The Romantic-Era Revival 1750-1850. Trade Cloth. Oxford University Press, Inc. New York, NY. 1999. 302p. ISBN:0-19-511561-9, ISBN13: 978-0-19-511561-1. Dewey:820.9. LCCN:97-051208.
Audience: **g,l,u,f.**

Fellowes, Edmund Horace **ML2631.F45 1972**
English Madrigal. Trade Cloth. Ayer Company Publishers, Inc. Manchester, NH. 1977. 111p. Select Bibliographies Reprint Ser. ISBN:0-8369-6929-4, ISBN13: 978-0-8369-6929-0. Dewey:784/.1. LCCN:72-006997.
Audience: **g,l,u,f.**

Ferguson, Margaret **PR1174.N6 2004**
The Norton Anthology of Poetry. Ed. 5. Trade Paper. W. W. Norton & Company, Inc. New York, NY. 2004. 2000p. ISBN:0-393-97920-2, ISBN13: 978-0-393-97920-6. Dewey:821.008. LCCN:2004-058100.
Audience: **g,l,u,f.**

Fowler, Alastair **PR545.C68C68 1994**
The Country House Poem: A Cabinet of Seventeenth-Century Estate Poems and Related Items. Trade Cloth. Edinburgh University Press. Edinburgh, 1994. 448p. ISBN:0-7486-0440-5, ISBN13: 978-0-7486-0440-1. Dewey:821/.408355. LCCN:94-159212.
Audience: **g,l,u,f.** *Choice, 1995.*

Fowler, Alistair (Editor) **PR1209 .N49 2002**
The New Oxford Book of Seventeenth-Century Verse. Trade Paper. Oxford University Press, Inc. New York, NY. 2002. 880p. Oxford Books of Verse ISBN:0-19-284087-8, ISBN13: 978-0-19-284087-5. Dewey:821/.408. LCCN:2002-282572.
Audience: **g,l,u,f.**

Fuller, John (Editor) **PR1195.S5O94 2002**
The Oxford Book of Sonnets. Trade Paper. Oxford University Press, Inc. New York, NY. 2003. 400p. Oxford Books of Verse ISBN:0-19-280389-1, ISBN13: 978-0-19-280389-4. Dewey:821/.04208.
Audience: **g,l,u,f.**

Fuller, John (Editor) **PR1195.S5O94 2000**
The Oxford Book of Sonnets. Trade Cloth. Oxford University Press, Inc. New York, NY. 2006. 400p. ISBN:0-19-214267-4, ISBN13: 978-0-19-214267-2. Dewey:821/.04208. LCCN:00-036757.
Audience: **g,l,u,f.**

Gardner, Helen (Editor, Introduction by) **PR1204**
The Metaphysical Poets. Ed. 3. Trade Paper. Penguin Group (USA) Inc. New York, NY. 1960. 336p. Penguin Classics Ser. ISBN:0-14-042038-X, ISBN13: 978-0-14-042038-8. Dewey:821.4/08.
Audience: **g,l,u,f.**

Garlick, Raymond & Mathias, Roland (Editors) **PR8964.A52 1993**
Anglo-Welsh Poetry 1480-1990. Ed. 2. Trade Paper. Seren Books. Bridgend, 1994. 377p. ISBN:1-85411-082-9, ISBN13: 978-1-85411-082-4. Dewey:821.008/09429. LCCN:95-184889.
Audience: **g,l,u,f.**

Gerrard, Christine **PR1215.E53 2004**
Eighteenth-Century Poetry: An Annotated Anthology. Ed. 2. David Fairer (Editor). Trade Cloth. Blackwell Publishing, Inc. Malden, MA. 2004. 600p. Blackwell Annotated Anthologies Ser. ISBN:1-4051-1318-9, ISBN13: 978-1-4051-1318-2. Dewey:821/.508. LCCN:2003-056027.
Audience: **l,u.**

Gray, Douglas (Editor) **PR1120.O93 1989**
The Oxford Book of Late Medieval Verse and Prose. Trade Paper. Oxford University Press, Inc. New York, NY. 1989. 608p. ISBN:0-19-282245-4, ISBN13: 978-0-19-282245-1. Dewey:820/.8/002. LCCN:88-023263.
Audience: **g,l,u,f.** B

Greene, Richard L. (Editor) **PR1195**
A Selection of English Carols. Trade Cloth. Greenwood Publishing Group, Inc. Portsmouth, NH. 1978. 279p. ISBN:0-313-20002-5, ISBN13: 978-0-313-20002-1. Dewey:821/.1/08. LCCN:77-013760.
Audience: **g,l,u,f.**

Greene, Richard Leighton (Author, Editor) **PR1195.C2G7**
The Early English Carols. Trade Paper. Books on Demand. Ann Arbor, MI. 612p. ISBN:0-598-78224-9, ISBN13: 978-0-598-78224-3. Dewey:PR1195.C2G7. LCCN:36-001733.
Audience: **g,l,u,f.**

Grierson, H. J. (Editor) **PR1209.M48 1995**
Metaphysical Lyrics and Poems of the Seventeenth Century: Donne to Butler. Ed. 2. Alastair Fowler (Revised by). Trade Paper. Oxford University Press, Inc. New York, NY. 1995. 352p. ISBN:0-19-282290-X, ISBN13: 978-0-19-282290-1. Dewey:821/.408. LCCN:94-026062.
Audience: **g,l,u,f.**

Gross, John (Editor) **PR1195.H8**
The Oxford Book of Comic Verse. Trade Paper. Oxford University Press, Inc. New York, NY. 2002. 546p. Oxford Books of Verse ISBN:0-19-284086-X, ISBN13: 978-0-19-284086-8. Dewey:821/.07/08.
Audience: **g,l,u,f.**

Hirsh, John C. (Editor) **PR1120.M375 2005**
Medieval Lyric: Middle English Lyrics, Ballads, and Carols. Trade Cloth. Blackwell Publishing, Inc. Malden, MA. 2004. 240p. ISBN:1-4051-1481-9, ISBN13: 978-1-4051-1481-3. Dewey:821.040801. LCCN:2003-026892.
Audience: **g,l,u,f.** *Choice, 2005.*

Jones, Emrys (Editor) **PR1205**
The New Oxford Book of Sixteenth-Century Verse. Trade Paper. Oxford University Press, Inc. New York, NY. 2002. 816p. Oxford Books of Verse ISBN:0-19-280195-3, ISBN13: 978-0-19-280195-1. Dewey:821.3/08.
Audience: **g,u,f.**

Karlin, Daniel (Editor) **PR1223.P46 1998**
Penguin Book of Victorian Verse. Trade Paper. Penguin Group (USA) Inc. New York, NY. 1999. 928p. Classics Ser. ISBN:0-14-044578-1, ISBN13: 978-0-14-044578-7. Dewey:821/.808. LCCN:99-461809.
Audience: **g,l,u,f.**

Kennelly, Brendan (Editor) **PR8851.P4 1981**
Penguin Book of Irish Verse. Ed. 2. Trade Paper. Penguin Group (USA) Inc. New York, NY. 1982. 480p. ISBN:0-14-042121-1, ISBN13: 978-0-14-042121-7. Dewey:821/.008. LCCN:82-139765.
Audience: **g,l,u,f.**

Kermode, Frank (Editor) **PR1195.P3**
English Pastoral Poetry, from the Beginnings to Marvell. Trade Cloth. Ayer Company Publishers, Inc. Manchester, NH. 1977. Granger Index Reprint Ser. ISBN:0-8369-6022-X, ISBN13: 978-0-8369-6022-8. Dewey:821/.008/014. LCCN:71-076938.
Audience: **g,l,u,f.** B

Leighton, Angela & Reynolds, Margaret (Editors) **PR1177.V53 1995**
Victorian Women Poets: An Anthology. Trade Cloth. Polity Press. Cambridge, 1995. 800p. Anthologies Ser. ISBN:0-631-17608-X, ISBN13: 978-0-631-17608-4. Dewey:821/.80809287. LCCN:95-002697.
Audience: **g,l,u,f.**

Levin, Phillis (Editor) **PR1195.S5P38 2001**
The Penguin Book of the Sonnet: 500 Years of a Classic Tradition in English. Trade Paper. Penguin Group (USA) Inc. New York, NY. 2001. 528p. ISBN:0-14-058929-5, ISBN13: 978-0-14-058929-0. Dewey:821/.04208. LCCN:00-062350.
Audience: **g,l,u,f.**

Lindsay, Maurice & Duncan, Lesley **PR8658**
Edinburgh Book of Twentieth-Century Scottish Poetry. Trade Cloth. Edinburgh University Press. Edinburgh, 2005. 384p. ISBN:0-7486-2015-X, ISBN13: 978-0-7486-2015-9. Dewey:821.9108. LCCN:2005-432732.
Audience: **g,l,u,f.**

Lonsdale, Roger (Editor) **PR1177.E34 1990**
Eighteenth Century Women Poets: An Oxford Anthology. Trade Paper. Oxford University Press, Inc. New York, NY. 1990. 602p. ISBN:0-19-282775-8, ISBN13: 978-0-19-282775-3. Dewey:821/.50809287. LCCN:90-007181.
Audience: **g,l,u,f.**

Lonsdale, Roger (Editor) **PR1215**
The New Oxford Book of Eighteenth Century Verse. Trade Paper. Oxford University Press, Inc. New York, NY. 2003. 912p. ISBN:0-19-280491-X, ISBN13: 978-0-19-280491-4. Dewey:821.508. LCCN:2003-272264.
Audience: **g,l,u,f.** B

Lord, George D. (Editor) **PR1195.H5**
1660-1678. Cloth over Boards. Yale University Press. Cumberland, RI. 1963. 536p. Poems on Affairs of State Ser., Vol. 1:Augustan Sati Ser. ISBN:0-300-00726-4, ISBN13: 978-0-300-00726-8. Dewey:821.070835809032.
Audience: **g,l,u,f.**

MacQueen, John & Scott, Tom (Editors) **PR8650.O84 1989**
The Oxford Book of Scottish Verse. Trade Paper. Oxford University Press, Inc. New York, NY. 1989. 672p. ISBN:0-19-282600-X, ISBN13: 978-0-19-282600-8. Dewey:821/.008/09263. LCCN:88-030855.
Audience: **g,l,u,f.**

McGann, Jerome J. (Editor) **PR1222.N48 2002**
The New Oxford Book of Romantic Period Verse. Trade Paper. Oxford University Press, Inc. New York, NY. 2002. 864p. Oxford Books of Verse ISBN:0-19-860432-7, ISBN13: 978-0-19-860432-7. Dewey:821/.7080145. LCCN:2002-511437.
Audience: **l,u.**

Morgan, Esther (Editor) **PS3019**
☐ The Poetry Archive.
http://www.poetryarchive.org
Bailey, Andrew (Editor).
Audience: **g,l,u,f.**

Morrison, Blake **PR1227.P38 1991**
Penguin Book of Contemporary British Verse. Trade Paper. Penguin Books, Ltd. London, 208p. ISBN:0-14-058552-4, ISBN13: 978-0-14-058552-0. Dewey:821.9/1408. LCCN:94-101442.
Audience: **g,l,u,f.**

Negri, Paul (Editor) **PR1223.E55 1999**
English Victorian Poetry: An Anthology. Trade Paper. Dover Publications, Inc. Mineola, NY. 1999. 256p. Thrift Editions Ser. ISBN:0-486-40425-0, ISBN13: 978-0-486-40425-7. Dewey:821/.808. LCCN:99-010649.
Audience: **g,l,u,f.**

Nicholson, D. H. & Lee, A. H. (Editors) **PR1191.O82 1997**
The Oxford Book of English Mystical Verse. Trade Cloth. Acropolis Books, Inc. Camarillo, CA. 1997. 648p. ISBN:1-889051-02-0, ISBN13: 978-1-889051-02-4. Dewey:821.008/0382. LCCN:96-043195.
Audience: **g,l,u,f.**

O'Gorman, Francis **PR1223.V535 2004**
Victorian Poetry: An Annotated Anthology. Trade Cloth. Blackwell Publishing, Inc. Malden, MA. 2004. 736p. Blackwell Annotated Anthologies Ser. ISBN:0-631-23435-7, ISBN13: 978-0-631-23435-7. Dewey:821/.808. LCCN:2003-020732.
Audience: **g,l,u,f.**

Opie, Iona & Opie, Peter **PR1195**
The Oxford Book of Narrative Verse. Trade Paper. Oxford University Press, Inc. New York, NY. 2004. 422p. Oxford Books of Verse ISBN:0-19-280196-1, ISBN13: 978-0-19-280196-8. Dewey:821/.03/08.
Audience: **g,l,u,f.** B

Ramazani, Jahan (Editor), et al. **PR1175**
The Norton Anthology of Modern and Contemporary Poetry. Ed. 3. Richard Ellman & Robert O'Clair (Editors). Trade Paper. W. W. Norton & Company, Inc. New York, NY. 2003. 2000p. ISBN:0-393-32429-X, ISBN13: 978-0-393-32429-7. Dewey:821.008.
Audience: **g,l,u,f.**

Ricks, Christopher (Editor) **PR1223**
The New Oxford Book of Victorian Verse. Trade Paper. Oxford University Press, Inc. New York, NY. 2002. 688p. Oxford Books of Verse ISBN:0-19-284084-3, ISBN13: 978-0-19-284084-4. Dewey:821/.808.
Audience: **g,l,u,f.**

Ricks, Christopher **PR1175.O897 1999**
The Oxford Book of English Verse. Trade Cloth. Oxford University Press, Inc. New York, NY. 1999. 742p. ISBN:0-19-214182-1, ISBN13: 978-0-19-214182-8. Dewey:821.008. LCCN:99-020831.
Audience: **g,l,u,f.**

Ricks, Christopher (Editor) **PR1205**
Metaphysical Poetry. Colin Burrow (Introduction by). Trade Paper. Penguin Group (USA) Inc. New York, NY. 2006. 304p. ISBN:0-14-042444-X, ISBN13: 978-0-14-042444-7. Dewey:821.3.
Audience: **g,l,u,f.**

Rudrum, Alan (Editor), et al. **PR1127.B76 2000**
The Broadview Anthology of Seventeenth-Century Verse and Prose. Joseph Black & Holly Nelson (Editors). Trade Paper. Broadview Press. Peterborough, ON. 2000. 1303p. Anthologies of English Literature Ser. ISBN:1-55111-053-9, ISBN13: 978-1-55111-053-0. Dewey:820.8/004. LCCN:2001-272401.
Audience: **g,l,u,f.**

Silkin, Jon (Editor) **PR1195.W65**
The Penguin Book of First World War Poetry. Ed. 2. Trade Paper. Penguin Group (USA) Inc. New York, NY. 1997. 356p. Twentieth Century Classics Ser. ISBN:0-14-118009-9, ISBN13: 978-0-14-118009-0. Dewey:821/.912/080358.
Audience: **g,l,u,f.**

Thomas, Donald (Editor) **PR1223**
The Everyman Book of Victorian Verse: The Pre-Raphaelites to the Nineties. Ed. 2. Trade Paper. Tuttle Publishing. Boston, MA. 1993. 240p. ISBN:0-460-87310-5, ISBN13: 978-0-460-87310-9. Dewey:821.808.
Audience: **g,l,u,f.**

Thomas, Donald (Editor) **PR1223**
The Everyman Book of Victorian Verse: The Post-Romantics. Trade Paper. Tuttle Publishing. Boston, MA. 1995. 288p. ISBN:0-460-87526-4, ISBN13: 978-0-460-87526-4. Dewey:821/.808.
Audience: **g,l,u,f.**

Tuma, Keith (Editor) **PR1225.O86 2001**
Anthology of Twentieth-Century British and Irish Poetry. Paper Text. Oxford University Press, Inc. New York, NY. 2001. 976p. ISBN:0-19-512894-X, ISBN13: 978-0-19-512894-9. Dewey:821/.9108. LCCN:00-041648.
Audience: **g,l,u,f.**

Turner, Michael R. **PR1223 .V5 1992**
Victorian Parlour Poetry: An Annotated Anthology. Trade Paper. Dover Publications, Inc. Mineola, NY. 1992. 325p. ISBN:0 486 27044 0, ISBN13: 978-0-486-27044-9. Dewey:821/.808. LCCN:91-037613.
Audience: **g,l,u,f.**

Untermeyer, Louis **PR1224 .U6**
Modern British Poetry. Trade Paper. Kessinger Publishing, LLC. Whitefish, MT. 2003. ISBN:0-7661-7593-6, ISBN13: 978-0-7661-7593-8. Dewey:821/.9/109.
Audience: **g,l,u,f.** B

Wain, John (Editor) **PR1175.O97 2003**
The Oxford Anthology of English Poetry: Spenser to Crabbe, Vol. I. Trade Paper. Oxford University Press, Inc. New York, NY. 2003. 684p. ISBN:0-19-280421-9, ISBN13: 978-0-19-280421-1. Dewey:821.008. LCCN:2003-267577.
Audience: **g,l,u,f.**

Wain, John (Editor) **PR1175.O97 2003**
The Oxford Anthology of English Poetry: Blake to Heaney. Trade Paper. Oxford University Press, Inc. New York, NY. 2003. 790p. ISBN:0-19-280422-7, ISBN13: 978-0-19-280422-8. Dewey:821.008. LCCN:2003-267577.
Audience: **g,l,u,f.**

Wordsworth, Jonathon & Wordsworth, Jessica (Contribution by) **PR1222**
The Penguin Book of Romantic Poetry. Trade Paper. Penguin Group (USA) Inc. New York, NY. 2006. 1056p. ISBN:0-14-043568-9, ISBN13: 978-0-14-043568-9. Dewey:821.708.
Audience: **g,l,u,f.**

Wu, Duncan (Editor) **PR1207.R46 2002**
Renaissance Poetry. Trade Cloth. Blackwell Publishing, Inc. Malden, MA. 2002. 208p. Blackwell Essential Literature Ser. ISBN:0-631-23009-2, ISBN13: 978-0-631-23009-0. Dewey:821/.308. LCCN:2002-022322.
Audience: **g,l,u,f.**

Wu, Duncan (Editor) **PR1222.R65 2002**
Romantic Poetry. Trade Cloth. Blackwell Publishing, Inc. Malden, MA. 2002. 192p. Blackwell Essential Literature Ser. ISBN:0-631-22973-6, ISBN13: 978-0-631-22973-5. Dewey:821/.7080145. LCCN:2002-020873.
Audience: **g,l,u,f.**

Wu, Duncan & DeMaria, Robert Jr. (Editors) **PR1217.P66 2002**
Poetry from 1660 to 1780: Civil War, Restoration, Revolution. Trade Cloth. Blackwell Publishing, Inc. Malden, MA. 2002. 192p. Blackwell Essential Literature Ser. ISBN:0-631-22981-7, ISBN13: 978-0-631-22981-0. Dewey:821/.509. LCCN:2002-023953.
Audience: **g,l,u,f.**

Wu, Duncan & Treharne, Elaine (Editors) **PR1203.O43 2002**
Old and Middle English Poetry. Trade Cloth. Blackwell Publishing, Inc. Malden, MA. 2002. 176p. Blackwell Essential Literature Ser. ISBN:0-631-23073-4, ISBN13: 978-0-631-23073-1. Dewey:829/.108. LCCN:2002-020868.
Audience: **l,u,f.**

Collections of British Literature > By Form > Drama

Barker, Simon & Hinds, Hilary (Editors) **PR1263.R68 2002**
Routledge Anthology of Renaissance Drama. Paper over Boards.

Routledge. New York, NY. 2002. 480p. ISBN:0-415-18733-8, ISBN13: 978-0-415-18733-6. Dewey:822/.308. LCCN:2002-026872.
Audience: **l,u,f.**

Bevington, David **PR1263.E56 2003**
English Renaissance Drama: A Norton Anthology. Lars Engle, Katharine Eisaman Maus & Eric Rasmussen (Editors). Trade Cloth. W. W. Norton & Company, Inc. New York, NY. 2002. 2400p. ISBN:0-393-97655-6, ISBN13: 978-0-393-97655-7. Dewey:822/.308. LCCN:2002-025074.
Audience: **l,u,f.**

Boucicault, Dion, et al. **PR1271.L66 2001**
London Assurance and Other Victorian Comedies. William S. Gilbert, Edward Bulwer-Lytton & Henry James (Authors), Klaus Stierstorfer & Michael Cordner (Editors). Trade Paper. Oxford University Press, Inc. New York, NY. 2001. 391p. Oxford English Drama Ser. ISBN:0-19-283296-4, ISBN13: 978-0-19-283296-2. Dewey:822/.05230808. LCCN:2001-275416.
Audience: **g,u,f.**

Harrington, John P. (Editor) **PR8869.M63 1991**
Modern Irish Drama. Trade Paper. W. W. Norton & Company, Inc. New York, NY. 1991. 592p. Critical Editions Ser. ISBN:0-393-96063-3, ISBN13: 978-0-393-96063-1. Dewey:822/.910809415. LCCN:90-038999.
Audience: **g,l,u,f.**

Pix, Mary, et al. **PR1269.E358 2001**
Eighteenth-Century Women Dramatists. Susanna Centlivre, Elizabeth Griffith & Hannah Cowley (Authors), Melinda C. Finberg (Editor). Trade Paper. Oxford University Press, Inc. New York, NY. 2001. 442p. Oxford English Drama Ser., :Oxford World's Classics ISBN:0-19-282729-4, ISBN13: 978-0-19-282729-6. Dewey:822/.50809287. LCCN:2001-035080.
Audience: **g,l,u,f.**

Von Sneidern, Maja-Lisa **PR1265.B76 2003**
The Broadview Anthology of Restoration and Early Eighteenth-Century Drama. J. Douglas Canfield (Editor). Trade Paper. Broadview Press. Peterborough, ON. 2003. xx, 1033p. Broadview Anthologies of English Literature Ser. ISBN:1-55111-581-6, ISBN13: 978-1-55111-581-8. Dewey:822/.408. LCCN:2003-464003.
Audience: **g,l,u,f.**

Wu, Duncan & Womersley, David (Editors) **PR1266.R35 2002**
Restoration Comedy. Duncan Wu (Introduction by). Trade Cloth. Blackwell Publishing, Inc. Malden, MA. 2002. 160p. Blackwell Essential Literature Ser. ISBN:0-631-23471-3, ISBN13: 978-0-631-23471-5. Dewey:822/.05230804. LCCN:2002-023954.
Audience: **l,u,f.**

Collections of British Literature > By Form > Prose

Addison, Joseph, et al. **PR1365.T23C66 1998**
The Commerce of Everyday Life: Selections from the Tatler and the Spectator (Bedford Cultural Editions). Richard Steele & Erin Mackie (Authors). Cloth over Boards. Palgrave Macmillan. New York, NY. 1998. 368p. Bedford Cultural Editions Ser. ISBN:0-312-16371-1, ISBN13: 978-0-312-16371-6. Dewey:824.508. LCCN:97-074950.
Audience: **g,l,u,f.** *Choice, 1998.*

Alden, Raymond MacDonald (Editor) **PR1301 .A4**
Readings in English Prose of the Nineteenth Century. Trade Paper. Kessinger Publishing, LLC. Whitefish, MT. 2005. ISBN:0-7661-9484-1, ISBN13: 978-0-7661-9484-7. Dewey:824.8080353.
Audience: **g.**

Broomfield, Andrea & Mitchell, Sally **PR1286.W6P76 1996**
Prose by Victorian Women: An Anthology. Cloth Text. Garland Publishing, Inc. New York, NY. 1995. 752p. Garland Reference Library of the Humanities, Vol. 1893: ISBN:0-8153-1970-3, ISBN13: 978-0-8153-1970-2. Dewey:828/.8080809287. LCCN:95-024400.
Audience: **g,l,u,f.** *Choice, 1996.*

Byatt, A. S. (Editor) **PR1309.S5088 2002**
The Oxford Book of English Short Stories. Trade Paper. Oxford University Press, Inc. New York, NY. 2003. 480p. Oxford Books of Prose ISBN:0-19-280376-X, ISBN13: 978-0-19-280376-4. Dewey:823/.01/08.
Audience: **g,l,u,f.**

Craig, Patricia (Editor) **PN6120.95.D45O95**
The Oxford Book of English Detective Stories. Trade Paper. Oxford University Press, Inc. New York, NY. 2003. 576p. Oxford Books of Prose ISBN:0-19-280375-1, ISBN13: 978-0-19-280375-7. Dewey:823/.087208. LCCN:2003-267606.
Audience: **g.**

Drake, Nathan **PR0099**
Essays, Biographical, Critical, and Historical, Illustrative of the Tatler, Spectator, and Guardian, Vol. 3. Trade Paper. Books on Demand. Ann Arbor, MI. 408p. ISBN:0-598-71414-6, ISBN13: 978-0-598-71414-5. Dewey:824/.5/09. LCCN:15-000234.
Audience: **g.**

Forkner, Benjamin (Editor) **PR8875.M6 1980**
Modern Irish Short Stories. Anthony Burgess (Preface by). Trade Cloth. Penguin Group (USA) Inc. New York, NY. 1980. 512p. ISBN:0-670-48324-9, ISBN13: 978-0-670-48324-2. Dewey:823/.01/08. LCCN:80-016071.
Audience: **g,l,u,f.**

Gross, John **PR1285.N48 1998**
The New Oxford Book of English Prose. Trade Cloth. Oxford University Press, Inc. New York, NY. 1998. 1054p. ISBN:0-19-214246-1, ISBN13: 978-0-19-214246-7. Dewey:828/.08. LCCN:97-049397.
Audience: **g.**

Gross, John (Editor) **PR1363**
The Oxford Book of Essays. Trade Paper. Oxford University Press, Inc. New York, NY. 2002. 704p. Oxford Books of Prose ISBN:0-19-284089-4, ISBN13: 978-0-19-284089-9. Dewey:824/.008.
Audience: **g,l,u,f.**

Kermode, Anita **PN6130**
The Oxford Book of Letters. Frank Kermode (Editor). Trade Paper. Oxford University Press, Inc. New York, NY. 2003. 584p. ISBN:0-19-280490-1, ISBN13: 978-0-19-280490-7. Dewey:808.8/6.
Audience: **g,l,u,f.**

Mish, Charles C. (Editor) **PR1295.M5**
Restoration Prose Fiction, 1666-1700: An Anthology of Representative Pieces. Trade Paper. Books on Demand. Ann Arbor, MI. 305p. ISBN:0-608-16534-4, ISBN13: 978-0-608-16534-9. Dewey:823/.4/08. LCCN:76-098095.
Audience: **g.**

Mundhenk, Rosemary J. **PR1304.V55 1999**
Victorian Prose: An Anthology. Trade Cloth. Columbia University Press. New York, NY. 1999. 496p. ISBN:0-231-11026-X, ISBN13: 978-0-231-11026-6. Dewey:828/.80808. LCCN:98-046151.
Audience: **g.**

Robinson, Solveig C. (Editor) **PR463.S47 2003**
A Serious Occupation: Literary Criticism by Victorian Women Writers. Trade Paper. Broadview Press. Peterborough, ON. 2003. xv, 307p. ISBN:1-55111-350-3, ISBN13: 978-1-55111-350-0. Dewey:820.9/08. LCCN:2003-277525.
Audience: **g,l,u,f.**

Salzman, Paul **PR1293**
An Anthology of Elizabethan Prose Fiction. Trade Paper. Oxford University Press, Inc. New York, NY. 1998. 464p. Oxford World's Classics Ser. ISBN:0-19-283901-2, ISBN13: 978-0-19-283901-5. Dewey:823/.3/08.
Audience: **g.**

Turner, Paul **PR461**
Victorian Poetry, Drama, and Miscellaneous Prose, 1832-1890. Trade Cloth. Oxford University Press, Inc. New York, NY. 1990. 532p. Oxford History of English Literature Ser., Vol. XIV ISBN:0-19-812239-X, ISBN13: 978-0-19-812239-5. Dewey:820.9008.
Audience: **g.**

Wilson, John D. **PR1293.W5 1969**
Life in Shakespeare's England: A Book of Elizabethan Prose. Trade Cloth. Barnes & Noble Books-Imports. Lanham, MD. 1969. xv, 291p. ISBN:0-389-01168-1, ISBN13: 978-0-389-01168-2. Dewey:942.05/5. LCCN:68-023765.
Audience: **g.**

Individual Authors and Works > Anglo-Saxon. Old and Middle English

PR1583.D6 1975
Beowulf: The Donaldson Translation, Backgrounds and Sources, Criticism. Trade Cloth. Norton. Farnborough, 1975. xvi, 205p. ISBN:0-393 04413-0, ISBN13: 978-0-393-04413-3. Dewey:829/.3. LCCN:75-017991.
Audience: **l,u.**

Ball, Catherine N. **DA130**
Old English Pages. http://www.georgetown.edu/faculty/ballc/oe/old_english.html Georgetown University.
Audience: **l,u,f.**

Bedingfield, Brad **DA130**
Anglo-Saxon England: A Guide to Online Resources. http://www.the-orb.net/encyclop/early/pre1000/asindex.html College of Staten Island, City University of New York.
Audience: **l,u,f.**

Bessinger, J. B. (Editor) **PR1506**
A Concordance to the Anglo-Saxon Poetic Records. Trade Cloth. Cornell University Press. Ithaca, NY. 1978. 1503p. Concordances Ser. ISBN:0-8014-1146-7, ISBN13: 978-0-8014-1146-5. Dewey:829/.1. LCCN:77-006186.
Audience: **u,f.**

Blair, Peter Hunter **PA8260 .H85 1990**
The World of Bede. Michael Lapidge (Foreword by). Cloth Text. Cambridge University Press. New York, NY. 1990. 354p. ISBN:0-521-39138-5, ISBN13: 978-0-521-39138-2. Dewey:274.2. LCCN:90-037684.
Audience: **u.**

Bolton, W. F. & Wrenn, C. L. (Editors) **PR1580**
Beowulf: With the Finnesburg Fragment. Ed. 3. Trade Paper. University of Exeter Press. Exeter, 1997. 304p. Exeter Medieval Texts and Studies ISBN:0-85989-518-1, ISBN13: 978-0-85989-518-7. Dewey:829.3.
Audience: **u.**

Borroff, Marie **PR1972.G35A35 2001**
Sir Gawain and the Green Knight: Patience, and Pearl: Verse Translations. Trade Paper. W. W. Norton & Company, Inc. New York, NY. 2001. 193p. ISBN:0-393-97658-0, ISBN13: 978-0-393-97658-8. Dewey:821/.1. LCCN:00-061616.
Audience: **u,f.**

Calder, Daniel G. **PR1664.C3**
Cynewulf. Library Binding. Thomson Gale. Farmington Hills, MI. 1981. 189p. English Authors Ser. ISBN:0-8057-6814-9, ISBN13: 978-0-8057-6814-5. Dewey:829/.4. LCCN:81-002343.
Audience: **u.**

Cartlidge, Neil (Editor) **PR2109.O7 A32 2001**
The Owl and the Nightingale: Text and Translation. Trade Cloth. University of Exeter Press. Exeter, 2001. 256p. Medieval Texts and Studies ISBN:0-85989-690-0, ISBN13: 978-0-85989-690-0. Dewey:821.1.
Audience: **u,f.**

Chickering, Howell D. **PR1583**
Beowulf: A Dual-Language Edition. Trade Paper. Knopf Publishing Group. New York, NY. 2006. 464p. ISBN:1-4000-9622-7, ISBN13: 978-1-4000-9622-0. Dewey:829.
Audience: **l,u.**

Doane, Alger N. **PR1611.A3.D6**
Genesis A: A New Edition. Trade Cloth. University of Wisconsin Press. Chicago, IL. 1978. 430p. ISBN:0-299-07430-7, ISBN13: 978-0-299-07430-2. Dewey:829/.1. LCCN:77-077437.
Audience: **u.**

Greenfield, Stanley B. (Translator) **PR1585**
A Readable "Beowulf": The Old English Epic Newly Translated. Alain Renoir (Introduction by). Trade Cloth. Southern Illinois University Press. Carbondale, IL. 1982. 173p. ISBN:0-8093-1060-0, ISBN13: 978-0-8093-1060-9. Dewey:829/.3. LCCN:81-016933.
Audience: **l,u.**

Hasenfratz, Robert J. (Editor) **PR1806 .H37 2000**
Ancrene Wisse. Trade Paper. Medieval Institute Publications. Kalamazoo, MI. 2005. xii + 690p. Middle English Texts Ser. ISBN:1-58044-070-3, ISBN13: 978-1-58044-070-7. Dewey:255/.901. LCCN:00-045252.
Audience: **u,f.**

Heaney, Seamus **PR1583.H43 2001**
Beowulf: A New Verse Translation. Trade Paper. W. W. Norton & Company, Inc. New York, NY. 2001. 224p. Critical Editions Ser. ISBN:0-393-97580-0, ISBN13: 978-0-393-97580-2. Dewey:829/.3. LCCN:2001-042554.
Audience: **g,l,u,f.**

Kiernan, Kevin **PR1580.K47 1999**
Electronic Beowulf. British Library. 1999. ISBN:0-7123-0494-0, ISBN13: 978-0-7123-0494-8.
Audience: **u,f.**

Klaeber **PR1580**
Beowulf and the Fight at Finnsburg. Ed. 3. Cloth Text. Houghton Mifflin College Division. Boston, MA. 1950. 471p. ISBN:0-669-21212-1, ISBN13: 978-0-669-21212-9. Dewey:829.3.
Audience: **u.**

Lehmann, Ruth P. M. (Translator) **PR1583.L38 1988**
Beowulf: An Imitative Translation. Trade Paper. University of Texas Press. Austin, TX. 1988. 127p. ISBN:0-292-70771-1, ISBN13: 978-0-292-70771-9. Dewey:829/.3. LCCN:88-010306.
Audience: **l.** *Choice, 1989.*

Millet, Bella **PR1808 .W48**
Ancrene Wisse/A Guide for Anchoresses: A Translation. Trade Paper. University of Exeter Press. Exeter, 2006. ISBN:0-85989-776-1, ISBN13: 978-0-85989-776-1. Dewey:255.901.
Audience: **u,f.**

Millett, Bella (Editor) **BX4213**
Ancrene Wisse, Vol. 1. Trade Cloth. Oxford University Press, Inc. New York, NY. 2006. 450p. Early English Text Society Original Ser. ISBN:0-19-722328-1, ISBN13: 978-0-19-722328-4. Dewey:248.8943.
Audience: **u,f.**

Simpson, James **PR2017.L38S56 1990**
Piers Plowman: An Introduction to the B-Text. Ed. 1. Cloth Text. Addison-Wesley Longman, Ltd. Harlow, 1990. 292p. ISBN:0-582-01392-5, ISBN13: 978-0-582-01392-6. Dewey:821/.1. LCCN:89-034272.
Audience: **u,f.** *Choice, 1991.*

Stanbury, Sarah (Editor) **PR2111.A2S73 2001**
Pearl. Consortium for the Teaching of the Middle Ages Staff (Contribution by). Trade Paper. Medieval Institute Publications. Kalamazoo, MI. 2003. viii + 112p. Middle English Texts Ser. ISBN:1-58044-033-9, ISBN13: 978-1-58044-033-2. Dewey:821/.1. LCCN:2001-044863.
Audience: **u,f.**

Vantuono, William (Translator) **PR2111.A28 1995**
Pearl: An Edition with Verse Translation. Paper Text. University of Notre Dame Press. Notre Dame, IN. 1995. 272p. ISBN:0-268-03811-2, ISBN13: 978-0-268-03811-3. Dewey:821/.1. LCCN:95-016890.
Audience: **u,f.** *Choice, 1996.*

Wada, Yoko (Editor) **PR1810.C657 2003**
A Companion to "Ancrene Wisse". Trade Cloth. Boydell & Brewer, Ltd. Woodbridge, 2003. 272p. ISBN:0-85991-762-2, ISBN13: 978-0-85991-762-9. Dewey:255/.901. LCCN:2002-155074.
Audience: **u,f.**

Williamson, Craig **PR1762.W5 1982**
A Feast of Creatures: Anglo-Saxon Riddle Songs. Trade Cloth. University of Pennsylvania Press. Philadelphia, PA. 1982. 240p. ISBN:0-8122-7843-7, ISBN13: 978-0-8122-7843-9. Dewey:829/.1. LCCN:82-004907.
Audience: **u.**

Individual Authors and Works > Anglo-Saxon. Old and Middle English > Criticism. Interpretation

Brodeur, Arthur Gilchrist **PR1585.B68**
The Art of Beowulf. Paper Text. Textbook Publishers. Temecula, CA. 2003. ix, 283p. ISBN:0-7581-2730-8, ISBN13: 978-0-7581-2730-3. Dewey:829.3.
Audience: **u,f.**

Chambers, R. W. **PR1585.C5**
Beowulf: An Introduction to the Study of the Poem with a Discussion of the Stories of Offa and Finn,. Paper Text. Textbook Publishers. Temecula, CA. 2003. xvii, 628p. ISBN:0-7581-1317-X, ISBN13: 978-0-7581-1317-7. Dewey:829.3.
Audience: **u.**

Clark, George (Editor) **PR1585.C55 1990**
Beowulf. Trade Cloth. Thomson Gale. Farmington Hills, MI. 1990. 308p. Twayne's English Authors Ser., No. 477 ISBN:0-8057-6996-X, ISBN13: 978-0-8057-6996-8. Dewey:829/.3. LCCN:89-077340.
Audience: **u,f.** *Choice, 1990.*

Creed, Robert P. **PR1588.C7 1990**
Reconstructing the Rhythm of Beowulf. Cloth Text. University of Missouri Press. Columbia, MO. 1990. 232p. ISBN:0-8262-0722-7, ISBN13: 978-0-8262-0722-7. Dewey:829/.3. LCCN:89-029252.
Audience: **u,f.** *Choice, 1991.*

Deskis, Susan E. **PR1587.P75D47 1996**
Beowulf and the Medieval Proverb Tradition. Trade Cloth. M R T S. Tempe, AZ. 1996. 192p. Medieval and Renaissance Texts and Studies, Vol. 155 ISBN:0-86698-195-0, ISBN13: 978-0-86698-195-8. Dewey:829/.3. LCCN:95-026147.
Audience: **u,f.** *Choice, 1997.*

Earl, James W. **PR1585.E37 1994**
Thinking about "Beowulf". Trade Cloth. Stanford University Press. Palo Alto, CA. 1994. xiv, 204p. ISBN:0-8047-1700-1, ISBN13: 978-0-8047-1700-7. Dewey:829.3. LCCN:93-047132.
Audience: **u.** *Choice, 1995.*

Fry, Donald K. **Z2012 .F83**
Beowulf and the Fight at Finnsburg: A Bibliography. Cloth Text. University Press of Virginia. Charlottesville, VA. 1969. xx, 222p. ISBN:0-8139-0268-1, ISBN13: 978-0-8139-0268-5. Dewey:016.829/3. LCCN:70-094760.
Audience: **u,f.**

Hasenfratz, Robert J. **Z2012.H23 1993**
Beowulf Scholarship: An Annotated Bibliography, 1979-1990. Cloth Text. Garland Publishing, Inc. New York, NY. 1993. 448p. Medieval Bibliographies Ser., Vol. 14 ISBN:0-8153-0084-0, ISBN13: 978-0-8153-0084-7. Dewey:016.8/293. LCCN:93-017683.
Audience: **u,f.** *Choice, 1994.*

Hudson, Marc **PR1585.H84 1990**
Beowulf: A Translation and Commentary. Trade Cloth. Bucknell University Press. Cranbury, NJ. 1990. 184p. ISBN:0-8387-5162-8, ISBN13: 978-0-8387-5162-6. Dewey:829/.3. LCCN:88-043407.
Audience: **u.** *Choice, 1991.*

Huppe, Bernard F. **PR1585.H86 1984**
The Hero in the Earthly City: A Reading of Beowulf. Trade Paper. M R T S. Tempe, AZ. 1984. 208p. Medieval and Renaissance Texts and Studies, Vol. 33 ISBN:0-86698-067-9, ISBN13: 978-0-86698-067-8. Dewey:829/.3. LCCN:84-000674.
Audience: **u,f.**

Irving, Edward B. Jr. **PR1585**
A Reading of Beowulf. Paper Text. Brigham Young University. Provo, UT. 1999. ISBN:0-8425-2452-5, ISBN13: 978-0-8425-2452-0. Dewey:829.3.
Audience: **u.**

Kiernan, Kevin S. **PR1585.K5 1996**
Beowulf and the Beowulf Manuscript. Katherine O. O'Keefe (Introduction by). Trade Paper. University of Michigan Press. Chicago, IL. 1997. 360p. ISBN:0-472-08412-7, ISBN13: 978-0-472-08412-8. Dewey:829/.3. LCCN:96-031025.
Audience: **u.**

Lee, Alvin **PR1585.L44 1998**
Gold-Hall and Earth-Dragon: Beowulf as Metaphor. Cloth over Boards. University of Toronto Press. Toronto, ON. 1999. 328p. ISBN:0-8020-4378-X, ISBN13: 978-0-8020-4378-8. Dewey:829/.3. LCCN:99-189724.
Audience: **u.** *Choice, 1999.*

Niles, John D. **PR1585.N54**
Beowulf: The Poem and Its Tradition. Trade Paper. Books on Demand. Ann Arbor, MI. 1983. 320p. ISBN:0-7837-2304-0, ISBN13: 978-0-7837-2304-4. Dewey:829/.3. LCCN:83-004308.
Audience: **u.**

Ogilvy, J. D. & Baker, Donald C. **PR1585**
Reading "Beowulf": An Introduction to the Poem, Its Background, and Its Style. Keith Baker (Illustrator). Trade Paper. University of Oklahoma Press. Norman, OK. 1986. 240p. ISBN:0-8061-2019-3, ISBN13: 978-0-8061-2019-5. Dewey:829/.3. LCCN:83-047835.
Audience: **l,u.**

Orchard, Andy **PR1585.O73 2003**
A Critical Companion to 'Beowulf'. Trade Cloth. Boydell & Brewer, Ltd. Woodbridge, 2004. 416p. ISBN:0-85991-766-5, ISBN13: 978-0-85991-766-7. Dewey:829.3. LCCN:2002-008049.
Audience: **u,f.** *Choice, 2003.*

Pearsall, Derek Albert **PN685.P43 2003**
Arthurian Romance: A Short Introduction. Trade Paper. Blackwell Publishing, Inc. Malden, MA. 2003. 192p. Blackwell Introductions to Literature Ser. ISBN:0-631-23320-2, ISBN13: 978-0-631-23320-6. Dewey:809/.93351. LCCN:2002-038486.
Audience: **u,f.** *Choice, 2003.*

Robinson, Fred C. **PR1588.R6 1985**
Beowulf and the Appositive Style. Cloth Text. University of Tennessee Press. Knoxville, TN. 1985. 120p. Hodges Lectures ISBN:0-87049-444-9, ISBN13: 978-0-87049-444-4. Dewey:829.3. LCCN:84-011889.
Audience: **u,f.** *Choice, 1985.*

Staver, Ruth Johnston **PR1585**
A Companion to Beowulf. Trade Cloth. Greenwood Publishing Group, Inc. Portsmouth, NH. 2005. 248p. ISBN:0-313-33224-X, ISBN13: 978-0-313-33224-1. Dewey:829.3. LCCN:2005-006568.
Audience: **l.** *Choice, 2006.*

Individual Authors and Works > Anglo-Saxon. Old and Middle English > Language

Barney, Stephen A. **PE274.B3 1985**
Word-Hoard: An Introduction to Old English Vocabulary. Ed. 2. Trade Paper. Yale University Press. Cumberland, RI. 1985. 86p. Yale Language Ser. ISBN:0-300-03506-3, ISBN13: 978-0-300-03506-3. Dewey:429/.81. LCCN:76-047003.
Audience: **l,u.**

Cassidy, F. J. & Ringler, R. **PE137**
Bright's Old English Grammar. Ed. 3. Cloth Text. Harcourt College Publishers. Fort Worth, TX. 1972. 494p. ISBN:0-03-084713-3, ISBN13: 978-0-03-084713-4. Dewey:429/.5. LCCN:76-179921.
Audience: **l,u.**

Diamond, Robert E. **PE135.D5 1989**
Old English: Grammar and Reader. Paper Text. Wayne State University Press. Detroit, MI. 1970. 304p. Waynebooks Ser., No. 38 ISBN:0-8143-1510-0, ISBN13: 978-0-8143-1510-1. Dewey:429/.82421. LCCN:89-005763.
Audience: **l,u.**

Hall, J. R. **PE279 .H3X 1984**
A Concise Anglo-Saxon Dictionary. Ed. 4. Herbert D. Meritt (Supplement by). Trade Paper. University of Toronto Press. Toronto, ON. 1984. 432p. Medieval Academy Reprints for Teaching Ser., No. 14 ISBN:0-8020-6548-1, ISBN13: 978-0-8020-6548-3. Dewey:429/.321. LCCN:87-673538.
Audience: **g.**

Jember, Gregory K. **PE279.J4**
English Old Eng. Old Eng. Dictionary. Trade Cloth. Westview Press. Boulder, CO. 1983. xxxiii, 178 pp. ISBN:0-89158-006-9, ISBN13: 978-0-89158-006-5. Dewey:429/.3/21. LCCN:75-030928.
Audience: **g.**

Marsden, Richard C. & Orchard, Andrew P. **PE137.M46 2003**
The Cambridge Old English Reader. Cloth Text. Cambridge University Press. New York, NY. 2004. 566p. ISBN:0-521-45426-3, ISBN13: 978-0-521-45426-1. Dewey:429/.86421. LCCN:2003-043579.
Audience: **u.** *Choice, 2004.*

Mitchell, Bruce & Robinson, Fred C. (Editors) **PE131.M5 2001**
A Guide to Old English. Ed. 6. Trade Paper. Blackwell Publishing, Inc. Malden, MA. 2001. 424p. ISBN:0-631-22636-2, ISBN13: 978-0-631-22636-9. Dewey:429/.82421. LCCN:00-046781.
Audience: **l,u,f.**

Robinson, Orrin W. **PD75**
Old English and Its Closest Relatives: A Survey of the Earliest Germanic Languages. Trade Paper. Stanford University Press. Palo Alto, CA. 1993. 304p. ISBN:0-8047-2221-8, ISBN13: 978-0-8047-2221-6. Dewey:430/.09.
Audience: **l,u,f.** *Choice, 1992.*

Individual Authors and Works > Anglo-Saxon. Old and Middle English > Metrical Romances

Benson, Larry D. (Editor) **PR2064.B4 1994**
King Arthur's Death: The Middle English Stanzaic Morte Arthur and Alliterative Morte Arthur. Edward E. Foster (Contribution by). Trade Paper. Medieval Institute Publications. Kalamazoo, MI. 2000. xii + 292p. Teams Middle English Text Ser. ISBN:1-879288-38-9, ISBN13: 978-1-879288-38-6. Dewey:821/.108. LCCN:94-026544.
Audience: **u,f.**

Borroff, Marie **PR2065.G31 B6**
Sir Gawain and the Green Knight: A Stylistic and Metrical Study. Paper Text. Textbook Publishers. Temecula, CA. 2003. xii, 295p. ISBN:0-7581-0137-6, ISBN13: 978-0-7581-0137-2. Dewey:821/.1.
Audience: **u,f.**

Brewer, Derek S. & Gibson, Jonathan (Editors) **PR321**
A Companion to the Gawain-Poet. Trade Paper. Boydell & Brewer, Ltd. Woodbridge, 2002. 452p. Arthurian Studies ISBN:0-85991-529-8, ISBN13: 978-0-85991-529-8. Dewey:821.1/09.
Audience: **u,f.** *Choice, 1997.*

Gordon, E. V. (Editor) **PR1203**
Sir Gawain and the Green Knight. Ed. 2. J. R. R. Tolkien (Translator). Paper Text. Oxford University Press, Inc. New York, NY. 1968. 260p. ISBN:0-19-811486-9, ISBN13: 978-0-19-811486-4. Dewey:821/.1/08.
Audience: **u,f.**

Kittredge, George Lyman **PR2065.G31K5**
A Study of Gawain and the Green Knight. Paper Text. Textbook Publishers. Temecula, CA. 2003. 323p. ISBN:0-7581-6785-7, ISBN13: 978-0-7581-6785-9. Dewey:821.1.
Audience: **u,f.**

Krishna, Valerie S. **PR2065.M3.A34 1983**
The Alliterative Morte Arthure: A New Verse Translation. Trade Cloth. University Press of America, Inc. Lanham, MD. 1983. 144p. ISBN:0-8191-3035-4, ISBN13: 978-0-8191-3035-8. Dewey:821/.1. LCCN:82-024838.
Audience: **u,f.**

Matthews, William **PR2065.M4M3**
The Tragedy of Arthur: A Study of the Alliterative Morte Arthure. Paper Text. Textbook Publishers. Temecula, CA. 2003. 230p. ISBN:0-7581-2748-0, ISBN13: 978-0-7581-2748-8. Dewey:821.1.
Audience: **u,f.**

Merwin, W. S. **PR2065.G3A35 2002**
Sir Gawain and the Green Knight: A New Verse Translation. Trade Cloth. Alfred A. Knopf Inc. New York, NY. 2002. 208p. ISBN:0-375-41476-2, ISBN13: 978-0-375-41476-3. Dewey:821/.1. LCCN:2002-020815.
Audience: **u,f.**

Sands, Donald B. (Editor) **PR2064.M46 1986**
Middle English Verse Romances. Trade Cloth. University of Exeter Press. Exeter, 1986. 408p. Medieval English Texts and Studies ISBN:0-85989-228-X, ISBN13: 978-0-85989-228-5. Dewey:821/.1/08. LCCN:88-168272.
Audience: **u,f.**

Individual Authors and Works > Anglo-Saxon. Old and Middle English > Individual Authors

Kempe, Margery **PR2007.K4A199 2001**
The Book of Margery Kempe. Trade Paper. W. W. Norton & Company, Inc. New York, NY. 2000. 328p. Critical Editions Ser. ISBN:0-393-97639-4, ISBN13: 978-0-393-97639-7. Dewey:248.2/2/092 B. LCCN:00-055455.
Audience: **g,l,u,f.**

Kempe, Margery B. **PR2007.K4A199 1996**
The Book of Margery Kempe. Lynn Staley (Editor). Trade Paper. Medieval Institute Publications. Kalamazoo, MI. 1998. viii, 263p. Middle English Texts ISBN:1-879288-72-9, ISBN13: 978-1-879288-72-0. Dewey:[B]. LCCN:96-027254.
Audience: **u,f.**

Individual Authors and Works > Anglo-Saxon. Old and Middle English > Individual Authors > Chaucer, Geoffrey

Ackroyd, Peter **PR1905**
Chaucer. UK-B Format Paperback. Knopf Publishing Group. New York, NY. 2005. 144p. ISBN:0-09-928748-X, ISBN13: 978-0-09-928748-3. Dewey:821/.1 B.
Audience: **g,l,u,f.**

Benson, C. David **PR1874 .B46 1986**
Chaucer's Drama of Style: Poetic Variety and Contrast in the Canterbury Tales. Trade Cloth. University of North Carolina Press. Chapel Hill, NC. 1986. 193p. ISBN:0-8078-1679-5, ISBN13: 978-0-8078-1679-0. Dewey:821/.1. LCCN:85-020849.
Audience: **u,f.**

Benson, C. David **PR1896.B46 1990**
Chaucer's Troilus and Criseyde. Trade Cloth. Routledge. New York, NY. 1990. 226p. ISBN:0-04-800085-X, ISBN13: 978-0-04-800085-9. Dewey:821/.1. LCCN:90-039824.
Audience: **u,f.**

Benson, C. David (Editor) **PR1924.C75 1991**
Critical Essays on Chaucer's Troilus and Criseyde and His Major Early Poems. Cloth Text. University of Toronto Press. Toronto, ON. 1991. 440p. ISBN:0-8020-5006-9, ISBN13: 978-0-8020-5006-9. Dewey:821/.1. LCCN:90-028318.
Audience: **u,f.**

Benson, Larry D., et al. **PR1851.B46 1987**
The Riverside Chaucer. Ed. 3. Geoffrey Chaucer, Robert Pratt & F. N. Robinson (Authors). Cloth Text. Houghton Mifflin College Division. Boston, MA. 1986. 1327p. ISBN:0-395-29031-7, ISBN13: 978-0-395-29031-6. Dewey:821/.1. LCCN:86-081304.
Audience: **u,f.** B

Boitani, Piero & Mann, Jill (Editors) **PR1924.C28 2003**
The Cambridge Companion to Chaucer. Ed. 2. Cloth Text. Cambridge University Press. New York, NY. 2004. 334p. Cambridge Companions to Literature Ser. ISBN:0-521-81556-8, ISBN13: 978-0-521-81556-7. Dewey:821/.1. LCCN:2003-051485.
Audience: **u,f.** *Choice, 2004, 1987.*

Bowden, Muriel **PR1851**
A Commentary on the General Prologue to the Canterbury Tales. Paper Text. Textbook Publishers. Temecula, CA. 2003. ix, 316p. ISBN:0-7581-9132-4, ISBN13: 978-0-7581-9132-8. Dewey:821.17.
Audience: **u,f.**

Bowden, Muriel **PR1924.B6 2001**
A Reader's Guide to Geoffrey Chaucer. Trade Paper. Syracuse University Press. Syracuse, NY. 2001. viii, 212p. Reader's Guide Ser. ISBN:0-8156-0696-6, ISBN13: 978-0-8156-0696-3. Dewey:821/.1. LCCN:00-053337.
Audience: **u,f.**

Brewer, Derek S. **PR1906.5.B68 1992**
Chaucer and His World. Trade Paper. Boydell & Brewer, Ltd. Woodbridge, 1996. 224p. ISBN.0-85991-366-X, ISBN13: 978-0-85991-366-9. Dewey:821/.1. LCCN:92-035873.
Audience: **u,f.**

Brewer, Derek S. **PR1924 .C44 1995**
Geoffrey Chaucer: 1837-1933. Paper over Boards. Routledge. New York, NY. 1996. 356p. Critical Heritage Ser., Vol. 1 ISBN:0-415-13398-X, ISBN13: 978-0-415-13398-2. Dewey:821.1.
Audience: **u,f.**

Brewer, Derek S. **PR1905.B72 1998**
A New Introduction to Chaucer: Longman Medieval and Renaissance. Ed. 2. Trade Paper. Longman Publishing Group. White Plains, NY. 1998. 416p. Longman Medieval and Renaissance Library ISBN:0-582-09348-1, ISBN13: 978-0-582-09348-5. Dewey:821.1. LCCN:97-043000.
Audience: **u,f.**

Brewer, Derek S. (Editor) **PR1924 .C44**
: 1385-1837, Vol. 1. Trade Cloth. Routledge. New York, NY. 1978. The Critical Heritage Ser. ISBN:0-7100-0223-8, ISBN13: 978-0-7100-0223-5. Dewey:821/.1.
Audience: **u,f.**

Brewer, Derek S. (Editor) **PR1924 .C44**
: 1837-1933, Vol. 2. Trade Cloth. Routledge. New York, NY. 1978. The Critical Heritage Ser. ISBN:0-7100-0224-6, ISBN13: 978-0-7100-0224-2. Dewey:821/.1.
Audience: **u,f.**

Brown, Peter (Editor) **PR1906.5 .C66 2002**
A Companion to Chaucer. Trade Paper. Blackwell Publishing, Inc. Malden, MA. 2002. 536p. ISBN:0-631-23590-6, ISBN13: 978-0-631-23590-3. Dewey:821.1.
Audience: **u,f.** *Choice, 2001.*

Cannon, Christopher **PR1940 .C36 1998**
The Making of Chaucer's English: A Study of Words. Trade Cloth. Cambridge University Press. New York, NY. 1999. 451p. Cambridge Studies in Medieval Literature, No. 39 ISBN:0-521-59274-7, ISBN13: 978-0-521-59274-1. Dewey:821/.1. LCCN:97-035262.
Audience: **u,f.**

Chaucer, Geoffrey **PR1866.R8 1983 PT.2**
The General Prologue. Trade Cloth. University of Oklahoma Press. Norman, OK. 1994. 326p. A Variorum Edition of the Works of Geoffrey Chaucer, The Canterbury Tales Ser., Pts. 1A-1B ISBN:0-8061-2552-7, ISBN13: 978-0-8061-2552-7. Dewey:821/.1. LCCN:93-034265.
Audience: **u,f.** *Choice, 1994.*

Chaucer, Geoffrey **PR1850**
Works: A Facsimile of the William Morris Kelmscott Chaucer, with the Original 87 Illus by Edward Burne: Jones, Together with an Introd. by John T. Winterich and a Glossary for the Modern Reader. Paper Text. Textbook Publishers. Temecula, CA. 2003. xixp. ISBN:0-7581-0258-5, ISBN13: 978-0-7581-0258-4. Dewey:821.17.
Audience: **u,f.**

Chaucer, Geoffrey **PR1924**
The Canterbury Tales. Donald C. Baker (Editor). Trade Cloth. University of Oklahoma Press. Norman, OK. 1983. 304p. A Variorum Edition of the Works of Geoffrey Chaucer, The Canterbury Tales Ser., Vol. II, Pt. 3 ISBN:0-8061-1785-0, ISBN13: 978-0-8061-1785-0. Dewey:822.92. LCCN:81-040286.
Audience: **u,f.** B

Chauncer, Geoffrey **PR1866.R8 1983,PT.10**
The Manciple's Tale. Donald C. Baker (Editor). Trade Cloth. University of Oklahoma Press. Norman, OK. 1984. 174p. A Variorum Edition of the Works of Geoffrey Chaucer, The Canterbury Tales Ser., Vol. 10 ISBN:0-8061-1872-5, ISBN13: 978-0-8061-1872-7. Dewey:821/.1. LCCN:83-014734.
Audience: **u,f.**

Chaucer, Geoffrey **PR1866.R8**
The Squire's Tale. Donald C. Baker (Editor). Trade Cloth. University of Oklahoma Press. Norman, OK. 1990. 302p. A Variorum Edition of the Works of Geoffrey Chaucer, The Canterbury Tales Ser., Vol. 12 ISBN:0-8061-2154-8, ISBN13: 978-0-8061-2154-3. Dewey:821/.1 s. LCCN:89-024928.
Audience: **u,f.**

Chaucer, Geoffrey **PR1868.W592B45 1996**
The Wife of Bath. Peter G. Beidler (Editor). Trade Paper. Bedford/Saint Martin's. New York, NY. 1995. 306p. Case Studies in Contemporary Criticism ISBN:0-312-11128-2, ISBN13: 978-0-312-11128-1. Dewey:821/.1. LCCN:95-080788.
Audience: **u,f.**

Chaucer, Geoffrey **PR2065.O3**
The Prioress's Tale. Beverly Boyd (Editor). Trade Cloth. University of Oklahoma Press. Norman, OK. 1987. 224p. A Variorum Edition of the Works of Geoffrey Chaucer, The Canterbury Tales Ser., Vol. 20 ISBN:0-8061-2045-2, ISBN13: 978-0-8061-2045-4. Dewey:821/.1. LCCN:86-025064.
Audience: **u,f.**

Chaucer, Geoffrey **PR1866.R8**
The Physician's Tale. Helen S. Corsa (Editor). Trade Cloth. University of Oklahoma Press. Norman, OK. 1987. 202p. A Variorum Edition of the Works of Geoffrey Chaucer, The Canterbury Tales Ser., Vol. 17 ISBN:0-8061-2038-X, ISBN13: 978-0-8061-2038-6. Dewey:821/.1. LCCN:79-033146.
Audience: **u,f.** *Choice, 1988.*

Chaucer, Geoffrey **PR1853 .P3 1982**
The Minor Poems, Pt. 1. Alfred David & George B. Pace (Editors). Trade Cloth. University of Oklahoma Press. Norman, OK. 1982. 252p. A Variorum Edition of the Works of Geoffrey Chaucer, The Canterbury Tales Ser., Vol. V ISBN:0-8061-1629-3, ISBN13: 978-0-8061-1629-7. Dewey:821/.1. LCCN:80-005943.
Audience: **u,f.**

Chaucer, Geoffrey & De Lorris, Guillaume **PR1888.D34 1999**
The Romaunt of the Rose and Le Roman de la Rose. Trade Cloth. University of Oklahoma Press. Norman, OK. 2000. 368p. Variorum Edition of the Works of Geoffrey Chaucer, Vol. 7 ISBN:0-8061-3147-0, ISBN13: 978-0-8061-3147-4. Dewey:821/.1. LCCN:98-037724.
Audience: **u,f.**

Chaucer, Geoffrey **PR1891.E45 2002**
A Treatise on the Astrolabe. Sigmund Eisner (Editor). Trade Cloth. University of Oklahoma Press. Norman, OK. 2002. 400p. ISBN:0-8061-3413-5, ISBN13: 978-0-8061-3413-0. Dewey:522/.4. LCCN:2001-052269.
Audience: **u,f.**

Chaucer, Geoffrey **PR1866.K64 1989**
The Canterbury Tales: Nine Tales and the General Prologue. V. A. Kolve & Glending Olson (Editors). Trade Paper. W. W. Norton & Company, Inc. New York, NY. 1989. 400p. Critical Editions Ser. ISBN:0-393-95245-2, ISBN13: 978-0-393-95245-2. Dewey:821/.1. LCCN:87-032084.
Audience: **l,u,f.**

Chaucer, Geoffrey **PR1865**
The Canterbury Tales, Vol. 1. Jill Mann (Notes by). Trade Paper. Penguin Group (USA) Inc. New York, NY. 2005. 1328p. ISBN:0-14-042234-X, ISBN13: 978-0-14-042234-4. Dewey:822.92.
Audience: **l,u,f.** B

Chaucer, Geoffrey **PR1866.R8 1983 PT. 9**
The Nun's Priest's Tale. Derek Albert Pearsall (Editor). Trade Cloth. University of Oklahoma Press. Norman, OK. 1984. 300p. A Variorum Edition of the Works of Geoffrey Chaucer, The Canterbury Tales Ser., Vol. II, Pt. 9 ISBN:0-8061-1779-6, ISBN13: 978-0-8061-1779-9. Dewey:821/.1. LCCN:83-005760.
Audience: **u,f.**

Chaucer, Geoffrey **PR1866.R8 1983 PT. 7**
The Summoner's Tale. John F. Plummer 3rd (Editor). Trade Cloth. University of Oklahoma Press. Norman, OK. 1995. 272p. Chaucer Variorium Ser., Vol. 2, Pt. 7 ISBN:0-8061-2744-9, ISBN13: 978-0-8061-2744-6. Dewey:821/.1 s. LCCN:94-038951.
Audience: **u,f.**

Chaucer, Geoffrey **PR1866 .R8 1979**
The Canterbury Tales: A Facsimile and Transcription of the Hengwrt Manuscript with Variants from the Ellesmere Manuscript. Paul G. Ruggiers (Editor), A. I. Doyle, M. B. Parkes & Donald C. Baker (Introduction by). Trade Cloth. University of Oklahoma Press. Norman, OK. 1979. 1078p. Chaucer Variorum Ser. ISBN:0-8061-1416-9, ISBN13: 978-0-8061-1416-3. Dewey:821/.1. LCCN:77-018611.
Audience: **u,f.**

Chaucer, Geoffrey **PR1868.K6 S6 1995**
The Knight's Tale. Ed. 2. A. C. Spearing (Editor, Contribution by), M. Hussey, J. Winny & J. E. Spearing (Contribution by). Trade Paper. Cambridge University Press. New York, NY. 1996. 254p. Selected Tales from Chaucer Ser. ISBN:0-521-49912-7, ISBN13: 978-0-521-49912-5. Dewey:821/.1. LCCN:94-044398.
Audience: **u,f.**

Chute, Marchette **PR1924**
Geoffrey Chaucer of England. Trade Cloth. Penguin Group (USA) Inc. New York, NY. 1946. ISBN:0-525-11257-X, ISBN13: 978-0-525-11257-0. Dewey:821/.1.
Audience: **g,l,u,f.** B

Cooper, Helen **PR1874.C64 1996**
Oxford Guides to Chaucer: The Canterbury Tales. Ed. 2. Paper Text. Oxford University Press, Inc. New York, NY. 1996. 452p. Oxford Guides to Chaucer Ser. ISBN:0-19-871155-7, ISBN13: 978-0-19-871155-1. Dewey:821/.1. LCCN:95-050434.
Audience: **u,f.** *Choice, 1990.*

Cooper, Helen **PR1874.C65 1984**
The Structure of the Canterbury Tales. Trade Cloth. University of Georgia Press. Athens, GA. 1984. 256p. ISBN:0-8203-0695-9, ISBN13: 978-0-8203-0695-7. Dewey:821/.1. LCCN:83-013997.
Audience: **u,f.**

Correale, Robert M. & Hamel, Mary (Editors) **PR1912.A2**
Sources and Analogues of the Canterbury Tales. Trade Paper. Boydell & Brewer, Ltd. Woodbridge, 2003. 638p. Chaucer Studies ISBN:0-85991-828-9, ISBN13: 978-0-85991-828-2. Dewey:821.1. LCCN:2001-037783.
Audience: **u,f.** *Choice, 2006, 2002.*

Correale, Robert M. & Hamel, Mary (Editors) **PR1912.A2S68 2002**
Sources and Analogues of the Canterbury Tales, Vol. II. Trade Cloth. Boydell & Brewer, Ltd. Woodbridge, 2005. 840p. Chaucer Studies ISBN:1-84384-048-0, ISBN13: 978-1-84384-048-0. Dewey:821.1. LCCN:2001-037783.
Audience: **u,f.** *Choice, 2006, 2002.*

Crane, Susan **PR1875.R65C73 1994**
Gender and Romance in Chaucer's Canterbury Tales. Paper Text. Princeton University Press. Princeton, NJ. 1994. 248p. ISBN:0-691-01527-9, ISBN13: 978-0-691-01527-9. Dewey:821/.1. LCCN:93-032421.
Audience: **u,f.** *Choice, 1995.*

David, Alfred **PR1924**
The Strumpet Muse: Art and Morals in Chaucer's Poetry. Trade Cloth. Indiana University Press. Bloomington, IN. 1977. 288p. ISBN:0-253-35517-6, ISBN13: 978-0-253-35517-1. Dewey:821/.1. LCCN:76-011939.
Audience: **u,f.**

Davis, Norman, et al. **PR1941**
A Chaucer Glossary. Douglas Gray & Patricia Ingham (Authors). Paper Text. Oxford University Press, Inc. New York, NY. 1979. 206p. ISBN:0-19-811171-1, ISBN13: 978-0-19-811171-9. Dewey:821/.1. LCCN:78-040245.
Audience: **g,l,u,f.**

Dinshaw, Carolyn **PR1933.S35D56 1989**
Chaucer's Sexual Poetics. Paper Text. University of Wisconsin Press. Chicago, IL. 1990. 272p. ISBN:0-299-12274-3, ISBN13: 978-0-299-12274-4. Dewey:821/.1. LCCN:89-040253.
Audience: **u,f.** *Choice, 1990.*

Edwards, Robert R. **PR1912.B6E39 2002**
Chaucer and Boccaccio: Antiquity and Modernity. Cloth over Boards. Palgrave Macmillan. New York, NY. 2002. 223p. ISBN:0-333-97008-X, ISBN13: 978-0-333-97008-9. Dewey:821/.1. LCCN:2001-050084.
Audience: **u,f.** *Choice, 2002.*

Ellis, Steve **PR1924**
Chaucer: An Oxford Guide. Paper Text. Oxford University Press, Inc. New York, NY. 2005. 668p. ISBN:0-19-925912-7, ISBN13: 978-0-19-925912-0. Dewey:821/.1. LCCN:2004-025110.
Audience: **g,l,u,f.**

Ellis, Steve (Editor) **PR1874 .C43 1998**
Chaucer: The Canterbury Tales. Trade Cloth. Longman Publishing Group. White Plains, NY. 1998. 256p. Longman Critical Readers Ser. ISBN:0-582-24880-9, ISBN13: 978-0-582-24880-9. Dewey:821.1.
Audience: **u,f.**

Glowka, Arthur W. **PR1951.G57 1991**
A Guide to Chaucer's Meter. Trade Cloth. University Press of America, Inc. Lanham, MD. 1991. 104p. ISBN:0-8191-8145-5, ISBN13: 978-0-8191-8145-9. Dewey:821/.1. LCCN:90-023781.
Audience: **u,f.** *Choice, 1992.*

Hansen, Elaine T. **PR1928.W64H36 1991**
Chaucer and the Fictions of Gender. Trade Cloth. University of California Press. Berkeley, CA. 1992. 385p. ISBN:0-520-07133-6, ISBN13: 978-0-520-07133-9. Dewey:823/.1. LCCN:91-013025.
Audience: **u,f.** *Choice, 1992.*

Hirsh, John **PR1905.H54 2002**
Chaucer and the Canterbury Tales: A Short Introduction. Trade Paper. Blackwell Publishing, Inc. Malden, MA. 2002. 192p. Introduction to Literature Ser. ISBN:0-631-22562-5, ISBN13: 978-0-631-22562-1. Dewey:821/.1 B. LCCN:2001-004356.
Audience: **l,u.**

Howard, Donald R. **PR1924**
Chaucer: His Life, His Works, His World. Trade Paper. Ballantine Books. New York, NY. 1989. 636p. ISBN:0-449-90341-9, ISBN13: 978-0-449-90341-4. Dewey:821/.1. LCCN:88-061354.
Audience: **g,u,f.** *Choice, 1988.*

Hussey, S. S. **PR1874**
Chaucer: An Introduction. Trade Cloth. Methuen & Company, Ltd. London, 1971. 244p. ISBN:0-416-14220-6, ISBN13: 978-0-416-14220-4. Dewey:821/.1. LCCN:78-869391.
Audience: **u,f.**

Jones, Terry **PR1868.K63J6 1985**
Chaucer's Knight: The Portrait of a Medieval Mercenary. Trade Paper. Routledge. New York, NY. 1985. 334p. ISBN:0-413-57510-1, ISBN13: 978-0-413-57510-4. Dewey:821/.1. LCCN:85-178737.
Audience: **u,f.**

Kolve, V. A. **PR1875.A44.K64 1984**
Chaucer and the Imagery of Narrative: The First Five Canterbury Tales. Trade Cloth. Stanford University Press. Palo Alto, CA. 1984. xvi, 551p. ISBN:0-8047-1161-5, ISBN13: 978-0-8047-1161-6. Dewey:821/.1. LCCN:80-050907.
Audience: **u,f.**

Leicester, Henry Marshall **PR1875.S45L45 1990**
The Disenchanted Self: Representing the Subject in the Canterbury Tales. Trade Cloth. University of California Press. Berkeley, CA. 1990. 463p. ISBN:0-520-06760-6, ISBN13: 978-0-520-06760-8. Dewey:821/.1. LCCN:89-005143.
Audience: **u,f.**

Lerer, Seth **PR1905.Y35 2006**
The Yale Companion to Chaucer. Cloth over Boards. Yale University Press. Cumberland, RI. 2006. 432p. ISBN:0-300-10929-6, ISBN13: 978-0-300-10929-0. Dewey:821/.1. LCCN:2005-025157.
Audience: **g,l,u,f.** *Choice, 2006.*

Mann, Jill **PR1868.P9 M3**
Chaucer and Medieval Estates Satire: The Literature of Social Classes and the General Prologue to the Canterbury Tales. Trade Paper. Cambridge University Press. New York, NY. 1973. 384p. ISBN:0-521-09795-9, ISBN13: 978-0-521-09795-6. Dewey:821/.1. LCCN:72-090490.
Audience: **u,f.**

Mann, Jill **PR1928.W64M36 2002**
Feminizing Chaucer. Trade Paper. Boydell & Brewer, Ltd. Woodbridge, 2002. 218p. Chaucer Studies, Vol. 30 ISBN:0-85991-613-8, ISBN13: 978-0-85991-613-4. Dewey:821/.1. LCCN:2002-074412.
Audience: **u,f.**

Martin, Priscilla **PR1928.W64M37 1990**
Chaucer's Women: Nuns, Wives and Amazons. Cloth Text. University of Iowa Press. Iowa City, IA. 1990. 270p. ISBN:0-87745-293-8, ISBN13: 978-0-87745-293-5. Dewey:821.1. LCCN:90-070034.
Audience: **u,f.** *Choice, 1991.*

Muscatine, Charles **PR1924**
Chaucer and the French Tradition: A Study in Style and Meaning. Paper Text. Textbook Publishers. Temecula, CA. 2003. 282p. ISBN:0-7581-2775-8, ISBN13: 978-0-7581-2775-4. Dewey:821/.1.
Audience: **u,f.** B

Owen, Charles A. (Editor) **PR1874 .O9 1978**
Discussions of the Canterbury Tales. Trade Cloth. Greenwood Publishing Group, Inc. Portsmouth, NH. 1978. 110p. ISBN:0-313-20012-2, ISBN13: 978-0-313-20012-0. Dewey:821/.1. LCCN:77-020278.
Audience: **u,f.**

Patterson, Lee **PR1933.H57P38 1991**
Chaucer and the Subject of History. Trade Paper. University of Wisconsin Press. Chicago, IL. 1991. 504p. ISBN:0-299-12834-2, ISBN13: 978-0-299-12834-0. Dewey:821/.1. LCCN:90-050651.
Audience: **u,f.** *Choice, 1992.*

Pearsall, Derek Albert **PR1905 .P43 1994**
The Life of Geoffrey Chaucer: A Critical Biography. Trade Paper. Blackwell Publishing, Inc. Malden, MA. 1995. 365p. ISBN:1-55786-665-1, ISBN13: 978-1-55786-665-3. Dewey:821.1.
Audience: **u,f.** *Choice, 1993.*

Pearsall, Derek Albert **PR1874.P43 1985**
The Canterbury Tales. Claude Rawson (Editor). Cloth Text. Routledge. New York, NY. 1985. 200p. Unwin Critical Library ISBN:0-04-800021-3, ISBN13: 978-0-04-800021-7. Dewey:821/.1. LCCN:85-006104.
Audience: **u,f.** B *Choice, 1986.*

Pearsall, Derek Albert & Wu, Duncan (Editors) **PR1203.P64 2002**
Poetry from Chaucer to Spenser. Trade Cloth. Blackwell Publishing, Inc. Malden, MA. 2002. 208p. Blackwell Essential Literature Ser. ISBN:0-631-22986-8, ISBN13: 978-0-631-22986-5. Dewey:821.008. LCCN:2002-023955.
Audience: **u,f.**

Phillips, Helen **PR1874.P48 1999**
An Introduction to the Canterbury Tales: Fiction, Writing, Context. Trade Paper. Palgrave Macmillan. New York, NY. 2000. 260p. ISBN:0-312-22740-X, ISBN13: 978-0-312-22740-1. Dewey:821/.1. LCCN:99-022268.
Audience: **u,f.** *Choice, 2000.*

Robertson, D. W. **PR1924.R58**
A Preface to Chaucer: Studies in Medieval Perspectives. Paper Text. Textbook Publishers. Temecula, CA. 2003. xvii, 519p. ISBN:0-7581-5765-7, ISBN13: 978-0-7581-5765-2. Dewey:821.1.
Audience: **l,u,f.**

Root, Robert Kilburn **PR1924 .R6**
The Poetry of Chaucer: A Guide to Its Study and Appreciation. Trade Paper. Kessinger Publishing, LLC. Whitefish, MT. 2005. ISBN:1-4179-2529-9, ISBN13: 978-1-4179-2529-2. Dewey:821.17.
Audience: **u,f.** B

Saunders, Corinne & Bradshaw, David (Editors) **PR1924.C59 2006**
A Concise Companion to Chaucer. Trade Cloth. Blackwell Publishing, Inc. Malden, MA. 2006. 304p. Concise Companions to Literature and Culture Ser. ISBN:1-4051-1387-1, ISBN13: 978-1-4051-1387-8. Dewey:821/.1. LCCN:2005-019821.
Audience: **g,l,u.**

Schoeck, Richard J. **PR1924.S37**
Chaucer Criticism: An Anthology,. Paper Text. Textbook Publishers. Temecula, CA. 2003. ISBN:0-7581-1817-1, ISBN13: 978-0-7581-1817-2. Dewey:821.1.
Audience: **u,f.**

Stillinger, Thomas C. (Editor) **PR1924.C77 1998**
Critical Essays on Geoffery Chaucer. Trade Cloth. Thomson Gale. Farmington Hills, MI. 1998. 272p. Critical Essays on British Literature Ser. ISBN:0-7838-0024-X, ISBN13: 978-0-7838-0024-0. Dewey:821/.1. LCCN:98-021545.
Audience: **u,f.**

Strohm, Paul **PR1924**
Social Chaucer. Trade Paper. Harvard University Press. Cambridge, MA. 1994. 236p. ISBN:0-674-81199-2, ISBN13: 978-0-674-81199-7. Dewey:821/.1.
Audience: **u,f.** *Choice, 1990.*

Thompson, N. S. **PR1874.T47 1996**
Chaucer, Boccaccio and the Debate of Love: A Comparative Study of the Decameron and the Canterbury Tales. Trade Cloth. Oxford University Press, Inc. New York, NY. 1996. 364p. ISBN:0-19-812378-7, ISBN13: 978-0-19-812378-1. Dewey:809.1/3. LCCN:96-014368.
Audience: **u,f.** *Choice, 1997.*

Wallace, David **PR1933.P64W35 1997**
Chaucerian Polity: Absolutist Lineages and Associational Forms in England and Italy. Trade Cloth. Stanford University Press. Palo Alto, CA. 1997. 576p. Figurae - Reading Medieval Culture Ser. ISBN:0-8047-2724-4, ISBN13: 978-0-8047-2724-2. Dewey:821/.1. LCCN:96-021911.
Audience: **u,f.** *Choice, 1997.*

Windeatt, Barry **PR1896.W56 1995**
Oxford Guides to Chaucer: Troilus and Criseyde. Trade Paper. Oxford University Press, Inc. New York, NY. 1995. 428p. Oxford Guides to Chaucer Ser. ISBN:0-19-811194-0, ISBN13: 978-0-19-811194-8. Dewey:821.1.
Audience: **u,f.** *Choice, 1993.*

Individual Authors and Works > Anglo-Saxon. Old and Middle English > Individual Authors > Langland, William

Alford, John A. **PR2015**
A Companion to Piers Plowman. Box or Slipcased. University of California Press. Berkeley, CA. 1988. xii, 286p. ISBN:0-520-06006-7, ISBN13: 978-0-520-06006-7. Dewey:821/.1. LCCN:87-024873.
Audience: **l,u,f.** *Choice, 1988.*

Benson, C. David **PR2015.B4 2003**
Public Piers Plowman: Modern Scholarship and Late Medieval English Culture. Trade Cloth. Pennsylvania State University Press. University Park, PA. 2005. 304p. ISBN:0-271-02315-5, ISBN13: 978-0-271-02315-1. Dewey:821/.1. LCCN:2003-009908.
Audience: **u,f.** *Choice, 2004.*

Bloomfield, Morton W. **PR2015.B5**
Piers Plowman As A: Century Apocalypse. Paper Text. Textbook Publishers. Temecula, CA. 2003. xi, 259p. ISBN:0-7581-4307-9, ISBN13: 978-0-7581-4307-5. Dewey:821.1.
Audience: **u,f.**

Godden, Malcolm R. **PR2015.G64 1990**
The Making of Piers Plowman. Ed. 1. Cloth Text. Addison-Wesley Longman, Ltd. Harlow, 1989. 236p. ISBN:0-582-05924-0, ISBN13: 978-0-582-05924-5. Dewey:821/.1. LCCN:89-037583.
Audience: **u,f.** *Choice, 1990.*

Harwood, Britton J. **PR2015 .H37 1994**
Piers Plowman and the Problem of Belief. Trade Paper. University of Toronto Press. Toronto, ON. 1995. 237p. ISBN:0-8020-7655-6, ISBN13: 978-0-8020-7655-7. Dewey:821.1.
Audience: **u,f.** *Choice, 1992.*

Kane, George (Editor) **PR2010.K3 1988**
Piers Plowman: The Three Versions. Trade Cloth. University of California Press. Berkeley, CA. 1988. 480p. ISBN:0-520-06229-9, ISBN13: 978-0-520-06229-0. Dewey:821/.1. LCCN:88-157167.
Audience: **u,f.** *Choice, 1988.*

Langland, William **PR2013.D6 2004**
Piers Plowman. Trade Paper. W. W. Norton & Company, Inc. New York, NY. 2004. 608p. A Norton Critical Edition Ser. ISBN:0-393-97559-2, ISBN13: 978-0-393-97559-8. Dewey:821/.1. LCCN:2004-057578.
Audience: **u,f.**

Langland, William **PR1924**
Piers Plowman: The Prologue and Passus I-VII of the B Text As Found in Bodleian Ms. Laud Misc. 581. Elizabeth D. Kirk & Judith H. Anderson (Editors), E. Talbot Donaldson (Translator). Trade Paper. W. W. Norton & Company, Inc. New York, NY. 1990. 288p. ISBN:0-393-96011-0, ISBN13: 978-0-393-96011-2. Dewey:821/.1. LCCN:89-003251.
Audience: **u,f.**

Langland, William **PR2010 .P4 1994**
Piers Plowman: An Edition of the C-Text. Derek Albert Pearsall (Editor). Trade Cloth. University of Exeter Press. Exeter, 1994. 416p. Exeter Medieval Texts and Studies ISBN:0-85989-429-0, ISBN13: 978-0-85989-429-6. Dewey:821.1.
Audience: **u,f.**

Langland, William **PR1924**
Piers Plowman: A New Translation of the B-Text. A. V. C. Schmidt (Translator). Trade Paper. Oxford University Press, Inc. New York, NY. 2001. 404p. Oxford World's Classics Ser. ISBN:0-19-283646-3, ISBN13: 978-0-19-283646-5. Dewey:821/.1.
Audience: **u,f.**

Simpson, James **PR2017.L38S56 1990**
Piers Plowman: An Introduction to the B-Text. Ed. 1. Paper Text. Addison-Wesley Longman, Ltd. Harlow, 1991. 288p. ISBN:0-582-01391-7, ISBN13: 978-0-582-01391-9. Dewey:821/.1. LCCN:89-034272.
Audience: **u,f.** *Choice, 1991.*

Individual Authors and Works > Anglo-Saxon. Old and Middle English > Individual Authors > Gower, John

Echard, Siân (Editor) **PR1987.C66 2004**
A Companion to Gower. Trade Cloth. Boydell & Brewer, Ltd. Woodbridge, 2005. 272p. ISBN:1-84384-000-6, ISBN13: 978-1-84384-000-8. Dewey:821/.1. LCCN:2003-017979.
Audience: **u,f.** *Choice, 2004.*

Gower, John & Othman, Ossama **PR1984**
[e] Confessio Amantis or Tales of the Seven Deadly Sins. E-Book. Kessinger Publishing, LLC. Whitefish, MT. 2004. ISBN:1-4192-1379-2, ISBN13: 978-1-4192-1379-3. Dewey:841/.1.
Audience: **g,l,u,f.**

Gower, John **PR1984 .C6 2000**
Confessio Amantis, Vol. 2. Russell A. Peck (Editor), Andrew Galloway (Translator). Trade Paper. Medieval Institute Publications. Kalamazoo, MI. 2005. viii + 418p. Middle English Texts Ser. ISBN:1-58044-047-9, ISBN13: 978-1-58044-047-9. Dewey:821/.1. LCCN:00-022403.
Audience: **u,f.**

Gower, John **PR1924**
Confessio Amantis, Vol. 3. Russell A. Peck (Editor), Andrew Galloway (Translator). Trade Paper. Medieval Institute Publications. Kalamazoo, MI. 2005. Middle English Texts Ser. ISBN:1-58044-092-4, ISBN13: 978-1-58044-092-9. Dewey:821/.1.
Audience: **u,f.**

Gower, John, et al. **PR1984.C6 2005**
Confessio Amantis. Ed. 2. Russell A. Peck & Andrew Galloway (Authors), Consortium for the Teaching of the Middle Ages Staff (Contribution by). Trade Cloth. Medieval Institute Publications. Kalamazoo, MI. 2005. ISBN:1-58044-102-5, ISBN13: 978-1-58044-102-5. Dewey:821/.1. LCCN:2005-030793.
Audience: **u,f.**

Nicholson, Peter **PR1984.C63N533 2005**
Love and Ethics in Gower's Confessio Amantis. Trade Cloth. University of Michigan Press. Chicago, IL. 2005. 472p. ISBN:0-472-11512-X, ISBN13: 978-0-472-11512-9. Dewey:821/.1. LCCN:2005-005832.
Audience: **l,u,f.** *Choice, 2006.*

Individual Authors and Works > Anglo-Saxon. Old and Middle English > Individual Authors > Malory, Thomas

Archibald, Elizabeth & Edwards, A. S. G. (Editors) **PR2045.C66**
A Companion to Malory. Trade Paper. Boydell & Brewer, Ltd. Woodbridge, 2000. 280p. Arthurian Studies ISBN:0-85991-520-4, ISBN13: 978-0-85991-520-5. Dewey:823.2.
Audience: **l,u,f.** *Choice, 1997.*

Benson, Larry D. **PR2045**
Malory's Morte d'Arthur: A 15th Century Chivalric Romance. Trade Cloth. Harvard University Press. Cambridge, MA. 1976. 268p. ISBN:0-674-54393-9, ISBN13: 978-0-674-54393-5. Dewey:823/.2. LCCN:75-019233.
Audience: **u,f.** B

Malory, Thomas **PR2041.M37 2002**
Le Morte d'Arthur. Trade Paper. W. W. Norton & Company, Inc. New York, NY. 2003. 752p. A Norton Critical Edition Ser. ISBN:0-393-97464-2, ISBN13: 978-0-393-97464-5. Dewey:823.2. LCCN:2002-026534.
Audience: **g,l,u,f.**

Malory, Thomas **PR2043 .C63 1998**
Le Morte Darthur: The Winchester Manuscript. Helen Cooper (Editor, Introduction by). Trade Paper. Oxford University Press, Inc. New York, NY. 1998. 610p. Oxford World's Classics Ser. ISBN:0-19-282420-1, ISBN13: 978-0-19-282420-2. Dewey:823.2. LCCN:97-018955.
Audience: **u,f.**

Malory, Thomas **PR2043**
Le Morte d'Arthur: King Arthur and the Legends of the Round Table. Robert Graves (Introduction by), Keith Baines (Contribution by). Mass Market. Penguin Group (USA) Inc. New York, NY. 2001. 512p. Signet Classics Ser. ISBN:0-451-52816-6, ISBN13: 978-0-451-52816-2. Dewey:823.2.
Audience: **g,l,u.**

Malory, Thomas **PR2041.V5 1990**
The Works of Sir Thomas Malory, Vol. II. Ed. 3. Eugene Vinaver (Editor), P. C. Field (Revised by). Cloth Text. Oxford University Press, Inc. New York, NY. 1990. 654p. Oxford English Texts ISBN:0-19-812345-0, ISBN13: 978-0-19-812345-3. Dewey:823/.2. LCCN:89-009272.
Audience: **u,f.**

Malory, Thomas **PR2041.V5 1990**
The Works of Sir Thomas Malory. Ed. 3. Eugene Vinaver (Editor), P. C. Field (Revised by). Cloth Text. Oxford University Press, Inc. New York, NY. 1990. 680p. Oxford English Texts, Vol. 3 ISBN:0-19-812346-9, ISBN13: 978-0-19-812346-0. Dewey:823/.2. LCCN:89-009272.
Audience: **u,f.**

Malory, Thomas **PR2041.V5 1990**
The Works of Sir Thomas Malory, Vol. I. Ed. 3. Eugene Vinaver (Editor), P. C. Field (Revised by). Cloth Text. Oxford University Press, Inc. New York, NY. 1990. 611p. Oxford English Texts ISBN:0-19-812344-2, ISBN13: 978-0-19-812344-6. Dewey:823/.2. LCCN:89-009272.
Audience: **u,f.**

McCarthy, Terence **PR2045.M36 1991**
An Introduction to Malory. Trade Paper. Boydell & Brewer, Ltd. Woodbridge, 2002. 192p. Arthurian Studies ISBN:0-85991-325-2, ISBN13: 978-0-85991-325-6. Dewey:823/.2. LCCN:90-029855.
Audience: **u,f.**

Parins, Marylyn **PR2045 .M35 1988**
Malory. Cloth Text. Routledge. New York, NY. 1988. 420p. The Critical Heritage Ser. ISBN:0-415-00223-0, ISBN13: 978-0-415-00223-3. Dewey:823/.2. LCCN:89-131045.
Audience: **u,f.** *Choice, 1989.*

Spisak, James W. & Matthews, William (Editors) **PR2045**
Caxton's Malory: A New Edition of Sir Thomas Malory's Le Mort d'Arthur, Based on the Pierpont Morgan Copy of William Caxton's Edition of 1485, Vol. Set. Bert Dillon (Contribution by). Trade Cloth. University of California Press. Berkeley, CA. 1983. 1100p. ISBN:0-520-03825-8, ISBN13: 978-0-520-03825-7. Dewey:823/.2. LCCN:81-007434.
Audience: **u,f.**

Individual Authors and Works > English Renaissance (1500-1640) Prose. Poetry

Anderson, Judith H. (Editor), et al. **PR2363.S65 1996**
Spenser's Life and the Subject of Biography. Donald Cheney & David A. Richardson (Editors). Cloth Text. University of Massachusetts Press. Amherst, MA. 1996. 232p. Massachusetts Studies in Early Modern Culture ISBN:1-55849-050-7, ISBN13: 978-1-55849-050-5. Dewey:821/.3 B. LCCN:96-019287.
Audience: **u,f.** *Choice, 1997.*

Ascham, R. **PR1293**
English Works. W. A. Wright (Editor). Trade Cloth. Cambridge University Press. Cambridge, 1970. 324p. ISBN:0-521-07768-0, ISBN13: 978-0-521-07768-2. Dewey:828/.2/08.
Audience: **g,l,u,f.**

Babb, Lawrence **PR2224**
Sanity in Bedlam: A Study of Robert Burton's Anatomy of Melancholy. Paper Text. Textbook Publishers. Temecula, CA. 2003. xi, 116p. ISBN:0-7581-8136-1, ISBN13: 978-0-7581-8136-7. Dewey:828.3.
Audience: **g.** B

Bacon, Francis **PR2205**
Francis Bacon: The Major Works. Brian Vickers (Editor). Trade Paper. Oxford University Press, Inc. New York, NY. 2002. 862p. Oxford World's Classics Ser. ISBN:0-19-284081-9, ISBN13: 978-0-19-284081-3. Dewey:824/.3. LCCN:2002-727711.
Audience: **g,l,u.**

Bevington, David & Hunter, George K. (Editors) **PR2659.L9**
Campaspe and Sappho and Phao: John Lyly. Trade Paper. Manchester University Press. Manchester, 1999. 328p. Revels Plays Ser. ISBN:0-7190-3100-1, ISBN13: 978-0-7190-3100-7. Dewey:822/.3.
Audience: **g.**

Bradner, Leicester **PR2363.B7**
Edmund Spenser and The Faerie Queene. Library Binding. University of Chicago Press. Chicago, IL. 1948. xi, 193 p. ;p. ISBN:0-226-07051-4, ISBN13: 978-0-226-07051-3. Dewey:821.31. LCCN:48-006359.
Audience: **g.** B

Breton, Nicholas **PR2214.B4**
Works in Verse and Prose. Paper Text. Classic Textbooks. Murrieta, CA. 1879. ISBN:1-4047-7193-X, ISBN13: 978-1-4047-7193-2. Dewey:821/.3.
Audience: **g.**

Burton, Robert **PR2223.A2F38 1989**
The Anatomy of Melancholy: Text. Nicolas K. Kiessling, Thomas C. Faulkner & Rhonda L. Blair (Editors). Trade Cloth. Oxford University Press, Inc. New York, NY. 1990. 452p. Oxford English Texts, Vol. 2 ISBN:0-19-812330-2, ISBN13: 978-0-19-812330-9. Dewey:828.308. LCCN:89-009396.
Audience: **g.** *Choice, 1991.*

Campion, Thomas **ML410.C3**
Campion's Work. Library Binding. Reprint Services Company. Temecula, CA. 1990. 400p. ISBN:0-7812-9056-2, ISBN13: 978-0-7812-9056-2. Dewey:782.4092.
Audience: **g.**

Carey, John **PR2248.C34 1990**
John Donne: Life, Mind and Art. Ed. 2. Trade Paper. Faber & Faber, Inc. New York, NY. 1991. 320p. ISBN:0-571-14337-7, ISBN13: 978-0-571-14337-5. Dewey:821/.3. LCCN:90-197663.
Audience: **g.** B

Daniel, Samuel **PR2241.D4A61998**
Samuel Daniel: Selected Poetry and a Defense of Rhyme. Geoffrey G. Hiller & Peter L. Groves (Editors). Trade Paper. Pegasus Press. Chandler, AZ. 1998. 251p. ISBN:1-889818-04-6, ISBN13: 978-1-889818-04-7. Dewey:821/.3. LCCN:98-023254.
Audience: **g.**

Davies, John **PR2242.D2**
e Orchestra. E-Book. Kessinger Publishing, LLC. Whitefish, MT. 2004. ISBN:1-4192-3912-0, ISBN13: 978-1-4192-3912-0. Dewey:821.35.
Audience: **g.**

Deloney, Thomas **PR2242 .D3**
The Works of Thomas Deloney. Paper Text. Classic Textbooks. Murrieta, CA. 1912. 600p. ISBN:1-4047-7202-2, ISBN13: 978-1-4047-7202-1. Dewey:821.3.
Audience: **g.** B

Donne, John **PR2245**
John Donne: Selected Poems. Ilona Bell & Christopher Ricks (Contribution by). Trade Paper. Penguin Group (USA) Inc. New York, NY. 2007. 304p. ISBN:0-14-042440-7, ISBN13: 978-0-14-042440-9. Dewey:821/.3.
Audience: **g.** *Choice, 1991.*

Donne, John **PR2248.A3 2004**
A Complete Concordance to the Poems of John Donne. Celia Floren (Editor). Trade Cloth. Georg Olms Verlag AG. Hildesheim, 2004. 1010p. ISBN:3-487-10326-5, ISBN13: 978-3-487-10326-6. Dewey:821/.3. LCCN:2004-450911.
Audience: **g.**

Donne, John **PR2246**
Elegies and the Songs and Sonnets. Helen Gardner (Editor). Trade Cloth. Oxford University Press, Inc. New York, NY. 2000. 372p. Oxford Scholarly Classics Ser. ISBN:0-19-811835-X, ISBN13: 978-0-19-811835-0. Dewey:821.3.
Audience: **g.** B

Donne, John **PR2246.M48**
The Epithalamions, Anniversaries and Epicedes. Wesley Milgate (Editor). Trade Cloth. Oxford University Press, Inc. New York, NY. 1978. 288p. Oxford English Texts ISBN:0-19-812729-4, ISBN13: 978-0-19-812729-1. Dewey:821/.3. LCCN:77-030423.
Audience: **g.** B

Donne, John **PR2246**
Satires, Epigrams and Verse Letters. Wesley Milgate (Editor). Trade Cloth. Oxford University Press, Inc. New York, NY. 1967. 380p. Oxford English Texts ISBN:0-19-811842-2, ISBN13: 978-0-19-811842-8. Dewey:821/.3.
Audience: **g.** B

Donne, John **PR2245.A5 P38 1991**
The Complete English Poems. C. A. Patrides (Introduction by). Trade Cloth. Knopf Publishing Group. New York, NY. 1991. 576p. ISBN:0-679-40558-5, ISBN13: 978-0-679-40558-0. Dewey:821/.3. LCCN:91-052975.
Audience: **g.**

Donne, John **BX5133.D61S5 2003**
John Donne's Sermons on the Psalms and Gospels: With a Selection of Prayers and Meditations. Evelyn M. Simpson (Editor). Trade Paper. University of California Press. Berkeley, CA. 2003. 246p. ISBN:0-520-23928-8, ISBN13: 978-0-520-23928-9. Dewey:220. LCCN:2003-276340.
Audience: **g.**

Douglas, Gavin **PR2250.A5S6**
The Poetical Works of Gavin Douglas, Bishop of Dunkeld, Vol. 4. John Small (Editor). Trade Paper. Books on Demand. Ann Arbor, MI. 360p. ISBN:0-598-84937-8, ISBN13: 978-0-598-84937-3. Dewey:821.24. LCCN:24-023127.
Audience: **g.**

Drayton, Michael **PR2255.A5**
The Complete Works of Michael Drayton, Now First Collected, Vol. 3. Richard Hooper (Introduction by). Trade Paper. Adamant Media. Chestnut Hill, MA. 2001. 313p. ISBN:1-4021-6559-5, ISBN13: 978-1-4021-6559-7. Dewey:821.
Audience: **g.**

Dunbar, William **PR2266**
William Dunbar: Selected Poems. Harriet Harvey Wood (Editor). Trade Paper. Routledge. New York, NY. 2003. 114p. Fyfield Bks. ISBN:0-415-96943-3, ISBN13: 978-0-415-96943-7. Dewey:821.2.
Audience: **g.**

Edwards, H. L. **PR2348**
Skelton, the Life and Times of an Early Tudor Poet. Paper Text. Classic Textbooks. Murrieta, CA. 1999. 232p. ISBN:1-4047-0060-9, ISBN13: 978-1-4047-0060-4. Dewey:821/.2.
Audience: **g.**

Fish, Stanley Eugene **PR2348 .F5 1976**
John Skelton's Poetry. Trade Cloth. Shoe String Press, Inc. North Haven, CT. 1976. viii, 268p. Yale Studies in English, Vol. 157 ISBN:0-208-01613-9, ISBN13: 978-0-208-01613-3. Dewey:821/.2. LCCN:76-020810.
Audience: **g.** B

Fletcher, Giles **PR2271**
Giles and Phineas Fletcher - Poetical Works. Paper Text. Classic Textbooks. Murrieta, CA. 1908. ISBN:1-4047-7208-1, ISBN13: 978-1-4047-7208-3. Dewey:821.
Audience: **g.** B

Fox, Ruth **PR2224**
The Tangled Chain: The Structure of Disorder in the Anatomy of Melancholy. Trade Cloth. University of California Press. Berkeley, CA. 1976. xiii, 282p. ISBN:0-520-03085-0, ISBN13: 978-0-520-03085-5. Dewey:828/.308. LCCN:75-017296.
Audience: **l,u,f.** B

Freeman, Rosemary **PR2358.F7**
The Faerie Queene; a Companion for Readers. Trade Cloth. University of California Press. Berkeley, CA. 1970. 350p. ISBN:0-520-01732-3, ISBN13: 978-0-520-01732-0. Dewey:821/.3. LCCN:70-116114.
Audience: **g.** B

Gascoigne, George **PR2277**
Complete Works, Set. Trade Cloth. Scholarly Press, Inc. Saint Clair Shores, MI. 1968. ISBN:0-403-00089-0, ISBN13: 978-0-403-00089-0. Dewey:821/.3.
Audience: **g.**

Gosse, Edmund William **PR2248 .G6**
The Life and Letters of John Donne. Paper Text. Classic Textbooks. Murrieta, CA. 1899. ISBN:1-4047-7204-9, ISBN13: 978-1-4047-7204-5. Dewey:821.3.
Audience: **g.**

Greville, Fulke **PR2215.A4 1968**
Selected Poems of Fulke Greville. Trade Cloth. Faber & Faber, Ltd. London, 1968. 159p. ISBN:0-571-08740-X, ISBN13: 978-0-571-08740-2. Dewey:821/.3. LCCN:68-143023.
Audience: **g,l,u,f.**

Hall, Joseph **PR2283.H7.A17 1971**
The Collected Poems of Joseph Hall, Bishop of Exeter and Norwich. Trade Cloth. Scholarly Press, Inc. Saint Clair Shores, MI. 1949. 309p. ISBN:0-403-01340-2, ISBN13: 978-0-403-01340-1. Dewey:821/.3. LCCN:75-161969.
Audience: **g.** B

Hamilton, A. C., et al. **PR2358.A3H27 2001**
Spenser: The Faerie Queene. Ed. 2. Shohachi Fukuda, Toshiyuki Suzuki & Hiroshi Yamashita (Authors). Trade Paper. Longman Publishing. Boston, MA. 2001. 848p. ISBN:0-582-09951-X, ISBN13: 978-0-582-09951-7. Dewey:821/.3. LCCN:2001-050514.
Audience: **g,l,u,f.**

Hangen, Eva C. **PR2403.A3**
Concordance to the Complete Poetical Works of Sir Thomas Wyatt. Trade Cloth. Johnson Reprint Corporation. New York, NY. 1969. English Literary Reference Ser. ISBN:0-384-21300-6, ISBN13: 978-0-384-21300-5. Dewey:821.27.
Audience: **g.**

Hankins, John E. **PR2358**
Source and Meaning in Spenser's Allegory: A Study of the Faerie Queene. Trade Cloth. Oxford University Press, Inc. New York, NY. 1972. 348p. ISBN:0-19-812013-3, ISBN13: 978-0-19-812013-1. Dewey:821/.3. LCCN:72-181312.
Audience: **g,l,u,f.** B

Harpsfield, Nicholas **923.242**
Life and Death of St Thomas More. Paper Text. Classic Textbooks. Murrieta, CA. 1932. ISBN:1-4047-0274-1, ISBN13: 978-1-4047-0274-5. Dewey:PR1119.
Audience: **g.**

Harris, Jesse W. **PR2209.B2.H28 1970**
John Bale. Trade Cloth. Ayer Company Publishers, Inc. Manchester, NH. 1977. 157p. Select Bibliographies Reprint Ser. ISBN:0-8369-5401-7, ISBN13: 978-0-8369-5401-2. Dewey:828/.2/09. LCCN:72-119958.
Audience: **g,l,u,f.** B

Heiserman, Arthur Ray **PR2348**
Skelton and Satire. Paper Text. Textbook Publishers. Temecula, CA. 2003. 326p. ISBN:0-7581-2592-5, ISBN13: 978-0-7581-2592-7. Dewey:827.2.
Audience: **g.** B

Herbert, Edward Herbert **PR2294**
Poems, English and Latin. Paper Text. Classic Textbooks. Murrieta, CA. 1923. 169p. ISBN:1-4047-7211-1, ISBN13: 978-1-4047-7211-3. Dewey:821.49.
Audience: **g.**

Hough, Graham Goulden **PR2358**
A Preface to the Faerie Queene. Paper Text. Textbook Publishers. Temecula, CA. 2003. 238p. ISBN:0-7581-7563-9, ISBN13: 978-0-7581-7563-2. Dewey:821.3.
Audience: **g.** B

Howard, Henry & Surrey, Henry Howard Earl of **PR2371**
Selected Poems: Henry Howard, Earl of Surrey. Dennis Keene (Editor). Trade Paper. Carcanet Press, Ltd. Manchester, 2006. 104p. ISBN:1-85754-699-7, ISBN13: 978-1-85754-699-6. Dewey:821/.2.
Audience: **g.**

Jones, Harry V. **PR2363**
Spenser Handbook. Trade Cloth. Irvington Publishers. New York, NY. ISBN:0-89197-423-7, ISBN13: 978-0-89197-423-9. Dewey:821.31.
Audience: **g.**

Lindsay, David **PR1119**
Works, Pts. I-IV. J. Small & F. Hall (Editors). Trade Cloth. Periodicals Service Company. Germantown, NY. 1974. EETS, OS Ser., Nos. 11, 19, 35, 37 ISBN:0-527-00013-2, ISBN13: 978-0-527-00013-4. Dewey:821.2.
Audience: **g.**

Lodge, Thomas **PR2297**
The Complete Works of Thomas Lodge. Paper Text. Classic Books. Murrieta, CA. 2001. ISBN:0-7426-8859-3, ISBN13: 978-0-7426-8859-9. Dewey:828.3.
Audience: **g.**

Lyly, John **PR2300**
Complete Works of John Lyly. Paper Text. Classic Textbooks. Murrieta, CA. 1902. ISBN:1-4047-7212-X, ISBN13: 978-1-4047-7212-0. Dewey:823.3.
Audience: **g.** B

MacCaffrey, Isabel G. **PR2358**
Spenser's Allegory: The Anatomy of Imagination. Trade Paper. Princeton University Press. Princeton, NJ. 1976. 464p. ISBN:0-691-10043-8, ISBN13: 978-0-691-10043-2. Dewey:821/.3. LCCN:75-030197.
Audience: **l,u,f.** B

Middleton, Thomas **PR2315.M5 G5; PR2714**
Ghost of Lucrece. Paper Text. Classic Textbooks. Murrieta, CA. 1937. 43p. ISBN:1-4047-0249-0, ISBN13: 978-1-4047-0249-3. Dewey:821.39.
Audience: **g.** B

Montgomery, Robert L. **PR2343.M63 1969**
Symmetry and Sense: The Poetry of Sir Philip Sidney. Library Binding. Greenwood Publishing Group, Inc. Portsmouth, NH. 1969. vii, 134p. ISBN:0-8371-2102-7, ISBN13: 978-0-8371-2102-4. Dewey:821/.3. LCCN:75-088911.
Audience: **g.** B

More, Thomas (Editor), et al. **JC71.P6**
Utopia. Edward Surtz & J. H. Hexter (Editors). Cloth over Boards. Yale University Press. Cumberland, RI. 1965. 750p. Complete Works of St. Thomas More, No. 4 ISBN:0-300-00982-8, ISBN13: 978-0-300-00982-8. Dewey:321/.07.
Audience: **g.** *Choice, 2001.*

More, Thomas **DA260**
The History of King Richard III and Selections from the English and Latin Poems. Richard S. Sylvester (Editor). Trade Paper. Yale University Press. Cumberland, RI. 1976. 192p. Selected Works of St. Thomas More ISBN:0-300-01925-4, ISBN13: 978-0-300-01925-4. Dewey:942.04/6/0924. LCCN:61-014944.
Audience: **g.**

Myrick, Kenneth **PR2343**
Sir Philip Sidney As a Literary Craftsman. Trade Paper. University of Nebraska Press. Lincoln, NE. 1966. x, 362p. ISBN:0-8032-5140-8, ISBN13: 978-0-8032-5140-3. Dewey:821.3. LCCN:35-013065.
Audience: **g.**

Niccols, Richard **PR2326.N4**
Sir Thomas Overbury's Vision, and Other English Sources of Nathaniel Hawthorne's The Scarlet Letter Facsimile Reproductions, with an Introd. Paper Text. Textbook Publishers. Temecula, CA. 2003. xviiip. ISBN:0-7581-4136-X, ISBN13: 978-0-7581-4136-1. Dewey:821.3.
Audience: **g.**

Osgood, Charles G. **PR2362**
Concordance to the Poems of Edmund Spenser. Trade Cloth. Peter Smith Publisher, Inc. Magnolia, MA. 1990. ISBN:0-8446-1332-0, ISBN13: 978-0-8446-1332-1. Dewey:821.3.
Audience: **g.**

Overbury, Thomas **PR2326.O5 A16 1977**
The Overburian Characters, to Which Is Added, a Wife. W. J. Paylor (Editor). Trade Cloth. A M S Press, Inc. New York, NY. ISBN:0-404-14580-9, ISBN13: 978-0-404-14580-4. Dewey:828/.3/07. LCCN:75-041207.
Audience: **g.** B

Quitslund, Jon A. **PR2358.Q58 2001**
Spenser's Supreme Fiction: Platonic Natural Philosophy and the Faerie Queene. Trade Cloth. University of Toronto Press. Toronto, ON. 2001. 716p. ISBN:0-8020-3505-1, ISBN13: 978-0-8020-3505-9. Dewey:821/.3. LCCN:2002-511088.
Audience: **g.** *Choice, 2002.*

Raleigh, Walter & Rudick, Michael **PR2334.A4 1999**
The Poems of Sir Walter Raleigh: An Historical Edition. Trade Cloth. M R T S. Tempe, AZ. 1999. 272p. Renaissance English Text Society Ser., Vol. 209 ISBN:0-86698-251-5, ISBN13: 978-0-86698-251-1. Dewey:821/.3. LCCN:99-054887.
Audience: **g.**

Rose, Mark **PR2358.R66**
Spenser's Art: A Companion to Book One of the Faerie Queen. Trade Cloth. Harvard University Press. Cambridge, MA. 1975. 160p. ISBN:0-674-83193-4, ISBN13: 978-0-674-83193-3. Dewey:821/.3. LCCN:74-021229.
Audience: **g.** B

Shire, Helena Mennie **PR2363.S5**
A Preface to Spenser. Trade Cloth. Longman Publishing Group. White Plains, NY. 1978. xii, 196p. ISBN:0-582-31511-5, ISBN13: 978-0-582-31511-2. Dewey:821/.3. LCCN:76-023272.
Audience: **g.** B

Sidney, Philip **PR2342.A5 1999**
The Countess of Pembroke's Arcadia: (The Old Arcadia). Trade Paper. Oxford University Press, Inc. New York, NY. 1999. 423p. Oxford World's Classics Ser. ISBN:0-19-283956-X, ISBN13: 978-0-19-283956-5. Dewey:823/.3. LCCN:00-265357.
Audience: **g.** B

Sidney, Philip **PR2340**
Sir Philip Sidney: The Major Works. Katherine Duncan-Jones (Editor). Trade Paper. Oxford University Press, Inc. New York, NY. 2002. 442p. Oxford World's Classics Ser. ISBN:0-19-284080-0, ISBN13: 978-0-19-284080-6. Dewey:821/.3. LCCN:2002-727712.
Audience: **g.**

Sisson, Charles Jasper (Editor) **PR2298 .S5**
Thomas Lodge and Other Elizabethans. Cloth Text. Taylor & Francis Group. Abingdon, 1967. 221p. ISBN:0-7146-1031-3, ISBN13: 978-0-7146-1031-3. Dewey:820.9003.
Audience: **g.** B

Skelton, John **PR1990.H4**
John Skelton (1460-1529): Selected Poems. Gerald Hammond (Editor). Trade Paper. Routledge. New York, NY. 2003. 144p. Fyfield Bks. ISBN:0-415-96963-8, ISBN13: 978-0-415-96963-5. Dewey:821/.2.
Audience: **g.**

Smith, A. J. **PR2248.J63 1996**
John Donne: The Critical Heritage. Catherine Phillips (Editor, Introduction by). Paper over Boards. Routledge. New York, NY. 1996. 552p. The Critical Heritage Ser. ISBN:0-415-07445-2, ISBN13: 978-0-415-07445-2. Dewey:821.3. LCCN:96-001910.
Audience: **g.** B

Southwell, Robert **PR2358**
Complete Poems. Paper Text. Classic Textbooks. Murrieta, CA. 1872. 232p. ISBN:1-4047-7221-9, ISBN13: 978-1-4047-7221-2. Dewey:821/.3.
Audience: **g.**

Spenser, Edmund **PR2352.B76 1995**
Edmund Spenser: Selected Short Poems. Ed. 1. Douglas Brooks-Davies (Editor). Cloth Text. Addison-Wesley Longman, Ltd. Harlow, 1995. xv, 438p. Annotated Texts Ser. ISBN:0-582-08912-3, ISBN13: 978-0-582-08912-9. Dewey:821/.3. LCCN:94-022616.
Audience: **g.**

Spenser, Edmund **PR2358**
The Fairy Queen. Douglas Brooks-Davies (Editor). Trade Paper. Tuttle Publishing. Boston, MA. 1996. 576p. ISBN:0-460-87572-8, ISBN13: 978-0-460-87572-1. Dewey:821.3.
Audience: **g.**

Spenser, Edmund **MLCS 91/12507 (P)**
The Faerie Queene. Thomas P. Roche & C. Patrick O'Donnell (Editors). Trade Paper. Penguin Group (USA) Inc. New York, NY. 1979. 1p. Classics Ser. ISBN:0-14-042207-2, ISBN13: 978-0-14-042207-8. Dewey:821.3. LCCN:88-166939.
Audience: **g.**

Spenser, Edmund **PR2350**
Poetical Works. J. C. Smith & Ernest De Selincourt (Editors). Paper Text. Oxford University Press, Inc. New York, NY. 1961. 808p. Oxford Standard Authors Ser. ISBN:0-19-281070-7, ISBN13: 978-0-19-281070-0. Dewey:821/.3.
Audience: **g.**

Stein, Arnold Sidney **PR2248**
John Donne's Lyrics: The Eloquence of Action. Paper Text. Textbook Publishers. Temecula, CA. 2003. 244p. ISBN:0-7581-2021-4, ISBN13: 978-0-7581-2021-2. Dewey:821.3.
Audience: **g.** B

Thomson, Patricia **PR2403**
Sir Thomas Wyatt and His Background. Trade Cloth. Stanford University Press. Palo Alto, CA. 1964. ISBN:0-8047-0229-2, ISBN13: 978-0-8047-0229-4. Dewey:821.2.
Audience: **g.** B

Thomson, Patricia (Editor) **PR2404**
Wyatt: The Critical Heritage. Trade Cloth. Routledge. New York, NY. 1974. 196p. The Critical Heritage Ser. ISBN:0-7100-7907-9, ISBN13: 978-0-7100-7907-7. Dewey:821/.2. LCCN:74-079362.
Audience: **g.** B

Warton, Thomas **PR2358**
Observations on the Fairy Queen of Spenser, Vol. 1. Trade Cloth. Greenwood Publishing Group, Inc. Portsmouth, NH. 1969. ISBN:0-8371-1784-4, ISBN13: 978-0-8371-1784-3. Dewey:821.3. LCCN:68-031011.
Audience: **g.** B

Watkins, John **PR2367.L5W38 1995**
The Specter of Dido: Spenser and Virgilian Epic. Cloth over Boards. Yale University Press. Cumberland, RI. 1995. 222p. ISBN:0-300-05883-7, ISBN13: 978-0-300-05883-3. Dewey:821/.3. LCCN:94-033643.
Audience: **g.** *Choice, 1995.*

Webber, Joan **PR2248**
Contrary Music: The Prose Style of John Donne. Trade Cloth. Greenwood Publishing Group, Inc. Portsmouth, NH. 1986. 238p. ISBN:0-313-25223-8, ISBN13: 978-0-313-25223-5. Dewey:828/.308. LCCN:86-018316.
Audience: **g.** B

Williams, Kathleen **PR2358 .W5 1973**
Spenser's World of Glass: A Reading of The Faerie Queen. Trade Cloth. University of California Press. Berkeley, CA. 1973. Library Reprint Ser., No. 34 ISBN:0-520-02369-2, ISBN13: 978-0-520-02369-7. Dewey:821/.3. LCCN:72-095300.
Audience: **g.** B

Wilson, John D. **PR2303.W5 1970**
John Lyly. Library Binding. M. S. G. Haskell House. Brooklyn, NY. 1969. vii, 148p. English Biography Ser., No. 31 ISBN:0-8383-0261-0, ISBN13: 978-0-8383-0261-3. Dewey:828/.3/09. LCCN:68-024926.
Audience: **g.**

Wither, George **PR2390.A2 1970**
Poetry of George Wither. Frank Sidgwick (Editor). Trade Cloth. Scholarly Press, Inc. Saint Clair Shores, MI. 1970. ISBN:0-403-00236-2, ISBN13: 978-0-403-00236-8. Dewey:821/.4. LCCN:71-107195.
Audience: **g.** B

Worden, Blair **PR2342.A6W67 1996**
The Sound of Virtue: Philip Sidney's Arcadia and Elizabethan Politics. Cloth over Boards. Yale University Press. Cumberland, RI. 1997. 432p. ISBN:0-300-06693-7, ISBN13: 978-0-300-06693-7. Dewey:823/.3. LCCN:96-018713.
Audience: **u,f.** *Choice, 1997.*

Wyatt, Thomas **PR2400.A5 R4 1978**
The Complete Poems: Sir Thomas Wyatt. R. A. Rebholz (Contribution by). Trade Paper. Penguin Group (USA) Inc. New York, NY. 1989. 560p. Penguin Classics Ser. ISBN:0-14-042227-7, ISBN13: 978-0-14-042227-6. Dewey:821/.2. LCCN:79-303373.
Audience: **g.**

Young, Richard B. **PR2342.A8.T5 1969**
Three Studies in the Renaissance: Sidney, Jonson, Milton. Trade Cloth. Shoe String Press, Inc. North Haven, CT. 1969. vii, 282p. Yale Studies in English, No. 138 ISBN:0-208-00780-6, ISBN13: 978-0-208-00780-3. Dewey:820.9/003. LCCN:69-015695.
Audience: **g.**

Individual Authors and Works > English Renaissance (1500-1640) Drama > B-C

Brome, Richard **PR2439.B5 A1**
Dramatic Works of Richard Brome. R. H. Shepherd (Editor). Trade Cloth. A M S Press, Inc. New York, NY. ISBN:0-404-01110-1, ISBN13: 978-0-404-01110-9. Dewey:822.3.
Audience: **g,l,u,f.**

Chapman, George **PR2243**
Plays and Poems. Trade Paper. Penguin Books, Ltd. London, 416p. ISBN:0-14-043636-7, ISBN13: 978-0-14-043636-5. Dewey:828.3/08.
Audience: **g,l,u,f.**

Chapman, George **PR2442**
Tragedies. Thomas M. Parrott (Editor). Trade Cloth. Russell & Russell Publishers. New York, NY. 1961. ISBN:0-8462-0150-X, ISBN13: 978-0-8462-0150-2. Dewey:822.3. LCCN:61-013786.
Audience: **g,l,u,f.**

Rees, Ennis **PR2454 .R4 1979**
The Tragedies of George Chapman. Library Binding. Hippocrene Books, Inc. New York, NY. 1979. ISBN:0-374-96767-9, ISBN13: 978-0-374-96767-3. Dewey:822/.3. LCCN:78-031846.
Audience: **l,u.**

Individual Authors and Works > English Renaissance (1500-1640) Drama > Beaumont, Francis, and John Fletcher

Beaumont, Francis & Fletcher, John **822.3**
The Dramatic Works in the Beaumont and Fletcher Canon. Paper Text. Classic Books. Murrieta, CA. 2001. Collected Works of Beaumont and Fletcher ISBN:0-7426-7063-5, ISBN13: 978-0-7426-7063-1. Dewey:PR2420.
Audience: **g,l,u,f.** *Choice, 1997.*

Beaumont, Francis & Fletcher, John **PR2426**
A King and No King. Paper Text. Classic Books. Murrieta, CA. 2001. Collected Works of Beaumont and Fletcher ISBN:0-7426-7045-7, ISBN13: 978-0-7426-7045-7. Dewey:822.3.
Audience: **g,l,u,f.**

Beaumont, Francis & Fletcher, John **PR2429.A12**
Philaster: Or, Love Lies A-Bleeding. Dora J. Ashe (Editor). Trade Cloth. University of Nebraska Press. Lincoln, NE. 1974. xxxii, 152p. Regents Renaissance Drama Ser. ISBN:0-8032-0291-1, ISBN13: 978-0-8032-0291-7. Dewey:822.3. LCCN:75-127980.
Audience: **g,l,u,f.**

Waith, Eugene M. **PR2434.W285 1969**
The Pattern of Tragicomedy in Beaumont and Fletcher. Trade Cloth. Shoe String Press, Inc. North Haven, CT. 1969. xiv, 212p. Yale Studies in English, No. 120 ISBN:0-208-00777-6, ISBN13: 978-0-208-00777-3. Dewey:822/.3/09. LCCN:69-015694.
Audience: **u,f.**

Wallis, Lawrence B. **PR2434**
Fletcher, Beaumont and Company. Library Binding. Hippocrene Books, Inc. New York, NY. 1968. ISBN:0-374-98208-2, ISBN13: 978-0-374-98208-9. Dewey:822/.3/09. LCCN:68-022292.
Audience: **l,u,f.**

Wilson, John H. **PR2434 .W5**
Influence of Beaumont and Fletcher on the Restoration Stage. Trade Cloth. Ayer Company Publishers, Inc. Manchester, NH. 1972. ISBN:0-405-09083-8, ISBN13: 978-0-405-09083-7. Dewey:822/.3/09. LCCN:67-028847.
Audience: **l,u.**

Individual Authors and Works > English Renaissance (1500-1640) Drama > D

Daniel, Samuel **PR2464.H96 1994**
Hymen's Triumph. John Pitcher (Editor). Cloth Text. Oxford University Press, Inc. New York, NY. 1995. 114p. Malone Society Ser., No. 155 ISBN:0-19-729032-9, ISBN13: 978-0-19-729032-3. Dewey:822/.3. LCCN:95-110546.
Audience: **g,l,u,f.**

D'Avenant, William **PR2471.M3**
Dramatic Works of William D'Avenant. James Maidment & W. H. Logan (Editors). Trade Cloth. Russell & Russell Publishers. New York, NY. 1989. ISBN:0-8462-0512-2, ISBN13: 978-0-8462-0512-8. LCCN:64-023459.
Audience: **g,l,u,f.**

Dekker, Thomas **PR2243 .G8**
The Gull's Hornbook. Paper Text. Classic Textbooks. Murrieta, CA. 1907. 126p. ISBN:1-4047-7199-9, ISBN13: 978-1-4047-7199-4. Dewey:824/.3.
Audience: **g,l,u,f.**

Dekker, Thomas **PR2486.A11998**
Honest Whore. Trade Paper. Routledge. New York, NY. 1999. 200p. Globe Quartos Ser. ISBN:0-87830-097-X, ISBN13: 978-0-87830-097-6. LCCN:00-701530.
Audience: **g,l,u,f.**

Dekker, Thomas **PR2243.P5 1971**
The Plague Pamphlets of Thomas Dekker. Trade Cloth. Scholarly Press, Inc. Saint Clair Shores, MI. 1925. 268p. ISBN:0-403-01319-4, ISBN13: 978-0-403-01319-7. Dewey:828/.3/08. LCCN:73-161963.
Audience: **u,f.**

Dekker, Thomas, et al. **PR739.F37**
The Witch of Edmonton. Ford & Rowley (Authors). Paper Text. W. W. Norton & Company, Inc. New York, NY. 1998. xlii, 115p. ISBN:0-393-90087-8, ISBN13: 978-0-393-90087-3. Dewey:822/.0523.
Audience: **g,l,u,f.**

Dekker, Thomas, et al. **PR1265.5.R63 2001**
The Roaring Girl and Other City Comedies. Ben Jonson, Thomas Middleton, George Chapman, John Marston & Eugene Giddens (Authors), James Knowles (Editor). Trade Paper. Oxford University Press, Inc. New York, NY. 2001. 474p. Oxford English Drama Ser., :Oxford World's Classics ISBN:0-19-282800-2, ISBN13: 978-0-19-282800-2. Dewey:822/.05230803. LCCN:2001-034363.
Audience: **g,l,u,f.**

Dekker, Thomas **PR2490**
The Shoemaker's Holiday. Peter J. Smith (Editor, Introduction by). Trade Paper. Theatre Communications Group, Inc. New York, NY. 2003. 128p. Drama Classics Ser. ISBN:1-85459-714-0, ISBN13: 978-1-85459-714-4. Dewey:822.3.
Audience: **g,l,u,f.**

Harbage, Alfred **PR2476.H3 1971**
Sir William Davenant, Poet Venturer, 1606-1668. Library Binding. Hippocrene Books, Inc. New York, NY. 1970. 317p. ISBN:0-374-93659-5, ISBN13: 978-0-374-93659-4. Dewey:821/.4. LCCN:75-120624.
Audience: **l,u,f.**

Price, George R. **PR2493**
Thomas Dekker. Library Binding. Irvington Publishers. New York, NY. 1969. Twayne's English Authors Ser. ISBN:0-8057-1148-1, ISBN13: 978-0-8057-1148-6. Dewey:822/.3. LCCN:68-017241.
Audience: **l,u.**

Rees, Joan **PR2241.Z5**
Samuel Daniel: A Critical and Biographical Study. Library Binding. Richard West. Philadelphia, PA. 1980. 184p. ISBN:0-8492-7654-3, ISBN13: 978-0-8492-7654-5. Dewey:821.3.
Audience: **l,u.**

Individual Authors and Works > English Renaissance (1500-1640) Drama > Ford, John

Anderson, Donald K. Jr. (Editor) **PR2527.C66 1986**
Concord in Discord: The Plays of John Ford, 1586-1986. Trade Cloth. A M S Press, Inc. New York, NY. 1986. Studies in the Renaissance, No. 17 ISBN:0-404-62287-9, ISBN13: 978-0-404-62287-9. Dewey:822/.3. LCCN:85-048063.
Audience: **u,f.** *Choice, 1987.*

Farr, Dorothy Mary **PR2528.S75.F3 1979**
John Ford and the Caroline Theatre. Trade Cloth. Barnes & Noble, Inc. New York, NY. 1979. ix, 184 p. ;p. ISBN:0-06-492065-8, ISBN13: 978-0-06-492065-0. Dewey:822/.3. LCCN:78-012679.
Audience: **l,u.**

Ford, John **PR2522**
Ford: Five Plays. Havelock Ellis (Editor). Trade Paper. Farrar, Straus & Giroux. New York, NY. 1957. ISBN:0-8090-0704-5, ISBN13: 978-0-8090-0704-2. Dewey:822.38.
Audience: **g,l,u,f.**

Ford, John **PR2524.T5 1997**
Tis Pity She's a Whore. Derek Roper (Editor). Trade Paper. Manchester University Press. Manchester, 1997. 144p. Revels Student Editions Ser. ISBN:0-7190-4359-X, ISBN13: 978-0-7190-4359-8. Dewey:822.3. LCCN:96-034810.
Audience: **g,l,u,f.**

Oliver, H. J. **PR2527**
The Problem of John Ford. Paper Text. Textbook Publishers. Temecula, CA. 2003. 146p. ISBN:0-7581-8363-1, ISBN13: 978-0-7581-8363-7. Dewey:822.3.
Audience: **g,l,u,f.**

Individual Authors and Works > English Renaissance (1500-1640) Drama > G-L

Greene, Robert **PR2541.C6 1970**
The Plays and Poems of Robert Greene. J. Churton Collins (Editor). Trade Cloth. Ayer Company Publishers, Inc. Manchester, NH. 1977. Select Bibliographies Reprint Ser. ISBN:0-8369-5400-9, ISBN13: 978-0-8369-5400-5. Dewey:823/.3/09. LCCN:79-119957.
Audience: **g,l,u,f.**

Jordan, John C. **PR2546**
Robert Greene. Library Binding. Hippocrene Books, Inc. New York, NY. 1965. ISBN:0-374-94408-3, ISBN13: 978-0-374-94408-7. Dewey:828.309.
Audience: **l,u.**

Kyd, Thomas **PR2411**
The Spanish Tragedy. Ed. 2. J. R. Mulryne (Editor). Paper Text. W. W. Norton & Company, Inc. New York, NY. 1989. The New Mermaids Ser. ISBN:0-393-90057-6, ISBN13: 978-0-393-90057-6. Dewey:822.3.
Audience: **g,l,u,f.**

Lindsay, David **PR2659.L5A7 1998**
The Three Estates: A Pleasant Satire in Commendation of Virtue and in Vituperation of Vice. Nigel Mace (Editor). Trade Cloth. Ashgate Publishing, Ltd. Aldershot, 1998. 221p. ISBN:1-84014-204-9, ISBN13: 978-1-84014-204-4. Dewey:822/.2. LCCN:97-042175.
Audience: **g,l,u,f.**

Individual Authors and Works > English Renaissance (1500-1640) Drama > Heywood, Thomas

Baines, Barbara J. **PR2577.B35 1984**
Thomas Heywood. Library Binding. Thomson Gale. Farmington Hills, MI. 1984. 178 p. :p. English Authors Ser., No. 388 ISBN:0-8057-6874-2, ISBN13: 978-0-8057-6874-9. Dewey:822/.3. LCCN:84-010768.
Audience: **l,u.** *Choice, 1985.*

Heywood, John **PR2564 .W6 1980**
John Heywood's Works and Miscellaneous Short Poems. Burton A. Milligan (Introduction by). Trade Cloth. Greenwood Publishing Group, Inc. Portsmouth, NH. 1980. xi, 297p. Illinois Studies in Language and Literature, Vol. 41 ISBN:0-8371-9075-4, ISBN13: 978-0-8371-9075-4. Dewey:822/.2. LCCN:80-012408.
Audience: **g,l,u,f.**

Heywood, Thomas **PR5818**
A Woman Killed with Kindness. R. W. Van Fossen (Editor). Trade Cloth. Johns Hopkins University Press. Baltimore, MD. 1969. 176p. Revels Plays Ser. ISBN:0-8018-2069-3, ISBN13: 978-0-8018-2069-4. Dewey:822/.8.
Audience: **g,l,u,f.**

Individual Authors and Works > English Renaissance (1500-1640) Drama > Jonson, Ben

Barton, Anne **PR2638**
Ben Jonson: Dramatist. Trade Paper. Cambridge University Press. New York, NY. 1984. 384p. ISBN:0-521-27748-5, ISBN13: 978-0-521-27748-8. Dewey:822/.3. LCCN:83-023196.
Audience: **u,f.**

Beaurline, Lester A. **PR2638.B4**
Jonson and Elizabethan Comedy: Essays in Dramatic Rhetoric. Trade Cloth. Huntington Library Press. San Marino, CA. 1978. 351p. ISBN:0-87328-071-7, ISBN13: 978-0-87328-071-6. Dewey:822/.3. LCCN:77-075148.
Audience: **l,u,f.**

Bryant, J. A. **PR2638.B7**
The Compassionate Satirist. Trade Cloth. University of Georgia Press. Athens, GA. 1973. 204p. ISBN:0-8203-0316-X, ISBN13: 978-0-8203-0316-1. Dewey:822/.3. LCCN:73-081623.
Audience: **u,f.**

Dessen, Alan C. **PR2638.D47**
Johnson's Moral Comedy. Cloth Text. Northwestern University Press. Evanston, IL. 1971. ix, 256p. ISBN:0-8101-0318-4, ISBN13: 978-0-8101-0318-4. Dewey:822/.3. LCCN:76-126900.
Audience: **u,f.**

Dutton, Richard **PR2642.L5.D88 1996**
Ben Jonson: Authority Criticism. Trade Cloth. Bow Historical Books. New Providence, NJ. 1996. xxiii, 249p. ISBN:0-333-62981-7, ISBN13: 978-0-333-62981-9. Dewey:821.3. LCCN:95-026794.
Audience: **u,f.**

Dutton, Richard **PR2638**
Ben Jonson: To the First Folio. Trade Paper. Cambridge University Press. New York, NY. 1983. 200p. British and Irish Authors Ser. ISBN:0-521-28596-8, ISBN13: 978-0-521-28596-4. Dewey:822/.3. LCCN:83-001819.
Audience: **u,f.**

Jonson, Ben **PR2602.A3 2001**
Ben Jonson's Plays and Masques. Ed. 2. Trade Paper. W. W. Norton & Company, Inc. New York, NY. 2001. 534p. Critical Editions Ser. ISBN:0-393-97638-6, ISBN13: 978-0-393-97638-0. Dewey:822/.3. LCCN:00-060906.
Audience: **g,l,u,f.**

Jonson, Ben **PR2625**
Complete Critical Edition: The Poems; The Prose Works, Vol. 8. C. H. Herford (Editor). Trade Cloth. Oxford University Press, Inc. New York, NY. 1947. 692p. ISBN:0-19-811359-5, ISBN13: 978-0-19-811359-1. Dewey:821.3.
Audience: **g,l,u,f.**

Jonson, Ben **PR2601**
Works, Vol. 1. C. H. Herford (Editor). Trade Cloth. Oxford University Press, Inc. New York, NY. 1924. 492p. ISBN:0-19-811352-8, ISBN13: 978-0-19-811352-2. Dewey:822.3.
Audience: **g,l,u,f.**

Jonson, Ben **PR2601**
Works, Vol. 11. C. H. Herford (Editor). Trade Cloth. Oxford University Press, Inc. New York, NY. 1952. ISBN:0-19-811362-5, ISBN13: 978-0-19-811362-1. Dewey:822.3.
Audience: **g,l,u,f.**

Jonson, Ben **PR2601**
Works, Vol. 2. C. H. Herford (Editor). Trade Cloth. Oxford University Press, Inc. New York, NY. 1925. 464p. ISBN:0-19-811353-6, ISBN13: 978-0-19-811353-9. Dewey:822.3.
Audience: **g,l,u,f.**

Jonson, Ben **PR2618**
Works, Vol. 7. C. H. Herford (Editor). Trade Cloth. Oxford University Press, Inc. New York, NY. 1941. 844p. ISBN:0-19-811358-7, ISBN13: 978-0-19-811358-4. Dewey:822.3.
Audience: **g,l,u,f.**

Jonson, Ben **PR2601**
Works: Cynthia's Revels, Poetaster, Sejanus His Fall, Eastward Ho. C. H. Herford (Editor). Trade Cloth. Oxford University Press, Inc. New York, NY. 1986. 636p. ISBN:0-19-811355-2, ISBN13: 978-0-19-811355-3. Dewey:822/.3.
Audience: **g,l,u,f.**

Jonson, Ben **PR2601**
Works: An Historical Survey of the Texts, the Stage History of the Plays, Commentary on the Plays. C. H. Herford (Editor). Trade Cloth. Oxford University Press, Inc. New York, NY. 1986. 752p. ISBN:0-19-811360-9, ISBN13: 978-0-19-811360-7. Dewey:822/.3.
Audience: **g,l,u,f.**

Jonson, Ben **PR2601**
Works, Vol. 10. C. H. Herford (Editor). Trade Cloth. Oxford University Press, Inc. New York, NY. 1950. 718p. ISBN:0-19-811361-7, ISBN13: 978-0-19-811361-4. Dewey:822.3.
Audience: **g,l,u,f.**

Jonson, Ben **PR2622**
Works, Vol. 5. C. H. Herford (Editor). Trade Cloth. Oxford University Press, Inc. New York, NY. 1967. 570p. ISBN:0-19-811356-0, ISBN13: 978-0-19-811356-0. Dewey:822.3.
Audience: **g,l,u,f.**

Jonson, Ben **PR2601**
Works: A Tale of a Tub, the Case Is Altered, Everyman Out of His Humour. C. H. Herford (Editor). Trade Cloth. Oxford University Press, Inc. New York, NY. 1986. 640p. ISBN:0-19-811354-4, ISBN13: 978-0-19-811354-6. Dewey:822/.3.
Audience: **g,l,u,f.**

Jonson, Ben **PR2601**
Works: Batholomew Fair; The Devil Is an Ass; The Staple of News; The New Inn; The Magnetic Lady. C. H. Herford (Editor). Trade Cloth. Oxford University Press, Inc. New York, NY. 1986. 616p. ISBN:0-19-811357-9, ISBN13: 978-0-19-811357-7. Dewey:822/.3.
Audience: **g,l,u,f.**

Jonson, Ben **PR2411**
Every Man in His Humour. Gabriele B. Jackson (Editor). Trade Paper. Yale University Press. Cumberland, RI. 1971. 260p. Ben Jonson Ser., No. 5 ISBN:0-300-01512-7, ISBN13: 978-0-300-01512-6. Dewey:822/.3.
Audience: **g,l,u,f.**

Jonson, Ben & Jonnes, Jill **PR2411**
Bartholomew Fair. F. A. Horsman (Editor). Trade Cloth. Johns Hopkins University Press. Baltimore, MD. 1981. 212p. The Revels Plays Ser. ISBN:0-8018-2070-7, ISBN13: 978-0-8018-2070-0. Dewey:822.3.
Audience: **g,l,u,f.**

Jonson, Ben **PR2358**
The Complete Poems: Jonson. George Parfitt (Contribution by). Trade Paper. Penguin Group (USA) Inc. New York, NY. 1988. 640p. Classics Ser. ISBN:0-14-042277-3, ISBN13: 978-0-14-042277-1. LCCN:88-196178.
Audience: **g,l,u,f.**

Miles, Rosalind **PR2638**
Ben Jonson: His Craft and Art. Trade Cloth. Routledge. New York, NY. 1990. 256p. ISBN:0-415-05578-4, ISBN13: 978-0-415-05578-9. Dewey:822/.3.
Audience: **l,u.** *Choice, 1991.*

Partridge, Edward B. **PR2638 .P3 1976**
The Broken Compass: A Study of the Major Comedies of Ben Jonson. Trade Cloth. Greenwood Publishing Group, Inc. Portsmouth, NH. 1976. 254p. ISBN:0-8371-8662-5, ISBN13: 978-0-8371-8662-7. Dewey:822/.3. LCCN:75-038386.
Audience: **u,f.**

Summers, Claude J. & Pebworth, Ted L. **PR2638.S69 1999**
Ben Jonson Revised. Trade Cloth. Thomson Gale. Farmington Hills, MI. 1999. xix, 293p. Twayne's English Authors Ser., Vol. 557 ISBN:0-8057-7062-3, ISBN13: 978-0-8057-7062-9. Dewey:822/.3. LCCN:99-040559.
Audience: **l,u.** *Choice, 2000.*

Trimpi, Wesley **PR2638**
Ben Jonson's Poems, a Study of the Plain Style. Paper Text. Textbook Publishers. Temecula, CA. 2003. 292p. ISBN:0-7581-3491-6, ISBN13: 978-0-7581-3491-2. Dewey:821.3.
Audience: **g,l,u,f.** B

Individual Authors and Works > English Renaissance (1500-1640) Drama > Marlowe, Christopher

Bakeless, John E. **PR2673.B32 1970**
The Tragicall History of Christopher Marlowe. Library Binding. Greenwood Publishing Group, Inc. Portsmouth, NH. 1970. ISBN:0-8371-3352-1, ISBN13: 978-0-8371-3352-2. Dewey:822/.3. LCCN:70-106681.
Audience: **g,l,u,f.** B

Bartels, Emily C. **PR2674.B37 1993**
Spectacles of Strangeness: Imperialism, Alienation, and Marlowe. Trade Cloth. University of Pennsylvania Press. Philadelphia, PA. 1993. 240p. ISBN:0-8122-3193-7, ISBN13: 978-0-8122-3193-9. Dewey:822/.3. LCCN:92-045865.
Audience: **u,f.** *Choice, 1994.*

Boas, Frederick Samuel **PR2673**
Marlowe and His Circle: A Biographical Survey. Paper Text. Classic Textbooks. Murrieta, CA. 1929. 159p. ISBN:1-4047-7249-9, ISBN13: 978-1-4047-7249-6. Dewey:822.32.
Audience: **u,f.**

Cole, Douglas **PR2674**
Christopher Marlowe and the Renaissance of Tragedy, 63. Trade Cloth. Greenwood Publishing Group, Inc. Portsmouth, NH. 1995. 200p. Contributions in Drama and Theatre Studies Ser., Vol. 63 ISBN:0-313-27516-5, ISBN13: 978-0-313-27516-6. Dewey:822/.3. LCCN:95-023019.
Audience: **u,f.** *Choice, 1996.*

Hotson, J. Leslie **PR2673 .H6**
Death of Christopher Marlowe. Trade Paper. Kessinger Publishing, LLC. Whitefish, MT. 2003. ISBN:0-7661-2928-4, ISBN13: 978-0-7661-2928-3. Dewey:821/.3.
Audience: **g,l,u,f.**

Kocher, Paul Harold **PR2673**
Christopher Marlowe: A Study of His Thought, Learning, and Character. Paper Text. Textbook Publishers. Temecula, CA. 2003. 344p. ISBN:0-7581-4465-2, ISBN13: 978-0-7581-4465-2. Dewey:822.3.
Audience: **l,u.**

Kuriyama, Constance Brown **PR2673.K87 2002**
Christopher Marlowe: A Renaissance Life. Trade Cloth. Cornell University Press. Ithaca, NY. 2002. 288p. ISBN:0-8014-3978-7, ISBN13: 978-0-8014-3978-0. Dewey:822/.3 B. LCCN:2001-007519.
Audience: **g,l,u,f.** *Choice, 2003.*

Marlowe, Christopher **PR2411**
Complete Plays and Poems. Trade Paper. Tuttle Publishing. Boston, MA. 1999. 416p. ISBN:0-460-87987-1, ISBN13: 978-0-460-87987-3. Dewey:822.3.
Audience: **g,l,u,f.**

Individual Authors and Works > English Renaissance (1500-1640) Drama > Massinger, Philip

Dunn, Thomas Alexander **PR2706**
Philip Massinger, the Man and the Playwright. Paper Text. Textbook Publishers. Temecula, CA. 2003. 284p. ISBN:0-7581-5303-1, ISBN13: 978-0-7581-5303-6. Dewey:822.37.
Audience: **l,u.**

Massinger, Philip **PR2701.5.M3 1976**
Plays and Poems of Philip Massinger. Philip Edwards & Colin Gibson (Editors). Trade Cloth. Oxford University Press, Inc. New York, NY. 1976. Oxford English Texts ISBN:0-19-811894-5, ISBN13: 978-0-19-811894-7. Dewey:822/.3. LCCN:76-378032.
Audience: **g,l,u,f.**

Massinger, Philip **PR2411**
Selected Plays: The Duke of Milan, the Roman Actor, A New Way to Pay Old Debts, the City Madam. Colin Gibson (Editor). Trade Cloth. Cambridge University Press. New York, NY. 1978. xiv, 387p. Plays by Renaissance and Restoration Dramatists Ser. ISBN:0-521-21728-8, ISBN13: 978-0-521-21728-6. Dewey:822/.3. LCCN:77-080835.
Audience: **g,l,u,f.**

Individual Authors and Works > English Renaissance (1500-1640) Drama > Middleton, Thomas

Heinemann, Margot **PR2411**
Puritanism and Theatre: Thomas Middleton and Opposition Drama Under the Early Stuarts. Trade Paper. Cambridge University Press. New York, NY. 1982. 309p. Past and Present Publications ISBN:0-521-27052-9, ISBN13: 978-0-521-27052-6. Dewey:822/.3. LCCN:79-014991.
Audience: **u,f.**

Middleton, Thomas **PR2714**
The Mayor of Queensborough, or Hengist King of Kent. Trade Paper. Routledge. New York, NY. 2005. 112p. Globe Quartos Ser. ISBN:0-87830-195-X, ISBN13: 978-0-87830-195-9. Dewey:822.3.
Audience: **g,l,u,f.**

Middleton, Thomas **PR2411 .S3**
The Second Maiden's Tragedy. Trade Paper. Kessinger Publishing, LLC. Whitefish, MT. 2004. ISBN:1-4191-8185-8, ISBN13: 978-1-4191-8185-6. Dewey:822/.3.
Audience: **g,l,u,f.**

Middleton, Thomas **PR2711 .B8**
Works of Thomas Middleton. Arthur H. Bullen (Editor). Trade Cloth. A M S Press, Inc. New York, NY. ISBN:0-404-04330-5, ISBN13: 978-0-404-04330-8. Dewey:822.3. LCCN:78-181958.
Audience: **g,l,u,f.**

Rowe, George E. Jr. **PR2717.R6**
Thomas Middleton and the New Comedy Tradition. Trade Cloth. University of Nebraska Press. Lincoln, NE. 1979. xii, 240p. ISBN:0-8032-3853-3, ISBN13: 978-0-8032-3853-4. Dewey:822/.3. LCCN:79-004289.
Audience: **u,f.**

Schoenbaum, Samuel **PR2717.S35 1970**
Middleton's Tragedies. Trade Cloth. Gordian Press, Inc. Staten Island, NY. 1970. 275p. ISBN:0-87752-132-8, ISBN13: 978-0-87752-132-7. Dewey:822/.3. LCCN:71-128191.
Audience: **u,f.**

Individual Authors and Works > English Renaissance (1500-1640) Drama > M-U

Braunmuller, A. R. **PR2737.B7 1983**
George Peele. Trade Cloth. Thomson Gale. Farmington Hills, MI. 1983. 163p. ISBN:0-8057-6842-4, ISBN13: 978-0-8057-6842-8. Dewey:822/.3. LCCN:83-000199.
Audience: **l,u.**

Caputi, Anthony **PR2696 .C3 1976**
John Marston, Satirist. Library Binding. Hippocrene Books, Inc. New York, NY. 1976. 289p. ISBN:0-374-91286-6, ISBN13: 978-0-374-91286-4. Dewey:822/.3. LCCN:75-038929.
Audience: **u,f.**

Colley, John Scott **PR2697**
John Marston's Theatrical Drama. Trade Cloth. Edwin Mellen Press, The. Lewiston, NY. 1974. 204p. ISBN:0-7734-0449-X, ISBN13: 978-0-7734-0449-6. Dewey:822/.3.
Audience: **l,u.**

Lucow, Ben **PR3147.L8 1981**
James Shirley. Library Binding. Thomson Gale. Farmington Hills, MI. 1981. 176p. English Authors Ser. ISBN:0-8057-6716-9, ISBN13: 978-0-8057-6716-2. Dewey:822/.4. LCCN:80-029503.
Audience: **l,u.**

Marston, John **PR2692.S78 1997**
The Malcontent and Other Plays. Keith Sturgess (Editor, Notes by). Trade Paper. Oxford University Press, Inc. New York, NY. 1997. 432p. Oxford World's Classics Ser. ISBN:0-19-282250-0, ISBN13: 978-0-19-282250-5. Dewey:822/.3. LCCN:96-048198.
Audience: **g,l,u,f.**

Nash, Thomas **PR2724**
The Unfortunate Traveller: Or, the Life of Jack Wilton. Paper Text. Textbook Publishers. Temecula, CA. 2003. 159p. ISBN:0-7581-5292-2, ISBN13: 978-0-7581-5292-3. Dewey:828.3.
Audience: **g,l,u,f.** B

Peele, George **PR2730**
The Life and Works of George Peele. Paper Text. Textbook Publishers. Temecula, CA. 2003. ISBN:0-7581-0131-7, ISBN13: 978-0-7581-0131-0. Dewey:822.3.
Audience: **g,l,u,f.** B

Scott, Michael **PR2697.S24 1978**
John Marston's Plays: Theme, Structure and Performance. Trade Cloth. Macmillan Publishers Ltd. London, 1978. 129p. ISBN:0-333-21909-0, ISBN13: 978-0-333-21909-6. Dewey:822/.3. LCCN:78-324255.
Audience: **l,u.**

Shirley, James **PR3141 .D8**
Dramatic Works and Poems, with Notes by William Gifford. Paper Text. Classic Textbooks. Murrieta, CA. 1833. ISBN:1-4047-7311-8, ISBN13: 978-1-4047-7311-0. Dewey:822.4.
Audience: **g,l,u,f.**

Tourneur, Cyril **PR3170.A5**
Works of Cyril Tourneur. Allardyce Nicoll (Editor). Trade Cloth. Russell & Russell Publishers. New York, NY. 1963. ISBN:0-8462-0399-5, ISBN13: 978-0-8462-0399-5. Dewey:822.39. LCCN:63-015185.
Audience: **g,l,u,f.**

Udall, Nicholas **PR3176.U3**
Dramatic Writings. Paper Text. Classic Textbooks. Murrieta, CA. 1906. 160p. ISBN:1-4047-7312-6, ISBN13: 978-1-4047-7312-7. Dewey:822.2.
Audience: **g,l,u,f.**

Individual Authors and Works > English Renaissance (1500-1640) Drama > Shakespeare

Boyce, Charles **PR2892 .B69**
Critical Companion to William Shakespeare: A Literary Reference to His Life and Work. Trade Paper. Facts On File, Inc. New York, NY. 2006. 1072p. Critical Companion To Ser. ISBN:0-8160-6518-7, ISBN13: 978-0-8160-6518-9. Dewey:822.3/3.
Audience: **g,l,u,f.**

Boyce, Charles **PR2892.B69 2005**
Critical Companion to William Shakespeare: A Literary Reference to His Life and Work. Ed. 2. Trade Cloth. Facts On File, Inc. New York, NY. 2005. 1088p. Critical Companion To Ser. ISBN:0-8160-5373-1, ISBN13: 978-0-8160-5373-5. Dewey:822.3/3. LCCN:2004-025769.
Audience: **g,l,u,f.** *Choice, 2005.*

Coye, Dale F. **PR3081**
Pronouncing Shakespeare's Words: A Guide from A to Zounds. Cloth Text. Greenwood Publishing Group, Inc. Portsmouth, NH. 1998. 744p. ISBN:0-313-30655-9, ISBN13: 978-0-313-30655-6. Dewey:822.3/3. LCCN:97-044868.
Audience: **g,l,u,f.** *Choice, 1998.*

Dobson, Michael & Wells, Stanley (Editors) **PR2892.O94 2001**
The Oxford Companion to Shakespeare. Trade Cloth. Oxford University Press, Inc. New York, NY. 2001. 576p. ISBN:0-19-811735-3, ISBN13: 978-0-19-811735-3. Dewey:822.3/3. LCCN:2001-277478.
Audience: **g,l,u,f.** *Choice, 2002.*

Gray, Terry **PR2754**
☐ Mr. William Shakespeare and the Internet. http://shakespeare.palomar.edu
Audience: **g,l,u,f.**

McDonald, Russ (Editor) **PR2894;**
Bedford Companion to Shakespeare: An Introduction with Documents. Ed. 2. Trade Cloth. Palgrave Macmillan. New York, NY. 2001. 480p. ISBN:0-312-23713-8, ISBN13: 978-0-312-23713-4. Dewey:822.33.
Audience: **g,l,u,f.**

Olsen, Kirstin **PR2892.O56 2002**
All Things Shakespeare: An Encyclopedia of Shakespeare's World, Vol. 1. Trade Cloth. Greenwood Publishing Group, Inc. Portsmouth, NH. 2002. xxiv, 804p. ISBN:0-313-32419-0, ISBN13: 978-0-313-32419-2. Dewey:822.3/3. LCCN:2002-069732.
Audience: **g,l,u,f.** *Choice, 2003.*

Olsen, Kirstin **PR2892.O56 2002**
All Things Shakespeare: An Encyclopedia of Shakespeare's World, Vol. 2. Trade Cloth. Greenwood Publishing Group, Inc. Portsmouth, NH. 2002. xxiv, 804p. ISBN:0-313-32420-4, ISBN13: 978-0-313-32420-8. Dewey:822.3/3. LCCN:2002-069732.
Audience: **g,l,u,f.** *Choice, 2003.*

Sutherland, John & Engel, Karl-Heinz **PR2997.P6S87 2000**
Henry V, War Criminal?: And Other Shakespeare Puzzles. Stephen Orgel (Introduction by). Trade Paper. Oxford University Press, Inc. New York, NY. 2000. 240p. Oxford World's Classics Ser. ISBN:0-19-283879-2, ISBN13: 978-0-19-283879-7. Dewey:822.3/3. LCCN:00-038597.
Audience: **g,l,u,f.**

Toropov, Brandon **PR2976**
Shakespeare for Beginners. Van Howell (Illustrator). Trade Paper. Writers & Readers Publishing, Inc. New York, NY. 1997. 176p. For Beginners Ser. ISBN:0-86316-228-2, ISBN13: 978-0-86316-228-2. Dewey:822.3/3.
Audience: **g,l,u.**

Individual Authors and Works > English Renaissance (1500-1640) Drama > Shakespeare > Individual Plays

Shakespeare, William **PR2976**
All's Well That Ends Well. Ed. 2. Library Binding. Thomson Learning EMEA, Ltd. London, 1999. Arden Shakespeare Third Ser. ISBN:0-17-443589-4, ISBN13: 978-0-17-443589-1. Dewey:822.3/3.
Audience: **g,l,u,f.**

Shakespeare, William **PR2804**
The Comedy of Errors. Ed. 3. Trade Cloth. Thomson Learning EMEA, Ltd. London, 1998. The Arden Shakespeare Ser. ISBN:0-17-443543-6, ISBN13: 978-0-17-443543-3. Dewey:822.33.
Audience: **g,l,u,f.**

Shakespeare, William **PR2805.A2R68**
Coriolanus. Ed. 3. Trade Cloth. Thomson Learning EMEA, Ltd. London, 2001. The Arden Shakespeare Ser. ISBN:0-17-443544-4, ISBN13: 978-0-17-443544-0. Dewey:791.4472.
Audience: **g,l,u,f.**

Shakespeare, William **PR2806.A2H59**
Cymbeline. Trade Cloth. Thomson Learning EMEA, Ltd. London, 2002. The Arden Shakespeare Ser. ISBN:0-17-443545-2, ISBN13: 978-0-17-443545-7. Dewey:791.4472.
Audience: **g,l,u,f.**

Shakespeare, William (Editor) **PR2976**
Julius Caesar. Ed. 3. Trade Cloth. Thomson Learning EMEA, Ltd. London, 1998. 412p. The Arden Shakespeare Ser. ISBN:0-17-443547-9, ISBN13: 978-0-17-443547-1. Dewey:822.3/3.
Audience: **g,l,u,f.**

Shakespeare, William **PR2976**
King Henry VI - Arden Shakespeare, Pt. 1. Ed. 3. Trade Cloth. Thomson Learning EMEA, Ltd. London, 2000. 345p. The Arden Shakespeare Ser. ISBN:0-17-443550-9, ISBN13: 978-0-17-443550-1. Dewey:822.3/3.
Audience: **g,l,u,f.**

Shakespeare, William **PR2976**
King Henry VI, part 2. Ed. 2. Trade Cloth. Thomson Learning. Independence, KY. 1957. liv, 197p. Arden Shakespeare Second Ser. ISBN:0-17-443607-6, ISBN13: 978-0-17-443607-2. Dewey:822.3/3.
Audience: **g,l,u,f.**

Shakespeare, William **PR2976**
King Henry VI, Part 3. Ed. 3. Trade Cloth. Thomson Learning EMEA, Ltd. London, 2002. The Arden Shakespeare Ser. ISBN:0-17-443552-5, ISBN13: 978-0-17-443552-5. Dewey:822.3/3.
Audience: **g,l,u,f.**

Shakespeare, William **PR2821**
King Richard III. Ed. 3. Trade Cloth. Thomson Learning EMEA, Ltd. London, 2001. The Arden Shakespeare Ser. ISBN:0-17-443556-8, ISBN13: 978-0-17-443556-3. Dewey:822.3/3.
Audience: **g,l,u,f.**

Shakespeare, William **PR2822.A2H5**
Love's Labour's Lost. Ed. 3. Trade Cloth. Thomson Learning EMEA, Ltd. London, 1998. xvii, 374p. The Arden Shakespeare Ser. ISBN:0-17-443557-6, ISBN13: 978-0-17-443557-0. Dewey:791.4472.
Audience: **g,l,u,f.**

Shakespeare, William **PR2976**
Macbeth. Ed. 9. Trade Cloth. Thomson Learning EMEA, Ltd. London, 2001. The Arden Shakespeare Ser. ISBN:0-17-443558-4, ISBN13: 978-0-17-443558-7. Dewey:822.3/3.
Audience: **l,u,f.** *Choice, 1996.*

Shakespeare, William **PR2824.A2H3**
Measure for Measure. Ed. 3. Trade Cloth. Thomson Learning EMEA, Ltd. London, 2002. The Arden Shakespeare Ser. ISBN:0-17-443559-2, ISBN13: 978-0-17-443559-4. Dewey:791.4472.
Audience: **g,l,u,f.**

Shakespeare, William **PR2976**
A Midsummer Night's Dream. Ed. 3. Trade Cloth. Thomson Learning EMEA, Ltd. London, 1999. The Arden Shakespeare Ser. ISBN:0-17-443562-2, ISBN13: 978-0-17-443562-4. Dewey:822.3/3.
Audience: **g,l,u,f.** *Choice, 1997, 1995.*

Shakespeare, William **PR2753 .F5**
A New Variorum Edition of Shakespeare, Set. Library Binding. Classic Books. Murrieta, CA. 1999. ISBN:1-58201-281-4, ISBN13: 978-1-58201-281-0. Dewey:822.3.
Audience: **g,l,u,f.**

Shakespeare, William **PR2831**
Romeo and Juliet. Ed. 3. Trade Cloth. Thomson Learning EMEA, Ltd. London, 2000. The Arden Shakespeare Ser. ISBN:0-17-443566-5, ISBN13: 978-0-17-443566-2. Dewey:822.3/3.
Audience: **g,l,u,f.** *Choice, 2006.*

Shakespeare, William **PR2976**
Shakespeare Made Easy. Ed. 3. Library Binding. Thomson Learning EMEA, Ltd. London, 1997. 425p. English Ser. ISBN:0-17-443465-0, ISBN13: 978-0-17-443465-8. Dewey:822.3/3.
Audience: **g,l,u,f.** *Choice, 2006.*

Shakespeare, William **PR2834**
Timon of Athens. Ed. 3. Trade Cloth. Thomson Learning EMEA, Ltd. London, 1999. The Arden Shakespeare Ser. ISBN:0 17 443569-X, ISBN13: 978-0-17-443569-3. Dewey:791.4472.
Audience: **g,l,u,f.**

Shakespeare, William **PR2836**
Troilus and Cressida. Ed. 3. Library Binding. Thomson Learning EMEA, Ltd. London, 1998. 491p. English Ser. ISBN:0-17-443570-3, ISBN13: 978-0-17-443570-9. Dewey:822.33.
Audience: **g,l,u,f.**

Shakespeare, William **PR2976**
Twelfth Night: Or, What You Will. Ed. 3. Trade Cloth. Thomson Learning EMEA, Ltd. London, 1999. The Arden Shakespeare Ser. ISBN:0-17-443571-1, ISBN13: 978-0-17-443571-6. Dewey:822.3/3.
Audience: **g,l,u,f.**

Shakespeare, William **PR2411**
The Two Noble Kinsmen. Ed. 3. Library Binding. Thomson Learning EMEA, Ltd. London, 1997. 411p. English Ser. ISBN:0-17-443463-4, ISBN13: 978-0-17-443463-4. Dewey:822/.3.
Audience: **g,l,u,f.** *Choice, 1990.*

Shakespeare, William **PR2839**
The Winter's Tale. Trade Cloth. Thomson Learning EMEA, Ltd. London, 2000. The Arden Shakespeare Ser. ISBN:0-17-443573-8, ISBN13: 978-0-17-443573-0. Dewey:822.33.
Audience: **g,l,u,f.**

Shakespeare, William **PR2976**
Titus Andronicus. Ed. 3. Jonathan Bate (Editor). Trade Cloth. Thomson Learning EMEA, Ltd. London, 1995. 336p. ISBN:1-904271-14-6, ISBN13: 978-1-904271-14-7. Dewey:822.3/3.
Audience: **g,l,u,f.**

Shakespeare, William **PR2976**
The Merchant of Venice: Texts and Contexts. Ed. 2. John Russell Brown (Editor). Library Binding. Thomson Learning EMEA, Ltd. London, 1999. 240p. Second Ser. ISBN:0-17-443580-0, ISBN13: 978-0-17-443580-8. Dewey:822.3/3.
Audience: **g,l,u,f.**

Shakespeare, William **PR2838.A2**
The Two Gentlemen of Verona. Ed. 3. William Carroll (Editor). Trade Cloth. Thomson Learning EMEA, Ltd. London, 2004. 400p. ISBN:1-903436-94-X, ISBN13: 978-1-903436-94-3. Dewey:791.4472.
Audience: **g,l,u,f.**

Shakespeare, William **PR2976**
King Henry V. Ed. 3. T. W. Craik (Editor). Trade Cloth. Thomson Learning EMEA, Ltd. London, 1995. 448p. ISBN:1-904271-07-3, ISBN13: 978-1-904271-07-9. Dewey:822.3/3.
Audience: **g,l,u,f.**

Shakespeare, William **PR2803.A2R64**
As You Like It. Ed. 3. Juliet Dusinberre (Editor). Trade Cloth. Thomson Learning EMEA, Ltd. London, 2006. ISBN:1-904271-21-9, ISBN13: 978-1-904271-21-5. Dewey:822.33.
Audience: **g,l,u,f.**

Shakespeare, William **PR2976**
The Riverside Shakespeare. Ed. 2. G. Blakemore Evans & J. M. M. Tobin (Editors). Trade Cloth. Houghton Mifflin Company Trade & Reference Division. Boston, MA. 1997. 2 eight-page color inserts, 3 eight-page black and white inserts, 50 black and white illustrations, 2 maps 2096p. ISBN:0-395-85822-4, ISBN13: 978-0-395-85822-6. Dewey:822.3/3.
Audience: **g,l,u,f.** B

Shakespeare, William **PR2976**
King Henry VIII. Ed. 2. R. A. Foakes (Editor). Library Binding. Thomson Learning EMEA, Ltd. London, 1999. Arden Shakespeare Second Ser. ISBN:0-17-443638-6, ISBN13: 978-0-17-443638-6. Dewey:822.3/3.
Audience: **g,l,u,f.**

Shakespeare, William **PR2976**
King Lear. Ed. 3. R. A. Foakes (Editor). Trade Cloth. Thomson Learning EMEA, Ltd. London, 1997. 455p. ISBN:1-903436-58-3, ISBN13: 978-1-903436-58-5. Dewey:822.3/3.
Audience: **g,l,u,f.** B *Choice, 1993, 1985.*

Shakespeare, William **PR2976**
King Richard II. Ed. 3. Charles R. Forker (Notes by, Foreword by). Trade Cloth. Thomson Learning EMEA, Ltd. London, 2002. 528p. Arden Shakespeare Third Ser. ISBN:1-903436-32-X, ISBN13: 978-1-903436-32-5. Dewey:822.3/3.
Audience: **g,l,u,f.**

Shakespeare, William **PR2830**
Pericles. Ed. 3. Suzanne Gossett (Editor). Trade Cloth. Thomson Learning EMEA, Ltd. London, 2004. 384p. ISBN:1-903436-84-2, ISBN13: 978-1-903436-84-4. Dewey:822.3/3.
Audience: **g,l,u,f.**

Shakespeare, William **PR2754.G74 1997**
The Norton Shakespeare: Based on the Oxford Edition. Stephen Greenblatt, Walter Cohen, Jean E. Howard & Katharine E. Maus (Editors), Andrew Gurr (Contribution by). Trade Cloth. W. W. Norton & Company, Inc. New York, NY. 1999. 3600p. ISBN:0-393-04107-7, ISBN13: 978-0-393-04107-1. Dewey:822.3/3. LCCN:97-007083.
Audience: **g,l,u,f.** *Choice, 1997.*

Shakespeare, William **PR2976**
The Taming of the Shrew. Ed. 3. Barbara Hodgdon (Editor). Trade Cloth. Thomson Learning EMEA, Ltd. London, 2005. 500p. ISBN:1-903436-92-3, ISBN13: 978-1-903436-92-9. Dewey:822.3/3.
Audience: **g,l,u,f.** *Choice, 1996.*

Shakespeare, William **PR2818.A2B7**
King John. Ed. 2. E. A. J. Honnigmann (Editor). Library Binding. Thomson Learning EMEA, Ltd. London, 1999. Arden Shakespeare Second Ser. ISBN:0-17-443639-4, ISBN13: 978-0-17-443639-3. Dewey:791.4472.
Audience: **g,l,u,f.** *Choice, 1990.*

Shakespeare, William **PR2976**
King Henry IV, Part 2. Ed. 2. A. R. Humphreys (Editor). Trade Paper. Thomson Learning EMEA, Ltd. London, 1967. i, 242p. ISBN:1-904271-06-5, ISBN13: 978-1-904271-06-2. Dewey:822.3/3.
Audience: **g,l,u,f.**

Shakespeare, William **PR2976**
King Henry IV, Pt. 1. Ed. 2. Arthur Raleigh Humphreys (Editor). Library Binding. Thomson Learning EMEA, Ltd. London, 1999. Second Ser. ISBN:0-17-443468-5, ISBN13: 978-0-17-443468-9. Dewey:822.3/3.
Audience: **g,l,u,f.**

Shakespeare, William **PR2810**
King Henry IV, Part 1. Ed. 3. David Scott Kastan (Editor). Trade Cloth. Thomson Learning EMEA, Ltd. London, 2002. 400p. ISBN:1-904271-34-0, ISBN13: 978-1-904271-34-5. Dewey:822.3/3.
Audience: **g,l,u,f.**

Shakespeare, William **PR2828.A2**
Much Ado about Nothing. Ed. 3. Claire McEachern (Editor). Trade Cloth. Thomson Learning EMEA, Ltd. London, 2005. 500p. ISBN:1-903436-82-6, ISBN13: 978-1-903436-82-0. Dewey:822.3/3.
Audience: **g,l,u,f.** *Choice, 1998.*

Shakespeare, William **PR2826.A2C7**
The Merry Wives of Windsor. Ed. 3. Giorgio Melchiori (Editor). Trade Cloth. Thomson Learning EMEA, Ltd. London, 1999. 364p. ISBN:1-904271-11-1, ISBN13: 978-1-904271-11-6. Dewey:822.3/3.
Audience: **g,l,u,f.**

Shakespeare, William **PR2802**
Antony and Cleopatra. Maurice R. Ridley (Editor). Trade Cloth. Routledge. New York, NY. 1954. 278p. Arden Shakespeare Ser. ISBN:0-416-47290-7, ISBN13: 978-0-416-47290-5. Dewey:822.3/3.
Audience: **g,l,u,f.**

Shakespeare, William **PR2976**
Hamlet. Ed. 3. Neil Taylor & Ann Thompson (Editors). Trade Cloth. Thomson Learning EMEA, Ltd. London, 2006. 440p. ISBN:1-904271-32-4, ISBN13: 978-1-904271-32-1. Dewey:822.3/3.
Audience: **g,l,u,f.** *Choice, 1999.*

Shakespeare, William **PR2833.A2V38 2000**
The Tempest. Ed. 3. Virginia Mason Vaughan & Alden T. Vaughan (Editors). Trade Cloth. Thomson Learning EMEA, Ltd. London, 1999. xx, 366p. Arden Shakespeare Third Ser. ISBN:1-903436-07-9, ISBN13: 978-1-903436-07-3. Dewey:822.3/3. LCCN:2001-615398.
Audience: **g,l,u,f.** *Choice, 2001.*

Shakespeare, William **PR2754.W45 1988**
William Shakespeare: The Complete Works. Stanley Wells, Gary Taylor, John Jowett & Bill Montgomery (Editors). Trade Cloth. Oxford University Press, Inc. New York, NY. 1988. 1348p. Oxford Shakespeare Ser. ISBN:0-19-811747-7, ISBN13: 978-0-19-811747-6. Dewey:822.3/3. LCCN:88-005231.
Audience: **g,l,u,f.** *Choice, 1987.*

Individual Authors and Works > English Renaissance (1500-1640) Drama > Shakespeare > Poems. Sonnets

Howard, Jean **PR2824**
A Companion to Shakespeare's Works: The Poems, Problem Comedies, Late Plays. Richard Dutton (Editor). Trade Paper. Blackwell Publishing, Inc. Malden, MA. 2005. 496p. ISBN:1-4051-3608-1, ISBN13: 978-1-4051-3608-2. Dewey:822.3/3. LCCN:2002-074602.
Audience: **g,l,u,f.**

Hubler, Edward **PR2848 .H8 1976**
The Sense of Shakespeare's Sonnets. Trade Cloth. Greenwood Publishing Group, Inc. Portsmouth, NH. 1976. 169p. Princeton Studies in English Ser. ISBN:0-8371-8815-6, ISBN13: 978-0-8371-8815-7. Dewey:821/.3. LCCN:76-003790.
Audience: **g,l,u,f.** B

Knight, George Wilson **PR2976**
The Mutual Flame: On Shakespeare's Sonnets and The Phoenix and the Turtle. Paper over Boards. Routledge. New York, NY. 2002. 328p. ISBN:0-415-29073-2, ISBN13: 978-0-415-29073-9. Dewey:821.3.
Audience: **g,l,u,f.**

Knight, George Wilson **PR2907.H3**
The Mutual Flame: On Shakespeare's Sonnets and the Phoenix and the Turtle. Paper Text. Textbook Publishers. Temecula, CA. 2003. 233p. ISBN:0-7581-8288-0, ISBN13: 978-0-7581-8288-3. Dewey:822.33.
Audience: **u,f.**

Leishman, J. B. **PR2848**
Themes and Variations in Shakespeare's Sonnets. Perfect, Paper over Boards. Routledge. New York, NY. 2005. 256p. ISBN:0-415-35295-9, ISBN13: 978-0-415-35295-6. Dewey:821.3.
Audience: **u,f.** B

Muir, Kenneth **PR2848**
Shakespeare's Sonnets. Perfect, Paper over Boards. Routledge. New York, NY. 2005. 200p. ISBN:0-415-35298-3, ISBN13: 978-0-415-35298-7. Dewey:821/.3.
Audience: **u,f.** B

Shakespeare, William **PR2358**
Poems. Ed. 3. Trade Cloth. Thomson Learning EMEA, Ltd. London, 2001. The Arden Shakespeare Ser. ISBN:0-17-443565-7, ISBN13: 978-0-17-443565-5. Dewey:821/.3.
Audience: **g,l,u,f.**

Shakespeare, William **PR2848.A2**
Shakespeare's Sonnets. Ed. 3. Library Binding. Thomson Wadsworth. Belmont, CA. 1997. 504p. Arden Shakespeare Third Ser. ISBN:0-17-443474-X, ISBN13: 978-0-17-443474-0. Dewey:270/.092/2 B.
Audience: **g,l,u,f.** B

Shakespeare, William **PR2750**
The Sonnets. Ed. 2. Gwynne Blakemore Evans (Editor), Anthony Hecht (Introduction by), Brian Gibbons & A. R.

Braunmuller (Contribution by). Cloth Text. Cambridge University Press. New York, NY. 2006. 292p. The New Cambridge Shakespeare Ser. ISBN:0-521-86118-7, ISBN13: 978-0-521-86118-2. Dewey:821.3.
Audience: **g,l,u,f.**

Wells, Stanley & Edmondson, Paul **PR2848**
Shakespeare's Sonnets. Trade Cloth. Oxford University Press, Inc. New York, NY. 2004. 208p. Oxford Shakespeare Topics Ser. ISBN:0-19-925610-1, ISBN13: 978-0-19-925610-5. Dewey:821/.3. LCCN:2005-271288.
Audience: **l,u,f.**

Individual Authors and Works > English Renaissance (1500-1640) Drama > Shakespeare > Concordances. Dictionaries

Bartlett, John **PR2892 .B34**
New and Complete Concordance of Shakespeare. Library Binding. Reprint Services Company. Temecula, CA. 1989. The Works of John Bartlett ISBN:0-7812-1905-1, ISBN13: 978-0-7812-1905-1. Dewey:822.33.
Audience: **g,l,u,f.**

Clark, Sandra (Editor) **PR2892.P45 1999**
Shakespeare Dictionary. Ed. 2. Trade Paper. Penguin Group (USA) Inc. New York, NY. 2000. 240p. ISBN:0-14-051421-X, ISBN13: 978-0-14-051421-6. Dewey:822.3/3. LCCN:00-702936.
Audience: **g,l,u,f.** *Choice, 2000.*

Coye, Dale F. **PR3081.C87 2002**
Pronouncing Shakespeare's Words: A Guide from A to Zounds. UK-B Format Paperback. Routledge. New York, NY. 2002. 360p. ISBN:0-415-94182-2, ISBN13: 978-0-415-94182-2. Dewey:822.3/3. LCCN:2002-009622.
Audience: **g,l,u,f.** *Choice, 1998.*

Crystal, David **PR2892.C78 2002**
Shakespeares Words: A Glossary and Language Companion. Trade Cloth. Penguin Group (USA) Inc. New York, NY. 2002. 676p. ISBN:0-14-100737-0, ISBN13: 978-0-14-100737-3. Dewey:822.3/3. LCCN:2002-489084.
Audience: **g,l,u,f.**

Onions, Charles T. **PR2892.O6 1986**
A Shakespeare Glossary. Ed. 3. Robert D. Eagleson (Editor). Trade Cloth. Oxford University Press, Inc. New York, NY. 1986. 360p. ISBN:0-19-811199-1, ISBN13: 978-0-19-811199-3. Dewey:822.3/3. LCCN:84-007912.
Audience: **g,l,u,f.** B

Shakespeare, William **PR2892**
The Arden Dictionary of Shakespeare Quotations. Ed. 3. Trade Cloth. Thomson Learning EMEA, Ltd. London, 1999. 396p. ISBN:0-17-443645-9, ISBN13: 978-0-17-443645-4. Dewey:822.33.
Audience: **g,l,u,f.**

Shakespeare, William, et al. **PR2892.F48 1998**
The Columbia Dictionary of Shakespeare Quotations. Mary Foakes & Reginald Foakes (Authors). Trade Cloth. Columbia University Press. New York, NY. 1998. 528p. ISBN:0-231-10434-0, ISBN13: 978-0-231-10434-0. Dewey:822.3/3. LCCN:97-044894.
Audience: **g,l,u,f.** *Choice, 1998.*

Spevack, Marvin (Editor) **PR2892 .S62 1973B**
The Harvard Concordance to Shakespeare. Library Binding. Georg Olms Verlag AG. Hildesheim, 1973. x, 1600p. Alpha-Omega, Reihe C Ser. ISBN:3-487-04852-3, ISBN13: 978-3-487-04852-9. Dewey:822.3/3. LCCN:74-193933.
Audience: **g,l,u,f.** B

Stokes, Francis G. **PR2892.S67**
A Dictionary of the Characters and Proper Names in the Works of Shakespeare. Library Binding. Reprint Services Company. Temecula, CA. 1988. ISBN:0-7812-0001-6, ISBN13: 978-0-7812-0001-1. Dewey:822.3/3.
Audience: **g,l,u,f.**

Wells, Stanley **PR2892.W43 2005**
A Dictionary of Shakespeare. Ed. 2. Trade Paper. Oxford University Press, Inc. New York, NY. 2005. 240p. Oxford Paperback Reference Ser. ISBN:0-19-280638-6, ISBN13: 978-0-19-280638-3. Dewey:822.3/3.
Audience: **g,l,u,f.**

Individual Authors and Works > English Renaissance (1500-1640) Drama > Shakespeare > Biography

Bentley, Gerald E. Jr. **PR2894 .B4 1986**
Shakespeare: A Biographical Handbook. Trade Cloth. Greenwood Publishing Group, Inc. Portsmouth, NH. 1986. 256p. Yale Shakespeare Supplements Ser. ISBN:0-313-25042-1, ISBN13: 978-0-313-25042-2. Dewey:822.3/3. LCCN:85-027246.
Audience: **u,f.**

Bradbrook, M. C. **PR2894**
Shakespeare: The Poet in His World. Paper over Boards. Routledge. New York, NY. 2005. 288p. ISBN:0-415-35274-6, ISBN13: 978-0-415-35274-1. Dewey:822.3/3.
Audience: **g,l,u,f.**

Chambers, Edmund K. **PR2893 .C5**
Sources for a Biography of Shakespeare. Trade Cloth. Somerset Publishers, Inc. Santa Barbara, CA. 1982. 80p. ISBN:0-403-04291-7, ISBN13: 978-0-403-04291-3. Dewey:928.2.
Audience: **u,f.**

Chambers, Edmund K. **PR2894.C44 1988**
William Shakespeare, Vol. II. Trade Cloth. Oxford University Press, Inc. New York, NY. 1989. 460p. ISBN:0-19-811774-4, ISBN13: 978-0-19-811774-2. Dewey:822.33. LCCN:88-031315.
Audience: **u,f.**

Chambers, Edmund K. **PR2894.C44 1988**
William Shakespeare: A Study of Facts and Problems, Vol. I. Trade Cloth. Oxford University Press, Inc. New York, NY. 1989. 596p. ISBN:0-19-811773-6, ISBN13: 978-0-19-811773-5. Dewey:822.3/3 B. LCCN:88-031315.
Audience: **u,f.**

Chambers, Edmund K. **PR2894 .C442**
Index to 'The Elizabethan Stage' and 'William Shakespeare' by Sir Edmund Chambers. Beatrice White (Editor). Trade Cloth. Ayer Company Publishers, Inc. Manchester, NH. 1972. ISBN:0-405-09067-6, ISBN13: 978-0-405-09067-7. Dewey:792.0942. LCCN:64-014701.
Audience: **u,f.**

Ellis-Fermor, Una **PR2899**
Shakespeare the Dramatist: And Other Papers. Kenneth Muir (Editor). Paper over Boards. Routledge. New York, NY. 2005. 208p. ISBN:0-415-35283-5, ISBN13: 978-0-415-35283-3. Dewey:822.3'3.
Audience: **g,l,u,f.**

Fraser, Russell A. **PR2894.F66 1991**
Shakespeare: The Later Years. Trade Cloth. Columbia University Press. New York, NY. 1992. 380p. ISBN:0-231-06766-6, ISBN13: 978-0-231-06766-9. Dewey:822.33. LCCN:91-031956.
Audience: **g,l,u,f.** *Choice, 1992.*

Fraser, Russell A. **PR2903.F7 1988**
Young Shakespeare. Trade Cloth. Columbia University Press. New York, NY. 1992. 247p. ISBN:0-231-06764-X, ISBN13: 978-0-231-06764-5. Dewey:822.3/3 B. LCCN:88-004959.
Audience: **g,l,u,f.** *Choice, 1989.*

Granville-Barker, Harley **PR2920.H65**
A Companion to Shakespeare Studies. Paper Text. Textbook Publishers. Temecula, CA. 2003. ISBN:0-7581-1308-0, ISBN13: 978-0-7581-1308-5. Dewey:792.094216.
Audience: **g,l,u,f.**

Greenblatt, Stephen **PR2976**
Will in the World: How Shakespeare Became Shakespeare. Trade Paper, Perfect. W. W. Norton & Company, Inc. New York, NY. 2005. 384p. ISBN:0-393-32737-X, ISBN13: 978-0-393-32737-3. Dewey:822.3/3 B.
Audience: **g,l,u,f.** *Choice, 2005.*

Harrison, George B. **PR2894**
Introducing Shakespeare. Library Binding. Reprint Services Company. Temecula, CA. 1988. ISBN:0-7812-0132-2, ISBN13: 978-0-7812-0132-2. Dewey:822.33.
Audience: **g,l,u,f.**

Harrison, George B. **PR2976.N5**
Shakespeare at Work 1592: 1603. Paper Text. Textbook Publishers. Temecula, CA. 2003. 325p. ISBN:0-7581-2102-4, ISBN13: 978-0-7581-2102-8. Dewey:822.33.
Audience: **g,l,u,f.**

Honan, Park **PR2894.H65 1998**
Shakespeare: A Life. Trade Cloth. Oxford University Press, Inc. New York, NY. 1999. 512p. ISBN:0-19-811792-2, ISBN13: 978-0-19-811792-6. Dewey:822.3/3 B. LCCN:98-022114.
Audience: **g,l,u,f.** *Choice, 1999.*

Schoenbaum, Samuel **PR2894.S33 1987**
William Shakespeare: A Compact Documentary Life. Ed. 2. Trade Paper. Oxford University Press, Inc. New York, NY. 1987. 405p. ISBN:0-19-505161-0, ISBN13: 978-0-19-505161-2. Dewey:822.3/3 B. LCCN:87-001729.
Audience: **g,l,u,f.**

Schoenbaum, Samuel **PR2893.S32 1981**
William Shakespeare: Records and Images. Trade Cloth. Oxford University Press, Inc. New York, NY. 1981. 296p. ISBN:0-19-520234-1, ISBN13: 978-0-19-520234-2. Dewey:822.3/3. LCCN:80-024538.
Audience: **g,l,u,f.**

Speaight, Robert **PR2894.S65 2000**
Shakespeare: The Man and His Achievement. Trade Paper. Cooper Square Publishers, Inc. New York, NY. 2000. 416p. ISBN:0-8154-1063-8, ISBN13: 978-0-8154-1063-8. Dewey:822.3/3. LCCN:00-026020.
Audience: **g,l,u,f.**

Wells, Stanley W. & Wells, Stanley **PR2894.W43 2003**
Shakespeare: For All Time. Trade Cloth. Oxford University Press, Inc. New York, NY. 2003. 480p. ISBN:0-19-516093-2, ISBN13: 978-0-19-516093-2. Dewey:822.3/3 B. LCCN:2002-027412.
Audience: **g,l,u,f.** *Choice, 2003.*

Individual Authors and Works > English Renaissance (1500-1640) Drama > Shakespeare > The Age of Shakespeare. Theaters

Gurr, Andrew **PR3095.G86 2004**
The Shakespeare Company, 1594-1642. Trade Cloth. Cambridge University Press. New York, NY. 2004. 356p. ISBN:0-521-80730-1, ISBN13: 978-0-521-80730-2. Dewey:792/.09421. LCCN:2003-055895.
Audience: **u,f.** *Choice, 2005.*

Harrison, G. B. **PR1125**
England in Shakespeare's Day. Perfect, Paper over Boards. Routledge. New York, NY. 2005. 256p. ISBN:0-415-35311-4, ISBN13: 978-0-415-35311-3. Dewey:820.8'0355.
Audience: **g,l,u,f.**

Hotson, Leslie **PS541.U5**
Shakespeare's Wooden O. Paper Text. Textbook Publishers. Temecula, CA. 2003. 335p. ISBN:0-7581-9110-3, ISBN13: 978-0-7581-9110-6. Dewey:811.082.
Audience: **g,l,u,f.**

Mulryne, Ronnie (Editor), et al. **NA6840.G72 L668 1997**
Shakespeare's Globe Rebuilt. Margaret Shewring & J. R. Mulryne (Editors). Trade Paper. Cambridge University Press. New York, NY. 1997. 192p. ISBN:0-521-59988-1, ISBN13: 978-0-521-59988-7. Dewey:725.8/22/09421. LCCN:97-178719.
Audience: **g,l,u,f.**

Orrell, John **NA6840.G72L66/**
The Quest for Shakespeare's Globe. Trade Cloth. Cambridge University Press. New York, NY. 1983. 203p. ISBN:0-521-24751-9, ISBN13: 978-0-521-24751-1. Dewey:725/.822/0942164. LCCN:82-009445.
Audience: **g,l,u,f.**

Schoenbaum, Samuel **PR2933.F64.S3**
Shakespeare, the Globe, and the World. Trade Cloth. Oxford University Press, Inc. New York, NY. 1979. 208 p. :p. ISBN:0-19-502645-4, ISBN13: 978-0-19-502645-0. Dewey:822.3/3. LCCN:79-003075.
Audience: **g,u,f.** BCL3

Wilson, Jean **PR2920.W55 1995**
The Archaeology of Shakespeare: The Material Legacy of Shakespeare's Theatre. Trade Cloth. Sutton Publishing, Ltd. Stroud, 1997. 224p. ISBN:0-7509-0926-9, ISBN13: 978-0-7509-0926-6. Dewey:792.9/5/09421. LCCN:96-161415.
Audience: **u,f.**

Individual Authors and Works > English Renaissance (1500-1640) Drama > Shakespeare > Criticism. Interpretation (General)

Baker, George P. **PR2995 .B3 1979**
Development of Shakespeare as a Dramatist. Trade Cloth. A M S Press, Inc. New York, NY. BCL Ser. I ISBN:0-404-00467-9, ISBN13: 978-0-404-00467-5. Dewey:822.3/3. LCCN:71-160010.
Audience: **u,f.**

Barker, Harley Granville **PR2976 .G673**
Prefaces to Shakespeare, Set. Book, Other. Heinemann. Portsmouth, NH. 1995. Prefaces to Shakespeare Ser. ISBN:0-435-08657-X, ISBN13: 978-0-435-08657-2. Dewey:822.3/3.
Audience: **g,l,u,f.**

Barton, Anne **PR2976 .B34 1994**
Essays, Mainly Shakespearean. Trade Cloth. Cambridge University Press. New York, NY. 1994. 406p. ISBN:0-521-40444-4, ISBN13: 978-0-521-40444-0. Dewey:822.33. LCCN:93-025374.
Audience: **u,f.**

Bell, Millicent **PR2983.B45 2002**
Shakespeare's Tragic Skepticism. Cloth over Boards. Yale University Press. Cumberland, RI. 2002. 304p. ISBN:0-300-09255-5, ISBN13: 978-0-300-09255-4. Dewey:822.3/3. LCCN:2002-003122.
Audience: **u,f.** *Choice, 2003.*

Bevington, David M. **PR2976.B44 2002**
Shakespeare: An Introduction. Trade Paper. Blackwell Publishing, Inc. Malden, MA. 2002. 264p. Blackwell Introductions to Literature Ser. ISBN:0-631-22719-9, ISBN13: 978-0-631-22719-9. Dewey:822.3/3. LCCN:2002-025358.
Audience: **l,u.** *Choice, 2003.*

Bowers, Fredson **HM73.P67**
On Editing Shakespeare and the Elizabethan Dramatists. Paper Text. Textbook Publishers. Temecula, CA. 2003. 131p. ISBN:0-7581-5546-8, ISBN13: 978-0-7581-5546-7. Dewey:390.
Audience: **u,f.**

Bullough, Geoffrey **PR2976**
Narrative and Dramatic Sources of Shakespeare. Paper Text. Textbook Publishers. Temecula, CA. 2003. ISBN:0-7581-4523-3, ISBN13: 978-0-7581-4523-9. Dewey:822.3/3.
Audience: **u,f.**

Burckhardt, Sigurd **PR2976 .B77**
Shakespearean Meanings. Trade Cloth. Princeton University Press. Princeton, NJ. 1968. ISBN:0-691-06146-7, ISBN13: 978-0-691-06146-7. Dewey:822.3/3. LCCN:68-015765.
Audience: **u.** BCL3

Callaghan, Dympna (Editor) **PR2991.F45 2000**
A Feminist Companion to Shakespeare. Book, Other. Blackwell Publishing, Inc. Malden, MA. 1999. 416p. Companions to Literature and Culture Ser. ISBN:0-631-20806-2, ISBN13: 978-0-631-20806-8. Dewey:822.3/3. LCCN:99-056237.
Audience: **u,f.** *Choice, 2000.*

Cavell, Stanley **PR2983.C38 2002**
Disowning Knowledge: In Seven Plays of Shakespeare. Ed. 2. Trade Cloth. Cambridge University Press. New York, NY. 2003. 270p. ISBN:0-521-82189-4, ISBN13: 978-0-521-82189-6. Dewey:822.3/3. LCCN:2002-034802.
Audience: **u,f.** *Choice, 2003.*

Champion, Larry S. **Z8811.C53 1993**
The Essential Shakespeare: An Annotated Bibliography of Major Modern Studies. Ed. 2. Trade Cloth. Thomson Gale. Farmington Hills, MI. 1993. 200p. Reference Publication in Literature Ser. ISBN:0-8161-7332-X, ISBN13: 978-0-8161-7332-7. Dewey:016.8223/3. LCCN:92-039078.
Audience: **u,f.** *Choice, 1993.*

Coleridge, Samuel Taylor **PR4480**
Lectures and Notes on Shakespeare and Other English Poets. Trade Paper. Kessinger Publishing, LLC. Whitefish, MT. 2005. ISBN:1-4179-7178-9, ISBN13: 978-1-4179-7178-7. Dewey:821.7.
Audience: **u,f.**

Colman, E. A. M. **PR2976.C57**
The Dramatic Use of Bawdy in Shakespeare. Trade Cloth. Longman Publishing Group. White Plains, NY. 1974. xi, 230p. ISBN:0-582-50456-2, ISBN13: 978-0-582-50456-1. Dewey:822.3/3. LCCN:73-086132.
Audience: **u,f.** BCL3

Curry, Walter C. **PR3001**
Shakespeare's Philosophical Patterns. Trade Cloth. Peter Smith Publisher, Inc. Magnolia, MA. 1990. ISBN:0-8446-0567-0, ISBN13: 978-0-8446-0567-8. Dewey:822.3/3.
Audience: **u,f.**

De Grazia, Margreta & Wells, Stanley (Editors) **PR2894 .C33 2001**
The Cambridge Companion to Shakespeare. Cloth Text. Cambridge University Press. New York, NY. 2001. 348p. Companions to Literature Ser. ISBN:0-521-65094-1, ISBN13: 978-0-521-65094-6. Dewey:822.3/3. LCCN:00-063002.
Audience: **g,l,u,f.** *Choice, 2001.*

de Sousa, Geraldo U. **PR3069.E87S68 1998**
Shakespeare's Cross-Cultural Encounters. Cloth over Boards. Palgrave Macmillan. New York, NY. 1999. 252p. ISBN:0-312-21721-8, ISBN13: 978-0-312-21721-1. Dewey:822.3/3. LCCN:98-034140.
Audience: **u,f.** *Choice, 1999.*

Dobson, Michael **PR2976**
The Making of the National Poet: Shakespeare, Adaptation and Authorship, 1660-1769. Trade Paper. Oxford University Press, Inc. New York, NY. 1995. 276p. ISBN:0-19-818323-2, ISBN13: 978-0-19-818323-5. Dewey:822.3/3. LCCN:92-012096.
Audience: **u,f.** *Choice, 1993.*

Dollimore, Jonathan & Sinfield, Alan (Editors) **PR3017.P59 1994**
Political Shakespeare: Essays in Cultural Materialism. Ed. 2. Trade Cloth. Cornell University Press. Ithaca, NY. 1994. 304p. ISBN:0-8014-3091-7, ISBN13: 978-0-8014-3091-6. Dewey:822.33. LCCN:94-015983.
Audience: **u,f.**

Dusinberre, Juliet **PR2991.D8 2003**
Shakespeare and the Nature of Women. Ed. 3. Trade Cloth. Palgrave Macmillan. New York, NY. 2003. 352p. ISBN:1-4039-1728-0, ISBN13: 978-1-4039-1728-7. Dewey:822.3/3. LCCN:2003-053271.
Audience: **u,f.** B

Dutton, Richard (Editor) **PR2824**
Companion to Shakespeare's Works, Vols. 1-4. Trade Cloth. Blackwell Publishing, Inc. Malden, MA. 2003. 1976p. ISBN:1-4051-0730-8, ISBN13: 978-1-4051-0730-3. Dewey:822.3/3. LCCN:2002-074602.
Audience: **g,l,u,f.** *Choice, 2004.*

Dutton, Richard (Editor), et al. **PR2894**
Theatre and Religion: Lancastrian Shakespeare. Alison Gail Findlay & Richard Wilson (Editors). Cloth over Boards. Manchester University Press. Manchester, 2004. 288p. ISBN:0-7190-6362-0, ISBN13: 978-0-7190-6362-6. Dewey:822.3/3. LCCN:2004-303523.
Audience: **u,f.** *Choice, 2004.*

Ellis-Fermor, Una **PR2976**
Shakespeare's Drama. Kenneth Muir (Editor). Paper over Boards. Routledge. New York, NY. 2005. 192p. ISBN:0-415-35284-3, ISBN13: 978-0-415-35284-0. Dewey:822.3/3.
Audience: **g,l,u,f.**

Evans, B. Ifor **PR3072**
The Language of Shakespeare's Plays. Paper over Boards. Routledge. New York, NY. 2005. 208p. ISBN:0-415-35285-1, ISBN13: 978-0-415-35285-7. Dewey:822.3/3.
Audience: **u,f.** B

Faber, Melvin D. (Editor) **PR3065 .D47 1983**
Design Within: Psychoanalytic Approaches to Shakespeare. Trade Cloth. Rowman & Littlefield Publishers, Inc. Lanham, MD. 1984. 576p. ISBN:0-87668-707-9, ISBN13: 978-0-87668-707-9. Dewey:822.33. LCCN:84-045232.
Audience: **u,f.**

Frye, Northrop **PR2976**
Northrop Frye on Shakespeare. Trade Paper. Yale University Press. Cumberland, RI. 1988. 186p. ISBN:0-300-04208-6, ISBN13: 978-0-300-04208-5. Dewey:822.3/3. LCCN:86-050485.
Audience: **l,u,f.** *Choice, 1987.*

Frye, Roland M. **PR2807**
The Renaissance Hamlet: Issues and Responses in 1600. Trade Cloth. Princeton University Press. Princeton, NJ. 1984. 368p. ISBN:0-691-06579-9, ISBN13: 978-0-691-06579-3. Dewey:822.3/3. LCCN:83-004255.
Audience: **u,f.** B

Garber, Marjorie **PR2976.G368 2004**
Shakespeare after All. Trade Cloth. Knopf Publishing Group. New York, NY. 2004. 1008p. ISBN:0-375-42190-4, ISBN13: 978-0-375-42190-7. Dewey:822.33. LCCN:2004-040063.
Audience: **g,l,u,f.** *Choice, 2005.*

Gless, Darryl J. **PR2824**
Measure for Measure, the Law and the Convent. Trade Cloth. Princeton University Press. Princeton, NJ. 1979. 304p. ISBN:0-691-06403-2, ISBN13: 978-0-691-06403-1. Dewey:822.3/3. LCCN:79-083990.
Audience: **u,f.** B

Goddard, Harold C. **PR2976**
The Meaning of Shakespeare, Vol. 1. Trade Paper. University of Chicago Press. Chicago, IL. 1960. 408p. ISBN:0-226-30041-2, ISBN13: 978-0-226-30041-2. Dewey:822.33. LCCN:51-002288.
Audience: **u,f.**

Greenblatt, Stephen **PR2807.G69 2001**
Hamlet in Purgatory. Trade Cloth. Princeton University Press. Princeton, NJ. 2001. 334p. ISBN:0-691-05873-3, ISBN13: 978-0-691-05873-3. Dewey:822.3/3. LCCN:00-060667.
Audience: **u,f.** *Choice, 2001.*

Greg, Walter W. **PR3071.G75 1972**
Principles of Emendation in Shakespeare. Trade Cloth. Scholarly Press, Inc. Saint Clair Shores, MI. 1971. 70p. ISBN:0-403-00613-9, ISBN13: 978-0-403-00613-7. Dewey:822.3/3. LCCN:73-131726.
Audience: **u,f.** B

Gurr, Andrew **PR3095.G86 2004**
The Shakespeare Company, 1594-1642. Trade Cloth. Cambridge University Press. New York, NY. 2004. 356p. ISBN:0-521-80730-1, ISBN13: 978-0-521-80730-2. Dewey:792/.09421. LCCN:2003-055895.
Audience: **u,f.** *Choice, 2005.*

Hansen, William F. **PR2807.A7**
Saxo Grammaticus and the Life of Hamlet: A Translation, History, and Commentary. Cloth Text. University of Nebraska Press. Lincoln, NE. 1983. 206p. ISBN:0-8032-2318-8, ISBN13: 978-0-8032-2318-9. Dewey:398/.352. LCCN:82-002671.
Audience: **u,f.** B

Hazlitt, William **PR2989**
Characters of Shakespeare's Plays. Trade Paper. Kessinger Publishing, LLC. Whitefish, MT. 2004. ISBN:1-4191-1258-9, ISBN13: 978-1-4191-1258-4. Dewey:822.33.
Audience: **u,f.**

Heilman, Robert B. **PR2819 .H4 1976**
This Great Stage: Image and Structure in King Lear. Trade Cloth. Greenwood Publishing Group, Inc. Portsmouth, NH. 1976. 339p. ISBN:0-8371-8523-8, ISBN13: 978-0-8371-8523-1. Dewey:822.3/3. LCCN:75-031365.
Audience: **u,f.**

Hyland, Peter **PR2984.H95 2002**
An Introduction to Shakespeare's Poems. Cloth over Boards. Palgrave Macmillan. New York, NY. 2003. 240p. ISBN:0-333-72592-1, ISBN13: 978-0-333-72592-4. Dewey:822.3/4. LCCN:2002-075255.
Audience: **l,u.** *Choice, 2003.*

Johnson, Samuel **PR3070 .J63**
Johnson on Shakespeare. Arthur Sherbo (Editor), Bertrand Bronson (Introduction by). Cloth over Boards. Yale University Press. Cumberland, RI. 1968. 1143p. Works of Samuel Johnson Ser., Vols. 7 & 8 ISBN:0-300-00605-5, ISBN13: 978-0-300-00605-6. Dewey:822.3/3.
Audience: **u,f.** B

Jorgensen, Paul A. **PR2823**
Our Naked Frailties: Sensational Art and Meaning in Macbeth. Trade Cloth. University of California Press. Berkeley, CA. 1971. x, 234p. ISBN:0-520-01915-6, ISBN13: 978-0-520-01915-7. Dewey:822.3/3. LCCN:70-145788.
Audience: **u,f.** B

Jorgensen, Paul A. **PR3069.M5J6**
Shakespeare's Military World. Paper Text. Textbook Publishers. Temecula, CA. 2003. 345p. ISBN:0-7581-2729-4, ISBN13: 978-0-7581-2729-7. Dewey:822.33.
Audience: **u,f.** B

Kermode, Frank **PR3095.K466 2004**
The Age of Shakespeare. Trade Cloth. Random House Adult Trade Publishing Group. New York, NY. 2004. 192p. ISBN:0-679-64244-7, ISBN13: 978-0-679-64244-2. Dewey:792/.0942/09031. LCCN:2003-044287.
Audience: **g,l,u.** *Choice, 2004.*

Kermode, Frank **PR3072.K47**
Shakespeare's Language. Trade Paper. Farrar, Straus & Giroux. New York, NY. 2001. 256p. ISBN:0-374-52774-1, ISBN13: 978-0-374-52774-7. Dewey:822.3/3.
Audience: **u,f.** *Choice, 2000.*

Kerrigan, William **PR2807.K46 1994**
Hamlet's Perfection. Trade Cloth. Johns Hopkins University Press. Baltimore, MD. 1994. 200p. ISBN:0-8018-4719-2, ISBN13: 978-0-8018-4719-6. Dewey:822.33. LCCN:93-020717.
Audience: **u,f.** *Choice, 1994.*

Kirkpatrick, Robin **PQ4050.E5K57 1995**
English and Italian Literature from Dante to Shakespeare: A Study of Sources, Analogy and Divergence. Trade Paper. Longman Publishing Group. White Plains, NY. 1995. 384p. Medieval and Renaissance Library ISBN:0-582-06558-5, ISBN13: 978-0-582-06558-1. Dewey:820.9. LCCN:94-021998.
Audience: **u,f.** *Choice, 1995.*

Kirschbaum, Leo **PR2989 .K5**
Character and Characterization in Shakespeare: Essays. Paper Text. Textbook Publishers. Temecula, CA. 2003. 168p. ISBN:0-7581-0641-6, ISBN13: 978-0-7581-0641-4. Dewey:822.33.
Audience: **u,f.**

Knight, G. Wilson **PR2979**
The Crown of Life: Essays in Interpretation of Shakespeare's Final Plays. Paper over Boards. Routledge. New York, NY. 2002. 344p. ISBN:0-415-29072-4, ISBN13: 978-0-415-29072-2. Dewey:822.33.
Audience: **g,l,u,f.**

Knight, G. Wilson **PR2976**
The Shakespearian Tempest: With a Chart of Shakespeare's Dramatic Universe. Paper over Boards. Routledge. New York, NY. 2002. 360p. ISBN:0-415-29071-6, ISBN13: 978-0-415-29071-5. Dewey:822.33.
Audience: **g,l,u,f.**

Knight, G. Wilson **PR2824**
The Sovereign Flower: On Shakespeare as the Poet of Royalism. Paper over Boards. Routledge. New York, NY. 2002. 248p. ISBN:0-415-29074-0, ISBN13: 978-0-415-29074-6. Dewey:822.33.
Audience: **g,l,u,f.**

Knights, L. C. **PR2899**
Some Shakespearean Themes and an Approach to "Hamlet". Trade Cloth. Stanford University Press. Palo Alto, CA. 1960. xii, 260p. ISBN:0-8047-0300-0, ISBN13: 978-0-8047-0300-0. Dewey:822.3/3.
Audience: **u,f.**

Kolin, Philip C. (Editor) **PR2829.O855 2001**
Othello: Critical Essays. Cloth Text. Garland Publishing, Inc. New York, NY. 2001. 432p. Shakespeare Criticism Ser., 25 ISBN:0-8153-3574-1, ISBN13: 978-0-8153-3574-0. Dewey:822.3/3. LCCN:2001-019475.
Audience: **u,f.** *Choice, 2002.*

Lenz, Carolyn R. (Editor), et al. **PR2976**
The Woman's Part: Feminist Criticism of Shakespeare. Gayle Greene & Carol T. Neely (Editors). Trade Paper. University of Illinois Press. Champaign, IL. 1984. 360p. ISBN:0-252-01016-7, ISBN13: 978-0-252-01016-3. Dewey:822.3/3. LCCN:79-026896.
Audience: **u,f.** B

Levin, Harry **PR2807 .L39**
Question of Hamlet. Trade Cloth. Oxford University Press, Inc. New York, NY. 1970. ISBN:0-19-500808-1, ISBN13: 978-0-19-500808-1. Dewey:822.3/3. LCCN:59-005784.
Audience: **u,f.**

Lloyd Evans, Gareth & Lloyd Evans, Barbara (Revised by) **PR2976**
The Upstart Crow: An Introduction to Shakespeare's Plays. Box or Slipcased. J. M. Dent & Sons. London, 1982. ix, 404p. ISBN:0-460-10256-7, ISBN13: 978-0-460-10256-8. Dewey:822.3/3. LCCN:82-186072.
Audience: **g,l,u,f.** B

Marder, Louis **PR2965 .M3**
His Exits and His Entrances, the Story of Shakespeare's Reputation. Library Binding. Arden Library. Darby, PA. 1983. 386p. ISBN:0-8495-3901-3, ISBN13: 978-0-8495-3901-5. Dewey:822.33.
Audience: **g,l,u,f.** B

McCrea, Scott **PR2937**
The Case for Shakespeare: The End of the Authorship Question. Trade Cloth. Greenwood Publishing Group, Inc. Portsmouth, NH. 2005. 296p. ISBN:0-275-98527-X, ISBN13: 978-0-275-98527-1. Dewey:822.3/3. LCCN:2004-017656.
Audience: **g,u,f.** *Choice, 2005.*

McDonald, Russ (Editor) **PR2970.S495 2004**
Shakespeare: An Anthology of Criticism and Theory, 1945-2000. Trade Cloth. Blackwell Publishing, Inc. Malden, MA. 2004. 952p. ISBN:0-631-23487-X, ISBN13: 978-0-631-23487-6. Dewey:822.3/3. LCCN:2003-012197.
Audience: **u,f.** *Choice, 2004.*

McKerrow, Ronald B. **PR3071 .M248 1977**
Prolegomena for the Oxford Shakespeare. Library Binding. Folcroft Library Editions. Folcroft, PA. 1939. ISBN:0-8414-6226-7, ISBN13: 978-0-8414-6226-7. Dewey:822.3/3. LCCN:77-022272.
Audience: **u,f.**

McKerrow, Ronald Brunlees **PR3071**
The Treatment of Shakespeare's Text by His Earlier Editors, 1709-1768. Trade Cloth. Ayer Company Publishers, Inc. Manchester, NH. 1977. Select Bibliographies Reprint Ser. ISBN:0-8369-5265-0, ISBN13: 978-0-8369-5265-0. Dewey:822.33. LCCN:79-109656.
Audience: **u,f.** B

Muir, Kenneth **PR2976.M754**
The Singularity of Shakespeare and Other Essays. Cloth Text. Barnes & Noble Books-Imports. Lanham, MD. 1977. 235p. English Texts and Studies Ser. ISBN:0-06-495018-2, ISBN13: 978-0-06-495018-3. Dewey:822.3/3. LCCN:77-007225.
Audience: **g,l,u,f.** B

Muir, Kenneth **PR2952.M84 1978**
The Sources of Shakespeare's Plays. Trade Cloth. Yale University Press. Cumberland, RI. 1978. vi, 320p. ISBN:0-300-02212-3, ISBN13: 978-0-300-02212-4. Dewey:822.3/3. LCCN:77-010295.
Audience: **g,l,u,f.** B

Orgel, Stephen **PR2965.O74 2003**
Imagining Shakespeare. Cloth over Boards. Palgrave Macmillan. New York, NY. 2003. 192p. ISBN:1-4039-1177-0, ISBN13: 978-1-4039-1177-3. Dewey:822.3/3. LCCN:2003-051778.
Audience: **u,f.** *Choice, 2003.*

Orgel, Stephen (Editor) **PR3071.S464 1999**
Shakespeare and the Editorial Tradition. Library Binding. Garland Publishing, Inc. New York, NY. 1999. 350p. The Scholarly Literature Ser. ISBN:0-8153-2965-2, ISBN13: 978-0-8153-2965-7. Dewey:822. LCCN:99-049782.
Audience: **u,f.**

Partridge, Eric **PR2892.P27 2001**
Shakespeare's Bawdy. Ed. 4. Trade Cloth. Routledge. New York, NY. 2001. 240p. Classics Ser. ISBN:0-415-25553-8, ISBN13: 978-0-415-25553-0. Dewey:822.3/3. LCCN:2001-041607.
Audience: **u,f.**

Pinciss, G. M. **PR658.R43P56 2000**
Forbidden Matter: Religion in the Drama of Shakespeare and His Contemporaries. Trade Cloth. University of Delaware Press. Newark, DE. 2000. 144p. ISBN:0-87413-706-3, ISBN13: 978-0-87413-706-4. Dewey:822/.3093823. LCCN:99-038700.
Audience: **u,f.** *Choice, 2000.*

Richman, David **PR2981.R47 1990**
Laughter, Pain, and Wonder: Shakespeare's Comedies and the Audience in the Theater. Trade Cloth. University of Delaware Press. Newark, DE. 1990. 200p. ISBN:0-87413-388-2, ISBN13: 978-0-87413-388-2. Dewey:822.3/3. LCCN:89-040413.
Audience: **u,f.** *Choice, 1991.*

Root, Robert K. **PR3009 .R72**
Classical Mythology in Shakespeare. Library Binding. Reprint Services Company. Temecula, CA. 1992. 134p. BCL1-PR English Literature Ser. ISBN:0-7812-7306-4, ISBN13: 978-0-7812-7306-0. Dewey:822.33.
Audience: **g,l,u,f.**

Rosenberg, Marvin **PR2829.R6 1992**
The Masks of Othello: The Search for the Identity of Othello, Iago, and Desdemona by Three Centuries of Actors and Critics. Trade Cloth. University of Delaware Press. Newark, DE. 1993. 328p. ISBN:0-87413-481-1, ISBN13: 978-0-87413-481-0. Dewey:822.3/3. LCCN:61-007521.
Audience: **u,f.** B

Rothwell, Kenneth S **PR3093**
A History of Shakespeare on Screen: A Century of Film and Television. Trade Cloth. Cambridge University Press. New York, NY. 1999. 366p. ISBN:0-521-59404-9, ISBN13: 978-0-521-59404-2. Dewey:791.43/6. LCCN:98-050547.
Audience: **u,f.** *Choice, 2000.*

Schanzer, Ernest **PR2808**
The Problem Plays of Shakespeare: A Study of Julius Caesar, Measure for Measure, Antony and Cleopatra. Paper over Boards. Routledge. New York, NY. 2005. 208p. ISBN:0-415-35305-X, ISBN13: 978-0-415-35305-2. Dewey:822.3'3.
Audience: **u,f.** B

Schwartz, Murray M. & Kahn, Coppelia **PR2976**
Representing Shakespeare: New Psychoanalytic Essays. Trade Cloth. Johns Hopkins University Press. Baltimore, MD. 1980. 320p. ISBN:0-8018-2302-1, ISBN13: 978-0-8018-2302-2. Dewey:822.3/3. LCCN:79-003682.
Audience: **u,f.** B

Shapiro, James **PR2825.S44 1996**
Shakespeare and the Jews. Trade Cloth. Columbia University Press. New York, NY. 1995. 332p. ISBN:0-231-10344-1, ISBN13: 978-0-231-10344-2. Dewey:822.33. LCCN:95-023260.
Audience: **u,f.** *Choice, 1996.*

Shaw, George Bernard **PR2976.S35 1971**
Shaw on Shakespeare. Edwin Wilson (Editor). Trade Cloth. Ayer Company Publishers, Inc. Manchester, NH. 1980. xxii, 284p. Essay Index Reprint Ser. ISBN:0-8369-2175-5, ISBN13: 978-0-8369-2175-5. Dewey:822.3/3. LCCN:77-134134.
Audience: **l,u,f.** BCL3

Speziale-Bagliacca, Roberto **PQ2246.M3S66 1998**
The King and the Adultress: A Psychoanalytical and Literary Reinterpretation of Madame Bovary and King Lear. Frank Kermode (Foreword by). Trade Cloth. Duke University Press. Durham, NC. 1998. xiv, 162p. ISBN:0-8223-2089-4, ISBN13: 978-0-8223-2089-0. Dewey:843/.8. LCCN:97-017772.
Audience: **u,f.** *Choice, 1998.*

Stock, R. D. **PR2975.J643 Z85**
Samuel Johnson and Neoclassical Dramatic Theory: The Intellectual Context of the "Preface to Shakespeare". Trade Cloth. University of Nebraska Press. Lincoln, NE. 1973. xxiv, 226p. ISBN:0-8032-0819-7, ISBN13: 978-0-8032-0819-3. Dewey:822.3/3. LCCN:72-077194.
Audience: **u,f.** BCL3

Stoll, Elmer E. **PR2989.S7**
Shakespeare's Young Lovers. Trade Cloth. A M S Press, Inc. New York, NY. ISBN:0-404-06282-2, ISBN13: 978-0-404-06282-8. Dewey:822.33. LCCN:75-182721.
Audience: **u,f.**

Taylor, Gary **PR2976**
Reinventing Shakespeare: A Cultural History from the Restoration to the Present. Trade Paper. Oxford University Press, Inc. New York, NY. 1991. 480p. ISBN:0-19-506679-0, ISBN13: 978-0-19-506679-1. Dewey:822.3/3.
Audience: **u,f.** *Choice, 1990.*

Taylor, Gary & Jowett, John **PR3095.T39 1993**
Shakespeare Reshaped, 1606-1623. Trade Cloth. Oxford University Press, Inc. New York, NY. 1993. 344p. Oxford Shakespeare Studies ISBN:0-19-812256-X, ISBN13: 978-0-19-812256-2. Dewey:822.3/3. LCCN:93-016328.
Audience: **u,f.** *Choice, 1994.*

Taylor, Mark **PR2997.I46T39 2002**
Shakespeare's Imitations. Trade Cloth. University of Delaware Press. Newark, DE. 2002. 192p. ISBN:0-87413-775-6, ISBN13: 978-0-87413-775-0. Dewey:822.3/3. LCCN:2002-018054.
Audience: **u,f.** *Choice, 2003.*

Thompson, Ann & McMullan, Gordon **PR3071**
In Arden: Editing Shakespeare - Arden Shakespeare. Trade Paper. Thomson Learning EMEA, Ltd. London, 2002. 288p. ISBN:1-904271-31-6, ISBN13: 978-1-904271-31-4. Dewey:822.33.
Audience: **u,f.**

Tillyard, Eustace M. **PR2981.5**
Shakespeare's Last Plays. Trade Paper. Continuum International Publishing Group, Ltd. London, 1938. 88p. ISBN:0-485-30017-6, ISBN13: 978-0-485-30017-8. Dewey:822.3/3.
Audience: **g,l,u,f.**

Tillyard, Eustace M. **PR2976.T57**
Shakespeare's Problem Plays. Trade Cloth. A M S Press, Inc. New York, NY. 1950. ISBN:0-404-20258-6, ISBN13: 978-0-404-20258-3. Dewey:822.33. LCCN:83-045901.
Audience: **g,l,u,f.**

Van Doren, Mark **PR2976.V25 2005**
Shakespeare. David Lehman (Foreword by). Trade Paper, Perfect. New York Review of Books, Incorporated, The. New York, NY. 2005. 302p. New York Review Books Classics ISBN:1-59017-168-3, ISBN13: 978-1-59017-168-4. Dewey:822.3/3. LCCN:2005-012785.
Audience: **g,l,u,f.** BCL3

Vaughan, Alden T. & Vaughan, Virginia M. **PR2833 .V38 1991**
Shakespeare's Caliban: A Cultural History. Trade Cloth. Cambridge University Press. New York, NY. 1991. 320p. ISBN:0-521-40305-7, ISBN13: 978-0-521-40305-4. Dewey:822.3/3. LCCN:90-028974.
Audience: **u,f.** *Choice, 1992.*

Vaughan, Virginia M. **PR2829.V38 1994**
Othello: A Contextual History. Cloth Text. Cambridge University Press. New York, NY. 1994. 257p. ISBN:0-521-46069-7, ISBN13: 978-0-521-46069-9. Dewey:822.3/3. LCCN:93-050148.
Audience: **u,f.** *Choice, 1995.*

Vickers, Brian **PR2970.V5 1993**
Appropriating Shakespeare: Contemporary Critical Quarrels. Trade Cloth. Yale University Press. Cumberland, RI. 1993. 528p. ISBN:0-300-05415-7, ISBN13: 978-0-300-05415-6. Dewey:822.33. LCCN:92-038549.
Audience: **u,f.** *Choice, 1993.*

Vikers, Brian (Editor) **PR2976**
Shakespeare: The Critical Heritage. Children's Board Books. Routledge. New York, NY. 1996. 3366p. Critical Heritage Ser. ISBN:0-415-13403-X, ISBN13: 978-0-415-13403-3. Dewey:822.33.
Audience: **u,f.**

Weimann, Robert **PR2976**
Shakespeare and the Popular Tradition in the Theater: Studies in the Social Dimension of Dramatic Form and Function. Robert Schwartz (Editor). Trade Paper. Johns Hopkins University Press. Baltimore, MD. 1974. 352p. ISBN:0-8018-3506-2, ISBN13: 978-0-8018-3506-3. Dewey:822.3/3. LCCN:77-013673.
Audience: **u,f.** BCL3

Wells, Stanley **PR3071 .W43 1984**
Re-Editing Shakespeare for the Modern Reader: Based on Lectures Given at the Folger Shakespeare Library, Washington, D. C. Trade Cloth. Oxford University Press, Inc. New York, NY. 1984. 144p. Oxford Shakespeare Studies ISBN:0-19-812934-3, ISBN13: 978-0-19-812934-9. Dewey:822.3/3. LCCN:84-016548.
Audience: **u,f.**

Wells, Stanley & Stanton, Sarah (Editors) **PR3091.C36 2002**
The Cambridge Companion to Shakespeare on Stage. Trade Paper. Cambridge University Press. New York, NY. 2002. 338p. Cambridge Companions to Literature Ser. ISBN:0-521-79711-X, ISBN13: 978-0-521-79711-5. Dewey:792.9/5. LCCN:2001-052447.
Audience: **g,l,u,f.**

Willbern, David **PR2997.P8W55 1997**
Poetic Will: Shakespeare and the Play of Language. Trade Cloth. University of Pennsylvania Press. Philadelphia, PA. 1997. xix, 237p. ISBN:0-8122-3389-1, ISBN13: 978-0-8122-3389-6. Dewey:822.3/3. LCCN:96-037484.
Audience: **u,f.** *Choice, 1997.*

Wilson, John Dover **PR2993.F2**
Fortunes of Falstaff. Trade Paper. Cambridge University Press. New York, NY. 1979. 151p. ISBN:0-521-09246-9, ISBN13: 978-0-521-09246-3. Dewey:822.3/3.
Audience: **u,f.**

Wilson, John Dover **PR2807.W48 1959**
What Happens in Hamlet. Ed. 3. Trade Paper. Cambridge University Press. New York, NY. 1951. 380p. ISBN:0-521-09109-8, ISBN13: 978-0-521-09109-1. Dewey:822.33. LCCN:59-065222.
Audience: **u,f.** B

Wilson, Richard **PR3024.W558 1993**
Will Power: Essays on Shakespearean Authority. Trade Paper. Wayne State University Press. Detroit, MI. 1993. 302p. ISBN:0-8143-2492-4, ISBN13: 978-0-8143-2492-9. Dewey:822.33. LCCN:93-060395.
Audience: **g,l,u,f.** *Choice, 1994.*

Individual Authors and Works > English Renaissance (1500-1640) Drama > Shakespeare > Comedies: Criticism. Interpretation

Barber, Cesar L. **PR2976**
Shakespeare's Festive Comedy. Ed. 2. Trade Paper. Princeton University Press. Princeton, NJ. 1972. 266p. ISBN:0-691-01304-7, ISBN13: 978-0-691-01304-6. Dewey:822.3/3.
Audience: **g,l,u,f.**

Charlton, H. B. **PR2981**
Shakespearian Comedy. Perfect, Paper over Boards. Routledge. New York, NY. 2005. 312p. ISBN:0-415-35267-3, ISBN13: 978-0-415-35267-3. Dewey:822.3'3.
Audience: **u,f.** B

Frye, Northrop **PR2981.F68 1993**
The Myth of Deliverance: Reflections of Shakespeare's Problem Comedies. A. C. Hamilton (Introduction by). Trade Paper. University of Toronto Press. Toronto, ON. 1993. 190p. ISBN:0-8020-7781-1, ISBN13: 978-0-8020-7781-3. Dewey:822.3/3. LCCN:94-161567.
Audience: **u,f.**

Howard, Jean **PR2824**
A Companion to Shakespeare's Works: The Comedies. Richard Dutton (Editor). Trade Paper. Blackwell Publishing, Inc. Malden, MA. 2005. 480p. ISBN:1-4051-3607-3, ISBN13: 978-1-4051-3607-5. Dewey:822.33. LCCN:2002-074602.
Audience: **g,l,u,f.**

Leggatt, Alexander (Editor) **PR2981 .C36 2002**
The Cambridge Companion to Shakespearean Comedy. Cloth Text. Cambridge University Press. New York, NY. 2001. 256p. Companions to Literature Ser. ISBN:0-521-77044-0, ISBN13: 978-0-521-77044-6. Dewey:822.33. LCCN:2001-025933.
Audience: **u,f.**

Newman, Karen **PR2981**
Shakespeare's Rhetoric of Comic Character: Dramatic Convention in Classical and Renaissance Comedy. Paper over Boards. Routledge. New York, NY. 2005. 168p. ISBN:0-415-35271-1, ISBN13: 978-0-415-35271-0. Dewey:822.3/3.
Audience: **u,f.** *Choice, 1985.*

Pettet, E. **PR2981 .P4 1976**
Shakespeare and the Romance Tradition. Library Binding. M. S. G. Haskell House. Brooklyn, NY. 1975. Studies in Shakespeare, No. 24 ISBN:0-8383-2081-3, ISBN13: 978-0-8383-2081-5. Dewey:822.3/3. LCCN:75-030806.
Audience: **u,f.**

Smith, Emma (Editor) **PR2981.S495 2003**
Shakespeare's Comedies: A Guide to Criticism. Trade Cloth. Blackwell Publishing, Inc. Malden, MA. 2003. 320p. Blackwell Guides to Criticism Ser. ISBN:0-631-22011-9, ISBN13: 978-0-631-22011-4. LCCN:2003-040322.
Audience: **u,f.**

Traversi, Derek **PR2981**
Shakespeare: The Last Phase. Trade Cloth. Stanford University Press. Palo Alto, CA. 1955. vii, 272p. ISBN:0-8047-0508-9, ISBN13: 978-0-8047-0508-0. Dewey:822.33.
Audience: **u,f.**

Wilson, John Dover **PR2981.W5**
Shakespeare's Happy Comedies. Paper Text. Textbook Publishers. Temecula, CA. 2003. 224p. ISBN:0-7581-7600-7, ISBN13: 978-0-7581-7600-4. Dewey:822.33.
Audience: **g,l,u,f.** B

Individual Authors and Works > English Renaissance (1500-1640) Drama > Shakespeare > Histories: Criticism. Interpretation

Berry, Edward I. **PR2982.B47**
Patterns of Decay: Shakespeare's Early Histories. Trade Cloth. University Press of Virginia. Charlottesville, VA. 1975. x, 130p. ISBN:0-8139-0595-8, ISBN13: 978-0-8139-0595-2. Dewey:822.3/3. LCCN:74-032400.
Audience: **u,f.** B

Campbell, Lily B. **PR2982**
Shakespeare's Histories: Mirrors of Elizabethan Policy. Paper over Boards. Routledge. New York, NY. 2005. 360p. ISBN:0-415-35310-6, ISBN13: 978-0-415-35310-6. Dewey:822.3'3.
Audience: **u,f.**

Hattaway, Michael (Editor) **PR2982.C29 2002**
The Cambridge Companion to Shakespeare's History Plays. Cloth Text. Cambridge University Press. New York, NY. 2002.

304p. Cambridge Companions to Literature Ser. ISBN:0-521-77277-X, ISBN13: 978-0-521-77277-8. Dewey:822.3/3. LCCN:2002-070873.
Audience: **u,f.** *Choice, 2003.*

Holderness, Graham **PR2982.H6 1985**
Shakespeare's History. Cloth Text. Palgrave Macmillan. New York, NY. 1985. 256p. ISBN:0-312-71581-1, ISBN13: 978-0-312-71581-6. Dewey:822.3/3. LCCN:85-002413.
Audience: **u,f.** B *Choice, 1985.*

Howard, Jean **PR2824**
A Companion to Shakespeare's Works: Shakespeare's Histories. Richard Dutton (Editor). Trade Paper. Blackwell Publishing, Inc. Malden, MA. 2005. 496p. ISBN:1-4051-3606-5, ISBN13: 978-1-4051-3606-8. Dewey:822.33. LCCN:2002-074602.
Audience: **l,u,f.**

Knowles, Ronald **PR3014.K58 2001**
Shakespeare's Arguments with History. Cloth over Boards. Palgrave Macmillan. New York, NY. 2002. 247p. ISBN:0-333-97021-7, ISBN13: 978-0-333-97021-8. Dewey:822.3/3. LCCN:2001-040660.
Audience: **l,u,f.** *Choice, 2002.*

Prior, Moody E. **PR2982.P7**
The Drama of Power. Trade Cloth. Northwestern University Press. Evanston, IL. 1973. xvi, 410p. ISBN:0-8101-0421-0, ISBN13: 978-0-8101-0421-1. Dewey:822.3/3. LCCN:73-076808.
Audience: **u,f.** B

Rackin, Phyllis **PR2982.R34**
Stages of History: Shakespeare's English Chronicles. Book, Other. Cornell University Press. Ithaca, NY. 1990. 264p. ISBN:0-8014-2430-5, ISBN13: 978-0-8014-2430-4. Dewey:822.3/3. LCCN:90-055196.
Audience: **l,u,f.** *Choice, 1991.*

Saccio, Peter **PR2982**
Shakespeare's English Kings: History, Chronicle, and Drama. Trade Cloth. Oxford University Press, Inc. New York, NY. 1977. "viii, 268"p. ISBN:0-19-281224-6, ISBN13: 978-0-19-281224-7. Dewey:822.3/3. LCCN:78-300593.
Audience: **l,u,f.** B

Smith, Emma (Editor) **PR2982**
Shakespeare's Histories: A Guide to Criticism. Trade Cloth. Blackwell Publishing, Inc. Malden, MA. 2003. 304p. Blackwell Guides to Criticism Ser. ISBN:0-631-22007-0, ISBN13: 978-0-631-22007-7. LCCN:2003-051818.
Audience: **u,f.**

Traversi, Derek **PR2982 .T7**
Shakespeare: From 'Richard II' to 'Henry V'. Trade Cloth. Stanford University Press. Palo Alto, CA. 1957. vii, 198p. ISBN:0-8047-0503-8, ISBN13: 978-0-8047-0503-5. Dewey:822.33.
Audience: **l,u,f.**

Traversi, Derek **PR2982**
Shakespeare: The Roman Plays. Trade Cloth. Stanford University Press. Palo Alto, CA. 1963. 280p. ISBN:0-8047-0182-2, ISBN13: 978-0-8047-0182-2. Dewey:822.33.
Audience: **l,u,f.**

Individual Authors and Works > English Renaissance (1500-1640) Drama > Shakespeare > Tragedies: Criticism. Interpretation

Barroll, J. Leeds **PR2802**
Shakespearean Tragedy: Genre, Tradition, and Change in Antony and Cleopatra. Trade Cloth. Folger Books. 1984. 312p. ISBN:0-918016-68-1, ISBN13: 978-0-918016-68-3. Dewey:822.3/3. LCCN:82-049309.
Audience: **u,f.** B

Bradley, A. C. **PR2983**
Shakespearean Tragedy: Lectures on Hamlet, Othello, King Lear and MacBeth. Trade Paper. Kessinger Publishing, LLC. Whitefish, MT. 2004. ISBN:1-4179-0408-9, ISBN13: 978-1-4179-0408-2. Dewey:822.33.
Audience: **u,f.**

Campbell, Lily G. **PR2983**
Shakespeare's Tragic Heroes: Slaves of Passion. Trade Cloth. Peter Smith Publisher, Inc. Magnolia, MA. 1960. ISBN:0-8446-1806-3, ISBN13: 978-0-8446-1806-7. Dewey:822.37.
Audience: **u,f.**

Farnham, Willard **PR2983**
Shakespeare's Tragic Frontier: The World of His Final Tragedies. Trade Cloth. Blackwell Publishing, Inc. Malden, MA. 289p. ISBN:0-631-15150-8, ISBN13: 978-0-631-15150-0. Dewey:822.3/3.
Audience: **u,f.** B

Harrison, G. B. **PR2983**
Shakespeare's Tragedies. Perfect, Paper over Boards. Routledge. New York, NY. 2005. 280p. ISBN:0-415-35321-1, ISBN13: 978-0-415-35321-2. Dewey:822.3'3.
Audience: **u,f.**

Holloway, John **PR2983**
The Story of the Night: Studies in Shakespeare's Major Tragedies. Paper over Boards. Routledge. New York, NY. 2005. 200p. ISBN:0-415-35323-8, ISBN13: 978-0-415-35323-6. Dewey:822.33.
Audience: **u,f.**

Honigmann, E. A. J. **PR2983.H628 2002**
Shakespeare: Seven Tragedies Revisited: The Dramatist's Manipulation of Response. Ed. 2. Trade Cloth. Palgrave Macmillan. New York, NY. 2002. ix, 275p. ISBN:0-333-99754-9, ISBN13: 978-0-333-99754-3. Dewey:822.3/3. LCCN:2001-059002.
Audience: **u,f.**

Howard, Jean **PR2824**
A Companion to Shakespeare's Works: The Tragedies. Richard Dutton (Editor). Trade Paper. Blackwell Publishing, Inc. Malden, MA. 2005. 504p. ISBN:1-4051-3605-7, ISBN13: 978-1-4051-3605-1. Dewey:822.3/3.
Audience: **g,l,u,f.**

Knight, G. Wilson **PR2983 .K58**
Imperial Theme: Further Interpretations of Shakespeare's Tragedies, Inlcuding the Roman Plays. Paper over Boards. Routledge. New York, NY. 2002. 392p. ISBN:0-415-29070-8, ISBN13: 978-0-415-29070-8. Dewey:822.33.
Audience: **u,f.**

Knight, G. Wilson **PR2983**
Shakespeare's Dramatic Challenge: On the Rise of Shakespeare's Tragic Heroes. Paper over Boards. Routledge. New York, NY. 2002. 184p. ISBN:0-415-29077-5, ISBN13: 978-0-415-29077-7. Dewey:822.33.
Audience: **u,f.**

Knight, G. Wilson **PR2976**
Wheel of Fire. Trade Cloth. Routledge. New York, NY. 1986. ISBN:0-416-50930-4, ISBN13: 978-0-416-50930-4. Dewey:822.3/3.
Audience: **u,f.**

Leggatt, Alexander **PR2983**
Shakespeare's Tragedies: Violation and Identity. Trade Paper. Cambridge University Press. New York, NY. 2005. 236p. ISBN:0-521-60863-5, ISBN13: 978-0-521-60863-3. Dewey:822.3/3. LCCN:2005-047128.
Audience: **l,u,f.** *Choice, 2005.*

Long, Michael **PR2983.L6**
The Unnatural Scene: A Study in Shakespearean Tragedy. Trade Cloth. Methuen & Company, Ltd. London, 1976. viii, 266p. ISBN:0-416-82130-8, ISBN13: 978-0-416-82130-7. Dewey:822.3/3. LCCN:76-360072.
Audience: **u,f.** B

Marsh, Derick R. C. **PR2983**
Passion Lends Them Power: A Study of Shakespeare's Love Tragedies. Trade Cloth. Bow Historical Books. New Providence, NJ. 1976. 240p. ISBN:0-06-494562-6, ISBN13: 978-0-06-494562-2. Dewey:822.3/3. LCCN:76-375729.
Audience: **u,f.** B

McEachern, Claire (Editor) **PR2983.C28 2002**
The Cambridge Companion to Shakespearean Tragedy. Cloth Text. Cambridge University Press. New York, NY. 2003. 292p. Cambridge Companions to Literature Ser. ISBN:0-521-79009-3, ISBN13: 978-0-521-79009-3. Dewey:822.3//3. LCCN:2002-067262.
Audience: **u,f.** *Choice, 2003.*

McEachern, Claire (Editor) **PR2983.C28 2002**
The Cambridge Companion to Shakespearean Tragedy. Trade Paper. Cambridge University Press. New York, NY. 2003. 292p. Cambridge Companions to Literature Ser. ISBN:0-521-79359-9, ISBN13: 978-0-521-79359-9. Dewey:822.3//3. LCCN:2002-067262.
Audience: **u,f.** *Choice, 2003.*

O'Toole, Fintan **PR2983 .O773 2002**
Shakespeare Is Hard, but So Is Life: A Radical Guide to Shakespearean Tragedy. Trade Paper. Granta. New York, NY. 2003. 128p. ISBN:1-86207-528-X, ISBN13: 978-1-86207-528-3. Dewey:822.3/3. LCCN:2004-426584.
Audience: **l,u.**

Rackin, Phyllis **PR2983.R27**
Shakespeare's Tragedies. Trade Cloth. Frederick Ungar A Book. Dulles, VA. 1978. 192p. Literature and Life Ser. ISBN:0-8044-2706-2, ISBN13: 978-0-8044-2706-7. Dewey:822.3/3. LCCN:75-034216.
Audience: **u,f.** B

Individual Authors and Works > English Renaissance (1500-1640) Drama > Webster, John

Berry, Ralph **PR3187**
The Art of John Webster. Trade Cloth. Oxford University Press, Inc. New York, NY. 1972. xiv, 174p. ISBN:0-19-812023-0, ISBN13: 978-0-19-812023-0. Dewey:822.3. LCCN:72-193341.
Audience: **u,f.** B

Bogard, Travis **PR3187**
The Tragic Satire of John Webster. Paper Text. Textbook Publishers. Temecula, CA. 2003. xii, 158p. ISBN:0-7581-4372-9, ISBN13: 978-0-7581-4372-3. Dewey:822.3.
Audience: **u,f.**

Boklund, Gunnar **PR3184.D83B6**
The Duchess of Malfi: Sources, Themes, Characters. Trade Paper. Books on Demand. Ann Arbor, MI. 1962. 199p. ISBN:0-7837-1673-7, ISBN13: 978-0-7837-1673-2. Dewey:822.3. LCCN:62-019212.
Audience: **l,u.** B

Hunter, G. K. **PR3187.H8 1969**
John Webster: A Critical Anthology. Trade Cloth. Penguin Group (USA) Inc. New York, NY. 1969. 328p. ISBN:0-14-080135-9, ISBN13: 978-0-14-080135-4. Dewey:822.3. LCCN:78-530038.
Audience: **g,l,u,f.** B

Leech, Clifford **PR3187.L4 1970**
John Webster. Library Binding. M. S. G. Haskell House. Brooklyn, NY. 1969. 122p. English Biography Ser., No. 31 ISBN:0-8383-0690-X, ISBN13: 978-0-8383-0690-1. Dewey:822/.3. LCCN:78-143481.
Audience: **g,l,u,f.** B

Webster, John **PR2411**
The Duchess of Malfi. Ed. 4. Paper Text. W. W. Norton & Company, Inc. New York, NY. 2001. The New Mermaids Ser. ISBN:0-393-90091-6, ISBN13: 978-0-393-90091-0. Dewey:822/.3.
Audience: **g,l,u,f.**

Webster, John **PR3184.W5 1996**
The White Devil. John R. Brown (Editor). Trade Paper. Manchester University Press. Manchester, 1996. 168p. Revels Student Editions Ser., Vol. 1 ISBN:0-7190-4355-7, ISBN13: 978-0-7190-4355-0. Dewey:822.3. LCCN:95-021693.
Audience: **g,l,u,f.**

Webster, John **PR3181**
Complete Works of John Webster, Set. F. L. Lucas (Editor). Trade Cloth. Gordian Press, Inc. Staten Island, NY. 1966. 1328p. ISBN:0-87752-119-0, ISBN13: 978-0-87752-119-8. Dewey:822.3. LCCN:66-020023.
Audience: **g,l,u,f.**

Webster, John **PR3182**
The Duchess of Malfi and Other Plays: The White Devil; The Duchess of Malfi; The Devil's Law-Case; A Cure for a Cuckold. Rene Weis (Editor, Introduction by). Trade Paper. Oxford University Press, Inc. New York, NY. 1998. 480p. Oxford World's Classics Ser. ISBN:0-19-283453-3, ISBN13: 978-0-19-283453-9. Dewey:822.3.
Audience: **g,l,u,f.**

Individual Authors and Works > 17th-18th C.

PR3291
The Adventures of Lindamira, a Lady of Quality. Library Binding. Garland Publishing, Inc. New York, NY. 1972. Foundations of the Novel Ser., Vol. 5 ISBN:0-8240-0517-1, ISBN13: 978-0-8240-0517-7. Dewey:823/.5. LCCN:79-170506.
Audience: **g,l,u,f.**

Individual Authors and Works > 17th-18th C. > Addison, Joseph

Addison, Joseph **PR3562**
Criticisms on Paradise Lost. Library Binding. Reprint Services Company. Temecula, CA. 1985. 200p. The Works of Joseph Addison ISBN:0-932051-91-X, ISBN13: 978-0-932051-91-2. Dewey:821/.4.
Audience: **g,l,u,f.**

Addison, Joseph **DA498 .A3**
The Freeholder: Or, Political Essays. Trade Cloth. Reprint Services Company. Temecula, CA. 1985. 311p. The Works of Joseph Addison ISBN:0-932051-53-7, ISBN13: 978-0-932051-53-0. Dewey:320.9/41/071.
Audience: **g,l,u,f.**

Addison, Joseph **PR3306**
Letters of Joseph Addison. Paper Text. Classic Textbooks. Murrieta, CA. 1941. 527p. ISBN:1-4047-0828-6, ISBN13: 978-1-4047-0828-0. Dewey:928.2.
Audience: **g,l,u,f.** B

Addison, Joseph **PR3301.G8 1978**
Miscellaneous Works of Joseph Addison. Trade Cloth. Scholarly Press, Inc. Saint Clair Shores, MI. 1971. :p. ISBN:0-403-00825-5, ISBN13: 978-0-403-00825-4. Dewey:824/.5. LCCN:71-148857.
Audience: **g,l,u,f.**

Addison, Joseph **PR3301**
Miscellaneous Works of Joseph Addison. Paper Text. Classic Textbooks. Murrieta, CA. 1914. ISBN:1-4047-0840-5, ISBN13: 978-1-4047-0840-2. Dewey:828.
Audience: **g,l,u,f.**

Addison, Joseph **PR3300**
The Works of Joseph Addison; Including the Whole Contents of B.P. Hurd's Edition, with Letters and Other Pieces Not Found in Any Previous Collection; and Macaulay's Essay on His Life and Works, ed., with Critical and Explanatory Notes, by George Washington Greene. Trade Cloth. Scholarly Publishing Office, University of Michigan Library. Ann Arbor, MI. 2004. ISBN:1-4181-0485-X, ISBN13: 978-1-4181-0485-6. Dewey:824.5.
Audience: **g,l,u,f.**

Addison, Joseph **PR1105**
The Works of the Right Honourable Joseph Addison. Trade Cloth. Scholarly Press, Inc. Saint Clair Shores, MI. 1976. ISBN:0-403-05790-6, ISBN13: 978-0-403-05790-0. Dewey:2.0750922.
Audience: **g,l,u,f.**

Addison, Joseph **PR3302**
Essays of Joseph Addison. Mabie Hamilton (Introduction by). Trade Paper. University Press of the Pacific. Miami, FL. 2004. 336p. ISBN:1-4102-1264-5, ISBN13: 978-1-4102-1264-1. Dewey:824.52.
Audience: **g,l,u,f.**

Addison, Joseph, et al. **PR1365.T23C66 1998**
The Commerce of Everyday Life: Selections from the Tatler and the Spectator (Bedford Cultural Editions). Richard Steele & Erin Mackie (Authors). Cloth over Boards. Palgrave Macmillan. New York, NY. 1998. 368p. Bedford Cultural Editions Ser. ISBN:0-312-16371-1, ISBN13: 978-0-312-16371-6. Dewey:824.508. LCCN:97-074950.
Audience: **g,l,u,f.** *Choice, 1998.*

Bloom, Edward A. & Bloom, Lillian D. **PR3706**
Joseph Addison's Sociable Animal: In the Market Place, on the Hustings, in the Pulpit. Trade Cloth. University Press of New England. Lebanon, NH. 1971. 290p. ISBN:0-87057-120-6, ISBN13: 978-0-87057-120-6. Dewey:824/.5. LCCN:73-111455.
Audience: **g,l,u,f.**

Courthope, William J. **PR3306**
Addison. John Morley (Editor). Library Binding. A M S Press, Inc. New York, NY. English Men of Letters Ser. ISBN:0-404-51707-2, ISBN13: 978-0-404-51707-6. Dewey:824.52. LCCN:68-058375.
Audience: **l,u.**

Finger, Charles J. **PR3306 .F5**
Joseph Addison and His Time. Trade Cloth. New Library Press.Net. Murrieta, CA. 1922. 94p. ISBN:0-7950-0337-4, ISBN13: 978-0-7950-0337-0. Dewey:824.5.
Audience: **g,l,u,f.**

Knight, Charles A. **Z8015.87.K55 1994**
Joseph Addison and Richard Steele: A Reference Guide, 1730-1991. Trade Cloth. Thomson Gale. Farmington Hills, MI. 1995. 584p. Reference Guide to Literature Ser. ISBN:0-8161-8980-3, ISBN13: 978-0-8161-8980-9. Dewey:016.824/5. LCCN:94-021458.
Audience: **l,u.** *Choice, 1995.*

Lannering, J. **PR3308.S8**
Studies in the Prose Style of Joseph Addison. Trade Paper. Periodicals Service Company. Germantown, NY. 1974. Essays and Studies on English Language and Literature, Vol. 9 ISBN:0-8115-0207-4, ISBN13: 978-0-8115-0207-8. Dewey:824.5.
Audience: **u,f.**

Otten, Robert M. **PR3307 .O8 1982**
Joseph Addison. Library Binding. Thomson Gale. Farmington Hills, MI. 1982. English Authors Ser. ISBN:0-8057-6824-6, ISBN13: 978-0-8057-6824-4. Dewey:824/.5. LCCN:82-001087.
Audience: **l,u.**

Smithers, Peter **PR3306.S55 1968**
The Life of Joseph Addison. Trade Cloth. Oxford University Press, Inc. New York, NY. 1968. xvi, 499p. ISBN:0-19-811658-6, ISBN13: 978-0-19-811658-5. Dewey:824/.5. LCCN:68-105168.
Audience: **g,l,u,f.** B

Individual Authors and Works > 17th-18th C. > Akenside, Mark

Akenside, Mark **PR3310.A5 D8**
The Poetical works of Mark Akenside. Ed. with A Life, by Rev. Alexander Dyce. Trade Cloth. Scholarly Publishing Office, University of Michigan Library. Ann Arbor, MI. 2004. ISBN:1-4181-0802-2, ISBN13: 978-1-4181-0802-1. Dewey:821.62.
Audience: **g,l,u,f.**

Akenside, Mark **PR3311.D59 1988**
The Poetical Manuscripts of Mark Akenside. Robin C. Dix (Introduction by). Trade Paper. Amherst College Press. Amherst, MA. 1988. 32p. ISBN:0-943184-02-9, ISBN13: 978-0-943184-02-9. Dewey:821/.6. LCCN:88-006200.
Audience: **g,l,u,f.**

Akenside, Mark **PR3310.A5 D8**
Poetical Works of Mark Akenside. Alexander Dyce (Editor). Trade Cloth. A M S Press, Inc. New York, NY. ISBN:0-404-00299-4, ISBN13: 978-0-404-00299-2. Dewey:821/.6. LCCN:71-094924.
Audience: **g,l,u,f.**

Dix, Robin (Editor) **PR3314.M37 2000**
Mark Akenside: A Reassessment. Trade Cloth. Fairleigh Dickinson University Press. Cranbury, NJ. 2000. 296p. ISBN:0-8386-3882-1, ISBN13: 978-0-8386-3882-8. Dewey:821/.6. LCCN:00-033571.
Audience: **u,f.**

Dix, Robin (Editor) **PR3310**
The Poetical Works of Mark Akenside. Trade Cloth. Fairleigh Dickinson University Press. Cranbury, NJ. 1996. 600p. ISBN:0-8386-3535-0, ISBN13: 978-0-8386-3535-3. Dewey:821/.6. LCCN:95-025560.
Audience: **g,l,u,f.**

Dix, Robin & Akenside, Mark **PR3314.D59 2006**
The Literary Career of Mark Akenside, Including an Edition of His Non-Medical Prose. Trade Cloth. Fairleigh Dickinson University Press. Cranbury, NJ. 2006. 416p. ISBN:0-8386-4097-4, ISBN13: 978-0-8386-4097-5. Dewey:824/.6. LCCN:2005-058520.
Audience: **g,l,u,f.**

Jung, Sandro **PR3314.J86 2003**
Poetic Meaning in the Eighteenth-Century Poems of Mark Akenside and William Shenstone. Trade Cloth. Edwin Mellen Press, The. Lewiston, NY. 2002. 280p. Mellen Studies in Literature, Vol. 159 ISBN:0-7734-6963-X, ISBN13: 978-0-7734-6963-1. Dewey:821/.509384. LCCN:2002-033718.
Audience: **u,f.**

Individual Authors and Works > 17th-18th C. > A-B

Astell, Mary **HQ1599.E5 A88X 1986B**
First English Feminist: Reflections upon Marriage and Other Writings. Bridget Hill (Editor). Trade Cloth. Ashgate Publishing, Ltd. Aldershot, 1986. "vii, 235"p. ISBN:0-566-05090-0, ISBN13: 978-0-566-05090-9. Dewey:828/.408. LCCN:89-206016.
Audience: **g,l,u,f.**

Astell, Mary, et al. **BV4817**
Letters Concerning the Love of God. John Norris, E. Derek Taylor & Melvyn New (Authors). Trade Cloth. Ashgate Publishing, Ltd. Aldershot, 2005. 272p. Early Modern Englishwoman, 1500-1750 Ser. ISBN:0-7546-0586-8, ISBN13: 978-0-7546-0586-7. Dewey:231/.6. LCCN:2004-009636.
Audience: **l,u,f.**

Astell, Mary **HQ1596**
A Serious Proposal to the Ladies, Pts. I-II. Patricia Springborg (Editor). Trade Paper. Broadview Press. Peterborough, ON. 2002. 300p. Broadview Literary Texts Ser. ISBN:1-55111-306-6, ISBN13: 978-1-55111-306-7. Dewey:305.42/0941/09033. LCCN:2003-267712.
Audience: **g,l,u,f.** B

Brome, Alexander **PR3326.B36A17 1982**
Poems. Roman R. Dubinski (Editor). Trade Cloth. University of Toronto Press. Toronto, ON. 1982. 560p. ISBN:0-8020-5535-4, ISBN13: 978-0-8020-5535-4. Dewey:821/.4. LCCN:83-107902.
Audience: **g,l,u,f.** B

Brooke, Frances **PR3326.B37B33 1997**
The Excursion. Paula R. Backscheider & Hope D. Cotton (Editors). Cloth Text. University Press of Kentucky. Lexington, KY. 1997. 224p. Eighteenth-Century Novels by Women Ser. ISBN:0-8131-1979-0, ISBN13: 978-0-8131-1979-3. Dewey:823/.6. LCCN:96-026708.
Audience: **g,l,u,f.**

Brooke, Frances **PR3326.B37**
The History of Emily Montague. Frederick Philip Grove (Contribution by). Trade Paper. McClelland & Stewart/Tundra Books. Plattsburgh, NY. 1995. 416p. New Canadian Library ISBN:0-7710-3457-1, ISBN13: 978-0-7710-3457-2. Dewey:823/.6.
Audience: **g,l,u,f.**

Brooke, Henry **PZ3.B7916 F4**
The Fool of Quality; or, The History of Henry, Earl of Moreland. by Henry Brooke. Trade Cloth. Scholarly Publishing Office, University of Michigan Library. Ann Arbor, MI. 2004. ISBN:1-4181-0971-1, ISBN13: 978-1-4181-0971-4. Dewey:823.6.
Audience: **g,l,u,f.**

Individual Authors and Works > 17th-18th C. > Behn, Aphra

Behn, Aphra **PR3317**
The Lover's Watch. Trade Paper. Hesperus Press. London, 2004. 104p. ISBN:1-84391-074-8, ISBN13: 978-1-84391-074-9. Dewey:823.4.
Audience: **g,l,u,f.**

Behn, Aphra **PR3317.L8 1984**
The Lucky Chance. Trade Paper. Heinemann. Portsmouth, NH. 1988. 69p. Royal Court Writers Ser. ISBN:0-413-57120-3, ISBN13: 978-0-413-57120-5. Dewey:822/.4. LCCN:84-185725.
Audience: **g,l,u,f.**

Behn, Aphra **PR3317 .A19 1990**
Behn: Five Plays. Maureen Duffy (Introduction by). Trade Paper. Methuen Publishing Ltd. London, 2004. 474p. Methuen World Dramatists Ser. ISBN:0-413-17090-X, ISBN13: 978-0-413-17090-3. Dewey:822/.4. LCCN:92-146508.
Audience: **l,u,f.**

Behn, Aphra **PR3364**
The Rover and Other Plays: The Rover; The Feigned Courtesans; The Lucky Chance; The Emperor of the Moon. Jane Spencer (Editor, Introduction by). Trade Paper. Oxford University Press, Inc. New York, NY. 2000. 430p. Oxford World's Classics Ser. ISBN:0-19-283451-7, ISBN13: 978-0-19-283451-5. Dewey:822.4.
Audience: **l,u,f.** *Choice, 1996.*

Behn, Aphra **PR3317**
The Complete Works of Aphra Behn: Love-Letters Between and Nobleman and His Sister. Janet Todd (Editor). Cloth Text. Ohio State University Press. Columbus, OH. 1993. 473p. ISBN:0-8142-0610-7, ISBN13: 978-0-8142-0610-2. Dewey:828/.409. LCCN:92-017972.
Audience: **l,u,f.**

Behn, Aphra **PR3364**
The Works of Aphra Behn. Janet Todd (Editor). Trade Cloth. Pickering & Chatto Publishers, Ltd. London, 1996. 3424p. ISBN:1-85196-018-X, ISBN13: 978-1-85196-018-7. Dewey:822.4.
Audience: **g,l,u,f.**

Behn, Aphra **PR3317**
Oroonoko. Janet M. Todd (Editor, Translator, Introduction by, Notes by). Trade Paper. Penguin Group (USA) Inc. New York, NY. 2004. 144p. ISBN:0-14-043988-9, ISBN13: 978-0-14-043988-5. Dewey:823.4.
Audience: **g,l,u,f.**

Goreau, Angeline **PR3317.Z5G6**
Reconstructing Aphra: A Social Biography of Aphra Behn. Trade Cloth. Penguin Group (USA) Inc. New York, NY. 1980. x, 339p. ISBN:0-8037-7478-8, ISBN13: 978-0-8037-7478-0. Dewey:822/.4. LCCN:80-011495.
Audience: **g,l,u,f.**

Hicks, Malcolm (Editor) **PR3562**
Aphra Behn (1640-1689): Selected Poems. Trade Paper. Carcanet Press, Ltd. Manchester, 128p. ISBN:1-85754-017-4, ISBN13: 978-1-85754-017-8. Dewey:821.4.
Audience: **g,l,u,f.**

Hughes, Derek & Todd, Janet (Editors) **PR3317.Z5C36 2004**
The Cambridge Companion to Aphra Behn. Trade Paper, Perfect. Cambridge University Press. New York, NY. 2004. 274p. Cambridge Companions to Literature Ser. ISBN:0-521-52720-1, ISBN13: 978-0-521-52720-0. Dewey:822/.4. LCCN:2004-049740.
Audience: **g,l,u,f.** *Choice, 2005.*

Individual Authors and Works > 17th-18th C. > Blake, William

Ackroyd, Peter **PR4146.A23 1996**
Blake: A Biography. Trade Cloth. Alfred A. Knopf Inc. New York, NY. 1996. 416p. ISBN:0-679-40967-X, ISBN13: 978-0-679-40967-0. Dewey:821.7. LCCN:96-075018.
Audience: **g,l,u,f.** *Choice, 1997.*

Beer, John **PR4146.B34 2005**
William Blake: A Literary Life. Trade Cloth. Palgrave Macmillan. New York, NY. 2005. 264p. Literary Lives Ser. ISBN:1-4039-3954-3, ISBN13: 978-1-4039-3954-8. Dewey:821/.7 B. LCCN:2005-043355.
Audience: **g,u,f.** *Choice, 2006.*

Behrendt, Stephen C. **ND1942.B55**
The Moment of Explosion: Blake and the Illustration of Milton. Cloth Text. University of Nebraska Press. Lincoln, NE. 1983. 235p. ISBN:0-8032-1169-4, ISBN13: 978-0-8032-1169-8. Dewey:759.2. LCCN:82-013561.
Audience: **u,f.**

Bentley, Gerald Eades **PR4146**
The Stranger from Paradise: A Biography of William Blake. Paul Mellon Centre for Studies in British Art Staff (Contribution by). Trade Paper. Yale University Press. Cumberland, RI. 2003. 632p. Paul Mellon Centre for Studies in Britis Ser. ISBN:0-300-10030-2, ISBN13: 978-0-300-10030-3. Dewey:821.7.
Audience: **g,l,u,f.**

Bindman, David **N6797.B57**
Blake as an Artist. Phaidon. 1977. ISBN:0-7148-1637-X, ISBN13: 978-0-7148-1637-1.
Audience: **u,f.**

Blake, William **PR4146**
The Blake Archive.
http://www.blakearchive.org/
Eaves, Morris (Editor); Essick, Robert (Editor); Viscomi, Joseph (Editor).
Audience: **g,l,u,f.**

Blake, William **PR4142.B78 2000**
William Blake: The Complete Illuminated Books. David Bindman (Introduction by). Trade Cloth. Thames & Hudson. New York, NY. 2000. 480p. ISBN:0-500-51014-8, ISBN13: 978-0-500-51014-8. Dewey:821/.7. LCCN:00-101383.
Audience: **g,l,u,f.**

Blake, William **PR4141.5 .J64 1979**
Blake's Poetry and Designs. Mary L. Johnson & John F. Grant (Editors). Paper Text. W. W. Norton & Company, Inc. New York, NY. 1979. 661p. Critical Editions Ser. ISBN:0-393-09083-3, ISBN13: 978-0-393-09083-3. Dewey:821/.7. LCCN:78-020958.
Audience: **g,u,f.**

Bloom, Harold **PR4147.B5 1970**
Blake's Apocalypse; a Study in Poetic Argument. Trade Cloth. Cornell University Press. Ithaca, NY. 1970. 454p. ISBN:0-8014-0568-8, ISBN13: 978-0-8014-0568-6. Dewey:821/.7. LCCN:70-011249.
Audience: **u,f.**

Bruder, Helen P. **PR4148.W6B78 1997**
William Blake and the Daughters of Albion. Trade Cloth. Palgrave Macmillan. New York, NY. 1997. 312p. ISBN:0-312-17481-0, ISBN13: 978-0-312-17481-1. Dewey:821.7. LCCN:97-007119.
Audience: **u,f.** *Choice, 1997.*

Butlin, Martin **N6797.B57.B87**
The Paintings and Drawings of William Blake. Trade Cloth Yale University Press. Cumberland, RI. 1981. 1408p. Paul Mellon Centre for Studies in British Art ISBN:0-300-02550-5, ISBN13: 978-0-300-02550-7. Dewey:760/.092/4. LCCN:80-006221.
Audience: **u,f.**

Damon, S. Foster **PR4146.A24 1988**
A Blake Dictionary: The Ideas and Symbols of William Blake. Morris Eaves (Foreword by). Trade Paper. University Press of New England. Lebanon, NH. 1988. 573p. ISBN:0-87451-436-3, ISBN13: 978-0-87451-436-0. Dewey:821/.7. LCCN:87-040509.
Audience: **u,f.** *Choice, 1989.*

Damrosch, Leopold Jr. **PR4147**
Symbol and Truth in Blake's Myth. Trade Cloth. Princeton University Press. Princeton, NJ. 1981. 504p. ISBN:0-691-06433-4, ISBN13: 978-0-691-06433-8. Dewey:821/.7. LCCN:80-007515.
Audience: **u,f.**

Eaves, Morris (Editor) **PR4147.C36 2002**
The Cambridge Companion to William Blake. Cloth Text. Cambridge University Press. New York, NY. 2003. 326p. Cambridge Companions to Literature Ser. ISBN:0-521-78147-7, ISBN13: 978-0-521-78147-3. Dewey:821/.7. LCCN:2002-067068.
Audience: **u,f.** *Choice, 2003.*

Eaves, Morris **PR4148.A35**
William Blake's Theory of Art. Trade Paper. Princeton University Press. Princeton, NJ. 1982. 216p. ISBN:0-691-00340-8, ISBN13: 978-0-691-00340-5. Dewey:700/.92/4. LCCN:81-047914.
Audience: **u,f.**

Erdman, David V. **PR4148.P6E7 1991**
Blake: Prophet Against Empire. Ed. 3. Trade Paper. Dover Publications, Inc. Mineola, NY. 1991. 608p. ISBN:0-486-26719-9, ISBN13: 978-0-486-26719-7. Dewey:821/.7. LCCN:90-026552.
Audience: **u,f.**

Erdman, David V. **NE642.B5A4 1992**
The Illuminated Blake: William Blake's Complete Illuminated Works with a Plate-by-Plate Commentary. Trade Paper. Dover Publications, Inc. Mineola, NY. 1992. 416p. ISBN:0-486-27234-6, ISBN13: 978-0-486-27234-4. Dewey:769.92. LCCN:92-009962.
Audience: **u,f.**

Erdman, David V. & Grant, John E. (Editors) **PR414**
Blake's Visionary Forms Dramatic. Princeton University Press. 1970. ISBN:0-691-06189-0, ISBN13: 978-0-691-06189-4.
Audience: **u,f.**

Erdman, David V. (ed.) **PR4146**
Blake Digital Text Project.
http://www.english.uga.edu/~wblake/home1.html
Audience: **g,l,u,f.**

Erdman, David V. & Blake, William **PR4141 .E7 1982**
The Complete Poetry and Prose of William Blake. Harold Bloom (Commentaries by). Trade Paper. Doubleday Publishing. New York, NY. 1997. 1024p. ISBN:0-385-15213-2, ISBN13: 978-0-385-15213-6. Dewey:821/.7. LCCN:79-007196.
Audience: **g,l,u,f.**

Ferber, Michael **PR4148.P6F4 1985**
The Social Vision of William Blake. Trade Cloth. Princeton University Press. Princeton, NJ. 1985. 288p. ISBN:0-691-08382-7, ISBN13: 978-0-691-08382-7. Dewey:821/.7. LCCN:85-000522.
Audience: **u,f.** *Choice, 1986.*

Frye, Northrop **PR4147.F7 1969**
Fearful Symmetry: A Study of William Blake. Trade Paper. Princeton University Press. Princeton, NJ. 1969. 472p. ISBN:0-691-01291-1, ISBN13: 978-0-691-01291-9. Dewey:821.7. LCCN:74-005945.
Audience: **g,l,u,f.**

Heppner, Christopher **NC978.5.B55 H46 1995**
Reading Blake's Designs. Cloth Text. Cambridge University Press. New York, NY. 1995. 320p. ISBN:0-521-47381-0, ISBN13: 978-0-521-47381-1. Dewey:741.6/4/092. LCCN:96-033926.
Audience: **u,f.**

Hobson, Christopher Z. **PR4148.P6H63 1999**
The Chained Boy: ORC and Blake's Idea of Revolution. Trade Cloth. Bucknell University Press. Cranbury, NJ. 1999. 416p. ISBN:0-8387-5385-X, ISBN13: 978-0-8387-5385-9. Dewey:821/.7. LCCN:98-044578.
Audience: **u,f.** *Choice, 2000.*

Klonsky, Milton **N6797.B57 K55 1977**
William Blake: The Seer and His Visions. Trade Cloth. Random House Value Publishing. New York, NY. 1988. ISBN:0-517-52939-4, ISBN13: 978-0-517-52939-3. Dewey:760/.092/4. LCCN:77-003979.
Audience: **u,f.**

Larrissy, Edward **PR4147.L37 1985**
William Blake. Trade Cloth. Blackwell Publishing, Inc. Malden, MA. 1985. 192p. ISBN:0-631-13485-9, ISBN13: 978-0-631-13485-5. Dewey:821/.7. LCCN:85-009105.
Audience: **l,u,f.** *Choice, 1986.*

Mee, Jon **PR4148.P6M44 1992**
Dangerous Enthusiasm: William Blake and the Culture of Radicalism in the 1790s. Trade Cloth. Oxford University Press, Inc. New York, NY. 1992. 268p. ISBN:0-19-812226-8, ISBN13: 978-0-19-812226-5. Dewey:821.7. LCCN:92-011156.
Audience: **u,f.**

Mitchell, W. J. **PR4147**
Blake's Composite Art: A Study of the Illuminated Poetry. Trade Paper. Princeton University Press. Princeton, NJ. 1983. 310p. ISBN:0-691-01402-7, ISBN13: 978-0-691-01402-9. Dewey:821/.7. LCCN:77-007116.
Audience: **u,f.**

Paley, Morton D. **PR4147.P3**
Energy and the Imagination: A Study of the Development of Blake's Thought. Trade Cloth. Oxford University Press, Inc. New York, NY. 1970. xiii, 272p. ISBN:0-19-811682-9, ISBN13: 978-0-19-811682-0. Dewey:760/.0924. LCCN:74-489414.
Audience: **u,f.**

Tannenbaum, Leslie **PR4148.B52 T3**
Biblical Tradition in Blake's Early Prophecies: The Great Code of Art. Trade Cloth. Princeton University Press. Princeton, NJ. 1982. 368p. ISBN:0-691-06490-3, ISBN13: 978-0-691-06490-1. Dewey:821/.7. LCCN:81-047158.
Audience: **u,f.**

Thompson, E. P. **F1038.S25**
Witness Against the Beast: William Blake and the Moral Law. Christopher Hill (Foreword by). Trade Paper. Cambridge University Press. New York, NY. 1994. 260p. ISBN:0-521-46977-5, ISBN13: 978-0-521-46977-7. Dewey:821.7.
Audience: **u,f.**

Viscomi, Joseph S. **NE642.B5V57 1993**
Blake and the Idea of the Book. Trade Cloth. Princeton University Press. Princeton, NJ. 1993. 456p. ISBN:0-691-06962-X, ISBN13: 978-0-691-06962-3. Dewey:769.92. LCCN:92-004261.
Audience: **u,f.** *Choice, 1994.*

Warner, Janet **PR4148.A75**
Blake and the Language of Art. Trade Cloth. McGill-Queen's University Press. Montreal, PQ. 1984. 231p. ISBN:0-7735-0435-4, ISBN13: 978-0-7735-0435-6. Dewey:760/.092/4.
Audience: **u,f.**

Webster, Brenda **PR4147.W36 1983**
Blake's Prophetic Psychology. Trade Cloth. University of Georgia Press. Athens, GA. 1983. 336p. ISBN:0-8203-0658-4, ISBN13: 978-0-8203-0658-2. Dewey:821/.7. LCCN:84-114638.
Audience: **u,f.**

Individual Authors and Works > 17th-18th C. > Boswell, James

Bloom, Harold (Introduction by) **PR3533.B7J34 1986**
James Boswell's Life of Samuel Johnson. Trade Cloth. Chelsea House Publishers. Langhorne, PA. 1986. 280p. Modern Critical Interpretations Ser. ISBN:0-87754-946-X, ISBN13: 978-0-87754-946-8. Dewey:828/.609 B. LCCN:85-026974.
Audience: **l,u.** *Choice, 1987.*

Boswell, James **PR3533**
Life of Johnson. Ed. 3. R. W. Chapman & J. D. Fleeman (Editors), Pat Rogers (Introduction by). Trade Paper. Oxford University Press, Inc. New York, NY. 1998. 1, 528p. Oxford World's Classics Ser. ISBN:0-19-283531-9, ISBN13: 978-0-19-283531-4. Dewey:828/.609.
Audience: **g,l,u,f.**

Boswell, James, et al. **PR3533**
Boswell's Life of Johnson: Together with Boswell's Journal of a Tour to the Hebrides, and Johnson's Diary of a Journey into North Wales. Ed. 2. Samuel Johnson, George Birkbeck Hill & Lawrence Fitzroy Powell (Authors). Trade Cloth. Oxford University Press, Inc. New York, NY. 1951. xxix, 596p. ISBN:0-19-811452-4, ISBN13: 978-0-19-811452-9. Dewey:828/.609.
Audience: **g,l,u,f.**

Boswell, James **PR3533 .B6 1994**
James Boswell's Life of Johnson: An Edition of the Original Manuscript. Bruce Redford & Elizabeth Goldring (Editors), Catherine Evtuhov (Translator). Cloth over Boards. Yale University Press. Cumberland, RI. 1999. 336p. Yale Editions of the Private Papers Jame Ser. ISBN:0-300-07969-9, ISBN13: 978-0-300-07969-2. Dewey:828/.609. LCCN:94-060557.
Audience: **g,l,u,f.**

Boswell, James, et al. **PR3325.A795 1993**
Boswell, Laird of Auchinleck: 1778-1782: The Yale Editions of the Private Papers of James Boswell. Joseph W. Reed & Frederick Albert Pottle (Authors). Trade Cloth. Edinburgh University Press. Edinburgh, 1993. xxxiv, 570p. ISBN:0-7486-0392-1, ISBN13: 978-0-7486-0392-3. Dewey:828/.609 B. LCCN:94-209865.
Audience: **g,l,u,f.**

Individual Authors and Works > 17th-18th C. > Browne, Thomas

Bennett **PR3327**
Sir Thomas Browne. Cloth Text. Cambridge University Press. New York, NY. 1962. 264p. ISBN:0-521-04159-7, ISBN13: 978-0-521-04159-1. Dewey:828.3.
Audience: **l,u.**

Bennett, Joan **PR3327**
Sir Thomas Browne, a Man of Achievement in Literature. Paper Text. Textbook Publishers. Temecula, CA. 2003. 254p. ISBN:0-7581-1295-5, ISBN13: 978-0-7581-1295-8. Dewey:828.3.
Audience: **l,u.**

Browne, Thomas **PR3327**
Works, Set. Geoffrey L. Keynes (Editor). Library Binding. Reprint Services Company. Temecula, CA. 1992. BCL1-PR English Literature Ser. ISBN:0-7812-7323-4, ISBN13: 978-0-7812-7323-7. Dewey:828.3.
Audience: **g,l,u,f.**

Browne, Thomas **PR3327 .A156**
Religio Medici, Hydriotaphia, and the Garden of Cyrus. R. H. Robbins (Editor). Paper Text. Oxford University Press, Inc. New York, NY. 1972. 224p. ISBN:0-19-871064-X, ISBN13: 978-0-19-871064-6. Dewey:828/.4/08. LCCN:72-170867.
Audience: **g,l,u,f.**

Individual Authors and Works > 17th-18th C. > Bunyan, John

Bunyan, John **PR3330.A2T48 2004**
The Pilgrim's Progress and Grace Abounding to the Chief of Sinners. Trade Paper. Knopf Publishing Group. New York, NY. 2004. 400p. Vintage Spiritual Classics Ser. ISBN:0-375-72568-7, ISBN13: 978-0-375-72568-5. Dewey:823/.4. LCCN:2003-062169.
Audience: **g,l,u,f.**

Bunyan, John **PR3329.L1 1988**
The Life and Death of Mr. Badman: Presented to the World in a Familiar Dialogue Between Mr. Wiseman and Mr. Attentive. James F. Forrest & Roger Sharrock (Editors). Trade Cloth. Oxford University Press, Inc. New York, NY. 1988. 232p. Oxford English Texts ISBN:0-19-812742-1, ISBN13: 978-0-19-812742-0. Dewey:823/.4. LCCN:87-029518.
Audience: **u,f.**

Bunyan, John **PR3329.H1 1980**
The Holy War. Roger Sharrock & James F. Forrest (Editors). Trade Cloth. Oxford University Press, Inc. New York, NY. 1980. xlviii, 288 pp. Oxford English Texts ISBN:0-19-811887-2, ISBN13: 978-0-19-811887-9. Dewey:828/.407. LCCN:79-040264.
Audience: **u,f.**

Bunyan, John **PR3331**
Grace Abounding to the Chief of Sinners. Roger Sharrock (Editor, Introduction by). Trade Cloth. Oxford University Press, Inc. New York, NY. 1966. Oxford Standard Authors Ser. ISBN:0-19-254159-5, ISBN13: 978-0-19-254159-8. Dewey:828.407.
Audience: **g,l,u,f.**

Bunyan, John **PR3317**
The Pilgrim's Progress. Ed. 2. James B. Wharey & Roger Sharrock (Editors). Trade Cloth. Oxford University Press, Inc. New York, NY. 1960. Oxford English Texts ISBN:0-19-811802-3, ISBN13: 978-0-19-811802-2. Dewey:823/.4.
Audience: **g,l,u,f.**

Greaves, Richard L. **PR3332.G66 2002**
Glimpses of Glory: John Bunyan and English Dissent. Trade Cloth. Stanford University Press. Palo Alto, CA. 2002. 720p. ISBN:0-8047-4530-7, ISBN13: 978-0-8047-4530-7. Dewey:828/.407. LCCN:2001-055039.
Audience: **u,f.** *Choice, 2003.*

Newey, Vincent (Editor) **PR3330.A9.P5 1980**
The Pilgrim's Progress: Critical and Historical Views. Trade Cloth. Barnes & Noble Books-Imports. Lanham, MD. 1980. 302p. English Texts and Studies ISBN:0-389-20016-6, ISBN13: 978-0-389-20016-1. Dewey:823/.4. LCCN:80-140328.
Audience: **l,u.**

Sharrock, Roger **PR3331**
John Bunyan. Trade Cloth. Greenwood Publishing Group, Inc. Portsmouth, NH. 1984. 163p. ISBN:0-313-24528-2, ISBN13: 978-0-313-24528-2. Dewey:828/.407. LCCN:84-006728.
Audience: **g,l,u,f.**

Tindall, William Y. **PR3331**
John Bunyan, Mechanick Preacher. Trade Cloth. Russell & Russell Publishers. New York, NY. 1964. ISBN:0-8462-0521-1, ISBN13: 978-0-8462-0521-0. Dewey:828/.407. LCCN:64-023462.
Audience: **g,l,u,f.**

Winslow, Ola Elizabeth **PR3331**
John Bunyan. Paper Text. Textbook Publishers. Temecula, CA. 2003. 242p. ISBN:0-7581-9113-8, ISBN13: 978-0-7581-9113-7. Dewey:828/.407.
Audience: **u,f.**

Individual Authors and Works > 17th-18th C. > Burney, Fanny

Burney, Fanny **PR3316**
Cecilia, or Memoirs of an Heiress. Trade Paper. Oxford University Press, Inc. New York, NY. 1999. 1,052p. Oxford World's Classics Ser. ISBN:0-19-283909-8, ISBN13: 978-0-19-283909-1. Dewey:823.6.
Audience: **g,l,u,f.**

Burney, Fanny **PR3316**
Camilla. Edward A. Bloom & Lillian D. Bloom (Editors). Trade Paper. Oxford University Press, Inc. New York, NY. 1999. 992p. Oxford World's Classics Ser. ISBN:0-19-283908-X, ISBN13: 978-0-19-283908-4. Dewey:823/.6.
Audience: **g,l,u,f.**

Burney, Fanny **PR3316**
Evelina: The History of a Young Lady's Entrance into the World. Ed. 2. Edward A. Bloom (Editor), Vivien Jones (Introduction by). Trade Paper. Oxford University Press, Inc. New York, NY. 2002. 499p. Oxford World's Classics Ser. ISBN:0-19-284031-2, ISBN13: 978-0-19-284031-8. Dewey:823/.6. LCCN:2003-265212.
Audience: **g,l,u,f.**

Burney, Fanny **PR3683**
Complete Plays of Frances Burney. Stewart Cooke, Geoffrey Sill & Paul Taylor (Editors). Trade Cloth. Pickering & Chatto Publishers, Ltd. London, 1995. 734p. ISBN:1-85196-073-2, ISBN13: 978-1-85196-073-6. Dewey:822.6.
Audience: **g,l,u,f.**

Burney, Fanny **PR3316.A4Z469 2002**
A Known Scribbler: Frances Burney on Literary Life. Justine Crump (Editor). Trade Paper. Broadview Press. Peterborough, ON. 2002. 380p. Broadview Literary Texts Ser. ISBN:1-55111-320-1, ISBN13: 978-1-55111-320-3. Dewey:823/.6 B. LCCN:2003-272455.
Audience: **u,f.**

Burney, Fanny **PR3316.A4Z/**
Selected Letters and Journals. Joyce Hemlow (Editor). Trade Paper. Oxford University Press, Inc. New York, NY. 1987. 410p. ISBN:0-19-281433-8, ISBN13: 978-0-19-281433-3. Dewey:823/.6.
Audience: **g,l,u,f.**

Burney, Fanny **PR3316.A4W58 1997**
The Witlings and the Woman Hater. Geoffrey M. Sill & Peter Sabor (Editors). Trade Cloth. Pickering & Chatto Publishers, Ltd. London, 1997. 204p. Pickering Woman's Classics Ser. ISBN:1-85196-360-X, ISBN13: 978-1-85196-360-7. Dewey:822/.6. LCCN:97-028194.
Audience: **g,l,u,f.**

Burney, Frances **PR3316.A4Z468 2001**
Journals and Letters. Peter Sabor & Lars E. Troide (Editors). Trade Paper. Penguin Group (USA) Inc. New York, NY. 2001. 608p. Classics Ser. ISBN:0-14-043624-3, ISBN13: 978-0-14-043624-2. Dewey:823/.6 B. LCCN:2001-277681.
Audience: **g,l,u,f.**

Doody, Margaret Anne **PR3316.A4Z63 1988**
Frances Burney: The Life in the Works. Cloth Text. Rutgers University Press. Piscataway, NJ. 1988. 528p. ISBN:0-8135-1309-X, ISBN13: 978-0-8135-1309-6. Dewey:823/.6 B. LCCN:88-001921.
Audience: **u,f.** *Choice, 1989.*

Hemlow, Joyce **PR3316.A4 Z647**
History of Fanny Burney. Trade Cloth. Oxford University Press, Inc. New York, NY. 1958. 544p. ISBN:0-19-811549-0, ISBN13: 978-0-19-811549-6. Dewey:928.2.
Audience: **g,l,u,f.**

Kilpatrick, Sarah **PR3316.A4Z664 1980**
Fanny Burney. Trade Cloth. David & Charles Publishers. Newton Abbot, 1980. 232p. ISBN:0-7153-7788-4, ISBN13: 978-0-7153-7788-8. Dewey:823/.8. LCCN:81-457894.
Audience: **g,l,u,f.**

Individual Authors and Works > 17th-18th C. > Butler, Samuel

Butler, Samuel **PR3338 .A15 1978**
Satires and Miscellaneous Poetry and Prose. Rene Lamar (Editor). Trade Cloth. A M S Press, Inc. New York, NY. BCL Ser. II ISBN:0-404-15301-1, ISBN13: 978-0-404-15301-4. Dewey:821/.4. LCCN:76-029457.
Audience: **g,l,u,f.**

Butler, Samuel **PR3338 .A7 1973**
Hudibras: And Selected Other Writings. John Wilders & Hugh De Quehen (Editors). Trade Cloth. Oxford University Press, Inc. New York, NY. 1973. xx, 316p. ISBN:0-19-871067-4, ISBN13: 978-0-19-871067-7. Dewey:821/.4. LCCN:73-172131.
Audience: **g,l,u,f.**

Wasserman, George **PR3338.W3 1989**
Samuel 'Hudibras' Butler. Cloth Text. Macmillan Publishing Company, Inc. Old Tappan, NJ. 1989. 184p. English Authors Ser., No. 193 ISBN:0-8057-6973-0, ISBN13: 978-0-8057-6973-9. Dewey:821/.4. LCCN:88-025906.
Audience: **l,u,f.**

Individual Authors and Works > 17th-18th C. > C

Ashley, Leonard R. **PR3347.A96 1989**
Colley Cibber. Trade Cloth. Thomson Gale. Farmington Hills, MI. 1988. 200p. ISBN:0-8057-6969-2, ISBN13: 978-0-8057-6969-2. Dewey:828/.509 B. LCCN:88-015618.
Audience: **l,u.**

Barker, Richard H. **PR3347 .B3**
Mr. Cibber of Drury Lane. Trade Cloth. A M S Press, Inc. New York, NY. ISBN:0-404-00654-X, ISBN13: 978-0-404-00654-9. Dewey:828.509. LCCN:71-160002.
Audience: **l,u.**

Bertonasco, Marc **PR3386 .B4**
Crashaw and the Baroque. Trade Cloth. University of Alabama Press. Tuscaloosa, AL. 1971. 158p. ISBN:0-8173-7308-X, ISBN13: 978-0-8173-7308-5. Dewey:821/.4. LCCN:70-148692.
Audience: **l,u.**

Boothby, F., et al. **PR1246.W65M57 2000**
Printed Writings 1641-1700: Miscellaneous Plays, Vol. 7. Ariadne, Susanna Centlivre & Stephanie Hodgson-Wright (Authors). Trade Cloth. Ashgate Publishing, Ltd. Aldershot, 2000. 280p. The Early Modern Englishwoman Ser., Vol. 7 ISBN:0-7546-0221-4, ISBN13: 978-0-7546-0221-7. Dewey:822/.40809287. LCCN:00-064300.
Audience: **g,l,u,f.**

Campbell, Thomas **PR4410.A5**
Complete Poetical Works of Thomas Campbell. J. Logie Robertson (Editor). Library Binding. M. S. G. Haskell House. Brooklyn, NY. 1969. Studies in Poetry, No. 38 ISBN:0-8383-0924-0, ISBN13: 978-0-8383-0924-7. Dewey:821.7. LCCN:68-024901.
Audience: **g,l,u,f.**

Carey, Henry **PR3339.C23**
Poems. Paper Text. Classic Textbooks. Murrieta, CA. 1930. 261p. ISBN:1-4047-7329-0, ISBN13: 978-1-4047-7329-5. Dewey:821.59.
Audience: **g,l,u,f.**

Centlivre, Susanna **PR3671.R5**
A Bold Stroke for a Wife. Ed. 2. Nancy Copeland (Editor). Trade Paper. Broadview Press. Peterborough, ON. 1995. 158p. Literary Texts Ser. ISBN:1-55111-021-0, ISBN13: 978-1-55111-021-9. Dewey:822.5.
Audience: **g,l,u,f.**

Centlivre, Susanna & O'Brien, John **PR1243**
The Wonder: A Woman Keeps a Secret. Trade Paper. Broadview Press. Peterborough, ON. 2003. 200p. Broadview Literary Texts Ser. ISBN:1-55111-454-2, ISBN13: 978-1-55111-454-5. Dewey:822/.5. LCCN:2004-444759.
Audience: **g,l,u,f.**

Chatterton, Thomas, et al. **PR3340.A2 1971**
The Complete Works of Thomas Chatterton: A Bicentenary Edition. Donald S. Taylor & Benjamin Beard Hoover (Authors). Trade Cloth. Oxford University Press, Inc. New York, NY. 1971. xlv, 1265p. ISBN:0-19-811848-1, ISBN13: 978-0-19-811848-0. Dewey:821/.6. LCCN:72-584147.
Audience: **g,l,u,f.**

Churchill, Charles **PR3346 .C8**
The Poetical works of Charles Churchill; with copious notes and a life of the author, by W. Tooke, F. R. S. In three Volumes. Trade Cloth. Scholarly Publishing Office, University of Michigan Library. Ann Arbor, MI. 2004. ISBN:1-4181-1046-9, ISBN13: 978-1-4181-1046-8. Dewey:821.6.
Audience: **g,l,u,f.**

Cibber, Colley **PR3347.A6 2000**
The Plays of Colley Cibber, Vol. 1. Trade Cloth. Fairleigh Dickinson University Press. Cranbury, NJ. 2000. 592p. ISBN:0-8386-3624-1, ISBN13: 978-0-8386-3624-4. Dewey:822/.5. LCCN:99-054768.
Audience: **g,l,u,f.**

Cibber, Colley **PR3347.A8 2000**
An Apology for the Life of Colley Cibber. Byrne R. S. Fone (Editor). Trade Paper. Dover Publications, Inc. Mineola, NY. 2000. 404p. Dover Books on Literature and Drama ISBN:0-486-41472-8, ISBN13: 978-0-486-41472-0. Dewey:828/.509 B. LCCN:00-043030.
Audience: **g,l,u,f.**

Cleland, John **PR3348.C65M45 2001**
Fanny Hill: Or Memoirs of a Woman of Pleasure. Gary Gautier (Introduction by). Trade Paper. Random House Adult Trade Publishing Group. New York, NY. 2001. 288p. Modern Library Classics ISBN:0-375-75808-9, ISBN13: 978-0-375-75808-9. Dewey:823/.6. LCCN:2001-030431.
Audience: **g,l,u,f.**

Collins, William **PR3350.A2 1979**
The Works of William Collins. Richard Wendorf & Charles Ryskamp (Editors). Trade Cloth. Oxford University Press, Inc. New York, NY. 1980. xxxvii, 234 pp. Oxford English Texts ISBN:0-19-812749-9, ISBN13: 978-0-19-812749-9. Dewey:821/.5. LCCN:78-040758.
Audience: **g,l,u,f.**

Collop, John **PR3356.C5**
The Poems of John Collop. Conrad Hilberry (Editor). Trade Cloth. University of Wisconsin Press. Chicago, IL. 1961. 240p. ISBN:0-299-02490-3, ISBN13: 978-0-299-02490-1. Dewey:821.4.
Audience: **g,l,u,f.**

Colman, George **PR3358.J4 1997**
Critical Edition of "The Jealous Wife" and "Polly Honeycombe" by George Colman the Elder (1732-1794). Thomas Price (Editor). Trade Cloth. Edwin Mellen Press, The. Lewiston, NY. 1997. 304p. Studies in British Literature Ser., Vol. 30 ISBN:0-7734-8626-7, ISBN13: 978-0-7734-8626-3. Dewey:822/.6. LCCN:97-012461.
Audience: **g,l,u,f.**

Crashaw, Richard **PR3386**
The Complete Poetry of Richard Crashaw. George W. Williams (Editor). Trade Cloth. New York University Press. New York, NY. 1972. 707p. ISBN:0-8147-9154-9, ISBN13: 978-0-8147-9154-7. Dewey:821/.4. LCCN:68-014177.
Audience: **g,l,u,f.**

Crowne, John **PR3388.C2**
City Politiques. John H. Wilson (Editor). Trade Cloth. University of Nebraska Press. Lincoln, NE. 1967. x, 159p. ISBN:0-8032-0355-1, ISBN13: 978-0-8032-0355-6. Dewey:999. LCCN:67-012641.
Audience: **u,f.**

Lock, F. P. **PR3339.C6.L6 1979**
Susanna Centlivre. Library Binding. Thomson Gale. Farmington Hills, MI. 1979. 155p. English Authors Ser. ISBN:0-8057-6744-4, ISBN13: 978-0-8057-6744-5. Dewey:822/.5. LCCN:78-024405.
Audience: **l,u.**

Page, Eugene R. **PR3358.Z5 P3**
George Colman, the Elder. Trade Cloth. A M S Press, Inc. New York, NY. ISBN:0-404-04857-9, ISBN13: 978-0-404-04857-0. Dewey:822.6. LCCN:74-181965.
Audience: **l,u.**

Smith, Raymond J. **PR3346.C8.S55**
Charles Churchill. Library Binding. Irvington Publishers. New York, NY. 1977. 156p. Twayne's English Authors Ser. ISBN:0-8057-6669-3, ISBN13: 978-0-8057-6669-1. Dewey:821/.6. LCCN:76-042988.
Audience: **l,u.**

Wendorf, Richard **PR3354.W46**
William Collins and Eighteenth-Century English Poetry. Trade Cloth. University of Minnesota Press. Minneapolis, MN. 1981. 256p. ISBN:0-8166-1058-4, ISBN13: 978-0-8166-1058-7. Dewey:823/.8. LCCN:81-014674.
Audience: **u,f.**

Individual Authors and Works > 17th-18th C. > Congreve, William

Avery, Emmett Langdon **PR3368.S8**
Congreve's Plays on the Century Stage. Paper Text. Textbook Publishers. Temecula, CA. 2003. viii, 226p. ISBN:0-7581-8096-9, ISBN13: 978-0-7581-8096-4. Dewey:822.46.
Audience: **l,u.**

Congreve, William **PR3361**
The Complete Works of William Congreve, Vol. 2. Trade Paper. Kessinger Publishing, LLC. Whitefish, MT. 2004. ISBN:0-7661-8739-X, ISBN13: 978-0-7661-8739-9.
Audience: **g,l,u,f.**

Congreve, William **PR3364**
The Mourning Bride, Poems and Miscellanies. Library Binding. Reprint Services Company. Temecula, CA. 1992. 540p. BCL1-PR English Literature Ser. ISBN:0-7812-7335-8, ISBN13: 978-0-7812-7335-0. Dewey:999.
Audience: **g,l,u,f.**

Congreve, William **PR3362**
Complete Plays of William Congreve. Herbert Davis (Editor). Library Binding. University of Chicago Press. Chicago, IL. 1967. ISBN:0-226-11485-6, ISBN13: 978-0-226-11485-9. Dewey:822.46. LCCN:66-020598.
Audience: **g,l,u,f.** B

Congreve, William **PR3360**
Way of the World and Other Plays. Eric S. Rump (Notes by). Trade Paper. Penguin Group (USA) Inc. New York, NY. 2006. 416p. ISBN:0-14-144185-2, ISBN13: 978-0-14-144185-6. Dewey:822.4.
Audience: **g,l,u,f.**

Holland, Norman Norwood Jr. **PR3432**
The First Modern Comedies: The Significance of Etherege, Wycherley and Congreve. Trade Cloth. Harvard University Press. Cambridge, MA. 1959. ISBN:0-674-30350-4, ISBN13: 978-0-674-30350-8. Dewey:822.409.
Audience: **l,u.** B

Love, Harold **PR3367.L6 1975**
Congreve. Trade Cloth. Rowman & Littlefield Publishers, Inc. Lanham, MD. 1975. 131p. Plays and Playwrights Ser. ISBN:0-87471-623-3, ISBN13: 978-0-87471-623-8. Dewey:822/.4. LCCN:74-023234.
Audience: **l,u.** B

Williams, Aubrey L. **PR3368.R4**
An Approach to Congreve. Cloth over Boards. Yale University Press. Cumberland, RI. 1979. 247p. ISBN:0-300-02304-9, ISBN13: 978-0-300-02304-6. Dewey:822/.4. LCCN:78-000381.
Audience: **l,u.** B

Individual Authors and Works > 17th-18th C. > Cowper, William

Cowper, William **PR3380 .A2 1980**
The Poems of William Cowper: 1785-1800. John D. Baird & Charles Ryskamp (Editors). Trade Cloth. Oxford University Press, Inc. New York, NY. 1996. 466p. Oxford English Texts ISBN:0-19-818296-1, ISBN13: 978-0-19-818296-2. Dewey:821.6. LCCN:78-040749.
Audience: **g,l,u,f.**

Cowper, William **PR3380.A2 1980**
The Poems of William Cowper, 1748-1782, Vol. I. John D. Baird & Charles Ryskamp (Editors). Trade Cloth. Oxford University Press, Inc. New York, NY. 1980. 642p. Oxford English Texts ISBN:0-19-811875-9, ISBN13: 978-0-19-811875-6. Dewey:821.6. LCCN:78-040749.
Audience: **g,l,u,f.** B

Cowper, William **PR4331**
The Poems of William Cowper, 1782-1785, Vol. II. John D. Baird & Charles Ryskamp (Editors). Trade Cloth. Oxford University Press, Inc. New York, NY. 1996. 484p. Oxford English Texts ISBN:0-19-812339-6, ISBN13: 978-0-19-812339-2. Dewey:821.6. LCCN:78-040749.
Audience: **g,l,u,f.**

Cowper, William **PR3383.A44 1989**
William Cowper: Selected Letters. James King & Charles Ryskamp (Editors). Trade Cloth. Oxford University Press, Inc. New York, NY. 1989. 268p. ISBN:0-19-818596-0, ISBN13: 978-0-19-818596-3. Dewey:821/.6 B. LCCN:88-028955.
Audience: **g,l,u,f.** *Choice, 1990.*

Cowper, William **PR4331**
The Poetical Works of William Cowper. Ed. 4. H. S. Milford (Editor). Trade Cloth. A M S Press, Inc. New York, NY. BCL Ser. II ISBN:0-404-14525-6, ISBN13: 978-0-404-14525-5. Dewey:821/.6. LCCN:75-041066.
Audience: **g,l,u,f.** B

Nicholson, Norman **PR3383 .N53**
William Cowper. Cloth Text. Richard West. Philadelphia, PA. 1980. 167p. ISBN:0-8492-1973-6, ISBN13: 978-0-8492-1973-3. Dewey:821.6.
Audience: **l,u.** B

Ryskamp, Charles **PR3383**
William Cowper of the Inner Temple, Esq: A Study of His Life and Works to the Year 1768. Paper Text. Textbook Publishers. Temecula, CA. 2003. xvii, 274p. ISBN:0-7581-1340-4, ISBN13: 978-0-7581-1340-5. Dewey:821.65.
Audience: **l,u.** B

Individual Authors and Works > 17th-18th C. > D-K

Denham, John **PR3562**
The Poetical Works of Sir John Denham. Trade Paper. Adamant Media. Chestnut Hill, MA. 2001. 180p. ISBN:1-4021-4838-0, ISBN13: 978-1-4021-4838-5. Dewey:821/.4.
Audience: **g,l,u,f.** B

Farquhar, George **PR3364**
The Recruiting Officer and Other Plays: The Constant Couple; The Twin Rivals; The Recruiting Officer; The Beaux' Stratagem.

William Myers (Editor). Trade Cloth. Oxford University Press, Inc. New York, NY. 1995. 428p. Oxford World's Classics Ser. ISBN:0-19-812153-9, ISBN13: 978-0-19-812153-4. Dewey:822.4. LCCN:95-002971.
Audience: **g,l,u,f.**

Graves, Richard **PZ3.G7873**
The Spiritual Quixote: A Comic Romance. Library Binding. Reprint Services Company. Temecula, CA. 1992. BCL1-PR English Literature Ser. ISBN:0-7812-7360-9, ISBN13: 978-0-7812-7360-2. Dewey:823/.6.
Audience: **g,l,u,f.**

Holcroft, Thomas **PR3515.H2 A8**
Anna St. Ives A Novel. Trade Paper. Kessinger Publishing, LLC. Whitefish, MT. 2004. ISBN:1-4191-0709-7, ISBN13: 978-1-4191-0709-2. Dewey:823/.6.
Audience: **g,l,u,f.**

Hurd, Richard **PN56.C53 H8**
Hurd's Letters on Chivalry and Romance. Library Binding. Reprint Services Company. Temecula, CA. 1992. 176p. BCL1-PR English Literature Ser. ISBN:0-7812-7365-X, ISBN13: 978-0-7812-7365-7. Dewey:820/.9.
Audience: **g,l,u,f.**

King, Henry **PR3539 .K65 1973**
The Poems of Bishop Henry King. John Sparrow (Editor). Library Binding. Folcroft Library Editions. Folcroft, PA. 1974. ISBN:0-8414-0645-6, ISBN13: 978-0-8414-0645-2. Dewey:821/.4. LCCN:72-010145.
Audience: **g,l,u,f.**

Underwood, Dale **PR3432.U5 1969**
Etherege and the Seventeenth-Century Comedy of Manners. Trade Cloth. Shoe String Press, Inc. North Haven, CT. 1969. ix, 165p. Yale Studies in English, No. 135 ISBN:0-208-00764-4, ISBN13: 978-0-208-00764-3. Dewey:822/.4. LCCN:69-015693.
Audience: **l,u,f.** B

Vaughn, Jack A. (Editor) **PR3431.D3.M27 1976**
Two Comedies by Thomas D'Urfey. Trade Cloth. Fairleigh Dickinson University Press. Cranbury, NJ. 1976. 301p. ISBN:0-8386-1478-7, ISBN13: 978-0-8386-1478-5. Dewey:822/.4. LCCN:73-021191.
Audience: **g,l,u,f.** B

Individual Authors and Works > 17th-18th C. > Defoe, Daniel

Backscheider, Paula R. **PR3406.B24 1989**
Daniel Defoe: His Life. Trade Cloth. Johns Hopkins University Press. Baltimore, MD. 1989. 688p. ISBN:0-8018-3785-5, ISBN13: 978-0-8018-3785-2. Dewey:823/.5 B. LCCN:88-026752.
Audience: **g,u,f.** *Choice, 1990.*

Backscheider, Paula R. **PR3407.B33 1986**
Daniel Defoe: Ambition and Innovation. Trade Cloth. University Press of Kentucky. Lexington, KY. 1986. 312p. ISBN:0-8131-1596-5, ISBN13: 978-0-8131-1596-2. Dewey:823/.5. LCCN:86-012076.
Audience: **u,f.** *Choice, 1987.*

Defoe, Daniel **PR3724.G8**
The History and Remarkable Life of the Truly Honourable Colonel Jacque, Commonly Called Colonel Jack. Trade Paper. University Press of the Pacific. Miami, FL. 2003. 600p. ISBN:1-4102-0802-8, ISBN13: 978-1-4102-0802-6. Dewey:823/.5.
Audience: **g,l,u,f.**

Defoe, Daniel **PR3404**
The Life, Adventures, and Piracies of the Famous Captain Singleton. Trade Paper. University Press of the Pacific. Miami, FL. 2002. 348p. ISBN:0-89875-914-5, ISBN13: 978-0-89875-914-3. Dewey:823.5.
Audience: **g,l,u,f.**

Defoe, Daniel **PR3724.G8**
Memoirs of a Cavalier, or, A Military Journal of the Wars in Germany and the Wars in England. Trade Paper. University Press of the Pacific. Miami, FL. 2002. 276p. ISBN:0-89875-958-7, ISBN13: 978-0-89875-958-7. Dewey:823/.5.
Audience: **g,l,u,f.**

Defoe, Daniel **PR3724.G8**
e Roxana: The Fortunate Mistress. E-Book. Penguin Group (USA) Inc. New York, NY. 2005. ISBN:0-7865-5676-5, ISBN13: 978-0-7865-5676-2. Dewey:823.5.
Audience: **g,l,u,f.**

Defoe, Daniel **QC944.D43 2005**
The Storm. Richard Hamblyn (Editor). Trade Paper. Penguin Group (USA) Inc. New York, NY. 2005. 272p. Penguin Classics Ser. ISBN:0-14-143992-0, ISBN13: 978-0-14-143992-1. Dewey:551.55/2/0941. LCCN:2005-276151.
Audience: **g,l,u,f.**

Defoe, Daniel & Rivero, Albert J. **PR3404.M63 2003**
Moll Flanders. Trade Paper. W. W. Norton & Company, Inc. New York, NY. 2003. 464p. A Norton Critical Edition Ser. ISBN:0-393-97862-1, ISBN13: 978-0-393-97862-9. Dewey:FIC. LCCN:2003-060948.
Audience: **g,l,u,f.**

Defoe, Daniel **PR3724.G8**
Robinson Crusoe: An Authoritative Text, Backgrounds and Sources, Criticism. Ed. 2. Michael Shinagel (Editor). Trade Paper. W. W. Norton & Company, Inc. New York, NY. 1993. 446p. Critical Editions Ser. ISBN:0-393-96452-3, ISBN13: 978-0-393-96452-3. Dewey:823.5. LCCN:93-012217.
Audience: **g,l,u,f.**

Defoe, Daniel **PR3404.J6**
A Journal of the Plague Year: Being Observations or Memorials of the Mosst Remarkable Occurence. Cynthia Wall (Notes by). Trade Paper. Penguin Group (USA) Inc. New York, NY. 2003. 336p. Penguin Classics Ser. ISBN:0-14-043785-1, ISBN13: 978-0-14-043785-0. LCCN:2003-276684.
Audience: **g,l,u,f.**

Green, Martin **PR3403.Z5G7 1990**
The Robinson Crusoe Story. Cloth Text. Pennsylvania State University Press. University Park, PA. 1991. 200p. ISBN:0-271-00705-2, ISBN13: 978-0-271-00705-2. Dewey:809/.93355. LCCN:90-030687.
Audience: **l,u,f.** *Choice, 1991.*

Lund, Roger D. **PR3407.L864 1997**
Critical Essays on Daniel Defoe. Trade Cloth. Thomson Gale. Farmington Hills, MI. 1997. 290p. Critical Essays on British Literature Ser. ISBN:0-7838-0007-X, ISBN13: 978-0-7838-0007-3. Dewey:823/.5. LCCN:96-046819.
Audience: **l,u.**

Novak, Maximillian E. **PR3406.N68 2001**
Daniel Defoe: His Life and Ideas. Trade Cloth. Oxford University Press, Inc. New York, NY. 2001. 768p. ISBN:0-19-812686-7, ISBN13: 978-0-19-812686-7. Dewey:823.5. LCCN:2002-276404.
Audience: **u,f.** *Choice, 2001.*

Phillips, Richard **PR830.A38P48 1997**
Mapping Men and Empire: A Geography of Adventure. Trade Paper. Routledge. New York, NY. 1996. 224p. ISBN:0-415-13772-1, ISBN13: 978-0-415-13772-0. Dewey:809.3/87. LCCN:96-010899.
Audience: **u,f.**

Richetti, John J. **PR3407.R48 1987**
Daniel Defoe. Trade Cloth. Thomson Gale. Farmington Hills, MI. 1987. 176p. English Authors Ser., No. 453 ISBN:0-8057-6955-2, ISBN13: 978-0-8057-6955-5. Dewey:823/.5. LCCN:87-008550.
Audience: **l,u.** *Choice, 1988.*

Seidel, Michael **PR3403.Z5S45 1991**
Robinson Crusoe: Island Myths and the Novel. Robert Lecker (Editor). Trade Paper. Thomson Gale. Farmington Hills, MI. 1991. 152p. Twayne's Masterwork Studies ISBN:0-8057-8120-X, ISBN13: 978-0-8057-8120-5. Dewey:823/.5. LCCN:90-043231.
Audience: **l,u.** *Choice, 1991.*

Individual Authors and Works > 17th-18th C. > Dryden, John

Bywaters, David **PR3427.P6B9 1991**
Dryden in Revolutionary England. Trade Cloth. University of California Press. Berkeley, CA. 1991. 208p. ISBN:0-520-07061-5, ISBN13: 978-0-520-07061-5. Dewey:821/.4. LCCN:90-038470.
Audience: **u,f.** *Choice, 1991.*

Dryden, John **PR3412 .G3**
The Prologues and Epilogues of John Dryden. Paper Text. Textbook Publishers. Temecula, CA. 2003. xxp. ISBN:0-7581-5336-8, ISBN13: 978-0-7581-5336-4. Dewey:821/.4.
Audience: **g,l,u,f.**

Dryden, John **PR3364**
Marriage a la Mode. Mark S. Auburn (Editor). Trade Cloth. University of Nebraska Press. Lincoln, NE. 1981. xxxii, 144p. Regents Restoration Drama Ser. ISBN:0-8032-0386-1, ISBN13: 978-0-8032-0386-0. Dewey:822/.4. LCCN:80-051043.
Audience: **g,l,u,f.**

Dryden, John **PR3412**
Poems and Fables of John Dryden. James Kinsley (Editor). Trade Cloth. Oxford University Press, Inc. New York, NY. 1970. xii, 864p. Oxford Standard Authors Ser. ISBN:0-19-281073-1, ISBN13: 978-0-19-281073-1. Dewey:821/.4.
Audience: **g,l,u,f.**

Dryden, John **PR3412**
The Major Works. Keith Walker (Editor). Trade Paper. Oxford University Press, Inc. New York, NY. 2003. 988p. Oxford World's Classics ISBN:0-19-284077-0, ISBN13: 978-0-19-284077-6. Dewey:821/.4. LCCN:2003-270051.
Audience: **g,l,u,f.**

Dryden, John **PR3423 .A45**
Letters. Charles E. Ward (Editor). Trade Cloth. A M S Press, Inc. New York, NY. ISBN:0-404-02186-7, ISBN13: 978-0-404-02186-3. Dewey:821/.4. LCCN:74-164791.
Audience: **g,l,u,f.**

Dryden, John **PR3562**
Selected Poems: Dryden. Steven N. Zwicker & David Bywaters (Editors), Steven N. Zwicker & David Bywaters (Introduction by, Notes by). Trade Paper. Penguin Group (USA) Inc. New York, NY. 2002. 608p. Classics Ser. ISBN:0-14-043914-5, ISBN13: 978-0-14-043914-4.
Audience: **g,l,u,f.**

Frost, William **PR3424.F74 1988**
John Dryden: Dramatist, Satirist, Translator. Trade Cloth. A M S Press, Inc. New York, NY. 1988. 288p. Studies in the Seventeenth Century, No. 3 ISBN:0-404-61723-9, ISBN13: 978-0-404-61723-3. Dewey:821/.4. LCCN:85-048003.
Audience: **u,f.** *Choice, 1988.*

Gelber, Michael Werth **PR3427.L5G45 2002**
The Just and the Lively: The Literary Criticism of John Dryden. Trade Cloth. Manchester University Press. Manchester, 1999. 342p. ISBN:0-7190-5414-1, ISBN13: 978-0-7190-5414-3. Dewey:821/.4. LCCN:2003-276360.
Audience: **u,f.** *Choice, 1999.*

Hughes, Derek **PR3427.H4.H8 1981**
Dryden's Heroic Plays. Trade Cloth. University of Nebraska Press. Lincoln, NE. 1980. xi, 195p. ISBN:0-8032-2314-5, ISBN13: 978-0-8032-2314-1. Dewey:822/.4. LCCN:80-019109.
Audience: **u,f.**

McFadden, George **PR3424**
Dryden the Public Writer, 1660-1685. Trade Cloth. Princeton University Press. Princeton, NJ. 1978. 320p. ISBN:0-691-06350-8, ISBN13: 978-0-691-06350-8. Dewey:821/.4. LCCN:77-085551.
Audience: **u,f.**

Miner, Earl **PR3424 .M53**
Dryden's Poetry. Trade Cloth. Indiana University Press. Bloomington, IN. 1967. 376p. ISBN:0-253-31835-1, ISBN13: 978-0-253-31835-0. Dewey:821/.4. LCCN:67-010108.
Audience: **l,u.**

Miner, Earl (Editor) **PR3424 .M54 1972B**
Writers and Their Background: John Dryden. Trade Cloth. Ohio University Press. Athens, OH. 1972. xxvi, 363p. Writers and Their Background Ser. ISBN:0-8214-0119-X, ISBN13: 978-0-8214-0119-4. Dewey:821/.4. LCCN:72-095818.
Audience: **l,u.**

Scott, Walter Sr. **PR3423 .S34**
The Life of John Dryden. Bernard Kreissman (Editor). Trade Paper. University of Nebraska Press. Lincoln, NE. 1963. xx, 471p. ISBN:0-8032-5177-7, ISBN13: 978-0-8032-5177-9. Dewey:821.4. LCCN:63-008121.
Audience: **g,l,u,f.**

Van Doren, Mark **PR3424 .V3 1969**
The Poetry of John Dryden. Library Binding. M. S. G. Haskell House. Brooklyn, NY. 1969. Studies in Dryden, No. 10 ISBN:0-8383-1207-1, ISBN13: 978-0-8383-1207-0. Dewey:821/.4. LCCN:79-095450.
Audience: **l,u.**

Ward, Charles E. **PR3423 .W3**
The Life of John Dryden. Paper Text. Textbook Publishers. Temecula, CA. 2003. 380p. ISBN:0-7581-1873-2, ISBN13: 978-0-7581-1873-8. Dewey:928.2.
Audience: **g,l,u,f.**

Winn, James A. **PR3423.W5 1987**
John Dryden and His World. Trade Cloth. Yale University Press. Cumberland, RI. 1987. 652p. ISBN:0-300-02994-2, ISBN13: 978-0-300-02994-9. Dewey:821.4. LCCN:87-002193.
Audience: **u,f.** *Choice, 1988.*

Wykes, David **PR3424**
A Preface to Dryden. Cloth Text. Longman Publishing Group. White Plains, NY. 1977. xix, 236p. Preface Bks. ISBN:0-582-35101-4, ISBN13: 978-0-582-35101-1. Dewey:821/.4. LCCN:76-012598.
Audience: **l,u.**

Zwicker, Steven N. (Editor) **PR3424.C36 2004**
The Cambridge Companion to John Dryden. Cloth Text. Cambridge University Press. New York, NY. 2004. 318p. Cambridge Companions to Literature Ser. ISBN:0-521-82427-3, ISBN13: 978-0-521-82427-9. Dewey:821/.4. LCCN:2003-065294.
Audience: **l,u,f.** *Choice, 2005.*

Zwicker, Steven N. **PR3427.P6Z94 1984**
Politics and Language in Dryden's Poetry. Cloth Text. Princeton University Press. Princeton, NJ. 1982. 265p. ISBN:0-691-06618-3, ISBN13: 978-0-691-06618-9. Dewey:821/.4. LCCN:84-004255.
Audience: **u,f.**

Individual Authors and Works > 17th-18th C. > Fielding, Henry

Bloom, Harold (Editor, Introduction by) **PR3457.H457 1987**
Henry Fielding. Library Binding. Chelsea House Publishers. Langhorne, PA. 1987. 272p. Modern Critical Views Ser. ISBN:1-55546-283-9, ISBN13: 978-1-55546-283-3. Dewey:823/.5. LCCN:87-010084.
Audience: **l,u.**

Fielding, Henry **PR3454.J67 1971**
The History of the Adventures of Joseph Andrews and of His Friend Mr. Abraham Adams; and, an Apology for the Life of Mrs. Shamela Andrews. Trade Cloth. Oxford University Press, Inc. New York, NY. 1970. xxviii, 394 pp. ISBN:0-19-255323-2, ISBN13: 978-0-19-255323-2. Dewey:823/.5. LCCN:78-548668.
Audience: **g,l,u,f.**

Fielding, Henry **PR3454.H5 1995**
Tom Jones a Foundling. Ed. 2. Trade Paper. W. W. Norton & Company, Inc. New York, NY. 1994. 810p. Critical Editions Ser. ISBN:0-393-96594-5, ISBN13: 978-0-393-96594-0. Dewey:823.5. LCCN:94-004512.
Audience: **g,l,u,f.**

Fielding, Henry **JC179.R9F37 1997**
Miscellanies by Henry Fielding, Esq.: Jonathan Wild. Hugh Amory (Editor), Bertrand A. Goldgar (Commentaries by, Introduction by). Library Binding. Wesleyan University Press. Middletown, CT. 1997. 414p. Works of Henry Fielding Ser. ISBN:0-8195-5298-4, ISBN13: 978-0-8195-5298-3. Dewey:320.092. LCCN:71-184366.
Audience: **g,l,u,f.**

Fielding, Henry & Fielding, Sarah **PR3724.G8**
The Correspondence of Henry and Sarah Fielding. Martin C. Battestin & Clive T. Probyn (Editors). Trade Cloth. Oxford University Press, Inc. New York, NY. 1993. 264p. ISBN:0-19-811273-4, ISBN13: 978-0-19-811273-0. Dewey:823.5. LCCN:92-027584.
Audience: **g,l,u,f.**

Fielding, Henry **PR3454.C5 1988**
The Covent-Garden Journal. Bertrand A. Goldgar (Editor). Library Binding. Wesleyan University Press. Middletown, CT. 1988. 563p. Works of Henry Fielding Ser. ISBN:0-8195-5167-8, ISBN13: 978-0-8195-5167-2. Dewey:824/.5. LCCN:87-027940.
Audience: **g,l,u,f.**

Fielding, Henry **PR3454.T6 1970**
The Tragedy of the Tragedies for the Life and Death of Tom Thumb the Great. James T. Hillhouse (Editor), H. Scribblerus Secundus (Annotations by). Trade Cloth. Scholarly Press, Inc. Saint Clair Shores, MI. 1971. viii, 223p. ISBN:0-403-00591-4, ISBN13: 978-0-403-00591-8. Dewey:822/.5. LCCN:71-131704.
Audience: **g,l,u,f.**

Fielding, Henry **PR3454**
Jonathan Wild. Claude Julien Rawson, Linda Bree & Hugh Amory (Editors). Trade Paper. Oxford University Press, Inc. New York, NY. 2004. 352p. Oxford World's Classics Ser. ISBN:0-19-280408-1, ISBN13: 978-0-19-280408-2. Dewey:823.5. LCCN:2004-270384.
Audience: **g,l,u,f.**

Hunter, J. Paul **PR3457**
Occasional Form: Henry Fielding and the Chains of Circumstance. Trade Cloth. Johns Hopkins University Press. Baltimore, MD. 1985. 248p. ISBN:0-8018-1672-6, ISBN13: 978-0-8018-1672-7. Dewey:823/.5. LCCN:75-011337.
Audience: **u,f.**

Lockwood, Thomas (Editor) **PR3452**
Henry Fielding: Plays, 1728-1731. Trade Cloth. Oxford University Press, Inc. New York, NY. 2004. 808p. The Wesleyan Edition of the Works of Henry Fielding ISBN:0-19-925789-2, ISBN13: 978-0-19-925789-8. Dewey:822/.5. LCCN:2004-047824.
Audience: **g,l,u,f.** *Choice, 2005.*

Miller, Henry Knight **PR3457**
Essays on Fielding's Miscellanies: A Commentary on Volume One. Paper Text. Textbook Publishers. Temecula, CA. 2003. xv, 474p. ISBN:0-7581-5790-8, ISBN13: 978-0-7581-5790-4. Dewey:828.5.
Audience: **l,u,f.**

Rawson, Claude **PR3457.R3 1991**
Henry Fielding and the Augustan Ideal under Stress. Trade Paper. Brill Academic Publishers, Inc. Boston, MA. 1991. 288p. ISBN:0-391-03711-0, ISBN13: 978-0-391-03711-3. Dewey:823/.5. LCCN:91-016182.
Audience: **u,f.**

Rivero, Albert J. **PR3457.C69 1998**
Critical Essays on Henry Fielding. Trade Cloth. Thomson Gale. Farmington Hills, MI. 1998. 245p. Critical Essays on British Literature Ser. ISBN:0-7838-0059-2, ISBN13: 978-0-7838-0059-2. Dewey:823/.5. LCCN:97-034644.
Audience: **l,u.**

Varey, Simon **PR3457.V37 1986**
Henry Fielding. Trade Cloth. Cambridge University Press. New York, NY. 1986. 164p. British and Irish Authors Ser. ISBN:0-521-26244-5, ISBN13: 978-0-521-26244-6. Dewey:823/.5. LCCN:85-028993.
Audience: **l,u.** *Choice, 1987.*

Individual Authors and Works > 17th-18th C. > Fielding, Sarah

Bree, Linda **PR3459.F3Z58 1996**
Sarah Fielding. Trade Cloth. Thomson Gale. Farmington Hills, MI. 1996. 176p. ISBN:0-8057-7051-8, ISBN13: 978-0-8057-7051-3. Dewey:823/.5. LCCN:96-012872.
Audience: **l,u.** *Choice, 1997.*

Fielding, Henry & Fielding, Sarah **PR3724.G8**
The Correspondence of Henry and Sarah Fielding. Martin C. Battestin & Clive T. Probyn (Editors). Trade Cloth. Oxford University Press, Inc. New York, NY. 1993. 264p. ISBN:0-19-811273-4, ISBN13: 978-0-19-811273-0. Dewey:823.5. LCCN:92-027584.
Audience: **g,l,u,f.**

Fielding, Sarah **PZ6.F5**
The Governess: [the Little Female Academy]. Library Binding. Sagebrush Education Resources. Caledonia, MN. 2002. ISBN:0-613-82818-6, ISBN13: 978-0-613-82818-5. Dewey:398.8.
Audience: **g,l,u,f.**

Fielding, Sarah **PR3459.F3 L5 1994**
The Lives of Cleopatra and Octavia. Christopher D. Johnson (Editor). Trade Cloth. Bucknell University Press. Cranbury, NJ. 1994. 200p. ISBN:0-8387-5257-8, ISBN13: 978-0-8387-5257-9. Dewey:823/.5. LCCN:92-056610.
Audience: **g,l,u,f.**

Fielding, Sarah **PR3459.F3**
The Adventures of David Simple: Containing an Account of His Travels Through the Cities of London and Westminster in the Search of a Real Friend. Malcolm Kelsall (Introduction by). Trade Paper. Oxford University Press, Inc. New York, NY. 1987. 466p. Oxford World's Classics Ser. ISBN:0-19-281766-3, ISBN13: 978-0-19-281766-2. Dewey:823/.6. LCCN:86-031217.
Audience: **g,l,u,f.**

Fielding, Sarah **PR3459.F3A7 1998**
The Adventures of David Simple and Volume the Last. Peter Sabor (Editor). Trade Cloth. University Press of Kentucky. Lexington, KY. 1998. 416p. Eighteenth-Century Novels by Women Ser. ISBN:0-8131-0945-0, ISBN13: 978-0-8131-0945-9. Dewey:823/.5. LCCN:97-050429.
Audience: **g,l,u,f.** *Choice, 1998.*

Fielding, Sarah **PR3459.F3H57 2004**
The History of Ophelia. Peter Sabor (Editor). Trade Paper. Broadview Press. Peterborough, ON. 2004. 320p. Broadview Editions Ser. ISBN:1-55111-120-9, ISBN13: 978-1-55111-120-9. Dewey:823/.5. LCCN:2004-444760.
Audience: **g,l,u,f.**

Individual Authors and Works > 17th-18th C. > Goldsmith, Oliver

Bloom, Harold (Editor, Introduction by) **PR3494.O45 1987**
Oliver Goldsmith. Library Binding. Chelsea House Publishers. Langhorne, PA. 1987. 184p. ISBN:1-55546-281-2, ISBN13: 978-1-55546-281-9. Dewey:828/.609. LCCN:87-005188.
Audience: **l,u.**

Dixon, Peter **PR3494.D58 1991**
Oliver Goldsmith Revisited. Trade Cloth. Thomson Gale. Farmington Hills, MI. 1991. 200p. Twayne's English Authors Ser., TEAS No. 487 ISBN:0-8057-7008-9, ISBN13: 978-0-8057-7008-7. Dewey:828/.609. LCCN:91-007819.
Audience: **l,u.**

Goldsmith, Oliver **PR3493**
Collected Letters. Paper Text. Classic Textbooks. Murrieta, CA. 1928. 189p. ISBN:1-4047-7357-6, ISBN13: 978-1-4047-7357-8. Dewey:826.6.
Audience: **u,f.**

Goldsmith, Oliver **PR3683**
She Stoops to Conquer. Ed. 2. Paper Text. W. W. Norton & Company, Inc. New York, NY. 2002. ISBN:0-393-90092-4, ISBN13: 978-0-393-90092-7. Dewey:822.6.
Audience: **g,l,u,f.**

Goldsmith, Oliver **PR9615.7**
The Complete Poetical Works of Oliver Goldsmith. Austin Dobson (Editor). Trade Cloth. IndyPublish.com. Cambridge, MA. 2002. 336p. ISBN:1-58827-277-X, ISBN13: 978-1-58827-277-5. Dewey:821.
Audience: **g,l,u,f.**

Goldsmith, Oliver **PR3480**
The Vicar of Wakefield. Arthur Friedman & Robert L. Mack (Editors). Trade Paper. Oxford University Press, Inc. New York, NY. 2006. 256p. Oxford World's Classics Ser. ISBN:0-19-280512-6, ISBN13: 978-0-19-280512-6. Dewey:823/.6. LCCN:2006-279246.
Audience: **g,l,u,f.**

Hadow, G. E., et al. **PR3482 .H25**
Essays on Goldsmith. C. B. Wheeler & Walter Scott Sr. (Authors). Trade Cloth. Richard West. Philadelphia, PA. 1973. ISBN:0-8274-0390-9, ISBN13: 978-0-8274-0390-1. Dewey:828.609.
Audience: **l,u.**

Rousseau, G. S. **PR3533**
Goldsmith: The Critical Heritage. Trade Paper. Routledge. New York, NY. 1985. 412p. ISBN:0-7102-0511-2, ISBN13: 978-0-7102-0511-7. Dewey:828/.609.
Audience: **l,u,f.**

Worth, Katharine **PR701.W67 1992**
Sheridan and Goldsmith. Cloth Text. Palgrave Macmillan. New York, NY. 1992. 176p. English Dramatists Ser. ISBN:0-312-08392-0, ISBN13: 978-0-312-08392-2. Dewey:822.609. LCCN:92-008838.
Audience: **u,f.** *Choice, 1993.*

Individual Authors and Works > 17th-18th C. > Gray, Thomas

Gray, Thomas **PR3503**
Correspondence. Trade Cloth. Somerset Publishers, Inc. Santa Barbara, CA. ISBN:0-403-04017-5, ISBN13: 978-0-403-04017-9. Dewey:821/.6.
Audience: **u,f.**

Gray, Thomas **PR3500.A5**
English Poems, Original and Translated from the Norse and Welsh. Paper Text. Classic Textbooks. Murrieta, CA. 1922. 293p. ISBN:1-4047-7361-4, ISBN13: 978-1-4047-7361-5. Dewey:821.6.
Audience: **g,l,u,f.**

Gray, Thomas **PR3501 .C7 1979**
Gray: Poetry and Prose. J. Crofts (Introduction by). Trade Cloth. A M S Press, Inc. New York, NY. ISBN:0-404-15304-6, ISBN13: 978-0-404-15304-5. Dewey:821/.6. LCCN:76-029472.
Audience: **g,l,u,f.**

Mack, Robert L. **PR3503.M23 2000**
Thomas Gray: A Life. Cloth over Boards. Yale University Press. Cumberland, RI. 2000. 736p. ISBN:0-300-08499-4, ISBN13: 978-0-300-08499-3. Dewey:821/.6 B. LCCN:00-104461.
Audience: **g,u,f.** *Choice, 2001.*

Individual Authors and Works > 17th-18th C. > Herbert, George

Bloch, Chana **PR3508.B5 1985**
Spelling the Word: George Herbert and the Bible. Trade Cloth. University of California Press. Berkeley, CA. 1985. xiv, 324p. ISBN:0-520-05121-1, ISBN13: 978-0-520-05121-8. Dewey:821/.3. LCCN:84-000123.
Audience: **u,f.** *Choice, 1985.*

Fish, Stanley Eugene **PR3508**
The Living Temple: George Herbert and Catechizing. Trade Cloth. University of California Press. Berkeley, CA. 1978. ix, 201p. ISBN:0-520-02657-8, ISBN13: 978-0-520-02657-5. Dewey:821/.3. LCCN:73-090664.
Audience: **u,f.**

Herbert, George **PR3507**
The Complete English Works: Poems and Other Writings. Trade Cloth. Alfred A. Knopf Inc. New York, NY. 1995. 592p. ISBN:0-679-44359-2, ISBN13: 978-0-679-44359-9. Dewey:828/.3.
Audience: **g,l,u,f.**

Malcolmson, Cristina **PR3508.M288 2003**
George Herbert: A Literary Life. Cloth over Boards. Palgrave Macmillan. New York, NY. 2004. 209p. Literary Lives Ser. ISBN:0-333-66978-9, ISBN13: 978-0-333-66978-5. Dewey:821/.3 B. LCCN:2003-054873.
Audience: **g,l,u,f.** *Choice, 2004.*

Patrides, G. A. (Editor) **PR3508**
George Herbert: The Critical Heritage. Trade Cloth. Routledge. New York, NY. 1983. 390p. The Critical Heritage Ser. ISBN:0-7100-9240-7, ISBN13: 978-0-7100-9240-3. Dewey:821/.3. LCCN:82-022959.
Audience: **l,u.**

Stein, Arnold **PR3508 .S7**
George Herbert's Lyrics. Trade Cloth. Johns Hopkins University Press. Baltimore, MD. 1968. 267p. ISBN:0-8018-0613-5, ISBN13: 978-0-8018-0613-1. Dewey:821/.3. LCCN:68-012898.
Audience: **l,u,f.**

Strier, Richard **PR2358**
Love Known: Theology and Experience in George Herbert's Poetry. Trade Paper. University of Chicago Press. Chicago, IL. 1997. xxii, 300p. ISBN:0-226-77717-0, ISBN13: 978-0-226-77717-7. Dewey:821/.3. LCCN:83-006798.
Audience: **u,f.**

Summers, Joseph H. **PR3508.S8 1981**
George Herbert: His Religion and Art. Trade Paper. Pegasus Press. Chandler, AZ. 1981. 250p. ISBN:0-86698-003-2, ISBN13: 978-0-86698-003-6. Dewey:821/.3. LCCN:96-133462.
Audience: **g,l,u,f.**

White, James B. **PR2358**
This Book of Starres: Learning to Read George Herbert. Trade Paper. University of Michigan Press. Chicago, IL. 1995. 320p. ISBN:0-472-08337-6, ISBN13: 978-0-472-08337-4. Dewey:821/.3. LCCN:93-046407.
Audience: **u,f.** *Choice, 1994.*

Individual Authors and Works > 17th-18th C. > Herrick, Robert

Coiro, Ann B. **PR3512.H43C6 1988**
Robert Herrick's Hesperides and the Epigram Book Tradition. Trade Cloth. Johns Hopkins University Press. Baltimore, MD. 1988. 280p. ISBN:0-8018-3571-2, ISBN13: 978-0-8018-3571-1. Dewey:821/.4. LCCN:87-022827.
Audience: **u,f.**

Herrick, Robert **PR3510.A5.M3**
Poetical Works. Trade Cloth. Oxford University Press, Inc. New York, NY. 1956. xl, 631p. ISBN:0-19-811813-9, ISBN13: 978-0-19-811813-8. Dewey:821/.4. LCCN:56-002924.
Audience: **g,l,u,f.** B

Moorman, Frederic William **PR3513**
Robert Herrick, a Biographical and Critical Study. Paper Text. Textbook Publishers. Temecula, CA. 2003. 343p. ISBN:0-7581-4404-0, ISBN13: 978-0-7581-4404-1. Dewey:821.4.
Audience: **l,u.**

Rollin, Roger B. **PR3514 .R64 1992**
Robert Herrick. Trade Cloth. Thomson Gale. Farmington Hills, MI. 1992. 180p. Twayne's English Authors Ser., No. 34 ISBN:0-8057-7012-7, ISBN13: 978-0-8057-7012-4. Dewey:821/.4. LCCN:91-033734.
Audience: **l,u.**

Individual Authors and Works > 17th-18th C. > Johnson, Samuel

Bate, Walter Jackson **PR3533**
The Achievement of Samuel Johnson. Paper Text. Textbook Publishers. Temecula, CA. 2003. xi, 248p. ISBN:0-7581-7108-0, ISBN13: 978-0-7581-7108-5. Dewey:828/.609.
Audience: **l,u.** B

Bate, Walter Jackson **PR3533.B334 1998**
Samuel Johnson. Trade Paper. Basic Books. New York, NY. 1998. 672p. ISBN:1-887178-76-7, ISBN13: 978-1-887178-76-1. Dewey:828/.609 B. LCCN:97-047734.
Audience: **g,l,u,f.** B

Clifford, James Lowry **PR3533**
Young Sam Johnson. Paper Text. Textbook Publishers. Temecula, CA. 2003. 377p. ISBN:0-7581-8742-4, ISBN13: 978-0-7581-8742-0. Dewey:928.2.
Audience: **l,u.** B

Clingham, Greg (Editor) **PR3534 .C34 1997**
The Cambridge Companion to Samuel Johnson. Trade Paper. Cambridge University Press. New York, NY. 1997. 284p. Companions to Literature Ser. ISBN:0-521-55625-2, ISBN13: 978-0-521-55625-5. Dewey:828.6/09. LCCN:96-051162.
Audience: **u,f.** *Choice, 1998.*

Clingham, Greg **PR3537.A9C58 2002**
Johnson, Writing, and Memory. Trade Cloth. Cambridge University Press. New York, NY. 2002. 234p. ISBN:0-521-81611-4, ISBN13: 978-0-521-81611-3. Dewey:828/.609. LCCN:2002-071580.
Audience: **u,f.** *Choice, 2003.*

Folkenflik, Robert **PR3537.B54**
Samuel Johnson, Biographer. Book, Other. Cornell University Press. Ithaca, NY. 1978. 224p. ISBN:0-8014-0968-3, ISBN13: 978-0-8014-0968-4. Dewey:828/.608. LCCN:78-058050.
Audience: **l,u,f.** B

Greene, Donald **PR3537.P6G7 1990**
The Politics of Samuel Johnson. Ed. 2. Trade Cloth. University of Georgia Press. Athens, GA. 1990. 440p. ISBN:0-8203-1204-5, ISBN13: 978-0-8203-1204-0. Dewey:828/.609. LCCN:89-038441.
Audience: **u,f.**

Greene, Donald **PR3534.G74 1989**
Samuel Johnson. Trade Cloth. Macmillan Publishing Company, Inc. Old Tappan, NJ. 1989. 224p. Twayne's English Authors Ser., No. 95 ISBN:0-8057-6962-5, ISBN13: 978-0-8057-6962-3. Dewey:828/.609. LCCN:89-033455.
Audience: **l,u.**

Johnson, Samuel **PR3521**
The Yale Edition of the Works of Samuel Johnson. Paper Text. Textbook Publishers. Temecula, CA. 2003. ISBN:0-7581-0111-2, ISBN13: 978-0-7581-0111-2. Dewey:828/.609.
Audience: **g,l,u,f.**

Johnson, Samuel **PR3522.G69 2000**
Samuel Johnson: The Major Works. Donald Greene (Editor). Trade Paper. Oxford University Press, Inc. New York, NY. 2000. 880p. Oxford World's Classics Ser. ISBN:0-19-284042-8, ISBN13: 978-0-19-284042-4. Dewey:828/.609. LCCN:2001-277128.
Audience: **g,l,u,f.**

Johnson, Samuel **PR9615.7**
Samuel Johnson: the Yale Anthology of His Prose and Poetry. Bruce Redford, Stephan Fix & Loren Rothschild (Editors). Cloth over Boards. Yale University Press. Cumberland, RI. 2007. ISBN:0-300-11303-X, ISBN13: 978-0-300-11303-7. Dewey:821.
Audience: **g,l,u,f.**

Johnson, Samuel **PR3634**
The Poems of Samuel Johnson. Ed. 2. David N. Smith & Edward McAdam (Editors), J. D. Fleeman (Revised by). Trade Cloth. Oxford University Press, Inc. New York, NY. 1974. 524p. Oxford English Texts ISBN:0-19-812702-2, ISBN13: 978-0-19-812702-4. Dewey:821/.5. LCCN:74-169404.
Audience: **g,l,u,f.** B

Johnson, Samuel **PR3529.A14 H2 1971**
The History of Rasselas, Prince of Abissinia. Geoffrey Tillotson & Brian Jenkins (Introduction by). Trade Cloth. Oxford University Press, Inc. New York, NY. 1971. xxx, 145p. ISBN:0-19-255342-9, ISBN13: 978-0-19-255342-3. Dewey:823/.6. LCCN:76-562416.
Audience: **g,l,u,f.** B

Kernan, Alvin **PR3534**
Samuel Johnson and the Impact of Print. Trade Paper. Princeton University Press. Princeton, NJ. 1989. 375p. ISBN:0-691-01475-2, ISBN13: 978-0-691-01475-3. Dewey:828.609. LCCN:86-042842.
Audience: **u,f.**

Lipking, Lawrence I. **PR3533.L56 1998**
Samuel Johnson: The Life of an Author. Trade Cloth. Harvard University Press. Cambridge, MA. 1998. 384p. ISBN:0-674-78777-3, ISBN13: 978-0-674-78777-3. Dewey:[B]. LCCN:98-018526.
Audience: **g,l,u,f.** *Choice, 1999.*

Mayhew, Robert J. **PR3537.L3M28 2004**
Landscape, Literature, and English Religious Culture, 1660-1800: Samuel Johnson and Languages of Natural Description. Cloth over Boards. Palgrave Macmillan. New York, NY. 2004. 416p. Studies in Modern History Ser. ISBN:0-333-99308-X, ISBN13: 978-0-333-99308-8. Dewey:828/.609. LCCN:2003-066389.
Audience: **u,f.** *Choice, 2004.*

Parker, Fred **PR448.S**
Scepticism and Literature: An Essay on Pope, Hume, Sterne, and Johnson. Trade Cloth. Oxford University Press, Inc. New York, NY. 2003. 304p. ISBN:0-19-925318-8, ISBN13: 978-0-19-925318-0. Dewey:820.9005. LCCN:2004-298260.
Audience: **u,f.** *Choice, 2004.*

Redford, Bruce (Editor) **PR3533 .A4**
The Letters of Samuel Johnson: Volume I: 1731-1772, Volume II: 1773-1776, Volume III: 1777-1781. Cloth Text. Princeton University Press. Princeton, NJ. 1994. 1909p. ISBN:0-691-03389-7, ISBN13: 978-0-691-03389-1. Dewey:828/.609.
Audience: **u,f.**

Rogers, Pat **PR3532**
The Samuel Johnson Encyclopedia. Cloth Text. Greenwood Publishing Group, Inc. Portsmouth, NH. 1996. 520p. ISBN:0-313-29411-9, ISBN13: 978-0-313-29411-2. Dewey:828/.609 B. LCCN:95-033072.
Audience: **g,l,u,f.** *Choice, 1996.*

Shaw, William & Piozzi, Hester Lynch **PR3533**
Memoirs of the Life and Writings of the Late Dr Samuel Johnson/[by] William Shaw ; [and], Anecdotes of the Late Samuel Johnson, LL.D. During the Last Twenty Years of His Life/[by] Hesther [i.e. Hester] Lynch Piozzi. Arthur Sherbo (Introduction by). Trade Cloth. Oxford University Press, Inc. New York, NY. 1974. xxii, 201p. ISBN:0-19-255416-6, ISBN13: 978-0-19-255416-1. Dewey:828/.609. LCCN:74-177118.
Audience: **g,l,u,f.** *B*

Sherbo, Arthur **PR3537.L5S54 1995**
Samuel Johnson's Critical Opinions: A Reexamination. Trade Cloth. University of Delaware Press. Newark, DE. 1995. 216p. ISBN:0-87413-547-8, ISBN13: 978-0-87413-547-3. Dewey:828/.609. LCCN:94-043846.
Audience: **u,f.**

Smallwood, Philip **PR3537.L5S63 2003**
Johnson's Critical Presence: Image, History, Judgment. Trade Cloth. Ashgate Publishing, Ltd. Aldershot, 2004. 190p. Studies in Early Modern English Literature ISBN:0-7546-3357-8, ISBN13: 978-0-7546-3357-0. Dewey:828/.609. LCCN:2003-065059.
Audience: **u,f.** *Choice, 2005.*

Venturo, David F. **PR3537.P58V46 1999**
Johnson the Poet: The Poetic Career of Samuel Johnson. Trade Cloth. University of Delaware Press. Newark, DE. 1999. 336p. ISBN:0-87413-676-8, ISBN13: 978-0-87413-676-0. Dewey:821/.6. LCCN:98-047239.
Audience: **g,u,f.** *Choice, 2000.*

Individual Authors and Works > 17th-18th C. > L-O

Cook, Richard I. **PR3545.M6.Z6**
Bernard Mandeville. Library Binding. Thomson Gale. Farmington Hills, MI. 1974. 174p. English Authors Ser. ISBN:0-8057-1371-9, ISBN13: 978-0-8057-1371-8. Dewey:192. LCCN:73-021513.
Audience: **l,u.** *B*

Ham, Roswell G. **PR3613**
Otway and Lee: Biography from a Baroque Age. Trade Cloth. Greenwood Publishing Group, Inc. Portsmouth, NH. 1969. 250p. ISBN:0-8371-0462-9, ISBN13: 978-0-8371-0462-1. Dewey:822.4. LCCN:69-013923.
Audience: **l,u.** *B*

Lee, Nathaniel **PR3540**
Works. Paper Text. Textbook Publishers. Temecula, CA. 2003. ISBN:0-7581-4161-0, ISBN13: 978-0-7581-4161-3. Dewey:822.49.
Audience: **g,l,u,f.** *B*

Lennox, Charlotte **PR3541**
The Female Quixote: Or the Adventures of Arabella. Trade Paper. Oxford University Press, Inc. New York, NY. 1998. 468p. Oxford World's Classics Ser. ISBN:0-19-283572-6, ISBN13: 978-0-19-283572-7. Dewey:823.6.
Audience: **g,l,u,f.**

Lennox, Charlotte **PR3541.L27L54 1995**
The Life of Harriot Stuart, Written by Herself. Susan Kubica (Editor, Introduction by). Trade Cloth. Fairleigh Dickinson University Press. Cranbury, NJ. 1995. 328p. ISBN:0-8386-3579-2, ISBN13: 978-0-8386-3579-7. Dewey:823/.6. LCCN:94-029387.
Audience: **g,l,u,f.**

Lillo, George **PR3671.R5**
The Dramatic Works of George Lillo: Including Silvia. James L. Steffensen & Richard Noble (Editors). Trade Cloth. Oxford University Press, Inc. New York, NY. 1993. 776p. Oxford English Texts ISBN:0-19-812714-6, ISBN13: 978-0-19-812714-7. Dewey:822.5. LCCN:91-038854.
Audience: **g,l,u,f.**

Lovelace, Richard **PR3542**
Poems, Set. C. H. Wilkinson (Editor). Library Binding. Reprint Services Company. Temecula, CA. 1992. BCL1-PR English Literature Ser. ISBN:0-7812-7369-2, ISBN13: 978-0-7812-7369-5. Dewey:821.45.
Audience: **g,l,u,f.**

MacKenzie, Henry **PR3543.M2M3 2001**
The Man of Feeling. Ed. 2. Brian Vickers (Editor), Stephen Bending & Stephen Bygrave (Introduction by). Trade Paper. Oxford University Press, Inc. New York, NY. 2002. 154p. Oxford World's Classics Ser. ISBN:0-19-284032-0, ISBN13: 978-0-19-284032-5. Dewey:823/.6. LCCN:2001-036926.
Audience: **g,l,u,f.** *B*

Mandeville, Bernard **HQ185.A5P44 2000**
A Modest Defence of Publick Stews: or An Essay upon Whoring, As It Is Now Practis'd in These Kingdoms. Richard I.

Cook (Introduction by). Trade Cloth. A M S Press, Inc. New York, NY. 1973. viii, 78p. The Augustan Reprints Ser., No. 162 ISBN:0-404-70162-0, ISBN13: 978-0-404-70162-8. Dewey:306.74/2/0942. LCCN:2001-265944.
Audience: **g,l,u,f.**

O'Keefe, John **PR3605.O3.A77 1977**
Wild Oats. Cloth Text. Harcourt Education. Oxford, 1977. 104p. ISBN:0-435-23722-5, ISBN13: 978-0-435-23722-6. Dewey:822/.6. LCCN:77-368276.
Audience: **g,l,u,f.** B

Oldham, John **PR3605.O4 A17 1987**
The Poems of John Oldham. Raman Seldon & Harold F. Brooks (Editors). Cloth Text. Oxford University Press, Inc. New York, NY. 1987. 760p. ISBN:0-19-812456-2, ISBN13: 978-0-19-812456-6. Dewey:821/.4. LCCN:88-153731.
Audience: **g,l,u,f.** *Choice, 1988.*

Otway, Thomas **PR3610.A5.G5 1968**
The Works of Thomas Otway; Plays, Poems, and Love-Letters. Trade Cloth. Oxford University Press, Inc. New York, NY. 1968. ISBN:0-19-811483-4, ISBN13: 978-0-19-811483-3. Dewey:822/.4. LCCN:68-133735.
Audience: **g,l,u,f.** B

Otway, Thomas **PR3612.O7 1976**
The Orphan. Aline M. Taylor (Editor). Trade Cloth. University of Nebraska Press. Lincoln, NE. 1976. xxx, 118p. Regents Restoration Drama Ser. ISBN:0-8032-0383-7, ISBN13: 978-0-8032-0383-9. Dewey:822/.4. LCCN:75-013067.
Audience: **g,l,u,f.** B

Saunders, Thomas B. **PR3544 .S2**
The Life and Letters of James MacPherson. Library Binding. Reprint Services Company. Temecula, CA. 1992. 327p. BCL1-PR English Literature Ser. ISBN:0-7812-7371-4, ISBN13: 978-0-7812-7371-8. Dewey:821/.6.
Audience: **u,f.**

Zigerell, James **PR3605.O4.Z98 1983**
John Oldham. Library Binding. Thomson Gale. Farmington Hills, MI. 1983. 162p. English Authors Ser., No. 372 ISBN:0-8057-6858-0, ISBN13: 978-0-8057-6858-9. Dewey:821/.4. LCCN:83-010722.
Audience: **l,u.** B

Individual Authors and Works > 17th-18th C. > Marvel, Andrew

Bloom, Harold (Introduction by) **PR3546.A865 1989**
Andrew Marvell. Andrew Marvell (Contribution by). Library Binding. Chelsea House Publishers. Langhorne, PA. 1990. 256p. Modern Critical Views Ser. ISBN:1-55546-320-7, ISBN13: 978-1-55546-320-5. Dewey:821/.4. LCCN:87-025697.
Audience: **l,u.**

Chernaik, Warren & Dzelzainis, Martin (Editors) **PR3546.M37 1999**
Marvell and Liberty. Cloth over Boards. Palgrave Macmillan. New York, NY. 1999. 381p. ISBN:0-312-22171-1, ISBN13: 978-0-312-22171-3. Dewey:821.4. LCCN:98-055451.
Audience: **u,f.**

Collins, Dan S. **Z8551.65.C64**
Andrew Marvell: A Reference Guide. Trade Cloth. Macmillan Publishing Company, Inc. Old Tappan, NJ. 1981. xiv, 449p. ISBN:0-8161-8017-2, ISBN13: 978-0-8161-8017-2. Dewey:016.821/4. LCCN:81-005017.
Audience: **l,u.**

Healy, Thomas **PE3546.A866 1998**
Andrew Marvel. Trade Paper. Longman Publishing Group. White Plains, NY. 1998. 224p. Longman Critical Readers Ser. ISBN:0-582-21907-8, ISBN13: 978-0-582-21907-6. Dewey:821.4. LCCN:98-012921.
Audience: **l,u.**

Hodge, R. I. **PR3546**
Foreshortened Time: Andrew Marvell and 17th-Century Revolutions. Trade Cloth. Boydell & Brewer, Inc. Rochester, NY. 1979. 179p. ISBN:0-85991-037-7, ISBN13: 978-0-85991-037-8. Dewey:821/.4.
Audience: **u,f.**

Marvell, Andrew **PR3546**
Marvell: Poems. Trade Cloth. Knopf Publishing Group. New York, NY. 2004. 256p. ISBN:1-4000-4252-6, ISBN13: 978-1-4000-4252-4. Dewey:821.
Audience: **g,l,u,f.**

Marvell, Andrew **PR3546.A6 2003**
The Prose Works of Andrew Marvell, 1672-1673, Vol. 1. Martin Dzelzainis & Annabel M. Patterson (Editors). Cloth over Boards. Yale University Press. Cumberland, RI. 2003. 544p. ISBN:0-300-09935-5, ISBN13: 978-0-300-09935-5. Dewey:828/.408. LCCN:2003-050055.
Audience: **g,l,u,f.** *Choice, 2004.*

Marvell, Andrew & Smith, Nigel **PR3546**
The Poems of Andrew Marvell: The Complete Works. Cloth Text. Longman Publishing. Boston, MA. 2003. 468p. ISBN:0-582-07770-2, ISBN13: 978-0-582-07770-6. Dewey:821.4.
Audience: **g,l,u,f.**

Murray, Nicholas **PR3546.M87 2000**
World Enough and Time: The Life of Andrew Marvell. Trade Cloth. St. Martin's Press. Gordonville, VA. 2000. 294p. ISBN:0-312-24277-8, ISBN13: 978-0-312-24277-0. Dewey:821.4. LCCN:99-088365.
Audience: **g,l,u,f.** *Choice, 2001.*

Patterson, Annabel **PR3546.P33 1999**
Marvell: The Writer in Public Life. Ed. 2. Trade Cloth. Longman Publishing Group. White Plains, NY. 1999. 200p. Medieval and Renaissance Library ISBN:0-582-35676-8, ISBN13: 978-0-582-35676-4. Dewey:821/.4. LCCN:99-039930.
Audience: **u,f.**

Ray, Robert H. **PR3546.R39 1999**
An Andrew Marvell Companion. Cloth Text. Garland Publishing, Inc. New York, NY. 1998. 224p. Reference Library of the Humanities, Vol. 1243 ISBN:0-8240-6248-5, ISBN13: 978-0-8240-6248-4. Dewey:821/.4 B. LCCN:97-034073.
Audience: **g,l,u,f.**

Smith, Nigel **PR3546**
Andrew Marvell: A Biography. Trade Cloth. Yale University Press. Cumberland, RI. 2006. 352p. ISBN:0-300-11221-1, ISBN13: 978-0-300-11221-4. Dewey:821.4.
Audience: **g,l,u,f.**

Wheeler, Thomas **PR3546.W4 1996**
Andrew Marvell Revisited. Trade Cloth. Thomson Gale. Farmington Hills, MI. 1996. xii, 187p. Twayne's English Authors Ser. ISBN:0-8057-7033-X, ISBN13: 978-0-8057-7033-9. Dewey:821/.4. LCCN:96-036040.
Audience: **l,u.**

Individual Authors and Works > 17th-18th C. > Milton, John

Behrendt, Stephen C. **ND1942.B55**
The Moment of Explosion: Blake and the Illustration of Milton. Cloth Text. University of Nebraska Press. Lincoln, NE. 1983. 235p. ISBN:0-8032-1169-4, ISBN13: 978-0-8032-1169-8. Dewey:759.2. LCCN:82-013561.
Audience: **u,f.**

Bridges, Robert S. **PR3597**
On the Prosody of Paradise Regained and Sampson Agonistes. Paper Text. Classic Books. Murrieta, CA. 2001. 32p. Collected Works of Robert Bridges ISBN:0-7426-7614-5, ISBN13: 978-0-7426-7614-5. Dewey:821.4.
Audience: **u,f.**

Crosman, Robert **PR3562.C68**
Reading Paradise Lost. Trade Cloth. Indiana University Press. Bloomington, IN. 1980. 276p. ISBN:0-253-15156-2, ISBN13: 978-0-253-15156-8. Dewey:821/.4. LCCN:79-003035.
Audience: **l,u,f.**

Crump, Galbraith M. **PR3562**
The Mystical Design of 'Paradise Lost'. Trade Cloth. Bucknell University Press. Cranbury, NJ. 1975. 194p. ISBN:0-8387-1519-2, ISBN13: 978-0-8387-1519-2. Dewey:821/.4. LCCN:74-000202.
Audience: **u,f.**

Danielson, Dennis (Editor) **PR3588 .C27 1999**
The Cambridge Companion to Milton. Ed. 2. Cloth Text. Cambridge University Press. New York, NY. 1999. 316p. Companions to Literature Ser. ISBN:0-521-65226-X, ISBN13: 978-0-521-65226-1. Dewey:821/.4. LCCN:99-010915.
Audience: **l,u,f.** *Choice, 1990.*

Danielson, Dennis **PR3562**
Milton's Good God: A Study in Literary Theodicy. Trade Cloth. Cambridge University Press. New York, NY. 1982. 303p. ISBN:0-521-23744-0, ISBN13: 978-0-521-23744-4. Dewey:821/.4. LCCN:81-015535.
Audience: **u,f.**

Darbishire, Helen **PR3562 .D3 1974**
Milton's Paradise Lost. Library Binding. Folcroft Library Editions. Folcroft, PA. 1951. ISBN:0-8414-3750-5, ISBN13: 978-0-8414-3750-0. Dewey:821/.4. LCCN:74-003031.
Audience: **l,u.**

Davies, Stevie **PR3562.D36 1983**
Images of Kinship in "Paradise Lost": Milton's Politics and Christian Liberty. Cloth Text. University of Missouri Press. Columbia, MO. 1983. 256p. ISBN:0-8262-0392-2, ISBN13: 978-0-8262-0392-2. Dewey:821/.4. LCCN:82-017485.
Audience: **u,f.**

Empson, William **PR3592**
Milton's God. Trade Cloth. Greenwood Publishing Group, Inc. Portsmouth, NH. 1979. 280p. ISBN:0-313-21021-7, ISBN13: 978-0-313-21021-1. Dewey:821/.4. LCCN:78-014409.
Audience: **l,u.**

Fallon, Robert T. **PR3592.P64F33 1995**
Divided Empire: Milton's Political Imagery. Trade Cloth. Pennsylvania State University Press. University Park, PA. 1996. 216p. ISBN:0-271-01460-1, ISBN13: 978-0-271-01460-9. Dewey:821/.4. LCCN:94-041636.
Audience: **u,f.** *Choice, 1996.*

Ferry, Anne **PR3562**
Milton's Epic Voice: The Narrator in Paradise Lost. Trade Paper. University of Chicago Press. Chicago, IL. 1983. 208p. ISBN:0-226-24468-7, ISBN13: 978-0-226-24468-6. Dewey:821/.4. LCCN:83-004839.
Audience: **l,u.**

Fiore, Peter A. **PR3562**
Milton and Augustine: Patterns of Augustinian Thought in Milton's Paradise Lost. Trade Cloth. Pennsylvania State University Press. University Park, PA. 1981. 144p. ISBN:0-271-00269-7, ISBN13: 978-0-271-00269-9. Dewey:821/.4. LCCN:80-017854.
Audience: **u,f.**

Fish, Stanley Eugene **PR3588.F57 2001**
How Milton Works. Trade Cloth. Harvard University Press. Cambridge, MA. 2001. 640p. ISBN:0-674-00465-5, ISBN13: 978-0-674-00465-8. Dewey:821/.4. LCCN:00-052977.
Audience: **u,f.** *Choice, 2001.*

Fish, Stanley Eugene **PR3562.F5 1998**
Surprised by Sin: The Reader in Paradise Lost. Ed. 2. Trade Paper. Harvard University Press. Cambridge, MA. 2003. 440p. ISBN:0-674-85747-X, ISBN13: 978-0-674-85747-6. Dewey:821.4. LCCN:97-038854.
Audience: **u,f.**

Fletcher, Harris F. **PR3594**
The Use of the Bible in Milton's Prose, with an Index of the Biblical Quotations and Citations Arranged in the Chronological Order of the Prose Works. Library Binding. Reprint Services Company. Temecula, CA. 1992. 176p. BCL1-PR English Literature Ser. ISBN:0-7812-7383-8, ISBN13: 978-0-7812-7383-1. Dewey:821.47.
Audience: **l,u,f.**

French, J. Milton (Editor) **PR3581 .F72**
Life Records of John Milton, 1608-1674, Set. Trade Cloth. Gordian Press, Inc. Staten Island, NY. 1966. 2368p. ISBN:0-87752-039-9, ISBN13: 978-0-87752-039-9. Dewey:828.403. LCCN:66-020024.
Audience: **u,f.**

Frye, Roland M. **PR3562**
Milton's Imagery and the Visual Arts: Iconographic Tradition in the Epic Poems. Trade Cloth. Princeton University Press. Princeton, NJ. 1978. 436p. ISBN:0-691-06349-4, ISBN13: 978-0-691-06349-2. Dewey:704.9/482/094. LCCN:77-024541.
Audience: **l,u,f.**

Hamlet, Desmond M **PR3562.H32**
One Greater Man: Justice and Damnation in Paradise Lost. Trade Cloth. Bucknell University Press. Cranbury, NJ. 1976. 224p. ISBN:0-8387-1674-1, ISBN13: 978-0-8387-1674-8. Dewey:821/.4. LCCN:74-027670.
Audience: **u,f.**

Hill, Christopher **PR3592.P64.H5 1978**
Milton and the English Revolution. Trade Cloth. Penguin Group (USA) Inc. New York, NY. 1978. xviii, 541p. ISBN:0-670-47612-9, ISBN13: 978-0-670-47612-1. Dewey:821.4. LCCN:77-021548.
Audience: **u,f.**

Hughes, Merritt Y. **PR3588**
The Variorum Commentary on the Poems of John Milton, Vol. 4. Trade Cloth. Columbia University Press. New York, NY. 1975. 379p. ISBN:0-231-08883-3, ISBN13: 978-0-231-08883-1. Dewey:821.4. LCCN:70-129962.
Audience: **u,f.**

Hunter, G. K. **PR3562**
Paradise Lost. Cloth Text. Routledge. New York, NY. 1980. 232p. Unwin Critical Library ISBN:0-04-800004-3, ISBN13: 978-0-04-800004-0. Dewey:821/.4. LCCN:79-041772.
Audience: **l,u.**

Kelley, Mark R. (Editor), et al. **PR3588.M476 2003**
Milton and the Grounds of Contention. Michael Lieb & John T. Shawcross (Editors), Joan Richardson, Ann Lauterback, Peter E. Medine, Lynne A. Greenberg, Susanne Woods, David Norbrook, Sharon Achinstein, Annabel Patterson, John Rogers & John P. Rumrich (Contribution by). Trade Cloth. Duquesne University Press. Pittsburgh, PA. 2003. 352p. Medieval and Renaissance Literary Studies ISBN:0-8207-0345-1, ISBN13: 978-0-8207-0345-9. Dewey:821/.4. LCCN:2003-008561.
Audience: **u,f.** *Choice, 2004.*

Knoppers, Laura L. **PR3592.P64K57 1994**
Historicizing Milton: Spectacle, Power and Poetry in Restoration England. Trade Cloth. University of Georgia Press. Athens, GA. 1994. xi, 209p. ISBN:0-8203-1594-X, ISBN13: 978-0-8203-1594-2. Dewey:821.4. LCCN:93-023007.
Audience: **u,f.** *Choice, 1995.*

Lewalski, Barbara **PR3581.L45 2001**
The Life of John Milton: A Critical Biography. Trade Cloth. Blackwell Publishing, Inc. Malden, MA. 2001. 816p. Blackwell Critical Biographies Ser. ISBN:0-631-17665-9, ISBN13: 978-0-631-17665-7. Dewey:821.4. LCCN:00-034320.
Audience: **g,l,u,f.** *Choice, 2001.*

Lewis, C. S. **PR3562.L4 1961**
A Preface to Paradise Lost: Being the Ballard Matthews Lectures Delivered at University College, North Wales 1941. Cloth Text. Oxford University Press, Inc. New York, NY. 1961. 154p. ISBN:0-19-500345-4, ISBN13: 978-0-19-500345-1. Dewey:821/.4. LCCN:96-181762.
Audience: **l,u,f.**

Lieb, Michael **PR3592.V56L54 1994**
Milton and the Culture of Violence. Book, Other. Cornell University Press. Ithaca, NY. 1994. 288p. ISBN:0-8014-2903-X, ISBN13: 978-0-8014-2903-3. Dewey:821/.4. LCCN:93-032279.
Audience: **u,f.** *Choice, 1995.*

Lieb, Michael **PR3562.L52**
Poetics of the Holy: A Reading of "Paradise Lost". Trade Cloth. University of North Carolina Press. Chapel Hill, NC. 1981. xxi, 442p. ISBN:0-8078-1479-2, ISBN13: 978-0-8078-1479-6. Dewey:821/.4. LCCN:80-029159.
Audience: **u,f.**

Lieb, Michael & Shawcross, John T. (Editors) **PR3581.L47**
Achievements of the Left Hand: Essays on the Prose of John Milton. Trade Cloth. University of Massachusetts Press. Amherst, MA. 1974. 404p. ISBN:0-87023-125-1, ISBN13: 978-0-87023-125-4. Dewey:824/.4. LCCN:73-079506.
Audience: **u,f.**

MacCaffrey, Isabel G. **PR3562**
Paradise Lost As Myth. Trade Cloth. Harvard University Press. Cambridge, MA. 1959. ISBN:0-674-65450-1, ISBN13: 978-0-674-65450-1. Dewey:821.4. LCCN:59-009282.
Audience: **l,u.**

Martz, Louis L. **PR3588.M376 1986**
Milton: Poet of Exile. Ed. 2. Trade Paper. Yale University Press. Cumberland, RI. 1986. 356p. ISBN:0-300-03736-8, ISBN13: 978-0-300-03736-4. Dewey:821/.4. LCCN:86-007772.
Audience: **g,l,u,f.**

McColley, Diane K. **PR3562.M34 1983**
Milton's Eve. Trade Cloth. University of Illinois Press. Champaign, IL. 1983. 247p. ISBN:0-252-00980-0, ISBN13: 978-0-252-00980-8. Dewey:821/.4. LCCN:83-001313.
Audience: **u,f.**

Miller, David M. **PR3588**
John Milton: Poetry. Trade Cloth. Macmillan Publishing Company, Inc. Old Tappan, NJ. 1978. 200p. English Authors Ser., No. 242 ISBN:0-8057-6724-X, ISBN13: 978-0-8057-6724-7. Dewey:821/.4. LCCN:78-018800.
Audience: **l,u.**

Milner, Andrew **PR3592.P64.M5 1981**
John Milton and the English Revolution: A Study in the Sociology of Literature. Trade Cloth. Barnes & Noble Books-Imports. Lanham, MD. 1981. 248p. ISBN:0-389-20123-5, ISBN13: 978-0-389-20123-6. Dewey:821/.4. LCCN:81-124809.
Audience: **u,f.**

Milton, John **PR3569**
The Complete Prose Works of John Milton. Trade Cloth. Yale University Press. Cumberland, RI. ISBN:0-318-56513-7, ISBN13: 978-0-318-56513-2.
Audience: **g,l,u,f.**

Milton, John **PR3562**
The Portable Milton. Douglas Bush (Editor, Introduction by). Trade Paper. Penguin Group (USA) Inc. New York, NY. 1976. 704p. Viking Portable Library ISBN:0-14-015044-7, ISBN13: 978-0-14-015044-5. Dewey:821/.4. LCCN:76-040946.
Audience: **g,l,u,f.**

Milton, John **PR3562**
Paradise Lost. Ed. 2. Scott Elledge (Editor). Trade Paper. W. W. Norton & Company, Inc. New York, NY. 1993. 698p. Critical Editions Ser. ISBN:0-393-96293-8, ISBN13: 978-0-393-96293-2. Dewey:821/.4. LCCN:92-009988.
Audience: **g,l,u,f.** *B*

Milton, John & Fowler, Alastair **PR3560 1998**
Milton: Paradise Lost. Ed. 2. Trade Paper. Longman Publishing. Boston, MA. 1998. 744p. Longman Annotated English Poets Ser. ISBN:0-582-21518-8, ISBN13: 978-0-582-21518-4. Dewey:811.4. LCCN:97-051835.
Audience: **l,u.**

Milton, John & Hughes, Merritt Y. (Editors) **PR3552.H74 2003**
The Complete Poems and Major Prose. Trade Cloth. Hackett Publishing Company, Inc. Indianapolis, IN. 2003. 1059p. ISBN:0-87220-678-5, ISBN13: 978-0-87220-678-6. Dewey:821/.4. LCCN:2002-191309.
Audience: **g,l,u,f.**

Milton, John **PR35602003**
Paradise Lost. Merritt Y. Hughes (Translator). Trade Cloth. Hackett Publishing Company, Inc. Indianapolis, IN. 2003. 324p. ISBN:0-87220-673-4, ISBN13: 978-0-87220-673-1. Dewey:821/.4. LCCN:2002-191310.
Audience: **g,l,u,f.** *B*

Milton, John **PR3569.P34 1985**
John Milton: Selected Prose. C. A. Patrides (Editor). Paper Text. University of Missouri Press. Columbia, MO. 1986. 464p. ISBN:0-8262-0484-8, ISBN13: 978-0-8262-0484-4. Dewey:824/.4. LCCN:85-001027.
Audience: **g,l,u,f.** *B*

Milton, John **PR3566. 1957**
Samson Agonistes. F. T. Prince (Editor). Trade Paper. Oxford University Press, Inc. New York, NY. 1970. 144p. ISBN:0-19-831910-X, ISBN13: 978-0-19-831910-8. Dewey:821.4. LCCN:57-003821.
Audience: **g,l,u,f.** *B*

Parker, William R. **PR3583.P3 1971**
Milton's Contemporary Reputation. Library Binding. M. S. G. Haskell House. Brooklyn, NY. 1970. ix, 299p. Studies in Milton, No. 22 ISBN:0-8383-1129-6, ISBN13: 978-0-8383-1129-5. Dewey:821/.4. LCCN:70-122996.
Audience: **u,f.** *B*

Parker, William R. **PR3562**
Milton: A Biographical Commentary. Ed. 2. Gordon Campbell (Commentaries by, Revised by). Trade Cloth. Oxford University Press, Inc. New York, NY. 1996. 878p. ISBN:0-19-812900-9, ISBN13: 978-0-19-812900-4. Dewey:821.4.
Audience: **l,u,f.**

Parker, William R. **PR3581.P27 1996**
Milton: A Biography. Ed. 2. Gordon Campbell (Commentaries by, Revised by). Trade Cloth. Oxford University Press, Inc. New York, NY. 1996. 690p. ISBN:0-19-812889-4, ISBN13: 978-0-19-812889-2. Dewey:821/.4 B. LCCN:96-016384.
Audience: **g,l,u,f.**

Radzinowicz, Mary A. **PR3566**
Toward Samson Agonistes: The Growth of Milton's Mind. Trade Cloth. Princeton University Press. Princeton, NJ. 1978. 464p. ISBN:0-691-06357-5, ISBN13: 978-0-691-06357-7. Dewey:821/.4. LCCN:77-085559.
Audience: **u,f.** *B*

Revard, Stella P. **PR3562**
The War in Heaven: Paradise Lost and the Tradition of Satan's Rebellion. Book, Other. Cornell University Press. Ithaca, NY. 1980. 320p. ISBN:0-8014-1138-6, ISBN13: 978-0-8014-1138-0. Dewey:821/.4. LCCN:79-023297.
Audience: **u,f.** *B*

Ricks, Christopher **PR3562**
Milton's Grand Style. Paper Text. Oxford University Press, Inc. New York, NY. 1978. 164p. ISBN:0-19-812090-7, ISBN13: 978-0-19-812090-2. Dewey:821/.4.
Audience: **l,u,f.**

Roston, Murray **PR3562.R6 1980**
Milton and the Baroque. Trade Cloth. University of Pittsburgh Press. Pittsburgh, PA. 1980. 201p. ISBN:0-8229-1138-8, ISBN13: 978-0-8229-1138-8. Dewey:821/.4. LCCN:79-021611.
Audience: **u,f.** *B*

Shawcross, John T. **PR3581.S5 1993**
John Milton: The Self and the World. Cloth Text. University Press of Kentucky. Lexington, KY. 2001. 368p. Studies in the English Renaissance ISBN:0-8131-1808-5, ISBN13: 978-0-8131-1808-6. Dewey:821/.4. LCCN:92-022037.
Audience: **u,f.** *Choice, 1993.*

Stavely, Keith W. **PR3592.P7**
The Politics of Milton's Prose Style. Trade Cloth. Yale University Press. Cumberland, RI. 1975. 180p. Studies in English, No. 185 ISBN:0-300-01804-5, ISBN13: 978-0-300-01804-2. Dewey:828/.408. LCCN:74-020086.
Audience: **u,f.** *B*

Stein, Arnold **PR3562 .S7**
Answerable Style: Essays on Paradise Lost. Trade Paper. University of Washington Press. Seattle, WA. 1967. ISBN:0-295-97878-3, ISBN13: 978-0-295-97878-9. Dewey:821.47. LCCN:53-005944.
Audience: **u,f.**

Summers, Joseph H. **PR3562.S8 1981**
The Muse's Method: An Introduction to Paradise Lost. Trade Cloth. Pegasus Press. Chandler, AZ. 1981. 230p. ISBN:0-86698-004-0, ISBN13: 978-0-86698-004-3. Dewey:821/.4. LCCN:96-133464.
Audience: **l,u,f.** *B*

Thorpe, James **PR3581.T49 1983**
John Milton: The Inner Life. Trade Cloth. Huntington Library Press. San Marino, CA. 1983. 200p. ISBN:0-87328-079-2, ISBN13: 978-0-87328-079-2. Dewey:821/.4. LCCN:83-012602.
Audience: **l,u,f.** *B*

Webber, Joan **PR3588**
Milton and His Epic Tradition. Trade Cloth. University of Washington Press. Seattle, WA. 1979. 260p. ISBN:0-295-95618-6, ISBN13: 978-0-295-95618-3. Dewey:821/.4. LCCN:78-004368.
Audience: **l,u,f.** *B*

Wittreich, Joseph **PR3566.W56 2002**
Shifting Contexts: Reinterpreting Samson Agonistes. Trade Cloth. Duquesne University Press. Pittsburgh, PA. 2002. 352p. Medieval and Renaissance Literary Studies ISBN:0-8207-0331-1, ISBN13: 978-0-8207-0331-2. Dewey:822/.4. LCCN:2002-001653.
Audience: **u,f.** *Choice, 2003.*

Individual Authors and Works > 17th-18th C. > Montagu, Lady Mary Wortley

Montagu, Lady Mary Wortley **DA501.M7**
Turkish Embassy Letters. Anita Desai & Malcolm Jack (Editors). Trade Cloth. Pickering & Chatto Publishers, Ltd. London, 1993. 256p. ISBN:1-85196-028-7, ISBN13: 978-1-85196-028-6. Dewey:826.5.
Audience: **g,l,u,f.**

Montagu, Lady Mary Wortley **PR3604.A6 1996**
Romance Writings. Isobel Grundy (Editor). Trade Cloth. Oxford University Press, Inc. New York, NY. 1996. 304p. ISBN:0-19-818319-4, ISBN13: 978-0-19-818319-8. Dewey:823/.5. LCCN:95-025046.
Audience: **g,l,u,f.**

Montagu, Lady Mary Wortley **DA501.M7**
The Complete Letters of Lady Mary Wortley Montagu. Robert Halsband (Editor). Other. Oxford University Press, Inc. New York, NY. ISBN:0-318-54813-5, ISBN13: 978-0-318-54813-5. Dewey:826/.5.
Audience: **g,l,u,f.**

Montagu, Lady Mary Wortley **PR3604.A6 1977**
Lady Mary Wortley Montagu: Essays and Poems and Simplicity, a Comedy. Robert Halsband & Isobel Grundy (Editors). Trade Cloth. Oxford University Press, Inc. New York, NY. 1977. 424p. ISBN:0-19-812444-9, ISBN13: 978-0-19-812444-3. Dewey:821/.5. LCCN:77-361583.
Audience: **g,l,u,f.** B

Individual Authors and Works > 17th-18th C. > P-Q

Clifford, James **PR3619.P5C5 1987**
Hester Lynch Piozzi. Ed. 2. Paper Text. Columbia University Press. New York, NY. 1987. 495p. ISBN:0-231-06389-X, ISBN13: 978-0-231-06389-0. Dewey:828/.609 B. LCCN:86-014749.
Audience: **l,u,f.**

Eves, Charles K. **PR3643.E9 1973**
Matthew Prior: Poet and Diplomatist. Library Binding. Hippocrene Books, Inc. New York, NY. 1973. 436p. ISBN:0-374-92646-8, ISBN13: 978-0-374-92646-5. Dewey:821/.5. LCCN:73-001151.
Audience: **l,u.** B

Ollard, Richard **DA445**
Pepys: A Biography. Trade Cloth. Allison & Busby, Ltd. London, 2003. 400p. ISBN:0-7490-0392-8, ISBN13: 978-0-7490-0392-0. Dewey:942.06/6/0924.
Audience: **g,l,u,f.**

Paltock, Robert **PR3615.P5L5 1990**
Peter Wilkins. Christopher Bentley (Editor), James G. Turner (Introduction by). Trade Paper. Oxford University Press, Inc. New York, NY. 1990. 430p. Oxford World's Classics Ser. ISBN:0-19-282704-9, ISBN13: 978-0-19-282704-3. Dewey:823/.6. LCCN:89-016306.
Audience: **g,l,u,f.**

Philips, Ambrose **PR3619.P2**
Poems of Ambrose Philips. Mary G. Segar (Editor). Trade Cloth. Russell & Russell Publishers. New York, NY. 1969. ISBN:0-8462-1370-2, ISBN13: 978-0-8462-1370-3. Dewey:821/.5. LCCN:71-080955.
Audience: **g,l,u,f.** B

Prior, Matthew **PR3640 .A2**
The Poetical works of Matthew Prior. with a life, by Rev. John Mitford. Trade Cloth. Scholarly Publishing Office, University of Michigan Library. Ann Arbor, MI. 2004. ISBN:1-4181-0809-X, ISBN13: 978-1-4181-0809-0. Dewey:821.
Audience: **g,l,u,f.**

Quarles, Francis **PR3650.A5**
Complete Works in Prose and Verse. Paper Text. Classic Textbooks. Murrieta, CA. 1880. ISBN:1-4047-7395-9, ISBN13: 978-1-4047-7395-0. Dewey:821/.4.
Audience: **g,l,u,f.**

Redford, Bruce **PR3533.B7R44 2002**
Designing the Life of Johnson. Trade Cloth. Oxford University Press, Inc. New York, NY. 2002. 198p. Lyell Lectures in Bibliography, Vols. 2001-2 ISBN:0-19-818739-4, ISBN13: 978-0-19-818739-4. Dewey:828/.609. LCCN:2001-058824.
Audience: **g,l,u,f.** *Choice, 2003.*

Individual Authors and Works > 17th-18th C. > Pope, Alexander

Bloom, Harold (Introduction by) **PR3634.A44 1986**
Alexander Pope. Trade Cloth. Chelsea House Publishers. Langhorne, PA. 1986. 189p. Modern Critical Views Ser. ISBN:0-87754-680-0, ISBN13: 978-0-87754-680-1. Dewey:821/.5. LCCN:85-029062.
Audience: **l,u.**

Bloom, Harold (Introduction by) **PR3629.A78 1988**
Alexander Pope's The Rape of the Lock. Library Binding. Chelsea House Publishers. Langhorne, PA. 1988. 152p. Modern Critical Interpretations Ser. ISBN:0-87754-422-0, ISBN13: 978-0-87754-422-7. Dewey:821/.5. LCCN:87-025607.
Audience: **l,u.**

Brower, Reuben A. **PR3637.A62B68 1986**
Alexander Pope: The Poetry of Allusion. Trade Paper. Oxford University Press, Inc. New York, NY. 1986. 384p. ISBN:0-19-881149-7, ISBN13: 978-0-19-881149-7. Dewey:821/.5. LCCN:86-008732.
Audience: **u,f.** B

Gordon, I. **PR3634**
A Preface to Pope. Trade Cloth. Longman Publishing Group. White Plains, NY. 1976. xiii, 195p. ISBN:0-582-31505-0, ISBN13: 978-0-582-31505-1. Dewey:821/.5. LCCN:75-025572.
Audience: **l,u.** B

Halsband, Robert **NC960**
The Rape of the Lock and Its Illustrations, 1714-1896. Trade Cloth. Oxford University Press, Inc. New York, NY. 1980. 176p. ISBN:0-19-812098-2, ISBN13: 978-0-19-812098-8. Dewey:741.64. LCCN:79 040481.
Audience: **u,f.** B

Hammond, Brean **PR3634**
Pope. Trade Cloth. Longman Publishing Group. White Plains, NY. 1996. 264p. Critical Readers Ser. ISBN:0-582-25539-2, ISBN13: 978-0-582-25539-5. Dewey:821.5.
Audience: **l,u.** *Choice, 1986.*

Jackson, Wallace & Yoder, R. Paul (Editors) **PR3634 .C75 1993**
Critical Essays on Alexander Pope. Trade Cloth. Thomson Gale. Farmington Hills, MI. 1993. 200p. Critical Essays on British Literature Ser. ISBN:0-8161-8862-9, ISBN13: 978-0-8161-8862-8. Dewey:821/.5. LCCN:93-007761.
Audience: **l,u.**

Mack, Maynard **PR3633**
Alexander Pope: A Life. Trade Paper. W. W. Norton & Company, Inc. New York, NY. 1988. ISBN:0-393-30529-5, ISBN13: 978-0-393-30529-6. Dewey:821/.5 B. LCCN:85-002941.
Audience: **g,l,u,f.** B *Choice, 1986.*

Mack, Maynard **PR3634**
Garden and the City: Retirement and Politics in the Later Poetry of Pope, 1731-1743. Trade Cloth. University of Toronto Press. Toronto, ON. 1969. xviii, 341p. Alexander Lectures Ser. ISBN:0-8020-5209-6, ISBN13: 978-0-8020-5209-4. Dewey:821.5. LCCN:69-018883.
Audience: **l,u,f.** B

Morris, David B. **PR3634**
Alexander Pope: The Genius of Sense. Trade Cloth. Harvard University Press. Cambridge, MA. 1984. 370p. ISBN:0-674-01522-3, ISBN13: 978-0-674-01522-7. Dewey:821/.5. LCCN:83-018577.
Audience: **u,f.** B

Parker, Fred **PR448.S**
Scepticism and Literature: An Essay on Pope, Hume, Sterne, and Johnson. Trade Cloth. Oxford University Press, Inc. New York, NY. 2003. 304p. ISBN:0-19-925318-8, ISBN13: 978-0-19-925318-0. Dewey:820.9005. LCCN:2004-298260.
Audience: **u,f.** *Choice, 2004.*

Pope, Alexander **PR3724.G8**
Scriblerus. Trade Paper. Hesperus Press. London, 2003. 112p. ISBN:1-84391-001-2, ISBN13: 978-1-84391-001-5. Dewey:823.5.
Audience: **g,l,u,f.**

Pope, Alexander **PR3622**
The Poems of Alexander Pope: A Reduced Revision of the Twickenham Text. John Butt (Editor). Trade Paper. Yale University Press. Cumberland, RI. 1966. 880p. ISBN:0-300-00030-8, ISBN13: 978-0-300-00030-6. Dewey:821.
Audience: **g,l,u,f.**

Pope, Alexander **PR3633.A4 2000**
Alexander Pope: Selected Letters. Howard Erskine-Hill (Editor). Cloth Text. Oxford University Press, Inc. New York, NY. 2000. 432p. ISBN:0-19-818565-0, ISBN13: 978-0-19-818565-9. Dewey:821/.5 B. LCCN:99-089798.
Audience: **g,l,u,f.** *Choice, 2001.*

Pope, Alexander **PN86**
Literary Criticism of Alexander Pope. Bertrand A. Goldgar (Editor). Trade Cloth. University of Nebraska Press. Lincoln, NE. 1965. xxxvi, 181p. Regents Critics Ser. ISBN:0-8032-0459-0, ISBN13: 978-0-8032-0459-1. Dewey:809. LCCN:64-017231.
Audience: **u,f.** B

Pope, Alexander **PR3634**
Pope: Selected Poetry. Douglas Grant (Selected by). Trade Paper. Penguin Group (USA) Inc. New York, NY. 1985. 224p. Penguin Poetry Library ISBN:0-14-058508-7, ISBN13: 978-0-14-058508-7. Dewey:821/.5.
Audience: **g,l,u,f.**

Pope, Alexander **PR3622.P7 2003**
The Rape of the Lock and Other Poems. Martin Price (Editor), Christopher R. Miller (Introduction by). Mass Market. Penguin Group (USA) Inc. New York, NY. 2003. 304p. Signet Classic Poetry Ser. ISBN:0-451-52877-8, ISBN13: 978-0-451-52877-3. Dewey:821/.5. LCCN:2002-031533.
Audience: **g,l,u,f.**

Sherburn, George Wiley **PR3633.S45 1968**
The Early Career of Alexander Pope. Trade Cloth. Oxford University Press, Inc. New York, NY. 1968. vi, 326p. ISBN:0-19-811675-6, ISBN13: 978-0-19-811675-2. Dewey:821/.5. LCCN:76-401360.
Audience: **u,f.** B

Individual Authors and Works > 17th-18th C. > R

Jenkins, Annibel **PR3671.R5.J4**
Nicholas Rowe. Library Binding. Thomson Gale. Farmington Hills, MI. 1977. 167p. English Authors Ser. ISBN:0-8057-6663-4, ISBN13: 978-0-8057-6663-9. Dewey:822/.5. LCCN:76-053826.
Audience: **l,u.** B

Martin, Burns **PR3657.M3 1973**
Allan Ramsay: A Study of His Life and Works. Library Binding. Greenwood Publishing Group, Inc. Portsmouth, NH. 1931. 203p. ISBN:0-8371-5830-3, ISBN13: 978-0-8371-5830-3. Dewey:821/.5. LCCN:72-000605.
Audience: **l,u.** B

Ramsay, Allan **PR8633**
Works. Paper Text. Textbook Publishers. Temecula, CA. 2003. ISBN:0-7581-5613-8, ISBN13: 978-0-7581-5613-6. Dewey:821.54.
Audience: **g,l,u,f.**

Reeve, Clara **PR3658.R5S3 2002**
The School for Widows. Jeanine M. Casler (Editor). Trade Cloth. University of Delaware Press. Newark, DE. 2002. 384p. ISBN:0-87413-804-3, ISBN13: 978-0-87413-804-7. Dewey:823/.6. LCCN:2002-075005.
Audience: **g,l,u,f.** *Choice, 2003.*

Reeve, Clara & Watt, James **PR3658.R5**
The Old English Baron. James Trainer (Editor). Trade Paper. Oxford University Press, Inc. New York, NY. 2004. 176p. Oxford World's Classics Ser. ISBN:0-19-280327-1, ISBN13: 978-0-19-280327-6. Dewey:823/.6. LCCN:2004-266914.
Audience: **g,l,u,f.**

Rowe, Nicholas **PR3671.R5A76**
Three Plays: Tamerlane, the Fair Penitent, Jane Shore. J. R. Sutherland (Editor). Trade Paper. Books on Demand. Ann Arbor, MI. 358p. ISBN:0-598-59090-0, ISBN13: 978-0-598-59090-9. Dewey:822.5. LCCN:29-020329.
Audience: **g,l,u,f.** B

Rymer, Thomas **PR3671.R7 1971**
Critical Works. Curt A. Zimansky (Editor). Library Binding. Greenwood Publishing Group, Inc. Portsmouth, NH. 1971. li, 299p. ISBN:0-8371-6157-6, ISBN13: 978-0-8371-6157-0. Dewey:822/.051. LCCN:70-156207.
Audience: **u,f.** B

Sennett, Herbert **PR3671.R5B8 2005**
Nicholas Rowe and the Beginnings of Feminism on the London Stage. Trade Cloth. Academica Press, LLC. Bethesda, MD. 2004. 312p. ISBN:1-930901-89-5, ISBN13: 978-1-930901-89-6. Dewey:822/.5. LCCN:2004-013562.
Audience: **u,f.**

Individual Authors and Works > 17th-18th C. > Richardson, Samuel

Castle, Terry **PR3664.C43**
Clarissa's Ciphers: Meaning and Disruption in Richarson's Clarissa. Book, Other. Cornell University Press. Ithaca, NY. 1982. 204p. ISBN:0-8014-1495-4, ISBN13: 978-0-8014-1495-4. Dewey:823/.6. LCCN:82-002460.
Audience: **u,f.** B

Eagleton, Terry **PR3664.C43 E2 1982**
The Rape of Clarissa: Writing, Sexuality and Class Struggle in Samuel Richardson. Trade Paper. University of Minnesota Press. Minneapolis, MN. 1982. 113p. ISBN:0-8166-1209-9, ISBN13: 978-0-8166-1209-3. Dewey:823/.6. LCCN:82-243008.
Audience: **u,f.** B

Eaves, Thomas Cary **PR3666**
Duncan & Kimpel, Ben
Samuel Richardson: A Biography. Trade Cloth. Oxford University Press, Inc. New York, NY. 1971. xvii, 728p. ISBN:0-19-812431-7, ISBN13: 978-0-19-812431-3. Dewey:823/.6. LCCN:78-027067.
Audience: **g,l,u,f.** B

Goldberg, Rita **PR3664.C43**
Sex and Enlightenment: Women in Richardson and Diderot. Trade Cloth. Cambridge University Press. New York, NY. 1984. 248p. ISBN:0-521-26069-8, ISBN13: 978-0-521-26069-5. Dewey:823/.6. LCCN:83-023210.
Audience: **u,f.** B

Ketcham, Michael G. **PR925.K38 1985**
Transparent Designs: Reading, Performance, and Form in the Spectator Papers. Trade Cloth. University of Georgia Press. Athens, GA. 1985. 224p. ISBN:0-8203-0771-8, ISBN13: 978-0-8203-0771-8. Dewey:824/.5/09. LCCN:84-024046.
Audience: **u,f.** B *Choice, 1985.*

Kinkead-Weekes, Mark **PR3667.K5 B**
Samuel Richardson, Dramatic Novelist. Trade Cloth. Routledge. New York, NY. 1973. ix, 506p. ISBN:0-416-02970-1, ISBN13: 978-0-416-02970-3. Dewey:823/.6. LCCN:74-159971.
Audience: **l,u,f.**

Richardson, Samuel **PR3664**
A Collection of the Moral and Instructive Sentiments, Maxims, Cautions and Reflections, Contained in the Histories of Pamela, Clarissa, and Sir Charles Grandison. J. Dussinger (Introduction by). Trade Cloth. A M S Press, Inc. New York, NY. 1992. The Clarissa Project Ser., Vol. 11 ISBN:0-404-64111-3, ISBN13: 978-0-404-64111-5. Dewey:828/.602. LCCN:92-009738.
Audience: **g,l,u.**

Richardson, Samuel & **PR3644.P2 1980**
Fielding, Henry
Pamela, Shamela. Mass Market. Penguin Group (USA) Inc. New York, NY. 1980. ISBN:0-451-51366-5, ISBN13: 978-0-451-51366-3. Dewey:823.5.
Audience: **g,l,u,f.**

Richardson, Samuel **PR3664.H5 1986**
Sir Charles Grandison. Jocelyn Harris (Editor, Introduction by). Trade Paper. Oxford University Press, Inc. New York, NY. 1986. 566p. Oxford World's Classics Ser. ISBN:0-19-281745-0, ISBN13: 978-0-19-281745-7. Dewey:823/.6. LCCN:86-002541.
Audience: **g,l,u,f.**

Richardson, Samuel **PR3664.P35 2001**
Pamela: Or Virtue Rewarded. Thomas Keymer & Alice Wakely (Editors). Trade Paper. Oxford University Press, Inc. New York, NY. 2001. 592p. Oxford World's Classics Ser. ISBN:0-19-282960-2, ISBN13: 978-0-19-282960-3. Dewey:823/.6. LCCN:2001-021704.
Audience: **g,l,u,f.**

Richardson, Samuel & Sherburn, George **PR3664.C4**
Clarissa. Ed. 1. Paper Text. Houghton Mifflin College Division. Boston, MA. 1962. 546p. ISBN:0-395-05164-9, ISBN13: 978-0-395-05164-1. Dewey:823.61. LCCN:62-052256.
Audience: **g,l,u,f.**

Warner, William B. **PR3664.C43**
Reading Clarissa: The Struggles of Interpretation. Cloth over Boards. Yale University Press. Cumberland, RI. 1979. 273p. ISBN:0-300-02321-9, ISBN13: 978-0-300-02321-3. Dewey:823/.6. LCCN:79-001475.
Audience: **u,f.**

Individual Authors and Works > 17th-18th C. > Rochester, John Wilmot, Earl of

Farley-Hills, David **PR3669.R2**
Rochester's Poetry. Trade Cloth. Rowman & Littlefield Publishers, Inc. Lanham, MD. 1978. 230p. ISBN:0-8476-6078-8, ISBN13: 978-0-8476-6078-0. Dewey:821/.4. LCCN:79-100289.
Audience: **l,u,f.**

Griffin, Dustin H. **PR3669.R2**
Satires Against Man: The Poems of Rochester. Trade Cloth. University of California Press. Berkeley, CA. 1974. xiii, 317p. ISBN:0-520-02394-3, ISBN13: 978-0-520-02394-9. Dewey:821/.4. LCCN:72-095304.
Audience: **u,f.**

Rochester, John W. **PR3669.R2**
The Complete Poems of John Wilmot, Earl of Rochester. Trade Paper. Books on Demand. Ann Arbor, MI. 325p. ISBN:0-8357-8077-5, ISBN13: 978-0-8357-8077-3. Dewey:821.4. LCCN:68-027768.
Audience: **g,l,u,f.**

Thormählen, Marianne **PR3669.R2 T47 1993**
Rochester: The Poems in Context. Trade Paper. Cambridge University Press. New York, NY. 2006. ISBN:0-521-02441-2, ISBN13: 978-0-521-02441-9. Dewey:821/.4.
Audience: **u,f.**

Treglown, Jeremy (Editor) **PR3669.R2.S65 1982**
Spirit of Wit: Reconsiderations of Rochester. Trade Cloth. Shoe String Press, Inc. North Haven, CT. 1982. 199p. ISBN:0-208-02012-8, ISBN13: 978-0-208-02012-3. Dewey:821/.4. LCCN:82-013751.
Audience: **l,u,f.**

Individual Authors and Works > 17th-18th C. > S

Savage, Richard **PR3671.S2**
Poetical Works. Paper Text. Textbook Publishers. Temecula, CA. 2003. 276p. ISBN:0-7581-1328-5, ISBN13: 978-0-7581-1328-3. Dewey:821.5.
Audience: **g,l,u,f.**

Scott, Sarah **PR3671.S33**
A Description of Millenium Hall, and the Country Adjacent, 1762. Library Binding. Garland Publishing, Inc. New York, NY. 1975. Flowering of the Novel Ser., Vol. 62 ISBN:0-8240-1161-9, ISBN13: 978-0-8240-1161-1. Dewey:823/.6. LCCN:74-016207.
Audience: **g,l,u,f.**

Scott, Sarah **PR3671.S33H577 1996**
The History of Sir George Ellison. Betty Rizzo (Editor). Trade Cloth. University Press of Kentucky. Lexington, KY. 1995. 288p. Eighteenth-Century Novels by Women Ser. ISBN:0-8131-1938-3, ISBN13: 978-0-8131-1938-0. Dewey:823/.6. LCCN:95-030288.
Audience: **g,l,u,f.**

Sedley, Charles **PR3671 .S4**
Poetical and Dramatic Works. Library Binding. Reprint Services Company. Temecula, CA. 1992. BCL1-PR English Literature Ser. ISBN:0-7812-7399-4, ISBN13: 978-0-7812-7399-2. Dewey:828/.4/09.
Audience: **g,l,u,f.**

Shadwell, Thomas **PR3671.S8**
The Virtuoso. Marjorie H. Nicolson & David S. Rodes (Editors). Paper Text. University of Nebraska Press. Lincoln, NE. 1966. 154p. Regents Restoration Drama Ser. ISBN:0-8032-5368-0, ISBN13: 978-0-8032-5368-1. Dewey:822.4. LCCN:65-019466.
Audience: **g,l,u,f.**

Sherbo, Arthur **PR3687.S7**
Christopher Smart: Scholar of the University. Trade Cloth. Michigan State University Press. East Lansing, MI. 1967. vi, 291p. ISBN:0-87013-110-9, ISBN13: 978-0-87013-110-3. Dewey:821/.6.
Audience: **g,l,u,f.**

Smart, Christopher **PR3687.S7 A6 1990**
Christopher Smart Selected Poems. Marcus Walsh & Karina Williamson (Editors). Trade Paper. Penguin Group (USA) Inc. New York, NY. 1991. 416p. Penguin Classics Ser. ISBN:0-14-042367-2, ISBN13: 978-0-14-042367-9. Dewey:821.6. LCCN:91-131408.
Audience: **g,l,u,f.**

Southern, Thomas **PR3699.S3**
Oroonoko: A Tragedy. Trade Cloth. Ayer Company Publishers, Inc. Manchester, NH. 1977. Black Heritage Library Collection ISBN:0-8369-8659-8, ISBN13: 978-0-8369-8659-4. Dewey:822. LCCN:75-093420.
Audience: **g,l,u,f.**

Squier, Charles L. **PR3718.Z5.S6**
Sir John Suckling. Trade Cloth. Thomson Gale. Farmington Hills, MI. 1978. 171 p. :p. English Authors Ser. ISBN:0-8057-6721-5, ISBN13: 978-0-8057-6721-6. Dewey:821/.4. LCCN:78-006429.
Audience: **l,u.**

Suckling, John **PR3718.A1 1971**
The Works of Sir John Suckling. Thomas Clayton (Commentaries by). Trade Cloth. Oxford University Press, Inc. New York, NY. 1971. xliv, 358p. ISBN:0-19-811850-3, ISBN13: 978-0-19-811850-3. Dewey:821/.4. LCCN:76-030160.
Audience: **g,l,u,f.**

Individual Authors and Works > 17th-18th C. > Shenstone, William

Humphreys, Arthur Raleigh **PR3677 .H8 1976**
William Shenstone: An Eighteenth-Century Portrait. Trade Cloth. A M S Press, Inc. New York, NY. ISBN:0-404-14673-2, ISBN13: 978-0-404-14673-3. Dewey:821/.5. LCCN:75-041146.
Audience: **l,u.**

Jung, Sandro **PR3314.J86 2003**
Poetic Meaning in the Eighteenth-Century Poems of Mark Akenside and William Shenstone. Trade Cloth. Edwin Mellen Press, The. Lewiston, NY. 2002. 280p. Mellen Studies in Literature, Vol. 159 ISBN:0-7734-6963-X, ISBN13: 978-0-7734-6963-1. Dewey:821/.509384. LCCN:2002-033718.
Audience: **u,f.**

Shenstone, William **PR3677**
Poetical Works. Library Binding. Reprint Services Company. Temecula, CA. 1992. 284p. BCL1-PR English Literature Ser. ISBN:0-7812-7400-1, ISBN13: 978-0-7812-7400-5. Dewey:821/.5.
Audience: **g,l,u,f.**

Individual Authors and Works > 17th-18th C. > Sheridan, Richard

Loftis, John C. **PR3684**
Sheridan and the Drama of Georgian England. Trade Cloth. Harvard University Press. Cambridge, MA. 1976. 186p. ISBN:0-674-80632-8, ISBN13: 978-0-674-80632-0. Dewey:828.6.
Audience: **l,u.**

Moore, Thomas **PR3683**
Memoirs of the Life of the Right Honorable Richard Brinsley Sheridan. Trade Cloth. Greenwood Publishing Group, Inc. Portsmouth, NH. 1969. ISBN:0-8371-9944-1, ISBN13: 978-0-8371-9944-3. Dewey:822.6. LCCN:69-014001.
Audience: **g,l,u,f.**

O'Toole, Fintan **PR3683.O86 1998**
A Traitor's Kiss: The Life of Richard Brinsley Sheridan. Cloth over Boards. Farrar, Straus & Giroux. New York, NY. 1998. 519p. ISBN:0-374-27931-4, ISBN13: 978-0-374-27931-8. Dewey:941/.07/092. LCCN:98-023261.
Audience: **g,l,u,f.** *Choice, 1999.*

Sheridan, Richard Brinsley **PR3683**
The School for Scandal and Other Plays. Michael Cordner (Editor). Trade Paper. Oxford University Press, Inc. New York, NY. 1998. 494p. Oxford World's Classics Ser. ISBN:0-19-282567-4, ISBN13: 978-0-19-282567-4. Dewey:822.6. LCCN:97-050491.
Audience: **g,l,u,f.**

Sheridan, Richard Brinsley **PR3680.A5 P7 1975**
Sheridan's Plays. Cecil Price (Editor). Trade Cloth. Oxford University Press, Inc. New York, NY. 1975. xxxiii, 442p. Oxford Standard Authors Ser. ISBN:0-19-254169-2, ISBN13: 978-0-19-254169-7. Dewey:822/.6. LCCN:75-330171.
Audience: **g,l,u,f.**

Sheridan, Richard Brinsley **PR3681.R8 1988**
The School for Scandal and Other Plays. Eric S. Rump (Notes by). Trade Paper. Penguin Group (USA) Inc. New York, NY. 1989. 288p. Classics Ser. ISBN:0-14-043240-X, ISBN13: 978-0-14-043240-4. Dewey:822.6. LCCN:89-132729.
Audience: **g,l,u,f.**

Worth, Katharine **PR701.W67 1992**
Sheridan and Goldsmith. Cloth Text. Palgrave Macmillan. New York, NY. 1992. 176p. English Dramatists Ser. ISBN:0-312-08392-0, ISBN13: 978-0-312-08392-2. Dewey:822.609. LCCN:92-008838.
Audience: **u,f.** *Choice, 1993.*

Individual Authors and Works > 17th-18th C. > Smith, Charlotte

Fry, Carrol L. **PR3688.S4Z64 1996**
Charlotte Smith. Trade Cloth. Thomson Gale. Farmington Hills, MI. 1996. xii, 170p. Twayne's English Authors Ser. ISBN:0-8057-7046-1, ISBN13: 978-0-8057-7046-9. Dewey:823/.6. LCCN:96-020000.
Audience: **l,u.**

Smith, Charlotte **PR3688**
Celestina. Loraine Fletcher (Editor). Trade Paper. Broadview Press. Peterborough, ON. 2004. 580p. Broadview Editions Ser. ISBN:1-55111-458-5, ISBN13: 978-1-55111-458-3. Dewey:823/.6. LCCN:2004-484854.
Audience: **g,l,u,f.**

Smith, Charlotte **PR3716**
Emmeline: The Orphan of the Castle. Loraine Fletcher (Editor). Trade Paper. Broadview Press. Peterborough, ON. 2003. 520p. ISBN:1-55111-359-7, ISBN13: 978-1-55111-359-3. Dewey:823/.6.
Audience: **g,l,u,f.**

Smith, Charlotte **PR3688.S4O5 2002**
The Old Manor House. Jacqueline M. Labbe (Editor). Trade Paper. Broadview Press. Peterborough, ON. 2002. 587p. Broadview Literary Texts Ser. ISBN:1-55111-213-2, ISBN13: 978-1-55111-213-8. Dewey:823/.6. LCCN:2003-265626.
Audience: **g,l,u,f.**

Smith, Charlotte, et al. **PR3716**
Desmond. Janet M. Todd & Antje Blank (Authors). Trade Paper. Broadview Press. Peterborough, ON. 2001. 488p. ISBN:1-55111-274-4, ISBN13: 978-1-55111-274-9. Dewey:823/.6.
Audience: **g,l,u,f.**

Individual Authors and Works > 17th-18th C. > Smollett, Tobias

Bold, Alan (Editor) **PR3697 .S57 1982**
Smollett: Author of the First Distinction. Cloth Text. Barnes & Noble Books-Imports. Lanham, MD. 1982. 240p. Critical Studies ISBN:0-389-20240-1, ISBN13: 978-0-389-20240-0. Dewey:823/.6. LCCN:82-167326.
Audience: **l,u.**

Jones, Claude E. **PR3696.J6 1970**
Smollett Studies. Trade Cloth. Phaeton Press, Inc. Staten Island, NY. 1970. 128p. ISBN:0-87753-048-3, ISBN13: 978-0-87753-048-0. Dewey:823/.6. LCCN:70-128188.
Audience: **l,u.**

Martz, Louis L. **PR3696 .M35**
The Later Career of Tobias Smollett. Trade Cloth. Shoe String Press, Inc. North Haven, CT. 1967. ix, 213p. Yale Studies in English, No. 97 ISBN:0-208-00208-1, ISBN13: 978-0-208-00208-2. Dewey:823/.6. LCCN:67-019508.
Audience: **u,f.**

Rousseau, George S. **PR3697**
Tobias Smollett. Trade Cloth. Continuum International Publishing Group, Ltd. London, 1982. 210p. ISBN:0-567-09330-1, ISBN13: 978-0-567-09330-1. Dewey:823/.6.
Audience: **l,u.**

Smollett, Tobias George **PR3694.R6 1995**
The Adventures of Roderick Random. David Blewett (Contribution by). Trade Paper. Penguin Group (USA) Inc. New York, NY. 1996. 512p. Penguin Classics Ser. ISBN:0-14-043332-5, ISBN13: 978-0-14-043332-6. Dewey:823.6. LCCN:96-164057.
Audience: **g,l,u,f.**

Smollett, Tobias George **PR3716**
The Adventures of Ferdinand Count Fathom. Paul-Gabriel Bouce (Contribution by). Trade Paper. Penguin Group (USA) Inc. New York, NY. 1990. 512p. Penguin Classics Ser. ISBN:0-14-043307-4, ISBN13: 978-0-14-043307-4. Dewey:823/.6.
Audience: **g,l,u,f.** *Choice, 1989.*

Smollett, Tobias George **PR3694.P/**
The Adventures of Peregrine Pickle. James L. Clifford (Editor), Paul-Gabriel Bouce (Revised by). Trade Paper. Oxford University Press, Inc. New York, NY. 1983. 840p. Oxford World's Classics Ser. ISBN:0-19-281663-2, ISBN13: 978-0-19-281663-4. Dewey:823/.6. LCCN:83-002454.
Audience: **g,l,u,f.**

Smollett, Tobias George **PR3694.L371 1973**
The Life and Adventures of Sir Launcelot Greaves. David Evans (Editor). Trade Cloth. Oxford University Press, Inc. New York, NY. 1973. xxvii, 234p. Oxford English Novels Ser. ISBN:0-19-255364-X, ISBN13: 978-0-19-255364-5. Dewey:823/.6. LCCN:74-162185.
Audience: **g,l,u,f.**

Smollett, Tobias George **DC25.S46 1999**
Travels Through France and Italy. Frank Felsenstein (Editor). Trade Paper. Oxford University Press, Inc. New York, NY. 1999. 464p. Oxford World's Classics Ser. ISBN:0-19-283634-X, ISBN13: 978-0-19-283634-2. Dewey:914.4/94140434. LCCN:99-217394.
Audience: **g,l,u,f.**

Smollett, Tobias George **PR3694.H8 1990**
The Expedition of Humphry Clinker. Thomas R. Preston (Editor). Trade Cloth. University of Georgia Press. Athens, GA. 1991. 544p. The Works of Tobias Smollett ISBN:0-8203-1203-7, ISBN13: 978-0-8203-1203-3. Dewey:823/.6. LCCN:89-036020.
Audience: **g,l,u,f.** *Choice, 1991.*

Spector, Robert D. **PR3698**
Smollet's Women: A Study in an Eighteenth-Century Masculine Sensibility. Trade Cloth. Greenwood Publishing Group, Inc. Portsmouth, NH. 1994. 208p. Contributions to the Study of World Literature Ser., No. 56 ISBN:0-313-28790-2, ISBN13: 978-0-313-28790-9. Dewey:823/.6. LCCN:93-049538.
Audience: **u,f.** *Choice, 1995.*

Individual Authors and Works > 17th-18th C. > Steele, Richard

Aitken, George **PR3706 .A7**
The Life of Richard Steele. Paper Text. Classic Textbooks. Murrieta, CA. 1889. ISBN:1-4047-7407-6, ISBN13: 978-1-4047-7407-0. Dewey:824/.5.
Audience: **l,u.**

Ketcham, Michael G. **PR925.K38 1985**
Transparent Designs: Reading, Performance, and Form in the Spectator Papers. Trade Cloth. University of Georgia Press. Athens, GA. 1985. 224p. ISBN:0-8203-0771-8, ISBN13: 978-0-8203-0771-8. Dewey:824/.5/09. LCCN:84-024046.
Audience: **u,f.** *Choice, 1985.*

Knight, Charles A. **Z8015.87.K55 1994**
Joseph Addison and Richard Steele: A Reference Guide, 1730-1991. Trade Cloth. Thomson Gale. Farmington Hills, MI. 1995. 584p. Reference Guide to Literature Ser. ISBN:0-8161-8980-3, ISBN13: 978-0-8161-8980-9. Dewey:016.824/5. LCCN:94-021458.
Audience: **l,u.** *Choice, 1995.*

Steele, Richard **PR3702**
Tracts and Pamphlets of Richard Steele. Rae Blanchard (Editor). Library Binding. Hippocrene Books, Inc. New York, NY. 1966. ISBN:0-374-90646-7, ISBN13: 978-0-374-90646-7. Dewey:828/.5/08.
Audience: **g,l,u,f.**

Steele, Richard **PR3701.K4**
The Plays of Richard Steele. Shirley S. Kenny (Editor). Trade Cloth. Oxford University Press, Inc. New York, NY. 1971. 460p. ISBN:0-19-812414-7, ISBN13: 978-0-19-812414-6. Dewey:822/.5. LCCN:79-027567.
Audience: **g,l,u,f.** B

Individual Authors and Works > 17th-18th C. > Sterne, Laurence

Keymer, Thomas (Editor) **PR3714.T73L385 2006**
Laurence Sterne's Tristram Shandy: A Casebook. Trade Cloth. Oxford University Press, Inc. New York, NY. 2006. 320p. Casebooks in Criticism Ser. ISBN:0-19-517560-3, ISBN13: 978-0-19-517560-8. Dewey:823/.6. LCCN:2005-022445.
Audience: **l,u.**

Kraft, Elizabeth **PR3716.K73 1996**
Laurence Sterne. Trade Cloth. Thomson Gale. Farmington Hills, MI. 1996. xviii, 163p. Twayne's English Authors Ser. ISBN:0-8057-7058-5, ISBN13: 978-0-8057-7058-2. Dewey:823/.6. LCCN:96-003082.
Audience: **l,u.** *Choice, 1997.*

Myer, Valerie G. (Editor) **PR3714.T73L38 1984**
Laurence Sterne: Riddles and Mysteries. Trade Cloth. Rowman & Littlefield Publishers, Inc. Lanham, MD. 1984. 184p. Critical Studies ISBN:0-389-20473-0, ISBN13: 978-0-389-20473-2. Dewey:823/.6. LCCN:84-002845.
Audience: **l,u.** B

New, Melvyn (Editor) **PR3716.C68 1998**
Critical Essays on Laurence Sterne. Trade Cloth. Thomson Gale. Farmington Hills, MI. 1998. 335p. Critical Essays on British Literature Ser. ISBN:0-7838-0040-1, ISBN13: 978-0-7838-0040-0. Dewey:823/.6. LCCN:97-034645.
Audience: **l,u.**

Parker, Fred **PR448.S**
Scepticism and Literature: An Essay on Pope, Hume, Sterne, and Johnson. Trade Cloth. Oxford University Press, Inc. New York, NY. 2003. 304p. ISBN:0-19-925318-8, ISBN13: 978-0-19-925318-0. Dewey:820.9005. LCCN:2004-298260.
Audience: **u,f.** *Choice, 2004.*

Ross, Ian Campbell **PR3716.R67 2001**
Laurence Sterne: A Life. Trade Cloth. Oxford University Press, Inc. New York, NY. 2001. 512p. ISBN:0-19-212235-5, ISBN13: 978-0-19-212235-3. Dewey:823/.6 B. LCCN:00-067753.
Audience: **g,l,u,f.**

Sterne, Laurence **PR3714.T7 2004**
The Life and Opinions of Tristram Shandy, Gentleman. Robert Folkenflik (Introduction by). Trade Paper. Random House Adult Trade Publishing Group. New York, NY. 2004. 704p. The Modern Library Classics ISBN:0-375-76119-5, ISBN13: 978-0-375-76119-5. Dewey:823/.6. LCCN:2004-559864.
Audience: **g,l,u,f.** B

Sterne, Laurence **PR3712**
Memoirs of Mr. Laurence Sterne, the Life and Opinions of Tristram Shandy, a Sentimental Journey, Selected Sermons and Letters. Douglas Grant (Editor). Trade Cloth. Harvard University Press. Cambridge, MA. 1950. The Reynard Library ISBN:0-674-56525-8, ISBN13: 978-0-674-56525-8. Dewey:823.6. LCCN:52-004996.
Audience: **g,l,u,f.**

Sterne, Laurence **PR3712.J3 1998**
A Sentimental Journey Through France and Italy by Mr. Yorick: With the Journal to Eliza and a Political Romance. Ian Jack (Editor, Introduction by, Notes by). Trade Paper. Oxford University Press, Inc. New York, NY. 1998. 272p. Oxford World's Classics Ser. ISBN:0-19-283522-X, ISBN13: 978-0-19-283522-2. Dewey:823/.6. LCCN:98-215901.
Audience: **g,l,u,f.**

Swearingen, James E. **PR3714.T73**
Reflexivity in Tristram Shandy: An Essay in Phenomenological Criticism. Trade Cloth. Yale University Press. Cumberland, RI. 1977. 272p. ISBN:0-300-02123-2, ISBN13: 978-0-300-02123-3. Dewey:823/.6. LCCN:77-005515.
Audience: **u,f.** B

Individual Authors and Works > 17th-18th C. > Swift, Jonathan

Barnett, Louise K. **PR3728.P58.B35**
Swift's Poetic Worlds. Trade Cloth. University of Delaware Press. Newark, DE. 1982. 224p. ISBN:0-87413-187-1, ISBN13: 978-0-87413-187-1. Dewey:821/.5. LCCN:80-054538.
Audience: **u,f.** B

Case, Arthur E. **PR3724.G8 C3**
Four Essays on Gulliver's Travels. Trade Cloth. Peter Smith Publisher, Inc. Magnolia, MA. 1990. ISBN:0-8446-1106-9, ISBN13: 978-0-8446-1106-8. Dewey:827.52.
Audience: **u,f.**

Davis, Herbert J. **PR3727 .D3 1979**
The Satire of Jonathan Swift. Trade Cloth. Greenwood Publishing Group, Inc. Portsmouth, NH. 1979. 109p. ISBN:0-313-22068-9, ISBN13: 978-0-313-22068-5. Dewey:827/.5. LCCN:79-017603.
Audience: **l,u.**

Downie, J. A. **PR3726**
Jonathan Swift: Political Writer. Paper Text. Routledge. New York, NY. 1986. 350p. ISBN:0-7102-0769-7, ISBN13: 978-0-7102-0769-2. Dewey:828/.509.
Audience: **u,f.** B

Ehrenpreis, Irvin **PR3726**
Swift: The Man, His Works, and the Age: Dr. Swift, Vol. II. Cloth Text. Harvard University Press. Cambridge, MA. 1983. 800p. ISBN:0-317-54487-X, ISBN13: 978-0-317-54487-9. Dewey:828.5.
Audience: **g,l,u,f.**

Fabricant, Carole **PR3728.S46F3 1995**
Swift's Landscape. Paper Text. University of Notre Dame Press. Notre Dame, IN. 1995. xxxv, 307p. ISBN:0-268-01754-9, ISBN13: 978-0-268-01754-5. Dewey:828/.509. LCCN:94-045617.
Audience: **u,f.**

Ferguson, Oliver Watkins **PR3727**
Jonathan Swift and Ireland. Paper Text. Textbook Publishers. Temecula, CA. 2003. viii, 217p. ISBN:0-7581-2257-8, ISBN13: 978-0-7581-2257-5. Dewey:828.5.
Audience: **u,f.**

Kelly, Ann Cline **PR3726.K45 2002**
Jonathan Swift and Popular Culture: Myth, Media and the Man. Cloth over Boards. Palgrave Macmillan. New York, NY. 2002. 256p. ISBN:0-312-23959-9, ISBN13: 978-0-312-23959-6. Dewey:828/.509 B. LCCN:2001-036569.
Audience: **u,f.** *Choice, 2002.*

Murry, John M. **PR3726**
Jonathan Swift, a Critical Biography. Paper Text. Textbook Publishers. Temecula, CA. 2003. 508p. ISBN:0-7581-7617-1, ISBN13: 978-0-7581-7617-2. Dewey:928.2.
Audience: **l,u,f.**

Rawson, Claude (Editor) **PR3727.C47 1983**
The Character of Swift's Satire: A Revised Focus. Trade Cloth. University of Delaware Press. Newark, DE. 1983. 344p. ISBN:0-87413-209-6, ISBN13: 978-0-87413-209-0. Dewey:828/.509. LCCN:81-072062.
Audience: **u,f.**

Swift, Jonathan **PR3724.G7 2005**
Gullivers Travels. Ed. 2. Trade Paper. Oxford University Press, Inc. New York, NY. 2005. 422p. Oxford World's Classics Ser. ISBN:0-19-280534-7, ISBN13: 978-0-19-280534-8. Dewey:823/.5. LCCN:2004-024295.
Audience: **g,l,u,f.**

Swift, Jonathan **PR3721**
Index to the Prose Writings. Herbert Davis & L. Landa (Editors). Cloth Text. Blackwell Publishing, Inc. Malden, MA. 1986. 400p. The Prose Writings of Jonathan Swift ISBN:0-631-00310-X, ISBN13: 978-0-631-00310-6. Dewey:821.5.
Audience: **g,l,u,f.**

Swift, Jonathan **PR3722.R64 1993**
Selected Poems: Swift. Pat Rogers (Contribution by). Trade Paper. Penguin Group (USA) Inc. New York, NY. 1993. 240p. ISBN:0-14-042377-X, ISBN13: 978-0-14-042377-8. LCCN:93-244477.
Audience: **g,l,u,f.**

Swift, Jonathan **PR3722**
The Major Works. Angus Ross & David Woolley (Editors). Trade Paper. Oxford University Press, Inc. New York, NY. 2003. 760p. Oxford World's Classics ISBN:0-19-284078-9, ISBN13: 978-0-19-284078-3. Dewey:828/.509. LCCN:2003-270050.
Audience: **g,l,u,f.**

Individual Authors and Works > 17th-18th C. > T-V

Hyde, Mary **PR3619.P5Z/**
The Thrales of Streatham Park. Trade Cloth. Harvard University Press. Cambridge, MA. 1977. 368p. ISBN:0-674-88746-8, ISBN13: 978-0-674-88746-6. Dewey:828/.609. LCCN:77-024922.
Audience: **g,l,u,f.**

Ross, Jan (Editor) **PR3736.T7A125 2005**
The Works of Thomas Traherne I: Inducements to Retiredness, a Sober View of Dr Twisses His Considerations, Seeds of Eternity or the Nature of the Soul, the Kingdom of God. Trade Cloth. Boydell & Brewer, Ltd. Woodbridge, 2005. 598p. Works of Thomas Traherne Ser. ISBN:1-84384-037-5, ISBN13: 978-1-84384-037-4. Dewey:821/.4. LCCN:2004-027955.
Audience: **g,l,u,f.** *Choice, 2005.*

Taylor, Jeremy **PR3729.T13 A6**
The Golden Grove: Selected Passages from the Sermons and Writings of Jeremy Taylor. Library Binding. Reprint Services Company. Temecula, CA. 1992. 330p. BCL1-PR English Literature Ser. ISBN:0-7812-7414-1, ISBN13: 978-0-7812-7414-2. Dewey:208.1.
Audience: **g,l,u,f.**

Thomson, James **PR3732.S4 1981**
The Seasons. James Sambrook (Editor). Trade Cloth. Oxford University Press, Inc. New York, NY. 1981. 512p. Oxford English Texts ISBN:0-19-812713-8, ISBN13: 978-0-19-812713-0. Dewey:821/.5. LCCN:79-041094.
Audience: **g,l,u,f.**

Vanbrugh, John **PR3737**
Complete Works. Bonamy Dobree & Geoffrey Webb (Editors). Trade Cloth. A M S Press, Inc. New York, NY. The Chertsey Worthies' Library ISBN:0-404-06760-3, ISBN13: 978-0-404-06760-1. Dewey:822.47. LCCN:28-018054.
Audience: **g,l,u,f.**

Vanbrugh, John **PR3737.A4 2004**
The Relapse and Other Plays. Brean S. Hammond (Introduction by, Notes by). Trade Paper. Oxford University Press, Inc. New York, NY. 2004. 432p. Oxford English Drama Ser. ISBN:0-19-283323-5, ISBN13: 978-0-19-283323-5. Dewey:822/.4. LCCN:2004-046162.
Audience: **g,l,u,f.**

Individual Authors and Works > 17th-18th C. > Vaughan, Henry

Blunden, Edmund **PR3744 .B6**
On the Poems of Henry Vaughan: Characteristics and Intimations. Library Binding. Reprint Services Company. Temecula, CA. 1992. 64p. BCL1-PR English Literature Ser. ISBN:0-7812-7416-8, ISBN13: 978-0-7812-7416-6. Dewey:821/.4.
Audience: **l,u.**

Bull, John **PR3738.B85 1998**
Vanbrugh and Farquhar. Trade Cloth. Macmillan Publishers Ltd. London, 1998. xviii, 158p. English Dramatists Ser. ISBN:0-333-46233-5, ISBN13: 978-0-333-46233-1. Dewey:822/.409. LCCN:97-032202.
Audience: **l,u.**

Hutchinson, F. E. **PR3743**
Henry Vaughan: A Life and Interpretation. Trade Paper. Kessinger Publishing, LLC. Whitefish, MT. 2005. ISBN:1-4179-9138-0, ISBN13: 978-1-4179-9138-9. Dewey:928.2.
Audience: **l,u.**

Individual Authors and Works > 17th-18th C. > W-Y

Fruchtman, Jack Jr. (Editor) **DC146.W67A4 1997**
An Eye-Witness Account of the French Revolution by Helen Maria Williams: Letters Containing a Sketch of the Politics of France. Trade Cloth. Peter Lang Publishing, Inc. New York, NY. 1997. 260p. The Age of Revolution and Romanticism Ser., Vol. 19 ISBN:0-8204-3120-6, ISBN13: 978-0-8204-3120-8. Dewey:944.04/092. LCCN:95-051554.
Audience: **u,f.**

Gilbert, Jack G. **PR3753.G5**
Edmund Waller. Library Binding. Thomson Gale. Farmington Hills, MI. 1979. 161p. English Authors Ser., No. 266 ISBN:0-8057-6763-0, ISBN13: 978-0-8057-6763-6. Dewey:821/.4. LCCN:78-031322.
Audience: **l,u.** B

Rogers, Katharine M. **PE3777**
William Wycherley. Library Binding. Thomson Gale. Farmington Hills, MI. 1983. English Authors Ser., No. 127 ISBN:0-8057-1584-3, ISBN13: 978-0-8057-1584-2. Dewey:822/.4.
Audience: **l,u.** B

Vance, John A. **PR3759.W2.Z93 1983**
Thomas and Joseph Warton. Trade Cloth. Thomson Gale. Farmington Hills, MI. 1983. 166p. English Authors Ser., No. 380 ISBN:0-8057-6866-1, ISBN13: 978-0-8057-6866-4. Dewey:821/.6/09. LCCN:83-006659.
Audience: **l,u.** B

Vance, John A. **PR3777.V36 2000**
William Wycherley and the Comedy of Fear. Trade Cloth. University of Delaware Press. Newark, DE. 2000. 259p. ISBN:0-87413-708-X, ISBN13: 978-0-87413-708-8. Dewey:822/.4. LCCN:99-089589.
Audience: **u,f.** *Choice, 2000.*

Waller, Edmund **PR3750.A1**
Poems, 1645, Together with Poems from Bodleian MS Don D 55. Trade Cloth. Scolar Press. Aldershot, 1971. [248]p. ISBN:0-85417-543-1, ISBN13: 978-0-85417-543-7. Dewey:821/.4. LCCN:72-185143.
Audience: **g,l,u,f.** B

Walpole, Horace **PR3757.W2**
The Castle of Otranto. Trade Paper. Dover Publications, Inc. Mineola, NY. 2004. 128p. Dover Thrift Editions Ser. ISBN:0-486-43412-5, ISBN13: 978-0-486-43412-4. Dewey:823/.6. LCCN:2003-070015.
Audience: **g,l,u,f.**

Walpole, Horace **PR3757.W2**
Horace Walpole's, Miscellany 1786-1795. Lars Troide (Editor). Cloth over Boards. Yale University Press. Cumberland, RI. 1978. 216p. Yale Studies in English, No. 188 ISBN:0-300-02105-4, ISBN13: 978-0-300-02105-9. Dewey:828/.609. LCCN:77-014117.
Audience: **g,l,u,f.** B

Wesley, Charles **BX8217.W47 2001**
The Sermons of Charles Wesley: A Critical Edition with Introduction and Notes. Kenneth G. C. Newport (Author, Editor). Trade Cloth. Oxford University Press, Inc. New York, NY. 2001. 422p. ISBN:0-19-826949-8, ISBN13: 978-0-19-826949-6. Dewey:252/.07. LCCN:00-068608.
Audience: **g,l,u,f.**

Wycherley, William **PR3771 .D59**
The Country Wife and Other Plays: Love in a Wood; The Gentleman Dancing-Master; The Country Wife; The Plain Dealer. Peter Dixon (Editor). Trade Paper. Oxford University Press, Inc. New York, NY. 2002. 520p. Oxford World's Classics Ser. ISBN:0-19-283454-1, ISBN13: 978-0-19-283454-6. Dewey:822/.4.
Audience: **g,l,u,f.**

Young, Edward **PR3780 .A2**
The Poetical works of Edward Young ... Trade Cloth. Scholarly Publishing Office, University of Michigan Library. Ann Arbor, MI. 2004. ISBN:1-4181-3080-X, ISBN13: 978-1-4181-3080-0. Dewey:821/.5.
Audience: **g,l,u,f.**

Individual Authors and Works > 19th C. > A-B

Ballantyne, R. M. **PR5684**
The Coral Island. Trade Paper. Kessinger Publishing, LLC. Whitefish, MT. 2004. ISBN:1-4192-5765-X, ISBN13: 978-1-4192-5765-0. Dewey:823/.8.
Audience: **g,l,u,f.**

Beckford, William **PR4091.V4 1970**
Vathek. Trade Cloth. Oxford University Press, Inc. New York, NY. 1970. xliii, 187p. ISBN:0-19-255337-2, ISBN13: 978-0-19-255337-9. Dewey:843/.5. LCCN:76-487817.
Audience: **g,l,u,f.** B

Boucicault, Dion **PR4161.B2**
Selected Plays. Andrew Parkin (Editor, Introduction by). Trade Cloth. Catholic University of America Press. Washington, DC. 1987. 407p. Irish Dramatic Texts Ser., No. 4 ISBN:0-8132-0616-2, ISBN13: 978-0-8132-0616-5. Dewey:822/.8. LCCN:85-031345.
Audience: **g,l,u,f.**

Braddon, Mary Elizabeth **PR4989**
Lady Audley's Secret. Trade Paper. Oxford University Press, Inc. New York, NY. 1998. 490p. Oxford World's Classics Ser. ISBN:0-19-283520-3, ISBN13: 978-0-19-283520-8. Dewey:823/.8.
Audience: **g,l,u,f.**

Wolff, Robert Lee **PR4989.M4.Z96**
Sensational Victorian: The Life and Fiction of Mary Elizabeth Braddon. Trade Cloth. Garland Publishing, Inc. New York, NY. 1979. xiv, 529p. ISBN:0-8240-1618-1, ISBN13: 978-0-8240-1618-0. Dewey:823/.8. LCCN:76-052717.
Audience: **g,l,u,f.**

Individual Authors and Works > 19th C. > Arnold, Matthew

ApRoberts, Ruth **PR4024**
Arnold and God. Trade Cloth. University of California Press. Berkeley, CA. 1983. 304p. ISBN:0-520-04747-8, ISBN13: 978-0-520-04747-1. Dewey:821/.8. LCCN:82-010847.
Audience: **u,f.**

Arnold, Matthew **LC72**
Complete Prose Works. Paper Text. Textbook Publishers. Temecula, CA. 2003. ISBN:0-7581-2043-5, ISBN13: 978-0-7581-2043-4. Dewey:999.
Audience: **g,l,u,f.**

Arnold, Matthew **PR4022.D5**
Discourses in America. Paper Text. Classic Books. Murrieta, CA. 2001. Collected Works of Matthew Arnold ISBN:0-7426-7176-3, ISBN13: 978-0-7426-7176-8. Dewey:809.
Audience: **g,l,u,f.**

Arnold, Matthew **PR4022**
Essays in Criticism: Second Series. Paper Text. Textbook Publishers. Temecula, CA. 2003. xviii, 243p. ISBN:0-7581-8850-1, ISBN13: 978-0-7581-8850-2. Dewey:824.8.
Audience: **u,f.**

Arnold, Matthew **PR4023**
The Letters of Matthew Arnold, 1848-1888, Set. Library Binding. Reprint Services Company. Temecula, CA. 1992. BCL1-PR English Literature Ser. ISBN:0-7812-7424-9, ISBN13: 978-0-7812-7424-1. Dewey:821.8.
Audience: **u,f.**

Arnold, Matthew **PA4037**
On Translating Homer. Paper Text. Classic Books. Murrieta, CA. 2001. 200p. ISBN:0-7426-9017-2, ISBN13: 978-0-7426-9017-2. Dewey:883/.01.
Audience: **u,f.**

Arnold, Matthew **PR4022 .N4**
Poems: A New Edition. Paper Text. Classic Books. Murrieta, CA. 2001. Collected Works of Matthew Arnold ISBN:0-7426-7154-2, ISBN13: 978-0-7426-7154-6. Dewey:123.
Audience: **g,l,u,f.**

Arnold, Matthew **PR4021.A46 1995**
Matthew Arnold. Miriam Allott (Editor). Trade Paper. Oxford University Press, Inc. New York, NY. 1995. 240p. Oxford Poetry Library ISBN:0-19-282273-X, ISBN13: 978-0-19-282273-4. Dewey:821.8. LCCN:94-029359.
Audience: **g,l,u,f.**

Arnold, Matthew **HN389.A72 1994**
Culture and Anarchy: Landmarks in the History of Education. Samuel Lipman (Editor), Maurice Cowling (Commentaries by). Cloth over Boards. Yale University Press. Cumberland, RI. 1994. 256p. Rethinking the Western Tradition Ser. ISBN:0-300-05866-7, ISBN13: 978-0-300-05866-6. Dewey:306.0941. LCCN:93-002427.
Audience: **u,f.**

Arnold, Matthew **PR5823**
The Portable Matthew Arnold. Lionel Trilling (Editor). Trade Paper. Penguin Group (USA) Inc. New York, NY. 1980. 672p. Portable Library ISBN:0-14-015045-5, ISBN13: 978-0-14-015045-2. Dewey:828/.809. LCCN:80-011582.
Audience: **g,l,u,f.**

Collini, Stefan **PR4024.C64 1988**
Arnold. Trade Paper. Oxford University Press, Inc. New York, NY. 1989. 144p. Past Masters Ser. ISBN:0-19-287660-0, ISBN13: 978-0-19-287660-7. Dewey:821/.8. LCCN:88-014174.
Audience: **u,f.** *Choice, 1989.*

Dawson, Carl (Editor) **PR4024**
Matthew Arnold: The Poetry. Paper over Boards. Routledge. New York, NY. 1996. 480p. Critical Heritage Ser. ISBN:0-415-13473-0, ISBN13: 978-0-415-13473-6. Dewey:821.8.
Audience: **u,f.**

Dawson, Carl (Editor) **PR4024**
Matthew Arnold: Prose Writings. Paper over Boards. Routledge. New York, NY. 1996. 476p. Critical Heritage Ser. ISBN:0-415-13472-2, ISBN13: 978-0-415-13472-9. Dewey:821.8.
Audience: **u,f.**

Dickstein, Morris **PS78.D5 1992**
The Critic and Society: From Matthew Arnold to the New Historicism. Trade Cloth. Oxford University Press, Inc. New York, NY. 1992. 240p. ISBN:0-19-507399-1, ISBN13: 978-0-19-507399-7. Dewey:801/.95/09730904. LCCN:91-043271.
Audience: **u,f.** *Choice, 1993.*

Hamilton, Ian **PR4023.H27 1999**
A Gift Imprisoned: The Poetic Life of Matthew Arnold. Cloth Text. Basic Books. New York, NY. 1999. 256p. ISBN:0-465-04421-2, ISBN13: 978-0-465-04421-4. Dewey:821.8. LCCN:00-687309.
Audience: **u,f.** *Choice, 1999.*

Honan, Park **PR4023 .H6 1983**
Matthew Arnold: A Life. Trade Paper. Harvard University Press. Cambridge, MA. 1983. 512p. ISBN:0-674-55465-5, ISBN13: 978-0-674-55465-8. Dewey:821/.8. LCCN:82-021234.
Audience: **g,l,u,f.**

MacHann, Clinton **PR4023.M28 1997**
Matthew Arnold: A Literary Life. Cloth over Boards. Palgrave Macmillan. New York, NY. 1998. 192p. Literary Lives Ser. ISBN:0-312-21031-0, ISBN13: 978-0-312-21031-1. Dewey:[B]. LCCN:97-018187.
Audience: **g,l,u,f.** *Choice, 1998.*

MacHann, Clinton & Burt, Forrest D. (Editors) **PR4024.M376 1988**
Matthew Arnold in His Time and Ours: Centenary Essays. Cloth Text. University Press of Virginia. Charlottesville, VA. 1988. 220p. ISBN:0-8139-1173-7, ISBN13: 978-0-8139-1173-1. Dewey:821/.8. LCCN:87-025271.
Audience: **u,f.** *Choice, 1988.*

Schneider, Mary W. **PR4024.S295 1989**
Poetry in the Age of Democracy: The Literary Criticism of Matthew Arnold. Trade Cloth. University Press of Kansas. Lawrence, KS. 1989. xii, 228p. ISBN:0-7006-0380-8, ISBN13: 978-0-7006-0380-0. Dewey:821/.8. LCCN:88-029096.
Audience: **u,f.** *Choice, 1989.*

Trilling, Lionel **PR4023 .T7 1977**
Matthew Arnold. Trade Cloth. Harcourt Trade Publishers. New York, NY. 1978. 480p. ISBN:0-15-158202-5, ISBN13: 978-0-15-158202-0. Dewey:821/.8. LCCN:77-025294.
Audience: **g,l,u,f.** B

Individual Authors and Works > 19th C. > Austen, Jane

Auerbach, Emily **PR4037.A93 2004**
Searching for Jane Austen. Trade Cloth. University of Wisconsin Press. Chicago, IL. 2004. 358p. ISBN:0-299-20180-5, ISBN13: 978-0-299-20180-7. Dewey:823/.7. LCCN:2004-005252.
Audience: **g,l,u,f.** *Choice, 2005.*

Austen, Jane **PR4034.N7 2004**
Northanger Abbey. Trade Paper. W. W. Norton & Company, Inc. New York, NY. 2004. 384p. A Norton Critical Edition Ser. ISBN:0-393-97850-8, ISBN13: 978-0-393-97850-6. Dewey:823/.7. LCCN:2004-054759.
Audience: **g,l,u,f.**

Austen, Jane **PR4034.P7 2001**
Pride and Prejudice. Ed. 3. Trade Paper. W. W. Norton & Company, Inc. New York, NY. 2000. 422p. Critical Editions Ser. ISBN:0-393-97604-1, ISBN13: 978-0-393-97604-5. Dewey:823/.7. LCCN:00-033956.
Audience: **g,l,u,f.**

Austen, Jane **PR4034**
Volume the Third. Library Binding. Folcroft Library Editions. Folcroft, PA. 1985. ISBN:0-8414-1678-8, ISBN13: 978-0-8414-1678-9. Dewey:823.7.
Audience: **g,l,u,f.**

Austen, Jane **PZ3**
The Watsons. Trade Cloth. Greenwood Publishing Group, Inc. Portsmouth, NH. 1973. 318p. ISBN:0-8371-6598-9, ISBN13: 978-0-8371-6598-1. Dewey:823/.7. LCCN:72-009808.
Audience: **g,l,u,f.**

Austen, Jane **PR4034.L6 1963**
Volume the Second. Southam, B.C.. Oxford, Clarendon Press. 1963.
Audience: **g,u,f.**

Austen, Jane **PR4030**
Volume the First. David Cecil (Foreword by). Cloth Text. Continuum International Publishing Group, Ltd. London, 1984. 142p. ISBN:0-485-10501-2, ISBN13: 978-0-485-10501-8. Dewey:828/.709.
Audience: **g.**

Austen, Jane **PR4034**
Lady Susan. R. W. Chapman (Editor). Trade Paper. Dover Publications, Inc. Mineola, NY. 2005. 80p. ISBN:0-486-44407-4, ISBN13: 978-0-486-44407-9. Dewey:823/.7. LCCN:2005-049221.
Audience: **g,l,u,f.**

Austen, Jane **PR4030**
The Oxford Illustrated Jane Austen, Set. Ed. 3. R. W. Chapman (Editor). Trade Cloth. Oxford University Press, Inc. New York, NY. 1988. 3, 184p. Oxford Illustrated Austen Ser. ISBN:0-19-254707-0, ISBN13: 978-0-19-254707-1. Dewey:823.7.
Audience: **g,u,f.**

Austen, Jane **PR4034.M3 1998**
Joseph Andrews. Claudia L. Johnson (Editor). Trade Paper. W. W. Norton & Company, Inc. New York, NY. 1998. 538p. Critical Editions Ser. ISBN:0-393-96791-3, ISBN13: 978-0-393-96791-3. Dewey:823/.7. LCCN:96-049462.
Audience: **g,l,u,f.**

Austen, Jane **PR4036.A4 1997**
Jane Austen's Letters. Ed. 3. Deirdre Le Faye (Editor). Trade Paper. Oxford University Press, Inc. New York, NY. 1997. 672p. ISBN:0-19-283297-2, ISBN13: 978-0-19-283297-9. Dewey:823/.7 B. LCCN:96-038253.
Audience: **g,l,u,f.** *Choice, 1995.*

Austen, Jane **PR4034.E5 2000**
Emma: Critical Edition. Ed. 3. Stephen M. Parrish (Editor). Trade Paper. W. W. Norton & Company, Inc. New York, NY. 2000. 464p. Critical Editions Ser. ISBN:0-393-97284-4, ISBN13: 978-0-393-97284-9. Dewey:823/.7. LCCN:99-048830.
Audience: **g,l,u,f.**

Austen, Jane **PR4034.P4 1995**
Persuasion. Patricia M. Spacks (Editor). Paper Text. W. W. Norton & Company, Inc. New York, NY. 1994. 316p. Critical Editions Ser. ISBN:0-393-96018-8, ISBN13: 978-0-393-96018-1. Dewey:823/.7. LCCN:94-004510.
Audience: **g,l,u,f.**

Austen, Jane **PR4036**
Love and Friendship: And Other Early Works. Fay Weldon (Introduction by). Trade Paper. Hesperus Press. London, 2003. 112p. Hesperus Classics Ser. ISBN:1-84391-060-8, ISBN13: 978-1-84391-060-2. Dewey:823.7.
Audience: **g,l,u,f.**

Austen-Leigh, James E. **PR4036.A8 2002**
A Memoir of Jane Austen: And Other Family Recollections. Kathryn Sutherland (Editor). Trade Paper. Oxford University Press, Inc. New York, NY. 2002. 340p. Oxford World's Classics Ser. ISBN:0-19-284074-6, ISBN13: 978-0-19-284074-5. Dewey:823/.7 B. LCCN:2002-029571.
Audience: **g,l,u,f.**

Babb, Howard S. **PR4037.B3 1967**
Jane Austen's Novels: The Fabric of Dialogue. Ed. 2. Archon Books. 1967.
Audience: **u,f.**

Bush, Douglas **PR4036.B8**
Jane Austen. New York, Macmillan Pub. Co. 1975. Masters of World Literature Series; 14 ISBN:0-02-519600-6, ISBN13: 978-0-02-519600-1.
Audience: **g,u,f.**

Butler, Marilyn **PR4037 .B8**
Jane Austen and the War of Ideas. Trade Cloth. Oxford University Press, Inc. New York, NY. 1975. 310p. ISBN:0-19-812068-0, ISBN13: 978-0-19-812068-1. Dewey:823/.7. LCCN:75-327777.
Audience: **u,f.**

Chapman, R. W. **PR4036.C5**
Jane Austen: Facts and Problems. Oxford, Clarendon Press. 1949. Clark Lectures
Audience: **g,l,u,f.**

Collins, Irene **PR4038.C53C64 1993**
Jane Austen and the Clergy. Trade Cloth. Continuum International Publishing Group, Ltd. London, 1994. 256p. ISBN:1-85285-114-7, ISBN13: 978-1-85285-114-9. Dewey:823.7. LCCN:94-002050.
Audience: **g,l,u,f.** *Choice, 1994.*

Copeland, Edward & McMaster, Juliet (Editors) **PR4036 .C3 1997**
The Cambridge Companion to Jane Austen. Cloth Text. Cambridge University Press. New York, NY. 1997. 267p. Companions to Literature Ser. ISBN:0-521-49517-2, ISBN13: 978-0-521-49517-2. Dewey:828.7. LCCN:96-023387.
Audience: **l,u.** *Choice, 1998.*

Fergus, Jan **PR4036.F47 1991**
Jane Austen: A Literary Life. Richard Dutton (Editor). Trade Cloth. Palgrave Macmillan. New York, NY. 1991. 208p. Literary Lives Ser. ISBN:0-312-05712-1, ISBN13: 978-0-312-05712-1. Dewey:823/.7 B. LCCN:90-047976.
Audience: **g,u,f.** *Choice, 1992.*

Galperin, William H. **PR4037.G35 2002**
The Historical Austen. Book, Other. University of Pennsylvania Press. Philadelphia, PA. 2002. 288p. ISBN:0-8122-3687-4, ISBN13: 978-0-8122-3687-3. Dewey:823/.7. LCCN:2002-074031.
Audience: **g,l,u,f.** *Choice, 2004.*

Gill, Richard & Gregory, Susan **PR4037.G54 2002**
Mastering the Novels of Jane Austen. Trade Paper. Palgrave Macmillan. New York, NY. 2003. 384p. Master Ser. ISBN:0 333-94898-X, ISBN13: 978-0-333-94898-9. Dewey:823/.7. LCCN:2002-028683.
Audience: **g,l,u,f.**

Grey, J. David (Editor) **PR4037.J35 1989**
Jane Austen's Beginnings: The Juvenilia and "Lady Susan". Trade Cloth. University of Rochester Press. Rochester, NY. 1991. 294p. Nineteenth-Century Studies ISBN:0-8357-1916-2, ISBN13: 978-0-8357-1916-2. Dewey:823/.7. LCCN:88-039518.
Audience: **l,u,f.** *Choice, 1989.*

Halperin, John **PR4036**
The Life of Jane Austen. Trade Paper. Johns Hopkins University Press. Baltimore, MD. 1996. 432p. ISBN:0-8018-5509-8, ISBN13: 978-0-8018-5509-2. Dewey:823/.7.
Audience: **g,u,f.**

Hardy, Barbara **PR4037**
A Reading of Jane Austen. Trade Paper. Continuum International Publishing Group, Ltd. London, 1997. 192p. ISBN:0-485-12032-1, ISBN13: 978-0-485-12032-5. Dewey:823/.7.
Audience: **g,l,u,f.**

Honan, Park **PR4036**
Jane Austen: Her Life. Trade Paper. Ballantine Books. New York, NY. 1989. 464p. ISBN:0-449-90319-2, ISBN13: 978-0-449-90319-3. Dewey:823/.7.
Audience: **g,l,u,f.** *Choice, 1988.*

Jenkins, Elizabeth **PR4036**
Jane Austen. Library Binding. Richard West. Philadelphia, PA. 1987. 286p. ISBN:0-8492-5614-3, ISBN13: 978-0-8492-5614-1. Dewey:823/.7.
Audience: **g,u,f.**

Johnson, Claudia L. **PR4038.P6J64**
Jane Austen: Women, Politics, and the Novel. Trade Paper. University of Chicago Press. Chicago, IL. 1990. 212p. ISBN:0-226-40139-1, ISBN13: 978-0-226-40139-3. Dewey:823.7.
Audience: **u,f.** *Choice, 1989.*

Johnson, Claudia L. **PR4034.S4 2002**
Sense and Sensibility. Trade Cloth. W. W. Norton & Company, Inc. New York, NY. 2001. xviii, 416p. Critical Editions Ser. ISBN:0-393-97751-X, ISBN13: 978-0-393-97751-6. Dewey:823/.7. LCCN:2001-042709.
Audience: **g,l,u,f.**

Knox-Shaw, Peter **PR4038.P5K68 2004**
Jane Austen and the Enlightenment. Trade Cloth. Cambridge University Press. New York, NY. 2004. 288p. ISBN:0-521-84346-4, ISBN13: 978-0-521-84346-1. Dewey:823/.7. LCCN:2004-049658.
Audience: **u,f.** *Choice, 2005.*

Lascelles, Mary **PR4037.L37 1995**
Jane Austen and Her Art. Trade Paper. Continuum International Publishing Group, Ltd. London, 1995. 240p. ISBN:0-485-12113-1, ISBN13: 978-0-485-12113-1. Dewey:823/.7. LCCN:94-044603.
Audience: **g,l,u,f.**

Liddell, Robert **PR4037.L5 1974**
The Novels of Jane Austen. Trade Cloth. Penguin Group (USA) Inc. New York, NY. 1974. iii-xiv,p. ISBN:0-7139-0729-0, ISBN13: 978-0-7139-0729-2. Dewey:823/.7. LCCN:75-300167.
Audience: **g,l,u,f.**

Litz, A. Walton **PR4037.L57**
Jane Austen, a Study of Her Artistic Development. Oxford University Press. 1965.
Audience: **u,f.**

Litz, Walton **PR4036 .J37 1986**
Jane Austen Handbook. David J. Grey & Brian Southam (Editors). Trade Cloth. Continuum International Publishing Group, Ltd. London, 1986. 528p. ISBN:0-485-11301-5, ISBN13: 978-0-485-11301-3. Dewey:823/.7. LCCN:86-194658.
Audience: **g,l,u,f.**

Looser, Devoney **PR4038.F44J36 1995**
Jane Austen and Discourses of Feminism. Cloth over Boards. Palgrave Macmillan. New York, NY. 1995. 208p. ISBN:0-312-12367-1, ISBN13: 978-0-312-12367-3. Dewey:823/.7. LCCN:95-022180.
Audience: **u,f.** *Choice, 1996.*

Lynch, Deidre (Editor) **PR4037.J39 2000**
Janeites: Austen's Disciples and Devotees. Trade Paper. Princeton University Press. Princeton, NJ. 2000. 244p. ISBN:0-691-05006-6, ISBN13: 978-0-691-05006-5. Dewey:823/.7. LCCN:00-021205.
Audience: **g,u,f.** *Choice, 2001.*

Miller, D. A. **PR4037.M55 2003**
Jane Austen, or the Secret of Style. Trade Cloth. Princeton University Press. Princeton, NJ. 2003. 136p. ISBN:0-691-09075-0, ISBN13: 978-0-691-09075-7. Dewey:813.7. LCCN:2002-193067.
Audience: **g,u,f.** *Choice, 2004.*

Moler, Kenneth L. **PR4034.P72M64 1989**
Pride and Prejudice: A Study in Artistic Economy. Trade Cloth. Thomson Gale. Farmington Hills, MI. 1988. 144p. Twayne's Masterworks Studies, No. 21 ISBN:0-8057-7983-3, ISBN13: 978-0-8057-7983-7. Dewey:823/.7. LCCN:88-016335.
Audience: **g,l,u,f.** *Choice, 1989.*

Morrison, Robert (Editor) **PR4034.P72J368 2005**
Pride and Prejudice: A Sourcebook. Paper over Boards. Routledge. New York, NY. 2005. 192p. Routledge Guides to Literature Ser. ISBN:0-415-26849-4, ISBN13: 978-0-415-26849-3. Dewey:823/.7. LCCN:2004-017563.
Audience: **g,l,u,f.**

Mudrick, Marvin **PR4038.I7 M8**
Jane Austen: Irony As Defense and Discovery. Paper Text. Textbook Publishers. Temecula, CA. 2003. 267p. ISBN:0-7581-5783-5, ISBN13: 978-0-7581-5783-6. Dewey:823/.7.
Audience: **g,l,u,f.** B

Olsen, Kirstin **PR4036**
All Things Austen: An Encyclopedia of Austen's World. Cloth Text. Greenwood Publishing Group, Inc. Portsmouth, NH. 2005. 876p. ISBN:0-313-33032-8, ISBN13: 978-0-313-33032-2. Dewey:823.7.
Audience: **g,l,u,f.** *Choice, 2005.*

Parrill, Sue **PR4038.F55P37 2002**
Jane Austen on Film and Television: A Critical Study of the Adaptations. Paper Text. McFarland & Company, Incorporated Publishers. Jefferson, NC. 2002. 229p. ISBN:0-7864-1349-2, ISBN13: 978-0-7864-1349-2. Dewey:791.43/6. LCCN:2002-000752.
Audience: **g,l,u,f.** *Choice, 2002.*

Poovey, Mary **PR469.W65P66 1985**
The Proper Lady and the Woman Writer: Ideology as Style in the Works of Mary Wollstonecraft, Mary Shelley, and Jane Austen. Catherine R. Stimpson (Foreword by). Trade Paper. University of Chicago Press. Chicago, IL. 1985. 250p. Women in Culture and Society Ser. ISBN:0-226-67528-9, ISBN13: 978-0-226-67528-2. Dewey:823.7093522. LCCN:83-003664.
Audience: **u,f.**

Pucci, Suzanne R. & Thompson, James (Editors) **PR4038.F55J33 2003**
Jane Austen and Co.: Remaking the Past in Contemporary Culture. Paper Text. State University of New York Press. Albany, NY. 2003. vi, 277p. ISBN:0-7914-5616-1, ISBN13: 978-0-7914-5616-3. Dewey:791.43/6. LCCN:2002-029235.
Audience: **u,f.** *Choice, 2003.*

Ross, Josephine **PR4038.E46R67 2003**
Jane Austen: A Companion. Trade Cloth. Rutgers University Press. Piscataway, NJ. 2003. 288p. ISBN:0-8135-3299-X, ISBN13: 978-0-8135-3299-8. Dewey:823/.7 B. LCCN:2002-036745.
Audience: **g,l,u,f.** *Choice, 2003.*

Ruoff, Gene W. **PR4034.S43 R86 1992**
Sense and Sensibility. Trade Paper. Palgrave Macmillan. New York, NY. 1992. Critical Studies of Key Texts Ser. ISBN:0-312-08599-0, ISBN13: 978-0-312-08599-5. Dewey:823/.7. LCCN:92-017361.
Audience: **g,l,u,f.**

Simons, Judy (Editor) **PR4034.M33M363 1997**
Mansfield Park and Persuasion. Cloth over Boards. Palgrave Macmillan. New York, NY. 1997. 234p. New Casebooks Ser. ISBN:0-312-17344-X, ISBN13: 978-0-312-17344-9. Dewey:823.7. LCCN:96-051471.
Audience: **g,l,u,f.** *Choice, 1997.*

Southam, B. C. **PR4037**
Jane Austen, 1811-1870, Vol. 1. Paper over Boards. Routledge. New York, NY. 1996. 286p. Critical Heritage Ser. ISBN:0-415-13456-0, ISBN13: 978-0-415-13456-9. Dewey:823.7.
Audience: **g,l,u,f.**

Southam, B. C. **PR4037**
Jane Austen, 1870-1940, Vol. 2. Paper over Boards. Routledge. New York, NY. 1996. 320p. Critical Heritage Ser. ISBN:0-415-13457-9, ISBN13: 978-0-415-13457-6. Dewey:823.7.
Audience: **g,l,u,f.**

Sulloway, Alison G. **PR4037.S85 1989**
Jane Austen and the Province of Womanhood. Trade Cloth. University of Pennsylvania Press. Philadelphia, PA. 1989. 252p. ISBN:0-8122-8171-3, ISBN13: 978-0-8122-8171-2. Dewey:823/.7. LCCN:88-038889.
Audience: **u,f.** *Choice, 1989.*

Sunderrajan & Park **PR4037**
Postcolonial Jane Austen. Trade Paper. Routledge. New York, NY. 2004. 272p. Postcolonial Literatures Ser. ISBN:0-415-34062-4, ISBN13: 978-0-415-34062-5. Dewey:823.7.
Audience: **u,f.**

Tandon, Bharat **PR4038.C575T36 2003**
Jane Austen and the Morality of Conversation. Trade Cloth. Wimbledon Publishing Company. London, 2003. 313p. Anthem Nineteenth Century Studies ISBN:1-84331-101-1, ISBN13: 978-1-84331-101-0. Dewey:823/.7. LCCN:2004-401265.
Audience: **u,f.** *Choice, 2004.*

Waldron, Mary **PR4037 .W29 1999**
Jane Austen and the Fiction of Her Time. Cloth Text. Cambridge University Press. New York, NY. 1999. 204p. ISBN:0-521-65130-1, ISBN13: 978-0-521-65130-1. Dewey:823/.7. LCCN:98-041681.
Audience: **g,l,u,f.** *Choice, 1999.*

Watt, Ian (Editor) **PR4037**
Jane Austen: A Collection of Critical Essays. Trade Paper. John Wiley & Sons, Inc. Hoboken, NJ. 1963. 192p. ISBN:0-13-053751-9, ISBN13: 978-0-13-053751-5. Dewey:823.7.
Audience: **g,l,u,f.**

Weldon, Fay **PR4037**
Letters to Alice: On First Reading Jane Austen. Jenifer Smith (Editor), Judith Baxter (Contribution by). Trade Paper. Cambridge University Press. New York, NY. 1998. 224p. Cambridge Literature Ser. ISBN:0-521-58928-2, ISBN13: 978-0-521-58928-4. Dewey:823.7.
Audience: **g,l,u.**

Wiltshire, John **PR4037 .W54 2001**
Recreating Jane Austen. Cloth Text. Cambridge University Press. New York, NY. 2001. 192p. ISBN:0-521-80246-6, ISBN13: 978-0-521-80246-8. Dewey:823.7. LCCN:2001-025451.
Audience: **g,l,u,f.** *Choice, 2002.*

Wright, Andrew **PR4036**
Jane Austen's Novels. Ed. 2. Trade Paper. Penguin Group (USA) Inc. New York, NY. 1972. 208p. ISBN:0-14-021483-6, ISBN13: 978-0-14-021483-3. Dewey:823/.7. LCCN:73-155270.
Audience: **g,l,u,f.**

Individual Authors and Works > 19th C. > Barrie, J. M.

Barrie, J. M. **PZ7.B27539PD 2004**
Peter Pan. F. D. Bedford (Illustrator), Anne McCaffrey (Introduction by). Trade Paper, Perfect. Random House, Inc. New York, NY. 2004. 192p. Modern Library Classics ISBN:0-8129-7297-X, ISBN13: 978-0-8129-7297-9. Dewey:[Fic]. LCCN:2004-049941.
Audience: **g,l,u,f.**

Barrie, J. M. **PR5366**
Peter Pan and Other Plays: The Admirable Crichton; Peter Pan; When Wendy Grew Up; What Every Woman Knows; Mary Rose. Peter Hollindale (Editor, Introduction by). Trade Paper. Oxford University Press, Inc. New York, NY. 1999. 374p. Oxford World's Classics Ser. ISBN:0-19-283919-5, ISBN13: 978-0-19-283919-0. Dewey:822.9/12.
Audience: **g,l,u,f.**

Barrie, J. M. & Phelps, William Lyon **PR4074**
The Representative Plays. Trade Paper. Kessinger Publishing, LLC. Whitefish, MT. 2005. ISBN:1-4179-3259-7, ISBN13: 978-1-4179-3259-7. Dewey:822.9.
Audience: **g,l,u,f.**

Birkin, Andrew **PR4076.B5 2003**
J. M. Barrie and the Lost Boys. Trade Paper. Yale University Press. Cumberland, RI. 2003. 344p. ISBN:0-300-09822-7, ISBN13: 978-0-300-09822-8. Dewey:828/.91209 B. LCCN:2004-273147.
Audience: **g,l,u,f.**

Wright, Allen **PR4076.W73**
J. M. Barrie: Glamour of Twilight. Trade Cloth. Ramsay Head Press. Edinburgh, 1976. 96p. ISBN:0-902859-37-4, ISBN13: 978-0-902859-37-1. Dewey:828/.9/1209. LCCN:77-363590.
Audience: **u,f.**

Individual Authors and Works > 19th C. > The Brontes

Allott, Miriam (Editor) **PR4168**
Brontes. Paper over Boards. Routledge. New York, NY. 1996. 496p. Critical Heritage Ser. ISBN:0-415-13461-7, ISBN13: 978-0-415-13461-3. Dewey:823.809.
Audience: **u,f.**

Barker, Juliet **PR4168.B763 1998**
The Brontes: A Life in Letters. Trade Cloth. Overlook Press, The. New York, NY. 1998. 448p. ISBN:0-87951-838-3, ISBN13: 978-0-87951-838-7. Dewey:823/.809. LCCN:97-024201.
Audience: **u,f.**

Bronte, Charlotte **PR4165.A4 1971**
Complete Poems of Charlotte Bronte. Trade Cloth. Scholarly Press, Inc. Saint Clair Shores, MI. 1972. 266p. Literature Ser. ISBN:0-403-00534-5, ISBN13: 978-0-403-00534-5. Dewey:821/.8. LCCN:73-131647.
Audience: **g,l,u,f.**

Bronte, Charlotte **PR4167.J3 2000**
Jane Eyre: Critical Edition. Ed. 3. Richard J. Dunn (Commentaries by). Trade Paper. W. W. Norton & Company, Inc. New York, NY. 2000. 548p. Critical Editions Ser. ISBN:0-393-97542-8, ISBN13: 978-0-393-97542-0. Dewey:823./8. LCCN:00-055450.
Audience: **g,l,u,f.**

Bronte, Charlotte **PR4167**
Jane Eyre. Jane Jack & Margaret Smith (Editors). Trade Cloth. Oxford University Press, Inc. New York, NY. 1969. xxxiii, 635p. Clarendon Edition of the Novels of the Brontes Ser. ISBN:0-19-811490-7, ISBN13: 978-0-19-811490-1. Dewey:FIC.
Audience: **l,u,f.**

Bronte, Charlotte **PR5684**
Shirley. Herbert Rosengarten & Margaret Smith (Editors). Cloth Text. Oxford University Press, Inc. New York, NY. 1979. 878p. Clarendon Edition of the Novels of the Brontes Ser. ISBN:0-19-812565-8, ISBN13: 978-0-19-812565-5. Dewey:823/.8. LCCN:78-040742.
Audience: **g,l,u,f.**

Bronte, Charlotte **PR4167.P7 1987**
The Professor. Margaret Smith & Herbert Rosengarten (Editors). Cloth Text. Oxford University Press, Inc. New York, NY. 1987. 400p. Clarendon Edition of the Novels of the Brontes Ser. ISBN:0-19-812694-8, ISBN13: 978-0-19-812694-2. Dewey:823/.8. LCCN:86-031152.
Audience: **g,l,u,f.** *Choice, 1988.*

Bronte, Charlotte **PR4167.V5 2000**
Villette. Ed. 2. Margaret Smith & Herbert Rosengarten (Editors), Margaret Smith (Introduction by). Trade Paper. Oxford University Press, Inc. New York, NY. 2001. 596p. Oxford World's Classics Ser. ISBN:0-19-283964-0, ISBN13: 978-0-19-283964-0. Dewey:823/.8. LCCN:00-040642.
Audience: **g,l,u,f.** *Choice, 1985.*

Bronte, Patrick Branwell **PR4174.B23A6**
The Poems of Patrick Branwell Bronte. Tom Winnifrith (Editor). Paper Text. New York University Press. New York, NY. 1991. 384p. ISBN:0-8147-9239-1, ISBN13: 978-0-8147-9239-1. Dewey:821/.8.
Audience: **g,l,u,f.**

Brontë, Anne **PR4162.A2**
Complete Poems of Anne Bronte. Trade Cloth. Scholarly Press, Inc. Saint Clair Shores, MI. 1971. ISBN:0-403-01758-0, ISBN13: 978-0-403-01758-4. Dewey:821.8.
Audience: **g,l,u,f.**

Brontë, Anne, et al. **PR4168**
The Bronte Sisters: Selected Poems of Charlotte, Emily and Anne Bronte. Charlotte Bronte & Emily Brontë (Authors). Cloth Text. Routledge. New York, NY. 2002. 128p. Fyfield Bks. ISBN:0-415-94089-3, ISBN13: 978-0-415-94089-4. Dewey:821.808.
Audience: **g,l,u,f.**

Brontë, Anne **PR4162.A54 1988**
Agnes Grey. Hilda Marsden & Robert Inglesfield (Editors). Trade Cloth. Oxford University Press, Inc. New York, NY. 1988. 252p. Clarendon Edition of the Novels of the Brontes Ser. ISBN:0-19-812693-X, ISBN13: 978-0-19-812693-5. Dewey:823/.8. LCCN:87-026952.
Audience: **g,l,u,f.** B *Choice, 1989.*

Brontë, Anne **PR4162.T4 1991**
The Tenant of Wildfell Hall. Herbert Rosengarten (Editor). Trade Cloth. Oxford University Press, Inc. New York, NY. 1992. 570p. Clarendon Edition of the Novels of the Brontes Ser. ISBN:0-19-812596-8, ISBN13: 978-0-19-812596-9. Dewey:FIC. LCCN:91-007263.
Audience: **g,l,u,f.** B

Brontë, Emily **PR4172.W7 2002**
Wuthering Heights. Ed. 4. Trade Paper. W. W. Norton & Company, Inc. New York, NY. 2002. 416p. A Norton Critical Edition Ser. ISBN:0-393-97889-3, ISBN13: 978-0-393-97889-6. Dewey:FIC. LCCN:2002-026531.
Audience: **g,l,u,f.** B

Brontë, Emily **PR4172.A4 1995B**
The Complete Poems of Emily Jane Brontë. C. W. Hatfield (Editor), Irene Tayler (Foreword by). Trade Paper. Columbia University Press. New York, NY. 1995. 262p. ISBN:0-231-10347-6, ISBN13: 978-0-231-10347-3. Dewey:821/.8. LCCN:97-100951.
Audience: **g,l,u,f.**

Brontë, Emily **PR4172.W7 1988**
Wuthering Heights. Hilda Marsden & Ian Jack (Editors). Trade Cloth. Oxford University Press, Inc. New York, NY. 1976. 554p. Clarendon Edition of the Novels of the Brontes Ser. ISBN:0-19-812511-9, ISBN13: 978-0-19-812511-2. Dewey:FIC.
Audience: **g,l,u,f.** B

Eagleton, Terry **PR871**
Myths of Power: A Marxist Study of the Brontes. Cloth over Boards. Palgrave Macmillan. New York, NY. 2005. 176p. ISBN:1-4039-4697-3, ISBN13: 978-1-4039-4697-3. Dewey:823/.809. LCCN:2004-061203.
Audience: **u,f.**

Edwards, Mike **PR4169.E39 1999**
Charlotte Bronte: The Novels. Cloth over Boards. Palgrave Macmillan. New York, NY. 1999. 240p. Analysing Texts Ser. ISBN:0-312-22364-1, ISBN13: 978-0-312-22364-9. Dewey:823.8. LCCN:99-018813.
Audience: **l,u.** *Choice, 2000.*

Gaskell, Elizabeth **PR4168**
The Life of Charlotte Bronte. Trade Paper. Oxford University Press, Inc. New York, NY. 2002. 624p. Oxford World's Classics Ser. ISBN:0-19-283805-9, ISBN13: 978-0-19-283805-6. Dewey:823.8.
Audience: **g,l,u,f.** B

Gates, Barbara T. **PR4169.C75 1990**
Critical Essays on Charlotte Bronte. Trade Cloth. Thomson Gale. Farmington Hills, MI. 1989. 304p. Critical Essays on British Literature Ser. ISBN:0-8161-8772-X, ISBN13: 978-0-8161-8772-0. Dewey:823/.8. LCCN:89-015647.
Audience: **u,f.** *Choice, 1990.*

Glen, Heather (Editor) **PR4168.C29 2002**
The Cambridge Companion to the Brontës. Cloth Text. Cambridge University Press. New York, NY. 2002. 270p. Cambridge Companions to Literature Ser. ISBN:0-521-77027-0, ISBN13: 978-0-521-77027-9. Dewey:823/.809. LCCN:2002-067052.
Audience: **u,f.** *Choice, 2003.*

Gérin, Winifred **PR4173**
Emily Brontë: A Biography. Trade Cloth. Oxford University Press, Inc. New York, NY. 1972. xviii, 290p. ISBN:0-19-812018-4, ISBN13: 978-0-19-812018-6. Dewey:823/.8. LCCN:79-881328.
Audience: **g,l,u,f.** B

Homans, Margaret **PR585.W6**
Women Writers and Poetic Identity: Dorothy Wordsworth, Emily Bronte and Emily Dickinson. Trade Cloth. Princeton University Press. Princeton, NJ. 1981. 272p. ISBN:0-691-06440-7, ISBN13: 978-0-691-06440-6. Dewey:821/.8/099287. LCCN:80-007527.
Audience: **l,u,f.**

Ingham, Patricia **PR4168**
The Brontes (Authors in Context). Trade Paper. Oxford University Press, Inc. New York, NY. 2006. 304p. Oxford World's Classics Ser. ISBN:0-19-284035-5, ISBN13: 978-0-19-284035-6. Dewey:823.809. LCCN:2006-296311.
Audience: **g,l,u,f.**

Michie, Elsie B. (Editor) **PR4167.J5C47 2006**
Charlotte Brontë's Jane Eyre: A Casebook. Trade Cloth. Oxford University Press, Inc. New York, NY. 2006. 224p. Casebooks in Criticism Ser. ISBN:0-19-517778-9, ISBN13: 978-0-19-517778-7. Dewey:823/.8. LCCN:2005-014213.
Audience: **g,l,u,f.**

Paddock, Lisa Olson & Rollyson, Carl E. **PR4168.P28 2002**
The Brontes A to Z. Trade Cloth. Facts On File, Inc. New York, NY. 2003. 272p. Literary A to Z Ser. ISBN:0-8160-4302-7, ISBN13: 978-0-8160-4302-6. Dewey:823/.809. LCCN:2002-075446.
Audience: **g,l,u,f.** *Choice, 2003.*

Peters, Margot **PR4168.P38**
Unquiet Soul: A Biography of Charlotte Bronte. Trade Cloth. Doubleday Publishing. New York, NY. 1975. xv, 460 p. :p. ISBN:0-385-06622-8, ISBN13: 978-0-385-06622-8. Dewey:823/.8. LCCN:74-009461.
Audience: **u,f.**

Pite, Ralph (Editor) **PR451**
Lives of Victorian Literary Figures II: The Brownings, the Brontes and the Rossettis by Their Contemporaries, Set. Trade Cloth. Pickering & Chatto Publishers, Ltd. London, 2004. 1432p. ISBN:1-85196-775-3, ISBN13: 978-1-85196-775-9. Dewey:820.9/008 B. LCCN:2003-022554.
Audience: **l,u,f.**

Shuttleworth, Sally **PR4169 .S48 1996**
Charlotte Bronte and Victorian Psychology. Gillian Beer (Contribution by). Trade Paper. Cambridge University Press. New York, NY. 2004. 304p. Cambridge Studies in Nineteenth-Century Literature and Culture Ser., Vol. 7 ISBN:0-521-61717-0, ISBN13: 978-0-521-61717-8. Dewey:823/.7. LCCN:2005-278193.
Audience: **u,f.**

Winnifrith, Tom **PR4168**
Charlotte and Emily Bronte: Literary Lives. Trade Paper. Palgrave Macmillan. New York, NY. 1994. Charlotte and Emily Bronte Ser., Vol. 1 ISBN:0-312-12227-6, ISBN13: 978-0-312-12227-0. Dewey:823/.8/09 B.
Audience: **u,f.** *Choice, 1989.*

Individual Authors and Works > 19th C. > Browning, Robert

PR4194 .C75
Critical Essays on Elizabeth Barrett Browning. Trade Cloth. Thomson Gale. Farmington Hills, MI. 1999. 10p. ISBN:0-7838-8461-3, ISBN13: 978-0-7838-8461-5. Dewey:821/.8.
Audience: **g.** *Choice, 1999.*

Bristow, Joseph **PR4238.B65 1991**
Robert Browning. Trade Cloth. Palgrave Macmillan. New York, NY. 1991. 178p. New Readings Ser. ISBN:0-312-06774-7, ISBN13: 978-0-312-06774-8. Dewey:821.8. LCCN:91-026837.
Audience: **g,l,u,f.**

Browning, Elizabeth Barrett **PR4185.A2 R49**
Aurora Leigh: Norton Critical Edition. Paper Text. W. W. Norton & Company, Inc. New York, NY. 2001. ISBN:0-393-94687-8, ISBN13: 978-0-393-94687-1. Dewey:821/.8.
Audience: **g.**

Browning, Elizabeth Barrett **PR4180**
Complete Poetical Works. Library Binding. Reprint Services Company. Temecula, CA. 1992. 1033p. BCL1-PR English Literature Ser. ISBN:0-7812-7458-3, ISBN13: 978-0-7812-7458-6. Dewey:821.82.
Audience: **g.**

Browning, Elizabeth Barrett **PR4189 .A1 1991**
Sonnets from the Portuguese. UK-Trade Paper. Doubleday Publishing. New York, NY. 1990. 112p. ISBN:0-385-41618-0, ISBN13: 978-0-385-41618-4. Dewey:821/.8. LCCN:90-003138.
Audience: **g.**

Browning, Robert **PR4231 .A3**
The Letters of Robert Browning and Eliza. Trade Paper. Kessinger Publishing, LLC. Whitefish, MT. 2005. ISBN:1-4179-0527-1, ISBN13: 978-1-4179-0527-0. Dewey:928.2.
Audience: **g.**

Browning, Robert **PR4803.H44**
Robert Browning's Poetry. Ed. 2. Paper Text. W. W. Norton & Company, Inc. New York, NY. 2005. 604p. ISBN:0-393-92600-1, ISBN13: 978-0-393-92600-2. Dewey:821/.8. LCCN:2006-047308.
Audience: **g.**

Browning, Robert **PR4803.H44**
The Works of Robert Browning, Set. Library Binding. Reprint Services Company. Temecula, CA. 1992. BCL1-PR English Literature Ser. ISBN:0-7812-7457-5, ISBN13: 978-0-7812-7457-9. Dewey:821.8.
Audience: **g.**

Browning, Robert & Barrett, Elizabeth Barrett **PR4803.H44**
The Letters of Robert Browning and Elizabeth Barrett Browning, 1845-1846, Vol. 2. Trade Paper. Kessinger Publishing, LLC. Whitefish, MT. 2005. ISBN:1-4179-0528-X, ISBN13: 978-1-4179-0528-7. Dewey:821/.8.
Audience: **g.**

Browning, Robert **PR4238**
The Major Works. Adam Roberts (Editor), Daniel Karllin (Introduction by). Trade Paper. Oxford University Press, Inc. New York, NY. 2005. 864p. Oxford World's Classics Ser. ISBN:0-19-280626-2, ISBN13: 978-0-19-280626-0. Dewey:821.8. LCCN:2006-277696.
Audience: **g.**

Carlin, Daniel **PR4242.H34K37 1993**
Browning's Hatreds. Trade Cloth. Oxford University Press, Inc. New York, NY. 1993. 288p. ISBN:0-19-811229-7, ISBN13: 978-0-19-811229-7. Dewey:821/.8. LCCN:93-002907.
Audience: **u,f.** *Choice, 1994.*

Hawlin, Stefan **PR4231.H39 2001**
The Complete Critical Guide to Robert Browning. Paper over Boards. Routledge. New York, NY. 2001. 240p. The Complete Critical Guides to English Literature Ser. ISBN:0-415-22231-1, ISBN13: 978-0-415-22231-0. Dewey:821/.8. LCCN:2001-032287.
Audience: **g.** *Choice, 2002.*

Honan, Park **PR4238.H6 1969**
Browning's Characters: A Study in Poetic Technique. Trade Cloth. Shoe String Press, Inc. North Haven, CT. 1969. xiv, 327p. ISBN:0-208-00793-8, ISBN13: 978-0-208-00793-3. Dewey:821/.8. LCCN:69-019215.
Audience: **g.** B

Jack, Ian **PR4238**
Browning's Major Poetry. Trade Cloth. Oxford University Press, Inc. New York, NY. 1973. xiv, 308p. ISBN:0-19-812048-6, ISBN13: 978-0-19-812048-3. Dewey:821/.8. LCCN:74-155507.
Audience: **g.** B

Litzinger, Boyd **PR4231.L58 1970**
Browning: The Critical Heritage. Trade Cloth. Barnes & Noble, Inc. New York, NY. 1970. xviii, 550p. ISBN:0-389-01024-3, ISBN13: 978-0-389-01024-1. Dewey:821/.8. LCCN:79-012803.
Audience: **g.** B

Mermin, Dorothy **PR4193.M43 1989**
Elizabeth Barrett Browning: The Origins of a New Poetry. Catherine R. Stimpson (Foreword by). Trade Cloth. University of Chicago Press. Chicago, IL. 1989. 326p. Women in Culture and Society Ser. ISBN:0-226-52038-2, ISBN13: 978-0-226-52038-4. Dewey:821/.8. LCCN:88-028680.
Audience: **u,f.** *Choice, 1989.*

Pite, Ralph (Editor) **PR451**
Lives of Victorian Literary Figures II: The Brownings, the Brontes and the Rossettis by Their Contemporaries, Set. Trade Cloth. Pickering & Chatto Publishers, Ltd. London, 2004. 1432p. ISBN:1-85196-775-3, ISBN13: 978-1-85196-775-9. Dewey:820.9/008 B. LCCN:2003-022554.
Audience: **l,u,f.**

Roberts, Adam **PR4238.R596 1996**
Robert Browning Revisited. Trade Cloth. Thomson Gale. Farmington Hills, MI. 1996. xi, 177p. ISBN:0-8057-4590-4, ISBN13: 978-0-8057-4590-0. Dewey:821/.8. LCCN:96-003324.
Audience: **g.** *Choice, 1997.*

Ryals, Clyde de L. **PR4231**
The Life of Robert Browning: A Critical Biography. Trade Paper. Blackwell Publishing, Inc. Malden, MA. 1996. 292p. Critical Biographies Ser., Vol. 3 ISBN:0-631-20093-2, ISBN13: 978-0-631-20093-2. Dewey:821.8.
Audience: **u,f.**

Stott, Rebecca & Avery, Simon **PR4182**
Elizabeth Barrett Browning. Trade Paper. Longman Publishing Group. White Plains, NY. 2003. 264p. ISBN:0-582-40470-3, ISBN13: 978-0-582-40470-0. Dewey:821.8.
Audience: **g.** *Choice, 2003.*

Tucker, Herbert F. **PR4238.T8**
Browning's Beginnings: The Art of Disclosure. Trade Cloth. University of Minnesota Press. Minneapolis, MN. 1980. 350p. ISBN:0-8166-0946-2, ISBN13: 978-0-8166-0946-8. Dewey:821/.8. LCCN:80-017727.
Audience: **u,f.** B

Washington, Peter (Editor) **PR4203**
The Brownings. Robert Browning & Elizabeth Barrett Browning (Based on a poem by). Trade Cloth. Knopf Publishing Group. New York, NY. 2003. Dewey:821.8.
Audience: **g.**

Woolford, John & Karlin, Daniel **PR4231.W66 1996**
Robert Browning. Ed. 1. Trade Cloth. Longman Publishing Group. White Plains, NY. 1996. 352p. Studies in Eighteenth and Nineteenth Century Literature ISBN:0-582-09614-6, ISBN13: 978-0-582-09614-1. Dewey:821.8. LCCN:95-044055.
Audience: **g.** *Choice, 1996.*

Individual Authors and Works > 19th C. > Burns, Robert

Bold, Alan N. **PR4331.B64 1990**
A Burns Companion. Cloth over Boards. Palgrave Macmillan. New York, NY. 1991. 447p. ISBN:0-312-04500-X, ISBN13: 978-0-312-04500-5. Dewey:821/.6 B. LCCN:89-070109.
Audience: **g.** *Choice, 1991.*

Burns, Robert **PA4229.L6**
The Complete Works of Robert Burns, Vol. 5. Trade Paper. Kessinger Publishing, LLC. Whitefish, MT. 2004. ISBN:1-4179-1553-6, ISBN13: 978-1-4179-1553-8. Dewey:824.6.
Audience: **g.**

Burns, Robert **PA4229.L6**
The Complete Works of Robert Burns, Vol. 2. Trade Paper. Kessinger Publishing, LLC. Whitefish, MT. 2004. ISBN:1-4179-1554-4, ISBN13: 978-1-4179-1554-5. Dewey:824.6.
Audience: **g.**

Burns, Robert **PA4229.L6**
The Complete Works of Robert Burns, Vol. 3. Trade Paper. Kessinger Publishing, LLC. Whitefish, MT. 2005. ISBN:0-7661-9834-0, ISBN13: 978-0-7661-9834-0. Dewey:824.6.
Audience: **g,l,u,f.**

Burns, Robert **PA4229.L6**
The Complete Works of Robert Burns, Vol. 4. Trade Paper. Kessinger Publishing, LLC. Whitefish, MT. 2004. ISBN:1-4179-4250-9, ISBN13: 978-1-4179-4250-3. Dewey:824.6.
Audience: **g.**

Burns, Robert **PR4300 1909.N25**
The Complete Works of Robert Burns, Vol. 1. Trade Paper. Kessinger Publishing, LLC. Whitefish, MT. 2004. ISBN:1-4179-4312-2, ISBN13: 978-1-4179-4312-8. Dewey:824.6.
Audience: **g.**

Hecht, Hans **PR4331**
Robert Burns: The Man and His Work. Paper Text. Alloway Publishing, Ltd. Darvel, 1999. 316p. ISBN:0-907526-51-9, ISBN13: 978-0-907526-51-3. Dewey:821/.6.
Audience: **g.**

McGuirk, Carol (Editor) **PR4338.C84 1998**
Critical Essays on Robert Burns. Trade Cloth. Thomson Gale. Farmington Hills, MI. 1998. 316p. Critical Essays on British Literature Ser. ISBN:0-7838-0045-2, ISBN13: 978-0-7838-0045-5. Dewey:821/.6. LCCN:98-030504.
Audience: **g.** *Choice, 1999.*

McIntyre, Ian **PR4331.M445 1995**
Dirt and Deity: A Life of Robert Burns. Trade Cloth. HarperCollins Publishers. New York, NY. 1996. 80p. ISBN:0-00-215964-3, ISBN13: 978-0-00-215964-7. Dewey:821/.6 B. LCCN:96-146135.
Audience: **u,f.** *Choice, 1996.*

Individual Authors and Works > 19th C. > Butler, Samuel

Butler, Samuel **PR4349.B7A16**
Essays on Life, Art and Science. E-Book. Kessinger Publishing, LLC. Whitefish, MT. 2004. ISBN:1-4192-1836-0, ISBN13: 978-1-4192-1836-1. Dewey:082.
Audience: **g,l,u,f.**

Butler, Samuel **PR4349 .B7**
The Note-Books of Samuel Butler. Trade Paper. Kessinger Publishing, LLC. Whitefish, MT. 2004. ISBN:1-4191-7573-4, ISBN13: 978-1-4191-7573-2. Dewey:828/.8/09 s 828/.8/0.
Audience: **g,l,u,f.**

Butler, Samuel **PR5684**
The Way of All Flesh. Trade Paper. Kessinger Publishing, LLC. Whitefish, MT. 2003. ISBN:0-7661-6990-1, ISBN13: 978-0-7661-6990-6. Dewey:823/.8.
Audience: **g,l,u,f.**

Butler, Samuel **PR3338.A76 1979**
Prose Observations. Hugh De Quehen (Editor). Trade Cloth. Oxford University Press, Inc. New York, NY. 1980. 470p. Oxford English Texts ISBN:0-19-812728-6, ISBN13: 978-0-19-812728-4. Dewey:823/.4. LCCN:77-030357.
Audience: **g,l,u,f.**

Butler, Samuel & Mumford, Lewis **PR4349.B7 E6**
Erewhon and Erewhon Revisited. Trade Paper. Kessinger Publishing, LLC. Whitefish, MT. 2005. ISBN:1-4179-0229-9, ISBN13: 978-1-4179-0229-3. Dewey:828.809.
Audience: **g,l,u,f.**

Individual Authors and Works > 19th C. > Byron, George Gordon, Lord

Blann, Robinson **PR4359.B53 1990**
Throwing the Scabbard Away: Byron's Battle Against the Censors of Don Juan. Cloth Text. Peter Lang Publishing, Inc. New York, NY. 1991. VIII, 179p. American University Studies, Ser. IV, Vol. 126:English Language and Literature ISBN:0-8204-1437-9, ISBN13: 978-0-8204-1437-9. Dewey:821/.7. LCCN:90-019402.
Audience: **u,f.** *Choice, 1992.*

Byron, George Gordon **PR4381**
Don Juan. Trade Cloth. Amereon, Ltd. Mattituck, NY. ISBN:0-89190-660-6, ISBN13: 978-0-89190-660-5. Dewey:821/.7.
Audience: **g.**

Byron, George Gordon **PR4372 .F7 1806AB**
Fugitive Pieces. Library Binding. M. S. G. Haskell House. Brooklyn, NY. 1972. Studies in Byron, No. 5 ISBN:0-8383-1553-4, ISBN13: 978-0-8383-1553-8. Dewey:821/.7. LCCN:72-003567.
Audience: **g.**

Byron, George Gordon **PR4383.H57**
His Very Self and Voice: Collected Conversations of Lord Byron. Paper Text. Textbook Publishers. Temecula, CA. 2003. xlvi, 676p. ISBN:0-7581-9127-8, ISBN13: 978-0-7581-9127-4. Dewey:821/.7.
Audience: **g.**

Byron, George Gordon **PR4381.A3 M8**
Lord Byron's Correspondence, Set. Library Binding. Reprint Services Company. Temecula, CA. 1992. BCL1-PR English Literature Ser. ISBN:0-7812-7474-5, ISBN13: 978-0-7812-7474-6. Dewey:B.
Audience: **g.**

Byron, George Gordon **PR4366**
Marino Faliero Doge of Venice: An Historical Tragedy and the Prophecy of Dante A Poem. Trade Paper. Kessinger Publishing, LLC. Whitefish, MT. 2004. ISBN:1-4179-5495-7, ISBN13: 978-1-4179-5495-7. Dewey:822.7.
Audience: **g.**

Byron, George Gordon **PR4381.A3 B4 1973**
Confessions of Lord Byron. W. A. Bettany (Editor). Library Binding. M. S. G. Haskell House. Brooklyn, NY. 1972. Studies in Byron, No. 5 ISBN:0-8383-1578-X, ISBN13: 978-0-8383-1578-1. Dewey:821/.7. LCCN:72-003739.
Audience: **u,f.**

Byron, George Gordon **PR4359.A1 1984**
Don Juan. Ed. 2. Louis Kronenberger (Introduction by). Trade Cloth. Random House, Inc. New York, NY. 1984. 515p. ISBN:0-394-60510-1, ISBN13: 978-0-394-60510-4. Dewey:821/.7. LCCN:84-004653.
Audience: **g.**

Byron, George Gordon **PR4381.A3.M35 1973**
Byron's Letters and Journals: 'In My Hot Youth', 1798-1810, Vol. 1. Ed. 2. Leslie A. Marchand (Editor). Trade Cloth. Harvard

University Press. Cambridge, MA. 1973. 298p. Byron's Letters and Journals ISBN:0-674-08940-5, ISBN13: 978-0-674-08940-2. Dewey:821/.7. LCCN:73-081853.
Audience: **g.**

Byron, George Gordon **PR4381.A3.M35 1973 V**
Famous in My Time, 1810-1812, Vol. 2. Leslie A. Marchand (Editor). Trade Cloth. Harvard University Press. Cambridge, MA. 1973. 308p. Byron's Letters and Journals ISBN:0-674-08941-3, ISBN13: 978-0-674-08941-9. Dewey:821/.7. LCCN:74-160825.
Audience: **g.**

Byron, George Gordon **PR4381**
The Flesh Is Frail, 1818-1819. Leslie A. Marchand (Editor). Trade Cloth. Harvard University Press. Cambridge, MA. 1976. 306p. Byron's Letters and Journals, Vol. VI ISBN:0-674-08946-4, ISBN13: 978-0-674-08946-4. Dewey:821/.7 s 821/.7 B.
Audience: **g.**

Byron, George Gordon **PR4381**
For Freedom's Battle, 1823-1824, Vol. XI. Leslie A. Marchand (Editor). Trade Cloth. Harvard University Press. Cambridge, MA. 1981. 256p. Byron's Letters and Journals, Vol. 11 ISBN:0-674-08953-7, ISBN13: 978-0-674-08953-2. Dewey:821/.7. LCCN:81-156653.
Audience: **g.**

Byron, George Gordon **PR4381**
The Complete Poetical Works of Byron: Childe Harold's Pilgrimage. Jerome J. McGann (Editor). Trade Paper. Oxford University Press, Inc. New York, NY. 1981. 350p. Oxford English Texts ISBN:0-19-812764-2, ISBN13: 978-0-19-812764-2. Dewey:821/.7. LCCN:78-041111.
Audience: **g.**

Byron, George Gordon **PR4351.M27**
The Complete Poetical Works. Jerome J. McGann & Barry Weller (Editors). Trade Cloth. Oxford University Press, Inc. New York, NY. 1993. 460p. Oxford English Texts, Vol. VII ISBN:0-19-812328-0, ISBN13: 978-0-19-812328-6. Dewey:821.7. LCCN:81-105172.
Audience: **g.**

Chew, Samuel C. **PR4388.C5**
The Dramas of Lord Byron, a Critical Study. Library Binding. Reprint Services Company. Temecula, CA. 1992. 181p. BCL1-PR English Literature Ser. ISBN:0-7812-7476-1, ISBN13: 978-0-7812-7476-0. Dewey:822/.7.
Audience: **g.**

Gleckner, Robert F. **PR4388.C75 1991**
Critical Essays on Lord Byron. Trade Cloth. Macmillan Publishing Company, Inc. Old Tappan, NJ. 1991. 200p. Critical Essays on British Literature Ser. ISBN:0-8161-8859-9, ISBN13: 978-0-8161-8859-8. Dewey:821/.7. LCCN:91-021926.
Audience: **g.**

Jack, Ian **PR457.J24**
English Literature, 1815-1832: Scott, Byron, and Keats. Trade Cloth. Oxford University Press, Inc. New York, NY. 1990. 656p. Oxford History of English Literature Ser., Vol XII ISBN:0-19-812238-1, ISBN13: 978-0-19-812238-8. Dewey:820.903. LCCN:63-025209.
Audience: **u,f.**

Marshall, William Harvey **PR4388.M3**
The Structure of Byron's Major Poems. Paper Text. Textbook Publishers. Temecula, CA. 2003. 191p. ISBN:0-7581-1659-4, ISBN13: 978-0-7581-1659-8. Dewey:821.7.
Audience: **g.**

McGann, Jerome J. **PR4392.R63 .M37 2002**
Byron and Romanticism. James Soderholm (Editor), Marilyn Butler & James Chandler (Contribution by). Cloth Text. Cambridge University Press. New York, NY. 2002. 326p. Cambridge Studies in Romanticism, Vol. 50 ISBN:0-521-80958-4, ISBN13: 978-0-521-80958-0. Dewey:821/.7. LCCN:2001-052891.
Audience: **u,f.**

Moore, Thomas **PR4381.A3 M6**
The Life, Letters and Journals of Lord Byron. Library Binding. Reprint Services Company. Temecula, CA. 735p. ISBN:0-7812-0248-5, ISBN13: 978-0-7812-0248-0. Dewey:821/.7 B.
Audience: **g.**

Nicolson, Harold G. **PR4382 .N5**
Byron, the Last Journey, April 1823-April 1824. Library Binding. Reprint Services Company. Temecula, CA. 1992. 288p. BCL1-PR English Literature Ser. ISBN:0-7812-7481-8, ISBN13: 978-0-7812-7481-4. Dewey:821/.7 B.
Audience: **u,f.**

Noel, Roden B. **PR4381**
Life of Lord Byron. Trade Cloth. Associated Faculty Press, Inc. New York, NY. 1971. 215p. ISBN:0-8046-1605-1, ISBN13: 978-0-8046-1605-8. Dewey:821/.7. LCCN:73-160773.
Audience: **g.**

Stabler, Jane **PR4392.H5S73 2002**
Byron, Poetics and History. Marilyn Butler & James Chandler (Contribution by). Trade Cloth. Cambridge University Press. New York, NY. 2002. 270p. Cambridge Studies in Romanticism, Vol. 52 ISBN:0-521-81241-0, ISBN13: 978-0-521-81241-2. Dewey:821/.7. LCCN:2002-022286.
Audience: **u,f.** *Choice, 2003.*

Thorslev, Peter Larsen **PR4389.T45**
The Byronic Hero: Types and Prototypes. Paper Text. Textbook Publishers. Temecula, CA. 2003. 228p. ISBN:0-7581-2000-1, ISBN13: 978-0-7581-2000-7. Dewey:821.7.
Audience: **g.**

Individual Authors and Works > 19th C. > C-D

Carleton, William **PR4036**
Traits and Stories of the Irish Peasantry, Vol. 2. Trade Paper. Oxford University Press, Inc. New York, NY. 2004. 464p. A Colin Smythe Publication ISBN:0-86140-173-5, ISBN13: 978-0-86140-173-4. Dewey:823/.7.
Audience: **g,l,u,f.**

Carleton, William **PR4036**
Traits and Stories of the Irish Peasantry, Vol. 1. Barbara Hayley (Foreword by). Trade Paper. Oxford University Press, Inc. New

York, NY. 2004. 496p. A Colin Smythe Publication ISBN:0-86140-172-7, ISBN13: 978-0-86140-172-7. Dewey:823/.7.

Audience: **g,l,u,f.**

Clare, John **PR4453.C6Z465 1996**
By Himself. David Powell & Eric Robinson (Editors). Trade Paper. Carcanet Press, Ltd. Manchester, 1997. 364p. ISBN:1-85754-288-6, ISBN13: 978-1-85754-288-2. Dewey:821/.7 B. LCCN:97-102496.

Audience: **g,l,u,f.** *Choice, 1997.*

Davidson, John **PR4525.D5.A17 1973**
The Poems of John Davidson. Trade Cloth. Scottish Academic Press. Kelso, Roxburghshire, 1973. xxxiv, 551p. ISBN:0-7011-1988-8, ISBN13: 978-0-7011-1988-1. Dewey:821/.8. LCCN:74-170500.

Audience: **g,l,u,f.**

Disraeli, Benjamin **PR5684**
Coningsby: Or, the New Generation. Trade Paper. Kessinger Publishing, LLC. Whitefish, MT. 2004. ISBN:1-4191-1388-7, ISBN13: 978-1-4191-1388-8. Dewey:823/.8.

Audience: **g,l,u,f.**

Disraeli, Benjamin **PR4084**
Lothair. Trade Paper. Kessinger Publishing, LLC. Whitefish, MT. 2004. ISBN:1-4191-3133-8, ISBN13: 978-1-4191-3133-2. Dewey:823/.8.

Audience: **g,l,u,f.**

Disraeli, Benjamin **PR4084**
Sybil: Or, the Two Nations. Trade Paper. Kessinger Publishing, LLC. Whitefish, MT. 2004. ISBN:1-4191-5015-4, ISBN13: 978-1-4191-5015-9. Dewey:823.8.

Audience: **g,l,u,f.**

Dowson, Ernest **PR4613.D5 A17**
The Poems and Prose of Ernest Dowson. Trade Paper. Kessinger Publishing, LLC. Whitefish, MT. 2004. ISBN:1-4191-7772-9, ISBN13: 978-1-4191-7772-9. Dewey:821.89.

Audience: **g,l,u,f.**

du Maurier, George **PR4634.T7 1998**
Trilby. Elaine Showalter (Editor). Trade Paper. Oxford University Press, Inc. New York, NY. 1999. 364p. Oxford World's Classics Ser. ISBN:0-19-283351-0, ISBN13: 978-0-19-283351-8. Dewey:823/.8. LCCN:98-034388.

Audience: **g,l,u,f.**

Feuchtwanger, Edgar **DA564.B3F48 2000**
Disraeli. Paper Text. Oxford University Press, Inc. New York, NY. 2000. 256p. Reputations Ser. ISBN:0-340-71910-9, ISBN13: 978-0-340-71910-7. Dewey:941.081/092 B. LCCN:00-712703.

Audience: **l,u.** *Choice, 2001.*

Townsend, James Benjamin **PR4525.D5Z83**
John Davidson, Poet of Armageddon. Paper Text. Textbook Publishers. Temecula, CA. 2003. 555p. ISBN:0-7581-0166-X, ISBN13: 978-0-7581-0166-2. Dewey:821/.8.

Audience: **u,f.**

Wolff, Robert Lee **PR4417.W6**
William Carleton, Irish Peasant Novelist: A Preface to His Fiction. Trade Cloth. Garland Publishing, Inc. New York, NY. 1980. 156p. ISBN:0-8240-3527-5, ISBN13: 978-0-8240-3527-3. Dewey:823/.7. LCCN:79-004399.

Audience: **g,l,u,f.**

Individual Authors and Works > 19th C. > Carlyle, Thomas

Ashton, Rosemary **PR4433.A74 2002**
Thomas and Jane Carlyle: The Portrait of a Marriage. Trade Cloth. Random House. London, 2002. 488p. ISBN:0-7011-6709-2, ISBN13: 978-0-7011-6709-7. Dewey:824/.8. LCCN:2002-391348.

Audience: **g,l,u,f.**

Carlyle, Jane W. **PR4419.C5 A83**
I Too Am Here: Selections from the Letters of Jane Welsh Carlyle. Trade Paper. Books on Demand. Ann Arbor, MI. 327p. ISBN:0-608-13406-6, ISBN13: 978-0-608-13406-2. Dewey:824/.8 B. LCCN:76-011093.

Audience: **g,l,u,f.**

Carlyle, Thomas **PN6222.P45**
Critical and Miscellaneous Essays: The W, Vol. 3. Trade Paper. Kessinger Publishing, LLC. Whitefish, MT. 2004. ISBN:0-7661-8758-6, ISBN13: 978-0-7661-8758-0. Dewey:824.

Audience: **g,l,u,f.**

Carlyle, Thomas **PR4420**
Critical and Miscellaneous Essays: The W, Vol. 2. Trade Paper. Kessinger Publishing, LLC. Whitefish, MT. 2004. ISBN:0-7661-8757-8, ISBN13: 978-0-7661-8757-3. Dewey:824.

Audience: **g,l,u,f.**

Carlyle, Thomas **PR4420**
Critical and Miscellaneous Essays: The W, Vol. 1. Trade Paper. Kessinger Publishing, LLC. Whitefish, MT. 2004. ISBN:0-7661-8755-1, ISBN13: 978-0-7661-8755-9. Dewey:824.

Audience: **g,l,u,f.**

Carlyle, Thomas **DL460 .C19**
Early Kings of Norway. Trade Paper. Kessinger Publishing, LLC. Whitefish, MT. 2004. ISBN:1-4191-1712-2, ISBN13: 978-1-4191-1712-1. Dewey:828.8.

Audience: **g,l,u,f.**

Carlyle, Thomas **DC161**
The French Revolution: The Works of Thom, Vol. 2. Trade Paper. Kessinger Publishing, LLC. Whitefish, MT. 2004. ISBN:0-7661-8764-0, ISBN13: 978-0-7661-8764-1. Dewey:944.04.

Audience: **g,l,u,f.**

Carlyle, Thomas **DC161**
The French Revolution: The Works of Thom, Vol. 1. Trade Paper. Kessinger Publishing, LLC. Whitefish, MT. 2004. ISBN:0-7661-8761-6, ISBN13: 978-0-7661-8761-0. Dewey:944.04.

Audience: **g,l,u,f.**

Carlyle, Thomas **DD404 .C3**
History of Friedrich the Second Called F. Trade Paper. Kessinger Publishing, LLC. Whitefish, MT. 2004. ISBN:0-7661-8759-4, ISBN13: 978-0-7661-8759-7. Dewey:923.143.
Audience: **g,l,u,f.**

Carlyle, Thomas **PR4425**
The Life of John Sterling; Latter Day Pamphlets: The Works of Thomas Carlyle. Trade Paper. Kessinger Publishing, LLC. Whitefish, MT. 2004. ISBN:0-7661-8756-X, ISBN13: 978-0-7661-8756-6. Dewey:854.
Audience: **g,l,u,f.**

Carlyle, Thomas **PR4420; DA426**
Oliver Cromwell's Letters and Speeches with Elucidations: The Works of Thomas Carlyle. Trade Paper. Kessinger Publishing, LLC. Whitefish, MT. 2004. ISBN:0-7661-8751-9, ISBN13: 978-0-7661-8751-1. Dewey:824/.8 s; 942.06/4/0.
Audience: **g,l,u,f.**

Carlyle, Thomas **PR4420; DA426**
Oliver Cromwell's Letters and Speeches with Elucidations: The Works of Thomas Carlyle. Trade Paper. Kessinger Publishing, LLC. Whitefish, MT. 2004. ISBN:0-7661-8752-7, ISBN13: 978-0-7661-8752-8. Dewey:824/.8 s; 942.06/4/0.
Audience: **g,l,u,f.**

Carlyle, Thomas **PR4430 .R4**
Reminiscences: Nineteenth-Century British Literature. Trade Paper. Oxford University Press, Inc. New York, NY. 1999. 512p. Oxford World's Classics Ser. ISBN:0-19-283889-X, ISBN13: 978-0-19-283889-6. Dewey:828/.8/03 B.
Audience: **g,l,u,f.**

Carlyle, Thomas, et al. **HN388 .C33 2005**
Past and Present. Joel J. Brattin & D. J. Trela (Authors), Chris Vanden Bossche (Introduction by, Notes by). Trade Cloth. University of California Press. Berkeley, CA. 2006. 871p. The Norman and Charlotte Strouse Edition of the Writings of Thomas Carlyle Ser. ISBN:0-520-24250-5, ISBN13: 978-0-520-24250-0. Dewey:941.081. LCCN:2005-040873.
Audience: **g,l,u,f.** B

Carlyle, Thomas **PR4426.A2.G65 1993**
On Heroes, Hero Worship and the Heroic in History. Michael K. Goldberg (Introduction by), Joel J. Brattin & Mark Engel (Contribution by). Trade Cloth. University of California Press. Berkeley, CA. 1993. 638p. Norman and Charlotte Strouse Edition of the Writings of Thomas Carlyle, Vol. 1 ISBN:0-520-07515-3, ISBN13: 978-0-520-07515-3. Dewey:920.02. LCCN:91-033937.
Audience: **g,l,u,f.** *Choice, 1993.*

Carlyle, Thomas, et al. **PR4429.A2 T37 2000**
Sartor Resartus: The Life and Opinions of Herr Teufelsdröckh. Rodger L. Tarr & Mark Engel (Authors). Trade Cloth. University of California Press. Berkeley, CA. 2000. 724p. Norman and Charlotte Strouse Edition of the Writings of Thomas Carlyle, Vol. 2 ISBN:0-520-20928-1, ISBN13: 978-0-520-20928-2. Dewey:823.8. LCCN:97-003100.
Audience: **g,l,u,f.** B

Carlyle, Thomas **PR4552**
A Carlyle Reader: Selections from the Writings of Thomas Carlyle. G. B. Tennyson (Editor). Paper Text. Copley Publishing Group. Acton, MA. 2000. ISBN:1-58390-008-X, ISBN13: 978-1-58390-008-6. Dewey:828/.808. LCCN:99-074754.
Audience: **g,l,u,f.** B

Carlyle, Thomas **D208 .C34 2002**
Historical Essays. Chris Vanden Bossche (Editor). Trade Cloth. University of California Press. Berkeley, CA. 2003. 1200p. The Norman and Charlotte Strouse Edition of the Writings of Thomas Carlyle Ser. ISBN:0-520-22061-7, ISBN13: 978-0-520-22061-4. Dewey:940. LCCN:2001-055534.
Audience: **g,l,u,f.**

Emerson, Ralph Waldo & Carlyle, Thomas **PS1631.A35C3**
The Correspondence of Emerson and Carlyle. Joseph Slater (Editor). Trade Paper. Books on Demand. Ann Arbor, MI. 632p. ISBN:0-8357-9063-0, ISBN13: 978-0-8357-9063-5. Dewey:816.3. LCCN:63-017539.
Audience: **g,l.** B

Fielding, K. J. & Sorensen, David (Editors) **PR4419.C5**
Jane Carlyle: Newly Selected Letters. Trade Cloth. Ashgate Publishing, Ltd. Aldershot, 2004. 380p. 19th Century Ser. ISBN:0-7546-0137-4, ISBN13: 978-0-7546-0137-1. Dewey:824/.8 B. LCCN:2003-048917.
Audience: **g,l,u,f.** *Choice, 2005.*

Froude, James A. **PR4433 .F74**
Thomas Carlyle: A History of His Life in London. Library Binding. Reprint Services Company. Temecula, CA. 1992. BCL1-PR English Literature Ser. ISBN:0-7812-7488-5, ISBN13: 978-0-7812-7488-3. Dewey:824/.8 B.
Audience: **g,l,u,f.** B

Froude, James A. **PR4433 .F73**
Thomas Carlyle: A History of the First Forty Years of His Life. Library Binding. Reprint Services Company. Temecula, CA. 1992. BCL1-PR English Literature Ser. ISBN:0-7812-7489-3, ISBN13: 978-0-7812-7489-0. Dewey:824/.8 B.
Audience: **g,l,u,f.**

Harrold, Charles Frederick **PR4434 .H3**
Carlyle and German Thought: 1819-1834. Paper Text. Classic Textbooks. Murrieta, CA. 1934. 340p. ISBN:1-4047-7490-4, ISBN13: 978-1-4047-7490-2. Dewey:828.8.
Audience: **g,l,u,f.** B

Heffer, Simon **PR4433.H44 1995**
Moral Desperado: A Life of Thomas Carlyle. Trade Cloth. Orion Books Ltd. London, 1996. 500p. ISBN:0-297-81564-4, ISBN13: 978-0-297-81564-8. Dewey:828.8/09. LCCN:95-203407.
Audience: **g,l,u,f.** *Choice, 1997.*

Jessop, Ralph **PR4437.P5J47 1997**
Carlylye and Scottish Thought. Ed. 1. Trade Cloth. Palgrave Macmillan. New York, NY. 1997. 220p. ISBN:0-312-17287-7, ISBN13: 978-0-312-17287-9. Dewey:824/.8. LCCN:96-044508.
Audience: **g,l,u,f.** *Choice, 1997.*

Kaplan, Fred **PR4552**
Thomas Carlyle: A Biography. Trade Paper. University of California Press. Berkeley, CA. 1993. 614p. ISBN:0-520-08200-1, ISBN13: 978-0-520-08200-7. Dewey:828/.808. LCCN:92-024439.
Audience: **g,l,u,f.**

LaValley, Albert J. **PR4434.L3**
Carlyle and the Idea of the Modern: Studies in Carlyle's Prophetic Literature and Its Relation to Blake, Nietzsche, Marx and Others. Trade Paper. Books on Demand. Ann Arbor, MI. 365p. ISBN:0-598-36526-5, ISBN13: 978-0-598-36526-2. Dewey:828/.8/08. LCCN:68-013916.
Audience: **g,l,u,f.**

Le Quesne, A. L. **PR781 .V54 1993**
Victorian Thinkers: Carlyle, Ruskin, Arnold, Morris. Trade Paper. Oxford University Press, Inc. New York, NY. 1993. 448p. ISBN:0-19-283104-6, ISBN13: 978-0-19-283104-0. Dewey:828.80809. LCCN:92-030091.
Audience: **g,l,u,f.**

Pite, Ralph (Editor), et al. **PR462.L585 2005**
Lives of Victorian Literary Figures III: The Carlyles, John Ruskin and Elizabeth Gaskell by their Contemporaries. Aileen Christianson, Simon Grimble & Sheila A. McIntosh (Editors). Trade Cloth. Pickering & Chatto Publishers, Ltd. London, 2005. 1200p. ISBN:1-85196-780-X, ISBN13: 978-1-85196-780-3. Dewey:820.9/008 B. LCCN:2004-025260.
Audience: **l,u,f.**

Siegel, Jules Paul (Editor) **PR4434**
Thomas Carlyle. Paper over Boards. Routledge. New York, NY. 1996. 544p. Critical Heritage Ser. ISBN:0-415-13470-6, ISBN13: 978-0-415-13470-5. Dewey:828.808.
Audience: **g,l,u,f.**

Trela, D. J. & Tarr, Rodger L. (Editors) **PR4434**
The Critical Response to Thomas Carlyle's Major Works. Cloth Text. Greenwood Publishing Group, Inc. Portsmouth, NH. 1997. 224p. Critical Responses in Arts and Letters Ser., Vol. 27 ISBN:0-313-29107-1, ISBN13: 978-0-313-29107-4. Dewey:824/.8. LCCN:96-050242.
Audience: **g,l,u,f.**

Individual Authors and Works > 19th C. > Carroll, Lewis (Dodgson)

Brooker, Will **PR4611.A73B76 2004**
Alice's Adventures: Lewis Carroll in Popular Culture. Trade Cloth. Continuum International Publishing Group, Ltd. London, 2005. 400p. ISBN:0-8264-1433-8, ISBN13: 978-0-8264-1433-5. Dewey:823/.8. LCCN:2004-001489.
Audience: **u,f.** *Choice, 2004.*

Carroll, Lewis **PR4611**
Jabberwocky and Other Nonsense Verse. Cloth Text. Penguin Group (USA) Inc. New York, NY. 9999. 56p. Classic Verse Ser. ISBN:0-7214-1755-8, ISBN13: 978-0-7214-1755-4. Dewey:821.8.
Audience: **g,l,u,f.**

Carroll, Lewis & Clark **PZ8.D666A**
Alice's Adventures in Wonderland. Trade Paper. Kessinger Publishing, LLC. Whitefish, MT. 2004. ISBN:1-4191-0552-3, ISBN13: 978-1-4191-0552-4. Dewey:[Fic].
Audience: **g,l,u,f.**

Carroll, Lewis **PR4611.A7 2000**
The Annotated Alice: Alice's Adventures in Wonderland and Through the Looking Glass. John Tenniel (Illustrator), Martin Gardner (Introduction by). Trade Cloth. W. W. Norton & Company, Inc. New York, NY. 1999. 384p. ISBN:0-393-04847-0, ISBN13: 978-0-393-04847-6. Dewey:823/.8. LCCN:99-035647.
Audience: **g,l,u,f.**

Cohen, Morton N. **PR4612.C588 1995**
Lewis Carroll: A Biography. Trade Cloth. Alfred A. Knopf Inc. New York, NY. 1995. 592p. ISBN:0-679-42298-6, ISBN13: 978-0-679-42298-3. Dewey:823.8. LCCN:95-002663.
Audience: **g,l,u,f.** *Choice, 1996.*

Robson, Catherine **PR468.G5R63 2003**
Men in Wonderland: The Lost Girlhood of the Victorian Gentleman. Trade Paper. Princeton University Press. Princeton, NJ. 2003. 264p. ISBN:0-691-11526-5, ISBN13: 978-0-691-11526-9. Dewey:820.9/352054.
Audience: **u,f.** *Choice, 2001.*

Individual Authors and Works > 19th C. > Chesterton, G. K.

Chesterton, G. K. **PR4453.C4I7 1998**
The Annotated Innocence of Father Brown. Trade Paper. Dover Publications, Inc. Mineola, NY. 1998. 320p. ISBN:0-486-29859-0, ISBN13: 978-0-486-29859-7. Dewey:823/.912. LCCN:97-020612.
Audience: **g.** *Choice, 1987.*

Chesterton, G. K. **PR6019.O9**
The Napoleon of Notting Hill. Paper Text. Classic Books. Murrieta, CA. 2001. 301p. Collected Works of G. K. Chesterton ISBN:0-7426-8008-8, ISBN13: 978-0-7426-8008-1. Dewey:823/.912.
Audience: **g.**

Chesterton, G. K. **BR121**
Orthodoxy. Paper Text. Classic Books. Murrieta, CA. 2001. 299p. Collected Works of G. K. Chesterton ISBN:0-7426-8013-4, ISBN13: 978-0-7426-8013-5. Dewey:239.
Audience: **g.**

Chesterton, G. K. **HN17.5**
What's Wrong with the World. Paper Text. Classic Books. Murrieta, CA. 2001. 293p. Collected Works of G. K. Chesterton ISBN:0-7426-8018-5, ISBN13: 978-0-7426-8018-0. Dewey:361.1.
Audience: **g.**

Chesterton, G. K. **PR4453.C4A6 2005**
Father Brown: The Essential Tales. P. D. James (Editor). Trade Paper. Random House, Inc. New York, NY. 2005. 288p. The Modern Library Classics ISBN:0-8129-7222-8, ISBN13: 978-0-8129-7222-1. Dewey:823/.912. LCCN:2004-059535.
Audience: **g.**

Ward, Maisie **PR4453.C4 Z84**
Gilbert Keith Chesterton. Trade Cloth. Rowman & Littlefield Publishers, Inc. Lanham, MD. 2005. 600p. ISBN:0-7425-5043-5, ISBN13: 978-0-7425-5043-8. Dewey:928.2.
Audience: **g.** B

Individual Authors and Works > 19th C. > Clare, John

Bate, Jonathan **PR4453.C6Z593 2003**
John Clare: A Biography. Cloth over Boards. Farrar, Straus & Giroux. New York, NY. 2003. 672p. ISBN:0-374-17990-5, ISBN13: 978-0-374-17990-8. Dewey:821/.7. LCCN:2003-044063.
Audience: **g.** *Choice, 2004.*

Clare, John **PR4453**
John Clare by Himself. Trade Paper. Routledge. New York, NY. 2002. 388p. ISBN:0-415-94234-9, ISBN13: 978-0-415-94234-8. Dewey:828.7.
Audience: **g.**

Clare, John **PR4453.C6.Z52 1970**
The Letters of John Clare. Trade Cloth. Barnes & Noble, Inc. New York, NY. 1970. 379p. ISBN:0-389-01021-9, ISBN13: 978-0-389-01021-0. Dewey:821/.7. LCCN:79-009747.
Audience: **g.** B

Clare, John **PR4453.C6.A16 1970**
The Prose of John Clare. Trade Cloth. Barnes & Noble, Inc. New York, NY. 1970. xii, 302p. ISBN:0-389-01022-7, ISBN13: 978-0-389-01022-7. Dewey:828/.8/08. LCCN:73-009846.
Audience: **g.** B

Clare, John **PR4453.C6**
Major Works. Eric Robinson & David Powell (Editors), Tom Paulin (Introduction by). Trade Paper. Oxford University Press, Inc. New York, NY. 2004. 566p. Oxford World's Classics Ser. ISBN:0-19-280563-0, ISBN13: 978-0-19-280563-8. Dewey:821/.7. LCCN:2004-275881.
Audience: **l,u,f.**

Haughton, Hugh (Editor), et al. **PR4453.C6 Z74 1994**
John Clare in Context. Adam Phillips & Geoffrey Summerfield (Editors). Trade Paper. Cambridge University Press. New York, NY. 2005. 329p. ISBN:0-521-02089-1, ISBN13: 978-0-521-02089-3. Dewey:821.7.
Audience: **g.**

Storey, Mark (Editor) **PR4453.C6 Z9 1995**
John Clare. Paper over Boards. Routledge. New York, NY. 1996. 472p. Critical Heritage Ser. ISBN:0-415-13449-8, ISBN13: 978-0-415-13449-1. Dewey:821.7.
Audience: **g.**

Individual Authors and Works > 19th C. > Clough, Arthur Hugh

Christiansen, Rupert **PR4458**
Voice of Victorian Sex: Arthur H. Clough, 1819-1861. Trade Paper. Faber & Faber, Ltd. London, 2001. 96p. Short Lives Ser. ISBN:0-571-20815-0, ISBN13: 978-0-571-20815-9. Dewey:821.8.
Audience: **g.**

Clough, Arthur Hugh **PR4456**
Arthur Hugh Clough: Selected Poems. Shirley Chew (Editor, Introduction by). Trade Paper. Routledge. New York, NY. 2003. 196p. Fyfield Bks. ISBN:0-415-96937-9, ISBN13: 978-0-415-96937-6. Dewey:821.8.
Audience: **g.**

Clough, Arthur Hugh **PR4456.M8**
The Poems of Arthur Hugh Clough. A. L. Norrington (Editor). Trade Cloth. Oxford University Press, Inc. New York, NY. 1968. Oxford Standard Authors Ser. ISBN:0-19-254162-5, ISBN13: 978-0-19-254162-8. Dewey:821.8.
Audience: **g.** B

Kenny, Anthony **PR4458**
Arthur Hugh Clough: A Poet's Life. Trade Cloth. Continuum International Publishing Group, Ltd. London, 2005. 256p. ISBN:0-8264-7382-2, ISBN13: 978-0-8264-7382-0. Dewey:821.8. LCCN:2006-361688.
Audience: **g.**

Thorpe, Michael (Editor) **PR4459 .T5**
Clough: The Critical Heritage. Trade Cloth. Routledge. New York, NY. 1972. xvii, 411p. ISBN:0-7100-7156-6, ISBN13: 978-0-7100-7156-9. Dewey:821/.8. LCCN:72-179695.
Audience: **g.** B

Individual Authors and Works > 19th C. > Coleridge, Samuel Taylor

Beer, John B. **PR4484 .B36 1978**
Coleridge the Visionary. Trade Cloth. Greenwood Publishing Group, Inc. Portsmouth, NH. 1978. 367p. ISBN:0-313-20360-1, ISBN13: 978-0-313-20360-2. Dewey:821/.7. LCCN:78-002445.
Audience: **u,f.**

Beer, John B. (Editor) **PR4470.F69**
The Collected Works of Samuel Taylor Coleridge: Aids of Reflection. Trade Cloth. Princeton University Press. Princeton, NJ. 1993. 726p. Bollingen Ser., Vol. LXXV, No. 9 ISBN:0-691-09876-X, ISBN13: 978-0-691-09876-0. Dewey:821.7. LCCN:92-000226.
Audience: **g.**

Beer, John B. **PR457.Q47 1995**
Questioning Romanticism. Trade Paper. Johns Hopkins University Press. Baltimore, MD. 1995. 328p. ISBN:0-8018-5053-3, ISBN13: 978-0-8018-5053-0. Dewey:820.9/145. LCCN:94-049331.
Audience: **u,f.** *Choice, 1996.*

Coburn, Kathleen & Harding, Anthony John (Editors) **PR4483**
The Notebooks of Samuel Taylor Coleridge: 1827-1834. Trade Cloth. Princeton University Press. Princeton, NJ. 2002. 2008p. Bollingen Ser. ISBN:0-691-09907-3, ISBN13: 978-0-691-09907-1. Dewey:821.
Audience: **g.**

Coleridge, Samuel Taylor **PR4470**
The Complete works of Samuel Taylor Coleridge. with an introductory essay upon his philosophical and theological opinions. Ed. by Professor Shedd. the Friend. Trade Cloth. Scholarly Publishing Office, University of Michigan Library. Ann Arbor, MI. 2004. ISBN:1-4181-0212-1, ISBN13: 978-1-4181-0212-8. Dewey:820.8.
Audience: **g.**

Coleridge, Samuel Taylor **PR4470.F69 VOL. 5**
Lectures, 1808-1819 on Literature. Trade Cloth. Bow Historical Books. New Providence, NJ. 1987. ISBN:0-7100-9382-9, ISBN13: 978-0-7100-9382-0. Dewey:828.708. LCCN:85-043198.
Audience: **g.**

Coleridge, Samuel Taylor **PR4483 A428 2000**
Letters, Vol. 3. Cloth Text. Oxford University Press, Inc. New York, NY. 2002. 596p. Oxford Scholarly Classics Ser. ISBN:0-19-818744-0, ISBN13: 978-0-19-818744-8. Dewey:821.7.
Audience: **g.**

Coleridge, Samuel Taylor **PR4470 .F69**
Philosophical Lectures, 1818-19. Trade Cloth. Philosophical Library, Inc. New York, NY. ISBN:0-8022-0281-0, ISBN13: 978-0-8022-0281-9. Dewey:821/.7 s 190.
Audience: **g.**

Coleridge, Samuel Taylor **PR4471**
The Poetical and Dramatic works of S. T. Coleridge, with a Memoir ... Trade Cloth. Scholarly Publishing Office, University of Michigan Library. Ann Arbor, MI. 2004. ISBN:1-4181-2285-8, ISBN13: 978-1-4181-2285-0. Dewey:821.7.
Audience: **g.**

Coleridge, Samuel Taylor **JC0224**
The Political Thought of Samuel Taylor Coleridge. Trade Paper. Books on Demand. Ann Arbor, MI. 274p. ISBN:0-598-98068-7, ISBN13: 978-0-598-98068-7. Dewey:320.81. LCCN:39-002662.
Audience: **g.**

Coleridge, Samuel Taylor **PR4472 .M67 1991**
On Religion and Psychology. John Beer (Editor). Cloth over Boards. Palgrave Macmillan. New York, NY. 2002. 288p. Coleridge's Writings, Vol. 4 ISBN:0-333-73490-4, ISBN13: 978-0-333-73490-2. Dewey:320/.01. LCCN:90-008673.
Audience: **g.**

Coleridge, Samuel Taylor **PR4472 .C6 1979**
Inquiring Spirit: A New Presentation of Coleridge from His Published and Unpublished Writings. Kathleen Coburn (Editor). Trade Cloth. Hyperion Press, Inc. Westport, CT. 1990. ISBN:0-88355-837-8, ISBN13: 978-0-88355-837-9. Dewey:828/.7/08. LCCN:78-065606.
Audience: **g.**

Coleridge, Samuel Taylor **OR4483**
Notebooks. Kathleen Coburn (Editor). Other. Princeton University Press. Princeton, NJ. Bollingen Ser., Vol. 50 ISBN:0-318-55361-9, ISBN13: 978-0-318-55361-0. Dewey:821.7. LCCN:56-013196.
Audience: **g.** B

Coleridge, Samuel Taylor **PR4381**
Biographia Literaria: Biographical Sketches of My Literary Life and Opinions, Vol. 7. K. Coburn & B. Winer (Editors). Trade Paper. Princeton University Press. Princeton, NJ. 1985. 866p. Bollingen Ser., Vol. 75 ISBN:0-691-01861-8, ISBN13: 978-0-691-01861-4. Dewey:821/.7. LCCN:68-010210.
Audience: **g.**

Coleridge, Samuel Taylor **PR4470**
Lectures, 1795: On Politics and Religion, Vol. 1. K. Coburn & B. Winer (Editors). Trade Cloth. Princeton University Press. Princeton, NJ. 1971. 512p. Collected Works of Samuel Taylor Coleridge, Vol. 1 ISBN:0-691-09861-1, ISBN13: 978-0-691-09861-6. Dewey:821/.7. LCCN:68-010210.
Audience: **g.**

Coleridge, Samuel Taylor **PR2976 .C55**
Notes and Lectures upon Shakespeare and Some of the Old Poets and Dramatists: With Other Literary Remains of S. T. Coleridge, Vol. 2. H. N. Coleridge (Editor). Trade Paper. Adamant Media. Chestnut Hill, MA. 2004. 379p. ISBN:1-4021-5003-2, ISBN13: 978-1-4021-5003-6. Dewey:822.3/3.
Audience: **g.**

Coleridge, Samuel Taylor **PR4479**
The Rime of the Ancient Mariner. Thomas Dilworth (Editor), David Jones (Illustrator). Trade Cloth. Enitharmon Press. London, 2006. 116p. ISBN:1-904634-14-1, ISBN13: 978-1-904634-14-0. Dewey:821.7.
Audience: **g.**

Coleridge, Samuel Taylor **PR4479.A2G37 2003**
The Annotated Ancient Mariner. Ed. 2. Gustave Doré (Illustrator), Martin Gardner (Introduction by, Notes by). Trade Cloth. Prometheus Books, Publishers. Amherst, NY. 2004. 210p. ISBN:1-59102-125-1, ISBN13: 978-1-59102-125-4. Dewey:821/.7. LCCN:2003-012747.
Audience: **g.**

Coleridge, Samuel Taylor **PR2976**
Coleridge's Criticism of Shakespeare. R.A. Foakes (Editor). Trade Cloth. Continuum International Publishing Group, Ltd. London, 196p. ISBN:0-485-11349-X, ISBN13: 978-0-485-11349-5. Dewey:822.3/3.
Audience: **g.**

Coleridge, Samuel Taylor & Jackson, J. R. **PR4470.F69**
Lectures, 1818-1819: On the History of Philosophy. Trade Cloth. Princeton University Press. Princeton, NJ. 2000. 1174p. Collected Works of Samuel Taylor Coleridge, Vol. 8 ISBN:0-691-09875-1, ISBN13: 978-0-691-09875-3. Dewey:821/.7 s 190. LCCN:99-030471.
Audience: **g.**

Coleridge, Samuel Taylor **PR4480 .W38**
The Watchman. Lewis Patton, K. Coburn & B. Winer (Editors). Trade Cloth. Princeton University Press. Princeton, NJ. 1970. 477p. Watchman Ser., Vol. 2 ISBN:0-691-09719-4, ISBN13: 978-0-691-09719-0. Dewey:824/.7. LCCN:68-010210.
Audience: **g.**

Coleridge, Samuel Taylor **PR4472**
The Friend, Vol. 4. B. Rooke, K. Coburn & B. Winer (Editors). Trade Cloth. Princeton University Press. Princeton, NJ. 1969. 1260p. Friend, Set Ser., Vol. 4 ISBN:0-691-09854-9, ISBN13: 978-0-691-09854-8. Dewey:824/.7. LCCN:68-010210.
Audience: **g.**

Coleridge, Samuel Taylor **PR4470.E53**
The Complete Works of Samuel Taylor Coleridge, Vol. 7. William Greenough Thayer Shedd (Editor). Trade Paper. Books on Demand. Ann Arbor, MI. 706p. ISBN:0-598-78088-2, ISBN13: 978-0-598-78088-1. Dewey:828.7. LCCN:12-031353.
Audience: **g.**

Coleridge, Samuel Taylor **PR4472.W37 1997**
Coleridge: Poems. Peter Washington (Selected by). Trade Cloth. Alfred A. Knopf Inc. New York, NY. 1997. 256p. Everyman's Library Pocket Poets ISBN:0-375-40072-9, ISBN13: 978-0-375-40072-8. Dewey:821/.7. LCCN:98-125159.
Audience: **g.**

Crawford, Walter B. **PR4484.R4**
Reading Coleridge: Approaches and Applications. Trade Paper. Books on Demand. Ann Arbor, MI. 288p. ISBN:0-608-08089-6, ISBN13: 978-0-608-08089-5. Dewey:821/.7. LCCN:79-007616.
Audience: **u,f.** B

Doughty, Oswald **PR4483**
Perturbed Spirit: The Life and Personality of Samuel Taylor Coleridge. Trade Cloth. Fairleigh Dickinson University Press. Cranbury, NJ. 1981. 365p. ISBN:0-8386-2353-0, ISBN13: 978-0-8386-2353-4. Dewey:821/.7. LCCN:78-066792.
Audience: **u,f.** B

Lowes, John L. **PR4484.L6**
The Road to Xanadu: A Study in the Ways of the Imagination. Library Binding. Reprint Services Company. Temecula, CA. 1992. 639p. BCL1-PR English Literature Ser. ISBN:0-7812-7501-6, ISBN13: 978-0-7812-7501-9. Dewey:821.7.
Audience: **g.**

Magnuson, Paul **PR4484.M28**
Coleridge and Wordsworth: A Lyrical Dialogue. Trade Paper. Books on Demand. Ann Arbor, MI. 345p. ISBN:0-608-06389-4, ISBN13: 978-0-608-06389-8. Dewey:821/.7/09. LCCN:87-026341.
Audience: **u,f.**

Matlak, Richard **PR5883.M34 1997**
The Poetry of Relationship: The Wordsworths and Coleridge, 1797-1800. Cloth over Boards. Palgrave Macmillan. New York, NY. 1997. 256p. ISBN:0-312-10166-X, ISBN13: 978-0-312-10166-4. Dewey:821/.709. LCCN:96-048921.
Audience: **g.** *Choice, 1998.*

Watkins, Daniel P. **PR590.W32 1996**
Sexual Power in British Romantic Poetry. Maxine L. Margolis & Martin F. Murphy (Editors). Trade Cloth. University Press of Florida. Gainesville, FL. 1996. 192p. ISBN:0-8130-1438-7, ISBN13: 978-0-8130-1438-8. Dewey:821/.7093538. LCCN:95-009219.
Audience: **g.** *Choice, 1996.*

Wordsworth, William & Coleridge, Samuel Taylor **PR5869 .L9 1969**
Lyrical Ballads, 1798. Ed. 2. W. J. Owen (Editor). Trade Cloth. Oxford University Press, Inc. New York, NY. 1970. 224p. ISBN:0-19-911006-9, ISBN13: 978-0-19-911006-3. Dewey:821/.7. LCCN:73-509900.
Audience: **g.**

Worthen, John **PR4483.W6 2001**
The Gang: Coleridge, the Hutchinsons and Wordsworths in 1802. Cloth over Boards. Yale University Press. Cumberland, RI. 2001. 352p. ISBN:0-300-08819-1, ISBN13: 978-0-300-08819-9. Dewey:821/.709 B. LCCN:00-043802.
Audience: **u,f.** *Choice, 2001.*

Individual Authors and Works > 19th C. > Collins, Wilkie

Collins, Wilkie **PR4494.D43**
The Dead Secret. A Novel. Trade Cloth. Scholarly Publishing Office, University of Michigan Library. Ann Arbor, MI. 2004. ISBN:1-4181-0218-0, ISBN13: 978-1-4181-0218-0. Dewey:826.
Audience: **g,l,u,f.**

Collins, Wilkie **PR5684**
The Moonstone. A novel. by Wilkie Collins. Trade Cloth. Scholarly Publishing Office, University of Michigan Library. Ann Arbor, MI. 2004. ISBN:1-4181-0195-8, ISBN13: 978-1-4181-0195-4. Dewey:823.8.
Audience: **g,l,u,f.**

Collins, Wilkie **PR4494.N6 1994**
No Name. Mark Ford (Notes by). Trade Paper. Penguin Group (USA) Inc. New York, NY. 1995. 640p. Classics Ser. ISBN:0-14-043397-X, ISBN13: 978-0-14-043397-5. Dewey:823/.8. LCCN:95-177962.
Audience: **g,l,u,f.** B

Collins, Wilkie **PR4494.B3 2000**
Basil. Dorothy Goldman (Editor). Trade Paper. Oxford University Press, Inc. New York, NY. 2000. 400p. Oxford World's Classics Ser. ISBN:0-19-283548-3, ISBN13: 978-0-19-283548-2. Dewey:823/.8. LCCN:00-268363.
Audience: **g,l,u,f.**

Collins, Wilkie **PR4494.M62 2002**
The Moonstone. Frederick R. Karl (Introduction by), Lillian Nayder (Afterword by). Mass Market. Penguin Group (USA) Inc. New York, NY. 2002. 512p. ISBN:0-451-52829-8, ISBN13: 978-0-451-52829-2. Dewey:823/.8. LCCN:2001-058524.
Audience: **g,l,u,f.**

Collins, Wilkie **PR4494**
The Woman in White. Trevor Nunn (Notes by). Trade Paper. Penguin Group (USA) Inc. New York, NY. 2005. 640p. ISBN:0-14-102031-8, ISBN13: 978-0-14-102031-0. Dewey:823/.8.
Audience: **g,l,u,f.**

Collins, Wilkie **PR4494**
Armadale. John Sutherland (Notes by). Trade Paper. Penguin Group (USA) Inc. New York, NY. 1995. 752p. Classics Ser. ISBN:0-14-043411-9, ISBN13: 978-0-14-043411-8. Dewey:823/.8.
Audience: **g,l,u,f.**

Nayder, Lillian **PR4586.N39 2001**
Unequal Partners: Charles Dickens, Wilkie Collins, and Victorian Authorship. Book, Other. Cornell University Press. Ithaca, NY. 2001. 240p. ISBN:0-8014-3925-6, ISBN13: 978-0-8014-3925-4. Dewey:823/.8. LCCN:2001-003445.
Audience: **u,f.** *Choice, 2002.*

Pite, Raloh (Editor), et al. **DA30**
Lives of Victorian Literary Figures V: Mary Elilzabeth Braddon, Wilkie Collins, William Thackeray by Their Contemporaries. Ed. 3. Judith Fisher, William Baker & Andrew Maunder (Editors). Trade Cloth. Pickering & Chatto Publishers, Ltd. London, 2007. 1200p. ISBN:1-85196-819-9, ISBN13: 978-1-85196-819-0. Dewey:941.
Audience: **l,u,f.**

Pykett, Lyn **PR4496.P94 2005**
Wilkie Collins. Trade Paper. Oxford University Press, Inc. New York, NY. 2005. 272p. Oxford World's Classics Ser. ISBN:0-19-284034-7, ISBN13: 978-0-19-284034-9. Dewey:823/.8 B. LCCN:2005-001541.
Audience: **u,f.**

Individual Authors and Works > 19th C. > Crabbe, George

Crabbe, George **PR4381**
The Borough. Trade Paper. Kessinger Publishing, LLC. Whitefish, MT. 2004. ISBN:1-4191-5485-0, ISBN13: 978-1-4191-5485-0. Dewey:821/.7.
Audience: **g.**

Crabbe, George
Inebriety and the Candidate. Trade Paper. Kessinger Publishing, LLC. Whitefish, MT. 2004. ISBN:1-4191-2646-6, ISBN13: 978-1-4191-2646-8.
Audience: **g.**

Crabbe, George **PR4513.L54**
The Life and Poetical Works of the Reverend George Crabbe. Trade Paper. Kessinger Publishing, LLC. Whitefish, MT. 2005. ISBN:1-4179-7268-8, ISBN13: 978-1-4179-7268-5. Dewey:824.
Audience: **g.**

Crabbe, George **PR4512**
Miscellaneous Poems. Trade Paper. Kessinger Publishing, LLC. Whitefish, MT. 2004. ISBN:1-4191-3445-0, ISBN13: 978-1-4191-3445-6. Dewey:821.
Audience: **g.**

Crabbe, George **PR4512**
Tales. Trade Paper. Kessinger Publishing, LLC. Whitefish, MT. 2004. ISBN:1-4191-5029-4, ISBN13: 978-1-4191-5029-6. Dewey:821.
Audience: **g.**

Crabbe, George **PR4512 .V5**
The Village and the Newspaper. Trade Paper. Kessinger Publishing, LLC. Whitefish, MT. 2004. ISBN:1-4191-8676-0, ISBN13: 978-1-4191-8676-9. Dewey:821.7.
Audience: **g.**

Pollard, Arthur (Editor) **PR4514 P65 1995**
George Crabbe. Paper over Boards. Routledge. New York, NY. 1996. 512p. Critical Heritage Ser. ISBN:0-415-13438-2, ISBN13: 978-0-415-13438-5. Dewey:821.7.
Audience: **g.**

Individual Authors and Works > 19th C. > DeQuincey, Thomas

Barrell, John **PR4538.O74B37 1991**
The Infection of Thomas De Quincey: The Psychopathology of Imperialism. Cloth over Boards. Yale University Press. Cumberland, RI. 1991. 288p. ISBN:0-300-04932-3, ISBN13: 978-0-300-04932-9. Dewey:828/.809. LCCN:90-049489.
Audience: **u,f.** *Choice, 1991.*

De Quincey, Thomas **PR4534**
The Avenger. Trade Paper. Kessinger Publishing, LLC. Whitefish, MT. 2004. ISBN:1-4191-5335-8, ISBN13: 978-1-4191-5335-8. Dewey:824.81.
Audience: **g,l,u,f.**

De Quincey, Thomas **PR4530**
Biographical Essays. Trade Paper. Kessinger Publishing, LLC. Whitefish, MT. 2004. ISBN:1-4191-1001-2, ISBN13: 978-1-4191-1001-6. Dewey:824.
Audience: **g,l,u,f.**

De Quincey, Thomas **PR4530.E54**
Confessions of an English Opium Eater. Trade Paper. Kessinger Publishing, LLC. Whitefish, MT. 2004. ISBN:1-4191-1383-6, ISBN13: 978-1-4191-1383-3. Dewey:824.81.
Audience: **g,l,u,f.**

De Quincey, Thomas **PR4534**
The English Mail Coach and Joan of Arc. Trade Paper. Kessinger Publishing, LLC. Whitefish, MT. 2004. ISBN:1-4191-6100-8, ISBN13: 978-1-4191-6100-1. Dewey:824.81.
Audience: **g,l,u,f.**

De Quincey, Thomas **PR4532**
On Murder Considered As One of the Fine Arts and Other Related Texts. Trade Paper. Kessinger Publishing, LLC. Whitefish, MT. 2004. ISBN:1-4191-3849-9, ISBN13: 978-1-4191-3849-2. Dewey:828.809.
Audience: **g,l,u,f.**

De Quincey, Thomas **PR4534**
Rhetoric and Style. Trade Paper. Kessinger Publishing, LLC. Whitefish, MT. 2004. ISBN:1-4191-4472-3, ISBN13: 978-1-4191-4472-1. Dewey:828.81.
Audience: **g,l,u,f.**

Individual Authors and Works > 19th C. > Dickens, Charles

PR4550

☐ The Dickens Project.
http://humwww.ucsc.edu:16080/dickens
Audience: **g,l,u,f.**

Ackroyd, Peter **PR5684**
Dickens: Public Life and Private Passion. Trade Cloth. Hylas Publishing. Irvington, NY. 2002. 192p. ISBN:1-59258-002-5, ISBN13: 978-1-59258-002-6. Dewey:823/.8 B.
Audience: **g,l,u,f.**

Andrews, Malcolm **PR4592.P74A53 1994**
Dickens and the Grown-Up Child. Cloth Text. University of Iowa Press. Iowa City, IA. 1994. 224p. ISBN:0-87745-449-3, ISBN13: 978-0-87745-449-6. Dewey:823/.8. LCCN:93-061155.
Audience: **u,f.** *Choice, 1995.*

Bowen, John **PR4588.B69 2003**
Other Dickens: Pickwick to Chuzzlewit. Trade Paper. Oxford University Press, Inc. New York, NY. 2003. 340p. ISBN:0-19-926140-7, ISBN13: 978-0-19-926140-6. Dewey:823/.8.
Audience: **g,u,f.** *Choice, 2000.*

Campbell, Elizabeth A. **PR4592.F38C36 2003**
Fortune's Wheel: Dickens and the Iconography of Women's Times. Trade Cloth. Ohio University Press. Athens, OH. 2003. 288p. ISBN:0-8214-1514-X, ISBN13: 978-0-8214-1514-6. Dewey:823/.8. LCCN:2003-049891.
Audience: **u,f.** *Choice, 2004.*

Chittick, Kathryn **PR4582.C48 1990**
Dickens and the Eighteen Thirties. Trade Cloth. Cambridge University Press. New York, NY. 1990. 222p. ISBN:0-521-38174-6, ISBN13: 978-0-521-38174-1. Dewey:823/.8 B. LCCN:90-001404.
Audience: **u,f.** *Choice, 1991.*

Clayton, Jay **PR451.C58 2003**
Charles Dickens in Cyberspace: The Afterlife of the Nineteenth Century in Postmodern Culture. Trade Cloth. Oxford University Press, Inc. New York, NY. 2003. 280p. ISBN:0-19-516051-7, ISBN13: 978-0-19-516051-2. Dewey:823/.8. LCCN:2002-011755.
Audience: **u,f.** *Choice, 2004.*

Collins, Philip **PR4588**
Dickens: The Critical Heritage. Trade Cloth. Routledge. New York, NY. 1971. xxi, 641p. The Critical Heritage Ser. ISBN:0-7100-6907-3, ISBN13: 978-0-7100-6907-8. Dewey:823/.8.
Audience: **g,l,u,f.**

Collins, Philip **PR4592.C7C6 1994**
Dickens and Crime. Ed. 3. Trade Paper. Palgrave Macmillan. New York, NY. 1995. 388p. ISBN:0-312-12327-2, ISBN13: 978-0-312-12327-7. Dewey:823/.8. LCCN:94-025477.
Audience: **u,f.**

Davis, Paul **PR4580.D38 1998**
Charles Dickens A to Z: The Essential Reference to His Life and Work. Trade Cloth. Facts On File, Inc. New York, NY. 1998. 448p. Literary A to Z Ser. ISBN:0-8160-2905-9, ISBN13: 978-0-8160-2905-1. Dewey:823/.8 B. LCCN:97-026237.
Audience: **g,l,u,f.** *Choice, 1999.*

Dickens, Charles **PR4567 .A1**
The Adventures of Oliver Twist. by Charles Dickens. Trade Cloth. Scholarly Publishing Office, University of Michigan Library. Ann Arbor, MI. 2004. ISBN:1-4181-0123-0, ISBN13: 978-1-4181-0123-7. Dewey:823/.8.
Audience: **g,l,u,f.**

Dickens, Charles **E165**
American Notes. Trade Cloth. Konemann. New York, NY. 2000. Cloth Bound Pocket Ser. ISBN:3-8290-5382-7, ISBN13: 978-3-8290-5382-2. Dewey:917.3/0458.
Audience: **g,l,u,f.**

Dickens, Charles **E165**
American Notes; and The Uncommercial Traveler. by Charles Dickens. Trade Cloth. Scholarly Publishing Office, University of Michigan Library. Ann Arbor, MI. 2004. ISBN:1-4181-0153-2, ISBN13: 978-1-4181-0153-4. Dewey:823.83.
Audience: **g,l,u,f.**

Dickens, Charles **PR4555**
Barnaby Rudge. by Charles Dickens. (Boz.) with ... illustrations from designs by George Cattermole and H. K. Browne. Trade Cloth. Scholarly Publishing Office, University of Michigan Library. Ann Arbor, MI. 2004. ISBN:1-4181-0156-7, ISBN13: 978-1-4181-0156-5. Dewey:823/.83.
Audience: **g,l,u,f.**

Dickens, Charles **PR4556**
Bleak House. by Charles Dickens. (Boz.) with ... illustrations, from designs by Phiz [pseud.] and Cruikshank. Trade Cloth. Scholarly Publishing Office, University of Michigan Library. Ann Arbor, MI. 2004. ISBN:1-4181-0159-1, ISBN13: 978-1-4181-0159-6. Dewey:823/.83.
Audience: **g,l,u,f.**

Dickens, Charles **PR4557**
Christmas Stories. by Charles Dickens. (Boz.) with ... illustrations. from designs by J. Leech and D. Maclise. Trade Cloth. Scholarly Publishing Office, University of Michigan Library. Ann Arbor, MI. 2004. ISBN:1-4181-0160-5, ISBN13: 978-1-4181-0160-2. Dewey:823.8.
Audience: **g,l,u,f.**

Dickens, Charles **PR5684**
David Copperfield. Trade Cloth. Konemann. New York, NY. 2000. ISBN:3-8290-5385-1, ISBN13: 978-3-8290-5385-3. Dewey:823/.8.
Audience: **g,l,u,f.**

Dickens, Charles **PR4558**
David Copperfield. by Charles Dickens. (Boz.) with ... illustrations from designs by H. K. Browne. Trade Cloth. Scholarly Publishing Office, University of Michigan Library. Ann Arbor, MI. 2004. ISBN:1-4181-0162-1, ISBN13: 978-1-4181-0162-6. Dewey:823/.8.
Audience: **g,l,u,f.**

Dickens, Charles **PR4559**
Dombey and Son. by Charles Dickens. (Boz). with ... illustrations. from designs of Phiz [pseud.] and Cruikshank. Trade Cloth. Scholarly Publishing Office, University of Michigan Library. Ann Arbor, MI. 2004. ISBN:1-4181-2484-2, ISBN13: 978-1-4181-2484-7. Dewey:823/.8.
Audience: **g,l,u,f.**

Dickens, Charles **PR4560 .C45**
Great Expectations: Norton Critical Editions. Ed. 3. Paper Text. W. W. Norton & Company, Inc. New York, NY. 2001. ISBN:0-393-94528-6, ISBN13: 978-0-393-94528-7. Dewey:823/.8.
Audience: **g,l,u,f.**

Dickens, Charles **PR5684**
Great Expectations. Trade Cloth. Konemann. New York, NY. 1999. Cloth Bound Pocket Ser. ISBN:3-8290-2968-3, ISBN13: 978-3-8290-2968-1. Dewey:823/.8.
Audience: **g,l,u,f.**

Dickens, Charles **PR4560**
Great Expectations. by Charles Dickens ... with ... illustrations. from original designs by John Mclenan. Trade Cloth. Scholarly Publishing Office, University of Michigan Library. Ann Arbor, MI. 2004. ISBN:1-4181-2488-5, ISBN13: 978-1-4181-2488-5. Dewey:823.
Audience: **g,l,u,f.**

Dickens, Charles **PR5684**
Hard Times. Trade Cloth. Konemann. New York, NY. 1998. 240p. Cloth Bound Pocket Ser. ISBN:3-89508-229-5, ISBN13: 978-3-89508-229-0. Dewey:FIC.
Audience: **g,l,u,f.**

Dickens, Charles **PR4563**
The Life and Adventures of Martin Chuzzlewit. by Chas. Dickens. Trade Cloth. Scholarly Publishing Office, University of Michigan Library. Ann Arbor, MI. 2004. ISBN:1-4181-0140-0, ISBN13: 978-1-4181-0140-4. Dewey:823.8.
Audience: **g,l,u,f.**

Dickens, Charles **PR4565**
The Life and Adventures of Nicholas Nickleby. by Charles Dickens ... with Illustrations. Trade Cloth. Scholarly Publishing Office, University of Michigan Library. Ann Arbor, MI. 2004. ISBN:1-4181-0119-2, ISBN13: 978-1-4181-0119-0. Dewey:823.8.
Audience: **g,l,u,f.**

Dickens, Charles **PR4562**
Little Dorrit. by Charles Dickens. (Boz.) with ... illustrations. from designs by Phiz [pseud.] and Cruikshank. Trade Cloth. Scholarly Publishing Office, University of Michigan Library. Ann Arbor, MI. 2004. ISBN:1-4181-2489-3, ISBN13: 978-1-4181-2489-2. Dewey:823.8.
Audience: **g,l,u,f.**

Dickens, Charles **PR4564**
The Mystery of Edwin Drood, Master Humphrey's clock, and Sketches by Boz. by Charles Dickens. Trade Cloth. Scholarly Publishing Office, University of Michigan Library. Ann Arbor, MI. 2004. ISBN:1-4181-0139-7, ISBN13: 978-1-4181-0139-8. Dewey:823.
Audience: **g,l,u,f.**

Dickens, Charles **PR4566 .A1**
The Old Curiosity Shop. by Charles Dickens. (Boz.) with ... illustrations. from designs by George Cattermole and H. K. Browne. Trade Cloth. Scholarly Publishing Office, University of Michigan Library. Ann Arbor, MI. 2004. ISBN:1-4181-0122-2, ISBN13: 978-1-4181-0122-0. Dewey:823/.8.
Audience: **g,l,u,f.**

Dickens, Charles **PR4567**
Oliver Twist. Trade Cloth. Konemann. New York, NY. 1999. Cloth Bound Pocket Ser. ISBN:3-8290-3004-5, ISBN13: 978-3-8290-3004-5. Dewey:823/.8.
Audience: **g,l,u,f.**

Dickens, Charles **PR4568 .A1; PZ3.D55**
Our Mutual Friend. by Charles Dickens (Boz.) with forty-one illustrations. from designs by Marcus Stone. Trade Cloth. Scholarly Publishing Office, University of Michigan Library. Ann Arbor, MI. 2004. ISBN:1-4181-0124-9, ISBN13: 978-1-4181-0124-4. Dewey:823/.8.
Audience: **g,l,u,f.**

Dickens, Charles **PR4569**
The Posthumous Papers of the Pickwick Club. by Charles Dickens. Trade Cloth. Scholarly Publishing Office, University of Michigan Library. Ann Arbor, MI. 2004. ISBN:1-4181-2493-1, ISBN13: 978-1-4181-2493-9. Dewey:823.83.
Audience: **g,l,u,f.**

Dickens, Charles **PZ3.D55**
Sketches by Boz, illustrative of every-day life and every-day people. by the author of the Pickwick Papers. Trade Cloth. Scholarly Publishing Office, University of Michigan Library. Ann Arbor, MI. 2004. ISBN:1-4181-1739-0, ISBN13: 978-1-4181-1739-9. Dewey:823.83.
Audience: **g,l,u,f.**

Dickens, Charles **PR4572 .S6**
Speeches: Literary and Social. Trade Paper. Kessinger Publishing, LLC. Whitefish, MT. 2004. ISBN:1-4191-4857-5, ISBN13: 978-1-4191-4857-6. Dewey:825.8.
Audience: **g,l,u,f.**

Dickens, Charles **PR4571**
A Tale of Two Cities. Trade Cloth. Konemann. New York, NY. 1998. Cloth Bound Pocket Ser. ISBN:3-8290-0880-5, ISBN13: 978-3-8290-0880-8. Dewey:FIC.
Audience: **g,l,u,f.**

Dickens, Charles **PZ3.D55**
A Tale of Two Cities ... Trade Cloth. Scholarly Publishing Office, University of Michigan Library. Ann Arbor, MI. 2004. ISBN:1-4181-1740-4, ISBN13: 978-1-4181-1740-5. Dewey:823/.8.
Audience: **g,l,u,f.**

Dickens, Charles **PR4567.A1 2005**
Oliver Twist. Frederick Busch (Introduction by), Edward Le Comte (Afterword by). Mass Market. Penguin Group (USA) Inc. New York, NY. 2005. 512p. ISBN:0-451-52971-5, ISBN13: 978-0-451-52971-8. Dewey:823/.8. LCCN:2004-026593.
Audience: **g,l,u,f.**

Dickens, Charles **PR5684**
Our Mutual Friend. Michael Cotsell (Editor, Introduction by, Notes by). Trade Paper. Oxford University Press, Inc. New York, NY. 1998. 878p. Oxford World's Classics Ser. ISBN:0-19-283523-8, ISBN13: 978-0-19-283523-9. Dewey:823/.8.
Audience: **g,l,u,f.**

Dickens, Charles **PR4569.A1 2004**
The Pickwick Papers. Jasper Fforde (Afterword by). Mass Market. Penguin Group (USA) Inc. New York, NY. 2004. 880p. ISBN:0-451-52938-3, ISBN13: 978-0-451-52938-1. Dewey:823/.8. LCCN:2003-070370.
Audience: **g,l,u,f.**

Dickens, Charles **PR4556.A2.F67**
Bleak House. George Ford & Sylvere Monod (Editors). Trade Cloth. W. W. Norton & Company, Inc. New York, NY. 1978. xx, 986 p., [p. Critical Editions Ser. ISBN:0-393-04374-6, ISBN13: 978-0-393-04374-7. Dewey:823/.8. LCCN:77-007783.
Audience: **g,l,u,f.** B

Dickens, Charles **PR4565.A2F67 2002**
Nicholas Nickleby. Mark Ford (Notes by), Douglas McGrath (Introduction by). Book, Other. Penguin Group (USA) Inc. New York, NY. 2002. 814p. ISBN:0-14-200275-5, ISBN13: 978-0-14-200275-9. Dewey:823.8. LCCN:2003-269677.
Audience: **g,l,u,f.**

Dickens, Charles **PR4572.M37 1981**
Charles Dickens' Book of Memoranda: A Photographic and Typographic Facsimile of the Notebook Begun in January 1855. Fred Kaplan (Editor). Trade Cloth. New York Public Library. New York, NY. 1981. 118p. Harcourt Brace Jovanovich Fund Ser., No. 2 ISBN:0-87104-279-7, ISBN13: 978-0-87104-279-8. Dewey:828/.803. LCCN:81-018872.
Audience: **g,l,u,f.** B

Dickens, Charles **PR4572.C68 2003**
The Annotated Christmas Carol: A Christmas Carol in Prose. John Leech (Illustrator), Michael Patrick Hearn (Introduction by). Trade Cloth. W. W. Norton & Company, Inc. New York, NY. 2003. 288p. ISBN:0-393-05158-7, ISBN13: 978-0-393-05158-2. Dewey:823/.8. LCCN:2003-044493.
Audience: **g,l,u,f.**

Dickens, Charles **PR4553.S58 1978**
Dickens on America and the Americans. Michael Slater (Editor). Trade Cloth. University of Texas Press. Austin, TX. 1978. 260p. ISBN:0-292-71517-X, ISBN13: 978-0-292-71517-2. Dewey:823/.8. LCCN:78-009313.
Audience: **g,l,u,f.** B

Dickens, Charles **PR4581.A3**
The Letters of Charles Dickens, Set. Kathleen Tillotson & Madeline House (Editors). Trade Cloth. Oxford University Press, Inc. New York, NY. 2002. British Academy Ser. ISBN:0-19-925808-2, ISBN13: 978-0-19-925808-6. Dewey:823.8.
Audience: **u,f.**

Dickens, Charles **PR4562**
Little Dorrit. Stephen Wall & Helen Small (Editors), Stephen Wall & Helen Small (Introduction by, Notes by). Trade Paper. Penguin Group (USA) Inc. New York, NY. 2004. 1024p. Penguin Classics Ser. ISBN:0-14-143996-3, ISBN13: 978-0-14-143996-9. Dewey:823/.8. LCCN:2004-269333.
Audience: **g,l,u,f.**

Frank, Lawrence **PR878.D4F73 2003**
Victorian Detective Fiction and the Nature of Evidence: The Scientific Investigations of Poe, Dickens and Doyle. Cloth over Boards. Palgrave Macmillan. New York, NY. 2003. 272p. Palgrave Studies in Nineteenth-Century Writing and Culture ISBN:1-4039-1139-8, ISBN13: 978-1-4039-1139-1. Dewey:823/.08720908. LCCN:2002-044800.
Audience: **u,f.** *Choice, 2004.*

Friedman, Stanley **PR4591.F75 2002**
Dickens' Fictions: Tapestries of Conscience. Trade Cloth. A M S Press. Pittsburgh, PA. 2002. xii, 195p. AMS Studies in the Nineteenth Century, No. 30 ISBN:0-404-64460-0, ISBN13: 978-0-404-64460-4. Dewey:823/.8. LCCN:2002-034241.
Audience: **u,f.** *Choice, 2004.*

Gay, Peter **PN3499**
Savage Reprisals: Bleak House, Madame Bovary, Buddenbrooks. Trade Paper. W. W. Norton & Company, Inc. New York, NY. 2003. 192p. ISBN:0-393-32509-1, ISBN13: 978-0-393-32509-6. Dewey:809.3/0094.
Audience: **g,u,f.** *Choice, 2003.*

Gissing, George R. **PR4588**
Charles Dickens: A Critical Study. Trade Paper. Kessinger Publishing, LLC. Whitefish, MT. 2004. ISBN:1-4191-1261-9, ISBN13: 978-1-4191-1261-4. Dewey:823/.8.
Audience: **g,l,u,f.**

Hayward, Jennifer P. **PN1992.8.S4H39 1997**
Consuming Pleasures: Active Audiences and Serial Fictions from Dickens to Soap Opera. Trade Cloth. University Press of Kentucky. Lexington, KY. 1997. 232p. ISBN:0-8131-2025-X, ISBN13: 978-0-8131-2025-6. Dewey:791.45/6. LCCN:97-016851.
Audience: **u,f.** *Choice, 1998.*

House, Humphry **PR4583.H65**
The Dickens World. Paper Text. Textbook Publishers. Temecula, CA. 2003. 231p. ISBN:0-7581-7172-2, ISBN13: 978-0-7581-7172-6. Dewey:823.8.
Audience: **g,l,u,f.**

John, Juliet **PR4589.J65 2003**
Dickens's Villains: Melodrama, Character, Popular Culture. Trade Paper. Oxford University Press, Inc. New York, NY. 2003. 272p. ISBN:0-19-926137-7, ISBN13: 978-0-19-926137-6. Dewey:823/.8.
Audience: **u,f.** *Choice, 2001.*

Johnson, Edgar **PR4581.J6**
Charles Dickens, His Tragedy and Triumph. Paper Text. Textbook Publishers. Temecula, CA. 2003. ISBN:0-7581-9716-0, ISBN13: 978-0-7581-9716-0. Dewey:928.2.
Audience: **g,l,u,f.** B

Jordan, John O. (Editor) **PR4588 .C26 2001**
The Cambridge Companion to Charles Dickens. Trade Paper. Cambridge University Press. New York, NY. 2001. 258p. Companions to Literature Ser. ISBN:0-521-66964-2, ISBN13: 978-0-521-66964-1. Dewey:823/.8. LCCN:00-065162.
Audience: **g,l,u,f.**

Kaplan, Fred **PR4581.K28 1998**
Dickens: A Biography. Trade Paper. Johns Hopkins University Press. Baltimore, MD. 1998. 640p. ISBN:0-8018-6018-0, ISBN13: 978-0-8018-6018-8. Dewey:823/.8 B. LCCN:98-021826.
Audience: **g,l,u,f.** *Choice, 1989.*

Langton, Robert **PR4582 .L3 1975**
The Childhood and Youth of Charles Dickens. Trade Cloth. A M S Press, Inc. New York, NY. ISBN:0-404-08875-9, ISBN13: 978-0-404-08875-0. Dewey:823/.8. LCCN:76-148809.
Audience: **g,l,u,f.**

Nayder, Lillian **PR4586.N39 2001**
Unequal Partners: Charles Dickens, Wilkie Collins, and Victorian Authorship. Book, Other. Cornell University Press. Ithaca, NY. 2001. 240p. ISBN:0-8014-3925-6, ISBN13: 978-0-8014-3925-4. Dewey:823/.8. LCCN:2001-003445.
Audience: **u,f.** *Choice, 2002.*

Patten, Robert & Bowen, John (Editors) **PR4588.P35 2005**
Palgrave Advances in Charles Dickens Studies. Cloth over Boards. Palgrave Macmillan. New York, NY. 2006. 368p. Palgrave Advances Ser. ISBN:1-4039-1285-8, ISBN13: 978-1-4039-1285-5. Dewey:823/.8. LCCN:2005-050044.
Audience: **g,l,u,f.** *Choice, 2006.*

Payne, David **PR868.P78P39 2005**
The Reenchantment of Nineteenth-Century Fiction: Dickens, Thackeray, George Eliot and Serialization. Saddle Stitched, Cloth over Boards, Dust Jacket. Palgrave Macmillan. New York, NY. 2005. 224p. Palgrave Studies in Nineteenth-Century Writing and Culture ISBN:1-4039-4774-0, ISBN13: 978-1-4039-4774-1. Dewey:823/.809. LCCN:2004-056954.
Audience: **u,f.** *Choice, 2006.*

Priestley, J. B. **PR4581.P67**
Charles Dickens, a Pictorial Biography. Paper Text. Textbook Publishers. Temecula, CA. 2003. 144p. ISBN:0-7581-0933-4, ISBN13: 978-0-7581-0933-0. Dewey:928.2.
Audience: **g,l,u,f.** B

Smiley, Jane **PR4581.S616 2002**
Charles Dickens. Trade Cloth. Penguin Group (USA) Inc. New York, NY. 2002. 224p. Penguin Lives Ser. ISBN:0-670-03077-5, ISBN13: 978-0-670-03077-4. Dewey:823/.8. LCCN:2001-045607.
Audience: **g,l,u,f.** *Choice, 2003, 2002.*

Vlock, Deborah **PR4592.P45 V58 1998**
Dickens, Novel Reading, and the Victorian Popular Theatre. Gillian Beer (Contribution by). Trade Paper. Cambridge University Press. New York, NY. 2006. 240p. Cambridge Studies in Nineteenth-Century Literature and Culture Ser. ISBN:0-521-02688 1, ISBN13: 978-0-521-02688-8. Dewey:823/.8.
Audience: **u,f.** *Choice, 1999.*

Welsh, Alexander **PR4592.C56 W45 1986**
The City of Dickens. Trade Paper. Harvard University Press. Cambridge, MA. 1986. 256p. ISBN:0-674-13185-1, ISBN13: 978-0-674-13185-9. Dewey:823/.8. LCCN:86-009963.
Audience: **u,f.** B

Welsh, Alexander **PR4556.W45 2000**
Dickens Redressed: The Art of Bleak House and Hard Times. Cloth over Boards. Yale University Press. Cumberland, RI. 2000. 248p. ISBN:0-300-08203-7, ISBN13: 978-0-300-08203-6. Dewey:823/.8. LCCN:99-087254.
Audience: **u,f.** *Choice, 2000.*

Individual Authors and Works > 19th C. > Doyle, Arthur Conan

Doyle, Arthur Conan **PR5684**
The Complete Sherlock Holmes, Pack. UK-Trade Paper. Bantam Books. New York, NY. 2004. ISBN:0-553-32825-5, ISBN13: 978-0-553-32825-7. Dewey:823/.8.
Audience: **g,l,u,f.** B

Doyle, Arthur Conan **PR4621**
New Annotated Sherlock Holmes, Vol. 1. Trade Cloth. W. W. Norton & Company, Inc. New York, NY. ISBN:0-393-05914-6, ISBN13: 978-0-393-05914-4. Dewey:823.8.
Audience: **g,l,u,f.**

Doyle, Arthur Conan **PR4622.L6 1998**
The Lost World: Being an Account of the Recent Amazing Adventures of Professor George E. Challenger, Lord John Roxton, Professor Summerlee, and Mr E. D. Malone of the Daily Gazette. Ian Duncan (Editor). Trade Paper. Oxford University Press, Inc. New York, NY. 1998. 230p. Oxford World's Classics Ser. ISBN:0-19-283352-9, ISBN13: 978-0-19-283352-5. Dewey:823.8. LCCN:97-032932.
Audience: **g,l,u,f.**

Doyle, Arthur Conan **PR4621.K55 2005**
The New Annotated Sherlock Holmes, Vols. 1 & 2. Leslie S. Klinger (Editor). Trade Cloth. W. W. Norton & Company, Inc. New York, NY. 2004. 650p. ISBN:0-393-05916-2, ISBN13: 978-0-393-05916-8. Dewey:823/.8. LCCN:2004-007890.
Audience: **g,l,u,f.**

Doyle, Arthur Conan **PR4620.K55 2005**
The New Annotated Sherlock Holmes: A Study in Scarlet; The Sign of the Four; The Hound of the Baskervilles; and the Valley of Fear. Leslie S. Klinger (Editor), Janet Byrne & Patricia J. Chui (Contribution by). Saddle Stitched, Cloth over Boards, Dust Jacket, Trade Cloth. W. W. Norton & Company, Inc. New York, NY. 2005. 992p. ISBN:0-393-05800-X, ISBN13: 978-0-393-05800-0. Dewey:823/.8. LCCN:2004-007890.
Audience: **g,l,u,f.**

Frank, Lawrence **PR878.D4F73 2003**
Victorian Detective Fiction and the Nature of Evidence: The Scientific Investigations of Poe, Dickens and Doyle. Cloth over Boards. Palgrave Macmillan. New York, NY. 2003. 272p. Palgrave Studies in Nineteenth-Century Writing and Culture ISBN:1-4039-1139-8, ISBN13: 978-1-4039-1139-1. Dewey:823/.08720908. LCCN:2002-044800.
Audience: **u,f.** *Choice, 2004.*

Individual Authors and Works > 19th C. > Edgeworth, Maria

Butler, Marilyn **PR4646**
Maria Edgeworth: A Literary Biography. Trade Cloth. Oxford University Press, Inc. New York, NY. 1972. x, 531p. ISBN:0-19-812017-6, ISBN13: 978-0-19-812017-9. Dewey:823/.7.
Audience: **g,l,u,f.**

Edgeworth, Maria **PR4644**
The Absentee. Trade Paper. Oxford University Press, Inc. New York, NY. 2002. 366p. Oxford World's Classics Ser. ISBN:0-19-283830-X, ISBN13: 978-0-19-283830-8. Dewey:823/.7.
Audience: **g,l,u,f.**

Edgeworth, Maria **PR4646**
The Life and Letters of Maria Edgeworth, Vol. 1. Trade Paper. Kessinger Publishing, LLC. Whitefish, MT. 2004. ISBN:1-4191-6936-X, ISBN13: 978-1-4191-6936-6. Dewey:823/.7 B.
Audience: **g,l,u,f.**

Edgeworth, Maria **PR4646**
The Life and Letters of Maria Edgeworth, Vol. 2. Trade Paper. Kessinger Publishing, LLC. Whitefish, MT. 2004. ISBN:1-4191-6937-8, ISBN13: 978-1-4191-6937-3. Dewey:823/.7 B.
Audience: **g,l,u,f.**

Edgeworth, Maria **PR4644**
Castle Rackrent. Ed. 2. George Watson (Editor), Kathryn J. Kirkpatrick (Introduction by). Trade Paper. Oxford University Press, Inc. New York, NY. 2000. 174p. Oxford World's Classics Ser. ISBN:0-19-283563-7, ISBN13: 978-0-19-283563-5. Dewey:823/.7. LCCN:94-048873.
Audience: **g,l,u,f.**

Kaufman, Heidi & Fauske, Christopher J. **PR4647.U53 2004**
An Uncomfortable Authority: Maria Edgeworth and Her Contexts. Ed. 2. Trade Cloth. University of Delaware Press. Newark, DE. 2004. 296p. ISBN:0-87413-878-7, ISBN13: 978-0-87413-878-8. Dewey:823/.7. LCCN:2004-002844.
Audience: **u,f.** *Choice, 2005.*

Individual Authors and Works > 19th C. > Eliot, George

Armitt, Lucie **PR4688.G377 2000**
George Eliot, Adam Bede, the Mill on the Floss, Middlemarch: Essays, Articles and Reviews. Trade Cloth. Columbia University Press. New York, NY. 2001. 208p. Critical Guides Ser. ISBN:0-231-12422-8, ISBN13: 978-0-231-12422-5. Dewey:823/.8. LCCN:2001-042377.
Audience: **l,u.**

Baker, William & Ross, J. C. **Z8259.B35 2002**
George Eliot: A Bibliographical History. Trade Cloth. Oak Knoll Press. New Castle, DE. 2002. 715p. ISBN:1-58456-069-X, ISBN13: 978-1-58456-069-2. Dewey:016.823/8. LCCN:2001-055442.
Audience: **u,f.** *Choice, 2003.*

Beer, Gillian **PR878.E95 B43 2000**
Darwin's Plots: Evolutionary Narrative in Darwin, George Eliot and Nineteenth-Century Fiction. Ed. 2. George Levine (Foreword by). Cloth Text. Cambridge University Press. New York, NY. 2000. 311p. ISBN:0-521-78008-X, ISBN13: 978-0-521-78008-7. Dewey:823.809356. LCCN:99-051377.
Audience: **u,f.**

Bodenheimer, Rosemarie **PR5684**
The Real Life of Mary Ann Evans: George Eliot, Her Letters and Fiction. Trade Paper. Cornell University Press. Ithaca, NY. 1996. 320p. ISBN:0-8014-8184-8, ISBN13: 978-0-8014-8184-0. Dewey:823.8.
Audience: **g,l,u,f.** *Choice, 1995.*

Carroll, David **PR4688.C3 1971**
George Eliot. Trade Cloth. Barnes & Noble Books-Imports. Lanham, MD. 1971. xv, 511p. The Critical Heritage Ser. ISBN:0-389-04073-8, ISBN13: 978-0-389-04073-6. Dewey:823/.8. LCCN:73-023395.
Audience: **g,l,u,f.**

David, Deirdre **PR469.F44D38 1987**
Intellectual Women and Victorian Patriarchy: Harriet Martineau, Elizabeth Barrett Browning, George Eliot. Trade Paper. Cornell University Press. Ithaca, NY. 1989. 265p. ISBN:0-8014-9414-1, ISBN13: 978-0-8014-9414-7. Dewey:820.9/9287. LCCN:86-023989.
Audience: **u,f.** *Choice, 1988.*

Eliot, George **NA737.A72**
Essays and Leaves from a Note-Book. Library Binding. Classic Books. Murrieta, CA. 1999. 400p. The Writings of George Eliot Ser., Vol. 21 ISBN:1-58201-088-9, ISBN13: 978-1-58201-088-5. Dewey:720.973.
Audience: **u,f.**

Eliot, George **PS3507.R55**
Essays and Uncollected Papers. Library Binding. Classic Books. Murrieta, CA. 1999. 400p. The Writings of George Eliot Ser., Vol. 22 ISBN:1-58201-089-7, ISBN13: 978-1-58201-089-2. Dewey:813/.5/2.
Audience: **u,f.**

Eliot, George **PR5684**
Middlemarch. Rosemary Ashton (Contribution by). Trade Paper. Penguin Group (USA) Inc. New York, NY. 2003. 880p. ISBN:0-14-143954-8, ISBN13: 978-0-14-143954-9. Dewey:823.8.
Audience: **g,l,u,f.** *Choice, 1988, 1987.*

Eliot, George **PR4668.A2B37 1996**
Romola. Dorothea Barrett (Editor, Introduction by). Trade Paper. Penguin Group (USA) Inc. New York, NY. 1997. 688p. Classics Ser. ISBN:0-14-043470-4, ISBN13: 978-0-14-043470-5. Dewey:823/.8. LCCN:97-184677.
Audience: **g,l,u,f.** *Choice, 1993.*

Eliot, George **PR4661.A1 2003**
The Mill on the Floss. A. S. Byatt (Contribution by). Trade Paper. Penguin Group (USA) Inc. New York, NY. 2003. 640p. Penguin Classics Ser. ISBN:0-14-143962-9, ISBN13: 978-0-14-143962-4. Dewey:823.8. LCCN:2003-286413.
Audience: **g,l,u,f.**

Eliot, George **PR4670**
Silas Marner. David Carroll (Editor, Introduction by), Q. D. Leavis (Preface by). Trade Paper. Penguin Group (USA) Inc. New York, NY. 2003. 272p. Penguin Classics Ser. ISBN:0-14-143975-0, ISBN13: 978-0-14-143975-4. Dewey:823/.8. LCCN:2003-269843.
Audience: **g,l,u,f.**

Eliot, George **PR4658.A2C38 1995**
Daniel Deronda. Terence Cave (Editor, Intro and Notes by). Trade Paper. Penguin Group (USA) Inc. New York, NY. 1996. 896p. Penguin Classics Ser. ISBN:0-14-043427-5, ISBN13: 978-0-14-043427-9. Dewey:823/.8. LCCN:96-130502.
Audience: **g,l,u,f.** *Choice, 1985.*

Eliot, George **PR4681.A3 C7 1970**
George Eliot's Life As Related in Her Letters and Journals. J. W. Cross (Editor, Arranged by). Trade Cloth. A M S Press, Inc. New York, NY. ISBN:0-404-01866-1, ISBN13: 978-0-404-01866-5. Dewey:823/.8. LCCN:78-111475.
Audience: **g,l,u,f.**

Eliot, George **PR4669.S3 1998**
Scenes of Clerical Life. Jennifer Gribble (Editor, Introduction by, Notes by). Trade Paper. Penguin Group (USA) Inc. New York, NY. 1999. 416p. Penguin Classics Ser. ISBN:0-14-043638-3, ISBN13: 978-0-14-043638-9. Dewey:823/.8. LCCN:99-462570.
Audience: **g,l,u,f.** *Choice, 1985.*

Eliot, George **PR4681 .A35 1998**
The Journals of George Eliot. Margaret Harris & Judith Johnston (Editors). Cloth Text. Cambridge University Press. New York, NY. 1999. 473p. ISBN:0-521-57412-9, ISBN13: 978-0-521-57412-9. Dewey:828/.803 B. LCCN:98-003679.
Audience: **g,l,u,f.** *Choice, 1999.*

Eliot, George **PR4656.A1 2004**
Adam Bede. F. R. Leavis (Foreword by), Regina Barrecca (Afterword by). Mass Market. Penguin Group (USA) Inc. New York, NY. 2004. 592p. ISBN:0-451-52942-1, ISBN13: 978-0-451-52942-8. Dewey:823/.8. LCCN:2004-044952.
Audience: **g,l,u,f.** *Choice, 2002.*

Eliot, George **PR4660.A1 1995**
Felix Holt, the Radical. Ed. 140. Lynda Mugglestone (Notes by). Trade Paper. Penguin Group (USA) Inc. New York, NY. 1995. 592p. Classics Ser. ISBN:0-14-043435-6, ISBN13: 978-0-14-043435-4. Dewey:823/.8. LCCN:96-111509.
Audience: **g,l,u,f.**

Eliot, George **PR4658**
The Lifted Veil and Brother Jacob. Sally Shuttleworth & Julia Briggs (Editors). Trade Paper. Penguin Group (USA) Inc. New York, NY. 2001. 160p. ISBN:0-14-043517-4, ISBN13: 978-0-14-043517-7. Dewey:823.8.
Audience: **g,l,u,f.**

Eliot, George **PR4652**
Eliot: Selected Essays, Poems and Others Writings. N. D. Warren (Editor), A. S. Byatt (Contribution by). Trade Paper. Penguin Group (USA) Inc. New York, NY. 1991. 544p. Penguin Classics Ser. ISBN:0-14-043148-9, ISBN13: 978-0-14-043148-3. Dewey:828.8/09.
Audience: **g,l,u,f.**

Haight, Gordon S. **PR4689.H27 1992**
George Eliot's Originals and Contemporaries: Essays in Victorian Literary History and Biography. Hugh Witemeyer (Editor). Trade Cloth. University of Michigan Press. Chicago, IL. 1992. 256p. ISBN:0-472-10264-8, ISBN13: 978-0-472-10264-8. Dewey:823.8. LCCN:91-028045.
Audience: **l,u,f.**

Henry, Nancy **PR4692.I46 H46 2002**
George Eliot and the British Empire. Gillian Beer (Contribution by). Trade Cloth. Cambridge University Press. New York, NY. 2002. 198p. Studies in Nineteenth-Century Literature and Culture, Vol. 34 ISBN:0-521-80845-6, ISBN13: 978-0-521-80845-3. Dewey:823.8. LCCN:2001-037576.
Audience: **u,f.** *Choice, 2002.*

Karl, Frederick R. **PR4681.K37 1995**
George Eliot - Voice of a Century: A Biography. Trade Cloth. W. W. Norton & Company, Inc. New York, NY. 1995. 250p. ISBN:0-393-03785-1, ISBN13: 978-0-393-03785-2. Dewey:823/.8 B. LCCN:94-037436.
Audience: **g,l,u,f.** *Choice, 1995.*

Levine, George (Editor) **PR4688 .C26 2001**
The Cambridge Companion to George Eliot. Cloth Text. Cambridge University Press. New York, NY. 2001. 266p. Companions to Literature Ser. ISBN:0-521-66267-2, ISBN13: 978-0-521-66267-3. Dewey:823/.8. LCCN:00-064235.
Audience: **l,u,f.** *Choice, 2001.*

Pangallo, Karen L. (Editor) **PR4688**
The Critical Response to George Eliot. Cloth Text. Greenwood Publishing Group, Inc. Portsmouth, NH. 1994. 256p. Critical Responses in Arts and Letters Ser., No. 11 ISBN:0-313-28773-2, ISBN13: 978-0-313-28773-2. Dewey:823/.8. LCCN:93-041224.
Audience: **l,u,f.** *Choice, 1994.*

Paris, Bernard J. **PR4692.P74P37 2003**
Rereading George Eliot: Changing Responses to Her Experiments in Life. Paper Text. State University of New York Press. Albany, NY. 2003. xiii, 224p. SUNY Series in Psychoanalysis and Culture ISBN:0-7914-5834-2, ISBN13: 978-0-7914-5834-1. Dewey:823/.8. LCCN:2002-036483.
Audience: **u,f.** *Choice, 2003.*

Payne, David **PR868.P78P39 2005**
The Reenchantment of Nineteenth-Century Fiction: Dickens, Thackeray, George Eliot and Serialization. Saddle Stitched, Cloth over Boards, Dust Jacket. Palgrave Macmillan. New York, NY. 2005. 224p. Palgrave Studies in Nineteenth-Century Writing and Culture ISBN:1-4039-4774-0, ISBN13: 978-1-4039-4774-1. Dewey:823/.809. LCCN:2004-056954.
Audience: **u,f.** *Choice, 2006.*

Rignall, John (Editor) **PR4680.O94 2001**
The Oxford Reader's Companion to George Eliot. Trade Paper. Oxford University Press, Inc. New York, NY. 2002. 528p. Reader's Companions Ser. ISBN:0-19-860422-X, ISBN13: 978-0-19-860422-8. Dewey:823/.8 B. LCCN:2001-044795.
Audience: **l,u,f.** *Choice, 2001.*

van den Broek, Antonie Gerard & Baker, William (Editors) **PR4666.A1 2005**
George Eliot Poetry. Trade Cloth. Pickering & Chatto Publishers, Ltd. London, 2005. 600p. Pickering Masters Ser. ISBN:1-85196-796-6, ISBN13: 978-1-85196-796-4. Dewey:821/.8. LCCN:2004-028463.
Audience: **g,l,u,f.** *Choice, 2005.*

Individual Authors and Works > 19th C. > G

Adams, Hazard **PR4728.G5 Z548**
Lady Gregory. Trade Cloth. Bucknell University Press. Cranbury, NJ. 1973. 106p. Irish Writers Ser. ISBN:0-8387-1085-9, ISBN13: 978-0-8387-1085-2. Dewey:822/.9/12. LCCN:72-003253.
Audience: **g,l,u,f.**

Gilbert, W. S. (William Schwenck) **PR4713**
Original Plays. Trade Cloth. Scholarly Publishing Office, University of Michigan Library. Ann Arbor, MI. 2004. ISBN:1-4181-3578-X, ISBN13: 978-1-4181-3578-2. Dewey:822.
Audience: **g,l,u,f.**

Godwin, William **PR4722**
Caleb Williams: Or Things As They Are. Maurice Hindle (Contribution by). Trade Paper. Penguin Group (USA) Inc. New York, NY. 2005. 448p. ISBN:0-14-144123-2, ISBN13: 978-0-14-144123-8.
Audience: **g,l,u,f.** B

Gregory, Isabella Augusta **PR5366**
Irish Folk-History Plays. Trade Paper. Kessinger Publishing, LLC. Whitefish, MT. 2003. ISBN:0-7661-4861-0, ISBN13: 978-0-7661-4861-1. Dewey:822/.9/12.
Audience: **g,l,u,f.** B

Gregory, Isabella Augusta **PR4728.G5**
Lady Gregory's Journals 1916 to 1930. Trade Paper. Kessinger Publishing, LLC. Whitefish, MT. 2005. ISBN:1-4179-9375-8, ISBN13: 978-1-4179-9375-8. Dewey:928.2.
Audience: **g,l,u,f.**

Gregory, Isabella Augusta **PR5366**
Seven Short Plays. Trade Paper. Kessinger Publishing, LLC. Whitefish, MT. 2005. ISBN:1-4179-6131-7, ISBN13: 978-1-4179-6131-3. Dewey:822/.9/12.
Audience: **g,l,u,f.**

Gregory, Isabella Augusta **PR4728.G5A6 1995**
Gregory: Selected Writings. Lucy McDiarmid & Maureen Waters (Contribution by). Trade Paper. Penguin Group (USA) Inc. New York, NY. 1996. 624p. Penguin Twentieth-Century Classics Ser. ISBN:0-14-018955-6, ISBN13: 978-0-14-018955-1. Dewey:822/.912. LCCN:96-133547.
Audience: **g,l,u,f.**

Kohfeldt, Mary L. **PR4728.G5Z625 1985**
Lady Gregory: The Woman Behind the Irish Renaissance. Trade Cloth. Simon & Schuster. New York, NY. 1985. 320p. ISBN:0-689-11486-9, ISBN13: 978-0-689-11486-1. Dewey:822/.914 B. LCCN:84-045044.
Audience: **g,l,u,f.** B

Individual Authors and Works > 19th C. > Gaskell, Elizabeth

Chapple, J. A. V. **PR4711.C55 1997**
Elizabeth Gaskell: The Early Years. Ed. 1. Cloth over Boards. Manchester University Press. Manchester, 1997. 492p. ISBN:0-7190-2550-8, ISBN13: 978-0-7190-2550-1. Dewey:[B]. LCCN:96-041960.
Audience: **g,l,u,f.** *Choice, 1997.*

Chapple, John A. & Sharps, J. G. **PR4711 .A4 1980**
Elizabeth Gaskell: A Portrait in Letters. Trade Cloth. Manchester University Press. Manchester, 1988. 168p. ISBN:0-7190-0799-2, ISBN13: 978-0-7190-0799-6. Dewey:823/.8. LCCN:81-107053.
Audience: **g,l,u,f.** B

Gaskell, Elizabeth **PR4168**
The Life of Charlotte Bronte. Trade Paper. Oxford University Press, Inc. New York, NY. 2002. 624p. Oxford World's Classics Ser. ISBN:0-19-283805-9, ISBN13: 978-0-19-283805-6. Dewey:823.8.
Audience: **g,l,u,f.** B

Gaskell, Elizabeth **PR5684**
Wives and Daughters. Angus Easson (Editor). Trade Paper. Oxford University Press, Inc. New York, NY. 2003. 784p. Oxford World's Classics Ser. ISBN:0-19-283839-3, ISBN13: 978-0-19-283839-1. Dewey:823/.8.
Audience: **g,l,u,f.** B

Gaskell, Elizabeth **PR4710.N6 1998**
North and South. Ed. 2. Angus Easson (Editor), Sally Shuttleworth (Introduction by). Trade Paper. Oxford University Press, Inc. New York, NY. 1998. 494p. Oxford World's Classics Ser. ISBN:0-19-283194-1, ISBN13: 978-0-19-283194-1. Dewey:823/.8. LCCN:98-013092.
Audience: **g,l,u,f.** B

Gaskell, Elizabeth **PR4710.M3 2006**
Mary Barton. Shirley Foster (Editor). Trade Paper. Oxford University Press, Inc. New York, NY. 2006. 480p. Oxford World's Classics Ser. ISBN:0-19-280562-2, ISBN13: 978-0-19-280562-1. Dewey:823/.8. LCCN:2005-021616.
Audience: **g,l,u,f.** B

Gaskell, Elizabeth **PR5684**
Ruth. Nancy Henry (Editor). Trade Paper. Tuttle Publishing. Boston, MA. 2001. 400p. ISBN:0-460-87660-0, ISBN13: 978-0-460-87660-5. Dewey:823/.8.
Audience: **g,l,u,f.**

Gaskell, Elizabeth **PR4710.C71998**
Cranford. Ed. 2. Elizabeth Porges Watson (Editor), Charlotte Mitchell (Introduction by, Notes by). Trade Paper. Oxford University Press, Inc. New York, NY. 1998. 226p. Oxford World's Classics Ser. ISBN:0-19-283209-3, ISBN13: 978-0-19-283209-2. Dewey:823/.8. LCCN:98-204713.
Audience: **g,l,u,f.**

Gerin, Winifred **PR4711.G4 1990**
Elizabeth Gaskell. Trade Cloth. Oxford University Press, Inc. New York, NY. 1980. xviii, 318p. Series K ISBN:0-19-281296-3, ISBN13: 978-0-19-281296-4. Dewey:823/.8 B. LCCN:90-041991.
Audience: **g,l,u,f.**

Pite, Ralph (Editor), et al. **PR462.L585 2005**
Lives of Victorian Literary Figures III: The Carlyles, John Ruskin and Elizabeth Gaskell by their Contemporaries. Aileen Christianson, Simon Grimble & Sheila A. McIntosh (Editors). Trade Cloth. Pickering & Chatto Publishers, Ltd. London, 2005. 1200p. ISBN:1-85196-780-X, ISBN13: 978-1-85196-780-3. Dewey:820.9/008 B. LCCN:2004-025260.
Audience: **l,u,f.**

Stitt, Megan P. **PR868.S34 S85 1998**
Metaphors of Change in the Language of Nineteenth-Century Fiction: Scott, Gaskell, and Kingsley. Trade Cloth. Oxford University Press, Inc. New York, NY. 1998. 218p. Oxford English Monographs ISBN:0-19-818442-5, ISBN13: 978-0-19-818442-3. Dewey:823.7/09. LCCN:97-044617.
Audience: **u,f.**

Stoneman, Patsy **PR4711.S76 1987**
Elizabeth Gaskell. Cloth Text. Indiana University Press. Bloomington, IN. 1987. 240p. Key Women Writers Ser. ISBN:0-253-30103-3, ISBN13: 978-0-253-30103-1. Dewey:823.8. LCCN:86-046239.
Audience: **u,f.**

Uglow, Jenny **PR4711**
Elizabeth Gaskell: A Habit of Stories. Trade Cloth. Farrar, Straus & Giroux. New York, NY. 1993. 8p. ISBN:0-374-14751-5, ISBN13: 978-0-374-14751-8. Dewey:823/.8 B. LCCN:92-082961.
Audience: **g,l,u,f.**

Individual Authors and Works > 19th C. > Gissing, George

Coustillas, Pierre (Editor) **PR4717**
George Gissing. Paper over Boards. Routledge. New York, NY. 1996. 584p. Critical Heritage Ser. ISBN:0-415-13468-4, ISBN13: 978-0-415-13468-2. Dewey:823.8.
Audience: **g,l,u,f.**

Gissing, George R. **PR4716.B6**
Born in Exile. Trade Paper. Kessinger Publishing, LLC. Whitefish, MT. 2004. ISBN:1-4191-1064-0, ISBN13: 978-1-4191-1064-1. Dewey:823.8.
Audience: **g,l,u,f.**

Gissing, George R. **PR5684**
The Emancipated. Trade Paper. Kessinger Publishing, LLC. Whitefish, MT. 2004. ISBN:1-4191-6081-8, ISBN13: 978-1-4191-6081-3. Dewey:823/.8.
Audience: **g,l,u,f.**

Gissing, George R. **PR5684**
In the Year of Jubilee. Trade Paper. Kessinger Publishing, LLC. Whitefish, MT. 2004. ISBN:1-4179-0431-3, ISBN13: 978-1-4179-0431-0. Dewey:823/.8.
Audience: **g,l,u,f.**

Gissing, George R. **PR4717 .A33**
The Letters of George Gissing to Eduard Bertz, 1887-1903. Paper Text. Textbook Publishers. Temecula, CA. 2003. 337p. ISBN:0-7581-4283-8, ISBN13: 978-0-7581-4283-2. Dewey:823/.8 B.
Audience: **g,l,u,f.**

Gissing, George R. **PR5684**
Letters of George Gissing to Members of His Family. Library Binding. Reprint Services Company. Temecula, CA. 1992. 414p. BCL1-PR English Literature Ser. ISBN:0-7812-7538-5, ISBN13: 978-0-7812-7538-5. Dewey:823/.8.
Audience: **g,l,u,f.**

Gissing, George R. **PR5684**
The Odd Women. Trade Paper. Oxford University Press, Inc. New York, NY. 2002. 408p. Oxford World's Classics Ser. ISBN:0-19-283312-X, ISBN13: 978-0-19-283312-9. Dewey:823/.8.
Audience: **g,l,u,f.**

Gissing, George R. **PR4716.P7 1987**
The Private Papers of Henry Ryecroft. Trade Paper. Oxford University Press, Inc. New York, NY. 1987. 240p. Oxford World's Classics Ser. ISBN:0-19-281749-3, ISBN13: 978-0-19-281749-5. Dewey:823/.8. LCCN:86-031105.
Audience: **g,l,u,f.**

Gissing, George R. **PR5684**
Sleeping Fires. Trade Paper. Kessinger Publishing, LLC. Whitefish, MT. 2004. ISBN:1-4191-4778-1, ISBN13: 978-1-4191-4778-4. Dewey:823/.8.
Audience: **g,l,u,f.**

Gissing, George R. **PR4716**
The Unclassed. Trade Paper. Kessinger Publishing, LLC. Whitefish, MT. 2004. ISBN:1-4191-8622-1, ISBN13: 978-1-4191-8622-6. Dewey:823/.8.
Audience: **g,l,u,f.**

Gissing, George R. **PR4716**
The Whirlpool. Trade Paper. Kessinger Publishing, LLC. Whitefish, MT. 2004. ISBN:1-4191-8771-6, ISBN13: 978-1-4191-8771-1. Dewey:823.8.
Audience: **g,l,u,f.**

Gissing, George R. **PR4716.W66 1985**
Workers in the Dawn. Pierre Coustillas (Editor). Trade Paper. Routledge. New York, NY. 1985. 920p. ISBN:0-416-01101-2, ISBN13: 978-0-416-01101-2. Dewey:823/.8.
Audience: **g,l,u,f.**

Gissing, George R. **PR4716.N48 1999**
The Nether World. Stephen Gill (Editor). Trade Paper. Oxford University Press, Inc. New York, NY. 1999. 438p. Oxford World's Classics Ser. ISBN:0-19-283767-2, ISBN13: 978-0-19-283767-7. Dewey:823.8.
Audience: **g,l,u,f.** BCL3

Gissing, George R. **PR4716.N48 1998**
New Grub Street. John Goode (Editor, Introduction by). Trade Paper. Oxford University Press, Inc. New York, NY. 1999. 568p. Oxford World's Classics Ser. ISBN:0-19-283658-7, ISBN13: 978-0-19-283658-8. Dewey:823/.8. LCCN:99-191923.
Audience: **g,l,u,f.** BCL3

Selig, Robert **PR4717.S4 1995**
George Gissing. Trade Cloth. Thomson Gale. Farmington Hills, MI. 1995. xiv, 156p. Twayne's English Authors Ser., 346 ISBN:0-8057-7061-5, ISBN13: 978-0-8057-7061-2. Dewey:823/.8. LCCN:94-022497.
Audience: **u,f.** *Choice, 1995.*

Individual Authors and Works > 19th C. > H

Blainey, Ann **PR4813.B55 1985**
Immortal Boy: A Portrait of Leigh Hunt. Cloth Text. Palgrave Macmillan. New York, NY. 1985. 256p. ISBN:0-312-40945-1, ISBN13: 978-0-312-40945-6. Dewey:828/.709. LCCN:84-027582.
Audience: **g,l,u,f.** BCL3 *Choice, 1985.*

Efrati, Carol **PR4809.H15E47 2002**
The Road to Danger, Guilt and Shame: The Lonely Way of A. E. Housman. Trade Cloth. Fairleigh Dickinson University Press. Cranbury, NJ. 2002. 376p. ISBN:0-8386-3906-2, ISBN13: 978-0-8386-3906-1. Dewey:821/.912. LCCN:2001-040225.
Audience: **u,f.** *Choice, 2002.*

Etherington, Norman **PR4732 .E86 1984**
Rider Haggard. Library Binding. Thomson Gale. Farmington Hills, MI. 1984. English Authors Ser., No. 383 ISBN:0-8057-6869-6, ISBN13: 978-0-8057-6869-5. Dewey:823/.8. LCCN:83-022883.
Audience: **l,u.**

Haggard, H. Rider **PR4731.K5 1998**
King Solomon's Mines. Dennis Butts (Editor, Introduction by, Notes by). Trade Paper. Oxford University Press, Inc. New York, NY. 1998. 366p. Oxford World's Classics Ser. ISBN:0-19-283485-1, ISBN13: 978-0-19-283485-0. Dewey:823/.8.
Audience: **g,l,u,f.**

Haggard, H. Rider **PR4731.S6 1991**
The Annotated She: A Critical Edition of H. Rider Haggard's Victorian Romance. Norman Etherington (Introduction by, Notes by). Trade Cloth. Indiana University Press. Bloomington, IN. 1991. 288p. ISBN:0-253-32072-0, ISBN13: 978-0-253-32072-8. Dewey:823/.8. LCCN:90-043751.
Audience: **g,l,u,f.**

Hallam, Arthur Henry **PR4735.H4**
Remains in Verse and Prose of Arthur Henry Hallam, with a Preface and Memoir ... Trade Cloth. Scholarly Publishing Office, University of Michigan Library. Ann Arbor, MI. 2004. ISBN:1-4181-1699-8, ISBN13: 978-1-4181-1699-6. Dewey:821.7.
Audience: **g,l,u,f.**

Hays, Mary & Opie, Amelia **PR4769.H6M4 2004**
The Memoirs of Emma Courtney and Adeline Mowbray; or the Mother and the Daughter. Miriam Wallace (Editor). Perfect. College Publishing. Glen Allen, VA. 2004. xiii, 645p. Eighteenth-Century Literature Ser. ISBN:0-9679121-9-9, ISBN13: 978-0-9679121-9-6. Dewey:823/.7. LCCN:2004-102757.
Audience: **g,l,u,f.**

Hays, Mary **PR4769.H6V5 1998**
The Victim of Prejudice. Ed. 2. Eleanor Ty (Editor), Edward Moore, Jean-Jacques Rousseau & Mary Wollstonecraft Sheley (Contribution by). Trade Paper. Broadview Press. Peterborough, ON. 1998. 260p. Literary Texts Ser. ISBN:1-55111-217-5, ISBN13: 978-1-55111-217-6. Dewey:823/.7. LCCN:99-169339.
Audience: **g,l,u,f.**

Henley, William Ernest **PR4783**
Poems by William Ernest Henley. Trade Paper. Kessinger Publishing, LLC. Whitefish, MT. 2005. ISBN:1-4179-3171-X, ISBN13: 978-1-4179-3171-2. Dewey:821.
Audience: **g,l,u,f.**

Henty, G. A. **PZ7.H4**
Ebook By Sheer Pluck A Tale of the Ashanti War. E-Book. Kessinger Publishing, LLC. Whitefish, MT. 2004. ISBN:1-4192-1141-2, ISBN13: 978-1-4192-1141-6. Dewey:87.1.
Audience: **g,l,u,f.**

Hoagwood, Terence A. **PR4809.H15H56 1995**
A. E. Housman Revisited. Trade Cloth. Thomson Gale. Farmington Hills, MI. 1995. 130p. Twayne's English Authors Ser., Vol. 514 ISBN:0-8057-7026-7, ISBN13: 978-0-8057-7026-1. Dewey:821/.912. LCCN:95-002015.
Audience: **l,u.** *Choice, 1996.*

Holden, Anthony **PR4813.H65 2005**
The Wit in the Dungeon: The Remarkable Life of Leigh Hunt--Poet, Revolutionary, and the Last of the Romantics. Trade Cloth. Little Brown & Company. New York, NY. 2005. 448p. ISBN:0-316-06752-0, ISBN13: 978-0-316-06752-2. Dewey:828/.709. LCCN:2005-044275.
Audience: **g,l,u,f.** *Choice, 2006.*

Hood, Thomas **PR4796 .M58; PN6175**
Hood's Own or Laughter from Year to Year. Trade Paper. Kessinger Publishing, LLC. Whitefish, MT. 2004. ISBN:1-4179-6219-4, ISBN13: 978-1-4179-6219-8. Dewey:827.72.
Audience: **g,l,u,f.**

Hood, Thomas **PR4795**
Humorous Poems by Thomas Hood. Trade Paper. Kessinger Publishing, LLC. Whitefish, MT. 2005. ISBN:1-4179-6221-6, ISBN13: 978-1-4179-6221-1. Dewey:828.7.
Audience: **g,l,u,f.**

Hood, Thomas **PR4795 .A2**
The Complete Poetical Works of Thomas Hood. Walter Jerrold (Editor). Trade Paper. Kessinger Publishing, LLC. Whitefish, MT. 2004. ISBN:1-4179-4554-0, ISBN13: 978-1-4179-4554-2. Dewey:821/.7.
Audience: **g,l,u,f.**

Housman, A. E. **PR4809.H15A17 1997**
The Poems of A. E. Housman. Archie Burnett (Editor). Trade Cloth. Oxford University Press, Inc. New York, NY. 1998. 640p. Oxford English Texts ISBN:0-19-812322-1, ISBN13: 978-0-19-812322-4. Dewey:821/.912. LCCN:97-016259.
Audience: **g,l,u,f.**

Hughes, Thomas **PR4809.H8T66 1999**
Tom Brown's Schooldays. Andrew Sanders (Editor). Trade Paper. Oxford University Press, Inc. New York, NY. 1999. 436p. Oxford World's Classics Ser. ISBN:0-19-283535-1, ISBN13: 978-0-19-283535-2. Dewey:823.8. LCCN:00-267040.
Audience: **g,l,u,f.**

Hunt, Leigh **PR4811**
Leigh Hunt: Selected Writings. David Jesson Dibley (Editor). Trade Paper. Routledge. New York, NY. 2003. 256p. Fyfield Bks. ISBN:0-415-96951-4, ISBN13: 978-0-415-96951-2. Dewey:828.709.
Audience: **g,l,u,f.**

Hunt, Leigh **PR4810 .A2 1978**
The Poetical Works of Leigh Hunt. H. S. Milford (Editor). Trade Cloth. A M S Press, Inc. New York, NY. ISBN:0-404-14556-6, ISBN13: 978-0-404-14556-9. Dewey:821/.7. LCCN:75-041147.
Audience: **g,l,u,f.**

Jerrold, Walter C. **PR4798.J5 1969**
Thomas Hood: His Life and Times. Library Binding. Greenwood Publishing Group, Inc. Portsmouth, NH. 1986. ix, 420p. ISBN:0-8371-1043-2, ISBN13: 978-0-8371-1043-1. Dewey:821/.7. LCCN:69-013953.
Audience: **l,u.**

Ricks, Christopher (Editor) **PR4809.H15R54**
A. E. Housman: A Collection of Critical Essays. Trade Paper. John Wiley & Sons, Inc. Hoboken, NJ. 1968. Twentieth Century Views Ser. ISBN:0-13-395905-8, ISBN13: 978-0-13-395905-5. Dewey:821/.9/12.
Audience: **l,u.**

Roe, Nicholas **PR4813**
Libertas: The Life of Leigh Hunt. Trade Cloth. Random House. London, 2006. 448p. ISBN:0-7126-0224-0, ISBN13: 978-0-7126-0224-2. Dewey:821.7. LCCN:2005-434342.
Audience: **g,l,u,f.** *Choice, 2006.*

Individual Authors and Works > 19th C. > Hardy, Thomas

Greenslade, William **PR4754**
Thomas Hardy's 'Facts' Notebook: A Critical Edition. Trade Cloth. Ashgate Publishing, Ltd. Aldershot, 2004. 402p. 19th Century Ser. ISBN:1-84014-235-9, ISBN13: 978-1-84014-235-8. Dewey:823/.8. LCCN:2002-042681.
Audience: **g.** *Choice, 2005.*

Halliday, F. E. **PR4753**
Thomas Hardy: His Life and Work. Trade Paper. House of Stratus, Inc. New York, NY. 2001. 199p. ISBN:1-84232-129-3, ISBN13: 978-1-84232-129-4. Dewey:823.8.
Audience: **g.**

Hardy, Emma & Hardy, Florence E. **PR4739.H77Z48 1996**
Letters of Emma and Florence Hardy. Michael Millgate (Editor). Trade Cloth. Oxford University Press, Inc. New York, NY. 1996. 390p. ISBN:0-19-818609-6, ISBN13: 978-0-19-818609-0. Dewey:820.9/008 B. LCCN:95-038304.
Audience: **u,f.**

Hardy, Florence E. **PR4753.H3**
The Early Life of Thomas Hardy: 1840-1891. Trade Cloth. Scholarly Press, Inc. Saint Clair Shores, MI. 1971. ISBN:0-403-00772-0, ISBN13: 978-0-403-00772-1. Dewey:823/.8 B.
Audience: **u,f.**

Hardy, Florence E. **PR4753**
The Later Years of Thomas Hardy, 1892-1928. Library Binding. Reprint Services Company. Temecula, CA. 1992. 286p. BCL1-PR English Literature Ser. ISBN:0-7812-7553-9, ISBN13: 978-0-7812-7553-8. Dewey:928.2391.
Audience: **u,f.**

Hardy, Thomas **PR4741**
Collected Poems. Paper Text. Classic Books. Murrieta, CA. 2001. 818p. Collected Works of Thomas Hardy ISBN:0-7426-7810-5, ISBN13: 978-0-7426-7810-1. Dewey:821.912.
Audience: **g,l,u,f.**

Hardy, Thomas **PR4750**
The Dynasts: An Epic Drama of the War with Napoleon Parts One and Two. Trade Paper. Kessinger Publishing, LLC. Whitefish, MT. 2004. ISBN:1-4179-0931-5, ISBN13: 978-1-4179-0931-5. Dewey:822.8.
Audience: **g.**

Hardy, Thomas **PR5684**
Far from the Madding Crowd. Trade Cloth. Random House Value Publishing. New York, NY. 2006. 496p. ISBN:0-517-22786-X, ISBN13: 978-0-517-22786-2. Dewey:823/.8.
Audience: **g,l,u,f.**

Hardy, Thomas **PR5684**
The Return of the Native. Trade Paper. Wordsworth Editions, Ltd. Ware, 1998. 400p. Classics Library ISBN:1-85326-238-2, ISBN13: 978-1-85326-238-8. Dewey:823/.8.
Audience: **g,l,u,f.**

Hardy, Thomas **PR4750.W39 1994**
Wessex Poems. Trade Cloth. Woodstock Books. Otley, 2003. 248p. Decadents, Symbolists, Anti-Decadents Ser. ISBN:1-85477-145-0, ISBN13: 978-1-85477-145-2. Dewey:821/.8. LCCN:93-041356.
Audience: **u,f.**

Hardy, Thomas **PR4748 .A2 1991**
Tess of the D'Urbervilles. Patricia Ingham (Introduction by). Trade Cloth. Knopf Publishing Group. New York, NY. 1991. 560p. ISBN:0-679-40586-0, ISBN13: 978-0-679-40586-3. Dewey:823.8.
Audience: **g,l,u,f.**

Hardy, Thomas **PR4746.A2T39 2002**
Jude the Obscure. Ed. 2. Patricia Ingham (Editor, Introduction by, Notes by). Trade Paper. Oxford University Press, Inc. New York, NY. 2003. 464p. Oxford World's Classics ISBN:0-19-280261-5, ISBN13: 978-0-19-280261-3. Dewey:823/.8. LCCN:2001-052326.
Audience: **g,l,u,f.**

Hardy, Thomas **PR4753**
The Collected Letters of Thomas Hardy: 1902-1908, Vol. 3. Richard L. Purdy (Editor). Trade Cloth. Oxford University Press, Inc. New York, NY. 1982. 378p. ISBN:0-19-812620-4, ISBN13: 978-0-19-812620-1. Dewey:823/.8. LCCN:77-030355.
Audience: **g.** B

Hardy, Thomas **PR4753**
The Collected Letters of Thomas Hardy, 1893-1901, Vol. 2. Richard L. Purdy (Editor). Trade Cloth. Oxford University Press, Inc. New York, NY. 1980. 320p. ISBN:0-19-812619-0, ISBN13: 978-0-19-812619-5. Dewey:823/.8. LCCN:79-042789.
Audience: **g.**

Hardy, Thomas **PR4753**
The Collected Letters of Thomas Hardy: 1914-1919, Vol. 5. Richard L. Purdy & Michael Millgate (Editors). Trade Cloth. Oxford University Press, Inc. New York, NY. 1985. 368p. ISBN:0-19-812622-0, ISBN13: 978-0-19-812622-5. Dewey:823/.8.
Audience: **g.**

Hardy, Thomas **PR4753**
The Collected Letters of Thomas Hardy: 1926-1927 (with Addenda, Corrigenda, and General Index), Vol. 7. Richard L. Purdy & Michael Millgate (Editors). Trade Cloth. Oxford University Press, Inc. New York, NY. 1988. 320p. ISBN:0-19-812624-7, ISBN13: 978-0-19-812624-9. Dewey:823/.8.
Audience: **g.**

Hardy, Thomas **PR4753**
The Collected Letters of Thomas Hardy: 1920-1925, Vol. 6. Richard L. Purdy & Michael Millgate (Editors). Cloth Text. Oxford University Press, Inc. New York, NY. 1987. 390p. ISBN:0-19-812623-9, ISBN13: 978-0-19-812623-2. Dewey:823/.8.
Audience: **g.**

Johnson, Lionel P. **PR4754 .J6 1973**
The Art of Thomas Hardy. Library Binding. M. S. G. Haskell House. Brooklyn, NY. 1969. Studies in Thomas Hardy, No. 14 ISBN:0-8383-0575-X, ISBN13: 978-0-8383-0575-1. Dewey:823/.8. LCCN:72-011548.
Audience: **g.**

Penguin Books Staff **PR9499.3.N3**
Jude the Obscure, Pride and Prejudice, Sons and Lovers, The Warden, Wuthering Heights, Vol. 2, Level 5. Cloth Text. Longman Publishing Group. White Plains, NY. 2000. 536p. Collected Classics, :Penguin Readers Ser. ISBN:0-582-34365-8, ISBN13: 978-0-582-34365-8. Dewey:823.
Audience: **g.**

Wolfreys, Julian (Editor) **PR4750.M3M38 2000**
The Mayor of Casterbridge. Cloth over Boards. Palgrave Macmillan. New York, NY. 2000. 223p. New Casebooks Ser. ISBN:0-312-23386-8, ISBN13: 978-0-312-23386-0. Dewey:823.8. LCCN:00-024308.
Audience: **g,l,u,f.**

Wright, Sarah Bird **PR4752.W75 2002**
Thomas Hardy A to Z: The Essential Reference to His Life and Work. Trade Cloth. Facts On File, Inc. New York, NY. 2002. 448p. Literary A to Z Ser. ISBN:0-8160-4289-6, ISBN13: 978-0-8160-4289-0. Dewey:823/.8. LCCN:2002-021481.
Audience: **g.** *Choice, 2003.*

Individual Authors and Works > 19th C. > Hazlitt, William

Hazlitt, William **PR4772**
Table Talk. Trade Paper. Kessinger Publishing, LLC. Whitefish, MT. 2004. ISBN:1-4191-5025-1, ISBN13: 978-1-4191-5025-8. Dewey:824.
Audience: **g,l,u,f.**

Hazlitt, William **PN2596.L6 H3 1979**
Hazlitt on Theatre: Selections from the View of the English Stage and Criticisms and Dramatic Essays. Robert Lowe (Editor), William Archer (Introduction by). Trade Cloth. Hyperion Press, Inc. Westport, CT. 1991. ISBN:0-88355-847-5, ISBN13: 978-0-88355-847-8. Dewey:792/.0941. LCCN:78-020469.
Audience: **g.**

Hazlitt, William & Wu, Duncan **PR4771.W8 1998**
The Selected Writings of William Hazlitt. Trade Cloth. Pickering & Chatto Publishers, Ltd. London, 1998. ISBN:1-85196-366-9, ISBN13: 978-1-85196-366-9. Dewey:824/.7. LCCN:98-010129.
Audience: **g.**

Hazlitt, William & Wu, Duncan **PR4771.W8 1998**
The Selected Writings of William Hazlitt. Trade Cloth. Pickering & Chatto Publishers, Ltd. London, 1998. ISBN:1-85196-362-6, ISBN13: 978-1-85196-362-1. Dewey:824/.7. LCCN:98-010129.
Audience: **g.**

Hazlitt, William & Wu, Duncan **PR4771.W8 1998**
The Selected Writings of William Hazlitt. Trade Cloth. Pickering & Chatto Publishers, Ltd. London, 1998. ISBN:1-85196-365-0, ISBN13: 978-1-85196-365-2. Dewey:824/.7. LCCN:98-010129.
Audience: **g.**

Hazlitt, William & Wu, Duncan **PR4771.W8 1998**
The Selected Writings of William Hazlitt. Trade Cloth. Pickering & Chatto Publishers, Ltd. London, 1998. ISBN:1-85196-368-5, ISBN13: 978-1-85196-368-3. Dewey:824/.7. LCCN:98-010129.
Audience: **g.**

Hazlitt, William & Wu, Duncan **PR4771.W8 1998**
The Selected Writings of William Hazlitt. Trade Cloth. Pickering & Chatto Publishers, Ltd. London, 1998. ISBN:1-85196-364-2, ISBN13: 978-1-85196-364-5. Dewey:824/.7. LCCN:98-010129.
Audience: **g.**

Hazlitt, William & Wu, Duncan **PR4771.W8 1998**
The Selected Writings of William Hazlitt. Trade Cloth. Pickering & Chatto Publishers, Ltd. London, 1998. ISBN:1-85196-363-4, ISBN13: 978-1-85196-363-8. Dewey:824/.7. LCCN:98-010129.
Audience: **g.**

Hazlitt, William & Wu, Duncan **PR4771.W8 1998**
The Selected Writings of William Hazlitt. Trade Cloth. Pickering & Chatto Publishers, Ltd. London, 1998. ISBN:1-85196-367-7, ISBN13: 978-1-85196-367-6. Dewey:824/.7. LCCN:98-010129.
Audience: **g.**

Jones, Stanley **PR4773.J66 1991**
Hazlitt: A Life: From Winterslow to Frith Street. Trade Paper. Oxford University Press, Inc. New York, NY. 1991. 416p. ISBN:0-19-282897-5, ISBN13: 978-0-19-282897-2. Dewey:824/.7 B. LCCN:91-012821.
Audience: **g.** *Choice, 1990.*

Kinnaird, John **PR4773**
William Hazlitt, Critic of Power. Cloth Text. Columbia University Press. New York, NY. 1978. 429p. ISBN:0-231-04600-6, ISBN13: 978-0-231-04600-8. Dewey:824/.7. LCCN:78-014523.
Audience: **g.** B

Paulin, Tom **PR4773**
The Day-Star of Liberty: William Hazlitt's Radical Style. Ed. 1. Trade Cloth. Faber & Faber, Inc. New York, NY. 1999. 400p. ISBN:0-571-17421-3, ISBN13: 978-0-571-17421-8. Dewey:824.7.
Audience: **g,l,u,f.**

Priestley, J. B. & Brett, R. L. **PR4773.P72 1994**
William Hazlitt. Michael Foot (Introduction by). Trade Cloth. Northcote House Publishers, Ltd. Tavistock, 1996. 80p. Writers and Their Work Ser. ISBN:0-7463-0745-4, ISBN13: 978-0-7463-0745-8. Dewey:824/.7 B. LCCN:95-218347.
Audience: **g.**

Individual Authors and Works > 19th C. > Hopkins, Gerard Manley

Allsopp, Michael E. & Sundermeier, Michael W. (Editors) **PR4803.H44Z6443 1989**
Gerard Manley Hopkins (1844-1889): New Essays on His Life, Writing and Place in English Literature. Trade Cloth. Edwin Mellen Press, The. Lewiston, NY. 1989. 304p. Studies in British Literature Ser., Vol. 1 ISBN:0-88946-928-8, ISBN13: 978-0-88946-928-0. Dewey:821/.8. LCCN:89-009309.
Audience: **g.** *Choice, 1989.*

Downes, David A. **PR4803.H44Z623 1990**
The Ignation Personality of Gerard Manley Hopkins. Trade Cloth. University Press of America, Inc. Lanham, MD. 1990. 234p. ISBN:0-8191-7664-8, ISBN13: 978-0-8191-7664-6. Dewey:821/.8. LCCN:89-024977.
Audience: **u,f.** *Choice, 1990.*

Ellis, Virginia R. **PR4803.H44Z625 1991**
Gerard Manley Hopkins and the Language of Mystery. Cloth Text. University of Missouri Press. Columbia, MO. 1991. 376p. ISBN:0-8262-0769-3, ISBN13: 978-0-8262-0769-2. Dewey:821/.8. LCCN:90-022095.
Audience: **u,f.** *Choice, 1991.*

Hartman, Geoffrey H. (editor) **PR4803.H44**
Hopkins; A Collection of Critical Essays. Prentice-Hall. 1966.
Audience: **g,l,u.**

Hollahan, Eugene (Editor) **PR4803.H44.Z6 1993**
Gerard Manley Hopkins and Critical Discourse. Trade Cloth. A M S Press, Inc. New York, NY. 1993. xiv, 372p. Georgia State Literary Studies, No. 11 ISBN:0-404-63211-4, ISBN13: 978-0-404-63211-3. Dewey:821/.8. LCCN:91-058149.
Audience: **u,f.**

Hopkins, Gerard Manley **PR4803.H44Z53**
Further Letters of Gerard Manley Hopkins, Including His Correspondence with Coventry Patmore. Paper Text. Textbook Publishers. Temecula, CA. 2003. xliii, 465p. ISBN:0-7581-7107-2, ISBN13: 978-0-7581-7107-8. Dewey:928.2.
Audience: **g.** B

Hopkins, Gerard Manley **PR4803.H44 Z55**
The Letters of Gerard Manley Hopkins to Robert Bridges. Paper Text. Textbook Publishers. Temecula, CA. 2003. xlvii, 324p. ISBN:0-7581-7181-1, ISBN13: 978-0-7581-7181-8. Dewey:928.2.
Audience: **g.** B

Hopkins, Gerard Manley **PR4803.H44**
A Hopkins reader. Pick, John (editor). Oxford University Press. 1953.
Audience: **g.**

Hopkins, Gerard Manley **PR4803.H44 A17**
Poems of Gerard Manley Hopkins. Ed. 4. W. H. Gardner & Norman H. MacKenzie (Editors). Trade Cloth. Oxford University Press, Inc. New York, NY. 1967. 426p. ISBN:0-19-500164-8, ISBN13: 978-0-19-500164-8. Dewey:821/.8.
Audience: **g.**

Hopkins, Gerard Manley **PR4803.H44A6 1991**
The Later Poetic Manuscripts of Gerard Manley Hopkins: From "The Wreck of the Deutschland" to the Final Dublin Sonnets in Facsimile. Norman H. MacKenzie (Editor). Cloth Text. Garland Publishing, Inc. New York, NY. 1991. 911031p. Gerard Manley Hopkins Ser. ISBN:0-8240-7444-0, ISBN13: 978-0-8240-7444-9. Dewey:821/.8. LCCN:91-003809.
Audience: **g.** *Choice, 1992.*

Hopkins, Gerard Manley **PR4803.H44A17 1989**
The Poetical Works of Gerard Manley Hopkins. Norman H. MacKenzie (Editor). Cloth Text. Oxford University Press, Inc. New York, NY. 1990. 624p. Oxford English Texts ISBN:0-19-811883-X, ISBN13: 978-0-19-811883-1. Dewey:821/.8. LCCN:88-029135.
Audience: **g.** *Choice, 1991.*

Hopkins, Gerard Manley **PR4803.H44Z48 1990**
Gerard Manley Hopkins: Selected Letters. Catherine Phillips (Editor). Trade Cloth. Oxford University Press, Inc. New York, NY. 1990. 384p. ISBN:0-19-818582-0, ISBN13: 978-0-19-818582-6. Dewey:821/.8 B. LCCN:89-015955.
Audience: **g.** *Choice, 1991.*

Loomis, Jeffrey B. **PR4803.H44Z7117 1988**
Dayspring in Darkness: Sacrament in Hopkins. Trade Cloth. Bucknell University Press. Cranbury, NJ. 1988. 224p. ISBN:0-8387-5138-5, ISBN13: 978-0-8387-5138-1. Dewey:821/.8. LCCN:87-047819.
Audience: **u,f.** *Choice, 1989.*

MacKenzie, Norman H. (Editor) **PR4803.H44A6 1989**
The Early Poetic Manuscripts and Notebooks of Gerard Manley Hopkins. Trade Cloth. Garland Publishing, Inc. New York, NY. 1989. 304p. Gerard Manley Hopkins Ser. ISBN:0-8240-3898-3, ISBN13: 978-0-8240-3898-4. Dewey:821/.8. LCCN:89-032239.
Audience: **g.** *Choice, 1990.*

MacKenzie, Norman H. **PR4803.H44.Z716**
A Reader's Guide to Gerard Manley Hopkins. Book, Other. Cornell University Press. Ithaca, NY. 1981. 256p. ISBN:0-8014-1349-4, ISBN13: 978-0-8014-1349-0. Dewey:821/.8. LCCN:80-069275.
Audience: **g.** B

Mariani, Paul L. **PR4803.H44.Z717**
Commentary on the Complete Poems of Gerard Manley Hopkins. Trade Cloth. Cornell University Press. Ithaca, NY. 1970. 372p. ISBN:0-8014-0553-X, ISBN13: 978-0-8014-0553-2. Dewey:821/.8. LCCN:74-105909.
Audience: **g,l,u,f.**

Martin, Robert B. **PR4803.H44Z71727**
Gerard Manley Hopkins: A Very Private Life. Trade Cloth. Penguin Group (USA) Inc. New York, NY. 1991. 352p. ISBN:0-399-13610-X, ISBN13: 978-0-399-13610-8. Dewey:821/.8 B. LCCN:91-006971.
Audience: **g.** *Choice, 1992.*

Nixon, Jude V. **PR4803.H44**
Gerald Manley Hopkins and His Contemporaries: Liddon, Newman, Darwin, and Pater. Cloth Text. Garland Publishing, Inc. New York, NY. 1993. 342p. Origins of Modernism Ser., Vol. 5 ISBN:0-8153-0386-6, ISBN13: 978-0-8153-0386-2. Dewey:821.8. LCCN:93-028007.
Audience: **u,f.** *Choice, 1994.*

Ong, Walter J. **PR4803.H44**
Hopkins, the Self and God. Cloth Text. University of Toronto Press. Toronto, ON. 1986. 194p. ISBN:0-8020-5688-1, ISBN13: 978-0-8020-5688-7. Dewey:821/.8. LCCN:92-177232.
Audience: **u,f.** *Choice, 1987.*

Phillips, Catherine (Editor) **PR4803.H44**
Gerard Manley Hopkins. Trade Cloth. Oxford University Press, Inc. New York, NY. 1987. 600p. The Oxford Authors Ser. ISBN:0-19-254190-0, ISBN13: 978-0-19-254190-1. Dewey:828/.809. LCCN:85-021405.
Audience: **g.** *Choice, 1988.*

Storey, Graham **PR4803.H44Z853 1992**
Preface to Hopkins. Ed. 2. Paper Text. Addison-Wesley Longman, Inc. Boston, MA. 1995. 256p. ISBN:0-582-08845-3, ISBN13: 978-0-582-08845-0. Dewey:821/.8 B. LCCN:91-022634.
Audience: **g.**

Sulloway, Alison G. **PR4803.H44C77 1990**
Critical Essays on Gerard Manley Hopkins. Trade Cloth. Thomson Gale. Farmington Hills, MI. 1989. 208p. Critical Essays on British Literature Ser. ISBN:0-8161-8773-8, ISBN13: 978-0-8161-8773-7. Dewey:821/.8. LCCN:89-015491.
Audience: **g.** *Choice, 1990.*

White, Norman **PR4803.H44Z924**
Hopkins: A Literary Biography. Trade Paper. Oxford University Press, Inc. New York, NY. 1995. 550p. ISBN:0-19-818350-X, ISBN13: 978-0-19-818350-1. Dewey:821.8.
Audience: **g.** *Choice, 1993.*

Zonneveld, Sjaak **PR4803.H44 Z98 1992**
Random Grim Forge: A Study of Social Ideas in the Work of Gerard Manley Hopkins. Trade Paper. Van Gorcum & Company B.V.. Assen, 1992. 200p. ISBN:90-232-2708-5, ISBN13: 978-90-232-2708-3. Dewey:821/.8. LCCN:92-231308.
Audience: **u,f.**

Individual Authors and Works > 19th C. > Keats, John

Bate, Walter Jackson **PR4836 .B3**
John Keats. Trade Paper. Harvard University Press. Cambridge, MA. 1979. 780p. Harvard Paperbacks Ser., No. 142 ISBN:0-674-47825-8, ISBN13: 978-0-674-47825-1. Dewey:821/.7. LCCN:63-017194.
Audience: **g.** B

Bate, Walter Jackson **PR4838.S8**
The Stylistic Development of Keats. Trade Cloth. A M S Press, Inc. New York, NY. ISBN:0-404-20019-2, ISBN13: 978-0-404-20019-0. Dewey:821.7. LCCN:83-048836.
Audience: **g.** B

Garrod, H. W. **PR4837 .G3**
Keats. Trade Paper. Kessinger Publishing, LLC. Whitefish, MT. 2003. ISBN:0-7661-4722-3, ISBN13: 978-0-7661-4722-5. Dewey:821.7.
Audience: **g.**

Gittings, Robert **PR4836**
John Keats. Trade Paper. Penguin Books Canada, Ltd. Toronto, ON. 2001. 528p. ISBN:0-14-139054-9, ISBN13: 978-0-14-139054-3. Dewey:821.7.
Audience: **g.**

Jack, Ian **PR457.J24**
English Literature, 1815-1832: Scott, Byron, and Keats. Trade Cloth. Oxford University Press, Inc. New York, NY. 1990. 656p. Oxford History of English Literature Ser., Vol XII ISBN:0-19-812238-1, ISBN13: 978-0-19-812238-8. Dewey:820.903. LCCN:63-025209.
Audience: **u,f.**

Keats, John **PR4830**
The Poetical Works of John Keats. with a Life. Trade Cloth. Scholarly Publishing Office, University of Michigan Library. Ann Arbor, MI. 2004. ISBN:1-4181-0151-6, ISBN13: 978-1-4181-0151-0. Dewey:821.7.
Audience: **g.**

Keats, John **PR4830**
The Poetical Works of John Keats. with A Memoir, by James Russell Lowell. Trade Cloth. Scholarly Publishing Office, University of Michigan Library. Ann Arbor, MI. 2004. ISBN:1-4181-0150-8, ISBN13: 978-1-4181-0150-3. Dewey:821.
Audience: **g.**

Keats, John **PR4832.C66 2001**
John Keats: The Major Works: Including Endymion, the Odes and Selected Letters. Elizabeth Cook (Editor). Trade Paper. Oxford University Press, Inc. New York, NY. 2001. 704p. Oxford World's Classics Ser. ISBN:0-19-284063-0, ISBN13: 978-0-19-284063-9. Dewey:821/.7. LCCN:2001-272404.
Audience: **g.**

Keats, John **PR4832.C66 1990**
John Keats. Elizabeth Cook (Editor). Trade Cloth. Oxford University Press, Inc. New York, NY. 1990. 704p. The Oxford Authors Ser. ISBN:0-19-254194-3, ISBN13: 978-0-19-254194-9. Dewey:821/.7. LCCN:89-049034.
Audience: **g.** *Choice, 1991.*

Keats, John **PR4836 .A56**
The Letters of John Keats. H. Buxton Forman (Editor). Trade Paper. Kessinger Publishing, LLC. Whitefish, MT. 2004. ISBN:1-4179-4563-X, ISBN13: 978-1-4179-4563-4. Dewey:826.7.
Audience: **g.**

Keats, John **PR4836.A4 1999**
The Letters of John Keats, 1814-1821. Hyder Edward Rollins (Editor). Trade Cloth. Harvard University Press. Cambridge, MA. 2002. 920p. ISBN:0-674-52702-X, ISBN13: 978-0-674-52702-7. Dewey:821/.7. LCCN:98-051920.
Audience: **g.**

Keats, John **PR4831.S75 1982**
John Keats: Complete Poems. Jack Stillinger (Editor). Trade Paper. Harvard University Press. Cambridge, MA. 1982. 528p. ISBN:0-674-15431-2, ISBN13: 978-0-674-15431-5. Dewey:821/.7. LCCN:82-006091.
Audience: **g.**

Keats, John **PR4831.S75 1978**
The Poems of John Keats. Jack Stillinger (Editor). Trade Cloth. Harvard University Press. Cambridge, MA. 1978. 792p. ISBN:0-674-67730-7, ISBN13: 978-0-674-67730-2. Dewey:821/.7. LCCN:78-004490.
Audience: **g.** B

Keats, John **PR4837 .S65**
The Texts of Keats' Poems. Jack Stillinger (Editor). Trade Cloth. Harvard University Press. Cambridge, MA. 1974. 320p. ISBN:0-674-87511-7, ISBN13: 978-0-674-87511-1. Dewey:821/.7. LCCN:73-086940.
Audience: **g.**

Matthews, G. M. (Editor) **PR4837.M27 1995**
John Keats. Paper over Boards. Routledge. New York, NY. 1996. 444p. Critical Heritage Ser. ISBN:0-415-13447-1, ISBN13: 978-0-415-13447-7. Dewey:821.7.
Audience: **g.**

Motion, Andrew **PR4381**
Keats. Trade Paper. University of Chicago Press. Chicago, IL. 1999. 656p. ISBN:0-226-54240-8, ISBN13: 978-0-226-54240-9. Dewey:821/.7 B. LCCN:98-041014.
Audience: **g.** *Choice, 1998.*

Murry, John M. **PR4837 .M8 1972**
Studies in Keats. Library Binding. M. S. G. Haskell House. Brooklyn, NY. 1969. Studies in Keats, No. 19 ISBN:0-8383-0671-3, ISBN13: 978-0-8383-0671-0. Dewey:821/.7. LCCN:78-185023.
Audience: **g.**

Pettet, E. C. **PR4837 .P4**
On the Poetry of Keats. Paper Text. Textbook Publishers. Temecula, CA. 2003. viii, 395p. ISBN:0-7581-1282-3, ISBN13: 978-0-7581-1282-8. Dewey:821/.7.
Audience: **g.**

Ridley, Maurice R. **PR4837**
Keats' Craftsmanship: A Study in Poetic Development. Library Binding. Reprint Services Company. Temecula, CA. 1992. 312p. BCL1-PR English Literature Ser. ISBN:0-7812-7574-1, ISBN13: 978-0-7812-7574-3. Dewey:821.7.
Audience: **u,f.**

Robinson, Jeffrey C. **PR4837.R54 1998**
Reception and Poetics in Keats: My Ended Poet. Cloth over Boards. Palgrave Macmillan. New York, NY. 1999. 221p. ISBN:0-312-21001-9, ISBN13: 978-0-312-21001-4. Dewey:821/.7. LCCN:97-031891.
Audience: **u,f.** *Choice, 1999.*

Roe, Nicholas **PR4838.P6R64 1997**
John Keats and the Culture of Dissent. Trade Cloth. Oxford University Press, Inc. New York, NY. 1997. 336p. ISBN:0-19-818396-8, ISBN13: 978-0-19-818396-9. Dewey:821/.7. LCCN:96-034554.
Audience: **u,f.**

Vendler, Helen H. **PR502**
Coming of Age as a Poet: Milton, Keats, Eliot, Plath. Trade Paper. Harvard University Press. Cambridge, MA. 2004. 192p. ISBN:0-674-01383-2, ISBN13: 978-0-674-01383-4. Dewey:820.9.
Audience: **g.** *Choice, 2003.*

Vendler, Helen H. **PR4837.V43**
The Odes of John Keats. Trade Paper. Harvard University Press. Cambridge, MA. 1983. 344p. Belknap Press Ser. ISBN:0-674-63076-9, ISBN13: 978-0-674-63076-5. Dewey:821/.7.
Audience: **g.** B

Walsh, John Evangelist **PR4836.W275 1999**
Darkling I Listen: Robert E. Lee's Army of Northern Virginia. Cloth over Boards. Palgrave Macmillan. New York, NY. 1999. 208p. ISBN:0-312-22255-6, ISBN13: 978-0-312-22255-0. Dewey:821/.7 B. LCCN:99-014213.
Audience: **g.** *Choice, 2000.*

Ward, Aileen **PR4836 .W3 1986**
John Keats: The Making of a Poet. Trade Paper. Farrar, Straus & Giroux. New York, NY. 1986. 488p. ISBN:0-374-52029-1, ISBN13: 978-0-374-52029-8. Dewey:821/.7. LCCN:86-080954.
Audience: **g.** B

Wolfson, Susan J. (Editor) **PR4837 .C27 2001**
The Cambridge Companion to Keats. Trade Paper. Cambridge University Press. New York, NY. 2001. 316p. Companions to Literature Ser. ISBN:0-521-65839-X, ISBN13: 978-0-521-65839-3. Dewey:821/.7. LCCN:00-064236.
Audience: **g.** *Choice, 2001.*

Individual Authors and Works > 19th C. > Kingsley, Charles

Kingsley, Charles **PR4840**
Hereward the Wake. Trade Paper. Kessinger Publishing, LLC. Whitefish, MT. 2003. ISBN:0-7661-7021-7, ISBN13: 978-0-7661-7021-6. Dewey:823/.8.
Audience: **g,l,u,f.**

Kingsley, Charles **PR4842**
Poems / by Charles Kingsley. Trade Cloth. Scholarly Publishing Office, University of Michigan Library. Ann Arbor, MI. 2004. ISBN:1-4181-2012-X, ISBN13: 978-1-4181-2012-2. Dewey:821.8.
Audience: **g,l,u,f.**

Kingsley, Charles **PR4842**
Westward Ho, Vol. 2. Trade Paper. Kessinger Publishing, LLC. Whitefish, MT. 2003. ISBN:0-7661-7016-0, ISBN13: 978-0-7661-7016-2. Dewey:823.85.
Audience: **g,l,u,f.**

Kingsley, Charles **PR4842**
Westward Ho, Vol. 1. Trade Paper. Kessinger Publishing, LLC. Whitefish, MT. 2003. ISBN:0-7661-7015-2, ISBN13: 978-0-7661-7015-5. Dewey:823.85.
Audience: **g,l,u,f.**

Kingsley, Charles **PZ3.K614**
Yeast: A Problem. Paper Text. Classic Books. Murrieta, CA. 2001. The Works of Charles Kingsley ISBN:0-7426-8588-8, ISBN13: 978-0-7426-8588-8. Dewey:823.
Audience: **g,l,u,f.**

Kingsley, Charles **PZ8.K619WAT 2006**
The Water Babies: A Fairy Tale for a Land-Baby. Warwick Goble (Illustrator). Trade Paper. Dover Publications, Inc. Mineola, NY. 2006. 160p. ISBN:0-486-45000-7, ISBN13: 978-0-486-45000-1. Dewey:[Fic]. LCCN:2005-046626.
Audience: **g,l,u,f.**

Kingsley, Charles & Hughes, Thomas **PZ3.E43**
Alton Locke, Vol. 1. Trade Paper. Kessinger Publishing, LLC. Whitefish, MT. 2004. ISBN:1-4179-2269-9, ISBN13: 978-1-4179-2269-7. Dewey:823.85.
Audience: **g,l,u,f.**

Stitt, Megan P. **PR868.S34 S85 1998**
Metaphors of Change in the Language of Nineteenth-Century Fiction: Scott, Gaskell, and Kingsley. Trade Cloth. Oxford University Press, Inc. New York, NY. 1998. 218p. Oxford English Monographs ISBN:0-19-818442-5, ISBN13: 978-0-19-818442-3. Dewey:823.7/09. LCCN:97-044617.
Audience: **u,f.**

Individual Authors and Works > 19th C. > Kipling, Rudyard

Gilmour, David **PR5823**
The Long Recessional: The Imperial Life of Rudyard Kipling. Trade Paper. Farrar, Straus & Giroux. New York, NY. 2003. 368p. ISBN:0-374-52896-9, ISBN13: 978-0-374-52896-6. Dewey:828/.809 B.
Audience: **g,l,u,f.** *Choice, 2003, 2002.*

Green, Roger Lancelyn (Editor) **PR4857**
Later Nineteenth and Early Twentieth Century English and European Novelists: Rudyard Kipling. Paper over Boards. Routledge. New York, NY. 1997. 428p. The Critical Heritage Ser. ISBN:0-415-15909-1, ISBN13: 978-0-415-15909-8. Dewey:809.3.
Audience: **g,l,u,f.**

Jarrell, Randall, et al. **PR4857.R77 1987**
Rudyard Kipling. Angus Wilson, Irving Howe, Donald Davie, Zohreh T. Sullivan, David Bromwich, Elliot L. Gilbert & Robert L. Caserio (Authors), Harold Bloom (Editor, Introduction by). Trade Cloth. Facts On File, Inc. New York, NY. 1988. 200p. Bloom's Modern Critical Views Ser. ISBN:0-87754-646-0, ISBN13: 978-0-87754-646-7. Dewey:828/.809. LCCN:86-021578.
Audience: **g,l,u,f.**

Kemp, Sandra **PR4858.I35K4 1988**
Kipling's Hidden Narratives. Cloth Text. Blackwell Publishing, Inc. Malden, MA. 1988. 192p. ISBN:0-631-15577-5, ISBN13: 978-0-631-15577-5. Dewey:823/.8. LCCN:87-034126.
Audience: **g,l,u,f.** *Choice, 1989.*

Kipling, Rudyard **PR4854**
Actions and Reactions. Trade Paper. Kessinger Publishing, LLC. Whitefish, MT. 2005. ISBN:1-4179-0439-9, ISBN13: 978-1-4179-0439-6. Dewey:813.
Audience: **g,l,u,f.**

Kipling, Rudyard **E168.K56**
American Notes. Trade Paper. Kessinger Publishing, LLC. Whitefish, MT. 2004. ISBN:1-4179-2815-8, ISBN13: 978-1-4179-2815-6. Dewey:320.
Audience: **g,l,u,f.**

Kipling, Rudyard **PR5684**
Captains Courageous. Trade Paper. Oxford University Press, Inc. New York, NY. 1999. 224p. Oxford World's Classics Ser. ISBN:0-19-283740-0, ISBN13: 978-0-19-283740-0. Dewey:823/.8.
Audience: **g,l,u,f.**

Kipling, Rudyard **PR4851**
Collected Verse of Rudyard Kipling. Trade Paper. Kessinger Publishing, LLC. Whitefish, MT. 2005. ISBN:1-4179-0750-9, ISBN13: 978-1-4179-0750-2. Dewey:821.
Audience: **g,l,u,f.**

Kipling, Rudyard **PZ3.K629DAY24**
The Day's Work. Trade Paper. Kessinger Publishing, LLC. Whitefish, MT. 2005. ISBN:1-4179-3391-7, ISBN13: 978-1-4179-3391-4. Dewey:823.8.
Audience: **g,l,u,f.**

Kipling, Rudyard **PR4852**
A Diversity of Creatures and Letters of. Trade Paper. Kessinger Publishing, LLC. Whitefish, MT. 2005. ISBN:1-4179-0359-7, ISBN13: 978-1-4179-0359-7. Dewey:823.
Audience: **g,l,u,f.**

Kipling, Rudyard **PR5823**
Life's Handicap. Trade Paper. Kessinger Publishing, LLC. Whitefish, MT. 2004. ISBN:1-4192-3044-1, ISBN13: 978-1-4192-3044-8. Dewey:828/.809.
Audience: **g,l,u,f.**

Kipling, Rudyard **PZ3.K629LIG27**
The Light that Failed. Trade Paper. Kessinger Publishing, LLC. Whitefish, MT. 2005. ISBN:0-7661-9464-7, ISBN13: 978-0-7661-9464-9. Dewey:823.
Audience: **g,l,u,f.**

Kipling, Rudyard **PR4854**
The Man Who Would Be King and Other Stories. Trade Paper. Oxford University Press, Inc. New York, NY. 1999. 352p. Oxford World's Classics Ser. ISBN:0-19-283629-3, ISBN13: 978-0-19-283629-8. Dewey:823/.8.
Audience: **g,l,u,f.**

Kipling, Rudyard **PR4854**
Plain Tales from the Hills. Trade Paper. Oxford University Press, Inc. New York, NY. 2001. 320p. Oxford World's Classics Ser. ISBN:0-19-283571-8, ISBN13: 978-0-19-283571-0. Dewey:823/.8. LCCN:2002-278329.
Audience: **g,l,u,f.**

Kipling, Rudyard **PR4852 .E45**
A Choice of Kipling's Verse. T. S. Eliot (Editor). Trade Paper. Faber & Faber, Inc. New York, NY. 1963. 304p. ISBN:0-571-05444-7, ISBN13: 978-0-571-05444-2. Dewey:821.8.
Audience: **g,l,u,f.** B

Kipling, Rudyard **PR4854,J83 K56 1998**
Just So Stories: For Little Children. Lisa Lewis (Editor), Rudyard Kipling (Illustrator), Lisa Lewis (Introduction by, Notes by). Trade Paper. Oxford University Press, Inc. New York, NY. 1998. 292p. Oxford World's Classics Ser. ISBN:0-19-283436-3, ISBN13: 978-0-19-283436-2. Dewey:823/.912. LCCN:98-205480.
Audience: **g,l,u,f.**

Kipling, Rudyard **PR4852 .M39**
Maugham's Choice of Kipling's Best. W. Somerset Maugham (Editor). Library Binding. Amereon, Ltd. Mattituck, NY. ISBN:0-88411-822-3, ISBN13: 978-0-88411-822-0. Dewey:823.89.
Audience: **g,l,u,f.**

Kipling, Rudyard **PR4854**
The Complete Stalky and Co. Isabel Quigly (Editor). Trade Paper. Oxford University Press, Inc. New York, NY. 1999. 362p. Oxford World's Classics Ser. ISBN:0-19-283859-8, ISBN13: 978-0-19-283859-9. Dewey:823.91.
Audience: **g,l,u,f.**

Kipling, Rudyard **PR4854**
The Jungle Books. W. W. Robson (Editor, Introduction by, Notes by). Trade Paper. Oxford University Press, Inc. New York, NY. 1998. 416p. Oxford World's Classics Ser. ISBN:0-19-283503-3, ISBN13: 978-0-19-283503-1. Dewey:823/.8.
Audience: **g,l,u,f.**

Kipling, Rudyard **PR4852.R87**
War Stories and Poems. Andrew Rutherford (Editor). Trade Paper. Oxford University Press, Inc. New York, NY. 1999. 404p. Oxford World's Classics Ser. ISBN:0-19-283686-2, ISBN13: 978-0-19-283686-1. Dewey:823.8.
Audience: **g,l,u,f.**

Kipling, Rudyard **PR4854**
Kim. Alan Sandison (Editor, Introduction by, Notes by). Trade Paper. Oxford University Press, Inc. New York, NY. 1998. 344p. Oxford World's Classics Ser. ISBN:0-19-283513-0, ISBN13: 978-0-19-283513-0. Dewey:823/.8. LCCN:86-016356.
Audience: **g,l,u,f.**

Kucich, John, et al. **PR1309.I46F53 2003**
Fictions of Empire: Heart of Darkness, The Man Who Would Be King and The Beach at Falesá. Joseph Conrad, Rudyard Kipling, Robert Louis Stevenson & Alan Richardson (Authors). Paper Text. Houghton Mifflin College Division. Boston, MA. 2002. 421p. New Riverside Editions Ser. ISBN:0-618-08488-6, ISBN13: 978-0-618-08488-3. Dewey:823/.809358. LCCN:2001-133336.
Audience: **g,l,u,f.**

Mallett, Phillip **PR4856.M24 2003**
Rudyard Kipling: A Literary Life. Cloth over Boards. Palgrave Macmillan. New York, NY. 2003. 256p. Literary Lives Ser. ISBN:0-333-55720-4, ISBN13: 978-0-333-55720-4. Dewey:828/.809 B. LCCN:2003-048286.
Audience: **g,l,u,f.** *Choice, 2004.*

Orel, Harold (Editor) **PR4857.C75 1989**
Critical Essays on Rudyard Kipling. Trade Cloth. Thomson Gale. Farmington Hills, MI. 1989. 248p. Critical Essays on British Literature Ser. ISBN:0-8161-8767-3, ISBN13: 978-0-8161-8767-6. Dewey:828/.809. LCCN:89-030750.
Audience: **g,u,f.**

Ricketts, Harry **PR4856.R54 2001**
Rudyard Kipling: A Life. Trade Paper. Avalon Publishing Group. New York, NY. 2000. 448p. ISBN:0-7867-0830-1, ISBN13: 978-0-7867-0830-7. Dewey:828/.809 B. LCCN:2002-277531.
Audience: **g,l,u,f.** *Choice, 2000.*

Sullivan, Zohreh T. **PR4858.I48 S85 1993**
Narratives of Empire: The Fictions of Rudyard Kipling. Trade Cloth. Cambridge University Press. New York, NY. 1993. 213p. ISBN:0-521-43425-4, ISBN13: 978-0-521-43425-6. Dewey:823.8. LCCN:92-017956.
Audience: **g,u,f.**

Wurgaft, Lewis D. **DS475 .W87**
The Imperial Imagination: Magic and Myth in Kipling's India. Trade Paper. Wesleyan University Press. Middletown, CT. 1986. 235p. ISBN:0-8195-6146-0, ISBN13: 978-0-8195-6146-6. Dewey:954.03. LCCN:82-023678.
Audience: **u,f.**

Young, W. Arthur **PR4856.A28**
A Dictionary of the Characters and Scenes in the Stories and Poems of Rudyard Kipling, 1886-1911. Library Binding. Reprint Services Company. Temecula, CA. 1992. 231p. BCL1-PR English Literature Ser. ISBN:0-7812-7583-0, ISBN13: 978-0-7812-7583-5. Dewey:828/.8/09.
Audience: **g,l,u,f.**

Individual Authors and Works > 19th C. > Lamb, Charles

Aaron, Jane **PR4864.A2 1991**
A Double Singleness: Gender and the Writings of Charles and Mary Lamb. Cloth Text. Oxford University Press, Inc. New York, NY. 1991. 230p. ISBN:0-19-812890-8, ISBN13: 978-0-19-812890-8. Dewey:824/.7. LCCN:90-027142.
Audience: **u,f.** *Choice, 1992.*

Barnett, George L. **PR4863 .B33 1972**
Charles Lamb: The Evolution of Elia. Library Binding. M. S. G. Haskell House. Brooklyn, NY. 1972. English Literature Ser., No. 33 ISBN:0-8383-1652-2, ISBN13: 978-0-8383-1652-8. Dewey:824/.7. LCCN:72-006858.
Audience: **u,f.**

Barnett, George L. **PR4863.B327**
Charles Lamb. Trade Cloth. Irvington Publishers. New York, NY. 1976. 172p. Twayne's English Authors Ser. ISBN:0-8057-6668-5, ISBN13: 978-0-8057-6668-4. Dewey:824/.7. LCCN:76-047526.
Audience: **l,u.**

Brown, John M. & Lamb, Charles **PR4860.A4 B7 1975**
The Portable Charles Lamb. Trade Cloth. Greenwood Publishing Group, Inc. Portsmouth, NH. 1975. 594p. ISBN:0-8371-8202-6, ISBN13: 978-0-8371-8202-5. Dewey:824/.7. LCCN:75-011488.
Audience: **g,l,u,f.**

Courtney, Winifred F. **PR4863.C6 1982**
Young Charles Lamb, 1775-1802. Trade Cloth. New York University Press. New York, NY. 1982. 411p. Gotham Library Ser. ISBN:0-8147-1382-3, ISBN13: 978-0-8147-1382-2. Dewey:824/.7. LCCN:81-014021.
Audience: **u,f.**

Hitchcock, Susan Tyler **PR4865.L2Z69 2005**
Mad Mary Lamb: Lunacy and Murder in Literary London. Trade Cloth. W. W. Norton & Company, Inc. New York, NY. 2005. 352p. ISBN:0-393-05741-0, ISBN13: 978-0-393-05741-6. Dewey:824/.7 B. LCCN:2004-019753.
Audience: **g,l,u,f.**

Lamb, Charles **PR4860.A4 G6 1978**
Charles Lamb: Prose and Poetry. Trade Cloth. Greenwood Publishing Group, Inc. Portsmouth, NH. 1978. 216p. The Clarendon Series of English Literature Ser. ISBN:0-313-20274-5, ISBN13: 978-0-313-20274-2. Dewey:824/.7. LCCN:77-028850.
Audience: **u,f.**

Lamb, Charles **PR4861.A2**
Essays of Elia: The Works of Charles Lamb, Vol. 1. Trade Paper. Kessinger Publishing, LLC. Whitefish, MT. 2005. ISBN:1-4179-1823-3, ISBN13: 978-1-4179-1823-2. Dewey:824.
Audience: **l,u,f.**

Lamb, Charles **PR4036**
Tales from Shakespeare. Library Binding. Sagebrush Education Resources. Caledonia, MN. 1986. ISBN:0-613-81941-1, ISBN13: 978-0-613-81941-1. Dewey:823.7.
Audience: **g,l,u,f.**

Lamb, Charles & Lamb, Mary **PR4860.A2 1971**
The Works of Charles and Mary Lamb, Set. E. V. Lucas (Editor). Trade Cloth. Scholarly Press, Inc. Saint Clair Shores, MI. 1970. ISBN:0-403-00366-0, ISBN13: 978-0-403-00366-2. Dewey:824/.7/08. LCCN:70-115252.
Audience: **l,u,f.**

Lamb, Charles **PR4860**
Charles Lamb: Selected Writings. J. E. Morpurgo (Editor, Introduction by). Trade Paper. Routledge. New York, NY. 2003. 96p. Fyfield Bks. ISBN:0-415-96955-7, ISBN13: 978-0-415-96955-0. Dewey:824.7.
Audience: **u,f.**

Lamb, Charles **PR4860.A3 1980**
Lamb As Critic. Roy Park (Editor). Trade Cloth. University of Nebraska Press. Lincoln, NE. 1980. xii, 367p. ISBN:0-8032-8700-3, ISBN13: 978-0-8032-8700-6. Dewey:809. LCCN:78-073572.
Audience: **u,f.**

McKenna, Wayne **PR4864.M3**
Charles Lamb and the Theatre. Trade Cloth. HarperCollins Publishers. New York, NY. 1977. 134p. ISBN:0-06-494707-6, ISBN13: 978-0-06-494707-7. Dewey:792/.092/4. LCCN:77-082139.
Audience: **g,l,u,f.**

Individual Authors and Works > 19th C. > M

Humpherys, Anne **PR4989.M48.Z687 1984**
Henry Mayhew. Trade Cloth. Thomson Gale. Farmington Hills, MI. 1984. 189p. English Authors Ser., No. 396 ISBN:0-8057-6882-3, ISBN13: 978-0-8057-6882-4. Dewey:808/.0092/4. LCCN:83-022729.
Audience: **g,l,u,f.**

Logan, Deborah Anna **PR4984.M5Z68 2002**
The Hour and the Woman: Harriet Martineau's "Somewhat Remarkable" Life. Trade Cloth. Northern Illinois University Press. DeKalb, IL. 2003. 343p. ISBN:0-87580-297-4, ISBN13: 978-0-87580-297-8. Dewey:823/.8 B. LCCN:2002-022608.
Audience: **g,l,u,f.** *Choice, 2003.*

Macaulay, Thomas Babington Macaulay, Baron **DA27**
Critical, historical, and miscellaneous essays and poems, by Lord Macaulay; with a memoir and Index. Trade Cloth. Scholarly Publishing Office, University of Michigan Library. Ann Arbor, MI. 2004. ISBN:1-4181-2222-X, ISBN13: 978-1-4181-2222-5. Dewey:824.8.
Audience: **g,l,u,f.**

Macaulay, Thomas Babington Macaulay, Baron **DA511.P6**
Life of William Pitt. by Lord Macaulay. Preceded by the life of the Earl of Chatham. Trade Cloth. Scholarly Publishing Office, University of Michigan Library. Ann Arbor, MI. 2004. ISBN:1-4181-0624-0, ISBN13: 978-1-4181-0624-9. Dewey:941.073.
Audience: **g,l,u,f.**

Macaulay, Thomas Babington Macaulay, Baron **DA536.M15**
Speeches by the Rt. Hon. Thomas Babington Macaulay. Trade Cloth. Scholarly Publishing Office, University of Michigan Library. Ann Arbor, MI. 2004. ISBN:1-4181-0628-3, ISBN13: 978-1-4181-0628-7. Dewey:825.
Audience: **g,l,u,f.**

MacDonald, George **PR5684**
At the Back of the North Wind. E-Book. Kessinger Publishing, LLC. Whitefish, MT. 2004. ISBN:1-4192-0800-4, ISBN13: 978-1-4192-0800-3. Dewey:823/.8.
Audience: **g,l,u,f.**

MacDonald, George **PR5684**
Phantastes. Trade Paper. Kessinger Publishing, LLC. Whitefish, MT. 2004. ISBN:1-4191-4121-X, ISBN13: 978-1-4191-4121-8. Dewey:823/.8.
Audience: **g,l,u,f.**

MacDonald, George **PZ8.M1754**
The Princess and the Goblin. Trade Paper. Kessinger Publishing, LLC. Whitefish, MT. 2004. ISBN:1-4192-7868-1, ISBN13: 978-1-4192-7868-6. Dewey:823/.8.
Audience: **g,l,u,f.**

Marryat, Frederick **E0165.M372**
Diary in America. Trade Paper. Kessinger Publishing, LLC. Whitefish, MT. 2004. ISBN:1-4191-1583-9, ISBN13: 978-1-4191-1583-7. Dewey:917.3.
Audience: **g,l,u,f.**

Marryat, Frederick **PR4036**
Masterman Ready. E-Book. Kessinger Publishing, LLC. Whitefish, MT. 2004. ISBN:1-4192-3321-1, ISBN13: 978-1-4192-3321-0. Dewey:823/.7.
Audience: **g,l,u,f.** B

Marryat, Frederick **PR4977**
Mr. Midshipman Easy. Trade Paper. Kessinger Publishing, LLC. Whitefish, MT. 2005. ISBN:1-4179-0822-X, ISBN13: 978-1-4179-0822-6. Dewey:823/.7.
Audience: **g,l,u,f.**

Martineau, Harriet **PR4984.M5 Z463**
Harriet Martineaus's Autobiography, Vol. 1. Trade Paper. Kessinger Publishing, LLC. Whitefish, MT. 2005. ISBN:1-4179-7016-2, ISBN13: 978-1-4179-7016-2. Dewey:823/.8.
Audience: **g,l,u,f.**

Martineau, Harriet **PR4984.M5 Z463**
Harriet Martineaus's Autobiography, Vol. 2. Trade Paper. Kessinger Publishing, LLC. Whitefish, MT. 2005. ISBN:1-4179-7017-0, ISBN13: 978-1-4179-7017-9. Dewey:823/.8.
Audience: **g,l,u,f.**

Martineau, Harriet **PR4803.H44Z48 1991**
Selected Letters. Valerie Sanders (Editor). Trade Paper. Oxford University Press, Inc. New York, NY. 1991. 384p. ISBN:0-19-282818-5, ISBN13: 978-0-19-282818-7. Dewey:821/.8 B. LCCN:90-025935.
Audience: **g,l,u,f.**

Maturin, Charles R. **PR4987.M7M42 2000**
Melmoth the Wanderer. Victor Sage (Editor). Trade Paper. Penguin Group (USA) Inc. New York, NY. 2001. 704p. Classics Ser. ISBN:0-14-044761-X, ISBN13: 978-0-14-044761-3. Dewey:823/.7. LCCN:2001-265474.
Audience: **g,l,u,f.**

Mayhew, Henry **HV4086.L66M38 2005**
The London Underworld in the Victorian Period: Authentic First-Person Accounts by Beggars, Thieves and Prostitutes. Trade Paper, Perfect. Dover Publications, Inc. Mineola, NY. 2005. 416p. ISBN:0-486-44006-0, ISBN13: 978-0-486-44006-4. Dewey:305.5/69/0942109034. LCCN:2005-041274.
Audience: **g,l,u,f.**

Mayhew, Henry **HV4086.L66 M38 1985**
London Labour and the London Poor. Victor Neuburg (Introduction by, Selected by). Trade Paper. Penguin Group (USA) Inc. New York, NY. 1986. 544p. Penguin Classics Ser. ISBN:0-14-043241-8, ISBN13: 978-0-14-043241-1. Dewey:305.5/69/09421. LCCN:86-111565.
Audience: **g,l,u,f.** B

Individual Authors and Works > 19th C. > Meredith, George

Beer, Gillian **PR5014.B4 1970**
Meredith: A Change of Masks. Trade Cloth. Continuum International Publishing Group, Ltd. London, 1970. x, 214 P.p. A Study of the Novels Ser. ISBN:0-485-11122-5, ISBN13: 978-0-485-11122-4. Dewey:823/.8. LCCN:70-546357.
Audience: **u,f.** B

Meredith, George **PR5684**
Evan Harrington, Pt. 2. Paper Text. Classic Books. Murrieta, CA. 2001. 320p. The Works of George Meredith, Vol. 4 ISBN:0-7426-5189-4, ISBN13: 978-0-7426-5189-0. Dewey:823/.8.
Audience: **g.**

Meredith, George **PR5684**
Evan Harrington, Pt. 1. Paper Text. Classic Books. Murrieta, CA. 2001. 316p. The Works of George Meredith, Vol. 3 ISBN:0-7426-5188-6, ISBN13: 978-0-7426-5188-3. Dewey:823/.8.
Audience: **g.**

Meredith, George **PR5007**
Poems by George Meredith. Trade Paper. Kessinger Publishing, LLC. Whitefish, MT. 2004. ISBN:1-4179-3069-1, ISBN13: 978-1-4179-3069-2. Dewey:821/.8.
Audience: **g.**

Meredith, George **PR5008.M6 1995**
Modern Love. Gillian Beer (Editor, Preface by). Trade Paper. Penguin Group (USA) Inc. New York, NY. 1996. 64p. Syrens Ser. ISBN:0-14-038909-1, ISBN13: 978-0-14-038909-8. Dewey:821/.8. LCCN:96-135550.
Audience: **g.**

Meredith, George **PR5013.A43 1970**
Letters of George Meredith. C. L. Cline (Editor). Trade Cloth. Oxford University Press, Inc. New York, NY. 1970. ISBN:0-19-811473-7, ISBN13: 978-0-19-811473-4. Dewey:823/.8. LCCN:79-499447.
Audience: **g.** B

Meredith, George **PR5684**
Diana of the Crossways. Nikki Lee Manos (Introduction by). Trade Cloth. Wayne State University Press. Detroit, MI. 2001. 448p. ISBN:0-8143-2976-4, ISBN13: 978-0-8143-2976-4. Dewey:823/.8.
Audience: **g.**

Meredith, George **PR5006.O7 1998**
The Ordeal of Richard Feverel: A History of a Father and Son. Edward Mendelson (Editor). Trade Paper. Penguin Group (USA) Inc. New York, NY. 1999. 560p. Penguin Classics Ser. ISBN:0-14-043483-6, ISBN13: 978-0-14-043483-5. Dewey:823.8. LCCN:99-461805.
Audience: **g.**

Meredith, George **PR5684**
The Egoist. Angus Wilson (Editor). Trade Paper. Penguin Group (USA) Inc. New York, NY. 1986. ISBN:0-452-00820-4, ISBN13: 978-0-452-00820-5. Dewey:823/.8.
Audience: **g.** B

Muendel, Renate **PR5014 .M84 1986**
George Meredith. Trade Cloth. Macmillan Publishing Company, Inc. Old Tappan, NJ. 1986. 160p. Twayne's English Authors Ser., No. 434 ISBN:0-8057-6932-3, ISBN13: 978-0-8057-6932-6. Dewey:823/.8. LCCN:86-012110.
Audience: **g.** *Choice, 1987.*

Priestley, J. B. **PR5684**
George Meredith. Library Binding. Reprint Services Company. Temecula, CA. 1992. 204p. BCL1-PR English Literature Ser. ISBN:0-7812-7597-0, ISBN13: 978-0-7812-7597-2. Dewey:823/.8.
Audience: **g.** B

Sassoon, Siegfried **PR5013 .S3**
Meredith. Trade Cloth. Associated Faculty Press, Inc. New York, NY. 1969. ISBN:0-8046-0404-5, ISBN13: 978-0-8046-0404-8. Dewey:823/.8 B. LCCN:68-026214.
Audience: **g.** B

Stevenson, Richard C. **PR5017.T4S74 2004**
The Experimental Impulse in George Meredith's Fiction. Trade Cloth. Bucknell University Press. Cranbury, NJ. 2004. 240p. ISBN:0-8387-5575-5, ISBN13: 978-0-8387-5575-4. Dewey:823/.8. LCCN:2004-002994.
Audience: **u,f.** *Choice, 2005.*

Wright, Walter F. **PR5014**
Art and Substance in George Meredith: A Study in Narrative. Trade Cloth. Greenwood Publishing Group, Inc. Portsmouth, NH. 1980. 211p. ISBN:0-313-22514-1, ISBN13: 978-0-313-22514-7. Dewey:823/.8. LCCN:80-014417.
Audience: **u.**

Individual Authors and Works > 19th C. > Moore, George

Frazier, Adrian **PR5043.F57 2000**
George Moore, 1852-1933. Cloth over Boards. Yale University Press. Cumberland, RI. 2000. 624p. ISBN:0-300-08245-2, ISBN13: 978-0-300-08245-6. Dewey:823/.8 B. LCCN:99-088360.
Audience: **u,f.** *Choice, 2000.*

Moore, George **PR5042 .C6; PZ3.M783**
Confessions of A Young Man. Trade Paper. Kessinger Publishing, LLC. Whitefish, MT. 2004. ISBN:1-4191-1382-8, ISBN13: 978-1-4191-1382-6. Dewey:828/.8/03.
Audience: **g,l,u,f.**

Moore, George **PR5042 .H3**
Hail and Farewell!, Vol. 1. Trade Paper. Kessinger Publishing, LLC. Whitefish, MT. 2005. ISBN:1-4179-3122-1, ISBN13: 978-1-4179-3122-4. Dewey:823.8.
Audience: **g,l,u,f.**

Moore, George **PR5042 .H3**
Hail and Farewell!, Vol. 2. Trade Paper. Kessinger Publishing, LLC. Whitefish, MT. 2005. ISBN:1-4179-3272-4, ISBN13: 978-1-4179-3272-6. Dewey:823.8.
Audience: **g,l,u,f.**

Moore, George **PR5042 .E8 1999**
Esther Waters. David Skilton (Editor). Trade Paper. Oxford University Press, Inc. New York, NY. 2001. 426p. Oxford World's Classics Ser. ISBN:0-19-283712-5, ISBN13: 978-0-19-283712-7. Dewey:823.8. LCCN:82-022330.
Audience: **g,l,u,f.**

Individual Authors and Works > 19th C. > Morris, William

Boos, Florence S. & Silver, Carole G. (Editors) **PR5087.S6S63 1990**
Socialism and the Literary Artistry of William Morris. Cloth Text. University of Missouri Press. Columbia, MO. 1990. 192p. ISBN:0-8262-0725-1, ISBN13: 978-0-8262-0725-8. Dewey:821/.8. LCCN:89-004834.
Audience: **u,f.** *Choice, 1991.*

Faulkner, Peter **PR5083**
Against the Age: An Introduction to William Morris. Cloth Text. Routledge. New York, NY. 1980. 192p. ISBN:0-04-809012-3, ISBN13: 978-0-04-809012-6. Dewey:709/.2/4. LCCN:80-040460.
Audience: **g.** B

Faulkner, Peter (Editor) **PR5084**
William Morris. Paper over Boards. Routledge. New York, NY. 1996. 480p. Critical Heritage Ser. ISBN:0-415-13474-9, ISBN13: 978-0-415-13474-3. Dewey:828.809.
Audience: **g.**

Faulkner, Peter & Preston, Peter (Editors) **PR5084.M67 1996**
William Morris: Centenary Essays. Trade Cloth. University of Exeter Press. Exeter, 1999. 300p. ISBN:0-85989-577-7, ISBN13: 978-0-85989-577-4. Dewey:821/.8. LCCN:2003-430249.
Audience: **g.**

Kirchhoff, Frederick **PR5087.M36K57 1990**
William Morris: The Construction of a Male Self, 1856-1872. Cloth Text. Ohio University Press. Athens, OH. 1990. 275p. ISBN:0-8214-0954-9, ISBN13: 978-0-8214-0954-1. Dewey:821/.8. LCCN:89-029000.
Audience: **u,f.** *Choice, 1991.*

MacCarthy, Fiona **PR5083.M23 1995**
William Morris: A Life for Our Time. Trade Cloth. Alfred A. Knopf Inc. New York, NY. 1995. 800p. ISBN:0-394-58531-3, ISBN13: 978-0-394-58531-4. Dewey:709.2. LCCN:95-035074.
Audience: **g.**

Morris, William **HX521 .M7**
Art and Socialism. Trade Paper. Kessinger Publishing, LLC. Whitefish, MT. 2004. ISBN:1-4191-0771-2, ISBN13: 978-1-4191-0771-9. Dewey:335.
Audience: **g.**

Morris, William **PR1105**
Chants for Socialists. Trade Paper. Kessinger Publishing, LLC. Whitefish, MT. 2004. ISBN:1-4191-1253-8, ISBN13: 978-1-4191-1253-9. Dewey:821.85.
Audience: **g.**

Morris, William **PR5078.D4**
The Defence of Guenevere, and Other Poems. Trade Paper. Books on Demand. Ann Arbor, MI. 556p. World's Classics Ser., Vol. 183 ISBN:0-598-58604-0, ISBN13. 978-0-598-58604-9. LCCN:41-003920.
Audience: **g,l,u,f.**

Morris, William **PR5079**
A Dream of John Ball and A King's Lesson. Trade Paper. Kessinger Publishing, LLC. Whitefish, MT. 2004. ISBN:1-4191-0104-8, ISBN13: 978-1-4191-0104-5. Dewey:823.8.
Audience: **g.**

Morris, William **PR5075**
The Earthy paradise, a poem. by William Morris. Trade Cloth. Scholarly Publishing Office, University of Michigan Library. Ann Arbor, MI. 2004. ISBN:1-4181-0819-7, ISBN13: 978-1-4181-0819-9. Dewey:821.8.
Audience: **g.**

Morris, William **N7445**
Hopes and Fears for Art. Trade Paper. Kessinger Publishing, LLC. Whitefish, MT. 2004. ISBN:1-4191-2460-9, ISBN13: 978-1-4191-2460-0. Dewey:701.
Audience: **g.**

Morris, William **PR5076**
The Life and Death of Jason. A poem by William Morris. Trade Cloth. Scholarly Publishing Office, University of Michigan Library. Ann Arbor, MI. 2004. ISBN:1-4181-0772-7, ISBN13: 978-1-4181-0772-7. Dewey:821.
Audience: **g.**

Morris, William **HX811**
News from Nowhere or an Epoch of Rest. Trade Paper. Kessinger Publishing, LLC. Whitefish, MT. 2004. ISBN:1-4191-3697-6, ISBN13: 978-1-4191-3697-9. Dewey:321.07.
Audience: **g.**

Morris, William **PR5078**
The Pilgrims of Hope. Trade Paper. Kessinger Publishing, LLC. Whitefish, MT. 2004. ISBN:1-4191-7747-8, ISBN13: 978-1-4191-7747-7. Dewey:821.85.
Audience: **g.**

Morris, William **PR5079 .R65**
The Roots of the Mountain Wherein is Told Somewhat of the Lives of the Men of Burgdale, Their Friends, Their Neighbours, Their Foemen and Their Fellows in Arms. Trade Paper. Kessinger Publishing, LLC. Whitefish, MT. 2004. ISBN:1-4191-8105-X, ISBN13: 978-1-4191-8105-4. Dewey:823/.8.
Audience: **g.**

Morris, William **HX246**
Signs of Change. Trade Paper. Kessinger Publishing, LLC. Whitefish, MT. 2004. ISBN:1-4191-4727-7, ISBN13: 978-1-4191-4727-2. Dewey:335.1.
Audience: **g.**

Morris, William **PR5684**
The Story of the Glittering Plain. Trade Paper. Kessinger Publishing, LLC. Whitefish, MT. 2004. ISBN:1-4191-8406-7, ISBN13: 978-1-4191-8406-2. Dewey:823/.8.
Audience: **g.**

Morris, William **PR5684**
The Water of the Wondrous Isles. Trade Paper. Kessinger Publishing, LLC. Whitefish, MT. 2004. ISBN:1-4191-8741-4, ISBN13: 978-1-4191-8741-4. Dewey:823/.8.
Audience: **g.**

Morris, William **PR5684**
The Well at the World's End. Trade Paper. Kessinger Publishing, LLC. Whitefish, MT. 2004. ISBN:1-4191-8758-9, ISBN13: 978-1-4191-8758-2. Dewey:823/.8.
Audience: **g.**

Morris, William **PR5684**
Wood Beyond the World. Trade Paper. Kessinger Publishing, LLC. Whitefish, MT. 2004. ISBN:1-4191-9485-2, ISBN13: 978-1-4191-9485-6. Dewey:823/.8.
Audience: **g.**

Morris, William O'Connor **DC149**
The French Revolution and First Empire: An Historical Sketch. by William O'Connor Morris. with an appendix upon the bibliography of the subject and a course of study by Hon. Andrew D. White. Trade Cloth. Scholarly Publishing Office, University of Michigan Library. Ann Arbor, MI. 2004. ISBN:1-4181-2173-8, ISBN13: 978-1-4181-2173-0. Dewey:944.04.
Audience: **g.**

Morris, William & Shankland, Graeme **PR5080 .N48 1986**
News from Nowhere and Selected Writings and Design. Asa Briggs (Editor). Trade Paper. Penguin Group (USA) Inc. New York, NY. 1984. 320p. English Library ISBN:0-14-043115-2, ISBN13: 978-0-14-043115-5. Dewey:082.
Audience: **g.**

Silver, Carole **PR5084 .S5 1982**
The Romance of William Morris. Trade Paper. Ohio University Press. Athens, OH. 1983. 251p. ISBN:0-8214-0706-6, ISBN13: 978-0-8214-0706-6. Dewey:821/.8. LCCN:82-002278.
Audience: **g.**

Thompson, E. P. **PR5083**
William Morris: Romantic to Revolutionary. Ed. 2. Trade Paper. Stanford University Press. Palo Alto, CA. 1988. 831p. ISBN:0-8047-1509-2, ISBN13: 978-0-8047-1509-6. Dewey:821/.8 B. LCCN:88-060490.
Audience: **g.**

Thompson, Paul (Editor) **PR5084.T46 1991**
The Work of William Morris. Ed. 3. Trade Cloth. Oxford University Press, Inc. New York, NY. 1992. 352p. ISBN:0-19-212279-7, ISBN13: 978-0-19-212279-7. Dewey:821/.8. LCCN:90-034792.
Audience: **g.**

Individual Authors and Works > 19th C. > P

Lazenby, Walter **PR5184 .L3**
Arthur Wing Pinero. Library Binding. Thomson Gale. Farmington Hills, MI. 1983. English Authors Ser., No. 150 ISBN:0-8057-1444-8, ISBN13: 978-0-8057-1444-9. Dewey:822/.8.
Audience: **l,u.** B

Mulvihill, James **PR5164.M85 1987**
Thomas Love Peacock. Trade Cloth. Thomson Gale. Farmington Hills, MI. 1987. 152p. Twayne's English Authors Ser., No. 456 ISBN:0-8057-6957-9, ISBN13: 978-0-8057-6957-9. Dewey:823/.7. LCCN:87-015003.
Audience: **l,u.** *Choice, 1988.*

Peacock, Thomas Love **PR5162**
Calidore. Trade Paper. Kessinger Publishing, LLC. Whitefish, MT. 2004. ISBN:1-4191-1159-0, ISBN13: 978-1-4191-1159-4. Dewey:843.54.
Audience: **g,l,u,f.**

Peacock, Thomas Love **PR4036**
Headlong Hall. Trade Paper. Kessinger Publishing, LLC. Whitefish, MT. 2004. ISBN:1-4191-2299-1, ISBN13: 978-1-4191-2299-6. Dewey:823.7.
Audience: **g,l,u,f.**

Peacock, Thomas Love **PR4036**
Maid Marian. Trade Paper. Kessinger Publishing, LLC. Whitefish, MT. 2004. ISBN:1-4191-3209-1, ISBN13: 978-1-4191-3209-4. Dewey:823.7.
Audience: **g,l,u,f.**

Peacock, Thomas Love **PZ3.P312**
Nightmare Abbey. Trade Paper. Kessinger Publishing, LLC. Whitefish, MT. 2004. ISBN:1-4191-3707-7, ISBN13: 978-1-4191-3707-5. Dewey:823/.7.
Audience: **g,l,u,f.**

Pinero, Arthur Wing **PR5181.R6 1985**
Plays. George Rowell (Editor). Trade Cloth. Cambridge University Press. New York, NY. 1986. 302p. British and American Playwrights Ser. ISBN:0-521-24103-0, ISBN13: 978-0-521-24103-8. Dewey:822/.8. LCCN:85-017504.
Audience: **g,l,u,f.**

Individual Authors and Works > 19th C. > Pater, Walter

Donoghue, Denis **PR5136.D66 1995**
Walter Pater: Lover of Strange Souls. Trade Cloth. Alfred A. Knopf Inc. New York, NY. 1995. 364p. ISBN:0-679-43753-3, ISBN13: 978-0-679-43753-6. Dewey:824/.8 B. LCCN:94-012843.
Audience: **u,f.**

Pater, Walter **PR5131.5**
Selected Writings of Walter Pater. Harold Bloom (Editor, Introduction by, Notes by). Cloth Text. Columbia University Press. New York, NY. 1982. 304p. A Morningside Bk. ISBN:0-231-05480-7, ISBN13: 978-0-231-05480-5. Dewey:824/.8. LCCN:81-017099.
Audience: **g,l,u,f.**

Pater, Walter **PR5132.B8 1986**
Walter Pater: Three Major Texts. William E. Buckler (Editor, Introduction by). Paper Text. New York University Press. New York, NY. 1986. 576p. ISBN:0-8147-1089-1, ISBN13: 978-0-8147-1089-0. Dewey:824/.8. LCCN:85-029738.
Audience: **u,f.**

Pater, Walter **NX542**
The Renaissance: Studies in Art and Poetry. Adam Phillips (Editor, Introduction by, Notes by). Trade Paper. Oxford University Press, Inc. New York, NY. 1998. 208p. Oxford World's Classics Ser. ISBN:0-19-283553-X, ISBN13: 978-0-19-283553-6. Dewey:700/.94. LCCN:86-016414.
Audience: **u,f.**

Pater, Walter **PR5134.M3 1986**
Marius the Epicurean: His Sensations and Ideas. Ian Small (Editor, Introduction by). Trade Paper. Oxford University Press, Inc. New York, NY. 1986. 304p. Oxford World's Classics Ser. ISBN:0-19-281705-1, ISBN13: 978-0-19-281705-1. Dewey:823/.8. LCCN:86-072605.
Audience: **u,f.**

Individual Authors and Works > 19th C. > R

Radcliffe, Ann **PR5202.M8 2001**
The Mysteries of Udolpho. Jacqueline Howard (Contribution by). Trade Paper. Penguin Group (USA) Inc. New York, NY. 2001. 704p. Classics Ser. ISBN:0-14-043759-2, ISBN13: 978-0-14-043759-1. Dewey:823/.6. LCCN:2001-277143.
Audience: **g,l,u,f.**

Reade, Charles **PR5214**
The Cloister and the Hearth A Tale of the Middle Ages. Trade Paper. Kessinger Publishing, LLC. Whitefish, MT. 2005. ISBN:1-4179-2675-9, ISBN13: 978-1-4179-2675-6. Dewey:823.89.
Audience: **g,l,u,f.**

Reade, Charles **PZ3.R222**
Hard Cash. Trade Paper. Kessinger Publishing, LLC. Whitefish, MT. 2004. ISBN:1-4191-2280-0, ISBN13: 978-1-4191-2280-4. Dewey:823.8.
Audience: **g,l,u,f.**

Individual Authors and Works > 19th C. > Rossetti, Dante Gabriel and Christina

Arseneau, Mary **PR5238.A77 2004**
Recovering Christina Rossetti: Female Community and Incarnational Poetics. Cloth over Boards. Palgrave Macmillan. New York, NY. 2004. 248p. ISBN:0-333-68395-1, ISBN13: 978-0-333-68395-8. Dewey:821/.8. LCCN:2003-065493.
Audience: **u,f.** *Choice, 2004.*

Arseneau, Mary **PR5238.C85 1999**
The Culture of Christina Rossetti: Female Poetics and Victorian Contexts. Lorraine J. Kooistra (Editor), Antony H. Harrison (Contribution by). Trade Cloth. Ohio University Press. Athens, OH. 1999. 373p. ISBN:0-8214-1243-4, ISBN13: 978-0-8214-1243-5. Dewey:821/.8. LCCN:98-049443.
Audience: **u,f.** *Choice, 2000.*

Battiscombe, Georgina **PR5238.B32 1981**
Christina Rossetti: A Divided Life. Trade Cloth. Henry Holt & Company. New York, NY. 1981. 256p. ISBN:0-03-059612-2, ISBN13: 978-0-03-059612-4. Dewey:821/.8. LCCN:81-047451.
Audience: **g.**

Bellas, Ralph A. **PR5238.B44 1977**
Christina Rossetti. Library Binding. Thomson Gale. Farmington Hills, MI. 1977. 139p. English Authors Ser., No.164 ISBN:0-8057-6671-5, ISBN13: 978-0-8057-6671-4. Dewey:821/.8. LCCN:76-029711.
Audience: **g.**

D'Amico, Diane **PR5238.D35 1999**
Christina Rossetti: Faith, Gender and Time. Cloth Text. Louisiana State University Press. Baton Rouge, LA. 1999. 200p. ISBN:0-8071-2375-7, ISBN13: 978-0-8071-2375-1. Dewey:821/.8. LCCN:99-028005.
Audience: **u,f.** *Choice, 2000.*

Dobbs, Brian & Dobbs, Judy **PR5246**
Dante Gabriel Rossetti: An Alien Victorian. Cloth Text. Brill Academic Publishers, Inc. Boston, MA. 1977. ISBN:0-686-86085-3, ISBN13: 978-0-686-86085-3. Dewey:759.2/092/4.
Audience: **u,f.**

Doughty, Oswald **PR5246.D6**
A Victorian Romantic, Dante Gabriel Rossetti. Paper Text. Textbook Publishers. Temecula, CA. 2003. 712p. ISBN:0-7581-7136-6, ISBN13: 978-0-7581-7136-8. Dewey:928.2.
Audience: **g.**

Howard, Ronnalie R. **PR5247**
The Dark Glass. Trade Cloth. Ohio University Press. Athens, OH. 1972. xiii, 218p. ISBN:0-8214-0099-1, ISBN13: 978-0-8214-0099-9. Dewey:821/.8. LCCN:70-158176.
Audience: **g.**

Kent, David A. (Editor) **PR4803.H44**
The Achievement of Christina Rossetti. Book, Other. Cornell University Press. Ithaca, NY. 1989. 402p. ISBN:0-8014-9677-2, ISBN13: 978-0-8014-9677-6. Dewey:821.8. LCCN:87-047548.
Audience: **g,l,u,f.** *Choice, 1988.*

Kent, David A. (Editor) **PR5238.A55 1987**
The Achievement of Christina Rossetti. Book, Other. Cornell University Press. Ithaca, NY. 1988. 402p. ISBN:0-8014-1937-9, ISBN13: 978-0-8014-1937-9. Dewey:821.8. LCCN:87-047548.
Audience: **g.** *Choice, 1988.*

Kooistra, Lorraine Janzen **PR5238.K66 2002**
Christina Rossetti and Illustration: A Publishing History. Trade Cloth. Ohio University Press. Athens, OH. 2002. 408p. ISBN:0-8214-1454-2, ISBN13: 978-0-8214-1454-5. Dewey:821/.8. LCCN:2002-072814.
Audience: **u,f.** *Choice, 2003.*

Marsh, Jan **PR5238.M37 1995**
Christina Rossetti: A Literary Biography. Trade Cloth. Penguin Group (USA) Inc. New York, NY. 1995. 640p. ISBN:0-670-83517-X, ISBN13: 978-0-670-83517-1. Dewey:821/.8 B. LCCN:95-016345.
Audience: **g.** *Choice, 1995.*

Marsh, Jan **PR5238.M37 1995**
Christina Rossetti: A Writer's Life. Viking. 1995. ISBN:0-670-83517-X, ISBN13: 978-0-670-83517-1.
Audience: **g.**

Mayberry, Katherine J. **PR5238.M38 1989**
Christina Rossetti and the Poetry of Discovery. Cloth Text. Louisiana State University Press. Baton Rouge, LA. 1989. 160p. ISBN:0-8071-1529-0, ISBN13: 978-0-8071-1529-9. Dewey:821/.8. LCCN:89-033163.
Audience: **g,l,u,f.** *Choice, 1990.*

Mayberry, Katherine J. **PR5238.M38 1989**
Christian Rossetti and the poetry of discovery. Louisiana State University Press. 1989. ISBN:0-8071-1529-0, ISBN13: 978-0-8071-1529-9.
Audience: **g.**

McGann, Jerome J.,(ed) **PR5241**
☐ The complete writings and pictures of Dante Gabriel Rossetti : A hypermedia research archive.
http://www.rossettiarchive.org
Institute for Advanced Technology in the Humanities at the University of Virginia.
Audience: **g.**

Palazzo, Lynda **PR5238.P35 2002**
Christina Rossetti's Feminist Theology. Cloth over Boards. Palgrave Macmillan. New York, NY. 2002. 184p. Cross-Currents in Religion and Culture Ser. ISBN:0-333-92033-3, ISBN13: 978-0-333-92033-6. Dewey:821/.8. LCCN:2001-056127.
Audience: **u,f.** *Choice, 2003.*

Pite, Ralph (Editor) **PR451**
Lives of Victorian Literary Figures II: The Brownings, the Brontes and the Rossettis by Their Contemporaries, Set. Trade Cloth. Pickering & Chatto Publishers, Ltd. London, 2004. 1432p. ISBN:1-85196-775-3, ISBN13: 978-1-85196-775-9. Dewey:820.9/008 B. LCCN:2003-022554.
Audience: **l,u,f.**

Richardson, James **PR0595.S44R5**
Vanishing Lives: Style and Self in Tennyson, D. G. Rossetti, Swinburne, and Yeats. Trade Paper. Books on Demand. Ann Arbor, MI. 1988. 251p. Virginia Victorian Studies ISBN:0-608-01438-9, ISBN13: 978-0-608-01438-8. Dewey:821/.8/09353. LCCN:87-025269.
Audience: **u,f.** *Choice, 1988.*

Riede, David **PR5247.R5 1992**
Dante Gabriel Rossetti Revisited. Trade Cloth. Thomson Gale. Farmington Hills, MI. 1992. 160p. Twayne's English Authors Ser. ISBN:0-8057-7027-5, ISBN13: 978-0-8057-7027-8. Dewey:821/.8. LCCN:92-008848.
Audience: **g.**

Riede, David G. **PR5247.C7 1992**
Critical Essays on Gabriel Rossetti. Trade Cloth. Macmillan Publishing Company, Inc. Old Tappan, NJ. 1992. 250p. Critical Essays on British Literature Ser. ISBN:0-8161-8863-7, ISBN13: 978-0-8161-8863-5. Dewey:821/.8. LCCN:92-000228.
Audience: **g.** *Choice, 1993.*

Rossetti, Christina Georgina **PR5238 .A3**
The Family Letters of Christina Georgina Rossetti. Paper Text. Classic Textbooks. Murrieta, CA. 1908. 242p. ISBN:1-4047-7624-9, ISBN13: 978-1-4047-7624-1. Dewey:826.8.
Audience: **g,l,u,f.**

Rossetti, Christina Georgina **PR5237.A1 1979**
Complete Poems of Christina Rossetti: A Variorum Edition, Vol. II. R. W. Crump (Editor). Cloth Text. Louisiana State University Press. Baton Rouge, LA. 1986. 525p. ISBN:0-8071-1246-1, ISBN13: 978-0-8071-1246-5. Dewey:821. LCCN:78-005571.
Audience: **g,l,u,f.** B *Choice, 1991, 1986.*

Rossetti, Christina Georgina **PR5237.A1 1979**
Complete Poems of Christina Rossetti: A Variorum Edition, Vol. I. R. W. Crump (Editor). Cloth Text. Louisiana State University Press. Baton Rouge, LA. 1979. xx, 332p. ISBN:0-8071-0358-6, ISBN13: 978-0-8071-0358-6. Dewey:821. LCCN:78-005571.
Audience: **g,l,u,f.** B *Choice, 1991, 1986.*

Rossetti, Christina Georgina **PR9639.3.C8 E3 1997**
Complete Poems of Christina Rossetti: A Variorum Edition, Vol. III. R. W. Crump (Editor). Cloth Text. Louisiana State University Press. Baton Rouge, LA. 1990. 784p. ISBN:0-8071-1530-4, ISBN13: 978-0-8071-1530-5. Dewey:821. LCCN:78-005571.
Audience: **g,l,u,f.** B *Choice, 1991, 1986.*

Rossetti, Christina Georgina **PR5237.A4 1998**
Selected Prose of Christina Rossetti. David A. Kent & P. G. Stanwood (Editors). Cloth over Boards. Palgrave Macmillan. New York, NY. 1998. 416p. ISBN:0-312-15903-X, ISBN13: 978-0-312-15903-0. Dewey:828/.808. LCCN:97-044885.
Audience: **g,l,u,f.** *Choice, 1999.*

Rossetti, Dante Gabriel **PQ4225.E8R65**
Dante and His Circle: With the Italian Poets Preceding Him. a Collection of Lyrics. Trade Paper. Books on Demand. Ann Arbor, MI. 326p. ISBN:0-598-86082-7, ISBN13: 978-0-598-86082-8. Dewey:851/.1/08. LCCN:17-013111.
Audience: **u,f.**

Rossetti, Dante Gabriel **PR5240 .F14**
Poems and Translations, 1850-1870, Together with the Prose Story "Hand and Soul". Library Binding. Reprint Services Company. Temecula, CA. 1992. 492p. BCL1-PR English Literature Ser. ISBN:0-7812-7627-6, ISBN13: 978-0-7812-7627-6. Dewey:851.
Audience: **g,l,u,f.**

Rossetti, Dante Gabriel **PR5241**
Poems, Ballads and Sonnets; Selections from the Posthumous Poems and from His Translations. Baum, Paul, (ed). Doubleday, Doran & Co.. 1937.
Audience: **g,l,u,f.**

Rossetti, Dante Gabriel **PR5241**
☐ The Complete Writings and Pictures of Dante Gabriel Rossetti.
http://www.rossettiarchive.org/
McGann, Jerome (editor).
Audience: **g,l,u,f.**

Rossetti, Dante Gabriel **PR5242.M38 2003**
Collected Poetry and Prose. Jerome J. McGann (Editor). Cloth over Boards. Yale University Press. Cumberland, RI. 2003. 464p. ISBN:0-300-09801-4, ISBN13: 978-0-300-09801-3. Dewey:821/.8. LCCN:2002-191017.
Audience: **g,l,u,f.**

Rossetti, Dante Gabriel **PR5240.E90**
The Collected Works of Dante Gabriel Rossetti, Vol. 1. William M. Rossetti (Notes by). Trade Paper. Books on Demand. Ann Arbor, MI. 576p. ISBN:0-608-34365-X, ISBN13: 978-0-608-34365-5. Dewey:821/.8. LCCN:31-005539.
Audience: **g,l,u,f.** B

Rossetti, William M. **PR5249.R2 A8 1970**
Some Reminiscences. Trade Cloth. A M S Press, Inc. New York, NY. 1975. 645p. ISBN:0-404-05440-4, ISBN13: 978-0-404-05440-3. Dewey:700/.924. LCCN:75-132386.
Audience: **g,l,u,f.**

Rossetti, William M. **PR5249.R2.A799 1977**
The Diary of W. M. Rossetti 1870-1873. Odette Bornand (Editor). Trade Cloth. Oxford University Press, Inc. New York, NY. 1978. 336p. ISBN:0-19-812458-9, ISBN13: 978-0-19-812458-0. Dewey:700/.92/4. LCCN:78-312738.
Audience: **g,l,u,f.** B

Smulders, Sharon **PR5238.S68 1996**
Christina Rossetti, Revisited. Trade Cloth. Macmillan Publishing Company, Inc. Old Tappan, NJ. 1996. 183p. ISBN:0-8057-7050-X, ISBN13: 978-0-8057-7050-6. Dewey:828.8/09. LCCN:95-040019.
Audience: **g.** *Choice, 1996.*

Individual Authors and Works > 19th C. > Ruskin,John

Batchelor, John **PR5263.B37 2000**
Life of Ruskin. Trade Cloth. Random House. London, 2000. xiv, 369p. ISBN:1-85619-580-5, ISBN13: 978-1-85619-580-5. Dewey:828/.809 B. LCCN:00-362827.
Audience: **g.**

Casteras, Susan P. & Gordon, Susan **N7483.R8J64 1993**
John Ruskin and the Victorian Eye. Trade Cloth. Phoenix Art Museum. Phoenix, AZ. 1993. 223p. ISBN:0-910407-27-4, ISBN13: 978-0-910407-27-4. Dewey:709/.2. LCCN:92-030289.
Audience: **g.** *Choice, 1993.*

Cate, George A. **Z8765.C28 1988**
John Ruskin: A Reference Guide. Trade Cloth. Macmillan Publishing Company, Inc. Old Tappan, NJ. 1988. xix, 146p. ISBN:0-8161-8908-0, ISBN13: 978-0-8161-8908-3. Dewey:016.828/809. LCCN:88-019158.
Audience: **g.** *Choice, 1989.*

Cook, Edward Tyas Sr. **PR5263**
The Life of John Ruskin, 1819-1860: Volume I, Vol. 1. Trade Paper. University Press of the Pacific. Miami, FL. 2003. 572p. ISBN:1-4102-0912-1, ISBN13: 978-1-4102-0912-2. Dewey:700/.924.
Audience: **g.**

Cook, Edward Tyas Sr. **PR5263**
The Life of John Ruskin, 1860-1900: Volume II, Vol. 2. Trade Paper. University Press of the Pacific. Miami, FL. 2003. 632p. ISBN:1-4102-0913-X, ISBN13: 978-1-4102-0913-9. Dewey:700/.924.
Audience: **g.**

Daley, Kenneth **PR5137.D35 2001**
The Rescue of Romanticism: Walter Pater and John Ruskin. Trade Cloth. Ohio University Press. Athens, OH. 2001. 181p. ISBN:0-8214-1382-1, ISBN13: 978-0-8214-1382-1. Dewey:824/.8. LCCN:2001-016308.
Audience: **g.** *Choice, 2002.*

Hilton, Tim **PR5823**
John Ruskin: The Early Years. Trade Paper. Yale University Press. Cumberland, RI. 2000. 320p. ISBN:0-300-08265-7, ISBN13: 978-0-300-08265-4. Dewey:828.8/09.
Audience: **g.**

Hilton, Tim **PR5823**
John Ruskin: The Later Years. Cloth over Boards. Yale University Press. Cumberland, RI. 2000. 688p. ISBN:0-300-08311-4, ISBN13: 978-0-300-08311-8. Dewey:828.8/09. LCCN:85-050177.
Audience: **g.** *Choice, 2000.*

Landow, George P. **PR5264.L3**
The Aesthetic and Critical Theories of John Ruskin. Trade Cloth. Princeton University Press. Princeton, NJ. 1971. xii, 468p. ISBN:0-691-06198-X, ISBN13: 978-0-691-06198-6. Dewey:828/.8/08. LCCN:76-120757.
Audience: **g.** B

O'Gorman, Francis **PR5823**
Late Ruskin. Trade Cloth. Ashgate Publishing, Ltd. Aldershot, 2001. 192p. The Nineteenth Century Ser. ISBN:1-84014-629-X, ISBN13: 978-1-84014-629-5. Dewey:828.8/09. LCCN:00-111524.
Audience: **g.**

Pite, Ralph (Editor), et al. **PR462.L585 2005**
Lives of Victorian Literary Figures III: The Carlyles, John Ruskin and Elizabeth Gaskell by their Contemporaries. Aileen Christianson, Simon Grimble & Sheila A. McIntosh (Editors). Trade Cloth. Pickering & Chatto Publishers, Ltd. London, 2005. 1200p. ISBN:1-85196-780-X, ISBN13: 978-1-85196-780-3. Dewey:820.9/008 B. LCCN:2004-025260.
Audience: **l,u,f.**

Rosenberg, John D. **PR5263.R6 1986**
The Darkening Glass. Trade Paper. Columbia University Press. New York, NY. 1986. 274p. ISBN:0-231-06387-3, ISBN13: 978-0-231-06387-6. Dewey:828/.809 B. LCCN:86-017148.
Audience: **u,f.**

Ruskin, John **PR5263.A3 2005**
Praeterita. Trade Cloth. Knopf Publishing Group. New York, NY. 2005. 632p. ISBN:1-4000-4317-4, ISBN13: 978-1-4000-4317-0. Dewey:828/.809 B. LCCN:2004-056447.
Audience: **g.**

Ruskin, John **PR5263.A37**
Ruskin's Letters from Venice 1851: 1852. Paper Text. Textbook Publishers. Temecula, CA. 2003. xx, 330p. ISBN:0-7581-0112-0, ISBN13: 978-0-7581-0112-9. Dewey:828/.8/09.
Audience: **g.**

Ruskin, John **PR5823**
Ruskin Today. Kenneth Clark (Editor). Trade Paper. Penguin Group (USA) Inc. New York, NY. 1983. 384p. ISBN:0-14-006326-9, ISBN13: 978-0-14-006326-4. Dewey:828/.809.
Audience: **g.**

Ruskin, John **PR5251**
The Works of John Ruskin. E. T. Cook & Alexander Wedderburn (Editors). Paper Text. Cambridge University Press. New York, NY. 1996. 36p. ISBN:0-521-56593-6, ISBN13: 978-0-521-56593-6. Dewey:825.
Audience: **g.**

Ruskin, John **PR5252.R64 1997**
The Genius of John Ruskin: Selections from His Writings. John D. Rosenberg (Editor), Herbert F. Tucker (Foreword by). Trade Paper. University Press of Virginia. Charlottesville, VA. 1998. 576p. Victorian Literature and Culture Ser. ISBN:0-8139-1789-1, ISBN13: 978-0-8139-1789-4. Dewey:828/.809. LCCN:97-031013.
Audience: **g,l,u,f.**

Ruskin, John **PR5263 .A327 1978**
The Gulf of Years: Letters from John Ruskin to Kathleen Olander. Rayner Unwin (Editor, Preface by), Kathleen Prynne (Commentaries by). Trade Cloth. Greenwood Publishing Group, Inc. Portsmouth, NH. 1978. 98p. ISBN:0-313-20188-9, ISBN13: 978-0-313-20188-2. Dewey:828/.8/09. LCCN:77-018837.
Audience: **g.**

Stoddart, Judith **HD8390.R93S76 1998**
Ruskin's Culture Wars: Fors Clarigera and the Crisis of Victorian Liberalism. Trade Cloth. University Press of Virginia. Charlottesville, VA. 1998. 224p. Victorian Literature and Culture Ser. ISBN:0-8139-1806-5, ISBN13: 978-0-8139-1806-8. Dewey:306/.0942/09034. LCCN:98-017583.
Audience: **u,f.** *Choice, 1999.*

Weltman, Sharon A. **PR5267.P6W45 1998**
Ruskin's Mythic Queen: Gender Subversion in Victorian Culture. Trade Cloth. Ohio University Press. Athens, OH. 1999. 225p. ISBN:0-8214-1235-3, ISBN13: 978-0-8214-1235-0. Dewey:828/.809. LCCN:98-023471.
Audience: **u,f.** *Choice, 1999.*

Individual Authors and Works > 19th C. > S

Kiely, David M. **PR5533.K53 1995**
John Millington Synge: A Biography. Trade Cloth. St. Martin's Press. Gordonville, VA. 1995. 320p. ISBN:0-312-13526-2, ISBN13: 978-0-312-13526-3. Dewey:822.912. LCCN:95-034750.
Audience: **g,l,u,f.**

Kopper, Edward A. Jr. (Editor) **PR5534**
J. M. Synge: Literary Companion. Cloth Text. Greenwood Publishing Group, Inc. Portsmouth, NH. 1988. 287p. ISBN:0-313-25173-8, ISBN13: 978-0-313-25173-3. Dewey:822/.912. LCCN:87-032295.
Audience: **u,f.** *Choice, 1989.*

McGann, Jerome J. **PR5514**
Swinburne: An Experiment in Criticism. Library Binding. University of Chicago Press. Chicago, IL. 1972. 352p. ISBN:0-226-55846-0, ISBN13: 978-0-226-55846-2. Dewey:821/.8. LCCN:72-077598.
Audience: **u,f.**

Stoker, Bram **PR6037.T617D7 1997**
Dracula: Authoritative Text, Contexts, Reviews and Reactions, Criticism, Dramatic and Film Variations. Nina Auerbach & David J. Skal (Editors). Paper Text. W. W. Norton & Company, Inc. New York, NY. 1996. xiii, 492p. Critical Editions Ser. ISBN:0-393-97012-4, ISBN13: 978-0-393-97012-8. Dewey:823/.8. LCCN:96-018985.
Audience: **g,l,u,f.**

Synge, John Millington **PR6031.O725**
The Aran Islands. Trade Paper. Kessinger Publishing, LLC. Whitefish, MT. 2004. ISBN:1-4191-5252-1, ISBN13: 978-1-4191-5252-8. Dewey:828/.91203 B.
Audience: **g,l,u,f.**

Synge, John Millington **PR5366**
The Complete Plays of Synge. T. R. Henn (Introduction by). Trade Paper. Methuen Publishing Ltd. London, 2004. Methuen World Dramatists Ser. ISBN:0-413-48520-X, ISBN13: 978-0-413-48520-5. Dewey:822.9/12.
Audience: **g,l,u,f.**

Individual Authors and Works > 19th C. > Scott, Sir Walter

Beiderwell, Bruce **PR5343.P68B45 1992**
Power and Punishment in Scott's Novels. Trade Cloth. University of Georgia Press. Athens, GA. 1992. 184p. ISBN:0-8203-1351-3, ISBN13: 978-0-8203-1351-1. Dewey:823/.7. LCCN:90-023277.
Audience: **g,l,u,f.** *Choice, 1992.*

Crawford, T. **PR5341.C66 1982**
Walter Scott. Trade Paper. Scottish Academic Press. Kelso, Roxburghshire, 1982. 132p. ISBN:0-7073-0305-2, ISBN13: 978-0-7073-0305-5. Dewey:828/.709. LCCN:82-227945.
Audience: **g,u,f.**

Dekker, George **PR858.T75D45 2004**
Fictions of Romantic Tourism. Trade Cloth. Stanford University Press. Palo Alto, CA. 2004. 352p. ISBN:0-8047-5008-4, ISBN13: 978-0-8047-5008-0. Dewey:823/.70932. LCCN:2004-013776.
Audience: **u,f.** *Choice, 2005.*

Hayden, John O. (Editor) **PR5341**
Walter Scott. Paper over Boards. Routledge. New York, NY. 1996. 552p. Critical Heritage Ser. ISBN:0-415-13427-7, ISBN13: 978-0-415-13427-9. Dewey:823.7.
Audience: **g,l,u,f.**

Jack, Ian **PR457.J24**
English Literature, 1815-1832: Scott, Byron, and Keats. Trade Cloth. Oxford University Press, Inc. New York, NY. 1990. 656p. Oxford History of English Literature Ser., Vol XII ISBN:0-19-812238-1, ISBN13: 978-0-19-812238-8. Dewey:820.903. LCCN:63-025209.
Audience: **u,f.**

Kerr, James L. **PR5343.H5 K47 1989**
Fiction Against History: Scott As Storyteller. Cloth Text. Cambridge University Press. New York, NY. 1989. 160p. ISBN:0-521-36425-6, ISBN13: 978-0-521-36425-6. Dewey:823/.7. LCCN:88-030511.
Audience: **g.** *Choice, 1990.*

McCracken-Flesher, Caroline **PR5343.S3**
Possible Scotlands: Walter Scott and the Story of Tomorrow. Trade Cloth. Oxford University Press, Inc. New York, NY. 2005. 239p. ISBN:0-19-516967-0, ISBN13: 978-0-19-516967-6. Dewey:823/.7. LCCN:2005-015446.
Audience: **l,u,f.** *Choice, 2006.*

Robertson, Fiona **PR5322.W43R63 1994**
Legitimate Histories: Scott, Gothic, and the Authorities of Fiction. Trade Cloth. Oxford University Press, Inc. New York, NY. 1994. 336p. Oxford English Monographs ISBN:0-19-811224-6, ISBN13: 978-0-19-811224-2. Dewey:823.7. LCCN:93-027024.
Audience: **u,f.** *Choice, 1994.*

Scott, Walter Sr. **PR5317.B3**
The Betrothed. Trade Paper. Kessinger Publishing, LLC. Whitefish, MT. 2004. ISBN:1-4191-5398-6, ISBN13: 978-1-4191-5398-3. Dewey:823.7.
Audience: **g.**

Scott, Walter Sr. **PZ3.S43**
The Talisman. Trade Paper. Kessinger Publishing, LLC. Whitefish, MT. 2004. ISBN:0-7661-8776-4, ISBN13: 978-0-7661-8776-4. Dewey:823.7.
Audience: **g.**

Scott, Walter Sr. **PR5320.L44**
A Legend of the Wars of Montrose. J. H. Alexander (Editor). Trade Cloth. Columbia University Press. New York, NY. 1996. 271p. ISBN:0-231-10570-3, ISBN13: 978-0-231-10570-5. Dewey:823/.7 s 823/.7. LCCN:96-148944.
Audience: **g.**

Scott, Walter Sr. **PR5322.W4**
Quentin Durward. J. H. Alexander & G. A. M. Wood (Editors). Trade Cloth. Edinburgh University Press. Edinburgh, 2001. 592p. Waverley Novels Ser. ISBN:0-7486-0579-7, ISBN13: 978-0-7486-0579-8. Dewey:823/.7. LCCN:95-229429.
Audience: **g.**

Scott, Walter Sr. **PR5319.A2A44 1993**
Kenilworth. John H. Alexander (Editor). Trade Cloth. Columbia University Press. New York, NY. 1993. 541p. ISBN:0-231-08472-2, ISBN13: 978-0-231-08472-7. Dewey:823.7. LCCN:93-011344.
Audience: **g.** *Choice, 1994.*

Scott, Walter Sr. **PR5305 .F72**
Selected Poems: Sir Walter Scott. Thomas Crawford (Editor). Trade Cloth. Oxford University Press, Inc. New York, NY. 1972. xxviii, 302p. ISBN:0-19-871059-3, ISBN13: 978-0-19-871059-2. Dewey:821/.7. LCCN:72-192883.
Audience: **g.** B

Scott, Walter Sr. **PR4036**
Rob Roy. Ian Duncan (Editor). Trade Paper. Oxford University Press, Inc. New York, NY. 1998. 560p. Oxford World's Classics Ser. ISBN:0-19-281763-9, ISBN13: 978-0-19-281763-1. Dewey:823/.7. LCCN:97-037480.
Audience: **g.**

Scott, Walter Sr. **PR5322.W4 1995 VOL.9**
The Monastery. Penny Fielding (Editor). Trade Cloth. Edinburgh University Press. Edinburgh, 2001. 354p. Waverley Novels Ser. ISBN:0-7486-0574-6, ISBN13: 978-0-7486-0574-3. Dewey:823/.7. LCCN:95-229429.
Audience: **g.**

Scott, Walter Sr. & Garside, P. D. **PR5317.G6 1999**
Guy Mannering. Trade Cloth. Edinburgh University Press. Edinburgh, 1999. 560p. Edinburgh Edition of the Waverley Novels Ser. ISBN:0-7486-0568-1, ISBN13: 978-0-7486-0568-2. Dewey:823/.7. LCCN:95-229429.
Audience: **g.**

Scott, Walter Sr. **PR5317.B53 1993**
The Black Dwarf. Peter D. Garside (Editor). Trade Cloth. Columbia University Press. New York, NY. 1993. 237p. ISBN:0-231-08474-9, ISBN13: 978-0-231-08474-1. Dewey:823.7. LCCN:93-011343.
Audience: **g.** *Choice, 1994.*

Scott, Walter Sr. **PR5334.A6 1971**
Letters of Sir Walter Scott. H. J. Grierson (Editor). Trade Cloth. A M S Press, Inc. New York, NY. 1971. ISBN:0-404-05650-4, ISBN13: 978-0-404-05650-6. Dewey:828/.7/09. LCCN:72-144431.
Audience: **g.** B

Scott, Walter Sr. & Hewitt, David **PR5322.W4 1995**
The Antiquary. Trade Cloth. Columbia University Press. New York, NY. 1995. 542p. ISBN:0-7486-0537-1, ISBN13: 978-0-7486-0537-8. Dewey:823/.7. LCCN:95-229429.
Audience: **g.**

Scott, Walter Sr. **PR5317**
The Heart of Midlothian. David Hewitt & Alison Lumsden (Editors). Trade Cloth. Edinburgh University Press. Edinburgh, 2004. 592p. Edinburgh Edition of the Waverley Novels ISBN:0-7486-0570-3, ISBN13: 978-0-7486-0570-5. Dewey:823/.7. LCCN:2004-381990.
Audience: **g.** *Choice, 2004.*

Scott, Walter Sr., et al. **PR5322.W4 1995**
The Fair Maid of Perth. Andrew Hook & Donald MacKenzie (Authors). Trade Cloth. Edinburgh University Press. Edinburgh, 2000. 532p. Edinburgh Edition of the Waverly Novels Ser. ISBN:0-7486-0585-1, ISBN13: 978-0-7486-0585-9. Dewey:823/.7. LCCN:95-229429.
Audience: **g.**

Scott, Walter Sr. **PR5322.W4**
The Abbot. Christopher Johnson (Editor). Trade Cloth. Edinburgh University Press. Edinburgh, 2001. 554p. Waverley Novels Ser. ISBN:0-7486-0575-4, ISBN13: 978-0-7486-0575-0. Dewey:823/.7. LCCN:95-229429.
Audience: **g.**

Scott, Walter Sr. **PR5341**
Fortunes of Nigel. Frank Jordan Jr. (Editor). Trade Cloth. Edinburgh University Press. Edinburgh, 1995. 688p. ISBN:0-7486-0577-0, ISBN13: 978-0-7486-0577-4. Dewey:823.7. LCCN:2005-363173.
Audience: **g.**

Scott, Walter Sr. **PR5322.W4 1995**
Chronicles of the Canongate. Claire Lamont (Editor). Trade Cloth. Edinburgh University Press. Edinburgh, 2001. 592p. Waverley Novels Ser. ISBN:0-7486-0584-3, ISBN13: 978-0-7486-0584-2. Dewey:823/.7. LCCN:95-229429.
Audience: **g.**

Scott, Walter Sr. **PR5322**
Waverley: Or 'Tis Sixty Years Since. Claire Lamont (Editor, Introduction by, Notes by). Trade Paper. Oxford University Press, Inc. New York, NY. 1998. 496p. Oxford World's Classics Ser. ISBN:0-19-283601-3, ISBN13: 978-0-19-283601-4. Dewey:823/.7. LCCN:85-015403.
Audience: **g.** B

Scott, Walter Sr. **PR5320.O4 1993**
The Tale of Old Mortality. Douglas S. Mack (Editor). Trade Cloth. Columbia University Press. New York, NY. 1993. 522p. ISBN:0-231-08470-6, ISBN13: 978-0-231-08470-3. Dewey:823/.7. LCCN:93-011345.
Audience: **g.** *Choice, 1994.*

Scott, Walter Sr. **BF1531.S5**
Letters on Demonology and Witchcraft. Henry Morley (Introduction by). Trade Paper. Kessinger Publishing, LLC. Whitefish, MT. 1994. 320p. ISBN:1-56459-430-0, ISBN13: 978-1-56459-430-3. Dewey:133.4/3/09411/09034.
Audience: **g.**

Scott, Walter Sr. **PR5318**
Ivanhoe. Graham Tulloch (Editor). Trade Cloth. Edinburgh University Press. Edinburgh, 1998. 560p. Edinburgh Edition of the Waverley Novels Ser. ISBN:0-7486-0573-8, ISBN13: 978-0-7486-0573-6. Dewey:823/.7. LCCN:95-229429.
Audience: **g.**

Scott, Walter Sr. **PR5322.W4**
St. Ronan's Well. Mark Weinstein (Editor). Trade Cloth. Columbia University Press. New York, NY. 1995. 508p. Edinburgh Edition of the Waverly Novels Ser. ISBN:0-231-10398-0, ISBN13: 978-0-231-10398-5. Dewey:823/.7. LCCN:95-229429.
Audience: **g.**

Scott, Walter Sr. **PR5322.W4**
The Pirate. Mark Weinstein & Alison Lumsden (Editors). Trade Cloth. Edinburgh University Press. Edinburgh, 2001. 592p. Waverley Novels Ser. ISBN:0-7486-0576-2, ISBN13: 978-0-7486-0576-7. Dewey:823/.7. LCCN:95-229429.
Audience: **g.**

Scott, Walter Sr. **PR5322.W4 VOL. 17**
Redgauntlet. G. A. Wood & David Hewitt (Editors). Trade Cloth. Columbia University Press. New York, NY. 1996. 528p. ISBN:0-231-10720-X, ISBN13: 978-0-231-10720-4. Dewey:823/.7. LCCN:95-229429.
Audience: **g.**

Shaw, Harry E. **PR5322.W43C74 1996**
Critical Essays on Sir Walter Scott. Trade Cloth. Thomson Gale. Farmington Hills, MI. 1996. 222p. Critical Essays on British Literature Ser. ISBN:0-7838-0005-3, ISBN13: 978-0-7838-0005-9. Dewey:823/.7. LCCN:96-034274.
Audience: **g.**

Stitt, Megan P. **PR868.S34 S85 1998**
Metaphors of Change in the Language of Nineteenth-Century Fiction: Scott, Gaskell, and Kingsley. Trade Cloth. Oxford University Press, Inc. New York, NY. 1998. 218p. Oxford English Monographs ISBN:0-19-818442-5, ISBN13: 978-0-19-818442-3. Dewey:823.7/09. LCCN:97-044617.
Audience: **u,f.**

Sutherland, John **PR5332.S87 1995**
The Life of Walter Scott: A Critical Biography. Claude Rawson (Editor). Trade Cloth. Blackwell Publishing, Inc. Malden, MA. 1995. 386p. Critical Biographies Ser. ISBN:1-55786-231-1, ISBN13: 978-1-55786-231-0. Dewey:828.7/09. LCCN:95-025769.
Audience: **g,l,u,f.**

Wagenknecht, Edward **PR5332.W34 1990**
Sir Walter Scott. Trade Cloth. Frederick Ungar A Book. Dulles, VA. 1990. 208p. Literature and Life Ser. ISBN:0-8264-0491-X, ISBN13: 978-0-8264-0491-6. Dewey:828/.709 B. LCCN:90-035182.
Audience: **g,l,u,f.** *Choice, 1991.*

Welsh, Alexander **PR5342.A2 W4**
The Hero of the Waverley Novels: With New Essays on Scott. Trade Cloth. Princeton University Press. Princeton, NJ. 1993. 268p. Literature in History Ser. ISBN:0-691-06958-1, ISBN13: 978-0-691-06958-6. Dewey:823/.7. LCCN:92-015744.
Audience: **g,l,u,f.**

Wilt, Judith **PR5341.W55 1985**
Secret Leaves: The Novels of Walter Scott. Library Binding. University of Chicago Press. Chicago, IL. 1994. x, 236p. ISBN:0-226-90160-2, ISBN13: 978-0-226-90160-2. Dewey:823/.7. LCCN:85-008615.
Audience: **g,l,u,f.** B *Choice, 1986.*

Individual Authors and Works > 19th C. > Shaw, George Bernard

Adams, Elsie B. **PR5367.C68 1991**
Critical Essay on George Bernard Shaw. Trade Cloth. Macmillan Publishing Company, Inc. Old Tappan, NJ. 1991. 200p. Critical

Essays on British Literature Ser. ISBN:0-8161-8858-0, ISBN13: 978-0-8161-8858-1. Dewey:822/.912. LCCN:91-013072.
Audience: **l,u.** *Choice, 1992.*

Baker, Stuart E. **PR5368.R4B26 2002**
Bernard Shaw's Remarkable Religion: A Faith That Fits the Facts. Trade Cloth. University Press of Florida. Gainesville, FL. 2002. xviii, 263p. The Florida Bernard Shaw Ser. ISBN:0-8130-2432-3, ISBN13: 978-0-8130-2432-5. Dewey:822/.912. LCCN:2001-043729.
Audience: **l,u,f.** *Choice, 2002.*

Dukore, Bernard Frank **PR5368.S75D85 2000**
Shaw's Theater. Trade Cloth. University Press of Florida. Gainesville, FL. 2000. 288p. Florida Bernard Shaw Ser. ISBN:0-8130-1757-2, ISBN13: 978-0-8130-1757-0. Dewey:792.9/5. LCCN:99-050695.
Audience: **u,f.** *Choice, 2000.*

Gahan, Peter **PR5367.G44 2005**
Shaw Shadows. Trade Cloth. University Press of Florida. Gainesville, FL. 2004. 352p. The Florida Bernard Shaw Ser. ISBN:0-8130-2769-1, ISBN13: 978-0-8130-2769-2. Dewey:822.912. LCCN:2004-051282.
Audience: **u,f.** *Choice, 2005.*

Gainor, J. Ellen **PR5368.W6G3 1991**
Shaw's Daughters: Dramatic and Narrative Constructions of Gender. Trade Cloth. University of Michigan Press. Chicago, IL. 1992. 296p. Theater Ser., :Theory - Text - Performance ISBN:0-472-10219-2, ISBN13: 978-0-472-10219-8. Dewey:822/.912. LCCN:91-031421.
Audience: **l,u,f.** *Choice, 1992.*

Gibbs, A. M. **PR5366**
Bernard Shaw: A Life. Saddle Stitched, Cloth over Boards, Dust Jacket. University Press of Florida. Gainesville, FL. 2005. 554p. The Florida Bernard Shaw Ser. ISBN:0-8130-2859-0, ISBN13: 978-0-8130-2859-0. Dewey:822/.912. LCCN:2005-045673.
Audience: **g,l,u,f.** *Choice, 2006.*

Gibbs, A. M. (Editor) **PR5366.S564 1990**
Shaw: Interviews and Recollections. Cloth Text. University of Iowa Press. Iowa City, IA. 1990. 584p. ISBN:0-87745-232-6, ISBN13: 978-0-87745-232-4. Dewey:822/.912. LCCN:88-051147.
Audience: **g,l,u,f.** *Choice, 1991.*

Gordon, David J. **PR5368.C56G67 1990**
Bernard Shaw and the Comic Sublime. Cloth Text. Palgrave Macmillan. New York, NY. 1990. 300p. ISBN:0-312-04067-9, ISBN13: 978-0-312-04067-3. Dewey:822.912. LCCN:89-024157.
Audience: **u,f.** *Choice, 1990.*

Griffith, Gareth **R5366**
Socialism and Superior Brains: The Political Thought of George Bernard Shaw. Trade Paper. Routledge. New York, NY. 1995. 320p. ISBN:0-415-12473-5, ISBN13: 978-0-415-12473-7. Dewey:822.912.
Audience: **g,u,f.**

Holroyd, Michael **PR5366**
Bernard Shaw: The One-Volume Definitive Edition. Trade Paper. W. W. Norton & Company, Inc. New York, NY. 2005. 864p. ISBN:0-393-32718-3, ISBN13: 978-0-393-32718-2. Dewey:822/.912 B.
Audience: **g,l,u,f.** *Choice, 1999.*

Holroyd, Michael **PR5366**
Bernard Shaw, Vol. 1. UK-Trade Paper. Knopf Publishing Group. New York, NY. 1998. xiv, 834p. ISBN:0-09-974901-7, ISBN13: 978-0-09-974901-1. Dewey:822/.912 B.
Audience: **g,l,u,f.**

Innes, Christopher (Editor) **PR5367 .C27 1998**
The Cambridge Companion to George Bernard Shaw. Charles Berst, Fred Marker & Fred Berg (Contribution by). Trade Paper. Cambridge University Press. New York, NY. 1998. 375p. Companions to Literature Ser. ISBN:0-521-56633-9, ISBN13: 978-0-521-56633-9. Dewey:822/.912. LCCN:97-042229.
Audience: **l,u,f.** *Choice, 1999.*

Michalos, Alex **PR5366.A4648 2002**
Bernard Shaw and the Webbs. Trade Cloth. University of Toronto Press. Toronto, ON. 2002. 600p. The Selected Correspondence of Bernard Shaw Ser. ISBN:0-8020-4123-X, ISBN13: 978-0-8020-4123-4. Dewey:822/.912 B. LCCN:2003-277889.
Audience: **g,l,u,f.** *Choice, 2003.*

Pagliaro, Harold E. **PR5368.S48.P34 2004**
Relations Between the Sexes in the Plays of George Bernard Shaw. Trade Cloth. Edwin Mellen Press, The. Lewiston, NY. 2004. 231p. Studies in British Literature Ser., Vol. 87 ISBN:0-7734-6365-8, ISBN13: 978-0-7734-6365-3. Dewey:822/.912. LCCN:2004-049851.
Audience: **l,u,f.** *Choice, 2005.*

Peters, Sally **PR5366**
Bernard Shaw: The Ascent of the Superman. Trade Paper. Yale University Press. Cumberland, RI. 1998. 344p. ISBN:0-300-07500-6, ISBN13: 978-0-300-07500-7. Dewey:822.9/12. LCCN:95-037248.
Audience: **u,f.** *Choice, 1996.*

Shaw, George Bernard **PR5361.B97 2002**
George Bernard Shaw's Plays: Mrs. Warren's Profession, Pygmalion, Man and Superman, Major Barbara: Contexts and Criticism. Ed. 2. Sandie Byrne (Editor). Trade Paper. W. W. Norton & Company, Inc. New York, NY. 2002. xii, 545p. A Norton Critical Edition Ser. ISBN:0-393-97753-6, ISBN13: 978-0-393-97753-0. Dewey:822/.912. LCCN:2001-044733.
Audience: **g,l,u,f.**

Shaw, George Bernard **PR5363.A3 2000**
Plays Unpleasant: Widowers' Houses; the Philanderer; Mrs Warren's Professsion. David Edgar (Introduction by). Trade Paper. Penguin Group (USA) Inc. New York, NY. 2001. 320p. Bernard Shaw Library ISBN:0-14-043793-2, ISBN13: 978-0-14-043793-5. LCCN:2001-266519.
Audience: **g,l,u,f.**

Shaw, George Bernard **PR5366**
Collected Letters, 1911-1925. Dan H. Laurence (Editor). Trade Cloth. Penguin Group (USA) Inc. New York, NY. 1985. 929p. ISBN:0-670-80543-2, ISBN13: 978-0-670-80543-3. Dewey:822/.912.
Audience: **g,l,u,f.**

Shaw, George Bernard **PR5361 .L3 1992**
Plays Extravagant: Too True to Be Good; the Simpleton of the Unexpected Isles; the Millionairess. Dan H. Laurence (Editor). Trade Paper. Penguin Group (USA) Inc. New York, NY. 1992. 320p. Shaw Library Ser. ISBN:0-14-045031-9, ISBN13: 978-0-14-045031-6. Dewey:822/.912. LCCN:92-187142.
Audience: **g,l,u,f.**

Shaw, George Bernard **PR5366**
Plays Political. Dan H. Laurence (Editor). Trade Paper. Penguin Group (USA) Inc. New York, NY. 1986. 464p. Shaw Library Ser. ISBN:0-14-045030-0, ISBN13: 978-0-14-045030-9. Dewey:822.9/12.
Audience: **g,l,u,f.**

Shaw, George Bernard **PR5366**
Saint Joan. Dan H. Laurence (Editor). Trade Paper. Penguin Group (USA) Inc. New York, NY. 1989. 160p. Penguin Plays Ser. ISBN:0-14-045023-8, ISBN13: 978-0-14-045023-1. Dewey:822/.912.
Audience: **g,l,u,f.**

Shaw, George Bernard **PR5363.A5 2000**
Three Plays for Puritans. Dan H. Laurence (Editor), Michael Billington (Introduction by). Trade Paper. Penguin Group (USA) Inc. New York, NY. 2001. 368p. Bernard Shaw Library ISBN:0-14-043792-4, ISBN13: 978-0-14-043792-8. Dewey:822/.912. LCCN:2001-266474.
Audience: **g,l,u,f.**

Shaw, George Bernard **PR5364.P7 1993**
The Complete Prefaces: 1889-1913. Dan H. Laurence & Daniel J. Leary (Editors). Trade Cloth. Penguin Group (USA) Inc. New York, NY. 1994. 672p. ISBN:0-7139-9056-2, ISBN13: 978-0-7139-9056-0. Dewey:824.912. LCCN:95-206877.
Audience: **g,l,u,f.** *Choice, 1994.*

Shaw, George Bernard **PR5364.P7 1993**
The Complete Prefaces: 1914-1929. Dan H. Laurence & Daniel J. Leary (Editors). Trade Cloth. Penguin Group (USA) Inc. New York, NY. 1995. 640p. ISBN:0-7139-9057-0, ISBN13: 978-0-7139-9057-7. Dewey:824.9/12. LCCN:95-206877.
Audience: **g,l,u,f.**

Shaw, George Bernard **PR5364.P7 1993**
The Complete Prefaces: 1930-1950. Dan H. Laurence & Daniel J. Leary (Editors). Trade Cloth. Penguin Group (USA) Inc. New York, NY. 1997. 640p. ISBN:0-7139-9058-9, ISBN13: 978-0-7139-9058-4. Dewey:824.9/12. LCCN:95-206877.
Audience: **g,l,u,f.**

Weintraub, Stanley **PR5366.W42 1996**
Shaw's People: Victoria to Churchill. Trade Cloth. Pennsylvania State University Press. University Park, PA. 1996. 632p. ISBN:0-271-01500-4, ISBN13: 978-0-271-01500-2. Dewey:822/.912 B. LCCN:95-015481.
Audience: **u,f.** *Choice, 1996.*

Individual Authors and Works > 19th C. > Shelley, Mary Wollstonecraft

Alexander, Meena **PR457.A45 1989**
Women in Romanticism: Mary Wollstonecraft, Dorothy Wordsworth and Mary Shelley. Trade Cloth. Rowman & Littlefield Publishers, Inc. Lanham, MD. 1989. 180p. ISBN:0-389-20884-1, ISBN13: 978-0-389-20884-6. Dewey:820.9/145. LCCN:89-007009.
Audience: **u,f.** *Choice, 1990.*

Bennett, Betty T. **PR4036**
Mary Wollstonecraft Shelley: An Introduction. Trade Paper. Johns Hopkins University Press. Baltimore, MD. 1998. 200p. ISBN:0-8018-5976-X, ISBN13: 978-0-8018-5976-2. Dewey:823/.7. LCCN:98-016237.
Audience: **u,f.** *Choice, 1999.*

Mellor, Anne K. **PR5398**
Mary Shelley: Her Life, Her Fiction, Her Monsters. Trade Cloth. Routledge. New York, NY. 1988. 350p. ISBN:0-415-02591-5, ISBN13: 978-0-415-02591-1. Dewey:823/.7 B.
Audience: **u,f.**

Poovey, Mary **PR469.W65P66 1985**
The Proper Lady and the Woman Writer: Ideology as Style in the Works of Mary Wollstonecraft, Mary Shelley, and Jane Austen. Catherine R. Stimpson (Foreword by). Trade Paper. University of Chicago Press. Chicago, IL. 1985. 250p. Women in Culture and Society Ser. ISBN:0-226-67528-9, ISBN13: 978-0-226-67528-2. Dewey:823.7093522. LCCN:83-003664.
Audience: **u,f.**

Schor, Esther (Editor) **PR5398.C36 2003**
The Cambridge Companion to Mary Shelley. Cloth Text. Cambridge University Press. New York, NY. 2003. 314p. Cambridge Companions to Literature Ser. ISBN:0-521-80984-3, ISBN13: 978-0-521-80984-9. Dewey:823/.7. LCCN:2003-046266.
Audience: **u,f.** *Choice, 2004.*

Seymour, Miranda **PR5398.S47 2000**
Mary Shelley. Trade Cloth. Grove/Atlantic, Inc. New York, NY. 2001. 672p. ISBN:0-8021-1702-3, ISBN13: 978-0-8021-1702-1. Dewey:823/.7 B. LCCN:2001-035094.
Audience: **g,l,u,f.** *Choice, 2002.*

Shelley, Mary Wollstonecraft **PR5397.F7 1998**
Frankenstein: Or, the Modern Prometheus: The 1818 Text. Marilyn Butler (Editor, Introduction by, Notes by). Trade Paper. Oxford University Press, Inc. New York, NY. 1998. 322p. Oxford World's Classics Ser. ISBN:0-19-283366-9, ISBN13: 978-0-19-283366-2. Dewey:823/.7. LCCN:98-203488.
Audience: **g,l,u,f.**

Shelley, Mary Wollstonecraft & Harper, Henry H. **PR5398 .A4**
Letters of Mary W. Shelley. Trade Paper. Kessinger Publishing, LLC. Whitefish, MT. 2005. ISBN:1-4179-9397-9, ISBN13: 978-1-4179-9397-0. Dewey:823/.7.
Audience: **u,f.**

Shelley, Mary Wollstonecraft **PR5397.F73M36 1996**
Frankenstein. J. Paul Hunter (Editor). Trade Paper. W. W. Norton & Company, Inc. New York, NY. 1995. 352p. Critical Editions Ser. ISBN:0-393-96458-2, ISBN13: 978-0-393-96458-5. Dewey:823/.7. LCCN:95-037928.
Audience: **g,l,u,f.**

Individual Authors and Works > 19th C. > Shelley, Percy Bysshe

Baker, Carlos **PR5438 .B26**
Shelley's Major Poetry: The Fabric of a Vision. Paper Text. Textbook Publishers. Temecula, CA. 2003. 307p. ISBN:0-7581-4426-1, ISBN13: 978-0-7581-4426-3. Dewey:821.7.
Audience: **l,u.** B

Bieri, James **PR5432.B54 2004**
Percy Bysshe Shelley: Youth's Unextinguished Fire, 1792-1816. Trade Cloth. University of Delaware Press. Newark, DE. 2004. 464p. ISBN:0-87413-870-1, ISBN13: 978-0-87413-870-2. Dewey:821/.7 B. LCCN:2004-002966.
Audience: **l,u,f.** *Choice, 2005.*

Bieri, James **PR5432.B538 2005**
Percy Bysshe Shelley: Exile of Unfulfilled Reknown, 1816-1822. Perfect, Dust Jacket. University of Delaware Press. Newark, DE. 2005. 441p. ISBN:0-87413-893-0, ISBN13: 978-0-87413-893-1. Dewey:821/.7 B. LCCN:2004-012679.
Audience: **l,u,f.** *Choice, 2005.*

Bloom, Harold **PR5438**
Shelley's Mythmaking. Paper Text. Textbook Publishers. Temecula, CA. 2003. 279p. ISBN:0-7581-0161-9, ISBN13: 978-0-7581-0161-7. Dewey:821.7.
Audience: **l,u.** B

Blunden, Edmund **PR5431.B5**
Shelley: A Life Story. Trade Paper. Books on Demand. Ann Arbor, MI. 402p. ISBN:0-598-59104-4, ISBN13: 978-0-598-59104-3. Dewey:928.2. LCCN:47-030070.
Audience: **l,u.** B

Cameron, Kenneth N. (Editor) **PR5431**
Shelley and His Circle, 1773-1822, Vols. 1 & 2. Trade Cloth, Box or Slipcased. Harvard University Press. Cambridge, MA. 1990. 1000p. ISBN:0-674-80610-7, ISBN13: 978-0-674-80610-8. Dewey:928.2. LCCN:60-005393.
Audience: **u,f.**

Cameron, Kenneth Neill **PR5431.C29**
Shelley: The Golden Years. Trade Cloth. Harvard University Press. Cambridge, MA. 1974. x, 669p. ISBN:0-674-03160-1, ISBN13: 978-0-674-03160-9. Dewey:821/.7. LCCN:73-080566.
Audience: **l,u,f.** B

Curran, Stuart **PR5438.C8**
Shelley's Annus Mirabilis: The Maturing of an Epic Vision. Trade Paper. Books on Demand. Ann Arbor, MI. 1975. 277p. ISBN:0-608-03173-9, ISBN13: 978-0-608-03173-6. Dewey:821/.7. LCCN:75-318514.
Audience: **l,u.** B

Hogg, Thomas J. **PR4381**
The Life of Percy Bysshe Shelley. Library Binding. Reprint Services Company. Temecula, CA. 1992. 585p. BCL1-PR English Literature Ser. ISBN:0-7812-7653-5, ISBN13: 978-0-7812-7653-5. Dewey:821/.7.
Audience: **l,u.** B

Ingpen, Roger **PR5431**
Shelley in England: New Facts and Letter. Trade Paper. Kessinger Publishing, LLC. Whitefish, MT. 2005. ISBN:1-4179-5593-7, ISBN13: 978-1-4179-5593-0. Dewey:821.7.
Audience: **l,u.**

King-Hele, Desmond G. **PR5438 .K5 1984**
Shelley: His Thought and Work. Ed. 3. Trade Cloth. Fairleigh Dickinson University Press. Cranbury, NJ. 1984. 416p. ISBN:0-8386-3199-1, ISBN13: 978-0-8386-3199-7. Dewey:821/.7. LCCN:83-014242.
Audience: **u,f.**

Maurois, Andre **PR5431**
Ariel or the Life of Shelley. Trade Paper. Kessinger Publishing, LLC. Whitefish, MT. 2003. ISBN:0-7661-4387-2, ISBN13: 978-0-7661-4387-6. Dewey:821.7.
Audience: **g,l,u,f.**

Morton, Timothy (Editor) **PR5438**
The Cambridge Companion to Shelley. Cloth Text. Cambridge University Press. New York, NY. 2006. 242p. Cambridge Companions to Literature Ser. ISBN:0-521-82604-7, ISBN13: 978-0-521-82604-4. Dewey:821.7.
Audience: **l,u,f.**

Norman, Sylva **PR5438 .N6**
Flight of the Skylark: The Development of Shelley's Reputation. Paper Text. Textbook Publishers. Temecula, CA. 2003. xiii, 304p. ISBN:0-7581-1753-1, ISBN13: 978-0-7581-1753-3. Dewey:928.2.
Audience: **l,u,f.**

Shelley, Percy Bysshe **PR5400**
The Complete Works of Shelley. Roger Ingpen & Walter E. Peck (Editors). Trade Cloth. Gordian Press, Inc. Staten Island, NY. 1965. 3984p. ISBN:0-87752-101-8, ISBN13: 978-0-87752-101-3. Dewey:828.7. LCCN:65-014696.
Audience: **g,l,u,f.**

Shelley, Percy Bysshe **PR5403.R4 2001**
Shelley's Poetry and Prose. Ed. 2. Donald Reiman (Editor). Trade Cloth. W. W. Norton & Company, Inc. New York, NY. 2002. xxii, 786p. Critical Editions Ser. ISBN:0-393-97752-8, ISBN13: 978-0-393-97752-3. Dewey:821/.7. LCCN:2001-030903.
Audience: **g,l,u,f.**

Shelley, Percy Bysshe **PR4381**
The Complete Poetry of Percy Bysshe Shelley, Vol. 2. Ed. 2. Donald H. Reiman & Neil Fraistat (Editors). Trade Cloth. Johns Hopkins University Press. Baltimore, MD. 2005. 920p. ISBN:0-8018-7874-8, ISBN13: 978-0-8018-7874-9. Dewey:821.7. LCCN:99-015163.
Audience: **g,l,u,f.**

Shelley, Percy Bysshe **PR54022000**
The Complete Poetry of Percy Bysshe Shelley, Vol. 1. Donald H. Reiman & Neil Fraistat (Editors). Trade Cloth. Johns Hopkins University Press. Baltimore, MD. 2000. 544p. ISBN:0-8018-6119-5, ISBN13: 978-0-8018-6119-2. Dewey:821/.7. LCCN:99-015163.
Audience: **g,l,u,f.**

Shelley, Percy Bysshe **PR4381**
Percy Bysshe Shelley. Timothy Webb (Editor). Trade Paper. Tuttle Publishing. Boston, MA. 1998. 128p. Everyman Paperback Classics Ser. ISBN:0-460-87944-8, ISBN13: 978-0-460-87944-6. Dewey:821.7.
Audience: **g,l,u,f.**

Wasserman, Earl R. & Bennett, Betty T. **PR4381**
Shelley: A Critical Reading. Stuart Curran (Editor). Trade Paper. Johns Hopkins University Press. Baltimore, MD. 1977. 512p. ISBN:0-8018-2017-0, ISBN13: 978-0-8018-2017-5. Dewey:821/.7. LCCN:70-138036.
Audience: **u,f.**

Wheatley, Kim **PR5438.W48 1999**
Shelley and His Readers: Beyond Paranoid Politics. Trade Cloth. University of Missouri Press. Columbia, MO. 1999. 296p. ISBN:0-8262-1221-2, ISBN13: 978-0-8262-1221-4. Dewey:821/.7. LCCN:99-025961.
Audience: **u,f.**

Individual Authors and Works > 19th C. > Stevenson, Robert Louis

Bell, Ian A. F. **PR5493.B4 1993**
Dreams of Exile: Robert Louis Stevenson, a Biography. Trade Cloth. Henry Holt & Company. New York, NY. 1993. 320p. ISBN:0-8050-2807-2, ISBN13: 978-0-8050-2807-2. Dewey:828/.809. LCCN:93-003792.
Audience: **g,l,u,f.** *Choice, 1994.*

Callow, Philip **PR5493.C28 2001**
Louis: A Life of Robert Louis Stevenson. Trade Cloth. Ivan R. Dee Publisher. Blue Ridge Summit, PA. 2001. 352p. ISBN:1-56663-343-5, ISBN13: 978-1-56663-343-7. Dewey:823.8. LCCN:00-063916.
Audience: **g,l,u,f.** *Choice, 2001.*

Colley, Ann C. **PR5497.R63 2004**
Robert Louis Stevenson and the Colonial Imagination. Trade Cloth. Ashgate Publishing, Ltd. Aldershot, 2004. 228p. ISBN:0-7546-3506-6, ISBN13: 978-0-7546-3506-2. Dewey:828/.809. LCCN:2003-025575.
Audience: **u,f.** *Choice, 2005.*

Gray, William **PR5493.G668 2004**
Robert Louis Stevenson: A Literary Life. Cloth over Boards. Palgrave Macmillan. New York, NY. 2004. 208p. Literary Lives Ser. ISBN:0-333-98400-5, ISBN13: 978-0-333-98400-0. Dewey:828/.809. LCCN:2003-070192.
Audience: **g,l,u,f.** *Choice, 2004.*

Kucich, John, et al. **PR1309.I46F53 2003**
Fictions of Empire: Heart of Darkness, The Man Who Would Be King and The Beach at Falesá. Joseph Conrad, Rudyard Kipling, Robert Louis Stevenson & Alan Richardson (Authors). Paper Text. Houghton Mifflin College Division. Boston, MA. 2002. 421p. New Riverside Editions Ser. ISBN:0-618-08488-6, ISBN13: 978-0-618-08488-3. Dewey:823/.809358. LCCN:2001-133336.
Audience: **g,l,u,f.**

Menikoff, Barry **PR5497.M46 2005**
Narrating Scotland: The Imagination of Robert Louis Stevenson. Trade Cloth. University of South Carolina Press. Columbia, SC. 2005. 240p. ISBN:1-57003-568-7, ISBN13: 978-1-57003-568-5. Dewey:828/.809. LCCN:2004-020593.
Audience: **u,f.** *Choice, 2005.*

Osbourne, Lloyd & Stevenson, Robert Louis **PR5484.E3 1995**
The Ebb-Tide: A Trio and Quartette. Peter Hinchcliffe & Catherine Kerrigan (Editors). Trade Cloth. Edinburgh University Press. Edinburgh, 1996. 178p. ISBN:0-7486-0476-6, ISBN13: 978-0-7486-0476-0. Dewey:823/.8. LCCN:96-222539.
Audience: **g,l,u,f.**

Stevenson, Robert Louis & Dury, Richard **PR5480**
Strange Case of Dr. Jekyll and Mr. Hyde. Trade Cloth. Edinburgh University Press. Edinburgh, 2004. 192p. ISBN:0-7486-1518-0, ISBN13: 978-0-7486-1518-6. Dewey:823.8.
Audience: **g,l,u,f.** *Choice, 2005.*

Stevenson, Robert Louis & Katz, Wendy R. **PR5486.A2K38 1998**
Treasure Island. Trade Cloth. Edinburgh University Press. Edinburgh, 1998. 288p. ISBN:0-7486-0837-0, ISBN13: 978-0-7486-0837-9. Dewey:[Fic]. LCCN:99-187045.
Audience: **g,l,u,f.**

Stevenson, Robert Louis **PR5489**
The Collected Poems of Robert Louis Stevenson. Roger Lewis (Editor). Trade Cloth. Edinburgh University Press. Edinburgh, 2004. 608p. Collected Works of Robert Louis Stevenson Ser. ISBN:0-7486-1557-1, ISBN13: 978-0-7486-1557-5. Dewey:821/.8. LCCN:2003-501305.
Audience: **g,l,u,f.**

Stevenson, Robert Louis **PR5484.K5 2005**
Kidnapped. Donald McFarlan (Notes by). Trade Paper, Perfect. Penguin Group (USA) Inc. New York, NY. 2005. 272p. Penguin Classics Ser. ISBN:0-14-303940-7, ISBN13: 978-0-14-303940-2. Dewey:[Fic]. LCCN:2005-047659.
Audience: **g,l,u,f.**

Stevenson, Robert Louis **PR5493.A3 1997**
Selected Letters of Robert Louis Stevenson. Ernest Mehew (Editor). Cloth over Boards. Yale University Press. Cumberland, RI. 1998. 640p. ISBN:0-300-07376-3, ISBN13: 978-0-300-07376-8. Dewey:[B]. LCCN:97-018029.
Audience: **g,l,u,f.** *Choice, 1998.*

Stevenson, Robert Louis **PR5484 .M2 1992**
The Master of Ballantrae and Weir of Hermiston. John Sutherland (Introduction by). Trade Cloth. Alfred A. Knopf Inc. New York, NY. 1992. xlix, 373p. Everyman's Library ISBN:0-679-41744-3, ISBN13: 978-0-679-41744-6. Dewey:823.8. LCCN:92-052909.
Audience: **g,l,u,f.**

Individual Authors and Works > 19th C. > Swinburne, Algernon Charles

Rooksby, Rikky & Shrimpton, Nicholas (Editors) **PR5514.W46 1993**
The Whole Music of Passion: New Essays on Swinburne. Trade Cloth. Ashgate Publishing, Ltd. Aldershot, 1993. 208p. ISBN:0-85967-925-X, ISBN13: 978-0-85967-925-1. Dewey:821/.8. LCCN:93-138156.
Audience: **u,f.** *Choice, 1993.*

Swinburne, Algernon Charles **PR4803.H44**
Selected Poems. Cloth Text. Routledge. New York, NY. 2002. 274p. ISBN:0-415-94237-3, ISBN13: 978-0-415-94237-9. Dewey:821/.8.
Audience: **g,l,u,f.**

Swinburne, Algernon Charles **PR5502.H39 2000**
Poems and Ballads and Atalanta in Calydon. Kenneth Haynes (Editor). Trade Paper. Penguin Group (USA) Inc. New York, NY. 2001. 448p. Classics Ser. ISBN:0-14-042250-1, ISBN13: 978-0-14-042250-4. Dewey:821/.8. LCCN:2002-275671.
Audience: **g,l,u,f.**

Swinburne, Algernon Charles & McGann, Jerome **PR5505**
Swinburne - The Major Poems and Selected Prose. Charles Sligh (Editor). Trade Paper. Yale University Press. Cumberland, RI. 2004. 528p. ISBN:0-300-10499-5, ISBN13: 978-0-300-10499-8. Dewey:821/.8. LCCN:2004-043062.
Audience: **g,l,u,f.**

Individual Authors and Works > 19th C. > Tennyson, Alfred

Baker, Arthur Ernest **PR5580 .B4**
A Tennyson Dictionary. Paper Text. Classic Textbooks. Murrieta, CA. 1916. 296p. ISBN:1-4047-7692-3, ISBN13: 978-1-4047-7692-0. Dewey:821/.8.
Audience: **l,u.**

Campbell, Matthew **PR595.W45 C36 1999**
Rhythm and Will in Victorian Poetry. Gillian Beer (Contribution by). Trade Cloth. Cambridge University Press. New York, NY. 1999. 288p. Studies in Nineteenth-Century Literature and Culture, No. 22 ISBN:0-521-64295-7, ISBN13: 978-0-521-64295-8. Dewey:821.809384. LCCN:98-038095.
Audience: **u,f.** *Choice, 2000.*

Hair, Donald S. **PR5594.H35 1991**
Tennyson's Language. Trade Cloth. University of Toronto Press. Toronto, ON. 1991. 440p. ISBN:0-8020-5905-8, ISBN13: 978-0-8020-5905-5. Dewey:821.8. LCCN:92-120072.
Audience: **u,f.** *Choice, 1992.*

Hood, James W. **PR5588.H66 2000**
Divining Desire: Tennyson and the Poetics of Transcendence. Trade Cloth. Ashgate Publishing, Ltd. Aldershot, 2000. xi, 209p. The Nineteenth Century Ser. ISBN:0-7546-0069-6, ISBN13: 978-0-7546-0069-5. Dewey:821/.8. LCCN:99-087286.
Audience: **l,u.**

Hughes, Linda K. **PR5592.D68H84 1987**
The Manyfaced Glass: Tennyson's Dramatic Monologues. Trade Cloth. Ohio University Press. Athens, OH. 1987. 320p. ISBN:0-8214-0853-4, ISBN13: 978-0-8214-0853-7. Dewey:821/.8. LCCN:86-023599.
Audience: **u,f.** *Choice, 1987.*

Levi, Peter **PR5581.L48 1993**
Tennyson. Trade Cloth. Simon & Schuster. New York, NY. 1994. 370p. ISBN:0-684-19662-X, ISBN13: 978-0-684-19662-6. Dewey:821.8. LCCN:93-011805.
Audience: **g,l,u.** *Choice, 1994.*

Markley, A. A. **PR5588.M37 2004**
Stateliest Measures: Tennyson and the Literature of Greece and Rome. Dust Jacket. University of Toronto Press. Toronto, ON. 2005. 270p. ISBN:0-8020-8937-2, ISBN13: 978-0-8020-8937-3. Dewey:821/.8. LCCN:2005-415822.
Audience: **u,f.** *Choice, 2005.*

Page, Norman **PR5581**
Tennyson: An Illustrated Life. Trade Cloth. Ivan R. Dee Publisher. Blue Ridge Summit, PA. 1990. 192p. ISBN:1-56131-060-3, ISBN13: 978-1-56131-060-9. Dewey:821.8.
Audience: **l,u.**

Pinion, Frank B. **PR5581.P47 1990**
A Tennyson Chronology. Trade Cloth. Macmillan Publishing Company, Inc. Old Tappan, NJ. 1990. 160p. Monograph Ser. ISBN:0-8161-1838-8, ISBN13: 978-0-8161-1838-0. Dewey:821/.8 B. LCCN:89-039749.
Audience: **l,u.** *Choice, 1990.*

Richardson, James **PR0595.S44R5**
Vanishing Lives: Style and Self in Tennyson, D. G. Rossetti, Swinburne, and Yeats. Trade Paper. Books on Demand. Ann Arbor, MI. 1988. 251p. Virginia Victorian Studies ISBN:0-608-01438-9, ISBN13: 978-0-608-01438-8. Dewey:821/.8/09353. LCCN:87-025269.
Audience: **u,f.** *Choice, 1988.*

Ricks, Christopher **PR5581.R54 1989**
Tennyson. Ed. 2. Trade Cloth. University of California Press. Berkeley, CA. 1989. 400p. ISBN:0-520-06784-3, ISBN13: 978-0-520-06784-4. Dewey:821/.8. LCCN:89-004833.
Audience: **l,u.**

Shaw, Marion **PR5592.S47S5 1988**
Alfred Lord Tennyson. Cloth Text. Brill Academic Publishers, Inc. Boston, MA. 1988. 160p. Feminist Readings Ser. ISBN:0-391-03526-6, ISBN13: 978-0-391-03526-3. Dewey:821/.8. LCCN:88-021169.
Audience: **l,u.** *Choice, 1989.*

Smith, Elton E. **PR5592.D7S65 1997**
Tennyson's Epic Drama. Trade Cloth. University Press of America, Inc. Lanham, MD. 1997. 160p. ISBN:0-7618-0875-2, ISBN13: 978-0-7618-0875-6. Dewey:822/.8. LCCN:97-029659.
Audience: **l.**

Tennyson, Alfred Lord **PR5562.A2G73 2003**
In Memoriam. Ed. 2. Trade Paper. W. W. Norton & Company, Inc. New York, NY. 2003. 272p. Norton Critical Edition Ser. ISBN:0-393-97926-1, ISBN13: 978-0-393-97926-8. Dewey:821/.8. LCCN:2003-051298.
Audience: **g,l,u,f.** B

Tennyson, Alfred Lord **PR5552.T5**
Tennyson's Suppressed Poems. Trade Paper. Kessinger Publishing, LLC. Whitefish, MT. 2005. ISBN:1-4179-6707-2, ISBN13: 978-1-4179-6707-0. Dewey:821.8.
Audience: **g,l,u,f.**

Tennyson, Alfred Lord **PR5558.A1 2003**
Idylls of the King and a Selection of Poems. Glenn D. Everett (Introduction by). Trade Paper. Penguin Group (USA) Inc. New York, NY. 2003. 384p. ISBN:0-451-52875-1, ISBN13: 978-0-451-52875-9. LCCN:2002-037868.
Audience: **g,l,u,f.**

Tennyson, Alfred Lord & Hill, Robert W. **PS3553.H5 1998**
Tennyson's Poetry. Ed. 2. Trade Paper. W. W. Norton & Company, Inc. New York, NY. 1999. 716p. Critical Editions Ser. ISBN:0-393-97279-8, ISBN13: 978-0-393-97279-5. Dewey:821.8. LCCN:98-021561.
Audience: **g,l,u,f.**

Tennyson, Alfred Lord **PR5581 .A4 1981**
The Letters of Alfred Lord Tennyson: 1871-1892, Vol. 3. Cecil Y. Lang & Edgar F. Shannon Jr. (Editors). Trade Cloth. Oxford University Press, Inc. New York, NY. 1991. 534p. ISBN:0-19-812692-1, ISBN13: 978-0-19-812692-8. Dewey:821/.8. LCCN:80-049924.
Audience: **l,u,f.**

Tennyson, Alfred Lord **PR5581.A4 1981**
The Letters of Alfred Lord Tennyson, 1821-1850. Cecil Y. Lang & Edgar F. Shannon Jr. (Editors). Trade Cloth. Harvard University Press. Cambridge, MA. 1981. 400p. Letters of Alfred Lord Tennyson, 1821-1850 Ser., Vol. I ISBN:0-674-52583-3, ISBN13: 978-0-674-52583-2. Dewey:821/.8. LCCN:80-025764.
Audience: **l,u,f.** B

Tennyson, Alfred Lord **PR5581 .A4**
The Letters of Alfred Lord Tennyson, 1851-1870, Vol. II. Cecil Y. Lang & Edgar F. Shannon Jr. (Editors). Trade Cloth. Harvard University Press. Cambridge, MA. 1987. 608p. ISBN:0-674-52584-1, ISBN13: 978-0-674-52584-9. Dewey:821/.8 B. LCCN:80-025764.
Audience: **l,u,f.** *Choice, 1987.*

Tennyson, Alfred Lord **PR5567.A2S53 1986**
Tennyson's Maud: A Definitive Edition. Susan Shatto (Editor). Trade Cloth. University of Oklahoma Press. Norman, OK. 1986. 320p. ISBN:0-8061-1986-1, ISBN13: 978-0-8061-1986-1. Dewey:821/.8. LCCN:85-026431.
Audience: **g,l,u,f.** *Choice, 1987.*

Tennyson, Alfred Lord **PR5562.A1 1982**
In Memoriam. Susan Shatto & Marion Shaw (Editors). Trade Cloth. Oxford University Press, Inc. New York, NY. 1982. 414p. ISBN:0-19-812747-2, ISBN13: 978-0-19-812747-5. Dewey:821/.8. LCCN:82-188984.
Audience: **g,l,u,f.** B

Tennyson, Alfred Tennyson, Baron **PR5556**
Enoch Arden, andc. by Alfred Tennyson. Trade Cloth. Scholarly Publishing Office, University of Michigan Library. Ann Arbor, MI. 2004. ISBN:1-4181-2454-0, ISBN13: 978-1-4181-2454-0. Dewey:821.81.
Audience: **g,l,u,f.**

Tennyson, Alfred Tennyson, Baron **PR5558**
Idyls of the King. by Alfred Tennyson, D. C. L., poet Laureate. Trade Cloth. Scholarly Publishing Office, University of Michigan Library. Ann Arbor, MI. 2004. ISBN:1-4181-2456-7, ISBN13: 978-1-4181-2456-4. Dewey:821.
Audience: **g,l,u,f.**

Tennyson, Alfred Tennyson, Baron **PR5562**
In Memoriam. Trade Cloth. Scholarly Publishing Office, University of Michigan Library. Ann Arbor, MI. 2004. ISBN:1-4181-2457-5, ISBN13: 978-1-4181-2457-1. Dewey:821/.8.
Audience: **g,l,u,f.**

Tennyson, Alfred Tennyson, Baron **PR5567**
Maud, and Other Poems, by Alfred Tennyson. Trade Cloth. Scholarly Publishing Office, University of Michigan Library. Ann Arbor, MI. 2004. ISBN:1-4181-2039-1, ISBN13: 978-1-4181-2039-9. Dewey:821.81.
Audience: **g,l,u,f.**

Tennyson, Alfred Tennyson, Baron **PR5567**
Maud, and Other Poems, by Alfred Tennyson. Trade Cloth. Scholarly Publishing Office, University of Michigan Library. Ann Arbor, MI. 2004. ISBN:1-4181-2036-7, ISBN13: 978-1-4181-2036-8. Dewey:821.81.
Audience: **g,l,u,f.**

Tennyson, Alfred Tennyson, Baron **PR5551**
Poems, by Alfred Tennyson. Trade Cloth. Scholarly Publishing Office, University of Michigan Library. Ann Arbor, MI. 2004. ISBN:1-4181-2447-8, ISBN13: 978-1-4181-2447-2. Dewey:821.8.
Audience: **g,l,u,f.**

Tennyson, Alfred Tennyson, Baron **PR5551**
Poems, by Alfred Tennyson. Trade Cloth. Scholarly Publishing Office, University of Michigan Library. Ann Arbor, MI. 2004. ISBN:1-4181-2446-X, ISBN13: 978-1-4181-2446-5. Dewey:821.8.
Audience: **g,l,u,f.**

Tennyson, Alfred Tennyson, Baron **PR5550**
The Poetical works of Alfred Tennyson, Poet Laureate, Etc. Complete in one Volume. Trade Cloth. Scholarly Publishing Office, University of Michigan Library. Ann Arbor, MI. 2004. ISBN:1-4181-2448-6, ISBN13: 978-1-4181-2448-9. Dewey:821.81.
Audience: **g,l,u,f.**

Tennyson, Alfred Tennyson, Baron **PR5550**
The Poetical Works of Alfred Tennyson, Poet Laureate, Etc. Two volumes in One. Trade Cloth. Scholarly Publishing Office, University of Michigan Library. Ann Arbor, MI. 2004. ISBN:1-4181-2450-8, ISBN13: 978-1-4181-2450-2. Dewey:821.81.
Audience: **g,l,u,f.**

Tennyson, Hallam **PR5581 .T4**
Alfred Lord Tennyson: A Memoir by His Son. Trade Paper. Kessinger Publishing, LLC. Whitefish, MT. 2005. ISBN:1-4179-7035-9, ISBN13: 978-1-4179-7035-3. Dewey:821/.8 B.
Audience: **g,l,u,f.**

Tennyson, Hallam **PR5581 .T4**
Alfred Lord Tennyson: A Memoir by His Son. Trade Paper. Kessinger Publishing, LLC. Whitefish, MT. 2005. ISBN:0-7661-8373-4, ISBN13: 978-0-7661-8373-5. Dewey:821/.8 B.
Audience: **g,l,u,f.**

Tucker, Herbert F. **PR5588 .C75 1993**
Critical Essays on Alfred Lord Tennyson. Trade Cloth. Thomson Gale. Farmington Hills, MI. 1993. 280p. Critical Essays on British Literature Ser. ISBN:0-8161-8864-5, ISBN13: 978-0-8161-8864-2. Dewey:821/.8. LCCN:92-038699.
Audience: **g,l,u,f.**

Individual Authors and Works > 19th C. > Thackeray, William Makepeace

Clarke, Micael M. **PR5642.W6C58 1995**
Thackeray and Women. Library Binding. Northern Illinois University Press. DeKalb, IL. 1995. 250p. ISBN:0-87580-197-8, ISBN13: 978-0-87580-197-1. Dewey:823/.8. LCCN:94-036979.
Audience: **u,f.** *Choice, 1996.*

Harden, Edgar F. **PR5638**
Thackeray the Writer: From Pendennis to Denis Duval. Cloth over Boards. Palgrave Macmillan. New York, NY. 2000. 252p. ISBN:0-312-22929-1, ISBN13: 978-0-312-22929-0. Dewey:823.8. LCCN:97-043870.
Audience: **u,f.** *Choice, 2000.*

Harden, Edgar F. **PR5618.H37 1995**
Vanity Fair. Trade Paper. Macmillan Publishing Company, Inc. Old Tappan, NJ. 1995. 127p. Twayne's Masterworks Studies, Vol. 157 ISBN:0-8057-4460-6, ISBN13: 978-0-8057-4460-6. Dewey:823/.8. LCCN:95-006208.
Audience: **g,l,u,f.**

Payne, David **PR868.P78P39 2005**
The Reenchantment of Nineteenth-Century Fiction: Dickens, Thackeray, George Eliot and Serialization. Saddle Stitched, Cloth over Boards, Dust Jacket. Palgrave Macmillan. New York, NY. 2005. 224p. Palgrave Studies in Nineteenth-Century Writing and Culture ISBN:1-4039-4774-0, ISBN13: 978-1-4039-4774-1. Dewey:823/.809. LCCN:2004-056954.
Audience: **u,f.** *Choice, 2006.*

Pite, Raloh (Editor), et al. **DA30**
Lives of Victorian Literary Figures V: Mary Elilzabeth Braddon, Wilkie Collins, William Thackeray by Their Contemporaries. Ed. 3. Judith Fisher, William Baker & Andrew Maunder (Editors). Trade Cloth. Pickering & Chatto Publishers, Ltd. London, 2007. 1200p. ISBN:1-85196-819-9, ISBN13: 978-1-85196-819-0. Dewey:941.
Audience: **l,u,f.**

Shillingsburg, Peter L. **PR5633.S5 1992**
Pegasus in Harness: Victorian Publishing and W. M. Thackeray. Cloth Text. University Press of Virginia. Charlottesville, VA. 1992. 320p. Victorian Literature and Culture Ser. ISBN:0-8139-1397-7, ISBN13: 978-0-8139-1397-1. Dewey:823.8. LCCN:92-002805.
Audience: **g,l,u,f.** *Choice, 1993.*

Shillingsburg, Peter L. **PR5631.S48 2001**
William Makepeace Thackeray: A Literary Life. Cloth over Boards. Palgrave Macmillan. New York, NY. 2001. 177p. Literary Lives Ser. ISBN:0-333-65092-1, ISBN13: 978-0-333-65092-9. Dewey:823/.8 B. LCCN:00-062602.
Audience: **u,f.** *Choice, 2001.*

Taylor, D. J. **PR5631**
Thackeray: The Life of a Literary Man. Trade Cloth. Avalon Publishing Group. New York, NY. 2001. 512p. ISBN:0-7867-0910-3, ISBN13: 978-0-7867-0910-6. Dewey:823/.8 BB.
Audience: **u,f.**

Thackeray, William Makepeace **PR5601**
The Adventures of Philip on His Way Through the World; Showing Who Robbed Him, Who Helped Him, and Who Passed Him By. by W. M. Thackeray. Trade Cloth. Scholarly Publishing Office, University of Michigan Library. Ann Arbor, MI. 2004. ISBN:1-4181-0145-1, ISBN13: 978-1-4181-0145-9. Dewey:823.82.
Audience: **g,l,u,f.**

Thackeray, William Makepeace **PR5611 .C7**
The Confessions of Fitz-Boodle; and Some Passages in the Life of Major Gahagan. by W. M. Thackeray. Trade Cloth. Scholarly Publishing Office, University of Michigan Library. Ann Arbor, MI. 2004. ISBN:1-4181-0141-9, ISBN13: 978-1-4181-0141-1. Dewey:823.
Audience: **g,l,u,f.**

Thackeray, William Makepeace **PR5602**
Early and Late Papers Hitherto Uncollected. by William Makepeace Thackeray. Trade Cloth. Scholarly Publishing Office, University of Michigan Library. Ann Arbor, MI. 2004. ISBN:1-4181-4596-3, ISBN13: 978-1-4181-4596-5. Dewey:828.
Audience: **g,l,u,f.**

Thackeray, William Makepeace **PR5616**
The History of Pendennis. His Fortunes and Misfortunes, His Friends and His Greatest Enemy. by William Maekpeace Thackeray. with illustrations on wood by the Author. Trade Cloth. Scholarly Publishing Office, University of Michigan Library. Ann Arbor, MI. 2004. ISBN:1-4181-0143-5, ISBN13: 978-1-4181-0143-5. Dewey:823/.8.
Audience: **g,l,u,f.**

Thackeray, William Makepeace **PR5614.A1**
The Newcomes. Library Binding. Classic Books. Murrieta, CA. 1999. The Complete Works of William Makepeace Thackeray, Vol. 14 ISBN:1-58201-395-0, ISBN13: 978-1-58201-395-4. Dewey:823.8.
Audience: **g,l,u,f.**

Thackeray, William Makepeace **PR5617**
Punch's Prize Novelists, The Fat Contributor, and Travels in London. by W. M. Thackeray. Trade Cloth. Scholarly Publishing Office, University of Michigan Library. Ann Arbor, MI. 2004. ISBN:1-4181-0146-X, ISBN13: 978-1-4181-0146-6. Dewey:Fic.
Audience: **g,l,u,f.**

Thackeray, William Makepeace **PR5617**
A Shabby Genteel Story, and Other Tales. by William M. Thackeray. Trade Cloth. Scholarly Publishing Office, University of Michigan Library. Ann Arbor, MI. 2004. ISBN:1-4181-0147-8, ISBN13: 978-1-4181-0147-3. Dewey:Fic.
Audience: **g,l,u,f.**

Thackeray, William Makepeace **PR5618**
Vanity fair. A novel without a hero. by William Makepeace Thackeray; with illustrations by the Author. Trade Cloth. Scholarly Publishing Office, University of Michigan Library. Ann Arbor, MI. 2004. ISBN:1-4181-0148-6, ISBN13: 978-1-4181-0148-0. Dewey:823.8.
Audience: **g,l,u,f.**

Thackeray, William Makepeace **PR5618**
Vanity Fair. John Carey (Editor). Trade Paper. Penguin Group (USA) Inc. New York, NY. 2003. 912p. ISBN:0-14-143983-1, ISBN13: 978-0-14-143983-9. Dewey:823/.8.
Audience: **g,l,u,f.**

Thackeray, William Makepeace **PR5612.A2 H37**
History of Henry Esmond. Edgar F. Harden (Editor). Trade Cloth. University of Michigan Press. Chicago, IL. 2004. 696p. ISBN:0-472-10746-1, ISBN13: 978-0-472-10746-9. Dewey:823/.8.
Audience: **g,l,u,f.**

Thackeray, William Makepeace **PR5608.A2S36 1999**
Barry Lyndon: The Memoirs of Barry Lyndon, Esq. Andrew Sanders (Editor, Introduction by). Trade Paper. Oxford University Press, Inc. New York, NY. 1999. 384p. Oxford World's Classics Ser. ISBN:0-19-283628-5, ISBN13: 978-0-19-283628-1. Dewey:823/.8. LCCN:00-267801.
Audience: **g,l,u,f.**

Thomas, Deborah A. **PR5642.S56.T48 1993**
Thackeray and Slavery. Trade Cloth. Ohio University Press. Athens, OH. 1993. 263p. ISBN:0-8214-1038-5, ISBN13: 978-0-8214-1038-7. Dewey:823/.8. LCCN:92-043257.
Audience: **u,f.** *Choice, 1993.*

Tillotson, Geoffrey (Editor) **PR5638**
William Thackeray. Paper over Boards. Routledge. New York, NY. 1996. 408p. Critical Heritage Ser. ISBN:0-415-13458-7, ISBN13: 978-0-415-13458-3. Dewey:823.8.
Audience: **u,f.**

Individual Authors and Works > 19th C. > Trollope, Anthony

ApRoberts, Ruth **PR5687.A6**
The Moral Trollope. Trade Cloth. Ohio University Press. Athens, OH. 1971. 203p. ISBN:0-8214-0089-4, ISBN13: 978-0-8214-0089-0. Dewey:823/.8. LCCN:75-141383.
Audience: **g,l,u,f.**

Cockshut, A. O. J. **PS3563.O6229**
Anthony Trollope: A Critical Study,. Paper Text. Textbook Publishers. Temecula, CA. 2003. 256p. ISBN:0-7581-7728-3, ISBN13: 978-0-7581-7728-5. Dewey:813.54.
Audience: **g,l,u,f.**

Edwards, P. D. **PR5687.E3 1978**
Anthony Trollope: His Art and Scope. Cloth Text. Palgrave Macmillan. New York, NY. 1978. x, 234 p. ;p. ISBN:0-312-04271-X, ISBN13: 978-0-312-04271-4. Dewey:823/.8. LCCN:77-027915.
Audience: **g,l,u,f.**

Gerould, Winifred **PR5686.A24 1970**
A Guide to Trollope. Trade Cloth. Greenwood Publishing Group, Inc. Portsmouth, NH. 1970. xxv, 256p. ISBN:0-8371-3034-4, ISBN13: 978-0-8371-3034-7. Dewey:823/.8. LCCN:70-100227.
Audience: **g,l,u,f.**

Glendinning, Victoria **PR5686.G58 1993**
Anthony Trollope. Trade Cloth. Alfred A. Knopf Inc. New York, NY. 1993. xxiii, 551p. ISBN:0-394-58268-3, ISBN13: 978-0-394-58268-9. Dewey:823/.8. LCCN:92-054275.
Audience: **g,l,u,f.** *Choice, 1993.*

Hall, N. John **PR5686 .H26 1993**
Trollope: A Biography. Trade Paper. Oxford University Press, Inc. New York, NY. 1993. 624p. ISBN:0-19-283071-6, ISBN13: 978-0-19-283071-5. Dewey:823/.8 B. LCCN:92-034889.
Audience: **g,l,u,f.** *Choice, 1992.*

Herbert, Christopher **PR5688.C56H47 1987**
Trollope and Comic Pleasure. Trade Cloth. University of Chicago Press. Chicago, IL. 1986. 253p. ISBN:0-226-32741-8, ISBN13: 978-0-226-32741-9. Dewey:823/.8. LCCN:86-011367.
Audience: **g,l,u,f.** *Choice, 1987.*

Kincaid, James R. **PR5687 .K55**
The Novels of Anthony Trollope. Trade Cloth. Oxford University Press, Inc. New York, NY. 1977. xiii, 302p. ISBN:0-19-812077-X, ISBN13: 978-0-19-812077-3. Dewey:823/.8. LCCN:77-368275.
Audience: **g,l,u,f.**

Markwick, Margaret **PR5688.W6M37 1997**
Trollope and Women. Trade Cloth. Continuum International Publishing Group, Ltd. London, 2003. 232p. ISBN:1-85285-152-X, ISBN13: 978-1-85285-152-1. Dewey:823/.8. LCCN:96-029451.
Audience: **g,l,u,f.**

Mullen, Richard **PR5686.M84 1992**
Anthony Trollope: A Victorian in His World. Trade Cloth. Frederic C. Beil Publisher, Inc. Savannah, GA. 1991. 767p. ISBN:0-913720-77-1, ISBN13: 978-0-913720-77-6. Dewey:823/.8 B. LCCN:91-016912.
Audience: **g,l,u,f.**

Mullen, Richard **PR5686.M85 1996**
Trollope Companion. Trade Paper. Penguin Group (USA) Inc. New York, NY. 1997. 576p. ISBN:0-14-023558-2, ISBN13: 978-0-14-023558-6. Dewey:823/.8 B. LCCN:97-152827.
Audience: **g,l,u,f.**

Nardin, Jane **PR5688.W6N37 1989**
He Knew She Was Right: The Independent Woman in the Novels of Anthony Trollope. Trade Cloth. Southern Illinois University Press. Carbondale, IL. 1989. 254p. Ad Feminam Ser. ISBN:0-8093-1484-3, ISBN13: 978-0-8093-1484-3. Dewey:823/.8. LCCN:88-015785.
Audience: **g,l,u,f.** *Choice, 1989.*

Nardin, Jane **PR5688.E8N37 1996**
Trollope and Vicorian Moral Philosophy. Trade Cloth. Ohio University Press. Athens, OH. 1996. 179p. ISBN:0-8214-1139-X, ISBN13: 978-0-8214-1139-1. Dewey:823/.8. LCCN:95-033251.
Audience: **g,l,u,f.** *Choice, 1996.*

Sadleir, Michael **PR5686 .S3 1975**
Trollope: A Commentary. Library Binding. Hippocrene Books, Inc. New York, NY. 1975. 435p. ISBN:0-374-97013-0, ISBN13: 978-0-374-97013-0. Dewey:823/.8 B. LCCN:75-011761.
Audience: **g,l,u,f.**

Smalley, Donald (Editor) **PR5684**
Anthony Trollope. Paper over Boards. Routledge. New York, NY. 1996. 592p. Critical Heritage Ser. ISBN:0-415-13460-9, ISBN13: 978-0-415-13460-6. Dewey:823.8.
Audience: **g,l,u,f.**

Snow, C. P. **PR5684**
Trollope: His Life and Art. Trade Cloth. House of Stratus, Inc. New York, NY. 2000. 202p. ISBN:1-84232-435-7, ISBN13: 978-1-84232-435-6. Dewey:823.8.
Audience: **g,l,u,f.**

Super, R. H. **PR5684**
The Chronicler of Barsetshire: A Life of Anthony Trollope. Trade Paper. University of Michigan Press. Chicago, IL. 1991. 528p. ISBN:0-472-08139-X, ISBN13: 978-0-472-08139-4. Dewey:823/.8.
Audience: **g,l,u,f.** *Choice, 1989.*

Terry, R. C. (Editor) **PR5686**
Oxford Reader's Companion to Trollope. Trade Paper. Oxford University Press, Inc. New York, NY. 2002. 640p. Reader's Companions Ser. ISBN:0-19-860420-3, ISBN13: 978-0-19-860420-4. Dewey:823.8.
Audience: **g,l,u,f.**

Trollope, Anthony **PR5684**
Ayala's Angel. Paper Text. Oxford University Press, Inc. New York, NY. 1998. ISBN:0-19-283775-3, ISBN13: 978-0-19-283775-2. Dewey:823/.8.
Audience: **g,l,u,f.** *B*

Trollope, Anthony **PR5684.C27 1994**
Can You Forgive Her? Trade Cloth. Alfred A. Knopf Inc. New York, NY. 1994. 960p. Everyman's Library ISBN:0-679-43595-6, ISBN13: 978-0-679-43595-2. Dewey:823/.8. LCCN:94-006553.
Audience: **g,l,u,f.**

Trollope, Anthony **PR5684**
Phineas Redux. Trade Paper. Oxford University Press, Inc. New York, NY. 2002. 768p. Oxford World's Classics Ser. ISBN:0-19-283559-9, ISBN13: 978-0-19-283559-8. Dewey:823/.8.
Audience: **g,l,u,f.** *B*

Trollope, Anthony **PR5684**
Rachel Ray. Trade Paper. Oxford University Press, Inc. New York, NY. 1998. 452p. Oxford World's Classics Ser. ISBN:0-19-283738-9, ISBN13: 978-0-19-283738-7. Dewey:823.8.
Audience: **g,l,u,f.** *B*

Trollope, Anthony **PR5684**
Phineas Finn: The Irish Member. Jacques Berthoud (Editor), T. L. Huskinson (Illustrator), Jacques Berthoud (Introduction by). Trade Paper. Oxford University Press, Inc. New York, NY. 1999. 780p. Oxford World's Classics Ser. ISBN:0-19-283533-5, ISBN13: 978-0-19-283533-8. Dewey:823.8.
Audience: **g,l,u,f.**

Trollope, Anthony **PR5682.B73**
The Complete Short Stories, Vol. I. Betty J. Breyer (Editor). Trade Cloth. Texas Christian University Press. Fort Worth, TX. 1979. 248p. ISBN:0-912646-56-X, ISBN13: 978-0-912646-56-5. Dewey:823/.8. LCCN:79-015520.
Audience: **g,l,u,f.** *B*

Trollope, Anthony **PR5684**
Framley Parsonage. P. D. Edwards (Introduction by). Trade Paper. Oxford University Press, Inc. New York, NY. 2002. 622p. Oxford World's Classics ISBN:0-19-283506-8, ISBN13: 978-0-19-283506-2. Dewey:823.8.
Audience: **g,l,u,f.** *B*

Trollope, Anthony **PR5684**
The Last Chronicle of Barset. Stephen Gill (Introduction by). Trade Paper. Oxford University Press, Inc. New York, NY. 2002. 928p. Oxford World's Classics Ser. ISBN:0-19-283534-3, ISBN13: 978-0-19-283534-5. Dewey:823/.8. LCCN:2002-278328.
Audience: **g,l,u,f.**

Trollope, Anthony **PR5686.A4 1983**
The Letters of Anthony Trollope, Set. N. John Hall & Nina Burgis (Editors). Trade Cloth. Stanford University Press. Palo Alto, CA. 1983. xxxviii, 1,082p. ISBN:0-8047-1076-7, ISBN13: 978-0-8047-1076-3. Dewey:823/.8. LCCN:79-064213.
Audience: **g,l,u,f.** *B*

Trollope, Anthony **PR5684**
The American Senator. John Halperin (Editor, Introduction by). Trade Paper. Oxford University Press, Inc. New York, NY. 1999. 596p. Oxford's World Classics Ser. ISBN:0-19-283714-1, ISBN13: 978-0-19-283714-1. Dewey:823/.8.
Audience: **g,l,u,f.** *B*

Trollope, Anthony **PR5684**
The Warden. Graham Handley (Introduction by). Trade Cloth. Random House, Inc. New York, NY. 1991. 240p. Everyman's Library ISBN:0-679-40551-8, ISBN13: 978-0-679-40551-1. Dewey:823/.8. LCCN:91-052985.
Audience: **g,l,u,f.**

Trollope, Anthony **PR5684 .W3**
Way We Live Now. Frank Kermode (Contribution by). Trade Paper. Penguin Group (USA) Inc. New York, NY. 2002. 816p. ISBN:0-14-243713-1, ISBN13: 978-0-14-243713-1. Dewey:823/.8.
Audience: **g,l,u,f.**

Trollope, Anthony **PR5684**
The Eustace Diamonds. W. J. McCormack (Editor), Blair Hughes-Stanton (Illustrator), W. J. McCormack (Introduction by). Trade Paper. Oxford University Press, Inc. New York, NY. 1998. 820p. Oxford World's Classics Ser. ISBN:0-19-283466-5, ISBN13: 978-0-19-283466-9. Dewey:823.8.
Audience: **g,l,u,f.** B

Trollope, Anthony **PR5681.S55**
Brown, Jones and Robinson. Juliet McMaster (Editor). Trade Cloth. Trollope Society. London, 2004. 176p. ISBN:1-870587-71-5, ISBN13: 978-1-870587-71-6. Dewey:823.8.
Audience: **g,l,u,f.**

Trollope, Anthony **PR5684**
Lady Anna. Stephen Orgel (Editor, Introduction by). Trade Paper. Oxford University Press, Inc. New York, NY. 1999. 544p. Oxford World's Classics Ser. ISBN:0-19-283718-4, ISBN13: 978-0-19-283718-9. Dewey:823/.8.
Audience: **g,l,u,f.**

Trollope, Anthony **PR5684**
Barchester Towers. Ed. 2. Michael Sadleir & Frederick Page (Editors), Edward Ardizzone (Illustrator), John Sutherland (Introduction by, Notes by). Trade Paper. Oxford University Press, Inc. New York, NY. 1998. 658p. Oxford World's Classics Ser. ISBN:0-19-283432-0, ISBN13: 978-0-19-283432-4. Dewey:823/.8.
Audience: **g,l,u,f.**

Trollope, Anthony & Skilton **PR5684**
Doctor Thorne. Trade Cloth. Trollope Society. London, 1996. 524p. ISBN:1-870587-58-8, ISBN13: 978-1-870587-58-7. Dewey:823/.8.
Audience: **g,l,u,f.**

Trollope, Anthony **PR5684**
Orley Farm. David Skilton (Editor). Trade Paper. Oxford University Press, Inc. New York, NY. 2001. 860p. Oxford World's Classics Ser. ISBN:0-19-283856-3, ISBN13: 978-0-19-283856-8. Dewey:823.8.
Audience: **g,l,u,f.** B

Trollope, Anthony **PR5684**
The Claverings. David Skilton (Editor, Introduction by, Notes by). Trade Paper. Oxford University Press, Inc. New York, NY. 1999. 560p. Oxford World's Classics Ser. ISBN:0-19-283707-9, ISBN13: 978-0-19-283707-3. Dewey:823.8.
Audience: **g,l,u,f.** B

Trollope, Anthony **PR5684**
An Autobiography. John Sutherland (Editor). Trade Cloth. Trollope Society. London, 2004. 176p. ISBN:1-870587-72-3, ISBN13: 978-1-870587-72-3. Dewey:823/.8 B.
Audience: **g,l,u,f.** B

Trollope, Anthony **PR5682.S88 1995**
Later Short Stories. John Sutherland (Editor). Trade Paper. Oxford University Press, Inc. New York, NY. 1995. 640p. Oxford World's Classics Ser. ISBN:0-19-282988-2, ISBN13: 978-0-19-282988-7. Dewey:823.8. LCCN:94-003459.
Audience: **g,l,u,f.**

Trollope, Anthony **PR5682.S88 1994**
Early Short Stories. John Sutherland (Editor, Introduction by). Trade Paper. Oxford University Press, Inc. New York, NY. 1995. 528p. Oxford World's Classics Ser. ISBN:0-19-282987-4, ISBN13: 978-0-19-282987-0. Dewey:823/.8. LCCN:94-002185.
Audience: **g,l,u,f.**

Trollope, Anthony **PR5684**
He Knew He Was Right. John Sutherland (Editor, Introduction by, Notes by). Trade Paper. Oxford University Press, Inc. New York, NY. 1998. 990p. Oxford World's Classics Ser. ISBN:0-19-283540-8, ISBN13: 978-0-19-283540-6. Dewey:823/.8.
Audience: **g,l,u,f.**

Trollope, Anthony **PR5684**
Cousin Henry. Julian F. Thompson (Editor). Trade Paper. Oxford University Press, Inc. New York, NY. 2000. 336p. Oxford World's Classics Ser. ISBN:0-19-283846-6, ISBN13: 978-0-19-283846-9. Dewey:823.8.
Audience: **g,l,u,f.**

Trollope, Anthony **PR5684**
The Prime Minister. Jennifer Uglow (Editor), Hector Whistler (Illustrator), John McCormick (Introduction by). Trade Paper. Oxford University Press, Inc. New York, NY. 2001. 864p. Oxford World's Classics Ser. ISBN:0-19-283532-7, ISBN13: 978-0-19-283532-1. Dewey:823/.8.
Audience: **g,l,u,f.**

Individual Authors and Works > 19th C. > W

Todd, Janet **PR5841**
Mary Wollstonecraft: A Revolutionary Life. Trade Paper. Columbia University Press. New York, NY. 2002. 544p. ISBN:0-231-12185-7, ISBN13: 978-0-231-12185-9. Dewey:828/.609 B.
Audience: **g,l,u,f.**

Wollstonecraft, Mary **PR5841.W8**
Letters on Sweden, Norway and Denmark. Trade Paper. Kessinger Publishing, LLC. Whitefish, MT. 2004. ISBN:1-4192-2996-6, ISBN13: 978-1-4192-2996-1. Dewey:828/.6/09 B.
Audience: **g,l,u,f.**

Wollstonecraft, Mary **JC571 .W87 1994**
A Vindication of the Rights of Men; A Vindication of the Rights of Woman; An Historical and Moral View of the French

Revolution. Trade Paper. Oxford University Press, Inc. New York, NY. 2004. 450p. Oxford World's Classics Ser. ISBN:0-19-283652-8, ISBN13: 978-0-19-283652-6. Dewey:323. LCCN:2004-559496.
Audience: **g,l,u,f.**

Wollstonecraft, Mary **PR5841.W8W76 2005**
Maria or the Wrongs of Woman. William S. Godwin (Preface by). Trade Paper. Dover Publications, Inc. Mineola, NY. 2005. 144p. ISBN:0-486-44503-8, ISBN13: 978-0-486-44503-8. Dewey:823/.6. LCCN:2005-049631.
Audience: **g,l,u,f.**

Wollstonecraft, Mary **PR5841.W8A6 1990**
A Wollstonecraft Anthology. Janet M. Todd (Editor). Cloth Text. Columbia University Press. New York, NY. 1990. 282p. ISBN:0-231-07250-3, ISBN13: 978-0-231-07250-2. Dewey:082. LCCN:89-022399.
Audience: **g,l,u,f.**

Wood, Ellen **PR5842.W8E3 2005**
East Lynne. Trade Paper. Oxford University Press, Inc. New York, NY. 2005. 694p. Oxford World's Classics Ser. ISBN:0-19-280462-6, ISBN13: 978-0-19-280462-4. Dewey:823/.8. LCCN:2004-024328.
Audience: **g,l,u,f.**

Individual Authors and Works > 19th C. > Wells, H. G.

Coren, Michael **PR5776.C58 1993**
The Invisible Man: The Life and Liberties of H. G. Wells. Lee Goerner (Editor). Children's Board Books. Macmillan Publishing Company, Inc. Old Tappan, NJ. 1993. 256p. ISBN:0-689-12119-9, ISBN13: 978-0-689-12119-7. Dewey:823/.912. LCCN:93-006907.
Audience: **g,l,u,f.** *Choice, 1994.*

Hammond, J. R. **PR5777.H3**
An H. G. Wells Companion: A Guide to the Novels, Romances, and Short Stories. Trade Cloth. Macmillan Publishers Ltd. London, 1979. xii, 288p. ISBN:0-333-24698-5, ISBN13: 978-0-333-24698-6. Dewey:823/.912. LCCN:80-457429.
Audience: **g,l,u,f.**

Hammond, John **PR5776.H375 2001**
A Preface to H. G. Wells. Trade Paper. Longman Publishing Group. White Plains, NY. 2001. 240p. ISBN:0-582-40472-X, ISBN13: 978-0-582-40472-4. Dewey:823.9/12.
Audience: **g,l,u,f.** *Choice, 2001.*

Kemp, Peter **PR5778.B55K4 1996**
H. G. Wells and the Culminating Ape: Biological Imperatives and Imaginative Obsessions. Trade Paper. Palgrave Macmillan. New York, NY. 1996. 242p. ISBN:0-312-16489-0, ISBN13: 978-0-312-16489-8. Dewey:823.9/12. LCCN:96-032352.
Audience: **u,f.**

MacKenzie, Norman & MacKenzie, Jeanne **PR5776.M3 1973**
H. G. Wells. Trade Cloth. Simon & Schuster. New York, NY. 1973. xvi, 487p. ISBN:0-671-21520-5, ISBN13: 978-0-671-21520-0. Dewey:823/.9/12. LCCN:73-001184.
Audience: **g,l,u,f.**

McConnell, Frank D. **PR5777 .M3 1981**
The Science Fiction of H. G. Wells. Trade Paper. Oxford University Press, Inc. New York, NY. 1981. 250p. Science Fiction Writers Ser., No. 622 ISBN:0-19-502812-0, ISBN13: 978-0-19-502812-6. Dewey:823/.912. LCCN:80-019675.
Audience: **g,l,u,f.**

Parrinder, Patrick (Editor) **PR5777.P37 1997**
Later Nineteenth and Early Twentieth Century English and European Novelists: H. G. Wells. Paper over Boards. Routledge. New York, NY. 1997. 368p. The Critical Heritage Ser. ISBN:0-415-15910-5, ISBN13: 978-0-415-15910-4. Dewey:809.3.
Audience: **g,l,u,f.**

Parrinder, Patrick **PR5777.P38 1995**
Shadows of the Future: H. G. Wells, Science Fiction, and Prophecy. Cloth Text. Syracuse University Press. Syracuse, NY. 1996. 170p. Utopianism and Communitarianism Ser. ISBN:0-8156-2691-6, ISBN13: 978-0-8156-2691-6. Dewey:823/.912. LCCN:95-021827.
Audience: **g,l,u,f.**

Reed, John R. **PR5778.P5.R4 1982**
The Natural History of H. G. Wells. Trade Cloth. Ohio University Press. Athens, OH. 1982. 304p. ISBN:0-8214-0628-0, ISBN13: 978-0-8214-0628-1. Dewey:823/.912. LCCN:81-011261.
Audience: **g,l,u,f.**

Scheick, William J. (Editor) **PR5777**
The Critical Response to H. G. Wells. Cloth Text. Greenwood Publishing Group, Inc. Portsmouth, NH. 1995. 256p. Critical Responses in Arts and Letters Ser., No. 17 ISBN:0-313-28859-3, ISBN13: 978-0-313-28859-3. Dewey:823/.912. LCCN:94-042119.
Audience: **g,l,u,f.** *Choice, 1995.*

Wagar, W. Warren **PR5770**
H. G. Wells: Traversing Time. Trade Cloth. Wesleyan University Press. Middletown, CT. 2004. 354p. The Wesleyan Early Classics of Science Fiction Ser. ISBN:0-8195-6725-6, ISBN13: 978-0-8195-6725-3. Dewey:823/.91209. LCCN:2004-303053.
Audience: **g,l,u,f.** *Choice, 2005.*

Wells, H. G. **PR6019.O9**
The Complete Short Stories of H. G. Wells. Ed. 22. Trade Cloth. St. Martin's Press. Gordonville, VA. 1988. 1038p. ISBN:0-317-64891-8, ISBN13: 978-0-317-64891-1. Dewey:823.9/12.
Audience: **g.**

Wells, H. G. **PR5774**
The Food of the Gods and How It Came to Earth. Trade Paper. Kessinger Publishing, LLC. Whitefish, MT. 2004. ISBN:1-4191-6257-8, ISBN13: 978-1-4191-6257-2. Dewey:823/.912.
Audience: **g.**

Wells, H. G. **PR5770**
A Modern Utopia. Gregory Claeys (Editor, Notes by), Francis Wheen (Introduction by). Trade Paper. Penguin Group (USA) Inc. New York, NY. 2006. 256p. ISBN:0-14-144112-7, ISBN13: 978-0-14-144112-2. Dewey:321.07.
Audience: **g.**

Wells, H. G. **PR5770**
The Shape of Things to Come. John Clute (Contribution by). Trade Paper. Penguin Group (USA) Inc. New York, NY. 2006. 448p. ISBN:0-14-144104-6, ISBN13: 978-0-14-144104-7. Dewey:823.9/12.
Audience: **g.**

Wells, H. G. **PR5774**
Kipps. Simon James (Editor, Notes by), David Lodge (Introduction by). Trade Paper. Penguin Group (USA) Inc. New York, NY. 2005. 320p. ISBN:0-14-144110-0, ISBN13: 978-0-14-144110-8. Dewey:823/.912.
Audience: **g.**

Wells, H. G. **PR5774**
The History of Mr Polly. Simon James (Editor, Notes by), John Sutherland (Introduction by, Notes by). Trade Paper. Penguin Group (USA) Inc. New York, NY. 2005. 272p. ISBN:0-14-144107-0, ISBN13: 978-0-14-144107-8. Dewey:823.912.
Audience: **g.**

Wells, H. G. **PR5774**
The First Men in the Moon. Steve Maclean (Editor), China Mieville (Introduction by), Steve McLean (Notes by), Patrick Parrinder (Introduction by). Trade Paper. Penguin Group (USA) Inc. New York, NY. 2005. 256p. ISBN:0-14-144108-9, ISBN13: 978-0-14-144108-5. Dewey:823/.912.
Audience: **g.**

Wells, H. G. **PR5774**
The War of the Worlds. Patrick Parrinder (Editor), Brian Aldiss (Introduction by), Andy Sawyer (Notes by). Trade Paper. Penguin Group (USA) Inc. New York, NY. 2005. 240p. Penguin Classics Ser. ISBN:0-14-144103-8, ISBN13: 978-0-14-144103-0. Dewey:[Fic].
Audience: **g.**

Wells, H. G. **PR5774**
Tono-Bungay. Patrick Parrinder (Editor), Edward Mendelson (Introduction by, Notes by). Trade Paper. Penguin Group (USA) Inc. New York, NY. 2005. 464p. ISBN:0-14-144111-9, ISBN13: 978-0-14-144111-5. Dewey:823/.912.
Audience: **g.**

Wells, H. G. **PR5774**
The Sleeper Awakes. Patrick Parrinder (Editor, Introduction by), Andy Sawyer (Notes by). Trade Paper. Penguin Group (USA) Inc. New York, NY. 2006. 288p. ISBN:0-14-144106-2, ISBN13: 978-0-14-144106-1. Dewey:823.912.
Audience: **g.**

Wells, H. G. **PR5770**
The Time Machine. Patrick Parrinder (Editor), Marina Warner (Introduction by), Steven McLean (Notes by). Trade Paper. Penguin Group (USA) Inc. New York, NY. 2005. 128p. Penguin Classics Ser. ISBN:0-14-143997-1, ISBN13: 978-0-14-143997-6. Dewey:[E].
Audience: **g.**

Wells, H. G. & Sawyer, Andy **PR5774**
The Invisible Man. Patrick Parrinder (Editor), Christopher Priest (Introduction by). Trade Paper, Perfect. Penguin Group (USA) Inc. New York, NY. 2005. 192p. ISBN:0-14-143998-X, ISBN13: 978-0-14-143998-3. Dewey:[Fic].
Audience: **g.**

Wells, H. G. **PR5774**
Ann Veronica. Sita Schutt (Editor), Margaret Drabble (Introduction by). Trade Paper. Penguin Group (USA) Inc. New York, NY. 2005. 352p. ISBN:0-14-144109-7, ISBN13: 978-0-14-144109-2. Dewey:823.912.
Audience: **g.**

Individual Authors and Works > 19th C. > Wilde, Oscar

Bartlett, Neil **PR5823**
Who Was That Man?: A Present for Mr. Oscar Wilde. Trade Cloth. Serpent's Tail Ltd. London, 1992. 256p. Masks Ser. ISBN:1-85242-123-1, ISBN13: 978-1-85242-123-6. Dewey:828/.809. LCCN:88-210069.
Audience: **g,l,u,f.**

Beardsley, Aubrey & Wilde, Oscar **PR5820.S2**
Salome. Alfred Douglas (Translator). Trade Paper. Dover Publications, Inc. Mineola, NY. 1967. 67p. ISBN:0-486-21830-9, ISBN13: 978-0-486-21830-4. Dewey:822/.8.
Audience: **g,l,u,f.**

Beckson, Karl (Editor) **PR5824**
Oscar Wilde. Paper over Boards. Routledge. New York, NY. 1997. 448p. The Critical Heritage Ser. ISBN:0-415-15952-0, ISBN13: 978-0-415-15952-4. Dewey:809.2.
Audience: **l,u,f.**

Beckson, Karl E. **PR5823.B34 1998**
The Oscar Wilde Encyclopedia. Trade Cloth. A M S Press, Inc. New York, NY. 1998. 456p. Studies in the Nineteenth Century ISBN:0-404-61498-1, ISBN13: 978-0-404-61498-0. Dewey:828/.809 B. LCCN:97-036303.
Audience: **l,u,f.** *Choice, 1998.*

Belford, Barbara **PR5823**
Oscar Wilde: A Certain Genius. Trade Paper. Random House Adult Trade Publishing Group. New York, NY. 2000. 400p. ISBN:0-8129-9261-X, ISBN13: 978-0-8129-9261-8. Dewey:828.8/09.
Audience: **l,u,f.** *Choice, 2001.*

Bristow, Joseph (Editor) **PR5814**
The Complete Works of Oscar Wilde: The Picture of Dorian Gray: the 1890 and 1891 Texts. Trade Cloth. Oxford University Press, Inc. New York, NY. 2005. 542p. The Complete Works of Oscar Wilde ISBN:0-19-818772-6, ISBN13: 978-0-19-818772-1. Dewey:821.8. LCCN:00-025689.
Audience: **g,l,u,f.**

Cohen, Philip K. **PR5827.R4**
The Moral Vision of Oscar Wilde. Trade Cloth. Fairleigh Dickinson University Press. Cranbury, NJ. 1978. 287p. ISBN:0-8386-2052-3, ISBN13: 978-0-8386-2052-6. Dewey:828/.809. LCCN:76-050283.
Audience: **u,f.**

Ellman, Richard **PR5823.E38**
Oscar Wilde. Trade Cloth. Random House Value Publishing. New York, NY. 1989. ISBN:0-517-69942-7, ISBN13: 978-0-517-69942-3. Dewey:828/.809.
Audience: **g,u,f.**

Freedman, Jonathan **PR5824.O83 1996**
Oscar Wilde: A Collection of Critical Essays. Ed. 1. Trade Paper. Prentice Hall PTR. Upper Saddle River, NJ. 1995. 257p. New Century Views Ser., Vol. 14 ISBN:0-13-146044-7, ISBN13: 978-0-13-146044-7. Dewey:828/.809. LCCN:95-012411.
Audience: **l,u.**

Gagnier, Regenia **PR5824.G34 1986**
Idylls of the Marketplace: Oscar Wilde and the Victorian Public. Trade Cloth. Stanford University Press. Palo Alto, CA. 1986. 272p. ISBN:0-8047-1334-0, ISBN13: 978-0-8047-1334-4. Dewey:828/.809. LCCN:86-001890.
Audience: **g,u,f.** *Choice, 1987.*

Gillespie, Michael P. **PR5827.A63G55 1996**
Oscar Wilde and the Poetics of Ambiguity. Trade Cloth. University Press of Florida. Gainesville, FL. 1996. 208p. ISBN:0-8130-1453-0, ISBN13: 978-0-8130-1453-1. Dewey:828/.809. LCCN:96-014579.
Audience: **u,f.** *Choice, 1997.*

Harris, Frank **PR5823 .H3**
Oscar Wilde, His Life and Confessions. Trade Cloth. 1st World Publishing, Inc. Fairfield, IA. 2005. 280p. ISBN:1-4218-0620-7, ISBN13: 978-1-4218-0620-4. Dewey:828.809. LCCN:2003-099616.
Audience: **g,l,u,f.**

Holland, Vyvyan **PR6029.R8**
Son of Oscar Wilde. Trade Paper. Avalon Publishing Group. New York, NY. 1999. 296p. ISBN:0-7867-0701-1, ISBN13: 978-0-7867-0701-0. Dewey:828/.91209 B. LCCN:00-267076.
Audience: **g,l,u,f.**

Holland, Vyvyan Beresford **PR5823**
Oscar Wilde, a Pictorial Biography. Paper Text. Textbook Publishers. Temecula, CA. 2003. 144p. ISBN:0-7581-0948-2, ISBN13: 978-0-7581-0948-4. Dewey:928.2.
Audience: **l,u.** B

Keane, Robert N. (Editor) **PR5823.O63 2000**
Oscar Wilde: The Man, His Writings, and His World. Trade Cloth. A M S Press. Pittsburgh, PA. 2002. xi, 278p. AMS Studies in the Nineteenth Century, No. 32 ISBN:0-404-64462-7, ISBN13: 978-0-404-64462-8. Dewey:828/.809. LCCN:2002-035640.
Audience: **l,u.** *Choice, 2004.*

Knox, Melissa **PR5824.K54 2001**
Oscar Wilde in the 1990s: The Critic As Creator. Trade Cloth. Camden House. Elizabethtown, NY. 2001. 230p. Literary Criticism in Perspective Ser. ISBN:1-57113-042-X, ISBN13: 978-1-57113-042-6. Dewey:828/.809. LCCN:2001-025587.
Audience: **l,u.** *Choice, 2002.*

Pearson, Hesketh **PR5823 .P4 1978**
The Life of Oscar Wilde. Trade Cloth. Greenwood Publishing Group, Inc. Portsmouth, NH. 1978. 399p. ISBN:0-313-20491-8, ISBN13: 978-0-313-20491-3. Dewey:828/.8/09. LCCN:78-006898.
Audience: **g,l,u.**

Raby, Peter (Editor) **PR5824 .C36 1997**
The Cambridge Companion to Oscar Wilde. Trade Paper. Cambridge University Press. New York, NY. 1997. 329p. Companions to Literature Ser. ISBN:0-521-47987-8, ISBN13: 978-0-521-47987-5. Dewey:828/.809. LCCN:96-037705.
Audience: **l,u,f.** *Choice, 1998.*

Roden, Frederick S. (Editor) **PR5824.P28 2004**
Palgrave Advances in Oscar Wilde Studies. Cloth over Boards. Palgrave Macmillan. New York, NY. 2005. 328p. Palgrave Advances Ser. ISBN:1-4039-2147-4, ISBN13: 978-1-4039-2147-5. Dewey:828/.809. LCCN:2004-046699.
Audience: **u,f.** *Choice, 2005.*

San Juan, E. **PR5824**
The Art of Oscar Wilde. Trade Cloth. Greenwood Publishing Group, Inc. Portsmouth, NH. 1978. 238p. ISBN:0-313-20211-7, ISBN13: 978-0-313-20211-7. Dewey:828/.8/09. LCCN:77-018910.
Audience: **l,u.** B

Sandulescu, C. George (Editor) **PR5824.R43 1994**
Rediscovering Oscar Wilde. Trade Cloth. Rowman & Littlefield Publishers, Inc. Lanham, MD. 1995. 464p. ISBN:0-86140-376-2, ISBN13: 978-0-86140-376-9. Dewey:828/.809. LCCN:95-237646.
Audience: **l,u.**

Small, Ian (Editor) **PR5814**
The Complete Works of Oscar Wilde: De Profundis; Epistola: In Carcere et Vinculis. Trade Cloth. Oxford University Press, Inc. New York, NY. 2005. 351p. The Complete Works of Oscar Wilde ISBN:0-19-811962-3, ISBN13: 978-0-19-811962-3. Dewey:821.8. LCCN:00-025689.
Audience: **g,l,u,f.**

Small, Ian **PR5823.S632 2000**
Oscar Wilde: Recent Research: A Supplement to 'Oscar Wilde Revalued'. Library Binding. E L T Press. Greensboro, NC. 2000. vii, 224p. 1880-1920 British Authors Ser., Vol. no. 15 ISBN:0-944318-14-2, ISBN13: 978-0-944318-14-0. Dewey:828/.809 B. LCCN:00-133041.
Audience: **l,u.** *Choice, 2001.*

Stokes, John **PR5823 .S68 1996**
Oscar Wilde: Myths, Miracles and Imitations. Trade Cloth. Cambridge University Press. New York, NY. 1996. 214p. ISBN:0-521-47537-6, ISBN13: 978-0-521-47537-2. Dewey:828.8/09. LCCN:95-032382.
Audience: **g,l,u,f.** *Choice, 1997.*

Wilde, Oscar **PR5812**
The Complete Works of Oscar Wilde. Ed. 5. Trade Cloth. HarperCollins Publishers Ltd. London, 2003. 1216p. ISBN:0-00-714435-0, ISBN13: 978-0-00-714435-8. Dewey:828.8/09.
Audience: **g,l,u,f.**

Wilde, Oscar **PR5818.D3 1998**
De Profundis. W. H. Auden (Editor), Rupert Hart-Davis (Notes by). Trade Paper. Overlook Press, The. New York, NY. 1998. 256p. ISBN:0-87951-870-7, ISBN13: 978-0-87951-870-7. Dewey:828/.803 B. LCCN:98-004790.
Audience: **g,l,u,f.** B

Wilde, Oscar **PR5812 .E4 1982**
The Artist as Critic: Critical Writings of Oscar Wilde. Richard Ellman (Editor). Trade Paper. University of Chicago Press. Chicago, IL. 1998. 474p. Phoenix Fiction Ser. ISBN:0-226-89764-8, ISBN13: 978-0-226-89764-6. Dewey:809. LCCN:82-013361.
Audience: **u,f.**

Wilde, Oscar **PR5810.G00 2000**
The Complete Works of Oscar Wilde: Poems and Poems in Prose. Bobby Fong & Karl Beckson (Editors). Trade Cloth. Oxford University Press, Inc. New York, NY. 2001. 366p. Oxford English Texts ISBN:0-19-811960-7, ISBN13: 978-0-19-811960-9. Dewey:828.809. LCCN:00-025689.
Audience: **g,l,u,f.** *Choice, 2001.*

Wilde, Oscar **PR5823.A4 2003**
Oscar Wilde: A Life in Letters. Merlin Holland (Selected by). Trade Cloth. HarperCollins Publishers. New York, NY. 2003. 416p. ISBN:0-00-716103-4, ISBN13: 978-0-00-716103-4. Dewey:828/.809. LCCN:2004-353187.
Audience: **l,u,f.**

Wilde, Oscar **PR5811.M87 2000**
Oscar Wilde - the Major Works: Including The Picture of Dorian Gray. Isobel Murray (Editor). Trade Paper. Oxford University Press, Inc. New York, NY. 2000. 662p. Oxford World's Classics Ser. ISBN:0-19-284054-1, ISBN13: 978-0-19-284054-7. Dewey:828/.809. LCCN:2001-278006.
Audience: **g,l,u,f.**

Wilde, Oscar **PR5823**
The Portable Oscar Wilde. Stanley Weintraub (Editor), Richard Aldington (Introduction by). Trade Paper. Penguin Group (USA) Inc. New York, NY. 1981. 752p. Portable Library ISBN:0-14-015093-5, ISBN13: 978-0-14-015093-3. Dewey:828/.809. LCCN:81-001349.
Audience: **g,l,u,f.**

Individual Authors and Works > 19th C. > Wordsworth, Dorothy

Alexander, Meena **PR457.A45 1989**
Women in Romanticism: Mary Wollstonecraft, Dorothy Wordsworth and Mary Shelley. Trade Cloth. Rowman & Littlefield Publishers, Inc. Lanham, MD. 1989. 180p. ISBN:0-389-20884-1, ISBN13: 978-0-389-20884-6. Dewey:820.9/145. LCCN:89-007009.
Audience: **u,f.** *Choice, 1990.*

Gittings, Robert & Manton, Jo **PR5849.G5 1985**
Dorothy Wordsworth. Trade Cloth. Oxford University Press, Inc. New York, NY. 1985. 208p. ISBN:0-19-818519-7, ISBN13: 978-0-19-818519-2. Dewey:821/.7 B. LCCN:85-174718.
Audience: **g,l,u,f.** *Choice, 1985.*

Gunn, Elizabeth **PR5849**
A passion for the particular : Dorothy Wordsworth : a portrait. Gollancz. 1981. ISBN:0-575-02700-2, ISBN13: 978-0-575-02700-8.
Audience: **l,u,f.**

Homans, Margaret **PR585.W6**
Women Writers and Poetic Identity: Dorothy Wordsworth, Emily Bronte and Emily Dickinson. Trade Cloth. Princeton University Press. Princeton, NJ. 1981. 272p. ISBN:0-691-06440-7, ISBN13: 978-0-691-06440-6. Dewey:821/.8/099287. LCCN:80-007527.
Audience: **l,u,f.**

Levin, Susan **PR5849**
Dorothy Wordsworth and Romanticism. Cloth Text. Rutgers University Press. Piscataway, NJ. 1987. 259p. The Douglass Series on Women's Lives and the Meaning of Gender ISBN:0-8135-1146-1, ISBN13: 978-0-8135-1146-7. Dewey:828/.709. LCCN:86-006711.
Audience: **u,f.** *Choice, 1987.*

Wordsworth, Dorothy **PR5849.A8 1987**
Journals of Dorothy Wordsworth. Ed. 2. Mary Moorman (Editor). Paper Text. Oxford University Press, Inc. New York, NY. 1971. 254p. Oxford Paperbacks Ser. ISBN:0-19-281103-7, ISBN13: 978-0-19-281103-5. Dewey:828/.703 B. LCCN:87-014133.
Audience: **g.**

Wordsworth, Dorothy **PR5849.A8 2002**
The Grasmere and Alfoxden Journals. Pamela Woof (Editor). Trade Paper. Oxford University Press, Inc. New York, NY. 2002. 362p. Oxford World's Classics Ser. ISBN:0-19-284062-2, ISBN13: 978-0-19-284062-2. Dewey:828.7/03. LCCN:2002-727710.
Audience: **g.**

Individual Authors and Works > 19th C. > Wordsworth, William

Abrams, M. H. (Editor) **PR4381**
Wordsworth: A Collection of Critical Essays. Trade Cloth. John Wiley & Sons, Inc. Hoboken, NJ. 1972. ISBN:0-685-03922-6, ISBN13: 978-0-685-03922-9. Dewey:821/.7.
Audience: **l,u,f.**

Averill, James H. **PR5892.S93**
Wordsworth and the Poetry of Human Suffering. Book, Other. Cornell University Press. Ithaca, NY. 1980. 318p. ISBN:0-8014-1249-8, ISBN13: 978-0-8014-1249-3. Dewey:821/.7. LCCN:79-021783.
Audience: **g,l,u,f.**

Barker, Juliet **PR5881.B27 2005**
Wordsworth: A Life. Trade Cloth. HarperCollins Publishers. New York, NY. 2005. 576p. ISBN:0-06-078731-7, ISBN13: 978-0-06-078731-8. Dewey:821/.7. LCCN:2005-047884.
Audience: **g,l,u,f.**

Bate, Jonathan **PR5892.N2B38 1991**
Romantic Ecology: Wordsworth and the Environmental Tradition. Cloth Text. Routledge. New York, NY. 1991. 144p. ISBN:0-415-06115-6, ISBN13: 978-0-415-06115-5. Dewey:821/.7. LCCN:90-024527.
Audience: **g,l,u,f.** *Choice, 1992.*

Bewell, Alan J. **PR5888.B47 1989**
Wordsworth and the Enlightenment: Nature, Man, and Society in the Experimental Poetry. Cloth over Boards. Yale University Press. Cumberland, RI. 1989. 352p. ISBN:0-300-04393-7, ISBN13: 978-0-300-04393-8. Dewey:821/.7. LCCN:88-020644.
Audience: **u,f.** *Choice, 1989.*

Blades, John **PR5869.L93B55 2004**
Wordsworth and Coleridge: Lyrical Ballads. Cloth over Boards. Palgrave Macmillan. New York, NY. 2005. 288p. Analysing Texts ISBN:1-4039-0479-0, ISBN13: 978-1-4039-0479-9. Dewey:821/.708. LCCN:2004-042103.
Audience: **g,l,u,f.**

Chandler, James K. **PR5892.P64C48 1984**
Wordsworth's Second Nature: A Study of the Poetry and Politics. Trade Paper. University of Chicago Press. Chicago, IL. 1984. 338p. ISBN:0-226-10081-2, ISBN13: 978-0-226-10081-4. Dewey:821/.7. LCCN:84-005979.
Audience: **g,l,u,f.**

Fay, Elizabeth A. **PR5892.A34F39 1995**
Becoming Wordsworthian: A Performative Aesthetic. Cloth Text. University of Massachusetts Press. Amherst, MA. 1995. 288p. ISBN:0-87023-960-0, ISBN13: 978-0-87023-960-1. Dewey:821/.7. LCCN:94-037565.
Audience: **l,u,f.**

Ferguson, Frances **PR5888**
Wordsworth : Language as Counter-Spirit. Yale University Press. 1977. ISBN:0-300-02063-5, ISBN13: 978-0-300-02063-2.
Audience: **g,l,u,f.**

Galperin, William H. **PR5888.G25 1989**
Revision and Authority in Wordsworth: The Interpretation of a Career. Trade Cloth. University of Pennsylvania Press. Philadelphia, PA. 1989. 256p. ISBN:0-8122-8140-3, ISBN13: 978-0-8122-8140-8. Dewey:821/.7. LCCN:88-030325.
Audience: **u,f.** *Choice, 1989.*

Garber, Frederick **PR5888**
Wordsworth and the Poetry of Encounter. Trade Cloth. University of Illinois Press. Champaign, IL. 1971. 207p. ISBN:0-252-00184-2, ISBN13: 978-0-252-00184-0. Dewey:821/.7. LCCN:71-157888.
Audience: **g,l,u,f.**

Gill, Stephen (Editor) **PR5888.C27 2003**
The Cambridge Companion to Wordsworth. Trade Paper. Cambridge University Press. New York, NY. 2003. 320p. Cambridge Companions to Literature Ser. ISBN:0-521-64681-2, ISBN13: 978-0-521-64681-9. Dewey:821/.7. LCCN:2002-034935.
Audience: **u,f.** *Choice, 2004.*

Gill, Stephen (Editor) **PR5888.C27 2003**
The Cambridge Companion to Wordsworth. Cloth Text. Cambridge University Press. New York, NY. 2003. 320p. Cambridge Companions to Literature Ser. ISBN:0-521-64116-0, ISBN13: 978-0-521-64116-6. Dewey:821/.7. LCCN:2002-034935.
Audience: **u,f.** *Choice, 2004.*

Gill, Stephen **PR5881**
William Wordsworth: A Life. Trade Paper. Oxford University Press, Inc. New York, NY. 1990. 544p. ISBN:0-19-282747-2, ISBN13: 978-0-19-282747-0. Dewey:821/.7 B.
Audience: **g,l,u,f.** *Choice, 1989.*

Gilpin, George H. Jr. **PR5888.G48 1990**
Critical Essays on William Wordsworth. Zack R. Bowen (Editor). Trade Cloth. Thomson Gale. Farmington Hills, MI. 1990. 360p. Critical Essays on British Literature Ser. ISBN:0-8161-8774-6, ISBN13: 978-0-8161-8774-4. Dewey:821/.7. LCCN:89-071694.
Audience: **u,f.**

Grob, Alan **PR5892.P5**
The Philosophic Mind: A Study of Wordsworth's Poetry and Thought, 1797-1805. Trade Cloth. Ohio State University Press. Columbus, OH. 1973. 291p. ISBN:0-8142-0178-4, ISBN13: 978-0-8142-0178-7. Dewey:821/.7. LCCN:72-012783.
Audience: **g,l,u,f.**

Hall, Spencer & Ramsey, Jonathan (Editors) **PR5888.A66 1986**
Approaches to Teaching Wordsworth's Poetry. Trade Cloth. Modern Language Association of America. New York, NY. 1986. "x, 182"p. Approaches to Teaching World Literature Ser., No. 11 ISBN:0-87352-495-0, ISBN13: 978-0-87352-495-7. Dewey:821/.7. LCCN:85-021762.
Audience: **f.**

Hamilton, Paul **PR5888.H36 1986**
Wordsworth: A Critical Introduction. Cloth Text. Brill Academic Publishers, Inc. Boston, MA. 1986. 172p. Harvester New Readings Ser. ISBN:0-391-03417-0, ISBN13: 978-0-391-03417-4. Dewey:821/.7. LCCN:86-000326.
Audience: **g,l,u,f.** *Choice, 1986.*

Hartman, Geoffrey H. **PR4381**
Wordsworth's Poetry, 1787-1814. Trade Cloth. Yale University Press. Cumberland, RI. 1964. ISBN:0-300-00538-5, ISBN13: 978-0-300-00538-7. Dewey:821/.7.
Audience: **g.**

Jacobus, Mary **PR5864.J27 1989**
Romanticism, Writing, and Sexual Difference: Essays on The Prelude. Trade Cloth. Oxford University Press, Inc. New York, NY. 1990. 328p. ISBN:0-19-812969-6, ISBN13: 978-0-19-812969-1. Dewey:821/.7. LCCN:89-008528.
Audience: **g,l,u,f.**

Johnston, Kenneth R. **PR5882.J65 1998**
The Hidden Wordsworth: Poet, Lover, Rebel, Spy. Trade Cloth. W. W. Norton & Company, Inc. New York, NY. 1998. 960p. ISBN:0-393-04623-0, ISBN13: 978-0-393-04623-6. Dewey:[B]. LCCN:97-040317.
Audience: **g,l,u,f.** *Choice, 1998.*

Johnston, Kenneth R. **PR5865**
Wordsworth and "The Recluse". Trade Cloth. Yale University Press. Cumberland, RI. 1984. 397p. ISBN:0-300-03108-4, ISBN13: 978-0-300-03108-9. Dewey:821/.7. LCCN:83-019713.
Audience: **g,l,u,f.**

Johnston, Kenneth R. & Ruoff, Gene W. (Editors) **PR5892.R63A34 1987**
The Age of William Wordsworth: Critical Essays on the Romantic Tradition. Cloth Text. Rutgers University Press. Piscataway, NJ. 1987. 380p. ISBN:0-8135-1243-3, ISBN13: 978-0-8135-1243-3. Dewey:821/.7. LCCN:87-000313.
Audience: **u,f.**

Jordan, John E. **PR5869.L93**
Why the Lyrical Ballads? Trade Cloth. University of California Press. Berkeley, CA. 1976. xii, 212p. ISBN:0-520-03124-5, ISBN13: 978-0-520-03124-1. Dewey:821/.7. LCCN:75-027926.
Audience: **g,l,u,f.**

Kroeber, Karl & Ruoff, Gene W. (Editors) **PR590.R59 1993**
Romantic Poetry: Recent Revisionary Criticism. Paper Text. Rutgers University Press. Piscataway, NJ. 1993. 450p. ISBN:0-8135-2010-X, ISBN13: 978-0-8135-2010-0. Dewey:821/.709. LCCN:93-017229.
Audience: **u,f.** *Choice, 1994.*

Levinson, Marjorie **PR5888.L48 1986**
Wordsworth's Great Period Poems: Four Essays. Trade Cloth. Cambridge University Press. New York, NY. 1986. 180p. ISBN:0-521-30829-1, ISBN13: 978-0-521-30829-8. Dewey:821/.7. LCCN:85-029119.
Audience: **g,l,u,f.**

Liu, Alan **PR5892.H5L5 1989**
Wordsworth: The Sense of History. Trade Cloth. Stanford University Press. Palo Alto, CA. 1989. 742p. ISBN:0-8047-1373-1, ISBN13: 978-0-8047-1373-3. Dewey:821/.7. LCCN:88-028382.
Audience: **g,u,f.** *Choice, 1990.*

Magnuson, Paul **PR4484.M28 1988**
Coleridge and Wordsworth: A Lyrical Dialogue. Trade Cloth. Princeton University Press. Princeton, NJ. 1988. 352p. ISBN:0-691-06732-5, ISBN13: 978-0-691-06732-2. Dewey:821/.7/09. LCCN:87-026341.
Audience: **g,l,u,f.**

McMaster, Graham (comp./editor) **PR5881**
Wiiliam Wordsworth : A Critical Anthology. Penguin Books. 1972. Penguin critical anthologies ISBN:0-14-080669-5, ISBN13: 978-0-14-080669-4.
Audience: **l,u,f.**

Moorman, Mary Trevelyan **PR5881**
The Early Years, 1770-1803, Vol. 1. Clarendon Press. 1957. William Wordsworth : a biography
Audience: **g,l,u,f.**

Moorman, Mary Trevelyan **PR4381**
The Later Years, 1803-1850, Vol. 2. Clarendon Press. 1965. William Wordsworth : a biography
Audience: **g,l,u,f.**

Newlyn, Lucy **PR590**
Coleridge, Wordsworth and the Language of Allusion. Trade Paper. Oxford University Press, Inc. New York, NY. 2001. 274p. ISBN:0-19-924259-3, ISBN13: 978-0-19-924259-7. Dewey:821.7/09.
Audience: **g,l,u,f.**

Page, Judith W. **PR5892.F45**
Wordsworth and the cultivation of women. University of California Press. 1994. ISBN:0-520-08493-4, ISBN13: 978-0-520-08493-3.
Audience: **g,l,u,f.**

Roe, Nicholas **PR590**
Wordsworth and Coleridge: The Radical Years. Trade Paper. Oxford University Press, Inc. New York, NY. 1990. 324p. Oxford English Monographs ISBN:0-19-811969-0, ISBN13: 978-0-19-811969-2. Dewey:821/.7/09. LCCN:87-015381.
Audience: **g,l,u,f.** *Choice, 1988.*

Ruoff, Gene W. **PR5888.R86 1989**
Wordsworth and Coleridge: The Making of the Major Lyrics, 1802-1804. Paper Text. Rutgers University Press. Piscataway, NJ. 1989. 320p. ISBN:0-8135-1399-5, ISBN13: 978-0-8135-1399-7. Dewey:821.709. LCCN:88-028292.
Audience: **g,l,u,f.** *Choice, 1990.*

Simpson, David **PR5892.H5**
Wordsworth's Historical Imagination : The Poetry of Displacement. Methuen. 1987. ISBN:0-416-03872-7, ISBN13: 978-0-416-03872-9.
Audience: **g,l,u,f.**

Stillinger, Jack **PR590.S75 2006**
Romantic Complexity: Keats, Coleridge, and Wordsworth. Trade Cloth. University of Illinois Press. Champaign, IL. 2006. 280p. ISBN:0-252-03062-1, ISBN13: 978-0-252-03062-8. Dewey:821/.709145. LCCN:2005-034422.
Audience: **g,l,u,f.**

Wolfson, Susan J. **PR4837.W65 1986**
The Questioning Presence: Wordsworth, Keats and the Interrogative Mode in Romantic Poetry. Book, Other. Cornell University Press. Ithaca, NY. 1986. 384p. ISBN:0-8014-1909-3, ISBN13: 978-0-8014-1909-6. Dewey:821/.7/09. LCCN:86-006407.
Audience: **u,f.**

Woof, Robert **PR5888.W44 2001**
William Wordsworth. Paper over Boards. Routledge. New York, NY. 2001. 1112p. The Critical Heritage Ser. ISBN:0-415-03441-8, ISBN13: 978-0-415-03441-8. Dewey:821/.7. LCCN:00-045941.
Audience: **l,u.**

Wordsworth, Jonathan **PR5881**
William Wordsworth: The Borders of Vision. Trade Paper. Oxford University Press, Inc. New York, NY. 1984. 514p. ISBN:0-19-812831-2, ISBN13: 978-0-19-812831-1. Dewey:821/.7.
Audience: **g,l,u,f.**

Wordsworth, William **PR5853.J33 2003**
Sonnet Series and Itinerary Poems, 1820-1845. Trade Cloth. Cornell University Press. Ithaca, NY. 2004. 1024p. The Cornell Wordsworth Ser. ISBN:0-8014-4196-X, ISBN13: 978-0-8014-4196-7. Dewey:821/.7. LCCN:2003-055659.
Audience: **g,l,u,f.**

Wordsworth, William **PR5851**
The Prose Works of William Wordsworth. Grosart, Alexander B. (Editor). Paperbackshop Co. UKLtd. - Echo Library. 2006. ISBN:1-84637-482-0, ISBN13: 978-1-84637-482-1.
Audience: **g.**

Wordsworth, William **PR4381**
An Evening Walk. James Averill (Editor). Book, Other. Cornell University Press. Ithaca, NY. 1984. 304p. Cornell Wordsworth Ser. ISBN:0-8014-1474-1, ISBN13: 978-0-8014-1474-9. Dewey:821/.7. LCCN:82-015196.
Audience: **g,l,u,f.**

Wordsworth, William **PR5869 .R8 1979**
The Ruined Cottage and the Pedlar. James Butler (Editor). Book, Other. Cornell University Press. Ithaca, NY. 1978. 512p. Cornell Wordsworth Ser. ISBN:0-8014-1153-X, ISBN13: 978-0-8014-1153-3. Dewey:821/.7. LCCN:78-058066.
Audience: **g,l,u,f.**

Wordsworth, William **PR5869.L9 1992**
Lyrical Ballads and Other Poems, 1797-1800. James Butler & Karen Green (Editors). Book, Other. Cornell University Press. Ithaca, NY. 1993. 872p. Cornell Wordsworth Ser. ISBN:0-8014-2572-7, ISBN13: 978-0-8014-2572-1. Dewey:821.7. LCCN:92-020343.
Audience: **g,l,u,f.** *Choice, 1993.*

Wordsworth, William & Coleridge, Samuel Taylor **PR5869 .L9 1969**
Lyrical Ballads, 1798. Ed. 2. W. J. Owen (Editor). Trade Cloth. Oxford University Press, Inc. New York, NY. 1970. 224p. ISBN:0-19-911006-9, ISBN13: 978-0-19-911006-3. Dewey:821/.7. LCCN:73-509900.
Audience: **g.**

Wordsworth, William **PR5853 .C8 1983**
Poems in Two Volumes and Other Poems, 1800-1807. Jared Curtis (Editor). Book, Other. Cornell University Press. Ithaca, NY. 1983. 760p. Cornell Wordsworth Ser. ISBN:0-8014-1445-8, ISBN13: 978-0-8014-1445-9. Dewey:821/.7. LCCN:81-003124.
Audience: **g,l,u,f.**

Wordsworth, William, et al. **PR5853.C8 1999**
Last Poems, 1821-1850. Jared R. Curtis, Apryl Lea Denny-Ferris & Jillian Heydt-Stevenson (Authors). Book, Other. Cornell University Press. Ithaca, NY. 1999. 944p. Cornell Wordsworth Ser. ISBN:0-8014-3625-7, ISBN13: 978-0-8014-3625-3. Dewey:821/.7. LCCN:99-030685.
Audience: **g,l,u,f.**

Wordsworth, William **PR5859 .H6 1977**
Home at Grasmere. Beth Darlington (Editor). Book, Other. Cornell University Press. Ithaca, NY. 1978. 472p. Cornell Wordsworth Ser. ISBN:0-8014-1055-X, ISBN13: 978-0-8014-1055-0. Dewey:821/.7. LCCN:76-028009.
Audience: **g,l,u,f.**

Wordsworth, William **PR5852 .G48 1975**
The Salisbury Plain Poems of William Wordsworth. Stephen Gill (Editor). Book, Other. Cornell University Press. Ithaca, NY. 1975. 352p. Cornell Wordsworth Ser. ISBN:0-8014-0892-X, ISBN13: 978-0-8014-0892-2. Dewey:821/.7. LCCN:74-004865.
Audience: **g,l,u,f.**

Wordsworth, William **PR4381**
William Wordsworth - the Major Works: Including The Prelude. Stephen Gill (Editor). Trade Paper. Oxford University Press, Inc. New York, NY. 2000. 784p. Oxford World's Classics Ser. ISBN:0-19-284044-4, ISBN13: 978-0-19-284044-8. Dewey:821.7. LCCN:83-017278.
Audience: **g.**

Wordsworth, William **PR5881**
The Letters of William Wordsworth: A New Selection. Alan G. Hill (Editor). Cloth Text. Oxford University Press, Inc. New York, NY. 1985. 360p. Oxford Letters and Memoirs Ser. ISBN:0-19-818529-4, ISBN13: 978-0-19-818529-1. Dewey:821/.7.
Audience: **g.**

Wordsworth, William **PR5853.K48 1989**
Shorter Poems, 1807-1820. Carl H. Ketcham (Editor). Book, Other. Cornell University Press. Ithaca, NY. 1990. 704p. Cornell Wordsworth Ser. ISBN:0-8014-2175-6, ISBN13: 978-0-8014-2175-4. Dewey:821/.7. LCCN:88-015969.
Audience: **g,l,u,f.** *Choice, 1990.*

Wordsworth, William **PR5853.L36 1997**
Early Poems and Fragments, 1785-1797. Carol Landon & Jared Curtis (Editors). Book, Other. Cornell University Press. Ithaca, NY. 1998. 873p. Wordsworth Ser. ISBN:0-8014-3318-5, ISBN13: 978-0-8014-3318-4. Dewey:821/.7. LCCN:97-040305.
Audience: **g,l,u,f.**

Wordsworth, William **PR1241**
The Borderers. Robert Osborn (Editor). Book, Other. Cornell University Press. Ithaca, NY. 1981. 784p. Cornell Wordsworth Ser. ISBN:0-8014-1283-8, ISBN13: 978-0-8014-1283-7. Dewey:822/.7. LCCN:80-011212.
Audience: **g,l,u,f.**

Wordsworth, William **PR5864.A2O94 1985**
The Fourteen-Book Prelude. W. J. Owen (Editor). Book, Other. Cornell University Press. Ithaca, NY. 1985. 1,240p. Cornell Wordsworth Ser. ISBN:0-8014-1687-6, ISBN13: 978-0-8014-1687-3. Dewey:821/.7. LCCN:84-007626.
Audience: **g,l,u,f.**

Wordsworth, William **PR5864.A2 P3**
The Prelude, 1798-1799. Stephen M. Parrish (Editor). Book, Other. Cornell University Press. Ithaca, NY. 1977. 324p. Cornell Wordsworth Ser. ISBN:0-8014-0854-7, ISBN13: 978-0-8014-0854-0. Dewey:821/.7. LCCN:76-008550.
Audience: **g,l,u,f.**

Wordsworth, William **PR4381**
The Prelude, 1799, 1805 and 1815. Jonathan Wordsworth (Editor). Trade Paper. W. W. Norton & Company, Inc. New York, NY. 1979. 684p. Critical Editions Ser. ISBN:0-393-09071-X, ISBN13: 978-0-393-09071-0. Dewey:821/.7. LCCN:79-013933.
Audience: **g.**

Wordsworth, William & Wordsworth, Mary **PR5881**
The Love Letters of William and Mary Wordsworth. Beth Darlington (Editor). Book, Other. Cornell University Press. Ithaca, NY. 1981. 248p. Cornell Wordsworth Ser. ISBN:0-8014-1261-7, ISBN13: 978-0-8014-1261-5. Dewey:821/.7. LCCN:81-067177.
Audience: **g.**

Worthen, John **PR4483.W6 2001**
The Gang: Coleridge, the Hutchinsons and Wordsworths in 1802. Cloth over Boards. Yale University Press. Cumberland, RI. 2001. 352p. ISBN:0-300-08819-1, ISBN13: 978-0-300-08819-9. Dewey:821/.709 B. LCCN:00-043802.
Audience: **u,f.** *Choice, 2001.*

Individual Authors and Works > 19th C. > Yeats, William Butler

Archibald, Douglas N. **PR5906 .A72 1983**
Yeats. Trade Cloth. Syracuse University Press. Syracuse, NY. 1983. 296p. Irish Studies ISBN:0-8156-2263-5, ISBN13: 978-0-8156-2263-5. Dewey:821/.8. LCCN:82-019638.
Audience: **g,l,u,f.** B

Bloom, Harold **PR5907**
Yeats. Trade Paper. Oxford University Press, Inc. New York, NY. 1972. 512p. ISBN:0-19-501603-3, ISBN13: 978-0-19-501603-1. Dewey:821/.8. LCCN:70-100365.
Audience: **g,l,u,f.** B

Eddins, Dwight **PR5907.E3**
Yeats: The Nineteenth Century Matrix. Trade Cloth. University of Alabama Press. Tuscaloosa, AL. 1971. 192p. ISBN:0-8173-7309-8, ISBN13: 978-0-8173-7309-2. Dewey:821/.8. LCCN:73-148693.
Audience: **g,l,u,f.** B

Ellmann, Richard **PS3509.L43**
The Identity of Yeats. Ed. 2. Trade Cloth. Oxford University Press, Inc. New York, NY. 1970. 368p. ISBN:0-19-501233-X, ISBN13: 978-0-19-501233-0. Dewey:821.912.
Audience: **g,l,u,f.** B

Ellmann, Richard **PR5906 .E4 1979**
Yeats the Man and the Masks. Trade Paper. W. W. Norton & Company, Inc. New York, NY. 2000. 356p. ISBN:0-393-00859-2, ISBN13: 978-0-393-00859-3. Dewey:821/.8. LCCN:79-018876.
Audience: **g,l,u,f.** B

Foster, R. F. **PR5906.F66 1997**
W. B. Yeats: A Life: The Apprentice Mage, 1865-1914, Vol. I. Trade Cloth. Oxford University Press, Inc. New York, NY. 1997. 672p. ISBN:0-19-211735-1, ISBN13: 978-0-19-211735-9. Dewey:821.8. LCCN:96-031671.
Audience: **g,l,u,f.** *Choice, 1997.*

Foster, R. F. **PR5906 .F66 1997**
W. B. Yeats: A Life: The Arch-Poet, 1915-1939. Trade Cloth. Oxford University Press, Inc. New York, NY. 2003. 822p. ISBN:0-19-818465-4, ISBN13: 978-0-19-818465-2. Dewey:821.8. LCCN:96-031671.
Audience: **g,l,u,f.** *Choice, 2004.*

Hall, James & Steinmann, Martin **PR5907 .H3**
Permanence of Yeats. Trade Cloth. Peter Smith Publisher, Inc. Magnolia, MA. 1980. ISBN:0-8446-2188-9, ISBN13: 978-0-8446-2188-3. Dewey:821.91.
Audience: **g,l,u,f.**

Harper, George M. **PR5907**
The Mingling of Heaven and Earth. Paper Text. Brill Academic Publishers, Inc. Boston, MA. 1975. 48p. New Yeats Papers Ser., No. 10 ISBN:0-85105-269-X, ISBN13: 978-0-85105-269-4. Dewey:792/.092/4. LCCN:76-356054.
Audience: **g,u,f.** B

Heaney, Seamus **PR503.H38 1995**
The Redress of Poetry. Trade Cloth. Farrar, Straus & Giroux. New York, NY. 1995. 212p. ISBN:0-374-24853-2, ISBN13: 978-0-374-24853-6. Dewey:821/.009. LCCN:95-019556.
Audience: **u,f.** *Choice, 1996.*

Jeffares, A. Norman **PR5907 .J39**
A Commentary on the Collected Poems of W. B. Yeats. Trade Cloth. Stanford University Press. Palo Alto, CA. 1968. ISBN:0-8047-0661-1, ISBN13: 978-0-8047-0661-2. Dewey:821. LCCN:68-009770.
Audience: **g,l,u,f.**

Jeffares, A. Norman **PR5907.J39 1984**
A New Commentary on the Poems of W. B. Yeats. Ed. 2. Trade Cloth. Stanford University Press. Palo Alto, CA. 1984. xl, 543p. ISBN:0-8047-1221-2, ISBN13: 978-0-8047-1221-7. Dewey:821/.8. LCCN:83-040105.
Audience: **g,l,u,f.** B

Jeffares, A. Norman (Editor) **PR5907**
W. B. Yeats: The Critical Heritage. Trade Cloth. Routledge. New York, NY. 1977. xvi, 483p. The Critical Heritage Ser. ISBN:0-7100-8480-3, ISBN13: 978-0-7100-8480-4. Dewey:821/.8. LCCN:77-030043.
Audience: **g,l,u,f.** B

Jeffares, A. Norman **PR5906**
W. B. Yeats: Man and Poet. Ed. 2. Trade Cloth. Routledge. New York, NY. 1949. 365p. ISBN:0-7100-1607-7, ISBN13: 978-0-7100-1607-2. Dewey:821.8.
Audience: **g,l,u,f.** *Choice, 1996.*

Koch, Vivienne **PR5907.K6 1969**
W. B. Yeats, the Tragic Phase; a Study of the Last Poems. Trade Cloth. Shoe String Press, Inc. North Haven, CT. 1969. 151p. ISBN:0-208-00805-5, ISBN13: 978-0-208-00805-3. Dewey:821. LCCN:69-019228.
Audience: **g,l,u,f.** B

Korg, Jacob **PS310.M57K67 1995**
Ritual and Experiment in Modern Poetry. Cloth over Boards. Palgrave Macmillan. New York, NY. 1995. 240p. ISBN:0-312-12453-8, ISBN13: 978-0-312-12453-3. Dewey:811/.5209. LCCN:94-025159.
Audience: **g,u,f.** *Choice, 1996.*

MacNeice, Louis **PR5907 .M25 1979**
The Poetry of W. B. Yeats. Trade Cloth. Greenwood Publishing Group, Inc. Portsmouth, NH. 1979. 242p. ISBN:0-313-22102-2, ISBN13: 978-0-313-22102-6. Dewey:821/.8. LCCN:79-017894.
Audience: **g,l,u,f.** B

Malins, Edward Greenway **PR5906.M296 1974**
A Preface to Yeats. Trade Cloth. Simon & Schuster. New York, NY. 1974. xii, 212 p. :p. ISBN:0-684-14076-4, ISBN13: 978-0-684-14076-6. Dewey:821/.8. LCCN:74-011930.
Audience: **g,l,u,f.** B

Murphy, William M. **PR5906.M87 1995**
Family Secrets: William Butler Yeats and His Relatives. Trade Cloth. Syracuse University Press. Syracuse, NY. 1995. 464p. Irish Studies ISBN:0-8156-0301-0, ISBN13: 978-0-8156-0301-6. Dewey:821/.8 B. LCCN:94-019006.
Audience: **g.** *Choice, 1995.*

O'Driscoll, Robert **PR5907**
Symbolism and Some Implications of the Symbolic Approach: W. B. Yeats During the Eighteen Nineties. Paper Text. Brill Academic Publishers, Inc. Boston, MA. 1975. 84p. New Yeats Papers Ser., No. 9 ISBN:0-85105-270-3, ISBN13: 978-0-85105-270-0. Dewey:821/.8. LCCN:76-355055.
Audience: **g,u,f.**

Richardson, James **PR0595.S44R5**
Vanishing Lives: Style and Self in Tennyson, D. G. Rossetti, Swinburne, and Yeats. Trade Paper. Books on Demand. Ann Arbor, MI. 1988. 251p. Virginia Victorian Studies ISBN:0-608-01438-9, ISBN13: 978-0-608-01438-8. Dewey:821/.8/09353. LCCN:87-025269.
Audience: **u,f.** *Choice, 1988.*

Stallworthy, Jon **PR5907**
Between the Lines: Yeats's Poetry in the Making. Trade Cloth. Oxford University Press, Inc. New York, NY. 1963. ISBN:0-19-811601-2, ISBN13: 978-0-19-811601-1. Dewey:821.912.
Audience: **g,l,u,f.**

Stead, C. K. **PR605.M63S7 1986**
Pound, Yeats, Eliot and the Modernist Movement. Cloth Text. Rutgers University Press. Piscataway, NJ. 1985. 300p. ISBN:0-8135-1075-9, ISBN13: 978-0-8135-1075-0. Dewey:821/.912/09. LCCN:84-029831.
Audience: **u,f.** *Choice, 1986.*

Sultan, Stanley **PR5907**
Yeats at His Last. Paper Text. Brill Academic Publishers, Inc. Boston, MA. 1975. 48p. New Yeats Papers Ser., No. 11 ISBN:0-85105-271-1, ISBN13: 978-0-85105-271-7. Dewey:821/.8. LCCN:76-355047.
Audience: **g,u,f.**

Unterecker, John E. **PR5907.U5 1971**
A Reader's Guide to William Butler Yeats. Trade Cloth. Farrar, Straus & Giroux. New York, NY. 1971. 310p. ISBN:0-374-98048-9, ISBN13: 978-0-374-98048-1. Dewey:821/.8. LCCN:72-154661.
Audience: **g,l,u,f.**

Unterecker, John E. (Editor) **PR4803.H44**
Yeats: A Collection of Critical Essays. Trade Cloth. Prentice-Hall. Upper Saddle, NJ. 1963. ISBN:0-13-971929-6, ISBN13: 978-0-13-971929-5. Dewey:821/.8.
Audience: **g,l,u,f.**

Ure, Peter **PR5980**
Towards a Mythology: Studies in the Poetry of W. B. Yeats. Trade Cloth. Greenwood Publishing Group, Inc. Portsmouth, NH. 1986. 123p. ISBN:0-313-25055-3, ISBN13: 978-0-313-25055-2. Dewey:821/.8. LCCN:85-024696.
Audience: **g,l,u,f.**

Ure, Peter **PR5907.U69**
Yeats and Anglo-Irish Literature: Critical Essays. Trade Cloth. Barnes & Noble, Inc. New York, NY. 1974. xvi, 292 p. ;p. ISBN:0-06-497112-0, ISBN13: 978-0-06-497112-6. Dewey:821/.8. LCCN:74-194800.
Audience: **g,l,u,f.**

Ure, Peter **PR5907 .U7**
Yeats the Playwright: A Commentary on Character and Design in the Major Plays. Trade Cloth, Box or Slipcased. Routledge. New York, NY. 1963. ISBN:0-7100-2351-0, ISBN13: 978-0-7100-2351-3. Dewey:822.912.
Audience: **g,l,u,f.**

Vendler, Helen H. **PR5904.V53 V4**
Yeat's Vision and the Later Plays. Trade Cloth. Harvard University Press. Cambridge, MA. 1963. ISBN:0-674-96541-8, ISBN13: 978-0-674-96541-6. Dewey:821.8. LCCN:63-009565.
Audience: **g.**

Yeats, W. B. **PR5906.A32 1987**
The Autobiography of William Butler Yeats: Consisting of Reveries over Chilhood and Youth, the Trembling of the Veil, and Dramatis Personae. Trade Cloth. Simon & Schuster. New York, NY. 1987. 416p. ISBN:0-02-632710-4, ISBN13: 978-0-02-632710-7. Dewey:821/.8 B. LCCN:87-014069.
Audience: **g,l,u,f.**

Yeats, W. B. **PR5900**
Collected Plays of William Butler Yeats. Trade Cloth. Simon & Schuster. New York, NY. 1953. 446p. ISBN:0-02-632630-2, ISBN13: 978-0-02-632630-8. Dewey:822.
Audience: **g,l,u,f.**

Yeats, W. B. **824.912**
Essays and Introductions. Trade Paper. Simon & Schuster. New York, NY. 1968. 544p. ISBN:0-02-055610-1, ISBN13: 978-0-02-055610-7. Dewey:PR5900.
Audience: **g.**

Yeats, W. B. **PR4433**
Explorations. Trade Paper. Macmillan Publishing Company, Inc. Old Tappan, NJ. 1973. ISBN:0-02-055630-6, ISBN13: 978-0-02-055630-5. Dewey:824/.8.
Audience: **g.**

Yeats, W. B. **PR5823**
Mythologies. Trade Paper. Simon & Schuster. New York, NY. 1998. 384p. ISBN:0-684-82621-6, ISBN13: 978-0-684-82621-9. Dewey:828/.809.
Audience: **g.**

Yeats, W. B. **PR5900.A3 1987**
The Variorum Edition of the Poems of W. B. Yeats. Peter Allt & Russell K. Alspach (Editors). Children's Board Books. Simon & Schuster. New York, NY. 1987. 928p. ISBN:0-02-632700-7, ISBN13: 978-0-02-632700-8. Dewey:821/.8. LCCN:87-014145.
Audience: **g,u,f.**

Yeats, W. B. **PR5900.A3 1997**
The Poems: The Collected Works of William Butler Yeats. Ed. 2. Richard J. Finneran (Editor). Trade Cloth. Simon & Schuster. New York, NY. 1997. 784p. Collected Works of W. B. Yeats, Vol. 1 ISBN:0-684-83935-0, ISBN13: 978-0-684-83935-6. Dewey:821/.8. LCCN:97-023065.
Audience: **g,l,u,f.**

Yeats, W. B. **PR5900.A5 1970**
Uncollected Prose: Early Reviews and Articles, 1897-1939, Vol. 1. John P. Frayne & Colton Johnson (Editors). Cloth Text. Columbia University Press. New York, NY. 1970. 437p. ISBN:0-231-02845-8, ISBN13: 978-0-231-02845-5. Dewey:828/.8/08. LCCN:74-101295.
Audience: **g.**

Yeats, W. B. **PR5900**
Uncollected Prose: Later Reviews, Articles and Other Miscellaneous Prose, 1897-1939, Vol. 2. John P. Frayne & Colton Johnson (Editors). Cloth Text. Columbia University Press. New York, NY. 1976. 543p. ISBN:0-231-03660-4, ISBN13: 978-0-231-03660-3. Dewey:828/.8/08. LCCN:74-101295.
Audience: **g.**

Yeats, W. B. **PR5907**
A Concordance to the Poems of W. B. Yeats. Stephen M. Parrish & James A. Painter (Editors). Book, Other. Cornell University Press. Ithaca, NY. 1963. 1004p. Cornell Concordances Ser. ISBN:0-8014-0328-6, ISBN13: 978-0-8014-0328-6. Dewey:821.912.
Audience: **g,l,u,f.**

Individual Authors and Works > 20th C. > A

Abse, Dannie **PR6051.B7**
New and Selected Poems. Trade Paper. Random House. London, 2003. 288p. ISBN:0-09-179518-4, ISBN13: 978-0-09-179518-4. Dewey:821.9/14.
Audience: **g,l,u,f.**

Adams, Richard **PR6019.O9**
Watership Down: A Novel. Trade Paper. Simon & Schuster. New York, NY. 2005. 496p. ISBN:0-7432-7770-8, ISBN13: 978-0-7432-7770-9. Dewey:823.91.
Audience: **g,l,u,f.**

Ambler, Eric **PR6001.M48U6 2001**
A Coffin for Dimitrios. Trade Paper. Knopf Publishing Group. New York, NY. 2001. 304p. ISBN:0-375-72671-3, ISBN13: 978-0-375-72671-2. Dewey:823/.912. LCCN:2001-025845.
Audience: **g,l,u,f.** B

Ambler, Eric **PR6001.M48E65 2002**
Epitaph for a Spy. Trade Paper. Knopf Publishing Group. New York, NY. 2002. 272p. ISBN:0-375-71324-7, ISBN13: 978-0-375-71324-8. Dewey:823/.912. LCCN:2001-039584.
Audience: **g,l,u,f.** B

Ambler, Eric **PR6001.M48J6 2002**
Journey into Fear. Trade Paper. Alfred A. Knopf Inc. New York, NY. 2002. 288p. Vintage Crime/Black Lizard Ser. ISBN:0-375-72672-1, ISBN13: 978-0-375-72672-9. Dewey:823/.912. LCCN:2002-725644.
Audience: **g,l,u,f.**

Ayckbourn, Alan **PR60651.Y35N6 1975**
The Norman Conquests: Table Manners, Living Together, Round and Round the Garden. Trade Paper. Grove/Atlantic, Inc. New York, NY. 1988. 224p. ISBN:0-8021-3134-4, ISBN13: 978-0-8021-3134-8. Dewey:822.9/14. LCCN:78-073501.
Audience: **g,l,u,f.** B

Cohen, Joseph (Editor) **PR6001.B7Z/**
The Poetry of Dannie Abse: Critical Essays and Reminiscences. Trade Cloth. Salem House Publishers. Scranton, PA. 1984. 187p. ISBN:0-86051-243-6, ISBN13: 978-0-86051-243-1. Dewey:821/.914. LCCN:83-200531.
Audience: **l,u,f.** B

Individual Authors and Works > 20th C. > Amis, Kingsley

Amis, Kingsley **PR6001.M6**
The Alteration. UK-B Format Paperback. Random House of Canada, Ltd. Mississauga, ON. 2004. 208p. ISBN:0-09-946108-0, ISBN13: 978-0-09-946108-1. Dewey:823/.9/1.
Audience: **g,l.**

Amis, Kingsley **PR6001.M6**
The Green Man. UK-B Format Paperback. Knopf Publishing Group. New York, NY. 2004. 176p. ISBN:0-09-946107-2, ISBN13: 978-0-09-946107-4. Dewey:823.9/14.
Audience: **g,l.**

Amis, Kingsley **PR6001.M6**
Jake's Thing. UK- A Format Paperback. Knopf Publishing Group. New York, NY. 2004. 285p. ISBN:0-09-946835-2, ISBN13: 978-0-09-946835-6. Dewey:823.9/14.
Audience: **g,l.**

Amis, Kingsley **PR6001.M5**
Kingsley Amis Poems. Trade Paper. Books on Demand. Ann Arbor, MI. 8p. ISBN:0-598-94444-3, ISBN13: 978-0-598-94444-3. Dewey:821.
Audience: **g,l.**

Amis, Kingsley **PR6001.M6**
Memoirs. UK-B Format Paperback. Random House of Canada, Ltd. Mississauga, ON. 2004. 346p. ISBN:0-09-946106-4, ISBN13: 978-0-09-946106-7. Dewey:828/.91409 B.
Audience: **g,l.**

Amis, Kingsley **PR6001.M6**
The Old Devils. UK-B Format Paperback. Knopf Publishing Group. New York, NY. 2004. 208p. ISBN:0-09-946105-6, ISBN13: 978-0-09-946105-0. Dewey:823.9/14.
Audience: **g,l.**

Amis, Kingsley **PR6015.I3**
The Russian Girl. Trade Paper. Penguin Group (USA) Inc. New York, NY. 1993. 304p. ISBN:0-14-014475-7, ISBN13: 978-0-14-014475-8. Dewey:823/.914.
Audience: **g,l.**

Amis, Kingsley **PR6001.M6**
Stanley and the Women. UK-B Format Paperback. Knopf Publishing Group. New York, NY. 2004. 320p. ISBN:0-09-946104-8, ISBN13: 978-0-09-946104-3. Dewey:823.9/14.
Audience: **g,l.**

Amis, Kingsley **PR6051**
You Can't Do Both. UK-B Format Paperback. Knopf Publishing Group. New York, NY. 2004. 306p. ISBN:0-09-946102-1, ISBN13: 978-0-09-946102-9. Dewey:823.9/14.
Audience: **g,l.**

Amis, Kingsley **PR6001.M6L8 1992**
Lucky Jim. David Lodge (Introduction by). Trade Paper. Penguin Group (USA) Inc. New York, NY. 1993. 272p. Twentieth Century Classics Ser. ISBN:0-14-018630-1, ISBN13: 978-0-14-018630-7. Dewey:823.9/14. LCCN:93-233719.
Audience: **g,l,u,f.**

Individual Authors and Works > 20th C. > Amis, Martin

Amis, Martin **PR6051.M5**
Collection of Short Stories. Trade Paper. Knopf Publishing Group. New York, NY. 2000. 208p. ISBN:0-375-70115-X, ISBN13: 978-0-375-70115-3. Dewey:FIC.
Audience: **g,l.**

Amis, Martin **PR6051.M5**
The Rachel Papers. UK-B Format Paperback. Knopf Publishing Group. New York, NY. 2003. 224p. ISBN:0-09-945542-0, ISBN13: 978-0-09-945542-4. Dewey:823/.9/1.
Audience: **g,l.**

Amis, Martin **PR6051.M5**
Time's Arrow: Or the Nature of the Offense. UK-B Format Paperback. Knopf Publishing Group. New York, NY. 2003. 176p. ISBN:0-09-945535-8, ISBN13: 978-0-09-945535-6. Dewey:823/.914.
Audience: **l,f.**

Amis, Martin **PR6051.M5W37 2002**
The War Against Cliche: Essays and Reviews, 1971-2000. Trade Paper. Random House, Inc. New York, NY. 2002. 528p. ISBN:0-375-72716-7, ISBN13: 978-0-375-72716-0. Dewey:824/.914. LCCN:2002-066155.
Audience: **g,l.**

Amis, Martin **PR6051.M5.Y45 2003**
Yellow Dog. Trade Cloth. Hyperion Press. New York, NY. 2003. 352p. ISBN:1-4013-5203-0, ISBN13: 978-1-4013-5203-5. Dewey:823/.914. LCCN:2004-266892.
Audience: **g,l.**

Individual Authors and Works > 20th C. > Auden, W. H.

Auden, W. H. **PR6001.U4J88 1994**
Juvenilia: Poems, 1922-1928. Katherine Bucknell (Editor). Cloth Text. Princeton University Press. Princeton, NJ. 1994. 336p. ISBN:0-691-03415-X, ISBN13: 978-0-691-03415-7. Dewey:811/.52. LCCN:93-035485.
Audience: **g,l,u,f.**

Auden, W. H. & Isherwood, Christopher **PR6001.U4A19 1988**
Plays and Other Dramatic Writings by W. H. Auden, 1928-1938, Vol. I. Edward Mendelson (Editor). Trade Cloth. Princeton University Press. Princeton, NJ. 1988. 720p. Complete Works of W.H. Auden ISBN:0-691-06740-6, ISBN13: 978-0-691-06740-7. Dewey:812/.52. LCCN:87-036616.
Audience: **g,l,u,f.** *Choice, 1989.*

Auden, W. H. & Kallman, Chester **PR6001.U4 A6 1993**
W. H. Auden and Chester Kallman: Libretti and Other Dramatic Writings by W. H. Auden, 1939-1973. Edward Mendelson (Editor). Trade Cloth. Princeton University Press. Princeton, NJ. 1993. 794p. Complete Works of W.H. Auden ISBN:0-691-03301-3, ISBN13: 978-0-691-03301-3. Dewey:812/.52. LCCN:92-018681.
Audience: **g,l,u,f.** *Choice, 1994.*

Auden, W. H. **PR6001.U4 A6 1996**
The Complete Works of W H Auden: Prose and Travel Books in Prose and Verse, 1926-1938. Edward Mendelson (Editor). Trade Cloth. Princeton University Press. Princeton, NJ. 1997. 876p. The Complete Works of W. H. Auden, Vol. 1 ISBN:0-691-06803-8, ISBN13: 978-0-691-06803-9. Dewey:818/.5208. LCCN:95-038162.
Audience: **g,l,u,f.**

Auden, W. H. **PR6001**
The Complete Works of W. H. Auden: Prose, 1939-1948. Edward Mendelson (Editor). Trade Cloth. Princeton University Press. Princeton, NJ. 2002. 568p. The Complete Works of W. H. Auden Ser. ISBN:0-691-08935-3, ISBN13: 978-0-691-08935-5. Dewey:828.9/12/08. LCCN:97-176233.
Audience: **g,l,u,f.** *Choice, 2003, 2002.*

Auden, W. H. **PR6001.U4 A17 1976**
W. H. Auden Collected Poems. Edward Mendelson (Editor). Trade Cloth. Random House, Inc. New York, NY. 1976. ISBN:0-394-40895-0, ISBN13: 978-0-394-40895-8. Dewey:811/.52. LCCN:76-014155.
Audience: **g,l,u,f.**

Davenport-Hines, Richard **PR6001.U4**
Auden. UK-B Format Paperback. Knopf Publishing Group. New York, NY. 2003. 352p. ISBN:0-09-944256-6, ISBN13: 978-0-09-944256-1. Dewey:821.9/12.
Audience: **g,l,u,f.**

Fuller, John **PS3531.O82**
W. H. Auden: A Commentary. Trade Paper. Princeton University Press. Princeton, NJ. 2000. 630p. ISBN:0-691-07049-0, ISBN13: 978-0-691-07049-0. Dewey:811/.52. LCCN:98-025234.
Audience: **g,l,u,f.** *Choice, 1999.*

Haffenden, John (Editor) **PR6001.U4Z/**
W. H. Auden: The Critical Heritage. Trade Cloth. Routledge. New York, NY. 1983. 500p. The Critical Heritage Ser. ISBN:0-7100-9350-0, ISBN13: 978-0-7100-9350-9. Dewey:821/.912. LCCN:83-003241.
Audience: **g,l,u,f.**

Hecht, Anthony **PR6001.U4Z73 1993**
The Hidden Law: The Poetry of W. H. Auden. Trade Cloth. Harvard University Press. Cambridge, MA. 1993. 496p. ISBN:0-674-39006-7, ISBN13: 978-0-674-39006-5. Dewey:821.912. LCCN:92-002549.
Audience: **g,l,u,f.** *Choice, 1993.*

Mendelson, Edward **PS3509.L43**
Early Auden. Trade Paper. Farrar, Straus & Giroux. New York, NY. 2000. 448p. ISBN:0-374-52695-8, ISBN13: 978-0-374-52695-5. Dewey:821/.912.
Audience: **g,l,u,f.**

Mendelson, Edward **PS3509.L43**
Later Auden. Trade Paper. Farrar, Straus & Giroux. New York, NY. 2000. 608p. ISBN:0-374-52699-0, ISBN13: 978-0-374-52699-3. Dewey:821.9/12.
Audience: **g,l,u,f.** *Choice, 1999.*

O'Neill, Michael & Reeves, Gareth **PR610.O54 1992**
Auden, MacNeice, Spender: The Thirties Poetry. Cloth Text.

Palgrave Macmillan. New York, NY. 1992. 264p. ISBN:0-312-06828-X, ISBN13: 978-0-312-06828-8. Dewey:821/.91209. LCCN:91-028970.
Audience: **u,f.** *Choice, 1992.*

Page, Norman **PR6001.U4Z765 1997**
Auden and Isherwood: The Berlin Years. Cloth over Boards. Palgrave Macmillan. New York, NY. 1998. 220p. ISBN:0-312-21173-2, ISBN13: 978-0-312-21173-8. Dewey:820.9/00912. LCCN:97-035010.
Audience: **g,l,u,f.** *Choice, 1999.*

Smith, Stan (Editor) **PR6001.U4Z634 2004**
The Cambridge Companion to W. H. Auden. Cloth Text. Cambridge University Press. New York, NY. 2005. 288p. Cambridge Companions to Literature Ser. ISBN:0-521-82962-3, ISBN13: 978-0-521-82962-5. Dewey:821/.912. LCCN:2004-051853.
Audience: **g,l,u,f.** *Choice, 2005.*

Individual Authors and Works > 20th C. > B

Bainbridge, Beryl **PR6052.A3195A97 1989**
An Awfully Big Adventure. Trade Cloth. Gerald Duckworth & Company, Ltd. London, 1989. 193p. ISBN:0-7156-2204-8, ISBN13: 978-0-7156-2204-9. Dewey:823.9/14. LCCN:91-226248.
Audience: **g,l,u,f.**

Bainbridge, Beryl **PR6015.I3**
The Birthday Boys. Trade Paper. Avalon Publishing Group. New York, NY. 1995. 192p. ISBN:0-7867-0207-9, ISBN13: 978-0-7867-0207-7. Dewey:823/.914. LCCN:00-269391.
Audience: **g,l,u,f.**

Bainbridge, Beryl **PR6052.A3195B68 1994**
The Bottle Factory Outing. Trade Paper. Avalon Publishing Group. New York, NY. 1994. 192p. ISBN:0-7867-0146-3, ISBN13: 978-0-7867-0146-9. Dewey:823.9/14. LCCN:94-019643.
Audience: **g,l,u,f.**

Bainbridge, Beryl **PR6052.A3195M8 1985**
Mum and Mr. Armitage: Selected Stories of Beryl Bainbridge. Trade Cloth. Gerald Duckworth & Company, Ltd. London, 1985. 144p. ISBN:0-7156-2080-0, ISBN13: 978-0-7156-2080-9. Dewey:823/.914. LCCN:86-136242.
Audience: **g,l,u,f.**

Bainbridge, Beryl **PR9619.3.B263Y68**
Young Adolf. Trade Paper. Avalon Publishing Group. New York, NY. 1995. 208p. ISBN:0-7867-0258-3, ISBN13: 978-0-7867-0258-9. Dewey:823.9/14. LCCN:96-157419.
Audience: **l,u,f.**

Ballard, J. G. **PR6015.I3**
Cocaine Nights. Trade Paper. Basic Books. New York, NY. 1999. 336p. ISBN:1-58243-017-9, ISBN13: 978-1-58243-017-1. Dewey:823/.914. LCCN:97-047739.
Audience: **g,l,u,f.**

Ballard, J. G. **PR6052.A46C7 2001**
Crash: A Novel. Trade Paper. Picador. New York, NY. 2001. 224p. ISBN:0-312-42033-1, ISBN13: 978-0-312-42033-8. Dewey:823/.914. LCCN:2001-053122.
Audience: **g,l,u,f.**

Ballard, J. G. **PR6019.O9**
The Crystal World. Trade Paper. Farrar, Straus & Giroux. New York, NY. 1988. 216p. ISBN:0-374-52096-8, ISBN13: 978-0-374-52096-0. Dewey:823/.9/1. LCCN:66-011685.
Audience: **g,l,u,f.**

Ballard, J. G. **PR6015.I3**
Empire of the Sun. Trade Paper. Simon & Schuster, Inc. New York, NY. 2005. 288p. ISBN:0-7432-6523-8, ISBN13: 978-0-7432-6523-2. Dewey:823/.914.
Audience: **g,l,u,f.**

Ballard, J. G. **PR6015.I3**
Best Short Stories of J. G. Ballard. Anthony Burgess (Introduction by). Trade Paper. Picador. New York, NY. 2001. 320p. ISBN:0-312-27844-6, ISBN13: 978-0-312-27844-1. Dewey:823/.914.
Audience: **g,l,u,f.**

Banville, John **PR6052.A57**
The Sea. Trade Cloth. Pan Macmillan. London, 2005. 200p. ISBN:0-330-48328-5, ISBN13: 978-0-330-48328-5. Dewey:813/.54.
Audience: **g,l,u,f.**

Barker, Pat **PR6052.A6488E97**
The Eye in the Door. Trade Paper. Penguin Group (USA) Inc. New York, NY. 1995. 288p. ISBN:0-452-27272-6, ISBN13: 978-0-452-27272-9. Dewey:823.914.
Audience: **g,l,u,f.**

Barker, Pat **PR6015.I3**
Ghost Road. Trade Paper. Penguin Group (USA) Inc. New York, NY. 1996. 288p. ISBN:0-452-27672-1, ISBN13: 978-0-452-27672-7. Dewey:823.9/14. LCCN:95-046863.
Audience: **g,l,u,f.**

Barker, Pat **PR6052.A6488**
Regeneration. Trade Paper. Penguin Group (USA) Inc. New York, NY. 1993. 256p. William Abrahams Book Ser. ISBN:0-452-27007-3, ISBN13: 978-0-452-27007-7. Dewey:823.914. LCCN:92-044872.
Audience: **g,l,u,f.**

Barker, Pat **PR6015.I3**
Union Street. Trade Cloth. Penguin Group (USA) Inc. New York, NY. 1983. 265p. ISBN:0-399-12880-8, ISBN13: 978-0-399-12880-6. Dewey:823/.914.
Audience: **g,l,u,f.**

Barnes, Djuna **PS3503.A614N5 2000**
Nightwood. Ed. 2. Dorothy Allison (Introduction by). Trade Cloth. Random House Adult Trade Publishing Group. New York, NY. 2000. 208p. Modern Library Ser. ISBN:0-679-64024-X, ISBN13: 978-0-679-64024-0. Dewey:813/.52. LCCN:99-056308.
Audience: **u,f.**

Beerbohm, Max **PR6013.R735**
Seven Men and Two Others. Trade Cloth. Prion. London, 2001. 288p. Humour Classics Ser. ISBN:1-85375-415-3, ISBN13: 978-1-85375-415-9. Dewey:828.9/12/08.
Audience: **g,l.**

Beerbohm, Max **PR6003.E4**
A Christmas Garland. N. John Hall (Editor). Cloth over Boards. Yale University Press. Cumberland, RI. 1993. 256p. ISBN:0-300-05809-8, ISBN13: 978-0-300-05809-3. Dewey:828.91208. LCCN:93-060824.
Audience: **g,l.**

Beerbohm, Max **PR6003**
The Illustrated Zuleika Dobson. N. John Hall (Introduction by). Trade Paper. Yale University Press. Cumberland, RI. 2002. 416p. ISBN:0-300-09732-8, ISBN13: 978-0-300-09732-0. Dewey:823.9/12.
Audience: **g,l.** *Choice, 1985.*

Beerbohm, Max **PR6003.E4A17 1994**
Max Beerbohm: Collected Verse. J. G. Riewald (Editor, Notes by). Trade Cloth. Shoe String Press, Inc. North Haven, CT. 1994. xxx, 222p. ISBN:0-208-02390-9, ISBN13: 978-0-208-02390-2. Dewey:821/.912. LCCN:93-036129.
Audience: **g,l.** *Choice, 1994.*

Bennett, Alan, et al. **PR6052.E5**
The Complete "Beyond the Fringe". Peter Cook, Jonathan Miller & Dudley Moore (Authors). Trade Paper. Heinemann. Portsmouth, NH. 1992. 159p. ISBN:0-413-14670-7, ISBN13: 978-0-413-14670-0. Dewey:828/.91409. LCCN:87-180612.
Audience: **g,l,u,f.**

Bentley, E. C. **PR6019.O9**
Trent Intervenes and Other Stories. Trade Cloth. House of Stratus, Inc. New York, NY. 2001. 242p. ISBN:0-7551-0326-2, ISBN13: 978-0-7551-0326-3. Dewey:823.9/12.
Audience: **g,l,u,f.**

Bentley, E. C. **PR6003.E7247T75 1997**
Trent's Last Case. Trade Paper. Dover Publications, Inc. Mineola, NY. 1997. 160p. Mystery Classics Ser. ISBN:0-486-29687-3, ISBN13: 978-0-486-29687-6. Dewey:823/.912. LCCN:96-053232.
Audience: **g,l,u,f.**

Betjeman, John **PR6003.E77**
Collected Poems. Frederick Winston Furneaux Smith Birkenhead (Translator, Introduction by). Trade Paper. John Murray. London, 2003. 448p. ISBN:0-7195-6546-4, ISBN13: 978-0-7195-6546-5. Dewey:821/.912.
Audience: **g,l,u,f.**

Blackwood, Algernon **PR6003.L3A83 2002**
Ancient Sorceries and Other Weird Stories. S. T. Joshi (Contribution by, Notes by). Trade Paper. Penguin Group (USA) Inc. New York, NY. 2002. 400p. Twentieth Century Classics Ser. ISBN:0-14-218015-7, ISBN13: 978-0-14-218015 0. Dewey:823/.912. LCCN:2002-072084.
Audience: **g,l,u,f.**

Bolt, Robert **PR6052.O39M3 1990**
A Man for All Seasons: A Play in Two Acts. Trade Paper. Knopf Publishing Group. New York, NY. 1990. 192p. Vintage International Ser. ISBN:0-679-72822-8, ISBN13: 978-0-679-72822-1. Dewey:822.914. LCCN:89-040518.
Audience: **g,l,u,f.**

Bolt, Robert **PR6052.O39 A6 2000**
Plays One. Trade Paper. Theatre Communications Group, Inc. New York, NY. 2001. 275p. ISBN:1-84002-157-8, ISBN13: 978-1-84002-157-8. Dewey:822.9/14. LCCN:2003-430293.
Audience: **g,l,u,f.**

Bolt, Robert **PR6066.I53**
Plays Two. Trade Paper. Theatre Communications Group, Inc. New York, NY. 2001. 272p. ISBN:1-84002-158-6, ISBN13: 978-1-84002-158-5. Dewey:822.9/14.
Audience: **g,l,u,f.**

Bradbury, Malcolm **PR6052.R246.R3 1983**
Rates of Exchange. Trade Cloth. Alfred A. Knopf Inc. New York, NY. 1983. 320p. ISBN:0-394-53268-6, ISBN13: 978-0-394-53268-4. Dewey:823.9/14. LCCN:83-047787.
Audience: **g,l,u,f.**

Brookner, Anita **PR6015.I3**
Hotel du Lac. Trade Paper. Knopf Publishing Group. New York, NY. 1995. 192p. ISBN:0-679-75932-8, ISBN13: 978-0-679-75932-4. Dewey:823/.914. LCCN:84-020641.
Audience: **g,l,u,f.**

Buchan, John **PR6019.O9**
Prester John. Trade Paper. Kessinger Publishing, LLC. Whitefish, MT. 2004. ISBN:1-4191-4289-5, ISBN13: 978-1-4191-4289-5. Dewey:823.9/12.
Audience: **g,l,u,f.**

Buchan, John **PR6019.O9**
The Four Adventures of Richard Hannay: The Thirty-Nine Steps; Greenmantle; Mr. Standfast; The Three Hostages. Robin Winks (Introduction by). Trade Paper. David R. Godine Publisher. Boston, MA. 2001. 672p. ISBN:0-87923-871-2, ISBN13: 978-0-87923-871-1. Dewey:823/.912.
Audience: **g,l,u,f.**

Bunting, Basil **PR6003.U36A17 2003**
Complete Poems of Basil Bunting. Trade Paper. New Directions Publishing Corporation. New York, NY. 2003. 256p. ISBN:0-8112-1563-6, ISBN13: 978-0-8112-1563-3. Dewey:821/.914. LCCN:2003-015465.
Audience: **g,l,u,f.**

Burnside, John **PR6052.U6683A94 2000**
The Asylum Dance. UK-B Format Paperback. Random House. London, 2000. 64p. ISBN:0-224-05938-6, ISBN13: 978-0-224-05938-1. Dewey:821/.914. LCCN:2001-326864.
Audience: **g,l,u,f.**

Byatt, A. S. **PR6052.Y2A83 1994**
Angels and Insects: Two Novellas. Trade Paper. Knopf Publishing Group. New York, NY. 1994. 352p. ISBN:0-679-75134-3, ISBN13: 978-0-679-75134-2. Dewey:823/.914. LCCN:93-043495.
Audience: **g,l,f.**

Byatt, A. S. **PR6052.Y2**
Babel Tower. UK-B Format Paperback. Knopf Publishing Group. New York, NY. 2000. 670p. ISBN:0-09-983940-7, ISBN13: 978-0-09-983940-8. Dewey:823.9/14.
Audience: **g,l,u,f.**

Byatt, A. S. **PR6052.Y2**
Possession: A Romance. Trade Paper. Knopf Publishing Group. New York, NY. 2002. 576p. ISBN:0-09-943184-X, ISBN13: 978-0-09-943184-8. Dewey:823.914.
Audience: **g,l,u,f.**

Byatt, A. S. **PR6052.Y2S7 1997**
Still Life. Trade Paper. Simon & Schuster. New York, NY. 1997. 400p. ISBN:0-684-83503-7, ISBN13: 978-0-684-83503-7. Dewey:823.9/14. LCCN:96-028801.
Audience: **g,l,u,f.**

Individual Authors and Works > 20th C. > Barnes, Julian

Barnes, Julian **PR6052.A6657A84 2006**
Arthur and George. Trade Cloth. Alfred A. Knopf Inc. New York, NY. 2006. 400p. ISBN:0-307-26310-X, ISBN13: 978-0-307-26310-0. Dewey:823/.914. LCCN:2005-048771.
Audience: **g,l,u,f.**

Barnes, Julian **PR6015.I3**
Cross Channel. Trade Cloth. Random House Value Publishing. New York, NY. 1997. RHVP-Remainder Ser. ISBN:0-517-19477-5, ISBN13: 978-0-517-19477-5. Dewey:823.9/14.
Audience: **g,l,u,f.**

Barnes, Julian **PR6052.A6657E54 1999**
England, England. Trade Cloth. Alfred A. Knopf Inc. New York, NY. 1999. 288p. ISBN:0-375-40582-8, ISBN13: 978-0-375-40582-2. Dewey:823.914. LCCN:98-046170.
Audience: **g,l,u,f.**

Barnes, Julian **PR6052.A6657F56 1990**
Flaubert's Parrot. Trade Paper. Random House, Inc. New York, NY. 1990. 192p. Vintage International Ser. ISBN:0-679-73136-9, ISBN13: 978-0-679-73136-8. Dewey:823.9/14. LCCN:90-050162.
Audience: **g,l,u,f.**

Barnes, Julian **PR6015.I3**
A History of the World in Ten and a Half Chapters. Trade Paper. Random House of Canada, Ltd. Mississauga, ON. 1990. ISBN:0-394-22179-6, ISBN13: 978-0-394-22179-3. Dewey:823.9/14.
Audience: **g,l,u,f.**

Individual Authors and Works > 20th C. > Beckett, Samuel

Ackerly, C. J. **PR6003.E282Z459 2004**
The Grove Companion to Samuel Beckett: A Reader's Guide to His Works, Life, and Thought. Trade Paper. Grove/Atlantic, Inc. New York, NY. 2004. 608p. ISBN:0-8021-4049-1, ISBN13: 978-0-8021-4049-4. Dewey:848/.91409. LCCN:2003-064617.
Audience: **g,l,u,f.**

Andonian, Cathleen C. (Editor) **PR6003**
The Critical Response to Samuel Beckett. Book, Other. Greenwood Publishing Group, Inc. Portsmouth, NH. 1998. 440p. Critical Responses in Arts and Letters Ser., Vol. 30 ISBN:0-313-28910-7, ISBN13: 978-0-313-28910-1. Dewey:848/.91409. LCCN:97-044888.
Audience: **l,u,f.** *Choice, 1998.*

Bair, Deirdre **PR6003.E282Z564 1990**
Samuel Beckett. Trade Paper. Simon & Schuster. New York, NY. 1990. 784p. ISBN:0-671-69173-2, ISBN13: 978-0-671-69173-8. Dewey:848/.91409 B. LCCN:89-026353.
Audience: **g,u,f.**

Beckett, Samuel **PR6003.E282A6 1991**
I Can't Go on, I'll Go On: A Samuel Beckett Reader. Trade Paper. Grove/Atlantic, Inc. New York, NY. 1994. 672p. ISBN:0-8021-3287-1, ISBN13: 978-0-8021-3287-1. Dewey:848/.91409. LCCN:91-021178.
Audience: **g,l,u,f.**

Beckett, Samuel **PQ2603.E378A6 1997**
Molloy; Malone Dies; The Unnamable: A Triology. Trade Cloth. Knopf Publishing Group. New York, NY. 1997. 528p. Everyman's Library, Vol. 236 ISBN:0-375-40070-2, ISBN13: 978-0-375-40070-4. Dewey:823/.912. LCCN:98-119494.
Audience: **g,l,u,f.**

Beckett, Samuel **PR6003.E282**
Waiting for Godot. Trade Cloth. Faber & Faber, Ltd. London, 2006. 208p. ISBN:0-571-22910-7, ISBN13: 978-0-571-22910-9. Dewey:842.9/12.
Audience: **g,l,u,f.**

Beckett, Samuel **PR6019.O9**
More Pricks Than Kicks. Trade Paper. Riverrun Press, Inc. Flemington, NJ. 1995. 204p. ISBN:0-7145-0705-9, ISBN13: 978-0-7145-0705-7. Dewey:823/.91.
Audience: **g,l,u,f.**

Beckett, Samuel **PR6003.E282A6 2006**
The Dramatic Works of Samuel Beckett: Volume III of the Grove Centenary Editions. Paul Auster (Editor), Edward Albee (Introduction by). Cloth over Boards. Grove/Atlantic, Inc. New York, NY. 2006. 520p. ISBN:0-8021-1819-4, ISBN13: 978-0-8021-1819-6. Dewey:848/.81409. LCCN:2005-055078.
Audience: **g,l,u,f.**

Beckett, Samuel **PR6003.E282A6 2006**
The Poems, Short Fiction and Criticism of Samuel Beckett, Vol. 4. Paul Auster (Editor), J. M. Coetzee (Introduction by). Cloth over Boards. Grove/Atlantic, Inc. New York, NY. 2006. 584p. ISBN:0-8021-1820-8, ISBN13: 978-0-8021-1820-2. Dewey:848/.81409. LCCN:2005-055078.
Audience: **g,l,u,f.**

Beckett, Samuel **PR6003.E282A6 2006**
The Novels of Samuel Beckett. Paul Auster (Editor), Salman Rushdie (Introduction by). Cloth over Boards. Grove/Atlantic, Inc. New York, NY. 2006. 536p. ISBN:0-8021-1818-6, ISBN13: 978-0-8021-1818-9. Dewey:848/.81409. LCCN:2005-055078.
Audience: **g,l,u,f.**

Beckett, Samuel **PR6003.E282A6 2006**
The Novels of Samuel Beckett: The Grove Centenary Editions. Paul Auster (Editor), Colm Toibin (Introduction by). Cloth over Boards. Grove/Atlantic, Inc. New York, NY. 2006. 496p. ISBN:0-8021-1817-8, ISBN13: 978-0-8021-1817-2. Dewey:848/.81409. LCCN:2005-055078.
Audience: **u,f.**

Beckett, Samuel **PR6003.E282**
Samuel Beckett: Waiting for Godot-Endgame. Peter Boxall (Editor). Trade Paper. Palgrave Macmillan. New York, NY. 2003. 206p. Readers' Guides to Essential Criticism Ser. ISBN:1-84046-082-2, ISBN13: 978-1-84046-082-7. Dewey:822.912.
Audience: **g,l,u,f.**

Beckett, Samuel **PR6003.E282A6 1995**
The Complete Short Prose of Samuel Beckett, 1929-1989. S. E. Gontarski (Editor, Introduction by). Trade Paper. Grove/Atlantic, Inc. New York, NY. 1997. 336p. ISBN:0-8021-3490-4, ISBN13: 978-0-8021-3490-5. Dewey:828.9/12/09. LCCN:95-013074.
Audience: **g,l,u,f.**

Beckett, Samuel, et al. **PR6003.E282Z57188**
Beckett Remembering, Remembering Beckett: A Centenary Celebration. James Knowlson & Elizabeth Knowlson (Authors). Trade Cloth. Arcade Publishing, Inc. New York, NY. 2006. 336p. ISBN:1-55970-772-0, ISBN13: 978-1-55970-772-5. Dewey:848/.91409. LCCN:2005-010308.
Audience: **u,f.**

Beckett, Samuel, et al. **PR6003.E282Z495 1998**
No Author Better Served: The Correspondence of Samuel Beckett and Alan Schneider. Alan Schneider & Maurice Harmon (Authors). Trade Cloth. Harvard University Press. Cambridge, MA. 1998. 512p. ISBN:0-674-62522-6, ISBN13: 978-0-674-62522-8. Dewey:848/.91409 B. LCCN:98-005207.
Audience: **g,l,u,f.** *Choice, 1999.*

Beckett, Samuel **PQ2603.E378E513 2006**
Waiting for Godot: A Tragicomedy in Two Acts. Roger Shepherd (Illustrator). Cloth over Boards. Grove/Atlantic, Inc. New York, NY. 2006. 368p. ISBN:0-8021-1821-6, ISBN13: 978-0-8021-1821-9. Dewey:842/.914. LCCN:2006-274520.
Audience: **g,l,u,f.**

Brater, Enoch **PR6003.E282**
The Essential Samuel Beckett: An Illustrated Biography. Ed. 2. Trade Paper. Thames & Hudson. New York, NY. 2003. 144p. ISBN:0-500-28411-3, ISBN13: 978-0-500-28411-7. Dewey:848/.91409 B. LCCN:2002-113522.
Audience: **g,l,u,f.**

Calder, John **PR6003.E282**
The Philosophy of Samuel Beckett. Trade Paper. Riverrun Press, Inc. Flemington, NJ. 2003. 152p. ISBN:0-7145-4283-0, ISBN13: 978-0-7145-4283-6. Dewey:828.91209.
Audience: **u,f.**

Cronin, Anthony **PR6003.E282Z6242**
Samuel Beckett: The Last Modernist. Trade Paper. Da Capo Press, Inc. Cambridge, MA. 1999. 480p. ISBN:0-306-80898-6, ISBN13: 978-0-306-80898-2. Dewey:848/.91409 B. LCCN:98-049249.
Audience: **l,u,f.**

Dukes, Gerry **PR6003.E282Z6275**
Samuel Beckett. Trade Paper. Penguin Group (USA) Inc. New York, NY. 2001. 176p. ISBN:0-14-029470-8, ISBN13: 978-0-14-029470-5. Dewey:842/.914 B. LCCN:2002-483117.
Audience: **g,l,u,f.**

Hasan, Ira **PR6003.E282Z6685**
Understanding Waiting for Godot by Samuel Beckett: Text and Critical Commentary. Trade Paper. Oxford University Press, Inc. New York, NY. 2002. 175p. ISBN:0-19-579515-6, ISBN13: 978-0-19-579515-8. Dewey:842/.914. LCCN:2002-343188.
Audience: **g,l,u,f.**

Knowlson, James R. **PR6003.E282Z764 2004**
Damned to Fame: The Life of Samuel Beckett. Trade Paper. Grove/Atlantic, Inc. New York, NY. 2004. 832p. ISBN:0-8021-4125-0, ISBN13: 978-0-8021-4125-5. Dewey:848/.91409 B. LCCN:2003-067583.
Audience: **g,l,u,f.**

Pattie, David **PR6003.E282Z7858**
The Complete Critical Guide to Samuel Beckett. Paper over Boards. Routledge. New York, NY. 2001. 240p. The Complete Critical Guides to English Literature Ser. ISBN:0-415-20253-1, ISBN13: 978-0-415-20253-4. Dewey:848/.91409. LCCN:00-055819.
Audience: **g,l,u,f.**

Individual Authors and Works > 20th C. > Behan, Brendan

Behan, Brendan **PR6066.I53**
Behan Complete Plays. Trade Paper. Methuen Publishing Ltd. London, 2004. 0p. Methuen World Classics Ser. ISBN:0-413-38780-1, ISBN13: 978-0-413-38780-6. Dewey:822.9/14.
Audience: **g,l,u,f.**

Behan, Brendan **PR6003.E417**
Borstal Boy. Benedict Kiely (Afterword by). Trade Paper. David R. Godine Publisher. Boston, MA. 1999. 386p. ISBN:1-56792-105-1, ISBN13: 978-1-56792-105-2. Dewey:365/.94264.
Audience: **g,l,u,f.** B

Behan, Brendan **PR6003.E417**
The Letters of Brendan Behan. E. H. Mikhail (Editor). Trade Cloth. McGill-Queen's University Press. Montreal, PQ. 1991. 272p. ISBN:0-7735-0888-0, ISBN13: 978-0-7735-0888-0. Dewey:822.914.
Audience: **g,l,u,f.**

Brannigan, John **PR6003.E417Z625 2002**
Brendan Behan: Cultural Nationalism and the Revisionist Writer. Trade Cloth. Four Courts Press. Dublin 8, 2002. 202p. ISBN:1-85182-669-6, ISBN13: 978-1-85182-669-8. Dewey:823.914. LCCN:2002-512363.
Audience: **g,l,u,f.** *Choice, 2003.*

O'Sullivan, Michael **PR6003.E417**
Brendan Behan: A Life. Trade Cloth. Roberts Rinehart Publishers. Boulder, CO. 1999. 354p. ISBN:1-56833-187-8, ISBN13: 978-1-56833-187-4. Dewey:822.914.
Audience: **g,l,u,f.** *Choice, 1999.*

Individual Authors and Works > 20th C. > Bennett, Arnold

Bennett, Arnold **PR6003.E6 D4 1975**
The Card: A Story of Adventure in the Five Towns. Trade Paper. Penguin Group (USA) Inc. New York, NY. 1991. 224p. Penguin Twentieth-Century Classics Ser. ISBN:0-14-018017-6, ISBN13: 978-0-14-018017-6. Dewey:823/.912. LCCN:92-115265.
Audience: **g,l,u,f.**

Bennett, Arnold **PR6019.O9**
The Card: A Story of Adventure in the Five Towns. Trade Paper. Penguin Group (USA) Inc. New York, NY. 1987. 224p. ISBN:0-14-003826-4, ISBN13: 978-0-14-003826-2. Dewey:823/.912.
Audience: **g,l,u,f.**

Bennett, Arnold **PR6003.E6G74 1992**
The Grim Smile of the Five Towns. Trade Paper. Penguin Group (USA) Inc. New York, NY. 1993. 192p. ISBN:0-14-018021-4, ISBN13: 978-0-14-018021-3. Dewey:823/.912. LCCN:93-197404.
Audience: **g,l,u,f.**

Bennett, Arnold **PR6019.O9**
Clayhanger. Andrew Lincoln (Contribution by). Trade Paper. Penguin Group (USA) Inc. New York, NY. 1989. 528p. ISBN:0-14-018269-1, ISBN13: 978-0-14-018269-9. Dewey:823/.9/1.
Audience: **g,l,u,f.**

Bennett, Arnold **PR6003.E6**
Anna of the Five Towns. Frank Swinnerton (Introduction by). Trade Paper. Penguin Group (USA) Inc. New York, NY. 1991. 240p. Penguin Twentieth-Century Classics Ser. ISBN:0-14-018015-X, ISBN13: 978-0-14-018015-2. Dewey:823.912.
Audience: **g,l,u,f.** B

Bennett, Arnold **PR6019.O9**
The Grand Babylon Hotel: A Fantasia on Modern Themes. Frank Swinnerton (Introduction by). Trade Paper. Penguin Group (USA) Inc. New York, NY. 1992. 224p. Penguin Twentieth-Century Classics Ser. ISBN:0-14-018019-2, ISBN13: 978-0-14-018019-0. Dewey:823/.9/1.
Audience: **g,l,u,f.**

Bennett, Arnold **PR6003.E6Z5**
Journals. Frank Swinnerton (Editor). Trade Paper. Penguin Group (USA) Inc. New York, NY. 1971. 608p. ISBN:0-14-003284-3, ISBN13: 978-0-14-003284-0. Dewey:823/.9/12. LCCN:70-874485.
Audience: **g,l,u,f.** B

Bennett, Arnold **PR6019.O9**
The Old Wives' Tale. John Wain (Introduction by, Notes by). Trade Paper. Penguin Group (USA) Inc. New York, NY. 1991. 624p. Penguin Twentieth-Century Classics Ser. ISBN:0-14-018255-1, ISBN13: 978-0-14-018255-2. Dewey:823.9/12.
Audience: **g,l,u,f.**

Individual Authors and Works > 20th C. > Bowen, Elizabeth

Bowen, E. **CS499.B7/**
Bowen's Court and Seven Windows. Trade Cloth. Random House, Inc. New York, NY. 1987. xvii, 459p. ISBN:0-86068-471-7, ISBN13: 978-0-86068-471-8. Dewey:941.8/350821/0924.
Audience: **g,u,f.**

Bowen, Elizabeth **PR6019.O9**
The Collected Stories of Elizabeth Bowen. Trade Paper. Knopf Publishing Group. New York, NY. 2006. 784p. ISBN:1-4000-9656-1, ISBN13: 978-1-4000-9656-5. Dewey:823/.912.
Audience: **g,l,u,f.**

Bowen, Elizabeth **PR6019.O9**
The Death of the Heart. Trade Paper. Random House Children's Books. New York, NY. 2000. 432p. ISBN:0-385-72017-3, ISBN13: 978-0-385-72017-5. Dewey:823.9/12.
Audience: **g,l,u,f.** B

Bowen, Elizabeth **PR6003.O6757E9 2003**
Eva Trout. Trade Paper. Knopf Publishing Group. New York, NY. 2003. 320p. ISBN:0-385-72131-5, ISBN13: 978-0-385-72131-8. Dewey:823/.912. LCCN:2003-265257.
Audience: **g,l,u,f.**

Bowen, Elizabeth **PR6003.O657H4 2002**
The Heat of the Day. Trade Paper. Knopf Publishing Group. New York, NY. 2002. 384p. ISBN:0-385-72128-5, ISBN13: 978-0-385-72128-8. Dewey:823/.912. LCCN:2002-727154.
Audience: **g,l,u,f.**

Bowen, Elizabeth **PR6003.O6757H6 2002**
The House in Paris. Trade Paper. Knopf Publishing Group. New York, NY. 2002. 288p. ISBN:0-385-72125-0, ISBN13: 978-0-385-72125-7. Dewey:823/.912. LCCN:2002-524066.
Audience: **g,l,u,f.** B

Bowen, Elizabeth **PR6003.O6757.A6 1986**
Irish Stories. Trade Paper. Poolbeg Press. Dublin, 1996. 136p. ISBN:0-905169-81-6, ISBN13: 978-0-905169-81-1. Dewey:823/.912. LCCN:98-115388.
Audience: **g,l,u,f.**

Bowen, Elizabeth **PR6003.O6757L38 2000**
The Last September. Trade Paper. Random House Children's Books. New York, NY. 2000. 320p. ISBN:0-385-72014-9, ISBN13: 978-0-385-72014-4. Dewey:823.9/12. LCCN:00-266311.
Audience: **g,l,u,f.** B

Bowen, Elizabeth **PR6003.O6757L5 2004**
The Little Girls. Trade Paper. Knopf Publishing Group. New York, NY. 2004. 320p. ISBN:1-4000-3479-5, ISBN13: 978-1-4000-3479-6. Dewey:823/.912. LCCN:2004-559883.
Audience: **g,l,u,f.** B

Bowen, Elizabeth **PR6019.O9**
To the North. Trade Paper. Knopf Publishing Group. New York, NY. 2006. 320p. ISBN:1-4000-9655-3, ISBN13: 978-1-4000-9655-8. Dewey:823.9/12.
Audience: **g,l,u,f.** B

Bowen, Elizabeth **PR6003.O6757W67 2003**
A World of Love. Trade Paper. Knopf Publishing Group. New York, NY. 2003. 160p. ISBN:1-4000-3105-2, ISBN13: 978-1-4000-3105-4. Dewey:823/.912. LCCN:2003-276411.
Audience: **g,l,u,f.**

Bowen, Elizabeth & Greene, Graham **PN45 .B62 1975**
Why Do I Write?: An Exchange of Views Between Elizabeth Bowen, Graham Greene and V. S. Pritchett. V. S. Pritchett (Preface by). Library Binding. M. S. G. Haskell House. Brooklyn, NY. 1975. English Literature Ser., No. 33 ISBN:0-8383-2094-5, ISBN13: 978-0-8383-2094-5. Dewey:801. LCCN:75-022190.
Audience: **g,l,u,f.**

Ellmann, Maud **PR6003.O6757**
Elizabeth Bowen: The Shadow Across the Page. Trade Paper. Edinburgh University Press. Edinburgh, 2005. 256p. ISBN:0-7486-1703-5, ISBN13: 978-0-7486-1703-6. Dewey:823/.912.
Audience: **g,l,u,f.** *Choice, 2004.*

Glendinning, Victoria **PR6019.O9**
Elizabeth Bowen. Mass Market. HarperCollins Publishers. New York, NY. 1986. ISBN:0-380-44354-6, ISBN13: 978-0-380-44354-3. Dewey:823.912.
Audience: **g,l,u,f.**

Lee, Hermione **PR6019.O9**
Elizabeth Bowen. UK-B Format Paperback. Knopf Publishing Group. New York, NY. 1999. 265p. ISBN:0-09-927715-8, ISBN13: 978-0-09-927715-6. Dewey:823.9/12.
Audience: **g,l,u,f.**

Individual Authors and Works > 20th C. > Boyd, William

Boyd, William **PR6015.I3**
Any Human Heart: A Novel. Trade Paper. Knopf Publishing Group. New York, NY. 2004. 512p. ISBN:1-4000-3100-1, ISBN13: 978-1-4000-3100-9. Dewey:823/.914.
Audience: **g,l,u,f.**

Boyd, William **PR6015.I3**
The Blue Afternoon, Vol. 1. Trade Paper. David McKay Company, Inc. New York, NY. 1997. 384p. ISBN:0-679-77260-X, ISBN13: 978-0-679-77260-6. Dewey:823/.914.
Audience: **l,u,f.**

Boyd, William **PR6015.I3**
Brazzaville Beach. Trade Paper. HarperCollins Publishers. New York, NY. 1995. 320p. ISBN:0-380-78049-6, ISBN13: 978-0-380-78049-5. Dewey:823.9/14.
Audience: **g,l,u,f.**

Boyd, William **PR6052.O9192G6 2003**
A Good Man in Africa: A Novel. Trade Paper. Knopf Publishing Group. New York, NY. 2003. 352p. ISBN:1-4000-3002-1, ISBN13: 978-1-4000-3002-6. Dewey:823/.914. LCCN:2003-265737.
Audience: **g,l,u,f.**

Boyd, William **PR6052.O9192I2 1999**
An Ice Cream War. Trade Paper. Knopf Publishing Group. New York, NY. 1999. 416p. ISBN:0-375-70502-3, ISBN13: 978-0-375-70502-1. Dewey:823/.914. LCCN:99-018313.
Audience: **g,l,u,f.**

Boyd, William **PR6052.O9192N4 2000**
The New Confessions: A Novel. Trade Paper. Knopf Publishing Group. New York, NY. 2000. 480p. Vintage International Ser. ISBN:0-375-70503-1, ISBN13: 978-0-375-70503-8. LCCN:00-036340.
Audience: **g,l,u,f.**

Individual Authors and Works > 20th C. > Brooke, Rupert

Brooke, Rupert **F1015.B87**
Letters from America. Henry James (Illustrator). Trade Paper. Turtle Point Press. New York, NY. 2002. 228p. ISBN:1-885586-69-8, ISBN13: 978-1-885586-69-8. Dewey:821/.912 B.
Audience: **g,l,u,f.**

Brooke, Rupert & Strachey, James **PR6003.R4Z483 1998**
Friends and Apostles: The Correspondence of Rupert Brooke and James Strachey, 1905-1914. Keith Hale (Editor). Cloth over Boards. Yale University Press. Cumberland, RI. 1998. 320p. ISBN:0-300-07004-7, ISBN13: 978-0-300-07004-0. Dewey:826.9/12/08. LCCN:98-007353.
Audience: **g,l,u,f.** *Choice, 1999.*

Brooke, Rupert & Woodberry, George Edward **PR6003.R4**
The Collected Poems of Rupert Brooke. Trade Paper. Kessinger Publishing, LLC. Whitefish, MT. 2005. ISBN:1-4179-1400-9, ISBN13: 978-1-4179-1400-5. Dewey:821/.912.
Audience: **g,l,u,f.**

Hassall, Christopher **PR6003.R4 Z67 1972**
Rupert Brooke: A Biography. Trade Paper. Faber & Faber, Ltd. London, 1972. 558p. ISBN:0-571-10196-8, ISBN13: 978-0-571-10196-2. Dewey:821/.9/12. LCCN:73-176138.
Audience: **l,u,f.**

Jones, Nigel **PR6003.R4Z683 1999**
Rupert Brooke: Life, Death and Myth. Trade Cloth. John Blake Publishing, Ltd. London, 2000. xvii, 462p. ISBN:1-86066-171-8, ISBN13: 978-1-86066-171-6. Dewey:821.9/12. LCCN:00-272929.
Audience: **l,u,f.**

Individual Authors and Works > 20th C. > Burgess, Anthony

Burgess, Anthony **PR6052.U638A65 1989**
Any Old Iron. Trade Cloth. Random House, Inc. New York, NY. 1989. ISBN:0-394-57484-2, ISBN13: 978-0-394-57484-4. Dewey:823/.914. LCCN:88-042682.
Audience: **g,l,u,f.**

Burgess, Anthony **PR6052.U638C5 1987**
A Clockwork Orange. Ed. 2. Trade Paper. W. W. Norton & Company, Inc. New York, NY. 1995. 208p. Norton Paperback Fiction Ser. ISBN:0-393-31283-6, ISBN13: 978-0-393-31283-6. Dewey:823.9/14. LCCN:89-023843.
Audience: **g,l,u,f.** *Choice, 1987.*

Burgess, Anthony **PR6015.I3**
The Complete Enderby. UK-Trade Paper. Knopf Publishing Group. New York, NY. 2002. 640p. ISBN:0-09-944259-0, ISBN13: 978-0-09-944259-2. Dewey:823.9/14.
Audience: **g,l,u,f.**

Burgess, Anthony **PR6052.U638E2 1994**
Earthly Powers. Trade Paper. Avalon Publishing Group. New York, NY. 1993. 608p. ISBN:0-7867-0026-2, ISBN13: 978-0-7867-0026-4. Dewey:823.9/14. LCCN:93-038767.
Audience: **g,l,u,f.**

Burgess, Anthony **PR6052.U638 E5 1983**
The End of the World News: An Entertainment. Cloth Text. McGraw-Hill Companies, The. New York, NY. 1983. 388p. ISBN:0-07-008965-5, ISBN13: 978-0-07-008965-5. Dewey:823/.914. LCCN:82-017159.
Audience: **g,l,u,f.**

Burgess, Anthony **PR6019.O9**
Honey for the Bears. Trade Paper. W. W. Norton & Company, Inc. New York, NY. 1996. 256p. ISBN:0-393-31441-3, ISBN13: 978-0-393-31441-0. Dewey:823/.9/1.
Audience: **g,l,u,f.**

Burgess, Anthony **PR6052.U638**
Little Wilson and Big God. UK-B Format Paperback. Knopf Publishing Group. New York, NY. 2002. 448p. ISBN:0-09-943705-8, ISBN13: 978-0-09-943705-5. Dewey:823.9/14.
Audience: **g,l,u,f.** *Choice, 1987.*

Burgess, Anthony **PR6015.I3**
Nothing Like the Sun: A Story of Shakespeare's Love-Life. Trade Cloth. W. W. Norton & Company, Inc. New York, NY. 1996. 240p. ISBN:0-393-31507-X, ISBN13: 978-0-393-31507-3. Dewey:823.9/14.
Audience: **g,l,u,f.**

Burgess, Anthony **PR6019.O9;**
Re Joyce. Trade Cloth. W. W. Norton & Company, Inc. New York, NY. 2000. 272p. ISBN:0-393-00445-7, ISBN13: 978-0-393-00445-8. Dewey:823.912. LCCN:65-018779.
Audience: **g,l,u,f.**

Burgess, Anthony **PR6052.U638**
The Wanting Seed. Trade Paper. W. W. Norton & Company, Inc. New York, NY. 1996. 288p. Norton Paperback Fiction Ser. ISBN:0-393-31508-8, ISBN13: 978-0-393-31508-0. Dewey:823/.914. LCCN:63-015877.
Audience: **g,l,u,f.**

Burgess, Anthony **PR6052.U638**
You've Had Your Time: The Second Part of the Confessions. UK-Trade Paper. Knopf Publishing Group. New York, NY. 2002. 400p. ISBN:0-09-943706-6, ISBN13: 978-0-09-943706-2. Dewey:823/914 B.
Audience: **g,l,u,f.** *Choice, 1991.*

Lewis, Roger **PR6052.U638Z695 2004**
Anthony Burgess: A Biography. Cloth over Boards. St. Martin's Press. Gordonville, VA. 2004. 480p. ISBN:0-312-32251-8, ISBN13: 978-0-312-32251-9. Dewey:823/.914 B. LCCN:2003-058774.
Audience: **g,l,u,f.** *Choice, 2004.*

Rostand, Edmond **PQ2653.O7C92 1990**
Cyrano de Bergerac. Anthony Burgess (Translator). Trade Paper. Knopf Publishing Group. New York, NY. 1990. 192p. ISBN:0-679-73413-9, ISBN13: 978-0-679-73413-0. Dewey:842/.8. LCCN:90-050435.
Audience: **g,l,u,f.** *Choice, 1995.*

Stinson, John J. **PR6052.U638Z89 1991**
Anthony Burgess Revisited. Trade Cloth. Thomson Gale. Farmington Hills, MI. 1991. 184p. Twayne's English Authors Ser., No. 482 ISBN:0-8057-7000-3, ISBN13: 978-0-8057-7000-1. Dewey:823/.914. LCCN:90-046003.
Audience: **g,l,u,f.** *Choice, 1991.*

Individual Authors and Works > 20th C. > C

Carter, Angela **PR6015.I3**
The Bloody Chamber. Trade Paper. Penguin Group (USA) Inc. New York, NY. 1990. 128p. ISBN:0-14-017821-X, ISBN13: 978-0-14-017821-0. Dewey:823.9/14.
Audience: **g,l,u,f.**

Carter, Angela **PR6053.A73**
Nights at the Circus. UK-B Format Paperback. Knopf Publishing Group. New York, NY. 1994. 368p. ISBN:0-09-938861-8, ISBN13: 978-0-09-938861-6. Dewey:823.9/14.
Audience: **g,l,u,f.**

Carter, Angela **PR6053.A73B87 1996**
Burning Your Boats: The Collected Short Stories. Salman Rushdie (Introduction by). Trade Cloth. Henry Holt & Company. New York, NY. 1996. 480p. ISBN:0-8050-4462-0, ISBN13: 978-0-8050-4462-1. Dewey:823/.914. LCCN:95-026312.
Audience: **g,l,u,f.**

Carter, Angela & Uglow, Jennifer S. **PR6053.A73S54 1997**
Shaking a Leg: Journalism and Writings. Trade Cloth. Random House. London, 1997. 641p. The Collected Angela Carter Ser. ISBN:0-7011-6336-4, ISBN13: 978-0-7011-6336-5. Dewey:828.9/14/08. LCCN:98-148778.
Audience: **g,l,u,f.**

Cartwright, Justin **PR6053.A746L43 1999**
Leading the Cheers. Trade Cloth. Avalon Publishing Group. New York, NY. 1999. 246p. ISBN:0-7867-0658-9, ISBN13: 978-0-7867-0658-7. Dewey:823/.914. LCCN:2001-268758.
Audience: **g,l,u,f.**

Childers, Erskine **PR6019.O9**
The Riddle of the Sands: A Record of Secret Service. Geoffrey Household (Foreword by). Trade Paper. Penguin Group (USA)

Inc. New York, NY. 2000. 336p. Classics Ser. ISBN:0-14-118165-6, ISBN13: 978-0-14-118165-3. Dewey:823/.9/1.

Audience: **g,l,u,f.**

Churchill, Caryl **PR6053.H786A19 1985**
Plays. Trade Paper. Methuen Publishing Ltd. London, 2004. Methuen Paperback Ser. ISBN:0-413-56670-6, ISBN13: 978-0-413-56670-6. Dewey:822.9/14. LCCN:85-186277.

Audience: **g,l,u,f.**

Churchill, Caryl **PR6066.I53**
Plays Two, Vol. 2. Trade Paper. Methuen Publishing Ltd. London, 2004. Methuen World Dramatists Ser. ISBN:0-413-62270-3, ISBN13: 978-0-413-62270-9. Dewey:822.9/14.

Audience: **l,u,f.**

Clarke, Arthur C. **PR6015.I3**
Childhood's End. Trade Cloth. Amereon, Ltd. Mattituck, NY. ISBN:0-8488-0157-1, ISBN13: 978-0-8488-0157-1. Dewey:823/.914.

Audience: **g,l,u,f.**

Clarke, Arthur C. **PR6005.L36A6 2000**
The Collected Stories of Arthur C. Clarke. Cloth over Boards. Tom Doherty Associates, LLC. New York, NY. 2001. 912p. ISBN:0-312-87821-4, ISBN13: 978-0-312-87821-4. Dewey:823/.914. LCCN:2002-275174.

Audience: **g,l,u,f.**

Clarke, Arthur C. & Kubrick, Stanley **PR6015.I3**
2001: A Space Odyssey. Library Binding. Buccaneer Books, Inc. Cutchogue, NY. 1994. ISBN:1-56849-417-3, ISBN13: 978-1-56849-417-3. Dewey:823/.914.

Audience: **g,l,u,f.**

Clarke, Austin **PR6005.L37.A17 1974**
Collected Poems. Trade Cloth. Bow Historical Books. New Providence, NJ. 1974. xvi, 568p. ISBN:0-19-211845-5, ISBN13: 978-0-19-211845-5. Dewey:821/.9/12. LCCN:75-314851.

Audience: **g,l,u,f.**

Clarke, Austin
Liberty Lane: A Ballad Play of Dublin in Two Acts with a Prologue. Dufour Editions, Inc. 1978. Dolmen Editions Ser. ISBN:0-85105-324-6, ISBN13: 978-0-85105-324-0.

Audience: **g,l,u,f.**

Clarke, Austin **GN652.B4**
Twice Round the Black Church: Early Memories of Ireland and England. Paper Text. Textbook Publishers. Temecula, CA. 2003. 178p. ISBN:0-7581-4592-6, ISBN13: 978-0-7581-4592-5. Dewey:572.968965.

Audience: **g,l,u,f.**

Clarke, Susanna **PR6103.L375J65 2004**
Jonathan Strange and Mr. Norrell: A Novel. Cloth over Boards. Bloomsbury Publishing. New York, NY. 2004. 800p. ISBN:1-58234-416-7, ISBN13: 978-1-58234-416-4. Dewey:823/.92. LCCN:2004-002402.

Audience: **g,l,u,f.**

Colum, Padraic **PR6005.O38A6 1989**
Selected Poems of Padraic Colum. Sanford Sternlicht (Editor). Cloth Text. Syracuse University Press. Syracuse, NY. 1989. 120p. Irish Studies ISBN:0-8156-2458-1, ISBN13: 978-0-8156-2458-5. Dewey:821/.912. LCCN:88-021962.

Audience: **g,l,u,f.**

Cope, Wendy **PR6053.O6535I36 2001**
If I Don't Know. Trade Cloth. Faber & Faber, Inc. New York, NY. 2001. 96p. ISBN:0-571-20767-7, ISBN13: 978-0-571-20767-1. Dewey:821/.914. LCCN:2001-536089.

Audience: **g,l,u,f.**

Crace, Jim **PR6015.I3**
Quarantine: A Novel, Set. Trade Paper. St. Martin's Press. Gordonville, VA. 1999. ISBN:0-312-20702-6, ISBN13: 978-0-312-20702-1. Dewey:823.9/14.

Audience: **g,l,u,f.**

Cronin, A. J. **PR6019.O9**
The Citadel. Trade Cloth. Little Brown & Company. New York, NY. 1983. ISBN:0-316-16158-6, ISBN13: 978-0-316-16158-9. Dewey:823.9/12.

Audience: **g,l,u,f.**

Sternlicht, Sanford (Editor) **PR6005.O38A6 1985**
Selected Short Stories of Padraic Colum. Cloth Text. Syracuse University Press. Syracuse, NY. 1985. 160p. Irish Studies ISBN:0-8156-2327-5, ISBN13: 978-0-8156-2327-4. Dewey:823/.912. LCCN:84-020522.

Audience: **g,l,u,f.**

Individual Authors and Works > 20th C. > Cary, Joyce

Adams, Hazard **PR6019.O9**
Joyce Cary's Trilogies: Pursuit of the Particular Real. Trade Paper. University Press of Florida. Gainesville, FL. 1986. 280p. ISBN:0-8130-0851-4, ISBN13: 978-0-8130-0851-6. Dewey:823/.912.

Audience: **u,f.**

Bloom, Robert
The Indeterminate World: A Study of the Novels of Joyce Cary. Textbook Publishers. 2003. ISBN:0-7581-1672-1, ISBN13: 978-0-7581-1672-7.

Audience: **u,f.**

Cary, Joyce **PR6005.A77**
An American Visitor. Trade Paper. Tuttle Publishing. Boston, MA. 1995. 224p. Paperback Classics ISBN:0-460-87586-8, ISBN13: 978-0-460-87586-8. Dewey:823.912.

Audience: **g,l,u,f.**

Cary, Joyce **PR6005.A77**
The Captive and the Free. Trade Cloth. House of Stratus, Inc. New York, NY. 2000. 440p. ISBN:1-84232-008-4, ISBN13: 978-1-84232-008-2. Dewey:823/.9/12.

Audience: **g,l,u,f.**

Cary, Joyce **DT20 .C3**
The Case for African Freedom, and Other Writings on Africa. Paper Text. Textbook Publishers. Temecula, CA. 2003. xiv, 241p. ISBN:0-7581-1557-1, ISBN13: 978-0-7581-1557-7. Dewey:960.
Audience: **u,f.**

Cary, Joyce **PR6019.O9**
Castle Corner. Trade Cloth. House of Stratus, Inc. New York, NY. 2000. 652p. ISBN:1-84232-009-2, ISBN13: 978-1-84232-009-9. Dewey:823.9/12.
Audience: **g,l,u,f.** B

Cary, Joyce **PR6019.O9**
Herself Surprised. Library Binding. Buccaneer Books, Inc. Cutchogue, NY. 1990. ISBN:0-89968-490-4, ISBN13: 978-0-89968-490-1. Dewey:823/.912.
Audience: **g,l,u,f.**

Cary, Joyce
Memoir of the Bobotes. Sterling Publishing Co., Inc. 2000. Phoenix Press Ser. ISBN:1-84212-102-2, ISBN13: 978-1-84212-102-3.
Audience: **g,l,u,f.**

Cary, Joyce **PR6019.O9**
Mister Johnson. Library Binding. Buccaneer Books, Inc. Cutchogue, NY. 1994. ISBN:1-56849-517-X, ISBN13: 978-1-56849-517-0. Dewey:823.9/12. LCCN:88-035710.
Audience: **g,l,u,f.**

Cary, Joyce **PR6005.A77N6 1985**
Not Honour More. Trade Paper. New Directions Publishing Corporation. New York, NY. 1985. 320p. Classics Ser., :Second Trilogy ISBN:0-8112-0966-0, ISBN13: 978-0-8112-0966-3. Dewey:823/.912. LCCN:85-010601.
Audience: **g,l,u,f.**

Cary, Joyce **PR6005.A77P7 1985**
Prisoner of Grace. Trade Paper. New Directions Publishing Corporation. New York, NY. 1985. 320p. Paperbook Ser. ISBN:0-8112-0964-4, ISBN13: 978-0-8112-0964-9. Dewey:823/.912. LCCN:85-010662.
Audience: **g,l,u,f.** B

Cary, Joyce **PR6019.O9**
Prisoner of Grace. Trade Cloth. House of Stratus, Inc. New York, NY. 2000. 438p. ISBN:1-84232-039-4, ISBN13: 978-1-84232-039-6. Dewey:823/.912.
Audience: **g,l,u,f.** B

Cary, Joyce **PR6005.A77H4 1999**
Herself Surprised, Vol. I. Brad Leithauser (Introduction by). Trade Paper. New York Review of Books, Incorporated, The. New York, NY. 1999. 300p. New York Review Books Classics Ser., Vol. 13 ISBN:0-940322-17-X, ISBN13: 978-0-940322-17-2. Dewey:823/.912. LCCN:99-015895.
Audience: **g,l,u,f.**

Cary, Joyce **PR6005.A77H6 1999**
The Horse's Mouth. Brad Leithauser (Introduction by). Trade Paper. New York Review of Books, Incorporated, The. New York, NY. 1999. 432p. ISBN:0-940322-19-6, ISBN13: 978-0-940322-19-6. Dewey:823/.91. LCCN:99-015898.
Audience: **g,l,u,f.**

Cary, Joyce **PR6005.A77T6 1999**
To Be a Pilgrim, Vol. 2. Brad Leithauser (Introduction by). Trade Paper. New York Review of Books, Incorporated, The. New York, NY. 1999. 400p. New York Review Books Classics Ser., Vol. 14 ISBN:0-940322-18-8, ISBN13: 978-0-940322-18-9. Dewey:823/.912. LCCN:99-015896.
Audience: **g,l,u,f.**

Closter, Susan V. **Z8150.8.V36 1985**
Joyce Cary and Lawrence Durrell: A Reference Guide. Trade Cloth. Macmillan Publishing Company, Inc. Old Tappan, NJ. 1985. 262p. Reference Guides to Literature Ser. ISBN:0-8161-8627-8, ISBN13: 978-0-8161-8627-3. Dewey:016.823/912. LCCN:85-005609.
Audience: **u,f.** *Choice, 1985.*

Cook, Cornelia **PR6005.A77 Z635**
Joyce Cary: Liberal Principles. Trade Cloth. University Press of America, Inc. Lanham, MD. 1981. 242p. Critical Studies ISBN:0-389-20201-0, ISBN13: 978-0-389-20201-1. Dewey:823/.912. LCCN:81-164790.
Audience: **u,f.**

Echeruo, Michael J. **PR6005.A77Z647 1979**
Joyce Cary and the Dimensions of Order. Trade Cloth. Macmillan Publishers Ltd. London, 1979. x, 175p. ISBN:0-333-24697-7, ISBN13: 978-0-333-24697-9. Dewey:823/.912. LCCN:79-308539.
Audience: **u,f.** B

Individual Authors and Works > 20th C. > Christie, Agatha

Cade, Jared **PR6065.H66**
Agatha Christie and the Eleven Missing Days. Trade Paper. Peter Owen Ltd. London, 2004. 26p. ISBN:0-7206-1112-1, ISBN13: 978-0-7206-1112-0. Dewey:823.912.
Audience: **g,l,u,f.**

Christie, Agatha **PR6005.H66A84 2004**
And Then There Were None. Trade Paper. St. Martin's Press. Gordonville, VA. 2004. 272p. ISBN:0-312-33087-1, ISBN13: 978-0-312-33087-3. Dewey:823/.912. LCCN:2004-041165.
Audience: **g,l,u,f.**

Christie, Agatha **PR6005.H66B7**
The Body in the Library. Mass Market. Penguin Group (USA) Inc. New York, NY. 2000. 224p. Miss Marple Mysteries Ser. ISBN:0-451-19987-1, ISBN13: 978-0-451-19987-4. Dewey:823.912.
Audience: **g,l,u,f.**

Christie, Agatha **PR6019.O9**
Miss Marple: The Complete Short Stories. Trade Paper. Penguin Group (USA) Inc. New York, NY. 1986. 352p. ISBN:0-425-09486-3, ISBN13: 978-0-425-09486-0. Dewey:823/.912.
Audience: **g,l,u,f.**

Christie, Agatha **PR5366**
The Mousetrap and Other Plays. Mass Market. Penguin Group (USA) Inc. New York, NY. 2000. 752p. Miss Marple Mysteries Ser. ISBN:0-451-20114-0, ISBN13: 978-0-451-20114-0. Dewey:822/.912.
Audience: **g,l,u,f.**

Christie, Agatha **PR6019.O9**
The Murder of Roger Ackroyd: A Hercule Poirot Mystery. Mass Market. Penguin Group (USA) Inc. New York, NY. 2004. 368p. ISBN:0-425-20047-7, ISBN13: 978-0-425-20047-6. Dewey:823.9/12.
Audience: **g,l,u,f.**

Christie, Agatha **PR6005.H66A6 2005**
Poirot in the Orient: Murder in Mesopotamia; Death on the Nile; Appointment with Death. Trade Paper. Penguin Group (USA) Inc. New York, NY. 2005. 608p. ISBN:0-425-20067-1, ISBN13: 978-0-425-20067-4. Dewey:823/.912. LCCN:2004-062290.
Audience: **g,l,u,f.**

Christie, Agatha **PR6019.O9**
The Secret Adversary. Mass Market. Penguin Group (USA) Inc. New York, NY. 2001. 256p. Tommy and Tuppence Mysteries Ser. ISBN:0-451-20120-5, ISBN13: 978-0-451-20120-1. Dewey:823.9/12.
Audience: **g,l,u,f.**

Christie, Agatha **CPB**
The Seven Dials Mystery. Val McDermid (Introduction by). Mass Market. St. Martin's Press. Gordonville, VA. 2001. 288p. St. Martin's Minotaur Mysteries Ser. ISBN:0-312-97977-0, ISBN13: 978-0-312-97977-5. Dewey:823.9/12. LCCN:2002-562711.
Audience: **g,l,u,f.**

Riley, Dick & McAllister, Pam **PR6005.H66 Z557**
The Bedside, Bathtub and Armchair Companion to Agatha Christie. Ed. 2. Trade Paper. Continuum International Publishing Group, Ltd. London, 2001. 384p. ISBN:0-8264-1375-7, ISBN13: 978-0-8264-1375-8. Dewey:823/.9/12.
Audience: **g,l,u,f.**

Individual Authors and Works > 20th C. > Compton-Burnett, Ivy

Baldanza, Frank **PR6005.O3895 Z585**
Ivy Compton-Burnett. Cloth Text. Irvington Publishers. New York, NY. 1964. 142p. Twayne's English Authors Ser. ISBN:0-8290-1728-3, ISBN13: 978-0-8290-1728-1. Dewey:823.912. LCCN:64-008325.
Audience: **g,l,u,f.**

Compton-Burnett, Ivy **PR6019.O9**
A Family and a Fortune. Trade Paper. Penguin Group (USA) Inc. New York, NY. 1983. 304p. Modern Classics Ser. ISBN:0-14-001713-5, ISBN13: 978-0-14-001713-7. Dewey:823/.9/1.
Audience: **g,l,u,f.**

Compton-Burnett, Ivy **PR6005.O3895**
First Omnibus. Trade Paper. Penguin Books, Ltd. London, 1994. 768p. ISBN:0-14-018662-X, ISBN13: 978-0-14-018662-8. Dewey:823.912.
Audience: **g,l,u,f.**

Compton-Burnett, Ivy **PR6005.O3895 T9**
Two Worlds and Their Ways. Trade Cloth. Victor Gollancz Ltd. London, 1969. 285p. ISBN:0-575-00280-8, ISBN13: 978-0-575-00280-7. Dewey:823/.912. LCCN:73-408339.
Audience: **g,l,u,f.**

Compton-Burnett, Ivy **PR6005.O3895M3 2001**
Manservant and Maidservant. Diane Johnson (Introduction by). Trade Paper. New York Review of Books, Incorporated, The. New York, NY. 2001. 328p. New York Review Books Classics Ser. ISBN:0-940322-63-3, ISBN13: 978-0-940322-63-9. Dewey:823/.91. LCCN:00-011547.
Audience: **g,l,u,f.**

Compton-Burnett, Ivy **PR6005.O3895H6 2001**
A House and Its Head. Francine Prose (Introduction by). Trade Paper. New York Review of Books, Incorporated, The. New York, NY. 2001. 304p. New York Review Books Classics Ser. ISBN:0-940322-64-1, ISBN13: 978-0-940322-64-6. Dewey:823/.91. LCCN:00-011546.
Audience: **g,l,u,f.**

Spurling, Hilary **PR6005.O3895Z915X**
Ivy When Young: The Early Life of I. Compton-Burnett, 1884-1919. Trade Cloth. Black Moss Press. Windsor, ON. 1983. 319 [16]p. ISBN:0-85031-504-2, ISBN13: 978-0-85031-504-2. Dewey:823/.912. LCCN:87-673549.
Audience: **g,l,u,f.**

Individual Authors and Works > 20th C. > Conrad, Joseph

Baines, Jocelyn **PR6005.O4**
Joseph Conrad. Trade Paper. Weidenfeld & Nicolson, Ltd. London, 1993. 520p. ISBN:0-297-81379-X, ISBN13: 978-0-297-81379-8. Dewey:823.912.
Audience: **l,u,f.**

Batchelor, John Calvin **PR6005.O4.Z557 1994**
The Life of Joseph Conrad: A Critical Biography. Trade Cloth. Blackwell Publishing, Inc. Malden, MA. 1993. 368p. Critical Biographies Ser. ISBN:0-631-16416-2, ISBN13: 978-0-631-16416-6. Dewey:823.9/12. LCCN:93-003674.
Audience: **l,u,f.** *Choice, 1994.*

Conrad, Jessie **PR6005.O4.Z58 1970**
Joseph Conrad As I Knew Him. Trade Cloth. Ayer Company Publishers, Inc. Manchester, NH. 1977. xxi, 162p. Select Bibliographies Reprint Ser. ISBN:0-8369-5497-1, ISBN13: 978-0-8369-5497-5. Dewey:823/.9/12. LCCN:76-128877.
Audience: **g,l,u,f.**

Conrad, Joseph **PR6005.O4A8 2003**
Almayer's Folly. Trade Paper. Dover Publications, Inc. Mineola, NY. 2003. 128p. Dover Thrift Editions Ser. ISBN:0-486-42677-7, ISBN13: 978-0-486-42677-8. Dewey:823/.912. LCCN:2002-035110.
Audience: **g,l,u,f.**

Conrad, Joseph **PR6005.O4**
Chance: A Tale in Two Parts. Trade Paper. Penguin Group (USA) Inc. New York, NY. 1993. 368p. Great Books of the 20th Century Ser. ISBN:0-14-018654-9, ISBN13: 978-0-14-018654-3. Dewey:823/.912. LCCN:75-320055.
Audience: **g,l,u,f.**

Conrad, Joseph **PR6005.O4H4 1999**
Heart of Darkness. Trade Paper. Penguin Group (USA) Inc. New York, NY. 1999. 160p. Penguin Great Books of the 20th Century Ser. ISBN:0-14-028163-0, ISBN13: 978-0-14-028163-7. Dewey:823/.912. LCCN:99-205953.
Audience: **g,l,u,f.** *Choice, 1989.*

Conrad, Joseph **PR6005.O4**
The Shadow-Line: A Confession. Jacques Berthoud (Contribution by, Notes by). Trade Paper. Penguin Group (USA) Inc. New York, NY. 1993. 160p. Penguin Great Books of the 20th Century Ser. ISBN:0-14-018097-4, ISBN13: 978-0-14-018097-8. Dewey:823.912.
Audience: **g,l,u,f.**

Conrad, Joseph **PR6005.O4.P7 1971**
Conrad's Prefaces to His Works. Edward Garnett (Introduction by). Trade Cloth. Ayer Company Publishers, Inc. Manchester, NH. 1977. viii, 218p. Select Bibliographies Reprint Ser. ISBN:0-8369-5831-4, ISBN13: 978-0-8369-5831-7. Dewey:823/.9/12. LCCN:72-160963.
Audience: **l,u,f.** B

Conrad, Joseph **PR6005.O4V5**
Victory: An Island Tale. Robert Hampson (Editor, Introduction by). Trade Paper. Penguin Group (USA) Inc. New York, NY. 1995. 416p. Penguin Great Books of the 20th Century Ser. ISBN:0-14-018978-5, ISBN13: 978-0-14-018978-0. Dewey:823.912.
Audience: **g,l,u,f.**

Conrad, Joseph **PR6019.O9**
Lord Jim: A Tale. Robert Hampson (Editor), Cedric P. Watts (Introduction by, Notes by). Trade Paper. Penguin Group (USA) Inc. New York, NY. 1989. 384p. Penguin Great Books of the 20th Century Ser. ISBN:0-14-018092-3, ISBN13: 978-0-14-018092-3. Dewey:823/.9/1.
Audience: **g,l,u,f.**

Conrad, Joseph **PR6005.O4H4 1988**
Heart of Darkness: An Authoritative Text, Backgrounds and Sources, Criticism. Ed. 3. Robert Kimbrough (Editor). Trade Paper. W. W. Norton & Company, Inc. New York, NY. 1987. 438p. Critical Editions Ser. ISBN:0-393-95552-4, ISBN13: 978-0-393-95552-1. Dewey:823/.912. LCCN:87-015645.
Audience: **u,f.**

Conrad, Joseph **PR6005.O4 N5638 1979**
The Nigger of the Narcissus. Ed. 3. Robert Kimbrough (Editor). Trade Paper. W. W. Norton & Company, Inc. New York, NY. 1979. 370p. Critical Editions Ser. ISBN:0-393-09019-1, ISBN13: 978-0-393-09019-2. Dewey:823/.912. LCCN:78-015249.
Audience: **l,u,f.** B

Conrad, Joseph **PR6005.O4U575 1996**
Under Western Eyes. Paul Kirschner (Notes by). Trade Paper. Penguin Group (USA) Inc. New York, NY. 1997. 432p. Great Books of the 20th Century Ser. ISBN:0-14-018849-5, ISBN13: 978-0-14-018849-3. Dewey:823/.912. LCCN:97-129058.
Audience: **g,l,u,f.**

Conrad, Joseph **PR6005.O4H476 2004**
Joseph Conrad's Heart of Darkness: A Casebook. Gene M. Moore (Editor). Trade Cloth. Oxford University Press, Inc. New York, NY. 2004. 288p. Casebooks in Criticism Ser. ISBN:0-19-515995-0, ISBN13: 978-0-19-515995-0. Dewey:823/.912. LCCN:2003-009868.
Audience: **l,u,f.**

Conrad, Joseph & Najder, Zdzislaw **PR6005.O4A6 1978**
Congo Diary and Other Uncollected Pieces. Trade Cloth. Doubleday Publishing. New York, NY. 1978. viii, 158p. ISBN:0-385-00771-X, ISBN13: 978-0-385-00771-9. Dewey:823/.9/12. LCCN:72-089333.
Audience: **g,l,u,f.** B

Conrad, Joseph **PR6005.O4Z/**
Conrad under Familial Eyes. Zdzislaw Najder (Editor), Halina Carroll Najder (Translator). Trade Cloth. Cambridge University Press. New York, NY. 1984. 304p. ISBN:0-521-25082-X, ISBN13: 978-0-521-25082-5. Dewey:823/.912. LCCN:83-005187.
Audience: **l,u,f.** B

Conrad, Joseph **PR6005.O4 H4 1997B**
Heart of Darkness and the Secret Sharer. Joyce Carol Oates (Introduction by). Mass Market. Penguin Group (USA) Inc. New York, NY. 1997. 176p. Signet Classics Ser. ISBN:0-451-52657-0, ISBN13: 978-0-451-52657-1. Dewey:823/.912. LCCN:97-066757.
Audience: **g,l,u,f.**

Conrad, Joseph **PR6019.O9**
Nostromo: A Tale of the Seaboard. Martin S. Smith (Editor, Introduction by). Trade Paper. Penguin Group (USA) Inc. New York, NY. 1990. 480p. Penguin Great Books of the 20th Century Ser. ISBN:0-14-018371-X, ISBN13: 978-0-14-018371-9. Dewey:823/.9/1.
Audience: **g,l,u,f.**

Conrad, Joseph **PR6005.O4; PZ3.C764**
The Secret Agent: A Simple Tale. Martin S. Smith (Editor, Introduction by). Trade Paper. Penguin Group (USA) Inc. New York, NY. 1990. 272p. Penguin Great Books of the 20th Century Ser. ISBN:0-14-018096-6, ISBN13: 978-0-14-018096-1. Dewey:823.
Audience: **g,l,u,f.**

Conrad, Joseph **PR6005.O4N6 2002**
Joseph Conrad: Notes on Life and Letters. J. H. Stape (Editor), S. W. Reid & M. H. Black (Contribution by), Andrew Busza (Assisted by), Bruce Harkness, Marion C. Michael & Norman Sherry (Contribution by). Trade Cloth. Cambridge University Press. New York, NY. 2004. 504p. The Cambridge Edition of the Works of Joseph Conrad Ser. ISBN:0-521-56163-9, ISBN13: 978-0-521-56163-1. Dewey:824/.912. LCCN:2002-020171.
Audience: **l,u,f.**

Conrad, Joseph **PR6019.O9**
Typhoon and Other Tales. Ed. 2. Cedric Watts (Editor). Trade Paper. Oxford University Press, Inc. New York, NY. 2003. 304p. Oxford World's Classics Ser. ISBN:0-19-280173-2, ISBN13: 978-0-19-280173-9. Dewey:823/.912.
Audience: **g,l,u,f.**

Conrad, Joseph **PR6005.O4**
The Nigger of the Narcissus. Cedric P. Watts (Notes by). Trade Paper. Penguin Group (USA) Inc. New York, NY. 1990. 208p. Penguin Great Books of the 20th Century Ser. ISBN:0-14-018094-X, ISBN13: 978-0-14-018094-7. Dewey:823/.912.
Audience: **g,l,u,f.**

Conrad, Joseph **PR6019.O9**
Portable Conrad. Morton D. Zabel & Frederick R. Karl (Editors). Trade Paper. Penguin Group (USA) Inc. New York, NY. 1976. 768p. Penguin Great Books of the 20th Century Ser., No. 33 ISBN:0-14-015033-1, ISBN13: 978-0-14-015033-9. Dewey:823/.9/1. LCCN:76-048272.
Audience: **g,l,u,f.**

Firchow, Peter E. **PR6005.O4H47645 2000**
Envisioning Africa: Racism and Imperialism in Conrad's Heart of Darkness. Trade Cloth. University Press of Kentucky. Lexington, KY. 1999. 288p. ISBN:0-8131-2128-0, ISBN13: 978-0-8131-2128-4. Dewey:823/.912. LCCN:99-012673.
Audience: **u,f.** *Choice, 2000.*

GoGwilt, Christopher Lloyd **PR6005.O4Z7275 1995**
The Invention of the West: Joseph Conrad and the Double-Mapping of Europe and Empire. Trade Cloth. Stanford University Press. Palo Alto, CA. 1995. 294p. ISBN:0-8047-2401-6, ISBN13: 978-0-8047-2401-2. Dewey:823.9/12. LCCN:94-032402.
Audience: **u,f.** *Choice, 1996.*

Griffith, John W. **PR6005.O4Z736 1995**
Joseph Conrad and the Anthropological Dilemma: 'Bewildered Traveller'. Trade Cloth. Oxford University Press, Inc. New York, NY. 1995. 258p. Oxford English Monographs ISBN:0-19-818300-3, ISBN13: 978-0-19-818300-6. Dewey:823/.912. LCCN:94-045316.
Audience: **u,f.** *Choice, 1996.*

Hand, Richard J. **PR6005.O4Z741874**
The Theatre of Joseph Conrad: Reconstructed Fictions. Cloth over Boards. Palgrave Macmillan. New York, NY. 2005. 240p. ISBN:1-4039-1899-6, ISBN13: 978-1-4039-1899-4. Dewey:823/.912. LCCN:2005-047040.
Audience: **u,f.**

Kaplan, Carola (Editor), et al. **PR6005.O4Z581154**
Conrad in the Twenty-First Century: Contemporary Approaches and Perspectives. Peter Mallios & Andrea White (Editors). UK-B Format Paperback. Routledge. New York, NY. 2004. 352p. ISBN:0-415-97165-9, ISBN13: 978-0-415-97165-2. Dewey:823/.912 B. LCCN:2004-015991.
Audience: **u,f.**

Knowles, Owen & Moore, Gene M. **PQ2631.E357**
Oxford Reader's Companion to Conrad. Trade Paper. Oxford University Press, Inc. New York, NY. 2002. 512p. Reader's Companions Ser. ISBN:0-19-860421-1, ISBN13: 978-0-19-860421-1. Dewey:823/.912 B.
Audience: **g,l,u,f.** *Choice, 2000.*

Krajka, W. **PR6005.O4Z7457 2004**
A Return to the Roots: Conrad, Poland and East- Central Europe. Trade Cloth. Columbia University Press. New York, NY. 2005. 312p. ISBN:0-88033-557-2, ISBN13: 978-0-88033-557-7. Dewey:823/.912. LCCN:2004-116245.
Audience: **u,f.**

Kucich, John, et al. **PR1309.I46F53 2003**
Fictions of Empire: Heart of Darkness, The Man Who Would Be King and The Beach at Falesá. Joseph Conrad, Rudyard Kipling, Robert Louis Stevenson & Alan Richardson (Authors). Paper Text. Houghton Mifflin College Division. Boston, MA. 2002. 421p. New Riverside Editions Ser. ISBN:0-618-08488-6, ISBN13: 978-0-618-08488-3. Dewey:823/.809358. LCCN:2001-133336.
Audience: **g,l,u,f.**

Meyers, Jeffrey **PR6005.O4Z778 2001**
Joseph Conrad: A Biography. Trade Paper. Cooper Square Publishers, Inc. New York, NY. 2001. 464p. ISBN:0-8154-1112-X, ISBN13: 978-0-8154-1112-3. Dewey:823/.912 B. LCCN:00-052314.
Audience: **g,l,u,f.** *Choice, 1991.*

Najder, Zdzislaw **PR6005.04Z78439 1997**
Conrad in Perspective: Essays on Art and Fidelity. Trade Paper. Cambridge University Press. New York, NY. 2005. 252p. ISBN:0-521-02146-4, ISBN13: 978-0-521-02146-3. Dewey:823/.912.
Audience: **u,f.** *Choice, 1998.*

Panichas, George A. **PR6005.O4Z784935**
Joseph Conrad: His Moral Vision. Saddle Stitched, Cloth over Boards, Dust Jacket. Mercer University Press. Macon, GA. 2005. 165p. ISBN:0-86554-936-2, ISBN13: 978-0-86554-936-4. Dewey:823.912. LCCN:2005-002536.
Audience: **u,f.**

Peters, John G. **PR6005.O4 Z784947 2**
Conrad and Impressionism. Trade Cloth. Cambridge University Press. New York, NY. 2001. 206p. ISBN:0-521-79173-1, ISBN13: 978-0-521-79173-1. Dewey:823.912. LCCN:00-031262.
Audience: **u,f.** *Choice, 2001.*

Ross, Stephen **PR6005**
Conrad and Empire. Trade Cloth. University of Missouri Press. Columbia, MO. 2004. 232p. ISBN:0-8262-1518-1, ISBN13: 978-0-8262-1518-5. Dewey:823/.912. LCCN:2003-025860.
Audience: **u,f.** *Choice, 2004.*

Sherry, Norman **PR6005.O4**
Conrad's Eastern World. Trade Paper. Cambridge University Press. New York, NY. 1977. 368p. ISBN:0-521-29120-8, ISBN13: 978-0-521-29120-0. Dewey:823.912.
Audience: **l,u,f.**

Sherry, Norman **PR6005.O4Z/**
Conrad's Western World. Trade Paper. Cambridge University Press. New York, NY. 1980. 478p. ISBN:0-521-29808-3, ISBN13: 978-0-521-29808-7. Dewey:823/.9/12. LCCN:70-130910.
Audience: **l,u,f.** BCL3

Stape, J. H. (Editor) **PR6005.O4 Z569 1996**
The Cambridge Companion to Joseph Conrad. Trade Paper. Cambridge University Press. New York, NY. 1996. 278p. Companions to Literature Ser. ISBN:0-521-48484-7, ISBN13: 978-0-521-48484-8. Dewey:823.9/12. LCCN:95-023461.
Audience: **g,l,u,f.**

Watt, Ian **PR6019.O9**
Conrad in the Nineteenth Century. Trade Cloth. University of California Press. Berkeley, CA. 1981. ISBN:0-520-04405-3, ISBN13: 978-0-520-04405-0. Dewey:823/.9/12.
Audience: **u,f.** BCL3

Watt, Ian P. **PR6005.O4 Z9232 2000**
Essays on Conrad. Trade Paper. Cambridge University Press. New York, NY. 2000. 226p. ISBN:0-521-78387-9, ISBN13: 978-0-521-78387-3. Dewey:823/.912. LCCN:99-056318.
Audience: **l,u,f.** *Choice, 2001.*

Individual Authors and Works > 20th C. > Coward, Noel

Coward, Noel **PR6005.O85**
Collected Plays, Vol. 5. Trade Paper. Methuen Publishing Ltd. London, 2004. Methuen World Classics: The Noel Coward Collection Ser. ISBN:0-413-51740-3, ISBN13: 978-0-413-51740-1. Dewey:821/.912.
Audience: **g,l,u,f.**

Coward, Noel **PR6005.O82**
Collected Plays, Vol. 3. Trade Paper. Methuen Publishing Ltd. London, 2004. ISBN:0-413-46100-9, ISBN13: 978-0-413-46100-1. Dewey:821/.912.
Audience: **g,l,u,f.**

Coward, Noel **PR5366**
Collected Plays: Hay Fever; the Vortex, Fallen Angels; Easy Virtue. Trade Paper. Methuen Publishing Ltd. London, 2004. ISBN:0-413-46060-6, ISBN13: 978-0-413-46060-8. Dewey:822.9/12.
Audience: **g,l,u,f.**

Coward, Noel **PR6005.O82**
Collected Plays, Vol. 4. Trade Paper. Methuen Publishing Ltd. London, 2004. ISBN:0-413-46120-3, ISBN13: 978-0-413-46120-9. Dewey:821/.912.
Audience: **g,l,u,f.**

Coward, Noel **PR6005.085**
Future Indefinite, Vol. 2. Trade Paper. Methuen Publishing Ltd. London, 2004. 352p. ISBN:0-413-77393-0, ISBN13: 978-0-413-77393-7. Dewey:792.092.
Audience: **g,l,u,f.** BCL3

Coward, Noel **PR5366**
Noel Coward Collected Plays: Semi Monde; Point Valaine; South Sea Bubble; Nude with Violin. Trade Paper. Methuen Publishing Ltd. London, 2004. Methuen World Classics: The Noel Coward Collection Ser. ISBN:0-413-73410-2, ISBN13: 978-0-413-73410-5. Dewey:822.9/12.
Audience: **g,l,u,f.**

Coward, Noel **PR5366**
Noel Coward Collected Plays: Private Lives; Bitter Sweet; The Marquise; Post Mortem. Trade Paper. Methuen Publishing Ltd. London, 2004. Methuen World Classics: The Noel Coward Collection Ser. ISBN:0-413-46080-0, ISBN13: 978-0-413-46080-6. Dewey:822.9/12.
Audience: **g,l,u,f.**

Coward, Noel **PR6005.O85Z5 2004**
Present Indicative, Vol. 1. Trade Paper. Methuen Publishing Ltd. London, 2004. 352p. ISBN:0-413-77413-9, ISBN13: 978-0-413-77413-2. Dewey:792/.092.
Audience: **g,l,u,f.** BCL3

Coward, Noel **PR5366**
Quadrille, Vol. 7. Trade Paper. Methuen Publishing Ltd. London, 2004. Methuen World Classics: The Noel Coward Collection Ser. ISBN:0-413-73400-5, ISBN13: 978-0-413-73400-6. Dewey:822.9/12.
Audience: **g,l,u,f.**

Coward, Noel **PR6005.O85**
Collected Verse. Martin Tickner & Graham Payn (Editors). Trade Paper. Methuen Publishing Ltd. London, 2004. ISBN:0-413-55150-4, ISBN13: 978-0-413-55150-4. Dewey:821/.912.
Audience: **g,l,u,f.**

Payn, Graham & Morley, Sheridan **PR6005**
Noel Coward Diaries. Trade Paper. Da Capo Press, Inc. Cambridge, MA. 2000. 712p. ISBN:0-306-80960-5, ISBN13: 978-0-306-80960-6. Dewey:828/.91203.
Audience: **g,l,u,f.**

Individual Authors and Works > 20th C. > D

Davie, Donald **PR6058.U37**
Donald Davie: Collected Poems. Trade Paper. Carcanet Press, Ltd. Manchester, 2002. 660p. ISBN:1-85754-406-4, ISBN13: 978-1-85754-406-0. Dewey:821.9/14.
Audience: **g,l,u,f.**

Day Lewis, Cecil **PS3509.L43**
The Complete Poems of C. Day Lewis. Trade Cloth. Stanford University Press. Palo Alto, CA. 1995. 768p. ISBN:0-8047-2073-8, ISBN13: 978-0-8047-2073-1. Dewey:821.9/12.
Audience: **g,l,u,f.** *Choice, 1993.*

Douglas, Keith **PR6007.O872.A17 1977**
Complete Poems. Desmond Graham (Editor). Trade Cloth. Oxford University Press, Inc. New York, NY. 1978. xiii, 145p. ISBN:0-19-211876-5, ISBN13: 978-0-19-211876-9. Dewey:821/.9/12. LCCN:77-030095.
Audience: **g,l,u,f.** *B*

Doyle, Roddy **PR6054.O95A6 1995**
The Barrytown Trilogy: The Commitments, the Snapper, the Van. Trade Paper. Penguin Group (USA) Inc. New York, NY. 1995. 640p. ISBN:0-14-025262-2, ISBN13: 978-0-14-025262-0. Dewey:823/.914. LCCN:95-012323.
Audience: **g,l,u,f.**

Doyle, Roddy **PR6015.I3**
Paddy Clarke Ha Ha Ha. Trade Paper. Penguin Group (USA) Inc. New York, NY. 1995. 288p. ISBN:0-14-023390-3, ISBN13: 978-0-14-023390-2. Dewey:823.9/14. LCCN:00-003988.
Audience: **g,l,u,f.**

Doyle, Roddy **PR6015.I3**
A Star Called Henry. Trade Paper. Penguin Group (USA) Inc. New York, NY. 2004. 402p. ISBN:0-14-303461-8, ISBN13: 978-0-14-303461-2. Dewey:823/.914.
Audience: **g,l,u,f.**

Doyle, Roddy **PR6015.I3**
The Woman Who Walked into Doors. Trade Paper. Penguin Group (USA) Inc. New York, NY. 1997. 240p. ISBN:0-14-025512-5, ISBN13: 978-0-14-025512-6. Dewey:823.914.
Audience: **g,l,u,f.**

Du Maurier, Daphne **PR6019.O9**
Frenchman's Creek. Library Binding. Bentley Publishers. Cambridge, MA. 1971. 320p. ISBN:0-8376-0412-5, ISBN13: 978-0-8376-0412-1. Dewey:823.9/12. LCCN:70-184730.
Audience: **g,l,u,f.**

Du Maurier, Daphne **PR6019.O9**
Jamaica Inn. Mass Market. HarperCollins Publishers. New York, NY. 1995. 304p. ISBN:0-380-72539-8, ISBN13: 978-0-380-72539-7. Dewey:823.9/12.
Audience: **g,l,u,f.**

Du Maurier, Daphne **PR6019.O9**
Don't Look Now. Trade Paper. Penguin Books Canada, Ltd. Toronto, ON. 1974. 272p. ISBN:0-14-003590-7, ISBN13: 978-0-14-003590-2. Dewey:823/.9/12.
Audience: **g,l,u,f.**

Du Maurier, Daphne **PR6019.O9**
Rebecca. Trade Cloth. Doubleday Publishing. New York, NY. 1948. 384p. ISBN:0-385-04380-5, ISBN13: 978-0-385-04380-9. Dewey:823.9/12. LCCN:93-000808.
Audience: **g,l,u,f.**

Dunn, Douglas **PR6054.U54E4 1985**
Elegies. Trade Paper. Faber & Faber, Ltd. London, 1985. 64p. ISBN:0-571-13469-6, ISBN13: 978-0-571-13469-4. Dewey:821.9/14. LCCN:84-025880.
Audience: **g,l,u,f.**

Gelpi, Albert **PR6007.A95Z68 1998**
Living in Time: The Poetry of C. Day Lewis. Trade Cloth. Oxford University Press, Inc. New York, NY. 1998. 256p. ISBN:0-19-509863-3, ISBN13: 978-0-19-509863-1. Dewey:821/.912. LCCN:96-045410.
Audience: **u,f.** *Choice, 1998.*

Holroyd, Michael (Introduction by) **CT788.D83**
The du Mauriers. Trade Paper, Perfect. Little, Brown Book Group Ltd. London, 2005. 336p. ISBN:1-84408-064-1, ISBN13: 978-1-84408-064-9. Dewey:929.2.
Audience: **g,l,u,f.**

Individual Authors and Works > 20th C. > Drabble, Margaret

Brownley, Martine Watson **PR9084.B76 2000**
Deferrals of Domain: Contemporary Women Novelists and the State. Cloth over Boards. Palgrave Macmillan. New York, NY. 2000. 304p. ISBN:0-312-22811-2, ISBN13: 978-0-312-22811-8. Dewey:823.9/1/09171241. LCCN:99-043175.
Audience: **u,f.** *Choice, 2000.*

Drabble, Margaret **PR6015.I3**
The Garrick Year. Trade Paper. Penguin Group (USA) Inc. New York, NY. 1984. ISBN:0-452-25590-2, ISBN13: 978-0-452-25590-6. Dewey:823/.914.
Audience: **g,l,u,f.** *B*

Drabble, Margaret **PR6015.I3**
The Gates of Ivory. Mass Market. McClelland & Stewart/Tundra Books. Plattsburgh, NY. 1992. ISBN:0-7710-2861-X, ISBN13: 978-0-7710-2861-8. Dewey:823.9/14.
Audience: **g,l,u,f.**

Drabble, Margaret **PR6015.I3**
The Ice Age. Trade Paper. Warner Books, Inc. New York, NY. 1983. 320p. ISBN:0-446-31118-9, ISBN13: 978-0-446-31118-2. Dewey:823/.914.
Audience: **g,l,u,f.** *B*

Drabble, Margaret **PR6015.I3**
A Natural Curiosity. Mass Market. McClelland & Stewart/Tundra Books. Plattsburgh, NY. 1990. ISBN:0-7710-2866-0, ISBN13: 978-0-7710-2866-3. Dewey:823/.914.
Audience: **g,l,u,f.**

Drabble, Margaret **PR6054.R25**
The Peppered Moth. Trade Paper. Harcourt Trade Publishers. New York, NY. 2002. 384p. ISBN:0-15-600719-3, ISBN13: 978-0-15-600719-1. Dewey:823/.914. LCCN:00-050568.
Audience: **g,l,u,f.**

Drabble, Margaret **PR6015.I3**
The Radiant Way. Mass Market. Ballantine Books. New York, NY. 1988. 384p. ISBN:0-8041-0365-8, ISBN13: 978-0-8041-0365-7. Dewey:823.9/14.
Audience: **g,l,u,f.**

Drabble, Margaret **PR6054.R25.R4**
The Realms of Gold. Trade Cloth. Alfred A. Knopf Inc. New York, NY. 1975. 354 p. ;p. ISBN:0-394-49877-1, ISBN13: 978-0-394-49877-5. Dewey:823/.9/1. LCCN:75-008229.
Audience: **g,l,u,f.** *B*

Drabble, Margaret **PR6054.R25W58 1997**
The Witch of Exmoor. Trade Cloth. Penguin Group (USA) Inc. New York, NY. 1997. 281p. ISBN:0-670-87276-8, ISBN13: 978-0-670-87276-3. Dewey:823.9/14. LCCN:97-010952.
Audience: **g,l,u,f.**

Individual Authors and Works > 20th C. > Durrell, Lawrence

Closter, Susan V. **Z8150.8.V36 1985**
Joyce Cary and Lawrence Durrell: A Reference Guide. Trade Cloth. Macmillan Publishing Company, Inc. Old Tappan, NJ. 1985. 262p. Reference Guides to Literature Ser. ISBN:0-8161-8627-8, ISBN13: 978-0-8161-8627-3. Dewey:016.823/912. LCCN:85-005609.
Audience: **u,f.** *Choice, 1985.*

Durrell, Lawrence **PR6007.U76B35 1991**
Balthasar. Trade Paper. Penguin Group (USA) Inc. New York, NY. 1991. 256p. Alexandria Quartet Ser. ISBN:0-14-015321-7, ISBN13: 978-0-14-015321-7. Dewey:828.91209. LCCN:93-106644.
Audience: **g,l,u,f.**

Durrell, Lawrence **PR6007.U76C55 1991**
Clea. Trade Paper. Penguin Group (USA) Inc. New York, NY. 1991. 288p. Alexandria Quartet Ser. ISBN:0-14-015322-5, ISBN13: 978-0-14-015322-4. Dewey:823/.912. LCCN:93-106626.
Audience: **g,l,u,f.**

Durrell, Lawrence **PR6019.O9**
Justine. Trade Paper. Penguin Group (USA) Inc. New York, NY. 1991. 256p. Alexandria Quartet Ser. ISBN:0-14-015319-5, ISBN13: 978-0-14-015319-4. Dewey:823/.912. LCCN:92-206253.
Audience: **g,l,u,f.**

Durrell, Lawrence **PR6007.U76M68 1991**
Mountolive. Trade Paper. Penguin Group (USA) Inc. New York, NY. 1991. 320p. Alexandria Quartet Ser. ISBN:0-14-015320-9, ISBN13: 978-0-14-015320-0. Dewey:823/.912. LCCN:93-106608.
Audience: **g,l,u,f.**

Durrell, Lawrence **PS3509.L43**
Collected Poems, 1931-1974. James A. Brigham (Editor). Trade Paper. DIANE Publishing Company. Collingdale, PA. 2004. 350p. ISBN:0-7567-7365-2, ISBN13: 978-0-7567-7365-6. Dewey:821/.912.
Audience: **g,l,u,f.** *B*

MacNiven, Ian S. **PR6007.U76.Z74 1998**
Lawrence Durrell: A Biography. Trade Cloth. Faber & Faber, Inc. New York, NY. 1998. 768p. ISBN:0-571-17248-2, ISBN13: 978-0-571-17248-1. Dewey:823.9/12.
Audience: **g,u,f.** *Choice, 1999.*

Moore, Harry Thornton **PR4681**
The World of Lawrence Durrell. Paper Text. Textbook Publishers. Temecula, CA. 2003. 239p. ISBN:0-7581-3668-4, ISBN13: 978-0-7581-3668-8. Dewey:920.
Audience: **g,u,f.**

Raper, Julius R. (Editor), et al. **PR6007.U76Z73 1995**
Lawrence Durrell: Comprehending the Whole. Melody L. Enscore & Paige M. Bynum (Editors). Cloth Text. University of Missouri Press. Columbia, MO. 1994. 224p. ISBN:0-8262-0982-3, ISBN13: 978-0-8262-0982-5. Dewey:828/.91209. LCCN:94-032938.
Audience: **u,f.**

Individual Authors and Works > 20th C. > F

Farley, Paul **PR6058.U37**
The Ice Age: A Collection of Poems. Trade Cloth. Pan Macmillan. London, 2002. 54p. ISBN:0-330-48453-2, ISBN13: 978-0-330-48453-4. Dewey:821.9/14.
Audience: **g,l,u,f.**

Fenton, James **PR6056.E53A6 1994**
Children in Exile: Poems 1968-1984. Trade Paper. Farrar, Straus & Giroux. New York, NY. 1994. 120p. ISBN:0-374-52406-8, ISBN13: 978-0-374-52406-7. Dewey:821/.914. LCCN:93-040177.
Audience: **g,l,u,f.**

Fenton, James
Out of Danger: Poems. Farrar, Straus & Giroux. 1995. ISBN:0-374-52437-8, ISBN13: 978-0-374-52437-1.
Audience: **g,l,u,f.**

Fitzgerald, Penelope **PR6056.I86O34 1998**
Offshore. Trade Paper. Houghton Mifflin Company Trade & Reference Division. Boston, MA. 1998. 144p. ISBN:0-395-47804-9, ISBN13: 978-0-395-47804-2. Dewey:823/.914. LCCN:97-050403.
Audience: **g,l,u,f.**

Fitzgerald, Penelope **PR6056.I86A6 2003**
The Bookshop; The Gate of Angels; The Blue Flower. Frank Kermode (Introduction by). Trade Cloth. Knopf Publishing Group. New York, NY. 2003. 512p. ISBN:1-4000-4126-0, ISBN13: 978-1-4000-4126-8. Dewey:823/.914. LCCN:2003-054595.
Audience: **g,l,u,f.**

Fleming, Ian **PR6056.L4C37 2002**
Casino Royale. Trade Paper. Penguin Group (USA) Inc. New York, NY. 2002. 192p. James Bond Ser. ISBN:0-14-200202-X, ISBN13: 978-0-14-200202-5. Dewey:823/.914. LCCN:2002-024602.
Audience: **g,l,u,f.**

Flynn, Leontia **PR6106**
These Days. Trade Paper. Random House. London, 2004. 64p. ISBN:0-224-07197-1, ISBN13: 978-0-224-07197-0. Dewey:821.92. LCCN:2005-440736.
Audience: **g,l,u,f.**

Foden, Giles **PR6015.I3**
The Last King of Scotland. Trade Paper. Alfred A. Knopf Inc. New York, NY. 1999. 352p. ISBN:0-375-70331-4, ISBN13: 978-0-375-70331-7. Dewey:823/.914. LCCN:98-036722.
Audience: **g,l,u,f.**

Forester, C. S. **PR6011.O56A69 1984**
The African Queen. Trade Paper. Little Brown & Company. New York, NY. 1984. 256p. ISBN:0-316-28910-8, ISBN13: 978-0-316-28910-8. Dewey:823/.912. LCCN:83-083340.
Audience: **g,l,u,f.**

Forester, C. S. **PR6011.O56M7 1998**
Mr. Midshipman Hornblower. Trade Paper. Little Brown & Company. New York, NY. 1984. 320p. Hornblower Ser., No. 1 ISBN:0-316-28912-4, ISBN13: 978-0-316-28912-2. Dewey:823/.912. LCCN:84-081020.
Audience: **g,l,u,f.**

Frayn, Michael **PR6015.I3**
Spies: A Novel. Trade Paper. Picador. New York, NY. 2003. 272p. ISBN:0-312-42117-6, ISBN13: 978-0-312-42117-5. Dewey:823/.914.
Audience: **g,l,u,f.**

Frayn, Michael **PR6056.R3T75 2002**
The Trick of It: A Novel. Trade Paper. Picador. New York, NY. 2002. 176p. ISBN:0-312-42144-3, ISBN13: 978-0-312-42144-1. Dewey:823/.914. LCCN:2003-265112.
Audience: **g,l,u,f.**

Individual Authors and Works > 20th C. > Ford, Ford Madox

Ford, Ford Madox **PR6011.O53G5 1999**
The Good Soldier: A Tale of Passion. Trade Paper. Oxford University Press, Inc. New York, NY. 1999. 352p. Oxford World's Classics Ser. ISBN:0-19-283620-X, ISBN13: 978-0-19-283620-5. Dewey:823/.912. LCCN:99-462450.
Audience: **g,l,u,f.**

Ford, Ford Madox **PR473.F63 2004**
The War Prose. Trade Cloth. New York University Press. New York, NY. 2004. 280p. ISBN:0-8147-2733-6, ISBN13: 978-0-8147-2733-1. Dewey:823/.912. LCCN:2004-044996.
Audience: **g,l,u,f.**

Ford, Ford Madox **PR6011.O53P35 2001**
Parade's End. Robie MacAulay (Introduction by). Trade Paper. Penguin Group (USA) Inc. New York, NY. 2001. 864p. ISBN:0-14-118661-5, ISBN13: 978-0-14-118661-0. Dewey:823/.912. LCCN:2001-021437.
Audience: **g,l,u,f.**

Ford, Ford Madox **PR6011.O53**
Selected Poems. Max Saunders (Editor). Trade Paper. Routledge. New York, NY. 2003. 176p. Fyfield Bks. ISBN:0-415-96947-6, ISBN13: 978-0-415-96947-5. Dewey:821.912.
Audience: **g,l,u,f.**

Ford, Ford Madox **PR6011.O53A6 2004**
Critical Essays. Max Saunders & Richard Stang (Editors). Trade Cloth. New York University Press. New York, NY. 2004. 340p. ISBN:0-8147-2734-4, ISBN13: 978-0-8147-2734-8. Dewey:823/.912. LCCN:2004-044997.
Audience: **u,f.**

Individual Authors and Works > 20th C. > Forster, E. M.

Beauman, Nicola **PR6011.O58Z62 1994**
E. M. Forster: A Biography of the Novelist E. M. Forster. Trade Cloth. Alfred A. Knopf Inc. New York, NY. 1994. x, 404p. ISBN:0-394-58381-7, ISBN13: 978-0-394-58381-5. Dewey:823/.912. LCCN:92-044378.
Audience: **g,l,u,f.** *Choice, 1994.*

Bradbury, Malcolm **PR6011.O58P3713**
E. M. Forster: A Passage to India. Trade Cloth. Macmillan Publishers Ltd. London, 1970. 252p. Casebook Ser. ISBN:0-333-01458-8, ISBN13: 978-0-333-01458-5. Dewey:823/.9/12. LCCN:71-515718.
Audience: **g,l,u,f.**

Crews, Frederick C. **E459.C35**
E M Forster: The Perils of Humanism. Paper Text. Textbook Publishers. Temecula, CA. 2003. 187p. ISBN:0-7581-5768-1, ISBN13: 978-0-7581-5768-3. Dewey:973.7/11.
Audience: **u,f.**

Edwards, Mike **PR6011.O58Z6538 2001**
E. M. Forster: The Novels. Cloth over Boards. Palgrave Macmillan. New York, NY. 2001. 236p. Analysing Texts Ser. ISBN:0-333-92253-0, ISBN13: 978-0-333-92253-8. Dewey:823/.912. LCCN:2001-027367.
Audience: **g,l,u,f.**

Forster, E. M. **PR6011.O58**
Abinger Harvest. Trade Paper. Harcourt Trade Publishers. New York, NY. 1950. 384p. ISBN:0-15-602610-4, ISBN13: 978-0-15-602610-9. Dewey:828. LCCN:36-010167.
Audience: **g,l,u,f.**

Forster, E. M. **PR6019.O9**
Maurice. Trade Paper, Perfect. W. W. Norton & Company, Inc. New York, NY. 1993. 256p. ISBN:0-393-31032-9, ISBN13: 978-0-393-31032-0. Dewey:823.9/12. LCCN:92-041161.
Audience: **g,l,u,f.**

Forster, E. M. **PR6011.O58P3 1989**
A Passage to India. Cloth over Boards. Harcourt Trade Publishers. New York, NY. 1989. 372p. HBJ Book Ser. ISBN:0-15-171141-0, ISBN13: 978-0-15-171141-3. Dewey:823.9/12. LCCN:43-001812.
Audience: **g,l,u,f.**

Forster, E. M. **PR6031.R6**
Two Cheers for Democracy. Trade Paper. Harcourt Trade Publishers. New York, NY. 1962. 384p. Harvest Book Ser. ISBN:0-15-692025-5, ISBN13: 978-0-15-692025-4. Dewey:824/.9/12. LCCN:51-013652.
Audience: **g,l,u,f.**

Forster, E. M. **PR6011.O58.W55 1993**
Where Angels Fear to Tread. Trade Paper. Dover Publications, Inc. Mineola, NY. 1993. 128p. Thrift Editions Ser. ISBN:0-486-27791-7, ISBN13: 978-0-486-27791-2. Dewey:823.9/12. LCCN:93-030717.
Audience: **g,l,u,f.**

Forster, E. M. **PR6011.O58H6 1998**
Howards End: Authoritative Text, Textual Appendix, Backgrounds and Contexts, Criticism. Paul B. Armstrong (Editor). Paper Text. W. W. Norton & Company, Inc. New York, NY. 1998. Critical Editions Ser. ISBN:0-393-97011-6, ISBN13: 978-0-393-97011-1. Dewey:823/.912. LCCN:97-009678.
Audience: **g,l,u,f.**

Forster, E. M. **PR6011.O58R6 2000**
A Room with a View. Malcolm Bradbury (Introduction by, Notes by). Trade Paper. Penguin Group (USA) Inc. New York, NY. 2000. 240p. Classics Ser. ISBN:0-14-118329-2, ISBN13: 978-0-14-118329-9. Dewey:823.9/12. LCCN:99-462172.
Audience: **g,l,u,f.**

Forster, E. M., et al. **PR6011.O58Z653**
E. M. Forster: A Human Exploration: Centenary Essays. G. K. Das & John B. Beer (Authors). Trade Cloth. Pan Macmillan. London, 1979. xvii, 314p. ISBN:0-333-25775-8, ISBN13: 978-0-333-25775-3. Dewey:823/.9/12. LCCN:79-319948.
Audience: **u,f.**

Forster, E. M. **PR6011.O58A6 2001**
Selected Stories of E. M. Forster. Mark Mitchell & David Leavitt (Contribution by). Trade Paper. Penguin Group (USA) Inc. New York, NY. 2001. 224p. Twentieth Century Classics Ser. ISBN:0-14-118619-4, ISBN13: 978-0-14-118619-1. Dewey:823/.912. LCCN:00-045664.
Audience: **g,l,u,f.**

Gardner, Philip (Editor) **PN3503**
E. M. Forster. Paper over Boards. Routledge. New York, NY. 1997. 520p. The Critical Heritage Ser. ISBN:0-415-15926-1, ISBN13: 978-0-415-15926-5. Dewey:809.3/04.
Audience: **u,f.**

Herz, Judith S. **PR6011.O58P3744 1992**
A Passage to India: Nation and Narration. Trade Paper. Thomson Gale. Farmington Hills, MI. 1992. 160p. Masterwork Studies ISBN:0-8057-8104-8, ISBN13: 978-0-8057-8104-5. Dewey:823/.912. LCCN:92-030294.
Audience: **g,u,f.** *Choice, 1993.*

Lago, Mary **PR6011.O58Z74 1995**
E. M. Forster: A Literary Life. Trade Cloth. Palgrave Macmillan. New York, NY. 1995. 170p. Literary Lives Ser., Vol. 1 ISBN:0-312-12178-4, ISBN13: 978-0-312-12178-5. Dewey:823.912. LCCN:94-009973.
Audience: **g,l,u,f.** *Choice, 1995.*

Medalie, David **PR6011.O58Z82267**
E. M. Forster's Modernism. Cloth over Boards. Palgrave Macmillan. New York, NY. 2002. 224p. ISBN:0-333-98782-9, ISBN13: 978-0-333-98782-7. Dewey:823/.912. LCCN:2001-056133.
Audience: **u,f.** *Choice, 2003.*

Shaheen, Mohammad **PR6011.O58Z8415 2004**
E. M. Forster and the Politics of Imperialism. Cloth over Boards. Palgrave Macmillan. New York, NY. 2004. 256p. ISBN:0-333-74136-6, ISBN13: 978-0-333-74136-8. Dewey:823/.912. LCCN:2003-060860.
Audience: **u,f.** *Choice, 2005.*

Wilde, Alan **PR6011.O58Z6514 1985**
Critical Essays on E. M. Forster. Trade Cloth. Thomson Gale. Farmington Hills, MI. 1985. 192p. British Literature Ser. ISBN:0-8161-8754-1, ISBN13: 978-0-8161-8754-6. Dewey:823/.912. LCCN:85-002763.
Audience: **u,f.** *Choice, 1986.*

Individual Authors and Works > 20th C. > Fowles, John

Foster, Thomas G. **PR6056.O85Z665 1994**
Understanding John Fowles. Cloth Text. University of South Carolina Press. Columbia, SC. 1994. 200p. ISBN:1-57003-003-0, ISBN13: 978-1-57003-003-1. Dewey:823/.914. LCCN:94-003215.
Audience: **u,f.** *Choice, 1995.*

Fowles, John **PR6056.O85**
The Collector. UK-B Format Paperback. Knopf Publishing Group. New York, NY. 2004. 288p. ISBN:0-09-947047-0, ISBN13: 978-0-09-947047-2. Dewey:823.9/14.
Audience: **g,l,u,f.**

Fowles, John **PR6015.I3**
The French Lieutenant's Woman. Trade Paper. Little Brown & Company. New York, NY. 1998. ISBN:0-316-18989-8, ISBN13: 978-0-316-18989-7. Dewey:823.9/14.
Audience: **g,l,u,f.**

Fowles, John **PR6056.O95Z465 2004**
The Journals, Vol. 1. UK-Trade Paper. Knopf Publishing Group. New York, NY. 2004. 600p. ISBN:0-09-944342-2, ISBN13: 978-0-09-944342-1. Dewey:823.9/14.
Audience: **u,f.**

Fowles, John **PR6015.I3**
A Maggot. Trade Paper. Little Brown & Company. New York, NY. 1998. 464p. ISBN:0-316-29049-1, ISBN13: 978-0-316-29049-4. Dewey:823.9/14. LCCN:98-191527.
Audience: **g,l,u,f.** B

Fowles, John **PR6015.I3**
The Magus. Trade Paper. Little Brown & Company. New York, NY. 2001. 656p. ISBN:0-316-29619-8, ISBN13: 978-0-316-29619-9. Dewey:823/.914.
Audience: **g,l,u,f.** B

Fowles, John **PR6056.O85W6 1998**
Wormholes: Essays and Occasional Writings. Cloth over Boards. Henry Holt & Company. New York, NY. 1998. 432p. ISBN:0-8050-5867-2, ISBN13: 978-0-8050-5867-3. Dewey:828.9/14/08. LCCN:97-042986.
Audience: **u,f.** *Choice, 1998.*

Individual Authors and Works > 20th C. > G

Crawford, Paul **PR6013.O35Z5968 2002**
Politics and History in William Golding: The World Turned Upside Down. Trade Paper. University of Missouri Press. Columbia, MO. 2002. 288p. ISBN:0-8262-1416-9, ISBN13: 978-0-8262-1416-4. Dewey:823/.914. LCCN:2002-027108.
Audience: **g,l,u,f.** *Choice, 2003.*

George, Peter Bryan **PR6015.I3**
Dr. Strangelove: Or How I Learned to Stop Worrying and Love the Bomb. Trade Paper. Prion. London, 1999. xi, 142p. The Film Ink Ser. ISBN:1-85375-310-6, ISBN13: 978-1-85375-310-7. Dewey:823.9/14.
Audience: **g,l,u,f.**

Godden, Rumer **PR6019.O9**
Black Narcissus. Library Binding. Yestermorrow, Inc. Princess Anne, MD. ISBN:1-56723-180-2, ISBN13: 978-1-56723-180-9. Dewey:823.9/12.
Audience: **g,l,u,f.**

Godden, Rumer **PR6013.O2I65 2005**
In This House of Brede. Phyllis Tickle (Introduction by). Trade Paper. Loyola Press. Chicago, IL. 2005. 368p. Loyola Classics ISBN:0-8294-2128-9, ISBN13: 978-0-8294-2128-6. Dewey:823/.912. LCCN:2004-025161.
Audience: **g,l,u,f.**

Golding, William **PR6015.I3**
Close Quarters. Ed. 1. Trade Paper. Farrar, Straus & Giroux. New York, NY. 1999. 281p. ISBN:0-374-52636-2, ISBN13: 978-0-374-52636-8. Dewey:823.9/14. LCCN:87-005351.
Audience: **g,l,u,f.**

Golding, William **PR6013.O35P3**
The Paper Men. Ed. 1. Trade Paper. Farrar, Straus & Giroux. New York, NY. 1999. 192p. ISBN:0-374-52639-7, ISBN13: 978-0-374-52639-9. Dewey:823.914. LCCN:84-001636.
Audience: **g,l,u,f.**

Golding, William **PR6015.I3**
Rites of Passage. Ed. 1. Trade Paper. Farrar, Straus & Giroux. New York, NY. 1999. 278p. ISBN:0-374-52640-0, ISBN13: 978-0-374-52640-5. Dewey:823.9/14. LCCN:80-016809.
Audience: **g,l,u,f.**

Golding, William **PR6013.O35L6 2003**
Lord of the Flies. Ed. 50. E. M. Forster (Introduction by). Trade Cloth. Penguin Group (USA) Inc. New York, NY. 2003. 336p. ISBN:0-399-52920-9, ISBN13: 978-0-399-52920-7. Dewey:823/.914. LCCN:2003-054825.
Audience: **g,l,u,f.**

Grahame, Kenneth **PZ10.3.G76 WI43**
The Wind in the Willows. Luanne Rice (Introduction by). Trade Paper. Penguin Group (USA) Inc. New York, NY. 2006. 240p. ISBN:0-451-53014-4, ISBN13: 978-0-451-53014-1. Dewey:Fic.
Audience: **g,l,u,f.**

Gray, Alasdair **PR6057.R3264P66 2002**
Poor Things. Janice Galloway (Introduction by). Trade Paper. Dalkey Archive Press. Normal, IL. 2002. 319p. British Literature Ser. ISBN:1-56478-307-3, ISBN13: 978-1-56478-307-3. Dewey:813.5/4. LCCN:2001-028783.
Audience: **g,l,u,f.**

Individual Authors and Works > 20th C. > Galsworthy, John

Dupre, Catherine **PR6013.A5.Z5655 1976**
John Galsworthy: A Biography. Other. Penguin Group (USA) Inc. New York, NY. 1976. 288p. ISBN:0-698-10715-2, ISBN13: 978-0-698-10715-1. Dewey:823/.9/12. LCCN:76-013473.
Audience: **g,l,u,f.**

Frechet, Alec **PR6013.A5.Z56613**
John Galsworthy: A Reassessment. Denis Mahaffey (Translator). Trade Cloth. Barnes & Noble Books-Imports. Lanham, MD. 1982. 242p. ISBN:0-389-20277-0, ISBN13: 978-0-389-20277-6. Dewey:823/.912. LCCN:81-022900.
Audience: **g,u,f.**

Galsworthy, John **PR6013**
Abracadabra, and Other Satires. Trade Paper. Fredonia Books. Miami, FL. 2004. 232p. ISBN:1-4101-0476-1, ISBN13: 978-1-4101-0476-2. Dewey:827.9.
Audience: **g,l,u,f.**

Galsworthy, John **PR6013.A5 E5**
Flowering Wilderness. Trade Paper. Fredonia Books. Miami, FL. 2004. 252p. ISBN:1-4101-0493-1, ISBN13: 978-1-4101-0493-9. Dewey:823.9.
Audience: **g,l,u,f.**

Galsworthy, John **PR6019.O9**
The Forsyte Saga. Trade Cloth. Replica Books. Bridgewater, NJ. 1999. 1122p. ISBN:0-7351-0122-1, ISBN13: 978-0-7351-0122-7. Dewey:823/.912.
Audience: **g,l,u,f.**

Galsworthy, John **R724**
The Little Man and Other Satires. Trade Paper. Fredonia Books. Miami, FL. 2004. 296p. ISBN:1-4101-0551-2, ISBN13: 978-1-4101-0551-6. Dewey:174.2.
Audience: **g,l,u,f.**

Galsworthy, John **PR6013.A5**
Maid in Waiting. Perfect. International Law & Taxation Publishers. Miami, FL. 2001. 372p. ISBN:1-58963-240-0, ISBN13: 978-1-58963-240-0. Dewey:823/.9/12.
Audience: **g,l,u,f.**

Galsworthy, John **PR6019.O9**
A Modern Comedy. Trade Paper. Kessinger Publishing, LLC. Whitefish, MT. 2005. ISBN:0-7661-9434-5, ISBN13: 978-0-7661-9434-2. Dewey:823/.912.
Audience: **g,l,u,f.**

Galsworthy, John **PR6013.A5**
On Forsyte 'Change. C. Scribner's Sons. 1930.
Audience: **g,u,f.**

Galsworthy, John **PR6013.A5**
One More River: Over the River. Trade Paper. Fredonia Books. Miami, FL. 2004. 376p. ISBN:1-4101-0543-1, ISBN13: 978-1-4101-0543-1. Dewey:823/.9/12.
Audience: **g,l,u,f.**

Galsworthy, John **PR6013.A5 A19**
The Plays of John Galsworthy. Trade Paper. Kessinger Publishing, LLC. Whitefish, MT. 2005. ISBN:1-4179-3905-2, ISBN13: 978-1-4179-3905-3. Dewey:822.91.
Audience: **g,l,u,f.**

Galsworthy, John & Baker, George P. **PR6013.A5**
Representative Plays. Trade Paper. Kessinger Publishing, LLC. Whitefish, MT. 2005. ISBN:1-4179-0657-X, ISBN13: 978-1-4179-0657-4. Dewey:822.
Audience: **g,l,u,f.** B

Smit, J. Henry **PR6013.A5Z74**
Short Stories of John Galsworthy. Trade Cloth. Richard West. Philadelphia, PA. 1989. ISBN:0-8274-3407-3, ISBN13: 978-0-8274-3407-3. Dewey:823.91.
Audience: **g,l,u,f.**

Sternlicht, Sanford **PR6013.A5Z75 1987**
John Galsworthy. Trade Cloth. Macmillan Publishing Company, Inc. Old Tappan, NJ. 1987. English Authors Ser., No. 447 ISBN:0-8057-6947-1, ISBN13: 978-0-8057-6947-0. Dewey:823/.912. LCCN:86-031815.
Audience: **g,l,u,f.** *Choice, 1987.*

Individual Authors and Works > 20th C. > Graves, Robert

Carter, D. N. **PR6013.R35Z63 1988**
Robert Graves: The Lasting Poetic Achievement. Trade Cloth. Rowman & Littlefield Publishers, Inc. Lanham, MD. 1988. 256p. ISBN:0-389-20818-3, ISBN13: 978-0-389-20818-1. Dewey:824.912. LCCN:88-029245.
Audience: **g,l,u,f.** *Choice, 1989.*

Graves, Richard P. **PR6013.R35Z7173 1995**
Robert Graves and the White Goddess, 1940-1985. Trade Cloth. Weidenfeld & Nicolson, Ltd. London, 1996. 400p. ISBN:0-297-81534-2, ISBN13: 978-0-297-81534-1. Dewey:821.9/12. LCCN:95-226987.
Audience: **g,l,u,f.** *Choice, 1997.*

Graves, Robert **PR6013.R35A17 1988**
Collected Poems, 1975. Trade Cloth. Oxford University Press, Inc. New York, NY. 1988. 624p. ISBN:0-19-505143-2, ISBN13: 978-0-19-505143-8. Dewey:821/.912. LCCN:87-018607.
Audience: **g,l,u,f.**

Graves, Robert **PR6019.O9**
Count Belisarius. Paper Text. Textbook Publishers. Temecula, CA. 2003. 421p. ISBN:0-7581-6547-1, ISBN13: 978-0-7581-6547-3. Dewey:823/.9/1.
Audience: **g,l,u,f.** B

Graves, Robert **PR6013 .R35 HE41**
Hercules, My Shipmate. Trade Cloth. Farrar, Straus & Giroux. New York, NY. 1982. 464p. ISBN:0-374-51677-4, ISBN13: 978-0-374-51677-2. Dewey:823.9.
Audience: **g,l,u,f.**

Graves, Robert **PR6013.R35I2 1998**
I, Claudius and Claudius the God. Richard Francis (Editor, Introduction by). Trade Cloth. Carcanet Press, Ltd. Manchester, 1998. 356p. ISBN:1-85754-279-7, ISBN13: 978-1-85754-279-0. Dewey:823/.912. LCCN:00-361286.
Audience: **g,l,u,f.**

Graves, Robert **PR6013.R35Z5 1990**
Good-Bye to All That: An Autobiography. Ed. 2. Paul Fussell (Preface by). Trade Paper. Doubleday Publishing. New York, NY. 1958. 368p. Anchor Bks. ISBN:0-385-09330-6, ISBN13: 978-0-385-09330-9. Dewey:821.9/12/09. LCCN:57-012294.
Audience: **g,l,u,f.**

Graves, Robert (Author, Editor) **PR6013.R35**
Wife to Mr. Milton and the Isles of Unwisdom. Simon Brittan (Editor), Robert Graves & Simon Brittan (Introduction by). Cloth over Boards. Carcanet Press, Ltd. Manchester, 2003. 860p. The Millennium Graves Ser. ISBN:1-85754-585-0, ISBN13: 978-1-85754-585-2. Dewey:823.9/12.
Audience: **g.**

Kersnowski, Frank L. (Editor) **PR6013.R35Z464 1989**
Conversations with Robert Graves. Trade Paper. University Press of Mississippi. Jackson, MS. 1989. 208p. Literary Conversations Ser. ISBN:0-87805-414-6, ISBN13: 978-0-87805-414-5. Dewey:821/.912. LCCN:89-032216.
Audience: **l,u,f.**

Kersnowski, Frank L. **PR6013.R35Z729 2002**
The Early Poetry of Robert Graves: The Goddess Beckons. Trade Cloth. University of Texas Press. Austin, TX. 2002. 192p. Literary Modernism Ser. ISBN:0-292-74343-2, ISBN13: 978-0-292-74343-4. Dewey:821/.912 B. LCCN:2001-053192.
Audience: **g,l,u,f.** *Choice, 2003.*

Kirkham, Michael **PR6013.R35 Z73 1969B**
Poetry of Robert Graves. Cloth Text. Brill Academic Publishers, Inc. Boston, MA. 1969. ix, 284p. ISBN:0-485-11103-9, ISBN13: 978-0-485-11103-3. Dewey:821/.9/12. LCCN:78-398179.
Audience: **g,l,u,f.** B

McPhail, Helen & Guest, Philip **PR6037.A86Z75 2001**
Robert Graves and Siegfried Sassoon. Trade Paper. Pen & Sword Books Ltd. Barnsley, 2001. 160p. Military History Ser. ISBN:0-85052-838-0, ISBN13: 978-0-85052-838-1. Dewey:821.912. LCCN:2002-391694.
Audience: **g,l,u,f.**

Individual Authors and Works > 20th C. > Greene, Graham

Allain, Marie-Francoise **PR6013.R44.Z4613**
The Other Man: Conversations with Graham Greene. Guido Waldman (Translator). Trade Cloth. Simon & Schuster. New

York, NY. 1983. 176p. ISBN:0-671-44767-X, ISBN13: 978-0-671-44767-0. Dewey:823/.912. LCCN:82-019652.
Audience: **g,l,u,f.**

Bloom, Harold (Introduction by) **PR6013.R44Z63345**
Graham Greene. Trade Cloth. Facts On File, Inc. New York, NY. 1988. 200p. Bloom's Modern Critical Views Ser. ISBN:0-87754-701-7, ISBN13: 978-0-87754-701-3. Dewey:823/.912. LCCN:86-024495.
Audience: **g,l,u,f.**

Bowen, Elizabeth & Greene, Graham **PN45 .B62 1975**
Why Do I Write?: An Exchange of Views Between Elizabeth Bowen, Graham Greene and V. S. Pritchett. V. S. Pritchett (Preface by). Library Binding. M. S. G. Haskell House. Brooklyn, NY. 1975. English Literature Ser., No. 33 ISBN:0-8383-2094-5, ISBN13: 978-0-8383-2094-5. Dewey:801. LCCN:75-022190.
Audience: **g,l,u,f.**

Cloetta, Yvonne **PR6013.R44**
In Search of a Beginning: My Life with Graham Greene. Euan Cameron (Translator), Marie-Francoise Allain (As told to). Trade Paper, Perfect. Bloomsbury Publishing Plc. London, 2005. 209p. ISBN:0-7475-7112-0, ISBN13: 978-0-7475-7112-4. Dewey:823/.912 B.
Audience: **g,l,u,f.**

DeVitis, A. A. **PR6013.R44.Z632 1986**
Graham Greene. Trade Cloth. Macmillan Publishing Company, Inc. Old Tappan, NJ. 1986. 248p. Twayne's English Authors Ser., 3 ISBN:0-8057-6911-0, ISBN13: 978-0-8057-6911-1. Dewey:823/.912. LCCN:85-017612.
Audience: **g,l,u,f.** *Choice, 1986.*

Diemert, Brian **PR6013.R44Z6322 1996**
Graham Greene's Thrillers and the 1930s. Trade Cloth. McGill-Queen's University Press. Montreal, PQ. 1996. 256p. ISBN:0-7735-1432-5, ISBN13: 978-0-7735-1432-4. Dewey:823/.912. LCCN:98-122715.
Audience: **g,l,u,f.**

Donaghy, Henry J. (Editor) **PR6013.R44 1992**
Conversations with Graham Greene. Trade Cloth. University Press of Mississippi. Jackson, MS. 1992. 208p. Literary Conversations Ser. ISBN:0-87805-550-9, ISBN13: 978-0-87805-550-0. Dewey:823.912. LCCN:91-033058.
Audience: **g,l,u,f.**

Falk, Quentin **PN1995**
Travels in Greeneland: The Complete Guide to the Cinema of Graham Greene. Ed. 3. Trade Paper. Reynolds & Hearn. Richmond, 2001. 192p. ISBN:1-903111-13-7, ISBN13: 978-1-903111-13-0. Dewey:791.4/375.
Audience: **g,l,u,f.**

Gaston, George M. A. **PR6013.R44Z6334 1984**
The Pursuit of Salvation: A Critical Guide to the Novels of Graham Greene. Trade Cloth. Whitston Publishing Company, Inc. Albany, NY. 1984. 170p. ISBN:0-87875-289-7, ISBN13: 978-0-87875-289-8. Dewey:823/.912. LCCN:84-050635.
Audience: **l,u,f.**

Greene, Graham **PR6013.R44**
Brighton Rock. Trade Paper. Knopf Publishing Group. New York, NY. 2004. 256p. ISBN:0-09-947016-0, ISBN13: 978-0-09-947016-8. Dewey:823/.912.
Audience: **g,l,u,f.**

Greene, Graham **PR6013.R44**
A Burnt-Out Case. UK-B Format Paperback. Knopf Publishing Group. New York, NY. 2004. 208p. ISBN:0-09-947843-9, ISBN13: 978-0-09-947843-0. Dewey:823/.9/1.
Audience: **g,l,u,f.**

Greene, Graham **PR6013.R44A19 2002**
Collected Plays. Trade Paper. Knopf Publishing Group. New York, NY. 2002. 414p. Vintage Classics Ser. ISBN:0-09-928625-4, ISBN13: 978-0-09-928625-7. Dewey:822/.912. LCCN:2002-483256.
Audience: **g,l,u,f.**

Greene, Graham **PR6013.R44**
The Comedians. UK-B Format Paperback. Knopf Publishing Group. New York, NY. 2005. 320p. ISBN:0-09-947837-4, ISBN13: 978-0-09-947837-9. Dewey:823/.914.
Audience: **g,l,u,f.**

Greene, Graham **PR6013.R44**
The Confidential Agent. UK-B Format Paperback. Knopf Publishing Group. New York, NY. 2002. 272p. ISBN:0-09-928619-X, ISBN13: 978-0-09-928619-6. Dewey:823/.9/1.
Audience: **g,l,u,f.**

Greene, Graham **PR6019.O9**
Dr. Fischer of Geneva or the Bomb Party. Trade Cloth. Penguin Group (USA) Inc. New York, NY. 1985. 160p. Uniform Editions Ser. ISBN:0-670-27522-0, ISBN13: 978-0-670-27522-9. Dewey:823.912.
Audience: **g,l,u,f.**

Greene, Graham **PR6019.O9**
The End of the Affair. Trade Paper. Penguin Group (USA) Inc. New York, NY. 1999. 192p. ISBN:0-14-029109-1, ISBN13: 978-0-14-029109-4. Dewey:823/.912.
Audience: **g,l,u,f.**

Greene, Graham **PR6019.O9**
England Made Me. Trade Paper. Penguin Group (USA) Inc. New York, NY. 1992. 208p. Penguin Twentieth-Century Classics Ser. ISBN:0-14-018551-8, ISBN13: 978-0-14-018551-5. Dewey:823.9/12.
Audience: **g,l,u,f.**

Greene, Graham **PR6031.R6**
Greene: Collected Essays. Trade Paper. Penguin Group (USA) Inc. New York, NY. 1993. 352p. Penguin Twentieth-Century Classics Ser. ISBN:0-14-018576-3, ISBN13: 978-0-14-018576-8. Dewey:824.912.
Audience: **g,l,u,f.**

Greene, Graham **PZ3.G8319HE6**
The Heart of the Matter. Trade Cloth. Heinemann. Portsmouth, NH. 1968. xiv, 266p. ISBN:0-435-29351-6, ISBN13: 978-0-435-29351-2. Dewey:823/.912. LCCN:72-404459.
Audience: **g,l,u,f.**

Greene, Graham **PR6013.R44H6 2000**
The Honorary Consul. Trade Cloth. Simon & Schuster. New York, NY. 2000. 288p. Simon and Schuster Classic Editions ISBN:0-684-87125-4, ISBN13: 978-0-684-87125-7. Dewey:823.9/12. LCCN:00-036587.
Audience: **g,l,u,f.**

Greene, Graham **PR6013.R44**
The Human Factor. UK-B Format Paperback. Knopf Publishing Group. New York, NY. 2000. 272p. ISBN:0-09-928852-4, ISBN13: 978-0-09-928852-7. Dewey:823.9/12.
Audience: **g,l,u,f.**

Greene, Graham **DT497**
In Search of a Character. Paper Text. Textbook Publishers. Temecula, CA. 2003. 93p. ISBN:0-7581-0937-7, ISBN13: 978-0-7581-0937-8. Dewey:916.7510424.
Audience: **g,l,u,f.**

Greene, Graham **PR6013.R44**
It's a Battlefield. Trade Paper. Knopf Publishing Group. New York, NY. 2002. 201p. ISBN:0-09-928222-4, ISBN13: 978-0-09-928222-8. Dewey:823.912.
Audience: **g,l,u,f.**

Greene, Graham **DA447.R6 G7**
Lord Rochester's Monkey. Trade Cloth. Penguin Group (USA) Inc. New York, NY. 1974. ISBN:0-670-44055-8, ISBN13: 978-0-670-44055-9. Dewey:942.06/6/0924. LCCN:73-017955.
Audience: **g,l,u,f.**

Greene, Graham **PR6013.R44**
Loser Takes All. Trade Paper. Knopf Publishing Group. New York, NY. 2002. 123p. ISBN:0-09-928622-X, ISBN13: 978-0-09-928622-6. Dewey:823.912.
Audience: **g,l,u,f.**

Greene, Graham **PR6013.R44 M6 1982**
Monsignor Quixote. Trade Cloth. Simon & Schuster. New York, NY. 1982. ISBN:0-671-45818-3, ISBN13: 978-0-671-45818-8. Dewey:823/.912. LCCN:82-005937.
Audience: **g,l,u,f.**

Greene, Graham **PR6019.O9**
Our Man in Havana. Trade Paper. Penguin Group (USA) Inc. New York, NY. 1991. 224p. Penguin Twentieth-Century Classics Ser. ISBN:0-14-018493-7, ISBN13: 978-0-14-018493-8. Dewey:823.9/12.
Audience: **g,l,u,f.**

Greene, Graham **PR6013.R44P6 2003**
The Power and the Glory. Trade Paper. Penguin Group (USA) Inc. New York, NY. 2003. 240p. Twentieth Century Classics Ser. ISBN:0-14-243730-1, ISBN13: 978-0-14-243730-8. Dewey:823/.912. LCCN:2002-034604.
Audience: **g,l,u,f.**

Greene, Graham **PR6013.R44Q5 2002**
The Quiet American. Trade Paper. Penguin Group (USA) Inc. New York, NY. 2002. 192p. ISBN:0-14-200138-4, ISBN13: 978-0-14-200138-7. Dewey:823/.912. LCCN:2001-052393.
Audience: **g,l,u,f.**

Greene, Graham **PR6019.O9**
The Tenth Man. Trade Paper. Simon & Schuster. New York, NY. 1998. 160p. ISBN:0-671-01909-0, ISBN13: 978-0-671-01909-9. Dewey:823/.912.
Audience: **g,l,u,f.**

Greene, Graham **PR6019.O9**
The Third Man and the Fallen Idol. UK-B Format Paperback. Knopf Publishing Group. New York, NY. 2002. 160p. ISBN:0-09-928623-8, ISBN13: 978-0-09-928623-3. Dewey:823/.912.
Audience: **g,l,u,f.**

Greene, Graham **PR6013.R44**
Ways of Escape and a Sort of Life. Trade Cloth. Penguin Group (USA) Inc. New York, NY. 1985. 320p. Uniform Editions Ser. ISBN:0-670-75262-2, ISBN13: 978-0-670-75262-1. Dewey:823/.912.
Audience: **g,l,u,f.**

Greene, Graham **PR6013.R44C28 2005**
The Captain and the Enemy. John Auchard (Introduction by). Trade Paper. Penguin Group (USA) Inc. New York, NY. 2005. 224p. Penguin Classics Ser. ISBN:0-14-303929-6, ISBN13: 978-0-14-303929-7. Dewey:823/.912. LCCN:2005-285186.
Audience: **g,l,u,f.**

Greene, Graham **PR6013.R44T7 1981**
Travels with My Aunt. Gloria Emerson (Introduction by). Trade Paper. Penguin Group (USA) Inc. New York, NY. 2004. 288p. Penguin Classics Ser. ISBN:0-14-303900-8, ISBN13: 978-0-14-303900-6. Dewey:823/.912. LCCN:2004-559272.
Audience: **g,l,u,f.**

Greene, Graham **PR6013.R44M5 2005**
The Ministry of Fear: An Entertainment. Alan Furst (Introduction by). Trade Paper. Penguin Group (USA) Inc. New York, NY. 2005. 224p. Penguin Classics Ser. ISBN:0-14-303911-3, ISBN13: 978-0-14-303911-2. Dewey:823/.912. LCCN:2004-063312.
Audience: **g,l,u,f.**

Greene, Graham **PR6013.R44S7 2004**
The Orient Express. Christopher Hitchens (Introduction by). Trade Paper. Penguin Group (USA) Inc. New York, NY. 2004. 224p. Penguin Classics Ser. ISBN:0-14-243791-3, ISBN13: 978-0-14-243791-9. Dewey:823/.912. LCCN:2004-559893.
Audience: **g,l,u,f.**

Greene, Graham **PR6013.R44T54 2005**
A Gun for Sale. Samuel Hynes (Introduction by). Trade Paper. Penguin Group (USA) Inc. New York, NY. 2005. 208p. Penguin Classics Ser. ISBN:0-14-303930-X, ISBN13: 978-0-14-303930-3. Dewey:823/.912. LCCN:2005-045802.
Audience: **g,l,u,f.**

Greene, Graham **PR6013.R44A6 2005**
Complete Short Stories. Pico Iyer (Introduction by). Trade Paper. Penguin Group (USA) Inc. New York, NY. 2005. 624p. Penguin Classics Ser. ISBN:0-14-303910-5, ISBN13: 978-0-14-303910-5. Dewey:823/.912. LCCN:2004-057255.
Audience: **g,l,u,f.**

Greene, Graham **F1215 .G82 2006**
The Lawless Roads. Ed. 60. David Rieff (Introduction by). Trade Paper. Penguin Group (USA) Inc. New York, NY. 2006. 240p. Penguin Classics Ser. ISBN:0-14-303973-3, ISBN13: 978-0-14-303973-0. Dewey:917.204/82. LCCN:2006-046024.
Audience: **l,u,f.**

Greene, Graham **PR6013.R44**
No Man's Land. James Sexton (Foreword by). Trade Cloth. Hesperus Press. London, 2005. 112p. ISBN:1-84391-414-X, ISBN13: 978-1-84391-414-3. Dewey:823.9/12.
Audience: **g,l,u,f.**

Greene, Graham **PR6013**
The Portable Graham Greene. Philip Stratford (Contribution by). Trade Paper. Penguin Group (USA) Inc. New York, NY. 2005. 672p. ISBN:0-14-303918-0, ISBN13: 978-0-14-303918-1. Dewey:823/.9/1.
Audience: **g,l,u,f.**

Greene, Graham **DT626.G7 2006**
Journey Without Maps. Paul Theroux (Introduction by). Trade Paper. Penguin Group (USA) Inc. New York, NY. 2006. 272p. ISBN:0-14-303972-5, ISBN13: 978-0-14-303972-3. Dewey:916.604/3. LCCN:2006-041982.
Audience: **g,l,u,f.**

Greene, Graham **PR6013.R44M26 2005**
The Man Within. Jonathan Yardley (Introduction by). Trade Paper. Penguin Group (USA) Inc. New York, NY. 2005. 240p. Penguin Classics Ser. ISBN:0-14-303921-0, ISBN13: 978-0-14-303921-1. Dewey:823/.912. LCCN:2005-273611.
Audience: **g,l,u,f.**

Kelly, Rosemary **PR6013.R44Z6346 1992**
Graham Greene: A Study of the Short Fiction. Trade Cloth. Macmillan Publishing Company, Inc. Old Tappan, NJ. 1992. 150p. Twayne's Studies in Short Fiction, Vol. 35 ISBN:0-8057-8342-3, ISBN13: 978-0-8057-8342-1. Dewey:823/.912. LCCN:91-045633.
Audience: **g,l,u,f.** *Choice, 1992.*

Sherry, Norman **PR6013.R44**
The Life of Graham Greene: 1955-1991. Book, Other. Penguin Group (USA) Inc. New York, NY. 2005. 944p. ISBN:0-14-303613-0, ISBN13: 978-0-14-303613-5. Dewey:823.912.
Audience: **g,l,u,f.**

Sherry, Norman **PR6013.R44**
The Life of Graham Greene, 1904-1939, Vol. I. Trade Paper. Penguin Group (USA) Inc. New York, NY. 2004. 816p. ISBN:0-14-200420-0, ISBN13: 978-0-14-200420-3. Dewey:823/.912.
Audience: **l,u,f.**

Sherry, Norman **PR6013.R44**
The Life of Graham Greene, 1939-1955, Vol. II. Trade Paper. Penguin Group (USA) Inc. New York, NY. 2004. 592p. ISBN.0-14-200421-9, ISBN13: 978-0-14-200421-0. Dewey:823.912.
Audience: **g,l,u,f.**

Sinyard, Neil **PR6013.R44Z847 2003**
Graham Greene: A Literary Life. Cloth over Boards. Palgrave Macmillan. New York, NY. 2004. 209p. Literary Lives Ser. ISBN:0-333-72986-2, ISBN13: 978-0-333-72986-1. Dewey:823/.912. LCCN:2003-053572.
Audience: **g,l,u,f.**

Walling, Gerald C. **PR6013.R44Z92 1991**
Graham Greene: A Study of Four Dramas. Cloth Text. Peter Lang Publishing, Inc. New York, NY. 1992. 199p. American University Studies, Ser. XXVI, Vol. 10:Theatre Arts ISBN:0-8204-1579-0, ISBN13: 978-0-8204-1579-6. Dewey:822/.912. LCCN:91-027455.
Audience: **l,u,f.**

Watts, Cedric T. **PR6013.R44Z925 1997**
A Preface to Greene. Ed. 1. Cloth Text. Addison-Wesley Longman, Ltd. Harlow, 1997. ix, 230p. Preface Bks. ISBN:0-582-25020-X, ISBN13: 978-0-582-25020-8. Dewey:823.9/12. LCCN:96-001729.
Audience: **g,l,u,f.**

Individual Authors and Works > 20th C. > H

Haddon, Mark **PZ7.H1165CU 2003**
The Curious Incident of the Dog in the Night-Time: A Novel. Trade Cloth. Doubleday Publishing. New York, NY. 2003. 240p. ISBN:0-385-50945-6, ISBN13: 978-0-385-50945-9. Dewey:[Fic]. LCCN:2002-031355.
Audience: **g,l,u,f.**

Hall, Radclyffe **PR6015.A33W43 1990**
The Well of Loneliness: A 1920s Classic of Lesbian Fiction. UK-Trade Paper. Doubleday Publishing. New York, NY. 1990. 448p. ISBN:0-385-41609-1, ISBN13: 978-0-385-41609-2. Dewey:823.9/12. LCCN:90-035904.
Audience: **g,l,u,f.**

Harris, Joanne **PR6058.A68826C46**
Chocolat: A Novel. Trade Paper. Penguin Group (USA) Inc. New York, NY. 2000. 320p. ISBN:0-14-100018-X, ISBN13: 978-0-14-100018-3. Dewey:823/.914. LCCN:98-021771.
Audience: **g,l,u,f.**

Hill, Selima **PR6058.I4494B86 2001**
Bunny. Trade Paper. Bloodaxe Books. Bala, 2002. 80p. ISBN:1-85224-507-7, ISBN13: 978-1-85224-507-8. Dewey:821/.914. LCCN:2002-421905.
Audience: **g,l,u,f.**

Hilton, James **PR6019.O9**
Goodbye, Mr. Chips. Library Binding. Buccaneer Books, Inc. Cutchogue, NY. 1982. ISBN:0-89966-413-X, ISBN13: 978-0-89966-413-2. Dewey:823.9/12.
Audience: **g,l,u,f.**

Hilton, James **PR6015.I53L6 2004**
Lost Horizon. Trade Paper. HarperCollins Publishers. New York, NY. 2004. 256p. ISBN:0-06-059452-7, ISBN13: 978-0-06-059452-7. Dewey:823/.92. LCCN:2004-046071.
Audience: **g,l,u,f.**

Hollinghurst, Alan **PR6058.O4467L56 2004**
The Line of Beauty: A Novel. Cloth over Boards. Bloomsbury Publishing. New York, NY. 2004. 400p. ISBN:1-58234-508-2, ISBN13: 978-1-58234-508-6. Dewey:823/.914. LCCN:2004-047660.
Audience: **g,l,u,f.**

Hornung, E. W. **PR6015.O687**
Raffles: The Amateur Cracksman. Richard Lancelyn Green (Notes by). Trade Paper. Penguin Group (USA) Inc. New York, NY. 2003. 240p. Penguin Classics Ser. ISBN:0-14-143933-5, ISBN13: 978-0-14-143933-4. Dewey:823.8. LCCN:2003-284079.
Audience: **g,l,u,f.**

Individual Authors and Works > 20th C. > Heaney, Seamus

Andrews, Elmer **PR6058.E2Z85 1998**
The Poetry of Seamus Heaney. Seamus Heaney (Contribution by). Trade Cloth. Columbia University Press. New York, NY. 2000. 192p. Columbia Critical Guides ISBN:0-231-11926-7, ISBN13: 978-0-231-11926-9. Dewey:821/.914. LCCN:99-041368.
Audience: **u,f.**

Heaney, Seamus (Translator) **PR1583.H43 2000**
Beowulf: A New Verse Translation. Cloth over Boards. Farrar, Straus & Giroux. New York, NY. 2000. 208p. ISBN:0-374-11119-7, ISBN13: 978-0-374-11119-9. Dewey:829/.3. LCCN:99-023209.
Audience: **g,l,u,f.**

Heaney, Seamus **PR6058.E2C74 1996**
Crediting Poetry: The Nobel Lecture. Cloth over Boards. Farrar, Straus & Giroux. New York, NY. 1996. 53p. ISBN:0-374-13138-4, ISBN13: 978-0-374-13138-8. Dewey:809.1. LCCN:96-000048.
Audience: **u,f.**

Heaney, Seamus **PR6058.E2D57 2006**
District and Circle: Poems. Cloth over Boards. Farrar, Straus & Giroux. New York, NY. 2006. 96p. ISBN:0-374-14092-8, ISBN13: 978-0-374-14092-2. Dewey:821/.914. LCCN:2005-044687.
Audience: **g,l,u,f.**

Heaney, Seamus **PR6058.U37**
Electric Light: Poems. Trade Paper. Farrar, Straus & Giroux. New York, NY. 2002. 112p. ISBN:0-374-52841-1, ISBN13: 978-0-374-52841-6. Dewey:821/.914.
Audience: **g,l,u,f.**

Heaney, Seamus **PR6058.E2F54 2002**
Finders Keepers: Selected Prose 1971-2001. Cloth over Boards. Farrar, Straus & Giroux. New York, NY. 2002. 432p. ISBN:0-374-15496-1, ISBN13: 978-0-374-15496-7. Dewey:828/.91408. LCCN:2002-101044.
Audience: **u,f.**

Heaney, Seamus **PR610**
The Government of the Tongue: Selected Prose, 1978-1987. Cloth over Boards. Farrar, Straus & Giroux. New York, NY. 1989. 200p. ISBN:0-374-16578-5, ISBN13: 978-0-374-16578-9. Dewey:821/.912/09.
Audience: **u,f.**

Heaney, Seamus **PR6058.E2H34 1987**
The Haw Lantern. Trade Cloth. Farrar, Straus & Giroux. New York, NY. 1987. 72p. ISBN:0-374-16837-7, ISBN13: 978-0-374-16837-7. Dewey:821/.914. LCCN:87-017705.
Audience: **g,l,u,f.**

Heaney, Seamus **PR6058.E2O65 1998**
Opened Ground: Selected Poems, 1966-1996. Cloth over Boards. Farrar, Straus & Giroux. New York, NY. 1998. 512p. ISBN:0-374-23517-1, ISBN13: 978-0-374-23517-8. Dewey:821/.914. LCCN:98-004331.
Audience: **g,l,u,f.**

Heaney, Seamus **PR503**
Preoccupations: Selected Prose, 1968-1978. Trade Cloth. Farrar, Straus & Giroux. New York, NY. 1981. 224p. ISBN:0-374-51650-2, ISBN13: 978-0-374-51650-5. Dewey:821/.009.
Audience: **g,l,u,f.**

Heaney, Seamus **PR503.H38 1995**
The Redress of Poetry. Trade Cloth. Farrar, Straus & Giroux. New York, NY. 1995. 212p. ISBN:0-374-24853-2, ISBN13: 978-0-374-24853-6. Dewey:821/.009. LCCN:95-019556.
Audience: **u,f.** *Choice, 1996.*

Heaney, Seamus **PR6058.E2S67 1996**
The Spirit Level: Poems. Cloth over Boards. Farrar, Straus & Giroux. New York, NY. 1996. 81p. ISBN:0-374-26779-0, ISBN13: 978-0-374-26779-7. Dewey:821.9/14. LCCN:95-042585.
Audience: **g,l,u,f.**

O'Brien, Eugene **PR6058.E2Z795 2003**
Seamus Heaney and the Place of Writing. Trade Cloth. University Press of Florida. Gainesville, FL. 2002. 160p. ISBN:0-8130-2582-6, ISBN13: 978-0-8130-2582-7. Dewey:821/.914. LCCN:2002-028933.
Audience: **u,f.** *Choice, 2003.*

Individual Authors and Works > 20th C. > Hughes, Ted

Aeschylus **PA3827.A7H84 1999**
The Oresteia of Aeschylus. Ted Hughes (Translator). Trade Cloth. Farrar, Straus & Giroux. New York, NY. 1999. 197p. ISBN:0-374-22721-7, ISBN13: 978-0-374-22721-0. Dewey:882/.01. LCCN:98-073704.
Audience: **g.** *Choice, 2000.*

Feinstein, Elaine **PR6058.U37Z69 2001**
Ted Hughes: The Life of a Poet. Trade Cloth. W. W. Norton & Company, Inc. New York, NY. 2001. 416p. ISBN:0-393-04967-1, ISBN13: 978-0-393-04967-1. Dewey:821.9/14. LCCN:2001-044925.
Audience: **g,l,u,f.** *Choice, 2002.*

Hughes, Ted **PR6058.U37**
Birthday Letters: Poems. Trade Cloth. Farrar, Straus & Giroux. New York, NY. 1998. ISBN:0-374-95806-8, ISBN13: 978-0-374-95806-0. Dewey:821.9/14.
Audience: **g,l,u,f.**

Hughes, Ted **PR6058.U37**
Collected Poems of Ted Hughes. Trade Cloth. Faber & Faber, Inc. New York, NY. 2003. 1376p. ISBN:0-571-21719-2, ISBN13: 978-0-571-21719-9. Dewey:821/.914. LCCN:2004-381498.
Audience: **g.**

Hughes, Ted **PR6015.I3**
Difficulties of a Bridegroom: Stories. Trade Paper. Picador. New York, NY. 1997. 176p. ISBN:0-312-16817-9, ISBN13: 978-0-312-16817-9. Dewey:823.9/14. LCCN:96-008307.
Audience: **g.**

Hughes, Ted **PR6058.U37A79 1999**
Euripides' Alcestis: A New Translation. Cloth over Boards. Farrar, Straus & Giroux. New York, NY. 1999. 128p. ISBN:0-374-14920-8, ISBN13: 978-0-374-14920-8. LCCN:99-042757.
Audience: **g,l,u,f.**

Hughes, Ted **PR6058.U37**
Lupercal. Trade Cloth. Faber & Faber, Ltd. London, 1960. ISBN:0-571-07035-3, ISBN13: 978-0-571-07035-0. Dewey:821/.9/14.
Audience: **g,l,u,f.**

Hughes, Ted **PR6058.U37 R35 1992**
Rain Charm for the Duchy and Other Laureate Poems. Trade Cloth. Faber & Faber, Inc. New York, NY. 1992. 96p. ISBN:0-571-16605-9, ISBN13: 978-0-571-16605-3. Dewey:821/.914. LCCN:92-206190.
Audience: **g.**

Hughes, Ted **PR6058.U37.A6 2002**
Selected Poems 1957-1994. Cloth over Boards. Farrar, Straus & Giroux. New York, NY. 2002. 352p. ISBN:0-374-25875-9, ISBN13: 978-0-374-25875-7. Dewey:821/.914. LCCN:2002-021603.
Audience: **g.**

Hughes, Ted **PR6058.U37Z67 1999**
Ted Hughes at 70. Cloth Text. Faber & Faber, Inc. New York, NY. 1999. 256p. ISBN:0-571-19686-1, ISBN13: 978-0-571-19686-9. Dewey:821/.914. LCCN:99-487878.
Audience: **g,l,u,f.**

Hughes, Ted **PR6013.O35**
Winter Pollen: Occasional Prose. William Scammell (Editor). Trade Cloth. Picador. New York, NY. 1996. ISBN:0-614-12884-6, ISBN13: 978-0-614-12884-0. Dewey:824/.914.
Audience: **g,l,u,f.**

Hughes, Ted **PZ7.H87398IQ 1988**
The Iron Giant. Dirk Zimmer (Illustrator). Trade Cloth. HarperCollins Publishers. New York, NY. 1988. 64p. ISBN:0-06-022638-2, ISBN13: 978-0-06-022638-1. Dewey:823.9/14. LCCN:87-045089.
Audience: **g.**

Middlebrook, Diane **PR6058.U37Z76 2003**
Her Husband: Hughes and Plath: Portrait of a Marriage. Trade Cloth. Penguin Group (USA) Inc. New York, NY. 2003. 384p. ISBN:0-670-03187-9, ISBN13: 978-0-670-03187-0. Dewey:821/.914 B. LCCN:2003-053768.
Audience: **g,l,u,f.**

Sagar, Keith **PR6058.U37Z875 2000**
The Laughter of Foxes: A Study of Ted Hughes. Trade Cloth. Liverpool University Press. Liverpool, 2000. 204p. Liverpool University Press - Liverpool English Texts and Studies ISBN:0-85323-565-1, ISBN13: 978-0-85323-565-1. Dewey:821/.914. LCCN:2001-411455.
Audience: **g,l,u,f.** *Choice, 2001.*

Sagar, Keith **PR6058.U37Z875 2000**
The Laughter of Foxes: A Study of Ted Hughes. Trade Paper. Liverpool University Press. Liverpool, 2005. 230p. Liverpool University Press - Liverpool English Texts and Studies ISBN:0-85323-575-9, ISBN13: 978-0-85323-575-0. Dewey:821/.914. LCCN:2001-411455.
Audience: **g,l,u,f.** *Choice, 2001.*

Wagner, Erica **PR6058.U37B5738 2001**
Ariel's Gift: Ted Hughes, Sylvia Plath, and the Story of the Birthday Letters. Trade Cloth. W. W. Norton & Company, Inc. New York, NY. 2001. 256p. ISBN:0-393-02009-6, ISBN13: 978-0-393-02009-0. Dewey:821/.914. LCCN:2001-018310.
Audience: **g,l,u,f.**

Individual Authors and Works > 20th C. > Huxley, Aldous

Bloom, Harold (Editor, Introduction by) **PR6015.U9B65 1996**
Aldous Huxley's Brave New World. Trade Paper. Chelsea House Publishers. Langhorne, PA. 1996. 90p. Bloom's Notes Ser. ISBN:0-7910-4084-4, ISBN13: 978-0-7910-4084-3. Dewey:823/.912. LCCN:95-045114.
Audience: **g,l,u,f.**

Firchow, Peter E. **PR6015.U9Z63 1972**
Aldous Huxley, Satirist and Novelist. Trade Cloth. University of Minnesota Press. Minneapolis, MN. 1972. viii, 203p. Monographs in the Humanities, : ISBN:0-8166-0635-8, ISBN13: 978-0-8166-0635-1. Dewey:823/.9/12. LCCN:74-187165.
Audience: **l,u,f.**

Firchow, Peter E. & Huxley, Aldous **PR6015.U9B67**
The End of Utopia: A Study of Aldous Huxley's Brave New World. Trade Cloth. Bucknell University Press. Cranbury, NJ. 1984. 160p. ISBN:0-8387-5058-3, ISBN13: 978-0-8387-5058-2. Dewey:823/.912. LCCN:82-074490.
Audience: **g,l,u,f.**

Huxley, Aldous **PR6015.U9 A77 1993**
After Many a Summer Dies the Swan. Trade Paper. Ivan R. Dee Publisher. Blue Ridge Summit, PA. 1993. 360p. ISBN:1-56663-018-5, ISBN13: 978-1-56663-018-4. Dewey:823.912. LCCN:92-043906.
Audience: **g,l,u,f.**

Huxley, Aldous **PR6015.U9**
Antic Hay. UK-B Format Paperback. Knopf Publishing Group. New York, NY. 2004. 256p. ISBN:0-09-945818-7, ISBN13: 978-0-09-945818-0. Dewey:823/.912.
Audience: **g,l,u,f.**

Huxley, Aldous **PR6015.U9B65 2004**
Brave New World and Brave New World Revisited. Trade Cloth. HarperCollins Publishers. New York, NY. 2004. 368p. ISBN:0-06-053526-1, ISBN13: 978-0-06-053526-1. Dewey:823/.912. LCCN:2004-040611.
Audience: **g.**

Huxley, Aldous **PR6015.U9 A6 1992**
Collected Short Stories. Trade Paper. Ivan R. Dee Publisher. Blue Ridge Summit, PA. 1992. 397p. ISBN:0-929587-81-2, ISBN13: 978-0-929587-81-3. Dewey:823/.912. LCCN:91-035171.
Audience: **g.** B

Huxley, Aldous **PR6015.U9**
Crome Yellow. UK-B Format Paperback. Knopf Publishing Group. New York, NY. 2004. 176p. ISBN:0-09-946189-7, ISBN13: 978-0-09-946189-0. Dewey:823/.912.
Audience: **g.** B

Huxley, Aldous **PR6015.U9**
Eyeless in Gaza. UK-B Format Paperback. Knopf Publishing Group. New York, NY. 2004. 464p. ISBN:0-09-945817-9, ISBN13: 978-0-09-945817-3. Dewey:823.912.
Audience: **g.** B

Huxley, Aldous **PR6015.U9**
Point Counter Point. UK-B Format Paperback. Random House of Canada, Ltd. Mississauga, ON. 2004. 464p. ISBN:0-09-945819-5, ISBN13: 978-0-09-945819-7. Dewey:823/.912.
Audience: **g.** B

Huxley, Aldous **PR6015.U9A6 2000**
Complete Essays, 1930-1935. Robert S. Baker & James Sexton (Editors). Trade Cloth. Ivan R. Dee Publisher. Blue Ridge Summit, PA. 2001. 480p. Collected Works of Aldous Huxley, Vol. 3 ISBN:1-56663-347-8, ISBN13: 978-1-56663-347-5. Dewey:824/.912. LCCN:00-034564.
Audience: **g.**

Huxley, Aldous **PR6015.U9A6 2000**
Complete Essays, 1920-1925, Vol. I. Robert S. Baker & James Sexton (Editors), Robert S. Baker & James Sexton (Commentaries by). Trade Cloth. Ivan R. Dee Publisher. Blue Ridge Summit, PA. 2000. 512p. ISBN:1-56663-322-2, ISBN13: 978-1-56663-322-2. Dewey:824/.912. LCCN:00-034564.
Audience: **g.** *Choice, 2001.*

Huxley, Aldous **PR6015.U9A6 2000**
Complete Essays, 1926-1930, Vol. II. Robert S. Baker & James Sexton (Editors), Robert S. Baker & James Sexton (Commentaries by). Trade Cloth. Ivan R. Dee Publisher. Blue Ridge Summit, PA. 2000. 608p. ISBN:1-56663-323-0, ISBN13: 978-1-56663-323-9. Dewey:824/.912. LCCN:00-034564.
Audience: **g.** *Choice, 2001.*

Huxley, Aldous **PR6015.U9A6 2000**
Complete Essays, 1936-1938, Vol. IV. Robert S. Baker & James Sexton (Editors), Robert S. Baker & James Sexton (Commentaries by). Trade Cloth. Ivan R. Dee Publisher. Blue Ridge Summit, PA. 2002. 416p. ISBN:1-56663-394-X, ISBN13: 978-1-56663-394-9. Dewey:824/.912. LCCN:00-034564.
Audience: **g.**

Huxley, Aldous **PR6015.U9A6 2000**
Complete Essays, 1938-1956, Vol. 5. Robert S. Baker & James Sexton (Editors), Robert S. Baker & James Sexton (Commentaries by). Trade Cloth. Ivan R. Dee Publisher. Blue Ridge Summit, PA. 2002. 448p. ISBN:1-56663-441-5, ISBN13: 978-1-56663-441-0. Dewey:824/.912. LCCN:00-034564.
Audience: **g.**

Huxley, Aldous **PR6015.U9T55 1998**
Time Must Have a Stop. Douglas Dutton (Preface by). Trade Paper. Dalkey Archive Press. Normal, IL. 1998. 264p. Coleman Dowell British Literature Ser. ISBN:1-56478-180-1, ISBN13: 978-1-56478-180-2. Dewey:823/.912. LCCN:97-051429.
Audience: **g.** B

Huxley, Aldous **PR6015.U9 Z53**
Letters of Aldous Huxley. Grover Smith (Editor). Trade Cloth. HarperCollins Publishers. New York, NY. 1970. ISBN:0-06-013937-4, ISBN13: 978-0-06-013937-7. Dewey:823/.9/12. LCCN:69-015263.
Audience: **g.** B

Huxley, Aldous **PR6015.U9.A17 1971**
Collected Poetry of Aldous Huxley. Donald Watt (Editor), R. Church (Introduction by). Trade Cloth. HarperCollins Publishers. New York, NY. 1971. 168p. Cass Canfield Bk ISBN:0-06-012051-7, ISBN13: 978-0-06-012051-1. Dewey:821/.9/12. LCCN:77-138736.
Audience: **g,l,u,f.** B

Kuehn, Robert E. (Editor) **PR6015.U9Z/**
Aldous Huxley: A Collection of Critical Essays. Trade Cloth. Prentice-Hall. Upper Saddle, NJ. 1974. 192p. Twentieth Century Views Ser. ISBN:0-13-448514-9, ISBN13: 978-0-13-448514-0. Dewey:823/.912. LCCN:74-011444.
Audience: **l,u.** B

May, Keith M. **PR6015.U9**
Aldous Huxley. Cloth Text. Brill Academic Publishers, Inc. Boston, MA. 1972. 256p. ISBN:0-236-17682-X, ISBN13: 978-0-236-17682-3. Dewey:823/.9/12. LCCN:73-162313.
Audience: **g,l,u,f.** B

Meckier, Jerome **PR6015.U9.Z76 1969**
Aldous Huxley; Satire and Structure. Trade Cloth. Barnes & Noble, Inc. New York, NY. 1969. 223p. ISBN:0-389-01031-6, ISBN13: 978-0-389-01031-9. Dewey:823/.9/12. LCCN:79-008451.
Audience: **g,l,u,f.** B

Meckier, Jerome (Editor) **PR6015.U9Z5956 1996**
Critical Essays on Aldous Huxley. Trade Cloth. Thomson Gale. Farmington Hills, MI. 1995. 192p. Critical Essays on British Literature Ser. ISBN:0-8161-8873-4, ISBN13: 978-0-8161-8873-4. Dewey:823/.912. LCCN:95-012209.
Audience: **g,l,u,f.**

Woodcock, George **PR6015.U9**
Dawn and the Darkest Hour: A Study of Aldous Huxley. Trade Cloth. Black Rose Books. Montreal, PQ. 2006. 295p. ISBN:1-55164-285-9, ISBN13: 978-1-55164-285-7. Dewey:823/.9/12.
Audience: **g,l,u,f.**

Wyatt, Donald **PR6015.U9**
Aldous Huxley. Trade Paper. Routledge. New York, NY. 1985. 320p. The Critical Heritage Ser. ISBN:0-7102-0591-0, ISBN13: 978-0-7102-0591-9. Dewey:823.912.
Audience: **g,l,u,f.**

Individual Authors and Works > 20th C. > I-J

Ishiguro, Kazuo **PR6015.I3**
An Artist of the Floating World. Trade Cloth. Peter Smith Publisher, Inc. Magnolia, MA. 2000. ISBN:0-8446-7123-1, ISBN13: 978-0-8446-7123-9. Dewey:823/.914.
Audience: **g,l,u,f.**

Ishiguro, Kazuo **PR6059.S5N48 2005**
Never Let Me Go. Trade Cloth. Alfred A. Knopf Inc. New York, NY. 2005. 304p. ISBN:1-4000-4339-5, ISBN13: 978-1-4000-4339-2. Dewey:823/.914. LCCN:2004-048966.
Audience: **g,l,u,f.**

Ishiguro, Kazuo **PR6059.S5R46**
The Remains of the Day. Trade Paper. Knopf Publishing Group. New York, NY. 1993. ISBN:0-394-25134-2, ISBN13: 978-0-394-25134-9. Dewey:823.
Audience: **g,l,u,f.** *Choice, 1990.*

Ishiguro, Kazuo **PR6059.S5W48**
When We Were Orphans. Trade Paper. Random House of Canada, Ltd. Mississauga, ON. 2001. 320p. ISBN:0-676-97306-X, ISBN13: 978-0-676-97306-8. Dewey:823.
Audience: **g,l,u,f.**

James, P. D. **PR6060**
Devices and Desires. Trade Paper. Knopf Publishing Group. New York, NY. 2004. 448p. ISBN:1-4000-7624-2, ISBN13: 978-1-4000-7624-6. Dewey:823.914.
Audience: **g,l,u,f.**

James, P. D. **PR6060.A467I5 2001**
Innocent Blood. Trade Paper. Simon & Schuster. New York, NY. 2001. 400p. ISBN:0-7432-1963-5, ISBN13: 978-0-7432-1963-1. Dewey:823/.914. LCCN:2001-034152.
Audience: **g,l,u,f.**

Jhabvala, Ruth Prawer **PR9499.3.J5E27 1998**
East into Upper East: Plain Tales from New York and New Delhi. Trade Cloth. Basic Books. New York, NY. 1998. 314p. ISBN:1-887178-50-3, ISBN13: 978-1-887178-50-1. Dewey:823. LCCN:98-034881.
Audience: **g,l,u,f.**

Jhabvala, Ruth Prawer **PR9499.3.J5H4 1999**
Heat and Dust. Trade Paper. Basic Books. New York, NY. 1999. 190p. ISBN:1-58243-015-2, ISBN13: 978-1-58243-015-7. Dewey:823.9/14. LCCN:99-020006.
Audience: **g,l,u,f.**

Jhabvala, Ruth Prawer **PR9499.3.J5M9 2004**
My Nine Lives: Chapters of a Possible Past. Trade Cloth. Shoemaker & Hoard. Emeryville, CA. 2004. 288p. ISBN:1-59376-028-0, ISBN13: 978-1-59376-028-1. Dewey:823/.914. LCCN:2004-302325.
Audience: **g,l,u,f.**

Jhabvala, Ruth Prawer **PR9499.3.J5T47 1999**
Three Continents. Trade Paper. Basic Books. New York, NY. 1999. 384p. ISBN:1-58243-032-2, ISBN13: 978-1-58243-032-4. Dewey:823. LCCN:99-016088.
Audience: **g,l,u,f.**

Johnson, Denis **PS3560.O3745H45 2002**
Shoppers: Two Plays by Denis Johnson. Trade Paper. HarperCollins Publishers. New York, NY. 2002. 224p. ISBN:0-06-093440-9, ISBN13: 978-0-06-093440-8. Dewey:813/.54. LCCN:2001-051933.
Audience: **g,l,u,f.**

Johnston, Jennifer **PR6060.O394.O4 1980**
The Old Jest. Trade Cloth. Doubleday Publishing. New York, NY. 1980. 203 p. ;p. ISBN:0-385-15447-X, ISBN13: 978-0-385-15447-5. Dewey:823/.914. LCCN:79-007518.
Audience: **g,l,u,f.**

Johnston, Jennifer **PR6060.O394.S5 1978**
Shadows on Our Skin. Trade Cloth. Doubleday Publishing. New York, NY. 1978. 198p. ISBN:0-385-13125-9, ISBN13: 978-0-385-13125-4. Dewey:823/.914. LCCN:77-072415.
Audience: **g,l,u,f.**

Individual Authors and Works > 20th C. > Isherwood, Christopher

Berg, James J. & Freeman, Chris (Editors) **PR6017.S5Z627 2001**
Conversations with Christopher Isherwood. Trade Cloth. University Press of Mississippi. Jackson, MS. 2001. 240p. Literary Conversations Ser. ISBN:1-57806-408-2, ISBN13: 978-1-57806-408-3. Dewey:823/.912 B. LCCN:2001-026735.
Audience: **g,l,u,f.**

Berg, James J. & Freeman, Chris (Editors) **PR6017.S5Z74 2000**
The Isherwood Century: Essays on the Life and Work of Christopher Isherwood. Armistead Maupin (Foreword by). Trade Cloth. University of Wisconsin Press. Chicago, IL. 1999. 296p. ISBN:0-299-16700-3, ISBN13: 978-0-299-16700-4. Dewey:823/.912 B. LCCN:99-006742.
Audience: **u,f.**

Isherwood, Christopher **PR6017.S5.A4**
All the Conspirators. Trade Paper. New Directions Publishing Corporation. New York, NY. 1979. 255p. ISBN:0-8112-0725-0, ISBN13: 978-0-8112-0725-6. Dewey:823.9/12. LCCN:58-012798.
Audience: **g,l,u,f.**

Isherwood, Christopher **PR6017**
The Berlin Stories. Trade Paper. New Directions Publishing Corporation. New York, NY. 1963. 207p. ISBN:0-8112-0070-1, ISBN13: 978-0-8112-0070-7. Dewey:823.912. LCCN:55-002508.
Audience: **g,l,u,f.**

Isherwood, Christopher **PR6017.S5Z498 2001**
Christopher and His Kind. Trade Paper. University of Minnesota Press. Minneapolis, MN. 2001. 352p. ISBN:0-8166-3863-2, ISBN13: 978-0-8166-3863-5. Dewey:823/.912 B. LCCN:2001-037031.
Audience: **u,f.**

Isherwood, Christopher **PR6072.A4**
Diaries, 1939-1960, Vol. 1. Trade Paper. HarperCollins Publishers. New York, NY. 1998. 1104p. ISBN:0-06-118018-1, ISBN13: 978-0-06-118018-7. Dewey:828/.91203 B.
Audience: **g,l,u,f.**

Isherwood, Christopher **PR6017.S5D6 1999**
Down There on a Visit. Trade Cloth. University of Minnesota Press. Minneapolis, MN. 1999. 318p. ISBN:0-8166-3367-3, ISBN13: 978-0-8166-3367-8. Dewey:823/.912. LCCN:99-011788.
Audience: **g,l,u,f.**

Isherwood, Christopher **PR6017.S5L5 2000**
Lions and Shadows: An Education in the Twenties. Trade Cloth. University of Minnesota Press. Minneapolis, MN. 2000. 312p. ISBN:0-8166-3604-4, ISBN13: 978-0-8166-3604-4. Dewey:823/.9/1. LCCN:99-059205.
Audience: **g,l,u,f.**

Isherwood, Christopher **PR6017.S5Z468 2000**
Lost Years: A Memoir, 1945-1951. Trade Cloth. HarperCollins Publishers. New York, NY. 2000. 432p. ISBN:0-06-118001-7, ISBN13: 978-0-06-118001-9. Dewey:823.9/12. LCCN:00-712869.
Audience: **g,l,u,f.**

Isherwood, Christopher **PR6017.S5M39 1999**
A Meeting by the River. Trade Paper. University of Minnesota Press. Minneapolis, MN. 1999. 160p. ISBN:0-8166-3368-1, ISBN13: 978-0-8166-3368-5. Dewey:823/.912. LCCN:99-028809.
Audience: **g,l,u,f.** B

Isherwood, Christopher **PR6017.S5M4 1999**
The Memorial: Portrait of a Family. Trade Paper. University of Minnesota Press. Minneapolis, MN. 1999. 296p. ISBN:0-8166-3369-X, ISBN13: 978-0-8166-3369-2. Dewey:823/.912. LCCN:98-054201.
Audience: **g,l,u,f.** B

Isherwood, Christopher **PR6017.S5P73 2000**
Prater Violet. Trade Paper. University of Minnesota Press. Minneapolis, MN. 2001. 144p. ISBN:0-8166-3861-6, ISBN13: 978-0-8166-3861-1. Dewey:823/.912. LCCN:00-054388.
Audience: **g,l,u,f.**

Isherwood, Christopher **PR6017.S5S5 2001**
A Single Man. Trade Cloth. University of Minnesota Press. Minneapolis, MN. 2001. 192p. ISBN:0-8166-3862-4, ISBN13: 978-0-8166-3862-8. Dewey:823/.912. LCCN:00-054389.
Audience: **g,l,u,f.**

Isherwood, Christopher **PR6013.R735**
Exhumations. Trade Paper. Random House. London, 1997. 254p. ISBN:0-413-56120-8, ISBN13: 978-0-413-56120-6. Dewey:828/.91208.
Audience: **g,l,u,f.**

Isherwood, Christopher **PR6017.S5W67 1999**
The World in the Evening. Trade Paper. University of Minnesota Press. Minneapolis, MN. 1999. 312p. ISBN:0-8166-3370-3, ISBN13: 978-0-8166-3370-8. Dewey:823/.912. LCCN:99-030769.
Audience: **g,l,u,f.**

Isherwood, Christopher **PR6017.S5Z464 1997**
Diaries, 1939-1960, Vol. 1. Katherine Bucknell (Editor, Introduction by). Trade Cloth. HarperCollins Publishers. New York, NY. 1997. 1104p. ISBN:0-06-118000-9, ISBN13: 978-0-06-118000-2. Dewey:828/.91203 B. LCCN:97-005501.
Audience: **g,l,u,f.**

Izzo, David Garrett **PR6017.S5Z745 2001**
Christopher Isherwood: His Era, His Gang, and the Legacy of the Truly Strong Man. Trade Cloth. University of South Carolina Press. Columbia, SC. 2001. 256p. ISBN:1-57003-403-6, ISBN13: 978-1-57003-403-9. Dewey:823/.912 B. LCCN:2001-000749.
Audience: **l,u,f.** *Choice, 2002.*

Izzo, David Garrett **PR6017.S5**
Christopher Isherwood Encyclopedia. Cloth Text. McFarland & Company, Incorporated Publishers. Jefferson, NC. 2005. 198p. ISBN:0-7864-1519-3, ISBN13: 978-0-7864-1519-9. Dewey:823/.912 B. LCCN:2004-025791.
Audience: **g,l,u,f.**

Page, Norman **PR6001.U4Z765 1997**
Auden and Isherwood: The Berlin Years. Cloth over Boards. Palgrave Macmillan. New York, NY. 1998. 220p. ISBN:0-312-21173-2, ISBN13: 978-0-312-21173-8. Dewey:820.9/00912. LCCN:97-035010.
Audience: **g,l,u,f.** *Choice, 1999.*

Parker, Peter **PR6017.S5Z79 2004**
Isherwood: A Life Revealed. Trade Cloth. Random House Adult Trade Publishing Group. New York, NY. 2004. 832p. ISBN:1-4000-6249-7, ISBN13: 978-1-4000-6249-2. Dewey:823/.912 B. LCCN:2004-053185.
Audience: **g,l,u,f.**

Wilde **PR6017.S5 Z9**
Christopher Isherwood. Trade Cloth. Thomson Gale. Farmington Hills, MI. 1971. ISBN:0-8057-0400-0, ISBN13: 978-0-8057-0400-6. Dewey:823/.9/12.
Audience: **l,u,f.**

Individual Authors and Works > 20th C. > Joyce, James

Adams, Robert Martin **PR6019.O9U515**
Surface and Symbol: The Consistancy of James Joyce's Ulysses. Paper Text. Textbook Publishers. Temecula, CA. 2003. 290p. ISBN:0-7581-7139-0, ISBN13: 978-0-7581-7139-9. Dewey:823.912.
Audience: **g.**

Atherton, James S. **PR6019.O9**
The Books at the Wake: A Study of Literary Allusions in James Joyce's "Finnegans Wake". Trade Cloth. Paul P. Appel Publisher. Scarsdale, NY. 314p. ISBN:0-911858-26-1, ISBN13: 978-0-911858-26-6. Dewey:823/.9/12. LCCN:74-005407.
Audience: **u,f.**

Attridge, Derek (Editor) **PR6019.O9.Z52637**
The Cambridge Companion to James Joyce. Ed. 2. Cloth Text. Cambridge University Press. New York, NY. 2004. 312p. Cambridge Companions to Literature Ser. ISBN:0-521-83710-3, ISBN13: 978-0-521-83710-1. Dewey:823/.912. LCCN:2003-062727.
Audience: **g.** *Choice, 1990.*

Attridge, Derek (Editor, Translator) **PR6019.O9U6583 2004**
James Joyce's Ulysses: A Casebook. Trade Cloth. Oxford University Press, Inc. New York, NY. 2004. 288p. Casebooks in Criticism Ser. ISBN:0-19-515830-X, ISBN13: 978-0-19-515830-4. Dewey:823/.912. LCCN:2003-007745.
Audience: **g.**

Beja, Morris & Norris, David (Editors) **PR6019.O9Z6343 1996**
Joyce in the Hibernian Metropolis: Essays. Cloth Text. Ohio State University Press. Columbus, OH. 1996. 312p. ISBN:0-8142-0685-9, ISBN13: 978-0-8142-0685-0. Dewey:823/.912. LCCN:95-050446.
Audience: **u,f.**

Benstock, Bernard (Editor) **PR6019.O9Z5276 1985**
Critical Essays on James Joyce. Trade Cloth. Thomson Gale. Farmington Hills, MI. 1985. 248p. Critical Essays on American Literature Ser. ISBN:0-8161-8751-7, ISBN13: 978-0-8161-8751-5. Dewey:823/.912. LCCN:84-012987.
Audience: **g.**

Benstock, Bernard **PR6019.O9U636 1989**
Critical Essays on James Joyce's "Ulysses". Trade Cloth. Thomson Gale. Farmington Hills, MI. 1989. 344p. Critical Essays on British Literature Ser. ISBN:0-8161-8766-5, ISBN13: 978-0-8161-8766-9. Dewey:823/.912. LCCN:88-026866.
Audience: **g.** *Choice, 1989.*

Benstock, Shari & Benstock, Bernard **PR6019.O9Z/**
Who's He When He's at Home: A James Joyce Directory. Trade Cloth. University of Illinois Press. Champaign, IL. 1980. 252p. ISBN:0-252-00756-5, ISBN13: 978-0-252-00756-9. Dewey:823/.912. LCCN:79-017947.
Audience: **g.**

Blamires, Harry **PR6019.O9U626 1996**
The New Bloomsday Book: A Guide Through Ulysses. Ed. 3. Paper over Boards. Routledge. New York, NY. 1996. 272p. ISBN:0-415-13857-4, ISBN13: 978-0-415-13857-4. Dewey:823.9/12. LCCN:95-044440.
Audience: **g.**

Bowen, Zack R. **PR6019.O9 Z52717 1984**
A Companion to Joyce Studies. Carens, James F.. Greenwood Press. 1984. ISBN:0-313-22832-9, ISBN13: 978-0-313-22832-2.
Audience: **g.**

Brandabur, Edward **PR6019.O9**
A Scrupulous Meanness: A Study of Joyce's Early Work. Trade Paper. Books on Demand. Ann Arbor, MI. 197p. ISBN:0-608-13883-5, ISBN13: 978-0-608-13883-1. Dewey:823/.9/12. LCCN:71-131057.
Audience: **g.**

Brown, Homer O. **PR6019.O9Z52634**
James Joyce's Early Fiction: The Biography of a Form. Trade Cloth. Press of Case Western Reserve University. Cleveland, OH. 1973. xii, 144p. ISBN:0-8295-0243-2, ISBN13: 978-0-8295-0243-5. Dewey:823/.9/12. LCCN:72-086350.
Audience: **g.**

Brunsdale, Mitzi M. **PR6019.O9.Z526355**
James Joyce: A Study of the Short Fiction. Trade Cloth. Macmillan Publishing Company, Inc. Old Tappan, NJ. 1993. 288p. Twayne's Studies in Short Fiction ISBN:0-8057-0854-5, ISBN13: 978-0-8057-0854-7. Dewey:823/.912. LCCN:92-039802.
Audience: **g.** *Choice, 1993.*

Burgess, Anthony **PR6019.O9 Z526364**
Joysprick: An Introduction to the Language of James Joyce. Trade Cloth. Blackwell Publishing, Inc. Malden, MA. 187p. ISBN:0-233-96264-6, ISBN13: 978-0-233-96264-1. Dewey:823/.9/12. LCCN:73-169764.
Audience: **g.**

Burgess, Anthony **PR6019.O9;**
Re Joyce. Trade Cloth. W. W. Norton & Company, Inc. New York, NY. 2000. 272p. ISBN:0-393-00445-7, ISBN13: 978-0-393-00445-8. Dewey:823.912. LCCN:65-018779.
Audience: **g,l,u,f.**

Carens, James F. & Brady, Philip (Editors) **PR6019.O9P64413 1998**
Critical Essays on Joyce's Portrait of the Artist As a Young Man. Trade Cloth. Thomson Gale. Farmington Hills, MI. 1998. 326p. ISBN:0-7838-0035-5, ISBN13: 978-0-7838-0035-6. Dewey:823/.912. LCCN:98-018912.
Audience: **g.**

Chace, William M. (Editor) **PR6019.O9Z/**
Joyce: A Collection of Critical Essays. Trade Cloth. Prentice-Hall. Upper Saddle, NJ. 1973. 192p. ISBN:0-13-511303-2, ISBN13: 978-0-13-511303-5. Dewey:823/.912. LCCN:73-018496.
Audience: **g.**

Connolly, Thomas E. (Editor) **PR6019.O9 P644**
Joyce's "Portrait": Criticisms and Critiques. Paper Text. Irvington Publishers. New York, NY. 1962. Goldentree Books in English Literature Ser. ISBN:0-89197-253-6, ISBN13: 978-0-89197-253-2. Dewey:823.912. LCCN:62-014861.
Audience: **g.**

Dalton, Jack P. (Author, Editor) **PR6019.O9F57**
Twelve and a Tilly: Essays on the Occasion of the 25th Anniversary of Finnegans Wake. Clive Hart (Editor). Trade Paper. Books on Demand. Ann Arbor, MI. 144p. ISBN:0-598-22614-1, ISBN13: 978-0-598-22614-3. Dewey:823.912. LCCN:65-027700.
Audience: **u,f.**

Ellmann, Richard **PR6019.O9Z/**
James Joyce. Ed. 2. Cloth Text. Oxford University Press, Inc. New York, NY. 1982. 906p. ISBN:0-19-503103-2, ISBN13: 978-0-19-503103-4. Dewey:823.9/12. LCCN:81-022455.
Audience: **g.** B

Ellmann, Richard **PR6019.O9**
Ulysses on the Liffey. Trade Paper. Oxford University Press, Inc. New York, NY. 1986. 256p. ISBN:0-19-501663-7, ISBN13: 978-0-19-501663-5. Dewey:823/.912.
Audience: **g.** B

Fargnoli, A. Nicholas & Gillespie, Michael P. **PR6019.O9Z533376**
James Joyce A to Z: The Essential Reference to His Life and Writings. Trade Cloth. Facts On File, Inc. New York, NY. 1995. 320p. Literary A to Z Ser. ISBN:0-8160-2904-0, ISBN13: 978-0-8160-2904-4. Dewey:823/.912. LCCN:94-034660.
Audience: **g.** *Choice, 1996.*

Gifford, Don **PR6019.O9D8**
Joyce Annotated: Notes for Dubliners and a Portrait of the Artist As a Young Man. Ed. 2. Trade Cloth. University of California Press. Berkeley, CA. 1981. 310p. ISBN:0-520-04189-5, ISBN13: 978-0-520-04189-9. Dewey:823/.912. LCCN:80-029448.
Audience: **g.** B

Gifford, Don **PR6019.O9**
Joyce Annotated: Notes for Dubliners and a Portrait of the Artist As a Young Man. Ed. 2. Trade Cloth. University of California Press. Berkeley, CA. 1982. 310p. ISBN:0-520-04610-2, ISBN13: 978-0-520-04610-8. Dewey:823/.912. LCCN:80-029448.
Audience: **g.** B

Gilbert, Stuart **PR6019.O9**
James Joyce's Ulysses. Mass Market. Knopf Publishing Group. New York, NY. 1955. 448p. James Joyce Ser., Vol. 13 ISBN:0-394-70013-9, ISBN13: 978-0-394-70013-7. Dewey:823.9/12.
Audience: **g.**

Gillespie, Michael Patrick & Gillespie, Paula **PR6019.O9U6522 2000**
Recent Criticism of James Joyce's Ulysses: An Analytical Review. Trade Cloth. Camden House. Elizabethtown, NY. 2002. 154p. Studies in English and American Literature, Linguistics and Culture ISBN:1-57113-217-1, ISBN13: 978-1-57113-217-8. Dewey:823/.912. LCCN:00-057213.
Audience: **g.** *Choice, 2001.*

Glasheen, Adaline **PR6019.O9F59**
A Second Census of Finnegans Wake: An Index of the Characters and Their Roles. Rev. and Expanded from the First Census. Trade Paper. Books on Demand. Ann Arbor, MI. 351p. ISBN:0-598-22622-2, ISBN13: 978-0-598-22622-8. Dewey:823.912. LCCN:63-007230.
Audience: **u,f.**

Gorman, Herbert **PR6019.O9 Z55 1974B**
James Joyce. Library Binding. M. S. G. Haskell House. Brooklyn, NY. 1974. Studies in Joyce, No. 96 ISBN:0-8383-2015-5, ISBN13: 978-0-8383-2015-0. Dewey:823/.9/12. LCCN:74-030368.
Audience: **g.**

Groden, Michael **PR6019.09U65**
Ulysses in Progress. Trade Paper. Books on Demand. Ann Arbor, MI. 251p. ISBN:0-8357-2787-4, ISBN13: 978-0-8357-2787-7. Dewey:823/.912. LCCN:77-001217.
Audience: **g.** B

Gunn, Ian & Hart, Clive **PR6019.09**
James Joyce's Dublin: A Topographical Guide to the Dublin of Ulysses. Trade Cloth. Thames & Hudson. New York, NY. 2004. 160p. ISBN:0-500-51159-4, ISBN13: 978-0-500-51159-6. Dewey:823/.912. LCCN:2003-096972.
Audience: **g.**

Hart, Clive **PR6019.O9 F592**
A Concordance to Finnegans Wake (1963). Trade Cloth. Paul P. Appel Publisher. Scarsdale, NY. 1963. 316p. ISBN:0-685-00472-4, ISBN13: 978-0-685-00472-2. Dewey:823.91.
Audience: **u,f.**

Hart, Clive & Hayman, David (Editors) **PR6019.O9U6**
James Joyce's Ulysses: Critical Essays. Trade Cloth. University of California Press. Berkeley, CA. 1974. xiv,433p. ISBN:0-520-02444-3, ISBN13: 978-0-520-02444-1. Dewey:823.9/12. LCCN:73-076108.
Audience: **g.** B

Hayman, David **PR6019.O9U6**
Ulysses: The Mechanics of Meaning. Ed. 2. University of Wisconsin Press. 1982. ISBN:0-299-09024-8, ISBN13: 978-0-299-09024-1.
Audience: **g.**

Healey, George H. (Editor) **PR6019.O9Z64**
Complete Dublin Diary of Stanislaus Joyce. Trade Paper. Books on Demand. Ann Arbor, MI. 205p. ISBN:0-8357-9076-2, ISBN13: 978-0-8357-9076-5. Dewey:828/.9/1203. LCCN:77-144033.
Audience: **g.**

Joyce, James **PR6019.O9.A19**
Collected Poems. Viking Press. 1957.
Audience: **g.**

Joyce, James **PZ3.J853FI8**
Shorter Finnegans Wake. Trade Cloth. Penguin Group (USA) Inc. New York, NY. 1967. ISBN:0-670-64270-3, ISBN13: 978-0-670-64270-0. Dewey:823.912.
Audience: **u,f.** B

Joyce, James **PR6019.O9 Z52 1975**
Selected Letters of James Joyce. Ellmann, Richard. Viking Press. 1975. ISBN:0-670-63190-6, ISBN13: 978-0-670-63190-2.
Audience: **g.**

Joyce, James **PR6019.O9.Z52**
Letters. Gilbert, Stuart. ; Ellmann, Richard.. Viking Press. 1966.
Audience: **g.**

Joyce, James **PR6019.O9 C5 1954**
Chamber Music. Tindall, William York. Columbia UP. 1954. Columbia Bicentennial Dditions and Studies
Audience: **g.**

Joyce, James **PR6019.O9**
A Portrait of the Artist As a Young Man: Text, Criticism, and Notes. Chester G. Anderson (Editor). Trade Paper. Penguin Group (USA) Inc. New York, NY. 1977. 576p. Critical Studies ISBN:0-14-015503-1, ISBN13: 978-0-14-015503-7. LCCN:67-030719.
Audience: **g.**

Joyce, James **PR6019.O9 E9 1973**
Exiles. Padraic Colum (Introduction by). Trade Paper. Penguin Group (USA) Inc. New York, NY. 1977. 192p. Plays Ser. ISBN:0-14-048126-5, ISBN13: 978-0-14-048126-6. Dewey:822/.912. LCCN:74-185801.
Audience: **g.**

Joyce, James **PR6019.O9**
Ulysses (Gabler Edition). Richard Ellmann (Introduction by). Trade Paper. Knopf Publishing Group. New York, NY. 1986. 680p. ISBN:0-394-74312-1, ISBN13: 978-0-394-74312-7. Dewey:823/.912. LCCN:85-028279.
Audience: **g.**

Joyce, James **PR6019.O9U4 1990**
Ulysses. Morris L. Ernst (Foreword by), John M. Woosley (Contribution by). Trade Paper. Knopf Publishing Group. New York, NY. 1990. 816p. ISBN:0 679-72276-9, ISBN13: 978-0-679-72276-2. Dewey:823/.912. LCCN:89-040555.
Audience: **g.** B

Joyce, James **PR6019.O9.P63 1993**
A Portrait of the Artist as a Young Man. Hans W. Gabler & Walter Hettche (Editors). Cloth Text. Garland Publishing, Inc. New York, NY. 1993. 366p. James Joyce Archive Ser. ISBN:0-8153-1278-4, ISBN13: 978-0-8153-1278-9. Dewey:823/.912. LCCN:93-019733.
Audience: **g.** *Choice, 1993.*

Joyce, James **PR6019.O9 D8 1993C**
Dubliners. John W. Jackson & Bernard MCGinley (Editors). Trade Cloth. St. Martin's Press. Gordonville, VA. 1993. ISBN:0-312-09790-5, ISBN13: 978-0-312-09790-5. Dewey:823.912. LCCN:93-017426.
Audience: **g.** *Choice, 1993.*

Joyce, James **PR6019.O9**
The Portable James Joyce. Harry T. Levin (Editor). Trade Paper. Penguin Group (USA) Inc. New York, NY. 1976. 768p. Portable Library, No. 30 ISBN:0-14-015030-7, ISBN13: 978-0-14-015030-8. Dewey:823/.9/1. LCCN:76-026850.
Audience: **g.**

Joyce, James **PR6019.O9A6 1989**
Critical Writings of James Joyce. Ellsworth Mason & Richard Ellmann (Editors), Guy Davenport (Foreword by). Trade Paper. Cornell University Press. Ithaca, NY. 1989. 288p. ISBN:0-8014-9587-3, ISBN13: 978-0-8014-9587-8. Dewey:824/.912. LCCN:88-043400.
Audience: **g.**

Joyce, James **PR6019.O9**
Ulysses: A Reader's Edition. Danis Rose (Editor). Trade Paper. Pan Macmillan. London, 1998. 826p. ISBN:0-330-35230-X, ISBN13: 978-0-330-35230-7. Dewey:823/.912.
Audience: **g.**

Joyce, James **PR6019.O9D8 1996**
Dubliners: Text and Criticism. Robert Scholes & A. Walton Litz (Editors). Trade Paper. Penguin Group (USA) Inc. New York, NY. 1996. 512p. The Viking Critical Library ISBN:0-14-024774-2, ISBN13: 978-0-14-024774-9. Dewey:823/.912. LCCN:96-002650.
Audience: **g.**

Joyce, James **PR6019.O9**
Stephen Hero. Theodore Spencer (Introduction by). Trade Paper. New Directions Publishing Corporation. New York, NY. 1963. 253p. ISBN:0-8112-0074-4, ISBN13: 978-0-8112-0074-5. Dewey:823.912. LCCN:63-014454.
Audience: **g.** B

Joyce, Stanislaus, et al. **PR6019.O9**
My Brother's Keeper: James Joyce's Early Years. Richard Ellmann & T. S. Eliot (Authors). Trade Paper. Da Capo Press, Inc. Cambridge, MA. 2003. 292p. ISBN:0-306-81210-X, ISBN13: 978-0-306-81210-1. Dewey:823.9/12.
Audience: **g.**

Kain, Richard Morgan **PR6019.O9.U67**
Fabulous voyager: James Joyce's Ulysses. University of Chicago Press. 1947.
Audience: **g.**

Kenner, Hugh **PR6019.O9Z67 1987**
Dublin's Joyce. Cloth Text. Columbia University Press. New York, NY. 1987. 384p. A Morningside Bk. ISBN:0-231-06632-5, ISBN13: 978-0-231-06632-7. Dewey:823/.912. LCCN:87-015863.
Audience: **g.** B

Kenner, Hugh **PR6019.O9.U672**
Joyce's Voices. University of California Press. 1978. ISBN:0-520-03206-3, ISBN13: 978-0-520-03206-4.
Audience: **g.**

Kenner, Hugh **PR6019.O9U6**
Ulysses. Ed. 2. Trade Paper. Johns Hopkins University Press. Baltimore, MD. 1979. 192p. ISBN:0-8018-3384-1, ISBN13: 978-0-8018-3384-7. Dewey:823/.912. LCCN:86-027773.
Audience: **g.** B

Levin, Harry **PR6019.O9**
James Joyce: A Critical Introduction. Trade Paper. New Directions Publishing Corporation. New York, NY. 1960. xiv, 256p. Paperbook Ser., Vol. 87 ISBN:0-8112-0089-2, ISBN13: 978-0-8112-0089-9. Dewey:823.91. LCCN:60-009222.
Audience: **g.** B

Litz, A. Walton **PR6019.O9U675**
The Art of James Joyce: Method and Design in Ulysses and Finnegans Wake. Paper Text. Textbook Publishers. Temecula, CA. 2003. 152p. ISBN:0-7581-7126-9, ISBN13: 978-0-7581-7126-9. Dewey:823.912.
Audience: **u,f.** B

Magalaner, Marvin **PR6019.O9Z7193**
A James Joyce Miscellany: Second Series. Paper Text. Textbook Publishers. Temecula, CA. 2003. 233p. ISBN:0-7581-3650-1, ISBN13: 978-0-7581-3650-3. Dewey:823.912.
Audience: **g.**

Magalaner, Marvin **PR6019.O9.Z7191**
A James Joyce Miscellany. James Joyce Society. 1957.
Audience: **g.**

Magalaner, Marvin **PR6019.O9.Z7193**
A James Joyce Miscellany. Third series. Southern Illinois UP. 1962.
Audience: **g.**

Magalaner, Marvin **PR6019.O9.Z725 1970**
Time of Apprenticeship: The Fiction of Young James Joyce. Trade Cloth. Ayer Company Publishers, Inc. Manchester, NH. 1977. 192p. Select Bibliographies Reprint Ser. ISBN:0-8369-5609-5, ISBN13: 978-0-8369-5609-2. Dewey:823/.9/12. LCCN:70-140366.
Audience: **g.**

Magalaner, Marvin **PR6019**
Time of Apprenticeship: The Fiction of Young James Joyce. Trade Paper. Books on Demand. Ann Arbor, MI. 194p. ISBN:0-598-55410-6, ISBN13: 978-0-598-55410-9. Dewey:823/.9/12. LCCN:59-006018.
Audience: **g.**

Magalaner, Marvin & Kain, Richard M. **PR6019.O9.Z72**
Joyce, the Man, the Work, the Reputation. New York UP. 1956.
Audience: **g.**

McCarthy, Jack **PR6019.O9U6834 1991**
Joyce's Dublin: A Walking Guide to Ulysses. Trade Cloth. St. Martin's Press. Gordonville, VA. 1991. ISBN:0-312-05885-3, ISBN13: 978-0-312-05885-2. Dewey:823/.912. LCCN:90-028408.
Audience: **g.**

McCarthy, P. **PR6019.O9.F5757 1992**
Critical Essays on Finnegans Wake. Trade Cloth. Macmillan Publishing Company, Inc. Old Tappan, NJ. 1992. 250p. Critical Essays on British Literature Ser. ISBN:0-8161-8870-X, ISBN13: 978-0-8161-8870-3. Dewey:821/.912. LCCN:92-004217.
Audience: **u,f.** *Choice, 1992.*

McHugh, Roland & Joyce, James **PR6019.O9F59357 2006**
Annotations to Finnegans Wake. Ed. 3. Trade Cloth. Johns Hopkins University Press. Baltimore, MD. 2006. 648p. ISBN:0-8018-8381-4, ISBN13: 978-0-8018-8381-1. Dewey:823/.912. LCCN:2005-024683.
Audience: **u,f.** B *Choice, 1992.*

Norris, Margot (Editor) **PR6019.O9U6375 1998**
Bedford Critical Companion to Joyce's Ulysses. Cloth over Boards. Palgrave Macmillan. New York, NY. 1998. 273p. ISBN:0-312-21067-1, ISBN13: 978-0-312-21067-0. Dewey:823/.912. LCCN:97-074966.
Audience: **g.** *Choice, 1998.*

Staley, Thomas F. (Author, Introduction by) **PR6019.O9U75**
Ulysses: Fifty Years. Trade Paper. Books on Demand. Ann Arbor, MI. 199p. ISBN:0-598-05383-2, ISBN13: 978-0-598-05383-1. Dewey:823/.912. LCCN:73-016538.
Audience: **g.** B

Steppe, Wolfhard & Gabler, Hans W. (Contribution by) **PR6019.O9 U725**
A Handlist to James Joyce's Ulysses: A Complete Alphabetical Index to the Critical Reading Text. Trade Paper. Garland Publishing, Inc. New York, NY. 1986. 310p. ISBN:0-8240-4749-4, ISBN13: 978-0-8240-4749-8. Dewey:823/.912.
Audience: **g.**

Sultan, Stanley **PR6019.O9**
The Argument of "Ulysses". Trade Cloth. Wesleyan University Press. Middletown, CT. 1987. 509p. ISBN:0-8195-5185-6, ISBN13: 978-0-8195-5185-6. Dewey:823/.912. LCCN:87-010653.
Audience: **g.**

Thornton, Weldon **PR6019.O9**
Allusions in Ulysses: An Annotated List. Trade Cloth. University of North Carolina Press. Chapel Hill, NC. 1982. 563p. ISBN:0-8078-4089-0, ISBN13: 978-0-8078-4089-4. Dewey:823/.9/12. LCCN:68-014359.
Audience: **g.** B

Tindall, William York **PR6019.O9Z833 1995**
A Reader's Guide to James Joyce. Trade Paper. Syracuse University Press. Syracuse, NY. 1995. 304p. Irish Studies ISBN:0-8156-0320-7, ISBN13: 978-0-8156-0320-7. Dewey:823/.9/12. LCCN:94-049335.
Audience: **g.** B

Individual Authors and Works > 20th C. > K-L

Keane, Molly **PR6021.E33**
Good Behaviour. Trade Paper. Little, Brown Book Group Ltd. London, 2006. 256p. ISBN:1-84408-324-1, ISBN13: 978-1-84408-324-4. Dewey:823.9/12.
Audience: **g,l,u,f.**

Kelman, James **PR6061.E518H69**
How Late It Was, How Late. Trade Paper, Perfect. W. W. Norton & Company, Inc. New York, NY. 2005. 384p. ISBN:0-393-32799-X, ISBN13: 978-0-393-32799-1. Dewey:823.914.
Audience: **g,l,u,f.**

Kneale, Matthew **PR6015.I3**
English Passengers: A Novel. Trade Paper. Doubleday Publishing. New York, NY. 2001. 464p. ISBN:0-385-49744-X, ISBN13: 978-0-385-49744-2. Dewey:823.9/14. LCCN:99-016402.
Audience: **g,l,u,f.**

Kureishi, Hanif **PR6061.U68B8 1991**
The Buddha of Suburbia. Trade Paper. Penguin Group (USA) Inc. New York, NY. 1991. 288p. ISBN:0-14-013168-X, ISBN13: 978-0-14-013168-0. Dewey:823.914. LCCN:90-021001.
Audience: **g,l,u,f.**

Kureishi, Hanif **PR6061.U68A6 2002**
My Beautiful Laundrette, Sammy and Rosie Get Laid: Collected Screenplays. Trade Paper. Faber & Faber, Inc. New York, NY. 2002. 400p. ISBN:0-571-21433-9, ISBN13: 978-0-571-21433-4. Dewey:791.43/75. LCCN:2003-427535.
Audience: **g,l,u,f.**

Kureishi, Hanif **PN1997**
My Son the Fanatic. Trade Cloth. Faber & Faber, Inc. New York, NY. 1999. 112p. ISBN:0-571-19234-3, ISBN13: 978-0-571-19234-2. Dewey:791.4/372.
Audience: **g,l,u,f.**

Lanchester, John **PR6015.I3**
The Debt to Pleasure. Trade Paper. St. Martin's Press. Gordonville, VA. 1998. 272p. ISBN:0-7710-4587-5, ISBN13: 978-0-7710-4587-5. Dewey:823/.914.
Audience: **g,l,u,f.**

Le Carré, John **PR6015.I3**
The Honourable Schoolboy: A Novel. Trade Paper. Simon & Schuster. New York, NY. 2002. 608p. ISBN:0-7434-5791-9, ISBN13: 978-0-7434-5791-0. Dewey:823.9/14.
Audience: **g,l,u,f.**

Le Carré, John **PR6015.I3**
Smiley's People: A Novel. Trade Paper. Simon & Schuster. New York, NY. 2002. 416p. ISBN:0-7434-5580-0, ISBN13: 978-0-7434-5580-0. Dewey:823.9/14.
Audience: **g,l,u,f.**

Le Carré, John **PR6015.I3**
The Spy Who Came in from the Cold. Trade Paper. Simon & Schuster. New York, NY. 2001. 224p. ISBN:0-7434-4253-9, ISBN13: 978-0-7434-4253-4. Dewey:823.9/14.
Audience: **g,l,u,f.**

Le Carré, John **PR6015.I3**
Tinker, Tailor, Soldier, Spy. Trade Paper. Simon & Schuster. New York, NY. 2002. 400p. ISBN:0-7434-5790-0, ISBN13: 978-0-7434-5790-3. Dewey:823.9/14.
Audience: **g,l,u,f.**

Le Fanu, J. Sheridan **PR5684**
The House by the Church-Yard. Elizabeth Bowen (Introduction by). Library Binding. Buccaneer Books, Inc. Cutchogue, NY. 1992. 500p. ISBN:0-89968-312-6, ISBN13: 978-0-89968-312-6. Dewey:823.8.
Audience: **g,l,u,f.**

Lebrecht, Norman **PR9619.3.L376**
The Song of Names. Trade Cloth. Knopf Publishing Group. New York, NY. Reading Group Guides ISBN:1-4000-3559-7, ISBN13: 978-1-4000-3559-5. Dewey:823/.92.
Audience: **g,l,u,f.**

Llewellyn, Richard **PR6023.L47H6 1997**
How Green Was My Valley. Trade Paper. Simon & Schuster. New York, NY. 1997. 512p. ISBN:0-684-82555-4, ISBN13: 978-0-684-82555-7. Dewey:FIC. LCCN:97-010174.
Audience: **g,l,u,f.**

Lodge, David **PR6015.I3**
Changing Places. Trade Paper. Penguin Group (USA) Inc. New York, NY. 1979. 256p. ISBN:0-14-017098-7, ISBN13: 978-0-14-017098-6. Dewey:823.9/14.
Audience: **g,l,u,f.**

Individual Authors and Works > 20th C. > Larkin, Philip

Bloomfield, B. C. **Z8483.98.B46 2001**
Philip Larkin: A Bibliography, 1933-1994. Library Binding. Oak Knoll Press. New Castle, DE. 2002. 224p. ISBN:1-58456-062-2, ISBN13: 978-1-58456-062-3. Dewey:016.821/914. LCCN:2001-047450.
Audience: **u,f.** *Choice, 2003.*

Cooper, Stephen **PR6023.A66**
Philip Larkin. Trade Cloth. Sussex Academic Press. Eastbourne, 2004. 208p. ISBN:1-84519-000-9, ISBN13: 978-1-84519-000-2. Dewey:821/.914. LCCN:2004-015674.
Audience: **u,f.** *Choice, 2005.*

Larkin, Philip **PR6023.A66J54 1984**
Jill. Trade Paper. Overlook Press, The. New York, NY. 1984. 256p. Tusk Bks. ISBN:0-87951-961-4, ISBN13: 978-0-87951-961-2. LCCN:75-027292.
Audience: **g,l,u,f.**

Larkin, Philip **PR6023.A66R4 1999**
Required Writing: Miscellaneous Pieces, 1955-1982. Trade Paper. University of Michigan Press. Chicago, IL. 1999. 328p. Poets on Poetry Ser. ISBN:0-472-08584-0, ISBN13: 978-0-472-08584-2. Dewey:821/.914. LCCN:98-053786.
Audience: **g,l,u,f.**

Larkin, Philip **PR6023.A66**
Selected Letters of Philip Larkin, 1940-1985. Trade Paper. Faber & Faber, Inc. New York, NY. 1999. 791p. ISBN:0-571-17048-X, ISBN13: 978-0-571-17048-7. Dewey:821.914.
Audience: **u,f.**

Larkin, Philip **PR6023.A66T76 2002**
Trouble at Willow Gables: And Other Fiction 1943-1953. Trade Cloth. Faber & Faber, Inc. New York, NY. 2002. 544p. ISBN:0-571-20347-7, ISBN13: 978-0-571-20347-5. Dewey:823/.914. LCCN:2002-483788.
Audience: **g,l,u,f.**

Larkin, Philip, et al. **ML3507.L42 2001**
Larkin's Jazz: Essays and Reviews, 1940-1984. Ed. 2. Richard Palmer & John White (Authors). Trade Paper. Continuum International Publishing Group, Ltd. London, 2001. 192p. ISBN:0-8264-5346-5, ISBN13: 978-0-8264-5346-4. Dewey:781.65/09. LCCN:00-047599.
Audience: **l,u,f.**

Larkin, Philip **PR6023.A66A17 2004**
Collected Poems. Anthony Thwaite (Editor). Trade Paper. Farrar, Straus & Giroux. New York, NY. 2004. 240p. ISBN:0-374-52920-5, ISBN13: 978-0-374-52920-8. Dewey:821/.914. LCCN:2003-060846.
Audience: **g,l,u,f.**

Individual Authors and Works > 20th C. > Lawrence, D. H.

Becket, Fiona **PR6023.A93Z56645**
Complete Critical Guide to D. H. Lawrence. Paper over Boards. Routledge. New York, NY. 2002. 208p. The Complete Critical Guides to English Literature Ser. ISBN:0-415-20251-5, ISBN13: 978-0-415-20251-0. Dewey:823/.912. LCCN:2001-048827.
Audience: **l,u.**

Black, Michael **PR6023.A93Z567 2001**
Lawrence's England: The Major Fiction 1913-20. Cloth over Boards. Palgrave Macmillan. New York, NY. 2002. 255p. ISBN:0-333-56626-2, ISBN13: 978-0-333-56626-8. Dewey:823/.912. LCCN:2001-036992.
Audience: **u,f.** *Choice, 2002.*

Bloom, Harold (Editor) **PR6023.A93Z62337**
D. H. Lawrence. Trade Cloth. Facts On File, Inc. New York, NY. 2001. 80p. Major Short Story Writers Ser. ISBN:0-7910-5947-2, ISBN13: 978-0-7910-5947-0. Dewey:823/.912. LCCN:2001-023094.
Audience: **l,u.**

Cushman, Keith & Ingersoll, Earl G. (Editors) **PR6023.A93Z623397**
D. H. Lawrence: New Worlds. Trade Paper. Fairleigh Dickinson University Press. Cranbury, NJ. 2003. 281p. ISBN:0-8386-3981-X, ISBN13: 978-0-8386-3981-8. Dewey:823/.912. LCCN:2002-154972.
Audience: **l,u,f.** *Choice, 2003.*

Ellis, David **PR6023.A93 Z62617 1**
The Cambridge Biography of D. H. Lawrence: Dying Game, 1922-1930. Cloth Text. Cambridge University Press. New York, NY. 1997. 816p. ISBN:0-521-25421-3, ISBN13: 978-0-521-25421-2. Dewey:823/.912 B. LCCN:96-052443.
Audience: **g,l,u,f.**

Ellis, David **PR6023.A93W6483 2005**
D. H. Lawrence's Women in Love: A Casebook. Trade Cloth. Oxford University Press, Inc. New York, NY. 2005. 304p. Casebooks in Criticism ISBN:0-19-517026-1, ISBN13: 978-0-19-517026-9. Dewey:823/.912. LCCN:2005-040652.
Audience: **l,u.**

Fernihough, Anne (Editor) **PR6023.A93 Z595 2001**
The Cambridge Companion to D. H. Lawrence. Cloth Text. Cambridge University Press. New York, NY. 2001. 312p. Companions to Literature Ser. ISBN:0-521-62339-1, ISBN13: 978-0-521-62339-1. Dewey:823/.912. LCCN:00-063001.
Audience: **l,u,f.** *Choice, 2001.*

Jackson, Dennis & Jackson, Fleda B. **PR6023.A93Z62325**
Critical Essays on D. H. Lawrence. Trade Cloth. Thomson Gale. Farmington Hills, MI. 1988. 240p. Critical Essays on British Literature Ser. ISBN:0-8161-8765-7, ISBN13: 978-0-8161-8765-2. Dewey:823/.912. LCCN:87-033111.
Audience: **l,u.** *Choice, 1988.*

Jackson, Rosie & Lawrence, Frieda **PR6029.R8**
Frieda Lawrence: Including Not I but the Wind by Frieda Lawrence. Ed. 2. Trade Paper. Rivers Oram Press/Pandora. London, 1995. 252p. ISBN:0-04-440939-7, ISBN13: 978-0-04-440939-7. Dewey:828.9/12/09.
Audience: **g,l,u,f.**

Kinkead-Weekes, Mark **PR6023.A93**
D. H. Lawrence: The Cambridge Biography of D. H. Lawrence. Cloth Text. Cambridge University Press. New York, NY. 1996. 989p. ISBN:0-521-25420-5, ISBN13: 978-0-521-25420-5. Dewey:823.9/12. LCCN:95-036102.
Audience: **g,l,u,f.** *Choice, 1996.*

Lawrence, D. H. **PR6019.O9**
Aaron's Rod. Library Binding. North Books. Wickford, RI. 2003. Twelve-Point Ser. ISBN:1-58287-258-9, ISBN13: 978-1-58287-258-2. Dewey:823.912.
Audience: **g,l,u,f.**

Lawrence, D. H. **PR6023.A93 L32 1973**
Apropos of Lady Chatterley's Lover. Library Binding. M. S. G. Haskell House. Brooklyn, NY. 1973. English Literature Ser., No. 33 ISBN:0-8383-1702-2, ISBN13: 978-0-8383-1702-0. Dewey:823/.9/12. LCCN:73-008959.
Audience: **g,l,u,f.**

Lawrence, D. H. **PR6019.O9**
Complete Short Stories of D. H. Lawrence, Vol. 2. Trade Paper. Penguin Group (USA) Inc. New York, NY. 1976. 596p. ISBN:0-14-004255-5, ISBN13: 978-0-14-004255-9. Dewey:823/.9/1.
Audience: **g,l,u,f.**

Lawrence, D. H. **PR6019.O9**
England, My England. Trade Cloth. Ayer Company Publishers, Inc. Manchester, NH. 1980. Short Story Index Reprint Ser. ISBN:0-8369-4153-5, ISBN13: 978-0-8369-4153-1. Dewey:823/.912. LCCN:72-003279.
Audience: **g,l,u,f.**

Lawrence, D. H. **PR6019.O9**
The Rainbow. Trade Cloth. Alfred A. Knopf Inc. New York, NY. 1993. 496p. Everyman's Library ISBN:0-679-42305-2, ISBN13: 978-0-679-42305-8. Dewey:823.9/12. LCCN:93-001860.
Audience: **g,l,u,f.**

Lawrence, D. H. **PR6019.O9**
The Virgin and the Gypsy. Trade Paper. Knopf Publishing Group. New York, NY. 1992. 160p. ISBN:0-679-74077-5, ISBN13: 978-0-679-74077-3. Dewey:823.9/12. LCCN:92-184943.
Audience: **g,l,u,f.**

Lawrence, D. H. **PR6019.O9**
The White Peacock. Paper Text. Classic Books. Murrieta, CA. 2001. Collected Works of D. H. Lawrence ISBN:0-7426-8147-5, ISBN13: 978-0-7426-8147-7. Dewey:823/.912.
Audience: **g,l,u,f.**

Lawrence, D. H. **PR6019.O9**
Women in Love. Trade Cloth. Knopf Publishing Group. New York, NY. 1992. ISBN:0-679-41326-X, ISBN13: 978-0-679-41326-4. Dewey:823/.912.
Audience: **g,l,u,f.**

Lawrence, D. H. **PS3509.L43**
The Works of D. H. Lawrence. Trade Paper. Wordsworth Editions, Ltd. Ware, 1998. 704p. Poetry Library ISBN:1-85326-417-2, ISBN13: 978-1-85326-417-7. Dewey:821.912.
Audience: **g,l,u,f.**

Lawrence, D. H. **PR6023.A93A6 2004**
D. H. Lawrence: Late Essays and Articles. James T. Boulton (Editor, Contribution by), M. H. Black, Lindeth Vasey & John Worthen (Contribution by). Trade Cloth. Cambridge University Press. New York, NY. 2004. 464p. The Cambridge Edition of the Works of D. H. Lawrence Ser. ISBN:0-521-58431-0, ISBN13: 978-0-521-58431-9. Dewey:824/.912. LCCN:2003-058437.
Audience: **g,l,u,f.** *Choice, 2004.*

Lawrence, D. H. **DG428.L37 1997**
D. H. Lawrence and Italy: Twilight in Italy, Sea and Sardinia, Etruscan Places. Anthony Burgess (Introduction by). Trade Paper. Penguin Group (USA) Inc. New York, NY. 1997. 512p. Twentieth Century Classics Ser. ISBN:0-14-118030-7, ISBN13: 978-0-14-118030-4. Dewey:914.5/0491. LCCN:97-178642.
Audience: **g,l,u,f.**

Lawrence, D. H. **PR6023.A93 P53 1987**
The Plumed Serpent. L. D. Clark (Editor), M. H. Black, James T. Boulton, Lindeth Vasey & John Worthen (Contribution by). Trade Paper. Cambridge University Press. New York, NY. 1987. 619p. Cambridge Edition of the Works of D. H. Lawrence ISBN:0-521-29422-3, ISBN13: 978-0-521-29422-5. Dewey:823/.912. LCCN:86-032674.
Audience: **g,l,u,f.**

Lawrence, D. H. **PR6023.A93L3 2003**
Lady Chatterley's Lover. Ed. 75. Geoff Dyer (Introduction by). Mass Market. Penguin Group (USA) Inc. New York, NY. 2003. 352p. ISBN:0-451-52888-3, ISBN13: 978-0-451-52888-9. Dewey:823/.912. LCCN:2002-045464.
Audience: **g,l,u,f.**

Lawrence, D. H. **PR6023.A93 B6 1990**
The Boy in the Bush. Paul Eggert & M. L. Skinner (Editors), M. H. Black, James T. Boulton, Lindeth Vasey & John Worthen (Contribution by). Trade Paper. Cambridge University Press. New York, NY. 2002. 562p. The Cambridge Edition of the Works of D. H. Lawrence Ser. ISBN:0-521-00714-3, ISBN13: 978-0-521-00714-6. Dewey:823/.912.
Audience: **g,l,u,f.**

Lawrence, D. H. **PR6019.O9**
Sons and Lovers. David Ellis (Introduction by). Trade Cloth. Random House, Inc. New York, NY. 1991. 432p. ISBN:0-679-40572-0, ISBN13: 978-0-679-40572-6. Dewey:823/.912.
Audience: **g,l,u,f.** *Choice, 1993.*

Lawrence, D. H. **PR6023.A93A6 1998**
Selected Critical Writings. Michael Herbert (Editor). Trade Paper. Oxford University Press, Inc. New York, NY. 2004. 396p. Oxford World's Classics Ser. ISBN:0-19-282364-7, ISBN13: 978-0-19-282364-9. Dewey:809. LCCN:98-003286.
Audience: **g,l,u,f.**

Lawrence, D. H. **BS2825.2**
Apocalypse and the Writings on Revelation. Mara Kalnins (Editor), M. H. Black, James T. Boulton, Lindeth Vasey & John Worthen (Contribution by). Trade Paper. Cambridge University Press. New York, NY. 2002. 263p. The Cambridge Edition of the Works of D. H. Lawrence Ser. ISBN:0-521-00706-2, ISBN13: 978-0-521-00706-1. Dewey:228/.06.
Audience: **u,f.** B

Lawrence, D. H. **PR6023.A93 L2 1999**
The First and Second Lady Chatterley Novels. Dieter Mehl & Christa Jansohn (Editors), M. H. Black, James T. Boulton, Lindeth Vasey & John Worthen (Contribution by). Trade Cloth. Cambridge University Press. New York, NY. 1999. 730p. The Works of D. H. Lawrence ISBN:0-521-47116-8, ISBN13: 978-0-521-47116-9. Dewey:823/.912. LCCN:98-030352.
Audience: **g,l,u,f.**

Lawrence, D. H. **PR6023.A93A6 1994**
The Fox, the Captain's Doll, the Ladybird. Dieter Miehl (Editor), David Ellis (Introduction by, Notes by). Trade Paper. Penguin Group (USA) Inc. New York, NY. 1995. 288p. Twentieth Century Classics Ser. ISBN:0-14-018779-0, ISBN13: 978-0-14-018779-3. Dewey:823/.914. LCCN:95-113748.
Audience: **g,l,u,f.**

Lawrence, D. H. **PR6023.A93A17 1993**
Complete Poems. F. Warren Roberts (Editor), Vivian De Sola Pinto (Compiled by, Introduction by, Notes by), F. Warren Roberts (Introduction by, Notes by). Trade Paper. Penguin Group (USA) Inc. New York, NY. 1994. 1088p. Twentieth Century Classics Ser. ISBN:0-14-018657-3, ISBN13: 978-0-14-018657-4. Dewey:821.912.
Audience: **g,l,u,f.**

Lawrence, D. H. **PR6023.A93L62 2003**
The Lost Girl. Lee Siegel (Introduction by). Book, Other. Random House Adult Trade Publishing Group. New York, NY. 2003. 400p. The Modern Library Classics ISBN:0-8129-6997-9, ISBN13: 978-0-8129-6997-9. Dewey:823/.912. LCCN:2003-053972.
Audience: **g,l,u,f.**

Lawrence, D. H. **PR6023.A93 K35 1994**
Kangaroo. Bruce Steele (Editor), M. H. Black, James T. Boulton, Lindeth Vasey & John Worthen (Contribution by). Trade Paper. Cambridge University Press. New York, NY. 2002. 549p. The Cambridge Edition of the Works of D. H. Lawrence Ser. ISBN:0-521-00711-9, ISBN13: 978-0-521-00711-5. Dewey:823.9/12.
Audience: **g,l,u,f.**

Lawrence, D. H. **BF173.L28 2003**
Psychoanalysis and the Unconscious and Fantasia of the Unconscious. Bruce Steele (Editor), M. H. Black, James T. Boulton, Lindeth Vasey & John Worthen (Contribution by). Trade Cloth. Cambridge University Press. New York, NY. 2004. 354p. The Cambridge Edition of the Works of D. H. Lawrence Ser. ISBN:0-521-32791-1, ISBN13: 978-0-521-32791-6. Dewey:150.19/5. LCCN:2003-063226.
Audience: **u,f.**

Lawrence, D. H. **PR6019.O9**
Portable D. H. Lawrence. Diana Trilling (Editor). Trade Paper. Penguin Group (USA) Inc. New York, NY. 1977. 704p. Portable Library, No. 28 ISBN:0-14-015028-5, ISBN13: 978-0-14-015028-5. Dewey:823/.9/1. LCCN:76-054705.
Audience: **g,l,u,f.** B

Marsh, Nicholas **PR6023.A93Z6777 2000**
D. H. Lawrence: The Novels. Cloth over Boards. Palgrave Macmillan. New York, NY. 2000. 272p. Analysing Texts Ser. ISBN:0-312-23284-5, ISBN13: 978-0-312-23284-9. Dewey:823/.912. LCCN:99-059195.
Audience: **l,u.** *Choice, 2000.*

Michelucci, Stefania **PR6023.A93Z68126**
Space and Place in the Works of D. H. Lawrence. Jill Franks (Translator). Paper Text. McFarland & Company, Incorporated Publishers. Jefferson, NC. 2002. 190p. ISBN:0-7864-1152-X, ISBN13: 978-0-7864-1152-8. Dewey:823/.912. LCCN:2001-056258.
Audience: **u,f.** *Choice, 2003, 2002.*

Sagar, Keith **PR6019.O9**
The Life of D. H. Lawrence: An Illustrated Biography. Ed. 2. Trade Cloth. Chaucer Press. London, 2004. 256p. ISBN:1-904449-18-2, ISBN13: 978-1-904449-18-8. Dewey:823.912.
Audience: **g,l,u,f.**

Salgado, Gamini **PR6019.O9**
A Preface to D. H. Lawrence. Trade Paper. Pearson Education. Boston, MA. 2000. 192p. Preface Ser ISBN:0-582-43766-0, ISBN13: 978-0-582-43766-1. Dewey:823.9/12. LCCN:00-061481.
Audience: **l,u.**

Squires, Michael & Talbot, Lynn K. **PR6023.A93Z92386**
Living at the Edge: A Biography of D. H. Lawrence and Frieda Von Richthofen. Trade Cloth. University of Wisconsin Press. Chicago, IL. 2002. 496p. ISBN:0-299-17750-5, ISBN13: 978-0-299-17750-8. Dewey:823/.912 B. LCCN:2001-005419.
Audience: **g,l,u,f.** *Choice, 2003.*

Worthen, James **PR6023.A93**
D. H. Lawrence: A Literary Life. Paper Text. Palgrave Macmillan. New York, NY. 1993. 222p. Literary Lives Ser. ISBN:0-312-08752-7, ISBN13: 978-0-312-08752-4. Dewey:823/.912.
Audience: **l,u.**

Worthen, John **PR6019.O9**
D. H. Lawrence: The Life of an Outsider. Trade Cloth. Basic Books. New York, NY. 2005. 560p. ISBN:1-58243-341-0, ISBN13: 978-1-58243-341-7. Dewey:823/.912.
Audience: **g,l,u,f.** *Choice, 2006.*

Worthen, John **PR6023.A93 Z957 1991**
D. H. Lawrence: The Early Years, 1885-1912, Vol. 1. Cloth Text. Cambridge University Press. New York, NY. 1991. 656p. ISBN:0-521-25419-1, ISBN13: 978-0-521-25419-9. Dewey:823/.912 B. LCCN:90-023423.
Audience: **g,l,u,f.** *Choice, 1992.*

Worthen, John & Harrison, Andrew **PR6023.A93S6675 2005**
D.H. Lawrence's Sons and Lovers: A Casebook. Trade Cloth. Oxford University Press, Inc. New York, NY. 2005. 320p. Casebooks in Criticism ISBN:0-19-517040-7, ISBN13: 978-0-19-517040-5. Dewey:823/.912. LCCN:2004-054702.
Audience: **l,u.**

Individual Authors and Works > 20th C. > Lessing, Doris

Greene, Gayle **PR6015.I3**
Doris Lessing: The Poetics of Change. Trade Paper. University of Michigan Press. Chicago, IL. 1997. 296p. ISBN:0-472-08433-X, ISBN13: 978-0-472-08433-3. Dewey:823/.914.
Audience: **g,l,u,f.** *Choice, 1995.*

Klein, Carole **PR6015.I3**
Doris Lessing: A Biography. Trade Cloth. Avalon Publishing Group. New York, NY. 2000. 296p. ISBN:0-7867-0806-9, ISBN13: 978-0-7867-0806-2. Dewey:823.9/14.
Audience: **g,l,u,f.** *Choice, 2001.*

Lessing, Doris **PR6015.I3**
Briefing for a Descent into Hell. Trade Paper. Knopf Publishing Group. New York, NY. 2003. 288p. ISBN:1-4000-7726-5, ISBN13: 978-1-4000-7726-7. Dewey:823.9/14.
Audience: **g,l,u,f.**

Lessing, Doris **PR6023.E833.D59 1983**
Documents Relating to the Sentimental Agents in the Volyen Empire. Trade Cloth. Alfred A. Knopf Inc. New York, NY. 1983. 178p. ISBN:0-394-52968-5, ISBN13: 978-0-394-52968-4. Dewey:823/.914. LCCN:82-048744.
Audience: **g,l,u,f.**

Lessing, Doris **PR6023.E833A6 1988**
The Doris Lessing Reader. Trade Cloth. Alfred A. Knopf Inc. New York, NY. 1989. 656p. ISBN:0-394-57307-2, ISBN13: 978-0-394-57307-6. Dewey:823/.914. LCCN:88-012689.
Audience: **g.**

Lessing, Doris **PR6023.E833F6 1995**
The Four-Gated City. Trade Paper. HarperCollins Publishers. New York, NY. 1995. 240p. Children of Violence Ser. ISBN:0-06-097667-5, ISBN13: 978-0-06-097667-5. Dewey:823/.914. LCCN:95-031487.
Audience: **g.**

Lessing, Doris **PR6023.E833G6 1999**
The Golden Notebook: Perennial Classics Edition. Trade Paper. HarperCollins Publishers. New York, NY. 1999. 672p. Perennial Classics Ser. ISBN:0-06-093140-X, ISBN13: 978-0-06-093140-7. LCCN:98-047608.
Audience: **g,l,u,f.**

Lessing, Doris **PR6023.E833G66 1986**
The Good Terrorist. Trade Paper. Knopf Publishing Group. New York, NY. 1986. 400p. ISBN:0-394-74629-5, ISBN13: 978-0-394-74629-6. Dewey:823/.914. LCCN:86-040142.
Audience: **g,l,u,f.**

Lessing, Doris **PR6023.E833G69 2004**
The Grandmothers: Four Short Novels. Trade Cloth. HarperCollins Publishers. New York, NY. 2004. 320p. ISBN:0-06-053010-3, ISBN13: 978-0-06-053010-5. Dewey:823/.914. LCCN:2003-056990.
Audience: **g.**

Lessing, Doris **PR6023.E833G7 2000**
The Grass Is Singing: A Novel. Trade Paper. HarperCollins Publishers. New York, NY. 2000. 256p. Perennial Classics Ser. ISBN:0-06-095346-2, ISBN13: 978-0-06-095346-1. Dewey:823/.914. LCCN:99-035316.
Audience: **g.**

Lessing, Doris **PR6023.E833L36 1995**
Landlocked. Trade Paper. HarperCollins Publishers. New York, NY. 1995. 352p. Children of Violence Ser., Vol. 4 ISBN:0-06-097665-9, ISBN13: 978-0-06-097665-1. Dewey:823.9/14. LCCN:95-031489.
Audience: **g.**

Lessing, Doris **PR6023.E833**
Learning How to Read. Trade Cloth. HarperCollins Publishers. New York, NY. 2004. 272p. ISBN:0-00-717985-5, ISBN13: 978-0-00-717985-5. Dewey:823/.914. LCCN:2005-360889.
Audience: **g.**

Lessing, Doris **PR6023.E833.M34 1982**
The Making of the Representative for Planet 8. Trade Cloth. Alfred A. Knopf Inc. New York, NY. 1982. 160p. ISBN:0-394-51906-X, ISBN13: 978-0-394-51906-7. Dewey:823.914. LCCN:80-029073.
Audience: **g.**

Lessing, Doris **PR6023.E833M357 1999**
Mara and Dann: An Adventure. Trade Cloth. HarperCollins Canada, Ltd. Scarborough, ON. 1998. 416p. ISBN:0-06-018294-6, ISBN13: 978-0-06-018294-6. Dewey:823/.914. LCCN:98-030782.
Audience: **g,l,u,f.**

Lessing, Doris **PR6023.E833.M3**
The Marriages Between Zones Three, Four and Five. Trade Cloth. Alfred A. Knopf Inc. New York, NY. 1980. 244p. ISBN:0-394-50914-5, ISBN13: 978-0-394-50914-3. Dewey:823.914. LCCN:79-016515.
Audience: **g,l,u,f.**

Lessing, Doris **PR6023.E833 M36 1981**
The Marriages Between Zones Three, Four and Five. Trade Paper. Knopf Publishing Group. New York, NY. 1981. 256p. ISBN:0-394-74978-2, ISBN13: 978-0-394-74978-5. Dewey:823.914. LCCN:81-040193.
Audience: **g,l,u,f.**

Lessing, Doris **PR6023.E833M38 1995**
Martha Quest. Trade Paper. HarperCollins Publishers. New York, NY. 1995. 240p. Children of Violence Ser., Vol. 1 ISBN:0-06-097666-7, ISBN13: 978-0-06-097666-8. Dewey:823/.914. LCCN:95-033106.
Audience: **g,l,u,f.**

Lessing, Doris **PR6023.E833P76 1995**
A Proper Marriage. Trade Paper. HarperCollins Publishers. New York, NY. 1995. 448p. Children of Violence Ser., Vol. 2 ISBN:0-06-097663-2, ISBN13: 978-0-06-097663-7. Dewey:823/.914. LCCN:95-033114.
Audience: **g,l,u,f.**

Lessing, Doris **PR6015.I3**
The Real Thing: Stories and Sketches. Trade Cloth. HarperCollins Publishers. New York, NY. 1992. 214p. ISBN:0-06-016853-6, ISBN13: 978-0-06-016853-7. Dewey:823/.914. LCCN:91-059932.
Audience: **g,l,u,f.**

Lessing, Doris **PR6023.E833R5 1995**
A Ripple from the Storm. Trade Paper. HarperCollins Publishers. New York, NY. 1995. 336p. Children of Violence Ser. ISBN:0-06-097664-0, ISBN13: 978-0-06-097664-4. Dewey:823/.914. LCCN:95-031488.
Audience: **g,l,u,f.**

Lessing, Doris **PR6015.I3**
The Sirian Experiments. Trade Paper. Knopf Publishing Group. New York, NY. 1982. 400p. ISBN:0-394-75195-7, ISBN13: 978-0-394-75195-5. Dewey:823.9/14. LCCN:81-052259.
Audience: **g,l,u,f.**

Lessing, Doris **PR6023.E833.Z52 1974**
A Small Personal Voice: Essays, Reviews, Interviews. Trade Cloth. Random House Children's Books. New York, NY. 1974. 192p. ISBN:0-394-49329-X, ISBN13: 978-0-394-49329-9. Dewey:823/.9/14. LCCN:74-007724.
Audience: **g,l,u,f.**

Lessing, Doris **PR6023.E833 S8**
Stories. Trade Cloth. Alfred A. Knopf Inc. New York, NY. 1978. 625 p. ;p. ISBN:0-394-50009-1, ISBN13: 978-0-394-50009-6. Dewey:823/.9/14. LCCN:77-020797.
Audience: **g.**

Lessing, Doris **PZ3.L56684 SU3**
The Summer Before the Dark. Trade Cloth. Random House Children's Books. New York, NY. 1973. ISBN:0-394-48428-2, ISBN13: 978-0-394-48428-0. Dewey:823.9/14. LCCN:72-011044.
Audience: **g.**

Lessing, Doris **PR6023.E833T56 2005**
Time Bites: Views and Reviews. Trade Cloth. HarperCollins Publishers. New York, NY. 2005. 384p. ISBN:0-06-083140-5, ISBN13: 978-0-06-083140-0. Dewey:809. LCCN:2005-046266.
Audience: **g.**

Lessing, Doris **PR6015.I3**
Under My Skin: My Autobiography, to 1949. Trade Paper. HarperCollins Publishers. New York, NY. 1995. 448p. ISBN:0-06-092664-3, ISBN13: 978-0-06-092664-9. Dewey:823.9/14. LCCN:94-020051.
Audience: **g.**

Lessing, Doris **PR6023.E833Z478 1997**
Walking in the Shade: 1949 to 1962. Trade Cloth. HarperCollins Publishers. New York, NY. 1997. 416p. ISBN:0-06-018295-4, ISBN13: 978-0-06-018295-3. Dewey:823.9/14. LCCN:97-009959.
Audience: **g.**

Rowe, Margaret M. **PR6023.E833Z85 1994**
Doris Lessing. Trade Cloth. Palgrave Macmillan. New York, NY. 1994. xii, 137p. Women Writers Ser., Vol. 1 ISBN:0-312-12192-X, ISBN13: 978-0-312-12192-1. Dewey:823/.914. LCCN:94-016871.
Audience: **g,l,u,f.** *Choice, 1995.*

Saxton, Ruth & Tobin, Jean (Editors) **PR888.W6W66 1994**
Woolf and Lessing: Breaking the Mold. Trade Cloth. Palgrave Macmillan. New York, NY. 1994. 224p. ISBN:0-312-12051-6, ISBN13: 978-0-312-12051-1. Dewey:823/.91099287. LCCN:94-015015.
Audience: **g,l,u,f.** *Choice, 1995.*

Sprague, Claire & Tiger, Virginia **PR6023.E833Z5895**
Critical Essays on Doris Lessing. Trade Cloth. Thomson Gale. Farmington Hills, MI. 1986. 225p. Critical Essays on British Literature Ser. ISBN:0-8161-8756-8, ISBN13: 978-0-8161-8756-0. Dewey:823/.914. LCCN:85-027097.
Audience: **g,l,u,f.** *Choice, 1986.*

Whittaker, Ruth **PR6023.E833Z/**
Doris Lessing. Trade Paper. Palgrave Macmillan. New York, NY. 1991. 154p. Modern Novelists Ser. ISBN:0-333-40753-9, ISBN13: 978-0-333-40753-0. Dewey:823/.914. LCCN:88-004416.
Audience: **g,l,u,f.** *Choice, 1989.*

Individual Authors and Works > 20th C. > Lewis, C. S.

Carpenter, Humphrey **PR6023.E926Z613 1978**
The Inklings: C. S. Lewis, J. R. R. Tolkien, Charles Williams, and Their Friends. Trade Cloth. Allen & Unwin Pty., Ltd. Crows Nest, NSW. 1978. 287p. ISBN:0-04-809011-5, ISBN13: 978-0-04-809011-9. Dewey:820/.9/00912. LCCN:78-040524.
Audience: **g,l,u.**

Green, Roger Lancelyn & Hooper, Walter **PR6023.E926Z6645**
C. S. Lewis: A Biography. Trade Paper. Harcourt Trade Publishers. New York, NY. 1994. 320p. Harvest Book Ser. ISBN:0-15-623205-7, ISBN13: 978-0-15-623205-0. Dewey:823/.912. LCCN:75-029425.
Audience: **g,l,u,f.**

Hannay, Margaret Patterson **PR6023.E926**
C. S. Lewis. Ungar. 1981. Modern literature series ISBN:0-8044-2341-5, ISBN13: 978-0-8044-2341-0.
Audience: **u,f.**

Lewis, C. S.
The Chronicles of Narnia: The Magician's Nephew; The Lion, the Witch and the Wardrobe; The Horse and His Boy; Prince Caspian; The Voyage of the Dawn Treader; The Silver Chair; The Last Battle. Trade Paper, Perfect. HarperCollins Publishers. New York, NY. 2005. The Chronicles of Narnia Ser. ISBN:0-06-084713-1, ISBN13: 978-0-06-084713-5.
Audience: **g,l,u,f.**

Lewis, C. S. **BJ1401.L4 2000**
The Great Divorce. Trade Paper. HarperCollins Publishers. New York, NY. 2001. 160p. ISBN:0-06-065295-0, ISBN13: 978-0-06-065295-1. Dewey:236/.2. LCCN:00-049859.
Audience: **g.** B

Lewis, C. S. **PR6019.O9**
Out of the Silent Planet. Trade Paper. Simon & Schuster. New York, NY. 2003. 160p. ISBN:0-7432-3490-1, ISBN13: 978-0-7432-3490-0. Dewey:823/.912.
Audience: **g,l,u,f.** B

Lewis, C. S. **PR6023.E926P47 1996**
Perelandra. Trade Cloth. Simon & Schuster. New York, NY. 1996. 192p. Scribner Classics Ser. ISBN:0-684-83365-4, ISBN13: 978-0-684-83365-1. Dewey:823.9/12. LCCN:96-020724.
Audience: **g,l,u,f.**

Lewis, C. S. **BV4935.L43A3 1995**
Surprised by Joy: The Shape of My Early Life. Cloth over Boards. Harcourt Trade Publishers. New York, NY. 1995. 240p. HBJ Book Ser. ISBN:0-15-100185-5, ISBN13: 978-0-15-100185-9. Dewey:[B]. LCCN:96-112306.
Audience: **g,l,u,f.** B

Lewis, C. S. **PR6023.E926T47 1996**
That Hideous Strength. Trade Cloth. Simon & Schuster. New York, NY. 1996. 384p. Scribner Classics Ser. ISBN:0-684-83367-0, ISBN13: 978-0-684-83367-5. Dewey:823/.912. LCCN:96-020722.
Audience: **g,l,u,f.**

Lewis, C. S. **PR6023.E926T54**
Till We Have Faces: A Myth Retold. Fritz Eichenberg (Illustrator). Trade Paper. Harcourt Trade Publishers. New York, NY. 1980. 324p. ISBN:0-15-690436-5, ISBN13: 978-0-15-690436-0. Dewey:823/.912. LCCN:79-024272.
Audience: **g,l,u,f.** B

Rumrich, John Peter **PR3562**
Matter of Glory : A New Preface to Paradise Lost. University of Pittsburgh Press. 1987. ISBN:0-8229-3564-3, ISBN13: 978-0-8229-3564-3.
Audience: **g,l,u,f.**

Sayer, George **PR6023.E926**
Jack: A Life of C. S. Lewis. Lyle W. Dorsett (Foreword by). Trade Paper, Perfect. Crossway Books. Wheaton, IL. 2005. 457p. ISBN:1-58134-739-1, ISBN13: 978-1-58134-739-5. Dewey:823/.912.
Audience: **g,l,u,f.**

Schakel, Peter J. (Editor) **PR6023.E926 Z79**
The Longing for a Form: Essays on the Fiction of C. S. Lewis. Trade Cloth. Kent State University Press. Kent, OH. 1977. 256p. ISBN:0-87338-204-8, ISBN13: 978-0-87338-204-5. Dewey:823/.9/12. LCCN:77-002586.
Audience: **l,u,f.**

Individual Authors and Works > 20th C. > Lewis, Wyndham

Edwards, Paul **NX547.6.L48E35 2000**
Wyndham Lewis: Painter and Writer. Cloth over Boards. Yale University Press. Cumberland, RI. 2000. 592p. Paul Mellon Centre for Studies in British Art ISBN:0-300-08209-6, ISBN13: 978-0-300-08209-8. Dewey:828/.91209. LCCN:99-048253.
Audience: **g,u,f.**

Jameson, Fredric **PR6023.E97Z/**
Fables of Aggression: Wyndham Lewis, the Modernist As Fascist. Trade Cloth. University of California Press. Berkeley, CA. 1979. ix, 190p. ISBN:0-520-03792-8, ISBN13: 978-0-520-03792-2. Dewey:823/.912. LCCN:78-064462.
Audience: **u,f.**

Lewis, Wyndham **AP4.E48 1994**
The Enemy: A Review of Art and Literature, Vol. 1. David P. Corbett (Contribution by). Trade Cloth. HarperCollins Publishers. New York, NY. 1994. 246p. ISBN:0-87685-948-1, ISBN13: 978-0-87685-948-3. Dewey:809.
Audience: **g,u,f.**

Lewis, Wyndham **PN80**
The Enemy: A Review of Art and Literature, Vol. 2. David P. Corbett (Contribution by). Trade Cloth. HarperCollins Publishers. New York, NY. 1994. 215p. ISBN:0-87685-951-1, ISBN13: 978-0-87685-951-3. Dewey:809.
Audience: **g,u,f.**

Lewis, Wyndham **PR1149**
Blast One. Bradford Morrow (Introduction by). Trade Paper. HarperCollins Publishers. New York, NY. 1997. 167p. Blast One Ser., Vol. 1 ISBN:0-87685-521-4, ISBN13: 978-0-87685-521-8. Dewey:820.8.
Audience: **g,l,u,f.**

Lewis, Wyndham **PR6023.E97**
Wyndham Lewis: Collected Poems and Plays. Alan Munton (Editor), C. H. Sisson (Introduction by). Trade Paper. Routledge. New York, NY. 2003. 144p. Fyfield Bks. ISBN:0-415-96953-0, ISBN13: 978-0-415-96953-6. Dewey:828/.91209.
Audience: **g,u,f.**

Lewis, Wyndham **PR6023.E97**
The Letters of Wyndham Lewis. W. K. Rose (Editor). Trade Cloth. New Directions Publishing Corporation. New York, NY. 1964. ISBN:0-8112-0305-0, ISBN13: 978-0-8112-0305-0. Dewey:826.912. LCCN:61-010121.
Audience: **g,u,f.**

Meyers, Jeffrey **PR6023.E97Z/**
The Enemy: A Biography of Wyndham Lewis. Trade Cloth. Routledge. New York, NY. 1982. 408p. ISBN:0-7100-0514-8, ISBN13: 978-0-7100-0514-4. Dewey:828/.91209. LCCN:81-169344.
Audience: **g,l,u,f.**

Individual Authors and Works > 20th C. > Lowry, Malcolm

Bareham, Tony **PR6023.O96Z567 1989**
Malcolm Lowry. Cloth Text. Palgrave Macmillan. New York, NY. 1989. 150p. Modern Novelists Ser. ISBN:0-312-02445-2, ISBN13: 978-0-312-02445-1. Dewey:813/.54. LCCN:88-023360.
Audience: **u,f.** *Choice, 1989.*

Bowker, Gordon **PR6023.O96**
Pursued by Furies: A Life of Malcolm Lowry. Trade Paper. Palgrave Macmillan. New York, NY. 1997. 696p. ISBN:0-312-16356-8, ISBN13: 978-0-312-16356-3. Dewey:823.912.
Audience: **g,l,u,f.** *Choice, 1996.*

Day, Douglas **PR6023.O96.Z598**
Malcolm Lowry: A Biography. Trade Cloth. Oxford University Press, Inc. New York, NY. 1973. xiii, 483p. ISBN:0-19-501711-0, ISBN13: 978-0-19-501711-3. Dewey:813/.54. LCCN:73-082665.
Audience: **g,u,f.**

Lowry, Malcolm **PR6023.O96**
Selected Poems. Trade Paper. City Lights Books. San Francisco, CA. 1962. 79p. Pocket Poets Ser., No. 17 ISBN:0-87286-030-2, ISBN13: 978-0-87286-030-8. Dewey:821.91.
Audience: **g,l,u,f.**

Lowry, Malcolm **PR6023.O96U5 2000**
Under the Volcano: A Novel. Trade Paper. HarperCollins Publishers. New York, NY. 2000. 432p. Perennial Classics Ser. ISBN:0-06-095522-8, ISBN13: 978-0-06-095522-9. Dewey:813/.54. LCCN:99-056296.
Audience: **g,l,u,f.**

Lowry, Malcolm **PR6023.O96U4 2005**
Ultramarine. Margerie B. Lowry (Introduction by). Trade Paper, Perfect. Overlook Press, The. New York, NY. 2005. 203p. Tusk Ivories Ser. ISBN:1-58567-695-0, ISBN13: 978-1-58567-695-8. Dewey:813.54. LCCN:2005-047319.
Audience: **g,l,u,f.**

Individual Authors and Works > 20th C. > M-N

Machen, Arthur **PR6025.A245G74 2005**
The Great God Pan and the Hill of Dreams. Trade Paper. Dover Publications, Inc. Mineola, NY. 2006. 240p. ISBN:0-486-44345-0, ISBN13: 978-0-486-44345-4. Dewey:823/.912. LCCN:2005-052032.
Audience: **g,l,u,f.**

MacInnes, Colin **PR6063.A239**
The London Novels. Trade Paper, Perfect. Allison & Busby, Ltd. London, 2005. 288p. ISBN:0-7490-8368-9, ISBN13: 978-0-7490-8368-7. Dewey:FIC.
Audience: **g,l,u,f.**

Mantel, Hilary **PR6063.A438F58 2000**
Fludd: A Novel. Trade Paper. Henry Holt & Company. New York, NY. 2000. 192p. ISBN:0-8050-6273-4, ISBN13: 978-0-8050-6273-1. Dewey:823.9/14. LCCN:99-049485.
Audience: **g,l,u,f.**

Mantel, Hilary **PR6015.I3**
The Giant O'Brien. Trade Paper. Doubleday Canada, Ltd. Toronto, ON. 1999. 208p. ISBN:0-385-25895-X, ISBN13: 978-0-385-25895-1. Dewey:823/.914.
Audience: **g,l,u,f.**

McEwan, Ian **PR6063.C4 A88 2002**
Atonement: A Novel. Trade Paper. Knopf Publishing Group. New York, NY. 2003. 368p. ISBN:0-385-72179-X, ISBN13: 978-0-385-72179-0. Dewey:823/.914. LCCN:2001-044291.
Audience: **g,l,u,f.**

McEwan, Ian **PR6063.C4**
The Comfort of Strangers. UK-B Format Paperback. Knopf Publishing Group. New York, NY. 2000. 144p. ISBN:0-09-975491-6, ISBN13: 978-0-09-975491-6. Dewey:823/.914.
Audience: **g,l,u,f.**

McEwan, Ian **PR6063.C4E53 1998**
Enduring Love. Trade Cloth. Doubleday Publishing. New York, NY. 1998. 272p. ISBN:0-385-49112-3, ISBN13: 978-0-385-49112-9. Dewey:823.914. LCCN:97-023029.
Audience: **g,l,u,f.**

McEwan, Ian **PR6063.C4S27 2005**
Saturday: A Novel. Trade Cloth. Doubleday Publishing. New York, NY. 2005. 304p. ISBN:0-385-51180-9, ISBN13: 978-0-385-51180-3. Dewey:823/.914. LCCN:2004-062127.
Audience: **g,l,u,f.**

Melville, Pauline **PR6015.I3**
The Ventriloquist's Tale. Cloth over Boards. Bloomsbury Publishing. New York, NY. 1998. 368p. ISBN:1-58234-009-9, ISBN13: 978-1-58234-009-8. Dewey:823/.914.
Audience: **g,l,u,f.**

Milne, A. A. **PZ7.M64 WI10**
Winnie the Pooh 80th Anniversary Edition. Ernest H. Shepard (Illustrator). Trade Cloth. Penguin Group (USA) Inc. New York, NY. 2006. 160p. ISBN:0-525-47768-3, ISBN13: 978-0-525-47768-6. Dewey:[Fic] 20.
Audience: **g,l,u,f.**

Moorcock, Michael **PR6063.O59**
Byzantium Endures. UK-B Format Paperback. Knopf Publishing Group. New York, NY. 2006. 416p. ISBN:0-09-948509-5, ISBN13: 978-0-09-948509-4. Dewey:823.914.
Audience: **g,l,u,f.**

Moorcock, Michael **PR6063.O59A6 2001**
The Cornelius Quartet: The Final Program; A Cure for Cancer; The English Assassin; The Condition of Muzak. Trade Paper. Avalon Publishing Group. New York, NY. 2001. 864p. ISBN:1-56858-183-1, ISBN13: 978-1-56858-183-5. Dewey:823/.914. LCCN:2001-023967.
Audience: **g,l,u,f.**

Neate, Patrick **PR6114.E25T86 2002**
Twelve Bar Blues. Trade Cloth. Grove/Atlantic, Inc. New York, NY. 2002. 416p. ISBN:0-8021-1727-9, ISBN13: 978-0-8021-1727-4. Dewey:823/.92. LCCN:2002-016443.
Audience: **g,l,u,f.**

Individual Authors and Works > 20th C. > MacDiarmid, Hugh

Glen, Duncan **PR6013.R735.Z67**
Hugh MacDiarmid; a Critical Survey. Trade Cloth. Barnes & Noble, Inc. New York, NY. 1972. ix, 241p. ISBN:0-06-492432-7, ISBN13: 978-0-06-492432-0. Dewey:821/.9/12. LCCN:73-161069.
Audience: **g,l,u,f.** B

MacDiarmid, Hugh **PR6013.R735 Z5 1972**
Lucky Poet: A Self-Study in Literature and Political Ideas Being the Autobiography of Hugh MacDiarmid. Trade Cloth. University of California Press. Berkeley, CA. 1972. ISBN:0-520-01852-4, ISBN13: 978-0-520-01852-5. Dewey:821/.9/12. LCCN:76-138287.
Audience: **g,l,u,f.**

MacDiarmid, Hugh **PR6013.R735 A17 2985**
The Complete Poems of Hugh MacDiarmid, Vol. 3. Michael Grieve & W. R. Aitken (Editors). Trade Paper. Penguin Group (USA) Inc. New York, NY. 1985. 752p. Nonfiction Ser. ISBN:0-14-007914-9, ISBN13: 978-0-14-007914-2. Dewey:821/.912. LCCN:85-150620.
Audience: **g.**

MacDiarmid, Hugh **PS3509.L43**
The Hugh MacDiarmid Anthology: Poems in Scots and English. Michael Grieve & Alexander Scott (Editors). Trade Cloth. Routledge. New York, NY. 1972. xxiii, 295p. The Scottish Ser. ISBN:0-7100-7432-8, ISBN13: 978-0-7100-7432-4. Dewey:821/.9/12. LCCN:72-083662.
Audience: **g,l,u,f.** B

MacDiarmid, Hugh, et al. **PR6013.R735**
The Revolutionary Art of the Future: Rediscovered Poems. John Manson, Dorian Grieve & Alan Riach (Authors). Trade Paper. Carcanet Press, Ltd. Manchester, 2004. 128p. ISBN:1-85754-733-0, ISBN13: 978-1-85754-733-7. Dewey:821/.912. LCCN:2004-478167.
Audience: **g,l,u,f.**

MacDiarmid, Hugh **PR6013.R735D7**
A Drunk Man Looks at the Thistle. John C. Weston (Editor). Trade Paper. University of Massachusetts Press. Amherst, MA. 1971. 136p. ISBN:0-87023-074-3, ISBN13: 978-0-87023-074-5. Dewey:821/.912. LCCN:70-103473.
Audience: **g,l,u,f.** B

Individual Authors and Works > 20th C. > MacNeice, Louis

MacNeice, Louis **PN1064.M3 1968**
Modern Poetry: A Personal Essay. Ed. 2. Trade Cloth. Oxford University Press, Inc. New York, NY. 1968. xxiii, 205p. ISBN:0-19-811674-8, ISBN13: 978-0-19-811674-5. Dewey:808.1. LCCN:79-376072.
Audience: **u,f.** B

MacNeice, Louis **PS3509.L43**
Collected Poems. Ed. 2. E. R. Dodds (Editor). Trade Paper. Faber & Faber, Inc. New York, NY. 1979. 598p. ISBN:0-571-11353-2, ISBN13: 978-0-571-11353-8. Dewey:821/.912.
Audience: **g,l,u,f.**

MacNeice, Louis **PR6025.A316A6 1990**
Selected Prose of Louis MacNeice. Alan Heuser (Editor). Trade Cloth. Oxford University Press, Inc. New York, NY. 1990. 328p. ISBN:0-19-818525-1, ISBN13: 978-0-19-818525-3. Dewey:828/.91208. LCCN:89-026469.
Audience: **u,f.**

MacNeice, Louis **PR6025.A316A6 1993**
Selected Plays of Louis MacNeice. Alan Heuser & Peter McDonald (Editors). Trade Cloth. Oxford University Press, Inc. New York, NY. 1994. 420p. ISBN:0-19-811245-9, ISBN13: 978-0-19-811245-7. Dewey:822.912. LCCN:93-019748.
Audience: **g,l,u,f.**

O'Neill, Michael & Reeves, Gareth **PR610.O54 1992**
Auden, MacNeice, Spender: The Thirties Poetry. Cloth Text. Palgrave Macmillan. New York, NY. 1992. 264p. ISBN:0-312-06828-X, ISBN13: 978-0-312-06828-8. Dewey:821/.91209. LCCN:91-028970.
Audience: **u,f.** *Choice, 1992.*

Stallworthy, Jon **PR6025.A316Z944 1995**
Louis MacNeice. Trade Cloth. W. W. Norton & Company, Inc. New York, NY. 1995. 608p. ISBN:0-393-03776-2, ISBN13: 978-0-393-03776-0. Dewey:821.9/12. LCCN:95-001785.
Audience: **g,u,f.** *Choice, 1995.*

Individual Authors and Works > 20th C. > Mansfield, Katherine

Dickson, Katherine M. **PR9639.3.M258Z6353**
Katherine Mansfield's New Zealand Stories. Trade Cloth. University Press of America, Inc. Lanham, MD. 1998. 120p. ISBN:0-7618-1072-2, ISBN13: 978-0-7618-1072-8. Dewey:823/.912. LCCN:98-010528.
Audience: **l,u,f.**

Kaplan, Sydney J. **PR9639.3.M258Z73**
Katherine Mansfield and the Origins of Modernist Fiction. Book, Other. Cornell University Press. Ithaca, NY. 1991. 248p. ISBN:0-8014-9915-1, ISBN13: 978-0-8014-9915-9. Dewey:823/.912. LCCN:90-045880.
Audience: **u,f.** *Choice, 1991.*

Mansfield, Katherine **PR6025.A57**
Journal of Katherine Mansfield. Trade Paper. Kessinger Publishing, LLC. Whitefish, MT. 2003. ISBN:0-7661-4433-X, ISBN13: 978-0-7661-4433-0. Dewey:928.2.
Audience: **g,l,u,f.**

Mansfield, Katherine **PR9639.3.M258**
Katherine Mansfield's Short Stories. Paper Text, Trade Paper. W. W. Norton & Company, Inc. New York, NY. 2005. 544p. A Norton Critical Edition Ser. ISBN:0-393-92533-1, ISBN13: 978-0-393-92533-3. Dewey:823/.912. LCCN:2005-051295.
Audience: **l,u,f.**

Mansfield, Katherine **PR9639.3.M258A6 1991**
Stories. Trade Paper. Knopf Publishing Group. New York, NY. 1991. 368p. Vintage Bks. ISBN:0-679-73374-4, ISBN13: 978-0-679-73374-4. Dewey:823/.912. LCCN:90-050474.
Audience: **g,l,u,f.**

Mansfield, Katherine **PR9639.3.M258Z494**
Letters Between Katherine Mansfield and John Middleton Murry. Cherry A. Hankin (Editor). Trade Paper. Ivan R. Dee Publisher. Blue Ridge Summit, PA. 1990. 432p. ISBN:0-941533-76-X, ISBN13: 978-0-941533-76-8. Dewey:823/.912 B. LCCN:90-040417.
Audience: **l,u,f.**

Mansfield, Katherine **PR9639.3.M258 Z48**
The Letters of Katherine Mansfield. John M. Murry (Editor). Trade Cloth. Howard Fertig Inc. New York, NY. 1975. 528p. ISBN:0-86527-271-9, ISBN13: 978-0-86527-271-2. Dewey:828 B. LCCN:74-016016.
Audience: **g,l,u,f.** B

Mansfield, Katherine **PR9639.3.M258Z48**
The Collected Letters of Katherine Mansfield: 1888-1917. Vincent O'Sullivan & Margaret Scott (Editors). Trade Cloth. Oxford University Press, Inc. New York, NY. 1984. 406p. ISBN:0-19-812613-1, ISBN13: 978-0-19-812613-3. Dewey:823. LCCN:83-012189.
Audience: **g,l,u,f.** B

Mansfield, Katherine **PR9639.3.M258Z48**
The Collected Letters of Katherine Mansfield: 1919-1920. Vincent O'Sullivan & Margaret Scott (Editors). Trade Cloth. Oxford University Press, Inc. New York, NY. 1993. 328p. ISBN:0-19-812615-8, ISBN13: 978-0-19-812615-7. Dewey:823. LCCN:83-012189.
Audience: **g,l,u,f.**

Mansfield, Katherine **PR9639.3.M258Z48**
The Collected Letters of Katherine Mansfield: 1918-September 1919. Vincent O'Sullivan & Margaret Scott (Editors). Trade Cloth. Oxford University Press, Inc. New York, NY. 1987. 382p. ISBN:0-19-812614-X, ISBN13: 978-0-19-812614-0. Dewey:823. LCCN:83-012189.
Audience: **g,l,u,f.**

Mansfield, Katherine **PR9639.3.M258A6**
The Katherine Mansfield Notebooks. Margaret Scott (Editor). Trade Paper. University of Minnesota Press. Minneapolis, MN. 2002. 712p. ISBN:0-8166-4236-2, ISBN13: 978-0-8166-4236-6. Dewey:823/.912. LCCN:2002-072648.
Audience: **g,l,u,f.**

Meyers, Jeffrey **PR9639.3.M258Z8 2002**
Katherine Mansfield: A Darker View. Trade Paper. Cooper Square Publishers, Inc. New York, NY. 2002. 344p. ISBN:0-8154-1197-9, ISBN13: 978-0-8154-1197-0. Dewey:823/.912 B. LCCN:2001-099924.
Audience: **u,f.**

Smith, Angela **PR9639.3.M258Z877**
Katherine Mansfield: A Literary Life. Trade Cloth. Palgrave Macmillan. New York, NY. 2000. x, 171p. ISBN:0-333-61878-5, ISBN13: 978-0-333-61878-3. Dewey:823/.912 B. LCCN:00-041495.
Audience: **l,u,f.** *Choice, 2001.*

Smith, Angela **PR9639.3.M258A6 2002**
Katherine Mansfield and Virginia Woolf: A Public of Two. Trade Cloth. Oxford University Press, Inc. New York, NY. 1999. 254p. ISBN:0-19-818398-4, ISBN13: 978-0-19-818398-3. Dewey:823/.912. LCCN:2001-054559.
Audience: **u,f.**

Tomalin, Claire **PR6025.A57Z/**
Katherine Mansfield: A Secret Life. Trade Cloth. Penguin Books, Ltd. London, 1987. 304p. ISBN:0-670-81392-3, ISBN13: 978-0-670-81392-6. Dewey:823/.912 B.
Audience: **l,u,f.** *Choice, 1988.*

Individual Authors and Works > 20th C. > Maugham, W. Somerset

Archer, Stanley **PR6025.A86.Z552 1993**
W. Somerset Maugham: A Study of the Short Fiction. Trade Cloth. Macmillan Publishing Company, Inc. Old Tappan, NJ. 1993. 152p. Twayne's Studies in Short Fiction, No. 44 ISBN:0-8057-0856-1, ISBN13: 978-0-8057-0856-1. Dewey:823/.912. LCCN:92-042071.
Audience: **l,u.** *Choice, 1993.*

Curtis, Anthony & Whitehead, John (Editors) **PR6025.A86**
W. Somerset Maugham. Trade Cloth. Routledge. New York, NY. 1987. 480p. ISBN:0-7100-9640-2, ISBN13: 978-0-7100-9640-1. Dewey:809.3/04. LCCN:86-017299.
Audience: **l,u.** *Choice, 1988.*

Maugham, W. Somerset **PR6019.O9**
Ashenden, or, The British Agent. Trade Cloth. Ayer Company Publishers, Inc. Manchester, NH. 1977. Works of W. Somerset Maugham ISBN:0-405-07805-6, ISBN13: 978-0-405-07805-7. Dewey:823.9/12. LCCN:75-025348.
Audience: **g,l,u,f.**

Maugham, W. Somerset **PR6025.A86C346 2000**
Cakes and Ale. Trade Paper. Knopf Publishing Group. New York, NY. 2000. 320p. ISBN:0-375-72502-4, ISBN13: 978-0-375-72502-9. Dewey:823.9/12. LCCN:00-033414.
Audience: **g,l,u,f.** B

Maugham, W. Somerset **PR6019.O9**
Catalina. UK-B Format Paperback. Knopf Publishing Group. New York, NY. 2001. 240p. ISBN:0-09-928684-X, ISBN13: 978-0-09-928684-4. Dewey:823.9/12.
Audience: **g,l,u,f.**

Maugham, W. Somerset **PR6025.A86**
The Collected Short Stories of W. Somerset Maugham, Vol. 3. UK-B Format Paperback. Knopf Publishing Group. New York, NY. 2002. 288p. ISBN:0-09-942885-7, ISBN13: 978-0-09-942885-5. Dewey:823/.9/1.
Audience: **g,l,u,f.**

Maugham, W. Somerset **PR6019.O9**
The Collected Short Stories of W. Somerset Maugham, Vol. 2. UK-Trade Paper. Knopf Publishing Group. New York, NY. 2002. 544p. ISBN:0-09-942884-9, ISBN13: 978-0-09-942884-8. Dewey:823/.9/1.
Audience: **g,l,u,f.**

Maugham, W. Somerset **PR6019.O9**
The Collected Short Stories of W. Somerset Maugham, Vol. 4. UK-Trade Paper. Knopf Publishing Group. New York, NY. 2002. 576p. ISBN:0-09-942886-5, ISBN13: 978-0-09-942886-2. Dewey:823/.9/1.
Audience: **g,l,u,f.**

Maugham, W. Somerset **PR6019.O9**
The Collected Short Stories of W. Somerset Maugham, Vol. 1. UK-B Format Paperback. Knopf Publishing Group. New York, NY. 2001. 536p. ISBN:0-09-928739-0, ISBN13: 978-0-09-928739-1. Dewey:823/.9/1.
Audience: **g,l,u,f.**

Maugham, W. Somerset **PR6019.O9**
Liza of Lambeth. Trade Paper. Knopf Publishing Group. New York, NY. 2000. 704p. ISBN:0-09-928274-7, ISBN13: 978-0-09-928274-7. Dewey:823.9/12.
Audience: **g.** B

Maugham, W. Somerset **PR6019.O9**
The Magician. Library Binding. North Books. Wickford, RI. 2005. Twelve-Point Ser. ISBN:1-58287-337-2, ISBN13: 978-1-58287-337-4. Dewey:823.9/12.
Audience: **g,l,u,f.**

Maugham, W. Somerset **PR5366**
Maugham Plays 2. Trade Paper. Methuen Publishing Ltd. London, 2003. 0p. Methuen World Classics Ser. ISBN:0-413-71310-5, ISBN13: 978-0-413-71310-0. Dewey:822.9/12.
Audience: **g,l,u,f.**

Maugham, W. Somerset **PR6019.O9**
The Moon and Sixpence. Trade Cloth. Ayer Company Publishers, Inc. Manchester, NH. 1977. Works of W. Somerset Maugham ISBN:0-405-07816-1, ISBN13: 978-0-405-07816-3. Dewey:823/.9/1. LCCN:75-025357.
Audience: **g,l,u,f.**

Maugham, W. Somerset **PR6019.O9**
Mrs. Craddock. Trade Cloth. Ayer Company Publishers, Inc. Manchester, NH. 1977. Works of W. Somerset Maugham ISBN:0-405-07817-X, ISBN13: 978-0-405-07817-0. Dewey:823.9/12. LCCN:75-025358.
Audience: **g,l,u,f.**

Maugham, W. Somerset **PR6019.O9**
The Narrow Corner. Trade Cloth. Ayer Company Publishers, Inc. Manchester, NH. 1977. Works of W. Somerset Maugham ISBN:0-405-07818-8, ISBN13: 978-0-405-07818-7. Dewey:823.9/12. LCCN:75-025359.
Audience: **g,l,u,f.**

Maugham, W. Somerset **PR6019.O9**
Of Human Bondage. Prebound. Turtleback Books. Madison, WI. 1915. ISBN:0-606-01173-0, ISBN13: 978-0-606-01173-0. Dewey:823/.912.
Audience: **g,l,u,f.**

Maugham, W. Somerset **PR6025.A86 P28**
The Painted Veil. Trade Paper. Knopf Publishing Group. New York, NY. 2006. 256p. ISBN:0-307-27777-1, ISBN13: 978-0-307-27777-0. Dewey:823/.912.
Audience: **g,l,u,f.**

Maugham, W. Somerset **PR5366**
Plays 1. Trade Paper. Methuen Publishing Ltd. London, 2003. 0p. Methuen World Classics Ser. ISBN:0-413-71300-8, ISBN13: 978-0-413-71300-1. Dewey:822.9/12.
Audience: **g,l,u,f.**

Maugham, W. Somerset **PR6031.R6**
Points of View: Five Essays. Trade Cloth. Ayer Company Publishers, Inc. Manchester, NH. 1977. Works of W. Somerset Maugham ISBN:0-405-07827-7, ISBN13: 978-0-405-07827-9. Dewey:824.9/12. LCCN:75-025374.
Audience: **g,l,u,f.** B

Maugham, W. Somerset **PR6025.A86**
The Razor's Edge. Trade Paper. Knopf Publishing Group. New York, NY. 2003. 320p. ISBN:1-4000-3420-5, ISBN13: 978-1-4000-3420-8. Dewey:951.05.
Audience: **g,l,u,f.**

Maugham, W. Somerset **PR6019.O9**
Theatre. UK-B Format Paperback. Knopf Publishing Group. New York, NY. 2001. 256p. ISBN:0-09-928683-1, ISBN13: 978-0-09-928683-7. Dewey:823.9/12.
Audience: **g,l,u,f.**

Maugham, W. Somerset **PR6019.O9**
Then and Now. Trade Cloth. Ayer Company Publishers, Inc. Manchester, NH. 1977. Works of W. Somerset Maugham ISBN:0-405-07822-6, ISBN13: 978-0-405-07822-4. Dewey:823.9/12. LCCN:75-025364.
Audience: **g,l,u,f.**

Maugham, W. Somerset **PR6019.O9**
Up at the Villa. Trade Cloth. Ayer Company Publishers, Inc. Manchester, NH. 1977. Works of W. Somerset Maugham ISBN:0-405-07824-2, ISBN13: 978-0-405-07824-8. Dewey:823/.912. LCCN:75-025366.
Audience: **g,l,u,f.**

Maugham, W. Somerset **PR6031.R6**
The Vagrant Mood. UK-B Format Paperback. Knopf Publishing Group. New York, NY. 2001. 208p. ISBN:0-09-928679-3, ISBN13: 978-0-09-928679-0. Dewey:824.9/12.
Audience: **g,l,u,f.**

Maugham, W. Somerset **PR6019.O9**
A Writer's Notebook. UK-B Format Paperback. Knopf Publishing Group. New York, NY. 2001. 352p. ISBN:0-09-928682-3, ISBN13: 978-0-09-928682-0. Dewey:823.9/12.
Audience: **g,l,u,f.**

Meyers, Jeffrey **PR6025.A86Z763 2004**
Somerset Maugham: A Life. Trade Cloth. Alfred A. Knopf Inc. New York, NY. 2004. 432p. ISBN:0-375-41475-4, ISBN13: 978-0-375-41475-6. Dewey:823/.912. LCCN:2003-056187.
Audience: **g,l,u,f.** *Choice, 2005.*

Meyers, Jeffrey **PR6025.A86A6 2003**
The W. Somerset Maugham Reader: Novels, Stories, Travel Writing. Trade Paper. Taylor Trade Publishing. Blue Ridge Summit, PA. 2004. 584p. ISBN:1-58979-072-3, ISBN13: 978-1-58979-072-8. Dewey:823/.912. LCCN:2003-020547.
Audience: **g,l,u,f.**

Individual Authors and Works > 20th C. > Mitford, Jessica and Nancy

Lovell, Mary S. **CT787.M57L68 2002**
The Sisters: The Saga of the Mitford Family. Trade Cloth. W. W. Norton & Company, Inc. New York, NY. 2002. 384p. ISBN:0-393-01043-0, ISBN13: 978-0-393-01043-5. Dewey:920.72/0941. LCCN:2001-044942.
Audience: **g,l,u,f.**

Mitford, Jessica **HD9999.U53**
The American Way of Death Revisited. Ed. 2. Trade Paper. Knopf Publishing Group. New York, NY. 2000. 320p. ISBN:0-679-77186-7, ISBN13: 978-0-679-77186-9. Dewey:393.9/0973.
Audience: **g,l,u,f.**

Mitford, Jessica **CT788**
Hons and Rebels. Christopher Hitchens (Introduction by). Trade Paper. New York Review of Books, Incorporated, The. New York, NY. 2004. 320p. New York Review Books Classics ISBN:1-59017-110-1, ISBN13: 978-1-59017-110-3. Dewey:973.9/092/4. LCCN:2004-016736.
Audience: **g,l,u,f.**

Mitford, Nancy **PR6025.I88**
The Blessing. Trade Paper. Avalon Publishing Group. New York, NY. 1998. 224p. ISBN:0-7867-0521-3, ISBN13: 978-0-7867-0521-4. Dewey:823.
Audience: **g,l,u,f.**

Mitford, Nancy **PR6019.O9**
Don't Tell Alfred. Trade Paper. Penguin Books, Ltd. London, 1977. 224p. ISBN:0-14-001976-6, ISBN13: 978-0-14-001976-6. Dewey:823.9/12.
Audience: **g,l,u,f.**

Mitford, Nancy **PR6015.I3**
The Pursuit of Love and Love in a Cold Climate: Two Novels. Trade Paper. Knopf Publishing Group. New York, NY. 2001. 480p. ISBN:0-375-71899-0, ISBN13: 978-0-375-71899-1. Dewey:823/.914.
Audience: **g,l,u,f.**

Mitford, Nancy **PR6025.I88**
Talent to Annoy: Selected Journalism. Charlotte Mosley (Editor). Trade Paper. Gibson Square Books Ltd. London, 2006. 304p. ISBN:1-903933-43-9, ISBN13: 978-1-903933-43-5. Dewey:828.9/1208.
Audience: **g,l,u,f.**

Thompson, Laura **PR6025.I88**
Life in a Cold Climate: A Portrait of a Contradictory Woman. Trade Paper. Headline Book Publishing. London, 2004. 432p. ISBN:0-7472-4575-4, ISBN13: 978-0-7472-4575-9. Dewey:823.9/12.
Audience: **g,l,u,f.**

Individual Authors and Works > 20th C. > Murdoch, Iris

Bayley, John **PR6015.I3**
Elegy for Iris. Trade Paper. Picador. New York, NY. 2001. 288p. ISBN:0-312-42111-7, ISBN13: 978-0-312-42111-3. Dewey:823/.914 B.
Audience: **g.**

Bloom, Harold (Introduction by) **PR6063.U7Z7 1986**
Iris Murdoch. Trade Cloth. Chelsea House Publishers. Langhorne, PA. 1986. 222p. ISBN:0-87754-705-X, ISBN13: 978-0-87754-705-1. Dewey:823/.914. LCCN:86-000947.
Audience: **g.**

Conradi, Peter J. **PR6063.U7Z629 2001**
Iris Murdoch: A Life. Trade Cloth. W. W. Norton & Company, Inc. New York, NY. 2001. 512p. ISBN:0-393-04875-6, ISBN13: 978-0-393-04875-9. Dewey:823/.914 B. LCCN:2001-032972.
Audience: **g.** *Choice, 2002.*

Murdoch, Iris **PR6063.U7**
An Accidental Man. UK-B Format Paperback. Random House. London, 2003. 384p. ISBN:0-09-943356-7, ISBN13: 978-0-09-943356-9. Dewey:823.9/14.
Audience: **g.**

Murdoch, Iris **PR6063.U7**
The Book and the Brotherhood. UK-B Format Paperback. Knopf Publishing Group. New York, NY. 2003. 608p. ISBN:0-09-943354-0, ISBN13: 978-0-09-943354-5. Dewey:823.9/14.
Audience: **g,l,u,f.**

Murdoch, Iris **PR6015.I3**
The Good Apprentice. Trade Paper. Penguin Group (USA) Inc. New York, NY. 2001. 528p. ISBN:0-14-118668-2, ISBN13: 978-0-14-118668-9. Dewey:823/.914.
Audience: **g.**

Murdoch, Iris **PR6063.U7.H45**
Henry and Cato. Trade Cloth. Penguin Group (USA) Inc. New York, NY. 1977. 375p. ISBN:0-670-36697-8, ISBN13: 978-0-670-36697-2. Dewey:823.9/14. LCCN:76-027653.
Audience: **g.**

Murdoch, Iris **PR6063.U7M47 1990**
The Message to the Planet. Trade Cloth. Penguin Group (USA) Inc. New York, NY. 1990. 640p. ISBN:0-670-82999-4, ISBN13: 978-0-670-82999-6. Dewey:823.9/14. LCCN:89-040352.
Audience: **g.**

Murdoch, Iris **PR6015.I3**
The Nice and the Good. Trade Paper. Penguin Group (USA) Inc. New York, NY. 1978. 368p. ISBN:0-14-003034-4, ISBN13: 978-0-14-003034-1. Dewey:823.9/14. LCCN:99-707250.
Audience: **g.**

Murdoch, Iris **PR6063.U7.P44 1983**
The Philosopher's Pupil. Trade Cloth. Penguin Group (USA) Inc. New York, NY. 1983. 576p. ISBN:0-670-55186-4, ISBN13: 978-0-670-55186-6. Dewey:823.9/14. LCCN:82-045901.
Audience: **g.**

Murdoch, Iris **PR6015.I3**
The Red and the Green. UK-B Format Paperback. Knopf Publishing Group. New York, NY. 2002. 320p. ISBN:0-09-942913-6, ISBN13: 978-0-09-942913-5. Dewey:823.9/14.
Audience: **g.**

Murdoch, Iris **PR6063.U7**
The Sacred and Profane Love Machine. UK-B Format Paperback. Random House. London, 2003. 336p. ISBN:0-09-943357-5, ISBN13: 978-0-09-943357-6. Dewey:823/.9/1.
Audience: **g.**

Murdoch, Iris **PR6063.U7**
The Sandcastle. UK-B Format Paperback. Knopf Publishing Group. New York, NY. 2003. 320p. ISBN:0-09-943358-3, ISBN13: 978-0-09-943358-3. Dewey:823.9/14.
Audience: **g.**

Murdoch, Iris **PR6015.I3**
A Severed Head. Paper Text. Textbook Publishers. Temecula, CA. 2003. 204p. ISBN:0-7581-6555-2, ISBN13: 978-0-7581-6555-8. Dewey:823.9/14.
Audience: **g.**

Murdoch, Iris **PR6015.I3**
A Word Child. UK-B Format Paperback. Knopf Publishing Group. New York, NY. 2002. 400p. ISBN:0-09-942912-8, ISBN13: 978-0-09-942912-8. Dewey:823.9/14.
Audience: **g.**

Murdoch, Iris **PR6063.U7N8 2002**
Nuns and Soldiers. Karen Armstrong (Introduction by). Trade Paper. Penguin Group (USA) Inc. New York, NY. 2002. 512p. Classics Ser. ISBN:0-14-218009-2, ISBN13: 978-0-14-218009-9. Dewey:823/.914. LCCN:2002-072563.
Audience: **g.**

Murdoch, Iris **PR6063.U7S25 2001**
The Sea, the Sea. Mary Kinzie (Introduction by). Trade Paper. Penguin Group (USA) Inc. New York, NY. 2001. 528p. Twentieth Century Classics Ser. ISBN:0-14-118616-X, ISBN13: 978-0-14-118616-0. Dewey:823/.914. LCCN:00-061132.
Audience: **g.**

Murdoch, Iris **PR6063.U7B5 2003**
The Black Prince. Martha C. Nussbaum (Introduction by). Trade Paper. Penguin Group (USA) Inc. New York, NY. 2003. 448p. Classics Ser. ISBN:0-14-218011-4, ISBN13: 978-0-14-218011-2. Dewey:823/.914. LCCN:2002-045043.
Audience: **g.**

Murdoch, Iris **PR6063.U7F3 2001**
A Fairly Honourable Defeat. Peter Reed (Introduction by). Trade Paper. Penguin Group (USA) Inc. New York, NY. 2001. 432p. Twentieth Century Classics Ser. ISBN:0-14-118617-8, ISBN13: 978-0-14-118617-7. Dewey:823/.914. LCCN:00-061138.
Audience: **g.**

Rowe **PR6063.U7 Z6295**
Iris Murdoch Revisited. Trade Cloth. Thomson Gale. Farmington Hills, MI. 1998. ISBN:0-8057-4620-X, ISBN13: 978-0-8057-4620-4. Dewey:823/.914.
Audience: **g.**

Individual Authors and Works > 20th C. > O-P

O'Brien, Edna **PR6015.I3**
The Country Girls. Trade Paper. Penguin Group (USA) Inc. New York, NY. 2002. 192p. ISBN:0-452-28343-4, ISBN13: 978-0-452-28343-5. Dewey:823.9/14.
Audience: **g,l,u,f.**

O'Brien, Edna **PR6065.B7H55 1995**
House of Splendid Isolation. Trade Paper. Penguin Group (USA) Inc. New York, NY. 1995. 240p. ISBN:0-452-27452-4, ISBN13: 978-0-452-27452-5. Dewey:823/.914. LCCN:94-047256.
Audience: **g,l,u,f.**

O'Brien, Flann **PR6029.N56 S8 1976**
O'Brien, Stories and Plays. Trade Cloth. Library of America, The. New York, NY. 1976. 240p. Richard Seaver Bks. ISBN:0-670-67206-8, ISBN13: 978-0-670-67206-6. Dewey:828/.9/1209. LCCN:75-041375.
Audience: **g,l,u,f.**

Paterson, Don **PR6116.A84L36 2005**
Landing Light: Poems. Cloth over Boards. Graywolf Press. St. Paul, MN. 2005. 88p. ISBN:1-55597-417-1, ISBN13: 978-1-55597-417-6. Dewey:821/.914. LCCN:2004-109267.
Audience: **g,l,u,f.**

Peake, Mervyn **PR6031.E183G64 1995**
The Gormenghast Novels: Titus Groan, Gormenghast, Titus Alone. Trade Paper. Overlook Press, The. New York, NY. 1995. 1168p. ISBN:0-87951-628-3, ISBN13: 978-0-87951-628-4. Dewey:823/.912. LCCN:95-016431.
Audience: **g,l,u,f.**

Pierre, D. B. C. **PR9619.4.P54V47**
Vernon God Little. Trade Paper. Harcourt Trade Publishers. New York, NY. 2004. 300p. ISBN:0-15-602998-7, ISBN13: 978-0-15-602998-8. Dewey:823/.92. LCCN:2004-003636.
Audience: **g,l,u,f.**

Powys, John Cowper **PR6019.O9**
A Glastonbury Romance. Trade Paper. Overlook Press, The. New York, NY. 2004. 1120p. ISBN:0-87951-681-X, ISBN13: 978-0-87951-681-9. Dewey:823.9/12. LCCN:87-005762.
Audience: **g,l,u,f.**

Powys, John Cowper **PR6031**
Weymouth Sands. Trade Cloth. Overlook Press, The. New York, NY. 1999. 567p. ISBN:0-87951-717-4, ISBN13: 978-0-87951-717-5. Dewey:823/.912. LCCN:99-010237.
Audience: **g,l,u,f.**

Pullman, Philip **PZ7.P968AM 2000**
The Amber Spyglass. Trade Cloth. Random House Children's Books. New York, NY. 2000. 544p. His Dark Materials Ser., Bk. 3 ISBN:0-679-87926-9, ISBN13: 978-0-679-87926-8. Dewey:[Fic]. LCCN:00-044776.
Audience: **g,l,u,f.**

Pullman, Philip **PZ7.P968GO 1996**
The Golden Compass. Trade Cloth. Random House Children's Books. New York, NY. 1996. 416p. His Dark Materials Ser., Bk. 1 ISBN:0-679-87924-2, ISBN13: 978-0-679-87924-4. Dewey:[Fic]. LCCN:95-033397.
Audience: **g,l,u,f.**

Pullman, Philip **PZ7.P968SU 1997**
The Subtle Knife. Trade Cloth. Random House Children's Books. New York, NY. 1997. 352p. His Dark Materials Ser., Bk. 2 ISBN:0-679-87925-0, ISBN13: 978-0-679-87925-1. Dewey:[Fic]. LCCN:97-000673.
Audience: **g,l,u,f.**

Individual Authors and Works > 20th C. > O'Brien, Flann

Asbee, Sue **PR6029.N56Z514 1991**
Flann O'Brien. Trade Cloth. Macmillan Publishing Company, Inc. Old Tappan, NJ. 1991. 160p. Twayne's English Authors Ser., No. 485 ISBN:0-8057-7001-1, ISBN13: 978-0-8057-7001-8. Dewey:828/.91209. LCCN:90-023666.
Audience: **u,f.** *Choice, 1991.*

O'Brien, Flann **PR6019.O9**
The Hard Life. Ed. 2. Trade Paper. Dalkey Archive Press. Normal, IL. 1996. 179p. ISBN:1-56478-141-0, ISBN13: 978-1-56478-141-3. Dewey:823/.912. LCCN:93-021207.
Audience: **g,l,u,f.**

O'Brien, Flann **PR6029.N56T48 1999**
The Third Policeman. Denis Donoghue (Introduction by). Trade Paper. Dalkey Archive Press. Normal, IL. 1999. 200p. John F. Byrne Irish Literature Ser. ISBN:1-56478-214-X, ISBN13: 978-1-56478-214-4. Dewey:823/.912. LCCN:98-052437.
Audience: **g,l,u,f.**

O'Brien, Flann **PR6029.N56A934 1998**
At Swim-Two-Birds. William H. Gass (Introduction by). Trade Paper. Dalkey Archive Press. Normal, IL. 1998. 316p. Irish Literature Ser. ISBN:1-56478-181-X, ISBN13: 978-1-56478-181-9. Dewey:823.9/12. LCCN:97-051424.
Audience: **g,l,u,f.**

O'Brien, Flann **PR6029.N56.F55 1978**
A Flann O'Brien Reader. Stephen Jones (Introduction by). Trade Cloth. Library of America, The. New York, NY. 1978. xxix, 447p. Richard Seaver Bks. ISBN:0-670-31740-3, ISBN13: 978-0-670-31740-0. Dewey:828/.9/1209. LCCN:76-046968.
Audience: **g,l,u,f.**

Individual Authors and Works > 20th C. > O'Casey, Sean

Kearney, Colbert **PR6029**
The Glamour of Grammar: Orality and Politics and the Emergence of Sean O'Casey. Trade Cloth. Greenwood Publishing Group, Inc. Portsmouth, NH. 2000. 160p. Contributions in Drama and Theatre Studies Ser., Vol. 92 ISBN:0-313-31303-2, ISBN13: 978-0-313-31303-5. Dewey:822/.914. LCCN:00-025110.
Audience: **u,f.** *Choice, 2001.*

O'Casey, Sean **PR6029.C33**
The Autobiographies of Sean O'Casey. Trade Paper. Hal Leonard Corporation. Milwaukee, WI. 2003. ISBN:0-634-03549-5, ISBN13: 978-0-634-03549-4. Dewey:822.91.
Audience: **g,l,u,f.**

O'Casey, Sean **BF408**
Behind the Green Curtains: Figuro in the Night. Paper Text. Textbook Publishers. Temecula, CA. 2003. 157p. ISBN:0-7581-3609-9, ISBN13: 978-0-7581-3609-1. Dewey:658.406.
Audience: **g,l,u,f.**

O'Casey, Sean **E840.8.O54**
The Drums of Father Ned. Paper Text. Textbook Publishers. Temecula, CA. 2003. 109p. ISBN:0-7581-3982-9, ISBN13: 978-0-7581-3982-5. Dewey:328.73/092/4.
Audience: **g,l,u,f.**

O'Casey, Sean **BQ1138**
Feathers from the Green Crow, Sean O'Casey 1905: 1925. Paper Text. Textbook Publishers. Temecula, CA. 2003. 342p. ISBN:0-7581-1949-6, ISBN13: 978-0-7581-1949-0. Dewey:294.3.
Audience: **g,l,u,f.** B

O'Casey, Sean
More Wren Songs. Paper Text. Classic Books. Murrieta, CA. 2001. Collected Works of Sean O'Casey ISBN:0-7426-8207-2, ISBN13: 978-0-7426-8207-8.
Audience: **g,l,u,f.**

O'Casey, Sean **DA965.A82**
The Story of Thomas Ashe. Paper Text. Classic Books. Murrieta, CA. 2001. 15p. Collected Works of Sean O'Casey ISBN:0-7426-8210-2, ISBN13: 978-0-7426-8210-8. Dewey:941.5082409.
Audience: **g,l,u,f.**

O'Casey, Sean **PR5366**
Three Dublin Plays: The Shadow of a Gunman; Juno and the Paycock, and the Plough and the Stars. Christopher Murray (Introduction by). Trade Paper. Faber & Faber, Inc. New York, NY. 2000. 272p. ISBN:0-571-19552-0, ISBN13: 978-0-571-19552-7. Dewey:822.9/12.
Audience: **g,l,u,f.**

Individual Authors and Works > 20th C. > O'Connor, Frank

O'Connor, Frank **DA965.C6O244 1998**
The Big Fellow: Michael Collins and the Irish Revolution. Ed. 1. Trade Paper. Picador. New York, NY. 1998. 224p. ISBN:0-312-18050-0, ISBN13: 978-0-312-18050-8. Dewey:941.5082/2. LCCN:97-033373.
Audience: **g,l,u,f.**

O'Connor, Frank (Editor) **PR8876.M63 1989**
Classic Irish Short Stories. Trade Paper. Oxford University Press, Inc. New York, NY. 1990. 352p. ISBN:0-19-281918-6, ISBN13: 978-0-19-281918-5. Dewey:823/.01/08/9415. LCCN:89-016111.
Audience: **g.**

O'Connor, Frank **PR6029.D58.A15 1981**
Collected Stories. Trade Cloth. Alfred A. Knopf Inc. New York, NY. 1981. 702p. ISBN:0-394-51602-8, ISBN13: 978-0-394-51602-8. Dewey:823/.912. LCCN:81-001253.
Audience: **g,l,u,f.** B

O'Connor, Frank **PR6029.D58**
My Father's Son. Trade Paper. Syracuse University Press. Syracuse, NY. 1999. 216p. Irish Studies ISBN:0-8156-0564-1, ISBN13: 978-0-8156-0564-5. Dewey:823/.912 B. LCCN:98-041806.
Audience: **g,l,u,f.** B

Individual Authors and Works > 20th C. > Orton, Joe

Lahr, John **PR6066.I53**
Prick Up Your Ears: The Biography of Joe Orton. Trade Paper. University of California Press. Berkeley, CA. 2000. 315p. ISBN:0-520-22666-6, ISBN13: 978-0-520-22666-1. Dewey:822.9/14. LCCN:00-028691.
Audience: **g,l,u,f.**

Orton, Joe **PR6015.I3**
Between Us Girls: A Novel. Trade Paper. Grove/Atlantic, Inc. New York, NY. 1999. 224p. ISBN:0-8021-3644-3, ISBN13: 978-0-8021-3644-2. Dewey:823.9/14.
Audience: **g,l,u,f.**

Orton, Joe **PR6065.R7**
The Complete Plays. Trade Cloth. Doubleday Direct. Garden City, NY. 1997. 448p. ISBN:1-56865-535-5, ISBN13: 978-1-56865-535-2. Dewey:822.914.
Audience: **g,l,u,f.**

Orton, Joe **PR6065.R7V57 1998**
The Visitors and Fred and Madge. Trade Paper. Grove/Atlantic, Inc. New York, NY. 1999. 192p. ISBN:0-8021-3628-1, ISBN13: 978-0-8021-3628-2. Dewey:822/.914. LCCN:99-030227.
Audience: **g,l,u,f.**

Orton, Joe **PR6065.R7Z467 1996**
Orton Diaries: Including the Correspondence of Edna Welthorpe and Others. John Lahr (Editor). Trade Paper. Da Capo Press, Inc. Cambridge, MA. 1996. 310p. ISBN:0-306-80733-5, ISBN13: 978-0-306-80733-6. Dewey:[B]. LCCN:96-018361.
Audience: **g,l,u,f.**

Individual Authors and Works > 20th C. > Orwell, George

Davison, Peter **PR6029.R8Z6279 1996**
George Orwell: A Literary Life. Cloth over Boards. Palgrave Macmillan. New York, NY. 1996. 205p. Literary Lives Ser. ISBN:0-312-12820-7, ISBN13: 978-0-312-12820-3. Dewey:828/.91209 B. LCCN:95-004652.
Audience: **g,l,u,f.** *Choice, 1996.*

Hitchens, Christopher **PR6029.R8**
Why Orwell Matters. Trade Paper. Basic Books. New York, NY. 2003. 224p. ISBN:0-465-03050-5, ISBN13: 978-0-465-03050-7. Dewey:828/.91209.
Audience: **g,l,u,f.**

Larkin, Emma **DS527.7.L37 2005**
Finding George Orwell in Burma: Travels in a Police State. Trade Cloth. Penguin Group (USA) Inc. New York, NY. 2005. 294p. ISBN:1-59420-052-1, ISBN13: 978-1-59420-052-6. Dewey:915.9104/53. LCCN:2004-065786.
Audience: **g,l,u,f.**

Meyers, Jeffrey **PR6029.R8Z736 2000**
Orwell: Wintry Conscience of a Generation. Trade Cloth. W. W. Norton & Company, Inc. New York, NY. 2000. 398p. ISBN:0-393-04792-X, ISBN13: 978-0-393-04792-9. Dewey:828/.91209 B. LCCN:00-038020.
Audience: **g,l,u,f.**

Newsinger, John **PR6019.O9**
Orwell's Politics. Trade Paper. Palgrave Macmillan. New York, NY. 2002. 190p. ISBN:0-333-96858-1, ISBN13: 978-0-333-96858-1. Dewey:823.9/12.
Audience: **g,u,f.** *Choice, 1999.*

Nussbaum, Martha (Editor), et al. **PR6029.R8N64326 2005**
On Nineteen Eighty-Four: Orwell and Our Future. Abbott Gleason & Jack Goldsmith (Editors). Trade Cloth. Princeton University Press. Princeton, NJ. 2005. 336p. ISBN:0-691-11360-2, ISBN13: 978-0-691-11360-9. Dewey:823/.912. LCCN:2004-059507.
Audience: **u,f.**

Orwell, George **PR6029.R8**
Burmese Days. Trade Paper. Harcourt Trade Publishers. New York, NY. 1974. 288p. Harbrace Paperbound Library ISBN:0-15-614850-1, ISBN13: 978-0-15-614850-4. Dewey:823.9/12. LCCN:73-012947.
Audience: **g,l,u,f.**

Orwell, George **PR6029.R8C58 1969**
A Clergyman's Daughter. Trade Paper. Harcourt Trade Publishers. New York, NY. 1950. 324p. Harvest Book Ser. ISBN:0-15-618065-0, ISBN13: 978-0-15-618065-8. Dewey:823.9/12. LCCN:60-010943.
Audience: **g,l,u,f.**

Orwell, George **PR6029.R8C66 1999**
Coming up for Air. Trade Paper. Harcourt Trade Publishers. New York, NY. 1969. 288p. Harvest Book Ser. ISBN:0-15-619625-5, ISBN13: 978-0-15-619625-3. Dewey:823/.912. LCCN:00-265573.
Audience: **g,l,u,f.**

Orwell, George **PR6029.R8 D5 1973**
Dickens, Dali and Others. Trade Paper. Harcourt Trade Publishers. New York, NY. 1970. 252p. ISBN:0-15-626053-0, ISBN13: 978-0-15-626053-4. Dewey:814. LCCN:63-022950.
Audience: **g,l,u,f.**

Orwell, George **DC715**
Down and Out in Paris and London. Trade Paper. Harcourt Trade Publishers. New York, NY. 1972. 228p. ISBN:0-15-626224-X, ISBN13: 978-0-15-626224-8. Dewey:362.5/09421/09043. LCCN:65-067354.
Audience: **g,l,u,f.**

Orwell, George **PR6029.R8**
Homage to Catalonia. Ed. 1. Trade Paper. Harcourt Trade Publishers. New York, NY. 1969. 264p. Harvest Book Ser. ISBN:0-15-642117-8, ISBN13: 978-0-15-642117-1. Dewey:946/.081. LCCN:52-006442.
Audience: **g,l,u,f.**

Orwell, George **PR6029.R8K44 1999**
Keep the Aspidistra Flying. Trade Paper. Harcourt Trade Publishers. New York, NY. 1969. 264p. Harvest Book Ser. ISBN:0-15-646899-9, ISBN13: 978-0-15-646899-2. Dewey:823/.912. LCCN:00-265574.
Audience: **g,l,u,f.**

Orwell, George **PR6029.R8**
Essays. John Carey (Introduction by). Trade Cloth. Alfred A. Knopf Inc. New York, NY. 2002. 1424p. ISBN:0-375-41503-3, ISBN13: 978-0-375-41503-6. Dewey:824.912.
Audience: **g,l,u,f.**

Orwell, George **HD8390.07 1958**
The Road to Wigan Pier. Victor Gollancz (Foreword by). Trade Paper. Harcourt Trade Publishers. New York, NY. 1972. 264p. ISBN:0-15-676750-3, ISBN13: 978-0-15-676750-7. Dewey:305.5/62/09428. LCCN:58-010888.
Audience: **g,l,u,f.**

Orwell, George **PR6029.R8 N49 1982**
Orwell's 1984: Text, Sources, Criticism. Ed. 2. Irving Howe & David Levin (Editors). Paper Text. Harcourt College Publishers. Fort Worth, TX. 1982. 450p. Harbrace Sourcebooks Ser. ISBN:0-15-565811-5, ISBN13: 978-0-15-565811-0. Dewey:823/.912. LCCN:81-081897.
Audience: **g,l,u,f.**

Orwell, George **PR6029.R8A6 2000**
The Collected Essays, Journalism and Letters of George Orwell: My Country Right or Left, 1940-1943. Sonia Orwell & Ian Angus (Editors). Trade Paper. David R. Godine Publisher. Boston, MA. 2000. 496p. Nonpareil Ser., Vol. 87 ISBN:1-56792-134-5, ISBN13: 978-1-56792-134-2. Dewey:828/.91209 B. LCCN:00-037540.
Audience: **g,l,u,f.**

Orwell, George **PR6029.R8A6 2000**
The Collected Essays, Journalism and Letters of George Orwell: An Age Like This, 1920-1940. Sonia Orwell & Ian Angus (Editors). Trade Paper. David R. Godine Publisher. Boston, MA. 2000. 600p. ISBN:1-56792-133-7, ISBN13: 978-1-56792-133-5. Dewey:828/.91209 B. LCCN:00-037540.
Audience: **g,l,u,f.**

Orwell, George **PR6029.R8A6 2000**
The Collected Essays, Journalism and Letters of George Orwell: In Front of Your Nose, 1945-1950. Sonia Orwell & Ian Angus (Editors). Trade Paper. David R. Godine Publisher. Boston, MA. 2000. 496p. Nonpareil Ser., Vol. 89 ISBN:1-56792-136-1, ISBN13: 978-1-56792-136-6. Dewey:828/.91209 B. LCCN:00-037540.
Audience: **g,l,u,f.**

Orwell, George **PR6029.R8A6 2000**
The Collected Essays, Journalism and Letters of George Orwell: As I Please, 1943-1945. Sonia Orwell & Ian Angus (Editors). Trade Paper. David R. Godine Publisher. Boston, MA. 2000. 496p. Nonpareil Ser., Vol. 88 ISBN:1-56792-135-3, ISBN13: 978-1-56792-135-9. Dewey:828/.91209 B. LCCN:00-037540.
Audience: **g,l,u,f.**

Orwell, George **PR6029.R8A63 2003**
Animal Farm: Centennial Edition. Ann Patchett (Foreword by). Trade Paper. Penguin Group (USA) Inc. New York, NY. 2003. 128p. ISBN:0-452-28424-4, ISBN13: 978-0-452-28424-1. Dewey:823/.912. LCCN:2003-274731.
Audience: **g,l,u,f.**

Orwell, George **PR6029.R8N647 2003**
Nineteen Eighty-Four. Thomas Pynchon (Foreword by), Erich Fromm (Afterword by). Trade Paper. Penguin Group (USA) Inc. New York, NY. 2003. 368p. ISBN:0-452-28423-6, ISBN13: 978-0-452-28423-4. Dewey:823/.912. LCCN:2003-273412.
Audience: **g,l,u,f.**

Patai, Daphne **PR6029.R8Z753 1984**
The Orwell Mystique: A Study in Male Ideology. Cloth Text. University of Massachusetts Press. Amherst, MA. 1984. 344p. ISBN:0-87023-446-3, ISBN13: 978-0-87023-446-0. Dewey:828/.91209. LCCN:84-008488.
Audience: **u,f.**

Rodden, John **PR6029.R8Z776 2001**
George Orwell: The Politics of Literary Reputation. Trade Paper. Transaction Publishers. Somerset, NJ. 2002. 510p. ISBN:0-7658-0896-X, ISBN13: 978-0-7658-0896-7. Dewey:828/.91209. LCCN:2001-048082.
Audience: **u,f.**

Smith, David **PR6019.O9**
Orwell for Beginners. Ed. 2. Michael Mosher (Illustrator). Trade Paper. Writers & Readers Publishing, Inc. New York, NY. 1999. 192p. ISBN:0-86316-292-4, ISBN13: 978-0-86316-292-3. Dewey:823.9/12.
Audience: **g,l,u.**

Stansky, Peter **PR6029.R8Z792 1994**
Unknown Orwell and Orwell: The Transformation. Trade Paper. Stanford University Press. Palo Alto, CA. 1994. 654p. ISBN:0-8047-2342-7, ISBN13: 978-0-8047-2342-8. Dewey:828/.91209 B. LCCN:94-065009.
Audience: **u,f.**

Taylor, D. J. **PR6029.R8**
Orwell: The Life. Trade Paper. Henry Holt & Company. New York, NY. 2004. 496p. ISBN:0-8050-7693-X, ISBN13: 978-0-8050-7693-6. Dewey:828/.91209 B.
Audience: **g,l,u,f.**

Voorhees, Richard J. **PR6029.R8 Z85**
The Paradox of George Orwell. Paper Text. Textbook Publishers. Temecula, CA. 2003. 127p. ISBN:0-7581-5300-7, ISBN13: 978-0-7581-5300-5. Dewey:928.2.
Audience: **g,u,f.**

Williams, Raymond **PR6029.R8 Z86**
George Orwell. Cloth Text. Columbia University Press. New York, NY. 1981. 112p. A Morningside Bk. ISBN:0-231-05374-6, ISBN13: 978-0-231-05374-7. Dewey:828/.91209. LCCN:61-006134.
Audience: **g,l,u,f.**

Woodcock, George **PR6029.R8**
Crystal Spirit: A Study of George Orwell. Trade Cloth. Black Rose Books. Montreal, PQ. 2005. 366p. ISBN:1-55164-269-7, ISBN13: 978-1-55164-269-7. Dewey:828/.91209.
Audience: **g,u,f.**

Individual Authors and Works > 20th C. > Osborne, John

Gilleman, Luc **PR6029.S39Z637 2001**
John Osborne: Vituperative Artist. Kimball King (Editor). Cloth Text. Garland Publishing, Inc. New York, NY. 2002. 260p. Casebooks in Modern Drama Ser., 13 ISBN:0-8153-2201-1, ISBN13: 978-0-8153-2201-6. Dewey:822/.914. LCCN:00-061736.
Audience: **u,f.** *Choice, 2003, 2002.*

Osborne, John **PR6065.S18**
Almost a Gentleman: An Autobiography, 1955-1956. Trade Paper. Faber & Faber, Inc. New York, NY. 1994. 304p. ISBN:0-571-16635-0, ISBN13: 978-0-571-16635-0. Dewey:822.914.
Audience: **g,l,u,f.**

Osborne, John **PR6029.S39**
A Better Class of Person: An Autobiography, 1929-1956. Trade Paper. Faber & Faber, Inc. New York, NY. 1994. 128p. ISBN:0-571-16399-8, ISBN13: 978-0-571-16399-1. Dewey:822.914.
Audience: **g,l,u,f.**

Osborne, John **PR6065.S18D36 1994**
Damn You, England: Collected Prose. Cloth Text. Faber & Faber, Inc. New York, NY. 1995. 268p. ISBN:0-571-16921-X, ISBN13: 978-0-571-16921-4. Dewey:828.9/14/08. LCCN:95-120430.
Audience: **g,u,f.**

Osborne, John **PR6066.I53**
John Osborne: The Entertainer-Hotel in Amsterdam-West of Suez. Trade Paper. Faber & Faber, Inc. New York, NY. 1998. 304p. ISBN:0-571-17846-4, ISBN13: 978-0-571-17846-9. Dewey:822.9/14.
Audience: **g,l,u,f.**

Osborne, John **PR6066.I53**
John Osborne Plays 1: Look Back in Anger; Epitaph for George Dillion; the World of Paul... Trade Paper. Faber & Faber, Inc. New York, NY. 1996. 289p. ISBN:0-571-17766-2, ISBN13: 978-0-571-17766-0. Dewey:822.9/14.
Audience: **g,l,u,f.**

Individual Authors and Works > 20th C. > Pinter, Harold

Billington, Michael **PR6066.I53**
The Life and Work of Harold Pinter. Trade Cloth. Faber & Faber, Inc. New York, NY. 1997. 384p. ISBN:0-571-17103-6, ISBN13: 978-0-571-17103-3. Dewey:822.9/14.
Audience: **g,u,f.** *Choice, 1997.*

Knowles, Ronald **PR6066.I53Z714 1995**
Understanding Harold Pinter. Cloth Text. University of South Carolina Press. Columbia, SC. 1995. 232p. Understanding Contemporary British Literature Ser. ISBN:1-57003-044-8, ISBN13: 978-1-57003-044-4. Dewey:822/.914. LCCN:95-004338.
Audience: **l,u.** *Choice, 1995.*

Pinter, Harold **PR6066.I53A9 1997**
Ashes to Ashes. Trade Paper. Grove/Atlantic, Inc. New York, NY. 1997. 96p. ISBN:0-8021-3510-2, ISBN13: 978-0-8021-3510-0. Dewey:822/.914. LCCN:97-001598.
Audience: **g,l,u,f.**

Pinter, Harold **PR6066.I53A6 1996**
Collected Poems and Prose. Trade Paper. Grove/Atlantic, Inc. New York, NY. 1995. 124p. ISBN:0-8021-3434-3, ISBN13: 978-0-8021-3434-9. Dewey:821/.914. LCCN:95-035957.
Audience: **g,l,u,f.**

Pinter, Harold **PR6066.I53 1990**
Complete Works: Birthday Party. Trade Paper. Grove/Atlantic, Inc. New York, NY. 1994. 256p. ISBN:0-8021-5096-9, ISBN13: 978-0-8021-5096-7. Dewey:822/.914. LCCN:90-013933.
Audience: **g,l,u,f.**

Pinter, Harold **PR6066.I53 1990**
Complete Works: The Homecoming, Vol. 3. Trade Paper. Grove/Atlantic, Inc. New York, NY. 1994. 256p. ISBN:0-8021-5049-7, ISBN13: 978-0-8021-5049-3. Dewey:822/.914. LCCN:90-013933.
Audience: **g,l,u,f.**

Pinter, Harold **PR6066.I53 1990**
Complete Works: The Caretaker, Vol. 2. Trade Paper. Grove/Atlantic, Inc. New York, NY. 1994. 256p. ISBN:0-8021-3237-5, ISBN13: 978-0-8021-3237-6. Dewey:822/.914. LCCN:90-013933.
Audience: **g,l,u,f.**

Pinter, Harold **PR6066.I53 1990**
Complete Works: Betrayal. Trade Paper. Grove/Atlantic, Inc. New York, NY. 1994. 384p. ISBN:0-8021-5050-0, ISBN13: 978-0-8021-5050-9. Dewey:822/.914. LCCN:90-013933.
Audience: **g,l,u,f.**

Pinter, Harold **GR342 .Z6 1979**
The Essential Pinter: Selections from the Work of Harold Pinter. Trade Paper. Grove/Atlantic, Inc. New York, NY. 2006. 416p. ISBN:0-8021-4269-9, ISBN13: 978-0-8021-4269-6. Dewey:822/.914. LCCN:2006-043518.
Audience: **g,l,u,f.**

Pinter, Harold **PN1997 A1 P5**
Five Screenplays: The Servant; The Pumpkin Eater; The Quiller Memorandum; Accident; The Go-Between. Trade Paper. Grove/Atlantic, Inc. New York, NY. 1994. 368p. ISBN:0-8021-5119-1, ISBN13: 978-0-8021-5119-3. Dewey:822/.9/14. LCCN:73-006220.
Audience: **g,l,u,f.**

Pinter, Harold **PR6066.I53 H65 1980**
The Hothouse. Trade Cloth. Grove/Atlantic, Inc. New York, NY. 1980. ISBN:0-394-51395-9, ISBN13: 978-0-394-51395-9. Dewey:822/.914.
Audience: **g,l,u,f.**

Pinter, Harold **PR6066.I53V37 1998**
Various Voices: Prose, Poetry, Politics, 1948-1998. Trade Cloth. Grove/Atlantic, Inc. New York, NY. 1999. 224p. ISBN:0-8021-1643-4, ISBN13: 978-0-8021-1643-7. Dewey:822/.914. LCCN:98-053371.
Audience: **g,u,f.**

Pinter, Harold, et al. **PN1997.3**
The Proust Screenplay. Joseph Losey & Barbara Bray (Authors). Trade Paper, Perfect. Grove/Atlantic, Inc. New York, NY. 1999. 177p. ISBN:0-8021-3646-X, ISBN13: 978-0-8021-3646-6. Dewey:822/.9/14.
Audience: **u,f.**

Prentice, Penelope **PR6066.I53Z75 2000**
The Pinter Ethic: The Erotic Aesthetic. Ed. 2. Trade Paper. Garland Publishing, Inc. New York, NY. 2000. 480p. Reference Library of the Humanities, Vol. 2237 ISBN:0-8153-3886-4, ISBN13: 978-0-8153-3886-4. Dewey:822/.914. LCCN:2001-265766.
Audience: **u,f.** *Choice, 1994.*

Raby, Peter (Editor) **PR6066.I53Z625520**
The Cambridge Companion to Harold Pinter. Cloth Text. Cambridge University Press. New York, NY. 2001. 292p. Companions to Literature Ser. ISBN:0-521-65123-9, ISBN13: 978-0-521-65123-3. Dewey:822/.914. LCCN:2001-022302.
Audience: **g,l,u,f.** *Choice, 2002.*

Individual Authors and Works > 20th C. > Powell, Anthony

Birns, Nicholas **PR6031.O74Z625 2004**
Understanding Anthony Powell. Trade Cloth. University of South Carolina Press. Columbia, SC. 2004. 448p. Understanding Contemporary British Literature Ser. ISBN:1-57003-549-0, ISBN13: 978-1-57003-549-4. Dewey:823/.912 B. LCCN:2004-004430.
Audience: **g,l,u,f.** *Choice, 2005.*

Powell, Anthony **PR6031.O74 D33**
A Dance to Music of Time: Second Movement. Trade Paper. University of Chicago Press. Chicago, IL. 1995. 746p. ISBN:0-226-67716-8, ISBN13: 978-0-226-67716-3. Dewey:823.912. LCCN:94-047228.
Audience: **g.**

Powell, Anthony **PR6031.O74 D34**
A Dance to the Music of Time: Fourth Movement. Trade Paper. University of Chicago Press. Chicago, IL. 1995. 804p. ISBN:0-226-67718-4, ISBN13: 978-0-226-67718-7. Dewey:823.912. LCCN:94-047228.
Audience: **g.**

Powell, Anthony **PR6031.074**
A Dance to the Music of Time: Third Movement. Trade Paper. University of Chicago Press. Chicago, IL. 1995. 731p. ISBN:0-226-67717-6, ISBN13: 978-0-226-67717-0. Dewey:Fic. LCCN:94-047228.
Audience: **g.** B

Powell, Anthony **PR6031.O74D33 1995**
A Dance to the Music of Time: First Movement. Trade Paper. University of Chicago Press. Chicago, IL. 1995. 732p. ISBN:0-226-67714-1, ISBN13: 978-0-226-67714-9. Dewey:823/.912. LCCN:94-047228.
Audience: **g.**

Powell, Anthony **PR6031.O74F57 2004**
The Fisher King. Trade Paper. University of Chicago Press. Chicago, IL. 2004. 256p. Phoenix Fiction Ser. ISBN:0-226-67700-1, ISBN13: 978-0-226-67700-2. Dewey:823/.912. LCCN:2004-048029.
Audience: **g.**

Powell, Anthony **PR6031.O74Z477 2001**
To Keep the Ball Rolling: The Memoirs of Anthony Powell. Trade Cloth. University of Chicago Press. Chicago, IL. 2001. 472p. ISBN:0-226-67721-4, ISBN13: 978-0-226-67721-7. Dewey:823/.912 B. LCCN:00-050780.
Audience: **g,l,u,f.** *Choice, 2001.*

Individual Authors and Works > 20th C. > Priestly, J. B.

Priestley, J. B. **PN1570**
The Art of the Dramatist: An Anthology of Writings on the Theatre. Trade Paper. Consortium Book Sales & Distribution. Saint Paul, MN. 2006. 232p. ISBN:1-84002-294-9, ISBN13: 978-1-84002-294-0. Dewey:808.2.
Audience: **u,f.**

Priestley, J. B. **PR6031.R53**
Collected Plays I. Trade Paper. Theatre Communications Group, Inc. New York, NY. 2003. 263p. ISBN:1-84002-292-2, ISBN13: 978-1-84002-292-6. Dewey:822.912.
Audience: **g,l,u,f.**

Priestley, J. B. **PR6031.R6**
Collected Plays Two. Trade Paper. Theatre Communications Group, Inc. New York, NY. 2004. 278p. ISBN:1-84002-293-0, ISBN13: 978-1-84002-293-3. Dewey:822.912.
Audience: **g,l,u,f.**

Priestley, J. B. **PR6031.R6.D38 1971**
Delight. Trade Cloth. Ayer Company Publishers, Inc. Manchester, NH. 1977. xvi, 170p. Essay Index Reprint Ser. ISBN:0-8369-2015-5, ISBN13: 978-0-8369-2015-4. Dewey:824/.9/12. LCCN:70-117828.
Audience: **g,l,u,f.** *B*

Priestley, J. B. **PR6031.R6M34 1996**
The Magicians. Trade Cloth. Frederic C. Beil Publisher, Inc. Savannah, GA. 1996. 160p. ISBN:0-913720-73-9, ISBN13: 978-0-913720-73-8. Dewey:823/.912. LCCN:90-043613.
Audience: **g,l,u,f.**

Priestley, J. B. **PR6031.R6 S3 1983**
Salt Is Leaving. Jacques Barzun & W. H. Taylor (Editors). Library Binding. Garland Publishing, Inc. New York, NY. 1983. 247p. Crime Fiction 1950-1975 Ser. ISBN:0-8240-4988-8, ISBN13: 978-0-8240-4988-1. Dewey:823.912. LCCN:81-047381.
Audience: **g,l,u,f.**

Priestley, J.B. **PR6019.O9**
Angel Pavement. Trade Paper. Kessinger Publishing, LLC. Whitefish, MT. 2005. ISBN:0-7661-9503-1, ISBN13: 978-0-7661-9503-5. Dewey:823/.9/1.
Audience: **g,l,u,f.**

Priestley, J.B. **PN6175**
Fools and Philosophers: A Gallery of Com. Trade Paper. Kessinger Publishing, LLC. Whitefish, MT. 2005. ISBN:1-4179-6579-7, ISBN13: 978-1-4179-6579-3. Dewey:827.
Audience: **g,l,u,f.**

Individual Authors and Works > 20th C. > Pritchett, V. S.

Bowen, Elizabeth & Greene, Graham **PN45 .B62 1975**
Why Do I Write?: An Exchange of Views Between Elizabeth Bowen, Graham Greene and V. S. Pritchett. V. S. Pritchett (Preface by). Library Binding. M. S. G. Haskell House. Brooklyn, NY. 1975. English Literature Ser., No. 33 ISBN:0-8383-2094-5, ISBN13: 978-0-8383-2094-5. Dewey:801. LCCN:75-022190.
Audience: **g,l,u,f.**

Pritchett, V. S. **PR6072.A4**
A Cab at the Door and Midnight Oil. Trade Paper. Random House Adult Trade Publishing Group. New York, NY. 1994. 432p. ISBN:0-8129-9183-4, ISBN13: 978-0-8129-9183-3. Dewey:828/.9/1203 B.
Audience: **g,l,u,f.**

Pritchett, V. S. **PR6031.R7 A6 1992**
Complete Collected Essays. Trade Cloth. Random House, Inc. New York, NY. 1992. ISBN:0-679-41112-7, ISBN13: 978-0-679-41112-3. Dewey:824/.912. LCCN:91-039919.
Audience: **u,f.**

Pritchett, V. S. **PR6019.O9**
Complete Collected Stories. Trade Paper. Knopf Publishing Group. New York, NY. 1992. ISBN:0-06-797389-2, ISBN13: 978-0-06-797389-9. Dewey:823/.912. LCCN:91-058068.
Audience: **g,l,u,f.**

Pritchett, V. S. **PR6031.R7**
The Essential Pritchett: Selected Writings. UK-Trade Paper. Knopf Publishing Group. New York, NY. 2004. 577p. ISBN:0-09-947459-X, ISBN13: 978-0-09-947459-3. Dewey:828.9/1209.
Audience: **g,l,u,f.**

Pritchett, V. S. **PR881**
The Pritchett Century. UK-B Format Paperback. Knopf Publishing Group. New York, NY. 1999. xxii, 577p. ISBN:0-09-975541-6, ISBN13: 978-0-09-975541-8. Dewey:823.9/12/09.
Audience: **u,f.**

Treglown, Jeremy **PR6031.R7Z897 2005**
V. S. Pritchett: A Working Life. Trade Cloth. Random House Adult Trade Publishing Group. New York, NY. 2005. 352p. ISBN:0-375-50853-8, ISBN13: 978-0-375-50853-0. Dewey:823/.912. LCCN:2004-053857.
Audience: **u,f.** *Choice, 2005.*

Individual Authors and Works > 20th C. > Pym, Barbara

Pym, Barbara **PR6015.I3**
Excellent Women. Trade Paper. Penguin Group (USA) Inc. New York, NY. 1988. 272p. ISBN:0-452-26730-7, ISBN13: 978-0-452-26730-5. Dewey:823/.914. LCCN:88-070110.
Audience: **g,l,u,f.**

Pym, Barbara **PR6015.I3**
Less Than Angels. Trade Paper. Moyer Bell. Kingston, RI. 2007. 256p. ISBN:1-55921-388-4, ISBN13: 978-1-55921-388-2. Dewey:823/.914.
Audience: **g,l,u,f.**

Pym, Barbara **PR6066.Y58 Q3 1978**
Quartet in Autumn. Trade Paper. Macmillan Publishing Company, Inc. Old Tappan, NJ. 1977. 218p. ISBN:0-333-22778-6, ISBN13: 978-0-333-22778-7. Dewey:823/.914. LCCN:77-379168.
Audience: **g,l,u,f.**

Pym, Barbara **PR6066.Y58S6 1999**
Some Tame Gazelle. Trade Paper. Moyer Bell. Kingston, RI. 1999. 252p. ISBN:1-55921-264-0, ISBN13: 978-1-55921-264-9. Dewey:823/.914. LCCN:98-028858.
Audience: **g,l,u,f.**

Pym, Barbara **PR6066.Y58**
Very Private Eye: An Autobiography in Diaries and Letters. Trade Paper. Moyer Bell. Kingston, RI. 2007. 380p. ISBN:1-55921-331-0, ISBN13: 978-1-55921-331-8. Dewey:823/.914 B.
Audience: **g,l,u,f.**

Salwak, Dale **Z8721.4.S25 1991**
Barbara Pym: A Reference Guide. Trade Cloth. Macmillan Publishing Company, Inc. Old Tappan, NJ. 1991. 193p. Reference Guides to Literature Ser. ISBN:0-8161-9076-3, ISBN13: 978-0-8161-9076-8. Dewey:016.823/914. LCCN:91-013044.
Audience: **g,l,u,f.**

Soule, George **Z2014.F4S68 1998**
Four British Women Novelists: Anita Brookner, Margaret Drabble, Iris Murdoch, Barbara Pym: An Annotated and Critical Secondary Bibliography. Trade Cloth. Scarecrow Press, Inc. Lanham, MD. 1998. 544p. Magill Bibliographies Ser. ISBN:0-8108-3505-3, ISBN13: 978-0-8108-3505-4. Dewey:016.823/914099287. LCCN:98-005992.
Audience: **g,l,u,f.** *Choice, 1998.*

Individual Authors and Works > 20th C. > R

Darlow, Michael **PR6035**
Terence Rattigan: The Man and His Work. Trade Cloth. Quartet Books, Ltd. London, 2000. 535p. ISBN:0-7043-7114-6, ISBN13: 978-0-7043-7114-9. Dewey:822.9/12.
Audience: **l,u,f.**

Rattigan, Terence **PR6035**
The Collected Plays of Terence Rattigan: The Later Plays, 1953-1977. Trade Cloth. Paper Tiger, The. Kerhonkson, NY. 2001. 729p. ISBN:1-889439-28-2, ISBN13: 978-1-889439-28-0. Dewey:822.912.
Audience: **g,l,u,f.**

Rattigan, Terence **PR6035**
The Collected Plays of Terence Rattigan: The Early Plays 1936-1952. Trade Cloth. Paper Tiger, The. Kerhonkson, NY. 2001. 652p. ISBN:1-889439-27-4, ISBN13: 978-1-889439-27-3. Dewey:822.912.
Audience: **g,l,u,f.**

Read, Herbert **PR6035.E24A6 1994**
Selected Poetry. Trade Cloth. Trafalgar Square. North Pomfret, VT. 1994. 288p. ISBN:1-85619-132-X, ISBN13: 978-1-85619-132-6. Dewey:821/.912. LCCN:93-241333.
Audience: **g,l,u,f.**

Read, Herbert E. **PN37 .R4**
Collected Essays in Literary Criticism. Trade Cloth. Hyperion Press, Inc. Westport, CT. 1985. ISBN:0-88355-811-4, ISBN13: 978-0-88355-811-9. Dewey:809. LCCN:78-014137.
Audience: **u,f.**

Read, Herbert Edward (Introduction by) **PR6035.E24T6 2002**
To Hell with Culture: And Other Essays on Art and Society. Ed. 2. Paper over Boards. Routledge. New York, NY. 2002. 240p. Routledge Classics Ser. ISBN:0-415-28992-0, ISBN13: 978-0-415-28992-4. Dewey:824/.912. LCCN:2002-031672.
Audience: **g,l,u,f.**

Rendell, Ruth **PR6068.E63**
Sins of the Fathers. Mass Market. Ballantine Books. New York, NY. 1986. 256p. ISBN:0-345-34253-4, ISBN13: 978-0-345-34253-9. Dewey:823.914.
Audience: **g,l,u,f.**

Rendell, Ruth **PR6015.I3**
Wexford: An Omnibus. Book, Other. Random House of Canada, Ltd. Mississauga, ON. 1994. 512p. ISBN:0-09-956640-0, ISBN13: 978-0-09-956640-3. Dewey:823/.914.
Audience: **g,l,u,f.**

Rohmer, Sax **PR6045.A37**
Fu Manchu Omnibuses: The Island of Fu Manchu; the Wrath of Fu Manchu and Other Stories, Vol. 5. Trade Paper. Allison & Busby, Ltd. London, 2001. 240p. Fu Manchu Omnibus Ser., Vol. 5 ISBN:0-7490-0520-3, ISBN13: 978-0-7490-0520-7. Dewey:823/.912.
Audience: **g,l,u,f.**

Individual Authors and Works > 20th C. > S

Sassoon, Siegfried **PR6037.A86**
Memoirs of a Fox-Hunting Man. Ed. 2. Trade Paper. Faber & Faber, Inc. New York, NY. 1960. 320p. ISBN:0-571-06454-X, ISBN13: 978-0-571-06454-0. Dewey:821.912.
Audience: **g,l,u,f.**

Sassoon, Siegfried **PR6019.O9**
Memoirs of an Infantry Officer. Trade Paper. Faber & Faber, Inc. New York, NY. 1965. 236p. ISBN:0-571-06410-8, ISBN13: 978-0-571-06410-6. Dewey:823/.912.
Audience: **g,l,u,f.** B

Sassoon, Siegfried **PR6037.A86**
Selected Poems. Trade Paper. Faber & Faber, Inc. New York, NY. 1968. 94p. ISBN:0-571-08540-7, ISBN13: 978-0-571-08540-8. Dewey:821.912.
Audience: **g,l,u,f.**

Sassoon, Siegfried **PR6037.A867**
The War Poems of Siegfried Sassoon. Rupert Hart-Davis (Editor). Trade Paper. Faber & Faber, Inc. New York, NY. 1983. 160p. ISBN:0-571-13015-1, ISBN13: 978-0-571-13015-3. Dewey:821.9/12. LCCN:82-024202.
Audience: **g,l,u,f.**

Self, Will **PR6069.E3654**
Grey Area. Trade Paper. Grove/Atlantic, Inc. New York, NY. 1997. 304p. ISBN:0-87113-673-2, ISBN13: 978-0-87113-673-2. Dewey:823.914. LCCN:95-000601.
Audience: **g,l,u,f.**

Self, Will **PR6015.I3**
How the Dead Live. Trade Paper. Grove/Atlantic, Inc. New York, NY. 2001. 416p. ISBN:0-8021-3848-9, ISBN13: 978-0-8021-3848-4. Dewey:823.9/14.
Audience: **g,l,u,f.**

Sillitoe, Alan **PR6015.I3**
The Loneliness of the Long-Distance Runner. Trade Paper. Penguin Group (USA) Inc. New York, NY. 1992. 176p. Plume Contemporary Fiction Ser. ISBN:0-452-26908-3, ISBN13: 978-0-452-26908-8. Dewey:823/.914. LCCN:92-053548.
Audience: **g,l,u,f.**

Sillitoe, Alan **PR6015.I3**
Saturday Night and Sunday Morning. Trade Paper. Penguin Group (USA) Inc. New York, NY. 1992. 256p. Plume Contemporary Fiction Ser. ISBN:0-452-26909-1, ISBN13: 978-0-452-26909-5. Dewey:823.9/14. LCCN:92-053549.
Audience: **g,l,u,f.** B

Smith, Zadie **PR6069.M59O5 2005**
On Beauty. Trade Cloth. Penguin Group (USA) Inc. New York, NY. 2005. 464p. ISBN:1-59420-063-7, ISBN13: 978-1-59420-063-2. Dewey:823/.92. LCCN:2006-272543.
Audience: **g,l,u,f.**

Smith, Zadie **PR6015.I3**
White Teeth. Trade Cloth. Knopf Publishing Group. New York, NY. ISBN:0-676-80899-9, ISBN13: 978-0-676-80899-5. Dewey:823/.914.
Audience: **g,l,u,f.**

Stevenson, Anne **PR6069.T45A6 1996**
The Collected Poems. Trade Paper. Oxford University Press, Inc. New York, NY. 1997. 288p. ISBN:0-19-283251-4, ISBN13: 978-0-19-283251-1. Dewey:811.5/4. LCCN:96-033690.
Audience: **g,l,u,f.**

Strachey, Lytton **DA562.S87 2003**
Eminent Victorians. John Sutherland (Editor). Trade Paper. Oxford University Press, Inc. New York, NY. 2003. 324p. Oxford World's Classics Ser. ISBN:0-19-280158-9, ISBN13: 978-0-19-280158-6. Dewey:941.081092/2 B.
Audience: **g,l,u,f.** B

Swift, Graham **PR6069.W47L3 1996**
Last Orders. Trade Paper. Knopf Publishing Group. New York, NY. 1997. 304p. ISBN:0-679-76662-6, ISBN13: 978-0-679-76662-9. Dewey:823/.914. LCCN:96-046858.
Audience: **g,l,u,f.**

Swift, Graham **PR6069.W47 L4 1992**
Learning to Swim and Other Stories. Trade Paper. Knopf Publishing Group. New York, NY. 1992. ISBN:0-679-73978-5, ISBN13: 978-0-679-73978-4. Dewey:823/.914. LCCN:91-050601.
Audience: **g,l,u,f.**

Swift, Graham **PR6015.I3**
Waterland. Trade Paper. Knopf Publishing Group. New York, NY. 1992. 368p. ISBN:0-679-73979-3, ISBN13: 978-0-679-73979-1. Dewey:823.9/14. LCCN:91-050600.
Audience: **g,l,u,f.**

Wilson, Jean M. **PR6037.A86Z9 1999**
Siegfried Sassoon: The Making of a War Poet, a Biography, 1886-1918. Paper over Boards. Routledge. New York, NY. 1999. 608p. ISBN:0-415-92325-5, ISBN13: 978-0-415-92325-5. Dewey:821/.912 B. LCCN:98-052081.
Audience: **g,l,u,f.**

Individual Authors and Works > 20th C. > Sackville-West, Vita

Glendinning, Victoria **PR6057.L43**
Vita: The Life of V. Sackville-West. Trade Paper. Phoenix House. London, 2005. 448p. ISBN:0-7538-1926-0, ISBN13: 978-0-7538-1926-5. Dewey:828.91209.
Audience: **g,l,u,f.**

Leaska, Mitchell A. & Phillips, John (Editors) **PR6039.R39.Z493 1990**
Violet to Vita: The Letters of Violet Trefusis to Vita Sackville-West, 1910-1921. Trade Paper. Penguin Group (USA) Inc. New York, NY. 1991. 320p. ISBN:0-14-015796-4, ISBN13: 978-0-14-015796-3. Dewey:823/.912. LCCN:90-050062.
Audience: **g,l,u,f.**

Nicolson, Nigel **PR6037.A35Z8 1998**
Portrait of a Marriage: Vita Sackville-West and Harold Nicolson. Trade Paper. University of Chicago Press. Chicago, IL. 1998. 278p. ISBN:0-226-58357-0, ISBN13: 978-0-226-58357-0. Dewey:823/.912 B. LCCN:98-023343.
Audience: **g,l,u,f.**

Sackville-West, Vita **PR6037.A35**
All Passion Spent. Library Binding. Buccaneer Books, Inc. Cutchogue, NY. 1990. 296p. ISBN:0-89966-745-7, ISBN13: 978-0-89966-745-4. Dewey:823/.910809287.
Audience: **g,l,u,f.**

Sackville-West, Vita **PR6037.A35**
The Edwardians. Library Binding. Buccaneer Books, Inc. Cutchogue, NY. 1990. ISBN:0-89968-549-8, ISBN13: 978-0-89968-549-6. Dewey:823.9.
Audience: **g,l,u,f.**

Sackville-West, Vita **PR6037.A35**
Land. Trade Cloth. Lincoln Frances Ltd. London, 2004. 108p. ISBN:0-7112-2359-9, ISBN13: 978-0-7112-2359-2. Dewey:821.9/12.
Audience: **g,l,u,f.**

Sackville-West, Vita **PR6037.A35**
No Signposts in the Sea. Trade Paper. Little, Brown Book Group Ltd. London, 2001. 156p. ISBN:0-86068-578-0, ISBN13: 978-0-86068-578-4. Dewey:823.9/12.
Audience: **g,l,u,f.**

Sackville-West, Vita **PR6037.A35A6 2002**
Vita Sackville-West: Selected Writings. Mary Ann Caws (Editor), Nigel Nicolson (Foreword by). Cloth over Boards. Palgrave Macmillan. New York, NY. 2002. 400p. ISBN:0-312-23760-X, ISBN13: 978-0-312-23760-8. Dewey:823/.912 B. LCCN:2002-283857.
Audience: **g,l,u,f.** *Choice, 2003.*

Individual Authors and Works > 20th C. > Saki (H. H. Munro)

Saki & Baring, Maurice **PR6025.U675**
The Unbearable Bassington. Trade Paper. Kessinger Publishing, LLC. Whitefish, MT. 2004. ISBN:1-4179-2368-7, ISBN13: 978-1-4179-2368-7. Dewey:823.7.
Audience: **g,l,u,f.**

Saki & Chesteron, G. K. **PR6025.U675**
The Toys of Peace and Other Papers. Trade Paper. Kessinger Publishing, LLC. Whitefish, MT. 2004. ISBN:1-4179-2261-3, ISBN13: 978-1-4179-2261-1. Dewey:823.912.
Audience: **g,l,u,f.**

Saki & Milne, A. A. **PR6025.U675**
The Chronicles of Clovis. Trade Paper. Kessinger Publishing, LLC. Whitefish, MT. 2004. ISBN:1-4179-2260-5, ISBN13: 978-1-4179-2260-4. Dewey:828/.9/12.
Audience: **g,l,u,f.**

Saki & Nevinson, H. W. **PZ3.M9274**
Beasts and Super Beasts. Trade Paper. Kessinger Publishing, LLC. Whitefish, MT. 2004. ISBN:1-4179-2262-1, ISBN13: 978-1-4179-2262-8. Dewey:823/.912.
Audience: **g,l,u,f.**

Saki & Squire, J. C. **PR6025.U675 S7**
The Square Egg and Other Sketches with Three Plays. Trade Paper. Kessinger Publishing, LLC. Whitefish, MT. 2005. ISBN:1-4179-3269-4, ISBN13: 978-1-4179-3269-6. Dewey:828/.912.
Audience: **g,l,u,f.**

Saki & Walpole, Hugh **PR6019.O9**
Reginald and Reginald in Russia. Trade Paper. Kessinger Publishing, LLC. Whitefish, MT. 2004. ISBN:1-4179-2367-9, ISBN13: 978-1-4179-2367-0. Dewey:823/.9/12.
Audience: **g,l,u,f.**

Individual Authors and Works > 20th C. > Sayers, Dorothy

Hannay, Margaret P. (Editor) **PR6037.A95.Z**
As Her Whimsey Took Her: Critical Essays on the Work of Dorothy L. Sayers. Trade Paper. Books on Demand. Ann Arbor, MI. 319p. ISBN:0-7837-0576-X, ISBN13: 978-0-7837-0576-7. Dewey:823/.9/12. LCCN:79-010933.
Audience: **g,u,f.** B

Hone, Ralph E. **PR6037.A95.Z73**
Dorothy L. Sayers: A Literary Biography. Trade Cloth. Kent State University Press. Kent, OH. 1979. 234p. ISBN:0-87338-228-5, ISBN13: 978-0-87338-228-1. Dewey:823/.9/12. LCCN:79-009783.
Audience: **g,l,u,f.** B

McGregor, Robert Kuhn & Lewis, Ethan **PR6037.A95Z78 2000**
Conundrums for the Long Weekend: England, Dorothy L. Sayers and Lord Peter Wimsey. Trade Cloth. Kent State University Press. Kent, OH. 2000. 272p. Lord Peter Wimsey Mystery Ser. ISBN:0-87338-665-5, ISBN13: 978-0-87338-665-4. Dewey:823/.912. LCCN:00-036876.
Audience: **g,l,u.** *Choice, 2001.*

Sayers, Dorothy L. **PR6019.O9**
Clouds of Witness. Trade Cloth. Random House Value Publishing. New York, NY. 1992. 746p. Lord Peter Wimsey Mystery Ser. ISBN:0-614-32007-0, ISBN13: 978-0-614-32007-7. Dewey:823.9/12.
Audience: **g,l,u,f.**

Sayers, Dorothy L. **PR6019.O9**
The Five Red Herrings. Library Binding. Buccaneer Books, Inc. Cutchogue, NY. 1994. Lord Peter Wimsey Mystery Ser. ISBN:1-56849-332-0, ISBN13: 978-1-56849-332-9. Dewey:823/.912.
Audience: **g,l,u,f.**

Sayers, Dorothy L. **PR6019.O9**
Gaudy Night. Trade Cloth. Random House Value Publishing. New York, NY. 1992. 746p. Lord Peter Wimsey Mystery Ser. ISBN:0-614-32009-7, ISBN13: 978-0-614-32009-1. Dewey:823.9/12.
Audience: **g,l,u,f.** B

Sayers, Dorothy L. **PR6019.O9**
Lord Peter: A Collection of All the Lord Peter Wimsey Stories. Trade Cloth. Amereon, Ltd. Mattituck, NY. Lord Peter Wimsey Mystery Ser. ISBN:0-8488-1153-4, ISBN13: 978-0-8488-1153-2. Dewey:823/.912.
Audience: **g,l,u,f.**

Sayers, Dorothy L. **PR6019.O9**
Murder Must Advertise. Trade Cloth. Random House Value Publishing. New York, NY. 1992. 746p. Lord Peter Wimsey Mystery Ser. ISBN:0-614-32008-9, ISBN13: 978-0-614-32008-4. Dewey:823.9/12.
Audience: **g,l,u,f.**

Sayers, Dorothy L. **PR6019.O9**
The Nine Tailors. Trade Cloth. Amereon, Ltd. Mattituck, NY. 320p. Lord Peter Wimsey Mystery Ser. ISBN:0-8488-2388-5, ISBN13: 978-0-8488-2388-7. Dewey:823.9/12.
Audience: **g,l,u,f.**

Sayers, Dorothy L. **PR6037.A95**
Whose Body? Trade Cloth. Random House Value Publishing. New York, NY. 1992. 746p. Lord Peter Wimsey Mystery Ser. ISBN:0-614-32006-2, ISBN13: 978-0-614-32006-0. Dewey:823.912.
Audience: **g,l,u,f.**

Individual Authors and Works > 20th C. > Scott, Paul

Haswell, Janis Tedesco **PR6069.C596Z69 2002**
Paul Scott's Philosophy of Place(s): The Fiction of Relationality. Trade Cloth. Peter Lang Publishing, Inc. New York, NY. 2002. 280p. Studies in Twentieth-Century British Literature, Vol. 5 ISBN:0-8204-5679-9, ISBN13: 978-0-8204-5679-9. Dewey:823/.914. LCCN:2001-034676.
Audience: **u,f.**

Scott, Paul **PR6069.C596J4 1998**
The Raj Quartet: The Jewel in the Crown. Trade Paper. University of Chicago Press. Chicago, IL. 1998. 472p. Raj Quartet Ser., Vol. 1 ISBN:0-226-74340-3, ISBN13: 978-0-226-74340-0. Dewey:823/.914. LCCN:98-010568.
Audience: **g,l,u,f.**

Scott, Paul **PR6069.C596D3 1998**
The Raj Quartet: The Day of the Scorpion. Trade Paper. University of Chicago Press. Chicago, IL. 1998. 493p. Raj Quartet Ser., Vol. 2 ISBN:0-226-74341-1, ISBN13: 978-0-226-74341-7. Dewey:823/.914. LCCN:98-010781.
Audience: **g,l,u,f.**

Scott, Paul **PR6069.C596D5 1998**
The Raj Quartet: A Division of Spoils. Trade Paper. University of Chicago Press. Chicago, IL. 1998. 608p. Phoenix Fiction Ser., Vol. 4 ISBN:0-226-74344-6, ISBN13: 978-0-226-74344-8. Dewey:823/.914. LCCN:98-010560.
Audience: **g,l,u,f.**

Scott, Paul **PR6069.C596T6 1998**
The Towers of Silence, Vol. 3. Trade Paper. University of Chicago Press. Chicago, IL. 1998. 399p. Raj Quartet Ser., Vol. 3 ISBN:0-226-74343-8, ISBN13: 978-0-226-74343-1. Dewey:823/.914. LCCN:98-010569.
Audience: **g,l,u,f.**

Spurling, Hilary **PR6069.C596Z857 1991**
Paul Scott: A Life of the Author of the Raj Quartet. Trade Cloth. W. W. Norton & Company, Inc. New York, NY. 1991. x, 438 p. :p. ISBN:0-393-02938-7, ISBN13: 978-0-393-02938-3. Dewey:823/.914 B. LCCN:91-011762.
Audience: **g,l,u,f.** *Choice, 1991.*

Individual Authors and Works > 20th C. > The Sitwells

Sitwell, Edith **PR610**
Aspects of Modern Poetry. Paper Text. Classic Textbooks. Murrieta, CA. 1999. 264p. ISBN:1-4047-0694-1, ISBN13: 978-1-4047-0694-1. Dewey:821/.9/1209PR610.S5.
Audience: **g.**

Sitwell, Edith **PS3509.L43**
Collected Poems. Paper Text. Textbook Publishers. Temecula, CA. 2003. L, 442p. ISBN:0-7581-1004-9, ISBN13: 978-0-7581-1004-6. Dewey:821.912.
Audience: **g.** B

Sitwell, Edith **CT782**
English Eccentrics. Paper Text. Textbook Publishers. Temecula, CA. 2003. 376p. ISBN:0-7581-0993-8, ISBN13: 978-0-7581-0993-4. Dewey:920/.042.
Audience: **g.**

Sitwell, Osbert **PR6037.I83Z518**
Tales My Father Taught Me: An Evocation of Extravagant Episodes. Paper Text. Textbook Publishers. Temecula, CA. 2003. 206p. ISBN:0-7581-9727-6, ISBN13: 978-0-7581-9727-6. Dewey:928.2.
Audience: **g.** B

Individual Authors and Works > 20th C. > Smith, Stevie

Civello, Catherine A. **PR6037.M43Z59 1997**
Patterns of Ambivalence: The Poetry and Fiction of Stevie Smith. Trade Cloth. Camden House. Elizabethtown, NY. 1997. 114p. Studies in English and American Literature, Linguistics, and Culture ISBN:1-57113-119-1, ISBN13: 978-1-57113-119-5. Dewey:828/.91209. LCCN:97-024267.
Audience: **u,f.** *Choice, 1998.*

Huk, Romana **PR6037.M43Z697 2005**
Stevie Smith: Between the Lines. Saddle Stitched, Cloth over Boards, Dust Jacket. Palgrave Macmillan. New York, NY. 2005. 344p. ISBN:0-333-54997-X, ISBN13: 978-0-333-54997-1. Dewey:828/.91209. LCCN:2004-054896.
Audience: **u,f.** *Choice, 2006.*

Smith, Stevie **PR6037.M43.A17 1976**
The Collected Poems of Stevie Smith [I. Trade Cloth. Oxford University Press, Inc. New York, NY. 1976. 591p. ISBN:0-19-519816-6, ISBN13: 978-0-19-519816-4. Dewey:821/.9/12. LCCN:75-004322.
Audience: **g,l,u,f.** B

Smith, Stevie **PR6037.M43A6 1988**
New Selected Poems of Stevie Smith. Trade Cloth. New Directions Publishing Corporation. New York, NY. 1988. 160p. ISBN:0-8112-1067-7, ISBN13: 978-0-8112-1067-6. Dewey:821/.912. LCCN:88-001428.
Audience: **g,l,u,f.**

Smith, Stevie **PT9876.17.U8K2913**
Novel on Yellow Paper. Trade Paper. New Directions Publishing Corporation. New York, NY. 1994. 256p. Revived Modern Classic Ser., Vol. 778 ISBN:0-8112-1239-4, ISBN13: 978-0-8112-1239-7. Dewey:823.9/12. LCCN:93-049827.
Audience: **g,l,u,f.**

Smith, Stevie **PR6037.M43A6 1995**
A Very Pleasant Evening with Stevie Smith: Selected Shorter Prose. Trade Paper. New Directions Publishing Corporation. New York, NY. 1995. 96p. ISBN:0-8112-1295-5, ISBN13: 978-0-8112-1295-3. Dewey:828/.91209. LCCN:95-002273.
Audience: **g,l,u,f.**

Smith, Stevie **PR6037.M43 A6 1982A**
Me Again: Uncollected Writings of Stevie Smith. Jack Barbera & William McBrien (Editors). Trade Cloth. Farrar, Straus & Giroux. New York, NY. 1982. 360p. ISBN:0-374-20494-2, ISBN13: 978-0-374-20494-5. Dewey:828/.91209. LCCN:82-005062.
Audience: **g,l,u,f.**

Smith, Stevie (Illustrator) **PR6037.M43A6 1985**
Stevie Smith: A Selection. Hermione Lee (Preface by). Trade Cloth. Faber & Faber, Ltd. London, 1985. 224p. ISBN:0-571-13029-1, ISBN13: 978-0-571-13029-0. Dewey:828/.91209. LCCN:84-028782.
Audience: **g,l,u,f.**

Individual Authors and Works > 20th C. > Spark, Muriel

Bold, Alan N. **PR6037.P29Z57 1986**
Muriel Spark. Trade Paper. Routledge. New York, NY. 1986. 96p. Contemporary Writers Ser. ISBN:0-416-40360-3, ISBN13: 978-0-416-40360-2. Dewey:823/.914. LCCN:86-012671.
Audience: **g,l,u,f.** *Choice, 1987.*

Hynes, Joseph (Editor) **PR6037.P29 Z62 1992**
Critical Essays on Muriel Spark. Trade Cloth. Macmillan Publishing Company, Inc. Old Tappan, NJ. 1992. 200p. Critical Essays on British Literature Ser. ISBN:0-8161-8869-6, ISBN13: 978-0-8161-8869-7. Dewey:823/.914. LCCN:92-019137.
Audience: **l,u,f.**

Spark, Muriel **PR6037.P25A65 1995**
The Abbess of Crewe. Trade Paper. New Directions Publishing Corporation. New York, NY. 1995. 108p. Bibelots Ser. ISBN:0-8112-1296-3, ISBN13: 978-0-8112-1296-0. Dewey:823.9/14. LCCN:95-001628.
Audience: **g,l,u,f.**

Spark, Muriel **PR6037.P29A6 2001**
All the Stories of Muriel Spark. Trade Paper. New Directions Publishing Corporation. New York, NY. 2001. 416p. ISBN:0-8112-1494-X, ISBN13: 978-0-8112-1494-0. Dewey:823/.914. LCCN:2001-042588.
Audience: **g,l,u,f.**

Spark, Muriel **PR6037.P29B29 1999**
The Bachelors. Trade Paper. New Directions Publishing Corporation. New York, NY. 1999. 192p. Classics Ser. ISBN:0-8112-1424-9, ISBN13: 978-0-8112-1424-7. Dewey:823/.914. LCCN:99-030688.
Audience: **g,l,u,f.**

Spark, Muriel **PR6037.P29B3 1999**
The Ballad of Peckham Rye. Trade Paper. New Directions Publishing Corporation. New York, NY. 1999. 143p. Classics Ser. ISBN:0-8112-1408-7, ISBN13: 978-0-8112-1408-7. Dewey:823/.914. LCCN:98-042457.
Audience: **g,l,u,f.**

Spark, Muriel **PR6037.P29C6 1994**
The Comforters. Trade Paper. New Directions Publishing Corporation. New York, NY. 1994. 208p. Revived Modern Classic Ser., Vol. 796 ISBN:0-8112-1285-8, ISBN13: 978-0-8112-1285-4. Dewey:823/.914. LCCN:94-012825.
Audience: **g,l,u,f.**

Spark, Muriel **PR6037.P29.A6 2001**
Complete Short Stories. Cloth Text. Penguin Group (USA) Inc. New York, NY. 2001. 432p. ISBN:0-670-91172-0, ISBN13: 978-0-670-91172-1. Dewey:823/.914. LCCN:2002-327525.
Audience: **g.**

Spark, Muriel **PR6015.I3**
A Far Cry from Kensington. Trade Paper. HarperCollins Publishers. New York, NY. 1990. 192p. ISBN:0-380-70786-1, ISBN13: 978-0-380-70786-7. Dewey:823/.914.
Audience: **g,l,u,f.**

Spark, Muriel **PR6037.P25**
The Finishing School: A Novel. Trade Cloth. Penguin Group (USA) Inc. New York, NY. 2004. 160p. ISBN:0-670-91173-9, ISBN13: 978-0-670-91173-8. Dewey:823/.914. LCCN:2004-381482.
Audience: **g.**

Spark, Muriel **PR6037.P29F56 2004**
The Finishing School. Trade Cloth. Doubleday Canada, Ltd. Toronto, ON. 2004. 192p. ISBN:0-385-51282-1, ISBN13: 978-0-385-51282-4. LCCN:2004-045533.
Audience: **g,l,u,f.**

Spark, Muriel **PR6037.P29A6 2003**
The Ghost Stories of Muriel Spark. Trade Paper. New Directions Publishing Corporation. New York, NY. 2003. 128p. ISBN:0-8112-1549-0, ISBN13: 978-0-8112-1549-7. Dewey:823/.914. LCCN:2003-014485.
Audience: **g,l,u,f.**

Spark, Muriel **PR6037.P29L6 2001**
Loitering with Intent. Trade Paper. New Directions Publishing Corporation. New York, NY. 2001. 224p. Classics Ser. ISBN:0-8112-1474-5, ISBN13: 978-0-8112-1474-2. Dewey:823/.914. LCCN:2001-030129.
Audience: **g,l,u,f.**

Spark, Muriel **PR6015.I3**
The Prime of Miss Jean Brodie. Trade Cloth. HarperCollins Publishers. New York, NY. 2000. ISBN:0-06-099587-4, ISBN13: 978-0-06-099587-4. Dewey:823/.914.
Audience: **g.**

Spark, Muriel **PR6037.P29A6 2004**
The Prime of Miss Jean Brodie; The Girls of Slender Means; The Driver's Seat; The Only Problem. Trade Cloth. Knopf Publishing Group. New York, NY. 2004. 512p. ISBN:1-4000-4206-2, ISBN13: 978-1-4000-4206-7. Dewey:8223/.914. LCCN:2003-069487.
Audience: **g,l,u,f.**

Spark, Muriel **PR6015.I3**
The Public Image. Trade Paper. New Directions Publishing Corporation. New York, NY. 1993. 160p. Revived Modern Classic Ser., Vol. 767 ISBN:0-8112-1246-7, ISBN13: 978-0-8112-1246-5. Dewey:823.9/14. LCCN:92-046593.
Audience: **g,l,u,f.**

Spark, Muriel **PR6015.I3**
Reality and Dreams. Trade Paper. Houghton Mifflin Company Trade & Reference Division. Boston, MA. 1998. 160p. ISBN:0-395-90133-2, ISBN13: 978-0-395-90133-5. Dewey:823.9/14. LCCN:96-052913.
Audience: **g,l,u,f.**

Spark, Muriel **PR6015.I3**
Aiding and Abetting. Trade Paper. Penguin Books, Ltd. London, 2002. 224p. ISBN:0-14-100990-X, ISBN13: 978-0-14-100990-2. Dewey:823.9/14.
Audience: **g,l,u,f.**

Spark, Muriel **PR6037.P25**
All the Poems: Collected Poems. Trade Cloth. Carcanet Press, Ltd. Manchester, 2004. 400p. ISBN:1-85754-773-X, ISBN13: 978-1-85754-773-3. Dewey:821.9/14.
Audience: **g,l,u,f.**

Spark, Muriel **PR6037.P29R6 2003**
Robinson. Trade Paper. New Directions Publishing Corporation. New York, NY. 2003. 176p. A New Directions Classics Ser. ISBN:0-8112-1518-0, ISBN13: 978-0-8112-1518-3. Dewey:823/.914. LCCN:2002-152801.
Audience: **g,l,u,f.**

Whittaker, Ruth **PR6037.P29Z97X**
The Faith and Fiction of Muriel Spark. Trade Cloth. Macmillan Publishers Ltd. London, 1982. 168p. ISBN:0-333-27297-8, ISBN13: 978-0-333-27297-8. Dewey:823/.914. LCCN:84-672274.
Audience: **u,f.**

Individual Authors and Works > 20th C. > Spender, Stephen

Leeming, David A. **PR6037.P47Z76 1999**
Stephen Spender: A Life in Modernism. Cloth over Boards. Henry Holt & Company. New York, NY. 1999. 320p. ISBN:0-8050-4249-0, ISBN13: 978-0-8050-4249-8. Dewey:821/.912 B. LCCN:99-020425.
Audience: **u,f.** *Choice, 2000.*

O'Neill, Michael & Reeves, Gareth **PR610.O54 1992**
Auden, MacNeice, Spender: The Thirties Poetry. Cloth Text. Palgrave Macmillan. New York, NY. 1992. 264p. ISBN:0-312-06828-X, ISBN13: 978-0-312-06828-8. Dewey:821/.91209. LCCN:91-028970.
Audience: **u,f.** *Choice, 1992.*

Spender, Stephen **PR6037.P47A17 1986**
Collected Poems, 1928-1985. Trade Cloth. Random House, Inc. New York, NY. 1986. 204p. ISBN:0-394-54601-6, ISBN13: 978-0-394-54601-8. Dewey:821/.912. LCCN:85-002323.
Audience: **g,l,u,f.** *Choice, 1986.*

Spender, Stephen **PR6037.P47.Z474 1986**
Journals, 1939-1983. Trade Paper. Oxford University Press, Inc. New York, NY. 1987. 512p. ISBN:0-19-505209-9, ISBN13: 978-0-19-505209-1. Dewey:828/.91203 B. LCCN:87-022276.
Audience: **g,l,u,f.** *Choice, 1986.*

Spender, Stephen **PR6019.O9**
The Temple. Trade Paper. Grove/Atlantic, Inc. New York, NY. 1997. 224p. ISBN:0-8021-3524-2, ISBN13: 978-0-8021-3524-7. Dewey:823/.912.
Audience: **g,l,u,f.**

Spender, Stephen **PR6037.P47.T5**
The Thirties and After: Essays. Trade Cloth. Random House, Inc. New York, NY. 1978. xiv, 236p. ISBN:0-394-50173-X, ISBN13: 978-0-394-50173-4. Dewey:824/.9/12. LCCN:78-023721.
Audience: **g,l,u,f.**

Spender, Stephen **PR6037.P47Z478 2001**
World Within World: The Autobiography of Stephen Spender. John Bayley (Introduction by). Trade Cloth. Random House Adult Trade Publishing Group. New York, NY. 2001. 432p. ISBN:0-679-64045-2, ISBN13: 978-0-679-64045-5. Dewey:821/.912 B. LCCN:00-064580.
Audience: **g,l,u,f.**

Sutherland, John **PR6037**
Stephen Spender: A Literary Life. Trade Cloth. Oxford University Press, Inc. New York, NY. 2005. 656p. ISBN:0-19-517816-5, ISBN13: 978-0-19-517816-6. Dewey:821/.912 B. LCCN:2004-009727.
Audience: **u,f.** *Choice, 2005.*

Individual Authors and Works > 20th C. > Stoppard, Tom

Fleming, John **PR6069.T6Z648 2003**
Stoppard's Theatre: Finding Order amid Chaos. Trade Paper. University of Texas Press. Austin, TX. 2003. 343p. Literary Modernism Ser. ISBN:0-292-72552-3, ISBN13: 978-0-292-72552-2. Dewey:822/.914.
Audience: **g,l,u,f.** *Choice, 2002.*

Kelly, Katherine E. (Editor) **PR6069.T6 Z615 2001**
The Cambridge Companion to Tom Stoppard. Cloth Text. Cambridge University Press. New York, NY. 2001. 260p. Companions to Literature Ser. ISBN:0-521-64178-0, ISBN13: 978-0-521-64178-4. Dewey:822/.914. LCCN:00-069777.
Audience: **g.** *Choice, 2002.*

Nadel, Ira B. **PR6069.T6Z784 2002**
Tom Stoppard: A Life. Trade Cloth. Palgrave Macmillan. New York, NY. 2002. 384p. ISBN:0-312-23778-2, ISBN13: 978-0-312-23778-3. Dewey:822/.8. LCCN:2002-510042.
Audience: **g,l,u,f.** *Choice, 2003.*

Stoppard, Tom **PR6069.T6**
The Plays for Radio, 1964-1991. Trade Cloth. Faber & Faber, Inc. New York, NY. 1994. 304p. ISBN:0-571-17208-3, ISBN13: 978-0-571-17208-5. Dewey:822.914.
Audience: **g.**

Stoppard, Tom **PR6066.I53**
Tom Stoppard: A Separate Peace, Teeth, Another Moon Called Earth, Neutral Ground, Professional Foul, Squaring the Circle. Ed. 3. Trade Paper. Faber & Faber, Inc. New York, NY. 1998. 272p. ISBN:0-571-19428-1, ISBN13: 978-0-571-19428-5. Dewey:822.9/14.
Audience: **g,l,u,f.**

Stoppard, Tom **PR6069.T6**
Tom Stoppard: Dalliance, Undiscovered Country, Rough Crossing, on the Razzle, The Seagull. Trade Paper. Faber & Faber, Inc. New York, NY. 2000. 480p. ISBN:0-571-19750-7, ISBN13: 978-0-571-19750-7. Dewey:822.9/14.
Audience: **g,l,u,f.**

Stoppard, Tom **PR6069.T6 A6 1996**
Tom Stoppard: The Dissolution of Dominic Boot; 'M' Is for Moon among Other Things; If You're Glad I'll Be Frank; Albert's Bridge; Where Are They Now?; Artist Descending a Staircase; The Dog It Was That Died; In the Native State. Trade Paper. Faber & Faber, Inc. New York, NY. 1997. 320p. ISBN:0-571-19008-1, ISBN13: 978-0-571-19008-9. Dewey:822/.914. LCCN:2003-447787.
Audience: **g,l,u,f.**

Stoppard, Tom **PR6066.I53**
Tom Stoppard: Arcadia, The Real Thing, Night and Day, Indian Ink, Hapgood. Trade Paper. Faber & Faber, Inc. New York, NY. 2000. 608p. ISBN:0-571-19751-5, ISBN13: 978-0-571-19751-4. Dewey:822.9/14.
Audience: **l,u,f.**

Stoppard, Tom **PR6069.T6Z47 1994**
Tom Stoppard in Conversation. Paul Delaney (Editor). Trade Paper. University of Michigan Press. Chicago, IL. 1994. 328p. Theater Ser., :Theory - Text - Performance ISBN:0-472-06561-0, ISBN13: 978-0-472-06561-5. Dewey:822/.914 B. LCCN:94-010262.
Audience: **g,l,u,f.**

Individual Authors and Works > 20th C. > T

Taylor, Helen (Introduction by) **PR6007.U43**
Myself When Young: The Shaping of a Writer. Trade Paper, Perfect. Little, Brown Book Group Ltd. London, 2005. 224p. ISBN:1-84408-096-X, ISBN13: 978-1-84408-096-0. Dewey:823.9/12.
Audience: **g,l,u,f.**

Thomas, Edward **PR6039.H55A17 2003**
The Poems of Edward Thomas. Trade Paper. Other Press, LLC. New York, NY. 2006. 208p. ISBN:1-59051-064-X, ISBN13: 978-1-59051-064-3. Dewey:821/.912. LCCN:2003-014933.
Audience: **g,l,u,f.**

Thomas, Edward **PR6039.H55**
A Language Not to Be Betrayed. Edna Longley (Editor). Trade Paper. Carcanet Press. New York, NY. 1986. 290p. ISBN:0-85635-670-0, ISBN13: 978-0-85635-670-4. Dewey:828/.91207.
Audience: **u,f.**

Tremain, Rose **PR6070.R364M87**
Music and Silence. Trade Paper. Simon & Schuster. New York, NY. 2001. 512p. ISBN:0-7434-1826-3, ISBN13: 978-0-7434-1826-3. Dewey:823.914.
Audience: **g,l,u,f.**

Trevor, William **PR6070.R4.S76**
The Story of Lucy Gault. Trade Paper. Penguin Group (USA) Inc. New York, NY. 2003. 240p. ISBN:0-14-200331-X, ISBN13: 978-0-14-200331-2. Dewey:823/.914. LCCN:2002-066381.
Audience: **g,l,u,f.**

Trevor, William **PR6070.R4A6 1993**
William Trevor: The Collected Stories. Trade Paper. Penguin Group (USA) Inc. New York, NY. 1993. 1280p. ISBN:0-14-023245-1, ISBN13: 978-0-14-023245-5. LCCN:93-032619.
Audience: **g,l,u,f.**

Trevor, William **PR6070.R4F6 2006**
Fools of Fortune. Francine Prose (Introduction by). Trade Paper. Penguin Group (USA) Inc. New York, NY. 2006. 208p. Penguin Classics Ser. ISBN:0-14-303962-8, ISBN13: 978-0-14-303962-4. Dewey:823/.914. LCCN:2005-058604.
Audience: **g,l,u,f.**

Individual Authors and Works > 20th C. > Thomas, Dylan

Ackerman, John **PR6039.H52 Z55**
Dylan Thomas: His Life and Work. Ed. 3. Trade Paper. St. Martin's Press. Gordonville, VA. 1996. 236p. ISBN:0-333-63404-7, ISBN13: 978-0-333-63404-2. Dewey:821/.912 B.
Audience: **u,f.**

Lycett, Andrew **PR6039.H52Z763 2004**
Dylan Thomas: A New Life. Trade Cloth. Overlook Press, The. New York, NY. 2004. 416p. ISBN:1-58567-541-5, ISBN13: 978-1-58567-541-8. Dewey:B. LCCN:2004-048319.
Audience: **g,u,f.**

Thomas, Dylan **PR6069.I5A65**
Adventures in the Skin Trade, and Other Stories. Paper Text. Textbook Publishers. Temecula, CA. 2003. 275p. ISBN:0-7581-7816-6, ISBN13: 978-0-7581-7816-9. Dewey:822/.9/14.
Audience: **g,l,u,f.**

Thomas, Dylan **PR6039.H52A6**
The Collected Poems of Dylan Thomas: 1934-1952. Trade Paper. DIANE Publishing Company. Collingdale, PA. 2004. 203p. ISBN:0-7567-8339-9, ISBN13: 978-0-7567-8339-6. Dewey:821/.914.
Audience: **g,l,u,f.**

Thomas, Dylan **PR6039.H52 A6 1993**
Eight Stories. Trade Paper. New Directions Publishing Corporation. New York, NY. 1993. 96p. Bibelots Ser. ISBN:0-8112-1245-9, ISBN13: 978-0-8112-1245-8. Dewey:823/.912. LCCN:93-000409.
Audience: **g,l,u,f.**

Thomas, Dylan **PR6039.H52 Z5 1968**
Portrait of the Artist As a Young Dog. Trade Paper. New Directions Publishing Corporation. New York, NY. 1956. 186p. ISBN:0-8112-0207-0, ISBN13: 978-0-8112-0207-7. Dewey:818.207. LCCN:40-034154.
Audience: **g,l,u,f.** *B*

Thomas, Dylan **PR6039.H52 A6**
Quite Early One Morning. Trade Paper. New Directions Publishing Corporation. New York, NY. 1960. ISBN:0-8112-0208-9, ISBN13: 978-0-8112-0208-4. Dewey:828.91. LCCN:54-012907.
Audience: **g,l,u,f.** *B*

Thomas, Dylan **PN1997.U45S5**
Under Milk Wood, a Play for Voices. Paper Text. Textbook Publishers. Temecula, CA. 2003. xiv, 107p. ISBN:0-7581-7817-4, ISBN13: 978-0-7581-7817-6. Dewey:823/.9/14.
Audience: **g,l,u,f.** *B*

Thomas, Dylan **PR6039.H52 A19**
Dylan Thomas: The Complete Screenplays. John Ackerman (Editor). Trade Cloth. Applause Theatre Book Publishers. New York, NY. 2000. 422p. ISBN:1-55783-226-9, ISBN13: 978-1-55783-226-9. Dewey:821.912. LCCN:95-080737.
Audience: **g,l,u,f.**

Thomas, Dylan **PR6039.H52C48 1995**
A Child's Christmas in Wales: And Five Poems. Fritz Eichenberg (Illustrator). Trade Cloth. New Directions Publishing Corporation. New York, NY. 1997. 64p. ISBN:0-8112-1308-0, ISBN13: 978-0-8112-1308-0. Dewey:828.9/1209. LCCN:77-088732.
Audience: **g,l,u,f.**

Thomas, Dylan **PR6019.O9**
The Collected Stories. Leslie Norris (Introduction by). Trade Paper. New Directions Publishing Corporation. New York, NY. 1986. 384p. ISBN:0-8112-0998-9, ISBN13: 978-0-8112-0998-4. Dewey:823/.912. LCCN:84-006822.
Audience: **g,l,u,f.** *B*

Tindall, William York **PR6039.H52Z865 1996**
A Reader's Guide to Dylan Thomas. Trade Paper. Syracuse University Press. Syracuse, NY. 1996. 305p. Reader's Guide Ser. ISBN:0-8156-0401-7, ISBN13: 978-0-8156-0401-3. Dewey:841/.912. LCCN:96-025794.
Audience: **g,l,u,f.** *B*

Individual Authors and Works > 20th C. > Tolkien, J. R. R.

Croft, Janet Brennan **PR6039**
War and the Works of J. R. R. Tolkien. Trade Cloth. Greenwood Publishing Group, Inc. Portsmouth, NH. 2004. 192p. Contributions to the Study of Science Fiction and Fantasy Ser., No. 106 ISBN:0-313-32592-8, ISBN13: 978-0-313-32592-2. Dewey:828/.91209. LCCN:2003-060425.
Audience: **g,l,u,f.** *Choice, 2005.*

Tolkien, J. R. R. **PR6019.O9**
The Fellowship of the Ring: Being the First Part of the Lord of the Rings. Trade Paper. Houghton Mifflin Company Trade & Reference Division. Boston, MA. 2005. 506p. The Lord of the Rings Ser., Bk. 1 ISBN:0-618-57494-8, ISBN13: 978-0-618-57494-0. Dewey:823/.912.
Audience: **g,l,u,f.**

Tolkien, J. R. R. **PR6039.O32H6**
The Hobbit: Or There and Back Again. Trade Paper. Houghton Mifflin Company Trade & Reference Division. Boston, MA. 2002. 365p. ISBN:0-618-26030-7, ISBN13: 978-0-618-26030-0. Dewey:[Fic].
Audience: **g,l,u,f.**

Tolkien, J. R. R. **PR6019.O9**
The Return of the King: Being the Third Part of the Lord of the Rings. Trade Paper. Houghton Mifflin Company Trade & Reference Division. Boston, MA. 2005. The Lord of the Rings Ser., Bk. 3 ISBN:0-618-57497-2, ISBN13: 978-0-618-57497-1. Dewey:823/.912.
Audience: **g,l,u,f.**

Tolkien, J. R. R. **PR6019.O9**
The Two Towers: Being the Second Part of the Lord of the Rings. Trade Paper. Houghton Mifflin Company Trade & Reference Division. Boston, MA. 2005. 412p. The Lord of the Rings Ser., Bk. 2 ISBN:0-618-57495-6, ISBN13: 978-0-618-57495-7. Dewey:823/.912.
Audience: **g,l,u,f.**

Individual Authors and Works > 20th C. > W

Wallace, Edgar **PR6019.O9**
The Four Just Men. Trade Paper. Kessinger Publishing, LLC. Whitefish, MT. 2005. ISBN:0-7661-9761-1, ISBN13: 978-0-7661-9761-9. Dewey:823/.912.
Audience: **g,l,u,f.**

Webb, Mary **PR6019.O9**
Precious Bane. Trade Cloth. Little, Brown Book Group Ltd. London, 2001. 288p. ISBN:0-86068-063-0, ISBN13: 978-0-86068-063-5. Dewey:823/.9/1.
Audience: **g,l,u,f.**

White, Antonia **PR6045.H15634 1984**
Beyond the Glass. Trade Cloth. Little, Brown Book Group Ltd. London, 2001. 288p. Modern Classics ISBN:0-86068-097-5, ISBN13: 978-0-86068-097-0. Dewey:823.9/12. LCCN:86-673227.
Audience: **g,l,u,f.**

White, T. H. **PR6019.O9**
The Once and Future King. Trade Cloth. Penguin Group (USA) Inc. New York, NY. 1958. 688p. ISBN:0-399-10597-2, ISBN13: 978-0-399-10597-5. Dewey:823/.912.
Audience: **g,l,u,f.** B

Williams, Charles **PR6019.O9**
All Hallows' Eve. Trade Paper. Regent College Publishing. Vancouver, BC. 2003. 296p. ISBN:1-57383-110-7, ISBN13: 978-1-57383-110-9. Dewey:823/.912.
Audience: **g,l,u,f.**

Williams, Charles **PR6019.O9**
The Greater Trumps. Trade Paper. Regent College Publishing. Vancouver, BC. 2003. 288p. ISBN:1-57383-111-5, ISBN13: 978-1-57383-111-6. Dewey:823/.9/1.
Audience: **g,l,u,f.** B

Winterson, Jeanette **PR6073.I55807 1987**
Oranges Are Not the Only Fruit. Trade Paper. Grove/Atlantic, Inc. New York, NY. 1997. 192p. ISBN:0-8021-3516-1, ISBN13: 978-0-8021-3516-2. Dewey:823.9/14. LCCN:87-014412.
Audience: **g,l,u,f.**

Winterson, Jeanette **PR6015.I3**
Written on the Body. Trade Paper. Random House of Canada, Ltd. Mississauga, ON. 1993. 192p. ISBN:0-394-28014-8, ISBN13: 978-0-394-28014-1. Dewey:823.9/14.
Audience: **g,l,u,f.**

Individual Authors and Works > 20th C. > Warner, Sylvia Townsend

Warner, Sylvia Townsend **PR6019.O9**
The Corner That Held Them. Trade Cloth. Little, Brown Book Group Ltd. London, 2001. 310p. Modern Classics ISBN:0-86068-878-X, ISBN13: 978-0-86068-878-5. Dewey:823.9/12.
Audience: **g,l,u,f.**

Warner, Sylvia Townsend **PR6045.A812A6 1988**
Selected Stories of Sylvia Townsend Warner. Trade Cloth. Penguin Group (USA) Inc. New York, NY. 1988. 464p. ISBN:0-670-82467-4, ISBN13: 978-0-670-82467-0. Dewey:823.912. LCCN:88-040099.
Audience: **g,l,u,f.**

Warner, Sylvia Townsend **PR6045.A812L65 1999**
Lolly Willowes: Or the Loving Huntsman. Alison Lurie (Introduction by). Trade Paper. New York Review of Books, Incorporated, The. New York, NY. 1999. 230p. New York Review Books Classics Ser., Vol. 5 ISBN:0-940322-16-1, ISBN13: 978-0-940322-16-5. Dewey:823/.9/1. LCCN:99-014569.
Audience: **g,l,u,f.**

Warner, Sylvia Townsend **PR6045.A812A6 1986**
Four in Hand: A Quartet of Novels. William Maxwell (Introduction by). Trade Cloth. W. W. Norton & Company, Inc. New York, NY. 1986. ISBN:0-393-02356-7, ISBN13: 978-0-393-02356-5. Dewey:823/.912. LCCN:86-005414.
Audience: **g,l,u,f.**

Warner, Sylvia Townsend **PR6045.A812M87 2001**
Music at the Long Verney: Twenty Stories. Michael Steinman (Editor), William Maxwell (Foreword by). Trade Cloth. Basic Books. New York, NY. 2000. 224p. ISBN:1-58243-112-4, ISBN13: 978-1-58243-112-3. Dewey:823/.912. LCCN:00-064460.
Audience: **g,l,u,f.**

Individual Authors and Works > 20th C. > Waugh, Evelyn

Beaty, Frederick L. **PR6019.O9**
The Ironic World of Evelyn Waugh: A Study of Eight Novels. Trade Paper. Northern Illinois University Press. DeKalb, IL. 1992. 250p. ISBN:0-87580-562-0, ISBN13: 978-0-87580-562-7. Dewey:823/.912. LCCN:92-001305.
Audience: **l,u,f.** *Choice, 1993.*

Crabbe, Katharyn W. **PR6045.A97Z628 1988**
Evelyn Waugh. Trade Cloth. Frederick Ungar A Book. Dulles, VA. 1988. 192p. Literature and Life Ser. ISBN:0-8044-2107-2, ISBN13: 978-0-8044-2107-2. Dewey:823/.912 B. LCCN:87-013927.
Audience: **l,u.** *Choice, 1988.*

Davie, Michael (Editor) **PR6045.A97.Z498 1977**
The Diaries of Evelyn Waugh. Trade Cloth. Little Brown & Company. New York, NY. 1977. 818 p. ;p. ISBN:0-316-17450-5, ISBN13: 978-0-316-17450-3. Dewey:823/.9/12. LCCN:77-016214.
Audience: **g,l,u,f.** B

Davis, Robert M. **PR6045.A97B734 1990**
Brideshead Revisited: The Past Redeemed. Trade Cloth. Thomson Gale. Farmington Hills, MI. 1990. 168p. Twayne's Masterwork Studies, No. 59 ISBN:0-8057-8092-0, ISBN13: 978-0-8057-8092-5. Dewey:823/.912. LCCN:90-004636.
Audience: **g,l,u,f.** *Choice, 1991.*

Hastings, Selina **PR6019.O9**
Evelyn Waugh: A Biography. Trade Cloth. DIANE Publishing Company. Collingdale, PA. 2000. 724p. ISBN:0-7881-9408-9, ISBN13: 978-0-7881-9408-5. Dewey:823/.912 B.
Audience: **g,l,u,f.** *Choice, 1995.*

Heath, Jeffrey M. **PR6019.O9**
The Picturesque Prison: Evelyn Waugh and His Writing. Trade Cloth. McGill-Queen's University Press. Montreal, PQ. 1983. ISBN:0-7735-0407-9, ISBN13: 978-0-7735-0407-3. Dewey:823/.912.
Audience: **l,u.** B

Patey, Douglas Lane **PR6019.O9**
The Life of Evelyn Waugh: A Critical Biography. Trade Paper. Blackwell Publishing, Inc. Malden, MA. 2001. 456p. Critical Biographies Ser. ISBN:0-631-23134-X, ISBN13: 978-0-631-23134-9. Dewey:823.9/12.
Audience: **l,u,f.**

Stannard, Martin **PR6045.A97Z79 1987**
Evelyn Waugh: The Early Years, 1903-1939. Trade Cloth. W. W. Norton & Company, Inc. New York, NY. 1987. 540p. ISBN:0-393-02450-4, ISBN13: 978-0-393-02450-0. Dewey:823/.912 B. LCCN:87-005750.
Audience: **g,l,u,f.** *Choice, 1988.*

Stannard, Martin (Editor) **PR6045.A97Z/**
Evelyn Waugh: The Critical Heritage. Trade Cloth. Routledge. New York, NY. 1984. 500p. The Critical Heritage Ser. ISBN:0-7100-9548-1, ISBN13: 978-0-7100-9548-0. Dewey:823/.912. LCCN:83-021172.
Audience: **g,l,u,f.** B

Stannard, Martin **PR6045.A97**
Evelyn Waugh: The Later Years, 1939-1966. Trade Cloth. W. W. Norton & Company, Inc. New York, NY. 1992. 512p. ISBN:0-393-03412-7, ISBN13: 978-0-393-03412-7. Dewey:823.912.
Audience: **g,l,u,f.** *Choice, 1993.*

Waugh, Evelyn **PR6019.O9**
Black Mischief. Trade Paper. Little Brown & Company. New York, NY. 2002. 304p. ISBN:0-316-91733-8, ISBN13: 978-0-316-91733-9. Dewey:823.9/12.
Audience: **g,l,u,f.** B

Waugh, Evelyn **PR6045.A97A6 1999**
The Complete Stories of Evelyn Waugh. Trade Cloth. Little Brown & Company. New York, NY. 1999. 536p. ISBN:0-316-92546-2, ISBN13: 978-0-316-92546-4. Dewey:823/.912. LCCN:99-020837.
Audience: **g,l,u,f.**

Waugh, Evelyn **PR6019.O9**
Decline and Fall. Trade Cloth. Alfred A. Knopf Inc. New York, NY. 1993. 224p. Everyman's Library ISBN:0-679-42041-X, ISBN13: 978-0-679-42041-5. Dewey:823.9/12. LCCN:92-054285.
Audience: **g,l,u,f.** B

Waugh, Evelyn **PR6045.A97L68 1999**
The Loved One. Trade Paper. Little Brown & Company. New York, NY. 1977. 176p. ISBN:0-316-92608-6, ISBN13: 978-0-316-92608-9. Dewey:823/.912. LCCN:00-269839.
Audience: **g,l,u,f.**

Waugh, Evelyn **PR6019.O9**
Put Out More Flags. Trade Paper. Little Brown & Company. New York, NY. 2002. 304p. ISBN:0-316-91605-6, ISBN13: 978-0-316-91605-9. Dewey:823.9/12.
Audience: **g,l,u,f.** B

Waugh, Evelyn **PR6045.A97S36 1999**
Scoop: A Novel about Journalists. Trade Paper. Little Brown & Company. New York, NY. 1977. 336p. ISBN:0-316-92610-8, ISBN13: 978-0-316-92610-2. Dewey:823.9/12. LCCN:00-269864.
Audience: **g,l,u,f.**

Waugh, Evelyn **PR6045.A97**
The Sword of Honour Trilogy. Trade Cloth. Alfred A. Knopf Inc. New York, NY. 1994. 768p. ISBN:0-679-43136-5, ISBN13: 978-0-679-43136-7. Dewey:823.912.
Audience: **g,l,u,f.**

Waugh, Evelyn **PR6045.A97.T3 1971**
Tactical Exercise. Trade Cloth. Ayer Company Publishers, Inc. Manchester, NH. 1980. 289p. Short Story Index Reprint Ser. ISBN:0-8369-3997-2, ISBN13: 978-0-8369-3997-2. Dewey:823/.9/12. LCCN:78-167471.
Audience: **g,l,u,f.** B

Waugh, Evelyn **PR6045.A97V55 1999**
Vile Bodies. Trade Paper. Little Brown & Company. New York, NY. 1977. 336p. ISBN:0-316-92611-6, ISBN13: 978-0-316-92611-9. Dewey:823.9/12. LCCN:00-269838.
Audience: **g,l,u,f.** B

Waugh, Evelyn **PR6045**
A Handful of Dust. William Boyd (Introduction by). Trade Cloth. Alfred A. Knopf Inc. New York, NY. 2002. 256p. ISBN:0-375-41420-7, ISBN13: 978-0-375-41420-6. Dewey:823/.912. LCCN:2002-283548.
Audience: **g,l,u,f.**

Waugh, Evelyn **PR6045.A97A6 2003**
Waugh Abroad: The Travel Writing of Evelyn Waugh. William Dalrymple & Nicholas Shakespeare (Introduction by). Trade Cloth. Knopf Publishing Group. New York, NY. 2003. 1152p. ISBN:1-4000-4076-0, ISBN13: 978-1-4000-4076-6. Dewey:828/.91203. LCCN:2003-053150.
Audience: **g,l,u,f.**

Waugh, Evelyn **PR6045.A97.A6 1983**
The Essays, Articles and Reviews of Evelyn Waugh. Donat Gallagher (Editor). Trade Cloth. Little Brown & Company. New York, NY. 1984. 672p. ISBN:0-316-92643-4, ISBN13: 978-0-316-92643-0. Dewey:828/.91208. LCCN:83-082436.
Audience: **g,l,u,f.** B

Waugh, Evelyn **PR6019.O9**
Brideshead Revisited. Frank Kermode (Introduction by). Trade Cloth. Alfred A. Knopf Inc. New York, NY. 1993. 368p. Everyman's Library, Vol. 172 ISBN:0-679-42300-1, ISBN13: 978-0-679-42300-3. Dewey:823/.912. LCCN:93-001854.
Audience: **g.**

Waugh, Evelyn **PR6045.A97H45 2005**
Helena. George Weigel (Introduction by). Trade Paper. Loyola Press. Chicago, IL. 2005. 256p. Loyola Classics ISBN:0-8294-2122-X, ISBN13: 978-0-8294-2122-4. Dewey:823/.912. LCCN:2004-026876.
Audience: **g,l,u,f.**

Individual Authors and Works > 20th C. > West, Rebecca

Lesinka, Zofia P. **PS228.W37L47 2002**
Perspectives of Four Women Writers on the Second World War: Gertrude Stein, Janet Flanner, Kay Boyle, and Rebecca West. Trade Cloth. Peter Lang Publishing, Inc. New York, NY. 2002. 200p. Studies in Literary Criticism and Theory Ser., Vol. 17 ISBN:0-8204-6103-2, ISBN13: 978-0-8204-6103-8. Dewey:810.9/358. LCCN:2002-023812.
Audience: **u,f.**

Rollyson, Carl **PR6045.E8Z85 1996**
Rebecca West: A Saga of the Century. Trade Cloth. Simon & Schuster. New York, NY. 1996. 512p. ISBN:0-684-19430-9, ISBN13: 978-0-684-19430-1. Dewey:828/.91209 B. LCCN:96-024231.
Audience: **g,l,u,f.** *Choice, 1997.*

Schweizer, Bernard **PR6045**
Rebecca West: Heroism, Rebellion, and the Female Epic. Trade Cloth. Greenwood Publishing Group, Inc. Portsmouth, NH. 2002. 184p. Contributions in Women's Studies, No. 199 ISBN:0-313-32360-7, ISBN13: 978-0-313-32360-7. Dewey:828/.91209. LCCN:2002-024480.
Audience: **u,f.** *Choice, 2003.*

West, Rebecca **PR6019.O9**
Cousin Rosamund. Trade Paper. Random House, Inc. New York, NY. 1988. 304p. ISBN:0-86068-829-1, ISBN13: 978-0-86068-829-7. Dewey:823.9/12.
Audience: **g,l,u,f.**

West, Rebecca **PR6045.E8Z464 1988**
Family Memories: An Autobiographical Journey. Trade Cloth. Penguin Group (USA) Inc. New York, NY. 1988. 272p. ISBN:0-670-81384-2, ISBN13: 978-0-670-81384-1. Dewey:828/.91209 B. LCCN:87-040317.
Audience: **g,l,u,f.** *Choice, 1988.*

West, Rebecca **PR6045.E8R4 2002**
The Return of the Soldier. Trade Paper. Dover Publications, Inc. Mineola, NY. 2002. 77p. Thrift Editions Ser. ISBN:0-486-42207-0, ISBN13: 978-0-486-42207-7. Dewey:823/.912. LCCN:2001-052742.
Audience: **g,l,u,f.**

West, Rebecca **PR6045.E8S86 1986**
Sunflower. Trade Cloth. Little, Brown Book Group Ltd. London, 1992. 276p. ISBN:0-86068-719-8, ISBN13: 978-0-86068-719-1. Dewey:823/.912. LCCN:87-111977.
Audience: **g,l,u,f.**

West, Rebecca **PR6045.E8**
This Real Night. Trade Cloth. Random House, Inc. New York, NY. 1987. 265p. ISBN:0-86068-669-8, ISBN13: 978-0-86068-669-9. Dewey:823.9/12.
Audience: **g,l,u,f.**

West, Rebecca **PR6013.R735**
Rebecca West: A Celebration. Samuel Hynes (Introduction by). Trade Paper. Penguin Group (USA) Inc. New York, NY. 1978. 800p. ISBN:0-14-004912-6, ISBN13: 978-0-14-004912-1. Dewey:828/.91208. LCCN:78-017429.
Audience: **g,l,u,f.**

West, Rebecca **PR6045.E8Z48 2000**
The Selected Letters of Rebecca West. Bonnie Kime Scott (Editor). Cloth over Boards. Yale University Press. Cumberland, RI. 2000. 546p. Henry McBride Series in Modernism and Modernity ISBN:0-300-07904-4, ISBN13: 978-0-300-07904-3. Dewey:828/.91209 B. LCCN:99-012240.
Audience: **u,f.** *Choice, 2000.*

Individual Authors and Works > 20th C. > Wilson, Angus

Drabble, Margaret **PR6045.I577Z63 1996**
Angus Wilson: A Biography. Trade Cloth. St. Martin's Press. Gordonville, VA. 1996. 740p. ISBN:0-312-14276-5, ISBN13: 978-0-312-14276-6. Dewey:823.9/14. LCCN:96-001479.
Audience: **g,l,u,f.** *Choice, 1997.*

Halio, Jay (Editor) **PR6045.I577.Z6 1985**
Critical Essays on Angus Wilson. Trade Cloth. Thomson Gale. Farmington Hills, MI. 1985. viii, 236p. Critical Essays on American Literature Ser. ISBN:0-8161-8691-X, ISBN13: 978-0-8161-8691-4. Dewey:823/.914. LCCN:84-015841.
Audience: **g,l,u,f.**

Wilson, Angus **PR6045.I577**
A Bit off the Map, and Other Stories. Paper Text. Textbook Publishers. Temecula, CA. 2003. 193p. ISBN:0-7581-0878-8, ISBN13: 978-0-7581-0878-4. Dewey:823.91.
Audience: **g,l,u,f.**

Wilson, Angus **PR6045.I577A15 1987**
The Collected Stories of Angus Wilson. Trade Cloth. Martin Secker & Warburg, Ltd. London, 1987. 413p. ISBN:0-436-57612-0, ISBN13: 978-0-436-57612-6. Dewey:823/.914. LCCN:88-124915.
Audience: **g,l,u,f.**

Wilson, Angus **PR6015.I3**
Hemlock and After. Paper Text. Textbook Publishers. Temecula, CA. 2003. 246p. ISBN:0-7581-3981-0, ISBN13: 978-0-7581-3981-8. Dewey:823.9/14.
Audience: **g,l,u,f.**

Wilson, Angus **PR6045.I577**
The Mulberry Bush, a Play in Three Acts. Paper Text. Textbook Publishers. Temecula, CA. 2003. 112p. ISBN:0-7581-3971-3, ISBN13: 978-0-7581-3971-9. Dewey:822.91.
Audience: **g,l,u,f.**

Wilson, Angus **PR6045.I577A75 2005**
Anglo-Saxon Attitudes. Jane Smiley (Introduction by). Trade Paper, Perfect. New York Review of Books, Incorporated, The. New York, NY. 2005. 346p. New York Review Books Classics ISBN:1-59017-142-X, ISBN13: 978-1-59017-142-4. Dewey:823/.914. LCCN:2004-027333.
Audience: **g,l,u,f.**

Individual Authors and Works > 20th C. > Wodehouse, P. G.

Connolly, Joseph **PR6045.O53**
P. G. Wodehouse. Trade Paper. Haus Publishing. London, 2005. 192p. ISBN:1-904341-68-3, ISBN13: 978-1-904341-68-0. Dewey:823.9/12.
Audience: **g,l,u,f.**

Connolly, Joseph **PR6045.O53.Z6**
P. G. Wodehouse: An Illustrated Biography: with Complete Bibliography and Collector's Guide. Trade Cloth. Publisher

Information Not Provided. Berkley, NJ. 1979. 160 p. :p. ISBN:0-85613-235-7, ISBN13: 978-0-85613-235-3. Dewey:823/.912. LCCN:80-451543.
Audience: **g,l,u,f.** B

McCrum, Robert **PR6045.O53Z98 2004**
Wodehouse: A Life. Trade Cloth. W. W. Norton & Company, Inc. New York, NY. 2004. 384p. ISBN:0-393-05159-5, ISBN13: 978-0-393-05159-9. Dewey:823/.912 B. LCCN:2004-018562.
Audience: **g,l,u,f.**

McIlvaine, Eileen, et al. **Z8430.2**
P. G. Wodehouse: A Comprehensive Bibliography and Checklist. Louise S. Sherby, James H. Heineman, Richard Usborne & Frances Donald (Authors), Peter Van Straaten (Illustrator). Trade Cloth. James H. Heineman Incorporated, Publisher. New York, NY. 1995. 544p. Wodehouse Monographs, No. 2 ISBN:0-87008-101-2, ISBN13: 978-0-87008-101-9. Dewey:016.823/912.
Audience: **g,l,u,f.**

Murphy, N. T. **PR110.B52**
In Search of Blandings: An Investigation into the Sources That Inspired P. G. Wodehouse. Tom Sharpe (Introduction by). Trade Cloth. Salem House Publishers. Scranton, PA. 1986. 256p. ISBN:0-88162-211-7, ISBN13: 978-0-88162-211-9. Dewey:823.
Audience: **g,l,u,f.** *Choice, 1986.*

Thompson, Kristin **PR6045.O53**
Wooster Proposes, Jeeves Disposes. Peter Van Straaten (Illustrator). Trade Cloth. James H. Heineman Incorporated, Publisher. New York, NY. 1995. ISBN:0-87008-139-X, ISBN13: 978-0-87008-139-2. Dewey:823.912.
Audience: **g,l,u,f.** *Choice, 1993.*

Usborne, Richard **PR6045.O53Z8895 2003**
Plum Sauce. Trade Cloth. Overlook Press, The. New York, NY. 2003. 240p. ISBN:1-58567-441-9, ISBN13: 978-1-58567-441-1. Dewey:823/.912. LCCN:2003-054931.
Audience: **g,l,u,f.**

Wodehouse, P. G. **PR6019.O9**
Blandings Castle. Trade Cloth. Overlook Press, The. New York, NY. 2002. 301p. ISBN:1-58567-338-2, ISBN13: 978-1-58567-338-4. Dewey:823.9/12.
Audience: **g,l,u,f.**

Wodehouse, P. G. **PR6045.O53C37 2003**
Carry On, Jeeves!. Trade Cloth. Overlook Press, The. New York, NY. 2003. 224p. ISBN:1-58567-392-7, ISBN13: 978-1-58567-392-6. Dewey:823/.912. LCCN:2003-286422.
Audience: **g,l,u,f.**

Wodehouse, P. G. **PR6045.O53C57 2002**
The Clicking of Cuthbert. Trade Cloth. Overlook Press, The. New York, NY. 2002. 224p. ISBN:1-58567-278-5, ISBN13: 978-1-58567-278-3. Dewey:823/.912. LCCN:2002-511932.
Audience: **g,l,u,f.**

Wodehouse, P. G. **PR6045.O53C6 2004**
Cocktail Time. Trade Cloth. Overlook Press, The. New York, NY. 2004. 304p. ISBN:1-58567-574-1, ISBN13: 978-1-58567-574-6. Dewey:823/.912. LCCN:2005-278226.
Audience: **g,l,u,f.**

Wodehouse, P. G. **PR6045.O53C63 2000**
The Code of the Woosters. Trade Cloth. Overlook Press, The. New York, NY. 2000. 224p. Collector's Wodehouse Ser. ISBN:1-58567-057-X, ISBN13: 978-1-58567-057-4. Dewey:823.9/12. LCCN:00-026870.
Audience: **g,l,u,f.**

Wodehouse, P. G. **PR6019.O9**
A Damsel in Distress. Trade Cloth. Overlook Press, The. New York, NY. 2003. 288p. ISBN:1-58567-430-3, ISBN13: 978-1-58567-430-5. Dewey:823.9/12.
Audience: **g,l,u,f.**

Wodehouse, P. G. **PR6045.O53G4 2003**
A Gentleman of Leisure. Trade Cloth. Overlook Press, The. New York, NY. 2003. 224p. ISBN:1-58567-391-9, ISBN13: 978-1-58567-391-9. Dewey:823/.912. LCCN:2004-266819.
Audience: **g,l,u,f.**

Wodehouse, P. G. **PR6045.O53H4 2001**
Heavy Weather. Trade Cloth. Overlook Press, The. New York, NY. 2002. 321p. ISBN:1-58567-230-0, ISBN13: 978-1-58567-230-1. Dewey:823/.912. LCCN:2002-278454.
Audience: **g,l,u,f.** B

Wodehouse, P. G. **PR6045.O53H59 2003**
Hot Water. Trade Cloth. Overlook Press, The. New York, NY. 2003. 224p. ISBN:1-58567-389-7, ISBN13: 978-1-58567-389-6. Dewey:823/.912. LCCN:2003-286421.
Audience: **g,l,u,f.**

Wodehouse, P. G. **PR6045.O53B4 2001**
Jeeves and the Feudal Spirit. Trade Cloth. Overlook Press, The. New York, NY. 2002. 231p. ISBN:1-58567-229-7, ISBN13: 978-1-58567-229-5. Dewey:823/.912. LCCN:2002-278453.
Audience: **g,l,u,f.**

Wodehouse, P. G. **PR6019.O9**
Jeeves in the Offing. Trade Cloth. Overlook Press, The. New York, NY. 2002. 200p. ISBN:1-58567-325-0, ISBN13: 978-1-58567-325-4. Dewey:823.9/12.
Audience: **g,l,u,f.**

Wodehouse, P. G. **PR6045.O53**
Jill the Reckless. Trade Cloth. Overlook Press, The. New York, NY. 2005. 290p. ISBN:1-58567-660-8, ISBN13: 978-1-58567-660-6. Dewey:823.912. LCCN:2005-278232.
Audience: **g,l,u,f.**

Wodehouse, P. G. **PR6045.O53J6 2002**
Joy in the Morning. Trade Cloth. Overlook Press, The. New York, NY. 2002. 296p. ISBN:1-58567-276-9, ISBN13: 978-1-58567-276-9. Dewey:823/.912. LCCN:2002-511440.
Audience: **g,l,u,f.**

Wodehouse, P. G. **PR6045.O53L38 2001**
Laughing Gas. Trade Cloth. Overlook Press, The. New York, NY. 2002. 286p. ISBN:1-58567-232-7, ISBN13: 978-1-58567-232-5. Dewey:823/.914. LCCN:2002-511126.
Audience: **g,l,u,f.**

Wodehouse, P. G. **PR6019.O9**
Leave It to Psmith. Trade Cloth. Overlook Press, The. New York, NY. 2003. 288p. ISBN:1-58567-432-X, ISBN13: 978-1-58567-432-9. Dewey:823.9/12.
Audience: **g,l,u,f.**

Wodehouse, P. G. **PR6045.O53C75 2002**
Lord Emsworth. Trade Cloth. Overlook Press, The. New York, NY. 2002. 268p. ISBN:1-58567-277-7, ISBN13: 978-1-58567-277-6. Dewey:823/.912. LCCN:2002-511446.
Audience: **g,l,u,f.**

Wodehouse, P. G. **PR6019.O9**
The Luck of the Bodkins. Trade Cloth. Overlook Press, The. New York, NY. 2002. 358p. ISBN:1-58567-336-6, ISBN13: 978-1-58567-336-0. Dewey:823.9/12.
Audience: **g,l,u,f.**

Wodehouse, P. G. **PR6045.O53M3 2001**
The Mating Season. Trade Cloth. Overlook Press, The. New York, NY. 2002. 272p. ISBN:1-58567-231-9, ISBN13: 978-1-58567-231-8. Dewey:823/.912. LCCN:2002-277855.
Audience: **g,l,u,f.**

Wodehouse, P. G. **PR6045.O53 M42 2002**
Meet Mr. Mulliner. Trade Cloth. Overlook Press, The. New York, NY. 2002. 203p. ISBN:1-58567-275-0, ISBN13: 978-1-58567-275-2. Dewey:823/.912. LCCN:2002-284109.
Audience: **g,l,u,f.**

Wodehouse, P. G. **PR6045.O53J4 2004**
Much Obliged Jeeves. Trade Cloth. Overlook Press, The. New York, NY. 2004. 208p. ISBN:1-58567-526-1, ISBN13: 978-1-58567-526-5. Dewey:823.912. LCCN:2004-557620.
Audience: **g,l,u,f.**

Wodehouse, P. G. **PR6019.O9**
Mulliner Nights. Trade Cloth. Overlook Press, The. New York, NY. 2003. 288p. ISBN:1-58567-433-8, ISBN13: 978-1-58567-433-6. Dewey:823/.912.
Audience: **g,l,u,f.**

Wodehouse, P. G. **PR6019.O9**
P. Smith in the City. Trade Cloth. Overlook Press, The. New York, NY. 2003. 208p. ISBN:1-58567-478-8, ISBN13: 978-1-58567-478-7. Dewey:823/.9/1.
Audience: **g,l,u,f.**

Wodehouse, P. G. **PR6045.O53P45 2004**
Picadilly Jim. Trade Cloth. Overlook Press, The. New York, NY. 2004. 302p. ISBN:1-58567-616-0, ISBN13: 978-1-58567-616-3. Dewey:823/.912. LCCN:2005-278231.
Audience: **g,l,u,f.**

Wodehouse, P. G. **PR6045.O53P5 2000**
Pigs Have Wings. Trade Cloth. Overlook Press, The. New York, NY. 2000. 224p. Collector's Wodehouse Ser. ISBN:1-58567-059-6, ISBN13: 978-1-58567-059-8. Dewey:823/.912. LCCN:00-026871.
Audience: **g,l,u,f.**

Wodehouse, P. G. **PR6045.O53B75 2000**
Right Ho, Jeeves. Trade Cloth. Overlook Press, The. New York, NY. 2000. 224p. Collector's Wodehouse Ser. ISBN:1-58567-058-8, ISBN13: 978-1-58567-058-1. Dewey:823/.912. LCCN:00-026872.
Audience: **g,l,u,f.**

Wodehouse, P. G. **PR6045.O53R4 2004**
Ring for Jeeves. Trade Cloth. Overlook Press, The. New York, NY. 2004. 208p. ISBN:1-58567-524-5, ISBN13: 978-1-58567-524-1. Dewey:823/.912. LCCN:2004-557107.
Audience: **g,l,u,f.**

Wodehouse, P. G. **PR6045.O53S69 2004**
Spring Fever. Trade Cloth. Overlook Press, The. New York, NY. 2004. 276p. ISBN:1-58567-575-X, ISBN13: 978-1-58567-575-3. Dewey:823/.912. LCCN:2005-278229.
Audience: **g,l,u,f.**

Wodehouse, P. G. **PR6045.O53**
Summer Lightning. Trade Cloth. Overlook Press, The. New York, NY. 2003. 272p. ISBN:1-58567-477-X, ISBN13: 978-1-58567-477-0. Dewey:823.9/12.
Audience: **g,l,u,f.** B

Wodehouse, P. G. **PR6045.O53S83 2003**
Summer Moonshine. Trade Cloth. Overlook Press, The. New York, NY. 2003. 224p. ISBN:1-58567-390-0, ISBN13: 978-1-58567-390-2. Dewey:823/.912. LCCN:2004-266917.
Audience: **g,l,u,f.** B

Wodehouse, P. G. **PR6019.O9**
Thank You, Jeeves. Trade Cloth. Overlook Press, The. New York, NY. 2003. 288p. ISBN:1-58567-434-6, ISBN13: 978-1-58567-434-3. Dewey:823.9/12.
Audience: **g,l,u,f.**

Wodehouse, P. G. **PR6019.O9**
Ukridge. Trade Cloth. Overlook Press, The. New York, NY. 2003. 272p. ISBN:1-58567-479-6, ISBN13: 978-1-58567-479-4. Dewey:823.9/12.
Audience: **g,l,u,f.**

Wodehouse, P. G. **PR6045.O53U58 2004**
Uncle Fred in the Springtime. Trade Cloth. Overlook Press, The. New York, NY. 2004. 208p. ISBN:1-58567-527-X, ISBN13: 978-1-58567-527-2. Dewey:823/.9/12. LCCN:2004-557649.
Audience: **g,l,u,f.**

Wodehouse, P. G. **PR6045.O53U6 2004**
Uneasy Money. Trade Cloth. Overlook Press, The. New York, NY. 2004. 298p. ISBN:1-58567-572-5, ISBN13: 978-1-58567-572-2. Dewey:823/.912. LCCN:2005-278230.
Audience: **g,l,u,f.**

Wodehouse, P. G. **PR6019.O9**
Young Men in Spats. Trade Cloth. Overlook Press, The. New York, NY. 2002. 259p. ISBN:1-58567-337-4, ISBN13: 978-1-58567-337-7. Dewey:823.9/12.
Audience: **g,l,u,f.**

Wodehouse, P. G., et al. **PR6045.O53A6 2003**
P. G. Wodehouse, in His Own Words. Barry Day & Tony Ring (Authors). Trade Cloth. Overlook Press, The. New York, NY. 2003. 320p. ISBN:1-58567-393-5, ISBN13: 978-1-58567-393-3. Dewey:823/.912. LCCN:2002-034610.
Audience: **g,l,u,f.**

Wodehouse, P. G. **PR6019.O9**
Yours, Plum: The Letters of P. G. Wodehouse. Frances Donaldson (Editor). Trade Cloth. James H. Heineman Incorporated, Publisher. New York, NY. 1995. 257p. The Letters of P. G. Wodehouse in Translation Ser. ISBN:0-87008-130-6, ISBN13: 978-0-87008-130-9. Dewey:823/.912 B.
Audience: **g,l,u,f.** *Choice, 1991.*

Individual Authors and Works > 20th C. > Woolf, Virginia

Abel, Elizabeth **PR6045.O72Z534 1989**
Virginia Woolf and the Fictions of Psychoanalysis. Catherine R. Stimpson (Foreword by). Trade Cloth. University of Chicago Press. Chicago, IL. 1989. 200p. Women in Culture and Society Ser. ISBN:0-226-00079-6, ISBN13: 978-0-226-00079-4. Dewey:823/.912. LCCN:89-004810.
Audience: **u,f.**

Bell, Quentin **PR6019.O9**
Virginia Woolf: A Biography. Trade Paper. Harcourt Trade Publishers. New York, NY. 1974. 576p. Harvest Book Ser. ISBN:0-15-693580-5, ISBN13: 978-0-15-693580-7. Dewey:823/.9/12. LCCN:73-012870.
Audience: **g,l,u,f.**

Brewster, Dorothy P. **PR6045.O72 Z563 1979**
Virginia Woolf's London. Trade Cloth. Greenwood Publishing Group, Inc. Portsmouth, NH. 1979. 120p. ISBN:0-313-20788-7, ISBN13: 978-0-313-20788-4. Dewey:823/.9/12. LCCN:78-026590.
Audience: **g,l,u,f.**

Briggs, Julia **PR6045.O72Z54359**
Virginia Woolf: An Inner Life. Cloth over Boards. Harcourt Trade Publishers. New York, NY. 2005. 544p. ISBN:0-15-101143-5, ISBN13: 978-0-15-101143-8. Dewey:823/.912. LCCN:2005-016048.
Audience: **g,l,u,f.** *Choice, 2006.*

Brosnan, Leila **PR6045.O72Z564 1997**
Reading Virginia Woolf's Essays and Journalism. Trade Cloth. Edinburgh University Press. Edinburgh, 1998. 200p. ISBN:0-7486-0852-4, ISBN13: 978-0-7486-0852-2. Dewey:823/.912. LCCN:98-131484.
Audience: **l,u,f.**

Cuddy-Keane, Melba **PR6045.O72Z57885**
Virginia Woolf, the Intellectual, and the Public Sphere. Trade Cloth. Cambridge University Press. New York, NY. 2003. 248p. ISBN:0-521-82867-8, ISBN13: 978-0-521-82867-3. Dewey:823/.912. LCCN:2003-043518.
Audience: **g,u,f.** *Choice, 2004.*

Curtis, Vanessa **PR6045.O72Z5789 2003**
Virginia Woolf's Women. Trade Cloth. University of Wisconsin Press. Chicago, IL. 2004. 224p. ISBN:0-299-18340-8, ISBN13: 978-0-299-18340-0. Dewey:823.9/12. LCCN:2002-075671.
Audience: **u,f.** *Choice, 2003.*

Daiches, David & Woolf, Virginia **PR6045.O72 Z58 1979**
Virginia Woolf. Trade Cloth. Greenwood Publishing Group, Inc. Portsmouth, NH. 1979. 169p. ISBN:0-313-21187-6, ISBN13: 978-0-313-21187-4. Dewey:823/.9/12. LCCN:78-012655.
Audience: **l,u,f.** B

DeSalvo, Louise & Leaska, Mitchell A. (Editors) **PR6037.A35**
The Letters of Vita Sackville-West and Virginia Woolf. Trade Paper. Cleis Press. San Francisco, CA. 2004. 480p. ISBN:1-57344-196-1, ISBN13: 978-1-57344-196-4. Dewey:823.9/12.
Audience: **g,l,u,f.**

Fleishman, Avrom **PR6019.O9**
Virginia Woolf: A Critical Reading. Trade Paper. Johns Hopkins University Press. Baltimore, MD. 1993. 248p. ISBN:0-8018-1958-X, ISBN13: 978-0-8018-1958-2. Dewey:823/.912. LCCN:74-024375.
Audience: **u,f.** B

Gordon, Lyndall **PR6019.O9**
Virginia Woolf: A Writer's Life. Trade Paper. W. W. Norton & Company, Inc. New York, NY. 2001. 360p. ISBN:0-393-32205-X, ISBN13: 978-0-393-32205-7. Dewey:823/.912 B.
Audience: **g,l,u,f.** B

Haule, James M. & Smith, Philip H. Jr. **PR6045.O72Z695 1991**
A Concordance to the Novels of Virginia Woolf. Trade Cloth. Garland Publishing, Inc. New York, NY. 1991. 3848p. ISBN:0-8240-6339-2, ISBN13: 978-0-8240-6339-9. Dewey:823/.912. LCCN:91-001218.
Audience: **u,f.** *Choice, 1991.*

Haule, James M. & Stape, J. H. (Editors) **PR6045.O72Z6267 2001**
Editing Virginia Woolf: Interpreting the Modernist Text. Cloth over Boards. Palgrave Macmillan. New York, NY. 2002. 214p. ISBN:0-333-77045-5, ISBN13: 978-0-333-77045-0. Dewey:823/.912. LCCN:2001-036187.
Audience: **u,f.**

Hussey, Mark **PR6045.O72Z729 1995**
Virginia Woolf A to Z: A Comprehensive Reference for Students, Teachers, and Common Readers to Her Life, Work and Critical Reception. Trade Cloth. Facts On File, Inc. New York, NY. 1995. 464p. Literary A to Z Ser. ISBN:0-8160-3020-0, ISBN13: 978-0-8160-3020-0. Dewey:823.9/12. LCCN:94-036500.
Audience: **g,l,u,f.** *Choice, 1996.*

Kelley, Alice V. **PR6045.O72Z/**
The Novels of Virginia Woolf. Trade Cloth. University of Chicago Press. Chicago, IL. 1973. vii, 279p. ISBN:0-226-42985-7, ISBN13: 978-0-226-42985-4. Dewey:823/.912. LCCN:73-077134.
Audience: **u,f.** B

King, Julia & Miletic-Vejzovic, Laila (Editors) **Z997.W92L53 2003**
The Library of Leonard and Virginia Woolf: A Short-Title Catalog. Julia King (Compiled by), Laila Miletic-Vejzovic (Compiled by, Foreword by), Diane Gillespie (Foreword by). Trade Cloth, Pictures or Photographs. Washington State University Press. Pullman, WA. 2004. 272p. ISBN:0-87422-270-2, ISBN13: 978-0-87422-270-8. Dewey:018/.2. LCCN:2003-021061.
Audience: **u,f.** *Choice, 2004.*

Lee, Hermione **PR6019.09**
Virginia Woolf. Trade Paper. Knopf Publishing Group. New York, NY. 1999. 944p. ISBN:0-375-70136-2, ISBN13: 978-0-375-70136-8. Dewey:823/.912 B.
Audience: **g,l,u,f.** *Choice, 1997.*

Little, Judy **PR830.W62**
Comedy and the Woman Writer: Woolf, Spark, and Feminism. Cloth Text. University of Nebraska Press. Lincoln, NE. 1983. 224p. ISBN:0-8032-2859-7, ISBN13: 978-0-8032-2859-7. Dewey:823/.912/099287. LCCN:82-019999.
Audience: **u,f.**

Love, Jean O. **PR6045.O72Z/**
Virginia Woolf: Sources of Madness and Art. Trade Cloth. University of California Press. Berkeley, CA. 1978. xiv, 379p. ISBN:0-520-03358-2, ISBN13: 978-0-520-03358-0. Dewey:823/.912. LCCN:76-048808.
Audience: **u,f.**

Love, Jean O. **PR6019.O9**
Worlds in Consciousness: Mythopoetic Thought in the Novels of Virginia Woolf. Trade Cloth. University of California Press. Berkeley, CA. 1970. "xvi, 268"p. ISBN:0-520-01606-8, ISBN13: 978-0-520-01606-4. Dewey:823/.9/12. LCCN:72-093185.
Audience: **u,f.**

Marcus, Jane (Editor) **PR6045.O72Z/**
Virginia Woolf: A Feminist Slant. Trade Cloth. University of Nebraska Press. Lincoln, NE. 1983. xvi, 281p. ISBN:0-8032-3081-8, ISBN13: 978-0-8032-3081-1. Dewey:823/.912. LCCN:82-024787.
Audience: **u,f.**

Marder, Herbert **PR6045.O72Z8152 2000**
The Measure of Life: Virginia Woolf's Last Years. Book, Other. Cornell University Press. Ithaca, NY. 2000. 432p. ISBN:0-8014-3729-6, ISBN13: 978-0-8014-3729-8. Dewey:823/.912 B. LCCN:00-020957.
Audience: **g,l,u,f.** *Choice, 2001.*

McNeillie, Andrew (Introduction by) **PR6045.O72 E7**
The Essays of Virginia Woolf: 1912-1918. Trade Cloth. Harcourt Trade Publishers. New York, NY. 1988. 448p. ISBN:0-15-129056-3, ISBN13: 978-0-15-129056-7. Dewey:824/.912.
Audience: **g,l,u,f.** *Choice, 1988.*

McNeillie, Andrew (Editor) **PR6045.O72 E7**
The Essays of Virginia Woolf: 1919-1924. Trade Cloth. Harcourt Trade Publishers. New York, NY. 1989. 544p. ISBN:0-15-129057-1, ISBN13: 978-0-15-129057-4. Dewey:824/.912.
Audience: **g,l,u,f.**

Moore, Madeline **PR6045.O72Z/**
The Short Season Between Two Silences. Allen & Unwin Pty., Ltd. 1984. ISBN:0-04-800022-1, ISBN13: 978-0-04-800022-4.
Audience: **l,u,f.**

Naremore, James **PR6045.O72**
The World Without a Self: Virginia Woolf and the Novel. Trade Cloth. Yale University Press. Cumberland, RI. 1973. 272p. ISBN:0-300-01594-1, ISBN13: 978-0-300-01594-2. Dewey:823/.9/12. LCCN:72-091315.
Audience: **u,f.**

Rosenberg, Beth C. & Dubino, Jeanne **PR6045.O72Z8923 1997**
Virginia Woolf and the Essay. Cloth over Boards. Palgrave Macmillan. New York, NY. 1997. 320p. ISBN:0-312-17233-8, ISBN13: 978-0-312-17233-6. Dewey:823/.912. LCCN:97-021442.
Audience: **l,u,f.** *Choice, 1998.*

Rosenfeld, Natania **PR6045.O72Z8672 2000**
Outsiders Together: Virginia and Leonard Woolf. Cloth Text. Princeton University Press. Princeton, NJ. 2000. 232p. ISBN:0-691-05884-9, ISBN13: 978-0-691-05884-9. Dewey:823/.912 B. LCCN:99-053742.
Audience: **g,l,u,f.** *Choice, 2000.*

Rosenfeld, Natania **PR6019.O9**
Outsiders Together: Virginia and Leonard Woolf. Trade Paper. Princeton University Press. Princeton, NJ. 2001. 230p. ISBN:0-691-08960-4, ISBN13: 978-0-691-08960-7. Dewey:823/.912 B.
Audience: **g,l,u,f.** *Choice, 2000.*

Silver, Brenda R. **PR6045.O72Z87633**
Virginia Woolf Icon. Trade Cloth. University of Chicago Press. Chicago, IL. 2000. 373p. Women in Culture and Society Ser. ISBN:0-226-75745-5, ISBN13: 978-0-226-75745-2. Dewey:823/.912. LCCN:99-036175.
Audience: **l,u,f.**

Silver, Brenda R. **PR6045.O72 Z8764**
Virginia Woolf's Reading Notebooks. Trade Cloth. Princeton University Press. Princeton, NJ. 1983. 450p. ISBN:0-691-06489-X, ISBN13: 978-0-691-06489-5. Dewey:828/.91203. LCCN:81-047156.
Audience: **l,u,f.**

Smith, Angela **PR9639.3.M258A6 2002**
Katherine Mansfield and Virginia Woolf: A Public of Two. Trade Cloth. Oxford University Press, Inc. New York, NY. 1999. 254p. ISBN:0-19-818398-4, ISBN13: 978-0-19-818398-3. Dewey:823/.912. LCCN:2001-054559.
Audience: **u,f.**

Squier, Susan M. **PR6045.O72Z8785 1985**
Virginia Woolf and London: The Sexual Politics of the City. Trade Cloth. University of North Carolina Press. Chapel Hill, NC. 1985. 232p. ISBN:0-8078-1637-X, ISBN13: 978-0-8078-1637-0. Dewey:823/.912. LCCN:84-017376.
Audience: **l,u,f.** *Choice, 1985.*

Steele, Elizabeth **Z8984.2.S743 1987**
Virginia Wolf's Rediscovered Essays: Sources and Allusions. Paper over Boards. Garland Publishing, Inc. New York, NY. 1987. 256p. Library of the Humanities ISBN:0-8240-8527-2, ISBN13: 978-0-8240-8527-8. Dewey:016.824/912. LCCN:86-005725.
Audience: **u,f.** *Choice, 1987.*

Willis, J. H. Jr. **Z232.H73W54 1992**
Leonard and Virginia Woolf As Publishers, 1917-1941: The Hogarth Press. Cloth Text. University Press of Virginia. Charlottesville, VA. 1992. 472p. ISBN:0-8139-1361-6, ISBN13: 978-0-8139-1361-2. Dewey:070.5092. LCCN:91-041505.
Audience: **l,u,f.** *Choice, 1993.*

Woolf, Virginia **PR6019.O9**
Between the Acts. Trade Paper. Harcourt Trade Publishers. New York, NY. 1970. 228p. ISBN:0-15-611870-X, ISBN13: 978-0-15-611870-5. Dewey:823.9/12. LCCN:41-051933.
Audience: **g,l,u,f.**

Woolf, Virginia **PN511.W72 2005**
The Common Reader. Trade Paper. Harcourt Trade Publishers. New York, NY. 2002. 288p. ISBN:0-15-602778-X, ISBN13: 978-0-15-602778-6. Dewey:820.9.
Audience: **g,l,u,f.**

Woolf, Virginia **PR6045.O72.Z494 1977**
The Diary of Virginia Woolf. Trade Cloth. Harcourt College Publishers. Fort Worth, TX. 1977. ISBN:0-15-125597-0, ISBN13: 978-0-15-125597-9. Dewey:828/.91203. LCCN:77-073111.
Audience: **g,l,u,f.** B

Woolf, Virginia **PR6019.O9**
Flush. Trade Paper. Oxford University Press, Inc. New York, NY. 1998. 184p. Oxford World's Classics Ser. ISBN:0-19-283328-6, ISBN13: 978-0-19-283328-0. Dewey:823/.9/12. LCCN:98-013090.
Audience: **g,l,u,f.**

Woolf, Virginia **PR6045.O72**
Haunted House and Other Short Stories. Trade Paper. Harcourt Trade Publishers. New York, NY. 2002. 168p. ISBN:0-15-602803-4, ISBN13: 978-0-15-602803-5. Dewey:823.912.
Audience: **g,l,u,f.** B

Woolf, Virginia **PR6019.O9**
Night and Day. Trade Paper. BookSurge, LLC. N Charleston, SC. 2002. 496p. ISBN:1-59109-040-7, ISBN13: 978-1-59109-040-3. Dewey:823.9/12.
Audience: **g,l,u,f.** B

Woolf, Virginia **PR99**
The Second Common Reader. Trade Paper. Harcourt Trade Publishers. New York, NY. 2003. 336p. ISBN:0-15-602816-6, ISBN13: 978-0-15-602816-5. Dewey:820/.9.
Audience: **g,l,u,f.** B

Woolf, Virginia **PR6045.O72**
A Writer's Diary. Trade Paper. Harcourt Trade Publishers. New York, NY. 2003. 372p. ISBN:0-15-602791-7, ISBN13: 978-0-15-602791-5. Dewey:823.912.
Audience: **g,l,u,f.**

Woolf, Virginia **PR6045.O72**
Essays of Virginia Woolf: 1912-8. Trade Cloth. Ebury Publishing. London, 1987. 448p. ISBN:0-7012-0667-5, ISBN13: 978-0-7012-0667-3. Dewey:824/.912.
Audience: **g,l,u,f.**

Woolf, Virginia **PR6019.O9**
Voyage Out. Trade Paper. Penguin Books Canada, Ltd. Toronto, ON. 2004. 432p. ISBN:0-14-118478-7, ISBN13: 978-0-14-118478-4. Dewey:823.912.
Audience: **g,l,u,f.** B

Woolf, Virginia **PR6045.O72**
A Room of One's Own and Three Guineas. Trade Paper. Oxford University Press. Oxford, 1998. 470p. ISBN:0-19-283484-3, ISBN13: 978-0-19-283484-3. Dewey:305.4/338/0942.
Audience: **g,l,u,f.**

Woolf, Virginia **PR6019.O9**
The Years. Trade Paper. Harcourt Trade Publishers. New York, NY. 1969. 444p. ISBN:0-15-699701-0, ISBN13: 978-0-15-699701-0. Dewey:823.9/12. LCCN:37-027268.
Audience: **g,l,u,f.**

Woolf, Virginia **PR6045.O72A15 1985**
The Complete Shorter Fiction of Victoria Woolf. Susan Dick (Editor). Trade Cloth. Harcourt Trade Publishers. New York, NY. 1986. 313p. ISBN:0-15-118983-8, ISBN13: 978-0-15-118983-0. Dewey:823/.912. LCCN:85-017719.
Audience: **g,l,u,f.** B

Woolf, Virginia **PR6045.O72A6 1989**
The Complete Shorter Fiction of Virginia Woolf. Ed. 2. Susan Dick (Editor). Trade Paper. Harcourt Trade Publishers. New York, NY. 1989. 360p. ISBN:0-15-621250-1, ISBN13: 978-0-15-621250-2. Dewey:823/.912. LCCN:89-002006.
Audience: **g,l,u,f.**

Woolf, Virginia **PR6045.O72O7 2006**
Orlando: A Biography. Mark Hussey (Editor). Trade Paper. Harcourt Trade Publishers. New York, NY. 2006. 384p. ISBN:0-15-603151-5, ISBN13: 978-0-15-603151-6. Dewey:823/.912. LCCN:2005-037769.
Audience: **g,l,u,f.**

Woolf, Virginia **PR6045.O72T5 2006**
Three Guineas. Mark Hussey (Editor). Trade Paper. Harcourt Trade Publishers. New York, NY. 2006. 352p. ISBN:0-15-603163-9, ISBN13: 978-0-15-603163-9. Dewey:823/.912. LCCN:2006-006360.
Audience: **g,l,u,f.**

Woolf, Virginia **PR6045.O72T6 2005**
To the Lighthouse. Mark Hussey (Preface by). Trade Paper, Perfect. Harcourt Trade Publishers. New York, NY. 2005. 312p. ISBN:0-15-603047-0, ISBN13: 978-0-15-603047-2. Dewey:823/.912. LCCN:2005-004201.
Audience: **g,l,u,f.**

Woolf, Virginia **PR6045.O72W3 2006**
The Waves. Mark Hussey (Editor). Trade Paper. Harcourt Trade Publishers. New York, NY. 2006. 348p. ISBN:0-15-603157-4, ISBN13: 978-0-15-603157-8. Dewey:823/.912. LCCN:2005-037770.
Audience: **g,l,u,f.**

Woolf, Virginia **PR6045.O72M7 2005**
Mrs. Dalloway. Mark Hussey (Editor), Bonnie Kime Scott (Introduction by). Trade Paper, Perfect. Harcourt Trade Publishers. New York, NY. 2005. 304p. ISBN:0-15-603035-7, ISBN13: 978-0-15-603035-9. Dewey:823/.912. LCCN:2005-003378.
Audience: **g,l,u,f.** B

Woolf, Virginia **PZ3.W884 PR6045.O72**
Jacob's Room. Regina Marler (Introduction by). Trade Paper. Penguin Group (USA) Inc. New York, NY. 2006. 224p. ISBN:0-451-53005-5, ISBN13: 978-0-451-53005-9. Dewey:823/.9/12.
Audience: **g,l,u,f.**

Woolf, Virginia **PR6045.O72**
Essays of Virginia Woolf: 1925-1928. A. McNeillie (Editor). Trade Cloth. Ebury Publishing. London, 1994. 576p. ISBN:0-7012-0669-1, ISBN13: 978-0-7012-0669-7. Dewey:824.912.
Audience: **g,l,u,f.**

Woolf, Virginia **PR6045.O72A6 1986**
The Essays of Virginia Woolf, Vol. 1. Andrew McNeillie (Editor). Trade Cloth. Harcourt Trade Publishers. New York, NY. 1987. 416p. ISBN:0-15-129055-5, ISBN13: 978-0-15-129055-0. Dewey:824/.912. LCCN:86-029520.
Audience: **g,l,u,f.** *Choice, 1987.*

Woolf, Virginia **PR6045.O72 Z525 1977**
The Letters of Virginia Woolf, 1888-1912, Vol. I. Nigel Nicolson & Joanne Trautmann (Editors). Trade Paper. Harcourt Trade Publishers. New York, NY. 1977. 566p. ISBN:0-15-650881-8, ISBN13: 978-0-15-650881-0. Dewey:823/.9/12. LCCN:76-040422.
Audience: **g,l,u,f.**

Woolf, Virginia **PR6045.O72**
The Letters of Virginia Woolf, 1911-1922, Vol. II. Nigel Nicolson & Joanne Trautmann (Editors). Trade Paper. Harcourt Trade Publishers. New York, NY. 1978. 672p. ISBN:0-15-650882-6, ISBN13: 978-0-15-650882-7. Dewey:823.912. LCCN:76-040422.
Audience: **g,l,u,f.**

Woolf, Virginia **PR6045.O72**
The Letters of Virginia Woolf, 1929-1931, Vol. IV. Nigel Nicolson & Joanne Trautmann (Editors). Trade Paper. Harcourt Trade Publishers. New York, NY. 1981. 480p. Letters of Virginia Woolf, 1929-1931 Ser., Vol. 4 ISBN:0-15-650884-2, ISBN13: 978-0-15-650884-1. Dewey:823.912. LCCN:76-040422.
Audience: **g,l,u,f.**

Woolf, Virginia **PR6045.O72**
The Letters of Virginia Woolf, 1932-1935, Vol. V. Nigel Nicolson & Joanne Trautmann (Editors). Trade Paper. Harcourt Trade Publishers. New York, NY. 1982. 504p. Letters of Virginia Woolf, 1932-1935 Ser., Vol. 5 ISBN:0-15-650886-9, ISBN13: 978-0-15-650886-5. Dewey:823.912. LCCN:75-025538.
Audience: **g,l,u,f.**

Woolf, Virginia **PR6045.O72**
The Letters of Virginia Woolf, 1936-1941, Vol. VI. Nigel Nicolson & Joanne Trautmann (Editors). Trade Paper. Harcourt Trade Publishers. New York, NY. 1982. 576p. ISBN:0-15-650887-7, ISBN13: 978-0-15-650887-2. Dewey:823.912. LCCN:75-025538.
Audience: **g,l,u,f.**

Woolf, Virginia & Prose, Francine **PR6045.O72M7 2003**
The Mrs. Dalloway Reader. Mark Hussey (Editor). Trade Paper. Harcourt Trade Publishers. New York, NY. 2004. 400p. ISBN:0-15-603015-2, ISBN13: 978-0-15-603015-1. Dewey:823/.912.
Audience: **g,l,u,f.**

Woolf, Virginia **PR6045.O72Z47 1985**
Moments of Being: Unpublished Autobiographical Writings. Ed. 2. Jeanne Schulkind (Editor). Trade Paper. Harcourt Trade Publishers. New York, NY. 1985. 240p. ISBN:0-15-661918-0, ISBN13: 978-0-15-661918-9. Dewey:823.9/12. LCCN:85-008521.
Audience: **g,l,u,f.**

CLASSICAL LANGUAGES AND LITERATURES

This section primarily covers the Greek and Latin languages and literatures; see also the sections on Greek and Roman history in the Ancient History section for additional coverage of classical cultures. The general and reference works category includes dictionaries of classical civilization, histories of literature, and similar works dealing with classical civilization and literature as a whole. Greek language and literature are covered, with various subsections covering major genres and individual authors. Latin language and literature receive similar treatment. Focus in these sections is on basic works for undergraduate education (including some more advanced works which will be used primarily by faculty in course preparation); these include editions, translations, commentaries, and key secondary works. I have preferred works in print whenever possible, although I have also included a few essential out-of-print works. Generally each listing for an individual author includes editions of major or commonly taught works, along with a single translation of each. An exception is made for a few authors, such Homer and the Greek tragedians, where multiple translations are included.

A separate subsection treats Medieval Latin. This includes introductory and bibliographical works, the most commonly used anthologies, and a limited selection of editions, commentaries, and translations of individual authors of value for undergraduate study.

—Fred Jenkins

General and Reference Works

PA3870

Bibliotheca Classica Selecta.
http://bcs.fltr.ucl.ac.be/default.htm

Audience: **f.**

The Classics Page at Ad Fontes Academy.
http://www.thelatinlibrary.com/classics

Audience: **g,l,u,f.**

HQ1127

Diotima: Materials for the Study of Women and Gender in the Ancient World.
http://www.stoa.org/diotima/

Audience: **g,l,u,f.**

PA3621

Internet Classics Archive.
http://classics.mit.edu/

Audience: **g,l,u,f.**

DF77

Perseus Digital Library.
http://www.perseus.tufts.edu/

Audience: **g,l,u,f.**

Halton, Thomas P. & O'Leary, Stella **DE59**
Classical Scholarship: An Annotated Bibliography. Trade Cloth. Kraus International Publications. Hackensack, NJ. 1986. 396p. ISBN:0-527-37436-9, ISBN13: 978-0-527-37436-5. Dewey:016.938. LCCN:82-048984.

Audience: **g,u,f.** *Choice, 1987.*

Harwin, Lorna **PA3003**
Reception Studies: New Surveys in the Classics. Lorna Harwick (Editor). Trade Paper. Oxford University Press, Inc. New York, NY. 2003. 136p. New Surveys in the Classics Ser., Vol. 33 ISBN:0-19-852865-5, ISBN13: 978-0-19-852865-4. Dewey:880/.09.

Audience: **g,u,f.**

Hornblower, Simon & Spawforth, Antony (Editors) **DE5**
The Oxford Classical Dictionary. Ed. 3. Trade Cloth. Oxford University Press, Inc. New York, NY. 2003. 1,696p. ISBN:0-19-860641-9, ISBN13: 978-0-19-860641-3. Dewey:938/.003. LCCN:2003-267385.

Audience: **g,l,u,f.** *Choice, 2003.*

Howatson, Margaret **PA31.H69 1989**
The Oxford Companion to Classical Literature. Ed. 2. Trade Cloth. Oxford University Press, Inc. New York, NY. 1989. 640p. ISBN:0-19-866121-5, ISBN13: 978-0-19-866121-4. Dewey:880.9/001. LCCN:88-027330.

Audience: **g,l,u,f.** *Choice, 1989.*

Jenkins, Fred W. **Z7016**
Classical Studies: A Guide to the Reference Literature. Ed. 2. Trade Paper. Libraries Unlimited, Inc. Westport, CT. 2006. 424p. Reference Sources in the Humanities Ser. ISBN:1 59158 119 2, ISBN13: 978-1-59158-119-2. Dewey:016.48. LCCN:2006-004705.

Audience: **g,l,u,f.** *Choice, 1996.*

Luce, T. James (Editor) **PA3009**
Ancient Writers: Greece and Rome, Set. Trade Cloth. Thomson Gale. Farmington Hills, MI. 1982. 1148p. Scribner Writers Ser., Vol. 1 ISBN:0-684-16595-3, ISBN13: 978-0-684-16595-0. Dewey:880/.09. LCCN:82-050612.

Audience: **g,l,u.**

McManus, Barbara F. **PA78.U6M38 1997**
Classics and Feminism: Gendering the Classics. Trade Cloth. Thomson Gale. Farmington Hills, MI. 1997. xv, 201p. Impact of Feminism on the Arts and Sciences Ser. ISBN:0-8057-9757-2, ISBN13: 978-0-8057-9757-2. Dewey:480/.07/073. LCCN:96-036021.

Audience: **u,f.** *Choice, 1997.*

Pfeiffer, Rudolph **AZ201 .P43**
History of Classical Scholarship from 1300 to 1850. Trade Cloth. Oxford University Press, Inc. New York, NY. 1976. 224p. ISBN:0-19-814364-8, ISBN13: 978-0-19-814364-2. Dewey:938/.007. LCCN:77-363045.

Audience: **u,f.**

Rabinowitz, Nancy S. & Richlin, Amy (Editors) **PA3009**
Feminist Theory and the Classics. UK-B Format Paperback. Routledge. New York, NY. 1993. 320p. Thinking Gender Ser. ISBN:0-415-90646-6, ISBN13: 978-0-415-90646-3. Dewey:880.09. LCCN:92-040745.

Audience: **u,f.**

Reynolds, Leighton D. & Wilson, N. G. **PA47.R4 1991**
Scribes and Scholars: A Guide to the Transmission of Greek and Latin Literature. Ed. 3. Trade Paper. Oxford University Press, Inc. New York, NY. 1991. 330p. ISBN:0-19-872146-3, ISBN13: 978-0-19-872146-8. Dewey:001.2. LCCN:90-041300.

Audience: **g,u,f.**

Russell, D. A. **PA3013**
Classical Literary Criticism. Trade Paper. Oxford University Press, Inc. New York, NY. 1998. 270p. Oxford World's Classics Ser. ISBN:0-19-283900-4, ISBN13: 978-0-19-283900-8. Dewey:880.09.

Audience: **g,u,f.**

Sandys, John Edwin **AZ106**
A History of Classical Scholarship from the Sixth Century B. C. to the 19th Century. Trade Cloth. Continuum International Publishing Group, Ltd. London, 1998. 1762p. ISBN:1-85506-595-9, ISBN13: 978-1-85506-595-6. Dewey:001.2/09.

Audience: **u,f.**

Thomas, Richard & Martindale, Charles (Editors) **PA3013.C597 2006**
Classics and the Uses of Reception. Trade Cloth. Blackwell Publishing, Inc. Malden, MA. 2006. 352p. Classical Receptions Ser. ISBN:1-4051-3146-2, ISBN13: 978-1-4051-3146-9. Dewey:880.09. LCCN:2005-030975.

Audience: **u,f.**

Greek > Greek Language

Blass, F. & Debrunner, A. **PA 813 B613**
Greek Grammar of the New Testament and Other Early Christian Literature. Robert W. Funk (Translator). Trade Cloth.

Zondervan. Grand Rapids, MI. 1990. 325p.
ISBN:0-310-24780-2, ISBN13: 978-0-310-24780-7.
Dewey:487.3.
Audience: **u,f.**

Goodwin, William W. **PA258**
A Greek Grammar. Trade Paper. Wipf & Stock Publishers. Eugene, OR. 2003. 488p. ISBN:1-59244-314-1, ISBN13: 978-1-59244-314-7. Dewey:485.
Audience: **u,f.**

Goodwin, William W. **PA369**
Syntax of the Moods and Tenses of the Greek Verb. Trade Cloth. William H. Allen -Bookseller. Philadelphia, PA. 1992. 472p. ISBN:0-9637069-1-8, ISBN13: 978-0-9637069-1-1. Dewey:485.
Audience: **u,f.**

Liddell, Henry G. & Scott, Robert (Compiled by) **PA445.E5**
An Intermediate Greek-English Lexicon: Founded upon the 7th Edition of Liddell and Scott's Greek-English Lexicon 1889. Cloth Text. Oxford University Press, Inc. New York, NY. 1945. 928p. ISBN:0-19-910206-6, ISBN13: 978-0-19-910206-8. Dewey:483.
Audience: **u,f.**

Morwood, James **PA258**
Oxford Grammar of Classical Greek. Trade Paper. Oxford University Press, Inc. New York, NY. 2003. 288p. ISBN:0-19-521851-5, ISBN13: 978-0-19-521851-0. Dewey:488.2/421.
Audience: **l,u,f.**

Palmer, L. R. **PA227 .P3**
The Greek Language. Cloth Text. Brill Academic Publishers, Inc. Boston, MA. 1980. Great Languages Ser. ISBN:0-391-01203-7, ISBN13: 978-0-391-01203-5. Dewey:480/.9. LCCN:79-026758.
Audience: **l,u.**

Scott, R. & Liddell, Henry G. **PA445.E5L6 1996**
A Greek-English Lexicon: With a Revised Supplement 1996. Ed. 9. P. G. Glare (Editor), Henry S. Jones (Revised by), Roderick McKenzie (Contribution by). Cloth Text. Oxford University Press, Inc. New York, NY. 1996. 2, 438p. ISBN:0-19-864226-1, ISBN13: 978-0-19-864226-8. Dewey:483.2/1. LCCN:95-032369.
Audience: **u,f.**

Sihler, Andrew L. **PA111.S54 1995**
New Comparative Grammar of Greek and Latin. Cloth Text. Oxford University Press, Inc. New York, NY. 1995. 720p. ISBN:0-19-508345-8, ISBN13: 978-0-19-508345-3. Dewey:485. LCCN:93-038929.
Audience: **l,u,f.**

Smyth, Herbert W. **PA254.S6 1968**
Greek Grammar. Ed. 2. Gordon M. Messing (Editor). Trade Cloth. Harvard University Press. Cambridge, MA. 1956. 812p. ISBN:0-674-36250-0, ISBN13: 978-0-674-36250-5. Dewey:485. LCCN:57-002203.
Audience: **l,u,f.** B

Greek > Greek Literature

Beye, Charles Rowan **PA3052.B4**
Ancient Greek Literature and Society. Trade Cloth. Knopf Publishing Group. New York, NY. 1975. 469p.p. ISBN:0-385-06443-8, ISBN13: 978-0-385-06443-9. Dewey:880/.9. LCCN:74-021235.
Audience: **g,l,u,f.** B

Dodds, Eric R. **BF1421 .D64**
The Greeks and the Irrational. Trade Cloth. Peter Smith Publisher, Inc. Magnolia, MA. 1990. ISBN:0-8446-6224-0, ISBN13: 978-0-8446-6224-4. Dewey:913.38.
Audience: **g,u,f.**

Dover, Kenneth J. **PA3557.D68 1997**
The Evolution of Greek Prose Style. Trade Cloth. Oxford University Press, Inc. New York, NY. 1997. 220p. ISBN:0-19-814028-2, ISBN13: 978-0-19-814028-3. Dewey:888/.010809. LCCN:97-002022.
Audience: **u,f.**

Dover, Kenneth J. **PA1057**
Greek Word Order. Paper Text. Textbook Publishers. Temecula, CA. 2003. 72p. ISBN:0-7581-1290-4, ISBN13: 978-0-7581-1290-3. Dewey:489.35.
Audience: **u,f.**

Easterling, P. E. (Editor) **PA3052 .G73 1985**
Greek Literature, Vol. 1. Bernard M. Knox (Editor, Contribution by), W. V. Clausen & E. J. Kenney (Contribution by). Trade Cloth. Cambridge University Press. New York, NY. 1985. 960p. The Cambridge History of Classical Literature Ser., Vol. 1 ISBN:0-521-21042-9, ISBN13: 978-0-521-21042-3. Dewey:880.09. LCCN:82-022048.
Audience: **g,l,u,f.** B

Ford, Andrew **PA3052**
The Origins of Criticism: Literary Culture and Poetic Theory in Classical Greece. Trade Paper. Princeton University Press. Princeton, NJ. 2004. 376p. ISBN:0-691-12025-0, ISBN13: 978-0-691-12025-6. Dewey:880.9/001.
Audience: **u,f.** *Choice, 2003.*

Gantz, Timothy **BL782**
Early Greek Myth: A Guide to Literary and Artistic Sources. Trade Paper. Johns Hopkins University Press. Baltimore, MD. 1996. 584p. ISBN:0-8018-5360-5, ISBN13: 978-0-8018-5360-9. Dewey:292.1/3. LCCN:92-026010.
Audience: **g,u,f.** *Choice, 1994.*

Gantz, Timothy **BL782.G34 1996**
Early Greek Myth: A Guide to Literary and Artistic Sources. Trade Paper. Johns Hopkins University Press. Baltimore, MD. 1996. 424p. ISBN:0-8018-5362-1, ISBN13: 978-0-8018-5362-3. Dewey:292.1/3. LCCN:92-026010.
Audience: **g,u,f.** *Choice, 1994.*

Hadas, Moses **PA3061**
History of Greek Literature. Trade Cloth. Columbia University Press. New York, NY. 1950. 327p. ISBN:0-231-01767-7, ISBN13: 978-0-231-01767-1. Dewey:880.9. LCCN:50-007015.
Audience: **g,l,u.** B

Lesky, Albin **PA3057.L413 1996**
A History of Greek Literature. James Willis & Cornelis De Heer (Translators). Trade Cloth. Hackett Publishing Company, Inc. Indianapolis, IN. 1996. 944p. ISBN:0-87220-351-4, ISBN13: 978-0-87220-351-8. Dewey:880.9. LCCN:96-078783.
Audience: **u,f.**

Rose, H. J. **PA3052.R6 1996**
A Handbook of Greek Literature: From Homer to the Age of Lucian. Ed. 5. Book, Other. Bolchazy-Carducci Publishers. Wauconda, IL. 1996. 463p. ISBN:0-86516-321-9, ISBN13: 978-0-86516-321-8. Dewey:880.9/001. LCCN:96-012099.
Audience: **g,l,u,f.** *B*

Rose, H. J. & Hard, Robin **BL783.H37 2003**
New Handbook of Greek Mythology. Ed. 7. Paper over Boards. Routledge. New York, NY. 2003. 776p. ISBN:0-415-18636-6, ISBN13: 978-0-415-18636-0. Dewey:292.1/3. LCCN:2003-046672.
Audience: **g,l,u.**

Said, Suzanne & Trede, Monique **PA3055.S25 1999**
Short History of Greek Literature. Paper over Boards. Routledge. New York, NY. 1999. 232p. ISBN:0-415-12271-6, ISBN13: 978-0-415-12271-9. Dewey:880.9/001. LCCN:99-019803.
Audience: **g,l,u.**

Taplin, Oliver (Editor) **PA3054.L58 2001**
Literature in the Greek World. Trade Paper. Oxford University Press, Inc. New York, NY. 2001. 328p. ISBN:0-19-289303-3, ISBN13: 978-0-19-289303-1. Dewey:880.9/001. LCCN:2001-276710.
Audience: **g,l,u,f.**

Turner, Eric G. **Z0113.8.T86**
Greek Manuscripts of the Ancient World. Trade Paper. Books on Demand. Ann Arbor, MI. 148p. ISBN:0-608-11349-2, ISBN13: 978-0-608-11349-4. Dewey:091/.0938. LCCN:79-148945.
Audience: **g,u,f.**

Whitmarsh, Tim **PA3052.W48 2004**
Ancient Greek Literature. Trade Paper. Polity Press. Cambridge, 2004. 296p. Cultural History of Literature Ser. ISBN:0-7456-2792-7, ISBN13: 978-0-7456-2792-2. Dewey:880.9/001. LCCN:2003-020332.
Audience: **g,u,f.**

Yunis, Harvey (Editor) **PA3009.W75 2002**
Written Text and the Rise of Literate Culture in Classical Greece. Trade Cloth. Cambridge University Press. New York, NY. 2003. 272p. ISBN:0-521-80930-4, ISBN13: 978-0-521-80930-6. Dewey:880.9/001. LCCN:2002-071492.
Audience: **u,f.**

Greek > Genres > Biography

Hagg, Tomas & Rousseau, Philip (Editors) **PA3043.G74 2000**
Greek Biography and Panegyric in Late Antiquity. Christian Hgel (Contribution by). Trade Cloth. University of California Press. Berkeley, CA. 2000. 302p. Transformation of the Classical Heritage Ser., Vol. 31 ISBN:0-520-22388-8, ISBN13: 978-0-520-22388-2. Dewey:888/.010809. LCCN:00-028710.
Audience: **u,f.** *Choice, 2001.*

Momigliano, Arnaldo D. **PA3043.M6 1993**
The Development of Greek Biography. Trade Paper. Harvard University Press. Cambridge, MA. 1993. 156p. ISBN:0-674-20041-1, ISBN13: 978-0-674-20041-8. Dewey:888.0109. LCCN:92-034861.
Audience: **u,f.**

Stuart, Duane R. **PA3043 .S8**
Epochs of Greek and Roman Biography. Trade Paper. Biblo & Tannen Booksellers & Publishers, Inc. Cheshire, CT. 1928. ISBN:0-8196-0193-4, ISBN13: 978-0-8196-0193-3. Dewey:880/.09. LCCN:67-019532.
Audience: **u,f.**

Greek > Genres > Drama

Arnott, Peter D. **PA3201.A77 1989**
Public and Performance in the Greek Theatre. Trade Cloth. Routledge. New York, NY. 1989. 224p. ISBN:0-415-02914-7, ISBN13: 978-0-415-02914-8. Dewey:792/.0938. LCCN:88-032156.
Audience: **u,f.** *Choice, 1990.*

Burnett, Anne P. **PA3136 .B79 1998**
Revenge in Attic and Later Tragedy. Trade Cloth. University of California Press. Berkeley, CA. 1998. 326p. Sather Classical Lectures, Vol. 62 ISBN:0-520-21096-4, ISBN13: 978-0-520-21096-7. Dewey:882/.0109. LCCN:97-022677.
Audience: **u,f.** *Choice, 1999.*

Easterling, P. E. (Editor) **PA3131 .C29 1997**
The Cambridge Companion to Greek Tragedy. Trade Paper. Cambridge University Press. New York, NY. 1997. 410p. Companions to Literature Ser. ISBN:0-521-42351-1, ISBN13: 978-0-521-42351-9. Dewey:882/.01/09. LCCN:96-037392.
Audience: **g,l,u,f.** *Choice, 1998.*

Goldhill, Simon **PA3131 .G54 1986**
Reading Greek Tragedy. Trade Paper. Cambridge University Press. New York, NY. 1986. 320p. ISBN:0-521-31579-4, ISBN13: 978-0-521-31579-1. Dewey:882/.01. LCCN:85-019004.
Audience: **g,l,u,f.**

Gregory, Justina (Editor) **PA3131.C56 2006**
A Companion to Greek Tragedy. Trade Cloth. Blackwell Publishing, Inc. Malden, MA. 2005. 576p. Blackwell Companions to the Ancient World Ser. ISBN:1-4051-0770-7, ISBN13: 978-1-4051-0770-9. Dewey:882/.0109. LCCN:2004-024920.
Audience: **u,f.** *Choice, 2006.*

Henderson, Jeffrey **PA3166.H4 1991**
The Maculate Muse: Obscene Language in Attic Comedy. Ed. 2. Paper Text. Oxford University Press, Inc. New York, NY. 1991. 288p. ISBN:0-19-506685-5, ISBN13: 978-0-19-506685-2. Dewey:882/.0109. LCCN:90-042489.
Audience: **u,f.**

Jones, John **PA3131.J6**
On Aristotle and Greek Tragedy. Paper Text. Textbook Publishers. Temecula, CA. 2003. 284p. ISBN:0-7581-7170-6, ISBN13: 978-0-7581-7170-2. Dewey:882/.01.
Audience: **u,f.**

Kitto, Humphrey D. **PA3131**
Greek Tragedy. Ed. 3. Trade Paper. Routledge. New York, NY. 1990. 416p. ISBN:0-415-05896-1, ISBN13: 978-0-415-05896-4. Dewey:882.00916.
Audience: **u,f.**

Lattimore, Richmond A. **PA3545.L38 2003**
The Poetry of Greek Tragedy. Trade Paper. Johns Hopkins University Press. Baltimore, MD. 2003. 160p. ISBN:0-8018-7260-X, ISBN13: 978-0-8018-7260-0. Dewey:882/.0109. LCCN:2002-043474.
Audience: **u,f.**

Lewis, David M. & Pickard-Cambridge, Arthur W. **PA3201.P5 1988**
The Dramatic Festivals of Athens. Ed. 2. John Gould (Revised by). Trade Cloth. Oxford University Press, Inc. New York, NY. 1989. 392p. ISBN:0-19-814258-7, ISBN13: 978-0-19-814258-4. Dewey:792/.0938. LCCN:89-164359.
Audience: **f.** B

Pickard-Cambridge, Arthur W. **PA3203**
Theatre of Dionysys in Athens. Trade Cloth. Oxford University Press, Inc. New York, NY. 1947. ISBN:0-19-814229-3, ISBN13: 978-0-19-814229-4. Dewey:792.
Audience: **f.**

Segal, Erich **PA3131**
Oxford Readings in Greek Tragedy. Trade Cloth. Oxford University Press, Inc. New York, NY. 1989. 460p. ISBN:0-19-872116-1, ISBN13: 978-0-19-872116-1. Dewey:882/.01/09.
Audience: **l,u,f.**

Taplin, Oliver **PA3131.T37 2003**
Greek Tragedy in Action. Ed. 2. Trade Paper. Routledge. New York, NY. 2002. 232p. ISBN:0-415-30251-X, ISBN13: 978-0-415-30251-7. Dewey:882/.01/09. LCCN:2004-275872.
Audience: **l,u,f.** B

Wiles, David **PA3201**
Tragedy in Athens: Performance Space and Theatrical Meaning. Trade Paper. Cambridge University Press. New York, NY. 1999. 240p. ISBN:0-521-66615-5, ISBN13: 978-0-521-66615-2. Dewey:792/.0938/5.
Audience: **u,f.** *Choice, 1998.*

Greek > Genres > Epic

Beye, Charles R. **PA4037 .B503 1976**
The Iliad, the Odyssey, and the Epic Tradition. Trade Cloth. Gordian Press, Inc. Staten Island, NY. 1976. 280p. ISBN:0-87752-187-5, ISBN13: 978-0-87752-187-7. Dewey:883/.01. LCCN:76-010726.
Audience: **g,l,u.**

Burgess, Jonathan S. **PA4037.B84 2001**
The Tradition of the Trojan War in Homer and the Epic Cycle. Trade Cloth. Johns Hopkins University Press. Baltimore, MD. 2001. 320p. ISBN:0-8018-6652-9, ISBN13: 978-0-8018-6652-4. Dewey:883/.01. LCCN:00-011637.
Audience: **u,f.** *Choice, 2002.*

Frame, Douglas **PA3107.F7**
The Myth of Return in Early Greek Epic. Trade Paper. Books on Demand. Ann Arbor, MI. 190p. ISBN:0-8357-8241-7, ISBN13: 978-0-8357-8241-8. Dewey:883/.01/09. LCCN:77-076306.
Audience: **u,f.**

Newman, John K. **PN56.E65N49 1986**
The Classical Epic Tradition. Cloth Text. University of Wisconsin Press. Chicago, IL. 1986. 576p. Studies in Classics ISBN:0-299-10510-5, ISBN13: 978-0-299-10510-5. Dewey:809.1/3. LCCN:85-040766.
Audience: **u,f.** *Choice, 1986.*

Thalmann, William G. **PA3092.T48**
Conventions of Form and Thought in Early Greek Epic Poetry. Trade Paper. Books on Demand. Ann Arbor, MI. 1984. 288p. ISBN:0-608-03660-9, ISBN13: 978-0-608-03660-1. Dewey:883/.01/09. LCCN:84-047944.
Audience: **u,f.**

Greek > Genres > History

Fornara, Charles W. **DE8.F67 1983**
The Nature of History in Ancient Greece and Rome. Trade Cloth. University of California Press. Berkeley, CA. 1983. 264p. Eidos Ser., No. 2:Studies in Classical Kinds ISBN:0-520-04910-1, ISBN13: 978-0-520-04910-9. Dewey:938/.007/2. LCCN:82-021888.
Audience: **g,u,f.** B

Hornblower, Simon (Editor) **DF211**
Greek Historiography. Trade Paper. Oxford University Press, Inc. New York, NY. 1996. 298p. ISBN:0-19-815072-5, ISBN13: 978-0-19-815072-5. Dewey:907.2/038. LCCN:93-045956.
Audience: **u,f.** *Choice, 1995.*

Luce, T. James **DF211.L83 1997**
The Greek Historians. Paper over Boards. Routledge. New York, NY. 1997. 168p. ISBN:0-415-10592-7, ISBN13: 978-0-415-10592-7. Dewey:938. LCCN:96-019960.
Audience: **g,l,u,f.**

Marincola, John **DF211**
Greek Historians. Oxford University Press. 2001. Greece & Rome. New Surveys in the Classics ISBN:0-19-922501-X, ISBN13: 978-0-19-922501-9.
Audience: **u,f.**

Pearson, Lionel **DG55.M3.P32 1987**
The Greek Historians of the West: Timaeus and His Predecessors. Trade Paper. Oxford University Press, Inc. New York, NY. 1988. 305p. American Philological Association Philological Monographs ISBN:1-55540-078-7, ISBN13: 978-1-55540-078-1. Dewey:945/.755. LCCN:87-004877.
Audience: **u,f.** *Choice, 1988.*

Greek > Genres > Lyric and Elegiac Poetry

Bowra, Maurice **PA3019.B6**
Greek Lyric Poetry from Alcman to Simonides. Ed. 2. Trade Cloth. Oxford University Press, Inc. New York, NY. 2001. 458p. Oxford Scholarly Classics Ser. ISBN:0-19-814329-X, ISBN13: 978-0-19-814329-1. Dewey:884.09.
Audience: **u,f.**

Campbell, D. A. **PA3433 .G74X 1982**
Greek Lyric Poetry: A Selection of Early Greek Lyric, Elegiac and Iambic Poetry. Trade Paper. Bristol Classical Press. London, 1982. 500p. Greek Texts Ser. ISBN:0-86292-008-6, ISBN13: 978-0-86292-008-1. Dewey:884/.01/08. LCCN:87-673438.
Audience: **u,f.**

Campbell, David A. **PA3622**
Greek Lyric: The New School of Poetry and Anonymous Songs and Hymns. Trade Cloth. Harvard University Press. Cambridge, MA. 1993. 496p. Loeb Classical Library Ser. ISBN:0-674-99559-7, ISBN13: 978-0-674-99559-8. Dewey:884.0108. LCCN:82-178982.
Audience: **g,l,u,f.**

Campbell, David A. (Translator) **PA3622**
Greek Lyric - Anacreon, Anacreontea, Choral Lyric from Olympus to Alcman, Vol. 2. Trade Cloth. Harvard University Press. Cambridge, MA. 1988. 560p. Greek Lyric Ser., No. 143 ISBN:0-674-99158-3, ISBN13: 978-0-674-99158-3. Dewey:808.8.
Audience: **g,l,u,f.**

Campbell, David A. (Translator) **PA3622 .C3 1982**
Greek Lyric - Sappho and Alcaeus, Vol. I. Trade Cloth. Harvard University Press. Cambridge, MA. 1982. 512p. Greek Lyric Ser., No. 142 ISBN:0-674-99157-5, ISBN13: 978-0-674-99157-6. Dewey:884/.01/08. LCCN:82-178982.
Audience: **g,l,u,f.**

Campbell, David A. (Editor, Translator) **PA3622**
Greek Lyric: Bacchylides, Corinna, and Others. Trade Cloth. Harvard University Press. Cambridge, MA. 1992. 432p. Greek Lyric Ser., No. 461 ISBN:0-674-99508-2, ISBN13: 978-0-674-99508-6. Dewey:884.0108. LCCN:82-178982.
Audience: **g,l,u,f.**

Gerber, Douglas E. (Editor) **PA3092.C66 1997**
A Companion to the Greek Lyric Poets. Trade Cloth. Brill Academic Publishers, Inc. Boston, MA. 1997. "viii, 292"p. Mnemosyne, Bibliotheca Classica Batava Ser., No. 173:Supplementum ISBN:90-04-09944-1, ISBN13: 978-90-04-09944-9. Dewey:884/.0109. LCCN:97-028625.
Audience: **u,f.**

Gerber, Douglas E. **PA3623.E44G75 1999**
Greek Elegiac Poetry: From the Seventh to the Fifth Centuries B. C. - Tyrtaeus, Solon, Theognis, and Others. Trade Cloth. Harvard University Press. Cambridge, MA. 1999. 512p. Loeb Classical Library, Vol. 258 ISBN:0-674-99582-1, ISBN13: 978-0-674-99582-6. Dewey:881/.0108. LCCN:98-026152.
Audience: **g,l,u,f.**

Hutchinson, G. O. **PA3110**
Greek Lyric Poetry: A Commentary on Selected Larger Pieces (Alcman, Stesichorus, Sappho, Alcaeus, Ibycus, Anacreon, Simonides, Bacchylides, Pindar, Sophocles, Euripides). Trade Paper. Oxford University Press, Inc. New York, NY. 2003. 552p. ISBN:0-19-926582-8, ISBN13: 978-0-19-926582-4. Dewey:884/.0109.
Audience: **u,f.**

Page, Denys L. (Editor) **PA3443**
Lyrica Graeca Selecta. Cloth Text. Oxford University Press, Inc. New York, NY. 1968. 276p. Oxford Classical Texts ISBN:0-19-814567-5, ISBN13: 978-0-19-814567-7. Dewey:880.81.
Audience: **u,f.**

Page, Denys L. (Editor) **PA3443**
Poetae Melici Graeci. Trade Cloth. Oxford University Press, Inc. New York, NY. 1962. 636p. ISBN:0-19-814333-8, ISBN13: 978-0-19-814333-8. Dewey:884/.01/08.
Audience: **u,f.**

Page, Denys L. (Editor) **PA3443 .S8 1974**
Supplementum Lyricum: Poetarum Lyricorum Graecorum Fragmenta Qua Recens Innotuerunt. Trade Cloth. Oxford University Press, Inc. New York, NY. 1974. 160p. ISBN:0-19-814002-9, ISBN13: 978-0-19-814002-3. Dewey:884/.01/08. LCCN:75-593704.
Audience: **u,f.**

Segal, Charles **PA3092.S44 1998**
Aglaia: The Poetry of Alcman, Sappho, Pindar, Bacchylides and Corinna. Book, Other. Rowman & Littlefield Publishers, Inc. Lanham, MD. 1998. 352p. Greek Studies, :Interdisciplinary Approaches ISBN:0-8476-8617-5, ISBN13: 978-0-8476-8617-9. Dewey:881/.0109. LCCN:97-034065.
Audience: **u,f.**

West, M. L. (Editor) **PA3443**
Delectus ex Iambis et Elegis Graecis. Cloth Text. Oxford University Press, Inc. New York, NY. 1980. 306p. Classical Monographs ISBN:0-19-814589-6, ISBN13: 978-0-19-814589-9. Dewey:884/.01/08. LCCN:77-030251.
Audience: **u,f.**

West, M. L. (Translator, Introduction by) **PA3622**
Greek Lyric Poetry. Trade Paper. Oxford University Press, Inc. New York, NY. 1999. 240p. Oxford World's Classics Ser. ISBN:0-19-283678-1, ISBN13: 978-0-19-283678-6. Dewey:884/.01/08.
Audience: **g,l,u.**

West, M. L. (Translator, Introduction by) **PA3622.W45 1994**
Greek Lyric Poetry: The Poems and Fragments of the Greek Iambic, Elegiac, and Melic Poets, Excluding Pindar and Bacchylides, down to 450 BC. Trade Paper. Oxford University Press, Inc. New York, NY. 1994. 240p. Oxford World's Classics Ser. ISBN:0-19-282360-4, ISBN13: 978-0-19-282360-1. Dewey:884/.0108. LCCN:94-005730.
Audience: **g,l,u.**

Greek > Genres > Medical and Scientific Writers

Galen **QP141.G25213 2000**
Galen on Food and Diet. Mark Grant (Translator). Paper over Boards. Routledge. New York, NY. 2000. 224p. ISBN:0-415-23232-5, ISBN13: 978-0-415-23232-6. Dewey:613.2. LCCN:00-036628.
Audience: **u,f.**

Hippocrates **R126.H7 L813 1998**
Hippocrates: Places in Man. Elizabeth M. Craik (Editor, Translator). Trade Cloth. Oxford University Press, Inc. New York, NY. 1998. 284p. ISBN:0-19-815227-2, ISBN13: 978-0-19-815227-9. Dewey:610. LCCN:98-002735.
Audience: **u,f.**

Hippocrates **PA3612**
Ancient Medicine, Airs, Waters, Places, Epidemics 1 and 3, the Oath, Precepts, Nutriment, Vol. 1. W. H. Jones (Translator). Trade Cloth. Harvard University Press. Cambridge, MA. 1923. 432p. Ancient Medicine, Airs, Waters, Places, Epidemics 1 and 2. Oat Ser., No. 147 ISBN:0-674-99162-1, ISBN13: 978-0-674-99162-0. Dewey:610.9.
Audience: **u,f.**

Hippocrates **R138**
Hippocratic Writings. G. E. Lloyd (Editor), J. Chadwick, W. N. Mann, E. T. Withington & I. M. Lonie (Translators). Trade Paper. Penguin Group (USA) Inc. New York, NY. 1984. 384p. Classics Ser. ISBN:0-14-044451-3, ISBN13: 978-0-14-044451-3. Dewey:610/.938.
Audience: **g,u,f.**

Hippocrates **PA3612**
Hippocrates: Diseases 3, Internal Affections, Regimen in Acute Diseases. Paul Potter (Translator). Trade Cloth. Harvard University Press. Cambridge, MA. 1988. 392p. Loeb Classical Library, No. 473 ISBN:0-674-99522-8, ISBN13: 978-0-674-99522-2. Dewey:610.
Audience: **u,f.**

Hippocrates **PA3612 .H65 1923**
Hippocrates: Places in Man - Glands, Fleshes. Prorrhetic 1-2, Physician, Use of Liquids, Ulcers, Haemorrhoids and Fistulas. Paul Potter (Editor, Translator). Trade Cloth. Harvard University Press. Cambridge, MA. 1995. 432p. Hippocrates Ser., Vol. 482 ISBN:0-674-99531-7, ISBN13: 978-0-674-99531-4. Dewey:610. LCCN:23-012030.
Audience: **u,f.**

Hippocrates **R126.H6E62513 1994**
Hippocrates: Epidemics 2, 4-6. Wesley Smith (Editor). Trade Cloth. Harvard University Press. Cambridge, MA. 1994. 432p. Loeb Classical Library, No. 477 ISBN:0-674-99526-0, ISBN13: 978-0-674-99526-0. Dewey:616. LCCN:93-019601.
Audience: **u,f.**

Hippocrates **PA3612**
On Wounds in the Head, in the Surgery, on Fractures, on Joints, Mochlikon, Vol. 3. E. T. Withington (Translator). Trade Cloth. Harvard University Press. Cambridge, MA. 1928. 488p. Loeb Classical Library, No.149 ISBN:0-674-99165-6, ISBN13: 978-0-674-99165-1. Dewey:610.9.
Audience: **u,f.**

Irby-Massie, Georgia L. & Keyser, Paul T. **Q127**
Greek Science of the Hellenistic Era: A Sourcebook. Paper over Boards. Routledge. New York, NY. 2001. 432p. ISBN:0-415-23847-1, ISBN13: 978-0-415-23847-2. Dewey:509.38.
Audience: **g,u.**

Jones, W. H. (Translator) **PA3612**
Heracleitus - On the Universe: Nature of Man, Regimen in Health, Humours, Amorphisms, Regimen 1-3, Dreams., Vol. 4. Trade Cloth. Harvard University Press. Cambridge, MA. 1931. 592p. Nature of Man, Regimen in Health, Humours, Amorphisms and Regim Ser., No. 150 ISBN:0-674-99166-4, ISBN13: 978-0-674-99166-8. Dewey:610.9.
Audience: **u,f.**

Jones, W. H. (Translator) **PA3612**
Prognostic, Regimen in Acute Diseases, the Sacred Disease, the Art, Breaths, Law, Decorum, Physician (Ch. 1), Dentition, Vol. 2. Trade Cloth. Harvard University Press. Cambridge, MA. 1923. 416p. Medical Works, No. 148 ISBN:0-674-99164-8, ISBN13: 978-0-674-99164-4. Dewey:610.9.
Audience: **u,f.**

Lloyd, G. E. R. **Q127.G7**
Greek Science after Aristotle. Trade Paper. W. W. Norton & Company, Inc. New York, NY. 1975. 208p. Ancient Culture and Society Ser. ISBN:0-393-00780-4, ISBN13: 978-0-393-00780-0. Dewey:509/.38. LCCN:72-011959.
Audience: **g,l,u,f.**

Lloyd, G. E. R. **R138**
In the Grip of Disease: Studies in the Greek Imagination. Trade Cloth. Oxford University Press, Inc. New York, NY. 2003. 280p. ISBN:0-19-925323-4, ISBN13: 978-0-19-925323-4. Dewey:610/.938. LCCN:2003-271017.
Audience: **g,u,f.**

Lloyd, G. E. R. **Q127.G7L59 1999**
Magic, Reason, and Experience: Studies in the Origins and Development of Greek Science. Trade Paper. Hackett Publishing Company, Inc. Indianapolis, IN. 1999. xii, 335p. ISBN:0-87220-528-2, ISBN13: 978-0-87220-528-4. Dewey:509.38. LCCN:99-075596.
Audience: **g,l,u,f.**

Lloyd, G. E. R. **Q127.G7**
Early Greek Science: Thales to Aristotle. Moses I. Finley (Editor). Trade Paper. W. W. Norton & Company, Inc. New York, NY. 1974. 174p. Ancient Culture and Society Ser. ISBN:0-393-00583-6, ISBN13: 978-0-393-00583-7. Dewey:509/.38.
Audience: **g,l,u,f.**

Longrigg, James (Editor) **R138.L649 1998**
Greek Medicine: From the Heroic to the Hellenistic Age: A Source Book. UK-B Format Paperback. Routledge. New York, NY. 1998. 256p. ISBN:0-415-92087-6, ISBN13: 978-0-415-92087-2. Dewey:610/.938. LCCN:98-015593.
Audience: **u,f.**

Longrigg, James **R138.L65 1993**
Greek Rational Medicine: Philosophy and Medicine from Alcmaeon to the Alexandrians. Paper over Boards. Routledge. New York, NY. 1993. 308p. ISBN:0-415-02594-X, ISBN13: 978-0-415-02594-2. Dewey:610.938. LCCN:92-028865.
Audience: **u,f.**

Rihll, Tracey-Elizabeth **Q127.G7R54 1999**
Greek Science: Greece and Rome, New Surveys in the Classics, Vol. 29. Trade Paper. Oxford University Press, Inc. New York, NY. 1999. 172p. Greece and Rome Studies, No. 29 ISBN:0-19-922395-5, ISBN13: 978-0-19-922395-4. Dewey:509.38. LCCN:00-710848.
Audience: **l,u,f.**

Soranus **R126.S623 1991**
Soranus' Gynecology. Owsei Temkin, Nicholson J. Eastman, Ludwig Edelstein & Alan F. Guttmacher (Translators). Trade Paper. Johns Hopkins University Press. Baltimore, MD. 1991. 312p. Softshell Bks. ISBN:0-8018-4320-0, ISBN13: 978-0-8018-4320-4. Dewey:618.1. LCCN:91-020791.
Audience: **g,l,u,f.**

Temkin, Owsei **R723**
Galenism: Rise and Decline of a Medical Philosophy. Trade Cloth. Cornell University Press. Ithaca, NY. 1973. 240p. History of Science Ser. ISBN:0-8014-0774-5, ISBN13: 978-0-8014-0774-1. Dewey:610/.92/4. LCCN:72-012411.
Audience: **u,f.**

Wolpert, Lewis **Q127.G7S364 2002**
Science and Mathematics in Ancient Greek Culture. C. J. Tuplin & T. E. Rihll (Editors). Trade Cloth. Oxford University Press, Inc. New York, NY. 2002. 396p. ISBN:0-19-815248-5, ISBN13: 978-0-19-815248-4. Dewey:509.38. LCCN:2003-265274.
Audience: **g,u,f.**

Greek > Genres > Oratory and Rhetoric

Antiphon & Andocides **PA3869.A3 1998**
Antiphon and Andocides. Michael Gagarin & Douglas M. MacDowell (Translators). Trade Cloth. University of Texas Press. Austin, TX. 1998. 202p. Oratory of Classical Greece Ser. ISBN:0-292-72808-5, ISBN13: 978-0-292-72808-0. Dewey:885/.01. LCCN:97-021207.
Audience: **l,u.** *Choice, 1998.*

Dionysius of Halicarnassus **PA3255**
Critical Essays: Ancient Orators, Lysias, Isocrates, Isaeus, Demosthenes, Thucydides. Stephen Usher (Translator). Trade Cloth. Harvard University Press. Cambridge, MA. 1974. 680p. Loeb Classical Library, No. 465 ISBN:0-674-99512-0, ISBN13: 978-0-674-99512-3. Dewey:888/.01/0809. LCCN:75-305450.
Audience: **l,u,f.** B

Jebb, Richard C. (Editor) **PA3479**
Selections from the Attic Orators: Antiphon, Andocides, Lysias, Isocrates and Isaeus. Trade Cloth. Aristide D. Caratzas Publisher. Athens, 1981. ISBN:0-89241-360-3, ISBN13: 978-0-89241-360-7. Dewey:885.01.
Audience: **u,f.**

Kennedy, George A. **PA3265.K4**
Art of Persuasion in Greece. Trade Paper. Books on Demand. Ann Arbor, MI. 362p. ISBN:0-8357-6027-8, ISBN13: 978-0-8357-6027-0. Dewey:808. LCCN:63-007070.
Audience: **u,f.**

Kennedy, George A. **PA3038.K46 1994**
A New History of Classical Rhetoric. Trade Paper. Princeton University Press. Princeton, NJ. 1994. 314p. ISBN:0-691-00059-X, ISBN13: 978-0-691-00059-6. Dewey:808/.04281. LCCN:94-011249.
Audience: **g,l,u,f.**

Porter, Stanley E. **PA3083.H36 1997**
Handbook of Classical Rhetoric in the Hellenistic Period (330 B.C.-A.D. 400). Trade Cloth. Brill Academic Publishers, Inc. Boston, MA. 1997. xvi, 901p. ISBN:90-04-09965-4, ISBN13: 978-90-04-09965-4. Dewey:808/.00938. LCCN:96-047335.
Audience: **u,f.**

Greek > Genres > Prose Fiction

Hagg, Tomas **PA3040**
The Novel in Antiquity. Trade Paper. University of California Press. Berkeley, CA. 1991. 276p. ISBN:0-520-07638-9, ISBN13: 978-0-520-07638-9. Dewey:883/.01/09. LCCN:84-045906.
Audience: **g,l,u,f.**

Perry, Ben Edwin **PA3040.P4**
The Ancient Romances: A Literary-Historical Account of Their Origins. Trade Cloth. University of California Press. Berkeley, CA. 1967. Sather Classical Lectures, No. 37 ISBN:0-520-01003-5, ISBN13: 978-0-520-01003-1. Dewey:880/.09.
Audience: **u,f.**

Reardon, B. P. (Editor) **PA3632**
Collected Ancient Greek Novels. Trade Paper. University of California Press. Berkeley, CA. 1997. 835p. ISBN:0-520-04306-5, ISBN13: 978-0-520-04306-0. Dewey:883/.01/08. LCCN:88-021093.
Audience: **g,l,u,f.** *Choice, 1990.*

Stephens, Susan A. & Winkler, John J. (Editors) **PA3632 .A53 1995**
Ancient Greek Novels - The Fragments: Introduction, Text, Translation, and Commentary. Trade Cloth. Princeton University Press. Princeton, NJ. 1995. 560p. ISBN:0-691-06941-7, ISBN13: 978-0-691-06941-8. Dewey:883.0108. LCCN:92-023526.
Audience: **u,f.**

Swain, Simon **PA3267.O94 1999**
Oxford Readings in the Greek Novel. Trade Cloth. Oxford University Press, Inc. New York, NY. 1999. 424p. ISBN:0-19-872189-7, ISBN13: 978-0-19-872189-5. Dewey:883/.0109. LCCN:98-045077.
Audience: **l,u,f.**

Greek > Individual Authors > Apollonius of Rhodes

Apollonius, Rhodius **PA3872**
Argonautica. Trade Cloth. Harvard University Press. Cambridge, MA. 1912. 448p. Loeb Classical Library, No. 1 ISBN:0-674-99001-3, ISBN13: 978-0-674-99001-2. Dewey:883/.01.
Audience: **g,l,u.**

Apollonius, Rhodius **PA3872.E5 1997**
The Argonautika: The Story of Jason and the Quest for the Golden Fleece. Peter Green (Translator). Trade Cloth. University of California Press. Berkeley, CA. 1997. 490p. Hellenistic Culture and Society Ser., Vol. 25 ISBN:0-520-07686-9, ISBN13: 978-0-520-07686-0. Dewey:883/.01. LCCN:96-024772.
Audience: **g,l,u.** *Choice, 1998.*

Hunter, R. L. **PA3872.Z4H78 2004**
The Argonautica of Apollonius. Trade Paper. Cambridge University Press. New York, NY. 2005. 216p. ISBN:0-521-60438-9, ISBN13: 978-0-521-60438-3. Dewey:883/.01. LCCN:2005-279340.
Audience: **u,f.**

Greek > Individual Authors > Polybius

Polybius **PA3612**
Histories, Bks. 1-2. Trade Cloth. Harvard University Press. Cambridge, MA. 1922. 448p. Loeb Classical Library, No. 128, 137-138, 159-161 ISBN:0-674-99142-7, ISBN13: 978-0-674-99142-2. Dewey:937.04.
Audience: **g,l,u,f.**

Polybius **PA4391**
Histories, Vol. 3. Trade Cloth. Harvard University Press. Cambridge, MA. 1923. 560p. Loeb Classical Library, No. 128, 137-138, 159-161 ISBN:0-674-99153-2, ISBN13: 978-0-674-99153-8. Dewey:937.04.
Audience: **g,l,u,f.**

Polybius **PA4391**
Histories, Vol. 5. Trade Cloth. Harvard University Press. Cambridge, MA. 1926. 544p. Loeb Classical Library, No. 128, 137-138, 159-161 ISBN:0-674-99176-1, ISBN13: 978-0-674-99176-7. Dewey:937.04.
Audience: **g,l,u,f.**

Polybius **PA4391**
Histories, Bks. 3-4. Trade Cloth. Harvard University Press. Cambridge, MA. 1922. 528p. Loeb Classical Library, No. 128, 137-138, 159-161 ISBN:0-674-99152-4, ISBN13: 978-0-674-99152-1. Dewey:937.04.
Audience: **g,l,u,f.**

Polybius **PA4391**
Histories, Bks. 9-15,Vol. 4. Trade Cloth. Harvard University Press. Cambridge, MA. 1925. 576p. Loeb Classical Library, No. 128, 137-138, 159-161 ISBN:0-674-99175-3, ISBN13: 978-0-674-99175-0. Dewey:937.04.
Audience: **g,l,u,f.**

Polybius **PA4391**
Histories, Bks. 28-39. Trade Cloth. Harvard University Press. Cambridge, MA. 1927. 480p. Loeb Classical Library, No. 128, 137-138, 159-161 ISBN:0-674-99178-8, ISBN13: 978-0-674-99178-1. Dewey:937.04.
Audience: **g,l,u,f.**

Walbank, F. W. **DG206.P65**
Polybius. Trade Cloth. University of California Press. Berkeley, CA. 1990. 201p. Sather Classical Lectures, Vol. 42:No. 30 ISBN:0-520-06981-1, ISBN13: 978-0-520-06981-7. Dewey:937/.007/2024. LCCN:72-189219.
Audience: **u,f.**

Walbank, F.W. **PA4393**
Historical Commentary on Polybius. Trade Cloth. Oxford University Press. Oxford, 1999. 2388p. ISBN:0-19-924023-X, ISBN13: 978-0-19-924023-4. Dewey:888.9.
Audience: **u,f.**

Greek > Individual Authors > Aeschylus

Aeschylus **PA3825.C5**
Aeschylus: Choephori. Anthony A. Bowen (Editor). Trade Paper. Bristol Classical Press. London, 1986. 196p. Greek Texts ISBN:0-86292-070-1, ISBN13: 978-0-86292-070-8. Dewey:882/.01.
Audience: **u.**

Aeschylus **PA3827.A8**
Agamemnon. John D. Denniston & Denys L. Page (Editors). Trade Cloth. Oxford University Press, Inc. New York, NY. 1957. ISBN:0-19-814102-5, ISBN13: 978-0-19-814102-0. Dewey:882.01.
Audience: **u,f.**

Aeschylus **PA3827.A8**
Agamemnon. Eduard Fraenkel (Editor). Cloth Text. Oxford University Press, Inc. New York, NY. 1950. 1, 070p. ISBN:0-19-814101-7, ISBN13: 978-0-19-814101-3. Dewey:882.01.
Audience: **u,f.**

Aeschylus **PA3626.A2**
Aeschylus, Vol. 1. David Grene & Richmond A. Lattimore (Editors). Trade Cloth. University of Chicago Press. Chicago, IL. 1992. 358p. Complete Greek Tragedies Ser. ISBN:0-226-30764-6, ISBN13: 978-0-226-30764-0. Dewey:882. LCCN:91-045936.
Audience: **g,l,u.**

Aeschylus **PA3825 .P8 1983**
Aeschylus: Prometheus Bound. Mark Griffith (Editor), P. E. Easterling, Philip Hardie, Richard Hunter & E. J. Kenney (Contribution by). Trade Paper. Cambridge University Press. New York, NY. 1983. 328p. Cambridge Greek and Latin Classics ISBN:0-521-27011-1, ISBN13: 978-0-521-27011-3. Dewey:882/.01. LCCN:82-001301.
Audience: **u,f.**

Aeschylus **PA3978**
Aeschylus: The Persians. Edith Hall (Editor, Translator). Trade Cloth. Aris & Phillips. Oxford, 1996. 201p. Classical Texts Ser. ISBN:0-85668-596-8, ISBN13: 978-0-85668-596-5. Dewey:882/.01.
Audience: **l,u.** *Choice, 1996.*

Aeschylus **PA3978**
Septem Quae Supersunt Tragoediae. Denys L. Page (Editor). Cloth Text. Oxford University Press, Inc. New York, NY. 1973. 348p. Oxford Classical Texts ISBN:0-19-814570-5, ISBN13: 978-0-19-814570-7. Dewey:882/.01.
Audience: **u,f.**

Aeschylus **PA3827.A7S53 2003**
The Oresteia. Alan Shapiro & Peter Burian (Editors). Trade Paper. Oxford University Press, Inc. New York, NY. 2004. 296p. Greek Tragedy in New Translations Ser. ISBN:0-19-513592-X, ISBN13: 978-0-19-513592-3. Dewey:882/.01. LCCN:2002-066272.
Audience: **g,l,u.**

Aeschylus **PA3825 .E7 1989**
Aeschylus: Eumenides. Alan H. Sommerstein (Editor). Cloth Text. Cambridge University Press. New York, NY. 1989. 320p. Cambridge Greek and Latin Classics ISBN:0-521-24084-0, ISBN13: 978-0-521-24084-0. Dewey:882/.01. LCCN:88-037095.
Audience: **u,f.**

Conacher, D. J. **PA3825.P8.C6**
Aeschylus' "Prometheus Bound": A Literary Commentary. Cloth Text. University of Toronto Press. Toronto, ON. 1980. 128p. ISBN:0-8020-2391-6, ISBN13: 978-0-8020-2391-9. Dewey:882/.01. LCCN:81-116850.
Audience: **l,u,f.**

Goldhill, Simon **PA3827.A7**
Aeschylus: The Oresteia. Ed. 2. Cloth Text. Cambridge University Press. New York, NY. 2004. 106p. Landmarks of World Literature Ser. ISBN:0-521-83229-2, ISBN13: 978-0-521-83229-8. Dewey:882/.01. LCCN:2004-556933.
Audiencc: **l,u.**

Hogan, James C. **PA3829**
A Commentary on the Complete Greek Tragedies: Aeschylus. Trade Cloth. University of Chicago Press. Chicago, IL. 1985. 332p. ISBN:0-226-34842-3, ISBN13: 978-0-226-34842-1. Dewey:882/.01. LCCN:84-002688.
Audience: **l,u,f.** *Choice, 1985.*

Otis, Brooks **PA3829.O8**
Cosmos and Tragedy: An Essay on the Meaning of Aeschylus. E. Christian Kopff (Editor). Trade Cloth. University of North Carolina Press. Chapel Hill, NC. 1981. xiii, 119p. ISBN:0-8078-1465-2, ISBN13: 978-0-8078-1465-9. Dewey:882/.01. LCCN:80-025320.
Audience: **u,f.**

Podlecki, Anthony J. **PA3978**
Political Background on Aeschylean Tragedy. Ed. 2. Trade Paper. Bristol Classical Press. London, xix, 188p. Bristol Classical Paperbacks Ser. ISBN:1-85399-573-8, ISBN13: 978-1-85399-573-6. Dewey:882/.01.
Audience: **u,f.**

Rosenmeyer, Thomas G. **PA3978**
The Art of Aeschylus. Trade Paper. University of California Press. Berkeley, CA. 1983. 393p. ISBN:0-520-04608-0, ISBN13: 978-0-520-04608-5. Dewey:882/.01. LCCN:81-001289.
Audience: **u,f.**

Stanford, William Bedell **PA3849.S8**
Aeschylus in His Style, a Study in Language and Personality. Trade Paper. Books on Demand. Ann Arbor, MI. 151p. ISBN:0-598-84113-X, ISBN13: 978-0-598-84113-1. Dewey:882/.01. LCCN:43-007642.
Audience: **u,f.**

Taplin, Oliver **PA3829**
The Stagecraft of Aeschylus: The Dramatic Use of Exits and Entrances in Greek Tragedy. Paper Text. Oxford University Press, Inc. New York, NY. 1990. 518p. ISBN:0-19-814486-5, ISBN13: 978-0-19-814486-1. Dewey:882/.01.
Audience: **u,f.**

Thalmann, William G. **PA3825.S4**
Dramatic Art in Aeschylus's Seven Against Thebes. Trade Cloth. Yale University Press. Cumberland, RI. 1978. 193p. Yale Classical Monographs, Vol. 1 ISBN:0-300-02219-0, ISBN13: 978-0-300-02219-3. Dewey:882/.01. LCCN:78-006585.
Audience: **u,f.**

Vellacott, Philip **PA3825.A6V37 1984**
The Logic of Tragedy: Morals and Integrity in Aeschylus' Oresteia. Cloth Text. Duke University Press. Durham, NC. 1984. ix, 190p. ISBN:0-8223-0597-6, ISBN13: 978-0-8223-0597-2. Dewey:882/.01. LCCN:84-004057.
Audience: **u,f.**

Greek > Individual Authors > Apollodorus

Apollodorus **BL782**
Apollodorus: The Library of Greek Mythology. Robin Hard (Translator, Introduction by, Notes by). Trade Paper. Oxford University Press, Inc. New York, NY. 1999. 326p. Oxford World's Classics Ser. ISBN:0-19-283924-1, ISBN13: 978-0-19-283924-4.
Audience: **g,l,u,f.**

Greek > Individual Authors > Lysias

Dover, Kenneth J. **PA4243 .D6**
Lysias and the Corpus Lysiacum. Trade Cloth. University of California Press. Berkeley, CA. 1968. Sather Classical Lectures, No. 39 ISBN:0-520-00351-9, ISBN13: 978-0-520-00351-4. Dewey:885/.01. LCCN:68-063337.
Audience: **u,f.**

Lysias **DF231.3**
Lysias: Selected Speeches. Charles D. Adams (Editor), A. J. Heisserer (Foreword by). Trade Paper. University of Oklahoma Press. Norman, OK. 1989. 408p. Oklahoma Series in Classical Culture, Vol. 3 ISBN:0-8061-1396-0, ISBN13: 978-0-8061-1396-8. Dewey:938/.5. LCCN:79-123339.
Audience: **l,u,f.**

Lysias **PA4241 .A3 1989**
Lysias: Selected Speeches. Christopher Carey (Editor), P. E. Easterling, Philip Hardie, Richard Hunter & E. J. Kenney (Contribution by). Trade Paper. Cambridge University Press. New York, NY. 1990. 244p. Cambridge Greek and Latin Classics ISBN:0-521-26988-1, ISBN13: 978-0-521-26988-9. Dewey:885/.01. LCCN:89-001041.
Audience: **u,f.**

Lysias **PA4242.E5T64 2000**
Lysias. S. C. Todd (Translator). Trade Cloth. University of Texas Press. Austin, TX. 2000. 432p. Oratory of Classical Greece Ser., Vol. 2 ISBN:0-292-78165-2, ISBN13: 978-0-292-78165-8. Dewey:885/.01. LCCN:99-006344.
Audience: **g,l,u.** B

Greek > Individual Authors > Aristotle

Aristotle **B407.S6 1984**
Complete Works of Aristotle: The Revised Oxford Translation, Set. Jonathan Barnes (Editor). Trade Cloth. Princeton University Press. Princeton, NJ. 1984. 2512p. Bollingen Ser., Vol. LXXI, No. 2 ISBN:0-691-09950-2, ISBN13: 978-0-691-09950-7. Dewey:185. LCCN:82-005317.
Audience: **g,l,u,f.** B

Aristotle **B430.A1 B28**
Ethica Nicomachea. Ingram Bywater (Editor). Trade Cloth. Oxford University Press, Inc. New York, NY. 1889. 272p. Oxford Classical Texts ISBN:0-19-814511-X, ISBN13: 978-0-19-814511-0. Dewey:171.3.
Audience: **f.**

Aristotle **PA3405.S8 A876**
Metaphysica. Werner Jaeger (Editor). Cloth Text. Oxford University Press, Inc. New York, NY. 1957. 336p. Oxford Classical Texts ISBN:0-19-814513-6, ISBN13: 978-0-19-814513-4. Dewey:110.
Audience: **f.**

Aristotle **PA3893**
De Arte Poetica Liber. Rudolf V. Kassee (Editor). Cloth Text. Oxford University Press, Inc. New York, NY. 1922. 94p. Oxford Classical Texts ISBN:0-19-814564-0, ISBN13: 978-0-19-814564-6. Dewey:808.1.
Audience: **f.**

Aristotle **PN173.A7K46 2006**
On Rhetoric: A Theory of Civic Discourse. Ed. 2. George A. Kennedy (Translator). Cloth Text. Oxford University Press, Inc. New York, NY. 2006. 352p. ISBN:0-19-530508-6, ISBN13: 978-0-19-530508-1. Dewey:808.5. LCCN:2005-055487.
Audience: **g,u,f.**

Aristotle **PA3893**
Ars Rhetorica. W. David Ross (Editor). Cloth Text. Oxford University Press, Inc. New York, NY. 1959. 224p. Oxford Classical Texts ISBN:0-19-814557-8, ISBN13: 978-0-19-814557-8. Dewey:171.3.
Audience: **f.**

Aristotle **PA3405.S8A875**
De Anima. W. David Ross (Editor). Trade Cloth. Oxford University Press, Inc. New York, NY. 1956. 120p. Oxford Classical Texts ISBN:0-19-814508-X, ISBN13: 978-0-19-814508-0. Dewey:591.
Audience: **f.**

Aristotle **PA3893**
Politica. W. David Ross (Editor). Cloth Text. Oxford University Press, Inc. New York, NY. 1957. 292p. Oxford Classical Texts ISBN:0-19-814515-2, ISBN13: 978-0-19-814515-8. Dewey:888.5.
Audience: **f.**

Aristotle **B430.A5R68 2002**
The Nicomachean Ethics. Christopher Rowe (Editor), Sarah Broadie (Introduction by). Paper Text. Oxford University Press, Inc. New York, NY. 2002. 480p. ISBN:0-19-875271-7, ISBN13: 978-0-19-875271-4. Dewey:170. LCCN:2002-283430.
Audience: **g,l,u,f.**

Aristotle **PA3893.E7 1991**
Ethica Eudemia. R. R. Walzer (Editor), J. M. Mingay (Editor, Preface by). Cloth Text. Oxford University Press, Inc. New York, NY. 1991. 182p. Oxford Classical Texts ISBN:0-19-814575-6, ISBN13: 978-0-19-814575-2. Dewey:171/.3. LCCN:90-015529.
Audience: **f.**

Barnes, Jonathan (Editor) **B485 .C35 1995**
The Cambridge Companion to Aristotle. Cloth Text. Cambridge University Press. New York, NY. 1995. 432p. Cambridge Companions to Philosophy Ser. ISBN:0-521-41133-5, ISBN13: 978-0-521-41133-2. Dewey:185. LCCN:94-000516.
Audience: **u,f.** *Choice, 1995.*

Jaeger, Werner W. **B485**
Aristotle: Fundamentals of the History of His Development. Ed. 2. Richard Robinson (Translator). Trade Cloth. A M S Press, Inc. New York, NY. ISBN:0-404-20131-8, ISBN13: 978-0-404-20131-9. Dewey:185.1. LCCN:83-045440.
Audience: **u,f.**

Rorty, Amelie O. (Editor) **PN1040.A53 R67 1992**
Essays on Aristotle's Poetics. Trade Paper. Princeton University Press. Princeton, NJ. 1992. 448p. ISBN:0-691-01498-1, ISBN13: 978-0-691-01498-2. Dewey:808.1. LCCN:91-043905.
Audience: **u,f.**

Ross, William David **B485**
Aristotle. Ed. 6. Trade Paper. Routledge. New York, NY. 2004. 336p. ISBN:0-415-32857-8, ISBN13: 978-0-415-32857-9. Dewey:185.
Audience: **g,u,f.**

Greek > Individual Authors > Bacchylides

Bacchylides **PA3943.A2 2003**
Bacchylides: A Selection. Herwig Maehler (Editor), P. E. Easterling, Philip Hardie, Richard Hunter & E. J. Kenney (Contribution by). Cloth Text. Cambridge University Press. New

York, NY. 2004. 292p. Cambridge Greek and Latin Classics Ser. ISBN:0-521-59036-1, ISBN13: 978-0-521-59036-5. Dewey:881/.01. LCCN:2003-055397.
Audience: **u,f.**

Bacchylides **PA3943.E5 1998**
Epinician Odes and Dithyrambs: Bacchylides. David R. Slavitt (Translator). Book, Other. University of Pennsylvania Press. Philadelphia, PA. 1998. 104p. ISBN:0-8122-3447-2, ISBN13: 978-0-8122-3447-3. Dewey:884/.01. LCCN:97-050450.
Audience: **g,l,u.**

Burnett, Anne P. **PA25.M3 VOL. 29**
The Art of Bacchylides. Trade Cloth. Harvard University Press. Cambridge, MA. 1985. 224p. Martin Classical Lectures, No. 29 ISBN:0-674-04666-8, ISBN13: 978-0-674-04666-5. Dewey:937 s. LCCN:84-010764.
Audience: **u,f.** B

Greek > Individual Authors > Demosthenes

Demosthenes **PA3951.E5 2003**
Demosthenes, Speeches 50-59. Victor Bers (Translator). Trade Cloth. University of Texas Press. Austin, TX. 2003. 224p. The Oratory of Classical Greece Ser., Vol. 6 ISBN:0-292-70921-8, ISBN13: 978-0-292-70921-8. Dewey:885/.01. LCCN:2002-012299.
Audience: **g,l,u.**

Demosthenes **PA3951 .E5 1985**
Demosthenes: Selected Private Speeches. Christopher Carey & R. A. Reid (Editors), P. E. Easterling, Philip Hardie, Richard Hunter & E. J. Kenney (Contribution by). Trade Paper. Cambridge University Press. New York, NY. 1985. 256p. Cambridge Greek and Latin Classics ISBN:0-521-28373-6, ISBN13: 978-0-521-28373-1. Dewey:885/.01. LCCN:84-021356.
Audience: **g,l,u.**

Demosthenes **PA3951.E5 2004**
Demosthenes, Speeches 27-38. Douglas M. MacDowell (Translator). Trade Cloth. University of Texas Press. Austin, TX. 2004. 254p. The Oratory of Classical Greece Ser., Vol. 8 ISBN:0-292-70253-1, ISBN13: 978-0-292-70253-0. Dewey:885/.01. LCCN:2003-023288.
Audience: **g,l,u.**

Demosthenes **PA3949 .A7 1972**
Demosthenes: Six Private Speeches. Lionel Pearson (Editor). Trade Paper. Oxford University Press, Inc. New York, NY. 1972. 296p. Philological Monographs, Vol. 1 ISBN:0-8061-0974-2, ISBN13: 978-0-8061-0974-9. Dewey:885/.01. LCCN:72-160502.
Audience: **u,f.**

Demosthenes **PA3950 .C6 2001**
Demosthenes: On the Crown. Harvey E. Yunis (Editor), P. E. Easterling, Philip Hardie, Richard Hunter & E. J. Kenney (Contribution by). Cloth Text. Cambridge University Press. New York, NY. 2001. 328p. Cambridge Greek and Latin Classics Ser. ISBN:0-521-62092-9, ISBN13. 978-0-521-62092-5. Dewey:885/.01. LCCN:00-063064.
Audience: **u,f.**

Demosthenes **PA3951.E5 2005**
Demosthenes, Speeches 18 and 19. Harvey Yunis (Translator, Introduction by, Notes by). Trade Cloth. University of Texas Press. Austin, TX. 2005. 254p. The Oratory of Classical Greece Ser., Vol. 9 ISBN:0-292-70577-8, ISBN13: 978-0-292-70577-7. Dewey:885/.01. LCCN:2004-008741.
Audience: **g,l,u.**

Pearson, Lionel **PA3964 .P4 1981**
The Art of Demosthenes. Trade Paper. Scholars Press. Atlanta, GA. 1982. American Philological Association Special Publications Ser. ISBN:0-89130-551-3, ISBN13: 978-0-89130-551-4. Dewey:885/.01. LCCN:81-016752.
Audience: **u,f.**

Worthington, Ian **PA3952.D68 2000**
Demosthenes: Statesman and Orator. Paper over Boards. Routledge. New York, NY. 2001. 304p. ISBN:0-415-20456-9, ISBN13: 978-0-415-20456-9. Dewey:885/.01 B. LCCN:00-031056.
Audience: **u,f.**

Greek > Individual Authors > Epicurus

Epicurus **B570.E5 1979**
The Extant Remains. Cyril Bailey (Translator, Notes by). Trade Cloth. Georg Olms Verlag AG. Hildesheim, 1990. 432p. ISBN:3-487-02865-4, ISBN13: 978-3-487-02865-1. Dewey:187.
Audience: **f.**

Epicurus **B570.E5I582 1994**
The Epicurus Reader: Selected Writings and Testimonia. Brad Inwood & Lloyd P. Gerson (Editors), Brad Inwood & Lloyd P. Gerson (Translators), D. S. Hutchinson (Introduction by). Trade Cloth. Hackett Publishing Company, Inc. Indianapolis, IN. 1994. 128p. HPC Classics Ser. ISBN:0-87220-242-9, ISBN13: 978-0-87220-242-9. Dewey:187. LCCN:93-044073.
Audience: **g,l,u.**

Rist, John M. **B573**
Epicurus: An Introduction. Trade Paper. Books on Demand. Ann Arbor, MI. 199p. ISBN:0-608-12496-6, ISBN13: 978-0-608-12496-4. Dewey:187. LCCN:70-177939.
Audience: **g,l,u,f.**

Greek > Individual Authors > Euripides

Barlow, Shirley A. **PA3992 .B3**
The Imagery of Euripides. Ed. 2. Trade Cloth. Associated University Presses. Cranbury, NJ. 1987. 192p. ISBN:0-8453-4513-3, ISBN13: 978-0-8453-4513-9. Dewey:882/.01.
Audience: **u,f.**

Burnett, Anne P. **PA3978.B8 1985**
Catastrophe Survived: Euripides' Plays of Mixed Reversal. Trade Paper. Oxford University Press, Inc. New York, NY. 1985. 244p. ISBN:0-19-814038-X, ISBN13: 978-0-19-814038-2. Dewey:882/.01. LCCN:85-002935.
Audience: **u,f.**

Clauss, James J. & Johnston, Sarah Iles (Editors) **BL820.M37M43 1997**
Medea: Essays on Medea in Myth, Literature, Philosophy, and Art. Trade Paper. Princeton University Press. Princeton, NJ. 1996. 378p. ISBN:0-691-04376-0, ISBN13: 978-0-691-04376-0. Dewey:292.2/13. LCCN:96-008537.
Audience: **g,u,f.**

Conacher, D. J. **PA3978.C74**
Euripidean Drama: Myth, Theme and Structure. Trade Paper. Books on Demand. Ann Arbor, MI. 371p. ISBN:0-598-16002-7, ISBN13: 978-0-598-16002-7. Dewey:882/.01. LCCN:68-076826.
Audience: **l,u,f.** B

Euripides **PA3975.T8B37 1986**
Euripides: Trojan Women. Shirley A. Barlow (Editor). Trade Cloth. Aris & Phillips. Oxford, 1986. 200p. Classical Texts Ser. ISBN:0-85668-228-4, ISBN13: 978-0-85668-228-5. Dewey:882/.01. LCCN:86-226985.
Audience: **u,f.** *Choice, 1987.*

Euripides **PA3973**
Hippolytus. W. S. Barrett (Editor). Trade Cloth. Oxford University Press, Inc. New York, NY. 1964. 470p. ISBN:0-19-814167-X, ISBN13: 978-0-19-814167-9. Dewey:882.
Audience: **u,f.**

Euripides **PA3975.A2 1998**
Women on the Edge: Four Plays. Ruby Blondell (Editor). Paper over Boards. Routledge. New York, NY. 1999. 512p. New Classical Canon Ser. ISBN:0-415-90773-X, ISBN13: 978-0-415-90773-6. Dewey:882.01. LCCN:98-003992.
Audience: **g,l,u,f.**

Euripides **PA3973.H5 1988**
Heracles. Godfrey W. Bond (Introduction by). Trade Paper. Oxford University Press, Inc. New York, NY. 1989. 468p. ISBN:0-19-814060-6, ISBN13: 978-0-19-814060-3. Dewey:882/.01. LCCN:88-025267.
Audience: **u,f.**

Euripides **PA3978**
Helen. Peter Burian (Editor). Trade Cloth. Aris & Phillips. Oxford, 2005. 200p. ISBN:0-85668-650-6, ISBN13: 978-0-85668-650-4. Dewey:882/.01.
Audience: **u,f.**

Euripides **PA3975.P6**
Euripides: Phoenecian Women. Elizabeth Craik (Editor). Trade Cloth. Aris & Phillips. Oxford, 1988. 296p. Classical Texts Ser. ISBN:0-85668-230-6, ISBN13: 978-0-85668-230-8. Dewey:882/.01.
Audience: **u,f.** *Choice, 1988.*

Euripides **PA3978**
Alcestis. A. M. Dale (Editor). Paper Text. Oxford University Press, Inc. New York, NY. 1978. 170p. Plays of Euripides Ser. ISBN:0-19-872097-1, ISBN13: 978-0-19-872097-3. Dewey:882/.01.
Audience: **u,f.**

Euripides **PA3975**
Euripides: Helen. A. M. Dale (Editor). Trade Paper. Bristol Classical Press. London, 1981. 216p. Greek Texts ISBN:0-906515-98-X, ISBN13: 978-0-906515-98-3. Dewey:882.01.
Audience: **u,f.**

Euripides & Denniston, John D. **PA3978**
Electra. Paper Text. Oxford University Press, Inc. New York, NY. 1979. 270p. Plays of Euripides Ser. ISBN:0-19-872094-7, ISBN13: 978-0-19-872094-2. Dewey:882/.01.
Audience: **u,f.**

Euripides **PA3973.B2 1986**
Bacchae. Ed. 2. E. R. Dodds (Editor). Paper Text. Oxford University Press, Inc. New York, NY. 1987. 320p. ISBN:0-19-872125-0, ISBN13: 978-0-19-872125-3. Dewey:882/.01. LCCN:85-029137.
Audience: **u,f.**

Euripides **PA3973.H3 1999**
Euripides' Hecuba: Introduction, Text and Commentary. Justina Gregory (Editor). Trade Cloth. Oxford University Press, Inc. New York, NY. 1999. 218p. American Philological Association Textbook Ser. ISBN:0-7885-0612-9, ISBN13: 978-0-7885-0612-3. Dewey:882/.01. LCCN:99-051956.
Audience: **l,u.**

Euripides **PA3626.A2**
Euripides, Vol. 4. David Grene & Richmond A. Lattimore (Editors). Trade Cloth. University of Chicago Press. Chicago, IL. 1992. 314p. Complete Greek Tragedies Ser., Vol. IV ISBN:0-226-30767-0, ISBN13: 978-0-226-30767-1. Dewey:882.2. LCCN:91-045936.
Audience: **g,l,u.** B

Euripides **PA3975.A1**
Euripides, Vol. 3. David Grene & Richmond A. Lattimore (Editors). Trade Cloth. University of Chicago Press. Chicago, IL. 1992. 672p. Complete Greek Tragedies Ser., Vol. III ISBN:0-226-30766-2, ISBN13: 978-0-226-30766-4. Dewey:882.2. LCCN:91-045936.
Audience: **g,l,u.** B

Euripides **PA3975.A2 1995**
Euripides: Children of Heracles, Hippolytus, Andromache, Hecuba. David Kovacs (Editor, Translator). Trade Cloth. Harvard University Press. Cambridge, MA. 1995. 528p. Loeb Classical Library, No. 484 ISBN:0-674-99533-3, ISBN13: 978-0-674-99533-8. Dewey:882/.01. LCCN:95-007619.
Audience: **g,l,u.**

Euripides **PA3975.A2 2002**
Euripides: Helen, Phoenician Women, Orestes. David Kovacs (Editor, Translator). Trade Cloth. Harvard University Press. Cambridge, MA. 2002. 624p. Loeb Classical Library, Vol. 11 ISBN:0-674-99600-3, ISBN13: 978-0-674-99600-7. Dewey:882/.01. LCCN:2001-047078.
Audience: **g,l,u.**

Euripides **PA3975.A2 1998**
Euripides: Suppliant Women, Electra, Heracles. David Kovacs (Editor, Translator). Trade Cloth. Harvard University Press. Cambridge, MA. 1998. 464p. Loeb Classical Library ISBN:0-674-99566-X, ISBN13: 978-0-674-99566-6. Dewey:82/.01. LCCN:97-036082.
Audience: **g,l,u.**

Euripides **PA3975.A2 2002**
Euripides: Bacchae, Iphigenia at Aulis, Rhesus. David Kovacs (Editor, Translator). Trade Cloth. Harvard University Press. Cambridge, MA. 2003. 464p. Loeb Classical Library, Vol. 495 ISBN:0-674-99601-1, ISBN13: 978-0-674-99601-4. Dewey:882/.01. LCCN:2002-068725.
Audience: **g,l,u.**

Euripides **PA3975.A2 1999**
The Trojan Women: Iphigenia among the Taurians, Ion. David Kovacs (Editor, Translator). Trade Cloth. Harvard University Press. Cambridge, MA. 1999. 520p. Loeb Classical Library, Vol. 10 ISBN:0-674-99574-0, ISBN13: 978-0-674-99574-1. Dewey:882/.01. LCCN:99-017693.
Audience: **g,l,u.**

Euripides **PA3973**
Euripides: Troades. K. H. Lee (Editor). Paper Text. St. Martin's Press. Gordonville, VA. 1976. 350p. Classical Ser. ISBN:0-312-26670-7, ISBN13: 978-0-312-26670-7. Dewey:882/.01. LCCN:75-013183.
Audience: **u,f.**

Euripides **PA3973.I6 1997**
Euripides: Ion. Kevin H. Lee (Translator). Trade Cloth. Aris & Phillips. Oxford, 1997. 338p. Classical Texts Ser. ISBN:0-85668-244-6, ISBN13: 978-0-85668-244-5. Dewey:882/.01. LCCN:95-182316.
Audience: **u,f.**

Euripides **PA3973.A5 2003**
Euripides' Alcestis. C. A. E. Luschnig & Hanna Roisman (Notes by, Commentaries by). Trade Paper. University of Oklahoma Press. Norman, OK. 2003. 304p. Oklahoma Series in Classical Culture, Vol. 29 ISBN:0-8061-3574-3, ISBN13: 978-0-8061-3574-8. Dewey:882/.01. LCCN:2002-045597.
Audience: **l,u.**

Euripides **PA3973 .M4 2002**
Euripides: Medea. Donald J. Mastronarde (Editor), P. E. Easterling, Philip Hardie, Richard Hunter & E. J. Kenney (Contribution by). Trade Paper. Cambridge University Press. New York, NY. 2002. 442p. Cambridge Greek and Latin Classics Ser. ISBN:0-521-64386-4, ISBN13: 978-0-521-64386-3. Dewey:882/.01. LCCN:2002-073768.
Audience: **l,u,f.**

Euripides **PA3973**
Euripides: Suppliant Women. James Morwood (Commentaries by). Trade Cloth. Aris & Phillips. Oxford, 2006. 200p. ISBN:0-85668-779-0, ISBN13: 978-0-85668-779-2. Dewey:882.01.
Audience: **u,f.**

Euripides **PA3973.M4**
Medea. Denys Page (Editor). Paper Text. Oxford University Press, Inc. New York, NY. 1976. 260p. Plays of Euripides Ser. ISBN:0-19-872092-0, ISBN13: 978-0-19-872092-8. Dewey:882.3.
Audience: **u,f.**

Euripides **PA3973.I8**
Iphigenia in Tauris. M. Platnauer (Editor). Trade Paper. Bristol Classical Press. London, 206p. Classic Commentaries Ser. ISBN:0-86292-038-8, ISBN13: 978-0-86292-038-8. Dewey:882.
Audience: **u,f.**

Euripides **PA3973.T8**
Cyclops. Richard Seaford (Editor). Trade Cloth. Oxford University Press, Inc. New York, NY. 1985. 240p. ISBN:0-19-814030-4, ISBN13: 978-0-19-814030-6. Dewey:882/.01. LCCN:83-026758.
Audience: **u,f.**

Euripides **PA3973.A6**
Andromache. P. T. Stevens (Editor). Paper Text. Oxford University Press, Inc. New York, NY. 1984. 264p. Plays of Euripides Ser. ISBN:0-19-872118-8, ISBN13: 978-0-19-872118-5. Dewey:882/.01.
Audience: **u,f.**

Euripides **PA3975.O7 1987**
Euripides: Orestes. M. L. West (Editor). Trade Cloth. Aris & Phillips. Oxford, 1987. 200p. Classical Texts Ser. ISBN:0-85668-310-8, ISBN13: 978-0-85668-310-7. Dewey:882/.01. LCCN:88-160645.
Audience: **u,f.** *Choice, 1987.*

Euripides **PA3973.H6 1993**
Euripides: Heraclidae. John Wilkins (Commentaries by, Introduction by). Cloth Text. Oxford University Press, Inc. New York, NY. 1993. 240p. ISBN:0-19-814758-9, ISBN13: 978-0-19-814758-9. Dewey:882.01. LCCN:92-032517.
Audience: **u,f.**

Gregory, Justina **PA3978**
Euripides and the Instruction of the Athenians. Trade Paper. University of Michigan Press. Chicago, IL. 1997. 224p. ISBN:0-472-08443-7, ISBN13: 978-0-472-08443-2. Dewey:882/.01.
Audience: **u,f.** *Choice, 1991.*

Ingram, R.Winnington **PA3973.B2**
Euripides and Dionysus: An Interpretation of the "Bacchae". Trade Paper. Bristol Classical Press. London, 204p. Bristol Classical Paperbacks Ser. ISBN:1-85399-524-X, ISBN13: 978-1-85399-524-8. Dewey:882.
Audience: **u,f.**

Kovacs, David & Euripides **PA3975 .A2 1994**
Euripides: Cyclops, Alcestis, Medea. Ed. 2. Trade Cloth. Harvard University Press. Cambridge, MA. 1994. 432p. Loeb Classical Library, No. L12 ISBN:0-674-99560-0, ISBN13: 978-0-674-99560-4. Dewey:882.01. LCCN:93-000821.
Audience: **g,l,u.**

Mitchell-Boyask, Robin (Editor) **PA3978.A66 2002**
Approaches to Teaching the Dramas of Euripides. Trade Cloth. Modern Language Association of America. New York, NY. 2002. xiii & 235p. Approaches to Teaching World Literature Ser., Vol. 73 ISBN:0-87352-769-0, ISBN13: 978-0-87352-769-9. Dewey:882/.01. LCCN:2001-059048.
Audience: **f.**

Mossman, Judith **PA3975.A6**
Oxford Readings in Euripides. Trade Cloth. Oxford University Press, Inc. New York, NY. 2003. 424p. Oxford Readings in Classical Studies ISBN:0-19-872185-4, ISBN13: 978-0-19-872185-7. Dewey:882/.01. LCCN:2002-192560.
Audience: **u,f.**

Rabinowitz, Nancy S. **PA3978**
Anxiety Veiled: Euripides and the Traffic in Women. Book, Other. Cornell University Press. Ithaca, NY. 1993. 264p. ISBN:0-8014-8091-4, ISBN13: 978-0-8014-8091-1. Dewey:882/.01. LCCN:93-017257.
Audience: **u,f.** *Choice, 1994.*

Segal, Charles **PA3978.S5 1993**
Euripides and the Poetics of Sorrow: Art, Gender, and Commemoration in "Alcestis," "Hippolytus," and "Hecuba". Cloth Text. Duke University Press. Durham, NC. 1993. 328p. ISBN:0-8223-1360-X, ISBN13: 978-0-8223-1360-1. Dewey:882.01. LCCN:93-015565.
Audience: **l,u,f.** *Choice, 1994.*

Greek > Individual Authors > Herodotus

Hartog, Francois **D58.H473H4713 1988**
The Mirror of Herodotus: The Representation of the Other in the Writing of History. Janet Lloyd (Translator). Trade Cloth. University of California Press. Berkeley, CA. 1988. 411p. The New Historicism Ser., No. 5:Studies in Cultural Poetics ISBN:0-520-05487-3, ISBN13: 978-0-520-05487-5. Dewey:930. LCCN:86-030913.
Audience: **u,f.** *Choice, 1989.*

Herodotus **PA4002.A39 2002**
Herodotus: Histories. Michael A. Flower & John Marincola (Editors), P. E. Easterling, Philip Hardie, Richard Hunter & E. J. Kenney (Contribution by). Cloth Text. Cambridge University Press. New York, NY. 2002. 374p. Cambridge Greek and Latin Classics Ser. ISBN:0-521-59368-9, ISBN13: 978-0-521-59368-7. Dewey:938/.03. LCCN:2002-017393.
Audience: **u,f.**

Herodotus **PA4002.A2**
History of the Persian Wars, Bks. 1-2. A. D. Godley (Translator). Trade Cloth. Harvard University Press. Cambridge, MA. 1986. 528p. Loeb Classical Library, No. 117-120 ISBN:0-674-99130-3, ISBN13: 978-0-674-99130-9. Dewey:880.8.
Audience: **g,l,u,f.**

Herodotus **PA4002.A2**
History of the Persian Wars, Bks. 5-7. A. D. Godley (Translator). Trade Cloth. Harvard University Press. Cambridge, MA. 1922. 592p. Loeb Classical Library, No. 117-120 ISBN:0-674-99133-8, ISBN13: 978-0-674-99133-0. Dewey:880.8.
Audience: **g,l,u,f.**

Herodotus **PA4002.A2**
History of the Persian Wars, 4. A. D. Godley (Translator). Trade Cloth. Harvard University Press. Cambridge, MA. 1925. 424p. Loeb Classical Library, No. 117-120 ISBN:0-674-99134-6, ISBN13: 978-0-674-99134-7. Dewey:880.8.
Audience: **g,l,u,f.**

Herodotus **PA4002.A2**
History of the Persian Wars, Bks. 3-4. A. D. Godley (Translator). Trade Cloth. Harvard University Press. Cambridge, MA. 1921. 448p. Loeb Classical Library, No. 117-120 ISBN:0-674-99131-1, ISBN13: 978-0-674-99131-6. Dewey:880.8.
Audience: **g,l,u,f.**

Herodotus **D58 .H4713 1987**
The History. David Grene (Translator). Trade Paper. University of Chicago Press. Chicago, IL. 1988. 710p. ISBN:0-226-32772-8, ISBN13: 978-0-226-32772-3. Dewey:930. LCCN:86-013635.
Audience: **g,l,u.**

Herodotus **PA4002 .A38**
Herodotus, Vol. 8. J. Enoch Powell (Editor). Trade Paper. Bristol Classical Press. London, 1991. 190p. Greek Texts Ser. ISBN:0-86292-004-3, ISBN13: 978-0-86292-004-3. Dewey:880.
Audience: **l,u,f.**

Herodotus **DF225.6**
Herodotus, Bk. 1. J. H. Sleeman (Editor, Introduction by, Notes by). Trade Paper. Bristol Classical Press. London, 384p. Greek Texts Ser. ISBN:1-85399-628-9, ISBN13: 978-1-85399-628-3. Dewey:938/.03.
Audience: **l,u,f.** B

Lateiner, Donald **D56.52.H45**
The Historical Method of Herodotus. Cloth over Boards. University of Toronto Press. Toronto, ON. 1989. 336p. Phoenix Supplementary Volumes Ser., No. 23 ISBN:0-8020-5793-4, ISBN13: 978-0-8020-5793-8. Dewey:938.03092.
Audience: **u,f.** *Choice, 1990.*

Marincola, John & Dewald, Carolyn (Editors) **PA4004**
The Cambridge Companion to Herodotus. Cloth Text. Cambridge University Press. New York, NY. 2006. 397p. Cambridge Companions to Literature Ser. ISBN:0-521-83001-X, ISBN13: 978-0-521-83001-0. Dewey:938.03092.
Audience: **g,l,u,f.**

McQueen, E. I. **PA4002**
A Commentary on Herodotus, Vol. 2. Trade Paper. Bristol Classical Press. London, 192p. Greek Texts Ser. ISBN:1-85399-586-X, ISBN13: 978-1-85399-586-6. Dewey:938.03.
Audience: **u,f.**

Powell, J. Enoch **PA4007**
A Lexicon to Herodotus. Library Binding. Georg Olms Verlag AG. Hildesheim, 1977. x, 392p. Olms Paperbacks Ser., Vol. 26 ISBN:3-487-00036-9, ISBN13: 978-3-487-00036-7. Dewey:881.
Audience: **l,u,f.**

Romm, James S. **D56.52.H45R66 1998**
Herodotus. Trade Paper. Yale University Press. Cumberland, RI. 1998. 232p. Hermes Bks. ISBN:0-300-07230-9, ISBN13: 978-0-300-07230-3. Dewey:938/.0072/02. LCCN:98-010983.
Audience: **g,l,u.** *Choice, 1999.*

Thomas, Rosalind **D58 .T46 2000**
Herodotus in Context: Ethnography, Science and the Art of Persuasion. Cloth Text. Cambridge University Press. New York, NY. 2000. 330p. ISBN:0-521-66259-1, ISBN13: 978-0-521-66259-8. Dewey:938.007202. LCCN:99-045516.
Audience: **u,f.** *Choice, 2001.*

Greek > Individual Authors > Hesiod

Clay, Jenny Strauss **PA4009.T5C48 2003**
Hesiod's Cosmos. Trade Cloth. Cambridge University Press. New York, NY. 2003. 214p. ISBN:0-521-82392-7, ISBN13: 978-0-521-82392-0. Dewey:881/.01. LCCN:2003-046175.
Audience: **u,f.** *Choice, 2004.*

Hesiod, ; West, M L **PA4010.E5.O7 1978**
Work and Days: With Prolegomena and Commentary. M. L. West (Editor). Oxford University Press, Inc. 1978. ISBN:0-19-814005-3, ISBN13: 978-0-19-814005-4.
Audience: **u,f.** B

Hesiod **PA4010.E5T5 2004**
Hesiod: Theogony, Works and Days, Shield. Ed. 2. Apostolos N. Athanassakis (Translator). Trade Paper. Johns Hopkins University Press. Baltimore, MD. 2004. 192p. ISBN:0-8018-7984-1, ISBN13: 978-0-8018-7984-5. Dewey:881/.01. LCCN:2004-002129.
Audience: **g,l,u.**

Hesiod **PA4010.E5 2004**
Works of Hesiod and the Homeric Hymns. Daryl Hine (Editor, Translator). Trade Cloth. University of Chicago Press. Chicago, IL. 2005. 230p. ISBN:0-226-32965-8, ISBN13: 978-0-226-32965-9. Dewey:881/.01. LCCN:2004-008778.
Audience: **g,l,u.** *Choice, 2005.*

Hesiod **PA4010**
Theogony and Works and Days. M. L. West (Editor). Trade Paper. Oxford University Press, Inc. New York, NY. 1999. 106p. Oxford World's Classics Ser. ISBN:0-19-283941-1, ISBN13: 978-0-19-283941-1. Dewey:881/.01.
Audience: **g,l,u.** *Choice, 1988.*

Hunter, Richard (Editor) **PA4009.Z5H47 2005**
The Hesiodic Catalogue of Women: Constructions and Reconstructions. Trade Cloth. Cambridge University Press. New York, NY. 2005. 360p. ISBN:0-521-83684-0, ISBN13: 978-0-521-83684-5. Dewey:881/.01. LCCN:2005-046969.
Audience: **u,f.**

Lamberton, Robert **PA4011.L36 1988**
Hesiod. Trade Paper. Yale University Press. Cumberland, RI. 1988. 192p. ISBN:0-300-04069-5, ISBN13: 978-0-300-04069-2. Dewey:881/.01. LCCN:87-010595.
Audience: **g,l,u.** *Choice, 1988.*

Pucci, Pietro **PA4011.P8**
Hesiod and the Language of Poetry. Trade Paper. Books on Demand. Ann Arbor, MI. 160p. ISBN:0-7837-1109-3, ISBN13: 978-0-7837-1109-6. Dewey:883/.01. LCCN:76-000234.
Audience: **u,f.**

Greek > Individual Authors > Homer

Autenreith, Georg **PA4209.Z5**
Homeric Dictionary. Trade Paper. Focus Publishing/R. Pullins Company, Inc. Newburyport, MA. 2000. 368p. Classical Reprints Ser. ISBN:1-58510-028-5, ISBN13: 978-1-58510-028-6. Dewey:883/.01.
Audience: **l,u,f.**

Brann, Eva **PA4037.B64 2002**
Homeric Moments: Clues to Delight in Reading the Odyssey and the Iliad. Trade Cloth. Paul Dry Books, Inc. Philadelphia, PA. 2002. 326p. ISBN:0-9679675-6-2, ISBN13: 978-0-9679675-6-1. Dewey:883/.01. LCCN:2002-006003.
Audience: **g,l,u,f.** *Choice, 2003.*

Cairns, Douglas L. (Editor) **PA4037.A5O94 2001**
Oxford Readings in Homer's Iliad. Trade Cloth. Oxford University Press, Inc. New York, NY. 2002. 516p. Oxford Readings in Classical Studies ISBN:0-19-872183-8, ISBN13: 978-0-19-872183-3. Dewey:883/.01. LCCN:2002-280922.
Audience: **u,f.**

Carpenter, Rhys **PA4037 .C28**
Folk Tale, Fiction and Saga in the Homeric Epics. Trade Cloth. University of California Press. Berkeley, CA. 1974. Sather Classical Lectures, No. 20 ISBN:0-520-02808-2, ISBN13: 978-0-520-02808-1. Dewey:883.1. LCCN:55-007555.
Audience: **g,u,f.**

Finley, M. I. **PA4037.F48 2002**
The World of Odysseus. Bernard Knox (Introduction by). Trade Paper. New York Review of Books, Incorporated, The. New York, NY. 2002. 232p. New York Review Books Classics Ser. ISBN:1-59017-017-2, ISBN13: 978-1-59017-017-5. Dewey:883/.01. LCCN:2002-002882.
Audience: **g,l,u,f.**

Foley, John Miles **PA4175.F65 1999**
Homer's Traditional Art. Trade Cloth. Pennsylvania State University Press. University Park, PA. 1999. 670p. ISBN:0-271-01870-4, ISBN13: 978-0-271-01870-6. Dewey:883/.01. LCCN:98-051850.
Audience: **u,f.** *Choice, 2000.*

Fowler, Robert (Editor) **PA4037.A5**
The Cambridge Companion to Homer. Cloth Text. Cambridge University Press. New York, NY. 2004. 444p. Cambridge Companions to Literature Ser. ISBN:0-521-81302-6, ISBN13: 978-0-521-81302-0. Dewey:883/.01. LCCN:2005-279822.
Audience: **g,l,u,f.** *Choice, 2005.*

Goodspeed, Edgar Johnson & Owen, William B. **PA4209 .Z5O8**
Homeric Vocabularies: Greek and English Word-Lists for the Study of Homer. Clyde Pharr (Foreword by). Trade Paper. University of Oklahoma Press. Norman, OK. 1969. 96p. ISBN:0-8061-0828-2, ISBN13: 978-0-8061-0828-5. Dewey:881/.01. LCCN:68-031669.
Audience: **l,u.**

Griffin, Jasper **PA4167**
Homer: The Odyssey. Ed. 2. Cloth Text. Cambridge University Press. New York, NY. 2003. 112p. Landmarks of World Literature Ser. ISBN:0-521-83211-X, ISBN13: 978-0-521-83211-3. Dewey:883/.01.
Audience: **g,l,u.**

Griffin, Jasper **PA4037**
Homer on Life and Death. Paper Text. Oxford University Press, Inc. New York, NY. 1983. 234p. ISBN:0-19-814026-6, ISBN13: 978-0-19-814026-9. Dewey:883/.01.
Audience: **u,f.**

Homer **PA4025**
The Homeric Hymns. Ed. 2. Apostolos N. Athanassakis (Translator). Trade Paper. Johns Hopkins University Press. Baltimore, MD. 2004. 128p. ISBN:0-8018-7983-3, ISBN13: 978-0-8018-7983-8. Dewey:883/.01. LCCN:2004-002130.
Audience: **g,l,u.** B

Homer **PA4025.A5F34 1996**
The Odyssey. Robert Fagles (Translator), Bernard Knox (Introduction by). Trade Cloth. Penguin Group (USA) Inc. New York, NY. 1996. 562p. ISBN:0-670-82162-4, ISBN13: 978-0-670-82162-4. Dewey:883/.01. LCCN:96-017280.
Audience: **g,l,u.**

Homer **PA4025.A2F33 1990**
Homer: The Iliad. Robert Fagles (Translator), Bernard M. Knox (Introduction by, Notes by). Trade Cloth. Penguin Group (USA) Inc. New York, NY. 1990. 704p. ISBN:0-670-83510-2, ISBN13: 978-0-670-83510-2. Dewey:883/.01. LCCN:89-040774.
Audience: **g,l,u.**

Homer **PA4037**
The Odyssey. Robert Fitzgerald (Translator), Seamus Heaney (Introduction by). Trade Cloth. Alfred A. Knopf Inc. New York, NY. 1992. 528p. ISBN:0-679-41047-3, ISBN13: 978-0-679-41047-8. Dewey:883/.01. LCCN:92-052903.
Audience: **g,l,u.**

Homer **PA4025.A2 F5 1992**
The Iliad. Robert Fitzgerald (Translator), Gregory Nagy (Introduction by). Trade Cloth. David McKay Company, Inc. New York, NY. 1992. 624p. Everyman's Library ISBN:0-679-41075-9, ISBN13: 978-0-679-41075-1. Dewey:883/.01. LCCN:91-053222.
Audience: **g,l,u.** B *Choice, 1997.*

Homer **PA4025.A6 G37 1994**
Odyssey, Bks. VI-VIII. A. F. Garvie, P. E. Easterling & E. J. Kenney (Editors), P. E. Easterling, Philip Hardie, Richard Hunter & E. J. Kenney (Contribution by). Trade Paper. Cambridge University Press. New York, NY. 1994. 376p. Cambridge Greek and Latin Classics ISBN:0-521-33840-9, ISBN13: 978-0-521-33840-0. Dewey:883/.01. LCCN:93-041169.
Audience: **u,f.**

Homer **PA4020.P9 1995**
Iliad Book IX. Jasper Griffin (Editor, Commentaries by, Introduction by). Trade Paper. Oxford University Press, Inc. New York, NY. 1995. 160p. ISBN:0-19-814130-0, ISBN13: 978-0-19-814130-3. Dewey:883.01. LCCN:94-044516.
Audience: **u,f.**

Homer **PA4025.A2L66 1997**
The Iliad. Stanley Lombardo (Translator, Contribution by), Sheila Murnaghan (Introduction by). Trade Cloth. Hackett Publishing Company, Inc. Indianapolis, IN. 1997. 584p. HPC Classics Ser. ISBN:0-87220-353-0, ISBN13: 978-0-87220-353-2. Dewey:883/.01. LCCN:96-053368.
Audience: **g,l,u.** B *Choice, 1997.*

Homer **PA4025.A5L66 2000**
The Odyssey. Stanley Lombardo (Translator), Sheila Murnaghan (Introduction by). Trade Cloth. Hackett Publishing Company, Inc. Indianapolis, IN. 2000. 478p. ISBN:0-87220-485-5, ISBN13: 978-0-87220-485-0. Dewey:883/.01. LCCN:99-054175.
Audience: **g,l,u.**

Homer **PA4020 .P24 1982**
Homer: The Iliad. Colin W. Macleod (Editor), P. E. Easterling, Philip Hardie, Richard Hunter & E. J. Kenney (Contribution by). Trade Paper. Cambridge University Press. New York, NY. 1982. 176p. Cambridge Greek and Latin Classics ISBN:0-521-28620-4, ISBN13: 978-0-521-28620-6. Dewey:883/.01. LCCN:81-012208.
Audience: **u,f.**

Homer **PA4021**
Homer: Odyssey I-XII. W. B. Stanford (Editor). Trade Paper. Bristol Classical Press. London, 1999. 528p. Greek Texts Ser. ISBN:1-85399-502-9, ISBN13: 978-1-85399-502-6. Dewey:883.1.
Audience: **l,u,f.**

Homer **PA4022**
Homer: Odyssey XIII-XXIV. W. Bedell Stanford (Editor). Trade Paper. Bristol Classical Press. London, 1996. 560p. Greek Texts Ser. ISBN:1-85399-512-6, ISBN13: 978-1-85399-512-5. Dewey:888.
Audience: **l,u,f.**

Homer **PA4020 .A1**
Homer: Iliad I-XII. Malcolm M. Wilcock (Editor). Trade Paper. Bristol Classical Press. London, 1996. 368p. Greek Texts Ser. ISBN:1-85399-507-X, ISBN13: 978-1-85399-507-1. Dewey:883/.01.
Audience: **l,u,f.**

Homer **PA4020**
Homer: Iliad XIII-XXIV. M. M. Willcock (Editor). Trade Paper. Bristol Classical Press. London, 1998. 368p. Greek Texts Ser. ISBN:1-85399-595-9, ISBN13: 978-1-85399-595-8. Dewey:883/.01.
Audience: **l,u,f.**

Kahane, Ahuvia (Editor), et al.
The Chicago Homer. Martin Mueller, Craig Berryman & Bill Parod (Editors), Richmond A. Lattimore & Daryl Hine (Translators). Library Binding. University of Chicago Press. Chicago, IL. 2000. ISBN:0-226-42246-1, ISBN13: 978-0-226-42246-6.
Audience: **g,l,u.**

Kirk, G. S. **PA4037.K46 2005**
The Songs of Homer. Trade Paper. Cambridge University Press. New York, NY. 2005. 454p. ISBN:0-521-61918-1, ISBN13: 978-0-521-61918-9. Dewey:883/.01. LCCN:2005-280224.
Audience: **l,u,f.** B

Latacz, Joachim **PA4037.L436 1996**
Homer: His Art and His World. James P. Holoka (Translator). Trade Paper. University of Michigan Press. Chicago, IL. 1998. 192p. ISBN:0-472-08353-8, ISBN13: 978-0-472-08353-4. Dewey:883/.01. LCCN:95-042481.
Audience: **u,f.** *Choice, 1996.*

Latacz, Joachim **DF221.T8**
Troy and Homer: Towards a Solution of an Old Mystery. Kevin Windle & Rosh Ireland (Translators). Trade Cloth. Oxford University Press, Inc. New York, NY. 2005. 362p. ISBN:0-19-926308-6, ISBN13: 978-0-19-926308-0. Dewey:939/.21. LCCN:2005-270131.
Audience: **u,f.** *Choice, 2005.*

Lord, Albert B. **PN1303.L62 2000**
The Singer of Tales. Ed. 2. Stephen A. Mitchell & Gregory Nagy (Editors). Trade Paper. Harvard University Press. Cambridge, MA. 2000. 352p. Harvard Studies in Comparative Literature, Vol. 24 ISBN:0-674-00283-0, ISBN13: 978-0-674-00283-8. Dewey:809.1/32. LCCN:00-021247.
Audience: **u,f.**

Morrison, James **PA4167**
A Companion to Homer's Odyssey. Cloth Text. Greenwood Publishing Group, Inc. Portsmouth, NH. 2003. 224p. ISBN:0-313-31854-9, ISBN13: 978-0-313-31854-2. Dewey:883/.01. LCCN:2002-075311.
Audience: **g,l,u.** *Choice, 2003.*

Nagy, Gregory **PA3015.H43N34 1999**
The Best of the Achaeans: Concepts of the Hero in Archaic Greek Poetry. Ed. 2. Trade Paper. Johns Hopkins University Press. Baltimore, MD. 1998. 424p. ISBN:0-8018-6015-6, ISBN13: 978-0-8018-6015-7. Dewey:883.0109. LCCN:98-022262.
Audience: **u,f.**

Nagy, Gregory **PA4037.N345 2003**
Homeric Questions. Trade Paper. University of Texas Press. Austin, TX. 1996. 192p. ISBN:0-292-75562-7, ISBN13: 978-0-292-75562-8. Dewey:883/.01. LCCN:95-039353.
Audience: **u,f.** *Choice, 1997.*

Nagy, Gregory **PA4037.N347 2003**
Homeric Responses. Trade Cloth. University of Texas Press. Austin, TX. 2004. 112p. ISBN:0-292-70553-0, ISBN13: 978-0-292-70553-1. Dewey:883/.01. LCCN:2003-008792.
Audience: **u,f.**

Owen, Eric Trevor **PA4037.O68 1989**
The Story of the Iliad. John H. Betts (Editor), Thom Kapheim (Illustrator). Book, Other. Bolchazy-Carducci Publishers. Wauconda, IL. 1989. 248p. ISBN:0-86516-235-2, ISBN13: 978-0-86516-235-8. Dewey:883/.01. LCCN:90-146790.
Audience: **g,l,u.**

Page, Denys L. **PA4167.P28**
Folktales in Homer's Odyssey. Trade Paper. Books on Demand. Ann Arbor, MI. 152p. Carl Newell Jackson Lectures, 1972 ISBN:0-608-10784-0, ISBN13: 978-0-608-10784-4. Dewey:883/.01. LCCN:73-075056.
Audience: **u,f.**

Page, Denys L. **PA4037 .P27**
History and the Homeric Iliad. Paper Text. Textbook Publishers. Temecula, CA. 2003. vi, 350p. ISBN:0-7581-2802-9, ISBN13: 978-0-7581-2802-7. Dewey:883.
Audience: **u,f.**

Parry, Milman **PA4175.P37 1987**
The Making of Homeric Verse: The Collected Papers of Milman Parry. Adam M. Parry (Editor). Trade Paper. Oxford University Press, Inc. New York, NY. 1987. 546p. ISBN:0-19-520560-X, ISBN13: 978-0-19-520560-2. Dewey:883/.01. LCCN:87-014702.
Audience: **f.** B

Pharr, Clyde & Wright, John **PA4179.P5 1985**
Homeric Greek. Trade Paper, Book, Other. University of Oklahoma Press. Norman, OK. 1986. 414p. ISBN:0-8061-1937-3, ISBN13: 978-0-8061-1937-3. Dewey:488.2/421. LCCN:84-040698.
Audience: **l.**

Powell, B. B. & Morris, I. **PA4037.N42 1996**
A New Companion to Homer. Trade Cloth. Brill Academic Publishers. Leiden, 1997. xviii, 755p. Mnemosyne Ser., Vol. 163:Supplements ISBN:90-04-09989-1, ISBN13: 978-90-04-09989-0. Dewey:883/.01. LCCN:96-038925.
Audience: **u,f.**

Powell, Barry B. **PA4037.P66 2004**
Homer. Trade Cloth. Blackwell Publishing, Inc. Malden, MA. 2003. 192p. Blackwell Introductions to the Classical World Ser. ISBN:0-631-23385-7, ISBN13: 978-0-631-23385-5. Dewey:883/.01. LCCN:2003-001873.
Audience: **g,l,u,f.** *Choice, 2004.*

Rayor, Diane J. (Translator) **PA4025.H8 R395 2004**
The Homeric Hymns: A Translation, with Introduction and Notes. Trade Cloth. University of California Press. Berkeley, CA. 2004. 178p. Joan Palevsky Imprint in Classical Literature Ser. ISBN:0-520-23991-1, ISBN13: 978-0-520-23991-3. Dewey:883/.01. LCCN:2003-005065.
Audience: **g,l,u.**

Rutherford, Richard **PA4037.R88 1996**
Homer. Oxford University Press. 1996. Greece & Rome. New Surveys in the Classics ISBN:0-19-922209-6, ISBN13: 978-0-19-922209-4.
Audience: **u,f.**

Taplin, Oliver **PA4037**
Homeric Soundings: The Shaping of the Iliad. Trade Paper. Oxford University Press, Inc. New York, NY. 1995. 326p. ISBN:0-19-815014-8, ISBN13: 978-0-19-815014-5. Dewey:883/.01. LCCN:91-018791.
Audience: **u,f.** *Choice, 1992.*

Tracy, Stephen V. **PA4167.T7 1990**
The Story of the Odyssey. Trade Paper. Princeton University Press. Princeton, NJ. 1990. 176p. ISBN:0-691-01494-9, ISBN13: 978-0-691-01494-4. Dewey:883/.01. LCCN:90-034573.
Audience: **g,l,u.** *Choice, 1991.*

Wace, A. J. B. **PA4037.W15**
A Companion to Homer. Paper Text. Textbook Publishers. Temecula, CA. 2003. xxix, 595p. ISBN:0-7581-8854-4, ISBN13: 978-0-7581-8854-0. Dewey:883.
Audience: **f.** B

West, M. L. (Editor, Translator) **PA4025.H8W47 2003**
Homeric Hymns, Homeric Apocrypha, Lives of Homer. Trade Cloth. Harvard University Press. Cambridge, MA. 2003. 480p. Loeb Classical Library, Vol. 496 ISBN:0-674-99606-2, ISBN13: 978-0-674-99606-9. Dewey:883/.0108. LCCN:2002-031814.
Audience: **g,l,u,f.**

Willcock, Malcolm M. **PA4037**
A Companion to the "Iliad". Trade Paper. University of Chicago Press. Chicago, IL. 1976. 302p. ISBN:0-226-89855-5, ISBN13: 978-0-226-89855-1. Dewey:883/.01. LCCN:75-020894.
Audience: **l,u,f.**

Wolf, Friedrich A. **PA4037.A2W68**
Prolegomena to Homer, 1795. Anthony Grafton & Glenn W. Most (Translators), Anthony Grafton, Glenn W. Most & James E. Zetzel (Contribution by, Introduction by). Trade Paper. Books on Demand. Ann Arbor, MI. 1985. 280p. ISBN:0-608-02739-1, ISBN13: 978-0-608-02739-5. Dewey:883/.01. LCCN:84-042907.
Audience: **f.**

Greek > Individual Authors > Longinus

Longinus **PR4472 .V35**
On the Sublime. Other. Harvard University Press. Cambridge, MA. Loeb Classical Library ISBN:0-318-53145-3, ISBN13: 978-0-318-53145-8. Dewey:809.
Audience: **g,l,u,f.**

Longinus **PA4229.L5E5 1991**
On Great Writing (On the Sublime). G. M. Grube (Translator, Introduction by). Trade Cloth. Hackett Publishing Company, Inc. Indianapolis, IN. 1991. 88p. ISBN:0-87220-081-7, ISBN13: 978-0-87220-081-4. Dewey:808. LCCN:90-049700.
Audience: **g,l,u,f.**

Greek > Individual Authors > Lucian

Branham, R. Bracht **PA4236.B73 1989**
Unruly Eloquence: Lucian and the Comedy of Traditions. Glen W. Bowersock (Editor). Trade Cloth. Harvard University Press. Cambridge, MA. 1989. 296p. Revealing Antiquity Ser., No. 2 ISBN:0-674-93035-5, ISBN13: 978-0-674-93035-3. Dewey:887/.01. LCCN:88-024297.
Audience: **g,l,u,f.** *Choice, 1989.*

Lucian **PA4230.A3 1976**
Lucian: Seventy Dialogues. Harry L. Levy (Introduction by). Trade Cloth. University of Oklahoma Press. Norman, OK. 1977. 341p. American Philological Association Ser., Vol. 4 ISBN:0-8061-1216-6, ISBN13: 978-0-8061-1216-9. Dewey:882/.01. LCCN:75-005652.
Audience: **l,u,f.**

Lucian **PA4231.A58 1991**
Lucian: A Selection. M. C. McLeod (Editor). Trade Cloth. Aris & Phillips. Oxford, 1991. 320p. Classical Texts Ser. ISBN:0-85668-415-5, ISBN13: 978-0-85668-415-9. Dewey:887/.01.
Audience: **l,u,f.**

Robinson, Christopher **PA4236.R6**
Lucian and His Influence in Europe. Trade Paper. Books on Demand. Ann Arbor, MI. 258p. ISBN:0-7837-3758-0, ISBN13: 978-0-7837-3758-4. Dewey:887/.01. LCCN:79-016580.
Audience: **g,l,u,f.** B

Turner, Paul **PA4231.A58 1990**
Lucian: Satirical Sketches. Trade Cloth. Indiana University Press. Bloomington, IN. 1990. 320p. ISBN:0-253-36097-8, ISBN13: 978-0-253-36097-7. Dewey:887/.01. LCCN:89-026834.
Audience: **g,l,u.**

Greek > Individual Authors > Menander

Goldberg, Sander M. **PA4247 .G58**
The Making of Meander's Comedy. Trade Cloth. Continuum International Publishing Group, Ltd. London, 160p. ISBN:0-485-11189-6, ISBN13: 978-0-485-11189-7. Dewey:882/.01. LCCN:80-513992.
Audience: **u,f.**

Menander **PA4246**
Comedies: Aspis - Georgos - Dis Exapaton - Dyskolos - Encheiridion - Epitrepontes. W. G. Arnott (Translator). Trade Cloth. Harvard University Press. Cambridge, MA. 1979. 592p. Loeb Classical Library, No. 132 ISBN:0-674-99147-8, ISBN13: 978-0-674-99147-7. Dewey:882/.01. LCCN:80-154351.
Audience: **g,l,u,f.**

Menander **PA4246 .E4 1979**
Menander - Heros, Theophoroumene, Karchedonios, Kitharistes, Kolax, Koneiazomenai, Leukadia, Misoumenos, Perikeiromene, Perinthia, Vol. 2. W. Geoffrey Arnott (Editor, Translator). Trade Cloth. Harvard University Press. Cambridge, MA. 1997. 512p. Loeb Classical Library ISBN:0-674-99506-6, ISBN13: 978-0-674-99506-2. Dewey:882.01. LCCN:80-154351.
Audience: **g,l,u,f.**

Menander **PA4246.E4 1979**
Menander: Samia, Sikyonioi, Synaristosai, Phasma, Unidentified Fragments. W. G. Arnott (Editor, Translator). Trade Cloth. Harvard University Press. Cambridge, MA. 2000. 656p. Loeb Classical Library, Vol. 3 ISBN:0-674-99584-8, ISBN13: 978-0-674-99584-0. Dewey:882/.01. LCCN:80-154351.
Audience: **g,l,u,f.**

Menander **PA4246.E4B35 2002**
Menander, the Plays and Fragments. Maurice Balme (Translator), Peter Brown (Introduction by). Trade Paper. Oxford University Press, Inc. New York, NY. 2002. 346p. Oxford World's Classics Ser. ISBN:0-19-283983-7, ISBN13: 978-0-19-283983-1. Dewey:822/.01. LCCN:2002-025760.
Audience: **g,l,u.**

Greek > Individual Authors > Pindar

Bowra, C. M. **PA4276.B78 2000**
Pindar. Trade Cloth. Oxford University Press, Inc. New York, NY. 2000. 464p. Oxford Scholarly Classics Ser. ISBN:0-19-814338-9, ISBN13: 978-0-19-814338-3. Dewey:884/.01. LCCN:2001-266326.
Audience: **u,f.**

Carne-Ross, D. S. **PA4276**
Pindar. Trade Paper. Yale University Press. Cumberland, RI. 1985. 216p. Hermes Bks. ISBN:0-300-03393-1, ISBN13: 978-0-300-03393-9. Dewey:884/.01. LCCN:84-040668.
Audience: **g,l,u.** *Choice, 1985.*

Kurke, Leslie **PA4276.K87 1991**
The Traffic in Praise: Pindar and the Poetics of Social Economy. Book, Other. Cornell University Press. Ithaca, NY. 1991. 304p. Myth and Poetics Ser. ISBN:0-8014-2350-3, ISBN13: 978-0-8014-2350-5. Dewey:884/.01. LCCN:90-055722.
Audience: **u,f.**

Nagy, Gregory **PA4276**
Pindar's Homer: The Lyric Possession of an Epic Past. Trade Paper. Johns Hopkins University Press. Baltimore, MD. 1994. 414p. ISBN:0-8018-4847-4, ISBN13: 978-0-8018-4847-6. Dewey:884/.0109. LCCN:89-019938.
Audience: **u,f.** *Choice, 1990.*

Pindar **PA4275.E5.R33 1997**
Pindar: Nemean Odes, Isthmian Odes, Fragments. William H. Race (Editor, Translator). Trade Cloth. Harvard University Press. Cambridge, MA. 1997. 464p. Loeb Classical Library® Ser. ISBN:0-674-99534-1, ISBN13: 978-0-674-99534-5. Dewey:884.01. LCCN:95-042927.
Audience: **g,l,u.**

Pindar **PA4275.E5R33 1997**
Pindar: Olympian Odes, Pythian Odes. William H. Race (Editor, Translator). Trade Cloth. Harvard University Press. Cambridge, MA. 1997. 400p. Loeb Classical Library, Vol. 56 & 485 ISBN:0-674-99564-3, ISBN13: 978-0-674-99564-2. Dewey:884.01. LCCN:95-042927.
Audience: **g,l,u.**

Pindar **PA4274.A5 1995**
Pindar: Olympians 2, 7 and 11; Nemean 4; Isthmians 3, 4 and 7. Malcolm M. Willcock (Editor). Cloth Text. Cambridge University Press. New York, NY. 1995. 189p. Cambridge Greek and Latin Classics ISBN:0-521-43055-0, ISBN13: 978-0-521-43055-5. Dewey:884.01. LCCN:94-013996.
Audience: **u,f.**

Greek > Individual Authors > Plato

Brickhouse, Thomas C. & Smith, Nicholas D. **B317**
Plato's Socrates. Trade Paper. Oxford University Press, Inc. New York, NY. 1996. 256p. ISBN:0-19-510111-1, ISBN13: 978-0-19-510111-9. Dewey:183.2.
Audience: **g,l,u.** *Choice, 1994.*

Brickhouse, Thomas C. & Smith, Nicholas D. **B316.B75 2002**
The Trial and Execution of Socrates: Sources and Controversies. Trade Paper. Oxford University Press, Inc. New York, NY. 2001. 296p. ISBN:0-19-511980-0, ISBN13: 978-0-19-511980-0. Dewey:183/.2. LCCN:2001-036915.
Audience: **g,l,u.** *Choice, 2002.*

Brisson, Luc **B398.M8B55 1999**
Plato the Myth Maker. Trade Cloth. University of Chicago Press. Chicago, IL. 1999. 244p. ISBN:0-226-07518-4, ISBN13: 978-0-226-07518-1. Dewey:184. LCCN:98-008641.
Audience: **u,f.**

Kraut, Richard (Editor) **B395 .C28 1992**
The Cambridge Companion to Plato. Cloth Text. Cambridge University Press. New York, NY. 1992. 576p. Cambridge Companions to Philosophy Ser. ISBN:0-521-43018-6, ISBN13: 978-0-521-43018-0. Dewey:184. LCCN:92-004991.
Audience: **g,u,f.** *Choice, 1993.*

Plato, et al. **B312.E5T75 2002**
The Trials of Socrates: Six Classic Texts. Aristophanes & Xenophon (Authors), C. D. C. Reeve (Editor). Trade Cloth. Hackett Publishing Company, Inc. Indianapolis, IN. 2002. 192p. ISBN:0-87220-590-8, ISBN13: 978-0-87220-590-1. Dewey:183/.2. LCCN:2001-051571.
Audience: **g,l,u.**

Plato **PA4279**
Euthyphro, Apology of Socrates, and Crito. John Burnet (Editor). Paper Text. Oxford University Press, Inc. New York, NY. 1977. 228p. ISBN:0-19-814015-0, ISBN13: 978-0-19-814015-3. Dewey:184.
Audience: **l,u.**

Plato **PA3405.S8**
Opera: Parmenides, Philebus, Symposium, Phaedrus, Alcibiades I and II, Hipparchus, Amatores, Vol. II. Ed. 2. John Burnet (Editor). Cloth Text. Oxford University Press, Inc. New York, NY. 1922. 410p. Oxford Classical Texts ISBN:0-19-814541-1, ISBN13: 978-0-19-814541-7. Dewey:184.
Audience: **f.**

Plato **PA3405.S8**
Opera: Clitopho, Respublica, Timaeus, Critias, Vol. IV. John Burnet (Editor). Trade Cloth. Oxford University Press, Inc. New York, NY. 1922. 554p. Oxford Classical Texts ISBN:0-19-814544-6, ISBN13: 978-0-19-814544-8. Dewey:184.
Audience: **f.**

Plato **PA 3405.S8**
Opera: Theages, Charmides, Laches, Lysis, Euthydemus, Protagoras, Gorgias, Meno, Hippias Maior, Hippas Minor, Io, Menexenus, Vol. III. John Burnet (Editor). Cloth Text. Oxford University Press, Inc. New York, NY. 1922. 524p. Oxford Classical Texts ISBN:0-19-814542-X, ISBN13: 978-0-19-814542-4. Dewey:184.
Audience: **f.**

Plato **PA4279**
Opera: Minos, Leges, Epinomis, Epistulae, Definitiones, Vol. V. John Burnet (Editor). Cloth Text. Oxford University Press, Inc. New York, NY. 1922. 610p. Oxford Classical Texts ISBN:0-19-814546-2, ISBN13: 978-0-19-814546-2. Dewey:184.
Audience: **f.**

Plato **B379.A2**
Phaedo. John Burnet (Editor). Paper Text. Oxford University Press, Inc. New York, NY. 1979. 218p. ISBN:0-19-814014-2, ISBN13: 978-0-19-814014-6. Dewey:184.
Audience: **l,u.** B

Plato **PA4279.A75 P58 2001**
Plato: Alcibiades. Nicholas Denyer (Editor), P. E. Easterling, Philip Hardie, Richard Hunter & E. J. Kenney (Contribution by). Cloth Text. Cambridge University Press. New York, NY. 2001. 266p. Greek and Latin Classics Ser. ISBN:0-521-63281-1, ISBN13: 978-0-521-63281-2. Dewey:184. LCCN:00-054375.
Audience: **u,f.**

Plato **B371.A5 D63 1990**
Gorgias. Ed. 2. E. R. Dodds (Editor), Eric Robertson (Illustrator). Trade Paper. Oxford University Press, Inc. New York, NY. 1990. 414p. ISBN:0-19-814495-4, ISBN13: 978-0-19-814495-3. Dewey:170. LCCN:89-029180.
Audience: **u,f.**

Plato **B385.A5 D68 1980**
Plato: Symposium. K. J. Dover (Editor), P. E. Easterling, Philip Hardie, Richard Hunter & E. J. Kenney (Contribution by). Trade Paper. Cambridge University Press. New York, NY. 1980. 196p. Cambridge Greek and Latin Classics ISBN:0-521-29523-8, ISBN13: 978-0-521-29523-9. Dewey:184. LCCN:78-067430.
Audience: **u,f.**

Plato **PA4279.A2 1993**
Platonis Opera: Euthyphro, Apologia Socratis, Crito, Phaedo, Cratylus, Sophista, Politicus, Theaetetus. Ed. 2. E. A. Duke, W. F. Hicken, W. S. M. Nicoll, D. B. Robinson & J. C. G. Strachan (Editors). Trade Cloth. Oxford University Press, Inc. New York, NY. 1995. 604p. Classical Monographs ISBN:0-19-814569-1, ISBN13: 978-0-19-814569-1. Dewey:184. LCCN:93-003754.
Audience: **f.**

Plato **B358**
The Collected Dialogues of Plato: Including the Letters. Edith Hamilton & Huntington Cairns (Editors). Cloth Text. Princeton University Press. Princeton, NJ. 1961. 1776p. Bollingen Ser., Vol. LXX, No. 1:LXXI Ser. ISBN:0-691-09718-6, ISBN13: 978-0-691-09718-3. Dewey:888. LCCN:61-011758.
Audience: **g,l,u,f.**

Plato **PA4279 .A3 1995**
Plato on Poetry: Ion; Republic 376e-398b9; Republic 595-608b10. Penelope Murray (Editor), P. E. Easterling, Philip Hardie, Richard Hunter & E. J. Kenney (Contribution by). Trade Paper. Cambridge University Press. New York, NY. 1996. 246p. Cambridge Greek and Latin Classics ISBN:0-521-34981-8, ISBN13: 978-0-521-34981-9. Dewey:881/.01. LCCN:95-013249.
Audience: **u,f.**

Plato **JC71.P513 2004**
Republic. Ed. 3. C. D. C. Reeve (Introduction by). Trade Cloth. Hackett Publishing Company, Inc. Indianapolis, IN. 2004. 358p. ISBN:0-87220-737-4, ISBN13: 978-0-87220-737-0. Dewey:321/.07. LCCN:2004-013418.
Audience: **g,l,u.** B *Choice, 2005.*

Plato **PA4279.P3 P39 1993**
Plato: Phaedo. C. J. Rowe (Editor), P. E. Easterling, Philip Hardie, Richard Hunter & E. J. Kenney (Contribution by). Trade Paper. Cambridge University Press. New York, NY. 1993. 313p. Cambridge Greek and Latin Classics ISBN:0-521-31318-X, ISBN13: 978-0-521-31318-6. Dewey:184. LCCN:92-033958.
Audience: **u,f.**

Plato **JC71**
Platonis Respublica. S. R. Slings (Editor). Trade Cloth. Oxford University Press, Inc. New York, NY. 2003. 452p. Oxford Classical Texts ISBN:0-19-924849-4, ISBN13: 978-0-19-924849-0. Dewey:321/.07.
Audience: **u,f.**

Rosen, Stanley **JC71.P6R67 2005**
Plato's Republic: A Study. Saddle Stitched, Cloth over Boards, Dust Jacket. Yale University Press. Cumberland, RI. 2005. 432p. ISBN:0-300-10962-8, ISBN13: 978-0-300-10962-7. Dewey:321/.07. LCCN:2005-044011.
Audience: **u,f.** *Choice, 2006.*

Taylor, A. E. **B395.T25 2001**
Plato: The Man and His Work. Trade Paper. Dover Publications, Inc. Mineola, NY. 2001. 574p. Dover Books on Western Philosophy ISBN:0-486-41605-4, ISBN13: 978-0-486-41605-2. Dewey:184 B. LCCN:00-065955.
Audience: **g,l,u,f.**

Greek > Individual Authors > Plutarch

Duff, Tim **DE7**
Plutarch's Lives: Exploring Virtue and Vice. Trade Paper. Oxford University Press, Inc. New York, NY. 2002. 448p. ISBN:0-19-925274-2, ISBN13: 978-0-19-925274-9. Dewey:920/.038. LCCN:98-040794.
Audience: **u,f.**

Lamberton, Robert **PA4382.L36 2002**
Plutarch. Cloth over Boards. Yale University Press. Cumberland, RI. 2002. 240p. Hermes Bks. ISBN:0-300-08810-8, ISBN13: 978-0-300-08810-6. Dewey:938/.007/202 B. LCCN:2001-002862.
Audience: **g,l,u.** *Choice, 2002.*

Plutarch **PA4368**
The Education of Children, How the Young Man Should Study Poetry, on Listening to Lectures, How to Tell a Flatterer from a Friend, How a Man May Become Aware of His Progress in Virtue. Trade Cloth. Harvard University Press. Cambridge, MA. 1927. 512p. Moralia Ser., Vol. 1 ISBN:0-674-99217-2, ISBN13: 978-0-674-99217-7. Dewey:885.
Audience: **g,l,u.**

Plutarch **PA4368**
Isis and Osiris, the E at Delphi, the Oracles at Delphi No Longer Given in Verse, the Obsolescence of Oracles. Trade Cloth. Harvard University Press. Cambridge, MA. 1936. 528p. Moralia Ser., Vol. 5 ISBN:0-674-99337-3, ISBN13: 978-0-674-99337-2. Dewey:888.8.
Audience: **g,l,u.**

Plutarch **PA4368**
On the Malice of Herodotus, Causes of Natural Phenomena, Vol. 11. Trade Cloth. Harvard University Press. Cambridge, MA. 1965. 256p. Moralia Ser., Vol. 11 ISBN:0-674-99469-8, ISBN13: 978-0-674-99469-0. Dewey:880.8.
Audience: **g,l,u.**

Plutarch **PA4369.A33**
Parallel Lives. Trade Cloth. Harvard University Press. Cambridge, MA. Loeb Classical Library, Nos. 46-47, 65, 80, 87, 98-103 ISBN:0-318-53133-X, ISBN13: 978-0-318-53133-5. Dewey:920.
Audience: **g,l,u.**

Plutarch **DF226.T45**
Plutarch: Life of Themistocles. John L. Marr (Editor, Translator, Introduction by). Trade Cloth. Aris & Phillips. Oxford, 1998. 172p. Classical Texts Ser. ISBN:0-85668-676-X, ISBN13: 978-0-85668-676-4. Dewey:938/.03/092 B. LCCN:99-225937.
Audience: **u.**

Plutarch **PA4369 .A73 1988**
Plutarch: Life of Antony. Christopher B. Pelling (Editor), P. E. Easterling, Philip Hardie, Richard Hunter & E. J. Kenney (Contribution by). Trade Cloth. Cambridge University Press. New York, NY. 1988. 352p. Cambridge Greek and Latin Classics Ser. ISBN:0-521-24066-2, ISBN13: 978-0-521-24066-6. Dewey:937/.05/0924. LCCN:87-003004.
Audience: **u,f.** *Choice, 1988.*

Plutarch **DG253.C3P5813 1989**
Plutarch: Lives of Aristides and Cato. David Sansone (Editor). Trade Cloth. Aris & Phillips. Oxford, 1989. 248p. Classical Texts Ser. ISBN:0-85668-421-X, ISBN13: 978-0-85668-421-0. Dewey:938/.03/092 B. LCCN:89-183580.
Audience: **u.**

Pomeroy, Sarah B. (Editor) **HQ731.P58 1999**
Plutarch's Advice to the Bride and Groom and a Consolation to His Wife: English Translations, Commentary, Interpretive Essays, and Bibliography. Trade Cloth. Oxford University Press, Inc. New York, NY. 1999. 240p. ISBN:0-19-512023-X, ISBN13: 978-0-19-512023-3. Dewey:306.81. LCCN:98-027968.
Audience: **u,f.**

Russell, D. **PA4382 .R8 1973**
Plutarch. Trade Cloth. Gerald Duckworth & Company, Ltd. London, 1986. 192p. ISBN:0-7156-0668-9, ISBN13: 978-0-7156-0668-1. Dewey:938/.007/2024. LCCN:73-157995.
Audience: **g,l,u.**

Stadter, Philip A. (Editor) **PA4385.P58 1992**
Plutarch and the Historical Tradition. Paper over Boards. Routledge. New York, NY. 1992. 196p. ISBN:0-415-07007-4, ISBN13: 978-0-415-07007-2. Dewey:920.038. LCCN:91-024831.
Audience: **u,f.**

Greek > Individual Authors > Sappho

Greene, Ellen (Editor) **PA4409.R474 1996**
Reading Sappho: Contemporary Approaches. Trade Cloth. University of California Press. Berkeley, CA. 1998. 316p. Classics and Contemporary Thought Ser., Vol. 2 ISBN:0-520-20195-7, ISBN13: 978-0-520-20195-8. Dewey:884/.01. LCCN:96-013702.
Audience: **l,u,f.** *Choice, 1998.*

Page, Denys L. **PA3861**
Sappho and Alcaeus: An Introduction to the Study of Ancient Lesbian Poetry. Paper Text. Oxford University Press, Inc. New York, NY. 1979. 350p. ISBN:0-19-814375-3, ISBN13: 978-0-19-814375-8. Dewey:884/.01/09.
Audience: **u,f.**

Rayor, Diane **PA3622.R39 1991**
Sappho's Lyre: Archaic Lyric and Women Poets of Ancient Greece. W. R. Johnson (Foreword by). Trade Cloth. University of California Press. Berkeley, CA. 1991. 234p. ISBN:0-520-07335-5, ISBN13: 978-0-520-07335-7. Dewey:884/.01089287. LCCN:90-048642.
Audience: **g,l,u,f.** *Choice, 1992.*

Sappho **PA4408.E5L6613 2002**
Poems and Fragments. Stanley Lombardo (Translator), Pamela Gordon (Introduction by). Trade Cloth. Hackett Publishing Company, Inc. Indianapolis, IN. 2002. 68p. ISBN:0-87220-592-4, ISBN13: 978-0-87220-592-5. Dewey:884/.01. LCCN:2001-051548.
Audience: **g,l,u,f.**

Snyder, Jane M. **PA4409.S64 1997**
Lesbian Desire in the Lyrics of Sappho. Trade Cloth. Columbia University Press. New York, NY. 1997. 278p. Between Men, Between Women Ser. ISBN:0-231-09994-0, ISBN13: 978-0-231-09994-3. Dewey:884/.01. LCCN:96-031981.
Audience: **u,f.** *Choice, 1997.*

Greek > Individual Authors > Sophocles

Hogan, James C. **PA4417.H64 1991**
A Commentary on the Plays of Sophocles. Trade Cloth. Southern Illinois University Press. Carbondale, IL. 1991. 396p. ISBN:0-8093-1665-X, ISBN13: 978-0-8093-1665-6. Dewey:882/.01. LCCN:90-036643.
Audience: **g,l,u,f.** *Choice, 1991.*

Kirkwood, G. M. **PA4417.K48 1994**
A Study of Sophoclean Drama. Book, Other. Cornell University Press. Ithaca, NY. 1994. 328p. Studies in Classical Philology ISBN:0-8014-8241-0, ISBN13: 978-0-8014-8241-0. Dewey:882/.01. LCCN:94-022808.
Audience: **u,f.**

Kitto, Humphrey D. **PA4417 .K5 1981**
Sophocles: Dramatist and Philosopher. Trade Cloth. Greenwood Publishing Group, Inc. Portsmouth, NH. 1981. 64p. ISBN:0-313-22625-3, ISBN13: 978-0-313-22625-0. Dewey:882/.01. LCCN:80-022360.
Audience: **g,l,u,f.**

Knox, Bernard M. **PA4417**
The Heroic Temper: Studies in Sophoclean Tragedy. Trade Paper. University of California Press. Berkeley, CA. 1965. 224p. Sather Classical Lectures, No. 35 ISBN:0-520-04957-8, ISBN13: 978-0-520-04957-4. Dewey:882/.01. LCCN:64-021864.
Audience: **u,f.**

Knox, Bernard M. **PA4413.O7K55 1998**
Oedipus at Thebes: Sophocles' Tragic Hero and His Time. Trade Paper. Yale University Press. Cumberland, RI. 1998. 300p. ISBN:0-300-07423-9, ISBN13: 978-0-300-07423-9. Dewey:882/.01. LCCN:97-018471.
Audience: **u,f.**

Reinhardt, Karl **PA3978**
Sophocles. Hazel Harvey & David Harvey (Translators), Hugh Lloyd-Jones (Introduction by). Cloth Text. Barnes & Noble Books-Imports. Lanham, MD. 1979. ISBN:0-06-495832-9, ISBN13: 978-0-06-495832-5. Dewey:882/.01. LCCN:78-018826.
Audience: **u,f.**

Segal, Charles **PA4413.O7S52 2001**
Oedipus Tyrannus: Tragic Heroism and the Limits of Knowledge. Ed. 2. Cloth Text. Oxford University Press, Inc. New York, NY. 2000. 208p. ISBN:0-19-513320-X, ISBN13: 978-0-19-513320-2. Dewey:882/.01. LCCN:00-032666.
Audience: **u,f.** *Choice, 1993.*

Segal, Charles **PA4417.S46 1995**
Sophocles' Tragic World: Divinity, Nature, Society. Trade Cloth. Harvard University Press. Cambridge, MA. 1995. 288p. ISBN:0-674-82100-9, ISBN13: 978-0-674-82100-2. Dewey:882/.01. LCCN:95-015249.
Audience: **u,f.** *Choice, 1996.*

Segal, Charles **PA4417.S47 1999**
Tragedy and Civilization: An Interpretation of Sophocles. Trade Paper. University of Oklahoma Press. Norman, OK. 1999. 528p. ISBN:0-8061-3136-5, ISBN13: 978-0-8061-3136-8. Dewey:882/.01. LCCN:98-044168.
Audience: **l,u,f.** B

Sophocles **PA4414.O7B44 1988**
Oedipus the King. Stephen Berg & Diskin Clay (Translators). Trade Paper. Oxford University Press, Inc. New York, NY. 1988. 128p. Greek Tragedy in New Translations Ser. ISBN:0-19-505493-8, ISBN13: 978-0-19-505493-4. Dewey:882/.01.
Audience: **g,l,u.**

Sophocles **PA4413.O7**
Sophocles: Oedipus Rex. Ed. 2. R. D. Dawe (Editor), P. E. Easterling, Philip Hardie, Richard Hunter & E. J. Kenney (Contribution by). Cloth Text. Cambridge University Press. New York, NY. 2006. 224p. Cambridge Greek and Latin Classics Ser. ISBN:0-521-85177-7, ISBN13: 978-0-521-85177-0. Dewey:882.01.
Audience: **u,f.**

Sophocles **PA4414.A7G53 2003**
Antigone. Reginald Gibbons & Charles Segal (Translators). Trade Cloth. Oxford University Press, Inc. New York, NY. 2003. 208p. Greek Tragedy in New Translations Ser. ISBN:0-19-514373-6, ISBN13: 978-0-19-514373-7. Dewey:882/.01. LCCN:2002-008966.
Audience: **g,l,u.**

Sophocles **PA4414.A5G65 1999**
Aias. Herbert Golder & Richard Pevear (Translators). Trade Paper. Oxford University Press, Inc. New York, NY. 1999. 128p. Greek Tragedy in New Translations Ser. ISBN:0-19-512819-2, ISBN13: 978-0-19-512819-2. Dewey:882/.01. LCCN:98-024421.
Audience: **g,l,u.**

Sophocles **PA4414.A1**
Sophocles, Vol. 2. David Grene & Richmond A. Lattimore (Editors). Trade Cloth. University of Chicago Press. Chicago, IL. 1992. 472p. Complete Greek Tragedies Ser., Vol. II ISBN:0-226-30765-4, ISBN13: 978-0-226-30765-7. Dewey:882.01. LCCN:91-045936.
Audience: **g,l,u.** B

Sophocles **PA4414.O5G74 2004**
Oedipus at Colonus. Eamon Grennan & Rachel Kitzinger (Translators). Trade Paper. Oxford University Press, Inc. New York, NY. 2004. 112p. Greek Tragedy in New Translations Ser. ISBN:0-19-513504-0, ISBN13: 978-0-19-513504-6. Dewey:882/.01. LCCN:2004-046500.
Audience: **g,l,u.**

Sophocles **PA4413 .A7 1999**
Antigone. Mark Griffith (Editor), P. E. Easterling, Philip Hardie, Richard Hunter & E. J. Kenney (Contribution by). Trade Paper. Cambridge University Press. New York, NY. 1999. 378p. Cambridge Greek and Latin Classics ISBN:0-521-33701-1, ISBN13: 978-0-521-33701-4. Dewey:882/.01. LCCN:98-035827.
Audience: **u,f.**

Sophocles **PA3978**
Sophocles: Electra. J. H. Kells (Editor), P. E. Easterling, Philip Hardie, Richard Hunter & E. J. Kenney (Contribution by). Trade Paper. Cambridge University Press. New York, NY. 1973. 263p. Cambridge Greek and Latin Classics ISBN:0-521-09796-7, ISBN13: 978-0-521-09796-3. Dewey:882/.01. LCCN:73-182028.
Audience: **u,f.**

Sophocles **PA4414.A1L56 1994**
Sophocles: Ajax, Electra, Oedipus Tyrannus. Hugh Lloyd-Jones (Editor, Translator). Trade Cloth. Harvard University Press. Cambridge, MA. 1994. 496p. Loeb Classical Library, Nos. 20-21 ISBN:0-674-99557-0, ISBN13: 978-0-674-99557-4. Dewey:882.01. LCCN:92-019295.
Audience: **g,l,u,f.**

Sophocles **PA4414.A1L56 1994**
Sophocles: Antigone, the Women of Trachis, Philoctetes, Oedipus at Colonus. Hugh Lloyd-Jones (Editor, Translator). Trade Cloth. Harvard University Press. Cambridge, MA. 1978. 608p. Loeb Classical Library, Vol. 2 ISBN:0-674-99558-9, ISBN13: 978-0-674-99558-1. Dewey:882.01. LCCN:92-019295.
Audience: **g,l,u,f.**

Sophocles **PA4414.A1L56 1994**
Sophocles - Fragments, Vol. 3. Hugh Lloyd-Jones (Editor, Translator). Trade Cloth. Harvard University Press. Cambridge, MA. 1996. 448p. Loeb Classical Library Ser. ISBN:0-674-99532-5, ISBN13: 978-0-674-99532-1. Dewey:882.01. LCCN:92-019295.
Audience: **g,l,u,f.**

Sophocles **PA4414.P5P48 2003**
Philoctetes. Carl Phillips & Diskin Clay (Editors), Carl Phillips (Translator), Diskin Clay (Introduction by, Notes by). Trade Paper. Oxford University Press, Inc. New York, NY. 2003. 128p. Greek Tragedy in New Translations Ser. ISBN:0-19-513657-8, ISBN13: 978-0-19-513657-9. Dewey:882.01. LCCN:2002-032763.
Audience: **g,l,u.**

Sophocles **PA4413**
Sophocles: Ajax. W. Bedell Stanford (Editor). Trade Paper. Bristol Classical Press. London, 1981. 384p. Greek Texts ISBN:0-86292-009-4, ISBN13: 978-0-86292-009-8. Dewey:882/.01.
Audience: **u,f.**

Steiner, George **PA4413.A7S76 1996**
Antigones: How the Antigone Legend Has Endured in Western Literature, Art, and Thought. Trade Paper. Yale University Press. Cumberland, RI. 1996. 328p. ISBN:0-300-06915-4, ISBN13: 978-0-300-06915-0. Dewey:882/.01. LCCN:96-060411.
Audience: **u,f.**

Winnington-Ingram, R. P. **PA4417.W55 1980**
Sophocles: An Interpretation. Trade Paper. Cambridge University Press. New York, NY. 1980. 358p. ISBN:0-521-29684-6, ISBN13: 978-0-521-29684-7. Dewey:882/.01. LCCN:79-050511.
Audience: **u,f.**

Greek > Individual Authors > Theocritus

Gutzwiller, Kathryn J. **PA4444.G8 1991**
Theocritus' Pastoral Analogies: The Formation of a Genre. Trade Paper. University of Wisconsin Press. Chicago, IL. 1991. 320p. Studies in Classics ISBN:0-299-12944-6, ISBN13: 978-0-299-12944-6. Dewey:884/.01. LCCN:91-007616.
Audience: **u,f.**

Theocritus **PA4442**
Theocritus: Select Poems. Kenneth J. Dover (Editor). Trade Paper. Bristol Classical Press. London, 1985. 400p. Greek Texts ISBN:0-86292-147-3, ISBN13: 978-0-86292-147-7. Dewey:881/.01.
Audience: **u,f.**

Theocritus **PA4442 .C617 2003**
Encomium of Ptolemy Philadelphus. R. L. Hunter (Translator, Commentaries by). Trade Cloth. University of California Press. Berkeley, CA. 2003. 244p. Hellenistic Culture and Society Ser., Vol. 38 ISBN:0-520-23560-6, ISBN13: 978-0-520-23560-1. Dewey:884/.01. LCCN:2002-073272.
Audience: **u,f.**

Theocritus **PA4442.A5 H86 1999**
Theocritus: Idylls 1, 3, 4, 6, 7, 10, 11 and 13. Richard L. Hunter (Editor). Cloth Text. Cambridge University Press. New York, NY. 1999. 320p. Cambridge Greek and Latin Classics ISBN:0-521-57416-1, ISBN13: 978-0-521-57416-7. Dewey:884/.01. LCCN:98-012922.
Audience: **u,f.**

Theocritus **PA4443.E5V47 2003**
Idylls. Anthony Verity (Translator), Richard L. Hunter (Introduction by). Trade Paper. Oxford University Press, Inc. New York, NY. 2003. 144p. Oxford World's Classics Ser. ISBN:0-19-283984-5, ISBN13: 978-0-19-283984-8. Dewey:884/.01.
Audience: **g,l,u.** *Choice, 1988.*

Greek > Individual Authors > Theophrastus

Theophrastus **PA4449.E5C5 2002**
Theophrastus - Characters: Herodas - Mimes: Sophron and Other Mime Fragments. Ed. 3. I. C. Cunningham (Editor, Translator). Trade Cloth. Harvard University Press. Cambridge, MA. 2003. 432p. Loeb Classical Library, Vol. 225 ISBN:0-674-99603-8, ISBN13: 978-0-674-99603-8. Dewey:888/.01/08. LCCN:2002-027603.
Audience: **g,l,u.**

Theophrastus **PA4449.E5C5 2004**
Theophrastus: Characters. James Diggle (Edited and Translated by, Contribution by), Neil Hopkinson, Jonathan Powell, Michael Reeve, David Sedley & Richard Tarrant (Contribution by). Trade Cloth. Cambridge University Press. New York, NY. 2004. 608p. Cambridge Classical Texts and Commentaries Ser., Vol. 41 ISBN:0-521-83980-7, ISBN13: 978-0-521-83980-8. Dewey:888/.0108. LCCN:2003-069706.
Audience: **f.**

Theophrastus **PA4448.A4E45 1993**
Theophrastus: Characters. R. G. Ussher (Editor). Trade Paper. Bristol Classical Press. London, 1993. 320p. Greek Texts ISBN:1-85399-188-0, ISBN13: 978-1-85399-188-2. Dewey:888/.0108. LCCN:93-156396.
Audience: **u.**

Greek > Individual Authors > Thucydides

Cameron, H. D. **PA4461.C28 2003**
Thucydides Book I: A Students' Grammatical Commentary. Trade Cloth. University of Michigan Press. Chicago, IL. 2003. 148p. ISBN:0-472-09847-0, ISBN13: 978-0-472-09847-7. Dewey:938/.05. LCCN:2003-055997.
Audience: **l,u.**

Cornford, Francis Macdonald **PA4461**
Thucydides: Mythistoricus. Trade Cloth. Bristol Classical Press. London, 2003. 272p. Bcpaperback Ser. ISBN:1-85399-665-3, ISBN13: 978-1-85399-665-8. Dewey:938/.05.
Audience: **g,u,f.**

Crane, Gregory **PA4461.C73 1996**
The Blinded Eye: Thucydides and the New Written Word. Trade Cloth. Rowman & Littlefield Publishers, Inc. Lanham, MD. 1996. 288p. Greek Studies, :Interdisciplinary Approaches ISBN:0-8476-8129-7, ISBN13: 978-0-8476-8129-7. Dewey:938/.05/072. LCCN:95-033520.
Audience: **u,f.**

Crane, Gregory **DF229.T6C88 1997**
Thucydides and the Ancient Simplicity: The Limits of Political Realism. Trade Cloth. University of California Press. Berkeley, CA. 1998. 362p. ISBN:0-520-20789-0, ISBN13: 978-0-520-20789-9. Dewey:938/.05. LCCN:96-029615.
Audience: **u,f.** *Choice, 1999.*

Rawlings, Hunter R. **PA4461.R3**
The Structure of Thucydides' History. Trade Paper. Books on Demand. Ann Arbor, MI. 293p. ISBN:0-8357-7898-3, ISBN13: 978-0-8357-7898-5. Dewey:938/.05/072. LCCN:80-008572.
Audience: **u,f.**

Stahl, Hans-Peter **DF229**
Thucydides: Man's Place in History. Trade Cloth. Classical Press of Wales, The. Swansea, 2002. 250p. ISBN:0-7156-3184-5, ISBN13: 978-0-7156-3184-3. Dewey:938/.05.
Audience: **u,f.**

Thucydides **DF229.T6**
Thucydides, Bk. 7. Kenneth J. Dover (Editor). Trade Cloth. Oxford University Press, Inc. New York, NY. 1965. ISBN:0-19-831829-4, ISBN13: 978-0-19-831829-3. Dewey:938/.05.
Audience: **u,f.**

Thucydides **DF229.T6**
Thucydides Book VI, Vol. 6. Kenneth J. Dover (Editor). Trade Paper. Bristol Classical Press. London, xxix, 104p. Greek Texts Ser. ISBN:1-85399-587-8, ISBN13: 978-1-85399-587-3. Dewey:938/.05.
Audience: **u,f.**

Thucydides **DF229.T5H6 1989**
The Peloponnesian War. Thomas Hobbes (Translator), David Grene (Commentaries by). Trade Paper. University of Chicago Press. Chicago, IL. 1989. 668p. ISBN:0-226-80106-3, ISBN13: 978-0-226-80106-3. Dewey:938/.05. LCCN:89-014647.
Audience: **g,l,u.**

Thucydides **PA3404**
Historiae, Vol. II, Bks. V-VIII. Ed. 2. H. S. Jones & J. Enoch Powell (Editors). Cloth Text. Oxford University Press, Inc. New York, NY. 1942. 328p. Oxford Classical Texts ISBN:0-19-814551-9, ISBN13: 978-0-19-814551-6. Dewey:881.
Audience: **f.**

Thucydides **PA3405.58.T7 1942**
Historiae, Vol. I, Bks. I-IV. Ed. 2. H. S. Jones & J. Enoch Powell (Editors). Cloth Text. Oxford University Press, Inc. New York, NY. 1942. 350p. Oxford Classical Texts ISBN:0-19-814550-0, ISBN13: 978-0-19-814550-9. Dewey:881. LCCN:43-001621.
Audience: **f.**

Thucydides **DF229.T5L38 1998**
The Peloponnesian War. Steven Lattimore (Translator, Introduction by, Notes by). Trade Cloth. Hackett Publishing Company, Inc. Indianapolis, IN. 1998. 530p. ISBN:0-87220-395-6, ISBN13: 978-0-87220-395-2. Dewey:938/.05 19. LCCN:97-046084.
Audience: **g,l,u.**

Thucydides **PA4461 .R87 1989**
The Peloponnesian War, Bk. II. J. S. Rusten (Editor). Trade Cloth. Cambridge University Press. New York, NY. 1989. 272p. Cambridge Greek and Latin Classics ISBN:0-521-32665-6, ISBN13: 978-0-521-32665-0. Dewey:938/.05 19. LCCN:88-002897.
Audience: **u,f.**

Zagorin, Perez **DF229.T6Z34 2005**
Thucydides: An Introduction for the Common Reader. Trade Cloth. Princeton University Press. Princeton, NJ. 2005. 216p. ISBN:0-691-12351-9, ISBN13: 978-0-691-12351-6. Dewey:938/.05/072. LCCN:2004-058635.
Audience: **g,l,u.** *Choice, 2006.*

Greek > Individual Authors > Xenophon

Anderson, J. K. **PA4236**
Xenophon. Trade Paper. Gerald Duckworth & Company, Ltd. London, 1986. 216p. ISBN:0-7156-1610-2, ISBN13: 978-0-7156-1610-9. Dewey:888/.01/09.
Audience: **u,f.**

Dillery, John **DF229.D55 1995**
Xenophon and the History of His Times. Paper over Boards. Routledge. New York, NY. 1995. 352p. ISBN:0-415-09139-X, ISBN13: 978-0-415-09139-8. Dewey:938/.007202. LCCN:94-030021.
Audience: **g,u,f.** *Choice, 1997.*

Miller, Walter (Translator) **PA4495**
Cyropaedia, Bks. 5-8. Trade Cloth. Harvard University Press. Cambridge, MA. 1994. 488p. Cyropaedia, Bks. 5-8, No. 51-52 ISBN:0-674-99058-7, ISBN13: 978-0-674-99058-6. Dewey:888.01. LCCN:73-164494.
Audience: **g,l,u,f.**

Xenophon **PA4495**
Cyropaedia, Bks. 1-4. Trade Cloth. Harvard University Press. Cambridge, MA. 1914. 416p. Cyropaedia, Bks. 1-4, No. 51-52 ISBN:0-674-99057-9, ISBN13: 978-0-674-99057-9. Dewey:888.01. LCCN:73-164494.
Audience: **g,l,u,f.**

Xenophon **PA4495**
Memorabilia and Oeconomicus, Symposium, and Apologia, Vol. 4. Trade Cloth. Harvard University Press. Cambridge, MA. 1923. 704p. Memorabilia and Oeconomicus, Symposium, and Apology Ser., No. 168 ISBN:0-674-99186-9, ISBN13: 978-0-674-99186-6. Dewey:888.01. LCCN:73-164494.
Audience: **g,l,u,f.**

Xenophon **PA4495**
Scripta Minora: Hiero, Agesilaus, Constitution of the Lacedaemonians, Ways and Means, Cavalry Commander, Art of Horsemanship, on Hunting, Constitution of the Athenians. Glen W. Bowersock (Translator). Trade Cloth. Harvard University Press. Cambridge, MA. 1925. 568p. Scripta Minora Ser., No. 183 ISBN:0-674-99202-4, ISBN13: 978-0-674-99202-3. Dewey:888.01. LCCN:73-164494.
Audience: **g,l,u,f.**

Xenophon **PA4495**
Hellenica, Bks. 5-7. C. L. Brownson (Editor). Trade Cloth. Harvard University Press. Cambridge, MA. 1921. 368p. Hellenica and Anabasis Bks., No. 88-90 ISBN:0-674-99099-4, ISBN13: 978-0-674-99099-9. Dewey:888.01. LCCN:73-164494.
Audience: **g,l,u,f.**

Xenophon **PA3612**
Hellenica, Bks. 1-4. C. L. Brownson (Translator). Trade Cloth. Harvard University Press. Cambridge, MA. 1918. 400p. Hellenica and Anabasis Bks., No. 88-90 ISBN:0-674-99098-6, ISBN13: 978-0-674-99098-2. Dewey:888.01. LCCN:73-164494.
Audience: **g,l,u,f.**

Xenophon **DF231.32.X413 1998**
Anabasis. Carleton L. Brownson (Editor). Trade Cloth. Harvard University Press. Cambridge, MA. 1998. 672p. Loeb Classical Library, Vol. 90 ISBN:0-674-99101-X, ISBN13: 978-0-674-99101-9. Dewey:938. LCCN:99-218930.
Audience: **g,l,u,f.**

Xenophon **PA4494.A5**
Xenophon's Anabasis, Bks. 1-4. Maurice W. Mather & Joseph W. Hewitt (Editors). Trade Paper, Book, Other. University of Oklahoma Press. Norman, OK. 1976. 522p. ISBN:0-8061-1347-2, ISBN13: 978-0-8061-1347-0. Dewey:488.64. LCCN:62-018051.
Audience: **l,u.**

Greek > Individual Authors > Aristophanes

Aristophanes **PA3875.R3**
Frogs. Trade Cloth. Oxford University Press, Inc. New York, NY. 1997. 266p. ISBN:0-19-872175-7, ISBN13: 978-0-19-872175-8. Dewey:882.01.
Audience: **u,f.** B

Aristophanes **PA3877 .A2**
Four Comedies: Lysistrata, the Congresswomen, the Acharnians, the Frogs. William Arrowsmith (Editor). Trade Paper. University of Michigan Press. Chicago, IL. 1969. 432p. Ann Arbor Paperbacks Ser. ISBN:0-472-06152-6, ISBN13: 978-0-472-06152-5. Dewey:882.01.
Audience: **g,l,u.**

Aristophanes **PA3877.A2**
Three Comedies: The Birds, the Clouds, the Wasps. William Arrowsmith (Editor). Trade Paper. University of Michigan Press. Chicago, IL. 1969. 408p. Ann Arbor Paperbacks Ser. ISBN:0-472-06153-4, ISBN13: 978-0-472-06153-2. Dewey:882.
Audience: **g,l,u.**

Aristophanes **PA3875.N8 1989**
Clouds. Kenneth J. Dover (Editor). Trade Paper. Oxford University Press, Inc. New York, NY. 1989. 414p. ISBN:0-19-814395-8, ISBN13: 978-0-19-814395-6. Dewey:882/.01. LCCN:88-035159.
Audience: **u,f.**

Aristophanes **PA3875**
Lysistrata. Jeffrey Henderson (Editor). Trade Paper. Oxford University Press, Inc. New York, NY. 1990. 308p. ISBN:0-19-814496-2, ISBN13: 978-0-19-814496-0. Dewey:882.01.
Audience: **g,l,u,f.**

Dover, Kenneth J. **PA3978**
Aristophanic Comedy. Trade Paper. University of California Press. Berkeley, CA. 1972. xiv, 253p. ISBN:0-520-02211-4, ISBN13: 978-0-520-02211-9. Dewey:882/.01. LCCN:70-182681.
Audience: **u,f.** B

Segal, Erich (Editor) **PA3879.O94 1996**
Oxford Readings in Aristophanes. Paper Text. Oxford University Press, Inc. New York, NY. 1996. 356p. ISBN:0-19-872157-9, ISBN13: 978-0-19-872157-4. Dewey:882/.01. LCCN:95-038110.
Audience: **u,f.** *Choice, 1997.*

Latin > Latin Language

Allen, J. H. & Greenough, J. B. **PA2087.A525 1979**
New Latin Grammar. George L. Kittredge, A. A. Howard & Benjamin L. D'Ooge (Editors). Library Binding. Aristide D. Caratzas Publisher. Athens, 1992. 490p. College Classical Ser. ISBN:0-89241-001-9, ISBN13: 978-0-89241-001-9. Dewey:478.2/421. LCCN:80-019039.
Audience: **g,l,u,f.**

Arnold, Thomas K. **PA2313.A76 2005**
Bradley's Arnold Latin Prose Composition. G. G. Bradley & J. F. Mountford (Revised by). Book, Other. Bolchazy-Carducci Publishers. Wauconda, IL. 2006. 450p. ISBN:0-86516-595-5, ISBN13: 978-0-86516-595-3. Dewey:808/.0471. LCCN:2004-029648.
Audience: **u.**

Baldi, Philip **PA2071.B35 1998**
The Foundations of Latin. Trade Cloth. Walter De Gruyter Inc. Ossining, NY. 1999. xviii, 534p. Trends in Linguistics Ser., Vol. 117 ISBN:3-11-016294-6, ISBN13: 978-3-11-016294-3. Dewey:475. LCCN:98-051324.
Audience: **u,f.**

Farrell, Joseph **PA2061.F395 2001**
e Latin Language and Latin Culture: From Ancient to Modern Times. E-Book. Cambridge University Press. New York, NY. ISBN:0-511-04081-4, ISBN13: 978-0-511-04081-8. Dewey:470.
Audience: **g,l,u,f.** *Choice, 2001.*

Gildersleeve, Basil L. & Lodge, Gonzalez **PA2087.G5 1997**
Gildersleeve's Latin Grammar. Ed. 3. Ward W. Briggs Jr. (Introduction by), William Wycislo (Contribution by). Book, Other. Bolchazy-Carducci Publishers. Wauconda, IL. 1997. 613p. ISBN:0-86516-353-7, ISBN13: 978-0-86516-353-9. Dewey:478.2/421. LCCN:97-017220.
Audience: **l,u,f.**

Glare, P. G. (Editor) **PA2365.E5**
Oxford Latin Dictionary. Cloth Text. Oxford University Press, Inc. New York, NY. 1983. 2, 150p. ISBN:0-19-864224-5, ISBN13: 978-0-19-864224-4. Dewey:473/.21. LCCN:82-008162.
Audience: **u,f.** B

Greenough, J. B. **PE1111.S487**
Allen and Greenough's New Latin Grammar. Anne Mahoney (Revised by). Trade Cloth. Focus Publishing/R. Pullins Company, Inc. Newburyport, MA. 2001. 512p. ISBN:1-58510-042-0, ISBN13: 978-1-58510-042-2. Dewey:425.
Audience: **l,u,f.**

Hammond, Mason **PA2057**
Latin: A Historical and Lingusitic Handbook. Trade Cloth. Harvard University Press. Cambridge, MA. 1976. 272p. ISBN:0-674-51290-1, ISBN13: 978-0-674-51290-0. Dewey:470. LCCN:75-033359.
Audience: **g,l,u,f.** B

Janson, Tore **PA2057**
A Natural History of Latin. Nigel Vincent & Merethe Damsgaard Sorensen (Translators). Trade Cloth. Oxford University Press, Inc. New York, NY. 2005. 316p. ISBN:0-19-926309-4, ISBN13: 978-0-19-926309-7. Dewey:470.9. LCCN:2004-276203.
Audience: **g,l,u,f.** *Choice, 2005.*

Latham, Ronald E. (Editor) **PA2891**
Revised Medieval Latin Word-List from British and Irish Sources. Cloth Text. Oxford University Press, Inc. New York, NY. 1965. 548p. British Academy Ser. ISBN:0-19-725891-3, ISBN13: 978-0-19-725891-0. Dewey:473.2.
Audience: **u,f.**

Lewis, Charlton T. & Short, Charles **PA2365.E5**
A Latin Dictionary: Founded on Andrews' Edition of Freund's Latin Dictionary. Cloth Text. Oxford University Press, Inc. New York, NY. 1956. 2, 048p. ISBN:0-19-864201-6, ISBN13: 978-0-19-864201-5. Dewey:473.21.
Audience: **u,f.**

Palmer, Leonard R. **PA2071.P26 1988**
The Latin Language. Trade Paper. University of Oklahoma Press. Norman, OK. 1988. 382p. ISBN:0-8061-2136-X, ISBN13: 978-0-8061-2136-9. Dewey:470. LCCN:87-040564.
Audience: **u,f.**

Simpson, D. P. **PA2365.E5C3 1977**
Cassell's Latin Dictionary: Latin-English, English-Latin. Trade Cloth. John Wiley & Sons, Inc. Hoboken, NJ. 1977. 912p. ISBN:0-02-522580-4, ISBN13: 978-0-02-522580-0. Dewey:433'.21. LCCN:77-007670.
Audience: **g,l.**

Traupman, John (Editor) **PA2365.E5S6 2000**
Smith's Copius and Critical English-Latin Dictionary. Trade Cloth. Wimbledon Publishing Company. London, 2001. 110p. Classics Ser. ISBN:1-898855-38-2, ISBN13: 978-1-898855-38-5. Dewey:423/.71. LCCN:2001-280590.
Audience: **g,l,u,f.**

Woodcock, E. C. **PA2285**
A New Latin Syntax. Book, Other. Bolchazy-Carducci Publishers. Wauconda, IL. 1987. xxiv, 268p. ISBN:0-86516-126-7, ISBN13: 978-0-86516-126-9. Dewey:475.
Audience: **u,f.**

Latin > General Works

Atchity, Kenneth J. (Editor) **PA6163.C58 1998**
The Classical Roman Reader: New Encounters with Ancient Rome. Trade Paper. Oxford University Press, Inc. New York, NY. 1998. 480p. ISBN:0-19-512740-4, ISBN13: 978-0-19-512740-9. Dewey:870.8/001. LCCN:98-029785.
Audience: **g,l,u.**

Auerbach, E. **PA8027**
Literary Language and Its Public in Late Latin Antiquity and in the Middle Ages. R. Manheim (Translator). Trade Cloth. Princeton University Press. Princeton, NJ. 1965. 456p. ISBN:0-691-09782-8, ISBN13: 978-0-691-09782-4. Dewey:879.
Audience: **u,f.**

Binns, J. W. (Editor) **PA6003**
Latin Literature of the Fourth Century. Trade Cloth. Routledge. New York, NY. 1974. x, 189p. Greek and Latin Studies ISBN:0-7100-7796-3, ISBN13: 978-0-7100-7796-7. Dewey:870/.9/001. LCCN:73-091031.
Audience: **g,u,f.**

Braund, Susanna Morton **PA6003.B73 2001**
Latin Literature. Paper over Boards. Routledge. New York, NY. 2001. 320p. Classical Foundations Ser. ISBN:0-415-19517-9, ISBN13: 978-0-415-19517-1. Dewey:870.9. LCCN:2001-031920.
Audience: **g,l,u,f.** *Choice, 2002.*

Conte, Gian Biagio **PA6003**
Latin Literature: A History. Ed. 2. Joseph B. Solodow (Translator), Don P. Fowler & Glen W. Most (Revised by). Trade Paper. Johns Hopkins University Press. Baltimore, MD. 1999. 864p. ISBN:0-8018-6253-1, ISBN13: 978-0-8018-6253-3. Dewey:870.9/001.
Audience: **g,l,u,f.** *Choice, 1994.*

Courtney, Edward **PA2510.C68 1999**
Archaic Latin Prose. Trade Cloth. Oxford University Press, Inc. New York, NY. 1999. 164p. American Philological Association American Classical Studies ISBN:0-7885-0544-0, ISBN13: 978-0-7885-0544-7. Dewey:477. LCCN:99-012849.
Audience: **u,f.**

Courtney, Edward **PA6045**
The Fragmentary Latin Poets: Edited with Commentary. Ed. 2. Trade Paper. Oxford University Press, Inc. New York, NY. 2003. 566p. ISBN:0-19-926579-8, ISBN13: 978-0-19-926579-4. Dewey:871.0109. LCCN:2004-268659.
Audience: **u,f.**

Duff, J. Wight **PA6003**
A Literary History of Rome: From the Origins to the Close of the Golden Age. Ed. 3. A.M. Duff (Editor). Barnes & Noble. 1953.
Audience: **g,u,f.**

Duff, John W. **PA6042 .D8 1979**
A Literary History of Rome in the Silver Age: From Tiberius to Hadrian. Ed. 3. A. M. Duff (Editor). Trade Cloth. Greenwood Publishing Group, Inc. Portsmouth, NH. 1979. 607p. ISBN:0-313-20939-1, ISBN13: 978-0-313-20939-0. Dewey:870/.9. LCCN:79-009906.
Audience: **u,f.**

Fantham, Elaine **PA6003.F36 1996**
Roman Literary Culture: From Cicero to Apuleius. Trade Cloth. Johns Hopkins University Press. Baltimore, MD. 1978. 352p. Ancient Society and History Ser. ISBN:0-8018-5204-8, ISBN13: 978-0-8018-5204-6. Dewey:870.9/001. LCCN:95-037599.
Audience: **g,u,f.** *Choice, 1996.*

Fowler, Don **PA6003.F68 2000**
Roman Constructions: Readings in Postmodern Latin. Trade Cloth. Oxford University Press, Inc. New York, NY. 2000. 366p. ISBN:0-19-815309-0, ISBN13: 978-0-19-815309-2. Dewey:870.9/001. LCCN:99-047632.
Audience: **u,f.**

Habinek, Thomas N. **PA2293.H3 1985**
The Colometry of Latin Prose. Trade Paper. University of California Press. Berkeley, CA. 1985. University of California Publications in Classical Studies, Vol. 25 ISBN:0-520-09689-4, ISBN13: 978-0-520-09689-9. Dewey:475. LCCN:85-001135.
Audience: **f.**

Habinek, Thomas N. **PA6029.P64H33 1998**
The Politics of Latin Literature: Writing, Identity and Empire in Ancient Rome. Cloth Text. Princeton University Press. Princeton, NJ. 1998. 248p. ISBN:0-691-06827-5, ISBN13: 978-0-691-06827-5. Dewey:870.9/001. LCCN:97-040074.
Audience: **u,f.** *Choice, 1998.*

Harrison, Stephen (Editor) **PA6004.C66 2004**
A Companion to Latin Literature. Trade Cloth. Blackwell Publishing, Inc. Malden, MA. 2005. 472p. Blackwell

Companions to the Ancient World Ser. ISBN:0-631-23529-9, ISBN13: 978-0-631-23529-3. Dewey:870.9/001. LCCN:2004-005855.
Audience: **g,u,f.** *Choice, 2005.*

Kenney, Edwin J. & Clausen, W. V. (Editors) **PA6003.L3**
The Cambridge History of Classical Literature: Latin Literature. Trade Cloth. Cambridge University Press. New York, NY. 1982. 974p. The Cambridge History of Classical Literature Ser. ISBN:0-521-21043-7, ISBN13: 978-0-521-21043-0. Dewey:880/.09. LCCN:79-000121.
Audience: **g,l,u,f.** *B*

Reynolds, Leighton D. (Editor) **PA6004.T49 1983**
Texts and Transmission: A Survey of the Latin Classics. Trade Cloth. Oxford University Press, Inc. New York, NY. 1984. 556p. ISBN:0-19-814456-3, ISBN13: 978-0-19-814456-4. Dewey:870/.9/001. LCCN:84-148890.
Audience: **f.**

Rose, H. J. **PA6003.R6**
A Handbook of Latin Literature. Trade Cloth. Biblo & Tannen Booksellers & Publishers, Inc. Cheshire, CT. 550p. ISBN:0-8196-0356-2, ISBN13: 978-0-8196-0356-2. Dewey:870.9.
Audience: **g,u,f.**

Taplin, Oliver (Editor) **PA6003.L58 2001**
Literature in the Roman World. Trade Paper. Oxford University Press, Inc. New York, NY. 2001. 320p. ISBN:0-19-289301-7, ISBN13: 978-0-19-289301-7. Dewey:880/.09. LCCN:2001-126090.
Audience: **g,l,u,f.**

Warmington, E. H. (Editor) **PA6156.A1 1935A**
Remains of Old Latin. Trade Cloth. Harvard University Press. Cambridge, MA. Loeb Classical Library, Nos. 294, 314, 329, 359 ISBN:0-318-53174-7, ISBN13: 978-0-318-53174-8. Dewey:870.82.
Audience: **u,f.**

Williams, Gordon **PA6019**
Change and Decline: Roman Literature in the Early Empire. Trade Cloth. University of California Press. Berkeley, CA. 1978. viii, 344p. Sather Classical Lectures, No. 45 ISBN:0-520-03333-7, ISBN13: 978-0-520-03333-7. Dewey:870.9/001. LCCN:76-024598.
Audience: **u,f.**

Williams, Gordon **PA6047**
Tradition and Originality in Roman Poetry. Cloth Text. Oxford University Press, Inc. New York, NY. 1987. 820p. ISBN:0-19-814347-8, ISBN13: 978-0-19-814347-5. Dewey:871/.01/09.
Audience: **u,f.**

Latin > Genres > Prose Fiction

Harrison, S. J. **PA6091.O94 1999**
Oxford Readings in the Roman Novel. Trade Paper. Oxford University Press, Inc. New York, NY. 1999. 378p. ISBN:0-19-872174-9, ISBN13: 978-0-19-872174-1. Dewey:873/.0109. LCCN:98-040793.
Audience: **u,f.**

Walsh, P. **PA6559**
Roman Novel. Ed. 2. Trade Paper. Bristol Classical Press. London, 1995. 286p. Classical Paperbacks Ser. ISBN:1-85399-450-2, ISBN13: 978-1-85399-450-0. Dewey:873.1/09.
Audience: **g,u,f.**

Latin > Genres > Drama

Beacham, Richard C. **PA6073.B44**
Roman Theatre and Its Audience. Trade Paper. Routledge. New York, NY. 1999. 288p. ISBN:0-415-12163-9, ISBN13: 978-0-415-12163-7. Dewey:792.0937.
Audience: **u,f.**

Beare, William **PA6067.B4**
The Roman Stage. Ed. 2. Trade Paper. Books on Demand. Ann Arbor, MI. 394p. ISBN:0-598-97264-1, ISBN13: 978-0-598-97264-4. Dewey:792.0937. LCCN:55-003218.
Audience: **u,f.**

Boyle, A. J. **PA6068.B69 2005**
Roman Tragedy. Paper over Boards. Routledge. New York, NY. 2005. 320p. ISBN:0-415-25102-8, ISBN13: 978-0-415-25102-0. Dewey:872/.0109. LCCN:2005-006892.
Audience: **u,f.**

Duckworth, George Eckel **PA6069 .D8 1994**
The Nature of Roman Comedy: A Study in Popular Entertainment. Ed. 2. R. L. Hunter (Foreword by). Trade Paper. University of Oklahoma Press. Norman, OK. 1994. 526p. ISBN:0-8061-2620-5, ISBN13: 978-0-8061-2620-3. Dewey:872/.0109. LCCN:93-027544.
Audience: **l,u,f.** *B*

Segal, Erich (Editor) **PA3028**
Oxford Readings in Menander, Plautus, and Terence. Trade Cloth. Oxford University Press, Inc. New York, NY. 2002. 308p. Oxford Readings in Classical Studies ISBN:0-19-872192-7, ISBN13: 978-0-19-872192-5. Dewey:872/.0109.
Audience: **u,f.**

Latin > Genres > Epic

Boyle, Anthony James **PA6054**
Roman Epic. Trade Paper. Routledge. New York, NY. 1996. 352p. ISBN:0-415-14357-8, ISBN13: 978-0-415-14357-8. Dewey:873/.009.
Audience: **g,l,u,f.**

Hardie, Philip **PA6054 .H28 1993**
The Epic Successors of Virgil: A Study in the Dynamics of a Tradition. Denis Feeney & Stephen Hinds (Contribution by). Trade Paper. Cambridge University Press. New York, NY. 1992. 141p. Roman Literature and Its Contexts Ser. ISBN:0-521-42562-X, ISBN13: 978-0-521-42562-9. Dewey:873.0109. LCCN:91-046846.
Audience: **u,f.**

Keith, A. M. **PA6054 .K44 2000**
Engendering Rome: Women in Latin Epic. Denis Feeney & Stephen Hinds (Contribution by). Trade Paper. Cambridge

University Press. New York, NY. 2000. 161p. Roman Literature and Its Contexts Ser. ISBN:0-521-55621-X, ISBN13: 978-0-521-55621-7. Dewey:873.0109352042. LCCN:99-023184.
Audience: **u,f.** *Choice, 2000.*

Latin > Genres > Epistolography

Levens, R. G. (Editor) **PA6139 .E7**
A Book of Latin Letters. Trade Paper. Blackwell Publishing, Inc. Malden, MA. 1989. 196p. Classical Texts Ser. ISBN:0-631-13867-6, ISBN13: 978-0-631-13867-9. Dewey:478.6421.
Audience: **l,u.**

Trapp, Michael (Editor) **PA3487.E4G74 2003**
Greek and Latin Letters: An Anthology with Translation. P. E. Easterling, Philip Hardie, Richard Hunter & E. J. Kenney (Contribution by). Cloth Text. Cambridge University Press. New York, NY. 2003. 358p. Cambridge Greek and Latin Classics Ser. ISBN:0-521-49597-0, ISBN13: 978-0-521-49597-4. Dewey:880. LCCN:2002-031214.
Audience: **u,f.**

Latin > Genres > History

Forsythe, Gary **DG206.P57F67 1994**
The Historian L. Calpurnius Piso Frugi and the Roman Annalistic Tradition. Trade Cloth. University Press of America, Inc. Lanham, MD. 1994. 564p. ISBN:0-8191-9742-4, ISBN13: 978-0-8191-9742-9. Dewey:937/.02/092. LCCN:94-034339.
Audience: **u,f.**

Kraus, Christina S. & Woodman, Anthony J. **DG206.A2**
Latin Historians. Oxford University Press. 1997. Greece & Rome. New Surveys in the Classics ISBN:0-19-922293-2, ISBN13: 978-0-19-922293-3.
Audience: **u,f.**

Laistner, Max L. **DG206.A2.L3**
The Greater Roman Historians. Trade Cloth. University of California Press. Berkeley, CA. 1947. Sather Classical Lectures, No. 21 ISBN:0-520-03365-5, ISBN13: 978-0-520-03365-8. Dewey:937.007.
Audience: **g,l,u,f.**

Mellor, Ronald **DG205.M45 1999**
The Roman Historians. Paper over Boards. Routledge. New York, NY. 1999. 224p. ISBN:0-415-11773-9, ISBN13: 978-0-415-11773-9. Dewey:937/.0072022. LCCN:98-027442.
Audience: **g,l,u,f.**

Plass, Paul **DG205.P53 1988**
Wit and the Writing of History: The Rhetoric of Historiography in Imperial Rome. Paper Text. University of Wisconsin Press. Chicago, IL. 1988. 204p. Studies in Classics ISBN:0-299-11804-5, ISBN13: 978-0-299-11804-4. Dewey:937/.0072. LCCN:88-040193.
Audience: **u,f.** *Choice, 1989.*

Potter, David S. **PA6021.P68 1999**
Literary Texts and the Roman Historian. Paper over Boards. Routledge. New York, NY. 1999. 232p. Approaching the Ancient World Ser. ISBN:0-415-08895-X, ISBN13: 978-0-415-08895-4. Dewey:870.9/358. LCCN:98-008690.
Audience: **u,f.**

Wiseman, T. P. **D13.5.R65**
Clio's Cosmetics. Trade Cloth. Bristol Phoenix Press. Exeter, 2004. 209p. Ignibus Paperback Ser. ISBN:1-904675-00-X, ISBN13: 978-1-904675-00-6. Dewey:907.2/037.
Audience: **u,f.**

Woodman, A. J. **PA181.W66 1988**
Rhetoric in Classical Historiography: Four Studies. E-Book. Taylor & Francis Group. Philadelphia, PA. ISBN:0-203-48053-8, ISBN13: 978-0-203-48053-3. Dewey:907/.2.
Audience: **u,f.** *Choice, 1988.*

Latin > Genres > Lyric and Elegiac Poetry

James, Sharon L. **PA6059.E6 J36 2003**
Learned Girls and Male Persuasion: Gender and Reading in Roman Love Elegy. Trade Cloth. University of California Press. Berkeley, CA. 2003. 368p. Joan Palevsky Imprint in Classical Literature Ser. ISBN:0-520-23381-6, ISBN13: 978-0-520-23381-2. Dewey:871/.01093543. LCCN:2002-010143.
Audience: **u,f.** *Choice, 2003.*

Kennedy, Duncan F. **PA6059.E6 K46 1992**
The Arts of Love: Five Studies in the Discourse of Roman Love Elegy. Cloth Text. Cambridge University Press. New York, NY. 1992. 119p. Roman Literature and Its Contexts Ser. ISBN:0-521-40422-3, ISBN13: 978-0-521-40422-8. Dewey:871.0109354. LCCN:91-046973.
Audience: **u,f.**

Luck, Georg **PA6059.E6.L8**
The Latin Love Elegy. Ed. 2. Trade Cloth. Methuen & Company, Ltd. London, 1969. 192p. ISBN:0-416-14230-3, ISBN13: 978-0-416-14230-3. Dewey:874/.01/09. LCCN:73-453406.
Audience: **l,u,f.**

Miller, Paul Allen **PA6127.L38 2002**
Latin Erotic Elegy: An Anthology and Reader. Paper over Boards. Routledge. New York, NY. 2002. 496p. ISBN:0-415-24371-8, ISBN13: 978-0-415-24371-1. Dewey:871/.01083543. LCCN:2001-048560.
Audience: **l,u,f.**

Putnam, Michael C. **PA6047.P8**
Essays on Latin Lyric, Elegy, and Epic. Trade Paper. Books on Demand. Ann Arbor, MI. 1982. 371p. Princeton Series of Collected Essays Ser. ISBN:0-608-02593-3, ISBN13: 978-0-608-02593-3. Dewey:871/.01/09. LCCN:81-047944.
Audience: **u,f.**

Rayor, Diane J. & Batstone, William W. (Editors) **PA6164.L38 1995**
Latin Lyric and Elegiac Poetry: An Anthology of New Translations. William S. Anderson (Introduction by). Cloth Text.

Garland Publishing, Inc. New York, NY. 1995. 384p.
ISBN:0-8153-0087-5, ISBN13: 978-0-8153-0087-8.
Dewey:871/.0108. LCCN:94-037902.
Audience: **g,l,u.** *Choice, 1995.*

Ross, D. O. **PA6047**
Backgrounds to Augustan Poetry, Gallus, Elegy and Rome. Trade Cloth. Cambridge University Press. New York, NY. 1975. 184p. ISBN:0-521-20704-5, ISBN13: 978-0-521-20704-1. Dewey:871/.01/09. LCCN:74-031782.
Audience: **u,f.**

Latin > Genres > Oratory and Rhetoric

Cicero, Marcus Tullius **PA6156**
Cicero: Rhetorica ad Herennium, A. Rhetorical Treatises. Harry Caplan (Translator). Trade Cloth. Harvard University Press. Cambridge, MA. 1981. 496p. Loeb Classical Library, Vol. 403 ISBN:0-674-99444-2, ISBN13: 978-0-674-99444-7. Dewey:876.01.
Audience: **g,u,f.**

Clarke, M. L. **PA6083.C6 1996**
Rhetoric at Rome: A Historical Survey. Ed. 3. D. H. Berry (Introduction by). Trade Paper. Routledge. New York, NY. 1996. 224p. Classical Studies ISBN:0-415-14156-7, ISBN13: 978-0-415-14156-7. Dewey:875/.009. LCCN:96-003816.
Audience: **g,u,f.**

Dominik, William J. (Editor) **PA6019.R66 1997**
Roman Eloquence: Rhetoric in Society and Literature. Paper over Boards. Routledge. New York, NY. 1997. 280p. ISBN:0-415-12544-8, ISBN13: 978-0-415-12544-4. Dewey:808/.00937. LCCN:96-052767.
Audience: **u,f.**

Kennedy, George A. **PA6085.K4**
The Art of Rhetoric in the Roman World, 300 B.C.-A.D. 300. Trade Paper. Books on Demand. Ann Arbor, MI. 674p. His a History of Rhetoric Ser., Vol. 2 ISBN:0-8357-3389-0, ISBN13: 978-0-8357-3389-2. Dewey:808/.047/1. LCCN:72-166380.
Audience: **g,l,u,f.**

Kennedy, George Alexander **PA3038.O73 2001**
The Orator in Action and Theory in Greece and Rome: Essays in Honor of George A. Kennedy. Cecil W. Wooten (Editor). Trade Cloth. Brill Academic Publishers, Inc. Boston, MA. 2001. "xviii, 174"p. Mnemosyne, Bibliotheca Classica Batava Ser., Vol. 224 ISBN:90-04-12213-3, ISBN13: 978-90-04-12213-0. Dewey:808.5/1/0938. LCCN:2001-043199.
Audience: **u,f.**

Latin > Genres > Satire

Braund, Susan H. **PA6056.B73 1992**
Roman Verse Satire. Oxford University Press. 1992. Greece & Rome. New Surveys in the Classics ISBN:0-19-922072-7, ISBN13: 978-0-19-922072-4.
Audience: **u,f.**

Coffey, M. **PA6056.C6 1989**
Roman Satire. Ed. 2. Trade Paper. Bristol Classical Press. London, 1989. 312p. Classical Paperbacks Ser. ISBN:1-85399-046-9, ISBN13: 978-1-85399-046-5. Dewey:877/.01/09. LCCN:90-129450.
Audience: **g,l,u,f.**

Dominick, William J. & Wehrle, William T. **PA6164.R638 1999**
Roman Verse Satirists Lucilius to Juvenal: A Selection. Book, Other. Bolchazy-Carducci Publishers. Wauconda, IL. 2000. 219p. ISBN:0-86516-442-8, ISBN13: 978-0-86516-442-0. Dewey:871/.070801. LCCN:99-051347.
Audience: **l,u.**

Freudenburg, Kirk (Editor) **PA6095.C36 2005**
The Cambridge Companion to Roman Satire. Cloth Text. Cambridge University Press. New York, NY. 2005. 372p. Cambridge Companions to Literature Ser. ISBN:0-521-80359-4, ISBN13: 978-0-521-80359-5. Dewey:877/.010932376. LCCN:2004-057024.
Audience: **g,l,u,f.** *Choice, 2006.*

Freudenburg, Kirk **PA6056.F74 2001**
The Satires of Rome: Threatening Poses from Lucilius to Juvenal. Cloth Text. Cambridge University Press. New York, NY. 2001. 308p. ISBN:0-521-80357-8, ISBN13: 978-0-521-80357-1. Dewey:871/.0109. LCCN:2001-025772.
Audience: **u,f.**

Highet, Gilbert **PN6149.S2H5**
The Anatomy of Satire. Paper Text. Textbook Publishers. Temecula, CA. 2003. 301p. ISBN:0-7581-5761-4, ISBN13: 978-0-7581-5761-4. Dewey:809.7.
Audience: **g,l,u,f.**

Knoche, Ulrich **PA6056.K613 1975**
Roman Satire. Edwin S. Ramage (Translator). Trade Cloth. Indiana University Press. Bloomington, IN. 1975. 320p. ISBN:0-253-35020-4, ISBN13: 978-0-253-35020-6. Dewey:877/.01/09. LCCN:74-025014.
Audience: **u,f.**

McKay, Alexander G. & Shepherd, D. M. (Editors) **PA6134**
Roman Satire: Horace, Juvenal, Persius, Petronius, and Seneca. Cloth Text. Palgrave Macmillan. New York, NY. 1976. ISBN:0-312-69090-8, ISBN13: 978-0-312-69090-8. Dewey:877/.01/08. LCCN:75-029860.
Audience: **l,u.**

Miller, Paul Allen (Editor) **PA6134.L38 2005**
Latin Verse Satire: An Anthology and Critical Reader. Paper over Boards. Routledge. New York, NY. 2005. 408p. ISBN:0-415-31715-0, ISBN13: 978-0-415-31715-3. Dewey:871/.070801. LCCN:2004-021780.
Audience: **u,f.**

Relihan, Joel C. **PA3033.R44 1993**
Ancient Menippean Satire. Trade Cloth. Johns Hopkins University Press. Baltimore, MD. 1993. 328p. ISBN:0-8018-4524-6, ISBN13: 978-0-8018-4524-6. Dewey:887.0109. LCCN:92-036271.
Audience: **u,f.** *Choice, 1994.*

Latin > Individual Authors > Caesar

Caesar, Julius **DG266**
The Civil War: With the Anonymous Alexandrian, African, and Spanish Wars. John Carter (Translator, Introduction by, Notes by). Trade Paper. Oxford University Press, Inc. New York, NY. 1999. 418p. Oxford World's Classics Ser. ISBN:0-19-283923-3, ISBN13: 978-0-19-283923-7. Dewey:937/.05.
Audience: **g,l,u.**

Caesar, Julius **PA6238**
Commentarii: De Bello Civili Cum Libris Incertorum Auctorum de Bello Alexandrino Africo Hispaniensi. R. L. Du Pontet (Editor). Cloth Text. Oxford University Press, Inc. New York, NY. 1922. 304p. Oxford Classical Texts ISBN:0-19-814603-5, ISBN13: 978-0-19-814603-2. Dewey:870.
Audience: **u,f.**

Caesar, Julius **PA6238**
Commentarii: Bello Gallico Cum A. Hirti Supplemento, Vol. I. R. L. Du Pontet (Editor). Cloth Text. Oxford University Press, Inc. New York, NY. 1968. 239p. Oxford Classical Texts ISBN:0-19-814602-7, ISBN13: 978-0-19-814602-5. Dewey:870.
Audience: **u,f.**

Caesar, Julius **PA6235**
Caesar: Gallic War I. C. Ewan (Introduction by). Trade Paper. Bristol Classical Press. London, 1985. 166p. Latin Texts ISBN:0-86292-177-5, ISBN13: 978-0-86292-177-4. Dewey:936.4.
Audience: **l,u.**

Caesar, Julius **DC62**
Seven Commentaries on the Gallic War. Carolyn Hammond (Translator), Aulus Hirtius (Commentaries by). Trade Paper. Oxford University Press, Inc. New York, NY. 1999. 314p. Oxford World's Classics Ser. ISBN:0-19-283582-3, ISBN13: 978-0-19-283582-6. Dewey:936.4/02.
Audience: **g,l,u.**

Gelzer, Matthias **DG261**
Caesar: Politician and Statesman. Trade Paper. Harvard University Press. Cambridge, MA. 1985. 368p. ISBN:0-674-09001-2, ISBN13: 978-0-674-09001-9. Dewey:937.050924.
Audience: **g,u,f.** B

Meier, Christian **DG261.M3713 1996**
Caesar. David McLintock (Translator). Paper Text. Basic Books. New York, NY. 1997. 528p. ISBN:0-465-00895-X, ISBN13: 978-0-465-00895-7. Dewey:937/.05/092. LCCN:95-030003.
Audience: **g,u,f.**

Latin > Individual Authors > Ammianus Marcellinus

Ammianus Marcellinus **PA6205**
Roman History. Trade Cloth. Harvard University Press. Cambridge, MA. Loeb Classical Library, No. 300, 315, 331 ISBN:0-318-53177-1, ISBN13: 978-0-318-53177-9. Dewey:937/.08.
Audience: **g,l,u.**

Ammianus Marcellinus **PA6203.A2 1980**
Ammianus Marcellinus: A Selection. R. C. Blockley (Selected by). Trade Cloth. Bristol Classical Press. London, 1981. 168p. ISBN:0-906515-07-6, ISBN13: 978-0-906515-07-5. Dewey:937/.06. LCCN:83-200632.
Audience: **u.**

Ammianus Marcellinus **DG316.7**
The Later Roman Empire A. D. 354-378. Walter Hamilton (Translator), Andrew W. Hadrill (Introduction by). Trade Paper. Penguin Group (USA) Inc. New York, NY. 1986. 512p. Classics Ser. ISBN:0-14-044406-8, ISBN13: 978-0-14-044406-3. Dewey:937/.08. LCCN:86-193724.
Audience: **g,l,u.**

Barnes, Timothy D. **DG316.B37 1998**
Ammianus Marcellinus and the Representation of Historical Reality. Book, Other. Cornell University Press. Ithaca, NY. 1998. 336p. Studies in Classical Philology ISBN:0-8014-3526-9, ISBN13: 978-0-8014-3526-3. Dewey:937/.007/202. LCCN:98-019791.
Audience: **u,f.** *Choice, 1999.*

Matthews, John F. **DG0316.7.M38**
The Roman Empire of Ammianus. Trade Paper. Books on Demand. Ann Arbor, MI. 1989. 623p. ISBN:0-608-03735-4, ISBN13: 978-0-608-03735-6. Dewey:937/.08. LCCN:89-045756.
Audience: **u,f.**

Latin > Individual Authors > Apuleius

Apuleius **PA6209.M3.H36 1989**
Metamorphoses, Bks. 7-11. J. Arthur Hanson (Translator). Trade Cloth. Harvard University Press. Cambridge, MA. 1990. 384p. Loeb Classical Library, Nos. 44 & 453 ISBN:0-674-99498-1, ISBN13: 978-0-674-99498-0. Dewey:873/.01. LCCN:89-015577.
Audience: **g,l,u.**

Apuleius **PA6209.M73 2002**
Apuleius: Rhetorical Works. S. J. Harrison (Editor), Stephen Harrison, John Hilton & Vincent Hunink (Translators), Stephen Harrison, John Hilton & Vincent Hunink (Annotations by). Cloth Text. Oxford University Press, Inc. New York, NY. 2001. 240p. ISBN:0-19-815292-2, ISBN13: 978-0-19-815292-7. Dewey:875/.01. LCCN:2001-021767.
Audience: **u,f.** *Choice, 2002.*

Apuleius **PA6207 .M4 1990**
Apuleius: Cupid and Psyche. Edwin J. Kenney (Editor), P. E. Easterling (Contribution by). Trade Cloth. Cambridge University Press. New York, NY. 1990. 253p. Greek and Latin Classics Ser. ISBN:0-521-26038-8, ISBN13: 978-0-521-26038-1. Dewey:873/.01. LCCN:90-001613.
Audience: **u,f.**

Apuleius **PA6825**
The Golden Ass. P. G. Walsh (Translator). Trade Paper. Oxford University Press, Inc. New York, NY. 1999. 332p. Oxford World's Classics Ser. ISBN:0-19-283888-1, ISBN13: 978-0-19-283888-9. Dewey:873./01.
Audience: **g,l,u.**

Hanson, J. Arthur (Translator) **PA6209.M3H36 1989**
Metamorphoses, Bks. 1-6. Apuleius (Selected by). Trade Cloth. Harvard University Press. Cambridge, MA. 1990. 392p. Loeb Classical Library, Nos. 44 & 453 ISBN:0-674-99049-8, ISBN13: 978-0-674-99049-4. Dewey:873/.01. LCCN:89-015577.
Audience: **g,l,u.**

Schlam, Carl C. **PA6217.S27 1992**
The Metamorphoses of Apuleius: On Making An Ass of Oneself. Trade Cloth. University of North Carolina Press. Chapel Hill, NC. 1992. 186p. ISBN:0-8078-2013-X, ISBN13: 978-0-8078-2013-1. Dewey:873/.01. LCCN:91-031412.
Audience: **u,f.** *Choice, 1992.*

Winkler, John J. **PA6825**
Auctor and Actor: A Narratological Reading of Apuleius' "The Golden Ass". Trade Paper. University of California Press. Berkeley, CA. 1991. 353p. ISBN:0-520-07639-7, ISBN13: 978-0-520-07639-6. Dewey:873/.01. LCCN:84-000182.
Audience: **u,f.** *Choice, 1986.*

Latin > Individual Authors > Augustine of Hippo

Augustine **PA6156**
Confessions, Bks. 1-8. Trade Cloth. Harvard University Press. Cambridge, MA. 1912. 480p. Loeb Classical Library, No. 26-27 ISBN:0-674-99029-3, ISBN13: 978-0-674-99029-6. Dewey:270.2092.
Audience: **g,l,u.**

Augustine **BR65.A52**
Select Letters. Trade Cloth. Harvard University Press. Cambridge, MA. 1930. 592p. Loeb Classical Library, No. 239 ISBN:0-674-99264-4, ISBN13: 978-0-674-99264-1. Dewey:281.4.
Audience: **g,l,u.**

Augustine (Editor) **BR65.A6**
Confessions. Henry Chadwick (Translator, Introduction by, Notes by). Trade Paper. Oxford University Press, Inc. New York, NY. 1998. 340p. Oxford World's Classics Ser. ISBN:0-19-283372-3, ISBN13: 978-0-19-283372-3. Dewey:270.2092.
Audience: **g,l,u.**

Augustine **BR65 .A6 1995**
Augustine: Confessions, Bks. I-IV. Gillian Clark (Editor), P. E. Easterling & E. J. Kenney (Contribution by). Cloth Text. Cambridge University Press. New York, NY. 1995. 208p. Cambridge Greek and Latin Classics - Imperial Library ISBN:0-521-49734-5, ISBN13: 978-0-521-49734-3. Dewey:270.2092. LCCN:95-003118.
Audience: **u,f.**

Augustine **BR65.A5**
City of God. Gill Evans (Editor), Henry Bettenson (Translator). Trade Paper. Penguin Group (USA) Inc. New York, NY. 2004. 1168p. ISBN:0-14-044894-2, ISBN13: 978-0-14-044894-8. Dewey:230/.01.
Audience: **g,l,u.**

Augustine **BR65.A64**
City of God Against the Pagans, Bks. 4-7. W. M. Green (Translator). Trade Cloth. Harvard University Press. Cambridge, MA. 1963. 544p. Loeb Classical Library, No. 411-417 ISBN:0-674-99453-1, ISBN13: 978-0-674-99453-9. Dewey:239/.3.
Audience: **g,l,u.**

Augustine **BR65.A64**
City of God Against the Pagans, Bks. 16-18. 35. W. M. Green (Translator). Trade Cloth. Harvard University Press. Cambridge, MA. 1965. 528p. Loeb Classical Library, No. 411-417 ISBN:0-674-99457-4, ISBN13: 978-0-674-99457-7. Dewey:239/.3.
Audience: **g,l,u.**

Augustine **BR65.A64**
City of God Against the Pagans, Bks. 21-22. W. M. Green (Translator). Trade Cloth. Harvard University Press. Cambridge, MA. 1972. 480p. Loeb Classical Library, No. 411-417 ISBN:0-674-99459-0, ISBN13: 978-0-674-99459-1. Dewey:239/.3.
Audience: **g,l,u.**

Augustine **PA6156**
City of God Against the Pagans, Bks. 18. 36-20. W. C. Greene (Translator). Trade Cloth. Harvard University Press. Cambridge, MA. 1960. 462p. Loeb Classical Library, No. 411-417 ISBN:0-674-99458-2, ISBN13: 978-0-674-99458-4. Dewey:239.3.
Audience: **g,l,u.**

Augustine **PA6156**
City of God Against the Pagans, Bks. 12-15. Philip Levine (Translator). Trade Cloth. Harvard University Press. Cambridge, MA. 1966. 592p. Loeb Classical Library, No. 411-417 ISBN:0-674-99456-6, ISBN13: 978-0-674-99456-0. Dewey:239.3.
Audience: **g,l,u.**

Augustine **BR65**
City of God Against the Pagans, Vol. 1. G. E. McCracken (Translator). Trade Cloth. Harvard University Press. Cambridge, MA. 1957. 496p. Loeb Classical Library, No. 411-417 ISBN:0-674-99452-3, ISBN13: 978-0-674-99452-2. Dewey:239.3.
Audience: **g,l,u.**

Augustine **BR65.A6 1992**
Confessions: Commentary. James J. O'Donnell (Editor). Cloth Text. Oxford University Press, Inc. New York, NY. 1992. 504p. ISBN:0-19-814074-6, ISBN13: 978-0-19-814074-0. Dewey:270.2092. LCCN:92-012361.
Audience: **u,f.**

Augustine **BR65.A6 1992**
Confessions: Text and Prolegomena. James J. O'Donnell (Editor). Cloth Text. Oxford University Press, Inc. New York, NY. 1992. 280p. ISBN:0-19-814378-8, ISBN13: 978-0-19-814378-9. Dewey:270.2092. LCCN:92-012361.
Audience: **u,f.**

Augustine **BR65.A6 1992**
Confessions: Commentary. James J. O'Donnell (Editor). Cloth Text. Oxford University Press, Inc. New York, NY. 1992. 496p. ISBN:0-19-814075-4, ISBN13: 978-0-19-814075-7. Dewey:270.2092. LCCN:92-012361.
Audience: **u,f.**

Augustine **PA6156**
Confessions, Bks. 9-13. W. Watts (Translator). Trade Cloth. Harvard University Press. Cambridge, MA. 1912. 496p. Loeb Classical Library, No. 26-27 ISBN:0-674-99030-7, ISBN13: 978-0-674-99030-2. Dewey:270.2092.
Audience: **g,l,u.**

Brown, Peter **BR1720.A9B7 2000**
Augustine of Hippo: A Biography with a New Epilogue. Trade Paper. University of California Press. Berkeley, CA. 2000. 562p. ISBN:0-520-22757-3, ISBN13: 978-0-520-22757-6. LCCN:2001-268207.
Audience: **g,l,u,f.**

MacCormack, Sabine **BR65.A9 M24 1998**
The Shadows of Poetry: Vergil in the Mind of Augustine. Trade Cloth. University of California Press. Berkeley, CA. 1998. 280p. Transformation of the Classical Heritage Ser., Vol. 26 ISBN:0-520-21187-1, ISBN13: 978-0-520-21187-2. Dewey:270.2/092. LCCN:97-045014.
Audience: **u,f.**

O'Donnell, James J. **BR1720.A9O36 2005**
Augustine: A New Biography. Trade Cloth. HarperCollins Publishers. New York, NY. 2005. 416p. ISBN:0-06-053537-7, ISBN13: 978-0-06-053537-7. Dewey:270.2/092 B. LCCN:2004-058347.
Audience: **g,l,u,f.**

Stump, Eleonore & Kretzmann, Norman (Editors) **B655.Z7C35 2001**
The Cambridge Companion to Augustine. Cloth Text. Cambridge University Press. New York, NY. 2001. 324p. Cambridge Companions to Philosophy Ser. ISBN:0-521-65018-6, ISBN13: 978-0-521-65018-2. Dewey:189/.2. LCCN:00-031173.
Audience: **g,l,u,f.** *Choice, 2002.*

Wiesen, David S. (Translator) **PA6156**
City of God Against the Pagans, Bks. 8-11. Trade Cloth. Harvard University Press. Cambridge, MA. 1968. 592p. Loeb Classical Library, No. 411-417 ISBN:0-674-99455-8, ISBN13: 978-0-674-99455-3. Dewey:239.3.
Audience: **g,l,u.**

Latin > Individual Authors > Catullus

Catullus, Gaius Valerius **PA6274.A2 2004**
The Student's Catullus. Ed. 3. Daniel H. Garrison (Editor). Trade Paper. University of Oklahoma Press. Norman, OK. 2004. 256p. Oklahoma Series in Classical Culture, Vol. 5 ISBN:0-8061-3635-9, ISBN13: 978-0-8061-3635-6. Dewey:874/.01. LCCN:2004-051734.
Audience: **l,u.**

Catullus, Gaius Valerius **PA6275.E5 G74 2005**
The Poems of Catullus: A Bilingual Edition. Peter Green (Translator). Trade Cloth. University of California Press. Berkeley, CA. 2005. 360p. ISBN:0-520-24264-5, ISBN13: 978-0-520-24264-7. Dewey:874/.01. LCCN:2004-013920.
Audience: **g,l,u.** *Choice, 2006.*

Catullus, Gaius Valerius **PA6105.S8 C26**
Carmina. Roger A. Mynors (Editor). Cloth Text. Oxford University Press, Inc. New York, NY. 1958. 136p. Oxford Classical Texts ISBN:0-19-814604-3, ISBN13: 978-0-19-814604-9. Dewey:937.0072.
Audience: **u,f.** B

Catullus, Gaius Valerius **PA6274.A2**
Catullus: Poems. Kenneth Quinn (Editor). Trade Paper. Bristol Classical Press. London, 1996. 334p. Latin Texts ISBN:1-85399-497-9, ISBN13: 978-1-85399-497-5. Dewey:874/.01.
Audience: **u,f.**

Catullus, Gaius Valerius **PA6276.T49 1997**
Catullus, Vol. 34. D. F. Thomson (Editor). Cloth over Boards. University of Toronto Press. Toronto, ON. 1996. 578p. Phoenix Supplementary Volumes Ser., Vol. 34 ISBN:0-8020-0676-0, ISBN13: 978-0-8020-0676-9. Dewey:874/.01. LCCN:97-181192.
Audience: **u,f.** *Choice, 1997.*

Ferguson, John **PA6276.F47 1988**
Catullus. Oxford University Press. 1988. Greece & Rome. New Surveys in the Classics
Audience: **u,f.**

Fitzgerald, William **PA6825**
Catullan Provocations: Lyric Poetry and the Drama of Position. Trade Paper. University of California Press. Berkeley, CA. 2000. 320p. Classics and Contemporary Thought Ser. ISBN:0-520-22156-7, ISBN13: 978-0-520-22156-7. Dewey:871/.01.
Audience: **u,f.**

Fordyce, C. J. **PA6276 .F55 1990**
Catullus. Trade Paper. Oxford University Press, Inc. New York, NY. 1990. 452p. ISBN:0-19-872147-1, ISBN13: 978-0-19-872147-5. Dewey:874/.01. LCCN:91-155742.
Audience: **u,f.**

Martin, Charles **PA6276.M37 1992**
Catullus. Cloth over Boards. Yale University Press. Cumberland, RI. 1992. 192p. Hermes Bks. ISBN:0-300-05199-9, ISBN13: 978-0-300-05199-5. Dewey:874.01. LCCN:91-040354.
Audience: **g,l,u.** *Choice, 1992.*

Quinn, Kenneth **PA6411**
The Catullan Revolution. Ed. 2. Trade Paper. Bristol Classical Press. London, 132p. Bristol Classical Paperbacks Ser. ISBN:1-85399-600-9, ISBN13: 978-1-85399-600-9. Dewey:874/.01.
Audience: **u,f.** B

Ross, David O. **PA6276.R57**
Style and Tradition in Catullus. Trade Cloth. Harvard University Press. Cambridge, MA. 1969. 200p. ISBN:0-674-85340-7, ISBN13: 978-0-674-85340-9. Dewey:871/.01. LCCN:69-018043.
Audience: **u,f.** B

Wheeler, Arthur L. **PA6276**
Catullus and the Traditions of Ancient Poetry. Trade Cloth. University of California Press. Berkeley, CA. 1974. Sather Classical Lectures, No. 9 ISBN:0-520-02640-3, ISBN13: 978-0-520-02640-7. Dewey:874.2.
Audience: **u,f.**

Wiseman, T. P. **PA6411**
Catullus and His World: A Reappraisal. Trade Paper. Cambridge University Press. New York, NY. 1986. 304p. ISBN:0-521-31968-4, ISBN13: 978-0-521-31968-3. Dewey:874/.01.
Audience: **u,f.** *Choice, 1986.*

Latin > Individual Authors > Cicero

Cerutti, Steven M. **PA6279.A93C47 1999**
Cicero Pro Archia Poeta Oratio: A Syntactic Analysis of the Speech and Companion to the Commentary. Book, Other. Bolchazy-Carducci Publishers. Wauconda, IL. 1999. 128p. ISBN:0-86516-439-8, ISBN13: 978-0-86516-439-0. Dewey:875/.01. LCCN:99-021314.
Audiencc: **l,u,f.**

Cicero, Marcus Tullius **PA6296**
Cicero Brutus, Orator: Rhetorical Treatises. Trade Cloth. Harvard University Press. Cambridge, MA. 1971. 544p. Loeb Classical Library, No. 342 ISBN:0-674-99377-2, ISBN13: 978-0-674-99377-8. Dewey:870.
Audience: **g,l,u,f.**

Cicero, Marcus Tullius **PA6308.D2 W66 2001**
Cicero: On Moral Ends. Julia Annas (Editor), Raphael Woolf (Translator), Karl Ameriks & Desmond M. Clarke (Contribution by). Cloth Text. Cambridge University Press. New York, NY. 2001. 200p. Texts in the History of Philosophy ISBN:0-521-66061-0, ISBN13: 978-0-521-66061-7. Dewey:171. LCCN:2002-265146.
Audience: **g,l,u,f.**

Cicero, Marcus Tullius **PA6279.C18 1988**
Pro M. Caelio Oratio. Ed. 3. Roland G. Austin (Editor). Trade Paper. Oxford University Press, Inc. New York, NY. 1988. 212p. ISBN:0-19-814062-2, ISBN13: 978-0-19-814062-7. Dewey:875/.01. LCCN:87-034985.
Audience: **u,f.**

Cicero, Marcus Tullius **PA6296.C2**
Cicero: On Old Age. Charles E. Bennett (Editor). Book, Other. Bolchazy-Carducci Publishers. Wauconda, IL. 2002. 326p. Textbook Ser. ISBN:0-86516-001-5, ISBN13: 978-0-86516-001-9. Dewey:878.
Audience: **l,u.**

Cicero, Marcus Tullius **PA6279 .A9 1998**
Cicero Pro Archia. Steven M. Cerutti (Introduction by, Commentaries by). Book, Other. Bolchazy-Carducci Publishers. Wauconda, IL. 1998. 160p. ISBN:0-86516-402-9, ISBN13: 978-0-86516-402-4. Dewey:875/.01. LCCN:97-041985.
Audience: **l,u.**

Cicero, Marcus Tullius **PA6308.T6**
Cicero: Tusculan Didputations I. A. E. Douglas (Editor). Trade Cloth. Aris & Phillips. Oxford, 1985. 200p. Classical Texts Ser. ISBN:0-85668-250-0, ISBN13: 978-0-85668-250-6. Dewey:878.
Audience: **l,u.**

Cicero, Marcus Tullius **BF637.S4**
Cicero: Tusculan Disputations II and V. A. E. Douglas (Editor). Trade Cloth. Aris & Phillips. Oxford, 1989. viii, 166p. Classical Texts Ser. ISBN:0-85668-432-5, ISBN13: 978-0-85668-432-6. Dewey:158/.1.
Audience: **l,u.** *Choice, 1990.*

Cicero, Marcus Tullius **PA6156**
Cicero: De Natura Deorum. Andrew R. Dyck (Editor), P. E. Easterling, Philip Hardie, Richard Hunter & E. J. Kenney (Contribution by). Cloth Text. Cambridge University Press. New York, NY. 2003. 246p. Cambridge Greek and Latin Classics Ser. ISBN:0-521-80360-8, ISBN13: 978-0-521-80360-1. Dewey:875/.01.
Audience: **u,f.**

Cicero, Marcus Tullius **PA6279 .A67 1993**
Cicero's Caesarian Speeches: A Stylistic Commentary. Harold C. Gotoff (Editor). Trade Cloth. University of North Carolina Press. Chapel Hill, NC. 1993. 360p. ISBN:0-8078-4407-1, ISBN13: 978-0-8078-4407-6. Dewey:875/.01. LCCN:92-050816.
Audience: **u,f.**

Cicero, Marcus Tullius **PA6279.C2**
Cicero: In Catilinam I and II. H. E. Gould & J. L. Whiteley (Editors). Trade Paper. Bristol Classical Press. London, 1982. 148p. Latin Texts ISBN:0-86292-014-0, ISBN13: 978-0-86292-014-2. Dewey:875.01.
Audience: **l,u.**

Cicero, Marcus Tullius **PA6307**
Cicero: Selected Political Speeches. Michael Grant (Translator, Introduction by). Trade Paper. Penguin Group (USA) Inc. New York, NY. 1977. 336p. Classics Ser. ISBN:0-14-044214-6, ISBN13: 978-0-14-044214-4. Dewey:875/.01. LCCN:70-445798.
Audience: **g,l,u.**

Cicero, Marcus Tullius **PA6279**
Murder Trials. Michael Grant (Translator, Introduction by). Trade Paper. Penguin Group (USA) Inc. New York, NY. 1975. 368p. Classics Ser. ISBN:0-14-044288-X, ISBN13: 978-0-14-044288-5. Dewey:875/.01. LCCN:82-211455.
Audience: **g,l,u.**

Cicero, Marcus Tullius **PA6308.T7G7313 2002**
Cicero on the Emotions: Tusculan Disputations 3 and 4. Margaret Graver (Translator). Trade Cloth. University of Chicago Press. Chicago, IL. 2002. 283p. ISBN:0-226-30577-5, ISBN13: 978-0-226-30577-6. Dewey:158/.1. LCCN:2001-003526.
Audience: **g,l,u,f.**

Cicero, Marcus Tullius **PA6282**
Cicero: Verrine V. R. G. Levens (Editor). Trade Paper. Bristol Classical Press. London, 1980. 256p. Latin Texts ISBN:0-906515-74-2, ISBN13: 978-0-906515-74-7. Dewey:871.
Audience: **l,u.**

Cicero, Marcus Tullius **PA6282.A5**
Cicero: Verrines II.1. T. N. Mitchell (Editor). Trade Cloth. Aris & Phillips. Oxford, 1986. vii, 229p. Classical Texts Ser. ISBN:0-85668-252-7, ISBN13: 978-0-85668-252-0. Dewey:875/.01.
Audience: **l,u.**

Cicero, Marcus Tullius **PA6308.L2P6 1990**
Cicero: Laelius on Friendship and the Dream of Scipio. I. G. F. Powell (Editor). Trade Cloth. Aris & Phillips. Oxford, 1991. 250p. Classical Texts Ser. ISBN:0-85668-440-6, ISBN13: 978-0-85668-440-1. Dewey:180.937.
Audience: **l,u.**

Cicero, Marcus Tullius **PA6296 .C2 1988**
Cicero: Cato Maior de Senectute. J. G. F. Powell & Kenneth Dover (Editors), Jonathan Powell, James Diggle, Neil Hopkinson, Michael Reeve, David Sedley & Richard Tarrant (Contribution by). Trade Cloth. Cambridge University Press. New York, NY. 1988. 320p. Cambridge Classical Texts and Commentaries Ser., No. 28 ISBN:0-521-33501-9, ISBN13: 978-0-521-33501-0. Dewey:305.2/6. LCCN:87-011772.
Audience: **u,f.** *Choice, 1988.*

Cicero, Marcus Tullius **PA6280**
Cicero: Philippics I-II. John T. Ramsey (Editor), P. E. Easterling, Philip Hardie, Richard Hunter & E. J. Kenney (Contribution by). Cloth Text. Cambridge University Press. New York, NY. 2003. 380p. Cambridge Greek and Latin Classics Ser. ISBN:0-521-41106-8, ISBN13: 978-0-521-41106-6. Dewey:875.01. LCCN:2003-273871.
Audience: **u,f.**

Cicero, Marcus Tullius **PA6297.A5**
Cicero: Letters to Atticus. D. R. Shackleton Bailey (Editor), James Diggle, Neil Hopkinson, Jonathan Powell, Michael Reeve, David Sedley & Richard Tarrant (Contribution by). Trade Paper. Cambridge University Press. New York, NY. 2004. 256p. Cambridge Classical Texts and Commentaries Ser. ISBN:0-521-60688-8, ISBN13: 978-0-521-60688-2. Dewey:876.1.
Audience: **u,f.**

Cicero, Marcus Tullius **PA6297**
Epistulae Ad Familiares: 62-47 B. C., Vol. 1. D. R. Shackleton Bailey (Editor), James Diggle, Neil Hopkinson, Jonathan Powell, Michael Reeve, David Sedley & Richard Tarrant (Contribution by). Trade Paper. Cambridge University Press. New York, NY. 2004. 553p. Cambridge Classical Texts and Commentaries Ser. ISBN:0-521-60697-7, ISBN13: 978-0-521-60697-4. Dewey:937/.05/0924.
Audience: **u,f.**

Cicero, Marcus Tullius **PA6297**
Epistulae Ad Familiares:47-43 B. C., Vol. 2. D. R. Shackleton Bailey (Editor), James Diggle, Neil Hopkinson, Jonathan Powell, Michael Reeve, David Sedley & Richard Tarrant (Contribution by). Trade Paper. Cambridge University Press. New York, NY. 2004. 640p. Cambridge Classical Texts and Commentaries Ser. ISBN:0-521-60698-5, ISBN13: 978-0-521-60698-1. Dewey:937/.05/0924.
Audience: **u,f.**

Cicero, Marcus Tullius **PA6297.A2**
Epistulae Ad Quintum Fratrem et M. Brutum. D. R. Shackleton Bailey (Editor), James Diggle, Neil Hopkinson, Jonathan Powell, Michael Reeve, David Sedley & Richard Tarrant (Contribution by). Trade Paper. Cambridge University Press. New York, NY. 2004. 286p. Cambridge Classical Texts and Commentaries Ser. ISBN:0-521-60700-0, ISBN13: 978-0-521-60700-1. Dewey:937.050924.
Audience: **u,f.**

Cicero, Marcus Tullius **PA6297.A5**
Letters to Atticus. D. R. Shackleton Bailey (Editor), James Diggle, Neil Hopkinson, Jonathan Powell, Michael Reeve, David Sedley & Richard Tarrant (Contribution by). Trade Paper. Cambridge University Press. New York, NY. 2004. 339p. Cambridge Classical Texts and Commentaries Ser. ISBN:0-521-60690-X, ISBN13: 978-0-521-60690-5. Dewey:876.1.
Audience: **u,f.**

Cicero, Marcus Tullius **PA6297**
Letters to Atticus. D. R. Shackleton Bailey (Editor), James Diggle, Neil Hopkinson, Jonathan Powell, Michael Reeve, David Sedley & Richard Tarrant (Contribution by). Trade Paper. Cambridge University Press. New York, NY. 2004. 487p. Cambridge Classical Texts and Commentaries Ser. ISBN:0-521-60692-6, ISBN13: 978-0-521-60692-9. Dewey:876/.01.
Audience: **u,f.**

Cicero, Marcus Tullius **PA6297.A5**
Letters to Atticus. D. R. Shackleton Bailey (Editor), James Diggle, Neil Hopkinson, Jonathan Powell, Michael Reeve, David Sedley & Richard Tarrant (Contribution by). Trade Paper. Cambridge University Press. New York, NY. 2004. 434p. Cambridge Classical Texts and Commentaries Ser. ISBN:0-521-60687-X, ISBN13: 978-0-521-60687-5. Dewey:876.1.
Audience: **u,f.**

Cicero, Marcus Tullius **PA6297 .A5**
Letters to Atticus. D. R. Shackleton Bailey (Editor), James Diggle, Neil Hopkinson, Jonathan Powell, Michael Reeve, David Sedley & Richard Tarrant (Contribution by). Trade Paper. Cambridge University Press. New York, NY. 2004. 440p. Cambridge Classical Texts and Commentaries Ser. ISBN:0-521-60689-6, ISBN13: 978-0-521-60689-9. Dewey:876.1.
Audience: **u,f.**

Cicero, Marcus Tullius **PA6297**
Letters to Atticus. D. R. Shackleton Bailey (Editor), James Diggle, Neil Hopkinson, Jonathan Powell, Michael Reeve, David Sedley & Richard Tarrant (Contribution by). Trade Paper. Cambridge University Press. New York, NY. 2004. 338p. Cambridge Classical Texts and Commentaries Ser. ISBN:0-521-60691-8, ISBN13: 978-0-521-60691-2. Dewey:876/.01.
Audience: **u,f.**

Cicero, Marcus Tullius **PA6297.A5**
Letters to Atticus: Indexes 1-6. D. R. Shackleton Bailey (Editor), James Diggle, Neil Hopkinson, Jonathan Powell, Michael Reeve, David Sedley & Richard Tarrant (Contribution by). Trade Paper. Cambridge University Press. New York, NY. 2004. 114p. Cambridge Classical Texts and Commentaries Ser. ISBN:0-521-60693-4, ISBN13: 978-0-521-60693-6. Dewey:876.1.
Audience: **u,f.**

Cicero, Marcus Tullius **PA6297.A23 1980**
Cicero: Select Letters. D. R. Shackleton Bailey (Editor), P. E. Easterling, Philip Hardie, Richard Hunter & E. J. Kenney (Contribution by). Trade Paper. Cambridge University Press. New York, NY. 1980. 244p. Cambridge Greek and Latin Classics ISBN:0-521-29524-6, ISBN13: 978-0-521-29524-6. Dewey:876/.01. LCCN:78-067430.
Audience: **l,u,f.**

Cicero, Marcus Tullius **PA6307.A4B35 1991**
Back from Exile: Six Speeches upon His Return. D. R. Shackleton Bailey (Translator, Introduction by, Notes by). Trade Cloth. Scholars Press. Atlanta, GA. 1991. 278p. ISBN:1-55540-626-2, ISBN13: 978-1-55540-626-4. Dewey:875/.01. LCCN:91-031383.
Audience: **g,l,u,f.**

Cicero, Marcus Tullius **PA6308.D5W26 2000**
On Obligations. P. G. Walsh (Translator). Trade Cloth. Oxford University Press, Inc. New York, NY. 2001. 278p. ISBN:0-19-924018-3, ISBN13: 978-0-19-924018-0. Dewey:171/.2. LCCN:99-056114.
Audience: **g,l,u,f.**

Cicero, Marcus Tullius **PA6308.D4W35 1997**
The Nature of the Gods. Patrick G. Walsh (Translator, Introduction by, Notes by). Trade Cloth. Oxford University Press, Inc. New York, NY. 1997. 286p. ISBN:0-19-815040-7, ISBN13: 978-0-19-815040-4. Dewey:292/.07. LCCN:96-034884.
Audience: **g,l,u,f.** *Choice, 1997.*

Cicero, Marcus Tullius **PA6156.C5**
On Invention, the Best Kind of Orator, Topics: Rhetorical Treatises. E. H. Warmington (Editor). Trade Cloth. Harvard University Press. Cambridge, MA. 1970. 496p. Loeb Classical Library, No. 386 ISBN:0-674-99425-6, ISBN13: 978-0-674-99425-6. Dewey:875.2.
Audience: **u,f.**

Cicero, Marcus Tullius **PA6296.D5 1994**
De Officiis. Michael Winterbottom (Editor). Trade Cloth. Oxford University Press, Inc. New York, NY. 1994. 192p. Classical Monographs ISBN:0-19-814673-6, ISBN13: 978-0-19-814673-5. Dewey:170. LCCN:93-039316.
Audience: **u,f.** B

Cicero, Marcus Tullius **PA6296 .D8 1995**
Cicero: De Re Publica, Selections. James E. G. Zetzel (Editor), P. E. Easterling, Philip Hardie, Richard Hunter & E. J. Kenney (Contribution by). Trade Paper. Cambridge University Press. New York, NY. 1995. 280p. Cambridge Greek and Latin Classics ISBN:0-521-34896-X, ISBN13: 978-0-521-34896-6. Dewey:320.1. LCCN:94-012714.
Audience: **u,f.**

Cicero, Marcus Tullius **JC81 .C613 1999**
Cicero: On the Commonwealth and on the Laws. James E. G. Zetzel (Edited and Translated by), Raymond Geuss & Quentin Skinner (Contribution by). Cloth Text. Cambridge University Press. New York, NY. 1999. 258p. Texts in the History of Political Thought ISBN:0-521-45344-5, ISBN13: 978-0-521-45344-8. Dewey:320.1. LCCN:98-049660.
Audience: **g,l,u,f.** *Choice, 2000.*

Dyck, Andrew R. **PA6296.D5D93 1996**
A Commentary on Cicero, De Officiis. Trade Cloth. University of Michigan Press. Chicago, IL. 1997. 760p. ISBN:0-472-10719-4, ISBN13: 978-0-472-10719-3. Dewey:171/.2. LCCN:96-045128.
Audience: **u,f.** *Choice, 1997.*

Gotoff, Harold C. **PA6279**
Cicero's Elegant Style: An Analysis of the Pro Archia. Trade Cloth. University of Illinois Press. Champaign, IL. 1979. 266p. ISBN:0-252-00730-1, ISBN13: 978-0-252-00730-9. Dewey:875/.01. LCCN:79-010245.
Audience: **u,f.**

Habicht, Christian **PA6320.H33**
Cicero the Politician. Trade Paper. Books on Demand. Ann Arbor, MI. 1990. 165p. Ancient Society and History Ser. ISBN:0-608-04051-7, ISBN13: 978-0-608-04051-6. Dewey:937/.05/092. LCCN:89-045485.
Audience: **g,l,u,f.** *Choice, 1990.*

Hutchinson, G. O. **PA6298.H87 1998**
Cicero's Correspondence: A Literary Study. Trade Cloth. Oxford University Press, Inc. New York, NY. 1998. 252p. ISBN:0-19-815066-0, ISBN13: 978-0-19-815066-4. Dewey:937/.05/092 B. LCCN:97-036304.
Audience: **u,f.** *Choice, 1999.*

Johnson, Walter Ralph **PA6357.J6**
Luxuriance and Economy: Cicero and the Alien Style. Trade Paper. Books on Demand. Ann Arbor, MI. 84p. University of California Publications: Classical Studies, Vol. 6 ISBN:0-598-20687-6, ISBN13: 978-0-598-20687-9. Dewey:875/.01. LCCN:75-633551.
Audience: **u,f.**

MacKendrick, Paul L. **B553.M33 1989**
The Philosophical Books of Cicero. Karen L. Singh (Contribution by). Cloth Text. Palgrave Macmillan. New York, NY. 1989. 400p. ISBN:0-312-03623-X, ISBN13: 978-0-312-03623-2. Dewey:186. LCCN:89-034979.
Audience: **g,l,u,f.** *Choice, 1990.*

May, James M. (Editor) **PA6285.B75 2002**
Brill's Companion to Cicero: Oratory and Rhetoric. Trade Cloth. Brill Academic Publishers. Leiden, 2002. xiv, 632p. ISBN:90-04-12147-1, ISBN13: 978-90-04-12147-8. Dewey:875/.01. LCCN:2002-066555.
Audience: **u,f.** *Choice, 2003.*

Mitchell, Thomas N. **DG260.C54**
Cicero. Trade Cloth. Yale University Press. Cumberland, RI. 1979. xii, 259p. ISBN:0-300-02277-8, ISBN13: 978-0-300-02277-3. Dewey:937/.05/0924. LCCN:78-031198.
Audience: **u,f.** B

Mitchell, Thomas N. **DG260.C53M58 1991**
Cicero: The Senior Statesman. Cloth over Boards. Yale University Press. Cumberland, RI. 1991. 360p. ISBN:0-300-04779-7, ISBN13: 978-0-300-04779-0. Dewey:937/.05/092 B. LCCN:90-038157.
Audience: **u,f.** *Choice, 1991.*

Powell, Jonathan & Paterson, Jeremy (Editors) **KJA2157**
Cicero the Advocate. Trade Cloth. Oxford University Press, Inc. New York, NY. 2004. 460p. ISBN:0-19-815280-9, ISBN13: 978-0-19-815280-4. Dewey:340.5/4/092. LCCN:2004-617292.
Audience: **u,f.** *Choice, 2005.*

Rawson, Elizabeth (Editor) **DG261**
Cicero: A Portrait. Trade Paper. Bristol Classical Press. London, 1994. 368p. Classical Paperbacks Ser. ISBN:0-86292-051-5, ISBN13: 978-0-86292-051-7. Dewey:937/.05/0924.
Audience: **g,l,u,f.** B

Stockton, David **DG260.C5/**
Cicero: A Political Biography. Paper Text. Oxford University Press, Inc. New York, NY. 1988. 376p. ISBN:0-19-872033-5, ISBN13: 978-0-19-872033-1. Dewey:937.050924.
Audience: **g,l,u,f.**

Latin > Individual Authors > Ennius

Ennius, Quintus **PA6382 .A2**
The Tragedies of Ennius: The Fragments. H. D. Jocelyn (Editor). Trade Paper. Books on Demand. Ann Arbor, MI. 481p. Cambridge Classical Texts and Commentaries Ser., No. 10 ISBN:0-608-14085-6, ISBN13: 978-0-608-14085-8. Dewey:872/.01. LCCN:67-011525.
Audience: **u,f.** B

Ennius, Quintus **PA6382.A3.E5 1985**
The Annals of Quintus Ennius. Otto Skutch (Editor). Cloth Text. Oxford University Press, Inc. New York, NY. 1985. 866p. ISBN:0-19-814448-2, ISBN13: 978-0-19-814448-9. Dewey:873.01. LCCN:83-008048.
Audience: **u,f.** B

Latin > Individual Authors > Horace

Anderson, William S. (Editor) **PA6411.W47 1999**
Why Horace?: A Collection of Interpretations. Book, Other. Bolchazy-Carducci Publishers. Wauconda, IL. 1999. 272p. ISBN:0-86516-434-7, ISBN13: 978-0-86516-434-5. Dewey:874/.01. LCCN:98-045905.
Audience: **g,l,u,f.**

Armstrong, David **PA6411.A77 1989**
Horace. Cloth over Boards. Yale University Press. Cumberland, RI. 1989. 192p. Hermes Bks. ISBN:0-300-04579-4, ISBN13: 978-0-300-04579-6. Dewey:874/.01. LCCN:89-009045.
Audience: **g,l,u,f.** *Choice, 1990.*

Commager, Steele **PA6825**
The Odes of Horace: A Critical Study. Paper Text. Textbook Publishers. Temecula, CA. 2003. xiv, 365p. ISBN:0-7581-0125-2, ISBN13: 978-0-7581-0125-9. Dewey:871/.01.
Audience: **u,f.**

Fraenkel, Eduard **PA6411 .F67 1980**
Horace. Paper Text. Oxford University Press, Inc. New York, NY. 1981. 478p. ISBN:0-19-814376-1, ISBN13: 978-0-19-814376-5. Dewey:874/.01. LCCN:80-041456.
Audience: **u,f.** B

Horace **PA6156**
Satires, Epistles, the Art of Poetry. Henry R. Fairclough (Translator). Trade Cloth. Harvard University Press. Cambridge, MA. 1926. 544p. Loeb Classical Library, No. 194 ISBN:0-674-99214-8, ISBN13: 978-0-674-99214-6. Dewey:878.
Audience: **g,l,u,f.**

Horace **PA6393 .C8 1995**
Epodes. David Mankin (Editor), P. E. Easterling, Philip Hardie, Richard Hunter & E. J. Kenney (Contribution by). Trade Paper. Cambridge University Press. New York, NY. 1995. 329p. Cambridge Greek and Latin Classics ISBN:0-521-39774-X, ISBN13: 978-0-521-39774-2. Dewey:871/.01. LCCN:94-038675.
Audience: **u,f.** *Choice, 1996.*

Horace **PA6393.E8 H67 1994**
Horace: Epistles. Roland Mayer (Editor). Cloth Text. Cambridge University Press. New York, NY. 1994. 299p. Cambridge Greek and Latin Classics ISBN:0-521-25898-7, ISBN13: 978-0-521-25898-2. Dewey:871.01. LCCN:93-042188.
Audience: **u,f.**

Horace **PA6394.A2 2005**
Horace, the Odes: New Translations by Contemporary Poets. J. D. McClatchy (Translator). Trade Paper. Princeton University Press. Princeton, NJ. 2005. 320p. Facing Pages Ser. ISBN:0-691-11981-3, ISBN13: 978-0-691-11981-6. Dewey:874.01.
Audience: **g,l,u.**

Horace **PA6395.W4 2002**
Horace Odes III Dulce Periculum: Text, Translation, and Commentary. David West (Translator). Trade Paper. Oxford University Press, Inc. New York, NY. 2002. 306p. ISBN:0-19-872165-X, ISBN13: 978-0-19-872165-9. Dewey:874/.01.
Audience: **g,l,u.**

Horace **PA6395.W43 1998**
Horace Odes II: Vatis Amici. David West (Editor, Translator). Trade Cloth. Oxford University Press, Inc. New York, NY. 1999. 180p. Classical Monographs ISBN:0-19-872162-5, ISBN13: 978-0-19-872162-8. Dewey:874/.01. LCCN:99-193696.
Audience: **g,l,u.**

Horace **PA6395.W4 1995**
Horace Odes I: Carpe Diem. David West (Translator, Commentaries by, Text by). Trade Paper. Oxford University Press, Inc. New York, NY. 1995. 216p. ISBN:0-19-872161-7, ISBN13: 978-0-19-872161-1. Dewey:874/.01. LCCN:94-044514.
Audience: **g,l,u.**

Mayer, Roland H. & Horace **PA6393 .E4 1989**
Horace: Epistles Book II and Ars Poetica. Niall Rudd (Editor), P. E. Easterling, Philip Hardie, Richard Hunter & E. J. Kenney (Contribution by). Trade Paper. Cambridge University Press. New York, NY. 1989. 256p. Cambridge Greek and Latin Classics ISBN:0-521-31292-2, ISBN13: 978-0-521-31292-9. Dewey:871.01. LCCN:89-007129.
Audience: **u,f.**

Nisbet, R. G. M. & Rudd, Niall **PA6411**
A Commentary on Horace: Odes. Trade Cloth. Oxford University Press, Inc. New York, NY. 2004. 424p. ISBN:0-19-926314-0, ISBN13: 978-0-19-926314-1. Dewey:874/.01. LCCN:2004-301651.
Audience: **u,f.** *Choice, 2005.*

Nisbet, Robin G. & Hubbard, Margaret **PA6411**
A Commentary on Horace: Odes, Book II. Paper Text. Oxford University Press, Inc. New York, NY. 1991. 372p. ISBN:0-19-814771-6, ISBN13: 978-0-19-814771-8. Dewey:874.01.
Audience: **u,f.**

Nisbet, Robin G. & Hubbard, Margaret **PA6411.N55 1989**
A Commentary on Horace: Odes, Bk. 1. Trade Paper. Oxford University Press, Inc. New York, NY. 1989. 498p. ISBN:0-19-814914-X, ISBN13: 978-0-19-814914-9. Dewey:874/.01. LCCN:89-009407.
Audience: **u,f.**

Rudd, Niall **PA6393.S8R8**
The Satires of Horace: A Study. Trade Paper. Books on Demand. Ann Arbor, MI. 330p. ISBN:0-608-12497-4, ISBN13: 978-0-608-12497-1. Dewey:877.01. LCCN:66-011031.
Audience: **u,f.**

Shackleton Bailey, D. R. **PA6411.B28 1982**
Profile of Horace. Trade Cloth. Harvard University Press. Cambridge, MA. 1982. 152p. ISBN:0-674-71325-7, ISBN13: 978-0-674-71325-3. Dewey:874/.01. LCCN:82-001010.
Audience: **g,l,u,f.**

Latin > Individual Authors > Juvenal

Highet, Gilbert **PA6448**
Juvenal the Satirist: A Study. Oxford University Press. 1961.
Audience: **g,u,f.**

Juvenal **PA6446 .A61 1996**
Juvenal: Satires. Susanna Morton Braund (Editor), P. E. Easterling, Philip Hardie, Richard Hunter & E. J. Kenney (Contribution by). Trade Paper. Cambridge University Press. New York, NY. 1996. 330p. Cambridge Greek and Latin Classics ISBN:0-521-35667-9, ISBN13: 978-0-521-35667-1. Dewey:871/.01. LCCN:95-011014.
Audience: **u,f.** *Choice, 1997.*

Juvenal & Persius **PA6447.E5B28 2004**
Juvenal and Persius. Susanna Morton Braund (Editor, Translator). Trade Cloth. Harvard University Press. Cambridge, MA. 2004. 560p. Loeb Classical Library, Vol. 91 ISBN:0-674-99612-7, ISBN13: 978-0-674-99612-0. Dewey:871.01. LCCN:2004-042213.
Audience: **g,l,u,f.**

Juvenal **PA6447.E5**
The Satires. Niall Rudd (Translator), William F. Barry (Introduction by). Trade Paper. Oxford University Press, Inc. New York, NY. 1999. 290p. Oxford World's Classics Ser. ISBN:0-19-283945-4, ISBN13: 978-0-19-283945-9. Dewey:877.
Audience: **g,l,u.**

Latin > Individual Authors > Livy

Gould, H. & Gould, J. Whiteley **PA6452**
Livy, Bk. 1. Trade Paper. Bristol Classical Press. London, 1993. 294p. Latin Texts ISBN:0-86292-296-8, ISBN13: 978-0-86292-296-2. Dewey:937.
Audience: **l,u.**

Livy **PA6452**
History of Roman: Summaries, Fragments, Julius Obsequens, General Index. Trade Cloth. Harvard University Press. Cambridge, MA. 1967. 592p. Loeb Classical Library, Vol. 14 ISBN:0-674-99445-0, ISBN13: 978-0-674-99445-4. Dewey:937.
Audience: **g,l,u,f.**

Livy **PA6156**
History of Rome: Books 5-7, Vol. 3. Trade Cloth. Harvard University Press. Cambridge, MA. 1978. 544p. Loeb Classical Library, Vol. 3:Latin Authors ISBN:0-674-99190-7, ISBN13: 978-0-674-99190-3. Dewey:937.
Audience: **g,l,u,f.**

Livy **PA6452**
History of Rome, Vol. 5. Trade Cloth. Harvard University Press. Cambridge, MA. 1977. 440p. Loeb Classical Library, Vol. 5 ISBN:0-674-99256-3, ISBN13: 978-0-674-99256-6. Dewey:937.
Audience: **g,l,u,f.**

Livy **PA6452**
History of Rome, Vol. 9. Trade Cloth. Harvard University Press. Cambridge, MA. 1970. 624p. Loeb Classical Library, Vol. 9 ISBN:0-674-99326-8, ISBN13: 978-0-674-99326-6. Dewey:937.
Audience: **g,l,u,f.**

Livy **PA6452**
History of Rome, Vol. 7. Trade Cloth. Harvard University Press. Cambridge, MA. 1970. 464p. Loeb Classical Library, Vol. 7 ISBN:0-674-99404-3, ISBN13: 978-0-674-99404-1. Dewey:937.
Audience: **g,l,u,f.**

Livy **PA6156**
History of Rome: Books 38-39, Vol. 11. Trade Cloth. Harvard University Press. Cambridge, MA. 1970. 426p. Loeb Classical Library, Vol. 11:Latin Authors ISBN:0-674-99346-2, ISBN13: 978-0-674-99346-4. Dewey:937.
Audience: **g,l,u,f.**

Livy **PA6452**
History of Rome: Books 43-45, Vol. 13. Trade Cloth. Harvard University Press. Cambridge, MA. 1951. 448p. Loeb Classical Library, Vol. 13:Latin Authors ISBN:0-674-99435-3, ISBN13: 978-0-674-99435-5. Dewey:937.
Audience: **g,l,u,f.**

Livy **PA6452**
History of Rome: Books 8-10, Vol. 4. Trade Cloth. Harvard University Press. Cambridge, MA. 1970. 592p. Loeb Classical Library, Vol. 4:Latin Authors ISBN:0-674-99210-5, ISBN13: 978-0-674-99210-8. Dewey:937.
Audience: **g,l,u,f.**

Livy **PA6452**
History of Rome: Books 28-30, Vol. 8. Trade Cloth. Harvard University Press. Cambridge, MA. 1971. 592p. Loeb Classical Library, Vol. 8:Latin Authors ISBN:0-674-99419-1, ISBN13: 978-0-674-99419-5. Dewey:937.
Audience: **g,l,u,f.**

Livy **PA6156**
History of Rome: Books 23-25, Vol. 6. Trade Cloth. Harvard University Press. Cambridge, MA. 1940. 530p. Loeb Classical Library, Vol. 6:Latin Authors ISBN:0-674-99392-6, ISBN13: 978-0-674-99392-1. Dewey:937.
Audience: **g,l,u,f.**

Livy **PA6452**
History of Rome, Vol. 10. Trade Cloth. Harvard University Press. Cambridge, MA. 1966. 512p. Loeb Classical Library, Vol. 10 ISBN:0-674-99332-2, ISBN13: 978-0-674-99332-7. Dewey:937.
Audience: **g,l,u,f.**

Livy **PA6452**
History of Rome: Books 40-42, Vol. 12. Trade Cloth. Harvard University Press. Cambridge, MA. 1991. 544p. Loeb Classical Library, Vol. 12:Latin Authors ISBN:0-674-99366-7, ISBN13: 978-0-674-99366-2. Dewey:937.
Audience: **g,l,u,f.**

Livy, Titus Livius **DG233 .L5813 1976**
History of Rome: Books 1-2, Vol. 1. B. O. Foster (Translator). Trade Cloth. Harvard University Press. Cambridge, MA. 1976. 488p. Loeb Classical Library, Vol. 114:Latin Authors ISBN:0-674-99126-5, ISBN13: 978-0-674-99126-2. Dewey:937. LCCN:88-211705.
Audience: **g,l,u,f.**

Livy **PA6452**
History of Rome: Books 3-4, Vol. 2. B. O. Foster (Translator). Trade Cloth. Harvard University Press. Cambridge, MA. 1970. 480p. Loeb Classical Library, Vol. 2:Latin Authors ISBN:0-674-99148-6, ISBN13: 978-0-674-99148-4. Dewey:937.
Audience: **g,l,u,f.**

Livy **DG247.L5513 2000**
The Dawn of the Roman Empire, Bks. 31-40. Waldemar Heckel (Editor), J. C. Yardley (Translator), Waldemar Heckel (Notes by). Trade Paper. Oxford University Press, Inc. New York, NY. 2000. 654p. Oxford World's Classics Ser. ISBN:0-19-283293-X, ISBN13: 978-0-19-283293-1. Dewey:937/.02. LCCN:00-036331.
Audience: **g,l,u.**

Livy **DG247**
Hannibal's War. Dexter Hoyos (Editor), J. C. Yardley (Translator). Trade Paper. Oxford University Press, Inc. New York, NY. 2006. 800p. Oxford World's Classics Ser. ISBN:0-19-283159-3, ISBN13: 978-0-19-283159-0. Dewey:937/.04092. LCCN:2006-275563.
Audience: **g,l,u.**

Livy **DG235 .L58 1994**
Livy: Ab Urbe Condita. Christina S. Kraus (Editor), P. E. Easterling, Philip Hardie, Richard Hunter & E. J. Kenney (Contribution by). Cloth Text. Cambridge University Press. New York, NY. 1994. 366p. Cambridge Greek and Latin Classics ISBN:0-521-41002-9, ISBN13: 978-0-521-41002-1. Dewey:937.04. LCCN:93-041170.
Audience: **u,f.**

Livy **DG233.L58213 1998**
The Rise of Rome, Bks. 1-5. T. James Luce Jr. (Editor, Translator). Trade Paper. Oxford University Press, Inc. New York, NY. 1999. 406p. Oxford World's Classics Ser., :Classics and Ancient Literature ISBN:0-19-282296-9, ISBN13: 978-0-19-282296-3. Dewey:937/.01. LCCN:98-011367.
Audience: **g,l,u.**

Luce, T. J. **DG207.L583**
Livy: The Composition of His History. Trade Cloth. Princeton University Press. Princeton, NJ. 1978. 352p. ISBN:0-691-03552-0, ISBN13: 978-0-691-03552-9. Dewey:937/.0072024. LCCN:77-072126.
Audience: **u,f.** B

Miles, Gary B. **DG207.L583M5**
Livy: Reconstructing Early Rome. Trade Paper. Cornell University Press. Ithaca, NY. 1997. 264p. ISBN:0-8014-8426-X, ISBN13: 978-0-8014-8426-1. Dewey:937.
Audience: **u,f.** *Choice, 1996.*

Ogilvie, Robert M. **PA6459**
A Commentary on Livy, Bks. I-V. Trade Cloth. Oxford University Press, Inc. New York, NY. 1965. 788p. ISBN:0-19-814432-6, ISBN13: 978-0-19-814432-8. Dewey:878.
Audience: **u,f.**

Walsh, P. G. **DG316**
Livy: His Historical Aims and Methods. Paper Text. Textbook Publishers. Temecula, CA. 2003. 300p. ISBN:0-7581-1326-9, ISBN13: 978-0-7581-1326-9. Dewey:937/.0072/02.
Audience: **u,f.** B

Walsh, P. G. (Editor) **PA6452.D9**
Livy XXXIX. Trade Cloth. Aris & Phillips. Oxford, 1994. 240p. ISBN:0-85668-625-5, ISBN13: 978-0-85668-625-2. Dewey:937.04.
Audience: **l,u.**

Latin > Individual Authors > Lucan

Ahl, Frederick **PA6480**
Lucan: An Introduction. Trade Cloth. Cornell University Press. Ithaca, NY. 1976. 400p. Cornell Studies in Classical Philology, Vol. XXXIX ISBN:0-8014-0837-7, ISBN13: 978-0-8014-0837-3. Dewey:873/.01. LCCN:75-016926.
Audience: **g,u,f.** B

Lucan **PA6156**
The Civil War (Pharsalia). J. D. Duff (Translator). Trade Cloth. Harvard University Press. Cambridge, MA. 1928. 656p. Loeb Classical Library, No. 220 ISBN:0-674-99242-3, ISBN13: 978-0-674-99242-9. Dewey:878.
Audience: **g,l,u.**

Lucan **PA6478 .A2 1992**
Lucan: De Bello Civili, Bk. II. Elaine Fantham (Editor). Cloth Text. Cambridge University Press. New York, NY. 1992. 256p. Cambridge Greek and Latin Classics ISBN:0-521-41010-X, ISBN13: 978-0-521-41010-6. Dewey:873/.01. LCCN:91-028313.
Audience: **u,f.**

Lucan **PA6478.A2**
Lucan: De Bello Civili I. R. Getty (Editor). Trade Paper. Bristol Classical Press. London, 1992. 224p. Latin Texts ISBN:1-85399-357-3, ISBN13: 978-1-85399-357-2. Dewey:873/.01.
Audience: **u.**

Masters, Jamie **PA6480 .M35 1992**
Poetry and Civil War in Lucan's "Bellum Civile". P. D. Garnsey, G. C. Horrocks, R. L. Hunter, M. Millett, R. G. Osborne, M. D. Reeve & D. N. Sedley (Contribution by). Trade Cloth. Cambridge University Press. New York, NY. 1992. 285p. Cambridge Classical Studies ISBN:0-521-41460-1, ISBN13: 978-0-521-41460-9. Dewey:873/.01. LCCN:91-017707.
Audience: **u,f.**

Morford, M. **PA6480**
The Poet Lucan. Trade Paper. Bristol Classical Press. London, 1996. 104p. Classical Paperbacks Ser. ISBN:1-85399-488-X, ISBN13: 978-1-85399-488-3. Dewey:873.01.
Audience: **g,u,f.**

Latin > Individual Authors > Lucretius

Clay, Diskin **B577.L64.C58 1983**
Lucretius and Epicurus. Book, Other. Cornell University Press. Ithaca, NY. 1983. 384p. ISBN:0-8014-1559-4, ISBN13: 978-0-8014-1559-3. Dewey:187. LCCN:83-045142.
Audience: **u,f.**

Johnson, W. R. **PA6485**
Lucretius in the Modern World. Trade Paper. Gerald Duckworth & Company, Ltd. London, 2000. 128p. Classical Inter/Faces Ser. ISBN:0-7156-2882-8, ISBN13: 978-0-7156-2882-9. Dewey:871.01.
Audience: **g,l,u,f.**

Lucretius Carus, ; Bailey, Cyril
De Rerum Natura: Titi Lucreti Cari de Rerum Natura: Libri Sex. Cyril Bailey (Editor). Oxford University Press, Inc. 1986. ISBN:0-19-814405-9, ISBN13: 978-0-19-814405-2.
Audience: **u,f.**

Lucretius Carus, Titus **PA6482**
Lucretius: De Rerum Natura. E. J. Kenney (Editor, Contribution by), P. E. Easterling, Philip Hardie & Richard Hunter (Contribution by). Trade Paper. Cambridge University Press. New York, NY. 1977. 256p. Cambridge Greek and Latin Classics Ser. ISBN:0-521-29177-1, ISBN13: 978-0-521-29177-4. Dewey:871.1.
Audience: **u,f.**

Lucretius Carus, Titus **PA6482**
De Rerum Natura: The Latin Text of Lucretius. William E. Leonard & Stanley B. Smith (Editors). Cloth Text. University of Wisconsin Press. Chicago, IL. 1942. 896p. ISBN:0-299-00362-0, ISBN13: 978-0-299-00362-3. Dewey:871.
Audience: **u,f.**

Lucretius Carus, Titus **PA6482**
De Rerum Natura: The Poem of Nature. C. H. Sisson (Translator, Introduction by). Trade Paper. Routledge. New York, NY. 2003. 196p. Fyfield Bks. ISBN:0-415-96957-3, ISBN13: 978-0-415-96957-4. Dewey:871/.01.
Audience: **g,l,u.**

Lucretius Carus, Titus **PA6483.E5S6 2001**
On the Nature of Things. Ed. 2. Martin Ferguson Smith (Translator). Trade Cloth. Hackett Publishing Company, Inc. Indianapolis, IN. 2001. 256p. Hackett Classics Ser. ISBN:0-87220-588-6, ISBN13: 978-0-87220-588-8. Dewey:871.01. LCCN:2001-026403.
Audience: **g,l,u.**

Sedley, David N. **PA6484 .S43 1998**
Lucretius and the Transformation of Greek Wisdom. Trade Cloth. Cambridge University Press. New York, NY. 1998. 252p. ISBN:0-521-57032-8, ISBN13: 978-0-521-57032-9. Dewey:187. LCCN:97-035277.
Audience: **u,f.**

West, David **PA6484.W4 1994**
The Imagery and Poetry of Lucretius. Trade Paper. University of Oklahoma Press. Norman, OK. 1994. viii, 152p. ISBN:0-8061-2639-6, ISBN13: 978-0-8061-2639-5. Dewey:871/.01. LCCN:93-044685.
Audience: **u,f.**

Latin > Individual Authors > Martial

Howell, P. **PA6507**
A Commentary on Book I of the Epigrams of Martial. Cloth Text. Continuum International Publishing Group, Ltd. London, 1980. 369p. ISBN:0-485-11191-8, ISBN13: 978-0-485-11191-0. Dewey:878/.0102.
Audience: **u,f.**

Martial **PA6502.H64 1995**
Martial: The Epigrams. Peter Howell (Editor, Translator). Trade Cloth. Aris & Phillips. Oxford, 1993. 176p. Classical Texts Ser. ISBN:0-85668-589-5, ISBN13: 978-0-85668-589-7. Dewey:878/.0102. LCCN:96-158902.
Audience: **u,f.** *Choice, 1996.*

Martial **PA6502**
Epigrams: Bks. 11-14, Vol. 2. D. R. Shackleton Bailey (Editor). Trade Cloth. Harvard University Press. Cambridge, MA. 1993. 432p. Loeb Classical Library, :Latin Authors ISBN:0-674-99556-2, ISBN13: 978-0-674-99556-7. Dewey:878/.0102. LCCN:92-008234.
Audience: **g,l,u,f.**

Martial **PA6502.B35 1993**
Epigrams: Bks. 11-14, Vol. 3. D. R. Shackleton Bailey (Editor). Trade Cloth. Harvard University Press. Cambridge, MA. 1993. 400p. Loeb Classical Library, Vol. 3:Latin Authors ISBN:0-674-99529-5, ISBN13: 978-0-674-99529-1. Dewey:878/.0102. LCCN:92-008234.
Audience: **g,l,u,f.**

Martial **PA6502.B35 1993**
Epigrams - Spectacles: Bks. 1-5, Vol. 1. D. R. Shackleton Bailey (Editor). Trade Cloth. Harvard University Press. Cambridge, MA. 1993. 440p. Loeb Classical Library, Vol. 1:Latin Authors ISBN:0-674-99555-4, ISBN13: 978-0-674-99555-0. Dewey:878/.0102. LCCN:92-008234.
Audience: **g,l,u,f.**

Martial **PA6501.A2 2003**
Martial: Select Epigrams. Lindsay Watson & Patricia Watson (Editors), P. E. Easterling, Philip Hardie, Richard Hunter & E. J. Kenney (Contribution by). Cloth Text. Cambridge University Press. New York, NY. 2003. 386p. Cambridge Greek and Latin Classics Ser. ISBN:0-521-55488-8, ISBN13: 978-0-521-55488-6. Dewey:878/.0102. LCCN:2002-034959.
Audience: **u,f.**

Martial **PA6502.W55 2003**
Martial's Epigrams, Bk. 2. Craig A. Williams (Editor, Translator, Commentaries by, Introduction by). Trade Cloth. Oxford University Press, Inc. New York, NY. 2004. 320p. ISBN:0-19-515531-9, ISBN13: 978-0-19-515531-0. Dewey:878/.0102. LCCN:2003-004244.
Audience: **u,f.**

Sullivan, J. P. **PA6507 .S85 1991**
Martial: The Unexpected Classic. Trade Cloth. Cambridge University Press. New York, NY. 1991. 414p. ISBN:0-521-26458-8, ISBN13: 978-0-521-26458-7. Dewey:878/.0102. LCCN:90-024794.
Audience: **u,f.** *Choice, 1992.*

Latin > Individual Authors > Ovid

Barchiesi, Alessandro **PA6537.B28 1997**
The Poet and the Prince: Ovid and Augustan Discourse. Trade Cloth. University of California Press. Berkeley, CA. 1997. 285p. ISBN:0-520-20223-6, ISBN13: 978-0-520-20223-8. Dewey:871/.01. LCCN:96-049230.
Audience: **u,f.** *Choice, 1998.*

Barsby, John **PA6537**
Ovid. Booth, Joan (addenda). Oxford University Press. 1991. Greece & Rome. New Surveys in the Classics ISBN:0-903035-08-1, ISBN13: 978-0-903035-08-8.
Audience: **u,f.**

Fantham, Elaine **PA6519.M9**
Ovid's Metamorphoses. Trade Cloth. Oxford University Press, Inc. New York, NY. 2004. 192p. Oxford Approaches Classical Literature Ser. ISBN:0-19-515409-6, ISBN13: 978-0-19-515409-2. Dewey:873/.01. LCCN:2003-016164.
Audience: **g,l,u.**

Hardie, Philip (Editor) **PA6537 .C28 2002**
The Cambridge Companion to Ovid. Cloth Text. Cambridge University Press. New York, NY. 2002. 424p. Companions to Literature Ser. ISBN:0-521-77281-8, ISBN13: 978-0-521-77281-5. Dewey:871/.01. LCCN:2001-037923.
Audience: **g,l,u,f.** *Choice, 2003.*

Hardie, Philip **PA6550 .H37 2002**
Ovid's Poetics of Illusion. Cloth Text. Cambridge University Press. New York, NY. 2002. 374p. ISBN:0-521-80087-0, ISBN13: 978-0-521-80087-7. Dewey:871/.01. LCCN:2001-037747.
Audience: **u,f.**

Jacobson, Howard **PA6519.H7.J3**
Ovid's Heroides. Trade Cloth. Princeton University Press. Princeton, NJ. 1974. 425p. ISBN:0-691-06271-4, ISBN13: 978-0-691-06271-6. Dewey:871/.01. LCCN:73-016754.
Audience: **u,f.** B

Mack, Sara **PA6537.M23 1988**
Ovid. John Herington (Editor). Trade Paper. Yale University Press. Cumberland, RI. 1988. 192p. Hermes Bks. ISBN:0-300-04295-7, ISBN13: 978-0-300-04295-5. Dewey:871/.01. LCCN:87-037157.
Audience: **g,l,u.** *Choice, 1989.*

Otis, Brooks **PA6519.M9**
Ovid As an Epic Poet. Ed. 2. Trade Cloth. Cambridge University Press. New York, NY. 1971. 460p. ISBN:0-521-07615-3, ISBN13: 978-0-521-07615-9. Dewey:873/.01. LCCN:75-096098.
Audience: **u,f.**

Ovid **PA6825**
Ovid's Metamorphoses, Bks. 6-10. William S. Anderson (Editor). Trade Paper, Book, Other. University of Oklahoma Press. Norman, OK. 1972. 540p. American Philological Association Ser., Vol. 2 ISBN:0-8061-1456-8, ISBN13: 978-0-8061-1456-9. Dewey:873/.01. LCCN:74-160488.
Audience: **l,u.**

Ovid **PA6519.M4A49 1996**
Ovid's Metamorphoses, Bks. 1-5. William S. Anderson (Editor, Commentaries by, Introduction by). Cloth Text. University of Oklahoma Press. Norman, OK. 1997. 584p. ISBN:0-8061-2845-3, ISBN13: 978-0-8061-2845-0. Dewey:873/.01. LCCN:96-011064.
Audience: **l,u.**

Ovid **PA6522; PA6519.A7**
Ovid: Amores I. J. Barsby (Editor). Trade Paper. Bristol Classical Press. London, 1991. 192p. Latin Texts ISBN:0-906515-45-9, ISBN13: 978-0-906515-45-7. Dewey:871/.01.
Audience: **l,u.**

Ovid **PA6519.F6 A4 1998**
Ovid: Fasti, Bk. IV. Elaine Fantham (Editor). Trade Cloth. Cambridge University Press. New York, NY. 1998. 301p. Cambridge Greek and Latin Classics, Bk. IV ISBN:0-521-44538-8, ISBN13: 978-0-521-44538-2. Dewey:871.01. LCCN:97-013724.
Audience: **u,f.**

Ovid **PA6522**
Ovid's Metamorphoses. Madeleine Forey (Editor), Arthur Golding (Translator). Trade Paper. Johns Hopkins University Press. Baltimore, MD. 2002. 576p. ISBN:0-8018-7060-7, ISBN13: 978-0-8018-7060-6. Dewey:871.
Audience: **u,f.**

Ovid **PA6825**
Fasti. Ed. 2. James George Frazer (Translator). Trade Cloth. Harvard University Press. Cambridge, MA. 1931. 496p. Loeb Classical Library, No. 253 ISBN:0-674-99279-2, ISBN13: 978-0-674-99279-5. Dewey:871/.01.
Audience: **g,l,u.**

Ovid **PA6522.A2 2005**
The Poems of Exile: Tristia and the Black Sea Letters. Peter Green (Translator, Introduction by, Notes by). Trade Paper. University of California Press. Berkeley, CA. 2005. 528p. ISBN:0-520-24260-2, ISBN13: 978-0-520-24260-9. Dewey:871/.01. LCCN:2004-055362.
Audience: **g,l,u.**

Ovid **PA6519.M6 A13 2000**
Ovid: Metamorphoses. Neil Hopkinson (Editor). Cloth Text. Cambridge University Press. New York, NY. 2000. 262p. Greek and Latin Classics Ser. ISBN:0-521-55421-7, ISBN13: 978-0-521-55421-3. Dewey:871.01. LCCN:99-087439.
Audience: **u,f.**

Ovid **PA6519 .H5 1995**
Ovid: Heroides: Select Epistles. Peter E. Knox (Editor). Cloth Text. Cambridge University Press. New York, NY. 1996. 339p. Cambridge Greek and Latin Classics ISBN:0-521-36279-2, ISBN13: 978-0-521-36279-5. Dewey:871/.01. LCCN:94-049341.
Audience: **u,f.** *Choice, 1996.*

Ovid **PA6522**
The Love Poems. A. D. Melville (Translator), E. J. Kenney (Introduction by, Notes by). Trade Paper. Oxford University Press, Inc. New York, NY. 1999. 304p. Oxford World's Classics Ser. ISBN:0-19-283633-1, ISBN13: 978-0-19-283633-5. Dewey:871.2.
Audience: **g,l,u.**

Ovid **PA6825**
Metamorphoses, Bks. 9-15. Ed. 2. Frank J. Miller (Translator). Trade Cloth. Harvard University Press. Cambridge, MA. 1916. 512p. Loeb Classical Library, No. 42-43 ISBN:0-674-99047-1, ISBN13: 978-0-674-99047-0. Dewey:871/.01.
Audience: **g,l,u.**

Ovid **PA6121.A7**
Ovid Metamorphoses: Books 1-8, Vol. 3. Frank J. Miller (Translator). Trade Cloth. Harvard University Press. Cambridge, MA. 1916. 496p. Loeb Classical Library ISBN:0-674-99046-3, ISBN13: 978-0-674-99046-3. Dewey:870.
Audience: **g,l,u.**

Ovid **PA6522.A8.M6 1979**
Art of Love, Cosmetics, Remedies for Love, Ibis, Walnut-Tree, Sea Fishing, Consolation, Vol. 2. Ed. 2. J. H. Mozley (Translator). Trade Cloth. Harvard University Press. Cambridge, MA. 1979. 400p. Loeb Classical Library, No. 232 ISBN:0-674-99255-5, ISBN13: 978-0-674-99255-9. Dewey:871/.01. LCCN:30-007535.
Audience: **g,l,u.**

Ovid **PA6522.F2N34 1995**
Ovid's Fasti: Roman Holidays. Betty R. Nagle (Notes by). Trade Paper. Indiana University Press. Bloomington, IN. 1995. 224p. ISBN:0-253-20933-1, ISBN13: 978-0-253-20933-7. Dewey:871/.01. LCCN:94-021660.
Audience: **g,l,u.** *Choice, 1995.*

Ovid **PA6522.A1 1977**
Heroides and Amores, Vol. 1. Ed. 2. Grant Showerman (Translator). Trade Cloth. Harvard University Press. Cambridge, MA. 1977. 536p. Loeb Classical Library, No. 41 ISBN:0-674-99045-5, ISBN13: 978-0-674-99045-6. Dewey:871/.01. LCCN:88-139567.
Audience: **g,l,u.**

Ovid **PA6522.M2S55 1994**
The Metamorphoses of Ovid. David R. Slavitt (Translator). Trade Paper. Johns Hopkins University Press. Baltimore, MD. 1994. 360p. ISBN:0-8018-4798-2, ISBN13: 978-0-8018-4798-1. Dewey:873/.01. LCCN:93-031580.
Audience: **g,l,u.**

Ovid **PA6156; PA6522**
Tristia, Ex Ponto, Vol. VI. A. L. Wheeler (Translator). Trade Cloth. Harvard University Press. Cambridge, MA. 1931. 560p. Loeb Classical Library, No. 151 ISBN:0-674-99167-2, ISBN13: 978-0-674-99167-5. Dewey:871.2.
Audience: **g,l,u.**

Syme, Ronald **DG279**
History in Ovid. Oxford University Press, Inc. 1979. ISBN:0-19-814825-9, ISBN13: 978-0-19-814825-8.
Audience: **u,f.**

Tissol, Garth **PA6519.M9T57 1997**
The Face of Nature: Wit, Narrative, and Cosmic Origins in Ovid's Metamorphoses. Trade Cloth. Princeton University Press. Princeton, NJ. 1996. 250p. ISBN:0-691-01102-8, ISBN13: 978-0-691-01102-8. Dewey:883/.01. LCCN:96-026943.
Audience: **u,f.** *Choice, 1997.*

Wilkinson, L. P. **PA6537**
Ovid Recalled. Trade Paper. Bristol Classical Press. London, 2003. 504p. Bcpaperback Ser. ISBN:1-85399-663-7, ISBN13: 978-1-85399-663-4. Dewey:871/.01.
Audience: **g,u,f.**

Latin > Individual Authors > Persius

Bramble, J. C. **PA6556**
Persius and the Programmatic Satire: A Study in Form and Imagery. P. D. Garnsey, G. C. Horrocks & R. L. Hunter (Contribution by). Trade Cloth. Cambridge University Press. New York, NY. 1974. 232p. Cambridge Classical Studies ISBN:0-521-08703-1, ISBN13: 978-0-521-08703-2. Dewey:871/.01. LCCN:72-083579.
Audience: **u,f.**

Dessen, Cynthia S. **PA6556**
The Satires of Persius. Ed. 2. Trade Cloth. Bristol Classical Press. London, 1996. 128p. Classical Paperbacks Ser. ISBN:1-85399-487-1, ISBN13: 978-1-85399-487-6. Dewey:877.01.
Audience: **u,f.**

Hooley, D. M. **PA6556.H66 1997**
The Knotted Thong: Structures of Mimesis in Persius. Trade Cloth. University of Michigan Press. Chicago, IL. 1998. 304p. ISBN:0-472-10792-5, ISBN13: 978-0-472-10792-6. Dewey:871/.01. LCCN:97-029415.
Audience: **u,f.** *Choice, 1998.*

Latin > Individual Authors > Petronius

Courtney, Edward **PA6559.C678 2001**
A Companion to Petronius. Trade Paper. Oxford University Press, Inc. New York, NY. 2002. 250p. ISBN:0-19-924594-0, ISBN13: 978-0-19-924594-9. Dewey:873/.01. LCCN:2002-280390.
Audience: **u,f.**

Petronius Arbiter **PA6825**
The Satyricon. William Arrowsmith (Translator). Cloth over Boards. University of Michigan Press. Chicago, IL. 1959. ISBN:0-472-72935-7, ISBN13: 978-0-472-72935-7. Dewey:873./01. LCCN:59-006026.
Audience: **g,l,u.**

Petronius Arbiter **PA6825**
The Satyrica. Daniel Kinney & R. Bracht Branham (Translators). Trade Paper. University of California Press. Berkeley, CA. 1997. 224p. ISBN:0-520-21118-9, ISBN13: 978-0-520-21118-6. Dewey:873/.01.
Audience: **g,l,u.** *Choice, 1996.*

Petronius Arbiter **PA6558.A5 1982**
Cena Trimalchionis. Martin S. Smith (Photographer). Paper Text. Oxford University Press, Inc. New York, NY. 1983. 270p. ISBN:0-19-814459-8, ISBN13: 978-0-19-814459-5. Dewey:873/.01. LCCN:83-235569.
Audience: **u,f.**

Slater, Niall W. **PA6559.S5 1990**
Reading Petronius. Trade Cloth. Johns Hopkins University Press. Baltimore, MD. 1990. 280p. ISBN:0-8018-3984-X, ISBN13: 978-0-8018-3984-9. Dewey:873/.01. LCCN:89-043484.
Audience: **u,f.** *Choice, 1991.*

Latin > Individual Authors > Plautus

Lindsay, W. M. **PA6605.L56 2002**
Syntax of Plautus. Trade Paper. Bristol Classical Press. London, 144p. ISBN:1-85399-648-3, ISBN13: 978-1-85399-648-1. Dewey:872/.01.
Audience: **u,f.**

Plautus, Titus Maccius **PA6568 .A6 2000**
Plautus: Amphitruo. David M. Christenson (Editor). Cloth Text. Cambridge University Press. New York, NY. 2000. 350p. Cambridge Greek and Latin Classics ISBN:0-521-45401-8, ISBN13: 978-0-521-45401-8. Dewey:872/.01. LCCN:99-043670.
Audience: **u,f.**

Plautus, Titus Maccius **PA6568 .M4 1993**
Plautus: Menaechmi. A. S. Gratwick (Editor). Cloth Text. Cambridge University Press. New York, NY. 1993. 286p. Cambridge Greek and Latin Classics ISBN:0-521-34162-0, ISBN13: 978-0-521-34162-2. Dewey:872.01. LCCN:92-017790.
Audience: **u,f.**

Plautus, Titus Maccius **PA6585**
Miles Gloriosus. Ed. 2. Mason Hammond (Editor). Trade Cloth. Harvard University Press. Cambridge, MA. 1963. 140p. ISBN:0-674-57436-2, ISBN13: 978-0-674-57436-6. Dewey:872/.01. LCCN:73-122213.
Audience: **l,u.**

Plautus, Titus Maccius & Terence **PA6165.F58 1999**
Five Comedies: Bacchides, Menaechmi, Miles Gloriosus, Hecyra, and Adelphoe. Deena Berg & Douglass Parker (Translators), Deena Berg & Douglass Parker (Introduction by). Trade Paper. Hackett Publishing Company, Inc. Indianapolis, IN. 1999. 424p. HPC Classics Ser. ISBN:0-87220-362-X, ISBN13: 978-0-87220-362-4. Dewey:872/.0108. LCCN:98-050732.
Audience: **g,l,u.**

Plautus, Titus Maccius **PA6585**
Plautus: Casina. Malcolm M. Willcock & W. T. Maccary (Editors), P. E. Easterling, Philip Hardie, Richard Hunter & E. J. Kenney (Contribution by). Trade Paper. Cambridge University Press. New York, NY. 1976. 241p. Cambridge Greek and Latin Classics ISBN:0-521-29022-8, ISBN13: 978-0-521-29022-7. Dewey:872/.01.
Audience: **u,f.**

Plautus, Titus Maccius **PA6568.C8 1993**
Plautus' Curculio. John Wright (Introduction by, Notes by). Trade Cloth. University of Oklahoma Press. Norman, OK. 1993. 176p. Series in Classical Culture, Vol. 17 ISBN:0-8061-2507-1, ISBN13: 978-0-8061-2507-7. Dewey:872/.01. LCCN:93-013385.
Audience: **l,u.**

Segal, Erich **PA6585.S4 1987**
Roman Laughter: The Comedy of Plautus. Ed. 2. Trade Paper. Oxford University Press, Inc. New York, NY. 1987. 268p. ISBN:0-19-504166-6, ISBN13: 978-0-19-504166-8. Dewey:872/.01. LCCN:86-023682.
Audience: **u,f.**

Latin > Individual Authors > Pliny the Elder

Beagon, Mary **Q143.P64B43 1992**
Roman Nature: The Thought of Pliny the Elder. Trade Cloth. Oxford University Press, Inc. New York, NY. 1992. 270p. Classical Monographs ISBN:0-19-814726-0, ISBN13: 978-0-19-814726-8. Dewey:509.37. LCCN:91-036006.
Audience: **u,f.**

Murphy, Trevor **QH41**
Pliny the Elder's Natural History: The Empire in the Encyclopedia. Trade Cloth. Oxford University Press, Inc. New York, NY. 2004. 320p. ISBN:0-19-926288-8, ISBN13: 978-0-19-926288-5. Dewey:937.06. LCCN:2004-300657.
Audience: **u,f.** *Choice, 2005.*

Pliny the Elder **PA6156**
Natural History: Index of Fishes, Vol. 8. Trade Cloth. Harvard University Press. Cambridge, MA. 1963. 608p. Loeb Classical Library, No. 392-394, 418-419 ISBN:0-674-99460-4, ISBN13: 978-0-674-99460-7. Dewey:870.
Audience: **g,l,u,f.**

Pliny the Elder **PA6156**
Natural History: Bks. 36-37, Vol. 10. Trade Cloth. Harvard University Press. Cambridge, MA. 1962. 368p. Loeb Classical Library, No. 392-394, 418-419 ISBN:0-674-99461-2, ISBN13: 978-0-674-99461-4. Dewey:870.
Audience: **g,l,u,f.**

Pliny the Elder **PA6156**
Natural History: Index of Plants, Vol. 7. Trade Cloth. Harvard University Press. Cambridge, MA. 1956. 576p. Loeb Classical Library, No. 392-394, 418-419 ISBN:0-674-99432-9, ISBN13: 978-0-674-99432-4. Dewey:870.
Audience: **g,l,u,f.**

Pliny the Elder **PA6156**
Natural History: Bks. 20-23, Vol. 6. W. H. Jones (Translator). Trade Cloth. Harvard University Press. Cambridge, MA. 1951. 560p. Loeb Classical Library ISBN:0-674-99431-0, ISBN13: 978-0-674-99431-7. Dewey:870.
Audience: **g,l,u,f.**

Pliny the Elder **PA6156**
Natural History: Bks. 33-35, Vol. 9. H. Rackham (Translator). Trade Cloth. Harvard University Press. Cambridge, MA. 1952. 432p. Loeb Classical Library, No. 392-394, 418-419 ISBN:0-674-99433-7, ISBN13: 978-0-674-99433-1. Dewey:870.
Audience: **g,l,u,f.**

Pliny the Elder **PA6156**
Natural History: Bks. 12-16, Vol. 4. E. H. Warmington (Editor). Trade Cloth. Harvard University Press. Cambridge, MA. 1945. 576p. Loeb Classical Library ISBN:0-674-99408-6, ISBN13: 978-0-674-99408-9. Dewey:870.
Audience: **g,l,u,f.**

Pliny the Elder **PA6156**
Natural History, Vol. 2. E. H. Warmington (Editor). Trade Cloth. Harvard University Press. Cambridge, MA. 1942. 672p. Loeb Classical Library ISBN:0-674-99388-8, ISBN13: 978-0-674-99388-4. Dewey:870.
Audience: **g,l,u,f.**

Pliny the Elder **PA6156**
Natural History, Vol. 1. E. H. Warmington (Editor). Trade Cloth. Harvard University Press. Cambridge, MA. 1938. 400p. Loeb Classical Library ISBN:0-674-99364-0, ISBN13: 978-0-674-99364-8. Dewey:870.
Audience: **g,l,u,f.**

Pliny the Elder **PA6156**
Natural History: Bks. 17-19, Vol. 5. E. H. Warmington (Editor). Trade Cloth. Harvard University Press. Cambridge, MA. 1950. 560p. Loeb Classical Library ISBN:0-674-99409-4, ISBN13: 978-0-674-99409-6. Dewey:870.
Audience: **g,l,u,f.**

Pliny the Elder **PA6156**
Natural History: Bks. 8-11, Vol. 3. E. H. Warmington (Editor). Trade Cloth. Harvard University Press. Cambridge, MA. 1940. 624p. Loeb Classical Library ISBN:0-674-99389-6, ISBN13: 978-0-674-99389-1. Dewey:870.
Audience: **g,l,u,f.**

Latin > Individual Authors > Pliny the Younger

Pliny the Younger **PA6156**
Letters and Panegyricus, Vol. 2, Bks. 8-10. Betty Radice (Translator). Trade Cloth. Harvard University Press. Cambridge, MA. 1969. 592p. Loeb Classical Library, No. 55, 59 ISBN:0-674-99066-8, ISBN13: 978-0-674-99066-1. Dewey:876/.01.
Audience: **g,l,u,f.**

Pliny the Younger **PA6156**
Pliny: Letters and Panegyricus, Vol. 1. Betty Radice (Editor). Trade Cloth. Harvard University Press. Cambridge, MA. 1969. 608p. Loeb Classical Library, No. 55, 59 ISBN:0-674-99061-7, ISBN13: 978-0-674-99061-6. Dewey:876/.01.
Audience: **g,l,u,f.**

Pliny the Younger **PA6638.A4 1967**
Fifty Letters of Pliny. Ed. 2. A. N. Sherwin-White (Editor). Trade Paper. Oxford University Press, Inc. New York, NY. 1969. 230p. ISBN:0-19-912010-2, ISBN13: 978-0-19-912010-9. Dewey:876/.01.
Audience: **l,u.**

Latin > Individual Authors > Propertius

Hubbard, Margaret **PA6646.H78 1975**
Propertius. Trade Cloth. Simon & Schuster. New York, NY. 1975. viii, 182 p.,p. ISBN:0-684-14464-6, ISBN13: 978-0-684-14464-1. Dewey:874/.01. LCCN:75-011481.
Audience: **g,u,f.**

Propertius **PA6644**
Propertius: Elegies. W. A. Camps (Editor). Trade Paper. Cambridge University Press. New York, NY. 1977. 112p. ISBN:0-521-29210-7, ISBN13: 978-0-521-29210-8. Dewey:874/.01.
Audience: **u,f.**

Propertius **PA6644.B2**
Propertius: Elegies, Bk. II. W. A. Camps (Editor). Trade Paper. Bristol Classical Press. London, 1985. 255p. Latin Texts ISBN:0-86292-148-1, ISBN13: 978-0-86292-148-4. Dewey:874.01.
Audience: **u,f.**

Propertius **PA6644.B3**
Propertius: Elegies III, Bk. III. W. A. Camps (Editor). Trade Paper. Bristol Classical Press. London, 1986. 188p. Latin Texts ISBN:0-86292-116-3, ISBN13: 978-0-86292-116-3. Dewey:874.4.
Audience: **u,f.**

Propertius **PA6644 .B4 1979**
Propertius: Elegies, Bk. IV. W. R. Connor & W. A. Camps (Editors). Library Binding. Ayer Company Publishers, Inc. Manchester, NH. 1979. Latin Texts and Commentaries Ser. ISBN:0-405-11597-0, ISBN13: 978-0-405-11597-4. Dewey:874/.01. LCCN:78-067126.
Audience: **u,f.**

Propertius **PA6645.E5K355 2004**
The Complete Elegies of Sextus Propertius. Vincent Katz (Translator, Introduction by, Notes by). Trade Cloth. Princeton University Press. Princeton, NJ. 2004. 488p. Lockert Library of Poetry in Translation ISBN:0-691-11581-8, ISBN13: 978-0-691-11581-8. Dewey:874/.01. LCCN:2003-057954.
Audience: **g,l,u.**

Propertius **PA6644.A2**
Elegies, I-IV: Propertius. L. Richardson Jr. (Editor). Trade Paper. Books on Demand. Ann Arbor, MI. 498p. American Philological Association Series of Classical Texts ISBN:0-598-17146-0, ISBN13: 978-0-598-17146-7. Dewey:874/.01. LCCN:76-026153.
Audience: **u,f.**

Sullivan, J. P. **PA6646**
Propertius: A Critical Introduction. Trade Cloth. Cambridge University Press. New York, NY. 1976. 185p. ISBN:0-521-20904-8, ISBN13: 978-0-521-20904-5. Dewey:874/.01. LCCN:75-010038.
Audience: **u,f.**

Latin > Individual Authors > Prudentius

Malamud, Martha A. **PA6648.P7M34 1989**
A Poetics of Transformation: Prudentius and Classical Mythology. Book, Other. Cornell University Press. Ithaca, NY. 1989. 224p. Cornell Studies in Classical Philology ISBN:0-8014-2249-3, ISBN13: 978-0-8014-2249-2. Dewey:871/.01. LCCN:88-043290.
Audience: **u,f.**

Prudentius **BR65**
Prudentius: Against Symmachus 2, Crowns of Martyrdom, Scenes from History, Epilogue, Vol. 2. Trade Cloth. Harvard University Press. Cambridge, MA. 1953. 400p. Loeb Classical Library ISBN:0-674-99438-8, ISBN13: 978-0-674-99438-6. Dewey:878.
Audience: **g,l,u.**

Prudentius **PA6648**
Works: Preface, Daily Round, Divinity of Christ, Origin of Sin, Fight for Mansoul, Against Symmachus 1, Vol. 1. Trade Cloth. Harvard University Press. Cambridge, MA. 1949. 432p. Loeb Classical Library, No. 387, 398 ISBN:0-674-99426-4, ISBN13: 978-0-674-99426-3. Dewey:871.
Audience: **g,l,u.**

Roberts, Michael **PA6648.P6P4773 1993**
Poetry and the Cult of the Martyrs: The Liber Peristephanon on Prudentius. Trade Cloth. University of Michigan Press. Chicago, IL. 1994. 232p. Recentiores: Later Latin Texts and Contexts Ser. ISBN:0-472-10449-7, ISBN13: 978-0-472-10449-9. Dewey:272/.1/0922. LCCN:93-031245.
Audience: **u,f.**

Latin > Individual Authors > Quintilian

Quintilian **PA6650.E5R87 2001**
The Orator's Education: Bks. 1-2, Vol. 1. Donald Russell (Editor, Translator). Trade Cloth. Harvard University Press. Cambridge, MA. 2002. 448p. Loeb Classical Library, Vols. 124-127 ISBN:0-674-99591-0, ISBN13: 978-0-674-99591-8. Dewey:808.5/1. LCCN:2001-016920.
Audience: **g,l,u,f.**

Quintilian **PA6650.E5R87 2001**
The Orator's Education: Bks. 9-10, Vol. 4. Donald Russell (Editor, Translator). Trade Cloth. Harvard University Press. Cambridge, MA. 2002. 416p. Loeb Classical Library, Vols. 124-127 ISBN:0-674-99594-5, ISBN13: 978-0-674-99594-9. Dewey:808.5/1. LCCN:2001-016920.
Audience: **g,l,u,f.**

Quintilian **PA6650.E5R87 2001**
The Orator's Education, Bks. 3-5,Vol. 2. Donald Russell (Editor, Translator). Trade Cloth. Harvard University Press. Cambridge, MA. 2002. 560p. Loeb Classical Library, Vols. 124-127 ISBN:0-674-99592-9, ISBN13: 978-0-674-99592-5. Dewey:808.5/1. LCCN:2001-016920.
Audience: **g,l,u,f.**

Quintilian **PA6650.E5R87 2001**
The Orator's Education: Bks. 6-8, Vol. 3. Donald Russell (Editor, Translator). Trade Cloth. Harvard University Press. Cambridge, MA. 2002. 496p. Loeb Classical Library, Vols. 124-127 ISBN:0-674-99593-7, ISBN13: 978-0-674-99593-2. Dewey:808.5/1. LCCN:2001-016920.
Audience: **g,l,u,f.**

Quintilian **PA6650.E5R87 2001**
The Orator's Education: Bks. 11-12, Vol. 5. Donald Russell (Editor, Translator). Trade Cloth. Harvard University Press. Cambridge, MA. 2002. 448p. Loeb Classical Library, Vols. 124-127 ISBN:0-674-99595-3, ISBN13: 978-0-674-99595-6. Dewey:808.5/1. LCCN:2001-016920.
Audience: **g,l,u,f.**

Latin > Individual Authors > Sallust

Earl, Donald C. **PA6656.E2**
The Political Thought of Sallust. Paper Text. Textbook Publishers. Temecula, CA. 2003. 132p. ISBN:0-7581-1334-X, ISBN13: 978-0-7581-1334-4. Dewey:878.
Audience: **u,f.**

Paul, G. M. **PA6653.A63 P3 1984**
A Historical Commentary on Sallust's Bellum Jugurthinum. Trade Cloth. Francis Cairns Publications, Ltd. Cambridge, 1984. 302p. ARCA (Classical and Medieval Texts, Papers and Monographs), No. 13 ISBN:0-905205-16-2, ISBN13: 978-0-905205-16-8. Dewey:939/.72. LCCN:84-152075.
Audience: **l,u,f.**

Rolfe, J. C. (Translator) **PA6654**
War with Catiline, War with Jugurtha - Selections from the Histories - Doubtful Works. Trade Cloth. Harvard University Press. Cambridge, MA. 1921. 560p. Loeb Classical Library, No. 116 ISBN:0-674-99128-1, ISBN13: 978-0-674-99128-6. Dewey:870.
Audience: **g,l,u.**

Sallust **PA6391**
The Jugurthine War and the Conspiracy of Catiline. S. A. Hanford (Translator, Introduction by). Trade Paper. Penguin Group (USA) Inc. New York, NY. 1964. 240p. Classics Ser. ISBN:0-14-044132-8, ISBN13: 978-0-14-044132-1. Dewey:878/.01.
Audience: **g,l,u.**

Sallust **PA6653.A4 R35 1984**
Sallust's Bellum Catilinae. J. T. Ramsey (Editor). Trade Paper. Oxford University Press, Inc. New York, NY. 1984. 272p. American Philological Association Textbook Ser. ISBN:0-89130-560-2, ISBN13: 978-0-89130-560-6. Dewey:937/.05. LCCN:81-021281.
Audience: **l,u,f.**

Sallust **PA6653 .A2 1991**
Catilina, Iugurtha, Historiarum Fragmenta Selecta; Appendix Sallustiana. L. D. Reynolds (Editor). Trade Cloth. Oxford University Press, Inc. New York, NY. 1991. 280p. Oxford Classical Texts ISBN:0-19-814667-1, ISBN13: 978-0-19-814667-4. Dewey:937.05. LCCN:94-132623.
Audience: **u,f.**

Syme, Ronald **PA6656 .S9 2002**
Sallust. Trade Paper. University of California Press. Berkeley, CA. 2002. 434p. Sather Classical Lectures, Vol. 33 ISBN:0-520-23479-0, ISBN13: 978-0-520-23479-6. Dewey:937/.05/092. LCCN:2002-018994.
Audience: **u,f.**

Latin > Individual Authors > Seneca the Elder

Seneca the Elder **PN4121**
Controversiae - Suasoriae, Fragments, Vol. 2. Michael Winterbottom (Translator). Trade Cloth. Harvard University Press. Cambridge, MA. 1974. 656p. Loeb Classical Library, No. 463-464 ISBN:0-674-99511-2, ISBN13: 978-0-674-99511-6. Dewey:808.5/1.
Audience: **u,f.**

Seneca the Elder **PA6156.S4.O7**
Seneca the Elder Declamations, Vol. 1. Michael Winterbottom (Translator). Trade Cloth. Harvard University Press. Cambridge, MA. 1974. 560p. Loeb Classical Library, No. 463-464 ISBN:0-674-99510-4, ISBN13: 978-0-674-99510-9. Dewey:080. LCCN:74-166313.
Audience: **u,f.**

Latin > Individual Authors > Seneca the Younger

Seneca, Lucius Annaeus **PA6664 .P5 1990**
Seneca: Phaedra. Michael Coffey & Roland Mayer (Editors), P. E. Easterling, Philip Hardie, Richard Hunter & E. J. Kenney (Contribution by). Cloth Text. Cambridge University Press. New York, NY. 1990. 229p. Cambridge Greek and Latin Classics Ser. ISBN:0-521-20085-7, ISBN13: 978-0-521-20085-1. Dewey:872/.01. LCCN:89-007267.
Audience: **u,f.**

Seneca, Lucius Annaeus **PA6665 .A9 1984**
Apocolocyntosis. P. T. Eden (Editor). Trade Cloth. Cambridge University Press. New York, NY. 1984. 192p. Cambridge Greek and Latin Classics ISBN:0-521-24617-2, ISBN13: 978-0-521-24617-0. Dewey:877/.01. LCCN:83-014344.
Audience: **u,f.**

Seneca, Lucius Annaeus **PA6661.E7**
Seneca: Select Letters. Walter C. Summers (Editor). Trade Paper. Bristol Classical Press. London, 1983. 500p. Latin Texts ISBN:0-86292-120-1, ISBN13: 978-0-86292-120-0. Dewey:878.5.
Audience: **u,f.**

Seneca, Lucius Annaeus **PA6664.T5**
Seneca's Thyestes. R. J. Tarrant (Editor). Paper Text. Oxford University Press, Inc. New York, NY. 1985. 288p. American Philological Association Textbook Ser. ISBN:0-89130-871-7, ISBN13: 978-0-89130-871-3. Dewey:872/.01.
Audience: **u,f.**

Seneca, Lucius Annaeus **PA6661.D6 2003**
Seneca: De Otio; de Brevitate Vitae. Gareth D. Williams (Editor), P. E. Easterling, Philip Hardie, Richard Hunter & E. J. Kenney (Contribution by). Cloth Text. Cambridge University Press. New York, NY. 2003. 286p. Cambridge Greek and Latin Classics Ser. ISBN:0-521-58223-7, ISBN13: 978-0-521-58223-0. Dewey:188.
Audience: **u,f.**

Latin > Individual Authors > Statius

Statius, Publius Papinius **PA6697.E5S5 2004**
The Silvae of Statius. Betty Rose Nagle (Translator, Introduction by, Notes by). Trade Cloth. Indiana University Press. Bloomington, IN. 2004. 176p. ISBN:0-253-34387-9, ISBN13: 978-0-253-34387-1. Dewey:871/.01. LCCN:2003-017927.
Audience: **g,l,u.**

Statius, Publius Papinius **PA6697**
The Thebaid: Seven Against Thebes. Charles Stanley Ross (Translator). Trade Cloth. Johns Hopkins University Press. Baltimore, MD. 2004. 432p. Johns Hopkins New Translations from Antiquity Ser. ISBN:0-8018-6908-0, ISBN13: 978-0-8018-6908-2. Dewey:871/.01. LCCN:2004-008928.
Audience: **g,l,u.** *Choice, 2005.*

Statius, Publius Papinius **PA6697.E5.T5 2003**
Thebaid: Achilleid, Books 8-12. D. R. Shackleton Bailey (Editor). Trade Cloth. Harvard University Press. Cambridge, MA. 2004. 448p. Loeb Classical Library, Vol. 498 ISBN:0-674-01209-7, ISBN13: 978-0-674-01209-7. Dewey:873/.01. LCCN:2003-051132.
Audience: **g,u,f.**

Statius, Publius Papinius **PA6697.E5T5 2003**
Thebaid: Bks. 1-7. D. R. Shackleton Bailey (Editor). Trade Cloth. Harvard University Press. Cambridge, MA. 2004. 472p. Loeb Classical Library, Vol. 207 ISBN:0-674-01208-9, ISBN13: 978-0-674-01208-0. Dewey:873/.01. LCCN:2003-051117.
Audience: **g,u,f.**

Latin > Individual Authors > Suetonius

Hurley, Donna W. **DG283.S83 H87 1993**
An Historical and Historiographical Commentary on Suetonius' Life of C. Caligula. Trade Cloth. Scholars Press. Atlanta, GA. 1993. 246p. American Philological Association, American Classical Studies, No. 32 ISBN:1-55540-880-X, ISBN13: 978-1-55540-880-0. Dewey:937/.07/092. LCCN:93-013723.
Audience: **u,f.**

Jones, Brian W. & Milns, R. D. **DG274**
Suetonius: The Flavian Emperors. Trade Paper. Bristol Classical Press. London, 256p. Classical Studies Ser. ISBN:1-85399-613-0, ISBN13: 978-1-85399-613-9. Dewey:937/.07/0922.
Audience: **u.**

Suetonius **DG277.S83**
Lives of the Caesars, 2. Trade Cloth. Harvard University Press. Cambridge, MA. 1914. 564p. Loeb Classical Library, No. 31, 38 ISBN:0-674-99042-0, ISBN13: 978-0-674-99042-5. Dewey:920.037.
Audience: **g,l,u.**

Suetonius **DG262**
Divus Julius Caesar. H. E. Butler & M. Cary (Editors). Trade Cloth. Oxford University Press, Inc. New York, NY. 1927. ISBN:0-19-814418-0, ISBN13: 978-0-19-814418-2. Dewey:292/.2/11.
Audience: **u,f.**

Suetonius **DG277.S83 2000**
Lives of the Caesars. Catharine Edwards (Editor). Trade Paper. Oxford University Press, Inc. New York, NY. 2001. 352p. Oxford World's Classics Ser. ISBN:0-19-283271-9, ISBN13: 978-0-19-283271-9. Dewey:920.037. LCCN:2001-275341.
Audience: **g,l,u.**

Suetonius **DG277**
The Twelve Caesars. Robert Graves (Translator), Michael Grant (Introduction by, Revised by). Trade Paper. Penguin Group (USA) Inc. New York, NY. 2003. 384p. Classics Ser. ISBN:0-14-044921-3, ISBN13: 978-0-14-044921-1. Dewey:937/.07/0922 B. LCCN:2003-267782.
Audience: **g,l,u.**

Suetonius **PA6700 .A35 2001**
Suetonius: Diuus Claudius. Donna W. Hurley (Editor), P. E. Easterling, Philip Hardie, Richard Hunter & E. J. Kenney (Contribution by). Cloth Text. Cambridge University Press. New York, NY. 2001. 282p. Cambridge Greek and Latin Classics Ser. ISBN:0-521-59325-5, ISBN13: 978-0-521-59325-0. Dewey:937/.07/092 B. LCCN:00-036299.
Audience: **u,f.**

Suetonius **PA6700**
Suetonius: Lives of Galba, Otho and Vitellius. David Shotter (Editor). Trade Cloth. Aris & Phillips. Oxford, 1993. 224p. ISBN:0-85668-537-2, ISBN13: 978-0-85668-537-8. Dewey:937.070922.
Audience: **u.**

Wallace-Hadrill, Andrew **DG206.G5**
Suetonius. Ed. 2. Trade Paper. Bristol Classical Press. London, 1995. 227p. Classical Paperbacks Ser. ISBN:1-85399-451-0, ISBN13: 978-1-85399-451-7. Dewey:937/.06/092.
Audience: **u,f.**

Latin > Individual Authors > Tacitus

Ash, Rhiannon **DG286.A84 1999**
Ordering Anarchy: Armies and Leaders in Tacitus' Histories. Trade Cloth. University of Michigan Press. Chicago, IL. 1999. 246p. ISBN:0-472-11113-2, ISBN13: 978-0-472-11113-8. Dewey:937/.07/092 B. LCCN:99-047172.
Audience: **u,f.** *Choice, 2001.*

Mellor, Ronald **DG206.T32M45 1994**
Tacitus. UK-B Format Paperback. Routledge. New York, NY. 1994. 200p. ISBN:0-415-91002-1, ISBN13: 978-0-415-91002-6. Dewey:937/.07/092. LCCN:94-028753.
Audience: **u,f.**

Syme, Ronald **DG206.T32**
Tacitus. Oxford University Press, Inc. 1980. ISBN:0-19-814327-3, ISBN13: 978-0-19-814327-7.
Audience: **u,f.** B

Tacitus, Cornelius **AC1**
Histories and Annals, Vols. II-V. Trade Cloth. Harvard University Press. Cambridge, MA. Loeb Classical Library, Nos. 111, 249, 312, 322 ISBN:0-318-53072-4, ISBN13: 978-0-318-53072-7. Dewey:878.6.
Audience: **g,l,u.**

Tacitus, Cornelius **DG291.7.A2T313 1999**
Agricola and Germany. Anthony Birley (Translator). Trade Paper. Oxford University Press, Inc. New York, NY. 1999. 216p. Oxford World's Classics Ser. ISBN:0-19-283300-6, ISBN13: 978-0-19-283300-6. Dewey:936.1/03. LCCN:98-034569.
Audience: **g,l,u.**

Tacitus, Cornelius **PA6705.H6B1 2003**
Tacitus: Histories, Vol. 1. Cynthia Damon (Editor). Cloth Text. Cambridge University Press. New York, NY. 2002. 338p. Cambridge Greek and Latin Classics Ser. ISBN:0-521-57072-7, ISBN13: 978-0-521-57072-5. Dewey:937/.05. LCCN:2002-073824.
Audience: **u,f.**

Tacitus, Cornelius **PA6105.S8**
Annales, Vol. I-VI, Bks. XI-XVI. C. D. Fisher (Editor). Cloth Text. Oxford University Press, Inc. New York, NY. 1922. 430p. Oxford Classical Texts ISBN:0-19-814633-7, ISBN13: 978-0-19-814633-9. Dewey:878.
Audience: **u,f.**

Tacitus, Cornelius **DG279**
Annals of Imperial Rome. Michael Grant (Introduction by). Trade Cloth. Dorset Press. New York, NY. 1985. 455p. ISBN:0-88029-024-2, ISBN13: 978-0-88029-024-1. Dewey:937/.07.
Audience: **g,l,u.**

Tacitus, Cornelius **PA6705.A6 B4 1989**
Tacitus IV: Annals. R. H. Martin & A. J. Woodman (Editors), P. E. Easterling, Philip Hardie, Richard Hunter & E. J. Kenney (Contribution by). Cloth Text. Cambridge University Press. New York, NY. 1990. 289p. Cambridge Greek and Latin Classics ISBN:0-521-30504-7, ISBN13: 978-0-521-30504-4. Dewey:937. LCCN:89-000545.
Audience: **u,f.**

Tacitus, Cornelius **PA6706.D5 T34 2001**
Tacitus: Dialogus de Oratoribus. Roland Mayer (Editor), P. E. Easterling, Philip Hardie, Richard Hunter & E. J. Kenney

(Contribution by). Cloth Text. Cambridge University Press. New York, NY. 2001. 238p. Greek and Latin Classics Ser. ISBN:0-521-47040-4, ISBN13: 978-0-521-47040-7. Dewey:878/.01/09. LCCN:00-062142.
Audience: **u,f.**

Tacitus, Cornelius **PA6705.A6**
Tacitus: Annals I. N. Miller (Editor). Trade Paper. Bristol Classical Press. London, 1989. 261p. Latin Texts ISBN:1-85399-358-1, ISBN13: 978-1-85399-358-9. Dewey:937.07.
Audience: **u.**

Tacitus, Cornelius **PA6707**
Agricola - Germania: Dialogue on Oratory, Vol. 1. R. M. Ogilvie & M. Winterbottom (Editors). Trade Cloth. Harvard University Press. Cambridge, MA. 1994. 384p. Loeb Classical Library, No. 35 ISBN:0-674-99039-0, ISBN13: 978-0-674-99039-5. Dewey:878.
Audience: **g,l,u.**

Tacitus, Cornelius **PA6307**
Opera Minora. Michael Winterbottom & R. M. Ogilive (Editors). Cloth Text. Oxford University Press, Inc. New York, NY. 1975. 124p. Oxford Classical Texts ISBN:0-19-814658-2, ISBN13: 978-0-19-814658-2. Dewey:878/.01/08.
Audience: **u,f.**

Tacitus, Cornelius **PA6705.A6**
Tacitus: Annals XIV. E. C. Woodcock (Editor). Trade Paper. Bristol Classical Press. London, 1992. 196p. Latin Texts ISBN:1-85399-315-8, ISBN13: 978-1-85399-315-2. Dewey:937.07092.
Audience: **u.**

Tacitus, Cornelius **DG207.T3W66 2001**
Annals. A. J. Woodman (Translator, Introduction by, Notes by). Trade Cloth. Hackett Publishing Company, Inc. Indianapolis, IN. 2004. 412p. ISBN:0-87220-559-2, ISBN13: 978-0-87220-559-8. Dewey:937/.07. LCCN:2004-047334.
Audience: **g,l,u.** *Choice, 2005.*

Woodman, A. J. **DG281.W66 1998**
Tacitus Reviewed. Trade Cloth. Oxford University Press, Inc. New York, NY. 1998. 268p. ISBN:0-19-815258-2, ISBN13: 978-0-19-815258-3. Dewey:937/.07. LCCN:98-027415.
Audience: **u,f.** *Choice, 1999.*

Latin > Individual Authors > Terence

Goldberg, Sander M. **PA6768.G65 1986**
Understanding Terence. Trade Cloth. Princeton University Press. Princeton, NJ. 1986. 232p. ISBN:0-691-03586-5, ISBN13: 978-0-691-03586-4. Dewey:872/.01. LCCN:85-043285.
Audience: **u,f.** *Choice, 1986.*

Terence **PA6756.A1B6 1992**
Terence: The Comedies. Palmer Bovie (Editor), Douglas Parker & Constance Carrier (Translators). Trade Paper. Johns Hopkins University Press. Baltimore, MD. 1975. 424p. Complete Roman Drama in Translation Ser. ISBN:0-8018-4354-5, ISBN13: 978-0-8018-4354-9. Dewey:872.01. LCCN:91-033984.
Audience: **g,l,u.**

Terence **PA6755.E8 T48 1999**
Terence: Eunuchus. Dave Brantley & John Barsby (Editors). Cloth Text. Cambridge University Press. New York, NY. 1999. 344p. Cambridge Greek and Latin Classics ISBN:0-521-45229-5, ISBN13: 978-0-521-45229-8. Dewey:872/.01. LCCN:98-013376.
Audience: **u,f.**

Terence **PA6585**
Terence: Adelphoe. R. H. Martin (Editor), P. E. Easterling, Philip Hardie, Richard Hunter & E. J. Kenney (Contribution by). Trade Paper. Cambridge University Press. New York, NY. 1976. 272p. Cambridge Greek and Latin Classics ISBN:0-521-29001-5, ISBN13: 978-0-521-29001-2. Dewey:872/.01. LCCN:75-036173.
Audience: **u,f.**

Latin > Individual Authors > Tibullus

Putnam, Michael C. **PA6789 .P8**
Tibullus: A Commentary. Trade Paper. University of Oklahoma Press. Norman, OK. 1979. 222p. American Philological Association Ser., Vol. 3 ISBN:0-8061-1560-2, ISBN13: 978-0-8061-1560-3. Dewey:478/.6/421.
Audience: **l,u,f.**

Tibullus **PA6787.A33**
Carminum Libri Tres. Ed. 2. J. P. Postgate (Editor). Cloth Text. Oxford University Press, Inc. New York, NY. 1924. 96p. Oxford Classical Texts ISBN:0-19-814637-X, ISBN13: 978-0-19-814637-7. Dewey:874.
Audience: **u,f.**

Yardley, John **PA6789**
Minor Authors of the Corpus Tibullianum. Paper Text. Bryn Mawr Commentaries. Bryn Mawr, PA. 1992. 57p. Latin Commentaries Ser. ISBN:0-929524-74-8, ISBN13: 978-0-929524-74-0. Dewey:874.01.
Audience: **u,f.**

Latin > Individual Authors > Vergil

Anderson, William Scovil **PA6825.A72 2005**
The Art of the Aeneid. Ed. 2. Book, Other. Bolchazy-Carducci Publishers. Wauconda, IL. 2005. viii + 121p. ISBN:0-86516-598-X, ISBN13: 978-0-86516-598-4. Dewey:883/.01. LCCN:2005-015595.
Audience: **g,l,u,f.**

Anderson, William Scovil & Quartarone, Lorina N. (Editors) **PA6825.A75 2002**
Approaches to Teaching Vergil's Aeneid. Trade Paper. Modern Language Association of America. New York, NY. 2002. xiii & 255p. Approaches to Teaching World Literature Ser., Vol. 74 ISBN:0-87352-772-0, ISBN13: 978-0-87352-772-9. Dewey:873/.01. LCCN:2002-022917.
Audience: **f.**

Camps, W. A. **PA6825**
An Introduction to Virgil's Aeneid. Paper Text. Oxford University Press, Inc. New York, NY. 1979. 176p. ISBN:0-19-872024-6, ISBN13: 978-0-19-872024-9. Dewey:873/.01.
Audience: **g,l,u,f.**

Clausen, Wendell (Editor, Commentaries by, Introduction by) **PA6825**
A Commentary on Virgil Eclogues. Paper Text. Oxford University Press, Inc. New York, NY. 1995. 358p. ISBN:0-19-815035-0, ISBN13: 978-0-19-815035-0. Dewey:873/.01.
Audience: **u,f.**

Comparetti, Domenico **PA6961.C63 1996**
Vergil in the Middle Ages. E. F. M. Benecke (Translator). Trade Paper. Princeton University Press. Princeton, NJ. 1996. 420p. ISBN:0-691-02678-5, ISBN13: 978-0-691-02678-7. Dewey:873/.01. LCCN:96-003403.
Audience: **g,l,u,f.** B

Hardie, Philip **PA6825**
Virgil: Greece and Rome, New Surveys in the Classics, No. 28. Trade Paper. Oxford University Press, Inc. New York, NY. 1998. 132p. ISBN:0-19-922342-4, ISBN13: 978-0-19-922342-8. Dewey:873/.01.
Audience: **u,f.**

Hardie, Philip R. **PA6825**
Virgil. Oxford University Press. 1998. Greece & Rome. New Surveys in the Classics ISBN:0-19-922342-4, ISBN13: 978-0-19-922342-8.
Audience: **u,f.**

Harrison, S. J. (Editor) **PA6825.O94 1990**
Oxford Readings in Vergil's Aeneid. Trade Paper. Oxford University Press, Inc. New York, NY. 1990. 488p. ISBN:0-19-814388-5, ISBN13: 978-0-19-814388-8. Dewey:873/.01. LCCN:89-025496.
Audience: **u,f.**

Harrison, S. J. (Editor) **PA6825.O94 1990**
Oxford Readings in Vergil's Aeneid. Cloth Text. Oxford University Press, Inc. New York, NY. 1990. 486p. ISBN:0-19-814389-3, ISBN13: 978-0-19-814389-5. Dewey:873/.01. LCCN:89-025496.
Audience: **g,u,f.**

Heinze, Richard **PA6825.H413 1993**
Virgil's Epic Technique. Hazel Harvey (Translator). Trade Cloth. University of California Press. Berkeley, CA. 1994. 396p. ISBN:0-520-06444-5, ISBN13: 978-0-520-06444-7. Dewey:873/.01. LCCN:93-005491.
Audience: **u,f.** *Choice, 1994.*

Lyne, R. O. **PA6825**
Further Voices in Vergil's Aeneid. Trade Paper. Oxford University Press, Inc. New York, NY. 1992. 262p. ISBN:0-19-814092-4, ISBN13: 978-0-19-814092-4. Dewey:873/.01. LCCN:86-016404.
Audience: **u,f.** *Choice, 1988.*

Lyne, R. O. **PA6825**
Words and the Poet: Characteristic Techniques of Style in Vergil's Aeneid. Trade Paper. Oxford University Press, Inc. New York, NY. 1998. 216p. ISBN:0-19-815261-2, ISBN13: 978-0-19-815261-3. Dewey:873/.01. LCCN:89-003086.
Audience: **u,f.**

Martindale, Charles (Editor) **PA6825 .C35 1997**
The Cambridge Companion to Virgil. Trade Cloth. Cambridge University Press. New York, NY. 1997. 388p. Companions to Literature Ser. ISBN:0-521-49539-3, ISBN13: 978-0-521-49539-4. Dewey:873/.01. LCCN:96-052447.
Audience: **g,l,u,f.** *Choice, 1998.*

Otis, Brooks **PA6825.O8 1995**
Virgil: A Study in Civilized Poetry. Ward A. Briggs Jr. (Foreword by). Trade Paper. University of Oklahoma Press. Norman, OK. 1995. 456p. Oklahoma Series in Classical Culture Ser., Vol. 20 ISBN:0-8061-2782-1, ISBN13: 978-0-8061-2782-8. Dewey:871/.01. LCCN:95-017062.
Audience: **u,f.** B

Perkell, Christine G. **PA6825.R38 1999**
Reading Vergil's Aeneid: An Interpretive Guide. Trade Cloth, Book, Other. University of Oklahoma Press. Norman, OK. 1999. 352p. Oklahoma Series in Classical Culture Ser., Vol. 23 ISBN:0-8061-3138-1, ISBN13: 978-0-8061-3138-2. Dewey:873/.01. LCCN:99-018499.
Audience: **g,l,u,f.**

Poschl, Viktor **PA6825**
The Art of Vergil: Image and Symbol in the "Aeneid". Gerda Seligson (Translator). Trade Cloth. Greenwood Publishing Group, Inc. Portsmouth, NH. 1986. 216p. ISBN:0-313-25053-7, ISBN13: 978-0-313-25053-8. Dewey:873/.01. LCCN:85-027077.
Audience: **u,f.**

Putnam, Michael C. **PA6825.P84 1995**
Virgil's Aeneid: Interpretation and Influence. Trade Cloth. University of North Carolina Press. Chapel Hill, NC. 1995. 352p. ISBN:0-8078-2191-8, ISBN13: 978-0-8078-2191-6. Dewey:873/.01. LCCN:94-019891.
Audience: **u,f.**

Quinn, Kenneth **PA6825**
Virgil's Aeneid: A Critical Description. Trade Cloth. Bristol Phoenix Press. Exeter, 2006. 460p. ISBN:1-904675-52-2, ISBN13: 978-1-904675-52-5. Dewey:873.01.
Audience: **u,f.**

Spence, Sarah (Editor) **PA6825.P545 2001**
Poets and Critics Read Vergil. Cloth over Boards. Yale University Press. Cumberland, RI. 2001. 240p. ISBN:0-300-08376-9, ISBN13: 978-0-300-08376-7. Dewey:871/.01. LCCN:00-033445.
Audience: **g,l,u,f.** *Choice, 2001.*

Thomas, Richard F. **PA6825.T517 1999**
Reading Virgil and His Texts: Studies in Intertextuality. Trade Cloth. University of Michigan Press. Chicago, IL. 2000. 360p. ISBN:0-472-10897-2, ISBN13: 978-0-472-10897-8. Dewey:871/.01. LCCN:99-033255.
Audience: **u,f.**

Thomas, Richard F. **PA6825 .T518 2001**
Virgil and the Augustan Reception. Cloth Text. Cambridge University Press. New York, NY. 2001. 344p. ISBN:0-521-78288-0, ISBN13: 978-0-521-78288-3. Dewey:871.01. LCCN:00-033712.
Audience: **g,u,f.**

Virgil **PA6801.A5/**
Aeneidos: Liber Quartus. Roland G. Austin (Editor). Paper Text. Oxford University Press, Inc. New York, NY. 1983. 232p. ISBN:0-19-872111-0, ISBN13: 978-0-19-872111-6. Dewey:873/.01.
Audience: **l,u,f.**

Virgil **PA6803.B26 A9 1986**
Aeneidos: Liber Sextus. Roland G. Austin (Commentaries by). Paper Text. Oxford University Press, Inc. New York, NY. 1986. 316p. ISBN:0-19-872128-5, ISBN13: 978-0-19-872128-4. Dewey:873/.01. LCCN:86-012757.
Audience: **l,u,f.**

Virgil **PA6803.B1**
Aeneidos: Liber Primus. Roland G. Austin (Editor). Paper Text. Oxford University Press, Inc. New York, NY. 1984. 264p. ISBN:0-19-872117-X, ISBN13: 978-0-19-872117-8. Dewey:873/.01.
Audience: **l,u,f.**

Virgil **PA6825**
Aeneidos: Liber Secundus. Roland G. Austin (Editor). Paper Text. Oxford University Press, Inc. New York, NY. 1980. 336p. ISBN:0-19-872106-4, ISBN13: 978-0-19-872106-2. Dewey:873/.01. LCCN:80-040078.
Audience: **l,u,f.**

Virgil **PA6807**
Appendix Vergiliana. W. V. Clausen, F. R. D. Goodyear, E. J. Kenney & J. A. Richmond (Editors). Cloth Text. Oxford University Press, Inc. New York, NY. 1966. 194p. Oxford Classical Texts ISBN:0-19-814648-5, ISBN13: 978-0-19-814648-3. Dewey:873.01.
Audience: **u,f.**

Virgil **PA6825**
Virgil: Eclogues. Robert Coleman (Editor), P. E. Easterling, Philip Hardie, Richard Hunter & E. J. Kenney (Contribution by). Trade Paper. Cambridge University Press. New York, NY. 1977. 320p. Cambridge Greek and Latin Classics ISBN:0-521-29107-0, ISBN13: 978-0-521-29107-1. Dewey:871/.01. LCCN:76-016917.
Audience: **u,f.**

Virgil **PA6807.A5 F53 1983**
The Aeneid. Robert Fitzgerald (Translator). Trade Cloth. Random House, Inc. New York, NY. 1983. ISBN:0-394-52827-1, ISBN13: 978-0-394-52827-4. Dewey:873/.01. LCCN:83-003101.
Audience: **g,l,u.**

Virgil **PA6803.B7**
Virgil: Aeneid VII and VIII. C. Fordyce (Editor). Trade Paper. Bristol Classical Press. London, 1985. 340p. Latin Texts ISBN:0-86292-171-6, ISBN13: 978-0-86292-171-2. Dewey:873/.01.
Audience: **u,f.**

Virgil **PA6803.B31 G73 1991**
Virgil: Aeneid. K. W. Grandsen & K. W. Gransden (Editors), P. E. Easterling, Philip Hardie, Richard Hunter & E. J. Kenney (Contribution by). Trade Paper. Cambridge University Press. New York, NY. 1991. 160p. Cambridge Greek and Latin Classics Ser. ISBN:0-521-27816-3, ISBN13: 978-0-521-27816-4. Dewey:883/.01. LCCN:90-023826.
Audience: **u,f.**

Virgil **PA6825**
Virgil's Aeneid: Cosmos and Imperium. Philip Hardie (Editor). Trade Paper. Oxford University Press, Inc. New York, NY. 1989. 416p. ISBN:0-19-814691-4, ISBN13: 978-0-19-814691-9. Dewey:873/.01.
Audience: **u,f.** *Choice, 1986.*

Virgil **PA6803.B29 H37 1994**
Virgil: The Aeneid. Philip Hardie (Editor, Contribution by), P. E. Easterling, Richard Hunter & E. J. Kenney (Contribution by). Trade Paper. Cambridge University Press. New York, NY. 1994. 267p. Cambridge Greek and Latin Classics, Bk. IX ISBN:0-521-35952-X, ISBN13: 978-0-521-35952-8. Dewey:873/.01. LCCN:93-044010.
Audience: **u,f.**

Virgil **PA6807.A5L58 2005**
Aeneid. Stanley Lombardo (Translator), W. R. Johnson (Introduction by). Trade Cloth. Hackett Publishing Company, Inc. Indianapolis, IN. 2005. 355p. ISBN:0-87220-732-3, ISBN13: 978-0-87220-732-5. Dewey:873/.01. LCCN:2004-022685.
Audience: **g,l,u.** *Choice, 2005, 1987.*

Virgil **PA6825**
The Aeneid of Virgil. Allen Mandelbaum (Translator), Barry Moser (Illustrator). Trade Paper. University of California Press. Berkeley, CA. 1996. 415p. ISBN:0-520-04550-5, ISBN13: 978-0-520-04550-7. Dewey:873/.01. LCCN:80-053773.
Audience: **g,l,u.**

Virgil **PA6825**
Georgics. Roger A. Mynors (Editor). Trade Paper. Oxford University Press, Inc. New York, NY. 1994. 440p. ISBN:0-19-814978-6, ISBN13: 978-0-19-814978-1. Dewey:873/.01.
Audience: **u,f.**

Virgil **PS3569.L3E28 1990**
Eclogues and Georgics of Virgil. David R. Slavitt (Editor, Translator). Trade Paper. Johns Hopkins University Press. Baltimore, MD. 1990. 176p. ISBN:0-8018-4111-9, ISBN13: 978-0-8018-4111-8. Dewey:811/.54. LCCN:90-005222.
Audience: **g,l,u.**

Virgil **PA6804**
Virgil: Eclogues and Georgics. R. D. Williams (Editor). Trade Paper. Bristol Classical Press. London, 1996. 240p. Latin Texts ISBN:1-85399-508-8, ISBN13: 978-1-85399-508-8. Dewey:871.01.
Audience: **l,u,f.**

Virgil **PA6802.A1**
Virgil: Aeneid I-VI. R. Deryck Williams (Editor). Trade Paper. Bristol Classical Press. London, 1996. 560p. Latin Texts ISBN:1-85399-496-0, ISBN13: 978-1-85399-496-8. Dewey:873.
Audience: **l,u,f.**

Virgil **PA6802.A7**
Virgil: Aeneid VII-XII. R. Deryck Williams (Editor). Trade Paper. Bristol Classical Press. London, 1996. 520p. Latin Texts ISBN:1-85399-500-2, ISBN13: 978-1-85399-500-2. Dewey:873/.01.
Audience: **l,u,f.**

Wilkinson, L. P. **PA6804.G4W5 1997**
The Georgics of Virgil: A Critical Survey. Niall Rudd (Foreword by). Trade Paper. University of Oklahoma Press. Norman, OK. 1997. 380p. ISBN:0-8061-2967-0, ISBN13: 978-0-8061-2967-9. Dewey:873/.01. LCCN:97-005682.
Audience: **u,f.**

Ziolkowski, Theodore J. **PA6825.Z56 1993**
Virgil and the Moderns. Cloth Text. Princeton University Press. Princeton, NJ. 1993. 296p. ISBN:0-691-03248-3, ISBN13: 978-0-691-03248-1. Dewey:871.01. LCCN:92-041209.
Audience: **g,u,f.** *Choice, 1994.*

Latin > Medieval Latin

Abelard, Peter & Heloise **PA8201.A4 2003**
Letters of Abelard and Heloise. Betty Radice (Translator), M. T. Clanchy (Revised by). Trade Paper. Penguin Group (USA) Inc. New York, NY. 2004. 384p. ISBN:0-14-044899-3, ISBN13: 978-0-14-044899-3. Dewey:189.4.
Audience: **g,l,u.**

Adcock, Fleur E. (Editor) **PA8347.H77 A23 1994**
Hugh Primas and the Archpoet. Peter Dronke (Contribution by). Trade Paper. Cambridge University Press. New York, NY. 2005. 151p. Cambridge Medieval Classics Ser. ISBN:0-521-39583-6, ISBN13: 978-0-521-39583-0. Dewey:881/.02.
Audience: **u,f.**

Auerbach, Erich **PA8027 .A813 1993**
Literary Language and Its Public in Late Latin Antiquity and in the Middle Ages. Ralph Manheim (Translator). Trade Paper. Princeton University Press. Princeton, NJ. 1993. 450p. Bollingen Ser., No. 74 ISBN:0-691-02468-5, ISBN13: 978-0-691-02468-4. Dewey:870.9/003. LCCN:92-037333.
Audience: **u,f.**

Bate, Keith (Editor) **PA8137 .T5**
Three Latin Comedies. Trade Paper. Pontifical Institute of Mediaeval Studies, Department of Publications. Toronto, ON. 1976. 104p. Toronto Medieval Latin Texts Ser., Vol. 6 ISBN:0-88844-455-9, ISBN13: 978-0-88844-455-4. Dewey:872/.03. LCCN:77-359301.
Audience: **u,f.**

Bede **BR746**
Bede's Historia Ecclesiastica. F. W. Garforth (Editor). Book, Other. Bolchazy-Carducci Publishers. Wauconda, IL. 1988. 158p. ISBN:0-86516-218-2, ISBN13: 978-0-86516-218-1. Dewey:274.2.
Audience: **l,u,f.**

Bede **PA6156**
Ecclesiastical History, Bks. 1-3. J. E. King (Translator). Trade Cloth. Harvard University Press. Cambridge, MA. 1930. 560p. Loeb Classical Library, No. 246, 248 ISBN:0-674-99271-7, ISBN13: 978-0-674-99271-9. Dewey:870.
Audience: **g,l,u.**

Bede **PA6156**
Ecclesiastical History - Lives of the Abbots, Letter to Egbert, Bks. 4-5,Vol. 2. J. E. King (Translator). Trade Cloth. Harvard University Press. Cambridge, MA. 1930. 528p. Loeb Classical Library, No. 246, 248 ISBN:0-674-99273-3, ISBN13: 978-0-674-99273-3. Dewey:878; 274.2.
Audience: **g,l,u.**

Bede **BR160.E4**
Ecclesiastical History, Bks. 6-10. J. E. Oulton (Translator). Trade Cloth. Harvard University Press. Cambridge, MA. 1932. 504p. Loeb Classical Library, No. 153, 265 ISBN:0-674-99293-8, ISBN13: 978-0-674-99293-1. Dewey:270.1.
Audience: **g,l,u.**

Beeson, Charles H. **PA2825.B44 1986**
A Primer of Medieval Latin: An Anthology of Prose and Poetry. Trade Paper. Catholic University of America Press. Washington, DC. 1986. 390p. ISBN:0-8132-0635-9, ISBN13: 978-0-8132-0635-6. Dewey:478.6/421. LCCN:86-008301.
Audience: **l,u,f.**

Benedict of Nursia **BX3004 .A2 1982**
The Rule of St. Benedict: The Abingdon Copy. John Chamberlin (Editor). Trade Paper. Pontifical Institute of Mediaeval Studies, Department of Publications. Toronto, ON. 1982. 95p. Toronto Medieval Latin Texts Ser., Vol. 13 ISBN:0-88844-463-X, ISBN13: 978-0-88844-463-9. Dewey:255/.106. LCCN:82-205899.
Audience: **u,f.**

Boethius **B659.A35**
Theological Tractates and the Consolation of Philosophy. E. K. Rand & S. J. Tester (Translators). Trade Cloth. Harvard University Press. Cambridge, MA. 1973. 464p. Loeb Classical Library, No. 74:Latin Authors ISBN:0-674-99083-8, ISBN13: 978-0-674-99083-8. Dewey:189/.4.
Audience: **g,l,u.**

Boethius **B659.C2E52 2001**
The Consolation of Philosophy. Joel C. Relihan (Translator, Introduction by, Notes by). Trade Cloth. Hackett Publishing Company, Inc. Indianapolis, IN. 2001. 240p. Hackett Classics Ser. ISBN:0-87220-584-3, ISBN13: 978-0-87220-584-0. Dewey:100. LCCN:2001-026401.
Audience: **g,l,u,f.** B

Bonfante, Larissa & Bonfante-Warren, Alexandra (Translators) **PA8340**
The Plays of Hrotswitha of Gandersheim. Larissa Bonfante (Introduction by). Book, Other. Bolchazy-Carducci Publishers. Wauconda, IL. 2000. 182p. ISBN:0-86516-178-X, ISBN13: 978-0-86516-178-8. Dewey:872/.03. LCCN:79-090053.
Audience: **g,l,u.** B

Curtius, Ernst Robert **PN671**
European Literature and the Latin Middle Ages. Paper Text. Textbook Publishers. Temecula, CA. 2003. xv, 662p. ISBN:0-7581-6680-X, ISBN13: 978-0-7581-6680-7. Dewey:809/.02.
Audience: **g,l,u,f.** B

Dante Alighieri **PQ4311 .D6 1996**
Dante: De Vulgari Eloquentia. Steven Botterill (Edited and Translated by), Peter Dronke (Contribution by). Trade Paper.

Cambridge University Press. New York, NY. 2005. 135p. Cambridge Medieval Classics Ser. ISBN:0-521-40923-3, ISBN13: 978-0-521-40923-0. Dewey:858.1/09. LCCN:2006-277899.

Audience: **u,f.**

Godman, Peter (Editor) **PA8164.P64 1985**
Poetry of the Carolingian Renaissance. Trade Cloth. University of Oklahoma Press. Norman, OK. 1985. 384p. ISBN:0-8061-1939-X, ISBN13: 978-0-8061-1939-7. Dewey:871/.03. LCCN:84-040699.

Audience: **u,f.**

Godman, Peter & Murray, Oswyn (Editors) **PA8050.L38 1990**
Latin Poetry and the Classical Tradition: Essays in Medieval and Renaissance Literature. Trade Cloth. Oxford University Press, Inc. New York, NY. 1991. 256p. Oxford-Warburg Studies ISBN:0-19-920174-9, ISBN13: 978-0-19-920174-7. Dewey:871/0309. LCCN:90-007727.

Audience: **u,f.**

Grosseteste, Robert **BX1913 .G76 1984**
Templum Dei: Edited from MS 27 of Emmanuel College, Cambridge. Joseph M. Goering & Frank A. C. Mantello (Editors). Trade Paper. Pontifical Institute of Mediaeval Studies, Department of Publications. Toronto, ON. 1984. 100p. Toronto Medieval Latin Texts Ser., Vol. 14 ISBN:0-88844-464-8, ISBN13: 978-0-88844-464-6. Dewey:253. LCCN:84-213830.

Audience: **u,f.**

Harrington, Karl P. & Pucci, Joseph M. **PA2825.M43 1997**
Medieval Latin. Ed. 2. Trade Cloth. University of Chicago Press. Chicago, IL. 1997. 702p. ISBN:0-226-31712-9, ISBN13: 978-0-226-31712-0. Dewey:477. LCCN:96-050254.

Audience: **u,f.**

Laistner, Max L. **CB351 .L27**
Thought and Letters in Western Europe, A. D. 500-900. Trade Cloth. Gordon Press Publishers. New York, NY. 1972. ISBN:0-8490-1207-4, ISBN13: 978-0-8490-1207-5. Dewey:809.4.

Audience: **g,l,u,f.**

Langton, Stephen **BX1756.L28 S44 1980**
Selected Sermons. Phyllis B. Roberts (Editor). Trade Paper. Pontifical Institute of Mediaeval Studies, Department of Publications. Toronto, ON. 1980. 107p. Toronto Medieval Latin Texts Ser., Vol. 10 ISBN:0-88844-460-5, ISBN13: 978-0-88844-460-8. Dewey:252/.02. LCCN:80-148603.

Audience: **u,f.**

Mantello, F. A. & Rigg, A. G. (Editors) **PA2802.M43 1996**
Medieval Latin: An Introduction and Bibliographical Guide. Trade Paper. Catholic University of America Press. Washington, DC. 1996. 774p. ISBN:0-8132-0842-4, ISBN13: 978-0-8132-0842-8. Dewey:016.477. LCCN:95-011339.

Audience: **g,l,u,f.** *Choice, 1997.*

Nigel of Canterbury **PA8445.W5 M57 1986**
Miracles of the Virgin Mary, in Verse: Miracula Sancte Dei Genitricis Virginis Marie, Versifice. Jan Ziolkowski (Editor). Trade Paper. Pontifical Institute of Mediaeval Studies, Department of Publications. Toronto, ON. 1986. 111p. Toronto Medieval Latin Texts Ser., Vol. 17 ISBN:0-88844-467-2, ISBN13: 978-0-88844-467-7. Dewey:873/.03. LCCN:87-130514.

Audience: **u,f.**

Norberg, Dag Ludvig **PA8051.N59 2003**
An Introduction to the Study of Medieval Latin Versification. Jan Ziolkowski (Editor, Introduction by). Trade Cloth. Catholic University of America Press. Washington, DC. 2003. 304p. ISBN:0-8132-1335-5, ISBN13: 978-0-8132-1335-4. Dewey:871/.0309. LCCN:2002-010003.

Audience: **u,f.**

Pascal, Paul **PA8340**
Hrotsvitha Dulcitius and Paphnutius. Paper Text. Bryn Mawr Commentaries. Bryn Mawr, PA. 1985. 83p. Latin Commentaries Ser. ISBN:0-929524-41-1, ISBN13: 978-0-929524-41-2. Dewey:872.03.

Audience: **l,u,f.**

Peter The Venerable **BX4705.P473 A43**
Selected Letters. Janet Martin & Giles Constable (Editors). Trade Paper. Pontifical Institute of Mediaeval Studies, Department of Publications. Toronto, ON. 1974. 115p. Toronto Medieval Latin Texts Ser., Vol. 3 ISBN:0-88844-452-4, ISBN13: 978-0-88844-452-3. Dewey:271.1022. LCCN:75-398160.

Audience: **u,f.**

Raby, F. J. E. **PA8056.R3 1953**
ⓔ A History of Christian-Latin Poetry from the Beginnings to the Close of the Middle Ages. Ed. 1997. E-Book. NetLibrary, Inc. Boulder, CO. 1997. ISBN:0-585-30457-2, ISBN13: 978-0-585-30457-1. Dewey:879.109.

Audience: **g,u,f.**

Raby, F. J. E. **PA8051.R3 1997**
ⓔ A History of Secular Latin Poetry in the Middle Ages. E-Book. NetLibrary, Inc. Boulder, CO. 1997. ISBN:0-585-33863-9, ISBN13: 978-0-585-33863-7. Dewey:879.109.

Audience: **g,u,f.**

Raby, Frederick J. (Editor) **PA8122**
Oxford Book of Medieval Latin Verse. Trade Cloth. Oxford University Press, Inc. New York, NY. 1959. 532p. ISBN:0-19-812119-9, ISBN13: 978-0-19-812119-0. Dewey:871/.008.

Audience: **u,f.**

Reynolds, Suzanne **PA2061 .R48 1996**
Medieval Reading: Grammar, Rhetoric and the Classical Text. Alastair Minnis, Patrick Boyde, John Burrow, Rita Copeland, Alan Deyermond, Peter Dronke, Nigel Palmer, Winthrop Wetherbee & B. Simon (Contribution by). Trade Paper. Cambridge University Press. New York, NY. 2004. 253p. Cambridge Studies in Medieval Literature Ser., Vol. 27 ISBN:0-521-60452-4, ISBN13: 978-0-521-60452-9. Dewey:809/.02.

Audience: **u,f.**

Rolle, Richard **BX2349**
Emendatio Vitae: Orationes ad Honorem Nominis Ihesu. Nicholas Watson (Editor). Trade Paper. Pontifical Institute of

Mediaeval Studies, Department of Publications. Toronto, ON. 1995. 96p. Toronto Medieval Latin Texts Ser., Vol. 21 ISBN:0-88844-471-0, ISBN13: 978-0-88844-471-4. Dewey:248.4/82. LCCN:98-108289.
Audience: **u,f.**

Sidwell, Keith C. **PA2825 .S53 1995**
Reading Medieval Latin. Trade Paper. Cambridge University Press. New York, NY. 1995. 416p. ISBN:0-521-44747-X, ISBN13: 978-0-521-44747-8. Dewey:477. LCCN:94-010864.
Audience: **l,u,f.**

Thorley, John **PA2825.T48 1998**
Documents in Medieval Latin. Trade Paper. University of Michigan Press. Chicago, IL. 1998. 199p. ISBN:0-472-08567-0, ISBN13: 978-0-472-08567-5. Dewey:477. LCCN:98-024457.
Audience: **g,u,f.**

Waddell, Helen **PA8065.S8W3 1989**
The Wandering Scholars. Trade Paper. University of Michigan Press. Chicago, IL. 1989. 332p. Ann Arbor Paperback Ser., Vol. 199 ISBN:0-472-06412-6, ISBN13: 978-0-472-06412-0. Dewey:871/.0309. LCCN:89-020267.
Audience: **g,l,u,f.**

Walsh, P. G. **PA8133.S8 C299 1976**
Thirty Poems from the Carmina Burana. Trade Cloth. Bristol Classical Press. London, 1993. 148p. ISBN:0-7049-0525-6, ISBN13: 978-0-7049-0525-2. Dewey:874/.03/08. LCCN:76-371990.
Audience: **u,f.**

Winterbottom, Michael (Editor) **BX4700.A27 W56**
Three Lives of English Saints. Trade Paper. Pontifical Institute of Mediaeval Studies, Department of Publications. Toronto, ON. 1972. 104p. Toronto Medieval Latin Texts Ser., Vol. 1 ISBN:0-88844-450-8, ISBN13: 978-0-88844-450-9. Dewey:270.3/092/2. LCCN:74-309195.
Audience: **u,f.**

FRENCH LANGUAGE AND LITERATURE

The French Language and Literature section provides a selection oftitles appropriate for language and literature study at theundergraduate level. The scope of this selection reflects the rapid,continuing growth of women's studies over the past two decades, andincludes major works of literature, literary history, biography, andcriticism. Particular emphasis has been given to the expansion ofthe francophone (outside of France) sections (especially Caribbeanand African) and to language, reflecting the growing importance ofthese fields in particular. The French section also includesaccessible critical guides and major works in English translation.

Where possible, works are recommended in their newest, most reliableeditions, with preference for compendious collected editions. Someworks are available only as reprints, while a few are out of print,though still recommended.

— Jeffry Larson

French Language

PC2640
Collins Robert comprehensive French dictionary. Ed. 2. Collins. 2006. ISBN:0-00-723249-7, ISBN13: 978-0-00-723249-9.
Audience: **g,l,u,f.**

Akehurst, F. R. & Davis, Judith M. (Editors) **PC3304.H36 1995**
A Handbook of the Troubadours. Trade Cloth. University of California Press. Berkeley, CA. 1995. 508p. Publications of the Center for Medieval and Renaissance Studies, Vol. 26 ISBN:0-520-07975-2, ISBN13: 978-0-520-07975-5. Dewey:849/.1209. LCCN:94-036018.
Audience: **u,f.** *Choice, 1996.*

Batchelor, R. E. & Offord, M. H. **PC2460 .B37 2000**
Using French: A Guide to Contemporary Usage. Ed. 3. Cloth Text. Cambridge University Press. New York, NY. 2000. 348p. ISBN:0-521-64177-2, ISBN13: 978-0-521-64177-7. Dewey:448.2/421. LCCN:00-269495.
Audience: **l,u.**

Battye, Adrian & Hintze, Marie-Anne **PC2105.B37 2000**
French Language Today: Linguistic Introduction. Ed. 2. Paper over Boards. Routledge. New York, NY. 2000. 360p. ISBN:0-415-19837-2, ISBN13: 978-0-415-19837-0. Dewey:440. LCCN:99-087392.
Audience: **g,u,f.**

Chiflet, Jean-Loup **PC2460**
Ciel!, Blake! = Sky!, Mortimer! : dictionnaire français-anglais des expressions courantes. Mots et cie. 2000. ISBN:2-913588-16-6, ISBN13: 978-2-913588-16-5.
Audience: **u,f.**

Chiflet, Jean-Loup & Jacobs, Edgar-P **PE1460**
Nom d'une pipe! : dictionnaire français-anglais des expressions courantes (2). Mots et Cie. 2004. ISBN:2-913588-58-1, ISBN13: 978-2-913588-58-5.
Audience: **u,f.**

Chiss, Jean-Louis, et al. **PC2073**
Introduction à la linguistique française. Filliolet, Jacques; Maingueneau, Dominique (Authors). Hachette. 2001. ISBN:2-01-145390-9, ISBN13: 978-2-01-145390-7.
Audience: **u,f.**

Colin, Jean-Paul, et al. **PC3741**
Dictionnaire de l'argot français et de ses origines. Mével, Jean-Pierre; Leclère, Christian (Authors). Larousse. 2001. ISBN:2-03-532046-1, ISBN13: 978-2-03-532046-9.
Audience: **g,u,f.**

Correard, Marie-Helene (Editor), et al. **PC2640.G684 2001**
The Oxford-Hachette French Dictionary. Ed. 3. Valerie Grundy, Jean-Benoit Ormal-Grenon & Natalie Pomier (Editors). Trade Cloth. Oxford University Press, Inc. New York, NY. 2001. 1,986p. ISBN:0-19-860363-0, ISBN13: 978-0-19-860363-4. Dewey:443/.21. LCCN:2001-272393.
Audience: **g,l,u,f.**

Elwert, W. Theodor **PC2505**
Traité de versification française des origines à nos jours. Klincksieck. 1965. Bibliothèque française et romane. Ser. A: Manuels et études linguistiques
Audience: **u,f.**

Etiemble **PC2582.E5**
Parlez-vous franglais? : fol en France, mad in France--la belle France, label France. Gallimard. 1991. ISBN:2-07-032635-7, ISBN13: 978-2-07-032635-8.
Audience: **u,f.**

Greimas, Algirdas Julien **PC2889**
Dictionnaire de l'ancien français. Larousse-Bordas/HER. 2001. ISBN:2-03-532048-8, ISBN13: 978-2-03-532048-3.
Audience: **u,f.**

Greimas, Algirdas-Julien; Keane, Teresa Mary **PC2889**
Dictionnaire du moyen français. Larousse-Bordas/HER. 2001. ISBN:2-03-532049-6, ISBN13: 978-2-03-532049-0.
Audience: **u,f.**

Grevisse, Maurice; Goosse, André **PC2073**
Le Bon usage : grammaire française. Ed. 13. Duculot. 2004. ISBN:2-8011-1045-0, ISBN13: 978-2-8011-1045-4.
Audience: **g,l,u,f.**

Harrap's Staff **PC2640 .H32**
Harrap's Unabridged French-English Dictionary. Trade Cloth. John Wiley & Sons, Inc. Hoboken, NJ. 1997. 2272p. ISBN:0-02-860570-5, ISBN13: 978-0-02-860570-8. Dewey:443/.21.
Audience: **g,l,u,f.**

Hawkins, Roger & Towell, Richard **PC2129.E5**
French Grammar and Usage. Ed. 2. Paper Text. McGraw-Hill Companies, The. New York, NY. 2001. 480p. ISBN:0-658-01798-5, ISBN13: 978-0-658-01798-8. Dewey:448.2/421.
Audience: **g,l,u.**

Hindley, Alan, et al. **PC2891 .H56 2000**
Old French-English Dictionary. Frederick W. Langley & Brian J. Levy (Authors). Trade Cloth. Cambridge University Press. New York, NY. 2000. 638p. ISBN:0-521-34564-2, ISBN13: 978-0-521-34564-4. Dewey:447/.01/03. LCCN:99-056328.
Audience: **u,f.**

Judge, Anne & Healey, Frederick G. **PC2105.J83 1995**
A Reference Grammar of Modern French. Ed. 2. Trade Paper. McGraw-Hill Companies, The. New York, NY. 1999. 528p. ISBN:0-8442-1631-3, ISBN13: 978-0-8442-1631-7. Dewey:448.2/421. LCCN:95-068973.
Audience: **g,l,u,f.**

Kibler, William W. **PC2823**
An Introduction to Old French. Trade Cloth. Modern Language Association of America. New York, NY. 1984. xxvii, 366p. Introduction to Older Languages Ser., No. 3 ISBN:0-87352-291-5, ISBN13: 978-0-87352-291-5. Dewey:822.3/3 s. LCCN:83-019368.
Audience: **u,f.**

Laroche-Claire, Yves **PC2582.E5**
Evitez le franglais, parlez français!. Albin Michel. 2004. ISBN:2-226-14382-3, ISBN13: 978-2-226-14382-2.
Audience: **u,f.**

Littré, Emile, et. al. **PC2625**
Dictionnaire de la langue française. Baudeneau, Jacques; Morhange-Bégué, Claude (Authors). Encyclopaedia Britannica France. 2001.
Audience: **u,f.**

Meney, Lionel **PC3643**
Dictionnaire québécois français. Guérin. 1999. ISBN:2-7601-5482-3, ISBN13: 978-2-7601-5482-7.
Audience: **g,u,f.**

Offord, Malcolm **PC2095**
Varieties of Contemporary French. Trade Cloth. Macmillan Education, Ltd. Oxford, 1990. 288p. ISBN:0-333-43248-7, ISBN13: 978-0-333-43248-8. Dewey:440.
Audience: **g,u,f.**

Price, Glanville **PC2112.P75 2002**
A Comprehensive French Grammar. Ed. 5. Trade Cloth. Blackwell Publishing, Inc. Malden, MA. 2002. 608p. Blackwell Reference Grammars Ser. ISBN:0-631-23562-0, ISBN13: 978-0-631-23562-0. Dewey:448.2/421. LCCN:2002-066636.
Audience: **g,l,u,f.**

Price, Glanville **PC2137.P75 2005**
An Introduction to French Pronunciation. Ed. 2. Trade Paper, Saddle Stitched. Blackwell Publishing, Inc. Malden, MA. 2005. 192p. Blackwell Reference Grammars Ser. ISBN:1-4051-3255-8, ISBN13: 978-1-4051-3255-8. Dewey:448.3421. LCCN:2004-029945.
Audience: **g,l,u,f.**

Rickard, Peter **PC2075**
A History of the French Language. Ed. 2. Trade Paper. Routledge. New York, NY. 1989. 192p. ISBN:0-415-10887-X, ISBN13: 978-0-415-10887-4. Dewey:440/.9. LCCN:89-005562.
Audience: **g,u,f.**

Robert, Paul & Rey, Alain **PC2625**
Le grand Robert de la langue française. Dictionnaires Le Robert. 2001. ISBN:2-85036-673-0, ISBN13: 978-2-85036-673-4.
Audience: **g,u,f.**

Robert, Paul & Rey-Debove, Josette **PC2625**
Le nouveau petit Robert : dictionnaire alphabétique et analogique de la langue française. Dictionnaires Le Robert. 2005. ISBN:2-84902-066-4, ISBN13: 978-2-84902-066-1.
Audience: **g,l,u,f.**

Vandeloise, Claude & Anselmo, Frank A. **PC2073**
Introduction to French Linguistics. LINCOM Europa. 2001. LINCOM Studies in Romance Linguistics ISBN:3-89586-780-2, ISBN13: 978-3-89586-780-4.
Audience: **u,f.**

Vinay, Jean-Paul & Darbelnet, Jean **PC2099.V513 1995**
Comparative Stylistics of French and English: A Methodology for Translation. Juan C. Sager & M.-J. Hamel (Editors), Juan C. Sager & M.-J. Hamel (Translators). Library Binding. John Benjamins Publishing Company. Philadelphia, PA. 1995. xx, 359p. Translation Library, Vol. 11 ISBN:1-55619-691-1, ISBN13: 978-1-55619-691-1. Dewey:445. LCCN:95-038277.
Audience: **l,u,f.**

White, Patrick, et al. **PC2640**
Harrap English/French Dictionary, Vol. 2. Anna Stevenson, Gearóid Cronin, Laurence Larroche, Georges Pilard & Lola Busuttil (Authors). Trade Cloth. Larousse Harrap Publishers. London, 1440p. ISBN:0-245-60702-1, ISBN13: 978-0-245-60702-8. Dewey:443.21.
Audience: **g,l,u,f.**

French Literature: History and Critcism > General

Barthes, Roland **PQ2063.S3B313 1997**
Sade, Fourier, Loyola. Trade Paper. Johns Hopkins University Press. Baltimore, MD. 1997. 184p. ISBN:0-8018-5526-8, ISBN13: 978-0-8018-5526-9. Dewey:840.9/3538. LCCN:96-042538.
Audience: **u,f.**

Beaumarchais, Jean-Pierre de et al. **PQ41 .B4 1998**
Dictionnaire des littératures de langue française, vol. 3. Couty, Daniel; Rey, Alain (Authors). Larousse-Bordas. 1998. ISBN:2-04-027244-5, ISBN13: 978-2-04-027244-9.
Audience: **u,f.**

Beaumarchais, Jean-Pierre de et al. **PQ41 .B4 1998**
Dictionnaire des littératures de langue française, vol. 4. Couty, Daniel; Rey, Alain (Authors). Larousse-Bordas. 1998. ISBN:2-04-027245-3, ISBN13: 978-2-04-027245-6.
Audience: **u,f.**

Beaumarchais, Jean-Pierre de et at. **PQ41 .B4 1998**
Dictionnaire des littératures de langue française, vol. 2. Couty, Daniel; Rey, Alain (Authors). Larousse-Bordas. 1998. ISBN:2-04-027243-7, ISBN13: 978-2-04-027243-2.
Audience: **u,f.**

Beaumarchais, Jean-Pierre de, et.al. **PQ41 .B4 1998**
Dictionnaire des littératures de langue française, vol. 1. Couty, Daniel; Rey, Alain (Authors). Larousse-Bordas. 1998. ISBN:2-04-027242-9, ISBN13: 978-2-04-027242-5.
Audience: **g,l,u,f.**

Bishop, Lloyd **PQ287.B57 1984**
The Romantic Hero and His Heirs in French Literature. Cloth Text. Peter Lang Publishing, Inc. New York, NY. 1984. 295p. American University Studies, Ser. II, Vol. 10:Romance, Languages and Literature ISBN:0-8204-0096-3, ISBN13: 978-0-8204-0096-9. Dewey:840/.9/145. LCCN:83-049351.
Audience: **l,u,f.**

Borgerhoff, Elbert B. **PQ245**
Freedom of French Classicism. Trade Cloth. Russell & Russell Publishers. New York, NY. 1968. ISBN:0-8462-1193-9, ISBN13: 978-0-8462-1193-8. Dewey:840.903. LCCN:68-027051.
Audience: **l,u,f.**

Bourdieu, Pierre **PN45**
The Rules of Art: Genesis and Structure of the Literary Field. Susan Emanuel (Translator). Trade Cloth. Stanford University Press. Palo Alto, CA. 1995. 288p. Meridian: Crossing Aesthetics Ser. ISBN:0-8047-2568-3, ISBN13: 978-0-8047-2568-2. Dewey:801. LCCN:94-074140.
Audience: **u,f.**

Braun, Sidney D. (Editor) **PQ41**
Dictionary of French Literature. Trade Cloth. Greenwood Publishing Group, Inc. Portsmouth, NH. 1971. 394p. ISBN:0-8371-5775-7, ISBN13: 978-0-8371-5775-7. Dewey:840/.9. LCCN:70-138576.
Audience: **g,l,u,f.**

Bree, Germaine **PQ149.B7**
Women Writers in France: Variations on a Theme. Trade Cloth. Rutgers University Press. Piscataway, NJ. 1973. 120p. ISBN:0-8135-0771-5, ISBN13: 978-0-8135-0771-2. Dewey:840/.9/9287. LCCN:73-013700.
Audience: **l,u,f.**

Brereton, Geoffrey **PQ119.B7 1976**
A Short History of French Literature. Ed. 2. Trade Paper. Penguin Group (USA) Inc. New York, NY. 1976. 368p. Pelican Ser. ISBN:0-14-020297-8, ISBN13: 978-0-14-020297-7. Dewey:840/.9. LCCN:76-366424.
Audience: **g,l,u,f.**

Brooks, Peter **PN3378.B76 1992**
Reading for the Plot: Design and Intention in Narrative. Trade Paper. Harvard University Press. Cambridge, MA. 1992. 392p. ISBN:0-674-74892-1, ISBN13: 978-0-674-74892-7. Dewey:809.3/923. LCCN:91-031007.
Audience: **u,f.**

Brooks, Peter **PR878.R4B76 2005**
Realist Vision. Cloth over Boards. Yale University Press. Cumberland, RI. 2005. 272p. ISBN:0-300-10680-7, ISBN13: 978-0-300-10680-0. Dewey:823/.80912. LCCN:2004-029501.
Audience: **u,f.** *Choice, 2005.*

Calin, William **PQ447.C35 1983**
A Muse for Heroes: Nine Centuries of the Epic in France. Cloth Text. University of Toronto Press. Toronto, ON. 1983. 527p. Romance Ser. ISBN:0-8020-5599-0, ISBN13: 978-0-8020-5599-6. Dewey:841/.03. LCCN:83-227864.
Audience: **l,u,f.**

Charvet, Patrick Edward **PQ103**
The Nineteenth and Twentieth Centuries, 1870-1940. Barnes and Noble Books. 1967.
Audience: **g,l.**

Charvet, Patrick Edward **PQ103**
The Nineteenth Century, 1789-1870. Benn. 1967.
Audience: **u,f.**

Cruickshank, John (Editor) **PQ226**
French Literature and Its Background. Trade Cloth. Oxford University Press, Inc. New York, NY. 1969. vi, 234p. ISBN:0-19-285028-8, ISBN13: 978-0-19-285028-7. Dewey:840.9.
Audience: **l,u.**

Cruickshank, John (Editor) **PQ139**
French Literature and Its Background, Vol. 4. Trade Cloth. Oxford University Press, Inc. New York, NY. 1969. 250p. ISBN:0-19-285029-6, ISBN13: 978-0-19-285029-4. Dewey:840.9.
Audience: **l,u.**

Cruickshank, John (Editor) **PQ226**
French Literature and Its Background, Vol. 5. Trade Cloth. Oxford University Press, Inc. New York, NY. 1969. 238p. ISBN:0-19-285033-4, ISBN13: 978-0-19-285033-1. Dewey:840.9.
Audience: **l,u.**

Cruickshank, John (Editor) **PQ139**
French Literature and Its Background, Vol. 6. Trade Cloth. Oxford University Press, Inc. New York, NY. 1970. 350p. ISBN:0-19-285043-1, ISBN13: 978-0-19-285043-0. Dewey:840.9.
Audience: **l,u.**

Cruickshank, John (Editor) **PQ139**
French Literature and Its Background, Vol. 3. Trade Cloth. Oxford University Press, Inc. New York, NY. 1968. 232p. ISBN:0-19-285021-0, ISBN13: 978-0-19-285021-8. Dewey:840.9.
Audience: **l,u.**

De Beaumarchais, Jean-Pierre **PQ41 .B4**
Dictionary of French Language Literature: Dictionnaire des Litteratures de Langue Francaise. Trade Cloth. French & European Publications, Inc. New York, NY. 1994. 3000p. ISBN:0-8288-1562-3, ISBN13: 978-0-8288-1562-8. Dewey:840/.3.
Audience: **u,f.**

Fox, John **PQ103**
The Middle Ages. Barnes and Nobel Books. 1974. ISBN:0-510-32201-8, ISBN13: 978-0-510-32201-4.
Audience: **u,f.**

France, Peter (Editor) **PQ41.N49 1995**
The New Oxford Companion to Literature in French. Trade Cloth. Oxford University Press, Inc. New York, NY. 1995. 916p. ISBN:0-19-866125-8, ISBN13: 978-0-19-866125-2. Dewey:840.9/0003. LCCN:95-225097.
Audience: **g,l,u,f.** *Choice, 1995.*

Grente, Georges (Editor) **PQ41**
Dictionnaire des lettres françaises, vol. 1. Fayard. 1994. ISBN:2-213-59340-X, ISBN13: 978-2-213-59340-1.
Audience: **u,f.**

Grente, Georges (Editor) **PQ41**
Dictionnaire des lettres françaises, vol. 2. Fayard. 1994. ISBN:2-213-59435-X, ISBN13: 978-2-213-59435-4.
Audience: **u,f.**

Grente, Georges (Editor) **PQ41**
Dictionnaire des lettres françaises, vol. 3. Fayard. 1994. ISBN:2-213-59543-7, ISBN13: 978-2-213-59543-6.
Audience: **u,f.**

Harvey, Paul H. & Heseltine, Janet E. (Editors) **PQ41**
Oxford Companion to French Literature. Trade Cloth. Oxford University Press, Inc. New York, NY. 1959. 786p. ISBN:0-19-866104-5, ISBN13: 978-0-19-866104-7. Dewey:840.3.
Audience: **g,l,u,f.**

Hollier, Denis (Editor) **PQ119.N48 1994**
A New History of French Literature. Trade Paper. Harvard University Press. Cambridge, MA. 1998. 1200p. ISBN:0-674-61566-2, ISBN13: 978-0-674-61566-3. Dewey:840.9. LCCN:95-139611.
Audience: **g,l,u,f.** *Choice, 1990.*

Hollier, Denis **PQ305.H6513 1997**
Absent Without Leave: French Literature under the Threat of War. Catherine Porter (Translator). Trade Cloth. Harvard University Press. Cambridge, MA. 1997. 244p. ISBN:0-674-21270-3, ISBN13: 978-0-674-21270-1. Dewey:840.9/00912. LCCN:97-016188.
Audience: **u,f.** *Choice, 1998.*

James, Henry **PQ139**
French Poets and Novelists. Library Binding. Reprint Services Company. Temecula, CA. 1992. Notable American Authors Ser. ISBN:0-7812-3456-5, ISBN13: 978-0-7812-3456-6. Dewey:840.9.
Audience: **l,u.**

Kamuf, Peggy **PN81.K338 1997**
The Division of Literature: Or the University in Deconstruction. Trade Cloth. University of Chicago Press. Chicago, IL. 1997. 268p. ISBN:0-226-42323-9, ISBN13: 978-0-226-42323-4. Dewey:807.1173. LCCN:96-020255.
Audience: **u,f.** *Choice, 1998.*

Kamuf, Peggy **PQ645**
Fictions of Feminine Desire: Disclosures of Heloise. Cloth Text. University of Nebraska Press. Lincoln, NE. 1982. xx, 170p. ISBN:0-8032-2705-1, ISBN13: 978-0-8032-2705-7. Dewey:843/.4/09352042. LCCN:81-010290.
Audience: **u,f.**

Lechte, John & Zournazi, Mary (Editors) **PN98.W64**
The Kristeva Critical Reader. Trade Paper. Edinburgh University Press. Edinburgh, 2004. 256p. ISBN:0-7486-1659-4, ISBN13: 978-0-7486-1659-6. Dewey:801.95.
Audience: **u,f.**

Lough, John **PQ146.L66**
Writer and Public in France: From the Middle Ages to the Present Day. Trade Cloth. Oxford University Press, Inc. New York, NY. 1978. 444p. ISBN:0-19-815749-5, ISBN13: 978-0-19-815749-6. Dewey:840/.9. LCCN:77-030365.
Audience: **u,f.**

McFarlane, I. D. **PQ103**
Renaissance France, 1470-1589. Barnes and Noble Books. 1974. ISBN:0-510-32205-0, ISBN13: 978-0-510-32205-2.
Audience: **u,f.**

Moore, Will Grayburn **PQ3913**
French Achievement in Literature. Trade Cloth. Bell & Hyman, Ltd. London, 1969. v, 135p. ISBN:0-7135-1508-2, ISBN13: 978-0-7135-1508-4. Dewey:840.
Audience: **l,u.**

Niklaus, Robert **PQ103**
The Eighteenth Century, 1715-1789. Barnes and Nobel Books. 1970. ISBN:0-389-03996-9, ISBN13: 978-0-389-03996-9.
Audience: **u,f.**

Peyre, Henri **PN56.S57**
Literature and Sincerity. Library Binding. Greenwood Publishing Group, Inc. Portsmouth, NH. 1978. Yale Romantic Studies, No. 9:Second Ser. ISBN:0-313-20454-3, ISBN13: 978-0-313-20454-8. Dewey:809/.933/53. LCCN:78-006243.
Audience: **u,f.**

Poulet, Georges **PQ145.6.T5**
The Interior Distance. Trade Cloth. Johns Hopkins University Press. Baltimore, MD. 1989. 302p. ISBN:0-8018-0537-6, ISBN13: 978-0-8018-0537-0. Dewey:840.9.
Audience: **u,f.**

Poulet, Georges **PQ145.6**
Studies in Human Time. Elliot Coleman (Translator). Trade Cloth. Greenwood Publishing Group, Inc. Portsmouth, NH. 1979. 363p. ISBN:0-8371-9348-6, ISBN13: 978-0-8371-9348-9. Dewey:840.9353. LCCN:78-013572.
Audience: **u,f.**

Reid, Joyce M. (Editor) **PQ41**
The Concise Oxford Dictionary of French Literature. Trade Paper. Oxford University Press, Inc. New York, NY. 1986. 700p. Oxford Paperback Reference Ser. ISBN:0-19-281200-9, ISBN13: 978-0-19-281200-1. Dewey:840/.9.
Audience: **g,l,u,f.**

Starobinski, Jean **PQ265.S7313 1993**
Blessings in Disguise: Or, the Morality of Evil. Arthur Goldhammer (Translator). Trade Cloth. Harvard University Press. Cambridge, MA. 1993. 244p. ISBN:0-674-07647-8, ISBN13: 978-0-674-07647-1. Dewey:840.9005. LCCN:92-017519.
Audience: **u,f.**

Starobinski, Jean **PN81.S6813 1989**
The Living Eye. Arthur Goldhammer (Translator). Trade Cloth. Harvard University Press. Cambridge, MA. 1989. 264p. Studies in Comparative Literature, No. 40 ISBN:0-674-53664-9, ISBN13: 978-0-674-53664-7. Dewey:809/.93353. LCCN:88-029398.
Audiencc: **u,f.**

Sullerot, Evelyne **PQ1113**
Women on Love: Eight Centuries of Feminine Writing. Box or Slipcased. Robert Hale Ltd. London, 1980. xi, 334p. ISBN:0-906908-13-2, ISBN13: 978-0-906908-13-6. Dewey:840.8/0354.
Audience: **l,u.**

Yarrow, Philip John **PQ103**
The Seventeenth Century, 1600-1715. Banres and Nobel Books. 1967.
Audience: **u,f.**

French Literature: History and Critcism > Special Periods > Medieval to 1500

Balmas, Enea Henri & Giraud, Yves **PQ196**
De Villon à Ronsard : XVe-XVIe siècles. Flammarion. 1997. ISBN:2-08-070958-5, ISBN13: 978-2-08-070958-5.
Audience: **u,f.**

Boase, Roger **GT2620**
The Origin and Meaning of Courtly Love. Trade Cloth. Rowman & Littlefield Publishers, Inc. Lanham, MD. 1977. 171p. ISBN:0-87471-950-X, ISBN13: 978-0-87471-950-5. Dewey:392/.6.
Audience: **l,u,f.**

Capellanus, Andreas **PA8250.A236D413 1990**
The Art of Courtly Love. John J. Parry (Introduction by). Trade Paper. Columbia University Press. New York, NY. 1990. 218p. Records of Civilization: Sources and Studies ISBN:0-231-07305-4, ISBN13: 978-0-231-07305-9. Dewey:306.7. LCCN:89-071284.
Audience: **l,u,f.**

Gaunt, Simon **PQ155.C74G38 2006**
Love and Death in Medieval French and Occitan Courtly Literature: Martyrs to Love. Trade Cloth. Oxford University Press, Inc. New York, NY. 2006. 256p. ISBN:0-19-927207-7, ISBN13: 978-0-19-927207-5. Dewey:841/.1093543. LCCN:2005-029729.
Audience: **u,f.**

Gaunt, Simon & Kay, Sarah (Editors) **PC3304 .T755 1999**
The Troubadours: An Introduction. Cloth Text. Cambridge University Press. New York, NY. 1999. 344p. ISBN:0-521-57388-2, ISBN13: 978-0-521-57388-7. Dewey:849/.1009. LCCN:98-011652.
Audience: **u,f.**

Kelly, Douglas **PQ155.L7**
Medieval Imagination: Rhetoric and the Poetry of Courtly Love. Trade Cloth. University of Wisconsin Press. Chicago, IL. 1978. 346p. ISBN:0-299-07610-5, ISBN13: 978-0-299-07610-8. Dewey:841/.1/09354. LCCN:78-003522.
Audience: **u,f.**

O'Neill, Mary **ML182.O54 2006**
Courtly Love Songs of Medieval France. Trade Cloth. Oxford University Press, Inc. New York, NY. 2006. 248p. Oxford Monographs on Music Ser. ISBN:0-19-816547-1, ISBN13: 978-0-19-816547-7. Dewey:849/.1209. LCCN:2005-027314.
Audience: **u,f.**

Payen, Jean Charles **PQ151**
Le Moyen âge. Flammarion. 1997. ISBN:2-08-070957-7, ISBN13: 978-2-08-070957-8.
Audience: **u,f.**

Pound, Ezra **PN681.P6 2005**
The Spirit of Romance. Richard Sieburth (Introduction by). Trade Paper. New Directions Publishing Corporation. New York, NY. 2005. 256p. ISBN:0-8112-1646-2, ISBN13: 978-0-8112-1646-3. Dewey:809.1/3. LCCN:2005-022154.
Audience: **g,l,u,f.**

Wilhelm, James J. **PC3315.W5**
Seven Troubadours: The Creators of Modern Verse. Trade Cloth. Pennsylvania State University Press. University Park, PA. 1970. 235p. ISBN:0-271-00099-6, ISBN13: 978-0-271-00099-2. Dewey:841/.1/09. LCCN:79-084668.
Audience: **u,f.**

French Literature: History and Critcism > Special Periods > Modern

Birkett, Jennifer & Kearns, James **PQ305.B524 1997**
A Guide to French Literature: Early Modern to Postmodernism. Trade Cloth. Palgrave Macmillan. New York, NY. 1997. 373p. ISBN:0-312-17475-6, ISBN13: 978-0-312-17475-0. Dewey:840.9. LCCN:97-001766.
Audience: **l,u.** *Choice, 1998.*

Bishop, Lloyd **PQ287.B58 1989**
Romantic Irony in French Literature: From Diderot to Beckett. Trade Cloth. Vanderbilt University Press. Nashville, TN. 1989. 256p. ISBN:0-8265-1233-X, ISBN13: 978-0-8265-1233-8. Dewey:840.9/18. LCCN:89-035563.
Audience: **u,f.**

Bloom, Harold (Introduction by) **PQ621.F74 1990**
French Prose and Criticism 1790 to World War II. Library Binding. Chelsea House Publishers. Langhorne, PA. 1990. 350p. The Critical Cosmos Ser. ISBN:1-55546-081-X, ISBN13: 978-1-55546-081-5. Dewey:848/.08. LCCN:87-028432.
Audience: **l,u.**

Crosland, Margaret **PQ149.C7**
Women of Iron and Velvet: French Women Writers After George Sand. Trade Cloth. Taplinger Publishing Company, Inc. Marlboro, NJ. 1976. 192p. ISBN:0-8008-8436-1, ISBN13: 978-0-8008-8436-9. Dewey:840/.9/9287. LCCN:75-008202.
Audience: **u,f.**

Décaudin, Michel & Leuwers, Daniel **PQ293**
De Zola à Guillaume Apollinaire, 1869-1920. Flammarion. 1996. ISBN:2-08-070964-X, ISBN13: 978-2-08-070964-6.
Audience: **u,f.**

Goldsmith, Elizabeth C. & Goodman, Dena **PQ149.G65 1995**
Going Public: Women and Publishing in Early Modern France. Book, Other. Cornell University Press. Ithaca, NY. 1995. 280p. Reading Women Writing Ser. ISBN:0-8014-2951-X, ISBN13: 978-0-8014-2951-4. Dewey:840.9/9287. LCCN:95-004889.
Audience: **u,f.** *Choice, 1996.*

Jeffery, Brian **PQ523.C/**
French Renaissance Comedy, 1552-1630. Trade Cloth. Oxford University Press, Inc. New York, NY. 1969. viii, 209p. ISBN:0-19-815391-0, ISBN13: 978-0-19-815391-7. Dewey:842.052.
Audience: **u,f.**

Krailsheimer, A. J. & Coupe, W. A. **PN731**
The Continental Renaissance, 1500-1600. Trade Cloth. Harvester Wheatsheaf. Harlow, 1978. 576p. ISBN:0-85527-671-1, ISBN13: 978-0-85527-671-3. Dewey:809/.031. LCCN:77-016643.
Audience: **g,l,u,f.**

Moore, Will Grayburn **PQ241**
French Classical Literature, an Essay. Paper Text. Textbook Publishers. Temecula, CA. 2003. 174p. ISBN:0-7581-7206-0, ISBN13: 978-0-7581-7206-8. Dewey:840.903.
Audience: **l,u,f.**

Morel, Jacques **PQ239**
De Montaigne à Corneille. Flammarion. 1997. ISBN:2-08-070959-3, ISBN13: 978-2-08-070959-2.
Audience: **u,f.**

Nadeau, Maurice **PQ305**
The History of Surrealism. Trade Cloth. Random House. London, 1968. 351p. ISBN:0-224-61390-1, ISBN13: 978-0-224-61390-3. Dewey:840.900912.
Audience: **u,f.**

Nurse, Peter H. **PQ526**
Classical Voices: Studies of Corneille, Racine, Molière, Mme de Lafayette. Trade Cloth. Larousse Harrap Publishers. London, 1971. 230p. ISBN:0-245-50566-0, ISBN13: 978-0-245-50566-9. Dewey:842/.4/09.
Audience: **l,u,f.**

Tieghem, Philippe van **PQ226**
Les grandes doctrines littéraires en France. Presses universitaires de France. 1990. ISBN:2-13-043151-8, ISBN13: 978-2-13-043151-0.
Audience: **u,f.**

French Literature: History and Critcism > Special Periods > Modern > 17th-19th C.

Adam, Antoine **PQ241**
Histoire de la littérature française au XVIIe siècle, vol. 1. A. Michel. 1997. ISBN:2-226-08910-1, ISBN13: 978-2-226-08910-6.
Audience: **u,f.**

Adam, Antoine **PQ241**
Histoire de la littérature française au XVIIe siècle, vol. 2. A. Michel. 1997. ISBN:2-226-08922-5, ISBN13: 978-2-226-08922-9.
Audience: **u,f.**

Adam, Antoine **PQ241**
Histoire de la littérature française au XVIIe siècle, vol. 3. A. Michel. 1997. ISBN:2-226-08923-3, ISBN13: 978-2-226-08923-6.
Audience: **u,f.**

Adam, Antoine & Tint, Herbert **PQ241**
Grandeur and Illusion: French Literature and Society, 1600-1715. Trade Cloth. Weidenfeld & Nicolson, Ltd. London, 1972. x, 312p. ISBN:0-297-76352-0, ISBN13: 978-0-297-76352-9. Dewey:840.9/004.
Audience: **l,u.**

Benichou, Paul **PQ265.B4413 1999**
The Consecration of the Writer, 1750-1830. Mark Jensen (Translator), Tzvetan Todorov (Preface by). Cloth Text. University of Nebraska Press. Lincoln, NE. 1999. 454p. European Horizons Ser. ISBN:0-8032-1291-7, ISBN13: 978-0-8032-1291-6. Dewey:840.9/382. LCCN:98-042381.
Audience: **u,f.** *Choice, 1999.*

Bénichou, Paul **PQ287**
Romantismes français, vol. 1. Gallimard. 2004. ISBN:2-07-076846-5, ISBN13: 978-2-07-076846-2.
Audience: **u,f.**

Bénichou, Paul **PQ287**
Romantismes français, vol. 2. Gallimard. 2004. ISBN:2-07-077244-6, ISBN13: 978-2-07-077244-5.
Audience: **u,f.**

Castex, Pierre Georges **PQ653**
Le cotne fantastique en France de Nodier a Maupassant. Corti. 1951.
Audience: **u,f.**

Cranston, Maurice **PN603.C73 1994**
The Romantic Movement. Jacques Le Goff (Introduction by). Trade Cloth. Blackwell Publishing, Inc. Malden, MA. 1994. 194p. The Making of Europe Ser. ISBN:0-631-17399-4, ISBN13: 978-0-631-17399-1. Dewey:809.9/145. LCCN:93-026713.
Audience: **l,u,f.**

Cyr, Myriam **PQ9113**
Letters of a Portuguese Nun: Uncovering the Mystery Behind a Seventeenth Century Forbidden Love. Trade Cloth. Hyperion Press. New York, NY. 2006. 256p. ISBN:0-7868-6911-9, ISBN13: 978-0-7868-6911-4. Dewey:946.9032092.
Audience: **u,f.**

Delon, Michel et al. **PQ261**
De l'Encyclopédie aux Méditations. Mauzi, Robert; Menant, Sylvain (Authors). Flammarion. 1998. ISBN:2-08-070962-3, ISBN13: 978-2-08-070962-2.
Audience: **u,f.**

Dolbow, Sandra W. **PQ41**
Dictionary of Modern French Literature: From the Age of Reason Though Realism. Cloth Text. Greenwood Publishing Group, Inc. Portsmouth, NH. 1986. 375p. ISBN:0-313-23784-0, ISBN13: 978-0-313-23784-3. Dewey:840/.3/21. LCCN:85-015492.
Audience: **g,l,u,f.** *Choice, 1986.*

Grimsley, Ronald (Editor) **PN751**
Age of Enlightenment, 1715-89. Trade Paper. Penguin Books, Ltd. London, 1979. 512p. ISBN:0-14-022140-9, ISBN13: 978-0-14-022140-4. Dewey:809/.033.
Audience: **u,f.**

Hammond, Nicholas **PQ241**
Creative Tensions: An Introduction to Seventeenth-Century French Literature. Duckworth. 1997. ISBN:0-7156-2801-1, ISBN13: 978-0-7156-2801-0.
Audience: **g,u,f.**

Hemmings, F. W. J. (Editor) **PN3499**
The Age of Realism. Trade Paper. Penguin Group (USA) Inc. New York, NY. 1974. 432p. Guide to European Lit Ser. ISBN:0-14-021779-7, ISBN13: 978-0-14-021779-7. Dewey:809.3/9/12.
Audience: **l,u.**

Krailsheimer, A. J. **PQ245**
Studies in Self-Interest: From Descartes to La Bruyère. Clarendon Press. 1962.
Audience: **u,f.**

Leigh, John **PQ263**
The Search for Enlightenment: An Introduction to Eighteenth-Century French Writing. Book, Other. Rowman & Littlefield Publishers, Inc. Lanham, MD. 1999. 176p. ISBN:0-7425-0047-0, ISBN13: 978-0-7425-0047-1. Dewey:840.9/005.
Audience: **u,f.**

Mason, Haydn **PQ261**
French Writers and Their Society, 1715-1800. Trade Cloth. Macmillan Publishers Ltd. London, 1982. 272p. ISBN:0-333-26465-7, ISBN13: 978-0-333-26465-2. Dewey:840.9/005.
Audience: **l,u,f.**

Milner, Max & Pichois, Claude **PQ281**
De Chateaubriand à Baudelaire, 1820-1869. Flammarion. 1996. ISBN:2-08-070963-1, ISBN13: 978-2-08-070963-9.
Audience: **u,f.**

Moore, Will Grayburn **PQ526.M6**
The Classical Drama of France. Trade Cloth. Oxford University Press, Inc. New York, NY. 1971. xi, 138p. ISBN:0-19-885055-7, ISBN13: 978-0-19-885055-7. Dewey:842/.4/09. LCCN:74-850453.
Audience: **l,u.**

Niklaus, Robert **PQ263**
The Eighteenth Century, 1715-1789. Trade Cloth. Ernest Benn Ltd. London, 1970. xx, 435p. ISBN:0-510-32231-X, ISBN13: 978-0-510-32231-1. Dewey:840.9/005.
Audience: **l,u.**

Richard, Jean-Pierre **PQ283**
Littérature et sensation. Editions du Seuil. 1990. ISBN:2-02-012493-9, ISBN13: 978-2-02-012493-5.
Audience: **u,f.**

Starobinski, Jean **N6756.S7313 1987**
The Invention of Liberty, 1700-1789. Trade Paper. Rizzoli International Publications, Inc. New York, NY. 1987. 220p. ISBN:0-8478-0846-7, ISBN13: 978-0-8478-0846-5. Dewey:709/.03/3. LCCN:87-009851.
Audience: **u,f.**

Starobinski, Jean **NX452.5.N4S713 1988**
1789: The Emblems of Reason. Barbara Bray (Translator). Trade Paper. MIT Press. Cambridge, MA. 1988. 304p. ISBN:0-262-69122-1, ISBN13: 978-0-262-69122-2. Dewey:709/.44. LCCN:88-019143.
Audience: **u,f.**

Zuber, Roger & Cuénin, Micheline **PQ241.Z82 1998**
Le Classicisme. Flammarion. 1998. ISBN:2-08-070960-7, ISBN13: 978-2-08-070960-8.
Audience: **u,f.**

French Literature: History and Critcism > Special Periods > Modern > 20th C.

Best, Victoria **PQ305**
An Introduction to Twentieth-Century French Literature. Trade Paper. Gerald Duckworth & Company, Ltd. London, 2002. 160p. New Readings Ser. ISBN:0-7156-3166-7, ISBN13: 978-0-7156-3166-9. Dewey:840.9/0091.
Audience: **l,u.**

Bree, Germaine **PQ305**
Twentieth-Century French Literature, 1920-1970. Louise Guiney (Translator). Trade Cloth. University of Chicago Press. Chicago, IL. 1983. 398p. ISBN:0-226-07195-2, ISBN13: 978-0-226-07195-4. Dewey:840.9/00912. LCCN:82-015980.
Audience: **u,f.**

Brée, Germaine & Morot-Sir, Edouard **PQ305**
Du surréalisme à l'empire de la critique. Flammarion. 1996. ISBN:2-08-070965-8, ISBN13: 978-2-08-070965-3.
Audience: **u,f.**

Gavronsky, Serge **PQ442**
Toward a New Poetics: Contemporary Writing in France. Trade Paper. University of California Press. Berkeley, CA. 1994. 382p. ISBN:0-520-08793-3, ISBN13: 978-0-520-08793-4. LCCN:94-002946.
Audience: **u,f.**

Hughes, Alex (Editor), et al. **PQ673.F74 1996**
French Erotic Fiction: Women's Desiring Writing, 1880-1990. Kate Ince & Jennifer Birkett (Editors). Trade Paper. Berg Publishers. Oxford, 1996. 191p. French Studies Ser. ISBN:1-85973-049-3, ISBN13: 978-1-85973-049-2. Dewey:843.9/093538. LCCN:96-000070.
Audience: **u,f.**

Lemaitre, Georges Edouard **PQ305**
From Cubism to Surrealism in French Literature. Trade Cloth. Greenwood Publishing Group, Inc. Portsmouth, NH. 1978. 256p. ISBN:0-313-20112-9, ISBN13: 978-0-313-20112-7. Dewey:840.90091. LCCN:77-018121.
Audience: **u,f.**

Picon, Gaetan **PQ305**
Contemporary French Literature: 1945 and after. Kelvin Scott & Graham Martin (Translators). Trade Cloth. Frederick Ungar A Book. Dulles, VA. 1974. 236p. ISBN:0-8044-3255-4, ISBN13: 978-0-8044-3255-9. Dewey:840/.9/00914. LCCN:72-089056.
Audience: **l,u,f.**

Sturrock, John **PQ305.S78 1998**
The Word from Paris: Essays on Modern French Writers and Thinkers. Trade Cloth. Analytical Psychology Club of San Francisco, Inc. San Francisco, CA. 1998. 256p. ISBN:1-85984-832-X, ISBN13: 978-1-85984-832-6. Dewey:840.9/00914. LCCN:99-237155.
Audience: **u,f.**

French Literature: History and Critcism > Special Forms

Balakian, Anna Elizabeth **PQ443.B3 1970**
Surrealism; the Road to the Absolute. Trade Cloth. Penguin Group (USA) Inc. New York, NY. 1970. 256p. ISBN:0-525-05103-1, ISBN13: 978-0-525-05103-9. Dewey:841/.91/091. LCCN:76-087200.
Audience: **u,f.**

French Literature: History and Critcism > Special Forms > Poetry

Balakian, Anna **PQ439**
Literary Origins of Surrealism: A New Mysticism in French Poetry. Trade Cloth. New York University Press. New York, NY. 1966. ISBN:0-8147-0024-1, ISBN13: 978-0-8147-0024-2. Dewey:841.109.
Audience: **u,f.**

Barzun, Jacques **PC2511.B37 1991**
An Essay on French Verse - for Readers of English Poetry. Trade Cloth. New Directions Publishing Corporation. New York, NY. 1991. 154p. ISBN:0-8112-1157-6, ISBN13: 978-0-8112-1157-4. Dewey:841.009. LCCN:90-048759.
Audience: **g,u,f.** *Choice, 1991.*

Bishop, Michael **PQ431.B57 1993**
Critical History of French Poetry. Trade Paper. Thomson Gale. Farmington Hills, MI. 1993. 384p. Twayne's Critical History of Poetry Ser. ISBN:0-8057-8453-5, ISBN13: 978-0-8057-8453-4. Dewey:841/.709. LCCN:93-027520.
Audience: **l,u.**

Bloom, Harold (Editor, Introduction by) **PQ405.F74 1990**
French Poetry: The Renaissance Through 1915. Trade Cloth. Chelsea House Publishers. Langhorne, PA. 1990. 478p. The Critical Cosmos Ser. ISBN:0-87754-997-4, ISBN13: 978-0-87754-997-0. Dewey:841/.009. LCCN:87-011767.
Audience: **l,u.**

Bonnefoy, Yves **PQ412.B66 1989**
The Act and the Place of Poetry: Selected Essays. John Naughton (Editor), Joseph Frank (Foreword by). Trade Cloth. University of Chicago Press. Chicago, IL. 1989. 196p. ISBN:0-226-06449-2, ISBN13: 978-0-226-06449-9. Dewey:841/.009. LCCN:88-021547.
Audience: **u,f.**

Bonnefoy, Yves **PR2881.5.F74B66 2004**
Shakespeare and the French Poet. John Naughton (Editor, Translator). Trade Cloth. University of Chicago Press. Chicago, IL. 2004. 304p. ISBN:0-226-06442-5, ISBN13: 978-0-226-06442-0. Dewey:822.3/3. LCCN:2003-023393.
Audience: **u,f.**

Brereton, Geoffrey **PQ401**
An Introduction to the French Poets: Villon to the Present Day. Ed. 2. Trade Cloth. Methuen & Company, Ltd. London, 1973. xii, 320p. ISBN:0-416-76620-X, ISBN13: 978-0-416-76620-2. Dewey:841/.009. LCCN:73-162190.
Audience: **l,u.**

Caws, Mary Ann **PQ443.C3**
The Poetry of Dada and Sur-Realism: Aragon, Breton, Tzara, Eluard and Desnos. Trade Cloth. Princeton University Press. Princeton, NJ. 1970. x, 226p. ISBN:0-691-06164-5, ISBN13: 978-0-691-06164-1. Dewey:841/.9/1209. LCCN:68-056304.
Audience: **l,u,f.**

Caws, Mary A. (Editor) **PQ443.C28**
About French Poetry from Dada to "Tel Quel": Text and Theory. Henri Peyre (Foreword by). Cloth Text. Wayne State University Press. Detroit, MI. 1974. 298p. ISBN:0-8143-1520-8, ISBN13: 978-0-8143-1520-0. Dewey:841/.9/1209. LCCN:74-010962.
Audience: **u,f.**

Coleman, Kathleen **PQ401.C65 1993**
Guide to French Poetry Explication. Trade Cloth. Thomson Gale. Farmington Hills, MI. 1993. 200p. G. K. Hall Reference Ser. ISBN:0-8161-9075-5, ISBN13: 978-0-8161-9075-1. Dewey:841.009. LCCN:92-022129.
Audience: **l,u.** *Choice, 1993.*

Fowlie, Wallace **PQ439**
Poem and Symbol: A Brief History of French Symbolism. Trade Paper. Pennsylvania State University Press. University Park, PA. 1990. 160p. ISBN:0-271-00696-X, ISBN13: 978-0-271-00696-3. Dewey:841/.00915. LCCN:89-016120.
Audience: **l,u,f.** *Choice, 1991.*

Gibson, Robert **PQ411 .G5**
Modern French Poets on Poetry: An Anthology. Trade Paper. Cambridge University Press. New York, NY. 303p. ISBN:0-521-09151-9, ISBN13: 978-0-521-09151-0. Dewey:841/.009.
Audience: **u,f.**

Greene, Robert W. **PQ441**
Six French Poets of Our Time: A Critical and Historical Study. Trade Cloth. Princeton University Press. Princeton, NJ. 1979. 216p. Essays in Literature Ser. ISBN:0-691-06390-7, ISBN13: 978-0-691-06390-4. Dewey:841/.912/09. LCCN:78-070927.
Audience: **l,u.**

Lewis, Roy **PN4151**
On Reading French Verse: A Study of Poetic Form. Trade Cloth. Oxford University Press, Inc. New York, NY. 1982. 272p. ISBN:0-19-815775-4, ISBN13: 978-0-19-815775-5. Dewey:841/.009.
Audience: **l,u.**

Lowell, Amy **PQ437**
Six French Poets: Studies in Contemporary Literature. Library Binding. Classic Books. Murrieta, CA. 1999. 488p. The Collected Works of Amy Lowell ISBN:1-58201-760-3, ISBN13: 978-1-58201-760-0. Dewey:841/.8/09.
Audience: **l,u,f.**

Michaud, Guy **PQ439**
Message poetique du symbolisme. Nizet. 1947.
Audience: **u,f.**

Peyre, Henri **PQ439.P413**
What Is Symbolism? Emmett Parker (Translator). Trade Cloth. University of Alabama Press. Tuscaloosa, AL. 1980. 224p. ISBN:0-8173-7004-8, ISBN13: 978-0-8173-7004-6. Dewey:841/.8/0915. LCCN:79-004686.
Audience: **l,u.**

Peyre, Henri **PQ287 .P5413**
What Is Romanticism? Roda P. Roberts (Translator). Trade Cloth. University of Alabama Press. Tuscaloosa, AL. 1977. ISBN:0-8173-7003-X, ISBN13: 978-0-8173-7003-9. Dewey:840/.9/14. LCCN:75-042374.
Audience: **l,u.**

Poulet, Georges **PQ2191.Z5**
Exploding Poetry: Baudelaire-Rimbaud. Francoise Meltzer (Translator). Trade Cloth. University of Chicago Press. Chicago, IL. 1997. 160p. ISBN:0-226-67650-1, ISBN13: 978-0-226-67650-0. Dewey:841/.8/09. LCCN:83-018062.
Audience: **u,f.**

Prendergast, Christopher (Editor) **PQ432 .N5 1990**
Nineteenth-Century French Poetry: Introductions to Close Reading. Trade Paper. Cambridge University Press. New York, NY. 1990. 270p. ISBN:0-521-34774-2, ISBN13: 978-0-521-34774-7. Dewey:841/.7/09. LCCN:89-031434.
Audience: **l,u.**

Raymond, Marcel **PQ437**
From Baudelaire to Surrealism. Trade Paper. Methuen & Company, Ltd. London, 1970. viii, 356p. ISBN:0-416-27950-3, ISBN13: 978-0-416-27950-4. Dewey:841/.8/09.
Audience: **l,u.**

Riffaterre, Hermine **PQ491**
The Prose Poem in France: Theory and Practice. Mary A. Caws (Editor). Trade Cloth. Columbia University Press. New York, NY. 1983. 237p. ISBN:0-231-05434-3, ISBN13: 978-0-231-05434-8. Dewey:841/.8/09. LCCN:82-020691.
Audience: **u,f.**

Scott, Clive **PQ471.F74S35 1990**
Vers Libre: The Emergence of Free Verse in France 1886-1914. Trade Cloth. Oxford University Press, Inc. New York, NY. 1990. 352p. ISBN:0-19-815159-4, ISBN13: 978-0-19-815159-3. Dewey:841/.809. LCCN:89-016059.
Audience: **u,f.**

Shaw, Mary **PQ401.S53 2003**
The Cambridge Introduction to French Poetry. Cloth Text. Cambridge University Press. New York, NY. 2003. 238p. Cambridge Introductions to Literature Ser. ISBN:0-521-80876-6, ISBN13: 978-0-521-80876-7. Dewey:841.009. LCCN:2002-041544.
Audience: **l,u.**

French Literature: History and Critcism > Special Forms > Drama

Benedikt, Wel **PQ1240.E5 B4**
Modern French Theatre: The Avant-Garde, Dada and Surrealism. Michael Benedikt & George E. Wellwarth (Editors), Michael Benedikt & George E. Wellwarth (Translators). Trade Paper. Penguin Group (USA) Inc. New York, NY. 1966. ISBN:0-525-47176-6, ISBN13: 978-0-525-47176-9. Dewey:842.91082.
Audience: **g,l,u,f.**

Borgerhoff, Joseph L. (Editor) **PQ1222**
Nineteenth Century French Plays. Trade Cloth. Irvington Publishers. New York, NY. 1978. ISBN:0-89197-319-2, ISBN13: 978-0-89197-319-5. Dewey:842/.009.
Audience: **l,u,f.**

Bradby, David **PQ556.B67 1991**
Modern French Drama, 1940-1990. Ed. 2. Trade Paper. Cambridge University Press. New York, NY. 1991. 345p. ISBN:0-521-40843-1, ISBN13: 978-0-521-40843-1. Dewey:842/.91409. LCCN:90-043073.
Audience: **l,u,f.**

Brereton, Geoffrey **PQ566**
French Comic Drama from the Sixteenth to the Eighteenth Century. Trade Cloth. Routledge. New York, NY. 1977. x, 290p. ISBN:0-416-78220-5, ISBN13: 978-0-416-78220-2. Dewey:842/.052. LCCN:77-359472.
Audience: **u,f.**

Brereton, Geoffrey **PQ561**
French Tragic Drama in the Sixteenth and Seventeenth Centuries. Trade Cloth. Routledge. New York, NY. 1973. 320p. ISBN:0-416-07630-0, ISBN13: 978-0-416-07630-1. Dewey:842/.051. LCCN:74-157940.
Audience: **u,f.**

Fowlie, Wallace **PQ556.F6**
Dionysus in Paris: A Guide to Contemporary French Theatre. Trade Cloth. Peter Smith Publisher, Inc. Magnolia, MA. 1990. ISBN:0-8446-0096-2, ISBN13: 978-0-8446-0096-3. Dewey:842/.9/109.
Audience: **u,f.** B

Frank, Grace **PQ511**
Medieval French Drama. Trade Cloth. Oxford University Press, Inc. New York, NY. 1954. 296p. ISBN:0-19-815317-1, ISBN13: 978-0-19-815317-7. Dewey:842.
Audience: **l,u,f.**

Grossvogel, David I. **PQ558**
20th Century French Drama. Trade Cloth. Gordian Press, Inc. Staten Island, NY. 1966. 384p. ISBN:0-87752-048-8, ISBN13: 978-0-87752-048-1. Dewey:842.9109. LCCN:68-016434.
Audience: **u,f.**

Guicharnaud, Jacques & Guicharnaud, June **PQ305**
Modern French Theatre: From Giraudoux to Genet. Trade Paper.

Yale University Press. Cumberland, RI. 1975. xiii, 383p. Romantic Studies, Second Ser., No. 7 ISBN:0-300-00106-1, ISBN13: 978-0-300-00106-8. Dewey:842/.9/1209. LCCN:67-026198.
Audience: **u,f.**

Knapp, Bettina L. **PQ556**
French Theatre, 1918-1939. Trade Paper. Macmillan Publishers Ltd. London, 1985. ISBN:0-333-37259-X, ISBN13: 978-0-333-37259-3. Dewey:842/.91209.
Audience: **l,u,f.**

Knapp, Bettina L. **PQ556 .K55**
French Theater since 1968. Library Binding. Thomson Gale. Farmington Hills, MI. 1995. ISBN:0-614-02580-X, ISBN13: 978-0-614-02580-4. Dewey:842/.91409.
Audience: **l,u.**

Knight, Alan E. **PQ511**
Aspects of Genre in Late Medieval French Drama. Cloth Text. Manchester University Press. Manchester, 1988. 190p. ISBN:0-7190-0862-X, ISBN13: 978-0-7190-0862-7. Dewey:842/.2/09. LCCN:82-062255.
Audience: **u,f.**

Pronko, Leonard C. **PQ558 .P7 1978**
Avant Garde: The Experimental Theater in France. Trade Cloth. Greenwood Publishing Group, Inc. Portsmouth, NH. 1978. 225p. ISBN:0-313-20096-3, ISBN13: 978-0-313-20096-0. Dewey:842/.9/1409. LCCN:77-026017.
Audience: **u,f.**

Schérer, Jacques **PQ526**
La dramaturgie classique en France. Nizet. 2001. ISBN:2-7078-1259-5, ISBN13: 978-2-7078-1259-9.
Audience: **u,f.**

Turnell, Martin **PQ527**
Classical Moment: Studies of Corneille, Moliere, and Racine. Trade Cloth. Greenwood Publishing Group, Inc. Portsmouth, NH. 1971. 261p. ISBN:0-8371-5803-6, ISBN13: 978-0-8371-5803-7. Dewey:842/.4/09. LCCN:79-138601.
Audience: **u,f.**

French Literature: History and Critcism > Special Forms > Prose. Prose Fiction

Adam, Antoine **PQ645**
Romanciers du XVIIe siècle: Sorel, Scarron, Furetière, Mme de La Fayette. Gallimard. 1998. ISBN:2-07-010479-6, ISBN13: 978-2-07-010479-6.
Audience: **u,f.**

Bloom, Harold (Introduction by) **PQ611.F74 1990**
French Prose and Criticism Through, 1789. Library Binding. Chelsea House Publishers. Langhorne, PA. 1990. 350p. The Critical Cosmos Ser. ISBN:1-55546-080-1, ISBN13: 978-1-55546-080-8. Dewey:848/.08. LCCN:87-018360.
Audience: **l,u.**

Brombert, Victor H. **PQ637.I5**
The Intellectual Hero: Studies in the French Novel 1880. Paper Text. Textbook Publishers. Temecula, CA. 2003. 255p. ISBN:0-7581-9858-2, ISBN13: 978-0-7581-9858-7. Dewey:843.9109.
Audience: **u,f.**

Brooks, Peter **PQ0648.B7**
The Novel of Worldliness: Crebillon, Marivaux, Laclos, Stendhal. Trade Paper. Books on Demand. Ann Arbor, MI. 305p. ISBN:0-608-17854-3, ISBN13: 978-0-608-17854-7. Dewey:843.509. LCCN:68-056303.
Audience: **l,u.**

Coulet, Henri **PQ631**
Le roman jusqu'à la Révolution. A. Colin. 2000. ISBN:2-200-25117-3, ISBN13: 978-2-200-25117-8.
Audience: **u,f.**

Girard, René **PN3491**
Deceit, Desire, and the Novel: Self and Other in Literary Structure. Yvonne Freccero (Translator). Trade Paper. Johns Hopkins University Press. Baltimore, MD. 1976. 328p. ISBN:0-8018-1830-3, ISBN13: 978-0-8018-1830-1. Dewey:809.3/9353. LCCN:65-028582.
Audience: **u,f.**

Levin, Harry **PQ283**
The Gates of Horn: A Study of Five French Realists. Paper Text. Oxford University Press, Inc. New York, NY. 1986. 576p. ISBN:0-19-500727-1, ISBN13: 978-0-19-500727-5. Dewey:843/.009/12. LCCN:63-012552.
Audience: **u,f.**

Lukács, György & Bostock, Anna **PN3331**
The Theory of the Novel: A Historico-Philosophical Essay on the Forms of Great Epic Literature. Trade Cloth. Merlin Press Ltd. London, 1971. 160p. ISBN:0-85036-139-7, ISBN13: 978-0-85036-139-1. Dewey:808.3.
Audience: **u,f.**

Mylne, Vivienne **PQ648**
The Eighteenth Century French Novel: Techniques of Illusion. Ed. 2. Trade Cloth. Cambridge University Press. New York, NY. 1981. 301p. ISBN:0-521-23864-1, ISBN13: 978-0-521-23864-9. Dewey:843/.5/09. LCCN:81-003911.
Audience: **u,f.**

Roudiez, S. Leon **PQ671.R64 1991**
French Fiction Revisited. Trade Cloth. Dalkey Archive Press. Normal, IL. 1991. 350p. ISBN:0-916583-73-2, ISBN13: 978-0-916583-73-6. Dewey:843/.9101. LCCN:90-014081.
Audience: **l,u.**

Showalter, English **PQ0645.S5**
The Evolution of the French Novel, 1641-1782. Trade Paper. Books on Demand. Ann Arbor, MI. 380p. ISBN:0-8357-2774-2, ISBN13: 978-0-8357-2774-7. Dewey:843.409. LCCN:78-037577.
Audience: **u,f.**

Turnell, Martin **PQ635**
The Art of French Fiction: Prevost, Standahl, Zola, Maupassant, Gide, Mauriac, Proust. Paper Text. Textbook Publishers. Temecula, CA. 2003. 394p. ISBN:0-7581-7795-X, ISBN13: 978-0-7581-7795-7. Dewey:843.809.
Audience: **l,u,f.**

Turnell, Martin **843/.03**
The Novel in France: Mme. de Lafayette, Laclos, Constant, Stendhal, Balzac, Flaubert, Proust. Trade Cloth. Ayer Company Publishers, Inc. Manchester, NH. 1977. Essay Index Reprint Ser. ISBN:0-8369-2831-8, ISBN13: 978-0-8369-2831-0. LCCN:72-000297.
Audience: **l,u,f.**

Turnell, Martin **PQ631.T83**
The Rise of the French Novel: Marivaux, Crebillon Fils, Rousseau, Stendhal, Flaubert, Alain-Fournier, Raymond Radiguet. Trade Cloth. New Directions Publishing Corporation. New York, NY. 1978. 309 p. ;p. ISBN:0-8112-0688-2, ISBN13: 978-0-8112-0688-4. Dewey:843/.03. LCCN:77-026792.
Audience: **l,u,f.**

Ullmann, Stephen **PQ635**
Style in the French Novel. Paper Text. Textbook Publishers. Temecula, CA. 2003. vii, 272p. ISBN:0-7581-1347-1, ISBN13: 978-0-7581-1347-4. Dewey:843.09.
Audience: **l,u,f.**

Unwin, Timothy (Editor) **PQ671 .C296 1997**
The Cambridge Companion to the French Novel: From 1800 to the Present. Cloth Text. Cambridge University Press. New York, NY. 1997. 305p. Companions to Literature Ser. ISBN:0-521-49563-6, ISBN13: 978-0-521-49563-9. Dewey:843.7/09. LCCN:96-052444.
Audience: **u,f.**

French Literature: History and Critcism > Special Forms > Prose. Prose Fiction > 20th C.

Babcock, Arthur E. **PQ671.B25 1997**
The French New Novel. Trade Cloth. Thomson Gale. Farmington Hills, MI. 1997. xii, 162p. Twayne's Critical History of the Novel Ser. ISBN:0-8057-7858-6, ISBN13: 978-0-8057-7858-8. Dewey:843/.91409. LCCN:96-039135.
Audience: **l,u.** *Choice, 1998.*

Cruickshank, John (Editor) **PQ671**
The Novelist As Philosopher: Studies in French Fiction, 1935-1960. Trade Cloth. Greenwood Publishing Group, Inc. Portsmouth, NH. 1978. 257p. ISBN:0-313-20271-0, ISBN13: 978-0-313-20271-1. Dewey:843.91409. LCCN:77-028882.
Audience: **u,f.**

Frohock, Wilbur M. **PQ0671.F7**
Style and Temper: Studies in French Fiction, 1925-1960. Trade Paper. Books on Demand. Ann Arbor, MI. 1967. 173p. ISBN:0-7837-4147-2, ISBN13: 978-0-7837-4147-5. Dewey:843.91409. LCCN:67-003155.
Audience: **l,u,f.**

Nadeau, Maurice **PQ671**
Le Roman français depuis la guerre. Le Passeur. 1992. ISBN:2-907913-12-3, ISBN13: 978-2-907913-12-6.
Audience: **u,f.**

Collections of French Literature

Gallica Classique.
http://gallica.bnf.fr/classique/
Audience: **u,f.**

Lagarde, André (Editor) **PQ1109**
Le Lagarde et Michard (set). Michard, Laurent (Editor). Ed. Bordas. 2003. ISBN:2-04-729822-9, ISBN13: 978-2-04-729822-0.
Audience: **l,u,f.**

Collections of French Literature > Poetry

Auster, Paul (Editor) **PQ1170.E6.R36 1982**
The Random House Book of Twentieth-Century French Poetry: With Translations by American and British Poets. Trade Cloth. Random House, Inc. New York, NY. 1982. 746p. ISBN:0-394-52197-8, ISBN13: 978-0-394-52197-8. Dewey:841/.91/08. LCCN:82-000280.
Audience: **g,l,u,f.**

Bergin, Thomas G., et al. **PC3322.A2**
Anthology of the Provencal Troubadours. Ed. 2. Susan Olson, William D. Paden & Nathaniel Smith (Authors). Trade Cloth. Yale University Press. Cumberland, RI. 1973. 512p. Romantic Studies, Second Ser., No. 23 ISBN:0-300-01405-8, ISBN13: 978-0-300-01405-1. Dewey:849/.1/04. LCCN:72-091287.
Audience: **u,f.**

Blackmore, A. M. & Blackmore, E. H. (Editors) **PQ1170.E6S534 2000**
Six Nineteenth Century French Poets: With Parallel French Text. Trade Paper. Oxford University Press, Inc. New York, NY. 2000. 384p. Oxford World's Classics Ser. ISBN:0-19-283973-X, ISBN13: 978-0-19-283973-2. Dewey:841/.708. LCCN:00-039210.
Audience: **g,l,u,f.**

Broome, Peter & Chesters, Graham (Editors) **PQ1183**
An Anthology of Modern French Poetry (1850-1950). Trade Paper. Cambridge University Press. New York, NY. 1976. 221p. ISBN:0-521-20929-3, ISBN13: 978-0-521-20929-8. Dewey:841/.8/08. LCCN:75-040769.
Audience: **g,l,u.**

Bruckner, Matilda Tomaryn (Editor), et al. **PC3365.E3**
Songs of the Women Troubadours. Laurie Shepard & Sarah White (Editors). Trade Paper. Taylor & Francis Group. Philadelphia, PA. 2000. 280p. ISBN:0-8153-3568-7, ISBN13: 978-0-8153-3568-9. Dewey:849.1/2/080/9287. LCCN:95-002961.
Audience: **u,f.**

Caws, Mary Ann (Editor) **PQ1170.E6Y35 2004**
The Yale Anthology of Twentieth-Century French Poetry. Cloth over Boards. Yale University Press. Cumberland, RI. 2004. 704p. ISBN:0-300-10010-8, ISBN13: 978-0-300-10010-5. Dewey:841/.9108. LCCN:2004-040695.
Audience: **g,l,u,f.** *Choice, 2005.*

Chauveau, Jean-Pierre (Editor) **PQ1165**
Anthologie de la poésie française, vol. 1. Gallimard. 2000. ISBN:2-07-011384-1, ISBN13: 978-2-07-011384-2.
Audience: **u,f.**

Chauveau, Jean-Pierre (Editor) **PQ1165**
Anthologie de la poésie française, vol. 2. Gallimard. 2000. ISBN:2-07-011599-2, ISBN13: 978-2-07-011599-0.
Audience: **u,f.**

Chedid, Andree **PQ1184**
Women's Poetry in France, 1965-1995: A Bilingual Anthology. Michael Bishop (Translator). Trade Paper. Wake Forest University Press. Winston-Salem, NC. 1997. 175p. Bilingual Editions of Contemporary French Poetry Ser. ISBN:0-916390-79-9, ISBN13: 978-0-916390-79-2. Dewey:841.08. LCCN:97-060922.
Audience: **g,l,u,f.** *Choice, 1998.*

Flores, Angel **PQ1170.E6F5 2000**
The Anchor Anthology of French Poetry: From Nerval to Valery in English Translation. Trade Paper. Doubleday Publishing. New York, NY. 2000. 480p. ISBN:0-385-49888-8, ISBN13: 978-0-385-49888-3. Dewey:841/.708. LCCN:00-268842.
Audience: **g,l,u,f.**

Gavronsky, Serge **PQ1184**
Poems and Texts: An Anthology of French Poems. Trade Cloth. October House. Preston, CT. 1969. ISBN:0-8079-0150-4, ISBN13: 978-0-8079-0150-2. Dewey:841/.9/109.
Audience: **g,l,u,f.**

Gavronsky, Serge (Translator) **PQ1170.E6S53 1997**
Six Contemporary French Women Poets: Theory, Practice and Pleasures. Trade Cloth. Southern Illinois University Press. Carbondale, IL. 1997. 144p. ISBN:0-8093-2115-7, ISBN13: 978-0-8093-2115-5. Dewey:841/.9140809287. LCCN:96-041759.
Audience: **u,f.**

Gibson, Robert (Compiled by) **PQ411**
Modern French Poets on Poetry: An Anthology. Trade Cloth. Cambridge University Press. New York, NY. 1979. 320p. ISBN:0-521-05078-2, ISBN13: 978-0-521-05078-4. Dewey:841/.009. LCCN:78-073241.
Audience: **g,l,u,f.**

Kelley, David & Khalfa, Jean (Translators) **PQ1170.E6N48 1996**
The New French Poetry. Trade Paper. Bloodaxe Books. Bala, 1996. 320p. ISBN:1-85224-260-4, ISBN13: 978-1-85224-260-2. Dewey:841/.914. LCCN:94-183725.
Audience: **g,l,u,f.**

Lucas, St. John & Jones, P. M. (Editors) **PQ1165 .O84**
Oxford Book of French Verse, Thirteenth Century to Twentieth Century. Ed. 2. Trade Cloth. Oxford University Press, Inc. New York, NY. 1957. ISBN:0-19-812109-1, ISBN13: 978-0-19-812109-1. Dewey:841.008.
Audience: **g,l,u,f.**

Newth, Michael (Translator) **PQ1310**
Heroes of the French Epic: A Selection of Chansons de Geste. Trade Paper. Boydell & Brewer, Ltd. Woodbridge, 2005. 714p. ISBN:1-84383-147-3, ISBN13: 978-1-84383-147-1. Dewey:841/.108. LCCN:2006-295909.
Audience: **g,l,u,f.**

Shapiro, Norman R. **PQ1170.E6L97 2002**
Lyrics of the French Renaissance: Marot, du Bellay and Ronsard. Hope H. Glidden (Introduction by). Cloth over Boards. Yale University Press. Cumberland, RI. 2002. 416p. ISBN:0-300-08759-4, ISBN13: 978-0-300-08759-8. Dewey:841.3. LCCN:2002-101820.
Audience: **g,l,u,f.**

Sorrell, Martin (Translator) **PQ1167 .E43 1995**
Elles: A Bilingual Anthology of Modern French Poetry by Women. Trade Paper. University of Exeter Press. Exeter, 1995. 268p. European Studies ISBN:0-85989-448-7, ISBN13: 978-0-85989-448-7. Dewey:841.9140809287. LCCN:96-140507.
Audience: **g,l,u,f.**

Terry, Patricia & Gavronsky, Serge **PQ1170./6**
Modern French Poetry: A Bilingual Anthology. Trade Cloth. Columbia University Press. New York, NY. 1975. xiii, 241p. ISBN:0-231-03957-3, ISBN13: 978-0-231-03957-4. Dewey:841/.8/08. LCCN:75-017893.
Audience: **g,l,u,f.**

Woledge, Brian (Editor), et al. **PQ1165**
Penguin Book of French Verse. Geoffrey Brereton & Anthony Hartley (Editors). Trade Paper. Penguin Group (USA) Inc. New York, NY. 1975. 704p. Penguin Poets Ser. ISBN:0-14-042182-3, ISBN13: 978-0-14-042182-8. Dewey:841/.008.
Audience: **g,l,u,f.**

Collections of French Literature > Drama. Fiction

Wald Lasowski, Patrick (Editor) **PQ1276.E75**
Romanciers libertins du XVIIIe siècle. Clerval, Alain (Editor). Gallimard. 2000. ISBN:2-07-011329-9, ISBN13: 978-2-07-011329-3.
Audience: **u,f.**

Bermel, Albert (Editor, Translator) **PQ1240.E8D69 1997**
A Dozen French Farces from the 15th to the 20th Centuries. Trade Paper. Hal Leonard Corporation. Milwaukee, WI. 1997. 403p. ISBN:0-87910-092-3, ISBN13: 978-0-87910-092-6. Dewey:842/.0523208. LCCN:97-003325.
Audience: **g,l,u,f.**

Castex, Pierre Georges **PN6071**
Anthologie du conte fantastique français. Corti. 2004.
ISBN:2-7143-0825-2, ISBN13: 978-2-7143-0825-2.
Audience: **u.**

Coleman, C. B. (Editor) **PQ1240.E7T495 1996**
Three French Comedies: Turcaret, the Triumph of Love, and Eating Crow. James Magruder (Translator, Introduction by). Cloth over Boards. Yale University Press. Cumberland, RI. 1996. 192p. ISBN:0-300-06275-3, ISBN13: 978-0-300-06275-5. Dewey:842/.052308. LCCN:95-040001.
Audience: **g,l,u,f.** *Choice, 1997.*

Corneille, Pierre, et al. **PQ1220**
Landmarks of French Classical Drama. Jean Racine, Moliere, Marivaux & Beaumarchais (Authors), David Bryer, Robert D. MacDonald, Christopher Hampton & John Fowles (Translators), David Bradby (Introduction by). Trade Paper. Heinemann. Portsmouth, NH. 1991. 393p. ISBN:0-413-63100-1, ISBN13: 978-0-413-63100-8. Dewey:842.4/08.
Audience: **l,u,f.**

Coulet, Henri (Editor) **PQ1268**
Nouvelles du XVIIIe siècle. Gallimard. 2002.
ISBN:2-07-011405-8, ISBN13: 978-2-07-011405-4.
Audience: **u,f.**

Coward, Richard (Translator) **PQ1278.S535 1999**
French. Trade Paper. Penguin Group (USA) Inc. New York, NY. 2001. 240p. New Penguin Parallel Texts Ser. ISBN:0-14-026543-0, ISBN13: 978-0-14-026543-9. Dewey:843/.0108. LCCN:2001-271159.
Audience: **g,l,u,f.**

Fallaize, Elizabeth (Editor) **PQ1278.O84 2002**
The Oxford Book of French Short Stories. Trade Paper. Oxford University Press, Inc. New York, NY. 2002. 374p. ISBN:0-19-288037-3, ISBN13: 978-0-19-288037-6. Dewey:843/.0108. LCCN:2002-510698.
Audience: **g,l,u,f.**

Feher, Michel **PQ1276.E75L53 1997**
The Libertine Reader: Eroticism and Enlightenment in Eighteenth-Century France. Trade Cloth. Zone Books. Brooklyn, NY. 1997. 1324p. ISBN:0-942299-42-6, ISBN13: 978-0-942299-42-7. Dewey:843/.50803538. LCCN:96-049079.
Audience: **g,l,u,f.**

Gratton, Johnnie & Le Juez, Brigitte (Editors) **PQ1275**
Modern French Short Fiction: An Anthology. Cloth Text. Manchester University Press. Manchester, 1994. 204p. ISBN:0-7190-4210-0, ISBN13: 978-0-7190-4210-2. Dewey:843.0108. LCCN:93-027932.
Audience: **g,l,u,f.**

Jourda, Pierre **PQ1275**
Conteurs français du XVIe siècle. Gallimard. 1971.
Audience: **u,f.**

Labiche, Eugene, et al. **PQ1240.E7**
Three French Farces. Sardou, Georges Feydeau, Gondinet & de Najac (Authors), Frederick Davies (Translator). Trade Paper. Penguin Group (USA) Inc. New York, NY. 1974. 288p. Penguin Classics Ser. ISBN:0-14-044292-8, ISBN13: 978-0-14-044292-2. Dewey:842/.052.
Audience: **g,l,u,f.**

Makward, Christiane P. & Miller, Judith G. (Editors) **PQ1240.E5P53 1994**
Plays by French and Francophone Women: A Critical Anthology. Trade Cloth. University of Michigan Press. Chicago, IL. 1995. 320p. ISBN:0-472-10263-X, ISBN13: 978-0-472-10263-1. Dewey:842/.91408. LCCN:95-020373.
Audience: **g,l,u,f.** *Choice, 1995.*

Peyre, Henri & Seronde, Joseph (Editors) **PQ1220**
Nine Classic French Plays. Ed. 2. Paper Text. Houghton Mifflin Company Trade & Reference Division. Boston, MA. 1974. ISBN:0-669-90241-1, ISBN13: 978-0-669-90241-9. Dewey:842/.4/08.
Audience: **g,l,u,f.**

Picard, Raymond (Editor) et al. Lafond, Jean (Editor), Cuénin, Micheline (Editor), Chupeau, Jacques (Editor) **PQ1267.N68**
Nouvelles du XVIIe siècle. Gallimard. 1997.
ISBN:2-07-011404-X, ISBN13: 978-2-07-011404-7.
Audience: **u,f.**

Shapiro, Norman R., et al. **PQ1240.E8F58 1994**
A Flea in Her Rear: or Ants in Her Pants: And Nine Other French Farces. Eugene Labiche, Henri Meilhac, Georges Feydeau, Allais, Courteline, Halevy & Sardou (Authors). Trade Paper. Applause Theatre Book Publishers. New York, NY. 1994. 480p. Tour de Farce Ser., Vol. 4 ISBN:1-55783-165-3, ISBN13: 978-1-55783-165-1. Dewey:842/.052308. LCCN:94-003164.
Audience: **g,l,u,f.** *Choice, 1994.*

Stabler, Arthur P. (Editor) **PQ1240.E5F58**
Four French Renaissance Plays: In Translation with Introduction and Notes, Preceded by an Essay on French Renaissance Drama. Trade Paper. Books on Demand. Ann Arbor, MI. 376p. ISBN:0-8357-8135-6, ISBN13: 978-0-8357-8135-0. Dewey:842/.3/08. LCCN:79-101203.
Audiencc: **g,l,u,f.**

Stone, Donald (Editor) **PQ1227 .S8**
Four Renaissance Tragedies. Paper Text. Harvard University Press. Cambridge, MA. 1966. xxx, 224p. ISBN:0-674-31550-2, ISBN13: 978-0-674-31550-1. Dewey:842.30816. LCCN:66-004592.
Audience: **g,l,u,f.**

Switzer, Richard (Editor) **PQ1553.C3**
Pathelin and Others Farces. Mirelle Guillet-Rydell (Translator). Library Binding. Garland Publishing, Inc. New York, NY. 1984. 300p. ISBN:0-8240-8917-0, ISBN13: 978-0-8240-8917-7. Dewey:843/.2. LCCN:84-048064.
Audience: **g,l,u,f.**

Old French Literature > Collections

Jonin, Pierre (Editor) **PQ1302**
Anthologie thématique de la poésie française du Moyen Age: traductions, introduction, préface. Champion. 1991.
ISBN:2-85203-207-4, ISBN13: 978-2-85203-207-1.
Audience: **u,f.**

Newth, Michael (Translator) **PQ1310**
Heroes of the French Epic: A Selection of Chansons de Geste. Trade Paper. Boydell & Brewer, Ltd. Woodbridge, 2005. 714p. ISBN:1-84383-147-3, ISBN13: 978-1-84383-147-1. Dewey:841/.108. LCCN:2006-295909.
Audience: **g,l,u,f.**

Pound, Ezra & Kehew, Robert (Editors) **PC3365.E3L37 2005**
Lark in the Morning: The Verses of the Troubadours. W. D. Snodgrass, Robert Kehew & W.D. Snodgrass (Translators). Trade Cloth. University of Chicago Press. Chicago, IL. 2005. 280p. ISBN:0-226-42932-6, ISBN13: 978-0-226-42932-8. Dewey:849/.1008. LCCN:2005-000956.
Audience: **u,f.** *Choice, 2006.*

Old French Literature > Individual Authors and Works to 1400

Bedier, Joseph **PQ1542.E5B5 1994**
The Romance of Tristan and Iseult. Hilaire Belloc (Translator). Trade Paper. Knopf Publishing Group. New York, NY. 1994. 224p. Vintage Bks. ISBN:0-679-75016-9, ISBN13: 978-0-679-75016-1. Dewey:843/.1. LCCN:93-042219.
Audience: **g,l,u,f.**

Beroul **PQ1537**
The Romance of Tristan: The Tale of Tristan's Madness. Alan S. Fedrick (Translator). Trade Paper. Penguin Group (USA) Inc. New York, NY. 1978. 176p. Classics Ser. ISBN:0-14-044230-8, ISBN13: 978-0-14-044230-4. Dewey:841.1. LCCN:72-020122.
Audience: **g,l,u,f.**

Brault, Gerard J. **841/.1**
La Chanson de Roland: Oxford Text and English Translation. Trade Paper. Pennsylvania State University Press. University Park, PA. 1984. 454p. ISBN:0-271-00375-8, ISBN13: 978-0-271-00375-7. Dewey:PQ1521.E5. LCCN:83-043223.
Audience: **u,f.**

Brault, Gerard J. (Editor) **PQ1521.E5.B7 1978**
The Song of Roland: An Analytical Edition - Introduction and Commentary, Vol. 1. Gerard Brault (Translator). Cloth Text. Pennsylvania State University Press. University Park, PA. 1978. 574p. ISBN:0-271-00516-5, ISBN13: 978-0-271-00516-4. Dewey:841/.1. LCCN:77-022946.
Audience: **l,u.**

Bromiley, Geoffrey N. **PQ203.5.A77**
Thomas' "Tristan" and the "Folie Tristan d'Oxford". Trade Cloth. Grant & Cutler. London, 1987. 97p. ISBN:0-7293-0257-1, ISBN13: 978-0-7293-0257-9. Dewey:841/.1/09351. LCCN:86-025650.
Audience: **u,f.**

Chretien de Troyes **PQ1447.E5K53 2005**
Arthurian Romances. William W. Kibler & Carleton W. Carroll (Translators), William W. Kibler (Introduction by). Trade Paper. Penguin Group (USA) Inc. New York, NY. 1991. 528p. Classics Ser. ISBN:0-14-044521-8, ISBN13: 978-0-14-044521-3. Dewey:841/.1. LCCN:91-171440.
Audience: **g,l,u,f.**

Chretien de Troyes **PQ1445.C5E5 1997**
Cligés. Burton Raffel (Translator). Cloth over Boards. Yale University Press. Cumberland, RI. 1997. 248p. ISBN:0-300-07020-9, ISBN13: 978-0-300-07020-0. Dewey:841/.1. LCCN:96-052694.
Audience: **g,l,u,f.**

Chretien de Troyes **PQ1445.L3E5 1997**
Lancelot: The Knight of the Cart. Burton Raffel (Translator). Cloth over Boards. Yale University Press. Cumberland, RI. 1997. 254p. ISBN:0-300-07120-5, ISBN13: 978-0-300-07120-7. Dewey:841.1. LCCN:97-014424.
Audience: **g,l,u,f.**

Chretien de Troyes **PQ1447.E5R34 1987**
Yvain: The Knight of the Lion. Burton Raffel (Translator). Cloth over Boards. Yale University Press. Cumberland, RI. 1987. 228p. ISBN:0-300-03837-2, ISBN13: 978-0-300-03837-8. Dewey:841/.1. LCCN:86-023346.
Audience: **g,l,u,f.** *Choice, 1987.*

Chretien de Troyes **PQ1447.E5R35 1999**
Perceval: The Story of the Grail. Burton Raffel (Translator), Joseph J. Duggan (Afterword by). Cloth over Boards. Yale University Press. Cumberland, RI. 1999. 320p. ISBN:0-300-07585-5, ISBN13: 978-0-300-07585-4. Dewey:841/.1. LCCN:98-018938.
Audience: **g,l,u,f.** *Choice, 1999.*

Chrétien de Troyes **PQ1528**
Erec and Enide. Dorothy Gilbert (Translator, Introduction by). Trade Cloth. University of California Press. Berkeley, CA. 1992. 285p. ISBN:0-520-07345-2, ISBN13: 978-0-520-07345-6. Dewey:841/.1. LCCN:91-043103.
Audience: **g,l,u,f.** *Choice, 1997.*

Chrétien de Troyes & Louis, Rene **PQ1528**
Erec et Enide. Trade Paper. French & European Publications, Inc. New York, NY. 1980. 187p. ISBN:0-7859-5236-5, ISBN13: 978-0-7859-5236-7. Dewey:841.1.
Audience: **u,f.**

Chrétien de Troyes **PQ1445.E6E5 1997**
Erec and Enide. Burton Raffel (Translator), Joseph J. Duggan (Afterword by). Cloth over Boards. Yale University Press. Cumberland, RI. 1997. 248p. ISBN:0-300-06770-4, ISBN13: 978-0-300-06770-5. Dewey:841/.1. LCCN:96-035477.
Audience: **g,l,u,f.** *Choice, 1997.*

Chrétien, de Troyes **PQ1443.P3**
OEuvres complètes. Gallimard. 1994. ISBN:2-07-011276-4, ISBN13: 978-2-07-011276-0.
Audience: **u,f.**

De Lorris, Guillaume & De Meun, Jean **PQ1528**
The Romance of the Rose. Frances Horgan (Translator). Trade Paper. Oxford University Press, Inc. New York, NY. 1999. 374p. Oxford World's Classics Ser. ISBN:0-19-283948-9, ISBN13: 978-0-19-283948-0. Dewey:841/.1.
Audience: **g,l,u,f.**

Dufournet, Jean **PQ1426.A3**
Aucassin et Nicolette. Ed. 2. Flammarion. 1997.
Audience: **u,f.**

Duggan, Joseph J. **PQ1448.D84 2001**
The Romances of Chretien de Troyes. Cloth over Boards. Yale University Press. Cumberland, RI. 2001. 408p. ISBN:0-300-08357-2, ISBN13: 978-0-300-08357-6. Dewey:841/.1. LCCN:00-011726.
Audience: **u,f.**

France, Marie de **PQ1494.L3**
The Lais of Marie de France. Ed. 2. Glyn S. Burgess & Keith Busby (Translators), Glyn S. Burgess & Keith Busby (Introduction by). Trade Paper. Penguin Group (USA) Inc. New York, NY. 1999. 176p. Penguin Classics Ser. ISBN:0-14-044759-8, ISBN13: 978-0-14-044759-0. Dewey:841.1.
Audience: **g,l,u,f.**

Frappier, Jean **PQ1448.F713**
Chretien de Troyes: The Man and His Work. Raymond J. Cormier (Translator). Library Binding. Ohio University Press. Athens, OH. 1982. xx, 241p. ISBN:0-8214-0603-5, ISBN13: 978-0-8214-0603-8. Dewey:841/.1. LCCN:81-009475.
Audience: **u,f.**

Guillaume, de Lorris **PQ1528**
Le Roman de la Rose. Flammarion. 1999. ISBN:2-08-071003-6, ISBN13: 978-2-08-071003-1.
Audience: **u,f.**

Guillaume, de Lorris & Jean, de Meun **PQ1528**
Le Roman de la Rose. Lanly, André (Translator). Champion. 1982.
Audience: **u,f.**

Hanning, Robert W. **PQ1494.L3 E5**
The Lais of Marie de France. Joan M. Ferrante (Editor, Translator). Trade Paper. Baker Academic. Ada, MI. 1995. 256p. ISBN:0-8010-2031-X, ISBN13: 978-0-8010-2031-5. Dewey:841/.1.
Audience: **g,l,u,f.**

Harrison, Robert (Translator) **PQ1521.E5**
The Song of Roland. Trade Paper. Penguin Group (USA) Inc. New York, NY. 2002. 192p. ISBN:0-451-52857-3, ISBN13: 978-0-451-52857-5. Dewey:841.1.
Audience: **g,l,u,f.**

Kay, Sarah **PQ1528**
"Romance of the Rose". Trade Cloth. Grant & Cutler. London, 1996. 125p. ISBN:0-7293-0382-9, ISBN13: 978-0-7293-0382-8. Dewey:841.1.
Audience: **l,u.**

Lacy, Norris J. (Editor) **PQ1535.E37 1999**
Early French Tristan Poems, Vol. II. Trade Cloth. Boydell & Brewer, Ltd. Woodbridge, 1998. 296p. Arthurian Archives Ser. ISBN:0-85991-542-5, ISBN13: 978-0-85991-542-7. Dewey:841/.109351. LCCN:98-033615.
Audience: **u,f.**

Lacy, Norris J. & Asher, Martha **PQ1475**
Lancelot-Grail: The Old French Arthurian Vulgate and Post-Vulgate in Translation. Cloth Text. Garland Publishing, Inc. New York, NY. 1996. 296p. Garland Reference Library of the Humanities Ser. ISBN:0-8153-0757-8, ISBN13: 978-0-8153-0757-0. Dewey:843.1. LCCN:92-001674.
Audience: **u,f.**

Lacy, Norris J. & Grimbert, Joan Tasker (Editors) **PQ1448.C65 2005**
A Companion to Chritien de Troyes. Trade Cloth. Boydell & Brewer, Ltd. Woodbridge, 2005. 260p. Arthurian Studies, Vol. 63 ISBN:1-84384-050-2, ISBN13: 978-1-84384-050-3. Dewey:841/.1. LCCN:2005-009926.
Audience: **u,f.** *Choice, 2006.*

Luria, Maxwell **PQ1528**
A Reader's Guide to the Roman de la Rose. Trade Cloth. Shoe String Press, Inc. North Haven, CT. 1982. xii, 282p. ISBN:0-208-01838-7, ISBN13: 978-0-208-01838-0. Dewey:841/.1. LCCN:81-022767.
Audience: **u,f.**

Maddox, Donald **PQ1573**
Semiotics of Deceit: Language, Drama, and Culture in Maistre Pierre Pathelin. Trade Cloth. Bucknell University Press. Cranbury, NJ. 1984. 232p. ISBN:0-8387-5040-0, ISBN13: 978-0-8387-5040-7. Dewey:842/.2. LCCN:82-074491.
Audience: **u,f.**

Marchello-Nizia, Christiane & Boyer, Régis **PQ1542**
Tristan et Yseut : les premières versions européennes. Galliamrd. 1995. ISBN:2-07-011335-3, ISBN13: 978-2-07-011335-4.
Audience: **u,f.**

Marie De France **PQ1494.L3**
Medieval Lays and Legends of Marie de France. Eugene Mason (Translator). Trade Paper. Dover Publications, Inc. Mineola, NY. 2003. 240p. ISBN:0-486-43137-1, ISBN13: 978-0-486-43137-6. Dewey:841.1. LCCN:2003-060008.
Audience: **g,l,u,f.**

Marie, de France **PQ1494**
Lais de Marie de France. Flammarion. 1994. ISBN:2-08-070759-0, ISBN13: 978-2-08-070759-8.
Audience: **u,f.**

Martin, Mary L. **PQ1494.F3**
The Fables of Marie de France: An English Translation. Ed. 2. Norris J. Lacy (Foreword by). Trade Cloth. Summa Publications, Inc. Birmingham, AL. 1984. 259p. ISBN:0-917786-34-3, ISBN13: 978-0-917786-34-1. Dewey:841.1.
Audience: **g,l,u,f.**

Merwin, W. S. **PQ1521.E5M413 2001**
The Song of Roland. Trade Paper. Random House Adult Trade Publishing Group. New York, NY. 2001. 160p. Modern Library Ser. ISBN:0-375-75711-2, ISBN13: 978-0-375-75711-2. Dewey:841/.1. LCCN:00-048989.
Audience: **g,l,u,f.**

Merwin, W. S. **PN6110.E6M4 1998**
Medieval Epics: Beowulf, the Song of Roland, the Nibelungenlied, and the Cid. William Alfred & Helen M.

Mustard (Translators). Trade Cloth. Random House, Inc. New York, NY. 1998. 640p. Modern Library Ser. ISBN:0-679-60301-8, ISBN13: 978-0-679-60301-6. Dewey:808.81/32. LCCN:98-004488.
Audience: **g,l,u,f.**

Mickel, Emanuel J. **PQ1495.M5**
Marie de France. Trade Cloth. Thomson Gale. Farmington Hills, MI. 1974. 189p. ISBN:0-8057-2591-1, ISBN13: 978-0-8057-2591-9. Dewey:841/.1. LCCN:73-017350.
Audience: **l,u.**

Noble, Peter S. **PQ1537**
Beroul's "Tristan" and the "Folie de Berne". Trade Cloth. Grant & Cutler. London, 1982. 109p. ISBN:0-7293-0128-1, ISBN13: 978-0-7293-0128-2. Dewey:841/.1.
Audience: **l,u.**

Norris, Lacy J. **PQ1537.A367 1989**
Beroul: The Romance of Tristan. Trade Cloth. Garland Publishing, Inc. New York, NY. 1989. 264p. Library of Medieval Literature, Vol. 36 ISBN:0-8240-8777-1, ISBN13: 978-0-8240-8777-7. Dewey:841/.1. LCCN:88-033475.
Audience: **g,l,u,f.** *Choice, 1989.*

Owen, Roy (Editor, Translator) **PQ1528**
The Romance of Reynard the Fox. Trade Paper. Oxford University Press, Inc. New York, NY. 1994. 296p. Oxford World's Classics Ser. ISBN:0-19-282801-0, ISBN13: 978-0-19-282801-9. Dewey:841.1.
Audience: **g,l,u,f.**

Poirion, Daniel (Editor) & Berthelot, Anne (Editor) **PQ1489**
Le livre du Graal. Gallimard. 2001. ISBN:2-07-011342-6, ISBN13: 978-2-07-011342-2.
Audience: **u,f.**

Segre, Cesare (Editor) **PQ1517**
La chanson de Roland. Tyssens, Madeleine (Editor); Guidot, Bernard (Editor). Droz. 2003. ISBN:2-600-00968-X, ISBN13: 978-2-600-00968-3.
Audience: **u,f.**

Spiegel, Harriet **PQ1494.F3 E5**
Marie de France: Fables. Trade Paper. University of Toronto Press. Toronto, ON. 1995. 282p. Medieval Academy Reprints for Teaching Ser., Vol. 32 ISBN:0-8020-7636-X, ISBN13: 978-0-8020-7636-6. Dewey:841/.1.
Audience: **g,l,u,f.**

Staines, David **PQ1447.E5S73 1990**
The Complete Romances of Chretien de Troyes. Trade Cloth. Indiana University Press. Bloomington, IN. 1991. 576p. ISBN:0-253-35440-4, ISBN13: 978-0-253-35440-2. Dewey:841/.1. LCCN:90-004060.
Audience: **g,l,u,f.** *Choice, 1991.*

Terry, Patricia (Translator) **PQ1508.E5T47 1992**
Renard the Fox. Trade Cloth. University of California Press. Berkeley, CA. 1992. 180p. ISBN:0-520-07683-4, ISBN13: 978-0-520-07683-9. Dewey:841/.1. LCCN:91-023051.
Audience: **g,l,u,f.**

Topsfield, L. T. **PQ1448**
Chretien de Troyes: A Study of the Arthurian Romances. Trade Cloth. Cambridge University Press. New York, NY. 1981. 375p. ISBN:0-521-23361-5, ISBN13: 978-0-521-23361-3. Dewey:841/.1. LCCN:80-049938.
Audience: **u,f.**

Uitti, Karl D. & Freeman, Michelle A. **PQ1448.U38 1995**
Chretien de Troyes Revisited. Trade Cloth. Thomson Gale. Farmington Hills, MI. 1994. 192p. Twayne's World Authors Ser., No. 841 ISBN:0-8057-4307-3, ISBN13: 978-0-8057-4307-4. Dewey:841.1. LCCN:94-033948.
Audience: **l,u.** *Choice, 1995.*

Vance, Eugène **PQ1522**
Reading the 'Song of Roland'. Trade Cloth. Prentice-Hall. Upper Saddle, NJ. 1970. ix, 118p. ISBN:0-13-753533-3, ISBN13: 978-0-13-753533-0. Dewey:841/.1. LCCN:74-097924.
Audience: **l,u.**

Old French Literature > Individual Authors and Works, 1400 to 1500

Altmann, Barbara K. & McGrady, Deborah L. (Editors) **PQ1575.Z5C464 2002**
Christine de Pizan: A Casebook. Paper over Boards. Routledge. New York, NY. 2002. 312p. Garland Medieval Casebooks Ser. ISBN:0-415-93909-7, ISBN13: 978-0-415-93909-6. Dewey:841/.2. LCCN:2002-068028.
Audience: **l,u.** *Choice, 2003.*

Charles, d'Orléans **PQ1553**
Charles d'Orléans poésies. Champion. 1983. ISBN:2-85203-104-3, ISBN13: 978-2-85203-104-3.
Audience: **u,f.**

Charles, d'Orleans **PQ1553.C5 1973**
The Poems of Charles of Orleans. Trade Cloth. Carcanet Press, Ltd. Manchester, 1973. 112p. ISBN:0-902145-68-1, ISBN13: 978-0-902145-68-9. Dewey:841/.2. LCCN:73-169450.
Audience: **g,l,u,f.**

Chartier, Alain **PQ1557.B3**
Alain Chartier: The Quarrel of the Belle Dame Sans Mercy. Joan E. McRae (Editor, Translator). Paper over Boards. C R C Press LLC. Boca Raton, FL. 2004. 512p. Routledge Medieval Texts ISBN:0-415-96611-6, ISBN13: 978-0-415-96611-5. Dewey:848/.208. LCCN:2003-025225.
Audience: **u,f.**

Christine de Pizan **PQ1575.A23 1997**
The Selected Writings of Christine de Pizan: New Translations, Criticism. Renate Blumenfeld-Kosinski (Editor). Paper Text. W. W. Norton & Company, Inc. New York, NY. 1997. 448p. Critical Editions Ser. ISBN:0-393-97010-8, ISBN13: 978-0-393-97010-4. Dewey:841/.2. LCCN:96-012764.
Audience: **g,l,u,f.**

Christine de Pizan **PQ1575.L56E5 1999**
The Book of the City of Ladies. Rosalind Brown-Grant (Translator, Introduction by). Trade Paper. Penguin Group (USA) Inc. New York, NY. 2000. 336p. Classics Ser. ISBN:0-14-044689-3, ISBN13: 978-0-14-044689-0. Dewey:843/.2. LCCN:00-267752.
Audience: **g,l,u,f.**

Christine de Pizan **HQ1613**
The Treasure of the City of Ladies. Sarah Lawson (Translator, Introduction by). Trade Paper. Penguin Group (USA) Inc. New York, NY. 2003. 240p. ISBN:0-14-044950-7, ISBN13: 978-0-14-044950-1. Dewey:305.4/2/0944/09024.
Audience: **g,l,u,f.**

Christine de Pizan & Willard, Charity C. **PQ1575.A27 1994**
The Writings of Christine de Pizan. Trade Paper. Persea Books, Inc. New York, NY. 1992. 400p. ISBN:0-89255-188-7, ISBN13: 978-0-89255-188-0. Dewey:841.2. LCCN:92-041941.
Audience: **u,f.**

Christine, de Pisan **PQ1575**
Le chemin de longue étude. Librairie générale française. 2000. ISBN:2-253-06671-0, ISBN13: 978-2-253-06671-2.
Audience: **u,f.**

Christine, de Pisan **PQ1575**
Le Livre de l'advision Cristine. Champion. 2001. ISBN:2-7453-0323-6, ISBN13: 978-2-7453-0323-3.
Audience: **u,f.**

Christine, de Pisan **PQ1575**
Le livre de la cité des dames. Stock. 2000.
Audience: **u,f.**

Christine, de Pizan **PQ1575**
Poésies d'amour : Poèmes. Aumage. 2003. ISBN:2-915070-07-5, ISBN13: 978-2-915070-07-1.
Audience: **u,f.**

Davis, A. H. (Translator)
Love and Loss: Selected Poems of Charles d'Orleans. Trade Paper. Small Poetry Press. Concord, CA. 2006. 84p. Select Poets Ser. ISBN:1-891298-31-3, ISBN13: 978-1-891298-31-8.
Audience: **g,l,u,f.**

Diner, Judith B. (Editor, Translator) **PQ1553.C3A225 1990**
One Hundred New Tales: Les Cents Nouvelles Nouvelles. Cloth Text. Garland Publishing, Inc. New York, NY. 1990. 394p. Library of Medieval Literature ISBN:0-8240-8510-8, ISBN13: 978-0-8240-8510-0. Dewey:843/.2. LCCN:89-023570.
Audience: **g,l,u,f.** *Choice, 1990.*

Fein, David A. **PQ1553.C5.F44 1983**
Charles d'Orleans. Trade Cloth. Thomson Gale. Farmington Hills, MI. 1983. 166 p. :p. World Authors Ser., No. 699 ISBN:0-8057-6546-8, ISBN13: 978-0-8057-6546-5. Dewey:841/.2. LCCN:83-005838.
Audience: **l,u.**

Fein, David A. **PQ1593.F45 1997**
Francois Villon Revisited. Trade Cloth. Thomson Gale. Farmington Hills, MI. 1997. xiii, 187p. ISBN:0-8057-4564-5, ISBN13: 978-0-8057-4564-1. Dewey:841/.2. LCCN:96-038633.
Audience: **l,u.** *Choice, 1998.*

Pathelin **PQ1381**
Maître pathelin. Droz. 1986. Recueil de farces, 1450-1550, vol. 7
Audience: **u,f.**

Pathelin, Pierre **PQ1573**
La Farce de maître. Dufournet, Jean (Translator). Flammarion. 1986.
Audience: **u,f.**

Villon, Francois **PQ1575.Z5**
The Poems of Francois Villon. Galway Kinnell (Translator, Introduction by, Notes by). Trade Paper. University Press of New England. Lebanon, NH. 1982. 270p. ISBN:0-87451-236-0, ISBN13: 978-0-87451-236-6. Dewey:841/.2. LCCN:81-071907.
Audience: **g,l,u,f.**

Villon, Francois **PQ1590.E5S27 1994**
Complete Poems: Francois Villon. Barbara N. Sargent-Baur (Editor). Cloth Text. University of Toronto Press. Toronto, ON. 1993. 346p. Medieval Texts and Translations Ser., No. 9 ISBN:0-8020-2946-9, ISBN13: 978-0-8020-2946-1. Dewey:841/.2. LCCN:95-108068.
Audience: **g,l,u,f.**

Villon, François **PQ1590**
OEuvres. Champion. 1992. ISBN:2-85203-213-9, ISBN13: 978-2-85203-213-2.
Audience: **u,f.**

Modern French Literature > 16th C. > A-M

Aubigné, Agrippa d' **PQ1603.A18**
OEuvres complètes. Champion. 2004. ISBN:2-7453-0988-9, ISBN13: 978-2-7453-0988-4.
Audience: **u,f.**

Buffum, Imbrie **PQ1603.A73**
Agrippa d'Aubigne's "Les Tragiques": A Study of the Baroque Style in Poetry. Trade Cloth. A M S Press, Inc. New York, NY. ISBN:0-404-14804-2, ISBN13: 978-0-404-14804-1. Dewey:841/.3. LCCN:75-041042.
Audience: **u,f.**

Cameron, Keith **PQ1603.C3**
Agrippa d'Aubigne. Trade Cloth. Irvington Publishers. New York, NY. 1977. 169p. Twayne's World Authors Ser. ISBN:0-8057-6280-9, ISBN13: 978-0-8057-6280-8. Dewey:841/.3. LCCN:77-000540.
Audience: **u,f.**

Cameron, Keith **PQ1628.L2Z6 1990**
Louise Labe. Cloth over Boards. Berg Publishers. Oxford, 1992. 252p. Women's Ser ISBN:0-85496-618-8, ISBN13: 978-0-85496-618-9. Dewey:841/.3 B. LCCN:89-018453.
Audience: **u,f.**

de Gournay, Marie Le Jars **PQ1799.G65A238 2002**
Apology for the Woman Writing and Other Works. Richard Hillman & Colette Quesnel (Editors), Richard Hillman &

Colette Quesnel (Translators). Trade Cloth. University of Chicago Press. Chicago, IL. 2002. 208p. The Other Voice in Early Modern Europe Ser. ISBN:0-226-30555-4, ISBN13: 978-0-226-30555-4. Dewey:848/.309. LCCN:2001-052272.
Audience: **u,f.**

De la Taille, Jean **PQ1628.L35.A6 1972**
Dramatic Works. Kathleen M. Hall & C. N. Smith (Editors). Cloth Text. Continuum International Publishing Group, Ltd. London, 1972. 212p. Renaissance Library ISBN:0-485-13804-2, ISBN13: 978-0-485-13804-7. Dewey:842/.3. LCCN:72-181388.
Audience: **g,u,f.**

Jones, K. R. **PQ1677 .J6**
Pierre de Ronsard. Library Binding. Irvington Publishers. New York, NY. 1970. Twayne's World Authors Ser. ISBN:0-8057-2778-7, ISBN13: 978-0-8057-2778-4. Dewey:841/.3. LCCN:75-120502.
Audience: **u,f.**

Joseph, George **PQ1635**
Clement Marot. Trade Cloth. Thomson Gale. Farmington Hills, MI. 1985. World Authors Ser. ISBN:0-8057-6600-6, ISBN13: 978-0-8057-6600-4. Dewey:841/.3.
Audience: **u,f.**

Labe, Louise **PQ1628.L2A23 2006**
Complete Poetry and Prose: A Bilingual Edition. Deborah Lesko Baker & Annie Finch (Translators). Trade Cloth. University of Chicago Press. Chicago, IL. 2006. 296p. The Other Voice in Early Modern Europe Ser. ISBN:0-226-46714-7, ISBN13: 978-0-226-46714-6. Dewey:841/.3. LCCN:2005-029665.
Audience: **g,u,f.**

Labé, Louise **PQ1628.L2**
OEuvres complètes. Droz. 1981.
Audience: **u,f.**

Marguerite, de Navarre **PQ1631.H3E5 1984**
The Heptameron. Paul A. Chilton (Translator, Introduction by). Trade Paper. Penguin Group (USA) Inc. New York, NY. 1984. 544p. Penguin Classics Ser. ISBN:0-14-044355-X, ISBN13: 978-0-14-044355-4. Dewey:843/.3. LCCN:84-186955.
Audience: **g,l,u,f.**

Marguerite, Queen consort of Henry II King of Navarre **PQ1631**
Heptaméron. Droz. 1999. ISBN:2-600-00368-1, ISBN13: 978-2-600-00368-1.
Audience: **u,f.**

Marot, Clément **PQ1365**
OEuvres complètes, vol. 1. Editions Slatkine. 1980. ISBN:2-05-101689-5, ISBN13: 978-2-05-101689-6.
Audience: **u,f.**

Marot, Clément **PQ1635**
OEuvres complètes, vol. 2. Editions Slatkine. 1980. ISBN:2-05-101690-9, ISBN13: 978-2-05-101690-2.
Audience: **u,f.**

Marot, Clément **PQ1635**
OEuvres complètes, vol. 3. Editions Slatkine. 1980. ISBN:2-05-101691-7, ISBN13: 978-2-05-101691-9.
Audience: **u,f.**

Marot, Clément **PQ1635**
OEuvres complètes, vol. 4. Editions Slatkine. 1980. ISBN:2-05-101692-5, ISBN13: 978-2-05-101692-6.
Audience: **u,f.**

Marot, Clément **PQ1635**
OEuvres complètes, vol. 5. Editions Slatkine. 1980. ISBN:2-05-101693-3, ISBN13: 978-2-05-101693-3.
Audience: **u,f.**

Marot, Clément **PQ1635**
OEuvres complètes, vol. 6. Editions Slatkine. 1980. ISBN:2-05-100179-0, ISBN13: 978-2-05-100179-3.
Audience: **u,f.**

Tetel, Marcel **PQ1631.H4**
Marguerite de Navarre's Heptameron: Themes, Language, and Structure. Trade Cloth. Duke University Press. Durham, NC. 1973. 214p. ISBN:0-8223-0279-9, ISBN13: 978-0-8223-0279-7. Dewey:843./3. LCCN:72-088735.
Audience: **u,f.**

Modern French Literature > 16th C. > Montaigne

Frame, Donald M. **PQ1643**
Montaigne: A Biography. Trade Paper. Farrar, Straus & Giroux. New York, NY. 1982. 432p. ISBN:0-86547-143-6, ISBN13: 978-0-86547-143-6. Dewey:844/.3. LCCN:83-063124.
Audience: **g,l,u,f.**

Frame, Donald M. **PQ1643**
Montaigne's Discovery of Man: The Humanization of a Humanist. Trade Cloth. Greenwood Publishing Group, Inc. Portsmouth, NH. 1983. 202p. ISBN:0-313-24120-1, ISBN13: 978-0-313-24120-8. Dewey:844.3. LCCN:83-012716.
Audience: **g,u,f.**

Friedrich, Hugo **PQ1643.F6913 1991**
Montaigne. Dawn Eng (Translator), Philippe Desan (Introduction by). Trade Cloth. University of California Press. Berkeley, CA. 1991. 433p. ISBN:0-520-07253-7, ISBN13: 978-0-520-07253-4. Dewey:844/.3. LCCN:90-047726.
Audience: **u,f.** *Choice, 1992.*

Langer, Ullrich (Editor) **B785.M74C36 2005**
The Cambridge Companion to Montaigne. Cloth Text. Cambridge University Press. New York, NY. 2005. 266p. Cambridge Companions to Philosophy Ser. ISBN:0-521-81953-9, ISBN13: 978-0-521-81953-4. Dewey:194. LCCN:2004-062841.
Audience: **l,u,f.** *Choice, 2006.*

Michel, De Montaigne **BJ1533.F8M65 2005**
On Friendship. M. A. Screech (Translator). Trade Paper. Penguin Group (USA) Inc. New York, NY. 2005. 128p. Great Ideas Ser. ISBN:0-14-303629-7, ISBN13: 978-0-14-303629-6. Dewey:177/.62. LCCN:2005-047718.
Audience: **g,l,u,f.**

Montaigne, Michel de **PQ1642.E5F7 2003**
The Complete Works. Trade Cloth. Knopf Publishing Group. New York, NY. 2003. 1392p. ISBN:1-4000-4021-3, ISBN13: 978-1-4000-4021-6. Dewey:844/.3. LCCN:2003-269762.
Audience: **g,l,u,f.**

Montaigne, Michel de **PQ1641**
Oeuvres complètes. Gallimard. 1992. ISBN:2-07-010363-3, ISBN13: 978-2-07-010363-8.
Audience: **u,f.**

Montaigne, Michel de & Florio, John **PQ1642.E5.F6**
The Essays. Trade Cloth. Ashgate Publishing, Ltd. Aldershot, 1969. 666p. ISBN:0-85417-105-3, ISBN13: 978-0-85417-105-7. Dewey:844/.3.
Audience: **g,u,f.**

Montaigne, Michel de **PQ1642.E5L6825 1999**
The Autobiography of Michel de Montaigne. Marvin Lowenthal (Editor, Translator, Selected by). Trade Paper. David R. Godine Publisher. Boston, MA. 1999. 408p. Nonpareil Bks., Vol. 80 ISBN:1-56792-098-5, ISBN13: 978-1-56792-098-7. Dewey:844/.3. LCCN:98-036153.
Audience: **g,l,u,f.**

Starobinski, Jean **PQ1643.S7413 1985**
Montaigne in Motion. Arthur Goldhammer (Translator). Paper Text. University of Chicago Press. Chicago, IL. 1993. xii, 348p. ISBN:0-226-77131-8, ISBN13: 978-0-226-77131-1. Dewey:844/.3. LCCN:85-001026.
Audience: **g,u,f.** *Choice, 1986.*

Tetel, Marcel **PQ1643.T4 1990**
Montaigne. Trade Cloth. Thomson Gale. Farmington Hills, MI. 1990. 168p. Twayne's World Authors Ser., No. 317 ISBN:0-8057-8259-1, ISBN13: 978-0-8057-8259-2. Dewey:844/.3. LCCN:89-077298.
Audience: **u,f.**

Modern French Literature > 16th C. > The Pleiade

Belleau, Remy **PQ1666**
OEuvres poétiques, vol. 1: Petites inventions. Odes d'Anacréon. OEuvres diverses (1554-1561). Champion. 1995. ISBN:2-85203-517-0, ISBN13: 978-2-85203-517-1.
Audience: **u,f.**

Belleau, Remy **PQ1666**
OEuvres poétiques, vol. 2: La Bergerie. Champion. 1995. ISBN:2-7453-0466-6, ISBN13: 978-2-7453-0466-7.
Audience: **u,f.**

Belleau, Remy **PQ1666**
OEuvres poétiques, vol. 3: Ode à Nogent. Dictamen metrificum de Bello Huguenotico. OEuvres diverses de 1565 à 1572. Champion. 1995. ISBN:2-85203-906-0, ISBN13: 978-2-85203-906-3.
Audience: **u,f.**

Belleau, Remy **PQ1666**
OEuvres poétiques, vol. 4: La Bergerie divisée en une Première et Seconde Iournée. Champion. 1995. ISBN:2-7453-0628-6, ISBN13: 978-2-7453-0628-9.
Audience: **u,f.**

Belleau, Remy **PQ1666**
OEuvres poétiques, vol. 5: 1573-1577, Odes d'Anacréon (1573-1574). Amours et nouveaux eschanges des pierres précieux. Poéies diverses. Tombeau de Belleau. Champion. 1995. ISBN:2-7453-0904-8, ISBN13: 978-2-7453-0904-4.
Audience: **u,f.**

Belleau, Remy **PQ1666**
OEuvres poétiques, vol. 6: OEuvres posthumes (1578). Champion. 1995. ISBN:2-7453-0843-2, ISBN13: 978-2-7453-0843-6.
Audience: **u,f.**

Cave, Terence **PQ1678**
Ronsard the Poet. Trade Cloth. Methuen & Company, Ltd. London, 1973. 360p. ISBN:0-416-08060-X, ISBN13: 978-0-416-08060-5. Dewey:841/.3. LCCN:73-177851.
Audience: **u,f.**

Du Bellay, Joachim **PQ1668**
Oeuvres complètes, vol. 1: La deffence, et illustration de la langue françoyse. Champion. 2003. ISBN:2-7453-0874-2, ISBN13: 978-2-7453-0874-0.
Audience: **u,f.**

Du Bellay, Joachim **PQ1668**
Oeuvres complètes, Vol. 2: Cinquante sonnetz à la louange de l'Olive. L'anterotique de la vieille, & de la jeune Amye. Vers lyriques. Champion. 2003. ISBN:2-7453-0864-5, ISBN13: 978-2-7453-0864-1.
Audience: **u,f.**

Du Bellay, Joachim **PQ1668.R4E5 2003**
The Regrets. David R. Slavitt (Translator, Translator). Trade Paper, Perfect. Northwestern University Press. Evanston, IL. 2004. 400p. European Poetry Classics Ser. ISBN:0-8101-1993-5, ISBN13: 978-0-8101-1993-2. Dewey:841/.3. LCCN:2003-007640.
Audience: **g,u,f.**

Jones, K. R. **PQ1677 .J6**
Pierre de Ronsard. Library Binding. Irvington Publishers. New York, NY. 1970. Twayne's World Authors Ser. ISBN:0-8057-2778-7, ISBN13: 978-0-8057-2778-4. Dewey:841/.3. LCCN:75-120502.
Audience: **u,f.**

Ronsard, Pierre de **PQ1674**
OEuvres complètes, Vol. 2. Gallimard. 1994. Pleiade Series ISBN:2-07-011337-X, ISBN13: 978-2-07-011337-8.
Audience: **u,f.**

Ronsard, Pierre de **PQ1674841.3**
Oeuvres completes, Vol. 1. Jean Cerard (Editor). Library Binding. French & European Publications, Inc. New York, NY. 1993. 1184p. ISBN:0-7859-3787-0, ISBN13: 978-0-7859-3787-6. Dewey:841.3.
Audience: **u,f.**

Ronsard, Pierre **PQ1674**
The Selected Poems of Ronsard. Malcolm Quainton & Elizabeth Vinestock (Translators). Trade Paper. Penguin Group (USA) Inc. New York, NY. 2002. 384p. ISBN:0-14-042424-5, ISBN13: 978-0-14-042424-9. Dewey:841.3.
Audience: **g,l,u,f.**

Shapiro, Norman R. **PQ1170.E6L97 2002**
Lyrics of the French Renaissance: Marot, du Bellay and Ronsard. Hope H. Glidden (Introduction by). Cloth over Boards. Yale University Press. Cumberland, RI. 2002. 416p. ISBN:0-300-08759-4, ISBN13: 978-0-300-08759-8. Dewey:841.3. LCCN:2002-101820.
Audience: **g,l,u,f.**

Modern French Literature > 16th C. > Rabelais

Bakhtin, Mikhail M. **PQ1694.B313 1984**
Rabelais and His World. Helene Iswolsky (Translator), Michael Holquist (Introduction by), Krystyna Pomorska (Foreword by). Trade Cloth. Indiana University Press. Bloomington, IN. 1984. 510p. ISBN:0-253-34830-7, ISBN13: 978-0-253-34830-2. Dewey:843/.3. LCCN:84-047792.
Audience: **u,f.** *Choice, 1985.*

Febvre, Lucien **PQ1694**
The Problem of Unbelief in the Sixteenth Century: The Religion of Rabelais. Beatrice Gottlieb (Translator). Trade Paper. Harvard University Press. Cambridge, MA. 1982. 552p. ISBN:0-674-70826-1, ISBN13: 978-0-674-70826-6. Dewey:843/.3.
Audience: **u,f.**

Rabelais, Francois **PQ1685.E5R34 1990**
Gargantua and Pantagruel. Burton Raffel (Translator). Trade Cloth. W. W. Norton & Company, Inc. New York, NY. 1990. xi, 623p. ISBN:0-393-02843-7, ISBN13: 978-0-393-02843-0. Dewey:843/.3. LCCN:89-025595.
Audience: **g,l,u,f.** *Choice, 1991.*

Rabelais, François **PQ1682**
OEuvres complètes. Gallimard. 1994. Pleiade Series ISBN:2-07-011340-X, ISBN13: 978-2-07-011340-8.
Audience: **u,f.**

Rabelais, François **PQ1682.Z5**
Les oeuvres romanesques : Gargantua, Pantagruel, le tiers livre, le quart livre, le cinquième livre. Joukovsky, Françoise (Translator). Champion. 1999. ISBN:2-7453-0089-X, ISBN13: 978-2-7453-0089-8.
Audience: **u,f.**

Rabelais, François **PQ1685.E5**
The Complete Works of Francois Rabelais. Donald M. Frame (Translator), Raymond C. La Charite (Foreword by). Trade Paper. University of California Press. Berkeley, CA. 1999. 1116p. ISBN:0-520-06401-1, ISBN13: 978-0-520-06401-0. Dewey:843/.3. LCCN:91-026198.
Audience: **g,l,u,f.** *Choice, 1992.*

Zegura, Elizabeth Chesney (Editor) **PQ1694**
The Rabelais Encyclopedia. Cloth Text. Greenwood Publishing Group, Inc. Portsmouth, NH. 2004. 320p. ISBN:0-313-31034-3, ISBN13: 978-0-313-31034-8. Dewey:843/.3. LCCN:2004-042479.
Audience: **g,l,u,f.** *Choice, 2005.*

Zegura, Elizabeth & Tetel, Marcel **PQ1694.C54 1993**
Rabelais Revisited. Trade Cloth. Thomson Gale. Farmington Hills, MI. 1993. 208p. Twayne's World Authors Ser., Vol. 837 ISBN:0-8057-8294-X, ISBN13: 978-0-8057-8294-3. Dewey:843/.3. LCCN:93-006761.
Audience: **u,f.** *Choice, 1994.*

Modern French Literature > 16th C. > S-Z

De Sponde, Jean **PQ1705.S7A275 2001**
Sonnets of Love and Death. David R. Slavitt (Translator). Trade Paper. Northwestern University Press. Evanston, IL. 2001. 83p. European Poetry Classics Ser. ISBN:0-8101-1840-8, ISBN13: 978-0-8101-1840-9. Dewey:841/.3. LCCN:2001-001090.
Audience: **g,u,f.**

Mulhauser, Ruth **PQ1705.S5.Z8**
Maurice Sceve. Library Binding. Irvington Publishers. New York, NY. 1977. 138p. Twayne's World Authors Ser. ISBN:0-8057-6264-7, ISBN13: 978-0-8057-6264-8. Dewey:841/.3. LCCN:76-028722.
Audience: **u,f.**

Sceve, Maurice **PQ1705.S5 D4 1984**
Delie. Trade Paper. Schoenhof's Foreign Books, Inc. Cambridge, MA. 1984. Poesie Ser. ISBN:2-07-032252-1, ISBN13: 978-2-07-032252-7. Dewey:841/.3.
Audience: **u,f.**

Sceve, Maurice & Sieburth, Richard **PQ1705.S5D4213 2002**
Emblems of Desire: Selections from "Delie". Trade Cloth. University of Pennsylvania Press. Philadelphia, PA. 2002. 232p. ISBN:0-8122-3694-7, ISBN13: 978-0-8122-3694-1. Dewey:841/.3. LCCN:2002-074227.
Audience: **g,u,f.** *Choice, 2003.*

Modern French Literature > 17th C. > A-B

Boileau Despréaux, Nicolas **PQ1719**
OEuvres complètes. Escal, Françoise (Editor). Gallimard. 1979. Pleiade Series
Audience: **u,f.**

Cyrano de Bergerac, Savinien **PQ1805.L5**
Other Worlds: The Comical History of the States and Empires of the Moon and Sun. Geoffrey Strachan (Introduction by). Trade Paper. Hodder General Publishing Division. London, 1976. 220p. ISBN:0-450-02995-6, ISBN13: 978-0-450-02995-0. Dewey:843/.4.
Audience: **g,l,u,f.**

De La Bruyere, Jean **PQ1803.A6E5 1992**
Characters. Henri Van Laun (Translator). Library Binding. Howard Fertig Inc. New York, NY. 1992. 494p. ISBN:0-86527-394-4, ISBN13: 978-0-86527-394-8. Dewey:844/.4. LCCN:89-023836.
Audience: **g,l,u,f.**

Knox, Edward C. **PQ1803.K5 1974**
Jean de la Bruyere. Library Binding. Irvington Publishers. New York, NY. 1973. 140p. Twayne's World Authors Ser. ISBN:0-8057-2507-5, ISBN13: 978-0-8057-2507-0. Dewey:848/.4/07. LCCN:73-015836.
Audience: **l,u.**

Modern French Literature > 17th C. > Corneille

Carlin, Claire L. **PQ1779.C37 1998**
Pierre Corneille Revisited. Trade Cloth. Thomson Gale. Farmington Hills, MI. 1998. xvii, 181p. Twayne's World Authors Ser., Vol. 874 ISBN:0-8057-4561-0, ISBN13: 978-0-8057-4561-0. Dewey:842/.4. LCCN:98-034788.
Audience: **l,u.** *Choice, 1999.*

Corneille, Pierre **PS758.A8**
Chief Plays. Paper Text. Textbook Publishers. Temecula, CA. 2003. 386p. ISBN:0-7581-5803-3, ISBN13: 978-0-7581-5803-1. Dewey:811/.2.
Audience: **l,u,f.**

Corneille, Pierre **PQ1860**
Polyeuctus, the Liar, Nicomedes. John Cairncross (Translator). Trade Paper. Penguin Group (USA) Inc. New York, NY. 1980. 320p. Penguin Classics Ser. ISBN:0-14-044349-5, ISBN13: 978-0-14-044349-3. Dewey:842/.4.
Audience: **g,l,u,f.**

Corneille, Pierre **PQ1745.E5.C3 1975**
The Cid, Cinna, the Theatrical Illusion. John Cairncross (Translator, Introduction by). Trade Paper. Penguin Group (USA) Inc. New York, NY. 1976. 288p. Classics Ser. ISBN:0-14-044312-6, ISBN13: 978-0-14-044312-7. Dewey:842/.4. LCCN:76-453793.
Audience: **g,l,u,f.**

Corneille, Pierre **PQ1749.E5C44 1987**
Le Cid: A Translation in Rhymed Couplets. Vincent J. Cheng (Translator). Trade Cloth. University of Delaware Press. Newark, DE. 1987. 208p. ISBN:0-87413-294-0, ISBN13: 978-0-87413-294-6. Dewey:842/.4. LCCN:85-040877.
Audience: **g,l,u,f.** *Choice, 1988.*

Corneille, Pierre **PQ1741**
Oeuvres Completes, Vol. 3. Georges Couton (Editor). Library Binding. French & European Publications, Inc. New York, NY. 1987. ISBN:0-7859-3878-8, ISBN13: 978-0-7859-3878-1. Dewey:842/.4.
Audience: **u,f.**

Corneille, Pierre & Couton, Georges (Editors) **PQ1741**
Oeuvres Completes, Vol. 2. Library Binding. French & European Publications, Inc. New York, NY. 1984. ISBN:0-7859-3868-0, ISBN13: 978-0-7859-3868-2. Dewey:842/.4.
Audience: **u,f.**

Corneille, Pierre **PQ1741**
Oeuvres Completes, Vol. 1. Georges Couton (Editor). Trade Cloth. French & European Publications, Inc. New York, NY. 1980. 1872p. ISBN:0-7859-3846-X, ISBN13: 978-0-7859-3846-0. Dewey:842/.4.
Audience: **u,f.**

Knight, R. C. **PQ1779.K65 1991**
Corneille's Tragedies: The Role of the Unexpected. Trade Cloth. Rowman & Littlefield Publishers, Inc. Lanham, MD. 1991. 144p. ISBN:0-389-20960-0, ISBN13: 978-0-389-20960-7. Dewey:842/.4. LCCN:91-026167.
Audience: **l,u.** *Choice, 1992.*

Nelson, Robert J. **PQ1782.N4**
Corneille: His Heroes and Their Worlds. Trade Cloth. University of Pennsylvania Press. Philadelphia, PA. 1963. 322p. ISBN:0-8122-7384-2, ISBN13: 978-0-8122-7384-7. Dewey:842.4. LCCN:63-007859.
Audience: **g,l,u,f.**

Watts, Derek A. **PQ1860**
Corneille: "Rodogune" and "Nicomede". Trade Cloth. Grant & Cutler. London, 1993. 93p. ISBN:0-7293-0346-2, ISBN13: 978-0-7293-0346-0. Dewey:842.4.
Audience: **l,u,f.**

Modern French Literature > 17th C. > C-G

Davis, James H. Jr. **PQ1796.D3**
Fenelon. Library Binding. Thomson Gale. Farmington Hills, MI. 1979. 186p. World Authors Ser. ISBN:0-8057-6384-8, ISBN13: 978-0-8057-6384-3. Dewey:848/.4/09. LCCN:78-031470.
Audience: **l,u.**

Fenelon, Francois de Salignac de La Mothe- **PQ1795.A16 1983**
OEuvres. Trade Cloth. Gallimard, Editions. Paris Cedex 07, 1983. ;p. ISBN:2-07-011017-6, ISBN13: 978-2-07-011017-9. Dewey:848/.409. LCCN:83-191310.
Audience: **u,f.**

Guilleragues, Gabriel Joseph de Lavergne **PQ1799**
Lettres portugaises. Droz. 1972.
Audience: **u,f.**

Modern French Literature > 17th C. > La Fontaine

Christofides, Koren (Editor) **PQ1806**
Fables of la Fontaine. Constantine Christofides & Christopher Carsten (Translators), Koren Christofides (Compiled by). Trade

Cloth. University of Washington Press. Seattle, WA. 2006. 172p. ISBN:0-295-98614-X, ISBN13: 978-0-295-98614-2. Dewey:841.4.
Audience: **g,l,u,f.**

La Fontaine, Jean De **PQ1806**
Oeuvres Completes. Other. Schoenhof's Foreign Books, Inc. Cambridge, MA. Pleiade Ser. ISBN:0-318-52142-3, ISBN13: 978-0-318-52142-8. Dewey:841.
Audience: **u,f.**

La Fontaine, Jean De **PQ1806**
Oeuvres Diverses, Tome II. Trade Cloth. Schoenhof's Foreign Books, Inc. Cambridge, MA. Pleiade Ser. ISBN:2-07-010297-1, ISBN13: 978-2-07-010297-6. Dewey:841.4.
Audience: **u,f.**

La Fontaine, Jean de **PQ1806**
OEuvres : sources et postérité d'Esope à l'Oulipo. Editions Complexe. 1995. ISBN:2-87027-562-5, ISBN13: 978-2-87027-562-7.
Audience: **u,f.**

La Fontaine, Jean De **PQ1811.E3S64 1988**
The Complete Fables of La Fontaine. Norman Spector (Editor). Trade Cloth. Northwestern University Press. Evanston, IL. 1988. 713p. ISBN:0-8101-0759-7, ISBN13: 978-0-8101-0759-5. Dewey:841/.4. LCCN:87-034843.
Audience: **g,l,u,f.** *Choice, 1988.*

La Fontaine, Jean De **PQ1812**
The Complete Tales in Verse: Jean de la Fontaine. Guido Waldman (Translator). Paper over Boards. Routledge. New York, NY. 2001. 208p. ISBN:0-415-93657-8, ISBN13: 978-0-415-93657-6. Dewey:841.4.
Audience: **g,l,u,f.**

Sweetser, Marie-Odile **PQ1812.S84 1987**
La Fontaine. Trade Cloth. Macmillan Publishing Company, Inc. Old Tappan, NJ. 1987. Twayne's World Authors Ser., No. 788 ISBN:0-8057-6639-1, ISBN13: 978-0-8057-6639-4. Dewey:841/.4. LCCN:86-018295.
Audience: **l,u.** *Choice, 1987.*

Modern French Literature > 17th C. > L-M

Beasley, Faith E. & Jensen, Katharine A. (Editors) **PQ1805.L5A737 1998**
Approaches to Teaching Lafayette's Princess of Cleves. Trade Cloth. Modern Language Association of America. New York, NY. 1998. xi, 211p. Approaches to Teaching World Literature Ser., Vol. 61 ISBN:0-87352-745-3, ISBN13: 978-0-87352-745-3. Dewey:843/.4. LCCN:98-035540.
Audience: **u,f.**

De La Bruyere, Jean **PQ1803.A63**
Les Caracteres. Trade Paper. Schoenhof's Foreign Books, Inc. Cambridge, MA. 1962. Folio Ser., No. 693 ISBN:2-07-036693-6, ISBN13: 978-2-07-036693-4. Dewey:848/.4/07.
Audience: **u,f.**

De La Bruyere, Jean **PQ1803.A1**
Oeuvres Completes. Julien Benda (Editor). Library Binding. French & European Publications, Inc. New York, NY. 1978. 768p. ISBN:0-7859-3760-9, ISBN13: 978-0-7859-3760-9. Dewey:844.4.
Audience: **u,f.**

De Lafayette, Madame **PQ1805.L5**
The Princess of Cleves. John Lyons (Editor). Trade Paper. W. W. Norton & Company, Inc. New York, NY. 1993. 314p. Critical Editions Ser. ISBN:0-393-96333-0, ISBN13: 978-0-393-96333-5. Dewey:843/.4. LCCN:92-042526.
Audience: **g,l,u,f.**

Haig, Stirling **PQ1805.L5 A756**
Madame de Lafayette. Library Binding. Irvington Publishers. New York, NY. 1970. Twayne's World Authors Ser. ISBN:0-8057-2508-3, ISBN13: 978-0-8057-2508-7. Dewey:843/.4. LCCN:71-079207.
Audience: **l,u.**

La Bruyère, Jean de **PQ1803**
Les caractères de Théophraste traduits du grec avec Les caractères ou Les moeurs de ce siècle. Escola, Marc (Editor). Champion. 1999. ISBN:2-7453-0084-9, ISBN13: 978-2-7453-0084-3.
Audience: **u,f.**

La Fayette, Madame de **PQ1805**
Romans et nouvelles. Niderst, Alain (editor). Dunod. 1997. ISBN:2-10-003276-3, ISBN13: 978-2-10-003276-1.
Audience: **u,f.**

La Rochefoucauld, Francois de **PQ1815**
Maxims. Leonard W. Tancock (Translator, Introduction by). Trade Paper. Penguin Group (USA) Inc. New York, NY. 1982. 128p. Classics Ser. ISBN:0-14-044095-X, ISBN13: 978-0-14-044095-9. Dewey:848/.402.
Audience: **g,l,u,f.**

Lafayette, Madame de **PQ1805.L5**
The Princesse de Cleves: The Princesse de Montpensier, The Comtesse de Tende. Terence Cave (Editor, Translator, Introduction by). Trade Paper. Oxford University Press, Inc. New York, NY. 1992. 280p. Oxford World's Classics Ser. ISBN:0-19-282687-5, ISBN13: 978-0-19-282687-9. Dewey:843.4. LCCN:91-034211.
Audience: **g,l,u,f.**

Lafayette, Marie-Madeleine **PQ1805.L5A7813 2006**
Zayde: A Spanish Romance. Nicholas D. Paige (Translator). Trade Cloth. University of Chicago Press. Chicago, IL. 2006. 248p. The Other Voice in Early Modern Europe Ser. ISBN:0-226-46851-8, ISBN13: 978-0-226-46851-8. Dewey:843/.4. LCCN:2006-012415.
Audience: **g,l,u,f.**

Malherbe **PQ1819**
Oeuvres: Poesies - Lettres. Library Binding. French & European Publications, Inc. New York, NY. 1971. ISBN:0-8288-3551-9, ISBN13: 978-0-8288-3551-0. Dewey:841.41.
Audience: **u,f.**

Rendall, Steven (Editor, Translator) **PQ1707.U7A622513**
Honore d'Urfe, Astrea. Trade Cloth. M R T S. Tempe, AZ.

1997. 416p. Medieval and Renaissance Texts and Studies, 134 ISBN:0-86698-142-X, ISBN13: 978-0-86698-142-2. Dewey:843/.4. LCCN:94-032421.
Audience: **u,f.** *Choice, 1995.*

Modern French Literature > 17th C. > Moliere

Gaines, James F. (Editor) **PQ1851**
The Moliere Encyclopedia. Cloth Text. Greenwood Publishing Group, Inc. Portsmouth, NH. 2002. 528p. ISBN:0-313-31255-9, ISBN13: 978-0-313-31255-7. Dewey:842/.4 B. LCCN:2002-016082.
Audience: **g,u,f.** *Choice, 2003.*

Hubert, Judd David **PQ1860**
Moliere and the Comedy of Intellect. Paper Text. Textbook Publishers. Temecula, CA. 2003. 275p. ISBN:0-7581-4481-4, ISBN13: 978-0-7581-4481-2. Dewey:842.4.
Audience: **u,f.**

Moliere, Jean-Baptiste **PQ1825.E5S58 2001**
The Misanthrope, Tartuffe, and Other Plays. Trade Paper. Oxford University Press, Inc. New York, NY. 2001. 400p. Oxford World's Classics Ser. ISBN:0-19-283341-3, ISBN13: 978-0-19-283341-9. Dewey:842/.4. LCCN:2002-276311.
Audience: **g,l,u,f.**

Moliere, Jean-Baptiste **PQ1821**
Oeuvres Completes, Vol. 2. Couton (Editor). Trade Cloth. Schoenhof's Foreign Books, Inc. Cambridge, MA. 1933. Pleiade Ser. ISBN:2-07-010361-7, ISBN13: 978-2-07-010361-4. Dewey:842.4.
Audience: **u,f.**

Moliere, Jean-Baptiste & Couton (Editors) **PQ1821**
Oeuvres Completes, Vol. 1. Trade Cloth. Schoenhof's Foreign Books, Inc. Cambridge, MA. 1933. Pleiade Ser. ISBN:2-07-010360-9, ISBN13: 978-2-07-010360-7. Dewey:842.4.
Audience: **u,f.**

Moliere, Jean-Baptiste **PQ1825.E5W583 2000**
The Miser and Other Plays: A New Selection. Ed. 2. David Coward & John Wood (Translators), David Coward (Introduction by, Notes by). Trade Paper. Penguin Group (USA) Inc. New York, NY. 2000. 336p. Classics Ser. ISBN:0-14-044728-8, ISBN13: 978-0-14-044728-6. Dewey:842/.4. LCCN:2001-278482.
Audience: **g,l,u,f.**

Moliere, Jean-Baptiste **PQ1825.E5.F68**
Tartuffe and Other Plays. Donald M. Frame (Translator, Introduction by). Trade Paper. Penguin Group (USA) Inc. New York, NY. 1960. 384p. Signet Classics Ser. ISBN:0-451-52454-3, ISBN13: 978-0-451-52454-6. Dewey:842. LCCN:67-016940.
Audience: **g,l,u,f.**

Moliere, Jean-Baptiste **PQ1860**
The Misanthrope and Other Plays. Donald M. Frame (Introduction by), Lewis Seifert (Afterword by). Trade Paper. Penguin Group (USA) Inc. New York, NY. 2005. 528p. ISBN:0-451-52987-1, ISBN13: 978-0-451-52987-9. Dewey:842/.4. LCCN:2006-276841.
Audience: **g,l,u,f.**

Moliere, Jean-Baptiste **PQ1860**
Les Femmes Savantes. Hugh Gaston Hall (Introduction by, Notes by). Trade Paper. Oxford University Press. Oxford, 1996. 206p. ISBN:0-19-832379-4, ISBN13: 978-0-19-832379-2. Dewey:842/.4.
Audience: **g,l,u,f.**

Moliere, Jean-Baptiste **PQ1860**
Don Juan: And Other Plays. Ian Maclean (Editor, Translator), George Graveley (Translator), Ian Maclean (Introduction by, Notes by). Trade Paper. Oxford University Press, Inc. New York, NY. 1998. 414p. Oxford World's Classics Ser. ISBN:0-19-283551-3, ISBN13: 978-0-19-283551-2. Dewey:842/.4.
Audience: **g,l,u,f.**

Moliere, Jean-Baptiste **PQ1831.A48 2001**
Don Juan. Richard Wilbur (Translator). Trade Paper. Harcourt Trade Publishers. New York, NY. 2001. 144p. Harvest Book Ser. ISBN:0-15-601310-X, ISBN13: 978-0-15-601310-9. Dewey:842/.4. LCCN:00-040749.
Audience: **g,l,u,f.**

Moliere, Jean-Baptiste **PQ1860**
The School for Husbands and Sganarelle: Or the Imaginary Cuckold. Richard Wilbur (Translator). Cloth over Boards. Harcourt Trade Publishers. New York, NY. 1992. 136p. ISBN:0-15-179577-0, ISBN13: 978-0-15-179577-2. Dewey:842.4. LCCN:91-039102.
Audience: **g,l,u,f.**

Moliere, Jean-Baptiste & Wilbur, Richard **PQ1825.E5**
The School for Wives and The Learned Ladies by Moliere: Two Comedies in an Acclaimed Translation. Trade Paper. Harcourt Trade Publishers. New York, NY. 1991. 324p. ISBN:0-15-679502-7, ISBN13: 978-0-15-679502-9. Dewey:842/.4. LCCN:91-035961.
Audience: **g,l,u,f.**

Moliere, Jean-Baptiste **PQ1842.A485 1997**
Tartuffe. Richard Wilbur (Translator). Cloth over Boards. Harcourt Trade Publishers. New York, NY. 1997. 240p. ISBN:0-15-100281-9, ISBN13: 978-0-15-100281-8. Dewey:842/.4. LCCN:96-047083.
Audience: **g,l,u,f.**

Moliere, Jean-Baptiste **PQ1827.A7E513 1995**
Amphitryon. Richard Wilbur (Translator, Afterword by). Trade Cloth. Harcourt Trade Publishers. New York, NY. 1995. 160p. ISBN:0-15-100156-1, ISBN13: 978-0-15-100156-9. Dewey:842/.4. LCCN:94-040640.
Audience: **g,l,u,f.**

Moore, Will Grayburn **PQ1860.M6 1968**
Moliere: A New Criticism. Trade Cloth. Oxford University Press, Inc. New York, NY. 1968. 147p. ISBN:0-19-815381-3, ISBN13: 978-0-19-815381-8. Dewey:842/.4. LCCN:68-120218.
Audience: **l,u.**

Scott, Virginia **PQ1852 .S44 2000**
Molière: A Theatrical Life. Cloth Text. Cambridge University Press. New York, NY. 2000. 343p. ISBN:0-521-78281-3, ISBN13: 978-0-521-78281-4. Dewey:842/.4 B. LCCN:00-021927.
Audience: **g,u,f.** *Choice, 2001.*

Walker, Hallam **PQ1860.W3 1990**
Moliere. Trade Cloth. Thomson Gale. Farmington Hills, MI. 1990. 200p. World Authors Ser. ISBN:0-8057-8258-3, ISBN13: 978-0-8057-8258-5. Dewey:842/.4. LCCN:89-024656.
Audience: **l,u.**

Modern French Literature > 17th C. > Pascal

Bloom, Harold (Introduction by) **B1903.B44 1989**
Blaise Pascal. Library Binding. Chelsea House Publishers. Langhorne, PA. 1989. 208p. Modern Critical Views Ser. ISBN:1-55546-373-8, ISBN13: 978-1-55546-373-1. Dewey:230/.2/0924. LCCN:87-018344.
Audience: **l,u.**

Cole, John R. **B1903.C64 1995**
Pascal: The Man and His Two Loves. Trade Cloth. New York University Press. New York, NY. 1995. 432p. ISBN:0-8147-1510-9, ISBN13: 978-0-8147-1510-9. Dewey:230/.2/092 B. LCCN:95-004381.
Audience: **u,f.** *Choice, 1996.*

Davidson, Hugh M. **B1903.D35 1983**
Blaise Pascal. Trade Cloth. Thomson Gale. Farmington Hills, MI. 1983. 165p. World Authors Ser., No. 701 ISBN:0-8057-6548-4, ISBN13: 978-0-8057-6548-9. Dewey:230/.2. LCCN:83-008438.
Audience: **g,l,u.** B

Hammond, Nicholas (Editor) **B1901.P43**
The Cambridge Companion to Pascal. Cloth Text. Cambridge University Press. New York, NY. 2003. 304p. Cambridge Companions to Philosophy Ser. ISBN:0-521-80924-X, ISBN13: 978-0-521-80924-5. Dewey:194. LCCN:2003-273207.
Audience: **u,f.**

Krailsheimer, A. J. **B1903**
Pascal. Oxford University Press. 1980. Past Masters Series ISBN:0-19-287513-2, ISBN13: 978-0-19-287513-6.
Audience: **l,u.**

Pascal, Blaise **B1900**
OEuvres complètes. Le Guern, Michel (Editor). Gallimard. 1998. Pleiade Series ISBN:2-07-011485-6, ISBN13: 978-2-07-011485-6.
Audience: **u,f.**

Pascal, Blaise **B1903**
The Provincial Letters. A. J. Krailsheimer (Translator, Introduction by). Trade Paper. Penguin Group (USA) Inc. New York, NY. 1982. 304p. ISBN:0-14-044196-4, ISBN13: 978-0-14-044196-3. Dewey:194.
Audience: **g,l,u,f.**

Pascal, Blaise **B1900**
Pensees. Alban J. Krailsheimer (Translator). Trade Paper. Penguin Group (USA) Inc. New York, NY. 2003. 368p. Penguin Classics Ser. ISBN:0-14-044645-1, ISBN13: 978-0-14-044645-6. Dewey:230/.2. LCCN:96-103500.
Audience: **g,l,u.**

Pascal, Blaise **BX1751.2**
Pensees and Other Writings. Honor Levi (Translator), Anthony Levi (Translator, Introduction by, Notes by). Trade Paper. Oxford University Press, Inc. New York, NY. 1999. 312p. Oxford World's Classics Ser. ISBN:0-19-283655-2, ISBN13: 978-0-19-283655-7. Dewey:230.2.
Audience: **g,l,u,f.**

Modern French Literature > 17th C. > Perrault

Perrault, Charles **PQ1877**
Contes. Soriano, Marc (Editor). Flammarion. 1989. ISBN:2-08-211541-0, ISBN13: 978-2-08-211541-4.
Audience: **u,f.**

Perrault, Charles **PZ8.P426**
Perrault's Complete Fairy Tales. W. Heath Robinson (Illustrator). Trade Paper. Penguin Group (USA) Inc. New York, NY. 2000. 192p. Puffin Classics Ser. ISBN:0-14-130651-3, ISBN13: 978-0-14-130651-3. Dewey:398.2/1/0944.
Audience: **g,l,u,f.**

Modern French Literature > 17th C. > Racine

Barthes, Roland **PQ1905.B313 1992**
On Racine. Richard Howard (Translator). Trade Paper. University of California Press. Berkeley, CA. 1992. 172p. ISBN:0-520-07824-1, ISBN13: 978-0-520-07824-6. Dewey:842/.4.
Audience: **u,f.**

Racine, Jean **PQ1885**
OEuvres complètes, Vol. 1. Forestier, Georges (Editor). Gallimard. 1999. ISBN:2-07-011561-5, ISBN13: 978-2-07-011561-7.
Audience: **u,f.**

Racine, Jean **PQ1898 .A34**
Phedre: A Play. Ted Hughes (Translator). Trade Paper. Farrar, Straus & Giroux. New York, NY. 2000. 96p. ISBN:0-374-52616-8, ISBN13: 978-0-374-52616-0. Dewey:842/.4. LCCN:98-074825.
Audience: **g,l,u,f.**

Racine, Jean **PQ1888.E5**
Four Greek Plays: Andromache, Iphigenia, Phaedra, Athaliah. R. C. Knight (Translator, Introduction by, Notes by). Cloth Text. Cambridge University Press. New York, NY. 1982. 239p. ISBN:0-521-24415-3, ISBN13: 978-0-521-24415-2. Dewey:842/.4.
Audience: **g,l,u,f.**

Racine, Jean **PR6066.I53**
Phaedra. Robert Lowell (Translator). Library Binding. Hippocrene Books, Inc. New York, NY. 1972. ISBN:0-374-95132-2, ISBN13: 978-0-374-95132-0. Dewey:822/.914.
Audience: **g,l,u,f.**

Racine, Jean **PQ1885**
Oeuvres Completes, Set. Picard (Editor). Trade Cloth. Schoenhof's Foreign Books, Inc. Cambridge, MA. Pleiade Ser. ISBN:0-685-34025-2, ISBN13: 978-0-685-34025-7. Dewey:842.49.
Audience: **u,f.**

Racine, Jean **PQ1860**
Phedre: Dual Language Edition. Margaret Rawlings (Translator, Foreword by). Trade Paper. Penguin Group (USA) Inc. New York, NY. 1992. 192p. Classics Ser. ISBN:0-14-044591-9, ISBN13: 978-0-14-044591-6. Dewey:842/.4. LCCN:92-143782.
Audience: **g,l,u,f.**

Racine, Jean **PQ1888.E5S56 1987**
Britannicus; Phaedra; Athaliah. Charles H. Sisson (Translator, Introduction by, Notes by). Trade Cloth. Oxford University Press, Inc. New York, NY. 1987. 240p. Oxford World's Classics Ser. ISBN:0-19-251037-1, ISBN13: 978-0-19-251037-2. Dewey:842/.4. LCCN:86-019977.
Audience: **g,l,u,f.**

Racine, Jean **PQ1860**
Andromache. Richard Wilbur (Translator), Igor Tulipanov (Illustrator). Trade Paper. Harcourt Trade Publishers. New York, NY. 1984. 120p. ISBN:0-15-607510-5, ISBN13: 978-0-15-607510-7. Dewey:842.4. LCCN:83-018439.
Audience: **g,l,u,f.**

Racine, Jean & Wilbur, Richard **PQ1898.A38 1986**
Phaedra, by Racine. Igor Tulipanov (Illustrator). Trade Paper. Harcourt Trade Publishers. New York, NY. 1987. 132p. ISBN:0-15-675780-X, ISBN13: 978-0-15-675780-5. Dewey:822/.914. LCCN:86-000413.
Audience: **g,l,u,f.**

Rohou, Jean **PQ1905**
Avez-vous lu Racine?: mise au point polémique. L'Harmattan. 2000. Collection Critiques littéraires ISBN:2-7384-8961-3, ISBN13: 978-2-7384-8961-6.
Audience: **u,f.**

Tobin, Ronald W. **PQ1905.T63 1999**
Jean Racine Revisited. Trade Cloth. Thomson Gale. Farmington Hills, MI. 1999. xiv, 195p. Twayne's World Authors Ser., Vol. 878 ISBN:0-8057-4605-6, ISBN13: 978-0-8057-4605-1. Dewey:842/.4. LCCN:98-037561.
Audience: **l,u.** *Choice, 1999.*

Modern French Literature > 17th C. > S-Z

De Mourgues, Odette **PQ1815**
Two French Moralists. Trade Cloth. Cambridge University Press. New York, NY. 1978. 220p. Major European Authors Ser. ISBN:0-521-21823-3, ISBN13: 978-0-521-21823-8. Dewey:848/.4/09. LCCN:77-082506.
Audience: **u,f.**

Farrell, Michele L. **PQ1925.F37 1991**
Performing Motherhood: The Sevigne Correspondence. Trade Paper. University Press of New England. Lebanon, NH. 1991. 312p. ISBN:0-87451-537-8, ISBN13: 978-0-87451-537-4. Dewey:846/.4. LCCN:91-013244.
Audience: **g,l,u,f.** *Choice, 1992.*

La Rochefoucauld, Francois de **PQ1815 .A7**
Maximes et Reflexions Diverses. Trade Cloth. French & European Publications, Inc. New York, NY. 1976. ISBN:0-318-63490-2, ISBN13: 978-0-318-63490-6. Dewey:848/.4/02.
Audience: **u,f.**

La Rochefoucauld, Francois de **PQ1815.A72 2002**
Moral Maxims. Irwin Primer (Editor, Notes by). Trade Cloth. University of Delaware Press. Newark, DE. 2002. 224p. ISBN:0-87413-820-5, ISBN13: 978-0-87413-820-7. Dewey:848/.402. LCCN:2002-075006.
Audience: **g,u,f.**

Moore, Will Grayburn **PQ1815.M59**
La Rochefoucauld: His Mind and Art. Trade Cloth. Oxford University Press, Inc. New York, NY. 1969. [9], 134p. ISBN:0-19-815384-8, ISBN13: 978-0-19-815384-9. Dewey:848/.4/02. LCCN:78-410844.
Audience: **l,u.**

Scudery, Madeleine de **PQ1922.A8E5 2003**
The Story of Sapho. Karen Newman (Editor, Translator). Trade Paper. University of Chicago Press. Chicago, IL. 2003. 186p. The Other Voice in Early Modern Europe Ser. ISBN:0-226-14399-6, ISBN13: 978-0-226-14399-6. Dewey:843/.7. LCCN:2002-043558.
Audience: **g,u,f.**

Sevigne, Mme De **PQ139**
Correspondance: Juillet 1675 - Septembre 1680, Vol. II. Trade Cloth. Gallimard, Editions. Paris Cedex 07, Pleiade Ser. ISBN:2-07-010525-3, ISBN13: 978-2-07-010525-0. Dewey:840.4.
Audience: **u,f.**

Sevigne, Mme De **PQ139**
Correspondance. Other. Schoenhof's Foreign Books, Inc. Cambridge, MA. Pleiade Ser. ISBN:0-318-51968-2, ISBN13: 978-0-318-51968-5. Dewey:840.4.
Audience: **u,f.**

Sevigne, Mme De **PQ1925**
: 1680-1696. Trade Cloth. Schoenhof's Foreign Books, Inc. Cambridge, MA. ISBN:2-07-010935-6, ISBN13: 978-2-07-010935-7. Dewey:846/.4.
Audience: **u,f.**

Sevigne, Mme De **PQ139**
Correspondance: Mars 1646 - Juillet 1675, Vol. I. Trade Cloth. Gallimard, Editions. Paris Cedex 07, Pleiade Ser. ISBN:2-07-010524-5, ISBN13: 978-2-07-010524-3. Dewey:840.4.
Audience: **u,f.**

Sevigne, Mme De **PQ1925.A27 1982**
Sevigne: Selected Letters. Leonard W. Tancock (Translator, Introduction by). Trade Paper. Penguin Group (USA) Inc. New York, NY. 1982. 1p. Classics Ser. ISBN:0-14-044405-X, ISBN13: 978-0-14-044405-6. Dewey:846/.4. LCCN:83-100182.
Audience: **g,l,u,f.**

Villedieu, Madame De **PQ1794.D5A6813 2004**
Memoirs of the Life of Henriette-Sylvie de Moliere: A Novel. Donna Kuizenga (Editor, Translator). Trade Cloth. University of Chicago Press. Chicago, IL. 2004. 225p. The Other Voice in Early Modern Europe Ser. ISBN:0-226-14419-4, ISBN13: 978-0-226-14419-1. Dewey:843/.4. LCCN:2003-022130.
Audience: **g,l,u,f.**

Watts, Derek A. **PQ1803**
La Rochefoucauld Maximes et Reflexions Diverses. Trade Paper. University of Glasgow. Glasgow, 1999. 96p. ISBN:0-85261-394-6, ISBN13: 978-0-85261-394-8. Dewey:848.407.
Audience: **u,f.**

Modern French Literature > 18th C. > A-C

Beaumarchais, Pierre De **PQ1956**
Oeuvres. Trade Cloth. Schoenhof's Foreign Books, Inc. Cambridge, MA. 1988. 1696p. Pleiade Ser. ISBN:2-07-011137-7, ISBN13: 978-2-07-011137-4. Dewey:842/.5.
Audience: **u,f.**

Beaumarchais, Pierre-Augustin Caron de **PQ1956**
The Figaro Trilogy: The Barber of Seville, the Marriage of Figaro, the Guilty Mother. David Coward (Translator). Trade Paper. Oxford University Press, Inc. New York, NY. 2003. 416p. Oxford World's Classics Ser. ISBN:0-19-280413-8, ISBN13: 978-0-19-280413-6. Dewey:842/.5. LCCN:2004-273020.
Audience: **g,l,u,f.**

Beaumarchais **PQ2003.Z5**
The Figaro Plays. John Leigh (Editor), John Wells (Translator). Trade Cloth. J. M. Dent & Sons. London, 290p. ISBN:0-460-87923-5, ISBN13: 978-0-460-87923-1. Dewey:842.5.
Audience: **g,l,u,f.**

Bretonne, Restif de la **PQ2025**
[romans], Vol. 1: Le pied de Fanchette ; Le paysan perverti ; Les contemporaines du commun, choix. Testud, Pierre (Editor). Laffont. 2002. ISBN:2-221-07172-7, ISBN13: 978-2-221-07172-4.
Audience: **u,f.**

Bretonne, Restif de la **PQ2025**
[romans], Vol. 2: La vie de mon père ; La La vie de mon père ; La femme de laboureur ; La femme infidèle ; Ingénue Saxancour ; L'épouse d'homme veuf ; La dernière aventure d'un homme de quarante-cinq ans ; La fille de mon hôtesse. Testud, Pierre (Editor). Laffont. 2002. ISBN:2-221-07173-5, ISBN13: 978-2-221-07173-1.
Audience: **u,f.**

Charriere, Isabelle De **PQ1963.C55**
Lettres de Mistriss Henley Publiees par son Amie. Philip Stewart (Editor), Joan H. Stewart (Introduction by). Trade Paper. Modern Language Association of America. New York, NY. 1993. xxx, 45p. MLA Texts and Translations Ser., No. 1a ISBN:0-87352-775-5, ISBN13: 978-0-87352-775-0. Dewey:843/.5. LCCN:93-026864.
Audience: **u,f.**

Charriere, Isabelle De **PQ1963.C55 1993**
Letters of Mistress Henley Published by Her Friend. Philip Stewart & Jean Vache (Translators). Trade Paper. Modern Language Association of America. New York, NY. 1993. xxix, 42p. MLA Texts and Translations Ser., No. 1b ISBN:0-87352-776-3, ISBN13: 978-0-87352-776-7. Dewey:843/.5. LCCN:93-026862.
Audience: **g,l,u,f.**

Chenier, Andre **PQ1965**
Oeuvres Completes. Laurent Walter (Editor). Library Binding. French & European Publications, Inc. New York, NY. 1940. 1120p. ISBN:0-7859-3750-1, ISBN13: 978-0-7859-3750-0. Dewey:843.59.
Audience: **u,f.**

Constant, Benjamin **PQ2211.C24A724 2001**
Adolphe. Patrick Coleman (Editor), Margaret Mauldon (Translator). Trade Paper. Oxford University Press, Inc. New York, NY. 2001. 120p. Oxford World's Classics Ser. ISBN:0-19-283927-6, ISBN13: 978-0-19-283927-5. Dewey:843/.6. LCCN:2001-269672.
Audience: **g,l,u,f.**

Dunkley, John **PQ2003.Z5**
Beaumarchais: "Le Barbier de Seville". Trade Cloth. Grant & Cutler. London, 1991. 92p. ISBN:0-7293-0331-4, ISBN13: 978-0-7293-0331-6. Dewey:842.5.
Audience: **l,u.**

Howarth, W. D. **PQ1956.H68 1995**
Beaumarchais. Paper over Boards. Routledge. New York, NY. 1995. 288p. ISBN:0-415-00751-8, ISBN13: 978-0-415-00751-1. Dewey:842/.5. LCCN:94-022876.
Audience: **l,u,f.**

Niklaus, Robert **PQ2003.Z5**
Beaumarchais: "Mariage de Figaro". Ed. 2. Roger Little (Editor). Trade Cloth. Grant & Cutler. London, 1995. 77p. ISBN:0-7293-0378-0, ISBN13: 978-0-7293-0378-1. Dewey:842/.5.
Audience: **l,u.**

Smernoff, Richard A. **PQ1965.S6**
Andre Chenier. Trade Cloth. Irvington Publishers. New York, NY. 1977. 168p. Twayne's World Authors Ser. ISBN:0-8057-6258-2, ISBN13: 978-0-8057-6258-7. Dewey:841/.5. LCCN:76-050038.
Audience: **l,u.**

Wood, Dennis **DC255.T3**
Benjamin Constant: A Biography. Paper over Boards. Routledge. New York, NY. 1993. 352p. ISBN:0-415-01937-0, ISBN13: 978-0-415-01937-8. Dewey:944.06092. LCCN:92-036696.
Audience: **g,l,u,f.**

Wood, Dennis **PQ2211.C24 A74 1987**
Constant: Adolphe. Trade Cloth. Cambridge University Press. New York, NY. 1987. 126p. Landmarks of World Literature Ser. ISBN:0-521-32822-5, ISBN13: 978-0-521-32822-7. Dewey:843/.6. LCCN:87-013101.
Audience: **l,u.**

Modern French Literature > 18th C. > Diderot

Diderot, Denis **PQ1979 .A8**
Lettres a Sophie Volland. Trade Paper. Schoenhof's Foreign Books, Inc. Cambridge, MA. 1984. 405p. Folio Ser., No. 1547 ISBN:2-07-037547-1, ISBN13: 978-2-07-037547-9. Dewey:034/.1/092.
Audience: **u,f.**

Diderot, Denis **PQ1979.A76E5 2005**
The Nun. Trade Paper, Perfect. Oxford University Press, Inc. New York, NY. 2005. 234p. Oxford World's Classics Ser. ISBN:0-19-280430-8, ISBN13: 978-0-19-280430-3. Dewey:843/.5. LCCN:2004-024150.
Audience: **g,l,u,f.**

Diderot, Denis **B2012.A2 1994**
Oeuvres. Trade Cloth. Robert Laffont. Paris, 1994. ISBN:2-221-05721-X, ISBN13: 978-2-221-05721-6. Dewey:194. LCCN:94-190347.
Audience: **u,f.**

Diderot, Denis & d'Alembert, Jean le Rond **AE25**
The Encyclopedia of Diderot and d'Alembert: A Collaborative Translation Project.
http://www.hti.umich.edu/d/did/
Audience: **g,l,u,f.**

Diderot, Denis **AE25**
Encyclopédie ou Dictionnaire raisonné des sciences, des arts et des métiers.
http://www.lib.uchicago.edu/efts/ARTFL/projects/encyc/
Robinet, Jean-Baptiste-René (Editor).
Audience: **u,f.**

Diderot, Denis **PQ1979.A227 2001**
Rameau's Nephew and Other Works. Jacques Barzun & Ralph H. Bowen (Translators). Trade Cloth. Hackett Publishing Company, Inc. Indianapolis, IN. 2001. 317p. ISBN:0-87220-487-1, ISBN13: 978-0-87220-487-4. Dewey:848/.509. LCCN:00-065036.
Audience: **g,l,u,f.**

Diderot, Denis **PQ1979.A6**
Oeuvres Romanesques. Henri Benac (Editor). Trade Cloth. French & European Publications, Inc. New York, NY. 1962. ISBN:0-8288-9953-3, ISBN13: 978-0-8288-9953-6. Dewey:843.5.
Audience: **u,f.**

Diderot, Denis **AE25 .E523**
Encyclopedia: Selections. Thomas Cassirer & Nelly S. Hoyt (Translators). Trade Paper. Macmillan Publishing Company, Inc. Old Tappan, NJ. 1965. ISBN:0-672-60479-5, ISBN13: 978-0-672-60479-9. Dewey:34.1. LCCN:65-026535.
Audience: **g,l,u,f.**

Diderot, Denis **PQ1979.A65E5 1999**
Jacques the Fatalist. David Coward (Editor). Trade Paper. Oxford University Press, Inc. New York, NY. 1999. 304p. Oxford World's Classics Ser. ISBN:0-19-283874-1, ISBN13: 978-0-19-283874-2. Dewey:843/.5. LCCN:98-031240.
Audience: **u,f.**

Diderot, Denis **PQ1979.A8**
Diderot's Letters to Sophie Volland: A Selection. Peter France (Translator). Trade Cloth. Oxford University Press, Inc. New York, NY. 1972. 225p. ISBN:0-19-212551-6, ISBN13: 978-0-19-212551-4. Dewey:194. LCCN:73-151601.
Audience: **g,l,u,f.**

Diderot, Denis **PQ1979.A25 1991**
This Is Not a Story and Other Stories. P. N. Furbank (Translator, Introduction by). Cloth Text. University of Missouri Press. Columbia, MO. 1991. 176p. ISBN:0-8262-0815-0, ISBN13: 978-0-8262-0815-6. Dewey:843/.5. LCCN:91-027703.
Audience: **g,l,u,f.** *Choice, 1992.*

Diderot, Denis **T9**
A Diderot Pictorial Encyclopedia of Trades and Industry: Manufacturing and the Technical Arts in Plates Selected from "L'Encyclopedie, ou Dictionnaire Raisonne des Sciences, des Arts et des Metiers". Ed. 2. Charles C. Gillispie (Introduction by, Notes by). Trade Paper. Dover Publications, Inc. Mineola, NY. 1993. 507p. Pictorial Archive Ser. ISBN:0-486-27429-2, ISBN13: 978-0-486-27429-4. Dewey:670. LCCN:92-031820.
Audience: **g,l,u,f.**

Diderot, Denis **N6846.D4613 1995**
Diderot on Art. John Goodman (Editor, Translator), Thomas Crow (Introduction by). Cloth over Boards. Yale University Press. Cumberland, RI. 1995. 312p. Salon of 1765 and Notes on Painting Ser., Vol. 1 ISBN:0-300-06248-6, ISBN13: 978-0-300-06248-9. LCCN:95-010638.
Audience: **g,l,u,f.** *Choice, 1996.*

Diderot, Denis **N6846.D4613 1995**
The Salon of 1767, Vol. 2. John Goodman (Editor, Translator), Thomas Crow (Introduction by). Cloth over Boards. Yale University Press. Cumberland, RI. 1995. 368p. ISBN:0-300-06249-4, ISBN13: 978-0-300-06249-6. Dewey:759.4/09033. LCCN:95-010638.
Audience: **g,l,u,f.** *Choice, 1996.*

Diderot, Denis **PQ1979**
The Indiscreet Jewels. Sophie Hawkes (Translator), Aram Vartanian (Introduction by). Trade Cloth. Marsilio Publishers. New York, NY. 1993. 320p. ISBN:0-941419-82-7, ISBN13: 978-0-941419-82-6. Dewey:843/.5. LCCN:92-062369.
Audience: **g,l,u,f.** *Choice, 1993.*

Diderot, Denis **B2012**
Selected Philosophical Writings. John Lough (Editor). Trade Cloth. Greenwood Publishing Group, Inc. Portsmouth, NH. 1987. 232p. ISBN:0-313-25228-9, ISBN13: 978-0-313-25228-0. Dewey:194. LCCN:86-025774.
Audience: **g,l,u,f.**

Diderot, Denis **BD581**
Thoughts on the Interpretation of Nature and Other Philosophical Works. Lorna Sandler (Translator). Cloth over Boards. Clinamen Press Ltd. Manchester, 2000. 200p. ISBN:1-903083-06-0, ISBN13: 978-1-903083-06-2. Dewey:113.
Audience: **g,l,u,f.**

Diderot, Denis **PQ1979**
Rameau's Nephew and D'Alembert's Dream. Leonard W. Tancock (Translator, Introduction by). Trade Paper. Penguin Group (USA) Inc. New York, NY. 1976. 240p. Classics Ser. ISBN:0-14-044173-5, ISBN13: 978-0-14-044173-4. Dewey:848.5/09. LCCN:77-357900.
Audience: **g,l,u,f.**

Diderot, Denis **JC179 .D46 1992**
Diderot: Political Writings. Robert Wokler & John H. Mason (Editors). Cloth Text. Cambridge University Press. New York, NY. 1992. 268p. Texts in the History of Political Thought ISBN:0-521-36044-7, ISBN13: 978-0-521-36044-9. Dewey:320.51.
Audience: **g,l,u,f.**

Fellows, Otise E. **PQ1979.F44 1989**
Diderot. Trade Cloth. Thomson Gale. Farmington Hills, MI. 1989. 232p. World Authors Ser., No. 425 ISBN:0-8057-8225-7, ISBN13: 978-0-8057-8225-7. Dewey:848/.509. LCCN:88-033276.
Audience: **l,u.**

Mortier, Roland & Trousson, Raymond **PQ1979**
Dictionnaire de Diderot. Champion. 1999. ISBN:2-7453-0067-9, ISBN13: 978-2-7453-0067-6.
Audience: **u,f.**

Wilson, Arthur M. **PQ1979 .W52**
Diderot. Trade Cloth. Oxford University Press, Inc. New York, NY. 1972. 936p. ISBN:0-19-501506-1, ISBN13: 978-0-19-501506-5. Dewey:194.
Audience: **g,l,u,f.**

Modern French Literature > 18th C. > D-R

Conroy, Peter V. Jr. **PQ2012.C66 1992**
Montesquieu Revisited. Trade Cloth. Thomson Gale. Farmington Hills, MI. 1992. 170p. World Authors Ser. ISBN:0-8057-8273-7, ISBN13: 978-0-8057-8273-8. Dewey:848/.509. LCCN:92-018575.
Audience: **l,u.** *Choice, 1993.*

Coward, David & Marivaux, Pierre Carlet de Chamblain de **PQ2003.V6**
Marivaux, la Vie de Marianne and le Paysan Parvenu. Trade Cloth. Grant & Cutler. London, 1982. 76p. ISBN:84-499-6036-3, ISBN13: 978-84-499-6036-9. Dewey:842/.5.
Audience: **u,f.**

De Montesquieu, Charles-Louis **PQ2011**
Oeuvres Completes. Roger Caillois (Editor). Trade Cloth. Schoenhof's Foreign Books, Inc. Cambridge, MA. Pleiade Ser., Vol. 1 ISBN:2-07-010365-X, ISBN13: 978-2-07-010365-2. Dewey:848.509.
Audience: **u,f.**

De Montesquieu, Charles-Louis **PQ2011**
Oeuvres Completes. Roger Caillois (Editor). Trade Cloth. Schoenhof's Foreign Books, Inc. Cambridge, MA. Pleiade Ser., Vol. 2 ISBN:2-07-010366-8, ISBN13: 978-2-07-010366-9. Dewey:848.509.
Audience: **u,f.**

De Montesquieu, Charles-Louis **JC179 .M74 1989**
The Spirit of the Laws. Anne M. Cohler, Basia C. Miller & Harold S. Stone (Editors). Cloth Text. Cambridge University Press. New York, NY. 1989. 808p. Texts in the History of Political Thought ISBN:0-521-36183-4, ISBN13: 978-0-521-36183-5. Dewey:320. LCCN:88-030006.
Audience: **u,f.**

Haac, Oscar A. **PQ2003.Z5.H3**
Marivaux. Library Binding. Irvington Publishers. New York, NY. 1974. 166p. Twayne's World Authors Ser. ISBN:0-8057-2593-8, ISBN13: 978-0-8057-2593-3. Dewey:842/.5. LCCN:73-017338.
Audience: **l,u.**

Laclos, Choderlos de **PQ1993**
Oeuvres Completes. Trade Cloth. Schoenhof's Foreign Books, Inc. Cambridge, MA. 1943. Pleiade Ser. ISBN:2-07-010937-2, ISBN13: 978-2-07-010937-1. Dewey:843/.6.
Audience: **u,f.**

Laclos, Choderlos de **PQ1993.L22**
Les Liaisons Dangereuses. Douglas Parmee (Editor), David Coward (Introduction by). Trade Paper. Oxford University Press, Inc. New York, NY. 1999. 442p. Oxford World's Classics Ser. ISBN:0-19-283867-9, ISBN13: 978-0-19-283867-4. Dewey:843/.6.
Audience: **g,l,u,f.**

Laclos, Choderlos de **PQ1993.L22L53 2003**
Les Liaisons Dangereuses. P. W. Stone (Translator, Introduction by). Trade Paper. Penguin Group (USA) Inc. New York, NY. 2003. 400p. Penguin Classics Ser. ISBN:0-14-044116-6, ISBN13: 978-0-14-044116-1. Dewey:843/.6.
Audience: **g,l,u,f.**

Malraux, André **PQ1993.L22**
Le Triangle Noir: Laclos, Goysa, Saint-Just. Trade Cloth. French & European Publications, Inc. New York, NY. ISBN:0-685-34272-7, ISBN13: 978-0-685-34272-5. Dewey:843.5.
Audience: **u,f.**

Marivaux, A. **PQ2003.A288 1999**
Marivaux: Three Plays. Stephen Wadsworth (Translator). Trade Paper. Smith and Kraus Publishers, Inc. Lyme, NH. 1999. x, 198p. Great Translations for Actors Ser. ISBN:1-57525-148-5, ISBN13: 978-1-57525-148-6. Dewey:842/.5. LCCN:98-038708.
Audience: **g,l,u,f.**

Marivaux, Pierre Carlet de Chamblain de **PQ2003**
Théâtre complet, Vol. 1. Gallimard. 1993. Pleiades Series ISBN:2-07-011259-4, ISBN13: 978-2-07-011259-3.
Audience: **u,f.**

Marivaux, Pierre Carlet de Chamblain de **PQ2003**
Théâtre complet, Vol. 2. Gallimard. 1994. Pleiades Series ISBN:2-07-011356-6, ISBN13: 978-2-07-011356-9.
Audience: **u,f.**

Marivaux, Pierre Carlet de Chamblain de **PQ2082.C3**
La vie de Marianne, ou, Les aventures de madame la comtesse de ***. Flammarion. 1997. ISBN:2-08-070309-9, ISBN13: 978-2-08-070309-5.
Audience: **u,f.**

Marivaux, Pierre Carlet de Chamblain de **PQ2105.A2**
Up from the Country: Infidelities - The Games of Love and Chance. David Cohen (Translator). Trade Paper. Penguin Group (USA) Inc. New York, NY. 1980. 368p. ISBN:0-14-044303-7, ISBN13: 978-0-14-044303-5. Dewey:848/.5/09.
Audience: **g,l,u,f.**

Marivaux **PQ2003.Z5**
Seven Comedies by Marivaux. Adrienne S. Mandel & Oscar Mandel (Editors). Trade Cloth. Irvington Publishers. New York, NY. 1968. 380p. ISBN:0-686-60850-X, ISBN13: 978-0-686-60850-9. Dewey:842/.5. LCCN:68-016386.
Audience: **g,l,u,f.**

Marivaux **PQ2082.C3**
Virtuous Orphan: or The Life of Marianne. Ronald Paulson (Editor). Library Binding. Garland Publishing, Inc. New York, NY. 1979. Novel 1720-1805 Ser. ISBN:0-8240-3652-2, ISBN13: 978-0-8240-3652-2. Dewey:843/.5. LCCN:78-060843.
Audience: **g,l,u,f.**

Marivaux **PQ2003.Z5**
Marivaux Plays. Claude Schumacher (Introduction by). Trade Paper. Methuen Publishing Ltd. London, 2004. 559p. Methuen World Dramatists Ser. ISBN:0-413-18560-5, ISBN13: 978-0-413-18560-0. Dewey:842/.5.
Audience: **l,u.**

Montesquieu, Charles de Secondat **PQ2011.L5E53 2004**
The Persian Letters. C. J. Betts (Translator, Introduction by). Trade Paper. Penguin Group (USA) Inc. New York, NY. 1973. 1p. Classics Ser. ISBN:0-14-044281-2, ISBN13: 978-0-14-044281-6. Dewey:843.5. LCCN:73-163802.
Audience: **g,l,u,f.**

Prevost, Abbe **PQ2082.C3**
Prevost: Manon Lescaut. Patrick Byrne (Editor). Trade Paper. Bristol Classical Press. London, 1999. 216p. Modern Language Ser. ISBN:1-85399-517-7, ISBN13: 978-1-85399-517-0. Dewey:843.5.
Audience: **g,l,u,f.**

Prevost, Abbe **PQ2021.M3A6 2004**
Manon Lescaut. Angela Scholar (Translator). Trade Paper. Oxford University Press, Inc. New York, NY. 2004. 208p. Oxford World's Classics Ser. ISBN:0-19-284065-7, ISBN13: 978-0-19-284065-3. Dewey:843/.5. LCCN:2004-299799.
Audience: **g,l,u,f.**

Rodmell, Graham E. & Marivaux, Pierre Carlet de Chamblain de **PQ2003.J4**
Le Jeu de L'amour et du Hasard and les Fausses Confidences. Trade Cloth. Grant & Cutler. London, 1982. 87p. ISBN:84-499-5686-2, ISBN13: 978-84-499-5686-7. Dewey:842/.5.
Audience: **l,u.**

Shklar, Judith N. **PQ2012.S53 1987**
Montesquieu. Trade Cloth. Oxford University Press, Inc. New York, NY. 1987. 144p. Past Masters Ser. ISBN:0-19-287649-X, ISBN13: 978-0-19-287649-2. Dewey:320.5/092/4. LCCN:87-005785.
Audience: **l,u.** *Choice, 1988.*

Smernoff, Richard A. **PQ2021.Z5S65 1985**
L' Abbe Prevost. Trade Cloth. Thomson Gale. Farmington Hills, MI. 1985. 137p. World Authors Ser. ISBN:0-8057-6594-8, ISBN13: 978-0-8057-6594-6. Dewey:843/.5. LCCN:84-022522.
Audience: **l,u.** *Choice, 1985.*

Thody, Phillip **PQ2082.C3**
Les Liaisons Dangereuses, Laclos: Critical Monographs in English. Ed. 3. Trade Paper. University of Glasgow, French & German Publications. Glasgow, 1993. 72p. ISBN:0-85261-317-2, ISBN13: 978-0-85261-317-7. Dewey:843.5.
Audience: **u,f.**

Modern French Literature > 18th C. > Rousseau

Conroy, Peter V. Jr. **PQ2053.C66 1998**
Jean Jacques Rousseau. Trade Cloth. Simon & Schuster. New York, NY. 1998. 171p. Twayne's World Authors Ser., Vol. 873 ISBN:0-8057-1616-5, ISBN13: 978-0-8057-1616-0. Dewey:848/.509. LCCN:98-023266.
Audience: **l,u.** *Choice, 1999.*

Cranston, Maurice **PQ2043**
Noble Savage Jean Jacques Rousseau. Cloth Text. Penguin Books Canada, Ltd. Toronto, ON. 1991. 416p. ISBN:0-7139-9051-1, ISBN13: 978-0-7139-9051-5. Dewey:194.
Audience: **g,l,u,f.**

Cranston, Maurice **PQ2045**
Jean Jacques: The Early Life and Work of Jean-Jacques Rosseau, 1712-1754. Trade Cloth. W. W. Norton & Company, Inc. New York, NY. 1983. 382p. ISBN:0-393-01744-3, ISBN13: 978-0-393-01744-1. Dewey:848/.509.
Audience: **g,l,u,f.**

Cranston, Maurice **PQ2047.C73 1997**
The Solitary Self: Jean-Jacques Rousseau in Exile and Adversity. Sanford Lakoff (Foreword by). Trade Cloth. University of Chicago Press. Chicago, IL. 1997. 267p. ISBN:0-226-11865-7, ISBN13: 978-0-226-11865-9. Dewey:194. LCCN:96-012922.
Audience: **g,u,f.** *Choice, 1997.*

Dent, N. J. **PQ2042.D46 1992**
A Rousseau Dictionary. Trade Cloth. Blackwell Publishing, Inc. Malden, MA. 1992. 260p. ISBN:0-631-17568-7, ISBN13: 978-0-631-17568-1. Dewey:194. LCCN:92-017607.
Audience: **g,l,u,f.** *Choice, 1993.*

Grimsley, Ronald **B2137**
The Philosophy of Rousseau. Trade Cloth. Oxford University Press. Oxford, 1973. 175p. ISBN:0-19-885062-X, ISBN13: 978-0-19-885062-5. Dewey:194.
Audience: **l,u.**

Grimsley, Ronald **B2137**
Jean-Jacques Rousseau. Trade Cloth. Barnes & Noble Books-Imports. Lanham, MD. 1983. 202p. ISBN:0-389-20378-5, ISBN13: 978-0-389-20378-0. Dewey:194. LCCN:82-024409.
Audience: **l,u.**

Rosseau, Jean-Jacques **B2132.E5 1988**
Rousseau: Selections: The Great Philosophers. Maurice Cranston (Editor). Paper Text. Prentice Hall PTR. Upper Saddle River, NJ. 1988. 364p. ISBN:0-02-325521-8, ISBN13: 978-0-02-325521-2. Dewey:194. LCCN:87-028151.
Audience: **g,l,u,f.**

Rousseau, Jean-Jacques **PQ2030**
Oeuvres complètes, Vol. 1: Les confessions. Autres textes autobiographiques. Gallimard. 1959. Pleiade Series
Audience: **u,f.**

Rousseau, Jean-Jacques **PQ2030**
Oeuvres complètes, Vol. 2: La nouvelle Héloïse. Théatre. Poésies. Essais littéraires. Gallimard. 1959. Pleiade Series
Audience: **u,f.**

Rousseau, Jean-Jacques **PQ2030**
Oeuvres complètes, Vol. 3: Du contrat social. Écrits politiques. Gallimard. 1959. Pleiade Series
Audience: **u,f.**

Rousseau, Jean-Jacques **PQ2030**
Oeuvres complètes, Vol. 4: Emile. Education-morale- botanique. Gallimard. 1959. Pleiade Series
Audience: **u,f.**

Rousseau, Jean-Jacques **ML3800**
Oeuvres complètes, vol. 5: Ecrits sur la musique, la langue et le théâtre. Gallimard. 1995. Pleiade Series ISBN:2-07-010693-4, ISBN13: 978-2-07-010693-6.
Audience: **u,f.**

Rousseau, Jean-Jacques, et al. **JC179.R7 1987**
Jean-Jacques Rousseau, Political Writings. Julia C. Bondanella & Alan Ritter (Authors). Trade Cloth. W. W. Norton & Company, Inc. New York, NY. 1987. ISBN:0-393-02479-2, ISBN13: 978-0-393-02479-1. Dewey:320. LCCN:87-024056.
Audience: **g,l,u,f.**

Rousseau, Jean-Jacques **PQ2034.A3 1990**
The Plan for Perpetual Peace, on the Government of Poland, and Other Writings on History and Politics. Judith Bush (Translator). Saddle Stitched, Cloth over Boards, Dust Jacket. University Press of New England. Lebanon, NH. 2005. 260p. Collected Writings of Rousseau Ser., Vol. 11 ISBN:1-58465-514-3, ISBN13: 978-1-58465-514-5. Dewey:320.94. LCCN:2005-014159.
Audience: **g,l,u,f.**

Rousseau, Jean-Jacques & Kelly, Christopher **PQ2034.A3 1990**
Letter to Beaumont, Letters Written from the Mountain, and Related Writings. Eve Grace (Editor). Library Binding. University Press of New England. Lebanon, NH. 2001. 356p. Collected Writings of Rousseau Ser., Vol. 9 ISBN:1-58465-164-4, ISBN13: 978-1-58465-164-2. Dewey:848/.509 s 848/.509. LCCN:2001-005385.
Audience: **g,l,u,f.**

Rousseau, Jean-Jacques **PQ2034.A3 1990**
The Reveries of the Solitary Walker, Botanical Writings and Letter to Franquieres. Christopher Kelly & Roger D. Masters (Editors), Charles Butterworth, Alexandra Cook & Terence E. Marshall (Translators). Library Binding. University Press of New England. Lebanon, NH. 2000. 377p. Collected Writings of Rousseau Ser., Vol. 8 ISBN:1-58465-007-9, ISBN13: 978-1-58465-007-2. Dewey:849/.509 s 848/.509. LCCN:99-039783.
Audience: **g,l,u,f.**

Rousseau, Jean-Jacques **PQ2034.A3**
The Confessions and Correspondence, Including the Letters to Malesherbes. Christopher Kelly, Roger D. Masters & Peter G. Stillmann (Editors), Christopher Kelly (Translator). Trade Cloth. University Press of New England. Lebanon, NH. 1995. 736p. Collected Writings of Rousseau, Vol. 5 ISBN:0-87451-707-9, ISBN13: 978-0-87451-707-1. Dewey:848/.509 s. LCCN:94-047021.
Audience: **g,l,u,f.**

Rousseau, Jean-Jacques **PQ2034.A3**
Discourse on the Sciences and Arts and Polemics. Roger D. Masters & Christopher Kelly (Editors), Roger D. Masters, Christopher Kelly & Judith R. Bush (Translators). Library Binding. University Press of New England. Lebanon, NH. 1992. 251p. Collected Writings of Rousseau, Vol. 2 ISBN:0-87451-580-7, ISBN13: 978-0-87451-580-0. Dewey:848/.509. LCCN:91-050820.
Audience: **g,l,u,f.** *Choice, 1994.*

Rousseau, Jean-Jacques **PQ2034.A3**
Rousseau, Judge of Jean-Jacques: Dialogues. Roger D. Masters & Christopher Kelly (Editors), Roger D. Masters, Christopher Kelly & Judith R. Bush (Translators). Library Binding. University Press of New England. Lebanon, NH. 1990. 309p. The Collected Writings of Rousseau, Vol. 1 ISBN:0-87451-495-9, ISBN13: 978-0-87451-495-7. Dewey:848/.509. LCCN:89-040234.
Audience: **g,l,u,f.** *Choice, 1994.*

Rousseau, Jean-Jacques **PQ2034.A3**
The Social Contract, Discourse on the Virtue Most Necessary for a Hero, Political Fragments and Geneva Manuscript. Roger D. Masters & Christopher Kelly (Editors), Roger D. Masters, Christopher Kelly & Judith R. Bush (Translators). Library

Binding. University Press of New England. Lebanon, NH. 1994. 306p. The Collected Writings of Rousseau, Vol. 4 ISBN:0-87451-646-3, ISBN13: 978-0-87451-646-3. Dewey:848/.509 s. LCCN:94-004496.

Audience: **g,l,u,f.**

Rousseau, Jean-Jacques **PQ2034.A3 1990 VOL.3**
Discourse on the Origin of Inequality, Polemics, and Political Economy. Roger D. Masters & Christopher Kelly (Editors), Roger D. Masters, Christopher Kelly, Judith R. Bush & Terence Marshall (Translators). Library Binding. University Press of New England. Lebanon, NH. 1993. 242p. Collected Writings of Rousseau, Vol. 3 ISBN:0-87451-603-X, ISBN13: 978-0-87451-603-6. Dewey:320.1/1. LCCN:92-053866.

Audience: **g,l,u,f.** *Choice, 1994.*

Rousseau, Jean-Jacques **PQ2034.A3**
Julie: Or the New Heloise: Letters of Two Lovers Who Live in a Small Town at the Foot of the Alps. Roger D. Masters, Christopher Kelly, Philip Stewart & Jean Vache (Editors), Philip Stewart & Jean Vache (Translators). Trade Cloth. University Press of New England. Lebanon, NH. 1997. 760p. Collected Writings of Rousseau, Vol. 6 ISBN:0-87451-824-5, ISBN13: 978-0-87451-824-5. Dewey:848/.509 s. LCCN:97-009172.

Audience: **g,l,u,f.** *Choice, 1998.*

Rousseau, Jean-Jacques **PQ2034.A3**
Essay on the Origin of Languages and Writings Related to Music. John T. Scott, Roger D. Masters & Christopher Kelly (Editors), John T. Scott (Translator). Trade Cloth. University Press of New England. Lebanon, NH. 1998. 656p. Collected Writings of Rousseau, Vol. 7 ISBN:0-87451-839-3, ISBN13: 978-0-87451-839-9. Dewey:780. LCCN:98-008043.

Audience: **g,l,u,f.** *Choice, 2000.*

Starobinski, Jean **B2137.S713 1988**
Jean-Jacques Rousseau: Transparency and Obstruction. Arthur Goldhammer (Translator), Robert Morrissey (Introduction by). Trade Cloth. University of Chicago Press. Chicago, IL. 1988. 460p. ISBN:0-226-77126-1, ISBN13: 978-0-226-77126-7. Dewey:848/.509. LCCN:87-019050.

Audience: **u,f.** *Choice, 1988.*

Starobinski, Jean **B2137.S713 1988**
Jean-Jacques Rousseau: Transparency and Obstruction. Arthur Goldhammer (Translator), Robert Morrissey (Introduction by). Paper Text. University of Chicago Press. Chicago, IL. 1997. xxxviii, 460p. ISBN:0-226-77128-8, ISBN13: 978-0-226-77128-1. Dewey:848/.509. LCCN:87-019050.

Audience: **u,f.** *Choice, 1988.*

Trousson, Raymond & Eigeldinger, Frédéric **PQ2030**
Dictionnaire de Jean-Jacques Rousseau. Champion. 1996. ISBN:2-85203-604-5, ISBN13: 978-2-85203-604-8.

Audience: **u,f.**

Modern French Literature > 18th C. > Sade

Blanchot, Maurice **PQ2220.D723Z613 2004**
Lautreamont and Sade. Trade Cloth. Stanford University Press. Palo Alto, CA. 2004. 200p. Meridian Ser., :Crossing Aesthetics Ser. ISBN:0-8047-4233-2, ISBN13: 978-0-8047-4233-7. Dewey:841/.8. LCCN:2004-006881.

Audience: **u,f.**

de Sade, Marquis **PQ2063.S3A65213 2005**
The Crimes of Love. Trade Paper. Oxford University Press, Inc. New York, NY. 2005. 388p. Oxford World's Classics Ser. ISBN:0-19-280507-X, ISBN13: 978-0-19-280507-2. Dewey:843/.6. LCCN:2004-026058.

Audience: **g,l,u,f.**

de Sade, Marquis **PQ2063**
Oeuvres Completes, Set. Trade Cloth. French & European Publications, Inc. New York, NY. ISBN:0-685-34060-0, ISBN13: 978-0-685-34060-8. Dewey:843/.6.

Audience: **u,f.**

de Sade, Marquis **PQ2063.S3A235 1992**
The Misfortunes of Virtue and Other Early Tales. David Coward (Translator). Trade Paper. Oxford University Press, Inc. New York, NY. 1999. 330p. Oxford World's Classics Ser. ISBN:0-19-283695-1, ISBN13: 978-0-19-283695-3. Dewey:843/.6. LCCN:91-038940.

Audience: **g,l,u,f.**

de Sade, Marquis **PQ2063.S3**
The Gothic Tales of the Marquis de Sade. Margaret Crosland (Translator). Trade Paper. Peter Owen Ltd. London, 2006. 183p. ISBN:0-7206-1251-9, ISBN13: 978-0-7206-1251-6. Dewey:843.6.

Audience: **g,l,u,f.**

de Sade, Marquis **PQ2063.S3**
The Passionate Philosopher: A Marquis de Sade Reader. Margaret Crosland (Translator, Introduction by). Trade Cloth. Peter Owen Ltd. London, 1991. 126p. ISBN:0-7206-0826-0, ISBN13: 978-0-7206-0826-7. Dewey:840.5.

Audience: **g,l,u,f.**

de Sade, Marquis **PN5006.T48**
Selected Letters of Marquis de Sade. Margaret Crosland (Introduction by), Jeremy Reed (Afterword by). Trade Paper. Peter Owen Ltd. London, 1992. 176p. ISBN:0-7206-0860-0, ISBN13: 978-0-7206-0860-1. Dewey:826.

Audience: **g,l,u,f.**

de Sade, Marquis **PQ2063.S3**
The 120 Days of Sodom and Other Writings. Austryn Wainhouse & Richard Seaver (Editors). Trade Paper. Grove/Atlantic, Inc. New York, NY. 1982. ISBN:0-394-17119-5, ISBN13: 978-0-394-17119-7. Dewey:843.6.

Audience: **g,l,u,f.**

de Sade, Marquis **PQ2063.S3A275 1990**
Justine, Philosophy in the Bedroom and Other Writings. Austryn Wainhouse & Richard Seaver (Translators), Jean Paulhan &

Maurice Blanchot (Introduction by). Trade Paper. Grove/Atlantic, Inc. New York, NY. 1994. 784p. ISBN:0-8021-3218-9, ISBN13: 978-0-8021-3218-5. Dewey:843/.6. LCCN:90-003153.
Audience: **g,l,u,f.**

Du Plessix Gray, Francine **PQ2063.S3**
At Home with the Marquis de Sade. UK-Trade Paper. Ebury Publishing. London, 2000. 495p. ISBN:0-7126-6522-6, ISBN13: 978-0-7126-6522-3. Dewey:843.6.
Audience: **g,l,u,f.**

Hood, Stuart **PQ2063.S3H66 1999**
Introducing Marquis de Sade. Ed. 2. Graham Crowley (Illustrator). Trade Paper. Totem Books. Cambridge, 1999. 176p. ISBN:1-84046-071-7, ISBN13: 978-1-84046-071-1. Dewey:843/.6. LCCN:99-071125.
Audience: **l,u.**

Lever, Maurice & Goldhammer, Arthur **PQ2063.S3L48 1994**
Sade: A Biography. Trade Paper. Harcourt Trade Publishers. New York, NY. 1994. 626p. Harvest Book Ser. ISBN:0-15-600111-X, ISBN13: 978-0-15-600111-3. Dewey:843.6. LCCN:94-015391.
Audience: **g,l,u,f.**

Paz, Octavio **PQ2063.S3P36513 1998**
An Erotic Beyond: Sade. Eliot Weinberger (Translator). Cloth over Boards. Harcourt Trade Publishers. New York, NY. 1998. 96p. ISBN:0-15-100352-1, ISBN13: 978-0-15-100352-5. Dewey:843/.6. LCCN:97-046048.
Audience: **u,f.**

Phillips, John **PQ2063.S3P45 2005**
How to Read Sade. Trade Paper. W. W. Norton & Company, Inc. New York, NY. 2005. 128p. ISBN:0-393-32822-8, ISBN13: 978-0-393-32822-6. Dewey:843/.6. LCCN:2005-019138.
Audience: **g,l,u.**

Phillips, John **PQ2063.S3**
The Marquis de Sade: A Very Short Introduction. Trade Paper. Oxford University Press, Inc. New York, NY. 2005. 144p. Very Short Introductions Ser., Vol. 124 ISBN:0-19-280469-3, ISBN13: 978-0-19-280469-3. Dewey:843/.6. LCCN:2005-299574.
Audience: **g,l,u,f.**

Schaeffer, Neil **PQ2063.S3**
The Marquis de Sade: A Life. Trade Paper. Harvard University Press. Cambridge, MA. 2000. 577p. ISBN:0-674-00392-6, ISBN13: 978-0-674-00392-7. Dewey:843.6.
Audience: **g,l,u,f.** *Choice, 2000.*

Modern French Literature > 18th C. > Voltaire

Knapp, Bettina L. **PQ2122.K63 2000**
Voltaire Revisited. Trade Cloth. Thomson Gale. Farmington Hills, MI. 2000. 170p. ISBN:0-8057-1634-3, ISBN13: 978-0-8057-1634-4. Dewey:848/.509. LCCN:99-053756.
Audience: **g,l,u.** *Choice, 2000.*

Mason, Haydn Trevos **PQ2099**
Voltaire: A Biography. Trade Cloth. Paul Elek Inc. Salem, NH. 1981. xiii, 194p. ISBN:0-236-40184-X, ISBN13: 978-0-236-40184-0. Dewey:848/.509.
Audience: **g,l,u,f.**

Pearson, Roger **PQ2099.P43 2005**
Voltaire Almighty: A Life in Pursuit of Freedom. Cloth over Boards. Bloomsbury Publishing. New York, NY. 2005. 384p. ISBN:1-58234-630-5, ISBN13: 978-1-58234-630-4. Dewey:848/.509 B. LCCN:2005-053027.
Audience: **g,l,u,f.** *Choice, 2006.*

Trousson, Raymond & Vercruysse, Jeroom **PQ2098**
Dictionnaire général de Voltaire. Champion. 2003. ISBN:2-7453-0765-7, ISBN13: 978-2-7453-0765-1.
Audience: **u,f.**

Voltaire **PQ2070**
Miracles and Idolatry. Trade Paper. Penguin Books Canada, Ltd. Toronto, ON. 2005. 144p. ISBN:0-14-102392-9, ISBN13: 978-0-14-102392-2. Dewey:844.5.
Audience: **g,l,u,f.**

Voltaire **PQ2084**
Correspondance choisie. Le Livre de poche. 1997. ISBN:2-253-13235-7, ISBN13: 978-2-253-13235-6.
Audience: **u,f.**

Voltaire, Francois **PQ2081.E5C84 2002**
Micromegas and Other Short Fictions. Theo Cuffe (Translator), Haydn Mason (Translator, Introduction by). Trade Paper. Penguin Group (USA) Inc. New York, NY. 2002. 208p. Classics Ser. ISBN:0-14-044686-9, ISBN13: 978-0-14-044686-9. Dewey:843.5. LCCN:2003-267176.
Audience: **g,l,u,f.**

Voltaire **B42**
Philosophical Dictionary. Theodore Besterman (Editor, Translator, Introduction by). Trade Paper. Penguin Group (USA) Inc. New York, NY. 1984. 400p. Classics Ser. ISBN:0-14-044257-X, ISBN13: 978-0-14-044257-1. Dewey:848.5/08. LCCN:72-187002.
Audience: **g,l,u,f.**

Voltaire **PQ2086.L4E5 1999**
Letters Concerning the English Nation. Nicholas Cronk (Editor, Introduction by, Notes by). Trade Paper. Oxford University Press, Inc. New York, NY. 1999. 233p. Oxford World's Classics Ser. ISBN:0-19-283708-7, ISBN13: 978-0-19-283708-0. Dewey:942.07. LCCN:00-265621.
Audience: **g,l,u,f.**

Voltaire **PQ2082.C3**
Romans et Contes. Frederic Deloffre (Editor). Library Binding. French & European Publications, Inc. New York, NY. 1979. ISBN:0-7859-3849-4, ISBN13: 978-0-7859-3849-1. Dewey:843.5.
Audience: **u,f.**

Voltaire **PQ2075 1998**
Candide and Other Stories. Roger Pearson (Translator, Introduction by, Notes by). Trade Paper. Oxford University

Press, Inc. New York, NY. 1998. 376p. Oxford World's Classics Ser. ISBN:0-19-283426-6, ISBN13: 978-0-19-283426-3. Dewey:843/.5. LCCN:98-219831.
Audience: **g,l,u,f.**

Voltaire **PQ1979**
The Portable Voltaire. Ben R. Redman (Editor). Trade Paper. Penguin Group (USA) Inc. New York, NY. 1977. 576p. Portable Library, No. 41 ISBN:0-14-015041-2, ISBN13: 978-0-14-015041-4. Dewey:848.508. LCCN:77-004746.
Audience: **g,l,u,f.**

Voltaire **PQ2073**
Melanges. Jacques Van den Heuvel (Editor). Trade Cloth. Schoenhof's Foreign Books, Inc. Cambridge, MA. 1961. Pleiade Ser. ISBN:2-07-010585-7, ISBN13: 978-2-07-010585-4. Dewey:848.509.
Audience: **u,f.**

Modern French Literature > 19th C. > Balzac

Balzac, Honore de **PQ2159**
La comédie humaine, vol. 1. Gallimard. 1976. ISBN:2-07-010851-1, ISBN13: 978-2-07-010851-0.
Audience: **u,f.**

Balzac, Honore de **PQ2159**
La comédie humaine, vol. 10. Gallimard. 1979. ISBN:2-07-010868-6, ISBN13: 978-2-07-010868-8.
Audience: **u,f.**

Balzac, Honore de **PQ2159**
La comédie humaine, vol. 11. Gallimard. 1980. ISBN:2-07-010876-7, ISBN13: 978-2-07-010876-3.
Audience: **u,f.**

Balzac, Honore de **PQ2159**
La comédie humaine, vol. 12. Gallimard. 1981. ISBN:2-07-010877-5, ISBN13: 978-2-07-010877-0.
Audience: **u,f.**

Balzac, Honore de **PQ2159**
La comédie humaine, vol. 2. Gallimard. 1976. ISBN:2-07-010852-X, ISBN13: 978-2-07-010852-7.
Audience: **u,f.**

Balzac, Honore de **PQ2159**
La comédie humaine, vol. 3. Gallimard. 1976. ISBN:2-07-010858-9, ISBN13: 978-2-07-010858-9.
Audience: **u,f.**

Balzac, Honore de **PQ2159**
La comédie humaine, vol. 4. Gallimard. 1976. ISBN:2-07-010862-7, ISBN13: 978-2-07-010862-6.
Audience: **u,f.**

Balzac, Honore de **PQ2159**
La comédie humaine, vol. 5. Gallimard. 1977. ISBN:2-07-010849-X, ISBN13: 978-2-07-010849-7.
Audience: **u,f.**

Balzac, Honore de **PQ2159**
La comédie humaine, vol. 6. Gallimard. 1977. ISBN:2-07-010850-3, ISBN13: 978-2-07-010850-3.
Audience: **u,f.**

Balzac, Honore de **PQ2159**
La comédie humaine, vol. 7. Gallimard. 1977. ISBN:2-07-010874-0, ISBN13: 978-2-07-010874-9.
Audience: **u,f.**

Balzac, Honore de **PQ2159**
La comédie humaine, vol. 8. Gallimard. 1978. ISBN:2-07-010866-X, ISBN13: 978-2-07-010866-4.
Audience: **u,f.**

Balzac, Honore de **PQ2159**
La comédie humaine, vol. 9. Gallimard. 1978. ISBN:2-07-010869-4, ISBN13: 978-2-07-010869-5.
Audience: **u,f.**

Balzac, Honore De **AC1 .E8**
Country Doctor: Quest of the Absolute and Other Novels. Trade Paper. Kessinger Publishing, LLC. Whitefish, MT. 2003. ISBN:0-7661-7117-5, ISBN13: 978-0-7661-7117-6. Dewey:81.
Audience: **g,l,u,f.**

Balzac, Honore De **PQ2178**
History of the Thirteen. Herbert J. Hunt (Editor, Translator). Trade Paper. Penguin Group (USA) Inc. New York, NY. 1975. 400p. Classics Ser. ISBN:0-14-044301-0, ISBN13: 978-0-14-044301-1. Dewey:843/.7. LCCN:74-195973.
Audience: **g,l,u,f.**

Balzac, Honoré de **PQ2161**
Atheist's Mass. Trade Paper. Penguin Group (USA) Inc. New York, NY. 1996. 96p. Classic Ser. ISBN:0-14-600199-0, ISBN13: 978-0-14-600199-4. Dewey:843.7.
Audience: **g,l,u,f.**

Balzac, Honoré de **PZ3.B22**
Cesar Birotteau. Trade Paper. Penguin Group (USA) Inc. New York, NY. 1994. 320p. ISBN:0-14-044600-1, ISBN13: 978-0-14-044600-5. Dewey:843.73.
Audience: **g,l,u,f.**

Balzac, Honoré de **PZ3.B22**
The Chouans. Trade Paper. Kessinger Publishing, LLC. Whitefish, MT. 2004. ISBN:1-4191-5665-9, ISBN13: 978-1-4191-5665-6. Dewey:843/.7.
Audience: **g,l,u,f.**

Balzac, Honoré de **PQ2178**
Droll Stories, Vol. 1. Trade Paper. Kessinger Publishing, LLC. Whitefish, MT. 2004. ISBN:1-4191-1696-7, ISBN13: 978-1-4191-1696-4. Dewey:843/.7.
Audience: **g,l,u,f.**

Balzac, Honoré de
Droll Stories, Vol. 2. Trade Paper. Kessinger Publishing, LLC. Whitefish, MT. 2004. ISBN:1-4191-1694-0, ISBN13: 978-1-4191-1694-0. Dewey:843/.7.
Audience: **g,l,u,f.**

Balzac, Honoré de **PQ2178**
Droll Stories, Vol. 3. Trade Paper. Kessinger Publishing, LLC. Whitefish, MT. 2004. ISBN:1-4191-1695-9, ISBN13: 978-1-4191-1695-7. Dewey:843/.7.
Audience: **g,l,u,f.**

Balzac, Honoré de **PQ2178**
The Black Sheep. Donald Adamson (Translator, Introduction by). Trade Paper. Penguin Group (USA) Inc. New York, NY. 1976. 352p. Penguin Classics Ser. ISBN:0-14-044237-5, ISBN13: 978-0-14-044237-3. Dewey:843/.7. LCCN:77-357255.
Audience: **g,l,u,f.**

Balzac, Honoré de **PQ2178**
Ursule Mirouet. Donald Adamson (Translator, Introduction by). Trade Paper. Penguin Group (USA) Inc. New York, NY. 1976. 272p. Penguin Classics Ser. ISBN:0-14-044316-9, ISBN13: 978-0-14-044316-5. Dewey:843/.7.
Audience: **g,l,u,f.**

Balzac, Honoré de & Brooks, Peter **PQ2168.A374 1998**
Le Pere Goriot: A New Translation: Responses, Contemporaries and Other Novelists, 20th Century Criticism. Burton Raffel (Translator). Trade Paper. W. W. Norton & Company, Inc. New York, NY. 1997. 384p. Critical Editions Ser. ISBN:0-393-97166-X, ISBN13: 978-0-393-97166-8. Dewey:843/.7. LCCN:97-019938.
Audience: **g,l,u,f.**

Balzac, Honoré de **PQ2178**
A Harlot High and Low. Rayner Heppenstall (Translator, Introduction by). Trade Paper. Penguin Group (USA) Inc. New York, NY. 1970. 560p. Classics Ser. ISBN:0-14-044232-4, ISBN13: 978-0-14-044232-8. Dewey:843/.7. LCCN:70-022523.
Audience: **g,l,u,f.**

Balzac, Honoré de **PQ2157**
Le Cousin Pons: Poor Relations. Herbert J. Hunt (Translator, Introduction by). Trade Paper. Penguin Group (USA) Inc. New York, NY. 1978. 336p. Classics Ser. ISBN:0-14-044205-7, ISBN13: 978-0-14-044205-2. LCCN:73-362884.
Audience: **g,l,u,f.**

Balzac, Honoré de **PQ2167.I6E5 2005**
Lost Illusions. Herbert J. Hunt (Translator, Introduction by). Trade Paper. Penguin Group (USA) Inc. New York, NY. 1976. 704p. Classics Ser. ISBN:0-14-044251-0, ISBN13: 978-0-14-044251-9. Dewey:843/.7. LCCN:79-029738.
Audience: **g,l,u,f.**

Balzac, Honoré de **PQ2178**
Murky Business. Herbert J. Hunt (Translator, Introduction by). Trade Paper. Penguin Group (USA) Inc. New York, NY. 1978. 224p. Penguin Classics Ser. ISBN:0-14-044271-5, ISBN13: 978-0-14-044271-7. Dewey:843/.7.
Audience: **g,l,u,f.**

Balzac, Honoré de **PQ2178**
The Wild Ass's Skin. Herbert J. Hunt (Translator, Introduction by). Trade Paper. Penguin Group (USA) Inc. New York, NY. 1977. 288p. Classics Ser. ISBN:0-14-044330-4, ISBN13: 978-0-14-044330-1. Dewey:843/.7. LCCN:78-302574.
Audience: **g,l,u,f.**

Balzac, Honoré de **PQ2178**
Pere Goriot. A. J. Krailsheimer (Translator). Trade Paper. Oxford University Press, Inc. New York, NY. 1999. 300p. Oxford World's Classics Ser. ISBN:0-19-283569-6, ISBN13: 978-0-19-283569-7. Dewey:843/.7.
Audience: **g,l,u,f.**

Balzac, Honoré de **PQ2166.A37 2003**
Eugenie Grandet. Christopher Prendergast (Editor), Sylvia Raphael (Translator). Trade Paper. Oxford University Press, Inc. New York, NY. 2003. 240p. Oxford World's Classics Ser. ISBN:0-19-280474-X, ISBN13: 978-0-19-280474-7. Dewey:843/.7. LCCN:2003-267578.
Audience: **g,l,u,f.**

Balzac, Honoré de **PQ2178**
Cousin Bette. Sylvia Raphael (Translator), David Bellos (Introduction by). Trade Paper. Oxford University Press, Inc. New York, NY. 1998. 528p. Oxford World's Classics Ser. ISBN:0-19-283668-4, ISBN13: 978-0-19-283668-7. Dewey:843/.7.
Audience: **g,l,u,f.**

Balzac, Honoré de **PQ2161.R3**
Balzac: Selected Short Stories. Sylvia Raphael (Translator, Introduction by). Trade Paper. Penguin Group (USA) Inc. New York, NY. 1977. 272p. Classics Ser. ISBN:0-14-044325-8, ISBN13: 978-0-14-044325-7. Dewey:843/.7. LCCN:77-366318.
Audience: **g,l,u,f.**

Balzac, Honoré de **PQ2168.A376 2004**
Pere Goriot. Henry Reed (Translator), Peter Brooks (Introduction by), Henry Reed (Afterword by). Mass Market. Penguin Group (USA) Inc. New York, NY. 2004. 320p. ISBN:0-451-52959-6, ISBN13: 978-0-451-52959-6. Dewey:843/.7. LCCN:2004-055329.
Audience: **g,l,u,f.**

Barthes, Roland **P99**
S/Z: An Essay. Richard Miller (Translator). Trade Paper. Blackwell Publishing, Inc. Malden, MA. 1990. 288p. ISBN:0-631-17607-1, ISBN13: 978-0-631-17607-7. Dewey:302.2.
Audience: **u,f.**

Butler, Ronnie **PQ2184.H55**
Balzac and the French Revolution. Trade Cloth. Rowman & Littlefield Publishers, Inc. Lanham, MD. 1983. 280p. ISBN:0-389-20406-4, ISBN13: 978-0-389-20406-0. Dewey:843/.7. LCCN:83-009926.
Audience: **u,f.**

Canfield, Arthur G. **PQ2159**
The Reappearing Characters in Balzac's Comedie Humaine. Edward B. Ham (Editor). Trade Cloth. Greenwood Publishing Group, Inc. Portsmouth, NH. 1977. 61p. Studies in Romance Languages and Literature, No. 37 ISBN:0-8371-9836-4, ISBN13: 978-0-8371-9836-1. Dewey:843.7. LCCN:77-014166.
Audience: **u,f.**

Hunt, Herbert James **PQ2159.C72**
Balzac's Comedie Humaine. Paper Text. Textbook Publishers. Temecula, CA. 2003. 506p. ISBN:0-7581-2155-5, ISBN13: 978-0-7581-2155-4. Dewey:843.7.
Audience: **l,u.**

Kanes, Martin **PQ2181.C75 1990**
Critical Essays on Honore de Balzac. Trade Cloth. Thomson Gale. Farmington Hills, MI. 1990. 248p. Critical Essays on World Literature Ser. ISBN:0-8161-8845-9, ISBN13: 978-0-8161-8845-1. Dewey:843/.7. LCCN:89-039239.
Audience: **l,u,f.** *Choice, 1990.*

Lukács, György **PN601**
Studies in European Realism: A Sociological Survey of the Writings of Balzac, Stendhal, Zola, Tolstoy, Gorki and Others. Trade Cloth. Merlin Press Ltd. London, 1972. 277p. ISBN:0-85036-146-X, ISBN13: 978-0-85036-146-9. Dewey:809/.91/2.
Audience: **l,u.**

Maurois, Andre **PQ2178**
Prometheus: The Life of Balzac. Trade Paper. Avalon Publishing Group. New York, NY. 1983. 573p. ISBN:0-88184-023-8, ISBN13: 978-0-88184-023-0. Dewey:848.7.
Audience: **g,l,u,f.**

Prendergast, Christopher **PQ2181.P68 1978**
Balzac: Fiction and Melodrama. Cloth Text. Holmes & Meier Publishers, Inc. Teaneck, NJ. 1979. 205p. ISBN:0-8419-0457-X, ISBN13: 978-0-8419-0457-6. Dewey:843/.7. LCCN:78-011267.
Audience: **l,u.**

Pritchett, V. S. **PQ2178**
Balzac. Trade Paper. Knopf Publishing Group. New York, NY. 2002. 272p. ISBN:0-09-942957-8, ISBN13: 978-0-09-942957-9. Dewey:843.7.
Audience: **l,u,f.**

Robb, Graham **PQ2178.R48 1994**
Balzac: A Life. Trade Cloth. W. W. Norton & Company, Inc. New York, NY. 1994. xvii, 521p. ISBN:0-393-03679-0, ISBN13: 978-0-393-03679-4. Dewey:843/.7 B. LCCN:94-018614.
Audience: **g,l,u,f.** *Choice, 1995.*

Stowe, William W. **PN3499**
Balzac, James and the Realistic Novel. Trade Cloth. Princeton University Press. Princeton, NJ. 1983. 224p. ISBN:0-691-06567-5, ISBN13: 978-0-691-06567-0. Dewey:809.3/1. LCCN:82-061388.
Audience: **u,f.**

Modern French Literature > 19th C. > Baudelaire

Baudelaire, Charles **PQ2191**
Oeuvres Completes, Tome 1. Trade Cloth. Schoenhof's Foreign Books, Inc. Cambridge, MA. 1975. 1604p. Pleiade Ser. ISBN:2-07-010829-5, ISBN13: 978-2-07-010829-9. Dewey:841.
Audience: **u,f.**

Baudelaire, Charles **PQ2191.Z5A3413 1995**
Intimate Journals. Norman Cameron (Translator), Richard Howard (Preface by). Trade Paper. Penguin Group (USA) Inc. New York, NY. 1996. 96p. Syrens Ser. ISBN:0-14-038911-3, ISBN13: 978-0-14-038911-1. Dewey:848/.803 B. LCCN:96-135511.
Audience: **g,l,u,f.**

Baudelaire, Charles **PQ2387.R5**
Les Fleurs du Mal. Graham Chesters (Editor). Trade Paper. Bristol Classical Press. London, 1995. 248p. French Texts ISBN:1-85399-344-1, ISBN13: 978-1-85399-344-2. Dewey:841.8.
Audience: **u,f.**

Baudelaire, Charles **PQ2387.R5**
Les Fleurs du Mal. Richard Howard (Translator), Michael Mazur (Illustrator). Trade Paper. David R. Godine Publisher. Boston, MA. 1983. 400p. ISBN:0-87923-462-8, ISBN13: 978-0-87923-462-1. Dewey:841.8. LCCN:81-013283.
Audience: **g,l,u,f.**

Baudelaire, Charles **PQ2191.Z5A42 2006**
Intimate Journals. Christopher Isherwood (Translator), W. H. Auden (Introduction by). Trade Paper. Dover Publications, Inc. Mineola, NY. 2006. 128p. ISBN:0-486-44778-2, ISBN13: 978-0-486-44778-0. Dewey:848/.803 B. LCCN:2006-040012.
Audience: **g,l,u,f.**

Baudelaire, Charles **PQ2191.S6E5 1989**
The Parisian Prowler: Le Spleen de Paris, Petits Poemes en Prose. Edward K. Kaplan (Translator). Trade Cloth. University of Georgia Press. Athens, GA. 1990. 168p. ISBN:0-8203-1162-6, ISBN13: 978-0-8203-1162-3. Dewey:841/.8. LCCN:89-004940.
Audience: **g,l,u,f.** *Choice, 1991.*

Baudelaire, Charles **PQ2191**
Oeuvres Completes. Le Dantec (Editor). Trade Cloth. Schoenhof's Foreign Books, Inc. Cambridge, MA. Pleiade Ser., Vol. 2 ISBN:2-07-010853-8, ISBN13: 978-2-07-010853-4. Dewey:841.
Audience: **u,f.**

Baudelaire, Charles **PQ2191.A244 1991**
The Prose Poems and La Fanfarlo. Rosemary Lloyd (Translator, Introduction by). Trade Paper. Oxford University Press, Inc. New York, NY. 1991. 160p. Oxford World's Classics Ser. ISBN:0-19-282703-0, ISBN13: 978-0-19-282703-6. Dewey:841/.8. LCCN:90-044124.
Audience: **g,l,u,f.**

Baudelaire, Charles **PQ2191.Z5A4 1986**
Selected Letters of Charles Baudelaire: The Conquest of Solitude. Rosemary Lloyd (Editor, Translator). Trade Cloth. University of Chicago Press. Chicago, IL. 1986. 300p. ISBN:0-226-03928-5, ISBN13: 978-0-226-03928-2. Dewey:841/.8. LCCN:85-016461.
Audience: **g,l,u,f.** *Choice, 1986.*

Baudelaire, Charles **841/.8**
Complete Poems: Charles Baudelaire. Walter Martin (Translator). Cloth Text. Routledge. New York, NY. 2002. 128p. Fyfield Bks. ISBN:0-415-94091-5, ISBN13: 978-0-415-94091-7. Dewey:PQ2191.
Audience: **g,l,u,f.**

Baudelaire, Charles **PQ2191.F6E5**
The Flowers of Evil. James McGowan (Translator, Notes by), Jonathan Culler (Introduction by). Trade Paper. Oxford University Press, Inc. New York, NY. 1998. 458p. Oxford World's Classics Ser. ISBN:0-19-283545-9, ISBN13: 978-0-19-283545-1. Dewey:841/.8. LCCN:92-028008.
Audience: **g,l,u,f.**

Benjamin, Walter **PQ2191.Z5B39713 2006**
The Writer of Modern Life: Essays on Charles Baudelaire. Michael W. Jennings (Editor), Howard Eiland, Edmund Jephcott, Rodney Livingstone & Harry Zohn (Translators). Trade Paper. Harvard University Press. Cambridge, MA. 2006. 320p. ISBN:0-674-02287-4, ISBN13: 978-0-674-02287-4. Dewey:841/.8. LCCN:2006-043584.
Audience: **u,f.**

Benjamin, Walter **PQ2191**
Charles Baudelaire: A Lyric Poet in the Era of High Capitalism. Harry Zohn (Translator). Trade Cloth. Analytical Psychology Club of San Francisco, Inc. San Francisco, CA. 1973. 192p. ISBN:0-902308-64-5, ISBN13: 978-0-902308-64-0. Dewey:841/.8. LCCN:73-176657.
Audience: **u,f.**

Hemmings, Frederic William John **PQ2191.Z5.H4 1982**
Baudelaire the Damned. Trade Cloth. Thomson Gale. Farmington Hills, MI. 1982. 256p. ISBN:0-684-17774-9, ISBN13: 978-0-684-17774-8. Dewey:841/.8. LCCN:82-010298.
Audience: **l,u.**

Leakey, F. W. **PQ2191.F63 L43 1992**
Baudelaire: Les Fleurs du Mal. Trade Cloth. Cambridge University Press. New York, NY. 1992. 142p. Landmarks of World Literature Ser. ISBN:0-521-36116-8, ISBN13: 978-0-521-36116-3. Dewey:841/.8. LCCN:91-019653.
Audience: **l,u.** *Choice, 1992.*

Lloyd, Rosemary **PQ2191.Z5L59 2002**
Baudelaire's World. Trade Cloth. Cornell University Press. Ithaca, NY. 2002. 320p. ISBN:0-8014-4026-2, ISBN13: 978-0-8014-4026-7. Dewey:841/.8. LCCN:2002-007299.
Audience: **g,u,f.** *Choice, 2003.*

Lloyd, Rosemary (Editor) **PQ2191.Z5C24 2005**
The Cambridge Companion to Baudelaire. Cloth Text. Cambridge University Press. New York, NY. 2006. 258p. Cambridge Companions to Literature Ser. ISBN:0-521-83094-X, ISBN13: 978-0-521-83094-2. Dewey:841/.8. LCCN:2005-012929.
Audience: **u,f.**

Sartre, Jean-Paul **PQ2387.R5**
Baudelaire. Martin Turnell (Translator). Trade Paper. New Directions Publishing Corporation. New York, NY. 1967. ISBN:0-8112-0189-9, ISBN13: 978-0-8112-0189-6. Dewey:841.8. LCCN:50-006845.
Audience: **g,l,u,f.**

Thompson, William J. (Editor) **PQ2387.R5**
Understanding "Les Fleurs du Mal" Critical Readings. Trade Paper. Vanderbilt University Press. Nashville, TN. 1997. 256p. ISBN:0-8265-1297-6, ISBN13: 978-0-8265-1297-0. Dewey:841/.8. LCCN:97-004698.
Audience: **l,u,f.** *Choice, 1997.*

Modern French Literature > 19th C. > B-D

Chateaubriand, Francois-Rene de **DC255.C4**
Memoires D'Outre-Tombe, Tombe 2. Trade Paper. Schoenhof's Foreign Books, Inc. Cambridge, MA. 1951. 1496p. Pleiade Ser. ISBN:2-07-010128-2, ISBN13: 978-2-07-010128-3. Dewey:840.
Audience: **u,f.**

Chateaubriand, Francois-Rene de **DC255.C4**
Memoires D'Outre-Tombe, Tome 1. Trade Paper. Schoenhof's Foreign Books, Inc. Cambridge, MA. 1951. 1232p. Pleiade Ser. ISBN:2-07-010127-4, ISBN13: 978-2-07-010127-6. Dewey:840.
Audience: **u,f.**

Chateaubriand, Francois-Rene de **PQ2205.A8**
Atala and René. Irving Putter (Translator). Trade Cloth. University of California Press. Berkeley, CA. 1952. ISBN:0-520-00223-7, ISBN13: 978-0-520-00223-4.
Audience: **g,l,u,f.**

Chénier, André **PQ1965**
OEuvres poétiques. Buisson, Georges (Editor). Paradigme. 2005. ISBN:2-86878-233-7, ISBN13: 978-2-86878-233-5.
Audience: **u,f.**

Daudet, Alphonse **PQ2216.T4**
Tartarin of Tarascon. Trade Paper. Kessinger Publishing, LLC. Whitefish, MT. 2004. ISBN:1-4191-5081-2, ISBN13: 978-1-4191-5081-4. Dewey:843.88.
Audience: **g,l,u,f.**

Painter, George D. **PQ2205.Z5.P34 1978**
Chateaubriand: The Longed-for Tempests, 1768-93, Vol. 1. Trade Cloth. Random House Children's Books. New York, NY. 1978. v. :p. ISBN:0-394-42658-4, ISBN13: 978-0-394-42658-7. Dewey:848/.6/09. LCCN:77-020366.
Audience: **g,l,u,f.**

Smethurst, Colin **PQ2063.S3**
Chateaubriand: "Atala" and "Rene". Trade Cloth. Grant & Cutler. London, 1996. 91p. ISBN:0-7293-0384-5, ISBN13: 978-0-7293-0384-2. Dewey:843.6.
Audience: **l,u.**

Switzer, Richard **PQ2205.Z5**
Chateaubriand. Library Binding. Irvington Publishers. New York, NY. 1971. Twayne's World Authors Ser. ISBN:0-8057-2208-4, ISBN13: 978-0-8057-2208-6. Dewey:848/.6/09. LCCN:71-125248.
Audience: **l,u.**

Modern French Literature > 19th C. > Dumas (pere et fils)

Dumas, Alexandre **PQ2222**
Les mousquetaires, Vol. 2. Schopp, Claude (Editor). Laffont. 1991. ISBN:2-221-06453-4, ISBN13: 978-2-221-06453-5.
Audience: **u,f.**

Dumas, Alexandre **PQ2222**
Les mousquetaires, Vol. 3. Schopp, Claude (Editor). Laffont. 1991. ISBN:2-221-06454-2, ISBN13: 978-2-221-06454-2.
Audience: **u,f.**

Dumas, Alexandre **PQ2178**
The Black Tulip. Trade Paper. Oxford University Press, Inc. New York, NY. 2000. 288p. Oxford World's Classics Ser. ISBN:0-19-283750-8, ISBN13: 978-0-19-283750-9. Dewey:843/.7.
Audience: **g,l,u,f.**

Dumas, Alexandre **PQ2231**
La Dame aux Camélias : le roman, le drame, La Traviata. Flammarion. 1999. ISBN:2-08-070381-1, ISBN13: 978-2-08-070381-1.
Audience: **u,f.**

Dumas, Alexandre **PQ2222**
Les mousquetaires, Vol. 1. Schopp, Claude (Editor). Laffont. 1991. ISBN:2-221-06452-6, ISBN13: 978-2-221-06452-8.
Audience: **u,f.**

Dumas, Alexandre **PQ2226**
The Count of Monte Cristo. Robin Buss (Translator, Introduction by, Notes by). Trade Paper. Penguin Group (USA) Inc. New York, NY. 2003. 1312p. Penguin Classics Ser. ISBN:0-14-044926-4, ISBN13: 978-0-14-044926-6. Dewey:847/.3. LCCN:2003-270054.
Audience: **g,l,u,f.**

Dumas, Alexandre **PQ2231.D2E5 2000**
La Dame aux Camelias. David Coward (Translator). Trade Paper. Oxford University Press, Inc. New York, NY. 2000. 244p. Oxford World's Classics Ser. ISBN:0-19-283638-2, ISBN13: 978-0-19-283638-0. Dewey:843/.7. LCCN:00-711204.
Audience: **g,l,u,f.**

Dumas, Alexandre **PQ2178**
La Reine Margot. David Coward (Editor). Trade Paper. Oxford University Press, Inc. New York, NY. 1999. 558p. Oxford World's Classics Ser. ISBN:0-19-283844-X, ISBN13: 978-0-19-283844-5. Dewey:843/.7.
Audience: **g,l,u,f.**

Dumas, Alexandre **PQ2229.V6E5 1998**
Twenty Years After. David Coward (Introduction by, Notes by). Trade Paper. Oxford University Press, Inc. New York, NY. 1998. 872p. Oxford World's Classics Ser. ISBN:0-19-283843-1, ISBN13: 978-0-19-283843-8. Dewey:843/.7. LCCN:99-188043.
Audience: **g,l,u,f.**

Dumas, Alexandre **PQ2178**
Louise de la Valliere. David Coward (Editor, Introduction by, Notes by). Trade Paper. Oxford University Press, Inc. New York, NY. 1998. 768p. Oxford World's Classics Ser. ISBN:0-19-283465-7, ISBN13: 978-0-19-283465-2. Dewey:843.7.
Audience: **g,l,u,f.**

Dumas, Alexandre **PQ2231.D2E5 2004**
Camille. Toril Moi (Introduction by). Trade Paper. Penguin Group (USA) Inc. New York, NY. 2004. 272p. ISBN:0-451-52920-0, ISBN13: 978-0-451-52920-6. Dewey:843.8. LCCN:2003-062212.
Audience: **g,l,u,f.**

Dumas, Alexandre **PQ2178**
The Three Musketeers. David A. Roach (Illustrator), Clare West (Contribution by). Trade Paper. Oxford University Press. Don Mills, ON. 2003. 64p. ISBN:0-19-424399-0, ISBN13: 978-0-19-424399-5. Dewey:843/.7.
Audience: **g,l,u,f.**

Dumas, Alexandre **PQ2228**
The Three Musketeers. Lord Sudley (Translator). Trade Paper. Penguin Group (USA) Inc. New York, NY. 1982. 720p. Penguin Classics Ser. ISBN:0-14-044025-9, ISBN13: 978-0-14-044025-6. Dewey:843/.7. LCCN:00-009173.
Audience: **g,l,u,f.**

Dumas, Alexandre **PE1119**
Dominoes. Clare West (Contribution by). Trade Paper. Oxford University Press. Oxford, 2004. 80p. ISBN:0-19-424343-5, ISBN13: 978-0-19-424343-8. Dewey:428.6.
Audience: **g,l,u,f.**

Dumas, Alexandre **PQ2227 .H6813**
The Man in the Iron Mask. Jack Zipes (Afterword by), Roger Celestin (Introduction by). Mass Market. Penguin Group (USA) Inc. New York, NY. 2006. 512p. ISBN:0-451-53013-6, ISBN13: 978-0-451-53013-4. Dewey:[Fic]. LCCN:2006-282421.
Audience: **g,l,u,f.**

Hemmings, F. W. J. **PQ2230**
The King of Romance: A Portrait of Alexandre Dumas. Trade Cloth. Penguin Books, Ltd. London, 1979. 231p. ISBN:0-241-10264-2, ISBN13: 978-0-241-10264-0. Dewey:843/.7.
Audience: **g,l,u,f.**

Maurois, Andre **PQ2230.M3313 1971**
Titans: A Three-Generation Biography of the Dumas. Library Binding. Greenwood Publishing Group, Inc. Portsmouth, NH. 1971. 508p. ISBN:0-8371-6151-7, ISBN13: 978-0-8371-6151-8. Dewey:840.9/007. LCCN:78-156201.
Audience: **g,l,u,f.**

Schopp, Claude **PQ2230.S3613 1988**
Alexandre Dumas: Genius of Life. Trade Cloth. Scholastic Library Publishing. Danbury, CT. 1988. vi, 506p. ISBN:0-531-15093-3, ISBN13: 978-0-531-15093-1. Dewey:843/.7. LCCN:88-026136.
Audience: **g,l,u,f.** *Choice, 1989.*

Stowe, Richard S. **PQ2230.S84**
Alexandre Dumas, pere. Library Binding. Thomson Gale. Farmington Hills, MI. 1976. 164p. World Authors Ser. ISBN:0-8057-6230-2, ISBN13: 978-0-8057-6230-3. Dewey:843/.7. LCCN:75-043919.
Audience: **l,u.**

Modern French Literature > 19th C. > F

France, Anatole **PQ2254.A62**
Novels of Anatole France: Penguin Island; the Crime of Sylvestre Bonnard and the Revolt of the Angels. Trade Paper. Kessinger Publishing, LLC. Whitefish, MT. 2005. ISBN:1-4191-5303-X, ISBN13: 978-1-4191-5303-7. Dewey:843/.8.
Audience: **g,l,u,f.**

France, Anatole — **PQ2469.Z5**
The Gods Will Have Blood. Frederick Davies (Translator, Introduction by). Trade Paper. Penguin Group (USA) Inc. New York, NY. 1990. 256p. Penguin Twentieth-Century Classics Ser. ISBN:0-14-018457-0, ISBN13: 978-0-14-018457-0. Dewey:843.8.
Audience: **g,l,u,f.**

France, Anatole — **PZ3.F844**
Thais. Robert B. Douglas (Translator). Trade Paper. Kessinger Publishing, LLC. Whitefish, MT. 2004. ISBN:1-4179-1709-1, ISBN13: 978-1-4179-1709-9. Dewey:843/.8.
Audience: **g,l,u,f.**

Fromentin, Eugene — **PQ2256.F5**
Dominique. Edward Marsh (Translator). Trade Paper. Soho Book Company. London, 1986. 250p. ISBN:0-948166-06-1, ISBN13: 978-0-948166-06-8. Dewey:843.89.
Audience: **g,l,u,f.**

Fromentin, Eugène — **PQ2256.F5**
Dominique, Vol. 1. Wright, Barbara (Editor). M. Didier. 1966.
Audience: **u,f.**

Fromentin, Eugène — **PQ2256.F5**
Dominique, Vol. 2. Wright, Barbara (Editor). M. DIdier. 1966.
Audience: **u,f.**

Wright, Barbara — **ND553.F8W75 2000**
Eugene Fromentin: A Life in Art and Letters. Alan Raitt (Editor). Trade Cloth. Peter Lang Publishing, Inc. New York, NY. 2000. 644p. Le Romantisme et Apres en France Ser., Vol. 5 ISBN:0-8204-4640-8, ISBN13: 978-0-8204-4640-0. Dewey:759.4 B. LCCN:99-088990.
Audience: **g,l,u,f.**

Modern French Literature > 19th C. > Flaubert

Bart, Benjamin F. — **PQ2247 .B3**
Flaubert. Trade Cloth. Syracuse University Press. Syracuse, NY. 1967. ISBN:0-8156-0057-7, ISBN13: 978-0-8156-0057-2. Dewey:843/.8. LCCN:67-027410.
Audience: **l,u.**

Berg, William J. & Martin, Laurey K. — **PQ2249.B43 1997**
Gustave Flaubert. Trade Cloth. Thomson Gale. Farmington Hills, MI. 1997. xxii, 179p. World Authors Ser., Vol. 866 ISBN:0-8057-8295-8, ISBN13: 978-0-8057-8295-0. Dewey:843/.8. LCCN:96-039866.
Audience: **l,u.**

Bloom, Harold (Introduction by) — **PQ2249.G84 1989**
Gustave Flaubert. Library Binding. Chelsea House Publishers. Langhorne, PA. 1990. 296p. Modern Critical Views Ser. ISBN:1-55546-302-9, ISBN13: 978-1-55546-302-1. Dewey:843/.8. LCCN:87-015488.
Audience: **l,u.**

Bloom, Harold (Introduction by) — **PQ2246.M3G87 1987**
Gustave Flaubert's Madame Bovary. Trade Cloth. Chelsea House Publishers. Langhorne, PA. 1987. Modern Critical Interpretations Ser. ISBN:1-55546-067-4, ISBN13: 978-1-55546-067-9. Dewey:843/.8. LCCN:87-015786.
Audience: **l,u.**

Brown, Frederick — **PQ2247.B685 2006**
Flaubert: A Biography. Trade Cloth. Little Brown & Company. New York, NY. 2006. 640p. ISBN:0-316-11878-8, ISBN13: 978-0-316-11878-1. Dewey:843/.8 B. LCCN:2005-017036.
Audience: **g,l,u,f.** *Choice, 2006.*

Flaubert, Gustave — **PQ2469.Z5**
Memoirs of a Madman. Trade Paper. Hesperus Press. London, 2003. 96p. ISBN:1-84391-000-4, ISBN13: 978-1-84391-000-8. Dewey:843.8.
Audience: **g,l,u,f.**

Flaubert, Gustave — **PQ2246**
OEuvres complètes, Vol. 1: Écrits de Jeunesse. Premiers romans. la tentation de saint Antoine. Madame Bovary. Salambo. Éditions du Seuil. 1964.
Audience: **u,f.**

Flaubert, Gustave — **PQ2246**
OEuvres complètes, Vol. 2: L'éducation sentimentale. Trois contes. Bouvard et Pécuchet. Théâtre. Voyages. Éditions du Seuil. 1964.
Audience: **u,f.**

Flaubert, Gustave — **PQ2246**
OEuvres complètes, Vol. 1. Gothot-Mersch, Claudine (Editor); Sagnes, Guy (Editor). Flammarion. 2001. Pleiade Series ISBN:2-07-011475-9, ISBN13: 978-2-07-011475-7.
Audience: **u,f.**

Flaubert, Gustave — **PQ2246**
Sentimental Education. Robert Baldick (Translator), Geoffrey Wall (Introduction by, Notes by, Revised by). Trade Paper. Penguin Group (USA) Inc. New York, NY. 2004. 512p. Penguin Classics Ser. ISBN:0-14-044797-0, ISBN13: 978-0-14-044797-2. Dewey:843/.8. LCCN:2004-557583.
Audience: **g,l,u,f.**

Flaubert, Gustave — **PQ2246.T4**
November: Fragments in a Nondescript Style. Andrew Brown (Translator). Trade Paper, Saddle Stitched. Hesperus Press. London, 2005. 106p. Hesperus Classics Ser. ISBN:1-84391-112-4, ISBN13: 978-1-84391-112-8. Dewey:843.8.
Audience: **g,l,u,f.**

Flaubert, Gustave — **PQ2246.M2E5 2004**
Madame Bovary. Ed. 2. Paul De Man (Editor, Translator), Eleanor Marx Aveling (Translator). Paper Text. W. W. Norton & Company, Inc. New York, NY. 2004. 688p. A Norton Critical Edition Ser. ISBN:0-393-97917-2, ISBN13: 978-0-393-97917-6. Dewey:843/.8. LCCN:2004-054771.
Audience: **g,l,u,f.**

Flaubert, Gustave **PQ2246.A25 1991**
Early Writings of Gustave Flaubert. Robert B. Griffin (Translator). Cloth Text. University of Nebraska Press. Lincoln, NE. 1991. 275p. ISBN:0-8032-1982-2, ISBN13: 978-0-8032-1982-3. Dewey:843/.8. LCCN:91-011715.
Audience: **g,l,u,f.** *Choice, 1992.*

Flaubert, Gustave **PQ2246.T4E5 2001**
The Temptation of St. Anthony. Lafcadio Hearn (Translator), Michel Foucault (Introduction by). Trade Paper. Random House Adult Trade Publishing Group. New York, NY. 2002. 288p. The Modern Library Classics ISBN:0-375-75912-3, ISBN13: 978-0-375-75912-3. Dewey:843/.8. LCCN:2001-044480.
Audience: **g,l,u,f.**

Flaubert, Gustave **PQ2247.A2 1993**
Flaubert-Sand: The Correspondence. Alphonse Jacobs (Editor), Francis Steegmuller & Barbara Bray (Translators), Francis Steegmuller (Foreword by, Notes by). Trade Cloth. Alfred A. Knopf Inc. New York, NY. 1993. xxxii, 428p. ISBN:0-679-41898-9, ISBN13: 978-0-679-41898-6. Dewey:843/.8. LCCN:92-016976.
Audience: **u,f.** *Choice, 1993.*

Flaubert, Gustave **PQ2469.Z5**
Three Tales. A. J. Krailsheimer (Translator, Introduction by, Notes by). Trade Paper. Oxford University Press, Inc. New York, NY. 1999. 140p. Oxford World's Classics Ser. ISBN:0-19-283631-5, ISBN13: 978-0-19-283631-1. Dewey:843/.8.
Audience: **g,l,u,f.**

Flaubert, Gustave **PQ3919.R74**
Salammbo. Alban J. Krailsheimer (Translator). Trade Paper. Penguin Group (USA) Inc. New York, NY. 1977. 288p. Penguin Classics Ser. ISBN:0-14-044328-2, ISBN13: 978-0-14-044328-8. Dewey:843. LCCN:77-569876.
Audience: **g,l,u,f.**

Flaubert, Gustave **PQ2246.B7E5 2005**
Bouvard and Pecuchet. Mark Polizzotti (Translator). Trade Cloth. Dalkey Archive Press. Normal, IL. 2005. 350p. ISBN:1-56478-393-6, ISBN13: 978-1-56478-393-6. Dewey:843/.8. LCCN:2004-063480.
Audience: **g,l,u,f.**

Flaubert, Gustave **PQ2469.Z5**
Madame Bovary. Francis Steegmuller (Translator). Trade Cloth. Random House. London, 1993. 384p. ISBN:1-85715-140-2, ISBN13: 978-1-85715-140-4. Dewey:843/.8.
Audience: **g,l,u,f.**

Flaubert, Gustave **PQ2247.A2**
The Letters of Gustave Flaubert, 1857-1880, Vol. II. Francis Steegmuller (Editor, Translator). Trade Cloth. Harvard University Press. Cambridge, MA. 1982. 336p. Letters of Gustave Flaubert, 1857-1880 Ser., Vol. II ISBN:0-674-52640-6, ISBN13: 978-0-674-52640-2. Dewey:843/.8. LCCN:79-013505.
Audience: **u,f.**

Flaubert, Gustave & Turgenev, Ivan **PQ2247.A2 1985**
Flaubert and Turgenev: A Friendship in Letters: The Complete Correspondence. Ed. 1. Barbara Beaumont (Editor). Trade Cloth. W. W. Norton & Company, Inc. New York, NY. 1985. 197p. ISBN:0-393-02206-4, ISBN13: 978-0-393-02206-3. Dewey:843/.8. LCCN:85-015250.
Audience: **u,f.** *Choice, 1986.*

Flaubert, Gustave **PQ2246.D53**
Dictionary of Received Ideas. Geoffrey Wall (Translator), Julian Barnes (Preface by). Trade Paper. Penguin Group (USA) Inc. New York, NY. 1995. 80p. Syrens Ser. ISBN:0-14-038904-0, ISBN13: 978-0-14-038904-3. Dewey:847/.8.
Audience: **g,l,u,f.**

Flaubert, Gustave **PQ2247.A2 1997**
Selected Letters. Geoffrey Wall (Translator, Introduction by). Trade Paper. Penguin Group (USA) Inc. New York, NY. 1998. 464p. Penguin Classics Ser. ISBN:0-14-044607-9, ISBN13: 978-0-14-044607-4. Dewey:843.8. LCCN:98-140276.
Audience: **g,l,u,f.**

Flaubert, Gustave **PQ2246**
Three Tales. Roger Whitehouse (Translator). Trade Paper, Perfect. Penguin Group (USA) Inc. New York, NY. 2005. 144p. ISBN:0-14-044800-4, ISBN13: 978-0-14-044800-9. Dewey:843/.8.
Audience: **g,l,u,f.**

Heath, Stephen C. **PQ2246.M3 H38 1992**
Flaubert: Madame Bovary. J. P. Stern (Contribution by). Trade Paper. Cambridge University Press. New York, NY. 1992. 179p. Landmarks of World Literature Ser. ISBN:0-521-31483-6, ISBN13: 978-0-521-31483-1. Dewey:843/.8. LCCN:91-019758.
Audience: **l,u.** *Choice, 1993.*

Lloyd, Rosemary **PQ2246.M3L5 1990**
Madame Bovary. Trade Cloth. Routledge. New York, NY. 1989. 336p. Unwin Critical Library ISBN:0-04-800084-1, ISBN13: 978-0-04-800084-2. Dewey:843/.8. LCCN:89-036516.
Audience: **l,u,f.** *Choice, 1991.*

Maraini, Dacia **PQ2246.M3M3713 1998**
Searching for Emma: Gustave Flaubert and Madame Bovary. Vincent J. Bertolini (Translator). Trade Cloth. University of Chicago Press. Chicago, IL. 1998. 156p. ISBN:0-226-50430-1, ISBN13: 978-0-226-50430-8. Dewey:843/.8. LCCN:97-023304.
Audience: **u,f.** *Choice, 1998.*

Nadeau, Maurice **PQ2247.N313**
The Greatness of Flaubert. Trade Cloth. Library Press, The. Randsburg, CA. 1972. 307p. ISBN:0-912050-09-8, ISBN13: 978-0-912050-09-6. Dewey:843/.8. LCCN:77-161408.
Audience: **l,u.**

Steegmuller, Francis **PQ2247.S8 2004**
Flaubert and Madame Bovary. Victor Brombert (Introduction by). Trade Paper. New York Review of Books, Incorporated, The. New York, NY. 2004. 400p. New York Review Books Classics ISBN:1-59017-116-0, ISBN13: 978-1-59017-116-5. Dewey:843/.8 B. LCCN:2004-017960.
Audience: **g,l,u,f.**

Unwin, Timothy (Editor) **PQ2249.C28 2004**
The Cambridge Companion to Flaubert. Trade Paper. Cambridge University Press. New York, NY. 2004. 254p. Cambridge Companions to Literature Ser. ISBN:0-521-89459-X, ISBN13: 978-0-521-89459-3. Dewey:843/.8. LCCN:2004-052833.
Audience: **l,u,f.** *Choice, 2005.*

Modern French Literature > 19th C. > G-H

Gaboriau, Emile **PQ2257.G2**
The Mystery of Orcival. Trade Paper. Kessinger Publishing, LLC. Whitefish, MT. 2005. ISBN:1-4179-0342-2, ISBN13: 978-1-4179-0342-9. Dewey:843.89.
Audience: **g,l,u,f.**

Gautier, Théophile **PQ2258**
OEuvres complètes. Montandon, Alain (Editor); Geisler-Szmulewicz, Anne (Editor). Champion. 2004. ISBN:2-7453-0966-8, ISBN13: 978-2-7453-0966-2.
Audience: **u,f.**

Gautier, Théophile **PQ2258**
Mademoiselle de Maupin. Helen Constantine (Translator), Patricia Duncker (Introduction by). Trade Paper. Penguin Group (USA) Inc. New York, NY. 2006. 384p. ISBN:0-14-044813-6, ISBN13: 978-0-14-044813-9. Dewey:843.7.
Audience: **g,l,u,f.**

Goncourt, Edmond L. & Goncourt, Jules A. **PQ2261**
Goncourt Journals, 1851-1870. Lewis Galantiere (Translator). Trade Cloth. Greenwood Publishing Group, Inc. Portsmouth, NH. 1969. 377p. ISBN:0-8371-0448-3, ISBN13: 978-0-8371-0448-5. Dewey:843.8. LCCN:69-010099.
Audience: **g,l,u,f.**

Grant, Richard B. **PQ2258.Z5**
Theophile Gautier. Library Binding. Thomson Gale. Farmington Hills, MI. 1975. World Authors Ser. ISBN:0-8057-6213-2, ISBN13: 978-0-8057-6213-6. Dewey:848/.7/09.
Audience: **l,u.**

Nerval, Gérard de **PQ2260**
OEuvres complètes, Vol. 3. Gallimard. 1984. ISBN:2-07-011262-4, ISBN13: 978-2-07-011262-3.
Audience: **u,f.**

Nerval, Gérard de **PQ2260.G36**
Oeuvres, Vol. 1. Beguin & Richer (Editors). Trade Cloth. Schoenhof's Foreign Books, Inc. Cambridge, MA. Pleiade Ser. ISBN:2-07-011067-2, ISBN13: 978-2-07-011067-4.
Audience: **u,f.**

Nerval, Gérard de **PQ2260**
Oeuvres, Vol. 2. Beguin & Richer (Editors). Trade Cloth. Schoenhof's Foreign Books, Inc. Cambridge, MA. Pleiade Ser. ISBN:2-07-011029-X, ISBN13: 978-2-07-011029-2.
Audience: **u,f.**

Nerval, Gérard de **PQ2178**
Aurelia Followed by Sylvie. Ed. 2. Kendall Lappin (Translator), Eric Basso (Introduction by, Notes by). Trade Paper. Leaping Dog Press. San Jose, CA. 1993. 160p. ISBN:1-878580-07-8, ISBN13: 978-1-878580-07-8. Dewey:843/.7.
Audience: **g,l,u,f.**

Nerval, Gérard de **PQ2326**
Chimeras. Derek Mahon (Translator). Trade Cloth. Northwestern University Press. Evanston, IL. 1996. ISBN:0-14-038929-6, ISBN13: 978-0-14-038929-6. Dewey:841/.7.
Audience: **g,l,u,f.**

Nerval, Gérard de **PQ2260.G36.C5 1973**
Les Chimeres. Norma Rinsler (Editor). Cloth Text. Continuum International Publishing Group, Ltd. London, 1973. 144p. French Poets Ser. ISBN:0-485-14702-5, ISBN13: 978-0-485-14702-5. Dewey:841/.7. LCCN:73-177864.
Audience: **u,f.**

Nerval, Gérard de **PQ2260.G36A25 1999**
De Nerval: Selected Writings. Richard Sieburth (Translator, Intro and Notes by). Trade Paper. Penguin Group (USA) Inc. New York, NY. 1999. 448p. Classics Ser. ISBN:0-14-044601-X, ISBN13: 978-0-14-044601-2. LCCN:00-265085.
Audience: **g,l,u,f.**

Nerval, Gérard de **PQ2326**
Les Chimeres. William Stone (Translator). Trade Paper. Menard Press, The. London, 1999. 64p. ISBN:1-874320-22-5, ISBN13: 978-1-874320-22-7. Dewey:841/.7.
Audience: **g,l,u,f.**

Rinsler, Norma **PQ2260.G36**
Gerard de Nerval. Trade Paper. Continuum International Publishing Group, Ltd. London, 1973. 163p. French Poets Ser. ISBN:0-485-12201-4, ISBN13: 978-0-485-12201-5. Dewey:841/.7.
Audience: **u,f.**

Modern French Literature > 19th C. > Hugo

Bloom, Harold (Editor, Introduction by) **PQ2301**
Victor Hugo. Library Binding. Chelsea House Publishers. Langhorne, PA. 1987. 256p. ISBN:1-55546-290-1, ISBN13: 978-1-55546-290-1. Dewey:848/.709.
Audience: **l,u.**

Brombert, Victor **PQ2304.M88.B76 1984**
Victor Hugo and the Visionary Novel. Trade Cloth. Harvard University Press. Cambridge, MA. 1984. 316p. ISBN:0-674-93550-0, ISBN13: 978-0-674-93550-1. Dewey:843/.7. LCCN:83-026584.
Audience: **l,u,f.**

Drouet, Juliette **PQ2295.D72313 2005**
My Beloved Toto: Letters from Juliette Drouet to Victor Hugo, 1833-1882. Evelyn Blewer (Editor), Victoria Tietze Larson (Translator), Jean Gaudon (Preface by). Saddle Stitched, Cloth over Boards. State University of New York Press. Albany, NY. 2005. 245p. SUNY Series, Women Writers in Translation ISBN:0-7914-6571-3, ISBN13: 978-0-7914-6571-4. Dewey:848/.709 B. LCCN:2004-065683.
Audience: **g,l,u,f.** *Choice, 2006.*

Halsall, Albert W. **PQ2301.H448 1998**
Victor Hugo and the Romantic Drama. Printed Dust Jacket. University of Toronto Press. Toronto, ON. 1998. 256p. ISBN:0-8020-4322-4, ISBN13: 978-0-8020-4322-1. Dewey:842/.7. LCCN:99-180921.
Audience: **u,f.** *Choice, 1999.*

Hugo, Victor **PQ2178**
Notre-Dame de Paris. Trade Paper. Oxford University Press, Inc. New York, NY. 1999. 592p. Oxford World's Classics Ser. ISBN:0-19-283701-X, ISBN13: 978-0-19-283701-1. Dewey:843/.7.
Audience: **g,l,u,f.**

Hugo, Victor **PQ2279**
Oeuvres complètes, Vol. 1. Laffont. 1985. ISBN:2-221-04687-0, ISBN13: 978-2-221-04687-6.
Audience: **u,f.**

Hugo, Victor **PQ2279**
Oeuvres complètes, Vol. 10. Laffont. 1985. ISBN:2-221-04698-6, ISBN13: 978-2-221-04698-2.
Audience: **u,f.**

Hugo, Victor **PQ2279**
Oeuvres complètes, Vol. 11. Laffont. 1985. ISBN:2-221-04700-1, ISBN13: 978-2-221-04700-2.
Audience: **u,f.**

Hugo, Victor **PQ2279**
Oeuvres complètes, Vol. 12. Laffont. 1985. ISBN:2-221-04687-0, ISBN13: 978-2-221-04687-6.
Audience: **u,f.**

Hugo, Victor **PQ2279**
Oeuvres complètes, Vol. 13. Laffont. 1985. ISBN:2-221-04699-4, ISBN13: 978-2-221-04699-9.
Audience: **u,f.**

Hugo, Victor **PQ2279**
Oeuvres complètes, Vol. 14. Laffont. 1985. ISBN:2-221-06427-5, ISBN13: 978-2-221-06427-6.
Audience: **u,f.**

Hugo, Victor **PQ2279**
Oeuvres complètes, Vol. 15. Laffont. 1985. ISBN:2-221-06427-5, ISBN13: 978-2-221-06427-6.
Audience: **u,f.**

Hugo, Victor **PQ2279**
Oeuvres complètes, Vol. 2. Laffont. 1985. ISBN:2-221-09671-1, ISBN13: 978-2-221-09671-0.
Audience: **u,f.**

Hugo, Victor **PQ2279**
Oeuvres complètes, Vol. 3. Laffont. 1985. ISBN:2-221-04690-0, ISBN13: 978-2-221-04690-6.
Audience: **u,f.**

Hugo, Victor **PQ2279**
Oeuvres complètes, Vol. 4. Laffont. 1985. ISBN:2-221-04691-9, ISBN13: 978-2-221-04691-3.
Audience: **u,f.**

Hugo, Victor **PQ2279**
Oeuvres complètes, Vol. 5. Laffont. 1985. ISBN:2-221-04692-7, ISBN13: 978-2-221-04692-0.
Audience: **u,f.**

Hugo, Victor **PQ2279**
Oeuvres complètes, Vol. 6. Laffont. 1985. ISBN:2-221-04693-5, ISBN13: 978-2-221-04693-7.
Audience: **u,f.**

Hugo, Victor **PQ2279**
Oeuvres complètes, Vol. 7. Laffont. 1985. ISBN:2-221-04694-3, ISBN13: 978-2-221-04694-4.
Audience: **u,f.**

Hugo, Victor **PQ2279**
Oeuvres complètes, Vol. 8. Laffont. 1985. ISBN:2-221-04695-1, ISBN13: 978-2-221-04695-1.
Audience: **u,f.**

Hugo, Victor **PQ2279**
Oeuvres complètes, Vol. 9. Laffont. 1985. ISBN:2-221-04696-X, ISBN13: 978-2-221-04696-8.
Audience: **u,f.**

Hugo, Victor **AC1 .E8**
The Toilers of the Sea: A Novel. with Two Engravings from Original Pictures by Gustave Doré. Trade Cloth. Scholarly Publishing Office, University of Michigan Library. Ann Arbor, MI. 2004. ISBN:1-4181-4626-9, ISBN13: 978-1-4181-4626-9. Dewey:081.
Audience: **g,l,u,f.**

Hugo, Victor **PQ2283**
Victor Hugo: Hernani, Marion de Lorme, Lucrece Borgia and Ruy Blas. Trade Paper. Methuen Publishing Ltd. London, 2004. 320p. ISBN:0-413-77269-1, ISBN13: 978-0-413-77269-5. Dewey:842.7.
Audience: **g,l,u,f.**

Hugo, Victor **PQ2283.B55 2004**
The Essential Victor Hugo. E. H. Blackmore & A. M. Blackmore (Editors). Trade Paper. Oxford University Press, Inc. New York, NY. 2004. 576p. Oxford World's Classics Ser. ISBN:0-19-280363-8, ISBN13: 978-0-19-280363-4. Dewey:848/.709. LCCN:2004-044092.
Audience: **g,l,u,f.**

Hugo, Victor **PQ2283.P24 2004**
Selected Poems of Victor Hugo: A Bilingual Edition. E. H. Blackmore & A. M. Blackmore (Translators). Trade Paper. University of Chicago Press. Chicago, IL. 2004. 664p. ISBN:0-226-35981-6, ISBN13: 978-0-226-35981-6. Dewey:841/.7.
Audience: **g,l,u,f.**

Hugo, Victor **PQ2283.P24 2002**
A Bilingual Edition of the Major Epics of Victor Hugo. E. H. Blackmore & A. M. Blackmore (Editors), E. H. Blackmore & A. M. Blackmore (Translators). Trade Cloth. Edwin Mellen Press, The. Lewiston, NY. 2002. 424p. ISBN:0-7734-7239-8, ISBN13: 978-0-7734-7239-6. Dewey:841/.7. LCCN:2001-044473.
Audience: **g,l,u,f.**

Hugo, Victor **PQ2286**
Les Miserables. Lee Fahnestock & Norman MacAfee (Translators). Mass Market. Penguin Group (USA) Inc. New York, NY. 1987. 1488p. Signet Classics Ser. ISBN:0-451-52526-4, ISBN13: 978-0-451-52526-0. Dewey:[Fic]. LCCN:86-062313.
Audience: **g,l,u,f.**

Hugo, Victor **PQ2283.A48 2002**
Selected Poems: Victor Hugo. Brooks Haxton (Translator). Trade Paper. Penguin Group (USA) Inc. New York, NY. 2002. 80p. Classics Ser. ISBN:0-14-243703-4, ISBN13: 978-0-14-243703-2. LCCN:2001-044802.
Audience: **g,l,u,f.**

Hugo, Victor **PQ2289.T7E5513 2002**
The Toilers of the Sea. James Hogarth (Translator), Graham Robb (Introduction by). Trade Paper. Random House Adult Trade Publishing Group. New York, NY. 2002. 480p. The Modern Library Classics ISBN:0-375-76132-2, ISBN13: 978-0-375-76132-4. Dewey:843/.7. LCCN:2002-022342.
Audience: **g,l,u,f.**

Hugo, Victor & Janc, John J. **PQ2285.H3 2001**
Hernani: Victor Hugo. Trade Cloth. University Press of America, Inc. Lanham, MD. 2001. 416p. ISBN:0-7618-2109-0, ISBN13: 978-0-7618-2109-0. Dewey:842/.7. LCCN:2001-048058.
Audience: **l,u.**

Hugo, Victor **PQ2288.A345 2002**
The Hunchback of Notre Dame. Catherine Liu (Translator), Elizabeth McCracken (Introduction by). Trade Paper. Random House Adult Trade Publishing Group. New York, NY. 2002. 432p. ISBN:0-679-64257-9, ISBN13: 978-0-679-64257-2. Dewey:843/.7. LCCN:2002-018917.
Audience: **g,l,u,f.**

Hugo, Victor **PQ2326**
Selected Poems. Steven Monte (Translator). Cloth Text. Routledge. New York, NY. 2002. 304p. Fyfield Bks. ISBN:0-415-94075-3, ISBN13: 978-0-415-94075-7. Dewey:841/.7.
Audience: **l,u.**

Hugo, Victor **PQ2286.A38 1997**
Les Miserables. Charles E. Wilbour (Translator), Peter Washington (Introduction by). Trade Cloth. Alfred A. Knopf Inc. New York, NY. 1998. 1472p. Everyman's Library ISBN:0-375-40317-5, ISBN13: 978-0-375-40317-0. Dewey:[Fic]. LCCN:98-156450.
Audience: **g,l,u,f.**

Richardson, Joanna **PQ2293.R5**
Victor Hugo. Trade Cloth. St. Martin's Press. Gordonville, VA. 1977. x, 334 p., [4p. ISBN:0-312-84035-7, ISBN13: 978-0-312-84035-8. Dewey:848/.7/09. LCCN:76-010564.
Audience: **g,l,u,f.**

Modern French Literature > 19th C. > Huysmans

Baldick, Robert **PQ2309.H4**
The Life of J-K Huysmans. Brendan King (Editor). Trade Paper. Dedalus, Ltd. Monroe, OR. 2006. 592p. ISBN:1-903517-43-5, ISBN13: 978-1-903517-43-7. Dewey:843.8.
Audience: **g,l,u,f.**

Huysmans, J. K. **PQ2469.Z5**
Cathedral. Trade Cloth. Dedalus Ltd. Sawtry, 1993. xii, 339p. ISBN:0-946626-49-9, ISBN13: 978-0-946626-49-6. Dewey:843.8.
Audience: **g,l,u,f.**

Huysmans, J. K. & Baldick, Robert **PQ2309.H4**
Downstream. Trade Paper. Turtle Point Press. New York, NY. 2005. 80p. ISBN:1-885586-35-3, ISBN13: 978-1-885586-35-3. Dewey:843.8.
Audience: **g,l,u,f.**

Huysmans, J. K. **PQ637.C37N45 1990**
The Road from Decadence: From Brothel to Cloister - Selected Letters of J. K. Huysmans. Barbara Beaumont (Editor, Translator, Introduction by). Cloth Text. Ohio State University Press. Columbus, OH. 1989. 273p. ISBN:0-8142-0492-9, ISBN13: 978-0-8142-0492-4. Dewey:843.009/23. LCCN:89-034065.
Audience: **l,u,f.** *Choice, 1989.*

Huysmans, J. K. **PQ2469.Z5**
En Route. David Blow (Editor), W. Fleming (Translator). Trade Paper. Dedalus, Ltd. Monroe, OR. 2002. 313p. Dedalus European Classics Ser. ISBN:1-873982-14-3, ISBN13: 978-1-873982-14-3. Dewey:843.8.
Audience: **g,l,u,f.**

Huysmans, J. K., et al. **PQ1276.D34D43 1998**
The Decadent Reader: Fiction, Fantasy, and Perversion from Fin-de-Siècle France. Barbey D'Aurevilly, Jean Lorrain, Guy de Maupassant & Adam Villiers de L'Isle (Authors), Asti Hustvedt (Editor). Trade Cloth. Zone Books. Brooklyn, NY. 1998. 1072p. ISBN:1-890951-06-4, ISBN13: 978-1-890951-06-1. Dewey:840.9/11. LCCN:97-053065.
Audience: **g,l,u,f.**

Huysmans, J. K. **PQ2309.H4L313 2001**
The Damned (La-Bas). Terry Hale (Translator, Introduction by, Notes by). Trade Paper. Penguin Group (USA) Inc. New York, NY. 2002. 320p. Classics Ser. ISBN:0-14-044767-9, ISBN13: 978-0-14-044767-5. Dewey:843.8. LCCN:2002-284558.
Audience: **g,l,u,f.**

Huysmans, Joris K. **PQ2309.H4**
En Route. Trade Paper. Hippocrene Books, Inc. New York, NY. 1990. 336p. Dedalus European Classics Ser. ISBN:0-87052-616-2, ISBN13: 978-0-87052-616-9. Dewey:843.8.
Audience: **g,l,u,f.**

Huysmans, Joris Karl **PQ2309.H4**
Against Nature. Robert Baldick (Translator), Patrick McGuiness (Introduction by, Notes by). Trade Paper. Penguin Group (USA) Inc. New York, NY. 2004. 288p. Penguin Classics Ser. ISBN:0-14-044763-6, ISBN13: 978-0-14-044763-7. Dewey:843/.8. LCCN:2004-270858.
Audience: **g,l,u,f.**

Huysmans, Joris K. **PQ2469.Z5**
Against the Grain. H. Ellis (Introduction by). Trade Paper. Dover Publications, Inc. Mineola, NY. 1969. 255p. ISBN:0-486-22190-3, ISBN13: 978-0-486-22190-8. Dewey:843/.8. LCCN:77-081802.
Audience: **g,l,u,f.**

Huysmans, Joris K. **PQ2469.Z5**
La Bas (Down There). Keene Wallace (Translator). Trade Paper. Dover Publications, Inc. Mineola, NY. 1972. 287p. ISBN:0-486-22837-1, ISBN13: 978-0-486-22837-2. Dewey:843/.8. LCCN:74-189352.
Audience: **g,l,u,f.**

Huysmans, Joris-Karl **PQ3919.R74**
La-Bas, Lower Depths. Trade Paper. Hippocrene Books, Inc. New York, NY. 1992. xiii, 287p. ISBN:0-7818-0007-2, ISBN13: 978-0-7818-0007-5. Dewey:843.
Audience: **g,l,u,f.**

Huysmans, Joris-Karl **PQ2469.Z5**
With the Flow. Trade Paper. Hesperus Press. London, 2003. 112p. ISBN:1-84391-050-0, ISBN13: 978-1-84391-050-3. Dewey:843.8.
Audience: **g,l,u,f.**

Huysmans, Joris-Karl **PQ2309**
Romans. Brunel, Pierre (Editor). Laffont. 2005. ISBN:2-221-09899-4, ISBN13: 978-2-221-09899-8.
Audience: **u,f.**

Huysmans, Joris-Karl **PQ2309.H4A6213 1998**
Against Nature: A Rebours. Nicholas White (Editor), Margaret Mauldon (Translator), Nicholas White (Introduction by, Notes by). Trade Paper. Oxford University Press, Inc. New York, NY. 1998. 272p. Oxford World's Classics Ser. ISBN:0-19-282367-1, ISBN13: 978-0-19-282367-0. Dewey:843.8. LCCN:97-047774.
Audience: **g,l,u,f.**

Lloyd, Christopher **PQ2309.H4**
J-K Huysmans and the Fin-de-Siecle Novel, Vol. 3. Trade Cloth. Edinburgh University Press. Edinburgh, 1991. ISBN:0-7486-0171-6, ISBN13: 978-0-7486-0171-4. Dewey:843/.8.
Audience: **u,f.**

Modern French Literature > 19th C. > L

De Lamartine, Alphonsc **PQ2327.A17**
Oeuvres Poetiques Completes. Jean Guyard (Editor). Trade Cloth. Schoenhof's Foreign Books, Inc. Cambridge, MA. 1963. Pleiade Ser. ISBN:2-07-010298-X, ISBN13: 978-2-07-010298-3. Dewey:841.7.
Audience: **u,f.**

De Lamartine, Alphonse **PQ2326**
Poetical Meditations - Meditations Poetiques. Gervase Hittle (Translator). Trade Cloth. Edwin Mellen Press, The. Lewiston, NY. 1993. 248p. Studies in French Literature, Vol. 14 ISBN:0-7734-9221-6, ISBN13: 978-0-7734-9221-9. Dewey:841.7. LCCN:92-043538.
Audience: **u,f.**

Fortescue, William **PQ2326**
Alphonse de Lamartine: A Political Biography. Cloth Text. Palgrave Macmillan. New York, NY. 1983. 304p. ISBN:0-312-02138-0, ISBN13: 978 0 312 02138-2. Dewey:841/.7. LCCN:82-042927.
Audience: **u,f.**

Holmes, Anne **PQ2323.L8Z67 1993**
Jules LaForgue and Poetic Innovation. Trade Cloth. Oxford University Press, Inc. New York, NY. 1993. 208p. ISBN:0-19-815876-9, ISBN13: 978-0-19-815876-9. Dewey:841/.8. LCCN:92-027745.
Audience: **u,f.** *Choice, 1993.*

Labiche, Eugene **PQ2619.A65**
Italian Straw Hat. Trade Paper. Nick Hern Books, Ltd. London, 2000. 96p. Drama Classics ISBN:1-85459-300-5, ISBN13: 978-1-85459-300-9. Dewey:842.8.
Audience: **g,l,u,f.**

Labiche, Eugène **PQ2321**
Théâtre, Vol. 1. Laffont. 1991. ISBN:2-221-06679-0, ISBN13: 978-2-221-06679-9.
Audience: **u,f.**

Labiche, Eugène **PQ2321**
Théâtre, Vol. 2. Laffont. 1991. ISBN:2-221-06680-4, ISBN13: 978-2-221-06680-5.
Audience: **u,f.**

Laforgue, Jules **PQ2323.L8**
Moral Tales. William J. Smith (Translator). Trade Cloth. New Directions Publishing Corporation. New York, NY. 1985. 224p. ISBN:0-8112-0942-3, ISBN13: 978-0-8112-0942-7. Dewey:841/.8. LCCN:84-025498.
Audience: **g,l,u,f.**

LaForgue, Jules **PQ2323**
Poems of Jules Laforgue. Patricia Terry (Translator), Henri Peyre (Introduction by). Trade Cloth. Greenwood Publishing Group, Inc. Portsmouth, NH. 1986. 217p. ISBN:0-313-25210-6, ISBN13: 978-0-313-25210-5. Dewey:841/.8. LCCN:86-004617.
Audience: **g,l,u,f.**

Lautreamont, Isidore de **PQ2220**
Oeuvres Completes. Trade Cloth. Schoenhof's Foreign Books, Inc. Cambridge, MA. Pleiade Ser. ISBN:2-07-010304-8, ISBN13: 978-2-07-010304-1. Dewey:843.8.
Audience: **u,f.**

Leconte de Lisle **PQ2332**
OEuvres de Leconte de Lisle, Vol. 1: Poèmes antiques. Pich, Edgard (Editor). Belles Lettres. 1976.
Audience: **u,f.**

Leconte de Lisle **PQ2332**
OEuvres de Leconte de Lisle, Vol. 2: Poèmes barbares. Pich, Edgard (Editor). Belles Lettres. 1976.
Audience: **u,f.**

Leconte de Lisle **PQ2332**
OEuvres de Leconte de Lisle, Vol. 3: Poèmes tragiques. Derniers poèmes. Pich, Edgard (Editor). Belles Lettres. 1976.
Audience: **u,f.**

Leconte de Lisle **PQ2332**
OEuvres de Leconte de Lisle, Vol. 4: OEuvres diverses. Pich, Edgard (Editor). Belles Lettres. 1978.
Audience: **u,f.**

Loti, Pierre & Cambon, M. Jules **PQ2472**
An Iceland Fisherman. Trade Paper. Kessinger Publishing, LLC. Whitefish, MT. 2005. ISBN:1-4179-3358-5, ISBN13: 978-1-4179-3358-7. Dewey:843.8.
Audience: **g,l,u,f.**

Modern French Literature > 19th C. > Mallarme

Bloom, Harold (Introduction by) **PQ2344.Z5S78 1987**
Stephane Mallarme. Library Binding. Chelsea House Publishers. Langhorne, PA. 1987. 256p. Modern Critical Views Ser. ISBN:1-55546-289-8, ISBN13: 978-1-55546-289-5. Dewey:841/.8. LCCN:87-008084.
Audience: **l,u.**

Cohn, Robert G. **PQ2344.D53C64 1990**
Mallarme's Divagations: A Guide and Commentary. Cloth Text. Peter Lang Publishing, Inc. New York, NY. 1991. x, 411p. American University Studies, Ser. II, Vol. 144:Romance, Languages and Literature ISBN:0-8204-1313-5, ISBN13: 978-0-8204-1313-6. Dewey:844/.8. LCCN:89-013832.
Audience: **l,u.**

Cohn, Robert G. **PQ2344.Z5C568 1987**
Mallarme's Prose Poems: A Critical Study. Trade Cloth. Cambridge University Press. New York, NY. 1987. 152p. Cambridge Studies in French, No. 19 ISBN:0-521-32552-8, ISBN13: 978-0-521-32552-3. Dewey:841/.8. LCCN:87-006580.
Audience: **u,f.** *Choice, 1988.*

Cohn, Robert G. & Gillespie, Gerald E. (Editors) **PQ2344.Z5M264 1999**
Mallarme in the Twentieth Century. Trade Cloth. Fairleigh Dickinson University Press. Cranbury, NJ. 1998. 304p. ISBN:0-8386-3795-7, ISBN13: 978-0-8386-3795-1. Dewey:841/.8. LCCN:98-002933.
Audience: **u,f.**

Fowlie, Wallace **PQ2344.Z5 F58**
Mallarme. Paper Text. Textbook Publishers. Temecula, CA. 2003. 299p. ISBN:0-7581-2586-0, ISBN13: 978-0-7581-2586-6. Dewey:841.8.
Audience: **l,u.**

Gill, Austin **PQ2344.Z/**
The Early Mallarme: Parentage, Early Years and Juvenilia. Trade Cloth. Oxford University Press, Inc. New York, NY. 1980. 286p. ISBN:0-19-815726-6, ISBN13: 978-0-19-815726-7. Dewey:841/.8. LCCN:79-041244.
Audience: **u,f.**

Lloyd, Rosemary **PQ2344.Z/**
Mallarmé, Poésies. Trade Cloth. Grant & Cutler. London, 1984. 83p. ISBN:84-499-7422-4, ISBN13: 978-84-499-7422-9. Dewey:841/.8.
Audience: **l,u.**

Lloyd, Rosemary **PQ2344.Z5L56 1999**
Mallarme: The Poet and His Circle. Trade Cloth. Cornell University Press. Ithaca, NY. 1999. 288p. ISBN:0-8014-3662-1, ISBN13: 978-0-8014-3662-8. Dewey:841/.8 B. LCCN:99-035644.
Audience: **u,f.** *Choice, 2000.*

Mallarmé, Stéphane **PQ2344.A128 1998**
Oeuvres Completes, Vol. 1. Trade Cloth. Gallimard, Editions. Paris Cedex 07, 1998. ;p. ISBN:2-07-011558-5, ISBN13: 978-2-07-011558-7. Dewey:841/.8.
Audience: **u,f.**

Mallarmé, Stéphane **PQ2344**
OEuvres complètes, Vol. 2. Gallimard. 2003. ISBN:2-07-011559-3, ISBN13: 978-2-07-011559-4.
Audience: **u,f.**

Mallarmé, Stéphane **PQ2344.P6E5 2005**
A Tomb for Anatole. Paul Auster (Translator). Trade Paper, Perfect. New Directions Publishing Corporation. New York, NY. 2005. 202p. ISBN:0-8112-1593-8, ISBN13: 978-0-8112-1593-0. Dewey:841.8. LCCN:2005-005538.
Audience: **g,l,u,f.**

Mallarmé, Stéphane **PQ2344**
Collected Poems and Other Verse. E. H. Blackmore, A. M. Blackmore & Elizabeth McCombie (Contribution by). Trade Paper. Oxford University Press, Inc. New York, NY. 2006. 320p. Oxford World's Classics Ser. ISBN:0-19-280362-X, ISBN13: 978-0-19-280362-7. Dewey:841.8. LCCN:2006-297077.
Audience: **g,l,u,f.**

Mallarmé, Stéphane **PQ2344.A2125 2001**
Mallarmé in Prose. Mary Ann Caws (Editor, Translator), Jill Anderson, Malcolm Bowie, Rosemary Lloyd, Richard Sieburth & Patricia Terry (Translators). Trade Paper. New Directions Publishing Corporation. New York, NY. 2001. 152p. ISBN:0-8112-1451-6, ISBN13: 978-0-8112-1451-3. Dewey:848/.808. LCCN:00-056065.
Audience: **g,l,u,f.**

Mallarmé, Stéphane **PQ2344.Z5A4 1988**
Selected Letters of Stephane Mallarme. Rosemary Lloyd (Editor, Translator). Trade Cloth. University of Chicago Press. Chicago, IL. 1988. 265p. ISBN:0-226-48841-1, ISBN13: 978-0-226-48841-7. Dewey:841/.8 B. LCCN:88-001351.
Audience: **g,l,u,f.** *Choice, 1989.*

Mallarmé, Stéphane **PQ2344.A286 1994**
Collected Poems of Stephane Mallarme. Henry Weinfield (Translator, Commentaries by). Trade Cloth. University of California Press. Berkeley, CA. 1995. 300p. ISBN:0-520-08188-9, ISBN13: 978-0-520-08188-8. Dewey:841.8. LCCN:94-026794.
Audience: **g,l,u,f.**

Mallarmé, Stéphane **PQ2344.A217 1996**
The Meaning of Mallarme: A Bilingual Edition of His Poesie and Un Coup de Des. John Young (Introduction by). Trade Paper. State Mutual Book & Periodical Service, Ltd. Bridgehampton, NY. 1990. 256p. ISBN:1-898218-29-3, ISBN13: 978-1-898218-29-6. Dewey:841.8. LCCN:95-221104.
Audience: **g,l,u,f.**

St. Aubyn, F. C. **PQ2344.Z5S2 1989**
Stephane Millarme. Trade Cloth. Macmillan Publishing Company, Inc. Old Tappan, NJ. 1989. 176p. World Authors Ser., No. 52 ISBN:0-8057-8254-0, ISBN13: 978-0-8057-8254-7. Dewey:841/.8. LCCN:89-030568.
Audience: **l,u.**

Modern French Literature > 19th C. > Maupassant

Fraser
Guy de Maupassant Revisited. Trade Cloth. Thomson Gale. Farmington Hills, MI. 1999. ISBN:0-8057-4565-3, ISBN13: 978-0-8057-4565-8.
Audience: **l,u.**

Greimas, Algirdas Julien & Maupassant, Guy de **PQ2349.D43**
Maupassant: The Semiotics of Text: Practical Exercises. Paul J. Perron (Translator). Trade Cloth. John Benjamins Publishing Company. Philadelphia, PA. 1988. xxxiv, 258p. Semiotic Crossroads Ser., Vol. 1 ISBN:1-55619-039-5, ISBN13: 978-1-55619-039-1. Dewey:843/.8. LCCN:88-009542.
Audience: **u,f.**

Maupassant, Guy de **PQ2349**
Boule de Suif. Trade Paper. Penguin Group (USA) Inc. New York, NY. 1996. 64p. Classic Ser. ISBN:0-14-600143-5, ISBN13: 978-0-14-600143-7. Dewey:843.8.
Audience: **g,l,u,f.**

Maupassant, Guy de **PQ2349**
Contes et Nouvelles, Tome 2. Trade Paper. Schoenhof's Foreign Books, Inc. Cambridge, MA. 1987. 1766p. Pleiade Ser. ISBN:2-07-010943-7, ISBN13: 978-2-07-010943-2. Dewey:843.8.
Audience: **u,f.**

Maupassant, Guy de **PQ2349**
Contes et Nouvelles, Tome 1. Trade Paper. Schoenhof's Foreign Books, Inc. Cambridge, MA. 1974. 1670p. Pleiade Ser. ISBN:2 07 010805-8, ISBN13: 978-2-07-010805-3. Dewey:843.8.
Audience: **u,f.**

Maupassant, Guy de **PQ2469.Z5**
Mademoiselle Fifi and Other Stories. Trade Paper. Oxford University Press, Inc. New York, NY. 1999. 278p. Oxford World's Classics Ser. ISBN:0-19-283752-4, ISBN13: 978-0-19-283752-3. Dewey:843.8.
Audience: **g,l,u,f.**

Maupassant, Guy de **PQ2349**
Maupassant: Short Stories. Trade Cloth. Penguin Group (USA) Inc. New York, NY. 1975. ISBN:0-460-01907-4, ISBN13: 978-0-460-01907-1. Dewey:843.89.
Audience: **g,l,u,f.**

Maupassant, Guy de **PQ2349.A4E5 1998**
A Day in the Country and Other Stories. David Coward (Translator). Trade Paper. Oxford University Press, Inc. New York, NY. 1998. 336p. Oxford World's Classics Ser. ISBN:0-19-283863-6, ISBN13: 978-0-19-283863-6. Dewey:843/.8. LCCN:99-186616.
Audience: **g,l,u,f.**

Maupassant, Guy de **PE1128**
A Night of Terror. Peter Kearney (Illustrator), Arnold Kellett (Adapted by). Trade Cloth. Oxford University Press, Inc. New York, NY. 1988. 106p. ISBN:0-19-580748-0, ISBN13: 978-0-19-580748-6. Dewey:428.6/4.
Audience: **g,l,u,f.**

Maupassant, Guy de **PQ2349.B3E5 2001**
Bel-Ami. Robert Lethbridge (Editor), Margaret Mauldon (Translator). Trade Paper. Oxford University Press, Inc. New York, NY. 2001. 368p. Oxford World's Classics Ser. ISBN:0-19-283683-8, ISBN13: 978-0-19-283683-0. Dewey:843/.8. LCCN:2001-276396.
Audience: **g,l,u,f.**

Maupassant, Guy de **PQ2349**
The Selected Stories of Guy de Maupassant. Andrew R. MacAndrew (Translator), Edward D. Sullivan (Introduction by). Trade Paper. Penguin Group (USA) Inc. New York, NY. 1984. 288p. ISBN:0-452-00686-4, ISBN13: 978-0-452-00686-7. Dewey:843.8.
Audience: **g,l,u,f.**

Maupassant, Guy de **PQ2349.P5E5 2001**
Pierre et Jean. Julie Mead (Translator), Robert Lethbridge (Introduction by, Notes by). Trade Paper. Oxford University Press, Inc. New York, NY. 2002. 208p. Oxford World's Classics Ser. ISBN:0-19-283147-X, ISBN13: 978-0-19-283147-7. Dewey:843/.8. LCCN:2001-045174.
Audience: **g,l,u,f.**

Maupassant, Guy de **PQ2349.A2**
A Parisian Affair and Other Stories. Sian Miles (Introduction by). Trade Paper. Penguin Group (USA) Inc. New York, NY. 2004. 352p. Penguin Classics Ser. ISBN:0-14-044812-8, ISBN13: 978-0-14-044812-2. Dewey:843/.8. LCCN:2004-275518.
Audience: **g,l,u,f.**

Maupassant, Guy de **PQ2349.V4E6 1999**
A Life: The Humble Truth. Roger Pearson (Translator). Trade Paper. Oxford University Press, Inc. New York, NY. 1999. 284p. Oxford World's Classics Ser. ISBN:0-19-283298-0, ISBN13: 978-0-19-283298-6. Dewey:843.8. LCCN:98-032139.
Audience: **g,l,u,f.**

Steegmuller, Francis **PQ2469.Z5**
Maupassant: A Lion in the Path. Trade Cloth. Ayer Company Publishers, Inc. Manchester, NH. 1977. Select Bibliographies Reprint Ser. ISBN:0-8369-6812-3, ISBN13: 978-0-8369-6812-5. Dewey:843/.8. LCCN:76-039210.
Audience: **g,l,u,f.**

Modern French Literature > 19th C. > M-R

Gould, Evlyn **PQ2362.C33G68 1996**
The Fate of Carmen. Trade Cloth. Johns Hopkins University Press. Baltimore, MD. 1996. 264p. Parallax Ser., :Re-Visions of Culture and Society ISBN:0-8018-5366-4, ISBN13: 978-0-8018-5366-1. Dewey:843/.7. LCCN:96-010772.
Audience: **u,f.** *Choice, 1997.*

Haac, Oscar A. **DC36.98.M5**
Jules Michelet. Library Binding. Thomson Gale. Farmington Hills, MI. 1982. World Authors Ser. ISBN:0-8057-6482-8, ISBN13: 978-0-8057-6482-6. Dewey:907/.2024.
Audience: **l,u.**

Maistre, Xavier de **PQ2342.M3A27 1994**
Voyage Around My Room: Selected Works of Xavier de Maistre. Stephen Sartarelli (Translator), Richard Howard (Introduction by). Trade Paper. New Directions Publishing Corporation. New York, NY. 1994. 192p. ISBN:0-8112-1280-7, ISBN13: 978-0-8112-1280-9. Dewey:843/.6. LCCN:94-017834.
Audience: **g,l,u,f.**

Musset, Alfred de **PQ2369**
Musset: Five Plays. Trade Paper. Methuen Publishing Ltd. London, 2004. 304p. Methuen Anthologies Ser., Vol. 5 ISBN:0-413-69240-X, ISBN13: 978-0-413-69240-5. Dewey:842.7.
Audience: **g,l,u,f.**

Musset, Alfred de & Meyer, Peter **PQ2369**
Seven Plays: Marianne, Fantasio, Don't Trifle with Love, the Candlestick, a Diversion, a Door Must Open or Shut, You Can't Think of Everything. Trade Paper. Oberon Books, Ltd. London, 2006. 279p. ISBN:1-84002-586-7, ISBN13: 978-1-84002-586-6. Dewey:842.7.
Audience: **g,l,u,f.**

Musset, Alfred de **PQ2369.A28 1994**
Comedies and Proverbs. David Sices (Editor, Translator), Alfred de Musset (Translator). Trade Cloth. Johns Hopkins University Press. Baltimore, MD. 1994. 264p. PAJ Bks. ISBN:0-8018-4682-X, ISBN13: 978-0-8018-4682-3. Dewey:842.7. LCCN:93-004371.
Audience: **g,l,u,f.** *Choice, 1994.*

Mérimée, Prosper **PQ2362**
Théâtre de Clara Gazul ; Romans et nouvelles. Gallimard. 1978.
Audience: **u,f.**

Mérimée, Prosper **PQ2362**
Carmen and Other Stories. Nicholas Jotcham (Translator, Introduction by, Notes by). Trade Paper. Oxford University Press, Inc. New York, NY. 1999. 396p. Oxford World's Classics Ser. ISBN:0-19-283722-2, ISBN13: 978-0-19-283722-6. Dewey:843.7.
Audience: **g,l,u,f.**

Rees, Margaret A. **PQ2370**
Alfred de Musset. Library Binding. Irvington Publishers. New York, NY. 1971. Twayne's World Authors Ser. ISBN:0-8057-2646-2, ISBN13: 978-0-8057-2646-6. Dewey:841/.7. LCCN:73-120495.
Audience: **l,u.**

Rostand, Edmond **PQ2635.O7C913 2003**
Cyrano de Bergerac: Heroic Comedy in Five Acts. Lowell Blair (Translator), Eteel Lawson (Introduction by). Trade Paper. Penguin Group (USA) Inc. New York, NY. 2003. 240p. ISBN:0-451-52892-1, ISBN13: 978-0-451-52892-6. Dewey:842/.8. LCCN:2003-045734.
Audience: **g,l,u,f.**

Rostand, Edmond **PQ2635.O7C913 1996**
Cyrano de Bergerac: A Heroic Comedy in Five Acts. Nicholas Cronk (Editor), Christopher Fry (Translator), Nicholas Cronk (Introduction by). Trade Paper. Oxford University Press, Inc. New York, NY. 1996. 192p. Oxford World's Classics Ser. ISBN:0-19-282424-4, ISBN13: 978-0-19-282424-0. Dewey:842.8. LCCN:95-045197.
Audience: **g,l,u,f.**

Modern French Literature > 19th C. > Rimbaud

Bloom, Harold (Editor, Introduction by) **PQ2387.R5Z55717 1988**
Arthur Rimbaud. Library Binding. Chelsea House Publishers. Langhorne, PA. 1987. 248p. Modern Critical Views Ser. ISBN:1-55546-292-8, ISBN13: 978-1-55546-292-5. Dewey:821/.8. LCCN:87-008007.
Audience: **l,u.**

Bonnefoy, Yves **PQ2387**
Rimbaud. Editions Seuil. 1994. ISBN:2-02-019830-4, ISBN13: 978-2-02-019830-1.
Audience: **u,f.**

Bonnefoy, Yves & Schmidt, Paul **PQ2387.R5Z/**
Rimbaud. Trade Paper. Harper & Row Ltd. London, 1973. 145p. ISBN:0-06-090297-3, ISBN13: 978-0-06-090297-1. Dewey:841/.8. LCCN:72-083824.
Audience: **l,u.**

Cohn, Robert G. **PN1261**
The Poetry of Rimbaud. Trade Cloth. Princeton University Press. Princeton, NJ. 1974. 416p. ISBN:0-691-06244-7, ISBN13: 978-0-691-06244-0. Dewey:809.1/034. LCCN:72-005377.
Audience: **u,f.**

Nicholl, Charles **PQ2387.R5Z7178 1999**
Somebody Else: Arthur Rimbaud in Africa 1880-1891. Trade Paper. University of Chicago Press. Chicago, IL. 1999. 352p. ISBN:0-226-58029-6, ISBN13: 978-0-226-58029-6. Dewey:841/.8 B. LCCN:98-051305.
Audience: **u,f.**

Rimbaud, Arthur **PQ2387**
OEuvres complètes, Vol. 1. Champion. 1999. ISBN:2-7453-0167-5, ISBN13: 978-2-7453-0167-3.
Audiencc: **u,f.**

Rimbaud, Arthur **PQ2387.R5A245 2005**
Rimbaud: Complete Works, Selected Letters. Wallace Fowlie (Translator), Seth Whidden (Revised by). Trade Cloth. University of Chicago Press. Chicago, IL. 2005. 496p. ISBN:0-226-71976-6, ISBN13: 978-0-226-71976-4. Dewey:841/.8. LCCN:2005-041859.
Audience: **g,l,u,f.**

Rimbaud, Arthur **PQ2387.R5**
Selected Poems and Letters of Arthur Rimbaud: Parallel Text Edition with Plain Prose Translations of Each Poem. Jeremy

Harding (Translator, Notes by, Introduction by). Trade Paper. Penguin Group (USA) Inc. New York, NY. 2005. 576p. Parallel Text, Penguin Ser. ISBN:0-14-044802-0, ISBN13: 978-0-14-044802-3. Dewey:841.8.
Audience: **g,l,u,f.**

Rimbaud, Arthur **PQ2387.R5A264 2002**
Rimbaud Complete. Wyatt Mason (Editor, Translator, Introduction by). Trade Cloth. Random House Adult Trade Publishing Group. New York, NY. 2002. 656p. ISBN:0-679-64230-7, ISBN13: 978-0-679-64230-5. Dewey:841/.8. LCCN:2001-051389.
Audience: **g,l,u,f.**

Rimbaud, Arthur **PQ2387.R5A285 2001**
Collected Poems. Martin Sorrell (Translator). Trade Paper. Oxford University Press, Inc. New York, NY. 2001. 373p. Oxford World's Classics Ser. ISBN:0-19-283344-8, ISBN13: 978-0-19-283344-0. Dewey:841/.8. LCCN:2001-021589.
Audience: **g,l,u,f.**

Robb, Graham **PQ2387.R5Z825 2000**
Rimbaud: A Biography. Trade Cloth. W. W. Norton & Company, Inc. New York, NY. 2000. 544p. ISBN:0-393-04955-8, ISBN13: 978-0-393-04955-8. Dewey:841/.8 B. LCCN:00-046534.
Audience: **g,l,u,f.** *Choice, 2001.*

St. Aubyn, F. C. **PQ2387.R5Z889 1988**
Arthur Rimbaud. Trade Cloth. Thomson Gale. Farmington Hills, MI. 1988. 184p. World Authors Ser., No. 369 ISBN:0-8057-8227-3, ISBN13: 978-0-8057-8227-1. Dewey:841/.8. LCCN:88-005186.
Audience: **l,u.**

Starkie, Enid **PQ2387.R5**
Arthur Rimbaud. Paper Text. Textbook Publishers. Temecula, CA. 2003. 491p. ISBN:0-7581-7808-5, ISBN13: 978-0-7581-7808-4. Dewey:841/.8.
Audience: **l,u.**

Modern French Literature > 19th C. > Sand

Atwood, William G. **PQ2414**
The Lioness and the Little One. Cloth Text. Columbia University Press. New York, NY. 1980. 352p. ISBN:0-231-04942-0, ISBN13: 978-0-231-04942-9. Dewey:786.1/092/4. LCCN:80-011288.
Audience: **u,f.**

Barry, Joseph (Editor) **PQ2397**
George Sand-in Her Own Words. Mass Market. Doubleday Publishing. New York, NY. 1979. ISBN:0-385-13346-4, ISBN13: 978-0-385-13346-3. Dewey:843/.7. LCCN:78-055845.
Audience: **g,l,u,f.**

Cate, Curtis **PQ2469.Z5**
George Sand: A Biography. Trade Cloth. Houghton Mifflin Company. New York, NY. 1975. 864p. ISBN:0-395-19954-9, ISBN13: 978-0-395-19954-1. Dewey:843/.8. LCCN:75-008680.
Audience: **g,l,u,f.**

Flaubert, Gustave **PQ2247.A2 1993**
Flaubert-Sand: The Correspondence. Alphonse Jacobs (Editor), Francis Steegmuller & Barbara Bray (Translators), Francis Steegmuller (Foreword by, Notes by). Trade Cloth. Alfred A. Knopf Inc. New York, NY. 1993. xxxii, 428p. ISBN:0-679-41898-9, ISBN13: 978-0-679-41898-6. Dewey:843/.8. LCCN:92-016976.
Audience: **u,f.** *Choice, 1993.*

Harlan, Elizabeth **PQ2412.H37 2004**
George Sand. Cloth over Boards. Yale University Press. Cumberland, RI. 2004. 400p. ISBN:0-300-10417-0, ISBN13: 978-0-300-10417-2. Dewey:843/.8 B. LCCN:2004-010315.
Audience: **g,l,u,f.**

Naginski, Isabelle H. **PQ2417.N34 1991**
George Sand: Writing for Her Life. Cloth Text. Rutgers University Press. Piscataway, NJ. 1991. 280p. ISBN:0-8135-1640-4, ISBN13: 978-0-8135-1640-0. Dewey:843/.7. LCCN:90-042140.
Audience: **g,l,u,f.**

Powell, David A. **PQ2417.P6 1990**
George Sand. Trade Cloth. Thomson Gale. Farmington Hills, MI. 1990. 176p. Twayne's World Authors Ser., No. 761 ISBN:0-8057-8260-5, ISBN13: 978-0-8057-8260-8. Dewey:843/.7. LCCN:90-030538.
Audience: **l,u.**

Sand, George **PQ2178**
Consuelo. Paper Text. Da Capo Press, Inc. Cambridge, MA. 1979. 225p. Quality Paperbacks Ser. ISBN:0-306-80102-7, ISBN13: 978-0-306-80102-0. Dewey:843/.7. LCCN:79-015632.
Audience: **g,l,u,f.**

Sand, George **PQ2401**
Lettres d'un voyageur. Flammarion. 2004. ISBN:2-08-071193-8, ISBN13: 978-2-08-071193-9.
Audience: **u,f.**

Sand, George **PQ2401**
Lettres d'une vie. Gallimard. 2004. ISBN:2-07-031471-5, ISBN13: 978-2-07-031471-3.
Audience: **u,f.**

Sand, George **PQ2394**
OEuvres autobiographiques, Vol. 1. Gallimard. 1992. Pleiade Series
Audience: **u,f.**

Sand, George **PQ2394**
OEuvres autobiographiques, Vol. 2. Gallimard. 1993. Pleiade Series
Audience: **u,f.**

Sand, George **PQ2394.F7**
Romans 1830. Omnibus. 1991. ISBN:2-258-03408-6, ISBN13: 978-2-258-03408-2.
Audience: **u,f.**

Sand, George **PQ2397.B56 2004**
The Devil's Pool and Other Stories. E. H. Blackmore, A. M. Blackmore & Francine Giguere (Translators). Cloth Text. State

University of New York Press. Albany, NY. 2004. 197p. SUNY Series, Women Writers in Translation ISBN:0-7914-6149-1, ISBN13: 978-0-7914-6149-5. Dewey:842/.7. LCCN:2003-060637.
Audience: **g,l,u,f.**

Sand, George **PQ2397.B55 2003**
Five Comedies. E. H. Blackmore, A. M. Blackmore & Francine Giguere (Translators). Cloth Text. State University of New York Press. Albany, NY. 2003. 272p. SUNY Series, Women Writers in Translation ISBN:0-7914-5711-7, ISBN13: 978-0-7914-5711-5. Dewey:842/.7. LCCN:2002-030448.
Audience: **g,l,u,f.**

Sand, George **PQ2469.Z5**
The Country Waif. Eirene Collis (Translator), Dorothy W. Zimmerman (Introduction by). Trade Cloth. University of Nebraska Press. Lincoln, NE. 1977. xxviii, 181p. ISBN:0-8032-0888-X, ISBN13: 978-0-8032-0888-9. Dewey:843/.8. LCCN:76-014125.
Audience: **g,l,u,f.**

Sand, George **PQ2469.Z5**
Lelia. Maria Espinosa (Translator). Trade Cloth. Indiana University Press. Bloomington, IN. 1978. 256p. ISBN:0-253-33318-0, ISBN13: 978-0-253-33318-6. Dewey:843/.8. LCCN:77-023639.
Audience: **g,l,u,f.**

Sand, George **DP302.B27 S213 1978**
Winter in Majorca. Robert Graves (Translator). Trade Cloth. Academy Chicago Publishers, Ltd. Chicago, IL. 1979. 216p. ISBN:0-915864-69-X, ISBN13: 978-0-915864-69-0. Dewey:914.6/75/0473/092.
Audience: **g,l,u,f.**

Sand, George **PQ2412.A2 E5**
My Life. Dan Hofstadter (Translator), Robert Phelps (Introduction by). Trade Cloth. HarperCollins Publishers. New York, NY. 1979. ISBN:0-06-013766-5, ISBN13: 978-0-06-013766-3. Dewey:843/.7. LCCN:77-003770.
Audience: **g,l,u,f.**

Sand, George **PZ3.S21**
She and He. George B. Ives (Translator). Trade Cloth. Academy Chicago Publishers, Ltd. Chicago, IL. 1978. 224p. ISBN:0-915864-84-3, ISBN13: 978-0-915864-84-3. Dewey:843/.8.
Audience: **g,l,u,f.**

Sand, George **PQ2412.A2E5 1991**
Story of My Life: The Autobiography of George Sand. Thelma Jurgrau (Editor). Cloth Text. State University of New York Press. Albany, NY. 1991. 1168p. SUNY Series, Women Writers in Translation ISBN:0-7914-0580-X, ISBN13: 978-0-7914-0580-2. Dewey:843/.7 B. LCCN:90-035172.
Audience: **g,l,u,f.**

Sand, George **PQ2411.S313 1989**
A Woman's Version of the Faust Legend: The Seven Strings of the Lyre. George A. Kennedy (Translator, Introduction by). Cloth Text. University of North Carolina Press. Chapel Hill, NC. 1989. x, 186p. ISBN:0-8078-1856-9, ISBN13: 978-0-8078-1856-5. Dewey:842/.7. LCCN:88-033796.
Audience: **g,l,u,f.** *Choice, 1990.*

Sand, George **PQ2407.M6E5 1994**
The Master Pipers. Rosemary Lloyd (Translator). Trade Paper. Oxford University Press, Inc. New York, NY. 1994. 368p. Oxford World's Classics Ser. ISBN:0-19-283097-X, ISBN13: 978-0-19-283097-5. Dewey:843/.7. LCCN:93-031046.
Audience: **g,l,u,f.**

Sand, George & Miles, Siân **PQ2409.M4**
Marianne. Box or Slipcased. Methuen & Company, Ltd. London, 1987. xv, 171p. ISBN:0-413-60370-9, ISBN13: 978-0-413-60370-8. Dewey:843/.7.
Audience: **g,l,u,f.**

Sand, George **PQ2412.A32E5 1987**
Lettres d'un Voyageur. Sasha Rabinovitch (Translator), Patricia Thomson (Introduction by). Trade Paper. Penguin Group (USA) Inc. New York, NY. 1988. 320p. Penguin Classics Ser. ISBN:0-14-044411-4, ISBN13: 978-0-14-044411-7. Dewey:843/.8. LCCN:88-160084.
Audience: **g,l,u,f.**

Sand, George **PQ2410.A37 1997**
Mauprat. Sylvia Raphael (Translator), Naomi Schor (Introduction by). Trade Paper. Oxford University Press, Inc. New York, NY. 1998. 336p. Oxford World's Classics Ser. ISBN:0-19-282434-1, ISBN13: 978-0-19-282434-9. Dewey:843/.7. LCCN:97-016248.
Audience: **g,l,u,f.**

Sand, George **PQ2404.A37 2000**
Indiana. Naomi Schor (Editor), Sylvia Raphael (Translator). Trade Paper. Oxford University Press, Inc. New York, NY. 2001. 306p. Oxford World's Classics Ser. ISBN:0-19-283797-4, ISBN13: 978-0-19-283797-4. Dewey:843/.8. LCCN:2001-274214.
Audience: **g,l,u,f.**

Winegarten, Renee **PQ2412**
The Double Life of George Sand. Trade Cloth. Basic Books. New York, NY. 1978. ISBN:0-465-01683-9, ISBN13: 978-0-465-01683-9. Dewey:843/.7. LCCN:78-054501.
Audience: **g,l,u,f.**

Modern French Literature > 19th C. > Stael

Besser, Gretchen R. **PQ2431.Z5B47 1994**
Germaine de Stael, Revisited. Trade Cloth. Macmillan Publishing Company, Inc. Old Tappan, NJ. 1994. 180p. Twayne's World Authors Ser., No. 849 ISBN:0-8057-8286-9, ISBN13: 978-0-8057-8286-8. Dewey:848/.609. LCCN:93-028437.
Audience: **l,u.** *Choice, 1994.*

Gutwirth, Madelyn **PQ2431.Z5.G87**
Madame de Stael, Novelist: The Emergence of the Artist As Woman. Trade Cloth. University of Illinois Press. Champaign, IL. 1978. 336p. ISBN:0-252-00676-3, ISBN13: 978-0-252-00676-0. Dewey:843/.6. LCCN:78-005836.
Audience: **l,u,f.**

Madame de Stael **PQ2431.C7E5 1998**
Corinne, or Italy. John Isbell (Editor), Sylvia Raphael (Translator). Trade Paper. Oxford University Press, Inc. New York, NY. 1999. 450p. Oxford World's Classics Ser. ISBN:0-19-282505-4, ISBN13: 978-0-19-282505-6. Dewey:843/.6. LCCN:98-010540.
Audience: **g,l,u,f.**

Stael, Germaine de & Berger, Morroe **PQ2431.A23 2000**
Politics, Literature and National Character. Trade Paper. Transaction Publishers. Somerset, NJ. 2000. 371p. ISBN:0-7658-0645-2, ISBN13: 978-0-7658-0645-1. Dewey:848/.609. LCCN:00-023400.
Audience: **g,l,u,f.**

Stael, Germaine de & Folkenflik, Vivian **PQ2205.Z5**
An Extraordinary Woman: Selected Writings of Germaine de Stael. Trade Paper. Eastern European Monographs. Bradenton, FL. 1992. 411p. ISBN:0-231-05587-0, ISBN13: 978-0-231-05587-1. Dewey:848.6/09.
Audience: **g,l,u,f.**

Stael, Germaine de **PQ2431.D4313 1995**
Delphine. Avriel Goldberger (Translator). Trade Paper. Northern Illinois University Press. DeKalb, IL. 1995. 550p. ISBN:0-87580-567-1, ISBN13: 978-0-87580-567-2. Dewey:843/.6. LCCN:94-045742.
Audience: **g,l,u,f.** *Choice, 1996.*

Stael, Germaine de **DC146.S7A25 2000**
Ten Years of Exile. Avriel H. Goldberger (Translator). Trade Cloth. Northern Illinois University Press. DeKalb, IL. 2003. 327p. ISBN:0-87580-255-9, ISBN13: 978-0-87580-255-8. Dewey:944.04/092 B. LCCN:99-023994.
Audience: **g,l,u,f.** *Choice, 2001.*

Staël, Madame de **PQ2431**
Corinne, ou, L'Italie. Balayé, Simone (Editor). Champion. 2000. ISBN:2-7453-0288-4, ISBN13: 978-2-7453-0288-5.
Audience: **u,f.**

Staël, Madame de **PQ2431**
Delphine. Balayé, SImone (Editor). Champion. 2004. ISBN:2-7453-0957-9, ISBN13: 978-2-7453-0957-0.
Audience: **u,f.**

Winegarten, Renee **PQ2431Z/**
Mme. de Stael. Trade Cloth. Berg Publishers. Oxford, 1992. 256p. Women's Ser ISBN:0-907582-87-7, ISBN13: 978-0-907582-87-8. Dewey:848.6/09. LCCN:85-013104.
Audience: **g,l,u,f.** *Choice, 1986.*

Modern French Literature > 19th C. > Stendahl

Alter, Robert & Cosman, Carol **PQ2436.A5 1986**
A Lion for Love: A Critical Biography of Stendhal. Trade Paper. Harvard University Press. Cambridge, MA. 1986. 304p. ISBN:0-674-53575-8, ISBN13: 978-0-674-53575-6. Dewey:848/.309 B. LCCN:86-011984.
Audience: **g,l,u,f.**

Ansel, Yves, et al. Berthier, Philippe, Nerlich, Michael **PQ2435**
Dictionnaire de Stendhal. Champion. 2003. ISBN:2-7453-0806-8, ISBN13: 978-2-7453-0806-1.
Audience: **u,f.**

Bloom, Harold (Introduction by) **PQ2435.R72S78 1988**
Stendhal's The Red and the Black. Trade Cloth. Chelsea House Publishers. Langhorne, PA. 1987. 160p. ISBN:1-55546-076-3, ISBN13: 978-1-55546-076-1. Dewey:843/.7. LCCN:87-009243.
Audience: **l,u.**

Bloom, Harold (Editor, Introduction by) **PQ2441.S69 2001**
Stendhal. Trade Cloth. Facts On File, Inc. New York, NY. 2001. 120p. Bloom's Major Novelists Ser. ISBN:0-7910-6351-8, ISBN13: 978-0-7910-6351-4. Dewey:843/.7. LCCN:2001-047495.
Audience: **l,u.**

Brombert, Victor H. **PQ2441 .B7**
Stendhal: A Collection of Critical Essays. Paper Text. Textbook Publishers. Temecula, CA. 2003. 171p. ISBN:0-7581-6121-2, ISBN13: 978-0-7581-6121-5. Dewey:843.7.
Audience: **l,u.**

Haig, Stirling **PQ2435.R72 H35 1989**
Stendhal: The Red and the Black. Cloth Text. Cambridge University Press. New York, NY. 1989. 128p. Landmarks of World Literature Ser. ISBN:0-521-34189-2, ISBN13: 978-0-521-34189-9. Dewey:843/.7. LCCN:88-039787.
Audience: **l,u.**

Keates, Jonathan **PQ2436**
Stendhal. Trade Paper. Avalon Publishing Group. New York, NY. 1998. 480p. ISBN:0-7867-0545-0, ISBN13: 978-0-7867-0545-0. Dewey:848/.709 B.
Audience: **l,u.**

Lukács, György **PN601**
Studies in European Realism: A Sociological Survey of the Writings of Balzac, Stendhal, Zola, Tolstoy, Gorki and Others. Trade Cloth. Merlin Press Ltd. London, 1972. 277p. ISBN:0-85036-146-X, ISBN13: 978-0-85036-146-9. Dewey:809/.91/2.
Audience: **l,u.**

Pearson, Roger **PQ2435.R72S77 1994**
Stendhal, the Red and the Black and the Charterhouse of Parma. Ed. 1. Trade Cloth. Addison-Wesley Longman, Ltd. Harlow, 1994. 256p. Modern Literatures in Perspective Ser. ISBN:0-582-09617-0, ISBN13: 978-0-582-09617-2. Dewey:843/.7. LCCN:93-030285.
Audience: **l,u.**

Stendhal **PQ2435.A2**
OEuvres intimes, Vol. 1. Gallimard. 1981.
Audience: **u,f.**

Stendhal **PQ2435.A2**
OEuvres intimes, Vol. 2. Gallimard. 1982.
Audience: **u,f.**

Stendhal **PQ2345**
OEuvres romanesques complètes, Vol. 1. Gallimard. 2005. ISBN:2-07-011714-6, ISBN13: 978-2-07-011714-7.
Audience: **u,f.**

Stendhal **PQ2435.R7E5 2003**
The Red and the Black: A Chronicle of 1830. Trade Cloth. W. W. Norton & Company, Inc. New York, NY. 2004. 352p. ISBN:0-87140-148-7, ISBN13: 978-0-87140-148-9. Dewey:843/.7.
Audience: **g,l,u,f.**

Stendhal **PQ2436.A2**
Voyages en France. Gallimard. 1992. ISBN:2-07-010696-9, ISBN13: 978-2-07-010696-7.
Audience: **u,f.**

Stendhal **DG426**
Voyages en Italie. Gallimard. 1996. ISBN:2-07-010697-7, ISBN13: 978-2-07-010697-4.
Audience: **u,f.**

Stendhal **PQ2441**
To the Happy Few: Selected Letters of Stendhal. E. Boudot-Lamotte (Editor), Norman Cameron (Translator), Cyril Connolly (Introduction by). Trade Paper. Soho Book Company. London, 1986. 384p. ISBN:0-948166-09-6, ISBN13: 978-0-948166-09-9. Dewey:843/.7.
Audience: **g,l,u,f.**

Stendhal **PQ2178**
Lucien Leuwen. Robin Buss (Editor), H. L. Edwards (Translator). Trade Paper. Penguin Group (USA) Inc. New York, NY. 1991. 560p. ISBN:0-14-044525-0, ISBN13: 978-0-14-044525-1. Dewey:843/.7.
Audience: **g,l,u,f.**

Stendhal **PQ2178**
Memoirs of an Egotist. David Ellis (Introduction by, Notes by). Trade Cloth. Random House. London, 1975. 160p. ISBN:0-7011-2100-9, ISBN13: 978-0-7011-2100-6. Dewey:843/.7.
Audience: **g,l,u,f.**

Stendhal **PQ2435.A3H69 1988**
The Pink and the Green with Mina de Vanghel. Richard Howard (Translator, Afterword by), Michel Deon (Introduction by). Trade Cloth. New Directions Publishing Corporation. New York, NY. 1988. 160p. ISBN:0-8112-1062-6, ISBN13: 978-0-8112-1062-1. Dewey:843/.7. LCCN:87-383210.
Audience: **g,l,u,f.**

Stendhal **PQ2435.C4E5 2000**
The Charterhouse of Parma. Richard Howard (Translator), Robert Andrew Parker (Introduction by). Trade Paper. Random House Adult Trade Publishing Group. New York, NY. 2000. 560p. Classics Ser. ISBN:0-679-78318-0, ISBN13: 978-0-679-78318-3. Dewey:843/.7. LCCN:00-033241.
Audience: **g,l,u,f.**

Stendhal & Knight, B. C. J. G. **PQ2435.D4E5 2004**
Love. Gilbert Sale & Suzanne Sale (Translators), Jean Stewart (Introduction by). Trade Paper. Penguin Group (USA) Inc. New York, NY. 1975. 336p. Classics Ser. ISBN:0-14-044307-X, ISBN13: 978-0-14-044307-3. Dewey:152.4/1. LCCN:76-359429.
Audience: **g,l,u,f.**

Stendhal **PQ2435.R7E5 2003**
The Red and the Black. Burton Raffel (Translator), Diane Johnson (Introduction by). Trade Cloth. Random House Adult Trade Publishing Group. New York, NY. 2003. 560p. ISBN:0-679-64284-6, ISBN13: 978-0-679-64284-8. Dewey:843/.7. LCCN:2002-040798.
Audience: **g,l,u,f.**

Stendhal **PQ2435.A3S37 1991**
Three Italian Chronicles. C. K. Scott-Moncrieff (Translator), Richard Howard (Introduction by). Trade Paper. New Directions Publishing Corporation. New York, NY. 1991. 208p. Revived Modern Classic Ser., Vol. 704 ISBN:0-8112-1150-9, ISBN13: 978-0-8112-1150-5. Dewey:843/.7. LCCN:90-035325.
Audience: **g,l,u,f.**

Stendhal **PQ2435.M4 E5**
Memoirs of a Tourist. Allan Seager (Translator). Trade Cloth. Northwestern University Press. Evanston, IL. 1962. ISBN:0-8101-0231-5, ISBN13: 978-0-8101-0231-6. Dewey:848.7.
Audience: **g,l,u,f.**

Stendhal **PQ2178**
The Life of Henry Brulard. John Sturrock (Translator, Introduction by). Trade Paper. Penguin Group (USA) Inc. New York, NY. 1995. ISBN:5-600-14044-4, ISBN13: 978-5-600-14044-8. Dewey:843/.7 B.
Audience: **g,l,u,f.**

Talbot, Emile J. **PQ2441.T35 1993**
Stendhal Revisited. Trade Cloth. Macmillan Publishing Company, Inc. Old Tappan, NJ. 1993. 192p. Twayne's World Authors Ser., Vol. 839 ISBN:0-8057-8288-5, ISBN13: 978-0-8057-8288-2. Dewey:848/.709. LCCN:93-019370.
Audience: **l,u,f.** *Choice, 1994.*

Modern French Literature > 19th C. > V

Fulvi, Philip A. (Translator) **PQ2474.C48E5 1990**
Alfred de Vigny's Chatterton: A 3-Act Play. Henry Paolucci (Introduction by). Trade Paper. Griffon House Publications. Smyrna, DE. 1990. 90p. ISBN:0-918680-45-X, ISBN13: 978-0-918680-45-7. Dewey:842/.7. LCCN:89-025933.
Audience: **g,l,u,f.**

Vigny, Alfred de **PQ2474.S4E5 1996**
Servitude and Grandeur of Arms. Roger Gard (Translator, Introduction by, Notes by). Trade Paper. Penguin Group (USA) Inc. New York, NY. 1997. 208p. Penguin Classics Ser. ISBN:0-14-044663-X, ISBN13: 978-0-14-044663-0. LCCN:97-129070.
Audience: **g,l,u,f.**

Villiers de l'Isle-Adam, Philippe A. **PQ24676.V4**
Axel. M. Gaddis Rose (Translator). Trade Paper. Soho Book Company. London, 1986. 175p. ISBN:0-948166-05-3, ISBN13: 978-0-948166-05-1. Dewey:843/.8.
Audience: **g,l,u,f.**

Villiers de l'Isle-Adam, P. **PQ2476.V4**
Cruel Tales. A. W. Raitt (Editor), Robert Baldick (Translator). Trade Paper. Oxford University Press, Inc. New York, NY. 1985. 320p. Oxford World's Classics Ser. ISBN:0-19-281696-9, ISBN13: 978-0-19-281696-2. Dewey:843/.8.
Audience: **g,l,u,f.**

Modern French Literature > 19th C. > Verlaine

Adam, Antoine **PQ2464**
The Art of Paul Verlaine. Carl Morse (Translator). Trade Cloth. New York University Press. New York, NY. 1963. ISBN:0-8147-0000-4, ISBN13: 978-0-8147-0000-6. Dewey:841.8. LCCN:63-019361.
Audience: **l,u,f.**

Schultz **PQ2464**
Paul Verlaine Revisited. Trade Cloth. Thomson Gale. Farmington Hills, MI. 1999. ISBN:0-8057-4603-X, ISBN13: 978-0-8057-4603-7. Dewey:841.8.
Audience: **g,l,u,f.**

Verlaine, Paul **PQ437**
The Cursed Poets. Trade Cloth. Penguin Group (USA) Inc. New York, NY. 2004. 150p. ISBN:1-931243-15-8, ISBN13: 978-1-931243-15-5. Dewey:841.809.
Audience: **g,l,u,f.**

Verlaine, Paul M.
Oeuvres Poetiques Completes. Jacques Borel (Editor). Library Binding. French & European Publications, Inc. New York, NY. 1938. ISBN:0-7859-3804-4, ISBN13: 978-0-7859-3804-0.
Audience: **u,f.**

Verlaine, Paul **PQ2463.A6 1948**
Selected Poems. C. F. MacIntyre (Translator). Trade Cloth. University of California Press. Berkeley, CA. 1948. 248p. ISBN:0-520-01298-4, ISBN13: 978-0-520-01298-1. Dewey:841/.8. LCCN:48-009157.
Audience: **g,l,u,f.**

Verlaine, Paul **PQ2463.A275 1999**
One Hundred and One Poems by Paul Verlaine: A Bilingual Edition. Norman R. Shapiro (Translator). Trade Cloth. University of Chicago Press. Chicago, IL. 1999. 309p. ISBN:0-226-85344-6, ISBN13: 978-0-226-85344-4. Dewey:841/.8. LCCN:98-029016.
Audience: **g,l,u,f.**

Verlaine, Paul **PQ2463.A277 1999**
Selected Poems. Martin Sorrell (Translator). Trade Paper. Oxford University Press, Inc. New York, NY. 2000. 356p. Oxford World's Classics Ser. ISBN:0-19-283332-4, ISBN13: 978-0-19-283332-7. Dewey:841/.8. LCCN:00-702554.
Audience: **g,l,u,f.**

Modern French Literature > 19th C. > Verne

Costello, Peter **PQ2469.Z5.C66 1978**
Jules Verne, Inventor of Science Fiction. Trade Cloth. Simon & Schuster. New York, NY. 1978. 239 p., [4] lp. ISBN:0-684-15824-8, ISBN13: 978-0-684-15824-2. Dewey:843/.8. LCCN:78-057528.
Audience: **l,u.**

Lottman, Herbert R. **PQ2469.Z5L65 1997**
Jules Verne: An Exploratory Biography. Cloth Text. St. Martin's Press. Gordonville, VA. 1996. 366p. ISBN:0-312-14636-1, ISBN13: 978-0-312-14636-8. Dewey:[B]. LCCN:96-030532.
Audience: **g,l,u,f.**

Lynch, L. **PQ2469.Z5L96 1992**
Jules Verne. Trade Cloth. Macmillan Publishing Company, Inc. Old Tappan, NJ. 1992. 160p. Twayne's World Authors Ser. ISBN:0-8057-8278-8, ISBN13: 978-0-8057-8278-3. Dewey:843.8. LCCN:92-006204.
Audience: **l,u.**

Verne, Jules **PQ2469.Z5**
From the Earth to the Moon. Trade Paper. Bantam Books. New York, NY. 1993. 208p. ISBN:0-553-21420-9, ISBN13: 978-0-553-21420-8. Dewey:843/.8.
Audience: **g,l,u,f.**

Verne, Jules **PQ2469.A24 1995**
Jules Verne, Five Complete Novels. Trade Cloth. Random House Value Publishing. New York, NY. 1995. 820p. ISBN:0-517-12250-2, ISBN13: 978-0-517-12250-1. Dewey:843/.8. LCCN:95-155109.
Audience: **g,l,u,f.**

Verne, Jules **PR4622**
Lost World Illustrated. Trade Paper. Penguin Group (USA) Inc. New York, NY. 1991. ISBN:0-425-12867-9, ISBN13: 978-0-425-12867-1. Dewey:823/.8.
Audience: **g,l,u,f.**

Verne, Jules **PQ2469**
Les romans de l'air. Omnibus. 2002. ISBN:2-258-05789-2, ISBN13: 978-2-258-05789-0.
Audience: **u,f.**

Verne, Jules **PQ2469**
Les romans de l'eau. Omnibus. 2002. ISBN:2-258-05788-4, ISBN13: 978-2-258-05788-3.
Audience: **u,f.**

Verne, Jules **PQ2469**
Les romans de la terre. Omnibus. 2002. ISBN:2-258-05855-4, ISBN13: 978-2-258-05855-2.
Audience: **u,f.**

Verne, Jules **PQ2469.Z5**
The Tribulations of a Chinese Gentleman. Trade Paper. Oxford University Press. Oxford, 1991. viii, 262p. ISBN:0-19-585374-1, ISBN13: 978-0-19-585374-2. Dewey:843.8.
Audience: **g,l,u,f.**

Verne, Jules **PQ2469**
Les romans du feu. Omnibus. 2002. ISBN:2-258-05856-2, ISBN13: 978-2-258-05856-9.
Audience: **u,f.**

Verne, Jules **PQ2469.I43E5 2004**
Mysterious Island. Isaac Asimov (Afterword by), Bruce Sterling (Introduction by). Trade Paper. Penguin Group (USA) Inc. New York, NY. 2004. 528p. ISBN:0-451-52941-3, ISBN13: 978-0-451-52941-1. Dewey:843/.8. LCCN:2004-045261.
Audience: **g,l,u,f.** *Choice, 2002.*

Verne, Jules **PQ2469.Z5**
20,000 Leagues under the Sea. Anthony Bonner (Translator), Ray Bradbury (Introduction by). Mass Market. Bantam Books. New York, NY. 1985. 448p. Bantam Classics Ser. ISBN:0-553-21252-4, ISBN13: 978-0-553-21252-5. Dewey:843/.8. LCCN:64-023657.
Audience: **g,l,u,f.**

Verne, Jules **PQ2469.V8E5 2005**
The Adventures of Captain Hatteras. William Butcher (Translator). Trade Paper, Perfect. Oxford University Press, Inc. New York, NY. 2005. 448p. Oxford World's Classics Ser. ISBN:0-19-280465-0, ISBN13: 978-0-19-280465-5. Dewey:843/.8. LCCN:2004-030781.
Audience: **g,l,u,f.**

Verne, Jules **PQ2469.Z5**
Adventures of the Rat Family. Evelyn Copeland (Translator), Felician Myrbach-Rheinfeld (Illustrator), Iona Opie (Introduction by). Trade Cloth. Oxford University Press, Inc. New York, NY. 1993. 72p. The Iona and Peter Opie Library of Children's Literature ISBN:0-19-508114-5, ISBN13: 978-0-19-508114-5. Dewey:843.8. LCCN:92-036983.
Audience: **g,l,u,f.**

Verne, Jules **PQ2469.Z5**
Around the World in Eighty Days. George M Towle (Translator). Mass Market. Bantam Books. New York, NY. 2005. 176p. ISBN:0-553-21356-3, ISBN13: 978-0-553-21356-0. Dewey:843/.8.
Audience: **g,l,u,f.**

Modern French Literature > 19th C. > Zola

Berg, W. & Martin, L. **PQ2538.B45 1992**
Emile Zola. Trade Cloth. Macmillan Publishing Company, Inc. Old Tappan, NJ. 1992. 160p. Twayne's World Authors Ser., Vol. 825 ISBN:0-8057-8271-0, ISBN13: 978-0-8057-8271-4. Dewey:843/.8. LCCN:91-034027.
Audience: **l,u.** *Choice, 1993.*

Brown, Frederick **PQ2528.B69 1996**
Zola: A Life. Trade Paper. Johns Hopkins University Press. Baltimore, MD. 1996. 888p. ISBN:0-8018-5463-6, ISBN13: 978-0-8018-5463-7. Dewey:843.8. LCCN:96-007498.
Audience: **g,l,u,f.**

Grant, Elliott M. **PQ2538.G7**
Emile Zola. Library Binding. Thomson Gale. Farmington Hills, MI. 1966. World Authors Ser. ISBN:0-8057-2996-8, ISBN13: 978-0-8057-2996-2.
Audience: **l,u.**

Hemmings, Frederic William John **PQ2528 .H44**
The Life and Times of Emile Zola. Trade Cloth. Thomson Gale. Farmington Hills, MI. 1977. ISBN:0-685-04565-X, ISBN13: 978-0-685-04565-7. Dewey:843/.8. LCCN:77-073899.
Audience: **g,l,u,f.**

Knapp, Bettina L. **PQ2538.K64**
Emile Zola. Trade Cloth. Frederick Ungar A Book. Dulles, VA. 1980. 186p. Literature and Life Ser. ISBN:0-8044-2482-9, ISBN13: 978-0-8044-2482-0. Dewey:843/.8. LCCN:79-048079.
Audience: **l,u.**

Lukács, György **PN601**
Studies in European Realism: A Sociological Survey of the Writings of Balzac, Stendhal, Zola, Tolstoy, Gorki and Others. Trade Cloth. Merlin Press Ltd. London, 1972. 277p. ISBN:0-85036-146-X, ISBN13: 978-0-85036-146-9. Dewey:809/.91/2.
Audience: **l,u.**

Smethurst, Colin (Editor) **PQ2469.Z5**
Zola: Germinal. Trade Paper. University of Glasgow. Glasgow, 1999. 64p. ISBN:0-85261-529-9, ISBN13: 978-0-85261-529-4. Dewey:843.8.
Audience: **l,u.**

Wilson, Angus **PQ2528**
Emile Zola, an Introductory Study of His Novels. Paper Text. Textbook Publishers. Temecula, CA. 2003. 148p. ISBN:0-7581-8039-X, ISBN13: 978-0-7581-8039-1. Dewey:843.89.
Audience: **l,u.**

Zola, Emile **PQ2489**
OEuvres complètes, vol. 10. Nouveau monde. 2002. ISBN:2-84736-042-5, ISBN13: 978-2-84736-042-4.
Audience: **u,f.**

Zola, Emile **PQ2489**
OEuvres complètes, vol. 12: Souffrance et révolte, 1884-1885. Nouveau monde. 2002. ISBN:2-84736-056-5, ISBN13: 978-2-84736-056-1.
Audience: **u,f.**

Zola, Emile **PQ2489**
OEuvres complètes, vol. 1: Les débuts, 1858-1865. Nouveau monde. 2002. ISBN:2-84736-015-8, ISBN13: 978-2-84736-015-8.
Audience: **u,f.**

Zola, Emile **PQ2489**
OEuvres complètes, vol. 2: Le feuilletoniste, 1866-1867. Nouveau monde. 2002. ISBN:2-84736-016-6, ISBN13: 978-2-84736-016-5.
Audience: **u,f.**

Zola, Emile **PQ2489**
OEuvres complètes, vol. 3: La naissance du naturalisme, 1868-1870. Nouveau monde. 2002. ISBN:2-84736-019-0, ISBN13: 978-2-84736-019-6.
Audience: **u,f.**

Zola, Emile **PQ2489**
OEuvres complètes, vol. 4: La guerre et la Commune (1870-1871). Nouveau monde. 2002. ISBN:2-84736-020-4, ISBN13: 978-2-84736-020-2.
Audience: **u,f.**

Zola, Emile **PQ2489**
OEuvres complètes, vol. 5. Nouveau monde. 2002. ISBN:2-84736-024-7, ISBN13: 978-2-84736-024-0.
Audience: **u,f.**

Zola, Emile **PQ2489**
OEuvres complètes, vol. 6. Nouveau monde. 2002. ISBN:2-84736-025-5, ISBN13: 978-2-84736-025-7.
Audience: **u,f.**

Zola, Emile **PQ2489**
OEuvres Complètes, Vol. 7: La République en Marche, 1875-1876. Nouveau monde. 2002.
Audience: **u,f.**

Zola, Emile **PQ2489**
OEuvres complètes, vol. 8: Le scandale de L'assommoir, 1877-1879. Nouveau monde. 2002. ISBN:2-84736-035-2, ISBN13: 978-2-84736-035-6.
Audience: **u,f.**

Zola, Emile **PQ2489**
OEuvres complètes, vol. 9. Nouveau monde. 2002. ISBN:2-84736-041-7, ISBN13: 978-2-84736-041-7.
Audience: **u,f.**

Zola, Emile **PQ2469.Z5**
Therese Raquin. Trade Paper. Oxford University Press, Inc. New York, NY. 1999. 252p. Oxford World's Classics Ser. ISBN:0-19-283676-5, ISBN13: 978-0-19-283676-2. Dewey:843/.8.
Audience: **g,l,u,f.**

Zola, Emile **PQ2504.A33 1998**
Germinal. Peter Collier (Translator), Robert Lethbridge (Introduction by). Trade Paper. Oxford University Press, Inc. New York, NY. 1998. 574p. Oxford World's Classics Ser. ISBN:0-19-283702-8, ISBN13: 978-0-19-283702-8. Dewey:843/.8. LCCN:98-204770.
Audience: **g,l,u,f.**

Zola, Emile **PQ2500.A33 2000**
La Debacle. Robert Lethbridge (Editor), Elinor Dorday (Translator). Trade Paper. Oxford University Press, Inc. New York, NY. 2000. 582p. Oxford World's Classics Ser. ISBN:0-19-282289-6, ISBN13: 978-0-19-282289-5. Dewey:843/.8. LCCN:99-053690.
Audience: **g,l,u,f.**

Zola, Emile **PQ2496.M38 1995**
L' Assommoir. Margaret Mauldon (Translator), Robert Lethbridge (Introduction by, Notes by). Trade Paper. Oxford University Press, Inc. New York, NY. 1995. 520p. Oxford World's Classics Ser. ISBN:0-19-282983-1, ISBN13: 978-0-19-282983-2. Dewey:843.8. LCCN:94-011779.
Audience: **g,l,u,f.**

Zola, Emile **PQ2499.C9**
The Kill. Brian Nelson (Translator). Trade Paper. Oxford University Press, Inc. New York, NY. 2005. 320p. Oxford World's Classics Ser. ISBN:0-19-280464-2, ISBN13: 978-0-19-280464-8. Dewey:843/.8. LCCN:2005-271660.
Audience: **g,l,u,f.**

Zola, Emile **PQ2514.P6E513 1999**
Pot Luck. Brian Nelson (Translator, Introduction by, Notes by). Trade Paper. Oxford University Press, Inc. New York, NY. 1999. 416p. Oxford World's Classics Ser. ISBN:0-19-283179-8, ISBN13: 978-0-19-283179-8. Dewey:843/.8. LCCN:98-019514.
Audience: **g,l,u,f.**

Zola, Emile **DC354.8 .Z6513**
The Dreyfus Affair: J'accuse and Other Writings. Alain Pages (Editor), Eleanor Levieux (Translator). Trade Paper. Yale University Press. Cumberland, RI. 1998. 244p. ISBN:0-300-07367-4, ISBN13: 978-0-300-07367-6. Dewey:944/.0812/092.
Audience: **g,l,u,f.**

Zola, Emile **PQ2493**
The Attack on the Mill and Other Stories. Douglas Parmee (Translator). Trade Paper. Oxford University Press, Inc. New York, NY. 2000. 400p. Oxford World's Classics Ser. ISBN:0-19-283661-7, ISBN13: 978-0-19-283661-8. Dewey:843.8.
Audience: **g,l,u,f.**

Zola, Emile **PQ2469.Z5**
The Earth. Douglas Parmee (Translator, Introduction by). Trade Paper. Penguin Group (USA) Inc. New York, NY. 1980. 512p. Classics Ser. ISBN:0-14-044387-8, ISBN13: 978-0-14-044387-5. Dewey:843/.8. LCCN:81-467802.
Audience: **g,l,u,f.**

Zola, Emile **PQ2469.Z5**
Nana. Douglas Parmee (Translator, Introduction by). Trade Paper. Oxford University Press, Inc. New York, NY. 1999. 462p. Oxford World's Classics Ser. ISBN:0-19-283670-6, ISBN13: 978-0-19-283670-0. Dewey:843/.8.
Audience: **g,l,u,f.**

Zola, Emile **PQ2469.Z5**
La Bete Humaine. Roger Pearson (Translator). Trade Paper. Oxford University Press, Inc. New York, NY. 1999. 424p. Oxford World's Classics Ser. ISBN:0-19-283814-8, ISBN13: 978-0-19-283814-8. Dewey:843.8. LCCN:95-047332.
Audience: **g,l,u,f.**

Zola, Emile **PQ2469.Z5**
The Masterpiece. Roger Pearson (Editor), Thomas Walton (Translator). Trade Paper. Oxford University Press, Inc. New York, NY. 1999. 458p. Oxford World's Classics Ser. ISBN:0-19-283963-2, ISBN13: 978-0-19-283963-3. Dewey:843.8.
Audience: **g,l,u,f.**

Zola, Émile **PQ2469.Z5**
The Ladies' Paradise. Brian Nelson (Translator, Translator, Notes by). Trade Paper. Oxford University Press, Inc. New York, NY. 1999. 470p. Oxford World's Classics Ser. ISBN:0-19-283602-1, ISBN13: 978-0-19-283602-1. Dewey:843.8.
Audience: **g,l,u,f.**

Modern French Literature > Individual Authors, 20th C., to 1960 > A

Alain-Fournier **PQ2611.O85**
Le Grand Meaulnes. Fayard. 1986. ISBN:2-213-01746-8, ISBN13: 978-2-213-01746-4.
Audience: **u,f.**

Aymé, Marcel **PQ2601.Y5 A15 1998**
OEuvres romanesques complètes, vol. 1. Gallimard. 1989. ISBN:2-07-011157-1, ISBN13: 978-2-07-011157-2.
Audience: **u,f.**

Aymé, Marcel **PQ2601.Y5 A15**
OEuvres romanesques complètes, vol. 2. Gallimard. 1989.
Audience: **u,f.**

Aymé, Marcel **PQ2601.Y5 A15**
OEuvres romanesques complètes, vol. 3. Gallimard. 1989. ISBN:2-07-011157-1, ISBN13: 978-2-07-011157-2.
Audience: **u,f.**

Modern French Literature > Individual Authors, 20th C., to 1960 > Anouilh

Anouilh, Jean **PQ2601.N67**
Pièces baroques. La Table ronde. 1974.
Audience: **u,f.**

Anouilh, Jean **PQ2601.N67 A6 1984b**
Pièces farceuses. Editions du Table ronde. 1984. ISBN:2-7103-0198-9, ISBN13: 978-2-7103-0198-1.
Audience: **u,f.**

Anouilh, Jean **PQ2601.N67**
Théâtre complet. Table ronde. 1966.
Audience: **u,f.**

Anouilh, Jean **PQ2601.N67A6 1987**
Anouilh Plays, Vol. 1. Christopher Fry, Barbara Broy & Timberlake Werterbaker (Translators), Ned Chaillet (Introduction by). Trade Paper. Methuen Publishing Ltd. London, 2004. 0p. Methuen's World Dramatists Ser. ISBN:0-413-14030-X, ISBN13: 978-0-413-14030-2. Dewey:842/.912. LCCN:88-134718.
Audience: **g,l,u,f.**

Anouilh, Jean **PQ2601.N67**
Becket. Frederic Raphael & Stephen Raphael (Translators). Trade Paper, Perfect. Methuen Publishing Ltd. London, 2005. 111p. ISBN:0-413-77492-9, ISBN13: 978-0-413-77492-7. Dewey:842.9.
Audience: **l,u,f.**

Anouilh, Jean **PQ2601.N67**
Anouilh Plays, Vol. 2. Jeremy Sams & Peter Meyer (Translators), Ned Chaillet (Introduction by). Trade Paper. Methuen Publishing Ltd. London, 2004. 0p. ISBN:0-413-72260-0, ISBN13: 978-0-413-72260-7. Dewey:842/.912.
Audience: **g,l,u,f.**

Pronko, Leonard C. **PQ2601.N67**
The World of Jean Anouilh. Paper Text. Textbook Publishers. Temecula, CA. 2003. 264p. ISBN:0-7581-2761-8, ISBN13: 978-0-7581-2761-7. Dewey:842.914.
Audience: **l,u.**

Modern French Literature > Individual Authors, 20th C., to 1960 > Apollinaire

Apollinaire, Guillaume **PQ2601.P6C313 2004**
Calligrammes: Poems of Peace and War, 1913-1916. Trade Cloth. University of California Press. Berkeley, CA. 2004. 525p. ISBN:0-520-24212-2, ISBN13: 978-0-520-24212-8. Dewey:841.912.
Audience: **g,l,u,f.**

Apollinaire, Guillaume **PQ3989.S47**
Oeuvres en prose complètes, vol. 1. Gallimard. 1993. ISBN:2-07-010828-7, ISBN13: 978-2-07-010828-2.
Audience: **u,f.**

Apollinaire, Guillaume **PQ601**
Oeuvres en prose complètes, vol. 2. Galliamrd. 1991. ISBN:2-07-011216-0, ISBN13: 978-2-07-011216-6.
Audience: **u,f.**

Apollinaire, Guillaume **PA2601.P6**
Oeuvres en prose complètes, vol. 3. Gallimard. 1993. ISBN:2-07-011321-3, ISBN13: 978-2-07-011321-7.
Audience: **u,f.**

Apollinaire, Guillaume **PQ2601.P6 A17**
Oeuvres poétiques complètes. Gallimard. 1987.
Audience: **u,f.**

Apollinaire, Guillaume **PQ2601.P6A713 1995**
Alcools. Donald Revell (Translator). Trade Paper. Wesleyan University Press. Middletown, CT. 1995. 185p. Wesleyan Poetry Ser. ISBN:0-8195-1228-1, ISBN13: 978-0-8195-1228-4. Dewey:841/.912. LCCN:95-002294.
Audience: **g,l,u,f.** *Choice, 1996.*

Apollinaire, Guillaume & Revell, Donald **PQ2601.P6A27 2004**
The Self-Dismembered Man: Selected Later Poems of Guillaume Apollinaire. Library Binding. Wesleyan University Press. Middletown, CT. 2004. 152p. ISBN:0-8195-6690-X, ISBN13: 978-0-8195-6690-4. Dewey:841/.912. LCCN:2003-026214.
Audience: **g,l,u,f.**

Apollinaire, Guillaume **PQ2601.P6**
Selected Writings of Apollinaire. Roger Shattuck (Translator). Trade Paper. New Directions Publishing Corporation. New York, NY. 1971. 284p. ISBN:0-8112-0003-5, ISBN13: 978-0-8112-0003-5. Dewey:841.91. LCCN:72-145928.
Audience: **g,l,u,f.**

Bates, Scott **PQ2601.P6Z55 1989**
Guillaume Apollinaire. Trade Cloth. Macmillan Publishing Company, Inc. Old Tappan, NJ. 1989. 200p. World Authors Ser. ISBN:0-8057-8246-X, ISBN13: 978-0-8057-8246-2. Dewey:841/.912. LCCN:88-024828.
Audience: **l,u.**

Steegmuller, Francis **PQ2601.P6**
Apollinaire: Poet among the Painters. Trade Cloth. Ayer Company Publishers, Inc. Manchester, NH. 1977. Biography Index Reprint Ser. ISBN:0-8369-8110-3, ISBN13: 978-0-8369-8110-0. Dewey:841/.912 B. LCCN:78-179742.
Audience: **l,u,f.**

Zufofsky, Louis & Zukofsky, Louis **PQ2601.P6Z9913 2003**
Style Apollinaire: The Writing of Guillaume Apollinaire. Serge Gavronsky (Editor). Library Binding. Wesleyan University Press. Middletown, CT. 2004. 296p. ISBN:0-8195-6619-5, ISBN13: 978-0-8195-6619-5. Dewey:841/.912. LCCN:2003-010102.
Audience: **u,f.**

Modern French Literature > Individual Authors, 20th C., to 1960 > Aragon

Aragon **PQ2601.R2 A15 1997**
OEuvres romanesques complètes, vol. 1. Gallimard. 1997. ISBN:2-07-011509-7, ISBN13: 978-2-07-011509-9.
Audience: **u,f.**

Aragon **PQ2601.R2 A15 1997**
OEuvres romanesques complètes, vol. 2. Gallimard. 1998. ISBN:2-07-011510-0, ISBN13: 978-2-07-011510-5.
Audience: **u,f.**

Aragon **PQ2601.R2 A15 1997**
OEuvres romanesques complètes, vol. 3. Gallimard. 2000. ISBN:2-07-011529-1, ISBN13: 978-2-07-011529-7.
Audience: **u,f.**

Aragon **PQ2601.R2**
Les yeux d'Elsa. Seghers. 2004. ISBN:2-232-12245-X, ISBN13: 978-2-232-12245-3.
Audience: **u,f.**

Modern French Literature > Individual Authors, 20th C., to 1960 > Arrabal, Artaud

Arrabal, Fernando **PQ2601.R65**
Baal Babylone : roman. C. Bourgois. 1975.
Audience: **u,f.**

Arrabal, Fernando **PQ2613.E53**
Guernica and Other Plays: The Labyrinth, The Tricycle, Picnic on the Battlefield, and They Put Handcuffs on the Flowers, The Architect and the Emperor of Assyria, Garden of Delights. Trade Paper. Grove/Atlantic, Inc. New York, NY. 1986. 392p. ISBN:0-8021-5122-1, ISBN13: 978-0-8021-5122-3. Dewey:842.9/12. LCCN:86-080293.
Audience: **g,l,u,f.**

Arrabal, Fernando **PQ2601.R65 A19 1968**
Théâtre. C. Bourgois. 1968. ISBN:2-267-00312-0, ISBN13: 978-2-267-00312-3.
Audience: **u,f.**

Arrabal, Fernando **PQ2601.R65**
Viva la Muerte (Baal Babylone). Trade Cloth. French & European Publications, Inc. New York, NY. ISBN:0-686-54477-3, ISBN13: 978-0-686-54477-7. Dewey:842.914.
Audience: **u,f.**

Arrabal, Fernando **PQ6601.R58T613 1991**
The Tower Struck by Lightning. Anthony Kerrigan (Translator). Trade Paper. Penguin Group (USA) Inc. New York, NY. 1991. 256p. ISBN:0-14-013021-7, ISBN13: 978-0-14-013021-8. Dewey:843/.914. LCCN:90-044248.
Audience: **g,l,u,f.** *Choice, 1988.*

Artaud, Antonin **PQ2601.R677**
OEuvres. Gallimard. 2004. ISBN:2-07-076507-5, ISBN13: 978-2-07-076507-2.
Audience: **u,f.**

Artaud, Antonin **PQ2601.P6**
Selected Writings of Artaud. Susan Sontag (Editor), Helen Weaver (Translator), Susan Sontag (Introduction by, Notes by), Don Levine (Notes by). Trade Paper. University of California Press. Berkeley, CA. 1988. 720p. ISBN:0-520-06443-7, ISBN13: 978-0-520-06443-0. Dewey:841/.9/12.
Audience: **g,l,u,f.**

Barber, Stephen **PQ2601.R677**
Blows and Bombs: Antonin Artaud: The Biography. Trade Paper. Creation Books. New York, NY. 2003. 224p. ISBN:1-84068-082-2, ISBN13: 978-1-84068-082-9. Dewey:848.91209.
Audience: **g,l,u,f.**

Esslin, Martin **PQ2601.P6**
Antonin Artaud. Trade Paper. Riverrun Press, Inc. Flemington, NJ. 2000. 127p. ISBN:0-7145-4204-0, ISBN13: 978-0-7145-4204-1. Dewey:841.9/12.
Audience: **l,u,f.**

Scheer, Edward **PQ2601.R677Z566 2003**
Antonin Artaud: A Critical Reader. Paper over Boards. Routledge. New York, NY. 2003. 224p. ISBN:0-415-28254-3, ISBN13: 978-0-415-28254-3. Dewey:848/.91209. LCCN:2003-005178.
Audience: **u,f.**

Stoppelman, Gabriela **N6853.P5**
Artaud for Beginners. Jorge Hardmeier (Illustrator). Trade Paper. Writers & Readers Publishing, Inc. New York, NY. 1999. 192p. ISBN:0-86316-291-6, ISBN13: 978-0-86316-291-6. Dewey:709.2.
Audience: **g,l,u.**

Modern French Literature > Individual Authors, 20th C., to 1960 > B

Barrès, Maurice **PQ2603**
Romans et voyages, vol. 1. R. Laffont. 1994.
ISBN:2-221-05943-3, ISBN13: 978-2-221-05943-2.
Audience: **u,f.**

Barrès, Maurice **PQ2603**
Romans et voyages, vol. 2. R. Laffont. 1994.
ISBN:2-221-05480-6, ISBN13: 978-2-221-05480-2.
Audience: **u,f.**

Beck, Béatrix **PQ2603.E368 Z465 1998**
Confidences de gargouille. B. Grasset. 1998.
ISBN:2-246-53231-0, ISBN13: 978-2-246-53231-6.
Audience: **u,f.**

Beck, Béatrix **PQ2603.E368 G85 1998**
Guidée par le songe : nouvelles (texte intégral). B. Grasset. 1998. ISBN:2-246-56001-2, ISBN13: 978-2-246-56001-2.
Audience: **u,f.**

Beck, Béatrix **PQ2603.E368**
Léon Morin, prêtre. Gallimard. 1996. ISBN:2-07-036217-5, ISBN13: 978-2-07-036217-2.
Audience: **u,f.**

Bernanos, Georges **PQ2637.A274**
The Diary of a Country Priest. Trade Paper. Avalon Publishing Group. New York, NY. 2001. 304p. ISBN:0-7867-0961-8, ISBN13: 978-0-7867-0961-8. Dewey:843/.9/1.
Audience: **g,l,u,f.**

Bernanos, Georges **PQ2603.E5875**
OEuvres romanesques ; suivies de, Dialogues des carmélites. Gallimard. 1997. ISBN:2-07-010067-7, ISBN13: 978-2-07-010067-5.
Audience: **u,f.**

Bernanos, Georges **PQ2603.E5875S613**
Under Satan's Sun. J. C. Whitehouse (Translator). Trade Cloth. University of Nebraska Press. Lincoln, NE. 2005. 257p. ISBN:0-8032-6180-2, ISBN13: 978-0-8032-6180-8. Dewey:843/.912. LCCN:00-053638.
Audience: **g,l,u,f.**

Brasillach, Robert **PQ2603.R315 S4**
Les sept couleurs. Godefroy de Bouillon. 1995.
ISBN:2-84191-003-2, ISBN13: 978-2-84191-003-8.
Audience: **u,f.**

Muron, Louis **PQ2603.E5875 Z7555 1996**
Bernanos. Flammarion. 1996. ISBN:2-08-067143-X, ISBN13: 978-2-08-067143-1.
Audience: **u,f.**

Modern French Literature > Individual Authors, 20th C., to 1960 > Beauvoir

Beauvoir, Simone de **PQ2603.E362 Z46613**
La force de l'âge. Gallimard. 1992.
Audience: **u,f.**

Beauvoir, Simone de **PQ2603.E362**
La force des choses. Gallimard. 1990. ISBN:2-07-036764-9, ISBN13: 978-2-07-036764-1.
Audience: **u,f.**

Beauvoir, Simone de **PQ2603.E362**
Hard Times: Force of Circumstance: The Autobiography of Simone de Beauvoir, 1952-1962. Trade Paper. Avalon Publishing Group. New York, NY. 1994. 384p. ISBN:1-56924-955-5, ISBN13: 978-1-56924-955-0. Dewey:848/.91409.
Audience: **g,l,u,f.**

Beauvoir, Simone de **PQ2603.E362 I5**
L'invitée. Gallimard. 1994.
Audience: **u,f.**

Beauvoir, Simone de **PQ2603.E362**
Lettres à Sartre, vol. 1. Gallimard. 2001. ISBN:2-07-071829-8, ISBN13: 978-2-07-071829-0.
Audience: **u,f.**

Beauvoir, Simone de **PQ2603.E362**
Lettres à Sartre, vol. 2. Gallimard. 2001. ISBN:2-07-071864-6, ISBN13: 978-2-07-071864-1.
Audience: **u,f.**

Beauvoir, Simone de **PQ2605.A3734**
Les Mandarins. Trade Paper. W. W. Norton & Company, Inc. New York, NY. 1999. 612p. Norton Paperback Fiction Ser. ISBN:0-393-31883-4, ISBN13: 978-0-393-31883-8. Dewey:843/.914. LCCN:91-000244.
Audience: **g,l,u.**

Beauvoir, Simone de **PQ2603.E362 M3**
Les mandarins. Gallimard. 1979.
Audience: **u,f.**

Beauvoir, Simone de **PQ2603.E362 Z523**
Memoirs of a Dutiful Daughter. Paper Text. Textbook Publishers. Temecula, CA. 2003. 382p. ISBN:0-7581-0210-0, ISBN13: 978-0-7581-0210-2. Dewey:843.914.
Audience: **g,l,u.**

Beauvoir, Simone de **PQ2603.E362 M6**
Une mort très douce. Gallimard. 1980.
Audience: **u,f.**

Beauvoir, Simone de **PQ2603.E362**
Mémoires dune jeune fille rangée. Gallimard. 1993.
ISBN:2-07-036786-X, ISBN13: 978-2-07-036786-3.
Audience: **u,f.**

Beauvoir, Simone de **PQ2603.E362**
The Prime of Life. Paper Text. Textbook Publishers. Temecula, CA. 2003. 479p. ISBN:0-7581-0255-0, ISBN13: 978-0-7581-0255-3. Dewey:848.914.
Audience: **g,l,u.**

Beauvoir, Simone de **PQ2603.E362**
Le sang des autres : roman. Gallimard. 1984.
ISBN:2-07-028023-3, ISBN13: 978-2-07-028023-0.
Audience: **u,f.**

Beauvoir, Simone de **PQ2603.E362I513 1990**
She Came to Stay. Trade Paper. W. W. Norton & Company, Inc. New York, NY. 1990. ISBN:0-393-30646-1, ISBN13: 978-0-393-30646-0. Dewey:843/.912. LCCN:89-022823.
Audience: **g,l,u,f.**

Beauvoir, Simone de **PQ2603.E362 T613**
Tous les hommes sont mortels. Gallimard. 1974.
Audience: **u,f.**

Beauvoir, Simone de **PQ2603.E362**
Tout compte fait. Galliamrd. 1989. ISBN:2-07-037022-4, ISBN13: 978-2-07-037022-1.
Audience: **u,f.**

Beauvoir, Simone de **PQ2603.E362T613 1992**
All Men Are Mortal. Leonard Friedman (Translator). Trade Paper. W. W. Norton & Company, Inc. New York, NY. 1992. 345p. ISBN:0-393-30845-6, ISBN13: 978-0-393-30845-7. Dewey:843.9/12. LCCN:92-006620.
Audience: **g,l,u,f.**

Beauvoir, Simone de **B2430.S34**
Adieux: A Farewell to Sartre. Patrick O'Brian (Translator). Trade Paper. Alfred A. Knopf Inc. New York, NY. 1985. ISBN:0-394-72898-X, ISBN13: 978-0-394-72898-8. Dewey:194.
Audience: **g,l,u,f.**

Beauvoir, Simone de **HV1451**
The Coming of Age. Patrick O'Brian (Translator). Trade Cloth. W. W. Norton & Company, Inc. New York, NY. 1996. 591p. ISBN:0-393-31443-X, ISBN13: 978-0-393-31443-4. Dewey:305.26.
Audience: **g,l,u,f.**

Modern French Literature > Individual Authors, 20th C., to 1960 > Beckett

Beckett, Samuel **PQ2603.E378**
Comment c'est. Éditions de Minuit. 1975. ISBN:2-7073-0019-5, ISBN13: 978-2-7073-0019-5.
Audience: **u,f.**

Beckett, Samuel **PR6003.E282**
Comédie et actes divers. Editions de Minuit. 1990. ISBN:2-7073-0225-2, ISBN13: 978-2-7073-0225-0.
Audience: **u,f.**

Beckett, Samuel **PR6003.E282A6 1991**
I Can't Go on, I'll Go On: A Samuel Beckett Reader. Trade Paper. Grove/Atlantic, Inc. New York, NY. 1994. 672p. ISBN:0-8021-3287-1, ISBN13: 978-0-8021-3287-1. Dewey:848/.91409. LCCN:91-021178.
Audience: **g,l,u,f.**

Beckett, Samuel **PQ2603.E378**
L'image. Éditions de Minuit. 1988. ISBN:2-7073-1169-3, ISBN13: 978-2-7073-1169-6.
Audience: **u,f.**

Beckett, Samuel **PQ2603.E378**
L'innommable. Editions de Minuit. 2004. ISBN:2-7073-1891-4, ISBN13: 978-2-7073-1891-6.
Audience: **u,f.**

Beckett, Samuel **PQ2603.E378 M3**
Malone meurt. Editions de Minuit. 2004. ISBN:2-7073-1890-6, ISBN13: 978-2-7073-1890-9.
Audience: **u,f.**

Beckett, Samuel **PR6003.E282**
Molloy. Editions de minuit. 1994. ISBN:2-7073-0628-2, ISBN13: 978-2-7073-0628-9.
Audience: **u,f.**

Beckett, Samuel **PQ2603.E378**
Nouvelles et textes pour rien. Éditions de Minuit. 1987. ISBN:2-7073-0010-1, ISBN13: 978-2-7073-0010-2.
Audience: **u,f.**

Beckett, Samuel **PR6003.E282**
Waiting for Godot. Trade Cloth. Faber & Faber, Ltd. London, 2006. 208p. ISBN:0-571-22910-7, ISBN13: 978-0-571-22910-9. Dewey:842.9/12.
Audience: **g,l,u,f.**

Beckett, Samuel **PQ2603.E378 T5**
Théâtre. Éditions de Minuit. 1971.
Audience: **u,f.**

Beckett, Samuel **PR6003.E282A6 2006**
The Dramatic Works of Samuel Beckett: Volume III of the Grove Centenary Editions. Paul Auster (Editor), Edward Albee (Introduction by). Cloth over Boards. Grove/Atlantic, Inc. New York, NY. 2006. 520p. ISBN:0-8021-1819-4, ISBN13: 978-0-8021-1819-6. Dewey:848/.81409. LCCN:2005-055078.
Audience: **g,l,u,f.**

Beckett, Samuel **PR6003.E282A6 2006**
The Poems, Short Fiction and Criticism of Samuel Beckett, Vol. 4. Paul Auster (Editor), J. M. Coetzee (Introduction by). Cloth over Boards. Grove/Atlantic, Inc. New York, NY. 2006. 584p. ISBN:0-8021-1820-8, ISBN13: 978-0-8021-1820-2. Dewey:848/.81409. LCCN:2005-055078.
Audience: **g,l,u,f.**

Beckett, Samuel **PR6003.E282A6 2006**
The Novels of Samuel Beckett. Paul Auster (Editor), Salman Rushdie (Introduction by). Cloth over Boards. Grove/Atlantic, Inc. New York, NY. 2006. 536p. ISBN:0-8021-1818-6, ISBN13: 978-0-8021-1818-9. Dewey:848/.81409. LCCN:2005-055078.
Audience: **g,l,u,f.**

Beckett, Samuel **PR6003.E282A6 2006**
The Novels of Samuel Beckett: The Grove Centenary Editions. Paul Auster (Editor), Colm Toibin (Introduction by). Cloth over Boards. Grove/Atlantic, Inc. New York, NY. 2006. 496p. ISBN:0-8021-1817-8, ISBN13: 978-0-8021-1817-2. Dewey:848/.81409. LCCN:2005-055078.
Audience: **u,f.**

Beckett, Samuel **PR6003.E282A6 1995**
The Complete Short Prose of Samuel Beckett, 1929-1989. S. E. Gontarski (Editor, Introduction by). Trade Paper. Grove/Atlantic, Inc. New York, NY. 1997. 336p. ISBN:0-8021-3490-4, ISBN13: 978-0-8021-3490-5. Dewey:828.9/12/09. LCCN:95-013074.
Audience: **g,l,u,f.**

Modern French Literature > Individual Authors, 20th C., to 1960 > Blanchot, Bonnefoy, Breton

Blanchot, Maurice **PQ2603.L3343**
Aminadab. Gallimard. 2004. ISBN:2-07-077029-X, ISBN13: 978-2-07-077029-8.
Audience: **u,f.**

Blanchot, Maurice **PQ2603.L3343**
L'arrêt de mort. Gallimard. 2003. ISBN:2-07-029699-7, ISBN13: 978-2-07-029699-6.
Audience: **u,f.**

Blanchot, Maurice **PQ2603.L3343**
L'écriture du désastre. Gallimard. 2003. ISBN:2-07-022248-9, ISBN13: 978-2-07-022248-3.
Audience: **u,f.**

Blanchot, Maurice **PQ2603.L3343**
Le pas au-delà. Gallimard. 2004. ISBN:2-07-028786-6, ISBN13: 978-2-07-028786-4.
Audience: **u,f.**

Blanchot, Maurice **PQ2603.L3343**
Thomas l'obscur : Première version, 1941 : roman. Gallimard. 2005. ISBN:2-07-077630-1, ISBN13: 978-2-07-077630-6.
Audience: **u,f.**

Blanchot, Maurice **PQ2603.L3343.A813**
Death Sentence. Lydia Davis (Translator). Paper Text. Barrytown/Station Hill Press. Barrytown, NY. 1997. 86p. ISBN:1-886449-41-4, ISBN13: 978-1-886449-41-1. Dewey:843.914. LCCN:98-019965.
Audience: **g,l,u,f.**

Blanchot, Maurice **PQ2631.R63**
When the Time Comes. Lydia Davis (Translator). Trade Paper. Barrytown/Station Hill Press. Barrytown, NY. 2002. 80p. ISBN:1-58177-097-9, ISBN13: 978-1-58177-097-1. Dewey:843/.912.
Audience: **g,l,u,f.**

Blanchot, Maurice **PQ2631.R63**
Thomas the Obscure. Robert Lamberton (Translator). Trade Paper. Barrytown/Station Hill Press. Barrytown, NY. 2002. 128p. ISBN:1-58177-098-7, ISBN13: 978-1-58177-098-8. Dewey:843/.912.
Audience: **g,l,u,f.**

Blanchot, Maurice **PQ2603.L3343A6 1998**
The Station Hill Blanchot Reader: Essays and Fiction. George Quasha (Editor), Paul Auster, Lydia Davis & Robert Lamberton (Translators). Trade Cloth. Barrytown/Station Hill Press. Barrytown, NY. 1995. 560p. ISBN:1-886449-17-1, ISBN13: 978-1-886449-17-6. Dewey:843/.912. LCCN:98-026242.
Audience: **g,l,u.**

Bonnefoy, Yves **PQ2603.O533**
Ce qui fut sans lumière ; suivi de Début et fin de la neige et de Là où retombe la flèche. Gallimard. 1995. ISBN:2-07-032825-2, ISBN13: 978-2-07-032825-3.
Audience: **u,f.**

Bonnefoy, Yves **PQ2603.O533 Z465**
Entretiens sur la poesie 1972-1990. Mercure de France. 1992.
Audience: **u,f.**

Bonnefoy, Yves **PQ2603.O533**
L'imaginaire métaphysique. Seuil. 2006. ISBN:2-02-086456-8, ISBN13: 978-2-02-086456-5.
Audience: **u,f.**

Bonnefoy, Yves **PQ2603.O533**
Poèmes. Gallimard. 1997. ISBN:2-07-032221-1, ISBN13: 978-2-07-032221-3.
Audience: **u,f.**

Bonnefoy, Yves **PQ2631.O643**
Early Poems, 1947-1959. Galway Kinnell & Richard Pevear (Contribution by). Trade Paper. Ohio University Press. Athens, OH. 1992. 300p. ISBN:0-8214-1048-2, ISBN13: 978-0-8214-1048-6. Dewey:841/.914. LCCN:89-072172.
Audience: **g,l,u,f.** *Choice, 1991.*

Bonnefoy, Yves **PQ2603.O533A2 1995**
New and Selected Poems. John T. Naughton & Anthony Rudolf (Editors), John T. Naughton & Anthony Rudolf (Translators). Trade Cloth. University of Chicago Press. Chicago, IL. 1995. 252p. ISBN:0-226-06458-1, ISBN13: 978-0-226-06458-1. Dewey:841.9/14. LCCN:95-010350.
Audience: **g,l,u,f.**

Bonnefoy, Yves **PQ2603.O533**
The Curved Planks: Poems / A Bilingual Edition. Hoyt Rogers (Translator), Richard Howard (Foreword by). Cloth over Boards. Farrar, Straus & Giroux. New York, NY. 2006. 256p. ISBN:0-374-18494-1, ISBN13: 978-0-374-18494-0. Dewey:841/.914.
Audience: **g,l,u,f.**

Breton, Andre **PQ2603.R35.A23 1982**
Poems of Andre Breton: A Bilingual Anthology. Jean-Pierre Cauvin & Mary A. Caws (Translators). Cloth Text. University of Texas Press. Austin, TX. 1982. 298p. ISBN:0-292-76476-6, ISBN13: 978-0-292-76476-7. Dewey:841/.912. LCCN:82-004846.
Audience: **g,l,u,f.**

Breton, Andre **PQ2603.R35P613 1999**
Break of Day. Mary Ann Caws & Mark Polizzotti (Translators). Trade Cloth. University of Nebraska Press. Lincoln, NE. 1999. 148p. French Modernist Library Ser. ISBN:0-8032-1259-3, ISBN13: 978-0-8032-1259-6. Dewey:844/.912. LCCN:99-018321.
Audience: **g,l,u,f.**

Breton, Andre **PQ2603.L3343**
Nadja. Richard Howard (Translator). Trade Paper. Grove/Atlantic, Inc. New York, NY. 1988. 160p. ISBN:0-8021-5026-8, ISBN13: 978-0-8021-5026-4. Dewey:848.9/12/07. LCCN:60-007639.
Audience: **g,l,u,f.**

Breton, Andre **PQ2603.R35**
André Breton: Selections. Mark Polizzotti (Editor). Trade Cloth. University of California Press. Berkeley, CA. 2003. 184p. Poets for the Millennium Ser. ISBN:0-520-23584-3, ISBN13: 978-0-520-23584-7. Dewey:841.9/12. LCCN:2003-041009.
Audience: **g,l,u,f.**

Breton, André **PQ2603**
OEuvres complètes, vol. 1. Gallimard. 1988.
ISBN:2-07-011138-5, ISBN13: 978-2-07-011138-1.
Audience: **u,f.**

Breton, André **PQ2603.R35 1988**
OEuvres complètes, vol. 2. Galliamrd. 1988.
ISBN:2-07-011234-9, ISBN13: 978-2-07-011234-0.
Audience: **u,f.**

Breton, André **PQ2603.R35 1988**
OEuvres complètes, vol. 3. Gallimard. 1999.
ISBN:2-07-011376-0, ISBN13: 978-2-07-011376-7.
Audience: **u,f.**

Béhar, Henri **PQ2603.R35**
André Breton : Le grand indésirable. Fayard. 2005.
ISBN:2-213-62602-2, ISBN13: 978-2-213-62602-4.
Audience: **u,f.**

Caws, Mary A. **PQ2603.R35Z6513 1996**
Andre Breton. Ed. 2. Trade Cloth. Thomson Gale. Farmington Hills, MI. 1996. 122p. Twayne's World Authors Ser. ISBN:0-8057-4623-4, ISBN13: 978-0-8057-4623-5. Dewey:848.9/12/09. LCCN:95-044929.
Audience: **l,u.**

Modern French Literature > Individual Authors, 20th C., to 1960 > Butor

Butor, Michel **PQ2603.U73 2006**
Oeuvres complètes de Michel Butor, vol. 2. Éditions de la Différence. 2006. ISBN:2-7291-1606-0, ISBN13: 978-2-7291-1606-4.
Audience: **u,f.**

Butor, Michel
Passing Time & A Change of Heart: Two Novels. Simon and Schuster. 1969.
Audiencc: **g,l,u,f.**

Butor, Michel **PQ2603**
OEuvres complètes de Michel Butor, vol. 1. Calle-Gruber, Mireille (Editor). Éditions de la Différence. 2006. ISBN:2-7291-1605-2, ISBN13: 978-2-7291-1605-7.
Audience: **u,f.**

Butor, Michel **PQ2603.U73P613 1995**
Portrait of the Artist as a Young Ape. Dominic Di Bernardi (Translator). Trade Cloth. Dalkey Archive Press. Normal, IL. 1995. 128p. ISBN:1-56478-077-5, ISBN13: 978-1-56478-077-5. Dewey:843/.914. LCCN:94-036953.
Audience: **g,l,u,f.** *Choice, 1996.*

Butor, Michel **PQ2603.U73D4413 2004**
Degrees. Richard Howard (Translator). Trade Cloth. Dalkey Archive Press. Normal, IL. 2005. 351p. ISBN:1-56478-340-5, ISBN13: 978-1-56478-340-0. Dewey:843/.914. LCCN:2004-052735.
Audience: **g,l,u,f.**

Butor, Michel **PQ2603.U73M613 2004**
Mobile. Richard Howard (Translator), John D'Agata (Introduction by). Trade Paper. Dalkey Archive Press. Normal, IL. 2004. 319p. ISBN:1-56478-343-X, ISBN13: 978-1-56478-343-1. Dewey:848/.914. LCCN:2003-070087.
Audience: **g,l,u,f.**

La Mothe, Jacques **PQ2603.U73 Z677 2002**
Butor en perspective. L'Harmattan. 2002. ISBN:2-7475-3445-6, ISBN13: 978-2-7475-3445-1.
Audience: **u,f.**

Oppenheim, Lois (Editor) **PQ2603.U73I4813 1996**
Improvisations on Butor: Transformation of Writing, by Michel Butor. Elinor S. Miller (Translator), S. E. Gontarski (Foreword by). Library Binding. University Press of Florida. Gainesville, FL. 1996. 224p. Crosscurrents Ser., :Comparative Studies in European Literature and Philosophy ISBN:0-8130-1378-X, ISBN13: 978-0-8130-1378-7. Dewey:844/.914. LCCN:95-030938.
Audience: **u,f.** *Choice, 1996.*

Spencer, M. C. **PQ2603.U73.Z89**
Michel Butor. Trade Cloth. Thomson Gale. Farmington Hills, MI. 1974. 187p. ISBN:0-8057-2186-X, ISBN13: 978-0-8057-2186-7. Dewey:848/.9/1409. LCCN:73-008071.
Audience: **l,u.**

Sturrock, John **PQ671.S76 1969**
The French New Novel: Claude Simon, Michel Butor, Alain Robbe-Grillet. Trade Cloth. Oxford University Press, Inc. New York, NY. 1969. [7], 244p. ISBN:0-19-212178-2, ISBN13: 978-0-19-212178-3. Dewey:843/.9/1409. LCCN:77-102633.
Audience: **u,f.**

Modern French Literature > Individual Authors, 20th C., to 1960 > Camus

Bree, Germaine **PQ2605.A3734**
Camus: A Collection of Critical Essays. Paper Text. Textbook Publishers. Temecula, CA. 2003. viii, 182p. ISBN:0-7581-6089-5, ISBN13: 978-0-7581-6089-8. Dewey:848.914.
Audience: **l,u.**

Camus, Albert **PQ2605.A3734**
Essais. Gallimard. 2000. ISBN:2-07-010105-3, ISBN13: 978-2-07-010105-4.
Audience: **u,f.**

Camus, Albert **PQ2605**
Oeuvres complètes, vol. 1. Gallimard. 2006.
ISBN:2-07-011702-2, ISBN13: 978-2-07-011702-4.
Audience: **u,f.**

Camus, Albert **PQ2605**
Oeuvres complètes, vol. 2. Gallimard. 2006.
ISBN:2-07-011703-0, ISBN13: 978-2-07-011703-1.
Audience: **u,f.**

Camus, Albert **PQ2605.A3734A23 2004**
The Plague, the Fall, Exile and the Kingdom, and Selected Essays. Trade Cloth. Knopf Publishing Group. New York, NY. 2004. 624p. ISBN:1-4000-4255-0, ISBN13: 978-1-4000-4255-5. Dewey:843/.914. LCCN:2004-050616.
Audience: **g,l,u,f.**

Camus, Albert **PQ2605.A3734M613**
Happy Death. Richard Howard (Translator), Jean Sarocchi (Afterword by, Notes by). Trade Paper. Random House, Inc. New York, NY. 1995. 208p. ISBN:0-679-76400-3, ISBN13: 978-0-679-76400-7. Dewey:843/.912. LCCN:95-215654.
Audience: **g,l,u,f.**

Camus, Albert **PQ2605.A3734M913**
The Myth of Sisyphus and Other Essays. Justin O'Brien (Translator). Trade Paper. Knopf Publishing Group. New York, NY. 1991. 224p. Vintage International Ser. ISBN:0-679-73373-6, ISBN13: 978-0-679-73373-7. Dewey:844/.914. LCCN:90-050476.
Audience: **g,l,u,f.**

Camus, Albert **PQ2605.A3734A25 1995**
Resistance, Rebellion, and Death: Essays. Justin O'Brien (Translator, Introduction by). Trade Paper. Random House, Inc. New York, NY. 1995. 288p. ISBN:0-679-76401-1, ISBN13: 978-0-679-76401-4. Dewey:844/.914. LCCN:95-215592.
Audience: **g,l,u,f.**

Camus, Albert **PQ2605.A3734**
The Stranger. Matthew Ward (Translator), Peter Dunwoodie (Introduction by). Trade Cloth. Alfred A. Knopf Inc. New York, NY. 1993. 160p. ISBN:0-679-42026-6, ISBN13: 978-0-679-42026-2. Dewey:843/.914. LCCN:92-054290.
Audience: **g,l,u,f.**

Cruickshank, John **PQ2605.A3734**
Albert Camus and the Literature of Revolt. Paper Text. Textbook Publishers. Temecula, CA. 2003. 248p. ISBN:0-7581-7150-1, ISBN13: 978-0-7581-7150-4. Dewey:840.81.
Audience: **l,u.**

Mairowitz, David Zane **PR6003.E282**
Introducing Camus. Ed. 2. Alain Korkos (Illustrator). Trade Paper. Totem Books. Cambridge, 2002. 176p. ISBN:1-84046-064-4, ISBN13: 978-1-84046-064-3. Dewey:848/.91409 B. LCCN:97-062431.
Audience: **g,l,u.**

McCarthy, Patrick **PQ2605.A37**
Camus: The Stranger. Ed. 2. Cloth Text. Cambridge University Press. New York, NY. 2004. 124p. Landmarks of World Literature Ser. ISBN:0-521-83210-1, ISBN13: 978-0-521-83210-6. Dewey:843/.914. LCCN:2004-271596.
Audience: **l,u.** *Choice, 1988.*

Todd, Olivier **PQ2605.O28**
Albert Camus: A Life. Trade Paper. Avalon Publishing Group. New York, NY. 2000. 448p. ISBN:0-7867-0739-9, ISBN13: 978-0-7867-0739-3. Dewey:848.9/12/09.
Audience: **g,l,u,f.**

Todd, Olivier **PQ2605.A3734**
Albert Camus : une vie. Gallimard. 1999. ISBN:2-07-041062-5, ISBN13: 978-2-07-041062-0.
Audience: **u,f.**

Modern French Literature > Individual Authors, 20th C., to 1960 > C

Caws, Mary A. **PQ2605.H3345.Z633**
Rene Char. Library Binding. Irvington Publishers. New York, NY. 1977. 174p. Twayne's World Authors Ser. ISBN:0-8057-6268-X, ISBN13: 978-0-8057-6268-6. Dewey:848/.9/1209. LCCN:76-050031.
Audience: **g,l.**

Cayrol, Jean **PQ2605.A873**
Les corps étrangers : roman. Editions du Seuil. 1987. ISBN:2-02-009477-0, ISBN13: 978-2-02-009477-1.
Audience: **u,f.**

Cayrol, Jean **PQ2605.A873**
Je vivrai l'amour des autres : roman. Éditions du Seuil. 1980. ISBN:2-02-005476-0, ISBN13: 978-2-02-005476-8.
Audience: **u,f.**

Cayrol, Jean **PQ2605.A873 P6 1995**
Poèmes de la nuit et du brouillard ; suivis de Larmes publiques. Editions du Seuil. 1995. ISBN:2-02-025795-5, ISBN13: 978-2-02-025795-4.
Audience: **u,f.**

Cendrars, Blaise **PQ2601.P6**
Blaise Cendrars - Complete Poems. Trade Paper. University of California Press. Berkeley, CA. 1993. 422p. ISBN:0-520-06580-8, ISBN13: 978-0-520-06580-2. LCCN:91-025903.
Audience: **l,u,f.**

Cendrars, Blaise **PQ2605.E55M613 2004**
Moravagine. Trade Paper. New York Review of Books, Incorporated, The. New York, NY. 2004. 256p. New York Review Books Classics ISBN:1-59017-063-6, ISBN13: 978-1-59017-063-2. Dewey:843/.912. LCCN:2004-015890.
Audience: **g,l,u.**

Cendrars, Blaise **PQ2605.E55**
Moravagine : roman. Ed. Grasset & Fasquelle. 2002. ISBN:2-246-10885-3, ISBN13: 978-2-246-10885-6.
Audience: **u,f.**

Cendrars, Blaise **PQ2605.E55**
Oeuvres complètes, vol. 1. Denoël. 1987.
Audience: **u,f.**

Cendrars, Blaise **PQ2605.E55**
Oeuvres complètes, vol. 2. Denoël. 1987.
Audience: **u,f.**

Cendrars, Blaise **PQ2605.E55**
Oeuvres complètes, vol. 3. Denoël. 1987.
Audience: **u,f.**

Cendrars, Blaise **PQ2605.E55**
Oeuvres complètes, vol. 4. Denoël. 1987.
Audience: **u,f.**

Cendrars, Blaise **PQ2605.E55**
Oeuvres complètes, vol. 5. Denoël. 1987.
Audience: **u,f.**

Cendrars, Blaise **PQ2605 .E55**
Oeuvres complètes, vol. 6. Denoël. 1987.
Audience: **u,f.**

Cendrars, Blaise **PQ2605.E55**
Oeuvres complètes, vol. 8. Denoël. 1987.
Audience: **u,f.**

Cendrars, Blaise **PQ2605.E55A225 1992**
Modernities and Other Writings. Monique Chefdor (Editor, Translator), Esther Allen (Translator), Monique Chefdor (Introduction by). Trade Cloth. University of Nebraska Press. Lincoln, NE. 1992. 134p. French Modernist Library Ser. ISBN:0-8032-1439-1, ISBN13: 978-0-8032-1439-2. Dewey:844.912. LCCN:91-043824.
Audience: **u,f.**

Cendrars, Blaise **PQ2605**
Films Without Images: Three Radio Plays. Mark Spitzer (Translator). Trade Paper. Green Integer. Los Angeles, CA. 2004. 300p. Green Integer Ser. ISBN:1-931243-83-2, ISBN13: 978-1-931243-83-4. Dewey:843.9.
Audience: **l,u,f.**

Cendrars, Miriam **PQ2605.E55**
Blaise Cendrars : l'or d'un poète. Gallimard. 1996. ISBN:2-07-058665-0, ISBN13: 978-2-07-058665-3.
Audience: **u,f.**

Char, René **PQ2605**
Oeuvres Completes. Trade Cloth. French & European Publications, Inc. New York, NY. 1983. Pleiade Ser. ISBN:0-8288-3457-1, ISBN13: 978-0-8288-3457-5. Dewey:841/.912.
Audience: **u,f.**

Char, René **PQ2605.H3345**
OEuvres complètes. Gallimard. 2004.
Audience: **u,f.**

Char, René **PQ2601.P6**
Selected Poems of Rene Char. Mary Ann Caws & Tina Jolas (Translators). Trade Cloth. New Directions Publishing Corporation. New York, NY. 1992. 160p. ISBN:0-8112-1191-6, ISBN13: 978-0-8112-1191-8. Dewey:841/.912. LCCN:92-006351.
Audience: **g,l,u,f.**

Char, René **PQ2605.H3345A25 2004**
The Smoke That Carried Us: Selected Poems of Rene Char. Susanne Dubroff (Translator). Trade Paper. White Pine Press. Buffalo, NY. 2004. 196p. ISBN:1-893996-70-0, ISBN13: 978-1-893996-70-0. Dewey:841/.912. LCCN:2003-116767.
Audience: **g,l,u,f.**

Cingria, Charles Albert **PQ2605.I6 G73 2000**
La grande ourse. Gallimard. 2000. ISBN:2-07-075874-5, ISBN13: 978-2-07-075874-6.
Audience: **u,f.**

Cingria, Charles-Albert **PQ2605.I6**
Le carnet du chat sauvage. Fata Morgana. 2000. ISBN:2-85194-533-5, ISBN13: 978-2-85194-533-4.
Audience: **u,f.**

Greilsamer, Laurent **PQ2605.H3345 Z695 2004**
L'éclair au front : la vie de René Char. Fayard. 2004. ISBN:2-213-60648-X, ISBN13: 978-2-213-60648-4.
Audience: **u,f.**

Modern French Literature > Individual Authors, 20th C., to 1960 > Claudel

Claudel, Paul **PQ2605.L2**
Cinq grandes odes : suivies d'un Processionnal pour saluer le siècle nouveau. Gallimard. 1999. ISBN:2-07-030074-9, ISBN13: 978-2-07-030074-7.
Audience: **u,f.**

Claudel, Paul **PQ2605.L2**
Cinq Grandes Odes, Processional Pour Saluer le Siecle Nouveau, la Cantate a Trois Voix. Trade Paper. French & European Publications, Inc. New York, NY. 1966. ISBN:0-8288-3850-X, ISBN13: 978-0-8288-3850-4. Dewey:848.91209.
Audience: **u,f.**

Claudel, Paul **PQ2605.L2 Z52**
Memoires Improvises. Trade Cloth. French & European Publications, Inc. New York, NY. 1969. 384p. ISBN:0-7859-1149-9, ISBN13: 978-0-7859-1149-4. Dewey:848/.91209.
Audience: **u,f.**

Claudel, Paul **PQ2605.L2 Z47 2001**
Mémoires improvisés : quarante et un entretiens avec Jean Amrouche. Gallimard. 2001. ISBN:2-07-076256-4, ISBN13: 978-2-07-076256-9.
Audience: **u,f.**

Claudel, Paul **PQ2605.L2 A13**
Oeuvres en prose. Gallimard. 1989. ISBN:2-07-010144-4, ISBN13: 978-2-07-010144-3.
Audience: **u,f.**

Claudel, Paul **PQ2635.O117**
Poésies. Gallimard. 1996. ISBN:2-07-030375-6, ISBN13: 978-2-07-030375-5.
Audience: **u,f.**

Claudel, Paul **PQ2605.L2 A19 1985**
Théâtre, vol. 1. Gallimard. 1992. ISBN:2-07-010141-X, ISBN13: 978-2-07-010141-2.
Audience: **u,f.**

Claudel, Paul **PQ2605.L2 A19 1985**
Théâtre, vol. 2. Gallimard. 1996. ISBN:2-07-010142-8, ISBN13: 978-2-07-010142-9.
Audience: **u,f.**

Claudel, Paul **PQ2605.L2**
Theatre, 2. Madaule (Editor). Trade Cloth. French & European Publications, Inc. New York, NY. 1966. Bibliotheque de la Pleiade Ser. ISBN:0-685-73336-X, ISBN13: 978-0-685-73336-3. Dewey:842.912.
Audience: **u,f.**

Claudel, Paul **PQ2605.L2**
Theatre, 1. Madaule (Editor). Trade Cloth. French & European Publications, Inc. New York, NY. 1966. Bibliotheque de la Pleiade Ser. ISBN:0-8288-9117-6, ISBN13: 978-0-8288-9117-2. Dewey:842.912.
Audience: **u,f.**

Claudel, Paul **PQ2605.L2**
Prose. Petit & Charles Galperine (Editors), Picon (Preface by). Trade Cloth. French & European Publications, Inc. New York, NY. 1965. Bibliotheque de la Pleiade Ser. ISBN:0-685-11455-4, ISBN13: 978-0-685-11455-1. Dewey:842.
Audience: **u,f.**

Modern French Literature > Individual Authors, 20th C., to 1960 > Cocteau

Arnaud, Claude **PQ2605.O15 Z565 2003**
Jean Cocteau. Gallimard. 2003. ISBN:2-07-075233-X, ISBN13: 978-2-07-075233-1.
Audience: **u,f.**

Cocteau, Jean **PQ2605.O15**
Les enfants terribles : roman. Grasset. 2002. ISBN:2-246-11253-2, ISBN13: 978-2-246-11253-2.
Audience: **u,f.**

Cocteau, Jean **PQ2613.E53**
The Infernal Machine and Other Plays. Trade Paper. New Directions Publishing Corporation. New York, NY. 1967. 409p. ISBN:0-8112-0022-1, ISBN13: 978-0-8112-0022-6. Dewey:842.9/12. LCCN:63-018631.
Audience: **g,l,u,f.**

Cocteau, Jean **PQ2605.O15 Z473 1983**
Le passé défini : journal. Gallimard. 1983. ISBN:2-07-070017-8, ISBN13: 978-2-07-070017-2.
Audience: **u,f.**

Cocteau, Jean **PQ2631.R63**
Thomas l'imposteur : histoire. Gallimard. 1995. ISBN:2-07-036480-1, ISBN13: 978-2-07-036480-0.
Audience: **u,f.**

Cocteau, Jean **PQ2605.O15 A19 2003**
Théâtre complet. Gallimard. 2003. ISBN:2-07-011540-2, ISBN13: 978-2-07-011540-2.
Audience: **u,f.**

Cocteau, Jean **PQ2631.R63**
Les Enfants Terribles. Rosamond Lehmann (Translator). Trade Cloth. Elysium Press. North Pomfret, VT. 1992. 120p. ISBN:0-9640399-0-7, ISBN13: 978-0-9640399-0-2. Dewey:843.9/12.
Audience: **g,l,u,f.**

Cocteau, Jean **PQ2605.O15P413 1994**
Les Parents Terribles. Jeremy Sams (Translator). Trade Paper. Theatre Communications Group, Inc. New York, NY. 1996. 96p. ISBN:1-85459-256-4, ISBN13: 978-1-85459-256-9. Dewey:842/.912. LCCN:95-129452.
Audience: **g,l,u,f.**

Knapp, Bettina L. **PQ2605.O15Z689 1989**
Jean Cocteau. Trade Cloth. Macmillan Publishing Company, Inc. Old Tappan, NJ. 1989. 176p. World Authors Ser., No. 84 ISBN:0-8057-8239-7, ISBN13: 978-0-8057-8239-4. Dewey:848/.91209. LCCN:88-037316.
Audience: **l,u.**

Modern French Literature > Individual Authors, 20th C., to 1960 > Collette

Colette **PQ2605**
OEuvres, vol. 1. Gallimard. 1984. Pleiade Ser. ISBN:2-07-011079-6, ISBN13: 978-2-07-011079-7.
Audience: **u,f.**

Colette **PQ2605**
OEuvres, vol. 2. Gallimard. 1986. Pleiade Ser. ISBN:2-07-011101-6, ISBN13: 978-2-07-011101-5.
Audience: **u,f.**

Colette **PQ2605**
OEuvres, vol. 3. Gallimard. 1991. Pleiade Ser. ISBN:2-07-011215-2, ISBN13: 978-2-07-011215-9.
Audience: **u,f.**

Colette **PQ2605.O28 1984**
OEuvres, vol. 4. Gallimard. 1991. Pleiade Ser. ISBN:2-07-011314-0, ISBN13: 978-2-07-011314-9.
Audience: **u,f.**

Colette **PQ2605.O28**
Chéri. Trade Cloth. Martin Secker & Warburg, Ltd. London, 1968. 154p. ISBN:0-436-10503-9, ISBN13: 978-0-436-10503-6. Dewey:843/.9/12. LCCN:71-364903.
Audience: **u,f.**

Colette **PQ2631.R63**
Six Novels. Paper Text. Textbook Publishers. Temecula, CA. 2003. 697p. ISBN:0-7581-8055-1, ISBN13: 978-0-7581-8055-1. Dewey:843/.912.
Audience: **g,l,u,f.**

Colette & McLeod, Enid **PQ2637.A274**
The Vagabond. Trade Cloth. Martin Secker & Warburg, Ltd. London, 1974. 223p. ISBN:0-436-10514-4, ISBN13: 978-0-436-10514-2. Dewey:843/.9/1.
Audience: **g,l,u,f.**

Colette **PQ2631.R63**
The Collected Stories of Colette. Robert G. Phelps (Editor), Matthew Ward, Antonia White & Anne-Marie Callimachi (Translators). Trade Paper. Farrar, Straus & Giroux. New York, NY. 1984. 605p. ISBN:0-374-51865-3, ISBN13: 978-0-374-51865-3. Dewey:843/.912. LCCN:83-016449.
Audience: **g,l,u,f.**

Colette, et al. **PQ2605.O28**
Earthly Paradise - Colette: An Autobiography Drawn from Her Lifetime Writings. Robert Phelps & Helen Beauclerk (Authors). Trade Paper. Cardinal Press. London, 1970. 444p. ISBN:0-7221-2433-3, ISBN13: 978-0-7221-2433-8. Dewey:843.912.
Audience: **g,l,u,f.**

Colette & Senhouse, Roger **PQ2605.O28**
The Ripening Seed. Trade Cloth. Martin Secker & Warburg, Ltd. London, 1969. 148p. ISBN:0-436-10512-8, ISBN13: 978-0-436-10512-8. Dewey:843.912. LCCN:75-460987.
Audience: **g,l,u,f.**

Colette & Senhouse, Roger **PQ2631.R63**
The Last of Chéri. Trade Cloth. Martin Secker & Warburg, Ltd. London, 1969. 144p. ISBN:0-436-10508-X, ISBN13: 978-0-436-10508-1. Dewey:843/.912.
Audience: **g,l,u,f.**

Colette **PQ2605.O28**
My Mother's House; and Sido. Judith Thurman (Introduction by). Trade Paper. DIANE Publishing Company. Collingdale, PA. 2005. 219p. ISBN:0-7567-9493-5, ISBN13: 978-0-7567-9493-4. Dewey:848/.9/1203.
Audience: **g,l,u,f.**

Modern French Literature > Individual Authors, 20th C., to 1960 > Desnos, Destouches (Celine)

Buckley, William K. (Editor) **PQ2607.E834Z57 1989**
Critical Essays on Louis-Ferdinand Celine. Trade Cloth. Thomson Gale. Farmington Hills, MI. 1988. 272p. Critical Essays on World Literature Ser. ISBN:0-8161-8841-6, ISBN13: 978-0-8161-8841-3. Dewey:843/.912. LCCN:88-013109.
Audience: **l,u.** *Choice, 1989.*

Celine, Louis-Ferdinand **PQ2607.E834**
Death on the Installment Plan. Ralph Manheim (Translator). Trade Paper. New Directions Publishing Corporation. New York, NY. 1971. ISBN:0-8112-0017-5, ISBN13: 978-0-8112-0017-2. Dewey:843. LCCN:48-006410.
Audience: **g,l,u,f.**

Celine, Louis-Ferdinand **PQ2607.E834N613 1996**
North. Ralph Manheim (Translator). Trade Paper. Dalkey Archive Press. Normal, IL. 1996. 454p. ISBN:1-56478-142-9, ISBN13: 978-1-56478-142-0. Dewey:843/.912. LCCN:96-015668.
Audience: **g,l,u,f.**

Céline, Louis-Ferdinand **PQ2635.O117**
Romans, vol. 1. Gallimard. 1981. ISBN:2-07-011000-1, ISBN13: 978-2-07-011000-1.
Audience: **u,f.**

Céline, Louis-Ferdinand **PQ2607.E834**
Romans, vol. 2. Gallimard. 1974. ISBN:2-07-010797-3, ISBN13: 978-2-07-010797-1.
Audience: **u,f.**

Céline, Louis-Ferdinand **PQ2607.E834.A6**
Romans, vol. 3. Gallimard. 1988. ISBN:2-07-011155-5, ISBN13: 978-2-07-011155-8.
Audience: **u,f.**

Céline, Louis-Ferdinand **PQ2607.E834 R6**
Romans, vol. 4. Gallimard. 1993. ISBN:2-07-011336-1, ISBN13: 978-2-07-011336-1.
Audience: **u,f.**

Céline, Louis-Ferdinand **PQ2607.E834V613 2006**
Journey to the End of the Night. Ralph Manheim (Translator), William T. Vollmann (Afterword by). Trade Paper. New Directions Publishing Corporation. New York, NY. 2006. 464p. ISBN:0-8112-1654-3, ISBN13: 978-0-8112-1654-8. Dewey:843/.912. LCCN:2005-036494.
Audience: **g,l,u,f.**

Desnos, Robert **PQ2607.E75 A114 1999**
OEuvres. Gallimard. 1999. ISBN:2-07-075427-8, ISBN13: 978-2-07-075427-4.
Audience: **u,f.**

Desnos, Robert, et al. **PQ1271**
The Automatic Muse: Surrealist Novels. Georges Limbour & Michel Leiris (Authors). Trade Cloth. Atlas Press. London, 1995. 150p. Atlas Anti-Classics Ser. ISBN:0-947757-79-1, ISBN13: 978-0-947757-79-3. Dewey:843.91208.
Audience: **u,f.**

Hewitt, Nicholas **PQ2607.E834Z697 1999**
The Life of Celine: A Critical Biography. Trade Cloth. Blackwell Publishing, Inc. Malden, MA. 1998. 392p. Blackwell Critical Biographies Ser., Vol. 11 ISBN:0-631-17615-2, ISBN13: 978-0-631-17615-2. Dewey:843/.912 B. LCCN:98-007229.
Audience: **g,l,u,f.** *Choice, 1999.*

O'Connell, David **PQ2607.E834.Z795**
Louis-Ferdinand Celine. Library Binding. Thomson Gale. Farmington Hills, MI. 1976. 175 p. :p. World Authors Ser. ISBN:0-8057-6256-6, ISBN13: 978-0-8057-6256-3. Dewey:843/.9/12. LCCN:76-026059.
Audience: **l,u.**

Modern French Literature > Individual Authors, 20th C., to 1960 > D-F

Alain-Fournier, Henri **PQ2637.A274**
Le Grand Meaulnes. Trade Cloth. French & European Publications, Inc. New York, NY. 1989. ISBN:0-7859-3562-2, ISBN13: 978-0-7859-3562-9. Dewey:843.91.
Audience: **u,f.**

Alain-Fournier, Henri **PQ2637.A274**
Le Grand Meaulnes. Frank Davison (Translator). Trade Paper. Penguin Group (USA) Inc. New York, NY. 1991. 208p. Penguin Twentieth-Century Classics Ser. ISBN:0-14-018282-9, ISBN13: 978-0-14-018282-8. Dewey:843.91.
Audience: **g,l,u,f.**

Crowley, Martin **PQ2607.U8245Z63365**
Duras, Writing, and the Ethical: Making the Broken Whole. Trade Cloth. Oxford University Press, Inc. New York, NY. 2001. 346p. Oxford Modern Languages and Literature Monographs ISBN:0-19-816013-5, ISBN13: 978-0-19-816013-7. Dewey:843/.912. LCCN:2001-269821.
Audience: **u,f.** *Choice, 2001.*

Drieu La Rochelle, Pierre **PQ2607.R5**
La comédie de Charleroi. Gallimard. 1996. ISBN:2-07-074586-4, ISBN13: 978-2-07-074586-9.
Audience: **u,f.**

Drieu La Rochelle, Pierre **PQ2607.R5**
Le feu follet : suivi de Adieu à Gonzague. Gallimard. 1997. ISBN:2-07-036152-7, ISBN13: 978-2-07-036152-6.
Audience: **u,f.**

Drieu La Rochelle, Pierre **PQ2607.R5**
Gilles. Gallimard. 2000. ISBN:2-07-036459-3, ISBN13: 978-2-07-036459-6.
Audience: **u,f.**

Duras, Marguerite **PQ2631.R63**
L' Amant. Trade Paper, Perfect. Editions de Minuit. Paris, 2005. 141p. ISBN:2-7073-0695-9, ISBN13: 978-2-7073-0695-1. Dewey:843/.912. LCCN:84-239371.
Audience: **u,f.**

Duras, Marguerite **PQ2631.R63**
L' Amante Anglaise. Trade Cloth. Alfred A. Knopf Inc. New York, NY. 1987. ISBN:0-394-55897-9, ISBN13: 978-0-394-55897-4. Dewey:843/.912.
Audience: **g,l,u,f.**

Duras, Marguerite **PQ2607.U8245**
Duras: Two Plays. Trade Paper. Theatre Communications Group, Inc. New York, NY. 1998. 240p. Oberon Bks. ISBN:1-870259-78-5, ISBN13: 978-1-870259-78-1. Dewey:843.912.
Audience: **l,u,f.**

Duras, Marguerite **PQ2613.E53**
Four Plays. Trade Paper. Theatre Communications Group, Inc. New York, NY. 1997. 183p. Oberon Bks. ISBN:1-870259-28-9, ISBN13: 978-1-870259-28-6. Dewey:842.912.
Audience: **l,u,f.**

Duras, Marguerite **PQ2607.U8245**
L'Amante anglaise. Gallimard. 1994. ISBN:2-07-070750-4, ISBN13: 978-2-07-070750-8.
Audience: **u,f.**

Duras, Marguerite **PQ2607.U8245A62613**
The Lover. Trade Paper. Knopf Publishing Group. New York, NY. 1998. 128p. ISBN:0-375-70052-8, ISBN13: 978-0-375-70052-1. Dewey:843/.912. LCCN:99-166709.
Audience: **g,l,u.**

Duras, Marguerite **PQ2607.U8245**
Moderato cantabile : suivi de Moderato cantabile et La Presse française. Éditions de Minuit. 1993. ISBN:2-7073-0314-3, ISBN13: 978-2-7073-0314-1.
Audience: **u,f.**

Duras, Marguerite **PQ2607.U8245**
Romans, cinéma, théâtre : un parcours, 1943-1993. Gallimard. 1997. ISBN:2-07-074491-4, ISBN13: 978-2-07-074491-6.
Audience: **u,f.**

Duras, Marguerite **PQ2607.U8245 A19**
Théâtre, vol. 1. Gallimard. 1998. ISBN:2-07-070188-3, ISBN13: 978-2-07-070188-9.
Audience: **u,f.**

Duras, Marguerite **PQ2607.U8245 A19**
Théâtre, vol. 2. Gallimard. 1968. ISBN:2-07-026964-7, ISBN13: 978-2-07-026964-8.
Audience: **u,f.**

Duras, Marguerite **PQ2607.U8245 A19**
Théâtre, vol. 3. Gallimard. 1984. ISBN:2-07-070175-1, ISBN13: 978-2-07-070175-9.
Audience: **u,f.**

Duras, Marguerite **PQ2607.U8245 A19**
Théâtre, vol. 4. Gallimard. 1999. ISBN:2-07-011314-0, ISBN13: 978-2-07-011314-9.
Audience: **u,f.**

Duras, Marguerite **PQ2637.A274**
Trilogy: The Square, 10:30 on a Summer Night, the Afternoon of M. Andesmas. Trade Paper. Riverrun Press, Inc. Flemington, NJ. 2000. 287p. ISBN:0-7145-3602-4, ISBN13: 978-0-7145-3602-6. Dewey:843/.9/1.
Audience: **g,l,u,f.**

Duras, Marguerite **PQ2607.U8245.D413**
Whole Days in the Trees. Anita Barrows (Translator). Trade Paper. Riverrun Press, Inc. Flemington, NJ. 2000. 157p. ISBN:0-7145-3854-X, ISBN13: 978-0-7145-3854-9. Dewey:843/.912. LCCN:84-181895.
Audience: **g,l,u,f.**

Duras, Marguerite **PQ2607.U8245Z46513**
Marguerite Duras. Edith Cohen & Peter Connor (Translators). Trade Cloth. City Lights Books. San Francisco, CA. 1987. 208p. ISBN:0-87286-198-8, ISBN13: 978-0-87286-198-5. Dewey:843/.912. LCCN:86-032702.
Audience: **g,l,u.**

Duras, Marguerite **PQ2607.U8245.C413**
No More. Richard Howard (Translator, Afterword by), Paul Otchakovsky-Laurens (Foreword by). Trade Cloth. Seven Stories Press. New York, NY. 2004. 0p. ISBN:1-888363-65-7, ISBN13: 978-1-888363-65-4. Dewey:848/.91203. LCCN:97-046209.
Audience: **g,l,u,f.**

Duras, Marguerite **PN1997 .D92513**
Hiroshima Mon Amour. Richard Seaver (Translator). Trade Paper. Grove/Atlantic, Inc. New York, NY. 1969. ISBN:0-394-17227-2, ISBN13: 978-0-394-17227-9. Dewey:791.437.
Audience: **g,l,u.**

Duras, Marguerite **PQ2631.R63**
Moderato Cantabile. Richard Seaver (Translator). Trade Paper. Riverrun Press, Inc. Flemington, NJ. 2002. 120p. ISBN:0-7145-0381-9, ISBN13: 978-0-7145-0381-3. Dewey:843.912.
Audience: **g,l,u,f.**

Eluard, Paul **PQ2609**
Oeuvres complètes, vol. 1. Gallimard. 1991. ISBN:2-07-010189-4, ISBN13: 978-2-07-010189-4.
Audience: **u,f.**

Eluard, Paul **PQ2609**
Oeuvres complètes, vol. 2. Gallimard. 1993. ISBN:2-07-010190-8, ISBN13: 978-2-07-010190-0.
Audience: **u,f.**

Eluard, Paul **PQ2609.L75**
Selected Writings. Paper Text. Textbook Publishers. Temecula, CA. 2003. xxxvi, 218p. ISBN:0-7581-7794-1, ISBN13: 978-0-7581-7794-0. Dewey:841.91.
Audience: **u,f.**

Eluard, Paul **PQ2609.L75A22 1988**
Selected Poems: Bilingual Edition. Gilbert Bowen (Translator). Trade Paper. Riverrun Press, Inc. Flemington, NJ. 1988. 128p. ISBN:0-7145-3995-3, ISBN13: 978-0-7145-3995-9. Dewey:841/.912. LCCN:87-012125.
Audience: **l,u,f.**

Feydeau, Georges **PQ2611.E86**
Feydeau, théâtre. Omnibus. 1994. ISBN:2-258-03743-3, ISBN13: 978-2-258-03743-4.
Audience: **u,f.**

Feydeau, Georges **PQ2619.A65**
Plays: One. Trade Paper. Methuen Publishing Ltd. London, 2004. 0p. ISBN:0-413-76170-3, ISBN13: 978-0-413-76170-5. Dewey:842.8.
Audience: **g,l,u.**

Feydeau, George & McLeish, Kenneth **PQ2619.A65**
Plays: Two. Ed. 2. Trade Paper. Methuen Publishing Ltd. London, 2004. 0p. ISBN:0-413-76920-8, ISBN13: 978-0-413-76920-6. Dewey:842.8.
Audience: **l,u,f.**

Hill, Leslie **PQ2631.R63**
Marguerite Duras: Apocalyptic Desires. Trade Paper. Routledge. New York, NY. 1993. 216p. ISBN:0-415-05048-0, ISBN13: 978-0-415-05048-7. Dewey:843.912. LCCN:92-034599.
Audience: **g,l,u.**

Lecarme, Jacques **PQ2607.R5 Z75 2001**
Drieu La Rochelle, ou, le bal des maudits. Presses universitaires de France. 2001. ISBN:2-13-049968-6, ISBN13: 978-2-13-049968-8.
Audience: **u,f.**

Nugent, Robert **PQ2609.L75.Z78**
Paul Eluard. Library Binding. Irvington Publishers. New York, NY. 1974. 153p. Twayne's World Authors Ser. ISBN:0-8057-2299-8, ISBN13: 978-0-8057-2299-4. Dewey:841/.9/12. LCCN:74-004132.
Audience: **g,l.**

Pronko, Leonard C. **PQ551**
Eugene Labiche and Georges Feydeau. Trade Paper. Grove/Atlantic, Inc. New York, NY. 1982. 192p. Modern Dramatists Ser. ISBN:0-394-17965-X, ISBN13: 978-0-394-17965-0. Dewey:842.912. LCCN:81-084703.
Audience: **l,u.**

Vircondelet, Alain **PQ2607.U8245Z9213**
Duras: A Biography. Thomas Buckley (Translator). Trade Cloth. Dalkey Archive Press. Normal, IL. 1994. xii, 378p. ISBN:1-56478-065-1, ISBN13: 978-1-56478-065-2. Dewey:843/.912 B. LCCN:94-008745.
Audience: **g,l,u,f.** *Choice, 1995.*

Modern French Literature > Individual Authors, 20th C., to 1960 > G

Ghelderode, Michel de **PQ2613.H17 A19**
Théâtre, vol. 1. Gallimard. 1957.
Audience: **u,f.**

Ghelderode, Michel de **PQ2613.H17 A19**
Théâtre, vol. 2. Gallimard. 1952. ISBN:2-07-022742-1, ISBN13: 978-2-07-022742-6.
Audience: **u,f.**

Ghelderode, Michel de **PQ2613.H17 A19**
Théâtre, vol. 3. Gallimard. 1953. ISBN:2-07-022743-X, ISBN13: 978-2-07-022743-3.
Audience: **u,f.**

Ghelderode, Michel de **PQ2613.H17 A19**
Théâtre, vol. 4. Gallimard. 1955. ISBN:2-07-022744-8, ISBN13: 978-2-07-022744-0.
Audience: **u,f.**

Ghelderode, Michel de **PQ2613.H17 A19**
Théâtre, vol. 5. Gallimard. 1957. ISBN:2-07-022745-6, ISBN13: 978-2-07-022745-7.
Audience: **u,f.**

Ghelderode, Michel de **PQ2613.H17 A19**
Théâtre, vol. 6. Gallimard. 1982. ISBN:2-07-023140-2, ISBN13: 978-2-07-023140-9.
Audience: **u,f.**

Giono, Jean **PQ2613.I57 A6**
OEuvres romanesques complètes, vol. 1. Gallimard. 1971. ISBN:2-07-010655-1, ISBN13: 978-2-07-010655-4.
Audience: **u,f.**

Giono, Jean **PQ2613.I57 A6**
OEuvres romanesques complètes, vol. 2. Gallimard. 1972. ISBN:2-07-010729-9, ISBN13: 978-2-07-010729-2.
Audience: **u,f.**

Giono, Jean **PQ2613.I57 A6**
OEuvres romanesques complètes, vol. 3. Gallimard. 1974. ISBN:2-07-010823-6, ISBN13: 978-2-07-010823-7.
Audience: **u,f.**

Giono, Jean **PQ2613.I57 A6**
OEuvres romanesques complètes, vol. 4. Gallimard. 1977. ISBN:2-07-010882-1, ISBN13: 978-2-07-010882-4.
Audience: **u,f.**

Giono, Jean **PQ2613.I57 A6**
OEuvres romanesques complètes, vol. 5. Gallimard. 1980. ISBN:2-07-010977-1, ISBN13: 978-2-07-010977-7.
Audience: **u,f.**

Giono, Jean **PQ2613.I57 1971**
OEuvres romanesques complètes, vol. 6. Gallimard. 1983. ISBN:2-07-011071-0, ISBN13: 978-2-07-011071-1.
Audience: **u,f.**

Giono, Jean **PQ2613.I57 A6 1989**
Récits et essais. Gallimard. 1989. ISBN:2-07-011156-3, ISBN13: 978-2-07-011156-5.
Audience: **u,f.**

Giraudoux, Jean **PQ2613.I74**
OEuvres romanesques complètes, vol. 1. Gallimard. 1990. ISBN:2-07-011185-7, ISBN13: 978-2-07-011185-5.
Audience: **u,f.**

Giraudoux, Jean **PQ2613.I74 A115 1982**
Théâtre complet. Gallimard. 1993. ISBN:2-07-010987-9, ISBN13: 978-2-07-010987-6.
Audience: **u,f.**

Giraudoux, Jean, **PQ2613.I74**
OEuvres romanesques complètes, vol. 2. Gallimard. 1990. ISBN:2-07-011357-4, ISBN13: 978-2-07-011357-6.
Audience: **u,f.**

Gracq, Julien **PQ2613.R124 1989**
OEuvres complètes, vol. 1. Gallimard. 1989. ISBN:2-07-011162-8, ISBN13: 978-2-07-011162-6.
Audience: **u,f.**

Gracq, Julien **PQ2613 .R124**
OEuvres complètes, vol. 2. Gallimard. 1995. ISBN:2-07-011162-8, ISBN13: 978-2-07-011162-6.
Audience: **u,f.**

Green, Julien **PQ2613**
OEuvres complètes, vol. 1. Gallimard. 1972. ISBN:2-07-010743-4, ISBN13: 978-2-07-010743-8.
Audience: **u,f.**

Green, Julien **PQ2613**
OEuvres complètes, vol. 2. Gallimard. 1972. ISBN:2-07-010770-1, ISBN13: 978-2-07-010770-4.
Audience: **u,f.**

Green, Julien **PQ2613**
OEuvres complètes, vol. 3. Gallimard. 1973. ISBN:2-07-010781-7, ISBN13: 978-2-07-010781-0.
Audience: **u,f.**

Green, Julien **PQ2613**
OEuvres complètes, vol. 4. Gallimard. 1973. ISBN:2-07-010822-8, ISBN13: 978-2-07-010822-0.
Audience: **u,f.**

Green, Julien **PQ2613**
OEuvres complètes, vol. 5. Gallimard. 1974. ISBN:2-07-010840-6, ISBN13: 978-2-07-010840-4.
Audience: **u,f.**

Green, Julien **PQ2613**
OEuvres complètes, vol. 6. Gallimard. 1975. ISBN:2-07-011187-3, ISBN13: 978-2-07-011187-9.
Audience: **u,f.**

Green, Julien **PQ2613**
OEuvres complètes, vol. 7. Gallimard. 1976. ISBN:2-07-011450-3, ISBN13: 978-2-07-011450-4.
Audience: **u,f.**

Green, Julien **PQ2613**
OEuvres complètes, vol. 8. Gallimard. 1977. ISBN:2-07-011550-X, ISBN13: 978-2-07-011550-1.
Audience: **u,f.**

Guillevic, Eugène **PQ2613.U46 A6 2001**
Art poétique : précédé de, Paroi ; et, suivi de, Le chant. Gallimard. 2001. ISBN:2-07-041758-1, ISBN13: 978-2-07-041758-2.
Audience: **u,f.**

Guillevic, Eugène **PQ2613.U46**
Du domaine, suivi de Euclidiennes. Gallimard. 2000. ISBN:2-07-032316-1, ISBN13: 978-2-07-032316-6.
Audience: **u,f.**

Guillevic, Eugène **PQ2613.U46**
Etier ; suivi de Autres. Gallimard. 1991. ISBN:2-07-032628-4, ISBN13: 978-2-07-032628-0.
Audience: **u,f.**

Guillevic, Eugène **PQ2613.U46**
Présent : poèmes, 1987-1997. Gallimard. 2004. ISBN:2-07-077021-4, ISBN13: 978-2-07-077021-2.
Audience: **u,f.**

Guillevic, Eugène **PQ2613.U46 T4**
Terraqué, suivi de Exécutoire. Gallimard. 1981.
Audience: **u,f.**

Murat, Michel **PQ2613.R124 Z7778 2004**
L'enchanteur réticent : essai sur Julien Gracq. J. Corti. 2004. ISBN:2-7143-0852-X, ISBN13: 978-2-7143-0852-8.
Audience: **u,f.**

Modern French Literature > Individual Authors, 20th C., to 1960 > Genet

Genet, Jean **PQ2613.E53Z46513**
The Declared Enemy: Texts and Interviews. Trade Cloth. Stanford University Press. Palo Alto, CA. 2004. 392p. Meridian: Crossing Aesthetics Ser. ISBN:0-8047-2944-1, ISBN13: 978-0-8047-2944-4. Dewey:840.9/0091. LCCN:2003-022583.
Audience: **u,f.** *Choice, 2004.*

Genet, Jean **PQ2613.E53F7313 2003**
Fragments of the Artwork. Trade Cloth. Stanford University Press. Palo Alto, CA. 2003. viii, 181p. Meridian, Crossing Aesthethics Ser. ISBN:0-8047-4286-3, ISBN13: 978-0-8047-4286-3. Dewey:844/.912. LCCN:2002-014202.
Audience: **u,f.**

Genet, Jean **PQ2613**
Théâtre Complet. Gallimard. 2002. ISBN:2-07-011491-0, ISBN13: 978-2-07-011491-7.
Audience: **u,f.**

Genet, Jean **PQ2613.E53Z46313**
Prisoner of Love. Barbara Bray (Translator). Trade Paper. New York Review of Books, Incorporated, The. New York, NY. 2003. 456p. ISBN:1-59017-028-8, ISBN13: 978-1-59017-028-1. Dewey:848/.91209. LCCN:2002-014859.
Audience: **g,l,u,f.**

Genet, Jean **PQ2613.E53**
The Balcony. Bernard Frechtman (Translator). Trade Paper. Grove/Atlantic, Inc. New York, NY. 1988. 112p. ISBN:0-8021-5034-9, ISBN13: 978-0-8021-5034-9. Dewey:842.912. LCCN:58-009490.
Audience: **g,l,u,f.**

Genet, Jean **PQ3919.2.T73**
The Blacks: A Clown Show. Bernard Frechtman (Translator). Trade Paper. Grove/Atlantic, Inc. New York, NY. 1988. 128p. ISBN:0-8021-5028-4, ISBN13: 978-0-8021-5028-8. Dewey:842. LCCN:60-006340.
Audience: **g,l,u,f.**

Genet, Jean **PQ2613 G285 F9**
Funeral Rites. Bernard Frechtman (Translator). Trade Paper. Grove/Atlantic, Inc. New York, NY. 1987. 272p. ISBN:0-8021-3087-9, ISBN13: 978-0-8021-3087-7. Dewey:843/.9/12. LCCN:68-058157.
Audience: **g,l,u,f.**

Genet, Jean **PQ3919.2.T73**
Maids and Deathwatch. Bernard Frechtman (Translator). Trade Paper. Grove/Atlantic, Inc. New York, NY. 1988. 168p. ISBN:0-8021-5056-X, ISBN13: 978-0-8021-5056-1. Dewey:842. LCCN:53-007149.
Audience: **g,l,u,f.**

Genet, Jean **PQ2613.E53**
Miracle of the Rose. Bernard Frechtman (Translator). Trade Paper. Grove/Atlantic, Inc. New York, NY. 1988. 344p. ISBN:0-8021-3088-7, ISBN13: 978-0-8021-3088-4. Dewey:842.912. LCCN:66-058157.
Audience: **g,l,u,f.**

Genet, Jean **PQ2613.E53**
The Screens. Bernard Frechtman (Translator). Trade Paper. Grove/Atlantic, Inc. New York, NY. 1987. 208p. ISBN:0-8021-5158-2, ISBN13: 978-0-8021-5158-2. Dewey:PQ2613.E53. LCCN:62-013055.
Audience: **g,l,u,f.**

Genet, Jean **PQ2613.E53N613 1991**
Our Lady of the Flowers. Bernard Frechtman (Translator), Jean-Paul Sartre (Introduction by). Trade Paper. Grove/Atlantic, Inc. New York, NY. 1987. 320p. ISBN:0-8021-3013-5, ISBN13: 978-0-8021-3013-6. Dewey:843.9/12. LCCN:87-000414.
Audience: **g,l,u,f.** B

Genet, Jean **PQ2613.E53J613 1987**
The Thief's Journal. Bernard Frechtman (Translator), Jean-Paul Sartre (Foreword by). Trade Paper. Grove/Atlantic, Inc. New York, NY. 1987. 272p. ISBN:0-8021-3014-3, ISBN13: 978-0-8021-3014-3. Dewey:843/.912. LCCN:87-012095.
Audience: **g,l,u,f.** B

Genet, Jean **PQ2613.E53**
Selected Writings of Jean Genet. Edmund White (Editor). Trade Paper. HarperCollins Publishers. New York, NY. 1995. 480p. Companions Ser. ISBN:0-88001-420-2, ISBN13: 978-0-88001-420-5. Dewey:842/.912.
Audience: **g,l,u,f.**

Knapp, Bettina L. **PQ2613.E53Z76 1989**
Jean Genet. Trade Cloth. Macmillan Publishing Company, Inc. Old Tappan, NJ. 1989. 200p. World Authors Ser., No. 44 ISBN:0-8057-8240-0, ISBN13: 978-0-8057-8240-0. Dewey:848/.91209. LCCN:88-021308.
Audience: **l,u.**

Redonnet, Marie **PQ2613.E53 Z867 2000**
Jean Genet, le poète travesti : Portrait d'une oeuvre. Grasset. 2000. ISBN:2-246-59281-X, ISBN13: 978-2-246-59281-5.
Audience: **u,f.**

Sartre, Jean-Paul **PQ2613.E53 Z883 1983**
Saint Genet: Actor and Martyr. Bernard Frechtman (Translator). Trade Paper. Knopf Publishing Group. New York, NY. 1983. 625p. ISBN:0-394-71583-7, ISBN13: 978-0-394-71583-4. Dewey:842/.912. LCCN:83-002460.
Audience: **u,f.**

White, Edmund **PQ2605.O28**
Genet: A Biography. Book, Other. Knopf Publishing Group. New York, NY. 1994. 800p. ISBN:0-679-75479-2, ISBN13: 978-0-679-75479-4. Dewey:848/.91209 B.
Audience: **g,l,u,f.** *Choice, 1994.*

Modern French Literature > Individual Authors, 20th C., to 1960 > Gide

Bree, Germaine **PQ2613**
Gide. Trade Cloth. Greenwood Publishing Group, Inc. Portsmouth, NH. 1985. 302p. ISBN:0-313-24797-8, ISBN13: 978-0-313-24797-2. Dewey:848/.91209. LCCN:84-027916.
Audience: **l,u.**

Cordle, Thomas **PQ2613.I2.Z6153 1993**
Andre Gide Revisited. Trade Cloth. Thomson Gale. Farmington Hills, MI. 1992. 160p. Twayne's World Authors Ser., Vol. 86 ISBN:0-8057-8283-4, ISBN13: 978-0-8057-8283-7. Dewey:848/.91209. LCCN:92-028708.
Audience: **l,u.** *Choice, 1993.*

Ferrere, E. L. **PC2025**
Andre Gide: L insaisissable protee, etude critique de l oeuvre de Gide. Trade Paper. French & European Publications, Inc. New York, NY. 2004. ISBN:0-320-04952-3, ISBN13: 978-0-320-04952-1. Dewey:843.9.
Audience: **u,f.**

Gide, Andre **PQ2613.I2**
The Counterfeiters. Trade Paper. Knopf Publishing Group. New York, NY. 1973. 480p. ISBN:0-394-71842-9, ISBN13: 978-0-394-71842-2. Dewey:843/.9/12. LCCN:72-008064.
Audience: **g,l,u,f.** B

Gide, Andre **PQ2613.I2 Z5213 2001**
If It Die: An Autobiography. Trade Paper. Knopf Publishing Group. New York, NY. 2001. 336p. Vintage International Ser. ISBN:0-375-72606-3, ISBN13: 978-0-375-72606-4. Dewey:848/.91209. LCCN:2004-266927.
Audience: **g,l,u,f.**

Gide, Andre **PQ2613.I2I4813 2003**
The Immoralist: A Dual-Language Book. Stanley Appelbaum (Editor, Translator). Trade Paper. Dover Publications, Inc. Mineola, NY. 2003. 208p. ISBN:0-486-42695-5, ISBN13: 978-0-486-42695-2. LCCN:2002-041030.
Audience: **g,l,u,f.**

Gide, Andre **HQ76.25.G5213 2000**
Corydon. Richard Howard (Translator). Trade Paper. University of Illinois Press. Champaign, IL. 2001. 160p. ISBN:0-252-07006-2, ISBN13: 978-0-252-07006-8. Dewey:306.76/6. LCCN:2001-027389.
Audience: **g,l,u,f.**

Gide, Andre **HV6963.N5313 2003**
Judge Not. Benjamin Ivry (Translator, Introduction by, Notes by). Trade Cloth. University of Illinois Press. Champaign, IL. 2003. 200p. ISBN:0-252-02844-9, ISBN13: 978-0-252-02844-1. Dewey:364.944. LCCN:2002-152245.
Audience: **g,l,u,f.**

Gide, Andre **PQ2613.I2Z56**
Self-Portraits, the Gide-Valery Letters, 1890-1942. Robert Mallet (Editor), June Guicharnaud (Translator). Trade Paper. Books on Demand. Ann Arbor, MI. 346p. ISBN:0-608-12555-5, ISBN13: 978-0-608-12555-8. Dewey:848.91209. LCCN:65-025125.
Audience: **g,l,u,f.**

Gide, Andre **PQ2613.I2Z465413**
Journals, 1889-1913, Vol. 1. Justin O'Brien (Translator), Richard Howard (Introduction by). Trade Paper. University of Illinois Press. Champaign, IL. 2000. 432p. ISBN:0-252-06929-3, ISBN13: 978-0-252-06929-1. Dewey:848/.91203 B. LCCN:00-037715.
Audience: **g,l,u,f.**

Gide, Andre **PQ2613.I2Z465413**
Journals, 1914-1927, Vol. 2. Justin O'Brien (Translator), Richard Howard (Introduction by). Trade Paper. University of Illinois Press. Champaign, IL. 2000. 496p. ISBN:0-252-06930-7, ISBN13: 978-0-252-06930-7. Dewey:848/.91203 B. LCCN:00-037715.
Audience: **g,l,u,f.**

Gide, Andre **PQ2613.I2Z465413**
Journals, 1928-1939, Vol. 3. Justin O'Brien (Translator), Richard Howard (Introduction by). Trade Paper. University of Illinois Press. Champaign, IL. 2000. 480p. ISBN:0-252-06931-5, ISBN13: 978-0-252-06931-4. Dewey:848/.91203 B. LCCN:00-037715.
Audience: **g,l,u,f.**

Gide, Andre **PQ2613.I2Z465413**
Journals, 1939-1949, Vol. 4. Justin O'Brien (Translator), Richard Howard (Introduction by). Trade Paper. University of Illinois Press. Champaign, IL. 2000. 368p. ISBN:0-252-06932-3, ISBN13: 978-0-252-06932-1. Dewey:848/.91203 B. LCCN:00-037715.
Audience: **g,l,u,f.**

Gide, André **PQ2613**
Les cahiers et les poésies d'André Walter : avec des fragments inédits du Journal. Gallimard. 1986. ISBN:2-07-032360-9, ISBN13: 978-2-07-032360-9.
Audience: **u,f.**

Gide, André **PQ2613.I2 A16 1999**
Essais critiques. Gallimard. 1999. ISBN:2-07-011504-6, ISBN13: 978-2-07-011504-4.
Audience: **u,f.**

Gide, André **PQ2613.I2**
Journal, vol. 1. Gallimard. 1996. ISBN:2-07-011395-7, ISBN13: 978-2-07-011395-8.
Audience: **u,f.**

Gide, André **PQ2613.I2**
Journal, vol. 2. Gallimard. 1997. ISBN:2-07-011396-5, ISBN13: 978-2-07-011396-5.
Audience: **u,f.**

Gide, André **PQ2613.I2 A6 1950**
Littérature engagée. Gallimard. 1950.
Audience: **u,f.**

Gide, André **PQ2613.I2**
Romans, récits et soties, oeuvres lyriques. Gallimard. 2001. ISBN:2-07-010225-4, ISBN13: 978-2-07-010225-9.
Audience: **u,f.**

Gide, André **PQ2613.I2 Z4775 2001**
Souvenirs et voyages. Gallimard. 2001. ISBN:2-07-011624-7, ISBN13: 978-2-07-011624-9.
Audience: **u,f.**

Gide, André **PQ2613.I2 A19**
Théâtre. Gallimard. 1969.
Audience: **u,f.**

Gide, André; Valéry, Paul **PQ2613.I2 Z52826**
André Gide - Paul Valéry : correspondance, 1890-1942. Gallimard. 1955.
Audience: **u,f.**

Sheridan, Alan **PQ2613.I2Z6916 1999**
Andre Gide: A Life in the Present. Trade Cloth. Harvard University Press. Cambridge, MA. 1999. 752p. ISBN:0-674-03527-5, ISBN13: 978-0-674-03527-0. Dewey:848.9/12/09. LCCN:98-073544.
Audience: **g,l,u,f.** *Choice, 1999.*

Modern French Literature > Individual Authors, 20th C., to 1960 > Ionesco

Ionesco, Eugène **PQ2617.O6**
Notes et contre-notes. Gallimard. 1992. ISBN:2-07-032744-2, ISBN13: 978-2-07-032744-7.
Audience: **u,f.**

Ionesco, Eugène **PQ2617.O6**
Journal en miettes. Gallimard. 1992. ISBN:2-07-032744-2, ISBN13: 978-2-07-032744-7.
Audience: **u,f.**

Ionesco, Eugène **PQ2617.O6 P7**
Présent passé, passé présent. Gallimard. 1976.
Audience: **u,f.**

Ionesco, Eugène **PQ2617.O6**
Théâtre complet. Gallimard. 2002. ISBN:2-07-011198-9, ISBN13: 978-2-07-011198-5.
Audience: **u,f.**

Modern French Literature > Individual Authors, 20th C., to 1960 > J

Jarry, Alfred **PQ2619.A65**
OEuvres complètes, vol. 1. Gallimard. 1988.
Audience: **u,f.**

Beaumont, Keith **PQ2619.A65Z58 1984**
Alfred Jarry: A Critical and Biographical Study. Cloth Text. Palgrave Macmillan. New York, NY. 1985. 396p. ISBN:0-312-01712-X, ISBN13: 978-0-312-01712-5. Dewey:842/.8. LCCN:84-040443.
Audience: **l,u,f.**

Jabès, Edmond **PQ2619.A112**
Le Livre des questions, vol. 1. Gallimard. 1988. ISBN:2-07-071194-3, ISBN13: 978-2-07-071194-9.
Audience: **u,f.**

Jabès, Edmond **PQ2619.A112**
Le Livre des questions, vol. 2. Gallimard. 1989. ISBN:2-07-071526-4, ISBN13: 978-2-07-071526-8.
Audience: **u,f.**

Jacob, Max **PQ2619.A17**
Le cornet à dés. Gallimard. 2003. ISBN:2-07-030437-X, ISBN13: 978-2-07-030437-0.
Audience: **u,f.**

Jacob, Max **PQ2619.A17**
Le laboratoire central. Gallimard. 1994. ISBN:2-07-032194-0, ISBN13: 978-2-07-032194-0.
Audience: **u,f.**

Jarry, Alfred **PQ2469.Z5**
Four Novels: Collected Works II. Trade Paper. Atlas Press. London, 2000. 400p. ISBN:1-900565-20-X, ISBN13: 978-1-900565-20-2. Dewey:843.8.
Audience: **g,l,u.**

Jarry, Alfred **PQ2619**
OEuvres complètes, vol. 2. Gallimard. 1988. ISBN:2-07-011127-X, ISBN13: 978-2-07-011127-5.
Audience: **u,f.**

Jarry, Alfred **PQ2619.A65**
OEuvres complètes, vol. 3. Gallimard. 1988.
Audience: **u,f.**

Jarry, Alfred **PQ2387.R5**
Adventures in Pataphysics: Collected Writings. Paul Edwards & Alastair Brotchie (Editors). Trade Paper. Atlas Press. London, 2001. 334p. ISBN:1-900565-25-0, ISBN13: 978-1-900565-25-7. Dewey:848.8/08.
Audience: **u,f.**

Jarry, Alfred **PQ2619.A65**
The Ubu Plays: Ubu Rex; Ubu Cuckolded; Ubu Enchained. Simon W. Taylor & Cyrill Connolly (Translators). Trade Paper. Grove/Atlantic, Inc. New York, NY. 1968. 160p. ISBN:0-8021-5010-1, ISBN13: 978-0-8021-5010-3. Dewey:812.1. LCCN:69-019439.
Audience: **g,l,u,f.**

LaBelle, Maurice M. **PQ2619.A65.Z72**
Alfred Jarry: Nihilism and the Theatre of the Absurd. Trade Cloth. New York University Press. New York, NY. 1980. ix, 194p. Gotham Library Ser. ISBN:0-8147-4995-X, ISBN13: 978-0-8147-4995-1. Dewey:842/.8. LCCN:79-003009.
Audience: **u,f.**

Modern French Literature > Individual Authors, 20th C., to 1960 > K-L

Jansiti, Carlo **PQ2623.E3657 Z73 1999**
Violette Leduc. B. Grasset. 1999. ISBN:2-246-57651-2, ISBN13: 978-2-246-57651-8.
Audience: **u,f.**

Kessel, Joseph **PQ2621.E77**
Belle de jour. Gallimard. 1996. ISBN:2-07-036125-X, ISBN13: 978-2-07-036125-0.
Audience: **u,f.**

Kessel, Joseph **PQ2621.E77**
Le lion. Gallimard. 1997. ISBN:2-07-036808-4, ISBN13: 978-2-07-036808-2.
Audience: **u,f.**

Larbaud, Valéry **PQ2623**
Oeuvres. Gallimard. 1989. ISBN:2-07-010300-5, ISBN13: 978-2-07-010300-3.
Audience: **u,f.**

Leduc, Violette **PQ2623.E3657**
La bâtarde. Gallimard. 1996. ISBN:2-07-074535-X, ISBN13: 978-2-07-074535-7.
Audience: **u,f.**

Leduc, Violette **PQ2623.E3657**
L'asphyxie. Gallimard. 1987. ISBN:2-07-071217-6, ISBN13: 978-2-07-071217-5.
Audience: **u,f.**

Leduc, Violette **PQ2623.E3657 T5 2000**
Thérèse et Isabelle : texte intégral. Gallimard. 2000. ISBN:2-07-075895-8, ISBN13: 978-2-07-075895-1.
Audience: **u,f.**

Leiris, Michel **PQ2623.E424**
L'Age d'homme : précédé de De la Littérature considérée comme une tauromachie. Gallimard. 2004. ISBN:2-07-036435-6, ISBN13: 978-2-07-036435-0.
Audience: **u,f.**

Leiris, Michel **PQ2623.E424 Z475 2003**
La règle du jeu. Gallimard. 2003. ISBN:2-07-011454-6, ISBN13: 978-2-07-011454-2.
Audience: **u,f.**

Lilar, Suzanne **PQ2623.I52**
La confession anonyme. Gallimard. 1983. ISBN:2-07-025106-3, ISBN13: 978-2-07-025106-3.
Audience: **u,f.**

Lilar, Suzanne **PQ2623.I52**
Une enfance gantoise. Éditions Labor. 1998. ISBN:2-8040-1202-6, ISBN13: 978-2-8040-1202-1.
Audience: **u,f.**

Lilar, Suzanne; Ronse, Henri **PQ2623.I52 Z6 1986**
Cahiers Suzanne Lilar. Gallimard. 1986. ISBN:2-07-070632-X, ISBN13: 978-2-07-070632-7.
Audience: **u,f.**

Modern French Literature > Individual Authors, 20th C., to 1960 > Maeterlinck

Maeterlinck, Maurice **PQ2625**
L'oiseau bleu : théâtre. Labor. 1998. ISBN:2-8040-1300-6, ISBN13: 978-2-8040-1300-4.
Audience: **u,f.**

Maeterlinck, Maurice **PQ2625.A5**
Pelléas et Mélisande. Labor. 2001. ISBN:2-8040-0204-7, ISBN13: 978-2-8040-0204-6.
Audience: **u,f.**

Modern French Literature > Individual Authors, 20th C., to 1960 > Malraux

Lebovics, Herman **DC33.7.L425 1999**
Mona Lisa's Escort: Andre Malraux and the Reinvention of French Culture. Book, Other. Cornell University Press. Ithaca, NY. 1999. 288p. ISBN:0-8014-3565-X, ISBN13: 978-0-8014-3565-2. Dewey:944.083. LCCN:98-030461.
Audience: **u,f.** *Choice, 1999.*

Lyotard, Jean François **PQ2625.A716 Z69658 1998**
Chambre sourde : l'antiesthétique de Malraux. Galilée. 1998. ISBN:2-7186-0489-1, ISBN13: 978-2-7186-0489-3.
Audience: **u,f.**

Malraux, Andre **PQ2625.A716C612 1992**
The Conquerors. Stephen Becker (Translator), Herbert R. Lottman (Foreword by). Trade Paper. University of Chicago Press. Chicago, IL. 1992. 212p. Phoenix Fiction Ser. ISBN:0-226-50290-2, ISBN13: 978-0-226-50290-8. Dewey:843/.912. LCCN:72-091594.
Audience: **g,u,f.**

Malraux, Andre **PQ2631.R63**
The Walnut Trees of Altenburg. A. W. Fielding (Translator), Conor C. O'Brien (Foreword by). Trade Paper. University of Chicago Press. Chicago, IL. 1992. 221p. Phoenix Fiction Ser. ISBN:0-226-50289-9, ISBN13: 978-0-226-50289-2. Dewey:843/.912. LCCN:88-037363.
Audience: **g,l,u,f.**

Malraux, André **PQ3919.R74**
Man's Fate. Trade Paper. Knopf Publishing Group. New York, NY. 1990. 368p. ISBN:0-679-72574-1, ISBN13: 978-0-679-72574-9. Dewey:843.
Audience: **u,f.**

Malraux, André **PQ2625**
Oeuvres complètes. Gallimard. 1989. ISBN:2-07-011142-3, ISBN13: 978-2-07-011142-8.
Audience: **u,f.**

Malraux, André **CB251.M313 1992**
The Temptation of the West. Robert Hollander (Translator), Jonathan D. Spence (Foreword by). Trade Paper. University of Chicago Press. Chicago, IL. 1998. 154p. ISBN:0-226-50291-0, ISBN13: 978-0-226-50291-5. Dewey:303.48/25104. LCCN:91-029981.
Audience: **u,f.**

Todd, Olivier **PQ2625.A716Z946513**
Malraux: A Life. Joseph West (Translator). Trade Cloth. Alfred A. Knopf Inc. New York, NY. 2005. 560p. ISBN:0-375-40702-2, ISBN13: 978-0-375-40702-4. Dewey:843/.912. LCCN:2004-044216.
Audience: **g,l,u,f.** *Choice, 2005.*

Modern French Literature > Individual Authors, 20th C., to 1960 > Martin du Gard, Mauriac

Alluin, Bernard **PQ2625.A823 Z54 1989**
Martin Du Gard, romancier. Aux Amateurs de livres. 1989. ISBN:2-87841-002-5, ISBN13: 978-2-87841-002-0.
Audience: **u,f.**

Martin Du Gard, Roger **PQ2625**
OEuvres complètes, vol. 1. Gallimard. 1995. ISBN:2-07-010343-9, ISBN13: 978-2-07-010343-0.
Audience: **u,f.**

Martin Du Gard, Roger **PQ2625**
OEuvres complètes, vol. 2. Gallimard. 1995. ISBN:2-07-010344-7, ISBN13: 978-2-07-010344-7.
Audience: **u,f.**

Mauriac, François **PQ2625.A93 A6**
OEuvres romanesques et théâtrales complètes, vol. 1. Gallimard. 1978. ISBN:2-07-010931-3, ISBN13: 978-2-07-010931-9.
Audience: **u,f.**

Mauriac, François **PQ2625.A93 A6**
OEuvres romanesques et théâtrales complètes, vol. 2. Gallimard. 1980.
Audience: **u,f.**

Mauriac, François **PQ2625.A93 A6**
OEuvres romanesques et théâtrales complètes, vol. 3. Gallimard. 1982.
Audience: **u,f.**

Mauriac, François **PQ2625.A93 A6**
OEuvres romanesques et théâtrales complètes, vol. 4. Gallimard. 1985.
Audience: **u,f.**

Modern French Literature > Individual Authors, 20th C., to 1960 > M-O

Bréchon, Robert **PQ2625.I2 Z578 2005**
Henri Michaux : la poésie comme destin : biographie. Aden. 2005. ISBN:2-84840-076-5, ISBN13: 978-2-84840-076-1.
Audience: **u,f.**

Michaux, Henri **PQ2625.I2 A113 1998**
OEuvres complètes, vol. 1. Gallimard. 1998. ISBN:2-07-011401-5, ISBN13: 978-2-07-011401-6.
Audience: **u,f.**

Michaux, Henri **PQ2625.I2**
OEuvres complètes, vol. 2. Gallimard. 1998.
ISBN:2-07-011402-3, ISBN13: 978-2-07-011402-3.
Audience: **u,f.**

Michaux, Henri **PQ2625.I2 A113 1998**
OEuvres complètes, vol. 3. Gallimard. 1998.
ISBN:2-07-011745-6, ISBN13: 978-2-07-011745-1.
Audience: **u,f.**

Montherlant, Henry de **PQ2625**
Essais. Gallimard. 1988. ISBN:2-07-010379-X, ISBN13: 978-2-07-010379-9.
Audience: **u,f.**

Montherlant, Henry de **PQ2625**
Romans : et oeuvres de fiction non théâtrales, vol. 1. Gallimard. 1982. ISBN:2-07-010376-5, ISBN13: 978-2-07-010376-8.
Audience: **u,f.**

Montherlant, Henry de **PQ2625**
Romans : et oeuvres de fiction non théâtrales, vol. 2. Gallimard. 1989. ISBN:2-07-011005-2, ISBN13: 978-2-07-011005-6.
Audience: **u,f.**

Montherlant, Henry de **PQ2625**
Théâtre. Gallimard. 1995. ISBN:2-07-010374-9, ISBN13: 978-2-07-010374-4.
Audience: **u,f.**

Obaldia, René de **PQ2629.B3 A19 2001**
Théâtre complet. B. Grasset. 2001. ISBN:2-246-62391-X, ISBN13: 978-2-246-62391-5.
Audience: **u,f.**

Modern French Literature > Individual Authors, 20th C., to 1960 > P

Castans, Raymond; Pagnol, Marcel **PQ2631.A26**
Il était une fois-- Marcel Pagnol. Editions de Fallois. 1995.
ISBN:2-87706-240-6, ISBN13: 978-2-87706-240-4.
Audience: **u,f.**

Marcel Pagnol **PQ2631.A26 1995**
OEuvres complètes, vol. 1. Editions de Fallois. 1995.
ISBN:2-87706-221-X, ISBN13: 978-2-87706-221-3.
Audience: **u,f.**

Pagnol, Marcel **PQ2631**
OEuvres complètes, vol. 3. Editions de Fallois. 1995.
ISBN:2-87706-223-6, ISBN13: 978-2-87706-223-7.
Audience: **u,f.**

Pagnol, Marcel **PQ2631**
OEuvres complètes, vol. 2. Editions de Fallois. 1995.
ISBN:2-87706-222-8, ISBN13: 978-2-87706-222-0.
Audience: **u,f.**

Perse, Saint-John **PQ2623**
OEuvres complètes. Gallimard. 1989. ISBN:2-07-010736-1, ISBN13: 978-2-07-010736-0.
Audience: **u,f.**

Pieyre de Mandiargues, André **PQ2631.I33 M3**
La marge. Gallimard. 1981.
Audience: **u,f.**

Pinget, Robert **PQ2631.I638**
L'inquisitoire. Editions de Minuit. 1986. ISBN:2-7073-1070-0, ISBN13: 978-2-7073-1070-5.
Audience: **u,f.**

Ponge, Francis **PQ2631.O643**
OEuvres complètes, vol. 1. Gallimard. 1999.
ISBN:2-07-011271-3, ISBN13: 978-2-07-011271-5.
Audience: **u,f.**

Ponge, Francis **PQ2631.O643 A113 1999**
OEuvres complètes, vol. 2. Gallimard. 2002.
ISBN:2-07-011493-7, ISBN13: 978-2-07-011493-1.
Audience: **u,f.**

Prévert, Jacques **PQ2631.R387 1992**
OEuvres complètes, vol. 1. Gallimard. 1992.
ISBN:2-07-011230-6, ISBN13: 978-2-07-011230-2.
Audience: **u,f.**

Prévert, Jacques **PQ2631.R387**
OEuvres complètes, vol. 2. Gallimard. 1996.
Audience: **u,f.**

Péguy, Charles **PQ2631.E25**
OEuvres en prose complètes, vol. 1. Gallimard. 1987.
ISBN:2-07-011114-8, ISBN13: 978-2-07-011114-5.
Audience: **u,f.**

Péguy, Charles **PQ3949.2.F7**
Oeuvres en prose complètes, vol. 2. Gallimard. 1992.
ISBN:2-07-011231-4, ISBN13: 978-2-07-011231-9.
Audience: **u,f.**

Péguy, Charles **PQ2631.P34**
OEuvres poétiques complètes. Gallimard. 1994.
ISBN:2-07-010438-9, ISBN13: 978-2-07-010438-3.
Audience: **u,f.**

Péret, Benjamin **PQ2631.E348**
Oeuvres complètes. J. Corti. 1987.
Audience: **u,f.**

Modern French Literature > Individual Authors, 20th C., to 1960 > Proust

Bales, Richard (Editor) **PQ2631.R63 Z54547 2**
The Cambridge Companion to Proust. Cloth Text. Cambridge University Press. New York, NY. 2001. 266p. Companions to Literature Ser. ISBN:0-521-66019-X, ISBN13: 978-0-521-66019-8. Dewey:843/.912. LCCN:00-045519.
Audience: **g,u,f.** *Choice, 2002.*

Carter, William C. **PQ2631.R63**
Marcel Proust: A Life. Trade Paper. Yale University Press. Cumberland, RI. 2002. 992p. Henry McBride Series in Modernism and Modernity ISBN:0-300-09400-0, ISBN13: 978-0-300-09400-8. Dewey:843/.912 B.
Audience: **g,l,u,f.** *Choice, 2000.*

Genette, Gerard **PN3331**
Narrative Discourse: An Essay in Method. Jane E. Lewin (Translator), Jonathan Culler (Foreword by). Trade Paper. Cornell University Press. Ithaca, NY. 1983. 288p. ISBN:0-8014-9259-9, ISBN13: 978-0-8014-9259-4. Dewey:809.3. LCCN:79-013499.
Audience: **u,f.**

Girard, Rene **PQ2631.R63**
Proust: A Collection of Critical Essays. Paper Text. Textbook Publishers. Temecula, CA. 2003. 182p. ISBN:0-7581-6113-1, ISBN13: 978-0-7581-6113-0. Dewey:843.912.
Audience: **u,f.**

Hindus, Milton **PQ2631.R63Z626 2001**
A Reader's Guide to Marcel Proust. Trade Paper. Syracuse University Press. Syracuse, NY. 2001. x, 275p. Reader's Guide Ser. ISBN:0-8156-0695-8, ISBN13: 978-0-8156-0695-6. Dewey:843/.914. LCCN:00-053171.
Audience: **g,l,u,f.**

Lee, Tanith & Caws, Mary Ann **PQ2631.R63Z545656**
Marcel Proust. Trade Cloth. Overlook Press, The. New York, NY. 2003. 160p. Overlook Illustrated Lives Ser. ISBN:1-58567-405-2, ISBN13: 978-1-58567-405-3. Dewey:843/.912. LCCN:2003-054929.
Audience: **g,l,u,f.**

Proust, Marcel **PQ2631.R63**
Contre Sainte-Beuve. Gallimard. 2000. ISBN:2-07-010651-9, ISBN13: 978-2-07-010651-6.
Audience: **u,f.**

Proust, Marcel **PQ2631.R63**
In Search of Lost Time, Set. Quantity Pack, Trade Paper. Random House Adult Trade Publishing Group. New York, NY. 2003. ISBN:0-8129-6964-2, ISBN13: 978-0-8129-6964-1. Dewey:843.9/12.
Audience: **g,l,u,f.**

Proust, Marcel **PQ2631.R63**
Jean Santeuil. Gallimard. 2001. ISBN:2-07-076185-1, ISBN13: 978-2-07-076185-2.
Audience: **u,f.**

Proust, Marcel **PQ2631.R63 Z48 2004**
Lettres : 1879-1922. Plon. 2004. ISBN:2-259-18505-3, ISBN13: 978-2-259-18505-9.
Audience: **u,f.**

Proust, Marcel **PQ2631.R63**
Marcel Proust on Art and Literature, 1896-1919. Paper Text. Textbook Publishers. Temecula, CA. 2003. 416p. ISBN:0-7581-8339-9, ISBN13: 978-0-7581-8339-2. Dewey:843/.912.
Audience: **u,f.**

Proust, Marcel **PQ2631.R63**
La recherche du temps perdu, vol. 1. Gallimard. 1987. ISBN:2-07-011126-1, ISBN13: 978-2-07-011126-8.
Audience: **u,f.**

Proust, Marcel **PQ2631.R63**
La recherche du temps perdu, vol. 2. Gallimard. 1987. ISBN:2-07-011136-9, ISBN13: 978-2-07-011136-7.
Audience: **u,f.**

Proust, Marcel **PQ2631.R63**
La recherche du temps perdu, vol. 3. Gallimard. 1987. ISBN:2-07-011143-1, ISBN13: 978-2-07-011143-5.
Audience: **u,f.**

Proust, Marcel **PQ2631.R63**
La recherche du temps perdu, vol. 4. Gallimard. 1987. ISBN:2-07-011164-4, ISBN13: 978-2-07-011164-0.
Audience: **u,f.**

Proust, Marcel **PQ2631.R63 D813**
Swann's Way: In Search of Lost Time. Lydia Davis (Translator, Introduction by, Notes by). Trade Paper. Penguin Group (USA) Inc. New York, NY. 2004. 496p. Penguin Classics Deluxe Edition Ser. ISBN:0-14-243796-4, ISBN13: 978-0-14-243796-4. Dewey:843/.912.
Audience: **g,l,u,f.**

Proust, Marcel **PQ2631.R63Z48 1988**
Marcel Proust: Selected Letters, 1880-1903. Philip Kolb (Editor), Ralph Manheim (Translator), J. M. Cocking (Introduction by). Paper Text. University of Chicago Press. Chicago, IL. 1997. xxviii, 376p. ISBN:0-226-68459-8, ISBN13: 978-0-226-68459-8. Dewey:843/.912 B. LCCN:88-014392.
Audience: **g,l,u,f.**

Proust, Marcel **PQ2631.R63**
In the Shadow of Young Girls in Flower: In Search of Lost Time. Christopher Prendergast (Editor), James Grieve (Translator, Introduction by, Notes by). Trade Paper. Penguin Group (USA) Inc. New York, NY. 2005. 576p. Penguin Classics Deluxe Edition Ser. ISBN:0-14-303907-5, ISBN13: 978-0-14-303907-5. Dewey:843.9/12.
Audience: **g,l,u,f.**

Proust, Marcel **PQ2631.R63 S6313**
Sodom and Gomorrah: In Search of Lost Time. John Sturrock (Translator). Trade Paper. Penguin Group (USA) Inc. New York, NY. 2005. 576p. Penguin Classics Deluxe Edition Ser. ISBN:0-14-303931-8, ISBN13: 978-0-14-303931-0. Dewey:843/.912.
Audience: **g,l,u,f.**

Proust, Marcel **PQ2631.R63**
On Reading. John Sturrock (Translator, Preface by). Trade Paper. Penguin Group (USA) Inc. New York, NY. 1995. 80p. Syrens Ser. ISBN:0-14-038903-2, ISBN13: 978-0-14-038903-6. Dewey:844/.9/12.
Audience: **u,f.**

Proust, Marcel **PQ2631.R63 C7413**
The Guermantes Way: In Search of Lost Time. Mark Treharne (Translator). Trade Paper. Penguin Group (USA) Inc. New York, NY. 2005. 640p. Penguin Classics Deluxe Edition Ser. ISBN:0-14-303922-9, ISBN13: 978-0-14-303922-8. Dewey:843.912.
Audience: **g,l,u,f.**

Shattuck, Roger **PQ2631.R63A883 2000**
Proust's Way: A Field Guide to 'In Search of Lost Time'. Trade Cloth. W. W. Norton & Company, Inc. New York, NY. 2000. 288p. ISBN:0-393-04914-0, ISBN13: 978-0-393-04914-5. Dewey:843/.912. LCCN:99-058472.
Audience: **g,l,u,f.** *Choice, 2000.*

Tadie, Jean-Yves **PQ2631.R63**
Marcel Proust: A Life. Euan Cameron (Translator). Trade Paper. Penguin Group (USA) Inc. New York, NY. 2001. 1016p. ISBN:0-14-100203-4, ISBN13: 978-0-14-100203-3. Dewey:843/.912 B.
Audience: **g,l,u,f.**

Modern French Literature > Individual Authors, 20th C., to 1960 > Q

Queneau, Raymond **PQ2633**
OEuvres complètes. Gallimard. 1987. ISBN:2-07-011168-7, ISBN13: 978-2-07-011168-8.
Audience: **u,f.**

Modern French Literature > Individual Authors, 20th C., to 1960 > R

Francis, R. A. **PQ2605.O28**
Romain Rolland. Cloth over Boards. Berg Publishers. Oxford, 1999. 256p. ISBN:1-85973-270-4, ISBN13: 978-1-85973-270-0. Dewey:848.9/12/09.
Audience: **g,l,u,f.** *Choice, 2000.*

Radiguet, Raymond **PQ2635.A25**
Le diable au corps ; suivi de, Le bal du comte d'Orgel : romans : texte intégral. Grasset. 2003. ISBN:2-246-15773-0, ISBN13: 978-2-246-15773-1.
Audience: **u,f.**

Renard, Jules **PQ2469.Z5**
OEuvres. Gallimard. 1987. ISBN:2-07-010474-5, ISBN13: 978-2-07-010474-1.
Audience: **u,f.**

Reverdy, Pierre **PQ2635.E85**
Main d'oeuvre : 1913-1949. Gallimard. 2000. ISBN:2-07-041260-1, ISBN13: 978-2-07-041260-0.
Audience: **u,f.**

Reverdy, Pierre **PQ2635 .E85A7**
Plupart du temps, 1915-1922. Gallimard. 1989. ISBN:2-07-032532-6, ISBN13: 978-2-07-032532-0.
Audience: **u,f.**

Robbe-Grillet, Alain **PQ2635.O117**
Djinn : un trou rouge entre les pavés disjoints. Editions de Minuit. 1985. ISBN:2-7073-1038-7, ISBN13: 978-2-7073-1038-5.
Audience: **u,f.**

Robbe-Grillet, Alain **PQ2635.O117**
Les gommes. Editions de Minuit. 1994. ISBN:2-7073-0256-2, ISBN13: 978-2-7073-0256-4.
Audience: **u,f.**

Robbe-Grillet, Alain **PQ2635.O117**
La Jalousie. Editions de Minuit. 1990. ISBN:2-7073-0054-3, ISBN13: 978-2-7073-0054-6.
Audience: **u,f.**

Robbe-Grillet, Alain **PQ2635.O117**
La Maison de rendez-vous. Editions de Minuit. 1980. ISBN:2-7073-0315-1, ISBN13: 978-2-7073-0315-8.
Audience: **u,f.**

Robbe-Grillet, Alain **PQ2635.O117**
Le miroir qui revient. Editions de Minuit. 1984. ISBN:2-7073-1007-7, ISBN13: 978-2-7073-1007-1.
Audience: **u,f.**

Robbe-Grillet, Alain **PR4887.M7 1952**
Repetition: A Novel. Trade Paper. Grove/Atlantic, Inc. New York, NY. 2004. 208p. ISBN:0-8021-4057-2, ISBN13: 978-0-8021-4057-9. Dewey:843/.914. LCCN:52-009057.
Audience: **g,l,u,f.**

Robbe-Grillet, Alain **PQ2635.O117**
Souvenirs du triangle d'or : roman. Editions de Minuit. 1985. ISBN:2-02-008612-3, ISBN13: 978-2-02-008612-7.
Audience: **u,f.**

Robbe-Grillet, Alain **PQ2635.O117**
Le voyeur. Éditions de Minuit. 1999.
Audience: **u,f.**

Robbe-Grillet, Alain **PQ2605.A3734**
The Erasers. Richard Howard (Translator). Trade Paper. Grove/Atlantic, Inc. New York, NY. 1994. 256p. ISBN:0-8021-5086-1, ISBN13: 978-0-8021-5086-8. Dewey:843/.914. LCCN:61-011766.
Audience: **g,l,u,f.**

Robbe-Grillet, Alain & Howard, Richard **PN3503**
For a New Novel: Essays on Fiction. Trade Paper. Northwestern University Press. Evanston, IL. 1992. 175p. ISBN:0-8101-0821-6, ISBN13: 978-0-8101-0821-9. Dewey:809.33.
Audience: **g,l,u,f.**

Robbe-Grillet, Alain **PZ4.R633**
Jealousy and In the Labyrinth. Richard Howard (Translator). Trade Paper. Grove/Atlantic, Inc. New York, NY. 1994. 320p. ISBN:0-8021-5106-X, ISBN13: 978-0-8021-5106-3. Dewey:843.9.
Audience: **g,l,u,f.**

Robbe-Grillet, Alain **PQ2635.O117**
The Voyeur. Richard Howard (Translator). Trade Paper. Grove/Atlantic, Inc. New York, NY. 1994. 224p. ISBN:0-8021-3165-4, ISBN13: 978-0-8021-3165-2. Dewey:843.914. LCCN:58-009912.
Audience: **g,l,u,f.**

Robbe-Grillet, Alain **PQ2635.O117A25 1987**
La Maison de Rendez-Vous and Djinn. Richard Howard, Yvone Lenard & Walter Wells (Translators). Trade Paper. Grove/Atlantic, Inc. New York, NY. 1987. 288p. ISBN:0-8021-3017-8, ISBN13: 978-0-8021-3017-4. Dewey:843/.914. LCCN:87-007387.
Audience: **g,l,u,f.**

Robbe-Grillet, Alain **PQ2635.O117Z47513**
Ghosts in the Mirror. Jo Levy (Translator). Trade Cloth. Grove/Atlantic, Inc. New York, NY. 1989. 160p. ISBN:0-8021-1036-3, ISBN13: 978-0-8021-1036-7. Dewey:843/.914 B. LCCN:88-006958.
Audience: **g,l,u,f.**

Robbe-Grillet, Alain **PQ2605.A3734**
Recollections of the Golden Triangle. J. A. Underwood (Translator). Trade Paper. Grove/Atlantic, Inc. New York, NY. 1986. 160p. ISBN:0-8021-5200-7, ISBN13: 978-0-8021-5200-8. Dewey:843/.914. LCCN:86-045233.
Audience: **g,l,u,f.**

Roblès, Emmanuel **PQ2635.O1845**
Cela s'appelle l'aurore : roman. Éditions du Seuil. 1980. ISBN:2-02-005506-6, ISBN13: 978-2-02-005506-2.
Audience: **u,f.**

Roblès, Emmanuel **PQ2635.O1845 A6 1985**
Théâtre, vol. 1. Grasset. 1985. ISBN:2-246-35591-5, ISBN13: 978-2-246-35591-5.
Audience: **u,f.**

Roblès, Emmanuel **PQ2635.O1845**
Théâtre, vol. 2. Grasset. 1985. ISBN:2-246-35591-5, ISBN13: 978-2-246-35591-5.
Audience: **u,f.**

Rolland, Romain **PQ2635.O5J313 1996**
Jean-Christophe. Louis Auchincloss (Introduction by). Cloth Text. Avalon Publishing Group. New York, NY. 1996. 1584p. ISBN:0-7867-0307-5, ISBN13: 978-0-7867-0307-4. Dewey:843.9/12. LCCN:96-014406.
Audience: **g,l,u,f.**

Romains, Jules
Les hommes de bonne volonté, Vol. 1. R. Laffont. 2003. Bouquins
Audience: **u,f.**

Romains, Jules **PQ2635.O52**
Les hommes de bonne volonté, Vol. 2. R. Laffont. 2003.
Audience: **u,f.**

Romains, Jules **PQ2635.O52**
Les hommes de bonne volonté, Vol. 3. R. Laffont. 2003.
Audience: **u,f.**

Romains, Jules **PQ2635.O52**
Les hommes de bonne volonté, Vol. 4. R. Laffont. 2003.
Audience: **u,f.**

Romains, Jules **PQ2635.O52**
Knock. Trade Paper. Schoenhof's Foreign Books, Inc. Cambridge, MA. 1972. Folio Ser., No. 60 ISBN:2-07-036060-1, ISBN13: 978-2-07-036060-4. Dewey:842.912.
Audience: **u,f.**

Rougemont, Denis de **PN682.C6**
Love in the Western World. Montgomery Belgion (Translator). Trade Paper. Princeton University Press. Princeton, NJ. 1983. 392p. ISBN:0-691-01393-4, ISBN13: 978-0-691-01393-0. Dewey:306.7/09181/2. LCCN:82-048560.
Audience: **g,l,u,f.**

Sturrock, John **PQ671.S76 1969**
The French New Novel: Claude Simon, Michel Butor, Alain Robbe-Grillet. Trade Cloth. Oxford University Press, Inc. New York, NY. 1969. [7], 244p. ISBN:0-19-212178-2, ISBN13: 978-0-19-212178-3. Dewey:843/.9/1409. LCCN:77-102633.
Audience: **u,f.**

Toesca, Maurice **PQ2635.E48 Z87 1977**
Jules Renard. A. Michel. 1976. ISBN:2-226-00414-9, ISBN13: 978-2-226-00414-7.
Audience: **u,f.**

Modern French Literature > Individual Authors, 20th C., to 1960 > S

Miller, Judith G. **PQ2633.U74Z76 1988**
Francoise Sagan. Cloth Text. Macmillan Publishing Company, Inc. Old Tappan, NJ. 1988. 152p. World Authors Ser., No. 797 ISBN:0-8057-8228-1, ISBN13: 978-0-8057-8228-8. Dewey:843/.914. LCCN:87-033114.
Audience: **l,u.**

Robinson, Joy M. **PQ2637.A274Z825 1984**
Antoine de Saint-Exupery. Trade Cloth. Thomson Gale. Farmington Hills, MI. 1984. 200p. World Authors Ser., No. 705 ISBN:0-8057-6552-2, ISBN13: 978-0-8057-6552-6. Dewey:848/.91209 B. LCCN:84-010769.
Audience: **l,u.**

Sagan, Francoise **PZ4.Q9**
Aimez-Vous Brahms? Trade Cloth. French & European Publications, Inc. New York, NY. 1963. ISBN:0-685-23930-6, ISBN13: 978-0-685-23930-8. Dewey:843.914.
Audience: **u,f.**

Sagan, Francoise **PQ2633.U74B613 2001**
Bonjour Tristesse. Diane Johnson (Introduction by). Trade Paper. HarperCollins Publishers. New York, NY. 2001. 144p. ISBN:0-06-621169-7, ISBN13: 978-0-06-621169-5. Dewey:843/.914. LCCN:2001-033145.
Audience: **u,f.**

Saint-Exupéry, Antoine de **PZ3**
The Little Prince. Trade Cloth. Harcourt Trade Publishers. New York, NY. 2003. ISBN:0-15-204730-1, ISBN13: 978-0-15-204730-6. Dewey:[Fic].
Audience: **g,l,u,f.**

Saint-Exupéry, Antoine de **PQ2637.A274**
Night Flight. Cloth Text. Amereon, Ltd. Mattituck, NY. 2000. ISBN:0-8488-2873-9, ISBN13: 978-0-8488-2873-8. Dewey:843/.9/1.
Audience: **u,f.**

Saint-Exupéry, Antoine de **PQ2613.I2**
Wind, Sand and Stars. Trade Paper. Harcourt Trade Publishers. New York, NY. 2002. 240p. ISBN:0-15-602749-6, ISBN13: 978-0-15-602749-6. Dewey:848.9/12/08.
Audience: **g,l,u,f.**

Schiff, Stacy **PQ2637.A274Z829 2006**
Saint Exupery. Trade Paper. Henry Holt & Company. New York, NY. 2006. 560p. ISBN:0-8050-7913-0, ISBN13: 978-0-8050-7913-5. Dewey:848/.91209 B. LCCN:2006-273417.
Audience: **g,l,u,f.**

Supervielle, Jules **PQ2637**
OEuvres poétiques complètes. Gallimard. 1996. ISBN:2-07-011438-4, ISBN13: 978-2-07-011438-2.
Audience: **u,f.**

Modern French Literature > Individual Authors, 20th C., to 1960 > Sarraute

Jefferson, Ann (Contribution by) **PQ2637.A783 Z72 2000**
Nathalie Sarraute, Fiction and Theory: Questions of Difference. Trade Cloth. Cambridge University Press. New York, NY. 2000. 230p. Cambridge Studies in French, No. 64 ISBN:0-521-77211-7, ISBN13: 978-0-521-77211-2. Dewey:843.914. LCCN:99-048651.
Audience: **u,f.** *Choice, 2001.*

Sarraute, Nathalie **PQ2637.A783.A24**
Collected Plays. Trade Cloth. George Braziller Inc. New York, NY. 1981. 107 p. ;p. ISBN:0-8076-0939-0, ISBN13: 978-0-8076-0939-2. Dewey:842/.9/14. LCCN:78-007111.
Audience: **g,l,u,f.**

Sarraute, Nathalie **PQ2637.A783**
OEuvres Completes. Gallimard. 1996. Pleiade Ser. ISBN:2-07-011434-1, ISBN13: 978-2-07-011434-4.
Audience: **u,f.**

Sarraute, Nathalie **PQ2637.A783V613 2004**
Do You Hear Them? Maria Jolas (Translator). Perfect. Dalkey Archive Press. Normal, IL. 2004. 147p. Coleman Dowell Ser. ISBN:1-56478-329-4, ISBN13: 978-1-56478-329-5. Dewey:843/.914. LCCN:2003-055103.
Audience: **g,l,u,f.**

Sarraute, Nathalie **PZ3.S247 GO**
The Golden Fruits. Maria Jolas (Translator). Trade Paper. Riverrun Press, Inc. Flemington, NJ. 1980. 143p. ISBN:0-7145-0259-6, ISBN13: 978-0-7145-0259-5. Dewey:813/.5/4.
Audience: **g,l,u,f.**

Sarraute, Nathalie **PQ2637.A783M313 2004**
Martereau. Maria Jolas (Translator). Trade Paper. Dalkey Archive Press. Normal, IL. 2004. 250p. ISBN:1-56478-348-0, ISBN13: 978-1-56478-348-6. Dewey:843/.914. LCCN:2003-070085.
Audience: **g,l,u,f.**

Sarraute, Nathalie **PQ2637.A783P5313**
The Planetarium. Maria Jolas (Translator). Trade Paper, Perfect. Dalkey Archive Press. Normal, IL. 2005. 246p. French Literature Ser. ISBN:1-56478-410-X, ISBN13: 978-1-56478-410-0. Dewey:FIC. LCCN:2005-049354.
Audience: **g,l,u,f.**

Sarraute, Nathalie **PQ2637.A783**
Tropisms. Maria Jolas (Translator). Trade Paper. George Braziller Inc. New York, NY. 1967. 71p. ISBN:0-8076-0412-7, ISBN13: 978-0-8076-0412-0. Dewey:843.914. LCCN:67-018211.
Audience: **g,l,u,f.**

Sarraute, Nathalie **PQ2637.A783T813 1990**
You Don't Love Yourself. Barbara Wright (Translator). Trade Cloth. George Braziller Inc. New York, NY. 1990. 216p. ISBN:0-8076-1254-5, ISBN13: 978-0-8076-1254-5. Dewey:843/.914. LCCN:90-044526.
Audience: **g,l,u,f.**

Modern French Literature > Individual Authors, 20th C., to 1960 > Sartre

Cohen-Solal, Annie **B2430.S34**
Sartre: A Life. Trade Paper. New Press, The. New York, NY. 2005. 592p. Lives of the Left Ser. ISBN:1-56584-974-4, ISBN13: 978-1-56584-974-7. Dewey:194.
Audience: **g,l,u.** *Choice, 1988.*

Halpern, Joseph **PQ2637.A82.Z725**
Critical Fictions: The Literary Criticism of Jean-Paul Sartre. Trade Cloth. Yale University Press. Cumberland, RI. 1976. 192p. Romantic Studies, No. 26 ISBN:0-300-01943-2, ISBN13: 978-0-300-01943-8. Dewey:840/.9. LCCN:75-018172.
Audience: **g,l,u,f.**

Kern, Edith **PQ2637.A82**
Sartre: A Collection of Critical Essays. Paper Text. Textbook Publishers. Temecula, CA. 2003. 179p. ISBN:0-7581-6115-8, ISBN13: 978-0-7581-6115-4. Dewey:848.914.
Audience: **l,u,f.**

Sartre, Jean-Paul **PQ2637.A82**
Les Mots. Trade Paper. French & European Publications, Inc. New York, NY. 1977. ISBN:0-8288-3749-X, ISBN13: 978-0-8288-3749-1. Dewey:848.914.
Audience: **u,f.**

Sartre, Jean-Paul **PQ2637.A82H82 1989**
No Exit and Three Other Plays. Trade Paper. Knopf Publishing Group. New York, NY. 1989. 288p. Vintage International Ser. ISBN:0-679-72516-4, ISBN13: 978-0-679-72516-9. Dewey:842/.914. LCCN:72-007484.
Audience: **g,l,u.**

Sartre, Jean-Paul **B2430.S34**
Life Situations: Essays Written and Spoken by Jean-Paul Sartre. Paul Auster & Lydia Davis (Translators). Trade Paper. Knopf Publishing Group. New York, NY. 1978. ISBN:0-394-73460-2, ISBN13: 978-0-394-73460-6. Dewey:194. LCCN:76-054561.
Audience: **g,l,u,f.**

Sartre, Jean-Paul **PQ2637.A82**
Oeuvres Romanesques. Michel Contat (Editor). Library Binding. French & European Publications, Inc. New York, NY. 1982. ISBN:0-7859-3855-9, ISBN13: 978-0-7859-3855-2. Dewey:843/.914.
Audience: **u,f.**

Sartre, Jean-Paul, et al. **PQ2637.A82**
Théâtre Complet. Michel Contat & Jacques Deguy (Authors). Trade Cloth. Gallimard, Editions. Paris Cedex 07, 2006. lxii, 1601p. ISBN:2-07-011528-3, ISBN13: 978-2-07-011528-0. Dewey:842.912.
Audience: **u,f.**

Sartre, Jean-Paul **PR6003.E282**
Sartre on Theater. Michel Contat & Michel Rybalka (Editors), Frank Jellinek (Translator). Trade Paper. Knopf Publishing Group. New York, NY. 1978. ISBN:0-394-73312-6, ISBN13: 978-0-394-73312-8. Dewey:848/.9/1409.
Audience: **g,l,u,f.**

Sartre, Jean-Paul **PR6003.E282**
The Words. Bernard Frechtman (Translator). Mass Market. Knopf Publishing Group. New York, NY. 1981. 256p. ISBN:0-394-74709-7, ISBN13: 978-0-394-74709-5. Dewey:848.9/14/09. LCCN:80-006136.
Audience: **g,l,u,f.**

Sartre, Jean-Paul **PN45.S245 1988**
What Is Literature? and Other Essays. Bernard Frechtman & Jeffrey Mehlman (Translators), Steven Ungar (Introduction by). Trade Paper. Harvard University Press. Cambridge, MA. 1988. 368p. ISBN:0-674-95084-4, ISBN13: 978-0-674-95084-9. Dewey:809. LCCN:87-037931.
Audience: **g,u,f.**

Sartre, Jean-Paul **PQ2605.A3734**
Troubled Sleep: A Novel. Gerard Manley Hopkins (Translator). Trade Paper. Knopf Publishing Group. New York, NY. 1992. 432p. Chemins de la Liberte = The Roads To Freedom Ser., Vol. 3 ISBN:0-679-74079-1, ISBN13: 978-0-679-74079-7. Dewey:843/.914. LCCN:91-050896.
Audience: **g,l,u,f.**

Sartre, Jean-Paul **PQ2631.R63**
The Age of Reason. Eric Sutton (Translator). Trade Paper. Knopf Publishing Group. New York, NY. 1992. 416p. Roads To Freedom = les Chemins de la Liberte Ser., Vol. 1 ISBN:0-679-73895-9, ISBN13: 978-0-679-73895-4. Dewey:843.9/12. LCCN:91-058067.
Audience: **g,l,u.**

Suhl, Benjamin **PQ2637.A82Z/**
Jean-Paul Sartre: The Philosopher As a Literary Critic. Cloth Text. Columbia University Press. New York, NY. 1973. 311p. ISBN:0-231-03338-9, ISBN13: 978-0-231-03338-1. Dewey:840.9. LCCN:71-116377.
Audience: **l,u,f.**

Thody, Philip **PQ2637.A82**
Jean-Paul Sartre: A Literary and Political Study. Paper Text. Textbook Publishers. Temecula, CA. 2003. 269p. ISBN:0-7581-9302-5, ISBN13: 978-0-7581-9302-5. Dewey:843.914.
Audience: **g,l,u.**

Thody, Philip & Read, Howard **B2430.S34**
Introducing Sartre. Richard Appignanesi (Editor). Trade Paper. Totem Books. Cambridge, 2003. 176p. ISBN:1-84046-066-0, ISBN13: 978-1-84046-066-7. Dewey:194. LCCN:97-062433.
Audience: **l,u.**

Modern French Literature > Individual Authors, 20th C., to 1960 > Valery

Gide, André; Valéry, Paul **PQ2613.I2 Z52826**
André Gide - Paul Valéry : correspondance, 1890-1942. Gallimard. 1955.
Audience: **u,f.**

Valéry, Paul
OEuvres, vol. 1. Gallimard. 1992. Pleiade Ser. ISBN:2-07-010576-8, ISBN13: 978-2-07-010576-2.
Audience: **u,f.**

Valéry, Paul
OEuvres, vol. 2. Gallimard. 1993. Pleiade Ser. ISBN:2-07-010577-6, ISBN13: 978-2-07-010577-9.
Audience: **u,f.**

Modern French Literature > Individual Authors, 1960- > A-L

Cardinal, Marie **PQ2663.A7 A75 1998**
Amour-- amours-- : roman. B. Grasset. 1998. ISBN:2-246-56101-9, ISBN13: 978-2-246-56101-9.
Audience: **u,f.**

Cardinal, Marie **PQ2663.A7**
Les grands désordres : roman. B. Grasset. 1987. ISBN:2-246-39921-1, ISBN13: 978-2-246-39921-6.
Audience: **u,f.**

Cardinal, Marie **PQ2663.A7**
Les mots pour le dire. Bristol Classical Press. 1993. ISBN:1-85399-336-0, ISBN13: 978-1-85399-336-7.
Audience: **u,f.**

Cardinal, Marie **PQ2605.A3734**
Words to Say It. Ed. 9. Pat Goodheart (Editor, Translator), Bruno Bettelheim (Afterword by, Preface by). Trade Paper. Van Vactor & Goodheart. Cambridge, MA. 1994. 308p. ISBN:0-941324-09-5, ISBN13: 978-0-941324-09-0. Dewey:843.9/14.
Audience: **g,l,u,f.**

Chawaf, Chantal **PQ2663.H379**
Elwina, le roman fée : roman. Flammarion. 1985. ISBN:2-08-064837-3, ISBN13: 978-2-08-064837-2.
Audience: **u,f.**

Chawaf, Chantal **PQ2663.H379.R4**
Retable; (la Reverie). Trade Cloth. Des Femmes. 75006 Paris, 1974. 165 p. :p. ISBN:2-7210-0010-1, ISBN13: 978-2-7210-0010-1. Dewey:843/.9/14. LCCN:75-504277.
Audience: **u,f.**

Chawaf, Chantal **PQ2663.H379**
Rédemption. Flammarion. 1989. ISBN:2-08-066242-2, ISBN13: 978-2-08-066242-2.
Audience: **u,f.**

Chawaf, Chantal **PQ2663.H379R413 1990**
Mother Love, Mother Earth. Monique F. Nagem (Translator). Cloth Text. Garland Publishing, Inc. New York, NY. 1992. 150p. Library of World Literature in Translation, Vol. 20 ISBN:0-8240-4399-5, ISBN13: 978-0-8240-4399-5. Dewey:843/.914. LCCN:90-003034.
Audience: **g,l,u,f.**

Chawaf, Chantal **PQ2663.H379R3813**
Redemption. Monique F. Nagem (Translator). Trade Cloth. Dalkey Archive Press. Normal, IL. 1992. 97p. ISBN:1-56478-003-1, ISBN13: 978-1-56478-003-4. Dewey:843.914. LCCN:92-000511.
Audience: **g,l,u,f.**

Chedid, Andrée **PQ2605.H4245**
La femme en rouge : et autres nouvelles. Editions J'ai lu. 2000. ISBN:2-290-30382-8, ISBN13: 978-2-290-30382-5.
Audience: **u,f.**

Chedid, Andrée **PQ2605.H4245 M47 2000**
Le message : roman. Flammarion. 2000. ISBN:2-08-068046-3, ISBN13: 978-2-08-068046-4.
Audience: **u,f.**

Chedid, Andrée **PQ2605.H4245**
Romans. Flammarion. 1998. ISBN:2-08-067642-3, ISBN13: 978-2-08-067642-9.
Audience: **u,f.**

Chedid, Andrée **PQ2605.H4245 R97 2003**
Rythmes : poèmes. Gallimard. 2003. ISBN:2-07-076774-4, ISBN13: 978-2-07-076774-8.
Audience: **u,f.**

Chedid, Andrée **PQ2605.H4245 T385 1999**
Territoires du souffle : poèmes. Flammarion. 1999.
Audience: **u,f.**

Chedid, Andrée **PQ2605.H4245 T49 1987**
Textes pour un poème, 1949-1970. Flammarion. 1987. ISBN:2-08-064987-6, ISBN13: 978-2-08-064987-4.
Audience: **u,f.**

Chessex, Jacques **PQ2663.H396**
L'ogre; roman. B. Grasset. 1973. ISBN:2-246-11143-9, ISBN13: 978-2-246-11143-6.
Audience: **u,f.**

Cixous, Helene **PQ2663.I9D413 1986**
Inside. Carol Barko (Translator). Trade Cloth. Knopf Publishing Group. New York, NY. 1986. 136p. ISBN:0-8052-4019-5, ISBN13: 978-0-8052-4019-1. Dewey:843/.914. LCCN:86-006611.
Audience: **g,l,u,f.**

Cixous, Helene **PQ2637.I547**
Angst. J. Levy (Translator). Trade Paper. Calder Publications Ltd. London, 1985. 219p. ISBN:0-7145-3905-8, ISBN13: 978-0-7145-3905-8. Dewey:843/.914. LCCN:85-018296.
Audience: **g,l,u,f.**

Cixous, Hélène **PQ2663.I9**
Angst. Des Femmes. 1998. ISBN:2-7210-0474-3, ISBN13: 978-2-7210-0474-1.
Audience: **u,f.**

Cixous, Hélène **PQ2663.I9**
Dedans. Des femmes. 1986. ISBN:2-7210-0298-8, ISBN13: 978-2-7210-0298-3.
Audience: **u,f.**

Cixous, Hélène **PQ2663.I9**
Théâtre. Des Femmes. 1986. ISBN:2-7210-0056-X, ISBN13: 978-2-7210-0056-9.
Audience: **u,f.**

Darrieussecq, Marie **PQ2664.A7214 B74 2001**
Bref séjour chez les vivants : roman. POL. 2001. ISBN:2-86744-844-1, ISBN13: 978-2-86744-844-7.
Audience: **u,f.**

Darrieussecq, Marie **PQ2664.A7214**
Truismes. Trade Paper. POL. Paris, 1998. ISBN:2-86744-527-2, ISBN13: 978-2-86744-527-9. Dewey:843.914.
Audience: **u,f.**

Darrieussecq, Marie **PQ2664.A7214**
A Brief Stay with the Living. Trade Cloth. Faber & Faber, Inc. New York, NY. 2003. 208p. ISBN:0-571-21494-0, ISBN13: 978-0-571-21494-5. Dewey:843/.914. LCCN:2003-363138.
Audience: **g,l,u,f.**

Darrieussecq, Marie **PQ2605.A3734**
Pig Tales: A Novel of Lust and Transformation. Linda Coverdale (Translator). Trade Cloth. New Press, The. New York, NY. 1997. 144p. ISBN:1-56584-361-4, ISBN13: 978-1-56584-361-5. Dewey:843.9/14. LCCN:97-065050.
Audience: **g,l,u,f.**

Deguy, Michel **PQ2664.E45 G57 1999**
Gisants : poèmes III, 1980-1995. Gallimard. 1999. ISBN:2-07-040786-1, ISBN13: 978-2-07-040786-6.
Audience: **u,f.**

Deguy, Michel **PQ2664.E48**
Ouï dire. Gallimard. 1966.
Audience: **u,f.**

Deguy, Michel **PQ2664.E45**
Poèmes II, 1970-1980. Gallimard. 1986. ISBN:2-07-032346-3, ISBN13: 978-2-07-032346-3.
Audience: **u,f.**

Deguy, Michel **PQ2664.E45G5713 2005**
Recumbents: With How to Name by Jacques Derrida. Library Binding. Wesleyan University Press. Middletown, CT. 2005. 268p. Wesleyan Poetry Ser. ISBN:0-8195-6747-7, ISBN13: 978-0-8195-6747-5. Dewey:841.914. LCCN:2004-022127.
Audience: **g,l,u,f.** *Choice, 2005.*

Deguy, Michel **PQ2664.E45A23 1984**
Given Giving: Selected Poems of Michel Deguy. Clayton Eshleman (Translator), Kenneth Koch (Introduction by). Trade Cloth. University of California Press. Berkeley, CA. 1984. 144p. ISBN:0-520-04728-1, ISBN13: 978-0-520-04728-0. Dewey:841/.914. LCCN:84-040332.
Audience: **g,l,u,f.**

Echenoz, Jean **PQ2665.C5 A8 1997**
Un an. Les Editions de Minuit. 1997. ISBN:2-7073-1587-7, ISBN13: 978-2-7073-1587-8.
Audience: **u,f.**

Echenoz, Jean **PQ2665.C5**
Lac. Éditions de Minuit. 1989. ISBN:2-7073-1304-1, ISBN13: 978-2-7073-1304-1.
Audience: **u,f.**

Echenoz, Jean **PQ2665.C5J413 2001**
I'm Gone. Mark Polizzotti (Translator). Trade Cloth. New Press, The. New York, NY. 2001. 208p. ISBN:1-56584-628-1, ISBN13: 978-1-56584-628-9. Dewey:843/.914. LCCN:00-064601.
Audience: **g,l,u,f.**

Echenoz, Jean & Waldman, Guido **PQ2665.C5L3313 1998**
Lake. Trade Cloth. Random House. London, 1998. 122p. ISBN:1-86046-449-1, ISBN13: 978-1-86046-449-2. Dewey:843/.914. LCCN:99-201955.
Audience: **g,l,u,f.**

Ernaux, Annie **PQ2665.R67**
La Femme Gelee. Trade Paper. Schoenhof's Foreign Books, Inc. Cambridge, MA. 1987. 181p. Folio Ser., No. 1818 ISBN:2-07-037818-7, ISBN13: 978-2-07-037818-0. Dewey:843.914.
Audience: **u,f.**

Ernaux, Annie **PQ2665.R67**
Passion simple. Gallimard. 1992. ISBN:2-07-072504-9, ISBN13: 978-2-07-072504-5.
Audience: **u,f.**

Ernaux, Annie **PQ2665.R67**
La Place. Trade Cloth. Gallimard, Editions. Paris Cedex 07, 2005. 113p. ISBN:2-07-070048-8, ISBN13: 978-2-07-070048-6. Dewey:843.914.
Audience: **u,f.**

Ernaux, Annie **PQ2665.R67P3713 1993**
Simple Passion. Trade Cloth. Avalon Publishing Group. New York, NY. 1993. 80p. ISBN:1-56858-003-7, ISBN13: 978-1-56858-003-6. Dewey:843/.914. LCCN:93-008702.
Audience: **g,l,u,f.**

Ernaux, Annie **PQ2605.A3734**
A Frozen Woman. Linda Covesdale (Translator). Trade Cloth. Seven Stories Press. New York, NY. 1996. 160p. ISBN:1-888363-14-2, ISBN13: 978-1-888363-14-2. Dewey:843/.914 B. LCCN:94-045795.
Audience: **g,l,u,f.**

Ernaux, Annie **PQ2605.A3734**
A Man's Place. Tanya Leslie (Translator). Trade Cloth. Seven Stories Press. New York, NY. 2004. 0p. ISBN:1-888363-19-3, ISBN13: 978-1-888363-19-7. Dewey:843/.914. LCCN:91-043106.
Audience: **g,l,u,f.**

Germain, Sylvie **PQ2667.E6845 M34 2005**
Magnus : roman. Albin Michel. 2005. ISBN:2-226-16734-X, ISBN13: 978-2-226-16734-7.
Audience: **u,f.**

Germain, Sylvie **PQ2605.A3734**
Days of Anger. Christine Donougher (Translator). Trade Paper. David R. Godine Publisher. Boston, MA. 2004. 192p. ISBN:1-56792-252-X, ISBN13: 978-1-56792-252-3. Dewey:843.914.
Audience: **g,l,u,f.**

Guyotat, Pierre **PQ2667.U9**
Tombeau pour cinq cent mille soldats : sept chants. Gallimard. 1987. ISBN:2-07-020722-6, ISBN13: 978-2-07-020722-0.
Audience: **u,f.**

Guyotat, Pierre **PQ2667.U9**
Éden, Éden, Éden. Gallimard. 1985. ISBN:2-07-070278-2, ISBN13: 978-2-07-070278-7.
Audience: **u,f.**

Guyotat, Pierre **PQ2667.U9**
Eden, Eden, Eden. Graham Fox (Translator). Trade Cloth. Creation Books. New York, NY. 2003. 192p. Modern Classics Ser., 2 ISBN:1-84068-063-6, ISBN13: 978-1-84068-063-8. Dewey:843.9/14.
Audience: **g,l,u,f.**

Guyotat, Pierre **PQ2667.U9**
Tomb for 500,000 Soldiers. Romain Slocombe (Translator). Trade Cloth. Creation Books. New York, NY. 2003. 512p. Modern Classics Ser. ISBN:1-84068-062-8, ISBN13: 978-1-84068-062-1. Dewey:843.9/14.
Audience: **g,l,u,f.**

Houellebecq, Michel **PQ2668.O77**
Extension du domaine de la lutte : roman. M. Nadeau. 1994. ISBN:2-86231-124-3, ISBN13: 978-2-86231-124-1.
Audience: **u,f.**

Houellebecq, Michel **PQ2668.O77**
Les particules élémentaires : roman. Flammarion. 1998. ISBN:2-08-067472-2, ISBN13: 978-2-08-067472-2.
Audience: **u,f.**

Houellebecq, Michel **PQ2668.O77**
Plateforme : roman. Flammarion. 2001. ISBN:2-08-068237-7, ISBN13: 978-2-08-068237-6.
Audience: **u,f.**

Houellebecq, Michel **PQ2605.A3734**
Whatever. Paul Hammond (Translator). Trade Paper. Serpent's Tail Ltd. London, 1998. 160p. ISBN:1-85242-584-9, ISBN13: 978-1-85242-584-5. Dewey:843.9/14. LCCN:98-086409.
Audience: **g,l,u,f.**

Houellebecq, Michel **PQ2668.O77P3713 2000**
The Elementary Particles. Frank Wynne (Translator). Trade Cloth. Alfred A. Knopf Inc. New York, NY. 2000. 272p. ISBN:0-375-40770-7, ISBN13: 978-0-375-40770-3. Dewey:843/.914. LCCN:00-040568.
Audience: **g,l,u,f.**

Houellebecq, Michel **PQ2668.O77P5313 2003**
Platform. Frank Wynne (Translator). Trade Cloth. Alfred A. Knopf Inc. New York, NY. 2003. 272p. ISBN:0-375-41462-2, ISBN13: 978-0-375-41462-6. Dewey:843/.914. LCCN:2002-040634.
Audience: **g,l,u,f.**

Jaccottet, Philippe **PQ2670.A225 C37 2001**
Carnets : 1995-1998. Gallimard. 2001. ISBN:2-07-076193-2, ISBN13: 978-2-07-076193-7.
Audience: **u,f.**

Jaccottet, Philippe **PQ2670.A225**
Poesie : 1946-1967. Gallimard. 1996. ISBN:2-07-031787-0, ISBN13: 978-2-07-031787-5.
Audience: **u,f.**

Jaccottet, Philippe **PQ2670.A225 S38 1996**
La seconde semaison : carnets, 1980-1994. Gallimard. 1996. ISBN:2-07-074399-3, ISBN13: 978-2-07-074399-5.
Audience: **u,f.**

Jaccottet, Philippe **PQ2670.A225 A6 1984**
A travers un verger ; suivi de, Les cormorans ; et de, Beauregard. Gallimard. 1984. ISBN:2-07-070221-9, ISBN13: 978-2-07-070221-3.
Audience: **u,f.**

Jaccottet, Philippe **PQ2670.A225**
À la lumière d'hiver : précédé de Leçons et de Chants d'en bas. Gallimard. 1984. ISBN:2-07-029716-0, ISBN13: 978-2-07-029716-0.
Audience: **u,f.**

Jaccottet, Philippe **PQ2670.A225.S413**
Seedtime. Andre Lefevere & Michael Hamburger (Translators). Trade Cloth. New Directions Publishing Corporation. New York, NY. 1977. 60p. ISBN:0-8112-0636-X, ISBN13: 978-0-8112-0636-5. Dewey:848/.91403. LCCN:76-045640.
Audience: **g,l,u,f.**

Jaccottet, Philippe **PQ2670.A225**
Selected Poems. D. Mahon (Translator). Trade Cloth. Penguin Books, Ltd. London, 1987. 160p. ISBN:0-670-81116-5, ISBN13: 978-0-670-81116-8. Dewey:841/.914.
Audience: **g,l,u,f.** *Choice, 1989.*

Jaccottet, Philippe **PQ2670.A225P46 1994**
Under Clouded Skies/Beauregard. Mark Treharne & David Constantine (Translators). Trade Paper. Bloodaxe Books. Bala, 1995. 160p. ISBN:1-85224-259-0, ISBN13: 978-1-85224-259-6. Dewey:841/.914. LCCN:94-162739.
Audience: **g,l,u,f.**

Kristeva, Julia **PQ2671.R547**
Possessions : roman. Fayard. 1996. ISBN:2-213-59678-6, ISBN13: 978-2-213-59678-5.
Audience: **u,f.**

Kristeva, Julia **PQ2671.R547 S2513**
Les samouraïs : roman. Fayard. 1990. ISBN:2-213-02492-8, ISBN13: 978-2-213-02492-9.
Audience: **u,f.**

Kristeva, Julia **PQ2671.R547 V53 1991**
Le vieil homme et les loups : roman. Fayard. 1991. ISBN:2-213-02762-5, ISBN13: 978-2-213-02762-3.
Audience: **u,f.**

Kristeva, Julia **PQ2671.R547V5313**
The Old Man and the Wolves: A Novel. Barbara Bray (Translator). Trade Cloth. Columbia University Press. New York, NY. 1994. 183p. ISBN:0-231-08020-4, ISBN13: 978-0-231-08020-0. Dewey:843/.914. LCCN:94-011795.
Audience: **g,l,u,f.**

Kristeva, Julia **PQ2671.R547.P6713**
Possessions: A Novel. Barbara Bray (Translator). Trade Cloth. Columbia University Press. New York, NY. 1998. 256p. ISBN:0-231-10998-9, ISBN13: 978-0-231-10998-7. Dewey:843/.914. LCCN:97-029554.
Audience: **g,l,u,f.**

Kristeva, Julia **PQ2671.R547S2513**
The Samurai: A Novel. Barbara Bray (Translator). Trade Cloth. Columbia University Press. New York, NY. 1992. 341p. ISBN:0-231-07542-1, ISBN13: 978-0-231-07542-8. Dewey:843.914. LCCN:92-022714.
Audience: **g,l,u,f.**

Kristeva, Julia **PQ2671.R547M4813**
Murder in Byzantium: A Novel. C. Jon Delogu (Translator). Trade Cloth. Columbia University Press. New York, NY. 2005. 264p. ISBN:0-231-13636-6, ISBN13: 978-0-231-13636-5. Dewey:843/.914. LCCN:2005-051851.
Audience: **g,l,u,f.**

Le Clezio, J. M. G. **PQ2672.E25O5513 1997**
Onitsha. Alison Anderson (Translator). Trade Cloth. University of Nebraska Press. Lincoln, NE. 1997. 206p. ISBN:0-8032-7966-3, ISBN13: 978-0-8032-7966-7. Dewey:843/.914. LCCN:96-032612.
Audience: **g,l,u,f.**

Le Clezio, J. M. G. **PQ2672.E25C4813 1993**
The Prospector. Carol Marks (Translator). Trade Cloth. David R. Godine Publisher. Boston, MA. 1993. 352p. Verba Mundi Ser. ISBN:0-87923-976-X, ISBN13: 978-0-87923-976-3. Dewey:843/.914. LCCN:93-036322.
Audience: **g,l,u,f.**

Le Clézio, J.-M. G. **PQ2672.E25**
Le chercheur d'or. Gallimard. 1985. ISBN:2-07-070247-2, ISBN13: 978-2-07-070247-3.
Audience: **u,f.**

Le Clézio, J.-M. G. **PQ2672.E25**
La Guerre. Gallimard. 1985. ISBN:2-07-027155-2, ISBN13: 978-2-07-027155-9.
Audience: **u,f.**

Le Clézio, J.-M. G. **PQ2672.E25**
Onitsha : roman. Gallimard. 1991. ISBN:2-07-072230-9, ISBN13: 978-2-07-072230-3.
Audience: **u,f.**

Le Clézio, J.-M. G. **PQ2673.E25**
Le procès-verbal. Gallimard. 1990. ISBN:2-07-023821-0, ISBN13: 978-2-07-023821-7.
Audience: **u,f.**

Le Clézio, J.-M. G. **PQ2672.E25 Z46 2004**
L'Africain. Mercure de Franc. 2004. ISBN:2-7152-2470-2, ISBN13: 978-2-7152-2470-4.
Audience: **u,f.**

Penrod, Lynn **PQ2663.I9Z8 1996**
Helene Cixious. Trade Cloth. Thomson Gale. Farmington Hills, MI. 1996. 176p. ISBN:0-8057-8284-2, ISBN13: 978-0-8057-8284-4. Dewey:305.4/2. LCCN:95-034509.
Audience: **l,u.**

Sellers, Susan (Editor) **PQ2663.I9A6 1994**
The Helene Cixous Reader. Jacques Derrida (Foreword by). Paper over Boards. Routledge. New York, NY. 1994. 272p. ISBN:0-415-04929-6, ISBN13: 978-0-415-04929-0. Dewey:848/.91409. LCCN:93-041292.
Audience: **u,f.**

Shiach, Morag **PQ2663.I9Z84 1991**
Helene Cixous: A Politics of Writing. Cloth Text. Routledge. New York, NY. 1991. 224p. ISBN:0-415-01333-X, ISBN13: 978-0-415-01333-8. Dewey:848/.91409. LCCN:91-009503.
Audience: **u,f.**

Smith, Anne Marie **PQ2671.R547Z85 1998**
Julia Kristeva: Speaking the Unspeakable. Trade Cloth. Pluto Press. London, 1998. 120p. Modern European Thinkers Ser. ISBN:0-7453-1058-3, ISBN13: 978-0-7453-1058-9. Dewey:843/.914. LCCN:98-003465.
Audience: **u,f.**

Thomas, Lyn **PQ2665.R67Z85 1999**
Annie Ernaux: An Introduction to the Writer and her Audience. Cloth over Boards. Berg Publishers. Oxford, 1999. 192p. New Directions in European Writing Ser. ISBN:1-85973-207-0, ISBN13: 978-1-85973-207-6. Dewey:843/.914. LCCN:99-208028.
Audience: **l,u,f.** *Choice, 2000.*

Wesemael, Sabine van **PQ2668.O77 Z94 2005**
Michel Houellebecq : le plaisir du texte. L'Harmattan. 2005. ISBN:2-7475-8079-2, ISBN13: 978-2-7475-8079-3.
Audience: **u,f.**

Modern French Literature > Individual Authors, 1960- > M-Z

Barthes, Roland **PQ2679.O4**
Writer Sollers. Trade Cloth. Continuum International Publishing Group, Ltd. London, 128p. ISBN:0-485-11337-6, ISBN13: 978-0-485-11337-2. Dewey:843/.914.
Audience: **u,f.** *Choice, 1988.*

Bellos, David **PQ2676.E67.Z53 1993**
Georges Perec, a Life in Words: A Biography. Trade Cloth. David R. Godine Publisher. Boston, MA. 1993. 832p. ISBN:0-87923-980-8, ISBN13: 978-0-87923-980-0. Dewey:848/.91409. LCCN:93-011604.
Audience: **g,l,u,f.** *Choice, 1994.*

Gascoigne, David **PQ2680.O83Z678 1996**
Michel Tournier. John Flower (Editor). Cloth over Boards. Berg Publishers. Oxford, 1996. 234p. New Directions in European Writing Ser. ISBN:1-85973-024-8, ISBN13: 978-1-85973-024-9. Dewey:843.9/14. LCCN:96-013677.
Audience: **g,l,u,f.**

Mansour, Joyce **PQ2673.A5**
Prose & poésie : oeuvre complète. Actes Sud. 1991. ISBN:2-86869-592-2, ISBN13: 978-2-86869-592-5.
Audience: **u,f.**

Mansour, Joyce **PQ2673.A5C7513 1995**
Screams. Serge Gavronsky (Translator, Introduction by). Trade Paper. Post-Apollo Press, The. Sausalito, CA. 1995. 100p. ISBN:0-942996-25-9, ISBN13: 978-0-942996-25-8. Dewey:841/.9/14. LCCN:95-017770.
Audience: **g,l,u,f.**

Modiano, Patrick **PQ2673.O3**
Les boulevards de ceinture. Gallimard. 1997. ISBN:2-07-037033-X, ISBN13: 978-2-07-037033-7.
Audience: **u,f.**

Modiano, Patrick **PQ2673.O3 P43 2005**
Un pedigree. Gallimard. 2005. ISBN:2-07-077333-7, ISBN13: 978-2-07-077333-6.
Audience: **u,f.**

Modiano, Patrick **PQ2673.O3**
Rue des Boutiques Obscures. Trade Paper. Schoenhof's Foreign Books, Inc. Cambridge, MA. 1982. 250p. Folio Ser., No. 1358 ISBN:2-07-037358-4, ISBN13: 978-2-07-037358-1. Dewey:843.914.
Audience: **u,f.**

Morris, Alan **PQ2673.O3M67 1996**
Patrick Modiano. John E. Flower (Editor). Cloth over Boards. Berg Publishers. Oxford, 1996. 228p. New Directions in European Writing Ser. ISBN:1-85973-098-1, ISBN13: 978-1-85973-098-0. Dewey:843.9/14. LCCN:96-000874.
Audience: **u,f.**

Ollier, Claude **PQ2675.L398**
Déconnection. Flammarion. 1988. ISBN:2-08-066243-0, ISBN13: 978-2-08-066243-9.
Audience: **u,f.**

Ollier, Claude **PQ2675.L398**
La mise en scène. Flammarion. 1982.
Audience: **u,f.**

Ollier, Claude **PQ2675.L398D4413**
Disconnection. Dominic Di Bernardi (Translator). Trade Cloth. Dalkey Archive Press. Normal, IL. 1989. 130p. ISBN:0-916583-47-3, ISBN13: 978-0-916583-47-7. Dewey:843/.914. LCCN:89-035215.
Audience: **g,l,u,f.** *Choice, 1990.*

Ollier, Claude **PQ2675.L398M513 2000**
The Mise-en-Scene. Dominic Di Bernardi (Translator, Afterword by). Trade Paper. Dalkey Archive Press. Normal, IL. 2000. 248p. ISBN:1-56478-232-8, ISBN13: 978-1-56478-232-8. Dewey:843/.914. LCCN:00-267329.
Audience: **l,u,f.**

Ostrovsky, Erika **PQ2683.I8Z8 1991**
A Constant Journey: The Fiction of Monique Wittig. Trade Cloth. Southern Illinois University Press. Carbondale, IL. 1991. 211p. ISBN:0-8093-1642-0, ISBN13: 978-0-8093-1642-7. Dewey:843/.914. LCCN:89-049482.
Audience: **l,u,f.** *Choice, 1991.*

Perec, Georges **PQ2676.E67**
Les choses : une histoire des années soixante. Julliard. 1997. ISBN:2-260-01471-2, ISBN13: 978-2-260-01471-3.
Audience: **u,f.**

Perec, Georges **PQ2676 .E67A7**
La disparition. Denoël. 2003. ISBN:2-07-071523-X, ISBN13: 978-2-07-071523-7.
Audience: **u,f.**

Perec, Georges **PQ2676.E67**
La vie mode d'emploi : roman. Hachette. 2000. ISBN:2-01-235557-9, ISBN13: 978-2-01-235557-6.
Audience: **u,f.**

Perec, Georges **PQ2637.A82**
W, ou, Le souvenir d'enfance. Gallimard. 1975. ISBN:2-07-073316-5, ISBN13: 978-2-07-073316-3.
Audience: **u,f.**

Perec, Georges
A Void. Gilbert Adair (Translator). Trade Cloth. HarperCollins Publishers. New York, NY. 1994. 256p. ISBN:0-00-271119-2, ISBN13: 978-0-00-271119-7. Dewey:843.9/14.
Audience: **g,l,u,f.**

Perec, Georges **PQ2605.A3734**
Life: A User's Manual. David Bellos (Translator). Trade Paper. David R. Godine Publisher. Boston, MA. 1987. 600p. ISBN:0-87923-751-1, ISBN13: 978-0-87923-751-6. Dewey:843.9/14. LCCN:87-008782.
Audience: **g,l,u,f.** *Choice, 1988.*

Perec, Georges **PQ2676**
W, or the Memory of Childhood. David Bellos (Translator). Trade Paper. David R. Godine Publisher. Boston, MA. 2002. 176p. ISBN:1-56792-158-2, ISBN13: 978-1-56792-158-8. Dewey:843/.914.
Audience: **g,l,u,f.** *Choice, 1989.*

Perec, Georges **PQ2676.E67A23 1990**
Things: A Story of the Sixties. David Bellos & Andrew Leak (Translators). Trade Cloth. David R. Godine Publisher. Boston, MA. 1990. 224p. ISBN:0-87923-857-7, ISBN13: 978-0-87923-857-5. Dewey:843/.914. LCCN:90-055284.
Audience: **g,l,u,f.** *Choice, 1991.*

Perec, Georges **PQ2676.E67A1613 1999**
53 Days. Harry Mathews & Jacques Roubaud (Editors), David Bellos (Translator). Trade Cloth. David R. Godine Publisher. Boston, MA. 1999. 272p. Verba Mundi Ser. ISBN:1-56792-088-8, ISBN13: 978-1-56792-088-8. Dewey:843/.914. LCCN:98-033645.
Audience: **g,l,u.**

Redonnet, Marie **PQ2678.E285**
Forever valley : roman. Minuit. 1987.
Audience: **u,f.**

Redonnet, Marie **PQ2678.E285**
Rose Mélie Rose : roman. Minuit. 1987. ISBN:2-7073-1133-2, ISBN13: 978-2-7073-1133-7.
Audience: **u,f.**

Redonnet, Marie **PQ2678.E285;**
Splendid Hôtel : roman. Editions de Minuit. 1986. ISBN:2-7073-1075-1, ISBN13: 978-2-7073-1075-0.
Audience: **u,f.**

Redonnet, Marie **PQ2678.E285F67 1994**
Forever Valley. Jordan Stump (Translator). Trade Cloth. University of Nebraska Press. Lincoln, NE. 1994. 117p. European Women Writers Ser. ISBN:0-8032-8951-0, ISBN13: 978-0-8032-8951-2. Dewey:843/.914. LCCN:94-001315.
Audience: **g,l,u,f.**

Redonnet, Marie **PQ2678.E285S65 1994**
Hotel Splendid. Jordan Stump (Translator). Trade Cloth. University of Nebraska Press. Lincoln, NE. 1994. 117p. European Women Writers Ser. ISBN:0-8032-8953-7, ISBN13: 978-0-8032-8953-6. Dewey:843/.914. LCCN:94-001314.
Audience: **g,l,u,f.**

Redonnet, Marie **PQ2678.E285R67 1994**
Rose Mellie Rose. Jordan Stump (Translator). Trade Cloth. University of Nebraska Press. Lincoln, NE. 1994. 123p. European Women Writers Ser. ISBN:0-8032-8952-9, ISBN13: 978-0-8032-8952-9. Dewey:843/.914. LCCN:94-001313.
Audience: **g,l,u,f.**

Réage, Pauline; Paulhan, Jean **PQ2678.E2**
Histoire d'O. Pauvert. 2002. ISBN:2-7202-0031-X, ISBN13: 978-2-7202-0031-1.
Audience: **u,f.**

Réage, Pauline **PQ2637.A274**
Story of O. John P. Hand (Translator). Trade Paper. Avalon Publishing Group. New York, NY. 1998. 186p. ISBN:1-56201-035-2, ISBN13: 978-1-56201-035-5. Dewey:843/.9/1.
Audience: **g,l,u,f.**

Sarrazin, Albertine **PQ2679.A7**
L'astragale: roman. Pauvert. 2001. ISBN:2-7202-1448-5, ISBN13: 978-2-7202-1448-6.
Audience: **u,f.**

Shaktini, Namascar (Editor) **PQ2683.I8Z78 2004**
On Monique Wittig: Theoretical, Political, and Literary Essays. Trade Cloth. University of Illinois Press. Champaign, IL. 2005. 248p. ISBN:0-252-02984-4, ISBN13: 978-0-252-02984-4. Dewey:843/.914. LCCN:2004-014401.
Audience: **u,f.** *Choice, 2005.*

Sollers, Philippe **PQ2679.O4**
Drame. Le Seuil. 1990. ISBN:2-07-071853-0, ISBN13: 978-2-07-071853-5.
Audience: **u,f.**

Sollers, Philippe **PQ2679.O4**
Femmes : roman. Gallimard. 1983. ISBN:2-07-024881-X, ISBN13: 978-2-07-024881-0.
Audience: **u,f.**

Sollers, Philippe **PQ2679.O4**
H. Gallimard. 2001. ISBN:2-07-075743-9, ISBN13: 978-2-07-075743-5.
Audience: **u,f.**

Sollers, Philippe **PQ2679.O4**
Parc. Trade Paper. Editions du Seuil. Paris, 1998. ISBN:2-02-005738-7, ISBN13: 978-2-02-005738-7. Dewey:843.914.
Audience: **u,f.**

Sollers, Philippe **PQ2679.O4**
L'étoile des amants : roman. Gallimard. 2002.
ISBN:2-07-076977-1, ISBN13: 978-2-07-076977-3.
Audience: **u,f.**

Sollers, Philippe **PQ2679.O4**
Event. Bruce Benderson & Ursule Molinaro (Translators), Roland Barthes (Contribution by). Trade Cloth. Red Dust, Inc. New York, NY. 1987. 104p. French Ser. ISBN:0-87376-046-8, ISBN13: 978-0-87376-046-1. Dewey:843/.914. LCCN:85-043078.
Audience: **g,l,u,f.** *Choice, 1987.*

Sollers, Philippe **PQ2605.A3734**
Women. B. Bray (Translator). Trade Cloth. Quartet Books, Ltd. London, 1991. 559p. ISBN:0-7043-2791-0, ISBN13: 978-0-7043-2791-7. Dewey:843.914.
Audience: **g,l,u,f.**

Sollers, Philippe **PQ2679.O4**
The Park. A. M. Sheridan-Smith (Translator). Trade Paper. Red Dust, Inc. New York, NY. 1969. 96p. French Ser. ISBN:0-87376-013-1, ISBN13: 978-0-87376-013-3. Dewey:843/.9/14. LCCN:76-090910.
Audience: **g,l,u,f.**

Tournier, Michel **PQ2680.O83 G3**
Gaspard, Melchior & Balthazar. Gallimard. 1980.
ISBN:2-07-023243-3, ISBN13: 978-2-07-023243-7.
Audience: **u,f.**

Tournier, Michel **PQ2680.O83 G6 1985**
La goutte d'or : roman. Gallimard. 1985. ISBN:2-07-070572-2, ISBN13: 978-2-07-070572-6.
Audience: **u,f.**

Tournier, Michel **PQ2680.O83**
Le roi des Aulnes : roman. Gallimard. 1989.
ISBN:2-07-027397-0, ISBN13: 978-2-07-027397-3.
Audience: **u,f.**

Tournier, Michel **PQ2605.A3734**
The Wind Spirit: An Autobiography. Trade Cloth. HarperCollins Publishers Ltd. London, 1989. 85p. ISBN:0-00-215922-8, ISBN13: 978-0-00-215922-7. Dewey:843/.914.
Audience: **l,u,f.**

Tournier, Michel **PQ2680.O83**
The Golden Droplet. Trade Cloth. HarperCollins Publishers Ltd. London, 1987. 192p. ISBN:0-00-223139-5, ISBN13: 978-0-00-223139-8. Dewey:843/.914.
Audience: **g,l,u,f.**

Tournier, Michel
Vendredi ; ou, Les limbes du Pacifique : roman. Gallimard. 1967. ISBN:2-07-026312-6, ISBN13: 978-2-07-026312-7.
Audience: **u,f.**

Tournier, Michel **PQ2680.O83R613 1997**
The Ogre. Barbara Bray (Translator). Trade Paper. Johns Hopkins University Press. Baltimore, MD. 1997. 384p. ISBN:0-8018-5590-X, ISBN13: 978-0-8018-5590-0. Dewey:843.9/14. LCCN:96-046778.
Audience: **g,l,u,f.**

Tournier, Michel **PQ2680.O83M413 1998**
Gemini. Ann Carter (Translator). Trade Paper. Johns Hopkins University Press. Baltimore, MD. 1998. 452p. ISBN:0-8018-5776-7, ISBN13: 978-0-8018-5776-8. Dewey:843/.914. LCCN:97-018469.
Audience: **u,f.**

Tournier, Michel **PQ2680.O83V413 1997**
Friday. Norman Denny (Translator). Trade Paper. Johns Hopkins University Press. Baltimore, MD. 1997. 240p. ISBN:0-8018-5592-6, ISBN13: 978-0-8018-5592-4. Dewey:843/.914. LCCN:96-045295.
Audience: **g,l,u,f.**

Tournier, Michel **PQ2680.O83G313 1997**
The Four Wise Men. Ralph Manheim (Translator). Trade Paper. Johns Hopkins University Press. Baltimore, MD. 1997. 264p. ISBN:0-8018-5733-3, ISBN13: 978-0-8018-5733-1. Dewey:843/.914. LCCN:97-012344.
Audience: **u,f.**

Wittig, Monique **PQ2683.I8**
Les Guerilleres. Trade Cloth. Penguin Group (USA) Inc. New York, NY. 1971. ISBN:0-670-42463-3, ISBN13: 978-0-670-42463-4. Dewey:843/.914. LCCN:70-158421.
Audience: **g,l,u,f.** B

Wittig, Monique **PQ2683.I8**
L'opoponax. Editions de Minuit. 1983. ISBN:2-7073-0662-2, ISBN13: 978-2-7073-0662-3.
Audience: **u,f.**

Wittig, Monique **PQ2637.A274**
Guerilleres. Trade Paper. Editions de Minuit. Paris, ISBN:2-7073-0042-X, ISBN13: 978-2-7073-0042-3. Dewey:843/.9/1.
Audience: **u,f.**

Wittig, Monique **PQ2683.I8 C6**
Corps Lesbien. Trade Paper. Editions de Minuit. Paris, 1973. ISBN:2-7073-0097-7, ISBN13: 978-2-7073-0097-3. Dewey:843.914.
Audience: **u,f.**

Wittig, Monique **PQ2683.I8**
Virgile, non. Editions de Minuit. 1985. ISBN:2-7073-1021-2, ISBN13: 978-2-7073-1021-7.
Audience: **u,f.**

Wittig, Monique **PQ2683.I8V5713 1987**
Across the Acheron. David Le Vay & Margaret Crosland (Translators). Trade Paper. Peter Owen Ltd. London, 1987. 119p. ISBN:0-7206-0664-0, ISBN13: 978-0-7206-0664-5. Dewey:843.914. LCCN:87-071417.
Audience: **g,l,u,f.** *Choice, 1987.*

Wittig, Monique **PQ2683.I8C613 1986**
The Lesbian Body. David Le Vay (Translator), Margaret Crosland (Introduction by). Trade Paper. Beacon Press. Boston, MA. 1986. 165p. Beacon Paperback Ser., Vol. 709 ISBN:0-8070-6307-X, ISBN13: 978-0-8070-6307-1. Dewey:843/.914. LCCN:85-047943.
Audience: **g,l,u,f.**

Worton, Michael **PQ2680.O83Z78 1995**
Michel Tournier. Ed. 1. Cloth Text. Addison-Wesley Longman, Ltd. Harlow, 1996. 232p. Modern Literatures in Perspective Ser. ISBN:0-582-08650-7, ISBN13: 978-0-582-08650-0. Dewey:843/.914. LCCN:95-018182.
Audience: **g,l,u.** *Choice, 1996.*

French Literature Outside France

Jack, Belinda **PQ3809.J33 1996**
Francophone Literatures: An Introductory Survey. Trade Cloth. Oxford University Press, Inc. New York, NY. 1996. 312p. ISBN:0-19-871507-2, ISBN13: 978-0-19-871507-8. Dewey:840.9. LCCN:96-017161.
Audience: **l,u.** *Choice, 1997.*

Kennedy, Ellen C. (Editor) **PQ3899.N4 1989**
The Negritude Poets: An Anthology of Black Poetry Translated from the French. Maya Angelou (Foreword by). Trade Paper. Avalon Publishing Group. New York, NY. 1993. 320p. Classic Reprint Ser. ISBN:0-938410-72-5, ISBN13: 978-0-938410-72-0. Dewey:841. LCCN:88-038513.
Audience: **g,l,u,f.**

Kesteloot, Lilyan **PQ3897.K3913 1991**
Black Writers in French: An Interpretive History. Trade Paper. Howard University Press. Washington, DC. 1990. xxxiii, 411 p.p. ISBN:0-88258-066-3, ISBN13: 978-0-88258-066-1. Dewey:840.9/896. LCCN:91-014178.
Audience: **u,f.** *Choice, 1991.*

Ndiaye, Christiane **PQ3809**
Introduction aux littératures francophones : Afrique, Caraïbe, Maghreb. Presses de l'Université de Montréal. 2004. ISBN:2-7606-1875-7, ISBN13: 978-2-7606-1875-6.
Audience: **u,f.**

Rouch, Alain & Clavreuil, Gérard **PQ3809.R75 1987**
Littératures nationales d'écriture française : Afrique noire, Caraïbes, océan Indien : histoire littéraire et anthologie. Bordas. 1987. ISBN:2-04-016881-8, ISBN13: 978-2-04-016881-0.
Audience: **u,f.**

Salhi, Kamal (Editor) **PQ3897.F73 2003**
Francophone Post-Colonial Cultures: Critical Essays. Trade Cloth. Lexington Books. Lanham, MD. 2003. 448p. After the Empire Ser. ISBN:0-7391-0567-1, ISBN13: 978-0-7391-0567-2. Dewey:840.9/917/541. LCCN:2002-151169.
Audience: **u,f.** *Choice, 2004.*

Senghor, Leopold S. **PQ3899**
Anthologie de la Nouvelle Poesie Negre et Malgache de Langue Francaise: Avec: Sartre, Jean-Paul. Orphee Noir. Ed. 4. Trade Paper. French & European Publications, Inc. New York, NY. 1985. ISBN:0-7859-1442-0, ISBN13: 978-0-7859-1442-6. Dewey:840.8.
Audience: **u,f.**

French Literature Outside France > Belgium

Bertrand, Jean-Pierre; Vrydaghs, David **PQ3814.H57 2003**
Histoire de la littérature belge francophone : 1830-2000. Fayard. 2003. ISBN:2-213-61709-0, ISBN13: 978-2-213-61709-1.
Audience: **u,f.**

Quaghebeur, Marc (Editor) **PQ3840**
Anthologie de la littérature française de Belgique : entre réel et surréel. Editions Racine. 2006. ISBN:2-87386-433-8, ISBN13: 978-2-87386-433-0.
Audience: **u,f.**

French Literature Outside France > West Indies

Depestre, René **PQ3809**
Hadriana in My Dreams. Heinemann International, Inc. 1995. ISBN:0-435-98937-5, ISBN13: 978-0-435-98937-8.
Audience: **g,l,u,f.**

Alexis, Jacques S. **PQ3949.A34 C6X 1982**
Compere General Soleil. Trade Paper. Schoenhof's Foreign Books, Inc. Cambridge, MA. 1985. 350p. L' Imaginaire Ser. ISBN:2-07-028730-0, ISBN13: 978-2-07-028730-7. Dewey:843.
Audience: **u.**

Alexis, Jacques S. **PQ3949.A34C6613 1999**
General Sun, My Brother. Carrol F. Coates (Translator). Trade Cloth. University Press of Virginia. Charlottesville, VA. 1999. 352p. ISBN:0-8139-1889-8, ISBN13: 978-0-8139-1889-1. Dewey:843. LCCN:99-023064.
Audience: **g,l,u,f.** *Choice, 2000.*

Arnold, A. James (Editor), et al. **PN849.C3H57 1994**
A History of Literature in the Caribbean: Hispanic and Francophone Regions. Julio Rodriguez-Luis & J. Michael Dash (Editors). Library Binding. John Benjamins Publishing Company. Philadelphia, PA. 1994. xviii, 579p. Comparative History of Literatures in European Languages Ser., Vol. No. 10 ISBN:1-55619-601-6, ISBN13: 978-1-55619-601-0. Dewey:809/.89729. LCCN:94-003353.
Audience: **u,f.**

Barbour, Sarah & Herndon, Gerise (Editors) **PQ3949.2.C65Z63 2005**
Emerging Perspectives on Maryse Conde: A Writer of Her Own. Trade Cloth. Africa World Press. Trenton, NJ. 2004. 320p. ISBN:1-59221-222-0, ISBN13: 978-1-59221-222-4. Dewey:843/.914. LCCN:2005-030952.
Audience: **l,u.**

Cesaire, Aime **PQ3949.C44A24 1990**
Lyric and Dramatic Poetry, 1946-82. Clayton Eshleman & Annette Smith (Translators), A. James Arnold (Introduction by). Cloth Text. University Press of Virginia. Charlottesville, VA. 1990. 235p. CARAF Bks. ISBN:0-8139-1256-3, ISBN13: 978-0-8139-1256-1. Dewey:841. LCCN:89-022415.
Audience: **g,l,u,f.** *Choice, 1991.*

Cesaire, Aime **PQ3949.C44C34 2000**
Cahier d'un Retour au Pays Natal. Ed. 2. Abiola Irele (Editor). Paper Text. Ohio State University Press. Columbus, OH. 2000. lxxiii, 158p. ISBN:0-8142-5020-3, ISBN13: 978-0-8142-5020-4. Dewey:841/.914. LCCN:99-032570.
Audience: **u,f.**

Chamoiseau, Patrick **PQ3919.R74**
Texaco: A Novel. Trade Paper. Knopf Publishing Group. New York, NY. 1998. 416p. ISBN:0-679-75175-0, ISBN13: 978-0-679-75175-5. Dewey:843.
Audience: **g,l,u,f.**

Chamoiseau, Patrick **PQ3949.2.C45 T49 1992**
Texaco : roman. Gallimard. 1992. ISBN:2-07-072750-5, ISBN13: 978-2-07-072750-6.
Audience: **u,f.**

Condé, Maryse **PQ3949.2.C65 D48 1997**
Desirada : roman. R. Laffont. 1997. ISBN:2-221-08466-7, ISBN13: 978-2-221-08466-3.
Audience: **u,f.**

Condé, Maryse **PQ3949.2.C65**
Moi, Tituba sorcière-- : noire de Salem. Mercure de France. 2005. ISBN:2-07-037929-9, ISBN13: 978-2-07-037929-3.
Audience: **u,f.**

Condé, Maryse **PQ3949.2.C65 S4413**
Segu. Trade Paper. Penguin Group (USA) Inc. New York, NY. 1996. 512p. ISBN:0-14-025949-X, ISBN13: 978-0-14-025949-0. Dewey:843.
Audience: **g,l,u.**

Condé, Maryse **PQ3949.2.C65 S44 1984**
Ségou, les murailles de terre : roman. R. Laffont. 1984. ISBN:2-221-01197-X, ISBN13: 978-2-221-01197-3.
Audience: **u,f.**

Condé, Maryse **PQ3949.2.C65V5413**
Tree of Life. Trade Cloth. Ballantine Books. New York, NY. 1992. 371p. ISBN:0-345-36074-5, ISBN13: 978-0-345-36074-8. Dewey:843. LCCN:91-058330.
Audience: **g,l,u,f.**

Condé, Maryse **PQ3949.2.C65**
La vie scélérate : roman. Seghers. 1987. ISBN:2-221-05251-X, ISBN13: 978-2-221-05251-8.
Audience: **u,f.**

Condé, Maryse **PQ3949.2.C65D4813**
Desirada. Richard Philcox (Translator). Trade Cloth. Soho Press, Inc. New York, NY. 2000. 260p. ISBN:1-56947-215-7, ISBN13: 978-1-56947-215-6. Dewey:843/.914. LCCN:00-030121.
Audience: **g,l,u,f.**

Condé, Maryse **PQ3949.2.C65M5613**
I, Tituba, Black Witch of Salem. Richard Philcox (Translator), Angela Y. Davis (Foreword by), Ann A. Scarboro (Afterword by). Cloth Text. University Press of Virginia. Charlottesville, VA. 1992. 248p. CARAF Ser. ISBN:0-8139-1398-5, ISBN13: 978-0-8139-1398-8. Dewey:843. LCCN:92-008134.
Audience: **g,l,u,f.** *Choice, 1993.*

Césaire, Aimé **PQ3949.C44 A17 1994**
La poésie. Éditions du Seuil. 1994. ISBN:2-02-021232-3, ISBN13: 978-2-02-021232-8.
Audience: **u,f.**

Césaire, Aimé **PQ2605.E74 S2**
Une saison au Congo : théâtre. Editions du Seuil. 2001. ISBN:2-02-048624-5, ISBN13: 978-2-02-048624-8.
Audience: **u,f.**

Césaire, Aimé **PQ2605.E74**
Une Tempête : Théâtre. Éditions du Seuil. 1997. ISBN:2-02-031431-2, ISBN13: 978-2-02-031431-2.
Audience: **u,f.**

Césaire, Aimé **PQ3949.C44**
La tragédie du roi Christophe : théâtre. Présence Africaine. 1988. ISBN:2-7087-0130-4, ISBN13: 978-2-7087-0130-4.
Audience: **u,f.**

Damas, Léon-Gontran **PQ3959.D3**
Pigments ; Névralgies. Présence africaine. 2003. ISBN:2-7087-0720-5, ISBN13: 978-2-7087-0720-7.
Audience: **u,f.**

Davis, Gregson **PQ3949.C44 Z65 1997**
Aimé Césaire. Abiola Irele (Contribution by). Trade Cloth. Cambridge University Press. New York, NY. 1997. 224p. Studies in African and Caribbean Literature, Vol. 5 ISBN:0-521-39072-9, ISBN13: 978-0-521-39072-9. Dewey:841. LCCN:96-051158.
Audience: **u,f.** *Choice, 1998.*

Depestre, Rene **PQ3949.D46**
Alleluia pour une Femme-Jardin. Trade Paper. Schoenhof's Foreign Books, Inc. Cambridge, MA. 1986. 215p. Folio Ser., No. 1713 ISBN:2-07-037713-X, ISBN13: 978-2-07-037713-8. Dewey:843.
Audience: **u,f.**

Depestre, Rene **PQ3949.D46M313 1990**
The Festival of the Greasy Pole. A. J. Arnold & K. Drame (Editors), Carrol F. Coates (Translator, Introduction by). Cloth Text. University Press of Virginia. Charlottesville, VA. 1990. 142p. CARAF Bks. ISBN:0-8139-1281-4, ISBN13: 978-0-8139-1281-3. Dewey:843. LCCN:89-078318.
Audience: **g,l,u,f.**

Depestre, Rene **PQ3949.D46.A813 1977**
A Rainbow for the Christian West. Joan Dayan (Translator). Trade Cloth. University of Massachusetts Press. Amherst, MA. 1977. 272p. ISBN:0-87023-229-0, ISBN13: 978-0-87023-229-9. Dewey:841. LCCN:76-045047.
Audience: **g,l,u,f.**

Depestre, René **PQ/3949/.D46/**
Alléluia pour une femme-jardin. Gallimard. 1998. ISBN:2-07-037713-X, ISBN13: 978-2-07-037713-8.
Audience: **u,f.**

Depestre, René **PQ3949.D46**
Hadriana dans tous mes rêves : roman. Gallimard. 1998. ISBN:2-07-071255-9, ISBN13: 978-2-07-071255-7.
Audience: **u,f.**

Depestre, René **PQ3949.D46**
Le mât de cocagne : roman. Gallimard. 1998.
ISBN:2-07-028760-2, ISBN13: 978-2-07-028760-4.
Audience: **u,f.**

Faustman, Jean **PQ2679.C43**
Le Creuset des Cultures: La Litterature Antillaise. Michael G. Paulson & Tamara Alvarez-Detrell (Editors). Trade Cloth. Peter Lang Publishing, Inc. New York, NY. 2004. 145p. Francophone Cultures and Literatures Ser. ISBN:0-8204-6732-4, ISBN13: 978-0-8204-6732-0. Dewey:843/.91409.
Audience: **u,f.**

Fowler, Carolyn **PQ3949.R73 Z66**
A Knot into the Thread: The Life and Work of Jacques Roumain. Trade Paper. Howard University Press. Washington, DC. 2003. 400p. ISBN:0-88258-221-6, ISBN13: 978-0-88258-221-4. Dewey:841.
Audience: **u,f.**

Gallagher, Mary **PQ3940**
Soundings in French Caribbean Writing, 1950-2000: The Shock of Space and Time. Trade Cloth. Oxford University Press, Inc. New York, NY. 2003. 302p. ISBN:0-19-815982-X, ISBN13: 978-0-19-815982-7. Dewey:840.9/729/09045. LCCN:2002-070205.
Audience: **u,f.** *Choice, 2003.*

Glissant, Edouard **PQ3949.2.G53.L49**
La Lezarde: Roman. Trade Cloth. Gallimard, Editions. Paris Cedex 07, 1997. 252p. ISBN:2-07-074623-2, ISBN13: 978-2-07-074623-1. LCCN:99-518731.
Audience: **u,f.**

Glissant, Edouard **PQ3949.2.G53.L49**
La Lézarde : roman. Gallimard. 1997. ISBN:2-07-074623-2, ISBN13: 978-2-07-074623-1.
Audience: **u,f.**

Glissant, Edouard **PQ3949.2.G53**
Monsieur Toussaint : version scénique. Gallimard. 1998.
ISBN:2-07-074621-6, ISBN13: 978-2-07-074621-7.
Audience: **u,f.**

Glissant, Edouard **PQ2667.L5**
Le sel noir ; Le sang rivé ; Boises. Gallimard. 1983.
ISBN:2-07-032240-8, ISBN13: 978-2-07-032240-4.
Audience: **u,f.**

Glissant, Edouard **PQ3949.2.G53L4913**
The Ripening. Michael Dash (Translator). Trade Paper. Heinemann. Portsmouth, NH. 1986. 195p. Caribbean Writers Ser. ISBN:0-435-98222-2, ISBN13: 978-0-435-98222-5. Dewey:843. LCCN:97-138272.
Audience: **g,l,u,f.** *Choice, 1986.*

Glissant, Edouard **PQ2617.O6**
Monsieur Toussaint. Joseph Foster & Barbara A. Franklin (Translators), Juris Silenieks (Introduction by). Trade Cloth. Lynne Rienner Publishers, Inc. Boulder, CO. 1981. 120p. ISBN:0-89410-128-5, ISBN13: 978-0-89410-128-1. Dewey:842/.914. LCCN:81-051665.
Audience: **g,l,u,f.**

Glissant, Edouard **PQ3949.2.G53 S4513**
Black Salt: Poems. Betsy Wing (Translator). Trade Cloth. University of Michigan Press. Chicago, IL. 1999. 168p. ISBN:0-472-09666-4, ISBN13: 978-0-472-09666-4. Dewey:841/.914.
Audience: **g,l,u,f.**

Haigh, Sam **PQ139**
An Introduction to Caribbean Francophone Writing: Guadeloupe and Martinique. Cloth over Boards. Berg Publishers. Oxford, 1999. 224p. French Studies Ser. ISBN:1-85973-293-3, ISBN13: 978-1-85973-293-9. Dewey:840.9.
Audience: **l,u.** *Choice, 2000.*

Jonassaint, Jean **PQ3948.5.H2**
Des Romans de Tradition Haitienne: Sur un Recit Tragique. Trade Cloth. Editions du CIDIHCA. Montreal, PQ. 2001. ISBN:2-7475-1672-5, ISBN13: 978-2-7475-1672-3. Dewey:843.009/97294.
Audience: **u,f.**

Kesteloot, Lilyan **PQ2605.E74 A6**
Aime Cesaire. Trade Paper. French & European Publications, Inc. New York, NY. Coll. Poetes d'aujourd'hui Ser. ISBN:0-8288-6090-4, ISBN13: 978-0-8288-6090-1. Dewey:842.91.
Audience: **u,f.**

Murdoch, H. Adlai **PQ3944.M87 2001**
Creole Identity in the French Caribbean Novel. Trade Cloth. University Press of Florida. Gainesville, FL. 2001. xi, 290p. ISBN:0-8130-1835-8, ISBN13: 978-0-8130-1835-5. Dewey:843.009/9729. LCCN:00-064908.
Audience: **u,f.** *Choice, 2001.*

Ormerod, Beverley **PQ3944.O76 1985**
An Introduction to the French Caribbean Novel. Trade Paper. Heinemann. Portsmouth, NH. 1985. viii, 160p. Studies in Caribbean Literature ISBN:0-435-91839-7, ISBN13: 978-0-435-91839-2. Dewey:843. LCCN:85-150162.
Audience: **l,u.** *Choice, 1985.*

Racine, Daniel L. **PQ3959.D3 Z86 1983**
Léon-Gontran Damas : l'homme et l'oeuvre. Présence africaine. 1983. ISBN:2-7087-0427-3, ISBN13: 978-2-7087-0427-5.
Audience: **u,f.**

Roumain, Jacques **PQ3949.R73**
Bois d'ébène ; suivi de Madrid. Mémoire d'encrier. 2003.
ISBN:2-923153-13-8, ISBN13: 978-2-923153-13-1.
Audience: **u,f.**

Roumain, Jacques **PQ3949.R73**
Gouverneurs de la rosée : roman. Mémoire d'encrier. 2004.
ISBN:2-923153-21-9, ISBN13: 978-2-923153-21-6.
Audience: **u,f.**

Roumain, Jacques **PQ3949.R73G613 1997**
Masters of the Dew. Trade Paper. Heinemann. Portsmouth, NH. 1978. 192p. Caribbean Writers Ser. ISBN:0-435-98745-3, ISBN13: 978-0-435-98745-9. Dewey:843/.9/1. LCCN:98-140605.
Audience: **g,l,u,f.**

Schwarz-Bart, Simone **PQ2679.C43**
Pluie et vent sur Télumée Miracle : roman. Éditions du Seuil. 1995. ISBN:2-02-023925-6, ISBN13: 978-2-02-023925-7.
Audience: **u,f.**

Schwarz-Bart, Simone **PQ2679.C43**
Ti Jean L'horizon : roman. Seuil. 1998. ISBN:2-02-033423-2, ISBN13: 978-2-02-033423-5.
Audience: **u,f.**

Schwarz-Bart, Simone; Schwarz-Bart, André
Un Plat de porc aux bananes vertes: roman. Éditions du Seuil. 1967.
Audience: **u,f.**

Schwarz-Bart, Simone **PQ2679.C43**
Between Two Worlds. Barbara Bray (Translator). Trade Paper. Heinemann. Portsmouth, NH. 1995. 212p. Caribbean Writers Ser. ISBN:0-435-98929-4, ISBN13: 978-0-435-98929-3. Dewey:843/.914.
Audience: **g,l,u,f.**

Schwarz-Bart, Simone **PQ2679.C43**
The Bridge of Beyond. Barbara Bray (Translator), Bridget Jones (Introduction by). Trade Paper. Heinemann. Portsmouth, NH. 1982. 174p. Caribbean Writers Ser. ISBN:0-435-98770-4, ISBN13: 978-0-435-98770-1. Dewey:843/.9/1.
Audience: **g,l,u,f.**

Warner, Keith Q. (Editor) **PQ3959.D3**
Critical Perspectives on Leon Gontran Damas. Trade Cloth. Lynne Rienner Publishers, Inc. Boulder, CO. 1988. 178p. Critical Perspectives Ser. ISBN:0-914478-57-5, ISBN13: 978-0-914478-57-7. Dewey:841.9. LCCN:80-053347.
Audience: **u,f.**

French Literature Outside France > Canada

Cogswell, Fred & Elder, Jo-Ann **PQ3917.M32**
Unfinished Dreams: Contemporary Poetry of Acadie. Goose Lane Editions. 1990. ISBN:0-86492-132-2, ISBN13: 978-0-86492-132-1.
Audience: **u,f.**

Lemire, Maurice **PQ3901.D5**
Dictionnaire des Oeuvres Littéraires du Québec, Vols. 1-7. Ed. 2. Fides. 1994.
Audience: **u,f.**

Mailhot, Laurent; Nepveu, Pierre **PQ3914**
La poésie québecoise des origines à nos jours. Montréal: Hexagone. 1990.
Audience: **u,f.**

French Literature Outside France > Canada > Individual Authors, to 1960

Aubert de Gaspé, Philippe **PQ1694**
Les Anciens Canadiens. Trade Cloth. Fides, Editions. Saint-Laurent, PQ. 2005. 357p. ISBN:2-7621-2625-8, ISBN13: 978-2-7621-2625-9. Dewey:843/.3.
Audience: **u,f.**

Blais, Marie-Claire **PQ3919.B6**
Une Saison dans la Vie d'Emmanuel. Trade Cloth. Fides, Editions. Saint-Laurent, PQ. 1994. ISBN:2-7621-1683-X, ISBN13: 978-2-7621-1683-0. Dewey:843/.54.
Audience: **u,f.**

Blais, Marie-Claire **PQ3919.B6**
Visions d'Anna. Trade Cloth. Editions du Boreal, Les. Montreal, PQ. 1990. 208p. ISBN:2-89052-375-6, ISBN13: 978-2-89052-375-3. Dewey:843/.54.
Audience: **u,f.**

Blais, Marie-Claire **PQ3919.B6**
Manuscrits de Pauline Archange: Vivre! Vivre! - Les Apparences. Trade Cloth. Editions du Boreal, Les. Montreal, PQ. 1991. 336p. ISBN:2-89052-417-5, ISBN13: 978-2-89052-417-0. Dewey:843/.54.
Audience: **u,f.**

Blais, Marie-Claire **PQ3919.B6**
Le Sourd dans la Ville. Trade Cloth. Editions du Boreal, Les. Montreal, PQ. 1996. 192p. ISBN:2-89052-794-8, ISBN13: 978-2-89052-794-2. Dewey:843/.54. LCCN:96-940812.
Audience: **u,f.**

Blais, Marie-Claire **PQ3919.B6**
Ceuvre Poetique, 1957-1996. Trade Cloth. Editions du Boreal, Les. Montreal, PQ. 1997. 192p. ISBN:2-89052-873-1, ISBN13: 978-2-89052-873-4. Dewey:841/.54. LCCN:97-941252.
Audience: **u,f.**

Blais, Marie-Claire **PR3919.B6**
Mad Shadows. Mass Market. McClelland & Stewart. Toronto, ON. 1990. 128p. New Canadian Library ISBN:0-7710-9867-7, ISBN13: 978-0-7710-9867-3. Dewey:C843/.54. LCCN:89-090758.
Audience: **g,l,u,f.**

Brochu, Andre **PQ2007.M6**
Anne Hebert: Le Secret de Vie et de Mort. Trade Cloth. University of Ottawa Press/Presses de l'Universite d'Ottawa. Ottawa, ON. 2000. 284p. ISBN:2-7603-0512-0, ISBN13: 978-2-7603-0512-0. Dewey:848/.5409.
Audience: **u,f.**

Clemente, Linda & Clemente, Bill **PQ3919.R74Z585 1997**
Gabrielle Roy: Creation and Memory. Trade Paper. ECW Press. Toronto, ON. 1997. 202p. ISBN:1-55022-287-2, ISBN13: 978-1-55022-287-6. Dewey:843 B. LCCN:97-141115.
Audience: **l,u,f.**

Garneau, Saint-Denys **PS8513.A75**
Regards et Jeux Dans l'Espace. Trade Cloth. Centre Educatif et Culturel. Anjou, PQ. 1996. 159p. ISBN:2-7617-1301-X, ISBN13: 978-2-7617-1301-6. Dewey:841/.52. LCCN:96-027173.
Audience: **u,f.**

Gilbert, Paula R. **PQ3919.R74Z76 1984**
The Literary Vision of Gabrielle Roy. Ed. 2. Trade Cloth. Summa Publications, Inc. Birmingham, AL. 1993. 335p. ISBN:0-917786-05-X, ISBN13: 978-0-917786-05-1. Dewey:843. LCCN:84-050323.
Audience: **u,f.**

Grandbois, Alain **PQ3919.G65**
Poemes. Trade Cloth. Editions de l'Hexagone, Les. Montreal, PQ. 2003. 216p. ISBN:2-89006-704-1, ISBN13: 978-2-89006-704-2. Dewey:841/.52.
Audience: **u,f.**

Groulx, Lionel **PQ3919.G76**
The Iron Wedge - (L'Appel de la Race), No. 136. Michel Gaulin (Editor). Trade Paper. McGill-Queen's University Press. Montreal, PQ. 212p. ISBN:0-88629-030-9, ISBN13: 978-0-88629-030-6. Dewey:843/.52.
Audience: **g,l,u,f.**

Guevremont, Germaine **PR 9277 U32 S8 2004**
Le Survenant. Trade Cloth. Fides, Editions. Saint-Laurent, PQ. 2004. 238p. ISBN:2-7621-2612-6, ISBN13: 978-2-7621-2612-9. Dewey:843/.52.
Audience: **u,f.**

Hébert, Anne **PQ3919.H37**
Ceuvre Poetique 1950-1990. Trade Paper. Editions du Boreal, Les. Montreal, PQ. 168p. ISBN:2-89052-520-1, ISBN13: 978-2-89052-520-7. Dewey:841/.914.
Audience: **u,f.**

Hébert, Anne **PQ3919.H37**
Les Fous des Bassan. Trade Paper. French & European Publications, Inc. New York, NY. 1984. ISBN:0-7859-2697-6, ISBN13: 978-0-7859-2697-9. Dewey:848.9971.
Audience: **u,f.**

Hébert, Anne **PS8515.E16**
Kamouraska. Trade Paper. Editions du Seuil. Paris, ISBN:2-02-031429-0, ISBN13: 978-2-02-031429-9.
Audience: **u,f.**

Hébert, Anne **PQ3919.H37**
The Torrent: Novellas and Short Stories. Trade Paper. Books on Demand. Ann Arbor, MI. 141p. French Writers of Canada Ser. ISBN:0-608-13585-2, ISBN13: 978-0-608-13585-4. Dewey:843. LCCN:73-083340.
Audience: **g,l,u,f.**

Hébert, Anne & Gallant, Mavis **PQ3919.H37**
Anne Hebert: Collected Later Novels. Sheila Fischman (Translator). Trade Paper. House of Anansi Press. Toronto, ON. 2003. 296p. ISBN:0-88784-671-8, ISBN13: 978-0-88784-671-7. Dewey:843/.54.
Audience: **g,l,u,f.**

Lemelin, Roger **PQ3919.L53**
Les Plouffe. Trade Cloth. Editions Internationales Alain Stanke, Limitee. Outremont, PQ. 1999. ISBN:2-7604-0671-7, ISBN13: 978-2-7604-0671-1. Dewey:843/.52.
Audience: **u,f.**

Nelligan, Emile, et al. **PQ1812**
Poesies Completes, 1896-1941. Rejean Robidoux & Paul Wyczynski (Authors). Trade Cloth. Fides, Editions. Saint-Laurent, PQ. 2004. 414p. ISBN:2-7621-2521-9, ISBN13: 978-2-7621-2521-4. Dewey:841/.4.
Audience: **u,f.**

Pallister, Janis L. (Editor) **PQ3919.H37Z54 2001**
The Art and Genius of Anne Hebert: Essays on Her Works: Night and the Day Are One. Trade Cloth. Fairleigh Dickinson University Press. Cranbury, NJ. 2001. 400p. ISBN:0-8386-3913-5, ISBN13: 978-0-8386-3913-9. Dewey:848/.91409. LCCN:2001-023282.
Audience: **l,u,f.**

Ricard, Francois **PQ3919.R74**
Gabrielle Roy: Une Vie. Trade Cloth. Editions du Boreal, Les. Montreal, PQ. 2000. 680p. ISBN:2-7646-0013-5, ISBN13: 978-2-7646-0013-9. Dewey:843/.54.
Audience: **u,f.**

Ringuet **PS8531.A48**
Trente Arpents. Trade Cloth. Editions Flammarion. Montreal, PQ. 2000. 288p. ISBN:2-89077-218-7, ISBN13: 978-2-89077-218-2. Dewey:843/.52.
Audicncc: **u,f.**

Roy, Gabrielle **PQ3919.R74**
La Detresse et l'Enchantement: Autobiographie. Ed. 3. Trade Cloth. Editions du Boreal, Les. Montreal, PQ. 1996. 518p. ISBN:2-89052-768-9, ISBN13: 978-2-89052-768-3. Dewey:843/.54.
Audience: **u,f.**

Roy, Gabrielle **PS8535.O95**
Rue Deschambault. Trade Cloth. Editions du Boreal, Les. Montreal, PQ. 1993. 270p. ISBN:2-89052-577-5, ISBN13: 978-2-89052-577-1. Dewey:843/.54.
Audience: **u,f.**

Roy, Gabrielle **PQ3919.R74**
Un Jardin au Bout du Monde. Trade Cloth. Editions du Boreal, Les. Montreal, PQ. 1994. 190p. ISBN:2-89052-595-3, ISBN13: 978-2-89052-595-5. Dewey:843/.54.
Audience: **u,f.**

Roy, Gabrielle **PQ3919.R74**
Bonheur d'Occasion. Trade Cloth. Editions du Boreal, Les. Montreal, PQ. 1993. 414p. ISBN:2-89052-575-9, ISBN13: 978-2-89052-575-7. Dewey:843/.54.
Audience: **u,f.**

Roy, Gabrielle **PQ3919.R74**
La Petite Poule d'Eau. Trade Cloth. Editions du Boreal, Les. Montreal, PQ. 1993. 276p. ISBN:2-89052-573-2, ISBN13: 978-2-89052-573-3. Dewey:843/.54.
Audience: **u,f.**

Roy, Gabrielle **PQ3919.R74**
Ces Enfants de Ma Vie. Trade Cloth. Editions du Boreal, Les. Montreal, PQ. 1993. 198p. ISBN:2-89052-574-0, ISBN13: 978-2-89052-574-0. Dewey:843/.54.
Audience: **u,f.**

Roy, Gabrielle **PQ3919.R74**
La Route d'Altamont. Trade Cloth. Editions du Boreal, Les. Montreal, PQ. 1993. 168p. ISBN:2-89052-572-4, ISBN13: 978-2-89052-572-6. Dewey:843/.54.
Audience: **u,f.**

Russell, Delbert W. **PQ3919.H37.Z86 1983**
Anne Hebert. Library Binding. Thomson Gale. Farmington Hills, MI. 1983. 155p. World Authors Ser. ISBN:0-8057-6531-X, ISBN13: 978-0-8057-6531-1. Dewey:848. LCCN:82-015798.
Audience: **l,u.**

Theriault, Yves **PQ3919.2.P7314**
Agaguk: Roman. Trade Cloth. Le Dernier Havre. Montreal, PQ. 2003. 394p. ISBN:2-89598-001-2, ISBN13: 978-2-89598-001-8. Dewey:843/.54.
Audience: **u,f.**

French Literature Outside France > Canada > Individual Authors, 1960-

Aquin, Hubert **PQ3919.2.P7314**
Prochain Episode. Trade Cloth. Bibliotheque Quebecoise. Saint-Laurent, PQ. 1995. ISBN:2-89406-117-X, ISBN13: 978-2-89406-117-6. Dewey:843/.54.
Audience: **u,f.**

Beauchemin, Yves **PQ3919.2.P7314**
Le Matou. Trade Cloth. Quebec Amerique. Montreal, PQ. 2001. 616p. ISBN:2-7644-0132-9, ISBN13: 978-2-7644-0132-3. Dewey:843/.54.
Audience: **u,f.**

Bessette, Gerard **PQ3919.2.B47**
Le Libraire. Trade Cloth. Editions Pierre Tisseyre. Saint-Laurent, PQ. 1993. 144p. ISBN:2-89051-500-1, ISBN13: 978-2-89051-500-0. Dewey:843/.54.
Audience: **u,f.**

Brault, Jacques **PQ3919.2.T6922**
Poemes. Trade Cloth. Editions du Noroit. Saint-Lambert, PQ. 2000. 402p. ISBN:2-89018-455-2, ISBN13: 978-2-89018-455-8. Dewey:841/.54.
Audience: **u,f.**

Brossard, Nicole **PQ3919.2.B75**
Le désert mauve. L'Hexagone. 1987. ISBN:2-89006-280-5, ISBN13: 978-2-89006-280-1.
Audience: **u,f.**

Carrier, Roch **PQ2605.A3734**
La Guerre, Yes Sir!. Trade Cloth. Editions Internationales Alain Stanke, Limitee. Outremont, PQ. 1998. ISBN:2-7604-0649-0, ISBN13: 978-2-7604-0649-0. Dewey:843.914.
Audience: **u,f.**

Chen, Ying **PQ3919.1.C532**
L' Ingratitutde: Roman. Trade Cloth. Lemeac Editeur, Inc. Montreal, PQ. 1995. 136p. ISBN:2-7609-1518-2, ISBN13: 978-2-7609-1518-3. Dewey:843/.54. LCCN:95-022641.
Audience: **u,f.**

Dalpe, Jean Marc **PQ3919.2.D246**
Un Vent Se le Qui Iparpille. Trade Paper. Prise de Parole, Inc. Sudbury, ON. 1999. ISBN:2-89423-094-X, ISBN13: 978-2-89423-094-7. Dewey:843/.914.
Audience: **u,f.**

David, Gilbert et al. **PQ3919.2.T73 Z77 1993**
des Belles-soeurs à Marcel poursuivi par les chiens. Lavoie, Pierre; Brochu, André (Authors). Cahiers de théâtre Jeu. 1993. ISBN:2-920999-02-8, ISBN13: 978-2-920999-02-2.
Audience: **u,f.**

Dube, Marcel **PQ3919.2.D76**
Zone. Trade Cloth. Lemeac Editeur, Inc. Montreal, PQ. 1968. 160p. ISBN:0-7761-0000-9, ISBN13: 978-0-7761-0000-5. Dewey:842.914.
Audience: **u,f.**

Ducharme, Réjean **PQ2664.U298**
L'Avalée des avalés. Gallimard. 1990. ISBN:2-07-037393-2, ISBN13: 978-2-07-037393-2.
Audience: **u,f.**

Ferron, Jacques **PQ3919.2.P7314**
Cotnoir. Trade Cloth. Editions Typo. Montreal, PQ. 2001. 109p. ISBN:2-89295-175-5, ISBN13: 978-2-89295-175-2. Dewey:843/.54.
Audience: **u,f.**

Godbout, Jacques **PQ3919.2.P7314**
Salut Galarneau!: Suivi de, le Temps des Galarneau. Trade Cloth. Fides, Editions. Saint-Laurent, PQ. 2000. ISBN:2-7621-2209-0, ISBN13: 978-2-7621-2209-1. Dewey:843/.54.
Audience: **u,f.**

Huston, Nancy **PQ3919.2.H87**
Cantique des Plaines: Roman. Trade Cloth. Lemeac Editeur, Inc. Montreal, PQ. 1995. 317p. ISBN:2-7427-0490-6, ISBN13: 978-2-7427-0490-3. Dewey:843/.54.
Audience: **u,f.**

Jasmin, Claude **PQ3919.2.P7314**
La Petite Patrie. Trade Cloth. Editions Typo. Montreal, PQ. 1999. ISBN:2-89295-157-7, ISBN13: 978-2-89295-157-8. Dewey:843/.54.
Audience: **u,f.**

Kattan, Naim **PQ3919.2.P7314**
Adieu Babylone. Trade Cloth. Lemeac Editeur, Inc. Montreal, PQ. 1986. 244p. ISBN:2-7609-3414-4, ISBN13: 978-2-7609-3414-6. Dewey:843/.54.
Audience: **u,f.**

Laberge, Marie **PQ3919.2.L12**
C'Etait Avant la Guerre a l'Anse-a-Gilles. Trade Cloth. Editions du Boreal, Les. Montreal, PQ. 168p. ISBN:2-89052-653-4, ISBN13: 978-2-89052-653-2. Dewey:842/.54.
Audience: **u,f.**

Laferriere, Dany **PQ3919.2.L163**
Eroshima, Vol. 132. Trade Cloth. Editions Typo. Montreal, PQ. 1998. ISBN:2-89295-145-3, ISBN13: 978-2-89295-145-5. Dewey:843/.54.
Audience: **u,f.**

Langevin, Andre **PQ2673.A762**
Poussiere Sur la Ville. Trade Cloth. Editions Pierre Tisseyre. Saint-Laurent, PQ. 216p. ISBN:0-7753-0090-X, ISBN13: 978-0-7753-0090-1. Dewey:843.
Audience: **u,f.**

Lapointe, Paul-Marie **PQ3919.2.L27**
L'espace de Vivre: Poemes 1968-2002. Trade Cloth. BPR Publishers. New Providence, NJ. 2004. 634p. Collection Rétrospectives ISBN:2-89006-724-6, ISBN13: 978-2-89006-724-0. Dewey:841/.54.
Audience: **u,f.**

Maillet, Antonine **PQ3919.2.M26**
La Sagouine. Trade Cloth. Lemeac Editeur, Inc. Montreal, PQ. 1994. 168p. ISBN:2-7609-0182-3, ISBN13: 978-2-7609-0182-7. Dewey:843.
Audience: **u,f.**

Maillet, Antonine **PQ3919.2.P7314**
Pelagie-la-Charrette. Trade Cloth. Bibliotheque Quebecoise. Saint-Laurent, PQ. 1999. ISBN:2-89406-177-3, ISBN13: 978-2-89406-177-0. Dewey:843/.54.
Audience: **u,f.**

Marchessault, Jovette **PQ3919.2.M2843**
La Saga des Poules Mouillees. Jacques Larue-Langlois (Introduction by). Trade Cloth. Lemeac Editeur, Inc. Montreal, PQ. 1989. 138p. ISBN:2-7609-0178-5, ISBN13: 978-2-7609-0178-0. Dewey:842/.54.
Audience: **u,f.**

Micone, Marco **PQ3919.2.M466**
Trilogia: Gens du Silence, Addolorata, Deja l'Agonie. Trade Cloth. Penguin Group (USA) Inc. New York, NY. 1996. ISBN:2-89005-647-3, ISBN13: 978-2-89005-647-3. Dewey:842/.54.
Audience: **u,f.**

Miron, Gaston **PQ3919.2.M5**
L' Homme Rapaille: Poemes. Ed. 3. Pierre Nepveu (Preface by). Trade Cloth. Editions Typo. Montreal, PQ. 1998. 252p. ISBN:2-89295-146-1, ISBN13: 978-2-89295-146-2. Dewey:841/.54. LCCN:98-003502.
Audience: **u,f.**

Poulin, Jacques **PQ3919.2.P7314**
Volkswagen Blues. Trade Cloth. Lemeac Editeur, Inc. Montreal, PQ. 1999. ISBN:2-7609-3224-9, ISBN13: 978-2-7609-3224-1. Dewey:843/.54.
Audience: **u,f.**

Robin, Regine **PQ3919.2.R5833**
La Quebecoite. Trade Cloth. X Y Z Publishing. Montreal, PQ. 1993. 232p. ISBN:2-89261-080-X, ISBN13: 978-2-89261-080-2. Dewey:843/.54.
Audience: **u,f.**

Tremblay, Michel **PQ3919.2.T73**
Theatre. Trade Cloth. Lemeac Editeur, Inc. Montreal, PQ. 1991. 448p. ISBN:2-7609-0194-7, ISBN13: 978-2-7609-0194-0. Dewey:842.
Audience: **u,f.**

Tremblay, Michel **PQ3919.2.T73**
La Duchesse et le Roturier. Trade Cloth. Lemeac Editeur, Inc. Montreal, PQ. 1982. 390p. ISBN:2-7609-3067-X, ISBN13: 978-2-7609-3067-4. Dewey:842.
Audience: **u,f.**

Tremblay, Michel **PQ3919.2.T73**
La Grosse Femme d'a Cote Est Enceinte: Roman. Trade Cloth. Lemeac Editeur, Inc. Montreal, PQ. 1995. 285p. ISBN:2-7609-1708-8, ISBN13: 978-2-7609-1708-8. Dewey:843/.54. LCCN:95-023368.
Audience: **u,f.**

Tremblay, Michel **PQ3919.2.T73**
Therese et Peirrette a l'Ecole des Saints-Anges: Roman. Trade Cloth. Lemeac Editeur, Inc. Montreal, PQ. 1995. 327p. ISBN:2-7609-1709-6, ISBN13: 978-2-7609-1709-5. Dewey:843/.54. LCCN:95-023097.
Audience: **u,f.**

Tremblay, Michel **PQ3919.2.T73**
C'ta ton Tour, Laura Cadieux. Trade Cloth. Bibliotheque Quebecoise. Saint-Laurent, PQ. 1997. ISBN:2-89406-106-4, ISBN13: 978-2-89406-106-0. Dewey:843/.54.
Audience: **u,f.**

Usmiani, Renate **PQ3919.2.T73**
Michel Tremblay. Trade Paper. Douglas & McIntyre, Ltd. Vancouver, BC. 1996. ISBN:0-88894-304-0, ISBN13: 978-0-88894-304-0. Dewey:842/.54.
Audience: **l,u,f.**

French Literature Outside France > Africa

Bjomson, Richard **PQ3988.5.C27B55 1991**
The African Quest for Freedom and Identity: Cameroonian Writing and the National Experience. Trade Cloth. Indiana University Press. Bloomington, IN. 1991. 528p. ISBN:0-253-31194-2, ISBN13: 978-0-253-31194-8. Dewey:840.9/96711. LCCN:90-039423.
Audience: **u,f.** *Choice, 1991.*

Bourgeacq, Jacques **PQ3985.5.E5V65 2001**
Voices from Madagascar: An Anthropology of Contemporary Francophone Literature. Liliane Ramarosoa (Contribution by). Trade Paper. Ohio University Press. Athens, OH. 2002. 339p. Research in International Studies, Vol. 75:Africa ISBN:0-89680-218-3, ISBN13: 978-0-89680-218-6. Dewey:840.8/09691/09045. LCCN:2001-016341.
Audience: **g,u,f.** *Choice, 2002.*

Dadie, Bernard B. **PQ3989.D28P313 1987**
The Black Cloth: A Collection of African Folk Tales. Karen C. Hatch (Translator), Es'kia Mphahlele (Foreword by). Trade Paper. University of Massachusetts Press. Amherst, MA. 1987. 176p. ISBN:0-87023-557-5, ISBN13: 978-0-87023-557-3. Dewey:843. LCCN:86-025043.
Audience: **g,l,u,f.** *Choice, 1987.*

D'Almeida, Irene A. **PQ3980.5.A46 1994**
Francophone African Women Writers: Destroying the Emptiness of Silence. Library Binding. University Press of Florida. Gainesville, FL. 1994. 208p. ISBN:0-8130-1302-X, ISBN13: 978-0-8130-1302-2. Dewey:840.9/9287/096. LCCN:94-026083.
Audience: **u,f.** *Choice, 1995.*

Jules-Rosette, Bennetta **PQ3981**
Black Paris: The African Writers' Landscape. Trade Paper. University of Illinois Press. Champaign, IL. 2000. 376p. ISBN:0-252-06935-8, ISBN13: 978-0-252-06935-2. Dewey:809/.8896/0904. LCCN:97-021068.
Audience: **u,f.** *Choice, 1998.*

Miller, Christopher L. **PQ3980.M548 1998**
Nationalists and Nomads: Essays on Francophone African Literature and Culture. Trade Cloth. University of Chicago Press. Chicago, IL. 1999. 272p. ISBN:0-226-52803-0, ISBN13: 978-0-226-52803-8. Dewey:840.9/896. LCCN:98-033698.
Audience: **u,f.** *Choice, 1999.*

Nkashama, Pius Ngandu **PQ3980.A52 P583 2002**
Ecritures littéraires : dictionnaire critique des oeuvres africaines de langue française, vol. 1. Presses universitaires du Nouveau Monde. 2002. ISBN:1-931948-01-1, ISBN13: 978-1-931948-01-2.
Audience: **u,f.**

Reed, John & Wake, Clive (Editors) **PQ3986.Z5**
French African Verse. Paper Text. Heinemann. Portsmouth, NH. 1972. xvi, 213p. African Writers Ser. ISBN:0-435-90106-0, ISBN13: 978-0-435-90106-6. Dewey:841. LCCN:73-156424.
Audience: **g,l,u,f.**

Woodhull, Winifred **PQ3988.N6.W66 1993**
Transfigurations of the Maghreb: Feminism, Decolonization, and Literatures. Book, Other. University of Minnesota Press. Minneapolis, MN. 1993. 260p. ISBN:0-8166-2054-7, ISBN13: 978-0-8166-2054-8. Dewey:840.9/9287/0961. LCCN:92-046725.
Audience: **g,u,f.** *Choice, 1994.*

French Literature Outside France > Africa > Individual Authors, to 1960

Dadie, Bernard Binlin **PQ3989.D28**
Pagne Noir. Trade Paper. Presence Africaine, Editions. Paris, 1990. ISBN:2-7087-0025-1, ISBN13: 978-2-7087-0025-3. Dewey:843.
Audience: **u,f.**

Dadie, Bernard Binlin **PQ3989.D28N413 1994**
An African in Paris. Karen C. Hatch (Translator). Trade Paper. University of Illinois Press. Champaign, IL. 1994. 184p. ISBN:0-252-06407-0, ISBN13: 978-0-252-06407-4. Dewey:843. LCCN:93-030915.
Audience: **g,l,u,f.** *Choice, 1995.*

Dadié, Bernard Binlin **PQ3989.D28**
Monsieur Thôgô-gnini : comédie. Présence africaine. 1996. ISBN:2-7087-0239-4, ISBN13: 978-2-7087-0239-4.
Audience: **u,f.**

Dadié, Bernard Binlin **PQ3989.D28**
Negre a Paris. Trade Paper. Presence Africaine, Editions. Paris, ISBN:2-7087-0618-7, ISBN13: 978-2-7087-0618-7. Dewey:896.83.
Audience: **u,f.**

Dadié, Bernard Binlin **PQ3989.D28**
Le pagne noir : contes africains. Présence Africaine. 1999. ISBN:2-7087-0025-1, ISBN13: 978-2-7087-0025-3.
Audience: **u,f.**

Dib, Mohammed **PQ3989.D52**
Cours sur la rive sauvage. Seuil. 2005. ISBN:2-02-081324-6, ISBN13: 978-2-02-081324-2.
Audience: **u,f.**

Dib, Mohammed **PQ3989.D52**
Grande Maison. Trade Paper. Editions du Seuil. Paris, 1996. ISBN:2-02-028312-3, ISBN13: 978-2-02-028312-0. Dewey:843.
Audience: **u,f.**

Dib, Mohammed **PQ3989.D52**
Le maître de chasse : roman. Seuil. 1997. ISBN:2-02-032642-6, ISBN13: 978-2-02-032642-1.
Audience: **u,f.**

Dib, Mohammed **PQ3989.D52N8513 2001**
The Savage Night. C. Dickson (Translator). Trade Cloth. University of Nebraska Press. Lincoln, NE. 2005. 191p. ISBN:0-8032-6620-0, ISBN13: 978-0-8032-6620-9. Dewey:843/.914. LCCN:00-059965.
Audience: **g,l,u,f.**

Dib, Mohammed **PQ3989.D52 O5**
Omneros. Carol Lettieri & Paul Vangelisti (Translators). Trade Paper. Invisible City/Red Hill Press. San Francisco, CA. 1978. ISBN:0-88031-050-2, ISBN13: 978-0-88031-050-5. Dewey:841.
Audience: **g,l,u,f.**

Dib, Mohammed **PQ3989.D52 Q51213**
Who Remembers the Sea. Louis Tremaine (Translator). Trade Cloth. Lynne Rienner Publishers, Inc. Boulder, CO. 1985. 122p. ISBN:0-89410-444-6, ISBN13: 978-0-89410-444-2. Dewey:843. LCCN:85-050529.
Audience: **g,l,u,f.**

Djian, Jean-Michel **PQ3989.S47 Z625 2005**
Léopold Sédar Senghor : genèse d'un imaginaire francophone ; suivi d'un entretien avec Aimé Césaire. Gallimard. 2005. ISBN:2-07-077601-8, ISBN13: 978-2-07-077601-6.
Audience: **u,f.**

Laye, Camara **PQ3989.C27**
L'enfant noir : roman. Plon. 1991. ISBN:2-266-02312-8, ISBN13: 978-2-266-02312-2.
Audience: **u,f.**

Laye, Camara **PQ3989.C27**
The Dark Child. Kirkup, James; Jones, Ernest (Translators). Noonday Press. 1994. ISBN:0-8090-1548-X, ISBN13: 978-0-8090-1548-1.
Audience: **g,l,u,f.**

Mezu, S. Okechukwu **PQ3989.S47**
The Poetry of Leopold Senghor. Library Binding. Black Academy Press, Inc. Baltimore, MD. 2000. 101p. ISBN:0-87831-135-1, ISBN13: 978-0-87831-135-4. Dewey:841.
Audience: **u,f.**

Oyono, Ferdinand **PQ3989.O9**
Chemin d'Europe. Club Afrique Loisir. 1980. ISBN:2-7236-0470-5, ISBN13: 978-2-7236-0470-3.
Audience: **u,f.**

Oyono, Ferdinand **PQ3989.O9**
Une vie de boy. Pocket. 2005. ISBN:2-266-02583-X, ISBN13: 978-2-266-02583-6.
Audience: **u,f.**

Oyono, Ferdinand **PQ3989.O9**
Le vieux nègre et la médaille : roman. Julliard. 2000. ISBN:2-264-00962-4, ISBN13: 978-2-264-00962-3.
Audience: **u,f.**

Oyono, Ferdinand **PQ3989.O9C513 1989**
Road to Europe. Richard Bjornson (Translator). Trade Paper. Lynne Rienner Publishers, Inc. Boulder, CO. 1989. 103p. ISBN:0-89410-591-4, ISBN13: 978-0-89410-591-3. Dewey:843. LCCN:86-051301.
Audience: **g,l,u,f.** *Choice, 1989.*

Oyono, Ferdinand **PQ3989.O9**
Houseboy. John Reed (Translator). Trade Paper. Heinemann. Portsmouth, NH. 1991. 144p. African Writers Ser. ISBN:0-435-90532-5, ISBN13: 978-0-435-90532-3. Dewey:843.914.
Audience: **g,l,u,f.**

Rabearivelo, Jean-Joseph **PQ3989.R23.A26 1975**
Translations from the Night. Paper Text. Heinemann. Portsmouth, NH. 1975. xxii, 73p. African Writers Ser. ISBN:0-435-90167-2, ISBN13: 978-0-435-90167-7. Dewey:841. LCCN:75-326551.
Audience: **g,l,u,f.**

Senghor, Leopold Sedar **PQ3989.S47;**
OEuvre poétique. Editions du Seuil. 1990. ISBN:2-02-012106-9, ISBN13: 978-2-02-012106-4.
Audience: **u,f.**

Senghor, Léopold Sédar **DT549.76.S46 A25 1964**
Liberté. Editions du Seuil. 1964. ISBN:2-02-005127-3, ISBN13: 978-2-02-005127-9.
Audience: **u,f.**

Senghor, Léopold Sédar **PQ3989.S47A24 1991**
Leopold Sedar Senghor: The Collected Poetry. Melvin Dixon (Translator, Introduction by). Cloth Text. University Press of Virginia. Charlottesville, VA. 1991. 704p. CARAF: Caribbean and African Literature Ser. ISBN:0-8139-1275-X, ISBN13: 978-0-8139-1275-2. Dewey:841. LCCN:91-008636.
Audience: **g,l,u,f.** *Choice, 1992.*

Spleth, Janice (Editor) **PQ3989.S47**
Critical Perspectives on Leopold Sedar Senghor. Trade Cloth. Lynne Rienner Publishers, Inc. Boulder, CO. 1993. 250p. ISBN:0-89410-548-5, ISBN13: 978-0-89410-548-7. Dewey:841.
Audience: **l,u,f.**

Spleth, Janice **PQ3989.S47Z89 1985**
Leopold Sedar Senghor. Trade Cloth. Thomson Gale. Farmington Hills, MI. 1985. 216p. Twayne's World Authors Ser., No. 765 ISBN:0-8057-6616-2, ISBN13: 978-0-8057-6616-5. Dewey:841. LCCN:85-008626.
Audience: **g,l,u,f.** *Choice, 1986.*

Vaillant, Janet G. **PQ3989.S47Z95 1990**
Black, French, and African: A Life of Leopold Sedar Senghor. Trade Cloth. Harvard University Press. Cambridge, MA. 1990. 416p. ISBN:0-674-07623-0, ISBN13: 978-0-674-07623-5. Dewey:841 B. LCCN:89-026767.
Audience: **g,u,f.** *Choice, 1991.*

French Literature Outside France > Africa > Individual Authors, 1960-

Arnold, Stephen H. (Editor) **PQ3989.2.B45Z62 1998**
Critical Perspectives on Mongo Beti. Library Binding. Lynne Rienner Publishers, Inc. Boulder, CO. 1998. 453p. ISBN:0-89410-586-8, ISBN13: 978-0-89410-586-9. Dewey:843. LCCN:97-014267.
Audience: **u,f.**

Azodo, Ada Uzoamaka (Editor) **PQ3989.2.B23Z65 2003**
Emerging Perspectives on Mariama Ba: Postcolonialism, Feminism, and Postmodernism. Trade Cloth. Africa World Press. Trenton, NJ. 2003. 650p. ISBN:1-59221-028-7, ISBN13: 978-1-59221-028-2. Dewey:843/.914. LCCN:2003-045191.
Audience: **u,f.**

Ba, Mariama **PQ3919.R74**
Scarlet Song. Ed. 1. Trade Paper. Longman Publishing Group. White Plains, NY. 1995. 171p. Longman African Writers Ser. ISBN:0-582-26455-3, ISBN13: 978-0-582-26455-7. Dewey:843.
Audience: **g,l,u,f.**

Ba, Mariama **PQ3989.2.B23**
Une Si Longue Lettre. Trade Paper. Nouvelles Editions Africaines. Abidjan, ISBN:2-7236-1042-X, ISBN13: 978-2-7236-1042-1. Dewey:896.321.
Audience: **u,f.**

Ba, Mariama **PQ3919.R74**
So Long a Letter. Modupe' Bode'-Thomas (Translator). Trade Paper. Heinemann. Portsmouth, NH. 1989. 96p. African Writers Ser. ISBN:0-435-90555-4, ISBN13: 978-0-435-90555-2. Dewey:843.
Audience: **g,l,u,f.**

Ben Jelloun, Tahar **PQ3989.2.J4**
Cette aveuglante absence de lumière : roman. Seuil. 2001. ISBN:2-02-041777-4, ISBN13: 978-2-02-041777-8.
Audience: **u,f.**

Ben Jelloun, Tahar **PQ3989.2.J4**
L'enfant de sable ; la nuit sacrée. Éditions du Seuil. 1987. ISBN:2-02-009965-9, ISBN13: 978-2-02-009965-3.
Audience: **u,f.**

Ben Jelloun, Tahar **PQ3989.2.J4N813 1989**
The Sacred Night. Trade Cloth. Harcourt Trade Publishers. New York, NY. 1989. 160p. ISBN:0-15-179150-3, ISBN13: 978-0-15-179150-7. Dewey:843. LCCN:88-030632.
Audience: **g,l,u,f.**

Ben Jelloun, Tahar **PQ3989.2.J4C4813**
This Blinding Absence of Light. Linda Coverdale (Translator). Trade Cloth. New Press, The. New York, NY. 2002. 208p. ISBN:1-56584-723-7, ISBN13: 978-1-56584-723-1. Dewey:843/.914. LCCN:2001-044122.
Audience: **g,l,u,f.**

Ben Jelloun, Tahar **PQ3989.2.J4E613 1987**
The Sand Child. Alan Sheridan (Translator). Trade Cloth. Harcourt Trade Publishers. New York, NY. 1987. ISBN:0-15-179287-9, ISBN13: 978-0-15-179287-0. Dewey:843. LCCN:87-007556.
Audience: **g,l,u,f.**

Beti, Mongo **PQ3989.2.B45 B73 2000**
Branle-bas en noir et blanc : roman. Julliard. 2000. ISBN:2-260-01510-7, ISBN13: 978-2-260-01510-9.
Audience: **u,f.**

Beti, Mongo **PQ3989.2.B45**
Mission to Kala. Trade Paper. Heinemann. Portsmouth, NH. 1964. 192p. African Writers Ser. ISBN:0-435-90013-7, ISBN13: 978-0-435-90013-7. Dewey:896.
Audience: **g,l,u,f.**

Beti, Mongo **PQ3989.2.B45**
Remember Ruben. L'Harmattan. 1982. ISBN:2-85802-230-5, ISBN13: 978-2-85802-230-4.
Audience: **u,f.**

Beti, Mongo **PR6019.O9**
The Poor Christ of Bomba. Gerald Moore (Translator). Paper Text. Waveland Press, Inc. Prospect Heights, IL. 2005. ISBN:1-57766-418-3, ISBN13: 978-1-57766-418-5. Dewey:823/.9/1.
Audience: **g,l,u,f.**

Beti, Mongo **PQ3919.R74**
Remember Ruben. Gerald Moore (Translator). Trade Paper. Heinemann. Portsmouth, NH. 1988. 252p. African Writers Ser. ISBN:0-435-90214-8, ISBN13: 978-0-435-90214-8. Dewey:843.
Audience: **g,l,u,f.**

Beyala, Calixthe **PQ3989.2.B48 A77 1994**
Assèze l'Africaine : roman. A. Michel. 1994. ISBN:2-226-06998-4, ISBN13: 978-2-226-06998-6.
Audience: **u,f.**

Beyala, Calixthe **PQ3989.2.B48 H66 1996**
Les honneurs perdus : roman. A. Michel. 1996. ISBN:2-226-08693-5, ISBN13: 978-2-226-08693-8.
Audience: **u,f.**

Beyala, Calixthe **PQ3989.2.B48 M36 1993**
Maman a un amant : roman. A. Michel. 1993. ISBN:2-226-06398-6, ISBN13: 978-2-226-06398-4.
Audience: **u,f.**

Clerc, Jeanne-Marie **PQ3989.2.D57 Z62 1997**
Assia Djebar : écrire, transgresser, résister. L'Harmattan. 1997. ISBN:2-7384-5253-1, ISBN13: 978-2-7384-5253-5.
Audience: **u,f.**

Diop, Birago **PQ3989.2.D55**
Leurres et lueurs : poèmes. Présence africaine. 2002. ISBN:2-7087-0619-5, ISBN13: 978-2-7087-0619-4.
Audience: **u,f.**

Diop, Birago **GR350**
Contes d'Amadou Koumba. Trade Paper. Presence Africaine, Editions. Paris, 1998. ISBN:2-7087-0167-3, ISBN13: 978-2-7087-0167-0. Dewey:848.996.
Audience: **u,f.**

Diop, Birago **PQ3989.2.D55**
Les Nouveaux contes d'Amadou Koumba. Présence africaine. 1994. ISBN:2-7087-0053-7, ISBN13: 978-2-7087-0053-6.
Audience: **u,f.**

Diop, David **PQ2631.O643**
Hammer Blows. Paper Text. Heinemann. Portsmouth, NH. 1975. x, 53p. African Writers Ser. ISBN:0-435-90174-5, ISBN13: 978-0-435-90174-5. Dewey:841/.914.
Audience: **g,l,u,f.**

Djebar, Assia **PQ3989.2.D57**
Les alouettes naïves : roman. Actes Sud. 1997. ISBN:2-7427-1169-4, ISBN13: 978-2-7427-1169-7.
Audience: **u,f.**

Djebar, Assia **PQ3919.R74**
Fantasia. Trade Cloth. Quartet Books, Ltd. London, 1993. 288p. ISBN:0-7043-2610-8, ISBN13: 978-0-7043-2610-1. Dewey:843.
Audience: **g,l,u,f.**

Djebar, Assia **PQ3989.2.D57**
Femmes d'Alger dans leur appartement : nouvelles. A. Michel. 2002. ISBN:2-253-06821-7, ISBN13: 978-2-253-06821-1.
Audience: **u,f.**

Djebar, Assia **PQ3982.2.D57**
L'amour, la fantasia : roman. A. Michel. 1994. ISBN:2-226-07748-0, ISBN13: 978-2-226-07748-6.
Audience: **u,f.**

Djebar, Assia **PQ3989.2.D57**
Ombre sultane : roman. A. Michel. 2006. ISBN:2-226-16991-1, ISBN13: 978-2-226-16991-4.
Audience: **u,f.**

Djebar, Assia **PQ3919.R74**
A Sister to Scheherazade. Trade Cloth. Quartet Books, Ltd. London, 1991. 170p. ISBN:0-7043-2670-1, ISBN13: 978-0-7043-2670-5. Dewey:843.
Audience: **g,l,u,f.**

Djebar, Assia **PQ3989.2.D57 V37 1995**
Vaste est la prison : roman. A. Michel. 1995. ISBN:2-226-07721-9, ISBN13: 978-2-226-07721-9.
Audience: **u,f.**

Djebar, Assia **PQ3989.2.D57E513**
Children of the New World: A Novel of the Algerian War. Marjolijn De Jager (Translator), Clarisse Zimra (Afterword by).

Trade Cloth. Feminist Press at The City University of New York. New York, NY. 2005. 224p. ISBN:1-55861-511-3, ISBN13: 978-1-55861-511-3. Dewey:843/.914. LCCN:2005-021564.
Audience: **g,l,u,f.**

Djebar, Assia **PQ3989.2.D57F413**
Women of Algiers in Their Apartment. Marjolijn de Jager (Translator), Clarisse Zimra (Afterword by). Cloth Text. University Press of Virginia. Charlottesville, VA. 1992. 224p. Caraf Bks. ISBN:0-8139-1402-7, ISBN13: 978-0-8139-1402-2. Dewey:[Fic]. LCCN:92-016856.
Audience: **g,l,u,f.** *Choice, 1993.*

Djebar, Assia **PQ3989.2.D57V3713**
So Vast the Prison. Betsy Wing (Translator). Trade Cloth. Seven Stories Press. New York, NY. 2004. ISBN:1-58322-009-7, ISBN13: 978-1-58322-009-2. Dewey:965/.046. LCCN:99-041329.
Audience: **g,l,u,f.**

Fall, Aminata Sow **PQ3989.2.F177**
La grève des bàttu, ou, Les dèchets humains : roman. Le Serpenta a Plumes. 2004. ISBN:2-84261-250-7, ISBN13: 978-2-84261-250-4.
Audience: **u,f.**

Fall, Aminata Sow **PQ3989.2.F177 A88 1993**
L'appel des arènes. Sépia. 1993. ISBN:2-907888-31-5, ISBN13: 978-2-907888-31-8.
Audience: **u,f.**

Kane, Cheikh H. **PQ2637.A274**
Ambiguous Adventure. Katherine Woods (Translator). Trade Paper. Heinemann. Portsmouth, NH. 1972. 186p. African Writers Ser. ISBN:0-435-90119-2, ISBN13: 978-0-435-90119-6. Dewey:843/.9/1.
Audience: **g,l,u,f.**

Kane, Hamidou **PQ3989.2.K3**
L'aventure ambiguë : récit. 10/18. 2002. ISBN:2-264-03693-1, ISBN13: 978-2-264-03693-3.
Audience: **u,f.**

Kateb, Yacine **PQ3989.2.Y28**
Nedjma : roman. Seuil. 1996. ISBN:2-02-028947-4, ISBN13: 978-2-02-028947-4.
Audience: **u,f.**

Kourouma, Ahmadou **PQ3989.2.K58**
Allah N'est Pas Oblige. Trade Cloth. Editions du Seuil. Paris, 2000. 232p. ISBN:2-02-042787-7, ISBN13: 978-2-02-042787-6. Dewey:843.
Audience: **u,f.**

Kourouma, Ahmadou **PQ3989.2.K58 E6 1998**
En attendant le vote des bêtes sauvages : roman. Editions du Seuil. 1998. ISBN:2-02-033142-X, ISBN13: 978-2-02-033142-5.
Audience: **u,f.**

Kourouma, Ahmadou **PQ3989.2.K58**
Allah Is Not Obliged. Trade Cloth. Random House. London, 2006. 224p. ISBN:0-434-00957-1, ISBN13: 978-0-434-00957-2. Dewey:843.9/14.
Audience: **g,l,u,f.**

Kourouma, Ahmadou **PQ3989.2.K58**
Waiting for the Wild Beasts to Vote. Trade Cloth. Ebury Publishing. London, 2003. 320p. ISBN:0-434-00814-1, ISBN13: 978-0-434-00814-8. Dewey:843.9/14.
Audience: **g,l,u,f.**

Kourouma, Ahmadou **PQ3989.2.K58**
Quand on refuse on dit non : roman. Seuil. 2004. ISBN:2-02-068022-X, ISBN13: 978-2-02-068022-6.
Audience: **u,f.**

Maalouf, Amin **PQ3979.2.M28 R63 1993**
Le rocher de Tanios : roman. B. Grasset. 1993. ISBN:2-246-46271-1, ISBN13: 978-2-246-46271-2.
Audience: **u,f.**

Sebbar, Leila **PQ3919.R74**
Sherazade. Dorothy S. Blair (Translator). Trade Cloth. Quartet Books, Ltd. London, 1991. 264p. ISBN:0-7043-2778-3, ISBN13: 978-0-7043-2778-8. Dewey:843.
Audience: **g,l,u,f.**

Sebbar, Leïla **PQ2679.E244**
Le Chinois vert d'Afrique. Eden. 2002. ISBN:2-913245-48-X, ISBN13: 978-2-913245-48-8.
Audience: **u,f.**

Sebbar, Leïla **PQ2679.E244**
La jeune fille au balcon : roman. Seuil. 2001. ISBN:2-02-051112-6, ISBN13: 978-2-02-051112-4.
Audience: **u,f.**

Sembene, Ousmane **PQ3989.S46**
Xala. Trade Paper. Presence Africaine, Editions. Paris, 1976. ISBN:2-7087-0589-X, ISBN13: 978-2-7087-0589-0. Dewey:843.
Audience: **u,f.**

Sembene, Ousmane **PQ3919.R74**
God's Bits of Wood. Trade Paper. Heinemann. Portsmouth, NH. 1996. 256p. ISBN:0-435-90959-2, ISBN13: 978-0-435-90959-8.
Audience: **g,l,u,f.**

Sembene, Ousmane **PQ3919.R74**
The Money-Order with White Genesis. Clive Wake (Translator). Trade Paper. Heinemann. Portsmouth, NH. 1987. 138p. African Writers Ser. ISBN:0-435-90894-4, ISBN13: 978-0-435-90894-2. Dewey:843.
Audience: **g,l,u,f.**

Sembene, Ousmane **PQ2637.A274**
Xala. Clive Wake (Translator). Trade Paper. Chicago Review Press, Inc. Chicago, IL. 1983. 110p. ISBN:1-55652-070-0, ISBN13: 978-1-55652-070-9. Dewey:843. LCCN:75-041811.
Audience: **g,l,u,f.**

Sembène, Ousmane **PQ3989.S46**
Vehi-Ciosane, ou, Blanche-Genèse : suivi du Mandat. Présence africaine. 2004. ISBN:2-7087-0170-3, ISBN13: 978-2-7087-0170-0.
Audience: **u,f.**

Tam'si, Tchicaya U
La main sèche. R. Laffont. 1980. ISBN:2-221-00545-7, ISBN13: 978-2-221-00545-3.
Audience: **u,f.**

Tam'si, Tchicaya U **PQ3989.2.T35 M3 1978**
Le mauvais sang ; suivi de Feu de brousse ; et, A triche-coeur. L'Harmattan. 1978. ISBN:2-85802-084-1, ISBN13: 978-2-85802-084-3.
Audience: **u,f.**

Tansi, Sony Lab'Ou **PQ3989.2.S64**
Les Sept solitudes de Lorsa Lopez : roman. Seuil. 1985. ISBN:2-02-008625-5, ISBN13: 978-2-02-008625-7.
Audience: **u,f.**

Tansi, Sony Labou **PQ3989.2.S64**
L'anté-peuple : roman. Editions du Seuil. 1983. ISBN:2-02-006542-8, ISBN13: 978-2-02-006542-9.
Audience: **u,f.**

Tansi, Sony Labou **PQ3989.2.S64**
La vie et demie : roman. Editions du Seuil. 1998. ISBN:2-02-035306-7, ISBN13: 978-2-02-035306-9.
Audience: **u,f.**

Tansi, Sony L. **PQ3989.2.S64A813**
The Antipeople. J. A. Underwood (Translator). Trade Cloth. Marion Boyars Publishers, Inc. New York, NY. 1987. 17p. ISBN:0-7145-2845-5, ISBN13: 978-0-7145-2845-8. Dewey:843. LCCN:86-029959.
Audience: **g,l,u,f.** *Choice, 1988.*

Tansi, Sony L. **PQ3989.2.S64S4713**
The Seven Solitudes of Lorsa Lopez. Clive Wake (Translator). Trade Paper. Heinemann. Portsmouth, NH. 1995. 129p. African Writers Ser. ISBN:0-435-90594-5, ISBN13: 978-0-435-90594-1. Dewey:843. LCCN:96-145817.
Audience: **g,l,u,f.**

Yacine, Kateb **PQ3989.2.Y28**
Nedjma. Trade Paper. Editions du Seuil. Paris, ISBN:2-02-028947-4, ISBN13: 978-2-02-028947-4. Dewey:848.996503.
Audience: **u,f.**

Yacine, Kateb **PQ3989.2.Y28N413**
Nedjma: Kateb Yacine. Richard Howard (Translator), Bernard Aresu (Introduction by). Cloth Text. University Press of Virginia. Charlottesville, VA. 1991. 400p. CARAF: Caribbean and African Literature Ser. ISBN:0-8139-1312-8, ISBN13: 978-0-8139-1312-4. Dewey:843. LCCN:90-028436.
Audience: **g,l,u,f.**

GENERAL LANGUAGE AND LITERATURE

This section contains works pertinent to the study of languages and literature in general, and includes works of literary theory and criticism which are not specific to a single national literature; works on linguistics and language (including the English language and its history and development); and works treating special topics allied to the study of literature, such as book history and translation.

Given the centrality of theoretical works to thc study of literature at the graduate level and to literary scholarship (though this tendency may have begun at last to ebb), this section contains more advanced works of criticism than were to be found in the various literature sections of BCL3. At the same time, it also attempts to present a balanced retrospective collection of criticism (e.g., works such as I. A. Richards' Practical Criticism), which are important to a historical understanding of criticism although they may be rarely cited in current scholarship.

Where possible, works are recommended in their newest, most reliable edition. Some works are available only as reprints, while a few are out of print, though still recommended.

— Marcus Elmore

Brunel, Pierre **PN56.M95D4813 1992**
Companion to Literary Myths: Heroes and Archetypes. Trade Cloth. Routledge. New York, NY. 1992. 864p. ISBN:0-415-06460-0, ISBN13: 978-0-415-06460-6. Dewey:809.93351. LCCN:92-028204.
Audience: **g,l,u,f.**

Bullock, Alan & Trombley, Stephen (Editors) **AG5.N76 1999**
The Norton Dictionary of Modern Thought. Trade Cloth. W. W. Norton & Company, Inc. New York, NY. 1999. xxiv, 933p. ISBN:0-393-04696-6, ISBN13: 978-0-393-04696-0. Dewey:032. LCCN:99-024581.
Audience: **g,l,u,f.** *Choice, 2000.*

Fraser, Michael (editor) **AZ101**
Humbul Humanities Hub.
http://www.humbul.ac.uk/index.html
Audience: **g,l,u,f.**

Harner, James L. **Z2011.H34 2002**
Literary Research Guide: An Annotated Listing of Reference Sources in English Literary Studies. Ed. 4. Trade Cloth. Modern Language Association of America. New York, NY. 2002. x & 820p. ISBN:0-87352-982-0, ISBN13: 978-0-87352-982-2. Dewey:016.8209. LCCN:2001-059649.
Audience: **g,l,u,f.** *Choice, 2003, 1999.*

Liu, Alan **PR20.5**
The Voice of the Shuttle.
http://vos.ucsb.edu
Audience: **g,l,u,f.**

Dictionaries, Encyclopedias

Abrams, M. H. & Harpham, Geoffrey G. **PN41.A184 2005**
A Glossary of Literary Terms. Ed. 8. Paper Text. Thomson Heinle. Boston, MA. 2004. 368p. ISBN:1-4130-0218-8, ISBN13: 978-1-4130-0218-8. Dewey:803. LCCN:2004-111345.
Audience: **g,l,u,f.** *Choice, 1993.*

Baldick, Chris **PN41.C67 2004**
A Concise Dictionary of Literary Terms. Ed. 2. Trade Paper. Oxford University Press, Inc. New York, NY. 2004. 290p. Oxford Paperback Reference Ser. ISBN:0-19-860883-7, ISBN13: 978-0-19-860883-7. Dewey:803. LCCN:2003-070163.
Audience: **g,l,u,f.**

Bowker Staff (Editor) **Z5916 .B785 PN3411**
Bowker's Guide to Characters in Fiction, 2006. Trade Cloth. R. R. Bowker LLC. New Providence, NJ. 2005. ISBN:0-8352-4748-1, ISBN13: 978-0-8352-4748-1. Dewey:016/.808/027.
Audience: **g,l,u,f.**

Cuddon, J. A. **PN41**
The Penguin Dictionary of Literary Terms and Literary Theory. Ed. 4. Trade Paper. Penguin Group (USA) Inc. New York, NY. 2000. 1024p. Dictionary, Penguin Ser. ISBN:0-14-051363-9, ISBN13: 978-0-14-051363-9. Dewey:803.
Audience: **g,l,u,f.**

Harmon, William **PN41.H355 2005**
A Handbook to Literature. Ed. 10. Trade Paper. Prentice Hall PTR. Upper Saddle River, NJ. 2005. 704p. ISBN:0-13-134442-0, ISBN13: 978-0-13-134442-6. Dewey:803. LCCN:2005-049285.
Audience: **g,l,u,f.**

Knowles, Elizabeth (Contribution by) **PE1630**
Oxford Dictionary of Phrase and Fable. Ed. 2. Trade Cloth. Oxford University Press, Inc. New York, NY. 2005. 806p. ISBN:0-19-860981-7, ISBN13: 978-0-19-860981-0. Dewey:422/.03. LCCN:2006-276426.
Audience: **g,l,u,f.**

Magill, Frank N. (Editor) **PN44.M33 1996**
Masterplots. Ed. 2. Laurence W. Mazzeno (Consultant Editor). Library Binding. Salem Press, Inc. Hackensack, NJ. 1996. 7382p. ISBN:0-89356-084-7, ISBN13: 978-0-89356-084-3. Dewey:809. LCCN:96-023382.
Audience: **g,l,u,f.**

Merriam-Webster, Inc. Staff **PE1460.M45 1994**
Merriam-Webster's Dictionary of English Usage. Ed. 2. Trade Cloth. Merriam-Webster, Inc. Springfield, MA. 1994. 992p. ISBN:0-87779-132-5, ISBN13: 978-0-87779-132-4. Dewey:428/.003. LCCN:93-019289.
Audience: **g,l,u,f.**

Murphy, Bruce **PN41.B4**
Benet's Reader's Encyclopedia. Ed. 4. Trade Cloth. HarperCollins Publishers. New York, NY. 1996. 1168p. ISBN:0-06-270110-X, ISBN13: 978-0-06-270110-7. Dewey:809. LCCN:96-217151.
Audience: **g,l,u,f.**

Room, Adrian & Ayto, John **PN43.B65 1999**
Brewer's Dictionary of Phrase and Fable. Ed. 16. Trade Cloth. HarperCollins Publishers. New York, NY. 2000. 1326p. Brewer's Dictionary Ser. ISBN:0-06-019653-X, ISBN13: 978-0-06-019653-0. Dewey:803. LCCN:00-267327.
Audience: **g,l,u,f.**

Language

P302
The Global Language Monitor.
http://www.languagemonitor.com/
Audience: **g,l,u,f.**

Crystal, David **P40.5.L33 C79 2002**
Language Death. Trade Paper. Cambridge University Press. New York, NY. 2002. 208p. Canto Refresh Your Ser. ISBN:0-521-01271-6, ISBN13: 978-0-521-01271-3. Dewey:417.7.
Audience: **l,u.** *Choice, 2001.*

Garry, Jane, et al. **P371.F33 2000**
Facts About the World's Languages: An Encyclopedia of the World's Major Languages, Past and Present. Rubino, Carl (Author). H. W. Wilson. 2001. ISBN:0-8242-0970-2, ISBN13: 978-0-8242-0970-4.
Audience: **g,l,u,f.**

Jackendoff, Ray **P151.J254 2002**
Foundations of Language: Brain, Meaning, Grammar, Evolution. Trade Cloth. Oxford University Press, Inc. New York, NY. 2002. 498p. ISBN:0-19-827012-7, ISBN13: 978-0-19-827012-6. Dewey:401.9. LCCN:2001-052066.
Audience: **u,f.**

Jakobson, Roman & Halle, Morris **P221 .J3**
Fundamentals of Language. Ed. 2. Trade Paper. Walter de Gruyter GmbH & Co. KG. Berlin, 2002. 96p. ISBN:3-11-017283-6, ISBN13: 978-3-11-017283-6. Dewey:414.
Audience: **l,u.** B

Martinich, A. P. **P106.P455 2001**
The Philosophy of Language. Ed. 4. Paper Text. Oxford University Press, Inc. New York, NY. 2000. 608p. ISBN:0-19-513543-1, ISBN13: 978-0-19-513543-5. Dewey:401. LCCN:00-025522.
Audience: **l,u.**

Napoli, Donna Jo **P107.N37 2003**
Language Matters: A Guide to Everyday Questions about Language. Trade Paper. Oxford University Press, Inc. New York, NY. 2003. 208p. ISBN:0-19-516048-7, ISBN13: 978-0-19-516048-2. Dewey:400. LCCN:2002-075810.
Audience: **g,l.**

Trudgill, Peter & Bauer, Laurie (Editors) **P106.L31755 1998**
Language Myths. Trade Paper. Penguin Group (USA) Inc. New York, NY. 1999. 208p. ISBN:0-14-026023-4, ISBN13: 978-0-14-026023-6. Dewey:400. LCCN:00-266856.
Audience: **g,l.**

Language > English

Burchfield, R. W. **PE1628.F65 2004**
Fowler's Modern English Usage. Ed. 3. Trade Cloth. Oxford University Press, Inc. New York, NY. 2004. 896p. ISBN:0-19-861021-1, ISBN13: 978-0-19-861021-2. Dewey:428/.003. LCCN:2005-271630.
Audience: **g,l,u,f.**

Gowers, Ernest **PE1421**
The Complete Plain Words. Sidney Greenbaum & Janet Whitcut (Revised by), Joseph Epstein (Introduction by). Trade Paper. David R. Godine Publisher. Boston, MA. 2002. 288p. ISBN:1-56792-203-1, ISBN13: 978-1-56792-203-5. Dewey:428.
Audience: **g,l,u,f.**

Language > English > Anglo-Saxon

Barney, Stephen A. **PE274.B3 1985**
Word-Hoard: An Introduction to Old English Vocabulary. Ed. 2. Trade Paper. Yale University Press. Cumberland, RI. 1985. 86p. Yale Language Ser. ISBN:0-300-03506-3, ISBN13: 978-0-300-03506-3. Dewey:429/.81. LCCN:76-047003.
Audience: **l,u.** B

Cassidy, F. J. & Ringler, R. **PE137**
Bright's Old English Grammar. Ed. 3. Cloth Text. Harcourt College Publishers. Fort Worth, TX. 1972. 494p. ISBN:0-03-084713-3, ISBN13: 978-0-03-084713-4. Dewey:429/.5. LCCN:76-179921.
Audience: **l,u.** B

Diamond, Robert E. **PE135.D5 1989**
Old English: Grammar and Reader. Paper Text. Wayne State University Press. Detroit, MI. 1970. 304p. Waynebooks Ser., No. 38 ISBN:0-8143-1510-0, ISBN13: 978-0-8143-1510-1. Dewey:429/.82421. LCCN:89-005763.
Audience: **l,u.** B

Hall, J. R. **PE279 .H3X 1984**
A Concise Anglo-Saxon Dictionary. Ed. 4. Herbert D. Meritt (Supplement by). Trade Paper. University of Toronto Press. Toronto, ON. 1984. 432p. Medieval Academy Reprints for Teaching Ser., No. 14 ISBN:0-8020-6548-1, ISBN13: 978-0-8020-6548-3. Dewey:429/.321. LCCN:87-673538.
Audience: **g.**

Jember, Gregory K. **PE279.J4**
English Old Eng. Old Eng. Dictionary. Trade Cloth. Westview Press. Boulder, CO. 1983. xxxiii, 178 pp. ISBN:0-89158-006-9, ISBN13: 978-0-89158-006-5. Dewey:429/.3/21. LCCN:75-030928.
Audience: **g.** B

Marsden, Richard C. & Orchard, Andrew P. **PE137.M46 2003**
The Cambridge Old English Reader. Cloth Text. Cambridge University Press. New York, NY. 2004. 566p. ISBN:0-521-45426-3, ISBN13: 978-0-521-45426-1. Dewey:429/.86421. LCCN:2003-043579.
Audience: **u.** *Choice, 2004.*

Mitchell, Bruce & Robinson, Fred C. (Editors) **PE131.M5 2001**
A Guide to Old English. Ed. 6. Trade Paper. Blackwell Publishing, Inc. Malden, MA. 2001. 424p. ISBN:0-631-22636-2, ISBN13: 978-0-631-22636-9. Dewey:429/.82421. LCCN:00-046781.
Audience: **l,u,f.** B

Robinson, Orrin W. **PD75**
Old English and Its Closest Relatives: A Survey of the Earliest Germanic Languages. Trade Paper. Stanford University Press. Palo Alto, CA. 1993. 304p. ISBN:0-8047-2221-8, ISBN13: 978-0-8047-2221-6. Dewey:430/.09.
Audience: **l,u,f.** *Choice, 1992.*

Language > English > Middle English

Brunner, Karl **PE531 .B713 1973**
An Outline of Middle English Grammar. Library Binding. Folcroft Library Editions. Folcroft, PA. 1974. ISBN:0-8414-1371-1, ISBN13: 978-0-8414-1371-9. Dewey:427/.02. LCCN:72-014364.
Audience: **u,f.** B

Burrow, J. A. & Turville-Petre, Thorlac **PE535.B87 2004**
A Book of Middle English. Ed. 3. Trade Cloth. Blackwell

Publishing, Inc. Malden, MA. 2004. 432p. ISBN:1-4051-1708-7, ISBN13: 978-1-4051-1708-1. Dewey:427/.02. LCCN:2004-047627.
Audience: **u,f.** *Choice, 1996.*

Jones, Charles **PE531**
Introduction to Middle English. Trade Cloth. Irvington Publishers. New York, NY. 1972. 256p. ISBN:0-03-084479-7, ISBN13: 978-0-03-084479-9. Dewey:427/.02. LCCN:77-155295.
Audience: **l,u.**

Kurath, Gertrude P. & Lewis, Robert E. (Editors) **PE679**
Middle English Dictionary, Vol. A. 1. Trade Paper. University of Michigan Press. Chicago, IL. 1956. 128p. Middle English Dictionary Ser. ISBN:0-472-01011-5, ISBN13: 978-0-472-01011-0. Dewey:427/.02/03.
Audience: **u,f.**

Mossé, Fernand **PE535**
A Handbook of Middle English. James A. Walker (Translator), Kemp Malone (Foreword by). Trade Paper. Johns Hopkins University Press. Baltimore, MD. 2001. 519p. ISBN:0-8018-6761-4, ISBN13: 978-0-8018-6761-3. Dewey:427.02. LCCN:68-017255.
Audience: **u,f.**

Turville-Petre, Thorlac **PE659.A6**
The Alliterative Revival. Trade Cloth. Boydell & Brewer, Ltd. Woodbridge, 1970. 159p. ISBN:0-85991-019-9, ISBN13: 978-0-85991-019-4. Dewey:426.
Audience: **u,f.**

Wardale, Edith E. **PE525 .W3 1977**
An Introduction to Middle English. Trade Cloth. A M S Press, Inc. New York, NY. ISBN:0-404-14626-0, ISBN13: 978-0-404-14626-9. Dewey:427/.02. LCCN:75-041289.
Audience: **l,u.**

Wright, Joseph & Wright, Elizabeth M. **PE531**
An Elementary Middle English Grammar. Ed. 2. Trade Cloth. Oxford University Press, Inc. New York, NY. 1979. 242p. ISBN:0-19-811941-0, ISBN13: 978-0-19-811941-8. Dewey:427/.02. LCCN:79-040340.
Audience: **u,f.**

Language > English > Modern English

Adams, Michael **PE3721**
Slayer Slang: A Buffy the Vampire Slayer Lexicon. Trade Paper. Oxford University Press, Inc. New York, NY. 2004. 320p. ISBN:0-19-517599-9, ISBN13: 978-0-19-517599-8. Dewey:791.45'72-dc21.
Audience: **g,l,u,f.**

Allen, Robert (Editor) **PE1628**
Pocket Fowler's Modern English Usage. Trade Paper. Oxford University Press, Inc. New York, NY. 2006. 632p. Oxford Paperback Reference Ser. ISBN:0-19-860947-7, ISBN13: 978-0-19-860947-6. Dewey:428/.003.
Audience: **g,l,u,f.**

Battistella, Edwin L. **P409.B38 2005**
Bad Language: Are Some Words Better than Others? Trade Cloth. Oxford University Press, Inc. New York, NY. 2005. 240p. ISBN:0-19-517248-5, ISBN13: 978-0-19-517248-5. Dewey:417/.2. LCCN:2005-040880.
Audience: **g,l,u,f.**

Baugh, John **PE3102.N42B37 2000**
Beyond Ebonics: Linguistic Pride and Racial Prejudice. Trade Cloth. Oxford University Press, Inc. New York, NY. 2000. 172p. ISBN:0-19-512046-9, ISBN13: 978-0-19-512046-2. Dewey:427/.973/08996073. LCCN:99-016833.
Audience: **g,l,u,f.** *Choice, 2000.*

Baugh, John **PE3102.N42B39 1999**
Out of the Mouths of Slaves: African American Language and Educational Malpractice. William Labov (Foreword by). Trade Paper. University of Texas Press. Austin, TX. 1999. 208p. ISBN:0-292-70873-4, ISBN13: 978-0-292-70873-0. Dewey:427/.973/08996. LCCN:98-028384.
Audience: **u,f.** *Choice, 2000.*

Bex, Tony & Watts, Richard J. **PE1074.7.S73 1999**
Standard English: The Widening Debate. Paper over Boards. Routledge. New York, NY. 1999. 324p. ISBN:0-415-19162-9, ISBN13: 978-0-415-19162-3. Dewey:428. LCCN:98-036167.
Audience: **u,f.**

Burchfield, R. W. **PE1072**
The English Language. Trade Paper. Oxford University Press, Inc. New York, NY. 2003. 222p. Oxford Language Classics Ser. ISBN:0-19-860403-3, ISBN13: 978-0-19-860403-7. Dewey:420.
Audience: **l,u,f.**

Carver, Craig M. **PE2846**
American Regional Dialects: A Word Geography. Paper Text. University of Michigan Press. Chicago, IL. 1987. 336p. ISBN:0-472-08103-9, ISBN13: 978-0-472-08103-5. Dewey:427/.973.
Audience: **g,l,u,f.** *Choice, 1987.*

Cheshire, Jenny (Editor, Introduction by) **PE1700 .E49 1991**
English Around the World: Sociolinguistic Perspectives. Trade Paper. Cambridge University Press. New York, NY. 1991. 700p. ISBN:0-521-39565-8, ISBN13: 978-0-521-39565-6. Dewey:420. LCCN:89-078085.
Audience: **l,u,f.**

Crowley, Tony **P368.C76 2003**
Standard English and the Politics of Language. Ed. 2. Cloth over Boards. Palgrave Macmillan. New York, NY. 2003. 304p. ISBN:0-333-99035-8, ISBN13: 978-0-333-99035-3. Dewey:428. LCCN:2002-042460.
Audience: **l,u,f.** *Choice, 2004, 1990.*

Crystal, David **PE1072**
The Cambridge Encyclopedia of the English Language. Ed. 2. Cloth Text. Cambridge University Press. New York, NY. 2003. 506p. ISBN:0-521-82348-X, ISBN13: 978-0-521-82348-7. Dewey:420. LCCN:2003-272259.
Audience: **l,u,f.** *Choice, 2004, 1995.*

Crystal, David **PE1087**
English as a Global Language. Ed. 2. Trade Paper. Cambridge University Press. New York, NY. 2003. 228p. ISBN:0-521-53032-6, ISBN13: 978-0-521-53032-3. Dewey:420. LCCN:2003-282119.
Audience: **u,f.** *Choice, 1998.*

Crystal, David **PE1072 .C7**
English Language: A Guided Tour of the Language. Ed. 2. Trade Paper. Penguin Group (USA) Inc. New York, NY. 2004. 336p. ISBN:0-14-100396-0, ISBN13: 978-0-14-100396-2. Dewey:420.
Audience: **g,l,u,f.**

Fabb, Nigel **PE1505 .F33 2002**
Language and Literary Structure: The Linguistic Analysis of Form in Verse and Narrative. Trade Paper. Cambridge University Press. New York, NY. 2002. 240p. ISBN:0-521-79698-9, ISBN13: 978-0-521-79698-9. Dewey:421.6. LCCN:2002-071569.
Audience: **u,f.**

Finegan, Edward & Rickford, John R. (Editors) **P377.L33 2004**
Language in the U. S. A.: Themes for the Twenty-First Century. Cloth Text. Cambridge University Press. New York, NY. 2004. 520p. ISBN:0-521-77175-7, ISBN13: 978-0-521-77175-7. Dewey:409/.73. LCCN:2003-055819.
Audience: **l,u,f.**

Garner, Bryan **PE2827.G37 2003**
Garner's Modern American Usage. Ed. 2. Trade Cloth. Oxford University Press, Inc. New York, NY. 2003. 928p. ISBN:0-19-516191-2, ISBN13: 978-0-19-516191-5. Dewey:423/.1. LCCN:2004-295114.
Audience: **g,l,u,f.** *Choice, 2004.*

Gelderen, Elly van **PE1106.G38 2002**
An Introduction to the Grammar of English: Syntactic Arguments and Socio-Historical Background. Trade Cloth. John Benjamins Publishing Company. Philadelphia, PA. 2002. xxiv, 200p. ISBN:1-58811-200-4, ISBN13: 978-1-58811-200-2. Dewey:428.2. LCCN:2002-021580.
Audience: **g,l,u,f.**

Glowka, Wayne & Lance, Donald M. (Editors) **PE1068.N55.L36 1993**
Language Variation in North American English: Research and Teaching. Trade Cloth. Modern Language Association of America. New York, NY. 1993. xvi, 417p. ISBN:0-87352-389-X, ISBN13: 978-0-87352-389-9. Dewey:428/.00707. LCCN:93-009451.
Audience: **l,u,f.** *Choice, 1994.*

Görlach, Manfred **PE821.G613 1991**
Introduction to Early Modern English. Trade Paper. Cambridge University Press. New York, NY. 1991. 488p. ISBN:0-521-31046-6, ISBN13: 978-0-521-31046-8. Dewey:420/.9/031. LCCN:89-077389.
Audience: **l,u.** *Choice, 1992.*

Hall, Joan Houston (Editor) **PE2843 .D52 1985**
Dictionary of American Regional English. Trade Cloth. Harvard University Press. Cambridge, MA. 2002. 1040p. Dictionary of American Regional English Ser., Vol. IV ISBN:0-674-00884-7, ISBN13: 978-0-674-00884-7. Dewey:427/.973. LCCN:84-029025.
Audience: **g,l,u,f.**

Jay, Timothy **PE3724.O3J38 1992**
Cursing in America: A Psycholinguistic Study of Dirty Language in the Courts, in the Movies, in the Schoolyards, and on the Streets. Trade Paper. John Benjamins Publishing Company. Philadelphia, PA. 1992. viii, 272p. ISBN:1-55619-452-8, ISBN13: 978-1-55619-452-8. Dewey:401/.9/0973. LCCN:92-006300.
Audience: **u,f.**

Lippi-Green, Rosina L. **PE2808.8.L57 1997**
English with an Accent. Paper over Boards. Routledge. New York, NY. 1997. 304p. ISBN:0-415-11476-4, ISBN13: 978-0-415-11476-9. Dewey:427.9/73. LCCN:96-033234.
Audience: **g,u,f.**

McArthur, Thomas **PE31 .O84 1992**
The Oxford Companion to the English Language. Trade Cloth. Oxford University Press, Inc. New York, NY. 1992. 1216p. ISBN:0-19-214183-X, ISBN13: 978-0-19-214183-5. Dewey:420/.3. LCCN:92-224249.
Audience: **g,l,u,f.** *Choice, 1993.*

McDavid, Raven I. Jr. **PE2841 .A75**
Needed Research in American English. Trade Paper. University of Alabama Press. Tuscaloosa, AL. 1984. iv, 76p. Publications of the American Dialect Society Ser., No. 71 ISBN:0-8173-0238-7, ISBN13: 978-0-8173-0238-2. Dewey:427.9.
Audience: **u,f.**

McMillan, James B. & Montgomery, Michael **Z1251.S7M37 1989**
ⓔ Annotated Bibliography of Southern American English. E-Book. NetLibrary, Inc. Boulder, CO. 1989. ISBN:0-585-20237-0, ISBN13: 978-0-585-20237-2. Dewey:016.427/975.
Audience: **g,l,u,f.**

McWhorter, John **PE2846**
Doing Our Own Thing: The Degradation of Language and Music and Why We Should, Like, Care. Trade Paper. Penguin Group (USA) Inc. New York, NY. 2004. 304p. ISBN:1-59240-084-1, ISBN13: 978-1-59240-084-3. Dewey:427/.973.
Audience: **g,l.** *Choice, 2004.*

McWhorter, John **PE2808.8 .M39 2000**
Word on the Street: Debunking the Myth of a Pure Standard English. Trade Paper. Basic Books. New York, NY. 2001. 302p. ISBN:0-7382-0446-3, ISBN13: 978-0-7382-0446-8. Dewey:306.44/0973. LCCN:2002-319306.
Audience: **g,u,f.**

Mencken, H. L. **PE1711**
The American Language. Ed. 4. Other. Alfred A. Knopf Inc. New York, NY. 1982. ISBN:0-318-54003-7, ISBN13: 978-0-318-54003-0. Dewey:427.
Audience: **g,l,u,f.**

Partridge, Eric **PE3711.P3 1970**
Slang to-Day and Yesterday, with a Short Historical Sketch and Vocabularies of English, American, and Australian Slang. Trade Cloth. Barnes & Noble, Inc. New York, NY. 1970. ix, 476p. ISBN:0-389-03977-2, ISBN13: 978-0-389-03977-8. Dewey:427.09. LCCN:72-016925.
Audience: **g,l,u,f.** B

Preston, Dennis Richard **PE2841.N44 2003**
Needed Research in American Dialects. Trade Cloth. Duke University Press. Durham, NC. 2004. 254p. Publication of the American Dialect Society Ser., No. 88 ISBN:0-8223-6594-4, ISBN13: 978-0-8223-6594-5. Dewey:427/.973. LCCN:2003-062715.
Audience: **u,f.**

Quirk, Randolph & Svartvik, Jan **P121**
Investigating Linguistic Acceptability. Paper Text. Walter de Gruyter GmbH & Co. KG. Berlin, 1966. Janua Linguarum, Ser. Minor, No. 54 ISBN:90-279-0585-1, ISBN13: 978-90-279-0585-7. Dewey:410.072.
Audience: **u,f.**

Raymond, James C. & Russell, I. Willis (Editors) **PE1072.J35 2004**
Essays in Linguistics: Dialectology, Grammar, and Lexicography in Honor of James B. McMillan. Trade Paper. University of Alabama Press. Tuscaloosa, AL. 2004. 208p. ISBN:0-8173-5121-3, ISBN13: 978-0-8173-5121-2. Dewey:420. LCCN:2003-070327.
Audience: **u,f.**

Ward, Ben **PE2841.A77 2006**
American Voices: How Dialects Differ from Coast to Coast. Walt Wolfram (Editor). Trade Paper. Blackwell Publishing, Inc. Malden, MA. 2005. 288p. ISBN:1-4051-2109-2, ISBN13: 978-1-4051-2109-5. Dewey:427/.973. LCCN:2005-017255.
Audience: **g,l,u,f.**

Wardhaugh, Ronald **PE1074.7.W37 1999**
e Proper English: Myths and Misunderstandings about Language. E-Book. Blackwell Publishing, Inc. Malden, MA. 1999. ISBN:0-631-22811-X, ISBN13: 978-0-631-22811-0. Dewey:428.
Audience: **g,l,u,f.**

Wheeler, Rebecca S. (Editor) **P51.L338 1999**
Language Alive in the Classroom. Paper Text. Greenwood Publishing Group, Inc. Portsmouth, NH. 1999. 240p. ISBN:0-275-96056-0, ISBN13: 978-0-275-96056-8. Dewey:410/.71. LCCN:98-053391.
Audience: **u,f.**

Wheeler, Rebecca S. (Editor) **P106.W663 1999**
The Workings of Language: From Prescriptions to Perspectives. Paper Text. Greenwood Publishing Group, Inc. Portsmouth, NH. 1999. 264p. ISBN:0-275-96246-6, ISBN13: 978-0-275-96246-3. Dewey:400. LCCN:98-050239.
Audience: **g,l,u,f.**

Willinsky, John **PE1617.O94W55 1994**
Empire of Words: The Reign of the O. E. D. Cloth Text. Princeton University Press. Princeton, NJ. 1994. 258p. ISBN:0-691-03719-1, ISBN13: 978 0 691 03719-6. Dewey:423/.028. LCCN:94-011247.
Audience: **g,l,u,f.** *Choice, 1995.*

Winchester, Simon **PE1617.O94W56 1998**
The Professor and the Madman: A Tale of Murder, Insanity, and the Making of the Oxford English Dictionary. Trade Cloth. HarperCollins Publishers. New York, NY. 1998. 256p. ISBN:0-06-017596-6, ISBN13: 978-0-06-017596-2. Dewey:423/.092. LCCN:98-010204.
Audience: **g,l,u,f.**

Wolfram, Walt & Schilling-Estes, Natalie **PE2846**
American English: Dialects and Variation. Book, Other. Blackwell Publishing, Inc. Malden, MA. 1998. 416p. Language in Society Ser., Vol. 24 ISBN:0-631-20486-5, ISBN13: 978-0-631-20486-2. Dewey:427.9/73. LCCN:97-037242.
Audience: **g,l,u,f.**

Language > English > Modern English > History

Aitchison, Jean (Author, Contribution by) **P142 .A37 2001**
Language Change: Progress or Decay? Ed. 3. Trade Paper. Cambridge University Press. New York, NY. 2000. 324p. Approaches to Linguistics Ser. ISBN:0-521-79535-4, ISBN13: 978-0-521-79535-7. Dewey:417.7.
Audience: **u,f.**

Algeo, John (Editor) **PE1072 .C36 1992**
English in North America. Richard M. Hogg (Contribution by). Cloth Text. Cambridge University Press. New York, NY. 2001. 662p. The Cambridge History of the English Language Ser., Vol. 6 ISBN:0-521-26479-0, ISBN13: 978-0-521-26479-2. Dewey:420/.9. LCCN:91-013881.
Audience: **l,u,f.** *Choice, 2002.*

Algeo, John & Pyles, Thomas **PE1075.A54 2004**
The Origins and Development of the English Language. Ed. 5. Cloth Text. Thomson Heinle. Boston, MA. 2004. 384p. ISBN:0-15-507055-X, ISBN13: 978-0-15-507055-4. Dewey:420/.9. LCCN:2003-114840.
Audience: **l,u,f.**

Bailey, Richard W. **PE1072.B33 2001**
Images of English: A Cultural History of the Language. Trade Paper. University of Michigan Press. Chicago, IL. 1993. 344p. ISBN:0-472-08242-6, ISBN13: 978-0-472-08242-1. Dewey:420/.9.
Audience: **g,l,u.** *Choice, 1992.*

Barber, Charles **PE821**
Early Modern English. Ed. 2. Trade Paper. Edinburgh University Press. Edinburgh, 1997. 304p. ISBN:0-7486-0835-4, ISBN13: 978-0-7486-0835-5. Dewey:420.9/031.
Audience: **l,u,f.**

Baron, Dennis E. **P119.32.U6B37 1990**
The English-Only Question: An Official Language for Americans. Cloth over Boards. Yale University Press. Cumberland, RI. 1990. 248p. ISBN:0-300-04852-1, ISBN13: 978-0-300-04852-0. Dewey:306.4/4973. LCCN:90-032041.
Audience: **u,f.** *Choice, 1991.*

Baron, Naomi S. **PE1075.B28 2000**
Alphabet to Email: How Written English Evolved and Where It's Headed. Paper over Boards. Routledge. New York, NY. 2000. 336p. ISBN:0-415-18685-4, ISBN13: 978-0-415-18685-8. Dewey:421/.1. LCCN:99-043735.
Audience: **g,l,u,f.** *Choice, 2000.*

Brinton, Laurel & Arnovick, Leslie **PE1075**
The English Language: A Linguistic History. Trade Paper. Oxford University Press, Inc. New York, NY. 2006. 542p. ISBN:0-19-542205-8, ISBN13: 978-0-19-542205-4. Dewey:420.9.
Audience: **g,l,u,f.**

Burchfield, Robert W. (Editor) **PE1072 .C36 1992**
English in Britain and Overseas: Origins and Development. Richard M. Hogg (Contribution by). Cloth Text. Cambridge University Press. New York, NY. 1994. 685p. The Cambridge History of the English Language Ser. ISBN:0-521-26478-2, ISBN13: 978-0-521-26478-5. Dewey:420.9. LCCN:91-013881.
Audience: **l,u,f.**

Burnley, David & Burnley, J. D. **PE1075.5.B87 2000**
The History of the English Language: A Source Book. Ed. 2. Trade Paper. Longman Publishing. Boston, MA. 2000. 440p. ISBN:0-582-31263-9, ISBN13: 978-0-582-31263-0. Dewey:420.9. LCCN:00-026239.
Audience: **l,u.** *Choice, 1992.*

Cassidy, Frederic G. (Editor) **PE2843.D52 1985**
Dictionary of American Regional English. Trade Cloth. Harvard University Press. Cambridge, MA. 1985. 1062p. Dictionary of American Regional English Ser., Vol. 1, A-C ISBN:0-674-20511-1, ISBN13: 978-0-674-20511-6. Dewey:427/.973. LCCN:84-029025.
Audience: **g,l,u,f.** B *Choice, 1986.*

Crawford, James (Editor) **P119.32.U6L36 1992**
Language Loyalties: A Source Book on the Official English Controversy. Trade Paper. University of Chicago Press. Chicago, IL. 1992. 532p. ISBN:0-226-12016-3, ISBN13: 978-0-226-12016-4. Dewey:306.4/4973. LCCN:91-029445.
Audience: **u,f.**

Crystal, David **PE1072 .C7**
English Language: A Guided Tour of the Language. Ed. 2. Trade Paper. Penguin Group (USA) Inc. New York, NY. 2004. 336p. ISBN:0-14-100396-0, ISBN13: 978-0-14-100396-2. Dewey:420.
Audience: **g,l,u,f.**

Crystal, David **PE1074.7.C79 2004**
The Stories of English. Trade Cloth. Overlook Press, The. New York, NY. 2004. 608p. ISBN:1-58567-601-2, ISBN13: 978-1-58567-601-9. Dewey:427. LCCN:2004-054727.
Audience: **g,l,u,f.**

Curzan, Anne **PE1211.C87 2003**
Gender Shifts in the History of English. Bas Aarts, John Algeo, Susan M. Fitzmaurice, Richard Hogg, Charles F. Meyer & Merja Kytö (Contribution by). Trade Cloth. Cambridge University Press. New York, NY. 2003. 240p. Studies in English Language Ser. ISBN:0-521-82007-3, ISBN13: 978-0-521-82007-3. Dewey:425. LCCN:2003-273210.
Audience: **u,f.** *Choice, 2003.*

Dillard, Joey L. **PE2809 .D544 1985**
Toward a Social History of American English. Trade Cloth. Walter de Gruyter GmbH & Co. KG. Berlin, 1985. xii, 301p. Contributions to the Sociology of Language Ser., No. 39 ISBN:3-11-010584-5, ISBN13: 978-3-11-010584-1. Dewey:420/.973. LCCN:84-020644.
Audience: **u,f.** B

Görlach, Manfred **PE821.G613 1991**
Introduction to Early Modern English. Trade Paper. Cambridge University Press. New York, NY. 1991. 488p. ISBN:0-521-31046-6, ISBN13: 978-0-521-31046-8. Dewey:420/.9/031. LCCN:89-077389.
Audience: **l,u.** *Choice, 1992.*

Hogg, Richard M. (Contribution by) **PE1075**
The Cambridge History of the English Language, Set. Cloth Text. Cambridge University Press. New York, NY. 2001. 4160p. The Cambridge History of the English Language Ser. ISBN:0-521-80758-1, ISBN13: 978-0-521-80758-6. Dewey:420.9.
Audience: **u,f.**

Hughes, Geoffrey **PE1571.H83 2000**
A History of English Words. Trade Paper. Blackwell Publishing, Inc. Malden, MA. 1999. 448p. The Language Library ISBN:0-631-18855-X, ISBN13: 978-0-631-18855-1. Dewey:423/.028. LCCN:99-034523.
Audience: **g,l,u,f.**

Jespersen, Otto **PE1075**
Growth and Structure of the English Language. Ed. 10. Randolph Quirk (Foreword by). Paper Text. University of Chicago Press. Chicago, IL. 1999. 256p. ISBN:0-226-39877-3, ISBN13: 978-0-226-39877-8. Dewey:420/.9. LCCN:81-022008.
Audience: **l,u,f.**

Knowles, Gerald **PE1075.K68 1997**
A Cultural History of the English Language. Trade Paper. Oxford University Press, Inc. New York, NY. 1997. 192p. A Hodder Arnold Publication ISBN:0-340-67680-9, ISBN13: 978-0-340-67680-6. Dewey:420/.9. LCCN:96-052280.
Audience: **u,f.**

Lass, Roger (Editor) **PE1072 .C36 1992**
1476-1776. Richard M. Hogg (Contribution by). Cloth Text. Cambridge University Press. New York, NY. 2000. 794p. The Cambridge History of the English Language Ser., Vol. 3 ISBN:0-521-26476-6, ISBN13: 978-0-521-26476-1. Dewey:420.9.
Audience: **l,u,f.** *Choice, 2000.*

Leith, Dick **PE1075 .L44 1997**
A Social History of English. Ed. 2. Paper over Boards. Routledge. New York, NY. 1997. 312p. ISBN:0-415-16456-7, ISBN13: 978-0-415-16456-6. Dewey:420.9.
Audience: **l,u,f.** B

Lounsbury, Thomas RaynesFord **PE1075 .L6**
History of the English Language. Paper Text. Classic Textbooks. Murrieta, CA. 1879. ISBN:1-4047-3864-9, ISBN13: 978-1-4047-3864-5. Dewey:420.9.
Audience: **g,l,u,f.**

McCrum, Robert, et al. **PE1075.M58 2003**
The Story of English. Ed. 3. William Cran & Robert MacNeil (Authors). Trade Paper. Penguin Group (USA) Inc. New York, NY. 2002. 496p. ISBN:0-14-200231-3, ISBN13: 978-0-14-200231-5. Dewey:420/.9. LCCN:2002-029818.
Audience: **g,l.** *Choice, 1987.*

Millward, C. M. **PE1075.M64 1996**
A Biography of the English Language. Ed. 2. Cloth Text. Thomson Heinle. Boston, MA. 1996. 464p. ISBN:0-15-501645-8, ISBN13: 978-0-15-501645-3. Dewey:420/.9. LCCN:96-148066.
Audience: **g,l,u,f.**

Milroy, James **PE1101.M55 1992**
Linguistic Variation and Change: On the Historical Sociolinguistics of English. Peter Trudgill (Preface by). Trade Paper. Blackwell Publishing, Inc. Malden, MA. 1991. 256p. Language in Society Ser. ISBN:0-631-14367-X, ISBN13: 978-0-631-14367-3. Dewey:306.4/4. LCCN:91-018703.
Audience: **u,f.** *Choice, 1992.*

Poplack, Shana (Editor) **PE3102.N42E54 1999**
The English History of African American English. Trade Paper. Blackwell Publishing, Inc. Malden, MA. 1999. 304p. Language and Society Ser., Vol. 28 ISBN:0-631-21262-0, ISBN13: 978-0-631-21262-1. Dewey:427/.08996073. LCCN:99-034522.
Audience: **g,l,u,f.**

Romaine, Suzanne (Editor) **PE1072 .C36 1992**
The Cambridge History of the English Language: 1776-1997. John Algeo, David Denison, Richard Coates, Michael K. MacMahon, Edward Finegan, Sylvia Adamson & Richard M. Hogg (Contribution by). Trade Cloth. Cambridge University Press. New York, NY. 1999. 816p. The Cambridge History of the English Language Ser., Vol. 4 ISBN:0-521-26477-4, ISBN13: 978-0-521-26477-8. Dewey:420.9. LCCN:91-013881.
Audience: **l,u,f.**

Smith, Jeremy **PE1075.S45 1996**
An Historical Study of English: A Dynamic Approach. Paper over Boards. Routledge. New York, NY. 1996. 248p. ISBN:0-415-13272-X, ISBN13: 978-0-415-13272-5. Dewey:420.9. LCCN:96-007566.
Audience: **u,f.**

Sturtevant, Edgar Howard **P121.S82**
Linguistic Change: An Introduction to the Historical Study of Language. Paper Text. Textbook Publishers. Temecula, CA. 2003. 185p. ISBN:0-7581-2595-X, ISBN13: 978-0-7581-2595-8. Dewey:409.
Audience: **u,f.**

Sweet, Henry **PE1101.S85**
A Short Historical English Grammar. Paper Text. Classic Textbooks. Murrieta, CA. 1892. 264p. ISBN:1-4047-0008-0, ISBN13: 978-1-4047-0008-6. Dewey:425.
Audience: **g,l,u.**

Visser, F. Th **PE1361.V5 2002**
An Historical Syntax of the English Language: Syntactical Units with One Verb; Syntactical Units with Two Verbs; Syntactical Units with Two and More Verbs. Ed. 4. Trade Cloth. Brill Academic Publishers. Leiden, 2002. 2636p. ISBN:90-04-07142-3, ISBN13: 978-90-04-07142-1. Dewey:425.2. LCCN:2002-282247.
Audience: **u,f.**

Visser, F. Th **PE1361.V5 2002**
An Historical Syntax of the English Language. Ed. 4. Trade Cloth. Brill Academic Publishers, Inc. Boston, MA. 2002. ISBN:90-04-05746-3, ISBN13: 978-90-04-05746-3. Dewey:425. LCCN:2002-282247.
Audience: **u,f.**

Williams, Joseph M. **PE1075**
Origins of the English Language: A Social and Linguistic History. Trade Paper. Simon & Schuster. New York, NY. 1986. 436p. ISBN:0-02-934470-0, ISBN13: 978-0-02-934470-5. Dewey:420/.9. LCCN:74-012596.
Audience: **u,f.**

Wolfram, Walt & Thomas, Erik R. **PE3102.N42W65 2002**
The Development of African American English. Trade Paper. Blackwell Publishing, Inc. Malden, MA. 2002. 256p. Language in Society Ser., Vol. 31 ISBN:0-631-23087-4, ISBN13: 978-0-631-23087-8. Dewey:427/.973/08996073. LCCN:2001-043959.
Audience: **l,u.** *Choice, 2002.*

Wright, Laura (Editor) **PE1074.7 .D48 2000**
The Development of Standard English, 1300-1800: Theories, Descriptions, Conflicts. Bas Aarts, John Algeo, Susan Fitzmaurice, Richard Hogg, Charles F. Meyer, B. Simon & Merja Kytö (Contribution by). Trade Cloth. Cambridge University Press. New York, NY. 2000. 248p. Studies in English Language ISBN:0-521-77114-5, ISBN13: 978-0-521-77114-6. Dewey:420/.9. LCCN:99-087473.
Audience: **l,u,f.**

Wyld, Henry Cecil Kennedy **PE1075.W8**
The Historical Study of the Mother Tongue: An Introduction to Philological Method. Trade Cloth. Classic Books. Murrieta, CA. 1969. xi, 412p. ISBN:0-7426-4064-7, ISBN13: 978-0-7426-4064-1. Dewey:420/.9.
Audience: **g,l,u,f.**

Language > English > Modern English > Grammar

Baker, C. L. **PE1361.B35 1995**
English Syntax. Ed. 2. Trade Paper. MIT Press. Cambridge, MA. 1995. 560p. ISBN:0-262-52198-9, ISBN13: 978-0-262-52198-7. Dewey:425. LCCN:94-048244.
Audience: **u,f.**

Balmuth, Miriam **PE1133.B26 2006**
The Roots of Phonics: A Historical Introduction. Trade Paper. PRO-ED, Inc. Austin, TX. 2006. ISBN:1-4164-0091-5, ISBN13: 978-1-4164-0091-2. Dewey:421/.5. LCCN:2005-047422.
Audience: **l,u.**

Burchfield, R. W. **PE1628.F65 2004**
Fowler's Modern English Usage. Ed. 3. Trade Cloth. Oxford University Press, Inc. New York, NY. 2004. 896p. ISBN:0-19-861021-1, ISBN13: 978-0-19-861021-2. Dewey:428/.003. LCCN:2005-271630.
Audience: **g,l,u,f.**

Burton-Roberts, Noel **PE1375.B87 1997**
Analyzing Sentences: An Introduction to English Syntax. Ed. 2. Trade Paper. Longman Publishing Group. White Plains, NY. 1997. 324p. Learning about Language Ser. ISBN:0-582-24876-0, ISBN13: 978-0-582-24876-2. Dewey:425. LCCN:96-048575.
Audience: **g,l,u.**

Chomsky, Noam & Halle, Morris **PE1133.C5 1991**
The Sound Pattern of English. Trade Cloth. MIT Press. Cambridge, MA. 1991. xiv, 470p. ISBN:0-262-03179-5, ISBN13: 978-0-262-03179-0. Dewey:421.5. LCCN:90-019232.
Audience: **l,u,f.** B

Coye, Dale F. **PR3081**
Pronouncing Shakespeare's Words: A Guide from A to Zounds. Cloth Text. Greenwood Publishing Group, Inc. Portsmouth, NH. 1998. 744p. ISBN:0-313-30655-9, ISBN13: 978-0-313-30655-6. Dewey:822.3/3. LCCN:97-044868.
Audience: **g,l,u,f.** *Choice, 1998.*

Dixon, R. M. W. **PE1112**
Semantic Approach to English Grammar. Ed. 2. Trade Cloth. Oxford University Press, Inc. New York, NY. 2005. 512p. Oxford Textbooks in Linguistics Ser. ISBN:0-19-928307-9, ISBN13: 978-0-19-928307-1. Dewey:425. LCCN:2005-283469.
Audience: **u,f.**

Dixon, R. M. W. **PE1112**
Semantic Approach to English Grammar. Ed. 2. Trade Paper. Oxford University Press, Inc. New York, NY. 2005. 512p. Oxford Textbooks in Linguistics Ser. ISBN:0-19-924740-4, ISBN13: 978-0-19-924740-0. Dewey:425.
Audience: **u,f.**

Ellis, Alexander J. **PE1133 .E45**
On Early English Pronunciation, with Especial Reference to Shakespeare and Chaucer, Set. Library Binding. M. S. G. Haskell House. Brooklyn, NY. 1969. Studies in Language, No. 41 ISBN:0-8383-0158-4, ISBN13: 978-0-8383-0158-6. Dewey:421/.52. LCCN:68-024964.
Audience: **l,u,f.**

Fischer, Phyllis E. **LB1573.3.F57 1993**
The Sounds and Spelling Patterns of English: Phonics for Teachers and Parents. Perfect. Oxton House, Publishers. Farmington, ME. 1993. 141p. ISBN:1-881929-01-9, ISBN13: 978-1-881929-01-7. Dewey:372.41/45. LCCN:93-213487.
Audience: **l,u,f.** *Choice, 1993.*

Garner, Bryan **PE2827.G37 2003**
Garner's Modern American Usage. Ed. 2. Trade Cloth. Oxford University Press, Inc. New York, NY. 2003. 928p. ISBN:0-19-516191-2, ISBN13: 978-0-19-516191-5. Dewey:423/.1. LCCN:2004-295114.
Audience: **g,l,u,f.** *Choice, 2004.*

Giegerich, Heinz J. **PE1133 .G47 1992**
English Phonology: An Introduction. S. R. Anderson, J. Bresnan, B. Comrie, W. Dressler & C. J. Ewen (Contribution by). Trade Paper. Cambridge University Press. New York, NY. 1992. 349p. Textbooks in Linguistics ISBN:0-521-33603-1, ISBN13: 978-0-521-33603-1. Dewey:421.5. LCCN:92-002744.
Audience: **l,u.**

Glowka, Wayne & Lance, Donald M. (Editors) **PE1068.N55.L36 1993**
Language Variation in North American English: Research and Teaching. Trade Cloth. Modern Language Association of America. New York, NY. 1993. xvi, 417p. ISBN:0-87352-389-X, ISBN13: 978-0-87352-389-9. Dewey:428/.00707. LCCN:93-009451.
Audience: **l,u,f.** *Choice, 1994.*

Greenbaum, Sidney **PE1112.G68 1989**
A College Grammar of English. Cloth Text. Longman Publishing Group. White Plains, NY. 1989. 340p. Longman English and Humanities Ser. ISBN:0-582-28597-6, ISBN13: 978-0-582-28597-2. Dewey:428.2. LCCN:88-014814.
Audience: **l,u.**

Greenbaum, Sidney **PE1106.G74 1996**
The Oxford English Grammar. Trade Cloth. Oxford University Press, Inc. New York, NY. 1996. 668p. ISBN:0-19-861250-8, ISBN13: 978-0-19-861250-6. Dewey:428.2. LCCN:95-111351.
Audience: **g,l,u,f.**

Greenbaum, Sidney & Nelson, Gerald **PE1112**
An Introduction to English Grammar. Ed. 2. Trade Paper. Pearson ESL. Boston, MA. 2002. 328p. ISBN:0-582-43741-5, ISBN13: 978-0-582-43741-8. Dewey:428.2.
Audience: **l,u.**

Hosler, Mary M. **PE1146.H77 1995**
20,000+ Words: Spelled and Divided for Quick Reference. Ed. 10. Trade Cloth. McGraw-Hill Higher Education. Burr Ridge, IL. 1995. ISBN:0-02-802158-4, ISBN13: 978-0-02-802158-4. Dewey:428.1. LCCN:95-036011.
Audience: **g,l,u,f.**

Huddleston, Rodney & Pullum, Geoffrey K. **PE1106 .H74 2002**
The Cambridge Grammar of the English Language. Trade Cloth. Cambridge University Press. New York, NY. 2002. 1860p. ISBN:0-521-43146-8, ISBN13: 978-0-521-43146-0. Dewey:425. LCCN:2001-025630.
Audience: **l,u.** *Choice, 2002.*

Huddleston, Rodney & Pullum, Geoffrey K. **PE1112**
A Student's Introduction to English Grammar. Cloth Text. Cambridge University Press. New York, NY. 2005. 320p. ISBN:0-521-84837-7, ISBN13: 978-0-521-84837-4. Dewey:428.2. LCCN:2005-280470.
Audience: **l,u.**

Hussey, Stanley **PE1101.H94 1995**
The English Language: Structure and Development. Cloth Text. Addison-Wesley Longman, Ltd. Harlow, 1995. 192p. ISBN:0-582-21762-8, ISBN13: 978-0-582-21762-1. Dewey:420.9. LCCN:95-005614.
Audience: **l,u.** *Choice, 1996.*

Jacobs, Roderick A. **PE1365.J33 1993**
English Syntax: A Grammar for English Language Professionals. Trade Paper. Oxford University Press, Inc. New York, NY. 1995. 392p. ISBN:0-19-434277-8, ISBN13: 978-0-19-434277-3. Dewey:428.2. LCCN:93-025121.
Audience: **u,f.**

Jespersen, Otto **PE1105 .J4**
Essentials of English Grammar. Trade Paper. University of Alabama Press. Tuscaloosa, AL. 1964. 392p. Alabama Linguistic and Philological Ser: V Ser. ISBN:0-8173-0452-5, ISBN13: 978-0-8173-0452-2. Dewey:425. LCCN:64-021942.
Audience: **l,u,f.**

Jespersen, Otto **PE1101 .J55**
A Modern English Grammar on Historical Principles. Cloth Text. Routledge. New York, NY. 1946. ISBN:0-04-425012-6, ISBN13: 978-0-04-425012-8. Dewey:425.
Audience: **l,u,f.**

Jespersen, Otto **P151 .J47 1992**
The Philosophy of Grammar. James D. McCawley (Foreword by). Trade Paper. University of Chicago Press. Chicago, IL. 1992. 372p. ISBN:0-226-39881-1, ISBN13: 978-0-226-39881-5. Dewey:415. LCCN:92-019138.
Audience: **u,f.**

Jones, Charles **PE1133.J6 1989**
A History of English Phonology. Paper Text. Longman Publishing Group. White Plains, NY. 1989. 384p. Linguistics Library ISBN:0-582-29156-9, ISBN13: 978-0-582-29156-0. Dewey:421/.5. LCCN:88-013610.
Audience: **u,f.** *Choice, 1990.*

Jones, Daniel **PE1137.J56 1956**
The Pronunciation of English. Ed. 4. Trade Paper. Cambridge University Press. New York, NY. 1956. 256p. ISBN:0-521-09369-4, ISBN13: 978-0-521-09369-9. Dewey:421.5. LCCN:57-000129.
Audience: **l,u,f.**

Kaplan, Jeffrey P. **PE1106.K37 1995**
English Grammar: Principles and Facts. Ed. 2. Cloth Text. Prentice Hall PTR. Upper Saddle River, NJ. 1994. 384p. ISBN:0-13-061565-X, ISBN13: 978-0-13-061565-7. Dewey:428.2. LCCN:94-016555.
Audience: **l,u.**

Kenyon, John S. **PE2815.K46 1994**
American Pronunciation. Ed. 12. Donald M. Lance & Stewart A. Kingsbury (Editors). Cloth Text. George Wahr Publishing Company. Ann Arbor, MI. 1997. 437p. ISBN:1-884739-08-3, ISBN13: 978-1-884739-08-8. Dewey:421/.52/0973. LCCN:94-061848.
Audience: **g,l,u,f.**

Klammer, Thomas P. **PC1106**
Analyzing English Grammar. Ed. 3. Paper Text. Allyn & Bacon, Inc. Boston, MA. 1999. ISBN:0-205-31552-6, ISBN13: 978-0-205-31552-9. Dewey:428.2.
Audience: **l,u.**

Lakoff, Robin Tolmach **HQ1206.L36 2004**
Language and Woman's Place: Text and Commentaries. Ed. 2. Mary Bucholtz (Editor). Trade Paper. Oxford University Press, Inc. New York, NY. 2004. 328p. Studies in Language and Gender, Vol. 3 ISBN:0-19-516757-0, ISBN13: 978-0-19-516757-3. Dewey:305.4. LCCN:2003-056479.
Audience: **u,f.** *Choice, 2005.*

Leech, Geoffrey N. & Svartvik, Jan **PE1128.L45 2002**
A Communicative Grammar of English. Ed. 3. Trade Paper. Pearson ESL. Boston, MA. 2003. 456p. ISBN:0-582-50633-6, ISBN13: 978-0-582-50633-6. Dewey:428.2/4.
Audience: **l,u.**

Lobeck, Anne **PE1112.M64 2001**
Discovering Grammar: An Introduction to English Sentence Structure. Ed. 3. Cloth Text. Oxford University Press, Inc. New York, NY. 2000. 384p. ISBN:0-19-512984-9, ISBN13: 978-0-19-512984-7. Dewey:428.2. LCCN:2001-021495.
Audience: **g,l,u.**

Lounsbury, Thomas RaynesFord **PE1137**
English Spelling and Spelling Reform. Trade Cloth. Classic Books. Murrieta, CA. 1970. xiii, 356p. ISBN:0-7426-4073-6, ISBN13: 978-0-7426-4073-3. Dewey:421/.52.
Audience: **l,u,f.**

McCawley, James D. **PE1361.M43 1988**
The Syntactic Phenomena of English. Trade Paper. University of Chicago Press. Chicago, IL. 1992. 384p. Syntactic Phenomena of English Ser., Vol. 1 ISBN:0-226-55624-7, ISBN13: 978-0-226-55624-6. Dewey:425. LCCN:88-014818.
Audience: **u,f.**

McCawley, James D. **PE1361.M43 1998**
The Syntactic Phenomena of English. Ed. 2. Trade Cloth. University of Chicago Press. Chicago, IL. 1998. 834p. ISBN:0-226-55627-1, ISBN13: 978-0-226-55627-7. Dewey:425. LCCN:97-011825.
Audience: **u,f.**

Merriam-Webster, Inc. Staff **PE1460.M45 1994**
Merriam-Webster's Dictionary of English Usage. Ed. 2. Trade Cloth. Merriam-Webster, Inc. Springfield, MA. 1994. 992p. ISBN:0-87779-132-5, ISBN13: 978-0-87779-132-4. Dewey:428/.003. LCCN:93-019289.
Audience: **g,l,u,f.**

Millward, C. M. **PE1075.M64 1996**
A Biography of the English Language. Ed. 2. Cloth Text. Thomson Heinle. Boston, MA. 1996. 464p. ISBN:0-15-501645-8, ISBN13: 978-0-15-501645-3. Dewey:420/.9. LCCN:96-148066.
Audience: **g,l,u,f.**

Morton, Jacqueline (Author, Editor) **PC2099.M67 2002**
English Grammar for Students of French: The Study Guide for Those Learning French. Ed. 5. Paper Text. Olivia & Hill Press, The. Ann Arbor, MI. 2002. 188p. English Grammar Ser. ISBN:0-934034-32-X, ISBN13: 978-0-934034-32-6. Dewey:445. LCCN:2001-097586.
Audience: **l,u.**

Nunberg, Geoffrey **PE1450.N78 1990**
The Linguistics of Punctuation. Trade Paper. C S L I Publications/Center for the Study of Language & Information. Stanford, CA. 1990. 160p. Lecture Notes, No. 18
ISBN:0-937073-46-6, ISBN13: 978-0-937073-46-9. Dewey:421/.52. LCCN:90-001411.
Audience: **u,f.**

Peters, Pam **PE1460**
The Cambridge Guide to English Usage. Cloth Text. Cambridge University Press. New York, NY. 2004. 620p.
ISBN:0-521-62181-X, ISBN13: 978-0-521-62181-6. Dewey:423/.1. LCCN:2004-301888.
Audience: **g,l,u,f.** *Choice, 2004.*

Poutsma, Hendrik **PE1105.P62**
A Grammar of Late Modern English, Vol. 4, Pt. 2. Ed. 2. Trade Paper. Books on Demand. Ann Arbor, MI. 377p.
ISBN:0-598-39737-X, ISBN13: 978-0-598-39737-9. Dewey:425. LCCN:39-020911.
Audience: **u,f.**

Quirk, Randolph **PE1106.G67**
A Grammar of Contemporary English. Trade Cloth. Longman Publishing Group. White Plains, NY. 1972. xii, 1120p.
ISBN:0-582-52444-X, ISBN13: 978-0-582-52444-6. Dewey:425. LCCN:74-155578.
Audience: **l,u.** B

Quirk, Randolph, et al. **PE1112**
A Comprehensive Grammar of the English Language. Ed. 1. Sidney Greenbaum, Geoffrey Leach & Jan Svartvik (Authors). Cloth Text. Longman Publishing Group. White Plains, NY. 1989. 1779p. ISBN:0-582-51734-6, ISBN13: 978-0-582-51734-9. Dewey:428.2. LCCN:84-027848.
Audience: **l,u,f.** B *Choice, 1986.*

Radford, Andrew **PE1361.R33 2004**
English Syntax: An Introduction. Cloth Text. Cambridge University Press. New York, NY. 2004. 396p.
ISBN:0-521-83499-6, ISBN13: 978-0-521-83499-5. Dewey:425. LCCN:2003-055386.
Audience: **u,f.**

Sledd, James **PL2840.M4**
A Short Introduction to English Grammar. Paper Text. Textbook Publishers. Temecula, CA. 2003. 346p. ISBN:0-7581-4103-3, ISBN13: 978-0-7581-4103-3. Dewey:895.135.
Audience: **g,l,u.**

Spinelli, Emily **PC4099**
English Grammar for Students of Spanish: The Study Guide for Those Learning Spanish. Ed. 5. Jacqueline Morton (Editor). Paper Text. Olivia & Hill Press, The. Ann Arbor, MI. 2003. 210p. English Grammar Ser. ISBN:0-934034-33-8, ISBN13: 978-0-934034-33-3. Dewey:428.2. LCCN:2002-115802.
Audience: **l,u.**

Sweet, Henry **PE1101.S85**
A Short Historical English Grammar. Trade Cloth. Classic Books. Murrieta, CA. 2001. 264p. ISBN:0-7426-4066-3, ISBN13: 978-0-7426-4066-5. Dewey:425.
Audience: **l,u.** B

Upton, Clive, et al. **PE1137.U68 2003**
Oxford Dictionary of Pronunciation for Current English. Ed. 2. William Kretzschmar & Rafal Konopka (Authors). Trade Paper. Oxford University Press, Inc. New York, NY. 2003. 1232p.
ISBN:0-19-860772-5, ISBN13: 978-0-19-860772-4. Dewey:423.1.
Audience: **g,l,u,f.**

Venezky, Richard L. **PE2817.V46 1999**
The American Way of Spelling: The Structure and Origins of American English Orthography. Cloth over Boards. Guilford Publications, Inc. New York, NY. 1999. 288p.
ISBN:1-57230-469-3, ISBN13: 978-1-57230-469-7. Dewey:421/.54. LCCN:99-018154.
Audience: **l,u,f.** *Choice, 2000.*

Wardhaugh, Ronald **PE1112.W29 2002**
Understanding English Grammar: A Linguistic Approach. Ed. 2. Trade Paper. Blackwell Publishing, Inc. Malden, MA. 2002. 296p. ISBN:0-631-23292-3, ISBN13: 978-0-631-23292-6. Dewey:428.2. LCCN:2002-066423.
Audience: **l,u,f.**

Wells, John C. **PE1137**
Accents of English: Beyond the British Isles. Trade Paper. Cambridge University Press. New York, NY. 1982. 226p.
ISBN:0-521-28541-0, ISBN13: 978-0-521-28541-4. Dewey:427. LCCN:81-010127.
Audience: **l,u,f.**

Wells, John C. **PE1137**
Accents of English, Vol. 2. Trade Paper. Cambridge University Press. New York, NY. 1982. 206p. ISBN:0-521-28540-2, ISBN13: 978-0-521-28540-7. Dewey:421/.52. LCCN:81-010127.
Audience: **l,u,f.** B

Wells, John C. **PE1711 .W4**
Accents of English, Vol. 1. Trade Paper. Cambridge University Press. New York, NY. 1982. 297p. ISBN:0-521-29719-2, ISBN13: 978-0-521-29719-6. Dewey:421/.52. LCCN:81-010127.
Audience: **l,u,f.** B

Wolfram, Walt & Johnson, Robert **PE1133.W64**
Phonological Analysis: Focus on American English. Ed. 1. Trade Paper. Prentice Hall PTR. Upper Saddle River, NJ. 1996. 224p.
ISBN:0-13-664988-2, ISBN13: 978-0-13-664988-5. Dewey:421.5.
Audience: **u,f.** B

Zorach, Cecile & Melin, Charlotte **PE1099.Z6 2001**
English Grammar for Students of German: A Study Guide for Those Studying German. Ed. 4. Jacqueline Morton (Editor). Paper Text. Olivia & Hill Press, The. Ann Arbor, MI. 2001. 190p. English Grammar Ser. ISBN:0-934034-31-1, ISBN13: 978-0-934034-31-9. Dewey:428.2/431. LCCN:00-104926.
Audience: **l,u.**

Linguistics

P302
☐ The Global Language Monitor.
http://www.languagemonitor.com/
Audience: **g,l,u,f.**

Aitchison, Jean (Author, Contribution by) **P142 .A37 2001**
Language Change: Progress or Decay? Ed. 3. Trade Paper. Cambridge University Press. New York, NY. 2000. 324p. Approaches to Linguistics Ser. ISBN:0-521-79535-4, ISBN13: 978-0-521-79535-7. Dewey:417.7.
Audience: **u,f.**

Andresen, Julie T. **P81.U5**
Linguistics in America, 1769-1924: A Critical History. Trade Paper. Routledge. New York, NY. 1996. 320p. History of Linguistic Thought Ser. ISBN:0-415-13259-2, ISBN13: 978-0-415-13259-6. Dewey:410/.973.
Audience: **u,f.** *Choice, 1991.*

Aronoff, Mark & Rees-Miller, Janie (Editors) **P121.H324 2001**
The Handbook of Linguistics. Book, Other. Blackwell Publishing, Inc. Malden, MA. 2000. 840p. Handbooks in Linguistics ISBN:0-631-20497-0, ISBN13: 978-0-631-20497-8. Dewey:410. LCCN:99-087401.
Audience: **l,u,f.** *Choice, 2001.*

Baker, Mark C. **P107.B35 2002**
The Atoms of Language: The Mind's Hidden Rules of Grammar. Trade Cloth. Oxford University Press, Inc. New York, NY. 2002. 288p. ISBN:0-19-860632-X, ISBN13: 978-0-19-860632-1. Dewey:400. LCCN:2002-074815.
Audience: **u,f.**

Barthes, Roland **P123 .B3813 1973**
Elements of Semiology. Trade Paper. Farrar, Straus & Giroux. New York, NY. 1977. 111p. ISBN:0-374-52146-8, ISBN13: 978-0-374-52146-2. Dewey:401.41.
Audience: **u,f.**

Berdichevsky, Norman **P35**
Nations, Language and Citizenship. Paper Text. McFarland & Company, Incorporated Publishers. Jefferson, NC. 2004. 288p. ISBN:0-7864-1710-2, ISBN13: 978-0-7864-1710-0. Dewey:306.44/9. LCCN:2003-025422.
Audience: **l,u.** *Choice, 2005.*

Bloomfield, Leonard **P121.B5 1984**
Language. Charles F. Hockett (Foreword by). Trade Paper. University of Chicago Press. Chicago, IL. 1984. 580p. ISBN:0-226-06067-5, ISBN13: 978-0-226-06067-5. Dewey:410. LCCN:84-008439.
Audience: **g,l,u,f.**

Burling, Robbins **P106.B778 1992**
Patterns of Language: Structure, Variation, Change. Paper Text. Elsevier Science & Technology Books. Saint Louis, MO. 1992. 461p. ISBN:0-12-144920-3, ISBN13: 978-0-12-144920-9. Dewey:410. LCCN:91-028918.
Audience: **u,f.**

Bynon, Theodora **P142**
Historical Linguistics. S. R. Anderson, J. Bresnan, B. Comrie, W. Dressler & C. J. Ewen (Contribution by). Trade Paper. Cambridge University Press. New York, NY. 1977. 280p. Textbooks in Linguistics ISBN:0 521-29188-7, ISBN13: 978-0-521-29188-0. Dewey:410. LCCN:76-062588.
Audience: **u,f.**

Campbell, Lyle **P140.C36 2004**
Historical Linguistics: An Introduction. Ed. 2. Trade Paper. MIT Press. Cambridge, MA. 2004. 472p. ISBN:0-262-53267-0, ISBN13: 978-0-262-53267-9. Dewey:417/.7. LCCN:2004-042637.
Audience: **l,u.**

Chafe, Wallace L. **P0121.C423**
Meaning and the Structure of Language. Trade Paper. Books on Demand. Ann Arbor, MI. 360p. ISBN:0-598-05669-6, ISBN13: 978-0-598-05669-6. Dewey:410. LCCN:79-114855.
Audience: **u,f.**

Chomsky, Noam **P123**
Cartesian Linguistics: A Chapter in the History of Rationalist Thought. Cloth Text. HarperCollins Publishers. New York, NY. 1966. ISBN:0-06-041275-5, ISBN13: 978-0-06-041275-3. Dewey:401.
Audience: **u,f.**

Chomsky, Noam **P121 .C47**
Current Issues in Linguistic Theory. Paper Text. Walter de Gruyter GmbH & Co. KG. Berlin, 1964. Janua Linguarum, Ser. Minor, No. 38 ISBN:90-279-0700-5, ISBN13: 978-90-279-0700-4. Dewey:407.8.
Audience: **u,f.**

Chomsky, Noam **P107**
Language and Mind. Ed. 3. Trade Cloth. Cambridge University Press. New York, NY. 2006. 208p. ISBN:0-521-85819-4, ISBN13: 978-0-521-85819-9. Dewey:401/.9.
Audience: **u,f.**

Chomsky, Noam **P291.C5 2002**
Syntactic Structures. Ed. 2. Trade Paper. Walter de Gruyter GmbH & Co. KG. Berlin, 2002. "xviii, 117"p. ISBN:3-11-017279-8, ISBN13: 978-3-11-017279-9. Dewey:415. LCCN:2002-043087.
Audience: **u,f.**

Chomsky, Noam **P107.C535 2004**
Rules and Representations. Norbert Hornstein (Foreword by). Trade Paper. Columbia University Press. New York, NY. 2005. 368p. Columbia Classics in Philosophy Ser. ISBN:0-231-13271-9, ISBN13: 978-0-231-13271-8. Dewey:401. LCCN:2004-061788.
Audience: **u,f.**

Clark, John, et al. **P217.C65 1995**
An Introduction to Phonetics and Phonology. Ed. 2. Colin Yallop & Janet Fletcher (Authors). Trade Paper. Blackwell Publishing, Inc. Malden, MA. 1995. 488p. Textbooks in Linguistics ISBN:0-631-19452-5, ISBN13: 978-0-631-19452-1. Dewey:414/.8. LCCN:94-043128.
Audience: **u.**

Cook, Vivian J. & Newson, Mark **P85.C47C66 1996**
Chomsky's Universal Grammar: An Introduction. Ed. 2. Trade Paper. Blackwell Publishing, Inc. Malden, MA. 1996. 384p. ISBN:0-631-19556-4, ISBN13: 978-0-631-19556-6. Dewey:415. LCCN:95-030630.
Audience: **u,f.**

Coulmas, Florian **Z40.C67 1996**
The Blackwell Encyclopedia of Writing Systems. Book, Other. Blackwell Publishing, Inc. Malden, MA. 1996. 640p. ISBN:0-631-19446-0, ISBN13: 978-0-631-19446-0. Dewey:411/.03. LCCN:94-047460.
Audience: **g,l,u,f.** *Choice, 1997.*

Crowley, Terry **P140 .C76 1997**
An Introduction to Historical Linguistics. Ed. 3. Paper Text. Oxford University Press, Inc. New York, NY. 1998. 342p. ISBN:0-19-558378-7, ISBN13: 978-0-19-558378-6. Dewey:417/.7. LCCN:97-200069.
Audience: **l,u.**

Crystal, David **P29.C65 2003**
A Dictionary of Linguistics and Phonetics. Ed. 5. Trade Paper. Blackwell Publishing, Inc. Malden, MA. 2003. 536p. The Language Library ISBN:0-631-22664-8, ISBN13: 978-0-631-22664-2. Dewey:410/.3. LCCN:2002-007797.
Audience: **l,u,f.** *Choice, 2003, 1997.*

Crystal, David **P40.5.L33 C79 2002**
Language Death. Trade Paper. Cambridge University Press. New York, NY. 2002. 208p. Canto Refresh Your Ser. ISBN:0-521-01271-6, ISBN13: 978-0-521-01271-3. Dewey:417.7.
Audience: **l,u.** *Choice, 2001.*

Crystal, David **P107.C79 2004**
The Language Revolution. Trade Cloth. Polity Press. Cambridge, 2004. 152p. Themes for the 21st Century Ser. ISBN:0-7456-3312-9, ISBN13: 978-0-7456-3312-1. Dewey:410. LCCN:2003-017872.
Audience: **u,f.**

Daniels, Peter T. & Bright, William (Editors) **P211.W714 1996**
The World's Writing Systems. Trade Cloth. Oxford University Press, Inc. New York, NY. 1996. 966p. ISBN:0-19-507993-0, ISBN13: 978-0-19-507993-7. Dewey:411. LCCN:95-002247.
Audience: **g,l,u,f.**

Davies, Alan & Elder, Catherine (Editors) **P129.H33 2004**
The Handbook of Applied Linguistics. Trade Cloth. Blackwell Publishing, Inc. Malden, MA. 2004. 888p. Blackwell Handbooks in Linguistics, Vol. 17 ISBN:0-631-22899-3, ISBN13: 978-0-631-22899-8. Dewey:418. LCCN:2003-021505.
Audience: **u,f.** *Choice, 2004.*

DeFrancis, John **P211.D36 1989**
Visible Speech: The Diverse Oneness of Writing Systems. Trade Cloth. University of Hawaii Press. Honolulu, HI. 1989. 328p. Asian Interactions and Comparisons Ser. ISBN:0-8248-1207-7, ISBN13: 978-0-8248-1207-2. Dewey:411. LCCN:89-004708.
Audience: **g,l,u.** *Choice, 1990.*

Duranti, Alessandro (Editor) **P35**
A Companion to Linguistic Anthropology. Trade Cloth. Blackwell Publishing, Inc. Malden, MA. 2004. 648p. Blackwell Companions to Anthropology Ser., Vol. 1 ISBN:0-631-22352-5, ISBN13: 978-0-631-22352-8. Dewey:306.44. LCCN:2003-056026.
Audience: **l,u,f.** *Choice, 2004.*

Eco, Umberto **P 106 .E2813 1995**
The Search for the Perfect Language. Jacques Le Goff (Editor), James Fentress (Translator). Trade Paper. Blackwell Publishing, Inc. Malden, MA. 1997. 400p. The Making of Europe Ser. ISBN:0-631-20510-1, ISBN13: 978-0-631-20510-4. Dewey:401.3.
Audience: **g,l,u.** *Choice, 1996.*

Fauconnier, Gilles & Sweetser, Eve (Editors) **P37.S63 1996**
Spaces, Worlds, and Grammar. Claudia M. Brugman, George Lakoff, Yo Matsumoto, Errapel Mejias-Bikandi, Laura A. Michaelis, Gisela Redeker & Jo Rubba (Contribution by). Trade Cloth. University of Chicago Press. Chicago, IL. 1996. 364p. Cognitive Theory of Language and Culture Ser. ISBN:0-226-23923-3, ISBN13: 978-0-226-23923-1. Dewey:401/.9. LCCN:96-012878.
Audience: **u,f.** *Choice, 1997.*

Frawley, William J. (Editor) **P29.I58 2003**
International Encyclopedia of Linguistics, Set. Ed. 2. Trade Cloth. Oxford University Press, Inc. New York, NY. 2003. 2,200p. ISBN:0-19-513977-1, ISBN13: 978-0-19-513977-8. Dewey:410/.3. LCCN:2003-000430.
Audience: **l,u,f.** *Choice, 2003.*

Garry, Jane, et al. **P371.F33 2000**
Facts About the World's Languages: An Encyclopedia of the World's Major Languages, Past and Present. Rubino, Carl (Author). H. W. Wilson. 2001. ISBN:0-8242-0970-2, ISBN13: 978-0-8242-0970-4.
Audience: **g,l,u,f.**

Goldsmith, John A. **P217.7.G65 1990**
Autosegmental and Metrical Phonology: An Introduction. Cloth Text. Blackwell Publishing, Inc. Malden, MA. 1989. 432p. ISBN:0-631-13675-4, ISBN13: 978-0-631-13675-0. Dewey:414/.6. LCCN:89-001007.
Audience: **u,f.**

Goldsmith, John A. (Editor) **P217 .H36 1996T**
The Handbook of Phonological Theory. Trade Paper. Blackwell Publishing, Inc. Malden, MA. 1996. 1000p. Blackwell Handbooks in Linguistics ISBN:0-631-20126-2, ISBN13: 978-0-631-20126-7. Dewey:414.
Audience: **u,f.**

Goldsmith, John A. (Editor) **P217.P486 1999**
Phonological Theory: The Essential Readings. Trade Cloth. Blackwell Publishing, Inc. Malden, MA. 1999. 448p. ISBN:0-631-20469-5, ISBN13: 978-0-631-20469-5. Dewey:414. LCCN:98-054654.
Audience: **u,f.**

Gordon, Raymond G., Jr. (Editor) **P371**
☐ Ethnologue: Languages of the World.
http://www.ethnologue.com/
Ed. 15. SIL International.
Audience: **g,l,u,f.**

Haley, Michael C. & Lunsford, Ronald F. **P85.C47H27 1994**
Noam Chomsky. Trade Cloth. Thomson Gale. Farmington Hills,

MI. 1993. 222p. Twayne's United States Authors Ser. ISBN:0-8057-4013-9, ISBN13: 978-0-8057-4013-4. Dewey:410.92. LCCN:93-026570.
Audience: **l,u.**

Halliday, M. A. K. **P149.H34**
Halliday: System and Function in Language: Selected Papers. Trade Cloth. Oxford University Press, Inc. New York, NY. 1976. xxi, 250 p. ;p. ISBN:0-19-437127-1, ISBN13: 978-0-19-437127-8. Dewey:415. LCCN:77-359080.
Audience: **u,f.**

Harris, Randy A. **P69**
The Linguistics Wars. Trade Paper. Oxford University Press, Inc. New York, NY. 1995. 368p. ISBN:0-19-509834-X, ISBN13: 978-0-19-509834-1. Dewey:410/.904.
Audience: **g,l,u.** *Choice, 1994.*

Hawkes, Terence **P146**
Structuralism and Semiotics. Ed. 2. Paper over Boards. Routledge. New York, NY. 2003. 192p. ISBN:0-415-32152-2, ISBN13: 978-0-415-32152-5. Dewey:801.9/5.
Audience: **l,u.**

Hockett, Charles Francis **P121.H63**
A Course in Modern Linguistics. Paper Text. Textbook Publishers. Temecula, CA. 2003. 621p. ISBN:0-7581-9272-X, ISBN13: 978-0-7581-9272-1. Dewey:400.
Audience: **g,l,u,f.**

Hoenigswald, Henry M. **P0123.H55**
Language Change and Linguistic Reconstruction. Trade Paper. Books on Demand. Ann Arbor, MI. 176p. Phoenix Bks. ISBN:0-608-18226-5, ISBN13: 978-0-608-18226-1. Dewey:410.
Audience: **u,f.**

Hopper, Paul J. & Traugott, Elizabeth Closs **P299.G73**
Grammaticalization. Ed. 2. S. R. Anderson, J. Bresnan, Bernard Comrie, W. Dressler & C. J. Ewen (Contribution by). Cloth Text. Cambridge University Press. New York, NY. 2003. 296p. Cambridge Textbooks in Linguistics Ser. ISBN:0-521-00948-0, ISBN13: 978-0-521-00948-5. Dewey:415. LCCN:2003-283548.
Audience: **u,f.**

International Phonetic Association Staff (Contribution by) **P227 .I52 1999**
Handbook of the International Phonetic Association: A Guide to the Use of the International Phonetic Alphabet. John Esling (Foreword by). Cloth Text. Cambridge University Press. New York, NY. 1999. 214p. ISBN:0-521-65236-7, ISBN13: 978-0-521-65236-0. Dewey:411. LCCN:98-032178.
Audience: **l,u,f.**

Jackendoff, Ray **P37.J254 2003**
Foundations of Language: Brain, Meaning, Grammar, Evolution. Trade Paper. Oxford University Press, Inc. New York, NY. 2003. 498p. ISBN:0-19-926437-6, ISBN13: 978-0-19-926437-7. Dewey:401.9.
Audience: **u,f.**

Jackendoff, Ray **P151.J254 2002**
Foundations of Language: Brain, Meaning, Grammar, Evolution. Trade Cloth. Oxford University Press, Inc. New York, NY. 2002. 498p. ISBN:0-19-827012-7, ISBN13: 978-0-19-827012-6. Dewey:401.9. LCCN:2001-052066.
Audience: **u,f.**

Jakobson, Roman & Halle, Morris **P221 .J3**
Fundamentals of Language. Ed. 2. Trade Paper. Walter de Gruyter GmbH & Co. KG. Berlin, 2002. 96p. ISBN:3-11-017283-6, ISBN13: 978-3-11-017283-6. Dewey:414.
Audience: **l,u.**

Jakobson, Roman **P121**
On Language. Monique Monville-Burston & Linda R. Waugh (Editors). Trade Paper. Harvard University Press. Cambridge, MA. 1995. 672p. ISBN:0-674-63536-1, ISBN13: 978-0-674-63536-4. Dewey:410.
Audience: **u,f.** *Choice, 1991.*

Jakobson, Roman & Waugh, Linda R. **P217 .J33 2002**
The Sound Shape of Language. Ed. 2. Trade Paper. Walter de Gruyter GmbH & Co. KG. Berlin, 2002. xvi, 335p. ISBN:3-11-017285-2, ISBN13: 978-3-11-017285-0. Dewey:414.
Audience: **u.**

Jakobson, Roman **P121.J27 1990**
On Language. Linda R. Waugh & Monique Monville-Burston (Editors). Trade Cloth. Harvard University Press. Cambridge, MA. 1990. 668p. ISBN:0-674-63535-3, ISBN13: 978-0-674-63535-7. Dewey:410. LCCN:89-078478.
Audience: **l,u.** *Choice, 1991.*

Jameson, Fredric **PN98.S7**
The Prison-House of Language: A Critical Account of Structuralism and Russian Formalism. Trade Paper. Princeton University Press. Princeton, NJ. 1975. 232p. Essays in Literature Ser. ISBN:0-691-01316-0, ISBN13: 978-0-691-01316-9. Dewey:801.9/5. LCCN:78-173757.
Audience: **u,f.**

Janda, Richard D. **P120.S48H36 2003**
The Handbook of Historical Linguistics. Brian D. Joseph (Editor). Trade Cloth. Blackwell Publishing, Inc. Malden, MA. 2003. 904p. Handbooks in Linguistics, Vol. 13 ISBN:0-631-19571-8, ISBN13: 978-0-631-19571-9. Dewey:417/.7. LCCN:2002-074363.
Audience: **l,u,f.** *Choice, 2003.*

Jespersen, Otto **P151 .J47 1992**
The Philosophy of Grammar. James D. McCawley (Foreword by). Trade Paper. University of Chicago Press. Chicago, IL. 1992. 372p. ISBN:0-226-39881-1, ISBN13: 978-0-226-39881-5. Dewey:415. LCCN:92-019138.
Audience: **u,f.**

Kager, Reni **P158.42 .K35 1999**
Optimality Theory. S. R. Anderson, J. Bresnan, B. Comrie, W. Dressler & C. J. Ewen (Contribution by). Cloth Text. Cambridge University Press. New York, NY. 1999. 400p. Textbooks in Linguistics ISBN:0-521-58019-6, ISBN13: 978-0-521-58019-9. Dewey:410.1. LCCN:98-039103.
Audience: **u,f.**

Kayne, Richard S. & Zanuttini, Raffaella (Editors) **P291**
Syntactic Theory: The Essential Readings. Trade Paper. Blackwell Publishing Ltd. Oxford, 2005. 608p. Linguistics Ser., :The Essential Readings ISBN:0-631-23589-2, ISBN13: 978-0-631-23589-7. Dewey:415.
Audience: **u,f.**

Kenstowicz, Michael J. **P217.6.K46 1994**
Phonology in Generative Grammar. Trade Paper. Blackwell Publishing, Inc. Malden, MA. 1993. 720p. ISBN:1-55786-426-8, ISBN13: 978-1-55786-426-0. Dewey:414. LCCN:92-037749.
Audience: **u,f.**

Kouwenberg, Silvia & Singler, John Victor (Editors) **PM7802**
The Handbook of Pidgins and Creoles. Trade Paper. Blackwell Publishing Ltd. Oxford, 2006. 288p. Blackwell Handbooks in Linguistics Ser. ISBN:0-631-22902-7, ISBN13: 978-0-631-22902-5. Dewey:417.2/2.
Audience: **u,f.**

Labov, William **P142**
Internal Factors. Trade Paper. Blackwell Publishing, Inc. Malden, MA. 1994. 672p. ISBN:0-631-17914-3, ISBN13: 978-0-631-17914-6. Dewey:417/.7.
Audience: **u,f.**

Labov, William **P142**
Social Factors. Trade Paper. Blackwell Publishing, Inc. Malden, MA. 2001. 592p. Language in Society Ser., Vol. 29 ISBN:0-631-17916-X, ISBN13: 978-0-631-17916-0. Dewey:417.7.
Audience: **u,f.**

Ladefoged, Peter **P221.L2 2006**
Course in Phonetics. Ed. 5. Paper Text. Thomson Heinle. Boston, MA. 2005. 320p. ISBN:1-4130-0688-4, ISBN13: 978-1-4130-0688-9. Dewey:414. LCCN:2005-924138.
Audience: **l,u,f.**

Ladefoged, Peter **P221.L244 2004**
Vowels and Consonants: An Introduction to the Sounds of Languages. Ed. 2. Trade Cloth, CD-ROM. Blackwell Publishing, Inc. Malden, MA. 2005. 224p. ISBN:1-4051-2458-X, ISBN13: 978-1-4051-2458-4. Dewey:414.
Audience: **u,f.**

Ladefoged, Peter & Maddieson, Ian **P221.L24 1996**
The Sounds of the World's Languages. Trade Paper. Blackwell Publishing, Inc. Malden, MA. 1996. 448p. Phonological Theory Ser. ISBN:0-631-19815-6, ISBN13: 978-0-631-19815-4. Dewey:414. LCCN:94-049209.
Audience: **l,u,f.**

Lakoff, George & Johnson, Mark **P106.L235 2003**
Metaphors We Live By. Ed. 2. Trade Paper. University of Chicago Press. Chicago, IL. 1981. 256p. ISBN:0-226-46801-1, ISBN13: 978-0-226-46801-3. Dewey:401. LCCN:2003-044774.
Audience: **u,f.** B

Lakoff, Robin Tolmach **HQ1206.L36 2004**
Language and Woman's Place: Text and Commentaries. Ed. 2. Mary Bucholtz (Editor). Trade Paper. Oxford University Press, Inc. New York, NY. 2004. 328p. Studies in Language and Gender, Vol. 3 ISBN:0-19-516757-0, ISBN13: 978-0-19-516757-3. Dewey:305.4. LCCN:2003-056479.
Audience: **u,f.** *Choice, 2005.*

Lehmann, Winfred P. **P140 .L44 1992**
Historical Linguistics. Ed. 3. Trade Paper. Routledge. New York, NY. 1993. 360p. ISBN:0-415-07243-3, ISBN13: 978-0-415-07243-4. Dewey:417.7. LCCN:92-045655.
Audience: **u,f.**

Lieberman, Philip & Blumstein, Sheila E. **QP306 .L53 1988**
Speech Physiology, Speech Perception, and Acoustic Phonetics. Trade Paper. Cambridge University Press. New York, NY. 1988. 272p. Cambridge Studies in Speech Science and Communication ISBN:0-521-31357-0, ISBN13: 978-0-521-31357-5. Dewey:612/.78. LCCN:87-013187.
Audience: **u,f.**

Lightfoot, David **P142.L54 1998**
The Development of Language: Acquisition, Change and Evolution. Book, Other. Blackwell Publishing, Inc. Malden, MA. 1999. 304p. Blackwell/Maryland Lectures in Language and Cognition Ser., Vol. 1 ISBN:0-631-21059-8, ISBN13: 978-0-631-21059-7. Dewey:401/.93. LCCN:98-028674.
Audience: **l,u.**

Lyons, John **P121 .L924 1991**
Natural Language and Universal Grammar: Essays in Linguistic Theory. Trade Paper. Cambridge University Press. New York, NY. 2006. 306p. ISBN:0-521-02309-2, ISBN13: 978-0-521-02309-2. Dewey:410.
Audience: **u,f.**

Macaulay, Ronald K. **P106**
The Social Art: Language and Its Uses. Paper Text. Oxford University Press, Inc. New York, NY. 1996. 256p. ISBN:0-19-510657-1, ISBN13: 978-0-19-510657-2. Dewey:400.
Audience: **g,l,u.**

Malmkjaer, Kirsten (Editor) **P29.L52 2001**
The Linguistics Encyclopedia. Ed. 2. Trade Paper. Routledge. New York, NY. 2004. 688p. ISBN:0-415-22210-9, ISBN13: 978-0-415-22210-5. Dewey:410/.3. LCCN:2001-019240.
Audience: **l,u,f.** *Choice, 1992.*

Martinich, A. P. **P106.P455 2001**
The Philosophy of Language. Ed. 4. Paper Text. Oxford University Press, Inc. New York, NY. 2000. 608p. ISBN:0-19-513543-1, ISBN13: 978-0-19-513543-5. Dewey:401. LCCN:00-025522.
Audience: **l,u.**

Matthews, Peter H. **P146 .M36 2001**
A Short History of Structural Linguistics. Trade Cloth. Cambridge University Press. New York, NY. 2001. 174p. ISBN:0-521-62367-7, ISBN13: 978-0-521-62367-4. Dewey:410/.1/8. LCCN:00-045524.
Audience: **u.** *Choice, 2001.*

Matthews, Peter H. **P121.J27**
Grammatical Theory in the United States: From Bloomfield to Chomsky. S. R. Anderson, J. Bresnan, B. Comrie, W. Dressler, C. J. Ewen & R. Huddleston (Contribution by). Trade Paper. Cambridge University Press. New York, NY. 1993. 286p. Studies in Linguistics, Vol. 67 ISBN:0-521-45847-1, ISBN13: 978-0-521-45847-4. Dewey:410.973. LCCN:92-041067.
Audience: **u,f.**

McMahon, April M. S. **P142 .M38 1994**
Understanding Language Change. Trade Paper. Cambridge University Press. New York, NY. 1994. 373p. ISBN:0-521-44665-1, ISBN13: 978-0-521-44665-5. Dewey:417.7. LCCN:93-008121.
Audience: **l,u.**

Meyerhoff, Miriam **P120.S48H36 2005**
The Handbook of Language and Gender. Janet Holmes (Editor). Trade Paper, Perfect. Blackwell Publishing, Inc. Malden, MA. 2005. 776p. ISBN:0-631-22503-X, ISBN13: 978-0-631-22503-4. Dewey:306.44. LCCN:2002-006515.
Audience: **g,l,u,f.** *Choice, 2003.*

Napoli, Donna Jo **P107.N37 2003**
Language Matters: A Guide to Everyday Questions about Language. Trade Paper. Oxford University Press, Inc. New York, NY. 2003. 208p. ISBN:0-19-516048-7, ISBN13: 978-0-19-516048-2. Dewey:400. LCCN:2002-075810.
Audience: **g,l.**

Nettle, Daniel & Romaine, Suzanne **P40.5.L33N48 2000**
Vanishing Voices: The Extinction of the World's Languages. Trade Cloth. Oxford University Press, Inc. New York, NY. 2000. 254p. ISBN:0-19-513624-1, ISBN13: 978-0-19-513624-1. Dewey:417/.7. LCCN:99-016979.
Audience: **g,l,u.** *Choice, 2001.*

Newmeyer, Frederick J. **P158.N4 1986**
Linguistic Theory in America. Ed. 2. Trade Cloth. Elsevier Science & Technology Books. Saint Louis, MO. 1986. 320p. ISBN:0-12-517151-X, ISBN13: 978-0-12-517151-9. Dewey:415. LCCN:86-010802.
Audience: **u,f.**

Newmeyer, Frederick J. (Editor) **P121**
Linguistics: Linguistic Theory: Extensions and Implications. Trade Paper. Cambridge University Press. New York, NY. 1989. 328p. ISBN:0-521-37581-9, ISBN13: 978-0-521-37581-8. Dewey:410.
Audience: **l,u.**

Newmeyer, Frederick J. (Editor) **P121**
Linguistics: Linguistic Theory: Foundations. Trade Paper. Cambridge University Press. New York, NY. 1989. 512p. ISBN:0-521-37580-0, ISBN13: 978-0-521-37580-1. Dewey:410.
Audience: **l,u.**

Newmeyer, Frederick J. (Editor) **P121 .L567 1988, VO**
Linguistics: The Cambridge Survey: Language: Psychological and Biological Aspects. Trade Cloth. Cambridge University Press. New York, NY. 1988. 366p. ISBN:0-521-30835-6, ISBN13: 978-0-521-30835-9. Dewey:401/.9. LCCN:87-025671.
Audience: **l,u.** *Choice, 1989.*

Newmeyer, Frederick J. (Editor) **P121.L567**
Linguistics: The Cambridge Survey: Language: the Socio-Cultural Context. Trade Cloth. Cambridge University Press. New York, NY. 1988. 304p. ISBN:0-521-30834-8, ISBN13: 978-0-521-30834-2. Dewey:410 s. LCCN:87-023876.
Audience: **l,u.** *Choice, 1989.*

O'Grady, William, et al. **P121.O35 2005**
Contemporary Linguistics: An Introduction. Ed. 5. John Archibald, Mark Aronoff & Janie Rees-Miller (Authors). Trade Paper. Bedford/Saint Martin's. New York, NY. 2004. 720p. ISBN:0-312-41936-8, ISBN13: 978-0-312-41936-3. Dewey:410. LCCN:2004-108139.
Audience: **l,u.**

Ostler, Nicholas **P107.O88 2005**
Empires of the Word: A Language History of the World. Trade Cloth. HarperCollins Publishers. New York, NY. 2005. 640p. ISBN:0-06-621086-0, ISBN13: 978-0-06-621086-5. Dewey:409. LCCN:2005-046010.
Audience: **g,l,u.** *Choice, 2005.*

Ouaknin, Marc-Alain **P211.O913 1999**
Mysteries of the Alphabet. Trade Cloth. Abbeville Press, Inc. New York, NY. 1999. 384p. ISBN:0-7892-0521-1, ISBN13: 978-0-7892-0521-6. Dewey:411. LCCN:98-044840.
Audience: **g,l,u.** *Choice, 1999.*

Piattelli-Palmarini, Massimo (Editor) **BF318**
Language and Learning: The Debate Between Jean Piaget and Noam Chomsky. Trade Paper. Harvard University Press. Cambridge, MA. 1984. 445p. ISBN:0-674-50941-2, ISBN13: 978-0-674-50941-2. Dewey:153.1/5.
Audience: **u,f.**

Pike, Kenneth L. **P219**
Phonemics: A Technique for Reducing Language to Writing. Charles Fries (Foreword by). Paper Text. University of Michigan Press. Chicago, IL. 1947. 274p. ISBN:0-472-08732-0, ISBN13: 978-0-472-08732-7. Dewey:411.
Audience: **u.** B

Pike, Kenneth L. **P221**
Phonetics: A Critical Analysis of Phonetic Theory and a Technic for the Practical Description of Sounds. Charles Fries (Foreword by). Paper Text. University of Michigan Press. Chicago, IL. 1943. 192p. ISBN:0-472-08733-9, ISBN13: 978-0-472-08733-4. Dewey:414.
Audience: **u.**

Pinker, Steven **P106**
The Language Instinct: How the Mind Creates Language. Trade Paper. HarperCollins Publishers. New York, NY. 2000. 544p. Perennial Classics Ser. ISBN:0-06-095833-2, ISBN13: 978-0-06-095833-6. Dewey:400.
Audience: **g,l,u.**

Pullum, Geoffrey K. & Ladusaw, William A. **P226.P85 1996**
Phonetic Symbol Guide. Ed. 2. Trade Cloth. University of Chicago Press. Chicago, IL. 1996. 358p. ISBN:0-226-68535-7, ISBN13: 978-0-226-68535-9. Dewey:414. LCCN:95-042773.
Audience: **l,u,f.**

Roca, Iggy M. & Johnson, Wyn **P217.R58 1999**
A Course in Phonology. Trade Cloth. Blackwell Publishing, Inc. Malden, MA. 1999. 752p. ISBN:0-631-21345-7, ISBN13: 978-0-631-21345-1. Dewey:414. LCCN:98-051941.
Audience: **u.**

Sampson, Geoffrey **P211.S36 1985**
Writing Systems: A Linguistic Introduction. Trade Cloth. Stanford University Press. Palo Alto, CA. 1985. 235p. ISBN:0-8047-1254-9, ISBN13: 978-0-8047-1254-5. Dewey:411/.09. LCCN:84-040708.
Audience: **l,u.** *Choice, 1986.*

Saussure, Ferdinand de **P121**
Course in General Linguistics. Paper Text. Textbook Publishers. Temecula, CA. 2003. 240p. ISBN:0-7581-6433-5, ISBN13: 978-0-7581-6433-9. Dewey:410.
Audience: **g,l,u,f.**

Sealey, Alison & Carter, Bob **P129**
Applied Linguistics as Social Science. Trade Cloth. Continuum International Publishing Group, Ltd. London, 2004. 224p. Advances in Applied Linguistics Ser. ISBN:0-8264-5519-0, ISBN13: 978-0-8264-5519-2. Dewey:418. LCCN:2004-301173.
Audience: **l,u.** *Choice, 2005.*

Stock, Brian **D123**
The Implications of Literacy: Written Language and Models of Interpretation in the 11th and 12th Centuries. Trade Paper. Princeton University Press. Princeton, NJ. 1987. 610p. ISBN:0-691-10227-9, ISBN13: 978-0-691-10227-6. Dewey:940.1/4. LCCN:82-047616.
Audience: **l,u.** B

Strazny, Philipp **P29.E483 2005**
Encyclopedia of Linguistics. Trade Cloth. Fitzroy Dearborn Publishers, Inc. Chicago, IL. 2004. ISBN:1-57958-450-0, ISBN13: 978-1-57958-450-4. Dewey:410/.3. LCCN:2004-014173.
Audience: **l,u,f.** *Choice, 2005.*

Sturtevant, Edgar Howard **P121.S82**
Linguistic Change: An Introduction to the Historical Study of Language. Paper Text. Textbook Publishers. Temecula, CA. 2003. 185p. ISBN:0-7581-2595-X, ISBN13: 978-0-7581-2595-8. Dewey:409.
Audience: **u,f.** B

Trask, R. L. (Editor) **P143**
Dictionary of Historical and Comparative Linguistics. Trade Cloth. Fitzroy Dearborn Publishers, Inc. Chicago, IL. 2001. 500p. ISBN:1-57958-218-4, ISBN13: 978-1-57958-218-0. Dewey:417.703.
Audience: **l,u,f.** *Choice, 2001.*

Trask, R. L. **P140.T74 1996**
Historical Linguistics. Trade Paper. Oxford University Press, Inc. New York, NY. 1996. 448p. A Hodder Arnold Publication ISBN:0-340-60758-0, ISBN13: 978-0-340-60758-9. Dewey:417.7. LCCN:96-017311.
Audience: **u.**

Trask, R. L. **P29.T687 1998**
Key Concepts in Language and Linguistics. Paper over Boards. Routledge. New York, NY. 1998. 400p. Key Concepts Ser. ISBN:0-415-15741-2, ISBN13: 978-0-415-15741-4. Dewey:410/.3. LCCN:98-024025.
Audience: **l,u,f.** *Choice, 1999.*

Trudgill, Peter & Bauer, Laurie (Editors) **P106.L31755 1998**
Language Myths. Trade Paper. Penguin Group (USA) Inc. New York, NY. 1999. 208p. ISBN:0-14-026023-4, ISBN13: 978-0-14-026023-6. Dewey:400. LCCN:00-266856.
Audience: **g,l.**

Weinreich, Uriel **P325 .W42**
On Semantics. Beatrice S. Weinreich (Editor), William Labov (Introduction by). Trade Cloth. University of Pennsylvania Press. Philadelphia, PA. 1979. ISBN:0-8122-7759-7, ISBN13: 978-0-8122-7759-3. Dewey:415. LCCN:78-065114.
Audience: **u,f.**

Composition and Rhetoric

Barnett, Robert W. & Blumner, Jacob S. **PE1404.B29 2001**
The Allyn and Bacon Guide to Writing Center: Theory and Practice. Trade Paper. Longman Publishing. Boston, MA. 2000. 592p. ISBN:0-205-32186-0, ISBN13: 978-0-205-32186-5. Dewey:808/.042/071. LCCN:00-062067.
Audience: **u,f.**

Berman, Jeffrey **PE1404.B465 2001**
Risky Writing: Self-Disclosure and Self-Transformation in the Classroom. Lynda Martin (Afterword by). Cloth Text. University of Massachusetts Press. Amherst, MA. 2001. 312p. ISBN:1-55849-337-9, ISBN13: 978-1-55849-337-7. Dewey:808/.042/0711. LCCN:2001-005765.
Audience: **u,f.** *Choice, 2002.*

Bizzell, Patricia **PE1404**
Academic Discourse and Critical Consciousness. Trade Paper. University of Pittsburgh Press. Pittsburgh, PA. 1993. 304p. Pittsburgh Series in Composition, Literacy, and Culture ISBN:0-8229-5485-0, ISBN13: 978-0-8229-5485-9. Dewey:808/.042/07. LCCN:92-011967.
Audience: **u,f.** *Choice, 1993.*

Blair, Hugh **PE1402.B6 2002**
Lectures on Rhetoric and Belles Lettres. Linda Ferreira-Buckley & S. Michael Halloran (Editors), Linda Ferreira-Buckley & S. Michael Halloran (Introduction by). Trade Cloth. Southern Illinois University Press. Carbondale, IL. 2003. 624p. Landmarks in Rhetoric and Public Address Ser. ISBN:0-8093-1754-0, ISBN13: 978-0-8093-1754-7. Dewey:808/.042/09033. LCCN:2001-049506.
Audience: **l,u,f.**

Booth, Wayne, et al. **Q180.55.M4B66 2003**
The Craft of Research. Ed. 2. Gregory G. Colomb & Joseph M. Williams (Authors). Trade Cloth. University of Chicago Press. Chicago, IL. 2003. 344p. Chicago Guides to Writing, Editing, and Publishing Ser. ISBN:0-226-06567-7, ISBN13: 978-0-226-06567-0. Dewey:001.4/2. LCCN:2002-015184.
Audience: **g,l,u,f.** *Choice, 1996.*

Carroll, Lee Ann **PE1404.C346 2002**
Rehearsing New Roles: How College Students Develop As Writers. Trade Cloth. Southern Illinois University Press. Carbondale, IL. 2002. 160p. Studies in Writing and Rhetoric ISBN:0-8093-2449-0, ISBN13: 978-0-8093-2449-1. Dewey:808/.042/0711. LCCN:2002-018755.
Audience: **u,f.** *Choice, 2003.*

Elbow, Peter **PE1409.5.E5 1998**
Writing Without Teachers. Ed. 2. Trade Paper. Oxford University Press, Inc. New York, NY. 1998. 240p. ISBN:0-19-512016-7, ISBN13: 978-0-19-512016-5. Dewey:808/.042/077. LCCN:97-045577.
Audience: **u,f.**

Gibaldi, Joseph **LB2369.G53 2003**
MLA Handbook for Writers of Research Papers. Ed. 6. Trade Paper. Modern Language Association of America. New York, NY. 2003. 361p. ISBN:0-87352-986-3, ISBN13: 978-0-87352-986-0. Dewey:808/.027. LCCN:2002-156363.
Audience: **g,l,u,f.** B *Choice, 1995.*

Gilyard, Keith & Schuster, Charles (Editors) **PE1405.U6R38 1999**
Race, Rhetoric, and Composition. Trade Paper. Heinemann. Portsmouth, NH. 1999. 158p. Crosscurrents Ser. ISBN:0-86709-484-2, ISBN13: 978-0-86709-484-8. Dewey:808/.042/07. LCCN:98-050204.
Audience: **u,f.**

Inman, James A. **PE1404.I46 2003**
Computers and Writing: The Cyborg Era. Cloth over Boards. Lawrence Erlbaum Associates, Inc. Mahwah, NJ. 2004. 304p. ISBN:0-8058-4160-1, ISBN13: 978-0-8058-4160-2. Dewey:808/.042/0285. LCCN:2002-192536.
Audience: **u,f.** *Choice, 2004.*

Kane, Thomas S. **PE1408 .K2728**
The Oxford Guide to Writing. Nancy Sommers (Editor). Trade Paper. Oxford University Press, Inc. New York, NY. 1983. ISBN:0-19-503297-7, ISBN13: 978-0-19-503297-0. Dewey:808/.042.
Audience: **g,l,u,f.**

Kennedy, Mary L. (Editor) **PE1404**
Theorizing Composition: A Critical Sourcebook of Theory and Scholarship in Contemporary Composition Studies. Cloth Text. Greenwood Publishing Group, Inc. Portsmouth, NH. 1998. 424p. ISBN:0-313-29927-7, ISBN13: 978-0-313-29927-8. Dewey:808/.042/07. LCCN:97-032005.
Audience: **u,f.** *Choice, 1998.*

Lawson, Bruce (Editor), et al. **PE1404.E47 1989**
Encountering Student Texts: Interpretive Issues in Reading Student Writing. Susan Sterr Ryan & W. Ross Winterowd (Editors). Trade Cloth. National Council of Teachers of English. Urbana, IL. 1989. "xvii, 242"p. ISBN:0-8141-1340-0, ISBN13: 978-0-8141-1340-0. Dewey:808/.042/07 20. LCCN:89-049574.
Audience: **u,f.**

Lindemann, Erika C. **PE1404.L53 2001**
A Rhetoric for Writing Teachers. Ed. 4. Trade Paper. Oxford University Press, Inc. New York, NY. 2001. 361p. ISBN:0-19-513045-6, ISBN13: 978-0-19-513045-4. Dewey:808/.042/071173. LCCN:00-046515.
Audience: **u,f.**

Monroe, Jonathan (Editor) **PE1405.U6W73 2002**
Writing and Revising the Disciplines. Trade Paper. Cornell University Press. Ithaca, NY. 2002. 208p. ISBN:0-8014-8751-X, ISBN13: 978-0-8014-8751-4. Dewey:808/.042/0710747. LCCN:2001-003247.
Audience: **u,f.**

Murphy, James J. (Editor) **PN183**
A Short History of Writing Instruction: From Ancient Greece to Twentieth-Century America. Trade Cloth. Lawrence Erlbaum Associates, Inc. Mahwah, NJ. 1990. 241p. ISBN:0-9611800-7-2, ISBN13: 978-0-9611800-7-2. Dewey:808.
Audience: **u,f.** *Choice, 1991.*

Rose, Mike **LC4823**
Lives on the Boundary: A Moving Account of the Struggles and Achievements of America's Educationally Underprepared. Trade Paper. Penguin Group (USA) Inc. New York, NY. 2005. 288p. ISBN:0-14-303546-0, ISBN13: 978-0-14-303546-6. Dewey:371.96/7. LCCN:2006-276271.
Audience: **g,l,u.**

Shaughnessy, Mina P. **PE1404**
Errors and Expectations: A Guide for the Teacher of Basic Writing. Paper Text. Oxford University Press, Inc. New York, NY. 1979. 324p. ISBN:0-19-502507-5, ISBN13: 978-0-19-502507-1. Dewey:808/.042/0711.
Audience: **u,f.** B

Smith, Adam **PE1407.S47 1971**
Lectures on Rhetoric and Belles Lettres. John M. Lothian (Editor). Trade Cloth. Southern Illinois University Press. Carbondale, IL. 1971. 248p. Landmarks in Rhetoric and Public Address Ser. ISBN:0-8093-0502-X, ISBN13: 978-0-8093-0502-5. Dewey:808. LCCN:72-145447.
Audience: **g,l,u,f.** B

Smitherman, Geneva & Villanueva, Victor (Editors) **PE1405.U6L36 2003**
Language Diversity in the Classroom: From Intention to Practice. Trade Cloth. Southern Illinois University Press. Carbondale, IL. 2003. 176p. Studies in Writing and Rhetoric Ser. ISBN:0-8093-2532-2, ISBN13: 978-0-8093-2532-0. Dewey:808/.042/071173. LCCN:2002-155100.
Audience: **u,f.**

Strunk, William Jr. & White, E. B. **PE1408.S772 1999**
The Elements of Style. Ed. 4. Trade Cloth. Longman Publishing Group. White Plains, NY. 1999. 85p. ISBN:0-205-31342-6, ISBN13: 978-0-205-31342-6. Dewey:808/.042. LCCN:99-016419.
Audience: **g,l,u,f.** B

Villanueva, Victor (Editor) **PE1404.C755 2003**
Cross-Talk in Comp Theory: A Reader. Ed. 2. Trade Paper. National Council of Teachers of English. Urbana, IL. 2003. 883p. ISBN:0-8141-0976-4, ISBN13: 978-0-8141-0976-2. Dewey:808/.042/071. LCCN:2002-156573.
Audience: **u,f.**

Williams, Joseph M. **PE1421.W5455 2005**
Style: The Basics of Clarity and Grace. Ed. 2. Trade Paper. Longman Publishing. Boston, MA. 2005. 160p. ISBN:0-321-33085-4, ISBN13: 978-0-321-33085-7. Dewey:808/.042. LCCN:2005-000458.
Audience: **g,l,u,f.**

Wolff, Janice M. (Editor) **PE1404.P658 2002**
Professing in the Contact Zone: Bringing Theory and Practice Together. Trade Paper. National Council of Teachers of English. Urbana, IL. 2002. xx, 312p. ISBN:0-8141-3740-7, ISBN13: 978-0-8141-3740-6. Dewey:808/.042/0711. LCCN:2001-054671.
Audience: **u,f.**

Study, Teaching, Literary Research

Z7006 .M64
MLA International Bibliography of Books and Articles on the Modern Languages and Literatures, Set. Trade Cloth. Modern Language Association of America. New York, NY. 2003. 1,000p. ISBN:0-87352-870-0, ISBN13: 978-0-87352-870-2. Dewey:016.8.
Audience: **g,l,u,f.**

Bloom, Harold **PN83.B57 2001**
How to Read and Why. Trade Paper. Simon & Schuster. New York, NY. 2001. 288p. ISBN:0-684-85907-6, ISBN13: 978-0-684-85907-1. Dewey:801/.9. LCCN:2001-049374.
Audience: **g,l,u.** *Choice, 2000.*

Booth, Wayne **PE68.U5**
The Vocation of a Teacher: Rhetorical Occasions, 1967-1988. Trade Paper. University of Chicago Press. Chicago, IL. 1991. 372p. ISBN:0-226-06582-0, ISBN13: 978-0-226-06582-3. Dewey:428/.007/1173. LCCN:88-014297.
Audience: **g,l,u,f.**

Booth, Wayne, et al. **Q180.55.M4B66 2003**
The Craft of Research. Ed. 2. Gregory G. Colomb & Joseph M. Williams (Authors). Trade Cloth. University of Chicago Press. Chicago, IL. 2003. 344p. Chicago Guides to Writing, Editing, and Publishing Ser. ISBN:0-226-06567-7, ISBN13: 978-0-226-06567-0. Dewey:001.4/2. LCCN:2002-015184.
Audience: **g,l,u,f.** *Choice, 1996.*

Elbow, Peter (Editor) **PE1408**
Landmark Essays on Voice and Writing. Trade Paper. Lawrence Erlbaum Associates, Inc. Mahwah, NJ. 1994. 272p. Landmark Essays Ser., Vol. 4 ISBN:1-880393-07-7, ISBN13: 978-1-880393-07-9. Dewey:808.042.
Audience: **g,u,f.**

Gibaldi, Joseph **LB2369 .G53 2003B**
MLA Handbook for Writers of Research Papers. Ed. 6. Trade Paper. Modern Language Association of America. New York, NY. 2006. xvii & 361p. ISBN:0-87352-987-1, ISBN13: 978-0-87352-987-7. Dewey:808/.027. LCCN:2003-001971.
Audience: **g,l,u,f.** B *Choice, 1995.*

Harner, James L. **Z2011.H34 2002**
Literary Research Guide: An Annotated Listing of Reference Sources in English Literary Studies. Ed. 4. Trade Cloth. Modern Language Association of America. New York, NY. 2002. x & 820p. ISBN:0-87352-982-0, ISBN13: 978-0-87352-982-2. Dewey:016.8209. LCCN:2001-059649.
Audience: **g,l,u,f.** *Choice, 2003, 1999.*

New York Times Staff **PN137.W734 2001**
Writers on Writing: Collected Essays from the New York Times. John Darnton (Editor). Cloth over Boards. Henry Holt & Company. New York, NY. 2001. 256p. ISBN:0-8050-6741-8, ISBN13: 978-0-8050-6741-5. Dewey:808/.02. LCCN:00-053509.
Audience: **g,l,u,f.**

Showalter, Elaine **PN59.S49 2003**
Teaching Literature. Trade Paper. Blackwell Publishing, Inc. Malden, MA. 2002. 176p. ISBN:0-631-22624-9, ISBN13: 978-0-631-22624-6. Dewey:807/.1/1. LCCN:2002-006133.
Audience: **g,l,u,f.** *Choice, 2003.*

Yancey, Kathleen Blake **PE68.U5Y36 2004**
Teaching Literature As Reflective Practice. Trade Cloth. National Council of Teachers of English. Urbana, IL. 2004. x, 123p. ISBN:0-8141-5116-7, ISBN13: 978-0-8141-5116-7. Dewey:807/.1/173. LCCN:2004-006586.
Audience: **g,u,f.**

Theory, Philosophy, Aesthetics

Adams, Hazard & Searle, Leroy (Editors) **PN94.C75 1986**
Critical Theory since 1965. Trade Paper. University Press of Florida. Gainesville, FL. 1986. 904p. ISBN:0-8130-0844-1, ISBN13: 978-0-8130-0844-8. Dewey:801/.95. LCCN:86-013216.
Audience: **g,u,f.**

Adams, Hazard & Searle, Leroy **PN49.C683 2005**
Critical Theory since Plato. Ed. 3. Hazard Adams & Leroy Searle (Editors). Cloth Text. Thomson Heinle. Boston, MA. 2004. 1568p. ISBN:0-15-505504-6, ISBN13: 978-0-15-505504-9. Dewey:801/.95. LCCN:2004-101932.
Audience: **g,u,f.** B

Aristotle **PA3621.A75 1995**
Poetics, On the Sublime, and On Style. Ed. 2. W. Hamilton Fyfe, Stephen Halliwell & Doreen C. Innes (Editors), W. Hamilton Fyfe, Stephen Halliwell, Doreen C. Innes & W. Rhys Roberts (Translators), Donald Russell (Revised by). Trade Cloth. Harvard University Press. Cambridge, MA. 1995. 544p. Loeb Classical Library, No. 199 ISBN:0-674-99563-5, ISBN13: 978-0-674-99563-5. Dewey:808.2. LCCN:94-005113.
Audience: **g,l,u,f.**

Bloom, Harold, et al. **PN94.D4 2004**
Deconstruction and Criticism. Paul De Man & Jacques Derrida (Authors). Trade Paper. Continuum International Publishing Group, Ltd. London, 2004. 224p. ISBN:0-8264-7692-9, ISBN13: 978-0-8264-7692-0. Dewey:801/.95/0904. LCCN:2005-272208.
Audience: **u,f.**

Bourdieu, Pierre **PN45**
The Rules of Art: Genesis and Structure of the Literary Field. Susan Emanuel (Translator). Trade Cloth. Stanford University Press. Palo Alto, CA. 1995. 288p. Meridian: Crossing Aesthetics Ser. ISBN:0-8047-2568-3, ISBN13: 978-0-8047-2568-2. Dewey:801. LCCN:94-074140.
Audience: **u,f.**

Croce, Benedetto **B3614.C73B7413 1995**
Guide to Aesthetics. Ed. 2. Patrick Romanell (Translator). Trade Cloth. Hackett Publishing Company, Inc. Indianapolis, IN. 1995. 128p. HPC Classics Ser. ISBN:0-87220-305-0, ISBN13: 978-0-87220-305-1. Dewey:111/.85. LCCN:94-043408.
Audience: **g,u,f.**

Culler, Jonathan **PN81.C857 2000**
Literary Theory: A Very Short Introduction. Trade Paper. Oxford University Press, Inc. New York, NY. 2000. 152p. Very Short Introductions Ser. ISBN:0-19-285383-X, ISBN13: 978-0-19-285383-7. Dewey:801.9/5. LCCN:97-017713.
Audience: **g,l,u.**

Derrida, Jacques **P105.D5313 1998**
Of Grammatology. Gayatri Chakravorty Spivak (Translator). Trade Paper. Johns Hopkins University Press. Baltimore, MD. 1998. 456p. ISBN:0-8018-5830-5, ISBN13: 978-0-8018-5830-7. Dewey:401. LCCN:76-017226.
Audience: **u,f.**

Eagleton, Terry **PN94.E2 1996**
Literary Theory: An Introduction. Ed. 2. Paper Text. University of Minnesota Press. Minneapolis, MN. 1996. 288p. ISBN:0-8166-1251-X, ISBN13: 978-0-8166-1251-2. Dewey:801. LCCN:97-125828.
Audience: **l,u.**

Felluga, Dino **PN86**
Introductory Guide to Critical Theory.
http://www.cla.purdue.edu/academic/engl/theory/
Audience: **l,u.**

Hartman, Geoffrey H. **PN81**
Saving the Text: Literature-Derrida-Philosophy. Trade Paper. Johns Hopkins University Press. Baltimore, MD. 1988. 216p. ISBN:0-8018-2453-2, ISBN13: 978-0-8018-2453-1. Dewey:801/.95. LCCN:80-021748.
Audience: **u,f.**

Iser, Wolfgang **PN81**
The Act of Reading: A Theory of Aesthetic Response. Trade Paper. Johns Hopkins University Press. Baltimore, MD. 1969. 224p. ISBN:0-8018-2371-4, ISBN13: 978-0-8018-2371-8. Dewey:801.9/5. LCCN:78-058296.
Audience: **u,f.**

Iser, Wolfgang **PN49.I77 2006**
How to Do Theory. Trade Paper. Blackwell Publishing, Inc. Malden, MA. 2005. 224p. How to Study Literature Ser. ISBN:1-4051-1580-7, ISBN13: 978-1-4051-1580-3. Dewey:801/.95. LCCN:2005-004140.
Audience: **g,u,f.** *Choice, 2006.*

Leitch, Vincent B. **PN81**
The Norton Anthology of Theory and Criticism. Cloth Text. W. W. Norton & Company, Inc. New York, NY. 2001. ISBN:0-393-94543-X, ISBN13: 978-0-393-94543-0. Dewey:801/.95.
Audience: **g,u,f.** *Choice, 2002.*

Lodge, David & Wood, Nigel **PN94.M57 1999**
Modern Criticism and Theory: A Reader. Ed. 2. Trade Paper. Longman Publishing. Boston, MA. 1999. 552p. ISBN:0-582-31287-6, ISBN13: 978-0-582-31287-6. Dewey:801/.95/0904. LCCN:99-021398.
Audience: **g,u,f.**

McGann, Jerome J. **PN98.E4M39 2001**
Radiant Textuality: Literature after the World Wide Web. Cloth over Boards. Palgrave Macmillan. New York, NY. 2001. 288p. ISBN:0-312-29352-6, ISBN13: 978-0-312-29352-9. Dewey:801/.959/0285. LCCN:2001-021795.
Audience: **u,f.** *Choice, 2002.*

Scholes, Robert **PN98.S7**
Structuralism in Literature: An Introduction. Trade Paper. Yale University Press. Cumberland, RI. 1975. 230p. ISBN:0-300-01850-9, ISBN13: 978-0-300-01850-9. Dewey:801.9/5. LCCN:73-090578.
Audience: **g,l,u,f.**

Silverman, Kaja **P99.S52 1983**
The Subject of Semiotics. Paper Text. Oxford University Press, Inc. New York, NY. 1984. 316p. ISBN:0-19-503178-4, ISBN13: 978-0-19-503178-2. Dewey:001.51.
Audience: **u,f.**

Sontag, Susan **PS3569.O6547 A6**
A Susan Sontag Reader. Elizabeth Hardwick (Introduction by). Trade Cloth. Farrar, Straus & Giroux. New York, NY. 1982. 446p. ISBN:0-374-27216-6, ISBN13: 978-0-374-27216-6. Dewey:818/.5409.
Audience: **u,f.**

Sturrock, John **B841.4.S927 2003**
Structuralism. Ed. 2. Trade Paper. Blackwell Publishing, Inc. Malden, MA. 2002. 176p. ISBN:0-631-23239-7, ISBN13: 978-0-631-23239-1. Dewey:149/.96. LCCN:2002-028112.
Audience: **u,f.**

Wellek, Rene & Warren, Austin **PN45 .W36**
Theory of Literature. Trade Paper. Harcourt Trade Publishers. New York, NY. 1964. 384p. ISBN:0-15-689084-4, ISBN13: 978-0-15-689084-7. Dewey:801.
Audience: **g,l,u,f.**

Criticism

Abrams, M. H. **PN751 .A2 1971**
The Mirror and the Lamp: Romantic Theory and the Critical Tradition. Paper Text. Oxford University Press, Inc. New York, NY. 1971. 406p. ISBN:0-19-501471-5, ISBN13: 978-0-19-501471-6. Dewey:801.950941.
Audience: **u,f.**

Abrams, M. H. **PN603 .A3 1973**
Natural Supernaturalism: Tradition and Revolution in Romantic Literature. Trade Paper. W. W. Norton & Company, Inc. New York, NY. 1973. 550p. ISBN:0-393-00609-3, ISBN13: 978-0-393-00609-4. Dewey:809/.9/14. LCCN:73-007855.
Audience: **u,f.**

Benstock, Shari, et al. **PR111.H36 2002**
A Handbook of Literary Feminisms. Suzanne Ferriss & Susanne Woods (Authors), Shari Benstock, Suzanne Ferriss & Susanne Woods (Editors). Paper Text. Oxford University Press, Inc. New York, NY. 2002. 304p. ISBN:0-19-510206-1, ISBN13: 978-0-19-510206-2. Dewey:820.9/9287. LCCN:2001-036415.
Audience: **g,l,u,f.**

Bogan, Louise **PN511**
Selected Criticism: Prose, Poetry. Paper Text. Textbook Publishers. Temecula, CA. 2003. 404p. ISBN:0-7581-7612-0, ISBN13: 978-0-7581-7612-7. Dewey:809.
Audience: **u,f.**

Booth, Wayne **PN98.M67B66 1988**
The Company We Keep: An Ethics of Fiction. Trade Paper. University of California Press. Berkeley, CA. 1989. 580p. ISBN:0-520-06210-8, ISBN13: 978-0-520-06210-8. Dewey:174/.98. LCCN:87-024610.
Audience: **g,l,u,f.** *Choice, 1989.*

Brooks, Cleanth **PR503**
The Well Wrought Urn: Studies in the Structure of Poetry. Trade Paper. Harcourt Trade Publishers. New York, NY. 1956. 324p. Harvest Book Ser. ISBN:0-15-695705-1, ISBN13: 978-0-15-695705-2. Dewey:821/.009. LCCN:47-003143.
Audience: **g,l,u,f.** B

Burke, Kenneth **PN511.B917**
Counter-Statement. Trade Cloth. University of California Press. Berkeley, CA. 1968. 244p. ISBN:0-520-00196-6, ISBN13: 978-0-520-00196-1. Dewey:804. LCCN:68-020356.
Audience: **u,f.** B

Damrosch, David **PN523.D36 2003**
What Is World Literature? Trade Cloth. Princeton University Press. Princeton, NJ. 2003. 336p. Translation/Transnation Ser. ISBN:0-691-04985-8, ISBN13: 978-0-691-04985-4. Dewey:809. LCCN:2002-029272.
Audience: **l,u,f.**

Eberle-Sinatra, Michael (Editor) **PN603**
☐ Romanticism on the Net.
http://www.ron.umontreal.ca/
Audience: **u,f.**

Eco, Umberto **PN85.E4313 2004**
On Literature. Martin McLaughlin (Translator). Cloth over Boards. Harcourt Trade Publishers. New York, NY. 2004. 352p. ISBN:0-15-100812-4, ISBN13: 978-0-15-100812-4. Dewey:809. LCCN:2004-010664.
Audience: **g,l,u,f.**

Empson, William **PN81**
Seven Types of Ambiguity. Trade Paper. New Directions Publishing Corporation. New York, NY. 1966. ISBN:0-8112-0037-X, ISBN13: 978-0-8112-0037-0. Dewey:801.9/5. LCCN:48-000078.
Audience: **g,l,u,f.** B

Fish, Stanley Eugene **PN45 .W36**
Is There a Text in This Class?: The Authority of Interpretive Communities. Trade Paper. Harvard University Press. Cambridge, MA. 1980. 408p. ISBN:0-674-46726-4, ISBN13: 978-0-674-46726-2. Dewey:801.
Audience: **g,u,f.** B

Frye, Northrop **PN81**
Anatomy of Criticism: Four Essays. Harold Bloom (Foreword by). Trade Paper. Princeton University Press. Princeton, NJ. 2000. 400p. ISBN:0-691-06999-9, ISBN13: 978-0-691-06999-9. Dewey:801.95. LCCN:56-008380.
Audience: **g,l,u,f.** B

Gallop, Jane **PN98.W64G33 2002**
Anecdotal Theory. Trade Cloth. Duke University Press. Durham, NC. 2002. 176p. ISBN:0-8223-3001-6, ISBN13: 978-0-8223-3001-1. Dewey:801/.95/09048. LCCN:2002-003918.
Audience: **u,f.** *Choice, 2003.*

Gramsci, Antonio **DG575.G69A25**
Selections from Cultural Writings. Geoffrey Nowell-Smith (Editor), William Boelhower (Translator), David Forgacs (Introduction by). Trade Paper. Harvard University Press. Cambridge, MA. 1991. 464p. ISBN:0-674-79986-0, ISBN13: 978-0-674-79986-8. Dewey:945.
Audience: **g,u,f.**

Hartman, Geoffrey H. & O'Hara, Daniel T. **PN75.H33A25 2004**
The Geoffrey Hartman Reader. Trade Cloth. Fordham University Press. Bronx, NY. 2004. 495p. ISBN:0-8232-2443-0, ISBN13: 978-0-8232-2443-2. Dewey:801/.95/0904. LCCN:2004-018940.
Audience: **u,f.**

Heath, Duncan, et al. **B836.5**
Introducing Romanticism. Judy Boreham & Richard Appignanesi (Authors). Trade Paper. Totem Books. Cambridge, 2006. 176p. ISBN:1-84046-671-5, ISBN13: 978-1-84046-671-3. Dewey:141.6.
Audience: **g,l,u,f.**

Jameson, Fredric **PN81 .J29**
The Political Unconscious: Narrative As a Socially Symbolic Act. Trade Paper. Cornell University Press. Ithaca, NY. 1982. 320p. ISBN:0-8014-9222-X, ISBN13: 978-0-8014-9222-8. Dewey:801/.95. LCCN:80-021459.
Audience: **u,f.**

Kaplan, Charles & Anderson, William (Editors) **PN81 .C85 1991**
Criticism: Major Statements. Ed. 3. Paper Text. St. Martin's Press. Gordonville, VA. 1991. 865p. ISBN:0-312-03502-0, ISBN13: 978-0-312-03502-0. Dewey:801/.95. LCCN:89-063905.
Audience: **g,l,u,f.**

Kermode, Frank **PN45.K44 2000**
The Sense of an Ending: Studies in the Theory of Fiction. Ed. 2. Trade Paper. Oxford University Press, Inc. New York, NY. 2000. 218p. ISBN:0-19-513612-8, ISBN13: 978-0-19-513612-8. Dewey:801. LCCN:99-043613.
Audience: **g,l,u,f.** B

Leavis, Frank R. (Editor) **PN94 .L37**
Towards Standards of Criticism: Selections from the Calendar of Modern Letters, 1925-1927. Trade Cloth. Johnson Reprint Corporation. New York, NY. 1969. Belles Letters in English Ser. ISBN:0-384-31925-4, ISBN13: 978-0-384-31925-7. Dewey:801/.95.
Audience: **g,l,u,f.**

Leitch, Vincent B. **PN81**
The Norton Anthology of Theory and Criticism. Cloth Text. W. W. Norton & Company, Inc. New York, NY. 2001. ISBN:0-393-94543-X, ISBN13: 978-0-393-94543-0. Dewey:801/.95.
Audience: **g,u,f.** *Choice, 2002.*

Lodge, David & Wood, Nigel **PN94.M57 1999**
Modern Criticism and Theory: A Reader. Ed. 2. Trade Paper. Longman Publishing. Boston, MA. 1999. 552p. ISBN:0-582-31287-6, ISBN13: 978-0-582-31287-6. Dewey:801/.95/0904. LCCN:99-021398.
Audience: **g,u,f.**

Marx, Karl & Engels, Friedrich **BH41**
Karl Marx and Friedrich Engels on Literature and Art: A Selection of Writings. Lee Baxandall (Editor), Stefan Morawski (Introduction by). Trade Cloth. International General. Amsterdam, 1974. 179p. Documents on Marxist Aesthetics Ser., Vol.I ISBN:0-88477-000-1, ISBN13: 978-0-88477-000-8. Dewey:700/.1.
Audience: **g,l,u,f.**

McGann, Jerome J. **P47**
A Critique of Modern Textual Criticism. David C. Greetham (Foreword by). Paper Text. University Press of Virginia. Charlottesville, VA. 1992. 160p. ISBN:0-8139-1418-3, ISBN13: 978-0-8139-1418-3. Dewey:801/.959. LCCN:92-014702.
Audience: **u,f.**

Mohl, Ruth **E210.A15**
The Three Estates in Medieval and Renaissance Literature. Paper Text. Textbook Publishers. Temecula, CA. 2003. xi, 425p. ISBN:0-7581-2939-4, ISBN13: 978-0-7581-2939-0. Dewey:973.311.
Audience: **u,f.**

Pound, Ezra **PN511.P63**
Make It New: Essays. Library Binding. Reprint Services Company. Temecula, CA. 1988. ISBN:0-7812-0195-0, ISBN13: 978-0-7812-0195-7. Dewey:809.
Audience: **g,l,u,f.**

Quiller-Couch, Arthur Thomas **PR99.Q5**
Adventures in Criticism. Trade Cloth. Scholarly Press, Inc. Saint Clair Shores, MI. 1969. ISBN:0-403-00064-5, ISBN13: 978-0-403-00064-7. Dewey:820.9. LCCN:12-037963.
Audience: **l,u,f.**

Rahv, Philip **PN761 .R25 1978**
Image and Idea: Fourteen Essays on Literary Themes. Trade Cloth. Greenwood Publishing Group, Inc. Portsmouth, NH. 1978. 164p. ISBN:0-313-20082-3, ISBN13: 978-0-313-20082-3. Dewey:809. LCCN:77-026061.
Audience: **u,f.**

Richards, I. A. **PN81**
Principles of Literary Criticism. Ed. 2. Trade Paper. Routledge. New York, NY. 2001. 296p. Classics Ser. ISBN:0-415-25402-7, ISBN13: 978-0-415-25402-1. Dewey:801.9/5.
Audience: **g,l,u,f.**

Roe, Nicholas **PR457.R4575 2005**
Romanticism: An Oxford Guide. Paper Text. Oxford University Press, Inc. New York, NY. 2005. 776p. ISBN:0-19-925840-6, ISBN13: 978-0-19-925840-6. Dewey:820.9/145. LCCN:2004-025235.
Audience: **g,l,u,f.**

Rollyson, Carl & Magill, Frank N. (Editors) **PN3451.C75 2000**
Critical Survey of Long Fiction. Ed. 2. Trade Cloth. Salem Press. Mississauga, ON. 2000. ;p. ISBN:0-89356-883-X, ISBN13: 978-0-89356-883-2. Dewey:809.3. LCCN:00-020195.
Audience: **g,l,u.** *Choice, 2001.*

Rushdie, Salman **PR6068.U757 I4 1991B**
Imaginary Homelands: Essays and Criticism 1981-1991. Trade Cloth. Penguin Group (USA) Inc. New York, NY. 1991. 432p. ISBN:0-14-014224-X, ISBN13: 978-0-14-014224-2. Dewey:828. LCCN:92-188054.
Audience: **l,u,f.** *Choice, 1991.*

Sontag, Susan **PN771**
Against Interpretation: And Other Essays. Trade Paper. Picador. New York, NY. 2001. 336p. ISBN:0-312-28086-6, ISBN13: 978-0-312-28086-4. Dewey:809/.04.
Audience: **u,f.**

Steiner, George **BD638**
Grammars of Creation: Originating in the Gifford Lectures of 1990. Trade Paper. Yale University Press. Cumberland, RI. 2002. 350p. ISBN:0-300-09729-8, ISBN13: 978-0-300-09729-0. Dewey:116.
Audience: **u,f.** *Choice, 2001.*

Stevens, David **PR468.R65**
Romanticism. Adrian Barlow (Contribution by). Trade Paper. Cambridge University Press. New York, NY. 2004. 128p. Cambridge Contexts in Literature Ser. ISBN:0-521-75372-4, ISBN13: 978-0-521-75372-2. Dewey:820.9/007.
Audience: **g,l.**

Trilling, Lionel **PN511**
The Opposing Self: Nine Essays in Criticism. Paper Text. Textbook Publishers. Temecula, CA. 2003. 232p. ISBN:0-7581-0894-X, ISBN13: 978-0-7581-0894-4. Dewey:820.9.
Audience: **g,l,u,f.**

Trilling, Lionel **PS3525.I5156**
The Moral Obligation to Be Intelligent: Selected Essays. Leon Wieseltier (Editor). Trade Paper. Farrar, Straus & Giroux. New York, NY. 2001. 592p. ISBN:0-374-52799-7, ISBN13: 978-0-374-52799-0. Dewey:812/.52.
Audience: **g,l,u,f.** *Choice, 2001.*

Warhol, Robyn R. & Herndl, Diane P. (Editors) **PN98.W64F366 1997**
Feminisms: An Anthology of Literary Theory and Criticism. Ed. 2. Trade Cloth. Rutgers University Press. Piscataway, NJ. 1997. 1,150p. ISBN:0-8135-2389-3, ISBN13: 978-0-8135-2389-7. Dewey:809.8/9/287. LCCN:96-031072.
Audience: **u,f.** *Choice, 1998.*

Warren, Austin **PN0511.W32**
Rage for Order: Essays in Criticism. Trade Paper. Books on Demand. Ann Arbor, MI. 164p. Ann Arbor Paperback Ser. ISBN:0-598-05480-4, ISBN13: 978-0-598-05480-7. Dewey:820.4.
Audience: **u,f.**

Watkins, Susan **PR888.F45W38 2001**
Twentieth-Century Women Novelists: Feminist Theory into Practice. Cloth over Boards. Palgrave Macmillan. New York, NY. 2001. 240p. ISBN:0-333-68345-5, ISBN13: 978-0-333-68345-3. Dewey:823/.91099287. LCCN:00-055676.
Audience: **u,f.**

Wilson, Edmund **PN771.W55 2004**
Axel's Castle: A Study of the Imaginative Literature of 1870-1930. Mary Gordon (Introduction by). Trade Paper. Farrar, Straus & Giroux. New York, NY. 2004. 272p. ISBN:0-374-52927-2, ISBN13: 978-0-374-52927-7. Dewey:809/.915. LCCN:2004-047062.
Audience: **u,f.**

Woolf, Virginia **PR6045.O72Z474 1991**
A Room of One's Own. Cloth over Boards. Harcourt Trade Publishers. New York, NY. 1991. 132p. HBJ Book Ser. ISBN:0-15-178733-6, ISBN13: 978-0-15-178733-3. Dewey:823/.912. LCCN:91-017953.
Audience: **g,l,u,f.**

Criticism > Special Approaches, Methods

Bakhtin, Mikhail M. **P47**
The Dialogic Imagination: Four Essays. Michael Holquist & Vadim Liapunov (Editors), Michael Holquist, Caryl Emerson, Kenneth Brostrom & Vadim Liapunov (Translators). Trade Paper. University of Texas Press. Austin, TX. 1982. 444p. Slavic Ser., No. 1 ISBN:0-292-71534-X, ISBN13: 978-0-292-71534-9. Dewey:801.9/59. LCCN:80-015450.
Audience: **g,u,f.**

Berman, Emanuel (Editor) **PN56.P92E87 1993**
Essential Papers on Literature and Psychoanalysis. Trade Paper. New York University Press. New York, NY. 1993. 504p. Essential Papers in Psychoanalysis ISBN:0-8147-1185-5, ISBN13: 978-0-8147-1185-9. Dewey:801.92. LCCN:92-028361.
Audience: **g,u,f.**

Blonsky, Marshall (Editor) **P99.O5 1985**
On Signs. Trade Paper. Johns Hopkins University Press. Baltimore, MD. 1985. 592p. ISBN:0-8018-3007-9, ISBN13: 978-0-8018-3007-5. Dewey:001.51. LCCN:84-047952.
Audience: **g,l,u,f.** *Choice, 1986.*

Bloom, Harold, et al. **PN94.D4 2004**
Deconstruction and Criticism. Paul De Man & Jacques Derrida (Authors). Trade Paper. Continuum International Publishing Group, Ltd. London, 2004. 224p. ISBN:0-8264-7692-9, ISBN13: 978-0-8264-7692-0. Dewey:801/.95/0904. LCCN:2005-272208.
Audience: **u,f.**

Brannigan, John **PN81.B663 1998**
New Historicism and Cultural Materialism. Cloth over Boards. Palgrave Macmillan. New York, NY. 1998. 272p. Transitions Ser. ISBN:0-312-21388-3, ISBN13: 978-0-312-21388-6. Dewey:801.9/5. LCCN:97-052610.
Audience: **u,f.** *Choice, 1998.*

Brooks, Peter **PN3378.B76 1992**
Reading for the Plot: Design and Intention in Narrative. Trade Paper. Harvard University Press. Cambridge, MA. 1992. 392p. ISBN:0-674-74892-1, ISBN13: 978-0-674-74892-7. Dewey:809.3/923. LCCN:91-031007.
Audience: **u,f.**

Culler, Jonathan **P85.B33C83 2002**
Barthes: A Very Short Introduction. Ed. 2. Trade Paper. Oxford University Press, Inc. New York, NY. 2002. 156p. Very Short Introductions Ser. ISBN:0-19-280159-7, ISBN13: 978-0-19-280159-3. Dewey:410/.92 B. LCCN:2002-514397.
Audience: **l,u.**

Culler, Jonathan **PN98.D43.C8 1982**
On Deconstruction: Theory and Criticism after Structuralism. Trade Cloth. Cornell University Press. Ithaca, NY. 1982. 312p. ISBN:0-8014-1322-2, ISBN13: 978-0-8014-1322-3. Dewey:801/.95. LCCN:82-007414.
Audience: **u,f.**

Culler, Jonathan **PN98.S7C8 2002**
Structuralist Poetics: Structuralism, Linguistics and the Study of Literature. Ed. 2. Paper over Boards. Routledge. New York, NY. 2002. 368p. Classics Ser. ISBN:0-415-28988-2, ISBN13: 978-0-415-28988-7. Dewey:801.95. LCCN:2002-031677.
Audience: **u,f.**

de Berg, Henk **PN56.P92**
Freud's Theory and Its Use in Literary and Cultural Studies: An Introduction. Trade Paper. Camden House. Elizabethtown, NY. 2004. 176p. Studies in German Literature, Linguistics, and Culture Ser. ISBN:1-57113-301-1, ISBN13: 978-1-57113-301-4. Dewey:809/.93353.
Audience: **u,f.** *Choice, 2003.*

De Man, Paul **PN85 .D37 1983**
Blindness and Insight: Essays in the Rhetoric of Contemporary Criticism. Ed. 2. Wlad Godzich (Introduction by). Trade Paper. University of Minnesota Press. Minneapolis, MN. 1983. 309p. Theory and History of Literature Ser., Vol. 7 ISBN:0-8166-1135-1, ISBN13: 978-0-8166-1135-5. Dewey:801/.95. LCCN:83-001379.
Audience: **u,f.**

Derrida, Jacques **P105.D5313 1998**
Of Grammatology. Gayatri Chakravorty Spivak (Translator). Trade Paper. Johns Hopkins University Press. Baltimore, MD. 1998. 456p. ISBN:0-8018-5830-5, ISBN13: 978-0-8018-5830-7. Dewey:401. LCCN:76-017226.
Audience: **u,f.** B

During, Simon (Editor) **HM101.C8928 1999**
The Cultural Studies Reader. Ed. 2. Paper over Boards. Routledge. New York, NY. 1999. 624p. ISBN:0-415-13753-5, ISBN13: 978-0-415-13753-9. Dewey:306. LCCN:98-051656.
Audience: **g,l,u,f.**

Eco, Umberto **P99**
A Theory of Semiotics. Trade Cloth. Indiana University Press. Bloomington, IN. 1976. 368p. Advances in Semiotics Ser. ISBN:0-253-35955-4, ISBN13: 978-0-253-35955-1. Dewey:001.51. LCCN:74-022833.
Audience: **u,f.** B

Gallagher, Catherine & Greenblatt, Stephen **PN81.G237 2000**
Practicing New Historicism. Trade Cloth. University of Chicago Press. Chicago, IL. 2000. 260p. ISBN:0-226-27934-0, ISBN13: 978-0-226-27934-3. Dewey:801.95. LCCN:99-042410.
Audience: **u,f.** *Choice, 2000.*

Gallop, Jane **BF175 .G33X 1982B**
The Daughter's Seduction: Feminism and Psychoanalysis. Trade Cloth. Cornell University Press. Ithaca, NY. 1982. 164p. ISBN:0-8014-1493-8, ISBN13: 978-0-8014-1493-0. Dewey:150.195. LCCN:84-672271.
Audience: **u,f.**

Hall, Stuart & du Gay, Paul (Editors) **HM101.Q47 1996**
Questions of Cultural Identity. Paper Text. SAGE Publications, Ltd. London, 1996. 208p. ISBN:0-8039-7883-9, ISBN13: 978-0-8039-7883-6. Dewey:306. LCCN:96-067699.
Audience: **l,u,f.**

Hartman, Geoffrey H. **PN81**
Saving the Text: Literature-Derrida-Philosophy. Trade Paper. Johns Hopkins University Press. Baltimore, MD. 1988. 216p. ISBN:0-8018-2453-2, ISBN13: 978-0-8018-2453-1. Dewey:801/.95. LCCN:80-021748.
Audience: **u,f.**

Holland, Norman N. **PN56.P92H6 1989**
Poems in Persons: An Introduction to the Psychoanalysis of Literature. Cloth Text. Columbia University Press. New York, NY. 1989. 192p. A Morningside Bk. ISBN:0-231-06982-0, ISBN13: 978-0-231-06982-3. Dewey:801/.92. LCCN:88-034193.
Audience: **u,f.**

Kristeva, Julia **PQ2607.E834Z/**
Powers of Horror: An Essay on Abjection. Leon S. Roudiez (Translator). Trade Paper. Edinburgh University Press. Edinburgh, 1984. 219p. ISBN:0-231-05347-9, ISBN13: 978-0-231-05347-1. Dewey:809.9/33/53. LCCN:82-004481.
Audience: **u,f.**

Kristeva, Julia, et al. **PN81**
Desire in Language: A Semiotic Approach to Literature and Art. Leon S. Roudiez & Alice A. Jardine (Authors), Thomas Gora (Translator). Trade Paper. Columbia University Press. New York, NY. 1982. 305p. ISBN:0-231-04807-6, ISBN13: 978-0-231-04807-1. Dewey:801.9/5. LCCN:80-010689.
Audience: **u,f.**

Moglen, Helene **PR858.F45 M64 2001**
The Trauma of Gender: A Feminist Theory of the English Novel. Trade Paper. University of California Press. Berkeley, CA. 2001. 228p. ISBN:0-520-22589-9, ISBN13: 978-0-520-22589-3. Dewey:823/.509353. LCCN:00-055965.
Audience: **g,u,f.** *Choice, 2001.*

Parry, Benita **PR9080.P366 2004**
Postcolonial Studies: A Materialist Critique. Paper over Boards. Routledge. New York, NY. 2004. 256p. Postcolonial Literatures Ser. ISBN:0-415-33599-X, ISBN13: 978-0-415-33599-7. Dewey:820.9/9171241. LCCN:2003-021140.
Audience: **u,f.**

Rosenblatt, Louise M. **PN59.R6 1995**
Literature As Exploration. Ed. 5. Wayne Booth (Foreword by). Trade Cloth. Modern Language Association of America. New York, NY. 1995. "xx, 321"p. ISBN:0-87352-567-1, ISBN13: 978-0-87352-567-1. Dewey:801/.95. LCCN:95-038208.
Audience: **g,u,f.**

Scholes, Robert **PN98.S46**
Semiotics and Interpretation. Trade Paper. Yale University Press. Cumberland, RI. 1983. 162p. ISBN:0-300-03093-2, ISBN13: 978-0-300-03093-8. Dewey:801. LCCN:81-015971.
Audience: **g,u,f.**

Scholes, Robert **PN98.S7**
Structuralism in Literature: An Introduction. Trade Paper. Yale University Press. Cumberland, RI. 1975. 230p. ISBN:0-300-01850-9, ISBN13: 978-0-300-01850-9. Dewey:801.9/5. LCCN:73-090578.
Audience: **g,l,u,f.**

Sebeok, Thomas A. **P99.S323 2001**
Global Semiotics. Trade Cloth. Indiana University Press. Bloomington, IN. 2001. 272p. Advances in Semiotics Ser. ISBN:0-253-33957-X, ISBN13: 978-0-253-33957-7. Dewey:401/.41. LCCN:00-143857.
Audience: **g,u,f.** *Choice, 2002.*

Silverman, Kaja **P99.S52 1983**
The Subject of Semiotics. Paper Text. Oxford University Press, Inc. New York, NY. 1984. 316p. ISBN:0-19-503178-4, ISBN13: 978-0-19-503178-2. Dewey:001.51.
Audience: **u,f.**

Sturrock, John **B841.4.S927 2003**
Structuralism. Ed. 2. Trade Paper. Blackwell Publishing, Inc. Malden, MA. 2002. 176p. ISBN:0-631-23239-7, ISBN13: 978-0-631-23239-1. Dewey:149/.96. LCCN:2002-028112.
Audience: **u,f.**

Veeser, Harold (Editor) **PN81.N43 1989**
The New Historicism. UK-B Format Paperback. Routledge. New York, NY. 1989. 272p. ISBN:0-415-90070-0, ISBN13: 978-0-415-90070-6. Dewey:901. LCCN:88-020935.
Audience: **u,f.**

Williams, Raymond **PN51**
Marxism and Literature. Paper Text. Oxford University Press, Inc. New York, NY. 1978. 224p. Marxist Introductions Ser. ISBN:0-19-876061-2, ISBN13: 978-0-19-876061-0. Dewey:335.43/8/80195.
Audience: **u,f.**

Criticism > Special Topics

Ashcroft, Bill, et al. **PR9080.A85 2002**
The Empire Writes Back: Theory and Practice in Post-Colonial Literatures. Ed. 2. Gareth Griffiths & Helen Tiffin (Authors). Paper over Boards. Routledge. New York, NY. 2002. 296p. New Accents Ser. ISBN:0-415-28019-2, ISBN13: 978-0-415-28019-8. Dewey:820.9/9171241. LCCN:2002-068034.
Audience: **u,f.** *Choice, 1990.*

Ashcroft, Bill (Editor), et al. **PR9080.P57 1995**
The Post-Colonial Studies Reader. Gareth Griffiths & Helen Tiffin (Editors). Cloth Text. Routledge. New York, NY. 1995. 384p. ISBN:0-415-09621-9, ISBN13: 978-0-415-09621-8. Dewey:820.9/358. LCCN:94-017829.
Audience: **u,f.**

Auerbach, Erich **PN56.R3A83 2003**
Mimesis: The Representation of Reality in Western Literature. Ed. 50. Willard R. Trask (Translator). Trade Paper. Princeton University Press. Princeton, NJ. 2003. 616p. ISBN:0-691-11336-X, ISBN13: 978-0-691-11336-4. Dewey:809.9/12. LCCN:2002-044721.
Audience: **g,l,u,f.**

Butler, Judith **HQ1154.B88 1999**
Gender Trouble: Feminism and the Subversion of Identity. Ed. 10. Trade Paper. Routledge. New York, NY. 1999. 256p. ISBN:0-415-92499-5, ISBN13: 978-0-415-92499-3. Dewey:305.3. LCCN:99-029349.
Audience: **u,f.** *Choice, 1990.*

Dettmar, Kevin J. H. **PR478.M6C65 2005**
Companion to Modernist Literature and Culture. David Bradshaw (Editor). Trade Cloth. Blackwell Publishing, Inc. Malden, MA. 2006. 616p. Blackwell Companions to Literature and Culture Ser., Vol. 39 ISBN:0-631-20435-0, ISBN13: 978-0-631-20435-0. Dewey:820.9/112. LCCN:2005-019721.
Audience: **u,f.** *Choice, 2006.*

Detweiler, Robert & Jasper, David (Editors) **PN49.D44 2000**
Religion and Literature: A Reader. Trade Paper. Westminster John Knox Press. Louisville, KY. 2000. 296p. ISBN:0-664-25846-8, ISBN13: 978-0-664-25846-7. Dewey:808.8/0382. LCCN:99-047561.
Audience: **g,l,u,f.**

Ferber, Michael (Editor) **PN603.C65 2005**
Companion to European Romanticism. Trade Cloth. Blackwell Publishing, Inc. Malden, MA. 2005. 600p. Blackwell Companions to Literature and Culture Ser., Vol. 38 ISBN:1-4051-1039-2, ISBN13: 978-1-4051-1039-6. Dewey:809/.9145. LCCN:2005-022100.
Audience: **u,f.**

Fletcher, Angus **PN56.A5 F5**
Allegory: The Theory of a Symbolic Mode. Book, Other. Cornell University Press. Ithaca, NY. 1982. 464p. ISBN:0-8014-9238-6, ISBN13: 978-0-8014-9238-9. Dewey:700. LCCN:64-011415.
Audience: **g,l,u,f.** B

Garrard, Greg **PR143.G37 2004**
Ecocriticism. Paper over Boards. Routledge. New York, NY. 2004. 224p. New Critical Idiom Ser. ISBN:0-415-19691-4, ISBN13: 978-0-415-19691-8. Dewey:820.9/36. LCCN:2004-003429.
Audience: **u,f.**

Iser, Wolfgang **PN81**
The Act of Reading: A Theory of Aesthetic Response. Trade Paper. Johns Hopkins University Press. Baltimore, MD. 1969. 224p. ISBN:0-8018-2371-4, ISBN13: 978-0-8018-2371-8. Dewey:801.9/5. LCCN:78-058296.
Audience: **u,f.** B

Jasper, David **BV4501.3.J37 2004**
The Sacred Desert: Religion, Literature, Art, and Culture. Trade Paper. Blackwell Publishing, Inc. Malden, MA. 2004. 232p. ISBN:1-4051-1975-6, ISBN13: 978-1-4051-1975-7. Dewey:248. LCCN:2003-019365.
Audience: **g,u,f.** *Choice, 2005.*

Langer, Lawrence L. **PN3418**
The Holocaust and the Literary Imagination. Trade Paper. Yale University Press. Cumberland, RI. 1977. 313p. ISBN:0-300-02121-6, ISBN13: 978-0-300-02121-9. Dewey:809.9/3358. LCCN:75-008443.
Audience: **g,l,u,f.**

Levenson, Michael (Editor) **PN56.M54C36 1999**
The Cambridge Companion to Modernism. Cloth Text. Cambridge University Press. New York, NY. 1999. 263p. Companions to Literature Ser. ISBN:0-521-49516-4, ISBN13: 978-0-521-49516-5. Dewey:809.9/112. LCCN:98-013355.
Audience: **u,f.** *Choice, 1999.*

Loomba, Ania **JV51.L66 2005**
Colonialism/Postcolonialism. Ed. 2. Saddle Stitched, Cloth over Boards. Routledge. New York, NY. 2005. 263p. The New Critical Idiom Ser. ISBN:0-415-35063-8, ISBN13: 978-0-415-35063-1. Dewey:325/.3. LCCN:2005-008207.
Audience: **u,f.**

Lukács, Georg **PN56.R3**
Essays on Realism. Rodney Livingstone (Editor), David Fernbach (Translator). Trade Paper. MIT Press. Cambridge, MA. 1983. 256p. ISBN:0-262-62042-1, ISBN13: 978-0-262-62042-0. Dewey:809/.912.
Audience: **u,f.**

Radway, Janice A. **PN4751**
Reading the Romance: Women, Patriarchy and Popular Literature. Ed. 2. Trade Cloth. University of North Carolina Press. Chapel Hill, NC. 1991. 306p. ISBN:0-8078-4349-0, ISBN13: 978-0-8078-4349-9. Dewey:302.2/32. LCCN:91-050284.
Audience: **g,l,u,f.**

Ricoeur, Paul **BL51.R43225 1995**
Figuring the Sacred: Religion, Narrative and Imagination. Mark I. Wallace (Editor), David Pellauer (Translator). Trade Paper. Augsburg Fortress, Publishers. Minneapolis, MN. 2003. 352p. ISBN:0-8006-2894-2, ISBN13: 978-0-8006-2894-9. Dewey:200. LCCN:95-005454.
Audience: **u,f.** *Choice, 1996.*

Said, Edward W. **PN761.S28 1994**
Culture and Imperialism. Trade Paper. Knopf Publishing Group. New York, NY. 1994. 416p. ISBN:0-679-75054-1, ISBN13: 978-0-679-75054-3. Dewey:809/.894. LCCN:93-043485.
Audience: **g,l,u,f.** *Choice, 1993.*

Said, Edward W. **DS32.8**
Orientalism: Western Concepts of the Orient. Trade Cloth. Routledge. New York, NY. 1979. 384p. ISBN:0-7100-0040-5, ISBN13: 978-0-7100-0040-8. Dewey:950/.07. LCCN:78-040534.
Audience: **g,l,u,f.**

Sedgwick, Eve K. **PN3352.A38**
Epistemology of the Closet. Trade Cloth. University of California Press. Berkeley, CA. 1991. 220p. ISBN:0-520-07874-8, ISBN13: 978-0-520-07874-1. Dewey:809.3/9353.
Audience: **u,f.**

Weinstein, Philip **PN3503.W393 2005**
Unknowing: The Work of Modernist Fiction. Trade Cloth. Cornell University Press. Ithaca, NY. 2005. 288p. ISBN:0-8014-4370-9, ISBN13: 978-0-8014-4370-1. Dewey:809.3/9112/0904. LCCN:2005-016066.
Audience: **u,f.** *Choice, 2006.*

Criticism > History of Criticism

Adams, Hazard & Searle, Leroy (Editors) **PN94.C75 1986**
Critical Theory since 1965. Trade Paper. University Press of Florida. Gainesville, FL. 1986. 904p. ISBN:0-8130-0844-1, ISBN13: 978-0-8130-0844-8. Dewey:801/.95. LCCN:86-013216.
Audience: **g,u,f.**

Adams, Hazard & Searle, Leroy **PN49.C683 2005**
Critical Theory since Plato. Ed. 3. Hazard Adams & Leroy Searle (Editors). Cloth Text. Thomson Heinle. Boston, MA. 2004. 1568p. ISBN:0-15-505504-6, ISBN13: 978-0-15-505504-9. Dewey:801/.95. LCCN:2004-101932.
Audience: **g,u,f.** B

Habib, M. A. R. **PN86**
History of Literary Criticism: From Plato to the Present. Trade Cloth. Blackwell Publishing, Inc. Malden, MA. 2005. 816p. ISBN:0-631-23200-1, ISBN13: 978-0-631-23200-1. Dewey:801/.95/09. LCCN:2005-004898.
Audience: **g,l,u,f.** *Choice, 2006.*

Wellek, Rene **PN86**
A History of Modern Criticism, 1750-1950: The First Half of the Twentieth Century: English and American. Trade Cloth. Yale University Press. Cumberland, RI. 1986. 345p. Modern Criticism Ser., Vol. 6 ISBN:0-300-03486-5, ISBN13: 978-0-300-03486-8. Dewey:801/.95/0903. LCCN:85-012005.
Audience: **g,l,u,f.** *Choice, 1986.*

Wellek, Rene **PN86**
A History of Modern Criticism, 1750-1950: French, Italian, and Spanish Criticism, 1900-1950. Cloth over Boards. Yale University Press. Cumberland, RI. 1992. 367p. History of Modern Criticism Ser., Vol. 8 ISBN:0-300-05451-3, ISBN13: 978-0-300-05451-4. Dewey:801.9509. LCCN:55-005989.
Audience: **g,l,u,f.**

Wellek, Rene **PN86**
A History of Modern Criticism, 1750-1950: The First Half of the Twentieth Century: English and American. Trade Cloth. Yale University Press. Cumberland, RI. 1986. 343p. Modern Criticism Ser., Vol. 5 ISBN:0-300-03378-8, ISBN13: 978-0-300-03378-6. Dewey:801/.95/0903. LCCN:85-012005.
Audience: **g,l,u,f.** *Choice, 1986.*

Wellek, Rene **PN86 .W415**
A History of Modern Criticism, 1750-1950: German, Russian, and East European Criticism, 1900-1950. Cloth over Boards. Yale University Press. Cumberland, RI. 1991. 488p. History of Modern Criticism Ser., Vol. 7 ISBN:0-300-05039-9, ISBN13: 978-0-300-05039-4. Dewey:801.9509. LCCN:55-005989.
Audience: **g,l,u,f.**

Reading

Adler, Mortimer J. & Van Doren, Charles **PN83.A43 1972**
How to Read a Book. Trade Paper. Simon & Schuster. New York, NY. 1972. 426p. ISBN:0-671-21209-5, ISBN13: 978-0-671-21209-4. Dewey:028. LCCN:72-081451.
Audience: **g,l,u.** B

Bloom, Harold **PN83.B57 2001**
How to Read and Why. Trade Paper. Simon & Schuster. New York, NY. 2001. 288p. ISBN:0-684-85907-6, ISBN13: 978-0-684-85907-1. Dewey:801/.9. LCCN:2001-049374.
Audience: **g,l,u.** *Choice, 2000.*

Cavallo, Guglielmo & Chartier, Roger (Editors) **Z1003.3.E85**
A History of Reading in the West. Lydia G. Cochrane (Translator). Trade Paper. University of Massachusetts Press. Amherst, MA. 2003. 488p. Studies in Print Culture and the History of the Book ISBN:1-55849-411-1, ISBN13: 978-1-55849-411-4. Dewey:028.9. LCCN:99-022447.
Audience: **g,l,u,f.**

Dirda, Michael **Z1035.A1D57 2004**
Bound to Please: An Extraordinary One-Volume Literary Education. Trade Cloth. W. W. Norton & Company, Inc. New York, NY. 2004. 608p. ISBN:0-393-05757-7, ISBN13: 978-0-393-05757-7. Dewey:081. LCCN:2004-054719.
Audience: **g,l,u,f.**

Iser, Wolfgang **PN81**
The Act of Reading: A Theory of Aesthetic Response. Trade Paper. Johns Hopkins University Press. Baltimore, MD. 1969. 224p. ISBN:0-8018-2371-4, ISBN13: 978-0-8018-2371-8. Dewey:801.9/5. LCCN:78-058296.
Audience: **u,f.** B

Manguel, Alberto **Z1003**
A History of Reading. Trade Paper. Penguin Group (USA) Inc. New York, NY. 1997. 384p. ISBN:0-14-016654-8, ISBN13: 978-0-14-016654-5. Dewey:028.9/09.
Audience: **g,l,u,f.** *Choice, 1997.*

Pound, Ezra **PN83**
ABC of Reading. Trade Paper. New Directions Publishing Corporation. New York, NY. 1960. 206p. ISBN:0-8112-0151-1, ISBN13: 978-0-8112-0151-3. Dewey:28. LCCN:2003-682220.
Audience: **g,l,u,f.** B

Turner, Mark **PN49 .T77**
The Literary Mind. Trade Paper. Oxford University Press, Inc. New York, NY. 1998. 198p. ISBN:0-19-512667-X, ISBN13: 978-0-19-512667-9. Dewey:401.9.
Audience: **g,u,f.** *Choice, 1997.*

Authorship

PN161
Literary Market Place 2005: The Directory of the American Book Publishing Industry. Trade Cloth. Information Today, Inc. Medford, NJ. 2004. 2,100p. ISBN:1-57387-203-2, ISBN13: 978-1-57387-203-4. Dewey:70.5.
Audience: **g,u,f.**

Alvarez, Al **PR6051.L9Z477 2005**
The Writer's Voice. Trade Cloth. W. W. Norton & Company, Inc. New York, NY. 2004. 128p. ISBN:0-393-05795-X, ISBN13: 978-0-393-05795-9. Dewey:809. LCCN:2004-012391.
Audience: **g,l,u,f.**

Bennett, Andrew **PN145.B429 2005**
Author. Trade Paper. Routledge. New York, NY. 2005. 160p. The New Critical Idiom Ser. ISBN:0-415-28164-4, ISBN13: 978-0-415-28164-5. Dewey:808/.02/09. LCCN:2004-013734.
Audience: **u,f.**

Bunge, Nancy L. **PN147.B798 2005**
Master Class: Lessons from Leading Writers. Trade Paper, Perfect. University of Iowa Press. Iowa City, IA. 2005. 216p. ISBN:0-87745-966-5, ISBN13: 978-0-87745-966-8. Dewey:808/.02. LCCN:2005-047012.
Audience: **g,u,f.**

Butcher, Judith, et al. **PN162.B86 2006**
Butcher's Copy-Editing: The Cambridge Handbook for Editors, Proofreaders and Copy-Editors. Ed. 4. Caroline Drake & Maureen Leach (Authors). Cloth Text. Cambridge University Press. New York, NY. 2006. 558p. ISBN:0-521-84713-3, ISBN13: 978-0-521-84713-1. Dewey:808/.027. LCCN:2005-032563.
Audience: **g,l,u,f.**

Delany, Samuel R. **PS3554.E437Z474 2005**
About Writing: Seven Essays, Four Letters, and Five Interviews. Library Binding. Wesleyan University Press. Middletown, CT. 2006. 432p. ISBN:0-8195-6715-9, ISBN13: 978-0-8195-6715-4. Dewey:813/.54. LCCN:2005-050758.
Audience: **g,u.**

Dufresne, John **PN3355**
The Lie That Tells a Truth: A Guide to Writing Fiction. Trade Paper. W. W. Norton & Company, Inc. New York, NY. 2004. 336p. ISBN:0-393-32581-4, ISBN13: 978-0-393-32581-2. Dewey:808.3.
Audience: **g,u,f.**

Gaskell, Philip **PN162.G3 1999**
From Writer to Reader: Studies in Editorial Method. Trade Cloth. Oak Knoll Press. New Castle, DE. 1999. 268p. ISBN:1-58456-000-2, ISBN13: 978-1-58456-000-5. Dewey:808/.02. LCCN:99-014971.
Audience: **u,f.** B

Koch, Stephen **PN3355.K59 2003**
The Modern Library Writer's Workshop: A Guide to the Craft of Fiction. Trade Paper. Random House Adult Trade Publishing Group. New York, NY. 2003. 320p. ISBN:0-375-75558-6, ISBN13: 978-0-375-75558-3. Dewey:808.3. LCCN:2002-032593.
Audience: **g,u,f.**

Lee, Maurice A. (Editor) **PN3373**
Writers on Writing: The Art of the Short Story. Trade Cloth. Greenwood Publishing Group, Inc. Portsmouth, NH. 2005. 270p. Contributions to the Study of World Literature Ser., No. 128 ISBN:0-313-31592-2, ISBN13: 978-0-313-31592-3. Dewey:808.3/1. LCCN:2005-001874.
Audience: **g,u,f.** *Choice, 2006.*

Ritter, R. M. & Hart, Horace **PN147**
New Hart's Rules: The Handbook of Style for Writers and Editors. Trade Cloth. Oxford University Press, Inc. New York, NY. 2005. 432p. ISBN:0-19-861041-6, ISBN13: 978-0-19-861041-0. Dewey:808.027. LCCN:2006-295388.
Audience: **g,l,u,f.**

Zinsser, William **PE1429**
On Writing Well: The Classic Guide to Writing Nonfiction. Ed. 30. Trade Paper. HarperCollins Publishers. New York, NY. 2006. 336p. ISBN:0-06-089154-8, ISBN13: 978-0-06-089154-1. Dewey:808/.042.
Audience: **g,l,u,f.**

Translating

Baker, Mona (Editor) **P306.E57 1997**
Routledge Encyclopedia of Translation Studies. Paper over Boards. Routledge. New York, NY. 1997. 680p. ISBN:0-415-09380-5, ISBN13: 978-0-415-09380-4. Dewey:418/.02/03. LCCN:96-044586.
Audience: **u,f.** *Choice, 1998.*

Bassnett, Susan **PN241**
Translation Studies. Ed. 3. Paper over Boards. Routledge. New York, NY. 2002. 192p. New Accents Ser. ISBN:0-415-28013-3, ISBN13: 978-0-415-28013-6. Dewey:418/.02. LCCN:2002-068174.
Audience: **u,f.**

Biguenet, John & Schulte, Rainer (Editors) **P306.T453 1992**
Theories of Translation: An Anthology of Essays from Dryden to Derrida. Trade Paper. University of Chicago Press. Chicago, IL. 1992. 260p. ISBN:0-226-04871-3, ISBN13: 978-0-226-04871-0. Dewey:418/.02/09. LCCN:91-022882.
Audience: **u,f.**

France, Peter (Editor) **PR131.O94 2001**
The Oxford Guide to Literature in English Translation. Trade Paper. Oxford University Press, Inc. New York, NY. 2001. 680p. ISBN:0-19-924784-6, ISBN13: 978-0-19-924784-4. Dewey:809. LCCN:00-025111.
Audience: **u,f.** *Choice, 2000.*

Venuti, Lawrence **P306.T7436 2004**
The Translation Studies Reader. Ed. 2. Paper over Boards. Routledge. New York, NY. 2004. 560p. ISBN:0-415-31919-6, ISBN13: 978-0-415-31919-5. Dewey:418/.02. LCCN:2003-022335.
Audience: **u,f.**

Literary History, Biography

Auden, W. H. **PR6001.U4D9 1989**
The Dyer's Hand and Other Essays. Trade Paper. Knopf Publishing Group. New York, NY. 1990. 544p. Vintage International Ser. ISBN:0-679-72484-2, ISBN13: 978-0-679-72484-1. Dewey:814/.52. LCCN:90-050192.
Audience: **g,u,f.** B

Barthes, Roland **AC25**
Mythologies. UK-B Format Paperback. Random House. London, 1993. 160p. ISBN:0-09-997220-4, ISBN13: 978-0-09-997220-4. Dewey:194.
Audience: **g,l,u,f.**

Barthes, Roland **PN203.B313**
Writing Degree Zero. Susan Sontag (Produced by). Trade Cloth. Peter Smith Publisher, Inc. Magnolia, MA. 2001. ISBN:0-8446-7169-X, ISBN13: 978-0-8446-7169-7. Dewey:808.02.
Audience: **g,u,f.**

Barzun, Jacques **CB358.B29 2003**
A Jacques Barzun Reader: Selections from His Works. Trade Paper. HarperCollins Publishers. New York, NY. 2003. 640p. Perennial Classics Ser. ISBN:0-06-093542-1, ISBN13: 978-0-06-093542-9. Dewey:909.8. LCCN:2003-040512.
Audience: **g,u,f.**

Benjamin, Walter **PN37.B4413 1986**
Illuminations. Hannah Arendt (Editor, Introduction by). Book, Other. Knopf Publishing Group. New York, NY. 1969. 288p. ISBN:0-8052-0241-2, ISBN13: 978-0-8052-0241-0. Dewey:834.912. LCCN:68-024382.
Audience: **g,u,f.**

Benjamin, Walter **PT2603.E455A26 1986**
Reflections: Essays, Aphorisms, Autobiographical Writings. Peter Demetz (Editor), Edmund Jephcott (Translator). UK-Trade Paper. Knopf Publishing Group. New York, NY. 1986. 400p. ISBN:0-8052-0802-X, ISBN13: 978-0-8052-0802-3. Dewey:834/.912. LCCN:85-026232.
Audience: **g,u,f.**

Boucquey, Thierry & Diamond, Marie Josephine **PN451.E55 2005**
Encyclopedia of World Writers, Beginnings to the Twentieth Century. Book Builders LLC Staff (Contribution by). Trade Cloth. Facts On File, Inc. New York, NY. 2005. 1440p. Encyclopedia of World Literature Ser. ISBN:0-8160-6143-2, ISBN13: 978-0-8160-6143-3. Dewey:809/.003 B. LCCN:2004-020551.
Audience: **g,l,u,f.** *Choice, 2005.*

Burke, Kenneth **PN511**
The Philosophy of Literary Form. Ed. 3. Trade Paper. University of California Press. Berkeley, CA. 1974. 463p. ISBN:0-520-02483-4, ISBN13: 978-0-520-02483-0. Dewey:801. LCCN:72-093526.
Audience: **g,u,f.**

Chesterton, G. K. **LB1028.R43**
A Handful of Authors: Essays on Books and Writers. Paper Text. Textbook Publishers. Temecula, CA. 2003. 214p. ISBN:0-7581-3930-6, ISBN13: 978-0-7581-3930-6. Dewey:370/.78/073.
Audience: **g,l,u,f.**

Hardwick, Elizabeth **PN471.H3 2001**
Seduction and Betrayal: Women and Literature. Joan Didion (Introduction by). Trade Paper. New York Review of Books, Incorporated, The. New York, NY. 2001. 224p. New York Review Books Classics Ser. ISBN:0-940322-78-1, ISBN13: 978-0-940322-78-3. Dewey:809/.89287. LCCN:2001-002540.
Audience: **g,l,u,f.**

Hyman, Stanley E. **PN94 .H9 1978**
The Armed Vision: A Study in the Methods of Modern Literary Criticism. Trade Cloth. Greenwood Publishing Group, Inc. Portsmouth, NH. 1978. 417p. ISBN:0-313-20273-7, ISBN13: 978-0-313-20273-5. Dewey:801/.95/0904. LCCN:77-029139.
Audience: **g,l,u,f.**

James, Henry **PN701**
Selected Literary Criticism. Morris Shapira (Editor), Frank R. Leavis (Preface by). Trade Paper. Cambridge University Press. New York, NY. 1981. 376p. ISBN:0-521-28365-5, ISBN13: 978-0-521-28365-6. Dewey:809/.03. LCCN:80-049685.
Audience: **g,l,u,f.**

Kazin, Alfred **PS29.K38A3 1995**
Writing Was Everything. Trade Cloth. Harvard University Press. Cambridge, MA. 1998. 160p. The William E. Massey Sr. Lectures in the History of American Civilization Ser., Vol. 1994 ISBN:0-674-96237-0, ISBN13: 978-0-674-96237-8. Dewey:809. LCCN:95-006625.
Audience: **g,l,u,f.**

Lewis, Wyndham **NX180.S6L48 1989**
Creatures of Habit and Creatures of Change: Essays on Art, Literature and Society, 1914-1956. Paul Edwards (Editor, Introduction by). Trade Paper. HarperCollins Publishers. New York, NY. 1989. 430p. ISBN:0-87685-769-1, ISBN13: 978-0-87685-769-4. Dewey:700/.1/03. LCCN:89-014999.
Audience: **g,l,u,f.**

Magill, Frank N. & Irons-Georges, Tracy (Editors) **PN451.M36 2003**
Cyclopedia of World Authors, Fourth Revised Edition, Volume 3: Joel Chandler Harris--Alessandro Manzoni. Ed. 4. Library Binding. Salem Press, Inc. Hackensack, NJ. 2003. ISBN:1-58765-125-4, ISBN13: 978-1-58765-125-0. Dewey:809 B. LCCN:2003-017382.
Audience: **g,l,u,f.**

Pound, Ezra **PN511**
Literary Essays. Paper Text. Textbook Publishers. Temecula, CA. 2003. xv, 464p. ISBN:0-7581-7807-7, ISBN13: 978-0-7581-7807-7. Dewey:804.
Audience: **g,l,u,f.**

Pound, Ezra **PN511.P63**
Make It New: Essays. Paper Text. Classic Textbooks. Murrieta, CA. 1999. 408p. ISBN:1-4047-0195-8, ISBN13: 978-1-4047-0195-3. Dewey:809.
Audience: **g,l,u,f.**

Quiller-Couch, Arthur Thomas **PR503**
Studies in Literature: Second Series. Paper Text. Classic Textbooks. Murrieta, CA. 1922. 301p. ISBN:1-4047-7019-4, ISBN13: 978-1-4047-7019-5. Dewey:821/.009.
Audience: **g,l,u,f.**

Read, Herbert Edward (Introduction by) **PR6035.E24T6 2002**
To Hell with Culture: And Other Essays on Art and Society. Ed. 2. Paper over Boards. Routledge. New York, NY. 2002. 240p. Routledge Classics Ser. ISBN:0-415-28992-0, ISBN13: 978-0-415-28992-4. Dewey:824/.912. LCCN:2002-031672.
Audience: **g,l,u,f.**

Santayana, George **PL898**
Essays in Literary Criticism of George Santayana. Paper Text. Textbook Publishers. Temecula, CA. 2003. xxviii, 414 pp. ISBN:0-7581-4080-0, ISBN13: 978-0-7581-4080-7. Dewey:791.538.
Audience: **g,u,f.**

Sartre, Jean-Paul **PN45.S245 1988**
What Is Literature? and Other Essays. Bernard Frechtman & Jeffrey Mehlman (Translators), Steven Ungar (Introduction by). Trade Paper. Harvard University Press. Cambridge, MA. 1988. 368p. ISBN:0-674-95084-4, ISBN13: 978-0-674-95084-9. Dewey:809. LCCN:87-037931.
Audience: **g,u,f.**

Stade, George & Jackson, William T. (Editors) **PN501 .E9 1983**
European Writers: The Middle Ages and the Renaissance. Trade Cloth. Thomson Gale. Farmington Hills, MI. 1983. 956p. ISBN:0-684-16594-5, ISBN13: 978-0-684-16594-3. Dewey:809/.894. LCCN:83-016333.
Audience: **g,l,u,f.** B

Steiner, George **PN511.S687 1998**
Language and Silence: Essays on Language, Literature, and the Inhuman. Trade Paper. Yale University Press. Cumberland, RI. 1998. 440p. ISBN:0-300-07471-9, ISBN13: 978-0-300-07471-0. Dewey:809. LCCN:97-032450.
Audience: **g,u,f.**

Tate, Allen **PR6029.C33A6**
Collected Essays. Paper Text. Textbook Publishers. Temecula, CA. 2003. ISBN:0-7581-3352-9, ISBN13: 978-0-7581-3352-6. Dewey:828.
Audience: **g,l,u,f.** B

Walcott, Derek **PR9272.9.W3 W48 1999**
What the Twilight Says: Essays. Ed. 1. Trade Paper. Farrar, Straus & Giroux. New York, NY. 1999. 256p. ISBN:0-374-52683-4, ISBN13: 978-0-374-52683-2. Dewey:814.
Audience: **g,l,u,f.**

Wilson, Edmund **PN56.S742W55 1997**
The Wound and the Bow: Seven Studies in Literature. Janet Groth (Contribution by). Trade Paper. Ohio University Press. Athens, OH. 1997. 260p. ISBN:0-8214-1189-6, ISBN13: 978-0-8214-1189-6. Dewey:809/.93353. LCCN:96-051164.
Audience: **g,l,u,f.** B

Woolf, Virginia **PR99**
The Common Reader, Vol. 2. UK-B Format Paperback. Knopf Publishing Group. New York, NY. 2003. 336p. ISBN:0-09-944367-8, ISBN13: 978-0-09-944367-4. Dewey:820.9.
Audience: **g,l,u,f.**

Woolf, Virginia **PR99**
The Common Reader, Vol. 1. UK-B Format Paperback. Knopf Publishing Group. New York, NY. 2003. 288p. ISBN:0-09-944366-X, ISBN13: 978-0-09-944366-7. Dewey:820.9.
Audience: **g,l,u,f.**

Book History

Altick, Richard D. **Z1003.5.G7A53 1998**
The English Common Reader: A Social History of the Mass Reading Public, 1800-1900. Ed. 2. Cloth Text. Ohio State University Press. Columbus, OH. 1998. 468p. ISBN:0-8142-0793-6, ISBN13: 978-0-8142-0793-2. Dewey:028/.9/0941. LCCN:98-019581.
Audience: **g,l,u,f.**

Chappell, Warren **Z124**
A Short History of the Printed Word. Trade Cloth. Dorset Press. New York, NY. 1990. 330p. Reprints Ser. ISBN:0-88029-324-1, ISBN13: 978-0-88029-324-2. Dewey:686.2/09.
Audience: **g,l,u,f.**

Eisenstein, Elizabeth L. **Z124 .E374 1993**
The Printing Revolution in Early Modern Europe. Trade Paper. Cambridge University Press. New York, NY. 1993. 314p. A Canto Book Ser. ISBN:0-521-44770-4, ISBN13: 978-0-521-44770-6. Dewey:686.2/094. LCCN:94-153513.
Audience: **g,l,u,f.** B

Feather, John P. **Z325 .F414 1988B**
A History of British Publishing. Trade Paper. Routledge. New York, NY. 1989. 304p. ISBN:0-415-02654-7, ISBN13: 978-0-415-02654-3. Dewey:070.5/0941. LCCN:88-028715.
Audience: **g,l,u,f.**

Febvre, Lucien **Z4**
The Coming of the Book: The Impact of Printing, 1450-1800. Trade Paper. Analytical Psychology Club of San Francisco, Inc. San Francisco, CA. 1997. 384p. Classics Ser. ISBN:1-85984-108-2, ISBN13: 978-1-85984-108-2. Dewey:002/.094.
Audience: **g,l,u,f.**

Finkelstein, David & McCleery, Alistair (Editors) **Z4.B647 2001**
The Book History Reader. Trade Paper. Routledge. New York, NY. 2001. 400p. ISBN:0-415-22658-9, ISBN13: 978-0-415-22658-5. Dewey:302.2/244/09. LCCN:2001-049226.
Audience: **g,l,u,f.**

Finkelstein, David & McCleery, Alistair **Z4.F49 2005**
An Introduction to Book History. Paper over Boards. Routledge. New York, NY. 2005. 168p. ISBN:0-415-31442-9, ISBN13: 978-0-415-31442-8. Dewey:002/.09. LCCN:2004-029350.
Audience: **g,l,u,f.**

Gaskell, Philip **Z1001**
A New Introduction to Bibliography. Oxford University Press, Inc. 1972. ISBN:0-19-818150-7, ISBN13: 978-0-19-818150-7.
Audience: **g,l,u,f.** B

Harris, William V. **PA53.H37 1989**
Ancient Literacy. Trade Cloth. Harvard University Press. Cambridge, MA. 1989. 406p. ISBN:0-674-03380-9, ISBN13: 978-0-674-03380-1. Dewey:302.2/244/0938. LCCN:89-007588.
Audience: **l,u,f.**

McKenzie, D. F. **Z1001 .M398 1999**
Bibliography and the Sociology of Texts. Cloth Text. Cambridge University Press. New York, NY. 1999. 136p. ISBN:0-521-64258-2, ISBN13: 978-0-521-64258-3. Dewey:na. LCCN:98-031000.
Audience: **u,f.**

McLuhan, Marshall **HM221**
The Gutenberg Galaxy: The Making of Typographic Man. Trade Paper. University of Toronto Press. Toronto, ON. 1962. 458p. ISBN:0-8020-6041-2, ISBN13: 978-0-8020-6041-9. Dewey:306.4/6. LCCN:62-004860.
Audience: **g,l,u,f.**

Petroski, Henry **Z685**
The Book on the Bookshelf. Trade Paper. Knopf Publishing Group. New York, NY. 2000. 304p. ISBN:0-375-70639-9, ISBN13: 978-0-375-70639-4. Dewey:022/.4/09. LCCN:99-014336.
Audience: **g,l,u,f.** *Choice, 2000.*

Radway, Janice A. **PN4751**
Reading the Romance: Women, Patriarchy and Popular Literature. Ed. 2. Trade Cloth. University of North Carolina Press. Chapel Hill, NC. 1991. 306p. ISBN:0-8078-4349-0, ISBN13: 978-0-8078-4349-9. Dewey:302.2/32. LCCN:91-050284.
Audience: **g,l,u,f.**

Steinberg, Sigfrid H. **Z124.S8 1996**
Five Hundred Years of Printing. Ed. 4. John Trevitt (Revised by), Beatrice Warde (Foreword by). Trade Cloth. Oak Knoll Press. New Castle, DE. 1996. 272p. ISBN:1-884718-19-1, ISBN13: 978-1-884718-19-9. Dewey:686.2/09. LCCN:96-012543.
Audience: **g,l,u,f.** B

Vincent, David **LC156.G72E58 1989**
Literacy and Popular Culture: England, 1750-1914. Peter Burke & Ruth Finnegan (Contribution by). Trade Paper. Cambridge University Press. New York, NY. 1993. 374p. Studies in Oral and Literate Culture, No. 19 ISBN:0-521-45771-8, ISBN13: 978-0-521-45771-2. Dewey:302.2/244/0942/09034.
Audience: **g,l,u,f.** *Choice, 1990.*

Special Forms of Literature

Cawelti, John G. **HM621.C39 2004**
Mystery, Violence, and Popular Culture: Essays. Trade Cloth. University of Wisconsin Press. Chicago, IL. 2004. 432p. ISBN:0-299-19630-5, ISBN13: 978-0-299-19630-1. Dewey:306. LCCN:2003-020569.
Audience: **g,u,f.**

Denning, Michael **PS377**
Mechanic Accents: Dime Novels and Working Class Culture of America. Ed. 2. Trade Paper. Analytical Psychology Club of San Francisco, Inc. San Francisco, CA. 1998. 288p. Haymarket Ser. ISBN:1-85984-250-X, ISBN13: 978-1-85984-250-8. Dewey:813.3/09.
Audience: **u,f.**

Frow, John **PN45.5.F76 2005**
Genre. Paper over Boards. Routledge. New York, NY. 2005. VIII, 176p. The New Critical Idiom Ser. ISBN:0-415-28062-1, ISBN13: 978-0-415-28062-4. Dewey:808. LCCN:2005-004673.
Audience: **g,u,f.**

Special Forms of Literature > Poetry

PS580
□ Academy of American Poets.
http://www.poets.org
Audience: **g,l,u,f.**

PS580
□ Library of Congress Poetry Center.
http://www.loc.gov/poetry/
Audience: **g,l,u,f.**

Aristotle **PA3621.A75 1995**
Poetics, On the Sublime, and On Style. Ed. 2. W. Hamilton Fyfe, Stephen Halliwell & Doreen C. Innes (Editors), W. Hamilton Fyfe, Stephen Halliwell, Doreen C. Innes & W. Rhys Roberts (Translators), Donald Russell (Revised by). Trade Cloth. Harvard University Press. Cambridge, MA. 1995. 544p. Loeb Classical Library, No. 199 ISBN:0-674-99563-5, ISBN13: 978-0-674-99563-5. Dewey:808.2. LCCN:94-005113.
Audience: **g,l,u,f.**

Lennard, John **PR502**
The Poetry Handbook. Ed. 2. Paper Text. Oxford University Press, Inc. New York, NY. 2006. 448p. ISBN:0-19-926538-0, ISBN13: 978-0-19-926538-1. Dewey:808.1. LCCN:2005-021580.
Audience: **g,l,u,f.**

Morgan, Esther (Editor) **PS3019**
□ The Poetry Archive.
http://www.poetryarchive.org
Bailey, Andrew (Editor).
Audience: **g,l,u,f.**

Paz, Octavio **PN1271.P39 1991**
The Other Voice: Essays on Modern Poetry. Helen Lane (Translator). Cloth over Boards. Harcourt Trade Publishers. New York, NY. 1991. 180p. ISBN:0-15-170449-X, ISBN13: 978-0-15-170449-1. Dewey:809.1. LCCN:91-004764.
Audience: **u,f.**

Special Forms of Literature > Poetry > Technique, Study, Teaching

Behn, Robin **PN1059.A9 P7 1992**
The Practice of Poetry: Writing Exercises from Poets Who Teach. Chase Twichell (Editor). Trade Paper. HarperCollins Publishers. New York, NY. 1992. 320p. ISBN:0-06-273024-X, ISBN13: 978-0-06-273024-4. Dewey:808.1. LCCN:92-052535.
Audience: **u,f.**

Fussell, Paul Jr. **PE1505.F78 1979**
Poetic Meter and Poetic Form. Paper Text. McGraw-Hill Higher Education. Burr Ridge, IL. 1979. 190p. ISBN:0-07-553606-4, ISBN13: 978-0-07-553606-2. Dewey:808.1.
Audience: **u,f.**

Gross, Harvey **PN1042.G7**
The Structure of Verse. Trade Paper. HarperCollins Publishers. New York, NY. 1979. 320p. ISBN:0-912946-59-8, ISBN13: 978-0-912946-59-7. Dewey:808.1. LCCN:78-006781.
Audience: **u,f.**

Hugo, Richard **PN1042.H8 2006**
The Triggering Town: Lectures and Essays on Poetry and Writing. Trade Paper. W. W. Norton & Company, Inc. New York, NY. 1992. 128p. ISBN:0-393-30933-9, ISBN13: 978-0-393-30933-1. Dewey:808.1.
Audience: **u,f.**

Lehman, David (Editor) **PS615.E374 1996**
Ecstatic Occasions, Expedient Forms: 85 Leading Contemporary Poets Select and Comment on Their Poems. Ed. 2. Trade Paper. University of Michigan Press. Chicago, IL. 1996. 228p. ISBN:0-472-06633-1, ISBN13: 978-0-472-06633-9. Dewey:811/.5408. LCCN:96-031099.
Audience: **u,f.**

Mayes, Frances **PN1042.M34 2001**
The Discovery of Poetry: A Field Guide to Reading and Writing Poems. Trade Paper. Harcourt Trade Publishers. New York, NY. 2001. 512p. ISBN:0-15-600762-2, ISBN13: 978-0-15-600762-7. Dewey:808.1. LCCN:2001-024958.
Audience: **g,l,u,f.**

Spiegelman, Willard **PS310.V57S67 2005**
How Poets See the World: The Art of Description in Contemporary Poetry. Trade Cloth. Oxford University Press, Inc. New York, NY. 2005. 256p. ISBN:0-19-517491-7, ISBN13: 978-0-19-517491-5. LCCN:2004-012519.
Audience: **g,l,u,f.** *Choice, 2005.*

Special Forms of Literature > Fiction

Armstrong, Nancy **PR821**
Desire and Domestic Fiction: A Political History of the Novel. Trade Paper. Oxford University Press, Inc. New York, NY. 1990. 310p. ISBN:0-19-506160-8, ISBN13: 978-0-19-506160-4. Dewey:823/.009. LCCN:86-016482.
Audience: **u,f.** *Choice, 1987.*

Booth, Wayne **PN3331**
The Rhetoric of Fiction. Ed. 2. Trade Paper. University of Chicago Press. Chicago, IL. 1983. 572p. ISBN:0-226-06558-8, ISBN13: 978-0-226-06558-8. Dewey:808.3. LCCN:82-013592.
Audience: **g,l,u,f.**

Girard, René **PN3491**
Deceit, Desire, and the Novel: Self and Other in Literary Structure. Yvonne Freccero (Translator). Trade Paper. Johns Hopkins University Press. Baltimore, MD. 1976. 328p. ISBN:0-8018-1830-3, ISBN13: 978-0-8018-1830-1. Dewey:809.3/9353. LCCN:65-028582.
Audience: **u,f.**

Hoffman, Michael J. **PN3331.E87 2005**
Essentials of the Theory of Fiction. Ed. 3. Trade Paper, Perfect. Duke University Press. Durham, NC. 2005. 568p. ISBN:0-8223-3521-2, ISBN13: 978-0-8223-3521-4. Dewey:809.3. LCCN:2004-024770.
Audience: **g,l,u,f.**

Hopkins, Gerard Manley **PN3499 .M33 1972**
The Art of Writing. Andre Maurois (Translator). Trade Cloth. Ayer Company Publishers, Inc. Manchester, NH. 1977. Essay Index Reprint Ser. ISBN:0-8369-2914-4, ISBN13: 978-0-8369-2914-0. Dewey:809.3. LCCN:72-003375.
Audience: **g,l,u,f.** B

Howells, William Dean **LB1555.K37**
Criticism and Fiction, and Other Essays. Paper Text. Textbook Publishers. Temecula, CA. 2003. xix, 413p. ISBN:0-7581-7719-4, ISBN13: 978-0-7581-7719-3. Dewey:372.
Audience: **g,l,u,f.**

James, Henry **PN3355.B464**
The Art of Fiction. Library Binding. Reprint Services Company. Temecula, CA. 1992. Notable American Authors Ser. ISBN:0-7812-3458-1, ISBN13: 978-0-7812-3458-0.
Audience: **g,l,u,f.**

James, Henry **PS2112**
The Art of the Novel. Library Binding. Reprint Services Company. Temecula, CA. 1993. 348p. BCL1-PS American Literature Ser. ISBN:0-7812-6975-X, ISBN13: 978-0-7812-6975-9. Dewey:813.46.
Audience: **g,l,u,f.**

James, Henry **PG503.R6C52**
The Future of the Novel: Essays on the Art of Fiction. Paper Text. Textbook Publishers. Temecula, CA. 2003. xviii, 286, [p. ISBN:0-7581-0823-0, ISBN13: 978-0-7581-0823-4. Dewey:891.709.
Audience: **g,l,u,f.** B

Maugham, W. Somerset **PN3495**
Ten Novels and Their Authors. UK-B Format Paperback. Knopf Publishing Group. New York, NY. 2001. 352p. ISBN:0-09-928678-5, ISBN13: 978-0-09-928678-3. Dewey:809.3.
Audience: **g,l,u,f.**

McKeon, Michael **PN3451.T49 2000**
Theory of the Novel: A Historical Approach. Trade Paper. Johns Hopkins University Press. Baltimore, MD. 2000. 968p. ISBN:0-8018-6397-X, ISBN13: 978-0-8018-6397-4. Dewey:809.3. LCCN:00-027120.
Audience: **g,u,f.** *Choice, 2001.*

McKeon, Michael (Author, Introduction by) **PR841.M3 2002**
The Origins of the English Novel, 1600-1740. Ed. 15. Trade Paper. Johns Hopkins University Press. Baltimore, MD. 2002. 560p. ISBN:0-8018-6959-5, ISBN13: 978-0-8018-6959-4. Dewey:823/.009. LCCN:2002-016072.
Audience: **g,l,u,f.** *Choice, 1987.*

Morrison, Jago **PR881.M67 2003**
Reading Contemporary Fiction. Paper over Boards. Routledge. New York, NY. 2003. 272p. ISBN:0-415-19455-5, ISBN13: 978-0-415-19455-6. Dewey:823/.91409. LCCN:2002-151162.
Audience: **g,l,u,f.**

O'Connor, Frank **PN3373.O36 2004**
The Lonely Voice: A Study of the Short Story. Trade Paper. Melville House Publishing. Hoboken, NJ. 2004. 224p. ISBN:0-9718659-9-X, ISBN13: 978-0-9718659-9-0. Dewey:809.3/1. LCCN:2004-008899.
Audience: **g,l,u,f.**

Robbe-Grillet, Alain & Howard, Richard **PN3503**
For a New Novel: Essays on Fiction. Trade Paper. Northwestern University Press. Evanston, IL. 1992. 175p. ISBN:0-8101-0821-6, ISBN13: 978-0-8101-0821-9. Dewey:809.33.
Audience: **g,l,u,f.**

Sarraute, Nathalie **PN3503.S313 1990**
The Age of Suspicion. Maria Jolas (Translator). Trade Paper. George Braziller Inc. New York, NY. 1990. 147p. ISBN:0-8076-1253-7, ISBN13: 978-0-8076-1253-8. Dewey:809.3/04. LCCN:90-044532.
Audience: **g,l,u,f.**

Smiley, Jane **PS3569.M39Z476 2005**
Thirteen Ways of Looking at the Novel. Trade Cloth. Alfred A. Knopf Inc. New York, NY. 2005. 608p. ISBN:1-4000-4059-0, ISBN13: 978-1-4000-4059-9. Dewey:813/.54 B. LCCN:2005-045181.
Audience: **g,l,u,f.**

Watt, Ian P. **PR851**
The Rise of the Novel. W. B. Carnochan (Foreword by). Trade Paper. University of California Press. Berkeley, CA. 2001. 339p. ISBN:0-520-23069-8, ISBN13: 978-0-520-23069-9. Dewey:823.509.
Audience: **g,l,u,f.**

Special Forms of Literature > Fiction > Technique, Study, Teaching

Booth, Wayne **PE68.U5**
The Vocation of a Teacher: Rhetorical Occasions, 1967-1988. Trade Paper. University of Chicago Press. Chicago, IL. 1991. 372p. ISBN:0-226-06582-0, ISBN13: 978-0-226-06582-3. Dewey:428/.007/1173. LCCN:88-014297.
Audience: **g,l,u,f.**

Burroway, Janet & Weinberg, Susan **PN3355.B79 2003**
Writing Fiction: A Guide to Narrative Craft. Ed. 6. Trade Paper. Longman Publishing. Boston, MA. 2002. 448p. ISBN:0-321-11795-6, ISBN13: 978-0-321-11795-3. Dewey:808.3. LCCN:2002-016220.
Audience: **g,l.**

Forster, E. M. **PN3353.F6 1985**
Aspects of the Novel. Trade Paper. Harcourt Trade Publishers. New York, NY. 1956. 192p. ISBN:0-15-609180-1, ISBN13: 978-0-15-609180-0. Dewey:823/.009. LCCN:27-023181.
Audience: **g,l,u,f.**

Nyren, Ron & Stone, Sarah **PN3355.S86 2005**
Deepening Fiction: A Practical Guide for Intermediate and Advanced Writers. Trade Paper. Longman Publishing Group. White Plains, NY. 2004. 448p. ISBN:0-321-19537-X, ISBN13: 978-0-321-19537-1. Dewey:808.3. LCCN:2004-053507.
Audience: **u,f.**

Stern, Jerome **PN3355.S78**
Making Shapely Fiction. Trade Paper. W. W. Norton & Company, Inc. New York, NY. 2000. 288p. ISBN:0-393-32124-X, ISBN13: 978-0-393-32124-1. Dewey:808.3.
Audience: **l,u.**

Warren, Robert Penn & Brooks, Cleanth **PN3355.B74 1979**
Understanding Fiction. Ed. 3. Trade Paper. Prentice Hall PTR. Upper Saddle River, NJ. 1998. 515p. ISBN:0-13-936690-3, ISBN13: 978-0-13-936690-1. Dewey:808.3. LCCN:78-027116.
Audience: **g,l,u.**

Special Forms of Literature > Special Topics and Types of Fiction

Fuchs, B **PN56.R6F83 2004**
Romance. Paper over Boards. Routledge. New York, NY. 2004. 160p. New Critical Idiom Ser. ISBN:0-415-21260-X, ISBN13: 978-0-415-21260-1. Dewey:809.3. LCCN:2004-003902.
Audience: **g,u,f.**

Special Forms of Literature > Special Topics and Types of Fiction > Detective Fiction

Albert, Walter **Z5917.D5**
Dective and Mystery Fiction: An International Bibliography of Secondary Sources. Ed. 3. Locus Press. 2003.
Audience: **g,l,u,f.**

Albert, Walter **Z5917.D5A43 1995**
Detective and Mystery Fiction: An International Bibliography of Secondary Sources. Ed. 2. Trade Cloth. Millefleurs. San Bernardino, CA. 1997. 672p. Brownstone Mystery Guides Ser., Vol. 10 ISBN:0-941028-15-1, ISBN13: 978-0-941028-15-8. Dewey:016.8093/872. LCCN:95-005335.
Audience: **g,l,u,f.** *Choice, 1985.*

Ashley, Mike (Editor) **PN3448.D4**
The Mammoth Encyclopedia of Modern Crime Fiction. Trade Paper. Avalon Publishing Group. New York, NY. 2002. 800p. ISBN:0-7867-1006-3, ISBN13: 978-0-7867-1006-5. Dewey:813/.0872/03.
Audience: **g,l,u,f.**

Barzun, Jacques & Taylor, Wendell H. **Z5917.D5B37 1989**
A Catalogue of Crime. Trade Cloth. HarperCollins Publishers. New York, NY. 1989. 864p. ISBN:0-06-010263-2, ISBN13: 978-0-06-010263-0. Dewey:016.80883/87208. LCCN:88-045884.
Audience: **g,l,u,f.** *Choice, 1990.*

Bleiler, Richard J. **Z5917.D5B59 2003**
The Reference and Research Guide to Mystery and Detective Fiction. Ed. 2. Trade Cloth. Libraries Unlimited, Inc. Westport, CT. 2004. 848p. Reference Sources in the Humanities Ser. ISBN:1-56308-924-6, ISBN13: 978-1-56308-924-4. Dewey:016.80883/872. LCCN:2003-058905.
Audience: **g,l,u,f.** *Choice, 2004.*

Contento, William G. & Greenberg, Martin H. **Z2014.F4C58 1991**
Index to Crime and Mystery Anthologies. Trade Cloth. Macmillan Publishing Company, Inc. Old Tappan, NJ. 1990. 760p. ISBN:0-8161-8629-4, ISBN13: 978-0-8161-8629-7. Dewey:016.813/087208. LCCN:90-043578.
Audience: **g,l,u,f.** *Choice, 1991.*

Cook, Michael L. **PN3448**
Mystery, Detective, and Espionage Magazines. Cloth Text. Greenwood Publishing Group, Inc. Portsmouth, NH. 1983. 793p. Historical Guides to the World's Periodicals and Newspapers ISBN:0-313-23310-1, ISBN13: 978-0-313-23310-4. Dewey:823/.0872. LCCN:82-020977.
Audience: **g,l,u,f.**

Herbert, Rosemary (Editor) **PN3448.D4H37 1999**
The Oxford Companion to Crime and Mystery Writing. Oxford University Press. 1999. ISBN:0-19-507239-1, ISBN13: 978-0-19-507239-6.
Audience: **g,l,u,f.**

Hubin, Allen J. **Z5917.D5**
CRIME FICTION IV: A Comprehensive Bibliography, 1749-2000. Locus Press. 2003.
Audience: **g,l,u,f.**

Kelleghan, Fiona (Editor) **PN3448.D4A16 2001**
100 Masters of Mystery and Detective Fiction, 2 vols. Library Binding. Salem Press, Inc. Hackensack, NJ. 2001. 757p. Magill's Choice Ser. ISBN:0-89356-958-5, ISBN13: 978-0-89356-958-7. Dewey:809.3/872. LCCN:2001-032834.
Audience: **g,l,u,f.** *Choice, 2002.*

Magill, Frank N. (Editor) **PN3448.D4C75 1988**
Critical Survey of Mystery and Detective Fiction, 4 vols. Library Binding. Salem Press, Inc. Hackensack, NJ. 1988. 1830p. ISBN:0-89356-486-9, ISBN13: 978-0-89356-486-5. Dewey:809.3/872. LCCN:88-028566.
Audience: **g,l,u,f.** *Choice, 1989.*

Montney, Charles **Z5917.D5S85 1997**
What Mystery Do I Read Next?: A Reader's Guide. Trade Cloth. Thomson Gale. Farmington Hills, MI. 1996. 550p. ISBN:0-7876-1592-7, ISBN13: 978-0-7876-1592-5. Dewey:016.80883/872. LCCN:96-047713.
Audience: **g,l,u,f.**

Priestman, Martin (Editor) **PR830.D4C36 2003**
The Cambridge Companion to Crime Fiction. Cloth Text. Cambridge University Press. New York, NY. 2003. 308p. Cambridge Companions to Literature Ser. ISBN:0-521-80399-3, ISBN13: 978-0-521-80399-1. Dewey:823/.087209. LCCN:2003-046056.
Audience: **g,l,u,f.** *Choice, 2004.*

Symons, Julian **PN3448.D4 S87 1993**
Bloody Murder: From the Detective Story to the Crime Novel. Ed. 3. Trade Cloth. Warner Books, Inc. New York, NY. 1993. 349p. ISBN:0-89296-496-0, ISBN13: 978-0-89296-496-3. Dewey:809.3/872. LCCN:92-054127.
Audience: **g,l,u,f.**

Van Dover, J. Kenneth **PR830.D4V36 2005**
We Must Have Certainty: Four Essays on the Detective Story. Trade Cloth. Susquehanna University Press. Cranbury, NJ. 2005. 224p. ISBN:1-57591-091-8, ISBN13: 978-1-57591-091-8. Dewey:823/.087209. LCCN:2004-028954.
Audience: **u,f.** *Choice, 2006.*

Winks, Robin W. (Editor) **PR830.D4**
Mystery and Suspense Writers: The Literature of Crime Detection and Espionage, Set. Library Binding. Thomson Gale. Farmington Hills, MI. 1998. 1296p. ISBN:0-684-80521-9, ISBN13: 978-0-684-80521-4. Dewey:823/.0872/09. LCCN:98-036812.
Audience: **g,l,u,f.** *Choice, 1999.*

Special Forms of Literature > Special Topics and Types of Fiction > Science Fiction

Ashley, Michael & Contento, William G. **Z5917**
The Supernatural Index: A Listing of Fantasy, Supernatural, Occult, Weird, and Horror Anthologies. Cloth Text. Greenwood Publishing Group, Inc. Portsmouth, NH. 1995. 952p. Bibliographies and Indexes in Science Fiction, Fantasy, and Horror Ser., No. 5 ISBN:0-313-24030-2, ISBN13: 978-0-313-24030-0. Dewey:016.80883/8738. LCCN:95-006290.
Audience: **g,l,u,f.** *Choice, 1995.*

Ashley, Mike **PS374.S35A78 2000**
The Time Machines: The Story of the Science-Fiction Pulp Magazines from the Beginning to 1950. Trade Cloth. Liverpool University Press. Liverpool, 2001. 320p. Liverpool Science Fiction Texts and Studies ISBN:0-85323-855-3, ISBN13: 978-0-85323-855-3. Dewey:813/.0876209. LCCN:2001-391450.
Audience: **g,l,u,f.**

Ashley, Mike **PS374.S35**
Transformations: The History of the Science Fiction Magazine 1950 to 1970. Trade Cloth. Liverpool University Press. Liverpool, 2005. 422p. Liverpool University Press - Liverpool Science Fiction Texts and Studies ISBN:0-85323-769-7, ISBN13: 978-0-85323-769-3. Dewey:809.38762.
Audience: **g,l,u,f.**

Barron, Neil **Z5917**
Anatomy of Wonder: A Critical Guide to Science Fiction. Ed. 5. Trade Cloth. Libraries Unlimited, Inc. Westport, CT. 2004. 1016p. ISBN:1-59158-171-0, ISBN13: 978-1-59158-171-0. Dewey:016.80883/8762. LCCN:2004-063249.
Audience: **g,l,u,f.** *Choice, 2005, 1995.*

Barron, Neil **Z6514.F35F35 1999**
Fantasy and Horror: A Critical and Historical Guide to Literature, Illustration, Film, T.V., Radio and the Internet. Trade

Cloth. Scarecrow Press, Inc. Lanham, MD. 1999. 832p. ISBN:0-8108-3596-7, ISBN13: 978-0-8108-3596-2. Dewey:700/.415. LCCN:98-046564.
Audience: **g,l,u,f.** *Choice, 2000.*

Bleiler, Everett F. **Z5917.S36B62 1990**
Science-Fiction: The Early Years. Trade Cloth. Kent State University Press. Kent, OH. 1990. 1,024p. ISBN:0-87338-416-4, ISBN13: 978-0-87338-416-2. Dewey:016.80883/8762. LCCN:90-004839.
Audience: **g,l,u,f.** *Choice, 1991.*

Bleiler, Everett F. & Bleiler, Richard J. **PS648.S3B57 1998**
Science-Fiction: The Gernsback Years. Trade Cloth. Kent State University Press. Kent, OH. 1998. 768p. ISBN:0-87338-604-3, ISBN13: 978-0-87338-604-3. Dewey:016.813/8762. LCCN:98-013374.
Audience: **g,l,u,f.** *Choice, 1999.*

Bleiler, Richard **PN3435.S96 2003**
Supernatural Fiction Writers, Set. Ed. 2. Library Binding. Thomson Gale. Farmington Hills, MI. 2002. 760p. The Scribner Writers Ser. ISBN:0-684-31250-6, ISBN13: 978-0-684-31250-7. Dewey:809.3/8738. LCCN:2002-011128.
Audience: **g,l,u,f.** *Choice, 2003.*

Burgess, Michael & Bartle, Lisa R. **Z5917.S36B87 2003**
Reference Guide to Science Fiction, Fantasy, and Horror. Ed. 2. Trade Cloth. Libraries Unlimited, Inc. Westport, CT. 2002. 598p. Reference Sources in the Humanities Ser. ISBN:1-56308-548-8, ISBN13: 978-1-56308-548-2. Dewey:016.8093/876. LCCN:2002-151707.
Audience: **g,l,u,f.** *Choice, 1992.*

Clute, John & Grant, John (Editors) **PN3435**
The Encyclopedia of Fantasy. Cloth over Boards. Palgrave Macmillan. New York, NY. 1997. 1100p. ISBN:0-312-15897-1, ISBN13: 978-0-312-15897-2. Dewey:809.3/8766/03. LCCN:96-037472.
Audience: **g,l,u,f.** *Choice, 1997.*

Clute, John & Nicholls, Peter **PN3433.4.E53 1995**
The Encyclopedia of Science Fiction. Trade Paper. St. Martin's Press. Gordonville, VA. 1995. ISBN:0-312-13486-X, ISBN13: 978-0-312-13486-0. Dewey:809.3/8762/03. LCCN:95-032883.
Audience: **g,l,u,f.** *Choice, 1993.*

Joshi, S. T. & Dziemianowicz, Stefan (Editors) **PN56**
Supernatural Literature of the World: An Encyclopedia. Cloth Text. Greenwood Publishing Group, Inc. Portsmouth, NH. 2005. 1556p. ISBN:0-313-32774-2, ISBN13: 978-0-313-32774-2. Dewey:809/.9337. LCCN:2005-008521.
Audience: **g,l,u,f.** *Choice, 2006.*

Miller, Stephen T., et. al. **PN3448.S45**
Science Fiction, Fantasy, and Weird Fiction Magazine Index (1890-2003). Contento, William G. (Author). Locus Press. 2003.
Audience: **g,l,u,f.**

Seed, David (Editor) **PN3433.5.C73 2005**
A Companion to Science Fiction. Trade Cloth. Blackwell Publishing, Inc. Malden, MA. 2005. 632p. Blackwell Companions to Literature and Culture Ser., Vol. 34 ISBN:1-4051-1218-2, ISBN13: 978-1-4051-1218-5. Dewey:809.3/8762. LCCN:2004-025185.
Audience: **g,l,u,f.** *Choice, 2006.*

Tymn, Marshall B. & Ashley, Mike (Editors) **PN3433**
Science Fiction, Fantasy, and Weird Fiction Magazines. Cloth Text. Greenwood Publishing Group, Inc. Portsmouth, NH. 1985. 970p. Historical Guides to the World's Periodicals and Newspapers ISBN:0-313-21221-X, ISBN13: 978-0-313-21221-5. Dewey:809.3/876. LCCN:84-011523.
Audience: **g,l,u,f.** *Choice, 1986.*

Westfahl, Gary (Editor) **PS374**
The Greenwood Encyclopedia of Science Fiction and Fantasy: Themes, Works, and Wonders. Cloth Text. Greenwood Publishing Group, Inc. Portsmouth, NH. 2005. 1612p. ISBN:0-313-32950-8, ISBN13: 978-0-313-32950-0. Dewey:813/.0876203. LCCN:2005-013677.
Audience: **g,l,u,f.** *Choice, 2006.*

Special Forms of Literature > Comic Books. Graphic Novels.

Carrier, David **PN6710.C35 2000**
The Aesthetics of Comics. Trade Cloth. Pennsylvania State University Press. University Park, PA. 2000. 478p. ISBN:0-271-01962-X, ISBN13: 978-0-271-01962-8. Dewey:741.5/01. LCCN:99-017980.
Audience: **l,u.** *Choice, 2000.*

Eisner, Will (Author, Illustrator) **NC1764 .E47**
Comics and Sequential Art. Ed. 16. Trade Paper. F & W Publications, Inc. Cincinnati, OH. 1994. 164p. ISBN:0-9614728-1-2, ISBN13: 978-0-9614728-1-8. Dewey:741.5. LCCN:85-061669.
Audience: **g,l,u,f.**

Fingeroth, Danny **PN6714.F54 2004**
Superman on the Couch: What Superheros Really Tell Us about Ourselves and Our Society. Trade Paper. Continuum International Publishing Group, Ltd. London, 2004. 192p. ISBN:0-8264-1540-7, ISBN13: 978-0-8264-1540-0. Dewey:741.5/9. LCCN:2003-020893.
Audience: **g,l,u,f.** *Choice, 2004.*

Harvey, Robert C. **PN6725.H37 1996**
The Art of the Comic Book: An Aesthetic History. Trade Cloth. University Press of Mississippi. Jackson, MS. 1996. 280p. Studies in Popular Culture ISBN:0-87805-758-7, ISBN13: 978-0-87805-758-0. Dewey:741.5/09. LCCN:95-000377.
Audience: **g,l,u,f.**

Klock, Geoff **PN6725.K59 2002**
How to Read Superhero Comics and Why. Trade Cloth. Continuum International Publishing Group, Ltd. London, 2002. 256p. ISBN:0-8264-1418-4, ISBN13: 978-0-8264-1418-2. Dewey:741.5/0973. LCCN:2002-005803.
Audience: **g,l,u,f.** *Choice, 2003.*

McCloud, Scott **PN6710.M335**
Understanding Comics. Trade Paper. HarperCollins Publishers. New York, NY. 1994. 224p. ISBN:0-06-097625-X, ISBN13: 978-0-06-097625-5. Dewey:741.5. LCCN:00-001910.
Audience: **g,l,u,f.**

Sabin, Roger **PN6725 .S33 1996**
Comics, Comix and Graphic Novels: A History of Comic Art. Trade Cloth. Phaidon Press. London, 1996. 240p. ISBN:0-7148-3008-9, ISBN13: 978-0-7148-3008-7. Dewey:741.5/0973. LCCN:2001-430396.
Audience: **g,l,u,f.**

Special Forms of Literature > Children's Literature

Bearne, Eve & Watson, Victor (Editors) **PR990.W47 2000**
Where Texts and Children Meet. Paper over Boards. Routledge. New York, NY. 2000. 248p. ISBN:0-415-20662-6, ISBN13: 978-0-415-20662-4. Dewey:820.9/9282. LCCN:99-036160.
Audience: **g,l,u,f.**

Bettelheim, Bruno **GR550 .B47 1989**
The Uses of Enchantment: The Meaning and Importance of Fairy Tales. Trade Paper. Knopf Publishing Group. New York, NY. 1989. 352p. Vintage Ser. ISBN:0-679-72393-5, ISBN13: 978-0-679-72393-6. Dewey:398.2.
Audience: **g,l,u,f.** B

Clark, Beverly Lyon & Higonnet, Margaret R. **PN1009.5.S48G57 2000**
Girls, Boys, Books, Toys: Gender in Children's Literature and Culture. Trade Paper. Johns Hopkins University Press. Baltimore, MD. 2000. 312p. ISBN:0-8018-6526-3, ISBN13: 978-0-8018-6526-8. Dewey:305.3/09.
Audience: **g,u,f.** *Choice, 2000.*

Hunt, Peter **PN1009.A1U44 2005**
Understanding Children's Literature. Ed. 2. Paper over Boards. Routledge. New York, NY. 2005. 232p. ISBN:0-415-37547-9, ISBN13: 978-0-415-37547-4. Dewey:809/.89282. LCCN:2005-002517.
Audience: **g,u,f.**

Lanes, Selma G. **PN1009.A1L33 2004**
Through the Looking Glass: Further Adventures and Misadventures in the Realm of Children's Literature. Trade Cloth. David R. Godine Publisher. Boston, MA. 2005. 256p. ISBN:1-56792-262-7, ISBN13: 978-1-56792-262-2. Dewey:809/.89282. LCCN:2004-016527.
Audience: **u,f.**

Lukens, Rebecca J. **PN1009.A1**
A Critical Handbook of Children's Literature. Ed. 6. Trade Cloth. Addison-Wesley Longman, Inc. Boston, MA. 2001. ISBN:0-201-66670-7, ISBN13: 978-0-201-66670-0. Dewey:809/.89282.
Audience: **g,l,u,f.**

Lundin, Anne H. **PS490.L86 2004**
Constructing the Canon of Children's Literature: Beyond Library Walls and Ivory Towers. Cloth Text. Routledge. New York, NY. 2004. 192p. Children's Literature and Culture Ser., Vol. 31 ISBN:0-8153-3841-4, ISBN13: 978-0-8153-3841-3. Dewey:810.9/9282. LCCN:2004-001366.
Audience: **g,u,f.**

Nikolajeva, Maria **PS490.N55 2005**
Aesthetic Approaches to Children's Literature: An Introduction. Trade Paper, Perfect. Scarecrow Press, Inc. Lanham, MD. 2005. 313p. ISBN:0-8108-5426-0, ISBN13: 978-0-8108-5426-0. Dewey:810.9/9282. LCCN:2004-024130.
Audience: **g,u,f.** *Choice, 2006.*

Paul, Lissa (Editor), et al. **PZ5 .N655 2005**
The Norton Anthology of Children's Literature: The Traditions in English. Lynne Vallone, Gillian Avery & Peter Hunt (Editors). Trade Paper, Perfect. W. W. Norton & Company, Inc. New York, NY. 2006. 2200p. ISBN:0-393-32776-0, ISBN13: 978-0-393-32776-2. Dewey:820.809282.
Audience: **g,l,u,f.**

Stahl, J. D., et al. **PN1009.A1**
Crosscurrents of Children's Literature: An Anthology of Texts and Criticism. Tina L. Hanlon & Elizabeth Lennox Keyser (Authors). Trade Paper. Oxford University Press, Inc. New York, NY. 2006. 800p. ISBN:0-19-513493-1, ISBN13: 978-0-19-513493-3. Dewey:820.8/09282. LCCN:2006-024446.
Audience: **g,u,f.**

Zipes, Jack D. **PN1009.A1Z57 2000**
Sticks and Stones: The Troublesome Success of Children's Literature from Slovenly Peter to Harry Potter. Paper over Boards. Routledge. New York, NY. 2000. 176p. ISBN:0-415-92811-7, ISBN13: 978-0-415-92811-3. Dewey:809/.89282/09045. LCCN:00-032318.
Audience: **g,u,f.** *Choice, 2001.*

Collections of Literature > Poetry

PS580
□ Academy of American Poets.
http://www.poets.org
Audience: **g,l,u,f.**

PS580
□ Library of Congress Poetry Center.
http://www.loc.gov/poetry/
Audience: **g,l,u,f.**

Bloom, Harold **PR1175.B4566 2004**
The Best Poems of the English Language: From Chaucer Through Frost. Trade Cloth. HarperCollins Publishers. New York, NY. 2004. 1008p. ISBN:0-06-054041-9, ISBN13: 978-0-06-054041-8. Dewey:821.008. LCCN:2003-051104.
Audience: **g,l,u.**

Ellman, Richard **PS613.N67 2003**
Norton Anthology of Modern and Contemporary Poetry, Vol. 1. Ed. 3. Trade Paper. W. W. Norton & Company, Inc. New York, NY. 2003. 1,100p. ISBN:0-393-97791-9, ISBN13: 978-0-393-97791-2. Dewey:821.008. LCCN:2002-037990.
Audience: **g,l,u,f.**

Feinstein, Sascha & Komunyakaa, Yusef (Editors) **PS595.J34J39 1991**
The Jazz Poetry Anthology. Trade Cloth. Indiana University Press. Bloomington, IN. 1991. 316p. ISBN:0-253-32163-8, ISBN13: 978-0-253-32163-3. Dewey:808.81/9357. LCCN:90-005237.
Audience: **g,l,u,f.**

Morgan, Esther (Editor) **PS3019**
The Poetry Archive.
http://www.poetryarchive.org
Bailey, Andrew (Editor).
Audience: **g,l,u,f.**

Pinter, Harold (Editor), et al. **PN6101.A15 1994**
Ninety-Nine Poems in Translation: An Anthology. Anthony Astbury & Geoffrey Godbert (Editors). Cloth Text. Grove/Atlantic, Inc. New York, NY. 1994. 149p. ISBN:0-8021-1557-8, ISBN13: 978-0-8021-1557-7. Dewey:808.81. LCCN:94-021546.
Audience: **g,l,u,f.**

Spiegelman, Willard **PS310.V57S67 2005**
How Poets See the World: The Art of Description in Contemporary Poetry. Trade Cloth. Oxford University Press, Inc. New York, NY. 2005. 256p. ISBN:0-19-517491-7, ISBN13: 978-0-19-517491-5. LCCN:2004-012519.
Audience: **g,l,u,f.** *Choice, 2005.*

Stallworthy, Jon (Editor) **PN6110.W28O93 2003**
The Oxford Book of War Poetry. Trade Paper. Oxford University Press, Inc. New York, NY. 2003. 390p. ISBN:0-19-280454-5, ISBN13: 978-0-19-280454-9. Dewey:808.8/19358.
Audience: **g,l,u,f.** B

Strand, Mark **PN6101.A163 2005**
100 Great Poems of the Twentieth Century. Trade Cloth. W. W. Norton & Company, Inc. New York, NY. 2005. 256p. ISBN:0-393-05894-8, ISBN13: 978-0-393-05894-9. Dewey:821/.9108. LCCN:2005-002150.
Audience: **g,l,u,f.**

Wordsworth, Jonathon & Wordsworth, Jessica (Contribution by) **PR1222**
The Penguin Book of Romantic Poetry. Trade Paper. Penguin Group (USA) Inc. New York, NY. 2006. 1056p. ISBN:0-14-043568-9, ISBN13: 978-0-14-043568-9. Dewey:821.708.
Audience: **g,l,u,f.**

Collections of Literature > Fiction

Chabon, Michael (Editor) **PS648.S5**
The Best American Short Stories 2005. Katrina Kenison (Contribution by). Trade Cloth. Houghton Mifflin Company Trade & Reference Division. Boston, MA. 2005. 320p. ISBN:0 618 42349-4, ISBN13: 978-0-618-42349-1. Dewey:813/.0108.
Audience: **g,l,u,f.**

Curtis, C. Michael (Editor) **PN6071.R4F35 2003**
Faith: Stories: Short Fiction on the Varieties and Vagaries of Faith. Trade Paper. Houghton Mifflin Company Trade & Reference Division. Boston, MA. 2003. 336p. ISBN:0-618-37824-3, ISBN13: 978-0-618-37824-1. Dewey:808.83/108382. LCCN:2003-056793.
Audience: **g,l,u,f.**

Gioia, Dana & Gwynn, R. S. **PN6120.2.A73 2006**
The Art of the Short Story: 52 Great Authors, Their Best Short Fiction, and Their Insights on Writing. Trade Paper. Longman Publishing Group. White Plains, NY. 2005. 320p. ISBN:0-321-33722-0, ISBN13: 978-0-321-33722-1. Dewey:808.83/1. LCCN:2005-351377.
Audience: **g,l,u.**

Gordimer, Nadine **PN6014.T34 2004**
Telling Tales. Trade Paper. Picador. New York, NY. 2004. 320p. ISBN:0-312-42404-3, ISBN13: 978-0-312-42404-6. Dewey:808.8/31. LCCN:2004-040124.
Audience: **g,l,u,f.**

Johnson-Davies, Denys **PJ7694.E8U53 2003**
Under the Naked Sky: Short Stories from the Arab World. Ed. 2. Trade Paper. American University in Cairo Press. New York, NY. 2003. 252p. ISBN:977-424-780-9, ISBN13: 978-977-424-780-4. Dewey:892.7/36/08. LCCN:2004-300602.
Audience: **g,l,u,f.**

Martin, Wendy **PN6120.2.A735 2006**
The Art of the Short Story. Paper Text. Houghton Mifflin College Division. Boston, MA. 2005. 1671p. ISBN:0-618-15575-9, ISBN13: 978-0-618-15575-0. Dewey:808.83/01. LCCN:2004-112191.
Audience: **g,l,u,f.**

Martin, Wendy **PS647.W6M67 2004**
More Stories We Tell: The Best Contemporary Short Stories by American Women. Trade Paper. Knopf Publishing Group. New York, NY. 2004. 384p. ISBN:0-375-71450-2, ISBN13: 978-0-375-71450-4. Dewey:813/.01089287. LCCN:2003-063208.
Audience: **g,l,u,f.**

Martin, Wendy **PS647.W6W4 1990**
We Are the Stories We Tell: The Best Short Stories by North American Women since 1945. Trade Paper. Knopf Publishing Group. New York, NY. 1990. 352p. ISBN:0-679-72881-3, ISBN13: 978-0-679-72881-8. Dewey:813/.01089287. LCCN:89-039587.
Audience: **g,l,u,f.**

McSweeney's Editors (Created by) **PS648.S5**
The Better of Mcsweeney's Volume One: Issues 1-10, Vol. 1. Trade Paper, Perfect. McSweeney's Publishing. San Francisco, CA. 2005. 361p. ISBN:1-932416-33-1, ISBN13: 978-1-932416-33-6. Dewey:820.8 B.
Audience: **g,l,u,f.**

Paris Review Staff **PN6014.P234**
The Paris Review Book: Of Heartbreak, Madness, Sex, Love, Betrayal, Outsiders, Intoxication, War, Whimsy, Horrors, God, Death, Dinner, Baseball, Travels, the Art of Writing, and

Everything Else in the World since 1953. George Plimpton (Introduction by). Trade Paper. Picador. New York, NY. 2004. 928p. ISBN:0-312-42239-3, ISBN13: 978-0-312-42239-4. Dewey:808.8.
Audience: **g,l,u,f.**

Remnick, David **PS549.N5W58 2000**
Wonderful Town: New York Stories from the New Yorker. Trade Cloth. Random House, Inc. New York, NY. 2000. 496p. ISBN:0-375-50356-0, ISBN13: 978-0-375-50356-6. LCCN:99-048838.
Audience: **g,l,u,f.**

Selvadurai, Shyam (Editor) **PS508.S67S76 2005**
Story-Wallah: Short Fiction from South Asian Writers. Trade Paper. Houghton Mifflin Company Trade & Reference Division. Boston, MA. 2005. 448p. ISBN:0-618-57680-0, ISBN13: 978-0-618-57680-7. Dewey:813/.01088911. LCCN:2004-060937.
Audience: **g,l,u,f.**

Collections of Literature > Essays

Lapham, Lewis H. & Rosenbush, Ellen (Editors) **PS509.U52A39 2000**
An American Album: One Hundred of Fifty Years of Harper's Magazine. Trade Cloth. Harper's Magazine Foundation. New York, NY. 2000. 760p. ISBN:1-879957-53-1, ISBN13: 978-1-879957-53-4. Dewey:810.8/04. LCCN:99-087125.
Audience: **g,l,u,f.**

Lopate, Phillip **PN6141.A78 1995**
The Art of the Personal Essay: An Anthology from the Classical Era to the Present. UK-Trade Paper. Doubleday Publishing. New York, NY. 1997. 832p. ISBN:0-385-42339-X, ISBN13: 978-0-385-42339-7. Dewey:808.8/4.
Audience: **g,l,u,f.** *Choice, 1994.*

New York Times Staff **PN137.W734 2001**
Writers on Writing: Collected Essays from the New York Times. John Darnton (Editor). Cloth over Boards. Henry Holt & Company. New York, NY. 2001. 256p. ISBN:0-8050-6741-8, ISBN13: 978-0-8050-6741-5. Dewey:808/.02. LCCN:00-053509.
Audience: **g,l,u,f.**

Orlean, Susan (Editor) **PS688**
The Best American Essays 2005. Robert Atwan (Contribution by). Trade Cloth. Houghton Mifflin Company Trade & Reference Division. Boston, MA. 2005. 320p. ISBN:0-618-35712-2, ISBN13: 978-0-618-35712-3. Dewey:814.008.
Audience: **g,l,u,f.**

Orwell, George **PR6029.R8**
Essays. John Carey (Introduction by). Trade Cloth. Alfred A. Knopf Inc. New York, NY. 2002. 1424p. ISBN:0-375-41503-3, ISBN13: 978-0-375-41503-6. Dewey:824.912.
Audience: **g,l,u,f.**

Paris Review Staff **PN6014.P234**
The Paris Review Book: Of Heartbreak, Madness, Sex, Love, Betrayal, Outsiders, Intoxication, War, Whimsy, Horrors, God, Death, Dinner, Baseball, Travels, the Art of Writing, and
Everything Else in the World since 1953. George Plimpton (Introduction by). Trade Paper. Picador. New York, NY. 2004. 928p. ISBN:0-312-42239-3, ISBN13: 978-0-312-42239-4. Dewey:808.8.
Audience: **g,l,u,f.**

Ulin, David L. (Editor) **PS572.L6A84 2001**
Another City: Writing from Los Angeles. Trade Paper. City Lights Books. San Francisco, CA. 2001. 240p. ISBN:0-87286-391-3, ISBN13: 978-0-87286-391-0. Dewey:820.8/03279494/09045. LCCN:2001-042122.
Audience: **g,l,u,f.**

Folklore

Ashliman, D. L. **Z5983**
A Guide to Folktales in the English Language: Based on the Aarne-Thompson Classification System. Cloth Text. Greenwood Publishing Group, Inc. Portsmouth, NH. 1987. 384p. Bibliographies and Indexes in World Literature Ser., No. 11 ISBN:0-313-25961-5, ISBN13: 978-0-313-25961-6. Dewey:016.3982/012. LCCN:87-015017.
Audience: **g,l,u,f.** *Choice, 1988.*

Dorson, Richard M. **GR50 .D63**
The British Folklorists: A History. Library Binding. University of Chicago Press. Chicago, IL. 1992. Folktales of the World Ser. ISBN:0-226-15863-2, ISBN13: 978-0-226-15863-1. Dewey:398./094200922. LCCN:68-016689.
Audience: **u,f.**

Dorson, Richard M. **BL315**
Folklore and Folklife: An Introduction. Trade Paper. University of Chicago Press. Chicago, IL. 1982. 572p. ISBN:0-226-15871-3, ISBN13: 978-0-226-15871-6. Dewey:398/.08. LCCN:77-189038.
Audience: **l,u.**

Dundes, Alan **GR42.D854 2002**
Bloody Mary in the Mirror: Essays in Psychoanalytic Folkloristics. Trade Cloth. University Press of Mississippi. Jackson, MS. 2002. 176p. ISBN:1-57806-461-9, ISBN13: 978-1-57806-461-8. Dewey:398/.01/9. LCCN:2002-020837.
Audience: **u,f.** *Choice, 2003.*

Dundes, Alan (Editor) **GR71.I46 1999**
International Folkloristics: Classic Contributions by the Founders of Folklore. Trade Paper. Rowman & Littlefield Publishers, Inc. Lanham, MD. 1999. 368p. ISBN:0-8476-9515-8, ISBN13: 978-0-8476-9515-7. Dewey:398. LCCN:99-029463.
Audience: **u,f.**

Dundes, Alan **GR45**
The Study of Folklore. Ed. 1. Trade Cloth. Prentice Hall PTR. Upper Saddle River, NJ. 1994. 479p. ISBN:0-13-858944-5, ISBN13: 978-0-13-858944-8. Dewey:398.072.
Audience: **u,f.**

Feintuch, Burt (Editor) **GR44.4.E44 2003**
Eight Words for the Study of Expressive Culture. Trade Cloth. University of Illinois Press. Champaign, IL. 2003. 248p. ISBN:0-252-02806-6, ISBN13: 978-0-252-02806-9. Dewey:398/.01/4. LCCN:2002-008284.
Audience: **u,f.** *Choice, 2004.*

Fine, Elizabeth C. **GR40 .F47**
The Folklore Text: From Performance to Print. Trade Paper. Indiana University Press. Bloomington, IN. 1994. 256p. ISBN:0-253-20922-6, ISBN13: 978-0-253-20922-1. Dewey:390/.01/8.
Audience: **u,f.** *Choice, 1985.*

Georges, Robert A. & Jones, Michael O. **GR40.G46 1995**
Folkloristics: An Introduction. Trade Cloth. Indiana University Press. Bloomington, IN. 1995. 352p. ISBN:0-253-32934-5, ISBN13: 978-0-253-32934-9. Dewey:398/.01. LCCN:95-014400.
Audience: **l,u.**

Ives, Edward D. **GR45.5.I93 1995**
The Tape-Recorded Interview: A Manual for Field Workers in Folklore and Oral History. Ed. 2. Trade Paper. University of Tennessee Press. Knoxville, TN. 1995. 128p. ISBN:0-87049-878-9, ISBN13: 978-0-87049-878-7. Dewey:390/.072. LCCN:94-018757.
Audience: **u,f.**

Leach, Maria **GR35 .F82 1984**
Funk and Wagnall's Standard Dictionary of Folklore, Mythology, and Legend. Jerome Fried (Editor). Trade Paper. HarperCollins Publishers. New York, NY. 1984. 1264p. ISBN:0-06-250511 4, ISBN13: 978-0-06-250511-8. Dewey:398/.042/03. LCCN:83-048421.
Audience: **g,l,u.**

Lindahl, Carl (Editor), et al. **GR35.M43 2002**
Medieval Folklore: A Guide to Myths, Legends, Tales, Beliefs, and Customs. John McNamara & John Lindow (Editors). Trade Cloth. Oxford University Press, Inc. New York, NY. 2002. 512p. ISBN:0-19-514771-5, ISBN13: 978-0-19-514771-1. Dewey:398/.094/0902. LCCN:2001-058814.
Audience: **g,l,u,f.**

MacDonald, Margaret Read (Editor) **GR72.3.T73 1999**
Traditional Storytelling Today: An International Sourcebook. Trade Cloth. Fitzroy Dearborn Publishers, Inc. Chicago, IL. 1999. 500p. ISBN:1-57958-011-4, ISBN13: 978-1-57958-011-7. Dewey:398. LCCN:00-551244.
Audience: **u,f.** *Choice, 2000.*

Oring, Elliott **GR66.F65 1986**
Folk Groups and Folklore Genres: An Introduction. Trade Paper. Utah State University Press. Logan, UT. 1986. 272p. ISBN:0-87421-128-X, ISBN13: 978-0-87421-128-3. Dewey:398. LCCN:86-015863.
Audience: **l,u.**

Paredes, Americo & Bauman, Dick (Editors) **GR550**
Toward New Perspectives in Folklore. Ed. 2. Perfect. Trickster Press. Bloomington, IN. 2000. 232p. ISBN:0-915305-47-X, ISBN13: 978-0-915305-47-6. Dewey:398/.042.
Audience: **u,f.**

Seal, Graham **GR35.S4 2001**
Encyclopedia of Folk Heroes. Library Binding. ABC-CLIO, Inc. Santa Barbara, CA. 2001. 347p. ISBN:1-57607-216-9, ISBN13: 978-1-57607-216-5. Dewey:398/.03. LCCN:2001-004423.
Audience: **g,l,u.** *Choice, 2002.*

Sims, Martha C. & Stephens, Martine **GR45.S56 2005**
Living Folklore: An Introduction to the Study of People and Their Traditions. Cloth Text. Utah State University Press. Logan, UT. 2005. 312p. ISBN:0-87421-611-7, ISBN13: 978-0-87421-611-0. Dewey:398/.072. LCCN:2005-011837.
Audience: **l,u.**

Thompson, Stith **GR72.56.T48 1989**
Motif-Index of Folk-Literature: A Classification of Narrative Elements in Folk Tales, Ballads, Myths, Fables, Mediaeval Romances, Exempla, Fabliaux, Jest-Books, and Local Legends. Trade Cloth. Indiana University Press. Bloomington, IN. 1958. 3564p. ISBN:0-253-33887-5, ISBN13: 978-0-253-33887-7. Dewey:025.4/63982. LCCN:55-008055.
Audience: **u,f.** B *Choice, 1995.*

Toelken, Barre **GR40.T63**
The Dynamics of Folklore. Cloth Text. Houghton Mifflin Company. New York, NY. 1979. xiii, 395p. ISBN:0-395-27068-5, ISBN13: 978-0-395-27068-4. Dewey:390/.01. LCCN:78-069536.
Audience: **u,f.** B

Zipes, Jack D. (Editor) **PN3437.O94 2002**
The Oxford Companion to Fairy Tales. Trade Paper. Oxford University Press, Inc. New York, NY. 2003. 640p. Library of Latin America ISBN:0-19-860509-9, ISBN13: 978-0-19-860509-6. Dewey:398.21. LCCN:2002-072251.
Audience: **g,l,u,f.** *Choice, 2000.*

Humor. Satire

Barreca, Regina **PR111.L27 1988**
Last Laughs: Perspectives on Women and Comedy. Paper over Boards. Gordon & Breach Publishing Group. New York, NY. 1988. 322p. Studies in Gender and Culture Ser. ISBN:0-677-22020-0, ISBN13: 978-0-677-22020-8. Dewey:820/.9/9287. LCCN:88-021225.
Audience: **u,f.**

Bergson, Henri **PN6149.P5B513 2005**
Laughter: An Essay on the Meaning of the Comic. Cloudesley Brereton & Fred Rothwell (Translators). Trade Paper. Dover Publications, Inc. Mineola, NY. 2005. 112p. ISBN:0-486-44380-9, ISBN13: 978-0-486-44380-5. Dewey:809/.917. LCCN:2005-047090.
Audience: **u,f.**

Cohen, Ted **PN6147.C56 1999**
Jokes: Philosophical Thoughts on Joking Matters. Trade Cloth. University of Chicago Press. Chicago, IL. 1999. 112p. ISBN:0-226-11230-6, ISBN13: 978-0-226-11230-5. Dewey:809.7. LCCN:99-012810.
Audience: **u,f.**

Freud, Sigmund **PN6149.P5.F7 1960**
Jokes and Their Relationship to the Unconscious. James Strachey (Translator). Trade Cloth. W. W. Norton & Company, Inc. New York, NY. 1990. 321p. Standard Edition of the Complete Psychological Works of Sigmund Freud ISBN:0-393-00145-8, ISBN13: 978-0-393-00145-7. Dewey:153.8. LCCN:91-114677.
Audience: **u,f.**

Rourke, Constance **PS430.R6 2004**
American Humor: A Study of the National Character. Greil Marcus (Introduction by). Trade Cloth. New York Review of Books, Incorporated, The. New York, NY. 2004. 380p. New York Review Books Classics Ser. ISBN:1-59017-079-2, ISBN13: 978-1-59017-079-3. Dewey:817.009/358. LCCN:2003-025878.
Audience: **g,l,u,f.** B

Wyndham-Lewis, D. B. & Lee, Charles (Editors) **PR1175.S784 2003**
The Stuffed Owl: An Anthology of Bad Verse. Billy Collins (Introduction by). Trade Paper. New York Review of Books, Incorporated, The. New York, NY. 2003. 328p. New York Review Books Classics Ser. ISBN:1-59017-038-5, ISBN13: 978-1-59017-038-0. Dewey:821.008. LCCN:2003-006580.
Audience: **g,l,u,f.**

GERMANIC LANGUAGES AND LITERATURES

The Germanic Languages and Literatures section includes titles for German studies from Germany, the former German Democratic Republic, Austria, and Switzerland. The scope of the section additionally includes titles on other Germanic and Scandinavian languages and literatures: Dutch, Flemish, Afrikaans, Old Icelandic, Old Norwegian, Modern Icelandic, Danish, Norwegian, and Swedish. Furthermore, the section provides dictionaries, other reference works and classic texts on language history, grammar, and etymology. Languages and literatures are treated chronologically from the earliest periods to the present. Each German literary period presents the original German works of pertinent authors, as well as English translations of these titles wherever possible. English critical works on most authors are listed as well. Other Germanic and Skandinavian languages and literatures are treated similarly.

Although the Germanic Languages and Literatures section is not intended to support the curriculum of a major in German, the titles listed in this most significant area of the section are well suited to the needs of undergraduates German majors. On the other hand, the other Germanic and Scandinavian areas are definitely not intended for majors, but instead afford a solid introduction to the subjects.

Works have been recommended in their latest editions. Some titles are available only in reprints, and, unfortunately, a number of key titles are out of print.

—Mark Padnos

German Literature > History. Criticism

Boesch, Bruno & Taylor, Ronald **PT85**
German Literature: A Critical Survey. Ed. 3. Trade Cloth. Methuen & Company, Ltd. London, 1971. 375p. ISBN:0-416-14940-5, ISBN13: 978-0-416-14940-1. Dewey:830.9. LCCN:77-882930.
Audience: **l,u.** *B*

Burger, Heinz Otto **PT85.B8 1971**
Annalen der Deutschen Literatur; eine Gemeinschaftsarbeit Zahlreicher Fachgelehrter. Trade Cloth. J. B. Metzler'sche Verlagsbuchhandlung & Carl Ernst Poeschel GmbH. Stuttgart, 1971. 838p. ISBN:3-476-00029-X, ISBN13: 978-3-476-00029-3. Dewey:830.9. LCCN:76-573146.
Audience: **u,f.** *B*

Garland, Henry & Garland, Mary **PT41.G3 1997**
The Oxford Companion to German Literature. Ed. 3. Trade Cloth. Oxford University Press, Inc. New York, NY. 1997. 968p. ISBN:0-19-815896-3, ISBN13: 978-0-19-815896-7. Dewey:830/.3. LCCN:96-053309.
Audience: **g,l,u,f.** *B* *Choice, 1998.*

Holub, Robert C. **PN99.G4**
Reception Theory: A Critical Introduction. Trade Cloth. Routledge. New York, NY. 1984. 189p. ISBN:0-416-33580-2, ISBN13: 978-0-416-33580-4. Dewey:801/.95/0943. LCCN:83-013385.
Audience: **u,f.** *B*

Linden, Walther **PT0085.L74**
Geschichte der Deutschen Literatur Von Den Anfangen Bis Zur Gegenwart. Trade Paper. Books on Demand. Ann Arbor, MI. 541p. ISBN:0-598-65929-3, ISBN13: 978-0-598-65929-3. Dewey:830.9. LCCN:38-000195.
Audience: **u,f.**

Martini, Fritz **PT85.M3 1984**
Deutsche Literaturgeschichte: Von Den Anfangen Bis Zur Gegenwart. Trade Cloth. Kroner, Alfred, Verlag GmbH & Company KG. Stuttgart, 1984. vii, 741p. ISBN:3-520-19618-2, ISBN13: 978-3-520-19618-7. Dewey:830/.9. LCCN:84-186373.
Audience: **u,f.** *B*

Merker, Paul & Stammler, Wolfgang **PT41.R4 1958**
Reallexikon der deutschen Literaturgeschichte. Begründet von Paul Merker und Wolfgang Stammler. Neu bearb. und unter redaktioneller Mitarbeit von Klaus Kanzog, sowie Mitwirkung zahlreicher Fachgelehrter. Hrsg. von Werner Kohlschmidt und Wolfgang Mohr. Berlin W. de Gruyter. 1958. ISBN:3-11-010085-1, ISBN13: 978-3-11-010085-3.
Audience: **u,f.**

Robertson, John George **PT91.R7 1970**
A History of German Literature. Ed. 6. Trade Cloth. Blackwood Publishing, Ltd. Walton On Thames, 1970. xxvii, 817p. ISBN:0-85158-103-X, ISBN13: 978-0-85158-103-3. Dewey:830.9. LCCN:74-552609.
Audience: **l,u.** *B*

Rose, Ernst **PT91.R75**
A History of German Literature. Trade Cloth. New York University Press. New York, NY. 1960. Gotham Library Ser. ISBN:0-8147-0362-3, ISBN13: 978-0-8147-0362-5. Dewey:830.9. LCCN:60-009405.
Audience: **g,l,u.** *B*

Schmitt, Fritz; Unter Mitarbeit von Gerhard Fricke **PT103.S4**
Deutsche Literaturgeschichte in Tabellen. Ed. 2. Frankfurt am Main, Athenäum-Verlag. 1960.
Audience: **u,f.**

German Literature > History. Criticism > Literary History by Period

Bernstein, Eckhard **PT251.B46 1983**
German Humanism. Trade Cloth. Thomson Gale. Farmington Hills, MI. 1983. 171p. World Authors Ser. ISBN:0-8057-6537-9, ISBN13: 978-0-8057-6537-3. Dewey:830/.9/003. LCCN:82-023324.
Audience: **l,u.** *B*

Ehrismann, Gustav **PT175.E3**
Geschichte der deutschen literatur bis zum ausgang des mittelalters. Beck, München, Germany. 1974. ISBN:3-406-01472-0, ISBN13: 978-3-406-01472-7.
Audience: **u,f.**

Hohendahl, Peter U. (Editor) **PT47.G4713 1988**
A History of German Literary Criticism, 1730-1980. Cloth Text. University of Nebraska Press. Lincoln, NE. 1988. 479p. Modern German Culture and Literature Ser. ISBN:0-8032-2340-4, ISBN13: 978-0-8032-2340-0. Dewey:801/.95/0943. LCCN:87-030178.
Audience: **u,f.**

Murdoch, Brian O. **PT183.M85 1983**
Old High German Literature. Trade Cloth. Thomson Gale. Farmington Hills, MI. 1983. 161 p. :p. World Authors Ser. ISBN:0-8057-6535-2, ISBN13: 978-0-8057-6535-9. Dewey:830/.9/001. LCCN:82-025478.
Audience: **l,u.** *B*

Salmon, Paul **PT175.S3x**
Literature in medieval Germany. Barnes & Noble. 1968.
Audience: **l,u,f.**

Taylor, Archer **PT245.T3**
The Literary History of Meistergesang. Modern Language Association of America. 1937.
Audience: **u,f.**

Walshe, Maurice O'C. (Maurice O'Connell) **PT175.W27**
Medieval German Literature : A Survey. Harvard University Press. 1962.
Audience: **u,f.**

Williams, Cedric E. **PT3818.W5 1974**
The Broken Eagle: The Politics of Austrian Literature from Empire to Anschluss. Trade Cloth. Barnes & Noble, Inc. New York, NY. 1974. xxii, 281p. ISBN:0-06-497713-7, ISBN13: 978-0-06-497713-5. Dewey:830/.9/9436. LCCN:74-180506.
Audience: **u,f.**

German Literature > History. Criticism > Literary History by Period > 18th-19th Centuries

Browning, Robert M. & Kerth, Thomas A. (Editors) **PT1265**
German Drama of the 18th Century: Lessing - Goethe - Lenz - Schiller - Kleist. Trade Paper. Brandywine Press, Inc. Naugatuck, CT. 2000. 592p. ISBN:1-881089-85-1, ISBN13: 978-1-881089-85-8. Dewey:832.608.
Audience: **u,f.**

Hatfield, Henry Caraway **PT313.H3**
Aesthetic Paganism in German Literature, from Winckelmann to the Death of Goethe. Harvard University Press. 1964.
Audience: **l,u,f.**

Korff, H. A. **PT285**
Geist der Goethezeit: Versuch einer Ideellen Entwicklung der klassisch-romantischen Literaturgeschichte. Darmstadt: Wissenschaftliche Buchgesellschaft. 1979.
Audience: **u,f.**

Lange, Victor **PT311.L26 1982**
The Classical Age of German Literature, 1740-1815. Holmes & Meier. 1982. ISBN:0-8419-0854-0, ISBN13: 978-0-8419-0854-3.
Audience: **g,l,u.**

Loewenthal, Erich & Schneider, Lambert (Editors) **PT317.L6**
Sturm und Drang; dramatische Schriften. Ed. 3. Heidelberg, Schneider. 1972.
Audience: **u,f.**

Pascal, Roy **PT317.P38 1967**
The German Sturm und Drang. Trade Cloth. Manchester University Press. Manchester, 1967. xvi, 347p. ISBN:0-7190-0194-3, ISBN13: 978-0-7190-0194-9. Dewey:830.9/006. LCCN:68-102695.
Audience: **u,f.**

German Literature > History. Criticism > Literary History by Period > 19th Century

Bernd, Clifford A. **PT345.B46**
German Poetic Realism. Library Binding. Thomson Gale. Farmington Hills, MI. 1981. 150p. World Authors Ser. ISBN:0-8057-6447-X, ISBN13: 978-0-8057-6447-5. Dewey:831/.8/0912. LCCN:80-023509.
Audience: **l,u.**

Koelb, Clayton & Downing, Eric (Editors) **PT341.G42 2005**
German Literature of the Nineteenth Century, 1832-1899. Trade Cloth. Camden House. Elizabethtown, NY. 2005. 360p. History of German Literature Ser., Vol. 9 ISBN:1-57113-250-3, ISBN13: 978-1-57113-250-5. Dewey:830.9007. LCCN:2004-027939.
Audience: **g,u,f.**

Mann, Thomas **PT343.M28**
Last Essays. Winston, Richard (translator); Winston, Clara (translator); Stern, James (translator); Stern, Tania (translator). Knopf. 1970.
Audience: **g,l,u,f.**

Martini, Fritz **PT391.M3 1981**
Deutsche Literatur Im Burgerlichen Realismus, 1848-1898. Trade Cloth. J. B. Metzler'sche Verlagsbuchhandlung & Carl Ernst Poeschel GmbH. Stuttgart, 1981. xxi, 992p. ISBN:3-476-00463-5, ISBN13: 978-3-476-00463-5. Dewey:830/.9/12. LCCN:81-104360.
Audience: **u,f.**

Seidlin, Oskar **PT343.S45**
Essays in German and Comparative Literature. University of North Carolina Press. 1961.
Audience: **u,f.**

Walzel, Oskar F. **PT361**
Deutsche Romantik. Paper Text. Classic Books. Murrieta, CA. 2001. ISBN:0-7426-9434-8, ISBN13: 978-0-7426-9434-7. Dewey:830.903.
Audience: **u,f.**

German Literature > History. Criticism > Literary History by Period > 20th Century

Best, Alan D. & Wolfshutz, Hans (Editors) **PT3818.M6 1980**
Modern Austrian Writing: Literature and Society after 1945. Trade Cloth. Rowman & Littlefield Publishers, Inc. Lanham, MD. 1980. 307p. ISBN:0-389-20038-7, ISBN13: 978-0-389-20038-3. Dewey:830/.9/9436. LCCN:80-508065.
Audience: **u,f.**

Demetz, Peter **PT405.D4**
Postwar German Literature: A Critical Introduction. Trade Paper. Knopf Publishing Group. New York, NY. 1988. 276p. ISBN:0-8052-0368-0, ISBN13: 978-0-8052-0368-4. Dewey:830.909. LCCN:73-114169.
Audience: **g,l,u.**

Huebener, Theodore **PT3705.H8**
Literature of East Germany. Trade Cloth. Continuum International Publishing Group, Ltd. London, 1970. ix, 134p. ISBN:0-8044-2401-2, ISBN13: 978-0-8044-2401-1. Dewey:830.9/0091. LCCN:75-114610.
Audience: **g,l,u,f.**

Jens, Walter **PT401**
Deutsche Literatur der Gegenwart; Themen, Stile, Tendenzen. Ed. 4. München, R. Piper. 1962.
Audience: **u,f.**

Ritchie, J. M **PT403.R54 1983**
German Literature under National Socialism. Trade Cloth. Rowman & Littlefield Publishers, Inc. Lanham, MD. 1983. 320p. ISBN:0-389-20418-8, ISBN13: 978-0-389-20418-3. Dewey:830.9/00912. LCCN:83-010557.
Audience: **g,l,u.**

Taylor, Ronald **PT401**
Literature and Society in Germany, 1918-1945. Trade Cloth. Barnes & Noble Books-Imports. Lanham, MD. 1980. 363p. Studies in Contemporary Literature and Culture ISBN:0-389-20036-0, ISBN13: 978-0-389-20036-9. Dewey:830.9/00912. LCCN:82-189886.
Audience: **l,u.**

German Literature > History. Criticism > Literary History, by Form > Poetry

Allen, Roy F. **PT553.A4**
German Expressionist Poetry. Library Binding. Thomson Gale. Farmington Hills, MI. 1979. 158 p. ;p. World Authors Ser. ISBN:0-8057-6386-4, ISBN13: 978-0-8057-6386-7. Dewey:831/.9/1209. LCCN:79-000493.
Audience: **l,u.**

Browning, Robert M. **PT531**
German Baroque Poetry, 1618-1723. Trade Cloth. Pennsylvania State University Press. University Park, PA. 1971. 292p. ISBN:0-271-01146-7, ISBN13: 978-0-271-01146-2. Dewey:831/.5/09. LCCN:77-136959.
Audience: **u,f.**

Browning, Robert M. **PT529**
German Poetry in the Age of the Enlightenment: From Brockes to Klopstock. Cloth Text. Pennsylvania State University Press. University Park, PA. 1978. 360p. Studies in German Literature ISBN:0-271-00541-6, ISBN13: 978-0-271-00541-6. Dewey:831/.5/09. LCCN:77-026832.
Audience: **u,f.**

Closs, August **PT0571.C6**
The Genius of the German Lyric: An Historic Survey of Its Formal and Metaphysical Values. Trade Paper. Books on Demand. Ann Arbor, MI. 492p. ISBN:0-598-81098-6, ISBN13: 978-0-598-81098-4. Dewey:831.04. LCCN:38-023394.
Audience: **l,u.**

Ermatinger, Emil **PT0537**
Die Deutsche Lyrik Seit Herder, Vol. 2. Ed. 2. Trade Paper. Books on Demand. Ann Arbor, MI. 294p. ISBN:0-598-91162-6, ISBN13: 978-0-598-91162-9. Dewey:831. LCCN:25-019084.
Audience: **u,f.**

Ermatinger, Emil **PT0537**
Die Deutsche Lyrik Seit Herder, Vol. 3. Ed. 2. Trade Paper. Books on Demand. Ann Arbor, MI. 332p. ISBN:0-598-91164-2, ISBN13: 978-0-598-91164-3. Dewey:831. LCCN:25-019084.
Audience: **u,f.**

Ermatinger, Emil **PT0537**
Die Deutsche Lyrik Seit Herder, Vol. 1. Ed. 2. Trade Paper. Books on Demand. Ann Arbor, MI. 330p. ISBN:0-598-91163-4, ISBN13: 978-0-598-91163-6. Dewey:831. LCCN:25-019084.
Audience: **u,f.**

Flores, John **PT3719.F5**
Poetry in East Germany: Adjustments, Visions and Provocations 1945-1970. Trade Cloth. Books on Demand. Ann Arbor, MI. 368p. Yale Germanic Studies, No. 5 ISBN:0-8357-9442-3, ISBN13: 978-0-8357-9442-8. Dewey:831/.9/1409. LCCN:77-115368.
Audience: **u,f.**

Gray, Ronald D. **PT501.G7 1976**
German Poetry: A Guide to Free Appreciation. Trade Cloth. Cambridge University Press. New York, NY. 1976. 144p. ISBN:0-521-20931-5, ISBN13: 978-0-521-20931-1. Dewey:831/.009. LCCN:75-020834.
Audience: **l,u.**

Holton, Milne & Kuhner, Herbert (Editors) **PT3824.Z5.A8 1985**
Austrian Poetry Today. Trade Cloth. Knopf Publishing Group. New York, NY. 1985. 384p. ISBN:0-8052-3903-0, ISBN13: 978-0-8052-3903-4. Dewey:831/.914/08. LCCN:83-020221.
Audience: **u,f.**

Meid, Volker **PT501**
Gedichte und Interpretationen. Stuttgart, Germany : P. Reclam. 1982. Universal-Bibliothek; Nr. 7890 [5]-7895 [5] ISBN:3-15-007890-3, ISBN13: 978-3-15-007890-7.
Audience: **u,f.**

German Literature > History. Criticism > Literary History, by Form > Drama

Bennett, Benjamin **PT641**
Modern Drama and German Classicism: Renaissance from Lessing to Brecht. Book, Other. Cornell University Press. Ithaca, NY. 1986. 360p. ISBN:0-8014-1189-0, ISBN13: 978-0-8014-1189-2. Dewey:832/.6/09. LCCN:79-014644.
Audience: **u,f.**

Huettich, H. G. **PT3721.H8**
Theater in the Planned Society: Contemporary Drama in the German Democratic Republic in its Historical, Political and Cultural Context. Trade Cloth. University of North Carolina Press. Chapel Hill, NC. 1978. xvi, 174p. Germanic Languages and Literatures Ser., No. 88 ISBN:0-8078-8088-4, ISBN13: 978-0-8078-8088-3. Dewey:832/.9/1409. LCCN:76-020606.
Audience: **u,f.**

Innes, Christopher **PT666**
Modern German Drama: A Study in Form. Trade Cloth. Cambridge University Press. New York, NY. 1979. 302p. ISBN:0-521-22576-0, ISBN13: 978-0-521-22576-2. Dewey:832/.914/09. LCCN:78-026597.
Audience: **l,u.**

Kistler, Mark O. **PT643.K5**
Drama of the Storm and Stress. Library Binding. Irvington Publishers. New York, NY. 1969. Twayne's World Authors Ser. ISBN:0-685-42219-4, ISBN13: 978-0-685-42219-9. Dewey:832/.6/09. LCCN:70-099550.
Audience: **l,u.**

Ritchie, J. M **PT668.R5**
German Expressionist Drama. Library Binding. Thomson Gale. Farmington Hills, MI. 1977. 198 p. :p. World Authors Ser. ISBN:0-8057-6261-2, ISBN13: 978-0-8057-6261-7. Dewey:832/.8/091. LCCN:76-046324.
Audience: **l,u.**

Wiese, Benno von **PT615**
Das deutsche Drama vom Barock bis zur Gegenwart: Interpretationen. Düsseldorf : A. Bagel. 1975. ISBN:3-513-02108-9, ISBN13: 978-3-513-02108-3.
Audience: **u,f.**

Wiese, Benno von **PT671.W5 1973**
Die deutsche Tragödie von Lessing bis Hebbel. Ed. 8. Hamburg : Hoffmann u. Campe. 1973. ISBN:3-455-09046-X, ISBN13: 978-3-455-09046-8.
Audience: **u,f.**

German Literature > History. Criticism > Literary History, by Form > Fiction

Bennett, Edwin K. **PT747.S6 B4**
A History of the German Novelle. Ed. 2. Trade Paper. Books on Demand. Ann Arbor, MI. 331p. ISBN:0-608-16412-7, ISBN13: 978-0-608-16412-0. Dewey:833.09.
Audience: **l,u.**

Berman, Russell A. **PT763**
Rise of the Modern German Novel: Crisis and Charisma. Trade Paper. iUniverse, Inc. Lincoln, NE. 1999. 324p. ISBN:1-58348-136-2, ISBN13: 978-1-58348-136-3. Dewey:833.709. LCCN:85-024770.
Audience: **u,f.**

Blackall, Eric A. **PT759.B55 1983**
The Novels of the German Romantics. Trade Cloth. Cornell University Press. Ithaca, NY. 1983. 315p. ISBN:0-8014-1523-3, ISBN13: 978-0-8014-1523-4. Dewey:833/.6/09145. LCCN:82-022104.
Audience: **l,u.** B

Emmel, Hildegard **PT741.E5413 1984**
History of the German Novel. Ellen Summerfield (Translator). Trade Cloth. Wayne State University Press. Detroit, MI. 1984. 398p. ISBN:0-8143-1770-7, ISBN13: 978-0-8143-1770-9. Dewey:833/.009. LCCN:88-005756.
Audience: **g,l,u.** B

Heitner, Robert R. (Editor) **PT772 .C6**
The Contemporary Novel in German: A Symposium. Trade Cloth. University of Texas Press. Austin, TX. 1967. 147p. Department of Germanic Languages Ser. ISBN:0-292-73670-3, ISBN13: 978-0-292-73670-2. Dewey:833/.9/109.
Audience: **u,f.**

Hewett-Thayer, Harvey W. **PT745 .H4**
The Modern German Novel: A Series of Studies and Appreciations. Trade Cloth. Ayer Company Publishers, Inc. Manchester, NH. 1977. Essay Index Reprint Ser. ISBN:0-8369-0537-7, ISBN13: 978-0-8369-0537-3. Dewey:833/.9/1209. LCCN:67-023232.
Audience: **u,f.**

Kontje, Todd **PT747.E6 K63 1993**
The German Bildungsroman: History of a Genre. Trade Cloth. Camden House. Elizabethtown, NY. 1993. 175p. LCGERM Ser. ISBN:1-879751-53-4, ISBN13: 978-1-879751-53-8. Dewey:833.009. LCCN:93-011688.
Audience: **u,f.**

Pascal, Roy **PT0741.P3**
The German Novel: Studies. Trade Paper. Books on Demand. Ann Arbor, MI. 354p. Canadian University Paperbooks Ser., No. 24 ISBN:0-8357-4164-8, ISBN13: 978-0-8357-4164-4. Dewey:833.009. LCCN:57-003904.
Audience: **l,u.** B

Ryan, Judith **PT772.R9 1983**
The Uncompleted Past: Postwar German Novels and the Third Reich. Trade Cloth. Wayne State University Press. Detroit, MI. 1983. 184p. ISBN:0-8143-1728-6, ISBN13: 978-0-8143-1728-0. Dewey:833/.914/09358. LCCN:83-006744.
Audience: **u,f.** B

Silz, Walter **PT763**
Realism and Reality: Studies in the German Novelle of Poetic Realism. Paper Text. Textbook Publishers. Temecula, CA. 2003. 168p. ISBN:0-7581-1863-5, ISBN13: 978-0-7581-1863-9. Dewey:833.09.
Audience: **u,f.**

Swales, Martin **PT747.E6**
The German Bildungsroman from Weiland to Hesse. Trade Cloth. Princeton University Press. Princeton, NJ. 1978. 184p. Essays in Literature Ser. ISBN:0-691-06359-1, ISBN13: 978-0-691-06359-1. Dewey:833/.009. LCCN:77-855681.
Audience: **l,u.**

Swales, Martin **PT763**
The German Novelle. Trade Cloth. Princeton University Press. Princeton, NJ. 1977. xi, 229p. ISBN:0-691-06331-1, ISBN13: 978-0-691-06331-7. Dewey:833/.009. LCCN:76-045913.
Audience: **l,u.** B

Wagener, Hans **PT756**
The German Baroque Novel. Library Binding. Thomson Gale. Farmington Hills, MI. 1983. World Authors Ser., No. 229 ISBN:0-8057-2356-0, ISBN13: 978-0-8057-2356-4. Dewey:833/.03.
Audience: **l,u.**

Wiese, Benno von **PT745.W5**
Der deutsche Roman vom Barock bis zur Gegenwart; Struktur und Geschichte. Düsseldorf, A. Bagel. 1963.
Audience: **u,f.**

German Literature > History. Criticism > Literary History, by Form > Folk Literature. Legends

Grimm, Jacob & Grimm, Wilhelm **PT921.G7z 1985**
Kinder- und Hausmärchen, gesammelt durch die Brüder Grimm: vollständige Ausgabe auf der Grundlage der dritten Auflage (1837). Rölleke, Heinz (Editor). Frankfurt am Main : Deutscher

Klassiker Verlag. 1985. Bibliothek deutscher Klassiker; 5; Variation: Bibliothek deutscher Klassiker (Frankfurt am Main, Germany); 5. ISBN:3-618-60660-5, ISBN13: 978-3-618-60660-4.

Audience: **u,f.**

Grimm, Jacob W., et al. **PT921.K5613 2003**
The Complete Fairy Tales of the Brothers Grimm. Ed. 3. Wilhelm K. Grimm & Johnny Gruelle (Authors), Jack D. Zipes (Translator, Introduction by). UK-Trade Paper. Knopf Publishing Group. New York, NY. 2003. 800p. Bantam Classics Ser. ISBN:0-553-38216-0, ISBN13: 978-0-553-38216-7. Dewey:398.2/0943. LCCN:2003-267061.

Audience: **g,l,u,f.**

Grimm, Jacob & Grimm, Wilhelm K. **PT915 .D44**
Werke: Abetilung III: Die Gemeinsamen Werke, Vol. 46. Trade Cloth. Georg Olms Verlag AG. Hildesheim, 2005. lxxvi/464p. ISBN:3-487-11651-0, ISBN13: 978-3-487-11651-8. Dewey:398.2/0943.

Audience: **u,f.**

Haile, Harry G. **PT0923.A8E5**
The History of Doctor Johann Faustus. Trade Paper. Books on Demand. Ann Arbor, MI. 144p. Illini Bks. ISBN:0-608-30086-1, ISBN13: 978-0-608-30086-3. Dewey:833.4. LCCN:65-019570.

Audience: **u,f.**

Oppenheimer, Paul (Translator) **PT941.E8**
A Pleasant Vintage of Till Eulenspiegel. Trade Cloth. Wesleyan University Press. Middletown, CT. 1972. 293p. ISBN:0-8195-4043-9, ISBN13: 978-0-8195-4043-0. Dewey:833.3. LCCN:73-184361.

Audience: **g,l,u,f.**

Rose, William (Editor) **PT923**
The History of the Damnable Life and Deserved Death of Doctor John Faustus. Library Binding. Arden Library. Darby, PA. 1982. 327p. ISBN:0-8495-1717-6, ISBN13: 978-0-8495-1717-4. Dewey:833.4.

Audience: **u,f.**

Rose, William **PT923.E5 1963**
Historia von Doctor Johann Fausten. English. The Historie of the Damnable Life and Deserved Death of Doctor John Faustus. Modernized, edited, and introduced by William Rose. Pfeiler, William Karl (Foreword to the American ed. by). Notre Dame, Ind., University of Notre Dame Press. 1963.

Audience: **g,l,u,f.**

Wiemken, Helmut & Schotus, Fridericus **PT923**
Doctor Fausti Weheklag; die Volksbücher von D. Johann Faust und Christoph Wagner. Nach den Erstdrucken neu bearb. und eingeleitet von Helmut Wiemken. Bremen, C. Schünemann. 1961. Sammlung Dieterich, Bd. 186

Audience: **u,f.**

German Literature > Collections of German Literature

Trahan, Elizabeth Welt **PF3117.T75**
Gruppe 47 [I. E. Siebenundvierzig], ein Querschnitt: An Anthology of Contemporary German Literature. Trade Paper. Books on Demand. Ann Arbor, MI. 282p. ISBN:0-598-05179-1, ISBN13: 978-0-598-05179-0. Dewey:438/.6/42.

Audience: **u,f.**

German Literature > Collections of German Literature > Poetry

Fischer-Dieskau, Dietrich **PT1160.E6.F5 1977**
The Fischer-Dieskau Book of Lieder. George Bird & Richard Stokes (Translators). Trade Cloth. Random House Children's Books. New York, NY. 1977. 435p. ISBN:0-394-49435-0, ISBN13: 978-0-394-49435-7. Dewey:784/.3/00943. LCCN:76-047955.

Audience: **g,l,u,f.**

Flores, Angel **PT1160.E5 F55 1965**
An Anthology of German Poetry from Hölderlin to Rilke in English Translation. Peter Smith, Gloucester, Mass.. 1965.

Audience: **g,l,u,f.**

Hamburger, Michael **PT3734.H3 1973**
East German Poetry: An Anthology. Trade Cloth. Penguin Group (USA) Inc. New York, NY. 1973. xxii, 213p. ISBN:0-525-09668-X, ISBN13: 978-0-525-09668-9. Dewey:831/.9/1208. LCCN:73-158584.

Audience: **g,l,u,f.**

Hamburger, Michael **PT1160.E5**
German Poetry, 1910-1975: An Anthology. Trade Cloth. Bow Historical Books. New Providence, NJ. 1976. xxxiii, 533p. ISBN:0-916354-08-3, ISBN13: 978-0-916354-08-4. Dewey:831/.9/1208. LCCN:76-021303.

Audience: **g,l,u,f.**

Prawer, Siegbert (Editor) **PT1174.P7**
Seventeen Modern German Poets. Trade Paper. Oxford University Press, Inc. New York, NY. 1971. 204p. Clarendon German Ser. ISBN:0-19-832474-X, ISBN13: 978-0-19-832474-4. Dewey:831/.9/108. LCCN:75-027732.

Audience: **g,l,u,f.**

Salinger, Herman (Editor) **PT1174**
Twentieth-century German Verse. Trade Cloth. Ayer Company Publishers, Inc. Manchester, NH. 1977. Granger Index Reprint Ser. ISBN:0-8369-6042-4, ISBN13: 978-0-8369-6042-6. Dewey:831.91082. LCCN:68-057065.

Audience: **g,u,f.**

Schoolfield, George C. (Editor) **PT1169.D96**
The German Lyric of the Baroque in English Translation. Trade Cloth. A M S Press, Inc. New York, NY. North Carolina University, Studies in the Germanic Languages and Literatures, No. 29 ISBN:0-404-50929-0, ISBN13: 978-0-404-50929-3. Dewey:831.082. LCCN:78-182711.

Audience: **g,l,u,f.**

Stahl, Ernest L. (Editor) **PT1155 .O8**
Oxford Book of German Verse, Twelfth to Twentieth Century. Ed. 3. Trade Cloth. Oxford University Press, Inc. New York, NY. 1968. ISBN:0-19-812132-6, ISBN13: 978-0-19-812132-9. Dewey:831/.008.
Audience: **g,l,u,f.**

Stein, Agnes (Editor, Translator) **PT1174**
Four German Poets: Gunter Eich, Hilde Domin, Erich Fried and Gunter Kunert. Gunter Eich, Hilde Domin, Erich Fried & Gunter Kunert (Contribution by). Trade Cloth. Red Dust, Inc. New York, NY. 1980. Contemporary Poets Ser. ISBN:0-87376-034-4, ISBN13: 978-0-87376-034-8. Dewey:831.08. LCCN:78-059474.
Audience: **g,l,u,f.**

German Literature > Collections of German Literature > Drama

Bennett, Benjamin **PT641**
Modern Drama and German Classicism: Renaissance from Lessing to Brecht. Book, Other. Cornell University Press. Ithaca, NY. 1986. 360p. ISBN:0-8014-1189-0, ISBN13: 978-0-8014-1189-2. Dewey:832/.6/09. LCCN:79-014644.
Audience: **u,f.**

Kerth, Thomas & Schoolfield, George (Editors) **PT636**
German Drama of the Baroque. Paper Text. Brandywine Press, Inc. Naugatuck, CT. 2006. ISBN:1-933385-12-X, ISBN13: 978-1-933385-12-9. Dewey:832/.4/09.
Audience: **u,f.**

Lohner, Edgar & Hannum, H. G. **PT1268 .L6**
Modern German Drama. Cloth Text. Houghton Mifflin Company. New York, NY. 1966. ISBN:0-395-04808-7, ISBN13: 978-0-395-04808-5. Dewey:832.9108. LCCN:66-003026.
Audience: **g,l,u.**

Russell, Douglas A. (Editor, Introduction by) **PT3826.D8**
An Anthology of Austrian Drama. Trade Cloth. Fairleigh Dickinson University Press. Cranbury, NJ. 1982. 450p. ISBN:0-8386-2003-5, ISBN13: 978-0-8386-2003-8. Dewey:832/.008/09436. LCCN:76-019836.
Audience: **u,f.**

German Literature > Collections of German Literature > Prose

Bates, Evan (Editor) **PT1327.G74 2003**
Great German Short Stories. Trade Paper. Dover Publications, Inc. Mineola, NY. 2003. 246p. Dover Thrift Editions Ser. ISBN:0-486-43205-X, ISBN13: 978-0-486-43205-2. Dewey:833/.0108. LCCN:2003-055218.
Audience: **g,l.**

Evans, Gerard **PT**
Short Stories in German, Erzahlungen auf Deutsch. Ernst Zillekens (Editor). Trade Paper. Penguin Group (USA) Inc. New York, NY. 2003. 208p. New Penguin Parallel Texts Ser. ISBN:0-14-026542-2, ISBN13: 978-0-14-026542-2. Dewey:833/.01080914. LCCN:2004-298956.
Audience: **g,l.**

Fiedler, Hermann Georg (Editor) **PT1305.O8**
Das Oxforder Buch deutscher Prosa von Luther bis Rilke. Oxford, Universitäts-verlag. 1959.
Audience: **u,f.**

Firchow, Peter E. & Firchow, Evelyn S. (Translators) **PT3740.E18**
East German Short Stories: An Introductory Anthology. Library Binding. Thomson Gale. Farmington Hills, MI. 1979. 251p. International Studies and Translations Ser. ISBN:0-8057-8159-5, ISBN13: 978-0-8057-8159-5. Dewey:833/.01. LCCN:78-021686.
Audience: **g,l,u,f.**

German Literature > Middle High German Literature

Brant, Sebastian **PT1509**
Ship of Fools. Trade Paper. Dover Publications, Inc. Mineola, NY. 1988. 399p. ISBN:0-486-25791-6, ISBN13: 978-0-486-25791-4. Dewey:831.3.
Audience: **u,f.**

Gentry, Francis G. (Editor) **PT1384.G47 1983**
German Medieval Tales. Thomas Berger (Foreword by). Trade Cloth. Continuum International Publishing Group, Ltd. London, 1982. 320p. German Library, Vol. 4 ISBN:0-8264-0272-0, ISBN13: 978-0-8264-0272-1. Dewey:830/.8/002. LCCN:82-022050.
Audience: **g,l,u,f.**

Goldin, Frederick **PT1673.G65 2002**
Walther von der Vogelweide: The Single-Stanza Lyrics. Paper over Boards. Routledge. New York, NY. 2002. 368p. Routledge Medieval Texts Ser., Vol. 2 ISBN:0-415-94337-X, ISBN13: 978-0-415-94337-6. Dewey:831/.21. LCCN:2002-068024.
Audience: **u,f.**

Gosse, Siegfried, et al. **PT1579.A1B37 1997**
Nibelungenlied. Mittelhochdeutsch / Neuhochdeutsch. Karl Bartsch & Helmut De Boor (Authors). Trade Paper. Philip Reclam jun., Verlag GmbH. Ditzingen, 1997. 1019p. ISBN:3-15-000644-9, ISBN13: 978-3-15-000644-3. Dewey:831/.21.
Audience: **u,f.**

Gottfried, von Strassburg, 13th cent. **PT1525.A2.M32**
Tristan und Isold. Ranke, Friedrich (Editor). Berlin, Weidmann. 1963.
Audience: **u,f.**

Grimmelshausen, Johann J. **PT1732**
Simplicissimus. Trade Paper. Bookking International. Paris, 1999. World Classic Literature Ser. ISBN:3-89507-006-8, ISBN13: 978-3-89507-006-8. Dewey:833.5.
Audience: **u,f.**

Hall, Clifton D. & Coleman, Samuel S. **PT1421.K68H35 1997**
Des Minnesangs Fruhling: A Complete Reference Work. Trade Cloth. University Press of Colorado. Boulder, CO. 1997. 512p. ISBN:0-87081-447-8, ISBN13: 978-0-87081-447-1. Dewey:831/.209. LCCN:97-022957.
Audience: **u,f.**

Hartmann Von Aue **PT1534.G8 Z49**
Gregorius: A Medieval Oedipus Legend. Trade Cloth. A M S Press, Inc. New York, NY. North Carolina University, Studies in the Germanic Languages and Literatures, No. 14 ISBN:0-404-50914-2, ISBN13: 978-0-404-50914-9. Dewey:831.2. LCCN:73-181903.
Audience: **g,l,u,f.**

Hartmann Von Aue **PT1526**
Iwein: The Knight with the Lion. J. W. Thomas (Translator, Introduction by). Paper Text. University of Nebraska Press. Lincoln, NE. 1979. 149p. ISBN:0-8032-7331-2, ISBN13: 978-0-8032-7331-3. Dewey:831/.2. LCCN:79-001139.
Audience: **g,l,u,f.**

Hatto, A. T. (Translator) **PT1579.A3**
The Nibelungenlied: Prose Translation. Trade Paper. Penguin Group (USA) Inc. New York, NY. 1965. 416p. Classics Ser. ISBN:0-14-044137-9, ISBN13: 978-0-14-044137-6. Dewey:833.2/1.
Audience: **g,l,u,f.**

Jackson, William T. **PT1526**
Anatomy of Love: The Tristan of Gottfried Von Strassburg. Trade Cloth. Columbia University Press. New York, NY. 1971. 280p. ISBN:0-231-03504-7, ISBN13: 978-0-231-03504-0. Dewey:831/.2. LCCN:70-154859.
Audience: **u,f.**

McConnell, Winder (Editor) **PT1589.C66 1998**
A Companion to the Nibelungenlied. Trade Cloth. Camden House. Elizabethtown, NY. 1998. 240p. Studies in German Literature, Linguistics, and Culture, :Literary Criticism in Perspective ISBN:1-57113-151-5, ISBN13: 978-1-57113-151-5. Dewey:831/.21. LCCN:98-021818.
Audience: **u,f.** *Choice, 1999.*

Ryder, Frank G. (Translator) **PT1579.A3**
Song of the Nibelungs: A Verse Translation from the Middle High German Nibelungenlied. Paper Text. Wayne State University Press. Detroit, MI. 1963. 436p. ISBN:0-8143-1192-X, ISBN13: 978-0-8143-1192-9. Dewey:831/.2. LCCN:82-017432.
Audience: **u,f.**

von Aue, Hartmann
Der Arme Heinrich. Ed. 10. Fischer Taschenbuch Verlag. 1997. ISBN:3-596-26488-X, ISBN13: 978-3-596-26488-9.
Audience: **u,f.**

Von Hartmann, Aue **PT1534.E8**
Erec. Michael Resler (Translator, Commentaries by, Introduction by). Trade Paper. Books on Demand. Ann Arbor, MI. 1987. 244p. Middle Ages Ser. ISBN:0-608-04811-9, ISBN13: 978-0-608-04811-6. Dewey:831/2. LCCN:87-012419.
Audience: **u,f.** *Choice, 1988.*

Weigand, Hermann J. **PT1688**
Wolfram's Parzival: Five Essays with an Introduction. Ursula Hoffmann (Editor). Trade Cloth. Cornell University Press. Ithaca, NY. 1969. 204p. ISBN:0-8014-0521-1, ISBN13: 978-0-8014-0521-1. Dewey:831/.2. LCCN:76-081597.
Audience: **u,f.**

Wolfram von Eschenbach **PT1682.P6**
Parzival: Text und Ubersetzung. Bernd Schirok & Peter Knecht (Contribution by). Trade Cloth. Walter de Gruyter GmbH & Co. KG. Berlin, 2003. clvii, 831p. ISBN:3-11-017859-1, ISBN13: 978-3-11-017859-3. Dewey:831.2.
Audience: **u,f.**

Wolfram, von Eschenbach **PT1682.W6.E56**
The Middle High German Poem of Willehalm. Passage, Charles E. (Translator). F. Ungar Pub. Co.. 1977. ISBN:0-8044-2183-8, ISBN13: 978-0-8044-2183-6.
Audience: **u,f.**

Wolfram, von Eschenbach **PT1682.P6 S8 1975**
Parzival. Stapel, Wilhelm (Translator). A. Langen, G. Müller. 1975. ISBN:3-7844-1212-2, ISBN13: 978-3-7844-1212-2.
Audience: **u,f.**

German Literature > German Literature: Individual Authors

Grimmelshausen, Hans Jakob Christoph von **PT1731.A7 E5 1986**
An Unabridged Translation of Simplicius Simplicissimus. University Press of America. 1986. ISBN:0-8191-5349-4, ISBN13: 978-0-8191-5349-4.
Audience: **g,l,u,f.**

Gryphius, Andreas **PT1734**
Andreas Gryphius/Catharina von Georgien: Sprachlich Modernisierter Text der Erstfassung von 1657/Herausgegeben von J. E. Oyler und A. H. Schulze. Trade Paper. Herbert Lang Et Compagnie AG, Buchhandlung, Antiquariat. Bern, 1978. 179p. Europaische Hochschulschriften Ser., Bd. 226 ISBN:3-261-03053-4, ISBN13: 978-3-261-03053-5. Dewey:832/.5.
Audience: **u,f.**

Gryphius, Andreas **PT1734.A1**
Werke in einem Band. Ed. 6. Szyrocki, Marian. Berlin : Aufbau-Verlag. 1987. ISBN:3-351-00631-4, ISBN13: 978-3-351-00631-0.
Audience: **u,f.**

Solbach, Andreas **PT756 .S65 1994**
Gesellschaftsethik und Romantheorie: Studien zu Grimmelshausen, Weise und Beer. Cloth Text. Peter Lang Publishing, Inc. New York, NY. 1995. IX, 284p. Renaissance and Baroque Studies and Texts, Vol. 8 ISBN:0-8204-2086-7, ISBN13: 978-0-8204-2086-8. Dewey:833/.509.
Audience: **u,f.**

Von Grimmelshausen, Hans J. **PT1731**
Courage, the Adventuress and the False Messiah. Hans Speier (Translator, Illustrator). Trade Paper. Princeton University Press. Princeton, NJ. 1964. ISBN:0-691-01255-5, ISBN13: 978-0-691-01255-1. Dewey:832/.509353.
Audience: **g,l,u,f.**

Weydt, Günther **PT1732.W37**
Nachahmung und Schöpfung im Barock; Studien um Grimmelshausen. Bern Francke. 1968.
Audience: **u,f.**

German Literature > German Literature: Individual Authors > 18th-19th Centuries (1700-1860/1870) > A-G

Arnim, Ludwig Achim, Freiherr von **PT1809.A15 M5 1962**
Sämtliche Romane und Erzählungen. Migge, Walther. C. Hanser. 1962.
Audience: **u,f.**

Benn, Maurice B. **PT1828.B6**
The Drama of Revolt: A Critical Study of Georg Büchner. Trade Paper. Cambridge University Press. New York, NY. 1979. 329p. Anglica Germanica Ser., No. 2 ISBN:0-521-29415-0, ISBN13: 978-0-521-29415-7. Dewey:832/.7. LCCN:75-003974.
Audience: **u,f.**

Brentano, Clemens **PT1825.A1**
Werke. Ed. 3. Frühwald, Wolfgang (Editor); Kemp, Friedhelm (Editor). Hanser. 1982.
Audience: **u,f.**

Buchner, Georg **BR60.A52**
Georg Buchner: Complete Plays and Prose. Carl Richard Mueller (Translator, Introduction by). Trade Paper. Farrar, Straus & Giroux. New York, NY. 1963. 224p. Mermaid Dramabook Ser. ISBN:0-8090-0727-4, ISBN13: 978-0-8090-0727-1. Dewey:281.1.
Audience: **g,l,u,f.**

Büchner, Georg **PT1828.B6 1967**
Sämtliche Werke und Briefe: historisch-kritische Ausgabe mit Kommentar. Lehmann, Werner R. (Editor). Wegner. 1967. ISBN:3-446-11670-2, ISBN13: 978-3-446-11670-2.
Audience: **u,f.**

Chamisso, Adelbert von **PT1834 .A1**
Werke, Set. Trade Cloth. A M S Press, Inc. New York, NY. 1976. BCL Ser., No. II ISBN:0-404-14850-6, ISBN13: 978-0-404-14850-8. Dewey:833.68. LCCN:75-041053.
Audience: **u,f.**

Chamisso, Adelbert von **PT1834.A1 1982**
Sämtliche Werke in zwei Bänden. Feudel, Werner (Editor); Laufer, Christel (Editor). Hauser. 1982. ISBN:3-446-13465-4, ISBN13: 978-3-446-13465-2.
Audience: **u,f.**

Cowen, Roy C. **PQ6398.G4**
Christian Dietrich Grabbe. Library Binding. Thomson Gale. Farmington Hills, MI. 1984. World Authors Ser. ISBN:0-8057-2396-X, ISBN13: 978-0-8057-2396-0. Dewey:868/.3/09.
Audience: **l,u.**

Droste-Hülshoff, Annette von **PT1848.A1 1994**
Sämtliche Werke in Zwei Bänden. Trade Cloth. Deutscher Klassiker Verlag GmbH. Frankfurt, 1994. ;p. ISBN:3-618-62015-2, ISBN13: 978-3-618-62015-0. Dewey:831/.7.
Audience: **u,f.**

Droste-Hülshoff, Annette von **PT1848.A1 1966**
Sämtliche Werke. Heselhaus, Clemens (Editor). C. Hanser. 1966.
Audience: **u,f.**

Eichendorff, Joseph **PT1856.A116 1985**
Werke in fünf Bänden. Trade Cloth. Deutscher Klassiker Verlag GmbH. Frankfurt, 1985. ISBN:3-618-60125-5, ISBN13: 978-3-618-60125-8. Dewey:838/.709.
Audience: **u,f.**

Eichendorff, Joseph, Freiherr von **PT1856.A1 1978**
Neue Gesamtausgabe der Werken und Schriften in vier Bänden. Ed. 3. Baumann, Gerhard (Editor); Grosse, Siegfried (Editor). Cotta. 1978. ISBN:3-7681-9906-1, ISBN13: 978-3-7681-9906-3.
Audience: **u,f.**

Fetzer, John F. **PT1825.Z5.F39**
Clemens Brentano. Trade Cloth. Thomson Gale. Farmington Hills, MI. 1981. 179p. World Authors Ser. ISBN:0-8057-6457-7, ISBN13: 978-0-8057-6457-4. Dewey:838/.609. LCCN:81-002314.
Audience: **l,u.** B

Fontane, Theodor **PT1863**
Effi Briest. Trade Paper. Penguin Group (USA) Inc. New York, NY. 2001. 256p. ISBN:0-14-044766-0, ISBN13: 978-0-14-044766-8. Dewey:833.8.
Audience: **u,f.**

Fontane, Theodor **PT1863.A1 1976**
Werke, Schriften und Briefe. Trade Cloth. Carl Hanser GmbH & Company. Muchen, 1976. ISBN:3-446-12205-2, ISBN13: 978-3-446-12205-5. Dewey:830.8. LCCN:78-341980.
Audience: **u,f.** B

Fontane, Theodor **PT1863.A4**
The woman Taken in Adultery and The Poggenpuhl Family. University of Chicago Press. 1979. ISBN:0-226-25680-4, ISBN13: 978-0-226-25680-1.
Audience: **g,l,u,f.**

Fontane, Theodor **PT2638.N5**
Short Novels and Other Writings. Peter Demetz (Editor), Peter Gay (Foreword by). Trade Cloth. Continuum International

Publishing Group, Ltd. London, 1982. 338p. German Library, Vol. 46 ISBN:0-8264-0250-X, ISBN13: 978-0-8264-0250-9. Dewey:833/.8. LCCN:81-040462.
Audience: **g,l,u,f.**

Garland, Henry **PT1863.Z7.G34**
The Berlin Novels of Theodor Fontane. Trade Cloth. Oxford University Press, Inc. New York, NY. 1980. 308p. ISBN:0-19-815765-7, ISBN13: 978-0-19-815765-6. Dewey:833/.8. LCCN:79-041386.
Audience: **u,f.**

Grabbe, Christian Dietrich **PT2253.G3 A6 1964**
Gesammelte Werke. Siefert, Fritz (Editor). S. Mohn. 1964.
Audience: **u,f.**

Grabbe, Christian D. **PT2253.G3**
Jest, Satire, Irony and Deeper Significance. Maurice Edwards (Translator). Trade Cloth. Continuum International Publishing Group, Ltd. London, 1966. ISBN:0-8044-2282-6, ISBN13: 978-0-8044-2282-6. Dewey:832.7. LCCN:66-019473.
Audience: **u,f.**

Grillparzer, Franz **PT2256.A1 1986**
Werke in Sechs Banden. Trade Cloth. Deutscher Klassiker Verlag GmbH. Frankfurt, 1986. ;p. ISBN:3-618-60620-6, ISBN13: 978-3-618-60620-8. Dewey:832/.6. LCCN:87-130963.
Audience: **u,f.**

Grillparzer, Franz **PT2256.A1 1969**
Sämtliche Werke: ausgewählte Briefe, Gespräche, Berichte. Frank, Peter (Editor); Pörnbacher, Karl (Editor). München: C. Hanser. 1969.
Audience: **u,f.**

Hauser, Ronald **PT1828.B6.H3**
Georg Buchner. Library Binding. Thomson Gale. Farmington Hills, MI. 1974. 161p. World Authors Ser. ISBN:0-8057-2183-5, ISBN13: 978-0-8057-2183-6. Dewey:831/.7. LCCN:73-017183.
Audience: **l,u.**

Hoermann, Roland **PT1809.Z5 H63 1984**
Achim von Arnim. Twayne. 1984. Twayne's World Authors Series; TWAS 722; German literature ISBN:0-8057-6569-7, ISBN13: 978-0-8057-6569-4.
Audience: **l,u.**

Richards, David G. **PT1828.B6.R5**
Georg Buchner and Birth of Modern Drama. Cloth Text. State University of New York Press. Albany, NY. 1977. xii, 289p. ISBN:0-87395-332-0, ISBN13: 978-0-87395-332-0. Dewey:831/.7. LCCN:76-000902.
Audience: **u,f.**

Schwarz, Egon **PT1856.Z5**
Joseph von Eichendorff. Library Binding. Thomson Gale. Farmington Hills, MI. 1984. World Authors Ser. ISBN:0-8057-2296-3, ISBN13: 978-0-8057-2296-3. Dewey:838/.7/09.
Audience: **l,u.**

Thompson, Bruce **PT2265.T5**
Franz Grillparzer. Twayne Publishers. 1981. Twayne's World Authors Series; TWAS 637; Germany ISBN:0-8057-6481-X, ISBN13: 978-0-8057-6481-9.
Audience: **l,u.**

Yates, W. E. **PT2265**
Grillparzer: A Critical Introduction. Trade Cloth. Cambridge University Press. New York, NY. 1972. 286p. ISBN:0-521-08241-2, ISBN13: 978-0-521-08241-9. Dewey:832/.6. LCCN:77-158550.
Audience: **u,f.**

German Literature > German Literature: Individual Authors > 18th-19th Centuries (1700-1860/1870) > Goethe

Blackall, Eric A. **PT1984**
Goethe and the Novel. Book, Other. Cornell University Press. Ithaca, NY. 1976. 344p. ISBN:0-8014-0978-0, ISBN13: 978-0-8014-0978-3. Dewey:833/.6. LCCN:75-038426.
Audience: **l,u,f.**

Boerner, Peter **PT2051**
Goethe. Trade Cloth. Haus Publishing. London, 2006. 192p. ISBN:1-904341-64-0, ISBN13: 978-1-904341-64-2. Dewey:831.6.
Audience: **u,f.**

Eckermann, Johann Peter, et al. **PT2049**
Conversations with Goethe. Johann Wolfgang von Goethe, John Oxenford & J. K. Moorhead (Authors). Trade Cloth. J. M. Dent & Sons. London, 1971. xxiv, 448p. ISBN:0-460-00851-X, ISBN13: 978-0-460-00851-8. Dewey:831/.6. LCCN:73-168675.
Audience: **l,u.**

Fairley, Barker **PT2049 .F33 1977**
A Study of Goethe. Trade Cloth. Greenwood Publishing Group, Inc. Portsmouth, NH. 1977. 280p. ISBN:0-8371-9330-3, ISBN13: 978-0-8371-9330-4. Dewey:831/.6. LCCN:76-056253.
Audience: **l,u,f.**

Goethe, Johann Wolfgang von **PT2026.A1 C83 1983**
[Works. English & German. 1983] Goethe edition. Suhrkamp/Insel Publishers. 1983. ISBN:3-518-03053-1, ISBN13: 978-3-518-03053-0.
Audience: **u,f.**

Goethe, Johann Wolfgang von **PT1891.C85 1985**
Sämtliche Werke: Briefe, Tagebücher und Gespräche. Trade Cloth. Deutscher Klassiker Verlag GmbH. Frankfurt, 1985. ISBN:3-618-60245-6, ISBN13: 978-3-618-60245-3. Dewey:831/.6.
Audience: **u,f.**

Goethe, Johann Wolfgang von **PT2005.A1**
Briefe an Goethe. Mandelkow, Karl Robert. Deutscher Taschenbuchverlag. 1988. ISBN:3-423-05917-6, ISBN13: 978-3-423-05917-6.
Audience: **u,f.**

Goethe, Johann Wolfgang von **PT2005.A1**
Goethes Briefe. Ed. 4. Mandelkow, Karl Robert; Gille, Klaus F.; Morawe, Bodo. Deutscher Taschenbuch Verlag. 1988. Goethes Briefe und Briefe an Goethe
Audience: **u,f.**

Hatfield, Henry C. **PT2177.H37**
Goethe: A Critical Introduction. Trade Paper. Books on Demand. Ann Arbor, MI. 255p. ISBN:0-7837-2270-2, ISBN13: 978-0-7837-2270-2. Dewey:838.6. LCCN:64-024031.
Audience: **l,u.**

Jantz, Harold **PT1930**
The Form of Faust: The Work of Art and Its Intrinsic Structures. Trade Cloth. Johns Hopkins University Press. Baltimore, MD. 1994. 224p. ISBN:0-8018-2080-4, ISBN13: 978-0-8018-2080-9. Dewey:832/.6. LCCN:78-001447.
Audience: **u,f.**

Staiger, Emil **PT2051.S67**
Goethe. Atlantis Verlag. 1952.
Audience: **u,f.**

Von Goethe, Johann Wolfgang **PT1891**
Goethe Set, Vol 1-10. Trade Cloth, Box or Slipcased. Konemann. New York, NY. 2000. Cloth Bound Pocket Ser. ISBN:3-8290-1300-0, ISBN13: 978-3-8290-1300-0. Dewey:831.6.
Audience: **u,f.**

Von Goethe, Johann Wolfgang **PT2027.A8 M6**
Goethe's Autobiography. Trade Cloth. Public Affairs Press. Washington, DC. 1949. ISBN:0-8183-0224-0, ISBN13: 978-0-8183-0224-4. Dewey:928.3.
Audience: **u,f.**

Von Goethe, Johann Wolfgang **PZ3.G552 W**
Wilhelm Meister's Apprenticeship. Trade Paper. Kessinger Publishing, LLC. Whitefish, MT. 2004. ISBN:1-4192-9418-0, ISBN13: 978-1-4192-9418-1. Dewey:833.6.
Audience: **u,f.**

Von Goethe, Johann Wolfgang **PT2026.A1C94 1994**
Goethe: Faust I and II, Vol. 2. Stuart Atkins (Editor, Translator). Paper Text. Princeton University Press. Princeton, NJ. 1994. 344p. ISBN:0-691-03656-X, ISBN13: 978-0-691-03656-4. Dewey:831/.6. LCCN:93-027617.
Audience: **u,f.**

Von Goethe, Johann Wolfgang **PT2026**
Goethe's Plays. Charles E. Passage (Translator). Trade Cloth. Frederick Ungar A Book. Dulles, VA. 1980. ISBN:0-8044-2258-3, ISBN13: 978-0-8044-2258-1. Dewey:832/.6. LCCN:79-004834.
Audience: **u,f.**

Von Goethe, Johann Wolfgang **PT2027.W3**
The Sufferings of Young Werther. Harry Steinhauer (Translator). Trade Paper. W. W. Norton & Company, Inc. New York, NY. 1969. ISBN:0-393-09880-X, ISBN13: 978-0-393-09880-8. Dewey:832.62.
Audience: **u,f.**

Williams, John **PT2049**
The Life of Goethe: A Critical Biography. Trade Paper. Blackwell Publishing, Inc. Malden, MA. 2001. 352p. Critical Biographies Ser. ISBN:0-631-23173-0, ISBN13: 978-0-631-23173-8. Dewey:831/.6.
Audience: **u,f.**

German Literature > German Literature: Individual Authors > 18th-19th Centuries (1700-1860/1870) > H-Z

Alt, A. Tilo **PT2528.Z5 A4**
Theodor Storm. Cloth Text. Irvington Publishers. New York, NY. 1973. 157p. Twayne's World Authors Ser. ISBN:0-8290-1757-7, ISBN13: 978-0-8290-1757-1. Dewey:833/.8. LCCN:72-002793.
Audience: **l,u.**

Arendt, Hannah **PT2546.V22**
Rahel Varnhagen: The Life of a Jewish Woman. Richard Winston & Clara Winston (Translators), Hannah Arendt (Preface by). Trade Paper. Harcourt Trade Publishers. New York, NY. 1974. 256p. ISBN:0-15-676100-9, ISBN13: 978-0-15-676100-0. Dewey:838/.6/08. LCCN:74-006478.
Audience: **g,l,u,f.** B

Bernd, Clifford A. **PD25 .N6 NO. 55**
Theodor Storm's Craft of Fiction. Trade Cloth. University of North Carolina Press. Chapel Hill, NC. 1966. Studies in Germanic Languages and Literatures Ser., No. 55 ISBN:0-8078-8055-8, ISBN13: 978-0-8078-8055-5. Dewey:833.8.
Audience: **u,f.**

Burkhard, Marianne **PT2432.Z9.B84 1978**
Conrad Ferdinand Meyer. Trade Cloth. Thomson Gale. Farmington Hills, MI. 1978. 175p. World Authors Ser. ISBN:0-8057-6321-X, ISBN13: 978-0-8057-6321-8. Dewey:831/.7. LCCN:77-028441.
Audience: **l,u.** B

Clark, Robert T.
Herder: His Life and Thought. Trade Cloth. University of California Press. Berkeley, CA. 1969. California Library Reprint Ser., No. 15 ISBN:0-520-01514-2, ISBN13: 978-0-520-01514-2.
Audience: **u,f.**

Daemmrich, Horst S. **PT2361.Z5D28**
The Shattered Self: E. T. A. Hoffmann's Tragic Vision. Trade Paper. Books on Demand. Ann Arbor, MI. 143p. ISBN:0-608-17805-5, ISBN13: 978-0-608-17805-9. Dewey:833/.6. LCCN:73-001490.
Audience: **u,f.**

Daemmrich, Horst S. **PT2451.Z5.D3**
Wilhelm Raabe. Library Binding. Thomson Gale. Farmington Hills, MI. 1981. 171 p. :p. World Authors Ser. ISBN:0-8057-6436-4, ISBN13: 978-0-8057-6436-9. Dewey:833/.8. LCCN:80-020982.
Audience: **l,u.**

Fairley, Barker **PT2340**
Heinrich Heine: An Interpretation. Trade Cloth. Greenwood Publishing Group, Inc. Portsmouth, NH. 1977. 176p. ISBN:0-8371-9338-9, ISBN13: 978-0-8371-9338-0. Dewey:831/.7. LCCN:77-000709.
Audience: **l,u.**

Folkers, George F. (Translator), et al. **PT2432.A15 1976**
The Complete Narrative Prose of Conrad Ferdinand Meyer. David B. Dickens & Marion W. Sonnenfeld (Translators). Trade Cloth. Bucknell University Press. Cranbury, NJ. 1976. 754p. ISBN:0-8387-1547-8, ISBN13: 978-0-8387-1547-5. Dewey:833/.7. LCCN:78-168824.
Audience: **l,u.**

Garland, Henry B. **PT2482 .G3 1976**
Schiller. Trade Cloth. Greenwood Publishing Group, Inc. Portsmouth, NH. 1977. 280p. ISBN:0-8371-9084-3, ISBN13: 978-0-8371-9084-6. Dewey:831/.6. LCCN:76-039809.
Audience: **l,u.**

Garland, Henry B. (Henry Burnand) **PT2406.G3 1963**
Lessing, the Founder of Modern German literature. Ed. 2. St. Martin's Press. 1963.
Audience: **u,f.**

Garland, Mary **PT2296.Z6**
Hebbel's Prose Tragedies. Trade Cloth. Cambridge University Press. New York, NY. 1973. 343p. Anglica Germanica Ser., No. 2 ISBN:0-521-20090-3, ISBN13: 978-0-521-20090-5. Dewey:832/.7. LCCN:72-088621.
Audience: **u,f.**

Gump, Margaret **PT2525.Z4.G8**
Adalbert Stifter. Library Binding. Thomson Gale. Farmington Hills, MI. 1974. 172p. World Authors Ser., No 274 ISBN:0-8057-2864-3, ISBN13: 978-0-8057-2864-4. Dewey:833/.7. LCCN:73-002367.
Audience: **l,u.**

Gundolf, Friedrich **PT2379.Z5 G8**
Heinrich Von Kleist. Paper Text. Classic Books. Murrieta, CA. 2001. 172p. ISBN:0-7426-9457-7, ISBN13: 978-0-7426-9457-6. Dewey:838609.
Audience: **u,f.**

Harich, Walther **PT2456.H28 1971**
Jean Paul. Trade Cloth. A M S Press, Inc. New York, NY. 1971. 860p. ISBN:0-404-03109-9, ISBN13: 978-0-404-03109-1. Dewey:838.609. LCCN:75-149661.
Audience: **u,f.**

Hauff, Wilhelm **PT2293.A1 1969**
Werke. Zeller, Bernhard (Editor). Insel-Verlag. 1969.
Audience: **u,f.**

Hebbel, Friedrich **PT2295.A1 1963**
Werke. Fricke, Gerhard (Editor). Hanser. 1963.
Audience: **u,f.**

Hebbel, Friedrich **PT2295.A2 E58 1974**
Three plays. Sonnenfeld, Marion (translator). Bucknell University Press. 1974. ISBN:0-8387-1239-8, ISBN13: 978-0-8387-1239-9.
Audience: **g,l,u,f.**

Hebel, Johann Peter **PT2298.H3 A2 1968**
Poetische Werke. Strauss, Emil. Tempel-Verlag. 1968.
Audience: **u,f.**

Heine, Heinrich **PT2301.A1 1973**
Historisch-Kritische Gesamtausgabe der Werke. Trade Cloth. Hoffman & Campe Verlag. Hamburg, 1973. ISBN:3-455-03006-8, ISBN13: 978-3-455-03006-8. Dewey:831/.6. LCCN:73-327285.
Audience: **u,f.**

Heine, Heinrich **PT2316.A4F4**
Lyric Poems and Ballads. Ernst Feise (Translator). Trade Paper. Books on Demand. Ann Arbor, MI. 1961. 221p. ISBN:0-608-00907-5, ISBN13: 978-0-608-00907-0. Dewey:831.7. LCCN:61-009402.
Audience: **g,l,u,f.**

Heine, Heinrich **PT2316.A3.H4 1982**
Poetry and Prose. Jost Hermand & Robert C. Holub (Editors), Alfred Kazin (Foreword by). Trade Cloth. Continuum International Publishing Group, Ltd. London, 1982. 320p. German Library, Vol. 32 ISBN:0-8264-0255-0, ISBN13: 978-0-8264-0255-4. Dewey:831/.7. LCCN:73-077054.
Audience: **g,l,u,f.**

Helbling, Robert E. **PT2379.Z5 H4 1975**
The Major Works of Heinrich von Kleist. New Directions. 1975. ISBN:0-8112-0563-0, ISBN13: 978-0-8112-0563-4.
Audience: **g,l,u,f.**

Herder, Johann Gottfried **PT2351.A1 1985**
Werke in Zehn Banden. Trade Cloth. Deutscher Klassiker Verlag GmbH. Frankfurt, 1985. ISBN:3-618-60710-5, ISBN13: 978-3-618-60710-6. Dewey:838/.609. LCCN:86-133179.
Audience: **u,f.**

Hoffmann, E. T. A. **PT2360.T48**
Three Marchen of E.T.A. Hoffman. Charles E. Passage (Translator). Trade Cloth. University of South Carolina Press. Columbia, SC. 1971. xxviii, 404p. ISBN:0-87249-188-9, ISBN13: 978-0-87249-188-5. Dewey:833/.6. LCCN:76-120580.
Audience: **g,l,u,f.**

Hoffmann, E. T. A. (Ernst Theodor Amadeus) **PT2360.T48**
Selected writings of E.T.A. Hoffmann. Kent, Leonard J. (Editor); Knight, Elizabeth C. (Editor). Chicago, University of Chicago Press. 1969.
Audience: **g,l,u,f.**

Hoffmann, E. T. A. (Ernst Theodor Amadeus) **PT2360.A1 1985**
Sämtliche Werke in sechs Bänden. Segebrecht, Wulf &

Steinecke, Hartmut (Editors). Deutscher Klassiker Verlag. 1985. Bibliothek deutscher Klassiker; 7 ISBN:3-618-60870-5, ISBN13: 978-3-618-60870-7.
Audience: **u,f.**

Holderlin, Friedrich **PT2359.H2 1975**
Samtliche Werke: Frankfurter Ausg. Trade Cloth. Bow Historical Books. New Providence, NJ. 1975. -6, 9-18p. ISBN:3-87877-079-0, ISBN13: 978-3-87877-079-4. Dewey:831.6. LCCN:76-454793.
Audience: **u,f.** B

Hölderlin, Friedrich **PT2359.H2A265 2004**
Poems of Friedrich Holderlin: The Fire of the Gods Drives Us to Set Forth by Day and by Night. James Mitchell (Translator, Selected by). Perfect. Ithuriel's Spear. San Francisco, CA. 2004. 64p. ISBN:0-9749502-0-3, ISBN13: 978-0-9749502-0-4. Dewey:831/.6. LCCN:2004-101926.
Audience: **u,f.**

Jean Paul **PT2454.A1x**
Werke. Miller, Norbert (Editor). C. Hanser. 1963.
Audience: **u,f.**

Keller, Gottfried **PT2374.A1 1985**
Sämtliche Werke in fünf Bänden. Trade Cloth. Deutscher Klassiker Verlag GmbH. Frankfurt, 1985. ISBN:3-618-60925-6, ISBN13: 978-3-618-60925-4. Dewey:838/.809.
Audience: **u,f.**

Keller, Gottfried **PT2374.A2 1982**
Stories. Ryder, Frank Glessner (Translator). Continuum. 1982. The German library, Vol. 44 ISBN:0-8264-0256-9, ISBN13: 978-0-8264-0256-1.
Audience: **g,l,u,f.**

Kleist, Heinrich von **PT2378.A2.E5**
The Marquise of O--, and other stories. Greenberg, Martin (Translator) (Introduction by); Mann, Thomas (Preface by). New York, Ungar. 1973. ISBN:0-8044-2478-0, ISBN13: 978-0-8044-2478-3.
Audience: **g,l,u,f.**

Kleist, Heinrich von **PT2378.A2 E5 1982**
Plays. Hinderer, Walter (Editor). Continuum. 1982. The German library, v. 25 ISBN:0-8264-0253-4, ISBN13: 978-0-8264-0253-0.
Audience: **g,l,u,f.**

Kleist, Heinrich von **PT2378.A1 1965**
Sämtliche Werke und Briefe. Ed. 4. Sembdner, Helmut (Editor). Carl Hanser. 1965.
Audience: **u,f.**

Klopstock, Freidrich G. **PT2381**
Klopstock, Friedrich Gottlieb: Werke und Briefe Historisch-Kritische Ausgabe. Horst Gronemeyer, Klaus Hurlebusch, Rose-Marie Hurlebusch & Elisabeth Hoepker-Herberg (Editors). Trade Cloth. Walter De Gruyter Inc. Ossining, NY. 1974. Section Werke Ser., Pt. 4, der Messias, Vol. 1, Text ISBN:3-11-004895-7, ISBN13: 978-3-11-004895-7. Dewey:831.6.
Audience: **u,f.**

Klopstock, Friedrich Gottlieb **PT2381.A3**
Ausgewählte Werke. Ed. 4. Schleiden, Karl August (Editor); Jünger, Friedrich Georg (Nachtwort von). C. Hanser. 1981.
Audience: **u,f.**

Lenau, Nicolaus **PT2393.A1 1989**
Werke und Briefe: Historisch-Kritische Gesamtausgabe. Trade Cloth. Bow Historical Books. New Providence, NJ. 1989. :p. ISBN:3-216-06874-9, ISBN13: 978-3-216-06874-3. Dewey:831/.7.
Audience: **u,f.**

Lenau, Nicolaus **PT2393.A1 1971**
Sämtliche Werke und Briefe. Dietze, Walter (Editor). Insel-Verl.. 1971.
Audience: **u,f.**

Lessing, Gotthold Ephraim **PT2396.A1 1985**
Werke und Briefe in Zwolf Banden. Trade Cloth. Deutscher Klassiker Verlag GmbH. Frankfurt, 1985. ISBN:3-618-61100-5, ISBN13: 978-3-618-61100-4. Dewey:832/.6. LCCN:86-132841.
Audience: **u,f.** B

Lessing, Gotthold Ephraim **PT2396.A1x**
Gesammelte Werke. Stammler, Wolfgang (Editor). C. Hanser. 1967.
Audience: **u,f.**

Lindsay, James M. **PT2374.Z4 L5**
Gottfried Keller: Life and Works. Trade Cloth. Dufour Editions, Inc. Chester Springs, PA. 1968. ISBN:0-8023-1205-5, ISBN13: 978-0-8023-1205-1. Dewey:838/.8/09. LCCN:69-014390.
Audience: **u,f.**

Mayo, Robert S. **PT2354 .M3**
Herder and the Beginnings of Comparative Literature. Trade Cloth. University of North Carolina Press. Chapel Hill, NC. 1969. vii, 153p. Studies in Comparative Literature, No. 48 ISBN:0-8078-7048-X, ISBN13: 978-0-8078-7048-8. Dewey:809.
Audience: **u,f.**

Meyer, Conrad Ferdinand **PT2432.A1 1982**
Werke in zwei Bänden. Engelhard, Hermann (Editor). Phaidon. 1982.
Audience: **u,f.**

Morike, Eduard Friedrich **PT2434.A1 1967**
Werke und Briefe. Trade Cloth. Ernst Klett Verlag fur Wirtschafts- und Bildungsservice GmbH. Stuttgart, 1968. ISBN:3-12-909340-0, ISBN13: 978-3-12-909340-5. Dewey:838/.709. LCCN:67-103010.
Audience: **u,f.**

Mörike, Eduard Friedrich **PT2434**
Poems. Bithell, Jethro (Introduction by); Cruickshank, Norah K. (Translator); Cunningham, Gilbert F. (Translator). Methuen. 1959.
Audience: **g,l,u,f.**

Mörike, Eduard Friedrich **PT2434.A6 1967**
Sämtliche Werke. Wiese, Benno von (Nachtwort von); Unger, Helga (Anmerkungen, Zeittafel und Bibliographie von). Winckler. 1967.
Audience: **u,f.**

Neubauer, John **PT2291.Z5**
Novalis. Twayne Publishers. 1980. Twayne's World Authors Series, Vol. 556 ISBN:0-8057-6398-8, ISBN13: 978-0-8057-6398-0.
Audience: **l,u.**

Novalis **PT2291.A1 1977**
Schriften: die Werke Friedrich von Hardenbergs. Kluckhohn, Paul (Editor); Samuel, R. H. (Richard H.) (Editor). W. Kohlhammer. 1977. ISBN:3-17-001299-1, ISBN13: 978-3-17-001299-8.
Audience: **u,f.**

Novalis **PT2291.H6E55 1984**
Hymns to the Night. Ed. 2. Dick Higgins (Translator). Trade Cloth. McPherson & Company. Kingston, NY. 1984. 56p. ISBN:0-914232-67-3, ISBN13: 978-0-914232-67-4. Dewey:831/.6. LCCN:84-004402.
Audience: **g,l,u,f.** B *Choice, 1985.*

Novalis **PZ3.H2175**
Henry Von Ofterdingen. Palmer Hilty (Translator). Trade Paper. Frederick Ungar A Book. Dulles, VA. 1964. ISBN:0-8044-6614-9, ISBN13: 978-0-8044-6614-1. Dewey:833.6. LCCN:64-015297.
Audience: **g,l,u,f.** B

Passage, Charles E. **PT2492.P3**
Friedrich Schiller. Trade Cloth. Frederick Ungar A Book. Dulles, VA. 1975. 192p. Literature and Life Ser. ISBN:0-8044-2734-8, ISBN13: 978-0-8044-2734-0. Dewey:831/.6. LCCN:74-076129.
Audience: **l,u.** B

Pilling, Claudia, et al. **PT2359.H2**
Schiller. Diana Schilling & Mirjam Springer (Authors), Angus McGeoch (Translator). Trade Paper, Saddle Stitched. Haus Publishing. London, 2005. 161p. ISBN:1-904341-65-9, ISBN13: 978-1-904341-65-9. Dewey:831.6.
Audience: **u,f.** *Choice, 2006.*

Purdie, Edna **PT2296.P8 1969**
Friedrich Hebbel: A Study of His Life and Work. Trade Cloth. Oxford University Press, Inc. New York, NY. 1969. 276p. ISBN:0-19-815390-2, ISBN13: 978-0-19-815390-0. Dewey:832/.7. LCCN:74-428330.
Audience: **l,u,f.** B

Raabe, W. **PT2451**
Werke. Trade Paper. Deutscher Taschenbuch Verlag GmbH & Co KG. München, ISBN:3-485-00395-6, ISBN13: 978-3-485-00395-7. Dewey:838.8.
Audience: **u,f.**

Raabe, Wilhelm **PT2451.A2 1983**
Novels. Volkmar Sander (Editor). Trade Paper. Continuum International Publishing Group, Ltd. London, 1992. 318p. Novels Ser., Vol. 45 ISBN:0-8264-0281-X, ISBN13: 978-0-8264-0281-3. Dewey:833/.8. LCCN:66-028139.
Audience: **u,f.** B

Rolleston, Thomas W. **PT1925**
Life of Gotthold Ephraim Lessing. Trade Paper. Adamant Media. Chestnut Hill, MA. 2004. 238p. ISBN:1-4021-4449-0, ISBN13: 978-1-4021-4449-3. Dewey:832/.6.
Audience: **g,l,u,f.**

Ross, C. R. **PT2406**
Lessing: His Life and Achievements. Trade Cloth. Foundation for Classical Reprints, The. Albuquerque, NM. 1992. 117p. ISBN:0-685-51059-X, ISBN13: 978-0-685-51059-9. Dewey:832/.6.
Audience: **g,u,f.**

Sammons, Jeffrey L. **PT2328**
Heinrich Heine. Trade Cloth. Princeton University Press. Princeton, NJ. 1980. 446p. ISBN:0-691-06321-4, ISBN13: 978-0-691-06321-8. Dewey:831/.7. LCCN:79-084015.
Audience: **u,f.**

Sammons, Jeffrey L. (Editor) **PT2451.Z5S2 1987**
Wilhelm Raabe: The Fiction of the Alternative Community. Cloth Text. Princeton University Press. Princeton, NJ. 1987. 435p. ISBN:0-691-06709-0, ISBN13: 978-0-691-06709-4. Dewey:833/.8. LCCN:86-030267.
Audience: **u,f.** *Choice, 1988.*

Schiller, Friedrich **PT1925**
Schiller: Five Plays. Trade Paper. Oberon Books, Ltd. London, 1998. 733p. Oberon Book Ser. ISBN:1-84002-036-9, ISBN13: 978-1-84002-036-6. Dewey:832.6.
Audience: **u,f.**

Schiller, Friedrich **PT2465.B60**
Sämtliche Werke. Göpfert, Herbert Georg (Editor); Alt, Peter-André (Editor); Meier, Albert (Editor); Riedel, Wolfgang (Editor). C. Hanser. 2004. ISBN:3-446-20501-2, ISBN13: 978-3-446-20501-7.
Audience: **u,f.**

Schiller, Friedrich **PT2473.K3.H5 1983**
Plays of Schiller. Walter Hinderer (Editor), Gordon A. Craig (Illustrator). Trade Cloth. Continuum International Publishing Group, Ltd. London, 1983. 354p. German Library, Vol. 15 ISBN:0-8264-0274-7, ISBN13: 978-0-8264-0274-5. Dewey:832/.6. LCCN:74-076129.
Audience: **g,l,u,f.** B

Schiller, Friedrich & Passage, Charles E. **PT2473.M3M4 2001**
Mary Stuart. Trade Paper. Dover Publications, Inc. Mineola, NY. 2001. 128p. Thrift Editions Ser. ISBN:0-486-41594-5, ISBN13: 978-0-486-41594-9. Dewey:832/.6. LCCN:00-047397.
Audience: **g,l,u,f.**

Schlegel, Friedrich **PA3093.S3413 2001**
On the Study of Greek Poetry. Book, Other. State University of New York Press. Albany, NY. 2001. ix, 146p. SUNY Series, Intersections, :Philosophy and Critical Theory ISBN:0-7914-4830-4, ISBN13: 978-0-7914-4830-4. Dewey:881/.0109. LCCN:00-048249.
Audience: **g,u,f.** *Choice, 2001.*

Schmidt, Hugo **PT2393.Z5 S3**
Nikolaus Lenau. Library Binding. Irvington Publishers. New York, NY. 1971. Twayne's World Authors Ser. ISBN:0-8057-2520-2, ISBN13: 978-0-8057-2520-9. Dewey:831/.7. LCCN:68-017227.
Audience: **l,u.** B

Simons, John D. **PT2492.S54**
Friedrich Schiller. Trade Cloth. Thomson Gale. Farmington Hills, MI. 1981. 163p. World Authors Ser. ISBN:0-8057-6445-3, ISBN13: 978-0-8057-6445-1. Dewey:831/.6. LCCN:81-004908.
Audience: **l,u.** B

Spencer, Hanna **PT2340.S64 1982**
Heinrich Heine. Library Binding. Thomson Gale. Farmington Hills, MI. 1982. 173 p., [1] pp. World Authors Ser. ISBN:0-8057-6516-6, ISBN13: 978-0-8057-6516-8. Dewey:831/.7. LCCN:82-009310.
Audience: **l,u.** B

Stanberry, D. Elaine **PR5438**
Love's Perplexing Obsession, Experienced by Two Geniuses: Heinrich Heine and Percy Bysshe Shelley. Trade Cloth. Vantage Press, Inc. New York, NY. 1981. ISBN:0-533-04826-5, ISBN13: 978-0-533-04826-7. Dewey:808.81.
Audience: **u,f.**

Stifter, Adalbert **PT2525.A1 1978**
Werke und Briefe: Historisch-Kritische Gesamtausgabe. Trade Cloth. W. Kohlammer GmbH. 70565 Stuttgart, 1978. , pt. 1-6p. ISBN:3-17-004232-7, ISBN13: 978-3-17-004232-2. Dewey:833.7. LCCN:79-383289.
Audience: **u,f.** B

Stifter, Adalbert **PT2525.A1**
Sämtliche Werke in fünf Einzelbänden. [Mit einem Nachwort von Fritz Krökel und Anmerkungen von Karl Pörnbacher.]. Krökel, Fritz; Pörnbacher, Karl. Winkler. 1979.
Audience: **u,f.**

Storm, Theodor **PT2528.A1x**
Werke: Gesamtausgabe in drei Bänden. Engelhard, Hermann (Editor). J.G. Cotta. 1958.
Audience: **u,f.**

Swales, Martin & Swales, Erika **PT2525.Z5**
Adalbert Stifter: A Critical Study. Trade Cloth. Cambridge University Press. New York, NY. 1984. 263p. Anglica Germanica Ser. ISBN:0-521-25972-X, ISBN13: 978-0-521-25972-9. Dewey:833/.7. LCCN:83-020914.
Audience: **u,f.** B

Tieck, Ludwig **PT2356.A1 1966**
Werke, in vier Bänden. Thalmann, Marianne (Editor). Winkler-Verlag. 1966.
Audience: **u,f.**

Tieck, Ludwig **PT2537.G8 1974**
Puss in Boots. Gerald Gillespie (Editor). Trade Cloth. University of Texas Press. Austin, TX. 1974. 138p. Edinburgh Bilingual Library, No. 8 ISBN:0-292-72702-X, ISBN13: 978-0-292-72702-1. Dewey:832/.7. LCCN:73-020869.
Audience: **g,l,u,f.** B

Uhland, Ludwig **PT2543.A33 1963**
Dichtungen, Briefe, Reden; eine Auswahl. Scheffler, Walter P. H. (Editor). Stuttgart, J.F. Steinkopf. 1963.
Audience: **u,f.**

Unger, Richard **PT2359.H2 U44 1984**
Friedrich Hölderlin. Twayne Publishers. 1984. Twayne's World Authors Series, Vol. 738 ISBN:0-8057-6585-9, ISBN13: 978-0-8057-6585-4.
Audience: **l,u.**

German Literature > German Literature: Individual Authors > 19th-20th Centuries (1860/70-1960)

PT1255
Horspiele: Aichinger, Bachmann, Boll, Eich, Hildesheimer Etc. Trade Paper. Fischer Taschenbuch Verlag. Frankfurt, ISBN:3-596-27010-3, ISBN13: 978-3-596-27010-1. Dewey:838.914.
Audience: **u,f.**

German Literature > German Literature: Individual Authors > 19th-20th Centuries (1860/70-1960) > A-B

Aichinger, Ilse **PT2601.I26.N3**
Nachricht vom Tag. Erzählungen. Fischer-Bücherei. 1970. ISBN:3-436-01294-7, ISBN13: 978-3-436-01294-6.
Audience: **u,f.**

Aichinger, Ilse **PT2601.I26**
Grossere Hoffnung. Trade Paper. Fischer Taschenbuch Verlag. Frankfurt, 1998. ISBN:3-596-11041-6, ISBN13: 978-3-596-11041-4. Dewey:833.91.
Audience: **u,f.**

Aichinger, Ilse **PT2601.I26.V47**
Verschenkter Rat: Gedichte. Trade Cloth. S. Fischer Verlag. 1978. 99p. ISBN:3-10-000509-0, ISBN13: 978-3-10-000509-0. Dewey:831/.9/14. LCCN:79-360584.
Audience: **u,f.** B

Aichinger, Ilse **PT2601.I26**
Selected Poetry and Prose. Allen H. Chappel (Translator), Lawrence Langer (Introduction by). Trade Paper. Logbridge-Rhodes, Inc. Waterford, VA. 1983. 141p. ISBN:0-937406-24-4, ISBN13: 978-0-937406-24-3. Dewey:833/.914. LCCN:83-014867.
Audience: **g,l,u,f.**

Aichinger, Ilse **PZ3.A2878**
Bound Man, and Other Stories. Eric Mosbacher (Translator). Trade Cloth. Ayer Company Publishers, Inc. Manchester, NH. 1977. Short Story Index Reprint Ser. ISBN:0-8369-3766-X, ISBN13: 978-0-8369-3766-4. Dewey:833/.9/14. LCCN:72-144151.
Audience: **g,l,u,f.**

Bachmann, Hugo **PT2603.A147**
Gestundete Zeit. Trade Paper. Piper Verlag GmbH. Munchen, 1998. ISBN:3-492-10306-5, ISBN13: 978-3-492-10306-0. Dewey:831.914.
Audience: **u,f.**

Bachmann, Ingeborg **PT2603.A147Ax**
Anrufung des grossen Bären: Gedichte. R. Piper. 1983. Serie Piper; Bd. 307 ISBN:3-492-00607-8, ISBN13: 978-3-492-00607-1.
Audience: **u,f.**

Bachmann, Ingeborg **PT2603.A147**
Complete Poems by Ingeborg Bachmann: Bilingual Edition. Peter Filkins (Translator). Trade Paper. Marsilio Publishers. New York, NY. 1994. 368p. ISBN:1-56886-010-2, ISBN13: 978-1-56886-010-7. Dewey:831.
Audience: **g,l,u,f.**

Barlach, Ernst **PT2603.A53 1956**
Das dichterische Werk. R. Piper. 1956.
Audience: **u,f.**

Barlach, Ernst **NB588.B35**
A Selftold Life. Naomi J. Groves (Translator). Trade Paper. Penumbra Press. Manotick, ON. 1990. 104p. ISBN:0-921254-07-5, ISBN13: 978-0-921254-07-2. Dewey:700/.92.
Audience: **u,f.**

Beer-Hofmann, Richard **PT2603.E27 1963**
Gesammelte Werke. S. Fischer. 1963.
Audience: **u,f.**

Beer-Hofmann, Richard **PT2603.E27 J32**
Jacob's Dream. Ida B. Wynn (Translator), Thornton Wilder (Introduction by). Trade Cloth. German Book Center, N. A., Inc. Mountaindale, NY. 1946. ISBN:0-917324-06-4, ISBN13: 978-0-917324-06-2. Dewey:832.91.
Audience: **g,l,u,f.**

Benn, Gottfried **PT2635.I65**
Ausgewahlte Gedichte. Trade Paper. Diogenes Verlag AG. Zurich, 1998. 111p. ISBN:3-257-20099-4, ISBN13: 978-3-257-20099-7. Dewey:831.912.
Audience: **u,f.**

Benn, Gottfried **PT2603.E46**
Gesammelte Werke. Wellershoff, Dieter (Editor). Limes Verlag. 1965.
Audience: **u,f.**

Benn, Gottfried **PT2603.E46A24 1987**
Prose, Essays, Poems. Richard Becker & Volkmar Sander (Editors), John Simon (Foreword by). Trade Paper. Continuum International Publishing Group, Ltd. London, 1987. 298p. German Library, Vol. 73 ISBN:0-8264-0311-5, ISBN13: 978-0-8264-0311-7. Dewey:831/.912. LCCN:87-000449.
Audience: **u,f.** *Choice, 1987.*

Borchert, Wolfgang **PT2603.O725.T7**
The Sad Geraniums, and Other Stories. Hamnett, Keith (Translator). Ecco Press. 1973. ISBN:0-912946-10-5, ISBN13: 978-0-912946-10-8.
Audience: **g,l,u,f.**

Borchert, Wolfgang & Meyer-Marwitz, Bernhard **PT2603**
Das Gesamtwerk. Trade Paper. Rowohlt Taschenbuch Verlag GmbH. Reinbek, 1999. ISBN:3-499-22509-3, ISBN13: 978-3-499-22509-3. Dewey:838.9.
Audience: **u,f.**

Borchert, Wolfgang **PT2601.L6**
The Man Outside. A. D. Porter (Translator). Trade Paper. New Directions Publishing Corporation. New York, NY. 1971. 270p. ISBN:0-8112-0011-6, ISBN13: 978-0-8112-0011-0. Dewey:838. LCCN:76-145929.
Audience: **u,f.**

Broch, Hermann **PT2603.R657.A1**
Gesammelte Werke. Rhein-Verlag. 1963.
Audience: **u,f.**

Broch, Hermann **PT2603.R657.S3**
The Sleepwalkers: A Trilogy. Muir, Willa (Translator); Muir, Edwin (Translator). Vintage Books. 1996. ISBN:0-679-76406-2, ISBN13: 978-0-679-76406-9.
Audience: **g,l,u,f.**

Broch, Hermann **PT2603.R657T613 1995**
The Death of Virgil. Jean S. Untermeyer (Translator), Hannah Arendt (Introduction by). Trade Paper. Knopf Publishing Group. New York, NY. 1995. 496p. ISBN:0-679-75548-9, ISBN13: 978-0-679-75548-7. Dewey:833/.912. LCCN:94-034712.
Audience: **u,f.**

Busch, Wilhelm **PT2603.U8.A22**
Das Gesamtwerk des Zeichners und Dichters. Werner, Hugo (Editor). Fackelverlag. 1959.
Audience: **u,f.**

Busch, Wilhelm **NC1509**
The Genius of Wilhelm Busch. Walter Arndt (Translator). Trade Cloth. University of California Press. Berkeley, CA. 1982. 450p. ISBN:0-520-03897-5, ISBN13: 978-0-520-03897-4. Dewey:741.5/943. LCCN:79-063545.
Audience: **u,f.**

Elstun, Esther N. **PT2603.E27Z/**
Richard Beer-Hofmann: His Life and Work. Trade Cloth. Pennsylvania State University Press. University Park, PA. 1983. 225p. Studies in German Literature ISBN:0-271-00335-9, ISBN13: 978-0-271-00335-1. Dewey:838/.91209. LCCN:82-014990.
Audience: **u,f.**

Keith-Smith, Brian **PT2603.O13.Z7**
Johannes Bobrowski. Trade Cloth. Wolff Publishing Company. Fairhope, AL. 1970. 119p. ISBN:0-85496-044-9, ISBN13: 978-0-85496-044-6. Dewey:838/.9/1409. LCCN:76-020446.
Audience: **u,f.**

Lotze, Dieter P. **PT2603.U8.Z725**
Wilhelm Busch. Library Binding. Thomson Gale. Farmington Hills, MI. 1979. 171 p., [6] lp. World Authors Ser. ISBN:0-8057-6365-1, ISBN13: 978-0-8057-6365-2. Dewey:831/.8. LCCN:78-014843.
Audience: **u,f.**

Ritchie, James McPherson **PT2603.E46.Z774**
Gottfried Benn: The Unreconstructed Expressionist. Trade Cloth. Wolff Publishing Company. Fairhope, AL. 1972. 126p. ISBN:0-85496-046-5, ISBN13: 978-0-85496-046-0. Dewey:831/.9/12. LCCN:73-152970.
Audience: **u,f.**

German Literature > German Literature: Individual Authors > 19th-20th Centuries (1860/70-1960) > Boll, Heinrich

Boll, Heinrich **PT2603.O394**
Gruppenbild Mit Dame. Trade Paper. Deutscher Taschenbuch Verlag GmbH & Co KG. München, ISBN:3-423-00959-4, ISBN13: 978-3-423-00959-1. Dewey:833.914.
Audience: **u,f.**

Böll, Heinrich **PT2603.O394**
Billard Um Halbzehn. Trade Paper. Deutscher Taschenbuch Verlag GmbH & Co KG. München, 327p. ISBN:3-423-00991-8, ISBN13: 978-3-423-00991-1. Dewey:833.914.
Audience: **u,f.**

Böll, Heinrich **PZ4.B6713**
Billiards at Half-Past Nine. Paper Text. McGraw-Hill Companies, The. New York, NY. 1963. 288p. ISBN:0-07-006401-6, ISBN13: 978-0-07-006401-0. Dewey:833.9. LCCN:62-015141.
Audience: **g,l,u,f.**

Böll, Heinrich **PT2603.O394.B7X 1980**
Das Brot der Fruhen Jahre: Erzahlung. Trade Cloth. Kiepenheuer & Witsch GmbH & Company KG. Koln, 1980. 141p. ISBN:3-462-01416-1, ISBN13: 978-3-462-01416-7. Dewey:833.9. LCCN:85-672869.
Audience: **u,f.**

Böll, Heinrich **PT2603.O394 A6 1967**
Erzählungen, Hörspiele, Aufsätze. Kiepenheuer & Witsch. 1967.
Audience: **u,f.**

Böll, Heinrich **PT2603.O394**
The Lost Honor of Katharina Blum. Cloth Text. McGraw-Hill Companies, The. New York, NY. 1975. ISBN:0-07-006425-3, ISBN13: 978-0-07-006425-6. Dewey:833/.9/14. LCCN:74-028138.
Audience: **g,l,u,f.**

Böll, Heinrich **PT2603.O394.V4**
Die Verlorene Ehre der Katharina Blum: Oder, Wie Gewalt Entstehen und Wohin Sie Fuhren Kann: Erzahlung. Trade Cloth. Kiepenheuer & Witsch GmbH & Company KG. Koln, 1974. 188p. ISBN:3-462-01033-6, ISBN13: 978-3-462-01033-6. Dewey:833.9. LCCN:74-351123.
Audience: **u,f.**

Böll, Heinrich **PT2603.O394**
Wo Warst Adam. Trade Paper. Deutscher Taschenbuch Verlag GmbH & Co KG. München, 140p. ISBN:3-423-00856-3, ISBN13: 978-3-423-00856-3. Dewey:833.914.
Audience: **u,f.**

Böll, Heinrich **PT2603.O394A28**
Missing Persons and Other Essays. Vennewitz, Leila (translator). McGraw-Hill. 1977. ISBN:0-07-006424-5, ISBN13: 978-0-07-006424-9.
Audience: **g,l,u,f.**

Böll, Heinrich **PT2603.O394W613 1994**
And Where Were You, Adam? Leila Vennewitz (Translator). Trade Paper. Northwestern University Press. Evanston, IL. 1994. 156p. European Classics Ser. ISBN:0-8101-1164-0, ISBN13: 978-0-8101-1164-6. Dewey:833/.914. LCCN:94-029297.
Audience: **g,l,u,f.**

Böll, Heinrich **PT2603.O394B713 1994**
The Bread of Those Early Years. Leila Vennewitz (Translator). Trade Cloth. Northwestern University Press. Evanston, IL. 1994. 144p. European Classics Ser. ISBN:0-8101-1178-0, ISBN13: 978-0-8101-1178-3. Dewey:833/.914. LCCN:94-010923.
Audience: **g,l,u,f.**

Böll, Heinrich **PZ33**
The Clown. Leila Vennewitz (Translator). Paper Text. McGraw-Hill Companies, The. New York, NY. 1978. ISBN:0-07-006420-2, ISBN13: 978-0-07-006420-1. Dewey:833/.9/1. LCCN:64-007935.
Audience: **g,l,u,f.**

Böll, Heinrich **PZ33**
Group Portrait with Lady. Leila Vennewitz (Translator). Cloth Text. McGraw-Hill Companies, The. New York, NY. 1973. 320p. ISBN:0-07-006423-7, ISBN13: 978-0-07-006423-2. Dewey:833/.9/1. LCCN:72-008835.
Audience: **g,l,u,f.**

Böll, Heinrich **DA978.B5613 1998**
Irish Journal. Leila Vennewitz (Translator). Trade Paper. Northwestern University Press. Evanston, IL. 1998. 127p. Marlboro Travel Ser. ISBN:0-8101-6062-5, ISBN13: 978-0-8101-6062-0. Dewey:838/.91403. LCCN:98-006903.
Audience: **g,l,u,f.**

Böll, Heinrich **PT2603.O394.A28 1995**
The Stories of Heinrich Boll. Leila Vennewitz (Translator). Trade Paper. Northwestern University Press. Evanston, IL. 1995. 690p. European Classics Ser. ISBN:0-8101-1207-8, ISBN13: 978-0-8101-1207-0. Dewey:833/.914. LCCN:95-038263.
Audience: **g,l,u,f.** *Choice, 1986.*

Böll, Heinrich & Vennewitz, Leila **PZ33**
Children Are Civilians Too. Trade Cloth. Martin Secker & Warburg, Ltd. London, 1973. 190p. ISBN:0-436-05446-9, ISBN13: 978-0-436-05446-4. Dewey:833/.9/1.
Audience: **g,l,u,f.**

Böll, Heinrich **PT2603.O394.Z47613**
What's to Become of the Boy?: Or, Something to Do with Books. Leila Vennewitz (Translator). Trade Cloth. Alfred A. Knopf Inc. New York, NY. 1984. 96p. ISBN:0-394-53016-0, ISBN13: 978-0-394-53016-1. Dewey:833/.914 B. LCCN:83-049087.
Audience: **g,l,u,f.**

Conard, Robert C. **PT2603.O394.Z596**
Heinrich Boll. Library Binding. Thomson Gale. Farmington Hills, MI. 1981. 228p. World Authors Ser. ISBN:0-8057-6464-X, ISBN13: 978-0-8057-6464-2. Dewey:833/.914. LCCN:81-002419.
Audience: **u,f.**

German Literature > German Literature: Individual Authors > 19th-20th Centuries (1860/70-1960) > Brecht, Bertolt

Brecht, Bertolt — **PT2603.R397.Z52513**
Diaries 1920-1922. Trade Cloth. Bow Historical Books. New Providence, NJ. 1979. xxiii, 182p. ISBN:0-312-07703-3, ISBN13: 978-0-312-07703-7. Dewey:838/.9/1203. LCCN:78-021345.
Audience: **g,l,u,f.** B

Brecht, Bertolt — **PT2603**
Ausgewaehlte Werke in Sechs Baenden. Trade Cloth. Suhrkamp Verlag. Frankfurt am Main, 1997. ISBN:3-518-40945-X, ISBN13: 978-3-518-40945-9. Dewey:832.9.
Audience: **u,f.**

Brecht, Bertolt — **PT2603.R397**
Gesammelte Werke. Suhrkamp. 1977.
Audience: **u,f.**

Brecht, Bertolt — **PT2603.R397.A28 1971**
Collected Plays. Manheim, Ralph (Editor); Willett, John (Editor). Pantheon Books. 1971. ISBN:0-394-40664-8, ISBN13: 978-0-394-40664-0.
Audience: **g,l,u,f.**

Brecht, Bertolt — **PT2603.R397 1967**
Gesammelte Werke: [Supplementbände]. Ramthun, Herta (Editor). Suhrkamp. 1982. ISBN:3-518-00944-3, ISBN13: 978-3-518-00944-4.
Audience: **u,f.**

Brecht, Bertolt — **PT2603.R397.A29 1979**
Poems, 1913-1956. John Willett, Ralph Manheim & Erich Fried (Editors). Trade Cloth. Routledge. New York, NY. 1987. 627p. ISBN:0-416-00081-9, ISBN13: 978-0-416-00081-8. Dewey:831.9/12. LCCN:79-009222.
Audience: **g,l,u,f.** B

Brecht, Bertolt — **PT2603.R397.A2 1983**
Short Stories, 1921-1946. John Willett & Ralph Manheim (Editors), Yvonne Knapp, Hugh Rorrison & Antony Tatlow (Translators). Trade Cloth. Routledge. New York, NY. 1983. xiii, 242p. ISBN:0-413-37050-X, ISBN13: 978-0-413-37050-1. Dewey:833/.912. LCCN:82-014095.
Audience: **g,l,u,f.** B

Demetz, Peter (Editor) — **PT2603.R397.Z587**
Brecht; A Collection of Critical Essays. Prentice-Hall. 1962. Twentieth Century Views
Audience: **u,f.**

Fuegi, John — **PT2603.R397.Z6193**
The Essential Brecht. Trade Cloth. Hennessey & Ingalls, Inc. Santa Monica, CA. 1972. 352p. University of Southern California Studies in Comparative Literature, No. 4 ISBN:0-912158-17-4, ISBN13: 978-0-912158-17-4. Dewey:832/.9/12. LCCN:79-188986.
Audience: **u,f.** B

Hayman, Ronald — **PT2603.R397Z6667**
Bertolt Brecht: The Plays. Trade Cloth. Barnes & Noble Books-Imports. Lanham, MD. 1984. 128p. Contemporary Playwrights Ser. ISBN:0-389-20492-7, ISBN13: 978-0-389-20492-3. Dewey:832/.912. LCCN:84-009261.
Audience: **u,f.** B

Hayman, Ronald — **PT2603.R397.Z6668**
Brecht: A Biography. Trade Cloth. Weidenfeld & Nicolson, Ltd. London, 1983. xxiv, 423p. ISBN:0-297-78206-1, ISBN13: 978-0-297-78206-3. Dewey:832/.912. LCCN:84-172755.
Audience: **u,f.** B

Hill, Claude — **PT2603.R397.Z677**
Bertolt Brecht. Library Binding. Thomson Gale. Farmington Hills, MI. 1975. 208p. World Authors Ser. ISBN:0-8057-2179-7, ISBN13: 978-0-8057-2179-9. Dewey:832/.9/12. LCCN:74-014610.
Audience: **l,u.** B

Lyon, James K. — **PT2603.R397Z/**
Bertolt Brecht in America. Trade Cloth. Princeton University Press. Princeton, NJ. 1980. 440p. ISBN:0-691-06443-1, ISBN13: 978-0-691-06443-7. Dewey:832/.912. LCCN:80-007543.
Audience: **u,f.** B

Mews, Siegfried & Knust, Herbert (Editors) — **PT2603.R397**
Essays on Brecht: Theatre and Politics. Trade Cloth. University of North Carolina Press. Chapel Hill, NC. 1974. xiii, 238p. Studies in Comparative Literature Ser., No. 79 ISBN:0-8078-8079-5, ISBN13: 978-0-8078-8079-1. Dewey:832/.9/12.
Audience: **u,f.**

German Literature > German Literature: Individual Authors > 19th-20th Centuries (1860/70-1960) > Canetti, Elias

Canetti, Elias — **PT2605.A58**
Die Blendung. Ed. 29. Trade Paper. Fischer Taschenbuch Verlag. Frankfurt, 1996. 512p. ISBN:3-596-20696-0, ISBN13: 978-3-596-20696-4. Dewey:833.912.
Audience: **u,f.**

Canetti, Elias — **PT2605.A58.Z513**
Die Fackel Im Ohr: Lebensgeschichte 1921-1931. Trade Cloth. Carl Hanser GmbH & Company. Muchen, 1980. 407p. ISBN:3-446-13138-8, ISBN13: 978-3-446-13138-5. Dewey:833/.912. LCCN:80-514183.
Audience: **u,f.** B

Canetti, Elias — **PT2605.A58.Z515 1977**
Die Gerettete Zunge: Geschichte Einer Jugend. Trade Cloth. Carl Hanser GmbH & Company. Muchen, 1977. 374p. ISBN:3-446-12335-0, ISBN13: 978-3-446-12335-9. Dewey:833.912. LCCN:77-481886.
Audience: **u,f.** B

Canetti, Elias **PT2605.A58.Z51513**
The Tongue Set Free: Remembrance of a European Childhood. Trade Cloth. The Seabury Press, Inc. New York, NY. 1979. viii, 268p. ISBN:0-8164-9103-8, ISBN13: 978-0-8164-9103-2. LCCN:79-018234.
Audience: **g,l,u,f.** B

Canetti, Elias **PT2605.A58G4513 1984**
The Conscience of Words. Joachim Neugroschel (Translator). Trade Cloth. Farrar, Straus & Giroux. New York, NY. 1984. 246p. ISBN:0-374-51881-5, ISBN13: 978-0-374-51881-3. Dewey:834/.912. LCCN:84-010163.
Audience: **u,f.**

Canetti, Elias **PT2605.A58.Z46513**
The Torch in My Ear. Joachim Neugroschel (Translator). Trade Cloth. Farrar, Straus & Giroux. New York, NY. 1982. 384p. ISBN:0-374-27847-4, ISBN13: 978-0-374-27847-2. Dewey:838.9/12/09. LCCN:82-007460.
Audience: **g,l,u,f.** B

German Literature > German Literature: Individual Authors > 19th-20th Centuries (1860/70-1960) > C-F

Carossa, Hans **PT2605.A65 1962**
Sämtliche Werke. Insel-Verlag. 1962.
Audience: **u,f.**

Celan, Paul **PT2605.E4.A1114 1983**
Gesammelte Werke in Funf Banden. Trade Cloth. Suhrkamp Publishers, New York, Inc. Lynchburg, TN. 1983. ISBN:3-518-04500-8, ISBN13: 978-3-518-04500-8. Dewey:831/.914. LCCN:84-105910.
Audience: **u,f.** B

Celan, Paul **PT2605.E4 A6**
Paul Celan: Poems. Michael Hamburger (Translator). Trade Paper. Persea Books, Inc. New York, NY. 1981. 286p. Poetry in Translation Ser. ISBN:0-89255-060-0, ISBN13: 978-0-89255-060-9. Dewey:831/.914. LCCN:79-009117.
Audience: **g,l,u,f.**

Celan, Paul **PT2605.E4A27 1986**
Collected Prose. Rosmarie Waldrop (Introduction by). Trade Cloth. Carcanet Press. New York, NY. 1986. 67p. ISBN:0-85635-645-X, ISBN13: 978-0-85635-645-2. Dewey:838.9/14/08. LCCN:86-181770.
Audience: **g,l,u,f.** *Choice, 1987.*

Dehmel, Richard **PT2607.E32**
Gesammelte Werke... Trade Cloth. Classic Books. Murrieta, CA. 1913. ISBN:0-7426-4462-6, ISBN13: 978-0-7426-4462-5. Dewey:831/.8.
Audience: **u,f.**

Ditzen, Rudolf & Fallada, Hans **PT2607.I6.K4**
Kleiner Mann, was nun?: Roman. Ed. 6. Aufbau-Verlag. 1980. Ausgewählte Werke in Einzelausgaben; 2
Audience: **u,f.**

Doblin, Alfred **PT2607.O35.B5 1977**
Berlin Alexanderplatz: Die Geschichte Von Franz Biberkopf. Trade Cloth. Walter De Gruyter Inc. Ossining, NY. 1977. 527p. ISBN:3-530-16645-6, ISBN13: 978-3-530-16645-3. Dewey:833/.9/12. LCCN:78-371086.
Audience: **u,f.** B

Durrenmatt, Friedrich **PT2607.U493A6 2006**
Friedrich Durrenmatt: Selected Writings. Trade Cloth. University of Chicago Press. Chicago, IL. 2006. 408p. ISBN:0-226-17429-8, ISBN13: 978-0-226-17429-7. Dewey:832/.914. LCCN:2006-013388.
Audience: **g,l,u,f.**

Durrenmatt, Friedrich **PH3241.H334**
The Visit. Patrick Bowles (Translator). Trade Paper. Grove/Atlantic, Inc. New York, NY. 1987. 112p. ISBN:0-8021-3066-6, ISBN13: 978-0-8021-3066-2. Dewey:832. LCCN:62-016341.
Audience: **g,l,u,f.**

Durrenmatt, Friedrich **PT2607.U493A6 2006**
Friedrich Durrenmatt: Selected Writings - Plays. Kenneth J. Northcott (Editor), Joel Agee (Translator). Trade Cloth. University of Chicago Press. Chicago, IL. 2006. 328p. ISBN:0-226-17426-3, ISBN13: 978-0-226-17426-6. Dewey:832/.914. LCCN:2006-013388.
Audience: **g,l,u,f.**

Durrenmatt, Friedrich **PT2607.U493A6 2006**
Friedrich Durrenmatt: Selected Writings - Essays. Kenneth J. Northcott (Editor), Joel Agee (Translator), Brian Evenson (Introduction by). Trade Cloth. University of Chicago Press. Chicago, IL. 2006. 184p. ISBN:0-226-17432-8, ISBN13: 978-0-226-17432-7. Dewey:832/.914. LCCN:2006-013388.
Audience: **g,l,u,f.**

Dürrenmatt, Friedrich **PT2607.U493 A19 1964**
Gesammelte Hörspiele. Verlag der Arche. 1964.
Audience: **u,f.**

Dürrenmatt, Friedrich **PT2607.U493.A19**
Komödien. Verlag der Arche. 1966.
Audience: **u,f.**

Dürrenmatt, Friedrich **PT2607.U493.A24**
Four plays: Romulus the Great. The Marriage of Mr. Mississippi. An Angel Comes to Babylon. The Physicists. Nellhaus, Gerhard (Translator). Grove Press. 1965.
Audience: **g,l,u,f.**

Enzensberger, Hans Magnus **PT2609.N9.L3**
Landessprache. Suhrkamp. 1963.
Audience: **u,f.**

Enzensberger, Hans Magnus **PT2609.N9**
Blindenschrift. Trade Paper. Suhrkamp Verlag. Frankfurt am Main, 1998. ISBN:3-518-10217-6, ISBN13: 978-3-518-10217-6. Dewey:831.91.
Audience: **u,f.**

Enzensberger, Hans Magnus **PT2605.E4**
Selected Poems. Trade Cloth. Bloodaxe Books. Bala, 1994. 256p. ISBN:1-85224-291-4, ISBN13: 978-1-85224-291-6. Dewey:831.914.
Audience: **g,l,u,f.** *Choice, 1995.*

Enzensberger, Hans Magnus **PT2609.N9.A24 1982**
Critical Essays of Enzensberger. Reinhold Grimm (Editor), John Simon (Foreword by). Trade Cloth. Continuum International Publishing Group, Ltd. London, 1982. 320p. German Library, Vol. 98 ISBN:0-8264-0258-5, ISBN13: 978-0-8264-0258-5. Dewey:834/.914. LCCN:81-019612.
Audience: **u,f.**

Fallada, Hans **PT2607.I6**
Kleiner Mann, Was Nun? Roy Reardon (Editor). Trade Paper. Routledge. New York, NY. 1987. 320p. ISBN:0-423-51680-9, ISBN13: 978-0-423-51680-7. Dewey:833/.912.
Audience: **u,f.**

Feuchtwanger, Lion **PT2611.E85 F34 1984**
Der falsche Nero: Roman. F. Taschenbuch Verlag. 1984. ISBN:3-596-25364-0, ISBN13: 978-3-596-25364-7.
Audience: **u,f.**

Feuchtwanger, Lion **PZ33**
The Ugly Duchess. Edwin Muir & Willa Muir (Translators). Trade Paper. Kessinger Publishing, LLC. Whitefish, MT. 2005. ISBN:1-4179-0637-5, ISBN13: 978-1-4179-0637-6. Dewey:833/.9/1.
Audience: **u,f.**

Tiusanen, Timo **PT2607.U493Z/**
Durrenmatt: A Study in Plays, Prose, Theory. Trade Cloth. Princeton University Press. Princeton, NJ. 1978. 504p. ISBN:0-691-06332-X, ISBN13: 978-0-691-06332-4. Dewey:832/.9/14. LCCN:76-045915.
Audience: **u,f.**

German Literature > German Literature: Individual Authors > 19th-20th Centuries (1860/70-1960) > Frisch, Max

Butler, Michael **PT2611.R814.Z634**
The Novels of Max Frisch. Trade Cloth. Publisher Information Not Provided. Berkley, NJ. 1976. 175p. ISBN:0-85496-059-7, ISBN13: 978-0-85496-059-0. Dewey:838/.9/1209. LCCN:76-054703.
Audience: **u,f.**

Butler, Michael **PT2611.R814Z635 1985**
The Plays of Max Frisch. Cloth Text. Palgrave Macmillan. New York, NY. 1985. 144p. ISBN:0-312-61680-5, ISBN13: 978-0-312-61680-9. Dewey:838/.91209. LCCN:84-017906.
Audience: **u,f.** *Choice, 1985.*

Frisch, Max **PT2611.R814S713 1994**
I'm Not Stiller. Trade Paper. Harcourt Trade Publishers. New York, NY. 1994. 384p. Harvest Book Ser. ISBN:0-15-684990-9, ISBN13: 978-0-15-684990-6. Dewey:843/.914. LCCN:94-004524.
Audience: **g,u,f.**

Frisch, Max **PT2611.R814 A19**
Stucke II. Trade Paper. Suhrkamp Verlag. Frankfurt am Main, ISBN:3-518-36581-9, ISBN13: 978-3-518-36581-6. Dewey:838.91209.
Audience: **u,f.**

Frisch, Max **PT2611.R814**
Stiller. Trade Paper. Suhrkamp Verlag. Frankfurt am Main, ISBN:3-518-36605-X, ISBN13: 978-3-518-36605-9. Dewey:838.91209.
Audience: **u,f.**

Frisch, Max **PT2611.R814 A19**
Stucke I. Trade Paper. Suhrkamp Verlag. Frankfurt am Main, ISBN:3-518-36570-3, ISBN13: 978-3-518-36570-0. Dewey:838.91209.
Audience: **u,f.**

Frisch, Max **PT2611.R814.M44**
Der Mensch Erscheint Im Holozan. Trade Cloth. Suhrkamp Publishers, New York, Inc. Lynchburg, TN. 1979. 142p. ISBN:3-518-02850-2, ISBN13: 978-3-518-02850-6. Dewey:833.912. LCCN:79-392262.
Audience: **u,f.**

Frisch, Max & Ackermann, Paul Kurt **PT2672.I4948**
Homo Faber. Ed. 1. Paper Text. Houghton Mifflin College Division. Boston, MA. 1973. 152p. ISBN:0-395-14402-7, ISBN13: 978-0-395-14402-2. Dewey:833/.9. LCCN:72-009379.
Audience: **u,f.**

Frisch, Max **PT2603.R397**
Three Plays. Michael Bullock & Geoffrey Skelton (Translators), Michael Bullock (Introduction by). Trade Paper. Heinemann. Portsmouth, NH. 1992. 257p. ISBN:0-413-66560-7, ISBN13: 978-0-413-66560-7. Dewey:832/.912.
Audience: **g,l,u,f.**

Frisch, Max **PT2611.R814**
Man in the Holocene: A Story. Geoffrey Skelton (Translator). Trade Cloth. Harcourt Trade Publishers. New York, NY. 1980. 120p. A Helen and Kurt Wolff Bk. ISBN:0-15-156931-2, ISBN13: 978-0-15-156931-1. Dewey:833/.912. LCCN:79-003351.
Audience: **g,l,u,f.**

Frisch, Max **PT2611.R814.Z513**
Montauk. Geoffrey Skelton (Translator). Trade Cloth. Harcourt Trade Publishers. New York, NY. 1976. 143p. A Helen and Kurt Wolff Bk. ISBN:0-15-162100-4, ISBN13: 978-0-15-162100-2. Dewey:838/.9/1209. LCCN:76-000070.
Audience: **g,l,u,f.**

German Literature > German Literature: Individual Authors > 19th-20th Centuries (1860/70-1960) > Grass, Gunter

Grass, Günter **PT2613.R338**
Aus dem Tagebuch Einer Schnecke. Trade Paper. Distribooks, Inc. Skokie, IL. 1999. 325p. ISBN:3-423-12593-4, ISBN13: 978-3-423-12593-2. Dewey:833.914.
Audience: **u,f.**

Grass, Günter **PT2613.R338**
Die Blechtrommel. Trade Paper. Deutscher Taschenbuch Verlag GmbH & Co KG. München, 1999. 778p. ISBN:3-423-11821-0, ISBN13: 978-3-423-11821-7. Dewey:833.914.
Audience: **u,f.**

Grass, Günter **PT2613.R338.B8**
Der Butt. Trade Cloth. Luchterhand Literaturverlag GmbH. Munchen, 1977. 693 p. ;p. ISBN:3-472-86069-3, ISBN13: 978-3-472-86069-3. Dewey:833.914. LCCN:77-564682.
Audience: **u,f.** B

Grass, Günter
Der Butt. Trade Paper. Deutscher Taschenbuch Verlag GmbH & Co KG. München, 1999. 702p. ISBN:3-423-11824-5, ISBN13: 978-3-423-11824-8. Dewey:833.914.
Audience: **u,f.**

Grass, Günter **PT2603.O394**
Cat and Mouse. UK-B Format Paperback. Random House of Canada, Ltd. Mississauga, ON. 1998. 192p. ISBN:0-7493-9480-3, ISBN13: 978-0-7493-9480-6. Dewey:833.9/14.
Audience: **u,f.**

Grass, Günter
The Flounder. Trade Paper. Harcourt Trade Publishers. New York, NY. 1989. 560p. A Helen and Kurt Wolff Bk. ISBN:0-15-631935-7, ISBN13: 978-0-15-631935-5. Dewey:833.9/14. LCCN:78-053891.
Audience: **u,f.**

Grass, Günter **PT2613.R338**
Hundejahre. Trade Cloth. Deutscher Taschenbuch Verlag GmbH & Co KG. München, 1999. 743p. ISBN:3-423-11823-7, ISBN13: 978-3-423-11823-1. Dewey:833.914.
Audience: **u,f.**

Grass, Günter **PT2603.O394**
Local Anaesthetic. Mass Market. Ballantine Books. New York, NY. 1981. ISBN:0-449-24257-9, ISBN13: 978-0-449-24257-5. Dewey:833/.914.
Audience: **g,l,u,f.**

Grass, Günter **PT2603.O394**
The Meeting at Telgte. Mass Market. Ballantine Books. New York, NY. 1982. 224p. ISBN:0-449-24504-7, ISBN13: 978-0-449-24504-0. Dewey:833/.914.
Audience: **g,l,u,f.**

Grass, Günter **PT2613.R338**
Ortlich Betaubt. Trade Cloth. Deutscher Taschenbuch Verlag GmbH & Co KG. München, 1998. 283p. ISBN:3-423-12069-X, ISBN13: 978-3-423-12069-2. Dewey:833.914.
Audience: **u,f.**

Grass, Günter
The Rat. Trade Paper. Harcourt Trade Publishers. New York, NY. 1989. 384p. ISBN:0-15-675830-X, ISBN13: 978-0-15-675830-7. Dewey:833/.914.
Audience: **u,f.**

Grass, Günter **PT2613.R338**
Die Rattin. Trade Paper. Deutscher Taschenbuch Verlag GmbH & Co KG. München, 1998. 486p. ISBN:3-423-12528-4, ISBN13: 978-3-423-12528-4. Dewey:833.914.
Audience: **u,f.**

Grass, Günter
Im Krebsgang. Trade Paper. C. Bange GmbH & Company KG. 96139 Hollfeld, 2005. 126p. ISBN:3-8044-1791-4, ISBN13: 978-3-8044-1791-5. Dewey:833.914.
Audience: **u,f.**

Grass, Günter
Unkenrufe. Trade Paper. Deutscher Taschenbuch Verlag GmbH & Co KG. München, 1998. 245p. ISBN:3-423-11846-6, ISBN13: 978-3-423-11846-0. Dewey:833.914.
Audience: **u,f.**

Grass, Günter **PT2613.R338.B5**
The Tin Drum. Manheim, Ralph (Translator). Pantheon Books. 1963.
Audience: **g,l,u,f.**

Grass, Günter **PT2603.O394**
Katz und Maus. H. F. Brookes & C. E. Fraenkel (Editors). Paper Text. Heinemann. Portsmouth, NH. 1971. 272p. ISBN:0-435-38370-1, ISBN13: 978-0-435-38370-1. Dewey:833.914.
Audience: **u,f.**

Grass, Günter **PT2613.R338U513 1992**
The Call of the Toad. Ralph Manheim (Translator). Trade Cloth. Harcourt Trade Publishers. New York, NY. 1992. 248p. ISBN:0-15-125743-4, ISBN13: 978-0-15-125743-0. Dewey:833.914. LCCN:92-020233.
Audience: **u,f.**

Grass, Günter **PT2613.R338H813 1989**
Dog Years. Ralph Manheim (Translator). Trade Paper. Harcourt Trade Publishers. New York, NY. 1989. 576p. ISBN:0-15-626112-X, ISBN13: 978-0-15-626112-8. Dewey:833.9/14. LCCN:89-038471.
Audience: **g,l,u,f.**

Grass, Günter **PZ4.G774FL**
The Flounder. Ralph Manheim (Translator). Trade Cloth. Harcourt Trade Publishers. New York, NY. 1978. xi, 547p. A Helen and Kurt Wolff Bk. ISBN:0-15-131486-1, ISBN13: 978-0-15-131486-7. Dewey:833.9/14. LCCN:78-053891.
Audience: **g,l,u,f.** B

Grass, Günter **PT2603.O394**
From the Diary of a Snail. Ralph Manheim (Translator). Trade Paper. Harcourt Trade Publishers. New York, NY. 1976. 310p. Harvest Book Ser. ISBN:0-15-633950-1, ISBN13: 978-0-15-633950-6. Dewey:833.9/14. LCCN:75-029309.
Audience: **g,l,u,f.**

Grass, Günter
Crabwalk. Krishna Winston (Translator). Trade Paper. Harcourt Trade Publishers. New York, NY. 2004. 252p. ISBN:0-15-602970-7, ISBN13: 978-0-15-602970-4. Dewey:833/.914.
Audience: **u,f.**

Hollington, Michael **PT2613.R338Z/**
Gunter Grass: The Writer in a Pluralist Society. Trade Cloth. Marion Boyars Publishers, Inc. New York, NY. 1980. 192p. ISBN:0-7145-2678-9, ISBN13: 978-0-7145-2678-2. Dewey:838/.91409. LCCN:79-056840.
Audience: **u,f.** B

Reddick, John **PT2613.R338.Z78 1975**
The Danzig Trilogy of Gunter Grass: A Study of the Tin Drum, Cat and Mouse, and Dog Years. Trade Cloth. Harcourt Trade Publishers. New York, NY. 1975. viii, 289p. ISBN:0-15-123815-4, ISBN13: 978-0-15-123815-6. Dewey:833.914. LCCN:74-011027.
Audience: **u,f.** B

German Literature > German Literature: Individual Authors > 19th-20th Centuries (1860/70-1960) > G-H

Bangerter, Lowell A. **PT2617.O47 Z7324**
Hugo Von Hofmannsthal. Trade Cloth. Frederick Ungar A Book. Dulles, VA. 1977. 192p. Literature and Life Ser. ISBN:0-8044-2028-9, ISBN13: 978-0-8044-2028-0. Dewey:831/.9/12. LCCN:76-020408.
Audience: **u,f.**

Coghlan, Brian **PT2617.O47 Z7354**
Hofmannsthal's Festival Dramas. Trade Cloth. Cambridge University Press. Cambridge, 1964. 420p. ISBN:0-521-04682-3, ISBN13: 978-0-521-04682-4. Dewey:832.912.
Audience: **u,f.**

George, Stefan **PT2613**
Gedichte. Trade Paper. Philip Reclam jun., Verlag GmbH. Ditzingen, 1998. ISBN:3-15-008444-X, ISBN13: 978-3-15-008444-1. Dewey:831.91.
Audience: **u,f.**

George, Stefan Anton **PT2613.E47 1968**
Werke. H. Küpper. 1968.
Audience: **u,f.**

George, Stefan **PT2613.E47.A25 1974**
The Works of Stefan George. Ed. 2. Olga Marx & Ernst Morwitz (Translators). Trade Cloth. University of North Carolina Press. Chapel Hill, NC. 1974. xxvi, 427p. Studies in the Germanic Languages and Literatures ISBN:0-8078-8078-7, ISBN13: 978-0-8078-8078-4. Dewey:831/.8. LCCN:73-016133.
Audience: **u,f.**

Hauptmann, Gerhart **PT2616.Z3**
The Dramatic Works of Gerhart Hauptmann. Trade Cloth. Classic Books. Murrieta, CA. 1912. ISBN:0-7426-4463-4, ISBN13: 978-0-7426-4463-2. Dewey:832.
Audience: **u,f.**

Hauptmann, Gerhart **PT2616.A1**
Sämtliche Werke. Hass, Hans-Egon (Editor); Machatzke, Martin (Editor); Bungies, Wolfgang (Editor). Propyläen Verlag. 1962.
Audience: **u,f.**

Hofmannsthal, Hugo von **PT2617.O47**
Poems and Verse Plays, Vol. 1. Pantheon Books. 1961. Bollingen ser.
Audience: **u,f.**

Hofmannsthal, Hugo von **PT2617.O47**
Selected Prose, Vol. 1. Pantheon Books. 1952. Bollingen ser.
Audience: **u,f.**

Hofmannsthal, Hugo von **PT2617.O47 1975**
Sämtliche Werke: krit. Ausg. Burger, Heinz Otto (Editor). S. Fischer. 1975.
Audience: **u,f.**

Hofmannsthal, Hugo von **PT2617.O47 A19 1953**
Dramen. Steiner, Herbert (Editor). S. Fischer. 1953. His Gesammelte Werke in Einzelausgaben
Audience: **u,f.**

Hofmannsthal, Hugo von **PT2617.O47**
Selected Plays and Libretti, Vol. 3. M. Hamburger (Editor). Trade Cloth. Princeton University Press. Princeton, NJ. 1963. 839p. Bollingen Ser. ISBN:0-691-09747-X, ISBN13: 978-0-691-09747-3. Dewey:832.912.
Audience: **u,f.**

Holz, Arno **PT2617.O72**
Phantasus. Trade Cloth. Johnson Reprint Corporation. New York, NY. 1968. ISBN:0-384-24100-X, ISBN13: 978-0-384-24100-8. Dewey:831.8.
Audience: **u,f.**

Holz, Arno **PT2617.O72 1961**
Werke. Emrich, Wilhelm (Editor); Holz, Anita (Editor). Luchterhand. 1961.
Audience: **u,f.**

Maurer, Warren **PT2616.Z9.M36 1982**
Gerhart Hauptmann. Library Binding. Thomson Gale. Farmington Hills, MI. 1982. 159p. World Authors Ser. ISBN:0-8057-6517-4, ISBN13: 978-0-8057-6517-5. Dewey:832/.8. LCCN:82-009358.
Audience: **u,f.**

Von Hofmannsthal, Hugo **PT2617 .O47**
Gedichte - Dramen I, (1891 - 1898). Ed. 8. Trade Paper. Fischer Taschenbuch Verlag. Frankfurt, 1996. 652p. ISBN:3-596-22159-5, ISBN13: 978-3-596-22159-2. Dewey:831.912.
Audience: **u,f.**

German Literature > German Literature: Individual Authors > 19th-20th Centuries (1860/70-1960) > Hesse, Herman

Hesse, Hermann **PT2617.E85.A1**
Gesammelte Schriften. Suhrkamp Verlag. 1987. ISBN:3-518-03108-2, ISBN13: 978-3-518-03108-7.
Audience: **u,f.**

Hesse, Hermann **PT2617.E85.Z54513**
The Hesse-Mann Letters: The Correspondence of Hermann Hesse and Thomas Mann, 1910-1955. Trade Cloth. Harper & Row Ltd. London, 1975. xxii, 196p. ISBN:0-06-010642-5, ISBN13: 978-0-06-010642-3. Dewey:838/.9/1209. LCCN:74-001818.
Audience: **g,l,u,f.**

Hesse, Hermann **PT2621.A26**
Steppenwolf. Mass Market. Bantam Books. New York, NY. 1983. ISBN:0-553-25533-9, ISBN13: 978-0-553-25533-1. Dewey:833.9/12.
Audience: **g,l,u,f.**

Hesse, Hermann **PT2617.E85D413 2000**
Demian. Stanley Appelbaum (Translator). Trade Paper. Dover Publications, Inc. Mineola, NY. 2000. 109p. Thrift Editions Ser. ISBN:0-486-41413-2, ISBN13: 978-0-486-41413-3. Dewey:833/.912. LCCN:00-064347.
Audience: **g,l,u,f.**

Hesse, Hermann **PT2617.E85S513 1999**
Siddhartha: An Indian Tale. Joachim Neugroschel (Translator), Ralph Freedman (Introduction by). Trade Paper. Penguin Group (USA) Inc. New York, NY. 2002. 176p. Penguin Classics Ser. ISBN:0-14-243718-2, ISBN13: 978-0-14-243718-6. Dewey:833/.912. LCCN:98-042928.
Audience: **g,l,u,f.**

Hesse, Hermann & Roloff, Michael **PT2617.E85P4 2003**
Peter Camenzind: A Novel. Trade Paper. Picador. New York, NY. 2003. 208p. ISBN:0-312-42263-6, ISBN13: 978-0-312-42263-9. Dewey:833/.912. LCCN:2003-058138.
Audience: **g,l,u,f.**

Hesse, Hermann & Vennewitz, Leila **PT2621.A26**
Narcissus and Goldmund. Trade Paper. Peter Owen Ltd. London, 1994. 253p. ISBN:0-7206-0876-7, ISBN13: 978-0-7206-0876-2. Dewey:833.912.
Audience: **g,l,u,f.**

Hesse, Hermann **PT2617.E85.K553**
Klingsor's Last Summer. Richard Winston & Clara Winston (Translators). Trade Cloth. Farrar, Straus & Giroux. New York, NY. 1970. 217p. ISBN:0-374-18166-7, ISBN13: 978-0-374-18166-6. Dewey:833/.9/1. LCCN:77-122825.
Audience: **g,l,u,f.** B

Hesse, Hermann **PT2617.E85G513 2002**
The Glass Bead Game: Magister Ludi. Richard Winston & Clara Winston (Translators), Theodore Ziolkowski (Foreword by). Trade Paper. Picador. New York, NY. 2002. 576p. ISBN:0-312-27849-7, ISBN13: 978-0-312-27849-6. Dewey:833/.9/12. LCCN:2002-035542.
Audience: **g,l,u,f.**

Hesse, Hermann **PT2635.I65**
Poems. Ed. 1. James Wright (Translator, Selected by). Trade Paper. Farrar, Straus & Giroux. New York, NY. 1999. 79p. ISBN:0-374-52641-9, ISBN13: 978-0-374-52641-2. Dewey:831/.912. LCCN:78-109558.
Audience: **g,l,u,f.**

Mileck, Joseph **PT2621.A26**
Hermann Hesse: Life and Art. Trade Paper. University of California Press. Berkeley, CA. 1981. 410p. ISBN:0-520-04152-6, ISBN13: 978-0-520-04152-3. Dewey:833/.9/12. LCCN:76-048020.
Audience: **u,f.** B

Otten, Anna (Editor) **PT2617.E85.Z85 1977**
Hesse Companion. Trade Paper. University of New Mexico Press. Albuquerque, NM. 1977. 476p. ISBN:0-8263-0440-0, ISBN13: 978-0-8263-0440-7. Dewey:833/.9/12. LCCN:76-057539.
Audience: **u,f.** B

Ziolkowski, Theodore J. **PT2617.E85 Z99**
Novels of Hermann Hesse: A Study in Theme and Structure. Trade Cloth. Princeton University Press. Princeton, NJ. 1965. 315p. ISBN:0-691-06084-3, ISBN13: 978-0-691-06084-2. Dewey:833.912.
Audience: **u,f.**

German Literature > German Literature: Individual Authors > 19th-20th Centuries (1860/70-1960) > J

Jünger, Ernst **PT2619**
Samtliche Werke. Trade Cloth. Klett, Ernst, Verlag GmbH. 70178 Stuttgart, 1978. ISBN:3-12-904111-7, ISBN13: 978-3-12-904111-6. Dewey:833.9.
Audience: **g,l,u,f.**

Jünger, Ernst **PT2619**
Werke. E. Klett. 1960.
Audience: **u,f.**

Jünger, Ernst **PT2621.A26**
On the Marble Cliffs. Stuart Hood (Translator), George Steiner (Introduction by). Trade Paper. Penguin Group (USA) Inc. New York, NY. 1984. 128p. ISBN:0-14-002985-0, ISBN13: 978-0-14-002985-7. Dewey:833/.9/12.
Audience: **g,l,u,f.**

German Literature > German Literature: Individual Authors > 19th-20th Centuries (1860/70-1960) > Kafka, Franz

Kafka, Franz **PT2621.A26**
Letters to Friends, Family and Editors. Trade Paper. Knopf Publishing Group. New York, NY. 1990. 509p. ISBN:0-8052-0949-2, ISBN13: 978-0-8052-0949-5. Dewey:833/.9/12.
Audience: **g,l,u,f.** B

Kafka, Franz **PT2621.A26**
Parables and Paradoxes: Parabeln und Paradoxe. Trade Paper. Knopf Publishing Group. New York, NY. 1961. ISBN:0-8052-0422-9, ISBN13: 978-0-8052-0422-3. Dewey:838.912. LCCN:61-014917.
Audience: **u,f.**

Kafka, Franz **PT2621.A26**
Das Urteil und andere Erzaehlungen. Trade Paper. Fischer Taschenbuch Verlag. Frankfurt, 1994. 189p. ISBN:3-596-20019-9, ISBN13: 978-3-596-20019-1. Dewey:833.912.
Audience: **u,f.**

Kafka, Franz **PT2621.A26 1947**
Gesammelte schriften. Brod, Max (Editor). Schocken Books. 1947.
Audience: **u,f.**

Kafka, Franz **PT2621.A26.P7**
The Castle. Muir, Edwin (translator); Muir, Willa (translator); Wilkins, Eithne (translator); Kaiser, Ernst (translator). Modern Library. 1969. Modern Library Books, 388
Audience: **g,l,u,f.**

Kafka, Franz, et al. **PF3117.E76**
Erzahlungen. Bertolt Brecht & Heinrich Böll (Authors), Charles W. Hoffman, Marjorie L. Hoover, Charles W. Hoffmann,

Richard Plant & Jack M. Stein (Editors). Paper Text. W. W. Norton & Company, Inc. New York, NY. 1970. 232p. ISBN:0-393-09937-7, ISBN13: 978-0-393-09937-9. Dewey:438.6421. LCCN:75-121183.
Audience: **u,f.**

Kafka, Franz **PT2621.A26**
I Am a Memory Come Alive: Autobiographical Writings. Nahum N. Glatzer (Editor). Trade Paper. Knopf Publishing Group. New York, NY. 1976. 277p. ISBN:0-8052-0428-8, ISBN13: 978-0-8052-0428-5. Dewey:833/.9/12. LCCN:74-008781.
Audience: **g,l,u,f.**

Kafka, Franz **PT2621.A26A2 1988**
The Complete Stories. Nahum N. Glatzer (Editor), John Updike (Foreword by). Trade Paper. Knopf Publishing Group. New York, NY. 1995. 512p. ISBN:0-8052-1055-5, ISBN13: 978-0-8052-1055-2. Dewey:833/.912. LCCN:88-018418.
Audience: **g,l,u,f.**

Kafka, Franz **PT2621.A6P7613 1998**
The Trial: A New Translation Based on the Restored Text. Breon Mitchell (Translator, Preface by). Trade Cloth. Knopf Publishing Group. New York, NY. 1998. 304p. ISBN:0-8052-4165-5, ISBN13: 978-0-8052-4165-5. Dewey:833/.912. LCCN:98-003447.
Audience: **g,l,u,f.**

Kafka, Franz
Der Prozess. Malcolm Pasley (Editor). Trade Paper. Fischer Taschenbuch Verlag. Frankfurt, 1994. 304p. ISBN:3-596-12443-3, ISBN13: 978-3-596-12443-5.
Audience: **u,f.**

Kafka, Franz
Das Schloss. Malcolm Pasley (Editor). Trade Paper. Fischer Taschenbuch Verlag. Frankfurt, 1994. 416p. ISBN:3-596-12444-1, ISBN13: 978-3-596-12444-2.
Audience: **u,f.**

Kafka, Franz
The Castle. J. A. Underwood (Translator), Idris Parry (Introduction by). Trade Paper. Penguin Books, Ltd. London, 2000. 280p. Twentieth Century Classics ISBN:0-14-018504-6, ISBN13: 978-0-14-018504-1. Dewey:833.9/12.
Audience: **g,l,u,f.**

Kuna, Franz **PT2621.A26.Z7666**
Franz Kafka: Literature As Corrective Punishment. Trade Cloth. Indiana University Press. Bloomington, IN. 1974. 196p. ISBN:0-253-33168-4, ISBN13: 978-0-253-33168-7. Dewey:833/.9/12. LCCN:74-004813.
Audience: **u,f.**

Pawel, Ernst **PT2621.A26.Z8155**
The Nightmare of Reason: A Life of Franz Kafka. Cloth over Boards. Farrar, Straus & Giroux. New York, NY. 1984. 496p. ISBN:0-374-22236-3, ISBN13: 978-0-374-22236-9. Dewey:833/.912. LCCN:83-025376.
Audience: **u,f.**

Politzer, Heinz **PT2621.A26 Z817**
Franz Kafka: Parable and Paradox. Book, Other. Cornell University Press. Ithaca, NY. 1966. 432p. ISBN:0-8014-0341-3, ISBN13: 978-0-8014-0341-5. Dewey:838.912. LCCN:62-020733.
Audience: **u,f.**

Sokel, Walter H. **PT2621.A26**
Franz Kafka. Trade Paper. Books on Demand. Ann Arbor, MI. 48p. Columbia Essays on Modern Writers Ser., No. 19 ISBN:0-608-18782-8, ISBN13: 978-0-608-18782-2. Dewey:833.912. LCCN:66-026005.
Audience: **u,f.**

German Literature > German Literature: Individual Authors > 19th-20th Centuries (1860/70-1960) > K-L

Kaiser, Georg **PT2621.A33 A6 1966**
Stücke, Erzählungen, Aufsätze, Gedichte. Huder, Walter (Editor). Kiepenheuer u. Witsch. 1966.
Audience: **u,f.**

Kaiser, Georg **PT2621.A33**
Coral: A Play. Winifred Katzin (Translator), V. Lange (Introduction by). Trade Paper. Frederick Ungar A Book. Dulles, VA. 1963. Coral Trilogy Ser., Pt. 1 ISBN:0-8044-6342-5, ISBN13: 978-0-8044-6342-3. Dewey:832.912. LCCN:63-012906.
Audience: **g,l,u,f.**

Kaiser, Georg **PT2621.A33**
Gas Two: A Play. Winifred Katzin (Translator), V. Lange (Introduction by). Trade Paper. Frederick Ungar A Book. Dulles, VA. 1963. Coral Trilogy Ser., Pt. 3 ISBN:0-8044-6344-1, ISBN13: 978-0-8044-6344-7. Dewey:832.912. LCCN:63-014962.
Audience: **g,l,u,f.**

Kaiser, Georg **PT2621.A33**
Gas One: A Play. Herman G. Scheffauer (Translator), V. Lange (Introduction by). Trade Paper. Frederick Ungar A Book. Dulles, VA. 1956. Coral Trilogy Ser., Pt. 2 ISBN:0-8044-6343-3, ISBN13: 978-0-8044-6343-0. Dewey:832. LCCN:56-012398.
Audience: **g,l,u,f.**

Kraus, Karl **PT2621.R27.A235 1977**
No Compromise: Selected Writings of Karl Kraus. Frederick Ungar (Editor), Sheema Z. Buehne (Translator). Trade Cloth. Frederick Ungar A Book. Dulles, VA. 1977. ix, 260p. ISBN:0-8044-2485-3, ISBN13: 978-0-8044-2485-1. Dewey:838/.9/1209. LCCN:76-015653.
Audience: **u,f.**

Kunert, Gunter **PT2621.U665.C35 1978**
Camera Obscura. Trade Cloth. Carl Hanser GmbH & Company. Muchen, 1978. 136p. ISBN:3-446-12597-3, ISBN13: 978-3-446-12597-1. Dewey:838/.9/1407. LCCN:78-389278.
Audience: **u,f.**

Le Fort, Gertrud von **PT2623.E26L413 2001**
Song at the Scaffold: A Novel of Horror and Holiness in the Reign of Terror. Trade Paper. Sophia Institute Press. Manchester, NH. 2001. 176p. ISBN:1-928832-34-2, ISBN13: 978-1-928832-34-8. Dewey:833/.912. LCCN:2001-034399.
Audience: **u,f.**

Le Fort, Gertrud, Freiin von **PT2623.E26 A15 1956**
Erzählende Schriften. Ehrenwirth. 1956.
Audience: **u,f.**

Lenz, Siegfried **PT2623.E583.D4**
Deutschstunde: Roman. Hoffmann und Campe. 1997. erkausgabe in Einzelbänden ;; Bd. 6; ISBN:3-455-04261-9, ISBN13: 978-3-455-04261-0.
Audience: **u,f.**

Lenz, Siegfried **PT2623.E583.H4**
Heimatmuseum: Roman. Trade Cloth. Hoffman & Campe Verlag. Hamburg, 1978. 654p. ISBN:3-455-04222-8, ISBN13: 978-3-455-04222-1. Dewey:833/.9/14. LCCN:79-340256.
Audience: **u,f.** B

Lenz, Siegfried **PT2623.E583.V6**
Das Vorbild: Roman. Trade Cloth. Hoffman & Campe Verlag. Hamburg, 1973. 526p. ISBN:3-455-04238-4, ISBN13: 978-3-455-04238-2. Dewey:833/.9/14. LCCN:73-354233.
Audience: **u,f.** B

Lenz, Siegfried **PT2623.E583.A6**
Gesammelte Erzählungen. Ed. 8. Russ, Colin (Nachtwort von). Hoffmann und Campe. 1979. ISBN:3-455-04215-5, ISBN13: 978-3-455-04215-3.
Audience: **u,f.**

Lenz, Siegfried **PT2623.E583.D413**
German Lesson. Ernst Kaiser & Eithne Wilkins (Translators). Trade Cloth. Farrar, Straus & Giroux. New York, NY. 1972. 471p. ISBN:0-8090-4907-4, ISBN13: 978-0-8090-4907-3. Dewey:833/.914. LCCN:77-163567.
Audience: **g,l,u,f.** B

Lenz, Siegfried **PT2623.E583.H413**
The Heritage. Krishna Winston (Translator). Trade Cloth. Farrar, Straus & Giroux. New York, NY. 1981. 464p. ISBN:0-8090-5466-3, ISBN13: 978-0-8090-5466-4. Dewey:833/.914. LCCN:80-084608.
Audience: **g,l,u,f.** B

Nordbruch, Claus **PT2623.E583**
Ubcr dic Pflicht: Eine Analyse des Werkes von Siegfried Lenz. Ed. 2. Trade Cloth. Georg Olms Verlag AG. Hildesheim, 2003. 252p. Germanistische Texte und Studien Ser., Vol. 53 ISBN:3-487-10078-9, ISBN13: 978-3-487-10078-4. Dewey:833.914.
Audience: **u,f.**

Schurer, Ernst **PT2621.A33**
Georg Kaiser. Library Binding. Irvington Publishers. New York, NY. 1971. 262p. Twayne's World Authors Ser. ISBN:0-8290-1744-5, ISBN13: 978-0-8290-1744-1. Dewey:832/.9/12. LCCN:70-161824.
Audience: **l,u.** B

Zohn, Harry **PT2621.R27**
Karl Kraus. Cloth Text. Irvington Publishers. New York, NY. 1971. 178p. Twayne's World Authors Ser. ISBN:0-8290-1742-9, ISBN13: 978-0-8290-1742-7. Dewey:838/.9/1209. LCCN:71-120020.
Audience: **l,u.** B

German Literature > German Literature: Individual Authors > 19th-20th Centuries (1860/70-1960) > Mann, Thomas

Dowden, Stephen D. (Editor) **PT2621.A26**
A Companion to Thomas Mann's Magic Mountain. Trade Paper. Camden House. Elizabethtown, NY. 2006. 272p. Studies in German Literature, Linguistics, and Culture Ser. ISBN:1-57113-248-1, ISBN13: 978-1-57113-248-2. Dewey:833.9/12. LCCN:98-021803.
Audience: **g,u,f.** *Choice, 1999.*

Gelley, Alexander (Editor) **PT2625.A44.Z53713**
Mythology and Humanism: The Correspondence of Thomas Mann and Karl Kerenyi. Trade Cloth. Cornell University Press. Ithaca, NY. 1975. 240p. ISBN:0-8014-0831-8, ISBN13: 978-0-8014-0831-1. Dewey:833/.9/12. LCCN:73-020796.
Audience: **u,f.** B

Hamilton, Nigel **PT2625.A43.Z647 1979**
The Brothers Mann: The Lives of Heinrich and Thomas Mann, 1871-1950 and 1875-1955. Trade Cloth. Yale University Press. Cumberland, RI. 1979. 422 p. ;p. ISBN:0-300-02348-0, ISBN13: 978-0-300-02348-0. Dewey:833/.912. LCCN:78-015114.
Audience: **u,f.** B

Mann, Thomas **PT2621.A26**
The Black Swan. Trade Cloth. Alfred A. Knopf Inc. New York, NY. 1954. ISBN:0-394-41708-9, ISBN13: 978-0-394-41708-0. Dewey:833/.912.
Audience: **g,l,u,f.**

Mann, Thomas **PT2621.A26**
Buddenbrooks. Trade Paper. Knopf Publishing Group. New York, NY. 1961. ISBN:0-394-70180-1, ISBN13: 978-0-394-70180-6. Dewey:833.9/12.
Audience: **u,f.** B

Mann, Thomas **PT2625.A44A16 1993**
Essays. Trade Cloth. S. Fischer Verlag. 1993. ;p. ISBN:3-10-048273-5, ISBN13: 978-3-10-048273-0. Dewey:834/.912.
Audience: **g,u,f.**

Mann, Thomas **PT2625.A44 A23**
Essays of Three Decades. Trade Cloth. Random House Children's Books. New York, NY. 1947. ISBN:0-394-42366-6, ISBN13: 978-0-394-42366-1. Dewey:834.91.
Audience: **g,l,u,f.** B

Mann, Thomas **PT2625.A44 1960**
Gesammelte Werke. S. Fischer. 1960.
Audience: **u,f.**

Mann, Thomas **PT2625.A44.A2**
Stories of a Lifetime. Secker & Warburg. 1961.
Audience: **g,l,u,f.**

Mann, Thomas **PZ3.M3184 ST7**
Stories of Three Decades. Trade Cloth. Alfred A. Knopf Inc. New York, NY. 1936. ISBN:0-394-44734-4, ISBN13: 978-0-394-44734-6. Dewey:932.
Audience: **g,l,u,f.**

Mann, Thomas **PT2625.A44.B42**
Confessions of Felix Krull, Confidence Man: The Early Years. Lindley, Denver (Translator). New York: Vintage Books. 1992. ISBN:0-679-73904-1, ISBN13: 978-0-679-73904-3.
Audience: **u,f.**

Mann, Thomas **PT2625.A44 Z523 1961**
Briefe. Mann, Erika (Editor). S. Fischer. 1961.
Audience: **u,f.**

Mann, Thomas **PT2621.A26**
Doctor Faustus: The Life of the German Composer, Adrian Leverkuhn, As Told by a Friend. H. T. Lowe-Porter (Translator). Trade Cloth. Alfred A. Knopf Inc. New York, NY. 1992. 580p. ISBN:0-679-40996-3, ISBN13: 978-0-679-40996-0. Dewey:833/.912.
Audience: **g,l,u,f.**

Mann, Thomas **DT61**
Stories of Three Decades. Helen T. Lowe-Porter (Translator). Trade Cloth. Random House, Inc. New York, NY. 1979. ISBN:0-394-60483-0, ISBN13: 978-0-394-60483-1. Dewey:932. LCCN:61-066696.
Audience: **g,l,u,f.**

Mann, Thomas **PT2625.A44E75 1992**
The Holy Sinner. Helen T. Lowe-Porter (Translator), Russell A. Berman (Introduction by). Trade Cloth. University of California Press. Berkeley, CA. 1992. 336p. ISBN:0-520-07672-9, ISBN13: 978-0-520-07672-3. Dewey:833/.912. LCCN:91-023118.
Audience: **g,l,u,f.**

Mann, Thomas **PT2625.A44L62 1990**
Lotte in Weimar: The Beloved Returns. Helen T. Lowe-Porter (Translator), Hayden V. White (Introduction by). Trade Cloth. University of California Press. Berkeley, CA. 1990. 475p. ISBN:0-520-07006-2, ISBN13: 978-0-520-07006-6. Dewey:833/.912. LCCN:90-010982.
Audience: **g,l,u,f.**

Mann, Thomas **PT2625.A44.B513 1983**
Reflections of a Nonpolitical Man. Walter D. Morris (Translator). Trade Cloth. Continuum International Publishing Group, Ltd. London, 1983. 600p. ISBN:0-8044-2585-X, ISBN13: 978-0-8044-2585-8. Dewey:833/.912. LCCN:82-040249.
Audience: **g,l,u,f.**

Mann, Thomas **PT2625.A44.Z46613**
Thomas Mann Diaries, 1918-1939. Richard Winston & Clara Winston (Translators), Hermann Kesten (Foreword by). Trade Cloth. Harry N. Abrams, Inc. New York, NY. 1982. 512p. ISBN:0-8109-1304-6, ISBN13: 978-0-8109-1304-2. Dewey:838/.91203. LCCN:81-022889.
Audience: **g,l,u,f.**

Mann, Thomas **PT2625.A44Z48 1990**
The Letters of Thomas Mann, 1889-1955. Richard Winston & Clara Winston (Editors), Richard Winston & Clara Winston (Translators). Trade Paper. University of California Press. Berkeley, CA. 1990. 482p. ISBN:0-520-06968-4, ISBN13: 978-0-520-06968-8. Dewey:833/.912 B. LCCN:89-020443.
Audience: **u,f.**

Mann, Thomas **PT2625.A44J7813 2004**
Joseph and His Brothers. John E. Woods (Translator). Trade Cloth. Knopf Publishing Group. New York, NY. 2005. 1536p. ISBN:1-4000-4001-9, ISBN13: 978-1-4000-4001-8. Dewey:823/.912. LCCN:2004-043226.
Audience: **g,l,u,f.**

Prater, Donald A. **PT2625.A44Z7658 1995**
Thomas Mann: A Life. Trade Cloth. Oxford University Press, Inc. New York, NY. 1995. 592p. ISBN:0-19-815861-0, ISBN13: 978-0-19-815861-5. Dewey:833.9/12. LCCN:94-044522.
Audience: **g,u,f.** *Choice, 1996.*

Prem, Boris **PT2625.A43**
Mann's "Der Untertan". Trade Paper. Langenscheidt Publishers Inc. Long Island City, NY. 2005. ISBN:3-580-63317-1, ISBN13: 978-3-580-63317-2. Dewey:833/.912.
Audience: **u,f.**

Reed, T. J. **PT2625.A44Z/**
Thomas Mann: The Uses of Tradition. Trade Cloth. Oxford University Press, Inc. New York, NY. 1974. xv, 433p. ISBN:0-19-815742-8, ISBN13: 978-0-19-815742-7. Dewey:833/.912. LCCN:74-182432.
Audience: **u,f.**

German Literature > German Literature: Individual Authors > 19th-20th Centuries (1860/70-1960) > M-R

Barker, Christine R. & Last, Rex W. **PT2635.E68 Z563**
Erich Maria Remarque. Cloth Text. Barnes & Noble Books-Imports. Lanham, MD. 1979. 174p. ISBN:0-06-490308-7, ISBN13: 978-0-06-490308-0. Dewey:833.912. LCCN:79-010837.
Audience: **u,f.**

De Mendelssohn, Peter **PT2625.A44.Z5446**
Der Zauberer: Das Leben des Deutschen Schriftstellers Thomas Mann. Trade Cloth. S. Fischer Verlag. 1975. ISBN:3-10-049402-4, ISBN13: 978-3-10-049402-3. Dewey:833.912. LCCN:75-512313.
Audience: **u,f.**

Hofacker, Erich **PT2625.O64.Z74**
Christian Morgenstern. Twayne Publishers. 1978. Twayne's World Authors Series, Vol. 508 ISBN:0-8057-6349-X, ISBN13: 978-0-8057-6349-2.
Audience: **l,u.**

Luft, David S. **PT2625.U8Z/**
Robert Musil and the Crisis of European Culture, 1880-1942. Trade Cloth. University of California Press. Berkeley, CA. 1980. 336p. ISBN:0-520-03852-5, ISBN13: 978-0-520-03852-3. Dewey:833/.912. LCCN:78-066008.
Audience: **u,f.** B

Mann, Heinrich **PT2625.A43.U5**
Die Jugend des Königs Henri Quatre. Reinbek bei Hamburg : Rowohlt Taschenbuch. 1985. ISBN:3-499-10689-2, ISBN13: 978-3-499-10689-7.
Audience: **u,f.**

Mann, Heinrich **PT2621.A26**
Henry, King of France. Trade Paper. Overlook Press, The. New York, NY. 1987. 800p. ISBN:0-87951-224-5, ISBN13: 978-0-87951-224-8. Dewey:833/.912. LCCN:84-022682.
Audience: **g,u,f.**

Mann, Heinrich **PT2625.A43.U5**
Der Untertan: Roman. S. Fischer. 1995. Gesammelte Werke in Einzelbänden / Heinrich Mann ISBN:3-10-047809-6, ISBN13: 978-3-10-047809-2.
Audience: **u,f.**

Morgenstern, Christian **PT2625.O64**
Gesammelte Werke in einem Band. Ed. 4. Piper. 1996. Serie Piper, 1067 ISBN:3-492-21067-8, ISBN13: 978-3-492-21067-6.
Audience: **u,f.**

Morgenstern, Christian **PT2625.O64**
Christian Morgenstern's Galgenlieder (Gallows Songs), Bilingual Edition. Max Knight (Translator, Introduction by). Trade Paper. University of California Press. Berkeley, CA. 1964. ISBN:0-520-00884-7, ISBN13: 978-0-520-00884-7.
Audience: **u,f.**

Musil, Robert **PT2625.U8**
Mann Ohne Eigenschaften. Trade Paper. Rowohlt Taschenbuch Verlag GmbH. Reinbek, 1998. ISBN:3-499-13463-2, ISBN13: 978-3-499-13463-0. Dewey:833/.912.
Audience: **u,f.**

Musil, Robert **PD25**
Die Verwirrungen des Zoglings Torless. Trade Cloth. McGraw-Hill/Contemporary. Lincolnwood, IL. 1978. ISBN:0-8442-2753-6, ISBN13: 978-0-8442-2753-5. Dewey:833/.912.
Audience: **u,f.**

Musil, Robert **PT2625.U8V413 2001**
The Confusions of Young Torless. Shaun Whiteside (Translator), J. M. Coetzee (Introduction by). Trade Paper. Penguin Group (USA) Inc. New York, NY. 2001. 176p. Twentieth Century Classics Ser. ISBN:0-14-218000-9, ISBN13: 978-0-14-218000-6. Dewey:833/.912. LCCN:2001-032735.
Audience: **u,f.**

Musil, Robert **PT2621.A26**
The Man Without Qualities. Sophie Wilkins & Burton Pike (Translators). Trade Paper. Knopf Publishing Group. New York, NY. 1996. 752p. Man Without Qualities Ser., Vol. 1 ISBN:0-679-76787-8, ISBN13: 978-0-679-76787-9. Dewey:833.9/12.
Audience: **g,l,u,f.**

Remarque, Erich Maria **PT2621.A26**
All Quiet on the Western Front. A. W. Wheen (Translator). Mass Market. Ballantine Books. New York, NY. 1987. 304p. ISBN:0-449-21394-3, ISBN13: 978-0-449-21394-0. Dewey:833.9/12.
Audience: **g,l,u,f.**

Roth, Joseph **PT2635.O84.R3X 1979**
Radetzkymarsch. Trade Cloth. Kiepenheuer & Witsch GmbH & Company KG. Koln, 1978. 382p. ISBN:3-462-01332-7, ISBN13: 978-3-462-01332-0. LCCN:84-672154.
Audience: **u,f.** B

Roth, Joseph **PT2635.O84R313 1995**
The Radetzky March. Joachim Neugroschel (Translator), Nadine Gordimer (Introduction by). Trade Cloth. Overlook Press, The. New York, NY. 1995. 320p. ISBN:0-87951-548-1, ISBN13: 978-0-87951-548-5. Dewey:833/.9/1. LCCN:94-018208.
Audience: **g,l,u,f.**

German Literature > German Literature: Individual Authors > 19th-20th Centuries (1860/70-1960) > Rilke, Ranier Maria

Leppmann, Wolfgang **PT2635.I65Z782313**
Rilke: A Life. Russell M. Stockman (Translator). Trade Cloth. Fromm International Publishing Corporation. New York, NY. 1995. 421p. ISBN:0-88064-014-6, ISBN13: 978-0-88064-014-5. Dewey:831/.912 B. LCCN:84-006062.
Audience: **u,f.** B

Rilke, Rainer Maria **PT2635.I65**
Die Aufzeichnungen des Malte Laurids Brigge. Trade Cloth. Insel Verlag Anton Kippenberg. Frankfurt am Main, ISBN:3-458-34391-1, ISBN13: 978-3-458-34391-2. Dewey:831.912.
Audience: **u,f.**

Rilke, Rainer Maria **PT2635.I65 1955**
Sämtliche Werke. Sieber-Rilke, Ruth (Editor). Insel-Verlag. 1955.
Audience: **u,f.**

Rilke, Rainer Maria **PT2635.I65L4513 1996**
Rilke: Poems. J. B. Leishman & Stephen Spender (Translators). Trade Paper. David McKay Company, Inc. New York, NY. 1996. 256p. Everyman's Library Pocket Poets Ser. ISBN:0-679-45098-X, ISBN13: 978-0-679-45098-6. Dewey:831.9/12. LCCN:96-019987.
Audience: **g,l,u,f.**

Rilke, Rainer Maria **PT2635.I65.A83 1983**
The Notebooks of Malte Laurids Brigge. Stephen Mitchell (Translator). Trade Cloth. Random House, Inc. New York, NY. 1983. 277p. ISBN:0-394-53011-X, ISBN13: 978-0-394-53011-6. Dewey:833/.912. LCCN:83-003432.
Audience: **g,l,u,f.** B

German Literature > German Literature: Individual Authors > 19th-20th Centuries (1860/70-1960) > S-Z

Best, Alan D. **PT2647.E26.Z57**
Frank Wedekind. Trade Cloth. Wolff Publishing Company. Fairhope, AL. 1975. 125p. ISBN:0-85496-054-6, ISBN13: 978-0-85496-054-5. Dewey:832/.8. LCCN:76-357909.
Audience: **u,f.** B

McCarthy, John A. **PT2569.M3**
Christoph Martin Wieland. Library Binding. Thomson Gale. Farmington Hills, MI. 1979. 192p. World Authors Ser. ISBN:0-8057-6369-4, ISBN13: 978-0-8057-6369-0. Dewey:838/.6/09. LCCN:78-014338.
Audience: **u,f.** B

Mews, Siegfried **PT2653.U33.Z77**
Carl Zuckmayer. Twayne. 1981. Twayne's World Authors Series, Vol. 610 ISBN:0-8057-6452-6, ISBN13: 978-0-8057-6452-9.
Audience: **g,l,u,f.**

Prater, Donald **PT2653.W42Z/**
European of Yesterday: A Biography of Stefan Zweig. Trade Cloth. Oxford University Press, Inc. New York, NY. 1972. xix, 390p. ISBN:0-19-815707-X, ISBN13: 978-0-19-815707-6. Dewey:838/.9/1209.
Audience: **u,f.**

Sachs, Nelly **PT2637.A4184 A6**
O the Chimneys: Selected Poems, Including the Verse Play, Eli. Michael Hamburger (Translator). Trade Cloth. Farrar, Straus & Giroux. New York, NY. 1967. ISBN:0-374-22380-7, ISBN13: 978-0-374-22380-9. Dewey:831/.9/14.
Audience: **g,l,u,f.** B

Sachs, Nelly **PT2637.A4184.A6 1970**
The Seeker and Other Poems. Matthew Mead (Translator). Trade Cloth. Farrar, Straus & Giroux. New York, NY. 1970. 399p. ISBN:0-374-25780-9, ISBN13: 978-0-374-25780-4. Dewey:831/.9/14. LCCN:79-137750.
Audience: **g,l,u,f.** B

Salamon, George **PT2653.W4.Z84**
Arnold Zweig. Library Binding. Thomson Gale. Farmington Hills, MI. 1975. 200p. World Authors Ser. ISBN:0-8057-6212-4, ISBN13: 978-0-8057-6212-9. Dewey:833/.9/12. LCCN:75-012736.
Audience: **u,f.**

Schnitzler, Arthur **PT2638.N5A22 2003**
Desire and Delusion: Three Novellas. Trade Cloth. Ivan R. Dee Publisher. Blue Ridge Summit, PA. 2003. 288p. ISBN:1-56663-542-X, ISBN13: 978-1-56663-542-4. Dewey:833/.8. LCCN:2003-053165.
Audience: **g,u,f.** *Choice, 2004.*

Schnitzler, Arthur **PT2638.N5**
Dream Story. Trade Cloth. Penguin Group (USA) Inc. New York, NY. 2004. 142p. Green Integer Ser. ISBN:1-931243-48-4, ISBN13: 978-1-931243-48-3. Dewey:833.8.
Audience: **g,l,u,f.**

Schnitzler, Arthur **PT2638.N5 1961**
Gesammelte werke. S. Fischer. 1961.
Audience: **u,f.**

Schnitzler, Arthur **PT2638.N5 A2 1982**
Plays and Stories. Schwarz, Egon (Editor). Continuum. 1982. The German Library. v. 55 ISBN:0-8264-0270-4, ISBN13: 978-0-8264-0270-7.
Audience: **g,l,u,f.**

Schnitzler, Arthur & Hutter, Catherine **PT2638.N5Z/**
My Youth in Vienna. Trade Cloth. Weidenfeld & Nicolson, Ltd. London, 1971. xiv, 304p. ISBN:0-297-00306-2, ISBN13: 978-0-297-00306-9. Dewey:832/.8.
Audience: **g,l,u,f.**

Seuffert, Bernhard & Kurrelmeyer, W. **PT2562**
Christoph Martin Wieland: Gesammelte Schriften. Arthur Hubner (Contribution by). Trade Cloth. Weidmann. 1987. 11946p. ISBN:3-615-00015-3, ISBN13: 978-3-615-00015-3. Dewey:833.6.
Audience: **u,f.**

Strittmatter, Erwin **PT2639.T833**
Der Laden: Roman. Aufbau-Verlag. 1987. ISBN:3-351-00392-7, ISBN13: 978-3-351-00392-0.
Audience: **u,f.**

Trakl, Georg **PT2642.R22.A17 1968**
Selected Poems. Trade Cloth. Random House. London, 1968. 125p. ISBN:0-224-61511-4, ISBN13: 978-0-224-61511-2. Dewey:831/.9/12. LCCN:74-367248.
Audience: **g,l,u,f.**

Trakl, Georg **PT2642.R22 1987**
Dichtungen und Briefe. Killy, Walther (Editor); Szklenar, Hans (Editor). O. Müller. 1987. ISBN:3-7160-2046-X, ISBN13: 978-3-7160-2046-3.
Audience: **u,f.**

Trakl, Georg **PT2635.I65**
Poems and Prose. Alexander Stillmark (Translator, Introduction by). Trade Cloth. Libris, Ltd. London, 2001. 192p. ISBN:1-870352-51-3, ISBN13: 978-1-870352-51-2. Dewey:831.912.
Audience: **u,f.**

Tucholsky, Kurt **PT2642.U4 1975**
Gesammelte Werke: In 10 Bd. Trade Cloth. Rowohlt Taschenbuch Verlag GmbH. Reinbek, 1975. ISBN:3-499-29001-4, ISBN13: 978-3-499-29001-5. Dewey:830.900.9. LCCN:76-455140.
Audience: **u,f.**

Tucholsky, Kurt **PT2642.U4 1960**
Gesammelte Werke. Gerold-Tucholsky, Mary (Editor); Raddatz, Fritz Joachim (Editor). Rowohlt. 1960.
Audience: **u,f.**

Urbach, Reinhard **PT2638.N5.Z913**
Arthur Schnitzler. Donald Daviau (Translator). Trade Cloth. Frederick Ungar A Book. Dulles, VA. 1973. 192p. Literature and Life Ser. ISBN:0-8044-2936-7, ISBN13: 978-0-8044-2936-8. Dewey:832/.8. LCCN:73-178165.
Audience: **u,f.** B

Wagener, Hans **PT2647.E77.Z84 1993**
Understanding Franz Werfel. Trade Cloth. University of South Carolina Press. Columbia, SC. 1993. 204p. Understanding Modern European and Latin American Literature Ser. ISBN:0-87249-883-2, ISBN13: 978-0-87249-883-9. Dewey:833/.912. LCCN:92-041141.
Audience: **g,u,f.** *Choice, 1993.*

Wedekind, Frank **PT2647.E26A6 1960**
Prosa, Dramen, Verse. A. Langen. 1968.
Audience: **u,f.**

Wedekind, Frank & Mueller, Carl Richard **PT2647.E26A26 2000**
Frank Wedekind: Four Major Plays. Trade Paper. Smith and Kraus Publishers, Inc. Lyme, NH. 2000. 288p. Great Translations of Plays Ser. ISBN:1-57525-209-0, ISBN13: 978-1-57525-209-4. Dewey:832/.8. LCCN:00-029708.
Audience: **u,f.**

Werfel, Franz **PT2647.E77**
The Forty Days of Musa Dagh. Trade Paper. Avalon Publishing Group. New York, NY. 2002. 824p. ISBN:0-7867-1138-8, ISBN13: 978-0-7867-1138-3. Dewey:833.912.
Audience: **g,u,f.**

Werfel, Franz **PT2621.A26**
The Song of Bernadette. Library Binding. Buccaneer Books, Inc. Cutchogue, NY. 1990. ISBN:0-89968-558-7, ISBN13: 978-0-89968-558-8. Dewey:833/.912.
Audience: **g,l,u,f.**

Werfel, Franz **PT2647.E77**
Die Dramen. Klarmann, Adolf D. (Editor). S. Fischer. 1959. His Gesammelte Werke; Variation: Werfel, Franz,; 1890-1945.; Gesammelte Werke.
Audience: **u,f.**

Zohn, Harry **PT2603.E455**
Germany? Germany!: A Kurt Tucholsky Reader. Trade Cloth. Carcanet Press, Ltd. Manchester, 256p. ISBN:0-85635-810-X, ISBN13: 978-0-85635-810-4. Dewey:838.91209.
Audience: **u,f.**

Zuckmayer, Carl **PT2653.U33 A19 1966**
Meisterdramen. G.B. Fischer. 1966. ISBN:3-10-696504-5, ISBN13: 978-3-10-696504-6.
Audience: **u,f.**

Zuckmayer, Carl **PT2653.U33**
Des Teufels General. Ed. 29. Trade Paper. Fischer Taschenbuch Verlag. Frankfurt, 1998. 156p. ISBN:3-596-27019-7, ISBN13: 978-3-596-27019-4. Dewey:832.912.
Audience: **u,f.**

Zweig, Arnold **PT2653.W4S713 1986**
The Case of Sergeant Grischa. Trade Paper. Penguin Group (USA) Inc. New York, NY. 1986. 464p. Modern Classics Ser. ISBN:0-14-007057-5, ISBN13: 978-0-14-007057-6. Dewey:833.9/12. LCCN:86-000742.
Audience: **g,l,u,f.**

Zweig, Stefan **PT2653.W42.Z48**
Die Welt von Gerstern: Erinnerungen eines Europäers. Fisher Taschenbuch Verlag. 1997. ISBN:3-596-21152-2, ISBN13: 978-3-596-21152-4.
Audience: **u,f.**

Zweig, Stefan **PT2653.W42 Z5 1964**
The World of Yesterday. Harry Zohn (Introduction by). Paper Text. University of Nebraska Press. Lincoln, NE. 1964. 463p. ISBN:0-8032-5224-2, ISBN13: 978-0-8032-5224-0. Dewey:838/.91209. LCCN:43-005821.
Audience: **g,l,u,f.**

German Literature > German Literature: Individual Authors > 20th Century (1961-2000) > A-F

Bernhard, Thomas **PT2662.E7.E79**
Die Erzahlungen. Trade Cloth. Suhrkamp Publishers, New York, Inc. Lynchburg, TN. 1979. 607p. ISBN:3-518-02142-7, ISBN13: 978-3-518-02142-2. Dewey:833/.914. LCCN:80-499572.
Audience: **u,f.** B

Bernhard, Thomas **PT2662.E7Z46413 1985**
Gathering Evidence: A Memoir. David McLintock (Translator). Trade Cloth. Alfred A. Knopf Inc. New York, NY. 1986. 340p. ISBN:0-394-54707-1, ISBN13: 978-0-394-54707-7. Dewey:838/.91409 B. LCCN:85-040393.
Audience: **g,l,u,f.** *Choice, 1986.*

Born, Nicolas **PT2662.O7**
The Deception. Trade Cloth. Little Brown & Company. New York, NY. 1983. ISBN:0-316-10273-3, ISBN13: 978-0-316-10273-5. Dewey:833/.914.
Audience: **g,l,u,f.**

Braun, Volker **PT2662.R34.U5 1972**
Das Ungezwungne Leben Kasts; Drei Berichte. Trade Cloth. Suhrkamp Publishers, New York, Inc. Lynchburg, TN. 1972. 149p. ISBN:3-518-02261-X, ISBN13: 978-3-518-02261-0. Dewey:838.9. LCCN:74-335486.
Audience: **u,f.** B

Braun, Volker **PT2662.R34.U5 1972**
Das ungezwungne Leben Kasts; drei Berichte. Suhrkamp. 1972. ISBN:3-518-02261-X, ISBN13: 978-3-518-02261-0.
Audience: **u,f.**

Braun, Volker **PT2662.R34 A6 1978**
Im Querschnitt Volker Braun: Gedichte, Prosa, Stücke, Aufsätze. Schubert, Holger J. (Editor); Schlenstedt, Dieter (Foreword by). Mitteldeutscher Verlag. 1978.
Audience: **u,f.**

Braun, Volker **PT2662.R34U5513 1988**
Unvollendete Geschichte. Andy Hollis (Editor). Trade Paper. Manchester University Press. Manchester, 1989. 120p. New German Texts Ser. ISBN:0-7190-2402-1, ISBN13: 978-0-7190-2402-3. Dewey:833/.914. LCCN:88-012740.
Audience: **u,f.**

De Bruyn, Günter **PT2662.R88.B8**
Buridans Esel: Roman. Fischer Taschenbuch Verlag. 1999. ISBN:3-596-14527-9, ISBN13: 978-3-596-14527-0.
Audience: **u,f.**

Kort, Wolfgang **PT2607.O35.Z718**
Alfred Döblin. Twayne Publishers. 1974. Twayne's World Authors Series, 290. Germany ISBN:0-8057-2266-1, ISBN13: 978-0-8057-2266-6.
Audience: **l,u.**

German Literature > German Literature: Individual Authors > 20th Century (1961-2000) > Handke, Peter

Handke, Peter **PT2668.A5.A8**
Die Angst des Tormanns beim Elfmeter. [Frankfurt am Main] Suhrkamp. 1970.
Audience: **u,f.**

Handke, Peter **PT2668.A5.L5 1979**
Die Linkshandige Frau: Erzahlung. Trade Cloth. Suhrkamp Publishers, New York, Inc. Lynchburg, TN. 1979. 130p. ISBN:3-518-03022-1, ISBN13: 978-3-518-03022-6. Dewey:833/.914. LCCN:81-161890.
Audience: **u,f.**

Handke, Peter **PT2668.A5.S85**
Die Stunde der Wahren Empfindung. Trade Cloth. Suhrkamp Publishers, New York, Inc. Lynchburg, TN. 1975. 166p. ISBN:3-518-03029-9, ISBN13: 978-3-518-03029-5. Dewey:833.9. LCCN:75-508138.
Audience: **u,f.**

Handke, Peter **PT2668.A5.G4**
Das Gewicht der Welt: Ein Journal (Nov. Trade Cloth. Residenz Verlag GmbH. Salzburg, 1977. 324p. ISBN:3-7017-0177-6, ISBN13: 978-3-7017-0177-3. Dewey:838/.91403. LCCN:78-344874.
Audience: **u,f.**

Handke, Peter **PT2668.A5.A8**
The Goalie's Anxiety at the Penalty Kick. Farrar, Straus and Giroux. 1972. ISBN:0-374-16376-6, ISBN13: 978-0-374-16376-1.
Audience: **g,l,u,f.**

Handke, Peter **PT2668.A5.L3 1979**
Langsame Heimkehr: Erzahlung. Trade Cloth. Suhrkamp Publishers, New York, Inc. Lynchburg, TN. 1979. 199p. ISBN:3-518-03021-3, ISBN13: 978-3-518-03021-9. Dewey:833/.914. LCCN:86-672114.
Audience: **u,f.**

Handke, Peter **PT2668.A5.L53**
The Left-Handed Woman. Ralph Manheim (Translator). Trade Cloth. Farrar, Straus & Giroux. New York, NY. 1978. 87p. ISBN:0-374-18497-6, ISBN13: 978-0-374-18497-1. Dewey:833/.9/1. LCCN:78-005568.
Audience: **g,l,u,f.**

Handke, Peter **PT2668.A5.S773**
A Moment of True Feeling. Ralph Manheim (Translator). Trade Cloth. Farrar, Straus & Giroux. New York, NY. 1977. 144p. ISBN:0-374-17291-9, ISBN13: 978-0-374-17291-6. Dewey:833/.9/14. LCCN:77-006616.
Audience: **g,l,u,f.**

Handke, Peter **PT2668.A5.K813**
Short Letter, Long Farewell. Ralph Manheim (Translator). Trade Cloth. Farrar, Straus & Giroux. New York, NY. 1974. 167p. ISBN:0-374-26318-3, ISBN13: 978-0-374-26318-8. Dewey:833/.9/1. LCCN:73-087695.
Audience: **g,l,u,f.**

Handke, Peter **PT2668.A5.A25 1985**
Slow Homecoming. Ralph Manheim (Translator). Cloth over Boards. Farrar, Straus & Giroux. New York, NY. 1985. 288p. ISBN:0-374-26635-2, ISBN13: 978-0-374-26635-6. Dewey:833/.914. LCCN:84-028597.
Audience: **g,l,u,f.** *Choice, 1985.*

Handke, Peter **PT2668.A5G413 1984**
The Weight of the World. Ralph Manheim (Translator). Cloth over Boards. Farrar, Straus & Giroux. New York, NY. 1984. 288p. ISBN:0-374-28745-7, ISBN13: 978-0-374-28745-0. Dewey:838/.91403. LCCN:84-004196.
Audience: **g,l,u,f.**

Klinkowitz, Jerome & Knowlton, James **PT2668.A5.Z75 1983**
Peter Handke and the Postmodern Transformation: The Goalie's Journey Home. Trade Paper. University of Missouri Press. Columbia, MO. 1983. 144p. Literary Frontiers Ser. ISBN:0-8262-0420-1, ISBN13: 978-0-8262-0420-2. Dewey:838/.91409. LCCN:83-006867.
Audience: **u,f.**

Schlueter, June **PT2668.A5Z/**
The Plays and Novels of Peter Handke. Trade Cloth. University of Pittsburgh Press. Pittsburgh, PA. 1981. 226p. Critical Essays in Modern Literature Ser. ISBN:0-8229-3443-4, ISBN13: 978-0-8229-3443-1. Dewey:838/.91409. LCCN:81-050242.
Audience: **u,f.**

German Literature > German Literature: Individual Authors > 20th Century (1961-2000) > H-T

Boulby, Mark **PT2670.O36.Z65**
Uwe Johnson. Trade Cloth. Frederick Ungar A Book. Dulles, VA. 1974. vii, 136p. Literature and Life Ser. ISBN:0-8044-2062-9, ISBN13: 978-0-8044-2062-4. Dewey:833/.9/14. LCCN:73-082315.
Audience: **u,f.**

Hermand, Jost **PT2685.E5**
Rethinking Peter Weiss, 32. Trade Paper. Peter Lang Publishing, Inc. New York, NY. 2001. 216p. German Life and Civilization Ser. ISBN:0-8204-5819-8, ISBN13: 978-0-8204-5819-9. Dewey:832/.914.
Audience: **u,f.**

Hochhuth, Rolf **DG428**
The Deputy. Richard Winston & Clara Winston (Translators), Albert Schweitzer (Introduction by). Trade Paper. Grove/Atlantic, Inc. New York, NY. 2006. 112p. ISBN:0-8021-4242-7, ISBN13: 978-0-8021-4242-9. Dewey:14.5/04/9.
Audience: **g,l,u,f.**

Johnson, Uwe **PT2670.O36.J3213**
Anniversaries: From the Life of Gesine Cresspahl. Trade Cloth. Harcourt College Publishers. Fort Worth, TX. 1975. 504p. ISBN:0-15-107560-3, ISBN13: 978-0-15-107560-7. Dewey:833/.9/1. LCCN:74-020942.
Audience: **g,l,u,f.**

Johnson, Uwe **PT2670.O36**
Mutmassungen Uber Jakob. Trade Paper. Suhrkamp Verlag. Frankfurt am Main, 1959. ISBN:3-518-11818-8, ISBN13: 978-3-518-11818-4. Dewey:833.914.
Audience: **u,f.**

Johnson, Uwe **PT2670.O36.J3**
Jahrestage: aus dem Leben von Gesine Cresspahl. Frankfurt am Main : Suhrkamp. 2000. ISBN:3-518-41165-9, ISBN13: 978-3-518-41165-0.
Audience: **u,f.**

Johnson, Uwe **PT2619.O56.M82**
Speculations about Jakob. Ursule Molinaro (Translator). Trade Paper. Harcourt Trade Publishers. New York, NY. 1972. 240p. ISBN:0-15-684719-1, ISBN13: 978-0-15-684719-3. Dewey:[Fic]. LCCN:62-017528.
Audience: **g,l,u,f.** B

Mann, Klaus
Mephisto. Trade Paper. Rowohlt Taschenbuch Verlag GmbH. Reinbek, ISBN:3-499-14821-8, ISBN13: 978-3-499-14821-7. Dewey:833.9/12.
Audience: **u,f.**

Mann, Klaus
Mephisto. Robin Smyth (Translator). Trade Paper. Penguin Group (USA) Inc. New York, NY. 1995. 272p. Penguin Twentieth-Century Classics Ser. ISBN:0-14-018918-1, ISBN13: 978-0-14-018918-6. Dewey:833.9/12.
Audience: **u,f.**

Morgner, Irmtraud **PT2673.O64.Z467 1984**
Die Hexe Im Landhaus: Gesprach in Solothurn. Trade Cloth. Rauhreif Verlag. Mohlin, 1984. 124p. ISBN:3-907764-03-X, ISBN13: 978-3-907764-03-9. Dewey:833/.914. LCCN:85-139512.
Audience: **u,f.** B

Muller, Heiner **PT2685.E5**
Hamletmachine and Other Texts for the Stage. Carl Weber (Translator). Trade Paper. P A J Publications. New York, NY. 1984. 140p. Paj Playscript Ser. ISBN:0-933826-45-1, ISBN13: 978-0-933826-45-8. Dewey:832/.914. LCCN:83-061193.
Audience: **g,l,u,f.** B

Plenzdorf **PT2676.L39.L37 1981**
Legende Vom Gluck Ohne Ende. Trade Paper. Suhrkamp Publishers, New York, Inc. Lynchburg, TN. 1981. 318p. ISBN:3-518-37222-X, ISBN13: 978-3-518-37222-7. Dewey:833/.914. LCCN:83-114031.
Audience: **u,f.** B

Plenzdorf, Ulrich **PT2676.L39**
The New Sufferings of Young W. Kenneth P. Wilcox (Translator). Paper Text. Waveland Press, Inc. Prospect Heights, IL. 1996. 84p. ISBN:0-88133-891-5, ISBN13: 978-0-88133-891-1. Dewey:832.914.
Audience: **u,f.**

Remarque, Erich Maria
Arc de Triomphe: Roman. Trade Paper. Kiepenheuer & Witsch GmbH & Company KG. Koln, 472p. ISBN:3-462-02723-9, ISBN13: 978-3-462-02723-5.
Audience: **u,f.**

Remarque, Erich Maria **PT2621.A26**
Im Western Nichts Neues. Trade Paper. Kiepenheuer & Witsch GmbH & Company KG. Koln, 2000. 494p. ISBN:3-462-02731-X, ISBN13: 978-3-462-02731-0. Dewey:833/.912.
Audience: **u,f.**

Remarque, Erich Maria
Weg Zuruck. Trade Paper. Kiepenheuer & Witsch GmbH & Company KG. Koln, 1998. ISBN:3-462-02050-1, ISBN13: 978-3-462-02050-2.
Audience: **u,f.**

Remarque, Erich Maria
The Road Back. Trade Paper. Simon Publications, Inc. 2002. 343p. ISBN:1-931541-74-4, ISBN13: 978-1-931541-74-9. Dewey:833/.9/1. LCCN:31-011921.
Audience: **u,f.**

Remarque, Erich Maria
Arch of Triumph. Walter Sorell & Denver Lindley (Translators). Trade Cloth. Simon Publications, Inc. 2001. 455p. ISBN:1-931313-64-4, ISBN13: 978-1-931313-64-3. Dewey:FIC.
Audience: **u,f.**

Sebald, W. G.
Ausgewanderten. Trade Paper. Fischer Taschenbuch Verlag. Frankfurt, 2006. 354p. ISBN:3-596-12056-X, ISBN13: 978-3-596-12056-7. Dewey:833.914.
Audience: **u,f.**

Sebald, W. G.
Nach der Anatur. Trade Paper. Fischer Taschenbuch Verlag. Frankfurt, 1999. ISBN:3-596-12055-1, ISBN13: 978-3-596-12055-0.
Audience: **u,f.**

Sebald, W. G. **PT2681.E18A95 2003**
Austerlitz. Trade Paper. Fischer Taschenbuch Verlag. Frankfurt, 420p. ISBN:3-596-14864-2, ISBN13: 978-3-596-14864-6. Dewey:833/.914.
Audience: **u,f.**

Sebald, W. G.
Austerlitz. Anthea Bell (Translator). Trade Paper. Random House Adult Trade Publishing Group. New York, NY. 2002. 304p. ISBN:0-375-75656-6, ISBN13: 978-0-375-75656-6. Dewey:833/.914. LCCN:2001-019785.
Audience: **u,f.**

Sebald, W. G.
After Nature. Michael Hamburger (Translator). Trade Paper. Random House Adult Trade Publishing Group. New York, NY. 2003. 128p. ISBN:0-375-75658-2, ISBN13: 978-0-375-75658-0. Dewey:833/.914.
Audience: **u,f.**

Sebald, W. G.
The Emigrants. Michael Hulse (Translator). Trade Paper. New Directions Publishing Corporation. New York, NY. 1997. 256p.

ISBN:0-8112-1366-8, ISBN13: 978-0-8112-1366-0. Dewey:833/.914. LCCN:96-022223.
Audience: **u,f.** *Choice, 1997.*

Strauss, Botho **PT2681.T6898.W5**
Die Widmung: Eine Erzahlung. Trade Cloth. Carl Hanser GmbH & Company. Muchen, 1977. 144 p. ;p. ISBN:3-446-12415-2, ISBN13: 978-3-446-12415-8. Dewey:833.914. LCCN:77-571419.
Audience: **u,f.** B

Strauss, Botho **PT2681.T6898**
Devotion. Sophie Wilkins (Translator). Trade Cloth. Farrar, Straus & Giroux. New York, NY. 1979. 128p. ISBN:0-374-13852-4, ISBN13: 978-0-374-13852-3. Dewey:833/.9/1. LCCN:79-009887.
Audience: **g,l,u,f.**

Weiss, Peter **PT2685.E5 A19 1991**
Dramen. Suhrkamp. 1991. Werke in sechs Bänden / Peter Weiss ;; Bd. 4-6 ISBN:3-518-40411-3, ISBN13: 978-3-518-40411-9.
Audience: **u,f.**

German Literature > German Literature: Individual Authors > 20th Century (1961-2000) > Walser, Martin

Walser, M. **PT2685.A48**
Das Einhorn. Trade Paper. Suhrkamp Verlag. Frankfurt am Main, 1995. 381p. ISBN:3-518-36659-9, ISBN13: 978-3-518-36659-2. Dewey:833.914.
Audience: **u,f.**

Walser, Martin **PT2685.A48.B7 1985**
Brandung: Roman. Trade Cloth. Suhrkamp Publishers, New York, Inc. Lynchburg, TN. 1985. 318p. ISBN:3-518-03570-3, ISBN13: 978-3-518-03570-2. Dewey:833/.914. LCCN:86-672328.
Audience: **u,f.** B

Walser, Martin **PT2685.A48.F48**
Ein Fliehendes Pferd: Novelle. Trade Cloth. Suhrkamp Publishers, New York, Inc. Lynchburg, TN. 1978. 150p. ISBN:3-518-04269-6, ISBN13: 978-3-518-04269-4. Dewey:833.9. LCCN:78-366616.
Audience: **u,f.** B

Walser, Martin **PT2685.A48.S35**
Das Schwanenhaus: Roman. Frankfurt am Main: Suhrkamp. 1980. ISBN:3-518-04640-3, ISBN13: 978-3-518-04640-1.
Audience: **u,f.**

Walser, Martin **PT2685.A48.S4**
Seelenarbeit: Roman. Trade Cloth. Suhrkamp Publishers, New York, Inc. Lynchburg, TN. 1979. 294p. ISBN:3-518-04630-6, ISBN13: 978-3-518-04630-2. Dewey:833/.9/14. LCCN:79-376187.
Audience: **u,f.** B

Walser, Martin **PT2603.O394**
The Swan Villa. Trade Paper. Henry Holt & Company. New York, NY. 1987. ISBN:0-8050-0358-4, ISBN13: 978-0-8050-0358-1. Dewey:833/.914.
Audience: **u,f.**

Walser, Martin **PT2685.A48**
The Unicorn. B. Ellis-Jones (Translator). Trade Paper. Marion Boyars Publishers, Inc. New York, NY. 1983. 283p. ISBN:0-7145-0886-1, ISBN13: 978-0-7145-0886-3. Dewey:833/.9/14.
Audience: **g,l,u,f.** B

Walser, Martin **PT2685.A48.S413 1985**
The Inner Man. Leila Vennewitz (Translator). Trade Cloth. Henry Holt & Company. New York, NY. 1985. 288p. ISBN:0-03-059373-5, ISBN13: 978-0-03-059373-4. Dewey:833/.914. LCCN:84-000672.
Audience: **g,l,u,f.** B

German Literature > German Literature: Individual Authors > 20th Century (1961-2000) > Wolf, Christa

Wolf, Christa **PT2685.O36**
Kassandra. Trade Paper. Deutscher Taschenbuch Verlag GmbH & Co KG. München, ISBN:3-423-11870-9, ISBN13: 978-3-423-11870-5. Dewey:833.914.
Audience: **u,f.**

Wolf, Christa **PT2685.O36.K5 1977**
Kindheitsmuster: Roman. Trade Cloth. Luchterhand Literaturverlag GmbH. Munchen, 1977. 480p. ISBN:3-472-86422-2, ISBN13: 978-3-472-86422-6. Dewey:833.9. LCCN:78-346954.
Audience: **u,f.** B

Wolf, Christa **PT2685.O36.N313 1989**
The Quest for Christa T. Trade Cloth. Farrar, Straus & Giroux. New York, NY. 1971. 185p. ISBN:0-374-23988-6, ISBN13: 978-0-374-23988-6. Dewey:833/.9/1. LCCN:78-133199.
Audience: **g,l,u,f.** B

Wolf, Christa **PT2685.O36.L413**
The Reader and the Writer. Trade Paper. International Publishers Company, Inc. New York, NY. 1978. 224p. ISBN:0-7178-0487-9, ISBN13: 978-0-7178-0487-0. Dewey:834/.9/14. LCCN:77-000905.
Audience: **g,l,u,f.** B

Wolf, Christa **PT2685.O36**
Nachdenken Uber Christa T. Trade Paper. Luchterhand Literaturverlag GmbH. Munchen, 2002. 203p. ISBN:3-630-62032-9, ISBN13: 978-3-630-62032-9. Dewey:833.914.
Audience: **u,f.**

Wolf, Christa **PT2685.O36 N32**
Nachdenken Uber Christa T. Trade Paper. Deutscher Taschenbuch Verlag GmbH & Co KG. München, ISBN:3-423-11834-2, ISBN13: 978-3-423-11834-7. Dewey:833.914.
Audience: **u,f.**

Wolf, Christa **PT2685.O36.K338 1983**
Voraussetzungen Einer Erzahlung, Kassandra: Frankfurter Poetik-Vorlesungen. Trade Cloth. Luchterhand Literaturverlag GmbH. Munchen, 1983. 160p. ISBN:3-472-61456-0, ISBN13: 978-3-472-61456-2. Dewey:838/.91409. LCCN:83-172398.
Audience: **u,f.**

Wolf, Christa **PT2685.O36K513 1984**
Patterns of Childhood. Ursule Molinaro & Hedwig Rappolt (Translators). Trade Cloth. Farrar, Straus & Giroux. New York, NY. 1984. 407p. ISBN:0-374-51844-0, ISBN13: 978-0-374-51844-8. Dewey:833/.914. LCCN:84-004135.
Audience: **g,l,u,f.**

Wolf, Christa **PT2685.O36K313 1984**
Cassandra: A Novel and Four Essays. Jan Van Heurck (Translator). Trade Cloth. Farrar, Straus & Giroux. New York, NY. 1984. 320p. ISBN:0-374-11956-2, ISBN13: 978-0-374-11956-0. Dewey:838/.91409. LCCN:84-008056.
Audience: **g,l,u,f.**

German Literature > Swiss Literature in German

Gunther, Werner **PT3868.G8**
Dichter der Neueren Schweiz. Trade Cloth. A. Francke AG. Bern, 1963. ISBN:3-317-01589-6, ISBN13: 978-3-317-01589-9. Dewey:830.9. LCCN:67-101690.
Audience: **u,f.**

Waidson, H. M. **PT1819.B6 Z95 1978**
Jeremias Gotthelf: An Introduction to the Swiss Novelist. Trade Cloth. Greenwood Publishing Group, Inc. Portsmouth, NH. 1978. 231p. Modern Language Studies ISBN:0-313-20231-1, ISBN13: 978-0-313-20231-5. Dewey:833/.7. LCCN:77-028429.
Audience: **l,u.**

German and Scandanavian Languages

Das Bedeutungsbuch. Trade Paper. Langenscheidt Publishers Inc. Long Island City, NY. 2005. 797p. Duden Ser., Vol. 10 ISBN:3-411-04103-X, ISBN13: 978-3-411-04103-9.
Audience: **u,f.**

Duden Ausspracheworterbuch. Trade Cloth. Bibliographisches Institut & F. A. Brockhaus AG. Mannheim, 1990. 794p. Duden Ser., Vol. 6 ISBN:3-411-00916-0, ISBN13: 978-3-411-00916-9.
Audience: **u,f.**

Duden Bildwörterbuch der deutschen Sprache. Trade Cloth. Bibliographisches Institut & F. A. Brockhaus AG. Mannheim, 1977. 672p. Duden Ser., Vol. 3 ISBN:3-411-00913-6, ISBN13: 978-3-411-00913-8.
Audience: **u,f.**

Pons Worterbuch der Deutschen Umgangssprache. Trade Cloth. Ernst Klett Verlag fur Wirtschafts- und Bildungsservice GmbH. Stuttgart, ISBN:3-12-570600-9, ISBN13: 978-3-12-570600-2.
Audience: **u,f.**

Oxford Duden-English Pictorial Dictionary. Trade Cloth. Insight Guides. Maspeth, NY. 1979. ISBN:3-411-01765-1, ISBN13: 978-3-411-01765-2.
Audience: **g,l,u.**

Bithell, Jethro **PF3131.B57**
German Pronunciation and Phonology. Methuen. 1952.
Audience: **l,u,f.**

Blackall, Eric A. **PF3083.B6**
The Emergence of German as a Literary Language, 1700-1775. Ed. 2. Cornell University Press. 1978. ISBN:0-8014-1170-X, ISBN13: 978-0-8014-1170-0.
Audience: **u,f.**

Brachin, Pierre **PF73**
The Dutch Language: A Survey. Paul Vincent (Translator, Adapted by). Trade Cloth. Nelson Thornes Ltd. Cheltenham, 1985. 160p. ISBN:0-85950-246-5, ISBN13: 978-0-85950-246-7. Dewey:439.3/1/09.
Audience: **g,l,u.**

Cassell Staff **PF3640**
Cassell's German English Dictionary. Charlotte Dixon, J. Horne & H. -C. Sasse (Compiled by). Trade Paper. John Wiley & Sons, Inc. Hoboken, NJ. 1986. 560p. ISBN:0-02-024850-4, ISBN13: 978-0-02-024850-7. Dewey:433/.21. LCCN:86-008286.
Audience: **g,l,u,f.**

Cassells Editors **PF640**
Cassell's New Dutch Dictionary: English-Dutch, Dutch-English. Ed. 2. Trade Cloth. John Wiley & Sons, Inc. Hoboken, NJ. 1982. 730p. ISBN:0-02-522940-0, ISBN13: 978-0-02-522940-2. Dewey:439.31.
Audience: **g,l,u,f.**

Drosdowski, Gunther & Duden, Konrad
Duden Fremdwörterbuch. Trade Cloth. Bibliographisches Institut & F. A. Brockhaus AG. Mannheim, 1990. 832p. Duden Ser., Vol. 5 ISBN:3-411-20915-1, ISBN13: 978-3-411-20915-6.
Audience: **u,f.**

Duden
Das Herkunftswoerterbuch, Vol. 7. Trade Paper. Langenscheidt Publishers Inc. Long Island City, NY. 2005. 844p. Duden Ser., Vol. 7 ISBN:3-411-04073-4, ISBN13: 978-3-411-04073-5.
Audience: **u,f.**

Duden
Redewendungen und Sprichwoertliche Redensarten. Trade Paper. Langenscheidt Publishers Inc. Long Island City, NY. 2005. 864p. Duden Ser., Vol. 11 ISBN:3-411-04112-9, ISBN13: 978-3-411-04112-1.
Audience: **u,f.**

Duden
Zitate und Ausspruече. Trade Paper. Langenscheidt Publishers Inc. Long Island City, NY. 2005. 832p. Duden Ser., Vol. 12 ISBN:3-411-04122-6, ISBN13: 978-3-411-04122-0.
Audience: **u,f.**

DUDEN Editors
Die Deutsche Rechtschreibung. Ed. 22. Trade Cloth. Langenscheidt Publishers Inc. Long Island City, NY. 2005. 1152p. Duden Ser., Vol. 1 ISBN:3-411-04012-2, ISBN13: 978-3-411-04012-4.
Audience: **u,f.**

DUDEN Editors
Duden, Grammatik der deutschen Gegenwartssprache. Trade Cloth. Langenscheidt Publishers Inc. Long Island City, NY. 1998. 912p. Duden Ser., Vol. 4 ISBN:3-411-04046-7, ISBN13: 978-3-411-04046-9.
Audience: **u,f.**

DUDEN Editors
Richtiges und Gutes Deutsch. Trade Paper. Langenscheidt Publishers Inc. Long Island City, NY. 2005. 803p. Duden Ser., Vol. 9 ISBN:3-411-04095-5, ISBN13: 978-3-411-04095-7.
Audience: **u,f.**

DUDEN Editors
Das Stilworterbuch. Trade Cloth. Langenscheidt Publishers Inc. Long Island City, NY. 1988. 864p. Duden Ser., Vol. 2 ISBN:3-411-20902-X, ISBN13: 978-3-411-20902-6.
Audience: **u,f.**

Farrell, R. B. **PF3591 .F37 1982**
Dictionary of German Synonyms. Ed. 3. Trade Paper. Cambridge University Press. New York, NY. 1977. 420p. ISBN:0-521-29068-6, ISBN13: 978-0-521-29068-5. Dewey:433/.2/1. LCCN:75-036175.
Audience: **g,l,u,f.**

Fox, Anthony **PF3139.5.F6 1984**
German Intonation: An Outline. Trade Cloth. Oxford University Press, Inc. New York, NY. 1984. 128p. ISBN:0-19-815794-0, ISBN13: 978-0-19-815794-6. Dewey:431/.6. LCCN:83-024399.
Audience: **l,u.**

Grimm, Jacob W. & Grimm, Wilhelm K. **PF3625.G86 1984**
Deutsches Woerterbuch, Set. Trade Paper. Adler's Foreign Books, Inc. Evanston, IL. 1984. ISBN:3-423-05945-1, ISBN13: 978-3-423-05945-9. Dewey:433.
Audience: **l,u.**

herausgegeben von der Dudenredaktion **PF3591**
Duden: das Synonymwörterbuch : ein Wörterbuch sinnverwandter Wörter. Ed. 3. [Bearbeitung, Christine Beil ... et al.]. Dudenverlag. 2004. Duden Series Vol. 8 ISBN:3-411-04083-1, ISBN13: 978-3-411-04083-4.
Audience: **u,f.**

Kluge, Friedrich **PF3580**
Etymologisches Worterbuch der Deutschen Sprache. Ed. 23. Elmar Seebold (Revised by). Trade Cloth. Walter De Gruyter Inc. Ossining, NY. 1999. lxiv, 921p. Jubilaums-Sonderausgabe Ser. ISBN:3-11-016392-6, ISBN13: 978-3-11-016392-6. Dewey:432/.03.
Audience: **u,f.**

Küpper, Heinz **PF3625.K8 1963**
Wörterbuch der deutschen Umgangssprache. Ed. 3. Claasen. 1963.
Audience: **u,f.**

Lederer, Herbert (Editor) **PF3105 .L43 1969**
Reference Grammar of the German Language. Trade Paper. Prentice Hall PTR. Upper Saddle River, NJ. 1969. 709p. ISBN:0-13-033705-6, ISBN13: 978-0-13-033705-4. Dewey:438/.2/42. LCCN:69-017352.
Audience: **g,l,u,f.**

Lexer, Matthias **PF4327.L42X 1981**
Matthias Lexers Mittelhochdeutsches Taschenworterbuch. Trade Cloth. S. Hirzel Verlag GmbH & Company. 70191 Stuttgart, 1981. viii, 504p. ISBN:3-7776-0359-7, ISBN13: 978-3-7776-0359-9. Dewey:437.02. LCCN:86-672397.
Audience: **u,f.**

Martin, W. & Tops, Guy A. **PF640.M37 1998**
Van Dale Groot Woordenboek Engels-Nederlands. Ed. 3. Trade Cloth. Wolter's Woordenboeken. 1998. xxix, 1763p. Woordenboeken Voor Hedendaags Taalgebruik Ser., : ISBN:90-6648-143-9, ISBN13: 978-90-6648-143-5. Dewey:423/.3931. LCCN:99-179338.
Audience: **u,f.**

Polenz, Peter Von **PF3075**
Geschichte der Deutschen Sprache. Ed. 9. Trade Cloth. Walter De Gruyter Inc. Ossining, NY. 1984. Sammlung Goeschen Ser., Vol. 2206 ISBN:3-11-007998-4, ISBN13: 978-3-11-007998-2. Dewey:430.9.
Audience: **u,f.**

Priebsch, Robert & Collinson, William Edward **PF3101.P67 1966**
The German language. Ed. 6. Faber. 1966.
Audience: **g,l,u.**

Russ, Charles V. **PF3131.R8**
Historical German Phonology and Morphology. Trade Cloth. Oxford University Press, Inc. New York, NY. 1979. 200p. Oxford History of the German Language Ser. ISBN:0-19-815727-4, ISBN13: 978-0-19-815727-4. Dewey:431/.5. LCCN:78-040248.
Audience: **u,f.**

Schemann, Hans **PF3460.S345 1995**
German/English Dictionary of Idioms. Paper over Boards. Routledge. New York, NY. 1996. 1280p. ISBN:0-415-14199-0, ISBN13: 978-0-415-14199-4. Dewey:433/.21. LCCN:96-001846.
Audience: **g,l,u,f.**

Siebs, Theodor **PF3137**
Deutsche Hochsprache; Bühnenaussprache. Ed. 18. Boor, Helmut de (Edited by); Diels, Paul (Edited by). deGruyter. 1961.
Audience: **u,f.**

Springer, Otto (Editor) **PF3640.L257**
Langenscheidt 's New Muret-Sanders Encyclopedic Dictionary of the English and German Languages. Langenscheidt. 1974.
Audience: **g,l,u,f.**

Van Dale **PF640 .M38 1986**
Van Dale'Woordenboek Dutch - Englis. Cloth Text. Nelson Thornes Ltd. Cheltenham, 1986. ISBN:90-6648-107-2, ISBN13: 978-90-6648-107-7. Dewey:439.3/1321. LCCN:86-221171.
Audience: **u,f.** B

Vandeputte, Omer **PF95.V3 1981**
Dutch, the Language of Twenty Million Dutch and Flemish People. Stichting Ons Erfdeel vzw. 1981.
Audience: **l,u.**

Wahrig, Gerhard **PF3625 .W2**
Deutsches Woerterbuch. Trade Cloth. French & European Publications, Inc. New York, NY. 1997. 1420p. ISBN:0-7859-9367-3, ISBN13: 978-0-7859-9367-4. Dewey:433.
Audience: **g,u,f.**

Waterman, John T. **PF3075**
A History of the German Language. Paper Text. Waveland Press, Inc. Prospect Heights, IL. 1991. 284p. ISBN:0-88133-590-8, ISBN13: 978-0-88133-590-3. Dewey:430.09.
Audience: **g,l,u,f.**

Wildhagen, Karl **PF3640 .W544**
Englisch-Deutsches, Deutsch-Englishes Woerterbuch: English - German. Ed. 2. Trade Cloth. French & European Publications, Inc. New York, NY. 1973. ISBN:0-685-57716-3, ISBN13: 978-0-685-57716-5. Dewey:433/.2/1.
Audience: **g,l,u,f.**

Wildhagen, Karl **PF3640 .W544**
English-Deutsches, Deutsch-Englisches Woerterbuch, Vol. 2. Ed. 2. Trade Cloth. Oscar Brandstetter (Verlag). Wiesbaden, 1972. ISBN:0-8288-6388-1, ISBN13: 978-0-8288-6388-9. Dewey:433/.2/1.
Audience: **g,l,u,f.**

Dutch Literature

Meijer, Reinder P. **PT5061**
Literature of the Low Countries. Trade Paper. Nelson Thornes Ltd. Cheltenham, 1978. 416p. ISBN:0-85950-094-2, ISBN13: 978-0-85950-094-4. Dewey:839.3/1/09. LCCN:79-308787.
Audience: **l,u,f.** B

Weevers, Theodor **PT5201 .W4**
Poetry of the Netherlands in Its European Context, 1170-1930. Cloth Text. Continuum International Publishing Group, Ltd. London, 1960. ISBN:0-485-11041-5, ISBN13: 978-0-485-11041-8. Dewey:839.31109.
Audience: **u,f.**

Dutch Literature > Collections

PT5411.C6
Reynard the Fox and Other Mediaeval Netherlands Secular Literature. Colledge, Edmund (Editor); Barnouw, Adriaan J. (Translator); Colledge, E. (Translator). London House & Maxwell. 1967.
Audience: **g,l,u,f.**

Barnouw, Adriaan Jacob (Translator) **PT5443.E4 E5 1971**
The Mirror of Salvation; A Moral Play of Everyman C. 1490. Nijhoff. 1971. ISBN:90-247-5095-4, ISBN13: 978-90-247-5095-5.
Audience: **g,l,u,f.**

Colledge, Edmund (Editor and Translator) **PT5445.E5.C6**
Mediaeval Netherlands Religious Literature. London House & Maxwell. 1965.
Audience: **g,l,u,f.**

Krispyn, Egbert (Editor) **PZ1.K893**
Modern Stories from Holland and Flanders. Library Binding. Thomson Gale. Farmington Hills, MI. 1973. International Studies and Translations Ser. ISBN:0-8057-3449-X, ISBN13: 978-0-8057-3449-2. Dewey:833.3/1/01.
Audience: **g,l,u,f.**

Smith, William J. & Holmes, James S. **PT5475.E5**
Dutch Interior: Postwar Poetry of the Netherlands and Flanders. Cees Buddingh' (Introduction by). Trade Cloth. Columbia University Press. New York, NY. 1984. 324p. ISBN:0-231-05746-6, ISBN13: 978-0-231-05746-2. Dewey:839.3/1164/08. LCCN:83-027332.
Audience: **g,l,u,f.**

Dutch Literature > Individual Authors, by Period

Blaman, Anna **PT5878.V85.O613X**
A Matter of Life and Death. Library Binding. Thomson Gale. Farmington Hills, MI. 1974. 235p. International Studies and Translations Ser. ISBN:0-8057-3441-4, ISBN13: 978-0-8057-3441-6. Dewey:839.3/1/362. LCCN:73-003955.
Audience: **g,l,u,f.** B

Brumble, H. David III (Translator) **PT5610.S613 1982**
G. A. Bredero, the Spanish Brabanter: A Seventeenth-Century Dutch Social Satire in Five Acts. Trade Cloth. M R T S. Tempe, AZ. 1982. 160p. Medieval and Renaissance Texts and Studies, Vol. 11 ISBN:0-86698-018-0, ISBN13: 978-0-86698-018-0. Dewey:839.3/123. LCCN:81-019004.
Audience: **g,l,u,f.** B

Coenen, Frans **PT5822.C55.O613**
The House on the Canal. Brockway, James (Translator) Oudshoorn, J. van (Alienation by); Clegg, N. C. (Translator). London House & Maxwell. 1965.
Audience: **g,l,u,f.**

Couperus, Louis **PZ3.C8341**
Old People and the Things that Pass. Teixeira de Mattos, Alexander (Translator). Sythoff. 1963.
Audience: **g,l,u,f.**

Erasmus, Desiderius **PA8514.E5 1994**
The Praise of Folly. John Wilson (Translator). Trade Cloth. Prometheus Books, Publishers. Amherst, NY. 1994. 196p. Great Minds Ser. ISBN:0-87975-885-6, ISBN13: 978-0-87975-885-1. Dewey:873/.04. LCCN:94-005475.
Audience: **g,u,f.**

Mulisch, Harry **PT5860.M85A6313 1985**
The Assault. Claire White (Translator). Trade Cloth. Knopf Publishing Group. New York, NY. 1985. 162p. ISBN:0-394-54245-2, ISBN13: 978-0-394-54245-4. Dewey:839.3/1364. LCCN:84-022623.
Audience: **g,l,u,f.**

Multatuli **PT5829.M3.E3 1982**
Max Havelaar: Or, the Coffee Auctions of the Dutch Trading Company. Roy Edwards (Translator), D. H. Lawrence (Introduction by), E. M. Beekman (Afterword by). Cloth Text. University of Massachusetts Press. Amherst, MA. 1982. 400p. Library of the Indies ISBN:0-87023-359-9, ISBN13: 978-0-87023-359-3. Dewey:839.3/18509. LCCN:82-002043.
Audience: **g,l,u,f.**

Van Eeden, Frederik **PT5831.V3**
Deeps of Deliverance. Margaret Robinson (Translator). Library Binding. Thomson Gale. Farmington Hills, MI. 1974. International Studies and Translations Ser. ISBN:0-8057-3419-8, ISBN13: 978-0-8057-3419-5. Dewey:839.3/1/35. LCCN:74-008923.
Audience: **g,l,u,f.**

Dutch Literature > Dutch Literature in Indonesia

Nieuwenhuys, Rob **PT5926.M46 1979**
Memory and Agony: Dutch Stories from Indonesia. Library Binding. Thomson Gale. Farmington Hills, MI. 1979. xxvii, 260p. International Studies and Translations Ser. ISBN:0-8057-8166-8, ISBN13: 978-0-8057-8166-3. Dewey:839.3/1/301. LCCN:79-013872.
Audience: **g,l,u,f.**

Nieuwenhuys, Rob **PT5911.N513 1982**
Mirror of the Indies: A History of Dutch Colonial Literature. E. M. Beekman (Editor), Frans Van Rosevelt (Translator). Cloth Text. University of Massachusetts Press. Amherst, MA. 1982. 368p. Library of the Indies ISBN:0-87023-368-8, ISBN13: 978-0-87023-368-5. Dewey:839.3/1/099598. LCCN:82-004755.
Audience: **u,f.**

Dutch Literature > Flemish Literature

Elsschot, Willem **PT6442.R5**
Villa des Roses. Trade Paper. Granta. New York, NY. 2003. 144p. ISBN:1-86207-616-2, ISBN13: 978-1-86207-616-7. Dewey:839.3/1362.
Audience: **u,f.**

Elsschot, Willem **PT6442.R5.T48**
Three novels: Soft Soap; The Leg; Will-o'-the-Wisp. Brotherton, A. (Translator). House & Maxwell. 1965. Bibliotheca Neerlandica [12]
Audience: **g,l,u,f.**

Gijsen, Marnix **PT6430.G67 K5513**
Lament for Agnes. W. James-Gerth (Translator). Library Binding. Thomson Gale. Farmington Hills, MI. 1975. 97p. International Studies and Translations Ser. ISBN:0-8057-8150-1, ISBN13: 978-0-8057-8150-2. Dewey:839.3/2/362. LCCN:74-034320.
Audience: **g,l,u,f.**

Insingel, Mark **PT6466.19.N7**
A Course of Time. Adrienne Dixon (Translator). Trade Cloth. Red Dust, Inc. New York, NY. 1977. ISBN:0-87376-029-8, ISBN13: 978-0-87376-029-4. Dewey:Fic. LCCN:76-056575.
Audience: **g,l,u,f.**

Ostaijen, Paul Van **PT6442.O8**
Feasts of Fear and Agony. Hidde Van Ameyden van Duym (Translator). Trade Paper. New Directions Publishing Corporation. New York, NY. 1976. 96p. ISBN:0-8112-0601-7, ISBN13: 978-0-8112-0601-3. Dewey:839.3/2/162. LCCN:75-026869.
Audience: **g,l,u,f.**

Dutch Literature > Afrikaans Literature

Breytenbach, Breyten **PT6592.12.R4Z475**
The True Confessions of an Albino Terrorist. Trade Cloth. Farrar, Straus & Giroux. New York, NY. 1985. 396p. ISBN:0-374-27935-7, ISBN13: 978-0-374-27935-6. Dewey:365/.45/0924. LCCN:84-025966.
Audience: **g,l,u,f.**

Brink, André **PR9499.3.N3**
Looking on Darkness: A Novel. UK-B Format Paperback. Random House. London, 1993. 400p. ISBN:0-7493-9987-2, ISBN13: 978-0-7493-9987-0. Dewey:823.
Audience: **g,l,u,f.**

Brink, André **PR9369.3.B7**
Praying Mantis. Trade Cloth. WaterBrook Press. Colorado Springs, CO. 2005. 224p. ISBN:0-436-20601-3, ISBN13: 978-0-436-20601-6. Dewey:823/.914. LCCN:2005-472906.
Audience: **g,l,u,f.**

Cope, Jack **PT6510.C65 1982**
The Adversary Within: Dissident Writers in Afrikaans. Trade Cloth. Bow Historical Books. New Providence, NJ. 1982. xi, 208p. ISBN:0-391-02697-6, ISBN13: 978-0-391-02697-1. Dewey:839.3/6/09. LCCN:83-148079.
Audience: **g,l,u,f.**

Rode, Linda & Gerwel, G. J. (Compiled by) **PR9367.32.I5 2001**
In the Rapids: New South African Stories. Trade Paper. Kwela Books. Roggebaai, 2002. 163p. ISBN:0-7957-0125-X, ISBN13: 978-0-7957-0125-2. Dewey:823/.0108968. LCCN:2002-403720.
Audience: **g,l,u,f.**

Scandanavia Literatures: General

Greenway, John L. **PT7048.G7**
The Golden Horns: Mythic Imagination and the Nordic Past. Trade Cloth. University of Georgia Press. Athens, GA. 1977. 232p. ISBN:0-8203-0384-4, ISBN13: 978-0-8203-0384-0. Dewey:839/.5/0937. LCCN:74-030676.
Audience: **g,l,u,f.**

Gustafson, Alrik (Introduction by) **PT7094.S4**
Scandinavian Plays of the Twentieth Century. Kraus Reprint Co.. 1971.
Audience: **g,l,u,f.**

Hallmundsson, Hallberg **PT7092.E5H3**
An Anthology of Scandinavian Literature, from the Viking Period to the Twentieth Century. Trade Paper. Books on Demand. Ann Arbor, MI. 386p. ISBN:0-598-35874-9, ISBN13: 978-0-598-35874-5. Dewey:839.508. LCCN:65-023076.
Audience: **g,l,u,f.** B

Marker, Frederick & Marker, Lise-Lone **PT7082.M3**
The Scandinavian Theatre. Trade Cloth. Rowman & Littlefield Publishers, Inc. Lanham, MD. 1975. 303p. Drama and Theatre Studies ISBN:0-87471-776-0, ISBN13: 978-0-87471-776-1. Dewey:792/.0948. LCCN:75-029017.
Audience: **l,u.** B

Rossel, Sven Hakon **PT7078.R6713 1982**
A History of Scandinavian Literature: 1870 to 1980. Anne C. Ulmer (Translator). Trade Cloth. University of Minnesota Press. Minneapolis, MN. 1982. 432p. Nordic Ser., Vol. 5 ISBN:0-8166-0906-3, ISBN13: 978-0-8166-0906-2. Dewey:839/.5. LCCN:81-014654.
Audience: **u,f.** B

Simonarson, Olafur H. **PT7094**
Drama Contemporary: Scandinavia. Trade Cloth. P A J Publications. New York, NY. 1990. 215p. ISBN:1-55554-050-3, ISBN13: 978-1-55554-050-0. Dewey:839.52/4.
Audience: **g,u,f.**

Weinstock, John M. & Rovinsky, Robert T. (Editors) **PT7063**
The Hero in Scandinavian Literature: From Peer Gynt to the Present. Trade Cloth. University of Texas Press. Austin, TX. 1975. 238p. Germanic Languages Symposia Ser. ISBN:0-292-73001-2, ISBN13: 978-0-292-73001-4. Dewey:839/.5. LCCN:74-026815.
Audience: **u,f.** B

Scandanavia Literatures: General > Old Icelandic. Old Norwegian

PT7235.E32 1983
Edda: A Collection of Essays. Trade Cloth. University of Manitoba Press. Winnipeg, MB. 1983. 332p. ISBN:0-88755-117-3, ISBN13: 978-0-88755-117-8. Dewey:839/.6/09. LCCN:83-191783.
Audience: **u.** B

Allen, Richard F. **PT7269.N5.A4**
Fire and Iron; Critical Approaches to Njals Saga. Trade Cloth. University of Pittsburgh Press. Pittsburgh, PA. 1971. xvi, 254p. ISBN:0-8229-3219-9, ISBN13: 978-0-8229-3219-2. Dewey:839/.63. LCCN:71-134493.
Audience: **u,f.** B

Anderson, George K. (Translator) **PT7287.V7.E52**
The Saga of the Volsungs. Trade Cloth. University of Delaware Press. Newark, DE. 1982. 272p. ISBN:0-87413-172-3, ISBN13: 978-0-87413-172-7. Dewey:839/.68. LCCN:80-065685.
Audience: **g,l,u,f.** B

Andersson, Theodore Murdock **PT7183.A45**
The Icelandic Family Saga; An Analytic Reading. Harvard University Press. 1967.
Audience: **u,f.**

Clover, Carol J. & Lindow, John (Editors) **PT7161.O4 1985**
Old Norse - Icelandic Literature: A Critical Guide. Book, Other. Cornell University Press. Ithaca, NY. 1985. 376p. Islandica Ser. ISBN:0-8014-1755-4, ISBN13: 978-0-8014-1755-9. Dewey:839/.6/09. LCCN:85-047697.
Audience: **u,f.** B *Choice, 1986.*

Fox, Denton & Palsson, Hermann (Translators) **PT7269.G7 E53**
Grettir's Saga. Trade Paper. University of Toronto Press. Toronto, ON. 1974. 195p. ISBN:0-8020-6165-6, ISBN13: 978-0-8020-6165-2. Dewey:839/.6/3. LCCN:72-090746.
Audience: **u,f.** B

Hallberg, Peter **PT7181.H313**
The Icelandic Saga. University of Nebraska Press. 1966.
Audience: **l,u.**

Hallberg, Peter **PT7172**
Old Icelandic Poetry: Eddic Lay and Skaldic Verse. Paul Schach & Sonja Lindgrenson (Translators), Paul Schach & Sonja Lindgrenson (Foreword by). Trade Paper. Books on Demand. Ann Arbor, MI. 1975. 231p. ISBN:0-7837-8882-7, ISBN13: 978-0-7837-8882-1. Dewey:839/.6/1009. LCCN:74-027186.
Audience: **u,f.** B

Halldór Hermannsson **PT7103.I7 v.13**
Bibliography of the Eddas. Kraus Reprint. 1966.
Audience: **g,l,u,f.**

Hannesson, Jóhann S. **PT7103.I7 v. 37**
Bibliography of the Eddas: A Supplement to Bibliography of the Eddas (Islandica XIII) by Halldór Hermannsson. Kraus Reprint Co.. 1973.
Audience: **g,l,u,f.**

Lönnroth, Lars **PT7269.N5.L6**
Njáls Saga: A Critical Introduction. University of California Press. 1976.
Audience: **u,f.**

Palsson, Hermann **PT7262.E5.P3**
Gautrek's Saga, and Other Medieval Tales. Trade Cloth.

University of London. London, 1968. 156p. ISBN:0-340-09396-X, ISBN13: 978-0-340-09396-2. Dewey:839.6808. LCCN:68-016829.
Audience: **u,f.**

Palsson, Hermann & Edwards, Paul (Translators) **PT7281.O7.E5 1978**
Orkneyinga Saga: The History of the Earls of Orkney. Trade Cloth. Salem House Publishers. Scranton, PA. 1978. 234p. ISBN:0-7012-0431-1, ISBN13: 978-0-7012-0431-0. Dewey:839/.68. LCCN:78-318053.
Audience: **g,l,u,f.**

Schlauch, Margaret (Translator) **PT7287.V7**
The Saga of the Volsungs, the Saga of Ragnar Lodbrook, Together with the Lay of Kraka. Trade Cloth. A M S Press, Inc. New York, NY. ISBN:0-404-14704-6, ISBN13: 978-0-404-14704-4. Dewey:839.6/3. LCCN:75-041284.
Audience: **u,f.**

Snorri Sturluson **PT7277.E5.L3**
Heimskringla: The Norse King Sagas. Laing, Samuel (translator). AMS Press. 1979. Everyman's Library
Audience: **g,l,u,f.**

Snorri Sturluson **PT7277.E5 L3 1979**
Heimskringla: Sagas of the Norse Kings. Samuel Laing (Translator). Trade Cloth. A M S Press, Inc. New York, NY. ISBN:0-404-14607-4, ISBN13: 978-0-404-14607-8. Dewey:839.6. LCCN:75-041259.
Audience: **u,f.**

Sturluson, Snorri **PT7313.E5.F38 1982**
Snorri Sturluson-Edda: Prologue and Gylfaginning. Anthony Faulkes (Editor). Trade Cloth. Oxford University Press, Inc. New York, NY. 1982. 212p. ISBN:0-19-811175-4, ISBN13: 978-0-19-811175-7. Dewey:839/.63. LCCN:79-041803.
Audience: **u,f.**

Sturluson, Snorri **PT7220**
King Harald's Saga: Harald Hardradi of Norway: from Snorri Sturluson's Heimskringla. Magnus Magnusson & Hermann Palsson (Translators), Magnus Magnusson & Hermann Palsson (Introduction by). Trade Paper. Penguin Group (USA) Inc. New York, NY. 1976. 192p. Classics Ser. ISBN:0-14-044183-2, ISBN13: 978-0-14-044183-3. Dewey:839/.68.
Audience: **u,f.**

Sturluson, Storri & Tiruvalluvar **PT7269.E3.E57 1976**
Egil's Saga. Paul Edwards & Hermann Palsson (Translators). Trade Paper. Penguin Group (USA) Inc. New York, NY. 1977. 256p. Classics Ser. ISBN:0-14-044321-5, ISBN13: 978-0-14-044321-9. Dewey:839/.6/1. LCCN:77-361577.
Audience: **u,f.**

Sveinsson, Einar Ol **PT7269.N5 E313**
Njals Saga: A Literary Masterpiece. Paul Schach (Editor). Trade Cloth. University of Nebraska Press. Lincoln, NE. 1971. ISBN:0-8032-0789-1, ISBN13: 978-0-8032-0789-9. Dewey:839/.6/3. LCCN:70-128914.
Audience: **l,u.**

Turville-Petre, E. O. **PT7172.T83**
Scaldic Poetry. Trade Cloth. Oxford University Press, Inc. New York, NY. 1976. lxxx, 102p. ISBN:0-19-812517-8, ISBN13: 978-0-19-812517-4. Dewey:839/.6/1009. LCCN:76-369573.
Audience: **u,f.**

Turville-Petre, Gabriel **PT7154 .T87**
Origins of Icelandic Literature. Trade Cloth. Oxford University Press, Inc. New York, NY. 1953. ISBN:0-19-811114-2, ISBN13: 978-0-19-811114-6. Dewey:839.609.
Audience: **l,u.**

Scandanavia Literatures: General > Modern Icelandic

Beck, Richard (Editor) **PT7459 .B4**
Icelandic Poems and Stories. Trade Cloth. Ayer Company Publishers, Inc. Manchester, NH. 1977. Short Story Index Reprint Ser. ISBN:0-8369-6001-7, ISBN13: 978-0-8369-6001-3. Dewey:839/.69/08003. LCCN:68-057059.
Audience: **g,u,f.**

Einarsson, Stefán **PT7103.I7 vol. 32-33**
History of Icelandic Prose Writers, 1800-1940. Cornell Univ. Press. 1948.
Audience: **u,f.**

Hallberg, Peter **PT7511.L3 Z713**
Halldor Laxness. Rory McTurk (Translator). Library Binding. Irvington Publishers. New York, NY. 1971. Twayne's World Authors Ser. ISBN:0-8057-2516-4, ISBN13: 978-0-8057-2516-2. Dewey:839/.69/34. LCCN:75-079208.
Audience: **l,u.**

Halldór Laxness **PT7511.L3.Q813**
A Quire of Seven. Boucher, Alan (Translator). Iceland Review Library. 1974.
Audience: **g,l,u,f.**

Laxness, Halldor Kiljan **PT7511.L3H413 2002**
World Light. Magnus Magnusson (Translator), Sven Birkerts (Introduction by). Book, Other. Knopf Publishing Group. New York, NY. 2002. 624p. ISBN:0-375-72757-4, ISBN13: 978-0-375-72757-3. Dewey:839/.6934. LCCN:2002-024994.
Audience: **u,f.**

Scandanavia Literatures: General > Danish

PZ1 .C766
Contemporary Danish Prose. Trade Paper. Kessinger Publishing, LLC. Whitefish, MT. 2004. ISBN:1-4192-1402-0, ISBN13: 978-1-4192-1402-8. Dewey:839.8/1/301.
Audience: **u,f.**

Billeskov-Jansen, F. J. & Mitchell, P. M. (Editors) **PT7965.B5 1972**
Anthology of Danish Literature. Trade Cloth. Southern Illinois

University Press. Carbondale, IL. 1971. ix, 606p. ISBN:0-8093-0487-2, ISBN13: 978-0-8093-0487-5. Dewey:839.8/108. LCCN:72-132475.
Audience: **g,l,u,f.** B

Ingwersen, Niels (Editor) **PT983.E5**
Seventeen Danish Poets: A Bilingual Anthology of Contemporary Danish Poetry. Trade Paper. Windflower Press. Lincoln, NE. 1982. 164p. ISBN:0-931534-10-0, ISBN13: 978-0-931534-10-2. Dewey:839.8/1174/08.
Audience: **u,f.**

Jensen, Line (Editor), et al. **PT7978.C6**
Contemporary Danish Poetry. Erik V. Jensen, Knud Mogensen & Alexander D. Taylor (Editors). Library Binding. Thomson Gale. Farmington Hills, MI. 1979. 343p. International Studies and Translations Ser. ISBN:0-8057-8157-9, ISBN13: 978-0-8057-8157-1. Dewey:839.8/1/17408. LCCN:77-002567.
Audience: **g,l,u,f.** B

Mitchell, P. M. & Ober, Kenneth H. (Translators) **PT8024.E5**
The Royal Guest and Other Classical Danish Narrative. Library Binding. University of Chicago Press. Chicago, IL. 1993. vi, 242p. ISBN:0-226-53213-5, ISBN13: 978-0-226-53213-4. Dewey:839.8/1/301. LCCN:77-078070.
Audience: **u,f.** B

Olrik, Axel (Editor) **PT7919.O5513 1968**
A Book of Danish Ballads. Smith-Dampier, E. M. (Translator). Books for Libraries Press. 1968.
Audience: **g,l,u,f.**

Rossel, Sven Hakon (Editor) **PT7660**
A History of Danish Literature. Trade Cloth. University of Nebraska Press. Lincoln, NE. 1992. 709p. A History of Scandinavian Literature Ser., Vol. 1 ISBN:0-8032-3886-X, ISBN13: 978-0-8032-3886-2. Dewey:839.8109. LCCN:91-046729.
Audience: **u,f.**

Scandanavia Literatures: General > Danish > Individual Authors

Andersen **PT8119**
Tales and Stories. Trade Paper. University of Washington Press. Seattle, WA. 1980. 316p. ISBN:0-295-95936-3, ISBN13: 978-0-295-95936-8. Dewey:839.8/136. LCCN:80-050867.
Audience: **g,l,u,f.** B

Bang, Herman **PT8123.B3T513 1984**
Tina. Paul Christopherson (Translator). Trade Cloth. Continuum International Publishing Group, Ltd. London, 1984. 224p. ISBN:0-485-11254-X, ISBN13: 978-0-485-11254-2. Dewey:839.8/136. LCCN:84-012286.
Audience: **g,l,u,f.** B

Branner, Hans Christian **PZ0003.B7384**
Two Minutes of Silence: Selected Short Stories. Trade Paper. Books on Demand. Ann Arbor, MI. 243p. Nordic Translation Ser. ISBN:0-8357-6776-0, ISBN13: 978-0-8357-6776-7. Dewey:839.81372. LCCN:66-022865.
Audience: **u,f.**

Bredsdorff, Elias & Andersen **PT8119.B6532 1994**
Hans Christian Andersen: The Story of His Life and Work 1805-75. Trade Paper. Farrar, Straus & Giroux. New York, NY. 1994. 376p. ISBN:0-374-52397-5, ISBN13: 978-0-374-52397-8. Dewey:839.8/136 B. LCCN:94-010851.
Audience: **g,l,u,f.**

Dinesen, Isak **PT8175.B545**
Anecdotes of Destiny. Trade Paper. Penguin Books Canada, Ltd. Toronto, ON. 1991. 256p. ISBN:0-14-018413-9, ISBN13: 978-0-14-018413-6. Dewey:839.8/1372.
Audience: **g,l,u,f.**

Dinesen, Isak **PT8175.B545**
Ehrengard. Trade Cloth. University of Chicago Press. Chicago, IL. 1976. 111p. ISBN:0-226-15293-6, ISBN13: 978-0-226-15293-6. Dewey:839.8/1/3/72.
Audience: **g,l,u,f.**

Dinesen, Isak **PT8175.B545**
Seven Gothic Tales. Trade Paper. Knopf Publishing Group. New York, NY. 1991. 448p. Vintage International Ser. ISBN:0-679-73641-7, ISBN13: 978-0-679-73641-7. Dewey:839.8/1372. LCCN:91-050030.
Audience: **g,l,u,f.**

Dinesen, Isak
Out of Africa. Mark Hannon (Illustrator). Library Binding. Buccaneer Books, Inc. Cutchogue, NY. 1993. ISBN:0-89968-444-0, ISBN13: 978-0-89968-444-4. Dewey:967.62.
Audience: **g,l,u,f.**

Dinesen, Isak **PT8175.B545**
Letters from Africa, 1914-1931. Frans Lasson (Editor), Anne Born (Translator). Trade Paper. University of Chicago Press. Chicago, IL. 1984. 516p. Phoenix Fiction Ser. ISBN:0-226-15311-8, ISBN13: 978-0-226-15311-7. Dewey:839.8/1372. LCCN:80-025856.
Audience: **g,l,u,f.** B

Gronbech, Bo **PT8120 .G74**
Hans Christian Andersen. Library Binding. Thomson Gale. Farmington Hills, MI. 1980. World Authors Ser. ISBN:0-8057-6454-2, ISBN13: 978-0-8057-6454-3. Dewey:839.8/136. LCCN:80-013621.
Audience: **l,u.** B

Hansen, Martin A. **PT8175.H33.L82**
Lucky Kristoffer. John J. Egglishaw (Translator). Library Binding. Irvington Publishers. New York, NY. 1974. 377p. Library of Scandinavian Literature ISBN:0-8057-3339-6, ISBN13: 978-0-8057-3339-6. Dewey:839.8/1/372. LCCN:73-009298.
Audience: **g,l,u,f.** B

Hansen, Martin A. **PT8175.B545**
The Liar. John J. Egglishaw (Translator), Eric Christiansen (Introduction by). Trade Paper. Sun & Moon Press. Los Angeles, CA. 1995. 208p. Sun and Moon Classics Ser., No. 111 ISBN:1-55713-243-7, ISBN13: 978-1-55713-243-7. Dewey:839.8/1372.
Audience: **u,f.**

Holberg, Ludvig **PT8085.N54 2004**
The Journey of Niels Klim to the World Underground. James I. McNelis Jr. (Translator, Introduction by), Peter Fitting (Preface by). Trade Cloth. University of Nebraska Press. Lincoln, NE. 2005. 280p. Bison Frontiers of Imagination Ser. ISBN:0-8032-7348-7, ISBN13: 978-0-8032-7348-1. Dewey:839.81/34. LCCN:2004-007401.
Audience: **g,l,u,f.**

Ingwersen, Faith & Ingwersen, Niels **PT8175.H33.Z7**
Martin A. Hansen. Cloth Text. Irvington Publishers. New York, NY. 1976. 197p. Twayne's World Authors Ser. ISBN:0-8057-6259-0, ISBN13: 978-0-8057-6259-4. Dewey:839.8/1/372. LCCN:76-021278.
Audience: **l,u.**

Ingwersen, Faith & Ingwersen, Niels **PT8175**
Quests for a Promised Land: The Works of Martin Andersen Nexo. Trade Cloth. Greenwood Publishing Group, Inc. Portsmouth, NH. 1985. 156p. Contributions to the Study of World Literature Ser., No. 8 ISBN:0-313-24469-3, ISBN13: 978-0-313-24469-8. Dewey:839.8/1372. LCCN:84-008916.
Audience: **l,u.**

Jacobsen, J. P. **PT8119**
Marie Grubbe. Anna A. Larson (Translator), Robert Raphael (Revised by). Trade Cloth. American-Scandinavian Foundation. Minneapolis, MN. 1975. Library of Scandinavian Literature, Vol. 30 ISBN:0-685-72816-1, ISBN13: 978-0-685-72816-1. Dewey:839.8/1/36.
Audience: **g,l,u,f.**

Jacobsen, Jens Peter **PT8140.N5E5 2006**
Niels Lyhne. Ed. 60. Tiina Nunnally (Translator), Eric Johannesson (Introduction by). Trade Paper. Penguin Group (USA) Inc. New York, NY. 2006. 208p. Penguin Classics Ser. ISBN:0-14-303981-4, ISBN13: 978-0-14-303981-5. Dewey:839.81/36. LCCN:2006-041636.
Audience: **u,f.**

Jansen, F. J. **PT8087.B48**
Ludvig Holberg. Library Binding. Irvington Publishers. New York, NY. 1974. 135p. Twayne's World Authors Ser. ISBN:0-8057-2431-1, ISBN13: 978-0-8057-2431-8. Dewey:839.8/1/8409. LCCN:74-002171.
Audience: **l,u.**

Jensen, Niels L. **PT8140.Z5.J4**
Jens Peter Jacobsen. Library Binding. Thomson Gale. Farmington Hills, MI. 1980. 187p. World Authors Ser. ISBN:0-8057-6415-1, ISBN13: 978-0-8057-6415-4. Dewey:839.8/136. LCCN:80-011521.
Audience: **l,u.**

Kierkegaard, Soren **PT8131.G9T6**
Two Ages: The Age of Revolution and the Present Age: A Literary Review. Howard V. Hong & Edna H. Hong (Edited and Translated by). Trade Cloth. Princeton University Press. Princeton, NJ. 1978. 208p. Kierkegaard's Writings, Vol. 14 ISBN:0-691-07226-4, ISBN13: 978-0-691-07226-5. Dewey:839.8/1/36. LCCN:77-071986.
Audience: **u,f.**

Kristensen, Tom **PZ0003.K8896**
Havoc. Carl Malmberg (Translator), Borge G. Madsen (Introduction by). Trade Paper. Books on Demand. Ann Arbor, MI. 1968. 445p. Nordic Translation Ser. ISBN:0-608-01887-2, ISBN13: 978-0-608-01887-4. Dewey:813.52. LCCN:68-014037.
Audience: **u,f.**

Nexo, Martin Anderson **PZ3.N49**
Ditte. Trade Cloth. Peter Smith Publisher, Inc. Magnolia, MA. 1979. ISBN:0-8446-1325-8, ISBN13: 978-0-8446-1325-3. Dewey:839.813.
Audience: **g,l,u,f.**

Thurman, Judith **PT8175.B545Z89 1995**
Isak Dinesen: The Life of a Storyteller. Trade Paper. Picador. New York, NY. 1995. 512p. ISBN:0-312-13525-4, ISBN13: 978-0-312-13525-6. Dewey:839.8/1372 b. LCCN:95-034769.
Audience: **g,l,u,f.**

Scandanavia Literatures: General > Norwegian > Literary History. Collections

Beyer, Harald **PT8360**
History of Norwegian Literature. Einar Ingvald Haugen (Editor). Trade Paper. American-Scandinavian Foundation. Minneapolis, MN. 1979. ISBN:0-89067-032-3, ISBN13: 978-0-89067-032-3. Dewey:839.8209. LCCN:56-006801.
Audience: **u,f.**

Johanssen, Terje (Editor) **PT8683.E5.J64 1984**
Twenty Contemporary Norwegian Poets: A Bilingual Anthology. Cloth Text. Palgrave Macmillan. New York, NY. 1984. 232p. ISBN:0-312-82422-X, ISBN13: 978-0-312-82422-8. Dewey:839.8/2174/08. LCCN:83-016002.
Audience: **u,f.**

McFarlane, James (Editor) **PT8721.S54 1982**
Slaves of Love and Other Norwegian Short Stories. Trade Cloth. Oxford University Press, Inc. New York, NY. 1982. xii, 265 p. ;p. ISBN:0-19-212601-6, ISBN13: 978-0-19-212601-6. Dewey:839.8/2301/08. LCCN:82-002269.
Audience: **g,l,u,f.**

McFarlane, James W. **PT8435 .M3 1979**
Ibsen and the Temper of Norwegian Literature. Library Binding. Hippocrene Books, Inc. New York, NY. 1979. ISBN:0-374-95479-8, ISBN13: 978-0-374-95479-6. Dewey:839.8/2/09.
Audience: **g,l,u,f.**

Scandanavia Literatures: General > Norwegian > Individual Authors, by Period

Beyer, Edward **PT8895**
Ibsen: The Man and His Work. Trade Paper. Taplinger Publishing Company, Inc. Marlboro, NJ. 1980. ISBN:0-8008-4056-9, ISBN13: 978-0-8008-4056-3. Dewey:839.8/2/26. LCCN:79-001917.
Audience: **l,u.**

Birn, Randi **PT8950**
Aksel Sandemose: Exile in Search of a Home, 2. Trade Cloth. Greenwood Publishing Group, Inc. Portsmouth, NH. 1984. 150p. Contributions to the Study of World Literature Ser., No. 2 ISBN:0-313-24163-5, ISBN13: 978-0-313-24163-5. Dewey:839.8/2372. LCCN:83-013034.
Audience: **u,f.** B

Bojer, Johan **PT8950.B6V562 1991**
The Emigrants. Ingeborg R. Kongslien (Introduction by). Trade Paper. Minnesota Historical Society Press. Saint Paul, MN. 1991. xii, 351p. Borealis Bks. ISBN:0-87351-260-X, ISBN13: 978-0-87351-260-2. Dewey:839.8/2372. LCCN:91-022742.
Audience: **u,f.**

Hamsun, Knut **PT8950.H3**
Growth of the Soil. Trade Paper. Kessinger Publishing, LLC. Whitefish, MT. 2004. ISBN:1-4192-2244-9, ISBN13: 978-1-4192-2244-3. Dewey:839.8/236.
Audience: **g,u,f.**

Hamsun, Knut **PT8950.H3**
Mysteries. Trade Paper. Farrar, Straus & Giroux. New York, NY. 1998. 352p. ISBN:0-374-52527-7, ISBN13: 978-0-374-52527-9. Dewey:839.8/236.
Audience: **g,l,u,f.** B

Hamsun, Knut **PT8950.H3.L33 1980**
Wayfarers. Trade Cloth. Farrar, Straus & Giroux. New York, NY. 1980. 459p. ISBN:0-374-28672-8, ISBN13: 978-0-374-28672-9. Dewey:839.8/236. LCCN:79-027034.
Audience: **g,l,u,f.** B

Hamsun, Knut **PT8950.H3**
Hunger. Robert Bly (Translator, Introduction by), Isaac Bashevis Singer (Introduction by). Trade Cloth. Gerald Duckworth & Company, Ltd. London, 1993. 232p. ISBN:0-7156-0761-8, ISBN13: 978-0-7156-0761-9. Dewey:839.8/236.
Audience: **g,l,u,f.**

Hamsun, Knut **PT8950.H3**
Pan: From Lieutenant Thomas Glahn's Papers. James W. McFarlane (Translator). Trade Paper. Farrar, Straus & Giroux. New York, NY. 1956. 192p. ISBN:0-374-50016-9, ISBN13: 978-0-374-50016-0. Dewey:839.
Audience: **u,f.** B

Hamsun, Knut **PT8950.H3 U593 1975**
The Wanderer. Oliver Stallybrass & Gunnvor Stallybrass (Translators). Trade Cloth. Farrar, Straus & Giroux. New York, NY. 1975. 288p. ISBN:0-374-28636-1, ISBN13: 978-0-374-28636-1. Dewey:839.8/236. LCCN:75-005915.
Audience: **g,l,u,f.** B

Ibsen, Henrick **PT8854.F5 1978**
Ibsen: The Complete Major Prose Plays. Rolf Fjelde (Translator). Trade Cloth. Farrar, Straus & Giroux. New York, NY. 1978. vi, 1143p. ISBN:0-374-17414-8, ISBN13: 978-0-374-17414-9. Dewey:839.8/2/26. LCCN:77-028349.
Audience: **g,l,u,f.** B

Ibsen, Henrik **PT8852.E5.M3**
The Oxford Ibsen. McFarlane, James Walter (Translator and Editor). Oxford University Press. 1960.
Audience: **g,l,u,f.**

Koht, Halvdan **PT8890 .K62**
Life of Ibsen. Einar Ingvald Haugen & A. E. Santaniello (Editors). Trade Cloth. Ayer Company Publishers, Inc. Manchester, NH. 1972. ISBN:0-405-08715-2, ISBN13: 978-0-405-08715-8. Dewey:839.8/2/26 B. LCCN:69-016322.
Audience: **g,l,u,f.** B

Meyer, Hans G. **PT8890 .M4413**
Henrik Ibsen. Helen Sebba (Translator). Trade Cloth. Continuum International Publishing Group, Ltd. London, 1981. World Dramatists Ser. ISBN:0-8044-2616-3, ISBN13: 978-0-8044-2616-9. Dewey:839.8/2/26. LCCN:72-163145.
Audience: **l,u.** B

Meyer, Michael **PT8890**
Ibsen. Trade Paper. Sutton Publishing, Ltd. Stroud, 2005. 656p. ISBN:0-7509-3738-6, ISBN13: 978-0-7509-3738-2. Dewey:839.8/226.
Audience: **g,l,u,f.**

Neass, Harald **PT8950.H3.Z745 1984**
Knut Hamsun. Trade Cloth. Thomson Gale. Farmington Hills, MI. 1984. 194p. World Authors Ser., No. 715 ISBN:0-8057-6562-X, ISBN13: 978-0-8057-6562-5. Dewey:839.8/236. LCCN:83-018343.
Audience: **l,u.** B

Northam, John **PT8897.D7.N6**
Ibsen's Dramatic Method: A Study of the Prose Dramas. Faber. 1979.
Audience: **u,f.**

Sandemose, Aksel **PT8950.S23V3713 2002**
The Werewolf. Ed. 2. Gustaf Lannestock (Translator), H. S. Naess (Introduction by). Trade Paper. University of Wisconsin Press. Chicago, IL. 2002. 394p. Library of World Fiction ISBN:0-299-03744-4, ISBN13: 978-0-299-03744-4. Dewey:839.8/2/372. LCCN:2003-265111.
Audience: **u,f.**

Shaw, George Bernard **PT8895.S53 1979**
Shaw and Ibsen: Bernard Shaw's The Quintessence of Ibsenism and Related Writings. J. L. Wisenthal (Editor, Introduction by). Trade Cloth. University of Toronto Press. Toronto, ON. 1979. viii, 268p. ISBN:0-8020-5454-4, ISBN13: 978-0-8020-5454-8. Dewey:839.8/2/26. LCCN:79-014858.
Audience: **u,f.** B

Undset, Sigrid, et al. **PT8950.U5**
Kristin Lavransdatter. Charles Archer & J. S. Scott (Authors). Trade Paper. Pan Macmillan. London, 1980. ISBN:0-330-25202-X, ISBN13: 978-0-330-25202-7. Dewey:839.82/372.
Audience: **g,l,u,f.**

Undset, Sigrid **PT8950.U5**
Four Stories. Naomi Walford (Translator). Library Binding. Greenwood Publishing Group, Inc. Portsmouth, NH. 1978. 245p. ISBN:0-313-20566-3, ISBN13: 978-0-313-20566-8. Dewey:839.8/2/372. LCCN:78-016903.
Audience: **g,l,u,f.** B

Scandanavia Literatures: General > Norwegian > Norwegian Literature in America

Reigstad, Paul **PT9150.R55Z8**
Rolvaag: His Life and Art. Trade Paper. Books on Demand. Ann Arbor, MI. 1972. 182p. ISBN:0-608-02041-9, ISBN13: 978-0-608-02041-9. Dewey:839.8/2/372. LCCN:70-175804.
Audience: **u,f.**

Rolvaag, Ole Edvart **PZ3.R6275**
Giants in the Earth: A Saga of the Prairie. Trade Paper. HarperCollins Publishers. New York, NY. 1999. 560p. Perennial Classics Ser. ISBN:0-06-093193-0, ISBN13: 978-0-06-093193-3. Dewey:[Fic)].
Audience: **g,l,u,f.**

Rolvaag, Ole Edvart **PT8950.U5**
Their Fathers' God. Trygve M. Ager (Translator). Trade Paper. University of Nebraska Press. Lincoln, NE. 1983. 338p. ISBN:0-8032-8911-1, ISBN13: 978-0-8032-8911-6. Dewey:839.8/2372. LCCN:82-017636.
Audience: **g,l,u,f.**

Rolvaag, Ole Edvart **PT8950.U5**
Peder Victorious: A Tale of the Pioneers 20 Years Later. Nora O. Solum (Translator), Gudrun H. Gvale (Introduction by). Trade Paper. University of Nebraska Press. Lincoln, NE. 1982. 325p. ISBN:0-8032-8906-5, ISBN13: 978-0-8032-8906-2. Dewey:839.8/2372. LCCN:81-016402.
Audience: **g,l,u,f.**

Rolvaag, Ole Edvart **PT9150.R55**
The Boat of Longing. Nora O. Solum (Translator), Einar Ingvald Haugen (Introduction by). Trade Paper. Minnesota Historical Society Press. Saint Paul, MN. 1985. xv, 304p. Borealis Bks. ISBN:0-87351-184-0, ISBN13: 978-0-87351-184-1. Dewey:839.8/2372. LCCN:84-029466.
Audience: **g,l,u,f.**

Scandanavia Literatures: General > Swedish > Literary History. Collections

Bly, Robert **PT9583.B62**
Friends, You Drank Some Darkness: Three Swedish Poets, Harry Martinson, Gunnar Ekelof, and Tomas Transtromer. Trade Cloth. Beacon Press. Boston, MA. 1975. xi, 267p. ISBN:0-8070-6390-8, ISBN13: 978-0-8070-6390-3. Dewey:839.7/1/708. LCCN:73-006244.
Audience: **g,l,u,f.**

Gustafson, Alrik **PT9263 .G8**
History of Swedish Literature. Trade Cloth. University of Minnesota Press. Minneapolis, MN. 1961. ISBN:0-8166-0236-0, ISBN13: 978-0-8166-0236-0. Dewey:839.709. LCCN:61-007722.
Audience: **u,f.**

Matthias, John & Printz-Pahlson, Goran (Translators) **PT9590.E5.C6**
Contemporary Swedish Poetry. Trade Cloth. Swallow Press. Athens, OH. 1980. 136p. ISBN:0-8040-0811-6, ISBN13: 978-0-8040-0811-2. Dewey:839.7/1/7408. LCCN:79-009655.
Audience: **u,f.**

Scandanavia Literatures: General > Swedish > Individual Authors, by Period

Bergman, Ingmar **PN1997**
Four Screenplays of Ingmar Bergman. Library Binding. Garland Publishing, Inc. New York, NY. 1985. 381p. Cinema Classics Ser. ISBN:0-8240-5752-X, ISBN13: 978-0-8240-5752-7. Dewey:791.43/72. LCCN:82-049277.
Audience: **g,l,u,f.**

Brandell, Gunnar **PT9815.B7213 1974**
Strindberg in Inferno. Barry Jacobs (Translator). Trade Cloth. Harvard University Press. Cambridge, MA. 1974. 352p. ISBN:0-674-84325-8, ISBN13: 978-0-674-84325-7. Dewey:839.7/2/6. LCCN:73-090851.
Audience: **u,f.**

Fridegard, Jan **PT9875.F788.J313**
I, Lars Hard. Robert E. Bjork (Translator). Cloth Text. University of Nebraska Press. Lincoln, NE. 1983. xvi, 105p. ISBN:0-8032-1963-6, ISBN13: 978-0-8032-1963-2. Dewey:839.7/372. LCCN:83-001098.
Audience: **g,l,u,f.**

Hakon, Sven & Stockenstrom, Goran (Editors) **PT9816**
August Strindberg and the Other: New Critical Approaches. Poul Houe (Directed By). Trade Paper. Rodopi. Kenilworth, NY. 2002. 203p. Internationale Forschungen Zur Allgemeinen und Vergleichenden Literaturwissenschaft Ser., 63 ISBN:90-420-1520-9, ISBN13: 978-90-420-1520-3. Dewey:839.726.
Audience: **g,u,f.**

Isaksson, Hans **PT9875.G95.Z74 1978**
Lars Gyllensten. Library Binding. Thomson Gale. Farmington Hills, MI. 1978. 194 p. :p. World Authors Ser. ISBN:0-8057-6314-7, ISBN13: 978-0-8057-6314-0. Dewey:839.7/3/74. LCCN:77-015551.
Audience: **l,u.**

Johannesson, Eric O. **PT9816.J55**
The Novels of August Strindberg: A Study in Theme and Structure. Trade Paper. Books on Demand. Ann Arbor, MI. 335p. ISBN:0-608-15841-0, ISBN13: 978-0-608-15841-9. Dewey:839.726. LCCN:68-029156.
Audience: **u,f.**

Johnson, Eyvind **PT9875.J6.S813**
Return to Ithaca, the Odyssey Retold as A Modern Novel. Van Doren, Mark (Preface by). Thames and Hudson. 1952.
Audience: **g,l,u,f.**

Lagercrantz, Olof **PT9815.L313 1984**
August Strindberg. Anselm Hollo (Translator). Trade Cloth. Farrar, Straus & Giroux. New York, NY. 1984. 400p. ISBN:0-374-10685-1, ISBN13: 978-0-374-10685-0. Dewey:839.7/26. LCCN:84-042803.
Audience: **g,l,u,f.**

Lagerkvist, Par **PT9875.L2B313 1989**
Barabbas. Alan Blair (Translator), Andre Gide (Contribution by), Lucien Maury (Produced by). Trade Paper. Knopf Publishing Group. New York, NY. 1989. 160p. Vintage International Ser. ISBN:0-679-72544-X, ISBN13: 978-0-679-72544-2. Dewey:839.7/372. LCCN:89-040100.
Audience: **u,f.**

Lagerkvist, Par **PT9875.L2.M3**
The Marriage Feast. Alan Blair & Carl E. Lindin (Translators). Trade Cloth. Farrar, Straus & Giroux. New York, NY. 1973. 222p. ISBN:0-8090-6786-2, ISBN13: 978-0-8090-6786-2. Dewey:839.7/3/72. LCCN:73-075187.
Audience: **g,l,u,f.**

Lagerkvist, Par **PT9875.L2 M6**
Modern Theatre: Seven Plays and an Essay. Thomas R. Buckman (Translator). Trade Cloth. University of Nebraska Press. Lincoln, NE. 1966. xxiv, 305p. ISBN:0-8032-0098-6, ISBN13: 978-0-8032-0098-2. Dewey:839.7272. LCCN:64-011582.
Audience: **g,l,u,f.**

Lagerkvist, Par **PT9875.L2**
The Dwarf. Alexandra Dick (Translator). Trade Paper. Farrar, Straus & Giroux. New York, NY. 1958. 288p. ISBN:0-374-52135-2, ISBN13: 978-0-374-52135-6. Dewey:839.736.
Audience: **u,f.**

Lagerkvist, Par **PZ3.L1354**
The Sibyl. Naomi Walford (Translator). Trade Paper. Knopf Publishing Group. New York, NY. 1963. 160p. ISBN:0-394-70240-9, ISBN13: 978-0-394-70240-7. Dewey:839.736.
Audience: **u,f.**

Lagerkvist, Par **PT9875.L2 H3813 1982**
The Holy Land. Naomi Walford (Translator), Emil Antonucci (Illustrator). Trade Paper. Knopf Publishing Group. New York, NY. 1982. 96p. ISBN:0-394-70819-9, ISBN13: 978-0-394-70819-5. Dewey:839.7/372. LCCN:81-068681.
Audience: **u,f.**

Lagerkvist, Pär **PT9875.L2.S913**
Pilgrim at Sea. Walford, Naomi (Translator); Antonucci, Emil (Drawings by). Random House. 1964.
Audience: **g,l,u,f.**

Lagerlöf, Selma **PT9767.G6E54 2004**
Gosta Berling's Saga. Trade Paper. Dover Publications, Inc. Mineola, NY. 2004. 368p. ISBN:0-486-43387-0, ISBN13: 978-0-486-43387-5. Dewey:839.73/72. LCCN:2003-064608.
Audience: **g,u,f.**

Lagerlöf, Selma **PT9875.L598**
Jerusalem. Trade Cloth. Classic Books. Murrieta, CA. 1970. viii, 396p. ISBN:0-7426-4477-4, ISBN13: 978-0-7426-4477-9. Dewey:839.7/3/72.
Audience: **g,u,f.**

Lamm, Martin **PT9816**
August Strindberg. Harry G. Carlson (Editor). Trade Cloth. Ayer Company Publishers, Inc. Manchester, NH. 1972. ISBN:0-405-08724-1, ISBN13: 978-0-405-08724-0. Dewey:839.7/2/6. LCCN:69-016323.
Audience: **u,f.**

Martinson, Harry **PT9875.M35A666213**
Aniara: An Epic Science Fiction Poem. Stephen Klass & Leif Sjoberg (Introduction by). Trade Paper. Story Line Press. Ashland, OR. 1998. 180p. ISBN:1-885266-63-4, ISBN13: 978-1-885266-63-7. Dewey:839.71/72. LCCN:98-007891.
Audience: **u,f.**

Moberg, Vilhelm **PT9875.M5**
Emigrants. Mass Market. Warner Books, Inc. New York, NY. 1984. ISBN:0-446-38115-2, ISBN13: 978-0-446-38115-4. Dewey:839.736.
Audience: **u,f.**

Moberg, Vilhelm **PT9875.L598**
The Last Letter Home. Mass Market. Warner Books, Inc. New York, NY. 1983. 288p. ISBN:0-446-31131-6, ISBN13: 978-0-446-31131-1. Dewey:839.73/72.
Audience: **u,f.**

Moberg, Vilhelm **PT9875.M5I613 1995**
Unto a Good Land. Trade Paper. Minnesota Historical Society Press. Saint Paul, MN. 1995. xxvii, 372p. Emigrant Novels Ser., Bk. 2 ISBN:0-87351-320-7, ISBN13: 978-0-87351-320-3. Dewey:839.73/72. LCCN:95-015847.
Audience: **u,f.**

Morgan, Margery **PT9811.A3**
August Strindberg. Bruce King & Adele King (Editors). Trade Paper. Grove/Atlantic, Inc. New York, NY. 1986. 172p. Modern Dramatists Ser. ISBN:0-394-62065-8, ISBN13: 978-0-394-62065-7. Dewey:839.7/26. LCCN:85-047546.
Audience: **u,f.**

Sprinchorn, Evert **PT9816**
Strindberg As Dramatist. Trade Cloth. Yale University Press. Cumberland, RI. 1982. 344p. ISBN:0-300-02731-1, ISBN13: 978-0-300-02731-0. Dewey:839.7/26. LCCN:81-023992.
Audience: **l,u.**

Stockenstrom, Goran (Editor) **PT9816.S698 1988**
Strindberg's Dramaturgy. Book, Other. University of Minnesota Press. Minneapolis, MN. 1988. xxii, 375p. Nordic Ser., Vol. 16 ISBN:0-8166-1612-4, ISBN13: 978-0-8166-1612-1. Dewey:839.7/26. LCCN:87-038090.
Audience: **u,f.** *Choice, 1989.*

Strindberg, August **PT9813.G5**
Getting Married. Trade Cloth. Penguin Group (USA) Inc. New York, NY. 1973. ISBN:0-670-33760-9, ISBN13: 978-0-670-33760-6. Dewey:839.7/3/6. LCCN:72-011063.
Audience: **g,l,u,f.**

Strindberg, August **PT9812.T5.E5 1979**
Plays of Confession and Therapy: To Damascus I, To Damascus II and To Damascus III. Trade Paper. University of Washington Press. Seattle, WA. 1979. 260p. ISBN:0-295-95567-8, ISBN13: 978-0-295-95567-4. Dewey:839.7/26. LCCN:78-020962.
Audience: **g,l,u,f.**

Strindberg, August **PT9811.A3.J56 1981**
Apologia and Two Folk Plays: The Great Highway, the Crownbridge, and Swanwhite. Walter Johnson (Translator). Trade Cloth. University of Washington Press. Seattle, WA. 1981. 244p. ISBN:0-295-95760-3, ISBN13: 978-0-295-95760-9. Dewey:839.7/26. LCCN:80-051072.
Audience: **g,l,u,f.** B

Strindberg, August **PT9811.A3.J6 1983**
Plays from the Cynical Life. Walter Johnson (Translator). Trade Cloth. University of Washington Press. Seattle, WA. 1983. 144p. ISBN:0-295-95980-0, ISBN13: 978-0-295-95980-1. Dewey:839.7/26. LCCN:82-013581.
Audience: **g,l,u,f.** B

Strindberg, August **PT9804**
The Vasa Trilogy. Walter Johnson (Translator). Trade Paper. University of Washington Press. Seattle, WA. 1966. 353p. ISBN:0-295-74057-4, ISBN13: 978-0-295-74057-7. Dewey:839.726. LCCN:59-006636.
Audience: **g,l,u,f.**

Strindberg, August (Translator) **PT9812.D6**
The Dance of Death. Stephen Mulrine (Translator, Introduction by). Trade Paper. Theatre Communications Group, Inc. New York, NY. 2004. 128p. Ser. ISBN:1-85459-750-7, ISBN13: 978-1-85459-750-2. Dewey:839.7/26.
Audience: **g,l,u,f.** B

Strindberg, August **PT9811.A3**
Eight Expressionist Plays. Arvid Paulson (Translator). Trade Paper. New York University Press. New York, NY. 1972. 512p. ISBN:0-8147-6558-0, ISBN13: 978-0-8147-6558-6. Dewey:839.7/2/6.
Audience: **g,l,u,f.**

Strindberg, August **PT9813.H4 A36**
The Natives of Hemso. Arvid Paulson (Translator). Trade Paper. Liveright Publishing Corporation. New York, NY. 1973. ISBN:0-87140-284-X, ISBN13: 978-0-87140-284-4. Dewey:839.736.
Audience: **u,f.**

Strindberg, August **PT9811.A3.P33**
Strindberg's One-Act Plays. Arvid Paulson (Translator), Barry Jacobs (Introduction by). Mass Market. Simon & Schuster. New York, NY. 1985. xxxii, 368p. ISBN:0-671-47490-1, ISBN13: 978-0-671-47490-4. Dewey:839.7/2/6. LCCN:79-004286.
Audience: **g,l,u,f.**

Strindberg, August **PT9814**
A Madman's Defense. Evert Sprinchorn (Introduction by). Trade Cloth. Peter Smith Publisher, Inc. Magnolia, MA. 1981. ISBN:0-8446-3025-X, ISBN13: 978-0-8446-3025-0. Dewey:839.7/3/6.
Audience: **u,f.**

Strindberg, August **PT9804 .S6**
Inferno: Alone and Other Writings. Evert Sprinchorn (Editor), E. Sprinchorn (Introduction by). Trade Cloth. Peter Smith Publisher, Inc. Magnolia, MA. 1983. ISBN:0-8446-3026-8, ISBN13: 978-0-8446-3026-7. Dewey:839.726.
Audience: **g,l,u,f.**

Strindberg, August **PT9813.T6**
Son of a Servant: The Story of the Evolution of a Human Being, 1849-1867. Evert Sprinchorn (Translator, Introduction by). Trade Cloth. Peter Smith Publisher, Inc. Magnolia, MA. 1979. xxi, 243p. ISBN:0-8446-3027-6, ISBN13: 978-0-8446-3027-4. Dewey:839.7209. LCCN:66-011748.
Audience: **u,f.**

Sundman, Per Olof & Sandbach, Mary **PZ4.S61953**
The Flight of the 'Eagle': A Documentary Novel. Trade Cloth. Martin Secker & Warburg, Ltd. London, 1970. 383p. ISBN:0-436-50502-9, ISBN13: 978-0-436-50502-7. Dewey:839.7/3/74.
Audience: **u,f.**

HISPANIC AND LUSO-BRAZILIAN LANGUAGES AND LITERATURES

This section provides a selection of titles appropriate for undergraduate study of the languages and literatures of Spain and Portugal and their former colonial possessions. The scope of this selection reflects the rapid, continuing growth of Iberian and Latin American studies over the past two decades, and includes major works of literature, literary history, biography, and criticism. Particular emphasis has been given to the expansion of the Latin American sections (Spanish America and Brazil) and to language, reflecting the growing importance of these fields in particular. With an eye toward greater integration across the curriculum, the Spanish and Portuguese section also includes accessible critical guides and major works in English translation.

— Heather Dubnick

Spanish Language

PC4591.G67 1987
Espasa Diccionario de Sinonimos y Antonimos. Ed. 3. Trade Cloth. Espasa Calpe, S.A.. Madrid, 1989. 1320p. ISBN:84-239-5919-8, ISBN13: 978-84-239-5919-8. Dewey:463/.1. LCCN:88-121952.
Audience: **u,f.**

PC4640.L39 1996
Larousse Diccionario Standard: Espanol-Ingles - English-Spanish. Trade Cloth. Larousse, Ediciones, S. A. de C. V.. Mexico, D. F., 1996. 717p. ISBN:970-607-584-4, ISBN13: 978-970-607-584-0. Dewey:863/.21. LCCN:95-076556.
Audience: **u,f.**

Azevedo, Milton M. **PC4073.A96 1992**
Introducción a la Lingüística Española. Cloth Text. Prentice Hall PTR. Upper Saddle River, NJ. 1991. 432p. ISBN:0-13-484031-3, ISBN13: 978-0-13-484031-4. Dewey:460. LCCN:91-014590.
Audience: **l,u,f.**

Barrutia, Richard & Schwegler, Armin **PC4137.B28 1994**
Fonética y fonología Españolas: Teoría y Práctica. Ed. 2. Trade Cloth. John Wiley & Sons, Inc. Hoboken, NJ. 1994. 464p. ISBN:0-471-30946-X, ISBN13: 978-0-471-30946-8. Dewey:468.3/421. LCCN:93-021202.
Audience: **l,u,f.**

Batchelor, R. E. & Pountain, Christopher J. **PC4128 .B3 1992**
Using Spanish: A Guide to Contemporary Usage. Cloth Text. Cambridge University Press. New York, NY. 1992. 334p. ISBN:0-521-42123-3, ISBN13: 978-0-521-42123-2. Dewey:468.2/421. LCCN:91-010240.
Audience: **g,l,u,f.**

Biblograf Editorial Staff (Compiled by) **PC4640.V694 2003**
Vox Modern Spanish and English Dictionary: English-Spanish/Spanish-English. Trade Cloth. McGraw-Hill Companies, The. New York, NY. 1986. 1072p. National Textbook Language Dictionaries Ser. ISBN:0-8442-7990-0, ISBN13: 978-0-8442-7990-9. Dewey:463/.21. LCCN:2002-045526.
Audience: **g,l,u,f.** *Choice, 1987.*

Bradley, Diarmuid & Butterfield, Jeremy **PC4640.C53 2004**
Collins Spanish-English, English-Spanish Dictionary = Collins Diccionario Español-Inglés, Inglés-Español. Ed. 5. Trade Cloth. HarperCollins Publishers. New York, NY. 2004. xvii, 1289p. ISBN:84-253-3843-3, ISBN13: 978-84-253-3843-4. Dewey:463.21. LCCN:2004-276405.
Audience: **g,l,u,f.**

Buitrago Jimenez, A. **PC**
Dictionary of Modern Expressions and Phrases. Trade Cloth. Espasa Calpe, S.A.. Madrid, 1997. 528p. ISBN:84-239-9227-6, ISBN13: 978-84-239-9227-0. Dewey:463/.1. LCCN:96-119171.
Audience: **g,l,u,f.**

Butt, John & Benjamin, Carmen **PC4112.B88 1994**
A New Reference Grammar of Modern Spanish. Ed. 2. Trade Cloth. Hodder Education. London, 1994. 592p. ISBN:0-340-58390-8, ISBN13: 978-0-340-58390-6. Dewey:468.2/4. LCCN:94-002090.
Audience: **g,l,u,f.** *Choice, 1989.*

Cotton, Christine E., et al. **PC4120.M3C68 2004**
A Su Salud!: Spanish for Health Professionals. Elizabeth Ely Tolman, Julia Cardona Mack & University of North Carolina Staff (Authors). Mixed Media, Trade Cloth, Compact Disc, DVD. Yale University Press. Cumberland, RI. 2004. 400p. ISBN:0-300-10363-8, ISBN13: 978-0-300-10363-2. Dewey:468.3/421/02461. LCCN:2004-046413.
Audience: **l,u,f.**

de Lucas Vallejo, Carmen **PC4460 .L83 1994**
Diccionario de Dudas. Trade Cloth. Edaf, Editorial S.A.. Madrid, 2002. 192p. ISBN:84-7640-789-0, ISBN13: 978-84-7640-789-9. Dewey:463. LCCN:94-204503.
Audience: **u,f.**

Elcock, W. D. **PC43.E55 1975**
The Romance Languages. Trade Cloth. Faber & Faber, Ltd. London, 1975. 589 p. :p. ISBN:0-571-04820-X, ISBN13: 978-0-571-04820-5. Dewey:440. LCCN:75-321068.
Audience: **l,u,f.**

Entwistle, W. J. **PC4075 .E5**
The Spanish Language, Together with Portuguese, Catalan and Basque. Library Binding. Gordon Press Publishers. New York, NY. 1975. ISBN:0-8490-1102-7, ISBN13: 978-0-8490-1102-3. Dewey:460.
Audience: **l,u,f.**

Equipo **PC4591.S56 2001**
Diccionario Avanzado de Sinonimos Yantonimos de la Lengua Española. Trade Cloth. Bow Historical Books. New Providence, NJ. 2001. 647p. ISBN:84-8332-181-5, ISBN13: 978-84-8332-181-2. Dewey:463/.1. LCCN:2001-446440.
Audience: **l,u,f.**

Escobar, Anna María, et al. **PC4073 .H83 2001**
Introducción a la lingüistica hispánica. José Ignacio Hualde & Antxon Olarrea (Authors). Cloth Text. Cambridge University Press. New York, NY. 2002. 384p. ISBN:0-521-80314-4, ISBN13: 978-0-521-80314-4. Dewey:468.2. LCCN:2002-524059.
Audience: **u,f.**

Espasa Staff (Editor) **PC**
Diccionario de Sinonimos y Antonimos. Ed. 13. Trade Cloth. Elliot's Books. Northford, CT. 1993. 808p. Espasa Bolsillo Ser. ISBN:84-239-9204-7, ISBN13: 978-84-239-9204-1. Dewey:463/.1. LCCN:94-238756.
Audience: **u,f.**

Foster, David William, et al. **PC4410.F68 1999**
The Writer's Reference Guide to Spanish: The Authoritative Handbook for Writers, Editors, Student. Daniel Altamiranda & Carmen De Urioste (Authors). Trade Cloth. University of Texas Press. Austin, TX. 2000. 284p. ISBN:0-292-72511-6, ISBN13: 978-0-292-72511-9. Dewey:808/.027. LCCN:99-006172.
Audience: **u,f.** *Choice, 2000.*

Gomex Torrego, L. **PC**
Manual de Español Correcto. Ed. 10. Trade Cloth. Acro Libros S.A.. Madrid, 1996. 824p. ISBN:84-7635-057-0, ISBN13: 978-84-7635-057-7. Dewey:468.2. LCCN:89-167608.
Audience: **u,f.**

Gomez Torrego, Leonardo **PC**
Como Escribir Bien en Espanol. Trade Cloth. Acro Libros S.A.. Madrid, 2002. 373p. ISBN:84-7635-327-8, ISBN13: 978-84-7635-327-1. Dewey:468.
Audience: **u,f.**

Gomez Torrego, Leonardo **PC4112 .G636 1998**
Gramatica Didactica del Espanol. Ed. 6. Trade Cloth. SM Ediciones. Madrid, 2002. 544p. ISBN:84-348-5440-6, ISBN13: 978-84-348-5440-6. Dewey:468.2. LCCN:99-492812.
Audience: **u,f.**

Gooch, Anthony & Pareded, Angela Garcia de **PC4640.C35 1987**
Cassell's Spanish-English English-Spanish Dictionary. Ed. 19. Edgar A. Peers (Editor). Trade Cloth. John Wiley & Sons, Inc. Hoboken, NJ. 1978. 1136p. ISBN:0-02-522910-9, ISBN13: 978-0-02-522910-5. Dewey:463'.21. LCCN:77-007403.
Audience: **g,l,u,f.**

HarperCollins Staff **PC4640.S595 2000**
Spanish Unabridged Dictionary. Ed. 6. Trade Cloth. HarperCollins Publishers. New York, NY. 2000. 1728p. ISBN:0-06-095691-7, ISBN13: 978-0-06-095691-2. Dewey:463/.21. LCCN:99-076607.
Audience: **l,u,f.**

Jarman, Beatriz Galimberti & Carvajal, Carol Styles **PC4640.O94 2003**
The Oxford Spanish Dictionary. Ed. 3. Roy Russell & Jane Horwood (Editors). Trade Cloth. Oxford University Press, Inc. New York, NY. 2003. 2,040p. ISBN:0-19-860475-0, ISBN13: 978-0-19-860475-4. Dewey:463/.21. LCCN:2003-272816.
Audience: **g,l,u,f.** *Choice, 2003.*

Kearon, John **PC4120.M3D5 2000**
Medical Spanish: A Conversational Approach. Ed. 2. Cloth Text. Harcourt College Publishers. Fort Worth, TX. 1999. xxviii, 288p. ISBN:0-03-026029-9, ISBN13: 978-0-03-026029-2. Dewey:468.3/421/02461. LCCN:99-060180.
Audience: **g,l,u,f.**

Klee, Carol A. & Ramos-Garcia, Luis A. (Editors) **PC4073.S6 1991**
Sociolinguistics of the Spanish-Speaking World: Iberia, Latin America, United States. Trade Cloth. Bilingual Press/Editorial Bilingue. Tempe, AZ. 1991. 368p. ISBN:0-927534-13-4, ISBN13: 978-0-927534-13-0. Dewey:306.4/4/0917561. LCCN:90-025750.
Audience: **u,f.**

Larousse Editors (Editor) **PC4640.L393 2004**
Larousse Unabridged Dictionary: Spanish-English / English-Spanish. Trade Cloth. Larousse, Editions. Paris, 2004. 1696p. Larousse Unabridged Ser. ISBN:2-03-542070-9, ISBN13: 978-2-03-542070-1. Dewey:463/.21.
Audience: **g,l,u,f.** *Choice, 2005.*

Leon, Victor **PC**
Diccionario de Argot Espanol. Ed. 2. Trade Cloth. Alianza Editorial, S. A.. Madrid, 264p. ISBN:84-206-1766-0, ISBN13: 978-84-206-1766-4. Dewey:467/.09. LCCN:80-131115.
Audience: **u,f.**

Lipski, John M. **PC4821.L56 1994**
Latin American Spanish. Ed. 1. Paper Text. Addison-Wesley Longman, Inc. Boston, MA. 1995. 380p. Longman Linguistics Library ISBN:0-582-08760-0, ISBN13: 978-0-582-08760-6. Dewey:467/.98. LCCN:93-031346.
Audience: **g,l,u,f.**

Lloyd, Paul **Q11 .P612 VOL. 173**
From Latin to Spanish. Trade Paper. American Philosophical Society. Canton, MA. 1987. 346p. Memoirs Ser., Vol. 173 ISBN:0-87169-173-6, ISBN13: 978-0-87169-173-6. Dewey:081. LCCN:86-072883.
Audience: **u,f.**

Mar-Molinero, Clare **PC4074.75.M38 1997**
The Spanish-Speaking World: A Practical Introduction to Sociolinguistic Issues. Paper over Boards. Routledge. New York, NY. 1997. 200p. Language in Society Ser. ISBN:0-415-12982-6, ISBN13: 978-0-415-12982-4. Dewey:306.4/4/0943. LCCN:96-043952.
Audience: **u,f.**

Menéndez Pidal, Ramón **PC**
Manual de Gramática Histórica Española. Ed. 22. Trade Cloth. Espasa Calpe, S.A.. Madrid, 1977. 368p. ISBN:84-239-4755-6, ISBN13: 978-84-239-4755-3. Dewey:465. LCCN:78-370944.
Audience: **u,f.** B

Moliner, Maria D. **PC**
Diccionario de Uso del Español. Ed. 2. Trade Cloth. Gredos, Editorial, S.A.. Madrid, 2002. ISBN:84-249-2310-3, ISBN13: 978-84-249-2310-5. Dewey:463.
Audience: **l,u,f.**

National Textbook Company Staff & Vox Staff **PC4640.V69 1994**
Vox Compact Spanish and English Dictionary. Ed. 2. Trade Cloth. McGraw-Hill Companies, The. New York, NY. 1994. 662p. National Textbook Language Dictionaries Ser. ISBN:0-8442-7985-4, ISBN13: 978-0-8442-7985-5. Dewey:463/.21. LCCN:2002-028804.
Audience: **g,l,u,f.**

Navarro Tomas, Tomás **PC**
Manual de Pronunciacion Espanola. Ed. 25. Trade Cloth. Consejo Superior de Investigaciones Científicas. Madrid, 1990. 328p. ISBN:84-00-07096-8, ISBN13: 978-84-00-07096-0. Dewey:468.1. LCCN:93-163301.
Audience: **l,u,f.**

Olivares, Rafael A. **PC4882**
NTC's Dictionary of Latin American Spanish. Trade Paper. McGraw-Hill Companies, The. New York, NY. 1999. 384p. ISBN:0-8442-7964-1, ISBN13: 978-0-8442-7964-0. Dewey:467.9/8/321.
Audience: **g,l,u,f.**

Passport Books Staff & Alcaraz, Daniel **PC4822.A38 1993**
Diccionario Practico de la Lengua Española del Nuevo Mundo. Trade Paper. McGraw-Hill Companies, The. New York, NY. 1993. 274p. ISBN:0-8442-7968-4, ISBN13: 978-0-8442-7968-8. Dewey:467/.98. LCCN:93-218252.
Audience: **u,f.**

Penny, Ralph **PC4101.P46 2002**
A History of the Spanish Language. Ed. 2. Cloth Text. Cambridge University Press. New York, NY. 2002. 418p. ISBN:0-521-80587-2, ISBN13: 978-0-521-80587-2. Dewey:460/.9. LCCN:2002-025671.
Audience: **u,f.** *Choice, 1992.*

Penny, Ralph **PC4074.7 .P46 2000**
Variation and Change in Spanish. Cloth Text. Cambridge University Press. New York, NY. 2000. 298p. ISBN:0-521-78045-4, ISBN13: 978-0-521-78045-2. Dewey:467.009. LCCN:00-023265.
Audience: **u,f.**

Pharies, David A., et al. **PC4640 .U5 2003**
The University of Chicago Spanish Dictionary: Spanish-English, English-Spanish. Ed. 5. María Irene Moyna & Gary K. Baker (Authors), Carlos Castillo & Otto Ferdinand Bond (Compiled by), University of Chicago Staff (Contribution by). Trade Cloth. Simon & Schuster, Ltd. London, 2003. xviii, 582p. ISBN:0-7434-9252-8, ISBN13: 978-0-7434-9252-2. Dewey:463/.21. LCCN:2004-558969.
Audience: **g,l,u,f.**

Real Academia Espanola Staff **PC4460.D5155**
Diccionario Panhispanico de Dudas. Trade Cloth. Alfaguara, Ediciones, S.A.- Grupo Santillana. 28043, Madrid, 2005. 848p. ISBN:958-704-368-5, ISBN13: 978-958-704-368-6. Dewey:468.
Audience: **u,f.**

Real Academia Espanola Staff **PC**
Ortografia de la Lengua Española. Trade Cloth. Espasa Calpe, S.A.. Madrid, 1999. 184p. ISBN:84-239-9250-0, ISBN13: 978-84-239-9250-8. Dewey:461/.52. LCCN:99-525880.
Audience: **l,u,f.**

Seco, Manuel **PC**
Diccionario de Dudas y Diflcultades. Trade Cloth. Espasa Calpe, S.A.. Madrid, 1998. 624p. ISBN:84-239-9425-2, ISBN13: 978-84-239-9425-0. Dewey:468.
Audience: **u,f.**

Stewart, Miranda **PC4087.S84 1999**
The Spanish Language Today. Paper over Boards. Routledge. New York, NY. 1999. 256p. ISBN:0-415-14258-X, ISBN13: 978-0-415-14258-8. Dewey:460/.9/049. LCCN:98-054089.
Audience: **g,l.**

Thompson, Stephen J. **PC4271.T483 1999**
15,000 Spanish Verbs: Fully Conjugated in All the Tenses Using Pattern Verbs. Ed. 2. Trade Cloth. Center For Innovative Language Learning. Washington, DC. 1999. iv, 203p. ISBN:0-9651418-2-9, ISBN13: 978-0-9651418-2-6. Dewey:465. LCCN:99-090213.
Audience: **g,l,u.**

Vox **PC4625**
Vox Diccionario de Uso del Español de America y Españ. Trade Cloth. McGraw-Hill Companies, The. New York, NY. 2004. 2022p. ISBN:0-07-142644-2, ISBN13: 978-0-07-142644-2. Dewey:463.
Audience: **u,f.**

Whitley, M. Stanley **PC4099.W45 1986**
Spanish-English Contrasts: An Introduction to Spanish Linguistics. Trade Cloth. Georgetown University Press. Washington, DC. 1986. 400p. Romance Languages and Linguistics Ser. ISBN:0-87840-095-8, ISBN13: 978-0-87840-095-9. Dewey:468.2/421. LCCN:86-022917.
Audience: **l,u.**

Zagona, Karen **PC4361 .Z34 2002**
The Syntax of Spanish. J. Bresnan, D. Lightfoot, I. Roberts, N. V. Smith & N. Vincent (Contribution by). Cloth Text. Cambridge University Press. New York, NY. 2002. 298p. Cambridge Syntax Guides Ser. ISBN:0-521-57177-4, ISBN13: 978-0-521-57177-7. Dewey:465. LCCN:2001-035092.
Audience: **u.**

Portuguese Language

PC5327.G73 1991
Grande Dicionário da Língua Portuguesa. Trade Cloth. Bow Historical Books. New Providence, NJ. 1991. ISBN:972-626-035-3, ISBN13: 978-972-626-035-6. Dewey:469.3. LCCN:93-191892.
Audience: **u,f.**

PC5333
Harrap's Portuguese Compact Dictionary. Trade Cloth. Larousse Harrap Publishers. London, 1290p. ISBN:0-245-60735-8, ISBN13: 978-0-245-60735-6. Dewey:469.3/21.
Audience: **g,l.**

HarperCollins Staff (Contribution by) **PC5333.C54 2001**
Collins Dicionario Ingles-Portugues, Portugues-Ingles. Ed. 3. Trade Paper. HarperCollins Publishers. New York, NY. 2001. xxiv, 615p. ISBN:0-00-472405-4, ISBN13: 978-0-00-472405-8. Dewey:469.3/21. LCCN:2002-391773.
Audience: **l,u,f.**

Hutchinson, Amelia P. & Lloyd, Janet **PC5067.3.H88 2003**
Portuguese: An Essential Grammar. Ed. 2. Paper over Boards. Routledge. New York, NY. 2003. 288p. Essential Grammars Ser. ISBN:0-415-30816-X, ISBN13: 978-0-415-30816-8. Dewey:469.82/421. LCCN:2003-005266.
Audience: **l,u,f.**

Hutchinson, Amélia P. & Lloyd, Janet **PC5067.3.H88 1996**
[e] Portuguese: An Essential Grammar. E-Book. Taylor & Francis Group. Philadelphia, PA. ISBN:0-203-97865-X, ISBN13: 978-0-203-97865-8. Dewey:469.82/421.
Audience: **l,u,f.**

Macedo, Donaldo P. & Koike, Dale A. **PC5064**
Romance Linguistics: The Portuguese Context. Trade Cloth. Greenwood Publishing Group, Inc. Portsmouth, NH. 1992. 216p. ISBN:0-89789-297-6, ISBN13: 978-0-89789-297-1. Dewey:469.86. LCCN:92-019868.
Audience: **u,f.**

Nitti, John J. & Ferreira, Michael J. **PC5145.A15 1995**
501 Portuguese Verbs. Trade Paper. Barron's Educational Series, Inc. Hauppauge, NY. 1995. 600p. ISBN:0-8120-9034-9, ISBN13: 978-0-8120-9034-5. Dewey:469.8/2/421. LCCN:94-073167.
Audience: **g,l,u,f.**

Taylor, James L. **PC5333.T3 1970**
A Portuguese-English Dictionary. Ed. 2. Trade Cloth. Stanford University Press. Palo Alto, CA. 1958. xxii, 662p. ISBN:0-8047-0480-5, ISBN13: 978-0-8047-0480-9. Dewey:469/.3/21. LCCN:72-026595.
Audience: **g,l,u,f.**

Tyson-Ward, Sue **PC5073**
Brazilian Portuguese. Ed. 2. Trade Paper. McGraw-Hill Trade. New York, NY. 2003. 256p. Teach Yourself Language Complete Courses Ser. ISBN:0-340-86032-4, ISBN13: 978-0-340-86032-8. Dewey:469.7/98.
Audience: **l,u.**

Tyson-Ward, Sue **PC5145.T97 1999**
Portuguese Verbs and Essentials of Grammar. Trade Paper. McGraw-Hill Companies, The. New York, NY. 1996. 144p. Verbs and Essentials of Ser. ISBN:0-8442-4698-0, ISBN13: 978-0-8442-4698-7. Dewey:469.82/421. LCCN:99-088831.
Audience: **l,u.**

Hispanic Literature

Pedrero, Paloma **PQ6666.E358**
El Color de Agosto. Trade Cloth. Machado, Antonio, Ediciones. Madrid, 1989. 76p. ISBN:84-7644-043-X, ISBN13: 978-84-7644-043-8. LCCN:90-871406.
Audience: **u,f.**

Hispanic Literature > History, Criticism

Alborg, J. L. **PQ**
Historia de la Literatura Espanola: El Siglo XVIII, Vol. 3. Trade Cloth. Elliot's Books. Northford, CT. 1993. 980p. ISBN:84-249-3130-0, ISBN13: 978-84-249-3130-8. Dewey:860.9.
Audience: **u,f.**

Alborg, J. L. **PQ**
Historia de la Literatura Espanola: Epoca Barroca, Vol. 2. Ed. 2. Trade Cloth. Elliot's Books. Northford, CT. 1993. 996p. ISBN:84-249-3128-9, ISBN13: 978-84-249-3128-5. Dewey:860.9.
Audience: **u,f.**

Alborg, J. L. **PQ**
Historia de la Literatura Espanola: Edad Media y Renacimiento, Vol. 1. Ed. 2. Trade Cloth. Elliot's Books. Northford, CT. 1993. 1082p. ISBN:84-249-3126-2, ISBN13: 978-84-249-3126-1. Dewey:860.9.
Audience: **u,f.**

Alborg, J. L. **PQ**
Historia de la Literatura Espanola: El Romanticismo, Vol. 4. Trade Cloth. Elliot's Books. Northford, CT. 1993. 952p. ISBN:84-249-3146-7, ISBN13: 978-84-249-3146-9. Dewey:860.9.
Audience: **u,f.**

Bleznick, Donald W. **Z2695.A2B55 1995**
A Sourcebook for Hispanic Literature and Language: A Selected Annotated Guide to Spanish, Spanish-American and United States Hispanic Bibliography, Literature, Linguistics, Journals, and Other Source Materials. Ed. 3. Trade Cloth. Scarecrow Press, Inc. Lanham, MD. 1995. 322p. ISBN:0-8108-2981-9, ISBN13: 978-0-8108-2981-7. Dewey:016.86. LCCN:94-047011.
Audience: **l,u,f.**

Chandler, Richard E. & Schwartz, Kessel **PQ6033.C45 1991**
A New History of Spanish Literature. Cloth Text. Louisiana State University Press. Baton Rouge, LA. 1991. 479p. ISBN:0-8071-1699-8, ISBN13: 978-0-8071-1699-9. Dewey:860.9. LCCN:91-002667.
Audience: **l,u,f.**

Davies, Catherine **CB226**
The Companion to Hispanic Studies. Trade Paper. Oxford University Press, Inc. New York, NY. 2002. 224p. A Hodder Arnold Publication ISBN:0-340-76298-5, ISBN13: 978-0-340-76298-1. Dewey:306.0896.
Audience: **l,u,f.**

Del Rio, Angel
Historia de la Lituratura Espanola. Trade Cloth. Holt, Rinehart & Winston, Inc. Austin, TX. 1984. ISBN:0-03-019075-4, ISBN13: 978-0-03-019075-9.
Audience: **u,f.**

Díaz-Plaja, Guillermo **PQ6032.D4913**
A History of Spanish Literature. Trade Cloth. New York University Press. New York, NY. 1971. xxii, 374p. ISBN:0-8147-1775-6, ISBN13: 978-0-8147-1775-2. Dewey:860.9. LCCN:70-124524.
Audience: **g,l,u,f.** B

Fox-Lockert, Lucia **PQ6055.F6**
Women Novelists in Spain and Spanish America. Trade Cloth. Scarecrow Press, Inc. Lanham, MD. 1979. 356p. ISBN:0-8108-1270-3, ISBN13: 978-0-8108-1270-3. Dewey:863/.009/9287. LCCN:79-023727.
Audience: **u,f.** B

Gies, David T. (Editor) **PQ6033.C36 2004**
The Cambridge History of Spanish Literature. Cloth Text. Cambridge University Press. New York, NY. 2005. 898p. ISBN:0-521-80618-6, ISBN13: 978-0-521-80618-3. Dewey:860.9. LCCN:2004-045601.
Audience: **u,f.** *Choice, 2005.*

Gullón, Ricardo **PQ6006.D6 1993**
Diccionario de Literatura Espanola e Hispanoamericana. Trade Cloth. Alianza Editorial, S. A.. Madrid, 1993. 936p. ISBN:84-206-5248-2, ISBN13: 978-84-206-5248-1. Dewey:860.9. LCCN:93-247192.
Audience: **l,u,f.**

Harris, Derek (Editor) **PQ6073.E94S67 1995**
The Spanish Avantgarde. Cloth Text. Manchester University Press. Manchester, 1995. xi, 223p. ISBN:0-7190-4341-7, ISBN13: 978-0-7190-4341-3. Dewey:700.9/46. LCCN:94-005409.
Audience: **u,f.**

Lapesa, Rafael **PC**
Historia de la Literatura HispanoAmericana. Ed. 9. Trade Cloth. Gredos, Editorial, S.A.. Madrid, 2002. 690p. ISBN:84-249-0072-3, ISBN13: 978-84-249-0072-4. Dewey:460/.9. LCCN:81-154525.
Audience: **u,f.** B

Moreno Gomez, Francisco **PQ**
Generacion del 27. Trade Paper. McGraw-Hill Higher Education. Burr Ridge, IL. 1999. 277p. ISBN:84-481-0994-5, ISBN13: 978-84-481-0994-3. LCCN:99-495314.
Audience: **u,f.**

Newmark, Maxim **PQ6006.N4**
Dictionary of Spanish Literature. Paper Text. Textbook Publishers. Temecula, CA. 2003. vii, 352p. ISBN:0-7581-6419-X, ISBN13: 978-0-7581-6419-3. Dewey:860/.9.
Audience: **l,u,f.**

Northup, George T. **PQ6037.N6**
An Introduction to Spanish Literature. Ed. 3. Nicholson B. Adams (Revised by). Trade Paper. Books on Demand. Ann Arbor, MI. 542p. ISBN:0-608-09027-1, ISBN13: 978-0-608-09027-6. Dewey:860.9. LCCN:60-008127.
Audience: **l,u,f.**

Perez, Janet & Horn, Paul W. **PQ6055.P4 1988**
Contemporary Women Writers of Spain. Trade Cloth. Thomson Gale. Farmington Hills, MI. 1988. 256p. World Authors Ser., No. 798 ISBN:0-8057-8229-X, ISBN13: 978-0-8057-8229-5. Dewey:860/.9/9287. LCCN:87-034830.
Audience: **g,l.** *Choice, 1989.*

Perez, Janet & Ihrie, Maureen (Editors) **PQ6055.F46 2002**
The Feminist Encyclopedia of Spanish Literature, Vol. 1. Library Binding. Greenwood Publishing Group, Inc. Portsmouth, NH. 2002. 1048p. ISBN:0-313-32444-1, ISBN13: 978-0-313-32444-4. Dewey:860.9/9287. LCCN:2002-019922.
Audience: **l,u,f.** *Choice, 2003.*

Soufas, Theresa Scott **PQ6066.S68 1990**
Melancholy and the Secular Mind in Spanish Golden Age Literature. Cloth Text. University of Missouri Press. Columbia, MO. 1990. 208p. ISBN:0-8262-0714-6, ISBN13: 978-0-8262-0714-2. Dewey:860.9/003. LCCN:89-004852.
Audience: **u,f.** *Choice, 1990.*

Surtz, Ronald E.
The Birth of a Theater. Trade Cloth. Castalia, Editorial S.A.. Madrid, 1979. 208p. ISBN:84-7039-303-0, ISBN13: 978-84-7039-303-7.
Audience: **u,f.**

Ticknor, George **PQ6033 .T5**
History of Spanish Literature, Vol. II. Cloth Text. Amereon, Ltd. Mattituck, NY. 2004. ISBN:0-8488-2971-9, ISBN13: 978-0-8488-2971-1. Dewey:860.9.
Audience: **g,l,u.**

Turner, Harriet S. & López de Martínez, Adelaida (Editors) **PQ6144**
The Cambridge Companion to the Spanish Novel: From 1600 to the Present. Cloth Text. Cambridge University Press. New York, NY. 2003. 344p. Cambridge Companions to Literature Ser. ISBN:0-521-77127-7, ISBN13: 978-0-521-77127-6. Dewey:863.009. LCCN:2004-299826.
Audience: **l,u.** *Choice, 2004.*

Valbuena Prat, Angel **PQ6032.V3 1982**
Historia de la Literatura Española obra Completa. Other. Gustavo Gili Editorial S.A.. Barcelona, 1981. ISBN:84-252-1071-2, ISBN13: 978-84-252-1071-6. Dewey:860/.9. LCCN:82-199254.
Audience: **u,f.** B

Valis, Noel & Maier, Carol (Editors) **PQ6055.I6 1990**
In the Feminine Mode: Essays on Hispanic Women Writers. Trade Cloth. Bucknell University Press. Cranbury, NJ. 1990. 288p. ISBN:0-8387-5160-1, ISBN13: 978-0-8387-5160-2. Dewey:860.9/9287. LCCN:88-043410.
Audience: **u,f.** *Choice, 1991.*

Walters, D. Gareth **PQ6076.W35 2002**
The Cambridge Introduction to Spanish Poetry: Spain and Spanish America. Cloth Text. Cambridge University Press. New York, NY. 2002. 236p. Cambridge Introductions to Literature Ser. ISBN:0-521-79122-7, ISBN13: 978-0-521-79122-9. Dewey:861.009. LCCN:2002-025670.
Audience: **g,l,u.** *Choice, 2003.*

Hispanic Literature > History, Criticism > Special Forms > Poetry

Debicki, Andrew P. **PQ6085.D398 1994**
Spanish Poetry of the Twentieth Century: Modernity and Beyond. Library Binding. University Press of Kentucky. Lexington, KY. 1994. 272p. Studies in Romance Languages, No. 37 ISBN:0-8131-1869-7, ISBN13: 978-0-8131-1869-7. Dewey:861/.609. LCCN:93-036928.
Audience: **u,f.** *Choice, 1995.*

Hart, Stephen M. **PQ6085.H37 1991**
Spanish, Catalan and Spanish-American Poetry from "Modernismo" to the Spanish Civil War: The Hispanic Connection. Trade Cloth. Edwin Mellen Press, The. Lewiston, NY. 1991. 216p. Hispanic Literature Ser., Vol. 11 ISBN:0-88946-697-1, ISBN13: 978-0-88946-697-5. Dewey:860.9/006. LCCN:90-024276.
Audience: **l,u,f.**

Menéndez Pidal, Ramón **PQ6088.M375 1974**
La Epopeya Castellana a Través de la Literatura Española. Trade Cloth. Espasa Calpe, S.A.. Madrid, 1974. 212p. ISBN:84-239-1561-1, ISBN13: 978-84-239-1561-3. Dewey:861/.03. LCCN:76-475638.
Audience: **u,f.** *B*

Soufas, C. Christopher **PQ6085.S65 1989**
Conflict of Light and Wind: The Spanish Generation of 1927 and the Ideology of Poetic Form. Trade Cloth. Wesleyan University Press. Middletown, CT. 1989. 296p. ISBN:0-8195-5219-4, ISBN13: 978-0-8195-5219-8. Dewey:861/.62/09. LCCN:89-005533.
Audience: **u,f.** *Choice, 1990.*

Terry, Arthur **PQ6081 .T47 1993**
Seventeenth-Century Spanish Poetry. Trade Cloth. Cambridge University Press. New York, NY. 1993. 316p. ISBN:0-521-44421-7, ISBN13: 978-0-521-44421-7. Dewey:361/.309. LCCN:92-040121.
Audience: **u,f.**

Walters, D. Gareth **PQ6076.W35 2002**
The Cambridge Introduction to Spanish Poetry: Spain and Spanish America. Cloth Text. Cambridge University Press. New York, NY. 2002. 236p. Cambridge Introductions to Literature Ser. ISBN:0-521-79122-7, ISBN13: 978-0-521-79122-9. Dewey:861.009. LCCN:2002-025670.
Audience: **g,l,u.** *Choice, 2003.*

Winfield, Jerry P. (Editor) **PQ6085.T88 1994**
Twentieth-Century Spanish Poets. Cloth Text. Thomson Gale. Farmington Hills, MI. 1993. 366p. Dictionary of Literary Biography Ser. ISBN:0-8103-5393-8, ISBN13: 978-0-8103-5393-0. Dewey:861.6. LCCN:93-026861.
Audience: **g,l,u.** *Choice, 1994.*

Hispanic Literature > History, Criticism > Special Forms > Drama

De Armas, Frederick A. **PQ6106.S73 1998**
A Star-Crossed Golden Age: Myth and the Spanish Comedia. Trade Cloth. Bucknell University Press. Cranbury, NJ. 1998. 248p. ISBN:0-8387-5376-0, ISBN13: 978-0-8387-5376-7. Dewey:862/.309. LCCN:97-039644.
Audience: **u,f.**

Edwards, Gwynne **PQ6115.E35 1985**
Dramatists in Perspective: Spanish Theatre in the Twentieth Century. Cloth Text. Palgrave Macmillan. New York, NY. 1985. 280p. ISBN:0-312-21950-4, ISBN13: 978-0-312-21950-5. Dewey:862/.6/09. LCCN:85-002216.
Audience: **u,f.** *B* *Choice, 1985.*

Holt, Marion P. **PQ6115.H65**
The Contemporary Spanish Theater, 1949-1972. Library Binding. Irvington Publishers. New York, NY. 1975. 189p. Twayne's World Authors Ser. ISBN:0-8057-2243-2, ISBN13: 978-0-8057-2243-7. Dewey:862/.6/409. LCCN:74-012472.
Audience: **l,u,f.** *B*

Larson, Catherine **PQ6105.L37 1991**
Language and the Comedia: Theory and Practice. Trade Cloth. Bucknell University Press. Cranbury, NJ. 1991. 181p. ISBN:0-8387-5180-6, ISBN13: 978-0-8387-5180-0. Dewey:862/.309. LCCN:89-046406.
Audience: **u,f.**

Mancing, Howard **PQ6105.G65 1994**
The Golden Age Comedia: Text, Theory and Performance. Charles Ganelin (Editor). Cloth Text. Purdue University Press. West Lafayette, IN. 1994. 422p. ISBN:1-55753-042-4, ISBN13: 978-1-55753-042-4. Dewey:862/.309. LCCN:93-001959.
Audience: **u,f.** *Choice, 1995.*

McKendrick, Melveena **PQ6105.M24 1989**
Theatre in Spain, 1490-1700. Cloth Text. Cambridge University Press. New York, NY. 1989. 352p. ISBN:0-521-35592-3, ISBN13: 978-0-521-35592-6. Dewey:862/.309. LCCN:89-031433.
Audience: **g,l,u,f.** *Choice, 1990.*

McKendrick, Melveena **PQ6102**
Woman and Society in the Spanish Drama of the Golden Age: A Study of the Mujer Varonil. Trade Cloth. Cambridge University Press. New York, NY. 1974. 384p. ISBN:0-521-20294-9, ISBN13: 978-0-521-20294-7. Dewey:862/.3/09355. LCCN:73-082457.
Audience: **u,f.**

Oriel, Charles **PQ6105.O7 1992**
Writing and Inscription in Golden Age Drama. Trade Cloth. Purdue University Press. West Lafayette, IN. 1992. 189p. Studies in Romance Literature ISBN:1-55753-019-X, ISBN13: 978-1-55753-019-6. Dewey:862/.309. LCCN:92-026368.
Audience: **u,f.** *Choice, 1993.*

Ruiz Ramón, Francisco **PQ**
Historia Del Teatro Español: Siglo XX. Ed. 10. Trade Cloth. Ediciones Cátedra. Madrid 1, 1995. 576p. ISBN:84-376-0049-9, ISBN13: 978-84-376-0049-9.
Audience: **u,f.**

Ruiz Ramón, Francisco **PQ**
Historia Del Teatro Español: (Desde Sus Orígenes Hasta 1900). Ed. 9. Trade Cloth. Ediciones Cátedra. Madrid 1, 1996. 392p. ISBN:84-376-0190-8, ISBN13: 978-84-376-0190-8.
Audience: **u,f.**

Simerka, Barbara (Editor) **PQ6105.A73 1996**
El Arte Nuevo de Estudiar Comedias: Literary Theory and Spanish Golden Age Drama. Trade Cloth. Bucknell University Press. Cranbury, NJ. 1996. 264p. ISBN:0-8387-5320-5, ISBN13: 978-0-8387-5320-0. Dewey:862/.309. LCCN:95-041299.
Audience: **u,f.**

Stoll, Anita K. & Smith, Dawn L. **PQ6106.G46 2000**
Gender, Identity and Representation in Spain's Golden Age. Trade Cloth. Bucknell University Press. Cranbury, NJ. 2000. 208p. ISBN:0-8387-5425-2, ISBN13: 978-0-8387-5425-2. Dewey:862/.309353. LCCN:99-024500.
Audience: **u,f.** *Choice, 2000.*

Stoll, Anita K. & Smith, Dawn L. (Editors) **PQ6105.P46 1991**
The Perception of Women in Spanish Theater of the Golden

Age. Trade Cloth. Bucknell University Press. Cranbury, NJ. 1991. 280p. ISBN:0-8387-5189-X, ISBN13: 978-0-8387-5189-3. Dewey:862/.309352042. LCCN:89-046402.
Audience: **u,f.** *Choice, 1992.*

Wilson, Margaret **PQ6105.W5 1969**
Spanish Drama of the Golden Age. Trade Cloth. Elsevier. New York, NY. 1969. xi, 221p. ISBN:0-08-013955-8, ISBN13: 978-0-08-013955-5. Dewey:862/.3/09. LCCN:74-078906.
Audience: **l,u,f.** B

Ziomek, Henryk **PQ6105.Z56 1984**
A History of Spanish Golden Age Drama. Trade Cloth. University Press of Kentucky. Lexington, KY. 1984. 256p. Studies in Romance Languages, No. 29 ISBN:0-8131-1506-X, ISBN13: 978-0-8131-1506-1. Dewey:862/.3/09. LCCN:83-023309.
Audience: **g,l,u.** B

Hispanic Literature > History, Criticism > Special Forms > Fiction

Boudreau, H. L. **PQ6144.I58 1998**
Intertextual Persuits: Literary Mediations in Modern Spanish Narrative. Jeanne P. Brownlow & John W. Kronik (Editors). Trade Cloth. Bucknell University Press. Cranbury, NJ. 1998. 272p. ISBN:0-8387-5370-1, ISBN13: 978-0-8387-5370-5. Dewey:860.9/006. LCCN:97-019958.
Audience: **u,f.** *Choice, 1999.*

Charnon-Deutsch, Lou **PQ6144.C429 1990**
Gender and Representation: Women in Spanish Realist Fiction. Trade Cloth. John Benjamins Publishing Company. Philadelphia, PA. 1990. xiv, 205p. Purdue University Monographs in Romance Languages, Vol. 32 ISBN:1-55619-083-2, ISBN13: 978-1-55619-083-4. Dewey:863/.509352042. LCCN:90-041865.
Audience: **u,f.**

Charnon-Deutsch, Lou **PQ6144.C427 1994**
Narratives of Desire: 19th-Century Spanish Fiction by Women. Trade Cloth. Pennsylvania State University Press. University Park, PA. 1994. 224p. Penn State Studies in Romance Literatures ISBN:0-271-01007-X, ISBN13: 978-0-271-01007-6. Dewey:863/.509352042. LCCN:93-017102.
Audience: **u,f.** *Choice, 1995.*

Dunn, Peter N. **PQ6147.P5.D82 1993**
Spanish Picaresque Fiction: A New Literary History. Trade Cloth. Cornell University Press. Ithaca, NY. 1993. 352p. ISBN:0-8014-2800-9, ISBN13: 978-0-8014-2800-5. Dewey:863.009/351. LCCN:92-036854.
Audience: **u,f.** *Choice, 1993.*

Gullón, Germán **PQ6144 .G85 1990**
La Novela Del XIX: Estudio Sobre Su Evolucion Formal. Trade Cloth. Rodopi. Kenilworth, NY. 1990. 135p. Teoría Literaria, Texto y Teoría Ser., Vol. 6 ISBN:90-5183-209-5, ISBN13: 978-90-5183-209-9. Dewey:863/.03. LCCN:91-163822.
Audience: **u,f.**

Herzberger, David K. **PQ6144.H47 1995**
Narrating the Past: Fiction and Historiography in Postwar Spain. Cloth Text. Duke University Press. Durham, NC. 1995. 192p. ISBN:0-8223-1582-3, ISBN13: 978-0-8223-1582-7. Dewey:863/.6409358. LCCN:94-024973.
Audience: **u,f.** *Choice, 1996.*

Ife, B. W. **PQ6147.P5I43 1985**
Reading and Fiction in Golden Age Spain: A Platonist Critique and Some Picaresque Replies. Trade Cloth. Cambridge University Press. New York, NY. 1985. 220p. Cambridge Iberian and Latin American Studies ISBN:0-521-30375-3, ISBN13: 978-0-521-30375-0. Dewey:863/.087/09. LCCN:85-004199.
Audience: **u,f.**

Johnson, Roberta **PQ6144.J58 1993**
Crossfire: Philosophy and the Novel in Spain, 1900-1934. Cloth Text. University Press of Kentucky. Lexington, KY. 1993. 248p. Studies in Romance Languages, Vol. 35 ISBN:0-8131-1824-7, ISBN13: 978-0-8131-1824-6. Dewey:863/.6209384. LCCN:92-038875.
Audience: **u,f.** *Choice, 1994.*

Johnson, Roberta **PQ6144.J585 2003**
Gender and Nation in the Spanish Modernist Novel. Trade Cloth. Vanderbilt University Press. Nashville, TN. 2003. 368p. ISBN:0-8265-1436-7, ISBN13: 978-0-8265-1436-3. Dewey:860.9/112. LCCN:2003-017647.
Audience: **u,f.** *Choice, 2004.*

Labanyi, Jo **PQ6144.L327 2000**
Gender and Modernization in the Spanish Realist Novel. Trade Cloth. Oxford University Press, Inc. New York, NY. 2006. 472p. Oxford Hispanic Studies ISBN:0-19-815178-0, ISBN13: 978-0-19-815178-4. Dewey:863/.50912. LCCN:2001-274441.
Audience: **u,f.** *Choice, 2001.*

Maiorino, Giancarlo (Editor) **PQ6147.P5P53 1996**
The Picaresque: Tradition and Displacement. Book, Other. University of Minnesota Press. Minneapolis, MN. 1996. 318p. Hispanic Issues Ser., Vol. 12 ISBN:0-8166-2722-3, ISBN13: 978-0-8166-2722-6. Dewey:863/.08709. LCCN:95-032079.
Audience: **u,f.**

Marti-Lopez, Elisa **PQ6144.M333 2002**
Borrowed Words: Translation, Imitation and the Making of the Nineteenth-Century Novel in Spain. Trade Cloth. Bucknell University Press. Cranbury, NJ. 2002. 200p. ISBN:0-8387-5520-8, ISBN13: 978-0-8387-5520-4. Dewey:863/.509. LCCN:2002-018406.
Audience: **u,f.**

Richardson, Nathan E. **PQ6140.R87R53 2002**
Postmodern Paletos: Immigration, Democracy and Globalization in Spanish Narrative and Film, 1950-2000. Trade Cloth. Bucknell University Press. Cranbury, NJ. 2002. 264p. ISBN:0-8387-5498-8, ISBN13: 978-0-8387-5498-6. Dewey:791.43/0946. LCCN:2001-037544.
Audience: **u,f.** *Choice, 2002.*

Rico, Francisco **PQ6147.P3**
The Spanish Picaresque Novel and the Point of View. Trade Cloth. Cambridge University Press. New York, NY. 1984. 159p.

Cambridge Iberian and Latin American Studies
ISBN:0-521-25370-5, ISBN13: 978-0-521-25370-3.
Dewey:863/.3/0917. LCCN:83-015040.
Audience: **u,f.**

Sieburth, Stephanie **PQ6144.S54 1994**
Inventing High and Low: Literature, Mass Culture and Uneven Modernity in Spain. Cloth Text. Duke University Press. Durham, NC. 1994. 296p. ISBN:0-8223-1444-4, ISBN13: 978-0-8223-1444-8. Dewey:863.009/355. LCCN:93-038920.
Audience: **u,f.** *Choice, 1995.*

Spires, Robert C. **PQ6144.S648 1984**
Beyond the Metafictional Mode: Directions in the Modern Spanish Novel. Trade Cloth. University Press of Kentucky. Lexington, KY. 1984. 168p. ISBN:0-8131-1520-5, ISBN13: 978-0-8131-1520-7. Dewey:863/.64/09. LCCN:84-007565.
Audience: **u,f.**

Spires, Robert C. **PQ6144.S65 1996**
Post-Totalitarian Spanish Fiction. Trade Cloth. University of Missouri Press. Columbia, MO. 1996. 280p.
ISBN:0-8262-1071-6, ISBN13: 978-0-8262-1071-5.
Dewey:863/.91409. LCCN:96-018447.
Audience: **u,f.** *Choice, 1997.*

Spires, Robert C. **PQ6144.S66 1988**
Transparent Simulacra: Spanish Fiction, 1902-1926. Cloth Text. University of Missouri Press. Columbia, MO. 1989. 192p.
ISBN:0-8262-0695-6, ISBN13: 978-0-8262-0695-4.
Dewey:863/.62/09. LCCN:88-004882.
Audience: **u,f.** *Choice, 1989.*

Thomas, Gareth **PQ6144 .T47 1990**
The Novel of the Spanish Civil War (1936-1975). Trade Cloth. Cambridge University Press. New York, NY. 1990. 285p.
ISBN:0-521-37158-9, ISBN13: 978-0-521-37158-2.
Dewey:863/.609358. LCCN:89-007352.
Audience: **l,u,f.** *Choice, 1990.*

Turner, Harriet S. & López de Martínez, Adelaida (Editors) **PQ6144**
The Cambridge Companion to the Spanish Novel: From 1600 to the Present. Cloth Text. Cambridge University Press. New York, NY. 2003. 344p. Cambridge Companions to Literature Ser.
ISBN:0-521-77127-7, ISBN13: 978-0-521-77127-6.
Dewey:863.009. LCCN:2004-299826.
Audience: **l,u.** *Choice, 2004.*

Hispanic Literature > Collections of Spanish Literature

Andres, Ramon **PQ6186.A66 1987**
Antologia Poetica del Romanticismo Espano (Poetic Anthology of the Spanish Romanticism). Trade Paper. GeoPlaneta, Editorial, S. A.. Barcelona, 1987. lxxxii, 264p.
ISBN:84-320-3973-X, ISBN13: 978-84-320-3973-7.
Dewey:861/.5/08. LCCN:88-164735.
Audience: **u,f.**

Appelbaum, Stanley (Editor) **PQ6267.E8S636 2006**
Spanish Stories of the Late Nineteenth Century: A Dual-Language Book. Trade Paper. Dover Publications, Inc. Mineola, NY. 2006. 240p. A Dual-Language Book Ser.
ISBN:0-486-44505-4, ISBN13: 978-0-486-44505-2.
Dewey:863/.010834. LCCN:2005-051879.
Audience: **g,l,u,f.**

Appelbaum, Stanley (Editor, Translator) **PQ6267.E4S63 2003**
Spanish Traditional Ballads: Romances Viejos Espanoles. Trade Paper. Dover Publications, Inc. Mineola, NY. 2003. 256p. A Dual-Language Book Ser. ISBN:0-486-42694-7, ISBN13: 978-0-486-42694-5. Dewey:861/.03308. LCCN:2003-041461.
Audience: **g,l,u,f.**

Barnstone, Willis (Editor, Translator) **PQ6176.B338 1993**
Six Masters of the Spanish Sonnet: Francisco de Quevedo, Sor Juana Ines de la Cruz, Antonia Machado, Federico Garcia Lorca, Jorge Luis Borges, Miguel Hernandez. Trade Cloth. Southern Illinois University Press. Carbondale, IL. 1993. 272p.
ISBN:0-8093-1772-9, ISBN13: 978-0-8093-1772-1.
Dewey:861/.04208. LCCN:92-012099.
Audience: **g,l,u,f.** *Choice, 1994.*

Benitez Claros, Rafael **PQ6219.B4**
Antologia Del Teatro Medieval. Trade Paper. Books on Demand. Ann Arbor, MI. 242p. Coleccion Del Estudiante; Textos Clasicos Espanoles Ser., Vol. 1 ISBN:0-598-88679-6, ISBN13: 978-0-598-88679-8. Dewey:862.08. LCCN:53-029509.
Audience: **l,u,f.**

Bordonada, Angela Ena (Translator) **MLCS 91/00399 (P)**
Novelas Breves de Escritoras Españolas: 1900-1936. Trade Cloth. Castalia, Editorial S.A.. Madrid, 1989. 497p.
ISBN:84-7039-570-X, ISBN13: 978-84-7039-570-3.
LCCN:91-743237.
Audience: **l,u,f.**

Buchanan, Milton Alexander **PQ6184.B8**
Spanish Poetry of the Golden Age. Ed. 2. Milton A. Buchanan (Editor). Trade Paper. Books on Demand. Ann Arbor, MI. 154p.
ISBN:0-598-15279-2, ISBN13: 978-0-598-15279-4.
Dewey:861.3082.
Audience: **g,l,u,f.**

Colón, Matilde **PQ6174.A86 1984**
Antologia de Literatura Hispanica Contemporanea, Vol. 1. Trade Cloth. University of Puerto Rico Press. Rio Piedras, PR. 1984. 240p. ISBN:0-8477-3511-7, ISBN13: 978-0-8477-3511-2.
Dewey:860/.8/006. LCCN:84-020849.
Audience: **u,f.**

Connell, G. **PQ6187**
Spanish Poetry of the Grupo Poetico de 1927. Trade Cloth. Pergamon Press. Kidlington, 1977. xv, 214p.
ISBN:0-08-016950-3, ISBN13: 978-0-08-016950-7.
Dewey:861/.6/208. LCCN:77-003297.
Audience: **l,u,f.**

Crow, John A. (Editor) **PQ6267.E2**
An Anthology of Spanish Poetry: From the Beginnings to the Present Day, Including Both Spain and Spanish America. Cloth Text. Louisiana State University Press. Baton Rouge, LA. 1979. 240p. ISBN:0-8071-0482-5, ISBN13: 978-0-8071-0482-8. Dewey:861/.008. LCCN:79-004619.
Audience: **g,l,u,f.**

Cummins, J. G. **PQ6175**
The Spanish Traditional Lyric. Cloth Text. Elsevier Science & Technology Books. Saint Louis, MO. 1977. xi, 179p. ISBN:0-08-018117-1, ISBN13: 978-0-08-018117-2. Dewey:861/.04. LCCN:76-001222.
Audience: **g,l,u,f.**

De Quevedo, Francisco **PQ6253**
Two Spanish Picaresque Novels. Michael Alpert (Translator, Introduction by). Trade Paper. Penguin Group (USA) Inc. New York, NY. 1969. 224p. Penguin Classics Ser. ISBN:0-14-044211-1, ISBN13: 978-0-14-044211-3. Dewey:863/.3/08.
Audience: **g,l,u,f.**

de Rojas, Fernando **PQ6253**
Celestina. John Clifford (Translator). Trade Paper. Theatre Communications Group, Inc. New York, NY. 2005. 128p. ISBN:1-85459-818-X, ISBN13: 978-1-85459-818-9. Dewey:862.2.
Audience: **g,l,u,f.**

Espie, Susan (Editor) **PQ6184.A67 1986**
Ant. Lirica Renacentista (Anthology - Renaissance Poetry). Other. Plaza & Janés Editories, S.A.. Barcelona, 419p. ISBN:84-01-90564-8, ISBN13: 978-84-01-90564-3. Dewey:861/.3/08. LCCN:86-181406.
Audience: **u,f.**

Flores, Angel (Editor) **PQ6267.E6S64 1991**
Great Spanish Plays: 16th-20th Century. Trade Paper. Dover Publications, Inc. Mineola, NY. 1991. 480p. ISBN:0-486-26898-5, ISBN13: 978-0-486-26898-9. Dewey:862/.008. LCCN:91-022776.
Audience: **g,l,u,f.**

Flores, Angel (Editor) **PQ6267.E2 1998**
Spanish Poetry: Poesia Espanola: A Dual-Language Anthology. Trade Paper. Dover Publications, Inc. Mineola, NY. 1998. 448p. ISBN:0-486-40171-5, ISBN13: 978-0-486-40171-3. Dewey:861.008. LCCN:97-044224.
Audience: **g,l,u,f.**

Flores, Angel **PQ6267.E8F6**
Spanish Writers in Exile. Trade Paper. Books on Demand. Ann Arbor, MI. 120p. ISBN:0-598-12118-8, ISBN13: 978-0-598-12118-9. Dewey:863/.01.
Audience: **u,f.**

Florit, Eugenio (Editor) **PQ6176.I68 1991**
Introduction to Spanish Poetry. Trade Paper. Dover Publications, Inc. Mineola, NY. 1991. 160p. ISBN:0-486-26712-1, ISBN13: 978-0-486-26712-8. Dewey:861.008. LCCN:90-023241.
Audience: **g,l,u,f.**

Foster, David W. **PQ6172.L543 1995**
Literatura Espanola: Una Antologia: De 1700 Hasta la Actualidad. Trade Paper. Garland Publishing, Inc. New York, NY. 1995. 640p. Reference Library of the Humanities, Vol. 2 ISBN:0-8153-2064-7, ISBN13: 978-0-8153-2064-7. Dewey:860.8. LCCN:95-019115.
Audience: **u,f.**

Foster, David W. **PQ6172.L543 1995**
Literatura Espanola: Una Antologia: De los Origenes Hasta 1700. Cloth Text. Garland Publishing, Inc. New York, NY. 1995. 904p. ISBN:0-8153-1755-7, ISBN13: 978-0-8153-1755-5. Dewey:860.8. LCCN:95-019115.
Audience: **u,f.**

Fotitch, Tatiana Zurunitch **PQ6174.A3F6**
An Anthology of Old Spanish. Trade Paper. Books on Demand. Ann Arbor, MI. 263p. ISBN:0-8357-5625-4, ISBN13: 978-0-8357-5625-9. Dewey:468.64. LCCN:70-083406.
Audience: **u,f.**

Gaos, Vicente **PQ6176 .D54**
Diez Siglos de Poesia Castelana. Trade Cloth. Alianza Editorial, S. A.. Madrid, 2000. 496p. ISBN:84-206-1581-1, ISBN13: 978-84-206-1581-3. Dewey:861.09. LCCN:76-465854.
Audience: **u,f.**

Greenfield, Sumner M. **PQ6174.G4 1997**
La Generacion de 1898 Ante Espana: Antologia de Literatura Moderna de Temas Nacionales y Universales. Ed. 2. Paper Text. Society of Spanish & Spanish-American Studies. Boulder, CO. 1997. 504p. Publications of the Society of Spanish and Spanish-American Studies ISBN:0-89295-088-9, ISBN13: 978-0-89295-088-1. Dewey:860.8. LCCN:97-067256.
Audience: **u,f.**

Hammer, Louis & Schyfter, Sara (Translators) **PQ6267.E2 1983**
Recent Poetry of Spain: A Bilingual Anthology. Louis Hammer & Sara Schyfter (Introduction by). Trade Cloth. Sachem Press. Old Chatham, NY. 1983. xxii, 340p. ISBN:0-937584-07-X, ISBN13: 978-0-937584-07-1. Dewey:861/.6/08. LCCN:83-011235.
Audience: **g,l,u,f.** B

Havard, Robert G. **PQ6187.H38 1988**
From Romanticism to Surrealism: Seven Spanish Poets. Trade Cloth. Rowman & Littlefield Publishers, Inc. Lanham, MD. 1988. 0p. ISBN:0-389-20810-8, ISBN13: 978-0-389-20810-5. Dewey:861/.62/09. LCCN:88-023244.
Audience: **l,u,f.** *Choice, 1989.*

Holt, Marion P. (Editor) **PQ6267.E6.H6**
Modern Spanish Stage: Four Plays. Trade Paper. Farrar, Straus & Giroux. New York, NY. 1970. 388p. ISBN:0-8090-0746-0, ISBN13: 978-0-8090-0746-2. Dewey:862/.6/208. LCCN:78-106966.
Audience: **g,l,u,f.** B

Ibarra, F. & Da Rosa, A. M. **PQ6172.A67 1992**
Antologia de Autores Espanoles: Modernos. Cloth Text. Prentice Hall PTR. Upper Saddle River, NJ. 1972. ISBN:0-13-087990-8, ISBN13: 978-0-13-087990-5. Dewey:468.6/421. LCCN:92-033678.
Audience: **u,f.**

Kaminsky, Amy K. (Editor) **PQ6173.W38 1996**
Water Lillies: An Anthology of Spanish Women Writers from the Fifteenth Through the Nineteenth Century. Book, Other. University of Minnesota Press. Minneapolis, MN. 1995. 592p. ISBN:0-8166-1944-1, ISBN13: 978-0-8166-1944-3. Dewey:860.8/09287. LCCN:95-000604.
Audience: **g,l,u,f.**

King, John R. **PQ6267.E8S56 1999**
Short Stories in Spanish. Trade Paper. Penguin Group (USA) Inc. New York, NY. 2001. 256p. New Penguin Parallel Texts Ser. ISBN:0-14-026541-4, ISBN13: 978-0-14-026541-5. Dewey:863/.0108064. LCCN:2001-274151.
Audience: **g,l,u,f.**

MacCurdy, Raymond R. **PQ6218.M3**
Spanish Drama of the Golden Age: Twelve Plays. Trade Cloth. Prentice Hall PTR. Upper Saddle River, NJ. 1971. ix, 634p. ISBN:0-390-58471-1, ISBN13: 978-0-390-58471-7. Dewey:862/.3/08. LCCN:77-136218.
Audience: **g,l,u,f.**

Marin, Diego **PQ6175.M187**
Lira Espanola: Representative Spanish Lyric Poets, 15th to 20th Centuries. Trade Paper. Books on Demand. Ann Arbor, MI. 389p. ISBN:0-598-75855-0, ISBN13: 978-0-598-75855-2. Dewey:861.008. LCCN:54-031884.
Audience: **l,u,f.**

Michael, Ian **PQ6181**
The Poem of the Cid. Rita Hamilton & Janet Perry (Translators). Cloth Text. Barnes & Noble Books-Imports. Lanham, MD. 1975. 242p. Manchester Medieval Classics Ser. ISBN:0-06-494799-8, ISBN13: 978-0-06-494799-2. Dewey:861/.1. LCCN:75-017168.
Audience: **g,l,u,f.** B

Mujica, Barbara **PQ6173.W66 2004**
Women Writers of Early Modern Spain: Sophia's Daughters. Trade Paper. Yale University Press. Cumberland, RI. 2003. 448p. Yale Language Ser. ISBN:0-300-09257-1, ISBN13: 978-0-300-09257-8. Dewey:860.8/09287/09031. LCCN:2003-008671.
Audience: **u,f.**

Mújica, Bárbara **PQ6174.A5A57 1991**
Antologia de la Literatura Espanola, Renacimiento y Siglo de Oro, Vol. 2. Trade Cloth. John Wiley & Sons, Inc. Hoboken, NJ. 1991. 640p. ISBN:0-471-53694-6, ISBN13: 978-0-471-53694-9. Dewey:860.8/003. LCCN:90-028274.
Audience: **u,f.**

Mújica, Bárbara **PQ6174.A3A58 1991**
Antología de la Literatura Española: Edad Media. Trade Cloth. John Wiley & Sons, Inc. Hoboken, NJ. 1991. 260p. ISBN:0-471-53693-8, ISBN13: 978-0-471-53693-2. Dewey:860.8/002. LCCN:90-028275.
Audience: **u,f.**

Mújica, Bárbara & Florensa, Eva **PQ6174.A855 1999**
Antologia de la Literatura Espanola: Siglos XVIII y XIX. Trade Paper. John Wiley & Sons, Inc. Hoboken, NJ. 1998. 522p. ISBN:0-471-25573-4, ISBN13: 978-0-471-25573-4. Dewey:860.8. LCCN:98-039978.
Audience: **u,f.**

Mújica, Bárbara & Zahareas, Anthony N. (Editors) **PQ6172**
Readings in Spanish Literature. Trade Cloth. Oxford University Press, Inc. New York, NY. 1975. x, 437p. ISBN:0-19-501845-1, ISBN13: 978-0-19-501845-5. Dewey:860/.8. LCCN:74-083994.
Audience: **u,f.**

O'Connor, Patricia W. **PQ6267.E6O26 1992**
Plays of the New Democratic Spain, 1975-1990. Trade Cloth. University Press of America, Inc. Lanham, MD. 1992. 500p. ISBN:0-8191-8441-1, ISBN13: 978-0-8191-8441-2. Dewey:862/.6408. LCCN:91-031120.
Audience: **u,f.**

O'Connor, Patricia W. & Pasquariello, Anthony M. (Editors) **PC4127.D7 C6**
Contemporary Spanish Theatre: Seven One-Act Plays. Paper Text. Thomson Gale. Farmington Hills, MI. 1980. ISBN:0-684-16500-7, ISBN13: 978-0-684-16500-4. Dewey:468.6/421. LCCN:79-026859.
Audience: **g,l,u,f.**

Patt, Beatrice P. & Nozick, Martin (Editors) **PQ6174.P35**
The Generation of 1898 and After: An Anthology for Students of Spanish. Trade Paper. Books on Demand. Ann Arbor, MI. 1960. 445p. ISBN:0-7837-8663-8, ISBN13: 978-0-7837-8663-6. Dewey:860.82. LCCN:60-053305.
Audience: **u,f.**

Pattison, Walter T. & Bleznick, Donald W. (Editors) **PQ6172**
Representative Spanish Authors: From the Middle Ages Through the Eighteenth Century. Ed. 3. Cloth Text. Oxford University Press, Inc. New York, NY. 1971. ix, 357p. ISBN:0-19-501326-3, ISBN13: 978-0-19-501326-9. Dewey:860.8. LCCN:78-139736.
Audience: **u,f.**

Pattison, Walter T. & Bleznick, Donald W. (Editors) **PQ6172**
Representative Spanish Authors, Vol. II. Ed. 3. Cloth Text. Oxford University Press, Inc. New York, NY. 1971. 500p. ISBN:0-19-501433-2, ISBN13: 978-0-19-501433-4. Dewey:860.8. LCCN:78-139736.
Audience: **u,f.**

Peers, Edgar A. (Editor) **PQ6176**
Critical Anthology of Spanish Verse. Trade Cloth. Greenwood Publishing Group, Inc. Portsmouth, NH. 1969. 1741p. ISBN:0-8371-0190-5, ISBN13: 978-0-8371-0190-3. Dewey:861/.008. LCCN:69-010145.
Audience: **g,l,u,f.**

Polt, John Herman Richard (Translator) **PQ6185 .P6**
Poesia del Siglo XVIII. Trade Cloth. Castalia, Editorial S.A.. Madrid, 416p. Clasicos Castalia, :Siglo XVIII ISBN:84-7039-216-6, ISBN13: 978-84-7039-216-0. Dewey:861.408. LCCN:76-460760.
Audience: **u,f.**

Ramos-Garcia, Luis A. (Editor) **PQ6187.B48 1997**
A Bilingual Anthology of Contemporary Spanish Poetry: The Generation of 1970. Dave Oliphant (Translator), Miguel Casado

(Introduction by). Trade Cloth. Edwin Mellen Press, The. Lewiston, NY. 1997. 364p. Hispanic Literature Ser., Vol. 43 ISBN:0-7734-8435-3, ISBN13: 978-0-7734-8435-1. Dewey:861/.6408. LCCN:97-032323.
Audience: **g,l,u,f.**

Resnick, Seymour & Pasmantier, Jeanne **PQ6172.R46 1994**
Nueve Siglos de Literatura Espanola (Nine Centuries of Spanish Literature): Bilingual Edition. Trade Paper. Dover Publications, Inc. Mineola, NY. 1994. 480p. ISBN:0-486-28271-6, ISBN13: 978-0-486-28271-8. Dewey:860.8. LCCN:94-019769.
Audience: **u,f.**

Reyes, Rogelio **PQ6185.P63 1988**
Poesia Espanola del Siglo XVIII. Trade Cloth. Ediciones Cátedra. Madrid 1, 432p. ISBN:84-376-0727-2, ISBN13: 978-84-376-0727-6. Dewey:861/.4/08. LCCN:88-160726.
Audience: **u,f.**

Rivers, Elias (Editor) **PQ6184.P574**
Poesia Lirica del Siglo de Oro (Lyric Poetry of the Golden Age). Trade Cloth. Ediciones Cátedra. Madrid 1, 368p. ISBN:84-376-0174-6, ISBN13: 978-84-376-0174-8. Dewey:861/.3/08. LCCN:80-119383.
Audience: **u,f.**

Sanchez-Romeralo, Antonio, et al. **PQ6172.A67 1992**
Antología de autores Españoles: Antiguos y Modernos. Fernando Ibarra & Antonio Sanchez-Romeraldo (Authors). Trade Paper. Prentice Hall PTR. Upper Saddle River, NJ. 1972. 395p. ISBN:0-13-033838-9, ISBN13: 978-0-13-033838-9. Dewey:468.6/421. LCCN:92-033678.
Audience: **u,f.**

Smith, C. **PQ6196.S5 1996**
Spanish Ballads. Ed. 2. Trade Paper. Bristol Classical Press. London, 1996. 224p. Spanish Texts Ser. ISBN:1-85399-445-6, ISBN13: 978-1-85399-445-6. Dewey:861/.044/08/03. LCCN:96-217338.
Audience: **g,l,u,f.**

St Martin, Hardie (Editor) **PQ6257**
Roots and Wings: Poetry from Spain 1900-1975. Trade Paper, Perfect. White Pine Press. Buffalo, NY. 2005. 528p. ISBN:1-893996-34-4, ISBN13: 978-1-893996-34-2. Dewey:861/.6.
Audience: **g,l,u.**

Turnbull, Eleanor L. **PQ6267E2 2002**
Ten Centuries of Spanish Poetry: An Anthology in English Verse with Original Texts, From the Eleventh Century to the Generation of 1898. Pedro Salinas (Introduction by). Trade Paper. Johns Hopkins University Press. Baltimore, MD. 2002. 468p. ISBN:0-8018-1042-6, ISBN13: 978-0-8018-1042-8. Dewey:861.008.
Audience: **u,f.**

Unamuno, Miguel de, et al. **PQ6267.E8S55 2004**
Short Stories by the Generation of 1898/Cuentos de la Generacion de 1898: A Dual-Language Book. Ramón del Valle-Inclán, Pio Baroja, Azorin & Vicente Blasco Ibanez (Authors), Stanley Appelbaum (Editor, Translator). Trade Paper. Dover Publications, Inc. Mineola, NY. 2004. 240p. A Dual-Language Book Ser. ISBN:0-486-43682-9, ISBN13: 978-0-486-43682-1. Dewey:863/.0108062. LCCN:2004-050191.
Audience: **g,l,u,f.**

Valbuena Prat, Angel **PQ6256.P5V3 1974**
La Novela Picaresca Espanola. Ed. 7. Other. Santillana USA Publishing Company, Inc. Doral, FL. 1974. ISBN:84-03-00958-5, ISBN13: 978-84-03-00958-5. Dewey:863.082. LCCN:75-571082.
Audience: **u,f.**

Vargas Llosa, Mario, et al. **PQ6267.E6**
The Methuen Book of Latin American Plays: La Chunga, Paper Flowers, Medea in the Mirror. Egon Wolff & Jose Triana (Authors). Trade Paper. Methuen Publishing Ltd. London, 2004. 320p. ISBN:0-413-77378-7, ISBN13: 978-0-413-77378-4. Dewey:862.6/408.
Audience: **g,l,u.**

Hispanic Literature > Spanish Literature: Individual Authors and Works > To 1700 > A-C

Aldana, Francisco **PQ6271.A8A6 1985**
Poesias Castellanas Completas. Trade Cloth. Ediciones Cátedra. Madrid 1, 516p. ISBN:84-376-0532-6, ISBN13: 978-84-376-0532-6. Dewey:861/.3. LCCN:85-239729.
Audience: **u,f.**

Appelbaum, Stanley (Editor) **PQ6367.E3A66 2005**
Poem of My Cid/Poema de Mio Cid: A Dual-Language Book. Trade Paper, Perfect. Dover Publications, Inc. Mineola, NY. 2005. 144p. A Dual-Language Book Ser. ISBN:0-486-44016-8, ISBN13: 978-0-486-44016-3. Dewey:861/.1. LCCN:2004-061767.
Audience: **g,l,u,f.**

Berceo, Gonzalo **PQ6397.M5 1986**
Milagros de Nuetras Sra (Miracles of Our Lady). Other. Plaza & Janés Editories, S.A.. Barcelona, 379p. ISBN:84-01-90569-9, ISBN13: 978-84-01-90569-8. Dewey:861/.3. LCCN:92-228381.
Audience: **u,f.**

Canavaggio, Jean **PQ6337.C2313 1990**
Cervantes. Joseph R. Jones (Translator). Trade Cloth. W. W. Norton & Company, Inc. New York, NY. 1990. 348p. ISBN:0-393-02812-7, ISBN13: 978-0-393-02812-6. Dewey:863/.3 B. LCCN:89-009462.
Audience: **g,l,u,f.** *Choice, 1990.*

De Berceo, Gonzalo **PQ6397.M513 1997**
Miracles of Our Lady. Richard T. Mount & Annette G. Cash (Translators). Trade Cloth. University Press of Kentucky. Lexington, KY. 1997. 176p. Studies in Romance Languages, 41 ISBN:0-8131-2019-5, ISBN13: 978-0-8131-2019-5. Dewey:861/.1. LCCN:97-002119.
Audience: **l,u,f.** *Choice, 1997.*

Fernández de Avellaneda, Alonso **PQ**
El Ingenioso Hidalgo Don Quijote de la Mancha. Luis Gómez Canseco (Editor). Trade Cloth. Biblioteca Nueva, Editorial, S.L.. Madrid, 2000. 800p. ISBN:84-7030-763-0, ISBN13: 978-84-7030-763-8. Dewey:863/.3. LCCN:2001-328092.
Audience: **u,f.**

Hamilton, Rita **PQ6366**
Poem of the Cid: Dual Language Edition. Trade Paper. Penguin Group (USA) Inc. New York, NY. 1985. 256p. Classics Ser. ISBN:0-14-044446-7, ISBN13: 978-0-14-044446-9. Dewey:861.1.
Audience: **g,l,u,f.**

John of the Cross **PQ6400.J8A23 2004**
A Bilingual Edition of Poems by St. John of the Cross: Spiritual Songs and Ballads. Kenneth Canatsey (Introduction by). Trade Cloth. Edwin Mellen Press, The. Lewiston, NY. 2003. 136p. ISBN:0-7734-6574-X, ISBN13: 978-0-7734-6574-9. Dewey:861/.3. LCCN:2003-066452.
Audience: **g,l,u,f.**

John of the Cross & Teresa of Avila **PQ6400.J8A235 2005**
Flame of Love: Poems of the Spanish Mystics. Loren G. Smith (Translator). Trade Cloth. Alba House. Staten Island, NY. 2005. xvi, 207p. ISBN:0-8189-0977-3, ISBN13: 978-0-8189-0977-1. Dewey:861/.30803824822. LCCN:2005-010978.
Audience: **g,l,u,f.**

Krabbenhoft, Ken (Translator) **PQ6400.J8A253 1999**
Poems of St. John of the Cross. Cloth over Boards. Harcourt Trade Publishers. New York, NY. 1999. 96p. ISBN:0-15-100327-0, ISBN13: 978-0-15-100327-3. Dewey:861/.3. LCCN:98-035251.
Audience: **g,l,u,f.**

Place, Edwin & Behm, Herbert (Translators) **PQ6275.E2 2003**
Amadis of Gaul. John E. Keller (Introduction by). Trade Paper. University Press of Kentucky. Lexington, KY. 2003. 688p. ISBN:0-8131-9034-7, ISBN13: 978-0-8131-9034-1. Dewey:863/.2. LCCN:2003-265405.
Audience: **g,l,u,f.**

Rodriguez de Montalvo, Garci **PQ6275.E1**
Amadis de Gaulle. Helen Moore (Editor), Anthony Munday (Translator). Trade Cloth. Ashgate Publishing, Ltd. Aldershot, 2004. 1062p. Non-Canonical Early Modern Popular Texts Ser. ISBN:0-7546-0727-5, ISBN13: 978-0-7546-0727-4. Dewey:863/.2. LCCN:2003-052345.
Audience: **l,u,f.**

Rodriquez de Montalvo, Garci **PQ6274.A1 1991**
Amadis de Gaula, I. Juan B. Avalle-Arce (Editor). Trade Cloth. Elliot's Books. Northford, CT. 1991. 750p. Nueva Austral Ser., Vol. 119 ISBN:84-239-1919-6, ISBN13: 978-84-239-1919-2. Dewey:863/.2. LCCN:91-225890.
Audience: **u,f.**

Smith, Colin J. **PQ6373**
The Making of the "Poema de Mio Cid". Trade Cloth. Cambridge University Press. New York, NY. 1983. 265p. ISBN:0-521-24992-9, ISBN13: 978-0-521-24992-8. Dewey:861/.1. LCCN:82-014663.
Audience: **u,f.**

Thompson, Colin P. **BV5080.J7755 T48**
The Poet and the Mystic: A Study of the Cantico Espiritual of San Juan de la Cruz. Trade Cloth. Oxford University Press, Inc. New York, NY. 1978. xi, 188p. Oxford Modern Languages and Literature Monographs ISBN:0-19-815531-X, ISBN13: 978-0-19-815531-7. Dewey:861/.3. LCCN:77-009326.
Audience: **u,f.**

Vogt, Eric W. **PQ6437.T3A28 1996**
The Complete Poetry of Teresa of Avila: A Bilingual Edition. Paper Text. University Press of the South, Inc. New Orleans, LA. 1996. 150p. Iberian Studies, No. 3 ISBN:1-889431-03-6, ISBN13: 978-1-889431-03-1. Dewey:861/.3. LCCN:96-061620.
Audience: **l,u,f.**

Whicker, Jules **PQ6431.R8Z94 2003**
The Plays of Juan Ruiz de Alarcón. Trade Cloth. Boydell & Brewer, Ltd. Woodbridge, 2003. 220p. Monografias A Ser. ISBN:1-85566-093-8, ISBN13: 978-1-85566-093-9. Dewey:862/.3. LCCN:2003-011729.
Audience: **g,l,u,f.**

Whitenack, Judith **PQ6272.Z5W46 1985**
The Impenitent Confession of Guzman de Alfarache. Trade Cloth. Hispanic Seminary of Medieval Studies. New York, NY. 1985. iv, 216p. ISBN:0-942260-53-8, ISBN13: 978-0-942260-53-3. Dewey:863/.3. LCCN:85-205951.
Audience: **u,f.**

Hispanic Literature > Spanish Literature: Individual Authors and Works > To 1700 > Calderon

Calderón de la Barca, Pedro **PQ6282.A4 1976**
El Alcalde de Zalamea. Trade Cloth. Castalia, Editorial S.A.. Madrid, 322p. Clasicos Castalia, :Siglo XVII ISBN:84-7039-237-9, ISBN13: 978-84-7039-237-5. Dewey:862/.3. LCCN:77-453523.
Audience: **u,f.**

Calderón de la Barca, Pedro **PQ6281.A3 1973**
Comedias de Capa y Espada: La Dama Duende; No Hay Cosa Como Callar. Trade Cloth. Espasa Calpe, S.A.. Madrid, 1973. xcii, 223p. ISBN:84-239-3137-4, ISBN13: 978-84-239-3137-8. Dewey:862/.3. LCCN:77-465786.
Audience: **u,f.**

Calderón de la Barca, Pedro **PQ6282.D3 1989**
La Dama Duende. Trade Cloth. GeoPlaneta, Editorial, S. A.. Barcelona, 1989. 304p. ISBN:84-320-4014-2, ISBN13: 978-84-320-4014-6. Dewey:862/.3. LCCN:90-167108.
Audience: **u,f.**

Calderón de la Barca, Pedro PQ6292.V5K5313 2004
Life's a Dream. Michael Kidd (Introduction by). Trade Cloth. University Press of Colorado. Boulder, CO. 2004. 159p. ISBN:0-87081-776-0, ISBN13: 978-0-87081-776-2. Dewey:862/.3. LCCN:2004-010260.
Audience: **g,l,u,f.**

Calderón de la Barca, Pedro PQ6292.A2 1985
Three Comedies. Kenneth Muir & Ann L. MacKenzie (Translators). Trade Cloth. University Press of Kentucky. Lexington, KY. 1985. 256p. Studies in Romance Languages, Vol. 31 ISBN:0-8131-1546-9, ISBN13: 978-0-8131-1546-7. Dewey:862/.3. LCCN:85-005369.
Audience: **g,l,u,f.** *Choice, 1986.*

Calderón de la Barca, Pedro & Porqueras Mayo, Alberto PQ6285.A1 1977
La Vida Es Sueno y El Alcalde de Zalamea. Trade Cloth. Espasa Calpe, S.A.. Madrid, 1977. 219p. ISBN:84-239-2023-2, ISBN13: 978-84-239-2023-5. Dewey:862.3. LCCN:77-557002.
Audience: **u,f.**

Cascardi, Anthony J. PQ6317.I44 C37 1984
The Limits of Illusion: A Critical Study of Calderon. A. R. D. Pagden, E. Pupo-Walker, P. E. Russell & Herbert S. Klein (Contribution by). Trade Cloth. Cambridge University Press. New York, NY. 1984. 196p. Cambridge Iberian and Latin American Studies ISBN:0-521-26281-X, ISBN13: 978-0-521-26281-1. Dewey:862/.3. LCCN:2006-273443.
Audience: **g,l,u,f.**

De Armas, Frederick A. (Editor), et al. PQ6312.C7
Critical Perspectives on Calderon de la Barca. David M. Gitlitz & Jose A. Madrigal (Editors). Trade Paper. Books on Demand. Ann Arbor, MI. 183p. ISBN:0-608-14801-6, ISBN13: 978-0-608-14801-4. Dewey:862.3. LCCN:80-053823.
Audience: **u,f.**

Greer, Margaret R. PQ6312.G74 1991
The Play of Power: Mythological Court Dramas of Calderon de la Barca. Cloth Text. Princeton University Press. Princeton, NJ. 1991. 310p. ISBN:0-691-06857-7, ISBN13: 978-0-691-06857-2. Dewey:862/.3. LCCN:90-044110.
Audience: **u,f.** *Choice, 1992.*

Kurtz, Barbara E. PQ6317.R4K87 1991
The Play of Allegory in the Autos Sacramentales of Pedro Calderon de la Barca. Cloth Text. Catholic University of America Press. Washington, DC. 1991. 250p. Contexts and Literature Ser., Vol. 2 ISBN:0-8132-0733-9, ISBN13: 978-0-8132-0733-9. Dewey:862.3. LCCN:90-036829.
Audience: **l,u,f.** *Choice, 1991.*

Maraniss, James E. PQ6312
On Calderon. Trade Cloth. University of Missouri Press. Columbia, MO. 1978. 144p. ISBN:0-8262-0237-3, ISBN13: 978-0-8262-0237-6. Dewey:862/.3. LCCN:77-014034.
Audience: **u,f.**

O'Connor, Thomas A. PQ6317.M84O26 1988
Myth and Mythology in the Theater of Pedro Calderon de la Barca. Trade Cloth. Trinity University Press. San Antonio, TX. 1988. 365p. ISBN:0-939980-21-5, ISBN13: 978-0-939980-21-5. Dewey:862/.3. LCCN:88-016057.
Audience: **g,l,u,f.** *Choice, 1989.*

Parker, Alexander A. PQ6312.P37 1988
The Mind and Art of Calderon: Essays on the Comedias. Trade Cloth. Cambridge University Press. New York, NY. 1989. 432p. Major European Authors Ser. ISBN:0-521-32334-7, ISBN13: 978-0-521-32334-5. Dewey:862/.3. LCCN:88-011851.
Audience: **u,f.** *Choice, 1989.*

Parker, Alexander Augustine PQ6312.P3
The Allegorical Dramas of Calderon: An Introduction to the Auto Sacramentales. Trade Paper. Books on Demand. Ann Arbor, MI. 232p. ISBN:0-598-71193-7, ISBN13: 978-0-598-71193-9. Dewey:862.35. LCCN:43-011230.
Audience: **u,f.**

Hispanic Literature > Spanish Literature: Individual Authors and Works > To 1700 > Cervantes

Arnoldo Mondadori editore Staff PQ6337.M613 1970
Cervantes; His Life, His Times, His Works. Trade Cloth. American Heritage Press. Camarillo, CA. 1970. 167p. ISBN:0-07-004854-1, ISBN13: 978-0-07-004854-6. Dewey:863/.3. LCCN:79-085204.
Audience: **l,u,f.**

Byron, William PQ6337.B9
Cervantes: A Biography. Trade Cloth. Doubleday Publishing. New York, NY. 1978. xiv, 583p. ISBN:0-385-00279-3, ISBN13: 978-0-385-00279-0. Dewey:863/.3. LCCN:74-033633.
Audience: **g,l,u,f.**

Cascardi, Anthony J. (Editor) PQ6351.C27 2002
The Cambridge Companion to Cervantes. Cloth Text. Cambridge University Press. New York, NY. 2002. 264p. Cambridge Companions to Literature Ser. ISBN:0-521-66321-0, ISBN13: 978-0-521-66321-2. Dewey:863/.3. LCCN:2002-017500.
Audience: **g,l,u,f.** *Choice, 2003.*

Castro, Americo PQ6337.C3
Cervantes. Trade Paper. Books on Demand. Ann Arbor, MI. 118p. ISBN:0-598-75420-2, ISBN13: 978-0-598-75420-2. Dewey:863.3. LCCN:32-003170.
Audience: **u,f.**

Castro, Americo PQ6351.C3
El Pensamiento de Cervantes, Por Americo Castro. Trade Paper. Books on Demand. Ann Arbor, MI. 416p. ISBN:0-598-90400-X, ISBN13: 978-0-598-90400-3. Dewey:863.3. LCCN:27-001984.
Audience: **u,f.**

Cervantes Saavedra, Miguel de PQ6324.A1 1982
Novelas Ejemplares I. Trade Cloth. Castalia, Editorial S.A.. Madrid, 318p. Clasicos Castalia, :Siglo XVII ISBN:84-7039-393-6, ISBN13: 978-84-7039-393-8. Dewey:863/.3. LCCN:82-206032.
Audience: **u,f.**

Cervantes Saavedra, Miguel de **PQ6325.A1 1987**
Teatro Completo. Trade Cloth. GeoPlaneta, Editorial, S. A.. Barcelona, 1987. 1072p. ISBN:84-320-3963-2, ISBN13: 978-84-320-3963-8. Dewey:862/.3. LCCN:88-124199.
Audience: **u,f.**

Cervantes Saavedra, Miguel de **PQ6329.A5 1999**
Selections from Don Quixote: A Dual-Language Book. Stanley Appelbaum (Translator, Introduction by). Trade Paper. Dover Publications, Inc. Mineola, NY. 1999. 256p. ISBN:0-486-40666-0, ISBN13: 978-0-486-40666-4. Dewey:863/.3. LCCN:99-012617.
Audience: **g,l,u,f.**

Cervantes Saavedra, Miguel de **PQ6329.A613 1992**
The Exemplary Novels, Vol. I. Carmen María Cervantes (Editor). Trade Cloth. Aris & Phillips. Oxford, 1992. 256p. ISBN:0-85668-555-0, ISBN13: 978-0-85668-555-2. Dewey:863/.3. LCCN:94-134893.
Audience: **g,l,u,f.**

Cervantes Saavedra, Miguel de **PQ6329.A2 2003**
Don Quixote. Edith Grossman (Translator), Harold Bloom (Translator, Introduction by). Trade Cloth. HarperCollins Publishers. New York, NY. 2003. 976p. ISBN:0-06-018870-7, ISBN13: 978-0-06-018870-2. Dewey:863.3. LCCN:2003-045216.
Audience: **g,l,u.** *Choice, 2004.*

Cervantes Saavedra, Miguel de **PQ6329.A613 1992**
Spanish Englishwoman: The Glass Graduate and the Power of Blood. B. W. Ife (Editor), R. M. Price (Translator). Trade Cloth. Aris & Phillips. Oxford, 1992. 100p. The Complete Exemplary Novels Ser., Vol. 2 ISBN:0-85668-493-7, ISBN13: 978-0-85668-493-7. Dewey:863/.3. LCCN:94-134893.
Audience: **g,l,u,f.**

Cervantes Saavedra, Miguel de **PQ6329.A2 1999**
Don Quixote de la Mancha. Charles Jarvis (Translator), Milan Kundera (Introduction by). Trade Cloth. Oxford University Press, Inc. New York, NY. 1999. 1126p. Oxford World's Classics Ser., Vol. 8 ISBN:0-19-210032-7, ISBN13: 978-0-19-210032-0. Dewey:863/.3. LCCN:99-461935.
Audience: **g,l,u,f.**

Cervantes Saavedra, Miguel de **PQ6329.A613 1992**
The Exemplary Novels, Vol. 4. Jones Staff & Macklin (Editors). Trade Cloth. Aris & Phillips. Oxford, 1992. 192p. ISBN:0-85668-497-X, ISBN13: 978-0-85668-497-5. Dewey:863/.3. LCCN:94-134893.
Audience: **g,l,u,f.**

Cervantes Saavedra, Miguel de **PQ6329.A6 P8 1982**
Three Exemplary Novels. Samuel Putnam (Translator), Luis Quintanilla (Illustrator). Trade Cloth. Greenwood Publishing Group, Inc. Portsmouth, NH. 1982. 232p. ISBN:0-313-23346-2, ISBN13: 978-0-313-23346-3. Dewey:863/.3. LCCN:81-020235.
Audience: **g,l,u,f.** B

Cervantes Saavedra, Miguel de **PQ6329.A2 1995**
The History of That Ingenious Gentleman, Don Quijote de la Mancha. Burton Raffel (Translator), Diana de Armas Wilson (Introduction by). Trade Cloth. W. W. Norton & Company, Inc. New York, NY. 1995. 800p. ISBN:0-393-03719-3, ISBN13: 978-0-393-03719-7. Dewey:863.3. LCCN:84-052573.
Audience: **g,l,u,f.** *Choice, 1996.*

Cervantes Saavedra, Miguel de **PQ6329.A2 1986**
The Adventures of Don Quixote de la Mancha. Tobias George Smollett (Translator), Carlos Fuentes (Introduction by). Trade Cloth. Farrar, Straus & Giroux. New York, NY. 1986. 845p. ISBN:0-374-14232-7, ISBN13: 978-0-374-14232-2. Dewey:863/.3. LCCN:85-002447.
Audience: **g,l,u,f.** B

Cervantes Saavedra, Miguel de **PQ6329.A613 1992**
The Exemplary Novels, Vol. 3. Thacker (Editor). Trade Cloth. Aris & Phillips. Oxford, 1992. 224p. ISBN:0-85668-495-3, ISBN13: 978-0-85668-495-1. Dewey:863/.3. LCCN:94-134893.
Audience: **g,l,u,f.**

Cervantes Saavedra, Miguel de **PQ6329.P4 1989**
The Trials of Persiles and Sigismunda: A Northern Story. Celia R. Weller & Clark A. Colahan (Translators). Trade Cloth. University of California Press. Berkeley, CA. 1989. 450p. ISBN:0-520-06315-5, ISBN13: 978-0-520-06315-0. Dewey:863/.3. LCCN:88-028187.
Audience: **g,l,u,f.** *Choice, 1990.*

Close, Anthony **PQ6352 .C615 1990**
Cervantes: "Don Quixote". Trade Cloth. Cambridge University Press. New York, NY. 1990. 146p. Landmarks of World Literature Ser. ISBN:0-521-32802-0, ISBN13: 978-0-521-32802-9. Dewey:863/.3. LCCN:89-022287.
Audience: **l,u,f.**

Close, Anthony **PQ6356.C66 2000**
Cervantes and the Comic Mind of His Age. Trade Cloth. Oxford University Press, Inc. New York, NY. 2000. 384p. ISBN:0-19-815998-6, ISBN13: 978-0-19-815998-8. Dewey:863/.3. LCCN:2001-265262.
Audience: **u,f.** *Choice, 2001.*

de Armas Wilson, Diana **PQ6353.W55 2000**
Cervantes, the Novel, and the New World. Trade Cloth. Oxford University Press, Inc. New York, NY. 2001. 270p. Oxford Hispanic Studies ISBN:0-19-816005-4, ISBN13: 978-0-19-816005-2. Dewey:863/.3. LCCN:2001-267036.
Audience: **u.** *Choice, 2002.*

Duran, Manuel & Rogg, Fay **PQ6352.D83 2006**
Fighting Windmills: Encounters with Don Quixote. Cloth over Boards. Yale University Press. Cumberland, RI. 2006. 288p. ISBN:0-300-11022-7, ISBN13: 978-0-300-11022-7. Dewey:863/.3. LCCN:2005-029715.
Audience: **u,f.**

Durán, Manuel **PQ6337.D84**
Cervantes. Trade Cloth. Thomson Gale. Farmington Hills, MI. 1974. 192p. World Authors Ser., No. 329 ISBN:0-8057-2206-8, ISBN13: 978-0-8057-2206-2. Dewey:863/.3. LCCN:74-007006.
Audience: **l,u,f.** B

El Saffar, Ruth **PQ6324.Z5**
Novel to Romance: A Study of Cervantes' Novelas Ejemplares. Trade Cloth. Johns Hopkins University Press. Baltimore, MD. 1984. 208p. ISBN:0-8018-1545-2, ISBN13: 978-0-8018-1545-4. Dewey:863/.3. LCCN:73-019332.
Audience: **u,f.** B

El Saffar, Ruth A. & Wilson, Diana D. (Editors) **PQ6358.P7.Q59 1993**
Quixotic Desire: Psychoanalytic Perspectives on Cervantes. Book, Other. Cornell University Press. Ithaca, NY. 1993. 352p. ISBN:0-8014-2823-8, ISBN13: 978-0-8014-2823-4. Dewey:863/.3. LCCN:93-013360.
Audience: **u,f.** *Choice, 1994.*

Fitzmaurice-Kelly, James **PQ6337.F54**
The Life of Miguel de Cervantes Saavedra: A Biographical, Literary and Historical Study. Trade Paper. Books on Demand. Ann Arbor, MI. 412p. ISBN:0-598-52519-X, ISBN13: 978-0-598-52519-2. Dewey:863/.3. LCCN:11-008640.
Audience: **g,l,u,f.**

Forcione, Alban K. **PQ6324.Z5**
Cervantes and the Humanist Vision: A Study of Four Exemplary Novels. Trade Cloth. Princeton University Press. Princeton, NJ. 1983. 700p. ISBN:0-691-06521-7, ISBN13: 978-0-691-06521-2. Dewey:863/.3. LCCN:82-047595.
Audience: **u,f.**

Forcione, Alban K. **PQ6324.C3**
Cervantes and the Mystery of Lawlessness: A Study of el Casamiento Enganoso y El Coloquio de los Perros. Trade Cloth. Princeton University Press. Princeton, NJ. 1984. 232p. ISBN:0-691-06588-8, ISBN13: 978-0-691-06588-5. Dewey:863/.3. LCCN:83-016129.
Audience: **u,f.**

Garces, Maria Antonia **PQ6338.A6G37 2002**
Cervantes in Algiers: A Captive's Tale. Trade Cloth. Vanderbilt University Press. Nashville, TN. 2002. 368p. ISBN:0-8265-1406-5, ISBN13: 978-0-8265-1406-6. Dewey:863/.3. LCCN:2002-004335.
Audience: **l,u,f.** *Choice, 2003.*

Gerli, E. Michael **PQ6356.G47 1995**
Refiguring Authority: Reading, Writing and Rewriting in Cervantes. Trade Cloth. University Press of Kentucky. Lexington, KY. 1996. 152p. ISBN:0-8131-1922-7, ISBN13: 978-0-8131-1922-9. Dewey:863/.3. LCCN:95-016577.
Audience: **u,f.** *Choice, 1996.*

Gilman, Stephen **PQ6353.G47 1989**
The Novel According to Cervantes. Roy H. Pearce (Foreword by). Trade Cloth. University of California Press. Berkeley, CA. 1989. 221p. ISBN:0-520-06231-0, ISBN13: 978-0-520-06231-3. Dewey:863/.3. LCCN:88-023458.
Audience: **u,f.** *Choice, 1990.*

Gonzalez Echevarria, Roberto (Editor) **PQ6352.C37 2005**
Cervantes' Don Quixote: A Casebook. Trade Cloth. Oxford University Press, Inc. New York, NY. 2005. 304p. Casebooks in Criticism Ser. ISBN:0-19-516937-9, ISBN13: 978-0-19-516937-9. Dewey:863/.3. LCCN:2004-063569.
Audience: **u,f.**

Gonzalez Echevarria, Roberto **PQ6351.G66 2005**
Love and the Law in Cervantes. Saddle Stitched, Cloth over Boards, Dust Jacket. Yale University Press. Cumberland, RI. 2005. 320p. ISBN:0-300-10992-X, ISBN13: 978-0-300-10992-4. Dewey:863/.3. LCCN:2005-041844.
Audience: **u,f.** *Choice, 2006.*

Hart, Thomas R. **PQ6324.Z5H37 1994**
Cervantes' Exemplary Fictions: A Study of the Novelas Ejemplares. Trade Cloth. University Press of Kentucky. Lexington, KY. 1993. 136p. Studies in Romance Languages, Vol. 36 ISBN:0-8131-1845-X, ISBN13: 978-0-8131-1845-1. Dewey:863/.3. LCCN:93-004867.
Audience: **u,f.**

Johnson, Carroll B. **PQ6352**
Madness and Lust: A Psychoanalytic Approach to Don Quixote. Trade Cloth. University of California Press. Berkeley, CA. 1983. 252p. ISBN:0-520-04752-4, ISBN13: 978-0-520-04752-5. Dewey:863/.3. LCCN:82-010916.
Audience: **u,f.**

Mancing, Howard **PQ6337**
The Cervantes Encyclopedia. Cloth Text. Greenwood Publishing Group, Inc. Portsmouth, NH. 2003. 864p. ISBN:0-313-30695-8, ISBN13: 978-0-313-30695 2. Dewey:863/.3. LCCN:2003-054725.
Audience: **g,l,u,f.** *Choice, 2004.*

Mancing, Howard **PQ6352.M24 2006**
Cervantes' Don Quixote: A Reference Guide. Trade Cloth. Greenwood Publishing Group, Inc. Portsmouth, NH. 2006. 248p. Greenwood Guides to Multicultural Literature Ser. ISBN:0-313-33347-5, ISBN13: 978-0-313-33347-7. Dewey:863/.3. LCCN:2005-037029.
Audience: **l,u,f.**

Nelson, L. **PQ6337 .N4**
Cervantes: A Collection of Critical Essays. Trade Cloth. Prentice-Hall. Upper Saddle, NJ. 1969. 176p. ISBN:0-13-123299-1, ISBN13: 978-0-13-123299-0. Dewey:863/.3. LCCN:77-090972.
Audience: **u,f.**

Presberg, Charles D. **PQ6353.P72 2003**
Adventures in Paradox: Don Quixote and the Western Tradition. Trade Paper. Pennsylvania State University Press. University Park, PA. 2003. 264p. ISBN:0-271-02364-3, ISBN13: 978-0-271-02364-9. Dewey:863.3.
Audience: **u,f.**

Quint, David **PQ6352.Q57 2005**
Cervante's Novel of Modern Times: A New Reading of Don Quijote. Trade Paper. Princeton University Press. Princeton, NJ. 2005. 192p. ISBN:0-691-12227-X, ISBN13: 978-0-691-12227-4. Dewey:863.3.
Audience: **u,f.**

Riley, E. C. **PQ6352.R48 1985**
Don Quixote. Claude Rawson (Editor). Cloth Text. Routledge. New York, NY. 1986. 192p. Unwin Critical Library ISBN:0-04-800009-4, ISBN13: 978-0-04-800009-5. Dewey:863/.3. LCCN:85-011179.
Audience: **u,f.**

Russell, P. E. **PQ6352.R87 1985**
Cervantes. Trade Cloth. Oxford University Press, Inc. New York, NY. 1985. 117p. Past Masters Ser. ISBN:0-19-287570-1, ISBN13: 978-0-19-287570-9. Dewey:863/.3. LCCN:85-010673.
Audience: **u,f.**

Saffar, Ruth E. **PQ6351.C75 1986**
Critical Essays on Cervantes. Trade Cloth. Thomson Gale. Farmington Hills, MI. 1986. 240p. Critical Essays on World Literature Ser. ISBN:0-8161-8825-4, ISBN13: 978-0-8161-8825-3. Dewey:863/.3. LCCN:85-024809.
Audience: **u,f.** *Choice, 1986.*

Wilson, Dianne **PQ6327.P5W55 1991**
Allegories of Love: Cervante's Persiles and Sigismunda. Trade Cloth. Princeton University Press. Princeton, NJ. 1991. 280p. ISBN:0-691-06854-2, ISBN13: 978-0-691-06854-1. Dewey:863/.3. LCCN:90-040841.
Audience: **u,f.** *Choice, 1991.*

Hispanic Literature > Spanish Literature: Individual Authors and Works > To 1700 > G-Q

Appelbaum, Stanley (Editor, Translator) **PQ6408.E5 2001**
Lazarillo de Tormes. Trade Paper. Dover Publications, Inc. Mineola, NY. 2001. 128p. A Dual-Language Book Ser. ISBN:0-486-41431-0, ISBN13: 978-0-486-41431-7. Dewey:863/.3. LCCN:00-064342.
Audience: **g,l,u,f.**

Arias, Joan **PQ6272.Z5 A7**
Guzman de Alfarache: The Unrepentant Narrator. Joseph Silverman (Preface by). Trade Cloth. Boydell & Brewer, Ltd. Woodbridge, 1977. 106p. Series A: Monagrafias, LVIII ISBN:0-7293-0033-1, ISBN13: 978-0-7293-0033-9. Dewey:863/.3. LCCN:78-377053.
Audience: **l,u,f.**

Aullón de Haro, Pedro **PQ6407.A1 1982**
Lazarillo de Tormes. Trade Cloth. Playor, Editorial, S.A.. Madrid, 1982. 136p. Clasicos Comentados Playor Ser., Vol. 7 ISBN:84-359-0290-0, ISBN13: 978-84-359-0290-8. Dewey:863/.3. LCCN:83-144877.
Audience: **u,f.**

De Leon, Fray Luis **PQ6410.L3.A5 1979**
The Unknown Light. Willis Barnstone (Editor). Cloth Text. State University of New York Press. Albany, NY. 1979. 175p. ISBN:0-87395-394-0, ISBN13: 978-0-87395-394-8. Dewey:861/.3. LCCN:79-015030.
Audience: **l,u,f.** B

De Manrique, Jorge **PQ6412.M5A17 1988**
Poesia Completa - Manrique. Trade Cloth. GeoPlaneta, Editorial, S. A.. Barcelona, 1988. 192p. ISBN:84-320-3985-3, ISBN13: 978-84-320-3985-0. Dewey:861/.2. LCCN:92-230124.
Audience: **u,f.**

De Molina, Tirso **PQ6435.E5**
Tirso de Molina: The Trickster of Seville and the Stone Guest. Edwards (Editor). Trade Cloth. Aris & Phillips. Oxford, 1986. 200p. Hispanic Classics Ser. ISBN:0-85668-300-0, ISBN13: 978-0-85668-300-8. Dewey:862/.3.
Audience: **g,l,u,f.**

De Molina, Tirso **PQ6434 .C613 1986**
Tirso de Molina: Damned for Despair. Ed. 2. Nicholas G. Round (Editor). Trade Paper. Aris & Phillips. Oxford, 2001. 200p. Hispanic Classics Ser. ISBN:0-85668-330-2, ISBN13: 978-0-85668-330-5. Dewey:862/.3. LCCN:87-131994.
Audience: **l,u,f.** *Choice, 1987.*

De Montemayor, Jorge **PQ6414.A35 1989**
The Diana. RoseAnna Mueller (Translator). Trade Cloth. Edwin Mellen Press, The. Lewiston, NY. 1989. 229p. Spanish Studies, Vol 1 ISBN:0-88946-735-8, ISBN13: 978-0-88946-735-4. Dewey:863/.3. LCCN:88-001730.
Audience: **l,u,f.**

De Quevedo, Francisco **PQ6422**
Sueños y discursos. Crosby, James (Editor). Editorial Castalia. 2002.
Audience: **u,f.**

De Quevedo, Francisco **PQ6422.A2 1989**
Francisco de Quevedo: Dreams and Discourses. R. K. Britton (Editor). Trade Cloth. Aris & Phillips. Oxford, 1989. 358p. Hispanic Classics Ser. ISBN:0-85668-352-3, ISBN13: 978-0-85668-352-7. Dewey:868/.307. LCCN:88-149645.
Audience: **g,l,u,f.**

Fiore, Robert L. **PQ6409.F56 1984**
Lazarillo de Tormes. Trade Cloth. Thomson Gale. Farmington Hills, MI. 1984. 150p. World Authors Ser., No. 714 ISBN:0-8057-6561-1, ISBN13: 978-0-8057-6561-8. Dewey:863/.3. LCCN:83-022633.
Audience: **l,u,f.** B

Gongora y Argote, Luis de **PQ6394.S6E5**
The Solitudes of Luis de Gongora. the Spanish Text, with an English Translation by Gilbert F. Cunningham. Pref. by A. A. Parker. Introd. by Elias L. Rivers. Trade Paper. Books on Demand. Ann Arbor, MI. 168p. ISBN:0-598-24685-1, ISBN13: 978-0-598-24685-1. Dewey:861/.3. LCCN:68-018492.
Audience: **u,f.**

Gracian, Baltasar **PQ6398**
The Art of Worldly Wisdom. Joseph Jacobs (Translator), Willis Barnstone (Introduction by). Trade Cloth. Shambhala Publications, Inc. Boston, MA. 2004. 208p. ISBN:1-59030-141-2, ISBN13: 978-1-59030-141-8. Dewey:868/.302.
Audience: **l,u,f.**

Gracian, Baltasar & Maurer, Christopher **PQ6398.G3A613 1996**
The Pocket Mirror of Heroes. Trade Cloth. Doubleday Publishing. New York, NY. 1995. 172p. ISBN:0-385-48021-0, ISBN13: 978-0-385-48021-5. Dewey:868/.309. LCCN:95-032754.
Audience: **l,u,f.**

Johnson, Carroll B. **PQ6272.Z5**
Inside Guzman De Alfarache. Trade Paper. University of California Press. Berkeley, CA. 1978. 258p. Publications in Modern Philology, Vol. 111 ISBN:0-520-09569-3, ISBN13: 978-0-520-09569-4. Dewey:863/.3. LCCN:76-055569.
Audience: **l,u,f.**

Manuel, Juan **PQ6401.Z85A9 1989**
Cinco Tratados. Reinaldo Ayerbe-Chaux (Editor). Trade Cloth. Hispanic Seminary of Medieval Studies. New York, NY. 1989. lxiv, 270p. Spanish Ser., No. 51 ISBN:0-940639-36-X, ISBN13: 978-0-940639-36-2. Dewey:863/.1. LCCN:89-180170.
Audience: **u,f.**

Manuel, Juan, et al. **PQ6401.E5**
The Book of Count Lucanor and Patronio: A Translation of Don Juan Manuel's El Conde Lucanor. John E. Keller & Louis Clark Keating (Authors). Trade Paper. Books on Demand. Ann Arbor, MI. 207p. Studies in Romance Languages, Vol. 16 ISBN:0-7837-5812-X, ISBN13: 978-0-7837-5812-1. Dewey:863.1. LCCN:76-024342.
Audience: **g,l,u,f.**

Mator, Carlos A. **PQ6272.Z5R74 1985**
El Narrador Picaro: Guzman de Alfarache. Trade Cloth. Hispanic Seminary of Medieval Studies. New York, NY. 1985. vi, 132p. ISBN:0-942260-51-1, ISBN13: 978-0-942260-51-9. Dewey:863.3. LCCN:85-180499.
Audience: **u,f.**

Montemayor, Jorge de **PQ6414.A2 1976**
Los Siete Libros de la Diana. Trade Cloth. Nacional, Editora. Madrid, 1976. lv, 277 p. ;p. ISBN:84-276-1296-6, ISBN13: 978-84-276-1296-9. Dewey:863/.3. LCCN:76-476593.
Audience: **u,f.**

Olivares, Julian **PQ6424.Z5**
The Love Poetry of Francisco de Quevedo: An Aesthetic and Existential Study. Trade Cloth. Cambridge University Press. New York, NY. 1983. 192p. Cambridge Iberian and Latin American Studies ISBN:0-521-24362-9, ISBN13: 978-0-521-24362-9. Dewey:861/.3. LCCN:82-014702.
Audience: **g,l,u,f.**

Ortega y Gasset, Jose **PQ6352.O67813 2000**
Meditations on Quixote: Translated from the Spanish by Evelyn Rugg and Diego Marin Introduction and Notes by Julian Marias. Evelyn Rugg & Diego Marin (Translators), Julian Marias (Introduction by, Notes by). Trade Paper. University of Illinois Press. Champaign, IL. 2000. 192p. ISBN:0-252-06895-5, ISBN13: 978-0-252-06895-9. Dewey:863/.3. LCCN:99-057812.
Audience: **l,u,f.**

Osuna, Alfonso J. Garcia (Editor) **PQ6408.E5 2005**
The Life of Lazarillo de Tormes: A Critical Edition Including the Original Spanish Text. Paper Text. McFarland & Company, Incorporated Publishers. Jefferson, NC. 2005. 160p. ISBN:0-7864-2134-7, ISBN13: 978-0-7864-2134-3. Dewey:863/.3. LCCN:2005-010592.
Audience: **l,u,f.**

Quevedo **PQ6421 .A5 1969**
An Anthology of Quevedo's Poetry. R. M. Price (Editor). Cloth Text. Manchester University Press. Manchester, 1988. 142p. Spanish Texts Ser. ISBN:0-7190-0384-9, ISBN13: 978-0-7190-0384-4. Dewey:861/.3. LCCN:70-494584.
Audience: **g,l,u,f.**

Scholberg, Kenneth R. **PQ6412.M3Z87 1984**
Introduccion a la Poesia de Gomez Manrique. Trade Cloth. Hispanic Seminary of Medieval Studies. New York, NY. 1983. iv, 110p. Spanish Ser., No. 14 ISBN:0-942260-40-6, ISBN13: 978-0-942260-40-3. Dewey:861/.2. LCCN:84-239829.
Audience: **u,f.**

Hispanic Literature > Spanish Literature: Individual Authors and Works > To 1700 > Rojas

Damiani, Bruno M. (Introduction by) **PQ6426.A1 1991**
La Celestina. Trade Cloth. Scripta Humanistica. Potomac, MD. 1990. 302p. ISBN:0-916379-86-8, ISBN13: 978-0-916379-86-5. Dewey:862/.2. LCCN:91-154147.
Audience: **u,f.**

Dunn, Peter N. **PQ6428.D8**
Fernando de Rojas. Trade Cloth. Thomson Gale. Farmington Hills, MI. 1975. 191 p. ;p. ISBN:0-8057-6218-3, ISBN13: 978-0-8057-6218-1. Dewey:868/.2/09. LCCN:75-009838.
Audience: **l,u,f.**

Gilman, Stephen **PQ6428.G5**
The Art of la Celestina. Trade Paper. Books on Demand. Ann Arbor, MI. 273p. ISBN:0-598-82164-3, ISBN13: 978-0-598-82164-5. Dewey:862.2. LCCN:55-009089.
Audience: **u,f.**

Gilman, Stephen **PQ6428.G53**
The Spain of Fernando de Rojas; the Intellectual and Social Landscape of la Celestina. Trade Cloth. Princeton University Press. Princeton, NJ. 1972. xv, 559p. ISBN:0-691-06202-1, ISBN13: 978-0-691-06202-0. Dewey:862/.2. LCCN:76-151530.
Audience: **u,f.**

Lida De Malkiel, Maria Rosa **PQ6430.L5**
Two Spanish Masterpieces: The Book of Good Love, and the Celestina. Trade Paper. Books on Demand. Ann Arbor, MI. 116p. Illinois University Language and Culture Ser., Vol. 49 ISBN:0-598-39368-4, ISBN13: 978-0-598-39368-5. Dewey:860.9. LCCN:61-062764.
Audience: **g,l,u,f.**

Rojas, Fernando de **PQ6426.A1 1974**
La Celestina: Tragicomedia de Calisto y Melibea. Ed. 3. Trade Cloth. Alianza Editorial, S. A.. Madrid, 272p. ISBN:84-206-1200 6, ISBN13: 978-84-206-1200-3. Dewey:862/.2. LCCN:76-459653.
Audience: **u,f.**

Rojas, Fernando de **PQ6426.A1 1985**
La Celestina: Tragicomedia de Calisto y Melibea: Edicion Critica. Miguel Marciales (Editor). Trade Cloth. University of Illinois Press. Champaign, IL. 1985. 320p. Illinois Medieval Monographs ISBN:0-252-01201-1, ISBN13: 978-0-252-01201-3. Dewey:862/.2. LCCN:85-008606.
Audience: **u,f.**

Rojas, Fernando de **PQ6426.A1 1985**
La Celestina: Tragicomedia de Calisto y Melibea: Introduccion. Miguel Marciales (Editor). Trade Cloth. University of Illinois Press. Champaign, IL. 1985. 398p. Illinois Medieval Monographs ISBN:0-252-01200-3, ISBN13: 978-0-252-01200-6. Dewey:862/.2. LCCN:85-008606.
Audience: **u,f.**

Rojas, Fernando de **PQ6427.E5**
Fernando Rojas: Celestina. Severin (Editor). Trade Cloth. Aris & Phillips. Oxford, 1987. 400p. Hispanic Classics Ser. ISBN:0-85668-344-2, ISBN13: 978-0-85668-344-2. Dewey:862/.2.
Audience: **u,f.**

Severin, Dorothy S. **PQ6428.S44 1989**
Tragicomedy and Novelistic Discourse in Celestina. Trade Cloth. Cambridge University Press. New York, NY. 1989. 160p. Cambridge Iberian and Latin American Studies ISBN:0-521-35085-9, ISBN13: 978-0-521-35085-3. Dewey:862/.2. LCCN:89-000496.
Audience: **u,f.** *Choice, 1990.*

Hispanic Literature > Spanish Literature: Individual Authors and Works > To 1700 > R-V

Larson, Donald R. **PQ6490.H7**
The Honor Plays of Lope De Vega. Trade Cloth. Harvard University Press. Cambridge, MA. 1978. 272p. ISBN:0-674-40628-1, ISBN13: 978-0-674-40628-5. Dewey:862/.3. LCCN:77-022950.
Audience: **u,f.** B

Lida De Malkiel, Maria Rosa **PQ6430.L5**
Two Spanish Masterpieces: The Book of Good Love, and the Celestina. Trade Paper. Books on Demand. Ann Arbor, MI. 116p. Illinois University Language and Culture Ser., Vol. 49 ISBN:0-598-39368-4, ISBN13: 978-0-598-39368-5. Dewey:860.9. LCCN:61-062764.
Audience: **g,l,u,f.** B

Ruiz de Alarcon, Juan **PQ7296.R8**
La Verdad Sospechosa. Trade Cloth. Oceano Grupo Editoria, S.A.. Barcelona, 2003. 152p. ISBN:84-7505-901-5, ISBN13: 978-84-7505-901-3. Dewey:862.
Audience: **u,f.**

Ruiz de Alarcón, Juan **PQ6431.R8V4 1976**
La Verdad Sospechosa. Trade Cloth. Ediciones Cátedra. Madrid 1, 144p. ISBN:84-376-0076-6, ISBN13: 978-84-376-0076-5. Dewey:862/.3. LCCN:77-451024.
Audience: **u,f.**

Ruiz, Juan **PQ6430.A5E5**
The Book of Good Love: Of the Archpriest of Hita, Juan Ruiz. Trade Paper. Books on Demand. Ann Arbor, MI. 344p. ISBN:0-598-88716-4, ISBN13: 978-0-598-88716-0. Dewey:861.1. LCCN:34-000277.
Audience: **u,f.**

Ruiz, Juan **PQ6430.A1 1992**
El Libro de Buen Amor. Trade Cloth. Ediciones Cátedra. Madrid 1, 736p. ISBN:84-376-1011-7, ISBN13: 978-84-376-1011-5. Dewey:861/.1. LCCN:94-192375.
Audience: **u,f.** B

Ruiz, Juan **PQ6430.A1 1972**
El Libro de Buen Amor. R. S. Willis (Introduction by). Trade Cloth. Princeton University Press. Princeton, NJ. 1972. 536p. ISBN:0-691-06086-X, ISBN13: 978-0-691-06086-6. Dewey:861/.1. LCCN:77-181876.
Audience: **u,f.** B

Ruiz, Juan **PQ6430.A1 1989**
El Libro del Arcipreste, Tambien Llamado Libro de Buen Amor: Edicion Sinoptica. Anthony N. Zahareas (Introduction by). Trade Cloth. Hispanic Seminary of Medieval Studies. New York, NY. 1989. lxvi, 230p. Spanish Ser., No. 44 ISBN:0-940639-28-9, ISBN13: 978-0-940639-28-7. Dewey:861/.1. LCCN:89-150788.
Audience: **u,f.**

Sieber, Harry **PQ6409.S53**
Language and Society in la Vida de Lazarillo de Tormes. Trade Paper. Books on Demand. Ann Arbor, MI. 128p. ISBN:0-608-06144-1, ISBN13: 978-0-608-06144-3. Dewey:863/.3. LCCN:78-008425.
Audience: **u,f.**

Hispanic Literature > Spanish Literature: Individual Authors and Works > To 1700 > Vega

Gicovate, Bernard **PQ6392.G5**
Garcilaso de la Vega. Library Binding. Thomson Gale. Farmington Hills, MI. 1975. 166p. World Authors Ser., No. 349 ISBN:0-8057-2342-0, ISBN13: 978-0-8057-2342-7. Dewey:861.3. LCCN:74-028304.
Audience: **u,f.** B

Heiple, Daniel L. **PQ6392.H45 1994**
Garcilaso de la Vega and the Italian Renaissance. Trade Cloth. Pennsylvania State University Press. University Park, PA. 1994. xv, 428p. Studies in Romance Literatures ISBN:0-271-01016-9, ISBN13: 978-0-271-01016-8. Dewey:861/.3. LCCN:93-014208.
Audience: **u,f.** *Choice, 1995.*

Vega, Garcilaso de la **E125.S7.G26**
The Florida of the Inca; A History of the Adelantado, Hernando de Soto, Governor and Captain General of the Kingdom of Florida, and of Other Heroic Spanish and Indian Cavaliers, Written by the Inca, Garcilaso de la Vega, An Officer of His Majesty, and a Native of the Great City of Cuzco, Capital of the Realms and Provinces of Peru University of Texas Press. 1951.
Audience: f.

Vega, Lope de **PQ6439.F75 1973**
Fuenteovejuna. Ed. 2. Trade Cloth. Castalia, Editorial S.A.. Madrid, 361p. Clasicos Castalia, :Siglo XVII ISBN:84-7039-083-X, ISBN13: 978-84-7039-083-8. Dewey:862/.3. LCCN:75-575377.
Audience: **u,f.**

Vega, Lope de **PQ6438.A2 1978**
El Mejor Alcalde, el Rey Fuenteovejuna. Trade Cloth. Espasa Calpe, S.A.. Madrid, 174p. ISBN:84-239-2043-7, ISBN13: 978-84-239-2043-3. Dewey:862/.3. LCCN:79-375327.
Audience: **u,f.**

Vega, Lope de **PQ6391 .A1 1984**
Obras Completas. Other. Plaza & Janés Editories, S.A.. Barcelona, 315p. ISBN:84-01-90522-2, ISBN13: 978-84-01-90522-3. Dewey:861.3. LCCN:92-180440.
Audience: **u,f.**

Vega, Lope de **PQ6439.F7513 1989**
Lope de Vega Carpio: Fuente Ovejuna. Victor Dixon (Editor). Trade Cloth. Aris & Phillips. Oxford, 1989. 223p. Hispanic Classics Ser. ISBN:0-85668-327-2, ISBN13: 978-0-85668-327-5. Dewey:862/.3. LCCN:90-126664.
Audience: **u,f.**

Vega, Lope de **PQ6459.A2 1999**
Three Major Plays. Gwynne Edwards (Translator). Trade Paper. Oxford University Press, Inc. New York, NY. 1999. 342p. Oxford World's Classics Ser. ISBN:0-19-283337-5, ISBN13: 978-0-19-283337-2. Dewey:862/.3. LCCN:98-026991.
Audience: **g,l,u.**

Vega, Lope de **PQ6439.C2**
The Knight of Olmedo/El Caballero de Olmedo. Willard F. King (Editor). Trade Paper. Books on Demand. Ann Arbor, MI. 214p. ISBN:0-7837-1466-1, ISBN13: 978-0-7837-1466-0. Dewey:862.3. LCCN:78-186118.
Audience: **g,l,u.**

Vega, Lope de & Zorrilla, Rojas **PQ6438**
Three Spanish Golden Age Plays: The Duchess of Amalfi's Steward/The Capulets and Montagues/Cleopatra. Gwynne Edwards (Translator). Trade Paper, Perfect. Methuen Publishing Ltd. London, 2005. 337p. ISBN:0-413-77475-9, ISBN13: 978-0-413-77475-0. Dewey:862.308.
Audience: **l,u,f.**

Hispanic Literature > Spanish Literature: Individual Authors and Works > To 1700 > S-Z

Zayas y Sotomayor, María de **PQ6498.Z5N6813 1990**
The Enchantments of Love: Amorous and Exemplary Novels. E-Book. NetLibrary, Inc. Boulder, CO. 1990. ISBN:0-585-30765-2, ISBN13: 978-0-585-30765-7. Dewey:863/.3.
Audience: **g,l,u,f.**

Zayas, Maria De **PQ6498.Z5N6813 1990**
The Enchantments of Love: Amorous and Exemplary Novels. H. Patsy Boyer (Translator). Trade Cloth. University of California Press. Berkeley, CA. 1990. 354p. ISBN:0-520-06671-5, ISBN13: 978-0-520-06671-7. Dewey:863/.3. LCCN:89-036559.
Audience: **g,l,u,f.**

Hispanic Literature > Spanish Literature: Individual Authors and Works > 1700-1868

Alarcón, Pedro Antonio de **PQ6502.A25 2001**
The Three-Cornered Hat and Captain Poison: A Dual Language Book. Stanley Appelbaum (Editor). Trade Paper. Dover Publications, Inc. Mineola, NY. 2002. 271p. A Dual-Language Book Ser. ISBN:0-486-41943-6, ISBN13: 978-0-486-41943-5. Dewey:863/.5. LCCN:2001-028751.
Audience: **g,l,u,f.**

Alas Leopoldo Clarín, Leopoldo (Clarin) **PQ6503.A4S8**
Su Unico Hijo. Trade Paper. Books on Demand. Ann Arbor, MI. 438p. ISBN:0-608-34414-1, ISBN13: 978-0-608-34414-0. Dewey:863.5. LCCN:45-000767.
Audience: **u,f.**

Alas Leopoldo Clarín, Leopoldo (Clarin) **PQ6503.A4.R313 1984**
La Regenta. John Rutherford (Translator). Trade Cloth. University of Georgia Press. Athens, GA. 1984. 736p. ISBN:0-8203-0700-9, ISBN13: 978-0-8203-0700-8. Dewey:863.5. LCCN:83-017886.
Audience: **g,l,u,f.**

Becquer, Gustavo Adolfo **PQ6503.B3A6 2006**
Rhymes and Legends (Selection) / Rimas y Leyendas (seleccion): A Dual-Language Book. Stanley Appelbaum (Editor). Trade Paper. Dover Publications, Inc. Mineola, NY. 2006. 224p. ISBN:0-486-44788-X, ISBN13: 978-0-486-44788-9. Dewey:861/.5. LCCN:2006-040178.
Audience: **g,l,u,f.**

Bécquer, Gustavo Adolfo **PQ6503.B3A6 1982**
Rimas ; Leyendas ; Cartas Desde Mi Celda. María del Pilar Palomo (Translator). Trade Cloth. Editorial Planeta, S. A.. Barcelona 8, 1982. 256p. Clasicos Universales Planeta Ser., Vol. 43 ISBN:84-320-3874-1, ISBN13: 978-84-320-3874-7. Dewey:861/.5. LCCN:87-672677.
Audience: **u,f.**

Bécquer, Gustavo Adolpho **PQ6503.B3L4 1979**
Leyendas. Trade Cloth. Alianza Editorial, S. A.. Madrid, 320p. ISBN:84-206-1745-8, ISBN13: 978-84-206-1745-9. Dewey:863/.5. LCCN:80-124702.
Audience: **u,f.**

Bécquer, Gustavo Adolpho **PQ6503.B3 R5 1975**
Rimas y Leyendas. Trade Cloth. Ediciones Cátedra. Madrid 1, 112p. ISBN:84-376-0052-9, ISBN13: 978-84-376-0052-9. Dewey:861.5. LCCN:76-480428.
Audience: **u,f.**

Bécquer, Gustavo Adolpho **PQ6503.B3L4 1988**
Leyendas. Ed. 2. Estrada F. Lopez (Editor). Trade Paper. Espasa Calpe, S.A.. Madrid, 1991. 358p. Nueva Austral Ser., No. 36 ISBN:84-239-1836-X, ISBN13: 978-84-239-1836-2. Dewey:863/.5. LCCN:89-124012.
Audience: **u,f.**

Cadalso, Jose **PQ6510.C3.C3 1975**
Cartas Marruecas. Trade Cloth. Nacional, Editora. Madrid, 1975. 284p. ISBN:84-276-1287-7, ISBN13: 978-84-276-1287-7. Dewey:868/.4/09. LCCN:76-473449.
Audience: **u,f.**

Campoamor, Ramón de **PQ6511.A17 1974**
Poesias. Trade Cloth. Ramon Sopena Editorial S.A.. Barcelona, 1974. ISBN:84-303-0549-1, ISBN13: 978-84-303-0549-0. Dewey:861/.5. LCCN:76-478221.
Audience: **u,f.**

Castro, Rosalia de, et al. **PQ6512.C226A23 1991**
Ⓔ Poems. Anna-Marie Aldaz, Barbara N. Gantt & Anne C. Bromley (Authors). E-Book. NetLibrary, Inc. Boulder, CO. 1991. ISBN:0-585-06935-2, ISBN13: 978-0-585-06935-7. Dewey:861/.5.
Audience: **g,l,u,f.**

Castro, Rosalia de **PQ6512.C226A23 1991**
Poems. Barbara N. Gantt (Editor), Anna-Marie Aldaz, Barbara N. Gantt & Anne C. Bromley (Translators), Anna-Marie Aldaz (Introduction by), Anne C. Bromley & Joseph Boles (Foreword by). Trade Cloth. State University of New York Press. Albany, NY. 1991. 216p. SUNY Series, Women Writers in Translation ISBN:0-7914-0582-6, ISBN13: 978-0-7914-0582-6. Dewey:861/.5. LCCN:90-009895.
Audience: **g,l,u,f.**

Castro, Rosalía de **PQ6512.C226E6 1978**
En Las Orillas Del Sar. Marina Mayoral (Translator). Trade Cloth. Castalia, Editorial S.A.. Madrid, 1978. 180p. Clasicos Castalia Ser., Vol. 90 ISBN:84-7039-279-4, ISBN13: 978-84-7039-279-5. Dewey:861/.5. LCCN:78-369291.
Audience: **u,f.**

Cox, R. Merritt **PQ6538.M5.Z62**
Juan Melendez Valdes. Library Binding. Thomson Gale. Farmington Hills, MI. 1974. 179p. World Authors Ser. ISBN:0-8057-2918-6, ISBN13: 978-0-8057-2918-4. Dewey:861/.4. LCCN:73-015583.
Audience: **l,u,f.** B

De Larra, Mariano J. **PQ6533.A84 1989**
Articulos de Costumbres. Luis F. Diaz Larios (Editor). Trade Cloth. Espasa Calpe, S.A.. Madrid, 1991. 456p. Nueva Austral Ser., Vol. 99 ISBN:84-239-1899-8, ISBN13: 978-84-239-1899-7. Dewey:863. LCCN:90-191065.
Audience: **u,f.**

De Torres Villarroel, Diego **PQ6570.T6Z478 1989**
Vida. Manuel M. Perez Lopez (Editor). Trade Cloth. Elliot's Books. Northford, CT. 1991. 328p. Nueva Austral Ser., Vol. 90 ISBN:84-239-1890-4, ISBN13: 978-84-239-1890-4. Dewey:868/.409 B. LCCN:90-145061.
Audience: **u,f.**

DeCoster, Cyrus **PQ6573.Z5.D4**
Juan Valera. Library Binding. Irvington Publishers. New York, NY. 1974. 186p. Twayne's World Authors Ser. ISBN:0-8057-2919-4, ISBN13: 978-0-8057-2919-1. Dewey:868/.5/09. LCCN:74-003058.
Audience: **l,u,f.** B

Galdós, Benito Pérez **PQ6555.F7E5 1986**
Fortunata and Jacinta: Two Stories of Married Women. Agnes M. Gullon (Translator). Trade Cloth. University of Georgia Press. Athens, GA. 1986. 840p. ISBN:0-8203-0783-1, ISBN13: 978-0-8203-0783-1. Dewey:863/.5. LCCN:84-028063.
Audience: **g,l,u,f.** B *Choice, 1987.*

Galdós, Benito Pérez **PQ6555.A25 1986**
Torquemada. Frances M. Lopez-Morillas (Translator). Cloth Text. Columbia University Press. New York, NY. 1986. 569p. ISBN:0-231-06228-1, ISBN13: 978-0-231-06228-2. Dewey:863/.5. LCCN:85-019560.
Audience: **g,l,u,f.** *Choice, 1986.*

Galdós, Benito Pérez **PQ6555.N413 1997**
Nazarin. Robert Rudder & Gloria Arjona (Translators). Paper Text. Latin American Literary Review Press. Pittsburgh, PA. 1997. 200p. Discoveries Ser. ISBN:0-935480-75-7, ISBN13: 978-0-935480-75-7. Dewey:863/.5. LCCN:97-017339.
Audience: **l,u,f.**

Galdós, Benito Pérez **PQ6555.A74513 1987**
Our Friend Manso. Robert H. Russell (Translator). Trade Cloth. Columbia University Press. New York, NY. 1987. 261p. ISBN:0-231-06404-7, ISBN13: 978-0-231-06404-0. Dewey:863/.5. LCCN:86-014758.
Audience: **l,u,f.** *Choice, 1987.*

Gilman, Stephen **PQ6555.Z5**
Galdos and the Art of the European Novel. Trade Cloth. Princeton University Press. Princeton, NJ. 1981. 416p. ISBN:0-691-06456-3, ISBN13: 978-0-691-06456-7. Dewey:863/.5. LCCN:80-008550.
Audience: **u,f.**

Gold, Hazel **PQ6555.Z5.G65 1993**
The Reframing of Realism: Galdos and the Discourses of the Nineteenth-Century Spanish Novel. Cloth Text. Duke University Press. Durham, NC. 1993. 255p. ISBN:0-8223-1334-0, ISBN13: 978-0-8223-1334-2. Dewey:863.5. LCCN:92-039376.
Audience: **u,f.** *Choice, 1994.*

Guillén, Jorge **PQ6503.B3A6**
La Poetica de Becquer. Trade Paper. Books on Demand. Ann Arbor, MI. 59p. ISBN:0-598-71530-4, ISBN13: 978-0-598-71530-2. Dewey:861.5.
Audience: **u,f.**

Klibbe, Lawrence H. **PQ6554.P3.Z7**
Jose Maria de Pereda. Library Binding. Thomson Gale. Farmington Hills, MI. 1975. 185p. World Authors Ser. ISBN:0-8057-2687-X, ISBN13: 978-0-8057-2687-9. Dewey:863/.5. LCCN:74-017390.
Audience: **g,l,u,f.** B

Melendez Valdes, Juan **PQ6538.M5 A17 1991**
Poesias. Cesar Real Ramos (Editor). Trade Cloth. Elliot's Books. Northford, CT. 1991. 328p. Nueva Austral Ser., Vol. 217 ISBN:84-239-7217-8, ISBN13: 978-84-239-7217-3. Dewey:861.4. LCCN:94-197960.
Audience: **u,f.**

Pattison, Walter T. **PQ6555.Z5.P28**
Benito Perez Galdos. Library Binding. Thomson Gale. Farmington Hills, MI. 1975. 181p. World Authors Ser., No. 341 ISBN:0-8057-2689-6, ISBN13: 978-0-8057-2689-3. Dewey:863/.5. LCCN:74-020650.
Audience: **u,f.** B

Pérez Galdós, Benito **PQ6555.A745**
El Amigo Manso. Ed. 3. Trade Paper. Books on Demand. Ann Arbor, MI. 372p. ISBN:0-598-80282-7, ISBN13: 978-0-598-80282-8. Dewey:863.5. LCCN:31-007650.
Audience: **l,u,f.**

Pérez Galdós, Benito **PQ6555.A8**
Angel Guerra, Vol. 1. Trade Paper. Books on Demand. Ann Arbor, MI. 374p. ISBN:0-598-53386-9, ISBN13: 978-0-598-53386-9. Dewey:863/.5. LCCN:31-007651.
Audience: **l,u,f.**

Pérez Galdós, Benito **PQ6555.M5**
Miau. Ricardo Gullon (Editor). Trade Paper. Books on Demand. Ann Arbor, MI. 691p. ISBN:0-598-75414-8, ISBN13: 978-0-598-75414-1. Dewey:863/.5. LCCN:61-025806.
Audience: **l,u,f.**

Rivas, Angel de Saavedra (Author, Editor) **PQ6560.A17 1976**
Romances. Ed. 7. Cipriano de Rivas Cherif (Editor), Angel de Saavedra Rivas & Cipriano de Rivas Cherif (Translators). Trade Cloth. Espasa Calpe, S.A.. Madrid, 1976. ;p. ISBN:84-239-6861-8, ISBN13: 978-84-239-6861-9. Dewey:862.5. LCCN:77-553010.
Audience: **u,f.**

Turner, Harriet S. **PQ6555**
Fortunata and Jacinta. J. P. Stern (Contribution by). Trade Paper. Cambridge University Press. New York, NY. 2005. 150p. Landmarks of World Literature Ser. ISBN:0-521-37868-0, ISBN13: 978-0-521-37868-0. Dewey:863.5.
Audience: **g,l,u,f.**

Valera, Juan **PQ6573.D6613 2002**
Dona Luz. Robert M. Fedorchek (Translator). Trade Cloth. Bucknell University Press. Cranbury, NJ. 2002. 184p. ISBN:0-8387-5536-4, ISBN13: 978-0-8387-5536-5. Dewey:863/.5. LCCN:2002-021539.
Audience: **g,l,u.** *Choice, 2003.*

Valis, Noel M. **PQ6503.A4R3**
Decadent Vision in Leopoldo Alas. Cloth Text. Louisiana State University Press. Baton Rouge, LA. 1981. xvi, 215p. ISBN:0-8071-0769-7, ISBN13: 978-0-8071-0769-0. Dewey:863/.5. LCCN:80-024108.
Audience: **u,f.**

Valis, Noël Maureen **PQ6503.A4EB.V35 2002**
e Leopoldo Alas (Clarin). E-Book. NetLibrary, Inc. Boulder, CO. 2002. ISBN:0-585-49094-5, ISBN13: 978-0-585-49094-6. Dewey:863.5.
Audience: **l,u,f.**

Zorilla, José **PQ6575.D613 2003**
A Translation of Jose Zorrilla's Don Juan Tenorio. Robert G. Trimble (Translator, Introduction by). Trade Cloth. Edwin Mellen Press, The. Lewiston, NY. 2003. 212p. Hispanic Literature Ser., Vol. 79 ISBN:0-7734-6732-7, ISBN13: 978-0-7734-6732-3. Dewey:862/.5. LCCN:2003-043006.
Audience: **u,f.**

Hispanic Literature > Spanish Literature: Individual Authors and Works > 1868-1960 > A-B

Alberti, Rafael **PQ6601.L2 A6 1980**
Antologia Poetica. Trade Cloth. Alianza Editorial, S. A.. Madrid, 264p. ISBN:84-206-1759-8, ISBN13: 978-84-206-1759-6. Dewey:861.62. LCCN:80-127786.
Audience: **u,f.**

Alberti, Rafael **PQ6601.L2 M3 1977**
Marinero en Tierra (Sailman at Shore). Trade Cloth. Editorial Lumen. Barcelona, 1995. 150p. ISBN:84-264-2717-0, ISBN13: 978-84-264-2717-5. Dewey:861.62. LCCN:77-481686.
Audience: **u,f.**

Alberti, Rafael **PQ6601.L2 R43**
Retorno de lo Vivo Lejano Obra Martiana (Return from the Life Distant). Trade Cloth. Editorial Seix Barral. Barcelona, 1979. 132p. ISBN:84-322-9531-0, ISBN13: 978-84-322-9531-7. Dewey:861.6. LCCN:79-112862.
Audience: **u,f.**

Alberti, Rafael **PQ6601.L2**
The Lost Grove: Autobiography of a Spanish Poet in Exile. Gabriel Berns (Editor, Translator). Trade Cloth. University of California Press. Berkeley, CA. 1977. 323p. ISBN:0-520-02786-8, ISBN13: 978-0-520-02786-2. Dewey:861/.6/2. LCCN:74-079760.
Audience: **l,u,f.**

Alberti, Rafael **PQ6601.L2S6313 1995**
Concerning the Angels. Christopher Sawyer-Lauçanno (Translator). Trade Cloth. City Lights Books. San Francisco, CA. 1995. 200p. ISBN:0-87286-297-6, ISBN13: 978-0-87286-297-5. Dewey:861/.62. LCCN:94-030722.
Audience: **l,u,f.**

Alberti, Rafael **PQ6601.L2A6213 1997**
To Painting: A Bilingual Collection. Carolyn L. Tipton (Translator, Introduction by). Trade Cloth. Northwestern University Press. Evanston, IL. 1997. 249p. ISBN:0-8101-1351-1, ISBN13: 978-0-8101-1351-0. Dewey:861.62. LCCN:97-035657.
Audience: **l,u,f.**

Aleixandre, V. **PQ6601.L26A6 1987**
Prosas Recobradas (Collected Prose Works). Trade Cloth. Plaza & Janés Editories, S.A.. Barcelona, 216p. ISBN:84-01-38113-4, ISBN13: 978-84-01-38113-3. Dewey:861/.62. LCCN:88-119693.
Audience: **u,f.**

Aleixandre, Vicente **PQ6601.L26D413 2000**
Destruction or Love: La Destruccibon O el Amor. Trade Cloth. Susquehanna University Press. Cranbury, NJ. 2000. 274p. ISBN:1-57591-051-9, ISBN13: 978-1-57591-051-2. Dewey:861/.62. LCCN:00-035780.
Audience: **l,u,f.**

Aleixandre, Vicente **PQ6601.L26S613 1987**
Shadow of Paradise: Sombra Del Paraiso. Hugh A. Harter (Translator), Claudio Rodriguez (Foreword by). Trade Cloth. University of California Press. Berkeley, CA. 1987. 232p. ISBN:0-520-05599-3, ISBN13: 978-0-520-05599-5. Dewey:861/.62. LCCN:86-006942.
Audience: **l,u,f.** *Choice, 1987.*

Aleixandre, Vicente **PQ6601.L26.A23 1979**
A Longing for the Light. Lewis Hyde (Editor). Trade Cloth. HarperCollins Publishers. New York, NY. 1979. xviii, 281p. ISBN:0-06-010059-1, ISBN13: 978-0-06-010059-9. Dewey:861/.6/2. LCCN:78-002113.
Audience: **l,u,f.** B

Ayala, Francisco **PQ6601.Y3C25 1978**
La Cabeza de Cordero. Trade Cloth. Ediciones Cátedra. Madrid 1, 288p. ISBN:84-376-0146-0, ISBN13: 978-84-376-0146-5. Dewey:863/.6/2. LCCN:79-340267.
Audience: **u,f.**

Ayala, Francisco **PQ6601.Y3U713 1985**
Usurpers. Carolyn Richmond (Translator). Trade Cloth. Knopf Publishing Group. New York, NY. 1987. 192p. ISBN:0-8052-3970-7, ISBN13: 978-0-8052-3970-6. Dewey:863.64. LCCN:84-023602.
Audience: **l,u,f.** *Choice, 1987.*

Azorin **PQ6623.A816V7 1973**
La Voluntad. Ed. 2. Trade Cloth. Castalia, Editorial S.A.. Madrid, 303p. Clasicos Castalia, :Siglo XX ISBN:84-7039-133-X, ISBN13: 978-84-7039-133-0. Dewey:863/.6/2. LCCN:75-576228.
Audience: **u,f.**

Azorín Catena, Elena (Translator) **PQ6623.A816D7 1973**
Doña Inés: Historia de Amor. Trade Cloth. Castalia Publishing Company. Eugene, OR. 1973. 248p. ISBN:84-7039-153-4, ISBN13: 978-84-7039-153-8. Dewey:863/.62. LCCN:73-363582.
Audience: **u,f.**

Baroja y Nessi, Pío **PQ6603.A7A9 1974**
El Arbol de la Ciencia. Ed. 5. Trade Paper. Alianza Editorial, S. A.. Madrid, 250p. ISBN:84-206-1050-X, ISBN13: 978-84-206-1050-4. Dewey:863.6. LCCN:75-557722.
Audience: **u,f.**

Baroja, Pio **PQ6603.A7**
Camino de Perfección. Paper Text. Textbook Publishers. Temecula, CA. 2003. 208p. ISBN:0-7581-9946-5, ISBN13: 978-0-7581-9946-1.
Audience: **u,f.**

Baroja, Pío **PQ**
Vidas Sombrías. José-Carlos Mainer (Translator). Trade Cloth. Biblioteca Nueva, Editorial, S.L.. Madrid, 1998. 219p. ISBN:84-7030-481-X, ISBN13: 978-84-7030-481-1. Dewey:863/.62. LCCN:98-140955.
Audience: **u,f.**

Benavente, Jacinto **PQ6603.E6A27**
Plays. John Garrett Underhill (Translator). Trade Paper. Books on Demand. Ann Arbor, MI. 332p. ISBN:0-598-50462-1, ISBN13: 978-0-598-50462-3. Dewey:862.6. LCCN:19-015598.
Audience: **g,l,u,f.**

Benavente, Jacinto **PQ6603.E6A26**
Plays. John Garrett Underhill (Translator). Trade Paper. Books on Demand. Ann Arbor, MI. 296p. ISBN:0-598-50459-1, ISBN13: 978-0-598-50459-3. Dewey:862.6. LCCN:17-014040.
Audience: **g,l,u,f.**

Benavente, Jacinto **PQ6603.E6A27**
Plays. John Garrett Underhill (Translator). Trade Paper. Books on Demand. Ann Arbor, MI. 258p. ISBN:0-598-50364-1, ISBN13: 978-0-598-50364-0. Dewey:862.6. LCCN:23-006267.
Audience: **g,l,u,f.**

Blasco Ibáñez, Vicente **PQ6603 .L2 1977**
Obras Completas: Con una Nota Biobibliográfica. Other. Santillana USA Publishing Company, Inc. Doral, FL. 1977. ISBN:84-03-00997-6, ISBN13: 978-84-03-00997-4. Dewey:863.5. LCCN:78-347764.
Audience: **u,f.**

Glenn, Kathleen M. **PQ6623.A816.Z597**
Azorin (Jose Martinez Ruiz). Library Binding. Thomson Gale. Farmington Hills, MI. 1981. 164p. World Authors Ser. ISBN:0-8057-6446-1, ISBN13: 978-0-8057-6446-8. Dewey:868/.62/09. LCCN:80-023267.
Audience: **u,f.** B

Vallejo, Antonio Buero **PQ6603.U4C6 1979**
El Concierto de San Ovidio; El Tragaluz. Trade Cloth. Castalia, Editorial S.A.. Madrid, 320p. Clasicos Castalia, :Siglo XX ISBN:84-7039-059-7, ISBN13: 978-84-7039-059-3. Dewey:862/.64. LCCN:80-117889.
Audience: **u,f.**

Vallejo, Antonio Buero **PQ6603.U4D413 1989**
A Dreamer for the People. Ed. 2. Trade Cloth. Aris & Phillips. Oxford, 1990. 240p. Hispanic Classics Ser. ISBN:0-85668-455-4, ISBN13: 978-0-85668-455-5. Dewey:862/.5/09145. LCCN:90-217914.
Audience: **g,l,u.**

Vallejo, Antonio Buero **PQ6603.U4A19 1987**
Historia de una Escalera (Story of Stairway - Meninas): Las Meninas. Ed. 13. Ricardo Domenech (Introduction by). Trade Cloth. Espasa Calpe, S.A.. Madrid, 232p. Nueva Austral Ser., No. 10 ISBN:84-239-1810-6, ISBN13: 978-84-239-1810-2. Dewey:862/.64. LCCN:90-188649.
Audience: **u,f.**

Vallejo, Antonio Buero **PQ6603.U4M8713 1994**
The Music Window (Musica Cercana). Martha T. Halsey (Editor), Marion P. Holt (Translator). Trade Paper. Estreno Plays. New Brunswick, NJ. 1994. xiv, 66p. Contemporary Spanish Plays Ser., Vol. 5 ISBN:0-9631212-4-3, ISBN13: 978-0-9631212-4-0. Dewey:862/.64. LCCN:93-074274.
Audience: **g,l,u,f.** *Choice, 1994.*

Vallejo, Antonio Buero **PQ6603.U4M413 1987**
Las Meninas: A Fantasia in Two Parts. Marion P. Holt (Translator). Trade Cloth. Trinity University Press. San Antonio, TX. 1987. 108p. ISBN:0-939980-17-7, ISBN13: 978-0-939980-17-8. Dewey:862/.64. LCCN:87-012524.
Audience: **g,l,u,f.** *Choice, 1988.*

Vallejo, Antonio Buero **PQ6603.U4A24 1985**
Three Plays: The Sleep of Reason, The Foundation, and In the Burning Darkness. Marion P. Holt (Translator). Trade Paper. Trinity University Press. San Antonio, TX. 179p. ISBN:0-939980-09-6, ISBN13: 978-0-939980-09-3. Dewey:862/.52. LCCN:85-001198.
Audience: **g,l,u,f.** *Choice, 1986.*

Vallejo, Antonio Buero **PQ6603.U4 M87 1990**
Musica Cercana. David Johnston (Introduction by). Trade Cloth. Elliot's Books. Northford, CT. 1991. 144p. Nueva Austral Ser., No. 132 ISBN:84-239-1932-3, ISBN13: 978-84-239-1932-1. Dewey:862.64. LCCN:90-200055.
Audience: **u,f.**

Vallejo, Antonio Buero **PQ6603.U4L38 1987**
Lazaro en el Laberinto. Mariano D. Paco (Editor). Trade Cloth. Elliot's Books. Northford, CT. 1991. 160p. Nueva Austral Ser., No. 29 ISBN:84-239-1829-7, ISBN13: 978-84-239-1829-4. Dewey:862.64. LCCN:92-199999.
Audience: **u,f.**

Hispanic Literature > Spanish Literature: Individual Authors and Works > 1868-1960 > C-D

Cela, Camilo Jose **PQ6605.E44C613 2001**
The Hive. J. M. Cohen & Arturo Barea (Translators). Trade Paper. Dalkey Archive Press. Normal, IL. 2001. 249p. ISBN:1-56478-268-9, ISBN13: 978-1-56478-268-7. Dewey:863.64. LCCN:2001-028041.
Audience: **g,l,u,f.**

Cela, Camilo José **PQ6605.E44F3 1975**
La Familia de Pascual Duarte. Trade Cloth. Destino Publishing, Inc. Auburn Hills, MI. 1975. 168p. ISBN:84-233-0733-6, ISBN13: 978-84-233-0733-3. Dewey:863/.62. LCCN:76-465996.
Audience: **u,f.**

Cela, Camilo José **PQ6605.E44M33 1983**
Mazurca para Dos Muertos. Trade Cloth. Ediciones del Norte. Hanover, NH. 1983. 272p. ISBN:84-322-0484-6, ISBN13: 978-84-322-0484-5. Dewey:863/.64. LCCN:84-103248.
Audience: **u,f.**

Cela, Camilo José **PQ6605.E44M3313 1992**
Mazurka for Two Dead Men. Patricia Haugaard (Translator). Trade Cloth. New Directions Publishing Corporation. New York, NY. 1992. 320p. ISBN:0-8112-1222-X, ISBN13: 978-0-8112-1222-9. Dewey:863/.64. LCCN:92-012618.
Audience: **g,l,u,f.** *Choice, 1993.*

Cela, Camilo José **PQ6605.E44F313 2004**
The Family of Pascual Duarte. Anthony Kerrigan (Translator). Trade Paper. Dalkey Archive Press. Normal, IL. 2004. 166p. Spanish Literature Ser. ISBN:1-56478-359-6, ISBN13: 978-1-56478-359-2. Dewey:863/.62. LCCN:2003-070066.
Audience: **g,l,u,f.**

Cela, Camilo José **PQ6605.E44A6 1991**
Paginas Escogidas. Dario Villanueva (Editor). Trade Cloth. Elliot's Books. Northford, CT. 1991. 288p. Nueva Austral Ser., Vol. 229 ISBN:84-239-7229-1, ISBN13: 978-84-239-7229-6. Dewey:863.62. LCCN:94-119036.
Audience: **u,f.**

Cernuda, Luis **PQ6605.E7A24 1999**
Selected Poems of Luis Cernuda. Reginald Gibbons (Editor, Translator). Trade Paper. Sheep Meadow Press, The. Riverdale-on-Hudson, NY. 1999. 227p. ISBN:1-878818-80-5, ISBN13: 978-1-878818-80-5. Dewey:861/.62. LCCN:99-058279.
Audience: **g,l,u,f.**

Cernuda, Luis **PQ6605.E7A245 2004**
Written in Water: The Collected Prose Poems. Stephen Kessler (Translator). Trade Paper. City Lights Books. San Francisco, CA. 2004. 128p. ISBN:0-87286-431-6, ISBN13: 978-0-87286-431-3. Dewey:861/.62. LCCN:2003-025653.
Audience: **g,l,u,f.**

Charlebois, Lucile C. **PQ6605.E44Z625 1998**
Understanding Camilo Jose Cela. Trade Cloth. University of South Carolina Press. Columbia, SC. 1998. 180p. ISBN:1-57003-151-7, ISBN13: 978-1-57003-151-9. Dewey:863.62. LCCN:96-051296.
Audience: **l,u,f.** *Choice, 1998.*

Perez, Janet **PQ6605.E44Z783 2000**
Camilo Jose Cela Revisited: Later Novels. Trade Cloth. Thomson Gale. Farmington Hills, MI. 2000. xviii, 189p. Twayne's World Authors Ser., Vol. 891 ISBN:0-8057-1640-8, ISBN13: 978-0-8057-1640-5. Dewey:863/.64. LCCN:00-030268.
Audience: **u,f.** *Choice, 2001.*

Hispanic Literature > Spanish Literature: Individual Authors and Works > 1868-1960 > G

Gaite, Carmen M. **PQ6623.A7657E513**
Behind the Curtains. Frances M. Lopez-Morillas (Translator). Trade Cloth. Columbia University Press. New York, NY. 1990. 279p. ISBN:0-231-06888-3, ISBN13: 978-0-231-06888-8. Dewey:863/.64. LCCN:89-029780.
Audience: **u,f.**

Goytisolo, Juan **PQ6613.O79M313 1993**
Makbara. Trade Paper. Serpent's Tail Ltd. London, 1994. 270p. Masks Ser. ISBN:1-85242-266-1, ISBN13: 978-1-85242-266-0. Dewey:863.64. LCCN:93-083062.
Audience: **u,f.**

Goytisolo, Juan **PQ6613.O79P25 1982**
Paisajes Despues de la Batalla. Trade Cloth. Ediciones del Norte. Hanover, NH. 1982. 196p. ISBN:84-85859-54-5, ISBN13: 978-84-85859-54-2. Dewey:863/.64. LCCN:85-239090.
Audience: **u,f.**

Goytisolo, Juan **PQ6613.O79**
Blind Rider. Peter Bush (Translator). Trade Paper. Serpent's Tail Ltd. London, 2005. 112p. ISBN:1-85242-863-5, ISBN13: 978-1-85242-863-1. Dewey:863/.64. LCCN:2006-365138.
Audience: **l,u,f.**

Goytisolo, Juan **PQ6613.O79C3913 2005**
A Cock-Eyed Comedy. Peter Bush (Translator). Trade Paper. City Lights Books. San Francisco, CA. 2005. 192p. ISBN:0-87286-450-2, ISBN13: 978-0-87286-450-4. Dewey:863/.64. LCCN:2005-029777.
Audience: **l,u,f.**

Goytisolo, Juan **PQ6613.O79**
Forbidden Territory and Realms of Strife: The Memoirs of Juan Goytisolo. Peter Bush (Translator). Trade Paper. Verso Books. London, 2003. 320p. ISBN:1-85984-555-X, ISBN13: 978-1-85984-555-4. Dewey:863/.64 B. LCCN:2003-053520.
Audience: **l,u,f.**

Goytisolo, Juan **PQ6613.O79C813 1994**
Quarantine. Peter Bush (Translator). Trade Cloth. Dalkey Archive Press. Normal, IL. 1994. 122p. ISBN:1-56478-044-9, ISBN13: 978-1-56478-044-7. Dewey:863/.64. LCCN:93-029198.
Audience: **l,u,f.** *Choice, 1994.*

Goytisolo, Juan **PQ6613.O79S5813 2002**
State of Siege. Helen Lane (Translator). Trade Paper. City Lights Books. San Francisco, CA. 2002. 144p. ISBN:0-87286-406-5, ISBN13: 978-0-87286-406-1. Dewey:863/.64. LCCN:2002-067609.
Audience: **u,f.**

Goytisolo, Juan **PQ6613.O79A25 1987**
Space in Motion. Helen R. Lane (Translator). Trade Paper. Lumen, Inc. Santa Fe, NM. 1988. 78p. ISBN:0-930829-03-4, ISBN13: 978-0-930829-03-2. Dewey:864/.64. LCCN:88-167013.
Audience: **l,u,f.** *Choice, 1988.*

Guillén, Jorge **PQ6613.U5A24 1999**
Horses in the Air and Other Poems. Cola Franzen (Translator). Trade Cloth. City Lights Books. San Francisco, CA. 2004. 248p. ISBN:0-87286-352-2, ISBN13: 978-0-87286-352-1. Dewey:861/.62. LCCN:99-019321.
Audience: **l,u,f.**

Guillén, Jorge **PQ6613.U5**
Guillen on Guillen: The Poetry and the Poet. Reginald Gibbons & Anthony L. Geist (Translators). Trade Cloth. Princeton University Press. Princeton, NJ. 1979. 220p. ISBN:0-691-06392-3, ISBN13: 978-0-691-06392-8. Dewey:861/.62. LCCN:78-070299.
Audience: **u,f.** B

Gómez de la Serna, Ramón, et al. **PQ6613.O4A27 2005**
Eight Novellas. Herlinda Charpentier Saitz & Robert L. Saitz (Authors). Trade Paper. Peter Lang Publishing, Inc. New York, NY. 2005. ix,261p. ISBN:0-8204-7435-5, ISBN13: 978-0-8204-7435-9. Dewey:863/.62. LCCN:2004-014116.
Audience: **u,f.**

Pope, Randolph D. **PQ6613.O79Z834 1995**
Understanding Juan Goytisolo. James Hardin (Editor). Cloth Text. University of South Carolina Press. Columbia, SC. 1995. 190p. Understanding Modern European and Latin American Literature Ser. ISBN:1-57003-069-3, ISBN13: 978-1-57003-069-7. Dewey:863/.64. LCCN:95-011606.
Audience: **l,u,f.** *Choice, 1996.*

Hispanic Literature > Spanish Literature: Individual Authors and Works > 1868-1960 > Garcia Lorca

García Lorca, Federico **PQ6613.A763**
Canciones (1921-1924). Trade Cloth. Alianza Editorial, S. A.. Madrid, 96p. ISBN:84-206-6106-6, ISBN13: 978-84-206-6106-3. Dewey:861/.62. LCCN:82-225901.
Audience: **u,f.**

García Lorca, Federico **PQ6613.A763A17 1975**
Canciones y Poemas para Ninos. Trade Cloth. Labor, Editorial S. A.. 08290 Cerdanyola (Barcelona), 96p. Coleccion Poemas Juvenil ISBN:84-335-8401-4, ISBN13: 978-84-335-8401-4. Dewey:861/.6/2. LCCN:76-478664.
Audience: **u,f.**

García Lorca, Federico **PQ6613.A763C4 1999**
House of Bernarda Alba. Trade Paper. Theatre Communications Group, Inc. New York, NY. 2000. 96p. ISBN:1-85459-459-1, ISBN13: 978-1-85459-459-4. Dewey:862.6/2.
Audience: **g,l,u,f.**

García Lorca, Federico **PQ6613.A763**
La Zapatera Prodigiosa. Trade Cloth. Alianza Editorial, S. A.. Madrid, 216p. ISBN:84-206-6107-4, ISBN13: 978-84-206-6107-0. Dewey:868/.6209 s 862/.62. LCCN:83-196845.
Audience: **u,f.**

García Lorca, Federico **PQ6613.A763A2115**
Book of Poems / Libro de Poemas: A Dual-Language Book. Stanley Appelbaum (Editor, Translator). Trade Paper. Dover Publications, Inc. Mineola, NY. 2004. 176p. A Dual-Language Book Ser. ISBN:0-486-43650-0, ISBN13: 978-0-486-43650-0. Dewey:861/.62. LCCN:2004-052893.
Audience: **g,l,u,f.**

García Lorca, Federico **PQ6613.A763A213 1988**
Ode to Walt Whitman and Other Poems. Carlos Bauer (Translator). Trade Cloth. City Lights Books. San Francisco, CA. 1988. 160p. ISBN:0-87286-219-4, ISBN13: 978-0-87286-219-7. Dewey:861/.62. LCCN:88-002586.
Audience: **g,l,u,f.** *Choice, 1989.*

García Lorca, Federico **PQ6613.A763A2265**
Four Major Plays. John Edmunds (Translator), Nicholas Round (Introduction by), Ann MacLaren (Notes by). Trade Paper. Oxford University Press, Inc. New York, NY. 2000. 288p. Oxford World's Classics Ser. ISBN:0-19-283938-1, ISBN13: 978-0-19-283938-1. Dewey:862/.62. LCCN:00-703215.
Audience: **l,u,f.**

García Lorca, Federico **PQ6613.A763.A227**
Plays One. Gwynne Edwards & Peter Luke (Translators), Gwynne Edwards (Introduction by). Trade Paper. Methuen Publishing Ltd. London, 2003. 0p. Methuen World Dramatists Ser. ISBN:0-413-15780-6, ISBN13: 978-0-413-15780-5. Dewey:862/.62. LCCN:87-209018.
Audience: **g,l,u,f.**

García Lorca, Federico **PQ6613.A763 1997**
Obras Completas. Miguel García-Posada (Editor). Trade Cloth. Bow Historical Books. New Providence, NJ. 1996. ISBN:84-226-6122-5, ISBN13: 978-84-226-6122-1. Dewey:868/.6209. LCCN:98-114899.
Audience: **u,f.**

García Lorca, Federico **PQ6613.A763**
Mariana Pineda. Robert G. Havard (Editor). Trade Cloth. Aris & Phillips. Oxford, 1987. 200p. Hispanic Classics Ser. ISBN:0-85668-333-7, ISBN13: 978-0-85668-333-6. Dewey:862/.62.
Audience: **u,f.** *Choice, 1987.*

García Lorca, Federico **PQ6613.A763**
Yerma. Mario Hernandez (Editor). Trade Cloth. Alianza Editorial, S. A.. Madrid, 196p. ISBN:84-206-6102-3, ISBN13: 978-84-206-6102-5. Dewey:862/.62. LCCN:81-169787.
Audience: **u,f.** *Choice, 1987.*

García Lorca, Federico **PQ6613.A763**
Libro de Poemas. Mario Hernandez (Editor, Introduction by, Notes by). Trade Cloth. Alianza Editorial, S. A.. Madrid, 280p. ISBN:84-206-6114-7, ISBN13: 978-84-206-6114-8. Dewey:868/.6209 s 861/.62. LCCN:85-191850.
Audience: **u,f.**

García Lorca, Federico **PQ6613.A763A235 1994**
Blood Wedding and Yerma. Ted Hughes & W. S. Merwin (Translators), Melia Benussen (Introduction by). Trade Cloth. Theatre Communications Group, Inc. New York, NY. 1994. 160p. TCG Translations Ser., Vol. 5 ISBN:1-55936-079-8, ISBN13: 978-1-55936-079-1. Dewey:862.62. LCCN:93-051498.
Audience: **g,l,u,f.**

García Lorca, Federico **PQ6613.A763**
Gypsy Ballads. Rolfe Humphries (Translator). Trade Paper. Books on Demand. Ann Arbor, MI. 64p. Indiana University Humanities Ser. ISBN:0-608-18252-4, ISBN13: 978-0-608-18252-0. Dewey:861.62. LCCN:53-009826.
Audience: **g,l,u,f.**

García Lorca, Federico & Jiménez, Juan Ramón **PQ6613.A763A222 1997**
Lorca and Jimenez: Selected Poems. Robert Bly (Editor). Trade Paper. Beacon Press. Boston, MA. 1997. 208p. ISBN:0-8070-6213-8, ISBN13: 978-0-8070-6213-5. Dewey:861/.6208. LCCN:96-052545.
Audience: **g,l,u,f.**

García Lorca, Federico **PQ6613.A763A6 1989**
Once Five Years Pass: And Other Dramatic Works. William B. Logan & Angel G. Orrios (Editors), William B. Logan & Angel G. Orrios (Translators), William B. Logan & Angel G. Orrios (Introduction by), Christopher Maurer (Foreword by). Trade Cloth. Barrytown/Station Hill Press. Barrytown, NY. 1989. 248p. ISBN:0-88268-070-6, ISBN13: 978-0-88268-070-5. Dewey:862/.62. LCCN:88-036815.
Audience: **g,l,u,f.** *Choice, 1990.*

García Lorca, Federico **PQ6613.A763A223 2005**
The Selected Poems of Federico Garcia Lorca. Francisco G. Lorca & Donald M. Allen (Editors), W. S. Merwin (Introduction by). Trade Paper. New Directions Publishing Corporation. New York, NY. 2005. 192p. ISBN:0-8112-1622-5, ISBN13: 978-0-8112-1622-7. Dewey:861/.62. LCCN:2005-002834.
Audience: **g,l,u,f.**

García Lorca, Federico **PQ6613.A763A17 1988**
Collected Poems. Christopher Maurer (Editor). Cloth over Boards. Farrar, Straus & Giroux. New York, NY. 1991. 248p. ISBN:0-374-12624-0, ISBN13: 978-0-374-12624-7. Dewey:861/.62. LCCN:87-033151.
Audience: **g,l,u,f.**

García Lorca, Federico **PQ6613.A763A225 2004**
Selected Verse. Christopher Maurer (Editor). Trade Paper. Farrar, Straus & Giroux. New York, NY. 2004. 432p. ISBN:0-374-52855-1, ISBN13: 978-0-374-52855-3. Dewey:861/.62. LCCN:2003-024286.
Audience: **g,l,u,f.**

García Lorca, Federico **PQ6613.A763A225 2001**
The Collected Poems: A Bilingual Edition. Christopher Maurer (Editor, Introduction by). Cloth over Boards. Farrar, Straus & Giroux. New York, NY. 2002. 960p. ISBN:0-374-12615-1, ISBN13: 978-0-374-12615-5. Dewey:861/.62. LCCN:2001-018779.
Audience: **g,l,u,f.**

García Lorca, Federico **PQ6613.A763A258 1998**
A Season in Granada: Uncollected Poems and Prose. Christopher Maurer (Editor, Translator). Trade Cloth. Anvil Press Poetry, Ltd. London, 1998. 128p. ISBN:0-85646-300-0, ISBN13: 978-0-85646-300-6. Dewey:861/.62. LCCN:98-234128.
Audience: **g,l,u,f.**

García Lorca, Federico **PQ6613.A763.P6313**
Poet in New York/Poeta en Nueva York: A Bilingual Edition. Christopher Maurer (Editor), Greg Simon & Steven F. White (Translators), Christopher Maurer (Introduction by). Trade Paper. Farrar, Straus & Giroux. New York, NY. 1998. 320p. ISBN:0-374-52540-4, ISBN13: 978-0-374-52540-8. Dewey:861/.62. LCCN:97-049953.
Audience: **g,l,u,f.**

García Lorca, Federico **PQ6613**
Five Plays: Comedies and Tragicomedies. Richard L. O'Connell & James Graham-Lujan (Translators). Trade Cloth. Greenwood Publishing Group, Inc. Portsmouth, NH. 1977. 246p. ISBN:0-8371-9583-7, ISBN13: 978-0-8371-9583-4. Dewey:862'.6'2. LCCN:77-004654.
Audience: **g,l,u,f.**

García Lorca, Federico **PQ6613.A763 C4 1983**
La Casa de Bernarda Alba. Herbert Ramsden (Editor). Trade Paper. Manchester University Press. Manchester, 1988. 120p. Spanish Texts Ser. ISBN:0-7190-0950-2, ISBN13: 978-0-7190-0950-1. Dewey:862/.62. LCCN:83-019936.
Audience: **u,f.**

García Lorca, Federico **PQ6613.A763**
Romancero Gitano. H. Ramsden (Introduction by, Notes by). Cloth Text. Manchester University Press. Manchester, 1988. 176p. Spanish Texts Ser. ISBN:0-7190-3007-2, ISBN13: 978-0-7190-3007-9. Dewey:861/.62. LCCN:87-038262.
Audience: **g,l,u,f.**

García Lorca, Federico **PQ6613.A763**
Romancero Gitano. H. Ramsden (Editor, Introduction by, Notes by). Trade Paper. Manchester University Press. Manchester, 1988. 160p. Spanish Texts Ser. ISBN:0-7190-1724-6, ISBN13: 978-0-7190-1724-7. Dewey:861/.62. LCCN:87-038262.
Audience: **u,f.**

García Lorca, Federico & Svich, Caridad **PQ6613.A763A6 2000**
Federico Garcia Lorca: Impossible Theater: Five Plays and Thirteen Poems. Trade Paper. Smith and Kraus Publishers, Inc. Lyme, NH. 2000. xix, 168p. ISBN:1-57525-228-7, ISBN13: 978-1-57525-228-5. Dewey:868/.6209. LCCN:00-044571.
Audience: **g,l,u,f.**

Gibson, Ian **PQ6613.A763Z64775**
Federico Garcia Lorca: A Life. Trade Cloth. Knopf Publishing Group. New York, NY. 1989. ISBN:0-394-50964-1, ISBN13: 978-0-394-50964-8. Dewey:868/.6209 B. LCCN:88-028871.
Audience: **l,u,f.**

Klein, Dennis A. **PQ6613.A763Z7347**
Blood Wedding, Yerma, and The House of Bernard Alba: Garcia Lorca's Tragic Trilogy. Trade Cloth. Thomson Gale. Farmington Hills, MI. 1991. 152p. Twayne's Masterwork Studies, No. 69 ISBN:0-8057-8351-2, ISBN13: 978-0-8057-8351-3. Dewey:862/.62. LCCN:90-021521.
Audience: **g,l,u,f.** *Choice, 1991.*

Lorca, Federico García **PQ6613.A763A225 2001**
Collected Poems. Christopher Maurer (Editor, Introduction by, Notes by). Trade Paper. Farrar, Straus & Giroux. New York, NY. 2002. 990p. ISBN:0-374-52691-5, ISBN13: 978-0-374-52691-7. Dewey:861/.62. LCCN:2001-018779.
Audience: **g,l,u,f.**

Newton, Candelas **PQ6613.A763Z7775**
Understanding Federico Garcia Lorca. Cloth Text. University of South Carolina Press. Columbia, SC. 1995. 190p. Understanding Modern European and Latin American Literature Ser. ISBN:1-57003-020-0, ISBN13: 978-1-57003-020-8. Dewey:868/.6209. LCCN:94-018708.
Audience: **l,u,f.** *Choice, 1995.*

Smith, Paul Julian **PQ6613.A763 Z88532**
The Theatre of García Lorca: Text, Performance, Psychoanalysis. Enrique Pupo-Walker (Contribution by). Trade Cloth. Cambridge University Press. New York, NY. 1998. 197p. Cambridge Studies in Latin American and Iberian Literature, No. 14 ISBN:0-521-62292-1, ISBN13: 978-0-521-62292-9. Dewey:862/.62. LCCN:97-038634.
Audience: **u,f.** *Choice, 1999.*

Stainton, Leslie **PQ6613.A763Z8856**
Lorca: A Dream of Life. Trade Cloth. Farrar, Straus & Giroux. New York, NY. 1999. 496p. ISBN:0-374-19097-6, ISBN13: 978-0-374-19097-2. Dewey:868.6/2/09. LCCN:98-051194.
Audience: **g,l,u,f.** *Choice, 2000.*

Hispanic Literature > Spanish Literature: Individual Authors and Works > 1868-1960 > H-Q

Fogelquist, Donald F. **PQ6619.I4.Z615**
Juan Ramon Jimenez. Trade Cloth. Thomson Gale. Farmington Hills, MI. 1976. 176p. ISBN:0-8057-6180-2, ISBN13: 978-0-8057-6180-1. Dewey:861/.6/2. LCCN:75-026547.
Audience: **l,u,f.** B

García Lorca, Federico & Jiménez, Juan Ramón **PQ6613.A763A222 1997**
Lorca and Jimenez: Selected Poems. Robert Bly (Editor). Trade Paper. Beacon Press. Boston, MA. 1997. 208p. ISBN:0-8070-6213-8, ISBN13: 978-0-8070-6213-5. Dewey:861/.6208. LCCN:96-052545.
Audience: **g,l,u,f.**

Jimenez, Juan Ramon & Harter, Hugh A. **PQ6619.I4D513 2004**
Diary of a Newlywed Poet: A Bilingual Edition of Diario de un Poeta Reciencasado. Michael P. Predmore (Introduction by). Trade Cloth. Susquehanna University Press. Cranbury, NJ. 2004. 504p. ISBN:1-57591-074-8, ISBN13: 978-1-57591-074-1. Dewey:861/.62. LCCN:2003-067340.
Audience: **l,u,f.** *Choice, 2004.*

Jimenez, Juan Ramon **PQ6619.I4**
Poesias Escogidas (Selected Poems) of Juan Ramon Jimenez. Salvador Ortiz-Carboneres (Editor). Trade Cloth. Aris & Phillips. Oxford, 2005. 96p. ISBN:0-85668-761-8, ISBN13: 978-0-85668-761-7. Dewey:861.62.
Audience: **l,u,f.**

Jiménez, Juan Ramón **PQ6619.I4 A17 1975**
Antologia Poetica. Trade Cloth. Ediciones Cátedra. Madrid 1, 192p. ISBN:84-376-0035-9, ISBN13: 978-84-376-0035-2. Dewey:861.62. LCCN:75-507776.
Audience: **u,f.**

Jiménez, Juan Ramón **PQ6619.I4P6 1988**
Platero y Yo. Richard A. Cardwell (Editor). Trade Cloth. Elliot's Books. Northford, CT. 1991. 288p. Nueva Austral Ser., Vol. 58 ISBN:84-239-1858-0, ISBN13: 978-84-239-1858-4. Dewey:861/.62. LCCN:89-170342.
Audience: **u,f.**

Jiménez, Juan Ramón **PQ6619.I4S613 1996**
Spiritual Sonnets: Sonetos Espirituales. Carl W. Cobb (Translator). Trade Cloth. Edwin Mellen Press, The. Lewiston, NY. 1996. 136p. Hispanic Literature Ser., Vol. 27 ISBN:0-7734-8889-8, ISBN13: 978-0-7734-8889-2. Dewey:861/.62. LCCN:95-009147.
Audience: **l,u,f.** *Choice, 1996.*

Jiménez, Juan Ramón **PQ6619.I4Z48 1992**
Cartas Antologia. Francisco Gardias (Editor). Trade Cloth. Elliot's Books. Northford, CT. 1991. 368p. Nueva Austral Ser., Vol. 251 ISBN:84-239-7251-8, ISBN13: 978-84-239-7251-7. Dewey:861/.62 B. LCCN:92-217783.
Audience: **u,f.**

Jiménez, Juan Ramón **PQ6619.I4.A22 1987**
Light and Shadows: Selected Poems and Prose of Juan Ramon Jimenez. James Wright, Robert Bly, Antonio T. de Nicolas,

Dennis Maloney & Clark M. Zlotchew (Translators). Trade Paper. White Pine Press. Buffalo, NY. 1987. 70p. ISBN:0-934834-72-5, ISBN13: 978-0-934834-72-8. Dewey:861/.62. LCCN:88-140980.
Audience: **l,u,f.** *Choice, 1988.*

Laforet, Carmen **PQ6621.A38**
La Niña y Otros Relatos. Trade Cloth. Magisterio Espanol, Editorial, S.A.. Fuenlabrada, 1983. 264p. ISBN:84-265-7065-8, ISBN13: 978-84-265-7065-9. Dewey:863.64.
Audience: **u,f.**

Laforet, Carmen **PQ6621.A38**
La Insolacion. Trade Cloth. Plaza & Janés Editories, S.A.. Barcelona, 1985. 272p. ISBN:84-01-90963-5, ISBN13: 978-84-01-90963-4. Dewey:863.
Audience: **u,f.**

Laforet, Carmen **PQ**
Nada. Other. Ediciones Destino. Barcelona, 2004. 295p. ISBN:84-233-3632-8, ISBN13: 978-84-233-3632-6. Dewey:863/.64.
Audience: **u,f.**

Machado y Ruiz, Antonio **PQ6623.A3A26 1987**
Solitudes, Galleries, and Other Poems. Richard L. Predmore (Translator), Michael Predmore (Introduction by). Cloth Text. Duke University Press. Durham, NC. 1987. ix, 237p. ISBN:0-8223-0713-8, ISBN13: 978-0-8223-0713-6. Dewey:861/.62. LCCN:86-032758.
Audience: **g,l,u,f.** *Choice, 1987.*

Machado, Antonio **PQ6623.A3A6 1981**
Yo Voy Sonando Caminos. Trade Cloth. Labor, Editorial S. A.. 08290 Cerdanyola (Barcelona), 96p. Coleccion Poemas Juvenil ISBN:84-335-8423-5, ISBN13: 978-84-335-8423-6. Dewey:861/.62. LCCN:81-199948.
Audience: **u,f.**

Machado, Antonio **PQ6623.A3A218 2003**
Border of a Dream: Selected Poems of Antonio Machado. Willis Barnstone (Translator). Trade Paper. Copper Canyon Press. Port Townsend, WA. 2003. 360p. ISBN:1-55659-198-5, ISBN13: 978-1-55659-198-3. Dewey:861/.62. LCCN:2003-016509.
Audience: **g,l,u,f.**

Machado, Antonio **PQ6623.A3.A245 1978**
Selected Poems of Antonio Machado. Betty J. Craige (Translator, Introduction by). Cloth Text. Louisiana State University Press. Baton Rouge, LA. 1978. 192p. ISBN:0-8071-0456-6, ISBN13: 978-0-8071-0456-9. Dewey:861/.6/2. LCCN:78-057504.
Audience: **g,l,u,f.**

Machado, Manuel **PQ6623.A34A17 1974**
Antologia. Emilio Miró (Prologue by). Trade Cloth. Plaza & Janes SA Edit. Argentina. Buenos Aires, 1974. 295p. ISBN:84-01-80938-X, ISBN13: 978-84-01-80938-5. Dewey:928.6. LCCN:75-591378.
Audience: **u,f.**

Manuel, Juan **PQ6401.E5 1987**
Le Conde Lucanor: A Collection of Mediaeval Spanish Stories. John England (Editor). Trade Cloth. Aris & Phillips. Oxford, 1987. x, 350p. Hispanic Classics Ser. ISBN:0-85668-325-6, ISBN13: 978-0-85668-325-1. Dewey:863/.1. LCCN:88-114350.
Audience: **g,l,u,f.**

Martín Gaite, Carmen **PQ6623.A7657C813**
The Back Room. Helen Lane (Translator). Trade Cloth. City Lights Books. San Francisco, CA. 2004. 216p. ISBN:0-87286-371-9, ISBN13: 978-0-87286-371-2. Dewey:863/.64. LCCN:99-088257.
Audience: **l,u,f.**

Marías, Javier **PQ6663.A7218**
Dark Back of Time. UK-B Format Paperback. Knopf Publishing Group. New York, NY. 2004. 336p. ISBN:0-09-928746-3, ISBN13: 978-0-09-928746-9. Dewey:863.6/4.
Audience: **l,u,f.**

Marías, Javier **PQ6663.A7218C6713**
A Heart So White. Margaret Jull Costa (Translator). Trade Cloth. New Directions Publishing Corporation. New York, NY. 2000. 288p. ISBN:0-8112-1452-4, ISBN13: 978-0-8112-1452-0. Dewey:863.6/4. LCCN:00-055021.
Audience: **l,u,f.**

Marías, Javier **PQ6663.A7218H613**
The Man of Feeling. Margaret Jull Costa (Translator). Trade Cloth. New Directions Publishing Corporation. New York, NY. 2003. 144p. ISBN:0-8112-1531-8, ISBN13: 978-0-8112-1531-2. Dewey:863/.64. LCCN:2002-153935.
Audience: **g,l,u,f.**

Marías, Javier **PQ6663.A7218T8313**
Your Face Tomorrow: Fever and Spear. Margaret Jull Costa (Translator). Trade Cloth. New Directions Publishing Corporation. New York, NY. 2005. 352p. ISBN:0-8112-1612-8, ISBN13: 978-0-8112-1612-8. Dewey:863/.64. LCCN:2005-000992.
Audience: **l,u,f.**

Matute, Ana M. **PQ6623.A89 T65 1980**
La Trampa. Trade Cloth. Ediciones Destino. Barcelona, 280p. ISBN:84-233-1069-8, ISBN13: 978-84-233-1069-2. Dewey:863. LCCN:81-128054.
Audience: **u,f.**

Molina, Antonio Munoz **PQ6663.U4795S4413**
Sepharad. Margaret Sayers Peden (Translator). Cloth over Boards. Harcourt Trade Publishers. New York, NY. 2003. 400p. ISBN:0-15-100901-5, ISBN13: 978-0-15-100901-5. Dewey:863/.64. LCCN:2003-005538.
Audience: **g,l,u,f.**

Nichols, Geraldine C. **PQ6615.E57.Z86**
Miguel Hernandez. Library Binding. Thomson Gale. Farmington Hills, MI. 1978. 201p. World Authors Ser. ISBN:0-8057-6301-5, ISBN13: 978-0-8057-6301-0. Dewey:861/.6/2. LCCN:77-019102.
Audience: **l,u,f.**

Olson, Paul R. **PQ6619.I4Z72**
Circle of Paradox: Time and Essence in the Poetry of Juan Ramon Jimenez. Trade Paper. Books on Demand. Ann Arbor, MI. 248p. ISBN:0-608-13739-1, ISBN13: 978-0-608-13739-1. Dewey:861.62. LCCN:67-021581.
Audience: **u,f.**

Ortega y Gasset, José **PQ6627.R8 1983**
Obras Completas. Trade Cloth. Alianza Editorial, S. A.. Madrid, 1983. 12560p. ISBN:84-206-4999-6, ISBN13: 978-84-206-4999-3. Dewey:868/.6209. LCCN:83-184268.
Audience: **u,f.**

Pardo Bazán, Emilia **PQ6629.A7P313 1992**
The House of Ulloa: A Novel by Emilia Pardo Bazan. Trade Cloth. University of Georgia Press. Athens, GA. 1992. 352p. ISBN:0-8203-1372-6, ISBN13: 978-0-8203-1372-6. Dewey:863/.5. LCCN:91-012757.
Audience: **g,l,u,f.** *Choice, 1992.*

Pardo Bazán, Emilia **PQ6629.A7 1973**
Obras Completas. Trade Cloth. Santillana USA Publishing Company, Inc. Doral, FL. 1973. :p. ISBN:84-03-00143-6, ISBN13: 978-84-03-00143-5. Dewey:868.6.
Audience: **u,f.**

Perez-Reverte, Arturo **PQ6666.E765L5613**
The Purity of Blood. Margaret Sayers Peden (Translator). Trade Cloth. Penguin Group (USA) Inc. New York, NY. 2006. 288p. ISBN:0-399-15320-9, ISBN13: 978-0-399-15320-4. Dewey:863/.64. LCCN:2005-050984.
Audience: **g,l,u,f.**

Pérez-Reverte, Arturo **PQ6666.E765P513 1998**
The Seville Communion. Sonia Soto (Translator). Cloth over Boards. Harcourt Trade Publishers. New York, NY. 1998. 400p. ISBN:0-15-100283-5, ISBN13: 978-0-15-100283-2. Dewey:863.6/4. LCCN:97-033050.
Audience: **g,l,u,f.**

Trueblood, Alan S. **PQ6613.U5**
Antonio Machado: Selected Poems. Trade Cloth. Harvard University Press. Cambridge, MA. 1982. 336p. ISBN:0-674-04065-1, ISBN13: 978-0-674-04065-6. Dewey:861/.62. LCCN:81-013481.
Audience: **g,l,u,f.**

Hispanic Literature > Spanish Literature: Individual Authors and Works > 1868-1960 > R-Z

del Valle-Inclán, Ramón **PQ6641.A47T5 1975**
Tirano Banderas. Trade Paper. Espasa Calpe, S.A.. Madrid, 240p. ISBN:84-239-2002-X, ISBN13: 978-84-239-2002-0. Dewey:863/.62. LCCN:76-460647.
Audience: **u,f.**

Mozick, Martin (Editor) **PQ6639.N3Z/**
Miguel de Unamuno: The Agony of Belief. Trade Cloth. Princeton University Press. Princeton, NJ. 1982. 238p. ISBN:0-691-06498-9, ISBN13: 978-0-691-06498-7. Dewey:868/.6209. LCCN:81-047966.
Audience: **l,u,f.**

Perez-Reverte, Arturo **PQ6666.E765C3813**
The Nautical Chart. Margaret Sayers Peden (Translator). Cloth over Boards. Harcourt Trade Publishers. New York, NY. 2001. 480p. ISBN:0-15-100534-6, ISBN13: 978-0-15-100534-5. Dewey:863/.64. LCCN:2001-039446.
Audience: **g,l,u,f.**

Ruiz Zafon, Carlos **PQ6668.U49S6613 2004**
The Shadow of the Wind: A Novel. Lucia Graves (Translator). Trade Paper. Penguin Group (USA) Inc. New York, NY. 2005. 496p. ISBN:0-14-303490-1, ISBN13: 978-0-14-303490-2. Dewey:863/.64. LCCN:2003-062376.
Audience: **g,l,u,f.**

Sevilla Arroyo, Florencio (Editor) **PQ6407.A1 1984**
Vida de Lazarillo de Tormes (Life of Lazarillo of Tormes). Other. Plaza & Janés Editories, S.A.. Barcelona, 246p. ISBN:84-01-90544-3, ISBN13: 978-84-01-90544-5. Dewey:863/.3. LCCN:86-218368.
Audience: **u,f.**

Unamuno, Miguel de **PQ6639.N3A26 1987**
3 Exemplary Novels. Trade Paper. Random House, Inc. New York, NY. 1987. ISBN:0-394-62366-5, ISBN13: 978-0-394-62366-5. Dewey:868/.6209. LCCN:86-033606.
Audience: **g,l,u,f.**

Unamuno, Miguel de **PQ6639.N3A7 1985**
Abel Sanchez. Trade Cloth. Castalia, Editorial S.A.. Madrid, 180p. Clásicos Castalia Ser., :Siglo XX ISBN:84-7039-458-4, ISBN13: 978-84-7039-458-4. Dewey:863/.62. LCCN:86-177181.
Audience: **u,f.**

Unamuno, Miguel de **PQ6639.N3A6 1992**
Antologia Poetica. Trade Cloth. Espasa Calpe, S.A.. Madrid, 312p. ISBN:84-239-7283-6, ISBN13: 978-84-239-7283-8. Dewey:861/.6/2. LCCN:93-231331.
Audience: **u,f.**

Unamuno, Miguel de **PQ6639.N3T513 2005**
Aunt Tula / la Tia Tula: A Dual-Language Book. Trade Paper. Dover Publications, Inc. Mineola, NY. 2005. 192p. A Dual-Language Book Ser. ISBN:0-486-44506-2, ISBN13: 978-0-486-44506-9. Dewey:863/.62. LCCN:2005-045539.
Audience: **g,l,u.**

Unamuno, Miguel de **PQ6639.N3N513 2000**
Mist: A Tragicomic Novel. Warner Fite (Translator). Trade Paper. University of Illinois Press. Champaign, IL. 2000. 352p. ISBN:0-252-06894-7, ISBN13: 978-0-252-06894-2. Dewey:863/.62. LCCN:99-055817.
Audience: **g,l,u,f.**

Unamuno, Miguel de **PQ6639.N3.A25**
Novela-Nivola. Anthony Kerrigan (Translator), Jean Cassou (Foreword by). Trade Paper. Princeton University Press. Princeton, NJ. 1987. 552p. Bollingen Ser., Vol. LXXXV, No. 6 ISBN:0-691-01875-8, ISBN13: 978-0-691-01875-1. Dewey:863/.62. LCCN:88-192370.
Audience: **g,l,u,f.**

Unamuno, Miguel de **PQ6639.N3.A25 VOL. 1**
Peace in War: A Novel: Selected Works of Miguel de Unamuno, Vol. 1. Anthony Kerrigan, Allen Lacy, Martin Nozick & Martin Nozicks (Translators). Trade Cloth. Princeton University Press. Princeton, NJ. 1983. 300p. Bollingen Ser., No. LXXXV-1 ISBN:0-691-09926-X, ISBN13: 978-0-691-09926-2. Dewey:863/.62. LCCN:82-061390.
Audience: **l,u,f.** B

Unamuno, Miguel de **PQ6639.N3A25**
The Agony of Christianity and Essays on Faith. Anthony Kerrigan (Translator), Martin Nozick (Contribution by). Trade

Paper. Books on Demand. Ann Arbor, MI. 1974. 314p. Selected Works of Miguel de Unamuno, Vol. 5 ISBN:0-608-02899-1, ISBN13: 978-0-608-02899-6. Dewey:868.6209. LCCN:67-022341.

Audience: **u,f.** B

Unamuno, Miguel de **PQ6639.N3A28 1996**
Abel Sanchez and Other Stories. Anthony Kerrigan (Translator), Mario J. Valdes (Introduction by). Trade Paper. Regnery Publishing, Incorporated, An Eagle Publishing Company. Washington, DC. 1996. 267p. ISBN:0-89526-707-1, ISBN13: 978-0-89526-707-8. Dewey:868/.6209. LCCN:96-020645.

Audience: **g,l,u.**

Unamuno, Miguel de **PQ6639.N3**
San Manuel Bueno Martir and la Novela de Don Sandalio. C. A. Longhurst (Editor). Trade Paper. Manchester University Press. Manchester, 1988. 160p. Spanish Texts Ser. ISBN:0-7190-1092-6, ISBN13: 978-0-7190-1092-7. Dewey:863/.62. LCCN:84-019415.

Audience: **u,f.**

Unamuno, Miguel de **PQ6639.N3A813 1996**
Love and Pedagogy. Michael Vande Berg (Translator). Cloth Text. Peter Lang Publishing, Inc. New York, NY. 1996. XXV, 187p. ISBN:0-8204-1725-4, ISBN13: 978-0-8204-1725-7. Dewey:863/.62. LCCN:92-036961.

Audience: **u,f.**

Valle-Inclán, Ramón del **PQ6641.A47A24 1993**
Valle-Inclan: Plays One. Trade Paper. Methuen Publishing Ltd. London, 2004. Methuen's World Dramatists Ser. ISBN:0-413-67090-2, ISBN13: 978-0-413-67090-8. Dewey:862.6/2. LCCN:96-128790.

Audience: **g,l,u.** *Choice, 1994.*

Valle-Inclán, Ramón del **PQ6641.A47.L813 1976**
Luces de Bohemia: Bohemian Lights. Anthony N. Zahareas & Gerald Gillespie (Translators). Trade Cloth. University of Texas Press. Austin, TX. 1976. 278p. Edinburgh Bilingual Library, No. 10 ISBN:0-292-74609-1, ISBN13: 978-0-292-74609-1. Dewey:862/.6/2. LCCN:75-036215.

Audience: **l,u,f.** B

Hispanic Literature > Spanish Literature: Individual Authors and Works > 1960-

Falcón, Lidia **PQ**
Cinco Obras de Teatro. Trade Cloth. Vindicacion Feminista, Publicaciones. Madrid, 1994. 150p. ISBN:84-88217-01-3, ISBN13: 978-84-88217-01-1.

Audience: **u,f.**

Olmo, Lauro **PQ6627.L54 C3**
Camisa English Spoken - S. Garcia. Ed. 3. Trade Paper. French & European Publications, Inc. New York, NY. 1986. 234p. ISBN:0-7859-5184-9, ISBN13: 978-0-7859-5184-1. Dewey:862.

Audience: **u,f.**

Perez-Reverte, Arturo **PQ6666.E765C3713**
Captain Alatriste. Margaret Sayers Peden (Translator). Trade Cloth. Penguin Group (USA) Inc. New York, NY. 2005. 272p. ISBN:0-399-15275-X, ISBN13: 978-0-399-15275-7. Dewey:863/.64. LCCN:2004-060210.

Audience: **g,l,u,f.**

Riera, Carmen **PQ**
Te Dejo el Mar. Luisa Cotoner (Translator, Introduction by). Trade Cloth. Elliot's Books. Northford, CT. 1991. 192p. Nueva Austral Ser., Vol. 211 ISBN:84-239-7211-9, ISBN13: 978-84-239-7211-1.

Audience: **u,f.**

Hispanic Literature > Hispanic-American Literature > History, Criticism

Andre, Maria Claudia (Editor) **PQ7081.C43 2001**
Chicanas and Latin American Women Writers Exploring the Realm of the Kitchen as a Self-Empowering Site. Trade Cloth. Edwin Mellen Press, The. Lewiston, NY. 2001. 180p. Women's Studies, Vol. 32 ISBN:0-7734-7344-0, ISBN13: 978-0-7734-7344-7. Dewey:860.9/9282/0980904. LCCN:2001-031591.

Audience: **g,l,u,f.**

Balderston, Daniel & Gonzalez, Mike (Editors) **PQ7081**
Encyclopedia of Twentieth-Century Latin American and Caribbean Literature, 1900-2003. Paper over Boards. Routledge. New York, NY. 2004. 560p. Encyclopedias of Contemporary Culture Ser. ISBN:0-415-30686-8, ISBN13: 978-0-415-30686-7. Dewey:860.9006. LCCN:2003-058528.

Audience: **g,l,u,f.**

Barnstone, Willis **PQ7087.E5L58 2003**
Literatures of Latin America: From Antiquity to the Present. Trade Paper. Prentice Hall PTR. Upper Saddle River, NJ. 2002. 475p. ISBN:0-13-061360-6, ISBN13: 978-0-13-061360-8. Dewey:808.8/0098. LCCN:2002-022667.

Audience: **l,u.**

Beverley, John **PQ7082.P76B48 2004**
Testimonio: On the Politics of Truth. Trade Cloth. University of Minnesota Press. Minneapolis, MN. 2004. 176p. ISBN:0-8166-2840-8, ISBN13: 978-0-8166-2840-7. Dewey:868/.6080998. LCCN:2003-025126.

Audience: **l,u,f.**

Cortes, Eladio & Barrea-Marlys, Mirta (Editors) **PQ7082**
Encyclopedia of Latin American Theater. Cloth Text. Greenwood Publishing Group, Inc. Portsmouth, NH. 2003. 552p. ISBN:0-313-29041-5, ISBN13: 978-0-313-29041-1. Dewey:862.009/98/03. LCCN:2003-049135.

Audience: **g.** *Choice, 2004.*

De la Campa, Romban **PQ7081.D262 1999**
Latin Americanism. Trade Paper. University of Minnesota Press. Minneapolis, MN. 1999. xiv, 223p. Cultural Studies of the Americas, Vol. 3 ISBN:0-8166-3117-4, ISBN13: 978-0-8166-3117-9. Dewey:868. LCCN:98-056167.

Audience: **u,f.** *Choice, 2000.*

Echevarría, Roberto González **PQ7082.N7 G68 1990**
Myth and Archive: A Theory of Latin American Narrative. Enrique Pupo-Walker (Contribution by). Trade Paper. Cambridge University Press. New York, NY. 2006. 259p. Cambridge Studies in Latin American and Iberian Literature Ser. ISBN:0-521-02399-8, ISBN13: 978-0-521-02399-3. Dewey:863.009/98.
Audience: **u,f.**

Foster, David W. & Altamiranda, Daniel (Editors) **PQ7081.A1F76 1997**
From Romanticism to Modernismo in Latin America. Library Binding. Garland Publishing, Inc. New York, NY. 1997. 448p. Spanish American Literature Ser., Vol. 3:A Collection of Essays ISBN:0-8153-2679-3, ISBN13: 978-0-8153-2679-3. Dewey:860.9/868. LCCN:97-040790.
Audience: **u,f.**

Foster, David W. & Altamiranda, Daniel (Editors) **PQ7081.A1T44 1997**
Theoretical Debates in Spanish American Literature. Library Binding. Garland Publishing, Inc. New York, NY. 1997. 448p. Spanish American Literature Ser., Vol. 1:A Collection of Essays ISBN:0-8153-2676-9, ISBN13: 978-0-8153-2676-2. Dewey:860.9/358. LCCN:97-040788.
Audience: **u,f.**

Foster, David W. & Altamiranda, Daniel (Editors) **PQ7081.A1T84 1997**
Twentieth-Century Spanish American Literature since 1960, Pt. 2. Library Binding. Garland Publishing, Inc. New York, NY. 1998. 416p. Spanish American Literature Ser., Vol. 5:A Collection of Essays ISBN:0-8153-2681-5, ISBN13: 978-0-8153-2681-6. Dewey:860.9/98/09045. LCCN:97-202999.
Audience: **u,f.**

Foster, David W. & Altamiranda, Daniel (Editors) **PQ7081.A1T842 1997**
Twentieth-Century Spanish American Literature to 1960, Pt. 1. Library Binding. Garland Publishing, Inc. New York, NY. 1997. 352p. Spanish Ser., Vol. 4:A Collection of Essays ISBN:0-8153-2680-7, ISBN13: 978-0-8153-2680-9. Dewey:860.9/98/09041. LCCN:97-041683.
Audience: **u,f.**

Foster, David W. & Altamiranda, Daniel (Editors) **PQ7081.A1W75 1997**
Writers of the Spanish Colonial Period. Library Binding. Garland Publishing, Inc. New York, NY. 1997. 456p. Spanish American Literature Ser., Vol. 2:A Collection of Essays ISBN:0-8153-2678-5, ISBN13: 978-0-8153-2678-6. Dewey:860.9/868. LCCN:97-040789.
Audience: **u,f.**

Franco, Jean **PQ7081 .F64 1994**
An Introduction to Spanish-American Literature. Ed. 3. Cloth Text. Cambridge University Press. New York, NY. 1995. 402p. ISBN:0-521-44479-9, ISBN13: 978-0-521-44479-8. Dewey:860.9/98. LCCN:94-016543.
Audience: **u,f.**

Garganigo, John F., et al. **PC4117 .H84**
Huellas de las literaturas Hispanoamericanas. Ed. 3. Rene de Costa, Alessandra Luiselli, Georgina Sabat-Rivers, Elzbieta Sklodowska & Ben A. Heller (Authors). Trade Paper. Prentice Hall PTR. Upper Saddle River, NJ. 2006. 768p. ISBN:0-13-195846-1, ISBN13: 978-0-13-195846-3. Dewey:468.6/421.
Audience: **u,f.**

Hart, Stephen M. **PQ7081.H353 1999**
A Companion to Spanish-American Literature. Trade Cloth. Boydell & Brewer, Ltd. Woodbridge, 2000. 216p. Monografias A Ser., Vol. 179 ISBN:1-85566-065-2, ISBN13: 978-1-85566-065-6. Dewey:860.9/868. LCCN:99-045411.
Audience: **l,u,f.** *Choice, 2000.*

Jackson, Richard **PQ7081.J2635 1997**
Black Writers and the Hispanic Canon. Trade Cloth. Thomson Gale. Farmington Hills, MI. 1997. xix, 139p. Twayne's World Authors Ser., Vol. 867 ISBN:0-8057-7801-2, ISBN13: 978-0-8057-7801-4. Dewey:860.9/89608. LCCN:97-006682.
Audience: **l,u,f.**

Jiménez, José Olivio **PQ7084.A475 1985**
Antologia Critica de la Poesia Modernista HispanoAmericana. Trade Cloth. Hiperión Ediciones. Madrid, 2002. 462p. ISBN:84-7517-149-4, ISBN13: 978-84-7517-149-4. Dewey:861/.008/01. LCCN:86-149126.
Audience: **u,f.**

Jrade, Cathy L. **PQ7081.J73 1998**
Modernismo, Modernity, and the Development of Spanish American Literature. Trade Paper. University of Texas Press. Austin, TX. 1998. 205p. Texas Pan American Ser. ISBN:0-292-74045-X, ISBN13: 978-0-292-74045-7. Dewey:860.9/112/098. LCCN:98-005890.
Audience: **u,f.** *Choice, 1999.*

Kristal, Efraín (Editor) **PQ7082.N7**
The Cambridge Companion to the Latin American Novel. Cloth Text. Cambridge University Press. New York, NY. 2005. 358p. Cambridge Companions to Literature Ser. ISBN:0-521-82533-4, ISBN13: 978-0-521-82533-7. Dewey:863.009/98. LCCN:2005-541467.
Audience: **l,u,f.** *Choice, 2005.*

Larousse Mexico Staff **PQ7081.3.A39**
Diccionario de Escritores Hispanoamericanos del Siglo XVI al Siglo XX. Trade Paper. Larousse, Ediciones, S. A. de C. V.. Mexico, D. F., 2003. 368p. ISBN:970-22-0442-9, ISBN13: 978-970-22-0442-8. Dewey:860.9/9803.
Audience: **u,f.** *Choice, 2004.*

Lindstrom, Naomi **PQ7082.N7L523 2004**
Early Spanish American Narrative. Trade Cloth. University of Texas Press. Austin, TX. 2004. 247p. ISBN:0-292-74720-9, ISBN13: 978-0-292-74720-3. Dewey:863.009/98. LCCN:2003-023303.
Audience: **u,f.** *Choice, 2005.*

Madrigal, Luis Íñigo & Ainsa, Fernando **PQ**
Historia de la Literatura Hispanoamericana: Tomo II. Del Neoclasicismo Al Modernismo. Ed. 2. Trade Cloth. Ediciones Cátedra. Madrid 1, 1993. 752p. ISBN:84-376-0643-8, ISBN13: 978-84-376-0643-9.
Audience: **u,f.**

Madrigal, Luis Íñigo & Alvar, Manuel **PQ**
Historia de la Literatura Hispanoamericana: Tomo I. Época Colonial. Ed. 3. Trade Cloth. Ediciones Cátedra. Madrid 1, 1987. 437p. Critica Y Estudios Literarios Ser. ISBN:84-376-0334-X, ISBN13: 978-84-376-0334-6. Dewey:860/.9/98. LCCN:82-197457.
Audience: **u,f.**

Salas, Susan (Editor) **PQ7081.A1H573**
Hispanic Literature Criticism, Set. Ed. 2. Trade Cloth. Thomson Gale. Farmington Hills, MI. 1999. 1163p. ISBN:0-7876-3755-6, ISBN13: 978-0-7876-3755-2. Dewey:860.9. LCCN:99-067761.
Audience: **u,f.**

Salgado, Maria Antonia (Editor) **PQ7082.P7M53 2003**
Modern Spanish American Poets. Trade Cloth. Thomson Gale. Farmington Hills, MI. 2003. xxxii, 460p. Dictionary of Literary Biography Ser., Vol. 283 ISBN:0-7876-6820-6, ISBN13: 978-0-7876-6820-4. Dewey:861/.60998 B. LCCN:2003-012071.
Audience: **u,f.**

Shaw, Donald L. **PQ7082.N7S495 2002**
A Companion to Modern Spanish American Fiction. Trade Cloth. Boydell & Brewer, Ltd. Woodbridge, 2001. 264p. Monografias A Ser. ISBN:1-85566-078-4, ISBN13: 978-1-85566-078-6. Dewey:863/.60998. LCCN:2001-044278.
Audience: **u,f.** *Choice, 2002.*

Shaw, Donald L. **PQ7082.N7S515 1998**
The Post-Boom in Spanish American Fiction. Trade Cloth. State University of New York Press. Albany, NY. 1998. 224p. Series in Latin American and Iberian Thought and Culture ISBN:0-7914-3825-2, ISBN13: 978-0-7914-3825-1. Dewey:863.6409868. LCCN:97-034102.
Audience: **u,f.** *Choice, 1998.*

Smith, Verity (Editor) **PQ7081.A1E56 2000**
Concise Encyclopedia of Latin American Literature. Trade Cloth. Fitzroy Dearborn Publishers, Inc. Chicago, IL. 2000. 700p. ISBN:1-57958-252-4, ISBN13: 978-1-57958-252-4. Dewey:860.9/98/03. LCCN:00-712296.
Audience: **g,l,u.** *Choice, 2001.*

Stavans, Ilan (Editor) **PQ7081.7**
The Cross and the Scroll: 1,000 Years of Jewish-Hispanic Literature. Paper over Boards. Routledge. New York, NY. 2002. 336p. ISBN:0-415-92930-X, ISBN13: 978-0-415-92930-1. Dewey:860.98924. LCCN:2003-271495.
Audience: **g,l,u.** *Choice, 2003.*

Valdes, Mario J. & Kadir, Djelal **PQ7081.A1L525 2004**
Literary Cultures of Latin America: A Comparative History: Institutional Modes and Cultural Modalities. Trade Cloth. Oxford University Press, Inc. New York, NY. 2004. ISBN:0-19-517541-7, ISBN13: 978-0-19-517541-7. Dewey:860.9/98. LCCN:2003-027353.
Audience: **g,l,u,f.**

Valdes, Mario J. & Kadir, Djelal **PQ7081.A1L525 2004**
Literary Cultures of Latin America: A Comparative History: Configurations of Literary Culture. Trade Cloth. Oxford University Press, Inc. New York, NY. 2004. ISBN:0-19-517540-9, ISBN13: 978-0-19-517540-0. Dewey:860.9/98. LCCN:2003-027353.
Audience: **g,l,u,f.**

Valdes, Mario J. & Kadir, Djelal **PQ7081.A1L525 2004**
Literary Cultures of Latin America: A Comparative History: Latin American Literary Culture. Trade Cloth. Oxford University Press, Inc. New York, NY. 2004. ISBN:0-19-517542-5, ISBN13: 978-0-19-517542-4. Dewey:860.9/98. LCCN:2003-027353.
Audience: **g,l,u,f.**

Versényi, Adam (Editor) **PQ7082.D7L373 2004**
Latin American Dramatists: First Series. Trade Cloth. Thomson Gale. Farmington Hills, MI. 2004. 400p. Dictionary of Literary Biography Ser., Vol. 305 ISBN:0-7876-6842-7, ISBN13: 978-0-7876-6842-6. Dewey:862/.609/03 B. LCCN:2004-017988.
Audience: **g,l,u,f.**

Williams, Raymond L. **PQ7082.N7W548 1998**
The Modern Latin American Novel. Trade Cloth. Thomson Gale. Farmington Hills, MI. 1998. 177p. Twayne's Critical History of the Novel Ser. ISBN:0-8057-1655-6, ISBN13: 978-0-8057-1655-9. Dewey:863. LCCN:98-025148.
Audience: **g,l.** *Choice, 1999.*

Williams, Raymond Leslie **PQ7082.N7W56 2005**
The Twentieth-Century Spanish American Novel. Trade Paper. University of Texas Press. Austin, TX. 2005. 280p. ISBN:0-292-70670-7, ISBN13: 978-0-292-70670-5. Dewey:863/.609868.
Audience: **g,l,u,f.** *Choice, 2003.*

Hispanic Literature > Hispanic-American Literature > Collections

Appelbaum, Stanley (Editor, Translator) **PQ7087.E5S65 2005**
Spanish-American Short Stories / Cuentos Hispanoamericanos: A Dual-Language Book. Trade Paper, Perfect. Dover Publications, Inc. Mineola, NY. 2005. 272p. Dual-Language Book Ser. ISBN:0-486-44123-7, ISBN13: 978-0-486-44123-8. Dewey:863/.010898/0904. LCCN:2005-042029.
Audience: **g,l,u,f.**

Bautista, Gloria (Editor) **PQ7083.V6 1995**
Voces Femeninas de Hispanoamerica. Trade Paper. University of Pittsburgh Press. Pittsburgh, PA. 1996. 321p. Pitt Latin American Ser. ISBN:0-8229-5558-X, ISBN13: 978-0-8229-5558-0. Dewey:860.8/09282/098. LCCN:95-016033.
Audience: **u,f.**

De Vallejo, Catharina V. **PQ7084.A484 1993**
Antologia de la Poesia del Romanticismo Hispanoamericano: (1820-1890). Trade Cloth. Ediciones Universal. Miami, FL. 2001. 406p. Coleccion Textos ISBN:0-89729-675-3, ISBN13: 978-0-89729-675-5. Dewey:861. LCCN:93-070446.
Audience: **u,f.**

Echevarría, Roberto González (Editor) **PQ7087.E5O9 1997**
The Oxford Book of Latin American Short Stories. Trade Cloth. Oxford University Press, Inc. New York, NY. 1997. 496p. ISBN:0-19-509590-1, ISBN13: 978-0-19-509590-6. Dewey:863/.010898. LCCN:97-005395.
Audience: **g,l,u,f.**

Fuentes, Carlos & Ortega, Julio (Editors) **PQ7087.E5V56 2000**
The Vintage Book of Latin American Stories. Carlos Fuentes & Julio Ortega (Introduction by). Trade Paper. Knopf Publishing Group. New York, NY. 2000. 400p. ISBN:0-679-77551-X, ISBN13: 978-0-679-77551-5. Dewey:863/.010898. LCCN:00-712739.
Audience: **g,l,u,f.**

Grünfeld, Mihai G. **PQ**
Antología de la Poesía Latinoamericana de Vanguardia (1916-1935). Trade Cloth. Hiperión Ediciones. Madrid, 1997. 558p. ISBN:84-7517-427-2, ISBN13: 978-84-7517-427-3. Dewey:861. LCCN:96-100558.
Audience: **u,f.**

Miller, Ingrid W. (Editor) **PQ7083.M55 1991**
Afro-Hispanic Literature: An Anthology of Hispanic Writers of Hispanic Ancestry. Richard L. Jackson (Introduction by). Trade Paper. Ediciones Universal. Miami, FL. 2001. 143p. Coleccion Ebano y Canela ISBN:0-89729-582-X, ISBN13: 978-0-89729-582-6. Dewey:860.8/089608. LCCN:91-084525.
Audience: **g,l,u,f.**

Monegal, Emir R. (Editor) **PQ7087.E5.B6**
The Borzoi Anthology of Latin American Literature, Vol. 1. Trade Paper. Alfred A. Knopf Inc. New York, NY. 1977. xv, 982p. ISBN:0-394-73301-0, ISBN13: 978-0-394-73301-2. Dewey:860/.8. LCCN:76-019126.
Audience: **g,l,u,f.**

Monegal, Emir R. (Editor) **PQ6172**
The Borzoi Anthology of Latin American Literature, Vol. 2. Trade Paper. Alfred A. Knopf Inc. New York, NY. 1977. ISBN:0-394-73366-5, ISBN13: 978-0-394-73366-1. Dewey:860/.8.
Audience: **g,l,u,f.**

Ortega, Julio & Fuentes, Carlos **PQ7087.E5P53 1999**
The Picador Book of Latin American Stories. Trade Paper. Pan Macmillan. London, 1999. xvii, 333p. ISBN:0-330-33955-9, ISBN13: 978-0-330-33955-1. Dewey:863/.010898/0904. LCCN:99-202438.
Audience: **g,l,u,f.**

Stavans, Ilan (Editor) **PQ7087.E5O89 1997**
The Oxford Book of Latin American Essays. Trade Cloth. Oxford University Press, Inc. New York, NY. 1997. 528p. ISBN:0-19-509234-1, ISBN13: 978-0-19-509234-9. Dewey:864.008/098. LCCN:97-010976.
Audience: **g,l,u.** *Choice, 1998.*

Hispanic Literature > Hispanic-American Literature > Individual Countries > Mexico

PQ7276.N68
La Novela de la Revolucion Mexicana. Other. Aguilar, S. A. de Ediciones-Grupo Santillana. 28043 Madrid, 1901. ISBN:84-03-00973-9, ISBN13: 978-84-03-00973-8. Dewey:863.6082.
Audience: **u,f.**

Agustin, Jose **PQ7298.1.G85**
Ciudades Desiertas (Deserted Cities). Trade Paper. Knopf Publishing Group. New York, NY. 1995. 184p. ISBN:0-679-76336-8, ISBN13: 978-0-679-76336-9. Dewey:863.
Audience: **l,u,f.**

Agustin, Jose **PQ7298.1.G85A6 2002**
Cuentos Completos. Trade Paper. Ediciones Joaquin Mortiz. 2002. 421p. ISBN:968-27-0822-2, ISBN13: 978-968-27-0822-0. Dewey:863/.64. LCCN:2002-496328.
Audience: **l,u,f.**

Altamirano, Ignacio Manuel **GT4814.A2**
Paisajes y Leyendas (Landscapes and Legends). Trade Cloth. Editorial Patria Cultural. ISBN:968-39-1030-0, ISBN13: 978-968-39-1030-1. Dewey:394.26972.
Audience: **u,f.**

Aridjis, Homero **PQ7297.A8365A6 1994**
Antologia Poetica: 1960-1994. Trade Cloth. Fondo de Cultura Economica USA. San Diego, CA. 1994. 503p. ISBN:968-16-4296-1, ISBN13: 978-968-16-4296-9. Dewey:861. LCCN:95-192194.
Audience: **l,u,f.**

Aridjis, Homero **PQ7297.A8365**
Hombre que Amaba el Sol. Trade Paper. Santillana USA Publishing Company, Inc. Doral, FL. 2005. 184p. ISBN:970-770-255-9, ISBN13: 978-970-770-255-4. Dewey:863.
Audience: **u,f.**

Aridjis, Homero **PQ7297.A8365 P59**
Los Poemas Solares. Trade Cloth. Fondo de Cultura Economica USA. San Diego, CA. 2005. 148p. ISBN:968-16-7201-1, ISBN13: 978-968-16-7201-0. Dewey:861/.64.
Audience: **u,f.**

Aridjis, Homero **PQ7297.A8365 M46**
Memorias del Nuevo Mundo. Trade Cloth. Harcourt Trade Publishers. New York, NY. 1996. ISBN:0-15-158872-4, ISBN13: 978-0-15-158872-5. Dewey:863.
Audience: **u,f.**

Aridjis, Homero **PQ7297.A8365**
La Montana de las Mariposas. Other. Santillana USA Publishing Company, Inc. Doral, FL. 2005. 336p. ISBN:84-663-0423-1, ISBN13: 978-84-663-0423-8. Dewey:863.
Audience: **u,f.**

Aridjis, Homero **PQ7297.A8365**
Ojos de Otro Mirar: Poesia 1960-2001. Trade Cloth. Fondo de Cultura Economica USA. San Diego, CA. 2004. 888p. Letras Mexicanas Ser. ISBN:968-16-6697-6, ISBN13: 978-968-16-6697-2. Dewey:863.
Audience: **u,f.**

Arreola, Juan José **PQ7297.A853**
Bestiario: Varia Invención. Trade Cloth. Fondo de Cultura Economica USA. San Diego, CA. 2004. Tezontle Ser. ISBN:968-16-6547-3, ISBN13: 978-968-16-6547-0. Dewey:868.9978.
Audience: **u,f.**

Azuela, Mariano **PQ7297.A9 L6**
Los De Abajo: Novela de la Revolucion Mexicana. Trade Cloth. French & European Publications, Inc. New York, NY. 2000. ISBN:0-320-03794-0, ISBN13: 978-0-320-03794-8. Dewey:468.6.
Audience: **u,f.**

Azuela, Mariano **PQ**
Mala Yerba/Esa Sangre. Trade Cloth. Fondo de Cultura Economica USA. San Diego, CA. 1958. 222p. ISBN:968-16-0910-7, ISBN13: 978-968-16-0910-8. Dewey:863.
Audience: **u,f.**

Azuela, Mariano **PQ7297.A9**
Tres Novelas de Mariano Azuela: La Malhora/El Desquite/La Luciernaga. Trade Cloth. Fondo de Cultura Economica. Mexico, DF 03100, 179p. ISBN:968-16-0426-1, ISBN13: 978-968-16-0426-4. Dewey:863.
Audience: **u,f.**

Azuela, Mariano **PQ7297.A9**
Three Novels by Mariano Azuela: The Trials of a Respectable Family; The Underdogs; The Firefly. Ed. 2. Frances K. Hendricks & Bernice Berler (Translators). Trade Cloth. Trinity University Press. San Antonio, TX. 373p. ISBN:0-911536-78-7, ISBN13: 978-0-911536-78-2. Dewey:863. LCCN:78-068663.
Audience: **l,u,f.**

Bellatin, Mario **PQ7298.12.E4**
La Escuela Del Dolor Humano de Sechuan. Trade Cloth. Tusquests Editores Mexico, S.A. de C.V.. Mexico, D.F., 2001. 104p. ISBN:970-699-035-6, ISBN13: 978-970-699-035-8. Dewey:863. LCCN:2002-393630.
Audience: **u,f.**

Bellatín, Mario **PQ7297 A9**
El Jardin de la Senora Murakami. Trade Cloth. Tusquets Editores. Barcelona, 2001. 196p. ISBN:84-8310-190-4, ISBN13: 978-84-8310-190-2. Dewey:863.
Audience: **u,f.**

Bellatín, Mario **PQ8498.12.E443**
Salon de Belleza. Trade Cloth. Tusquets Editores. Barcelona, 2000. 176p. ISBN:84-8310-142-4, ISBN13: 978-84-8310-142-1. Dewey:868.972.
Audience: **u,f.**

Campobello, Nellie **PQ7297.C24448 C37**
Cartucho: Relatos de la Lucha en el Norte de Mexico. Other. Ediciones Era. México D. F., 2000. 171p. ISBN:968-411-455-9, ISBN13: 978-968-411-455-5. Dewey:972.
Audience: **u,f.**

Campobello, Nellie **PQ7297.C24448C3713**
Cartucho and My Mother's Hands. Doris Meyer & Irene Matthews (Translators), Elena Poniatowska (Introduction by). Trade Paper. University of Texas Press. Austin, TX. 1988. 143p. Texas Pan American Ser. ISBN:0-292-71111-5, ISBN13: 978-0-292-71111-2. Dewey:863. LCCN:87-025462.
Audience: **u,f.**

De la Cruz, Sor Juana Ines **PQ7296**
Obras Completas. Trade Paper. French & European Publications, Inc. New York, NY. 1997. 948p. ISBN:0-320-06670-3, ISBN13: 978-0-320-06670-2. Dewey:868.
Audience: **u,f.**

Esquivel, Laura **PQ7298.15.S638**
Como Agua para Chocolate. Trade Paper. Knopf Publishing Group. New York, NY. 2001. 256p. ISBN:0-385-72123-4, ISBN13: 978-0-385-72123-3. Dewey:863.
Audience: **u,f.**

Esquivel, Laura **PQ7082.N7**
The Law of Love. UK-Trade Paper. Random House Value Publishing. New York, NY. 1997. 288p. ISBN:0-609-80127-9, ISBN13: 978-0-609-80127-7. Dewey:863.
Audience: **g,l,u,f.**

Esquivel, Laura **PQ7082.N7**
La Ley del Amor. Trade Paper, Compact Disc. Crown Publishing Group. New York, NY. 1997. 288p. ISBN:0-609-80149-X, ISBN13: 978-0-609-80149-9. Dewey:863.
Audience: **u,f.**

Esquivel, Laura **BF535**
El Libro de las Emociones: Son de la Razon Sin Corazon. Mass Market. Random House, Inc. New York, NY. 2002. 144p. ISBN:1-4000-0118-8, ISBN13: 978-1-4000-0118-7. Dewey:152.4.
Audience: **u,f.**

Esquivel, Laura **PQ7298.15.S638M35**
Malinche Spanish Version: Novela. Trade Cloth. Simon & Schuster. New York, NY. 2006. 208p. ISBN:0-7432-9034-8, ISBN13: 978-0-7432-9034-0. Dewey:863/.64. LCCN:2005-058161.
Audience: **u,f.**

Esquivel, Laura **PQ6613.O79**
Swift as Desire. Trade Paper. Knopf Publishing Group. New York, NY. 2002. 208p. ISBN:0-385-72151-X, ISBN13: 978-0-385-72151-6. Dewey:863/.64.
Audience: **g,l,u,f.**

Esquivel, Laura **PQ7298.15.S638**
Tan Veloz Como el Deseo. UK-Trade Paper. Random House Children's Books. New York, NY. 2001. 224p. ISBN:0-385-72163-3, ISBN13: 978-0-385-72163-9. Dewey:863/.64. LCCN:2002-523096.
Audience: **u,f.**

Esquivel, Laura **PQ7298.15.S638M3513**
Malinche. Ernesto Mestre-Reed (Translator). Trade Cloth. Simon & Schuster. New York, NY. 2006. 208p. ISBN:0-7432-9033-X, ISBN13: 978-0-7432-9033 3. Dewey:863.64. LCCN:2005-057124.
Audience: **u,f.**

Fuentes, Carlos **PQ7297.F793**
Los Anos con Laura Diaz. Trade Paper. Santillana USA Publishing Company, Inc. Doral, FL. 1999. 600p. ISBN:968-19-0531-8, ISBN13: 978-968-19-0531-6. Dewey:863/.64.
Audience: **u,f.**

Fuentes, Carlos **N6679.B6**
Botero Mujeres. Cloth over Boards. Villegas Editores Ltda. Bogota, 2005. 224p. ISBN:958-8156-45-9, ISBN13: 978-958-8156-45-3. Dewey:709.
Audience: **u,f.**

Fuentes, Carlos **PQ7297.F793**
La Campana. Trade Paper. Santillana USA Publishing Company, Inc. Doral, FL. 2005. 326p. ISBN:968-19-1107-5, ISBN13: 978-968-19-1107-2. Dewey:863.
Audience: **u,f.**

Fuentes, Carlos **PQ7297.F793**
Carlos Fuentes. Trade Paper. Santillana USA Publishing Company, Inc. Doral, FL. 2005. 152p. ISBN:968-19-0815-5, ISBN13: 978-968-19-0815-7. Dewey:863/.64.
Audience: **u,f.**

Fuentes, Carlos **PQ**
Constancia y Otras Novelas para Virgenes. Trade Paper. Santillana USA Publishing Company, Inc. Doral, FL. 2005. 448p. ISBN:968-19-0872-4, ISBN13: 978-968-19-0872-0. Dewey:863.
Audience: **u,f.**

Fuentes, Carlos **PQ7297.F793 F76 1995**
La Frontera de Cristal. Trade Paper. Santillana USA Publishing Company, Inc. Doral, FL. 2005. 298p. ISBN:968-19-0268-8, ISBN13: 978-968-19-0268-1. Dewey:863. LCCN:96-166267.
Audience: **u,f.**

Fuentes, Carlos **PQ7297.F793 I665**
Inquieta Compania. Trade Paper, Perfect. Suma de Letras, S.L.. Madrid, 2005. 295p. ISBN:84-663-1577-2, ISBN13: 978-84-663-1577-7. Dewey:863/.64.
Audience: **u,f.**

Fuentes, Carlos **PQ7297.F793 M8 1995**
La Muerte de Artemio Cruz. Trade Cloth. Ediciones Cátedra. Madrid 1, 2001. 418p. ISBN:84-376-1393-0, ISBN13: 978-84-376-1393-2. Dewey:863. LCCN:96-140211.
Audience: **u,f.**

Fuentes, Carlos **PQ7297.F793 S55 2003**
La Silla del Águila. Trade Paper. Santillana USA Publishing Company, Inc. Doral, FL. 2005. 416p. ISBN:968-19-1202-0, ISBN13: 978-968-19-1202-4. Dewey:863/.64. LCCN:2003-423638.
Audience: **u,f.**

Fuentes, Carlos **PQ7297.F793T413 2003**
Terra Nostra. Margaret Sayers Peden (Translator), Milan Kundera (Afterword by). Trade Paper. Dalkey Archive Press. Normal, IL. 2003. 786p. Latin American Literature Ser. ISBN:1-56478-287-5, ISBN13: 978-1-56478-287-8. Dewey:863/.64. LCCN:2002-041570.
Audience: **l,u,f.**

Goytisolo, Jose Agustin **PQ**
Palabras para Julia y Otros Poemas. Ed. 2. Trade Cloth. Plaza & Janés Editories, S.A.. Barcelona, 2000. 96p. ISBN:84-01-59011-6, ISBN13: 978-84-01-59011-5. Dewey:861.64.
Audience: **u,f.**

Guzmán, Martín Luis **PQ**
El Águila y la Serpiente. Trade Cloth. Casiopea. Barcelona, 2001. 416p. ISBN:84-95446-05-7, ISBN13: 978-84-95446-05-3.
Audience: **u,f.**

Guzmán, Martín Luis **PQ**
La Sombra del Caudillo. Rafael Olea Franco (Editor). Trade Cloth. Association Archives de la Litterature Latino-Americaines des Caraibes et Africaine du XXe Siecle.. Madrid, 2003. 912p. ISBN:84-89666-63-6, ISBN13: 978-84-89666-63-4.
Audience: **u,f.**

Monterroso, Augusto, et al. **PQ7475 .C46 2002**
Los Centroamericanos. José Agustín & Francisco Hinojosa (Authors). Trade Paper. Santillana USA Publishing Company, Inc. Doral, FL. 376p. ISBN:99922-788-0-3, ISBN13: 978-99922-788-0-2. Dewey:863/.01089728. LCCN:2003-555490.
Audience: **u,f.**

Paz, Octavio **PQ7297.P285 C53 1996**
Claridad Errante: Poesia y Prosa. Trade Paper. Fondo de Cultura Economica USA. San Diego, CA. 1996. 93p. Fondo 2000 Ser. ISBN:968-16-5121-9, ISBN13: 978-968-16-5121-3. Dewey:868. LCCN:97-184289.
Audience: **u,f.**

Paz, Octavio **F**
El Laberinto de la Soledad. Ed. 5. Trade Cloth. Ediciones Cátedra. Madrid 1, 2000. 592p. ISBN:84-376-1168-7, ISBN13: 978-84-376-1168-6. Dewey:306/.0896872. LCCN:93-217368.
Audience: **u,f.**

Paz, Octavio **PQ7297.P285 A6 1988**
Libertad Bajo Palabra: Obras Poetica, 1935-1957. Ed. 4. Trade Cloth. Ediciones Cátedra. Madrid 1, 1998. 384p. ISBN:84-376-0775-2, ISBN13: 978-84-376-0775-7. Dewey:861/.6. LCCN:89-108551.
Audience: **u,f.**

Paz, Octavio **F1210**
The Labyrinth of Solitude: The Other Mexico and Return to the Labyrinth of Solitude and The U. S. A. and The Philanthropic Ogre. Lysander Kemp (Translator). Trade Paper. Grove/Atlantic, Inc. New York, NY. 1994. 408p. ISBN:0-8021-5042-X, ISBN13: 978-0-8021-5042-4. Dewey:864. LCCN:82-047999.
Audience: **g,l,u,f.**

Paz, Octavio **PQ7297.P285**
La Rama. Tetsuo Kitora (Illustrator). Trade Paper. Centro de Informacion y Desarrollo de la Comunicacion y la Literatura. Mexico, D.F., 2005. ISBN:968-494-046-7, ISBN13: 978-968-494-046-8. Dewey:861.
Audience: **u,f.**

Paz, Octavio & Paz, Marie Jose **PQ7297.P285F5413**
Figures and Figurations. Trade Cloth. New Directions Publishing

Corporation. New York, NY. 2002. 64p. ISBN:0-8112-1524-5, ISBN13: 978-0-8112-1524-4. Dewey:861/.62. LCCN:2002-008697.

Audience: **l,u,f.**

Paz, Octavio **PN1161.P3 1991**

Children of the Mire: Modern Poetry from Romanticism to the Avant-Garde. Ed. 2. Rachael Phillips (Read by). Trade Paper. Harvard University Press. Cambridge, MA. 1991. 192p. The Charles Eliot Norton Lectures, Vol. 1971 ISBN:0-674-11629-1, ISBN13: 978-0-674-11629-0. Dewey:809.1/03. LCCN:90-026837.

Audience: **g,l,u,f.**

Paz, Octavio **PQ8097.N4**

The Collected Poems of Octavio Paz, 1957-1987: Bilingual Edition. Eliot Weinberger (Editor, Translator), Elizabeth Bishop, Paul Blackburn & Lysander Kemp (Translators). Trade Paper. New Directions Publishing Corporation. New York, NY. 1991. 688p. ISBN:0-8112-1173-8, ISBN13: 978-0-8112-1173-4. Dewey:861. LCCN:87-023989.

Audience: **l,u,f.** *Choice, 1988.*

Puga, María Luisa **PQ7298.26.U48**

Panico O Peligro. Trade Cloth. Fondo de Cultura Economica USA. San Diego, CA. 2004. 459p. Coleccion Popular Ser. ISBN:968-16-6686-0, ISBN13: 978-968-16-6686-6. Dewey:868.75.

Audience: **l,u,f.**

Reyes, Alfonso (Editor, Prologue by) **PQ**

Cuentos. Trade Cloth. Editorial Oceano De Mexico, S.A. DE C.V.. 11560 Mexico D.F., 2001. 252p. ISBN:970-651-412-0, ISBN13: 978-970-651-412-7. Dewey:863/.62.

Audience: **u,f.**

Rulfo, Juan **PS7297.R89**

Aire de las Colinas: Cartas a Clara. Trade Cloth. Plaza & Janés Editories, S.A.. Barcelona, 2000. 336p. ISBN:84-01-01377-1, ISBN13: 978-84-01-01377-5. Dewey:866.

Audience: **u,f.**

Rulfo, Juan **PQ**

El Llano en Llamas. Ed. 12. Trade Cloth. Ediciones Cátedra. Madrid 1, 2000. 184p. ISBN:84-376-0512-1, ISBN13: 978-84-376-0512-8. Dewey:863.

Audience: **u,f.**

Rulfo, Juan **PQ**

Pedro Paramo. Trade Cloth. Plaza & Janés Editories, S.A.. Barcelona, 2000. 144p. ISBN:84-01-01375-5, ISBN13: 978-84-01-01375-1. Dewey:863/.64.

Audience: **u,f.**

Rulfo, Juan, et al. **PQ7297.R89I5 1983**

Inframundo: El Mexico de Juan Rulfo. Ed. 2. Fernando Benitez, Gabriel García Márquez & Carlos Fuentes (Authors), Juan J. Bremer (Editor). Paper Text. Ediciones del Norte. Hanover, NH. 1983. 160p. ISBN:0-910061-15-7, ISBN13: 978-0-910061-15-5. Dewey:863. LCCN:84-108695.

Audience: **u,f.**

Rulfo, Juan **PQ7297.R89P413 2002**

Pedro Paramo. Margaret Sayers Peden (Translator), Josephine Sacabo (Photographer), Elena Poniatowska (Contribution by). Trade Cloth. University of Texas Press. Austin, TX. 2002. 164p. Wittliff Gallery Ser. ISBN:0-292-77121-5, ISBN13: 978-0-292-77121-5. Dewey:863/.64. LCCN:2002-001054.

Audience: **g,l,u,f.**

Taibo, Paco Ignacio II **PQ7298.3.A58**

Algunas Nubes/No Habra Final Feliz. Trade Cloth. Planeta Mexicana Editorial S. A. de C. V.. Mexico D.F., 2003. 247p. ISBN:970-690-965-6, ISBN13: 978-970-690-965-7. Dewey:863.

Audience: **u,f.**

Taibo, Paco Ignacio II **PQ7298.3.A57**

Cosa Facil. Trade Cloth. Planeta Mexicana Editorial S. A. de C. V.. Mexico D.F., 2003. 222p. ISBN:970-690-963-X, ISBN13: 978-970-690-963-3. Dewey:863.

Audience: **u,f.**

Taibo, Paco Ignacio II **PQ7298.3.A58**

Dias de Combate. Trade Cloth. Planeta Mexicana Editorial S. A. de C. V.. Mexico D.F., 2003. 225p. ISBN:970-690-964-8, ISBN13: 978-970-690-964-0. Dewey:863.

Audience: **u,f.**

Taibo, Paco Ignacio II **PQ7082.N7**

Life Itself. Beth Henson (Translator). Trade Paper. Warner Books, Inc. New York, NY. 1995. 208p. ISBN:0-446-40331-8, ISBN13: 978-0-446-40331-3. Dewey:863.

Audience: **g,l,u,f.**

Taibo, Paco Ignacio II **PQ7298.3.A58D413**

Just Passing Through. Martin Michael Roberts (Translator). Trade Cloth. Cinco Puntos Press. El Paso, TX. 2000. 170p. ISBN:0-938317-47-4, ISBN13: 978-0-938317-47-0. Dewey:863. LCCN:99-033494.

Audience: **g,l,u,f.**

Usigli, Rodolfo **PQ7297.U85**

Corona de Luz. Trade Cloth. Fondo de Cultura Economica USA. San Diego, CA. 232p. ISBN:968-16-0432-6, ISBN13: 978-968-16-0432-5. Dewey:862/.6.

Audience: **u,f.**

Usigli, Rodolfo **PQ7297.U85G413 2005**

The Impostor: A Play for Demagogues. Ramon Layera (Translator). Trade Paper, Perfect. Latin American Literary Review Press. Pittsburgh, PA. 2005. 127p. Discoveries Ser. ISBN:1-891270-22-2, ISBN13: 978-1-891270-22-2. Dewey:862.64. LCCN:2005-017882.

Audience: **g,l,u,f.**

Villaurrutia, Xavier & Paz, Octavio **PQ7297.V6.N5813 1993**

Nostalgia for Death and Hieroglyphs of Desire: Poetry. Eliot Weinberger (Editor, Translator), Esther Allen (Translator). Trade Paper. Copper Canyon Press. Port Townsend, WA. 1993. 144p. ISBN:1-55659-053-9, ISBN13: 978-1-55659-053-5. Dewey:861. LCCN:92-017926.

Audience: **g,l,u,f.** *Choice, 1993.*

Yanez, Agustin **PQ7297.Y3**

Al Filo Del Agua. Paper Text. Textbook Publishers. Temecula, CA. 2003. xiii, 387p. ISBN:0-7581-6324-X, ISBN13: 978-0-7581-6324-0. Dewey:863.

Audience: **u,f.**

Yanez, Agustin **PQ7297.Y3 C7 1986**
La Creacion (The Creation). Trade Cloth. Fondo de Cultura Economica USA. San Diego, CA. 1992. 314p. ISBN:968-16-2380-0, ISBN13: 978-968-16-2380-7. Dewey:863. LCCN:88-170232.
Audience: **u,f.**

Yanez, Agustin **PQ7297.Y3**
Las Tierras Flacas. Trade Cloth. Ediciones Joaquin Mortiz. 2003. 361p. ISBN:968-27-0896-6, ISBN13: 978-968-27-0896-1. Dewey:863.
Audience: **u,f.**

Hispanic Literature > Hispanic-American Literature > Individual Countries > Cuba

Alberto, Eliseo **PQ7390.A375C3713**
Caracol Beach. Edith Grossman (Translator). Trade Cloth. Alfred A. Knopf Inc. New York, NY. 2000. 304p. ISBN:0-375-40540-2, ISBN13: 978-0-375-40540-2. Dewey:863. LCCN:99-058954.
Audience: **l,u,f.**

Arenas, Reinaldo **PQ7390.A72 A7 1984**
Arturo, la Estrella Mas Brillante. Other. Montesinos Editor, S.A.. Barcelona, 94p. ISBN:84-85859-96-0, ISBN13: 978-84-85859-96-2. Dewey:863/.64. LCCN:94-120020.
Audience: **u,f.**

Arenas, Reinaldo **PQ7390.A72P613 1991**
The Doorman: A Novel. Trade Cloth. Grove/Atlantic, Inc. New York, NY. 1991. ISBN:0-8021-1109-2, ISBN13: 978-0-8021-1109-8. Dewey:863. LCCN:90-028775.
Audience: **g,l,u,f.**

Arenas, Reinaldo **PQ7390.A72A813 1994**
The Assault. Andrew Hurley (Translator). Trade Cloth. Penguin Group (USA) Inc. New York, NY. 1994. 160p. ISBN:0-670-84066-1, ISBN13: 978-0-670-84066-3. Dewey:863. LCCN:93-032554.
Audience: **g,l,u,f.**

Arenas, Reinaldo **PQ7390.A72C5513 2000**
The Color of Summer: Or the New Garden of Earthly Delight. Andrew Hurley (Translator). Trade Cloth. Penguin Group (USA) Inc. New York, NY. 2000. 544p. ISBN:0-670-84065-3, ISBN13: 978-0-670-84065-6. Dewey:863. LCCN:99-055698.
Audience: **g,l,u,f.**

Arenas, Reinaldo **PQ7390.A72P3413 1990**
The Palace of the White Skunks. Andrew Hurley (Translator). Trade Cloth. Penguin Group (USA) Inc. New York, NY. 1991. 384p. ISBN:0-670-81510-1, ISBN13: 978-0-670-81510-4. Dewey:863. LCCN:89-040688.
Audience: **g,l,u,f.**

Arenas, Reinaldo **PQ7390.A72O813 1987**
Farewell to the Sea: A Novel of Cuba. Andrew Hurley (Translator), Thomas Colchie (Introduction by). Trade Paper. Penguin Group (USA) Inc. New York, NY. 1987. 448p. Pentagonia Ser. ISBN:0-14-006636-5, ISBN13: 978-0-14-006636-4. Dewey:863. LCCN:86-021227.
Audience: **g,l,u,f.**

Arenas, Reinaldo **PQ7390.A72C413 1988**
Singing from the Well. Andrew Hurley (Translator), Thomas Colchie (Introduction by). Trade Paper. Penguin Group (USA) Inc. New York, NY. 1988. 240p. King Penguin Ser. ISBN:0-14-009444-X, ISBN13: 978-0-14-009444-2. Dewey:863. LCCN:87-029183.
Audience: **g,l,u,f.** *Choice, 1987.*

Arenas, Reinaldo **PQ7390**
Before Night Falls: A Memoir. Dolores Koch (Translator). Trade Cloth. Penguin Group (USA) Inc. New York, NY. 1993. 336p. ISBN:0-670-84078-5, ISBN13: 978-0-670-84078-6. Dewey:863. LCCN:92-050743.
Audience: **g,l,u,f.**

Arenas, Reinaldo **PQ7390.A72A24 2001**
Mona and Other Tales. Dolores Koch (Translator). Trade Paper. Knopf Publishing Group. New York, NY. 2001. 208p. ISBN:0-375-72730-2, ISBN13: 978-0-375-72730-6. Dewey:863/.64. LCCN:2001-026552.
Audience: **g,l,u,f.**

Arenas, Reinaldo **PQ7390.A72A6 1989**
Old Rosa: A Novel in Two Stories. Ann T. Slater & Andrew Hurley (Translators). Trade Cloth. Grove/Atlantic, Inc. New York, NY. 1989. 112p. ISBN:0-8021-1092-4, ISBN13: 978-0-8021-1092-3. Dewey:863. LCCN:88-021421.
Audience: **g,l,u,f.**

Baquero, Gastón **PQ**
Poesía Completa. Trade Cloth. Verbum, Editorial S.L.. Madrid, 1998. 400p. ISBN:84-7962-121-4, ISBN13: 978-84-7962-121-6. Dewey:861/.64. LCCN:98-171522.
Audience: **u,f.**

Barnet, Miguel **PQ7390.B3.R3 1991**
Rachel's Song: A Novel. W. Nick Hill (Translator). Trade Paper. Curbstone Press. Willimantic, CT. 1991. 128p. ISBN:0-915306-87-5, ISBN13: 978-0-915306-87-9. Dewey:863. LCCN:91-055412.
Audience: **l,u,f.** *Choice, 1992.*

Benítez Rojo, Antonio **PQ7390.B42A6 1997**
Antologia Personal. Trade Cloth. University of Puerto Rico Press. Rio Piedras, PR. 1997. 256p. ISBN:0-8477-0299-5, ISBN13: 978-0-8477-0299-2. Dewey:863. LCCN:96-049316.
Audience: **u,f.**

Benítez Rojo, Antonio & Maraniss, James E. **PQ7390.B42A26 1998**
[Ebook] A View from the Mangrove. E-Book. NetLibrary, Inc. Boulder, CO. 1998. ISBN:0-585-08313-4, ISBN13: 978-0-585-08313-1. Dewey:863.
Audience: **l,u,f.**

Benítez Rojo, Antonio **PQ7390.B42M313 1990**
Sea of Lentils. James E. Maraniss (Translator), Sydney Lea (Introduction by). Cloth Text. University of Massachusetts Press. Amherst, MA. 1990. 216p. ISBN:0-87023-723-3, ISBN13: 978-0-87023-723-2. Dewey:863. LCCN:90-031381.
Audience: **l,u,f.** *Choice, 1991.*

Bueno, Salvador **PQ7378.B9**
Medio Siglo de Literatura Cubana, 1902-1952. Trade Paper. Books on Demand. Ann Arbor, MI. 235p. ISBN:0-598-88688-5, ISBN13: 978-0-598-88688-0. Dewey:860.997291. LCCN:53-026134.
Audience: **u,f.**

Bush, Peter R. (Editor) **PQ7386.V65 1998**
The Voice of the Turtle: An Anthology of Cuban Stories. Trade Paper. Grove/Atlantic, Inc. New York, NY. 1998. 400p. ISBN:0-8021-3555-2, ISBN13: 978-0-8021-3555-1. Dewey:863/.010897291. LCCN:97-038169.
Audience: **l,u,f.**

Cabrera, Lydia **PQ7389.C22 C84**
Cuentos para Adultos Ninos y Retrasados Mentales. Trade Cloth. Ediciones Universal. Miami, FL. 2001. 233p. Coleccion del Chichereku ISBN:0-89729-763-6, ISBN13: 978-0-89729-763-9. Dewey:863. LCCN:83-080058.
Audience: **u,f.**

Cabrera, Lydia **GR121.C8C3213 2004**
Afro-Cuban Tales. Alberto Hernandez-Chiroldes & Lauren Yoder (Translators), Isabel Castellanos (Introduction by). Trade Cloth. University of Nebraska Press. Lincoln, NE. 2005. 169p. ISBN:0-8032-6438-0, ISBN13: 978-0-8032-6438-0. Dewey:398.2/097291. LCCN:2004-048089.
Audience: **l,u,f.**

Cabrera, Lydia **PQ**
Cuentos Negros de Cuba. Ed. 3. Fernando Ortiz (Introduction by). Trade Cloth. Ediciones Universal. Miami, FL. 2001. 175p. Coleccion del Chichereku ISBN:0-89729-671-0, ISBN13: 978-0-89729-671-7. Dewey:398.2/0899607291.
Audience: **l,u,f.**

Carlson, Lori Marie & Hijuelos, Óscar (Editors) **PQ7383.5.E5B87 2006**
Burnt Sugar Cana Quemada: Contemporary Cuban Poetry in English and Spanish. Trade Paper. Simon & Schuster. New York, NY. 2006. 144p. ISBN:0-7432-7662-0, ISBN13: 978-0-7432-7662-7. Dewey:861/.608097291. LCCN:2005-058027.
Audience: **g,l,u,f.**

Carpentier, Alejo **PQ7389.C263S513 2001**
Explosion in a Cathedral. Trade Paper. University of Minnesota Press. Minneapolis, MN. 2001. 360p. ISBN:0-8166-3808-X, ISBN13: 978-0-8166-3808-6. Dewey:863/.64. LCCN:00-054390.
Audience: **g,l,u,f.**

Carpentier, Alejo **PQ7389.C263P313 2001**
The Lost Steps. Trade Paper. University of Minnesota Press. Minneapolis, MN. 2001. 296p. ISBN:0-8166-3807-1, ISBN13: 978-0-8166-3807-9. Dewey:863/.6. LCCN:00-069052.
Audience: **g,l,u,f.**

Carpentier, Alejo **PQ7389.C263P3 1985**
Los Pasos Perdidos. Trade Cloth. Ediciones Cátedra. Madrid 1, 336p. ISBN:84-376-0502-4, ISBN13: 978-84-376-0502-9. Dewey:863. LCCN:88-125907.
Audience: **u,f.** B

Carpentier, Alejo **PQ7389.C263R413 2006**
The Kingdom of This World: A Novel. Harriet de Onis (Translator), Edwidge Danticat (Introduction by). Trade Paper. Farrar, Straus & Giroux. New York, NY. 2006. 190p. FSG Classics Ser. ISBN:0-374-53011-4, ISBN13: 978-0-374-53011-2. Dewey:863/.64. LCCN:2005-056813.
Audience: **g,l,u,f.**

Casey, Calvert & Stavans, Ilan **PQ7390.C3A6 1998**
Calvert Casey: The Collected Stories. John H. Polt (Translator). Trade Cloth. Duke University Press. Durham, NC. 1998. 224p. ISBN:0-8223-2153-X, ISBN13: 978-0-8223-2153-8. LCCN:97-032272.
Audience: **g,l,u,f.** *Choice, 1998.*

Codina, Norberto **PQ**
Poesía Cubana del Siglo XX: Antología. Jesús J. Barquet (Prologue by). Trade Cloth. Fondo de Cultura Economica USA. San Diego, CA. 2004. 558p. Tierra Firme Ser. ISBN:968-16-6761-1, ISBN13: 978-968-16-6761-0.
Audience: **u,f.**

Del Casal, Julian **PQ7389.C266A**
Poesias Completas. Trade Paper. Books on Demand. Ann Arbor, MI. 356p. Cuadernos de Cultura, Septima Serie Ser., Vol. 1 ISBN:0-598-77967-1, ISBN13: 978-0-598-77967-0. Dewey:861.5. LCCN:47-017901.
Audience: **u,f.**

Del Casal, Julian **PQ7389.C266A**
The Poetry of Julian Del Casal: A Critical Edition, Vol. 1. Robert J. Glickman (Editor). Trade Paper. Books on Demand. Ann Arbor, MI. 1976. 304p. ISBN:0-7837-4878-7, ISBN13: 978-0-7837-4878-8. Dewey:861.5. LCCN:76-022800.
Audience: **u,f.**

Del Casal, Julian **PQ7389.C266A**
The Poetry of Julian Del Casal: A Critical Edition, Vol. 2. Robert J. Glickman (Editor). Trade Paper. Books on Demand. Ann Arbor, MI. 1978. 486p. ISBN:0-7837-4879-5, ISBN13: 978-0-7837-4879-5. Dewey:861.5. LCCN:76-022800.
Audience: **u,f.**

Echevarria, Roberto Gonzalez **PQ7389.C263Z/**
Alejo Carpentier: The Pilgrim at Home. Book, Other. Cornell University Press. Ithaca, NY. 1977. 304p. ISBN:0-8014-1029-0, ISBN13: 978-0-8014-1029-1. Dewey:863. LCCN:76-028013.
Audience: **u,f.**

Firmat, Gustavo Perez **PQ7378 .P47 1989**
The Cuban Condition: Translation and Identity in Modern Cuban Literature. Enrique Pupo-Walker (Contribution by). Trade Cloth. Cambridge University Press. New York, NY. 1989. 196p. Cambridge Studies in Latin American and Iberian Literature ISBN:0-521-32747-4, ISBN13: 978-0-521-32747-3. Dewey:860/.9/97291. LCCN:88-023454.
Audience: **u,f.** *Choice, 1990.*

García, Cristina (Editor, Introduction by) **PQ7383.5.E5C83 2003**
Cubanisimo!: The Vintage Book of Contemporary Cuban Literature. Trade Paper. Knopf Publishing Group. New York, NY. 2003. 400p. ISBN:0-385-72137-4, ISBN13: 978-0-385-72137-0. Dewey:860.8/097291. LCCN:2002-038076.
Audience: **g,l,u,f.**

Guillén, Nicolas **PQ7389.G84**
Yoruba from Cuba: Selected Poems of Nicolás Guillén. Salvador Ortiz-Carboneres (Translator, Preface by), Alistair Hennessy (Foreword by). Trade Paper. Peepal Tree Press, Ltd. Leeds, 2005. 240p. ISBN:1-900715-97-X, ISBN13: 978-1-900715-97-3. Dewey:861.6/2.
Audience: **l,u,f.**

Guillén, Nicolás **PQ**
Songoro Cosongo Y Othros Poemas. Trade Cloth. Alianza Editorial, S. A.. Madrid, 2002. 368p. ISBN:84-206-1815-2, ISBN13: 978-84-206-1815-9. Dewey:861. LCCN:81-188921.
Audience: **u,f.**

Guillén, Nicolás **PQ7389.G84S5**
Cuba Libre: Poems. Langston Hughes & Ben Frederic Carruthers (Translators). Trade Paper. Books on Demand. Ann Arbor, MI. 114p. ISBN:0-598-51998-X, ISBN13: 978-0-598-51998-6. Dewey:861. LCCN:49-013581.
Audience: **l,u,f.**

Guillén, Nicolás **PQ7389.G84**
The Great Zoo and Other Poems. Robert Márquez (Editor, Translator). Trade Cloth. Monthly Review Press. New York, NY. 1973. 224p. ISBN:0-85345-256-3, ISBN13: 978-0-85345-256-0. Dewey:861. LCCN:72-081758.
Audience: **l,u,f.**

Hernández, Rafael & Rojas, Rafael **F1787.E57 2002**
Ensayo Cubano del Siglo XX: Antología. Trade Cloth. Fondo de Cultura Economica USA. San Diego, CA. 2004. 738p. Tierra Firme Ser. ISBN:968-16-6720-4, ISBN13: 978-968-16-6720-7. Dewey:972.9106.
Audience: **u,f.**

Huidobro, Matias M. **PQ7390.M65 D413 1992**
Qwert and the Wedding Gown: A Novel. John Mitchell & Ruth M. De Aguilar (Translators). Trade Cloth. Plover Press. Kailua, HI. 1992. 163p. ISBN:0-917635-12-4, ISBN13: 978-0-917635-12-0. Dewey:863. LCCN:92-006005.
Audience: **u,f.**

Infante, Guillermo Cabrena **PQ7389.C233H313 2005**
Infante's Inferno. Trade Paper, Perfect. Dalkey Archive Press. Normal, IL. 2005. 410p. ISBN:1-56478-384-7, ISBN13: 978-1-56478-384-4. Dewey:869/.64. LCCN:2004-063485.
Audience: **l,u,f.**

Infante, Guillermo Cabrera **PQ7389.C233T713 2004**
Three Trapped Tigers. Donald Gardner & Suzanne Jill Levine (Translators). Trade Cloth. Dalkey Archive Press. Normal, IL. 2004. 487p. ISBN:1-56478-379-0, ISBN13: 978-1-56478-379-0. Dewey:863/.64. LCCN:2004-053775.
Audience: **g,l,u,f.**

Kutzinski, Vera M. **PQ7378.K87 1993**
Sugar's Secrets: Race and the Erotics of Cuban Nationalism. Cloth Text. University Press of Virginia. Charlottesville, VA. 1993. 280p. New World Studies, : ISBN:0-8139-1466-3, ISBN13: 978-0-8139-1466-4. Dewey:860.9355. LCCN:93-007644.
Audience: **u,f.** *Choice, 1994.*

Lezama Lima, Jose **PQ7389.L49P313 2000**
Paradiso. Gregory Rabassa (Translator). Trade Paper. Dalkey Archive Press. Normal, IL. 1999. 478p. ISBN:1-56478-228-X, ISBN13: 978-1-56478-228-1. Dewey:863. LCCN:99-035090.
Audience: **l,u,f.** B

Lezama Lima, José (Editor) **PQ**
Antología de la Poesía Cubana: Obra Completa. Trade Cloth. Verbum, Editorial S.L.. Madrid, 2002. 1892p. ISBN:84-7962-236-9, ISBN13: 978-84-7962-236-7.
Audience: **u,f.**

Lima, Jose Lezama **PQ7389.L49 A25 2005**
Jose Lezama Lima: Selections. Ernesto Livon-Grosman (Editor). Trade Paper. University of California Press. Berkeley, CA. 2005. 240p. Poets for the Millennium Ser., Vol. 4 ISBN:0-520-23476-6, ISBN13: 978-0-520-23476-5. Dewey:861/.62. LCCN:2004-044063.
Audience: **l,u,f.**

Martí, José **PQ7389.M2A6 2002**
Selected Writings. Esther Allen (Translator), Roberto Gonzalez Echevarria (Introduction by). Trade Paper. Penguin Group (USA) Inc. New York, NY. 2002. 496p. Classics Ser. ISBN:0-14-243704-2, ISBN13: 978-0-14-243704-9. Dewey:861/.5. LCCN:2001-054865.
Audience: **l,u,f.**

Martí, José **PQ7389.M2.A27 1982**
Jose Marti: Major Poems. Philip S. Foner (Editor), Elinor Randall (Translator). Trade Paper. Holmes & Meier Publishers, Inc. Teaneck, NJ. 1982. 200p. ISBN:0-8419-0834-6, ISBN13: 978-0-8419-0834-5. Dewey:861. LCCN:81-020016.
Audience: **g,l,u,f.** B

Martí, José **PQ7389.M2V4513 2005**
Versos Sencillos. Anne Fountain (Translator), Pete Seeger (Foreword by). Trade Paper, Perfect. McFarland & Company, Incorporated Publishers. Jefferson, NC. 2005. 130p. Latino and Latin American Studies ISBN:0-7864-2386-2, ISBN13: 978-0-7864-2386-6. Dewey:861. LCCN:2005-020841.
Audience: **u,f.**

Martí, José **PQ7389.M2V4513 1997**
Versos Sencillos. Manuel A. Tellechea (Translator). Trade Cloth. Arte Publico Press. Houston, TX. 1997. 128p. Recovering the U.S.-Hispanic Literary Heritage Ser. ISBN:1-55885-218-2, ISBN13: 978-1-55885-218-1. Dewey:861. LCCN:97-022189.
Audience: **l,u,f.**

Martínez, Julio A. (Editor) **PQ7378**
Dictionary of Twentieth-Century Cuban Literature. Cloth Text. Greenwood Publishing Group, Inc. Portsmouth, NH. 1990. 549p. ISBN:0-313-25185-1, ISBN13: 978-0-313-25185-6. Dewey:860/.9/97291. LCCN:88-035805.
Audience: **g,l,u.** *Choice, 1990.*

Montes Huidobro, Matías **PQ7390.M65F86 1990**
Funeral en Teruel. Francesca M. Colecchia (Introduction by). Trade Paper. Editorial Persona. Honolulu, HI. 1989. 96p. Teatro Ser. ISBN:0-945791-05-4, ISBN13: 978-0-945791-05-8. LCCN:89-080701.
Audience: **u,f.**

Montes Huidobro, Matías **PQ7390.M65O26 1991**
Obras en un Acto. Ana M. Montes (Illustrator). Trade Paper. Editorial Persona. Honolulu, HI. 1989. 128p. Teatro Ser. ISBN:0-945791-06-2, ISBN13: 978-0-945791-06-5. LCCN:89-080700.
Audience: **u,f.**

Nelson, Ardis L. **PQ7389.C233Z66 1999**
Guillermo Cabrera Infante. Trade Cloth. Thomson Gale. Farmington Hills, MI. 1999. xxv, 242p. ISBN:0-8057-1644-0, ISBN13: 978-0-8057-1644-3. Dewey:863. LCCN:98-049188.
Audience: **l,u,f.** *Choice, 1999.*

Piñera, Virgilio **PQ7389.P49A6X 1983**
Cuentos. Trade Cloth. Alfaguara, Ediciones, S.A.- Grupo Santillana. 28043, Madrid, 1983. 320p. ISBN:84-204-2145-6, ISBN13: 978-84-204-2145-2. LCCN:87-673876.
Audience: **u,f.**

Piñera, Virgilio **PQ7389.P49 A59 1990**
Aire Frio. Trade Cloth. Asociacin de Directores de Escena. Madrid, 1901. 176p. ISBN:84-87591-05-1, ISBN13: 978-84-87591-05-1. Dewey:862.
Audience: **u,f.**

Prieto, Jose Manuel **PQ7390.P76L5813 2000**
Nocturnal Butterflies of the Russian Empire: A Novel. Thomas Christensen & Carol Christensen (Translators). Trade Cloth. Grove/Atlantic, Inc. New York, NY. 2000. 322p. ISBN:0-8021-1665-5, ISBN13: 978-0-8021-1665-9. Dewey:863. LCCN:00-042957.
Audience: **g,l,u,f.**

Pérez Sarduy, Pedro & Stubbs, Jean **PQ7382.A48 1998**
Afrocuba: Una Antología de Escritos Cubanos Sobre Raza, Política y Cultura. Trade Cloth. University of Puerto Rico Press. Rio Piedras, PR. 1998. 336p. ISBN:0-8477-0302-9, ISBN13: 978-0-8477-0302-9. Dewey:305.8/0097291. LCCN:97-040779.
Audience: **u,f.**

Sarduy, Severo **PQ7390.S28M3**
Maitreya. Trade Cloth. Editorial Seix Barral. Barcelona, 1978. 192p. ISBN:84-322-1378-0, ISBN13: 978-84-322-1378-6. Dewey:863. LCCN:79-357717.
Audience: **u,f.** *Choice, 1988.*

Sarduy, Severo **PQ7390.S28D413 1994**
From Cuba with a Song. Suzanne J. Levine (Translator). Trade Paper. Sun & Moon Press. Los Angeles, CA. 1994. 104p. Sun and Moon Classics Ser., No. 52 ISBN:1-55713-158-9, ISBN13: 978-1-55713-158-4. Dewey:863. LCCN:94-028405.
Audience: **l,u,f.**

Sarduy, Severo **PQ7390.S28C713 1995**
Christ on the Rue Jacob. Suzanne J. Levine & Carol Maier (Translators). Trade Paper. Mercury House. San Francisco, CA. 1995. 176p. ISBN:1-56279-075-7, ISBN13: 978-1-56279-075-2. Dewey:864. LCCN:94-037259.
Audience: **l,u,f.**

Sarduy, Severo **PQ7390.S28A6 1995**
Cobra and Maitreya. Suzanne J. Levine (Translator), James McCourt (Introduction by). Trade Cloth. Dalkey Archive Press. Normal, IL. 1995. 288p. ISBN:1-56478-076-7, ISBN13: 978-1-56478-076-8. Dewey:863. LCCN:94-025167.
Audience: **l,u,f.**

Shaw, Donald L. **PQ7389.C263.Z88 1985**
Alejo Carpentier. Trade Cloth. Thomson Gale. Farmington Hills, MI. 1985. 150p. World Authors Ser., No. 756 ISBN:0-8057-6606-5, ISBN13: 978-0-8057-6606-6. Dewey:863. LCCN:84-025297.
Audience: **l,u,f.** B *Choice, 1985.*

Smorkaloff, Pamela Maria **PQ7382.S66 1999**
Contemporary Cuban Writers. Trade Cloth. Thomson Gale. Farmington Hills, MI. 1999. xxiii, 100p. ISBN:0-8057-1617-3, ISBN13: 978-0-8057-1617-7. Dewey:863. LCCN:99-027604.
Audience: **l,u.** *Choice, 2000.*

Soto, Gary **PQ7390.A72Z87 1998**
Reinaldo Arenas. Trade Cloth. Thomson Gale. Farmington Hills, MI. 1998. 185p. World Authors Ser., Vol. 870 ISBN:0-8057-4554-8, ISBN13: 978-0-8057-4554-2. Dewey:863. LCCN:98-021201.
Audience: **g,l.** *Choice, 1999.*

Valdés, Zoé **PQ7082.N7**
Cafe Nostalgia. Trade Cloth. Editorial Planeta, S. A.. Barcelona 8, 2001. 160p. ISBN:84-08-03933-4, ISBN13: 978-84-08-03933-4. Dewey:863.
Audience: **u,f.**

Valdés, Zoé **PQ7390.V342T313 1999**
I Gave You All I Had. Nadia Benabid (Translator). Trade Cloth. Arcade Publishing, Inc. New York, NY. 1999. 320p. ISBN:1-55970-477-2, ISBN13: 978-1-55970-477-9. Dewey:863/.64. LCCN:00-269034.
Audience: **g,l,u,f.**

Villaverde, Cirilo **PQ7389.V55C413 2004**
Cecilia Valdes or el Angel Hill. Sibylle Fischer (Editor), Helen Lane (Translator). Trade Cloth. Oxford University Press, Inc. New York, NY. 2005. 542p. Library of Latin America ISBN:0-19-514394-9, ISBN13: 978-0-19-514394-2. Dewey:863/.5. LCCN:2003-058232.
Audience: **g,l,u.**

Yanez, Mirta (Editor) **PQ7386.C835 1998**
Cubana: Contemporary Fiction by Cuban Women. Dick Cluster & Cindy Schuster (Translators), Ruth Behar (Introduction by). Trade Cloth. Beacon Press. Boston, MA. 1998. 240p. ISBN:0-8070-8336-4, ISBN13: 978-0-8070-8336-9. Dewey:863/.01089287/097291. LCCN:97-045924.
Audience: **g,l,u,f.** *Choice, 1998.*

Hispanic Literature > Hispanic-American Literature > Individual Countries > Central America

Ak'abal, Humberto **PQ7499.2.A3584**
Ajyuq', el Animalero. Trade Cloth. Piedra Santa, Editorial. Guatemala, 1995. 55p. ISBN:84-89451-16-8, ISBN13: 978-84-89451-16-2.
Audience: **u,f.**

Alegría, Claribel **PQ7539.A47**
El Nino Que Buscaba a Ayer. Paper Text. Donars Spanish Books. Lafayette, CO. 1997. Encuento/Literary Encounters Ser. ISBN:968-494-072-6, ISBN13: 978-968-494-072-7. Dewey:428.
Audience: **u,f.**

Alegría, Claribel & Flakoll, Darwin J. **PQ7539.A47**
Ashes of Izalco. Trade Paper. Curbstone Press. Willimantic, CT. 1998. 192p. ISBN:0-915306-84-0, ISBN13: 978-0-915306-84-8. Dewey:861. LCCN:89-062125.
Audience: **u,f.** *Choice, 1990.*

Alegría, Claribel **PQ8097.N4**
Luisa in Realityland: A Novel. Darwin J. Flakoll (Translator). Trade Paper. Curbstone Press. Willimantic, CT. 1988. 154p. ISBN:0-915306-69-7, ISBN13: 978-0-915306-69-5. Dewey:861. LCCN:87-071705.
Audience: **l,u,f.** *Choice, 1988.*

Alegría, Claribel **PQ7539.A47A24 1997**
Thresholds (Umbrales): Poems. Darwin J. Flakoll (Translator). Trade Paper. Curbstone Press. Willimantic, CT. 1996. 70p. ISBN:1-880684-36-5, ISBN13: 978-1-880684-36-8. Dewey:861. LCCN:96-021329.
Audience: **l,u,f.**

Alegría, Claribel **PQ7539.A47M813 1989**
Woman of the River. Darwin J. Flakoll (Translator). Trade Paper. University of Pittsburgh Press. Pittsburgh, PA. 1989. 112p. Pitt Poetry Ser. ISBN:0-8229-5409-5, ISBN13: 978-0-8229-5409-5. Dewey:811. LCCN:88-004775.
Audience: **l,u,f.** *Choice, 1989.*

Alegría, Claribel **PQ7539.A47S67 1999**
Sorrow. Carolyn Forche (Translator, Introduction by). Trade Paper. Curbstone Press. Willimantic, CT. 1999. 104p. Curbstone Press Contemporary Poets Ser. ISBN:1-880684-63-2, ISBN13: 978-1-880684-63-4. Dewey:861. LCCN:99-027585.
Audience: **l,u,f.**

Alegría, Claribel **MLCS 93/08014 (P)**
Family Album: Three Novellas. Amanda Hopkinson (Translator). Trade Paper. Curbstone Press. Willimantic, CT. 1991. 192p. ISBN:0-915306-94-8, ISBN13: 978-0-915306-94-7. Dewey:863. LCCN:91-055413.
Audience: **l,u,f.**

Alegría, Claribel **PQ7539.A47S7613 2003**
Soltando Amarras: Casting Off. Margaret Sayers Peden (Translator). Trade Paper. Curbstone Press. Willimantic, CT. 2003. 114p. ISBN:1-880684-98-5, ISBN13: 978-1-880684-98-6. Dewey:861/.64. LCCN:2002-035165.
Audience: **l,u,f.**

Arango, Luis Alfredo **PQ7499.2.A68**
Con barro del Corazon: Ruk' Kach' Ulew Re Uk'Ux Jun. Trade Cloth. Fondo de Cultura Economica de Guatemala. Guatemala, 2004. Intercultural Ser. ISBN:99922-48-02-5, ISBN13: 978-99922-48-02-7. Dewey:863.64.
Audience: **u,f.**

Arango, Luis Alfredo **PQ7499.2.A68**
A vuelo de Pajaro: Chi xik'anik Tz'ikin. Trade Cloth. Fondo de Cultura Economica de Guatemala. Guatemala, 2004. Intercultural Ser. ISBN:99922-48-15-7, ISBN13: 978-99922-48-15-7. Dewey:863.64.
Audience: **u,f.**

Argueta, Manlio **PQ7539.2.A68D513**
One Day of Life. Bill Brow (Translator). Trade Paper. Knopf Publishing Group. New York, NY. 1991. 224p. Vintage International Ser. ISBN:0-679-73243-8, ISBN13: 978-0-679-73243-3. Dewey:863. LCCN:90-050213.
Audience: **g,l,u,f.**

Argueta, Manlio **PQ7539.2.A68**
A Place Called Milagro de la Paz. Michael B. Miller (Translator). Trade Paper. Curbstone Press. Willimantic, CT. 2000. 160p. ISBN:1-880684-68-3, ISBN13: 978-1-880684-68-9. Dewey:863/.64. LCCN:99-086710.
Audience: **g,l,u,f.**

Arias, Arturo **PQ7499.2.A73S66 2002**
Sopa de Caracol. Trade Paper. Santillana USA Publishing Company, Inc. Doral, FL. 2005. 402p. ISBN:99922-3-197-1, ISBN13: 978-99922-3-197-5. Dewey:863/.64. LCCN:2003-555487.
Audience: **u,f.**

Arias, Arturo **PQ7499.2.A73C3713**
Rattlesnake. Sean Higgins & Jill Robbins (Translators). Trade Paper. Curbstone Press. Willimantic, CT. 2003. 228p. ISBN:1-931896-01-1, ISBN13: 978-1-931896-01-6. Dewey:863/.64. LCCN:2003-016402.
Audience: **g,l,u,f.**

Arias, Arturo **PQ7499.2.A73.D4713**
After the Bombs: A Novel. Asa Zatz (Translator). Trade Cloth. Curbstone Press. Willimantic, CT. 1990. 224p. ISBN:0-915306-88-3, ISBN13: 978-0-915306-88-6. Dewey:863. LCCN:90-081428.
Audience: **g,l,u,f.** *Choice, 1991.*

Asturias, Miguel Ángel **PQ7499.A75**
El Arbol de la Cruz. Trade Cloth. Fondo de Cultura Economica. Mexico, DF 03100, 306p. Coleccion Archivos de Ediciones Criticas ISBN:84-88344-05-8, ISBN13: 978-84-88344-05-2. Dewey:863.6.
Audience: **u,f.**

Asturias, Miguel Ángel **PQ7499.A75**
Hombres de Maize. Trade Cloth. Alianza Editorial, S. A.. Madrid, 368p. ISBN:84-206-1413-0, ISBN13: 978-84-206-1413-7. Dewey:863.
Audience: **u,f.**

Asturias, Miguel Ángel **PQ7499 A75 L4 1999**
Leyendas de Guatemala. Trade Cloth. Ediciones Cátedra. Madrid 1, 2002. 240p. ISBN:84-376-1353-1, ISBN13: 978-84-376-1353-6. Dewey:398.4.
Audience: **u,f.**

Asturias, Miguel Ángel **PQ7499.A75**
El Senor Presidente. Library Binding. Sagebrush Education Resources. Caledonia, MN. 1998. ISBN:0-613-80721-9, ISBN13: 978-0-613-80721-0. Dewey:863.
Audience: **u,f.**

Asturias, Miguel Ángel **PZ4.A843**
El Senor Presidente (The Honorable Mister President). Trade Paper. Editorial Voluntad S.A.. Coleccion Centro Literario ISBN:958-02-0495-0, ISBN13: 978-958-02-0495-4. Dewey:863.
Audience: **u,f.**

Asturias, Miguel Ángel **F1434.2.R3A7713 1997**
The Mirror of Lida Sal: Tales Based on Mayan Myths and Guatemalan Legends. Gilbert Alter-Gilbert (Translator). Trade Paper. Latin American Literary Review Press. Pittsburgh, PA. 1997. 126p. ISBN:0-935480-83-8, ISBN13: 978-0-935480-83-2. Dewey:398.2/097281. LCCN:96-035864.
Audience: **g,l,u,f.**

Benedetti, Mario **PQ8519.B292A23 1997**
Blood Pact and Other Stories. Claribel Alegría & Darwin J. Flakoll (Editors). Trade Paper. Curbstone Press. Willimantic, CT. 1997. 214p. ISBN:1-880684-39-X, ISBN13: 978-1-880684-39-9. Dewey:863. LCCN:96-021343.
Audience: **g,l,u,f.**

Cardenal, Ernesto **PQ7519.C34A6 1978**
Antología. Trade Cloth. Laia, Editorial S. A.. Barcelona 14, 1978. 280p. ISBN:84-7222-354-X, ISBN13: 978-84-7222-354-7. Dewey:861. LCCN:78-369220.
Audience: **u,f.**

Cardenal, Ernesto **PQ8097.N4**
Golden UFOs: The Indian Poems Los Ovnis de Oro: Poemas Indios. Cloth Text. Indiana University Press. Bloomington, IN. 1992. 480p. ISBN:0-253-31302-3, ISBN13: 978-0-253-31302-7. Dewey:861. LCCN:91-033638.
Audience: **l,u,f.**

Cardenal, Ernesto **PQ**
Vida Perdida. Trade Cloth. GeoPlaneta, Editorial, S. A.. Barcelona, 1999. 464p. ISBN:84-322-0832-9, ISBN13: 978-84-322-0832-4. Dewey:861/.64 B. LCCN:99-509099.
Audience: **u,f.**

Cardenal, Ernesto **PQ7519**
Cosmic Canticle. John Lyons (Translator). Trade Paper. Curbstone Press. Willimantic, CT. 2002. 490p. ISBN:1-880684-93-4, ISBN13: 978-1-880684-93-1. Dewey:861.
Audience: **u,f.** *Choice, 1994.*

Cardenal, Ernesto **PQ7519.C34E813 1995**
The Doubtful Strait. John Lyons & Tamara R. Williams (Translators). Trade Paper. Indiana University Press. Bloomington, IN. 1995. 224p. ISBN:0-253-20903-X, ISBN13: 978-0-253-20903-0. Dewey:861. LCCN:94-000633.
Audience: **g,l,u,f.** *Choice, 1995.*

Cardoza y Aragon, Luis **PQ7499.C34**
El Rio: Novelas de Caballeria. Book, Other. Fondo de Cultura Economica USA. San Diego, CA. ISBN:968-16-5037-9, ISBN13: 978-968-16-5037-7. Dewey:868.6409.
Audience: **u,f.**

Carrera, Margarita **PQ6613.O79**
En la mirilla del Jaguar: Biografia novelada de monsenor Gerardi. Trade Cloth. Fondo de Cultura Economica de Guatemala. Guatemala, 2004. Coleccion Escritores Centroamericanos Ser. ISBN:99922-48-20-3, ISBN13: 978-99922-48-20-1. Dewey:863/.64. LCCN:2002-527104.
Audience: **u,f.**

Castillo, Otto Rene **PQ7499.2.C38**
Let's Go!. Perfect. Azul Editions. Washington, DC. 2006. ISBN:1-885214-36-7, ISBN13: 978-1-885214-36-2. Dewey:861.
Audience: **g,l,u,f.**

Dalton, Roque **PQ8097.N4**
Clandestine Poems--Poemas Clandestinos: Bilingual Edition. Barbara Paschke & Eric Weaver (Editors), Jack Hirschman (Translator), Margaret Randall (Introduction by). Trade Paper. New Americas Press. San Francisco, CA. 1984. 224p. ISBN:0-942638-07-7, ISBN13: 978-0-942638-07-3. Dewey:861. LCCN:83-051488.
Audience: **l,u,f.**

Dalton, Roque **PQ7539.2.D3**
Clandestine Poems (Poemas Clandestinos). Barbara Paschke & Jack Weaver (Editors), Jack Hirschman (Translator), Margaret Randall (Introduction by). Trade Paper. Curbstone Press. Willimantic, CT. 1998. 184p. ISBN:0-915306-91-3, ISBN13: 978-0-915306-91-6. Dewey:861. LCCN:83-051488.
Audience: **l,u,f.**

Dalton, Roque **HX148.8.M37**
Miguel Marmol. Kathleen Ross & Richard Schaaf (Translators), Margaret Randall (Preface by), Manlio Argueta (Introduction by). Trade Paper. Curbstone Press. Willimantic, CT. 1988. 506p. ISBN:0-915306-67-0, ISBN13: 978-0-915306-67-1. Dewey:324.27284/075/0924. LCCN:87-071397.
Audience: **l,u,f.** *Choice, 1987.*

Dalton, Roque **PQ7539.2.D3A6 1996**
Small Hours of the Night: Selected Poems of Roque Dalton. Hardie St. Martin (Editor), Jonathan Cohen (Translator), Ernesto Cardenal & Claribel Alegría (Introduction by). Trade Paper. Curbstone Press. Willimantic, CT. 1996. 228p. ISBN:1-880684-35-7, ISBN13: 978-1-880684-35-1. Dewey:861. LCCN:96-000867.
Audience: **l,u,f.**

Darío, Rubén **PQ7519.D3A225 2001**
Selected Poems of Ruben Dario: A Bilingual Anthology. Alberto Acereda & Will Derusha (Editors), Alberto Acereda & Will Derusha (Translators), Alberto Acereda & Will Derusha (Introduction by). Trade Cloth. Bucknell University Press. Cranbury, NJ. 2001. 268p. ISBN:0-8387-5461-9, ISBN13: 978-0-8387-5461-0. Dewey:861/.5. LCCN:2001-018450.
Audience: **l,u,f.** *Choice, 2002.*

Darío, Rubén **PQ7519.D3A228 2005**
Selected Writings (Dario, Ruben). Andrew Hurley, Greg Simon & Steven White (Translators), Ilan Stavans (Introduction by). Trade Paper. Penguin Group (USA) Inc. New York, NY. 2005. 736p. Penguin Classics Ser. ISBN:0-14-303936-9, ISBN13: 978-0-14-303936-5. Dewey:861/.5. LCCN:2005-045224.
Audience: **l,u,f.**

Darío, Rubén **PQ7519.D3 A17 1952B**
Poesias Completas. Alfonso Mendez Plancarte & Helene Westbrook Harrison (Contribution by). Trade Cloth. Information Handling Services. Englewood, CO. 1952. "lxiv, 1450"p. ISBN:0-910972-02-8, ISBN13: 978-0-910972-02-4. Dewey:869.31. LCCN:78-129774.
Audience: **u,f.**

Gonzalez, Otto-Raul **PQ7499.G63**
Coctel de Frutas: Yuja'n Uwach Che'. Trade Cloth. Fondo de Cultura Economica de Guatemala. Guatemala, 2004. Intercultural Ser. ISBN:99922-48-07-6, ISBN13: 978-99922-48-07-2. Dewey:861.
Audience: **u,f.**

Gonzalez, Otto-Raul **PQ7499.G63 A6 1998**
Huitzil Uan Tuxtli: Colibri y Conejo - Medio Siglo de Poesia. Trade Paper. Fondo de Cultura Economica USA. San Diego, CA. 1998. ISBN:968-16-5218-5, ISBN13: 978-968-16-5218-0. Dewey:861. LCCN:98-204815.
Audience: **u,f.**

Lars, Claudia **PQ7539.B7Z47613 2003**
Land of Childhood. Trade Paper. iUniverse, Inc. Lincoln, NE. 2003. 114p. ISBN:0-595-27353-X, ISBN13: 978-0-595-27353-9. Dewey:861/.64 B. LCCN:2003-384055.
Audience: **l,u,f.**

Liano, Dante **PQ7499.L48**
El hijo de Casa. Trade Paper. Roca Editorial De Libros. Barcelona, ISBN:84-96284-17-4, ISBN13: 978-84-96284-17-3. Dewey:863.
Audience: **u,f.**

Lindo, Hugo **PQ7539.L5**
Only the Voice. Elizabeth G. Miller (Translator). Trade Paper. Mundus Artium Press. Richardson, TX. 1984. 110p. ISBN:0-939378-04-3, ISBN13: 978-0-939378-04-3. Dewey:861.64.
Audience: **u,f.**

Lindo, Hugo **PQ7539.L5 A25 1986**
The Ways of Rain: And Other Poems by Hugo Lindo. Yvette E. Miller (Editor), Elizabeth G. Miller (Translator), Rainer Schulte (Foreword by). Trade Paper. Latin American Literary Review Press. Pittsburgh, PA. 1986. 160p. Discoveries Ser. ISBN:0-935480-24-2, ISBN13: 978-0-935480-24-5. Dewey:861. LCCN:86-018577.
Audience: **l,u,f.** *Choice, 1987.*

Lobo, Tatiana **PQ7489.2.L58A7313**
Assault on Paradise. Asa Zatz (Translator). Trade Paper. Curbstone Press. Willimantic, CT. 1998. 298p. ISBN:1-880684-46-2, ISBN13: 978-1-880684-46-7. Dewey:863. LCCN:97-047572.
Audience: **l,u,f.** *Choice, 1999.*

Lyra, Carmen **PQ7489.L9A6 2000**
The Subversive Voice of Carmen Lyra: Selected Works. Elizabeth Rosa Horan (Editor, Translator, Introduction by). Trade Cloth. University Press of Florida. Gainesville, FL. 2000. xvi, 225p. ISBN:0-8130-1767-X, ISBN13: 978-0-8130-1767-9. Dewey:863. LCCN:99-087011.
Audience: **l,u,f.** *Choice, 2001.*

Menchu, Rigoberta **F1465.2.Q5M373 1998**
Crossing Borders: An Autobiography. Trade Cloth. Analytical Psychology Club of San Francisco, Inc. San Francisco, CA. 1998. 242p. ISBN:1-85984-893-1, ISBN13: 978-1-85984-893-7. Dewey:972.8/1052/092. LCCN:98-030118.
Audience: **u,f.** *Choice, 1999.*

Menchu, Rigoberta **F1465.2.Q5 M386 1998**
Rigoberta: La Nieta de Los Mayas. Trade Cloth. Santillana USA Publishing Company, Inc. Doral, FL. 1998. 264p. ISBN:84-03-59526-3, ISBN13: 978-84-03-59526-2. Dewey:972.8105/2/092. LCCN:98-171338.
Audience: **l,u,f.**

Menchu, Rigoberta **F1465.3.S62**
I, Rigoberta Menchu: An Indian Woman in Guatemala. Elizabeth Burgos-Debray (Editor), Ann Wright (Translator), Elizabeth Burgos-Debray (Introduction by). Trade Paper. Verso Books. London, 1987. 252p. ISBN:0-86091-788-6, ISBN13: 978-0-86091-788-5. Dewey:972.81/00497. LCCN:84-157775.
Audience: **l,u,f.**

Monteforte Toledo, Mario **PQ7499.M56**
La isla de las Navajas: Ri Utukel Ulew Re Ri Ch'ich'. Trade Cloth. Fondo de Cultura Economica de Guatemala. Guatemala, 2004. Intercultural Ser. ISBN:99922-48-06-8, ISBN13: 978-99922-48-06-5. Dewey:863.
Audience: **u,f.**

Naranjo, Carmen **PQ7489.2.N3N8413**
There Never Was a Once upon a Time. Yvette E. Miller (Editor), Linda Britt (Translator, Introduction by). Trade Paper. Latin American Literary Review Press. Pittsburgh, PA. 1989. 94p. ISBN:0-935480-41-2, ISBN13: 978-0-935480-41-2. Dewey:863. LCCN:89-012822.
Audience: **l,u,f.**

Recinos, Adrian (Translator) **F1465**
Popol Vuh: Las Antiguas Historias Del Quiche (Indigenous Legends). Trade Cloth. Piedra Santa, Editorial. Guatemala, 1997. 270p. ISBN:84-8377-093-8, ISBN13: 978-84-8377-093-1. Dewey:299.784.
Audience: **u,f.**

Recinos, Adrian (Translator), et al. **F1465**
Popol Vuh: The Sacred Book of the Ancient Quiche Maya: Spanish Version of the Original Maya. Delia Goetz & Aylvanus G. Morley (Translators). Trade Paper. University of Oklahoma Press. Norman, OK. 1991. 288p. Civilization of the American Indian Ser., No. 29 ISBN:0-8061-2266-8, ISBN13: 978-0-8061-2266-3. Dewey:913.7281. LCCN:50-006643.
Audience: **g,l,u,f.**

Rodas, Ana Maria **PQ7499.2.R58**
La Monja: Ixoq rusamajel Ajaw. Trade Cloth. Fondo de Cultura Economica de Guatemala. Guatemala, 2004. Intercultural Ser. ISBN:99922-48-14-9, ISBN13: 978-99922-48-14-0. Dewey:861.
Audience: **u,f.**

Ruz, Alberto & Cardoza y Aragón, Luis **GN**
El Pueblo Maya. Ed. 2. Trade Cloth. Promotora Editorial, S.A. de C.V.. 11570 Mexico D.F., 1992. 346p. ISBN:970-611-244-8, ISBN13: 978-970-611-244-6. Dewey:972.81/01.
Audience: **u,f.**

Solorzano, Carlos **PQ7499.S6 C6 1993**
Crossroads, and Other Plays by Carlos Solorzano. Francesca Colecchia (Editor, Translator). Trade Cloth. Fairleigh Dickinson University Press. Cranbury, NJ. 1993. 148p. ISBN:0-8386-3485-0, ISBN13: 978-0-8386-3485-1. Dewey:862. LCCN:91-058941.
Audience: **g,l,u,f.**

Tedlock, Dennis **F1465.2.Q5T45 1997**
Breath on the Mirror: Mythic Voices and Visions of the Living Maya. Trade Paper. University of New Mexico Press. Albuquerque, NM. 1997. 260p. ISBN:0-8263-1823-1, ISBN13: 978-0-8263-1823-7. Dewey:299/.72. LCCN:97-001378.
Audience: **g,l,u,f.**

Tedlock, Dennis **PM4231.Z95**
Rabinal Achi: A Mayan Drama of Sacrifice. Trade Paper. Oxford University Press, Inc. New York, NY. 2005. 382p. ISBN:0-19-513975-5, ISBN13: 978-0-19-513975-4. Dewey:897.42.
Audience: **g,l,u,f.**

Zamora, Daisy **PQ7519.2.Z35V513**
The Violent Foam: New and Selected Poems. George Evans (Translator). Trade Paper. Curbstone Press. Willimantic, CT. 2002. 162p. ISBN:1-880684-88-8, ISBN13: 978-1-880684-88-7. Dewey:861/.64. LCCN:2002-004255.
Audience: **g,l,u,f.**

Zamora, Daisy **PQ8097.N4**
Riverbed of Memory. Barbara Paschke (Translator). Trade Cloth. City Lights Books. San Francisco, CA. 1993. 120p. Pocket Poets Ser., No. 49 ISBN:0-87286-273-9, ISBN13: 978-0-87286-273-9. Dewey:861. LCCN:92-034355.
Audience: **g,l,u,f.**

Zamora, Daisy **PQ7519.2.Z35**
Clean Slate: New and Selected Poems. Margaret Randall & Elinor Randall (Translators). Trade Paper. Curbstone Press. Willimantic, CT. 1993. 192p. ISBN:1-880684-09-8, ISBN13: 978-1-880684-09-2. Dewey:861. LCCN:93-004848.
Audience: **g,l,u,f.**

Hispanic Literature > Hispanic-American Literature > Individual Countries > Argentina

Bell-Villada, Gene H. **PQ7797.B635Z6342**
Borges and His Fiction: A Guide to His Mind and Art. Trade Cloth. University of Texas Press. Austin, TX. 2000. 351p. Texas Pan American Ser. ISBN:0-292-70877-7, ISBN13: 978-0-292-70877-8. Dewey:868. LCCN:99-020938.
Audience: **g,l,u,f.**

Bloom, Harold (Introduction by) **PQ7797.B635Z7383**
Jorge Luis Borges. Trade Cloth. Facts On File, Inc. New York, NY. 2004. 112p. Bloom's BioCritiques Ser. ISBN:0-7910-7872-8, ISBN13: 978-0-7910-7872-3. Dewey:868/.6209. LCCN:2003-023937.
Audience: **g,l,u,f.**

Bloom, Harold (Editor) **PQ7797.C7145Z5947**
Julio Cortazar. Trade Cloth. Facts On File, Inc. New York, NY. 2005. 300p. Bloom's Modern Critical Views Ser. ISBN:0-7910-8134-6, ISBN13: 978-0-7910-8134-1. Dewey:863/.64. LCCN:2004-026652.
Audience: **g,l,u,f.**

Bloom, Harold (Editor, Translator, Introduction by) **PQ7797.C7145Z7149**
Julio Cortazar. Trade Cloth. Facts On File, Inc. New York, NY. 2003. 80p. Bloom's Major Short Story Writers Ser. ISBN:0-7910-7592-3, ISBN13: 978-0-7910-7592-0. Dewey:863/.64. LCCN:2003-012277.
Audience: **g,l,u,f.**

Borges, Jorge Luis **PQ**
Obras Completas, Vol. 3. Other. Emecé Editores S.A.. Buenos Aires, 1996. ISBN:950-04-0949-6, ISBN13: 978-950-04-0949-0. Dewey:868.
Audience: **u,f.**

Borges, Jorge Luis **PQ**
Obras Completas, Vol. 2. Other. Emecé Editores S.A.. Buenos Aires, 1996. ISBN:950-04-0948-8, ISBN13: 978-950-04-0948-3. Dewey:868.
Audience: **u,f.**

Borges, Jorge Luis **PQ**
Obras Completas, Vol. 4. Trade Cloth. Emecé Editores S.A.. Buenos Aires, 1996. ISBN:950-04-2259-X, ISBN13: 978-950-04-2259-8. Dewey:868.
Audience: **u,f.**

Borges, Jorge Luis **PQ**
Obras Completas, Vol. 1. Trade Cloth. Emecé Editores S.A.. Buenos Aires, 1996. ISBN:950-04-0947-X, ISBN13: 978-950-04-0947-6. Dewey:868.
Audience: **u,f.**

Borges, Jorge Luis **PQ7797.B635A2 1999**
Selected Poems. Andrew Coleman & Alexander Coleman (Editors). Trade Cloth. Penguin Group (USA) Inc. New York, NY. 1999. 576p. ISBN:0-670-84941-3, ISBN13: 978-0-670-84941-3. Dewey:861. LCCN:99-010318.
Audience: **g,l,u,f.** *Choice, 1999.*

Borges, Jorge Luis **PQ7797.B635A24 1998**
Collected Fictions, Vol. 3. Andrew Hurley (Translator), Jorge Luis Borges (Preface by). Trade Cloth. Penguin Group (USA) Inc. New York, NY. 1998. 576p. ISBN:0-670-84970-7, ISBN13: 978-0-670-84970-3. Dewey:863. LCCN:98-021217.
Audience: **g,l,u,f.**

Borges, Jorge Luis **PQ7797.B635B5213**
The Library of Babel. Andrew Hurley (Translator), Erik Desmazieres (Illustrator). Trade Cloth. David R. Godine Publisher. Boston, MA. 2000. 48p. Pocket Paragon Ser. ISBN:1-56792-123-X, ISBN13: 978-1-56792-123-6. Dewey:868/.6209. LCCN:00-034836.
Audience: **g,l,u,f.**

Borges, Jorge Luis **PQ7797.B635A24 2004**
The Aleph and Other Stories. Andrew Hurley (Author, Notes by). Trade Paper. Penguin Group (USA) Inc. New York, NY. 2004. 224p. Penguin Classics Ser. ISBN:0-14-243788-3, ISBN13: 978-0-14-243788-9. Dewey:863/.62. LCCN:2004-276122.
Audience: **g,l,u,f.**

Borges, Jorge Luis **PQ7797.B635H513 2004**
Universal History of Iniquity. Andrew Hurley (Author, Notes by). Trade Paper. Penguin Group (USA) Inc. New York, NY. 2004. 112p. Penguin Classics Ser. ISBN:0-14-243789-1, ISBN13: 978-0-14-243789-6. Dewey:868. LCCN:2004-301813.
Audience: **g,l,u,f.**

Borges, Jorge Luis **PQ7797.B635.F513**
Fictions. Anthony Kerrigan (Editor, Introduction by). Trade Paper. Riverrun Press, Inc. Flemington, NJ. 1991. 160p. ISBN:0-7145-4083-8, ISBN13: 978-0-7145-4083-2. Dewey:863. LCCN:87-672380.
Audience: **g,l,u,f.**

Borges, Jorge Luis **PQ7797.B635A22 1999**
Selected Non-Fictions. Eliot Weinberger (Editor), Esther Allen, Suzane Jill Levine & Andrew Hurley (Translators). Trade Cloth. Penguin Group (USA) Inc. New York, NY. 1999. 560p. ISBN:0-670-84947-2, ISBN13: 978-0-670-84947-5. Dewey:864. LCCN:99-012386.
Audience: **g,l,u,f.**

Cortazar, Julio **PQ7797.C7145**
Bestiario. Trade Cloth. Suma de Letras, S.L.. Madrid, 2005. 176p. ISBN:84-663-0227-1, ISBN13: 978-84-663-0227-2. Dewey:863.64.
Audience: **u,f.**

Cortazar, Julio **PQ7797.C7145**
Final Del Juego. Trade Cloth. Suma de Letras, S.L.. Madrid, 2005. 240p. ISBN:84-663-1180-7, ISBN13: 978-84-663-1180-9. Dewey:863.64.
Audience: **u,f.**

Cortazar, Julio **PQ7797.C7145**
Rayuela. Other. Santillana USA Publishing Company, Inc. Doral, FL. 2005. 711p. ISBN:84-663-0463-0, ISBN13: 978-84-663-0463-4. Dewey:863.64.
Audience: **u,f.** B

Di Giovanni, Norman Thomas **PQ7797.B635**
The Lesson of the Master: On Borges and His Work. Trade Paper. Continuum International Publishing Group, Ltd. London, 2004. 208p. ISBN:0-8264-7625-2, ISBN13: 978-0-8264-7625-8. Dewey:868/.6209. LCCN:2005-274901.
Audience: **g,l,u,f.**

Dragon, Osvaldo **PQ7797.D736 T4**
Historias para Ser Contadas - Stories for the Theatre. Joe Rosenberg & Graciella Rosenberg (Translators). Trade Paper. Encore Performance Publishing. Orem, UT. 1994. 21p. Multicultural Theatre Ser. ISBN:1-57514-101-9, ISBN13: 978-1-57514-101-5. Dewey:863.
Audience: **l,u,f.**

Fares, Gustavo C., et al. **PQ7776.2.W65.E713**
e Contemporary Argentinean Women Writers: A Critical Anthology. Linda Britt & Eliana Cazaubon Hermann (Authors). E-Book. University Press of Florida. Gainesville, FL. 1998. ISBN:0-8130-2245-2, ISBN13: 978-0-8130-2245-1. Dewey:860.99287.
Audience: **g,l,u,f.**

Foster, David W. **PQ7703.F6**
Currents in the Contemporary Argentine Novel: Arlt, Mallea, Sabato, and Cortazar. Trade Cloth. University of Missouri Press. Columbia, MO. 1975. 168p. ISBN:0-8262-0176-8, ISBN13: 978-0-8262-0176-8. Dewey:863/.03. LCCN:74-030083.
Audience: **u,f.** B

Gambaro, Griselda **PQ7797.G253**
Teatro. Trade Cloth. Grupo Editorial Norma. Buenos Aires, 2002. 191p. ISBN:987-545-065-0, ISBN13: 978-987-545-065-3. Dewey:862. LCCN:2003-400083.
Audience: **u,f.**

Gorostiza, Carlos, et al. **PQ7769.T42 1992**
Teatro Argentino Contemporaneo: Antologia. Carlos Somigliana & Aide Bortnik (Authors). Trade Cloth. Fondo de Cultura Economica USA. San Diego, CA. 1992. 1216p. ISBN:84-375-0324-8, ISBN13: 978-84-375-0324-0. Dewey:862. LCCN:93-141057.
Audience: **u,f.**

Güiraldes, Ricardo **PQ7797.G75D613 1995**
Don Segundo Sombra. Patricia O. Steiner (Translator). Cloth Text. University of Pittsburgh Press. Pittsburgh, PA. 1994. 336p. Latin American Literature Ser. ISBN:0-8229-3851-0, ISBN13: 978-0-8229-3851-4. Dewey:863. LCCN:94-012900.
Audience: **l,u,f.** *Choice, 1995.*

Hernández, José **PQ7797.H3**
Martin Fierro. Cloth over Boards. Edimat Libros, S. A.. Arganda del Rey, 2004. 256p. Clásicos Selección Ser. ISBN:84-8403-570-0, ISBN13: 978-84-8403-570-1. Dewey:861.
Audience: **u,f.**

Kerrigan, Anthony (Editor) **PQ7797.B635**
Ficciones. Jorge Luis Borges & Anthony Kerrigan (Introduction by). Trade Paper. Grove/Atlantic, Inc. New York, NY. 1987. 176p. ISBN:0-8021-3030-5, ISBN13: 978-0-8021-3030-3. Dewey:868. LCCN:62-013054.
Audience: **g,l,u,f.**

Lindstrom, Naomi **PQ7797.B635Z7735**
Jorge Luis Borges. Trade Cloth. Thomson Gale. Farmington Hills, MI. 1990. 208p. Twayne's Studies in Short Fiction ISBN:0-8057-8327-X, ISBN13: 978-0-8057-8327-8. Dewey:863. LCCN:90-004155.
Audience: **l,u,f.** *Choice, 1991.*

Lugones, Leopoldo **PQ7797.L85A6 1989**
Leopoldo Lugones, Cuento, Poesia y Ensayo. Perfect. Colihue. Buenos Aires, 1989. 204p. ISBN:950-581-082-2, ISBN13: 978-950-581-082-6. Dewey:861. LCCN:90-134645.
Audience: **u,f.**

Marmol, Jose **PQ7797.M27A713 2001**
Amalia. Dorris Sommer (Editor), Helen Lane (Translator). Trade Paper. Oxford University Press, Inc. New York, NY. 2001. 688p. Library of Latin America ISBN:0-19-512277-1, ISBN13: 978-0-19-512277-0. Dewey:836/.5. LCCN:2001-021380.
Audience: **l,u,f.**

Puig, Manuel **PQ7798.26.U4A2313**
Kiss of the Spider Woman and Two Other Plays. Allan Baker & Ronald J. Christ (Contribution by). Trade Paper. W. W. Norton

& Company, Inc. New York, NY. 1994. 192p. ISBN:0-393-31148-1, ISBN13: 978-0-393-31148-8. Dewey:862. LCCN:94-006549.
Audience: **g,l,u,f.**

Samuels, Steven **PQ7797.B635Z77344**
Jorge Luis Borges: Argentine Writer. Library Binding. Chelsea House Publishers. Langhorne, PA. 1992. 120p. Hispanics of Achievement Ser. ISBN:0-7910-1236-0, ISBN13: 978-0-7910-1236-9. Dewey:868 B. LCCN:91-017667.
Audience: **u,f.**

Stabb, Martin S. **PQ7797.B635Z9178**
Borges Revisited (Argentina). Trade Cloth. Thomson Gale. Farmington Hills, MI. 1991. 168p. World Authors Ser. ISBN:0-8057-8263-X, ISBN13: 978-0-8057-8263-9. Dewey:868. LCCN:90-048714.
Audience: **g,l.** *Choice, 1991.*

Standish, Peter **PQ7797.C7145Z793**
Understanding Julio Cortazar. Trade Cloth. University of South Carolina Press. Columbia, SC. 2001. xvii, 222p. Understanding Modern European and Latin American Literature Ser. ISBN:1-57003-390-0, ISBN13: 978-1-57003-390-2. Dewey:863/.64. LCCN:00-012030.
Audience: **g,l,u,f.**

Stavans, Ilan **PQ7797.C7145Z795**
Julio Cortazar: A Study of the Short Fiction. Trade Cloth. Thomson Gale. Farmington Hills, MI. 1996. 160p. Twayne's Studies in Short Fiction ISBN:0-8057-8293-1, ISBN13: 978-0-8057-8293-6. Dewey:863. LCCN:95-032554.
Audience: **g,l.** *Choice, 1996.*

Williamson, Edwin **PQ7797.B635Z953 2004**
Borges: A Life. Trade Cloth. Penguin Group (USA) Inc. New York, NY. 2004. 416p. ISBN:0-670-88579-7, ISBN13: 978-0-670-88579-4. Dewey:868/.62 B. LCCN:2004-041290.
Audience: **g,l,u.** *Choice, 2005.*

Woodall, James **PQ7797.B635Z965 1996**
Borges: A Life. Ed. 3. Cloth Text. Basic Books. New York, NY. 1997. 368p. ISBN:0-465-04361-5, ISBN13: 978-0-465-04361-3. Dewey:868 B. LCCN:96-047671.
Audience: **g,l,u.**

Hispanic Literature > Hispanic-American Literature > Individual Countries > Chile

Agosín, Marjorie **PQ8098.1.G6A27 1994**
Toward the Splendid City: Poems. Richard Schaaf (Translator). Trade Cloth. Bilingual Press/Editorial Bilingue. Tempe, AZ. 1994. 192p. ISBN:0-927534-46-0, ISBN13: 978-0-927534-46-8. Dewey:861. LCCN:94-006216.
Audience: **l,u,f.**

Allende, Isabel **PQ8098.1.L54C84 1990**
Cuentos de Eva Luna. Trade Cloth. Editorial Sudamericana S.A.. Buenos Aires, 1989. 283p. ISBN:950-07-0586-9, ISBN13: 978-950-07-0586-8. Dewey:863. LCCN:90-166361.
Audience: **u,f.**

Allende, Isabel **PQ8098.1.L54C313**
The House of the Spirits. Trade Cloth. Knopf Publishing Group. New York, NY. 2005. 528p. ISBN:1-4000-4318-2, ISBN13: 978-1-4000-4318-7. Dewey:863.6/4. LCCN:2004-064939.
Audience: **g,l,u,f.**

Allende, Isabel **PQ8098.1.L54C8413**
The Stories of Eva Luna. Trade Paper. Simon & Schuster. New York, NY. 2001. 352p. ISBN:0-7432-1718-7, ISBN13: 978-0-7432-1718-7. Dewey:863.6/4. LCCN:2002-278377.
Audience: **g,l,u,f.**

Allende, Isabel **PQ8098.1.L54Z467**
My Invented Country: A Nostalgic Journey Through Chile. Margaret Sayers Peden (Translator). Trade Cloth. HarperCollins Publishers. New York, NY. 2003. 224p. ISBN:0-06-054564-X, ISBN13: 978-0-06-054564-2. Dewey:863/.64. LCCN:2002-191267.
Audience: **g,l,u,f.**

Allende, Isabel **PQ8098.1.L54R4813**
Portrait in Sepia: A Novel. Margaret Sayers Peden (Translator). Trade Cloth. HarperCollins Publishers. New York, NY. 2001. 320p. ISBN:0-06-621161-1, ISBN13: 978-0-06-621161-9. Dewey:863.6/4. LCCN:00-054127.
Audience: **g,l,u,f.**

Bloom, Harold (Introduction by) **PQ8097.N4Z719 1989**
Pablo Neruda. Library Binding. Chelsea House Publishers. Langhorne, PA. 1989. 360p. Modern Critical Views Ser. ISBN:1-55546-298-7, ISBN13: 978-1-55546-298-7. Dewey:861. LCCN:87-027686.
Audience: **g,l,u,f.**

Bolaño, Roberto **PQ8098.12.O38E813**
Distant Star. Trade Paper. New Directions Publishing Corporation. New York, NY. 2004. 160p. ISBN:0-8112-1586-5, ISBN13: 978-0-8112-1586-2. Dewey:863/.64. LCCN:2004-019033.
Audience: **l,u,f.**

Bolaño, Roberto **PQ8098.12.O38A2 2006**
Last Evenings on Earth. Chris Andrews (Translator). Trade Cloth. New Directions Publishing Corporation. New York, NY. 2006. 256p. ISBN:0-8112-1634-9, ISBN13: 978-0-8112-1634-0. Dewey:863/.64. LCCN:2006-003819.
Audience: **l,u,f.**

Cox, Karen Castellucci **PQ8098**
Isabel Allende: A Critical Companion. Cloth Text. Greenwood Publishing Group, Inc. Portsmouth, NH. 2003. 200p. Critical Companions to Popular Contemporary Writers Ser. ISBN:0-313-31695-3, ISBN13: 978-0-313-31695-1. Dewey:863/.64. LCCN:2002-192778.
Audience: **l,u,f.**

Donoso, José **MLCS 90/10075 (P)**
Casa de Campo. Trade Cloth. Editorial Seix Barral. Barcelona, 1995. 504p. Europe Today Ser. ISBN:84-322-0344-0, ISBN13: 978-84-322-0344-2. Dewey:863. LCCN:90-872570.
Audience: **u,f.**

Donoso, José **PQ8097**
The Obscene Bird of Night. Hardie St. Martin & Leonard Marcus (Translators). Trade Paper. David R. Godine Publisher. Boston, MA. 1979. 448p. Verba Mundi Ser. ISBN:1-56792-046-2, ISBN13: 978-1-56792-046-8. Dewey:861.62.
Audience: **g,l,u,f.**

Dorfman, Ariel **PR9309.9.D67B5818**
Blake's Therapy. Trade Cloth. Seven Stories Press. New York, NY. 2004. 0p. ISBN:1-58322-070-4, ISBN13: 978-1-58322-070-2. Dewey:813/.54. LCCN:00-051016.
Audience: **g,l,u,f.**

Dorfman, Ariel **PR9309.9.D67M37 2004**
Mascara: A Novel. Trade Paper. Seven Stories Press. New York, NY. 2004. 128p. ISBN:1-58322-641-9, ISBN13: 978-1-58322-641-4. Dewey:863/.64. LCCN:2004-012308.
Audience: **g,l,u,f.**

Dorfman, Ariel
La Muerte y la Doncella. Trade Paper. Seven Stories Press. New York, NY. 2004. 184p. ISBN:1-58322-078-X, ISBN13: 978-1-58322-078-8.
Audience: **u,f.**

Dorfman, Ariel **PR9309.9.D67N36 2003**
The Nanny and the Iceberg. Trade Paper. Seven Stories Press. New York, NY. 2004. 0p. ISBN:1-58322-567-6, ISBN13: 978-1-58322-567-7. Dewey:813/.54. LCCN:2003-010780.
Audience: **g,l,u,f.**

Dorfman, Ariel **PQ8098.14.O7A6 2004**
Other Septembers, Many Americas: Selected Provocations, 1980-2004. Trade Paper. Seven Stories Press. New York, NY. 2004. 256p. ISBN:1-58322-632-X, ISBN13: 978-1-58322-632-2. Dewey:864/.64. LCCN:2004-007935.
Audience: **g,u,f.**

Dorfman, Ariel **PQ8098.14.O7Z46818**
Rumbo al Sur, Deseando el Norte: Un Romance en Dos Lenguas. Trade Cloth. Thorndike Press. Waterville, ME. 2003. ISBN:0-7862-5035-6, ISBN13: 978-0-7862-5035-6. Dewey:863/.64 B. LCCN:2002-072143.
Audience: **u,f.**

Dorfman, Ariel
Terapia. Trade Paper. Seven Stories Press. New York, NY. 2004. 256p. ISBN:1-58322-071-2, ISBN13: 978-1-58322-071-9. Dewey:813/.54. LCCN:00-050526.
Audience: **u,f.**

Dorfman, Ariel **PQ8098.14.O7V513**
Widows. Trade Paper. Seven Stories Press. New York, NY. 2004. 0p. ISBN:1-58322-483-1, ISBN13: 978-1-58322-483-0. Dewey:863/.64. LCCN:2002-008915.
Audience: **g,l,u,f.**

Edwards, Jorge **PN**
Los Convidados de Piedra. Eva Valcárcel (Editor). Trade Cloth. Ediciones Cátedra. Madrid 1, 2001. 440p. ISBN:84-376-1892-4, ISBN13: 978-84-376-1892-0. LCCN:2001-405630.
Audience: **u,f.**

Erskine, Robertson (Editor) **PQ8098.1.L54Z695**
Isabel Allende. Trade Cloth. Facts On File, Inc. New York, NY. 2002. 200p. Bloom's Modern Critical Views Ser. ISBN:0-7910-7039-5, ISBN13: 978-0-7910-7039-0. Dewey:863/.64. LCCN:2002-009105.
Audience: **g,l,u,f.**

Goodnough, David **PQ8097.N4Z6483 1998**
Pablo Neruda: Nobel Prize-Winning Poet. Library Binding. Enslow Publishers, Inc. Berkeley Heights, NJ. 1998. 128p. Hispanic Biographies Ser. ISBN:0-7660-1042-2, ISBN13: 978-0-7660-1042-0. Dewey:861 B. LCCN:97-032888.
Audience: **g,l,u,f.**

Huidobro, Vicente **PQ8097.H8**
Manifestos Manifest. Gilbert Alter-Gilbert (Translator). Trade Paper. Green Integer. Los Angeles, CA. 1999. 250p. Green Integer Bks., No. 20 ISBN:1-892295-08-3, ISBN13: 978-1-892295-08-8. Dewey:861.62.
Audience: **l,u,f.**

Huidobro, Vicente **PQ8097.H8.A24 1981**
The Selected Poetry of Vicente Huidobro. David M. Guss (Editor), Stephen Fredman, Carlos Hagan & W. S. Merwin (Translators). Trade Cloth. New Directions Publishing Corporation. New York, NY. 1982. 288p. ISBN:0-8112-0804-4, ISBN13: 978-0-8112-0804-8. Dewey:861. LCCN:81-004305.
Audience: **l,u,f.** B

Huidobro, Vicente **PQ8097.H8A813 2003**
Altazor. Eliot Weinberger (Translator). Trade Paper. University Press of New England. Lebanon, NH. 2004. 176p. Wesleyan Poetry Ser. ISBN:0-8195-6678-0, ISBN13: 978-0-8195-6678-2. Dewey:861/.62. LCCN:2003-018839.
Audience: **g,l,u,f.**

Levine, Linda Gould **PQ8098.1.L54Z72 2002**
Isabel Allende. Trade Cloth. Thomson Gale. Farmington Hills, MI. 2002. 220p. Twayne's World Authors Ser., Vol. 893 ISBN:0-8057-1689-0, ISBN13: 978-0-8057-1689-4. Dewey:863/.64. LCCN:2001-008661.
Audience: **l,u,f.** *Choice, 2002.*

Main, Mary **PQ8098.1.L54Z76 2005**
Isabel Allende: Award-Winning Latin American Author. Library Binding. Enslow Publishers, Inc. Berkeley Heights, NJ. 2005. 128p. Latino Biography Library ISBN:0-7660-2488-1, ISBN13: 978-0-7660-2488-5. Dewey:863/.64 B. LCCN:2004-027541.
Audience: **g,l,u,f.**

McMurray, George R. **PQ8097.D617.Z77**
Jose Donoso. Library Binding. Thomson Gale. Farmington Hills, MI. 1979. 178p. World Authors Ser. ISBN:0-8057-6358-9, ISBN13: 978-0-8057-6358-4. Dewey:863. LCCN:78-015574.
Audience: **l,u,f.** B

Mistral, Gabriela, et al. **PQ8097.G6**
Gabriela Mistral: Selected Poems. Paul Burns & Salvador Ortiz-Carboneres (Authors). Trade Paper. Aris & Phillips. Oxford, 2005. 220p. ISBN:0-85668-764-2, ISBN13: 978-0-85668-764-8. Dewey:861.62.
Audience: **g,l,u,f.**

Mistral, Gabriela **PQ8097.G6A23 1992**
A Gabriela Mistral Reader. Maria Jacketti (Translator). Trade Paper. White Pine Press. Buffalo, NY. 1997. 230p. ISBN:1-877727-18-0, ISBN13: 978-1-877727-18-4. Dewey:861. LCCN:94-176598.
Audience: **g,l,u,f.**

Mistral, Gabriela **PQ8097.G6A28 2002**
Selected Prose and Prose-Poems. Stephen Tapscott (Edited and Translated by). Trade Cloth. University of Texas Press. Austin, TX. 2002. 304p. Texas Pan American Literature in Translation Ser. ISBN:0-292-75260-1, ISBN13: 978-0-292-75260-3. Dewey:861/.62. LCCN:2002-003306.
Audience: **g,l,u,f.**

Neruda, Pablo **PQ8097.N4C17 1990**
Canto General. Trade Cloth. Ediciones Cátedra. Madrid 1, 2002. 656p. ISBN:84-376-0930-5, ISBN13: 978-84-376-0930-0. Dewey:861. LCCN:91-113816.
Audience: **l,u,f.** *Choice, 1991.*

Neruda, Pablo **PQ8097.N4C5 1977**
Cien Sonetos de Amor. Trade Cloth. Editorial Seix Barral. Barcelona, 2000. 128p. Biblioteca Breve Ser., Vol. 407:Poesia ISBN:84-322-0311-4, ISBN13: 978-84-322-0311-4. Dewey:861.62. LCCN:78-346980.
Audience: **l,u,f.**

Neruda, Pablo **PQ8097.N4R613 2005**
The Separate Rose/la Rosa Separada. Ed. 2. Trade Paper, Perfect. Copper Canyon Press. Port Townsend, WA. 2005. 58p. Kage-an Bks. ISBN:1-55659-225-6, ISBN13: 978-1-55659-225-6. Dewey:861/.62. LCCN:2005-003262.
Audience: **g,l,u,f.**

Neruda, Pablo **PQ8097.N4A913 2005**
Still Another Day/aun. Ed. 2. Trade Paper, Perfect. Copper Canyon Press. Port Townsend, WA. 2005. 62p. Kage-an Bks. ISBN:1-55659-224-8, ISBN13: 978-1-55659-224-9. Dewey:861/.62. LCCN:2005-003263.
Audience: **l,u,f.**

Neruda, Pablo **PQ8097.N4A235 2004**
The Essential Neruda: Selected Poems. Mark Eisner (Editor), Lawrence Ferlinghetti (Preface by). Trade Paper. City Lights Books. San Francisco, CA. 2004. 200p. ISBN:0-87286-428-6, ISBN13: 978-0-87286-428-3. Dewey:861/.64. LCCN:2003-025360.
Audience: **g,l,u,f.**

Neruda, Pablo **PQ8097**
Canto General. Ed. 50. Jack Schmitt (Translator), Roberto Gonzalez Echevarria (Introduction by). Trade Paper. University of California Press. Berkeley, CA. 2000. 423p. Latin American Literature and Culture Ser. ISBN:0-520-22709-3, ISBN13: 978-0-520-22709-5. Dewey:861.
Audience: **g,l,u,f.** *Choice, 1991.*

Neruda, Pablo **PQ8097.N4Z/**
Memoirs. Hardie St. Martin (Translator). Trade Paper. Penguin Group (USA) Inc. New York, NY. 1978. 384p. ISBN:0-14-004661-5, ISBN13: 978-0-14-004661-8. Dewey:861. LCCN:77-014170.
Audience: **g,l,u,f.**

Neruda, Pablo **PQ8097.N4A2 2003**
The Poetry of Pablo Neruda. Ilan Stavans (Editor, Introduction by). Trade Cloth. Farrar, Straus & Giroux. New York, NY. 2003. 1040p. ISBN:0-374-29995-1, ISBN13: 978-0-374-29995-8. Dewey:861/.62. LCCN:2002-032548.
Audience: **g,l,u,f.**

Neruda, Pablo **PQ8097.N4C513 1986**
One Hundred Love Sonnets/Cien Sonetos de Amor. Stephen Tapscott (Translator). Trade Cloth. University of Texas Press. Austin, TX. 1986. 232p. Texas Pan American Ser. ISBN:0-292-76029-9, ISBN13: 978-0-292-76029-5. Dewey:861. LCCN:85-026421.
Audience: **g,l,u,f.**

Neruda, Pablo **PQ8097.N4E79 2006**
Spain in Our Hearts/Espana en el Corazon: Hymn to the Glories of the People at War/Himno a Las Glorias del Pueblo en la Guerra. Donald D. Walsh (Translator). Trade Paper, Perfect. New Directions Publishing Corporation. New York, NY. 2005. 65p. A New Directions Bibelot Ser. ISBN:0-8112-1642-X, ISBN13: 978-0-8112-1642-5. Dewey:861.62. LCCN:2005-023640.
Audience: **g,l,u,f.**

Neruda, Pablo & Walsh, Donald Devenish **PQ8097.N4R413 2004**
Residence on Earth. Trade Paper. New Directions Publishing Corporation. New York, NY. 2004. 352p. ISBN:0-8112-1581-4, ISBN13: 978-0-8112-1581-7. Dewey:861/.62. LCCN:2003-028143.
Audience: **g,l,u,f.**

Hispanic Literature > Hispanic-American Literature > Individual Countries > Colombia

Baldwin, Stanley P. **PQ8180.17.A73Z585**
Gabriel Garcia Marquez: His Life and Works. Cloth over Boards. Spark Publishing Group. New York, NY. 2003. 144p. Library of Great Authors ISBN:1-58663-837-8, ISBN13: 978-1-58663-837-5. Dewey:863/.64. LCCN:2003-007806.
Audience: **g,l,u,f.**

Bell-Villada, Gene H. (Editor) **PQ8180.17.A73Z467**
Conversations with Gabriel Garcia Marquez. Saddle Stitched, Cloth over Boards. University Press of Mississippi. Jackson, MS. 2005. 200p. Literary Conversations Ser. ISBN:1-57806-783-9, ISBN13: 978-1-57806-783-1. Dewey:863/.64. LCCN:2005-005457.
Audience: **g,l,u,f.**

Bell-Villada, Gene H. (Editor) **PQ8180.17.A73C5323**
Gabriel Garcia Marquez's One Hundred Years of Solitude: A Casebook. Trade Paper. Oxford University Press, Inc. New York, NY. 2002. 192p. Casebooks in Criticism Ser. ISBN:0-19-514455-4, ISBN13: 978-0-19-514455-0. Dewey:863/.64. LCCN:2001-035849.
Audience: **g,l,u,f.**

Bell-Villada, Gene H. **89-16474**
Garcia Marquez: The Man and His Work. Trade Paper. University of North Carolina Press. Chapel Hill, NC. 1990. 266p. ISBN:0-8078-4264-8, ISBN13: 978-0-8078-4264-5. Dewey:863 B. LCCN:89-016474.
Audience: **g,l,u,f.** *Choice, 1990.*

Benatar, Raquel; Torrecilla, Pablo; Petersen, Patricia; Benatar, Raquel; Torrecilla, Pablo; Petersen, Patricia **PQ8180.17.A73Z595**
Gabriel Garcia Marquez and His Magical Universe. Raquel Benatar (Translator) ; Patricia Petersen (Translator) ; Pablo Torrecilla (Illustrator). Arte Pï'blico Press. 2002. ISBN:1-56492-340-1, ISBN13: 978-1-56492-340-0.
Audience: **g,l,u,f.**

Bloom, Harold (Introduction by) **PQ8180.17.A73Z6734**
Gabriel Garcia Marquez. Trade Cloth. Facts On File, Inc. New York, NY. 1989. 222p. Bloom's Modern Critical Views Ser. ISBN:1-55546-297-9, ISBN13: 978-1-55546-297-0. Dewey:863. LCCN:87-022774.
Audience: **g,l,u,f.**

Bloom, Harold **PQ8180.17.A73.C5287**
Gabriel Garcia Marquez's One Hundred Years of Solitude. Trade Cloth. Chelsea House Publishers. Langhorne, PA. 1988. Modern Critical Interpretations Ser. ISBN:1-55546-338-X, ISBN13: 978-1-55546-338-0. Dewey:863. LCCN:87-028755.
Audience: **g,l,u,f.**

Bloom, Harold **PQ8180.17.A73Z598**
Gabriel García Márquez. Trade Cloth, Laminated. Facts On File, Inc. New York, NY. 2005. 152p. Bloom's Biocritiques Ser. ISBN:0-7910-8115-X, ISBN13: 978-0-7910-8115-0. Dewey:863/.64. LCCN:2005-008632.
Audience: **g,l,u,f.**

Bloom, Harold (Editor) **PQ8180.17.A73A8345**
Love in the Time of Cholera. Trade Cloth. Facts On File, Inc. New York, NY. 2005. 144-176p. ISBN:0-7910-8120-6, ISBN13: 978-0-7910-8120-4. Dewey:863/.64. LCCN:2004-023882.
Audience: **g,l,u,f.**

De Gonzalez, Nelly S. (Compiled by) **PQ8180**
Bibliographic Guide to Gabriel Garcia Marquez, 1986-1992. Ed. 2. Cloth Text. Greenwood Publishing Group, Inc. Portsmouth, NH. 1994. 464p. Bibliographies and Indexes in World Literature Ser., Vol. 42 ISBN:0-313-28832-1, ISBN13: 978-0-313-28832-6. Dewey:016.863/64. LCCN:93-045321.
Audience: **u,f.** *Choice, 1994.*

De Valdes, Maria E. & Valdes, Mario J. (Editors) **PQ8180.17.A73C527**
Approaches to Teaching Garcia Marquez's One Hundred Years of Solitude. Trade Cloth. Modern Language Association of America. New York, NY. 1990. x, 156p. Approaches to Teaching World Literature Ser., No. 31 ISBN:0-87352-535-3, ISBN13: 978-0-87352-535-0. Dewey:863. LCCN:90-006555.
Audience: **f.**

Fahy, Thomas Richard **PQ8180.17.A73A834**
Gabriel Garcia Marquez's Love in the Time of Cholera: A Reader's Guide. Trade Paper. Continuum International Publishing Group, Ltd. London, 2003. 96p. Continuum Contemporaries Ser. ISBN:0-8264-1475-3, ISBN13: 978-0-8264-1475-5. Dewey:863/.62. LCCN:2003-003727.
Audience: **l,u,f.**

Fiddian, Robin (Editor, Introduction by) **PQ8180.17.A73Z67495**
Garcia Marquez. Ed. 1. Cloth Text. Addison-Wesley Longman, Ltd. Harlow, 1995. ix, 244p. Modern Literatures in Perspective Ser. ISBN:0-582-21405-X, ISBN13: 978-0-582-21405-7. Dewey:863. LCCN:94-041418.
Audience: **l,u,f.**

Garcia Marquez, Gabriel **PQ8180**
Gabriel Garcia Marquez: An Annotated Bibliography, 1947-1979. Margaret E. Fau (Compiled by). Cloth Text. Greenwood Publishing Group, Inc. Portsmouth, NH. 1980. 198p. ISBN:0-313-22224-X, ISBN13: 978-0-313-22224-5. Dewey:016.863. LCCN:80-000784.
Audience: **u,f.**

García Márquez, Gabriel **PQ8180.17.A73A8 1985**
Amor en los Tiempos del Colera. Trade Paper. Editorial Sudamericana S.A.. Buenos Aires, 451p. ISBN:950-07-0320-3, ISBN13: 978-950-07-0320-8. Dewey:863. LCCN:86-136755.
Audience: **u,f.**

García Márquez, Gabriel **PQ8180.17.A73D45**
Del Amor y Otros Demonios. Trade Paper. Editorial Sudamericana S.A.. Buenos Aires, 201p. ISBN:950-07-0928-7, ISBN13: 978-950-07-0928-6. Dewey:863. LCCN:95-101807.
Audience: **u,f.**

García Márquez, Gabriel **PQ8180.17.A73G4**
El General en Su Laberinto. Trade Cloth. Oveja Negra, Editorial. Santafe de Bogota Cundinamarca, 284p. ISBN:958-06-0006-6, ISBN13: 978-958-06-0006-0. Dewey:[Fic]. LCCN:89-168486.
Audience: **u,f.**

García Márquez, Gabriel **PQ8180.17.A73G413**
The General in His Labyrinth. Trade Cloth. Knopf Publishing Group. New York, NY. 2004. 288p. ISBN:1-4000-4333-6, ISBN13: 978-1-4000-4333-0. Dewey:863/.64. LCCN:2004-050083.
Audience: **g,l,u,f.** *Choice, 1991.*

García Márquez, Gabriel **PQ8180.17.A73A27**
Innocent Erendira: And Other Stories. Trade Paper. HarperCollins Publishers. New York, NY. 2005. 192p. Perennial Classics Ser. ISBN:0-06-075158-4, ISBN13: 978-0-06-075158-6. Dewey:863/.64. LCCN:2004-051257.
Audience: **g,l,u,f.**

García Márquez, Gabriel **PQ8180.17.A73A27**
Leaf Storm: And Other Stories. Trade Paper. HarperCollins Publishers. New York, NY. 2005. 160p. Perennial Classics Ser. ISBN:0-06-075155-X, ISBN13: 978-0-06-075155-5. Dewey:863/.64. LCCN:2004-051255.
Audience: **g,l,u,f.**

García Márquez, Gabriel **PQ8180.17.A73A23**
No One Writes to the Colonel: And Other Stories. Trade Paper. HarperCollins Publishers. New York, NY. 2005. 192p. Perennial Classics Ser. ISBN:0-06-075157-6, ISBN13: 978-0-06-075157-9. Dewey:863/.64. LCCN:2004-051256.
Audience: **g,l,u,f.**

García Márquez, Gabriel **PQ8180.17.A73C513**
One Hundred Years of Solitude. Trade Cloth. Alfred A. Knopf Inc. New York, NY. 1995. 448p. ISBN:0-679-44465-3, ISBN13: 978-0-679-44465-7. Dewey:863. LCCN:95-234911.
Audience: **g,l,u,f.**

García Márquez, Gabriel **PQ8180.17.A73T6**
Todos Los Cuentos de Gabriel Garcia Marquez (1947-1972). Trade Cloth. Plaza & Janés Editories, S.A.. Barcelona, 1975. 320p. Novelistas Del Dia Ser. ISBN:84-01-30159-9, ISBN13: 978-84-01-30159-9. Dewey:863. LCCN:75-511402.
Audience: **u,f.**

García Márquez, Gabriel **PQ8180.17.A73Z47813**
Vivir para Contarla. Trade Cloth. Knopf Publishing Group. New York, NY. 2002. 592p. ISBN:1-4000-4106-6, ISBN13: 978-1-4000-4106-0. Dewey:863/.64 B. LCCN:2003-058924.
Audience: **u,f.**

García Márquez, Gabriel **PQ8180.17.A73Z47813**
Living to Tell the Tale. Edith Grossman (Translator). Trade Cloth. Alfred A. Knopf Inc. New York, NY. 2003. 496p. ISBN:1-4000-4134-1, ISBN13: 978-1-4000-4134-3. Dewey:863/.64 B. LCCN:2003-058924.
Audience: **g,l,u,f.** *Choice, 2004.*

García Márquez, Gabriel **PQ8180.17.A73M4613**
Memories of My Melancholy Whores. Edith Grossman (Translator). Trade Cloth. Alfred A. Knopf Inc. New York, NY. 2005. 128p. ISBN:1-4000-4460-X, ISBN13: 978-1-4000-4460-3. Dewey:863/.64. LCCN:2005-043591.
Audience: **g,l,u,f.**

García Márquez, Gabriel **PQ8180.17.A73D4513**
Of Love and Other Demons. Edith Grossman (Translator). Trade Cloth. Alfred A. Knopf Inc. New York, NY. 1995. 160p. ISBN:0-679-43853-X, ISBN13: 978-0-679-43853-3. Dewey:863. LCCN:94-042904.
Audience: **g,l,u,f.**

García Márquez, Gabriel **PQ8180.17.A73D6313**
Strange Pilgrims. Edith Grossman (Translator). Trade Cloth. Alfred A. Knopf Inc. New York, NY. 1993. xiii, 188p. ISBN:0-679-42566-7, ISBN13: 978-0-679-42566-3. Dewey:823. LCCN:93-012257.
Audience: **g,l,u,f.**

García Márquez, Gabriel **PQ8180.17.A73A813**
Love in the Time of Cholera. Edith Grossman (Translator), Nicholas Shakespeare (Introduction by). Trade Cloth. Alfred A. Knopf Inc. New York, NY. 1997. 464p. Everyman's Library, Vol. 235 ISBN:0-375-40069-9, ISBN13: 978-0-375-40069-8. Dewey:863. LCCN:98-119521.
Audience: **g,l,u,f.** *Choice, 1988.*

García Márquez, Gabriel **MLCS 81/1887**
El Coronel No Tiene Quien le Escriba. Giovanni Pontiero (Editor). Trade Paper. Manchester University Press. Manchester, 1988. 90p. ISBN:0-7190-0836-0, ISBN13: 978-0-7190-0836-8. Dewey:863. LCCN:81-194415.
Audience: **u,f.**

García Márquez, Gabriel **PQ8180.17.A73O813**
The Autumn of the Patriarch. Gregory Rabassa (Translator). Trade Paper. HarperCollins Publishers. New York, NY. 1999. 272p. Perennial Classic Ser. ISBN:0-06-093267-8, ISBN13: 978-0-06-093267-1. Dewey:863. LCCN:99-034253.
Audience: **g,l,u,f.**

García Márquez, Gabriel **PQ8180.17.A73C6813**
Chronicle of a Death Foretold. Gregory Rabassa (Translator). Trade Cloth. Alfred A. Knopf Inc. New York, NY. 1983. 128p. ISBN:0-394-53074-8, ISBN13: 978-0-394-53074-1. Dewey:[Fic]. LCCN:82-048884.
Audience: **g,l,u,f.**

García Márquez, Gabriel **PQ8180.17.A73A27**
Collected Novellas. Gregory Rabassa (Translator). Trade Paper. HarperCollins Publishers. New York, NY. 1999. 288p. Perennial Classics Ser. ISBN:0-06-093266-X, ISBN13: 978-0-06-093266-4. Dewey:863. LCCN:99-034271.
Audience: **g,l,u,f.**

García Márquez, Gabriel **PQ8180.17.A73A27**
Collected Stories. Gregory Rabassa & B. J. Bernstein (Translators). Trade Cloth. HarperCollins Publishers. New York, NY. 1984. vi, 311 p. ;p. ISBN:0-06-015364-4, ISBN13: 978-0-06-015364-9. Dewey:863. LCCN:84-047826.
Audience: **g,l,u,f.**

Isaacs, Jorge **PQ8179.I8M3**
Maria: Novela Americana. Ralph Hayward Keniston (Editor). Trade Paper. Books on Demand. Ann Arbor, MI. 223p. ISBN:0-598-74253-0, ISBN13: 978-0-598-74253-7. Dewey:863.5.
Audience: **l,u,f.**

Janes, Regina **PQ8180.17.A73C5325**
One Hundred Years of Solitude: Modes of Reading. Trade Cloth. Thomson Gale. Farmington Hills, MI. 1991. 136p. Twayne's Masterwork Studies, No. 70 ISBN:0-8057-7989-2, ISBN13: 978-0-8057-7989-9. Dewey:863. LCCN:90-028481.
Audience: **l,u,f.** *Choice, 1991.*

McGuirk, Bernard & Cardwell, Richard (Editors) **PQ8180.17.A73Z/**
Gabriel Garcia Marquez: New Readings. Trade Cloth. Cambridge University Press. New York, NY. 1987. 240p. Cambridge Iberian and Latin American Studies ISBN:0-521-32836-5, ISBN13: 978-0-521-32836-4. Dewey:863. LCCN:86-024424.
Audience: **l,u,f.** *Choice, 1988.*

McMurray, George R. (Editor) **PQ8180.17.A73Z653**
Critical Essays on Gabriel Garcia Marquez. Trade Cloth. Macmillan Publishing Company, Inc. Old Tappan, NJ. 1987. 224p. Critical Essays Ser. ISBN:0-8161-8834-3, ISBN13: 978-0-8161-8834-5. Dewey:863. LCCN:86-033717.
Audience: **l,u,f.** *Choice, 1987.*

McMurray, George R. **PQ8180.17.A73Z/**
Gabriel Garcia Marquez. Trade Cloth. Frederick Ungar A Book. Dulles, VA. 1977. x, 182p. Literature and Life Ser. ISBN:0-8044-2620-1, ISBN13: 978-0-8044-2620-6. Dewey:863. LCCN:76-020409.
Audience: **l,u,f.**

McNerney, Kathleen **PQ8180.17.A73Z724**
Understanding Gabriel Garcia Marquez. James N. Hardin (Editor). Cloth Text. University of South Carolina Press. Columbia, SC. 1989. 192p. Understanding Contemporary European and Latin Literature Ser. ISBN:0-87249-563-9, ISBN13: 978-0-87249-563-0. Dewey:863. LCCN:88-027829.
Audience: **l,u,f.** *Choice, 1989.*

Mellen, Joan **PQ8180.17.A73Z732**
Literary Masters: Gabriel Garcia Marquez. Children's Board Books. Thomson Gale. Farmington Hills, MI. 1999. 176p. Literary Masters Ser., Vol. 5 ISBN:0-7876-3970-2, ISBN13: 978-0-7876-3970-9. Dewey:863/.64. LCCN:2001-266791.
Audience: **l,u,f.**

Mellen, Joan **PQ8180.17.A73C532**
Literary Masterpieces: One Hundred Years of Solitude. Thomson Gale Staff (Editor). Trade Cloth. Thomson Gale. Farmington Hills, MI. 1999. 210p. Gale Study Guides to Great Literature Ser., Vol. 5 ISBN:0-7876-3971-0, ISBN13: 978-0-7876-3971-6. Dewey:863/.64. LCCN:2001-266794.
Audience: **l,u,f.**

Minta, Stephen **PQ8180.17.A73Z74**
Garcia Marquez: Writer of Colombia. Trade Cloth. HarperCollins Publishers. New York, NY. 1987. 208p. ISBN:0-06-435755-4, ISBN13: 978-0-06-435755-5. Dewey:863. LCCN:86-045671.
Audience: **g,l,u,f.**

Mutis, Alvaro **PQ8180.23.U8E6613**
Maqroll. Edith Grossman (Translator), Francisco Goldman (Introduction by). Trade Paper. New York Review of Books, Incorporated, The. New York, NY. 2002. 720p. New York Review Books Classics Ser. ISBN:0-940322-91-9, ISBN13: 978-0-940322-91-2. Dewey:863/.64. LCCN:2001-006229.
Audience: **g,l,u,f.**

Oberhelman, Harvey D. **PQ8180.17.A73Z6735**
Gabriel Garcia Marquez: A Study of the Short Fiction. Trade Cloth. Macmillan Publishing Company, Inc. Old Tappan, NJ. 1991. 168p. Twayne's Studies in Short Fiction, No. 24 ISBN:0-8057-8333-4, ISBN13: 978-0-8057-8333-9. Dewey:863. LCCN:91-009679.
Audience: **g,l,u,f.**

Ortega, Julio (Editor) **PQ8180.17.A73Z6736**
Gabriel Garcia Marquez and the Powers of Fiction. Trade Cloth. University of Texas Press. Austin, TX. 1988. 104p. Texas Pan American Ser. ISBN:0-292-72740-2, ISBN13: 978-0-292-72740-3. Dewey:863. LCCN:88-001370.
Audience: **u,f.** *Choice, 1989.*

Pelayo, Ruben **PQ8180**
Gabriel Garcia Marquez: A Critical Companion. Cloth Text. Greenwood Publishing Group, Inc. Portsmouth, NH. 2002. 200p. Critical Companions to Popular Contemporary Writers Ser. ISBN:0-313-32619-3, ISBN13: 978-0-313-32619-6. Dewey:863/.64.
Audience: **l,u,f.**

Shaw, Bradley A. & Vera-Godwin, Nova (Editors) **PQ8180.17.A7**
Critical Perspectives on Gabriel Garcia Marquez. Trade Paper. Books on Demand. Ann Arbor, MI. 159p. ISBN:0-608-15673-6, ISBN13: 978-0-608-15673-6. Dewey:863. LCCN:83-051008.
Audience: **u,f.**

Silva, José Asunción **PQ8179.S5A17**
Poesias: Jose Asuncion Silva, Edicion Critica de Hector H. Orjuela. Trade Paper. Books on Demand. Ann Arbor, MI. 354p. Biblioteca Colombiana Ser., Vol. 8 ISBN:0-598-12814-X, ISBN13: 978-0-598-12814-0. Dewey:861. LCCN:80-110813.
Audience: **u,f.**

Silva, José Asunción **PQ8179.S5D413 2005**
After-Dinner Conversation: The Diary of a Decadent. Kelly Washbourne (Translator, Intro and Notes by). Trade Cloth. University of Texas Press. Austin, TX. 2005. 280p. Texas Pan American Literature in Translation Ser. ISBN:0-292-70698-7, ISBN13: 978-0-292-70698-9. Dewey:863/.64. LCCN:2004-030275.
Audience: **g,l,u,f.**

Strathern, Paul **PQ8180.17.A73Z936**
Garcia Marquez in 90 Minutes. Trade Cloth. Ivan R. Dee Publisher. Blue Ridge Summit, PA. 2004. 128p. Great Writers Series... Ser. ISBN:1-56663-623-X, ISBN13: 978-1-56663-623-0. Dewey:863/.64. LCCN:2004-048614.
Audience: **u,f.**

Welsch, Gabe **PQ8180.17.A73C535**
One Hundred Years of Solitude: Essays. Harold Bloom (Editor, Introduction by). Trade Cloth. Facts On File, Inc. New York, NY. 2002. 150p. Bloom's Modern Critical Interpretations Ser. ISBN:0-7910-7046-8, ISBN13: 978-0-7910-7046-8. Dewey:863/.64. LCCN:2002-009603.
Audience: **u,f.**

Williams, Raymond L. **PQ8172.W47 1991**
The Colombian Novel, 1844-1987. Cloth Text. University of Texas Press. Austin, TX. 1991. 295p. Texas Pan American Ser. ISBN:0-292-75542-2, ISBN13: 978-0-292-75542-0. Dewey:863. LCCN:90-044902.
Audience: **g,l,u,f.** *Choice, 1992.*

Williams, Raymond L. **PQ8180.17.A73Z95**
Gabriel Garcia Marquez. Trade Cloth. Macmillan Publishing Company, Inc. Old Tappan, NJ. 1984. 192p. Twayne's World Authors Ser., No. 749 ISBN:0-8057-6597-2, ISBN13: 978-0-8057-6597-7. Dewey:863. LCCN:84-006754.
Audience: **g,l,u,f.**

Wood, Michael **PQ8180.17.A73Z96**
Garcia Marquez: "One Hundred Years of Solitude". Cloth Text. Cambridge University Press. New York, NY. 1990. 130p. Landmarks of World Literature Ser. ISBN:0-521-32823-3, ISBN13: 978-0-521-32823-4. Dewey:863. LCCN:89-022332.
Audience: **g,l,u,f.**

Hispanic Literature > Hispanic-American Literature > Individual Countries > Ecuador

Icaza, Jorge **PQ7082.N7**
Huasipungo. Trade Cloth. Plaza & Janés Editories, S.A.. Barcelona, 2001. 192p. ISBN:84-01-00298-2, ISBN13: 978-84-01-00298-4. Dewey:863.
Audience: **u,f.**

Hispanic Literature > Hispanic-American Literature > Individual Countries > Peru

Arguedas, Jose M. **PQ8497.A65Z4313 2000**
The Fox from up Above and the Fox from down Below. Julio Ortega (Editor), Frances Horning Barraclough (Translator). Cloth Text. University of Pittsburgh Press. Pittsburgh, PA. 2000. xxxiii, 326p. Coleccion Archivos Ser. ISBN:0-8229-4117-1, ISBN13: 978-0-8229-4117-0. Dewey:863/.62. LCCN:00-009251.
Audience: **g,l,u,f.**

Bryce-Echenique, Alfredo **PQ8498.12.R94A6 1995**
Antologia Personal de Alfredo Bryce Echenique. Trade Cloth. University of Puerto Rico Press. Rio Piedras, PR. 1995. 496p. ISBN:0-8477-0216-2, ISBN13: 978-0-8477-0216-9. Dewey:863. LCCN:94-027868.
Audience: **u,f.**

Castro-Klaren, Sara **PQ8498.32.A65Z644**
Understanding Mario Vargas Llosa. James Hardin (Editor). Cloth Text. University of South Carolina Press. Columbia, SC. 1990. 258p. Understanding Modern European and Latin American Literature Ser. ISBN:0-87249-668-6, ISBN13: 978-0-87249-668-2. Dewey:863. LCCN:89-070449.
Audience: **g,l,u,f.** *Choice, 1991.*

Gerdes, Dick **PQ8498.32.A65Z668**
Mario Vargas Llosa. Trade Cloth. Thomson Gale. Farmington Hills, MI. 1985. 232p. Twayne World Authors Ser., No. 762 ISBN:0-8057-6612-X, ISBN13: 978-0-8057-6612-7. Dewey:863. LCCN:85-005447.
Audience: **l,u,f.** *Choice, 1986.*

Higgins, J. (Editor) **PQ8497.V35**
Cesar Vallejo: An Anthology of Poetry. Trade Cloth. Pergamon Press. Kidlington, 1970. ix, 183p. ISBN:0-08-015762-9, ISBN13: 978-0-08-015762-7. Dewey:861.
Audience: **g,l,u,f.**

Kristal, Efrain **PQ8498.32.A65Z697**
Temptation of the Word: The Novels of Mario Vargas Llosa. Trade Cloth. Vanderbilt University Press. Nashville, TN. 1998. 276p. ISBN:0-8265-1301-8, ISBN13: 978-0-8265-1301-4. Dewey:863. LCCN:97-021194.
Audience: **g,l,u,f.** *Choice, 1998.*

Matto de Turner, Clorinda **PQ8497.M3**
Aves Sin Nido. Trade Paper. Books on Demand. Ann Arbor, MI. 300p. ISBN:0-598-88370-3, ISBN13: 978-0-598-88370-4. Dewey:863.
Audience: **u,f.**

Matto de Turner, Clorinda **PQ8497.M3A913 1996**
Birds without a Nest: A Novel. J. G. Hudson (Translator), Naomi Lindstrom (Contribution by). Trade Cloth. University of Texas Press. Austin, TX. 1996. 205p. Texas Pan American Ser. ISBN:0-292-75194-X, ISBN13: 978-0-292-75194-1. Dewey:863. LCCN:95-044768.
Audience: **g,l,u,f.** *Choice, 1997.*

Ribeyro, Julio Ramon **PQ8497.R47 A6**
Cuentos Completos. Trade Cloth. Alfaguara, Ediciones, S.A.-Grupo Santillana. 28043, Madrid, 1998. 752p. ISBN:84-204-8424-5, ISBN13: 978-84-204-8424-2. Dewey:863/.64.
Audience: **u,f.**

Rowe, William (Editor) **PQ8497.A65.R5 1973**
Jose M. Arguedas: Los Rios Profundos. Trade Cloth. Elsevier Science & Technology Books. Saint Louis, MO. 1973. 288p. ISBN:0-08-017014-5, ISBN13: 978-0-08-017014-5. Dewey:863/.6. LCCN:73-004524.
Audience: **u,f.**

Vallejo, César **PQ8497.V35A17 1978**
Poesía Completa. Trade Cloth. Barral Editores, S.A.. Barcelona, 1978. 932p. ISBN:84-211-3008-0, ISBN13: 978-84-211-3008-7. Dewey:861. LCCN:78-377010.
Audience: **u,f.**

Vallejo, César **PQ8497.V35T713 2000**
Trilce. Clayton Eshleman (Translator), Julio Ortega (Contribution by), Americo Ferrari (Introduction by). Trade Paper. Wesleyan University Press. Middletown, CT. 2000. 304p. Wesleyan Poetry Series ISBN:0-8195-6421-4, ISBN13: 978-0-8195-6421-4. Dewey:861/.62. LCCN:00-040418.
Audience: **g,l,u,f.** *Choice, 1993.*

Vallejo, César, et al. **PQ8497.V35**
César Vallejo: Autógrafos Olvidados. Juan Fló & Stephen M. Hart (Authors). Trade Cloth. Boydell & Brewer, Ltd. Woodbridge, 2003. 192p. Textos B Ser. ISBN:1-85566-084-9, ISBN13: 978-1-85566-084-7. Dewey:861.6/2.
Audience: **u,f.**

Vallejo, César & Fogden, Barry **PQ8497.V35H413 1995**
The Black Heralds: Los Heraldos Negros. Trade Cloth. Allardyce, Barnett, Publishers. Lewes, 112p. ISBN:0-907954-23-5, ISBN13: 978-0-907954-23-1. Dewey:861. LCCN:96-133459.
Audience: **g,l,u,f.**

Vargas Llosa, Mario **PQ8498.32.A65C413**
The Green House. Trade Paper. HarperCollins Publishers. New York, NY. 2005. 416p. ISBN:0-06-073279-2, ISBN13: 978-0-06-073279-0. Dewey:863/.64. LCCN:2004-063259.
Audience: **g,l,u,f.**

Vargas Llosa, Mario **PQ8498.32.A65G8 1981**
La Guerra del Fin del Mundo. Trade Cloth. Editorial Seix Barral. Barcelona, 1981. 542p. ISBN:84-322-0396-3, ISBN13: 978-84-322-0396-1. Dewey:863. LCCN:82-150225.
Audience: **u,f.**

Vargas Llosa, Mario **PQ8498.32.A65J4 1978**
Los Jefes, los Cachorros. Trade Cloth. Alianza Editorial, S. A.. Madrid, 152p. ISBN:84-206-1700-8, ISBN13: 978-84-206-1700-8. Dewey:863. LCCN:79-396890.
Audience: **u,f.**

Vargas Llosa, Mario **PQ8498.32.A65T5 1977**
La Tia Julia y el Escribidor. Trade Cloth. Editorial Seix Barral. Barcelona, 1977. 452p. ISBN:84-322-0323-8, ISBN13: 978-84-322-0323-7. Dewey:863. LCCN:77-574603.
Audience: **u,f.**

Vargas Llosa, Mario **PQ8498.32.A65F5413**
The Feast of the Goat: A Novel. Edith Grossman (Translator). Cloth over Boards. Farrar, Straus & Giroux. New York, NY. 2001. 416p. ISBN:0-374-15476-7, ISBN13: 978-0-374-15476-9. Dewey:863/.64. LCCN:2001-033480.
Audience: **g,l,u,f.**

Vargas Llosa, Mario & Grossman, Edith **PQ8498.32.A65C8213**
The Notebooks of Don Rigoberto. Mario Vargas Llosa (Translator). Trade Cloth. Farrar, Straus & Giroux. New York, NY. 1998. 400p. ISBN:0-374-22327-0, ISBN13: 978-0-374-22327-4. Dewey:863. LCCN:98-070961.
Audience: **g,l,u,f.**

Vargas Llosa, Mario **PQ8498.32.A65.A25**
Making Waves: Essays. John King III (Editor, Translator). Trade Cloth. Farrar, Straus & Giroux. New York, NY. 1997. 338p. ISBN:0-374-20038-6, ISBN13: 978-0-374-20038-1. Dewey:863. LCCN:97-000267.
Audience: **u,f.**

Vargas Llosa, Mario **PQ8498.32.A65.T513**
Aunt Julia and the Scriptwriter. Helen Lane (Translator). Trade Cloth. Farrar, Straus & Giroux. New York, NY. 1982. 374p. ISBN:0-374-10691-6, ISBN13: 978-0-374-10691-1. Dewey:863. LCCN:82-005159.
Audience: **g,l,u,f.**

Vargas Llosa, Mario **PQ8498.32.A65P4913**
A Fish in the Water: A Memoir. Helen Lane (Translator). Trade Cloth. Farrar, Straus & Giroux. New York, NY. 1994. 532p. ISBN:0-374-15509-7, ISBN13: 978-0-374-15509-4. Dewey:863. LCCN:93-042603.
Audience: **u,f.**

Vargas Llosa, Mario **PQ8498.32.A65E413**
In Praise of the Stepmother. Helen Lane (Translator). Trade Cloth. Farrar, Straus & Giroux. New York, NY. 1990. 149p. ISBN:0-374-17583-7, ISBN13: 978-0-374-17583-2. Dewey:863. LCCN:90-003018.
Audience: **g,l,u,f.**

Vargas Llosa, Mario **PQ8498.32.A65H3413**
The Storyteller: A Novel. Ed. 1. Helen Lane (Translator). Cloth over Boards. Farrar, Straus & Giroux. New York, NY. 1989. 224p. ISBN:0-374-27085-6, ISBN13: 978-0-374-27085-8. Dewey:863/.64. LCCN:89-007452.
Audience: **g,l,u,f.** *Choice, 1990.*

Vargas Llosa, Mario **PQ8498.32.A65G813**
The War of the End of the World. Helen Lane (Translator). Cloth over Boards. Farrar, Straus & Giroux. New York, NY. 1984. 576p. ISBN:0-374-28651-5, ISBN13: 978-0-374-28651-4. Dewey:863. LCCN:84-010187.
Audience: **g,l,u,f.**

Vargas Llosa, Mario **PQ8498.32.A65A5 1990**
A Writer's Reality. Ed. 1. Myron Lichtblau (Introduction by). Trade Cloth. Syracuse University Press. Syracuse, NY. 1990. 164p. ISBN:0-8156-0253-7, ISBN13: 978-0-8156-0253-8. Dewey:863. LCCN:90-043036.
Audience: **g,l,u,f.** *Choice, 1991.*

Vargas Llosa, Mario **PQ8498.32.A65.C63**
Conversation in the Cathedral. Gregory Rabassa (Translator). Trade Cloth. HarperCollins Publishers. New York, NY. 1983. 608p. ISBN:0-06-014502-1, ISBN13: 978-0-06-014502-6. Dewey:863/.64. LCCN:74-001892.
Audience: **g,l,u,f.**

Williams, Raymond L. **PQ8498.32.A65Z94**
Mario Vargas Llosa. Trade Cloth. Frederick Ungar A Book. Dulles, VA. 1987. 230p. Literature and Life Ser. ISBN:0-8044-2978-2, ISBN13: 978-0-8044-2978-8. Dewey:863. LCCN:86-025016.
Audience: **u,f.** *Choice, 1987.*

Hispanic Literature > Hispanic-American Literature > Individual Countries > Uruguay

Benedetti, Mario **PQ8519.B292A15 1986**
Cuentos Completos. Trade Cloth. Alianza Editorial, S. A.. Madrid, 1986. 536p. Alianza Tres Ser., Vol. 197 ISBN:84-206-3187-6, ISBN13: 978-84-206-3187-5. Dewey:863. LCCN:87-155821.
Audience: **u,f.**

Benedetti, Mario **PQ8519.B292A23 1997**
Blood Pact and Other Stories. Claribel Alegría & Darwin J. Flakoll (Editors). Trade Paper. Curbstone Press. Willimantic, CT. 1997. 214p. ISBN:1-880684-39-X, ISBN13: 978-1-880684-39-9. Dewey:863. LCCN:96-021343.
Audience: **g,l,u,f.**

Benedetti, Mario **PQ8519.B292A24 2003**
Little Stones at My Window: Selected Poems. Charles Dean Hatfield (Translator, Introduction by). Trade Paper. Curbstone Press. Willimantic, CT. 2003. 400p. ISBN:1-880684-90-X, ISBN13: 978-1-880684-90-0. Dewey:861/.64. LCCN:2002-072863.
Audience: **g,l,u,f.**

Hernandez, Felisberto **PQ8519.H34A215 2002**
Lands of Memory. Esther Allen (Translator). Trade Cloth. New Directions Publishing Corporation. New York, NY. 2002. 192p. ISBN:0-8112-1483-4, ISBN13: 978-0-8112-1483-4. Dewey:863/.62. LCCN:2001-042589.
Audience: **u,f.**

Ibarbourou, Juana **PQ8519.I 3A6**
Antologia Poetica. Other. Cultura Hispánica, Ediciones. Madrid, 1901. ISBN:84-7232-086-3, ISBN13: 978-84-7232-086-4. Dewey:861.6.
Audience: **u,f.**

Onetti, Juan Carlos **PQ8519.O59G66 1990**
Goodbyes and Stories. Daniel Balderston (Translator). Cloth Text. University of Texas Press. Austin, TX. 1990. 190p. Texas Pan American Ser. ISBN:0-292-72743-7, ISBN13: 978-0-292-72743-4. Dewey:863. LCCN:89-039745.
Audience: **g,l,u,f.** *Choice, 1990.*

Onetti, Juan Carlos **PQ8519.O59J813 1991**
Body Snatcher. Alfred MacAdam (Translator). Trade Cloth. Knopf Publishing Group. New York, NY. 1991. 320p. ISBN:0-679-40178-4, ISBN13: 978-0-679-40178-0. Dewey:863. LCCN:90-053411.
Audience: **l,u,f.**

Onetti, Juan Carlos **PQ8519.O59A6 1994**
Juan Carlos Onetti: Selected Short Stories. Peter Turton (Introduction by, Notes by). Cloth Text. Manchester University Press. Manchester, 1994. 119p. Hispanic Texts ISBN:0-7190-4212-7, ISBN13: 978-0-7190-4212-6. Dewey:863. LCCN:93-047157.
Audience: **g,l,u,f.**

Quiroga, Horacio **PQ8519.Q5A6 1989**
A la Deriva y Otros Cuentos. Perfect. Colihue. Buenos Aires, 1988. 244p. ISBN:950-581-081-4, ISBN13: 978-950-581-081-9. Dewey:863. LCCN:89-171856.
Audience: **u,f.**

Quiroga, Horacio **PQ8519.Q5C8 1997**
Cuentos de Amor de Locura y de Muerte. Trade Paper. Penguin Group (USA) Inc. New York, NY. 1997. 160p. Penguin Ediciones Ser. ISBN:0-14-026631-3, ISBN13: 978-0-14-026631-3. Dewey:863. LCCN:96-054877.
Audience: **u,f.**

Quiroga, Horacio **PQ8519.Q5A23 1987**
The Exiles and Other Stories. J. David Danielson (Translator). Trade Cloth. University of Texas Press. Austin, TX. 1987. 168p. Texas Pan American Ser. ISBN:0-292-72050-5, ISBN13: 978-0-292-72050-3. Dewey:863. LCCN:86-030722.
Audience: **l,u,f.** *Choice, 1988.*

Quiroga, Horacio **PQ8519.Q5A26 2004**
The Decapitated Chicken and Other Stories. Margaret Sayers Peden (Editor), Sarah Margaret Peden (Translator), Ed Lindlof (Illustrator), Jean Franco (Introduction by). Trade Paper. University of Wisconsin Press. Chicago, IL. 2004. 192p. The Americas Ser. ISBN:0-299-19834-0, ISBN13: 978-0-299-19834-3. Dewey:863/.62. LCCN:2004-041930.
Audience: **g,l,u,f.**

Rodo, Jose E. **PQ8519.R6A713 1988**
Ariel. Margaret Sayers Peden (Translator), Carlos Fuentes (Prologue by). Trade Cloth. University of Texas Press. Austin, TX. 1988. 156p. ISBN:0-292-70395-3, ISBN13: 978-0-292-70395-7. Dewey:864. LCCN:87-019202.
Audience: **g,l,u,f.** *Choice, 1988.*

Hispanic Literature > Hispanic-American Literature > Individual Countries > Venezuela

Bello, Andres **PQ8549.B3A6 1997**
Selected Writings of Andres Bello. Ivan Jaksic (Editor), Frances Lopez-Morillas (Translator). Trade Cloth. Oxford University Press, Inc. New York, NY. 1997. 352p. Library of Latin America ISBN:0-19-510545-1, ISBN13: 978-0-19-510545-2. Dewey:868. LCCN:96-044127.
Audience: **l,u,f.**

Gallegos, Rómulo **PQ8549.G24**
Dona Barbara: Translated into English. Robert Malloy (Translator). Trade Paper. Books on Demand. Ann Arbor, MI. 444p. ISBN:0-598-47524-9, ISBN13: 978-0-598-47524-4. Dewey:863. LCCN:31-020843.
Audience: **l,u,f.**

Murillo, Fernando **PQ8549.B3 Z735 1987**
Andres Bello: Venezuelan Author. Other. Informacion y Revistas. Madrid, 153p. ISBN:84-7679-043-0, ISBN13: 978-84-7679-043-4. Dewey:861. LCCN:90-175083.
Audience: **u,f.**

Rizal, Jose **PQ8897.R5N513 1997**
Noli Me Tangere. Raul L. Locsin (Editor), Ma. S. Lacson-Locsin (Translator). Trade Cloth. University of Hawaii Press. Honolulu, HI. 1997. 472p. SHAPS Library of Translations ISBN:0-8248-1916-0, ISBN13: 978-0-8248-1916-3. Dewey:893. LCCN:96-050256.
Audience: **u,f.**

Shaw, D.L. **PQ8549.G24.D6297**
Gallegos: "Dona Barbara". Trade Cloth. Grant & Cutler. London, 1972. 84p. ISBN:0-900411-37-6, ISBN13: 978-0-900411-37-3. Dewey:863. LCCN:73-158874.
Audience: **u,f.**

Luso-Brazilian Literature > History, Criticism

De Laguna, Asela R. (Editor) **PQ9003.G66 2001**
Global Impact of the Portuguese Language. Trade Cloth. Transaction Publishers. Somerset, NJ. 2001. 284p. ISBN:0-7658-0059-4, ISBN13: 978-0-7658-0059-6. Dewey:869.09. LCCN:2001-027888.
Audience: **l,u,f.**

Macedo, Helder & De Melo e Castro, E. M. (Editors) **PQ9163.E6**
Contemporary Portuguese Poetry: An Anthology in English. John Brook-Smith, Susan Dos Santos, Michael Schmidt & Alan Sillitoe (Translators). Trade Cloth. Brill Academic Publishers, Inc. Boston, MA. 1979. 270p. Translation Ser. ISBN:0-85635-244-6, ISBN13: 978-0 85635-244-7. Dewey:869.1/42/08. LCCN:78-326236.
Audience: **g,l,u,f.**

Luso-Brazilian Literature > Individual Authors

Antunes, Antonio Lobo **PQ9263.N77M3613 2003**
The Inquisitors' Manual. Richard Zenith (Translator). Trade Cloth. Grove/Atlantic, Inc. New York, NY. 2002. 448p. ISBN:0-8021-1732-5, ISBN13: 978-0-8021-1732-8. Dewey:869.3/42. LCCN:2002-033858.
Audience: **g,l,u,f.**

Barreno, Maria Isabel **PQ9264.A74.N613**
The Three Marias: New Portuguese Letters. Trade Cloth. Doubleday Publishing. New York, NY. 1975. 432 p. ;p. ISBN:0-385-01853-3, ISBN13: 978-0-385-01853-1. Dewey:869/.08/09287. LCCN:74-002826.
Audience: **l,u,f.**

Camoes, Luis de **PQ9199.A5 2005**
Selected Sonnets: A Bilingual Edition. William Baer (Translator). Trade Cloth. University of Chicago Press. Chicago, IL. 2005. 176p. ISBN:0-226-09266-6, ISBN13: 978-0-226-09266-9. Dewey:869.1/2. LCCN:2004-058521.
Audience: **g,l,u,f.** *Choice, 2006.*

Camoes, Luiz de **PQ9199.A2F3**
The Lusiad, by Luis de Camoens, Translated by Richard Fanshawe. Richard Fanshawe (Translator). Trade Paper. Books on Demand. Ann Arbor, MI. 343p. ISBN:0-598-96951-9, ISBN13: 978-0-598-96951-4. Dewey:869.12. LCCN:40-014762.
Audience: **g,l,u,f.**

Camões, Luiz de **PQ9198.A2 1973**
Os Lusiadas. Frank Pierce (Introduction by, Notes by). Trade Cloth. Oxford University Press, Inc. New York, NY. 1973. xlvii, 271p. ISBN:0-19-815737-1, ISBN13: 978-0-19-815737-3. Dewey:869/.1/2. LCCN:73-175327.
Audience: **l,u,f.**

Camões, Luís de **PQ9199.A3 2001**
Sulcando o Mar: Poemas de Os LusíAdas. Trade Cloth. Bow Historical Books. New Providence, NJ. 116p. ISBN:972-8087-85-3, ISBN13: 978-972-8087-85-2. Dewey:869.12. LCCN:2004-403145.
Audience: **u,f.**

Coleman, Alexander **PQ9261.E3.Z617**
Eca de Queiros and European Realism. Trade Cloth. New York University Press. New York, NY. 1980. x, 330 p. ;p. Gotham Library Ser. ISBN:0-8147-1378-5, ISBN13: 978-0-8147-1378-5. Dewey:869/.3/3. LCCN:79-003011.
Audience: **u,f.**

De Sena, Jorge **PQ9261.S337A6 1989**
By the Rivers of Babylon and Other Stories. Daphne Patai (Editor). Trade Cloth. Rutgers University Press. Piscataway, NJ. 1989. 155p. ISBN:0-8135-1388-X, ISBN13: 978-0-8135-1388-1. Dewey:869.3/42. LCCN:88-021100.
Audience: **l,u,f.**

Eca de Queiros, Jose Maria **PQ9261.E3C713 2003**
The Crime of Father Amaro. Margaret Jull Costa (Translator, Introduction by). Trade Cloth. New Directions Publishing Corporation. New York, NY. 2003. 480p. ISBN:0-8112-1532-6, ISBN13: 978-0-8112-1532-9. Dewey:869.3/3. LCCN:2002-153488.
Audience: **g,l,u,f.**

Eca de Queiros, Jose Maria **PQ9261.E3**
The Relic. Ed. 2. Margaret Jull Costa (Editor, Translator). Trade Paper. Dedalus, Ltd. Monroe, OR. 2003. 28p. European Classics Ser. ISBN:0-946626-94-4, ISBN13: 978-0-946626-94-6. Dewey:869.3.
Audience: **g,l,u,f.**

Eca de Queiros, Jose Maria **PQ9261.E3M313 1998**
Maias. Patricia McGowan Pinheiro & Ann Stevens (Translators). Trade Paper. Penguin Group (USA) Inc. New York, NY. 1999. 656p. Penguin Classics Ser. ISBN:0-14-044694-X, ISBN13: 978-0-14-044694-4. Dewey:869.3/3. LCCN:99-228033.
Audience: **g,l,u,f.**

Lobo Antunes, Antonio **PQ9263.N77F313 1990**
Fado Alexandrino. Gregory Rabassa (Translator). Trade Cloth. Grove/Atlantic, Inc. New York, NY. 1990. 512p. ISBN:0-8021-1299-4, ISBN13: 978-0-8021-1299-6. Dewey:869.3/42. LCCN:89-025981.
Audience: **l,u,f.** *Choice, 1991.*

Lobo Antunes, Antonio **PQ9263.N77E9713 1991**
An Explanation of the Birds: A Novel. Richard Zenith (Translator). Trade Cloth. Grove/Atlantic, Inc. New York, NY. 1991. 256p. ISBN:0-8021-1339-7, ISBN13: 978-0-8021-1339-9. Dewey:869.3/42. LCCN:91-004471.
Audience: **l,u,f.** *Choice, 1992.*

Lobo Antunes, Antonio **PQ9263.N77O7313 2000**
The Natural Order of Things. Richard Zenith (Translator). Trade Cloth. Grove/Atlantic, Inc. New York, NY. 2000. 320p. ISBN:0-8021-1658-2, ISBN13: 978-0-8021-1658-1. Dewey:869.3/42. LCCN:99-040063.
Audience: **l,u,f.**

Pessoa, Fernando **PQ9261.P417A26 1988**
Always Astonished: Selected Prose. Edwin Honig (Translator). Trade Cloth. City Lights Books. San Francisco, CA. 1988. 160p. ISBN:0-87286-228-3, ISBN13: 978-0-87286-228-9. Dewey:869.4/41. LCCN:88-016863.
Audience: **l,u,f.**

Pessoa, Fernando **PQ9261.P417A262 1998**
The Poems of Fernando Pessoa. Edwin Honig & Susan M. Brown (Editors). Trade Cloth. City Lights Books. San Francisco, CA. 1998. 236p. ISBN:0-87286-342-5, ISBN13: 978-0-87286-342-2. Dewey:869.1/41. LCCN:98-011043.
Audience: **l,u,f.**

Pessoa, Fernando **PQ9261.P417Q3313**
A Critical, Dual-Language Edition of Quadras Ao Gosta Popular/Quatrains in the Popular Style. Philip Krummrich (Translator). Trade Cloth. Edwin Mellen Press, The. Lewiston, NY. 2003. 166p. Hispanic Literature Ser., Vol. 82 ISBN:0-7734-6586-3, ISBN13: 978-0-7734-6586-2. Dewey:869.1/41. LCCN:2003-059653.
Audience: **u,f.**

Pessoa, Fernando **PQ9261.P417Z46213**
The Book of Disquiet. Richard Zenith (Editor, Translator). Trade Paper. Penguin Group (USA) Inc. New York, NY. 2002. 544p. Classics Ser. ISBN:0-14-118304-7, ISBN13: 978-0-14-118304-6. Dewey:869.1/41 B. LCCN:2002-035485.
Audience: **g,l,u,f.** *Choice, 1997, 1992.*

Pessoa, Fernando **PQ9261.P417A288 1998**
Fernando Pessoa and Co.: Selected Poems. Richard Zenith (Editor, Translator). Trade Cloth. Grove/Atlantic, Inc. New York, NY. 1998. 304p. ISBN:0-8021-1628-0, ISBN13: 978-0-8021-1628-4. Dewey:869. LCCN:97-050201.
Audience: **g,l,u,f.**

Pessoa, Fernando **PQ9261.P417A288 2001**
The Selected Prose of Fernando Pessoa. Richard Zenith (Editor, Translator). Trade Cloth. Grove/Atlantic, Inc. New York, NY. 2001. xxi, 342p. ISBN:0-8021-1694-9, ISBN13: 978-0-8021-1694-9. Dewey:869.8/4108. LCCN:2001-018997.
Audience: **g,l,u.**

Queiros, Eca de **PQ9261.E3**
Cousin Bazilio. Trade Paper. Dedalus, Ltd. Monroe, OR. 2004. 421p. Dedalus European Classics Ser. ISBN:1-903517-08-7, ISBN13: 978-1-903517-08-6. Dewey:869.33.
Audience: **u,f.**

Queiros, Eca de **PQ9261.E3A6 1993**
The Yellow Sofa. Trade Cloth. Carcanet Press, Ltd. Manchester, 1994. 180p. ISBN:1-85754-034-4, ISBN13: 978-1-85754-034-5. Dewey:869.3/3 F. LCCN:94-126982.
Audience: **l,u,f.**

Sadlier, Darlene J. **PQ9261.P417Z835 1998**
e An Introduction to Fernando Pessoa: Modernism and the Paradoxes of Authorship. E-Book. University Press of Florida. Gainesville, FL. ISBN:0-8130-2390-4, ISBN13: 978-0-8130-2390-8. Dewey:869.1/41.
Audience: **u,f.** *Choice, 1998.*

Vicente, Gil **PQ9251.A6E6 1997**
Gil Vicente: Three Discovery Plays: Auto da Barca do Inferno, Exortacao da Guerra, Auto da India. A. J. Lappin (Editor, Translator). Trade Cloth. Aris & Phillips. Oxford, 1997. 300p. Hispanic Classics Ser. ISBN:0-85668-665-4, ISBN13: 978-0-85668-665-8. Dewey:869.2/2. LCCN:97-150556.
Audience: **g,l,u.**

Luso-Brazilian Literature > Lusophone Literature > Brazil

Alencar, Jose de **PQ9697.A53I813 2000**
Iracema. Alcides Villaca & Naomi Lindstrom (Editors), Clifford E. Landers (Translator). Trade Cloth. Oxford University Press, Inc. New York, NY. 2000. 176p. Library of Latin America ISBN:0-19-511547-3, ISBN13: 978-0-19-511547-5. Dewey:869.3. LCCN:99-045927.
Audience: **l,u,f.**

Alves, Miriam **PQ9653.E54 1995**
Onfim Nos...Finally Us...: Escritoras Negras Brasileviras Contemporaneas - Contemporary Black Brazilian Women Writers. Carolyn R. Durham (Translator). Trade Cloth. Lynne Rienner Publishers, Inc. Boulder, CO. 1995. 260p. ISBN:0-89410-789-5, ISBN13: 978-0-89410-789-4. Dewey:869.1. LCCN:94-045735.
Audience: **u,f.**

Amado, Jorge
Dona Flor and Her Two Husbands. Trade Paper. Knopf Publishing Group. New York, NY. 2006. 576p. ISBN:0-307-27664-3, ISBN13: 978-0-307-27664-3.
Audience: **g,l,u,f.**

Amado, Jorge
Gabriela, Clove and Cinnamon. Trade Paper. Knopf Publishing Group. New York, NY. 2006. 448p. ISBN:0-307-27665-1, ISBN13: 978-0-307-27665-0. Dewey:869.3.
Audience: **g,l,u,f.**

Amado, Jorge
Los Santos, Guia de Calles Y. Ed. 10. Trade Cloth. Losada. Buenos Aires, 2002. 376p. ISBN:950-03-7665-2, ISBN13: 978-950-03-7665-5.
Audience: **u,f.**

Amado, Jorge
Sea of Death. Gregory Rabassa (Translator). Trade Paper. HarperCollins Publishers. New York, NY. 1989. 288p. ISBN:0-380-75478-9, ISBN13: 978-0-380-75478-6. Dewey:869.3.
Audience: **g,l,u,f.**

Amado, Jorge **PQ9697.A647S7913**
The War of the Saints. Gregory Rabassa (Translator). Trade Cloth. Bantam Books. New York, NY. 1993. 368p. ISBN:0-553-09537-4, ISBN13: 978-0-553-09537-1. Dewey:869.3. LCCN:93-005310.
Audience: **g,l,u,f.**

Andrade Muricy, Jose Candido de **PQ9644**
A Nova Literatura Brasileira: Critica e Antologia. Trade Paper. Books on Demand. Ann Arbor, MI. 429p. ISBN:0-598-38107-4, ISBN13: 978-0-598-38107-1. Dewey:869/.08/0981. LCCN:41-003871.
Audience: **u,f.**

Bishop, Elizabeth & Brasil, Emanuel (Editors) **PQ9658.B5**
An Anthology of Twentieth-Century Brazilian Poetry. Elizabeth Bishop & Emanuel Brasil (Introduction by). Trade Paper. Wesleyan University Press. Middletown, CT. 1972. 203p. Wesleyan Poetry Classics Ser. ISBN:0-8195-6023-5, ISBN13: 978-0-8195-6023-0. Dewey:869/.1. LCCN:75-184359.
Audience: **u,f.**

Brasil, Emanuel & Smith, William J. (Editors) **PQ9663.E5B72 1983**
Brazilian Poetry (1950-1980). Trade Cloth. Wesleyan University Press. Middletown, CT. 1983. 197p. Wesleyan Poetry in Translation Ser. ISBN:0-8195-5075-2, ISBN13: 978-0-8195-5075-0. Dewey:869.1. LCCN:83-199745.
Audience: **g,l,u,f.**

Brookshaw, David **PQ9523.B57B713 1986**
Race and Color in Brazilian Literature. Trade Cloth. Scarecrow Press, Inc. Lanham, MD. 1986. 356p. ISBN:0-8108-1880-9,

ISBN13: 978-0-8108-1880-4. Dewey:869/.09/981.
LCCN:86-000961.
Audience: **u,f.** *Choice, 1987.*

Brower, Keith H., et al. **PQ9697.A647Z465 2000**
Jorge Amado: New Critical Essays. Earl Fitz & Enrique Martinez-Vidal (Authors). Cloth Text. Garland Publishing, Inc. New York, NY. 2001. 300p. Latin American Studies, Vol. 18 ISBN:0-8153-2083-3, ISBN13: 978-0-8153-2083-8. Dewey:869.3/41. LCCN:00-061735.
Audience: **l,u,f.**

Buarque, Chico **PQ9698.18.O35B8313**
Budapest: A Novel. Alison Entrekin (Translator). Trade Cloth. Grove/Atlantic, Inc. New York, NY. 2004. 192p. ISBN:0-8021-1782-1, ISBN13: 978-0-8021-1782-3. Dewey:869/.342. LCCN:2004-052299.
Audience: **l,u,f.**

Buarque, Chico **PQ9698.18.O35B4613**
Benjamin. Clifford E. Landers (Translator). Trade Cloth. Bloomsbury Publishing Plc. London, 1997. 150p. ISBN:0-7475-3015-7, ISBN13: 978-0-7475-3015-2. Dewey:869.3. LCCN:98-117761.
Audience: **l,u,f.**

Buarque, Chico **PQ9698.18.O35E7713**
Turbulence: A Novel. Alfred MacAdam (Translator). Trade Cloth. Knopf Publishing Group. New York, NY. 1993. 176p. ISBN:0-679-41264-6, ISBN13: 978-0-679-41264-9. Dewey:869.3. LCCN:91-050837.
Audience: **l,u,f.**

Cabral de Melo Neto, Joao **PQ9697.M463A26 1994**
Selected Poetry, 1937-1990. Djelal Kadir (Editor), Elizabeth Bishop (Translator). Library Binding. Wesleyan University Press. Middletown, CT. 1994. 214p. Wesleyan Poetry Ser. ISBN:0-8195-2217-1, ISBN13: 978-0-8195-2217-7. Dewey:869.1. LCCN:94-017252.
Audience: **g,l,u,f.**

Caldwell, Helen **PQ9697.M18.Z573**
Machado de Assis: The Brazilian Master and His Novels. Trade Cloth. University of California Press. Berkeley, CA. 1970. 270p. ISBN:0-520-01608-4, ISBN13: 978-0-520-01608-8. Dewey:869.3. LCCN:76-089891.
Audience: **g,l,u,f.**

Chamberlain, Bobby J. **PQ9697.A647Z585 1990**
Jorge Amado (Brazi). Trade Cloth. Macmillan Publishing Company, Inc. Old Tappan, NJ. 1990. 152p. Twayne's World Authors Ser., No. 767 ISBN:0-8057-8261-3, ISBN13: 978-0-8057-8261-5. Dewey:869.3. LCCN:90-034428.
Audience: **g,l,u,f.** *Choice, 1991.*

Cixous, Helene, et al. **PQ9697.L585Z58 1990**
Ⓔ Reading with Clarice Lispector. Clarice Lispector & Verena Andermatt Conley (Authors). E-Book. NetLibrary, Inc. Boulder, CO. 1990. ISBN:0-585-38621-8, ISBN13: 978-0-585-38621-8. Dewey:869.3.
Audience: **l,u,f.**

Coelho, Paulo **PQ9698.13.O3456A4513**
The Alchemist: A Fable about Following Your Dream. Alan R. Clarke (Translator). Library Binding. Thomson Gale. Farmington Hills, MI. 1995. 165p. ISBN:0-7838-1195-0, ISBN13: 978-0-7838-1195-6. Dewey:823.9/14. LCCN:94-042789.
Audience: **g,l,u,f.**

Coelho, Paulo **PQ9698.13.O3546Z3413**
The Zahir: A Novel of Obsession. Margaret Jull Costa (Translator). Trade Cloth. HarperCollins Publishers. New York, NY. 2005. 320p. ISBN:0-06-082521-9, ISBN13: 978-0-06-082521-8. Dewey:869/.342. LCCN:2005-040377.
Audience: **g,l,u,f.**

De Almeida, Manuel Antonio **PQ9697.A6M413 1999**
Memoirs of a Militia Sergeant. Ronald W. Sousa (Translator), Thomas H. Holloway (Foreword by), Flora Sussekind (Afterword by). Trade Cloth. Oxford University Press, Inc. New York, NY. 2000. 208p. Library of Latin America ISBN:0-19-511549-X, ISBN13: 978-0-19-511549-9. Dewey:869.3. LCCN:98-048751.
Audience: **g,l,u,f.**

Drummond, Carlos **PQ9697.A7185A24 1986**
Traveling in Family. Trade Paper. Random House, Inc. New York, NY. 1986. ISBN:0-394-74751-8, ISBN13: 978-0-394-74751-4. Dewey:869.1. LCCN:86-010009.
Audience: **l,u,f.** *Choice, 1987.*

Ferreira-Pinto, Cristina **PQ9676.U73 1999**
Urban Voices: Contemporary Short Stories from Brazil. Trade Cloth. University Press of America, Inc. Lanham, MD. 1999. 282p. ISBN:0-7618-1379-9, ISBN13: 978-0-7618-1379-8. Dewey:869.3/0108981. LCCN:99-020083.
Audience: **g,l,u,f.** *Choice, 2000.*

Fitz, Earl E. **PQ9597.F58 2004**
Brazilian Narrative Traditions in a Comparative Context. Trade Cloth. Modern Language Association of America. New York, NY. 2006. viii & 303p. World Literature Reimagined Ser., Vol. 1 ISBN:0-87352-587-6, ISBN13: 978-0-87352-587-9. Dewey:869.3/009981. LCCN:2004-017526.
Audience: **u,f.** *Choice, 2005.*

Fitz, Earl E. **PQ9697.L585Z66 1985**
Clarice Lispector. Trade Cloth. Thomson Gale. Farmington Hills, MI. 1985. 188p. World Authors Ser. ISBN:0-8057-6605-7, ISBN13: 978-0-8057-6605-9. Dewey:869.3. LCCN:84-025199.
Audience: **l,u,f.** *Choice, 1985.*

Fitz, Earl E. **PQ9697.M18Z633 1989**
Machado de Assis. Trade Cloth. Thomson Gale. Farmington Hills, MI. 1989. 160p. World Authors Ser. ISBN:0-8057-8244-3, ISBN13: 978-0-8057-8244-8. Dewey:869.3. LCCN:88-025925.
Audience: **l,u,f.** *Choice, 1989.*

Graham, Richard (Editor) **PQ9697.M18D636 1999**
Machado de Assis: Reflections on a Brazilian Master Writer. Trade Cloth. University of Texas Press. Austin, TX. 1999. 150p. Critical Reflections on Latin America Ser. ISBN:0-292-72821-2, ISBN13: 978-0-292-72821-9. Dewey:869.3. LCCN:99-012681.
Audience: **l,u,f.** *Choice, 2000.*

Haberly, David T. **PQ9522.N27**
Three Sad Races: Racial Identity and National Consciousness in Brazilian Literature. Trade Cloth. Cambridge University Press. New York, NY. 1983. 208p. ISBN:0-521-24722-5, ISBN13: 978-0-521-24722-1. Dewey:869.09/981. LCCN:82-004467.
Audience: **u,f.**

Hatoum, Milton **PQ9698.18.A86D6513**
The Brothers. John Gledson (Translator). Cloth over Boards. Farrar, Straus & Giroux. New York, NY. 2002. 240p. ISBN:0-374-14118-5, ISBN13: 978-0-374-14118-9. Dewey:869.3/42. LCCN:2002-017054.
Audience: **g,l,u,f.**

Hulet, Claude L.
Brazilian Literature: 1920-1960, Vol. 3. Trade Paper. Georgetown University Press. Washington, DC. 1975. Brazilian Literature Ser., Vol. 3 ISBN:0-87840-038-9, ISBN13: 978-0-87840-038-6. LCCN:74-016331.
Audience: **u,f.**

Hulet, Claude L.
Brazilian Literature: 1880-1920, Vol. 2. Trade Paper. Georgetown University Press. Washington, DC. 1974. 297p. Brazilian Literature Ser., Vol. 2 ISBN:0-87840-034-6, ISBN13: 978-0-87840-034-8. Dewey:869.09981. LCCN:74-016331.
Audience: **u,f.**

Hulet, Claude L. **PQ9635.H8**
Brazilian Literature: 1500-1880. Trade Paper. Georgetown University Press. Washington, DC. 1974. 395p. Brazilian Literature Ser., Vol. 1 ISBN:0-87840-033-8, ISBN13: 978-0-87840-033-1. Dewey:869.09981. LCCN:74-016331.
Audience: **u,f.**

Jackson, K. David **PQ9676.O94 2006**
Oxford Anthology of the Brazilian Short Story. Trade Cloth. Oxford University Press, Inc. New York, NY. 2006. 542p. ISBN:0-19-516759-7, ISBN13: 978-0-19-516759-7. Dewey:869.3/0108981. LCCN:2005-028860.
Audience: **g,l,u,f.**

Lins, Osman **PQ9697.L555N613 1995**
Nine, Novena. Adria Frizzi (Translator). Trade Paper. Sun & Moon Press. Los Angeles, CA. 1995. 250p. Sun and Moon Classics Ser., No. 104 ISBN:1-55713-229-1, ISBN13: 978-1-55713-229-1. Dewey:869.3. LCCN:95-035738.
Audience: **l,u,f.**

Lins, Osman **PQ9697.L555R313 1995**
The Queen of the Prisons of Greece. Adria Frizzi (Translator). Trade Cloth. Dalkey Archive Press. Normal, IL. 1995. 192p. ISBN:1-56478-056-2, ISBN13: 978-1-56478-056-0. Dewey:869. LCCN:94-007326.
Audience: **u,f.**

Lispector, Clarice **PQ9697**
Agua Viva: Ficcao. Ed. 2. Trade Paper. Books on Demand. Ann Arbor, MI. 123p. ISBN:0-598-26094-3, ISBN13: 978-0-598-26094-9. Dewey:869.3.
Audience: **u,f.**

Lispector, Clarice **PQ9697.L585**
Apple in the Dark. Trade Cloth. Random House, Inc. New York, NY. 1992. xv, 361p. ISBN:0-86068-550-0, ISBN13: 978-0-86068-550-0. Dewey:869.3.
Audience: **u,f.**

Lispector, Clarice **PQ9697.L585V**
A Via Crucis Do Corpo. Trade Paper. Books on Demand. Ann Arbor, MI. 98p. ISBN:0-598-19109-7, ISBN13: 978-0-598-19109-0. Dewey:869.95. LCCN:74-233913.
Audience: **u,f.**

Lispector, Clarice **PQ9697.L585D4713**
Selected Cronicas. Giovanni Pontiero (Translator). Trade Cloth. New Directions Publishing Corporation. New York, NY. 1996. 296p. ISBN:0-8112-1340-4, ISBN13: 978-0-8112-1340-0. Dewey:869.4. LCCN:96-023768.
Audience: **l,u,f.**

Lispector, Clarice **PQ9697.L585L413 1992**
The Foreign Legion. Giovanni Pontiero (Translator, Afterword by). Trade Paper. New Directions Publishing Corporation. New York, NY. 1992. 224p. Paperbook Ser., Vol. 732 ISBN:0-8112-1189-4, ISBN13: 978-0-8112-1189-5. Dewey:869.3. LCCN:91-029992.
Audience: **l,u,f.**

Lispector, Clarice **PQ9697.L585H6713**
The Hour of the Star. Giovanni Pontiero (Translator, Afterword by). Trade Paper. New Directions Publishing Corporation. New York, NY. 1992. 96p. Paperbook Ser., Vol. 733 ISBN:0-8112-1190-8, ISBN13: 978-0-8112-1190-1. Dewey:869.3. LCCN:91-029995.
Audience: **l,u,f.**

Lispector, Clarice **PQ9697.L585P413 1990**
Near to the Wild Heart. Giovanni Pontiero (Translator, Afterword by). Trade Cloth. New Directions Publishing Corporation. New York, NY. 1990. 192p. ISBN:0-8112-1139-8, ISBN13: 978-0-8112-1139-0. Dewey:869.3. LCCN:90-033455.
Audience: **l,u,f.**

Machado de Assis. **PQ9697.M18.Q513 1999**
[e] Quincas Borba: A Novel. E-Book. Oxford University Press, Inc. New York, NY. ISBN:1-4237-4101-3, ISBN13: 978-1-4237-4101-5. Dewey:869.3.
Audience: **g,l,u,f.**

Machado de Assis, Joaquim Maria **PQ9697.M18D613 1991**
Dom Casmurro. Helen Caldwell (Translator), Carlos Fuentes (Introduction by). Trade Cloth. Farrar, Straus & Giroux. New York, NY. 1991. 288p. ISBN:0-374-52303-7, ISBN13: 978-0-374-52303-9. Dewey:869.3. LCCN:91-019838.
Audience: **g,l,u,f.**

Machado de Assis, Joaquim Maria **PQ9697.M18Q513 1998**
Quincas Borba. Celso Favaretto & David T. Haberly (Editors), Gregory Rabassa (Translator). Trade Cloth. Oxford University Press, Inc. New York, NY. 1998. 320p. Library of Latin America ISBN:0-19-510681-4, ISBN13: 978-0-19-510681-7. Dewey:869.3. LCCN:97-027706.
Audience: **g,l,u,f.**

Machado de Assis, Joaquim Maria **PQ9697.M18E713 2000**
Esau and Jacob. Carlos Felipe Moises & Dain Borges (Editors), Elizabeth Lowe (Translator). Trade Cloth. Oxford University Press, Inc. New York, NY. 2000. 304p. Library of Latin America ISBN:0-19-510810-8, ISBN13: 978-0-19-510810-1. Dewey:869.3/3. LCCN:00-036330.
Audience: **g,l,u,f.** *Choice, 2001.*

Machado de Assis, Joaquim Maria **PQ9697.M18M513 1997**
The Posthumous Memoirs of Bras Cubas. Gregory Rabassa (Translator), Gilberto Pinheiro Passos (Afterword by, Foreword by). Trade Cloth. Oxford University Press, Inc. New York, NY. 1997. 240p. Library of Latin America ISBN:0-19-510169-3, ISBN13: 978-0-19-510169-0. Dewey:869.3. LCCN:96-044125.
Audience: **g,l,u,f.** *Choice, 1998.*

Machado de Assis **PQ9697.M18**
The Wager. Robert L. Scott-Buccleuch (Translator, Introduction by). Trade Paper. Peter Owen Ltd. London, 2005. 165p. ISBN:0-7206-1230-6, ISBN13: 978-0-7206-1230-1. Dewey:869.3.
Audience: **g,l,u,f.**

MacHado, Ana Maria & Delicado, Federico **PQ9698.23.A182.B47**
Besos Mágicos. E-Book. NetLibrary, Inc. Boulder, CO. ISBN:1-4175-6639-6, ISBN13: 978-1-4175-6639-6. Dewey:863.
Audience: **u,f.**

March, Kathleen N. (Editor) **PQ9466.A56 1991**
An Anthology of Galician Short Stories: Asi Vai o Conto. Trade Cloth. Edwin Mellen Press, The. Lewiston, NY. 1991. 248p. Hispanic Literature Ser., Vol. 13 ISBN:0-7734-9749-8, ISBN13: 978-0-7734-9749-8. Dewey:869.3/0108. LCCN:91-025884.
Audience: **u,f.**

Marotti, Giorgio **PQ9607.B53M3713 1987**
Black Characters in the Brazilian Novel. Maria O. Marotti & Harry Lawton (Translators). Trade Cloth. C A A S Publications. Los Angeles, CA. 1987. 448p. Afro-American Culture and Society Monographs, Vol. 6 ISBN:0-934934-24-X, ISBN13: 978-0-934934-24-4. Dewey:869.3/093520396. LCCN:86-016041.
Audience: **u,f.** *Choice, 1987.*

Marting, Diane E. (Editor) **PQ9697**
Clarice Lispector: A Bio-Bibliography, 2. Cloth Text. Greenwood Publishing Group, Inc. Portsmouth, NH. 1993. 368p. Bio-Bibliographies in World Literature Ser., Vol. 2 ISBN:0-313-27803-2, ISBN13: 978-0-313-27803-7. Dewey:016.8693. LCCN:93-028537.
Audience: **l,u,f.** *Choice, 1994.*

Martins, Wilson **PQ9555 .M313 1979**
The Modernist Idea: A Critical Survey of Brazilian Writing in the Twentieth Century. Jack E. Tomlins (Translator). Trade Cloth. Greenwood Publishing Group, Inc. Portsmouth, NH. 1979. 345p. ISBN:0-313-20811-5, ISBN13: 978-0-313-20811-9. Dewey:869. LCCN:78-024232.
Audience: **u,f.**

Peixoto, Afranio **PQ9635**
Panorama de Literatura Brasileira: Introducoes e Notas de Afranio Peixoto. Trade Paper. Books on Demand. Ann Arbor, MI. 559p. Livros Do Brasil; Colecuo de Obras-Primas Da Da Literatura Nacional, Dirigida Por A. Peixoto Ser., Vol. 2 ISBN:0-598-62993-9, ISBN13: 978-0-598-62993-7. Dewey:869.09. LCCN:41-024037.
Audience: **u,f.**

Perrone, Charles A. **PQ9571.P47 1996**
Seven Faces: Brazilian Poetry since Modernism. Cloth Text. Duke University Press. Durham, NC. 1996. 280p. ISBN:0-8223-1807-5, ISBN13: 978-0-8223-1807-1. Dewey:869.1. LCCN:96-000078.
Audience: **u,f.** *Choice, 1997.*

Pinon, Nelida **PQ9698.26.I5D613**
Caetana's Sweet Song. Trade Cloth. Alfred A. Knopf Inc. New York, NY. 1992. ISBN:0-394-58997-1, ISBN13: 978-0-394-58997-8. Dewey:869.3. LCCN:91-026409.
Audience: **g,l,u,f.**

Pinon, Nelida **PQ9698.26.I5R413**
The Republic of Dreams. Trade Cloth. Alfred A. Knopf Inc. New York, NY. 1989. ISBN:0-394-55525-2, ISBN13: 978-0-394-55525-6. Dewey:869.3. LCCN:88-008290.
Audience: **g,l,u,f.**

Poeta Movima **PQ9691.A494L58 2004**
Literary Amazonia: Modern Writing by Amazonian Authors. Nicomedes Suarez-Arauz (Editor). Trade Cloth. University Press of Florida. Gainesville, FL. 2004. 216p. ISBN:0-8130-2728-4, ISBN13: 978-0-8130-2728-9. Dewey:869.09/9811/0904. LCCN:2003-070508.
Audience: **u,f.** *Choice, 2004.*

Pontiero, G. **PQ9658 .P65 1969**
An Anthology of Brazilian Modernist Poetry. Trade Cloth. Pergamon Press. Kidlington, 1969. xiii, 245p. ISBN:0-08-013327-4, ISBN13: 978-0-08-013327-0. Dewey:869/.1/008. LCCN:68-055563.
Audience: **g,l,u,f.**

Putnam, Samuel **PQ9511.P8 1971**
Marvelous Journey: A Survey of Four Centuries of Brazilian Writing. Library Binding. Hippocrene Books, Inc. New York, NY. 1971. xvi, 269, xiip. ISBN:0-374-96703-2, ISBN13: 978-0-374-96703-1. Dewey:869/.009. LCCN:73-159250.
Audience: **u,f.**

Rector, Monica **PQ9506.B73 2004**
Dictionary of Literary Biography, Vol. 307. Trade Cloth. Thomson Gale. Farmington Hills, MI. 2004. 400p. Dictionary of Literary Biography Ser., Vol. 307 ISBN:0-7876-6844-3, ISBN13: 978-0-7876-6844-0. Dewey:869.09/981/03 B. LCCN:2004-018640.
Audience: **g,l,u,f.**

Rheda, Regina **PQ9698.28.H43A24**
First World Third Class and Other Tales of the Global Mix. Adria Frizzi, David Coles, Charles A. Perrone & Reyoung (Editors), Christopher Dunn (Introduction by). Trade Cloth. University of Texas Press. Austin, TX. 2005. 304p. Texas Pan American Literature in Translation Ser. ISBN:0-292-70648-0, ISBN13: 978-0-292-70648-4. Dewey:869.3/42. LCCN:2005-001637.
Audience: **u,f.**

Rivas, Manuel **PQ9469.2.R5L3713**
The Carpenter's Pencil. Jonathan Dunne (Translator). Trade Cloth. Overlook Press, The. New York, NY. 2001. 160p. ISBN:1-58567-145-2, ISBN13: 978-1-58567-145-8. Dewey:869.3/42. LCCN:2001-021101.
Audience: **g,l,u,f.**

Sadlier, Darlene J. (Editor, Translator) **PQ9677.E5O56 1992**
One Hundred Years after Tomorrow: Brazilian Women's Fiction in the Twentieth Century. Cloth Text. Indiana University Press. Bloomington, IN. 1992. 260p. ISBN:0-253-35045-X, ISBN13: 978-0-253-35045-9. Dewey:869.3. LCCN:91-022132.
Audience: **u,f.** *Choice, 1992.*

Santiago, Silviano **PQ9697.S2732S7413**
Stella Manhattan. George Yudice (Translator). Cloth Text. Duke University Press. Durham, NC. 1994. 224p. ISBN:0-8223-1486-X, ISBN13: 978-0-8223-1486-8. Dewey:869.3. LCCN:94-009342.
Audience: **u,f.**

Schwarz, Roberto **PQ9697.M18M537 2001**
A Master on the Periphery of Capitalism: Machado de Assis. John A. Gledson (Translator, Introduction by). Trade Cloth. Duke University Press. Durham, NC. 2001. 264p. Post-Contemporary Interventions Latin America in Translation en Traduccion em Traducao Ser. ISBN:0-8223-2210-2, ISBN13: 978-0-8223-2210-8. Dewey:869.3/3. LCCN:2001-033782.
Audience: **u,f.** *Choice, 2002.*

Scliar, Moacyr **PQ9698.29.C54E8713**
Strange Nation of Rafael Mende. Trade Cloth. Crown Publishing Group. New York, NY. 1988. ISBN:0-517-56776-8, ISBN13: 978-0-517-56776-0. Dewey:869.3. LCCN:87-017598.
Audience: **g,l,u,f.**

Scliar, Moacyr & Giacomelli, Eloah F. **PQ9698.29.C54**
[e] The Collected Stories of Moacyr Scliar. E-Book. NetLibrary, Inc. Boulder, CO. 1999. ISBN:0-585-25076-6, ISBN13: 978-0-585-25076-2. Dewey:869.3.
Audience: **g,l,u,f.**

Scliar, Moacyr **PQ9698.29.C54A24**
The Collected Stories of Moacyr Scliar. Ilan Stavans (Introduction by). Trade Cloth. University of New Mexico Press. Albuquerque, NM. 1999. 400p. Jewish Latin America Ser., Vol. 7: ISBN:0-8263-1911-4, ISBN13: 978-0-8263-1911-1. Dewey:869.3. LCCN:99-032298.
Audience: **g,l,u,f.** *Choice, 2000.*

Stern, Irwin (Contribution by) **PQ9501**
Dictionary of Brazilian Literature. Cloth Text. Greenwood Publishing Group, Inc. Portsmouth, NH. 1988. 452p. ISBN:0-313-24932-6, ISBN13: 978-0-313-24932-7. Dewey:869/.09/981. LCCN:87-017744.
Audience: **g,l,u,f.** *Choice, 1988.*

Suarez, Jose I. & Tomlins, Jack E. **PQ9697.A72Z897 2000**
Mario de Andrade: The Creative Works. Trade Cloth. Bucknell University Press. Cranbury, NJ. 2000. 195p. ISBN:0-8387-5426-0, ISBN13: 978-0-8387-5426-9. Dewey:869.8. LCCN:99-041817.
Audience: **l,u,f.** *Choice, 2000.*

Verissimo, Erico **PQ9512 .V4 1969**
Brazilian Literature: An Outline. Trade Cloth. Greenwood Publishing Group, Inc. Portsmouth, NH. 1970. 184p. ISBN:0-8371-2319-4, ISBN13: 978-0-8371-2319-6. Dewey:869.09. LCCN:78-088987.
Audience: **g,l.**

Luso-Brazilian Literature > Lusophone Literature > Africa

Burness, Donald **PQ9900.S43 2003**
Seasons of Harvest: Essays on the Literature of Lusophone Africa. Trade Cloth. Africa World Press. Trenton, NJ. 2000. 262p. ISBN:0-86543-845-5, ISBN13: 978-0-86543-845-3. Dewey:869.09/96. LCCN:2003-008505.
Audience: **l,u,f.**

Chabal, Patrick (Editor) **PQ9900.P67 1996**
The Post-Colonial Literature of Lusophone Africa. Trade Cloth. Northwestern University Press. Evanston, IL. 1996. 314p. ISBN:0-8101-1422-4, ISBN13: 978-0-8101-1422-7. Dewey:869/.09/004. LCCN:95-053848.
Audience: **u,f.**

Hamilton, Russell G. **PQ9900.H3**
Voices from an Empire: A History of Afro-Portuguese Literature. Trade Cloth. University of Minnesota Press. Minneapolis, MN. 1975. 320p. ISBN:0-8166-0745-1, ISBN13: 978-0-8166-0745-7. Dewey:869/.09. LCCN:74-024416.
Audience: **u,f.**

ITALIAN LANGUAGE AND LITERATURE

The Italian Language and Literature section provides a selection of titles appropriate for language and literature study at the undergraduate level. It is not intended to support the curriculum of a major in Italian.

The scope of this selection reflects the rapid, continuing growth of women's and gay studies over the past two decades, and includes major works of literature, literary history, biography, and criticism. Particular emphasis has been given to those authors who have influenced the traditions of other western national literatures. The Italian section also includes accessible critical guides and major works in English translation.

Where possible, works are recommended in their newest, most reliable editions, with preference for compendious collected editions. Some works are available only as reprints, while a few are out of print, though still recommended.

— Jeffry Larson

Italian Literature: History and Criticism

Ardissino, Erminia **PQ4037**
Il Seicento. Battistini, Andrea (Editor). Il mulino. 2005. Storia della Letteratura Italiana, Vol. 3 ISBN:88-15-10651-0, ISBN13: 978-88-15-10651-3.
Audience: **u,f.**

Arico, Santo L. (Editor) **PQ4055.W6C66 1990**
Contemporary Women Writers in Italy: A Modern Renaissance. Cloth Text. University of Massachusetts Press. Amherst, MA. 1990. 248p. ISBN:0-87023-710-1, ISBN13: 978-0-87023-710-2. Dewey:850.9/9287/09045. LCCN:89-028436.
Audience: **u,f.** *Choice, 1991.*

Battistini, Andrea (Editor) **PQ4037**
Il Duecento e il Trecento. Il mulino. 2005. Storia della Letteratura Italiana, Vol. 1 ISBN:88-15-10608-1, ISBN13: 978-88-15-10608-7.
Audience: **u,f.**

Beniscelli, Alberto **PQ4037**
Il Settecento. Battistini, Andrea (Editor). Il mulino. 2005. Storia della Letteratura Italiana. Vol. 4
Audience: **u,f.**

Bonavita, Riccardo **PQ4037**
L'Ottocento. Battistini, Andrea (Editor). Il mulino. 2005. Storia della Letteratura Italiana, Vol. 5 ISBN:88-15-10629-4, ISBN13: 978-88-15-10629-2.
Audience: **u,f.**

Bondanella, Peter C. & Shiffman, Jody R. (Editors) **PQ4006**
Dictionary of Italian Literature. Ed. 2. Julia R. Bondanella (Editor-In-Chief). Cloth Text. Greenwood Publishing Group, Inc. Portsmouth, NH. 1996. 736p. ISBN:0-313-27745-1, ISBN13: 978-0-313-27745-0. Dewey:850/.3. LCCN:95-033077.
Audience: **g,l,u,f.** *Choice, 1997.*

Bondanella, Peter & Ciccarelli, Andrea (Editors) **PQ4170.C36 2003**
The Cambridge Companion to the Italian Novel. Cloth Text. Cambridge University Press. New York, NY. 2003. 266p. Cambridge Companions to Literature Ser. ISBN:0-521-66018-1, ISBN13: 978-0-521-66018-1. Dewey:853.009. LCCN:2002-041706.
Audience: **g,u,f.**

Borsellino, Nino & Pedullà, Walter **PQ4087**
Letteratura Italiana del Novecento Rizzoli Larousse, Vol. 1: La Nascita del Moderno, dalla Crisi del Naturalismo alle Avanguardie, 1900-1930. Rizzoli. 2000.
Audience: **u,f.**

Borsellino, Nino & Pedullà, Walter **PQ4087**
Letteratura Italiana del Novecento Rizzoli Larousse, Vol. 2: Le Forme del Realismo, dal Realismo Magico al Neorealismo, 1930-1960. Rizzoli. 2000.
Audience: **u,f.**

Borsellino, Nino & Pedullà, Walter **PQ4087**
Letteratura Italiana del Novecento Rizzoli Larousse, Vol. 3: Sperimentalismo e Tradizione del Nuovo dalla Contestazione al Postmoderno, 1960-2000. Rizzoli. 2000.
Audience: **u,f.**

Brand, Peter & Pertile, Lino (Editors) **PQ4038 .C35 1999**
The Cambridge History of Italian Literature. Cloth Text. Cambridge University Press. New York, NY. 1997. 735p. ISBN:0-521-43492-0, ISBN13: 978-0-521-43492-8. Dewey:850.9. LCCN:00-265436.
Audience: **u,f.** *Choice, 1998.*

Bruscagli, Riccardo **PQ4037**
Il Quattrocento e il Cinquecento. Battistini, Andrea (Editor). Il mulino. 2005. Storia della Letteratura Italiana, Vol. 2 ISBN:88-15-10650-2, ISBN13: 978-88-15-10650-6.
Audience: **u,f.**

Calvino, Italo **PQ4199.E5**
Italian Fables. Collier. 1961.
Audience: **g,l,u,f.**

Calvino, Italo **PQ4865.C6**
Six Memos for the Next Millennium. Trade Paper. Knopf Publishing Group. New York, NY. 1993. 144p. The Charles Eliot Norton Lectures ISBN:0-679-74237-9, ISBN13: 978-0-679-74237-1. Dewey:854.9/14. LCCN:92-050641.
Audience: **g,u,f.** *Choice, 1988.*

Calvino, Italo **PN37.C3513 1986**
The Uses of Literature: Essays. Patrick Creagh & William Weaver (Translators). Trade Cloth. Harcourt Trade Publishers. New York, NY. 1986. 352p. ISBN:0-15-193205-0, ISBN13: 978-0-15-193205-4. Dewey:800. LCCN:86-004753.
Audience: **g,u,f.**

Cary, Joseph **PQ4113.C37 1993**
Three Modern Italian Poets: Saba, Ungaretti, Montale. Ed. 2. Trade Paper. University of Chicago Press. Chicago, IL. 1993. 396p. ISBN:0-226-09527-4, ISBN13: 978-0-226-09527-1. Dewey:851.91209. LCCN:93-012940.
Audience: **u,f.**

Casadei, Alberto **PQ4037**
Il Novecento. Battistini, Andrea (Editor). Il Mulino. 2005. Storia della Letteratura Italiana, Vol. 6
Audience: **u,f.**

Chiarelli, Luigi, et al. **PQ4145.I73 2001**
Italian Grotesque Theater. Luigi Antonelli & Enrico Cavacchioli (Authors), Michael Vena (Translator, Introduction by). Trade Cloth. Fairleigh Dickinson University Press. Cranbury, NJ. 2001. 194p. ISBN:0-8386-3894-5, ISBN13: 978-0-8386-3894-1. Dewey:852/.912/08. LCCN:2001-018952.
Audience: **u,f.** *Choice, 2001.*

Contini, Gianfranco **PQ4204**
Letteratura dell'Italia unità : 1861-1968. Sansoni. 1994. ISBN:88-383-1611-2, ISBN13: 978-88-383-1611-1.
Audience: **u,f.**

Cope, Jackson I. **PQ4149.C67 1996**
Secret Sharers in Italian Comedy: From Machiavelli to Goldoni. Cloth Text. Duke University Press. Durham, NC. 1996. 232p. ISBN:0-8223-1760-5, ISBN13: 978-0-8223-1760-9. Dewey:852/.052309353. LCCN:95-049319.
Audience: **u,f.** *Choice, 1997.*

Croce, Benedetto **PQ4037**
Storia dell'età barocca in Italia : pensiero, poesia e letteratura, vita morale. Adelphi. 1993. ISBN:88-459-1019-9, ISBN13: 978-88-459-1019-7.
Audience: **u,f.**

De Sanctis, Francesco **PQ4037**
History of Italian Literature. Barnes & Noble Books. 1968.
Audience: **g,u,f.**

Ghidetti, Enrico; Luti, Giorgio **PQ4057**
Dizionario critico della letteratura italiana del Novecento. Editori riuniti. 1997. ISBN:88-359-4132-6, ISBN13: 978-88-359-4132-3.
Audience: **u,f.**

Godman, Peter **DG737.55.G63 1998**
From Poliziano to Machiavelli: Florentine Humanism in the High Renaissance. Trade Cloth. Princeton University Press. Princeton, NJ. 1998. 384p. ISBN:0-691-01746-8, ISBN13: 978-0-691-01746-4. Dewey:945/.51. LCCN:97-044320.
Audience: **u,f.** *Choice, 1999.*

Hainsworth, Peter, et al. **PN2**
Italy: Fiction, Theater, Poetry, Film Since 1950. Joseph Farrell, Charles Klopp, John Picchione, Rinaldina Russell, Joseph Francese, Ellen V. Nerenberg & Peter Bondanella (Authors), Robert A. Dombroski (Editor). Trade Paper. Griffon House Publications. Smyrna, DE. 2000. 164p. Review of National Literatures Ser. ISBN:0-918680-90-5, ISBN13: 978-0-918680-90-7. Dewey:850.9.
Audience: **g,u,f.**

Jensen, Frede (Editor) **PQ4225.E8J46 1986**
The Poetry of the Sicilian School. Library Binding. Garland Publishing, Inc. New York, NY. 1986. 336p. ISBN:0-8240-8722-4, ISBN13: 978-0-8240-8722-7. Dewey:851/.1/08. LCCN:85-025213.
Audience: **u,f.**

Keenoy, Ray & Brown, Saskia (Editors) **PQ4174.K44 1995**
Babel Guide to Italian Fiction in Translation. Trade Paper. Boulevard/Babel, Ltd. Oxford, 183p. Babel Guides ISBN:1-899460-00-4, ISBN13: 978-1-899460-00-7. Dewey:853/.91409. LCCN:98-114865.
Audience: **g,l,u,f.**

Pacifici, Sergio **PQ4087**
A Guide to Contemporary Italian Literature, from Futurism to Neorealism. Paper Text. Textbook Publishers. Temecula, CA. 2003. 352p. ISBN:0-7581-0241-0, ISBN13: 978-0-7581-0241-6. Dewey:850.904.
Audience: **u,f.**

Pacifici, Sergio **PQ4173**
The Modern Italian Novel: From Pea to Moravia. Trade Cloth. Southern Illinois University Press. Carbondale, IL. 1979. 288p. Crosscurrents-Modern Critiques Ser. ISBN:0-8093-0873-8, ISBN13: 978-0-8093-0873-6. Dewey:853/.009. LCCN:67-013047.
Audience: **u,f.**

Parati, Graziella **PQ4203.5.I55M43 1999**
Mediterranean Crossroads: Migration Literature in Italy. Trade Cloth. Fairleigh Dickinson University Press. Cranbury, NJ. 1999. 224p. ISBN:0-8386-3813-9, ISBN13: 978-0-8386-3813-2. Dewey:853/.0108920691. LCCN:99-019418.
Audience: **g,u,f.**

Rebay, Luciano (Editor) **PQ4208.I68 1991**
Introduction to Italian Poetry. Trade Paper. Dover Publications, Inc. Mineola, NY. 1991. 160p. ISBN:0-486-26715-6, ISBN13: 978-0-486-26715-9. Dewey:851.008. LCCN:90-023243.
Audience: **g,u,f.**

Wilkins, Ernest H. **PQ4038.W5 1974**
A History of Italian Literature. Thomas G. Bergin (Revised by). Trade Cloth. Harvard University Press. Cambridge, MA. 1974. 570p. ISBN:0-674-39701-0, ISBN13: 978-0-674-39701-9. Dewey:850/.9. LCCN:74-080444.
Audience: **u,f.**

Wood, Sharon **PQ4055.W6W66 1995**
Italian Women's Writing, 1860-1994. Trade Cloth. Continuum International Publishing Group, Ltd. London, 1995. 280p. Women in Context Ser., :Women's Writing 1850-1990 ISBN:0-485-91002-0, ISBN13: 978-0-485-91002-5. Dewey:850.9/9287. LCCN:95-038269.
Audience: **u,f.** *Choice, 1996.*

Italian Language

Bacchelli, Gabriella (Contribution by) **PC1640**
HarperCollins Italian-English, English-Italian Dictionary. Trade Cloth. HarperCollins Publishers. New York, NY. 1995. 1440p. ISBN:0-06-275517-X, ISBN13: 978-0-06-275517-9. Dewey:453.21. LCCN:94-042350.
Audience: **g,l,u,f.**

Clivio, Gianrenzo P. & Danesi, Marcel **PC1073.C65 2000**
Sounds, Forms and Uses of Italian: An Introduction to Italian Linguistics. Cloth over Boards. University of Toronto Press. Toronto, ON. 2000. 256p. Italian Studies, : ISBN:0-8020-4800-5, ISBN13: 978-0-8020-4800-4. Dewey:450. LCCN:00-712147.
Audience: **g,l,u,f.**

De Mauro, Tullio **PC1625**
Grande dizionario italiano dell'uso. UTET. 2003. ISBN:88-02-06057-6, ISBN13: 978-88-02-06057-6.
Audience: **g,l,u,f.**

Devoto, Giacomo **PC1075**
The Languages of Italy. V. Louise Katainen (Translator). Library Binding. University of Chicago Press. Chicago, IL. 1978. xvi, 357p. History and Structure of Languages Ser.
ISBN:0-226-14368-6, ISBN13: 978-0-226-14368-2.
Dewey:470/.09. LCCN:78-003391.
Audience: **g,u,f.**

Lepschy, Anna Laura & Lepschy, Giulio C. **PC1087.L46 1988**
The Italian Language Today. Ed. 2. Trade Paper. Ivan R. Dee Publisher. Blue Ridge Summit, PA. 1990. 272p.
ISBN:0-941533-22-0, ISBN13: 978-0-941533-22-5.
Dewey:458.2/421. LCCN:88-005320.
Audience: **g,u,f.**

Macchi, Vladimiro **PC1640**
English-Italian, Italian-English. Rizzoli Larousse. 2003.
ISBN:0-06-081774-7, ISBN13: 978-0-06-081774-9.
Audience: **g,l,u,f.**

Maiden, Martin **PC1075.M35 1995**
A Linguistic History of Italian. Trade Cloth. Addison-Wesley Longman, Ltd. Harlow, 1994. 352p. Longman Linguistics Library ISBN:0-582-05929-1, ISBN13: 978-0-582-05929-0.
Dewey:450/.9. LCCN:93-046832.
Audience: **u,f.**

Maiden, Martin, et al. **PC2129.E5H39 2001**
Reference Grammar of Modern Italian. Ed. 2. Cecilia Robustelli & Roger Hawkins (Authors). Trade Paper. McGraw-Hill Companies, The. New York, NY. 2000. 544p.
ISBN:0-658-00430-1, ISBN13: 978-0-658-00430-8.
Dewey:448.2/421. LCCN:2001-022319.
Audience: **g,l,u,f.**

Migliorini, Bruno **PC1075.M513X 1984**
Italian Language. Cloth Text. Faber & Faber, Ltd. London, 1984. 553p. ISBN:0-571-18073-6, ISBN13: 978-0-571-18073-8.
Dewey:450/.9. LCCN:87-673380.
Audience: **g,u,f.**

Reynolds, Barbara (Editor) **PC1640**
Cambridge-Signorelli Italian-English-English-Italian Dictionary. Trade Cloth. Cambridge University Press. New York, NY. 1986. 2278p. ISBN:0-521-32702-4, ISBN13: 978-0-521-32702-2.
Dewey:453/.21.
Audience: **g,l,u,f.** *Choice, 1986.*

Collections of Italian Literature

☐ La Biblioteca Italiana.
http://www.bibliotecaitaliana.it/
Audience: **u,f.**

Bentley, Eric **PQ4244.E5S4 1986**
The Servant of Two Masters: And Other Italian Classics. Trade Paper. Applause Theatre Book Publishers. New York, NY. 1986. 268p. Eric Bentley's Dramatic Repertoire Ser.
ISBN:0-936839-20-1, ISBN13: 978-0-936839-20-2.
Dewey:852/.008. LCCN:86-017252.
Audience: **g,l,u,f.**

Bohn, Willard **PQ4225.E8B64 2005**
Italian Futurist Poetry. Dust Jacket. University of Toronto Press. Toronto, ON. 2005. 270p. ISBN:0-8020-3948-0, ISBN13: 978-0-8020-3948-4. Dewey:851/.912080114.
LCCN:2005-283187.
Audience: **u,f.**

Contini, Gianfranco (Editor) **PQ4213**
Poeti del Duecento, vol. 1, bk. 1. R. Ricciardi. 1995.
ISBN:88-7817-102-6, ISBN13: 978-88-7817-102-2.
Audience: **u,f.**

Contini, Gianfranco (Editor) **PQ4213**
Poeti del Duecento, vol. 1, bk. 2. R. Ricciardi. 1995.
ISBN:88-7817-105-0, ISBN13: 978-88-7817-105-3.
Audience: **u,f.**

Contini, Gianfranco (Editor) **PQ4213**
Poeti del Duecento, vol. 2, bk. 1. R. Ricciardi. 1995.
ISBN:88-7817-106-9, ISBN13: 978-88-7817-106-0.
Audience: **u,f.**

Contini, Gianfranco (Editor) **PQ4213**
Poeti del Duecento, vol. 2, bk. 2. R. Ricciardi. 1995.
ISBN:88-7817-101-8, ISBN13: 978-88-7817-101-5.
Audience: **u,f.**

Cucchi, Maurizio **PQ4214**
Poeti Italiani del Secondo Novecento, 1945-1995. Ed. 4. Giovanardi, Stefano (Editor). A. Mondadori. 2001.
ISBN:88-04-40077-3, ISBN13: 978-88-04-40077-6.
Audience: **u,f.**

Cutrufelli, Maria Rosa (Editor) **PQ4249.6.E75N4513**
In the Forbidden City: An Anthology of Erotic Fiction by Italian Women. Vincent J. Bertolini (Translator). Trade Cloth. University of Chicago Press. Chicago, IL. 2000. 170p.
ISBN:0-226-13223-4, ISBN13: 978-0-226-13223-5.
Dewey:853/.01083538/082. LCCN:00-024265.
Audience: **g,u,f.**

Giannetti, Laura & Ruggiero, Guido **PQ4244.E6G534 2003**
Five Comedies from the Italian Renaissance. Trade Paper. Johns Hopkins University Press. Baltimore, MD. 2003. 368p.
ISBN:0-8018-7258-8, ISBN13: 978-0-8018-7258-7.
Dewey:852/.05230802. LCCN:2002-009446.
Audience: **u,f.**

House, Jane & Attisani, Antonio (Editors) **PQ4244.E5T83 1994**
Twentieth-Century Italian Drama: An Anthology, the First Fifty Years. Trade Cloth. Columbia University Press. New York, NY. 1995. 622p. ISBN:0-231-07118-3, ISBN13: 978-0-231-07118-5.
Dewey:852/.91208. LCCN:94-029111.
Audience: **l,u,f.**

Jensen, Frede (Editor, Translator) **PQ4213.A2T87 1994**
Tuscan Poetry of the Duecento: An Anthology. Cloth Text. Garland Publishing, Inc. New York, NY. 1994. 392p. Garland Library of Medieval Literature Ser., No. 99A
ISBN:0-8153-1625-9, ISBN13: 978-0-8153-1625-1.
Dewey:851/.10809455. LCCN:94-003346.
Audience: **u,f.**

Kay, George R. **PQ4225.E5**
The Penguin Book of Italian Verse. Paper Text. Textbook Publishers. Temecula, CA. 2003. xxxiii, 424 pp. ISBN:0-7581-6611-7, ISBN13: 978-0-7581-6611-1. Dewey:851.008.
Audience: **g,l,u,f.**

Lind, Levi Robert **PQ4208**
Lyric Poetry of the Italian Renaissance: An Anthology with Verse Translations. Paper Text. Textbook Publishers. Temecula, CA. 2003. xxvii, 334p. ISBN:0-7581-0193-7, ISBN13: 978-0-7581-0193-8. Dewey:851.04.
Audience: **u,f.**

Lind, Levi Robert **PQ4214.L5 1974**
Twentieth-Century Italian Poetry; a Bilingual Anthology. Trade Cloth. Macmillan Publishing Company, Inc. Old Tappan, NJ. 1974. xxxi, 400p. ISBN:0-672-51409-5, ISBN13: 978-0-672-51409-8. Dewey:851/.9/108. LCCN:73-011343.
Audience: **u,f.**

McKendrick, Jamie **PQ4113**
20th-Century Italian Poems. Trade Paper. Faber & Faber, Ltd. London, 2004. 192p. ISBN:0-571-19700-0, ISBN13: 978-0-571-19700-2. Dewey:851.9109. LCCN:2005-360982.
Audience: **u,f.**

Mengaldo, Pier von **PQ4214**
Poeti Italiani Del Novecento. Trade Paper. Mondadori. Segrate (Milano), 1995. ISBN:88-04-38731-9, ISBN13: 978-88-04-38731-2. Dewey:851.91408.
Audience: **u,f.**

O'Brien, Catherine (Editor) **PQ4209**
Italian Women Poets of the Twentieth Century. Irish Academic Press. 1996. ISBN:0-7165-2603-4, ISBN13: 978-0-7165-2603-2.
Audience: **g,u,f.**

O'Brien, Catherine **PQ4209.I88 1996**
Italian Women Poets. Trade Cloth. Taylor & Francis Group. Abingdon, 1996. 200p. ISBN:0-7165-2603-4, ISBN13: 978-0-7165-2603-2. Dewey:851/.910809287. LCCN:96-227726.
Audience: **g,u,f.** *Choice, 1997.*

Penman, Bruce (Editor) **PQ4244.E5**
Five Italian Renaissance Comedies. Trade Paper. Penguin Group (USA) Inc. New York, NY. 1978. 448p. Penguin Classics Ser. ISBN:0-14-044338-X, ISBN13: 978-0-14-044338-7. Dewey:852/.052. LCCN:79-304949.
Audience: **u,f.**

Picchione, John & Smith, Lawrence R. (Editors) **PQ4214**
Twentieth-Century Italian Poetry: An Anthology. Trade Paper. University of Toronto Press. Toronto, ON. 1992. 536p. Italian Studies, : ISBN:0-8020-7368-9, ISBN13: 978-0-8020-7368-6. Dewey:851.9108. LCCN:94-136401.
Audience: **u,f.**

Prunster, N. & Victoria University Staff **PQ4253.A5R65 2000**
Romeo and Juliet Before Shakespeare: Four Early Stories of Star-Crossed Love. Trade Paper. BPR Publishers. New Providence, NJ. 2000. 127p. Renaissance and Reformation Texts in Translation Ser., Vol. 8 ISBN:0-7727-2015-0, ISBN13: 978-0-7727-2015-3. Dewey:853/.0850803. LCCN:2001-326347.
Audience: **u,f.**

Roberts, Nick **PQ4257.E5S56 1999**
Short Stories in Italian. Trade Paper. Penguin Group (USA) Inc. New York, NY. 2001. 192p. New Penguin Parallel Texts Ser. ISBN:0-14-026540-6, ISBN13: 978-0-14-026540-8. Dewey:853/.0108. LCCN:2001-274159.
Audience: **g,l,u,f.**

Rossetti, Dante Gabriel **PQ4225.E8R65**
Dante and His Circle: With the Italian Poets Preceding Him. a Collection of Lyrics. Trade Paper. Books on Demand. Ann Arbor, MI. 326p. ISBN:0-598-86082-7, ISBN13: 978-0-598-86082-8. Dewey:851/.1/08. LCCN:17-013111.
Audience: **u,f.**

Segre, Cesare & Ossola, Carlo **PQ4207**
Antologia della Poesia Italiana, vol. 1. Einaudi. 1997. ISBN:88-446-0008-0, ISBN13: 978-88-446-0008-2.
Audience: **u,f.**

Segre, Cesare & Ossola, Carlo **PQ4207**
Antologia della Poesia Italiana, vol. 2. Einaudi. 1998. ISBN:88-446-0067-6, ISBN13: 978-88-446-0067-9.
Audience: **u,f.**

Segre, Cesare & Ossola, Carlo **PQ4207**
Antologia della Poesia Italiana, vol. 3. Einaudi. 1999. ISBN:88-446-0076-5, ISBN13: 978-88-446-0076-1.
Audience: **u,f.**

Silone, Ignazio, et al. **PQ4257.E5O64 1999**
Open City: Seven Writers in Postwar Rome. Giorgio Bassani, Alberto Moravia, Elsa Morante, Natalia Ginzgurg, Carlo Levi & Carlo E. Gadda (Authors), William Weaver (Editor). Trade Paper. Steerforth Press. Hanover, NH. 1999. 462p. Steerforth Italia Ser. ISBN:1-883642-82-5, ISBN13: 978-1-883642-82-2. Dewey:853/.91408. LCCN:99-015666.
Audience: **g,l,u,f.**

Smith, Lawrence R. (Editor) **PQ4214**
The New Italian Poetry, Nineteen Forty-Five to the Present: A Bilingual Anthology. Trade Cloth. University of California Press. Berkeley, CA. 1981. 491p. ISBN:0-520-03859-2, ISBN13: 978-0-520-03859-2. Dewey:851/.914/08. LCCN:78-066014.
Audience: **u,f.**

Swinburne, Algernon Charles, et al. **PR5502.M35 2004**
Italian Tales: An Anthology of Contemporary Italian Fiction. Jerome J. McGann, Charles L. Sligh & Massimo Riva (Authors). Cloth over Boards. Yale University Press. Cumberland, RI. 2005. 296p. Italian Literature and Thought Ser. ISBN:0-300-09530-9, ISBN13: 978-0-300-09530-2. Dewey:853/.0108092. LCCN:2004-042281.
Audience: **g,u,f.**

Individual Authors and Works > To 1400

Consoli, Joseph P. & Wilhelm, James J. (Editors) **PQ4253.A4E5 1997**
The Novellino or One Hundred Ancient Tales: A Edition and Translation Based on the 1525 Gualteruzzi Editio Princeps. Joseph P. Consoli (Translator). Cloth Text. Garland Publishing,

Inc. New York, NY. 1997. 224p. Garland Library of Medieval Literature Ser., Vol. 105A ISBN:0-8153-1080-3, ISBN13: 978-0-8153-1080-8. Dewey:853/.0108. LCCN:96-041562.
Audience: **u,f.** *Choice, 1997.*

Iacopone da Todi **PQ4472.J3 A62**
Laude. GLF editori Laterza. 2006. ISBN:88-420-7970-7, ISBN13: 978-88-420-7970-5.
Audience: **u,f.**

Individual Authors and Works > To 1400 > Boccaccio

Bergin, Thomas G. **PQ4286.B4**
Boccaccio. Trade Cloth. Penguin Group (USA) Inc. New York, NY. 1981. 448p. ISBN:0-670-17735-0, ISBN13: 978-0-670-17735-6. Dewey:858/.109. LCCN:81-065281.
Audience: **g,l,u,f.**

Boccaccio, Giovanni **PQ4266**
Elegia di madonna Fiammetta. Mursia. 1987.
Audience: **u,f.**

Boccaccio, Giovanni **PQ4266**
Filostrato. Mursia. 1990. ISBN:88-425-0494-7, ISBN13: 978-88-425-0494-8.
Audience: **u,f.**

Boccaccio, Giovanni **PQ4266**
Ninfale fiesolano. Mursia. 1991. ISBN:88-425-0906-X, ISBN13: 978-88-425-0906-6.
Audience: **u,f.**

Boccaccio, Giovanni **PQ4267**
Decameron. Ed. 8. Branca, Vittore (Editor). A. Mondadori. 2001. ISBN:88-04-24872-6, ISBN13: 978-88-04-24872-9.
Audience: **u,f.**

Boccaccio, Giovanni **PQ4266**
Il Corbaccio. Natali, Giulia (Editor). Mursia. 1992. ISBN:88-425-1204-4, ISBN13: 978-88-425-1204-2.
Audience: **u,f.**

Boccaccio, Giovanni **PQ4274.D5E5 2001**
Famous Women. Virginia Brown (Editor). Trade Cloth. Harvard University Press. Cambridge, MA. 2001. 560p. The I Tatti Renaissance Library ISBN:0-674-00347-0, ISBN13: 978-0-674-00347-7. Dewey:920.72 B. LCCN:00-053492.
Audience: **u,f.** *Choice, 2001.*

Boccaccio, Giovanni **PQ4272.E5.C6 1975**
The Corbaccio. Anthony K. Cassell (Editor, Translator). Trade Cloth. University of Illinois Press. Champaign, IL. 1975. 216p. ISBN:0-252-00479-5, ISBN13: 978-0-252-00479-7. Dewey:853/.1. LCCN:75-009844.
Audience: **g,l,u,f.**

Boccaccio, Giovanni **PQ4272.E5 N5 1974**
The Nymph of Fiesole. Daniel J. Donno (Translator), Angela Conner (Illustrator). Library Binding. Greenwood Publishing Group, Inc. Portsmouth, NH. 1974. 149p. ISBN:0-8371-7500-3, ISBN13: 978-0-8371-7500-3. Dewey:851/.1. LCCN:74-005781.
Audience: **g,l,u,f.**

Boccaccio, Giovanni **PQ4272.E5A357 2003**
The Decameron. Ed. 2. G. H. McWilliam (Translator, Introduction by, Notes by). Trade Paper. Penguin Group (USA) Inc. New York, NY. 2003. 1072p. ISBN:0-14-044930-2, ISBN13: 978-0-14-044930-3. Dewey:853.1.
Audience: **g,l,u,f.**

Boccaccio, Giovanni **PQ4272.E5.A357 1983**
The Decameron. Mark Musa & Peter E. Bondanella (Translators), Thomas G. Bergin (Introduction by). Trade Cloth. W. W. Norton & Company, Inc. New York, NY. 1983. ix, 689p. Critical Editions Ser. ISBN:0-393-01754-0, ISBN13: 978-0-393-01754-0. Dewey:853.1. LCCN:82-024674.
Audience: **g,l,u,f.**

Boccaccio, Giovanni **PQ4272.E5 A36 1982**
Decameron: The John Payne Translation, Set. John Payne (Translator), Charles S. Singleton (Revised by). Trade Cloth. University of California Press. Berkeley, CA. 1983. 444p. ISBN:0-520-03557-7, ISBN13: 978-0-520-03557-7. Dewey:853/.1. LCCN:77-083112.
Audience: **g,l,u,f.**

Boccaccio, Giovanni **PQ4272.E5A95 1985**
L' Ameto. Judith Serafini-Sauli (Translator). Library Binding. Garland Publishing, Inc. New York, NY. 1984. xxix, 171p. Library of Medieval Literature ISBN:0-8240-8918-9, ISBN13: 978-0-8240-8918-4. Dewey:853/.1. LCCN:84-048066.
Audience: **u,f.**

Boccaccio, Giovanni & Traversa, Vincenzo **PQ4272.E5T4 2003**
Giovanni Boccaccio: Theseid of the Nuptials of Emilia. Trade Cloth. Peter Lang Publishing, Inc. New York, NY. 2002. 608p. Currents in Comparative Romance Languages and Literatures Ser., Vol. 116 ISBN:0-8204-6106-7, ISBN13: 978-0-8204-6106-9. Dewey:851/.1. LCCN:2002-005786.
Audience: **u,f.**

Boccaccio, Giovanni **PQ4272.E5 A38 1998**
The Decameron. Jonathan Usher (Editor), Guido Waldman (Translator), Jonathan Usher (Introduction by, Notes by). Trade Paper. Oxford University Press, Inc. New York, NY. 1999. 738p. Oxford World's Classics Ser. ISBN:0-19-283691-9, ISBN13: 978-0-19-283691-5. Dewey:853.1. LCCN:99-462697.
Audience: **g,l,u,f.**

Boccaccio, Giovanni **PQ4272.E5F5 1986**
Giovanni Boccaccio: Il Filostrato. James J. Wilhelm & Lowry Nelson Jr. (Editors), Robert Roberts & Anna B. Seldis (Translators), Robert Roberts & Anna B. Seldis (Introduction by). Library Binding. Garland Publishing, Inc. New York, NY. 1986. 512p. Library of Medieval Literature, Vol. 53-A ISBN:0-8240-8705-4, ISBN13: 978-0-8240-8705-0. Dewey:851/.1. LCCN:86-007611.
Audience: **u,f.** *Choice, 1987.*

Branca, Vittore **PQ4277**
Boccaccio: The Man and His Works. Dennis J. McCauliffe (Editor, Translator), Richard Monges (Translator). Cloth Text. New York University Press. New York, NY. 1976. 341p. ISBN:0-8147-0953-2, ISBN13: 978-0-8147-0953-5. Dewey:858/.1/09. LCCN:71-081830.
Audience: **l,u,f.**

Edwards, Robert R. **PR1912.B6E39 2002**
Chaucer and Boccaccio: Antiquity and Modernity. Cloth over Boards. Palgrave Macmillan. New York, NY. 2002. 223p. ISBN:0-333-97008-X, ISBN13: 978-0-333-97008-9. Dewey:821/.1. LCCN:2001-050084.
Audience: **u,f.** *Choice, 2002.*

Lee, A. Collingwood **F229**
The Decameron, Its Sources and Analogues. Paper Text. Classic Books. Murrieta, CA. 2001. 363p. ISBN:0-7426-9355-4, ISBN13: 978-0-7426-9355-5. Dewey:975.5/01/0924.
Audience: **u,f.**

Wallace, David J. **PQ4287 .W35 1991**
Boccaccio: Decameron. J. P. Stern (Contribution by). Trade Paper. Cambridge University Press. New York, NY. 1991. 131p. Landmarks of World Literature Ser. ISBN:0-521-38851-1, ISBN13: 978-0-521-38851-1. Dewey:853/.1. LCCN:90-028232.
Audience: **u,f.**

Individual Authors and Works > To 1400 > Cavalcanti

Anderson, D. **PQ4829.O565**
Pound's Cavalcanti: An Edition of the Translations, Notes and Essays. Trade Cloth. Princeton University Press. Princeton, NJ. 1983. 336p. ISBN:0-691-06519-5, ISBN13: 978-0-691-06519-9. Dewey:851/.912. LCCN:82-047581.
Audience: **u,f.**

Ardizzone, Maria Luisa **PQ4299.C2A84 2002**
Guido Cavalcanti: The Other Middle Ages. Printed Dust Jacket. University of Toronto Press. Toronto, ON. 2002. 272p. Toronto Italian Studies ISBN:0-8020-3591-4, ISBN13: 978-0-8020-3591-2. Dewey:851/.1. LCCN:2002-510483.
Audience: **u,f.** *Choice, 2003.*

Cavalcanti, Guido **PQ4299**
Rime. 8879894080. Donzelli. 1998.
Audience: **u,f.**

Cavalcanti, Guido **PQ4299.C2 1992**
The Complete Poems. Marc A. Cirigliano (Translator, Introduction by). Trade Paper. Italica Press. New York, NY. 1992. 200p. ISBN:0-934977-27-5, ISBN13: 978-0-934977-27-2. Dewey:851/.1. LCCN:92-012123.
Audience: **g,l,u,f.** *Choice, 1993.*

Individual Authors and Works > To 1400 > Dante

Dante Alighieri **PQ4302**
Commedia, vol. 1: Inferno. A. Mondadori. 1991. ISBN:88-04-34004-5, ISBN13: 978-88-04-34004-1.
Audience: **u,f.**

Dante Alighieri **PQ4302**
Commedia, vol. 2: Purgatorio. A. Mondadori. 1991.
Audience: **u,f.**

Dante Alighieri **PQ4302**
Commedia, vol. 3: Paradiso. A. Mondadori. 1997. ISBN:88-04-42268-8, ISBN13: 978-88-04-42268-6.
Audience: **u,f.**

Dante Alighieri **PQ4309**
Rime. Edizioni del Galluzzo per la Fondazione Ezio Franceschini. 2005. ISBN:88-8450-152-0, ISBN13: 978-88-8450-152-3.
Audience: **u,f.**

Dante Alighieri **PQ4300**
Tutte le opere. Sansoni. 1992. ISBN:88-383-1402-0, ISBN13: 978-88-383-1402-5.
Audience: **u,f.**

Dante Alighieri **PQ4309**
Dante's Lyric Poetry. Foster, Kenelm (Translator); Boyde, Patrick (Translator). Clarendon Press. 1967.
Audience: **u,f.**

Dante Alighieri **PQ4315**
Dante Alighieri's Divine Comedy, Vol. 5. Paradise: Italian Text with Verse Translation. Musa, Mark (Translator). Indiana University Press. 2005. ISBN:0-253-34141-8, ISBN13: 978-0-253-34141-9.
Audience: **g,l,u,f.**

Dante Alighieri **PQ4315**
Dante Alighieri's Divine Comedy, Vol. 3: Purgatory. Italian Text and Verse Translation. Musa, Mark (Translator). Indiana University Press. 2000. ISBN:0-253-33649-X, ISBN13: 978-0-253-33649-1.
Audience: **g,l,u,f.**

Dante Alighieri **PQ4311 .D6 1996**
Dante: De Vulgari Eloquentia. Steven Botterill (Edited and Translated by), Peter Dronke (Contribution by). Trade Paper. Cambridge University Press. New York, NY. 2005. 135p. Cambridge Medieval Classics Ser. ISBN:0-521-40923-3, ISBN13: 978-0-521-40923-0. Dewey:858.1/09. LCCN:2006-277899.
Audience: **u,f.**

Dante Alighieri **PQ4315.58.C47 1995**
La Vita Nuova. Dino S. Cervigni & Edward Vasta (Translators). Cloth Text. University of Notre Dame Press. Notre Dame, IN. 1995. 339p. ISBN:0-268-01925-8, ISBN13: 978-0-268-01925-9. Dewey:851/.1. LCCN:95-002300.
Audience: **u,f.** *Choice, 1996.*

Dante Alighieri **PQ4315.C5 2003**
The Divine Comedy: The Inferno, the Purgatorio and the Paradiso. John Ciardi (Translator). Trade Paper. Penguin Group (USA) Inc. New York, NY. 2003. 928p. ISBN:0-451-20863-3, ISBN13: 978-0-451-20863-7. Dewey:851/.1. LCCN:2002-037963.
Audience: **g,l,u,f.**

Dante Alighieri **PQ4390**
The Divine Comedy. John Ciardi (Translator). Trade Cloth. W. W. Norton & Company, Inc. New York, NY. 1977. 602p. ISBN:0-393-04472-6, ISBN13: 978-0-393-04472-0. Dewey:851/.1.
Audience: **g,l,u,f.**

Dante Alighieri **PQ4315.D87 1996**
The Divine Comedy of Dante Alighieri: Inferno, Vol. 1. Robert M. Durling (Editor, Translator), Robert Turner (Illustrator), Robert M. Durling (Notes by), Ronald L. Martinez (Introduction by, Notes by). Trade Cloth. Oxford University Press, Inc. New York, NY. 1996. 672p. ISBN:0-19-508740-2, ISBN13: 978-0-19-508740-6. Dewey:851.1. LCCN:95-012740.
Audience: **g,l,u,f.** *Choice, 1996.*

Dante Alighieri **PQ4390**
The Divine Comedy of Dante Alighieri: Purgatorio. Robert M. Durling (Editor), Robert Turner (Illustrator), Ronald L. Martinez (Introduction by). Trade Paper. Oxford University Press, Inc. New York, NY. 2004. 720p. ISBN:0-19-508745-3, ISBN13: 978-0-19-508745-1. Dewey:851/.1.
Audience: **g,l,u,f.**

Dante Alighieri **PQ4315.2.E76 2002**
Inferno. Anthony M. Esolen (Translator), Gustave Dore (Illustrator). Trade Cloth. Random House Adult Trade Publishing Group. New York, NY. 2002. 528p. ISBN:0-679-64261-7, ISBN13: 978-0-679-64261-9. Dewey:741.944. LCCN:2002-029511.
Audience: **g,l,u,f.** *Choice, 2003.*

Dante Alighieri **PQ4315.3**
Purgatory. Anthony M. Esolen (Editor, Translator), Gustave Dore (Illustrator), Anthony M. Esolen (Introduction by). Trade Cloth. Random House Adult Trade Publishing Group. New York, NY. 2003. 544p. ISBN:0-679-64268-4, ISBN13: 978-0-679-64268-8. Dewey:851.1. LCCN:2002-045187.
Audience: **g,l,u,f.** *Choice, 2004.*

Dante Alighieri **PQ4302**
La Divina Commedia. C. H. Grandgent (Editor), Charles S. Singleton (Revised by). Trade Cloth. Harvard University Press. Cambridge, MA. 1972. 988p. ISBN:0-674-21290-8, ISBN13: 978-0-674-21290-9. Dewey:851/.1. LCCN:72-078429.
Audience: **u,f.**

Dante Alighieri **PQ4315.2.H28 1993**
Dante's Inferno. Daniel Halpern (Editor), James Merrill (Introduction by), Giuseppe Mazzotta (Afterword by). Trade Cloth. HarperCollins Publishers. New York, NY. 1998. xiii, 199p. ISBN:0-88001-291-9, ISBN13: 978-0-88001-291-1. Dewey:851/.1. LCCN:92-028061.
Audience: **g,l,u,f.**

Dante Alighieri **PQ4315.2.H65 2000**
The Inferno. Robert Hollander & Jean Hollander (Translators). Trade Cloth. Doubleday Publishing. New York, NY. 2000. 672p. ISBN:0-385-49697-4, ISBN13: 978-0-385-49697-1. Dewey:851/.1. LCCN:00-034531.
Audience: **g,l,u,f.** *Choice, 2001.*

Dante Alighieri **PQ4310.C213 1990**
Dante's II Convivio. Richard H. Lansing (Translator). Trade Cloth. Garland Publishing, Inc. New York, NY. 1990. 312p. Library of Medieval Literature ISBN:0-8240-5797-X, ISBN13: 978-0-8240-5797-8. Dewey:851/.1. LCCN:88-023719.
Audience: **u,f.** *Choice, 1990.*

Dante Alighieri **PQ4390**
La Vita Nuova. Mark Musa (Editor). Trade Paper. Oxford University Press, Inc. New York, NY. 1999. 122p. Oxford World's Classics Ser. ISBN:0-19-283935-7, ISBN13: 978-0-19-283935-0. Dewey:851/.1.
Audience: **u,f.** *Choice, 1996.*

Dante Alighieri **PQ4315.2.M77 1996**
Dante Alighieri's Divine Comedy: Inferno, Italian Text and Translation, Vol. 1. Mark Musa (Translator, Commentaries by). Cloth Text. Indiana University Press. Bloomington, IN. 1997. 352p. ISBN:0-253-32968-X, ISBN13: 978-0-253-32968-4. Dewey:851/.1. LCCN:96-012746.
Audience: **g,l,u,f.**

Dante Alighieri **PQ4315.62.S5313 1995**
Dante: Monarchia. Prue Shaw (Editor). Trade Cloth. Cambridge University Press. New York, NY. 1995. 232p. Cambridge Medieval Classics, No. 4 ISBN:0-521-48272-0, ISBN13: 978-0-521-48272-1. Dewey:320.01. LCCN:94-024397.
Audience: **u,f.** *Choice, 1996.*

Dante Alighieri (Editor) **PQ4315.S57 1992**
The Divine Comedy. C. H. Sisson (Translator), David N. Higgins (Introduction by, Notes by). Trade Paper. Oxford University Press, Inc. New York, NY. 1998. 742p. Oxford World's Classics Ser. ISBN:0-19-283502-5, ISBN13: 978-0-19-283502-4. Dewey:851/.1. LCCN:92-000553.
Audience: **g,l,u,f.**

Hollander, Robert (Editor) **PQ4300**
The Princeton Dante Project.
http://etcweb.princeton.edu/dante/index.html
Audience: **g,l,u,f.**

Individual Authors and Works > To 1400 > Dante > Biography. Criticism

Auerbach, Erich **PQ4390**
Dante: Poet of the Secular World. Theodore Silverstein (Editor), Ralph Manheim (Translator). Paper Text. University of Chicago Press. Chicago, IL. 1992. 204p. ISBN:0-226-03205-1, ISBN13: 978-0-226-03205-4. Dewey:851.5.
Audience: **u,f.**

Barolini, Teodolinda **PQ4409.P64B37 1984**
Dante's Poets: Textuality and Truth in the Comedy. Princeton. 1984. ISBN:0-691-06609-4, ISBN13: 978-0-691-06609-7.
Audience: **u,f.**

Barolini, Teodolinda **PQ4416.B37 1992**
The Undivine Comedy: Detheologizing Dante. Princeton Univ. Press. 1992. ISBN:0-691-06953-0, ISBN13: 978-0-691-06953-1.
Audience: **u,f.**

Bergin, Thomas Goddard **PQ4390**
Dante's 'Divine Comedy'. Trade Cloth. Prentice-Hall. Upper Saddle, NJ. 1971. xi, 116p. ISBN:0-13-197434-3, ISBN13: 978-0-13-197434-0. Dewey:851/.1. LCCN:73-151516.
Audience: **l,u,f.**

Bloom, Harold (Introduction by) **PQ4390.D273 2004**
Dante Alighieri. Trade Cloth. Facts On File, Inc. New York, NY. 2003. 150p. Bloom's Modern Critical Views Ser. ISBN:0-7910-7658-X, ISBN13: 978-0-7910-7658-3. Dewey:851/.1. LCCN:2003-023902.
Audience: **l,u,f.**

Bloom, Harold (Editor, Introduction by) **PQ4443.D36 1996**
Dante's Divine Comedy: The Inferno. Trade Cloth. Facts On File, Inc. New York, NY. 1996. 90p. Bloom's Notes Ser. ISBN:0-7910-4057-7, ISBN13: 978-0-7910-4057-7. Dewey:851/.1. LCCN:95-045101.
Audience: **l,u,f.**

Boccaccio, Giovanni **PQ4338.B6E44 1990**
Giovanni Boccaccio: The Life of Dante. Library Binding. Garland Publishing, Inc. New York, NY. 1989. 350p. Library of Medieval Literature ISBN:0-8240-8873-5, ISBN13: 978-0-8240-8873-6. Dewey:851/.1 B. LCCN:84-005405.
Audience: **u,f.** *Choice, 1990.*

Boyde, Patrick **PQ4412 .B63 1993**
Perception and Passion in Dante's Comedy. Trade Paper. Cambridge University Press. New York, NY. 2006. 362p. ISBN:0-521-02855-8, ISBN13: 978-0-521-02855-4. Dewey:851.1.
Audience: **u,f.** *Choice, 1994.*

Cachey, Theodore J. (Editor) **PQ4383.D36 1995**
Dante Now. Trade Cloth. University of Notre Dame Press. Notre Dame, IN. 1996. xxi, 283p. William and Katherine Devers Series in Dante Studies, Vol. 1 ISBN:0-268-00879-5, ISBN13: 978-0-268-00879-6. Dewey:851.1. LCCN:94-039220.
Audience: **u,f.**

Caesar, Michael **PQ4390.A2D36 1989**
Dante. Trade Cloth. Routledge. New York, NY. 1989. 624p. The Critical Heritage Ser. ISBN:0-415-02822-1, ISBN13: 978-0-415-02822-6. Dewey:851/.1. LCCN:88-014886.
Audience: **g,l,u.** *Choice, 1989.*

Cogan, Marc **PQ4390.C68 1999**
The Design in the Wax: The Structure of the Divine Comedy and Its Meaning. Trade Paper. University of Notre Dame Press. Notre Dame, IN. 1999. 432p. William and Katherine Devers Series in Dante Studies, Vol. 3 ISBN:0-268-00887-6, ISBN13: 978-0-268-00887-1. Dewey:851/.1. LCCN:98-054915.
Audience: **u,f.** *Choice, 1999.*

Croce, Benedetto **PQ4390.C8 1971**
The Poetry of Dante 1922. Trade Cloth. Paul P. Appel Publisher. Scarsdale, NY. 1971. 319p. ISBN:0-911858-12-1, ISBN13: 978-0-911858-12-9. Dewey:851/.1. LCCN:74-162490.
Audience: **l,u,f.**

Dante Alighieri **PQ4315**
Dante Alighieri's Divine Comedy, vol. 4: Purgatory. Commentary. Musa, Mark (Editor). Indiana University Press. 2000. ISBN:0-253-33651-1, ISBN13: 978-0-253-33651-4.
Audience: **g,l,u,f.**

Dante Alighieri **PQ4315**
Dante Alighieri's Divine Comedy, Vol. 6. Paradise: Notes and Commentary. Musa, Mark (Translator. Indiana University Press. 2005. ISBN:0-253-34141-8, ISBN13: 978-0-253-34141-9.
Audience: **g,l,u,f.**

Dante Alighieri **PQ4315.2.M77 1996**
Dante Alighieri's Divine Comedy: Inferno, Commentary, Vol. 2. Mark Musa (Translator, Commentaries by). Cloth Text. Indiana University Press. Bloomington, IN. 1997. 470p. ISBN:0-253-32967-1, ISBN13: 978-0-253-32967-7. Dewey:851/.1. LCCN:96-012746.
Audience: **g,l,u,f.**

Freccero, John **PQ4390.F82 1986**
Dante: The Poetics of Conversion. Harvard University Press. 1986. ISBN:0-674-19225-7, ISBN13: 978-0-674-19225-6.
Audience: **l,u,f.**

Gilson, Etienne **PQ4412 .G55**
Dante and Philosophy. David Moore (Translator). Trade Cloth. Peter Smith Publisher, Inc. Magnolia, MA. 1990. ISBN:0-8446-0645-6, ISBN13: 978-0-8446-0645-3. Dewey:851/.1.
Audience: **u,f.**

Hawkins, Peter & Jacoff, Rachel (Editors) **PQ4381.2.P64 2001**
The Poets' Dante: Essays on Dante by Twentieth-Century Poets. Trade Cloth. Farrar, Straus & Giroux. New York, NY. 2001. xxvi, 406p. ISBN:0-374-23536-8, ISBN13: 978-0-374-23536-9. Dewey:851/.1. LCCN:00-033552.
Audience: **g,u,f.**

Hollander, Robert **PQ4335.H63 2001**
Dante: A Life in Works. Cloth over Boards. Yale University Press. Cumberland, RI. 2001. 240p. ISBN:0-300-08494-3, ISBN13: 978-0-300-08494-8. Dewey:851/.1 B. LCCN:00-049539.
Audience: **g,u,f.** *Choice, 2001.*

Iannucci, Amilcare (Editor) **PQ4390**
Dante: Contemporary Perspectives. Trade Paper. University of Toronto Press. Toronto, ON. 1997. 256p. Italian Studies, No. 2: ISBN:0-8020-7736-6, ISBN13: 978-0-8020-7736-3. Dewey:851.1.
Audience: **u,f.** *Choice, 1997.*

Jacoff, Rachel (Editor) **PQ4335.C36 1993**
The Cambridge Companion to Dante. Trade Paper. Cambridge University Press. New York, NY. 1993. 290p. Companions to Literature Ser. ISBN:0-521-42742-8, ISBN13: 978-0-521-42742-5. Dewey:851.1. LCCN:92-017126.
Audience: **u,f.**

Kirkpatrick, Robin **PQ4315**
Dante: The Divine Comedy. Ed. 2. Trade Paper. Cambridge University Press. New York, NY. 2004. 130p. Landmarks of World Literature Ser. ISBN:0-521-53994-3, ISBN13: 978-0-521-53994-4. Dewey:851/.1. LCCN:2004-271597.
Audience: **l,u.** *Choice, 1987.*

Lansing, Richard (Editor) **PQ4333.D36 2000**
The Dante Encyclopedia. Trade Cloth. Garland Publishing, Inc. New York, NY. 2000. 800p. Reference Library of the Humanities, Vol. 1836 ISBN:0-8153-1659-3, ISBN13: 978-0-8153-1659-6. Dewey:851/.1 B. LCCN:00-021203.
Audience: **g,l,u,f.** *Choice, 2000.*

Lansing, Richard H. (Editor) **PQ4390.D2834 2002**
Dante. Paper over Boards. Routledge. New York, NY. 2002. 3466p. ISBN:0-415-94093-1, ISBN13: 978-0-415-94093-1. Dewey:851/.1. LCCN:2002-031850.
Audience: **u,f.**

Mazzaro, Jerome **PQ4310.V4**
The Figure of Dante: An Essay on the Vita Nuova. Trade Cloth. Princeton University Press. Princeton, NJ. 1981. 192p. Essays in Literature Ser. ISBN:0-691-06474-1, ISBN13: 978-0-691-06474-1. Dewey:851/.1. LCCN:81-047146.
Audience: **u,f.**

Mazzotta, Giuseppe **PQ4390.C788 1991**
Critical Essays on Dante. Trade Cloth. Macmillan Publishing Company, Inc. Old Tappan, NJ. 1991. 232p. Critical Essays in World Literature Ser. ISBN:0-8161-8849-1, ISBN13: 978-0-8161-8849-9. Dewey:851/.1. LCCN:90-020307.
Audience: **u,f.** *Choice, 1991.*

Mazzotta, Giuseppe **PQ4392.M39 1993**
Dante's Vision and the Circle of Knowledge. Princeton. 1992. ISBN:0-691-06966-2, ISBN13: 978-0-691-06966-1.
Audience: **u,f.**

Mazzotta, Giuseppe **PQ4390**
Dante, Poet of the Desert: History and Allegory in the Divine Comedy. Trade Cloth. Princeton University Press. Princeton, NJ. 1979. 360p. ISBN:0-691-06399-0, ISBN13: 978-0-691-06399-7. Dewey:851/.1. LCCN:78-027468.
Audience: **u,f.**

Payton, Rodney J. **PQ4443.P38 1992**
A Modern Reader's Guide to Dante's Inferno. Trade Paper. Peter Lang Publishing, Inc. New York, NY. 1993. 264p. American University Studies, Ser. II, Vol. 191:Romance, Languages and Literature ISBN:0-8204-1827-7, ISBN13: 978-0-8204-1827-8. Dewey:851/.1. LCCN:91-043149.
Audience: **g,l,u,f.** *Choice, 1993.*

Reynolds, Barbara **PQ4335.R49 2006**
Dante: The Poet, the Political Thinker, the Man. Cloth over Boards. Shoemaker & Hoard. Emeryville, CA. 2006. 448p. ISBN:1-59376-124-4, ISBN13: 978-1-59376-124-0. Dewey:851/.1 B. LCCN:2006-023882.
Audience: **g,u,f.**

Scott, John A. **PQ4390.S464 2003**
Understanding Dante. Trade Paper. University of Notre Dame Press. Notre Dame, IN. 2004. 504p. The William and Katherine Devers Series in Dante Studies, Vol. 6 ISBN:0-268-04451-1, ISBN13: 978-0-268-04451-0. Dewey:851/.1. LCCN:2003-050728.
Audience: **g,u,f.** *Choice, 2005.*

Tambling, Jeremy **PQ4390**
Dante. Trade Paper. Longman Publishing Group. White Plains, NY. 1998. 224p. Longman Critical Readers Ser. ISBN:0-582-31265-5, ISBN13: 978-0-582-31265-4. Dewey:851.1.
Audience: **u,f.**

Took, J. F. **PQ4308.T66 1990**
Dante: An Introduction to the Minor Works. Trade Cloth. Oxford University Press, Inc. New York, NY. 1991. 248p. ISBN:0-19-815158-6, ISBN13: 978-0-19-815158-6. Dewey:851/.1. LCCN:90-006888.
Audience: **u,f.** *Choice, 1991.*

Toynbee, Paget **PQ4335.T7 2005**
Dante Alighieri: His Life and Works. Robert Hollander (Introduction by). Trade Paper, Perfect. Dover Publications, Inc. Mineola, NY. 2005. 316p. ISBN:0-486-44340-X, ISBN13: 978-0-486-44340-9. Dewey:851/.1 B. LCCN:2005-045176.
Audience: **g,u,f.**

Williams, Charles **PQ4390**
The Figure of Beatrice: A Study in Dante. Paper Text. Textbook Publishers. Temecula, CA. 2003. 236p. ISBN:0-7581-7632-5, ISBN13: 978-0-7581-7632-5. Dewey:851/.1.
Audience: **u,f.**

Individual Authors and Works > To 1400 > Petrarca

Bergin, Thomas G. **PQ4505**
Petrarch. Library Binding. Thomson Gale. Farmington Hills, MI. 1984. World Authors Ser., No. 81 ISBN:0-8057-2694-2, ISBN13: 978-0-8057-2694-7. Dewey:851/.1.
Audience: **l,u,f.**

Bishop, Morris **PQ4505**
Petrarch and His World. Trade Cloth. Associated Faculty Press, Inc. New York, NY. 1973. 400p. ISBN:0-8046-1730-9, ISBN13: 978-0-8046-1730-7. Dewey:851/.1. LCCN:72-085320.
Audience: **u,f.**

Bloom, Harold (Introduction by) **PQ4505.P4 1989**
Petrarch. Library Binding. Chelsea House Publishers. Langhorne, PA. 1989. 184p. Modern Critical Views Ser. ISBN:1-55546-308-8, ISBN13: 978-1-55546-308-3. Dewey:851/.1. LCCN:87-017826.
Audience: **l,u,f.**

Cook, James W. (Translator) **PQ4496.E23C66 1995**
Petrarch's Songbook: Rerum Vulgarium Fragmenta. A Verse Translation. Germaine Warkentin (Introduction by). Trade Cloth. M R T S. Tempe, AZ. 1995. 464p. Medieval and Renaissance Texts and Studies, Vol. 151 ISBN:0-86698-191-8, ISBN13: 978-0-86698-191-0. Dewey:851/.1. LCCN:95-035500.
Audience: **u,f.** *Choice, 1996.*

Foster, Kenelm **PQ4540**
Petrarch: Poet and Humanist. Trade Cloth. Edinburgh University Press. Edinburgh, 1984. xii, 241p. ISBN:0-85224-485-1, ISBN13: 978-0-85224-485-2. Dewey:851/.1. LCCN:84-231563.
Audience: **u,f.**

Hainsworth, Peter **PQ4478.H35 1988**
Petrarch the Poet: An Introduction to the Rerum Vulgarium Fragmenta. Library Binding. Routledge. New York, NY. 1988. 256p. ISBN:0-415-00270-2, ISBN13: 978-0-415-00270-7. Dewey:851/.1. LCCN:88-009681.
Audience: **u,f.** *Choice, 1989.*

Mann, Nicholas **PQ4540.M3 1984**
Petrarch. Trade Cloth. Oxford University Press, Inc. New York, NY. 1984. 121p. Past Masters Ser. ISBN:0-19-287610-4, ISBN13: 978-0-19-287610-2. Dewey:851/.1. LCCN:84-004404.
Audience: **l,u,f.** *Choice, 1985.*

Mazzotta, Giuseppe **PQ4390**
The Worlds of Petrarch. Cloth Text. Duke University Press. Durham, NC. 1993. 248p. Monographs in Medieval and Renaissance Studies, Vol. 14 ISBN:0-8223-1363-4, ISBN13: 978-0-8223-1363-2. Dewey:851.1. LCCN:93-019793.
Audience: **u,f.**

Petrarca, Francesco **PQ4489**
Canzoniere: Rerum Vulgarium Fragmenta. Einaudi. 2005. ISBN:88-06-16889-4, ISBN13: 978-88-06-16889-6.
Audience: **u,f.**

Petrarca, Francesco **PQ4489**
Epistole. Unione tipografico-editrice torinese. 1978.
Audience: **u,f.**

Petrarca, Francesco **PQ4275**
Opere italiane, vol. 1. Mondadori. 1996. ISBN:88-04-41022-1, ISBN13: 978-88-04-41022-5.
Audience: **u,f.**

Petrarca, Francesco **PQ4275**
Opere italiane, vol. 2. Mondadori. 1996. ISBN:88-04-41402-2, ISBN13: 978-88-04-41402-5.
Audience: **u,f.**

Petrarca, Francesco **PQ4489**
Rime e trionfi. Unione tipografico-editrice torinese. 1968.
Audience: **u,f.**

Petrarca, Francesco **PQ4496**
Triumphs. Wilkins, Ernest (Translator). University of Chicago Press. 1962.
Audience: **u,f.**

Petrarch, Francesco **PQ4496.E21 2003**
Invectives. David Marsh (Editor, Translator). Trade Cloth. Harvard University Press. Cambridge, MA. 2004. 560p. The I Tatti Renaissance Library, Vol. 11 ISBN:0-674-01154-6, ISBN13: 978-0-674-01154-0. Dewey:874/.01. LCCN:2003-056663.
Audience: **u,f.**

Petrarch, Francesco **PQ4496 .E23**
The Portable Petrarch. Mark Musa (Translator). Trade Paper. Penguin Group (USA) Inc. New York, NY. 2004. 592p. ISBN:0-14-200084-1, ISBN13: 978-0-14-200084-7. Dewey:851/.1.
Audience: **g,l,u,f.**

Petrarch, Francesco **PQ4496**
Selections from the Canzoniere and Other Works. Mark Musa (Editor). Trade Paper. Oxford University Press, Inc. New York, NY. 1999. 128p. Oxford World's Classics Ser. ISBN:0-19-283951-9, ISBN13: 978-0-19-283951-0. Dewey:858/.109.
Audience: **g,l,u,f.**

Petrarch, Francesco **PQ4496.E23M8 1996**
Canzoniere. Mark Musa (Translator, Commentaries by, Introduction by, Notes by), Barbara Manfredi (Introduction by), Petrarch Canzoniere (Commentaries by, Notes by). Cloth Text. Indiana University Press. Bloomington, IN. 1996. 800p. ISBN:0-253-33944-8, ISBN13: 978-0-253-33944-7. Dewey:851/.1. LCCN:95-035943.
Audience: **g,u,f.** *Choice, 1996.*

Petrarch, Francesco **PQ4496.E23 2004**
The Poetry of Petrarch. David Young (Translator). Cloth over Boards. Farrar, Straus & Giroux. New York, NY. 2004. 320p. ISBN:0-374-23532-5, ISBN13: 978-0-374-23532-1. Dewey:851/.1. LCCN:2003-060844.
Audience: **g,l,u,f.**

Wilkins, Ernest Hatch **PQ4505**
Life of Petrarch. Paper Text. Textbook Publishers. Temecula, CA. 2003. viii, 275p. ISBN:0-7581-2352-3, ISBN13: 978-0-7581-2352-7. Dewey:928.5.
Audience: **g,u,f.**

Individual Authors and Works > 1400-1700 > Aretino

Aretino, Pietro **PQ4563**
Edizione nazionale delle opere di Pietro Aretino, vol. 1. Salerno editrice. 1992. ISBN:88-8402-095-6, ISBN13: 978-88-8402-095-6.
Audience: **u,f.**

Aretino, Pietro **PQ4563**
Edizione nazionale delle opere di Pietro Aretino, vol. 2. Salerno editrice. 1992.
Audience: **u,f.**

Aretino, Pietro **PQ4563**
Edizione nazionale delle opere di Pietro Aretino, vol. 3. Salerno editrice. 1992.
Audience: **u,f.**

Aretino, Pietro **PQ4563**
Edizione nazionale delle opere di Pietro Aretino, vol. 4. Salerno editrice. 1992.
Audience: **u,f.**

Aretino, Pietro **PQ4563**
Edizione nazionale delle opere di Pietro Aretino, vol. 5. Salerno editrice. 1992.
Audience: **u,f.**

Aretino, Pietro **PQ4563**
Edizione nazionale delle opere di Pietro Aretino, vol. 6. Salerno editrice. 1992.
Audience: **u,f.**

Aretino, Pietro **PQ4563**
Edizione nazionale delle opere di Pietro Aretino, vol. 7. Salerno editrice. 1992.
Audience: **u,f.**

Aretino, Pietro **PQ4563**
Edizione nazionale delle opere di Pietro Aretino, vol. 8. Salerno editrice. 1992.
Audience: **u,f.**

Aretino, Pietro **PQ4563**
Edizione nazionale delle opere di Pietro Aretino, vol. 9. Salerno editrice. 1992.
Audience: **u,f.**

Aretino, Pietro **PQ4563.R2.E5 1970**
The Ragionamenti: The Lives of Nuns, the Lives of Married Women, the Lives of Courtesans. Trade Cloth. Odyssey Press. Mesa, AZ. 1970. xvii, 185p. ISBN:0-85095-030-9, ISBN13: 978-0-85095-030-4. Dewey:853/.3. LCCN:76-496211.
Audience: **g,l,f.**

Aretino, Pietro **PQ4564.A4.E5 1976**
Aretino: Selected Letters. George Bull (Translator). Trade Paper. Penguin Group (USA) Inc. New York, NY. 1977. 256p. Penguin Classics Ser. ISBN:0-14-044317-7, ISBN13: 978-0-14-044317-2. Dewey:856/.3. LCCN:76-380093.
Audience: **u,f.**

Aretino, Pietro **PQ4619.C9**
Aretino's Dialogues. Margaret Rosenthal (Translator). Dust Jacket. University of Toronto Press. Toronto, ON. 2005. 420p. Lorenzo Da Ponte Italian Library ISBN:0-8020-9004-4, ISBN13: 978-0-8020-9004-1. Dewey:855/.3. LCCN:2006-276701.
Audience: **g,l,u,f.**

Waddington, Raymond B. **PQ4564**
Aretino's Satyr: Sexuality, Satire, and Self-Projection in Sixteenth-Century Literature and Art. Trade Cloth. University of Toronto Press. Toronto, ON. 2003. 320p. Toronto Italian Studies ISBN:0-8020-8814-7, ISBN13: 978-0-8020-8814-7. Dewey:858/.309. LCCN:2004-299279.
Audience: **u,f.**

Individual Authors and Works > 1400-1700 > Ariosto

Ariosto, Lodovico **PQ4567**
Orlando furioso. Arnoldo Mondadori. 2001. ISBN:88-17-16804-1, ISBN13: 978-88-17-16804-5.
Audience: **u,f.**

Ariosto, Ludovico **PQ4582.E5**
Sir John Harington's Translation of Orlando Furioso. Paper Text. Textbook Publishers. Temecula, CA. 2003. xi, 579p. ISBN:0-7581-3670-6, ISBN13: 978-0-7581-3670-1. Dewey:851.3.
Audience: **u,f.**

Ariosto, Ludovico **PQ1**
The Comedies of Ariosto. Edmond Beame & Leonard G. Sbrocchi (Editors). Cloth Text. University of Chicago Press. Chicago, IL. 1975. xlvi, 322p. ISBN:0-226-02649-3, ISBN13: 978-0-226-02649-7. Dewey:852/.3. LCCN:74-005739.
Audience: **g,l,u,f.**

Ariosto, Ludovico, et al. **PQ4103 .L83**
Le Rime. Pietro Bembo & Giovanni D. Casa (Authors). Trade Cloth. Georg Olms Verlag AG. Hildesheim, 1995. 692p. ISBN:3-487-10056-8, ISBN13: 978-3-487-10056-2. Dewey:016.851/408.
Audience: **u,f.**

Ariosto, Ludovico **PQ4582.E5.A368 1975**
Orlando Furioso, Pt. 1. Barbara Reynolds (Translator, Introduction by). Trade Paper. Penguin Group (USA) Inc. New York, NY. 1975. 832p. Classics Ser. ISBN:0-14-044311-8, ISBN13: 978-0-14-044311-0. Dewey:851.3. LCCN:75-327748.
Audience: **g,l,u,f.**

Ariosto, Ludovico **PQ4569**
Orlando Furioso: The Frenzy of Orlando: A Romantic Epic. Barbara Reynolds (Translator, Introduction by). Trade Paper. Penguin Group (USA) Inc. New York, NY. 1977. 800p. Classics Ser., Vol. 2 ISBN:0-14-044310-X, ISBN13: 978-0-14-044310-3. Dewey:851.3.
Audience: **g,l,u,f.**

Ariosto, Ludovico **PQ4582**
Orlando Furioso. Guido Waldman (Translator, Introduction by). Trade Paper. Oxford University Press, Inc. New York, NY. 1999. 646p. Oxford World's Classics Ser. ISBN:0-19-283677-3, ISBN13: 978-0-19-283677-9. Dewey:851.3.
Audience: **g,l,u,f.**

Beecher, Donald, et al. **PQ4587.A75 2003**
Ariosto Today: Contemporary Perspectives. Massimo Ciavolella & Roberto Fedi (Authors). Trade Cloth. University of Toronto Press. Toronto, ON. 2003. 272p. ISBN:0-8020-2967-1, ISBN13: 978-0-8020-2967-6. Dewey:851/.3. LCCN:2003-273407.
Audience: **u,f.** *Choice, 2003.*

Cavallo, Jo Ann **PQ4117.C38 2004**
The Romance Epics of Boiardo, Ariosto, and Tasso: From Public Duty to Private Pleasure. Dust Jacket. University of Toronto Press. Toronto, ON. 2004. 300p. Toronto Italian Studies ISBN:0-8020-8915-1, ISBN13: 978-0-8020-8915-1. Dewey:851/.03209. LCCN:2004-275933.
Audience: **u,f.**

Finucci, Valeria **PQ4569.R46 1999**
Renaissance Transactions: Ariosto and Tasso. Trade Paper. Duke University Press. Durham, NC. 1999. 296p. Duke Monographs in Medieval and Renaissance Studies, Vol. 17 ISBN:0-8223-2295-1, ISBN13: 978-0-8223-2295-5. Dewey:851/.309. LCCN:98-023344.
Audience: **u,f.** *Choice, 2000.*

Individual Authors and Works > 1400-1700 > B-V

Banti, Anna **PQ4827**
Artemisia. Shirley D. Caracciolo (Translator), Susan Sontag (Introduction by). Trade Cloth. University of Nebraska Press.

Lincoln, NE. 2005. 232p. European Women Writers Ser. ISBN:0-8032-6213-2, ISBN13: 978-0-8032-6213-3. Dewey:853/.912. LCCN:2004-270289.
Audience: **l,u,f.**

Bembo, Pietro **PQ4608.A6 1971**
Gli Asolani. Rudolf B. Gottfried (Translator). Trade Cloth. Ayer Company Publishers, Inc. Manchester, NH. 1977. xx, 200p. Select Bibliographies Reprint Ser. ISBN:0-8369-5941-8, ISBN13: 978-0-8369-5941-3. Dewey:858/.3/07. LCCN:76-168501.
Audience: **g,l,u,f.**

Boiardo, Matteo Maria **PQ4612**
Opere. R. Ricciardi. 1999. ISBN:88-7817-003-8, ISBN13: 978-88-7817-003-2.
Audience: **u,f.**

Boiardo, Matteo M. **PQ4612.A3 1989**
Orlando Innamorato. Charles L. Ross (Introduction by, Notes by). Trade Cloth. University of California Press. Berkeley, CA. 1989. 416p. Biblioteca Italiana Ser., No. 6 ISBN:0-520-05978-6, ISBN13: 978-0-520-05978-8. Dewey:851.2. LCCN:88-001084.
Audience: **u,f.** *Choice, 1990.*

Buonarroti, Michelangelo & Nims, John F. **PQ4615.B6A25 1998**
The Complete Poems of Michelangelo. Trade Cloth. University of Chicago Press. Chicago, IL. 1998. 208p. ISBN:0-226-08033-1, ISBN13: 978-0-226-08033-8. Dewey:851/.4. LCCN:98-007704.
Audience: **g,l,u,f.** *Choice, 1999.*

Castiglione, Baldassarre, conte **BJ1604**
Il libro del cortegiano. Einaudi. 1998. ISBN:88-06-13205-9, ISBN13: 978-88-06-13205-7.
Audience: **u,f.**

Castilgione, Baldesar **BJ1604.C43 2002**
Book of the Courtier. Trade Paper. W. W. Norton & Company, Inc. New York, NY. 2002. 512p. Critical Editions Ser. ISBN:0-393-97606-8, ISBN13: 978-0-393-97606-9. Dewey:170/.44. LCCN:2001-044867.
Audience: **g,l,u,f.**

di Lodovico Buonarroti Simoni, Michelangelo **N6923.B9M549 1999**
Michelangelo: Life, Letters, and Poetry. Trade Paper. Oxford University Press, Inc. New York, NY. 1999. 206p. Oxford World's Classics Ser. ISBN:0-19-283770-2, ISBN13: 978-0-19-283770-7. Dewey:709/.2 B. LCCN:00-502341.
Audience: **g,l,u,f.**

Guarini, Battista **PQ4626**
Il pastor fido. Marsilio. 1999. ISBN:88-317-7299-6, ISBN13: 978-88-317-7299-0.
Audience: **u,f.**

Marino, Giambattista **PQ4628**
La galeria. La finestra. 2005.
Audience: **u,f.**

Marino, Giambattista **PQ4628**
L'Adone. La finestra. 2004.
Audience: **u,f.**

Marino, Giambattista **PQ4628**
La sampogna : con le Egloghe boscarecce. La finestra. 2006. ISBN:88-88097-15-5, ISBN13: 978-88-88097-15-2.
Audience: **u,f.**

Poliziano, Angelo
Poesie. Unione tipografico editrice torinese. 2006. Classici italiani ISBN:88-02-07351-1, ISBN13: 978-88-02-07351-4.
Audience: **u,f.**

Poliziano, Angelo **PQ4630**
Poesie volgari, vol. 1: Testi. Vecchiarelli. 1997. ISBN:88-85316-93-X, ISBN13: 978-88-85316-93-5.
Audience: **u,f.**

Poliziano, Angelo **PQ4630**
Poesie volgari, vol. 2: Commento. Vecchiarelli. 1997.
Audience: **u,f.**

Poliziano, Angelo **PQ4630**
Silvae. L.S. Olschki. 1997. ISBN:88-222-4489-3, ISBN13: 978-88-222-4489-5.
Audience: **u,f.**

Poliziano, Angelo **PA8563.S9513 2004**
Silvae. Charles Fantazzi (Editor, Translator). Trade Cloth. Harvard University Press. Cambridge, MA. 2004. 240p. The I Tatti Renaissance Library, Vol. 14 ISBN:0-674-01480-4, ISBN13: 978-0-674-01480-0. Dewey:871/.04. LCCN:2004-040516.
Audience: **u,f.**

Poliziano, Angelo **PQ4630**
A Translation of the Orpheus of Angelo Politian and the Aminta of Torquato Tasso. Louis E. Lord (Introduction by). Trade Cloth. Greenwood Publishing Group, Inc. Portsmouth, NH. 1986. 182p. ISBN:0-313-25211-4, ISBN13: 978-0-313-25211-2. Dewey:852/.2. LCCN:86-003172.
Audience: **u,f.**

Poliziano, Angelo **PQ4630.P5.A713 1979**
The "Stanze" of Angelo Poliziano. David Quint (Editor). Trade Cloth. University of Massachusetts Press. Amherst, MA. 1979. 128p. ISBN:0-87023-145-6, ISBN13: 978-0-87023-145-2. Dewey:851/.2. LCCN:78-053180.
Audience: **g,l,u,f.**

Pulci, Luigi **PQ4631.M3 1984**
Il Morgante. Trade Cloth. U T E T SpA. Torino, 1984. :p. ISBN:88-02-03826-0, ISBN13: 978-88-02-03826-1. Dewey:851/.2. LCCN:84-248051.
Audience: **u,f.**

Pulci, Luigi **PQ4631.M3E5 1998**
Morgante: The Epic Adventures of Orlando and His Giant Friend Morgante. Joseph Tusiani (Translator), Edoardo A. L'Bano (Introduction by, Notes by). Trade Cloth. Indiana University Press. Bloomington, IN. 1998. 975p. Indiana Masterpiece Editions Ser. ISBN:0-253-33399-7, ISBN13: 978-0-253-33399-5. Dewey:851/.2. LCCN:97-044991.
Audience: **g,l,u,f.** *Choice, 1999.*

Ryan, Christopher **PQ4615**
The Poetry of Michelangelo: An Introduction. Fairleigh Dickinson University Press. 1998. ISBN:0-8386-3802-3, ISBN13: 978-0-8386-3802-6.
Audience: **l,u.**

Saslow, James M. **PQ4615.B6A265 1991**
The Poetry of Michelangelo: An Annotated Translation. Trade Cloth. Yale University Press. Cumberland, RI. 1991. 576p. ISBN:0-300-04960-9, ISBN13: 978-0-300-04960-2. Dewey:851/.4. LCCN:90-048480.
Audience: **g,l,u,f.** *Choice, 1991.*

Sheridan, Thomas **PQ4626.P313 1989**
The Faithful Shepherd: A Translation of Battista Guarini's Il Pastor Fido. Robert T. Hogan & Edward A. Nickerson (Editors). Trade Cloth. University of Delaware Press. Newark, DE. 1990. 192p. ISBN:0-87413-375-0, ISBN13: 978-0-87413-375-2. Dewey:852/.5. LCCN:88-040583.
Audience: **g,l,u,f.** *Choice, 1990.*

Vico, Giambattista **B3580**
Opere. Ed. 3. A. Mondadori. 2001. ISBN:88-04-46928-5, ISBN13: 978-88-04-46928-5.
Audience: **u,f.**

Vico, Giambattista **B3580.E5**
Vico: Selected Writings. Leon Pompa (Editor, Translator). Trade Cloth. Cambridge University Press. New York, NY. 1982. 296p. ISBN:0-521-23514-6, ISBN13: 978-0-521-23514-3. Dewey:195. LCCN:81-012215.
Audience: **u,f.**

Individual Authors and Works > 1400-1700 > Machiavelli

Machiavelli, Niccolo **JC143**
The Prince. Ed. 2. Robert M. Adams (Editor, Translator). Trade Paper. W. W. Norton & Company, Inc. New York, NY. 1992. 288p. Critical Editions Ser. ISBN:0-393-96220-2, ISBN13: 978-0-393-96220-8. Dewey:320/.01. LCCN:91-032538.
Audience: **g,l,u,f.**

Machiavelli, Niccolo **JC143.M16313 1996**
Discourses on Livy. Harvey C. Mansfield Jr. & Nathan Tarcov (Translators). Trade Cloth. University of Chicago Press. Chicago, IL. 1996. 424p. ISBN:0-226-50035-7, ISBN13: 978-0-226-50035-5. Dewey:937/.02. LCCN:95-050910.
Audience: **g,l,u,f.** *Choice, 1996.*

Machiavelli, Niccolo **PQ4627.M2A25**
The Comedies of Machiavelli: The Woman from Andros, The Mandrake, Clizia. David Sices & James B. Atkinson (Translators). Trade Paper. Books on Demand. Ann Arbor, MI. 416p. ISBN:0-608-21991-6, ISBN13: 978-0-608-21991-2. Dewey:852/.3. LCCN:84-040595.
Audience: **g,l,u,f.**

Machiavelli, Niccolò **DG713.5**
Opere, vol. 1. Einaudi-Gallimard. 1997. ISBN:88-446-0016-1, ISBN13: 978-88-446-0016-7.
Audience: **u,f.**

Machiavelli, Niccolò **DG731.5**
Opere, vol. 2. Einaudi-Gallimard. 1997. ISBN:88-446-0084-6, ISBN13: 978-88-446-0084-6.
Audience: **u,f.**

Machiavelli, Niccolò **DG731.5**
Opere, vol. 3. Einaudi-Gallimard. 1997. ISBN:88-446-0070-6, ISBN13: 978-88-446-0070-9.
Audience: **u,f.**

Ridolfi, Roberto **DG0738.14.M2**
The Life of Niccolo Machiavelli. Cecil Grayson (Translator). Trade Paper. Books on Demand. Ann Arbor, MI. 351p. ISBN:0-598-22154-9, ISBN13: 978-0-598-22154-4. Dewey:320.1/092. LCCN:62-015048.
Audience: **g,l,u,f.**

Ruffo-Fiore, Silvia **PQ4627.M2**
Niccolo Machiavelli. Trade Cloth. Thomson Gale. Farmington Hills, MI. 1982. World Authors Ser. ISBN:0-8057-6499-2, ISBN13: 978-0-8057-6499-4. Dewey:858/.309.
Audience: **l,u.**

Individual Authors and Works > 1400-1700 > Tasso

Brand, C. P. **PQ4655**
Torquato Tasso: A Study of the Poet and of his Contribution to English Literature. Trade Cloth. Cambridge University Press. New York, NY. 1965. 356p. ISBN:0-521-04311-5, ISBN13: 978-0-521-04311-3. Dewey:851.4.
Audience: **l,u.**

Cavallo, Jo Ann **PQ4117.C38 2004**
The Romance Epics of Boiardo, Ariosto, and Tasso: From Public Duty to Private Pleasure. Dust Jacket. University of Toronto Press. Toronto, ON. 2004. 300p. Toronto Italian Studies ISBN:0-8020-8915-1, ISBN13: 978-0-8020-8915-1. Dewey:851/.03209. LCCN:2004-275933.
Audience: **u,f.**

Finucci, Valeria **PQ4569.R46 1999**
Renaissance Transactions: Ariosto and Tasso. Trade Paper. Duke University Press. Durham, NC. 1999. 296p. Duke Monographs in Medieval and Renaissance Studies, Vol. 17 ISBN:0-8223-2295-1, ISBN13: 978-0-8223-2295-5. Dewey:851/.309. LCCN:98-023344.
Audience: **u,f.** *Choice, 2000.*

Poliziano, Angelo **PQ4630**
A Translation of the Orpheus of Angelo Politian and the Aminta of Torquato Tasso. Louis E. Lord (Introduction by). Trade Cloth. Greenwood Publishing Group, Inc. Portsmouth, NH. 1986. 182p. ISBN:0-313-25211-4, ISBN13: 978-0-313-25211-2. Dewey:852/.2. LCCN:86-003172.
Audience: **u,f.**

Stampino, Maria Galli **PQ4639.A3S73 2005**
Staging the Pastoral: Tasso's Aminta and the Emergence of Modern Western Theater. Book, Other. Arizona State University, Arizona Center for Medieval & Renaissance Studies. Tempe, AZ. 2005. ISBN:0-86698-323-6, ISBN13: 978-0-86698-323-5. Dewey:792.9/5. LCCN:2005-027846.
Audience: **u,f.**

Tasso, Torquato **PQ4640**
Dialoghi, vol. 1. Classici Rizzoli. 1998. ISBN:88-17-18934-0, ISBN13: 978-88-17-18934-7.
Audience: **u,f.**

Tasso, Torquato **PQ4640**
Dialoghi, vol. 2. Classici Rizzoli. 1998. ISBN:88-17-18935-9, ISBN13: 978-88-17-18935-4.
Audience: **u,f.**

Tasso, Torquato **PQ4638**
Gerusalemme liberata. Ed. 4. A. Mondadori. 1999. ISBN:88-04-16192-2, ISBN13: 978-88-04-16192-9.
Audience: **u,f.**

Tasso, Torquato **PQ4642.E21E84 2000**
Jerusalem Delivered (Gerusalemme Liberata). Anthony M. Esolen (Author, Translator). Trade Paper. Johns Hopkins University Press. Baltimore, MD. 2000. 512p. ISBN:0-8018-6323-6, ISBN13: 978-0-8018-6323-3. Dewey:851/.4. LCCN:99-055723.
Audience: **g,l,u,f.** *Choice, 2001.*

Tasso, Torquato **PQ4624**
Aminta. C. E. Griffiths (Editor). Cloth Text. Manchester University Press. Manchester, 1988. 168p. Italian Texts Ser. ISBN:0-7190-0522-1, ISBN13: 978-0-7190-0522-0. Dewey:852/.4.
Audience: **u,f.**

Tasso, Torquato **PQ4642.E22J47 2000**
Aminta: A Pastoral Play. Charles Jernigan & Irene Marchegiani Jones (Editors), Charles Jernigan & Irene Marchegiani Jones (Translators), Charles Jernigan & Irene Marchegiani Jones (Introduction by). Trade Paper. Italica Press. New York, NY. 2000. xxxiii, 180p. Dual-Language Poetry Ser. ISBN:0-934977-65-8, ISBN13: 978-0-934977-65-4. Dewey:852/.4. LCCN:00-063221.
Audience: **g,l,u,f.**

Tasso, Torquato **PQ4642.E2 1982**
Tasso's Dialogues: A Selection, with the "Discourse on the Art of the Dialogue". Carnes Lord & Dain A. Trafton (Translators). Trade Cloth. University of California Press. Berkeley, CA. 1983. 288p. Biblioteca Italiana Ser., No. 4 ISBN:0-520-04464-9, ISBN13: 978-0-520-04464-7. Dewey:858/.408. LCCN:81-012937.
Audience: **g,l,u,f.**

Individual Authors and Works > 1701-1900 > A-G

D'Annunzio, Gabriele **PQ4803**
Prose di ricerca. A. Mondadori. 2005. ISBN:88-04-52370-0, ISBN13: 978-88-04-52370-3.
Audience: **u,f.**

Alfieri, Vittorio **PQ4677**
Vittorio Alfieri. Ferrucci, Franco (Editor). Istituto poligrafico e Zecca dello Stato. 1995.
Audience: **u,f.**

Belli, G. G. **PQ4683.B43**
The Roman Sonnets. Harold Norse (Translator), William Carlos Williams (Preface by), Alberto Moravia (Introduction by). Trade Paper. Jargon Society, Incorporated, The. Winston-Salem, NC. 1960. ISBN:0-912330-72-4, ISBN13: 978-0-912330-72-3. Dewey:851.7. LCCN:60-009955.
Audience: **u,f.**

Belli, Giuseppe G. **PQ4683.B43.A28**
Sonnets of Giuseppe Belli. Miller Williams (Translator). Cloth Text. Louisiana State University Press. Baton Rouge, LA. 1981. xx, 164p. ISBN:0-8071-0762-X, ISBN13: 978-0-8071-0762-1. Dewey:851/.7. LCCN:80-024331.
Audience: **g,l,u,f.**

Cambon, Glauco **PQ4691**
Ugo Foscolo: Poet of Exile. Trade Cloth. Princeton University Press. Princeton, NJ. 1980. 360p. ISBN:0-691-06424-5, ISBN13: 978-0-691-06424-6. Dewey:851/.6. LCCN:79-003193.
Audience: **u,f.**

Carducci, Giosuè **PQ4686**
Opere scelte di Giosue Carducci, vol. 1. Unione tipografico-editrice torinese. 1993. ISBN:88-02-04616-6, ISBN13: 978-88-02-04616-7.
Audience: **u,f.**

Carducci, Giosuè **PQ4686**
Opere scelte di Giosue Carducci, vol. 2. Unione tipografico-editrice torinese. 1993. ISBN:88-02-04775-8, ISBN13: 978-88-02-04775-1.
Audience: **u,f.**

Collodi, Carlo & Castellani Pollidori, Ornella **PZ44.C64**
Le Avventure di Pinocchio. Fondazione Nazionale Carlo Collodi. 1983.
Audience: **u,f.**

Collodi, Carlo **PQ4841.C482**
The Adventures of Pinocchio. Ann Lawson Lucas (Translator). Trade Paper. Oxford University Press, Inc. New York, NY. 2002. 248p. Oxford World's Classics Ser. ISBN:0-19-280150-3, ISBN13: 978-0-19-280150-0. Dewey:853/.8. LCCN:96-001472.
Audience: **g,l,u,f.**

Foscolo, Ugo **PQ4689**
Opere, vol. 1. Einaudi-Gallimard. 1994. ISBN:88-446-0017-X, ISBN13: 978-88-446-0017-4.
Audience: **u,f.**

Foscolo, Ugo **PQ4689**
Opere, vol. 2. Einaudi-Gallimard. 1995. ISBN:88-446-0025-0, ISBN13: 978-88-446-0025-9.
Audience: **u,f.**

Foscolo, Ugo **PQ4689**
Last Letters of Jacopo Ortis. Douglas Radcliff-Umstead (Translator). Trade Paper. University of North Carolina Press. Chapel Hill, NC. 1970. Studies in the Romance Languages and Literatures, No. 89 ISBN:0-8078-9089-8, ISBN13: 978-0-8078-9089-9. Dewey:853.6.
Audience: **g,u,f.**

Gozzi, Carlo **PQ4703.A6 1989**
Five Tales for the Theatre: The Raven, The King Stag, Turandot, The Serpent Woman, and The Green Bird. Albert Bermel & Ted Emery (Editors), Albert Bermel & Ted Emery (Translators). Trade Cloth. University of Chicago Press. Chicago, IL. 1989. 320p. ISBN:0-226-30579-1, ISBN13: 978-0-226-30579-0. Dewey:852/.914. LCCN:89-030641.
Audience: **g,l,u,f.**

Umstead, Douglas R. **PQ4691**
Ugo Foscolo. Trade Cloth. Thomson Gale. Farmington Hills, MI. 1984. World Authors Ser. ISBN:0-8057-2320-X, ISBN13: 978-0-8057-2320-5. Dewey:858/.6.
Audience: **u,f.**

Individual Authors and Works > 1701-1900 > Goldoni

Goldoni, Carlo **PQ4693**
Opere. Ed. 6. Mursia. 1993.
Audience: **u,f.**

Goldoni, Carlo **PQ4695 .E5 1979**
Three Comedies: Mine Hostess, the Boors, and the Fan. Clifford Bax, I. M. Rawson, Eleanor Farjeon & Herbert Farjeon (Translators), Gabriele Baldini (Introduction by). Trade Cloth. Greenwood Publishing Group, Inc. Portsmouth, NH. 1979. 293p. ISBN:0-313-21259-7, ISBN13: 978-0-313-21259-8. Dewey:852/.6. LCCN:79-004666.
Audience: **g,l,u,f.**

Goldoni, Carlo **PQ4695**
The Holiday Trilogy. Anthony Oldcorn (Translator). Trade Cloth. Marsilio Publishers. New York, NY. 1994. 300p. ISBN:0-941419-60-6, ISBN13: 978-0-941419-60-4. Dewey:852. LCCN:92-082643.
Audience: **g,l,u,f.** *Choice, 1995.*

Goldoni, Carlo **PQ4695 .E5 1978**
The Comedies of Goldoni. Helen Zimmern (Editor, Introduction by). Trade Cloth. Hyperion Press, Inc. Westport, CT. 1986. Library of World Literature Ser. ISBN:0-88355-544-1, ISBN13: 978-0-88355-544-6. Dewey:852/.6. LCCN:77-005358.
Audience: **g,l,u,f.**

Riedt, Heinz **PQ4699.R513**
Carlo Goldoni. Ursule Molinaro (Translator). Trade Cloth. Continuum International Publishing Group, Ltd. London, 1974. 160p. World Dramatists Ser. ISBN:0-8044-2729-1, ISBN13: 978-0-8044-2729-6. Dewey:852/.6. LCCN:73-085411.
Audience: **u,f.**

Individual Authors and Works > 1701-1900 > Leopardi

Barricelli, Gian P. **PQ4710.B328 1986**
Giacomo Leopardi. Trade Cloth. Thomson Gale. Farmington Hills, MI. 1986. 224p. Twayne's World Authors Ser., No.753 ISBN:0-8057-6602-2, ISBN13: 978-0-8057-6602-8. Dewey:851/.7. LCCN:86-003140.
Audience: **u,f.** *Choice, 1987.*

Leopardi, Giacomo **PQ4708**
Poesie e prose, vol. 1. Ed. 7. A. Mondadori. 1996. ISBN:88-04-30264-X, ISBN13: 978-88-04-30264-3.
Audience: **u,f.**

Leopardi, Giacomo **PQ4708**
Poesie e prose, vol. 2. Ed. 5. A. Mondadori. 1998. ISBN:88-04-30455-3, ISBN13: 978-88-04-30455-5.
Audience: **u,f.**

Leopardi, Giacomo **PQ4709.E5**
Thoughts. Trade Paper. Hesperus Press. London, 2003. 112p. ISBN:1-84391-012-8, ISBN13: 978-1-84391-012-1. Dewey:858.708.
Audience: **g,u,f.**

Leopardi, Giacomo **PQ4708**
Zibaldone, vol. 1: 1. Autografo 1-2341. Ed. 3. A. Mondadori. 2003.
Audience: **u,f.**

Leopardi, Giacomo **PQ4708**
Zibaldone, vol. 2: Autografo 2342-4526. Ed. 3. A. Mondadori. 2003.
Audience: **u,f.**

Leopardi, Giacomo **PQ4708**
Zibaldone, vol. 3: Commento. Bibliografia. Indice analittico. Indici filologici. Ed. 3. A. Mondadori. 2003.
Audience: **u,f.**

Leopardi, Giacomo **PQ4709.E5.A1 1981**
A Leopardi Reader. Ottavio M. Casale (Editor). Trade Cloth. University of Illinois Press. Champaign, IL. 1981. 300p. ISBN:0-252-00824-3, ISBN13: 978-0-252-00824-5. Dewey:858/.709. LCCN:80-029068.
Audience: **g,u,f.**

Leopardi, Giacomo **PQ4709.E5**
Operette Morali: Essays and Dialogues. Giovanni Del Cecchetti (Translator). Trade Paper. University of California Press. Berkeley, CA. 1983. 672p. Biblioteca Italiana Ser., No. 3 ISBN:0-520-04928-4, ISBN13: 978-0-520-04928-4. Dewey:858/.708. LCCN:82-002627.
Audience: **u,f.**

Leopardi, Giacomo **PQ4709.E5A13 1997**
Leopardi: Selected Poems. Eamon Grennan (Translator). Trade Paper. Princeton University Press. Princeton, NJ. 1997. 118p. The Lockert Library of Poetry in Translation ISBN:0-691-01644-5, ISBN13: 978-0-691-01644-3. Dewey:851/.7. LCCN:96-047721.
Audience: **g,l,u,f.**

Leopardi, Giacomo **PQ4708 .Z3213 1992**
Zibaldone: A Selection by Giacomo Leopardi. Martha King (Editor, Introduction by), Daniela Bini (Introduction by). Cloth Text. Peter Lang Publishing, Inc. New York, NY. 1993. XXII, 209p. Studies in Italian Culture Ser., Vol. 8:Literature in History ISBN:0-8204-1723-8, ISBN13: 978-0-8204-1723-3. Dewey:858/.703. LCCN:91-043276.
Audience: **u,f.**

Leopardi, Giacomo **PQ4709.E5A3 1998**
The Canti with a Selection of His Prose: The Centenary Edition. J. G. Nichols (Translator). Trade Paper. Carcanet Press, Ltd. Manchester, 1998. 192p. ISBN:1-85754-359-9, ISBN13: 978-1-85754-359-9. Dewey:851.7. LCCN:99-222036.
Audience: **g,u,f.**

Leopardi, Giacomo **PQ4709.E5 A2**
Giacomo Leopardi, Poems: Poems: Bilingual. Ed. 2. Arturo Vivante (Translator, Introduction by). Perfect. Delphinium Press. Wellfleet, MA. 1994. 76p. ISBN:0-9620305-0-3, ISBN13: 978-0-9620305-0-5. Dewey:851.7.
Audience: **u,f.**

Individual Authors and Works > 1701-1900 > Manzoni

Barricelli, Gian P. **PQ4715**
Alessandro Manzoni. Cloth Text. Irvington Publishers. New York, NY. 1976. 194p. Twayne's World Authors Ser. ISBN:0-8057-6251-5, ISBN13: 978-0-8057-6251-8. Dewey:853/.7. LCCN:76-016481.
Audience: **u,f.**

Chandler, S. B. **PQ4715**
Manzoni. Trade Cloth. Edinburgh University Press. Edinburgh, 1974. 139p. ISBN:0-85224-247-6, ISBN13: 978-0-85224-247-6. Dewey:853/.7.
Audience: **u,f.**

Manzoni, Alessandro **PQ4713**
I Romanzi. A. Mondadori. 2002. ISBN:88-04-47904-3, ISBN13: 978-88-04-47904-8.
Audience: **u,f.**

Manzoni, Alessandro **PQ4713**
Opere, vol. 1. Unione tipografico-editrice torinese. 1990. ISBN:88-02-01841-3, ISBN13: 978-88-02-01841-6.
Audience: **u,f.**

Manzoni, Alessandro **PQ4713**
Opere, vol. 2. Unione tipografico-editrice torinese. 1990. ISBN:88-02-01842-1, ISBN13: 978-88-02-01842-3.
Audience: **u,f.**

Manzoni, Alessandro **PQ4713**
Opere, vol. 3. Unione tipografico-editrice torinese. 1990. ISBN:88-02-04379-5, ISBN13: 978-88-02-04379-1.
Audience: **u,f.**

Manzoni, Alessandro **PQ4713**
Tutte le opere, Volume primo. Sansoni. 1990.
Audience: **u,f.**

Manzoni, Alessandro **PQ4713**
Tutte le opere, Volume secondo. Sansoni. 1990.
Audience: **u,f.**

Manzoni, Alessandro **PN3441**
On the Historical Novel. Sandra Bermann (Translator). Cloth Text. University of Nebraska Press. Lincoln, NE. 1984. 134p. ISBN:0-8032-3084-2, ISBN13: 978-0-8032-3084-2. Dewey:809.3/81. LCCN:83-010583.
Audience: **u,f.**

Manzoni, Alessandro **PQ4714.A24 2004**
Alessandro Manzoni's the Count of Carmagnola and Adelchis. Federica Brunori Deigan (Translator). Trade Cloth. Johns Hopkins University Press. Baltimore, MD. 2004. 360p. ISBN:0-8018-7881-0, ISBN13: 978-0-8018-7881-7. Dewey:853/.7. LCCN:2003-018059.
Audience: **u,f.** *Choice, 2005.*

Manzoni, Alessandro **PQ4714**
The Betrothed: (I Promessi Sposi). Bruce Penman (Translator, Introduction by). Trade Paper. Penguin Group (USA) Inc. New York, NY. 1984. 720p. Classics Ser. ISBN:0-14-044274-X, ISBN13: 978-0-14-044274-8. Dewey:853.7. LCCN:73-165908.
Audience: **g,l,u,f.**

Individual Authors and Works > 1701-1900 > M-P

Metastasio, Pietro **PQ4717**
Drammi per musica, vol. 1. Marsilio. 2000. ISBN:88-317-8122-7, ISBN13: 978-88-317-8122-0.
Audience: **u,f.**

Metastasio, Pietro **PQ4717**
Drammi per musica, vol. 2. Marsilio. 2003. ISBN:88-317-8314-9, ISBN13: 978-88-317-8314-9.
Audience: **u,f.**

Metastasio, Pietro **PQ4718.A1**
Three Melodramas. Joseph G. Fucilla (Translator). Trade Cloth. University Press of Kentucky. Lexington, KY. 1981. 164p. Studies in Romance Languages, No. 24 ISBN:0-8131-1400-4, ISBN13: 978-0-8131-1400-2. Dewey:852/.5. LCCN:80-051017.
Audience: **g,l,u,f.**

Nievo, Ippolito
Le confessioni d'un italiano. Unione tipografico editrice torinese. 2006. ISBN:88-02-07350-3, ISBN13: 978-88-02-07350-7.
Audience: **u,f.**

Nievo, Ippolito **PZ3**
Castle of Fratta. Lovett F. Edwards (Translator). Trade Cloth. Greenwood Publishing Group, Inc. Portsmouth, NH. 1974. 589p. ISBN:0-8371-7660-3, ISBN13: 978-0-8371-7660-4. Dewey:853/.7. LCCN:74-010017.
Audience: **g,l,u,f.**

Porta, Carlo Antonio Melchiore Filippo **PQ4730**
Poesie. A. Mondadori. 2000. ISBN:88-04-47162-X, ISBN13: 978-88-04-47162-2.
Audience: **u,f.**

Individual Authors and Works > 1701-1900 > Verga

Bergin, Thomas G. **PQ4734.V5 Z6**
Giovanni Verga. Library Binding. Greenwood Publishing Group, Inc. Portsmouth, NH. 1985. ISBN:0-8371-2851-X, ISBN13: 978-0-8371-2851-1. Dewey:853/.8. LCCN:77-098816.
Audience: **u,f.**

Cecchetti, Giovanni **PQ4734.V5.Z6527**
Giovanni Verga. Trade Cloth. Thomson Gale. Farmington Hills, MI. 1978. 172p. World Authors Ser., No. 489 Italy ISBN:0-8057-6330-9, ISBN13: 978-0-8057-6330-0. Dewey:853/.8. LCCN:77-019342.
Audience: **u,f.**

Verga, Giovanni **PQ4734.V5**
I Malavoglia. Edizioni Il Polifilo. 1995. ISBN:88-7050-436-0, ISBN13: 978-88-7050-436-1.
Audience: **u,f.**

Verga, Giovanni **PQ4841.C482**
Life in the Country. Trade Paper. Hesperus Press. London, 2003. 128p. ISBN:1-84391-042-X, ISBN13: 978-1-84391-042-8. Dewey:853.8.
Audience: **g,l,u,f.**

Verga, Giovanni **PQ4734**
Mastro-don Gesualdo : edizione critica. Le Monnier. 1993. ISBN:88-00-81172-8, ISBN13: 978-88-00-81172-9.
Audience: **u,f.**

Verga, Giovanni **PQ4734**
Opere di Giovanni Verga. Mursia. 1988.
Audience: **u,f.**

Verga, Giovanni **PQ4734**
Tutte le novelle. Ed. 6. A. Mondadori. 2001. ISBN:88-04-16023-3, ISBN13: 978-88-04-16023-6.
Audience: **u,f.**

Verga, Giovanni **PQ4734.V5A22 2001**
Sicilian Stories (Novelle Siciliane): A Dual-Language Book. Stanley Appelbaum (Editor, Translator). Trade Paper. Dover Publications, Inc. Mineola, NY. 2002. 256p. ISBN:0-486-41945-2, ISBN13: 978-0-486-41945-9. Dewey:853/.8. LCCN:2001-042396.
Audience: **u,f.**

Verga, Giovanni & Lan, David **PQ4804**
La Lupa. Trade Paper. Methuen Publishing Ltd. London, 2004. Methuen Modern Plays Ser. ISBN:0-413-75450-2, ISBN13: 978-0-413-75450-9. Dewey:852.8.
Audience: **g,l,u,f.**

Verga, Giovanni **PQ4734.V5N613 2000**
Little Novels of Sicily. Ed. 3. D. H. Lawrence (Translator). Trade Cloth. Steerforth Press. Hanover, NH. 2004. 200p. Steerforth Italia Ser. ISBN:1-883642-54-X, ISBN13: 978-1-883642-54-9. Dewey:853/.8. LCCN:99-043311.
Audience: **g,l,u,f.**

Verga, Giovanni **PZ3**
Mastro Don Gesualdo. D. H. Lawrence (Translator). Trade Cloth. Greenwood Publishing Group, Inc. Portsmouth, NH. 1976. 454p. ISBN:0-8371-8198-4, ISBN13: 978-0-8371-8198-1. Dewey:853/.8. LCCN:75-011486.
Audience: **g,u,f.**

Verga, Giovanni **PQ4734.V5A27 1999**
Cavalleria Rusticana and Other Stories. G. H. McWilliam (Translator, Introduction by). Trade Paper. Penguin Group (USA) Inc. New York, NY. 2000. 272p. Classics Ser. ISBN:0-14-044741-5, ISBN13: 978-0-14-044741-5. Dewey:853/.8. LCCN:00-267751.
Audience: **g,l,u,f.**

Verga, Giovanni **PQ4841.C482**
The House by the Medlar Tree. Raymond Rosenthal (Translator), Giovanni Cecchetti (Introduction by). Trade Cloth. University of California Press. Berkeley, CA. 1984. 275p. ISBN:0-520-04846-6, ISBN13: 978-0-520-04846-1. Dewey:853/.8. LCCN:83-003466.
Audience: **g,l,u,f.**

Individual Authors and Works > 1901-1960 > A-C

Aleramo, Sibilla **PZ3.M7962**
A Woman. Rosalind Delmar (Translator), Richard Drake (Introduction by). Trade Cloth. University of California Press. Berkeley, CA. 1980. 220p. ISBN:0-520-04108-9, ISBN13: 978-0-520-04108-0. Dewey:853/.9/1.
Audience: **g,l,u,f.**

Bacchelli, Riccardo **PQ4807.A23**
The Mill on the Po. Frances Frenaye (Translator). Library Binding. Greenwood Publishing Group, Inc. Portsmouth, NH. 1975. 591p. ISBN:0-8371-8077-5, ISBN13: 978-0-8371-8077-9. Dewey:853/.9/12. LCCN:75-003800.
Audience: **g,l,u,f.**

Bassani, Giorgio **PQ4807.A79.C513**
Five Stories of Ferrara. Trade Cloth. Harcourt Trade Publishers. New York, NY. 1971. 216p. A Helen and Kurt Wolff Bk. ISBN:0-15-131400-4, ISBN13: 978-0-15-131400-3. Dewey:853/.9/14. LCCN:76-153681.
Audience: **g,l,u,f.**

Bassani, Giorgio **PQ4807.A79**
The Smell of Hay. Trade Cloth. Harcourt Trade Publishers. New York, NY. 1975. 193p. A Helen and Kurt Wolff Bk. ISBN:0-15-183146-7, ISBN13: 978-0-15-183146-3. Dewey:853/.9/14. LCCN:75-016222.
Audience: **g,l,u,f.**

Bassani, Giorgio **PQ4807.A79G513 2005**
The Garden of the Finzi-Continis. William Weaver (Translator), Tim Parks (Introduction by). Trade Cloth. Knopf Publishing Group. New York, NY. 2005. 280p. ISBN:1-4000-4422-7, ISBN13: 978-1-4000-4422-1. Dewey:853/.914. LCCN:2004-063119.
Audience: **g,l,u,f.**

Betti, Ugo **PQ4807**
Three plays. Hill and Wang. 1966.
Audience: **g,l,u,f.**

Campana, Dino **PQ4809.A52.C313 1984**
Orphic Songs. Charles Wright (Translator), Jonathan Galassi (Introduction by). Trade Cloth. Oberlin College Press. Oberlin, OH. 2003. 130p. Field Translation Ser. ISBN:0-932440-16-9, ISBN13: 978-0-932440-16-7. Dewey:851/.912. LCCN:83-063448.
Audience: **g,u,f.**

Individual Authors and Works > 1901-1960 > Calvino

Bolongaro, Eugenio **PQ4809.A45Z647 2003**
Italo Calvino and the Compass of Literature. Trade Cloth. University of Toronto Press. Toronto, ON. 2003. 240p. Toronto Italian Studies ISBN:0-8020-8763-9, ISBN13: 978-0-8020-8763-8. Dewey:853/.914. LCCN:2004-268221.
Audience: **u,f.**

Calvino, Italo (Editor) **PJ7846.A46**
Fantastic Tales: Visionary and Everyday. Trade Paper. Knopf Publishing Group. New York, NY. 1998. 608p. ISBN:0-679-75544-6, ISBN13: 978-0-679-75544-9. Dewey:808.3/8766. LCCN:93-012824.
Audience: **g,l,u,f.**

Calvino, Italo **PQ4809.A45**
If on a Winter's Night a Traveler. Trade Cloth. Alfred A. Knopf Inc. New York, NY. 1993. 304p. Everyman's Library ISBN:0-679-42025-8, ISBN13: 978-0-679-42025-5. Dewey:853.914. LCCN:92-054302.
Audience: **g,l,u,f.**

Calvino, Italo **PQ4809.A45**
Invisible Cities. UK-B Format Paperback. Knopf Publishing Group. New York, NY. 2002. 165p. ISBN:0-09-942983-7, ISBN13: 978-0-09-942983-8. Dewey:853.9/14.
Audience: **g,l,u,f.**

Calvino, Italo **PQ4809.A45S413 2000**
The Path to the Spiders' Nests. Trade Paper. HarperCollins Publishers. New York, NY. 2000. 192p. ISBN:0-06-095658-5, ISBN13: 978-0-06-095658-5. Dewey:853.9/14. LCCN:00-028150.
Audience: **g,l,u,f.**

Calvino, Italo **PQ4809.A45**
The Road to San Giovanni. Trade Paper. Knopf Publishing Group. New York, NY. 1994. 160p. ISBN:0-679-74348-0, ISBN13: 978-0-679-74348-4. Dewey:853.9/14.
Audience: **g,l,u,f.**

Calvino, Italo **PQ4809**
Romanzi E Racconti. A. Mondadori. 1995.
Audience: **u,f.**

Calvino, Italo **PQ4809**
Saggi : 1945-1985. Ed. 3. Mondadori. 2001. ISBN:88-04-40404-3, ISBN13: 978-88-04-40404-0.
Audience: **u,f.**

Calvino, Italo **PQ4865.C6**
The Literature Machine: Essays. Trade Paper. Random House. London, 1997. 15p. ISBN:0-7493-9994-5, ISBN13: 978-0-7493-9994-8. Dewey:854.9/14.
Audience: **g,l,u,f.**

Calvino, Italo **PN511**
Why Read the Classics? Trade Cloth. Knopf Publishing Group. New York, NY. 1999. 288p. ISBN:0-676-59283-X, ISBN13: 978-0-676-59283-2. Dewey:809.
Audience: **g,l,u,f.**

Calvino, Italo **PQ4809.A45**
The Baron in the Trees. Archibald Colquhoun (Translator). Trade Paper. Harcourt Trade Publishers. New York, NY. 1977. 228p. Harbrace Paperbound Library ISBN:0-15-610680-9, ISBN13: 978-0-15-610680-1. Dewey:853/.9/14. LCCN:76-039704.
Audience: **g,l,u,f.**

Calvino, Italo **PQ4809.A45**
The Nonexistent Knight and the Cloven Viscount. J. Ferrone & H. Wolff (Editors). Trade Paper. Harcourt Trade Publishers. New York, NY. 1977. 264p. Harbrace Paperbound Library ISBN:0-15-665975-1, ISBN13: 978-0-15-665975-8. Dewey:853/.9/14. LCCN:76-039699.
Audience: **g,l,u,f.**

Calvino, Italo **GR176.C3413**
Italian Folktales. George Martin (Translator). Cloth over Boards. Harcourt Trade Publishers. New York, NY. 1990. 800p. A Helen and Kurt Wolff Bk. ISBN:0-15-145770-0, ISBN13: 978-0-15-145770-0. Dewey:398.2/0945. LCCN:80-011879.
Audience: **g,l,u,f.**

Calvino, Italo **PQ4809.A45Z465 2003**
The Hermit in Paris: Autobiographical Writings. Martin McLaughlin (Translator). Trade Cloth. Knopf Publishing Group. New York, NY. 2003. 272p. ISBN:0-375-42184-X, ISBN13: 978-0-375-42184-6. Dewey:853/.914. LCCN:2002-075965.
Audience: **g,l,u,f.**

Calvino, Italo **PQ4809.A45P713 1995**
Numbers in the Dark and Other Stories. Tim Parks (Translator). Trade Cloth. Knopf Publishing Group. New York, NY. 1995. 288p. ISBN:0-679-44205-7, ISBN13: 978-0-679-44205-9. Dewey:853.9/14. LCCN:95-024359.
Audience: **g,l,u,f.**

Calvino, Italo **PQ4809.A45**
The Castle of Crossed Destinies. William Weaver (Translator). Trade Paper. Harcourt Trade Publishers. New York, NY. 1979. 144p. Harvest Book Ser. ISBN:0-15-615455-2, ISBN13: 978-0-15-615455-0. Dewey:853.9/14. LCCN:78-023588.
Audience: **g,l,u,f.**

Calvino, Italo **PZ3.M7962**
Cosmicomics. William Weaver (Translator). Trade Paper. Harcourt Trade Publishers. New York, NY. 1976. 168p. Harbrace Paperbound Library, Vol. 69 ISBN:0-15-622600-6, ISBN13: 978-0-15-622600-4. Dewey:853/.91. LCCN:76-014795.
Audience: **g,l,u,f.**

Calvino, Italo **PQ4809.A45**
Marcovaldo: Or the Seasons in the City. William Weaver (Translator). Trade Cloth. Harcourt Trade Publishers. New York, NY. 1983. 121p. A Helen and Kurt Wolff Bk. ISBN:0-15-157081-7, ISBN13: 978-0-15-157081-2. Dewey:853.9/14. LCCN:83-004372.
Audience: **g,l,u,f.**

Calvino, Italo **PQ4809.A45P313 1985**
Mr. Palomar. William Weaver (Translator). Trade Cloth. Harcourt Trade Publishers. New York, NY. 1985. 144p. A Helen and Kurt Wolff Bk. ISBN:0-15-162835-1, ISBN13: 978-0-15-162835-3. Dewey:853/.914. LCCN:85-005490.
Audience: **g,l,u,f.**

Calvino, Italo **PQ4809.A45A6 1988**
Under the Jaguar Sun. William Weaver (Translator). Trade Cloth. Harcourt Trade Publishers. New York, NY. 1988. 96p. ISBN:0-15-192820-7, ISBN13: 978-0-15-192820-0. Dewey:853.9/14. LCCN:88-000835.
Audience: **g,l,u,f.**

Calvino, Italo **PZ3.C13956**
The Watcher and Other Stories. William Weaver & Archibald Colquhoun (Translators). Trade Paper. Harcourt Trade Publishers. New York, NY. 1975. 192p. Harbrace Paperbound Library ISBN:0-15-694952-0, ISBN13: 978-0-15-694952-1. Dewey:853/.9/14. LCCN:75-009829.
Audience: **g,l,u,f.**

Calvino, Italo **PQ4809.A45A813 1984**
Difficult Loves. William Weaver, Archibald Colquhoun & Peggy Wright (Translators). Trade Cloth. Harcourt Trade Publishers. New York, NY. 1984. A Helen and Kurt Wolff Bk. ISBN:0-15-125610-1, ISBN13: 978-0-15-125610-5. Dewey:853.9/14. LCCN:84-000685.
Audience: **g,l,u,f.**

Jeannet, Angela M. **PQ4809.A45Z765 2000**
Under the Radiant Sun and Crescent Moon. Printed Dust Jacket. University of Toronto Press. Toronto, ON. 2000. 224p. Italian Studies, : ISBN:0-8020-4724-6, ISBN13: 978-0-8020-4724-3. Dewey:853/.914. LCCN:00-700461.
Audience: **g,l,u,f.** *Choice, 2001.*

McLaughlin, Martin L. **PQ4809.A45**
Italo Calvino. Trade Cloth. Edinburgh University Press. Edinburgh, 1998. 240p. Writers of Italy Ser. ISBN:0-7486-0917-2, ISBN13: 978-0-7486-0917-8. Dewey:853.914.
Audience: **u,f.**

Ricci, Franco (Editor) **PQ4809.A45Z677 1988**
Calvino Revisited. Trade Paper. Dovehouse Editions Canada. Ottawa, ON. 1989. 230p. ISBN:0-919473-71-7, ISBN13: 978-0-919473-71-3. Dewey:853/.914. LCCN:89-199255.
Audience: **u,f.**

Weiss, Beno **PQ4809.A45**
Understanding Italo Calvino. Trade Cloth. University of South Carolina Press. Columbia, SC. 1993. 244p. Understanding Modern European and Latin American Literature Ser. ISBN:0-87249-858-1, ISBN13: 978-0-87249-858-7. Dewey:853/.914. LCCN:92-040941.
Audience: **u,f.**

Individual Authors and Works > 1901-1960 > D-L

De Filippo, Eduardo **PQ4815.I48A2 1992**
Four Plays. Carlo Ardito & Peter Tinniswood (Translators). Trade Paper. Methuen Publishing Ltd. London, 2003. World Dramatists Ser. ISBN:0-413-66620-4, ISBN13: 978-0-413-66620-8. Dewey:852.9/12. LCCN:93-136278.
Audience: **g,l,u,f.**

De Filippo, Eduardo **PQ4815.I48A225 2004**
Theater Neapolitan Style: Five One-Act Plays. Mimi D'Aponte (Introduction by). Trade Cloth. Fairleigh Dickinson University Press. Cranbury, NJ. 2004. 128p. ISBN:0-8386-4035-4, ISBN13: 978-0-8386-4035-7. Dewey:852/.912. LCCN:2004-001343.
Audience: **g,l,u,f.**

Fenoglio, Beppe **PQ4809.A45**
Johnny the Partisan. Trade Cloth. Quartet Books, Ltd. London, 1995. 429p. ISBN:0-7043-7078-6, ISBN13: 978-0-7043-7078-4. Dewey:853.9/14.
Audience: **g,l,u,f.**

Fenoglio, Beppe **PQ4815.E63**
Ruin. John Shepley (Translator). Trade Cloth. Northwestern University Press. Evanston, IL. 1995. 94p. ISBN:0-910395-83-7, ISBN13: 978-0-910395-83-0. Dewey:853/.914. LCCN:92-080362.
Audience: **g,l,u,f.**

Fenoglio, Beppe **PQ4815.E63V413 2002**
The Twenty-Three Days of the City of Alba: Stories. John Shepley (Translator). Trade Cloth. Steerforth Press. Hanover, NH. 2004. 176p. Steerforth Italia Ser. ISBN:1-58642-040-2, ISBN13: 978-1-58642-040-6. Dewey:853/.914. LCCN:2001-057751.
Audience: **g,l,u,f.**

Gadda, Carlo Emilio **PZ3.M7962**
Acquainted with Grief. Trade Paper. George Braziller Inc. New York, NY. 1985. 244p. ISBN:0-8076-1115-8, ISBN13: 978-0-8076-1115-9. Dewey:853.91. LCCN:69-012804.
Audience: **g,l,u,f.**

Gadda, Carlo Emilio **PQ4817.A33.Q413 1984**
That Awful Mess on Via Merulana. William Weaver (Translator), Italo Calvino (Introduction by). Trade Paper. George Braziller Inc. New York, NY. 1984. 392p. ISBN:0-8076-1093-3, ISBN13: 978-0-8076-1093-0. Dewey:853/.912. LCCN:84-002848.
Audience: **g,l,u,f.**

Gozzano, Guido **PQ4817.O9C6213 1987**
The Colloquies and Selected Letters. J. G. Nichols (Introduction by). Trade Paper. Carcanet Press, Ltd. Manchester, 1987. 141p. ISBN:0-85635-628-X, ISBN13: 978-0-85635-628-5. Dewey:851/.912 B. LCCN:86-181777.
Audience: **g,l,u,f.** *Choice, 1987.*

Levi, Primo **PQ4809.A45**
The Periodic Table. Trade Paper. Knopf Publishing Group. New York, NY. 1995. 240p. ISBN:0-8052-1041-5, ISBN13: 978-0-8052-1041-5. Dewey:853.9/14. LCCN:54-000053.
Audience: **g,l,u,f.**

Luzi, Mario **PQ4827.U9**
After Many Years. Trade Cloth. Dedalus Press, The. Dublin 13, 1990. ISBN:0-948268-77-8, ISBN13: 978-0-948268-77-9. Dewey:851.912.
Audience: **g,l,u,f.**

Luzi, Mario **PQ4827.U9**
Earthly and Heavenly Journey of Simone Martini. Trade Cloth. Penguin Group (USA) Inc. New York, NY. 2004. 407p. Green Integer Ser. ISBN:1-931243-53-0, ISBN13: 978-1-931243-53-7. Dewey:851.912.
Audience: **g,u,f.**

Luzi, Mario **PQ4827.U9**
For the Baptism of Our Fragments. Trade Paper. Guernica Editions, Inc. Tonawanda, NY. 1992. 190p. Essential Poets Ser., No. 46 ISBN:0-920717-55-1, ISBN13: 978-0-920717-55-4. Dewey:851/.912.
Audience: **g,u,f.**

Luzi, Mario **PQ4827**
Tutte le poesie. Garzanti. 2001. ISBN:88-11-66914-6, ISBN13: 978-88-11-66914-2.
Audience: **u,f.**

Luzi, Mario **PQ4829.O565**
Phrases and Passages of a Salutary Song. Luigi Bonaffini (Translator). Trade Paper. Guerilla Poetics, Inc. Amherst, MA. 1999. 150p. ISBN:1-77051-077-X, ISBN13: 978-1-77051-077-7. Dewey:851/.912.
Audience: **g,u,f.**

Luzi, Mario **PQ4827.U9 S68**
Under Human Species. Luigi Bonaffini (Translator). Trade Paper. Green Integer. Los Angeles, CA. 2005. 400p. ISBN:1-933382-04-X, ISBN13: 978-1-933382-04-3. Dewey:851.912.
Audience: **g,u,f.**

Luzi, Mario **PQ4827.U9.I5**
In the Dark Body of Metamorphosis and Other Poems. I. L. Salomon (Translator). Trade Cloth. W. W. Norton & Company, Inc. New York, NY. 1975. 110p. ISBN:0-393-04391-6, ISBN13: 978-0-393-04391-4. Dewey:851/.9/12. LCCN:74-011122.
Audience: **g,u,f.**

Malaparte, Curzio **PQ4829.A515 A6 1997**
Opere scelte. A. Mondadori. 1997. ISBN:88-04-43436-8, ISBN13: 978-88-04-43436-8.
Audience: **u,f.**

Individual Authors and Works > 1901-1960 > D'Annunzio

D'Annunzio, Gabriele **PQ4803**
Prose di ricerca, vol. 1. A. Mondadori. 2005. ISBN:88-04-52370-0, ISBN13: 978-88-04-52370-3.
Audience: **u,f.**

D'Annunzio, Gabriele **PQ4803**
Prose di Ricerca, Vol. 2. A. Mondadori. 2005. ISBN:88-04-52370-0, ISBN13: 978-88-04-52370-3.
Audience: **u,f.**

D'Annunzio, Gabriele **PQ4803.Z3L46 2003**
The Book of the Virgins. Trade Paper. Hesperus Press. London, 2003. 120p. 100 Pages Ser. ISBN:1-84391-052-7, ISBN13: 978-1-84391-052-7. Dewey:853.8. LCCN:2005-412023.
Audience: **g,l,u,f.**

D'Annunzio, Gabriele **PQ4829.O62**
Flame. Paper Text. Marsilio Publishers. New York, NY. 1999. 312p. ISBN:1-56886-062-5, ISBN13: 978-1-56886-062-6. Dewey:853.912.
Audience: **g,l,u,f.**

D'Annunzio, Gabriele **PQ4841.C482**
The Child of Pleasure. Ed. 2. Georgina Harding (Translator). Trade Paper. Dedalus, Ltd. Monroe, OR. 1999. 311p. Decadence Ser. ISBN:0-946626-60-X, ISBN13: 978-0-946626-60-1. Dewey:853/.8.
Audience: **g,l,u,f.**

D'Annunzio, Gabriele **PQ4841.C482**
L' Innocente (The Victim). Ed. 2. Georgina Harding (Translator). Trade Paper. Dedalus, Ltd. Monroe, OR. 1997. 333p. Decadence Ser. ISBN:0-946626-64-2, ISBN13: 978-0-946626-64-9. Dewey:853.8.
Audience: **g,l,u,f.**

D'Annunzio, Gabriele **PQ4829.O62**
The Triumph of Death. Ed. 2. Georgina Harding (Translator). Trade Paper. Dedalus, Ltd. Monroe, OR. 1999. 320p. Decadence Ser. ISBN:0-946626-62-6, ISBN13: 978-0-946626-62-5. Dewey:853.912.
Audience: **g,l,u,f.**

D'Annunzio, Gabriele **PQ4835.A3**
Halcyon. J. G. Nichols (Translator). Trade Paper. Carcanet Press, Ltd. Manchester, 2006. 264p. ISBN:1-85754-693-8, ISBN13: 978-1-85754-693-4. Dewey:851/.8.
Audience: **g,l,u,f.**

D'Annunzio, Gabriele **PQ4803.Z3 F89**
Francesca Da Rimini. Arthur Symons (Translator). Trade Paper. Kessinger Publishing, LLC. Whitefish, MT. 2005. ISBN:1-4179-0288-4, ISBN13: 978-1-4179-0288-0. Dewey:852.8.
Audience: **g,l,u,f.**

D'Annunzio, Gabrielle **PQ4841.C482**
Nocturne and Five Tales of Love and Death. Raymond Rosenthal (Translator). Trade Cloth. Northwestern University Press. Evanston, IL. 1988. 264p. ISBN:0-910395-40-3, ISBN13: 978-0-910395-40-3. Dewey:853/.8. LCCN:88-060729.
Audience: **g,l,u,f.**

Klopp, Charles **PQ4804.K55 1988**
Gabriele D'Annunzio. Trade Cloth. Macmillan Publishing Company, Inc. Old Tappan, NJ. 1988. 176p. ISBN:0-8057-8243-5, ISBN13: 978-0-8057-8243-1. Dewey:858/.809. LCCN:88-012385.
Audience: **g,u,f.**

Valesio, Paolo **PQ4804.V35 1992**
Gabriele D'Annunzio: The Dark Flame. Marilyn Migiel (Translator). Cloth over Boards. Yale University Press. Cumberland, RI. 1992. 288p. ISBN:0-300-04871-8, ISBN13: 978-0-300-04871-1. Dewey:858/.809. LCCN:91-029491.
Audience: **g,u,f.** *Choice, 1992.*

Woodhouse, John **PQ4804.W66 1998**
Gabriele D'Annunzio: Defiant Archangel. Cloth Text. Oxford University Press, Inc. New York, NY. 1998. 424p. ISBN:0-19-815945-5, ISBN13: 978-0-19-815945-2. Dewey:853.9/12. LCCN:97-033335.
Audience: **u,f.** *Choice, 1998.*

Individual Authors and Works > 1901-1960 > Deledda

Deledda, Grazia **PQ4811**
Romanzi e novell. Ed. 7. Mondadori. 1994.
ISBN:88-04-09674-8, ISBN13: 978-88-04-09674-0.
Audience: **u,f.**

Deledda, Grazia **PQ4811.E6N313 1995**
After the Divorce. Susan Ashe (Translator). Trade Cloth. Northwestern University Press. Evanston, IL. 1995. 174p. European Classics Ser. ISBN:0-8101-1248-5, ISBN13: 978-0-8101-1248-3. Dewey:853/.8. LCCN:95-012351.
Audience: **g,l,u,f.** *Choice, 1986.*

Deledda, Grazia **PQ4811.E6C6413 1988**
Cosima. Martha King (Introduction by). Trade Paper. Italica Press. New York, NY. 1988. 153p. ISBN:0-934977-06-2, ISBN13: 978-0-934977-06-7. Dewey:853/.8. LCCN:87-045355.
Audience: **g,l,u,f.**

Deledda, Grazia **PQ4811.E6E513 1995**
Elias Portolu. Martha King (Translator). Trade Cloth. Northwestern University Press. Evanston, IL. 1995. 194p. European Classics Ser. ISBN:0-8101-1250-7, ISBN13: 978-0-8101-1250-6. Dewey:853/.8. LCCN:95-012332.
Audience: **g,l,u,f.**

Deledda, Grazia **PQ4811.E6C213 1998**
Reeds in the Wind. Martha King (Translator), Dolores Turchi (Introduction by). Trade Paper. Italica Press. New York, NY. 1999. 224p. Italian Fiction in Translation Ser. ISBN:0-934977-63-1, ISBN13: 978-0-934977-63-0. Dewey:853/.8. LCCN:97-032515.
Audience: **g,l,u,f.**

Deledda, Grazia & Kozma, Janice M. **PQ4811.E6C313 2004**
Ashes. Trade Cloth. Fairleigh Dickinson University Press. Cranbury, NJ. 2004. 224p. ISBN:0-8386-4003-6, ISBN13: 978-0-8386-4003-6. Dewey:853/.8. LCCN:2003-010577.
Audience: **g,l,u,f.**

Deledda, Grazia **PQ4811.E6M313 2006**
Marianna Sirca. Janice M. Kozma (Introduction by). Trade Cloth. Fairleigh Dickinson University Press. Cranbury, NJ. 2006. 176p. ISBN:0-8386-4068-0, ISBN13: 978-0-8386-4068-5. Dewey:853/.8. LCCN:2005-032927.
Audience: **g,l,u,f.**

Deledda, Grazia **PQ4811.E615**
La Madre: The Woman and the Priest. Ed. 2. D. M. Lawrence & Eric Lane (Editors), M. G. Steegman (Translator). Trade Paper. Dedalus, Ltd. Monroe, OR. 1999. 224p. European Classics Ser. ISBN:0-946626-20-0, ISBN13: 978-0-946626-20-5. Dewey:853/.912.
Audience: **g,l,u,f.**

Deledda, Grazia **PQ4811.E6C4513 2002**
The Church of Solitude. E. Ann Matter (Translator). Cloth Text. State University of New York Press. Albany, NY. 2002. 176p. ISBN:0-7914-5457-6, ISBN13: 978-0-7914-5457-2. Dewey:853/.8. LCCN:2002-020092.
Audience: **g,l,u,f.**

King, Martha **PQ4811**
Grazia Deledda : a legendary life. Troubador. 2005.
ISBN:1-904744-67-2, ISBN13: 978-1-904744-67-2.
Audience: **g,u,f.**

Individual Authors and Works > 1901-1960 > Ginzburg

Ginzburg, Natalia **PQ4817**
Opere, vol. 1. Ed. 3. A. Mondadori. 1995. ISBN:88-04-25910-8, ISBN13: 978-88-04-25910-7.
Audience: **u,f.**

Ginzburg, Natalia **PQ4817**
Opere, vol. 2. Ed. 3. A. Mondadori. 1995. ISBN:88-04-30060-4, ISBN13: 978-88-04-30060-1.
Audience: **u,f.**

Ginzburg, Natalia **PQ4829.O62**
Voices in the Evening. Trade Cloth. Random House Value Publishing. New York, NY. 1995. ISBN:0-517-13812-3, ISBN13: 978-0-517-13812-0. Dewey:853/.912.
Audience: **g,l,u,f.**

Ginzburg, Natalia **PQ4817.I5**
No Way. Sheila Cudahy (Translator). Trade Cloth. Harcourt Trade Publishers. New York, NY. 1974. 168p. A Helen and Kurt Wolff Bk. ISBN:0-15-167674-7, ISBN13: 978-0-15-167674-3. Dewey:853/.9/12. LCCN:74-007069.
Audience: **g,l,u,f.**

Ginzburg, Natalia **PQ4817.I5P513 1986**
The Little Virtues. Dick David (Translator). Trade Cloth. Henry Holt & Company. New York, NY. 1986. 110p. ISBN:0-8050-0077-1, ISBN13: 978-0-8050-0077-1. Dewey:854/.912. LCCN:86-013488.
Audience: **g,l,u,f.**

Ginzburg, Natalia **PQ4809.A45**
All Our Yesterdays. Angus Davidson (Translator). Trade Cloth. Carcanet Press. New York, NY. 1985. 300p. ISBN:0-85635-593-3, ISBN13: 978-0-85635-593-6. Dewey:853.9/14.
Audience: **g,l,u,f.**

Ginzburg, Natalia **PQ4817.I5C513 1987**
The City and the House. Dick Davis (Translator). Trade Cloth. Henry Holt & Company. New York, NY. 1987. ISBN:0-8050-0392-4, ISBN13: 978-0-8050-0392-5. Dewey:853/.914. LCCN:86-031563.
Audience: **g,l,u,f.**

Ginzburg, Natalia **PQ4715.G4713 1987**
The Manzoni Family. Marie Evans (Translator). Trade Cloth. Henry Holt & Company. New York, NY. 1987. 358p. ISBN:0-8050-0613-3, ISBN13: 978-0-8050-0613-1. Dewey:853/.914. LCCN:87-009892.
Audience: **g,l,u,f.** *Choice, 1988.*

Ginzburg, Natalia **PQ4817.I5A6 1990**
The Road to the City: Two Novellas. Frances Frenaye (Translator). Trade Cloth. Arcade Publishing, Inc. New York, NY. 1990. 149p. ISBN:1-55970-052-1, ISBN13: 978-1-55970-052-8. Dewey:853/.912. LCCN:89-038521.
Audience: **g,l,u,f.**

Ginzburg, Natalia **PQ4817.I5Z463513**
It's Hard to Talk about Yourself. Cesare Garboli & Lisa Ginzburg (Editors), Louise Quirke (Translator). Trade Cloth. University of Chicago Press. Chicago, IL. 2003. 248p. ISBN:0-226-29688-1, ISBN13: 978-0-226-29688-3. Dewey:853/.912. LCCN:2002-153254.
Audience: **g,l,u,f.**

Ginzburg, Natalia **PQ4817.I5A27 2002**
A Place to Live: And Other Selected Essays of Natalia Ginzburg. Lynne Sharon Schwartz (Translator). Trade Cloth. Seven Stories Press. New York, NY. 2004. ISBN:1-58322-474-2, ISBN13: 978-1-58322-474-8. Dewey:854/.912. LCCN:2002-001559.
Audience: **g,u,f.**

Ginzburg, Natalia **PQ4809.A45**
The Things We Used to Say. Judith Woolf (Translator, Introduction by). Trade Cloth. Arcade Publishing, Inc. New York, NY. 1999. 224p. ISBN:1-55970-467-5, ISBN13: 978-1-55970-467-0. Dewey:853.9/14. LCCN:98-073501.
Audience: **g,l,u,f.**

Jeannet, Angela M. & Sanguinetti Katz, Giuliana (Editors) **PQ4817.I5Z7748 2000**
Natalia Ginzburg: Voice of the Twentieth Century. Printed Dust Jacket. University of Toronto Press. Toronto, ON. 2000. 256p. Italian Studies, : ISBN:0-8020-4722-X, ISBN13: 978-0-8020-4722-9. Dewey:853/.912. LCCN:00-710173.
Audience: **u,f.**

Individual Authors and Works > 1901-1960 > Marinetti

Blum, Cinzia S. **PQ4829.A76Z57 1996**
The Other Modernism: F. T. Marinetti's Futurist Fiction of Power. Trade Paper. University of California Press. Berkeley, CA. 1996. 224p. ISBN:0-520-20049-7, ISBN13: 978-0-520-20049-4. Dewey:858/.91209. LCCN:96-003604.
Audience: **u,f.** *Choice, 1996.*

Chamberlain, Lesley & Marinetti, Filippo Tommaso **TX723.M32913 1989**
The Futurist Cookbook. Sue Brill (Translator). Trade Cloth. Chronicle Books LLC. San Francisco, CA. 1991. 176p. ISBN:0-938491-30-X, ISBN13: 978-0-938491-30-9. Dewey:641.5945. LCCN:89-017705.
Audience: **g,l,u,f.**

Marinetti, Filippo Tommaso **PQ4829**
Gli indomabili : con un'antologia di scritti futuristi sull'arte meccanica e d'avanguardia. A. Mondadori. 2000.
Audience: **u,f.**

Marinetti, Filippo Tommaso **PQ4829**
Les mots en liberté futuristes. A. Mondadori. 1986.
Audience: **u,f.**

Marinetti, Filippo Tommaso **PQ4829**
Scritti francesi. A. Mondadori. 1983.
Audience: **u,f.**

Marinetti, Filippo Tommaso **PQ4829**
Teoria e invenzione futurista. A. Mondadori. 2001. ISBN:88-04-22037-6, ISBN13: 978-88-04-22037-4.
Audience: **u,f.**

Marinetti, Filippo Tommaso **PQ4829.A76**
The Untameables. Arthur A. Coppotelli (Translator), Luigi Ballerini (Introduction by). Trade Paper. Sun & Moon Press. Los Angeles, CA. 1993. 88p. Sun and Moon Classics Ser., No. 28 ISBN:0-685-66684-0, ISBN13: 978-0-685-66684-5. Dewey:858.91209.
Audience: **g,u,f.**

Marinetti, Filippo Tommaso **PQ2625.A78719**
Mafarka the Futurist. Carol Diethe & Steve Cox (Translators). Trade Paper. Middlesex University Press. London, 1998. 240p. ISBN:1-898253-10-2, ISBN13: 978-1-898253-10-5. Dewey:853/.912.
Audience: **g,l,u,f.**

Marinetti, Filippo Tommaso **NX600.F8**
Let's Murder the Moonshine: Selected Writings. R. W. Flint & Arthur A. Coppotelli (Translators). Trade Paper. Sun & Moon Press. Los Angeles, CA. 1990. 288p. Sun and Moon Classics Ser., No. 12 ISBN:1-55713-101-5, ISBN13: 978-1-55713-101-0. Dewey:700.904.
Audience: **g,l,u,f.**

Marinetti, Filippo Tommaso **PQ4829.A78A255 1996**
Selected Poems and Related Prose. Elizabeth R. Napier & Barbara R. Studholme (Translators), Paolo Valesio (Introduction by), Luce Marinetti (Selected by). Cloth over Boards. Yale University Press. Cumberland, RI. 2002. 272p. ISBN:0-300-04103-9, ISBN13: 978-0-300-04103-3. Dewey:841/.912. LCCN:96-011140.
Audience: **g,u,f.**

Individual Authors and Works > 1901-1960 > Montale

Becker, Jared **PQ4829.O565Z5684**
Eugenio Montale. Trade Cloth. Macmillan Publishing Company, Inc. Old Tappan, NJ. 1986. 224p. Twayne's World Authors Ser., No. 778 ISBN:0-8057-6633-2, ISBN13: 978-0-8057-6633-2. Dewey:851/.912. LCCN:86-000225.
Audience: **u,f.** *Choice, 1987.*

Cambon, Glauco **PQ4829.O565Z/**
Eugenio Montale's Poetry: A Dream in Reason's Presence. Trade Cloth. Princeton University Press. Princeton, NJ. 1983. 270p. ISBN:0-691-06520-9, ISBN13: 978-0-691-06520-5. Dewey:851/.912. LCCN:82-047584.
Audience: **u,f.**

Montale, Eugenio **PQ4829.O565.A24**
Selected Poems of Eugenio Montale. Trade Cloth. Penguin Group (USA) Inc. New York, NY. 1969. 126p. ISBN:0-14-042099-1, ISBN13: 978-0-14-042099-9. Dewey:851.914. LCCN:75-454634.
Audience: **g,l,u,f.**

Montale, Eugenio **PQ4829.O565**
Modern Classics Poems. Trade Paper. Penguin Books Canada, Ltd. Toronto, ON. 2002. 224p. ISBN:0-14-118102-8, ISBN13: 978-0-14-118102-8. Dewey:851.9/12.
Audience: **g,l,u,f.**

Montale, Eugenio **PQ4829**
Tutte le poesie. Ed. 12. Tutte le poesie. 2001. ISBN:88-04-24072-5, ISBN13: 978-88-04-24072-3.
Audience: **u,f.**

Montale, Eugenio **PQ4829.O565**
Cuttlefish Bones. William Arrowsmith (Translator). Trade Paper. W. W. Norton & Company, Inc. New York, NY. 1994. 296p. ISBN:0-393-31171-6, ISBN13: 978-0-393-31171-6. Dewey:851/.912.
Audience: **g,l,u,f.** *Choice, 1994.*

Montale, Eugenio **PQ4829.O565O313 1987**
The Occasions. William Arrowsmith (Translator, Preface by, Commentaries by). Trade Paper. W. W. Norton & Company, Inc. New York, NY. 1987. 169p. ISBN:0-393-30324-1, ISBN13: 978-0-393-30324-7. Dewey:851/.912. LCCN:86-016269.
Audience: **g,l,u,f.** *Choice, 1987.*

Montale, Eugenio **PQ4829.O565B813 1986**
The Storm and Other Things. William Arrowsmith (Translator, Preface by, Commentaries by). Trade Cloth. W. W. Norton & Company, Inc. New York, NY. 1986. ISBN:0-393-01996-9, ISBN13: 978-0-393-01996-4. Dewey:851/.912. LCCN:85-011407.
Audience: **g,l,u,f.** *Choice, 1986.*

Montale, Eugenio **PQ4829.O565.A7813**
Otherwise: Last and First Poems of Eugenio Montale. Jonathan Galassi (Translator). Trade Cloth. Knopf Publishing Group. New York, NY. 1984. 192p. ISBN:0-394-52963-4, ISBN13: 978-0-394-52963-9. Dewey:851/.912. LCCN:84-042533.
Audience: **g,l,u,f.**

Montale, Eugenio **PQ4829.O565A244 2000**
Collected Poems 1920-1954: Bilingual Edition. Jonathan Galassi (Translator, Annotations by). Trade Paper. Farrar, Straus & Giroux. New York, NY. 2000. 624p. ISBN:0-374-52625-7, ISBN13: 978-0-374-52625-2. Dewey:851/.912. LCCN:00-035456.
Audience: **g,u,f.**

Montale, Eugenio **PQ4829.O565**
Posthumous Diary: Diario Postumo. Jonathan Galassi (Translator, Introduction by). Trade Paper. Turtle Point Press. New York, NY. 2001. 206p. ISBN:1-885586-22-1, ISBN13: 978-1-885586-22-3. Dewey:851.91.
Audience: **u,f.**

Montale, Eugenio & Reed, Jeremy **PQ4829.O565**
Coast Guard's House. Trade Paper. Bloodaxe Books. Bala, 1990. 224p. ISBN:1-85224-100-4, ISBN13: 978-1-85224-100-1. Dewey:851.912.
Audience: **g,l,u,f.** *Choice, 1992.*

Montale, Eugenio **PQ4829.O565**
It Depends: A Poet's Notebook. G. Singh (Translator, Introduction by). Trade Cloth. New Directions Publishing Corporation. New York, NY. 1980. 192p. ISBN:0-8112-0773-0, ISBN13: 978-0-8112-0773-7. Dewey:851/.912. LCCN:80-016629.
Audience: **g,u,f.**

Montale, Eugenio **PQ4829.O565.S3313**
Satura. Rosanna Warren (Editor), William Arrowsmith (Translator, Notes by), Claire de C. L. Huffman (Preface by). Trade Cloth. W. W. Norton & Company, Inc. New York, NY. 1998. 240p. ISBN:0-393-04647-8, ISBN13: 978-0-393-04647-2. Dewey:851/.912. LCCN:97-032720.
Audience: **g,l,u,f.**

West, Rebecca J. **PQ4829.O565Z/**
Eugenio Montale: Poet on the Edge. Trade Cloth. Harvard University Press. Cambridge, MA. 1981. 210p. ISBN:0-674-26910-1, ISBN13: 978-0-674-26910-1. Dewey:851/.912. LCCN:81-004119.
Audience: **u,f.**

Individual Authors and Works > 1901-1960 > Morante. Moravia

Morante, Elsa **PQ4829.O615.S813**
History: A Novel. Trade Cloth. Alfred A. Knopf Inc. New York, NY. 1977. ix, 561p. ISBN:0-394-49802-X, ISBN13: 978-0-394-49802-7. Dewey:853/.912. LCCN:76-045755.
Audience: **g,l,u,f.**

Morante, Elsa **PQ4829.O615I813 2002**
Arturo's Island: A Novel. Isabel Quigley (Translator). Trade Cloth. Steerforth Press. Hanover, NH. 2004. 384p. ISBN:1-58642-041-0, ISBN13: 978-1-58642-041-3. Dewey:853/.912. LCCN:2001-057752.
Audience: **g,l,u,f.**

Morante, Elsa **PQ4829.O615A8813**
Aracoeli. William Weaver (Translator). Trade Cloth. Random House, Inc. New York, NY. 1984. 320p. ISBN:0-394-53518-9, ISBN13: 978-0-394-53518-0. Dewey:853/.912. LCCN:84-042524.
Audience: **g,l,u,f.**

Moravia, Alberto **PQ4829.O62**
The Conformist. Other. Penguin Group (USA) Inc. New York, NY. 1982. 320p. ISBN:0-86721-069-9, ISBN13: 978-0-86721-069-9. Dewey:853/.912. LCCN:81-085375.
Audience: **g,l,u,f.**

Moravia, Alberto **PQ4829**
Opere : romanzi e racconti, vol. 1. Bompiani. 2000. ISBN:88-452-4414-8, ISBN13: 978-88-452-4414-8.
Audience: **u,f.**

Moravia, Alberto **PQ4829**
Opere : romanzi e racconti, vol. 2. Bompiani. 2000. ISBN:88-452-5191-8, ISBN13: 978-88-452-5191-7.
Audience: **u,f.**

Moravia, Alberto **PQ4829**
Opere : romanzi e racconti, vol. 3. Bompiani. 2000. ISBN:88-452-3299-9, ISBN13: 978-88-452-3299-2.
Audience: **u,f.**

Moravia, Alberto **PQ4829.O62I5513 2000**
The Time of Indifference: A Novel. Tami Calliope (Translator). Trade Paper. Steerforth Press. Hanover, NH. 2004. 310p. Steerforth Italia Ser. ISBN:1-58642-005-4, ISBN13: 978-1-58642-005-5. Dewey:853/.912. LCCN:00-044580.
Audience: **g,l,u,f.**

Moravia, Alberto **PQ4829.O62D513 2005**
Contempt. Ed. 2. Angus Davidson (Translator), Tim Parks (Introduction by). Trade Paper. New York Review of Books, Incorporated, The. New York, NY. 2004. 272p. ISBN:1-59017-122-5, ISBN13: 978-1-59017-122-6. Dewey:853.9/12.
Audience: **g,l,u,f.**

Moravia, Alberto **PQ4829.O62N613 2005**
Boredom. Ed. 2. Angus Davidson (Translator), William Weaver (Introduction by). Trade Paper. New York Review of Books, Incorporated, The. New York, NY. 2004. 352p. ISBN:1-59017-121-7, ISBN13: 978-1-59017-121-9. Dewey:853.9/12.
Audience: **g,l,u,f.**

Individual Authors and Works > 1901-1960 > P-R

Lajolo, Davide **PQ4835.A846**
An Absurd Vice: A Biography of Cesare Pavese. Mario Pietralunga & Mark Pietralunga (Translators). Trade Paper. New Directions Publishing Corporation. New York, NY. 1983. 288p. ISBN:0-8112-0851-6, ISBN13: 978-0-8112-0851-2. Dewey:853/.912. LCCN:82-014482.
Audience: **u,f.**

O'Healy, Anne-Marie **PQ4835.A846Z76645**
Cesare Pavese. Trade Cloth. Thomson Gale. Farmington Hills, MI. 1988. 192p. Twayne World Authors Ser., No. 785 ISBN:0-8057-8242-7, ISBN13: 978-0-8057-8242-4. Dewey:853/.912. LCCN:88-014682.
Audience: **u,f.** *Choice, 1989.*

Pascoli, Giovanni **PQ4835**
Poesie e prose scelte. A. Mondadori. 2001. ISBN:88-04-50428-5, ISBN13: 978-88-04-50428-3.
Audience: **u,f.**

Pascoli, Giovanni **PQ4835.A3 A17 1983**
Selected Poems: Pascoli. P. R. Horne (Editor). Cloth Text. Manchester University Press. Manchester, 1988. 192p. Italian Texts Ser. ISBN:0-7190-0870-0, ISBN13: 978-0-7190-0870-2. Dewey:851/.8. LCCN:82-134879.
Audience: **u,f.**

Pavese, Cesar **PQ4835**
Le poesie. Einaudi. 1998. ISBN:88-06-14781-1, ISBN13: 978-88-06-14781-5.
Audience: **u,f.**

Pavese, Cesare **PQ4835.A84**
Among Women Only. Trade Paper. Peter Owen Ltd. London, 2004. 198p. Peter Owen Modern Classics Ser. ISBN:0-7206-1214-4, ISBN13: 978-0-7206-1214-1. Dewey:853.912. LCCN:2004-478625.
Audience: **g,l,u,f.**

Pavese, Cesare **PQ4835.A846**
The Political Prisoner. Trade Paper. Peter Owen Ltd. London, 2006. 176p. ISBN:0-7206-1262-4, ISBN13: 978-0-7206-1262-2. Dewey:853.912.
Audience: **g,l,u,f.**

Pavese, Cesare **PQ4835**
Tutti i racconti, vol. 1. Einaudi. 2002. ISBN:88-06-60081-8, ISBN13: 978-88-06-60081-5.
Audience: **u,f.**

Pavese, Cesare **PQ4835**
Tutti i racconti, vol. 2. Einaudi. 2002. ISBN:88-446-0081-1, ISBN13: 978-88-446-0081-5.
Audience: **u,f.**

Pavese, Cesare **PQ4835.A846**
Comrade. Trade Cloth. Peter Owen Ltd. London, ISBN:0-7206-1751-0, ISBN13: 978-0-7206-1751-1. Dewey:853.91.
Audience: **g,l,u,f.**

Pavese, Cesare **PQ4835**
Tutti i romanzi. Einaudi. 2000. ISBN:88-446-0079-X, ISBN13: 978-88-446-0079-2.
Audience: **u,f.**

Pavese, Cesare **PQ4835.A846.D513**
Dialogues with Leuco. William Arrowsmith (Translator), Juan Garcia Ponce (Introduction by). Trade Cloth. Marsilio Publishers. New York, NY. 1989. 201p. ISBN:0-941419-38-X, ISBN13: 978-0-941419-38-3. Dewey:858.912. LCCN:89-083807.
Audience: **g,l,u,f.**

Pavese, Cesare **PQ4835.A846A23 2002**
Disaffections: Complete Poems 1930-1950. Geoffrey Brock (Translator). Trade Paper. Copper Canyon Press. Port Townsend, WA. 2002. 300p. ISBN:1-55659-174-8, ISBN13: 978-1-55659-174-7. Dewey:851/.912. LCCN:2001-007425.
Audience: **g,l,u,f.**

Pavese, Cesare **PQ4835.A846A238 2001**
Selected Works. R. W. Flint (Introduction by). Trade Paper. New York Review of Books, Incorporated, The. New York, NY. 2001. 424p. New York Review Books Classics Ser. ISBN:0-940322-85-4, ISBN13: 978-0-940322-85-1. Dewey:853/.912. LCCN:2001-005156.
Audience: **g,l,u,f.**

Pavese, Cesare **PQ4835.A846L813 2003**
The Moon and the Bonfires. R. W. Flint (Translator), Mark Rudman (Introduction by). Trade Paper. New York Review of Books, Incorporated, The. New York, NY. 2002. 176p. New York Review Books Classics Ser. ISBN:1-59017-021-0, ISBN13: 978-1-59017-021-2. Dewey:853/.912. LCCN:2002-009792.
Audience: **g,l,u,f.**

Pavese, Cesare **PQ4835.A846**
Festival Night. A.E. Murch (Translator). Trade Cloth. Peter Owen Ltd. London, 212p. ISBN:0-7206-3280-3, ISBN13: 978-0-7206-3280-4. Dewey:853.91.
Audience: **g,l,u,f.**

Thompson, Doug & Thompson, A. D. **PQ4835.A846Z/**
Cesare Pavese: A Study of the Major Novels and Poems. Cloth Text. Cambridge University Press. New York, NY. 1982. 302p. ISBN:0-521-23602-9, ISBN13: 978-0-521-23602-7. Dewey:858/.91209. LCCN:81-015467.
Audience: **u,f.**

Individual Authors and Works > 1901-1960 > Pasolini

Baranski, Zymunt G. (Editor) **PQ4835.A48Z8345 1999**
Pasolini Old and New: Surveys and Studies. Joseph Francese, Robert Gordon, Sam Rohdie, Patrick Rumble, David Ward, Angela Meekins, Michael Caesar, Tullio De Mauro, Christopher Wagstaff & John Welle (Contribution by). Trade Cloth, Box or Slipcased. Four Courts Press. Dublin 8, 1999. 420p. Publications of the Foundation for Italian Studies, University College Dublin ISBN:1-85182-436-7, ISBN13: 978-1-85182-436-6. Dewey:858/.91409. LCCN:99-495135.
Audience: **u,f.**

Friedrich, Pia **PQ4835.A48**
Pier Paolo Pasolini. Trade Cloth. Thomson Gale. Farmington Hills, MI. 1982. World Authors Ser. ISBN:0-8057-6500-X, ISBN13: 978-0-8057-6500-7. Dewey:858/.91409.
Audience: **g,l,u,f.**

Gordon, Robert S. **PQ4835.A48Z6885 1996**
Pasolini: Forms of Subjectivity. Trade Cloth. Oxford University Press, Inc. New York, NY. 1996. 336p. ISBN:0-19-815905-6, ISBN13: 978-0-19-815905-6. Dewey:858.9/12/09. LCCN:96-026835.
Audience: **u,f.** *Choice, 1997.*

Pasolini, Pier Paolo **PQ4835**
Per il cinema. A. Mondadori. 2001. ISBN:88-04-48941-3, ISBN13: 978-88-04-48941-2.
Audience: **u,f.**

Pasolini, Pier Paolo **PQ4879.E74**
Poems. Trade Paper. Farrar, Straus & Giroux. New York, NY. 1996. 256p. ISBN:0-374-52469-6, ISBN13: 978-0-374-52469-2. Dewey:851/.914. LCCN:81-048293.
Audience: **g,l,u,f.**

Pasolini, Pier Paolo **PQ4835**
Romanzi e racconti, vol. 1. Ed. 3. A. Mondadori. 1999.
Audience: **u,f.**

Pasolini, Pier Paolo **PQ4835**
Romanzi e racconti, vol. 2. Ed. 3. A. Mondadori. 1999. ISBN:88-04-45292-7, ISBN13: 978-88-04-45292-8.
Audience: **u,f.**

Pasolini, Pier Paolo **PQ4835**
Saggi sulla letteratura e sull'arte. A. Mondadori. 1999. ISBN:88-04-45686-8, ISBN13: 978-88-04-45686-5.
Audience: **u,f.**

Pasolini, Pier Paolo **PQ4835**
Saggi sulla politica e sulla società. A. Mondadori. 1999. ISBN:88-04-45687-6, ISBN13: 978-88-04-45687-2.
Audience: **u,f.**

Pasolini, Pier Paolo **PQ4835**
Teatro. A. Mondadori. 2001. ISBN:88-04-48942-1, ISBN13: 978-88-04-48942-9.
Audience: **u,f.**

Pasolini, Pier Paolo **PQ4879.E74**
The Ashes of Gramsci. Trade Paper. Spectacular Diseases. Peterborough, 1982. 12p. ISBN:0-9506316-7-1, ISBN13: 978-0-9506316-7-7. Dewey:851/.914.
Audience: **g,l,u,f.**

Pasolini, Pier Paolo **PQ4835**
Tutte le poesie. Mondadori. 2003. ISBN:88-04-51041-2, ISBN13: 978-88-04-51041-3.
Audience: **u,f.**

Pasolini, Pier Paolo **PQ4835.A48A23 1986**
Roman Poems. Lawrence Ferlinghetti & Francesca Valente (Translators), Alberto Moravia (Preface by). Trade Cloth. City Lights Books. San Francisco, CA. 1986. 96p. Pocket Poets Ser., No. 41 ISBN:0-87286-187-2, ISBN13: 978-0-87286-187-9. Dewey:851/.914. LCCN:86-002643.
Audience: **g,l,u,f.**

Pasolini, Pier Paolo **PQ4835.A48S7613 2003**
Stories from the City of God: Roman Stories and Chronicles, 1950-1966. Marina Harss (Translator). Trade Cloth. Other Press, LLC. New York, NY. 2006. 272p. ISBN:1-59051-048-8, ISBN13: 978-1-59051-048-3. Dewey:853/.914. LCCN:2003-040462.
Audience: **g,l,u,f.**

Pasolini, Pier Paolo **DG451.P3613 1983**
Lutheran Letters. Stuart Hood (Translator). Trade Cloth. Carcanet Press. New York, NY. 1983. 129p. ISBN:0-85635-410-4, ISBN13: 978-0-85635-410-6. Dewey:945.092. LCCN:83-124290.
Audience: **g,l,u,f.**

Pasolini, Pier Paolo **PQ4835.A48P313 1999**
The Savage Father. Pasquale Verdicchio (Translator). Trade Paper. Guernica Editions, Inc. Tonawanda, NY. 1999. 128p. Drama Ser., Vol. 18 ISBN:1-55071-081-8, ISBN13: 978-1-55071-081-6. Dewey:852/.914. LCCN:99-064481.
Audience: **g,l,u,f.**

Rumble, Patrick & Testa, Bart (Editors) **PQ4835.A48Z8626 1994**
Pier Paolo Pasolini: Contemporary Perspectives. Trade Cloth. University of Toronto Press. Toronto, ON. 1993. 530p. Toronto Italian Studies ISBN:0-8020-2966-3, ISBN13: 978-0-8020-2966-9. Dewey:858/.91409. LCCN:95-120658.
Audience: **l,u,f.**

Schwartz, Barth D. **PN1998.3.P367S39**
Pasolini Requiem. Trade Cloth. Knopf Publishing Group. New York, NY. 1992. 800p. ISBN:0-394-57744-2, ISBN13: 978-0-394-57744-9. Dewey:858/.91409 B. LCCN:90-053403.
Audience: **u,f.** *Choice, 1993.*

Siciliano, Enzo **PQ4835.A48.Z8813**
Pasolini. Trade Cloth. Random House, Inc. New York, NY. 1982. 433p. ISBN:0-394-52299-0, ISBN13: 978-0-394-52299-9. Dewey:791.43/0233/0924. LCCN:81-048294.
Audience: **g,l,u,f.**

Ward, David **PQ4835.A48Z96 1995**
A Poetics of Resistance: Narrative and the Writings of Pier Paolo Pasolini. Trade Cloth. Fairleigh Dickinson University Press. Cranbury, NJ. 1995. 216p. ISBN:0-8386-3585-7, ISBN13: 978-0-8386-3585-8. Dewey:858/.91409. LCCN:95-006297.
Audience: **u,f.**

Individual Authors and Works > 1901-1960 > Pirandello

Bassanese, Fiora A. **PQ4835.I7Z53478 1997**
Understanding Luigi Pirandello. James N. Hardin (Editor). Trade Cloth. University of South Carolina Press. Columbia, SC. 1997. 200p. Understanding Modern European and Latin American Literature Ser. ISBN:1-57003-081-2, ISBN13: 978-1-57003-081-9. Dewey:858.9/12/09. LCCN:96-025198.
Audience: **u,f.** *Choice, 1997.*

Biasin, Gian-Paolo & Gieri, Manuela (Editors) **PQ4835.I7Z66525 1999**
Luigi Pirandello: Contemporary Perspectives. Cloth over Boards. University of Toronto Press. Toronto, ON. 1998. 256p. Italian Studies, : ISBN:0-8020-4387-9, ISBN13: 978-0-8020-4387-0. Dewey:852/.912. LCCN:99-475905.
Audience: **u,f.** *Choice, 1999.*

Lorch, Jennifer **PQ4835.I7S4348 2004**
Pirandello: Six Characters in Search of an Author. Michael Robinson (Contribution by). Trade Paper. Cambridge University Press. New York, NY. 2004. 272p. Plays in Production Ser. ISBN:0-521-64618-9, ISBN13: 978-0-521-64618-5. Dewey:852/.912. LCCN:2004-045817.
Audience: **g,l,u,f.**

Paolucci, Anne **PQ4835.I7Z722 2005**
Selected Essays on the Plays and Fiction of Luigi Pirandello. Trade Cloth. Harvard University Press. Cambridge, MA. 2005. ISBN:1-932107-13-4, ISBN13: 978-1-932107-13-5. Dewey:852/.912. LCCN:2005-046255.
Audience: **u,f.**

Pirandello, Luigi **PQ4835**
Collected plays, vol. 3: The rules of the game, Each in his own way, Grafted, The other son. Calder. 1992. ISBN:0-7145-4181-8, ISBN13: 978-0-7145-4181-5.
Audience: **g,l,u,f.**

Pirandello, Luigi **PQ4835**
Maschere nude, vol. 1. Ed. 3. A. Mondadori. 1994. ISBN:88-04-24481-X, ISBN13: 978-88-04-24481-3.
Audience: **u,f.**

Pirandello, Luigi **PQ4835**
Maschere nude, vol. 2. A. Mondadori. 1993. ISBN:88-04-33278-6, ISBN13: 978-88-04-33278-7.
Audience: **u,f.**

Pirandello, Luigi **PQ4835**
Maschere nude, vol. 3. A. Mondadori. 2004. ISBN:88-04-52375-1, ISBN13: 978-88-04-52375-8.
Audience: **u,f.**

Pirandello, Luigi **PQ4835**
Novelle per un anno, vol. 1, bk. 1. Ed. 5. A. Mondadori. 1996.
Audience: **u,f.**

Pirandello, Luigi **PQ4835**
Novelle per un anno, vol. 1, bk. 2. Ed. 5. A. Mondadori. 1996.
Audience: **u,f.**

Pirandello, Luigi **PQ4835**
Novelle per un anno, vol. 2, bk. 1. Ed. 5. A. Mondadori. 1996. ISBN:88-04-21192-X, ISBN13: 978-88-04-21192-1.
Audience: **u,f.**

Pirandello, Luigi **PQ4835**
Novelle per un anno, vol. 2, bk. 2. Ed. 5. A. Mondadori. 1996.
Audience: **u,f.**

Pirandello, Luigi **PQ4835**
Novelle per un anno, vol. 3, bk. 1. Ed. 5. A. Mondadori. 1997. ISBN:88-04-33872-5, ISBN13: 978-88-04-33872-7.
Audience: **u,f.**

Pirandello, Luigi **PQ4835**
Novelle per un anno, vol. 3, bk. 2. Ed. 5. A. Mondadori. 1997.
Audience: **u,f.**

Pirandello, Luigi **PQ4835**
Tutti i romanzi, vol. 1. Ed. 11. A. Mondadori. 2003.
Audience: **u,f.**

Pirandello, Luigi **PQ4835**
Tutti i romanzi, vol. 2. Ed. 11. A. Mondadori. 2003.
Audience: **u,f.**

Pirandello, Luigi **PQ4835.I7S7713 2000**
Her Husband. Martha King & Mary Ann Frese Witt (Translators). Trade Cloth. Duke University Press. Durham, NC. 2000. 264p. ISBN:0-8223-2600-0, ISBN13: 978-0-8223-2600-7. Dewey:853/.912. LCCN:00-030868.
Audience: **g,l,u,f.** *Choice, 2001.*

Pirandello, Luigi & Reed, Henry **PQ4835.I7A2 1988**
Plays: Contains: Henry IV; Right You Are If You Think You Are; Lazarus; the Man with the Flower in His Mouth. Tradc Paper. Riverrun Press, Inc. Flemington, NJ. 1986. 236p. ISBN:0-7145-4110-9, ISBN13: 978-0-7145-4110-5. Dewey:852/.912. LCCN:86-027977.
Audience: **g,l,u,f.**

Pirandello, Luigi **PR4835.P664**
Plays: Contains: No One Knows Why; Cap and Bells; the Jar; I Haven't Yet Chosen. Robert Rietti (Editor). Trade Paper. Riverrun Press, Inc. Flemington, NJ. 2004. ISBN:0-7145-4289-X, ISBN13: 978-0-7145-4289-8. Dewey:852.912.
Audience: **g,l,u,f.**

Pirandello, Luigi **PQ4835.I7**
Plays: Contains: As You Desire Me; Think It over Giaccomino!; This Time It Will Be Different; the Imbecile. Robert Rietti (Editor). Trade Paper. Riverrun Press, Inc. Flemington, NJ. 1999. 216p. ISBN:0-7145-4271-7, ISBN13: 978-0-7145-4271-3. Dewey:852.912.
Audience: **g,l,u,f.**

Pirandello, Luigi **PQ4835.I7**
Collected Plays: Six Characters in Search of an Author, All for the Best, Clothe the Naked and Limes from Sicily, Vol. 2. Robert Rietty (Editor), Bullock & Reed (Translators). Trade Paper. Riverrun Press, Inc. Flemington, NJ. 1989. 224p. ISBN:0-7145-3984-8, ISBN13: 978-0-7145-3984-3. Dewey:852/.912. LCCN:86-027977.
Audience: **g,l,u,f.**

Individual Authors and Works > 1901-1960 > S-Z

Leake, Elizabeth **PQ4841.I4Z655 2003**
The Reinvention of Ignazio Silone. Trade Cloth. University of Toronto Press. Toronto, ON. 2003. 224p. Toronto Italian Studies ISBN:0-8020-8767-1, ISBN13: 978-0-8020-8767-6. Dewey:853/.912. LCCN:2004-270203.
Audience: **g,u,f.**

Paynter, Maria Nicolai **PQ4841.I4Z765 2000**
Ignazio Silone: Beyond the Tragic Vision. Trade Cloth. University of Toronto Press. Toronto, ON. 2000. 594p. Italian Studies, : ISBN:0-8020-0705-8, ISBN13: 978-0-8020-0705-6. Dewey:853.912. LCCN:00-269219.
Audience: **u,f.** *Choice, 2000.*

Saba, Umberto **PQ4841**
Tutte le prose. A. Mondadori. 2001. ISBN:88-04-48936-7, ISBN13: 978-88-04-48936-8.
Audience: **u,f.**

Silone, Ignazio **PQ4841**
Romanzi e saggi, vol. 1. A. Mondadori. 1998. ISBN:88-04-43585-2, ISBN13: 978-88-04-43585-3.
Audience: **u,f.**

Silone, Ignazio **PQ4841**
Romanzi e saggi, vol. 2. A. Mondadori. 1999. ISBN:88-04-45778-3, ISBN13: 978-88-04-45778-7.
Audience: **u,f.**

Silone, Ignazio **PQ4841.I4A6 2000**
The Abruzzo Trilogy: Fontamara, Bread and Wine, The Seed Beneath the Snow. Eric Mosbacher (Translator), Alexander Stille (Introduction by). Trade Paper. Steerforth Press. Hanover, NH. 2000. 960p. Steerforth Italia Ser. ISBN:1-58642-006-2, ISBN13: 978-1-58642-006-2. Dewey:853/.912. LCCN:00-061882.
Audience: **g,l,u,f.**

Tomasi di Lampedusa, Giuseppe **PQ4843**
Opere. Ed. 5. A. Mondadori. 2004. ISBN:88-04-53177-0, ISBN13: 978-88-04-53177-7.
Audience: **u,f.**

Tomasi Di Lampedusa, Giuseppe **PZ3.M7962**
The Leopard. David Gilmour (Introduction by). Trade Cloth. Knopf Publishing Group. New York, NY. 1991. 240p. Everyman's Library ISBN:0-679-40757-X, ISBN13: 978-0-679-40757-7. Dewey:853/.91. LCCN:91-052980.
Audience: **g,l,u,f.**

Ungaretti, Giuseppe **PQ4845**
Vita d'un uomo : tutte le poesie. Ed. 17. A. Mondadori. 2000. ISBN:88-04-08597-5, ISBN13: 978-88-04-08597-3.
Audience: **u,f.**

Ungaretti, Giuseppe **PQ4845.N4A23 2002**
Selected Poems: A Bilingual Edition. Andrew Frisardi (Translator). Cloth over Boards. Farrar, Straus & Giroux. New York, NY. 2002. 320p. ISBN:0-374-26075-3, ISBN13: 978-0-374-26075-0. Dewey:851/.912. LCCN:2002-020134.
Audience: **g,u,f.**

Vittorini, Elio **PZ3.V83**
A Vittorini Omnibus: The Twilight of the Elephant, in Sicily, La Garibaldina. Cinina Brescia, Wilfrid David & Frances Keene (Translators). Trade Paper. New Directions Publishing Corporation. New York, NY. 1973. 320p. Book Ser. ISBN:0-8112-0499-5, ISBN13: 978-0-8112-0499-6. Dewey:853/.9/12. LCCN:73-078790.
Audience: **g,l,u,f.**

Individual Authors and Works > 1901-1960 > Schmitz (Italo Svevo)

Svevo, Italo **PQ4841**
Tutte le opere, vol. 1. A. Mondadori. 2004. ISBN:88-04-52367-0, ISBN13: 978-88-04-52367-3.
Audience: **u,f.**

Svevo, Italo **PW4841**
Tutte le opere, vol. 2. A. Mondadori. 2004. ISBN:88-04-52369-7, ISBN13: 978-88-04-52369-7.
Audience: **u,f.**

Svevo, Italo **PQ4841**
Tutte le opere, vol. 3. A. Mondadori. 2004. ISBN:88-04-52368-9, ISBN13: 978-88-04-52368-0.
Audience: **u,f.**

Svevo, Italo **PQ4841.C482S8413**
Emilio's Carnival: Or Senilita. Beth Archer Brombert (Translator, Introduction by), Victor Brombert (Introduction by). Trade Paper. Yale University Press. Cumberland, RI. 2001. 264p. Henry McBride Series in Modernism and Modernity ISBN:0-300-09049-8, ISBN13: 978-0-300-09049-9. Dewey:853/.8. LCCN:2001-000914.
Audience: **g,l,u,f.**

Svevo, Italo **PQ4841.C482S8413**
As a Man Grows Older. Beryl de Zoete (Translator), James Lasdun (Introduction by). Trade Paper. New York Review of Books, Incorporated, The. New York, NY. 2001. 256p. New York Review Books Classics Ser. ISBN:0-940322-84-6, ISBN13: 978-0-940322-84-4. Dewey:853/.8. LCCN:2001-004884.
Audience: **g,l,u,f.**

Svevo, Italo **PQ4841.C482C613 2001**
Zeno's Conscience. William Weaver (Translator), Elizabeth Hardwick (Produced by). Trade Cloth. Alfred A. Knopf Inc. New York, NY. 2001. 496p. ISBN:0-375-41330-8, ISBN13: 978-0-375-41330-8. Dewey:853/.8. LCCN:2001-040821.
Audience: **g,l,u,f.**

Weiss, Beno **PQ4841.C482.Z95 1987**
Italo Svevo. Trade Cloth. Macmillan Publishing Company, Inc. Old Tappan, NJ. 1987. 160p. World Authors Ser., No. 795 ISBN:0-8057-6649-9, ISBN13: 978-0-8057-6649-3. Dewey:853/.8. LCCN:87-017714.
Audience: **u,f.** *Choice, 1988.*

Individual Authors and Works > 1961-

Behan, Tom **PQ4866.O2Z597 2000**
Dario Fo: Revolutionary Theatre. Trade Cloth. Pluto Press. London, 1999. 192p. ISBN:0-7453-1362-0, ISBN13: 978-0-7453-1362-7. Dewey:852/.914. LCCN:99-042772.
Audience: **u,f.** *Choice, 2000.*

Eco, Umberto **PQ4809.A45**
The Name of the Rose. William Weaver (Translator). Trade Cloth. Harcourt Trade Publishers. New York, NY. 1995. ISBN:0-15-100213-4, ISBN13: 978-0-15-100213-9. Dewey:853/.914.
Audience: **g,l,u,f.**

Eco, Umberto **PQ4865.C6T7 1986**
Travels in Hyper Reality: Essays. Kurt H. Wolff & Helen Wolff (Editors), William Weaver (Translator). Trade Cloth. Harcourt Trade Publishers. New York, NY. 1986. 236p. ISBN:0-15-191079-0, ISBN13: 978-0-15-191079-3. Dewey:854/.914. LCCN:85-024810.
Audience: **g,l,u,f.**

Farrell, Joseph & Scuderi, Antonio **PQ4866.O2Z63 2000**
Dario Fo: Stage, Text and Tradition. Trade Cloth. Southern Illinois University Press. Carbondale, IL. 2000. 208p. ISBN:0-8093-2335-4, ISBN13: 978-0-8093-2335-7. Dewey:852/.914. LCCN:00-038785.
Audience: **u,f.** *Choice, 2001.*

Fo, Dario **PQ4866.O2**
Plays 1. Trade Paper. Methuen Publishing Ltd. London, 2004. ISBN:0-413-15420-3, ISBN13: 978-0-413-15420-0. Dewey:852.9/14.
Audience: **l,u,f.**

Fo, Dario **PQ4866.O2 A6 1997**
Plays 2. Trade Paper. Methuen Publishing Ltd. London, 2004. 0p. ISBN:0-413-68020-7, ISBN13: 978-0-413-68020-4. Dewey:852/.914. LCCN:98-133581.
Audience: **l,u,f.**

Fo, Dario **PQ4866**
Teatro. G. Einaudi. 2000. ISBN:88-06-15615-2, ISBN13: 978-88-06-15615-2.
Audience: **u,f.**

Fo, Dario **PN2061**
The Tricks of the Trade. Cloth Text. Routledge. New York, NY. 1991. 224p. ISBN:0-87830-007-4, ISBN13: 978-0-87830-007-5. Dewey:792.028.
Audience: **l,u,f.** *Choice, 1992.*

OTHER LITERATURES IN ENGLISH

This section in comprised of titles appropriate for the study of literature in English outside the usual rubric of British Literature and/or American Literature. For each of the several national literatures represented in this section, titles have been selected in a balance of primary and secondary works that represent the various major genres of poetry, drama, short fiction, and the novel; the traditionally defined literary periods, with particular attention to colonial and post-colonial distinctions; and what might be considered "hot" or current themes that were not covered in BCL3, such as queer studies.

— James Bracken

General and Reference Sources

Ashcroft, Bill, et al. **PR9080.A85 2002**
The Empire Writes Back: Theory and Practice in Post-Colonial Literatures. Ed. 2. Gareth Griffiths & Helen Tiffin (Authors). Paper over Boards. Routledge. New York, NY. 2002. 296p. New Accents Ser. ISBN:0-415-28019-2, ISBN13: 978-0-415-28019-8. Dewey:820.9/9171241. LCCN:2002-068034.
Audience: **u,f.** *Choice, 1990.*

Barker, Francis (Editor), et al. **PN51**
Colonial Discourse: PostColonial Theory. Peter Hulme & Margeret Iversen (Editors). Trade Paper. Manchester University Press. Manchester, 1996. 300p. Essex Symposia Ser. ISBN:0-7190-4876-1, ISBN13: 978-0-7190-4876-0. Dewey:809.9/3358.
Audience: **u,f.**

Benson, Eugene & Conolly, L. W. (Editors) **PR478**
Encyclopedia of Post-Colonial Literatures in English. Ed. 2. Paper over Boards. Routledge. New York, NY. 2005. 2096p. ISBN:0-415-27885-6, ISBN13: 978-0-415-27885-0. Dewey:820.9917142109045.
Audience: **g,l,u,f.** *Choice, 2005, 1995.*

Bery, Ashok & Murray, Patricia (Editors) **PN56.C63C66 2000**
Comparing Postcolonial Literatures: Dislocations. Cloth over Boards. Palgrave Macmillan. New York, NY. 2000. 298p. ISBN:0-312-22781-7, ISBN13: 978-0-312-22781-4. Dewey:809.9/33/58. LCCN:99-043179.
Audience: **u,f.**

Boehmer, Elleke **PR149**
Colonial and Postcolonial Literature. Ed. 2. Paper Text. Oxford University Press, Inc. New York, NY. 2005. 368p. ISBN:0-19-925371-4, ISBN13: 978-0-19-925371-5. Dewey:820.9/9171241. LCCN:2005-019306.
Audience: **u,f.**

Boehmer, Elleke **PN56.5.W64**
Stories of Women: Gender and Narrative in the Postcolonial Nation. Cloth over Boards. Manchester University Press. Manchester, 2005. 256p. ISBN:0-7190-6878-9, ISBN13: 978-0-7190-6878-2. Dewey:809.93358. LCCN:2005-296314.
Audience: **l,u.**

Cheyfitz, Eric **PS169.I45C4 1997**
The Poetics of Imperialism: Translation and Colonization from the Tempest to Tarzan. Book, Other. University of Pennsylvania Press. Philadelphia, PA. 1997. 272p. ISBN:0-8122-1609-1, ISBN13: 978-0-8122-1609-7. Dewey:325/.32/091821. LCCN:96-045596.
Audience: **g,l,u,f.** *Choice, 1991.*

Childs, Peter (Editor, Introduction by) **PR25.P66 1999**
Post-Colonial Theory and English Literature: A Reader. Trade Cloth. Edinburgh University Press. Edinburgh, 2000. 456p. ISBN:0-7486-1069-3, ISBN13: 978-0-7486-1069-3. Dewey:820.9. LCCN:00-344427.
Audience: **u,f.**

Gandhi, Leela **JV51.G36 1998**
Postcolonial Theory: A Critical Introduction. Trade Paper. Columbia University Press. New York, NY. 1998. 192p. ISBN:0-231-11273-4, ISBN13: 978-0-231-11273-4. Dewey:301. LCCN:97-032402.
Audience: **u,f.**

Gilbert, Helen (Editor) **PR9087.P67 2001**
Post-Colonial Plays: An Anthology. Paper over Boards. Routledge. New York, NY. 2001. 496p. ISBN:0-415-16448-6, ISBN13: 978-0-415-16448-1. Dewey:822/.92080358. LCCN:2001-031226.
Audience: **g,l,u,f.**

Goonetilleke, D. C. R. A. (Editor) **PR9080.5 .P47 2001**
Perspectives on Post-Colonial Literature. Trade Paper. Skoob Books Publishing, Ltd. London, 212p. ISBN:1-871438-28-4, ISBN13: 978-1-871438-28-4. Dewey:809.04.
Audience: **u,f.**

Griffiths, Gareth, et al. **PR9080.P57 2005**
The Post-Colonial Studies Reader. Ed. 2. Helen Tiffin & Bill Ashcroft (Authors). Paper over Boards. Routledge. New York, NY. 2005. 544p. ISBN:0-415-34564-2, ISBN13: 978-0-415-34564-4. Dewey:820.9/358. LCCN:2005-012943.
Audience: **u,f.**

Hawley, John C. (Editor) **PN849**
Encyclopedia of Postcolonial Studies. Cloth Text. Greenwood Publishing Group, Inc. Portsmouth, NH. 2001. 520p. ISBN:0-313-31192-7, ISBN13: 978-0-313-31192-5. Dewey:809/.891724. LCCN:2001-023317.
Audience: **u,f.** *Choice, 2002.*

King, Bruce **PR85**
The Oxford English Literary History, 1948-2000: The Internationalization of English Literature. Trade Cloth. Oxford University Press, Inc. New York, NY. 2004. 400p. Oxford English Literary History Ser., Vol. 13 ISBN:0-19-818428-X, ISBN13: 978-0-19-818428-7. Dewey:820.9/920693. LCCN:2004-273375.
Audience: **g,l,u,f.**

Lawson, Alan, et al. **Z2000.9.P67 1997**
Post-Colonial Literatures in English: General Theoretical Comparative, 1970-1993. Tiffin & Shane Rowland (Authors). Trade Cloth. Thomson Gale. Farmington Hills, MI. 1997. 374p. Reference Publication in Literature Ser. ISBN:0-8161-7358-3, ISBN13: 978-0-8161-7358-7. Dewey:016.8209/9171241. LCCN:97-003559.
Audience: **u,f.**

Liu, Alan **PR20.5**
The Voice of the Shuttle.
http://vos.ucsb.edu
Audience: **g,l,u,f.**

Mohanram, Radhika & Rajan, Gita (Editors) **PR9080**
English Postcoloniality: Literatures from Around the World. Book, Other. Greenwood Publishing Group, Inc. Portsmouth, NH. 1996. 232p. Contribution to the Study of World Literature Ser., No. 66 ISBN:0-313-28854-2, ISBN13: 978-0-313-28854-8. Dewey:820.9/9171241. LCCN:95-033071.
Audience: **u,f.** *Choice, 1996.*

Mongia, Padmini **PN771.C595 1996**
Contemporary Postcolonial Theory: A Reader. Padmini Mongia (Editor). Hodder Arnold. 1996. A Hodder Arnold Publication ISBN:0-340-65288-8, ISBN13: 978-0-340-65288-6.
Audience: **g,l,u,f.**

Moore-Gilbert, Bart **B3209.B754N68 1997**
Postcolonial Theory: Contexts, Practices, Politics. Trade Paper. Analytical Psychology Club of San Francisco, Inc. San Francisco, CA. 1997. 243p. ISBN:1-85984-034-5, ISBN13: 978-1-85984-034-4. Dewey:193. LCCN:97-016324.
Audience: **u,f.** *Choice, 1997.*

Parini, Jay (Editor) **PR9080.5.W67 2003**
World Writers in English. Trade Cloth. Thomson Gale. Farmington Hills, MI. 2003. 1100p. The Scribner Writers Ser. ISBN:0-684-31290-5, ISBN13: 978-0-684-31290-3. Dewey:820.9/9171241. LCCN:2003-014873.
Audience: **l,u,f.** *Choice, 2004.*

Rajan, Gita & Mohanram, Radhika (Editors) **PN56**
Postcolonial Discourse and Changing Cultural Contexts: Theory and Criticism. Trade Cloth. Greenwood Publishing Group, Inc. Portsmouth, NH. 1995. 240p. Contributions to the Study of World Literature Ser., Vol. 64 ISBN:0-313-29693-6, ISBN13: 978-0-313-29693-2. Dewey:809/.93358. LCCN:95-016019.
Audience: **u,f.** *Choice, 1996.*

Ross, Robert (Editor) **PR9088 .C65**
Colonial and Postcolonial Fiction: An Anthology. Patrick White, David Malouf, Margaret Atwood, Anita Desai, Janet Frame & Nadine Gordimer (Contribution by). Trade Paper. Garland Publishing, Inc. New York, NY. 1999. 472p. Reference Library of the Humanities ISBN:0-8153-3320-X, ISBN13: 978-0-8153-3320-3. Dewey:823.008/091712.
Audience: **g,l,u,f.**

Sharpe, Jenny **PR830.W6.S5 1993**
Allegories of Empire: The Figure of Woman in the Colonial Text. Book, Other. University of Minnesota Press. Minneapolis, MN. 1993. 199p. ISBN:0-8166-2059-8, ISBN13: 978-0-8166-2059-3. Dewey:823.009/352042. LCCN:92-045112.
Audience: **l,u,f.** *Choice, 1993.*

Vann, J. Don & VanArsdel, Rosemary T. (Editors) **PN5124.P4P47 1996**
Periodicals of Queen Victoria's Empire: An Exploration. Printed Dust Jacket. University of Toronto Press. Toronto, ON. 1996. 372p. ISBN:0-8020-0810-0, ISBN13: 978-0-8020-0810-7. Dewey:052/.09171241. LCCN:97-103839.
Audience: **u,f.**

Warwick, Ronald **Z2013.5.C/**
Commonwealth Literature Periodicals: A Bibliography, Including Periodicals of Former Commonwealth Countries, with Locations in the United Kingdom. Ronald Warwick (Compiled by). Continuum International Publishing Group, Ltd. 1979. ISBN:0-7201-0800-4, ISBN13: 978-0-7201-0800-2.
Audience: **u,f.**

Wisker, Gina **PN7605**
Key Concepts in Postcolonial Literature. Trade Paper. Palgrave Macmillan. New York, NY. 2007. 240p. Palgrave Key Concepts Ser. ISBN:1-4039-4448-2, ISBN13: 978-1-4039-4448-1. Dewey:809.
Audience: **g,l,f.**

Canada > Literary History and Criticism

PR9184.6
☐ The Canadian Association for Commonwealth Literature and Language Studies.
http://www.carleton.ca/caclals/
Ottowa, Ontario: Carleton University.
Audience: **u,f.**

PR9080
☐ Canadian Literature & Culture in the Postcolonial and Postimperial Literature in English.
http://www.postcolonialweb.org/
National University of Singapore.
Audience: **g,l,u,f.**

Armstrong, Jeannette (Editor) **PR9185.6.I5L66 1993**
Looking at the Words of Our People: An Anthology of First Nation Literary Criticism. Trade Paper. Theytus Books, Ltd. Penticton, BC. 1993. 215p. ISBN:0-919441-52-1, ISBN13: 978-0-919441-52-1. Dewey:810.9/897. LCCN:95-138549.
Audience: **g,l,u,f.**

Atwood, Margaret **PR9199.3.A8 N44 2002**
Negotiating with the Dead: A Writer on Writing. Cloth Text. Cambridge University Press. New York, NY. 2002. 248p. The Empson Lectures ISBN:0-521-66260-5, ISBN13: 978-0-521-66260-4. Dewey:808.3. LCCN:2001-025135.
Audience: **g,l,u,f.** *Choice, 2002.*

Atwood, Margaret **PR9184.3.A8**
Survival: A Thematic Guide to Canadian Literature. Trade Paper. McClelland & Stewart. Toronto, ON. 2004. 320p. ISBN:0-7710-0872-4, ISBN13: 978-0-7710-0872-6. Dewey:810.9.
Audience: **g,l,u,f.**

Atwood, Margaret Eleanor **PR918.2**
Strange Things: The Malevolent North in Canadian Literature. Oxford University Press. 1995. ISBN:0-19-811976-3, ISBN13: 978-0-19-811976-0.
Audience: **u,f.**

Baker, Ray Palmer **PR9111**
A History of the English-Canadian Literature to the Confederation: Its Relation to the Literature of Great Britain and the United States. Trade Paper. Books on Demand. Ann Arbor, MI. 210p. ISBN:0-598-63717-6, ISBN13: 978-0-598-63717-8. Dewey:810.9. LCCN:21-000385.
Audience: **u,f.**

Ballstadt, Carl (Editor) **PR9184.6.S4**
The Search for English-Canadian Literature: An Anthology of Critical Articles from the Nineteenth and Early Twentieth Centuries. Trade Paper. Books on Demand. Ann Arbor, MI. 263p. Literature of Canada, Poetry and Prose in Reprint Ser., No. 16 ISBN:0-608-12792-2, ISBN13: 978-0-608-12792-7. Dewey:810/.9/971. LCCN:75-015779.
Audience: **g,l,u,f.**

Benson, Eugene ; Conolly, L. W. **PN230**
The Oxford Companion to Canadian Theatre. Oxford University Press. 1989. ISBN:0-19-540672-9, ISBN13: 978-0-19-540672-6.
Audience: **g,l,u,f.**

Benson, Eugene & Toye, William (Editors) **PR9180.2.O94 1997**
The Oxford Companion to Canadian Literature. Ed. 2. Trade Cloth. Oxford University Press, Inc. New York, NY. 1998. 1,216p. ISBN:0-19-541167-6, ISBN13: 978-0-19-541167-6. Dewey:810.9/971/03 B. LCCN:98-162071.
Audience: **g,l,u,f.** *Choice, 1998.*

Birney, Earle **PR9199.3.B44.Z477**
Spreading Time: Remarks on Canadian Writing and Writers, 1904-1949. Trade Cloth. Vehicule Press. Montreal, PQ. 1980. v. :p. ISBN:0-919890-24-5, ISBN13: 978-0-919890-24-4. Dewey:810/.9/005. LCCN:81-120888.
Audience: **g,l,u,f.** B

Clarke, George Elliott (Editor) **PR9188.2.B57C57 2002**
Odysseys Home: Mapping African-Canadian Literature. Cloth over Boards. University of Toronto Press. Toronto, ON. 2002. 376p. ISBN:0-8020-4376-3, ISBN13: 978-0-8020-4376-4. Dewey:810.9/896071. LCCN:2003-277283.
Audience: **g,l,u,f.**

Cohen, Mark **PR9192.6.C33C64 2001**
Censorship in Canadian Literature. Trade Cloth. McGill-Queen's University Press. Montreal, PQ. 2001. xii, 205p. ISBN:0-7735-2214-X, ISBN13: 978-0-7735-2214-5. Dewey:813/.5409. LCCN:2002-514916.
Audience: **g,l,u,f.**

Conolly, L. W. (Editor) **PR9191.5.C32 1995**
Canadian Drama and the Critics. Trade Paper. Talonbooks, Ltd. Vancouver, BC. 1995. 384p. ISBN:0-88922-359-9, ISBN13: 978-0-88922-359-2. Dewey:812/.5409971. LCCN:96-108170.
Audience: **g,l,u,f.**

Davidson, Arnold E. (Editor) **PR9184.6.S77 1990**
Studies on Canadian Literature: Introductory and Critical Essays. Library Binding. Modern Language Association of America. New York, NY. 1991. v, 371p. ISBN:0-87352-199-4, ISBN13: 978-0-87352-199-4. Dewey:810.9/971. LCCN:90-006529.
Audience: **l,u.** *Choice, 1991.*

Dudek, Louis; Michael Gnarowski **PR9171.D8**
The Making of Modern Poetry in Canada: Essential Articles on Contemporary Canadian Poetry in English. Ryerson Press. 1967.
Audience: **u,f.**

Frye, Northrop **PR9153.F7**
The Bush Garden: Essays on the Canadian Imagination. Trade Paper. House of Anansi Press. Toronto, ON. 1971. 208p. ISBN:0-88784-707-2, ISBN13: 978-0-88784-707-3. Dewey:810.9/971. LCCN:71-152412.
Audience: **g,l,u,f.**

Gerson, Carole **PR9188**
Canada's Early Women Writers. http://www.lib.sfu.ca/researchtools/databases/dbofdb.htm?DatabaseID=424 University of British Columbia and Simon Fraser University.
Audience: **g,l,u,f.**

Goldie, Terry **PN3426.I53 G65 1993**
Fear and Temptation: The Image of the Indigene in Canadian, Australian and New Zealand Literatures. Trade Paper. McGill-Queen's University Press. Montreal, PQ. 1993. 288p. ISBN:0-7735-1102-4, ISBN13: 978-0-7735-1102-6. Dewey:820.935203.
Audience: **u,f.**

Hamilton, A. C. **PN75.F7 H3 1990**
Northrop Frye: Anatomy of His Criticism. Cloth Text. University of Toronto Press. Toronto, ON. 1991. 652p. ISBN:0-8020-2697-4, ISBN13: 978-0-8020-2697-2. Dewey:801/.95/092. LCCN:92-120191.
Audience: **u,f.**

Hart, Jonathan **PN75.F7H37 1994**
Northrop Frye: The Theoretical Imagination. Cloth Text. Routledge. New York, NY. 1994. 336p. Critics of the Twentieth Century Ser. ISBN:0-415-07536-X, ISBN13: 978-0-415-07536-7. Dewey:801.95092. LCCN:93-028764.
Audience: **u,f.**

Heble, Ajay (Editor), et al. **PR9114**
New Contexts of Canadian Criticism. Donna P. Pennee & J. R. Struthers (Editors). Trade Paper. Broadview Press. Peterborough, ON. 1997. 407p. ISBN:1-55111-106-3, ISBN13: 978-1-55111-106-3. Dewey:801.9/5/0971. LCCN:96-932119.
Audience: **u,f.**

Howells, Coral Ann **PR9188.H68 1987**
Private and Fictional Words: Canadian Women Novelists of the 1970's and 1980's. Trade Cloth. Methuen & Company, Ltd. London, 1987. 200p. ISBN:0-416-37640-1, ISBN13: 978-0-416-37640-1. Dewey:813/.54/099287. LCCN:87-001580.
Audience: **u,f.**

Hutcheon, Linda **PR9192.5.H88 1988**
The Canadian Postmodern: A Study of Contemporary Canadian Fiction. Trade Paper. Oxford University Press, Inc. New York, NY. 1989. 248p. ISBN:0-19-540668-0, ISBN13: 978-0-19-540668-9. Dewey:813/.5409. LCCN:89-191936.
Audience: **u,f.** *Choice, 1989.*

Jeffrey M. Heath (Editor) **PR9184.3**
Profiles in Canadian Literature. Canada: Dundurn Group, The. 2004.
Audience: **g,l.**

Jones, Douglas G. **PR9111.J6**
Butterfly on Rock: A Study of Themes and Images in Canadian Literature. Trade Cloth. University of Toronto Press. Toronto, ON. 1970. x, 197p. ISBN:0-8020-5230-4, ISBN13: 978-0-8020-5230-8. Dewey:810.9. LCCN:75-133438.
Audience: **g,l.**

Kamboureli, Smaro **PR918.2**
Scandalous Bodies: Diasporic Literature in English Canada. Oxford University Press. 2000. ISBN:0-19-541450-0, ISBN13: 978-0-19-541450-9.
Audience: **u,f.**

Ketterer, David **PR9192.6.S34K4 1992**
Canadian Science Fiction and Fantasy. Cloth Text. Indiana University Press. Bloomington, IN. 1992. 228p. ISBN:0-253-33122-6, ISBN13: 978-0-253-33122-9. Dewey:813/.087609971. LCCN:91-025710.
Audience: **g,l,u,f.** *Choice, 1992.*

Klinck, Carl Frederick **PR918.3**
Literary History of Canada: Canadian Literature in English. Ed. 2. University of Toronto Press. 1976. ISBN:0-8020-2211-1, ISBN13: 978-0-8020-2211-0.
Audience: **g,l,u,f.**

Klinck, Carl F. & Bailey, Alfred G. (Editors) **PR9184.3.K5**
Literary History of Canada: Canadian Literature in English. Trade Paper. Books on Demand. Ann Arbor, MI. 959p. ISBN:0-8357-6362-5, ISBN13: 978-0-8357-6362-2. Dewey:810/.9/005. LCCN:65-001360.
Audience: **g,l,u,f.** B

Kroetsch, Robert **PR9189.6.K76 1989**
The Lovely Treachery of Words: Essays Selected and New. Trade Paper. Oxford University Press, Inc. New York, NY. 1989. 216p. ISBN:0-19-540694-X, ISBN13: 978-0-19-540694-8. Dewey:810.9971. LCCN:89-177743.
Audience: **u,f.** *Choice, 1989.*

Kröller, Eva-Marie (Editor) **PR9184.3.C34 2003**
The Cambridge Companion to Canadian Literature. Cloth Text. Cambridge University Press. New York, NY. 2004. 324p. Cambridge Companions to Literature Ser. ISBN:0-521-81441-3, ISBN13: 978-0-521-81441-6. Dewey:810.9/971. LCCN:2003-055128.
Audience: **g,l,u,f.**

Lecker, Robert (Editor) **PR9184.4.C36 1991**
Canadian Canons: Essays in Literary Value. Cloth Text. University of Toronto Press. Toronto, ON. 1992. 520p. ISBN:0-8020-5826-4, ISBN13: 978-0-8020-5826-3. Dewey:810.9. LCCN:91-004869.
Audience: **g,l,u,f.**

Lecker, Robert (Editor), et al. **PR9184.3**
Canadian Writers and Their Works: Fiction. Jack David & Ellen Quigley (Editors), Isaac Bickerstaff (Illustrator). Trade Cloth. ECW Press. Toronto, ON. 1991. 298p. ISBN:1-55022-052-7, ISBN13: 978-1-55022-052-0. Dewey:810/.9/971.
Audience: **g,l,u.** B *Choice, 1990.*

Lecker, Robert (Editor), et al. **PR9192.2**
Canadian Writers and Their Works: Neil Bissoondath, Austin Clarke, Joy Kogawa, Rohinton Mistry and Josef Skvorecky, Vol. 11. Jack David & Ellen Quigley (Editors), George Woodcock (Introduction by). Trade Cloth. ECW Press. Toronto, ON. 1996. 300p. ISBN:1-55022-213-9, ISBN13: 978-1-55022-213-5. Dewey:810/.9/971.
Audience: **g,l,u.**

Lecker, Robert (Editor), et al. **PR9192.2 .C38**
Canadian Writers and Their Works: Dennis Cooley, Christopher Dewdney, Steve McCaffery, Fred Wah and Tom Wayman, Vol. XII. Jack David & Ellen Quigley (Editors), George Woodcock (Introduction by). Trade Cloth. ECW Press. Toronto, ON. 300p. ISBN:1-55022-219-8, ISBN13: 978-1-55022-219-7. Dewey:810/.9/971.
Audience: **g,l,u.**

Lecker, Robert (Editor), et al. **PR9192.2**
Canadian Writers and Their Works: Sandra Birdsell, Timothy Findley, W. P. Kinsella and David Adams Richards. Jack David & Ellen Quigley (Editors), George Woodcock (Introduction by). Trade Cloth. ECW Press. Toronto, ON. 1996. 350p. ISBN:1-55022-215-5, ISBN13: 978-1-55022-215-9. Dewey:810/.9/971.
Audience: **g,l,u.** *Choice, 1996.*

Lecker, Robert (Editor), et al. **PR9192.2**
Canadian Writers and Their Works: Roo Borson, Lorna Crozier, Mary di Michele, Erin Moure and Sharon Thesen. Jack David & Ellen Quigley (Editors), George Woodcock (Introduction by). Trade Cloth. ECW Press. Toronto, ON. 1995. 340p. ISBN:1-55022-217-1, ISBN13: 978-1-55022-217-3. Dewey:810/.9/971.
Audience: **g,l,u.** *Choice, 1996.*

New, W. H. **PR9180.2.C38 1990**
99 Canadian Writers Before 1890. Cloth Text. Thomson Gale. Farmington Hills, MI. 1990. 400p. ISBN:0-8103-4579-X, ISBN13: 978-0-8103-4579-9. Dewey:810.9/003 B. LCCN:90-043445.
Audience: **g,l,u.**

New, W. H. (Editor) **PR9186.2.C36 1986**
Canadian Writers since 1960, First Series. Cloth Text. Thomson Gale. Farmington Hills, MI. 1986. 445p. Dictionary of Literary Biography Ser., Vol. 53 ISBN:0-8103-1731-1, ISBN13: 978-0-8103-1731-4. Dewey:810/.9/0054. LCCN:86-014892.
Audience: **g,l,u.** *Choice, 1987.*

New, W. H. (Editor) **PR9186.2.C363 1987**
Canadian Writers since 1960, Second Series. Ed. 2. Cloth Text. Thomson Gale. Farmington Hills, MI. 1987. 416p. Dictionary of Literary Biography Ser., Vol. 60 ISBN:0-8103-1738-9, ISBN13: 978-0-8103-1738-3. Dewey:810/.9/0054. LCCN:87-014351.
Audience: **g,l,u.**

New, W. H. (Editor) **PR9180.2.C37 1990**
Canadian Writers, 1890-1920. Cloth Text. Thomson Gale. Farmington Hills, MI. 1990. 487p. Dictionary of Library Biography Ser., Vol. 92 ISBN:0-8103-4572-2, ISBN13: 978-0-8103-4572-0. Dewey:810.9/0003 B. LCCN:89-048355.
Audience: **g,l,u.** *Choice, 1990.*

New, W. H. **PS8015**
Encyclopedia of Literature in Canada. Trade Cloth. University of Toronto Press. Toronto, ON. 2002. "1,000"p. ISBN:0-8020-0761-9, ISBN13: 978-0-8020-0761-2. Dewey:810.9/971/03. LCCN:2003-279602.
Audience: **g,l,u,f.** *Choice, 2003.*

New, W. H. **PS8061.N48 2003**
A History of Canadian Literature. Ed. 2. Trade Paper. McGill-Queen's University Press. Montreal, PQ. 2003. 464p. ISBN:0-7735-2597-1, ISBN13: 978-0-7735-2597-9. Dewey:809/.811. LCCN:2004-555150.
Audience: **u,f.** *Choice, 1989.*

Ondaatje, Michael **PS3566.L27**
Running in the Family. Trade Paper. McClelland & Stewart. Toronto, ON. 1999. 208p. ISBN:0-7710-6883-2, ISBN13: 978-0-7710-6883-6. Dewey:811/.54.
Audience: **g,l,u,f.**

Petrone, Penny **PM23**
Native Literature in Canada from the Oral Tradition to the Present. Oxford University Press. 1990. ISBN:0-19-540796-2, ISBN13: 978-0-19-540796-9.
Audience: **u,f.**

Stouck, David **PR9184.3.S84 1988**
Major Canadian Authors: A Critical Introduction to Canadian Literature in English. Ed. 2. Paper Text. University of Nebraska Press. Lincoln, NE. 1988. 330p. ISBN:0-8032-9188-4, ISBN13: 978-0-8032-9188-1. Dewey:810/.9/971. LCCN:87-038089.
Audience: **g,l,u.**

Stouck, David (Editor) **PR9199.3.R599**
Sinclair Ross' As for Me and My House: Five Decades of Criticism. Cloth Text. University of Toronto Press. Toronto, ON. 1991. 520p. ISBN:0-8020-5897-3, ISBN13: 978-0-8020-5897-3. Dewey:813/.52.
Audience: **l,u.**

Toye, William (Editor) **PR9180.2.C66 2001**
The Concise Oxford Companion to Canadian Literature. Ed. 2. Cloth Text. Oxford University Press, Inc. New York, NY. 2001. 536p. ISBN:0-19-541523-X, ISBN13: 978-0-19-541523-0. Dewey:810.9/971/03. LCCN:2001-273878.
Audience: **g,l,u,f.** *Choice, 2002.*

Wagner, Anton; Bryan, Bonita J. Orosz **PR9191.2**
The Brock Bibliography of Published Canadian Plays in English, 1766-1978. Playwrights Press. 1980. ISBN:0-88754-157-7, ISBN13: 978-0-88754-157-5.
Audience: **u,f.**

Waterston, Elizabeth **PR9193.9.W37 1992**
Children's Literature in Canada. Trade Cloth. Thomson Gale. Farmington Hills, MI. 1992. 200p. Twayne's World Authors Ser., No. 823 ISBN:0-8057-8264-8, ISBN13: 978-0-8057-8264-6. Dewey:810.9/9282. LCCN:92-024079.
Audience: **l,u.** *Choice, 1993.*

Zimmerman, Cynthia **PR9188**
Playwriting Women: Female Voices in English Canada. Christopher Innes (Editor). Trade Paper. Simon & Pierre Publishing Company, Ltd. Toronto, ON. 2004. 236p. ISBN:0-88924-258-5, ISBN13: 978-0-88924-258-6. Dewey:812/.5409/9287.
Audience: **u,f.** *Choice, 1995.*

Canada > Collections

PR9194.4
The Canadian Literature Archive.
http://www.umanitoba.ca/canlit/
University of Manitoba.
Audience: **g,l,u,f.**

PR9190.2.C35
Canadian Poetry.
http://www.library.utoronto.ca/canpoetry/index.html
University of Toronto Library.
Audience: **g,l,u,f.**

PR9190.2.C35
Canadian Poets Online: Writing Canada into the Millenium.
http://www.ucalgary.ca/UofC/faculties/HUM/ENGL/canada/
University of Calgary.
Audience: **g,l,u,f.**

Acorn, Milton (Contribution by), et al. **PR9195.7.A35 2004**
After the Eclipse: Poems. Herb Barrett & Marty Flomen (Contribution by). Perfect. Mekler & Deahl Publishers. Hamilton, ON. 2004. 89p. ISBN:1-896367-25-9, ISBN13: 978-1-896367-25-5. Dewey:811/.54080971. LCCN:2004-463013.
Audience: **g,l,u,f.**

Atwood, Margaret Eleanor **PR919.25**
The New Oxford Book of Canadian Verse in English. Oxford University Press. 1982. ISBN:0-19-540396-7, ISBN13: 978-0-19-540396-1.
Audience: **g,l,u,f.**

Atwood, Margaret Eleanor; Weaver, Robert **PR919.32**
The New Oxford Book of Canadian Short Stories in English. Oxford University Press. 1995. ISBN:0-19-541025-4, ISBN13: 978-0-19-541025-9.
Audience: **g,l,u,f.**

Ballstadt, Carl (Editor) **PR9199.2.M65Z49 1993**
Letters of Love and Duty: The Correspondence of Susanna and John Moodie. Cloth Text. University of Toronto Press. Toronto, ON. 1993. 740p. ISBN:0-8020-5708-X, ISBN13: 978-0-8020-5708-2. Dewey:813/.3 B. LCCN:92-095697.
Audience: **g,l,u,f.** *Choice, 1994.*

Campbell, Sandra (Editor) **PR919.33**
New Women: Short Stories by Canadian Women, 1900-1920. McMullen, Lorraine (Editor). University of Ottawa Press. 1991. Canadian Short Story Library, No. 14 ISBN:0-7766-0323-X, ISBN13: 978-0-7766-0323-0.
Audience: **g,l,u,f.**

Dagg, Anne Innis (Editor) **Z8313**
The Feminine Gaze: A Canadian Compendium of Non-Fiction Women Authors and Their Books, 1836-1945. Trade Cloth. Wilfrid Laurier University Press. Waterloo, ON. 2001. 354p. ISBN:0-88920-355-5, ISBN13: 978-0-88920-355-6. Dewey:016.818/08.
Audience: **g,l,u,f.** *Choice, 2002.*

Fiorentino, Jon Paul (Editor) **PR9195.72**
Post-Prairie: An Anthology of New Poetry. Robert Kroetsch (Editor). Talonbooks, Ltd. 2005. ISBN:0-88922-523-0, ISBN13: 978-0-88922-523-7.
Audience: **g,l,u,f.**

Gerson, Carole **PR9192.4.G47 1989**
A Purer Taste: The Reading and Writing of Fiction in English in Nineteenth-Century Canada. Cloth Text. University of Toronto Press. Toronto, ON. 1989. 224p. ISBN:0-8020-5820-5, ISBN13: 978-0-8020-5820-1. Dewey:813/.409/971. LCCN:89-175134.
Audience: **u,f.**

King, Thomas (Editor) **PR9197.33.I53**
All My Relations: An Anthology of Contemporary Canadian Native Fiction. University of Oklahoma Press. 1992. American Indian Literature and Critical Studies Ser., Vol. 4 ISBN:0-8061-2429-6, ISBN13: 978-0-8061-2429-2.
Audience: **g,l,u,f.**

Moses, Daniel D. (Editor) **PR9194.5.I5A58 1998**
An Anthology of Canadian Native Literature in English. Terry Goldie (Editor). Oxford University Press. 1998. ISBN:0-19-541282-6, ISBN13: 978-0-19-541282-6.
Audience: **g,l,u,f.**

Ondaatje, Michael **PR9197.32.F77 1995**
From Ink Lake: Canadian Stories. Trade Paper. Random House of Canada, Ltd. Mississauga, ON. 1995. 736p. ISBN:0-394-28138-1, ISBN13: 978-0-394-28138-4. Dewey:813/.0108971. LCCN:96-121539.
Audience: **g,l,u,f.** *Choice, 1991.*

Sullivan, Rosemary (Editor) **PR919.33**
The Oxford Book of Stories by Canadian Women in English. Oxford University Press. 1999. ISBN:0-19-541426-8, ISBN13: 978-0-19-541426-4.
Audience: **g,l,u,f.**

Canada > Individual Authors > 19th C.

Crawford, Isabella Valancy **PR4518.C17**
Collected Poems. Trade Paper. Books on Demand. Ann Arbor, MI. 352p. Literature of Canada, Poetry and Prose in Reprint Ser. ISBN:0-608-12843-0, ISBN13: 978-0-608-12843-6. Dewey:811/.4. LCCN:72-091689.
Audience: **g,l,u,f.**

Crawford, Isabella Valancy **PR9199.2.C83**
Old Spookses' Pass. Trade Paper. Kessinger Publishing, LLC. Whitefish, MT. 2004. ISBN:1-4191-3817-0, ISBN13: 978-1-4191-3817-1. Dewey:811.4.
Audience: **g,l,u,f.**

De Mille, James **PS2124**
A Strange Manuscript Found in a Copper Cylinder. Trade Paper. McGill-Queen's University Press. Montreal, PQ. ISBN:0-7735-2167-4, ISBN13: 978-0-7735-2167-4. Dewey:813/.4.
Audience: **l,u,f.**

Grove, Frederick Philip **PR919.3**
In Search of Myself. McClelland and Stewart. 1946. New Canadian Library, No. 94 ISBN:0-7710-9194-X, ISBN13: 978-0-7710-9194-0.
Audience: **u,f.**

Grove, Frederick Philip **F596 .G88**
Over Prairie Trails. Trade Paper. Kessinger Publishing, LLC. Whitefish, MT. 2004. ISBN:1-4191-3973-8, ISBN13: 978-1-4191-3973-4. Dewey:912.12704/2.
Audience: **g,l,u,f.**

Haliburton, Thomas Chandler **PR4735.H25**
The Letter-bag of the Great Western. Trade Cloth. Scholarly Publishing Office, University of Michigan Library. Ann Arbor, MI. 2004. ISBN:1-4181-0028-5, ISBN13: 978-1-4181-0028-5. Dewey:817.3.
Audience: **u,f.**

Haliburton, Thomas Chandler **PR4735.H25**
The Sayings and Doings of Samuel Slick Together with His Opinion on Matrimony. Trade Cloth. Scholarly Publishing Office, University of Michigan Library. Ann Arbor, MI. 2004. ISBN:1-4181-0048-X, ISBN13: 978-1-4181-0048-3. Dewey:817/.3.
Audience: **u,f.**

Heavysege, Charles **PR9199.2.H4**
Saul and Selected Poems. Sandra Djwa (Introduction by). Trade Paper. University of Toronto Press. Toronto, ON. 1976. Literature of Canada Ser. ISBN:0-8020-6262-8, ISBN13: 978-0-8020-6262-8. Dewey:811/.3. LCCN:76-017038.
Audience: **u,f.**

Lampman, Archibald **PR919.2**
Selected Poetry of Archibald Lampman. Gnarowski, Michael (Editor). Tecumseh Press. 1990. ISBN:0-919662-14-5, ISBN13: 978-0-919662-14-8.
Audience: **g,l,u,f.**

Lampman, Archibald **PR9199.3.L29**
The Poems of Archibald Lampman (Including at the Long Sault). Whitridge, Margaret Coulby (Introduction by). University of Toronto Press. 1974. Literature of Canada Ser., Vol. 12 ISBN:0-598-15266-0, ISBN13: 978-0-598-15266-4.
Audience: **g,l,u,f.**

Lampman, Archibald **PR9199.3.L29.A6 1974**
The Poems of Archibald Lampman. Margaret C. Whitridge (Introduction by). Trade Cloth. University of Toronto Press. Toronto, ON. 1974. xxxviii, xxv,p. ISBN:0-8020-2074-7, ISBN13: 978-0-8020-2074-1. Dewey:811/.4. LCCN:73-092517.
Audience: **g,l,u,f.** B

Mair, Charles **PR4972.M35**
Tecumseh, A Drama and Canadian Poems. Trade Paper. Kessinger Publishing, LLC. Whitefish, MT. 2005. ISBN:1-4179-0276-0, ISBN13: 978-1-4179-0276-7. Dewey:819.
Audience: **g,l,u,f.**

Moodie, Susanna **F1057**
Roughing It in the Bush; or, Life in Canada, Pt. 2. Trade Cloth. Scholarly Publishing Office, University of Michigan Library. Ann Arbor, MI. 2004. ISBN:1-4181-5765-1, ISBN13: 978-1-4181-5765-4. Dewey:917.13/042.
Audience: **g,l,u,f.**

Moodie, Susanna **F1057**
Roughing It in the Bush; or, Life in Canada, Pt. 1. Trade Cloth. Scholarly Publishing Office, University of Michigan Library. Ann Arbor, MI. 2004. ISBN:1-4181-5764-3, ISBN13: 978-1-4181-5764-7. Dewey:917.13/042.
Audience: **g,l,u,f.**

O'Hagan, Howard **PR9199.3.O35**
Tay John. Mass Market. McClelland & Stewart/Tundra Books. Plattsburgh, NY. 1996. 272p. New Canadian Library ISBN:0-7710-9850-2, ISBN13: 978-0-7710-9850-5. Dewey:813.54.
Audience: **g,l,u,f.**

Richardson, John **PR9199.2.R53**
Wacousta: The Prophecy. Mass Market. McClelland & Stewart/Tundra Books. Plattsburgh, NY. 1991. 552p. New Canadian Library ISBN:0-7710-9877-4, ISBN13: 978-0-7710-9877-2. Dewey:C813/.3.
Audience: **g,l,u,f.**

Richardson, John **HF1002.D4923**
The Canadian Brothers: or The Prophecy Fulfilled: A Tale of the Late American War. Donald Stephens (Editor). Trade Paper. McGill-Queen's University Press. Montreal, PQ. 541p. ISBN:0-88629-171-2, ISBN13: 978-0-88629-171-6. Dewey:330/.03.
Audience: **g,l,u,f.**

Sangster, Charles & Johnston, Gordon **PR5299.S27**
The St. Lawrence and the Saguenay and Other Poems. Trade Paper. University of Toronto Press. Toronto, ON. 1972. Literature of Canada Ser. ISBN:0-8020-6169-9, ISBN13: 978-0-8020-6169-0. Dewey:811/.3. LCCN:72-091692.
Audience: **g,l,u,f.**

Thurston, John **PR9199.2.M65Z88 1996**
The Work of Words: The Writing of Susanna Strickland Moodie. Trade Cloth. McGill-Queen's University Press. Montreal, PQ. 1996. 280p. ISBN:0-7735-1287-X, ISBN13: 978-0-7735-1287-0. Dewey:813/.3. LCCN:97-159446.
Audience: **l,u.**

Traill, Catharine Parr **F1057**
The Backwoods of Canada, No. 11. Michael A. Peterman (Editor). Trade Paper. McGill-Queen's University Press. Montreal, PQ. ISBN:0-88629-306-5, ISBN13: 978-0-88629-306-2. Dewey:917.1304/2. LCCN:96-900895.
Audience: **g,l,u,f.**

Canada > Individual Authors > 20th C. > A-C

Acorn, Milton **PR9199.3.A18 A6 1983**
Dig up My Heart: Selected Poems 1952-83. Trade Paper. McClelland & Stewart/Tundra Books. Plattsburgh, NY. 1983. Modern Canadian Poets Ser. ISBN:0-7710-0003-0, ISBN13: 978-0-7710-0003-4. Dewey:813/.54. LCCN:83-181698.
Audience: **g,l,u,f.**

Aquin, Hubert **PQ3919.2.P7314**
Prochain Episode. Mass Market. McClelland & Stewart. Toronto, ON. 1972. ISBN:0-7710-9184-2, ISBN13: 978-0-7710-9184-1. Dewey:843/.54.
Audience: **g,l,u,f.**

Armstrong, Jeannette **PR9199.3.A546**
Slash. Ed. 3. Trade Paper. Theytus Books, Ltd. Penticton, BC. 1985. 254p. ISBN:0-919441-29-7, ISBN13: 978-0-919441-29-3. Dewey:813/.54.
Audience: **g,l,u,f.**

Avison, Margaret **PR9199.3.A92A79 2003**
Always Now: The Collected Poems. Porcupine's Quill, Inc. 2005. The Collected Poems of Margaret Avison Ser. ISBN:0-88984-261-2, ISBN13: 978-0-88984-261-8.
Audience: **g,l,u,f.**

Birdsell, Sandra **PR9199.3.B4385A35**
Agassiz: A Novel in Stories. R. W. Scholes (Illustrator). Trade Cloth. Milkweed Editions. Minneapolis, MN. 1993. 352p. ISBN:0-915943-61-1, ISBN13: 978-0-915943-61-6. Dewey:813/.54. LCCN:90-022663.
Audience: **g,l,u,f.** *Choice, 1991.*

Birney, Earle **PR9199.3.B44 A6 1975**
Collected Poems. Trade Cloth. McClelland & Stewart/Tundra Books. Plattsburgh, NY. 1975. ISBN:0-7710-1474-0, ISBN13: 978-0-7710-1474-1. Dewey:811/.5/2. LCCN:75-307130.
Audience: **g,l,u,f.**

Birney, Earle **PR6003.I775 D3**
David, and Other Poems. The Ryerson Press. 1942.
Audience: **g,l,u,f.**

Bissoondath, Neil **PR9199.3B68**
Digging up the Mountains: Selected Stories. Trade Paper. General Distribution Services, Inc. Niagara Falls, NY. 1986. 247p. ISBN:0-7715-9246-9, ISBN13: 978-0-7715-9246-1. Dewey:813.54.
Audience: **g,l,u,f.**

Buckler, Ernest **PR9199.3.B763**
Mountain and the Valley. Robert Gibbs (Afterword by). Mass Market. McClelland & Stewart/Tundra Books. Plattsburgh, NY. 1996. 304p. New Canadian Library ISBN:0-7710-9952-5, ISBN13: 978-0-7710-9952-6. Dewey:C813/.54. LCCN:89-093678.
Audience: **g,l,u,f.**

Carr, Emily **E78.B9C37 2004**
Klee Wyck. Trade Paper. Douglas & McIntyre, Ltd. Vancouver, BC. 2004. 144p. The World of Emily Carr Ser. ISBN:1-55365-027-1, ISBN13: 978-1-55365-027-0. Dewey:971.1004/97. LCCN:2003-055793.
Audience: **g,l,u,f.**

Clarke, George Elliott **PS3568.O243**
George and Rue. Trade Cloth. Avalon Publishing Group. New York, NY. 2006. 240p. ISBN:0-7867-1620-7, ISBN13: 978-0-7867-1620-3. Dewey:813/.54.
Audience: **g,l,u,f.**

Clarke, George Elliott **PR9199.3.C5265W47**
Whylah Falls. Ed. 10. Trade Cloth. Raincoast Book Distribution. Vancouver, BC. 2000. 208p. ISBN:1-896095-52-6, ISBN13: 978-1-896095-52-3. Dewey:812/.54.
Audience: **g,l,u,f.**

Cohen, Leonard **PQ3919.R74**
Beautiful Losers. Trade Cloth. Penguin Group (USA) Inc. New York, NY. 1966. ISBN:0-670-15291-9, ISBN13: 978-0-670-15291-9. Dewey:813/.54.
Audience: **g,l,u,f.**

Cohen, Leonard **PR9199.3.C57S74 1993**
Stranger Music: Selected Poems and Songs. Trade Cloth. Knopf Publishing Group. New York, NY. 1993. 415p. ISBN:0-679-42729-5, ISBN13: 978-0-679-42729-2. Dewey:811/.54. LCCN:93-000751.
Audience: **g,l,u,f.**

Cohen, Matt **PS3568.O243**
Elizabeth and After: A Novel. Trade Cloth. DIANE Publishing Company. Collingdale, PA. 2005. 370p. ISBN:0-7567-9528-1, ISBN13: 978-0-7567-9528-3. Dewey:813/.54.
Audience: **g,l,u,f.**

Schaffer, Dylan **RC265.6.S275S33 2006**
Life, Death and Bialys: A Father/Son Baking Story. Cloth over Boards. Bloomsbury Publishing. New York, NY. 2006. 272p. ISBN:1-59691-192-1, ISBN13: 978-1-59691-192-5. Dewey:362.196/9940092 B. LCCN:2006-003185.
Audience: **g,l,u,f.**

Canada > Individual Authors > 20th C. > Atwood, Margaret

Arnold E. Davidson, Cathy Davidson (Editor) **PR9199.3.A8.Z54**
The Art of Margaret Atwood: Essays in Criticism. Anansi Productions. 1981. ISBN:0-88784-080-9, ISBN13: 978-0-88784-080-7.
Audience: **l,u,f.**

Atwood, Margaret **PR9199.3.A8B55 2000**
The Blind Assassin. Trade Cloth. Doubleday Publishing. New York, NY. 2000. 544p. ISBN:0-385-47572-1, ISBN13: 978-0-385-47572-3. Dewey:813/.54. LCCN:99-462109.
Audience: **g,l,u,f.**

Atwood, Margaret **PS3568.O243**
Bluebeard's Egg. Mass Market. Seal Books. Toronto, ON. 1999. 272p. ISBN:0-7704-2819-3, ISBN13: 978-0-7704-2819-8. Dewey:813/.54.
Audience: **g,l,u,f.**

Atwood, Margaret **PR9199.3.A8C38 1998**
Cat's Eye. Trade Paper. Doubleday Publishing. New York, NY. 1998. 480p. ISBN:0-385-49102-6, ISBN13: 978-0-385-49102-0. Dewey:813.5/4.
Audience: **g,l,u,f.**

Atwood, Margaret **PR9199.3.A8H3 1998**
The Handmaid's Tale. Trade Paper. Anchor Books. Two Harbors, MN. 1998. 320p. ISBN:0-385-49081-X, ISBN13: 978-0-385-49081-8. Dewey:813/.54. LCCN:97-042966.
Audience: **g,l,u,f.** B *Choice, 1986.*

Atwood, Margaret **PR9199.3.A8**
☐ O.W. Toad: Margaret Atwood Reference Site. http://www.owtoad.com/
Audience: **g,l,u,f.**

Atwood, Margaret **PR9199.3.A8O79 2003**
Oryx and Crake. Trade Cloth. Doubleday Publishing. New York, NY. 2003. 400p. ISBN:0-385-50385-7, ISBN13: 978-0-385-50385-3. Dewey:813/.54. LCCN:2002-073290.
Audience: **g,l,u,f.**

Atwood, Margaret **PR9199.3.A8P46 2005**
The Penelopiad: The Myth of Penelope and Odysseus. Trade Cloth. Knopf Canada. Toronto, ON. 2005. 216p. ISBN:0-676-97418-X, ISBN13: 978-0-676-97418-8. Dewey:813/.54. LCCN:2006-373544.
Audience: **g,l,u,f.**

Atwood, Margaret **PR9199.3.A8A6 1987**
Selected Poems: 1965-1975. Houghton Mifflin Company Trade & Reference Division. 1987. ISBN:0-395-40422-3, ISBN13: 978-0-395-40422-5.
Audience: **g,l,u,f.**

Atwood, Margaret **PS3568.O243**
Wilderness Tips. Trade Paper. Doubleday Publishing. New York, NY. 1998. 240p. ISBN:0-385-49111-5, ISBN13: 978-0-385-49111-2. Dewey:813/.54. LCCN:91-017086.
Audience: **g,l,u,f.**

Atwood, Margaret **PR9199.3.A8W75 2005**
Writing with Intent: Essays, Reviews, Personal Prose: 1983-2005. Trade Cloth. Avalon Publishing Group. New York, NY. 2005. 464p. ISBN:0-7867-1535-9, ISBN13: 978-0-7867-1535-0. Dewey:818/.5409. LCCN:2005-042086.
Audience: **g,l,u,f.**

Atwood, Margaret **PR9199.3.A8 A17 1987**
Selected Poems II: 1976 - 1986. Houghton Mifflin Company Trade & Reference Division. 1987. ISBN:0-395-45406-9, ISBN13: 978-0-395-45406-0.
Audience: **g,l,u,f.**

Atwood, Margaret **PR9199.3.A8 C57 1978**
The Circle Game. Sherrill E. Grace (Introduction by). Trade Paper. House of Anansi Press. Toronto, ON. 1978. 95p. ISBN:0-88784-070-1, ISBN13: 978-0-88784-070-8. Dewey:811/.54. LCCN:00-500039.
Audience: **g,l,u,f.**

Howells, Coral Ann (Editor) **PR9199.3.A8Z565 2006**
The Cambridge Companion to Margaret Atwood. Cloth Text. Cambridge University Press. New York, NY. 2006. 222p. Cambridge Companions to Literature Ser. ISBN:0-521-83966-1, ISBN13: 978-0-521-83966-2. Dewey:818/.5409. LCCN:2005-024381.
Audience: **g,l,u,f.**

Howells, Coral Ann **PR9199.3.A8Z695 2005**
Margaret Atwood. Ed. 2. Palgrave Macmillan. 2005. ISBN:1-4039-2200-4, ISBN13: 978-1-4039-2200-7.
Audience: **l,u.**

Van Spanckeren, Kathryn & Castro, Jan G. (Editors) **PR9199.3.A8Z76 1988**
Margaret Atwood: Vision and Forms. Margaret Atwood (Foreword by). Cloth Text. Southern Illinois University Press. Carbondale, IL. 1988. 302p. Ad Feminam: Women and Literature Ser. ISBN:0-8093-1408-8, ISBN13: 978-0-8093-1408-9. Dewey:818/.5409. LCCN:88-006452.
Audience: **u,f.** *Choice, 1989.*

Canada > Individual Authors > 20th C. > D-F

Davies, Robertson **PR9199.3.D3C6 1992**
The Cornish Trilogy: The Rebel Angels; What's Bred in the Bone; The Lyre of Orpheus. Trade Paper. Penguin Group (USA) Inc. New York, NY. 1992. 1152p. ISBN:0-14-015850-2, ISBN13: 978-0-14-015850-2. Dewey:813/.54. LCCN:91-050242.
Audience: **g,l,u,f.**

Davies, Robertson **PR9199.3.D3**
The Deptford Trilogy. Trade Cloth. Penguin Group (USA) Inc. New York, NY. 1988. 864p. ISBN:0-670-81790-2, ISBN13: 978-0-670-81790-0. Dewey:813/.54.
Audience: **g,l,u,f.**

Davies, Robertson **PR9199.3.D3**
Fortune, My Foe and Eros at Breakfast: Two Plays. Trade Paper. Simon & Pierre Publishing Company, Ltd. Toronto, ON. 2004. 124p. ISBN:0-88924-241-0, ISBN13: 978-0-88924-241-8. Dewey:812/.54.
Audience: **g,l,u,f.**

Davies, Robertson **PS3568.O243**
The Salterton Trilogy: Tempest-Tost; Leaven of Malice; A Mixture of Frailties. Trade Paper. Penguin Group (USA) Inc. New York, NY. 1991. 816p. ISBN:0-14-015910-X, ISBN13: 978-0-14-015910-3. Dewey:813/.54. LCCN:86-227292.
Audience: **g,l,u,f.**

Dudek, Louis **PR9199.3.D83A6 1998**
The Poetry of Louis Dudek: Definitive Edition. Trade Paper. Golden Dog Press. Kemptville, ON. 1998. 256p. ISBN:0-919614-82-5, ISBN13: 978-0-919614-82-6. Dewey:811/.52. LCCN:00-303701.
Audience: **g,l,u,f.**

Findley, Timothy **PR9199.3.F52N6 1984**
Not Wanted on the Voyage. Trade Cloth. Dell Publishing. New York, NY. 1985. 368p. ISBN:0-385-29415-8, ISBN13: 978-0-385-29415-7. Dewey:813/.54. LCCN:85-000897.
Audience: **g,l,u,f.**

Canada > Individual Authors > 20th C. > G-H

Gallant, Mavis **PS3568.O243**
Across the Bridge. Trade Cloth. McClelland & Stewart/Tundra Books. Plattsburgh, NY. 1993. 208p. ISBN:0-7710-3305-2, ISBN13: 978-0-7710-3305-6. Dewey:813/.54.
Audience: **g,l,u,f.**

Gallant, Mavis **PS3568.O243**
The Selected Stories of Mavis Gallant. Trade Paper. McClelland & Stewart. Toronto, ON. 1997. 912p. ISBN:0-7710-3330-3, ISBN13: 978-0-7710-3330-8. Dewey:813.5/4.
Audience: **g,l,u,f.**

Gallant, Mavis **PR9199.3.G26A6 2004**
Montreal Stories. Russell Banks (Editor). Trade Paper. McClelland & Stewart. Toronto, ON. 2004. 344p. ISBN:0-7710-3277-3, ISBN13: 978-0-7710-3277-6. Dewey:813/.54. LCCN:2004-380986.
Audience: **g,l,u,f.**

Glassco, John **PR9199.3.G574Z46**
Memoirs of Montparnasse. Mavis Gallant (Introduction by). Trade Paper. New York Review of Books, Incorporated, The. New York, NY. 2007. 296p. New York Review Books Classics ISBN:1-59017-184-5, ISBN13: 978-1-59017-184-4. Dewey:818/5409 B. LCCN:2005-036203.
Audience: **g,l,u,f.**

Harrison, Charles **PZ3.H3184**
Generals Die in Bed: A Story from the Trenches. Trade Cloth. Annick Press, Ltd. Toronto, ON. 2002. 180p. ISBN:1-55037-731-0, ISBN13: 978-1-55037-731-6. Dewey:813.52.
Audience: **g,l,u,f.**

Canada > Individual Authors > 20th C. > K

Klein, A. M. **PR9199.3.K48**
A. M. Klein - Complete Poems: Original Poems, 1926-1934; Original Poems, 1937-1955 and Poetry Translations, Vol. 2. Zailig Pollock (Editor). Trade Cloth. University of Toronto Press. Toronto, ON. 1990. 2211p. Collected Works of A. M. Klein ISBN:0-8020-5802-7, ISBN13: 978-0-8020-5802-7. Dewey:C811/.52.
Audience: **g,l,u,f.** *Choice, 1991.*

Klein, A. M. **PR9199.3.K48A6 1997**
Selected Poems. Zailig Pollock, Seymour Mayne & Usher Caplan (Editors). Trade Cloth. University of Toronto Press. Toronto, ON. 1997. 500p. Collected Works of A. M. Klein ISBN:0-8020-0734-1, ISBN13: 978-0-8020-0734-6. Dewey:811/.52. LCCN:97-193763.
Audience: **g,l,u,f.**

Kogawa, Joy **PR9199.3.K63I87 1994**
Itsuka. Trade Paper. Alfred A. Knopf Inc. New York, NY. 1993. 352p. ISBN:0-385-46885-7, ISBN13: 978-0-385-46885-5. Dewey:813/.54. LCCN:93-026076.
Audience: **g,l,u,f.**

Kogawa, Joy **PS3568.O243**
Obasan. UK-Trade Paper. Knopf Publishing Group. New York, NY. 1993. 320p. ISBN:0-385-46886-5, ISBN13: 978-0-385-46886-2. Dewey:813/.54. LCCN:93-026081.
Audience: **g,l,u,f.**

Kroetsch, Robert **PR9199.3.K7S78 2004**
The Studhorse Man. Ed. 10. Aritha Van Herk (Introduction by). Trade Paper. University of Alberta Press. Georgetown, ON. 2004. 224p. Currents: An Interdisciplinary Ser. ISBN:0-88864-425-6, ISBN13: 978-0-88864-425-1. Dewey:813/.54. LCCN:2004-463305.
Audience: **g,l,u,f.**

Canada > Individual Authors > 20th C. > L

Lau, Evelyn **PR9199.3.L3287F7**
Fresh Girls and Other Stories. Trade Cloth. Hyperion Press. New York, NY. 1995. 128p. ISBN:0-7868-6058-8, ISBN13: 978-0-7868-6058-6. Dewey:813/.54. LCCN:94-007565.
Audience: **g,l,u,f.**

Lau, Evelyn **CT1138.L4**
Runaway: Diary of a Street Kid. Trade Paper. Coach House Press, Inc. Woodstock, IL. 1995. 276p. ISBN:0-88910-491-3, ISBN13: 978-0-88910-491-4. Dewey:362.74/092.
Audience: **g,l,u,f.**

Laurence, Margaret **PR9199.3.L33.B57**
A Bird in the House. Trade Paper. University of Chicago Press. Chicago, IL. 1993. 192p. Phoenix Fiction Ser. ISBN:0-226-46934-4, ISBN13: 978-0-226-46934-8. LCCN:93-012154.
Audience: **g,l,u,f.** B

Laurence, Margaret **PS3568.O243**
The Stone Angel. Ed. 40. Trade Paper. McClelland & Stewart. Toronto, ON. 2004. 344p. ISBN:0-7710-4708-8, ISBN13: 978-0-7710-4708-4. Dewey:813/.54.
Audience: **g,l,u,f.**

Laurence, Margaret **PR9199.3.L33D58 1993**
The Diviners. Margaret Atwood (Afterword by). Trade Paper. University of Chicago Press. Chicago, IL. 1993. 397p. Phoenix Fiction Ser. ISBN:0-226-46935-2, ISBN13: 978-0-226-46935-5. Dewey:813.5/4. LCCN:93-016183.
Audience: **g,l,u,f.**

Laurence, Margaret **PR9199.3.L33 J4 1993**
A Jest of God. Margaret Atwood (Afterword by). Trade Paper. University of Chicago Press. Chicago, IL. 1993. 218p. Phoenix Fiction Ser. ISBN:0-226-46952-2, ISBN13: 978-0-226-46952-2. Dewey:813/.54. LCCN:93-008034.
Audience: **g,l,u,f.** B

Layton, Irving **PS3566.L27**
The Improved Binoculars. Saddle Stitched. Porcupine's Quill, Inc. Erin, ON. 1990. 128p. ISBN:0-88984-101-2, ISBN13: 978-0-88984-101-7. Dewey:811/.54. LCCN:92-220557.
Audience: **g,l,u,f.**

Layton, Irving **C811/.54**
A Wild Peculiar Joy: The Selected Poems. Trade Paper. McClelland & Stewart. Toronto, ON. 2004. 368p. ISBN:0-7710-4948-X, ISBN13: 978-0-7710-4948-4. Dewey:PR9199.3.L35A6.
Audience: **g,l,u,f.**

Layton, Irving **PR9199.3.L35F66 1992**
Fornalutx: Selected Poems, 1928-1990. Brian Trehearne (Introduction by). Trade Cloth. McGill-Queen's University Press. Montreal, PQ. 1992. 208p. ISBN:0-7735-0952-6, ISBN13: 978-0-7735-0952-8. Dewey:811/.54. LCCN:93-210370.
Audience: **g,l,u,f.**

Leacock, Stephen **PR6023.E15**
Arcadian Adventures with the Idle Rich. Trade Paper. Kessinger Publishing, LLC. Whitefish, MT. 2004. ISBN:1-4191-0740-2, ISBN13: 978-1-4191-0740-5. Dewey:817.59.
Audience: **g,l,u,f.**

Leacock, Stephen **PR6023.E15**
Literary Lapses. Trade Paper. Kessinger Publishing, LLC. Whitefish, MT. 2004. ISBN:1-4191-3067-6, ISBN13: 978-1-4191-3067-0. Dewey:817/.5/2.
Audience: **u,f.**

Leacock, Stephen **PR6023.E15.N7 1971**
Nonsense Novels. Trade Cloth. Dover Publications, Inc. Mineola, NY. 1971. 102p. ISBN:0-486-22759-6, ISBN13: 978-0-486-22759-7. Dewey:818/.5/207. LCCN:78-166423.
Audience: **g,l,u,f.** B

Leacock, Stephen **PS3511.A86**
Sunshine Sketches of a Little Town. Trade Paper. Kessinger Publishing, LLC. Whitefish, MT. 2004. ISBN:1-4191-4999-7, ISBN13: 978-1-4191-4999-3. Dewey:813/.52.
Audience: **g,l,u,f.**

Livesay, Dorothy **PR9199.3.L56**
Beginnings. Trade Paper. Peguis Publishers, Ltd. Grand Forks, ND. 1997. ISBN:0-920541-94-1, ISBN13: 978-0-920541-94-4. Dewey:813/.52. LCCN:89-131949.
Audience: **g,l,u,f.**

Canada > Individual Authors > 20th C. > M

Mandel, Eli **PS3566.L27**
The Other Harmony: The Collected Poetry of Eli Mandel. Judy Lea Chapman & Andrew James Stubbs (Editors). Trade Cloth. Canadian Plains Research Center. Regina, SK. 2003. 760p. ISBN:0-88977-138-3, ISBN13: 978-0-88977-138-3. Dewey:811/.54.
Audience: **g,l,u,f.**

Michaels, Anne **PS3568.O243**
Fugitive Pieces. Trade Cloth. McClelland & Stewart. Toronto, ON. 2006. 312p. ISBN:0-7710-5886-1, ISBN13: 978-0-7710-5886-8. Dewey:FIC.
Audience: **g,l,u,f.**

Mitchell, W. O. **PS3568.O243**
According to Jake and the Kid. Trade Cloth. McClelland & Stewart/Tundra Books. Plattsburgh, NY. 1989. ISBN:0-7710-6073-4, ISBN13: 978-0-7710-6073-1. Dewey:813/.54. LCCN:90-115469.
Audience: **g,l,u,f.**

Montgomery, L. M. **PR9199.3.M6A75 2003**
Anne of Green Gables. Jennifer Lee Carroll (Afterword by). Mass Market. Penguin Group (USA) Inc. New York, NY. 2003. 320p. ISBN:0-451-52882-4, ISBN13: 978-0-451-52882-7. Dewey:813/.52. LCCN:2003-041503.
Audience: **g,l,u,f.**

Waterston, Elizabeth **PR9199.3.M6**
Kindling Spirit: Lucy Maud Montgomery's Anne of Green Gables. Trade Paper. ECW Press. Toronto, ON. 1993. Canadian Fiction Studies, No. 19 ISBN:1-55022-113-2, ISBN13: 978-1-55022-113-8. Dewey:C813/.52.
Audience: **l,u.**

Canada > Individual Authors > 20th C. > Munro, Alice

Howells, Coral Ann **PR9199.3.M8Z7 1998**
Alice Munro. Trade Paper. Manchester University Press. Manchester, 1998. 208p. Contemporary World Writers Ser. ISBN:0-7190-4559-2, ISBN13: 978-0-7190-4559-2. Dewey:813.5/4. LCCN:98-018302.
Audience: **g,l,u.** *Choice, 1999.*

Munro, Alice **PR9199.3.M8W47 1991**
The Beggar Maid: Stories of Flo and Rose. Trade Paper. David McKay Company, Inc. New York, NY. 1991. 224p. Vintage Contemporaries Ser. ISBN:0-679-73271-3, ISBN13: 978-0-679-73271-6. Dewey:813.5/4. LCCN:90-050492.
Audience: **g,l,u,f.** B

Munro, Alice **PR9199.3.M8F7 1991**
Friend of My Youth. Trade Paper. Random House, Inc. New York, NY. 1991. 288p. Vintage Contemporaries Ser. ISBN:0-679-72957-7, ISBN13: 978-0-679-72957-0. Dewey:813.5/4. LCCN:90-050495.
Audience: **g,l,u,f.**

Munro, Alice **PS3568.O243**
Hateship, Friendship, Courtship, Loveship, Marriage: Stories. Trade Paper. Alfred A. Knopf Inc. New York, NY. 2002. 336p. ISBN:0-375-72743-4, ISBN13: 978-0-375-72743-6. Dewey:813/.54.
Audience: **g,l,u,f.**

Munro, Alice **PR9199.3.M8L58 2001**
Lives of Girls and Women. UK-Trade Paper. Knopf Publishing Group. New York, NY. 2001. 288p. ISBN:0-375-70749-2, ISBN13: 978-0-375-70749-0. Dewey:813/.54. LCCN:00-063412.
Audience: **g,l,u,f.**

Munro, Alice **PR9199.3.M8M66 1991**
The Moons of Jupiter: Stories. Trade Paper. Random House Adult Trade Publishing Group. New York, NY. 1991. 256p. Vintage Contemporaries Ser. ISBN:0-679-73270-5, ISBN13: 978-0-679-73270-9. Dewey:813.5/4. LCCN:90-050493.
Audience: **g,l,u,f.** B

Munro, Alice **PS3568.O243**
Open Secrets: Stories. Trade Paper. Knopf Publishing Group. New York, NY. 1995. 304p. ISBN:0-679-75562-4, ISBN13: 978-0-679-75562-3. Dewey:813/.54.
Audience: **g,l,u,f.**

Munro, Alice **PR9199.3.M8P7 2000**
The Progress of Love. Trade Paper. Knopf Publishing Group. New York, NY. 2000. 320p. Vintage Contemporaries Ser. ISBN:0-375-72470-2, ISBN13: 978-0-375-72470-1. Dewey:813.5/4. LCCN:00-712806.
Audience: **g,l,u,f.**

Munro, Alice **PS3568.O243**
Runaway: Stories. Trade Paper. Knopf Publishing Group. New York, NY. 2005. 352p. ISBN:1-4000-7791-5, ISBN13: 978-1-4000-7791-5. Dewey:813.54. LCCN:2005-284533.
Audience: **g,l,u,f.**

Munro, Alice **PR9199.3.M8A6 1996**
Selected Stories. Trade Cloth. Alfred A. Knopf Inc. New York, NY. 1996. 544p. ISBN:0-679-44627-3, ISBN13: 978-0-679-44627-9. Dewey:813.5/4. LCCN:96-004145.
Audience: **g,l,u,f.**

Canada > Individual Authors > 20th C. > Ondaatje, Michael

Ondaatje, Michael **PR9199.3.O5.A84 2000**
Anil's Ghost. Trade Cloth. Thorndike Press. Waterville, ME. 2000. 443p. ISBN:0-7540-1494-0, ISBN13: 978-0-7540-1494-2. Dewey:813.5/4. LCCN:00-042351.
Audience: **g,l,u,f.**

Ondaatje, Michael **PR9199.3.O5C5 1997**
The Cinnamon Peeler: Selected Poems. Trade Paper. Knopf Publishing Group. New York, NY. 1997. 208p. ISBN:0-679-77913-2, ISBN13: 978-0-679-77913-1. Dewey:811/.54. LCCN:97-111363.
Audience: **g,l,u,f.**

Ondaatje, Michael **PR9199.3.O5C6 1996**
The Collected Works of Billy the Kid. Trade Paper. Knopf Publishing Group. New York, NY. 1996. 128p. ISBN:0-679-76786-X, ISBN13: 978-0-679-76786-2. Dewey:818/.5407. LCCN:95-046415.
Audience: **g,l,u,f.**

Ondaatje, Michael **PR9199.3.O5E54 1992**
The English Patient. Trade Cloth. Alfred A. Knopf Inc. New York, NY. 1992. 320p. ISBN:0-679-41678-1, ISBN13: 978-0-679-41678-4. Dewey:813.5/4. LCCN:92-053089.
Audience: **g,l,u,f.**

Ondaatje, Michael **PR9199.3.O5H36 1999**
Handwriting: Poems. Trade Cloth. Alfred A. Knopf Inc. New York, NY. 1999. 96p. ISBN:0-375-40559-3, ISBN13: 978-0-375-40559-4. Dewey:811/.54. LCCN:98-041731.
Audience: **g,l,u,f.**

Ondaatje, Michael **PR9199.3.O5I5 1997**
In the Skin of a Lion: A Novel. Trade Paper. David McKay Company, Inc. New York, NY. 1997. 256p. ISBN:0-679-77266-9, ISBN13: 978-0-679-77266-8. Dewey:813/.54. LCCN:97-111370.
Audience: **g,l,u,f.**

Solecki, Sam **PR9199.3.O5Z866 2003**
Ragas of Longing: The Poetry of Michael Ondaatje. Cloth over Boards. University of Toronto Press. Toronto, ON. 2003. 256p. ISBN:0-8020-3763-1, ISBN13: 978-0-8020-3763-3. Dewey:811/.54. LCCN:2004-272590.
Audience: **g,l,u,f.** *Choice, 2004.*

Totosy de Zepetnek, Steven **PR9199.3.O5Z63 2005**
Comparative Cultural Studies and Michael Ondaatje's Writing. Trade Paper. Purdue University Press. West Lafayette, IN. 2005. 147p. Comparative Cultural Studies ISBN:1-55753-378-4, ISBN13: 978-1-55753-378-4. Dewey:818/.5409. LCCN:2004-013298.
Audience: **u,f.**

Canada > Individual Authors > 20th C. > P

Page, P. K. **PR6031.A24 G53**
The Glass Air: Poems Selected and New. Trade Paper. Oxford University Press, Inc. New York, NY. 1986. 200p. ISBN:0-19-540506-4, ISBN13: 978-0-19-540506-4. Dewey:811.5.
Audience: **g,l,u,f.**

Page, P. K. **PS3566.L27**
The Hidden Room. Trade Paper. David R. Godine Publisher. Boston, MA. 2003. ISBN:1-56792-225-2, ISBN13: 978-1-56792-225-7. Dewey:811/.54.
Audience: **g,l,u,f.**

Pollock, Sharon **PR9199.3.P57D63 2003**
Doc. Trade Paper. Broadview Press. Peterborough, ON. 2002. 90p. Broadview Drama Ser. ISBN:1-55111-525-5, ISBN13: 978-1-55111-525-2. Dewey:812/.54. LCCN:2003-270964.
Audience: **g,l,u,f.**

Pratt, E. J. **PR9199.3.P7A6 1995**
Pursuits Amateur and Academic: The Selected Prose of E. J. Pratt. Cloth Text. University of Toronto Press. Toronto, ON. 1995. 760p. Collected Works of E. J. Pratt ISBN:0-8020-2907-8, ISBN13: 978-0-8020-2907-2. Dewey:818/.5208. LCCN:95-184864.
Audience: **u,f.**

Pratt, E. J. **PR9199.3.P7**
E. J. Pratt: Complete Poems, Pts. I & II. Sandra Djwa & R. G. Moyles (Editors). Trade Cloth. University of Toronto Press. Toronto, ON. 1989. 1786p. ISBN:0-8020-5775-6, ISBN13: 978-0-8020-5775-4. Dewey:811/.52.
Audience: **g,l,u,f.** *Choice, 1989.*

Pratt, E. J. (Author, Editor) **PR9199.3.P7A6 2000**
Selected Poems: E. J. Pratt. Sandra Djwa & W. J. Keith (Editors). Trade Cloth. University of Toronto Press. Toronto, ON. 2000. 538p. ISBN:0-8020-4335-6, ISBN13: 978-0-8020-4335-1. Dewey:811/.52. LCCN:2001-280486.
Audience: **g,l,u,f.** *Choice, 2001.*

Purdy, Al **PR9199.3.P8A17 2000**
Beyond Remembering: The Collected Poems of Al Purdy. Sam Solecki (Editor). Trade Cloth. Harbour Publishing Company, Ltd. Madeira Park, BC. 2000. 608p. ISBN:1-55017-225-5, ISBN13: 978-1-55017-225-6. Dewey:811/.54. LCCN:2001-320717.
Audience: **g,l,u,f.**

Canada > Individual Authors > 20th C. > R

Ricci, Nino **PR9199.3.R512B66**
Lives of the Saints. Trade Paper. Picador. New York, NY. 1995. ISBN:0-312-13441-X, ISBN13: 978-0-312-13441-9. Dewey:813/.54. LCCN:95-021022.
Audience: **g,l,u,f.**

Richards, David Adams **PR9199.3.R465**
The Coming of Winter. Mass Market. McClelland & Stewart/Tundra Books. Plattsburgh, NY. 1992. 328p. New Canadian Library ISBN:0-7710-9885-5, ISBN13: 978-0-7710-9885-7. Dewey:C813/.54.
Audience: **g,l,u,f.**

Richards, David Adams **PR9199.3.R465R63**
River of the Brokenhearted. Trade Cloth. Arcade Publishing, Inc. New York, NY. 2004. 400p. ISBN:1-55970-712-7, ISBN13: 978-1-55970-712-1. Dewey:813/.54. LCCN:2003-020368.
Audience: **g,l,u,f.**

Richler, Mordecai **PR6019.O9**
The Apprenticeship of Duddy Kravitz The Apprenticeship of Duddy Kravitz. Trade Cloth, Trade Cloth. McClelland & Stewart McClelland & Stewart. Toronto, ON. 2006 2006. 376p. ISBN:0-7710-7535-9, ISBN13: 978-0-7710-7535-3. Dewey:813/.54.
Audience: **g,l,u,f.**

Richler, Mordecai **PS3568.O243**
Barney's Version. Trade Paper. Random House of Canada, Ltd. Mississauga, ON. 1998. 432p. ISBN:0-676-97174-1, ISBN13: 978-0-676-97174-3. Dewey:813/.54.
Audience: **g,l,u,f.**

Richler, Mordecai **PS3568.O243**
Son of a Smaller Hero. Roy Smith (Afterword by). Mass Market. McClelland & Stewart/Tundra Books. Plattsburgh, NY. 1996. 208p. New Canadian Library ISBN:0-7710-9970-3, ISBN13: 978-0-7710-9970-0. Dewey:813/.54.
Audience: **g,l,u,f.**

Roberts, Charles G. D. **PR5231 .I5**
In Divers Tones. Trade Paper. Kessinger Publishing, LLC. Whitefish, MT. 2004. ISBN:1-4191-2570-2, ISBN13: 978-1-4191-2570-6. Dewey:811.49.
Audience: **g,l,u,f.**

Ross, Sinclair **PR9199.3.R599**
As for Me and My House. Mass Market. McClelland & Stewart/Tundra Books. Plattsburgh, NY. 1989. 224p. New Canadian Library ISBN:0-7710-9997-5, ISBN13: 978-0-7710-9997-7. Dewey:813/.54. LCCN:88-094952.
Audience: **g,l,u,f.**

Ross, Sinclair **PR9199.3.R599**
The Lamp at Noon and Other Stories. Mass Market. McClelland & Stewart/Tundra Books. Plattsburgh, NY. 1996. 144p. New Canadian Library ISBN:0-7710-9996-7, ISBN13: 978-0-7710-9996-0. Dewey:C813/.54. LCCN:88-094202.
Audience: **g,l,u,f.** B

Canada > Individual Authors > 20th C. > S-V

Shields, Carol **PR9199.3.S514S43**
Small Ceremonies. Trade Paper. Penguin Group (USA) Inc. New York, NY. 1996. 194p. ISBN:0-14-025145-6, ISBN13: 978-0-14-025145-6. Dewey:813.54. LCCN:95-030647.
Audience: **g,l,u,f.**

Shields, Carol **PR9199.3.S514S76**
The Stone Diaries. Trade Paper. Penguin Group (USA) Inc. New York, NY. 1995. 400p. ISBN:0-14-023313-X, ISBN13: 978-0-14-023313-1. Dewey:813.5/4. LCCN:93-030239.
Audience: **g,l,u,f.**

Souster, Raymond **PR9199.3.S6T87 2003**
Twenty-Three New Poems. Oberon. 2003. ISBN:0-7780-1217-4, ISBN13: 978-0-7780-1217-7.
Audience: **g,l,u,f.**

Urquhart, Jane **PS3568.O243**
Away. Trade Cloth. McClelland & Stewart. Toronto, ON. 2006. 368p. ISBN:0-7710-8653-9, ISBN13: 978-0-7710-8653-3. Dewey:813/.54.
Audience: **g,l,u,f.**

Urquhart, Jane **PS3568.O243**
A Map of Glass. Trade Cloth. McClelland & Stewart. Toronto, ON. 2005. 384p. ISBN:0-7710-8727-6, ISBN13: 978-0-7710-8727-1. Dewey:813/.54.
Audience: **g,l,u,f.**

Van Herk, Aritha **PR6019.O9**
Judith. Trade Cloth. Little Brown & Company. New York, NY. 1978. ISBN:0-316-89696-9, ISBN13: 978-0-316-89696-2. Dewey:823/.9/1. LCCN:78-060696.
Audience: **g,l,u,f.**

Van Herk, Aritha **PR9199.3.V359 T4**
The Tent Peg: A Novel. Trade Cloth. McClelland & Stewart/Tundra Books. Plattsburgh, NY. 1981. ISBN:0-7710-8702-0, ISBN13: 978-0-7710-8702-8. Dewey:813/.54. LCCN:81-125119.
Audience: **g,l,u,f.**

Vanderhaeghe, Guy **PS3568.O243**
The Englishman's Boy. Trade Cloth. McClelland & Stewart. Toronto, ON. 1996. 344p. ISBN:0-7710-8693-8, ISBN13: 978-0-7710-8693-9. Dewey:813.54. LCCN:97-015518.
Audience: **g,l,u,f.**

Vanderhaeghe, Guy **PR9199.3.V384M3 1985**
Man Descending: Selected Stories. Trade Paper. Houghton Mifflin Company. New York, NY. 1985. 230p. ISBN:0-89919-385-4, ISBN13: 978-0-89919-385-4. Dewey:813/.54. LCCN:85-002758.
Audience: **g,l,u,f.**

Canada > Individual Authors > 20th C. > W

Waddington, Miriam **PR9199.3.W3 A6 1986**
Collected Poems. Paper Text. Oxford University Press, Inc. New York, NY. 1987. 440p. ISBN:0-19-540535-8, ISBN13: 978-0-19-540535-4. Dewey:811/.54. LCCN:87-210302.
Audience: **g,l,u,f.**

Webb, Phyllis **PS3566.L27**
Selected Poems: The Vision Tree. Trade Paper. Talonbooks, Ltd. Vancouver, BC. 1982. 160p. ISBN:0-88922-202-9, ISBN13: 978-0-88922-202-1. Dewey:811/.54. LCCN:83-154809.
Audience: **g,l,u,f.**

Wiebe, Rudy **PS3568.O243**
The Temptations of Big Bear. Mass Market. McClelland & Stewart/Tundra Books. Plattsburgh, NY. 1995. 408p. ISBN:0-7710-3454-7, ISBN13: 978-0-7710-3454-1. Dewey:813/.54.
Audience: **g,l,u,f.**

Wilson, Ethel **PR9199.3.W4984**
The Equations of Love. Mass Market. McClelland & Stewart/Tundra Books. Plattsburgh, NY. 1996. 264p. New Canadian Library ISBN:0-7710-8954-6, ISBN13: 978-0-7710-8954-1. Dewey:813/.52.
Audience: **g,l,u,f.**

Wilson, Ethel **PR6045.1593**
Hetty Dorval. Mass Market. McClelland & Stewart/Tundra Books. Plattsburgh, NY. 1996. 112p. New Canadian Library ISBN:0-7710-8953-8, ISBN13: 978-0-7710-8953-4. Dewey:823.914.
Audience: **g,l,u,f.**

Wilson, Ethel **PR9199.3.W4984**
The Innocent Traveller. Mass Market. McClelland & Stewart/Tundra Books. Plattsburgh, NY. 1996. 245p. New Canadian Library ISBN:0-7710-8955-4, ISBN13: 978-0-7710-8955-8. Dewey:813/.52.
Audience: **g,l,u,f.**

Wilson, Ethel **PR9199.3.W4984**
Swamp Angel. Mass Market. McClelland & Stewart/Tundra Books. Plattsburgh, NY. 1996. 224p. New Canadian Library ISBN:0-7710-8958-9, ISBN13: 978-0-7710-8958-9. Dewey:C813/.54.
Audience: **g,l,u,f.**

Wiseman, Adele **PR9199.3.W54C7 1993**
Crackpot. Trade Cloth. University of Nebraska Press. Lincoln, NE. 1993. 300p. ISBN:0-8032-9753-X, ISBN13: 978-0-8032-9753-1. Dewey:813/.54. LCCN:93-008476.
Audience: **g,l,u,f.**

Wiseman, Adele **PS3568.O243**
The Sacrifice. Trade Cloth. Penguin Group (USA) Inc. New York, NY. 1956. ISBN:0-670-61449-1, ISBN13: 978-0-670-61449-3. Dewey:813/.54.
Audience: **g,l,u,f.**

Australia/New Zealand > Literary History and Criticism

PR9634.3

☐ New Zealand Literature File.
http://www.library.auckland.ac.nz/subjects/nzp/nzlit2/authors.htm
University of Auckland.
Audience: **g,l,u,f.**

PR9634.3

☐ New Zealand Writer Files.
http://www.bookcouncil.org.nz/writers/index.html
New Zealand Book Council.
Audience: **g,l,u,f.**

AustLit **PR9604.3**
☐ AustLit Online Database : The Resource for Australian Literature.
http://www.austlit.edu.au/
AustLit.
Audience: **g,l,u,f.**

Bennett, Bruce **PR9612.52.B46 2002**
Australian Short Fiction: A History. Eileen Scarff (Editor). Trade Paper. University of Queensland Press. Saint Lucia, QLD. 2002. 400p. UQP Studies in Australian Literature Ser. ISBN:0-7022-3301-3, ISBN13: 978-0-7022-3301-2. Dewey:823/.0109994. LCCN:2003-427378.
Audience: **u,f.**

Bennett, Bruce & Strauss, Jennifer (Editors) **PR9604.3.O93 1998**
The Oxford Literary History of Australia. Trade Cloth. Oxford University Press, Inc. New York, NY. 1999. 496p. ISBN:0-19-553737-8, ISBN13: 978-0-19-553737-6. Dewey:820.9/994. LCCN:98-193279.
Audience: **u,f.** *Choice, 1999.*

Blackford, Russell, et al. **PR9612**
Strange Constellations: A History of Australian Science Fiction. Van Ikin & Sean McMullen (Authors). Trade Cloth. Greenwood Publishing Group, Inc. Portsmouth, NH. 1999. 264p. Contributions to the Study of Science Fiction and Fantasy Ser., Vol. 80 ISBN:0-313-25112-6, ISBN13: 978-0-313-25112-2. Dewey:823/.0876209994. LCCN:98-037716.
Audience: **u,f.**

Brooks, David & Walker, Brenda (Editors) **PR9614 .P66 1989**
Poetry and Gender: Statements and Essays on Australian Women Poets. Trade Paper. University of Queensland Press. Saint Lucia, QLD. 1989. 256p. ISBN:0-7022-2240-2, ISBN13: 978-0-7022-2240-5. Dewey:A821.0099287. LCCN:90-109439.
Audience: **u,f.**

Bulman-May, James **PR9624.3**
New Zealand Multicultural Writing. Trade Paper. Aarhus Universitetsforlag. DK-8200 Aarhus N, 2003. 320p. The/Dolphin Ser., No. 34 ISBN:87-7934-008-3, ISBN13: 978-87-7934-008-4. Dewey:820.9993.
Audience: **u,f.**

Clancy, Laurie **PR9612.2.C53 1992**
A Reader's Guide to Australian Fiction. Trade Paper. Oxford University Press, Inc. New York, NY. 1993. 386p. ISBN:0-19-554620-2, ISBN13: 978-0-19-554620-0. Dewey:823. LCCN:93-215654.
Audience: **g,l,u,f.**

Dixon, Robert & Lee, Christopher **PR9604.3.A88 2000**
Authority and Influence: Australian Literary Criticism 1950-2000. Delys Bird (Editor). Trade Paper. University of Queensland Press. Saint Lucia, QLD. 2001. 448p. ISBN:0-7022-3203-3, ISBN13: 978-0-7022-3203-9. Dewey:801/.95/0994. LCCN:2001-430471.
Audience: **u,f.**

Evans, Patrick **PR9624.3 .E94 1990**
Penguin History of NZ Literature. Trade Paper. Penguin Group New Zealand, Ltd. Albany, Auckland, 1990. 288p. ISBN:0-14-011371-1, ISBN13: 978-0-14-011371-6. Dewey:820.9/993. LCCN:91-174802.
Audience: **u,f.**

Ferrier, Carole (Editor) **PR9608 .G46 1986**
Gender, Politics and Fiction: Twentieth Century Australian Women's Novels. Paper Text. University of Queensland Press. Saint Lucia, QLD. 1987. 262p. ISBN:0-7022-2007-8, ISBN13: 978-0-7022-2007-4. Dewey:823. LCCN:85-029543.
Audience: **u,f.** *Choice, 1986.*

Goetzfridt, Nicholas J. **PN849**
Indigenous Literature of Oceania: A Survey of Criticism and Interpretation. Cloth Text. Greenwood Publishing Group, Inc. Portsmouth, NH. 1995. 368p. Bibliographies and Indexes in World Literature Ser., Vol. 47 ISBN:0-313-29173-X, ISBN13: 978-0-313-29173-9. Dewey:809/.899. LCCN:94-037081.
Audience: **u,f.** *Choice, 1995.*

Goldie, Terry **PN3426.I53 G65 1993**
Fear and Temptation: The Image of the Indigene in Canadian, Australian and New Zealand Literatures. Trade Paper. McGill-Queen's University Press. Montreal, PQ. 1993. 288p. ISBN:0-7735-1102-4, ISBN13: 978-0-7735-1102-6. Dewey:820.935203.
Audience: **u,f.**

Goodwin, Kenneth **PR9609.6**
A History of Australian Literature. Trade Paper. Palgrave Macmillan. New York, NY. 1987. 333p. ISBN:0-312-01135-0, ISBN13: 978-0-312-01135-2. Dewey:820/.9/994. LCCN:85-022190.
Audience: **u,f.** *Choice, 1986.*

Haynes, Roslynn D. **GB618.89 .H39 1998**
Seeking the Centre: The Australian Desert in Literature, Art and Film. Cloth Text. Cambridge University Press. New York, NY. 1999. 364p. ISBN:0-521-57111-1, ISBN13: 978-0-521-57111-1. Dewey:551.41/5/0994. LCCN:98-025121.
Audience: **u,f.** *Choice, 1999.*

Healy, J. J. **PR9605.6.A88H4 1989**
Literature and the Aborigine in Australia. Ed. 2. Trade Paper. University of Queensland Press. Saint Lucia, QLD. 1989. 314p. UQP Studies in Australian Literature Ser. ISBN:0-7022-2150-3, ISBN13: 978-0-7022-2150-7. Dewey:820.9/352039915. LCCN:89-162347.
Audience: **u,f.**

Hergenhan, Laurie (Editor) **PR9604.3 .P4 1988**
The Penguin New Literary History of Australia. Trade Paper. Penguin Group Australia. Scoresby, VIC. 1988. 640p. ISBN:0-14-007514-3, ISBN13: 978-0-14-007514-4. Dewey:820.9/994. LCCN:89-140340.
Audience: **u,f.**

Hergenhan, Laurie **PR9612.6.P74H47 1993**
Unnatural Lives: Studies in Australian Convict Fiction. Trade Paper. University of Queensland Press. Saint Lucia, QLD. 1993. 248p. ISBN:0-7022-2258-5, ISBN13: 978-0-7022-2258-0. Dewey:823. LCCN:93-176023.
Audience: **u,f.**

Hodge, Bob & Mishra, Vijay **PR9605.2 .H63 1991**
Dark Side of the Dream: Australian Literature and the Postcolonial Mind. Trade Paper. Allen & Unwin Pty., Ltd. Crows Nest, NSW. 1992. 280p. ISBN:0-04-442346-2, ISBN13: 978-0-04-442346-1. Dewey:820.9/994. LCCN:92-178851.
Audience: **u,f.** *Choice, 1992.*

Jones, Lawrence **PR9632.5**
Barbed Wire and Mirrors: Essays on New Zealand Prose. Ed. 2. Trade Paper. Otago University Press. Dunedin, 1990. 392p. ISBN:0-908569-53-X, ISBN13: 978-0-908569-53-3. Dewey:823.
Audience: **u,f.**

Knight, Stephen **PR9612.6.D48K58 1997**
Continent of Mystery: A Thematic History of Australian Crime Fiction. Trade Paper. Melbourne University Publishing. Carlton, VIC. 1997. 236p. ISBN:0-522-84659-9, ISBN13: 978-0-522-84659-1. Dewey:823/.087209994. LCCN:98-170612.
Audience: **u,f.**

Lees, Stella **PR9613.9.L44 1993**
The Oxford Companion to Australian Children's Literature. Trade Cloth. Oxford University Press, Inc. New York, NY. 1993. vii, 485p. ISBN:0-19-553592-8, ISBN13: 978-0-19-553592-1. Dewey:820.9/9282/0994. LCCN:93-197195.
Audience: **g,l,u,f.** *Choice, 1994.*

Lever, Richard, et al. **Z4021.L48 1996**
Post-Colonial Literatures in English: Australia, 1970-1992. James Wieland & Scott Findlay (Authors). Trade Cloth. Thomson Gale. Farmington Hills, MI. 1996. 361p. Reference Publication in Literature Ser. ISBN:0-8161-7375-3, ISBN13: 978-0-8161-7375-4. Dewey:016.8209/994. LCCN:95-044820.
Audience: **u,f.** *Choice, 1997.*

Lucas, Rosemary & McCredden, Lyn **PR9608.L83 1996**
Bridgings: Readings in Australian Women's Poetry. Trade Paper. Oxford University Press, Inc. New York, NY. 1997. 240p. ISBN:0-19-553595-2, ISBN13: 978-0-19-553595-2. Dewey:821. LCCN:96-218824.
Audience: **u,f.** *Choice, 1997.*

McAuley, James (Editor) **PR9615.7**
A Map of Australian Verse: The Twentieth Century. Trade Paper. Oxford University Press, Inc. New York, NY. 1977. 352p. ISBN:0-19-550474-7, ISBN13: 978-0-19-550474-3. Dewey:821.
Audience: **u,f.**

Milne, Geoffrey **PN3014**
Theatre Australia (Un)limited: Australian Theatre since the 1950s. Trade Paper. Rodopi. Kenilworth, NY. 2004. 444p. Australian Playwrights, Vol. 10:A Series of Monographs and Video Programmes ISBN:90-420-0930-6, ISBN13: 978-90-420-0930-1. Dewey:792.0994.
Audience: **u,f.**

Murray, Stuart (Contribution by) **PR9629.6.M87 1998**
Never a Soul at Home: New Zealand Literary Nationalism and the 1930's. Trade Cloth. Victoria University Press. Wellington, 1998. 300p. ISBN:0-86473-341-0, ISBN13: 978-0-86473-341-2. Dewey:820.9/993/0904. LCCN:99-194246.
Audience: **u,f.** *Choice, 1999.*

Ojinmah, Umelo **PR9639.3.I5Z8 1993**
Witi Ihimaera: A Changing Vision. Trade Paper. Otago University Press. Dunedin, 1996. 146p. ISBN:0-908569-57-2, ISBN13: 978-0-908569-57-1. Dewey:823. LCCN:93-130290.
Audience: **u,f.**

Parsons, Philip & Chance, Victoria (Editors) **PN3011**
Companion to Theatre in Australia. Trade Cloth. Currency Press. Strawberry Hills, NSW. 1995. 704p. ISBN:0-86819-357-7, ISBN13: 978-0-86819-357-1. Dewey:792.0994. LCCN:95-119287.
Audience: **g,l,u,f.**

Robinson, Roger & Wattie, Nelson (Editors) **PR9620.2.O88 1998**
The Oxford Companion to New Zealand Literature. Trade Cloth. Oxford University Press, Inc. New York, NY. 1999. 624p. ISBN:0-19-558348-5, ISBN13: 978-0-19-558348-9. Dewey:820.9/993/03. LCCN:99-200843.
Audience: **g,l,u,f.** *Choice, 1999.*

Schafer, William J. **PR9624.3.S33 1998**
Mapping the Godzone: A Primer on New Zealand Literature and Culture. Trade Paper. University of Hawaii Press. Honolulu, HI. 1998. 216p. Latitude 20 Book Ser. ISBN:0-8248-2016-9, ISBN13: 978-0-8248-2016-9. Dewey:820.9/993. LCCN:98-010181.
Audience: **g,l,u,f.** *Choice, 1999.*

Schurmann-Zeggel, Heinz **Z4023.5.A87S38 2000**
Black Australian Literature: A Bibliography of Fiction, Poetry, Drama, Oral Traditions and Non-Fiction, Including Critical Commentary, 1900-1991. Trade Paper. Peter Lang Publishing, Inc. New York, NY. 2000. 322p. German-Australian Studies, Vol. 11 ISBN:0-8204-5057-X, ISBN13: 978-0-8204-5057-5. Dewey:016.8208/089915. LCCN:00-026882.
Audience: **u,f.**

Sheridan, Susan **PR9608.2.A96S47 1995**
Along the Faultlines: Sex, Race and Nation in Australian Women's Writing. Trade Paper. Allen & Unwin Pty., Ltd. Crows Nest, NSW. 1996. 208p. ISBN:1-86373-867-3, ISBN13: 978-1-86373-867-5. Dewey:820.9/9287/0994. LCCN:95-196032.
Audience: **u,f.**

Shoemaker, Adam **PR9608.2.A96S48 2004**
Black Words White Page: Aboriginal Literature 1929-1988. Trade Paper. BPR Publishers. New Providence, NJ. 2004. 326p. ISBN:0-9751229-5-9, ISBN13: 978-0-9751229-5-2. Dewey:820.989915. LCCN:2005-415510.
Audience: **u,f.**

Spender, Dale **PR9608.S64 1988**
Writing a New World: Two Centuries of Australian Women Writers. Trade Paper. Pandora Press. London, 1988. 332p. ISBN:0-86358-172-2, ISBN13: 978-0-86358-172-4. Dewey:820.9/9287. LCCN:90-148253.
Audience: **u,f.**

Sturm, Terry (Editor) **PR9624.3 .O94 1991**
The Oxford History of New Zealand Literature. Cloth Text. Oxford University Press, Inc. New York, NY. 1991. 768p. ISBN:0-19-558211-X, ISBN13: 978-0-19-558211-6. Dewey:820.9/993. LCCN:91-171488.
Audience: **u,f.** *Choice, 1992.*

Taylor, Andrew **PR9610.T38 1987**
Reading Australian Poetry. Trade Paper. University of Queensland Press. Saint Lucia, QLD. 1988. 218p. ISBN:0-7022-2062-0, ISBN13: 978-0-7022-2062-3. Dewey:821. LCCN:86-027246.
Audience: **l,u,f.**

Webby, Elizabeth (Editor) **PR9604.3 .C36 2000**
The Cambridge Companion to Australian Literature. Cloth Text. Cambridge University Press. New York, NY. 2000. 348p. Cambridge Companions to Literature Ser. ISBN:0-521-65122-0, ISBN13: 978-0-521-65122-6. Dewey:820.9/994. LCCN:00-031234.
Audience: **u,f.**

Wilde, William H. **PR9600.2 .W55 1985**
Oxford Companion to Australian Literature. Trade Cloth. Oxford University Press, Inc. New York, NY. 1986. 760p. ISBN:0-19-554233-9, ISBN13: 978-0-19-554233-2. Dewey:820/.9/944. LCCN:86-146201.
Audience: **g,l,u,f.** *Choice, 1986.*

Wilding, Michael **PR9612.2 .W45 1997**
Studies in Classic Australian Fiction. Trade Paper. Sydney Studies. Leichhardt, NSW. 1997. 231p. ISBN:0-949405-13-2, ISBN13: 978-0-949405-13-5. Dewey:823.009/994. LCCN:2001-430936.
Audience: **u,f.**

Williams, Mark **Z3008.L58W55 1996**
Post-Colonial Literatures in English: Southeast Asia, New Zealand, and the Pacific, 1970-1992. Trade Cloth. Thomson Gale. Farmington Hills, MI. 1996. 370p. Reference Publication in Literature Ser. ISBN:0-8161-7353-2, ISBN13: 978-0-8161-7353-2. Dewey:016.895. LCCN:95-044859.
Audience: **u,f.** *Choice, 1997.*

Williams, Mark & Leggott, Michele (Editors) **PR9629.6.O64 1995**
Opening the Book: New Essays on New Zealand Writing. Trade Paper. Auckland University Press. Auckland, 1995. 336p. ISBN:1-86940-115-8, ISBN13: 978-1-86940-115-3. Dewey:820.9/993. LCCN:95-180524.
Audience: **u,f.**

Australia/New Zealand > Collections

PR9604.3
☐ Australian Literary and Historical Texts.
http://setis.library.usyd.edu.au/oztexts/ozlit.html
University of Sidney.
Audience: **g,l,u,f.**

PR9634.8
☐ Early New Zealand Books.
http://www.enzb.auckland.ac.nz/
University of Auckland.
Audience: **g,l,u,f.**

☐ New Zealand Electronic Text Centre.
http://www.nzetc.org/
Victoria University of Wellington.
Audience: **g,l,u,f.**

PR9604.3
☐ Project Gutenberg of Australia.
http://www.gutenberg.net.au/pgaus.html
Project Gutenberg.
Audience: **g,l,u,f.**

Ackland, Michael **PR9614.8.P46 1993**
Penguin Book of 19th Century Australian Literature. Trade Paper. Penguin Group Australia. Scoresby, VIC. 1993. 400p. ISBN:0-14-015703-4, ISBN13: 978-0-14-015703-1. Dewey:820.9/994/09034. LCCN:93-178995.
Audience: **g,l,u,f.**

Bennett, Warwick & Hudson, Patrick L. (Editors) **PR9637.35.S33R88**
Rutherford's Dreams: A New Zealand Science Fiction Collection. Trade Paper. IPL Books. Wellington, 240p. ISBN:0-908876-87-4, ISBN13: 978-0-908876-87-7. Dewey:823/.08762089993. LCCN:95-189482.
Audience: **g,l,u,f.**

Bornholdt, Jenny (Editor), et al. **PR9635.25 .A58 1997**
An Anthology of New Zealand Poetry in English. Gregory O'Brien & Mark Williams (Editors). Trade Paper. Oxford University Press, Inc. New York, NY. 1998. 584p. ISBN:0-19-558355-8, ISBN13: 978-0-19-558355-7. Dewey:821.008/0993. LCCN:97-131546.
Audience: **g,l,u,f.** *Choice, 1998.*

Dessaix, Robert (Editor) **PR9614.5.G38**
Australian Gay and Lesbian Writing: An Anthology. Trade Paper. Oxford University Press, Inc. New York, NY. 1995. 392p. ISBN:0-19-553686-X, ISBN13: 978-0-19-553686-7. Dewey:820.8/092/0664.
Audience: **g,l,u,f.**

Gilbert, Kevin (Editor) **PR9608.2.A96I57 1988**
Inside Black Australia: An Anthology of Aboriginal Poetry. Trade Paper. Penguin Group (USA) Inc. New York, NY. 1989. 240p. ISBN:0-14-011126-3, ISBN13: 978-0-14-011126-2. Dewey:821. LCCN:88-212000.
Audience: **g,l,u,f.**

Hergenhan, Laurie (Author, Editor) **PR9617.32**
The Australian Short Story. Trade Paper. University of Queensland Press. Saint Lucia, QLD. 2002. 304p. ISBN:0-7022-3290-4, ISBN13: 978-0-7022-3290-9. Dewey:823/.0108994.
Audience: **g,l,u,f.**

Kramer, Leonie & Mitchell, Adrian (Editors) **PR9614.4.O85 1985**
The Oxford Anthology of Australian Literature. Trade Cloth. Oxford University Press, Inc. New York, NY. 1985. 589p. ISBN:0-19-554477-3, ISBN13: 978-0-19-554477-0. Dewey:820/.8/0994. LCCN:85-228185.
Audience: **g,l,u,f.**

Leggott, Michele and Brian Flaherty **PR9645.23**
New Zealand Electronic Poetry Centre. http://www.nzepc.auckland.ac.nz/ University of Auckland.
Audience: **g,l,u,f.**

Lever, Susan **PR9615.3.O94 1995**
The Oxford Book of Australian Women's Verse. Trade Paper. Oxford University Press, Inc. New York, NY. 1996. 280p. ISBN:0-19-553505-7, ISBN13: 978-0-19-553505-1. Dewey:821/.008/09287. LCCN:96-102276.
Audience: **g,l,u,f.**

Murray, Les A. **PR9615.25.N49 1996**
The New Oxford Book of Australian Verse. Ed. 3. Cloth Text. Oxford University Press, Inc. New York, NY. 1996. 464p. ISBN:0-19-553994-X, ISBN13: 978-0-19-553994-3. Dewey:821/.008. LCCN:97-109053.
Audience: **g,l,u,f.** *Choice, 1986.*

O'Sullivan, Vincent (Editor) **PR9634 .A58 1987**
An Anthology of Twentieth Century New Zealand Poetry. Ed. 3. Trade Paper. Oxford University Press, Inc. New York, NY. 1987. 460p. ISBN:0-19-558163-6, ISBN13: 978-0-19-558163-8. Dewey:821. LCCN:88-102358.
Audience: **g,l,u,f.**

O'Sullivan, Vincent (Selected by) **PR9637.32.O94 1994**
The Oxford Book of New Zealand Short Stories. Trade Paper. Oxford University Press, Inc. New York, NY. 1994. 464p. ISBN:0-19-558291-8, ISBN13: 978-0-19-558291-8. Dewey:823/.01/08/993. LCCN:94-148963.
Audience: **g,l,u,f.**

Sabbioni, Jennifer (Editor), et al. **PR9614.5.A94I53 1998**
Indigenous Australian Voices: A Reader. Kay Schaffer & Sidonie Smith (Editors). Trade Cloth. Rutgers University Press. Piscataway, NJ. 1998. lviii, 310p. ISBN:0-8135-2491-1, ISBN13: 978-0-8135-2491-7. Dewey:820.8/089915. LCCN:97-030812.
Audience: **g,l,u,f.** *Choice, 1999.*

Salusineszky, Imre (Editor) **PR9617.7 .O94 1997**
The Oxford Book of Australian Essays. Cloth Text. Oxford University Press, Inc. New York, NY. 1998. 304p. Oxford Books of Prose ISBN:0-19-553739-4, ISBN13: 978-0-19-553739-0. Dewey:824. LCCN:98-108128.
Audience: **g,l,u,f.** *Choice, 1998.*

Tranter, John **PR9615.7 .P44 1991**
The Penguin Book of Modern Australian Poetry. Philip Mead (Editor). Trade Paper. Penguin Books Canada, Ltd. Toronto, ON. 1991. 512p. ISBN:0-14-058649-0, ISBN13: 978-0-14-058649-7. Dewey:821. LCCN:92-179408.
Audience: **g,l,u,f.**

Tranter, John & Mead, Philip (Editors) **PR9615.7.P44 1994**
The Bloodaxe Book of Modern Australian Poetry. Trade Paper. Bloodaxe Books. Bala, 1995. 474p. ISBN:1-85224-315-5, ISBN13: 978-1-85224-315-9. Dewey:821. LCCN:95-183398.
Audience: **g,l,u,f.**

Wedde, Ian & McQueen, Harvey (Editors) **PR9635.25.P4 1986**
The Penguin Book of New Zealand Verse. Trade Paper. Penguin Group (USA) Inc. New York, NY. 1986. 575p. Penguin Poetry Ser. ISBN:0-14-042333-8, ISBN13: 978-0-14-042333-4. Dewey:821/.008/09931. LCCN:86-160779.
Audience: **g,l,u,f.**

Wilding, Michael (Editor) **PR9617.32.O94 1994**
The Oxford Book of Australian Short Stories. Trade Cloth. Oxford University Press, Inc. New York, NY. 1995. 368p. ISBN:0-19-553610-X, ISBN13: 978-0-19-553610-2. Dewey:823/.0108994. LCCN:94-235754.
Audience: **g,l,u,f.**

Williamson, David (Editor), et al. **PR9611.5**
Contemporary Australian Plays. Hannie Rayson, Keith Robinson, Tony Taylor, Wesley Enoch, Deborah Mailman & Russell Vanderbroucke (Editors). Trade Paper. Methuen Publishing Ltd. London, 2004. ISBN:0-413-76760-4, ISBN13: 978-0-413-76760-8. Dewey:822.
Audience: **g,l,u,f.**

Australia/New Zealand > Individual Authors > A

Ackland, Michael **PR9610.4.A28 1994**
That Shining Band. Trade Paper. University of Queensland Press. Saint Lucia, QLD. 243p. ISBN:0-7022-2686-6, ISBN13: 978-0-7022-2686-1. Dewey:821. LCCN:94-204426.
Audience: **u,f.**

Ashton-Warner, Sylvia **PR9639.3.A8Z/**
I Passed This Way. Trade Cloth. Little, Brown Book Group Ltd. London, 1980. ix, 499p. ISBN:0-86068-160-2, ISBN13: 978-0-86068-160-1. Dewey:823.
Audience: **g,l,u,f.**

Ashton-Warner, Sylvia **PR9639.3.A8S65**
Spinster, a Novel. Paper Text. Textbook Publishers. Temecula, CA. 2003. 242p. ISBN:0-7581-3833-4, ISBN13: 978-0-7581-3833-0. Dewey:823.
Audience: **g,l,u,f.**

Astley, Thea **PR9619.3.A75**
It's Raining in Mango. Trade Cloth. Penguin Group Australia. Scoresby, VIC. 1988. 208p. ISBN:0-670-82065-2, ISBN13: 978-0-670-82065-8. Dewey:823.
Audience: **g,l,u,f.**

Astley, Thea **PR9619.3.A75**
Vanishing Points. Trade Cloth. Random House Australia. Scoresby, VIC. 1992. 242p. ISBN:0-85561-478-1, ISBN13: 978-0-85561-478-2. Dewey:823.
Audience: **g,l,u,f.**

Astley, Thea **PR9619.3.A75**
The Slow Natives. Trade Paper. Penguin Group Australia. Scoresby, VIC. 1999. 224p. ISBN:0-14-013411-5, ISBN13: 978-0-14-013411-7. Dewey:A823.3.
Audience: **g,l,u,f.**

Australia/New Zealand > Individual Authors > B

Baxter, James K. **PR9639.3.B3A17 2004**
The Collected Poems of James K. Baxter. John E. Weir & John Weir (Editors). Trade Cloth. Oxford University Press, Inc. New York, NY. 2004. 688p. ISBN:0-19-558489-9, ISBN13: 978-0-19-558489-9. Dewey:821/.914. LCCN:2004-401784.
Audience: **g,l,u,f.**

Baynton, Barbara **PR9499.3.N3**
Bush Studies. Trade Paper. Kessinger Publishing, LLC. Whitefish, MT. 2004. ISBN:1-4191-1129-9, ISBN13: 978-1-4191-1129-7. Dewey:823.
Audience: **g,l,u,f.**

Bethell, Ursula & O'Sullivan, Vincent **PR9639.3.B43A17 1997**
Collected Poems. Trade Cloth. Victoria University Press. Wellington, 1997. xxiii, 112p. ISBN:0-86473-307-0, ISBN13: 978-0-86473-307-8. Dewey:821. LCCN:98-155702.
Audience: **g,l,u,f.**

Boyd, Martin **PR9619.3.B63L8 1985**
Lucinda Brayford. Dorothy Green (Introduction by). Trade Paper. Penguin Group (USA) Inc. New York, NY. 1985. 552p. Fiction Ser. ISBN:0-14-007231-4, ISBN13: 978-0-14-007231-0. Dewey:823/.912. LCCN:85-179109.
Audience: **g,l,u,f.**

Brasch, Charles **PR9639.3.B67A17 1984**
Charles Brasch Collected Poems. Alan Roddick (Editor). Trade Paper. Oxford University Press, Inc. New York, NY. 1984. xiv, 256p. ISBN:0-19-558105-9, ISBN13: 978-0-19-558105-8. Dewey:821. LCCN:84-199930.
Audience: **g,l,u,f.** B

Australia/New Zealand > Individual Authors > C

Carey, Peter **PR9619.3.C36I45 1996**
Illywhacker. Trade Paper. Knopf Publishing Group. New York, NY. 1996. 608p. ISBN:0-679-76790-8, ISBN13: 978-0-679-76790-9. Dewey:823.3. LCCN:95-043450.
Audience: **g,l,u,f.**

Carey, Peter **PR9619.3.C36O73 1997**
Oscar and Lucinda. Trade Paper. Knopf Publishing Group. New York, NY. 1997. 448p. ISBN:0-679-77750-4, ISBN13: 978-0-679-77750-2. Dewey:823.3. LCCN:97-006669.
Audience: **g,l,u,f.** *Choice, 1988.*

Carey, Peter **PR9619.3.C36 T7**
True History of the Kelly Gang: A Novel. Trade Paper. Knopf Publishing Group. New York, NY. 2001. 384p. ISBN:0-375-72467-2, ISBN13: 978-0-375-72467-1. Dewey:823.
Audience: **g,l,u,f.**

Cross, Ian **PR6939.3**
The God Boy. Trade Paper. Penguin Books, Ltd. London, 2004. 192p. ISBN:0-14-118744-1, ISBN13: 978-0-14-118744-0. Dewey:823/.9/1.
Audience: **g,l,u,f.**

Curnow, Allen **PR9615.7**
Early Days Yet: New and Collected Peoms 1941-1997. Trade Paper. Carcanet Press, Ltd. Manchester, 1997. 320p. ISBN:1-85754-297-5, ISBN13: 978-1-85754-297-4. Dewey:821.
Audience: **g,l,u,f.**

Australia/New Zealand > Individual Authors > D

Dark, Eleanor **PR6019.O9**
The Timeless Land. Trade Paper. HarperCollins Publishers Australia. Pymble, NSW. 1982. 447p. ISBN:0-207-14266-1, ISBN13: 978-0-207-14266-6. Dewey:823/.9/1.
Audience: **g,l,u,f.**

Duff, Alan **PR9639.3.D792O5 1995**
Once Were Warriors. Trade Paper. Knopf Publishing Group. New York, NY. 1995. 208p. ISBN:0-679-76181-0, ISBN13: 978-0-679-76181-5. Dewey:823. LCCN:93-043507.
Audience: **g,l,u,f.**

Duff, Alan **PR9639.3.D792**
What Becomes of the Broken Hearted. Trade Paper. Random House Australia. Scoresby, VIC. 1998. ISBN:0-09-183421-X, ISBN13: 978-0-09-183421-0. Dewey:NZ823.2.
Audience: **g,l,u,f.**

Duff, Alan **PR9639.3.D792O53**
One Night Out Stealing. Trade Paper. University of Hawaii Press. Honolulu, HI. 1995. 192p. Talanoa Ser. ISBN:0-8248-1684-6, ISBN13: 978-0-8248-1684-1. Dewey:823. LCCN:95-013244.
Audience: **g,l,u,f.**

Australia/New Zealand > Individual Authors > F

Fitzgerald, Robert D. **PR9619.3.F48A6 1987**
Robert D. Fitzgerald. Julian Croft (Editor). Paper Text. University of Queensland Press. Saint Lucia, QLD. 1987. 239p. UQP Australian Authors Ser. ISBN:0-7022-1917-7, ISBN13: 978-0-7022-1917-7. Dewey:821. LCCN:85-032300.
Audience: **l,u,f.**

Flanagan, Richard **PR9619.3.F525G68**
Gould's Book of Fish: A Novel in Twelve Fish. Trade Cloth. Grove/Atlantic, Inc. New York, NY. 2002. 416p. ISBN:0-8021-1711-2, ISBN13: 978-0-8021-1711-3. Dewey:823.9/14. LCCN:2001-055747.
Audience: **g,l,u,f.**

Flanagan, Richard **PR619.3.F525**
Death of a River Guide. Trade Paper. Atlantic Books, Ltd. London, 2004. 336p. ISBN:1-84354-219-6, ISBN13: 978-1-84354-219-3. Dewey:823.914.
Audience: **g,l,u,f.**

Flanagan, Richard **PR9619.3.F525S68**
The Sound of One Hand Clapping. Trade Paper. Grove/Atlantic, Inc. New York, NY. 2001. 432p. ISBN:0-8021-3784-9, ISBN13: 978-0-8021-3784-5. Dewey:823.3.
Audience: **g,l,u,f.**

Franklin, Miles **PR9619.3.F68M9**
My Brilliant Career. Trade Paper. Kessinger Publishing, LLC. Whitefish, MT. 2004. ISBN:1-4191-3596-1, ISBN13: 978-1-4191-3596-5. Dewey:823.
Audience: **g,l,u,f.**

Furphy, Joseph **DU105**
e Such Is Life: Being Certain Extracts from the Diary of Tom Collins. E-Book. Kessinger Publishing, LLC. Whitefish, MT. 2004. ISBN:1-4192-4991-6, ISBN13: 978-1-4192-4991-4. Dewey:919.4.
Audience: **g,l,u,f.** E

Roe, Jill & Bettison, Margaret **PR9619.3.F68A6 2001**
A Gregarious Culture: Topical Writings of Miles Franklin. Trade Paper. University of Queensland Press. Saint Lucia, QLD. 2001. 251p. UQP Australian Authors Ser. ISBN:0-7022-3237-8, ISBN13: 978-0-7022-3237-4. Dewey:824/.912. LCCN:2001-431761.
Audience: **g,l,u,f.**

Australia/New Zealand > Individual Authors > Frame, Janet

Frame, Janet **PR9639.3.F7C3**
The Carpathians. Trade Paper. George Braziller Inc. New York, NY. 1993. ISBN:0-8076-1298-7, ISBN13: 978-0-8076-1298-9. Dewey:823. LCCN:92-035601.
Audience: **g,l,u,f.**

Frame, Janet **PR9499.3.N3**
The Edge of the Alphabet. Trade Paper. George Braziller Inc. New York, NY. 1991. 303p. ISBN:0-8076-1270-7, ISBN13: 978-0-8076-1270-5. Dewey:823. LCCN:62-016268.
Audience: **g,l,u,f.**

Frame, Janet **PR9639.3.F7 F3 1982**
Faces in the Water. Trade Paper. George Braziller Inc. New York, NY. 1982. 256p. ISBN:0-8076-0957-9, ISBN13: 978-0-8076-0957-6. Dewey:823. LCCN:79-025441.
Audience: **g,l,u,f.** E

Frame, Janet **PN6056.R26**
Intensive Care. Trade Paper. George Braziller Inc. New York, NY. 1994. 352p. ISBN:0-8076-1341-X, ISBN13: 978-0-8076-1341-2. Dewey:823.
Audience: **g,l,u,f.** E

Frame, Janet **PR9639.3.F7 O94 1982**
Owls Do Cry. Trade Paper. George Braziller Inc. New York, NY. 1982. 211p. ISBN:0-8076-0956-0, ISBN13: 978-0-8076-0956-9. Dewey:823. LCCN:79-028167.
Audience: **g,l,u,f.** E

Frame, Janet **PR9639.3.F7 A6**
The Pocket Mirror. Trade Paper. George Braziller Inc. New York, NY. 1991. 121p. ISBN:0-8076-1272-3, ISBN13: 978-0-8076-1272-9. Dewey:NZ823.2. LCCN:67-018210.
Audience: **g,l,u,f.**

Frame, Janet **PR9639.3.F7**
The Reservoir: Stories and Sketches. Trade Paper. George Braziller Inc. New York, NY. 1993. 182p. ISBN:0-8076-1305-3, ISBN13: 978-0-8076-1305-4. Dewey:Fic.
Audience: **g,l,u,f.**

Frame, Janet **PR9639.3.F7**
Scented Gardens for the Blind. Trade Paper. George Braziller Inc. New York, NY. 1980. 252p. ISBN:0-8076-0985-4, ISBN13: 978-0-8076-0985-9. Dewey:823. LCCN:64-010786.
Audience: **g,l,u,f.**

Frame, Janet **PR9639.3.F7**
The Envoy from Mirror City: An Autobiography. Trade Paper. Random House New Zealand. Glenfield, Auckland, 1991. 152p. ISBN:1-86941-131-5, ISBN13: 978-1-86941-131-2. Dewey:823.
Audience: **g,l,u,f.** E

Frame, Janet **PR9639.3.F7**
An Angel at My Table: The Complete Autobiography. Book, Other. Women's Press, Limited, The. London, 2002. 434p. ISBN:0-7043-4693-1, ISBN13: 978-0-7043-4693-2. Dewey:823.
Audience: **g,l,u,f.**

Frame, Janet **PR9639.3.F7.Z4**
To the Is-Land: An Autobiography, Vol. 1. Trade Cloth. George Braziller Inc. New York, NY. 1982. 253p. ISBN:0-8076-1042-9, ISBN13: 978-0-8076-1042-8. Dewey:823. LCCN:82-001350.
Audience: **g,l,u,f.** E

Mercer, Gina **PR9639.3.F7**
Janet Frame: Subversive Fictions. Trade Paper. Otago University Press. Dunedin, 2000. 304p. ISBN:0-908569-82-3, ISBN13: 978-0-908569-82-3. Dewey:823.
Audience: **u,f.**

Panny, Judith Dell **PR9639.3.F7 Z83 1993**
I Have What I Gave: The Fiction of Janet Frame. Trade Paper. George Braziller Inc. New York, NY. 1993. 194p. ISBN:0-8076-1309-6, ISBN13: 978-0-8076-1309-2. Dewey:823. LCCN:93-016386.
Audience: **u,f.**

Australia/New Zealand > Individual Authors > G

Gee, Maurice **PR9639.3.G4**
Plumb. Ed. 4. Trade Paper. Penguin Books Canada, Ltd. Toronto, ON. 2000. 264p. ISBN:0-14-029562-3, ISBN13: 978-0-14-029562-7. Dewey:823.
Audience: **g,l,u,f.**

Glover, Denis **PR9639.3.G5A6 1995**
Denis Glover: Selected Poems. Bill Manhire (Editor). Trade Paper. Victoria University Press. Wellington, 1995. 128p. ISBN:0-86473-292-9, ISBN13: 978-0-86473-292-7. Dewey:821. LCCN:96-148986.
Audience: **g,l,u,f.**

Grace, Patricia **PR9639.3.G7P6 1995**
Potiki. Trade Paper. University of Hawaii Press. Honolulu, HI. 1995. 192p. Talanoa Ser. ISBN:0-8248-1706-0, ISBN13: 978-0-8248-1706-0. Dewey:823. LCCN:94-045651.
Audience: **g,l,u,f.**

Grenville, Kate **PR9619.3**
Joan Makes History. Trade Paper. University of Queensland Press. Saint Lucia, QLD. 2002. 288p. ISBN:0-7022-3330-7, ISBN13: 978-0-7022-3330-2. Dewey:823. LCCN:2004-540809.
Audience: **g,l,u,f.**

Grenville, Kate **PR9619.3.G73L5 1994**
Lilian's Story. Trade Paper. Harcourt Trade Publishers. New York, NY. 1994. 240p. Harvest Book Ser. ISBN:0-15-600123-3, ISBN13: 978-0-15-600123-6. Dewey:823.9/14. LCCN:94-027261.
Audience: **g,l,u,f.**

Australia/New Zealand > Individual Authors > H

Handel, Henry **PR2045**
Fortunes of Richard Mahoney. Trade Cloth. Text Publishing Company. Melbourne, VIC. ISBN:1-876485-70-1, ISBN13: 978-1-876485-70-2. Dewey:823.2.
Audience: **g,l,u,f.**

Hulme, Keri **PR9639.3.H75S76 2004**
Stonefish. Trade Paper. BPR Publishers. New Providence, NJ. 2004. 225p. ISBN:1-86969-088-5, ISBN13: 978-1-86969-088-5. Dewey:823.2. LCCN:2005-363392.
Audience: **g,l,u,f.**

Hulme, Keri **PR9639.3.H75S77 1992**
Strands. Oxford University Press, Inc. 1992. ISBN:1-86940-068-2, ISBN13: 978-1-86940-068-2.
Audience: **g,l,u,f.**

Hulme, Keri **PR9639.3.H75T4 1987**
Te Kaihau: The Windeater. Trade Cloth. George Braziller Inc. New York, NY. 1987. ISBN:0-8076-1168-9, ISBN13: 978-0-8076-1168-5. Dewey:823. LCCN:86-031760.
Audience: **g,l,u,f.**

Hulme, Keri (Author, Preface by) **PR9639.3.H75B6 2005**
The Bone People. Trade Cloth. Louisiana State University Press. Baton Rouge, LA. 2005. 472p. ISBN:0-8071-3072-9, ISBN13: 978-0-8071-3072-8. Dewey:823.9/14. LCCN:2005-272650.
Audience: **g,l,u,f.** B *Choice, 1986.*

Hyde, Robin **PR9639.3.H94G6 2001**
The Godwits Fly. Patrick Sandbrook (Editor, Introduction by). Trade Paper. Auckland University Press. Auckland, 2001. 260p. ISBN:1-86940-245-6, ISBN13: 978-1-86940-245-7. Dewey:823/.912. LCCN:2001-326646.
Audience: **g,l,u,f.**

Australia/New Zealand > Individual Authors > I

Ihimaera, Witi **PZ7.I273WH 2003**
The Whale Rider. Cloth over Boards. Harcourt Children's Books. New York, NY. 2003. 152p. ISBN:0-15-205017-5, ISBN13: 978-0-15-205017-7. Dewey:[Fic]. LCCN:2003-003943.
Audience: **g,l,u,f.**

Ihimaera, Witi **PR9639.3.I5**
Nights in the Gardens of Spain. Ed. 3. Trade Paper. Reed Publishing (NZ), Ltd. Auckland, 1995. 304p. ISBN:0-7900-0406-2, ISBN13: 978-0-7900-0406-8. Dewey:823.
Audience: **g,l,u,f.**

Ihimaera, Witi **PR9639.3.I5**
Pounamu Pounamu. Trade Paper. Reed Publishing (NZ), Ltd. Auckland, 2003. 160p. ISBN:1-877348-02-3, ISBN13: 978-1-877348-02-0. Dewey:823.
Audience: **g,l,u,f.**

Ihimaera, Witi **PR9639.3.I5**
The Matriarch. Trade Paper. Reed Publishing (NZ), Ltd. Auckland, 1996. 458p. ISBN:0-7900-0513-1, ISBN13: 978-0-7900-0513-3. Dewey:823.914.
Audience: **g,l,u,f.**

Ihimaera, Witi **PR9639.3.I5W6 2000**
Woman Far Walking. Trade Paper. Huia Publishers. Wellington, 2000. 112p. ISBN:1-877241-51-2, ISBN13: 978-1-877241-51-2. Dewey:822/.914. LCCN:00-691141.
Audience: **g,l,u,f.**

Australia/New Zealand > Individual Authors > K

Keneally, Thomas **PR9619.3.K46F3**
A Family Madness. Trade Paper. Simon & Schuster. New York, NY. 1993. 336p. ISBN:0-671-88512-X, ISBN13: 978-0-671-88512-0. Dewey:823.
Audience: **g,l,u,f.**

Keneally, Thomas **PR9619.3**
Schindler's List. Trade Cloth. Simon & Schuster. New York, NY. 1994. 400p. ISBN:0-671-51688-4, ISBN13: 978-0-671-51688-8. Dewey:823. LCCN:82-010489.
Audience: **g,l,u,f.**

Kidman, Fiona
The Book of Secrets. Pan Macmillan. 1988.
ISBN:0-330-27140-7, ISBN13: 978-0-330-27140-0.
Audience: **g,l,u,f.**

Kinsella, John **PR9619.3.K55**
Peripheral Light: Selected and New Poems. Trade Paper. W. W. Norton & Company, Inc. New York, NY. 2005. 224p. ISBN:0-393-32705-1, ISBN13: 978-0-393-32705-2. Dewey:821/.914.
Audience: **g,l,u,f.**

Koch, C. J. **PR6019.O9**
The Year of Living Dangerously. Trade Paper. Penguin Group (USA) Inc. New York, NY. 1983. 288p. ISBN:0-14-006535-0, ISBN13: 978-0-14-006535-0. Dewey:823/.9/1. LCCN:82-012259.
Audience: **g,l,u,f.**

Australia/New Zealand > Individual Authors > L

Kiernan, Brian (Editor) **PR9691.2.L3**
Henry Lawson. Trade Paper. University of Queensland Press. Saint Lucia, QLD. 1976. 394p. UQP Australian Authors Ser. ISBN:0-7022-1231-8, ISBN13: 978-0-7022-1231-4. Dewey:828.
Audience: **l,u,f.**

Lawson, Henry **MLCS 91/12220 (P)**
Collected Stories of Henry Lawson. Trade Cloth. Penguin Group Australia. Scoresby, VIC. 1987. 856p. ISBN:0-670-90019-2, ISBN13: 978-0-670-90019-0. Dewey:823/.2. LCCN:88-125182.
Audience: **g,l,u,f.**

Lawson, Henry **PR6045.R44 A6 1971**
Collected Verse of Henry Lawson. Colin Roderick (Introduction by, Notes by). Trade Cloth. Angus & Robertson, Ltd. London, 1969. xxxvii, 491p. ISBN:0-207-95090-3, ISBN13: 978-0-207-95090-2. Dewey:821.
Audience: **g,l,u,f.**

Australia/New Zealand > Individual Authors > M

Malouf, David **PR9619.3.M265**
The Great World. Trade Paper. Knopf Publishing Group. New York, NY. 1993. 340p. ISBN:0-679-74836-9, ISBN13: 978-0-679-74836-6. Dewey:823. LCCN:93-015510.
Audience: **g,l,u,f.**

Malouf, David **PR9619.3.M265H3**
Harland's Half Acre. UK-B Format Paperback. Knopf Publishing Group. New York, NY. 1999. 230p. ISBN:0-09-927383-7, ISBN13: 978-0-09-927383-7. Dewey:823.
Audience: **g,l,u,f.** B

Malouf, David **PR9619.3.M265R4**
Remembering Babylon. Trade Paper. Knopf Publishing Group. New York, NY. 1994. 224p. ISBN:0-679-74951-9, ISBN13: 978-0-679-74951-6. Dewey:823.
Audience: **g,l,u,f.**

Malouf, David **PR9499.3.N3**
David Malouf: Johnno, Short Stories, Poems, Essays and Interviews. James Tulip (Editor). Trade Paper. University of Queensland Press. Saint Lucia, QLD. 1991. 364p. ISBN:0-7022-2310-7, ISBN13: 978-0-7022-2310-5. Dewey:823. LCCN:90-203350.
Audience: **g,l,u,f.**

Mander, Jane **PR9639.3.M25**
The Story of a New Zealand River. Trade Paper. Random House New Zealand. Glenfield, Auckland, 1999. ISBN:1-86941-389-X, ISBN13: 978-1-86941-389-7. Dewey:823.
Audience: **g,l,u,f.**

Manning, Frederic **PR6025.A45**
Her Privates We. William Boyd (Introduction by). Trade Paper. Serpent's Tail Ltd. London, 1999. 288p. ISBN:1-85242-717-5, ISBN13: 978-1-85242-717-7. Dewey:823. LCCN:99-063332.
Audience: **g,l,u,f.**

Martin, Catherine **PR9619.2.M385A97**
An Australian Girl. Graham Tulloch (Editor), Amanda Nettlebeck (Introduction by). Trade Paper. Oxford University Press, Inc. New York, NY. 1999. 518p. Oxford World's Classics Ser. ISBN:0-19-283922-5, ISBN13: 978-0-19-283922-0. Dewey:823. LCCN:98-041802.
Audience: **g,l,u,f.**

McCullough, Colleen **PR9619.3.M32T5 1998**
The Thorn Birds. Trade Cloth. Random House Value Publishing. New York, NY. 1998. 704p. Modern Classics Ser. ISBN:0-517-20165-8, ISBN13: 978-0-517-20165-7. Dewey:823/.9/1. LCCN:97-050349.
Audience: **g,l,u,f.**

Mudrooroo **PQ1745.E5L6**
Wild Cat Falling. UK-B Format Paperback. Angus & Robertson, Ltd. London, 2001. 152p. ISBN:0-207-19732-6, ISBN13: 978-0-207-19732-1. Dewey:842.41.
Audience: **g,l,u,f.**

Mulgan, John **PR6025**
Man Alone. Trade Paper. Penguin Books Canada, Ltd. Toronto, ON. 2002. 208p. ISBN:0-14-302001-3, ISBN13: 978-0-14-302001-1. Dewey:821.91.
Audience: **g,l,u,f.**

Australia/New Zealand > Individual Authors > O

O'Sullivan, Vincent
Selected Poems. Oxford University Press. 1992. Oxford Poets Ser. ISBN:0-19-558242-X, ISBN13: 978-0-19-558242-0.
Audience: **g,l,u,f.**

O'Sullivan, Vincent **PR9639.3.O7**
Let the River Stand. Trade Paper. Penguin Books, Ltd. London, 1993. 304p. ISBN:0-14-023217-6, ISBN13: 978-0-14-023217-2. Dewey:823.
Audience: **g,l,u,f.**

O'Sullivan, Vincent **PR9639.3.O7**
Billy. Trade Paper. Victoria University Press. Wellington, 1990. 64p. ISBN:0-86473-205-8, ISBN13: 978-0-86473-205-7. Dewey:823.
Audience: **g,l,u,f.**

Australia/New Zealand > Individual Authors > P-R

Paterson, Andrew Barton 'Banjo' **PR6031.A75 M3**
The Man from Snowy River and Other Verse. Trade Paper. Kessinger Publishing, LLC. Whitefish, MT. 2004. ISBN:1-4191-7146-1, ISBN13: 978-1-4191-7146-8. Dewey:A821/.2.
Audience: **g,l,u,f.**

Pilkington, Doris & Garimara, Nugi **PR9619.3.P535F65**
Follow the Rabbit-Proof Fence. Trade Paper. University of Queensland Press. Saint Lucia, QLD. 1996. 140p. ISBN:0-7022-2709-9, ISBN13: 978-0-7022-2709-7. Dewey:823. LCCN:96-144585.
Audience: **g,l,u,f.**

Porter, Hal **PR9619.3.P56Z477**
The Watcher on the Cast-Iron Balcony. Trade Paper. University of Queensland Press. Saint Lucia, QLD. 1993. 264p. ISBN:0-7022-2558-4, ISBN13: 978-0-7022-2558-1. Dewey:823 B. LCCN:93-169962.
Audience: **g,l,u,f.**

Richardson, Henry Handel **PR9619.3.R5**
The Fortunes of Richard Mahony. Trade Paper. Penguin Group Australia. Scoresby, VIC. 1982. 840p. ISBN:0-14-006139-8, ISBN13: 978-0-14-006139-0. Dewey:823.
Audience: **g,l,u,f.**

Richardson, Henry Handel **PR9619.3.R5A6 1997**
Henry Handel Richardson: The Getting of Wisdom, Stories, Selected Prose and Correspondence. Susan Lever & Catherine Pratt (Editors). Trade Paper. University of Queensland Press. Saint Lucia, QLD. 1997. 268p. ISBN:0-7022-2918-0, ISBN13: 978-0-7022-2918-3. Dewey:823. LCCN:97-169585.
Audience: **g,l,u,f.**

Australia/New Zealand > Individual Authors > S

Sargeson, Frank **PR9639.3.S3**
Stories of Frank Sargeson. Trade Paper. Penguin Books Canada, Ltd. Toronto, ON. 1986. 360p. ISBN:0-14-006068-5, ISBN13: 978-0-14-006068-3. Dewey:823.
Audience: **g,l,u,f.**

Satchell, William **PR9639.3**
Land of the Lost. Trade Paper. Auckland University Press. Auckland, 1972. 222p. ISBN:0-19-647593-7, ISBN13: 978-0-19-647593-6. Dewey:823.912.
Audience: **g,l,u,f.**

Shadbolt, Maurice **PR9639.3.S5**
The New Zealand Wars Trilogy: House of Strife, Monday's Warriors, Season of the Jew. Trade Paper. David Ling Publishing Ltd. Birkenhead, Auckland, 2005. 986p. ISBN:0-908990-99-5, ISBN13: 978-0-908990-99-3. Dewey:823. LCCN:2005-391691.
Audience: **g,l,u,f.**

Slessor, Kenneth **PR9619.3.S534**
Selected Poems. UK-B Format Paperback. HarperCollins Publishers Australia. Pymble, NSW. 1994. 160p. ISBN:0-207-18298-1, ISBN13: 978-0-207-18298-3. Dewey:821.
Audience: **g,l,u,f.**

Australia/New Zealand > Individual Authors > Stead, C. K.

Blake, Ann **PR9619.3.S75Z55 1999**
Christina Stead's Politics of Place. Trade Paper. University of Western Australia Press. Crawley, W.A.. 1999. 182p. ISBN:1-876268-35-2, ISBN13: 978-1-876268-35-0. Dewey:823/.912. LCCN:2001-339495.
Audience: **u,f.**

Brydon, Diana **PR9619.3.S75Z57 1987**
Christina Stead. Trade Cloth. Rowman & Littlefield Publishers, Inc. Lanham, MD. 1987. 176p. Women Writers Ser. ISBN:0-389-20689-X, ISBN13: 978-0-389-20689-7. Dewey:823. LCCN:86-022307.
Audience: **l,u,f.** *Choice, 1987.*

Rowley, Hazel **PR9619.3.S75Z87 1993**
Christina Stead. Trade Cloth. Random House Australia. Scoresby, VIC. 1993. 656p. ISBN:0-85561-384-X, ISBN13: 978-0-85561-384-6. Dewey:823 B. LCCN:93-177831.
Audience: **g,l,u,f.**

Stead, C. K. **PR9629.6.S745 2002**
Kin of Place: Essays on New Zealand Writers. Trade Paper. Auckland University Press. Auckland, 2002. 352p. ISBN:1-86940-272-3, ISBN13: 978-1-86940-272-3. Dewey:820/.9/9931. LCCN:2002-416752.
Audience: **g,l,u,f.**

Stead, C. K. **PR6019.O9**
Miss Herbert. Trade Cloth. Random House, Inc. New York, NY. 1992. 320p. ISBN:0-86068-319-2, ISBN13: 978-0-86068-319-3. Dewey:823/.9/1.
Audience: **g,l,u,f.**

Stead, C. K. **PR9639.3.S7S56 1994**
The Singing Whakapapa. Trade Paper. Penguin Books, Ltd. London, 1994. 312p. ISBN:0-14-023853-0, ISBN13: 978-0-14-023853-2. Dewey:823. LCCN:95-131800.
Audience: **g,l,u,f.**

Stead, C. K. **PR9639.3.S7R43 2004**
The Red Tram. Trade Paper. Auckland University Press. Auckland, 2005. 80p. ISBN:1-86940-330-4, ISBN13: 978-1-86940-330-0. Dewey:821.2. LCCN:2005-391052.
Audience: **g,l,u,f.**

Stead, Christina **PR6019.O9**
For Love Alone. Trade Paper. ETT Imprint. Petersham, NSW. 1999. 256p. ISBN:1-875892-59-1, ISBN13: 978-1-875892-59-4. Dewey:823/.9/1.
Audience: **g,l,u,f.**

Stead, Christina **PR6037.T225 H67**
House of All Nations. Trade Cloth. Holt, Rinehart & Winston. Austin, TX. 1972. viii, 787p. ISBN:0-03-001946-X, ISBN13: 978-0-03-001946-3. Dewey:823/.9/1. LCCN:72-080210.
Audience: **g,l,u,f.** B

Stead, Christina **PR9619.3.S75**
A Little Tea, a Little Chat. Trade Cloth. Random House, Inc. New York, NY. 1987. 288p. ISBN:0-86068-176-9, ISBN13: 978-0-86068-176-2. Dewey:823. LCCN:86-672293.
Audience: **g,l,u,f.** B

Stead, Christina **PR6019.O9**
The Man Who Loved Children. Trade Cloth. Alfred A. Knopf Inc. New York, NY. 1995. 529p. ISBN:0-679-44364-9, ISBN13: 978-0-679-44364-3. Dewey:823/.9/1.
Audience: **g,l,u,f.** B

Stead, Christina **PR9499.3.N3**
The Little Hotel. Paper Text. Richmond. Crows Nest, NSW. 2004. 142p. ISBN:1-920688-13-7, ISBN13: 978-1-920688-13-4. Dewey:823.
Audience: **g,l,u,f.**

Stead, Christina **PR9619.3.S75**
The Salzburg Tales. Trade Paper. ETT Imprint. Petersham, NSW. 2004. 504p. ISBN:0-207-16798-2, ISBN13: 978-0-207-16798-0. Dewey:A823.2.
Audience: **g,l,u,f.** B

Stead, Christina **PR9619.3.S75**
Seven Poor Men of Sydney. Trade Paper. ETT Imprint. Petersham, NSW. 1999. ISBN:1-875892-60-5, ISBN13: 978-1-875892-60-0. Dewey:823.91.
Audience: **g,l,u,f.**

Stead, Christina **PR9619.3.S75O25 1985**
An Ocean of Story. R. G. Geering (Editor, Afterword by). Trade Cloth. Penguin Group (USA) Inc. New York, NY. 1986. 560p. ISBN:0-670-80996-9, ISBN13: 978-0-670-80996-7. Dewey:823. LCCN:86-159098.
Audience: **g,l,u,f.** B

Stead, C.K. **PR6069.T37**
All Visitors Ashore. UK-B Format Paperback. Random House. London, 2002. 160p. ISBN:1-86046-936-1, ISBN13: 978-1-86046-936-7. Dewey:823.
Audience: **g,l,u,f.**

Australia/New Zealand > Individual Authors > T-U

Tuwhare, Hone (Contribution by) **PR9639.3.T8S43 1997**
Shape-Shifter. Trade Cloth. Steele Roberts Publishing Ltd. Wellington, 1997. 120p. ISBN:0-9583712-1-0, ISBN13: 978-0-9583712-1-6. Dewey:821. LCCN:98-174173.
Audience: **g,l,u,f.**

Tuwhare, Hone **PR9639.3.T8A6 1994**
Deep River Talk: Collected Poems. Frank Stewart (Introduction by). Trade Paper. University of Hawaii Press. Honolulu, HI. 1994. 209p. Talano Ser. ISBN:0-8248-1607-2, ISBN13: 978-0-8248-1607-0. Dewey:821. LCCN:93-047103.
Audience: **g,l,u,f.**

Upfield, Arthur **PR9619.3.U6**
Death of a Lake. Trade Paper. Pan Macmillan. London, 1984. 174p. ISBN:0-330-27056-7, ISBN13: 978-0-330-27056-4. Dewey:823.
Audience: **g,l,u,f.**

Australia/New Zealand > Individual Authors > W

Walker, Shirley **PR9612.6.W6 W48 1983**
Who Is She? Trade Paper. University of Queensland Press. Saint Lucia, QLD. 1983. xi, 219p. ISBN:0-7022-1693-3, ISBN13: 978-0-7022-1693-0. Dewey:823. LCCN:82-021794.
Audience: **u,f.**

Warung, Price **PZ3.A852**
Tales of the Early Days. Trade Paper. Sydney University Press. Sydney, NSW. 2004. 114p. ISBN:1-920897-58-5, ISBN13: 978-1-920897-58-1. Dewey:823.6.
Audience: **g,l,u,f.**

Winton, Tim **PR9619.3.W585C58**
Cloudstreet: A Novel. Trade Paper. Simon & Schuster. New York, NY. 2002. 432p. ISBN:0-7432-3441-3, ISBN13: 978-0-7432-3441-2. Dewey:823/.914. LCCN:2002-022376.
Audience: **g,l,u,f.**

Winton, Tim **PR9619.3.W585D57**
Dirt Music: A Novel. Trade Paper. Simon & Schuster. New York, NY. 2003. 416p. ISBN:0-7432-2848-0, ISBN13: 978-0-7432-2848-0. Dewey:823/.914. LCCN:2003-045515.
Audience: **g,l,u,f.**

Wright, Judith **PR9619.3.W7**
Collected Poems. UK-B Format Paperback. HarperCollins Publishers Australia. Pymble, NSW. 1994. 435p. ISBN:0-207-18135-7, ISBN13: 978-0-207-18135-1. Dewey:821.
Audience: **g,l,u,f.**

Australia/New Zealand > Individual Authors > White, Patrick

Marr, David **PR9499.3.N3**
Patrick White: A Life. Trade Paper. Random House Australia. Scoresby, VIC. 1992. 744p. ISBN:0-09-182722-1, ISBN13: 978-0-09-182722-9. Dewey:823 B.
Audience: **g,l,u,f.** *Choice, 1992.*

Smith, Vivian & Hubber, Brian **Z8970.7**
Patrick White: A Bibliography. Trade Cloth. Oak Knoll Press. New Castle, DE. 2004. 348p. ISBN:1-58456-143-2, ISBN13: 978-1-58456-143-9. Dewey:016.8233. LCCN:2005-363405.
Audience: **u,f.**

Tacey, David J. **PR9619.3.W5Z89 1988**
Patrick White: Fiction and the Unconscious. Trade Cloth. Oxford University Press, Inc. New York, NY. 1988. 296p. ISBN:0-19-554867-1, ISBN13: 978-0-19-554867-9. Dewey:823. LCCN:88-150815.
Audience: **u,f.** *Choice, 1989.*

White, Patrick **PR9619.3.W5**
The Cockatoos: Shorter Novels and Stories. Trade Paper. Penguin Group (USA) Inc. New York, NY. 1993. 288p. Penguin Twentieth-Century Classics Ser. ISBN:0-14-018582-8, ISBN13: 978-0-14-018582-9. Dewey:823.
Audience: **g,l,u,f.**

White, Patrick **PR9619.3.W5A19 1994**
Collected Plays, Vol. 2. Trade Paper. Currency Press. Strawberry Hills, NSW. 1994. 248p. Australian Dramatists Ser. ISBN:0-86819-305-4, ISBN13: 978-0-86819-305-2. Dewey:822. LCCN:94-174766.
Audience: **g,l,u,f.**

White, Patrick **PR9619.3.W5S65**
The Solid Mandala. Trade Paper. Penguin Group (USA) Inc. New York, NY. 1983. 320p. ISBN:0-14-002975-3, ISBN13: 978-0-14-002975-8. Dewey:823.
Audience: **g,l,u,f.**

White, Patrick **PR6019.O9**
The Eye of the Storm. UK-Trade Paper. Random House. London, 1996. 608p. ISBN:0-09-932421-0, ISBN13: 978-0-09-932421-8. Dewey:823/.9/1.
Audience: **g,l,u,f.**

White, Patrick **PR9619.3.W5**
Voss. UK-B Format Paperback. Random House. London, 1994. 448p. ISBN:0-09-932471-7, ISBN13: 978-0-09-932471-3. Dewey:823.
Audience: **g,l,u,f.**

White, Patrick **PR9619.3.W5**
The Aunt's Story. UK-B Format Paperback. Random House. London, 1994. 287p. ISBN:0-09-932401-6, ISBN13: 978-0-09-932401-0. Dewey:823.
Audience: **g,l,u,f.**

White, Patrick **PR9619.3.W5**
The Collected Plays, Vol. 1. Trade Paper. Currency Press. Strawberry Hills, NSW. 1985. 364p. ISBN:0-86819-124-8, ISBN13: 978-0-86819-124-9. Dewey:822.
Audience: **g,l,u,f.**

White, Patrick **PR9619.3.W5**
The Tree of Man. UK-B Format Paperback. Random House. London, 1994. 480p. ISBN:0-09-932451-2, ISBN13: 978-0-09-932451-5. Dewey:823.
Audience: **g,l,u,f.** B

White, Patrick **PR9619.3.W5**
The Vivisector. UK-Trade Paper. Random House. London, 1994. 617p. ISBN:0-09-932461-X, ISBN13: 978-0-09-932461-4. Dewey:823.
Audience: **g,l,u,f.**

White, Patrick **PR9619.3.W5**
The Twyborn Affair. Trade Paper. Penguin Group (USA) Inc. New York, NY. 1993. 432p. ISBN:0-14-018606-9, ISBN13: 978-0-14-018606-2. Dewey:823.
Audience: **g,l,u,f.** B

White, Patrick **PR9619.3.W5R533 2002**
Riders in the Chariot. David Malouf (Introduction by). Trade Paper. New York Review of Books, Incorporated, The. New York, NY. 2002. 656p. New York Review Books Classics Ser. ISBN:1-59017-002-4, ISBN13: 978-1-59017-002-1. Dewey:823/.912. LCCN:2002-000742.
Audience: **g,l,u,f.** B

Williams, Mark **PR9619.3.W5**
Patrick White. Trade Cloth. Palgrave Macmillan Ltd. Basingstoke, 1993. 192p. ISBN:0-333-51714-8, ISBN13: 978-0-333-51714-7. Dewey:823.
Audience: **u,f.** *Choice, 1993.*

Africa

Gikandi, Simon (Editor) **PL8010.E63 2002**
Encyclopedia of African Literature. Paper over Boards. Routledge. New York, NY. 2002. 648p. ISBN:0-415-23019-5, ISBN13: 978-0-415-23019-3. Dewey:809/.896/03. LCCN:2002-072757.
Audience: **g,l,u,f.**

Killam, Douglas & Rowe, Ruth (Editors) **PR9340**
The Companion to African Literatures. Trade Cloth. Jo Ann Curry. Seminole, FL. 2001. 336p. ISBN:0-85255-549-0, ISBN13: 978-0-85255-549-1. Dewey:820.9/96/03 B. LCCN:99-030001.
Audience: **g,l.**

Africa > Literary History and Criticism

Attridge, Derek & Jolly, Rosemary (Editors) **PL8014.S6 W75 1998**
Writing South Africa: Literature, Apartheid, and Democracy, 1970-1995. Derek Attridge, Rosemary Jolly, André Brink, Peter Horn, Elleke Boehmer, Graham Pechey & Lewis Nkosi (Contribution by). Trade Cloth. Cambridge University Press. New York, NY. 1998. 306p. ISBN:0-521-59218-6, ISBN13: 978-0-521-59218-5. Dewey:809/.8968. LCCN:97-017217.
Audience: **l,u,f.** *Choice, 1998.*

Banham, Martin, et al. **PN2969.A37 1999**
African Theatre in Development. James Gibbs, Femi Osofisan & Jane Plastow (Authors). Trade Paper. Indiana University Press. Bloomington, IN. 1999. 192p. ISBN:0-253-21341-X, ISBN13: 978-0-253-21341-9. Dewey:792/.096. LCCN:99-029414.
Audience: **g,l,u,f.** *Choice, 2000.*

Barber, Karin (Editor) **PL8010.R43 1997**
Readings in African Popular Culture. Trade Cloth. Indiana University Press. Bloomington, IN. 1997. viii, 184p. ISBN:0-253-33294-X, ISBN13: 978-0-253-33294-3. Dewey:306/.096. LCCN:97-011211.
Audience: **l,u,f.**

Barber, Karin, et al. **PN2979.B37 1997**
West African Popular Theatre. John Collins & Alian Ricard (Authors). Cloth Text. Indiana University Press. Bloomington, IN. 1997. 542p. Drama and Performance Studies ISBN:0-253-33204-4, ISBN13: 978-0-253-33204-2. Dewey:792/.0966. LCCN:96-042321.
Audience: **g,l,u,f.** *Choice, 1998.*

Booker, M. Keith **PR9344.B66 1998**
The African Novel in English: An Introduction. Trade Paper. Greenwood Publishing Group, Inc. Portsmouth, NH. 1998. 240p. Studies in African Literature ISBN:0-325-00030-1, ISBN13: 978-0-325-00030-5. Dewey:823/.009/96. LCCN:97-031166.
Audience: **l,u,f.** *Choice, 1998.*

Conteh-Morgan, John & Olaniyan, Tejumola **PN2969.A34 2004**
e African Drama and Performance. E-Book. Indiana University Press. Bloomington, IN. 2004. 280p. African Expressive Cultures Ser. ISBN:0-253-34439-5, ISBN13: 978-0-253-34439-7. Dewey:791/.096/0904. LCCN:2004-000688.
Audience: **g,l,u,f.**

Fung, Karen **PR9340**
Africa South of the Sahara: African Literature and Writers on the Internet.
http://www-sul.stanford.edu/depts/ssrg/africa/lit.html
Audience: **g,l,u,f.**

Gikandi, Simon **PL8010.6.G55 1987**
Reading the African Novel. Trade Paper. Heinemann. Portsmouth, NH. 1987. 186p. Studies in African Literature ISBN:0-435-08018-0, ISBN13: 978-0-435-08018-1. Dewey:809.3. LCCN:86-14998.
Audience: **u,f.** *Choice, 1988.*

Gover, Daniel (Editor), et al. **PL8010.P584 2000**
The Post-Colonial Condition of African Literature. John Conteh-Morgan & Jane Bryce (Editors). Trade Cloth. Africa World Press. Trenton, NJ. 1999. 149p. Annual Selected Papers of the ALA, Vol. 6 ISBN:0-86543-771-8, ISBN13: 978-0-86543-771-5. Dewey:809/.896. LCCN:99-015295.
Audience: **l,u,f.**

Griffiths, Gareth **PR9340.G75 2000**
African Literatures in English: East and West. Trade Cloth. Longman Publishing Group. White Plains, NY. 2000. 432p. Longman Literature in English Ser. ISBN:0-582-08925-5, ISBN13: 978-0-582-08925-9. Dewey:820.9/96. LCCN:99-053636.
Audience: **l,u,f.**

Hay, Margaret Jean (Editor) **PL8010.6.A34 2000**
African Novels in the Classroom. Library Binding. Lynne Rienner Publishers, Inc. Boulder, CO. 2000. vi, 314p. ISBN:1-55587-853-9, ISBN13: 978-1-55587-853-5. Dewey:809.3/0096. LCCN:00-022780.
Audience: **f.** *Choice, 2001.*

Irele, F. Abiola & Gikandi, Simon **PN841.I74 2003**
The Cambridge History of African and Caribbean Literature, Set. Quantity Pack, Cloth Text. Cambridge University Press. New York, NY. 2004. 954p. ISBN:0-521-59434-0, ISBN13: 978-0-521-59434-9. Dewey:809/.8896. LCCN:2003-046121.
Audience: **l,u,f.** *Choice, 2004.*

Jemi, Onwuchekwa & Madubuike, Ihechukwu **PL8010**
Toward the Decolonization of African Literature: African Fiction and Poetry and Their Critics. Trade Cloth. Kegan Paul International, Ltd. London, 1998. 320p. ISBN:0-7103-0123-5, ISBN13: 978-0-7103-0123-9. Dewey:896.
Audience: **g,l,u,f.**

Landow, George **PR9340**
African Postcolonial Literature.
http://www.postcolonialweb.org/misc/africov.html
Audience: **g,l,u,f.**

Lindfors, Bernth **Z3508.L5L562 1989**
Black African Literature in English, 1982-1986. Library Binding. Hans Zell Publishers. East Grinstead, 1989. 550p. ISBN:0-905450-75-2, ISBN13: 978-0-905450-75-9. Dewey:820.9/896. LCCN:89-007537.
Audience: **l,u,f.**

Lindfors, Bernth **Z3508.L5L563 1995**
Black African Literature in English, 1987-1991. Trade Cloth. Hans Zell Publishers. East Grinstead, 1995. 682p. Bibliographical Research in African Literature Ser., No. 3 ISBN:1-873836-16-3, ISBN13: 978-1-873836-16-3. Dewey:820.9/896. LCCN:97-189537.
Audience: **l,u,f.** *Choice, 1995.*

Lindfors, Bernth **PR9340 .L455 2000**
Black African Literature in English, 1992-1996. Trade Cloth. James Currey Ltd. Oxford, 2000. 704p. ISBN:0-85255-565-2, ISBN13: 978-0-85255-565-1. Dewey:016.8/2/08/0896.
Audience: **l,u,f.** *Choice, 2002.*

Lindfors, Bernth **PR9340 .L56**
Popular Literatures in Africa. Trade Cloth. Africa World Press. Trenton, NJ. 1996. 136p. ISBN:0-86543-220-1, ISBN13: 978-0-86543-220-8. Dewey:820.9.
Audience: **l,u,f.** *Choice, 1991.*

Lindfors, Bernth & Sander, Reinhard W. (Editors) **PR9205.A52T893 1996**
Twentieth-Century Caribbean and Black African Writers. Cloth Text. Thomson Gale. Farmington Hills, MI. 1995. 400p. Dictionary of Literary Biography Ser., Vol. 157 ISBN:0-8103-9352-2, ISBN13: 978-0-8103-9352-3. Dewey:810.9/9729. LCCN:95-032083.
Audience: **l,u,f.** *Choice, 1996.*

Nazareth, Peter **PR9340.5.N3**
An African View of Literature. Trade Paper. Books on Demand. Ann Arbor, MI. 238p. ISBN:0-598-21333-3, ISBN13: 978-0-598-21333-4. Dewey:820/.9/96. LCCN:73-086065.
Audience: **l,u,f.**

Ogunjimi, Bayo & Na'allah, Abdul Rasheed **GR350.O367 2003**
Introduction to African Oral Literature and Performance. Trade Cloth. Africa World Press. Trenton, NJ. 2004. 146p. ISBN:1-59221-150-X, ISBN13: 978-1-59221-150-0. Dewey:398/.096. LCCN:2005-013840.
Audience: **l,u,f.**

Okpewho, Isidore **GR350.O37 1992**
African Oral Literature: Backgrounds, Character and Continuity. Cloth Text. Indiana University Press. Bloomington, IN. 1992. 408p. ISBN:0-253-34167-1, ISBN13: 978-0-253-34167-9. Dewey:398.2/096. LCCN:91-025671.
Audience: **l,u,f.** *Choice, 1993.*

Owomoyela, Oyekan (Editor) **PL8010.H57 1993**
A History of Twentieth-Century African Literatures. Trade Paper. University of Nebraska Press. Lincoln, NE. 1993. 411p. ISBN:0-8032-8604-X, ISBN13: 978-0-8032-8604-7. Dewey:809.8896. LCCN:92-037874.
Audience: **g,l,u,f.** *Choice, 1994.*

Parker, Michael & Starkey, Roger (Editors) **PR9080**
Postcolonial Literatures: Achebe, Ngugi, Desai, Walcott. Trade Cloth. Palgrave Macmillan Ltd. Basingstoke, 1995. ix, 288p. ISBN:0-333-60802-X, ISBN13: 978-0-333-60802-9. Dewey:820.9/9171241.
Audience: **u,f.**

Reboussin, Dan **PR9340**
☐ African Writers: Voices of Change. http://web.uflib.ufl.edu/cm/africana/writers.htm
Audience: **g,l,u,f.**

Scanlon, Paul A. **PR9350.2.S68 2000B**
South African Writers. Cloth Text. Thomson Gale. Farmington Hills, MI. 2000. xx, 526p. Dictionary of Literary Biography Ser., Vol. 225 ISBN:0-7876-3134-5, ISBN13: 978-0-7876-3134-5. Dewey:820.9/968/03 B. LCCN:00-035446.
Audience: **g,l,u,f.**

Wright, Derek **PR9344.W75 1997**
New Directions in African Literature, 1970-1990. Trade Cloth. Thomson Gale. Farmington Hills, MI. 1997. 201p. Twayne's World Authors Ser., Vol. 869 ISBN:0-8057-4556-4, ISBN13: 978-0-8057-4556-6. Dewey:823. LCCN:97-020634.
Audience: **g,l,u,f.**

Africa > Collections

Bruner, Charlotte (Editor) **PR9348.H44 1993**
The Heinemann Book of African Women's Writing. Trade Paper. Heinemann. Portsmouth, NH. 1993. 224p. ISBN:0-435-90673-9, ISBN13: 978-0-435-90673-3. Dewey:820.8/09287/096. LCCN:94-101587.
Audience: **g,l,u,f.** *Choice, 1993.*

Bruner, Charlotte **PR9347.5**
Unwinding Threads: Writing by Women in Africa. Ed. 2. Trade Paper. Heinemann. Portsmouth, NH. 1994. 224p. African Writers Ser. ISBN:0-435-90989-4, ISBN13: 978-0-435-90989-5. Dewey:808.899287.
Audience: **g,l,u,f.**

Courlander, Harold (Editor) **GR350**
A Treasury of African Folklore: The Oral Literature, Traditions, Myths, Legends, Epics, Tales, Recollections, Wisdom, Sayings, and Humor of Africa. Ed. 2. Trade Paper. Avalon Publishing Group. New York, NY. 2001. 640p. ISBN:1-56924-536-3, ISBN13: 978-1-56924-536-1. Dewey:398.2/096.
Audience: **g,l,u,f.**

Graver, David (Editor) **PL8014.S62D73 1999**
Drama for a New South Africa: Seven Plays. Trade Cloth. Indiana University Press. Bloomington, IN. 1999. 240p. Drama and Performance Studies ISBN:0-253-33570-1, ISBN13: 978-0-253-33570-8. Dewey:822. LCCN:99-025444.
Audience: **g,l,u,f.** *Choice, 2000.*

Jeyifo, Biodun **PR9347.M63 2001**
Modern African Drama. Trade Paper. W. W. Norton & Company, Inc. New York, NY. 2002. 608p. A Norton Critical Edition Ser. ISBN:0-393-97529-0, ISBN13: 978-0-393-97529-1. Dewey:822.008/096. LCCN:2001-044667.
Audience: **g,l,u,f.**

Larson, Charles R. (Editor, Introduction by) **PL8011**
Under African Skies: Modern African Stories. Trade Paper. Farrar, Straus & Giroux. New York, NY. 1998. 336p. ISBN:0-374-52550-1, ISBN13: 978-0-374-52550-7. Dewey:808.8/31/0896.
Audience: **g,l,u,f.** *Choice, 1998.*

Ojaide, Tanure & Sallah, Tijan M. (Editors) **PL8013.E5N478**
The New African Poetry: An Anthology. Trade Paper. Lynne Rienner Publishers, Inc. Boulder, CO. 2000. 233p. ISBN:0-89410-891-3, ISBN13: 978-0-89410-891-4. Dewey:896.
Audience: **g,l,u,f.**

Vera, Yvonne **PL8011.O64 1999**
Opening Spaces: An Anthology of Contemporary African Women's Writings. Book, Other. Heinemann. Portsmouth, NH. 1999. 186p. African Writers Ser. ISBN:0-435-91010-8, ISBN13: 978-0-435-91010-5. Dewey:896. LCCN:99-031512.
Audience: **g,l,u,f.** *Choice, 2000.*

Africa > Individual Authors > A

Aidoo, Ama Ata **PR6051.I33**
Dilemma of a Ghost and Anowa. Trade Paper. Longman Publishing. Boston, MA. 1995. 124p. African Writers Ser. ISBN:0-582-27602-0, ISBN13: 978-0-582-27602-4. Dewey:822.
Audience: **g,l,u,f.**

Aidoo, Ama Ata **PR9379.9.A35**
Our Sister Killjoy: Longman African Writers. Trade Paper. Longman Publishing. Boston, MA. 1997. 134p. ISBN:0-582-30845-3, ISBN13: 978-0-582-30845-9. Dewey:823.
Audience: **g,l,u,f.**

Aidoo, Ama Ata **PR9379.9.A35**
Changes: A Love Story. Tuzyline Allan (Afterword by). Trade Cloth. Feminist Press at The City University of New York. New York, NY. 1993. 208p. Women Writing Africa Ser. ISBN:1-55861-064-2, ISBN13: 978-1-55861-064-4. Dewey:823. LCCN:93-029102.
Audience: **g,l,u,f.**

Armah, Ayi Kwei **PZ4.A725 Be3 PR9379.9.A7**
The Beautyful Ones Are Not yet Born. Heinemann. 1969. ISBN:0-435-90625-9, ISBN13: 978-0-435-90625-2.
Audience: **g,l,u,f.**

Armah, Ayi Kwei **PR6051.R55**
The Healers: A Novel. Per Ankh. 2000. ISBN:2-911928-04-0, ISBN13: 978-2-911928-04-8.
Audience: **g,l,u,f.**

Azodo, Ada U. & Wilentz, Gay (Editors) **PR9379.9.A35Z65 1998**
Emerging Perspectives on Ama Ata Aidoo. Trade Cloth. Africa World Press. Trenton, NJ. 1998. 500p. ISBN:0-86543-580-4, ISBN13: 978-0-86543-580-3. Dewey:828. LCCN:98-007823.
Audience: **l,u,f.**

Odamtten, Vincent O. **PR9379.9.A35Z8 1994**
The Art of Ama Ata Aidoo: Polylectics and Reading Against Neocolonialism. Trade Cloth. University Press of Florida. Gainesville, FL. 1994. 216p. ISBN:0-8130-1276-7, ISBN13: 978-0-8130-1276-6. Dewey:828. LCCN:93-035009.
Audience: **l,u,f.** *Choice, 1994.*

Wilson-Tagoe, Nana **PR9379.9.A35 Z8**
Ama Ata Aidoo. Trade Cloth. Northcote House Publishers, Ltd. Tavistock, 2004. ISBN:0-7463-1033-1, ISBN13: 978-0-7463-1033-5. Dewey:828.
Audience: **l,u,f.**

Africa > Individual Authors > Achebe, Chinua

Achebe, Chinua **PR9387.9.A3A17 2004**
Collected Poems. Trade Paper. Knopf Publishing Group. New York, NY. 2004. 96p. ISBN:1-4000-7658-7, ISBN13: 978-1-4000-7658-1. Dewey:821/.914. LCCN:2004-040986.
Audience: **g,l,u,f.**

Achebe, Chinua **PR9387.9.A3Z467 2000**
Home and Exile. Trade Paper. Oxford University Press, Inc. New York, NY. 2000. 127p. ISBN:0-19-513506-7, ISBN13: 978-0-19-513506-0. Dewey:823.9/14. LCCN:99-462124.
Audience: **g,l,u,f.**

Achebe, Chinua **PR9387.9.A3T5 1992**
Things Fall Apart. Anthony Appiah (Introduction by). Trade Cloth. Alfred A. Knopf Inc. New York, NY. 1995. 272p. ISBN:0-679-44623-0, ISBN13: 978-0-679-44623-1. Dewey:823.9/14. LCCN:97-103913.
Audience: **g,l,u,f.**

Booker, M. Keith (Editor) **2003049203**
The Chinua Achebe Encyclopedia. Cloth Text. Greenwood Publishing Group, Inc. Portsmouth, NH. 2003. 344p. ISBN:0-325-07063-6, ISBN13: 978-0-325-07063-6. Dewey:823/.914. LCCN:2003-049203.
Audience: **l,u,f.** *Choice, 2004.*

Emenyonu, Ernest N. & Uko, Iniobong (Editors) **PR9387.9.A3 Z655**
Emerging Perspectives on Chinua Achebe: ISINKA, the Artistic Purpose: Chinua Achebe and the Theory of African Literature, Vol. 2. Trade Cloth. Africa World Press. Trenton, NJ. 2004. 396p. ISBN:0-86543-877-3, ISBN13: 978-0-86543-877-4. Dewey:823.9/14.
Audience: **l,u,f.**

Gikandi, Simon **PR9387.9.A3Z68 1991**
Reading Chinua Achebe: Language and Ideology in Fiction. Trade Paper. Heinemann. Portsmouth, NH. 1991. 165p. Studies in African Literature ISBN:0-435-08057-1, ISBN13: 978-0-435-08057-0. Dewey:823. LCCN:90-26560.
Audience: **u,f.** *Choice, 1992.*

Lindfors, Bernth (Editor) **PR9387.9.A3Z58 1997**
Conversations with Chinua Achebe. Trade Paper. University Press of Mississippi. Jackson, MS. 1997. 199p. Literary Conversations Ser. ISBN:0-87805-999-7, ISBN13: 978-0-87805-999-7. Dewey:[B]. LCCN:97-006953.
Audience: **l,u,f.**

Ogbaa, Kalu **PR9387**
Understanding Things Fall Apart: A Student Casebook to Issues, Sources and Historical Documents. Cloth Text. Greenwood Publishing Group, Inc. Portsmouth, NH. 1999. 256p. Literature in Context Ser. ISBN:0-313-30294-4, ISBN13: 978-0-313-30294-7. Dewey:823. LCCN:98-022902.
Audience: **l,u,f.**

Okpewho, Isidore (Editor) **PR9387.9.A3T52397**
Chinua Achebe's Things Fall Apart: A Casebook. Trade Cloth. Oxford University Press, Inc. New York, NY. 2003. 288p. Casebooks in Criticism Ser. ISBN:0-19-514763-4, ISBN13: 978-0-19-514763-6. Dewey:823/.914. LCCN:2002-013555.
Audience: **l,u,f.**

Africa > Individual Authors > Coetzee, J. M.

Attwell, David **PR9369.3.C58Z635**
J. M. Coetzee: South Africa and the Politics of Writing. Trade Cloth. University of California Press. Berkeley, CA. 1993. ix, 147p. Perspectives on Southern Africa Ser., Vol. 48 ISBN:0-520-07810-1, ISBN13: 978-0-520-07810-9. Dewey:823. LCCN:92-013468.
Audience: **l,u,f.** *Choice, 1993.*

Coetzee, J. M. **PR9369.3.C58A7**
Age of Iron. Trade Paper. Penguin Group (USA) Inc. New York, NY. 1998. 208p. ISBN:0-14-027565-7, ISBN13: 978-0-14-027565-0. Dewey:823. LCCN:90-008310.
Audience: **g,l,u,f.** *Choice, 1991.*

Coetzee, J. M. **PR9369.3.C58Z463**
Boyhood: Scenes from Provincial Life. Trade Paper. Penguin Group (USA) Inc. New York, NY. 1998. 176p. ISBN:0-14-026566-X, ISBN13: 978-0-14-026566-8. Dewey:823. LCCN:97-012360.
Audience: **g,l,u,f.**

Coetzee, J. M. **PR9369.3.C58F6 1987**
Foe. Trade Paper. Penguin Group (USA) Inc. New York, NY. 1988. 160p. King Penguin Ser. ISBN:0-14-009623-X, ISBN13: 978-0-14-009623-1. Dewey:823. LCCN:87-011913.
Audience: **g,l,u,f.**

Coetzee, J. M. **PR9369.3**
In the Heart of the Country. UK-B Format Paperback. Knopf Publishing Group. New York, NY. 2004. 160p. ISBN:0-09-946594-9, ISBN13: 978-0-09-946594-2. Dewey:823.
Audience: **g,l,u,f.**

Coetzee, J. M. **PR9499.3.N3**
The Master of Petersburg. Trade Paper. Penguin Group (USA) Inc. New York, NY. 1995. 256p. ISBN:0-14-023810-7, ISBN13: 978-0-14-023810-5. Dewey:823. LCCN:94-009947.
Audience: **g,l,u,f.**

Coetzee, J. M. **PR9369.3.C58L43 2004**
The Nobel Lecture in Literature 2003. Trade Paper. Penguin Group (USA) Inc. New York, NY. 2004. 32p. ISBN:0-14-303453-7, ISBN13: 978-0-14-303453-7. Dewey:823/.914. LCCN:2004-058274.
Audience: **g,l,u,f.**

Coetzee, J. M. **PR9369.3.C58S56 2005**
Slow Man. Trade Cloth. Penguin Group (USA) Inc. New York, NY. 2005. 208p. ISBN:0-670-03459-2, ISBN13: 978-0-670-03459-8. Dewey:823.3. LCCN:2005-054693.
Audience: **g,l,u,f.**

Coetzee, J. M. **PR6013.O35**
Stranger Shores: Literary Essays, 1986-1999. UK-B Format Paperback. Knopf Publishing Group. New York, NY. 2002. 272p. ISBN:0-09-942262-X, ISBN13: 978-0-09-942262-4. Dewey:824/.914.
Audience: **u,f.**

Coetzee, J. M. **PR9369.3W3 2004**
Waiting for the Barbarians. UK-B Format Paperback. Knopf Publishing Group. New York, NY. 2004. 176p. ISBN:0-09-946593-0, ISBN13: 978-0-09-946593-5. Dewey:823/.914.
Audience: **g,l,u,f.**

Coetzee, J. M. **PR9369.3.C58Y68 2002**
Youth: Scenes from Provincial Life II. Trade Cloth. Penguin Group (USA) Inc. New York, NY. 2002. 176p. ISBN:0-670-03102-X, ISBN13: 978-0-670-03102-3. Dewey:823/.914. LCCN:2002-016879.
Audience: **g,l,u,f.**

Head, Dominic **PR9369.3.C58 Z68 19**
J. M. Coetzee. Abiola Irele (Contribution by). Trade Cloth. Cambridge University Press. New York, NY. 1998. 208p. Studies in African and Caribbean Literature, Vol. 6 ISBN:0-521-48232-1, ISBN13: 978-0-521-48232-5. Dewey:823. LCCN:97-006959.
Audience: **l,u,f.** *Choice, 1998.*

Kossew, Sue **PR9369.3.C58Z637**
Critical Essays on J. M. Coetzee. Trade Cloth. Thomson Gale. Farmington Hills, MI. 1998. 242p. Critical Essays on World Literature Ser. ISBN:0-7838-0053-3, ISBN13: 978-0-7838-0053-0. Dewey:823. LCCN:97-036417.
Audience: **l,u,f.** *Choice, 1998.*

Africa > Individual Authors > D-E

Dangarembga, Tsitsi **PR9390.9.D36N47 2004**
Nervous Conditions. Trade Paper. Avalon Publishing Group. New York, NY. 2005. 256p. ISBN:1-58005-134-0, ISBN13: 978-1-58005-134-7. Dewey:823/.914. LCCN:2005-277344.
Audience: **g,l,u,f.** *Choice, 1989.*

Emecheta, Buchi **PR9387.9.E36**
The Joys of Motherhood. Trade Paper. George Braziller Inc. New York, NY. 1980. 244p. ISBN:0-8076-0950-1, ISBN13: 978-0-8076-0950-7. Dewey:823. LCCN:78-024640.
Audience: **g,l,u,f.**

Emecheta, Buchi **PR6019.O9**
Second-Class Citizen. Trade Paper. George Braziller Inc. New York, NY. 1983. 175p. ISBN:0-8076-1066-6, ISBN13: 978-0-8076-1066-4. Dewey:823/.9/1. LCCN:82-024355.
Audience: **g,l,u,f.**

Fishburn, Katherine **PR9387**
Reading Buchi Emecheta: Cross-Cultural Conversations. Trade Cloth. Greenwood Publishing Group, Inc. Portsmouth, NH. 1995. 224p. Contributions to the Study of World Literature Ser., Vol. 61 ISBN:0-313-29589-1, ISBN13: 978-0-313-29589-8. Dewey:823. LCCN:94-039245.
Audience: **l,u,f.** *Choice, 1995.*

Sougou, Omar **PR9387.9.E36**
Writing Across Cultures: Gender Politics and Difference in the Fiction of Buchi Emecheta. Trade Cloth. Rodopi. Kenilworth, NY. 2002. ix, 243p. Cross-Cultures Ser., Vol. 51 ISBN:90-420-1308-7, ISBN13: 978-90-420-1308-7. Dewey:823.
Audience: **l,u,f.**

Umeh, Marie (Editor) **PR9387.9.E36**
Emerging Perspectives of Buchi Emecheta. Trade Cloth. Africa World Press. Trenton, NJ. 1995. 532p. ISBN:0-86543-454-9, ISBN13: 978-0-86543-454-7. Dewey:823. LCCN:95-010357.
Audience: **l,u,f.**

Africa > Individual Authors > F

Farah, Nuruddin **PR9396.9.F3F76 2006**
From a Crooked Rib. Trade Paper. Penguin Group (USA) Inc. New York, NY. 2006. 176p. ISBN:0-14-303726-9, ISBN13: 978-0-14-303726-2. Dewey:823/.914. LCCN:2005-058670.
Audience: **g,l,u,f.**

Farah, Nuruddin **PR9396.9.F3**
Gifts. Trade Paper. Penguin Group (USA) Inc. New York, NY. 2000. 256p. ISBN:0-14-029642-5, ISBN13: 978-0-14-029642-6. Dewey:823.
Audience: **g,l,u,f.**

Farah, Nuruddin **PR6015.I3**
Links. Trade Paper. Penguin Group (USA) Inc. New York, NY. 2005. 352p. ISBN:0-14-303484-7, ISBN13: 978-0-14-303484-1. Dewey:823/.914.
Audience: **g,l,u,f.**

Fugard, Athol **PR9369.3.F8A6 1991**
Blood Knot and Other Plays. Trade Paper. Theatre Communications Group, Inc. New York, NY. 1991. 240p. ISBN:1-55936-020-8, ISBN13: 978-1-55936-020-3. Dewey:822. LCCN:90-029029.
Audience: **g,l,u,f.**

Fugard, Athol **PR9369.3.F8.A19 1978**
Boesman and Lena and Other Plays. Trade Cloth. Oxford University Press, Inc. New York, NY. 1978. xxv, 299p. ISBN:0-19-281242-4, ISBN13: 978-0-19-281242-1. Dewey:822. LCCN:77-030721.
Audience: **g,l,u,f.**

Fugard, Athol **PR9369.3.F8E95 2006**
Exits and Entrances. Trade Paper. Theatre Communications Group, Inc. New York, NY. 2005. 104p. ISBN:1-55936-269-3, ISBN13: 978-1-55936-269-6. Dewey:822/.914. LCCN:2006-013099.
Audience: **g,l,u,f.**

Fugard, Athol **PR9369.3.F8M3 1984**
Master Harold and the Boys. Trade Paper. Penguin Group (USA) Inc. New York, NY. 1984. 64p. Plays Ser. ISBN:0-14-048187-7, ISBN13: 978-0-14-048187-7. Dewey:822. LCCN:84-001008.
Audience: **g,l,u,f.**

Fugard, Athol
Statements: Three Plays. Trade Cloth. Oxford University Press, Inc. New York, NY. 1979. 109p. ISBN:0-19-281170-3, ISBN13: 978-0-19-281170-7. Dewey:822.
Audience: **g,l,u,f.**

Fugard, Athol, et al. **PR9369.3.F8 M3 1997**
Master Harold. Laurie G. Kirszner & Stephen R. Mandell (Authors). Paper Text. Thomson Heinle. Boston, MA. 1997. 192p. Harcourt Brace Casebook Series in Literature Ser. ISBN:0-15-505483-X, ISBN13: 978-0-15-505483-7. Dewey:822. LCCN:97-070035.
Audience: **l,u,f.**

Ngaboh-Smart, Francis **PR9344**
Beyond Empire and Nation: Postnational Arguments in the Fiction of Nuruddin Farah and B. Kojo Laing. Trade Cloth. Rodopi. Kenilworth, NY. 2004. 168p. Cross/Cultures: Readings in the Post/Colonial Literatures in English Ser., Vol. 70 ISBN:90-420-0980-2, ISBN13: 978-90-420-0980-6. Dewey:823.
Audience: **l,u,f.**

Wertheim, Albert **PR9369.3.F8Z95 2000**
(e) The Dramatic Art of Athol Fugard: From South Africa to the World. E-Book. Indiana University Press. Bloomington, IN. 2000. xv, 273p. ISBN:0-253-33823-9, ISBN13: 978-0-253-33823-5. Dewey:822/.914. LCCN:00-039627.
Audience: **l,u,f.** *Choice, 2001.*

Wright, Derek (Editor) **PR9396.9.F3Z66 2002**
Emerging Perspectives on Nuruddin Farah. Trade Cloth. Africa World Press. Trenton, NJ. 2002. 768p. ISBN:0-86543-918-4, ISBN13: 978-0-86543-918-4. Dewey:823/.914. LCCN:2002-010371.
Audience: **g,l,u,f.**

Africa > Individual Authors > Gordimer, Nadine

Gordimer, Nadine **PR9499.3.N3**
Crimes of Conscience: Selected Short Stories. Trade Paper. Heinemann. Portsmouth, NH. 1991. 122p. African Writers Ser. ISBN:0-435-90668-2, ISBN13: 978-0-435-90668-9. Dewey:823.
Audience: **g,l,u,f.**

Gordimer, Nadine **PR9369.3.G6G48 2005**
Get a Life: A Novel. Saddle Stitched, Cloth over Boards, Dust Jacket. Farrar, Straus & Giroux. New York, NY. 2005. 208p. ISBN:0-374-16170-4, ISBN13: 978-0-374-16170-5. Dewey:823/.914. LCCN:2005-007199.
Audience: **g,l,u,f.**

Gordimer, Nadine **PR9499.3.N3**
The House Gun. Trade Paper. Penguin Group (USA) Inc. New York, NY. 1999. 304p. ISBN:0-14-027820-6, ISBN13: 978-0-14-027820-0. Dewey:823. LCCN:97-028787.
Audience: **g,l,u,f.**

Gordimer, Nadine **PR9499.3.N3**
July's People. Trade Cloth. Addison-Wesley Longman, Ltd. Harlow, 1991. 184p. ISBN:0-582-06011-7, ISBN13: 978-0-582-06011-1. Dewey:823.
Audience: **g,l,u,f.**

Gordimer, Nadine **D421**
Living in Hope and History: Notes from Our Century. Trade Paper. Farrar, Straus & Giroux. New York, NY. 2000. 256p. ISBN:0-374-52752-0, ISBN13: 978-0-374-52752-5. Dewey:909.8/2.
Audience: **g,l,u,f.**

Gordimer, Nadine **PR9369.3.G6L66 2003**
Loot: And Other Stories. Cloth over Boards. Farrar, Straus & Giroux. New York, NY. 2003. 256p. ISBN:0-374-19090-9, ISBN13: 978-0-374-19090-3. Dewey:823/.914. LCCN:2002-042601.
Audience: **g,l,u,f.**

Gordimer, Nadine **PR9369.3.G6 P53 2001**
The Pickup: A Novel. Trade Paper. Penguin Group (USA) Inc. New York, NY. 2002. 288p. ISBN:0-14-200142-2, ISBN13: 978-0-14-200142-4. Dewey:823/.914. LCCN:2001-023041.
Audience: **g,l,u,f.**

Gordimer, Nadine **PR9369.3.G6 A6 1993**
Why Haven't You Written?: Selected Stories, 1950-1970. Trade Paper. Penguin Group (USA) Inc. New York, NY. 1993. 240p. ISBN:0-14-017657-8, ISBN13: 978-0-14-017657-5. Dewey:823.
Audience: **g,l,u,f.**

Gordimer, Nadine **PN771.G67 1995**
Writing and Being. Trade Cloth. Harvard University Press. Cambridge, MA. 1998. 160p. The Charles Eliot Norton Lectures ISBN:0-674-96232-X, ISBN13: 978-0-674-96232-3. Dewey:809/.04. LCCN:96-021843.
Audience: **g,l,u,f.**

Uledi-Kamanga, Brighton J. **PR9369.3.G6Z92 2000**
Cracks in the Wall: Nadine Gordimer's Fiction and the Irony of Apartheid. Trade Cloth. Africa World Press. Trenton, NJ. 2000. 242p. ISBN:0-86543-827-7, ISBN13: 978-0-86543-827-9. Dewey:823. LCCN:99-059945.
Audience: **l,u,f.**

Uraizee, Joya F. (Contribution by) **PR9344.U7 2000**
This Is No Place for a Woman: Nadine Gordimer, Nayantara Sahgal, Buchi Emecheta, and the Politics of Gender. Cloth Text. Africa World Press. Trenton, NJ. 1999. 272p. ISBN:0-86543-766-1, ISBN13: 978-0-86543-766-1. Dewey:820.9/9287/096. LCCN:99-028635.
Audience: **l,u,f.**

Africa > Individual Authors > H

Brown, Coreen **PR9369.3.H4Z58 2003**
The Creative Vision of Bessie Head. Trade Paper. Fairleigh Dickinson University Press. Cranbury, NJ. 2003. 244p. ISBN:0-8386-3982-8, ISBN13: 978-0-8386-3982-5. Dewey:823/.914. LCCN:2002-014380.
Audience: **l,u,f.** *Choice, 2003.*

Head, Bessie **PR9369.3.H4**
Maru. Trade Paper. Heinemann. Portsmouth, NH. 1997. 128p. ISBN:0-435-90963-0, ISBN13: 978-0-435-90963-5. Dewey:823.9/14.
Audience: **g,l,u,f.**

Head, Bessie **PR9369.3.H4**
When Rain Clouds Gather. Trade Paper. Heinemann. Portsmouth, NH. 1996. 188p. African Writers Ser. ISBN:0-435-90961-4, ISBN13: 978-0-435-90961-1. Dewey:896.39.
Audience: **g,l,u,f.**

Ibrahim, Huma (Editor) **PR9369.3.H4Z66 2003**
Emerging Perspectives on Bessie Head. Trade Cloth. Africa World Press. Trenton, NJ. 2003. 326p. ISBN:1-59221-073-2, ISBN13: 978-1-59221-073-2. Dewey:823/.914. LCCN:2003-024705.
Audience: **l,u,f.**

MacKenzie, Craig **PR9369.3.H4Z77 1999**
Bessie Head. Trade Cloth. Thomson Gale. Farmington Hills, MI. 1998. 12p. ISBN:0-8057-1629-7, ISBN13: 978-0-8057-1629-0. Dewey:823. LCCN:98-055671.
Audience: **l,u,f.** *Choice, 1999.*

Africa > Individual Authors > M-N

Mda, Zakes **PR6015.I3**
The Heart of Redness: A Novel. Trade Paper. Picador. New York, NY. 2003. 288p. ISBN:0-312-42174-5, ISBN13: 978-0-312-42174-8. Dewey:823/.914.
Audience: **g,l,u,f.**

Mda, Zakes **PR6015.I3**
The Madonna of Excelsior: A Novel. Trade Paper. Picador. New York, NY. 2005. 272p. ISBN:0-312-42382-9, ISBN13: 978-0-312-42382-7. Dewey:823/.914.
Audience: **g,l,u,f.**

Mda, Zakes **PR9369.3.M4S48 2004**
She Plays with the Darkness: A Novel. Trade Paper. Picador. New York, NY. 2004. 224p. ISBN:0-312-42325-X, ISBN13: 978-0-312-42325-4. Dewey:823/.914. LCCN:2003-060830.
Audience: **g,l,u,f.**

Mda, Zakes **PR9369.3.M4W47 2005**
The Whale Caller: A Novel. Cloth over Boards. Farrar, Straus & Giroux. New York, NY. 2005. 240p. ISBN:0-374-28785-6, ISBN13: 978-0-374-28785-6. Dewey:823/.914. LCCN:2005-014196.
Audience: **g,l,u,f.**

Mphahlele, Ezekiel **PR6019.O9**
The Wanderers. Trade Cloth. Macmillan Publishers Ltd. London, 1972. 315p. ISBN:0-333-13594-6, ISBN13: 978-0-333-13594-5. Dewey:823/.9/1.
Audience: **g,l,u,f.**

Nwapa, Flora **PR9387.9.N933**
Efuru. Trade Paper. Heinemann. Portsmouth, NH. 1966. 288p. African Writers Ser. ISBN:0-435-90026-9, ISBN13: 978-0-435-90026-7. Dewey:823.
Audience: **g,l,u,f.**

Nwapa, Flora **PR9387.9.N933W48**
Wives at War and Other Stories. Trade Cloth. Africa World Press. Trenton, NJ. 1992. 125p. ISBN:0-86543-327-5, ISBN13: 978-0-86543-327-4. Dewey:823. LCCN:93-148880.
Audience: **g,l,u,f.**

Africa > Individual Authors > O-R

Fraser, Robert **PR6015.I3**
Ben Okri: Towards the Invisible City. Trade Cloth. Northcote House Publishers, Ltd. Tavistock, 2004. 144p. Writers and Their Works Ser. ISBN:0-7463-0993-7, ISBN13: 978-0-7463-0993-3. Dewey:823.9/14.
Audience: **l,u,f.**

Mazrui, Ali A. **PR6063.A96**
The Trial of Christopher Okigbo. Trade Paper. Heinemann. Portsmouth, NH. 1971. 145p. African Writers Ser. ISBN:0-435-90097-8, ISBN13: 978-0-435-90097-7. Dewey:823. LCCN:72-175700.
Audience: **g,l,u,f.**

Nwoga, Donatus I. (Editor) **PR9387.9.O378 Z65**
Critical Perspectives on Christopher Okigbo. Obiora Udechukwu (Illustrator). Trade Cloth. Lynne Rienner Publishers, Inc. Boulder, CO. 1985. 367p. Critical Perspectives Ser. ISBN:0-89410-258-3, ISBN13: 978-0-89410-258-5. Dewey:821. LCCN:80-053349.
Audience: **l,u,f.** *Choice, 1985.*

Okafor, Dubem **PR9387.9.O378 1998**
The Dance of Death: Nigerian History and Christopher Okigbo's Poetry. Trade Cloth. Africa World Press. Trenton, NJ. 1997. 232p. ISBN:0-86543-555-3, ISBN13: 978-0-86543-555-1. Dewey:821. LCCN:97-015056.
Audience: **l,u,f.**

Okigbo, Christopher **PR9387.9.O378.A17**
Collected Poems. Trade Paper. Heinemann Educational Books. London, 1986. xxviii, 99p. ISBN:0-434-53220-7, ISBN13: 978-0-434-53220-9. Dewey:821. LCCN:88-154171.
Audience: **g,l,u,f.**

Okri, Ben **PR6015.I3**
The Famished Road. Trade Paper. Random House Children's Books. New York, NY. 1993. 512p. ISBN:0-385-42513-9, ISBN13: 978-0-385-42513-1. Dewey:823.9/14. LCCN:92-044168.
Audience: **g,l,u,f.**

Osofisan, Femi **PR9387.9.O85 A66**
Another Raft. Trade Cloth. Malthouse Press Ltd, Nigeria. Lagos, 1999. 86p. ISBN:978-2601-08-X, ISBN13: 978-978-2601-08-7. Dewey:822.914.
Audience: **g,l,u,f.**

Osofisan, Femi **PR9387.O86 1999**
The Nostalgic Drum. Trade Cloth. Africa World Press. Trenton, NJ. 1999. 368p. ISBN:0-86543-806-4, ISBN13: 978-0-86543-806-4. Dewey:820.9/9669. LCCN:99-050317.
Audience: **g,l,u,f.**

Osofisan, Femi **PR9387.9.O83**
Once upon Four Robbers. Trade Cloth. Heinemann Educational Books (Nigeria), Ltd. Ibadan, Oyo State, 1998. 107p. ISBN:978-129-179-6, ISBN13: 978-978-129-179-1. Dewey:822.
Audience: **g,l,u,f.**

Osofisan, Femi **PR9387.9.O85O75 1995**
The Oriki of a Grasshopper, and Other Plays. Abiola Irele (Introduction by). Trade Paper. Howard University Press. Washington, DC. 1995. 196p. ISBN:0-88258-181-3, ISBN13: 978-0-88258-181-1. Dewey:822. LCCN:95-006636.
Audience: **g,l,u,f.**

P'Bitek, Okot **PL8041**
Song of Lawino and Song of Ocol. Frank Horley (Illustrator), G. A. Heron (Introduction by). Trade Paper. Heinemann. Portsmouth, NH. 1984. 158p. African Writers Ser., No. 266 ISBN:0-435-90266-0, ISBN13: 978-0-435-90266-7. Dewey:896/.5. LCCN:84-186416.
Audience: **g,l,u,f.**

p'Bitek, Okot & Liyong, Taban lo **PL8041.9.P3W413 2001**
The Defence of Lawino. Trade Cloth. Fountain Publishers Ltd. Kampala, 2001. 132p. ISBN:9970-02-269-5, ISBN13: 978-9970-02-269-4. Dewey:821/.914. LCCN:2001-295082.
Audience: **g,l,u,f.**

Rotimi, Ola **PR6068.O843 G6**
The Gods Are Not to Blame. Trade Paper. Oxford University Press. Oxford, 1971. 72p. ISBN:0-19-211358-5, ISBN13: 978-0-19-211358-0. Dewey:822. LCCN:75-028492.
Audience: **g,l,u,f.**

Africa > Individual Authors > S-T

Lindfors, Bernth (Editor) **PR9387.9.T8.Z6**
Critical Perspectives on Amos Tutuola. Nic Clapp & Susan Trumpower (Illustrators). Trade Cloth. Lynne Rienner Publishers, Inc. Boulder, CO. 1975. 318p. ISBN:0-914478-05-2, ISBN13: 978-0-914478-05-8. Dewey:823. LCCN:75-013706.
Audience: **l,u,f.**

Owomoyela, Oyekan **PR9387.9.T8Z83 1999**
Amos Tutuola Revisited. Trade Cloth. Thomson Gale. Farmington Hills, MI. 1999. xii, 174p. Twayne's World Authors Ser., Vol. 880 ISBN:0-8057-4610-2, ISBN13: 978-0-8057-4610-5. Dewey:823. LCCN:99-014327.
Audience: **l,u,f.** *Choice, 1999.*

Schreiner, Olive **PR9369.2.S37S7 1998**
The Story of an African Farm. Joseph Bristow (Editor, Introduction by). Trade Paper. Oxford University Press, Inc. New York, NY. 1999. 322p. Oxford World's Classics Ser. ISBN:0-19-283664-1, ISBN13: 978-0-19-283664-9. Dewey:823/.8. LCCN:99-461826.
Audience: **g,l,u,f.**

Tutuola, Amos **PZ4**
Palm-Wine Drinkard and His Dead Palm-Wine Tapster in the Dead's Town. Trade Cloth. Greenwood Publishing Group, Inc. Portsmouth, NH. 1970. 130p. ISBN:0-8371-4044-7, ISBN13: 978-0-8371-4044-5. Dewey:823. LCCN:78-104255.
Audience: **g,l,u,f.**

Tutuola, Amos **PR9387.9.T8W45 1989**
The Wild Hunter in the Bush of the Ghosts: Standard Edition. Bernth Lindfors (Editor). Trade Cloth. Lynne Rienner Publishers, Inc. Boulder, CO. 1989. 126p. ISBN:0-89410-452-7, ISBN13: 978-0-89410-452-7. Dewey:823. LCCN:84-051444.
Audience: **g,l,u,f.**

Africa > Individual Authors > Soyinka, Wole

Gates, Henry Louis Jr. (Editor) **ND237.R725A93 1983**
In the House of Osubgo: Critical Essays on Wole Soyinka. Trade Cloth. Oxford University Press, Inc. New York, NY. 2000. 288p. ISBN:0-19-503349-3, ISBN13: 978-0-19-503349-6. Dewey:759.13. LCCN:83-002268.
Audience: **u,f.**

Gibbs, James **PR9387.9.S6Z/**
Wole Soyinka. Trade Paper. Macmillan Education, Ltd. Oxford, 1986. ix, 170p. ISBN:0-333-30528-0, ISBN13: 978-0-333-30528-7. Dewey:822.
Audience: **g,l,u,f.**

Jeyifo, Biodun (Editor) **PR9387.9.S6Z464 2001**
Conversations with Wole Soyinka. Trade Cloth. University Press of Mississippi. Jackson, MS. 2001. xxii, 242p. Literary Conversations Ser. ISBN:1-57806-337-X, ISBN13: 978-1-57806-337-6. Dewey:822/.914 B. LCCN:00-049526.
Audience: **g,l,u,f.** *Choice, 2001.*

Jeyifo, Biodun (Editor) **PR9387.9.S6Z83 2001**
Perspectives on Wole Soyinka: Freedom and Complexity. Trade Cloth. University Press of Mississippi. Jackson, MS. 2001. 248p. ISBN:1-57806-335-3, ISBN13: 978-1-57806-335-2. Dewey:822/.914. LCCN:00-051334.
Audience: **u,f.**

Jeyifo, Biodun **PR9387.9.S6Z675 2003**
Wole Soyinka: Politics, Poetics, and Postcolonialism. Abiola Irele (Contribution by). Trade Cloth. Cambridge University Press. New York, NY. 2003. 356p. Cambridge Studies in African and Caribbean Literature Ser., Vol. 9 ISBN:0-521-39486-4, ISBN13: 978-0-521-39486-4. Dewey:822/.914. LCCN:2003-053200.
Audience: **u,f.** *Choice, 2004.*

Soyinka, Wole
The Burden of Memory, the Muse of Forgiveness. Trade Paper. Oxford University Press, Inc. New York, NY. 2000. 224p. The W. E. B. Du Bois Institute Ser. ISBN:0-19-513428-1, ISBN13: 978-0-19-513428-5. Dewey:960.3/2.
Audience: **u,f.** *Choice, 1999.*

Soyinka, Wole
Collected Plays, Vol. 2. Paper Text. Oxford University Press, Inc. New York, NY. 1975. 282p. ISBN:0-19-281164-9, ISBN13: 978-0-19-281164-6. Dewey:822.
Audience: **g,l,u,f.**

Soyinka, Wole **PR9387.9.S6 1973**
Collected Plays, Vol. 1. Paper Text. Oxford University Press, Inc. New York, NY. 1973. 320p. ISBN:0-19-281136-3, ISBN13: 978-0-19-281136-3. Dewey:822. LCCN:74-156793.
Audience: **g,l,u,f.**

Soyinka, Wole **PR9387.9.S6D4 2002**
Death and the King's Horseman. Trade Paper. W. W. Norton & Company, Inc. New York, NY. 2002. xxv, 228p. Critical Editions Ser. ISBN:0-393-97761-7, ISBN13: 978-0-393-97761-5. Dewey:822/.914. LCCN:2002-026539.
Audience: **g,l,u,f.**

Soyinka, Wole
Madmen and Specialists. Trade Paper. Methuen Publishing Ltd. London, 2003. 0p. ISBN:0-416-18760-9, ISBN13: 978-0-416-18760-1. Dewey:822.
Audience: **g,l,u,f.**

Soyinka, Wole **DT49 .W516**
The Essential Soyinka: A Reader. Henry Louis Gates Jr. (Author, Introduction by). Trade Cloth. Knopf Publishing Group. New York, NY. 1997. 416p. ISBN:0-679-43990-0, ISBN13: 978-0-679-43990-5. Dewey:330.9662605.
Audience: **g,l,u,f.**

Soyinka, Wole
The Interpreters. Eldred Jones (Introduction by, Notes by). Trade Paper. Heinemann. Portsmouth, NH. 1984. 260p. African Writers Ser. ISBN:0-435-90076-5, ISBN13: 978-0-435-90076-2. Dewey:823.
Audience: **g,l,u,f.**

Soyinka, Wole
Poetry of Wole Soyinka. Tanure Ojaide (Editor). Trade Cloth. Malthouse Press Ltd, Nigeria. Lagos, 2002. 140p. ISBN:978-023-006-8, ISBN13: 978-978-023-006-7. Dewey:823.
Audience: **g,l,u,f.** *Choice, 1996.*

Wright, Derek **PR9387.9.S6Z97 1993**
Wole Soyinka. Trade Cloth. Macmillan Publishing Company, Inc. Old Tappan, NJ. 1992. 160p. Twayne's World Authors Ser. ISBN:0-8057-8279-6, ISBN13: 978-0-8057-8279-0. Dewey:822. LCCN:92-024088.
Audience: **g,l,u,f.** *Choice, 1993.*

Africa > Individual Authors > Thiongo, Ngugi Wa

Cantalupo, Charles (Editor) **PR9381.9.N45Z776**
Ngugi Wa Thiong'o: Text and Contexts. Trade Cloth. Africa World Press. Trenton, NJ. 1995. 390p. ISBN:0-86543-444-1, ISBN13: 978-0-86543-444-8. Dewey:823. LCCN:95-021818.
Audience: **l,u,f.**

Cantalupo, Charles (Editor) **PR9381.9.N45 Z95**
The World of Ngugi Wa Thiong'o. Trade Cloth. Africa World Press. Trenton, NJ. 1996. 248p. ISBN:0-86543-458-1, ISBN13: 978-0-86543-458-5. Dewey:828.91408.
Audience: **g,l,u,f.**

Cook, David & Okenimkpe, Michael **PR9381.9.N45.Z562**
Ngugi Wa Thiong'o: An Exploration of His Writings. Ed. 2. Trade Paper. Heinemann. Portsmouth, NH. 1997. 283p. Studies in African Literature ISBN:0-435-07430-X, ISBN13: 978-0-435-07430-2. Dewey:823. LCCN:97-219198.
Audience: **g,l,u,f.** B

Gikandi, Simon **PR9381.9.N45 Z67 20**
Ngugi wa Thiong'o. Abiola Irele (Contribution by). Cloth Text. Cambridge University Press. New York, NY. 2000. 340p. Cambridge Studies in African and Caribbean Literature, No. 8 ISBN:0-521-48006-X, ISBN13: 978-0-521-48006-2. Dewey:823. LCCN:99-043662.
Audience: **l,u,f.** *Choice, 2001.*

Lindfors, Bernth (Editor), et al. **PR9381.9.N45Z473**
Ngugi Wa Thiong'o Speaks: Interviews with the Kenyan Writer. Lynette Cintron & Sander Reinhard (Editors). Trade Cloth. Africa World Press. Trenton, NJ. 2004. 376p. ISBN:1-59221-265-4, ISBN13: 978-1-59221-265-1. Dewey:823/.914. LCCN:2005-017732.
Audience: **g,l,u,f.**

Lovesey, Oliver **PR9381.9.N45Z76 2000**
Ngugi Wa Thiongo. Trade Cloth. Thomson Gale. Farmington Hills, MI. 2000. 164p. ISBN:0-8057-1695-5, ISBN13: 978-0-8057-1695-5. Dewey:823. LCCN:99-050023.
Audience: **l,u,f.** *Choice, 2000.*

Nazareth, Peter **PR9381.9.N45Z568**
The Critical Essays on Ngugi wa Thiong'o. Trade Cloth. Thomson Gale. Farmington Hills, MI. 2000. xi, 341p. Critical Essays on World Literature Ser. ISBN:0-7838-0456-3, ISBN13: 978-0-7838-0456-9. Dewey:823/.914. LCCN:00-044318.
Audience: **l,u,f.** *Choice, 2001.*

Ngugi wa Thiong'o **PR6019.O9**
Secret Lives: And Other Stories. Trade Paper. Heinemann. Portsmouth, NH. 1992. 144p. ISBN:0-435-90150-8, ISBN13: 978-0-435-90150-9. Dewey:823/.9/1.
Audience: **g,l,u,f.**

Ngugi wa Thiong'o **PR9381.9.N45P436**
Petals of Blood. Moses Isegawa (Introduction by). Trade Paper. Penguin Group (USA) Inc. New York, NY. 2005. 432p. Penguin Classics Ser. ISBN:0-14-303917-2, ISBN13: 978-0-14-303917-4. Dewey:823. LCCN:2005-271659.
Audience: **g,l,u,f.**

Ngugi wa Thiong'o **PL8379.9.N4M3713**
Matigari. Wangaui wa Goro (Translator). Trade Cloth. Africa World Press. Trenton, NJ. 1996. 160p. ISBN:0-86543-360-7, ISBN13: 978-0-86543-360-1. Dewey:896/.39. LCCN:96-044440.
Audience: **g,l,u,f.** *Choice, 1990.*

Ogude, James **PR9381.9.N45Z82 1999**
Ngugi's Novels and African History: Narrating the Nation. Trade Paper. Pluto Press. London, 1999. 192p. ISBN:0-7453-1431-7, ISBN13: 978-0-7453-1431-0. Dewey:823. LCCN:99-023065.
Audience: **l,u,f.** *Choice, 2000.*

Thiongo, Ngugi Wa **PL8010.N48 1986**
Decolonising the Mind: The Politics of Language in African Literature. Trade Paper. Heinemann. Portsmouth, NH. 1986. 114p. Studies in African Literature ISBN:0-435-08016-4, ISBN13: 978-0-435-08016-7. Dewey:809/.889/6. LCCN:86-4683.
Audience: **l,u,f.**

Africa > Individual Authors > V

Vassanji, M. G. **PS3568.O243**
The Book of Secrets: A Novel. Trade Paper. Picador. New York, NY. 1996. 337p. ISBN:0-312-15068-7, ISBN13: 978-0-312-15068-6. Dewey:813/.54. LCCN:95-044948.
Audience: **g,l,u,f.**

Vera, Yvonne **PR9390.9.V47B88 2000**
Butterfly Burning: A Novel. Trade Paper. Farrar, Straus & Giroux. New York, NY. 2000. 144p. ISBN:0-374-29186-1, ISBN13: 978-0-374-29186-0. Dewey:823/.914. LCCN:00-028834.
Audience: **g,l,u,f.**

Vera, Yvonne **PR6015.I3**
The Stone Virgins: A Novel. Trade Paper. Farrar, Straus & Giroux. New York, NY. 2004. 192p. ISBN:0-374-52894-2, ISBN13: 978-0-374-52894-2. Dewey:823/.914.
Audience: **g,l,u,f.**

Asia

Ahmad, Aijaz **PN849.U43 A36 1994**
In Theory: Nations, Classes, Literature. Trade Paper. Analytical Psychology Club of San Francisco, Inc. San Francisco, CA. 1994. 368p. ISBN:0-86091-677-4, ISBN13: 978-0-86091-677-2. Dewey:820.991724.
Audience: **u,f.**

Bahri, Deepika & Vasudeva, Mary (Editors) **E184.S69B48 1996**
Between the Lines: South Asians and Postcoloniality. Library Binding. Temple University Press. Philadelphia, PA. 1996. 400p. Asian American History and Culture Ser. ISBN:1-56639-467-8, ISBN13: 978-1-56639-467-3. Dewey:973/.04914. LCCN:95-052972.
Audience: **u,f.**

Benson, Eugene & Conolly, L. W. (Editors) **PR478**
Encyclopedia of Post-Colonial Literatures in English. Ed. 2. Paper over Boards. Routledge. New York, NY. 2005. 2096p. ISBN:0-415-27885-6, ISBN13: 978-0-415-27885-0. Dewey:820.9917142109045.
Audience: **g,l,u,f.** *Choice, 2005, 1995.*

Bhabha, Homi K. **PN56.N19N38 1990**
Nation and Narration. Trade Paper. Routledge. New York, NY. 1990. 352p. ISBN:0-415-01483-2, ISBN13: 978-0-415-01483-0. Dewey:809/.93358. LCCN:89-024051.
Audience: **u,f.**

Bhadra, Gautam (Editor), et al. **DS463**
Subaltern Studies: Writings on South Asian History and Society. Gyan Prakash & Susie Tharu (Editors). Cloth Text. Oxford University Press, Inc. New York, NY. 1999. 264p. ISBN:0-19-564570-7, ISBN13: 978-0-19-564570-5. Dewey:954/.03.
Audience: **u,f.**

Bien, Gloria, et al. **PN70.C66 1996**
Contemporary Literature of Asia. Ed. 1. Vinay Dharwadker & Arthur W. Biddle (Authors). Trade Paper. Prentice Hall PTR. Upper Saddle River, NJ. 1996. 531p. ISBN:0-13-373259-2, ISBN13: 978-0-13-373259-7. Dewey:895. LCCN:95-044124.
Audience: **g,l,u,f.**

Breckenridge, Carol A. (Editor) **DS423.C577 1995**
Consuming Modernity: Public Culture in a South Asian World. Cloth Text. University of Minnesota Press. Minneapolis, MN. 1995. 224p. ISBN:0-8166-2305-8, ISBN13: 978-0-8166-2305-1. Dewey:306/.0954. LCCN:94-046772.
Audience: **u,f.**

Brians, Paul **PR9484**
Modern South Asian Literature in English. Cloth Text. Greenwood Publishing Group, Inc. Portsmouth, NH. 2003. 264p. Literature As Windows to World Cultures Ser. ISBN:0-313-32011-X, ISBN13: 978-0-313-32011-8. Dewey:820.9/954. LCCN:2003-052842.
Audience: **g,l,u,f.** *Choice, 2004.*

Chan, Mimi & Harris, Roy (Editors) **PR9410.A515**
Asian Voices in English. Trade Cloth. Hong Kong University Press. Hong Kong, 1991. 224p. ISBN:962-209-282-9, ISBN13: 978-962-209-282-2. Dewey:820.995.
Audience: **g,l,u,f.**

De Mel, Neloufer **HQ1236.5.S72**
Women and the Nation's Narrative: Gender and Nationalism in Twentieth Century Sri Lanka. Kali for Women Staff (Contribution by). Trade Paper. Rowman & Littlefield Publishers, Inc. Lanham, MD. 2001. 304p. ISBN:0-7425-1807-8, ISBN13: 978-0-7425-1807-0. Dewey:305.42/095493.
Audience: **u,f.**

Francia, Luis H. (Editor, Introduction by) **PR9550.5.B76 1993**
Brown River, White Ocean: An Anthology of Twentieth-Century Philippine Literature in English. Trade Paper. Rutgers University Press. Piscataway, NJ. 1993. 279p. ISBN:0-8135-1999-3, ISBN13: 978-0-8135-1999-9. Dewey:820.809. LCCN:92-046381.
Audience: **g,l,u,f.**

Goonetilleke, D. C. R. A. **PR9440.7 M63 1991**
Modern Sri Lankan Drama. Cloth Text. South Asia Books. Columbia, MO. 1991. 228p. Sri Lanka Studies, No. 15 ISBN:81-7030-251-X, ISBN13: 978-81-7030-251-3. Dewey:822. LCCN:91-907487.
Audience: **g,l,u,f.**

Gunesekera, Romesh **PR6015.I3**
The Sandglass. Trade Cloth. New Press, The. New York, NY. 1998. 288p. ISBN:1-56584-484-X, ISBN13: 978-1-56584-484-1. Dewey:823.9/14.
Audience: **g,l,u,f.**

Hamid, Mohsin **PS3558.A12M68**
Moth Smoke: A Novel. Trade Paper. Picador. New York, NY. 2001. 256p. ISBN:0-312-27323-1, ISBN13: 978-0-312-27323-1. Dewey:813.
Audience: **g,l,u,f.**

Jain, Jasbir & Singh, Veena (Editors) **PR9484.6 .C63 2000**
Contesting Postcolonialisms. Trade Cloth. Rawat Publications. Jaipur, 2000. 271p. ISBN:81-7033-550-7, ISBN13: 978-81-7033-550-4. Dewey:820.9954. LCCN:99-952802.
Audience: **u,f.**

Kanaganayakam, Chelva **PR9418.5.A785.K36**
Configurations of Exile: The South Asian Writers and Their World. Trade Paper. T S A R Publications. Toronto, ON. 160p. ISBN:0-920661-47-5, ISBN13: 978-0-920661-47-5. Dewey:820.9/954. LCCN:96-120400.
Audience: **g,l,u,f.**

Khwaja, Waqas A. (Editor) **PK2211.E8**
Pakistani Short Stories. Cloth Text. UBS Publishers Distributors (P), Ltd. New Delhi, 1992. ISBN:81-85674-45-0, ISBN13: 978-81-85674-45-2. Dewey:891.439308.
Audience: **g,l,u,f.**

Kim, Richard E. **PS3561.I415 Z473**
Lost Names: Scenes from Korean Boyhood. Trade Paper. University of California Press. Berkeley, CA. 1998. 208p. ISBN:0-520-21424-2, ISBN13: 978-0-520-21424-8. Dewey:813/.54; B. LCCN:97-046168.
Audience: **g,l,u,f.**

Kirpal, Viney **PR9492.5.N49 1990**
The New English Novel in English: A Study of the 1980s. Trade Cloth. Allied Publishers Private, Ltd. New Delhi, 1990. ISBN:81-7023-256-2, ISBN13: 978-81-7023-256-8. Dewey:823. LCCN:90-907144.
Audience: **u,f.**

Kuruvilla, M I
Studies in World Literature. Apt Books, Inc. 1984. ISBN:0-86590-271-2, ISBN13: 978-0-86590-271-8.
Audience: **u,f.**

Lim, Catherine
Little Ironies: Stories of Singapore. Heinemann. 1978. Writing in Asia Ser. ISBN:0-435-00224-4, ISBN13: 978-0-435-00224-4.
Audience: **g,l,u,f.**

Lim, Catherine
Or Else, the Lightning God and Other Stories. Heinemann. 1980. Writing in Asia Ser. ISBN:0-435-00251-1, ISBN13: 978-0-435-00251-0.
Audience: **g,l,u,f.**

Mukherjee, Dipika (Editor), et al. **PR9570.S52M47 2002**
Merlin and the Hibiscus: Contemporary Short Stories from Singapore and Malaysia. Kirpal Singh & M.A. Quayum (Editors). Trade Paper. Penguin Group (USA) Inc. New York, NY. 2002. 256p. ISBN:0-14-302812-X, ISBN13: 978-0-14-302812-3. Dewey:823.01080914. LCCN:2002-293684.
Audience: **g,l,u,f.**

Nandy, Ashis **DS442.5**
The Intimate Enemy: Loss and Recovery of Self under Colonialism. Paper Text. Oxford University Press, Inc. New York, NY. 1989. 142p. ISBN:0-19-562237-5, ISBN13: 978-0-19-562237-9. Dewey:325/.341/0954.
Audience: **u,f.**

Nasta, Susheila **PR129.A785N37 2001**
Home Truths: Fictions of the South Asian Diaspora in Britain. Cloth over Boards. Palgrave Macmillan. New York, NY. 2002. 319p. ISBN:0-333-67005-1, ISBN13: 978-0-333-67005-7. Dewey:823/.910895. LCCN:2001-133053.
Audience: **u,f.**

Nkrumah, Kwame
Neo-Colonialism: The Last Stage of Imperialism. Brill Academic Publishers, Inc. 1965. ISBN:0-901787-33-7, ISBN13: 978-0-901787-33-0.
Audience: **u,f.** B

Nor Faridah Abdul Manaf & Quayum, Mohammad A. **PR9530.N67 2003**
Colonial to Global: Malaysian Women's Writing in English, 1940s-1990s. Ed. 2. Trade Cloth. International Islamic University, Ahmad Ibrahim Kulliyah of Laws, The Law Centre. Kuala Lumpur, 2003. 449p. ISBN:983-9727-83-4, ISBN13: 978-983-9727-83-8. Dewey:820. LCCN:2003-534782.
Audience: **g,l,u,f.**

Papayanis, Marilyn A. **PR125.P37 2004**
Writing in the Margins: The Ethics of Expatriation from Lawrence to Ondaatje. Cloth Text. Vanderbilt University Press. Nashville, TN. 2005. 305p. ISBN:0-8265-1468-5, ISBN13: 978-0-8265-1468-4. Dewey:820.9/358. LCCN:2004-017372.
Audience: **u,f.** *Choice, 2005.*

Pollock, Sheldon I. (Editor) **PK2903 .L47 2003**
Literary Cultures in History: Reconstructions from South Asia. Trade Cloth. University of California Press. Berkeley, CA. 2003. 1108p. ISBN:0-520-22821-9, ISBN13: 978-0-520-22821-4. Dewey:891.4. LCCN:2001-027673.
Audience: **u,f.** *Choice, 2004.*

Ponzanesi, Sandra **PR9488.P66 2004**
Paradoxes of Postcolonial Culture: Contemporary Women Writers of the Indian and Afro-Italian Diaspora. Cloth Text. State University of New York Press. Albany, NY. 2004. 288p. Explorations in Postcolonial Studies ISBN:0-7914-6201-3, ISBN13: 978-0-7914-6201-0. Dewey:820.9/9287/0954. LCCN:2004-045295.
Audience: **l,u,f.** *Choice, 2005.*

Selvadurai, Shyam **PR9440.9.S42C56 2000**
Cinnamon Gardens: A Novel. Trade Paper. Harcourt Trade Publishers. New York, NY. 2000. 368p. Harvest Book Ser. ISBN:0-15-601328-2, ISBN13: 978-0-15-601328-4. Dewey:813.5/4. LCCN:99-049987.
Audience: **g,l,u,f.**

Shamsie, Muneeza (Editor) **PR9540.5.D73 1997**
A Dragonfly in the Sun: An Anthology of Pakistani Writing in English. Trade Cloth. Oxford University Press, Inc. New York, NY. 1997. 630p. Jubilee Ser. ISBN:0-19-577784-0, ISBN13: 978-0-19-577784-0. Dewey:820.8/095491. LCCN:98-107360.
Audience: **g,l,u,f.**

Shirwadkar, Meena **PR9492.6.W65**
Image of Women in Indo-Anglian Novel. Trade Cloth. Asia Book Corporation of America. Flushing, NY. 1979. 169p. ISBN:0-318-37056-5, ISBN13: 978-0-318-37056-9. Dewey:823/.009/9287.
Audience: **l,u,f.**

Singh, Kirpal (Editor) **PL3508**
The Writer's Sense of the Past: Essays on Southeast Asian and Australasian Literature. Trade Paper. Singapore University Press Proprietary, Ltd. Singapore, 1987. 250p. ISBN:9971-69-108-6, ISBN13: 978-9971-69-108-0. Dewey:809.8959.
Audience: **u,f.**

Spivak, Gayatri Chakravorty **HM101.S773 1988**
In Other Worlds: Essays in Cultural Politics. UK-B Format Paperback. Routledge. New York, NY. 1987. 336p. ISBN:0-415-90002-6, ISBN13: 978-0-415-90002-7. Dewey:306. LCCN:87-037676.
Audience: **u,f.**

Wijesinha, Rajiva **PR9440.9.W657**
Acts of Faith. Trade Paper. Navarang Publishers & Booksellers. New Delhi, 1986. 181p. ISBN:81-7013-032-8, ISBN13: 978-81-7013-032-1. Dewey:823. LCCN:85-910841.
Audience: **g,l,u,f.**

Williams, Mark **Z3008.L58W55 1996**
Post-Colonial Literatures in English: Southeast Asia, New Zealand, and the Pacific, 1970-1992. Trade Cloth. Thomson Gale. Farmington Hills, MI. 1996. 370p. Reference Publication in Literature Ser. ISBN:0-8161-7353-2, ISBN13: 978-0-8161-7353-2. Dewey:016.895. LCCN:95-044859.
Audience: **u,f.** *Choice, 1997.*

Xu, Xi & Ingham, Mike (Editors) **PR9450.5**
City Voices: Hong Kong Writing in English, 1945-Present. Trade Cloth. Hong Kong University Press. Hong Kong, 2003. 420p. ISBN:962-209-604-2, ISBN13: 978-962-209-604-2. Dewey:820.8/095125. LCCN:2003-475436.
Audience: **g,l,u,f.**

Yeo, Robert
Singular Stories, Vol. One: Tales from Singapore. Robert Yeo (Editor). Lynne Rienner Publishers, Inc. 1993. ISBN:0-89410-758-5, ISBN13: 978-0-89410-758-0.
Audience: **g,l,u,f.**

Zaman, Niaz **PK5423**
A Divided Legacy: The Partition in Selected Novels of India, Pakistan, and Bangladesh. Trade Cloth. Oxford University Press, Inc. New York, NY. 2001. 358p. ISBN:0-19-579535-0, ISBN13: 978-0-19-579535-6. Dewey:891.4/371/09358.
Audience: **u,f.**

Zapanta-Manlapaz, Edna **PR9550.5**
Filipino Women Writers in English: Their Story: 1905-2002. Trade Cloth. Ateneo de Manila University Press. Manila, 2004. 270p. ISBN:971-550-451-5, ISBN13: 978-971-550-451-5. Dewey:820.8/09287/09599.
Audience: **g,l,u,f.**

Asia > India > Literary History and Criticism

Afzal-Khan, Fawzia **PR9492.2 .A4 1993**
Cultural Imperialism and the Indo-English Novel: Genre and Ideology in the Novels of R. K. Narayan, Anita Desai, Kamala Markandaya, and Salman Rushdie. Trade Paper. Pennsylvania State University Press. University Park, PA. 1993. 200p. ISBN:0-271-01013-4, ISBN13: 978-0-271-01013-7. Dewey:823. LCCN:92-029782.
Audience: **u,f.** *Choice, 1994.*

Allen, Richard & Trivedi, Harish (Editors) **PR129.I5L58 2000**
Literature and Nation: Britain and India 1800-1990. Paper over Boards. Routledge. New York, NY. 2001. 400p. ISBN:0-415-21206-5, ISBN13: 978-0-415-21206-9. Dewey:820.9/3254. LCCN:00-042205.
Audience: **u,f.**

Burton, Antoinette M. & Burton, Antoinette **PR9492.6.W6B87 2003**
Dwelling in the Archive: Women Writing House, Home, and History in Late Colonial India. Trade Paper. Oxford University Press, Inc. New York, NY. 2003. 216p. ISBN:0-19-514425-2, ISBN13: 978-0-19-514425-3. Dewey:820.9/355. LCCN:2002-070077.
Audience: **u,f.** *Choice, 2003.*

Chavan, Sunanda P **PR9488.C48 1984**
The Fair Voice: A Study of Indian Women Poets in English. Apt Books, Inc. 1984. ISBN:0-86590-591-6, ISBN13: 978-0-86590-591-7.
Audience: **u,f.**

Dodiya, Jaydipsinh & Surendran, K. V. (Editors) **PK5421.I53 2000**
Indian English Drama: Critical Perspectives. Trade Cloth. Sarup & Sons Publishers. New Delhi, 2000. xi, 121p.
ISBN:81-7625-110-0, ISBN13: 978-81-7625-110-5.
Dewey:822/.9109954. LCCN:00-289378.
Audience: **l,u,f.**

Dwivedi, A. N. **PR9492.52 .S78 1991**
Studies in Contemporary Indian-English Short Story: A Collection of Critical Essays. Trade Cloth. B. R. Publishing Corporation. New Delhi, 1991. New World Ser., No. 38
ISBN:81-7018-658-7, ISBN13: 978-81-7018-658-8.
Dewey:823/.0109954. LCCN:92-902482.
Audience: **g,l,u,f.**

Ezekiel, Nissim, et al. **PR9489.6**
Mapping Cultural Spaces: Postcolonial Indian Literature in English: Essays in Honour of Nissim Ezekiel. Nilufer E. Bharucha & Vrinda Nabar (Authors). Trade Cloth. Vision. New Delhi, 1998. 376p. ISBN:81-7094-311-6, ISBN13: 978-81-7094-311-2. Dewey:820.9/954/0904. LCCN:98-917124.
Audience: **u,f.**

Gorra, Michael **PR888.I6G67 1997**
After Empire: Scott, Naipaul, Rushdie. Trade Paper. University of Chicago Press. Chicago, IL. 1997. 218p.
ISBN:0-226-30475-2, ISBN13: 978-0-226-30475-5.
Dewey:823/.91409358. LCCN:96-023769.
Audience: **u,f.** *Choice, 1997.*

Jain, Jasbir & Amin, Amina (Editors) **PR9492.6.P87M37 1995**
Margins of Erasure: Purdah in the Subcontinental Novel in English. Trade Cloth. Sterling Publishers Pvt., Limited,. New Delhi, 1995. 248p. ISBN:81-207-1744-9, ISBN13: 978-81-207-1744-2. Dewey:823/.009/355. LCCN:95-901722.
Audience: **u,f.**

Joshi, Priya **PR9492.2.J68 2002**
In Another Country: Colonialism, Culture, and the English Novel in India. Trade Cloth. Columbia University Press. New York, NY. 2002. 368p. ISBN:0-231-12584-4, ISBN13: 978-0-231-12584-0. Dewey:823/.809954. LCCN:2001-047921.
Audience: **u,f.** *Choice, 2003, 2002.*

Kanaganayakam, Chelva **PR9492.5**
Counterrealism and Indo-Anglian Fiction. Trade Cloth. Wilfrid Laurier University Press. Waterloo, ON. 2002. 192p.
ISBN:0-88920-398-9, ISBN13: 978-0-88920-398-3. Dewey:823.
Audience: **u,f.** *Choice, 2003.*

Kaushik, Asha **PR9492.6.P64◇38**
Politics Aesthetics and Culture: A Study of Indo-Anglian Political Novel. Trade Cloth. Manohar Publications. New Delhi, 1988. ISBN:81-85054-47-9, ISBN13: 978-81-85054-47-6.
Dewey:823.009/358.
Audience: **u,f.** *Choice, 1989.*

Kirpal, Viney **PR9080.K55 1989**
A Third World Novel of Expatriation: A Study of Emigre Fiction by Indian, West African and Caribbean Writers. Apt Books, Inc. 1989. ISBN:81-207-0904-7, ISBN13: 978-81-207-0904-1.
Audience: **u,f.**

Mehrotra, Arvind Krishna **PR9489.6.H57 2002**
History of Indian Literature in English. Trade Cloth. Columbia University Press. New York, NY. 2003. 320p.
ISBN:0-231-12810-X, ISBN13: 978-0-231-12810-0.
Dewey:820.9/954/0904. LCCN:2002-025978.
Audience: **g,l,u,f.** *Choice, 2003.*

Moore-Gilbert, Bart (Editor) **PR9489.4.W75 1996**
Writing India, 1757-1990: The Literature of British India. Cloth Text. Manchester University Press. Manchester, 1996. 256p.
ISBN:0-7190-4265-8, ISBN13: 978-0-7190-4265-2.
Dewey:820.9. LCCN:95-031538.
Audience: **u,f.** *Choice, 1996.*

Mukherjee, Meenakshi **PR9484.6**
The Perishable Empire: Essays on Indian Writing in English. Trade Paper. Oxford University Press, Inc. New York, NY. 2003. 228p. ISBN:0-19-566270-9, ISBN13: 978-0-19-566270-2.
Dewey:820.9/954.
Audience: **u,f.** *Choice, 2001.*

Naik, M. K. **PR9484.3 .N35**
A History of Indian English Literature. Trade Cloth. Sahitya Akademy, Rabindra Bhawan. New Delhi, 1998.
ISBN:81-7201-840-1, ISBN13: 978-81-7201-840-5.
Dewey:820/.9/954.
Audience: **g,l,u,f.**

Narasimhaiah, C. D. **PR9484.6.N38 1999**
Swan and the Eagle: Essays on Indian English Literature. Ed. 3. Trade Paper. Vision. New Delhi, 1999. 295p.
ISBN:81-7094-338-8, ISBN13: 978-81-7094-338-9.
Dewey:820.9954.
Audience: **u,f.**

Natarajan, Nalini (Editor) **PK5416**
Handbook of Twentieth-Century Literatures of India. Cloth Text. Greenwood Publishing Group, Inc. Portsmouth, NH. 1996. 448p.
ISBN:0-313-28778-3, ISBN13: 978-0-313-28778-7.
Dewey:891/.1. LCCN:95-020938.
Audience: **u,f.** *Choice, 1997.*

Nelson, Emmanuel S. (Editor) **PR9485**
Writers of the Indian Diaspora: A Bio-Bibliographical Critical Sourcebook. Cloth Text. Greenwood Publishing Group, Inc. Portsmouth, NH. 1993. 504p. ISBN:0-313-27904-7, ISBN13: 978-0-313-27904-1. Dewey:820.9891411. LCCN:92-027898.
Audience: **g,l,u,f.** *Choice, 1994.*

Ramamurti, K S
Rise of the Indian Novel in English. Apt Books, Inc. 1987.
ISBN:81-207-0642-0, ISBN13: 978-81-207-0642-2.
Audience: **u,f.**

Sarma, G P
Nationalism in Indo-Anglican Fiction. Apt Books, Inc. 1990.
ISBN:81-207-1222-6, ISBN13: 978-81-207-1222-5.
Audience: **l,u,f.**

Singh, Jyotsna G. **PR129.I5S46 1996**
Colonial Narratives/Cultural Dialogues: Discoveries of India in the Language of Colonialism. Paper over Boards. Routledge. New York, NY. 1996. 208p. ISBN:0-415-08518-7, ISBN13: 978-0-415-08518-2. Dewey:820.9/358. LCCN:96-007428.
Audience: **u,f.**

Suleri, Sara **PR9484.3.S85 1992**
The Rhetoric of English India. Trade Paper. University of Chicago Press. Chicago, IL. 1993. 240p. ISBN:0-226-77983-1, ISBN13: 978-0-226-77983-6. Dewey:820.9/3254. LCCN:91-013014.
Audience: **u,f.** *Choice, 1992.*

Vanita, Ruth (Editor) **HQ76.2.I4Q84 2001**
Queering India: Same-Sex Love and Eroticism in Indian Culture and Society. Paper over Boards. Routledge. New York, NY. 2001. 256p. ISBN:0-415-92949-0, ISBN13: 978-0-415-92949-3. Dewey:306.76/6/0954. LCCN:2001-019111.
Audience: **u,f.**

Verma, K. D. **PR9489.6.V46 2000**
The Indian Imagination: Critical Essays on Indian Writing in English. Cloth over Boards. Palgrave Macmillan. New York, NY. 2000. 288p. ISBN:0-312-21139-2, ISBN13: 978-0-312-21139-4. Dewey:820.9/954. LCCN:99-057757.
Audience: **u,f.** *Choice, 2001.*

Viswanathan, Gauri
Masks of Conquest: Literary Study and British Rule in India. Oxford University Press, Inc. 1998. ISBN:0-19-564640-1, ISBN13: 978-0-19-564640-5.
Audience: **g,u,f.**

Walsh, William **PR9484.4.W35 1990**
Indian Literature in English: Longman Literature in English Series. Ed. 1. Paper Text. Longman Publishing Group. White Plains, NY. 1990. 272p. Literature in English Ser. ISBN:0-582-49480-X, ISBN13: 978-0-582-49480-0. Dewey:820.9/954. LCCN:89-034271.
Audience: **g,l,u.**

Williams, A. **PR9489.2**
Indo-Anglian Literature, 1880-1970: A Survey. Trade Cloth. South Asia Books. Columbia, MO. 1977. ISBN:0-88386-996-9, ISBN13: 978-0-88386-996-3. Dewey:820/.9.
Audience: **u,f.**

Asia > India > Collections

Butalia, Urashi (Editor) **PR9494.5.W66 I6 1992**
In Other Words: New Writing by Indian Women. Cloth Text. Kali for Women. New Delhi, 1992. 204p. ISBN:81-85107-48-3, ISBN13: 978-81-85107-48-6. Dewey:823. LCCN:92-906358.
Audience: **g,l,u,f.**

Chaudhuri, Amit **PR9494.9.V57 2002**
The Vintage Book of Modern Indian Literature. Trade Paper. Knopf Publishing Group. New York, NY. 2004. 688p. ISBN:0-375-71300-X, ISBN13: 978-0-375-71300-2. Dewey:820.8/0954/0904. LCCN:2002-071389.
Audience: **g,l,u,f.**

Cowasjee, Saros (Editor) **PR9497.32.O94 1998**
The Oxford Anthology of Raj Stories. Cloth Text. Oxford University Press, Inc. New York, NY. 1999. 360p. ISBN:0-19-564279-1, ISBN13: 978-0-19-564279-7. Dewey:823/.01083254. LCCN:98-909291.
Audience: **g,l,u,f.** *Choice, 2000.*

de Souza, Eunice (Editor) **PR9494.3**
Nine Indian Women Poets: An Anthology. Paper Text. Oxford University Press, Inc. New York, NY. 2001. 108p. ISBN:0-19-565847-7, ISBN13: 978-0-19-565847-7. Dewey:821/.008/09287.
Audience: **g,l,u,f.**

Holmstrom, Lakshmi
The Inner Courtyard: Stories by Indian Women. Lakshmi Holmstrom (Editor). Trafalgar Square. 1992. ISBN:1-85381-044-4, ISBN13: 978-1-85381-044-2.
Audience: **g,l,u,f.**

Hoskote, Ranjit (Editor) **PR9495.25**
Reasons for Belonging: Fourteen Contemporary Indian Poets. Trade Cloth. Penguin Group (USA) Inc. New York, NY. 2002. xxviii, 148p. ISBN:0-670-89094-4, ISBN13: 978-0-670-89094-1. Dewey:821.91. LCCN:2002-293036.
Audience: **g,l,u,f.**

Iyengar, K Srinivasa
Indian Writing in English. Ed. 5. Apt Books, Inc. 1984. ISBN:0-86590-447-2, ISBN13: 978-0-86590-447-7.
Audience: **g,l,u,f.**

King, Bruce **PR9490.2**
Modern Indian Poetry in English. Ed. 2. Trade Paper. Oxford University Press, Inc. New York, NY. 2005. 428p. Oxford India Paperbacks Ser. ISBN:0-19-567197-X, ISBN13: 978-0-19-567197-1. Dewey:821.9109954. LCCN:2006-270047.
Audience: **g,l,u,f.** *Choice, 1988.*

Rushdie, Salman & West, Elizabeth (Editors) **PR9494.9.V56 1997**
Mirrorwork: 50 Years of Indian Writing, 1947-1997. Trade Paper. Henry Holt & Company. New York, NY. 1997. 560p. ISBN:0-8050-5710-2, ISBN13: 978-0-8050-5710-2. Dewey:820.8/0954. LCCN:97-019595.
Audience: **g,l,u,f.**

Sarang, Vilas **PR9495.7.I48 1990**
Indian English Poetry: Since Nineteen Fifty: An Anthology. Vilas Sarang (Editor). Apt Books, Inc. 1990. ISBN:0-86311-167-X, ISBN13: 978-0-86311-167-9.
Audience: **g,l,u,f.**

Sukthankar, Ashwini **PK2978.E5F33 1999**
Facing the Mirror: Lesbian Writing from India. Trade Cloth. Penguin Group (USA) Inc. New York, NY. 1999. xli, 409p. ISBN:0-14-028309-9, ISBN13: 978-0-14-028309-9. Dewey:810.809206643. LCCN:99-933297.
Audience: **u,f.**

Tharu, Susie J. & Lalita, K. (Editors) **PK2978.E5W57**
Women Writing in India: The Twentieth Century. Trade Paper. Feminist Press at The City University of New York. New York, NY. 1993. 688p. ISBN:1-55861-029-4, ISBN13: 978-1-55861-029-3. Dewey:891/.1. LCCN:90-003788.
Audience: **g,l,u,f.** *Choice, 1993.*

Tharu, Susie J. & Lalita, K. (Editors) **PK2978.E5W57 1990**
Women Writing in India: 600 BC to the Present, Vol. I. Trade

Paper. Feminist Press at The City University of New York. New York, NY. 1991. 576p. Women Writing in India Ser., Vol. 1 ISBN:1-55861-027-8, ISBN13: 978-1-55861-027-9. Dewey:891/.1. LCCN:90-003788.
Audience: **g,l,u,f.**

Asia > India > Individual Authors > A-D

Anand, Mulk Raj **PR6019.O9**
Untouchable. E. M. Forster (Introduction by). Trade Paper. Penguin Group (USA) Inc. New York, NY. 1990. 160p. Penguin Twentieth-Century Classics Ser. ISBN:0-14-018395-7, ISBN13: 978-0-14-018395-5. Dewey:823.
Audience: **g,l,u,f.**

Chandra, Vikram **PS3553.H27165.L68**
Love and Longing in Bombay. Trade Cloth. Little Brown & Company. New York, NY. 1997. 288p. ISBN:0-316-13307-8, ISBN13: 978-0-316-13307-4. Dewey:823. LCCN:96-042520.
Audience: **g,l,u,f.**

Chandra, Vikram **PR9499.3.N3**
Red Earth and Pouring Rain. Trade Cloth. Little Brown & Company. New York, NY. 1995. ISBN:0-316-13266-7, ISBN13: 978-0-316-13266-4. Dewey:823. LCCN:94-048841.
Audience: **g,l,u,f.**

Chatterjee, Upamanyu **PR9499.3.C4665E54**
English, August: An Indian Story. Akhil Sharma (Introduction by). Trade Paper. New York Review of Books, Incorporated, The. New York, NY. 2006. 336p. New York Review Books Classics ISBN:1-59017-179-9, ISBN13: 978-1-59017-179-0. Dewey:823/.914. LCCN:2005-022842.
Audience: **g,l,u,f.**

Chaudhuri, Amit **PR9499.3.C4678.F74**
Freedom Song: Three Novels. Trade Paper. Alfred A. Knopf Inc. New York, NY. 2000. 448p. ISBN:0-375-70400-0, ISBN13: 978-0-375-70400-0. Dewey:823. LCCN:98-035260.
Audience: **g,l,u,f.**

Chaudhuri, Amit **PR9499.3.C4678R43**
Real Time: Stories and a Reminiscence. Trade Paper. Picador. New York, NY. 2003. 192p. ISBN:0-312-42114-1, ISBN13: 978-0-312-42114-4. Dewey:823/.914. LCCN:2003-041624.
Audience: **g,l,u,f.**

Desai, Anita **PR9499.3.D465B38**
Baumgartner's Bombay. Trade Paper. Houghton Mifflin Company Trade & Reference Division. Boston, MA. 2000. 240p. ISBN:0-618-05680-7, ISBN13: 978-0-618-05680-4. Dewey:823/.914. LCCN:00-037024.
Audience: **g,l,u,f.**

Desai, Anita **PR6015.I3**
Clear Light of Day. UK-B Format Paperback. Knopf Publishing Group. New York, NY. 2001. 192p. ISBN:0-09-927618-6, ISBN13: 978-0-09-927618-0. Dewey:823/.914.
Audience: **g,l,u,f.**

Desai, Anita **PR9499.3.D465**
Games at Twilight. UK-B Format Paperback. Knopf Publishing Group. New York, NY. 2001. 137p. ISBN:0-09-942853-9, ISBN13: 978-0-09-942853-4. Dewey:823.
Audience: **g,l,u,f.**

Desai, Anita **PR9499.3.D465**
In Custody. Trade Paper. Knopf Publishing Group. New York, NY. 2001. 225p. ISBN:0-09-942849-0, ISBN13: 978-0-09-942849-7. Dewey:823.
Audience: **g,l,u,f.**

Divakaruni, Chitra Banerjee **PS3568.O243**
Arranged Marriage: Stories. Trade Paper. Random House Children's Books. New York, NY. 1996. 320p. ISBN:0-385-48350-3, ISBN13: 978-0-385-48350-6. Dewey:813.5/4. LCCN:94-037210.
Audience: **g,l,u,f.**

Divakaruni, Chitra Banerjee **PS3554.I86S57 1999**
Sister of My Heart. Trade Paper. Random House Children's Books. New York, NY. 2000. 336p. ISBN:0-385-48951-X, ISBN13: 978-0-385-48951-5. Dewey:813.54. LCCN:98-030254.
Audience: **g,l,u,f.**

Asia > India > Individual Authors > G-K

Ghosh, Amitav **PR9499.3.G536C35**
The Calcutta Chromosome: A Novel of Fevers, Delirium and Discovery. Trade Paper. HarperCollins Publishers. New York, NY. 2001. 320p. ISBN:0-380-81394-7, ISBN13: 978-0-380-81394-0. Dewey:823.
Audience: **g,l,u,f.**

Ghosh, Amitav **PR9499.3.G536G58**
The Glass Palace. Trade Paper. Random House Adult Trade Publishing Group. New York, NY. 2002. 512p. ISBN:0-375-75877-1, ISBN13: 978-0-375-75877-5. Dewey:823.
Audience: **g,l,u,f.**

Ghosh, Amitav **PR9499.3.G536S53**
The Shadow Lines: A Novel. Trade Paper. Houghton Mifflin Company Trade & Reference Division. Boston, MA. 2005. 256p. ISBN:0-618-32996-X, ISBN13: 978-0-618-32996-0. Dewey:823/.914. LCCN:2005-040384.
Audience: **g,l,u,f.**

Hossain, Rokeya S. **PR9420.9.R65S86 1988**
Sultana's Dream: And Selections from the Secluded Ones. Roushan Jahan (Editor, Translator), Hanna Papanek (Afterword by). Trade Cloth. Feminist Press at The City University of New York. New York, NY. 1988. 104p. ISBN:0-935312-98-6, ISBN13: 978-0-935312-98-0. Dewey:823. LCCN:88-011033.
Audience: **g,l,u,f.**

Asia > India > Individual Authors > M

Mishra, Pankaj **PR9499.3.M538R65**
The Romantics: A Novel. Trade Cloth. RST Indiaink Publishing. New Delhi, 2000. 277p. ISBN:81-86939-05-9, ISBN13: 978-81-86939-05-5. Dewey:823. LCCN:99-947830.
Audience: **g,l,u,f.**

Mistry, Rohinton **PR9199.3.M494F56**
A Fine Balance: A Novel. Trade Paper. Knopf Publishing Group. New York, NY. 2001. 624p. ISBN:1-4000-3065-X, ISBN13: 978-1-4000-3065-1. Dewey:813/.54. LCCN:95-049317.
Audience: **g,l,u,f.** *Choice, 1996.*

Mistry, Rohinton **PR9199.3.M494 1992**
Such a Long Journey. Trade Paper. Knopf Publishing Group. New York, NY. 1992. 352p. ISBN:0-679-73871-1, ISBN13: 978-0-679-73871-8. Dewey:823. LCCN:91-058052.
Audience: **g,l,u,f.**

Mukherjee, Bharati **PR9499.3.M77D47 2002**
Desirable Daughters. Trade Cloth. Hyperion Press. New York, NY. 2002. 310p. ISBN:0-7868-6598-9, ISBN13: 978-0-7868-6598-7. Dewey:813.54. LCCN:2001-053061.
Audience: **g,l,u,f.**

Mukherjee, Bharati **PS3568.O243**
Jasmine. Trade Paper. Grove/Atlantic, Inc. New York, NY. 1999. 256p. ISBN:0-8021-3630-3, ISBN13: 978-0-8021-3630-5. Dewey:813.5/4.
Audience: **g,l,u,f.**

Nelson, Emmanuel S. (Editor) **PR9499.3.M77**
Bharati Mukherjee: Critical Perspectives. Paper over Boards. Garland Publishing, Inc. New York, NY. 1993. 256p. Garland Reference Library of the Humanities, Vol. 1663 ISBN:0-8153-1173-7, ISBN13: 978-0-8153-1173-7. Dewey:813.54. LCCN:93-018145.
Audience: **l,u.** *Choice, 1994.*

Asia > India > Individual Authors > Narayan, R. K.

Kain, Geoffrey R. (Editor) **PR9499.3.N3Z842 1993**
R. K. Narayan: Contemporary Critical Perspectives. Trade Cloth. Michigan State University Press. East Lansing, MI. 1993. 200p. ISBN:0-87013-330-6, ISBN13: 978-0-87013-330-5. Dewey:823. LCCN:93-029080.
Audience: **g,l,u,f.** *Choice, 1994.*

Narayan, R. K. **PR9499.3.N3**
The Guide: A Novel. Trade Paper. Penguin Group (USA) Inc. New York, NY. 1992. 224p. Twentieth Century Classics Ser. ISBN:0-14-018547-X, ISBN13: 978-0-14-018547-8. Dewey:891.46.
Audience: **g,l,u,f.**

Narayan, R. K. **PR9499.3.N3M3 2000**
The Mahabharata: A Shortened Modern Prose Version of the Indian Epic. Trade Paper. University of Chicago Press. Chicago, IL. 2000. 192p. ISBN:0-226-56822-9, ISBN13: 978-0-226-56822-5. Dewey:294.5/923. LCCN:00-033776.
Audience: **g,l,u,f.**

Narayan, R. K. **PR9499.3.N3M34 1984**
Malgudi Days. Trade Paper. Penguin Group (USA) Inc. New York, NY. 1995. 256p. Twentieth Century Classics Ser. ISBN:0-14-018543-7, ISBN13: 978-0-14-018543-0. Dewey:823. LCCN:95-113767.
Audience: **g,l,u,f.**

Narayan, R. K. **PR6027.A68**
The Man-Eater of Malgudi. Trade Paper. Penguin Group (USA) Inc. New York, NY. 1993. 176p. Twentieth Century Classics Ser. ISBN:0-14-018548-8, ISBN13: 978-0-14-018548-5. Dewey:823.912.
Audience: **g,l,u,f.**

Narayan, R. K. **PR9499.3.N3M5 1981**
Mr. Sampath: The Printer of Malgudi. Trade Paper. University of Chicago Press. Chicago, IL. 1981. 220p. Phoenix Fiction Ser. ISBN:0-226-56839-3, ISBN13: 978-0-226-56839-3. Dewey:823. LCCN:80-027352.
Audience: **g,l,u,f.**

Narayan, R. K. **PR9499.3.N3 Z52 1999**
My Days. Trade Cloth. HarperCollins Publishers. New York, NY. 1999. 192p. ISBN:0-88001-625-6, ISBN13: 978-0-88001-625-4. Dewey:823. LCCN:98-014082.
Audience: **g,l,u,f.**

Narayan, R. K. **PR9499.3.N3 G6 1993**
Gods, Demons, and Others. R. K. Laxman (Illustrator). Trade Paper. University of Chicago Press. Chicago, IL. 1993. 252p. ISBN:0-226-56825-3, ISBN13: 978-0-226-56825-6. Dewey:823. LCCN:92-043997.
Audience: **g,l,u,f.**

Sharan, Nagendra N. **PR9499.3.N3**
Critical Study of the Novels of R. K. Narayan. Trade Cloth. Classics India Publications. Delhi, 1993. ISBN:81-7054-171-9, ISBN13: 978-81-7054-171-4. Dewey:823. LCCN:92-911762.
Audience: **l,u.**

Walsh, William **PR9499.3.N3 Z94 1982**
R. K. Narayan: A Critical Appreciation. Trade Cloth. University of Chicago Press. Chicago, IL. 1982. 184p. ISBN:0-226-87213-0, ISBN13: 978-0-226-87213-1. Dewey:823. LCCN:82-040320.
Audience: **g,l,u,f.**

Asia > India > Individual Authors > R

Rangel-Ribeiro, Victor **PS3568.A566T58 1998**
Tivolem. Trade Cloth. Milkweed Editions. Minneapolis, MN. 1998. 400p. Milkweed National Fiction Prize Ser. ISBN:1-57131-019-3, ISBN13: 978-1-57131-019-4. Dewey:813/.54. LCCN:97-043264.
Audience: **l,u,f.** *Choice, 1998.*

Rao, Raja **PZ3**
Kanthapura. Trade Paper. New Directions Publishing Corporation. New York, NY. 1967. ISBN:0-8112-0168-6, ISBN13: 978-0-8112-0168-1. Dewey:823. LCCN:63-018637.
Audience: **g,l,u,f.** B

Roy, Arundhati **HD1698.I42G8565 1999**
The Cost of Living. Trade Paper. Random House, Inc. New York, NY. 1999. 144p. Modern Library Ser. ISBN:0-375-75614-0, ISBN13: 978-0-375-75614-6. Dewey:333.91/15/095475. LCCN:99-041156.
Audience: **g,l,u,f.**

Roy, Arundhati **PR9499.3.R59G63 1998**
The God of Small Things. Trade Paper. HarperCollins Publishers. New York, NY. 1998. 336p. ISBN:0-06-097749-3, ISBN13: 978-0-06-097749-8. Dewey:823. LCCN:97-032562.
Audience: **g,l,u,f.** *Choice, 1998.*

Asia > India > Individual Authors > Rushdie, Salman

Cundy, Catherine **PR6068.U757Z6 1996**
Salman Rushdie. Cloth Text. Manchester University Press. Manchester, 1997. 320p. Contemporary World Writers Ser. ISBN:0-7190-4408-1, ISBN13: 978-0-7190-4408-3. Dewey:823/.914. LCCN:96-009826.
Audience: **g,l,u,f.**

Hassumani, Sabrina **PR6068.U757Z64 2002**
Salman Rushdie: A Postmodern Reading of His Major Works. Trade Cloth. Fairleigh Dickinson University Press. Cranbury, NJ. 2002. 160p. ISBN:0-8386-3934-8, ISBN13: 978-0-8386-3934-4. Dewey:823/.914. LCCN:2001-054479.
Audience: **u,f.**

Maitland, Sara & Appignanesi, Lisa (Editors) **PR6068.U757S2736**
The Rushdie File. Trade Paper. Syracuse University Press. Syracuse, NY. 1990. 256p. Contemporary Issues in the Middle East Ser. ISBN:0-8156-0248-0, ISBN13: 978-0-8156-0248-4. Dewey:823. LCCN:89-048413.
Audience: **g,l,u,f.** *Choice, 1990.*

Reder, Michael R. (Editor) **PR6068.U757Z465 2000**
Conversations with Salman Rushdie. Trade Cloth. University Press of Mississippi. Jackson, MS. 2000. xvi, 238p. Literary Conversations Ser. ISBN:1-57806-185-7, ISBN13: 978-1-57806-185-3. Dewey:823/.914 B. LCCN:99-057120.
Audience: **g,l,u,f.**

Rushdie, Salman **PR6068.U757E27 1996**
East, West: Stories. Trade Paper. Knopf Publishing Group. New York, NY. 1995. 224p. ISBN:0-679-75789-9, ISBN13: 978-0-679-75789-4. Dewey:823/.914. LCCN:96-119558.
Audience: **g,l,u,f.**

Rushdie, Salman **PR6068.U757 I4 1991B**
Imaginary Homelands: Essays and Criticism 1981-1991. Trade Cloth. Penguin Group (USA) Inc. New York, NY. 1991. 432p. ISBN:0-14-014224-X, ISBN13: 978-0-14-014224-2. Dewey:828. LCCN:92-188054.
Audience: **l,u,f.** *Choice, 1991.*

Rushdie, Salman **PR6068.U757M66 1996B**
The Moor's Last Sigh. Trade Paper. Random House of Canada, Ltd. Mississauga, ON. 1996. 448p. ISBN:0-394-28197-7, ISBN13: 978-0-394-28197-1. Dewey:823.
Audience: **g,l,u,f.**

Rushdie, Salman **PR6068.U757S27385**
The Satanic Verses: A Novel. Trade Paper. Picador. New York, NY. 2000. 576p. ISBN:0-312-27082-8, ISBN13: 978-0-312-27082-7. Dewey:823/.914. LCCN:97-000795.
Audience: **g,l,u,f.**

Rushdie, Salman **PR6068.U757S5**
Shame. Trade Paper. Picador. New York, NY. 2000. 320p. ISBN:0-312-27093-3, ISBN13: 978-0-312-27093-3. Dewey:823.
Audience: **g,l,u,f.**

Rushdie, Salman **PR6068.U757M5 1995**
Midnight's Children. Anita Desai (Introduction by). Trade Cloth. Alfred A. Knopf Inc. New York, NY. 1995. 624p. ISBN:0-679-44462-9, ISBN13: 978-0-679-44462-6. Dewey:823/.914. LCCN:95-234890.
Audience: **g,l,u,f.** B

Asia > India > Individual Authors > S-T

Selvadurai, Shyam **PR9440.9.S42F86 1997**
Funny Boy: A Novel in Six Stories. Trade Paper. Harcourt Trade Publishers. New York, NY. 1997. 320p. Harvest Book Ser. ISBN:0-15-600500-X, ISBN13: 978-0-15-600500-5. Dewey:813. LCCN:97-006782.
Audience: **g,l,u,f.**

Seth, Vikram **PR9499.3.S38S83**
A Suitable Boy: A Novel. Trade Paper. HarperCollins Publishers. New York, NY. 1994. 1488p. ISBN:0-06-092500-0, ISBN13: 978-0-06-092500-0. Dewey:823. LCCN:92-054744.
Audience: **g,l,u,f.**

Sidhwa, Bapsi **PR9540.9.S53I34**
Cracking India: A Novel. Trade Paper. Milkweed Editions. Minneapolis, MN. 2006. 296p. ISBN:1-57131-048-7, ISBN13: 978-1-57131-048-4. Dewey:823.
Audience: **g,l,u,f.** *Choice, 1992.*

Singh, Khushwant **PR9499.3.S53**
Train to Pakistan. Trade Paper. Grove/Atlantic, Inc. New York, NY. 1994. 192p. ISBN:0-8021-3221-9, ISBN13: 978-0-8021-3221-5. Dewey:823. LCCN:80-008920.
Audience: **g,l,u,f.**

Suri, Manil **PS3569.U725D43 2002**
The Death of Vishnu: A Novel. Trade Paper. HarperCollins Publishers. New York, NY. 2002. 304p. ISBN:0-06-000438-X, ISBN13: 978-0-06-000438-5. Dewey:813/.6. LCCN:2001-036961.
Audience: **g,l,u,f.**

Syal, Meera **PR9499.3.S975L54**
Life Isn't All Ha Ha Hee Hee. Trade Cloth. New Press, The. New York, NY. 2000. 336p. ISBN:1-56584-614-1, ISBN13: 978-1-56584-614-2. Dewey:823.9/14. LCCN:99-054390.
Audience: **g,l,u,f.**

Tagore, Rabindranath **PK1723 .C4913 1993**
Quartet. Trade Paper. Heinemann. Portsmouth, NH. 1994. 96p. Asian Writers Ser. ISBN:0-435-95086-X, ISBN13: 978-0-435-95086-6. Dewey:891.4435.
Audience: **g,l,u,f.**

Tharoor, Shashi **PR9499.3.T535G7**
The Great Indian Novel. Trade Paper. Arcade Publishing, Inc. New York, NY. 1993. 423p. ISBN:1-55970-194-3, ISBN13: 978-1-55970-194-5. Dewey:823.
Audience: **g,l,u,f.**

Tharoor, Shashi **PR9499.3.T535R56**
Riot: A Love Story. Trade Cloth. Arcade Publishing, Inc. New York, NY. 2001. 272p. ISBN:1-55970-605-8, ISBN13: 978-1-55970-605-6. Dewey:823/.914. LCCN:2001-033311.
Audience: **g,l,u,f.**

West Indies

Bloom, Harold **PR9205.05.C37**
Caribbean Women Writers. Library Binding. Sagebrush Education Resources. Caledonia, MN. 1997. ISBN:0-613-86159-0, ISBN13: 978-0-613-86159-5. Dewey:810.9/9287/09729 B.
Audience: **l,u,f.**

Booker, M. Keith **PR9205**
The Caribbean Novel in English: An Introduction. Dubravka Juraga. Heinemann. 2001. ISBN:0-325-00212-6, ISBN13: 978-0-325-00212-5.
Audience: **l,u.**

Bouson, J. Brooks **PR9275.A583K564 2005**
Jamaica Kincaid: Writing Memory, Writing Back to the Mother. Cloth Text. State University of New York Press. Albany, NY. 2005. 256p. ISBN:0-7914-6523-3, ISBN13: 978-0-7914-6523-3. Dewey:813/.54. LCCN:2004-027305.
Audience: **g,l,u,f.** *Choice, 2006.*

Braithwaite, Kamau **PR9230.9.B68B5 1995**
Black and Blues. Trade Paper. New Directions Publishing Corporation. New York, NY. 1995. 70p. Paperbook Ser., Vol. 815 ISBN:0-8112-1313-7, ISBN13: 978-0-8112-1313-4. Dewey:811. LCCN:95-034695.
Audience: **g,l,u,f.**

Brathwaite, Kamau **PR9230.9.B68A57 2001**
Ancestors. Trade Paper. New Directions Publishing Corporation. New York, NY. 2001. 544p. ISBN:0-8112-1448-6, ISBN13: 978-0-8112-1448-3. Dewey:811/.54. LCCN:00-055023.
Audience: **g,l,u,f.**

Brathwaite, Kamau **PR9230.9.B68.A6 1973**
The Arrivants: A New World Trilogy. Trade Paper. Oxford University Press, Inc. New York, NY. 2004. 275p. ISBN:0-19-281154-1, ISBN13: 978-0-19-281154-7. Dewey:821. LCCN:73-181354.
Audience: **g,l,u,f.** B

Brown, Stewart (Author, Editor) **PR9205.8**
The Oxford Book of Caribbean Short Stories. Ed. 2. John Wickham (Editor). Trade Paper. Oxford University Press, Inc. New York, NY. 2002. 512p. Oxford Books of Prose ISBN:0-19-280229-1, ISBN13: 978-0-19-280229-3. Dewey:813/.01089729.
Audience: **g,l,u,f.**

Conde, Mary & Lonsdale, Thorunn (Editors) **PR9205.4.C37 1998**
Caribbean Women Writers: Fiction in English. Trade Paper. Palgrave Macmillan. New York, NY. 1999. 245p. ISBN:0-312-21863-X, ISBN13: 978-0-312-21863-8. Dewey:813/.0099287. LCCN:98-028418.
Audience: **l,u,f.** *Choice, 1999.*

Denniston, Dorothy H. **PS3563.A7223Z64 1995**
The Fiction of Paule Marshall: Reconstructions of History, Culture, and Gender. Cloth Text. University of Tennessee Press. Knoxville, TN. 1995. 216p. ISBN:0-87049-838-X, ISBN13: 978-0-87049-838-1. Dewey:813/.54. LCCN:94-018767.
Audience: **l,u,f.** *Choice, 1996.*

Donnell, Alison
Una Marson and Louise Bennett. Trade Paper. Northcote House Publishers, Ltd. Tavistock, 2004. ISBN:0-7463-0990-2, ISBN13: 978-0-7463-0990-2.
Audience: **l,u,f.**

Donnell, Alison **PR9205.5**
Twentieth Century Caribbean Literature. Paper over Boards. Routledge. New York, NY. 2005. X, 278p. ISBN:0-415-26199-6, ISBN13: 978-0-415-26199-9. Dewey:820.9/9729/0904. LCCN:2005-009603.
Audience: **l,u,f.**

Donnell, Alison & Welsh, Sarah L. (Compiled by) **PR9205.5.R68 1996**
The Routledge Reader in Caribbean Literature. Paper over Boards. Routledge. New York, NY. 1996. 560p. ISBN:0-415-12048-9, ISBN13: 978-0-415-12048-7. Dewey:810.9/9729. LCCN:95-048494.
Audience: **g,l,u,f.** *Choice, 1997.*

Figueredo, D. H. **PN849.C3E53 2006**
Encyclopedia of Caribbean Literature. Trade Cloth. Greenwood Publishing Group, Inc. Portsmouth, NH. 2005. ISBN:0-313-32743-2, ISBN13: 978-0-313-32743-8. Dewey:809/.89729. LCCN:2005-025483.
Audience: **g,l,u,f.**

Hathaway, Heather **PS3525.A24785Z69**
Caribbean Waves: Relocating Claude Mckay and Paule Marshall. Trade Cloth. Indiana University Press. Bloomington, IN. 1999. 232p. Blacks in the Diaspora Ser. ISBN:0-253-33569-8, ISBN13: 978-0-253-33569-2. Dewey:810.9/896073. LCCN:99-013329.
Audience: **l,u,f.** *Choice, 2000.*

James, Cynthia **PR9205**
The Maroon Narrative: Caribbean Literature in English Across Boundaries, Ethnicities and Centuries. Trade Cloth. Greenwood Publishing Group, Inc. Portsmouth, NH. 2002. 144p. Studies in Caribbean Literature ISBN:0-325-07099-7, ISBN13: 978-0-325-07099-5. Dewey:810.9/3520625. LCCN:2001-059383.
Audience: **l,u,f.**

Kincaid, Jamaica **PR9275.A583**
Annie John: A Novel. Trade Paper. Farrar, Straus & Giroux. New York, NY. 1997. 148p. ISBN:0-374-52510-2, ISBN13: 978-0-374-52510-1. Dewey:813.54. LCCN:84-028630.
Audience: **g,l,u,f.**

Kincaid, Jamaica **PR9275.A583.K.5636**
The Autobiography of My Mother. Trade Paper. Penguin Group (USA) Inc. New York, NY. 1997. 240p. ISBN:0-452-27466-4, ISBN13: 978-0-452-27466-2. Dewey:813. LCCN:96-029478.
Audience: **g,l,u,f.**

Kincaid, Jamaica **PS3568.O243**
Mr. Potter. Trade Paper. Random House of Canada, Ltd. Mississauga, ON. 2003. 208p. ISBN:0-676-97470-8, ISBN13: 978-0-676-97470-6. Dewey:813/.54.
Audience: **g,l,u,f.**

Lamming, George **PR9230.9.L25E47 1994**
The Emigrants. Trade Paper. University of Michigan Press. Chicago, IL. 1994. 344p. Ann Arbor Paperback Ser. ISBN:0-472-06470-3, ISBN13: 978-0-472-06470-0. Dewey:813. LCCN:94-002141.
Audience: **g,l,u,f.** B

Lamming, George **PR9230.9.L25.I5 1991**
In the Castle of My Skin. Trade Paper. University of Michigan Press. Chicago, IL. 1991. 314p. Ann Arbor Paperback Ser. ISBN:0-472-06468-1, ISBN13: 978-0-472-06468-7. Dewey:823/.91. LCCN:91-042068.
Audience: **g,l,u,f.** B *Choice, 1992.*

Marshall, Paule **PS3563.A7223F57 2001**
The Fisher King: A Novel. Library Binding. Center Point Large Print. Thorndike, ME. 2001. 256p. ISBN:1-58547-074-0, ISBN13: 978-1-58547-074-7. Dewey:813/.54. LCCN:00-047444.
Audience: **g,l,u,f.**

Marshall, Paule **PS3568.O243**
Praisesong for the Widow. Trade Paper. Penguin Group (USA) Inc. New York, NY. 1984. 256p. Contemporary Fiction Ser. ISBN:0-452-26711-0, ISBN13: 978-0-452-26711-4. Dewey:813/.54.
Audience: **g,l,u,f.**

Marshall, Paule **PS3563.A7223B7 2006**
Brown Girl, Brownstones. Edwidge Danticat (Foreword by). Trade Paper. Consortium Book Sales & Distribution. Saint Paul, MN. 2006. 304p. ISBN:1-55861-498-2, ISBN13: 978-1-55861-498-7. Dewey:813/.54. LCCN:2005-029191.
Audience: **g,l,u,f.**

McDonald, Ian & Brown, Stewart **PR9205.6.H45 1992**
The Heinemann Book of Caribbean Poetry. Trade Paper. Heinemann. Portsmouth, NH. 1992. 256p. Caribbean Writers Ser. ISBN:0-435-98817-4, ISBN13: 978-0-435-98817-3. Dewey:811/.00809729. LCCN:93-159094.
Audience: **g,l,u,f.**

Mistron, Deborah **PR9275.A583 K563436**
e Understanding Jamaica Kincaid's Annie John: A Student Casebook to Issues, Sources, and Historical Documents. E-Book. Greenwood Publishing Group, Inc. Portsmouth, NH. 2003. 232p. Literature in Context Ser. ISBN:0-313-01044-7, ISBN13: 978-0-313-01044-6. Dewey:813. LCCN:98-012158.
Audience: **l,u,f.**

Nair, Supriya **PR9230.9.L25Z79 1996**
Caliban's Curse: George Lamming and the Revisioning of History. Trade Cloth. University of Michigan Press. Chicago, IL. 1996. 184p. ISBN:0-472-10717-8, ISBN13: 978-0-472-10717-9. Dewey:813. LCCN:96-010322.
Audience: **l,u,f.** *Choice, 1997.*

Olaniyan, Tejumola **PS338.N4O43 1995**
Scars of Conquest/Masks of Resistance: The Invention of Cultural Identities in African, African-American, and Caribbean Drama. Trade Cloth. Oxford University Press, Inc. New York, NY. 1995. 208p. ISBN:0-19-509405-0, ISBN13: 978-0-19-509405-3. Dewey:809.2/008996073. LCCN:94-033238.
Audience: **l,u,f.**

Paravisini-Gebert, Lizabeth **PR9275.A583K566**
Jamaica Kincaid: A Critical Companion. Cloth Text. Greenwood Publishing Group, Inc. Portsmouth, NH. 2002. 200p. Critical Companions to Popular Contemporary Writers Ser. ISBN:0-313-32630-4, ISBN13: 978-0-313-32630-1. Dewey:813.
Audience: **l,u,f.** *Choice, 2000.*

Pettis, Joyce **PS3563.A7223Z83 1995**
Toward Wholeness in Paule Marshall's Fiction. Cloth Text. University Press of Virginia. Charlottesville, VA. 1995. 192p. ISBN:0-8139-1614-3, ISBN13: 978-0-8139-1614-9. Dewey:813/.54. LCCN:94-048916.
Audience: **l,u,f.** *Choice, 1996.*

Pollard, Charles W. **PR9272.9.W3Z82 2004**
New World Modernisms: T. S. Eliot, Derek Walcott, and Kamau Brathwaite. Trade Cloth. University Press of Virginia. Charlottesville, VA. 2004. 240p. New World Studies ISBN:0-8139-2277-1, ISBN13: 978-0-8139-2277-5. Dewey:811/.54099729. LCCN:2003-026773.
Audience: **l,u,f.**

Reiss, Timothy J. (Editor) **PR9230.9.B68Z68 2001**
For the Geography of a Soul: Emerging Perspectives on Kamau Brathwaite. Cloth Text. Africa World Press. Trenton, NJ. 2001. 420p. ISBN:0-86543-904-4, ISBN13: 978-0-86543-904-7. Dewey:811/.54. LCCN:2001-002550.
Audience: **l,u,f.**

Williams, Emily Allen **PR9230**
The Critical Response to Kamau Brathwaite. Trade Cloth. Greenwood Publishing Group, Inc. Portsmouth, NH. 2004. 368p. Critical Responses in Arts and Letters Ser., No. 41 ISBN:0-275-97957-1, ISBN13: 978-0-275-97957-7. Dewey:811/.54. LCCN:2004-044375.
Audience: **l,u,f.** *Choice, 2005.*

West Indies > Naipaul, V. S.

Barnouw, Dagmar **PR9272.9.N32Z57 2003**
Naipaul's Strangers. Trade Paper. Indiana University Press. Bloomington, IN. 2003. 240p. ISBN:0-253-21579-X, ISBN13: 978-0-253-21579-6. Dewey:823/.914. LCCN:2002-014599.
Audience: **u,f.** *Choice, 2003.*

Gorra, Michael **PR888.I6G67 1997**
After Empire: Scott, Naipaul, Rushdie. Trade Paper. University of Chicago Press. Chicago, IL. 1997. 218p. ISBN:0-226-30475-2, ISBN13: 978-0-226-30475-5. Dewey:823/.91409358. LCCN:96-023769.
Audience: **u,f.** *Choice, 1997.*

Naipaul, V. S. **PR6015.I3**
A Bend in the River. Trade Paper. Random House of Canada, Ltd. Mississauga, ON. 2002. 288p. ISBN:0-676-97513-5, ISBN13: 978-0-676-97513-0. Dewey:823/.914.
Audience: **g,l,u,f.**

Naipaul, V. S. **PR6015.I3**
Guerrillas. Trade Paper. Random House of Canada, Ltd. Mississauga, ON. 2001. 256p. ISBN:0-676-97506-2, ISBN13: 978-0-676-97506-2. Dewey:823/.914.
Audience: **g,l,u,f.**

Naipaul, V. S. **PR9272.9.N32H55 2001**
Half a Life. Trade Cloth. Alfred A. Knopf Inc. New York, NY. 2001. 224p. ISBN:0-375-40737-5, ISBN13: 978-0-375-40737-6. Dewey:823/.914. LCCN:2001-033730.
Audience: **g,l,u,f.**

Naipaul, V. S. **PR9272.9.N32H6 2001**
A House for Mr. Biswas: A Novel. Trade Paper. Knopf Publishing Group. New York, NY. 2001. 576p. ISBN:0-375-70716-6, ISBN13: 978-0-375-70716-2. Dewey:823/.914. LCCN:00-049056.
Audience: **g,l,u,f.**

Naipaul, V. S. **PR9272.9.N32L5**
Literary Occasions: Essays. Trade Paper. Knopf Publishing Group. New York, NY. 2004. 240p. ISBN:1-4000-3130-3, ISBN13: 978-1-4000-3130-6. Dewey:809.
Audience: **g,l,u,f.**

Naipaul, V. S. **PR9272.9.N32M49 2004**
Magic Seeds. Trade Cloth. Knopf Publishing Group. New York, NY. 2004. 288p. ISBN:0-375-40736-7, ISBN13: 978-0-375-40736-9. Dewey:823/.914. LCCN:2004-048964.
Audience: **g,l,u,f.**

Naipaul, V. S. **PR9272.9.N32M55 2001**
The Mimic Men: A Novel. Trade Paper. Knopf Publishing Group. New York, NY. 2001. 304p. ISBN:0-375-70717-4, ISBN13: 978-0-375-70717-9. Dewey:823/.914. LCCN:00-052753.
Audience: **g,l,u,f.**

Naipaul, V. S. **PR6015.I3**
A Way in the World. UK-Trade Paper. Random House, Inc. New York, NY. 1995. 400p. ISBN:0-679-76166-7, ISBN13: 978-0-679-76166-2. Dewey:823/.914.
Audience: **g,l,u,f.**

Naipaul, V. S. **PR6013.O35**
The Writer and the World: Essays. Trade Paper. Knopf Publishing Group. New York, NY. 2003. 544p. ISBN:0-375-70730-1, ISBN13: 978-0-375-70730-8. Dewey:824/.914.
Audience: **g,l,u,f.**

West Indies > Rhys, Jean

Burrows, Victoria **PR9205.4.B87 2004**
Whiteness and Trauma: The Mother-Daughter Knot in the Fiction of Jean Rhys, Jamaica Kincaid and Toni Morrison. Cloth over Boards. Palgrave Macmillan. New York, NY. 2004. 240p. ISBN:1-4039-2198-9, ISBN13: 978-1-4039-2198-7. Dewey:813/.540935252. LCCN:2003-060958.
Audience: **l,u,f.** *Choice, 2004.*

Maurel, Sylvie **PR6035.H96Z794 1998**
Jean Rhys. Cloth over Boards. Palgrave Macmillan. New York, NY. 1999. 194p. Women Writers Ser. ISBN:0-312-21687-4, ISBN13: 978-0-312-21687-0. Dewey:813. LCCN:98-021227.
Audience: **u,f.** *Choice, 1999.*

Rhys, Jean **PR6035.H96**
After Leaving Mr. MacKenzie. Trade Paper. W. W. Norton & Company, Inc. New York, NY. 1997. 192p. ISBN:0-393-31547-9, ISBN13: 978-0-393-31547-9. Dewey:823.912. LCCN:79-160658.
Audience: **g,l,u,f.**

Rhys, Jean **PR6035.H96G6 1986**
Good Morning, Midnight. Ed. 2. Trade Paper. W. W. Norton & Company, Inc. New York, NY. 1999. 192p. Shoreline Bks. ISBN:0-393-30394-2, ISBN13: 978-0-393-30394-0. Dewey:813. LCCN:86-012669.
Audience: **g,l,u,f.**

Rhys, Jean **PR6035.H96P67**
Quartet. Trade Paper. W. W. Norton & Company, Inc. New York, NY. 1997. 192p. Norton Paperback Fiction Ser. ISBN:0-393-31546-0, ISBN13: 978-0-393-31546-2. Dewey:813. LCCN:77-138795.
Audience: **g,l,u,f.**

Rhys, Jean **PR6035.H96S58 1979**
Sleep It off Lady: Stories. Trade Paper. Penguin Group (USA) Inc. New York, NY. 1995. 176p. Penguin Twentieth-Century Classics Ser. ISBN:0-14-018345-0, ISBN13: 978-0-14-018345-0. Dewey:823/.912. LCCN:95-224829.
Audience: **g,l,u,f.**

Rhys, Jean **PR6035.H96T5 1972**
Tigers are Better-Looking: With a selection from the Left Bank. Trade Paper. Penguin Group (USA) Inc. New York, NY. 1996. 224p. Penguin Twentieth-Century Classics Ser. ISBN:0-14-018346-9, ISBN13: 978-0-14-018346-7. Dewey:823/.912. LCCN:96-184625.
Audience: **g,l,u,f.**

Rhys, Jean **PR6035.H96**
Voyage in the Dark. Trade Paper. W. W. Norton & Company, Inc. New York, NY. 1994. Norton Paperback Fiction Ser. ISBN:0-393-31146-5, ISBN13: 978-0-393-31146-4. Dewey:813.
Audience: **g,l,u,f.**

Rhys, Jean **PR6035.H96 A6 1987**
The Collected Short Stories. Diana Athill (Introduction by). Trade Cloth. W. W. Norton & Company, Inc. New York, NY. 1987. ISBN:0-393-02375-3, ISBN13: 978-0-393-02375-6. Dewey:823/.912. LCCN:88-138678.
Audience: **g,l,u,f.**

Rhys, Jean & Bronte, Charlotte **PR6035.H96W5 1999**
Wide Sargasso Sea. Judith L. Raiskin (Editor). Trade Paper. W. W. Norton & Company, Inc. New York, NY. 1998. 284p. Critical Editions Ser. ISBN:0-393-96012-9, ISBN13: 978-0-393-96012-9. Dewey:823/.912. LCCN:98-014266.
Audience: **g,l,u,f.**

Savory, Elaine **PR6035.H96 Z86 1999**
Jean Rhys. Abiola Irele (Contribution by). Cloth Text. Cambridge University Press. New York, NY. 1999. 330p.

Cambridge Studies in African and Caribbean Literature, No. 6 ISBN:0-521-47434-5, ISBN13: 978-0-521-47434-4. Dewey:823.912. LCCN:99-211215.
Audience: **u,f.** *Choice, 1999.*

Simpson, Anne B. **PR6035.H96Z865 2005**
Territories of the Psyche: The Fiction of Jean Rhys. Cloth over Boards. Palgrave Macmillan. New York, NY. 2005. 192p. ISBN:1-4039-6613-3, ISBN13: 978-1-4039-6613-1. Dewey:823/.912. LCCN:2004-050530.
Audience: **l,u,f.** *Choice, 2005.*

West Indies > Walcott, Derek

Baer, William (Editor) **PR9272.9.W3Z477 1996**
Conversations with Derek Walcott. Trade Cloth. University Press of Mississippi. Jackson, MS. 1996. 211p. Literary Conversations Ser. ISBN:0-87805-855-9, ISBN13: 978-0-87805-855-6. Dewey:811. LCCN:95-044262.
Audience: **g,l,u,f.**

Baugh, Edward **PR9272.9.W3Z54 2006**
Derek Walcott. Abiola Irele (Contribution by). Trade Cloth. Cambridge University Press. New York, NY. 2006. 270p. Cambridge Studies in African and Caribbean Literature Ser., Vol. 10 ISBN:0-521-55358-X, ISBN13: 978-0-521-55358-2. Dewey:811/.54. LCCN:2005-022418.
Audience: **l,u,f.**

Breslin, Paul **PR9272.9.W3Z545 2001**
Nobody's Nation: Reading Derek Walcott. Trade Cloth. University of Chicago Press. Chicago, IL. 2001. 340p. ISBN:0-226-07426-9, ISBN13: 978-0-226-07426-9. Dewey:811/.54. LCCN:2001-002128.
Audience: **l,u,f.**

Hamner, Robert D. **PR9272.9.W3.O4434**
Epic of the Dispossessed: Derek Walcott's Omeros. Trade Cloth. University of Missouri Press. Columbia, MO. 1997. 200p. ISBN:0-8262-1124-0, ISBN13: 978-0-8262-1124-8. Dewey:811. LCCN:97-013099.
Audience: **l,u,f.**

Martinez-Duenas Espejo, Jose Luis & Perez Fernandez, Jose Maria **PR9272.9.W3Z53 2001**
Approaches to the Poetics of Derek Walcott. Trade Cloth. Edwin Mellen Press, The. Lewiston, NY. 2001. 204p. Caribbean Studies, Vol. 9 ISBN:0-7734-7475-7, ISBN13: 978-0-7734-7475-8. Dewey:811/.54. LCCN:00-069058.
Audience: **l,u,f.**

Walcott, Derek
Collected Poems, 1948-1984. Trade Paper. Farrar, Straus & Giroux. New York, NY. 1987. 516p. ISBN:0-374-52025-9, ISBN13: 978-0-374-52025-0. Dewey:811.
Audience: **g,l,u,f.**

Walcott, Derek
Dream on Monkey Mountain and Other Plays. Trade Paper. Farrar, Straus & Giroux. New York, NY. 1971. 326p. ISBN:0-374-50860-7, ISBN13: 978-0-374-50860-9. LCCN:74-122827.
Audience: **g,l,u,f.**

Walcott, Derek **PR9272.9.W3H35 2001**
The Haitian Trilogy: Plays: Henri Christophe, Drums and Colours, and The Haytian Earth. Trade Paper. Farrar, Straus & Giroux. New York, NY. 2002. 448p. ISBN:0-374-52813-6, ISBN13: 978-0-374-52813-3. Dewey:812/.54. LCCN:2001-023158.
Audience: **g,l,u,f.**

Walcott, Derek **PR9272.9.W3 O44 1992**
Omeros. Trade Paper. Farrar, Straus & Giroux. New York, NY. 1992. 325p. ISBN:0-374-52350-9, ISBN13: 978-0-374-52350-3. Dewey:811.
Audience: **g,l,u,f.**

Walcott, Derek **PR9272.9.W3 P76**
The Prodigal: A Poem. Trade Paper. Farrar, Straus & Giroux. New York, NY. 2006. 112p. ISBN:0-374-53016-5, ISBN13: 978-0-374-53016-7. Dewey:811/.54.
Audience: **g,l,u,f.**

Walcott, Derek **PR9272.9.W3 W35 2002**
Walker and Ghost Dance: Plays. Trade Paper. Farrar, Straus & Giroux. New York, NY. 2002. 144p. ISBN:0-374-52814-4, ISBN13: 978-0-374-52814-0. Dewey:812/.54. LCCN:2002-101069.
Audience: **l,u,f.**

RUSSIAN AND EASTERN EUROPEAN LANGUAGES AND LITERATURES

The treatment of Slavic languages and literatures at the undergraduate level traditionally focuses on an introductory study of the language and the classic literary works of major authors. The selections in this section are intended to support such programs. BCL3 focused on Russian language literature and language. To some extent, this was a necessity, as much of the literature available in English translation at the time was by Russian authors. However, changes in the region have increased the interest in the other countries of the regions and, consequently, the availability of English translations of their literary works.

In BCL3 the treatment of the languages of the region was uneven. In selecting titles for RCL, we have included bilingual dictionaries and grammars for each of the languages of the region wherever possible. In general, the goal was to provide a broader treatment of the East European countries.

The coverage of classic Russian literature was especially thorough in BCL3. We sought to update and supplement what had been listed in BCL3. The reader is referred to BCL3 publication for a more comprehensive list of Russian titles.

Websites presented unique considerations. Along with the usual concerns of authority and longevity, breadth and quality of coverage were also issues. The majority of works available online are translations of Russian texts. There are a number of excellent websites and databases available for literature and languages in general which are not listed in this section, as they are not primarily focused on Slavic materials. These include lists of large numbers of language dictionaries, translations of Slavic works and their critical literatures. Some of them are fee-based sources such as questia.com or NetLibrary.com. Others, like Project Gutenberg (http://www.gutenberg.org/browse/loccs/pg) and YourDictionary (http://www.yourdictionary.com/languages/slavic.html) are freely available.

Sites that are specific to Slavic literatures, authors or languages have been included in those cases where they include quality translations of major works or major linguistic resources. Portals such as RUSSNET, with links to a variety of language resources have also been included when the authority was clear.

New editions of older works have been included for the most important literary works and where a new translation or interpretive content is available.

Selections were made with the intention of providing broader coverage of the literature of the region in English translation. A larger number of titles have been selected to provide a better overview of the literary development of all the countries of the region.

Émigré publications are not included with one exception, the inclusion of major publications by an author before his or her emigration.

— Helen Sullivan

Z2483

American Bibliography of Slavic and East European Studies.
http://www.library.uiuc.edu/absees/
EBSCO / American Association for the Advancement of Slavic Studies.

Audience: **g,l,u,f.**

Z2483

European Bibliography of Slavic and East European Studies.
http://www2.msh-paris.fr/betuee/BD_Bibl_Est_accueil_angl.htm

Audience: **u,f.**

Slavic Languages

Slavic & Baltic Languages.
http://polyglot.lss.wisc.edu/lss/lang/slavic.html
University of Wisconsin.

Audience: **l.**

PG38.U6

Slavic and East European Language Resource Center.
http://www.seelrc.org
Duke University.

Audience: **l,u,f.**

Stefanllari, Ilo **PG9591.S737 2000**
English Albanian Dictionary of Idioms. Trade Paper. Hippocrene Books, Inc. New York, NY. 1999. 500p. ISBN:0-7818-0783-2, ISBN13: 978-0-7818-0783-8. Dewey:423/.91991. LCCN:99-046942.

Audience: **g,l,u,f.**

Slavic Languages > General > Reference

Comrie, Bernard (Editor) **P381.E83**
The Major Languages of Eastern Europe. Routledge. 1990. The Major Languages ISBN:0-415-05771-X, ISBN13: 978-0-415-05771-4.

Audience: **u,f.**

Slavic Languages > Baltic Languages > Dictionaries

Baltrusaityte, Jurgita **PG8679.B27 2004**
Lithuanian-English Dictionary and Phrasebook. Trade Paper. Hippocrene Books, Inc. New York, NY. 2003. 274p. New Dictionary and Phrasebooks Ser. ISBN:0-7818-1009-4, ISBN13: 978-0-7818-1009-8. Dewey:491/.92321. LCCN:2004-042465.

Audience: **g,l.**

Benyukh, Ksenia **PH625.B39 2002**
Estonian Dictionary and Phrasebook. Trade Paper. Hippocrene Books, Inc. New York, NY. 2002. 272p. ISBN:0-7818-0931-2, ISBN13: 978-0-7818-0931-3. Dewey:494/.545321. LCCN:2002-032851.

Audience: **l.**

Piesarskas, Bronius & Svecevicius, Bronius **PG8679.P52 1995**
Lithuanian Dictionary: English-Lithuanian, Lithuanian-English. Ed. 2. Trade Paper. Routledge. New York, NY. 1995. 848p. ISBN:0-415-12857-9, ISBN13: 978-0-415-12857-5. Dewey:491.9/2/3/21. LCCN:95-018213.

Audience: **l,u.** *Choice, 1996.*

Saagpakk, Paul F. **PH625**
Estonian-English Dictionary. Trade Cloth. Yale University Press. Cumberland, RI. 1982. 1216p. Yale Linguistic Ser. ISBN:0-300-02849-0, ISBN13: 978-0-300-02849-2. Dewey:494/.545321. LCCN:81-043606.

Audience: **l,u.**

Silvet, J. **PH625**
Estonian-English Dictionary. Library Binding. French & European Publications, Inc. New York, NY. 1993. 507p. ISBN:0-8288-2631-5, ISBN13: 978-0-8288-2631-0. Dewey:423.9454.

Audience: **l,u.**

Sosare, M. & Birzvalka, I. **PG8979**
Latvian-English - English-Latvian Practical Dictionary. Trade Paper. Hippocrene Books, Inc. New York, NY. 1993. 474p. ISBN:0-7818-0059-5, ISBN13: 978-0-7818-0059-4. Dewey:491.93321.

Audience: **l,u.**

Slavic Languages > Baltic Languages > Reference

Benyukh, Ksenia **PH625.B39 2002**
Estonian Dictionary and Phrasebook. Trade Paper. Hippocrene Books, Inc. New York, NY. 2002. 272p. ISBN:0-7818-0931-2, ISBN13: 978-0-7818-0931-3. Dewey:494/.545321. LCCN:2002-032851.

Audience: **l.**

Mathiassen, Terje **PG8831.M38 1997**
A Short Grammar of Latvian. Trade Paper. Slavica Publishers. Bloomington, IN. 1997. 236p. ISBN:0-89357-270-5, ISBN13: 978-0-89357-270-9. Dewey:491/.9382421. LCCN:97-190866.

Audience: **l.**

Mathiassen, Terje **PG8531.M38 1996**
A Short Grammar of Lithuanian. Trade Paper. Slavica Publishers. Bloomington, IN. 1996. 256p. ISBN:0-89357-267-5, ISBN13: 978-0-89357-267-9. Dewey:491/.925. LCCN:96-212621.

Audience: **l.**

Press, Ian & Ramoniene, Meilute **PG3859.5.E5P74 1996**
Colloquial Lithuanian: A Complete Language Course. Trade Paper. Routledge. New York, NY. 1996. 400p. Colloquial Ser. ISBN:0-415-12103-5, ISBN13: 978-0-415-12103-3. Dewey:491.9/2/83421. LCCN:95-039835.

Audience: **l.**

Slavic Languages > Bulgarian > Dictionaries

Boianova, Snezhana **PG979**
Angliisko-Bulgarski Rechnik - English-Bulgarian Dictionary. Ed. 3. Gaberoff. 2001. ISBN:954-9607-41-0, ISBN13: 978-954-9607-41-3.
Audience: **l,u,f.**

Boianova, Snezhana, et al. **PG979**
Bulgarsko-Angliiski Rechnik - Bulgarian-English Dictionary. Ed. 4. Ilieva, Lena; Kilovski, Vakrilen (Authors). Gaberoff. 2003. ISBN:954-9607-50-X, ISBN13: 978-954-9607-50-5.
Audience: **l,u,f.**

Georgieva, Ana Ivanova **PG979.A474 2000**
Angliisko-Bulgarski I Bulgarsko-Angliiski Kartinen Rechnik Duden-Trud. Knigoizdatelska Kushta Trud. 2000. Rechnitsi Duden-Trud ISBN:954-528-115-4, ISBN13: 978-954-528-115-0.
Audience: **l,u.**

Rakudzhiev, Rumen, et al. **PG979.A47 1995**
Angliisko-Bulgarski Frazeologichen Rechnik: Okolo 25 000 Idioma: A-Z. Ilieva, Liubov (Author). Mag-77. 1995. ISBN:954-531-016-2, ISBN13: 978-954-531-016-4.
Audience: **u.**

Slavic Languages > Bulgarian > Grammars

Hauge, Kjetil Ra **PG831.R3 1999**
A Short Grammar of Contemporary Bulgarian. Slavica. 1999. ISBN:0-89357-276-4, ISBN13: 978-0-89357-276-1.
Audience: **l.**

Raykov, Mariana **PG835.5 R39X 2005**
Beginners Bulgarian. Trade Paper. Hippocrene Books, Inc. New York, NY. 2006. 208p. ISBN:0-7818-1101-5, ISBN13: 978-0-7818-1101-9. Dewey:491.8183421.
Audience: **l.**

Scatton, Ernest A. **PG831.S25 1984**
A Reference Grammar of Modern Bulgarian. Slavica Publishers. 1984. ISBN:0-89357-123-7, ISBN13: 978-0-89357-123-8.
Audience: **u.**

Slavic Languages > Croatian > Dictionaries

Benson, Morton **PG1376**
Standard English-SerboCroatian, SerboCroatian-English Dictionary: A Dictionary of Bosnian, Croatian, and Serbian Standards. Trade Paper. Cambridge University Press. New York, NY. 1998. 344p. ISBN:0-521-64553-0, ISBN13: 978-0-521-64553-9. Dewey:491.8/2321.
Audience: **l,u.**

Bogadek, F. A. **PG1376**
New Croatian - English Dictionary. Trade Cloth. Laurier Books, Ltd. Ottawa, ON. 2000. 498p. ISBN:81-206-1436-4, ISBN13: 978-81-206-1436-9. Dewey:491.82321.
Audience: **l,u.**

Bogadek, F. Y. **PG1376**
New English - Croatian Dictionary. Trade Cloth. Laurier Books, Ltd. Ottawa, ON. 2000. 532p. ISBN:81-206-1437-2, ISBN13: 978-81-206-1437-6. Dewey:491.82321.
Audience: **l,u.**

eSipka, Danko **PG1377.S56 2002**
Dictionary of Serbian, Croatian, and Bosnian New Words. Trade Cloth. Dunwoody Press. Hyattsville, MD. 2002. 132p. ISBN:1-881265-86-2, ISBN13: 978-1-881265-86-3. Dewey:491.8/2321. LCCN:2002-108790.
Audience: **f.**

Slavic Languages > Czech > Dictionaries

Fronek, Josef **PG4640**
Velky Cesko-Anglicky Slovnik. Leda. 2000. ISBN:80-85927-54-3, ISBN13: 978-80-85927-54-2.
Audience: **l,u.**

Hais, Karel, et al. **PG4640.H343 1997**
Velky Anglicko-Cesky Slovnik. Hodek, Bretislav (Author). Praha: Leda: Academia. 1997. ISBN:80-85927-37-3, ISBN13: 978-80-85927-37-5.
Audience: **l,u.**

Slavic Languages > Czech > Grammars

J., Naughton **PG4129.E5**
Czech: An Essential Grammar. Paper over Boards. Routledge. New York, NY. 2005. 288p. Essential Grammars Ser. ISBN:0-415-28784-7, ISBN13: 978-0-415-28784-5. Dewey:491.8682421.
Audience: **l.**

Janda, Laura A.; Townsend, Charles Edward **PG4112.J36 2000**
Czech. Lincom Europa. 2000. Languages of the World; Materials, No. 125 ISBN:3-89586-142-1, ISBN13: 978-3-89586-142-0.
Audience: **u.**

Townsend, Charles Edward **PG4771.P7.T69**
A Description of Spoken Prague Czech. Slavica Publishers. 1990. ISBN:0-89357-211-X, ISBN13: 978-0-89357-211-2.
Audience: **u.**

Slavic Languages > Hungarian > Dictionaries

Magay, Tamas & Orszagh, Laszlo **PH2640**
A Concise Hungarian-English Dictionary. Ed. 3. Trade Cloth. Akademiai Kiado. Budapest, 1993. 1152p. ISBN:963-05-6547-1, ISBN13: 978-963-05-6547-9. Dewey:494.511321.
Audience: **l,u.**

Orszagh, Laszlo **PH2640**
English to Hungarian Classical Comprehensive Dictionary. Trade Cloth. French & European Publications, Inc. New York, NY. 1998. 2000p. ISBN:0-320-00000-1, ISBN13: 978-0-320-00000-3. Dewey:494.511321.
Audience: **l,u.**

Orszagh, Laszlo **PH2640**
English-Hungarian Comprehensive Dictionary. Ed. 11. Trade Cloth. French & European Publications, Inc. New York, NY. 1992. 2319p. ISBN:0-7859-8856-4, ISBN13: 978-0-7859-8856-4. Dewey:494.511.
Audience: **l,u.**

Slavic Languages > Hungarian > Grammars

Rounds, Carol **PH2105.R68 2001**
Hungarian: An Essential Grammar. Paper over Boards. Routledge. New York, NY. 2001. 336p. Routledge Grammars Ser. ISBN:0-415-22611-2, ISBN13: 978-0-415-22611-0. Dewey:494/.51182421. LCCN:2001-016014.
Audience: **l.**

Rounds, Carol & Solyom, Erika **PH2065.R68 2002**
Colloquial Hungarian: The Complete Course for Beginners. Ed. 2. Trade Paper. Routledge. New York, NY. 2002. 336p. Colloquial Ser. ISBN:0-415-24256-8, ISBN13: 978-0-415-24256-1. Dewey:494/.51182421. LCCN:2002-069783.
Audience: **l.**

Slavic Languages > Macedonian > Dictionaries

Crvenkovski **PG1175.E5**
Standard English - Macedonian, Macedonian - English Dictionary. Trade Cloth. French & European Publications, Inc. New York, NY. 1990. 1000p. ISBN:0-8288-8225-8, ISBN13: 978-0-8288-8225-5. Dewey:491.8/19321.
Audience: **l,u,f.**

Slavic Languages > Macedonian > Grammars

Kramer, Christina E. **PG1159**
Macedonian: A Course for Beginning and Intermediate Students. Ed. 2. Trade Paper. University of Wisconsin Press. Chicago, IL. 2003. 542p. ISBN:0-299-18804-3, ISBN13: 978-0-299-18804-7. Dewey:491.8/1982421. LCCN:2003-050144.
Audience: **l,u.**

Slavic Languages > Polish > Dictionaries

Stanislawski, Jan **PG6640**
Wielki Slownik Angielsko-Polski - The Great English-Polish Dictionary. Trade Paper. Szwede Slavic Books. Palo Alto, CA. 1993. ISBN:83-85840-34-6, ISBN13: 978-83-85840-34-3. Dewey:423.91851.
Audience: **l,u.**

Stanislawski, Jan **LPG6640**
Wielki Slownik Polsko-Angielski - The Great Polish-English Dictionary. Trade Paper. Szwede Slavic Books. Palo Alto, CA. 1993. ISBN:83-214-0956-3, ISBN13: 978-83-214-0956-6. Dewey:491.8/5/321.
Audience: **l,u.**

Slavic Languages > Polish > Grammars

Bialec, Dana **PG6129.E5**
Basic Polish: Grammar. Trade Paper. Routledge. New York, NY. 2001. 248p. Grammar Workbooks Ser. ISBN:0-415-22437-3, ISBN13: 978-0-415-22437-6. Dewey:491.8/5824/21.
Audience: **l.**

Bielec, Dana **PG6129.E5B54 1998**
Polish: An Essential Grammar. Trade Paper. Routledge. New York, NY. 1998. 312p. Grammar Ser. ISBN:0-415-16406-0, ISBN13: 978-0-415-16406-1. Dewey:491.8/582421. LCCN:97-044254.
Audience: **u.**

Mazur, Bolesaw W. **PG6129.E5M384 2001**
Colloquial Polish: The Complete Course for Beginners. Ed. 2. Trade Paper. Routledge. New York, NY. 2001. 336p. Colloquials Ser. ISBN:0-415-15752-8, ISBN13: 978-0-415-15752-0. Dewey:491.8/582421. LCCN:2001-016218.
Audience: **l.**

Swan, Oscar E. **PG6105.S89 2002**
A Grammar of Contemporary Polish. Trade Cloth. Slavica Publishers. Bloomington, IN. 2002. 496p. ISBN:0-89357-296-9, ISBN13: 978-0-89357-296-9. Dewey:491.8/582421. LCCN:2002-026654.
Audience: **l,u.**

Slavic Languages > Russian

American Council for International Education
☐ Russnet.
http://www.russnet.org
Audience: **l,u,f.**

Boyle, Eloise M. & Gerhart, Genevra (Editors) **P35.5.R9R87 2002**
The Russian Context: The Context Behind the Language. Trade Paper. Slavica Publishers. Bloomington, IN. 2002. 732p. ISBN:0-89357-287-X, ISBN13: 978-0-89357-287-7. Dewey:306.44/0947. LCCN:2002-002613.
Audience: **l.**

Slavic Languages > Russian > Dictionaries

Margulis, Alexander & Kholodnaya, Asya (Editors) **PN6505.S5M34 2000**
Russian-English Dictionary of Proverbs and Sayings. Cloth Text. McFarland & Company, Incorporated Publishers. Jefferson, NC. 2000. 495p. ISBN:0-7864-0703-4, ISBN13: 978-0-7864-0703-3. Dewey:398.9/9171/03. LCCN:99-58987.
Audience: **g,u,f.** *Choice, 2000.*

Shapiro, Norman **PG2640.S45 1998**
The Oxford Picture Dictionary: English/Russian Edition. Trade Paper. Oxford University Press, Inc. New York, NY. 1998. 240p. The Oxford Picture Dictionary Program Ser. ISBN:0-19-435192-0, ISBN13: 978-0-19-435192-8. Dewey:423/.9171. LCCN:98-010026.
Audience: **l.**

Wheeler, Marcus (Editor), et al. **PG2640.W5 2000**
The Oxford Russian Dictionary. Ed. 2. Boris Unbegaun, Paul Falla & Della Thompson (Editors). Trade Cloth. Oxford University Press, Inc. New York, NY. 2000. 1,320p. ISBN:0-19-860160-3, ISBN13: 978-0-19-860160-9. Dewey:491.73/21. LCCN:00-708887.
Audience: **l,u,f.** *Choice, 2001.*

Slavic Languages > Russian > Grammars

Brown, N. **PG2129.E5**
Russian: An Essential Grammar. Trade Paper. Routledge. New York, NY. 2005. 224p. Grammar Ser. ISBN:0-415-13710-1, ISBN13: 978-0-415-13710-2. Dewey:491.782/421.
Audience: **l.**

Gerhart, Genevra **PG2121.G43 2001**
The Russian's World. Ed. 3. Trade Paper. Slavica Publishers. Bloomington, IN. 2000. 420p. ISBN:0-89357-293-4, ISBN13: 978-0-89357-293-8. Dewey:491.783/421. LCCN:2002-727740.
Audience: **l.**

Mahota, William J. **PG2271.M234 1996**
Russian Motion Verbs for Intermediate Students. Trade Paper. Yale University Press. Cumberland, RI. 1996. 148p. Yale Language Ser. ISBN:0-300-06413-6, ISBN13: 978-0-300-06413-1. Dewey:491.7/82421. LCCN:95-048780.
Audience: **u.**

Rojavin, Marina & Reid, Allan **PG2129.E5R64 2004**
A Guide to Russian Words and Expressions That Cause Difficulties. Trade Cloth. Edwin Mellen Press, The. Lewiston, NY. 2004. 242p. Studies in Slavic Language and Literature, Vol. 23 ISBN:0-7734-6302-X, ISBN13: 978-0-7734-6302-8. Dewey:491.783/421. LCCN:2004-050486.
Audience: **l,u.**

Seifrid, Thomas **P107.S45 2005**
The Word Made Self: Russian Writings on Language, 1860-1930. Book, Other. Cornell University Press. Ithaca, NY. 2005. 272p. ISBN:0-8014-4316-4, ISBN13: 978-0-8014-4316-9. Dewey:400. LCCN:2004-023506.
Audience: **u,f.** *Choice, 2005.*

Smyth, Sarah & Crosbie, Elena V. **PG2129.E5 S65 2001**
Rus': A Comprehensive Course in Russian. Trade Paper. Cambridge University Press. New York, NY. 2002. 718p. ISBN:0-521-64555-7, ISBN13: 978-0-521-64555-3. Dewey:491.782/421. LCCN:00-067440.
Audience: **l,u.**

Wade, Terence R. **PG2106.W33 2000**
A Comprehensive Russian Grammar. Ed. 2. Trade Paper. Blackwell Publishing, Inc. Malden, MA. 2000. 640p. Blackwell Reference Grammars Ser. ISBN:0-631-20757-0, ISBN13: 978-0-631-20757-3. Dewey:491.782/421. LCCN:99-047633.
Audience: **l,u.** *Choice, 1992.*

Slavic Languages > Serbian > Dictionaries

Brkic, Svetozar **PG1377**
English-Serbian and Serbian-English Dictionary. Trade Cloth. Beogradski izdava mko-grafimki zavod. Beograd, 2001. 749p. ISBN:86-13-00981-6, ISBN13: 978-86-13-00981-8. Dewey:491.82321.
Audience: **l,u,f.**

eSipka, Danko **PG1377.S56 2002**
Dictionary of Serbian, Croatian, and Bosnian New Words. Trade Cloth. Dunwoody Press. Hyattsville, MD. 2002. 132p. ISBN:1-881265-86-2, ISBN13: 978-1-881265-86-3. Dewey:491.8/2321. LCCN:2002-108790.
Audience: **f.**

Heaney, Duska Radosavljevic & Awde, Nicholas **PG1376.A947 2004**
Serbian-English/English-Serbian Dictionary and Phrasebook: Romanized. Trade Paper. Hippocrene Books, Inc. New York, NY. 2004. 175p. New Dictionary and Phrasebooks Ser. ISBN:0-7818-1049-3, ISBN13: 978-0-7818-1049-4. Dewey:491.8/2. LCCN:2004-059657.
Audience: **l.**

Ignjatic, Zdravko **PG1377**
English-Serbian and Serbian-English Dictionary and Grammar. Trade Cloth. Institut za strane jezike. Beograd, 2002. 1324p. ISBN:86-7147-054-7, ISBN13: 978-86-7147-054-4. Dewey:491.82321.
Audience: **l.**

Slavic Languages > Serbian > Grammars

Hammond, Lila **PG1239.5.E5H25 2005**
Serbian: An Essential Grammar. Trade Paper. Routledge. New York, NY. 2005. 336p. Essential Grammars Ser. ISBN:0-415-28641-7, ISBN13: 978-0-415-28641-1. Dewey:491.8/282421. LCCN:2004-010094.
Audience: **l.**

Ignjatic, Zdravko **PG1377**
English-Serbian and Serbian-English Dictionary and Grammar. Trade Cloth. Institut za strane jezike. Beograd, 2002. 1324p. ISBN:86-7147-054-7, ISBN13: 978-86-7147-054-4. Dewey:491.82321.
Audience: **l.**

Slavic Languages > Slovak > Dictionaries

Canikova, Andrea **PG5379.S635 2002**
Slovensko-Anglicky Slovnik. Ed. 2. Slovak Academic Press. 2002. ISBN:80-88908-96-5, ISBN13: 978-80-88908-96-8.
Audience: **l,u.**

Cániková, Andrea **PG5379.A83 1998**
Anglicko-Slovensky Slovnik. Slovak Academic Press. 1998. ISBN:80-88908-14-0, ISBN13: 978-80-88908-14-2.
Audience: **l,u,f.**

Slavic Languages > Slovak > Grammars

Mistrík, Jozef **PG5233**
A Grammar of Contemporary Slovak. Ed. 2. Bratislava : Slovenské pedagogické nakladatel'stvo. 1988.
Audience: **l,u.**

Swan, Oscar E., et al. **PG5239.5.E5 S93 1990**
Beginning Slovak: A Course for the Individual or Classroom Learner. Galova-Lorinc, Sylvia (Author). Slavica Publishers. 1990. ISBN:0-89357-214-4, ISBN13: 978-0-89357-214-3.
Audience: **l.**

Slavic Languages > Slovenian > Dictionaries

Snoj, Nina **PG1891**
Slovene-English/English-Slovene Dictionary and Phrasebook. Trade Paper. Hippocrene Books, Inc. New York, NY. 2006. 180p. New Dictionary and Phrasebooks Ser. ISBN:0-7818-1047-7, ISBN13: 978-0-7818-1047-0. Dewey:491.8/4321.
Audience: **l.**

Slavic Languages > Slovenian > Grammars

Derbyshire, William W. **PG1823.D47 1993**
A Basic Reference Grammar of Slovene. Paper Text. Slavica Publishers. Bloomington, IN. 1993. 154p. ISBN:0-89357-236-5, ISBN13: 978-0-89357-236-5. Dewey:491.8/482421. LCCN:94-130906.
Audience: **l.**

Herrity, Peter **PG1827.5.E5H47 2000**
Slovene: A Comprehensive Grammar. Paper over Boards. Routledge. New York, NY. 2000. 384p. Grammars Ser. ISBN:0-415-23147-7, ISBN13: 978-0-415-23147-3. Dewey:491.8/482421. LCCN:00-028085.
Audience: **l,u.**

Slavic Languages > Ukranian > Dictionaries

Benyuch, Oleg **PG3891 .B45**
Ukrainian-English - English-Ukrainian Standard Dictionary. Trade Paper. Hippocrene Books, Inc. New York, NY. 1995. 590p. Hippocrene Dictionaries Ser. ISBN:0-7818-0374-8, ISBN13: 978-0-7818-0374-8. Dewey:491.79321.
Audience: **l,u.**

Mladen, Davidovic **PG3891**
Ukrainian-English - English-Ukrainian. Trade Paper. Hippocrene Books, Inc. New York, NY. 1996. 448p. ISBN:0-7818-0498-1, ISBN13: 978-0-7818-0498-1. Dewey:491.79/03.
Audience: **l,u.**

Slavic Languages > Ukranian > Grammars

Bekh, Olena & Dingley, James **DK508**
Teach Yourself Ukrainian: A Complete Course for Beginners. Book, Other. McGraw-Hill Trade. New York, NY. 1998. 320p. ISBN:0-8442-3852-X, ISBN13: 978-0-8442-3852-4. Dewey:491.7983421.
Audience: **l.**

Press, Ian & Pugh, Stefan **PG3823**
Colloquial Ukrainian. Quantity Pack. Routledge. New York, NY. 1994. 384p. Colloquial Ser. ISBN:0-415-30626-4, ISBN13: 978-0-415-30626-3. Dewey:491.7/982421.
Audience: **l,u.**

Pugh, Stefan M. & Press, J. Ian **PG3819.P84 1999**
Ukrainian: A Comprehensive Grammar. Trade Paper. Routledge. New York, NY. 1999. 336p. Routledge Grammar Ser. ISBN:0-415-15030-2, ISBN13: 978-0-415-15030-9. Dewey:491.7/982421. LCCN:98-032358.
Audience: **l.**

Smyrniw, Walter **PG3875 .S56**
Ukrainian Prose Manual: A Text for Intermediate Language Studies. Trade Paper. Mosaic Press. Niagara Falls, NY. 1990. 192p. ISBN:0-88962-052-0, ISBN13: 978-0-88962-052-0. Dewey:491.7/9/82421.
Audience: **u.**

Slavic Languages > Albanian

Hysa, Ramazan John **PG9591.H96 1999**
English-Albanian Comprehensive Dictionary. Trade Cloth. Hippocrene Books, Inc. New York, NY. 1999. 1000p. Hippocrene Dictionaries Ser. ISBN:0-7818-0792-1, ISBN13: 978-0-7818-0792-0. Dewey:423/.91991. LCCN:2001-269889.
Audience: **l,u,f.**

Newmark, Leonard D. **PG9591**
Oxford Albanian-English Dictionary. Trade Paper. Oxford University Press, Inc. New York, NY. 2000. 1,056p. ISBN:0-19-860322-3, ISBN13: 978-0-19-860322-1. Dewey:491.9/913/21.
Audience: **l,u,f.**

Orel, Vladimir E. **PG9519.O74 2000**
A Concise Historical Grammar of the Albanian Language: Reconstruction of Proto-Albanian. Trade Cloth. Brill Academic Publishers, Inc. Boston, MA. 2000. "xxii, 332"p. ISBN:90-04-11647-8, ISBN13: 978-90-04-11647-4. Dewey:491/.9915. LCCN:99-053799.
Audience: **u,f.**

Zymberi, Isa **PG9501**
Colloquial Albanian: The Complete Course for Beginners. Ed. 2. Trade Paper, Audio Cassette, Compact Disc. Routledge. New York, NY. 2004. 384p. Colloquial Ser. ISBN:0-415-30753-8, ISBN13: 978-0-415-30753-6. Dewey:491.991.
Audience: **l,u,f.**

Slavic Languages > Romanian > Dictionaries

Levitchi, Leon **PC779**
Dictionar roman-englez: 60,000 de cuvinte. Teora. 2005. ISBN:973-20-0582-3, ISBN13: 978-973-20-0582-8.
Audience: **l,u.**

Levitchi, Leon; Bantas, Andrei **PC779**
Dictionar englez-roman: b 70,000 cuvinte. Teora. 2005. ISBN:973-20-0058-9, ISBN13: 978-973-20-0058-8.
Audience: **l,u.**

Slavic Languages > Romanian > Gramamrs

Augerot, James E. **PC635.A77 2000**
Romanian/Limba Romana: A Course in Modern Romanian. Center for Romanian Studies. 1999. ISBN:973-98392-0-7, ISBN13: 978-973-98392-0-4.
Audience: **l,u.**

Deletant, Dennis & Alexandrescu, Yvonne **PC779**
Teach Yourself Romanian Complete Course. Ed. 3. Trade Paper, Mixed Media. McGraw-Hill Companies, The. New York, NY. 2004. 256p. ISBN:0-07-142474-1, ISBN13: 978-0-07-142474-5. Dewey:459.321.
Audience: **l.**

Slavic Languages > Yugoslav > Dictionaries

eSipka, Danko **PG1377.S56 2002**
Dictionary of Serbian, Croatian, and Bosnian New Words. Trade Cloth. Dunwoody Press. Hyattsville, MD. 2002. 132p. ISBN:1-881265-86-2, ISBN13: 978-1-881265-86-3. Dewey:491.8/2321. LCCN:2002-108790.
Audience: **f.**

Slavic Literatures > General

Baker, William **PG564.S684 1997**
South Slavic Writers since World War II. Cloth Text. Thomson Gale. Farmington Hills, MI. 1997. 400p. Dictionary of Literary Biography Ser., Vol. 181 ISBN:0-7876-1070-4, ISBN13: 978-0-7876-1070-8. Dewey:[B]. LCCN:97-015112.
Audience: **l,u,f.**

Chitnis, Rajendra A. **PG512.C49 2004**
Literature in Post-Communist Russia and Eastern Europe: The Russian, Czech and Slovak Fiction of the Changes, 1988-98. Trade Cloth. Routledge. New York, NY. 2004. 272p. BASEES/RoutledgeCurzon Series on Russian and East European Studies, Vol. 16 ISBN:0-415-35557-5, ISBN13: 978-0-415-35557-5. Dewey:891.8. LCCN:2004-011265.
Audience: **u,f.**

Efimov, Nina, et al. **PG504.5.C75 1998**
Critical Essays on the Prose and Poetry of Modern Slavic Women Writers. Christine D. Tomei & Richard L. Chapple (Authors). Trade Cloth. Edwin Mellen Press, The. Lewiston, NY. 1998. 224p. Studies in Slavic Language and Literature ISBN:0-7734-8363-2, ISBN13: 978-0-7734-8363-7. Dewey:891.8. LCCN:98-024712.
Audience: **u,f.** *Choice, 1999.*

Gorup, Radmila J. & Rakic, Bogdan (Editors) **PG4099.T6 2000**
In a Foreign Harbor: Essays in Honor of Vasa D. Mihailovich. Trade Cloth. Slavica Publishers. Bloomington, IN. 2000. 250p. ISBN:0-89357-289-6, ISBN13: 978-0-89357-289-1. Dewey:891.8/09. LCCN:2001-404803.
Audience: **u,f.**

Kalinowska, Izabela **PG7020.A8K35 2004**
Between East and West: Polish and Russian Nineteenth-Century Travel to the Orient. Trade Cloth. University of Rochester Press. Rochester, NY. 2004. 216p. Rochester Studies in Central Europe Ser. ISBN:1-58046-172-7, ISBN13: 978-1-58046-172-6. Dewey:891.709/325. LCCN:2004-017410.
Audience: **u,f.**

Karcz, Andrzej **PG7008.K36 2002**
The Polish Formalist School and Russian Formalism. Trade Cloth. University of Rochester Press. Rochester, NY. 2004. 230p. Rochester Studies in Central Europe ISBN:1-58046-110-7, ISBN13: 978-1-58046-110-8. Dewey:891.8/509. LCCN:2002-022559.
Audience: **u,f.**

Naum, Gellu **PC840.24.A8Z3513**
Zenobia. James Brook & Sasha Vlad (Translators). Trade Cloth. Northwestern University Press. Evanston, IL. 1995. 192p. Writings from an Unbound Europe ISBN:0-8101-1254-X, ISBN13: 978-0-8101-1254-4. Dewey:859/.334. LCCN:95-010848.
Audience: **g,l,u,f.** *Choice, 1996.*

Tschizewskij, Dmitrij **LC89.W5**
On Romanticism in Slavic Literature. Paper Text. Textbook Publishers. Temecula, CA. 2003. 63p. ISBN:0-7581-7986-3, ISBN13: 978-0-7581-7986-9. Dewey:379.
Audience: **u.**

Zlatar, Zdenko **PG1658.G8O8395 1995**
The Slavic Epic: Gundulic's Osman. Cloth Text. Peter Lang Publishing, Inc. New York, NY. 1995. XXX, 598p. Balkan Studies, Vol. 4 ISBN:0-8204-2380-7, ISBN13: 978-0-8204-2380-7. Dewey:891.8/212. LCCN:93-045754.
Audience: **u,f.**

Slavic Literatures > General > Anthologies

Efimov, Nina, et al. **PG504.5.C75 1998**
Critical Essays on the Prose and Poetry of Modern Slavic Women Writers. Christine D. Tomei & Richard L. Chapple (Authors). Trade Cloth. Edwin Mellen Press, The. Lewiston, NY. 1998. 224p. Studies in Slavic Language and Literature ISBN:0-7734-8363-2, ISBN13: 978-0-7734-8363-7. Dewey:891.8. LCCN:98-024712.
Audience: **u,f.** *Choice, 1999.*

Slavic Literatures > General > Bibliographies

Nisula, Dasha Culic **Z7041.N57 2001**
Bibliography of Slavic Literature. Trade Cloth. Scarecrow Press, Inc. Lanham, MD. 2001. 296p. Area Bibliographies Ser., Vol. 20 ISBN:0-8108-4005-7, ISBN13: 978-0-8108-4005-8. Dewey:016.8918. LCCN:00-068761.
Audience: **l,f.** *Choice, 2002.*

Serafin, Steven (Editor) **Z2483.T883 2001**
Twentieth-Century Eastern European Writers. Trade Cloth. Thomson Gale. Farmington Hills, MI. 2000. xxiii, 483p. Dictionary of Literary Biography Ser., Vol. 232 ISBN:0-7876-4649-0, ISBN13: 978-0-7876-4649-3. Dewey:809/.8947. LCCN:00-059334.
Audience: **l,u,f.**

Slavic Literatures > General > Biography

Baker, William **PG564.S684 1997**
South Slavic Writers since World War II. Cloth Text. Thomson Gale. Farmington Hills, MI. 1997. 400p. Dictionary of Literary Biography Ser., Vol. 181 ISBN:0-7876-1070-4, ISBN13: 978-0-7876-1070-8. Dewey:[B]. LCCN:97-015112.
Audience: **l,u,f.**

Milhailovich, Vasa D. (Editor) **PG564.S68 1995**
DLB 147: South Slavic Writers Before World War II. Cloth Text. Thomson Gale. Farmington Hills, MI. 1994. 368p. Dictionary of Literary Biography Ser., Vol. 147 ISBN:0-8103-5708-9, ISBN13: 978-0-8103-5708-2. Dewey:891.81/009 B. LCCN:94-079482.
Audience: **l,u,f.** *Choice, 1995.*

Serafin, Steven (Editor) **Z2483.T883 2001**
Twentieth-Century Eastern European Writers. Trade Cloth. Thomson Gale. Farmington Hills, MI. 2000. xxiii, 483p. Dictionary of Literary Biography Ser., Vol. 232 ISBN:0-7876-4649-0, ISBN13: 978-0-7876-4649-3. Dewey:809/.8947. LCCN:00-059334.
Audience: **l,u,f.**

Slavic Literatures > General > Dictionaries

Segel, Harold B. **Z2483.S444 2002**
The Columbia Guide to the Literatures of Eastern Europe Since 1945. Trade Cloth. Columbia University Press. New York, NY. 2003. 776p. ISBN:0-231-11404-4, ISBN13: 978-0-231-11404-2. Dewey:809/.8947. LCCN:2002-025661.
Audience: **l,u.** *Choice, 2003.*

Slavic Literatures > Bulgarian > Anthologies

Butler, Thomas **PG13.M46**
Monumenta Bulgarica: A Bilingual Anthology of Bulgarian Texts from the 9th to the 19th Centuries. Michigan Slavic Publications. 2004. Michigan Slavic Materials, No. 41
Audience: **g,l,u,f.**

Harteis, Richard; Meredith, William **PG1145.E3 W56 1992**
Window on the Black Sea: Bulgarian Poetry in Translation. Carnegie Mellon University Press. 1992. ISBN:0-88748-141-8, ISBN13: 978-0-88748-141-3.
Audience: **g,l,u,f.**

Kirilov, Nikolai; Kirk, Frank **PZ1.K583 In PG1145**
Introduction to Modern Bulgarian Literature: An Anthology of Short Stories. Twayne Publishers. 1969. Twayne's Introductions to World Literature Series
Audience: **g,l,u,f.**

Meredith, William **PG1145.E3 P64 1986**
Poets of Bulgaria. Balaban, John (Translator). Unicorn Press. 1986. ISBN:0-87775-189-7, ISBN13: 978-0-87775-189-2.
Audience: **g,l,u,f.**

Sapinkopf, Lisa **PG1145.E3 C57 1992**
Clay and Star: Contemporary Bulgarian Poets. Belev, Georgi (Author). Milkweed Editions. 1992. ISBN:0-915943-85-9, ISBN13: 978-0-915943-85-2.
Audience: **g,l,u,f.**

Tonchev, Belin **PG1145.E3 Y6 1990**
Young Poets of a New Bulgaria: An Anthology. Petsin, Peter (il.); Barker, Sebastian (intro.). Forest Books. 1990. ISBN:0-948259-71-X, ISBN13: 978-0-948259-71-5.
Audience: **g,l,u,f.**

Slavic Literatures > Bulgarian > Biography

Markov, Georgi **PG1038.23 .A74 Z474 1984**
The Truth That Killed. Ticknor & Fields. 1984. ISBN:0-89919-296-3, ISBN13: 978-0-89919-296-3.
Audience: **l,u.**

Slavov, Atanas **DR91.S57 1986**
With the Precision of Bats. Occidental Press. 1986. ISBN:0-911050-59-0, ISBN13: 978-0-911050-59-2.
Audience: **l,u.**

Slavic Literatures > Bulgarian > Dictionary

Matejic, Mateja, et al. **Z2898.L5 B56 1982**
A Biobibliographical Handbook of Bulgarian Authors. Black, Karen L. (Author). Slavica. 1982. ISBN:0-89357-091-5, ISBN13: 978-0-89357-091-0.
Audience: **l,u.**

Slavic Literatures > Bulgarian > History and Criticism

Moser, Charles A. **PG1001.M67**
A History of Bulgarian Literature 865-1944. Mouton. 1972. Slavistic Printings and Reprintings, No. 112
Audience: **l,u.**

Slavov, Atanas **PG1008.S53**
The Thaw in Bulgarian Literature. Boulder: East European Monographs. 1981. East European Monographs, no. 74 ISBN:0-914710-78-8, ISBN13: 978-0-914710-78-3.
Audience: **u,f.**

Slavic Literatures > Bulgarian > Individual Authors

Dimitrova, Blaga, et al. **PG1037.D5 A25 2002**
Scars. Popova-Wightman, Ludmilla G.; Shurbanov, Aleksandur (Authors). Ivy Press. 2002. Bulgarian Poetry in Translation, Vol. 3 ISBN:1-930214-03-0, ISBN13: 978-1-930214-03-3.
Audience: **g,l,u,f.**

Dimitrova, Blaga **PZ4.D583 Jo PG1037.D5**
Journey to Oneself. Pridham, Radost (tr.). Cassell. 1969. ISBN:0-304-93293-0, ISBN13: 978-0-304-93293-1.
Audience: **g,l,u,f.**

Donchev, Anton **PZ4.D68.Ti3**
Time of Parting: A Novel. Morrow. 1968.
Audience: **g,l,u,f.**

Khaitov, Nikolai **PG1037.K45.D513**
Wild Tales. Owen. 1979. UNESCO Collection of Representative Works; European Series ISBN:0-7206-0543-1, ISBN13: 978-0-7206-0543-3.
Audience: **g,l,u,f.**

Pavlov, Konstantin; Popova-Wightman, Ludmilla G. **PG1038.26.A88 A27 2003**
Capriccio for Goya. Ivy Press. 2003. Bulgarian Poetry in Translation, Vol. 6 ISBN:1-930214-07-3, ISBN13: 978-1-930214-07-1.
Audience: **g,l,u,f.**

Vazov, Ivan Minchov **PZ3.V48 U7 PG1037.V3**
Under the Yoke. Alexieva, Marguerite and Theodora Atanassova (Translater); Zabriskie, Lilla Lyon (Editor). Twayne Publishers. 1971.
Audience: **g,l,u,f.**

Slavic Literatures > Baltic

Rubulis, Aleksis **PH302**
Baltic Literature: A Survey of Finnish, Estonian, Latvian, and Lithuanian Literatures. Trade Cloth. University of Notre Dame Press. Notre Dame, IN. 1970. xv, 215p. ISBN:0-268-00393-9, ISBN13: 978-0-268-00393-7. Dewey:891.9. LCCN:79-105728.
Audience: **g,l,f.** B

Slavic Literatures > Baltic > Anthologies

Cedrins, Inara (Editor) **PG9145.E3C66 1984**
Contemporary Latvian Poetry. Trade Paper. University of Iowa Press. Iowa City, IA. 1984. 224p. Iowa Translations Ser. ISBN:0-87745-128-1, ISBN13: 978-0-87745-128-0. Dewey:891/.9313/08. LCCN:84-008800.
Audience: **g,l,u,f.**

Ezergailis, Inta M. **PG9007.5.W65E97 1998**
Nostalgia and Beyond: Eleven Latvian Women Writers. Trade Cloth. University Press of America, Inc. Lanham, MD. 1997. 280p. ISBN:0-7618-0996-1, ISBN13: 978-0-7618-0996-8. Dewey:891/.93099287/0904. LCCN:97-039065.
Audience: **g,l,u,f.**

Kelertas, Violeta (Editor) **PG8771.E8 C6 1992**
Come into My Time: Lithuania in Prose Fiction, 1970-90. Trade Cloth. University of Illinois Press. Champaign, IL. 1992. 264p. ISBN:0-252-01881-8, ISBN13: 978-0-252-01881-7. Dewey:891/.923010803.
Audience: **g,l,u,f.**

Matthews, W. K. **PH671.E5M3**
Anthology of Modern Estonian Poetry. Paper Text. Textbook Publishers. Temecula, CA. 2003. 161p. ISBN:0-7581-2305-1, ISBN13: 978-0-7581-2305-3. Dewey:894.5451082.
Audience: **g,l,u,f.**

Moseley, Christopher **PN6120.2.F76 1994**
From Baltic Shores: Short Stories from Denmark, Estonia, Finland, Latvia, Lithuania, Sweden. Norvik Press. 1995. ISBN:1-870041-25-9, ISBN13: 978-1-870041-25-6.
Audience: **g,l,u,f.**

Reddaway, Darlene & Pruul, Kajar (Editors) **PH671.E5E874 1996**
Estonian Short Stories. Ritva Poom (Translator). Trade Cloth. Northwestern University Press. Evanston, IL. 1996. 277p. Writings from an Unbound Europe ISBN:0-8101-1240-X, ISBN13: 978-0-8101-1240-7. Dewey:894/.54530108. LCCN:95-040096.
Audience: **g,l,u,f.** *Choice, 1996.*

Slavic Literatures > Baltic > History and Criticism

Straumanis, Alfreds **PG8103 .B34**
Baltic Drama: A Handbook and Bibliography. Waveland Press, Inc. 1981. ISBN:0-917974-63-8, ISBN13: 978-0-917974-63-2.
Audience: **u,f.**

Slavic Literatures > Baltic > Individual Authors

Alisanka, Eugenijus **PG8722.1.L53P4513**
City of Ash. H. L. Hix (Translator, Introduction by). Trade Paper. Northwestern University Press. Evanston, IL. 2000. 62p. Writings from an Unbound Europe Ser. ISBN:0-8101-1784-3, ISBN13: 978-0-8101-1784-6. Dewey:891/.9314. LCCN:00-008902.
Audience: **g,l,u,f.**

Onnepalu, Tonu **PH666.3.O33P5513**
Border State. Madli Puhvel (Translator). Trade Cloth. Northwestern University Press. Evanston, IL. 2000. 100p. Writings from an Unbound Europe Ser. ISBN:0-8101-1779-7, ISBN13: 978-0-8101-1779-2. Dewey:894/.54533. LCCN:99-462232.
Audience: **g,l,u,f.**

Smuul, Juhan **G860**
Antaractica Ahoy!. University Press of the Pacific. 2000. ISBN:0-89875-068-7, ISBN13: 978-0-89875-068-3.
Audience: **g,l,u,f.**

Venclova, Thomas **PN849.E9**
Forms of Hope: Essays. Sheep Meadow Press. 2002. ISBN:1-931357-11-0, ISBN13: 978-1-931357-11-1.
Audience: **g,l,u,f.**

Slavic Literatures > Czech > Anthologies

Buchler, Alexandra **PG5145.E8 T48 1996**
This Side of Reality: Modern Czech Writing. London; New York, NY : Serpent's Tail. 1996. ISBN:1-85242-378-1, ISBN13: 978-1-85242-378-0.
Audience: **g,l,u,f.**

Cejka, Jaroslav & Cernik, Michal **PG5025.C36 1988**
The New Czech Poetry. Trade Paper. Bloodaxe Books. Bala, 1988. 64p. ISBN:1-85224-066-0, ISBN13: 978-1-85224-066-0. Dewey:891.861508. LCCN:88-051309.
Audience: **g,l,u,f.**

French, Alfred **PG5025.F68**
Anthology of Czech Poetry. Czechoslovak Society of Arts and Sciences in America. 1973. Michigan Slavic Translations; No. 2
Audience: **g,l,u,f.**

Goetz-Stankiewicz, Marketa **PG5145.E1 G66 1992**
Good-Bye, Samizdat: Twenty Years of Czechoslovak Underground Writing. Evanston, Ill.: Northwestern University Press. 1992. ISBN:0-8101-1010-5, ISBN13: 978-0-8101-1010-6.
Audience: **g,l,u,f.**

Goetz-Stankiewicz, Marketa **PG5145.E5 V38 1987**
The Vanek Plays: Four Authors, One Character. University of British Columbia Press. 1987. ISBN:0-7748-0280-4, ISBN13: 978-0-7748-0280-2.
Audience: **g,l,u,f.**

Harkins, William Edward **PG5145.E8 C95 1983**
Czech Prose: An Anthology. Michigan Slavic Publications, Dept. of Slavic Languages and Literatures, University of Michigan. 1983. Michigan Slavic Translations, No. 6 ISBN:0-930042-51-4, ISBN13: 978-0-930042-51-6.
Audience: **g,l,u,f.**

Lappin, Elena **PG5145.E8 D39 1997**
Daylight in Nightclub Inferno : Czech Fiction from the Post-Kundera generation. North Haven, Conn.: Catbird Press. 1997. ISBN:0-945774-33-8, ISBN13: 978-0-945774-33-4.
Audience: **g,l,u,f.**

Schamschula, Walter (Editor) **PG5145.E1A58 1990**
An Anthology of Czech Literature: 1st Period: From the Beginnings until 1410. Trade Paper. Peter Lang Publishing, Inc. New York, NY. 1991. 255p. West Slavic Contributions, Vol. 2 ISBN:3-631-43044-2, ISBN13: 978-3-631-43044-6. Dewey:891.8/608. LCCN:90-020248.
Audience: **g,l,u,f.**

Slavic Literatures > Czech > Bibliography

Serafin, Steven (Editor) **Z2483.T883 2001**
Twentieth-Century Eastern European Writers. Trade Cloth. Thomson Gale. Farmington Hills, MI. 2000. xxiii, 483p. Dictionary of Literary Biography Ser., Vol. 232 ISBN:0-7876-4649-0, ISBN13: 978-0-7876-4649-3. Dewey:809/.8947. LCCN:00-059334.
Audience: **l,u,f.**

Slavic Literatures > Czech > Biography

Havel, Vaclav **PG5039.18.A9 Z48413 1989**
Letters to Olga: June 1979-September 1982. New York: H. Holt. 1989. ISBN:0-8050-0973-6, ISBN13: 978-0-8050-0973-6.
Audience: **u.**

Serafin, Steven (Editor) **Z2483.T883 2001**
Twentieth-Century Eastern European Writers. Trade Cloth. Thomson Gale. Farmington Hills, MI. 2000. xxiii, 483p. Dictionary of Literary Biography Ser., Vol. 232 ISBN:0-7876-4649-0, ISBN13: 978-0-7876-4649-3. Dewey:809/.8947. LCCN:00-059334.
Audience: **l,u,f.**

Slavic Literatures > Czech > History and Criticism

French, A. **PG5007.F73 1982**
Czech Writers and Politics, 1945-1969. Boulder: East European Monographs; New York: Distributed by Columbia University Press. 1982. East European monographs; No. 94 ISBN:0-914710-88-5, ISBN13: 978-0-914710-88-2.
Audience: **u,f.**

French, Alfred **PG5008.F7**
The Poets of Prague: Czech Poetry Between the Wars. Oxford U. P.. 1969. ISBN:0-19-211286-4, ISBN13: 978-0-19-211286-6.
Audience: **u,f.**

Goetz-Stankiewicz, Marketa **PG5009.G9**
The Silenced Theatre: Czech Playwrights Without a Stage. University of Toronto Press. 1979. ISBN:0-8020-5426-9, ISBN13: 978-0-8020-5426-5.
Audience: **u,f.**

Hruby, Peter **PG5007.H66 1990**
Daydreams and Nightmares: Czech Communist and Ex-Communist Literature 1917-1987. East European Monographs. 1990. East European Monographs, No. 290 ISBN:0-88033-187-9, ISBN13: 978-0-88033-187-6.
Audience: **u,f.**

Novak, Arne; Harkins, et al. **PG5001.N6313 1986**
Czech Literature. Harkins, William Edward (Author). Ann Arbor: Michigan Slavic Publications. 1986. The Joint Committee on Eastern Europe Publication Ser., No. 4 ISBN:0-930042-64-6, ISBN13: 978-0-930042-64-6.
Audience: **u,f.**

Porter, Robert **PG5011.P67 2001**
An Introduction to Twentieth-Century Czech Fiction: Comedies of Defiance. Brighton; Portland, Or.; Sussex Academic Press. 2001. ISBN:1-902210-80-8, ISBN13: 978-1-902210-80-3.
Audience: **u.**

Souckova, Milada **PG5006.S59**
The Czech Romantics. Mouton. 1958. Slavistic Printings and Reprintings; No. 17
Audience: **u,f.**

Steiner, Peter **PG5011.S74 2000**
The deserts of Bohemia: Czech Ffiction and Its Social Context. Ithaca, NY: Cornell University Press. 2000. ISBN:0-8014-3717-2, ISBN13: 978-0-8014-3717-5.
Audience: **u,f.**

Thomas, Alfred **PG5005.5.S62 T48 1998**
Anne's Bohemia: Czech Literature and Society, 1310-1420. Minneapolis: University of Minnesota Press. 1998. Medieval Cultures; Vol. 13 ISBN:0-8166-3053-4, ISBN13: 978-0-8166-3053-0.
Audience: **u,f.**

Thomas, Alfred **PG5003.2.T77 T48 1995**
The Labyrinth of the Word: Truth and Representation in Czech Literature. R. Oldenbourg. 1995. Veroffentlichungen des Collegium Carolinum; Bd. 78 ISBN:3-486-55997-4, ISBN13: 978-3-486-55997-2.
Audience: **u,f.**

Trensky, Paul I. **PG5009.T7 1981**
Czech Drama since World War II. M. E. Sharpe. 1981. Columbia Slavic Sudies
Audience: **u.**

Wellek, Rene **PG5003.W4**
Essays on Czech Literature. Demetz, Peter (Introduction). Mouton. 1963. Slavistic Printings and Reprintings; No. 43
Audience: **u,f.**

Slavic Literatures > Czech > Individual Authors

Aji, Aron **PG5039.21.U6 Z78 1992**
Milan Kundera and the Art of Fiction: Critical Essays. New York: Garland. 1992. Garland Reference Library of the Humanities; Vol. 1156 ISBN:0-8153-0038-7, ISBN13: 978-0-8153-0038-0.
Audience: **g,l,u,f.**

Bloom, Harold **PG5039.21.U6 Z779 2003**
Milan Kundera. Chelsea House Publishers. 2003. Bloom's Modern Critical Views ISBN:0-7910-7043-3, ISBN13: 978-0-7910-7043-7.
Audience: **g,l,u,f.**

Capek, Karel **PG5038.C3**
War with the Newts. Evanston, IL: Northwestern University Press. 1996. European Classics Ser. ISBN:0-8101-1468-2, ISBN13: 978-0-8101-1468-5.
Audience: **g,l,u,f.**

Capek, Karel, et al. **PG5038.C3 K613 1997**
Apocryphal Tales: With a Selection of Fables and Would-Be Tales. Comrada, Norma (Author). Catbird Press. 1997. ISBN:0-945774-34-6, ISBN13: 978-0-945774-34-1.
Audience: **g,l,u,f.**

Capek, Karel, et al. **PG5038.C3 A25 1990**
Toward the Radical Cente: A Karel Capek Rader. Kussi, Peter (Author). Highland Park, NJ: Catbird Press. 1990. ISBN:0-945774-06-0, ISBN13: 978-0-945774-06-8.
Audience: **g,l,u,f.**

Capek, Karel **PG5038.C3T613 2005**
The Absolute at Large. Stephen Baxter (Introduction by). Trade Paper. University of Nebraska Press. Lincoln, NE. 2006. 256p. Bison Frontiers of the Imagination Ser. ISBN:0-8032-6459-3, ISBN13: 978-0-8032-6459-5. LCCN:2005-041874.
Audience: **g,l,u,f.**

Fischerova, Daniela **PG5039.16.I82P7713**
Fingers Pointing Somewhere Else. Neil Bermel (Translator). Trade Cloth. Catbird Press. North Haven, CT. 2000. 175p. ISBN:0-945774-44-3, ISBN13: 978-0-945774-44-0. Dewey:891.8/636. LCCN:99-016409.
Audience: **g,l,u,f.** *Choice, 2000.*

Goetz-Stankiewicz, Marketa, et al. **DB2241.H38 C75 1999**
Critical Essays on Vaìclav Havel. Carey, Phyllis (Author). New York: G.K. Hall: Twayne. 1999. Critical Essays on World Literature Ser. ISBN:0-7838-8463-X, ISBN13: 978-0-7838-8463-9.
Audience: **g,l,u,f.**

Grusa, Jiri **PG5039.17.R87 D613 2000**
The Questionnaire. Normal, IL: Dalkey Archive Press. 2000. Eastern European Literature Ser. ISBN:1-56478-227-1, ISBN13: 978-1-56478-227-4.
Audience: **g,l,u,f.**

Hasek, Jaroslav **PG5038.H28 O713 1993**
The Good Soldier Svejk: And His Fortunes in the World War. New York: Knopf: Distributed by Random House. 1993. Everyman's library; 151 ISBN:0-679-42036-3, ISBN13: 978-0-679-42036-1.
Audience: **g,l,u,f.**

Hasek, Jaroslav **PG5038.H28A25 1991**
The Bachura Scandal: And Other Stories and Sketches. Alan Menhennet (Translator). Trade Paper. Angel Books. London, 1991. 160p. ISBN:0-946162-41-7, ISBN13: 978-0-946162-41-3. Dewey:891.8/635. LCCN:93-242061.
Audience: **g,l,u,f.**

Havel, Vaclav **PG5039.18.A9 A2 1993**
The Garden Party and Other Plays. New York: Grove Press. 1993. ISBN:0-8021-3307-X, ISBN13: 978-0-8021-3307-6.
Audience: **g,l,u,f.**

Hirsal, Josef **PG5038.H525.P5713**
A Bohemian Youth. Michael H. Heim (Translator). Trade Cloth. Northwestern University Press. Evanston, IL. 1997. 85p. Writings from an Unbound Europe ISBN:0-8101-1223-X, ISBN13: 978-0-8101-1223-0. Dewey:891.8/6354. LCCN:97-040411.
Audience: **g,l,u,f.**

Holub, Miroslav **PG5038.H64**
Intensive Care: Selected and New Poems. Trade Cloth. Oberlin College Press. Oberlin, OH. 2003. 205p. Field Translation Ser., No. 22 ISBN:0-932440-75-4, ISBN13: 978-0-932440-75-4. Dewey:891.8/6154. LCCN:96-067483.
Audience: **g,l,u,f.**

Holub, Miroslav, et al. **PG5038.H64**
Interferon, or On Theater. Young, David; Habova, Dana (Authors). [Oberlin, Ohio]: Oberlin College. 1982. Field Translation Ser. Vol. 7 ISBN:0-932440-12-6, ISBN13: 978-0-932440-12-9.
Audience: **g,l,u,f.**

Holubova, Miloslava **PG5039.18.O44V5313**
More Than One Life. Alex Zucker, Lyn Coffin & Zdenka Brodska (Translators). Trade Cloth. Northwestern University Press. Evanston, IL. 1999. 104p. ISBN:0-8101-1705-3, ISBN13: 978-0-8101-1705-1. Dewey:891.8/6354. LCCN:99-013058.
Audience: **g,l,u,f.**

Hrabal, Bohumil **PG5039.18.R2**
I Served the King of England. London: Vintage. 2006. ISBN:0-09-949289-X, ISBN13: 978-0-09-949289-4.
Audience: **g,l,u,f.**

Hrabal, Bohumil, et al. **PG5039.18.R2 0813 1995**
Closely Watched Trains. Pargeter, Edith; Skvorecky, Josef (Authors). Northwestern University Press. 1995. European Classics Ser. ISBN:0-8101-1278-7, ISBN13: 978-0-8101-1278-0.
Audience: **g,l,u,f.**

Jirasek, Alois **GR154.J5713 1992**
Old Czech Legends. Forest Books. 1992. UNESCO Collection of Representative Works; European Series ISBN:1-85610-020-0, ISBN13: 978-1-85610-020-5.
Audience: **g,l,u,f.**

Klima, Ivan, et al. **PG5039.21.L5 S6813 2002**
Judge on Trial. Brain, A. G. (Author). Vintage. 2002. ISBN:0-09-942959-4, ISBN13: 978-0-09-942959-3.
Audience: **g,l,u,f.**

Klima, Ivan, et al. **PG5039.21.L5 P6413 1997**
The Ultimate Intimacy. Brain, A. G. (Author). New York: Grove Press. 1997. ISBN:0-8021-1625-6, ISBN13: 978-0-8021-1625-3.
Audience: **g,l,u,f.**

Klima, Ivan **PG5038.C3Z752413**
Karel Capek: Life and Work. Norma Comrada (Translator), Robert Wechsler (Preface by). Trade Cloth. Catbird Press. North Haven, CT. 2002. 266p. ISBN:0-945774-53-2, ISBN13: 978-0-945774-53-2. Dewey:891.8/6252 B. LCCN:2002-001594.
Audience: **g,l,u,f.** *Choice, 2002.*

Kohout, Pavel **PG5038.K64.U213**
Poor Murderer: A Play. Viking Press. 1977. ISBN:0-670-56445-1, ISBN13: 978-0-670-56445-3.
Audience: **g,l,u,f.**

Kohout, Pavel **PG5038.K64 S6413 1995**
I Am Snowing: The Confessions of a Woman of Prague. Bermel, Neil (Translator). Harcourt Brace. 1995. Harvest in Translation Ser. ISBN:0-15-600187-X, ISBN13: 978-0-15-600187-8.
Audience: **g,l,u,f.**

Kundera, Milan **PG5039.21.U6 N413 2004**
The Unbearable Lightness of Being. Heim, Michael Henry (Author). New York: HarperCollins. 2004. ISBN:0-06-059718-6, ISBN13: 978-0-06-059718-4.
Audience: **g,l,u,f.**

Kundera, Milan, et al. **PG5039.21.U6 N3413 2001**
Immortality. Kussi, Peter (Author). Faber and Faber. 2001. ISBN:0-571-20918-1, ISBN13: 978-0-571-20918-7.
Audience: **g,l,u,f.**

Kundera, Milan **PG5039.21.U6**
The Joke. Heim, Michael Henry (Translator). Faber and Faber. 1992. ISBN:0-571-16693-8, ISBN13: 978-0-571-16693-0.
Audience: **g,l,u,f.**

Kundera, Milan **PG5039.21.U6 S58413 1999**
Laughable Loves. Rappaport, Suzanne (Translator). Harper Perennial. 1999. ISBN:0-06-099703-6, ISBN13: 978-0-06-099703-8.
Audience: **g,l,u,f.**

Lustig, Arnost **PG5038.L85 A2 2001**
The Bitter Smell of Almonds: Selected Fiction. Evanston, Ill.: Northwestern University Press. 2001. Jewish Lives Ser. ISBN:0-8101-1902-1, ISBN13: 978-0-8101-1902-4.
Audience: **g,l,u,f.**

Nemcova, Bozena **PZ3.N341.Gr5**
Granny: Scenes from Country Life. Pargeter, Edith (Translator). Greenwood Press. 1976. ISBN:0-8371-9355-9, ISBN13: 978-0-8371-9355-7.
Audience: **g,l,u,f.**

Neruda, Jan, et al. **PG5038.N45 P613 1999**
Prague Tales. Heim, Michael Henry; Klima, Ivan (Authors). Central European University Press. 1999. Central European Classics Ser. ISBN:963-9116-23-8, ISBN13: 978-963-9116-23-8.
Audience: **g,l,u,f.**

Nezval, Vitezslav **PG5038.N47**
Antilyrik and Other Poems. Milos Sovak & Jerome Rothenberg (Translators). Trade Paper. Green Integer. Los Angeles, CA. 2000. 136p. Green Integer Bks., Vol. 86 ISBN:1-892295-75-X, ISBN13: 978-1-892295-75-0. Dewey:891.8615.
Audience: **g,l,u,f.**

Nezval, Vitezslav **PG5038.N47A6413 2001**
Alphabet: Abeceda. Jindrich Toman & Matthew Witkovski (Translators). Trade Cloth. Michigan Slavic Publications. Ann Arbor, MI. 2001. 72p. Czech Translations Ser., Vol. 3 ISBN:0-930042-88-3, ISBN13: 978-0-930042-88-2. Dewey:891.8/6152. LCCN:2001-044458.
Audience: **g,l,u,f.**

Olbracht, Ivan **PG5038.Z35N513 2001**
Nikola the Outlaw. Marie K. Holecek (Translator). Trade Paper. Northwestern University Press. Evanston, IL. 2001. 220p. Literature in Translation Ser. ISBN:0-8101-1827-0, ISBN13: 978-0-8101-1827-0. Dewey:891.8/6352. LCCN:2001-000907.
Audience: **g,l,u,f.**

Rocamora, Carol **PG5039.18.A9 Z87 2005**
Acts of Courage: Vaclav Havel's Life in the Theater. Smith and Kraus. 2005. ISBN:1-57525-344-5, ISBN13: 978-1-57525-344-2.
Audience: **g,l,u,f.**

Seifert, Jaroslav **PG5038.S45A25**
The Poetry of Jaroslav Seifert. George Gibian (Editor), Ewald Osers & George Gibian (Translators). Trade Cloth. Catbird Press. North Haven, CT. 1998. 256p. ISBN:0-945774-39-7, ISBN13: 978-0-945774-39-6. Dewey:891.8/6152. LCCN:97-040802.
Audience: **g,l,u,f.**

Skvorecky, Josef, et al. **PG5038.S527 P6813 1999**
The Engineer of Human Souls. Wilson, Paul R. (Author). Normal, IL: Dalkey Archive Press. 1999. ISBN:1-56478-199-2, ISBN13: 978-1-56478-199-4.
Audience: **g,l,u,f.**

Skvorecky, Josef, et al. **PG5038.S527 T313 1993**
The Republic of Whores: A Fagment from the Time of the Cults. Wilson, Paul R. (Author). Hopewell, N.J.: Ecco Press. 1993. ISBN:0-88001-371-0, ISBN13: 978-0-88001-371-0.
Audience: **g,l,u,f.**

Skvorecky, Josef, et al. **PG5038.S527**
The Cowards. Nemcova, Jeanne (Author). Vintage Books. 1995. ISBN:0-394-28058-X, ISBN13: 978-0-394-28058-5.
Audience: **g,l,u,f.**

Topol, Jachym **PG5039.3.O648S4713**
City, Sister, Silver. Alex Zucker (Translator). Trade Cloth. Catbird Press. North Haven, CT. 2001. 512p. ISBN:0-945774-45-1, ISBN13: 978-0-945774-45-7. Dewey:891.8/636. LCCN:99-016410.
Audience: **g,l,u,f.** *Choice, 2000.*

Trensky, Paul I., et al. **PG5038.S527 Z89 1991**
The Fiction of Josef Skvorecky. Harnick, Michaela (Author). New York: St. Martin's Press. 1991. ISBN:0-312-05336-3, ISBN13: 978-0-312-05336-9.
Audience: **g,l,u,f.**

Vaculik, Ludvik **PZ4.V117 Gu PG5039.32.A2**
The Guinea Pigs. Northwestern University Press. 1986. ISBN:0-8101-0726-0, ISBN13: 978-0-8101-0726-7.
Audience: **g,l,u,f.**

Vaculik, Ludvik **PG5039.32.A2 S413 1994**
The Axe. Northwestern University Press. 1994. European Classics ISBN:0-8101-1018-0, ISBN13: 978-0-8101-1018-2.
Audience: **g,l,u,f.**

Weil, Jiri, et al. **PG5038.W4**
Life with a Star. Klimova, Rita.; Schloss, Roslyn (Authors). Penguin. 2002. Penguin Classics Ser. ISBN:0-14-118695-X, ISBN13: 978-0-14-118695-5.
Audience: **g,l,u,f.**

Slavic Literatures > Hungarian

Konrad, George **DB958.3.K6613 1995**
The Melancholy of Rebirth: Essays from Post-Communist Central Eruope, 1989-1994. Trade Paper. Harcourt Trade Publishers. New York, NY. 1995. 176p. ISBN:0-15-600252-3, ISBN13: 978-0-15-600252-3. Dewey:943.905/3. LCCN:94-039650.
Audience: **u.**

Slavic Literatures > Hungarian > Anthologies

Alvarez, A. **PZ1**
Hungarian Short Stories. Oxford University Press. 1967.
Audience: **g,l,u,f.**

Hungarian National Library
Hungarian texts in translation.
http://www.mek.iif.hu/porta/szint/human/szepirod/forditas/
Audience: **g,l,u,f.**

Illes, Lajos (ed.) **PZ1.F748 PH3441.E8**
44 Hungarian Short Stories. Snow, C. P.. Corvina. 1979.
ISBN:963-13-6510-7, ISBN13: 978-963-13-6510-8.
Audience: **g,l,u,f.**

Jones, D. Mervyn **PH3308**
Five Hungarian Writers. Oxford University Press. 1966.
Audience: **g,l,u,f.**

Suleiman, Susan Rubin & Forgacs, Eva (Editors) **PH3138.J48C66 2003**
Contemporary Jewish Writing in Hungary: An Anthology. Trade Cloth. University of Nebraska Press. Lincoln, NE. 2005. 520p. Jewish Writing in the Contemporary World Ser.
ISBN:0-8032-9304-6, ISBN13: 978-0-8032-9304-5.
Dewey:894/.511098924/09045. LCCN:2003-044750.
Audience: **g,l,u,f.**

Szakolczay, Lajos **PH3441.E8**
Give or Take a Day: Contemporary Hungarian Short Stories. Trade Paper. Corvina Books. 1999. 224p. ISBN:963-13-4287-5, ISBN13: 978-963-13-4287-1. Dewey:894.5113011.
Audience: **g,l,u,f.**

Serafin, Steven (Editor) **Z2483.T883 2001**
Twentieth-Century Eastern European Writers. Trade Cloth. Thomson Gale. Farmington Hills, MI. 2000. xxiii, 483p. Dictionary of Literary Biography Ser., Vol. 232
ISBN:0-7876-4649-0, ISBN13: 978-0-7876-4649-3.
Dewey:809/.8947. LCCN:00-059334.
Audience: **l,u,f.**

Slavic Literatures > Hungarian > Bibliography

Serafin, Steven (Editor) **Z2483.T883 2001**
Twentieth-Century Eastern European Writers. Trade Cloth. Thomson Gale. Farmington Hills, MI. 2000. xxiii, 483p. Dictionary of Literary Biography Ser., Vol. 232
ISBN:0-7876-4649-0, ISBN13: 978-0-7876-4649-3.
Dewey:809/.8947. LCCN:00-059334.
Audience: **l,u,f.**

Slavic Literatures > Hungarian > Biography

Ozsvbath, Zsuzsanna & Radnboti, Miklbos **PH3321.R27Z67 2000**
In the Footsteps of Orpheus: The Life and Times of Miklbos Radnboti. Trade Cloth. Indiana University Press. Bloomington, IN. 2001. xvi, 264p. Jewish Literature and Culture Ser.
ISBN:0-253-33801-8, ISBN13: 978-0-253-33801-3.
Dewey:894/.511132 B. LCCN:00-038909.
Audience: **u,f.** *Choice, 2001.*

Slavic Literatures > Hungarian > History and Criticism

Czigany, Lorant **PH3012**
The Oxford History of Hungarian Literature from the Earliest Times to the Present. Oxford University Press. 1984.
ISBN:0-19-815781-9, ISBN13: 978-0-19-815781-6.
Audience: **u,f.**

Klaniczay, Tibor **PH3012.M31413 1982**
A History of Hungarian Literature. Corvina. 1982.
ISBN:963-13-1542-8, ISBN13: 978-963-13-1542-4.
Audience: **u,f.**

Ozsvbath, Zsuzsanna & Radnboti, Miklbos **PH3321.R27Z67 2000**
In the Footsteps of Orpheus: The Life and Times of Miklbos Radnboti. Trade Cloth. Indiana University Press. Bloomington, IN. 2001. xvi, 264p. Jewish Literature and Culture Ser.
ISBN:0-253-33801-8, ISBN13: 978-0-253-33801-3.
Dewey:894/.511132 B. LCCN:00-038909.
Audience: **u,f.** *Choice, 2001.*

Slavic Literatures > Hungarian > Individual Authors

Dery, Tibor **PH3213.D53**
The Portuguese Princess and Other Stories. Kathleen Szasz (Translator). Trade Paper. Northwestern University Press. Evanston, IL. 1987. 224p. ISBN:0-8101-0766-X, ISBN13: 978-0-8101-0766-3. Dewey:894.51.
Audience: **g,l,u,f.**

Dery, Tibor **PH3213.D53A6 2005**
Love and Other Stories. George Szirtes (Introduction by). Trade Paper. New Directions Publishing Corporation. New York, NY. 2005. 272p. ISBN:0-8112-1625-X, ISBN13: 978-0-8112-1625-8. Dewey:894/.511/33. LCCN:2005-000995.
Audience: **g,l,u,f.**

Gomori, George & Szirtes, George (Editors) **PH3441.E3C65 1996**
The Colonnade of Teeth: Modern Hungarian Poetry. Trade Paper. Bloodaxe Books. Bala, 1997. 270p. ISBN:1-85224-331-7, ISBN13: 978-1-85224-331-9. Dewey:894.5111308. LCCN:96-224963.
Audience: **g,l,u,f.** *Choice, 1997.*

Illyes, Gyula **PH3241.I55A6 2000**
Charon's Ferry: Fifty Poems. Bruce Berlind (Translator). Trade Cloth. Northwestern University Press. Evanston, IL. 2000. 75p. Writings from an Unbound Europe ISBN:0-8101-1798-3, ISBN13: 978-0-8101-1798-3. Dewey:894/.511132. LCCN:00-010142.
Audience: **g,l,u,f.**

Jozsef, Attila **PH3281.J64**
Sixty poems. Mariscat. 2001. ISBN:0-946588-30-9, ISBN13: 978-0-946588-30-5.
Audience: **g,l,u,f.**

Jozsef, Attila **PH3281.J64**
Winter Night: Selected Poems of Attila Jozsef. John Batki (Translator). Trade Paper. Oberlin College Press. Oberlin, OH. 2003. 127p. Field Translation Ser., Vol. 23 ISBN:0-932440-78-9, ISBN13: 978-0-932440-78-5. Dewey:894/.511132. LCCN:97-066615.
Audience: **g,l,u,f.**

Jozsef, Attila **PH3281.J64A17 1999**
The Iron-Blue Vault: Selected Poems. Zsuzsanna Ozsvath & Frederick Turner (Translators). Trade Paper. Bloodaxe Books. Bala, 2000. 160p. ISBN:1-85224-503-4, ISBN13: 978-1-85224-503-0. Dewey:894/.511132. LCCN:00-421372.
Audience: **g,l,u,f.**

Kertész, Imre **PH3281.K3815 S6713**
Fateless. Christopher Wilson & Katharina Wilson (Translators). Trade Cloth. Northwestern University Press. Evanston, IL. 1992. 200p. ISBN:0-8101-1024-5, ISBN13: 978-0-8101-1024-3. Dewey:894/.511334.
Audience: **g,l,u,f.**

Kosztolanyi, D. **PN99.U5P69**
Skylark. Trade Cloth. Central European University Press. Herndon, VA. 1999. 240p. Central European Classics Ser. ISBN:963-9116-66-1, ISBN13: 978-963-9116-66-5. Dewey:801.
Audience: **g,l,u,f.**

Krasznahorkai, Laszlo **PH3281.K8866**
The Melancholy of Resistance. George Szirtes (Translator). Trade Paper. Quartet Books, Ltd. London, 2000. 272p. ISBN:0-7043-8009-9, ISBN13: 978-0-7043-8009-7. Dewey:894/.51134.
Audience: **g,l,u,f.**

Krudy, Gyula **PH3281.K89**
Sunflower. John Batki (Translator), John Lukacs (Introduction by). Trade Paper. Corvina Books. 1999. 208p. ISBN:963-13-4332-4, ISBN13: 978-963-13-4332-8. Dewey:894/.511332. LCCN:98-181527.
Audience: **g,l,u,f.**

Krudy, Gyula & Szirtes, George **PH3281.K89**
The Adventures of Sindbad. Trade Cloth. Central European University Press. Herndon, VA. 1998. 232p. Central European Classics Ser., Vol. 5 ISBN:963-9116-12-2, ISBN13: 978-963-9116-12-2. Dewey:894.51133.
Audience: **g,l,u,f.**

Molnar, Ferenc **PH3287.P3 E5**
The Paul Street Boys. Trade Paper. Corvina Books. 1999. 208p. ISBN:963-13-4803-2, ISBN13: 978-963-13-4803-3. Dewey:894.51123.
Audience: **g,l,u,f.**

Moricz, Zsigmond **PH3291.M5R613 1997**
Relations. Trade Paper. Corvina Books. 1999. 240p. ISBN:963-13-4289-1, ISBN13: 978-963-13-4289-5. Dewey:894/.511332. LCCN:98-142137.
Audience: **g,l,u,f.**

Márai, Sándor **PH3281.M35 G94**
[Ebook] Embers. E-Book. Knopf Publishing Group. New York, NY. 2003. ISBN:1-4000-7774-5, ISBN13: 978-1-4000-7774-8. Dewey:894/.511334.
Audience: **g,l,u,f.**

Petofi, Sandor **PH3304**
John the Valiant. John Ridland (Translator). Trade Paper. Hesperus Press. London, 2004. 152p. ISBN:1-84391-084-5, ISBN13: 978-1-84391-084-8. Dewey:894.51112.
Audience: **g,l,u,f.**

Radnoti, Miklos **PH3321.R27T313 2003**
Clouded Sky. Steven Polgar, Stephen Berg & S. J. Marks (Translators). Trade Paper. Sheep Meadow Press, The. Riverdale-on-Hudson, NY. 2003. 128p. ISBN:1-931357-12-9, ISBN13: 978-1-931357-12-8. Dewey:894/.511132. LCCN:2003-008562.
Audience: **g,l,u,f.**

Szabo, Magda **PH3351.S592A7413**
The Door. Stefan Draughon (Translator). Trade Cloth. Eastern European Monographs. Bradenton, FL. 1995. 280p. ISBN:0-88033-304-9, ISBN13: 978-0-88033-304-7. Dewey:894.511332. LCCN:94-061341.
Audience: **g,l,u,f.**

Tandori, Dezso **PH3351.T335A23 1986**
Birds and Other Relations: Selected Poetry of Dezso Tandori. Princeton University Press. 1986. ISBN:0-691-06685-X, ISBN13: 978-0-691-06685-1.
Audience: **g,l,u,f.**

Weores, Sandor **PH3381.W4**
If All the World Were a Blackbird: Poems. Aberdeen University Press. 1985. ISBN:0-08-032440-1, ISBN13: 978-0-08-032440-1.
Audience: **g,l,u,f.**

Weores, Sandor, et al. **PH3381.W4**
Eternal Moment. Miklos Vajda & William J. Smith (Authors). Trade Cloth. Anvil Press Poetry, Ltd. London, 1988. 152p. ISBN:0-85646-185-7, ISBN13: 978-0-85646-185-9. Dewey:894/.51113.
Audience: **g,l,u,f.**

Slavic Literatures > Macedonian > Anthologies

Osers, Ewald (Editor, Translator) **PG1198.E3 C66 1991**
Contemporary Macedonian Poetry. Trade Paper. Forest Books. London, 1992. 223p. ISBN:0-948259-67-1, ISBN13: 978-0-948259-67-8. Dewey:891.819108. LCCN:91-070144.
Audience: **g,l,u,f.**

Slavic Literatures > Macedonian > Individual Authors

Basevski, Dimitar & Brownjohn, Alan **PG1196.12.A68T46**
Temporal Stay: Poems. Trade Paper. Forest Books. London, 1998. 68p. ISBN:1-85610-043-X, ISBN13: 978-1-85610-043-4. Dewey:891.8/191. LCCN:96-061885.
Audience: **g,l,u,f.**

Jovanovski, Meto **PG1195.J6A23 1992**
Faceless Men: And Other Macedonian Stories. J. Folks & D. Holton (Translators). Trade Paper. Forest Books. London, 1993. 82p. ISBN:1-85610-007-3, ISBN13: 978-1-85610-007-6. Dewey:891.8/193. LCCN:92-070451.
Audience: **g,l,u,f.**

Smilevski, Goce **PG1196.29.M58R3913**
Conversation with Spinoza: A Cobweb Novel. Filip Korzenski (Translator). Trade Cloth. Northwestern University Press. Evanston, IL. 2006. 152p. Writings from an Unbound Europe Ser. ISBN:0-8101-2375-4, ISBN13: 978-0-8101-2375-5. Dewey:891.81936. LCCN:2005-036780.
Audience: **g,l,u,f.**

Slavic Literatures > Polish

Old Polish Literature Online.
http://www.staropolska.gimnazjum.com.pl/ang/info/index.html
Audience: **l,f.**

Andrzejewski, Jerzy **PG7158.A7P613 1991**
Ashes and Diamonds. David J. Welsch (Translator), Heinrich Böll (Introduction by), Barbara Niemczyk (Foreword by). Trade Paper. Northwestern University Press. Evanston, IL. 1984. 239p. ISBN:0-8101-0856-9, ISBN13: 978-0-8101-0856-1. Dewey:891.8/537. LCCN:91-008061.
Audience: **g,l,u,f.** B

Gillon, Adam & Krzyzanowski, Ludwik (Editors) **PG7445.E1**
Introduction to Modern Polish Literature. Ed. 2. Trade Paper. Hippocrene Books, Inc. New York, NY. 1981. 480p. ISBN:0-88254-516-7, ISBN13: 978-0-88254-516-5. Dewey:891.8/5/08007. LCCN:81-086230.
Audience: **u.** B

Gombrowicz, Witold **PG7158.G669**
Cosmos and Pornografia. Trade Paper. Grove/Atlantic, Inc. New York, NY. 1994. 192p. ISBN:0-8021-5159-0, ISBN13: 978-0-8021-5159-9. Dewey:891.85. LCCN:85-081780.
Audience: **g,l,u,f.**

Gombrowicz, Witold **PG7158.L39**
Trans-Atlantyk. Carolyn French & Nina Karsov (Translators). Trade Paper. Yale University Press. Cumberland, RI. 1995. 152p. ISBN:0-300-06503-5, ISBN13: 978-0-300-06503-9. Dewey:891.8537.
Audience: **g,l,u,f.**

Goscilo, Helena (Editor, Translator) **PG3276.R87 1985**
Russian and Polish Women's Fiction. Paper Text. University of Tennessee Press. Knoxville, TN. 1985. 360p. ISBN:0-87049-472-4, ISBN13: 978-0-87049-472-7. Dewey:891.73/008/09287. LCCN:84-020915.
Audience: **u.** B

Slavic Literatures > Polish > Anthologies

Baranczak, Stanislaw & Cavanagh, Clare (Editors) **PG7445.E3P64 1991**
Polish Poetry of the Last Two Decades of Communist Rule: Spoiling Cannibals' Fun. Stanislaw Baranczak & Clare Cavanagh (Translators), Helen H. Vendler (Foreword by). Trade Cloth. Northwestern University Press. Evanston, IL. 1991. 196p. ISBN:0-8101-0968-9, ISBN13: 978-0-8101-0968-1. Dewey:891.8/51708. LCCN:91-003253.
Audience: **g,l,u,f.**

Karasek, Krzysztof, et al. **PG7445.E3 H8 1982**
Humps and Wings: Polish Poetry Since '68. Stanislaw Baranczak, Julian Kornhauser, Adam Zagajewski & Antoni Pawlak (Authors), Tadeusz Nyczek (Editor), Boguslaw Rostworowski (Translator), Jan Sawka (Illustrator). Trade Paper. Invisible City/Red Hill Press. San Francisco, CA. 1982. 80p. Invisible City Ser., No. 1 ISBN:0-88031-059-6, ISBN13: 978-0-88031-059-8. Dewey:891.8/517/08. LCCN:82-080896.
Audience: **g,l,u,f.**

Kott, Jan (Editor) **PG7445.E8F68 1990**
Four Decades of Polish Essays. Jadwiga Kosicka, Lillian Vallee, Jaroslaw Anders, Michael Kott, Ronald Strom & Daniel Gerould (Translators). Trade Cloth. Northwestern University Press. Evanston, IL. 1990. 403p. ISBN:0-8101-0862-3, ISBN13: 978-0-8101-0862-2. Dewey:891.8/547. LCCN:90-034265.
Audience: **g,l,u,f.**

Mayewski, Pawel **PG7445.E1 M3**
The Broken Mirror: A Collection of Writings from Contemporary Poland,. Paper Text. Textbook Publishers. Temecula, CA. 2003. 209p. ISBN:0-7581-5058-X, ISBN13: 978-0-7581-5058-5. Dewey:891.85082.
Audience: **g,l,u,f.**

Mikos, Michael J. (Translator) **PG7445.E1M43 1991**
Medieval Literature of Poland: An Anthology. Paper over

Boards. Garland Publishing, Inc. New York, NY. 1992. 286p. Library of Medieval Literature, Vol. 82B ISBN:0-8153-0408-0, ISBN13: 978-0-8153-0408-1. Dewey:891.8/509002. LCCN:91-024676.
Audience: **g,l,u,f.**

Mikos, Michael J. **PG7445.E1M55 1995**
Polish Renaissance Literature: An Anthology. Trade Cloth. Slavica Publishers. Bloomington, IN. 1995. 275p. ISBN:0-89357-257-8, ISBN13: 978-0-89357-257-0. Dewey:891.8/508003. LCCN:95-182289.
Audience: **g,l,u,f.**

Mikos, Michael J. (Translator) **PG7445.E1P65 2002**
Polish Romantic Literature: An Anthology. Trade Cloth. Slavica Publishers. Bloomington, IN. 2002. vi, 216p. ISBN:0-89357-281-0, ISBN13: 978-0-89357-281-5. Dewey:891.8/5080145. LCCN:2002-075851.
Audience: **g,l,u,f.**

Polonsky, Antony & Adamczyk-Garbowska, Monika (Editors) **PG7135.5.J48C66 2001**
Contemporary Jewish Writing in Poland: An Anthology. Cloth Text. University of Nebraska Press. Lincoln, NE. 2001. 349p. Jewish Writing in the Contemporary World Ser. ISBN:0-8032-3721-9, ISBN13: 978-0-8032-3721-6. Dewey:891.8/50808924/09045. LCCN:00-059971.
Audience: **g,l,u,f.** *Choice, 2002.*

Schenker, Alexander M. **PG6117**
Fifteen Modern Polish Short Stories: An Annotated Reader and a Glossary. Trade Paper. Yale University Press. Cumberland, RI. 1970. 200p. Linguistic Ser ISBN:0-300-01326-4, ISBN13: 978-0-300-01326-9. Dewey:491.858/6/421. LCCN:74-123394.
Audience: **g,l,u,f.**

Segel, Harold B. (Editor) **PG7445.E5**
Polish Romantic Drama: Three Plays in English Translation. Ed. 2. Trade Paper. Gordon & Breach Publishing Group. New York, NY. 1997. 304p. Polish Theatre Archive Ser. ISBN:90-5702-088-2, ISBN13: 978-90-5702-088-9. Dewey:891.8/5/2/6/08.
Audience: **g,l,u,f.**

Smith, Teresa H. **PG7445.E8**
The Eagle and the Crow: Modern Polish Short Stories. Teresa Halikowska & George Hyde (Editors), Wiesiek Powaga & Basia Pletanek (Translators), Teresa Halikowska & George Hyde (Introduction by). Trade Paper. Serpent's Tail Ltd. London, 1996. 304p. ISBN:1-85242-356-0, ISBN13: 978-1-85242-356-8. Dewey:891.8/5/301/0807. LCCN:96-069161.
Audience: **g,l,u,f.**

Slavic Literatures > Polish > Bibliography

Maciuszko, Jerzy J. **Z2528.T7 M33**
Polish Short Story in English: A Guide and Critical Bibliography. Trade Cloth. Wayne State University Press. Detroit, MI. 1968. ISBN:0-8143-1342-6, ISBN13: 978-0-8143-1342-8. Dewey:016.8918/5/3. LCCN:68-012253.
Audience: **u.**

Serafin, Steven (Editor) **Z2483.T883 2001**
Twentieth-Century Eastern European Writers. Trade Cloth. Thomson Gale. Farmington Hills, MI. 2000. xxiii, 483p. Dictionary of Literary Biography Ser., Vol. 232 ISBN:0-7876-4649-0, ISBN13: 978-0-7876-4649-3. Dewey:809/.8947. LCCN:00-059334.
Audience: **l,u,f.**

Slavic Literatures > Polish > Biography

Serafin, Steven (Editor) **Z2483.T883 2001**
Twentieth-Century Eastern European Writers. Trade Cloth. Thomson Gale. Farmington Hills, MI. 2000. xxiii, 483p. Dictionary of Literary Biography Ser., Vol. 232 ISBN:0-7876-4649-0, ISBN13: 978-0-7876-4649-3. Dewey:809/.8947. LCCN:00-059334.
Audience: **l,u,f.**

Slavic Literatures > Polish > Dictionary

Czerwinski, E. J. (Editor) **PG7007**
Dictionary of Polish Literature. Cloth Text. Greenwood Publishing Group, Inc. Portsmouth, NH. 1994. 504p. ISBN:0-313-26222-5, ISBN13: 978-0-313-26222-7. Dewey:891.8/509/0003. LCCN:93-049540.
Audience: **l,u,f.** *Choice, 1995.*

Slavic Literatures > Polish > History and Criticism

Baranczak, Stanislaw **PG7167.E64Z5913 1987**
A Fugitive from Utopia: The Poetry of Zbigniew Herbert. Trade Cloth. Harvard University Press. Cambridge, MA. 1987. 176p. ISBN:0-674-32685-7, ISBN13: 978-0-674-32685-9. Dewey:891.8/517. LCCN:86-025818.
Audience: **u,f.** *Choice, 1988.*

Borkowska, Grazyna **PG7098.4.B6713 2001**
Alienated Women: A Study on Polish Women's Fiction. Trade Cloth. Central European University Press. Herndon, VA. 2001. 340p. ISBN:963-9241-03-2, ISBN13: 978-963-9241-03-9. Dewey:891.8/53099287/09034. LCCN:2001-028229.
Audience: **u,f.** *Choice, 2002.*

Cioffi, Kathleen **PN2859.P6**
Alternative Theatre in Poland: 1954-1989. Cloth Text. Gordon & Breach Publishing Group. New York, NY. 1996. 288p. Polish Theatre Archive Ser., Vol. 2 ISBN:3-7186-5853-4, ISBN13: 978-3-7186-5853-4. Dewey:792/.022/09438.
Audience: **u,f.**

Czerniawski, Adam (Editor) **PG7070.M375 1991**
The Mature Laurel: Essays on Modern Polish Poetry. Trade Cloth. Dufour Editions, Inc. Chester Springs, PA. 1990. 326p. ISBN:0-8023-1292-6, ISBN13: 978-0-8023-1292-1. Dewey:891.8/51709. LCCN:90-024814.
Audience: **u,f.** *Choice, 1992.*

Dadlez, Anna R. **PG7099.5.P65**
Political and Social Issues in Poland, as Reflected in the Polish Novel. Trade Cloth. Eastern European Monographs. Bradenton, FL. 1989. 289p. ISBN:0-88033-166-6, ISBN13: 978-0-88033-166-1. Dewey:973.8/4. LCCN:89-083890.
Audience: **u,f.**

Eile, Stanislaw **PG7053.N27E38 2000**
Literature and Nationalism in Partitioned Poland, 1795-1918. Cloth over Boards. Palgrave Macmillan. New York, NY. 2000. 248p. Studies in Russia and East Europe ISBN:0-312-23159-8, ISBN13: 978-0-312-23159-0. Dewey:891.8/5/09358. LCCN:99-056329.
Audience: **u.** *Choice, 2001.*

Kalinowska, Izabela **PG7020.A8K35 2004**
Between East and West: Polish and Russian Nineteenth-Century Travel to the Orient. Trade Cloth. University of Rochester Press. Rochester, NY. 2004. 216p. Rochester Studies in Central Europe Ser. ISBN:1-58046-172-7, ISBN13: 978-1-58046-172-6. Dewey:891.709/325. LCCN:2004-017410.
Audience: **u,f.**

Karcz, Andrzej **PG7008.K36 2002**
The Polish Formalist School and Russian Formalism. Trade Cloth. University of Rochester Press. Rochester, NY. 2004. 230p. Rochester Studies in Central Europe ISBN:1-58046-110-7, ISBN13: 978-1-58046-110-8. Dewey:891.8/509. LCCN:2002-022559.
Audience: **u,f.**

Kraszewski, Charles S. **PG7167.E64Z76 2003**
Essays on the Dramatic Works of Polish Poet Zbigniew Herbert. Trade Cloth. Edwin Mellen Press, The. Lewiston, NY. 2002. 176p. ISBN:0-7734-7062-X, ISBN13: 978-0-7734-7062-0. Dewey:891.8/527. LCCN:2002-070333.
Audience: **u,f.**

Mikos, Michael J. **PG7445.E1M54 1996**
Polish Baroque and Enlightenment Literature: An Anthology. Trade Cloth. Slavica Publishers. Bloomington, IN. 1996. 382p. ISBN:0-89357-266-7, ISBN13: 978-0-89357-266-2. Dewey:891.8/508004. LCCN:97-155106.
Audience: **u.**

Milosz, Czeslaw **PG7012**
The History of Polish Literature. Ed. 2. Trade Paper. University of California Press. Berkeley, CA. 1983. 570p. ISBN:0-520-04477-0, ISBN13: 978-0-520-04477-7. Dewey:891.8/5/09. LCCN:82-020227.
Audience: **u.**

Prokop-Janiec, Eugenia **PG7035.J48P7613 2003**
Polish-Jewish Literature in the Interwar Years. Trade Cloth. Syracuse University Press. Syracuse, NY. 2003. xix, 314p. Judaic Traditions in Literature, Music, and Art Ser. ISBN:0-8156-2984-2, ISBN13: 978-0-8156-2984-9. Dewey:891.8/5098924/09042. LCCN:2002-044583.
Audience: **u.** *Choice, 2003.*

Segel, Harold B. (Editor) **PG7445.E1S77 1996**
Stranger in Our Midst: Images of the Jew in Polish Literature. Book, Other. Cornell University Press. Ithaca, NY. 1996. 432p. ISBN:0-8014-2865-3, ISBN13: 978-0-8014-2865-4. Dewey:891.8/50935203924. LCCN:95-050480.
Audience: **u,f.** *Choice, 1997.*

Wilczek, Piotr **PG7015.W55 2006**
Mis and Mis: Polish Literature in the Context of Cross-Cultural Communication. Trade Paper. Peter Lang Publishing, Inc. New York, NY. 2005. 164p. Literary and Cultural Theory Ser., Vol. 22 ISBN:0-8204-9817-3, ISBN13: 978-0-8204-9817-1. Dewey:891.8/509. LCCN:2005-057920.
Audience: **u,f.**

Slavic Literatures > Polish > Individual Authors

Henryk Sienkiewicz.
http://info-poland.buffalo.edu/classroom/sienkiewicz.html
University of Buffalo.
Audience: **g,l,u,f.**

Andrzejewski, Jerzy **PG7158.A7P613 1991**
Ashes and Diamonds. David J. Welsch (Translator), Heinrich Böll (Introduction by), Barbara Niemczyk (Foreword by). Trade Paper. Northwestern University Press. Evanston, IL. 1984. 239p. ISBN:0-8101-0856-9, ISBN13: 978-0-8101-0856-1. Dewey:891.8/537. LCCN:91-008061.
Audience: **g,l,u,f.**

Baczynski, Krzysztof Kamil **PG7158.B313**
White Magic and Other Poems. Bill Johnson (Translator). Trade Paper. Green Integer. Los Angeles, CA. 2004. 120p. Green Integer Ser. ISBN:1-931243-81-6, ISBN13: 978-1-931243-81-0. Dewey:891.85172.
Audience: **g,l,u,f.**

Borowski, Tadeusz **PG7158.L39**
This Way for the Gas, Ladies and Gentlemen. Barbara Vedder (Editor, Translator), Michael Kandel (Translator), Jan Kott (Introduction by). Trade Paper. Penguin Group (USA) Inc. New York, NY. 1992. 1p. Penguin Twentieth-Century Classics Ser. ISBN:0-14-018624-7, ISBN13: 978-0-14-018624-6. Dewey:891.8/537. LCCN:92-204852.
Audience: **g,l,u,f.**

Chwin, Stefan **PG7162.H84H3613 2004**
Death in Danzig. Philip Boehm (Translator). Cloth over Boards. Harcourt Trade Publishers. New York, NY. 2004. 272p. ISBN:0-15-100805-1, ISBN13: 978-0-15-100805-6. Dewey:891.8538. LCCN:2004-002099.
Audience: **g,l,u,f.**

Czerniawski, Adam (Translator) **PG7157.K6**
Treny: The Laments of Kochanowski. Donald Davie (Introduction by). Trade Paper. European Humanities Research Centre. Oxford, 2001. 74p. Studies in Comparative Literature Ser. ISBN:1-900755-55-6, ISBN13: 978-1-900755-55-9. Dewey:891.8513.
Audience: **g,l,u,f.**

Ficowski, Jerzy **PR9275.A583**
Waiting for the Dog to Sleep. Soren Gauger & Marcin Piekoszewski (Translators). Trade Paper. Twisted Spoon Press. Prague 5, 2006. 188p. Contemporary Writing from Central Europe Ser. ISBN:80-86264-24-6, ISBN13: 978-80-86264-24-0. Dewey:813.
Audience: **g,l,u,f.**

Goerke, Natasza **PG7166.O34**
Farewells to Plasma. W. Martin (Translator), Jeffrey Young (Illustrator, Designed by). Trade Cloth. Twisted Spoon Press. Prague 5, 2001. 132p. Contemporary Writing from Central Europe Ser. ISBN:80-86264-15-7, ISBN13: 978-80-86264-15-8. Dewey:813.
Audience: **g,l,u,f.**

Gombrowicz, Witold **PG7158.G669F4713**
Ferdydurke. Danuta Borchardt (Translator), Susan Sontag (Foreword by). Cloth over Boards. Yale University Press. Cumberland, RI. 2000. 320p. ISBN:0-300-08239-8, ISBN13: 978-0-300-08239-5. Dewey:891.8/5273. LCCN:99-058269.
Audience: **g,l,u,f.**

Herbert, Zbigniew **PG7167.E64A2 2006**
The Collected Poems: 1956-1998. Trade Cloth. HarperCollins Publishers. New York, NY. 2007. 608p. ISBN:0-06-078390-7, ISBN13: 978-0-06-078390-7. Dewey:891.8/5173. LCCN:2006-040856.
Audience: **g,l,u,f.**

Herling, Gustaw **PG7158.H446**
The Island: Three Tales. Ronald Strom (Translator). Trade Paper. Penguin Group (USA) Inc. New York, NY. 1994. 160p. ISBN:0-14-023279-6, ISBN13: 978-0-14-023279-0. Dewey:891.8537.
Audience: **g,l,u,f.** *Choice, 1991.*

Herling-Grudzinski, Gustaw **PG7158.H446A25 2003**
Noonday Cemetery and Other Stories. Bill Johnston (Translator). Trade Cloth. New Directions Publishing Corporation. New York, NY. 2003. 256p. ISBN:0-8112-1529-6, ISBN13: 978-0-8112-1529-9. Dewey:891.8/537. LCCN:2003-000358.
Audience: **g,l,u,f.**

Hlasko, Marek **PG7158.H55O7813 1994**
The Eighth Day of the Week. Norbert Guterman (Translator). Trade Paper. Northwestern University Press. Evanston, IL. 1994. 123p. European Classics Ser. ISBN:0-8101-1119-5, ISBN13: 978-0-8101-1119-6. Dewey:891.857. LCCN:93-049838.
Audience: **g,l,u,f.**

Hlasko, Marek **PG7158.H55K55 1990**
Killing the Second Dog. Tomasz Mirkowicz (Translator). Trade Paper. Cane Hill Press. New York, NY. 1990. 117p. ISBN:0-943433-04-5, ISBN13: 978-0-943433-04-2. Dewey:891.857. LCCN:89-081158.
Audience: **g,l,u,f.**

Hlasko, Marek **PG7158.H55**
All Backs Were Turned. Tomasz Mirkowicz (Translator), Thompson Bradley (Introduction by). Trade Paper. Cane Hill Press. New York, NY. 1991. 118p. ISBN:0-943433-07-X, ISBN13: 978-0-943433-07-3. Dewey:891.8537. LCCN:90-084230.
Audience: **g,l,u,f.**

Huelle, Pawel **PG7167.U86A25 1995**
Moving House and Other Stories. Antonia Lloyd-Jones (Translator). Trade Cloth. Harcourt Trade Publishers. New York, NY. 1995. 248p. ISBN:0-15-162731-2, ISBN13: 978-0-15-162731-8. Dewey:891.8/537. LCCN:93-048587.
Audience: **g,l,u,f.**

Konwicki, Tadeusz **PG7158.K6513N4813**
New World Avenue and Vicinity. Walter Arndt (Translator). Cloth over Boards. Farrar, Straus & Giroux. New York, NY. 1991. 224p. ISBN:0-374-22182-0, ISBN13: 978-0-374-22182-9. Dewey:891.8/537. LCCN:90-048492.
Audience: **g,l,u,f.** *Choice, 1991.*

Konwicki, Tadeusz **PG7158.K6513.K613**
The Polish Complex. Richard Lourie (Translator, Introduction by). Trade Paper. Dalkey Archive Press. Normal, IL. 1998. 224p. American Literature Ser. ISBN:1-56478-201-8, ISBN13: 978-1-56478-201-4. Dewey:891.8/537373. LCCN:98-023365.
Audience: **g,l,u,f.**

Krall, Hanna **D804.3.K724 2005**
The Woman from Hamburg: And Other True Stories. Madeline G. Levine (Translator). Trade Cloth. Other Press, LLC. New York, NY. 2006. 264p. ISBN:1-59051-136-0, ISBN13: 978-1-59051-136-7. Dewey:940.53/18/092 B. LCCN:2004-022648.
Audience: **g,l,u,f.**

Krasicki, Ignacy **PG7157.K7B28213 1997**
Polish Fables: Bilingual Edition. Gerard Kapolka (Translator), Barbara Swiozinska (Illustrator). Trade Cloth. Hippocrene Books, Inc. New York, NY. 1997. 106p. ISBN:0-7818-0548-1, ISBN13: 978-0-7818-0548-3. Dewey:891.8515. LCCN:97-031161.
Audience: **g,l,u,f.**

Krasinski, Zygmunt **PG7158**
The Un-Divine Comedy. Harriette Kennedy & Zofia Uminska (Translators). Trade Cloth. Greenwood Publishing Group, Inc. Portsmouth, NH. 1976. 111p. ISBN:0-8371-7513-5, ISBN13: 978-0-8371-7513-3. Dewey:891.8526. LCCN:74-005774.
Audience: **g,l,u,f.**

Lem, Stanislaw **PG7158.L39**
The Cyberiad. Trade Paper. Harcourt Trade Publishers. New York, NY. 2002. 312p. ISBN:0-15-602759-3, ISBN13: 978-0-15-602759-5. Dewey:891.8/537.
Audience: **g,l,u,f.**

Lem, Stanislaw **PG7158.L39S613 1987**
Solaris. Joanna Kilmartin & Steve Cox (Translators). Trade Paper. Harcourt Trade Publishers. New York, NY. 2002. 204p. ISBN:0-15-602760-7, ISBN13: 978-0-15-602760-1. Dewey:891.8/537. LCCN:86-031938.
Audience: **g,l,u,f.**

Lesmian, Boreslaw **PN6727.W475**
Sinbad the Sailor. Krystina Boron (Translator). Trade Cloth. Pomegranate Press. Cambridge, MA. 1980. ISBN:0-686-64726-2, ISBN13: 978-0-686-64726-3. Dewey:741.5/973.
Audience: **g,l,u,f.**

Lipska, Ewa **PG7171.I63.A26 1991**
Poet? Criminal? Madman?: Poems. B. Plebanek & T. Howard (Translators), A. Czerniawski (Introduction by). Trade Paper. Forest Books. London, 1991. 96p. ISBN:1-85610-011-1, ISBN13: 978-1-85610-011-3. Dewey:891.8517. LCCN:91-072165.
Audience: **g,l,u,f.** *Choice, 1993.*

Lloyd-Jones, Antonia (Translator) **PG7158.I8A25 2002**
The Birch Grove and Other Stories. Leszek Kolakowski (Introduction by). Trade Cloth. Central European University Press. Herndon, VA. 2002. 286p. Central European Classics Ser. ISBN:963-9241-45-8, ISBN13: 978-963-9241-45-9. Dewey:891.8/5373. LCCN:2002-003353.
Audience: **g,l,u,f.**

Maslowska, Dorota **PG7213.A84W6513 2005**
Snow White and Russian Red. Benjamin Paloff (Translator). Trade Paper. Grove/Atlantic, Inc. New York, NY. 2005. 304p. ISBN:0-8021-7001-3, ISBN13: 978-0-8021-7001-9. Dewey:891.8/538. LCCN:2004-042352.
Audience: **g,l,u,f.**

Mickiewicz, Adam **PG7158.M5 A25**
Selected Poetry and Prose. Paper Text. Textbook Publishers. Temecula, CA. 2003. 191p. ISBN:0-7581-6328-2, ISBN13: 978-0-7581-6328-8. Dewey:891.851.
Audience: **g,l,u,f.**

Mickiewicz, Adam **PG7158.M5P312 1992**
Pan Tadeusz. Kennety R. Mackenzie (Translator). Trade Paper. Hippocrene Books, Inc. New York, NY. 1992. 598p. ISBN:0-7818-0033-1, ISBN13: 978-0-7818-0033-4. LCCN:93-195891.
Audience: **g,l,u,f.**

Mikos, Michael J. (Translator) **PG7445.E1M43 1991**
Medieval Literature of Poland: An Anthology. Paper over Boards. Garland Publishing, Inc. New York, NY. 1992. 286p. Library of Medieval Literature, Vol. 82B ISBN:0-8153-0408-0, ISBN13: 978-0-8153-0408-1. Dewey:891.8/509002. LCCN:91-024676.
Audience: **g,l,u,f.**

Mrozek, Slawomir **PG7172.R65A2 2004**
The Mrozek Reader. Daniel Gerould (Editor). Trade Paper. Grove/Atlantic, Inc. New York, NY. 2004. 352p. ISBN:0-8021-4066-1, ISBN13: 978-0-8021-4066-1. Dewey:891.8/527. LCCN:2003-067760.
Audience: **g,l,u,f.**

Nalkowska, Zofia **PG7158.N34M3413 2000**
Medallions. Diana Kuprel (Translator). Trade Cloth. Northwestern University Press. Evanston, IL. 2000. 49p. Jewish Lives Ser. ISBN:0-8101-1742-8, ISBN13: 978-0-8101-1742-6. Dewey:940.53/174386. LCCN:99-048758.
Audience: **g,l,u,f.**

Norwid, Cyprian Kamil & Czerniawski, Adam **PG7158.N57**
Selected Poems of Cyprian Norwid. Book, Other. Anvil Press Poetry, Ltd. London, 2004. 96p. ISBN:0-85646-369-8, ISBN13: 978-0-85646-369-3. Dewey:891.8516. LCCN:2005-434736.
Audience: **g,l,u,f.**

Pasek, Jan Chryzostom **DK4312.P3A35**
Memoirs of the Polish Baroque: The Writings of Jan Chryzostom Pasek, a Squire of the Commonwealth of Poland and Lithuania. Catherine S. Leach (Editor). Trade Paper. Books on Demand. Ann Arbor, MI. 415p. ISBN:0-608-17277-4, ISBN13: 978-0-608-17277-4. Dewey:943.8/02/0924. LCCN:74-077731.
Audience: **g,l,u,f.** B

Pilch, Jerzy **PG7175.I49I5613 2002**
His Current Woman. Bill Johnston (Translator). Trade Paper. Northwestern University Press. Evanston, IL. 2002. 136p. ISBN:0-8101-1918-8, ISBN13: 978-0-8101-1918-5. Dewey:891.8/538. LCCN:2001-006877.
Audience: **g,l,u,f.** *Choice, 2003, 2002.*

Potocki, Jan **PQ2063.S3**
The Manuscript Found in Saragossa. Ian Maclean (Translator, Introduction by). Trade Paper. Penguin Group (USA) Inc. New York, NY. 1996. 656p. Classics Ser. ISBN:0-14-044580-3, ISBN13: 978-0-14-044580-0. Dewey:843/.6.
Audience: **g,l,u,f.**

Prus, Bolesiaw **PG7158.S4**
The Doll. Trade Paper. Hippocrene Books, Inc. New York, NY. 1993. 700p. ISBN:0-7818-0158-3, ISBN13: 978-0-7818-0158-4. Dewey:891.8/536.
Audience: **g,l,u,f.**

Prus, Boleslav **PG7158.G6A25 1996**
The Sins of Childhood and Other Stories. Bill Johnston (Translator). Trade Paper. Northwestern University Press. Evanston, IL. 1997. 247p. European Classics Ser. ISBN:0-8101-1462-3, ISBN13: 978-0-8101-1462-3. Dewey:891.8/536. LCCN:96-042276.
Audience: **g,l,u,f.** *Choice, 1997.*

Rozewicz, Tadeusz **PG7158.R63A24 1998**
Reading the Apocalypse in Bed: Selected Works. Trade Paper. Marion Boyars Publishers, Inc. New York, NY. 1998. 297p. ISBN:0-7145-3037-9, ISBN13: 978-0-7145-3037-6. Dewey:891.8/5273. LCCN:98-025180.
Audience: **g,l,u,f.**

Rozewicz, Tadeusz **PG7158.R63**
The Trap. Adam Czerniawski (Translator). Trade Cloth. Gordon & Breach Publishing Group. New York, NY. 1997. 115p. Polish Theatre Archive Ser. ISBN:3-7186-5855-0, ISBN13: 978-3-7186-5855-8. Dewey:891.8/5/2/7.
Audience: **g,l,u,f.**

Schulz, Bruno, et al. **PR6066.I53**
Street of Crocodiles. Simon McBurney & Mark Wheatley (Authors). Trade Paper. Methuen Publishing Ltd. London, 2004. 0p. ISBN:0-413-73870-1, ISBN13: 978-0-413-73870-7. Dewey:822.9/14.
Audience: **g,l,u,f.**

Sienkiewicz, Henryka **PG7158.S4 A27**
Selected Tales. Ed. 2. Trade Cloth. American Institute of Polish Culture. Miami, FL. 1979. 311p. ISBN:1-881284-10-7, ISBN13: 978-1-881284-10-9. Dewey:891.8/536.
Audience: **g,l,u,f.**

Sienkiewicz, Henryka **PZ3.S57 Y**
Yanko the Musician and Other Stories. Jeremiah Curtin (Translator). Trade Paper. Fredonia Books. Miami, FL. 2003. 288p. ISBN:1-4101-0307-2, ISBN13: 978-1-4101-0307-9. Dewey:891.8536.
Audience: **g,l,u,f.**

Sienkiewicz, Henryka **PG7158.S4Q43 1997**
Quo Vadis? W. S. Kuniczak (Translator). Trade Paper. Hippocrene Books, Inc. New York, NY. 1997. 579p. ISBN:0-7818-0550-3, ISBN13: 978-0-7818-0550-6. Dewey:891.8/5/3/6. LCCN:97-002694.
Audience: **g,l,u,f.**

Slowacki, Juliusz **PG7158.S6**
Mary Stuart, a Romantic Drama. Arthur P. Coleman & Marion M. Coleman (Translators). Trade Cloth. Greenwood Publishing Group, Inc. Portsmouth, NH. 1978. 106p. ISBN:0-8371-7712-X, ISBN13: 978-0-8371-7712-0. Dewey:891.8526. LCCN:74-011993.
Audience: **g,l,u,f.**

Stasiuk, Andrzej **PG7179.U45**
White Raven. Trade Paper. Serpent's Tail Ltd. London, 2001. 256p. ISBN:1-85242-667-5, ISBN13: 978-1-85242-667-5. Dewey:891.8/538. LCCN:00-102182.
Audience: **g,l,u,f.**

Stasiuk, Andrzej **PG7178.T28**
Tales of Galicia. Margarita Nafpaktitis (Translator, Afterword by). Trade Cloth. Twisted Spoon Press. Prague 5, 2003. 140p. Contemporary Writing from Central Europe Ser. ISBN:80-86264-05-X, ISBN13: 978-80-86264-05-9. Dewey:891.8517.
Audience: **g,l,u,f.**

Szewc, Piotr **PG7178.Z39Z2513 1999**
Annihilation. Ewa Hryniewicz-Yarbrough (Translator). Trade Cloth. Dalkey Archive Press. Normal, IL. 1999. 107p. Coleman Dowell Ser. ISBN:1-56478-205-0, ISBN13: 978-1-56478-205-2. Dewey:891.8/5373. LCCN:00-266178.
Audience: **g,l,u,f.**

Szymborska, Wislawa **PG7158.M553**
Miracle Fair: Selected Poems of Wislawa Szymborska. Trade Paper. W. W. Norton & Company, Inc. New York, NY. 2002. 176p. ISBN:0-393-32385-4, ISBN13: 978-0-393-32385-6. Dewey:891.8/517.
Audience: **g,l,u,f.**

Szymborska, Wislawa **PG7158.M553**
Poems New and Collected. Trade Paper. Harcourt Trade Publishers. New York, NY. 2000. 296p. ISBN:0-15-601146-8, ISBN13: 978-0-15-601146-4. Dewey:891.8517.
Audience: **g,l,u,f.**

Szymborska, Wislawa **PG7178.Z9A222 2005**
Monologue of a Dog. Stanislaw Baranczak & Clare Cavanagh (Translators), Billy Collins (Foreword by). Cloth over Boards. Harcourt Trade Publishers. New York, NY. 2005. 112p. ISBN:0-15-101220-2, ISBN13: 978-0-15-101220-6. Dewey:895.8/5173. LCCN:2005-016084.
Audience: **g,l,u,f.**

Szymborska, Wislawa **PG7178.Z9A222 2002**
Nonrequired Reading: Prose Pieces. Clare Cavanagh (Translator). Cloth over Boards. Harcourt Trade Publishers. New York, NY. 2002. 256p. ISBN:0-15-100660-1, ISBN13: 978-0-15-100660-1. Dewey:028.1. LCCN:2002-002440.
Audience: **g,l,u,f.**

Tulli, Magdalena **PG7179.U45T7913 2005**
Moving Parts. Bill Johnston (Translator). Saddle Stitched, Cloth over Boards, Dust Jacket. Archipelago Books. Brooklyn, NY. 2005. 133p. ISBN:0-9763950-0-2, ISBN13: 978-0-9763950-0-3. Dewey:891.8/538. LCCN:2005-016693.
Audience: **g,l,u,f.**

Tulli, Magdelena **PG7179.U45S5813 2004**
Dreams and Stones. Bill Johnston (Translator). Trade Cloth. Archipelago Books. Brooklyn, NY. 2004. 130p. ISBN:0-9728692-6-3, ISBN13: 978-0-9728692-6-3. Dewey:891.8/538. LCCN:2003-020335.
Audience: **g,l,u,f.**

Wat, Aleksander **PG7158.W282**
My Century. Czeslaw Milosz (Introduction by). Trade Cloth. New York Review of Books, Incorporated, The. New York, NY. 2003. 448p. New York Review Books Classics ISBN:1-59017-065-2, ISBN13: 978-1-59017-065-6. Dewey:891.8/517 B. LCCN:2003-023592.
Audience: **g,l,u,f.**

Witkiewicz, Stanislaw I. **PG7158.W52A24 1988**
The Madman and the Nun and the Crazy Locomotive: Three Plays (Including "The Water Hen"). Daniel Gerould & C. S. Durer (Editors), Jan Kott (Foreword by). Trade Paper. Applause Theatre Book Publishers. New York, NY. 1988. 110p. ISBN:0-936839-83-X, ISBN13: 978-0-936839-83-7. Dewey:891.8/527. LCCN:88-007715.
Audience: **g,l,u,f.**

Witkiewicz, Stanislaw I. **PG7158.W52 A24 1992**
A Witkiewicz Reader: The Life and Work of Stanislaw Ignacy Witkiewicz. Daniel Gerould (Editor, Translator). Trade Paper. Northwestern University Press. Evanston, IL. 1992. 359p. ISBN:0-8101-0994-8, ISBN13: 978-0-8101-0994-0. Dewey:891.8/527. LCCN:92-019031.
Audience: **g,l,u,f.**

Witkiewicz, Stanislaw I. **PG7158.W52N513 1996**
Insatiability: A Novel. Louis Iribarne (Translator). Trade Cloth. Northwestern University Press. Evanston, IL. 1996. 534p. ISBN:0-8101-1133-0, ISBN13: 978-0-8101-1133-2. Dewey:891.8/537. LCCN:96-004251.
Audience: **g,l,u,f.**

Wyspianski, Stanislaw **PG7158.W8W413 1990**
The Wedding. Gerald T. Kapolka (Editor). Trade Cloth. Ardis Publishers. Woodstock, NY. 1990. 200p. ISBN:0-88233-556-1, ISBN13: 978-0-88233-556-8. Dewey:891.8/526. LCCN:89-006648.
Audience: **g,l,u,f.**

Zeromski, Stefan **PG7158.Z4W5514 2002**
The Faithful River. Bill Johnston (Translator). Trade Paper. Northwestern University Press. Evanston, IL. 1999. 179p. European Classics Ser. ISBN:0-8101-1596-4, ISBN13: 978-0-8101-1596-5. Dewey:891.8/536. LCCN:99-027010.
Audience: **g,l,u,f.**

Slavic Literatures > Russian

TK5105.875.I57
☐ Friends & Partners Russian Literature Site. http://www.fplib.org/literature/
Audience: **l,u,f.**

Cornwell, Neil (Editor) **PG2951.R68 2001**
Routledge Companion to Russian Literature. Trade Paper. Routledge. New York, NY. 2001. 288p. Routledge Companions Ser. ISBN:0-415-23366-6, ISBN13: 978-0-415-23366-8. Dewey:891.709. LCCN:2001-019769.
Audience: **l,u,f.** *Choice, 2002.*

Geldern, James von & McReynolds, Louise (Editors) **DK32.E6 1998**
Entertaining Tsarist Russia: Tales, Songs, Plays, Movies, Jokes, Ads, and Images from Russian Urban Life, 1779-1917. Trade Paper. Indiana University Press. Bloomington, IN. 1998. 464p. Indiana-Michigan Series in Russian and East European Studies ISBN:0-253-21195-6, ISBN13: 978-0-253-21195-8. Dewey:306/.0947/09034. LCCN:97-052597.
Audience: **l,u.** *Choice, 1999.*

Hammarberg, Gitta **PG3314.Z9 S44 1991**
From the Idyll to the Novel: Karamzin's Sentimentalist Prose. Catriona Kelly, Anthony Cross, Caryl Emerson, Barbara Heldt, Malcolm Jones, Donald Rayfield, G. S. Smith & Victor Terras (Contribution by). Trade Paper. Cambridge University Press. New York, NY. 2006. 348p. Cambridge Studies in Russian Literature Ser. ISBN:0-521-02560-5, ISBN13: 978-0-521-02560-7. Dewey:891.78/209.
Audience: **u,f.**

Haney, Jack V. (Editor) **GR202.C645 1999**
Russian Animal Tales. Trade Cloth. M. E. Sharpe Inc. Armonk, NY. 2000. 296p. The Complete Russian Folktale Ser., Vol. 2 ISBN:1-56324-490-X, ISBN13: 978-1-56324-490-2. Dewey:398.2/0947. LCCN:98-030059.
Audience: **u,f.**

Haney, Jack V. (Editor) **GR202.C645 2003**
Russian Legends. Trade Cloth. M. E. Sharpe Inc. Armonk, NY. 2003. 240p. Complete Russian Folktale Ser., Vol. 5 ISBN:1-56324-493-4, ISBN13: 978-1-56324-493-3. Dewey:398.2/0947. LCCN:98-030059.
Audience: **u,f.**

Ivanits, Linda J. **GR203.R88I93 1989**
Russian Folk Belief. Trade Cloth. M. E. Sharpe Inc. Armonk, NY. 1989. 276p. ISBN:0-87332-422-6, ISBN13: 978-0-87332-422-9. Dewey:398/.0947. LCCN:87-032067.
Audience: **u,f.** *Choice, 1990.*

Jones, Malcolm V. & Miller, Robin Feuer (Editors) **PG3098.3.C33 1998**
The Cambridge Companion to the Classic Russian Novel. Malcolm V. Jones, Robert Maguire, Hugh McLean, Gareth Jones & Lesley Milne (Contribution by). Trade Paper. Cambridge University Press. New York, NY. 1998. 338p. Companions to Literature Ser. ISBN:0-521-47909-6, ISBN13: 978-0-521-47909-7. Dewey:891.73/009. LCCN:97-033220.
Audience: **l,u,f.** *Choice, 1998.*

Ledkovsky, Marina (Editor), et al. **PG2997**
Dictionary of Russian Women Writers. Charlotte Rosenthal & Mary F. Zirin (Editors). Cloth Text. Greenwood Publishing Group, Inc. Portsmouth, NH. 1994. 960p. ISBN:0-313-26265-9, ISBN13: 978 0 313 26265-4. Dewey:891.709928703. LCCN:93-013012.
Audience: **l,u,f.** *Choice, 1994.*

Nabokov, Vladimir (Translator) **PG3300.S6**
The Song of Igor's Campaign. Trade Cloth. Ardis Publishers. Woodstock, NY. 1989. 128p. ISBN:0-87501-061-X, ISBN13: 978-0-87501-061-8. Dewey:891.711.
Audience: **g,l,u,f.**

Ogden, J. Alexander & Kalb, Judith E. **PG3098.3.R874 2001**
Russian Novelists in the Age of Tolstoy and Dostoevsky. Trade Cloth. Thomson Gale. Farmington Hills, MI. 2001. xxvii, 469p. Dictionary of Literary Biography Ser., Vol. 238 ISBN:0-7876-4655-5, ISBN13: 978-0-7876-4655-4. Dewey:891.73/3/03 B. LCCN:00-053515.
Audience: **l,u,f.**

Riordan, James **GR345.R55 1990**
The Sun Maiden and the Crescent Moon: Siberian Folk Tales. Trade Cloth. Interlink Publishing Group, Inc. Northampton, MA. 1991. 224p. International Folk Tales Ser. ISBN:0-940793-66-0, ISBN13: 978-0-940793-66-8. Dewey:398.2/1/0957. LCCN:90-042586.
Audience: **u,f.**

Seifrid, Thomas **P107.S45 2005**
The Word Made Self: Russian Writings on Language, 1860-1930. Book, Other. Cornell University Press. Ithaca, NY. 2005. 272p. ISBN:0-8014-4316-4, ISBN13: 978-0-8014-4316-9. Dewey:400. LCCN:2004-023506.
Audience: **u,f.** *Choice, 2005.*

Terras, Victor **PG3056.T44 1998**
Poetry of the Silver Age: The Various Voices of Russian Modernism. Alexander Landman (Translator), Horst-Jurgen Gerigk (Preface by). Trade Cloth. Dresden University Press. Dresden, 1998. 480p. ISBN:3-931828-71-9, ISBN13: 978-3-931828-71-4. Dewey:891.71/409. LCCN:00-269235.
Audience: **u,f.** *Choice, 1999.*

Van Deusen, Kira **GR203.2.C5V36 1999**
Raven and the Rock: Storytelling in Chukotka. Trade Cloth. University of Washington Press. Seattle, WA. 1999. xvii, 190p. ISBN:0-295-97842-2, ISBN13: 978-0-295-97842-0. Dewey:398.2/0957/7. LCCN:99-031842.
Audience: **l,f.**

Wachtel, Michael **PG3041.W328 2004**
The Cambridge Introduction to Russian Poetry. Trade Paper. Cambridge University Press. New York, NY. 2004. 178p. Cambridge Introductions to Literature Ser. ISBN:0-521-00493-4, ISBN13: 978-0-521-00493-0. Dewey:891.71/009. LCCN:2003-065619.
Audience: **g,l,u.** *Choice, 2005.*

Slavic Literatures > Russian > Anthologies

Afanas'ev, Aleksandr Nikolaevich **GR202.A6613 2006**
Russian Fairy Tales. UK-Trade Paper. Knopf Publishing Group. New York, NY. 1976. 672p. Fairy Tale and Folklore Library ISBN:0-394-73090-9, ISBN13: 978-0-394-73090-5. Dewey:398.20947. LCCN:2006-271176.
Audience: **g,l,u,f.**

Balina, Marina (Editor), et al. **GR138**
Politicizing Magic: An Anthology of Russian and Soviet Fairy Tales. Helena Goscilo & Mark Lipovetsky (Editors). Trade Cloth. Northwestern University Press. Evanston, IL. 2005. 432p. ISBN:0-8101-2031-3, ISBN13: 978-0-8101-2031-0. Dewey:398.2/0947. LCCN:2005-010140.
Audience: **g,l,u,f.** *Choice, 2006.*

Brown, Clarence (Contribution by, Notes by) **PG3213 .P67 1993**
The Portable Twentieth-Century Russian Reader. Trade Paper. Penguin Group (USA) Inc. New York, NY. 2003. 640p. ISBN:0-14-243757-3, ISBN13: 978-0-14-243757-5. Dewey:891.708/004. LCCN:2003-283124.
Audience: **g,l,u,f.**

Freeborn, Richard (Editor), et al. **PG2925 .I5 1974**
Russian and Slavic Literature. Robin R. Milner-Gulland & Charles A. Ward (Editors). Trade Paper. Slavica Publishers. Bloomington, IN. 1976. ISBN:0-89357-038-9, ISBN13: 978-0-89357-038-5. Dewey:891.8. LCCN:80-118299.
Audience: **g,l,u,f.**

Goscilo, Helena (Introduction by) **PG3213.L58 1995**
Lives in Transit: A Collection of Recent Russian Women's Writing. Trade Cloth. Ardis Publishers. Woodstock, NY. 1995. 327p. ISBN:0-87501-100-4, ISBN13: 978-0-87501-100-4. Dewey:891.708/09287. LCCN:93-022986.
Audience: **g,l,u,f.** *Choice, 1995.*

Goscilo, Helena (Editor) **PG3276.G54 1990**
Glasnost: An Anthology of Russian Literature under Gorbachev. Byron Lindsey (Introduction by). Trade Paper. Knopf Publishing Group. New York, NY. 1990. 466p. Contemporary Russian Prose Ser. ISBN:0-679-73008-7, ISBN13: 978-0-679-73008-8. Dewey:891.78/440808. LCCN:89-018525.
Audience: **g,l,u,f.**

Hoisington, Thomas H. (Editor, Translator) **PG3286.O89 1998**
Out Visiting and Back Home: Russian Stories on Aging. Trade Cloth. Northwestern University Press. Evanston, IL. 1998. 230p. ISBN:0-8101-1470-4, ISBN13: 978-0-8101-1470-8. Dewey:891.73/0108354. LCCN:97-048552.
Audience: **g,l,u,f.**

Kelly, Catriona (Editor) **PG3213.U87 1999**
Snap Shots of the Century Utopias: Russian Modernist Texts, 1905-1940. Trade Paper. Penguin Group (USA) Inc. New York, NY. 2000. 416p. ISBN:0-14-118081-1, ISBN13: 978-0-14-118081-6. Dewey:891.708/0112/09041. LCCN:00-709371.
Audience: **g,l,u,f.**

Kharms, Daniil & Vvedensky, Alexander **PG3213.M26 1997**
The Man with the Black Coat: Russia's Literature of the Absurd. George Gibian (Editor, Translator). Trade Paper. Northwestern University Press. Evanston, IL. 1997. 258p. European Classics Ser. ISBN:0-8101-1573-5, ISBN13: 978-0-8101-1573-6. Dewey:891.708/0384. LCCN:97-017494.
Audience: **g,l,u,f.**

Langen, Timothy & Weir, Justin (Editors) **PG3245.E38 2000**
Eight Twentieth-Century Russian Plays. Trade Paper. Northwestern University Press. Evanston, IL. 2000. 354p. European Drama Classics Ser. ISBN:0-8101-1374-0, ISBN13: 978-0-8101-1374-9. Dewey:891.72/408. LCCN:00-008680.
Audience: **g,l,u,f.**

Luker, Nicholas (Editor) **PG3266.F76 1988**
From Furmanov to Sholokhov: An Anthology of the Classics of Socialist Realism. Nicholas Luder (Introduction by). Paper Text. Ardis Publishers. Woodstock, NY. 1988. ISBN:0-87501-037-7, ISBN13: 978-0-87501-037-3. Dewey:891.78/42/08012. LCCN:88-016635.
Audience: **g,l,u,f.** *Choice, 1989.*

Ostashevsky, Eugene (Editor) **PG3213.O24 2005**
Oberiu: An Anthology of Russian Absurdism. Susan Sontag (Foreword by). Trade Paper. Northwestern University Press. Evanston, IL. 2006. 296p. ISBN:0-8101-2293-6, ISBN13: 978-0-8101-2293-2. Dewey:891.7080384. LCCN:2005-023271.
Audience: **g,l,u,f.**

Perova, Natasha (Editor) **PG3286**
Captives: Selected Short Stories. Trade Paper, Saddle Stitched. Glas. Moskva 119517, 2005. 270p. ISBN:5-7172-0072-2, ISBN13: 978-5-7172-0072-1. Dewey:891.730108044.
Audience: **g,l,u,f.**

Perova, Natasha & Tait, Arch (Editors) **PG3213**
Soviet Grotesque. Trade Paper. Ivan R. Dee Publisher. Blue Ridge Summit, PA. 1991. 240p. Glas Ser., No. 2 ISBN:0-939010-47-X, ISBN13: 978-0-939010-47-9. Dewey:891.708.
Audience: **g,l,u,f.**

Polukhina, Valentina & Weissbort, Daniel (Editors) **PG3230.7.W65A58 2005**
An Anthology of Contemporary Russian Women Poets. Stephanie Sandler (Preface by). Trade Cloth. University of Iowa Press. Iowa City, IA. 2005. 292p. ISBN:0-87745-947-9, ISBN13: 978-0-87745-947-7. Dewey:891.71/40809287. LCCN:2004-066089.
Audience: **g,l,u,f.** *Choice, 2006.*

Proffer, Carl & Proffer, Ellendea C. (Editors) **PG3056**
The Ardis Anthology of Russian Futurism. Trade Paper. Ardis Publishers. Woodstock, NY. 1980. 413p. ISBN:0-686-77801-4, ISBN13: 978-0-686-77801-1. Dewey:891.71/42/08.
Audience: **g,l,u,f.** B

Reynolds, Andrew **PG3276.P46 1995**
The Penguin Book of New Russian Writing. Victor Erofeyev (Editor). Trade Paper. Penguin Group (USA) Inc. New York, NY. 1996. 416p. ISBN:0-14-015963-0, ISBN13: 978-0-14-015963-9. Dewey:891.73. LCCN:96-133612.
Audience: **g,l,u,f.**

Riordan, James (Translator) **PZ8.1**
Russian Gypsy Tales. Yefim Druts & Alexei Gessler (Compiled by). Trade Cloth. Interlink Publishing Group, Inc. Northampton,

MA. 2004. 160p. International Folk Tales Ser. ISBN:1-56656-442-5, ISBN13: 978-1-56656-442-7. Dewey:398.2/1/08991497047.
Audience: **g,l,u,f.**

Rydel, Christine (Editor, Translator) **PG3213**
The Ardis Anthology of Russian Romanticism. John Mersereau Jr. (Afterword by). Trade Paper. Ardis Publishers. Woodstock, NY. 1984. ISBN:0-88233-742-4, ISBN13: 978-0-88233-742-5. Dewey:891.7/08/03.
Audience: **g,l,u,f.** B

Rzhevsky, Nicholas (Editor) **PG3213.A56 1996**
An Anthology of Russian Literature from Earliest Writings to Modern Fiction: Introduction to a Culture. Cloth Text. M. E. Sharpe Inc. Armonk, NY. 1996. 608p. ISBN:1-56324-421-7, ISBN13: 978-1-56324-421-6. Dewey:891.708. LCCN:95-042684.
Audience: **g,l,u,f.**

Schweikert, Harry C. (Editor) **PG3276**
Russian Short Stories. Trade Paper. University Press of the Pacific. Miami, FL. 2004. 456p. ISBN:1-4102-1623-3, ISBN13: 978-1-4102-1623-6. Dewey:891.7/3/01.
Audience: **g,l,u,f.**

Segel, Harold B. **PG3086**
Twentieth-Century Russian Drama: From Gorky to the Present. Trade Cloth. Johns Hopkins University Press. Baltimore, MD. 1993. 544p. PAJ Bks., :Art and Performance ISBN:0-8018-4690-0, ISBN13: 978-0-8018-4690-8. Dewey:891.72409. LCCN:93-010350.
Audience: **g,l,u,f.**

Seltzer, Thomas (Editor) **PG3286**
Best Russian Short Stories. Trade Paper. Kessinger Publishing, LLC. Whitefish, MT. 2004. ISBN:1-4179-1585-4, ISBN13: 978-1-4179-1585-9. Dewey:891.7.
Audience: **g,l,u,f.**

Shrayer, Maxim D. (Editor) **PG3213.A55 2006**
An Anthology of Jewish-Russian Literature. Cloth Text. M. E. Sharpe Inc. Armonk, NY. 2006. 992p. ISBN:0-7656-0521-X, ISBN13: 978-0-7656-0521-4. Dewey:891.708/08924/009034. LCCN:2005-012792.
Audience: **g,l,u,f.**

Smith, Melissa T. (Translator) **PG3485.8.R35**
The Russian Mirror: Three Plays by Russian Women. Cloth Text. Gordon & Breach Publishing Group. New York, NY. 1998. 112p. Russian Theatre Archive Ser. ISBN:90-5755-024-5, ISBN13: 978-90-5755-024-9. Dewey:891.7/25.
Audience: **g,l,u,f.**

Townsend, R. S. (Translator) **PG3286.R894 1992**
Russian Short Stories. John Bayley (Introduction by). Trade Paper. Tuttle Publishing. Boston, MA. 1992. 190p. ISBN:0-460-87164-1, ISBN13: 978-0-460-87164-8. Dewey:891.73/0108. LCCN:93-157126.
Audience: **g,l,u,f.**

Zenkovsky, Serge A. (Editor) **PG3213**
Medieval Russian Epics, Chronicles, and Tales. Trade Paper. Penguin Group (USA) Inc. New York, NY. 1974. 544p. ISBN:0-452-01086-1, ISBN13: 978-0-452-01086-4. Dewey:891.708.
Audience: **g,l,u,f.**

Slavic Literatures > Russian > Bibliography

Cornwell, Neil (Editor) **PG2951.R68 2001**
Routledge Companion to Russian Literature. Trade Paper. Routledge. New York, NY. 2001. 288p. Routledge Companions Ser. ISBN:0-415-23366-6, ISBN13: 978-0-415-23366-8. Dewey:891.709. LCCN:2001-019769.
Audience: **l,u,f.** *Choice, 2002.*

Cross, A. G. ; Smith, G. S. **Z2504.T8C98 1984**
Eighteenth Century Russian Literature Culture and Thought: A Bibliography of English-Language Scholarship and Translations. Oriental Research Partners. 1984. ISBN:0-89250-334-3, ISBN13: 978-0-89250-334-6.
Audience: **l,u.**

Palmer, Gene V. **Z2501.R88 2002**
Russian Literature--Overview and Bibliography. Trade Cloth. Nova Science Publishers, Inc. Hauppauge, NY. 2002. 241p. ISBN:1-59033-289-X, ISBN13: 978-1-59033-289-4. Dewey:016.8917. LCCN:2002-728408.
Audience: **l.**

Proffer, Carl R. (Compiled by) **Z2503.P76 1990**
Nineteenth-Century Russian Literature in English: A Bibliography of Criticism and Translations. Trade Cloth. Ardis Publishers. Woodstock, NY. 1990. 260p. ISBN:0-88233-943-5, ISBN13: 978-0-88233-943-6. Dewey:891.709/003. LCCN:89-018589.
Audience: **u.** *Choice, 1990.*

Stevanovic, Bosiljka & Wertsman, Vladimir **Z2500.S8 1987**
Free Voices in Russian Literature, 1950s-1980s: A Bio-Bibliographical Guide to over 900 Authors. Trade Cloth. Russica Publishers. New York, NY. 1987. 500p. Russica Bibliography Ser., No. 4 ISBN:0-89830-090-8, ISBN13: 978-0-89830-090-1. Dewey:891.709/0044. LCCN:84-061344.
Audience: **u,f.** *Choice, 1988.*

Slavic Literatures > Russian > Biography

PG3476.A324
☐ Anna Akhmatova.
http://www.poets.org/poet.php/prmPID/1
Academy of American Poets.
Audience: **g,l,u,f.**

PG3328.Z6

☐ FyodorDostoevsky.com. http://www.fyodordostoevsky.com/
Audience: **g,l,u,f.**

Bruccoli, Matthew J. (Editor), et al. **Z2504.P7R87 1999**
Russian Literature in the Age of Pushkin and Gogol. Richard Layman & C. E. Clark (Editors). Cloth Text. Thomson Gale. Farmington Hills, MI. 1999. 400p. Dictionary of Literary Biography Ser., Vol. 205 ISBN:0-7876-3099-3, ISBN13: 978-0-7876-3099-7. Dewey:016.89171/308. LCCN:98-053956.
Audience: **l,u.** *Choice, 1999.*

Cornwell, Neil (Editor) **PG2951.R68 2001**
Routledge Companion to Russian Literature. Trade Paper. Routledge. New York, NY. 2001. 288p. Routledge Companions Ser. ISBN:0-415-23366-6, ISBN13: 978-0-415-23366-8. Dewey:891.709. LCCN:2001-019769.
Audience: **l,u,f.** *Choice, 2002.*

Dinega, Alyssa W. (Editor) **PG3012.R78 2003**
Russian Literature in the Age of Realism. Trade Cloth. Thomson Gale. Farmington Hills, MI. 2003. 400p. Dictionary of Literary Biography Ser., Vol. 277 ISBN:0-7876-6021-3, ISBN13: 978-0-7876-6021-5. Dewey:891.709/003 B. LCCN:2003-004002.
Audience: **l,u.**

Ignashev, Diane M. & Krive, Sarah (Editors) **PN1993.5.I8B27 1988**
Women and Writing in Russia and the U. S. S. R.: A Bibliography of English-Language Sources. Paper over Boards. Garland Publishing, Inc. New York, NY. 1992. 341p. ISBN:0-8240-3647-6, ISBN13: 978-0-8240-3647-8. Dewey:016.79143/75/0954. LCCN:92-009246.
Audience: **l,u.** *Choice, 1993, 1989.*

Ledkovsky, Marina (Editor), et al. **PG2997**
Dictionary of Russian Women Writers. Charlotte Rosenthal & Mary F. Zirin (Editors). Cloth Text. Greenwood Publishing Group, Inc. Portsmouth, NH. 1994. 960p. ISBN:0-313-26265-9, ISBN13: 978-0-313-26265-4. Dewey:891.709928703. LCCN:93-013012.
Audience: **l,u,f.** *Choice, 1994.*

Levitt, Marcus C. (Editor) **Z2500.E17 1995**
Early Modern Russian Writers: Late Seventeenth and Eighteenth Centuries. Cloth Text. Thomson Gale. Farmington Hills, MI. 1995. 465p. Dictionary of Literary Biography Ser., Vol. 150 ISBN:0-8103-5711-9, ISBN13: 978-0-8103-5711-2. Dewey:891.709/001 B. LCCN:95-001711.
Audience: **u,f.** *Choice, 1996.*

Lipoveetiskiaei, M. N. **Z2500.R85 2003**
Russian Writers since 1980. Marina Balina (Editor). Trade Cloth. Thomson Gale. Farmington Hills, MI. 2003. xxvii, 456p. Dictionary of Literary Biography Ser., Vol. 285 ISBN:0-7876-6822-2, ISBN13: 978-0-7876-6822-8. Dewey:891.709/0044. LCCN:2003-014684.
Audience: **l,u.**

Ogden, J. Alexander & Kalb, Judith E. **PG3098.3.R874 2001**
Russian Novelists in the Age of Tolstoy and Dostoevsky. Trade Cloth. Thomson Gale. Farmington Hills, MI. 2001. xxvii, 469p. Dictionary of Literary Biography Ser., Vol. 238 ISBN:0-7876-4655-5, ISBN13: 978-0-7876-4655-4. Dewey:891.73/3/03 B. LCCN:00-053515.
Audience: **l,u,f.**

Rydel, Christine (Editor) **PG3094.R867 2002**
Russian Prose Writers Between the World Wars. Trade Cloth. Thomson Gale. Farmington Hills, MI. 2002. xxiii, 580p. Dictionary of Literary Biography Ser., Vol. 272 ISBN:0-7876-6016-7, ISBN13: 978-0-7876-6016-1. Dewey:891.78/420803 B. LCCN:2002-151196.
Audience: **l,u.**

Stevanovic, Bosiljka & Wertsman, Vladimir **Z2500.S8 1987**
Free Voices in Russian Literature, 1950s-1980s: A Bio-Bibliographical Guide to over 900 Authors. Trade Cloth. Russica Publishers. New York, NY. 1987. 500p. Russica Bibliography Ser., No. 4 ISBN:0-89830-090-8, ISBN13: 978-0-89830-090-1. Dewey:891.709/0044. LCCN:84-061344.
Audience: **u,f.** *Choice, 1988.*

Tomei, Christine D. (Editor) **PG3203.W64.R868 1999**
Russian Women Writers. Trade Cloth. Garland Publishing, Inc. New York, NY. 1999. 1608p. Women Writers of the World Ser., No. 3 ISBN:0-8153-1797-2, ISBN13: 978-0-8153-1797-5. Dewey:891.70809287. LCCN:98-048028.
Audience: **u,f.** *Choice, 1999.*

Slavic Literatures > Russian > Dictionary

Chapple, Richard **PG3328.A09.C5 1983**
A Dostoevsky Dictionary. Ardis. 1983. ISBN:0-88233-616-9, ISBN13: 978-0-88233-616-9.
Audience: **u.**

Cornwell, Neil (Editor) **PG2940.R44 1998**
Reference Guide to Russian Literature. Trade Cloth. Fitzroy Dearborn Publishers, Inc. Chicago, IL. 1998. 972p. ISBN:1-884964-10-9, ISBN13: 978-1-884964-10-7. Dewey:891.7/03. LCCN:97-169924.
Audience: **l,u,f.** *Choice, 1998.*

Kasack, Wolfgang **Z2500.K3513 1988**
Dictionary of Russian Literature since 1917. Maria Carlson & Jane T. Hedges (Translators), Rebecca Atack (Revised by). Cloth Text. Columbia University Press. New York, NY. 1988. 500p. ISBN:0-231-05242-1, ISBN13: 978-0-231-05242-9. Dewey:891.7/09/004 B. LCCN:87-020838.
Audience: **l,u.** *Choice, 1989.*

Ledkovsky, Marina (Editor), et al. **PG2997**
Dictionary of Russian Women Writers. Charlotte Rosenthal & Mary F. Zirin (Editors). Cloth Text. Greenwood Publishing Group, Inc. Portsmouth, NH. 1994. 960p. ISBN:0-313-26265-9, ISBN13: 978-0-313-26265-4. Dewey:891.709928703. LCCN:93-013012.
Audience: **l,u,f.** *Choice, 1994.*

Orwin, Donna T. (Editor) **PG3409.5**
The Cambridge Companion to Tolstoy. Cloth Text. Cambridge University Press. New York, NY. 2002. 288p. Cambridge Companions to Literature Ser. ISBN:0-521-79271-1, ISBN13: 978-0-521-79271-4. Dewey:891.73/3.
Audience: **g,l,u,f.** *Choice, 2003.*

Terras, Victor **PG2940**
Handbook of Russian Literature. Trade Paper. Yale University Press. Cumberland, RI. 1990. 578p. ISBN:0-300-04868-8, ISBN13: 978-0-300-04868-1. Dewey:891.7/03/21.
Audience: **l,u.** B *Choice, 1985.*

Slavic Literatures > Russian > History and Criticism

Adlam, Carol **PG2997 .A35**
Women in Russian Literature after Glasnot: Female Alternatives. Perfect, Paper over Boards. European Humanities Research Centre. Oxford, 2004. 135p. Legenda Ser. ISBN:1-900755-92-0, ISBN13: 978-1-900755-92-4. Dewey:891.7090352209049. LCCN:2006-277242.
Audience: **u,f.**

Anderson, Roger B. & Debreczeny, Paul (Editors) **PG3015.5.A73R87 1994**
Russian Narrative and Visual Art: Varieties of Seeing. Trade Cloth. University Press of Florida. Gainesville, FL. 1994. 216p. ISBN:0-8130-1255-4, ISBN13: 978-0-8130-1255-1. Dewey:891.73/309. LCCN:93-034786.
Audience: **u,f.** *Choice, 1994.*

Bakhtin, Mikhail M. **PG3328.Z6**
Problems of Dostoevsky's Poetics. Caryl Emerson (Editor, Translator), Wayne Booth (Introduction by). Trade Paper. University of Minnesota Press. Minneapolis, MN. 1984. 333p. Theory and History of Literature Ser., Vol. 8 ISBN:0-8166-1228-5, ISBN13: 978-0-8166-1228-4. Dewey:891.73/3. LCCN:83-012348.
Audience: **u,f.**

Bakhtin, Mikhail M. **P49.B2813 1986**
Speech Genres and Other Late Essays. Caryl Emerson & Michael Holquist (Editors), Vern W. McGee (Translator). Trade Cloth. University of Texas Press. Austin, TX. 1987. 203p. University of Texas Press Slavic Ser., No. 8 ISBN:0-292-72046-7, ISBN13: 978-0-292-72046-6. Dewey:410. LCCN:86-011399.
Audience: **u,f.** *Choice, 1987.*

Bakhtin, Mikhail M. **BH39.B29 1990**
Art and Answerability: Early Philosophical Essays. Michael Holquist (Editor), Vadim Liapunov (Editor, Translator), Kenneth Brostrom (Translator). Cloth Text. University of Texas Press. Austin, TX. 1990. 384p. Slavic Ser., No. 9 ISBN:0-292-70411-9, ISBN13: 978-0-292-70411-4. Dewey:111/.85. LCCN:89-070718.
Audience: **u,f.**

Barker, Adele Marie & Gheith, Jehanne M. (Editors) **PG2997**
e A History of Women's Writing in Russia. E-Book. Cambridge University Press. New York, NY. 2005. ISBN:0-511-03851-8, ISBN13: 978-0-511-03851-8. Dewey:891.7099287.
Audience: **l,u,f.** *Choice, 2003.*

Bristol, Evelyn **PG3041.B67 1990**
A History of Russian Poetry. Cloth Text. Oxford University Press, Inc. New York, NY. 1991. 368p. ISBN:0-19-504659-5, ISBN13: 978-0-19-504659-5. Dewey:891.71009. LCCN:89-026602.
Audience: **u,f.**

Bunin, Ivan A. **PG3410.B813 2001**
The Liberation of Tolstoy: A Tale of Two Writers. Thomas Gaiton Marullo (Translator), Vladimir T. Khmelkov (Introduction by). Trade Cloth. Northwestern University Press. Evanston, IL. 2001. 364p. Studies in Russian Literature and Theory ISBN:0-8101-1752-5, ISBN13: 978-0-8101-1752-5. Dewey:891.73/3. LCCN:00-011025.
Audience: **u,f.** *Choice, 2002.*

Catteau, Jacques **PG3326**
Dostoyevsky and the Process of Literary Creation. Audrey Littlewood (Translator), Catriona Kelly, Anthony Cross, Caryl Emerson, Barbara Heldt, Malcolm Jones, Donald Rayfield, G. S. Smith & Victor Terras (Contribution by). Trade Paper. Cambridge University Press. New York, NY. 2005. 567p. Cambridge Studies in Russian Literature Ser. ISBN:0-521-02278-9, ISBN13: 978-0-521-02278-1. Dewey:891.73/3. LCCN:2006-277346.
Audience: **u,f.** *Choice, 1989.*

Chances, Ellen **PG3479.4.I8 Z6 1993**
Andrei Bitov: The Ecology of Inspiration. Catriona Kelly, Anthony Cross, Caryl Emerson, Barbara Heldt, Malcolm Jones, Donald Rayfield, G. S. Smith & Victor Terras (Contribution by). Trade Paper. Cambridge University Press. New York, NY. 2006. 350p. Cambridge Studies in Russian Literature Ser. ISBN:0-521-02527-3, ISBN13: 978-0-521-02527-0. Dewey:891.7344. LCCN:2006-279872.
Audience: **u,f.** *Choice, 1994.*

Chitnis, Rajendra A. **PG512.C49 2004**
Literature in Post-Communist Russia and Eastern Europe: The Russian, Czech and Slovak Fiction of the Changes, 1988-98. Trade Cloth. Routledge. New York, NY. 2004. 272p. BASEES/RoutledgeCurzon Series on Russian and East European Studies, Vol. 16 ISBN:0-415-35557-5, ISBN13: 978-0-415-35557-5. Dewey:891.8. LCCN:2004-011265.
Audience: **u,f.**

Clark, Katerina **PG3098.4.C4 2000**
The Soviet Novel: History As Ritual. Ed. 3. Library Binding. Indiana University Press. Bloomington, IN. 2000. xv, 320p. ISBN:0-253-33703-8, ISBN13: 978-0-253-33703-0. Dewey:891.73/40912. LCCN:00-038290.
Audience: **u,f.**

Davidson, Pamela **PG2987.D45R87 2000**
Russian Literature and Its Demons. Trade Cloth. Berghahn Books, Inc. New York, NY. 2000. xiv, 530p. Studies in Slavic Literature, Culture and Society, Vol. 6 ISBN:1-57181-758-1, ISBN13: 978 1 57181 758 7. Dewey:891.709/37. LCCN:99-045400.
Audience: **l,u,f.** *Choice, 2001.*

Dunham, Vera Sandomirsky **PG3095.D8 1990**
In Stalin's Time: Middleclass Values in Soviet Fiction. Ed. 2. Jerry F. Hough (Introduction by). Paper Text. Duke University Press. Durham, NC. 1990. 320p. Studies of the Harriman Institute ISBN:0-8223-1085-6, ISBN13: 978-0-8223-1085-3. Dewey:891.73/4209355. LCCN:90-042414.
Audience: **u,f.**

Erlich, Victor **PG3022.E74 1994**
Modernism and Revolution: Russian Literature in Transition. Trade Cloth. Harvard University Press. Cambridge, MA. 1994. 328p. ISBN:0-674-58070-2, ISBN13: 978-0-674-58070-1. Dewey:891.7090042. LCCN:93-024159.
Audience: **u,f.** *Choice, 1994.*

Freeborn, Richard **PG3096.R48**
The Russian Revolutionary Novel: Turgenev to Pasternak. Catriona Kelly, Anthony Cross, Caryl Emerson, Barbara Heldt, Malcolm Jones, Donald Rayfield, G. S. Smith & Victor Terras (Contribution by). Trade Paper. Cambridge University Press. New York, NY. 1985. 318p. Cambridge Studies in Russian Literature Ser. ISBN:0-521-31737-1, ISBN13: 978-0-521-31737-5. Dewey:891.73/009/358.
Audience: **u,f.**

Goscilo, Helena (Editor) **PG2997**
Fruits of Her Plume: Essays on Contemporary Russian Women's Culture. Cloth Text. M. E. Sharpe Inc. Armonk, NY. 1993. 320p. ISBN:1-56324-125-0, ISBN13: 978-1-56324-125-3. Dewey:891.70992870904. LCCN:93-022088.
Audience: **u,f.**

Hoisington, Sona S. **PG3096.W6P57 1995**
A Plot of Her Own: The Female Protagonist in Russian Literature. Trade Paper. Northwestern University Press. Evanston, IL. 1995. 164p. Studies in Russian Literature and Theory ISBN:0-8101-1298-1, ISBN13: 978-0-8101-1298-8. Dewey:891.709/352042. LCCN:95-001989.
Audience: **u,f.** *Choice, 1995.*

Holmgren, Beth **PG2981.P6H65 1998**
[e] Rewriting Capitalism: Literature and the Market in Late Tsarist Russia and the Kingdom of Poland. E-Book. NetLibrary, Inc. Boulder, CO. 1998. ISBN:0-585-04402-3, ISBN13: 978-0-585-04402-6. Dewey:891.709/003.
Audience: **u,f.**

Holmgren, Beth (Editor) **PG3091.9.A93R97 2003**
The Russian Memoir: History and Literature. Trade Cloth. Northwestern University Press. Evanston, IL. 2003. 256p. Studies in Russian Literature and Theory ISBN:0-8101-1929-3, ISBN13: 978-0-8101-1929-1. Dewey:891.709/492. LCCN:2002-154753.
Audience: **u,f.** *Choice, 2004.*

Holmgren, Beth **PG2997**
[e] Women's Works in Stalin's Time: On Lidiia Chukovskaia and Nadezhda Mandelstam. E-Book. Indiana University Press. Bloomington, IN. 1993. 240p. ISBN:0-253-20829-7, ISBN13: 978-0-253-20829-3. Dewey:891.709/9287. LCCN:92-046343.
Audience: **u,f.** *Choice, 1994.*

Hutchings, Stephen C. **PG3096.M35 H88 1997**
Russian Modernism: The Transfiguration of the Everyday. Catriona Kelly, Anthony Cross, Caryl Emerson, Barbara Heldt, Malcolm Jones, Donald Rayfield, G. S. Smith & Victor Terras (Contribution by). Trade Paper. Cambridge University Press. New York, NY. 2006. 295p. Cambridge Studies in Russian Literature Ser. ISBN:0-521-02449-8, ISBN13: 978-0-521-02449-5. Dewey:891.7309/112. LCCN:2006-280127.
Audience: **u,f.** *Choice, 1998.*

Jones, Malcolm V. & Miller, Robin Feuer (Editors) **PG3098.3.C33 1998**
The Cambridge Companion to the Classic Russian Novel. Malcolm V. Jones, Robert Maguire, Hugh McLean, Gareth Jones & Lesley Milne (Contribution by). Trade Paper. Cambridge University Press. New York, NY. 1998. 338p. Companions to Literature Ser. ISBN:0-521-47909-6, ISBN13: 978-0-521-47909-7. Dewey:891.73/009. LCCN:97-033220.
Audience: **l,u,f.** *Choice, 1998.*

Kalinowska, Izabela **PG7020.A8K35 2004**
Between East and West: Polish and Russian Nineteenth-Century Travel to the Orient. Trade Cloth. University of Rochester Press. Rochester, NY. 2004. 216p. Rochester Studies in Central Europe Ser. ISBN:1-58046-172-7, ISBN13: 978-1-58046-172-6. Dewey:891.709/325. LCCN:2004-017410.
Audience: **u,f.**

Karcz, Andrzej **PG7008.K36 2002**
The Polish Formalist School and Russian Formalism. Trade Cloth. University of Rochester Press. Rochester, NY. 2004. 230p. Rochester Studies in Central Europe ISBN:1-58046-110-7, ISBN13: 978-1-58046-110-8. Dewey:891.8/509. LCCN:2002-022559.
Audience: **u,f.**

Kelly, Aileen **DK209.6.H4K45 1999**
Views from the Other Shore: Essays on Herzen, Chekhov and Bakhtin. Cloth over Boards. Yale University Press. Cumberland, RI. 1999. 272p. Russian Literature and Thought Ser. ISBN:0-300-07486-7, ISBN13: 978-0-300-07486-4. Dewey:947/.073/0922. LCCN:98-052435.
Audience: **u,f.**

Kelly, Catriona **PG2997**
A History of Russian Women's Writing 1820-1992. Trade Paper. Oxford University Press, Inc. New York, NY. 1998. 512p. ISBN:0-19-815964-1, ISBN13: 978-0-19-815964-3. Dewey:891.7/09003.
Audience: **u,f.**

Kelly, Catriona **PG2950.K45 2001**
Russian Literature: A Very Short Introduction. Trade Paper. Oxford University Press, Inc. New York, NY. 2001. 182p. Very Short Introductions Ser., Vol. 53 ISBN:0-19-280144-9, ISBN13: 978-0-19-280144-9. Dewey:891.709. LCCN:2001-036418.
Audience: **g,l,u,f.**

Kelly, Catriona & Lovell, Stephen (Editors) **PG3020.5.M6 R79 2000**
Russian Literature, Modernism and the Visual Arts. Catriona Kelly, Anthony Cross, Caryl Emerson, Barbara Heldt, Malcolm Jones, Donald Rayfield, G. S. Smith & Victor Terras (Contribution by). Trade Cloth. Cambridge University Press. New York, NY. 2000. 332p. Cambridge Studies in Russian Literature ISBN:0-521-66191-9, ISBN13: 978-0-521-66191-1. Dewey:891.709/112. LCCN:99-023185.
Audience: **u,f.**

Kornblatt, Judith D. **PG2989.H4.K67 1992**
The Cossack Hero in Russian Literature: A Study in Cultural Mythology. Trade Cloth. University of Wisconsin Press.

Chicago, IL. 1993. 244p. Studies of the Harriman Institute, Columbia University ISBN:0-299-13520-9, ISBN13: 978-0-299-13520-1. Dewey:891.7093520391714. LCCN:92-050254.
Audience: **u,f.** *Choice, 1993.*

Kropotkin, Petr Alekseevich **PG3012**
Ideals and Realities in Russian Literature. Paper Text. Classic Books. Murrieta, CA. 2001. 341p. ISBN:0-7426-9094-6, ISBN13: 978-0-7426-9094-3. Dewey:891.7/09/003.
Audience: **l,u,f.**

Laird, Sally (Editor) **PG3021**
Voices of Russian Literature: Interviews with Ten Contemporary Writers. Trade Cloth. Oxford University Press, Inc. New York, NY. 1999. 259p. ISBN:0-19-815181-0, ISBN13: 978-0-19-815181-4. Dewey:891.7/090044.
Audience: **l,u,f.** *Choice, 1999.*

Layton, Susan **PG3015.5.C3 L39 1994**
Russian Literature and Empire: Conquest of the Caucasus from Pushkin to Tolstoy. Catriona Kelly, Anthony Cross, Caryl Emerson, Barbara Heldt, Malcolm Jones, Donald Rayfield, G. S. Smith & Victor Terras (Contribution by). Trade Paper. Cambridge University Press. New York, NY. 2005. 370p. Cambridge Studies in Russian Literature Ser. ISBN:0-521-02001-8, ISBN13: 978-0-521-02001-5. Dewey:891.709/32479/09034. LCCN:2005-284538.
Audience: **u,f.**

Marsh, Rosalind J. (Editor) **PG2997 .G4 1996**
Gender and Russian Literature: New Perspectives. Trade Cloth. Cambridge University Press. New York, NY. 1996. 372p. Studies in Russian Literature ISBN:0-521-55258-3, ISBN13: 978-0-521-55258-5. Dewey:891.7/099287. LCCN:95-030646.
Audience: **u,f.**

Marsh, Rosalind J. **PG2975.M34 1995**
History and Literature in Contemporary Russia. Trade Cloth. New York University Press. New York, NY. 1995. 288p. ISBN:0-8147-5527-5, ISBN13: 978-0-8147-5527-3. Dewey:891.7/09358. LCCN:94-039054.
Audience: **u,f.** *Choice, 1996.*

Masing-Delic, Irene **PG3022.M37 1992**
Abolishing Death: A Salvation Myth of Russian Twentieth-Century Literature. Trade Cloth. Stanford University Press. Palo Alto, CA. 1992. 376p. ISBN:0-8047-1935-7, ISBN13: 978-0-8047-1935-3. Dewey:891.7/40938. LCCN:92-013992.
Audience: **u,f.** *Choice, 1993.*

Mathewson, Rufus W. Jr. **PG2989.H4M3 1999**
The Positive Hero in Russian Literature. Ed. 2. Trade Paper. Northwestern University Press. Evanston, IL. 2000. 369p. Srlt Ser. ISBN:0-8101-1716-9, ISBN13: 978-0-8101-1716-7. Dewey:891.73/409352. LCCN:99-049407.
Audience: **u,f.**

McMillin, Arnold (Editor) **PG3022.R43 2000**
Reconstructing the Canon: Russian Writing in the 1980's. Cloth Text. Gordon & Breach Publishing Group. New York, NY. 2000. 336p. Studies in Russian and European Literature, Vol. 3 ISBN:90-5702-593-0, ISBN13: 978-90-5702-593-8. Dewey:891.709/004. LCCN:2002-421316.
Audience: **u,f.**

Mirsky, Dimitry S. **PC794.M65**
History of Russian Literature: From Its Beginnings to 1900. Francis J. Whitfield (Editor). Trade Paper. Knopf Publishing Group. New York, NY. 1958. ISBN:0-394-70720-6, ISBN13: 978-0-394-70720-4. Dewey:891.7/009.
Audience: **l,u,f.**

Morris, Marcia A. **PG2989.H4.M6 1993**
Saints and Revolutionaries: The Ascetic Hero in Russian Fiction. Cloth Text. State University of New York Press. Albany, NY. 1993. 256p. ISBN:0-7914-1299-7, ISBN13: 978-0-7914-1299-2. Dewey:891.709/27. LCCN:92-000279.
Audience: **u,f.** *Choice, 1993.*

Moser, Charles A. (Editor) **PG2951.C36 1989**
The Cambridge History of Russian Literature. Cloth Text. Cambridge University Press. New York, NY. 1989. 704p. ISBN:0-521-30994-8, ISBN13: 978-0-521-30994-3. Dewey:891.709. LCCN:88-025999.
Audience: **l,u.** *Choice, 1990.*

Nabokov, Vladimir **PG551.E3**
Lectures on Russian Literature. Trade Paper. Harcourt Trade Publishers. New York, NY. 2002. 352p. ISBN:0-15-602776-3, ISBN13: 978-0-15-602776-2. Dewey:891.7.
Audience: **u,f.**

Olcott, Anthony **PG3098.D46O43 2001**
Russian Pulp: The Detektiv and the Russian Way of Crime. Book, Other. Rowman & Littlefield Publishers, Inc. Lanham, MD. 2001. 240p. ISBN:0-7425-1140-5, ISBN13: 978-0-7425-1140-8. Dewey:891.73/08720904. LCCN:2001-018060.
Audience: **g,l,u,f.** *Choice, 2002.*

Parthe, Kathleen **PG2987.P58P37 2004**
Russia's Dangerous Texts: Politics Between the Lines. Cloth over Boards. Yale University Press. Cumberland, RI. 2004. 304p. ISBN:0-300-09851-0, ISBN13: 978-0-300-09851-8. Dewey:891.709/358. LCCN:2004-042031.
Audience: **u,f.** *Choice, 2005.*

Parthé, Kathleen **PG3096.C68P37 1992**
e Russian Village Prose: The Radiant Past. E-Book. Princeton University Press. Princeton, NJ. ISBN:1-4008-1294-1, ISBN13: 978-1-4008-1294-3. Dewey:891.73/4409321734.
Audience: **u,f.**

Patterson, David **PJ5049.R8P3 1999**
Hebrew Novel in Czarist Russia: A Portrait of Jewish Life in the Nineteenth Century. Book, Other. Rowman & Littlefield Publishers, Inc. Lanham, MD. 1999. 348p. ISBN:0-8476-9338-4, ISBN13: 978-0-8476-9338-2. Dewey:892.4/3509355. LCCN:98-044399.
Audience: **u,f.**

Roberts, Graham **PG3026.O24 R63 1997**
The Last Soviet Avant-Garde: OBERIU - Fact, Fiction, Metafiction. Catriona Kelly, Anthony Cross, Caryl Emerson, Barbara Heldt, Malcolm Jones, Donald Rayfield, G. S. Smith & Victor Terras (Contribution by). Trade Paper. Cambridge University Press. New York, NY. 2006. 291p. Cambridge Studies in Russian Literature Ser. ISBN:0-521-02834-5, ISBN13: 978-0-521-02834-9. Dewey:891.709/0042.
Audience: **u,f.**

Ryan-Hayes, Karen L. **PG3026.S3 R94 1995**
Contemporary Russian Satire: A Genre Study. Catriona Kelly, Anthony Cross, Caryl Emerson, Barbara Heldt, Malcolm Jones, Donald Rayfield, G. S. Smith & Victor Terras (Contribution by). Trade Paper. Cambridge University Press. New York, NY. 2006. 303p. Cambridge Studies in Russian Literature Ser. ISBN:0-521-02626-1, ISBN13: 978-0-521-02626-0. Dewey:891.7/8/44/02.
Audience: **u,f.**

Sandler, Stephanie **PG3043.R47 1999**
Rereading Russian Poetry. Cloth over Boards. Yale University Press. Cumberland, RI. 1999. 384p. Russian Literature and Thought Ser. ISBN:0-300-07149-3, ISBN13: 978-0-300-07149-8. Dewey:891.71009. LCCN:98-007700.
Audience: **u,f.** *Choice, 2000.*

Schonle, Andreas **PG3091.9.T73S36 2000**
Authenticity and Fiction in the Russian Literary Journey, 1790-1840. Trade Cloth. Harvard University Press. Cambridge, MA. 2000. 304p. Russian Research Center Studies, Vol. 92 ISBN:0-674-00232-6, ISBN13: 978-0-674-00232-6. Dewey:891.78/30809355. LCCN:00-020359.
Audience: **u,f.**

Shneidman, N N **PG3098.4.S47 1995**
Russian Literature, 1988-1994: The End of an Era. University of Toronto Press. 1995. ISBN:0-8020-7466-9, ISBN13: 978-0-8020-7466-9.
Audience: **u,f.**

Shneidman, N. N. **PG3098.4**
Soviet Literature in the 1980s: Decade of Transition. Cloth Text. University of Toronto Press. Toronto, ON. 1989. 256p. ISBN:0-8020-5812-4, ISBN13: 978-0-8020-5812-6. Dewey:891.734409. LCCN:90-039327.
Audience: **u,f.** *Choice, 1990.*

Sicher, Efraim **PG2998.J4 S5 1995**
Jews in Russian Literature after the October Revolution: Writers and Artists between Hope and Apostasy. Catriona Kelly, Anthony Cross, Caryl Emerson, Barbara Heldt, Malcolm Jones, Donald Rayfield, G. S. Smith & Victor Terras (Contribution by). Trade Paper. Cambridge University Press. New York, NY. 2006. 306p. Cambridge Studies in Russian Literature Ser. ISBN:0-521-02599-0, ISBN13: 978-0-521-02599-7. Dewey:891.7/098924. LCCN:2006-277082.
Audience: **l,u,f.**

Smeliansky, Anatoly **PN2724 .S515 1999**
The Russian Theatre after Stalin. Patrick Miles (Translator), Laurence Senelick (Foreword by), David Bradby (Contribution by). Trade Paper. Cambridge University Press. New York, NY. 1999. 270p. Studies in Modern Theatre ISBN:0-521-58794-8, ISBN13: 978-0-521-58794-5. Dewey:792/.0947/09045. LCCN:00-709380.
Audience: **u,f.** *Choice, 2000.*

Terras, Victor **PG3328.Z6T397 1998**
Reading Dostoevsky. Trade Cloth. University of Wisconsin Press. Chicago, IL. 1998. 184p. ISBN:0-299-16050-5, ISBN13: 978-0-299-16050-0. Dewey:891.73/3. LCCN:98-023342.
Audience: **u,f.**

Terras, Victor **PG3056.T44 1998**
Poetry of the Silver Age: The Various Voices of Russian Modernism. Alexander Landman (Translator), Horst-Jurgen Gerigk (Preface by). Trade Cloth. Dresden University Press. Dresden, 1998. 480p. ISBN:3-931828-71-9, ISBN13: 978-3-931828-71-4. Dewey:891.71/409. LCCN:00-269235.
Audience: **u,f.** *Choice, 1999.*

Tomei, Christine D. (Editor) **PG3203.W64.R868 1999**
Russian Women Writers. Trade Cloth. Garland Publishing, Inc. New York, NY. 1999. 1608p. Women Writers of the World Ser., No. 3 ISBN:0-8153-1797-2, ISBN13: 978-0-8153-1797-5. Dewey:891.70809287. LCCN:98-048028.
Audience: **u,f.** *Choice, 1999.*

Trotsky, Leon **PG3026.P64T7613 2005**
Literature and Revolution. Trade Cloth. Haymarket Books. Chicago, IL. 2005. 300p. ISBN:1-931859-21-3, ISBN13: 978-1-931859-21-9. Dewey:986.106/35. LCCN:2004-021412.
Audience: **u,f.**

Tschizewskij, Dmitrij **PG3012**
History of Nineteenth-Century Russian Literature. Serge A. Zenkovsky (Editor), Richard N. Porter (Translator). Trade Cloth. Greenwood Publishing Group, Inc. Portsmouth, NH. 1986. 498p. ISBN:0-313-25274-2, ISBN13: 978-0-313-25274-7. Dewey:891.7/09/003. LCCN:86-022739.
Audience: **u,f.**

Wachtel, Andrew B. **PG2975.W33 1994**
An Obsession with History: Russian Writers Confront the Past. Trade Cloth. Stanford University Press. Palo Alto, CA. 1994. 274p. ISBN:0-8047-2246-3, ISBN13: 978-0-8047-2246-9. Dewey:891.709/358. LCCN:93-014174.
Audience: **u,f.** *Choice, 1994.*

Slavic Literatures > Russian > Individual Authors

PG3476.A324
☐ Anna Akhmatova.
http://www.poets.org/poet.php/prmPID/1
Academy of American Poets.
Audience: **g,l,u,f.**

PG3328.Z6
☐ FyodorDostoevsky.com.
http://www.fyodordostoevsky.com/
Audience: **g,l,u,f.**

Akhmadulina, Bella **PG3478.K45A27 1990**
The Garden: New and Selected Poetry. F. D. Reeve (Translator). Trade Cloth. Henry Holt & Company. New York, NY. 1990. 160p. ISBN:0-8050-1249-4, ISBN13: 978-0-8050-1249-1. Dewey:891.71/44. LCCN:90-004396.
Audience: **g,l,u,f.**

Akhmatova, Anna Andreevena **PG3476.A324**
The Complete Poems of Anna Akhmatova. Ed. 3. Roberta Reeder (Editor), Judith Hemschemeyer (Translator), Roberta Reeder (Introduction by). Trade Paper. Zephyr Press. Brookline, MA. 2000. 948p. ISBN:0-939010-27-5, ISBN13: 978-0-939010-27-1. Dewey:891.7/1/42. LCCN:92-062648.
Audience: **g,l,u,f.** *Choice, 1993, 1990.*

Aksakov, Sergei **SH633.A5713 1997**
Notes on Fishing. Thomas P. Hodge (Translator). Trade Cloth. Northwestern University Press. Evanston, IL. 1997. 232p. Srlt Ser. ISBN:0-8101-1366-X, ISBN13: 978-0-8101-1366-4. Dewey:799.1. LCCN:97-014128.
Audience: **g,l,u,f.**

Aksakov, Sergei **SK316.R9A3913 1998**
Notes of a Provincial Wildfowler. Kevin Windle (Translator). Trade Cloth. Northwestern University Press. Evanston, IL. 1998. 304p. Studies in Russian Literature and Theory ISBN:0-8101-1391-0, ISBN13: 978-0-8101-1391-6. Dewey:799.2/44/0947. LCCN:98-016062.
Audience: **g,l,u,f.**

Aksyonov, Vassily **PG3478.K7**
Generations of Winter. Trade Paper. Knopf Publishing Group. New York, NY. 1995. 608p. ISBN:0-679-76182-9, ISBN13: 978-0-679-76182-2. Dewey:891.73/44.
Audience: **g,l,u,f.**

Aksyonov, Vassily **PG3478.K7A27 1991**
The Destruction of Pompeii and Other Stories. Lena Karpov (Introduction by). Trade Paper. Knopf Publishing Group. New York, NY. 1991. 183p. Contemporary Russian Prose Ser. ISBN:0-679-73441-4, ISBN13: 978-0-679-73441-3. Dewey:891.73/44. LCCN:90-028781.
Audience: **g,l,u,f.** *Choice, 1991.*

Alexandrov, Vladimir E. **PG3326**
Andrei Bely: The Major Symbolist Fiction. Trade Paper. iUniverse, Inc. Lincoln, NE. 1999. 240p. Russian Research Center Studies, Vol. 83 ISBN:1-58348-449-3, ISBN13: 978-1-58348-449-4. Dewey:891.73/3. LCCN:99-090969.
Audience: **u,f.** *Choice, 1986.*

Andreev, Leonid Nikolaevich **PG3452**
Plays: The Black Maskers, the Life of Man, the Sabine Women. Paper Text. Classic Books. Murrieta, CA. 2001. 214p. ISBN:0-7426-9107-1, ISBN13: 978-0-7426-9107-0. Dewey:891.72.
Audience: **g,l,u,f.**

Babel, Isaac **PG3476.B2A23 2001**
The Complete Works of Isaac Babel. Nathalie Babel (Editor), Peter Constantine (Translator), Cynthia Ozick (Introduction by). Trade Cloth. W. W. Norton & Company, Inc. New York, NY. 2001. 992p. ISBN:0-393-04846-2, ISBN13: 978-0-393-04846-9. Dewey:891.73/42. LCCN:2001-044036.
Audience: **g,l,u,f.**

Bagby, Lewis (Editor) **PG3337.L4G49 2001**
Lermontov's A Hero of Our Time: A Critical Companion. Paper Text. Northwestern University Press. Evanston, IL. 2002. 206p. AATSEEL Critical Companions to Russian Literature Ser. ISBN:0-8101-1680-4, ISBN13: 978-0-8101-1680-1. Dewey:891.73/3. LCCN:2001-001122.
Audience: **u,f.**

Bakhtin, Mikhail M. **PG3328.Z6**
Problems of Dostoevsky's Poetics. Caryl Emerson (Editor, Translator), Wayne Booth (Introduction by). Trade Paper. University of Minnesota Press. Minneapolis, MN. 1984. 333p. Theory and History of Literature Ser., Vol. 8 ISBN:0-8166-1228-5, ISBN13: 978-0-8166-1228-4. Dewey:891.73/3. LCCN:83-012348.
Audience: **u,f.**

Bely, Andrei **PG3453.B84K6513 1999**
Kotik Letaev. Gerald J. Janecek (Translator, Introduction by). Trade Paper. Northwestern University Press. Evanston, IL. 1999. 268p. European Classics Ser. ISBN:0-8101-1626-X, ISBN13: 978-0-8101-1626-9. Dewey:891.73/3. LCCN:99-019486.
Audience: **g,l,u,f.**

Bitov, Andrei **PG3479.4.I8**
A Captive of the Caucasus. Trade Paper. Zondervan. Grand Rapids, MI. 1994. 323p. ISBN:0-00-271668-2, ISBN13: 978-0-00-271668-0. Dewey:891.78/4403.
Audience: **g,l,u,f.**

Bitov, Andrei **PG3479.4.I8P813 1998**
Pushkin House. Susan Brownsberger (Translator). Trade Paper. Dalkey Archive Press. Normal, IL. 1998. 371p. American Literature Ser. ISBN:1-56478-200-X, ISBN13: 978-1-56478-200-7. Dewey:891.73/44. LCCN:98-023360.
Audience: **g,l,u,f.**

Blok, Aleksandr **PG3453.B6A26 2000**
Selected Poems. Trade Paper. Carcanet Press, Ltd. Manchester, 2000. 128p. Poetry Pleiade Ser. ISBN:1-85754-473-0, ISBN13: 978-1-85754-473-2. Dewey:891.71/3. LCCN:2001-326565.
Audience: **g,l,u,f.**

Blok, Aleksandr Aleksandrovich **PG3453**
Aleksandr Blok's Trilogy of Lyric Drama. Routledge. 2003. ISBN:0-415-28050-8, ISBN13: 978-0-415-28050-1.
Audience: **g,l,u,f.**

Bulgakov, Mikhail Afanasevich **PG3476.B78**
The Fatal Eggs. Hugh Aplin (Translator), Doris Lessing (Introduction by). Trade Paper. Hesperus Press. London, 2003. 112p. ISBN:1-84391-063-2, ISBN13: 978-1-84391-063-3. Dewey:891.7342.
Audience: **g,l,u,f.**

Bulgakov, Mikhail Afanasevich **PG3476.B78B513 1987**
The White Guard. Michael Gleeny (Translator). Trade Cloth. Academy Chicago Publishers, Ltd. Chicago, IL. 2000. 319p. ISBN:0-89733-246-6, ISBN13: 978-0-89733-246-0. Dewey:891.73/42. LCCN:86-032299.
Audience: **g,l,u,f.**

Bulgakov, Mikhail Afanasevich **DK265**
Heart of a Dog. Michael Glenay (Translator). Trade Paper. Random House. London, 1997. 128p. ISBN:1-86046-083-6, ISBN13: 978-1-86046-083-8. Dewey:947/.0841.
Audience: **g,l,u,f.**

Bulgakov, Mikhail Afanasevich **PG3476.S52**
The Master and Margarita. Richard Pevear & Larissa

Volokhonsky (Translators), Richard Pevear (Introduction by). Trade Paper. Penguin Group (USA) Inc. New York, NY. 2001. 432p. ISBN:0-14-118014-5, ISBN13: 978-0-14-118014-4. Dewey:891.73/42.
Audience: **g,l,u,f.**

Bulgakov, Mikhail Afanasevich **PG3476.B78Z3513 1996**
Zoyka's Apartment: A Tragic Farce in Three Acts. Nicholas Saunders & Frank Dwyer (Translators). Trade Paper. Smith and Kraus Publishers, Inc. Lyme, NH. 1996. 128p. Great Translations for Actors Ser. ISBN:1-880399-93-8, ISBN13: 978-1-880399-93-4. Dewey:891.72/42. LCCN:95-045899.
Audience: **g,l,u,f.**

Bulgakov, Mikhail Afanasevich **PG3476.B78M3353 1996**
The Master and Margarita: A Critical Companion. Laura D. Weeks (Editor). Paper Text. Northwestern University Press. Evanston, IL. 1996. 252p. Northwestern/Aatseel Critical Companions to Russian Literature Ser. ISBN:0-8101-1212-4, ISBN13: 978-0-8101-1212-4. Dewey:891.7342. LCCN:95-045958.
Audience: **u,f.**

Bunin, Ivan **PZ3.B8835**
The Gentleman from San Francisco. Trade Paper. Kessinger Publishing, LLC. Whitefish, MT. 2004. ISBN:1-4192-6348-X, ISBN13: 978-1-4192-6348-4. Dewey:891.73.
Audience: **g,l,u,f.**

Bunin, Ivan A. **PG3410.B813 2001**
The Liberation of Tolstoy: A Tale of Two Writers. Thomas Gaiton Marullo (Translator), Vladimir T. Khmelkov (Introduction by). Trade Cloth. Northwestern University Press. Evanston, IL. 2001. 364p. Studies in Russian Literature and Theory ISBN:0-8101-1752-5, ISBN13: 978-0-8101-1752-5. Dewey:891.73/3. LCCN:00-011025.
Audience: **u,f.** *Choice, 2002.*

Bunin, Ivan **PG3453.B9**
Night of Denial: Stories and Novellas. Robert Bowie (Translator). Trade Paper. Northwestern University Press. Evanston, IL. 2006. 640p. European Classics Ser. ISBN:0-8101-1403-8, ISBN13: 978-0-8101-1403-6. Dewey:891.73/3. LCCN:2006-011310.
Audience: **g,l,u,f.**

Catteau, Jacques **PG3326**
Dostoyevsky and the Process of Literary Creation. Audrey Littlewood (Translator), Catriona Kelly, Anthony Cross, Caryl Emerson, Barbara Heldt, Malcolm Jones, Donald Rayfield, G. S. Smith & Victor Terras (Contribution by). Trade Paper. Cambridge University Press. New York, NY. 2005. 567p. Cambridge Studies in Russian Literature Ser. ISBN:0-521-02278-9, ISBN13: 978-0-521-02278-1. Dewey:891.73/3. LCCN:2006-277346.
Audience: **u,f.** *Choice, 1989.*

Cavanagh, Clare **PG3476.M355Z59 1995**
(e) Osip Mandelstam and the Modernist Creation of Tradition. E-Book. Princeton University Press. Princeton, NJ. ISBN:1-4008-1120-1, ISBN13: 978-1-4008-1120-5. Dewey:891.71/3.
Audience: **u,f.**

Chances, Ellen **PG3479.4.I8 Z6 1993**
Andrei Bitov: The Ecology of Inspiration. Catriona Kelly, Anthony Cross, Caryl Emerson, Barbara Heldt, Malcolm Jones, Donald Rayfield, G. S. Smith & Victor Terras (Contribution by). Trade Paper. Cambridge University Press. New York, NY. 2006. 350p. Cambridge Studies in Russian Literature Ser. ISBN:0-521-02527-3, ISBN13: 978-0-521-02527-0. Dewey:891.7344. LCCN:2006-279872.
Audience: **u,f.** *Choice, 1994.*

Chekhov, Anton **PG3456.A15 1979**
Anton Chekhov's Short Stories. Ralph E. Matlaw (Editor), Constance Garnett (Translator). Trade Paper. W. W. Norton & Company, Inc. New York, NY. 1979. 369p. Critical Editions Ser. ISBN:0-393-09002-7, ISBN13: 978-0-393-09002-4. Dewey:891.7/3/3. LCCN:78-017052.
Audience: **g,l,u,f.**

Chekhov, Anton **PG3456.A13P48 2004**
The Complete Short Novels. Richard Pevear & Larissa Volokhonsky (Translators). Trade Cloth. Knopf Publishing Group. New York, NY. 2004. 600p. ISBN:1-4000-4049-3, ISBN13: 978-1-4000-4049-0. Dewey:891.73/3. LCCN:2003-064595.
Audience: **g,l,u,f.**

Chekhov, Anton **PG3455**
The Complete Plays. Laurence Senelick (Editor). Trade Cloth. W. W. Norton & Company, Inc. New York, NY. 2005. 992p. ISBN:0-393-04885-3, ISBN13: 978-0-393-04885-8. Dewey:891.72/3. LCCN:2005-024362.
Audience: **g,l,u,f.**

Clayton, J. Douglas **PG3343.B64C57 2002**
Dimitry's Shade: A Reading of Alexander Pushkin's Boris Godunov. Trade Cloth. Northwestern University Press. Evanston, IL. 2004. 216p. Studies in Russian Literature and Theory ISBN:0-8101-1938-2, ISBN13: 978-0-8101-1938-3. Dewey:891.72/3. LCCN:2002-012283.
Audience: **u,f.**

Cornwell, Neil **PG3337.O3Z62 1997**
Vladimir Odoevsky and Romantic Poets. Trade Cloth. Berghahn Books, Inc. New York, NY. 1998. 174p. ISBN:1-57181-907-X, ISBN13: 978-1-57181-907-9. Dewey:891.78/309. LCCN:97-028797.
Audience: **u,f.**

Danow, David K. **PG3328.Z7 T435 1991**
The Dialogic Sign: Essays on the Major Novels of Dostojefsky. Cloth Text. Peter Lang Publishing, Inc. New York, NY. 1992. 219p. Studies in Russian Language and Literature ISBN:0-8204-1628-2, ISBN13: 978-0-8204-1628-1. Dewey:891.73/3. LCCN:91-033847.
Audience: **u,f.**

Dobychin, Leonid **PG3476**
Encounters with Lise and Other Stories. Richard C. Borden (Editor, Translator), Natalia Belova (Translator), Richard C. Borden (Introduction by). Trade Paper. Northwestern University Press. Evanston, IL. 2005. 192p. European Classics Ser. ISBN:0-8101-1972-2, ISBN13: 978-0-8101-1972-7. Dewey:891.73/42. LCCN:2005-001544.
Audience: **g,l,u,f.**

Dostoevsky, Fyodor **PG3326**
The Adolescent. Trade Paper. W. W. Norton & Company, Inc. New York, NY. 2003. 634p. ISBN:0-393-32490-7, ISBN13: 978-0-393-32490-7. Dewey:891.73/3.
Audience: **g,l,u,f.**

Dostoevsky, Fyodor **PG3326**
The Gambler. Trade Paper. W. W. Norton & Company, Inc. New York, NY. 1997. 184p. ISBN:0-393-31649-1, ISBN13: 978-0-393-31649-0. Dewey:891.733. LCCN:81-001494.
Audience: **g,l,u,f.**

Dostoevsky, Fyodor **PG3326.Z4 2001**
Notes from the Underground. Ed. 2. Trade Cloth. W. W. Norton & Company, Inc. New York, NY. 2000. xiv, 258p. Critical Editions Ser. ISBN:0-393-97612-2, ISBN13: 978-0-393-97612-0. Dewey:891.73/3. LCCN:00-037985.
Audience: **g,l,u,f.**

Dostoevsky, Fyodor M. **PG3326.P7 1989**
Crime and Punishment. Ed. 3. George Gibian (Editor). Trade Paper. W. W. Norton & Company, Inc. New York, NY. 1989. 704p. Critical Editions Ser. ISBN:0-393-95623-7, ISBN13: 978-0-393-95623-8. Dewey:891.73/3. LCCN:88-025502.
Audience: **g,l,u,f.**

Dostoyevsky, Fyodor **AC1**
The Brothers Karamazov: Norton Critical Edtion. Paper Text. W. W. Norton & Company, Inc. New York, NY. 2001. ISBN:0-393-94692-4, ISBN13: 978-0-393-94692-5. Dewey:891.734.
Audience: **g,l,u,f.**

Dostoyevsky, Fyodor **PG3326**
Devils. Michael R. Katz (Translator). Trade Paper. Oxford University Press, Inc. New York, NY. 2000. 790p. Oxford World's Classics Ser. ISBN:0-19-283829-6, ISBN13: 978-0-19-283829-2. Dewey:891.7/33.
Audience: **g,l,u,f.**

Egan, David **PG338**
Leo Tolstoy: an annotated bibliography of English language sources from 1978-2003. Scarecrow Press, Inc. 2005. ISBN:0-8108-5411-2, ISBN13: 978-0-8108-5411-6.
Audience: **g,l,u,f.**

Erofeev, Venedikt **PG3479.7.R59M613**
Moscow to the End of the Line. H. William Tjalsma (Translator). Trade Paper. Northwestern University Press. Evanston, IL. 1992. 164p. European Classics Ser. ISBN:0-8101-1200-0, ISBN13: 978-0-8101-1200-1. Dewey:891.73/44. LCCN:94-020616.
Audience: **g,l,u,f.**

Erofeyev, Victor **PG3479.7.R58Z3613**
Life with an Idiot. Trade Paper. Penguin Group (USA) Inc. New York, NY. 2004. 256p. ISBN:0-14-023621-X, ISBN13: 978-0-14-023621-7. Dewey:891.73/44. LCCN:2004-053393.
Audience: **g,l,u,f.**

Erofeyev, Victor **PG3488.O4**
Russian Beauty. Andrew Reynolds (Translator). Trade Paper. Penguin Group (USA) Inc. New York, NY. 1994. 352p. ISBN:0-14-023731-3, ISBN13: 978-0-14-023731-3. Dewey:891.7/344.
Audience: **g,l,u,f.**

Farber, Vreneli **PG3489.3.A45Z663**
The Prose of Aleksandr Vampilov. Trade Cloth. Peter Lang Publishing, Inc. New York, NY. 2003. vii, 189p. Middlebury Studies in Russian Language and Literature, Vol. 29 ISBN:0-8204-6813-4, ISBN13: 978-0-8204-6813-6. Dewey:891.74/44. LCCN:2003-005863.
Audience: **u,f.**

Fonvizin, I **PG3313.F6 N4**
Fonvizin: The Minor. W. Harrison (Editor). Trade Paper. International Publishers Marketing. Herndon, VA. 1995. 168p. Russian Texts Ser. ISBN:0-900186-51-8, ISBN13: 978-0-900186-51-6. Dewey:891.722.
Audience: **g,l,u,f.**

Fusso, Susanne **PG3332.M43.F87 1993**
Designing Dead Souls: An Anatomy of Disorder in Gogol. Trade Cloth. Stanford University Press. Palo Alto, CA. 1993. 216p. ISBN:0-8047-2049-5, ISBN13: 978-0-8047-2049-6. Dewey:891.73/3. LCCN:92-021749.
Audience: **u,f.** *Choice, 1993.*

Fusso, Susanne **PG3328.Z7S494 2006**
Discovering Sexuality in Dostoevsky. Trade Cloth. Northwestern University Press. Evanston, IL. 2006. 128p. Studies in Russian Literature and Theory ISBN:0-8101-2107-7, ISBN13: 978-0-8101-2107-2. Dewey:891.733. LCCN:2006-002652.
Audience: **u,f.**

Ginzburg, Eugenia S. **DK268.3 .G513**
Journey into the Whirlwind. Ed. 1. Trade Paper. Harcourt Trade Publishers. New York, NY. 2002. 432p. ISBN:0-15-602751-8, ISBN13: 978-0-15-602751-9. Dewey:365/.6/0924.
Audience: **g,l,u,f.**

Givens, John **PG3487.U5Z67 2000**
Prodigal Son: Vasilii Shukshin in Soviet Russia Culture. Trade Cloth. Northwestern University Press. Evanston, IL. 2000. 267p. Studies in Russian Literature and Theory ISBN:0-8101-1770-3, ISBN13: 978-0-8101-1770-9. Dewey:891.73/44. LCCN:00-008699.
Audience: **u,f.**

Gladkov, Fyodor Vasilievich **PG3476.G53T813 1994**
Cement. A. S. Arthur & C. Ashleigh (Translators). Trade Cloth. Northwestern University Press. Evanston, IL. 1994. 312p. European Classics Ser. ISBN:0-8101-1175-6, ISBN13: 978-0-8101-1175-2. Dewey:891.73/42. LCCN:94-022785.
Audience: **g,l,u,f.**

Gogol, Nikolai **PG3332**
Dead Souls. Trade Paper. Penguin Group (USA) Inc. New York, NY. 2004. 512p. Penguin Classics Ser. ISBN:0-14-044807-1, ISBN13: 978-0-14-044807-8. Dewey:891.73/3. LCCN:2004-275517.
Audience: **g,l,u,f.** *Choice, 1996.*

Gogol, Nikolai **PG3458**
Three Plays: The Marriage; The Gamblers; The Government Inspector. Stephen Mulrine (Translator). Trade Paper. Methuen Publishing Ltd. London, 2004. 0p. World Classics Ser. ISBN:0-413-73340-8, ISBN13: 978-0-413-73340-5. Dewey:891.7/2/3.
Audience: **g,l,u,f.**

Gogol, Nikolai **PG3332**
Diary of a Madman, the Government Inspector and Selected Stories. Ronald Wilks (Translator), Robert Maguire (Introduction by). Trade Paper. Penguin Group (USA) Inc. New York, NY. 2006. 368p. ISBN:0-14-044907-8, ISBN13: 978-0-14-044907-5. Dewey:891.733.
Audience: **g,l,u,f.**

Goncharov, Ivan A. **PG3326**
Oblomov. Natalie Duddington (Translator). Library Binding. Buccaneer Books, Inc. Cutchogue, NY. 1990. ISBN:0-89966-685-X, ISBN13: 978-0-89966-685-3. Dewey:891.73/3.
Audience: **g,l,u,f.**

Gorky, Maxim **PZ3.G678**
Stories of the Steppe. Trade Paper. University Press of the Pacific. Miami, FL. 2003. 60p. ISBN:1-4102-0572-X, ISBN13: 978-1-4102-0572-8.
Audience: **g,l,u,f.**

Gorky, Maxim **PG3463.N2C6 1999**
The Lower Depths. William-Alan Landes (Editor), Jennie Covan (Translator). Trade Paper. Players Press, Inc. Studio City, CA. 2003. 64p. Players Press Classic Plays Ser. ISBN:0-88734-815-7, ISBN13: 978-0-88734-815-0. Dewey:891.72/3. LCCN:99-051846.
Audience: **g,l,u,f.**

Gorky, Maxim **PG3463.M35**
Mother. Ed. 4. Margaret Wettlin (Translator). Trade Paper. University Press of the Pacific. Miami, FL. 2000. 424p. ISBN:0-89875-116-0, ISBN13: 978-0-89875-116-1.
Audience: **g,l,u,f.**

Gorky, Maxim **PG3335.Z8**
My Childhood. Ronald Wilks (Translator, Introduction by). Trade Paper. Penguin Group (USA) Inc. New York, NY. 1991. 240p. Penguin Twentieth-Century Classics Ser. ISBN:0-14-018285-3, ISBN13: 978-0-14-018285-9. Dewey:891.78309.
Audience: **g,l,u,f.**

Goscilo, Helena **PG3476.T58Z67 1996**
The Explosive World of Tatyana N. Tolstaya's Fiction. Cloth Text. M. E. Sharpe Inc. Armonk, NY. 1996. 240p. Writers' Worlds Ser. ISBN:1-56324-858-1, ISBN13: 978-1-56324-858-0. Dewey:891.73/44. LCCN:96-014577.
Audience: **u,f.** *Choice, 1997.*

Gottlieb, Vera & Allain, Paul (Editors) **PG3458.Z8 C36 2000**
The Cambridge Companion to Chekhov. Cloth Text. Cambridge University Press. New York, NY. 2000. 328p. Companions to Literature Ser. ISBN:0-521-58117-6, ISBN13: 978-0-521-58117-2. Dewey:891.72/3. LCCN:99-055578.
Audience: **l,u,f.** *Choice, 2001.*

Grekova, I. **PG3481.4.E43S5 1994**
The Ship of Widows. Cathy Porter (Translator), Helena Goscilo (Foreword by). Trade Paper. Northwestern University Press. Evanston, IL. 1994. 179p. European Classics Ser. ISBN:0-8101-1144-6, ISBN13: 978-0-8101-1144-8. Dewey:891.73/44. LCCN:93-049837.
Audience: **g,l,u,f.**

Grossman, Vasily Semenovich **PG3476.G7Z3513 2006**
Life and Fate. Robert Chandler (Introduction by). Trade Paper. New York Review of Books, Incorporated, The. New York, NY. 2006. 896p. New York Review Books Classics ISBN:1-59017-201-9, ISBN13: 978-1-59017-201-8. Dewey:891.73/42. LCCN:2005-022739.
Audience: **g,l,u,f.**

Grossman, Vasily **D764.G772 2006**
A Writer at War: Vasily Grossman with the Red Army, 1941-1945. Antony Beevor (Editor), Luba Vinogradova (Translator). Trade Cloth. Knopf Publishing Group. New York, NY. 2006. 400p. ISBN:0-375-42407-5, ISBN13: 978-0-375-42407-6. Dewey:940.54/217/092 B. LCCN:2005-051033.
Audience: **g,l,u,f.** *Choice, 2006.*

Grossman, Vasily **PG3476.G7V813 1997**
Forever Flowing. Thomas P. Whitney (Translator). Trade Paper. Northwestern University Press. Evanston, IL. 1997. 247p. European Classics Ser. ISBN:0-8101-1503-4, ISBN13: 978-0-8101-1503-3. Dewey:891.73/42. LCCN:96-051009.
Audience: **g,l,u,f.**

Hammarberg, Gitta **PG3314.Z9 S44 1991**
From the Idyll to the Novel: Karamzin's Sentimentalist Prose. Catriona Kelly, Anthony Cross, Caryl Emerson, Barbara Heldt, Malcolm Jones, Donald Rayfield, G. S. Smith & Victor Terras (Contribution by). Trade Paper. Cambridge University Press. New York, NY. 2006. 348p. Cambridge Studies in Russian Literature Ser. ISBN:0-521-02560-5, ISBN13: 978-0-521-02560-7. Dewey:891.78/209.
Audience: **u,f.**

Hippius, Zinaida **PG3460.G5**
Selected Works of Zinaida Hippius. Temira Pachmuss (Editor). Trade Cloth. University of Illinois Press. Champaign, IL. 1972. 324p. ISBN:0-252-00260-1, ISBN13: 978-0-252-00260-1. Dewey:891.7/1/3. LCCN:72-188447.
Audience: **g,l,u,f.** B

Hobson, Mary (Author, Translator) **PG3337.G7G666 2005**
Aleksandr Griboedov's 'Woe from Wit': A Commentary and Translation. Trade Cloth. Edwin Mellen Press, The. Lewiston, NY. 2005. 622p. Studies in Slavic Language and Literature ISBN:0-7734-6146-9, ISBN13: 978-0-7734-6146-8. Dewey:891.72/3. LCCN:2005-046173.
Audience: **g,l,u,f.**

Holmgren, Beth **PG2997**
e Women's Works in Stalin's Time: On Lidiia Chukovskaia and Nadezhda Mandelstam. E-Book. Indiana University Press. Bloomington, IN. 1993. 240p. ISBN:0-253-20829-7, ISBN13: 978-0-253-20829-3. Dewey:891.709/9287. LCCN:92-046343.
Audience: **u,f.** *Choice, 1994.*

Ivanov, Viacheslav **PG3467.I8A23 2001**
Selected Essays: Viacheslav Ivanov. Michael Wachtel (Editor), Robert Bird (Translator). Trade Paper. Northwestern University Press. Evanston, IL. 2003. 352p. SRLT ISBN:0-8101-2083-6, ISBN13: 978-0-8101-2083-9. Dewey:891.70915. LCCN:2001-000081.
Audience: **g,l,u,f.** *Choice, 2004.*

Jackson, Robert L. & Nelson, Lowry Jr. (Editors) **PG3476.M355**
Vyacheslav Ivanov: Poet, Critic and Philosopher. Trade Cloth. Yale Russian & East European Publications. New Haven, CT. 1986. 455p. Yale Russian and East European Publications, No. 8 ISBN:0-936586-08-7, ISBN13: 978-0-936586-08-3. Dewey:891.71/3. LCCN:85-051637.
Audience: **u,f.**

Kataev, Valentin **PG3476.K4V713 1995**
Time, Forward!. Charles Malamuth (Translator), Edward J. Brown (Foreword by). Trade Paper. Northwestern University Press. Evanston, IL. 1995. 345p. European Classics Ser. ISBN:0-8101-1247-7, ISBN13: 978-0-8101-1247-6. Dewey:891.7/3/4. LCCN:95-023933.
Audience: **g,l,u,f.**

Khlebnikov, Velimir **PG3476.K485A23 1987**
Collected Works of Velimir Khlebnikov: Letters and Theoretical Writings, Vol. I. Charlotte Douglas (Editor), Paul Schmidt (Translator). Trade Cloth. Harvard University Press. Cambridge, MA. 1987. 464p. ISBN:0-674-14045-1, ISBN13: 978-0-674-14045-5. Dewey:891.71/3 B. LCCN:87-008399.
Audience: **u,f.** *Choice, 1988.*

Khlebnikov, Velimir **PG3335.Z8**
The King of Time: Selected Writings of the Russian Futurian. Charlotte Douglas (Editor), Paul Schmidt (Translator). Trade Paper. Harvard University Press. Cambridge, MA. 1990. 270p. ISBN:0-674-50516-6, ISBN13: 978-0-674-50516-2. Dewey:891.78309.
Audience: **g,l,u,f.**

Khlebnikov, Velimir **PG3335.Z8**
Collected Works of Velimir Khlebnikov: Prose, Plays, and Supersagas, Vol. II. Ronald Vroon (Editor), Paul Schmidt (Translator). Trade Cloth. Harvard University Press. Cambridge, MA. 1989. 384p. Collected Works of Velimir Khlebnikov, Vol. 2:Vol. 2 ISBN:0-674-14046-X, ISBN13: 978-0-674-14046-2. Dewey:891.78309. LCCN:87-008399.
Audience: **g,l,u,f.** *Choice, 1990.*

Kropotkin, Petr Alekseevich **PG3012**
Ideals and Realities in Russian Literature. Paper Text. Classic Books. Murrieta, CA. 2001. 341p. ISBN:0-7426-9094-6, ISBN13: 978-0-7426-9094-3. Dewey:891.7/09/003.
Audience: **l,u,f.**

Kuprin, Aleksandr I. **PG3467.K8**
The Duel. Trade Cloth. Hyperion Press, Inc. Westport, CT. 1987. Classics of Russian Literature Ser. ISBN:0-88355-491-7, ISBN13: 978-0-88355-491-3. Dewey:891.7/3/3. LCCN:76-023881.
Audience: **g,l,u,f.**

Lantz, Kenneth **PG**
The Dostoevsky Encyclopedia. Greenwood Press. 2004. ISBN:0-313-30384-3, ISBN13: 978-0-313-30384-5.
Audience: **g,l,u,f.**

Leatherbarrow, William J. (Editor) **PG3328.Z6 C27 2002**
The Cambridge Companion to Dostoevsky. Cloth Text. Cambridge University Press. New York, NY. 2002. 260p. Cambridge Companions to Literature Ser. ISBN:0-521-65253-7, ISBN13: 978-0-521-65253-7. Dewey:891.73/3. LCCN:2002-067684.
Audience: **l,u,f.** *Choice, 2003.*

Leatherbarrow, William J. **PG3325.B63D67 1999**
Dostoevsky's the Devils: A Critical Companion. Paper Text. Northwestern University Press. Evanston, IL. 1999. 164p. Northwestern/Aatseel Critical Companions to Russian Literature Ser. ISBN:0-8101-1444-5, ISBN13: 978-0-8101-1444-9. Dewey:891.73/3. LCCN:99-027505.
Audience: **u,f.**

Leatherbarrow, William J. **PG3325.B73 L4 1992**
Dostoyevsky: The Brothers Karamazov. J. P. Stern (Contribution by). Trade Paper. Cambridge University Press. New York, NY. 1992. 129p. Landmarks of World Literature Ser. ISBN:0-521-38601-2, ISBN13: 978-0-521-38601-2. Dewey:891.733. LCCN:91-043123.
Audience: **u,f.** *Choice, 1993.*

Leighton, Lauren G. **Z8165.4.L45 2005**
A Bibliography of Anton Chekhov in English. Trade Cloth. Edwin Mellen Press, The. Lewiston, NY. 2004. 561p. Studies in Slavic Language and Literature, 24 ISBN:0-7734-6285-6, ISBN13: 978-0-7734-6285-4. Dewey:016.89172/3. LCCN:2004-063179.
Audience: **g,l,u,f.**

Lermontov, Mikhail **PG3326**
A Hero of Our Time. Trade Cloth. Knopf Publishing Group. New York, NY. 1992. 224p. Everyman's Library ISBN:0-679-41327-8, ISBN13: 978-0-679-41327-1. Dewey:891.73/3. LCCN:91-058692.
Audience: **g,l,u,f.**

Lermontov, Mikhail **PG3337.L4A24**
The Demon, and Other Poems. Eugene M. Kayden (Translator), Maurice Bowra (Introduction by). Trade Paper. Books on Demand. Ann Arbor, MI. 225p. Classics of Russian Poetry Ser. ISBN:0-598-21232-9, ISBN13: 978-0-598-21232-0. Dewey:891.713. LCCN:62-021070.
Audience: **g,l,u,f.**

Leskov, N. S. **PG3337.L5A247 2003**
The Enchanted Wanderer: Selected Tales. David Magarshack (Translator). Trade Paper. Random House Adult Trade Publishing Group. New York, NY. 2003. 320p. ISBN:0-8129-6696-1, ISBN13: 978-0-8129-6696-1. Dewey:891.73/3. LCCN:2002-032580.
Audience: **g,l,u,f.**

Lowe, David A. (Editor) **PG3443.C7 1988**
Critical Essays on Ivan Turgenev. Trade Cloth. Thomson Gale. Farmington Hills, MI. 1988. 176p. Critical Essays on World Literature Ser. ISBN:0-8161-8842-4, ISBN13: 978-0-8161-8842-0. Dewey:891.73/3. LCCN:88-016312.
Audience: **u,f.** *Choice, 1989.*

Mandelshtam, Osip **PG3476.M355.A243**
The Complete Critical Prose and Letters. Trade Cloth. Ardis Publishers. Woodstock, NY. 1979. 725 p., [2] lp. ISBN:0-88233-163-9, ISBN13: 978-0-88233-163-8. Dewey:891.7/8/308. LCCN:78-064999.
Audience: **g,l,u,f.**

Mandelshtam, Osip **PG3476.M355**
Mandelshtam: Selected Poems. James Greene (Translator), Donald Rayfield (Introduction by), Nadezhda Mandelstam & Donald Davie (Foreword by). Trade Paper. Penguin Group (USA) Inc. New York, NY. 1992. 144p. Classics Ser. ISBN:0-14-018474-0, ISBN13: 978-0-14-018474-7. Dewey:891.713. LCCN:92-211686.
Audience: **g,l,u,f.**

Mandelshtam, Osip **PG3476.M355**
Tristia. Kevin J. Kinsella (Translator). Trade Paper. Green Integer. Los Angeles, CA. 2005. 130p. ISBN:1-933382-07-4, ISBN13: 978-1-933382-07-4. Dewey:891.7/1/3.
Audience: **g,l,u,f.**

Mandelstam, Nadezhda **PG3476.M355Z813 1999**
Hope Against Hope: A Memoir. Max Hayward (Translator), Clarence Brown (Introduction by). Trade Paper. Random House, Inc. New York, NY. 1999. 480p. Modern Library Ser. ISBN:0-375-75316-8, ISBN13: 978-0-375-75316-9. LCCN:98-047833.
Audience: **g,l,u,f.**

Martinsen, Deborah A. **PG3328.Z7S526 2003**
Surprised by Shame: Dostoevsky's Liars and Narrative Exposure. Trade Cloth. Ohio State University Press. Columbus, OH. 2003. xvii, 273p. The Theory and Interpretation of Narrative Ser. ISBN:0-8142-0921-1, ISBN13: 978-0-8142-0921-9. Dewey:891.73/3. LCCN:2002-153881.
Audience: **u,f.** *Choice, 2003.*

Mayakovsky, Vladimir **PG3476.A324**
The Bedbug and Selected Poetry. Patricia Blake (Editor), Max Hayward & George Reavey (Translators). Trade Paper. Indiana University Press. Bloomington, IN. 1975. 320p. ISBN:0-253-20189-6, ISBN13: 978-0-253-20189-8. Dewey:891.7/1/42. LCCN:75-010805.
Audience: **g,l,u,f.** B

Mayakovsky, Vladimir **PG3476.M3A24 1995**
Mayakovsky--Plays. Guy Daniels (Translator), Robert Payne (Introduction by). Trade Paper. Northwestern University Press. Evanston, IL. 1995. 276p. European Drama Classics Ser. ISBN:0-8101-1339-2, ISBN13: 978-0-8101-1339-8. Dewey:891.7/242. LCCN:95-023932.
Audience: **g,l,u,f.**

Nabokov, Vladimir (Translator) **PG3300.S6**
The Song of Igor's Campaign. Trade Cloth. Ardis Publishers. Woodstock, NY. 1989. 128p. ISBN:0-87501-061-X, ISBN13: 978-0-87501-061-8. Dewey:891.711.
Audience: **g,l,u,f.**

Odoevsky, Vladimir Fedorovich **PG3337.O3R813 1997**
Russian Nights. Olga Koshansky-Olienikov & Ralph E. Matlaw (Translators). Trade Paper. Northwestern University Press. Evanston, IL. 1997. 264p. European Classics Ser. ISBN:0-8101-1520-4, ISBN13: 978-0-8101-1520-0. Dewey:891.73/3. LCCN:96-052851.
Audience: **g,l,u,f.**

Odoevsky, Vladimir F. **PG3337.O3**
The Salamander and Other Gothic Tales. Neil Cornwell (Editor, Translator, Introduction by). Trade Paper. Northwestern University Press. Evanston, IL. 1992. 215p. ISBN:0-8101-1062-8, ISBN13: 978-0-8101-1062-5. Dewey:891.73/3. LCCN:92-025756.
Audience: **g,l,u,f.**

Olesha, Yuri **PG3476.O37Z213 2004**
Envy. Marian Schwartz (Translator), Ken Kalfus (Introduction by). Trade Paper. New York Review of Books, Incorporated, The. New York, NY. 2004. 178p. New York Review Books Classics Ser. ISBN:1-59017-086-5, ISBN13: 978-1-59017-086-1. Dewey:891.73/42. LCCN:2004-004060.
Audience: **g,l,u,f.**

Orwin, Donna T. (Editor) **PG3409.5**
The Cambridge Companion to Tolstoy. Cloth Text. Cambridge University Press. New York, NY. 2002. 288p. Cambridge Companions to Literature Ser. ISBN:0-521-79271-1, ISBN13: 978-0-521-79271-4. Dewey:891.73/3.
Audience: **g,l,u,f.** *Choice, 2003.*

Ostrovsky, Aleksandr Nikolaevich **PG3337.O8A28**
Plays. Paper Text. Classic Books. Murrieta, CA. 2001. 305p. ISBN:0-7426-9102-0, ISBN13: 978-0-7426-9102-5. Dewey:891.7/2/3.
Audience: **g,l,u,f.**

Pasternak, Boris Leonidovich **PG3476.P27S413 2001**
My Sister--Life. Mark Rudman & Bohdan Boychuk (Translators). Trade Paper. Northwestern University Press. Evanston, IL. 2001. 116p. European Poetry Classics Ser. ISBN:0-8101-1909-9, ISBN13: 978-0-8101-1909-3. Dewey:891.71/42. LCCN:2001-034544.
Audience: **g,l,u,f.**

Pasternak, Boris **PG3476.P27D63 1991**
Doctor Zhivago. John Bayley (Introduction by). Trade Paper. Knopf Publishing Group. New York, NY. 1997. 592p. ISBN:0-679-77438-6, ISBN13: 978-0-679-77438-9. Dewey:891.7/342. LCCN:90-053445.
Audience: **g,l,u,f.**

Pasternak, Boris **PG3476.P27A248 2003**
Second Nature: Poems. Andre Navrozov (Translator). Trade Paper. Peter Owen Ltd. London, 2003. 83p. ISBN:0-7206-1192-X, ISBN13: 978-0-7206-1192-2. Dewey:891.71/42. LCCN:2004-381404.
Audience: **g,l,u,f.**

Pattison, George & Thompson, Diane Oenning (Editors) **PG3328.Z7 R4233 2001**
Dostoevsky and the Christian Tradition. Anthony Cross, Caryl Emerson, Barbara Heldt, Malcolm Jones, Catriona Kelly, Donald Rayfield, G. S. Smith & Victor Terras (Contribution by). Trade Cloth. Cambridge University Press. New York, NY. 2001. 294p. Studies in Russian Literature ISBN:0-521-78278-3, ISBN13: 978-0-521-78278-4. Dewey:891.73/3. LCCN:00-065988.
Audience: **u,f.**

Pelevin, Victor **PG3488.O4**
The Life of Insects: A Novel. Andrew Bromfield (Translator). Trade Paper. Penguin Group (USA) Inc. New York, NY. 1999. 192p. ISBN:0-14-027972-5, ISBN13: 978-0-14-027972-6. Dewey:891.73/44. LCCN:97-011106.
Audience: **g,l,u,f.**

Pelevin, Victor **PG3488.O4**
A Werewolf Problem in Central Russia and Other Stories. Andrew Bromfield (Translator). Trade Paper. New Directions Publishing Corporation. New York, NY. 2003. 224p. ISBN:0-8112-1543-1, ISBN13: 978-0-8112-1543-5. Dewey:891.73/44.
Audience: **g,l,u,f.**

Petrov, Evgeni I. & Ilf, Ilya **PG3476.I44D913 1997**
The Twelve Chairs. John H. Richardson (Translator), Maurice Friedberg (Introduction by). Trade Paper. Northwestern University Press. Evanston, IL. 1997. 395p. European Classics Ser. ISBN:0-8101-1484-4, ISBN13: 978-0-8101-1484-5. Dewey:891.73/42. LCCN:96-029783.
Audience: **g,l,u,f.**

Petrushevskaya, Ludmilla **PG3485.E724T56 1994**
The Time . . . Night. Sally Laird (Translator). Trade Cloth. Knopf Publishing Group. New York, NY. 1994. 155p. ISBN:0-679-43616-2, ISBN13: 978-0-679-43616-4. Dewey:891.73/44. LCCN:94-009076.
Audience: **g,l,u,f.**

Pilniak, Boris **PZ3.V86 TAM10**
Tales of the Wilderness. Trade Paper. Kessinger Publishing, LLC. Whitefish, MT. 2004. ISBN:1-4191-5069-3, ISBN13: 978-1-4191-5069-2. Dewey:891.7/3/42.
Audience: **g,l,u,f.**

Platonov, Andrei **PG3476.P543A23 2000**
The Fierce and Beautiful World. Joseph Barnes (Translator), Tatyana Tolstaya (Introduction by). Trade Paper. New York Review of Books, Incorporated, The. New York, NY. 2000. 264p. New York Review Books Classics Ser. ISBN:0-940322-33-1, ISBN13: 978-0-940322-33-2. Dewey:891.73/42. LCCN:99-046036.
Audience: **g,l,u,f.**

Platonov, Andrey **PG3476.S52**
The Foundation Pit. Book, Other. Random House. London, 1997. 192p. ISBN:1-86046-050-X, ISBN13: 978-1-86046-050-0. Dewey:891.7/342.
Audience: **g,l,u,f.**

Platonov, Andrey **PG3476.P543**
Soul. UK-Trade Paper. Random House. London, 2003. 208p. ISBN:1-84343-038-X, ISBN13: 978-1-84343-038-4.
Audience: **g,l,u,f.**

Popov, Evgeny **PG3485.2.P557Z35213**
Merry-Making in Old Russia: And Other Stories. Robert Porter (Translator). Trade Cloth. Northwestern University Press. Evanston, IL. 1997. 218p. Writings from an Unbound Europe ISBN:0-8101-1326-0, ISBN13: 978-0-8101-1326-8. Dewey:891.7/344. LCCN:97-012449.
Audience: **g,l,u,f.**

Pushkin, Alexander **PG3347.E8**
Eugene Onegin: A Novel in Verse. Trade Paper. Penguin Group (USA) Inc. New York, NY. 2003. 320p. Penguin Classics Ser. ISBN:0-14-044803-9, ISBN13: 978-0-14-044803-0. Dewey:891.71/3. LCCN:2003-269446.
Audience: **g,l,u,f.** B *Choice, 1991.*

Pushkin, Alexandr **PG3326**
The Queen of Spades. Trade Paper. Kessinger Publishing, LLC. Whitefish, MT. 2004. ISBN:1-4192-7959-9, ISBN13: 978-1-4192-7959-1. Dewey:891.73/3.
Audience: **g,l,u,f.**

Pushkin, Alexandr **PG3347.A17 2002**
Collected Narrative and Lyrical Poetry. Walter Arndt (Translator). Trade Cloth. Ardis Publishers. Woodstock, NY. 1984. 472p. ISBN:0-88233-826-9, ISBN13: 978-0-88233-826-2. Dewey:891.71/3. LCCN:2003-269477.
Audience: **g,l,u,f.**

Pushkin, Alexandr & Brett, Simon **PG3347.A2 2005**
The Gypsies and Other Narrative Poems. Antony Wood (Introduction by, Notes by). Trade Cloth. David R. Godine Publisher. Boston, MA. 2005. xl, 116p. ISBN:1-56792-305-4, ISBN13: 978-1-56792-305-6. Dewey:891.71/3. LCCN:2005-023014.
Audience: **g,l,u,f.** *Choice, 2006.*

Pushkin, Alexandr **PG3326**
Alexander Pushkin: Complete Prose Fiction. Paul Debreczeny (Translator). Trade Paper. Stanford University Press. Palo Alto, CA. 1983. 557p. ISBN:0-8047-1800-8, ISBN13: 978-0-8047-1800-4. Dewey:891.73/3. LCCN:81-085450.
Audience: **g,l,u,f.**

Pushkin, Alexandr, et al. **PG3230.5 .P86 1991**
Pushkin, Plus . . .: Lyric Poems of Eight Russian Poets. Ivan Krylov, Mikhail Lermontov, Nikolai Nekrasov, Alexander Blok, Fedor Sologub, Osip Mandelstam & Sergei Yesenin (Authors), Vassar W. Smith (Translator, Introduction by, Notes by). Trade Paper. Hot Biscuit Productions, Inc. Memphis, TN. 1997. 100p. ISBN:1-880964-02-3, ISBN13: 978-1-880964-02-6. Dewey:891.71008. LCCN:92-090674.
Audience: **g,l,u,f.**

Radishchev, Alexander **HN525**
Journey from Petersburg to Moscow. Trade Paper. Bookking International. Paris, 1999. World Classic Literature Ser. ISBN:2-87714-258-2, ISBN13: 978-2-87714-258-8. Dewey:891.7/4/2.
Audience: **u,f.**

Rasputin, Valentin **PG3485.5.A85P7613**
Farewell to Matyora: A Novel. Ed. 2. Antonina W. Bouis (Translator), Kathleen Parthe (Foreword by). Trade Paper. Northwestern University Press. Evanston, IL. 1995. 227p. European Classics Ser. ISBN:0-8101-1329-5, ISBN13: 978-0-8101-1329-9. Dewey:891.73/44. LCCN:95-021830.
Audience: **g,l,u,f.**

Rasputin, Valentin **PG3485.5.A85A24 1989**
Siberia on Fire: Stories and Essays by Valentin Rasputin. Gerald Mikkelson & Margaret Winchell (Translators), Gerald Mikkelson & Margaret Winchell (Introduction by). Trade Paper.

Northern Illinois University Press. DeKalb, IL. 1989. 252p. ISBN:0-87580-547-7, ISBN13: 978-0-87580-547-4. Dewey:891.73/44. LCCN:89-016024.
Audience: **g,l,u,f.** *Choice, 1990.*

Rasputin, Valentin **DK761**
Siberia, Siberia. Margaret Winchell & Gerald Mikkelson (Translators). Trade Paper. Northwestern University Press. Evanston, IL. 1997. 438p. ISBN:0-8101-1575-1, ISBN13: 978-0-8101-1575-0. Dewey:957. LCCN:96-007098.
Audience: **g,l,u,f.** *Choice, 1997.*

Rayfield, Donald **PG3458.Z8R39 1999**
Understanding Chekhov: A Critical Study of Chekhov's Prose and Drama. Trade Paper. University of Wisconsin Press. Chicago, IL. 1999. 224p. ISBN:0-299-16314-8, ISBN13: 978-0-299-16314-3. Dewey:891.72/3. LCCN:99-010704.
Audience: **u,f.** *Choice, 2000.*

Ronshin, Valery **PG3485.6.N73**
Living a Life: Absurd Tales. Jose Alaniz & Kathleen Cook (Translators). Trade Paper. Northwestern University Press. Evanston, IL. 2002. 208p. ISBN:5-7172-0060-9, ISBN13: 978-5-7172-0060-8. Dewey:891.7.
Audience: **g,l,u,f.**

Ryan-Hayes, Karen (Editor) **PG3479.7.R59.M638**
Venedikt Erofeev's Moscow - Petushki: Critical Perspectives. Cloth Text. Peter Lang Publishing, Inc. New York, NY. 1997. X, 231p. Middlebury Studies in Russian Languages and Literature, Vol. 14 ISBN:0-8204-3666-6, ISBN13: 978-0-8204-3666-1. Dewey:891.73/44. LCCN:96-034896.
Audience: **u,f.**

Saltykov-Shchedrin, Mikhail Evgrafovich **PG3361.S3**
The Golovyov Family. Natalie Duddington (Translator). Trade Cloth. Hyperion Press, Inc. Westport, CT. 1989. Classics of Russian Literature Ser. ISBN:0-88355-514-X, ISBN13: 978-0-88355-514-9. Dewey:891.7/3/3. LCCN:76-023897.
Audience: **g,l,u,f.**

Saltykov-Shchedrin, Mikhail Evgrafovich **PZ3.S182; PG3361.S3**
Fables. Vera Velkhovsky (Translator). Trade Paper. Hyperion Press, Inc. Westport, CT. 1977. Classics of Russian Literature Ser. ISBN:0-88355-517-4, ISBN13: 978-0-88355-517-0. Dewey:891.7/3/3. LCCN:76-023898.
Audience: **g,l,u,f.**

Seifrid, Thomas **PG3476.P543 Z778 19**
Andrei Platonov: Uncertainties of Spirit. Catriona Kelly, Anthony Cross, Caryl Emerson, Barbara Heldt, Malcolm Jones, Donald Rayfield, G. S. Smith & Victor Terras (Contribution by). Trade Paper. Cambridge University Press. New York, NY. 2006. 288p. Cambridge Studies in Russian Literature Ser. ISBN:0-521-02675-X, ISBN13: 978-0-521-02675-8. Dewey:891.73/42.
Audience: **u,f.**

Shalamov, Varlam **PG3487.A592**
Kolyma Tales. John Glad (Translator, Foreword by). Trade Paper. Penguin Group (USA) Inc. New York, NY. 1995. 528p. Twentieth Century Classics Ser. ISBN:0-14-018695-6, ISBN13: 978-0-14-018695-6. Dewey:891.73/42.
Audience: **g,l,u,f.**

Shneidman, N. N. **PG3098.4.S473 2004**
Russian Literature, 1995-2002: On the Threshold of the New Millennium. Cloth over Boards. University of Toronto Press. Toronto, ON. 2004. 240p. ISBN:0-8020-8724-8, ISBN13: 978-0-8020-8724-9. Dewey:891.73/509. LCCN:2004-484717.
Audience: **u,f.**

Sholokhov, Mikhail **PG3476.S52T4813 1996**
Quiet Flows the Don. Brian Murphy (Editor), Robert Daglish (Translator), Brian Murphy (Revised by). Cloth Text. Avalon Publishing Group. New York, NY. 1996. 1376p. ISBN:0-7867-0360-1, ISBN13: 978-0-7867-0360-9. Dewey:891.7/3/42. LCCN:96-030926.
Audience: **g,l,u,f.**

Shukshin, Vasily **PG3487.U5A26 1996**
Stories from a Siberian Village. John Givens & Laura Michael (Translators), Kathleen F. Parthe (Foreword by). Trade Paper. Northern Illinois University Press. DeKalb, IL. 2003. 304p. ISBN:0-87580-572-8, ISBN13: 978-0-87580-572-6. Dewey:891.73/44. LCCN:95-046643.
Audience: **g,l,u,f.** *Choice, 1997.*

Sologub, Fedor **PG3470.T4 M413 1983**
The Petty Demon. Samuel D. Cioran (Translator). Trade Cloth. Ardis Publishers. Woodstock, NY. 1983. 352p. ISBN:0-88233-808-0, ISBN13: 978-0-88233-808-8. Dewey:891.73/3. LCCN:83-002723.
Audience: **g,l,u,f.** B

Solzhenitsyn, Aleksandr **PG3488.O4**
Cancer Ward. UK-B Format Paperback. Knopf Publishing Group. New York, NY. 2003. 576p. ISBN:0-09-957551-5, ISBN13: 978-0-09-957551-1. Dewey:891.7/344.
Audience: **g,l,u,f.**

Solzhenitsyn, Aleksandr **HV9713.S6413 2002**
The Gulag Archipelago, 1918-1956. Trade Paper. HarperCollins Publishers. New York, NY. 2002. 512p. Perennial Classics Ser. ISBN:0-06-000776-1, ISBN13: 978-0-06-000776-8. Dewey:365/.45/0947. LCCN:2001-046504.
Audience: **g,l,u,f.**

Solzhenitsyn, Aleksandr **PG3476.B425**
Stories and Prose Poems. Ed. 2. Michael Glenny (Translator). Trade Paper. Farrar, Straus & Giroux. New York, NY. 1974. ISBN:0-374-51116-0, ISBN13: 978-0-374-51116-6. Dewey:891.734. LCCN:74-148708.
Audience: **g,l,u,f.**

Solzhenitsyn, Aleksandr **PG3488.O4V23 1997**
The First Circle. Thomas P. Whitney (Translator). Trade Paper. Northwestern University Press. Evanston, IL. 1997. 580p. European Classics Ser. ISBN:0-8101-1590-5, ISBN13: 978-0-8101-1590-3. Dewey:891.7/3/44. LCCN:97-023067.
Audience: **g,l,u,f.**

Solzhenitsyn, Aleksandr **PG3488.O4O3313 2005**
One Day in the Life of Ivan Denisovich: A Novel. H. T. Willetts (Translator). Trade Paper. Farrar, Straus & Giroux. New York, NY. 2005. 188p. ISBN:0-374-52952-3, ISBN13: 978-0-374-52952-9. Dewey:891.73/44. LCCN:2004-062824.
Audience: **g,l,u,f.**

Swift, Mark Stanley **PG3458.Z9R447 2003**
Biblical Subtexts and Religious Themes in Works of Anton Chekhov. Trade Cloth. Peter Lang Publishing, Inc. New York, NY. 2004. 207p. Middlebury Studies in Russian Language and Literature, Vol. 18 ISBN:0-8204-3875-8, ISBN13: 978-0-8204-3875-7. Dewey:891.72/3. LCCN:2003-001220.
Audience: **u,f.**

Terras, Victor **PG3325**
A Karamazov Companion: Commentary on the Genesis, Language, and Style of Dostoevsky's Novel. Trade Paper. University of Wisconsin Press. Chicago, IL. 2002. 496p. ISBN:0-299-08314-4, ISBN13: 978-0-299-08314-4. Dewey:891.73/3. LCCN:80-005117.
Audience: **u,f.**

Terras, Victor **PG3328.Z6T397 1998**
Reading Dostoevsky. Trade Cloth. University of Wisconsin Press. Chicago, IL. 1998. 184p. ISBN:0-299-16050-5, ISBN13: 978-0-299-16050-0. Dewey:891.73/3. LCCN:98-023342.
Audience: **u,f.**

Thorlby, Anthony **PG3365.A63 T48 1987**
Tolstoy: Anna Karenina. J. P. Stern (Contribution by). Trade Paper. Cambridge University Press. New York, NY. 1987. 128p. Landmarks of World Literature Ser. ISBN:0-521-31325-2, ISBN13: 978-0-521-31325-4. Dewey:891.73/3.
Audience: **u,f.**

Tolstaya, Tatyana **PG3476.T58**
Sleepwalker in a Fog. Trade Cloth. Random House Value Publishing. New York, NY. 1998. ISBN:0-517-32862-3, ISBN13: 978-0-517-32862-0. Dewey:891.73/44.
Audience: **g,l,u,f.**

Tolstaya, Tatyana **PG3476.T58A24 2003**
Pushkin's Children: Writing on Russia and Russians. Jamey Gambrell (Translator), Alma Guillermoprieto (Introduction by). Trade Paper. Houghton Mifflin Company Trade & Reference Division. Boston, MA. 2003. 256p. ISBN:0-618-12500-0, ISBN13: 978-0-618-12500-5. Dewey:891.73/44. LCCN:2002-027610.
Audience: **g,l,u,f.**

Tolstoy, Alexei **PZ3.T58**
The Ordeal: A Trilogy - Book Two: 1918, Vol. 2. Trade Paper. University Press of the Pacific. Miami, FL. 2000. 416p. ISBN:0-89875-127-6, ISBN13: 978-0-89875-127-7. Dewey:891.734.
Audience: **g,l,u,f.**

Tolstoy, Alexei **PZ3.T58**
The Ordeal: A Trilogy - Book Three: Bleak Morning, Vol. 3. Tatiana Litvinov & Ivy Litvinov (Translators). Trade Paper. University Press of the Pacific. Miami, FL. 2000. 516p. ISBN:0-89875-128-4, ISBN13: 978-0-89875-128-4. Dewey:891.734.
Audience: **g,l,u,f.**

Tolstoy, Alexei **PZ3.T58**
The Ordeal: A Trilogy: The Sisters, Vol. 1. Tatiana Litvinov & Ivy Litvinov (Translators). Trade Paper. University Press of the Pacific. Miami, FL. 2000. 384p. ISBN:0-89875-126-8, ISBN13: 978-0-89875-126-0. Dewey:891.734.
Audience: **g,l,u,f.**

Tolstoy, Leo **PG3366.A13M3 2001**
Collected Shorter Fiction, Vol. I. Maude, Louise Shanks; Maude, Aylmer. New York: Knopf. 2001. Everyman's Library, 243 ISBN:0-375-41172-0, ISBN13: 978-0-375-41172-4.
Audience: **g,l,u,f.**

Tolstoy, Leo **PG3366.A6 1995**
Anna Karenina: Backgrounds and Sources Criticism. Ed. 2. George Gibian (Editor), Aylmer Maude (Translator). Trade Paper. W. W. Norton & Company, Inc. New York, NY. 1995. 874p. Critical Editions Ser. ISBN:0-393-96642-9, ISBN13: 978-0-393-96642-8. Dewey:891.73/3. LCCN:94-025857.
Audience: **g,l,u,f.**

Tolstoy, Leo **PG3366**
War and Peace. Henry Gifford (Editor), Louise Maude & Aylmer Maude (Translators), Henry Gifford (Introduction by, Notes by). Trade Paper. Oxford University Press, Inc. New York, NY. 1998. 1,386p. Oxford World's Classics Ser. ISBN:0-19-283398-7, ISBN13: 978-0-19-283398-3. Dewey:891.73/3.
Audience: **g,l,u,f.**

Tolstoy, Leo **PG3326**
Resurrection. Richard F. Gustafson (Introduction by). Trade Paper. Oxford University Press, Inc. New York, NY. 2000. 526p. Oxford World's Classics Ser. ISBN:0-19-283642-0, ISBN13: 978-0-19-283642-7. Dewey:891.73/3.
Audience: **g,l,u,f.**

Tolstoy, Leo **PG3366.A13M3 2001**
The Collected Shorter Fiction, Vol. II. Aylmer Maude & Nigel J. Cooper (Translators), John Bayley (Introduction by). Trade Cloth. Alfred A. Knopf Inc. New York, NY. 2001. ISBN:0-375-41287-5, ISBN13: 978-0-375-41287-5. Dewey:891.73/3. LCCN:00-053487.
Audience: **g,l,u,f.**

Tolstoy, Leo **PG3366.A6 2001**
Anna Karenina. Richard Pevear & Larissa Volokhonsky (Translators). Trade Paper. Penguin Group (USA) Inc. New York, NY. 2004. 862p. Oprah's Book Club Ser., Bk. 5 ISBN:0-14-303500-2, ISBN13: 978-0-14-303500-8. Dewey:891.73/3. LCCN:00-043356.
Audience: **g,l,u,f.**

Tolstoy, Leo **BH39.T62413 1995**
What Is Art? Richard Pevear & Larissa Volokhonsky (Translators), Richard Pevear (Preface by). Trade Paper. Penguin Group (USA) Inc. New York, NY. 1996. 240p. Classics Ser. ISBN:0-14-044642-7, ISBN13: 978-0-14-044642-5. Dewey:700.1. LCCN:60-009557.
Audience: **g,l,u,f.**

Trifonov, Yuri **PG3489.R5D713 1999**
Another Life and The House on the Embankment. Michael Glenny (Translator), John Updike (Foreword by). Trade Paper. Northwestern University Press. Evanston, IL. 1999. 350p. European Classics Ser. ISBN:0-8101-1570-0, ISBN13: 978-0-8101-1570-5. Dewey:891.73/44. LCCN:99-042542.
Audience: **g,l,u,f.**

Trifonov, Yuri **PG3489.R5A26 2001**
The Exchange and Other Stories. Ellendea C. Proffer, Helen P. Burlingame, Jim Somers & Byron Lindsey (Translators),

Ellendea C. Proffer & Ronald Meyer (Introduction by). Trade Paper. Northwestern University Press. Evanston, IL. 2002. 192p. European Classics Ser. ISBN:0-8101-1860-2, ISBN13: 978-0-8101-1860-7. Dewey:891.73/44. LCCN:2001-042566.
Audience: **g,l,u,f.**

Tsvetaeva, Marina I. **PG3476.T75A24 2002**
Earthly Signs: Moscow Diaries, 1917-1922. Jamey Gambrell (Editor, Translator, Introduction by). Cloth over Boards. Yale University Press. Cumberland, RI. 2002. 288p. Russian Literature and Thought Ser. ISBN:0-300-06922-7, ISBN13: 978-0-300-06922-8. Dewey:891.71/4208. LCCN:2002-004498.
Audience: **g,l,u,f.** *Choice, 2003.*

Turgenev, Ivan **PG3326**
First Love and The Diary of a Superfluous Man. Trade Paper. University Publishing House, Inc. Mannford, OK. 2001. 149p. ISBN:1-57002-168-6, ISBN13: 978-1-57002-168-8. Dewey:891.73/3.
Audience: **g,l,u,f.**

Turgenev, Ivan **PG3421**
Sketches from a Hunter's Album: The Complete Edition. Ed. 2. Richard Freeborn (Translator, Introduction by, Notes by). Trade Paper. Penguin Group (USA) Inc. New York, NY. 1990. 416p. Classics Ser. ISBN:0-14-044522-6, ISBN13: 978-0-14-044522-0. Dewey:891.733. LCCN:91-143098.
Audience: **g,l,u,f.**

Turgenev, Ivan **PG3420.O8E5 1996**
Fathers and Sons. Michael R. Katz (Editor, Translator). Trade Paper. W. W. Norton & Company, Inc. New York, NY. 1995. 352p. Critical Editions Ser. ISBN:0-393-96752-2, ISBN13: 978-0-393-96752-4. Dewey:891.73/3. LCCN:95-005395.
Audience: **g,l,u,f.** *Choice, 1994.*

Ulitskaya, Ludmila **PG3489.2.L58**
The Funeral Party: A Novel. Trade Paper. Knopf Publishing Group. New York, NY. 2002. 160p. ISBN:0-8052-1132-2, ISBN13: 978-0-8052-1132-0. Dewey:891.735.
Audience: **g,l,u,f.**

Ulitskaya, Ludmila **PG3489.2.L58A28 2005**
Sonechka: A Novella and Stories. Arch Tait (Translator). Trade Cloth. Knopf Publishing Group. New York, NY. 2005. 256p. ISBN:0-8052-4195-7, ISBN13: 978-0-8052-4195-2. Dewey:891.73/5. LCCN:2004-059154.
Audience: **g,l,u,f.**

Vasilenko, Svetlana **PG3489.3.A747A23**
Shamara and Other Writings. Helena Goscilo (Editor, Translator), Andrew Bromfield, Elisabeth Jezierski, Daria A. Kirjanov, Elena V. Prokhorova & Benjamin Sutcliffe (Translators). Trade Paper. Northwestern University Press. Evanston, IL. 1999. 245p. Writings from an Unbound Europe ISBN:0-8101-1722-3, ISBN13: 978-0-8101-1722-8. Dewey:891.73/5. LCCN:99-056625.
Audience: **g,l,u,f.**

Verbitskaya, Anastasya **PG3470.V4K413 1999**
Keys to Happiness. Beth Holmgren & Helena Goscilo (Editors), Beth Holmgren & Helena Goscilo (Translators). Trade Paper. Indiana University Press. Bloomington, IN. 1999. 336p. ISBN:0-253-21299-5, ISBN13: 978-0-253-21299-3. Dewey:891.73/3. LCCN:98-048993.
Audience: **g,l,u,f.** *Choice, 2000.*

Woll, Josephine **PG3489.R5Z96 1991**
Invented Truth: Soviet Reality and the Literary Imagination of Iurii Trifonov. Cloth Text. Duke University Press. Durham, NC. 1991. 180p. ISBN:0-8223-1151-8, ISBN13: 978-0-8223-1151-5. Dewey:891.73/44. LCCN:90-027834.
Audience: **u,f.** *Choice, 1992.*

Woodward, J. (Editor) **PG3476.M355**
Blok: Selected Poems. Trade Paper. Bristol Classical Press. London, 1992. 196p. Russian Texts Ser. ISBN:1-85399-311-5, ISBN13: 978-1-85399-311-4. Dewey:891.713.
Audience: **g,l,u,f.**

Yefremov, Ivan, et al. **PN6071.S33**
The Heart of the Serpent: Soviet Science Fiction. Strugatsky Arkady, Victor Separin, Boris Strugatsky & Valentina Zhuravleva (Authors). Trade Paper. Fredonia Books. Miami, FL. 2002. 272p. ISBN:1-4101-0041-3, ISBN13: 978-1-4101-0041-2. Dewey:891.73.
Audience: **g,l,u,f.**

Yevtushenko, Yevgeny **PG3479.4.R64**
The Face Behind the Face. Arthur Boyars & Simon Franklin (Translators). Trade Paper. Marion Boyars Publishers, Inc. New York, NY. 1990. 208p. ISBN:0-7145-2617-7, ISBN13: 978-0-7145-2617-1. Dewey:891.71/44.
Audience: **g,l,u,f.**

Zamiatin, Eugene & Zamiatin, Yevgeny **PG3476.Z34**
We. Trade Paper. Penguin Group (USA) Inc. New York, NY. 1991. 256p. ISBN:0-14-016710-2, ISBN13: 978-0-14-016710-8. Dewey:Fic.
Audience: **g,l,u,f.**

Zoshchenko, Mikhail **PG3476.S52**
The Wonderful Dog and Other Tales. E. Fen (Translator). Trade Cloth. Hyperion Press, Inc. Westport, CT. 1973. 179p. Soviet Literature in English Translation Ser. ISBN:0-88355-029-6, ISBN13: 978-0-88355-029-8. Dewey:891.7/3/42. LCCN:72-090320.
Audience: **g,l,u,f.**

Slavic Literatures > Serbian > Anthologies

Gorup, Radmilla & Obradovic, Nadezda (Editors) **PG1595.E8P75 1998**
The Prince of Fire: An Anthology of Contemporary Serbian Short Stories. Cloth Text. University of Pittsburgh Press. Pittsburgh, PA. 1998. 335p. Pitt Series in Russian and East European Studies ISBN:0-8229-4058-2, ISBN13: 978-0-8229-4058-6. Dewey:891.8/230108. LCCN:97-045345.
Audience: **g,l,u,f.** *Choice, 1998.*

Holton, Milne & Mihailovich, Vasa D. **PG1595.E3H65**
Serbian Poetry from the Beginnings to the Present: An Historical Anthology. Trade Cloth. Yale Russian & East European Publications. New Haven, CT. 1989. 472p. Yale Russian and East European Publications, No. 11 ISBN:0-936586-11-7, ISBN13: 978-0-936586-11-3. Dewey:891.8/21008. LCCN:88-050322.
Audience: **g,l,u,f.** *Choice, 1989.*

Holton, Milne & Mihailovich, Vasa D. (Editors) **PG1465.S66 1997**
Songs of the Serbian People: From the Collection of Vuk Karadzic. Milne Holton & Vasa D. Mihailovich (Translators). Trade Paper. University of Pittsburgh Press. Pittsburgh, PA. 1997. 310p. Pitt Series in Russian and East European Studies ISBN:0-8229-5609-8, ISBN13: 978-0-8229-5609-9. Dewey:891.8/21008. LCCN:97-004561.
Audience: **g,u.**

Mihailovich, Vasa D. (Editor, Translator) **PG1418.D77P468 2003**
Songs of the Sun, Love and Death: Selected Poems. Perfect. Serbian Classics Press, The. New York, NY. 2004. 134p. ISBN:0-9678893-2-4, ISBN13: 978-0-9678893-2-0. Dewey:491.7. LCCN:2003-113063.
Audience: **g,l,u,f.**

Simic, Charles **PG1595.E3 H67 1992**
Horse Has Six Legs: Contemporary Serbian Poetry. Trade Paper. Graywolf Press. St. Paul, MN. 1992. 224p. ISBN:1-55597-165-2, ISBN13: 978-1-55597-165-6. Dewey:891.8/21508. LCCN:92-007759.
Audience: **g,l,u,f.**

Slavic Literatures > Serbian > History and Criticism

Milojkovic-Djuric, Jelena **DR2008.M55 1988**
Tradition and Avante-Garde: Literature and Arts in Serbian Culture, 1900-1918. Trade Cloth. Eastern European Monographs. Bradenton, FL. 1988. 227p. East European Monographs, No. 234 ISBN:0-88033-131-3, ISBN13: 978-0-88033-131-9. Dewey:949.7/1015. LCCN:87-082407.
Audience: **u,f.**

Slavic Literatures > Serbian > Individual Authors

Bazdulj, Muharem **PG1420.12.A93D7813**
The Second Book. Oleg Andric & Andrew Baruch Wachtel (Translators). Trade Cloth. Northwestern University Press. Evanston, IL. 2005. 152p. Writings from an Unbound Europe Ser. ISBN:0-8101-1935-8, ISBN13: 978-0-8101-1935-2. Dewey:FIC. LCCN:2004-010430.
Audience: **g,l,u,f.**

Cosic, Bora **PG1418.C59U413 1997**
My Family's Role in the World Revolution: And Other Prose. Ann C. Bigelow (Translator). Trade Cloth. Northwestern University Press. Evanston, IL. 1997. 250p. Writings from an Unbound Europe ISBN:0-8101-1367-8, ISBN13: 978-0-8101-1367-1. Dewey:891.8/2354. LCCN:97-015118.
Audience: **g,l,u,f.**

Jergovic, Miljenko **PG1419.2.E74S2713**
Sarajevo Marlboro. Stela Tomasevic (Translator), Aamiel Alcalay (Introduction by). Trade Paper. Archipelago Books. Brooklyn, NY. 2004. 180p. ISBN:0-9728692-2-0, ISBN13: 978-0-9728692-2-5. Dewey:891.8/2354. LCCN:2003-013678.
Audience: **g,l,u,f.**

Kis, Danilo **PG1419.21.I8B313**
Garden, Ashes. William J. Hannaher (Translator), Aleksandar Hemon (Introduction by). Trade Paper. Dalkey Archive Press. Normal, IL. 2003. 170p. ISBN:1-56478-326-X, ISBN13: 978-1-56478-326-4. Dewey:891.8/2354. LCCN:2003-055104.
Audience: **g,l,u,f.**

Kis, Danilo **PG1419.21.I8P413**
Hourglass. Ralph Manheim (Translator). Trade Paper. Northwestern University Press. Evanston, IL. 1998. 274p. European Classics Ser. ISBN:0-8101-1513-1, ISBN13: 978-0-8101-1513-2. Dewey:891.8/2/354. LCCN:97-026746.
Audience: **g,l,u,f.**

Lalic, Ivan V. & Jones, Francis R. **PG1419.22.A4A24 1995**
A Rusty Needle. Trade Paper. Anvil Press Poetry, Ltd. London, 2002. 200p. ISBN:0-85646-241-1, ISBN13: 978-0-85646-241-2. Dewey:891.8/215. LCCN:96-135484.
Audience: **g,l,u,f.**

Lazic, Radmila **PG1419.22.A939A6**
A Wake for the Living: Poems. Charles Simic (Translator). Trade Paper. Graywolf Press. St. Paul, MN. 2003. 144p. ISBN:1-55597-390-6, ISBN13: 978-1-55597-390-2. Dewey:891.8216. LCCN:2003-101173.
Audience: **g,l,u,f.**

Pavic, Milorad **PG1418.A6**
Landscape Painted with Tea. Trade Paper. Alfred A. Knopf Inc. New York, NY. 1991. 352p. Vintage International Ser. ISBN:0 679-73344-2, ISBN13: 978-0-679-73344-7. Dewey:891.8/235. LCCN:91-050009.
Audience: **g,l,u,f.** *Choice, 1991.*

Pavic, Milorad **PG1419.26.A78H3213**
Dictionary of the Khazars: Female Edition. Christina Pribicevic-Zoric (Translator). Trade Paper. Knopf Publishing Group. New York, NY. 1989. 352p. Vintage International Ser. ISBN:0-679-72754-X, ISBN13: 978-0-679-72754-5. Dewey:891.8/235. LCCN:89-016680.
Audience: **l,u.**

Pavic, Milorad **PG1419.26.A78H313**
Dictionary of the Khazars: Male Edition. Christina Pribicevic-Zoric (Translator). Trade Paper. Knopf Publishing Group. New York, NY. 1989. 352p. Vintage International Ser. ISBN:0-679-72461-3, ISBN13: 978-0-679-72461-2. Dewey:891.8/235. LCCN:89-040142.
Audience: **l,u.**

Pekic, Borislav **PG1419.26.E5V713**
The Time of Miracles: A Legend. Lovett F. Edwards (Translator). Trade Paper. Northwestern University Press. Evanston, IL. 1994. 320p. Writings from an Unbound Europe ISBN:0-8101-1117-9, ISBN13: 978-0-8101-1117-2. Dewey:891.73/44. LCCN:93-045889.
Audience: **g,l,u,f.**

Pekic, Borislav **PG1419.26.E5H613**
The Houses of Belgrade. Bernard Johnson (Translator). Trade Paper. Northwestern University Press. Evanston, IL. 1994. 212p. Writings from an Unbound Europe ISBN:0-8101-1141-1, ISBN13: 978-0-8101-1141-7. Dewey:891.8/235. LCCN:93-047920.
Audience: **g,l,u,f.**

Selimovic, Mesa **PG1419.29.E43T913**
The Fortress. Edward D. Goy & Jasna Levinger-Goy (Translators). Trade Cloth. Northwestern University Press. Evanston, IL. 1999. 406p. Writings from an Unbound Europe ISBN:0-8101-1712-6, ISBN13: 978-0-8101-1712-9. Dewey:891.8/2354. LCCN:99-027539.
Audience: **g,l,u,f.**

Selimovic, Mesa **PG1419.29.E43D413**
Death and the Dervish. Bogdan Rakic & Stephen Dickey (Translators). Trade Cloth. Northwestern University Press. Evanston, IL. 1996. 469p. Writings from an Unbound Europe ISBN:0-8101-1296-5, ISBN13: 978-0-8101-1296-4. Dewey:891.8. LCCN:96-017300.
Audience: **g,l,u,f.**

Tisma, Aleksandar **PG1419.21.I8**
The Book of Blam. Trade Paper. Harcourt Trade Publishers. New York, NY. 2000. 240p. ISBN:0-15-600841-6, ISBN13: 978-0-15-600841-9. Dewey:891.8/2354.
Audience: **g,l,u,f.**

Zivkovic, Zoran **PG1419.36.I954V7413**
Time Gifts. Alice Copple-Tosic (Translator). Trade Paper. Northwestern University Press. Evanston, IL. 2000. 81p. Writings from an Unbound Europe ISBN:0-8101-1782-7, ISBN13: 978-0-8101-1782-2. Dewey:891.8/2354. LCCN:00-008926.
Audience: **g,l,u,f.**

Slavic Literatures > Slovak > Anthologies

Cincura, Andrew **PG5545.E. A5**
An Anthology of Slovak Literature. University Hardcovers. 1976.
Audience: **g,l,u,f.**

Hudík, Pavol, et al. **PG5545.E8 I5 2002**
In Search of Homo Sapiens: Twenty-Five Contemporary Slovak Short Stories. Trebatická, Heather; Bednár, Lucy (Authors). Bolchazy-Carducci. 2002. ISBN:0-86516-532-7, ISBN13: 978-0-86516-532-8.
Audience: **g,l,u,f.**

Slavic Literatures > Slovak > History and Criticism

Petro, Peter **PG5401.P48 1996**
A History of Slovak Literature. McGill-Queen's University Press. 1996. ISBN:0-7735-1402-3, ISBN13: 978-0-7735-1402-7.
Audience: **u,f.**

Rudinsky, Norma, et al. **PG5404.8 .W65 R84 1991**
Incipient Feminists: Women Writers in the Slovak National Revival. Pridavkova-Minarikova, Marianna (Authors). Slavica Publishers. 1991. Slovak Language and Literature, No. 3 ISBN:0-89357-220-9, ISBN13: 978-0-89357-220-4.
Audience: **u,f.**

Slavic Literatures > Slovak > Individual Authors

Mnacko, Ladislav **PZ4.M6937 Tas**
The Taste of Power. Stevenson, Paul (Translator); Hayward, Max (Forward). Praeger. 1967.
Audience: **g,l,u,f.**

Simecka, Martin M. **PG5439.29.I37 Z313 1996**
The Year of the Frog: A Novel. Petro, Peter (Translator); Havel, Vaclav (Forward). Simon & Schuster. 1996. ISBN:0-684-81367-X, ISBN13: 978-0-684-81367-7.
Audience: **g,l,u,f.**

Vilikovsky, Pavel **PG5439.32.I4V413**
Ever Green Is...: Selected Prose. Andrew Baruch Wachtel (Editor), Charles Sabatos (Translator). Trade Paper. Northwestern University Press. Evanston, IL. 2002. 195p. Writings from an Unbound Europe ISBN:0-8101-1908-0, ISBN13: 978-0-8101-1908-6. Dewey:891.8/73. LCCN:2001-007413.
Audience: **g,l,u,f.** *Choice, 2003.*

Slavic Literatures > Slovenian > Anthologies

Cooper, Henry R. (Editor) **PG1961.E1B55 2003**
A Bilingual Anthology of Slovene Literature. Trade Paper. Slavica Publishers. Bloomington, IN. 2003. 333p. An Anthology of South Slavic Literatures Ser., Vol. 1 ISBN:0-89357-309-4, ISBN13: 978-0-89357-309-6. Dewey:891.8/4008. LCCN:2003-010016.
Audience: **u,f.**

Jackson, Richard (Editor) **PG1961.E3D68 1993**
Double Vision: Four Slovene Poets. Michael Biggins & Ales Debeljak (Translators). Trade Paper. Poetry Miscellany. Chattanooga, TN. 1992. 110p. ISBN:1-881489-04-3, ISBN13: 978-1-881489-04-7. Dewey:891.8/41508. LCCN:98-158759.
Audience: **g,l,u,f.**

Slavic Literatures > Slovenian > History and Criticism

Zawacki, Andrew (Editor) **PG1961.E1A37 1999**
Afterwards: Slovenian Writing, 1945-1995. Trade Paper. White Pine Press. Buffalo, NY. 1999. 242p. Terra Incognita Ser., Vol. 4 ISBN:1-877727-97-0, ISBN13: 978-1-877727-97-9. Dewey:891.8/408005. LCCN:99-043487.
Audience: **g,l,u,f.**

Slavic Literatures > Slovenian > Individual Authors

Blatnik, Andrej **PG1919.12.L38M4613**
Skinswaps. Tamara Soban (Translator). Trade Cloth. Northwestern University Press. Evanston, IL. 1998. 109p.

Writings from an Unbound Europe ISBN:0-8101-1656-1, ISBN13: 978-0-8101-1656-6. Dewey:891.8/435. LCCN:98-034133.

Audience: **g,l,u,f.**

Jancar, Drago **PG1919.2.A54P6713**
Mocking Desire. Michael Biggins (Translator). Trade Cloth. Northwestern University Press. Evanston, IL. 1998. 267p. Writings from an Unbound Europe ISBN:0-8101-1553-0, ISBN13: 978-0-8101-1553-8. Dewey:891.8/435. LCCN:98-015527.

Audience: **g,l,u,f.**

Jancar, Drago **PG1919.2.A54S4813**
Northern Lights. Michael Biggins (Translator). Trade Paper. Northwestern University Press. Evanston, IL. 2001. 257p. Writings from an Unbound Europe ISBN:0-8101-1839-4, ISBN13: 978-0-8101-1839-3. Dewey:891.8/435. LCCN:00-012337.

Audience: **g,l,u,f.**

Kocbek, Edvard **PG1918.K58A27 2004**
Nothing Is Lost: Selected Poems. Michael Scammell (Editor, Translator), Veno Taufer (Translator), Michael Scammell (Introduction by), Charles Simic (Foreword by). Trade Cloth. Princeton University Press. Princeton, NJ. 2004. 176p. The Lockert Library of Poetry in Translation ISBN:0-691-11839-6, ISBN13: 978-0-691-11839-0. Dewey:891.8/415. LCCN:2003-062203.

Audience: **g,l,u,f.**

Salamun, Tomaz **PG1919.29.A5K6513**
The Book for My Brother. Trade Paper. Harcourt Trade Publishers. New York, NY. 2006. 108p. ISBN:0-15-603205-8, ISBN13: 978-0-15-603205-6. Dewey:891.8/415. LCCN:2005-031614.

Audience: **g,l,u,f.**

Salamun, Tomaz **PG1919.29.A5**
Poker. Matvei Yankelevich (Editor), Tomaz Salamun & Joshua Beckman (Translators), Peter Kruty Editions & McNaughton Gunn (Produced by), Jeremy Mickel (Designed by). Trade Paper. Ugly Duckling Presse. Brooklyn, NY. 2003. 88p. Eastern European Poets Ser., No. 3 ISBN:0-9727684-2-4, ISBN13: 978-0-9727684-2-9. Dewey:891.8/415.

Audience: **g,l,u,f.**

Taufer, Veno (Author, Translator) **PG1919.3.A9V6413**
Waterlings. Milne Holton (Translator). Trade Cloth. Northwestern University Press. Evanston, IL. 2000. 109p. ISBN:0-8101-1810-6, ISBN13: 978-0-8101-1810-2. Dewey:891.8/415. LCCN:00-009921.

Audience: **g,l,u,f.**

Slavic Literatures > Ukranian > Anthologies

PG3931
From Three Worlds: New Ukrainian Writing. Hogan, Ed (Editor). Zephyr Press. 1996. ISBN:0-939010-53-1, ISBN13: 978-0-939010-53-0.

Audience: **g,l,u,f.**

Franklin, Simon (Translator) **BX513**
Sermons and Rhetoric of Kievan Rus'. Trade Cloth. Harvard Ukrainian Research Institute. Cambridge, MA. 1991. Library of Early Ukrainian Literature: English Translations, Vol. 5 ISBN:0-916458-42-3, ISBN13: 978-0-916458-42-3. Dewey:252/.01947.

Audience: **u,f.**

Hryhorenko, Hrytsko & Ukrainka, Lesya **PG3948.H699**
From Heart to Heart. Sonia Morris (Editor), Roma Z. Franko (Translator), Raissa Chol (Illustrator). Trade Paper. Language Lanterns Publications, Inc. S. Surrey, BC. 1999. 480p. Women's Voices in Ukrainian Literature, Vol. 4 ISBN:0-9683899-3-7, ISBN13: 978-0-9683899-3-5.

Audience: **g,l,u,f.**

Kobylianska, Olha & Yaroshynska, Yevheniya **PG3948.K55**
But... The Lord Is Silent. Sonia Morris (Editor), Roma Franko (Translator), Raissa Choi (Illustrator). Trade Paper. Language Lanterns Publications, Inc. S. Surrey, BC. 1999. 470p. Women's Voices in Ukrainian Literature Ser., Vol. III ISBN:0-9683899-2-9, ISBN13: 978-0-9683899-2-8. Dewey:891.7/93/01089287.

Audience: **g,l,u,f.**

Luckyj, George S. (Editor) **PG3986.E8M63 1995**
Modern Ukrainian Short Stories. Ed. 1. Library Binding. Libraries Unlimited, Inc. Westport, CT. 1995. 230p. ISBN:1-56308-391-4, ISBN13: 978-1-56308-391-4. Dewey:891.7/930108. LCCN:95-019552.

Audience: **g,l,u,f.**

Pchilka, Olena, et al. **PG3932.5.W65W37 2000**
Warm the Children, O Sun. Nataliya Kobrynska, Lyubov Yanovska, Hrytsko Hryhorenko, Olha Kobylianska & Lesya Ukrainka (Authors), Sonia Morris (Editor), Roma Franko (Translator), Raissa Choi (Illustrator). Trade Paper. Language Lanterns Publications, Inc. S. Surrey, BC. 2000. 480p. Women's Voices in Ukrainian Literature Ser., Vol. V ISBN:0-9683899-4-5, ISBN13: 978-0-9683899-4-2. Dewey:891.7/9301089287. LCCN:2002-392742.

Audience: **g,l,u,f.**

Pchilka, Olena, et al. **PG3932.5.W65F67 2000**
For a Crust of Bread. Nataliya Kobrynska, Lyubov Yanovska, Olha Kobylianska, Yevheniya Yaroshynska, Hrytsko Hryhorenko & Lesya Ukrainka (Authors), Sonia Morris (Editor), Roma Franko (Translator), Raissa Choi (Illustrator). Trade Paper. Language Lanterns Publications, Inc. S. Surrey, BC. 2000. 480p. Women's Voices in Ukrainian Literature Ser., Vol. 6 ISBN:0-9683899-5-3, ISBN13: 978-0-9683899-5-9. Dewey:891.7/9301089287. LCCN:2002-391250.

Audience: **g,l,u,f.**

Slavic Literatures > Ukranian > Bibliography

Luckyj, George S. **PG3916.2 .L83 1992**
Ukrainian Literature in the Twentieth Century: A Reader's Guide. Paper Text. University of Toronto Press. Toronto, ON.

1992. 230p. ISBN:0-8020-6003-X, ISBN13: 978-0-8020-6003-7. Dewey:891.7/9003. LCCN:92-191722.
Audience: **u,f.** *Choice, 1992.*

Piaseckyj, Oksana **Z2514.U5P52 1989**
Bibliography of Ukrainian Literature in English and French: Translations and Critical Works, 1950-1986. University of Ottawa Press. 1989. University of Ottawa Ukrainian Studies; 10 ISBN:0-7766-0264-0, ISBN13: 978-0-7766-0264-6.
Audience: **u,f.**

Slavic Literatures > Ukranian > Biography

Luckyj, George S. **PG3948.K8562 L8 1983**
Panteleimon Kulish: A Sketch of His Life and Times. Trade Cloth. Eastern European Monographs. Bradenton, FL. 1983. 229p. ISBN:0-88033-016-3, ISBN13: 978-0-88033-016-9. Dewey:891.7/912. LCCN:82-083522.
Audience: **g,l,u,f.**

Taras H. Shevchenko Museum and Memorial Park Foundation
☐ Taras Shevchenko Museum.
http://www.infoukes.com/shevchenkomuseum/poetry
Audience: **g,l,u,f.**

Slavic Literatures > Ukranian > History and Criticism

Cyzevs'kyj, Dmytro & Luckyj, George S. **PG3905.C513 1996**
A History of Ukrainian Literature: From the 11th to the End of the 19th Century. Ed. 2. Dolly Ferguson, Doreen Gorsline & Ulana Petyk (Translators). Library Binding. Libraries Unlimited, Inc. Westport, CT. 1997. 800p. ISBN:1-56308-522-4, ISBN13: 978-1-56308-522-2. Dewey:891.7/909. LCCN:96-025814.
Audience: **l,u,f.**

Ilnytzkyj, O. S. **PG3906.F87I45 1997**
Ukrainian Futurism: 1914-1930: A Historical and Critical Study. Cambridge, Mass: Harvard University Press. 1997. Harvard Series in Ukrainian Studies ISBN:0-916458-56-3, ISBN13: 978-0-916458-56-0.
Audience: **u,f.**

Lindheim, Ralph & Luckyj, George S. (Editors) **DK508.4.T68 1996**
Towards an Intellectual History of Ukraine: An Anthology of Ukrainian Thought, 1710-1993. Trade Paper. University of Toronto Press. Toronto, ON. 1996. 660p. ISBN:0-8020-7855-9, ISBN13: 978-0-8020-7855-1. Dewey:947.7. LCCN:97-123145.
Audience: **u,f.**

Luckyj, George S. **PN849.R9**
Discordant Voices: The Non-Russian Soviet Literatures, 1952-1973. Trade Paper. Mosaic Press. Niagara Falls, NY. 1986. 160p. ISBN:0-88962-014-8, ISBN13: 978-0-88962-014-8. Dewey:809/.8947.
Audience: **u,f.**

Luckyj, George S. **PG3916.2 .L83 1992**
Ukrainian Literature in the Twentieth Century: A Reader's Guide. Paper Text. University of Toronto Press. Toronto, ON. 1992. 230p. ISBN:0-8020-6003-X, ISBN13: 978-0-8020-6003-7. Dewey:891.7/9003. LCCN:92-191722.
Audience: **u,f.** *Choice, 1992.*

Pritsak, Omeljan **DK70 .O43 1990**
The Old Rus' Kievan and Galician-Volhynian Chronicles: The Ostroz'kyj (Xlebnikov) and akCetvertyns'kyj (Pogodin) Codices. Trade Cloth. Harvard University Press. Cambridge, MA. 1991. 761p. Library of Ukrainian Literature Texts, No. 8 ISBN:0-916458-37-7, ISBN13: 978-0-916458-37-9. Dewey:891.7981.
Audience: **u,f.**

Slavic Literatures > Ukranian > Individual Authors

Andrukhovych, Yuri **PG3949.1.N296P4713**
Perverzion. Michael M. Naydan (Translator). Trade Paper, Perfect. Northwestern University Press. Evanston, IL. 2005. 344p. Writings from an Unbound Europe ISBN:0-8101-1964-1, ISBN13: 978-0-8101-1964-2. Dewey:891.7/934. LCCN:2003-010985.
Audience: **g,l,u,f.**

Dibrova, Volodymyr & Melnyczuk, Askold **PG3949.14.I27A25 199**
Peltse and Pentameron. Halyna Hryn (Translator). Trade Cloth. Northwestern University Press. Evanston, IL. 1996. 198p. Writings from an Unbound Europe ISBN:0-8101-1219-1, ISBN13: 978-0-8101-1219-3. Dewey:891.7/933. LCCN:96-027239.
Audience: **g,l,u,f.**

Duknovych, Aleksandr **PG3948.D85D613 1994**
Virtue Is More Important Than Riches. Elaine Rusinko (Editor, Translator). Trade Cloth. Eastern European Monographs. Bradenton, FL. 1995. 85p. ISBN:0-88033-290-5, ISBN13: 978-0-88033-290-3. Dewey:891.72/3. LCCN:93-074055.
Audience: **g,l,u,f.**

Franko, Ivan **PG3948.F7 A26 1987**
Moses and Other Poems. New York: Vantage Press. 1987. ISBN:0-533-07262-X, ISBN13: 978-0-533-07262-0.
Audience: **g,l,u,f.**

Ivan Franko National University of Lviv
☐ Ivan Franko.
http://www.lnu.edu.ua/ifranko/franko_eng.html
Audience: **g,l,u,f.**

Klekh, Igor **PG3482.6.L42A26 2003**
A Land the Size of Binoculars. Michael Naydan & Slava Yastremski (Translators), Michael Naydan & Slava Yastremski (Foreword by), Andrei Bitov (Introduction by). Trade Cloth. Northwestern University Press. Evanston, IL. 2004. 272p. Writings from an Unbound Europe ISBN:0-8101-1942-0, ISBN13: 978-0-8101-1942-0. Dewey:891.7/934. LCCN:2002-154470.
Audience: **g,l,u,f.**

Myrnyi, I. P. **PG3948.M84**
Do Oxen Low When Mangers Are Full?: Novel. Kiev, Dnipro. 1990.
Audience: **g,l,u,f.**

Shevchenko, T. **PG3948.S5 A2 1989**
Selected Poetry. Kyiv: Dnipro Publishers. 1989.
Audience: **g,l,u,f.**

Shevchenko, Taras **PG3948.S5**
Selections: Poetry, Prose. Kiev: Dnipro. 1988.
ISBN:5-308-00224-X, ISBN13: 978-5-308-00224-6.
Audience: **g,l,u,f.**

Taras H. Shevchenko Museum and Memorial Park Foundation
Taras Shevchenko Museum.
http://www.infoukes.com/shevchenkomuseum/poetry
Audience: **g,l,u,f.**

Slavic Literatures > Albanian

Camaj, Martin **PG9621.C3A25 1990**
Selected Poetry. Cloth Text. New York University Press. New York, NY. 1990. 220p. Studies in Near Eastern Civilization, No. 14 ISBN:0 8147-1444-7, ISBN13: 978-0-8147-1444-7. Dewey:891/.9911. LCCN:90-006032.
Audience: **g,l,u,f.**

Elsie, Robert **PG9603.E438 2005**
Albanian Literature: A Short History. Cloth over Boards. I. B. Tauris & Company, Ltd. London, 2006. 372p. ISBN:1-84511-031-5, ISBN13: 978-1-84511-031-4. Dewey:891/.99109. LCCN:2006-273055.
Audience: **g,l,u,f.**

Elsie, Robert **PG9602**
Dictionary of Albanian Literature. Cloth Text. Greenwood Publishing Group, Inc. Portsmouth, NH. 1986. 178p. ISBN:0-313-25186-X, ISBN13: 978-0-313-25186-3. Dewey:891/.991/03. LCCN:85-031693.
Audience: **g,l,u,f.**

Elsie, Robert **PG9603.E44 1995**
History of Albanian Literature. Trade Cloth. Eastern European Monographs. Bradenton, FL. 1993. 1054p. ISBN:0-88033-276-X, ISBN13: 978-0-88033-276-7. Dewey:891/.99109. LCCN:95-060870.
Audience: **g,l,u,f.**

Elsie, Robert **PG9606 .E46**
Studies in Modern Albanian Literature and Culture. Trade Cloth. Eastern European Monographs. Bradenton, FL. 1996. 200p. ISBN:0-88033-352-9, ISBN13: 978-0-88033-352-8. Dewey:891/.99109.
Audience: **g,l,u,f.**

Elsie, Robert (Editor, Translator) **PG9621.C3**
An Anthology of Modern Albanian Poetry: An Elusive Eagle Soars. Trade Paper. Forest Books. London, 1993. 240p. UNESCO Library of World Poetry ISBN:1-85610-017-0, ISBN13: 978 1 85610 017-5. Dewey:891.9911. LCCN:92-075076.
Audience: **g,l,u,f.**

Fishta, Gjergj **PG9621.F5**
The Highland Lute: The Albanian National Epic. Robert Elsie & Janice Mathie-Heck (Translators). Cloth over Boards. I. B. Tauris & Company, Ltd. London, 2006. 256p. ISBN:1-84511-118-4, ISBN13: 978-1-84511-118-2. Dewey:891/.9911. LCCN:2006-296290.
Audience: **g,l,u,f.**

Gjecovi, Shtjefen & Logoreci, Anton (Editors) **KJG138.N672 1989**
The Code of Leke Dukagjini. Martin Camaj (Translator). Trade Cloth. Gjonlekaj Publishing Company. Bronx, NY. 1992. 269p. ISBN:0-9622141-0-8, ISBN13: 978-0-9622141-0-3. Dewey:340.5/094965. LCCN:89-011226.
Audience: **g,l,u,f.**

Kadare, Ismail **PG9621.K3**
Chronicle in Stone. Trade Cloth. Ivan R. Dee Publisher. Blue Ridge Summit, PA. 1987. 277p. ISBN:0-941533-00-X, ISBN13: 978-0-941533-00-3. Dewey:891/.9913. LCCN:87-005530.
Audience: **g,l,u,f.**

Kadare, Ismail **PG9621.K3T7513 2000**
Elegy for Kosovo: Stories. Peter Constantine (Translator). Trade Cloth. Arcade Publishing, Inc. New York, NY. 2000. 128p. ISBN:1-55970-528-0, ISBN13: 978-1-55970-528-8. Dewey:891/.9913. LCCN:00-026610.
Audience: **g,l,u,f.**

Lleshanaku, Luljeta **PG9621.L54A25 2002**
Fresco: Selected Poetry of Luljeta Lleshanaku. Henry Israeli (Editor, Translator, Afterword by), Peter Constantine (Introduction by). Trade Paper. New Directions Publishing Corporation. New York, NY. 2002. 96p. ISBN:0-8112-1511-3, ISBN13: 978-0-8112-1511-4. Dewey:891/.9911. LCCN:2001-052140.
Audience: **g,l,u,f.**

Pipa, Arshi **PG9606.P56 1991**
Contemporary Albanian Literature. Trade Cloth. Eastern European Monographs. Bradenton, FL. 1991. 175p. ISBN:0-88033-202-6, ISBN13: 978-0-88033-202-6. Dewey:891/.99109. LCCN:91-071093.
Audience: **u,f.**

Zhiti, Visar **PG9621.Z52**
The Condemned Apple: Selected Poetry. Robert Elsie (Translator). Trade Paper, Perfect. Green Integer. Los Angeles, CA. 2004. 314p. ISBN:1-931243-72-7, ISBN13: 978-1-931243-72-8. Dewey:891/.9913.
Audience: **g,l,u,f.**

Slavic Literatures > Romanian > Anthologies

Cartianu, Ana & Johnston, R. C. (Editors) **PC839.E5**
Selected Works of Ion Creanga and Mihai Eminescu. Ana Cartianu & R. C. Johnston (Translators). Trade Cloth. Eastern European Monographs. Bradenton, FL. 1993. 307p. Classics of Romanian Literature Ser., Vol. 1 ISBN:0-88033-224-7, ISBN13: 978-0-88033-224-8. Dewey:859.12. LCCN:91-072148.
Audience: **g,l,u,f.**

Stoica, Ion (Editor) **PC871.E3S7 1991**
Young Poets of a New Romania. B. Walker (Translator), Alan Brownjohn (Introduction by). Trade Paper. Forest Books. London, 1991. 160p. ISBN:0-948259-89-2, ISBN13: 978-0-948259-89-0. Dewey:859/.13408. LCCN:90-071088.
Audience: **g,l,u,f.**

Treptow, Kurt W. (Editor, Translator) **PC834.2.A58 1994**
An Anthology of Romanian Women Poets. Adam J. Sorkin (Translator). Trade Cloth. Eastern European Monographs. Bradenton, FL. 1994. 157p. ISBN:0-88033-294-8, ISBN13: 978-0-88033-294-1. Dewey:859/.100809287. LCCN:94-072037.
Audience: **g,l,u,f.**

Slavic Literatures > Romanian > History and Criticism

Calinescu, George **PC801**
History of Romanian Literature. Ed. 4. Nagard-UNESCO. 1988.
Audience: **u.**

Cioranescu, Alexandre **PC839.B33 Z63**
Ion Barbu. Trade Cloth. Thomson Gale. Farmington Hills, MI. 1981. World Authors Ser. ISBN:0-8057-6432-1, ISBN13: 978-0-8057-6432-1. Dewey:859/.132. LCCN:81-004184.
Audience: **u.**

Orlich, Ileana Alexandra **PC803.8.W6O75 2002**
Silent Bodies: Rediscovering the Women of Romanian Short Fiction. Trade Cloth. Eastern European Monographs. Bradenton, FL. 2002. 128p. ISBN:0-88033-499-1, ISBN13: 978-0-88033-499-0. Dewey:859/.301093522. LCCN:2002-110853.
Audience: **u.**

Parvu, Sorin **PC812.P37 1994**
The Romanian Novel. Trade Cloth. Eastern European Monographs. Bradenton, FL. 1994. 161p. ISBN:0-88033-226-3, ISBN13: 978-0-88033-226-2. Dewey:859/.3009.
Audience: **u.**

Slavic Literatures > Romanian > Individual Authors

Arghezi, Tudor **PC839.B55**
Selected Poems of Tudor Arghezi. Michael Impey & Brian Swann (Translators). Trade Paper. Princeton University Press. Princeton, NJ. 1976. 258p. The Lockert Library of Poetry in Translation ISBN:0-691-01328-4, ISBN13: 978-0-691-01328-2. Dewey:859/.1/32. LCCN:75-030185.
Audience: **g,l,u,f.**

Blaga, Lucian **PC839.B55Z3513 2001**
Zalmoxis. Doris Platnus-Runey (Translator), Keith Hitchins (Introduction by). Trade Cloth. Center for Romanian Studies, The. Iali, 2000. 114p. ISBN:973-9432-17-4, ISBN13: 978-973-9432-17-7. Dewey:859/.232. LCCN:2001-524364.
Audience: **g,l,u,f.**

Blaga, Lucian **PC839.B55A28 2001**
Complete Poetical Works of Lucian Blaga. Brenda Walker (Translator). Trade Cloth. Center for Romanian Studies, The. Iali, 2001. 624p. UNESCO Collection of Representative Works ISBN:973-9432-23-9, ISBN13: 978-973-9432-23-8. Dewey:859/.132. LCCN:2002-278780.
Audience: **g,l,u,f.**

Buzura, Augustin **PC840.12.U94R4413**
Refuges. Trade Cloth. Eastern European Monographs. Bradenton, FL. 1994. 461p. ISBN:0-88033-296-4, ISBN13: 978-0-88033-296-5. Dewey:859/.334. LCCN:94-071277.
Audience: **g,l,u,f.**

Buzura, Augustin **PC840.12.U95**
Requiem for Fools and Beasts. Trade Cloth. Columbia University Press. New York, NY. 2004. 570p. ISBN:0-88033-559-9, ISBN13: 978-0-88033-559-1. Dewey:859.334. LCCN:2004-112564.
Audience: **g,l,u,f.**

Cartarescu, Mircea **PC840.13.A86N6713**
Nostalgia. Andrei Codrescu (Introduction by). Trade Paper, Perfect. New Directions Publishing Corporation. New York, NY. 2005. 322p. ISBN:0-8112-1588-1, ISBN13: 978-0-8112-1588-6. Dewey:859/.335. LCCN:2005-018927.
Audience: **g,l,u,f.**

Crasnaru, Daniela **PC840.13.R34M313**
The Grand Prize and Other Stories. Northwestern University Press. 2004. Writings from an Unbound Europe ISBN:0-8101-1849-1, ISBN13: 978-0-8101-1849-2.
Audience: **g,l,u,f.**

Crasnaru, Daniela **PC840.13.R34M313**
The Grand Prize and Other Stories. Adam J. Sorkin (Translator). Trade Cloth. Northwestern University Press. Evanston, IL. 2005. 128p. Writings from an Unbound Europe ISBN:0-8101-1849-1, ISBN13: 978-0-8101-1849-2. Dewey:859/.334. LCCN:2004-004724.
Audience: **g,l,u,f.**

Danilov, Nichita **PC840.14.A57**
Second-Hand Souls: Selected Writing. Sean Cotter (Translator, Introduction by). Trade Cloth. Twisted Spoon Press. Prague 5, 2003. 148p. Contemporary Writing from Central Europe Ser. ISBN:80-86264-08-4, ISBN13: 978-80-86264-08-0. Dewey:859.135.
Audience: **g,l,u,f.**

Deletant, A. & Walker, B. (Translators) **PC840.19.D5**
Exile on a Peppercorn: The Poetry of Mircea Dinescu. Trade Paper. Forest Books. London, 1990. 82p. ISBN:0-948259-00-0, ISBN13: 978-0-948259-00-5. Dewey:859/.134. LCCN:85-080387.
Audience: **g,l,u,f.**

Eliade, Mircea **PC839.E38 N6513**
Two Strange Tales. Trade Paper. Shambhala Publications, Inc. Boston, MA. 2001. 144p. ISBN:1-57062-663-4, ISBN13: 978-1-57062-663-0. Dewey:859/.334. LCCN:86-013026.
Audience: **g,l,u,f.**

Eliade, Mircea **PC839.E38 M97 1992**
Mystic Stories: The Sacred and the Profane. Ana Cartianu (Translator). Trade Cloth. Eastern European Monographs. Bradenton, FL. 1993. 280p. ISBN:0-88033-227-1, ISBN13: 978-0-88033-227-9. Dewey:859/.334. LCCN:91-072637.
Audience: **g,l,u,f.**

Eliade, Mircea **PC839.E38A26 1988**
Youth Without Youth and Other Novellas. Mac L. Ricketts (Translator), Matei Calinescu (Introduction by). Trade Cloth. Ohio State University Press. Columbus, OH. 1988. 256p. ISBN:0-8142-0457-0, ISBN13: 978-0-8142-0457-3. Dewey:859/.334. LCCN:87-037576.
Audience: **g,l,u,f.**

Eliade, Mircea **PC839.E38 N613**
The Forbidden Forest. Mac L. Ricketts & Mary P. Stevenson (Translators). Cloth Text. University of Notre Dame Press. Notre Dame, IN. 1978. ISBN:0-268-00943-0, ISBN13: 978-0-268-00943-4. Dewey:859/.3/34. LCCN:76-051618.
Audience: **g,l,u,f.**

Eliade, Mircea **PC839.E38M313**
Bengal Nights: A Novel. Catherine Spencer (Translator). Trade Paper. University of Chicago Press. Chicago, IL. 1995. 184p. ISBN:0-226-20419-7, ISBN13: 978-0-226-20419-2. Dewey:859.334.
Audience: **g,l,u,f.**

Eminescu, Mihai **PC839.E5**
Poems and Prose. Center for Romanian Studies. 2000. ISBN:973-9432-10-7, ISBN13: 978-973-9432-10-8.
Audience: **g,l,u,f.**

Eminescu, Mihai **PC839.E5 A255 1989**
Poems. Translated by Cornelia M. Popescu. Bucharest. 1989. ISBN:973-23-0082-5, ISBN13: 978-973-23-0082-4.
Audience: **g,l,u,f.**

Eminescu, Mihai **PC839.E5 Z478 2000**
Up to the Star: The Life and Work of the Romanina Poet Mihai Eminescu. Bantas, Andrei; Net, Mariana. Clusium. 2000. ISBN:973-555-290-6, ISBN13: 978-973-555-290-9.
Audience: **g,l,u,f.**

Goma, Paul **PC839.E38**
My Childhood at the Gate of Unrest: A Romanian Memoir. Angela Clark (Translator). Trade Cloth. Readers International. Columbia, LA. 1990. 250p. ISBN:0-930523-73-3, ISBN13: 978-0-930523-73-2. Dewey:859.334. LCCN:89-064268.
Audience: **g,l,u,f.**

Manea, Norman **PC840.23.A47A24 1994**
Compulsory Happiness. Linda Coverdale (Translator). Trade Paper. Northwestern University Press. Evanston, IL. 1994. 259p. Writings from an Unbound Europe ISBN:0-8101-1190-X, ISBN13: 978-0-8101-1190-5. Dewey:859/.334. LCCN:94-017021.
Audience: **g,l,u,f.**

Rebreanu, Liviu **PC839.R4**
Adam and Eve. Minerva Publishing House. 1986.
Audience: **g,l,u,f.**

Rebreanu, Liviu **PC839.R4 I623**
Ion. Ralph M. Aderman (Editor). Trade Cloth. Irvington Publishers. New York, NY. 1967. ISBN:0-8057-5695-7, ISBN13: 978-0-8057-5695-1. Dewey:859/.3/32. LCCN:67-025190.
Audience: **g,l,u,f.**

Rebreanu, Liviu **PB839.R4**
The Uprising. P. Crandjean & S. Hartauer (Translators). Trade Cloth. Peter Owen Ltd. London, 1964. 384p. ISBN:0-7206-9382-9, ISBN13: 978-0-7206-9382-9. Dewey:859.3.
Audience: **g,l,u,f.**

Sadoveanu, Mihail (Translator) **PC839.S3 A23 1991**
The Hatchet: The Life of Stephen the Great. Trade Cloth. Eastern European Monographs. Bradenton, FL. 1994. 280p. ISBN:0-88033-237-9, ISBN13: 978-0-88033-237-8. Dewey:859/.332. LCCN:91-076234.
Audience: **g,l,u,f.**

Simion, Eugen **PC839.E38Z87 2001**
Mircea Eliade: The Mythical Narrative. Trade Cloth. Eastern European Monographs. Bradenton, FL. 2001. 320p. ISBN:0-88033-436-3, ISBN13: 978-0-88033-436-5. Dewey:859/.334. LCCN:2001-131201.
Audience: **g,l,u,f.**

Sorescu, Marin **PC840.29.O74**
The Thirst of the Salt Mountain: A Trilogy of Plays. Andrea Deletant & Brenda Walker (Translators). Trade Paper. Forest Books. London, 1990. 112p. ISBN:0-9509487-5-6, ISBN13: 978-0-9509487-5-1. Dewey:859/.234. LCCN:85-070248.
Audience: **g,l,u,f.**

Sorescu, Marin **PC840.29.O74**
Let's Talk about the Weather. A. Deletant & B. Walker (Translators), J. Silkin (Introduction by). Trade Paper. Forest Books. London, 1987. 84p. ISBN:0-9509487-8-0, ISBN13: 978-0-9509487-8-2. Dewey:859/.134. LCCN:85-070247.
Audience: **g,l,u,f.**

Sorescu, Marin **PC840.29.O74 A24**
Hands Behind My Back: Selected Poems. Gabriela Dragnea, Stuart Friebert & Adriana Varga (Translators), Seamus Heaney (Introduction by). Trade Cloth. Oberlin College Press. Oberlin, OH. 2003. 168p. Field Translation Ser., No. 18 ISBN:0-932440-58-4, ISBN13: 978-0-932440-58-7. Dewey:859.1. LCCN:91-061274.
Audience: **g,l,u,f.**

Stanescu, Nichita **PC840.29.T345A23**
Bas-Relief with Heroes: Selected Poems, 1960-1982. Thomas C. Carlson & Vasile Poenaru (Translators), Benedict Ganescu (Illustrator), Dumitri R. Popa (Introduction by). Trade Cloth. Memphis State University Press. Memphis, TN. 1988. 156p. ISBN:0-87870-214-8, ISBN13: 978-0-87870-214-5. Dewey:859/.134. LCCN:88-023527.
Audience: **g,l,u,f.**

Teodoreanu, Ionel **PC839.T4 L313 1992**
One Moldavian Summer. Eugenia Farca (Translator). Trade Cloth. Eastern European Monographs. Bradenton, FL. 1993. 267p. ISBN:0 88033 238-7, ISBN13: 978-0-88033-238-5. Dewey:859/.332. LCCN:91-078020.
Audience: **g,l,u,f.**

Voiculescu, Vasile **PC839.V6**
Tales of Fantasy and Magic. Minerva. 1986.
Audience: **g,l,u,f.**

Slavic Literatures > Croatian > Anthologies

Hawkesworth, Celia **PG1404.9.W65H39 2000**
Voices in the Shadows. Trade Cloth. Central European University Press. Herndon, VA. 2000. 292p. ISBN:963-9116-62-9, ISBN13: 978-963-9116-62-7. Dewey:891.8/2099287. LCCN:00-022648.
Audience: **g,l,u,f.** *Choice, 2000.*

Slavic Literatures > Croatian > History and Criticism

Lekic, Anita **PG1419.26.O48**
The Poetry of Vasko Popa. Cloth Text. Peter Lang Publishing, Inc. New York, NY. 1993. XIV, 178p. Balkan Studies, Vol. 2 ISBN:0-8204-1777-7, ISBN13: 978-0-8204-1777-6. Dewey:891.8/215. LCCN:92-007285.
Audience: **u,f.**

Slavic Literatures > Croatian > Individual Authors

Drakulic, Slavenka **DR1313**
They Would Never Hurt a Fly: War Criminals on Trial in the Hague. Trade Paper. Penguin Group (USA) Inc. New York, NY. 2005. 224p. ISBN:0-14-303542-8, ISBN13: 978-0-14-303542-8. Dewey:949.703.
Audience: **g,l,u,f.**

Drakulic, Slavenka **PG1419.21.I8**
S.: A Novel about the Balkans. Marko Ivic (Translator). Trade Paper. Penguin Group (USA) Inc. New York, NY. 2001. 224p. ISBN:0-14-029844-4, ISBN13: 978-0-14-029844-4. Dewey:891.8/2354.
Audience: **g,l,u,f.**

Krleza, Miroslav **PG1618.K69N33 1995**
On the Edge of Reason. Zora Depolo (Translator), Jeremy Catto (Introduction by). Trade Paper. New Directions Publishing Corporation. New York, NY. 1995. 188p. Revived Modern Classic Ser. ISBN:0-8112-1306-4, ISBN13: 978-0-8112-1306-6. Dewey:891.8/235. LCCN:95-037589.
Audience: **g,l,u,f.**

Krleza, Miroslav **PG1618.K69B3413 2002**
The Banquet in Blitva. Edward Dennis Goy & Jasna Levinger-Goy (Translators). Trade Paper. Northwestern University Press. Evanston, IL. 2004. 376p. Literature in Translation Ser. ISBN:0-8101-1862-9, ISBN13: 978-0-8101-1862-1. Dewey:891.8/235. LCCN:2002-012089.
Audience: **g,l,u,f.**

Nuhanovic, Gordan **PG1620.24.U28**
The Survival League. Julienne Eden Busic (Translator). Trade Paper. Ooligan Press. Portland, OR. 2005. 126p. New Croatia Ser. ISBN:1-932010-06-8, ISBN13: 978-1-932010-06-0. Dewey:891.8/236.
Audience: **g,l,u,f.**

Ugresic, Dubravka **PG1619.31.G7M8913**
The Museum of Unconditional Surrender. Celia Hawkesworth (Translator). Trade Paper. New Directions Publishing Corporation. New York, NY. 2002. xi, 238p. ISBN:0-8112-1493-1, ISBN13: 978-0-8112-1493-3. Dewey:891.8/2354.
Audience: **g,l,u,f.**

Vrkljan, Irena **PG1619.32.R53Z4713**
The Silk, the Shears and Marina. Sibelan Forrester & Celia Hawkesworth (Translators). Trade Cloth. Northwestern University Press. Evanston, IL. 1999. 185p. Writings from an Unbound Europe ISBN:0-8101-1603-0, ISBN13: 978-0-8101-1603-0. Dewey:891.8/285409 B. LCCN:98-046976.
Audience: **g,l,u,f.**

Slavic Literatures > Yugoslav > Anthologies

Labon, Joanna (Editor) **PG584.E1B35 1995**
Balkan Blues: Writing Out of Yugoslavia. Trade Paper. Northwestern University Press. Evanston, IL. 1995. 268p. Writings from an Unbound Europe ISBN:0-8101-1325-2, ISBN13: 978-0-8101-1325-1. Dewey:891.808/09497. LCCN:95-025082.
Audience: **u,f.**

Wiener, Leo (Compiled by) **PN6014**
Specimens of Slavonic Literature: Croatian, Serbian, Slovak, Little Russian, Bohemian, Slovene. Trade Paper. University Press of the Pacific. Miami, FL. 2005. 116p. ISBN:1-4102-1985-2, ISBN13: 978-1-4102-1985-5. Dewey:808.
Audience: **g,u,f.**

Slavic Literatures > Yugoslav > History and Criticism

Barac, Antun **PG561 .B313**
A History of Yugoslav Literature. Trade Cloth. Michigan Slavic Publications. Ann Arbor, MI. 1972. Joint Committee on Eastern Europe Publication Ser., No. 1 ISBN:0-930042-19-0, ISBN13: 978-0-930042-19-6. Dewey:891.8.
Audience: **l,u,f.** B

Bogert, Ralph **PG1618.K69 Z594 1991**
The Writer As Naysayer: Miroslav Krleza and the Aesthetic of Interwar Central Europe. Trade Cloth. Slavica Publishers. Bloomington, IN. 1991. 266p. UCLA Slavic Studies, Vol. 20 ISBN:0-89357-212-8, ISBN13: 978-0-89357-212-9. Dewey:891.8/28509. LCCN:91-213461.
Audience: **u,f.**

Lord, Albert B. **PN1303.L62 2000**
The Singer of Tales. Ed. 2. Stephen A. Mitchell & Gregory Nagy (Editors). Trade Paper. Harvard University Press. Cambridge, MA. 2000. 352p. Harvard Studies in Comparative Literature, Vol. 24 ISBN:0-674-00283-0, ISBN13: 978-0-674-00283-8. Dewey:809.1/32. LCCN:00-021247.
Audience: **u,f.**

Wachtel, Andrew **DR1228.W33 1998**
The Failure of Multi-Culturalism in One Country: Literature and Literary Politics in the Rise and Fall of Yugoslavia. Trade Cloth. Stanford University Press. Palo Alto, CA. 1998. 320p. ISBN:0-8047-3180-2, ISBN13: 978-0-8047-3180-5. Dewey:306/.09497. LCCN:98-004438.
Audience: **g,u,f.**

Slavic Literatures > Yugoslav > Individual Authors

Andric, Ivo **PG1418.A6 A2 1992**
The Damned Yard and Other Stories. Celia Hawkesworth (Editor, Translator). Trade Paper. Forest Books. London, 1993. 198p. ISBN:1-85610-022-7, ISBN13: 978-1-85610-022-9. Dewey:891.8235. LCCN:92-072469.
Audience: **g,l,u,f.**

Andric, Ivo **PG1418.A6T713 1992**
The Days of the Consuls. Celia Hawkesworth & Bogdan Rakic (Translators). Trade Paper. Forest Books. London, 1993. 416p. ISBN:1-85610-024-3, ISBN13: 978-1-85610-024-3. Dewey:891.8/235. LCCN:92-072470.
Audience: **g,l,u,f.** *Choice, 1993.*

Andric, Ivo **PG1418.A6 T713 1993**
The Bosnian Chronicle. Joseph Hitreck (Translator). Trade Paper. Arcade Publishing, Inc. New York, NY. 1993. 432p. ISBN:1-55970-236-2, ISBN13: 978-1-55970-236-2. LCCN:93-008695.
Audience: **g,l,u,f.**

Author Index

A

C

D

E

F

G

H

I

J

K

L

N

O

P

Q

R

S

T

U

W

X

Y

Z

Title Index

A

B

C

D

E

F

G

H

I

J

K

L

M

N

O

P

Q

R

S

T

U

V

W

X

Y

Z

Numeric Titles